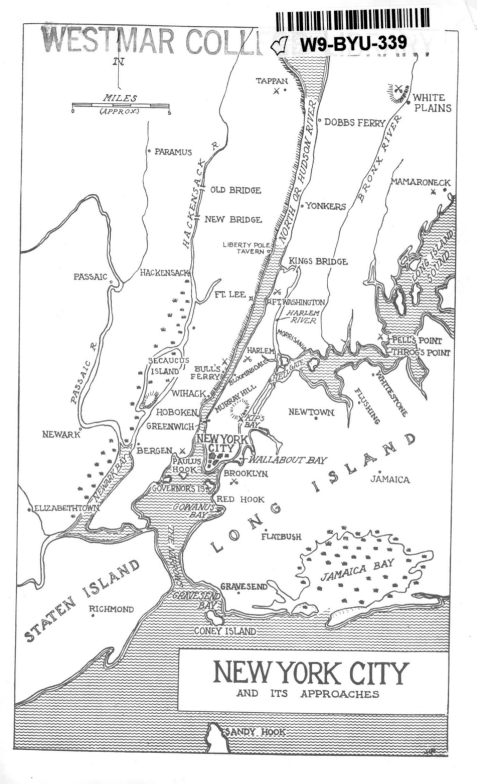

NEW YORK CITY

AND ITS APPROACHES

ENCYCLOPEDIA OF
THE AMERICAN REVOLUTION

By the same author

CIVIL WAR DICTIONARY

MILITARY CUSTOMS AND TRADITIONS

LANDMARKS OF THE AMERICAN REVOLUTION

Encyclopedia
of the
AMERICAN
REVOLUTION

by

Mark Mayo Boatner III

★

Bicentennial Edition

★

David McKay Company, Inc.
New York

Bicentennial Edition, Revised and Expanded
ENCYCLOPEDIA OF THE AMERICAN REVOLUTION

COPYRIGHT © 1974, 1966 BY MARK MAYO BOATNER III

Library of Congress Catalog Card Number: 73-91868
ISBN: 0-679-50440-0

MANUFACTURED IN THE UNITED STATES OF AMERICA

PERMISSIONS

The author would like to express his indebtedness to the innumerable authors and publishers whose works have been consulted and quoted in *The Encyclopedia of the American Revolution.*
Written permission has been received from the following publishers:

American Heritage Publishing Co., Inc.: excerpts from J. H. Plumb, "Our Last King," *American Heritage Magazine,* June 1960; and A. B. Tourtellot's comments on Harold Murdock's "Nineteenth of April 1775," *American Heritage Magazine,* August 1959; and various excerpts from *The American Heritage Book of the Revolution.*
Department of the Army, Office of the Quartermaster General: excerpts from Erna Risch, *Quartermaster Support of the Army: A History of the Corps, 1775–1939* (Washington, D.C., 1962).
The Bobbs-Merrill Company, Inc.: Henry Steele Commager and Richard B. Morris, *The Spirit of 'Seventy-Six* (Indianapolis and New York, 1958).
The University of Chicago Press: excerpts from Edmund S. Morgan, *Birth of the Republic, 1763–89,* © 1956.
Columbia University Press: excerpts from Howard Swiggett, *War Out of Niagara,* © 1933.
Encyclopaedia Britannica: excerpts from 11th edition.
Harper & Row, Publishers: excerpts from John R. Alden, *The American Revolution,* © 1954; from Lynn Montross, *Rag, Tag and Bobtail: The Story of the Continental Army, 1775–1783,* © 1952; and from *The Reluctant Rebels: The Story of the Continental Congress, 1774–1784,* © 1950.
Harvard University Press: excerpt from Allen French, *The Taking of Ticonderoga in 1775 . . . ,* © 1928.
Holt, Rinehart and Winston, Inc.: excerpts from Samuel Flagg Bemis, *A Diplomatic History of the United States,* 3rd edition, copyright 1950.
Houghton Mifflin Company: excerpts from C. H. Van Tyne, *War of Independence,* © 1929.
Illinois State Historical Library: excerpts from James A. James (ed.), "George Rogers Clark Papers, 1771–1781," *Collections,* Volume 8, 1912.
Little, Brown and Company: excerpts from Louise Hall Tharp, *The Baroness and the General,* © 1962 by Louise Hall Tharp, used by permission of the publisher.
Louisiana State University Press: excerpts from John Richard Alden, *General Gage in America,* © 1948, and *The South in the Revolution, 1763–1789,* © 1957.
The Macmillan Company: excerpts from Christopher Ward, *The War of the Revolution,* © 1952.
The University of Michigan Press: excerpt from *Lexington to Fallen Timbers,* © 1942.
The University of North Carolina Library: excerpts from the Davie-Weems Historical Notes in the Southern Historical Collection (item No. 2540).

To my personal link with the American Revolution
EMILY NELSON GUNNELL
(1869–1969)
my grandmother and
great-granddaughter of
THOMAS NELSON, JR.
(1739–1789)

ACKNOWLEDGMENTS

I would like to express appreciation to Professor Hugh F. Rankin, Professor of History, Tulane University, for reading and commenting on the manuscript and the galleys of this entire book. Professor Richard B. Morris, Gouverneur Morris Professor of History, Columbia University, was kind enough to examine the completed galleys and arrange for "updating the scholarship" in several areas. The latter was done by Mr. Thomas J. Archdeacon with painstaking thoroughness for which I would like to add a special note of thanks.

Mr. Howard H. Peckham and Professor Bernhard A. Uhlendorf checked my articles on Colonial military affairs and German participation. Brigadiers C. N. Barclay and R. G. Thurburn rallied to my call for assistance in straightening out biographical details about British officers. Mr. La Dow Johnston and Mr. Carl Pipert helped me correct traditional errors about the Kentucky Rifle, and Mr. James C. Risk rendered the same service on the subject of coins in America. Colonel F. B. Nihart furnished material about the U.S. Marine Corps.

Most of the maps were rendered from my full-scale sketches by David M. Prior and Larry N. Tumlinson. Several were done by Douglas V. Koch; William D. Dunstan and Bruce H. Gilmer each contributed an important one.

My publisher, Mr. Kennett L. Rawson, has shown generosity, patience, and personal interest that transcend the normal demands of business, and the book is a better one for his pains.

To my wife, Patricia, whose literary collaboration since production of *The Civil War Dictionary* has progressively been diverted by production of three sons, I wish to express appreciation and acknowledgment of her work on many biographical sketches.

Let me add the customary note that the persons listed above deserve credit for many of the good things in this book while I alone am responsible for its errors and imperfections.

MARK M. BOATNER III

Penrith Plantation
Jackson, Louisiana

CONTENTS

INTRODUCTION

The scope and general organization of this book will be apparent to the reader who digs into it and who reads the explanation of my system of cross referencing (see below). I would, however, like to say a few words here for the benefit of the casual reader who may pick up the book in a library and for the reviewer who may be in a hurry.

As for *scope,* while the book deals primarily with American history during the period 1763–83, it is not confined to a vacuum of nationality or time. A conscious effort has been made to cover British, French, and German participation; this means that the American reader may find that some ancestor has been eliminated to make room for a foreigner who (in my opinion) should have the space. As for time, I have found it necessary to go back from 1763 and forward from 1783 to provide essential background and to round out the stories of persons and issues of the Revolution. While the battles of Culloden and Fontenoy have no real place in the history of the American Revolution, they did figure in the earlier lives of participants and help explain tactics of the Revolution. "Assumption" and the Republican Party emerged after the American Revolution, but I found it useful to include them as articles, even though there was no need to add an article on the Constitutional Convention.

The reader will find other peculiar inclusions and omissions, particularly insofar as the background of the Revolution and the postwar period are concerned. Although I do not claim infallibility in the decisions involved, I would like to point out a mechanical problem that may not occur to the reader: the need to avoid retelling the same story or presenting the same set of facts in several places. I found, for example, that several men were involved with the issue of "Assumption"; rather than define this in each biographical sketch I made it a separate entry for cross reference. Some pre-Revolutionary individuals are included only because their names had a way of cropping up in the literature of the Revolution (e.g., James Wolfe, George Whitefield, and Gov. Norborne Botetourt), whereas other more important individuals have been omitted for the opposite reason (e.g., Gov. William Berkeley, William Penn).

For this work to be useful not only to serious scholars and researchers but also to general readers and toilers in the high school library, it contains details and explanations that are valuable to some readers but not to others.

From my source citations it is apparent that this book is based on recognized secondary works and authorities. I have taken particular pains to note results of the most recent scholarship, much of which revises traditional views of the American Revolution.

Since this is a *reference* book, it was necessary to fragment the history of an era and to tie the fragments together with "cover articles" and cross references. Cross references are indicated by SMALL CAPITALS, *but only when there is some reason for you to consult this cross reference for pertinent information*. In other words, I have not mechanically put in small capitals every name or topic for which there happens to be a separate article. As an example, here is an excerpt from the entry on Gen. Gold S. Silliman: "During the N.Y. Camp'n. he had commanded his regiment at Long Island and White Plains. In 1777 he saw action in the DANBURY RAID. Captured by the Loyalists, he was paroled on Long Island and exchanged a year later for his Yale classmate Thomas JONES." Now, there are articles on the N.Y. Camp'n., the battles of Long Island and White Plains, and on Loyalists; but these have not been cross referenced because they say nothing about Silliman. And does the intelligent reader have to be told that this book contains articles on these subjects? On the other hand, cross reference *is* made to the DANBURY RAID and Thomas JONES because these articles do contain information about Silliman.

To summarize my plan of "cover articles" let's assume that you are cast ashore on a desert isle with this book and decide you want to reconstruct a history of the American Revolution from its fragments. You would start with the article entitled BACKGROUND AND ORIGINS . . . ; this would refer you to another major "cover article," COLONIAL WARS, and to minor articles on such topics as MERCANTILISM, the NAVIGATION ACTS, ROYAL GOVERNMENT IN AMERICA, etc., etc.

The three major aspects of the Revolution itself, political, diplomatic, and military, are dealt with under:

CONTINENTAL CONGRESS
DIPLOMACY OF THE AMERICAN REVOLUTION
MILITARY AFFAIRS

Common sense would lead you to such headings and most others in this book, but other headings of what might be called topical articles are necessarily arbitrary. In this Bicentennial Edition I have therefore included an abbreviated index of major cover articles and of certain topical articles I would like to bring to the reader's attention. This index starts on page 1289.

Maps and sketches are placed throughout the text where they are most convenient for reference and as visual aids. The Index of Maps, starting on page 1275, gives not only the page location of these maps (indicated in SMALL CAPITALS) but also indexes the major place names on these maps.

As for bibliography, a main list is at the back of the book and classified bibliographies follow many individual articles. Much new scholarship has been published since this encyclopedia appeared in 1966, and there should be a great outpouring during the bicentennial years. It would be futile to attempt with each new printing of my book to update the bibliographies—those accompanying individual articles and the main one at the end of this book—but it is possible to identify the works cited in revised articles and to point out some of the most significant new historical works recently published and in preparation. This information appears in an addendum following the main bibliography (see page 1273).

Much valuable information has been furnished me by correspondents, particularly genealogists and family historians. I have been disappointed, hovever, by the fact that more users of this book have not found errors. It would be reassuring to believe that this is because my book has few errors remaining in it after two reprintings, but I know the main reason is that so much work remains to be done by scholars in the field of Revolutionary War history and biography. This somewhat surprising fact has been brought home to me during the four years I have labored to produce a guide to historic sites (*Landmarks of the American Revolution*). I ask that readers who detect errors in this book will send corrections that will enable me to keep improving it as future printings are undertaken.

I fervently hope that a new generation will be inspired by the bicentennial years to take an intelligent interest in the history of our national origins and that this book will have some modest part in stimulating that interest.

September, 1973

M M B
2343 S. Nash Street
Arlington, Virginia 22202

LIST OF ABBREVIATIONS

(Also used but not listed are months, compass directions, colonies and states, universities, etc. A number in parentheses following the name of a warship indicates the number of guns.)

A.A.G. . . . Assistant Adjutant General
A.D.C. . . . Aide de Camp
A.G. . . . . Adjutant General
A.W.O.L. . . Absent (Absence) Without Leave
Adj. . . . . Adjutant
Adm. . . Admiral
Arty. . . Artillery
Asst. . . . Assistant
Assy. . . Assembly
Atty. . . . Attorney

b. . . . . Born
B.G. . . . Brigadier General
Bn. . . . Battalion
Br. . . . Bridge
Brig. . . . Brigade
Btry. . . . Battery (of Artillery)
Bvt. . . . Brevet

c. . . . . *Circa* (about)
C. in C. . Commander in Chief
C.G. . . . Commanding General
C.H. . . . Court House
C.R. . . . Cross Roads
Ch. . . . Church
Cal. . . . Caliber
Capt. . . Captain
Capt.-Lt. . Captain-Lieutenant (a rank between these two)
Cav. . . . Cavalry
Chev. . . Chevalier [see article]
C.O. . . . Commanding Officer
Co. . . . Company
co. . . . County
Comm. of Corresp. . Committee of Correspondence
Comm. of Safety . Committee of Safety
Commiss. . Commissary
Cong. . . Congress
Cont'l(s). . Continental(s)

Cont'l.
Cong. . . . Continental Congress
Cpl. . . . . Corporal

d. . . . . Penny, pence; died
D.O.W. . . Died of Wounds
Decl. of Indep. . Declaration of Independence
Dep. . . . Deputy
Dept. . . Department
Div. . . . Division

Engr(s). . Engineer(s)
Exped. . . Expedition

Ft. . . . Fort

G.C.B. . . (Knight), Grand Cross of the Bath
G.H.Q. . . General Headquarters
G.O. . . . General Orders
Gen. . . . General
Gov. . . . Governor

H.M.S. . . His Majesty's Ship
Hq. . . . Headquarters

I.G. . . . Inspector General
Ibid. . . . *Ibidem* (used in a source citation to refer to the work mentioned in the preceding citation)
Indep. . . Independent, independence
Inf. . . . Infantry

J.A.G. . . Judge Advocate General
J.O.P. . . Justice of the Peace

xvii

K.C.B. . . . Knight Commander of the Bath
K.I.A. . . . Killed in Action

L.D. . . . . Line of Departure
L. of C. . . Line of Communications (see article)
Lt. . . . . . Lieutenant, Light (Artillery, Infantry, etc.)

m. . . . . . Married
M.A. . . . Master of Arts
M.D. . . . Doctor of Medicine
M.P. . . . . Member of Parliament
Maj. . . . . Major
Med. . . . Medical
Mil. . . . . Military

N.C.O. . . . Noncommissioned Officer
N.S. . . . . New Style (see also O.S.)
N.Y.C. . . . New York City

O.S. . . . . Old Style (see article on CALENDARS. . . .)
Op. cit. . . *Opere citato*, "in the work cited" (used in a source citation to refer to a specified author's work that has been named earlier in the article)
Opns. . . . Operations (of a military force)
Ord. . . . . Ordnance (branch of the Army)

Ph.D. . . . Doctor of Philosophy
Post . . . . Posterior, "later" (used in a source citation to indicate that the specified author's work is listed later in the article)
P.M. . . . . Provost Marshal
P.O.W. . . . Prisoner(s) of War
Prov. . . . Province, Provincial
Pt. . . . . . Point (used in maps)
Pvt. . . . . Private (soldier)

Q.M. . . . Quartermaster
Q.M.G. . . Quartermaster General

R. . . . . . River
Regt. . . . Regiment
Res. . . . . Reserve(s)
Rev. . . . . Revolution

s. . . . . . Shilling
Sec. . . . . Secretary
Sgt. . . . . Sergeant
Supt. . . . Superintendent
Surg. . . . Surgeon

Treas. . . . Treasury

U.S. . . . . United States

Vols. . . . Volunteers

W.I.A. . . . Wounded in Action

ENCYCLOPEDIA OF
THE AMERICAN REVOLUTION

A

AACHEN, Treaty of. 18 Oct. 1748. This ended the War of the AUSTRIAN SUCCESSION and restored Louisburg to France. (Aachen is known also as Aix-la-Chapelle.)

ABATIS (ah'bah tee). An obstacle formed of trees felled toward the enemy.

ABENAKI. More correctly called Abnaki, and known to the Puritans as Tarrateens (*Handbook of American Indians,* "Abnaki"), they were a loose confederacy of Algonkian (or Algonquin) tribes located in what now is the state of Maine and southern New Brunswick. Under the influence of a strong French mission, centered at Norridgewock on the Kennebec, the Abenaki and French raided the northern New England settlements during the Colonial Wars, particularly King William's War, 1689–97. Resumption of French-inspired attacks after the latter war led New Englanders to organize an expedition in 1724 that destroyed Norridgewock. The Kennebec Indians were dispersed, mainly into Canada, and their new capital was located on the St. Francis River near its junction with the St. Lawrence. The Penobscot, Passamaquoddy, and Malecite did not migrate, however, and in 1749 the former tribe made peace with the English. Some other Indians returned to Norridgewock, but this place was raided again in 1749 and in 1754 its inhabitants returned to St. Francis. There they were attacked by Robert ROGERS and virtually eliminated as a military threat. (*Concise D.A.H.,* "Indian Tribes")

ABERCROMBIE. The British officers famous for their association with the American Revolution are listed in *D.N.B.* under the spelling ABERCROMBY.

ABERCROMBY, James. ?–1775. British officer. A.D.C. to Amherst in 1759, he was promoted to Lt. Col. in 1770. He died of wounds on 24 June '75 after leading the grenadiers in the assaults at Bunker Hill. Brother of Ralph and Robert ABERCROMBY, he is not the son of James ABERCROMBY (1706–1781), as is sometimes stated (e.g., Appleton's).

ABERCROMBY, James. 1706–1781. British officer. Born into a wealthy family, he was a Col. in 1746, Maj. Gen. in 1756. During the COLONIAL WARS he commanded a large force until relieved on 9 Nov. '58 after his fiasco at Ticonderoga (7 July '58). In the merry tradition of the degenerate British military service of the period he went on to become a Lt. Gen. in '59 and a full Gen. in '72. Understandably, he is not in *D.N.B.*

ABERCROMBY, Sir Ralph. 1734–1801. British officer. This British officer figures in the American Revolution only as the famous brother of Robert (1740–1827) and James (?–1775). By opposing the government's coercion of the colonies, Ralph forfeited his own chances for military advancement in 1775–82. He nevertheless became a Maj. Gen. in 1787, distinguished himself in Flanders, and went on to become the top soldier of his generation. With Sir John Moore he is credited with revitalizing the British Army. (*D.N.B.*)

1

He was mortally wounded in Egypt while leading a successful campaign against Napoleon's troops.

ABERCROMBY, Sir Robert. 1740–1827. British officer. After outstanding service in the French and Indian War (Ticonderoga, Niagara, Montreal), he became a Capt. in 1761 and retired two years later on half pay. In 1772 he became a Maj. and the next year was Lt. Col. of the 37th Foot. *D.N.B.* cites his "distinguished service" at Long Island (Aug. '76), Brandywine and Germantown (Sept. and Oct. '77), on the Charleston Expedition ('80), and at Yorktown ('81). Appleton's comments on his expedition to destroy American shipping on the Delaware in May, '78, his attack at CROOKED BILLET, Pa., his wound at Monmouth (28 June '78), and his action at Yorktown. (See "Abercromby's Sortie" in the article on YORKTOWN.) In 1782 he was promoted to Col. and made A.D.C. to the King. He distinguished himself in nine years of fighting in India, becoming a Maj. Gen. in 1790, succeeding Cornwallis as C. in C. in '93. An eye disease forced him to return to England in Apr. '97, and he died at the age of 87 as the oldest general in the British Army. Less of a leader than his brother Ralph (see above), he still ranks among Britain's greatest generals; with his fame as a soldier he returned from India with a reputation for incorruptibility. (*D.N.B.*) See also RIFLEMEN.

ABNAKI. See ABENAKI.

ABOVILLE, François Marie, Count d'. 1730–1817. French officer. Commander of French artillery at YORKTOWN. A B.G. in 1788, he commanded the French Army in the North in 1792, was governor of Brest in 1807, and as Lt. Gen. became a peer after the Bourbon restoration.

ABRAHAM, Plains of (Quebec). See PLAINS OF ABRAHAM, 13 Sept. 1759, 15 Nov. '75, and 6 May '76.

ACADIA (Nova Scotia). Named for the Greek region that the French call *Acadie* and the British call Arcadia, the word was spelled Acadia or Arcadia in accordance with the two derivations. When first mentioned in a French grant of 1603, Acadia stretched from Cape Breton to the latitude of Philadelphia. Since the British not only claimed but also occupied the region as far north as the present state of Maine, Acadia soon came to mean the area now known as New Brunswick and Nova Scotia, or the country actually occupied by the Acadians. In 1621 the British crown granted Acadia—with its undefined boundaries—to Sir Wm. Alexander and renamed it Nova Scotia. The area was restored to France in 1632, captured by New England colonials in 1654, and returned to France in 1670. When England regained it in 1713 (Treaty of Utrecht) the agreement gave them "all Nova Scotia with its ancient boundaries." The French maintained that this meant only the peninsula of Nova Scotia. Since only the latter area was colonized (pop. 10,000 in 1755), and since its settlers were known as Acadians, the names Acadia and Nova Scotia can be considered synonymous after 1713. (Expulsion of the Acadians, dramatized by Longfellow's *Evangeline,* started 8 Oct. '55, during the French and Indian War; it was prompted by British fears that since many Acadians refused to swear loyalty to England they might constitute a "fifth column.")

ACHARD DE BONVOULOIR, Julien. 1749–1783. French secret agent. On 8 Sept. '75 this man sailed for America from London with instructions from the French ambassador, the

Comte de Guines, to send back secret reports on the situation in the colonies and the possibilities of covertly supporting the rebels. Masquerading as a merchant of Antwerp, and instructed by Guines never even to *pronounce* the word *French,* he arranged a meeting with Benjamin Franklin and three other members of the Secret Committee. Although the personable French gentleman disclaimed any official connections and said that he was there only to explore the possibilities of making some private deals to supply the Americans with munitions, the committeemen sensed his real mission. This is apparent from the record of questions they submitted to him in writing: could the gentleman inform them of the official French attitude toward the colonists, and if they were favorable how could this be authenticated? How could they go about getting two qualified engineers? Would it be possible to get arms and other war supplies directly from France, paid for in American products, and would French ports be open for such an exchange? Although Bonvouloir reported to his superiors that he had stoutly maintained his position as a private citizen, and promised only that he would present their requests where they might be satisfied, the seed of secret aid was planted in Philadelphia and in Paris. Bonvouloir's report of 28 Dec. '75 came at a time when American military fortunes were high enough for France to feel the rebels were strong enough to be worth backing against England: the Boston garrison was bottled up; Montreal had fallen; and Quebec was menaced. Congress saw through Bonvouloir's sham and on 3 Mar. '76 named Silas Deane its emissary to find out what he could do in Paris to get French aid. This led to the establishment of HORTALEZ & CIE. The French were afraid that Bonvouloir had been

so transparent in the accomplishment of his mission that he would embarrass the court officially, and on 13 June '76 Vergennes, who had reluctantly approved the mission, wrote to Guines: "I strongly hope M. de Bonvouloir has been sufficiently prudent (*avisé*) to undertake his return voyage." The foreign minister, not at all pleased with the way the agent had handled his difficult task, willingly sent the ambassador 200 louis Bonvouloir needed to get home, the latter having exhausted his advance of 4,800 livres. (Lasseray, 117)

Who was this man? When de Guines wrote Vergennes on 28 July '75 to recommend that he be sent on this mission he submitted the following information: "M. de Bonvouloir, French gentleman, cousin-german of M. le marquis de Lambert [a close friend of Count C. F. de Broglie], one of whose brothers is a captain in the regiment of the Commissary General and another is in the Lyonnais [Regt.], was a volunteer in the Cape Regiment; due to sickness he left San Domingo for a change of air; he has been in all the English colonies; he has just come from there; he was given an offer to join the rebel army; he has established sources of information there.... He has given me excellent reports on all he has seen and would like nothing better than to return there." During his travels in America in 1774 Bonvouloir had represented himself as being a French officer; Vergennes agreed to de Guines' request that he be given a commission as Lt. of Inf. for such use as he might find for it during his secret mission, but the Foreign Minister pointed out that the official records had nothing to indicate that this man had ever been associated with the Cape Regt. (Lasseray, 113, 114, and *n.*) After his book had gone to press Commander Lasseray was able to add the following information:

Julien Achard de Bonvouloir was born in what is now the Dept. of Orne (in Normandy), was a *lieutenant de frégate* on 10 July '79, became a *lieutenant d'artillerie,* and on 30 Sept. '81 was made *aide-major* in the expeditionary corps in India. He died 18 Apr. '83 near Pondichéry. (*Op. cit.,* 650)

ACLAND,* John Dyke. d. 1778. British politician and officer. In the Parliament of 1774 he became a prominent advocate of vigorous action against the American colonies, and in the same year he joined the 33d Foot as an ensign (23 Mar.). He later became Maj. of the 20th Foot. In 1776 he went to Canada and served under Guy Carleton before taking part in Burgoyne's Offensive as commander of the grenadiers. His remarkable young wife, whom he married in Sept. '70, accompanied him to America and became a famous camp follower. Lady Harriet (Christian Henrietta Caroline, 1750–1815) was the daughter of the Earl of Ilchester. She had been painted by Sir Joshua Reynolds as a girl standing at her mother's knee and again in 1771–72 (*D.N.B.*). Throwing herself into the life of the American wilderness, she nursed her husband through a serious illness at Chambly and at Skenesboro, N.Y., tended the wounds he sustained at Hubbardton, 7 July '77. Just before Burgoyne crossed the Hudson, Maj. Acland and Lady Harriet narrowly escaped from their burning tent after a pet dog knocked over a candle. At the Second Battle of SARATOGA, 7 Oct. '77, Acland was shot through both legs and abandoned when the Americans overran the redoubt his grenadiers had been defending. James Wilkinson saved him from a murderous boy who was about

* Although spelled Ackland in most American histories, the name in *D.N.B.* is Acland.

to kill him as he lay helpless, and had him evacuated to the quarters of Gen. Poor. His valet is alleged to have been wounded while searching for his master. When Lady Harriet learned that her husband was alive but seriously wounded she got Burgoyne's permission to try to join him. About sunset on 9 Oct. she started down the Hudson with her maid, the valet, Chaplain Brudenell, and a remarkable note from Burgoyne asking GATES' protection for this magnificent camp follower. (See Lossing, I, 67 *n.*) After a hazardous trip through a storm the boat was hailed by an American sentinel. When "the clear, silvery tones of a woman's voice" answered from the darkness, the soldier was "filled . . . with superstitious fear," says Lossing (*Op. cit.*). He and a comrade refused to let the boat land until Maj. Henry Dearborn arrived. Burgoyne later said she was kept waiting "seven or eight dark and cold hours," a version British writers are inclined to believe (*D.N.B.*), but American writers say the delay was a matter of a few minutes. Lady Harriet was chivalrously received and joined her husband the next morning.

Back in England on parole Acland resumed his tempestuous parliamentary career. He died on 22 Nov. '78 from the effects of a cold brought on by exposure during a duel. The oft-repeated story that he died defending American courage, that Lady Harriet "became a maniac, and remained so two years" (Lossing, *op. cit.*), and that she then married Chaplain Brudenell, "has no foundation in fact," according to *D.N.B.* The latter source does not mention the cause of the duel nor the fate of the opponent, but there may well be some truth to the story that the duel resulted from a dinner party argument with a Lt. Lloyd, who made supercilious remarks about the quality of British military opposition in America, and that he was killed in the encounter. (Lossing, *op. cit.,* 68 *n.*)

ACTIVE CASE. As explained in the biographical sketch of George Ross, the Cont'l. Cong. annulled the verdict of a Pa. court and ruled that the *Active* was the prize of Olmsted and his associates. Meanwhile, Benedict Arnold, commander in Philadelphia, had made a secret agreement with Olmsted that in return for one-half interest he would advance funds for the appeal and would use his influence with Cong. on their behalf. When the Pa. verdict was overruled, Arnold had an aide sell the prize, pay the $280 in costs and charges, and turn the rest of the money over to Olmsted *et al.* On failure of Judge Ross to yield, however, state authorities got possession of the £47,981 for which the cargo—not yet the sloop—had been sold, and Cong. did not feel justified in protesting. In 1809 the U.S. Supreme Court ordered the state of Pa. to pay all that the Cont'l. Cong. had awarded him. (Van Doren, *Secret History,* 177).

ACTS OF 1651, 1660, and 1663. See NAVIGATION ACTS.

ADAMS, John. 1735–1826. Patriot statesman, Signer, V.P. under Washington and 2d U.S. Pres. Mass. Great-great-grandson of Henry Adams, who reached America in 1640 (Page Smith, *Adams,* 3), he was the son of John (1691–1760) and Susanna Boylston Adams. Farmers, maltsters, and local officials, the Adams had been undistinguished beyond their village of Braintree (originally Mount Wollaston, now Quincy). John, the subject of this sketch, said in later years that his father's marriage into the prominent Boylston family had lifted the Adams from small-town obscurity. (*Ibid.*) Young John graduated from Harvard in 1755, was admitted to the Boston bar three years later, and slowly built up a law practice. In Oct. '64 he married the delightful Abigail, daughter of Rev. Wm. and Elizabeth Quincy Smith, which not only brought him a wife who would prove to be a lively and worthy partner as he rose to fame but who also gave him wide connections with prominent Mass. families.

Soon after graduating from Harvard, Adams had taken an interest in local politics and started writing for the newspapers. The Stamp Act crisis brought him into prominence as author of the resolutions of protest sent by Braintree to its representatives in the legislature and which were used by other towns as a model. This led to his association with Jeremiah Gridley and James Otis in presenting Boston's memorial on the closing of the courts and started Adams' long contest with Lt. Gov. Thos. Hutchinson. Early in 1768 he moved to Boston, where he enlarged his practice and became even more prominent in political affairs. He defended John Hancock on charges of smuggling and after the BOSTON "MASSACRE," 5 Mar. '70, he and Josiah Quincy defended the British guard commander and his men. Unlike his radical cousin Sam Adams, John disapproved of the Stamp Act riots and other violence but based his opposition to the mother country's coercive policy on strictly legal grounds. He claimed to have the only complete set of British statutes-at-large in the colonies. (W. C. Ford in *D.A.B.*)

He was offered the post as advocate general in the court of admiralty but saw that this was an attempt to break his association with the patriot leaders and declined. In the spring of 1771 ill health caused him to leave Boston and return to Braintree, but swiftly moving political developments soon brought him back to Boston. He heartily approved the Boston Tea Party, but continued to oppose mob violence. Although he saw that independence was a possibility, he dreaded it. (*D.A.B.*) On 14 June '74 he was chosen a delegate to the Cont'l. Cong., and sat with each succeeding Congress through the election of 4 Dec. '77. (See below) In the 1st Cong. he helped draft the declaration to the King and a declaration of rights. In the 2d Cong. he unsuccessfully opposed further petitions to the King; he was largely responsible for Washington's selection as C. in C., a move calculated to draw Va. into closer support of the Revolution. Having come around to the conviction that independence was desirable, on 7 June '76 he seconded the resolution of Richard Henry Lee to this end. The next day he was appointed on the committee that drafted the Decl. of Indep. and Thos. Jefferson, the principal author, credited Adams with getting the document approved by Congress. Although he had no important part in writing the Decl. of Indep. (*D.A.B.*), Adams did draft a plan of treaties with foreign powers. On 13 June he was placed on the newly created Board of War, where his duties were onerous. He took part in the PEACE CONF. ON STATEN IS., 11 Sept. '76. Worn down by his duties and having business at home, he left Philadelphia on 13 Oct. and rejoined Congress 1 Feb. '77, when they were at Baltimore. Here he continued to be involved in the most important and vexatious affairs of the delegates: the problems of foreign officers, the loss of Ticonderoga, the Saratoga Convention, the squabbling of American officers for advancement and recognition, the problems of prices, currency, and loans. He was not involved in the CONWAY CABAL, but did not consider Washington irreplaceable.

John Adams left Congress on 26 Oct.

'77 never, as it turned out, to return. On 28 Nov. he was elected to succeed Silas Deane as commissioner to France, and on 13 Feb. '78 he and his 10-year-old son, John Quincy Adams (who would be 6th U.S. Pres.), sailed for Bordeaux. The New England Yankee did not like France, the French, or his fellow commissioners. In May he drafted a plan for reducing the squabbling commission to a single representative. This was agreed to by Franklin—with whom Adams lived—was eventually approved by Congress, and on 22 Mar. '79 Adams embarked at Nantes to sail home. The French government detained him until the middle of June so that he might accompany the French minister. Adams and Gérard reached Boston on 2 Aug. aboard the *Sensible.* A week later Adams was named to represent Braintree in the convention called to draw up the state constitution, and this document was largely his.

On 25 Sept. '79 Adams and Jay were nominated to negotiate a peace treaty, but on the 27th Jay was given the mission of negotiating a treaty with Spain, and Adams was named minister plenipotentiary for drawing up a treaty of peace and of commerce with Great Britain. Embarking on the *Sensible,* 13 Nov., with his sons John and Charles, Adams landed at El Ferrol (N.W. tip of Spain) on 8 Dec. and reached Paris 5 Feb. '80 after an overland voyage. Not believing that it was the moment to initiate peace negotiations, the French government got Adams, against his judgment, to keep his mission a secret. This put him in a delicate position with Franklin, who was not informed of Adams' mission. Adams was soon at loggerheads with Vergennes and without French agreement he went to Holland on 27 July to look into securing a loan for the U.S. Although Congress endorsed Vergennes' position that the peace mission of Adams should not yet be made known to Great Britain, this body refused to accept the minister's request that Adams be placed under French direction. On 29 Dec. he was made minister to the United Province (Holland) as successor to Henry Laurens and was authorized to join the new Armed Neutrality League. Adams made valuable connections in Holland but the country had no material assistance to offer the U.S.

On 15 June '81 Congress established a five-man commission, including Adams, to handle the treaty negotiations originally entrusted to Adams alone, and on 12 July they revoked his powers to treat with Great Britain on commerce. After securing Dutch recognition of the U.S. (19 Apr. '82), arranging a loan, and bringing about a treaty of amity and commerce (Oct. '82), Adams reached Paris on 26 Oct. '82 to take a key part in the PEACE NEGOTIATIONS that resulted in the final PEACE TREATY, 3 Sept. '83.

In the summer of 1784 Adams took a house in Auteuil and Mrs. Adams joined him with their daughter. On 24 Feb. '85 he was appointed envoy to the Court of St. James. He went to London in May and was received by GEORGE III. Criticism by European writers led him to publish in 1787 a three-volume *Defense of the Constitution of the United States*. While this ably refuted the criticism in Europe and was favorably received in America because the convention for framing a Federal constitution was then assembling, it offended many Americans with its aristocratic overtones. In one sentence, for example, he suggested that the country should have a senate composed of "the rich, the well-born and the able." Feeling that his task in London was done, Adams asked for recall and letters were sent to him in Feb. '88.

In the election of 1789 John Adams received 34 out of 69 votes for vice president and won what he called in a letter to Abigail, "the most insignificant office that ever the invention of man contrived or his imagination conceived." His only means of exerting influence was by a deciding vote when the Senate was equally divided, but it happened that this situation arose no fewer than 20 times—more frequently than at any time since. As political parties formed out of the controversies of the next few years, Adams became second only to Alexander Hamilton in the Federalist hierarchy.

In 1796 he defeated Thos. Jefferson to become president, despite the scheme of Alexander HAMILTON that might, under the pretext of assuring Jefferson's defeat, have made Thos. Pinckney our second president. After an administration marked by domestic intrigues that embittered his later life and by complex problems of foreign policy, Adams was defeated by Thos. Jefferson and did not serve a second term. He lived to see his son, John Quincy, become president in 1824. In retirement he wrote of the history he had helped make, and although much of his work is valuable it is marred by a notoriously bad memory. A widower since 28 Oct. 1818, John Adams died on the 50th anniversary of the Decl. of Indep. His last words are said to have been "Thomas Jefferson still survives," but the latter had passed on a few hours earlier.

Of average height, vigorous and florid, he became corpulent as he got older. Portraits by Peale (who called him "a tender, soft, affectionate creature"), Copley, and John Trumbull show a high brow and a round face in which kindliness and a trace of humor seem to compete with a feeling that he should look stern and unbending for posterity. Completely honest and outspoken, he was not made for big-league politics or diplomacy. Jefferson wrote of him in 1787, "He is vain, irritable, and a bad calculator of the force and probable effect of the motives which govern men. This is all the ill which can possibly be said of him."

A recent biography is Page Smith, *John Adams*, 2 vols., 1962. *D.A.B.* lists 21 of what W. C. Ford calls his more important published writings. Among these are *Letters . . . to his Wife* (1841), which constitute Vol. III and Vol. IV supplementing *Letters of Abigail Adams* (1841), the two series being republished in 1876 as *Familiar Letters of John Adams and his wife Abigail Adams*. His grandson, Charles Francis Adams, edited the 10-vol. *Works* (1850–56) of which the first volume is a biography. See also Catherine D. Bowen, *John Adams and the American Revolution*, 1950 and Gilbert Chinard, *Honest John Adams*, 1933.

His son, John Quincy (1767–1848), was 6th Pres. The latter's son, Charles Francis (1807–1886), was a diplomat, statesman, and historical writer. The sons of Charles Francis were also distinguished men: C. F. (Jr.), 1835–1915, was a railroad expert, Civil War Union officer, economist, and historian; Henry (Brooks), 1838–1918, was a historian and man of letters who is best remembered for his *Education of Henry Adams* (1907).

John was a second cousin of Samuel ADAMS.

ADAMS, Samuel. 1722–1803. Radical patriot, political agitator, master propagandist, Signer. Mass. He rose from obscurity in 1765 with the Stamp Act crisis, and he fell from eminence as the chief figure of the Revolution when Congress got down to the business of constructive statesmanship after the Decl. of Indep. in 1776. But during the decade that intervened, Sam Adams

was "truly the Man of the Revolution," as Thos. Jefferson called him.

He and John Adams were second cousins, both being great-great-grandsons of Henry, who established the Adams family in Braintree (later Quincy), and being great-grandsons of Joseph Adams (b. 1626). Old Samuel Adams, the father of our Sam, was a deacon in Old South Church in Boston and was instrumental in establishing New South Church. Deacon Adams served at various times as justice of the peace, selectman, and member from Boston in the House of Representatives. Young Sam graduated from Harvard in 1740. He then "studied law to please his father, but gave it up to please his mother." (Carl Lotus Becker in *D.A.B.*) After a few months in the counting house of Thos. Cushing, he borrowed £1,000 from his father to start his own business, loaned half of this to a friend who could not repay it, and promptly lost the remaining half. He then joined his father in the family brewery, "where it may be supposed he did little good for lack of capacity, and little harm from lack of responsibility." (*Ibid.*)

Deacon Adams died in 1748. A short time later Sam's mother died and he found himself in possession of a considerable estate that included the fine family home on Purchase Street, Boston, and the thriving brewery. Within 10 years, however, he had dissipated this inheritance and an unsuccessful attempt was made by creditors to seize his house. During the period 1756–64 he was tax collector, and in this post he accumulated an arrears of about £8,000 in uncollected back taxes. With this record of failure in managing his own affairs, the 42-year-old Sam Adams stepped onto the stage of history to manage the American Revolution.

Some years before 1764, when the

end of Salutary Neglect marked the start of Adams' political career, he had been identified with the popular party. Lt. Gov. Thos. Hutchinson was the outstanding figure in the wealthy, socially prominent, and exclusive group of families that ruled the province. (Leaders of the "popular party," incidentally, included some of the wealthiest men in Mass.)

Adams' zest for the task of discrediting the opposition party was heightened by personal reasons for wanting revenge against Hutchinson, who had caused Deacon Adams to take a large financial loss when Hutchinson led the movement to dissolve the Land Bank (1741), and who held that Adams had "made defalcation" in the matter of Boston's taxes. In 1764 Adams drafted instructions for Boston's representatives in the legislature. (Cousin John took his first step toward national prominence in doing the same thing for Braintree.) In 1765 Sam Adams again wrote the instructions for the "Boston Seat," and on 27 Sept. he was elected to fill the vacancy left by Oxenbridge Thatcher in the House. The night of 26–27 Aug. a Boston mob sacked the splendid home of HUTCHINSON. In 1766 the radicals gained control of the House of Representatives, five prominent conservatives including Hutchinson, Andrew Oliver, and Peter Oliver being excluded. Adams was re-elected in 1766 and served continuously until 1774. He rapidly assumed the leadership of this body, used his influence to bring about the recall of Gov. Bernard, and then massed his political artillery on Lt. Gov. Hutchinson. Adams organized the opposition against the Townshend Acts, helped form the Non-Importation Association of 1768, drafted the famous "Circular Letter" to the assemblies of other provinces and that for the "Convention" of the patriot party held in Boston in 1768.

(*D.A.B.*) Previously he had sparked the formation of the Sons of Liberty. In 1747 he had helped found a political club, and by 1763 he had joined the influential Caucus Club.

While not credited with being an original political thinker, Adams had remarkable skill not only in organizing political strength but also in writing polemics. He based most of his arguments against the mother country on Natural Law and "universal Reason," and he wrote extensively to prominent leaders on both sides of the Atlantic as well as for the newspapers. His main task, however, was to get the patriots mad at the British and keep them mad; there were times when this was by no means easy. Although writers continue to maintain that Adams "never openly countenanced violence" (*D.A.B.*), whenever mob action took place around Boston you did not have to look far behind the scenes to find him. He could deplore the sacking of Hutchinson's mansion and the Boston "Massacre," but his innocence in these affairs is somewhat academic.

For two years following the repeal of the Townshend Revenue Act, 12 Apr. '70, Adams was virtually alone as guardian of the Revolutionary flame. "Yet it was during these years of declining interest that Adams made what was perhaps his chief contribution to the Revolution by keeping the dying controversy alive." (*D.A.B.*) In 1771 Hutchinson, now Gov. of Mass., wrote "I doubt whether there is a greater incendiary in the King's dominion. . . ."

Adams worked during this period to set up a revolutionary organization. On 2 Nov. '72 the Boston Town Meeting, on his motion, appointed "a committee of correspondence . . . to state the rights of the Colonists and of this Province in particular, as men, as Christians, and as Subjects; and to communicate the same to the several towns and to the world." Adams had already written to the towns about this project; now he urged them to follow Boston's lead. In this matter he may be credited with initiating revolutionary government in Mass. (*Ibid.*) and sowing the seed in the other colonies. Bringing about the HUTCHINSON LETTERS AFFAIR he not only weakened his old political foes further but also aroused public opinion against the crown officials. His next triumph was the BOSTON TEA PARTY, 16 Dec. '73. He took the lead in opposing the Intolerable Acts (1774). Learning that other colonies were unwilling to adopt nonintercourse measures independently, Adams concluded that an intercolonial congress was an "absolute necessity." On 17 June '74 he moved that the House of Representatives appoint delegates to such a congress; this was adopted, and he was chosen one of the five representatives. Before this congress convened in Philadelphia he had an active part in organizing the convention that adopted the SUFFOLK RESOLVES, Sept. '74. Reaching Philadelphia for the 2d Cont'l. Cong., he favored immediate independence, proposed a confederation of colonies that were ready for independence, supported the resolution that independent state governments be formed, and supported adoption of the Decl. of Indep. (There is some question as to whether Adams provoked the killings at Lexington and whether the actions at LEXINGTON AND CONCORD, 19 Apr. '75, were prompted by an effort by the British to capture Sam Adams and John Hancock. These two were on the scene, however. Both were specifically excluded from the offer of pardon issued to the "infatuated multitude" by Gage on 12 June '75. [This was written by BURGOYNE and is mentioned also under BOSTON SIEGE.])

When he signed the Decl. of Indep.

for which he had worked so long and so effectively, Samuel Adams in effect signed his resignation from Revolutionary leadership. Although he served in the Cont'l. Cong. from 1774 until 1781 he showed no talent for constructive statesmanship; his influence was destructive. "His career in Congress was marred by factiousness, intrigue and broils," comments a recent biographer. "His weaknesses are most apparent in his attempts to control the American army during the war and in the protracted feuds he carried on with his political enemies in Congress." (Miller, *Adams,* 344) Although *D.A.B.* says Adams was not, as charged by Hancock, implicated in the CONWAY CABAL to remove Washington as C. in C., Miller says he was involved but "carefully covered up all traces of his work...." (*Ibid.,* 349)

In Apr. '81 he returned to Boston, where he never recovered his former influence. He sat with the convention that drafted the state constitution (1779-80), and became state senator and council member. Much to his surprise and irritation he could never win the governorship from the popular John Hancock, but he was Lt. Gov. from 1789 to 1793, became Gov. on Hancock's death, and was elected to the office during the period 1794-97. Despite his popular sympathies he opposed Shays's Rebellion. As a member of the convention in 1788 to ratify the Constitution, he first opposed but finally supported it.

A grandson, Wm. V. Wells, who wrote the laudatory but carefully and thoroughly researched *Life and Public Services of Samuel Adams* (3 vols., 1865), gives this description: "His stature was a little above the medium height. * * * His gestures were animated, and in conversation there was a slight tremulous motion of the head. His complexion was florid, and his eyes dark blue. The eyebrows were heavy, almost to bushiness, and contrasted remarkably with the clear forehead, which, at the age of seventy, had but few wrinkles. The face had a benignant but care-worn expression, blended with a native dignity (some have said majesty) of countenance which never failed to impress strangers." (Quoted in Appleton's) Copley's portrait of Adams, painted about 1770, is in the Boston Museum of Fine Arts.

Standard works, in addition to that of Wells mentioned above, are: H. A. Cushing (ed.), *The Writings of ...*, 4 vols. (1904–8); James K. Hosmer, *Samuel Adams* (1885); Ralph Volney Harlow, *Samuel Adams, Promoter of the American Revolution* (1923); and John C. Miller, *Sam Adams, Pioneer in Propaganda* (1936 and 1960). Becker says Hosmer generally follows Wells but is more discriminating; Harlow is "Freudian" and not always accurate in detail; Harlow ends up being as biased against Adams as grandson Wells is in favor of. (*D.A.B.*)

Second cousin of John ADAMS.

"ADDITIONAL CONT'L. REGTS." The Congressional resolution of 27 Dec. '76 authorized the raising of 16 regiments "at large." These were not numbered but, except for the "German" Regt., were known by the name of their colonels. The following information is from Heitman:

Col. David Forman assumed command of his regiment on 12 Jan. '77. The unit was never fully recruited, and on 1 July '78 was disbanded, personnel going mainly to the N.J. Line.

Col. Nathaniel Gist commanded his regiment from 11 Jan. '77 to 1 Jan. '81, absorbing Grayson's Regt. and Thruston's on 22 Apr. '79. (See below)

Col. Wm. Grayson's Regt. existed 11 Jan. '77–22 Apr. '79. (See Gist's Regt., above)

Col. Thos. Hartley commanded his regiment 1 Jan. '77–16 Dec. '78, at which time it became the 11th Pa.

Col. David Henley's Regt. was formed 1 Jan. '77 and on 22 Apr. '79 was consolidated with Henry Jackson's Regt. (below).

Col. Henry Jackson's Regt., 12 Jan. '77–23 July '80, became the 16th Mass. on the latter date.

Col. Wm. R. Lee's Regt., 1 Jan. '77–24 Jan. '78, was consolidated with Henry Jackson's Regt. on the latter date.

Col. Wm. Malcolm's Regt., 30 Apr. '77–22 Apr. '79, was consolidated with Spencer's Regt. on 22 Apr. '79. (See below)

Col. John Patton's Regt., 11 Jan. '77–13 Jan. '79, was commanded by Lt. Col. John Park after 3 Feb. '78, and (presumably) by Maj. Joseph Prowell to 13 Jan. '79. It then was broken up, part of its personnel going to the 11th Pa. and the rest to the Del. Regt.

Col. Moses Rawlings' Regt. was commanded by Rawlings from 12 Jan. '77 to 2 June '79. Its Lt. Col. has not been identified, if the regiment had one. Maj. Alexander Smith served with it from 11 Sept. '77 to 6 Sept. '80. No unit records have been found and Heitman believes it never was fully organized. Originally raised in 1776 in Va. and Md. as Stephenson's Md. and Va. Rifle Regt., it was reorganized in 1777 to become one of the "additional regiments."

Col. Henry Sherburne's Regt. was in existence 12 Jan. '77–1 Jan. '81.

Col. Oliver Spencer's Regt. was under his command during its existence, 15 Jan. '77–1 Jan. '81.

Col. Chas. M. Thruston's Regt. appears not to have been fully organized. Thruston commanded it 15 Jan. '77–1 Jan. '78. Its other regimental officers are not known. On 22 Apr. '79 the unit was merged with Gist's Regt.

Col. Seth Warner's Regt. was organized under the 5 July '76 resolve of Congress; not being attached to any state, it was regarded in 1777 as one of the 16 "additional regiments." Warner commanded until 1 Jan. '81.

Col. Sam'l. B. Webb commanded his regiment 1 Jan. '77–1 Jan. '81, on which date it was transferred to the Conn. Line and designated the 3d Conn.

German Regt. or Battalion was organized under the Congressional resolution of 25 May '76. Raised in Md. and Pa., but having no state identity, it was considered one of the 16 "additional regiments." It was commanded by Col. Nicholas Haussegger 17 July '76–19 Mar. '77, and by Col. (Baron) DeArendt from the latter date to 1 Jan. '81.

Unless otherwise noted, I have assumed that the regiments ceased to exist on the date Heitman shows their colonel no longer in command. Only the German Battalion (or Regt.) was commanded by two colonels in succession.

"ADDRESSERS." When 23 citizens of Marblehead, Mass., signed an address to retiring Gov. Hutchinson, and another 100 subscribed to another one welcoming Gen. Gage to Boston, the Whigs published the names of these "Addressers," along with those of "PROTESTERS" and "MANDAMUS COUNCILLORS." This marked them for persecution by the radicals.

ADJUTANTS. In the British Army staff as organized by Marlborough (1650–1722) the Adjutant began to assume more important duties at higher level as well as at the regimental level. He was an all-purpose staff officer and seems in some ways to have been the principal assistant of the regimental major, who was the operations officer.

In the higher staffs he stayed at the general's elbow and saw that orders were properly transmitted through the aides de camp; he was charged with the supervision of outposts and with security. (J. D. Hittle, *The Military Staff, Its History and Development,* 3d ed., Harrisburg, Pa., 1961, p. 138) "They not only controlled the personnel administration of the units, but much of their prestige was attributable to the fact that they were the staff officers through whom most of the general orders were issued." (*Ibid.,* 180)

The American Army adopted the British staff system and Horatio GATES became its first Adjutant General (A.G.) on 17 June '75. As evidence of the importance attached to this post, it is worth noting that Gates was the senior B.G. in the Cont'l. Army. Successive A.G.s (with their dates of appointment) were Col. Joseph Reed (5 June '76), B.G. Arthur St. Clair (22 Jan. '77), B.G. George Weedon (20 Feb. '77), Col. Morgan Connor (19 Apr. '77), Col. Timothy Pickering (18 June '77), Col. Alexander Scammell (5 Jan. '78), B.G. Edward Hand (8 Jan. '81–3 Nov. '83). (*A.A.,* 67)

John André was A.G. of Clinton's army during his negotiations with Benedict Arnold, having succeeded Lord Rawdon in Sept. '79. A.G. Baurmeister of the Hessian forces left the valuable *Journals* so often cited in accounts of the Revolution.

The Cont'l. Army (and others) had only one A.G.; the officer holding the comparable post in the other major field commands was known as a deputy A.G. and his immediate subordinate would be an assistant A.G.

ADMIRAL WARREN, The. Name used in many contemporary accounts for WARREN TAVERN, Pa.

ADMIRALS, "Colored." The 17th-century British navy was divided into operating squadrons known as the Red, White, and Blue. These squadrons subsequently became formal terms for designating seniority of the top flag officers in the following pecking order: Adm. of the Fleet (there was no Adm. of the Red), Adm. of the White, Adm. of the Blue, Vice-Adm. of the Red, Vice-Adm. of the White, and so on down to Rear-Adm. of the Blue. When a Capt. was first promoted to flag rank for active service he became Rear-Adm. of the Blue, and he would subsequently be promoted to Rear-Adm. of the White, etc. Although promotion to flag rank was generally by seniority, if an officer jumped over the heads of senior captains to become Rear-Adm. of the Blue these other captains were made Rear-Adms. on the retired list and were familiarily said to have been "yellowed," that is, to have become Rear-Adms. of a fictitious Yellow squadron. (David Hannay in *E.B.*, "Navy....")

ADMIRALTY COURTS. The Anglo-American branch of law dealing with maritime matters is known as admiralty law, the words *maritime* and *admiralty* being synonymous in this connotation. (F. R. Sandborn in *Ency. of Soc. Sc.*, IX-X, "Maritime Law") The High Court of Admiralty, raised in the 14th cent. to equal importance with the common law courts at Westminster Hall, spawned local or regional courts known as vice-admiralty courts. This last term comes from the fact that the courts existed in a district headed by a vice-admiral; when the court was set up in Halifax under the Act of 1764, for example, the Earl of Northumberland was appointed vice-admiral.

Although attempts to establish vice-admiralty courts in America date from early colonial days, these were long unsuccessful; most admiralty (i.e., maritime) cases were tried in ordinary civil courts. In 1678, however, the first of a long series of admiralty commissions was received by New York's governor, and as early as 1696 a vice-admiralty court was sitting in N.Y.C. In 1697, resulting from the Navigation Act of 1696, vice-admiralty courts were systematically organized in America. Their jurisdiction was wider than that of their English counterparts and had to do particularly with enforcing the unpopular Acts of Trade. (Sandborn, *op. cit.*) By an act of 1708 this jurisdiction was extended to include prize cases, and by the act of 1722 ("broad arrow policy") to include timber. Appeal was to the High Court of Admiralty at first; after 1748 this jurisdiction was shared with the Privy Council until the latter assumed sole appellate jurisdiction in 1766. (Morris, *E.A.H.*, 58)

The Townshend Acts (1767) extended the system, establishing vice-admiralty courts at Halifax, Boston, Philadelphia, and Charleston. The older courts remained in existence, but the new ones took over the appellate jurisdiction; the best authorities now say further appeal to England *was* permitted.

Vice-admiralty courts figured prominently in the background and origins of the Revolution. They were unpopular with the Americans first because their purpose was to enforce British revenue measures—to back up CUSTOMS COMMISSIONERS, prosecute smugglers, and help enforce the NAVIGATION ACTS.

Furthermore, these courts exercised summary jurisdiction and did not have trial by jury. Andrews points out, however, that the coercive and oppressive aspects of the vice-admiralty courts in the history of the colonies has been overstressed while their usefulness has been neglected. See C. M. Andrews, *Background....*

AFFLECK, Edmund. 1723?–1788. British commodore. He served throughout the Seven Years' War but had no opportunity to gain distinction. In 1757 he was promoted to Capt. In 1778 he sailed with the *Bedford* (74) to America with Adm. Byron, but his ship was shattered by a storm in Oct. and he returned to England. In 1779 he served under Sir Charles Hardy in the inglorious campaign in the Channel, but he distinguished himself in the action off Cape St. Vincent, 16 Jan. '80, as part of Sir George Rodney's command in the relief of Gibraltar. Sailing back to America with Adm. Graves, he took part in the action off CHESAPEAKE BAY, 16 Mar. '81, but since the peculiar tactics of Adm. Arbuthnot put him at the rear of the line he had no effective part in the battle. After this engagement and through the summer he was commissioner of the port of N.Y. Promoted to commodore, he resumed command of the *Bedford* and on 12 Nov. '81 sailed with Adm. Samuel Hood for the West Indies. Distinguishing himself at St. Kitts, 26 Jan. '82, and at Saints Passage in Apr. (see WEST INDIES . . .), he was made a baronet. At the end of the war he returned to England and was subsequently promoted to Rear Adm. of the Blue (see ADMIRALS, "Colored"), "but never hoisted his flag." (*D.N.B.*) A supporter of Pitt the Younger, he was an M.P. from 1782 until his death on 19 Nov. '88.

His brother Philip (1726–1799) served as a naval Capt. in the West Indies, where he commanded the *Triumph* (74). He was Adm. of the White when he died on 21 Dec. '99.

"AFRICAN ARROWS." This exotic term is used in Revolutionary War literature for the ancient technique of setting fire to defended places by the use of flaming arrows. The reason they were called *African* arrows is probably because a West Indian bow—presumably of African origin or design—happened to be available for use at FT. MOTTE,

S.C., 12 May '81, when the technique was employed with well-publicized success by Marion and "Light-Horse Harry" Lee. Flaming arrows were sometimes fired from muskets (see NINETY-SIX, 22 May. . . .).

AGITATION. To arouse, organize, and direct colonial action against British authority, political agitators played a vital role in events leading to the American Revolution. Whereas many colonists were loyal to the mother country, many others were politically indifferent. Various British acts prior to the STAMP ACT (1765) antagonized certain elements of colonial America. (See BACKGROUND. . . .) In Boston, hotbed of the Revolution, Samuel Adams emerged from obscurity to become the dean of agitators in opposing the Stamp Act. Repeal of this act led to relaxation of tensions, but Sam ADAMS saw to it that the SONS OF LIBERTY were ready to act when conditions again were ripe for agitation and provocation. The TOWNSHEND ACTS (1767) furnished the atmosphere within which agitation could be revived. After the 'LIBERTY AFFAIR and events associated with the MASS. CIRC. LTR., James OTIS asserted his influence (particularly with the rural element) to defeat the proposal of Sam Adams that armed resistance be used to prevent British troops from landing to garrison Boston. The BOSTON "MASSACRE," Mar. '70, was just what the agitators needed to mobilize popular resentment against the British, but another distressing interlude of political peace soon occurred. Then came the Tea Act, and the BOSTON TEA PARTY (1773) was the next triumph of Sam Adams. The INTOLERABLE ACTS (1774) so mobilized colonial ire that the agitators had relatively little difficulty from then on, although Sam Adams deserves credit not only for masterminding the "incidents" that turned the American masses against authority but also in organizing the small, hard-core cadres to exploit to the fullest the resulting disorders. As farfetched as it might seem, there is evidence that he contrived the situation on Lexington Green so as to provoke another British "atrocity." (This is discussed in the article on LEXINGTON AND CONCORD in the section headed "Who Fired First?")

See also NONIMPORTATION and PROPAGANDA.

AIX-LA-CHAPELLE, Treaty of. 18 Oct. 1748. Also called the Treaty of Aachen, this ended the War of the AUSTRIAN SUCCESSION, and restored Louisburg to France.

ALAMANCE, Battle of the, 16 May 1771. Climaxing the troubles with the REGULATORS of N.C., Gov. Tryon took the field and moved from New Bern toward Hillsboro. Gen. Hugh Waddell led a second column to Salisbury, and the plan was for him to link up with Tryon at Hillsboro. When Tryon reached his objective, without opposition, he learned that Waddell had been confronted by large numbers of Regulators and had not advanced. On 11 May Tryon started toward Salisbury, and on the 14th he reached the Alamance River. The Regulators were camped five miles away. Although they numbered 2,000 to Tryon's 1,000, the Regulators had no leader, no artillery, and many were unarmed. On 16 May Tryon formed in two lines outside the enemy encampment and demanded submission. Still without proper leadership, and divided among themselves as to whether they would do battle or merely make a show of resistance to gain concessions from the royal governor, the Regulators formed a crude line of defense. Tryon opened fire with his artillery, ordered in his infantry, and after something more than an hour of spo-

radic and uneven resistance he drove the insurgents from the field in disorder. Nine were killed on each side, and Tryon had 61 wounded. (Alden, *South,* 160. According to the *Concise D.A.H.* the Regulators had about 20 killed.) See REGULATORS for subsequent events.

ALBANY CONVENTION AND PLAN. 1754. At the request of British authorities, delegates from seven colonies (N.Y., Md., Pa., and the New England provinces) convened at Albany, N.Y., 19 June–10 July, ostensibly to make a single treaty with the Iroquois, whose traditional allegiance was shifting from the English to the French camp. Although the delegates did agree on a plan of union (see below), neither the British government nor the individual colonies found it acceptable. The convention is therefore cited as evidence that the American colonies were incapable of acting in concert against a common enemy, the French and Indians. The convention was significant, however, as a precedent for the later Cont'l. Cong.

The Albany Plan of Union was based on a plan drawn up in 1751 by Benj. Franklin, and probably contained modifications by Thos. Hutchinson. Although rejected, the plan deserves attention because it left its mark on many later schemes for confederation. All colonies except Georgia and Nova Scotia were to be united under a president general appointed and paid by the crown. The colonies would elect a grand council whose legislative power would be subject to approval by the president general and the crown; representation on this council would vary between two and seven delegates from each colony, depending on each colony's contribution to the general treasury. The president general and grand council were to have jurisdiction over Indian affairs, including new land purchases outside existing colonial boundaries.

ALEXANDER, Mr. Code name of Wm. RANKIN.

ALEXANDER ("Stirling"), William. 1726–1783. Cont'l. general. N.Y.–N.J. His father, James (1691–1756), fled from Scotland after serving with some distinction under the Old Pretender in 1715; in N.Y.C. he became a prominent lawyer and patriot, married the widow of a prosperous merchant, and was disbarred for a year because of his defense of John Peter Zenger. The son, William, received a good education, became an excellent mathematician and astronomer like his father, and was associated with his mother in the provision business she had carried on after the death of her first husband. At the start of the French and Indian War he served on the military staff of Mass. Gov. Shirley and in 1756 accompanied him to England, where the next year he defended him in Commons against charges of mismanaging military operations in 1755. While in England, Alexander undertook to claim the earldom of Stirling. Although he was unable to secure official claim to the title—hence I have called him "Alexander"—he and his wife were known to American contemporaries as Lord and Lady Stirling; their daughter was called Lady Kitty. Soon after returning to America in 1762 he moved ʋo Basking Ridge, N.J., where he established an elegant home. (It was ʋurned in 1920.) D. S. Freeman accepts the story that Alexander heard James GRANT make his arrogant boast in the House of Commons on 2 Feb. '75. (See GRANT) (*Washington*, IV, 377 and *n.*, citing Stryker) This is questionable inasmuch as it seems unlikely that Alexander revisited England after 1762. When the Revolution started he was a prominent Whig, a man of great wealth and social position who had

married the sister of Gov. Livingston, become a member of the N.J. Provincial Council, surveyor-gen., and had been one of the early governors of Kings College (now Columbia). "In either country he would have been distinguished for a fine, martial appearance and for his social arts if not for his intellect," writes D. S. Freeman, who also quotes Lafayette as judging him "braver than wise," (*Washington,* III, 322 and IV, 241A), yet on behalf of Alexander's mind it should be mentioned that he wrote a report on the transit of Venus in 1769 (*D.A.B.*).

Commissioned Col. 1st N.J. Regt. on 7 Nov. '75, he soon won distinction in capturing the BLUE MOUNTAIN VALLEY, although more of the credit may be due to Elias Dayton. On 1 Mar. '76 Alexander was appointed B.G. and on the 7th succeeded Chas. Lee as commander in N.Y.C., in which post he directed the construction of works including Forts Lee and Washington as well as the fortifications on Brooklyn Heights.

At LONG ISLAND, 27 Aug. '76, Gen. Alexander had his finest hour. Taken prisoner, he was exchanged the next month for Gov. Montfort BROWNE and Cortlandt Skinner and rejoined Washington in Westchester co. for the remaining phases of the N.Y. Campaign. At TRENTON, 26 Dec. '76, he performed well and on 19 Feb. '77 was one of five promoted to Maj. Gen.

After his outpost action at SHORT HILLS, N.J., 26 June '77, he spent a short period of time in the Hudson Highlands and rejoined the main army to fight at BRANDYWINE and GERMANTOWN. His report to Washington of Wilkinson's indiscreet remarks brought the CONWAY CABAL into the open. At MONMOUTH, 28 June '78, his handling of the artillery on the left wing was particularly commendable. He presided

over the LEE COURT MARTIAL, 4 July–
12 Aug. '78. After getting the thanks
of Congress for his support of Henry
Lee's raid on Paulus Hook, he directed
the mismanaged STATEN ISLAND EX-
PEDITION, 14–15 Jan. '80, and sat on
John André's board of inquiry. He then
served in N.J. and Pa., and in Oct. '81
took command of the Northern Dept.
With headquarters at Albany he prepared plans for resisting an expected
attack from Canada. He died of gout
(Appleton's) at Albany on 15 Jan. '83
before reaching his 57th birthday.

"Lord Stirling," as he signed himself
and was known to his republican countrymen, "was brave, intelligent, energetic and yet cautious; a good organizer
and military engineer," says Edmund
Kimball Alden in D.A.B. Although
Alexander is characterized as "hard-
drinking," Freeman says "it never was
even whispered that he was drunk when
Henry Knox's guns were barking, or the
rattle of the skirmishers' muskets was
heard in woods." (Washington, IV,
241A) In his inimitable style, the
biographer of Washington goes on to
give this judgment:

"For some reason, a field operation
entrusted to Stirling was apt to get
snarled. Neither he nor his Chief would
know exactly why plans went astray,
but they did.* * * The category of Stirling was one of the largest in an army
—the comprehensive class of those a
Commander-in-Chief never would think
of demoting—or of advancing." (Ibid.)

Stirling Papers are in the NYPL and
the Lib. of Cong. Freeman says "it
may be worth a student's time to check
the list in 7 NJHSP (I) p. 138. Many
of his letters are lost altogether." (Ibid.,
IV, 663)

Biographies are: W. A. Duer (his
grandson), Life . . . (1847); Ludwig
Schumacher, Earl of Stirling (1897);
C. A. Ditmas, Life. . . . (1920).

ALFRED–GLASGOW ENCOUN-
TER (Block Island, N.Y.), 6 Apr. '76.
Five Cont'l. ships totaling 90 guns, under Esek HOPKINS, were returning from
their successful NASSAU raid when the
British frigate Glasgow (20) sailed into
their midst between midnight and 1
A.M. In a remarkable three-hour night
action British Capt. Tryingham Howe
inflicted 24 casualties while sustaining
only four killed and wounded. With a
lucky shot he had knocked out the
wheel block of the Alfred (24) and
then raked her several times. Although
badly mauled, the Glasgow escaped.
During the engagement her Capt. had
taken the precaution of throwing overboard some dispatches he was carrying from Gen. Howe in Halifax to
Gen. Clinton, who was engaged in his
Charleston Expedition of 1776 (Clinton, American Rebellion, 372).

ALLEN, Ethan. 1738–1789. American officer. N.H. (Vt.) Born in Conn.,
by 1769 he probably had moved to
the N.H. Grants, and the next year was
named "colonel commandant" of the
Green Mountain Boys, a rough-and-
ready force organized in the dispute
between N.Y. and N.H. over the region
that became Vt. Little about Allen's
life until this time is known; he is said
to have been preparing for college when
his father died (1755) and is known to
have served at Ft. Wm. Henry in 1757.
(Gilbert H. Doane in D.A.B.) Allen's
prominence in the intercolonial dispute
is indicated by the fact that Gov. Tryon
of N.Y. in Dec. '71 offered £20 for
his capture but raised the price to
£100 in Mar. '74. After leading the
force that took TICONDEROGA, 10 May
'75, he was voted out of command of
the Green Mountain Boys. Operating
in Canada ahead of Montgomery's invading army, he was captured after his
premature attack on MONTREAL, 25
Sept. '75. Identified as the captor of

Ticonderoga, Allen was sent in irons to England and lodged in Pendennis Castle. But the goverment feared reprisals if they hanged Allen, so they returned him to America. He reached Halifax in June '76 and in Oct. was paroled in N.Y.C. Capt. Alexander Graydon wrote in his *Memoirs:* "I have seldom met a man possessing ... a stronger mind, or whose mode of expression was more vehement and oratorical. His style was a singular compound of local barbarisms, scriptural phrases and oriental wildness; and although unclassical and sometimes ungrammatical, it was highly animated and forcible. ..." (Quoted in Ward, *W.O.R.,* 930–31) A brother brought him money and Allen lived comfortably at N.Y.C. until jailed for parole violation, a charge he admitted was "partly true." (*Ibid.*) On 6 May '78 he was exchanged for Col. Archibald Campbell and reported to Washington at Valley Forge. On 14 May he was breveted Col., Cont'l. Army, "in reward of his fortitude, firmness and zeal in the cause of his country, manifested during his long and cruel captivity, as well as on former occasions." (Heitman)

Back in Vt. he resumed his activity and in Sept. submitted the Vt. claims to Congress. This body was in no position to get involved in a dispute between N.Y. and N.H., and Allen's mission failed. Appointed Maj. Gen. of Vt. militia in 1779, he launched what *D.A.B.* calls "a petty warfare" against the N.Y. settlers. Egerton expresses the long-standing suspicion of Allen's patriotism when he speaks of him as "the Vermont adventurer, who was coquetting ... with the British with the view of safeguarding the interests of his state. ..." The British realized their opportunities for capitalizing on the situation in Vt. and in July '80 Allen received a letter from Beverley ROBIN-SON that led to a correspondence between Allen and HALDIMAND. Some writers still question whether Allen really considered a deal with the enemy to make Vt. a province of Britain or whether he was using this as a threat in order to get favorable consideration by Congress. In his *Secret History* Carl Van Doren traces the British strategy and renders this judgment:

"Although Allen and a few other Vermont politicians continued their complex horse-trading with Congress and the governor of Canada, and in time may have come to think that an alliance with Great Britain would be more profitable than admission to the United States, they seem never to have gone beyond claims to independence of either country till after the treaty which ended the war. So far as treacherous assistance was concerned, Robinson had no more success with Allen than DeLancey had with either Parsons or Sullivan." (p. 414)

Allen published *A Narrative of Col. Allen's Captivity* in 1779 (see "GREAT JEHOVAH ...") and was the author of several books and pamphlets. One of these, *Reason the Only Oracle of Man ...*, is in the "rare" category: most of the copies were burned in a fire at the printer's, and practically all others were destroyed by the printer because he considered the book atheistic. (*D.A.B.*)

John Pell's *Ethan Allen* (1932) was the first satisfactory biography of this legendary figure.

ALLIANCE–SYBILLE ENGAGEMENT, Jan. 1783. Accompanied by another Cont'l. ship, the *Duc de Lauzun* (20), John Barry sailed from Havana in the *Alliance* (32) with a large amount of specie for delivery to Congress. Several days later they were sighted and pursued by three British frigates. The *Alliance* was getting away when Barry

saw that the *Lauzun* was being overtaken, so he turned to assist the smaller
and slower ship. While Barry was in-
structing Capt. Green of the *Lauzun* to
jettison his guns and run for it, a 50-
gun French ship from Havana bore
down on the scene. Two of the British
frigates, meanwhile, remained at a distance, and the French ship also failed to
join Barry. The *Alliance* engaged the
third British ship, *Sybille*, in a 45-minute
action before the latter withdrew. According to the account of John Kessler,
mate on the *Alliance,* the enemy's guns
were silenced and "she appeared very
much injured in her hull." (C. & M.,
962) He estimates American losses as
three killed, three died of wounds, and
another eight wounded. This has been
called the last naval action of the war
save for some privateering exploits.
(*Ibid.*, 960)

ALSOP, John. d. 1794. Congressman. Conn.–N.Y. Born in Middletown,
Conn., according to the brief notice in
Appleton's "he was a prosperous merchant of unquestioned patriotism and
integrity, and was a worthy member of
the first American congress in 1774–
'76." Characterized by John Adams as
"a soft, sweet man," he is remembered
primarily for his opposition to the Decl.
of Indep. On 16 July '76 he wrote to
the N.Y. Convention that since the proposed declaration "closed the door of
reconciliation" he could no longer serve
as a delegate. When the British occupied N.Y.C. he withdrew to Middletown until the war was over. He died
in Newton, Long Island. One son, Richard (1761–1815), formed the "Hartford
Wits." Another, John (1776–1841), was
a poet.

ALTAMAHAW FORD. The action
generally known as Haw River (Pyle's
Defeat), N.C., 25 Feb. '81, is referred
to by Kenneth Roberts in his *Oliver
Wiswell* as Altamahaw Ford in the text

and as Attamahaw Ford on the end
paper map.

AMBOY, N. J. Contemporary British
and American writers did not show any
consistent usage of the names Amboy,
Perth Amboy, and South Amboy. According to Freeman the safest assumption is that any of the three forms referred to the area of modern Raritan
Bay. (*Washington,* IV, 303 *n.*)

"AMERICAN." For comment on usage see "United States. . . ."

AMERICAN FLAG. See Flag,
American.

AMERICAN LEGION. See Legion
for the four units so called.

AMERICAN REVENUE ACT of
1764. See Navigation Acts.

AMHERST, Jeffery. 1717–1797. British general. His father's neighbor in
Kent took young Jeffery as a page and
in 1731 got him an ensigncy in the
Guards. After serving as A.D.C. to
Gen. Ligonier, C. in C. in Germany,
he moved to the Duke of Cumberland's
staff and in 1756 had become Lt. Col.
of the 15th Regt. Pitt overruled the
king's objections and in 1758 made Amherst a Maj. Gen. in command of an
expedition being sent to retrieve British
fortunes against the French in America. On 26 July he captured Louisburg
after a dashing assault made by James
Wolfe (another of Pitt's selections) and
in Sept. he succeeded the inept James
Abercromby (one of the king's choices)
as C. in C.

"Amherst, a tall, thin gentleman with
an aquiline nose, was never a popular
man [writes Alden]. He was grave,
formal, cautious, taciturn, and cold to
strangers, especially cold to those who
had not chosen English parents of the
right stock; nor was he an educated
man. He was, nevertheless, intelligent,
devoted to his profession, and thor-

oughly honest. Unscrupulous contractors, cunning politicians, and wirepullers heartily disliked him . . . No genius in the art of war, Amherst was a good administrator; he compensated for his lack of inspiration in the field by a dogged perseverance; and he was grimly determined to shatter French Canada." (Alden, *Gage,* 47–48)

In Nov. '58 he captured Ft. Duquesne and then prepared to implement the strategy drawn up by Pitt for the final conquest of Canada. Expressing pride in the achievements of 1758 he wrote to Gage, "We must keep the ball rolling, one campaign will do all." (*Ibid.*) The next year he personally led the column that captured Ticonderoga and Crown Point while Wolfe took Quebec and Prideaux captured Niagara. (Both of the latter were killed.) In Sept. '60 the three columns converged on Montreal, took the place without firing a shot, and the French were through in Canada. After signing the articles of capitulation with Vaudreuil on 8 Sept., Amherst made a hasty inspection of Quebec and went to N.Y.C. to take up his new position as Gov. Gen. of British North America.

Amherst's fame is based on his performance during these three years, and the rest is a long, pathetic contrast. His inept Indian policies led to PONTIAC'S WAR, 1763–1764, and to his recall to England in 1763.* (*D.N.B.*) But as the conqueror of Canada he was tremendously popular with the people of England, a fact that became dramati-

---

* Amherst proposed starting a smallpox epidemic among the Indians (see "GERM WARFARE"). He heartily approved Bouquet's idea that dogs be used to hunt the Indians down, but wrote him: "England is at too great a distance to think of that at present." (Peckham, *Pontiac,* 227)

---

cally apparent in 1770 when the king tried to have Amherst retire on a pension so that his sinecures of absentee Gov. of Va. and Col. of the 60th ("Royal American") Regt. could be passed on to the impecunious Lord Bottetourt; the king not only backed down but gave Amherst an additional colonelcy, that of the 3d ("Buffs") Regt. Promoted to Lt. Gen. in 1772 he became officiating C. in C. of the forces. He supported the king's coercive policy toward the Americans, an attitude which, with his tremendous popular following, made him a valuable asset to the government.

During the Revolution his chief services were as advisor to the government and in suppressing the Gordon Riots in 1780. In 1776 he became Lord Amherst and two years later was a full general. Advent of the Rockingham ministry in 1782 necessitated his leaving the government, but in 1783 he again became officiating C. in C. Although he was responsible for innumerable abuses that grew up in the army it was not until 1795, long after he was too old for the post, that he could be induced to resign and make way for the Duke of York. At the king's insistence he was made Field Marshal in 1796.

Lord Jeffery Amherst was one of seven brothers, only one of whom, Lt. Gen. William Amherst (bapt. 1732–1781), had any children. Another brother was Vice Adm. John Amherst (1718–1778). The other Jeffery AMHERST (d. 1815) was no kin to this family.

For the student of military biography Amherst is an interesting case: selected on the basis of merit by Pitt, over the heads of seniors, he more than lived up to expectations in an important command for the next three years; for the next 30 years he was a military vegetable and did great damage to the British Army before he could be removed from the scene.

AMHERST, Jeffery (No.2). d. 1815. British officer. No kin to Lord Jeffery AMHERST, he may have been from the Amherst family of Kenilworth, Warwickshire (Collins' *Peerage; D.N.B.*). He became an Ensign in the 60th Foot on 3 June '71. With the local rank of Maj. in 1781 he was A.D.C. to Gen. James Robertson and is mentioned in Clinton's memoirs as the officer sent on the *Jupiter* from N.Y.C. (20 Mar. '81) with dispatches for Cornwallis (*American Rebellion,* 286). He was promoted to the regular rank of Maj. in the 60th Foot on 1 Oct. '82, transferred to the 10th Foot on 8 Aug. '83, and reached the grade of Maj. Gen. on 1 Jan. '98.

AMUSE. In the 17th and 18th centuries the usual sense of this word was "to divert the attention of" or "to mislead" (*O.U.D.*). When a tactician of the period sent out a force to amuse the enemy his intentions were no more humorous than those of today's commander who plans a diversion. See also WORDS, Archaic.

AMUSETTE. A light field cannon invented by Marshal Maurice de Saxe (1696–1750). The word passed into the English language in 1761 (*O.U.D.*).

ANDERSON, Enoch. d. 1820. Remembered for his *Personal Recollections . . .* of the DELAWARE CONTINENTALS.

ANDERSON, John. John ANDRÉ'S pseudonym in ARNOLD'S TREASON.

ANDRÉ, John. 1751–1780. British officer and spy. Son of a Swiss merchant from Geneva who settled in London, he was educated in Geneva and commissioned in the army on 4 Mar. '71. He went to America in 1774 as Lt. in the 7th Regt., was captured at St. Johns in Nov. '75, and spent a year on parole in the interior of Pa. Becoming a Capt. in the 26th Regt., he was A.D.C. to Gen. Grey during the British sojourn in Philadelphia. Here the ambitious, industrious, capable, and engaging young officer was active in organizing dramatic performances, became a friend of Peggy Shippen, and staged the MISCHIANZA, 18 May '78. On Grey's recommendation André became A.D.C. to Sir Henry Clinton in N.Y. and was entrusted with handling Clinton's correspondence with his secret agents and informers. (Van Doren, *Secret History,* 125) In this capacity he became involved in Benedict Arnold's treasonable overtures in May '79. After an absence from N.Y. to accompany the Charleston Expedition of 1780 as Clinton's A.G. he again was charged with negotiations with Arnold.

Under ARNOLD'S TREASON is the story of how a series of mishaps led to his execution as a spy on 2 Oct. '80. The British Army went into mourning for his death, a monument was erected in Westminster Abbey, and his body was moved there in 1821. Washington's refusal either to pardon André or grant his pathetic request to die before a firing squad rather than on the gallows have both been defended by historians. Writing in *D.N.B.* R. E. Graves says: "Washington and André deserve equal honour: André for having accepted a terrible risk for his country and borne the consequences of failure with unshrinking courage; and Washington for having performed his duty to his own country at a great sacrifice of his feelings." As was the case with Nathan Hale, André's death was mourned by both sides.

He was an officer of exceptional ability, which is perhaps best indicated by his being appointed deputy A.G. with the rank of Maj. on 23 Oct. '79 at the age of 28 and, in the absence of an A.G., in actually handling all the duties of that office during Clinton's Charleston Expedition of 1780. In addition to being a social charmer, he showed real artistic talent in his sketch of Peggy Shippen, the sketch he did of himself while awaiting execution, and in his verses. Excerpts from his "Cow Chace" are under BULL'S FERRY.

His portrait by Sir Joshua Reynolds was first published in Van Doren's *Secret History,* where the Arnold-André correspondence also appears for the first time. *Major André's Journal; Operations of the British Army . . . June, 1777, to November 1778 . . .* was copyrighted in 1904 and republished in 1930.

ANDRUSTOWN, N.Y., 18 July 1778. (BORDER WARFARE) This settlement of seven families, six miles S.E. of German Flats, was plundered and burned by Indians under Joseph Brant. An unknown number of persons were killed and captured. (Lossing, I, 255; Swiggett, *Niagara,* 136)

ANNA. As part of the 1780 CHARLESTON EXPED., the British transport *Anna* was crippled by the storms that started when the convoy was two days out of N.Y. She was taken in tow by the *Renown* (50), but the cable broke and the *Anna* eventually drifted clear across the Atlantic to Cornwall. (See Lowell, 243–44 and von Eelking, 63–64) Various references in Uhlendorf's *Siege of Charleston* (pp. 13 *n.,* 25, 105 *n.,* 106 *n.,* 143) state that her passengers were Capt. Geo. Hanger and his company of 120 Hessian and Anspach chasseurs (or jägers), Althausen's 35 riflemen, and (possibly) some 30 of Ewald's jägers who were distributed among other ships when their transport, *Fan,* was damaged before leaving N.Y. As shown in the sketch of HANGER, however, this officer did not share the fate of his company.

ARBUTHNOT, Marriot. 1711–1794. British admiral. Nothing of certainty is known about his birth, parentage, or youth, according to *D.N.B.,* although some sources indicate that he was a nephew of the famous poet John Arbuthnot (1667–1735). Becoming a Lt., R.N., at the advanced age of 28, he was a Capt. in 1747. From 1775 until Jan. '78 he was naval commissioner at Halifax. Recalled to England on his promotion to flag rank, he was appointed C. in C. on the American station early in 1779. Sailing on 1 May, he reached N.Y. on 25 Aug. and CLINTON, who had been clamoring for a competent admiral, considered the assignment of this old and undistinguished naval person a deliberate affront. The admiral's performance turned out to be worse than his reputation: "old, inconsistent, unreliable" (Fisher, *Struggle,* II, 456), he also was thoroughly uncooperative. The threat presented by d'Estaing's movement toward American waters from the West Indies caused Arbuthnot to remain in the North until it became clear that the enemy's objective was SAVANNAH (9 Oct. '79). He and Clinton then worked in sufficient harmony to win the crushing victory at CHARLESTON in 1780, although the limited naval cooperation provided during the siege is credited to the remarkable Elphinstone. Returning north with the forces Clinton took back to N.Y., Arbuthnot posted his fleet at Gardiner's Bay, at the eastern end of Long Island Sound, to bottle up the French fleet that had landed Rochambeau at Newport, R.I., on 10 July '80. When Adm. George Rodney reached Sandy Hook in Sept. '80 from the Leeward Islands to counter a threat expected from a French fleet under de Guichen, he informed Arbuthnot that as the senior admiral he was assuming over-all command. Arbuthnot drew up a violent protest to being superseded; Rodney merely forwarded the case to the Admiralty. When the latter supported Rodney, Arbuthnot submitted his resignation on the grounds of ill health. The French threat failed to materialize, and on 16 Nov. Rodney sailed for his regular post. After his battle off CHESAPEAKE BAY, 16 Mar. '81, Arbuthnot was succeeded by Adm. Thos. Graves, and on 4 July '81 he sailed home. On 1 Feb. '93 he was made Admiral of the Blue (see ADMIRALS, "Colored") and became clinically dead the next year. Professionally, he had been dead for years. Sir John Knox Laughton's sketch in *D.N.B.* comments that his ignorance of naval discipline was proved in his altercation with Rodney, and his ignorance of naval tactics was shown off Chesapeake Bay. "He appears in contemporary stories...as a coarse, blustering, foul-mouthed bully and in history as an example of the extremity to which the maladministration of Lord Sandwich had reduced the navy." (*Ibid.*)

ARCADIA. Alternate spelling of ACADIA.

ARMAND, Charles. See TUFFIN.

ARMED NEUTRALITY. Conceived and phrased by the Danes, proclaimed by Catherine the Great on 29 Feb. '80, and subscribed to also by Sweden, Armed Neutrality is recognized by American diplomatic and naval historians as a notable set of principles. (Bemis, *Diplomatic History of the U.S.*, 38; Mahan, *Sea Power,* 405) England's claim of the right to seize enemy goods carried in neutral ships had become intolerable to the neutrals who wanted to make money out of the war. Russia, Denmark, and Sweden therefore drew up a defensive treaty for the protection of neutral shipping in wartime and invited the belligerents, France, Spain,

and Great Britain, to accept them. The principles were:

(1) That neutral vessels may navigate freely from port to port and along the coasts of the nations at war.

(2) That the effects belonging to subjects of the said Powers at war shall be free on board neutral vessels, with the exception of contraband merchandise. (In other words, "free ships make free goods.")

(3) That, as to the specification of the above-mentioned merchandise [contraband], the Empress holds to what is enumerated in the 10th and 11th articles of her treaty of commerce [of 1766] with Great Britain, extending her obligations to all the Powers at war. (That treaty did not include naval stores or ships' timbers as contraband.)

(4) That to determine what constitutes a blockaded port, this designation shall apply only to a port where the attacking Power has stationed its vessels sufficiently near and in such a way as to render access thereto clearly dangerous.

(5) That these principles shall serve as a rule for proceedings and judgments as to the legality of prizes.

Spain and France immediately accepted these principles. Great Britain, which could submit to the first and third principles as a matter of policy but could not recognize them as "rights," decided on the course of simply disregarding the Armed Neutrality, a decision endorsed even by the bitter Opposition of the day. (Mahan, *op. cit.*, 406) When later invited to join the League of Armed Neutrals, the principal European nations did so, although Portugal joined 24 July '82, after peace negotiations had started, and the Two Sicilies joined 21 Feb. '83, after the peace had been signed. The DUTCH, to their sorrow, were the first to join; the States General voted on 18 Nov. '80 to adhere, and they formally ratified the treaty on 4 Jan. '81. Armed Neutrality accomplished so little that Catherine called it an "Armed Nullity."

ARMSTRONG, James. Cont'l. officer. N.C. A Capt. in the 2d N.C. on 1 Sept. '75, and Col. of the 8th N.C. on 26 Nov. '76, he retired 1 June '78. He later became Col. of a militia regiment and was wounded at Stono Ferry, 20 June '79. (Heitman)

Another James Armstrong was Lt. of N.C. Dragoons from Oct. '77 to Jan. '81. A third James Armstrong was from Pa. and served in Lee's Legion (see below). Appleton's has another James Armstrong from Pa., but almost certainly has this man confused with *John* ARMSTRONG.

ARMSTRONG, James. Cont'l. officer. Pa. According to Heitman, James Armstrong of Pa. became Q.M. of the 2d Pa. on 20 Feb. '76, 2d Lt. on 21 May '76, 1st Lt. of the 2d Cav. on 1 Apr. '77, was promoted to Capt. on 1 Jan. '79, captured at Dorchester, S.C., on 13 Dec. '81, and was a prisoner until the end of the war. The last part of this service record fits the description of the Capt. Armstrong mentioned throughout Lee's *Memoirs*. Of his capture, Lee says "Armstrong was one of the most gallant of the brave, too apt to bury in the confidence he reposed in his sword, those considerations which prudence suggested. [He was] the first and only horse-officer of the Legion captured during the war." (*Op. cit.,* 538. "How he was admired, and how handsomely he was treated by his captors, see GARDEN'S Anecdotes, page 125," adds Lee in a footnote.) A Lt. James Armstrong "of Lee's dragoons" led one of the forlorn hopes at PAULUS HOOK, 19 Aug. '79, and although Heitman shows the man by this name promoted to Capt. on 1 Jan. '79, presumably he

is the same. See preceding article for three other James Armstrongs.

ARMSTRONG, John (Sr.). 1717–1795.* Cont'l. B.G.; Pa. Maj. Gen. Ireland–Pa. During the French and Indian War he commanded the 300-man force of Pa. troops that destroyed the Indian settlements at Kittanning, Pa. (8 Sept. '56) and was honored by the corporation of Philadelphia. He was the senior Pa. officer in Forbes' expedition to Duquesne (1758) and became a close friend of Washington. Col. Armstrong also served in Pontiac's War (1763). Although an elderly man and suffering from chronic rheumatism, he was named a Cont'l. B.G. on 1 Mar. '76; he might well have been given a higher rank if Washington had not advised Congress against it, despite his faith in and friendship for his old comrade in arms. (Freeman, *Washington,* IV, 73) Gen. Armstrong took part in the successful defense of Charleston (June '76), but as commander of S.C. troops at Haddrell's Point was not engaged with the enemy. During the N.J. Campaign he was useful to Washington in trying to "stir up the people" in his part of Pa. (around Carlisle) and in establishing magazines. (*Ibid.,* 280) Dissatisfied with his lot as a regular, he resigned as a Cont'l. B.G. on 4 Apr. '77 and the next day was appointed to the same grade in the state militia. At Brandywine (11 Sept. '77) he commanded Pa. militia posted at Pyle's Ford, a point where no enemy threat was expected and where none materialized. At Germantown (4 Oct. '77) he led the militia that constituted the right flank of Washington's complicated attack and although he made contact with the enemy the battle was lost before his command became seriously engaged.

* The dates 1720 and 1725 are also given for Armstrong's birth.

He was named Maj. Gen. on 9 Jan. '78 and held this militia rank the rest of the war. After the Wyoming "massacre" (July '78) he led part of the relief forces sent to the scene but saw no action. A member of Congress in 1778–80 and 1787–88, he also held many local public offices. Father of John ARMSTRONG (1758–1843).

ARMSTRONG, John (Jr.). 1758–1843. American officer; prominent postwar politician. Pa. A student at Princeton when the war started, he was a volunteer A.D.C. to Gen. Mercer until that officer was mortally wounded (3 Jan. '77) at Princeton; he then served Gates in the same capacity until the end of the war. He is the aide sent by Gates to recall Arnold during the Second Battle of SARATOGA (7 Oct. '77). Maj. Armstrong composed the NEWBURGH ADDRESSES (1783). After the Revolution he had a long political career—U.S. Senator 1800–4, Minister to France 1804–10—that culminated in his becoming Sec. of War to Pres. Madison in Jan. 1813. Blamed for failure of the expedition against Montreal and for the British capture of Washington, he was forced to resign. He wrote an apologia in his *Notices of the War of 1812*. Other works were biographies of Montgomery and Wayne and treatises on agriculture and gardening. He was the brother-in-law of Robt. Livingston, whose sister, he married in 1789, and was a son of John ARMSTRONG (1717–1795).

ARNOLD, Benedict. 1741–1801. Cont'l. general and traitor. Conn. Great-grandson of a R.I. governor, Arnold was born in Norwich, Conn., received a fair education, and at the age of 14 was apprenticed to a druggist. The next year, in Mar. '58, he ran off, enlisted in a N.Y. company, was advertised as a deserter in May '59, and through the efforts of his austere, pious, and domi-

neering mother was brought back to Norwich. In Mar. '60 he enlisted again, served briefly in upper N.Y., and again deserted. He made his way home alone through the wilderness and completed his apprenticeship. After the death of his parents the 21-year-old Arnold sold the family property and went with his sister Hannah to New Haven, where he opened a shop to sell drugs and books. He became a successful merchant and started sailing his own ships to the West Indies and Canada. One of his activities was horse-trading, a business which took him to Montreal and Quebec. Like others who had the opportunity, Arnold undoubtedly engaged in smuggling as well. In 1767 he married Margaret Mansfield and had three sons in five years.

Having been elected Capt. of militia in Dec. '74, he reached Cambridge with his company 10 days after the "Lexington alarm." The wayward scholar, apprentice, and recruit had grown into a successful businessman and trader with considerable knowledge of the sea. Tremendously energetic and restless, he was a man about 5 feet 9 inches tall, thick set, unusually strong, and possessing great stamina. Ice-gray eyes were set off by black hair and a swarthy complexion. While no authentic portrait is known to exist, a black lead drawing from life by du Simitière in July '77 shows a beak-nosed man with a heavy, jutting jaw and a sloping brow. (Freeman, *Washington*, III, 373B and V, 123B)

Almost immediately upon his arrival in the Boston lines Arnold talked the authorities into letting him lead a bold enterprise. Mass. appointed him a militia Col. on 3 May and he took part with Ethan Allen in the capture of TICONDEROGA, 10 May '75. Using captured boats he raided ST. JOHNS, Can., 17 May, and on 1 June was instructed by Mass. authorities to take temporary command of all American forces on Lake Champlain. On the 14th, Mass. sent a committee with instructions to put all American troops in his area under a leader from Conn. Arnold took violent exception to being superseded and after withdrawing with a body of supporters to the captured vessels off Crown Point he appeared to be ready to defy the order. The committee prevailed on his men to recognize their authority and a mutiny was avoided. On 5 July Arnold left the lakes and reached Cambridge the end of the month to face accusations of mishandling funds entrusted to him for the expedition. Benj. Church (!) headed a committee of investigation, and the Mass. legislature eventually paid the official expenses Arnold had incurred. Meanwhile, Arnold's wife had died on 19 June. Carl Van Doren writes:

"This first chapter of Arnold's Revolutionary history was an epitome of the whole. As a soldier he was original and audacious, quick in forming plans, quick in putting them into vigorous execution. He led his soldiers, not drove them, and won and held the devotion of the rank and file. He had a gift for command when the objective was clear and his imperious will could be fully bent upon it.* * * But in the conflict of instructions and of officers of rank equal or nearly equal with his, Arnold was restive and arrogant. He could not turn philosopher and patiently endure small irritations day by day. He was passionate and personal in almost all his judgments. * * * At the same time, Arnold was a whirlwind hero who could not be bothered with keeping track of small expenses. Spend what had to be spent, and figure the amount up later." (*Secret History,* 150)

ARNOLD'S MARCH TO QUEBEC, 13 Sept.–9 Nov. '75, was the next episode in the career of the "whirlwind hero." Badly wounded in the right knee in the unsuccessful attack on QUEBEC, 31 Dec. '75, he was appointed B.G. on 10 Jan. Early in Apr. '76 he surrendered command of the pathetic little army outside Quebec to David Wooster and established his headquarters at Montreal. In May he sallied forth to release the prisoners taken in the actions at the CEDARS, and he was the last American to leave Canada. (See CANADA INVASION)

At VALCOUR ISLAND, 11–13 Oct. '76, he commanded a remarkable action of great strategic importance.

During this period he maintained good relations with his superiors Schuyler and Gates, but he clashed with three officers who were junior to him. Capt. Jacobus Wynkoop of the Navy had been sent by Schuyler to take charge of the fleet on Lake Champlain; when he challenged Arnold's authority as over-all commander he was arrested and, with the backing of Gates, removed. Moses Hazen was charged by Arnold with negligence in handling the stores evacuated from Montreal, but Arnold made himself so offensive to the court-martial that the latter acquitted Hazen and ordered Arnold arrested. Gates dissolved the court and on 2 Dec. a board cleared Hazen of Arnold's charges. John Brown proved to be a more tenacious enemy. His grievance was that Arnold had not honored Montgomery's promise to promote him to Lt. Col. Arnold justified his action on the ground that Brown had violated the articles of capitulation by plundering the baggage of British officers captured at Sorel. Brown denied this and accused Arnold of appropriating for himself goods seized at Montreal. Brown's request for a court of inquiry was referred from Arnold to Wooster to Schuyler to Gates to the Board of War, where it apparently was pigeonholed. On 1 Dec. Brown submitted 13 charges against Arnold, but these also were shelved.

Arnold, meanwhile, reached Albany from Lake Champlain on 27 Nov., faced the inquiry on the Hazen affair, and went to join Washington in N.J. On 23 Dec. he was sent to Providence to help Joseph Spencer plan an operation to oust the British from Newport, a place they had just occupied. While in New England he was outraged to learn that on 19 Feb. Congress had promoted five officers over his head to Maj. Gen. All of them were junior to him in service and in ability. (They were, in order of their new seniority, Alexander, Mifflin, St. Clair, Stephen, and Lincoln.) He wrote Washington that Congress must have intended this as "a very civil way of requesting my resignation." Washington, who had not been consulted on this list and who had the highest opinion of Arnold, urged him to remain in the service while he attempted to have the injustice righted. Frustrated in his efforts to raise troops and supplies for the Newport operation, incensed by the failure of federal authorities to recognize his military accomplishments to date, and worried about the neglected state of his personal affairs at New Haven, Arnold has been described as "sulking in his tent like some rustic Achilles" when an opportunity suddenly arose for him to display his whirlwind generalship. This was in connection with the DANBURY RAID, 23–28 Apr. '77. Again the popular hero, he was promoted to Maj. Gen. on 2 May, but Congress did not remove the principal grievance: he was still junior to those five second-raters on the 19 Feb. list.

John Brown, also a good man at pressing a grievance, had meanwhile renewed his personal offensive. On 12 May he published an attack on Arnold that ended with the prophetic words: "Money is this man's god, and to get enough of it he would sacrifice his country." Exactly a month later, after Arnold had reached Morristown, Washington wrote Congress asking that a committee investigate the matters Arnold wanted settled: his public accounts, Brown's charges, and his seniority. In Philadelphia on 20 May Arnold sent Congress Brown's handbill of 12 May and reiterated the request for an inquiry. The Board of War was given the latter duty and on 23 May reported that Brown's charges were groundless. Some delegates still wanted an accounting for $55,000 of the $67,000 Congress had advanced him for operations in Canada, but Arnold was sent on 14 June to take charge of militia forces on the Delaware where the enemy started their perplexing maneuvers that preceded the Philadelphia Campaign. Arnold returned to resume his arguments with Congress, but the same day that he finally submitted his resignation—11 July '77—Congress received Washington's request that he be assigned to command militia of the Northern Dept. in opposing Burgoyne's Offensive. Arnold asked that his resignation be suspended and headed north. On 8 Aug. a motion to backdate Arnold's commission to 19 Feb. was defeated in Congress by 16 votes to six.

Arnold's first assignment in the north was to lead the relief expedition that ended ST. LEGER'S EXPEDITION. He sided with Schuyler in the factionalism that rent the Northern army, and was almost immediately at odds with Gates when that general succeeded Schuyler. In the First and Second Battles of SARATOGA, 19 Sept. and 7 Oct., he played a prominent and controversial part.

Seriously wounded in the latter action, he was incapacitated for many months. But Congress again was forced to acknowledge his contribution to the cause: they officially thanked him along with Gates and Lincoln for the defeat of Burgoyne, and on 29 Nov. they resolved that Washington should adjust his date of rank. A new commission made him a Maj. Gen. as of 17 Feb. '77, which finally gave him seniority over those other five. The slate of his grievances now virtually erased, Benedict Arnold entered a new phase of his career. Because his leg had not healed sufficiently for him to lead troops in the field, he was directed on 28 May '78 to take command in Philadelphia when the expected British evacuation took place. On 19 June he was in the city.

Since Philadelphia was the seat of the state as well as the federal government, Arnold had two sets of civil authorities over him. Furthermore, the city was divided into factions: patriots who returned, Loyalists and collaborators who remained, and neutralists. Any military commander in such a situation would have trouble, but few could have gotten into it any faster than Arnold. Almost from the start he was suspected of using his official position for personal speculation. He heightened suspicion and alienated townspeople in all walks of life by ostentatious living, far beyond his known means of legitimate income. Joseph Reed, president of the Pa. Council and of the state, soon became his principal enemy and in early Feb. '79 presented Congress with eight charges of misconduct against him. Arnold immediately demanded an investigation, and in Mar. a committee of Congress reported that he should be cleared of all charges. Reed would not quit, however, and in Apr. Congress referred four of the charges to a court-martial, having dropped the others. A

14-man court, including Gens. Robt. Howe, Smallwood, Henry Knox, Wm. Woodward, and Wm. Irvine, six colonels, and three lieutenant colonels met at Middlebrook, N.J., on 1 June but was almost immediately adjourned because the British had started an expedition up the Hudson. It was not able to reconvene until Dec., by which time Gens. Smallwood, Woodward, and Irvine had been replaced by Wm. Maxwell and Mordecai Gist. Only two of the colonels remained on the court. The prosecution was handled by Col. John Laurance, and Arnold took charge of his own defense.

Although documents brought to light long after the trial prove that Arnold's dishonesty as the military commander of Philadelphia was far worse than the state authorities suspected, the latter were unable to assemble adequate evidence to support their case. (Carl Van Doren, *Secret History, passim*) Hence they had had to resort to such charges as "imposing menial offices upon the sons of freemen of this state." There was more substance to the other three charges that were presented at the trial, although proof was lacking. After hearing Arnold argue his case with admirable skill, on 26 Jan. '80 the court gave the closest thing to a "whitewash" possible without insulting the accusers. They dismissed two of the charges entirely—those having to do with his purchasing goods for personal speculation during the period he had closed all shops in Philadelphia, and the business about "menial offices upon the sons of freemen"—but they found him guilty of improperly issuing a pass for the *Charming Nancy* to leave the city while other vessels were temporarily quarantined and guilty of using public wagons for private purposes. The sentence, however, was merely a reprimand from the C. in C. Although Washington's reprimand was written almost as a commendation, Arnold was furious that he did not receive a complete acquittal.

Arnold had not waited to finish his protracted battle with the Pa. authorities before making the decision that launched him into the adventure for which he is known in history. On 8 Apr. '79 he had married the 19-year-old Peggy Shippen, a prominent Philadelphia belle whose pert face survives in a sketch made by John André during the British occupation of the city and whose father had been chief justice of the colony. (Arnold was 38 at the time, twice the age of his bride, but hardly an old man.) The next month Arnold took the first step in the sequence of events covered in detail under ARNOLD'S TREASON.

Although he had failed to deliver West Point, the British made good their promises to reward him for his effort and compensate him for his losses in coming over to their side. He was commissioned B.G. of the British Army and given the associated perquisites (pension, etc.). He was awarded £6,315 for his property losses. In the spring of 1782 Peggy was awarded a yearly pension of £500 and £100 per year was eventually given to each of her children. Arnold also was given a command and started raising a legion of Tories and deserters. After escaping an attempt by Sgt. John CHAMPE to kidnap him in N.Y., Arnold led the raids described under VIRGINIA, MILITARY OPERATIONS IN and NEW LONDON, Sept. '81. The British officers in America did not welcome this provincial traitor as a bosom companion in arms, and the high command did not really trust him. Furthermore, his success in assembling his legion of deserters was not impressive. Although deserters and Loyalists were plentiful and Arnold offered a bounty of three guineas gold and could promise his recruits the same food, clothing, and pay as British regulars, at the end of a year he had attracted only 212 men and was short 684 needed to complete his legion. (Montross, *Rag, Tag,* 390) Having had little opportunity to distinguish himself as a British commander, Arnold went to London in Dec. '81. Here he was consulted on American affairs by the king and his ministers, but was offered no field command and felt himself the victim of scorn and neglect.

"Arnold was obsessed by a desire to make some large, quick fortune which would satisfy his terrible restlessness and bring security to his family," writes Van Doren. "Without military or official employment, he turned to commerce. . . ." (*Op. cit.,* 424) Toward the end of 1785 he established himself as a merchant-shipper at St. John, New Brunswick, and re-entered the West Indies trade. He also produced an illegitimate son, John Sage, who was born about 1786 to an unknown woman, whom he probably found at St. John. (*Ibid.*) The next year he brought Peggy and her children to Canada, and his sister Hannah arrived from Conn. with the sons of his first marriage to join the household. But the Tory refugees at St. John were hostile, Peggy was snubbed by her Philadelphia acquaintances when she hazarded a visit in late 1789, and the traitor moved back to England in 1791. His sister and three eldest sons remained in America. On 1 July '92 he fought a duel with the Earl of Lauderdale, who had accurately impugned Arnold's character during a debate in the House of Lords. Arnold shot and missed; Lauderdale held his fire; and after more discussion Lauderdale apologized. (*Ibid.,* 425) During the war with France Arnold was actively engaged in fitting out privateers, but lost more than he gained.

Trevelyan ends volume I of *George the Third and Charles Fox* with these words:

"Arnold's courage at last gave way; and he fell into melancholy, and deep dejection, which certain sentimental writers have pleased themselves by attributing to repentance and remorse, but which arose from the chagrin of pecuniary distress, and the consciousness of a hopelessly mismanaged life. He was attacked by a nervous disease; sleep fled from him; and in June 1801 he died a broken man, leaving his family a heritage of debts and lawsuits.* * * . . . the name of Benedict Arnold, which once promised to be only less renowned and honoured than that of George Washington, was regarded by three generations of his fellow-countrymen as a by-word for treachery." (p. 342)

Peggy Shippen Arnold (1760–1804) did not survive him long. Her four sons served in the British Army, one of them, James Robertson Arnold, becoming a Lt. Gen. A grandson, Wm. Trail Arnold, was killed in 1855 at Sevastopol, and a great-grandson, Theodore Stephenson, was a Maj. Gen. in World War I. The eldest of Arnold's sons by his first wife, and his namesake, was mortally wounded in the West Indies in 1795 while serving as an artillery officer.

A standard biography is Isaac N. Arnold, *The Life of Benedict Arnold: His Patriotism and His Treason,* Chicago, 1880. It is based on a thorough study of all sources available at the time, and although the author was a distant relative of his subject he was not an apologist. The *Proceedings* of Arnold's court-martial were published in 1780. The last word on Arnold's treason, which was not possible until the complete Arnold-André correspondence became available in the 1920's and

early 1930's, is Carl Van Doren's *Secret History.* Malcom Decker's *Benedict Arnold: Son of the Havens* (1932) contains material not in Isaac Arnold's biography. James Flexner's *Traitor and the Spy* (1953) and Willard Wallace's *Traitorous Hero* (1954) are favored by some modern historians.

ARNOLD LEGEND. During the century and a half between Arnold's treason and the discovery of new source material (see biographical sketch above) biographers went from the extreme of picturing "a monster who found delight during his boyhood in robbing birds' nests and mangling the fledglings" to "awarding him a martyr's crown as the bravest and best American soldier of the war, forced into treason because he was neglected and misunderstood." (Montross, *Rag, Tag,* 19) The new facts show Arnold to have been "bold, crafty, unscrupulous, unrepentant: the Iago of traitors," says Van Doren in the preface to his *Secret History.*

Yet there still is disagreement as to his true worth as a field commander, and there is not likely to be new source material to assist in clearing this up. "Greene, Wayne, Morgan, Knox, Stirling [Alexander], Sullivan and a dozen other generals made a greater contribution and risked their lives on more fields," says Montross in a statement that I would not like to defend. "The best explanation of the Arnold legend is probably to be found in the timeless popular preference for the glory hunter as compared to the soldier of cerebral capacity," he continues, on somewhat safer ground, in my opinion. (*Op. cit.,* 390)

It is amusing, however, that while some writers credit Arnold with winning the two battles of Saratoga almost singlehanded, others question whether he even was on the field in the first battle and maintain that the second was won before he charged in to lead a costly, useless attack. These matters are discussed under SARATOGA, 19 Sept., and SARATOGA, 7 Oct. '77. If he has been given too much credit, particularly by British writers, the cause may be that "Burgoyne said his defeat was all Arnold's 'doing,' and Germain got from official reports the impression that Arnold was 'the most enterprising man among the rebels.' " (Van Tyne, *War of Indep.,* 430)

The glorification of Arnold by Kenneth Roberts in his magnificent historical novels, *Arundel* and *Rabble in Arms,* has undoubtedly done much to misshape the popular image of the traitor as a paragon of military leadership and a victim of petty, jealous men. The Arnold legend ends with the improbable story that on his deathbed he asked to be clothed in his Cont'l. uniform, saying: "God forgive me for ever putting on any other."

ARNOLD'S MARCH TO QUEBEC.
13 Sept.–9 Nov. 1775. Although the CANADA INVASION had been ordered by Congress, "the cooperation of Arnold through an advance on Quebec had been Washington's own design." (Freeman, *Washington,* IV, 10) The proposed route up the Kennebec River and down the Chaudière to Quebec had been repeatedly mapped and described —particularly by British army engineer Capt. John Montresor, who made it seem a feasible avenue of approach; Col. Jonathan Brewer had proposed using it in the spring of 1775 to threaten Quebec; but Washington and Arnold were ignorant of its difficulties, especially in winter. (Ward, *W.O.R.,* 163)

Reuben Colburn, a Kennebec boatbuilder who happened to be in Cambridge when the expedition was conceived, was approached by Arnold on 21 Aug. about furnishing 200 light BATEAUX. On 3 Sept., Washington gave

Colburn orders to provide them. Two days later, notice of the expedition appeared in general orders, and a call went out for volunteers.

ORGANIZATION OF ARNOLD'S COMMAND

According to Ward (*op. cit.*), Arnold's command of about 1,100 men was organized as follows. Three companies of riflemen, the units chosen by lot, were Capt. Dan Morgan's Virginians and the Pennsylvanians of Captains William Hendricks and Matthew Smith. The first battalion, headed by Lt. Col. Roger Enos and with Maj. Return Jonathan Meigs as his assistant, comprised the companies of Captains Thomas Williams, Henry Dearborn, Oliver Hanchet, William Goodrich, and a certain Scott (who is not further identified). The second battalion was led by Lt. Col. Christopher Greene and Maj. Timothy Bigelow; company commanders were Captains Samuel Ward Jr., Simeon Thayer, John Topham, Jonas Hubbard, and Samuel McCobb. (Alden says these two battalions totaled only seven companies. *Amer. Rev.,* 53) A detachment of 50 artificers, led by Capt. Colburn, joined on the Kennebec.

The expedition had a surgeon (Isaac SENTER), a surgeon's mate and two assistants, two adjutants (Christian FEBIGER was brigade major), two quartermasters, and a chaplain (Samuel Spring). Five "unattached volunteers" were Aaron BURR, Matthias Ogden, Eleazer Oswald, Charles Porterfield, and John McGuire.

Although Washington's G.O. specified that members of the expedition should be "active woodsmen and well acquainted with batteaus [*sic*]," most of them—other than the riflemen—turned out to be farmers with little knowledge of the wilderness or of boats. Nor were they all volunteers, since Washington had been realist enough to provide that if enough men did not volunteer the rest would be assigned. Discipline of Arnold's command was up to standards of the day: the three captains of riflemen refused to subordinate themselves to a superior officer, Greene, and Arnold had to abandon his plan of organizing them into a single corps; just before the expedition was to leave Cambridge, some men refused to march until they received a month's pay.

THE DEPARTURE

Led by the riflemen on 11 Sept., the last of Arnold's troops marched from Cambridge on the 13th. They sailed from Newburyport on the 19th, and reached Gardinerstown, on the Kennebec below Ft. Western, on 22 Sept. Arnold found his 200 bateaux waiting. Considering that Colburn had had 18 days from the time he received the order in Cambridge, this was a remarkable achievement, but the boats were of green lumber (the only available) and many were poorly constructed and smaller than specified. Arnold accepted the boats, having no alternative, and ordered another 20. Colburn had been charged also with assembling flour and meat for the expedition, and for furnishing information about the route. His two scouts, Getchell and Berry, went as far as the Dead River and returned with ominous news that the British appeared to expect an invasion from this direction: they had met an Abenaki Indian named Natanis who said he was being paid to warn the British of the expected American advance, and that a British outpost was located on the Chaudière.

On 25 Sept., the expedition left Ft. Western (now Augusta, Me.) and started up the Kennebec. They were preceded by two reconnaissance patrols led by Lts. Archibald Steele and Church. The main body took two days to cover the first 18 miles to Ft. Halifax. The first real portage was at Ticonic Falls, where the 400-pound bateaux and about 65 tons of matériel were carried half a mile. Then came Five Mile Ripples (or Falls), the dangerous half-mile approach to Skowhegan Falls, the falls, the Bombazee Rips, and the three Norridgewock Falls. Until now the expedition had passed through a region dotted with an occasional settlement, where they could get some assistance in the form of supplies and labor; thereafter, until they were well down the Chaudière into Canada, the route was through the wilderness. Having spent three days passing Norridgewock Falls, repairing their badly battered boats, and finding many provisions already spoiled by water, on 9 Oct. the column pushed on. Curritunk Falls required the next major portage. On 11 Oct., Arnold and an advance element reached the Great Carrying Place, where eight miles of portage and four miles of rowing across three ponds took the expedition to the Dead River (actually the west branch of the Kennebec). The route then involved 30 miles of rowing up the Dead River, followed by a four-mile carry across the Height of Land—the watershed between the Kennebec and Chaudière—to a treacherous stream that meandered through swamps to Lake Megantic.

For many days before reaching the Great Carrying Place, however, it had been apparent that the expedition was faced with unforeseen hazards. First, no woodsman in his right mind would have considered the route passable for bateaux, particularly in winter. Second, Arnold had miscalculated the length of his march (see Summary, below); food was running out for this reason and also because much was spoiled when water got into the broken casks. Finally, the weather was against them: from the beginning it had been cold enough to take a toll among men who had to spend their days struggling in the water to manhandle the boats past obstacles in the river; but the temperature dropped further, and continuous, heavy rains started falling. When they were on Dead River a hurricane of historic proportions struck, on 21 Oct., to swell the river from 60 to 200 yards in width.

About this time, Morgan's Virginians contrived to replenish their supplies in a manner employed by soldiers since the dawn of warfare. Having heretofore led the van, with the primary mission of clearing the way across the Great Carrying Place, they then—unaccountably, at the time—relinquished the lead to Christopher Greene's division of three companies; while these companies passed through Morgan's men at the Great Carrying Place, the Virginians stole their flour. Nobody could prove this—then or now—but Arnold gave Morgan pointed instructions to stay at the head of the column thereafter. Greene's troops had to camp and await resupply from the reserves supposed to be with Enos' division, which was bringing up the rear, but two barrels of flour were all Greene got. The four companies of Meigs's third division followed Morgan, but when Enos caught up with Greene on 25 Oct. these two commanders were ordered to send on only those who could be given 15 days' provisions.

THE "DEFECTION" OF ENOS

After a COUNCIL OF WAR, Greene's men staggered on toward Quebec with a meager two and a half barrels of flour from Enos' stocks, whereas Enos started to the rear with about 300 men: his own division plus stragglers and the sick from other divisions. (This retreat was accomplished in 11 days of relatively easy travel.) A court-martial found Enos not guilty of "quitting his commanding officer without leave." Many have defended Enos' unheroic conduct on the grounds that Arnold and his 700 men could not have gone on without the provisions sent forward from the last division; this is the essence of a statement by Gen. Sullivan about six months later, and Gen. William Heath joined 24 other officers in a testimonial that Enos deserved "applause rather than censure." (Freeman, op. cit., III, 574 n.) But the judgment "cowardly defection" of some modern historians (e.g., Peckham, War of Indep., 30) reflects that of Enos' contemporaries, and this officer left the service less than a month after his acquittal by a court-martial.

ARNOLD STRUGGLES ON

Up the flooded Dead River, over four and a half miles of portage to Seven Mile Stream, the remaining 700 gaunt survivors then floundered through icy swamps to find Lake Megantic. On 31 Oct., Arnold's main body was assembled on the Chaudière. By now they had only a few bateaux left, several of the surviving ones having been wrecked in the dangerous rapids and falls of this last river. "Our greatest luxuries now consisted of a little water, stiffened with flour," wrote Senter on 1 Nov. They killed and ate a pet dog that had hitherto survived the hazards of the wilderness. "Nor did the shaving soap, pomatum, and even the lip salve, leather of their shoes, cartridge boxes, etc., share any better fate." (Senter, Journal, cited in C. & M., 199 ff.)

Arnold had forged ahead with an advance party to get provisions, and on 30 Oct. came to the first Canadian house. He sent back provisions that reached his men on 2 Nov.

The Indian Natanis, whom Arnold had ordered killed or captured on sight, joined the expedition at Sartigan, the first Indian settlement. Whether he had never been on the British side—as Kenneth Roberts portrays him in *Arundel*—or merely wanted the expedition to keep out of his hunting grounds is uncertain; however, he had shadowed the Americans from the Great Carrying Place until he could safely show himself. "His subsequent conduct indicated no unfriendliness to the expedition. On the other hand, he may simply have inclined toward whichever party was, at the moment, the more useful to him." (Ward, *op. cit.*, 448 *n*.) He and 50 other Indians joined Arnold with their canoes.

At St. Mary's the expedition left the river and marched north to reach the St. Lawrence at Point Levis, opposite Quebec, on 9 Nov. '75. Within a day, the aggressive Arnold had found Indian canoes and dugouts, had prepared scaling ladders, had gotten flour, and was preparing to cross the mile-wide St. Lawrence—which was full of British naval craft. This attempt was, however, delayed by a gale that lasted until the 13th. Arnold then started across. Owing to the shortage of boats, only three quarters of the small (about 700-man) force got across the first night. When the rest crossed the second night, bringing the scaling ladders, Arnold led them onto the Plains of Abraham. Meanwhile, the defenders of Quebec had been alerted. Arnold wisely decided against attempting an assault. See CANADA INVASION and QUEBEC for subsequent events.

SUMMARY

In a truly remarkable operation, Arnold had started from Ft. Western with 1,100 men and led them in 45 days across 350 miles of wilderness to arrive at the gates of Quebec, in midwinter with 675 survivors. There was enough fight left in them to push across the St. Lawrence and throw 1,200 defenders of the citadel into considerable consternation.

As for numbers and losses, the basic authority, Justin Smith (see below) says almost exactly 1,050 left Cambridge, about 50 (Colburn's carpenters) joined on the Kennebec, and Arnold drew clothing for 675 survivors on 5 Dec. Ward points out that if this large a number actually survived, and knowing that 300 returned with Enos and another 70 were sent back from Dead River, only 55 could have died, deserted, or turned back as escorts with the invalids. (The original 1,100 minus the 675 survivors, minus 300 with Enos, minus 70 evacuated from Dead River, would leave 55.) Finding it "incredible that no more than 55 were lost otherwise," Ward says, "It seems probable that the arrivals were not much more than half of the original party." (*op. cit.*, 450 *n*.) Speaking as a soldier, I wonder why these scholars appear innocent of the tendency some soldiers have to "pad" strength figures when they are submitted as a basis for drawing supplies.

On the other hand, one un-American historian writes, "The stories of the hardships that were endured may be rejected as fables." (Whitton, 399 *n*., citing Kingsford, *History of Canada*, V, 480, 481) Suspicion is also stimulated by such comments as these: "One of the most wonderful things about it is that so many simple, hungry, sick, miserable men had time to keep journals" (C. & M., 192); "Probably no other expedition of similar length made by so few men has produced so many contemporary records." (Ward, *op. cit.*, 448)

AUTHORITIES

The works of Justin H. Smith, the basic authority on this subject, are *Arnold's March to Quebec* (New York, 1903) and *Our Struggle for the Fourteenth Colony* (2 vols., New York, 1907). John Codman, *Arnold's Expedition to Quebec* (New York, 1902), is "more readable but not so accurate in detail," according to Ward. Kenneth Roberts, *March to Quebec* (New York, 1938; revised 1940) is a valuable collection and annotation of the more important journals and documents; his *Arundel* (New York, 1929) is accurate historical fiction.

ARNOLD'S RAID IN VA., 1781. See VIRGINIA, MILITARY OPERATIONS IN.

ARNOLD'S TREASON, May 1779–25 Sept. 1780.* Early in May '79 Maj. Gen. Benedict Arnold, then military commander at Philadelphia, decided to offer his services to the British. He sent for Joseph STANSBURY, a Tory whose mild nature and cautious conduct had enabled him to continue living in the city, and said he was ready either to join the British outright or to undertake secret dealings. With the knowledge and probably the help of a N.Y.C. Loyalist, the Rev. Jonathan ODELL, Stansbury met on 10 May with Capt. (later Maj.) John André, Clinton's aide. The British accepted Arnold's offer and decided it would be best for him to remain in his present post; meanwhile, secret channels were established for correspondence between Arnold and André through Stansbury. Arnold started sending information almost immediately. He used the code name "Moore" during most of the 16-month conspiracy. One important item of information Arnold sent the British was that Rochambeau's

* A note on sources is at the end of this article.

expeditionary force was expected, and this intelligence influenced the SPRINGFIELD, N.J., RAID of Knyphausen.

The 19-year-old Peggy Shippen, whom the 38-year-old Arnold had married 8 Apr. '79, was a partner in his treason from the beginning. There is no reason to believe, however, that she instigated it, or that Arnold was won over by British agents. The romantic theory that Peggy and André had fallen in love during the British occupation of Philadelphia, and that this had something to do with the treason, is also unsupported. Arnold's defection came after a long series of grievances had been accumulated by this complicated man. (See ARNOLD)

Various plans for cooperation between Arnold and the British were considered. Clinton proposed (sometime in June '79) that he "join the army, accept a command, be cut off"; the British would pay two guineas a head for the soldiers he surrendered. Relations broke down shortly thereafter when Clinton refused to meet Arnold's demand for £10,000, regardless of his specific service to the British, to compensate him for the losses he would suffer if the Americans discovered his double dealing. When Arnold reopened negotiations, apparently in May '80, he was still involved in the drawn-out courtmartial for his corruption in Philadelphia. (See ARNOLD) Meanwhile he had been working to get command of West Point. On 15 June he wrote the enemy that he expected this assignment and exactly a month later, having received from Clinton a vague response to another letter dealing with his proposed arrangements for the surrender of West Point, Arnold pressed Clinton for an agreement on the price: he wanted £10,000, win, lose, or draw, and £20,000 "If I point out a plan of cooperation by which Sir Henry shall possess himself of West Point, the garrison, etc., etc., etc." In this coded letter of 15 July, he concluded: "I expect a full and explicit answer. The 20th I set off for West Point. A personal interview with an officer that you can confide in is absolutely necessary to plan matters. In the meantime I shall communicate to our mutual friend Stansbury. . . ."

Because of a breakdown of their communications, it was more than five weeks before Arnold learned that Clinton would pay the £20,000 if the British got possession of West Point, its garrison of 3,000 men, its artillery, and its stores. He would not agree to Arnold's price for cooperation "whether services are performed or not," but he did assure the traitor that if the plot failed he would not be "left a victim." Meanwhile, however, Arnold sent the British bits and pieces of information, including these as "innocent confidences" to his wife (in Philadelphia), who relayed them through Stansbury to Odell to André. Since Washington and Rochambeau were working out plans for what became the YORKTOWN CAMPAIGN this intelligence was extremely valuable. As late as 1 Aug. Arnold was slated to command a wing of the allied army in this campaign, but he pleaded physical disability (his three-year-old wound) and on 3 Aug. he received command of West Point. On 5 Aug. he wrote the British from West Point that departure of Cont'l. troops had reduced the garrison to 1,500 Mass. militia and that these were "in want of tents, provisions and almost everything."

Arnold's new command comprised not only West Point proper but also Stony Point and Verplancks Point some 10 miles (air line) to the south, the outpost at Fishkill somewhat less than the same distance to the north, and the infantry-cavalry force "on the Lines" at North Castle, which was roughly the

same distance east of Verplancks. The traitor immediately started preparations for cooperation with the British. Instead of establishing headquarters at West Point, he selected the house of Col. Beverley ROBINSON, across the river. Over the objections of Col. John Lamb, who commanded the West Point garrison, he detached 200 men from that place to cut wood under the direction of Col. Udny Hay, who commanded at Fishkill; Lamb was particularly critical of this weakening of his force since he had already sent Hay 200 militia for guard duty. Although Arnold did not, as he has been charged, take up or partially dismantle the chain across the Hudson that had been laid to block enemy ships, he w·is able to accomplish his end merel by neglecting repairs he knew were necessary.

The traitor also went to work immediately to set up a net of secret agents. He had tried unsuccessfully to get the names of rebel spies operating in N.Y., but he promptly established contact with Joshua Hett SMITH. This Smith lived a short distance below Kings Ferry in the country house of his brother, William, who was royal chief justice of N.Y. and now a refugee in N.Y.C. Joshua was known as an active Whig and while Robt. Howe commanded at West Point he had handled the latter's secret agents. Arnold had · met Smith in Philadelphia, and Howe may have suggested that Arnold use him for intelligence work. In any event, Arnold immediately established contact with Smith, and the latter offered to make his home available as an overnight stop for Peggy when she came through to join Arnold at Robinson's.

Arnold's intimacy with Smith was one of several factors that led to a tense atmosphere in his military household. Col. Richard VARICK and Maj.

David Franks did not conceal their disapproval of their chief's dealing with a man whose brother was a famous Tory; yet until the end they never suspected that Arnold was up to anything more dishonorable than profiteering. Arnold, as a matter of fact, used the latter as a cover plan for his business of treason.

On about 24 Aug. Arnold finally got Clinton's letter of 24 July in answer to his letter of 15 July. He still maintained that his initial £10,000 fee was reasonable and urged that Clinton send a representative to make further plans. After a number of possibilities had been considered, the conspirators worked out the following scheme: Col. Robinson would request a meeting with Arnold ostensibly to discuss arrangements about the Tory's household property; John André would come along, and an opportunity would be found for him to discuss with Arnold plans for the surrender of West Point. Clinton's emissaries would use the armed sloop *Vulture*, which was regularly stationed at Spuyten Duyvil and occasionally sent boats up the Hudson on reconnaissance. After unsuccessful attempts to meet on 11 and 20 Sept., Smith was rowed to the *Vulture* before midnight of 21 Sept. and returned with a certain John Anderson for a clandestine meeting between that person and Arnold. "Anderson," of course, was John André. As far as Joshua Smith knew, however, he was a merchant who wore a British army officer's blouse under his blue topcoat because of some peculiar desire to pretend he was an officer.

At this point no definite plans had been worked out either for the André-Arnold meeting or for the actual surrender. Smith boarded the *Vulture* with several documents. One, which put him in the status of a "flag" and would get him past any American guard boats he might encounter on the river, was an open letter from Arnold to Robinson saying Smith would conduct him to "a place of safety" where Arnold and Robinson could discuss whatever proposals the latter had in mind. Another pass authorized Smith and Mr. John Anderson to "pass and repass the guards near Kings Ferry at all times." Since no single pass mentioned both Robinson and André (that is to say, Anderson), and since—for reasons unknown to Robinson—Arnold seemed anxious to meet André, Robinson agreed to André's going ashore alone.

By the time Arnold and André had completed their conference in the woods (about 4 A.M.) it was too late for the British officer to be returned under cover of darkness to the ship.* He was therefore taken to Smith's house, about four miles away, to wait until Friday night (22–23 Sept.). About dawn, however, Col. James Livingston, who commanded American forces in this area, on his own initiative attacked the *Vulture* with two cannon he had moved to Tellers Point (on the east shore). Arnold must have been horrified as he watched from a window of Smith's house, and after the battered *Vulture* finally managed to escape downstream he apparently decided that André would have to make his escape overland.

* "Nothing is positively known about the topics and decisions of the interview," points out Van Doren (*post*, 332). On 19 Sept. Clinton had completed preparations for the attack on West Point to the extent possible before André should return with details from Arnold. "It should be added that the fall of West Point to the British would by no means have brought an end to the war," comments Alden. (*Amer. Rev.*, 210 *n*.)

André was getting in deeper and deeper. Although his going ashore under an assumed name was a risk he had accepted from the start, Clinton had prescribed that he not go in disguise, that he not enter the enemy lines, and (although Clinton did not state this restriction until later) that he not carry any papers. At Smith's he was within the American lines. During the meeting the previous night Arnold had given him documents containing all the information about the Highland defenses that an enemy might want. (These are listed below.) Unless he could be rowed back to the *Vulture* during the hours of darkness, André would certainly have to shed his red coat. Under the circumstances, however, he had no choice but to follow the plan that Arnold now devised. According to André, Arnold made him put the papers between his stockings and his feet. Arnold prescribed that Smith act as guide, and he made out passes that would serve either for a boat trip to Dobbs Ferry—the route André expected to be followed—or to get "John Anderson" through the American guards at White Plains.

Arnold left in his barge to return to Robinson's House. Smith accompanied him to Stony Point and then returned to inform André that the overland route would be used. Whether this decision was on Smith's own initiative or on instructions from Arnold, the young British officer was surprised and alarmed; but he had no choice. If Smith had known who John Anderson really was he might have decided differently: although the water route was actually no safer than the one overland, it had the essential advantage of not requiring that André remove his uniform. Smith and "Anderson" stopped for a drink with some officers at Stony Point,

crossed Kings Ferry, visited Col. Livingston at Verplancks and stopped for the night near Crompond (about eight miles from the river). André had intended to ride straight on to White Plains but a militia captain, "solicitous or suspicious," pointed out the dangers of meeting Loyalist partisans.

Before dawn on the 23d (Saturday) André and Smith moved on. When they reached the vicinity of Pine's Bridge over the Croton River André was left to cover the remaining 15 miles alone; he was now beyond the normal range of patriot patrols (but had Arnold's pass to cover this eventuality) and Smith did not want to run the risk of meeting a Loyalist patrol. At Pleasantville André learned that rebel patrols were on the road ahead, so he turned toward Tarrytown. About 9 or 10 A.M. he was stopped by three men at the bridge just outside the latter place.

"The legend of André's capture is classic," says Carl Van Doren, "but the facts are obscure." When he was challenged by John Paulding, Isaac Van Wart, and David Williams, André made the mistake of assuming they were Loyalists. He did not produce his pass until they had decided to search him. These three men were "volunteer militiamen" operating under a recent N.Y. act permitting them to claim property found on a captured enemy. While the loftiest of patriotic motives were subsequently attributed to their actions, their real interest probably was loot.

The prisoner was taken to North Castle, where Lt. Col. John Jameson commanded American troops "on the Line." Arnold had previously issued instructions that a John Anderson might come into the lines from N.Y.C. and had ordered that he be sent to his headquarters on the Hudson. Jameson was puzzled by the fact that "Anderson" had been brought to him from *behind the lines*, and also by the papers, which he subsequently characterized as being "of a very dangerous tendency." The American outpost commander came up with an interesting compromise decision: he sent the prisoner to Arnold, as called for by his instructions, but sent the papers to Washington, who was believed to be around Danbury enroute to Peekskill.

Maj. Benjamin TALLMADGE returned to North Castle later in the day, learned of what had happened, and immediately suspected the truth. Although he could not talk the good, gray Col. Jameson out of reporting the capture to Arnold, Tallmadge did succeed in having "John Anderson" called back. When the latter returned to North Castle and learned that the incriminating papers had been sent to Washington, he revealed his true identity. André did not mention his connection with Arnold, but wrote Washington that he had come between the lines to "meet a person who was to give me intelligence" and had subsequently been "betrayed . . . into the vile condition of an enemy in disguise within your posts."

After this almost unbelievable situation had been set up on Saturday, nothing happened on Sunday. Washington had not been found at Danbury; the messenger returned to North Castle, added André's letter to his papers, and headed for Robinson's House, where Washington was known to be traveling. Earlier in the day the other messenger, having returned with André, departed with Jameson's report to Arnold. It was a race to see whether Washington or Arnold would get the word first, but for some reason neither messenger reached Robinson's House until Monday morning.

The most exciting event at Robin-son's House on Sunday was an exchange of incivilities at the dinner table between Arnold's aides (Varick and Franks) and his guest, Smith. The aides still suspected that Smith's dealings with their chief meant nothing more improper than some sort of war profiteering, but they could not be polite to a man whose brother was a famous Tory. Arnold reprimanded his aides for their bad manners to a guest but promised to have less to do with Smith in the future. Washington, meanwhile, had changed his route and sent word that after spending the night at Fishkill (instead of Peekskill) he would reach the Robinson House in time for breakfast on Monday. By a strange coincidence Smith went on from Arnold's headquarters to Fishkill, from which place he wanted to move his family to his brother's house (near Tarrytown), and he had dinner in the house where Washington spent Sunday night.

THE CLIMAX

On Monday, 25 Sept., things happened fast. About 9 A.M. two officers from Washington's party reached the Robinson House to say he would be late. While Arnold's household was at breakfast Jameson's first message was delivered to the traitor. Arnold told the militia lieutenant who brought it not to say anything to the others and, without showing his alarm, went upstairs to give Peggy the bad news before he made his own escape. He was coming back down when Franks informed him Washington was about to arrive! Arnold ordered a horse, left word for his chief that he had urgent business at West Point for about an hour, hurried to his barge, and started down the Hudson to the *Vulture*.

Washington arrived about 10:30 with a party that included Lafayette, Henry

Knox, and Alexander Hamilton. After eating breakfast they were rowed over to West Point to inspect the works and meet Arnold. Franks then learned about the message from Jameson and the fact that the bearer had been ordered to keep quiet about it. For the first time suspicion began to dawn on the two aides, but they quickly agreed this was "uncharitable and unwarranted," as Varick explained later. Even when they heard that Arnold had headed down the river and not across to West Point they were not alarmed.

Peggy Arnold now went into an act that fooled not only the people on the scene but generations of eminent historians. She sent for Varick and hysterically accused him of ordering her child killed! The 27-year-old bachelor, who had been sick for three days, and whom Peggy had nursed tenderly the preceding day, must have thought his fever had affected his reason: he found an insane woman, "her hair dishevelled and flowing about her neck," too scantily dressed "to be seen even by gentlemen of the family," who fell on her knees "with prayers and entreaties to spare her innocent babe." Varick tried to lift her to her feet but was too weak from his own illness. When Franks and Dr. Eustis, Arnold's headquarters surgeon, finally arrived, Varick said "we carried her to her bed, raving mad."

Washington returned at 4 P.M., already beginning to have vague misgivings about Arnold's long absence, and saw the first set of papers forwarded by Jameson with a note that these had been found on a man called John Anderson. The documents included a summary of the army's strength, a report of the troops at West Point and vicinity, an estimate of the forces needed to garrison the defenses properly, a return of the ordnance on hand, the plan of artillery deployment in the event of an alarm, a copy of the minutes Washington had sent Arnold on an important council of war held 6 Sept., and a report by Arnold on the defects of the West Point defenses. Washington was then handed the letter identifying Anderson as John André. When he then was told that Arnold had received a message at the breakfast table just before his sudden departure, Washington knew the worst. Although the bird had more than six hours' head start, Hamilton was directed to ride down the Hudson and try to intercept his flight to the *Vulture.* Before Hamilton could return from Verplancks Point to confirm the traitor's escape, Washington was given a letter written by Arnold aboard the ship and sent ashore under a flag. "Love to my country actuates my present conduct," said this astounding communication, which was the start of a long apologia. Peggy was "good and innocent as an angel," he lied, but added a truthful footnote saying that Varick, Franks, and Smith "are totally ignorant of any transactions of mine, that they had reason to believe were injurious to the public."

Meanwhile, Washington had been faced with the task of "correcting mistakes deliberately made to expose an American stronghold to successful attack," writes D. S. Freeman. "Arnold had been careful to be careless." Perhaps the enemy was already advancing, and by 7 P.M. Washington had learned enough about the "friendly situation" to start issuing orders: detachments were recalled from Fishkill (the woodcutters and militia guards); Greene was directed to send his closest division immediately to Kings Ferry, and the rest of the main army was alerted for movement; since Washington had reason to fear that some of Arnold's subordinate commanders were in on the plot, he took steps to see that reliable officers were on duty. These, and other precautions, turned out to be unnecessary.

ANDRÉ'S FATE

Washington ordered André brought under heavy guard to Robinson's House. He then ordered Col. Livingston, commandant at Kings Ferry, brought to him for questioning, and Col. Lamb was sent to command Livingston's important post. Livingston's innocence was quickly established. Meanwhile, Washington had no alternative but to tell Varick and Franks to consider themselves under house arrest, a precaution which they accepted without resentment. Lt. Gouvion was sent to Fishkill to arrest Smith, who was found and hurried (on foot) to Robinson's House, where he arrived before 8 P.M. on Monday (25 Sept.). From this glib and voluble individual Washington finally was able to get details from which he could see Arnold's conspiracy with some perspective. He realized that but for "a most providential interposition" that led to André's capture, Arnold would have delivered a vital American citadel to the enemy. ("To Lafayette, it seemed that Arnold's scheme was to invite the enemy's attack and then to pretend that he had been overwhelmed by a surprise," says D. S. Freeman.)

Maj. John André reached Robinson's House the morning of the 26th after a long night ride in the rain with a strong escort of dragoons commanded by Tallmadge. Washington declined to see André but he did get the details of his capture and of the disagreement between Jameson and Tallmadge as to how this should be reported. André was then sent to West Point, taken by barge to Stony Point on the 28th, and imprisoned at Mabie's Tavern in Tappan. Smith accompanied him, but the two were not allowed to communicate. On Friday, 29 Sept., a board met to examine André as speedily as possible and "report a precise state of his case, together with your opinion of the light in which he ought to be considered and the punishment that ought to be inflicted." Nathanael Greene was president of the board that included Maj. Gens. Alexander ("Stirling"), Lafayette, Steuben, St. Clair, and Robt. Howe; and Brig. Gens. James Clinton, John Glover, Edw. Hand, John Stark, S. H. Parsons, Henry Knox, and Jedidiah Huntington. The only record of the trial is the abstract made by John Laurance. The board interrogated André and then heard letters from Beverley Robinson, Arnold, and Sir Henry Clinton. The most damning testimony was André's honest admission that he could not pretend that he came ashore under a flag. The letters, on the other hand, insisted that André had come ashore under a flag, had acted on Arnold's orders while within the American lines, and therefore could not be considered a spy subject to the usual penalty. After the single day's hearing ("the unhappy prisoner gave us no trouble in calling witnesses," commented Steuben to an aide, "he confessed everything"), the board concluded that André's coming ashore "in a private and secret manner" and his subsequent movements behind the American lines "under a feigned name, and in a disguised habit" made him a spy and that he should be executed. Washington issued a G.O. quoting the board's report and directing "the execution of the above sentence in the usual way [by hanging] this afternoon [1 Oct.] at 5 o'clock precisely." About 1 P.M. of the day for which the execution was scheduled Washington received Sir Henry Clinton's request for a delay until Maj. Gen. James Robertson and two others could arrive "to give you a true state of facts. . . ." Although Washington suspected that Clinton had nothing to add to the case he postponed the execution until noon of the next day. Meanwhile he had received André's appeal to be shot as a soldier and not hanged, a pathetic request that Washington could not grant and did not even answer. It is also possible that some of his officers, unknown to Washington, were trying to see whether Clinton would exchange Arnold for André: although Van Doren is fairly certain that Hamilton wrote Clinton on 30 Sept. in a disguised hand to this effect, Freeman believes this is unlikely. Clinton's emissary, as suspected, had no new facts; Gen. Robertson ended up presenting what, in effect, was a plea that André be released as a personal favor to Clinton. As for the possible exchange of Arnold for André, Clinton could not consider it, André rejected the possibility when it was suggested to him, and there was always the problem of catching Arnold if everybody else had agreed to the trade.

John André was hanged on 2 Oct. Suffice it here to say that he died like a man and that Americans as well as British wished that in the case of this engaging young officer—as in the case of Nathan Hale—there could be some relaxation of the traditional attitude toward spies. The British author of the article on André in the *D.N.B.* has this to say:

"Washington has been unreasonably censured for not having granted him a more honourable death. To have done so would have implied a doubt as to the justice of his conviction. . . . Washington and André deserve equal honour: André for having accepted a terrible risk for his country and borne the consequences of failure with unshrinking courage; and Washington for having performed his duty to his own country at a great sacrifice of his feelings." (R. E. Graves, quoted in C. & M., 759)

For the subsequent career of Arnold and the story of Peggy and her progeny, see ARNOLD. Col. Varick called a court of inquiry and on 2 Nov. was unanimously cleared of any suspicion; for his later difficulties, however, see VARICK. Franks testified but was not himself suspected of any complicity. Although Schuyler and Robert R. Livingston had used their influence to help Arnold get the assignment to West Point, neither was suspected of treason. Joshua Smith was acquitted by a court-martial but subsequently imprisoned by state authorities; see SMITH for his subsequent experiences. Those three dubious patriots, PAULDING, VAN WART, and WILLIAMS, were each given the thanks of Congress, a silver medal, and an annual dole of $200 in specie. When Paulding applied to Congress in 1817 for an increase, ex-Maj. Benjamin Tallmadge, then a member of the House of Representatives, presented evidence (based on his interrogation of André after the capture) that the heroes had been motivated by greed and not patriotism and had been more than compensated for their accidental contribution to the American cause. (Lossing II, 206 *n.*)

Note on sources: Some of the basic facts on Arnold's treason were unknown until the British Headquarters files became available to scholars in the 1920's. These papers, part of the Clements Collection, include the Arnold-André correspondence which, in turn, led to other unknown or neglected sources and resulted in the publication in 1941 of Carl Van Doren's *Secret History of the American Revolution.* This work is the definitive study on Arnold's conspiracy and the basis for the present article; the book is so well indexed that I have omitted specific citations. Freeman's *Washington* includes valuable material to supplement Van

Doren, and the two authorities disagree on certain facts and opinions. Commager and Morris in their *Spirit of 'Seventy-Six* include excerpts of basic source documents.

ARTICLES OF CONFEDERATION. (Adopted by Congress 15 Nov. 1777; Ratified 1 Mar. '81) Proposed by Richard Henry Lee on 7 June '76 when he offered his resolution for independence, the idea of confederation was then studied by a committee under John Dickinson. On 12 July '76, exactly a month after the latter's appointment to head this committee, the "Articles of Confederation and Perpetual Union" were presented to Congress. After more than a year of intermittent debate the 13 articles were formally adopted on 15 Nov. '77 and sent two days later to the states for ratification. Congress had finally adopted the articles on the basis that states would pay their share of governmental expenses in proportion to their land area. Ratification was delayed by Md. because she refused to act until states with western land claims ("three-sided states") ceded them to the U.S. Va. yielded on 2 Jan. '81, Md. signed on 27 Feb., and final ratification took place 1 Mar. '81. This ended the 2d Cont'l. Congress in name; on 2 Mar. it became "The United States in Congress Assembled." The country was governed under these articles until ratification of the Federal Constitution on 21 Nov. '88; on 10 Oct. '88 the last Congress under the Articles transacted its last business, and on 4 Mar. '89 the first Congress under the Constitution met in N.Y.C.

The book which lent its title to the period is John Fiske, *The Critical Period of American History, 1783–1789* (Boston & N.Y., 1888). More balanced, but basically in agreement with Fiske's unfavorable description of the period, is Andrew C. McLaughlin, *The Confederation and the Constitution, 1783– 1789,* in *The American Nation: A History,* edited by Albert Bushnell Hart, vol. X (N.Y., 1905). A widely divergent view is presented by Merrill Jensen in *The New Nation: a History of the United States During the Confederation* (N.Y., 1905) and in *The Articles of Confederation: an Interpretation of the Social-constitutional History of the American Revolution, 1774– 1781* (Madison, Wisc., 1948).

ARTIFICERS were soldier craftsmen, technicians, and skilled laborers who operated military depots and accompanied troops in the field. Separate companies and smaller detachments existed from the earliest days of the Revolution, some performing quartermaster duties or constructing fortifications, others working as gunsmiths and artillery technicians, and many serving as carpenters, wheelwrights, blacksmiths, and bateauxmen.

According to Heitman there were two artillery artificer regiments, commanded by Cols. Benjamin FLOWER and Jeduthan BALDWIN. (*Historical Register,* 15, 83, & 230) But Berg makes clear the distinction between artillery and quartermaster artificers, pointing out further that only Flower's "Regiments of Artillery Artificers" actually existed as a regiment. The companies raised by Baldwin were quartermaster artificers, 11 companies of which (mostly from Conn.) were in service by 1779. Plans to "regiment" these units were never carried out, and in 1781 another effort to form a regiment of artificers, apparently artillery and quartermaster, also failed. (See F. A. Berg, *Ency. of Cont'l. Army Units,* 11–12 & 115–16)

ARTILLERY OF THE 18TH CENTURY. The first use of gunpowder, which had become widespread by the end of the 14th century, was not in small, hand weapons but in artillery. It took many improvements in metals and powder to "miniaturize" the cannon into a musket. It was not until the advent of Gustavus Adolphus (1594–1632) that guns were made sufficiently mobile to become field artillery; until then their role had been in the attack and defense of fortresses. At Breitenfeld, in 1631, Gustavus proved the soundness of his ideas and marked the birth of true field artillery by using light guns to smash the Spanish infantry squares. Gunners had been civilian technicians until 1671, when Louis XIV of France raised the first artillery unit and established schools, but French artillery officers did not receive military rank until 1732, and in some countries drivers were "contract civilians" as late as the 1790's. (Manucy, *post,* 7–8)

During the Colonial Wars artillery had to be water-borne; its use was limited to the defense and siege of forts, and to war (or privateering) at sea. The British—and Provincials—used field artillery, probably for the first time in America, in the capture of Louisburg in 1745. In 1775 the Cont'l. Army started the war with only the cannon, ammunition, and gunpowder they could capture from British forts and ships, plus what was in the hands of the colonial militia. British raids to SALEM, Mass., 26 Feb. '75, and to LEXINGTON AND CONCORD, less than two months later, had the mission of confiscating ordnance reported to be in the possession of the rebels. To overcome their lack of siege artillery, the Americans brought in KNOX'S "NOBLE TRAIN" from captured Ticonderoga and drove the British from Boston.

In the "linear tactics" described under MUSKETS AND MUSKETRY there was little use for field artillery, and its employment was further restricted by the problems of land transportation in North America (an "underdeveloped country" at that time!). GRASSHOPPERS were sometimes used. The British artillery hero of Minden, William PHILLIPS, made effective use of his guns on Burgoyne's Offensive, particularly at TICONDEROGA, July '77, and the first battle of SARATOGA, 19 Sept. '77, proving that artillery could be moved by inland waterways well into the interior. In Aug. '76 only about 500 American artillerymen were present for duty, as compared with four times that number of British gunners in Gen. Howe's army who were "perfectly equipped and disciplined." (Trevelyan, *American Revolution,* VI, 205) The colonists had started casting cannon and making carriages by 1775, and some French field pieces—made obsolete by the GRIBEAUVAL system—were brought to America during the war.

"The mobile guns of Washington's army ranged from 3- to 24-pounders, with 5½- and 8-inch howitzers. They were usually bronze. A few iron siege guns of 18-, 24-, and 32-pounder caliber were on hand. The guns used round shot, grape, and case shot; mortars fired bombs and carcasses. 'Side boxes' on each side of the carriage held 21 rounds of ammunition. . . . Horses or oxen, with hired civilian drivers, formed the transport. On the battlefield the cannoneers manned drag ropes to maneuver the guns into position." (Manucy, *post,* 10)

Maximum effective range of artillery —even fairly large-caliber guns firing solid shot—was about 1,200 yards, and with untrained gunners using imperfect weapons and ammunition the range was about 400 yards. During the Boston Siege the British delivered one cannonade at short range that inflicted only one slight casualty in the American lines. British artillery did succeed in destroying Roxbury, at a range of about a mile from their positions at Boston Neck; they also lobbed mortar shells into Cambridge, more than two miles away, but due to faulty ammunition this fire did little damage.

American chief of artillery was Henry KNOX, and his remarkable job in organizing that arm is outlined under his biographical sketch. Units of the American army were "Gridley's and Knox's Regt. of Arty.," commanded by Col. Richard Gridley from 19 May to 17 Nov. '75, and by Knox until its disbandment the end of 1776. John LAMB was a Maj. in this organization after 9 Jan. '76, and John Crane served with it in this grade from 10 Dec. '75 to 1 Jan. '77 (Heitman, 14). Four numbered regiments of Cont'l. Arty. were in existence during the Revolution: the 1st Regt., Col. Charles Harrison, 30 Nov. '76–17 June '83; the 2d Arty., Col. John Lamb, 1 Jan. '77–17 June '83; the 3d Arty., Col. John Crane, 1 Jan. '77–17 June '83; and the 4th Arty., Col. Thomas Proctor, 5 Feb. '77–18 Apr. '81. The "Corps of Arty." was created after the hostilities ended; Col. John Crane was in command from 17 June '83 to 3 Nov. '83, and Maj. Sebastian Bauman was the second in command until 20 June '84. By its resolution of 4 June '84 Congress had reduced the army to "25 privates to guard the stores at Fort Pitt and 55 to guard the stores at West Point . . . , no officers to remain in service above the rank of captain."

"Picture them at West Point, all that remained of Alexander Hamilton's battery, oiling the trunnions of three and six pounders, mowing grass on the magazines and doing their turn at guard. The army—a few watchmen not even glori-

fied." (Ganoe, *U.S. Army*, 91. "Hamilton's Battery" became Battery F, 4th Regt. of Arty., and now exists as Battery D, 5th Field Arty., the only U.S. Army unit whose lineage is traced to the Cont'l. Army.)

Two regiments of artillery artificers existed and were known by the names of their commanders: Col. Jeduthan Baldwin, 3 Sept. '76–29 Mar. '81; and Col. Benjamin Flower, 16 July '76–28 Apr. '81.

See Albert Manucy, *Artillery Through the Ages: A Short Illustrated History of Cannon, Emphasizing Types Used in America* (1949).

ASGILL, Charles. 1762 or '63–1823. British officer in HUDDY–ASGILL AFFAIR. Only son of the first Sir Charles Asgill, he entered the army on 27 Feb. '78 as an ensign in the 1st Foot Guards. He was captured at Yorktown, 3 Feb. '81. When Moses Hazen was directed by Washington to select an officer by lot to be executed in retaliation for the hanging of Huddy, "By negligence or misunderstanding, Hazen failed to observe the requirement that the victim be a prisoner who had no claim to protection," which Asgill had under the terms of Cornwallis' capitulation. (Freeman, *Washington*, V, 414) Washington did not feel he could release Asgill nor, apparently, did he see fit to have another victim selected. The initiative of Asgill's mother resulted in the solution: Lady Asgill went to Paris and presented to Vergennes a plea so moving that he showed it to the king and queen. At their request Vergennes wrote Washington (29 July '82), Washington sent the letter to Congress, Congress voted that Asgill be released, and Washington gladly ordered it. (See HUDDY–ASGILL for further detail.)

Asgill, who was only 19 or 20 years old in 1782, succeeded to his father's baronetcy on 15 Sept. '88. On 4 June

1814 he became a full Gen. in the British Army. (*D.N.B.*)

ASHE, John. *c.* 1720–1781. Politician and militia B.G. N.C. Son of John Baptista Ashe, and sometimes confused with a nephew of that name (1748–1802), he probably was born in Brunswick co. He married his cousin Rebecca, sister of Judge Maurice and Gen. James Moore. During the French and Indian War he was an officer in the militia, and in the politics preceding the Revolution he became prominent as a patriot leader: in 1762–65 he was speaker of the Colonial Assembly; he played a conspicuous part in the Stamp Act crisis, leading the mob to Brunswick on 18 Feb. '66. (Alden, *South,* 88) Siding with the government against the REGULATORS in 1771, either he or his nephew namesake was captured and whipped. (*D.A.B.*) At the start of the civil war in the Carolinas that characterized the struggle in the South, in Mar. '75 he organized and drilled the patriot militia of New Hanover co. while Robt. Howe did the same in Brunswick co. "When some citizens of Wilmington displayed reluctance to engage in economic reprisal against Britain, Ashe convinced them of its wisdom by appearing in the town at the head of 500 armed men." (Alden, *op. cit.,* 182) On 18 July '75, Ashe, Howe, and Cornelius Harnett led the militia into Ft. Johnston in a futile attempt to seize the royal Gov. Josiah Martin.

Appointed Col. of state troops in 1775 and B.G. on 23 Apr. '76, he was given command of the Wilmington district. Until this time the politically able Ashe had been spared the danger of showing his military inaptitude. With the start of active military operations in the South, however, his good luck ran out. He was badly defeated at BRIAR CREEK, 3 Mar. '79, tried by court-martial (Gen. Moultrie presiding), and severely censured for "want of sufficient vigilance." In justice to Ashe, he was on the receiving end of an exceptionally able and daring attack; few other American generals would have done much better. A man of high character and of demonstrated patriotism, he was greatly depressed by his experience. When the British overran his part of the Carolinas he went into hiding. Betrayed to the enemy in 1781, he was paroled but died in Oct. '81 of smallpox. (*D.A.B.*)

ASSOCIATED LOYALISTS. While this name was adopted by various Tory organizations, it is most commonly associated with two specific ones. During the British occupation of R.I., Col. Edw. Winslow Jr. formed the "Associated Loyalists of New England," also called the "Loyal Association of Refugees," to revenge losses and indignities suffered at the hands of the patriots. They made several raids to Long Island, capturing vessels, cattle, and people. (*D.A.H.* article by W. H. Siebert, "Associated Loyalists. . . .") The better-known organization grew out of a meeting held in London on 29 May '80 with Sir Wm. Pepperrell as chairman and Joseph Galloway on the committee to draw up an address to the king. Wm. Franklin, son of Benj. Franklin, became the head of this organization, whose purpose, apart from revenge and plunder, was to give the Tories some sort of legitimate status in dealing with the British and American governments. In Nov. '80 the Associated Loyalists were given authority by Clinton to make war under their own officers, but Sir Henry viewed the body with a lack of enthusiasm and withheld some of the powers requested by its board. In connection with the Yorktown surrender the Board of Associated Loyalists informed Clinton in great alarm that they considered themselves "abandoned to the power of an inveterate, implacable enemy" (Clinton's words) by the 10th article of the capitulation, in which the Americans refused to promise that the Tory prisoners at Yorktown would not be punished for joining the British. (Clinton, *Amer. Reb.*, 352) Clinton was unable to give them any satisfaction on this particular matter, but their influence was sufficiently strong for him to feel obliged to pacify them by directing that British commanders in the future would "pay the same attention . . . to the interests and security of the loyalists within their respective districts that they did to those of the King's troops. . . ." (*Ibid.*, 353) The HUDDY–ASGILL AFFAIR led Clinton to deprive the Associated Loyalists of all their powers, and in Aug. '82 Franklin left for England.

See Van Doren, *Secret History, passim.*

ASSOCIATED REFUGEES. See FANNING'S REGT.

ASSOCIATION. Various "associations" of Loyalists as well as of Patriots were created during the pre-Revolutionary period as a means of organizing and testing political strength. Members were known as "associators."

The Virginia Association was adopted 18 May '69 as a NONIMPORTATION agreement banning British goods on which a duty was charged (except paper), slaves (after 1 Nov.), and many European luxuries. A Maryland provisional convention on 22 June drew up a similar association, but added a provision for boycotting those who would not make a similar compact. Other colonies and individual port towns followed suit.

The Continental Association ("The Association"), signed by the first Cont'l. Congress 20 Oct. '74, was modeled after the Virginia Association. After expressing loyalty and enumerating grievances, the document states:

"To obtain redress of these grievances, which threaten destruction to the lives, liberty, and property of his majesty's subjects, in North-America, we are of opinion, that a non-importation, non-consumption, and non-exportation agreement, faithfully adhered to, will prove the most speedy, effectual, and peaceable measure: . . ." (Commager, *Docs.*, 85) Nonimportation was to be effective 1 Dec. '74, and nonexportation on 10 Sept. '75. The document included provisions for enforcement by committees of correspondence, discontinuation of the slave trade, development of American agriculture and industry, and called for austerity. By April the Association was operating in 12 colonies; Georgia adopted a modified version 23 Jan. '75. Evidence of its effectiveness is the decrease of over 90 per cent in the value of English imports by the American colonies between 1774 and 1775. Desperate English merchants put pressure on the government for reconciliation with the colonies; they were worried not only by the decline in business but also by the fact that if war broke out they would never collect the large sums owed them by American planters. "There was more to the Association than met the eye," points out Montross; it was actually "the crude political forerunner of the Confederation and the Constitution." (Montross, *Reluctant Rebels,* 58) Commager quotes the historian R. Hildreth as saying, "The signature of the Association may be considered as the commencement of the American Union."

Other associations of a different nature began to be organized in early 1775. Unlike those created for commercial retaliation, these promoted armed opposition to England. "In these associations the spirit of war appears for the first time." (Van Tyne, *Loyalists,* 75–76)

ASSOCIATORS. As mentioned at the end of the preceding article, certain "associations" were military rather than political. Among these were the "Philadelphia Associators" who reinforced Washington in the dark days of Dec. '76. (See NEW JERSEY CAMPAIGN)

According to *The Army Lineage Book, Volume II: Infantry* (Washington, 1953) this militia organization was constituted 7 Dec. '47 by official recognition of The Associators, who had been founded 21 Nov. '47 in Philadelphia by Benj. Franklin. Organized 29 Dec. '47 as the "Associated Regiment of Foot of Philadelphia," they were reorganized in 1775 as the "Associators of the City & Liberties of Philadelphia," with five battalions. In 1777 they were reorganized as the "Philadelphia Brigade of Militia" under command of John Cadwalader. On 11 Apr. '93 they were again reorganized as volunteer infantry elements of the 1st Brig., 1st Div., Pa. militia. The modern 111th Inf. Regt. of the Pa. National Guard traces its lineage to the Associators. (*Op. cit.,* 307)

"ASSUMPTION" was a political issue that arose when Sec. of the Treas. Hamilton proposed that the federal government "assume" some $18,000,000 of state debts incurred during the Revolution. At the same time there was a controversy over the site for the national capital. Alexander White and Richard Bland LEE of Va., both opposed to assumption, attended the meeting engineered by Jefferson with Hamilton in July '89. In return for Hamilton's consent to the choice of a site on the Potomac for what is now Washington, D.C., White and Lee endorsed assumption. Gale and Daniel Carroll of Md. also changed sides; assumption was passed and the Potomac River site was selected. (*D.A.B.,* "R. B. Lee"; *D.A.H.,* "Assumption . . .")

ATLANTIC CROSSING. Allowing for calms and storms, it normally took an 18th-century sailing vessel a month to cross from America to England and twice that time to return. (Westerly winds prevailed.) Four months would be a reasonable time for a British official to wait for a reply to a dispatch sent to America. Instances of faster communication can be cited, but on the other hand the last dispatches from England that Gen. Howe received in Boston before evacuating that place on 17 Mar. '76 were dated 22 Oct. '75. Not a single supply ship reached Boston during this 148-day period. The reason for this was the exceptionally bad weather that winter.

Convoy movement, made necessary because of privateers, was much slower because the slowest ship dictated the pace. Van Tyne writes:

"The passage was dangerous, too, as the safe passage of only one supply ship during three months of the Siege of Boston testified.* * * In the seven years of the American war seventy-six ships foundered or were wrecked. Some had hulls leaky and worm-eaten, others had bows that might be wave-crushed." [In another work the same author elaborates as follows:] "As a result of embezzlement, thievery, swindling, or at the best, of official carelessness in the dockyards, the transports were often little better than floating charnel houses. Of thirty-four ships, said by the Admiralty to be in prime condition, Keppel on one occasion found only six 'fit to meet a seaman's eye.' " (*Eng. and America,* 120–21; *War of Indep.,* 97)

The ordeal of this transatlantic crossing was a great deterrent to RECRUITING IN GREAT BRITAIN, according to Van Tyne:

"Current stories of a soldier's life on a transport were enough to deter the stoutest English patriot from enlistment.* * * Press gangs justled him on ship-board where the cat, the rattan, and the rope's-end cowed him into obedience. There he and his fellows were 'pressed and packed like sardines' in bunks between decks, so that in storm, with portholes made tight, they gasped for air as if 'buried alive in coffins.'

"These were the horrors of the night, but the day was often worse. Kicked and caned by the mate or sergeant, branded, pilloried and starved, the soldier arrived at the voyage's end only to be robbed by the purser or paymaster. If he rioted or protested against this beastly treatment it was attributed to the unrest of his wicked heart.* * * For food, the soldier on a transport had oatmeal, often sour and weevily, boiled in ship water full of worms. . . . His daily bread was often full of vermin, his bacon sometimes four or five years old. War profiteers furnished meat that had lain in salt for years. It was under such conditions that English armies must be flung three thousand miles to fight their fellow subjects." (*Eng. and America,* 124; the same general material is in *War of Indep.,* 97 *ff.*) (See also CHARLESTON EXPED. of Clinton in 1780 for horrors of the 38-day coastal trip and unscheduled voyage of the ANNA.)

ATTAINDER, Acts of. These were passed by American states to extinguish the civil rights and confiscate the property of Loyalists on the grounds of treason. In many instances they outlawed the individual not only in the sense that he could not sue or testify in court but also in the sense that his life was *ipso facto* forfeited. An attainted individual could neither receive nor transmit by inheritance. See LOYALISTS. The Constitution provided that no *bill* of attainder would be legal and that no act of attainder could affect relatives. (A bill of attainder is one that attaints an individual without a judicial trial.)

ATTAMAHAW. See ALTAMAHAW.

ATTUCKS, Crispus. *c.* 1723–1770. Agitator. The leader of the mob that precipitated the BOSTON "MASSACRE," 5 Mar. '70, and one of the three Americans killed outright, he is generally believed to have been a gigantic, knock-kneed mulatto slave who ran away from Deacon William Browne of Framingham, Mass., in 1750. (E. K. Alden in *D.A.B.*) A strong argument also has been presented to prove that he was an Indian, and there is evidence that he may have been of mixed Indian and Negro blood. (*Ibid.*)

AUGSBURG, WAR OF THE LEAGUE OF. See King William's War (1689–97) under COLONIAL WARS.

AUGUSTA, Ga., 29 Jan.–13 Feb. '79. Occupied by British under Col. Archibald Campbell. See SOUTHERN THEATER, Mil. Opns. in.

AUGUSTA, Ga., 14–18 Sept. '80. Clarke's abortive attack. While Ferguson led Tory operations that culminated in his annihilation at KINGS MOUNTAIN, Col. Elijah Clarke and Lt. Col. James McCall undertook to wipe out the important Tory stronghold at Augusta. McCall recruited only 80 of the 500 men he hoped to get with the assistance of Pickens in the neighborhood of Ninety-Six. In his home territory of Wilkes County, Ga., Clarke assembled 350, and McCall joined forces with him at Soap Creek, 40 miles N.W. of Augusta. In three columns the rebels approached their objective on 14 Sept. without having been detected. The left column, under Maj. Samuel Taylor, surprised an Indian camp near Hawk's Creek and chased the savages into the White House, a strongly fortified trading post a mile and a half west of Augusta. When Cols. Thos. Brown and Grierson

left the town to join the Indians and
Capt. Johnson's company of King's
Rangers at the White House, Clarke
and McCall captured Forts Cornwallis
and Grierson in Augusta. Leaving detachments to hold these forts, the rebels
concentrated their fire on the White
House from 11 A.M. until darkness.
The next day (15 Sept.) two guns from
Ft. Grierson were brought into action,
but Capt. Martin of S.C. was the only
qualified artillerist among the besiegers
and he was killed early in the day.
Clarke's force cut off the enemy's water
supply early on the 15th when they
drove an Indian outpost from the river
bank, and that night they stopped an attempt by 50 well-armed Indians to reinforce the garrison. But the rebels were
not strong enough to take the position by assault and Brown, although
wounded early in the action and suffering severely from thirst, was not a
man to give up. When Col. John Cruger appeared on the S.C. side of the
river the morning of the 18th with the
expected relief column from Ninety-
Six, Clarke abandoned the siege about
10 A.M. and headed west for the safety
of the mountains.

The patriots lost about 60 killed and
wounded; many others deserted during
the siege with plunder from the forts.
Capt. Ashby and 28 others were hanged
on the stairway of the White House.
Aside from 20 Indians killed, Tory
losses are not known.

"It was a reckless, ill-advised expedition," says Fisher. (*Struggle,* II, 347)
Failing to accomplish its purpose, it
caused an outburst of Tory vindictive-
ness in the region, and 400 women and
children were forced to flee with the
300 survivors of Clarke's expedition
toward N.C. (Ward, *W.O.R.,* 739) Attempts by Ferguson to intercept this column figured prominently in the events
preceding KINGS MOUNTAIN, 7 Oct.

AUGUSTA, Ga., 22 May–5 June '81.
(SOUTHERN CAMPAIGNS OF GREENE) As
the main rebel army moved against
Ninety-Six, Harry Lee was detached
with his Legion and the newly raised
N.C. militia of Maj. Pinketham Eaton
to support the 1,300 militia of Pickens
and Elijah Clarke besieging Augusta.
Col. Thos. Brown with 330 Tory militia and 300 Creek Indians were holding
Ft. Cornwallis, on the N.W. side of the
town, 150 yards from the Savannah
River, and the smaller post about half
a mile west that was called Ft. Grierson. Augusta had been invested since
16 Apr. About the middle of May,
Clarke had resumed command of the
Ga. militia around Augusta, and a detachment of mountaineers under Isaac
Shelby and Ga. troops under Patrick
Carr had been sent by him to block
a Tory relief column; at Walker's
Bridge, on Briar Creek, Shelby and
Carr stopped and drove back the Tory
force of Maj. Dill. (Lossing, II, 717)
This and other little successes encouraged Clarke to believe that Augusta
could be taken by assault, and it was
at this stage that Pickens and Lee
were ordered by Greene to undertake
this operation. Lee's capture of FT.
GALPHIN, 21 May, was an important
preliminary action that deprived Brown
of a considerable body of reserves (two
Tory companies) and supplies.

Lee's cavalry, under Maj. Egleston,
were the first to join the militia around
Augusta. Egleston informed Brown that
strong reinforcements were on the way
from Greene's army and summoned the
Tory commander to surrender; Brown
refused. Lee's main body arrived the
morning of the 23d, and the rebels immediately surrounded Col. Grierson's
fort, attacked from three sides, and captured it with little difficulty. When the
80 defenders tried to fight their way
half a mile east to Ft. Cornwallis they

were overwhelmed and brutally chopped up: 30 were killed and almost all the others wounded and captured. Col. Grierson was murdered by Capt. Samuel Alexander of the Ga. militia almost as soon as he was captured. (*Ibid.,* 718 and *n.*) Among the few rebel casualties at Ft. Grierson was Maj. Eaton. An attempt by Brown to make a sortie in support of Grierson was checked by Lee.

Ft. Cornwallis was a harder nut to crack. The only available artillery was the little 3-pdr. of Capt. Finley (Lee's Legion) and an old iron 5-pdr. that Clarke had picked up. One of the two guns captured from Grierson was later brought into action. Meanwhile, Lee and Pickens had to undertake regular approaches. On Lee's suggestion a Maham Tower was started. Brown tried to drive the builders off with fire from his two heaviest guns, and he launched two determined but unsuccessful sorties. He then secretly moved powder into a frame house that stood between the fort and the tower. According to Lossing, Brown then sent a wily Scot to masquerade as a deserter and talk the attackers into burning the house to clear their field of observation. According to Ward, the "deserter's" mission was to burn the tower, and the house was mined with a view to blowing it up when rebel riflemen entered it to support their expected attack. In any event, Lee suspected the motives of the deserter and had him locked up before he could do any harm either by his acts or advice, and the house was prematurely blown up by the defenders without damage either to the tower or the rebel troops. (Lossing, 718; Ward, 815)

On 31 May, Brown refused a second surrender summons. That night a captured 6-pdr. from Ft. Grierson was mounted in the tower and the next morning the rebels started an effective cannon and small arms fire from it. After riflemen had driven the enemy gun crews away from their pieces, the 6-pdr. dismounted the two cannon that had been firing on the tower.

On 4 June the attackers were formed for the final assault when Brown agreed to consider a conditional surrender. After a day of negotiations the Tories laid down their arms and were marched off under guard to be paroled in Savannah. A strong guard of regulars had to protect Brown from Grierson's fate. Lee marched with the prisoners to NINETY-SIX. Pickens followed later, but was then sent with the cavalry of Lee and Washington to oppose the relief column led by Rawdon to Ninety-Six.

Rebel losses were about 40 during the siege. (Ward, 815) The Tories had 52 killed and 334 captured. (Lossing, II, 719)

AUSTRIAN SUCCESSION, War of the. 1740–48. Caused by Frederick the Great of Prussia's rejection of the Pragmatic Sanction (by which Charles VI decreed in 1713 that his territories should pass to his daughter Maria Theresa if there were no male heir) and by Austria's invasion of Silesia (Dec. '40), this war started with France, Spain, Saxony, and Sardinia supporting the Bavarian claim to the imperial title in 1741. Each of the allies coveted a portion of the Hapsburg dominions. Britain arranged a peace between Austria and Prussia in 1742. George II led Anglo-Prussian forces in operations that resulted in French defeat at Dettingen, 27 June '43, and French withdrawal from German soil. In 1743 an alliance of Britain, Austria, and Sardinia was formed to drive France and Spain from Italy. France, Spain, and Prussia joined forces in 1744. After the French victory of Marshal de Saxe at FONTENOY, which gave them control of Flanders, Prussia withdrew from the alliance, retaining

Silesia. In 1746 the Bourbons were driven from northern Italy.

France declared war on England in 1744, which touched off the Second Jacobite Rebellion; the latter was crushed at CULLODEN. The European conflict evolved into a struggle for maritime and colonial supremacy, and the American phase was King George's War. The British captured Louisburg in 1745, the French took Madras in 1746, and England gained control of the seas. (The War of Jenkins' Ear, 1739–42, was related to the War of the Austrian Succession; see COLONIAL WARS.)

The treaty of Aachen, 18 Oct. '48, restored all conquests, including Louisburg—much to the disgust of Americans. Prussia retained Silesia, Holland regained her frontier fortresses, the Pragmatic Sanction was guaranteed, Francis I (Maria Theresa's consort and coregent) was recognized as emperor of Austria, Parma and Piacenza went to Spain, Savoy and Nice became part of Sardinia, France was to expel the Young Pretender.

The war forms part of the background of the American Revolution. It is of interest also because many officers who served in the conflict were later involved in the Revolution.

B

BACKGROUND AND ORIGINS OF THE REVOLUTION. 1560–1775. While the era of the American Revolution may be considered to start around 1763, any study of this era must include military, economic, and political events prior to 1763. This article is intended as a summary of and also as a topical and chronological index to the "background" topics covered in this book.

The critical year 1763 saw the COLONIAL WARS end. The Treaty of PARIS, signed in this year, left England the undisputed victor over a humiliated France and an impotent Spain. Not immediately apparent, however, were England's serious weaknesses: a crushing debt, world-wide commitments, lack of allies, and a weak home government. George III had acceded to the throne in 1760 with the determination to "be a King," but with few qualifications for achieving this ambition. Although "the court of George III was clean, and his conduct worthy of an Englishman, a Christian, and a King" (Van Tyne, *War of Independence,* 162–63), English society and government of the period were decadent and corrupt.

MERCANTILISM, translated into statute law by the Acts of Trade and Navigation (see NAVIGATION ACTS), was a philosophy that exerted a strong influence on Anglo-American relations before the Revolution. Although the basic Navigation Acts dated from 1651, it was not until England's economic crisis of 1763 and George III's assumption of leadership that she abandoned the policy of SALUTARY NEGLECT and turned to her colonies for desperately needed revenue.

The Americans, however, were in a particularly unsympathetic mood at this time. Economically, they had their own troubles in the form of a postwar depression. Militarily, elimination of the traditional French and Indian threat made them feel less dependent on British troops for protection; this dependence had been one of the firmest ties between the colonies and the mother country. Politically, the colonists had scored an impressive series of victories against the Crown during the French and Indian War (1755–63), and the colonial assemblies, full of their own strength, were ready for battle. (Miller, *Origins of the American Revolution,* 37–39)

Almost from the beginning, English colonists had the institutions and political outlook that made for strong feelings of personal liberty and hatred of arbitrary government. Their jealousy of inherited "English rights" had been encouraged and fostered by the home country to stimulate settlement. Among the many things that combined to permit growth of an independent spirit in America were distance from England and lack of a strong central administration of colonial affairs. (See Board of TRADE) The English Civil War (1642–46), which started just when Charles I was about to "apply the rod to Puritans overseas" (Miller, *op. cit.,* 29), and subsequent preoccupations in England during Cromwell's Commonwealth (1649–60), gave the colonists a long period of virtual independence. Enactment of the NAVIGATION ACTS (1650–96) did not bother the colonists at first, since the previously mentioned policy of SALUTARY NEGLECT was long followed.

Although the Crown gradually supplanted charter and proprietary governments with ROYAL GOVERNMENTS in the colonies, most royal governors were incompetent political appointees, dominated by the colonial assemblies. Even if the governor had been capable, he had the impossible task of trying to execute royal instructions through an elected colonial assembly that appointed many of the administrative officers, initiated all laws, made appropriations, and controlled the colonial purse strings, including payment of his own salary.

The existence of representative assemblies in all the colonies by 1776 was an "institutional affinity [that] laid the foundations for the concerted resistance without which the American Revolution would have been impossible." (Miller, *op. cit.,* 31)

At a distance of almost two centuries we may also lose sight of the fact that the "English at home and in the colonies were wholly different types." (Egerton, *Causes,* 13) It is surprising to find that James Otis, a prominent colonial politician before the Revolution, was a fifth-generation American; on the other hand, this helps explain Egerton's statement. The colonists argued that they were "better Englishmen than the English, sounder interpreters of the British constitution than George III, and more consistent defenders of the fundamental laws of nature than the sovereign Parliament." (Pollard, *Factors,* 19)

When Americans had exhausted the resources of accepted legal and political arguments in their quarrel with the British government they invoked NATURAL LAW and developed new political theories. They also showed a genius for PROPAGANDA.

The background and origins of the American Revolution constitute a complex and controversial field in which historians continue to produce new interpretations and arrive at varying conclusions. The preceding discussion has attempted to include the high lights. The following chronology presents additional background and will serve as an index to entries to be found in alphabetical order throughout this book.

A selected bibliography follows the chronology.

Chronological Index of Events Leading to the American Revolution

c.1560–1760	COLONIAL WARS
1651–73	Basic NAVIGATION ACTS implement MERCANTILISM but are mitigated by policy of SALUTARY NEGLECT
1696–1782	Colonial affairs directed by Board of TRADE
1696	Vice-ADMIRALTY COURTS established
1733	Molasses Act (see NAVIGATION ACTS)
1740–48	War of AUSTRIAN SUCCESSION (see this article for some important background of European affairs)
1749	OHIO COMPANY
1754	ALBANY CONVENTION and Plan of Union
1755–63	French and Indian War (last of COLONIAL WARS)
1760	GEORGE III ascends throne
	WRITS OF ASSISTANCE widely applied
1763	Treaty of PARIS
	PONTIAC'S WAR
	PROCLAMATION OF 1763
	PARSON'S CAUSE
	Grenville's Ministry starts
1764	SALUTARY NEGLECT ends
	Sugar Act (see NAVIGATION ACTS)
	Colonial CURRENCY ACT
1765	STAMP ACT
	SONS OF LIBERTY formed
	TAR AND FEATHERS
	NONIMPORTATION
	QUARTERING ACTS
1765 (cont'd.)	VIRGINIA RESOLVES (May)
	Stamp Act CONGRESS called (June)
	Declaration of Rights and Grievances (see STAMP ACT)
	Rockingham's Ministry succeeds Grenville's (July)
1766	Stamp Act repealed
	DECLARATORY ACT
	Chatham's Ministry (1766–68)
1767	TOWNSHEND ACTS
	Nonimportation revived
1768	MASSACHUSETTS CIRCULAR LETTER
	FARMER'S LETTERS
	LIBERTY AFFAIR (June)
	British troops arrive in Boston (Oct.)
	Grafton's Ministry (1768–70)
1770	BOSTON "MASSACRE" (March)
	GOLDEN HILL
	North's Ministry
	Townshend Duties, except on tea, repealed
	Agitation at a lull; nonimportation discontinued
1771	Battle of ALAMANCE
1772	GASPÉE AFFAIR
	Committees of Correspondence (see SONS OF LIBERTY)
1773	TEA ACT
	BOSTON TEA PARTY
	HUTCHINSON LETTERS AFFAIR
1774	INTOLERABLE ACTS (March)
	QUEBEC ACT
	SUFFOLK RESOLVES
(cont'd.)	Cont'l. CONGRESS assembles

1774 (cont'd) GALLOWAY PLAN OF UNION
Cont'l. ASSOCIATION adopted

1775 Conciliation proposed by North
SALEM Bridge Affair
LEXINGTON AND CONCORD
2d Cont'l. Congress assembles
Washington commander in chief
BUNKER HILL
BOSTON SIEGE (July '75–Mar. '76)
CANADA INVASION

1776 COMMON SENSE published
INDEPENDENCE voted by Congress

Works devoted entirely or primarily to the causes and origins of the Revolution are those by Andrews, Egerton, Gipson, Howard, Knollenberg, Miller, Van Tyne, and Wahlke. See also the special studies by Beers (British colonial policy), E. B. Greene (provincial America), Jameson (*The American Revolution Considered as a Social Movement*),* Labaree (royal government), Osgood (American colonies in 17th and 18th centuries), Eric Robson (political and military aspects of the Revolution), Sachse (colonial Americans in England), and L. B. Wright (cultural aspects).

BAHAMAS. New Providence (now Nassau) was twice captured by American naval forces: see two entries headed NASSAU. Spanish forces captured the defenseless islands in the summer of 1782.

* Jameson's thesis that the Revolution had very democratizing political and economic effects is no longer entirely accepted by most historians.

BALDWIN, Jeduthan. 1732–1788. Cont'l. officer. Mass. Born in Woburn and undoubtedly related to Loammi BALDWIN, he later established his home in Brookfield. After commanding a company in the French and Indian War and serving in the Mass. Prov. Cong., 1774–75, he entered the Cont'l. Army on 16 Mar. '76 as Capt. Assist. Engineer. Charged with constructing fortifications for the Boston Siege, his *Journal* (*post*) is a valuable source of details on that campaign. On 3 Sept. '76 he was promoted to Col. of Engrs. after having been active in constructing the defenses of N.Y.C. The next year he worked with Kosciuszko, under St. Clair's command, in the fortification of Ticonderoga, and in 1780 he was associated with the same two men in constructing the works at West Point. In what presumably was a concurrent assignment, Baldwin raised several companies of quartermaster ARTIFICERS.

"Colonel Jeduthan Baldwin of Brookfield could not have passed a test in theory but he knew how to get the most in practice from country lads working with pick and spade under fire," writes Montross in his *Rag, Tag and Bobtail* (p. 81). He apparently possessed the temperament to work harmoniously with Kosciuszko, who had the technical qualifications that Baldwin lacked. His *Revolutionary Journal*, edited by Thomas J. Baldwin, was published in Bangor, Me., 1906.

BALDWIN, Loammi. 1740–1807. Civil engineer, Cont'l. officer. Mass. Born in Woburn and descended from a founder of that town, he became a cabinetmaker. He was ambitious for higher learning and several times a week would walk to Cambridge with his friend Benjamin THOMPSON to attend lectures on mathematics and physics by Prof. John Winthrop of Harvard. Progressing from surveyor, he had become a civil engineer by the time the war started. He became Maj. of militia and was at Concord, 19 Apr. '75. (Heitman) On 19 May he became Lt. Col. of Gerrish's Mass. Regt., succeeded him as commander when Gerrish was cashiered 19 Aug. (Heitman, 246; the *D.A.B.* sketch of Baldwin says "on Gerrish's retirement.") When the regiment was redesignated the 26th Cont'l. on 1 Jan. '76 and increased from eight to 10 companies, Baldwin was promoted to Col. He served through the Boston Siege, went to N.Y. with the main army, saw action at PELL'S POINT, took part in the retreat to the Delaware, and led his regiment at Trenton, 26 Dec. '76. Because of continued ill health (*D.A.B.*) he resigned on 31 Dec. '76. (Heitman)

After holding a number of political posts he returned to a full-time pursuit of civil engineering as a leading projector and chief engineer of the Middlesex Canal joining the Charles and Merrimac Rivers. While so engaged he got into a project that made his name a household word: finding a seedling apple tree whose fruit was exceptionally good, he grafted it to his own trees and developed what we know as the "Baldwin" apple. This has been called "the standard winter apple of Eastern America," it might be pointed out for the benefit of the reader who remains unimpressed.

His son Loammi (1780–1838) has been called the "Father of Civil Engineering in America."

BALFOUR, Nisbet. 1743–1832. British officer. Of a noble Scottish family—not, as is sometimes said, the son of a bookseller—he entered the army in 1761 as an ensign in the 4th Regt. By 1770 he had reached the grade of Capt., but had had no combat experience. He was badly wounded at Bunker Hill and saw action at Long Island, 27 Aug. '76. His services had been so conspicuous

that he was sent home with the dispatches of victory and breveted Maj. After taking part in the Philadephia Campaign, he was appointed Lt. Col. of the 23d Regt. in 1778. Moving south with Clinton, he took part in the Charleston Expedition of 1780. When the British pushed inland to secure their hold on the South, Balfour was put in command of the isolated and strategic post of Ninety-Six, where he had three battalions of Royal Provincials and some light infantry. (Ward, *W.O.R.*, 704) Here he assisted Ferguson in raising 4,000 Tory militia. Before Cornwallis left Charleston around mid-Aug. '80 to take command of Rawdon's forces for the Camden Campaign he called Balfour back to be commandant of Charleston. In this capacity he supported the subsequent operations of Cornwallis and Rawdon, both of whom held him in highest esteem. (Balfour was actually senior to Rawdon. See RAWDON-HASTINGS.) His execution of Isaac HAYNE was considered by the patriots to mark Balfour's character "with the foul stain of dishonor and savage cruelty"—to be the act of "a proud, vain, and ambitious man ... [who] knew that the surest road to distinction was rigor toward the rebels." (Lossing, II, 774 and *n.*) Cornwallis, on the other hand, commended him for following his instructions and for showing the courage to accept responsibility. (*D.N.B.*)

Balfour was rewarded for his war service by promotion to Col. and the appointment as A.D.C. to the King. He and a lawyer were selected to award to Loyalists the money granted by Parliament to compensate them for their losses. In 1790 he was elected to Parliament. Three years later, when the war started against the French, Balfour was promoted to Maj. Gen. and took part in the operations of

RAWDON. He remained to serve under Ralph Abercromby in Flanders until Dec. '94, which ended his active military duty. Meanwhile he had been made Col. of the 93d Regt. in 1793 and of the 39th the next year. Named Lt. Gen. in 1798, returned to Parliament in 1802, and promoted to full Gen. in 1803, he was the sixth ranking general in the British Army when he died at the age of 80, 62 years after starting his military career.

BALME. See MOTTIN DE LA BALME.

BANCROFT, Edward. 1744–1820. Double agent, writer, inventor. Born at Westfield, Mass., he led an adventurous life as a sailor and colonist in Dutch Guiana before settling in London. Here he wrote on American subjects for the *Monthly Review*, published his *Essay on the Natural History of Guiana* (1769), *Remarks on the Review of the Controversy between Great Britain and Her Colonies* (1769), and *Charles Wentworth* (1770), a novel attacking Christianity. Despite a lack of regular schooling in his early years, he had become a well-educated man, had studied medicine in England, was a scientific observer while living in Guiana, and in London he became a friend of Benjamin Franklin. A natural intriguer, he served as Franklin's spy in London and later performed in the same role for Silas Deane. These two Americans never suspected Bancroft, who also gained the confidence of John Paul Jones. In Dec. '76 he became a spy for the British, assuming the name Edwards. With a pay of £400 initially, increased to £1,000 a year, and promised the post of regius professor of divinity at King's (Columbia) College when N.Y. was returned to British control, Bancroft was given the mission of spying on the American commissioners in Paris. His reports were sent to Paul Wentworth, another double spy, in Lon-

don. Using his secret information, he speculated on war news such as Burgoyne's defeat and peace negotiations, although he sometimes suffered losses. As an inventor he made important discoveries in the field of textile dyes. His *Experimental Researches Concerning the Philosophy of Permanent Colours* was published in 1794 and expanded in 1813. (*D.A.B.*)

Although his treachery did not come to light for nearly 70 years after his death, Edward Bancroft "continued to be a British subject after the Revolution and from time to time furnished later ministers advice and information that seemed to indicate his enduring fidelity." (Van Doren, *Secret History*, 431) See Einstein, *Divided Loyalties* (1933) and Prof. Boyd's article cited under Silas DEANE.

BARBÉ-MARBOIS, François, Marquis de. 1745–1837. French politician. Accompanying Luzerne to Philadelphia in 1779 as his secretary, he soon married a local girl. From his vantage point in the French legation he felt he had acquired information on which to base a history of Arnold's treason: his *Complot d'Arnold . . .*, published in 1816, is "Lively but full of conjectures and melodramatic inventions. English version by Robert Walsh in *American Register*, II, 15–63." (Van Doren, *Secret History*, 496) His interesting American diary and letters for the period 1779–85 was published as E. P. Chase, *Our Revolutionary Forefathers, The Letters of François, Marquis de Barbé-Marbois* (New York, 1929).

After leaving Philadelphia he became intendant of San Domingo, returning to France at the close of 1789, and served in diplomatic positions under the revolutionary government. His loyalty having been under suspicion on two previous occasions, he was arrested after the coup d'état of 4 Sept. '97, transported to French Guiana, and freed by Napoleon in 1799. In 1803 he negotiated the Louisiana Purchase. Noted for his servility, he survived the vicissitudes of French politics under six governments. (*E.B.*) He published several books on his experiences.

BARRAS, Jacques-Melchior Saint-Laurent, Comte de. Died *c.* 1800. French admiral. As commander of the French squadron at Newport at the start of the YORKTOWN CAMPAIGN, he was somewhat of a problem to Washington and Rochambeau because of his independent views: unwillingness to convoy the French army into the Chesapeake, unwillingness to move to Boston when the French army left Newport (which would have created a requirement to leave American troops to protect his anchorage at Newport), his desire to undertake a raid against British shipping off Newfoundland at a time when his support was needed in the Yorktown Campaign, and his hesitation about cooperating with the lower-ranking de Grasse around Yorktown. (See UNITY OF COMMAND.) He eventually cooperated with the allied armies, however, and safely entered the harbor of Yorktown on 10 Sept. '81, after the battle off CHESAPEAKE CAPES, 5 Sept. '81. In 1782 he especially distinguished himself in the West Indies by capturing Montserrat from the British. (Appleton's) The next year he retired from active service with the grade of Lt. Gen. of the Navy. (*Ibid.*)

I have followed the form of his name in the index to Chastellux, *Travels....* He is indexed in Clinton, *American Rebellion,* as Barras de Saint-Laurent, Louis, Comte de, and is listed in Appleton's as Barras, Count Louis de. Freeman wisely avoids the issue by indexing him merely as Barras, Comte de.

Rochambeau described him to Washington, before the Wethersfield Con-

ference, as "above 60 years of age, a particular friend of Count d'Estaing; he commanded his vanguard when he forced the entry of this harbor [of NEWPORT, 5–8 Aug. '78]." Chastellux privately—if inaccurately—assured Washington, "The Admiral is a good, plain dealing gentleman who will give no difficulty." (Quoted in Freeman, *Washington,* V, 286–87 and *n.*)

BARRÉ, Isaac. 1762–1802. British officer and politician. Famous in America as a champion of their rights, Isaac Barré was the son of a French refugee who had become a prominent merchant in Dublin. Isaac was educated at Trinity College in Dublin, took his degrees in 1745, and despite his parents' desires that he become an attorney had entered the army as an ensign the next year. During the unsuccessful attack on Rochefort in 1757 he won the high regard of James Wolfe and Lord Shelburne, the latter being Col. of his regiment. He was with Wolfe when the latter was killed at Quebec and is in the famous picture by West. At Quebec Barré received a disfiguring wound, a bullet remaining lodged in his cheek to give his swarthy face a "savage glare." (W. P. Courtney in *D.N.B.*) Pitt turned down his application for advancement in 1760, but he was Lt. Col. in command of the 106th Foot from 1761 to 1763.

Through Shelburne's influence he entered Parliament on 5 Dec. '61 and five days later delivered a vehement speech against Pitt. (*Ibid.*) On 7 Feb. '65 he blasted the proposal to tax the American colonists and referred to them as "sons of liberty." The patriots adopted this name for the groups opposing the Stamp Act. Almost without rival as an opposition orator, he was a hero in America, a terror to the government, and second in unpopularity with George III only to John Wilkes. Wilkes-Barre,

Pa., was named after these two. When news of Bunker Hill reached England, Barré accused the troops of misbehavior. "Barré had a real grievance, since he had been unjustly deprived of his commission for political reasons," comments Fortescue, "but such a speech as this makes one ashamed that he should ever have held a commission at all." (*British Army,* III, 172–73) He went blind about 1783 but remained in Parliament until forced out in 1790 after a disagreement with Shelburne. His brother was captured under amusing circumstances at EUTAW SPRINGS.

BARREN HILL, Pa., 20 May '78. When spies brought the unexpected information that the British appeared to be preparing to evacuate Philadelphia and return to N.Y.C., Washington detached a strong force from Valley Forge in the direction of Philadelphia. The oversized outpost had three missions: to cover Valley Forge, to harass foraging parties the enemy would have to dispatch to prepare for their change of base, and to gather information that would indicate as soon as possible the enemy's movement from the city. (Freeman, *Washington,* V, 7)

For this task Washington assigned 2,200 men and five guns, a sizable portion of his effective strength and some of his best troops. Lafayette was given command of the operation, probably as a way of honoring the new French Alliance (*ibid.,* 8), and also because the young Major General had been pining for a chance to command troops in combat. With detailed instructions that emphasized the importance of his task, the value of the troops assigned, and the need for security, Lafayette left camp on 18 May, crossed the Schuykill at Swede's Ford, turned south and took up a good position at Barren Hill, near Matson's Ford. Here, at the juncture of several important roads, he was mid-

way between the two armies: 11 miles from Philadelphia and 12 from Valley Forge. (Writing in about 1850, Lossing commented that Barren Hill could be distinctly seen from the highest point of the Valley Forge camp.)

Poor's Brig. and the guns were posted on high ground just west of the church on Barren Hill and facing south; their right flank was protected by steep bluffs that drop off to the Schuykill, and their left was anchored on two or three stone houses along the Ridge Road. (Lossing, II, 328) Allen McLANE's independent company and 50 Oneida Indians outposted the Ridge Road to the south toward Philadelphia, and James Potter's Pa. militia were sent to guard the road that led west from White Marsh.

That night, the 18th, Lafayette settled down in this position while the British celebrated their MISCHIANZA, but the enemy had already learned of his expedition and planned to gobble up his isolated force.

THE BRITISH PLAN

Grant was to leave Philadelphia at 10:30 the night of 19 May with 5,000 men and 15 guns to take a circuitous route leading to the junction of the White Marsh and Ridge roads, a mile and a half north of Barren Hill; this would cut off Lafayette's retreat along Ridge Road to Matson's or Swede's Ford. Grey would lead 2,000 grenadiers and a small troop of dragoons up the road from Germantown and then along the road that led to Lafayette's left (east) flank. Clinton and Howe would lead a strong force up the Ridge Road and go into position close to Poor's front. Having thus encircled Lafayette with greatly superior forces on three sides, trapping him against the river, the British would close in the morning of the 20th to capture or annihilate his entire command. It looked like such a sure thing that Howe planned a dinner party for the evening of the 20th "to meet the Marquis de La Fayette." (Ward, 565)

THE ACTION

Potter's militia scattered before Grant's advance without offering any resistance and without furnishing Lafayette any information of the enemy's advance; both Grant and Grey took up their planned positions. On Ridge Road to the south, however, McLane's men picked up two British grenadiers at Three Mile Run and learned of the British plan. Sending Capt. Parr with a company of riflemen to make contact with Clinton's column and fight a delaying action, McLane raced back to warn Lafayette at dawn of the situation. About this time the sound of firing from Parr's direction and the report of a local patriot that enemy troops were on the road from White Marsh confirmed McLane's intelligence.

Lafayette had chosen his position with care, however, and he already knew (according to Freeman) or soon learned (according to Ward) something about the terrain that the enemy did not know: there was another road leading down to Matson's Ford that would bypass Grant's force. Furthermore, it ran along low ground that would conceal his troops from enemy observation. The situation was still perilous, however, and Lafayette's escape was due not only to the enemy's stupidity and overconfidence as well as his own skill and coolness under pressure, but also to Steuben's recent training at Valley Forge.

"It was really a victory of the new drill [says Lynn Montross]. In the past the rebels had marched in an 'Indian file' so extended that the head of a column ran the risk of being overwhelmed before the tail got into action. * * * Under the old system, with all its confusion and delays, hundreds of rebels would doubtless have been trapped at Barren Hill. As it proved, they owed their salvation to a swift retreat of compact platoon columns which made their way over the river without the customary disorder and straggling." (*Rag, Tag,* 280)

While the professionals delayed to reconnoiter, Lafayette coolly set up a small rear guard around the church, sent patrols to simulate an attack against Grant, calmed down the men who were showing symptoms of panic —and slipped away with only a few casualties.

The unsuspecting Clinton moved on to Barren Hill to meet—the scouts of Grant's column moving cautiously down from the north. "Toward evening," reported Baurmeister, "General Grant's troops returned to their quarters. The weather was hot, and a fruitless march totaling forty English miles fatigued the men very much." (*Journals,* 176) The others had gotten back about 2 P.M. (*Ibid.*) The guest of honor did not mess with them that evening, but reoccupied Barren Hill until his return to Washington's table on 23 May.

COMMENT

Although the Americans had a good laugh over Lafayette's artful escape, "this expedition was as useless as it was perilous": too small to furnish any real protection to the main body at Valley Forge, it was unnecessarily large for its intelligence mission. (Ward, *W.O.R.,* 562) Washington was lucky not to have paid dearly for his poor judgment in sending it out, particularly under an untried commander.

BARRY, John. 1745–1803. Cont'l. naval officer. Ireland. After going to sea at an early age he settled in Philadelphia around 1760 and became a wealthy shipmaster and owner. Early in the war he was given command of the brig *Lexington*. In taking the tender *Edward,* on 17 Apr. '76, he made "the first capture in actual battle of a British war-ship by a regularly commissioned American cruiser." (*D.A.B.*) Placed seventh on the 10 Oct. '76 list of captains, he soon took command of the *Effingham* (32) but was bottled up in the Delaware during the Philadelphia Campaign and unable to put to sea. After distinguishing himself in a number of operations in the river before his ship was burned to prevent her capture, Barry took command of the *Raleigh* (32). He lost this ship in a gallant fight against superior forces but saved most of his crew from capture. In 1781 he commanded the *Alliance* (32), in which he took many prizes before being severely wounded in the attack and capture of the *Atalanta* and *Trepassy.* Later in the year he took Lafayette back to France. In the indecisive but well-conducted ALLIANCE– SYBILLE ENGAGEMENT, Jan. '83, he fought the last important naval action of the war.

In 1794 he was named senior captain and placed in command of the *United States* (44) when Congress ordered six frigates built for the Barbary Coast operations. He saw no combat in the years that followed. In his *History of the Navy,* James Fenimore Cooper places Barry second only to John Paul Jones among the naval officers of the Revolution. (*Op. cit.,* I, 252, cited in *D.A.B.*). See Martin I. J. Griffin, *Commodore John Barry* (1897), John Frost, *American Naval Biography* (1844).

BARTLETT, Josiah. 1729–1795. Signer. Mass. After a classical education, he started the study of medicine at 16 and five years later began practicing in Kingston, N.H. A successful doctor who introduced many medical reforms, he entered the provincial assembly in 1765 and served continuously until the Revolution. He was named J.O.P. in 1767 and in 1770 took command of a militia regiment. Gov. Wentworth dismissed him from both posts in Feb. '75 for his open opposition to the Crown. In 1774 he became a member of the committee of correspondence and was sent to the first provincial congress. He had been elected to the 1774 Cont'l. Congress but was unable to accept when his house, apparently maliciously, was burned down. In 1775 he was again elected and served until 1777 when he resigned for poor health. He signed the Decl. of Indep. in 1776. In 1777 he was with Stark at Bennington as agent of the state in providing the N.H. troops with medical supplies and was Col. of militia 1777–79. He was re-elected to Congress in March '78 and voted in 1781 for the Articles of Confederation, which he had helped write. He served on many major committees and, worn physically by Congress's many moves in 1778–79, he refused re-election. Appointed chief justice of the N.H. court of common pleas, he continued in the legal field when, in 1782, he was named assoc. justice of the superior court. In 1788 he was made chief justice, serving two years. He helped ratify the Federal Constitution in 1788, and he was chief executive (then called president) of N.H. 1790–92. In 1793, when the title was changed, he was elected first governor and served for another year. He organized and was first president of the N.H. Medical Society in 1791, the year after he was given an honorary M.D. degree by Dartmouth.

BARTON, William. 1748–1831. Militia officer, captor of Gen. Richard

PRESCOTT. R.I. A hatter by trade, he became Adj. of Richmond's R.I. Regt. on 3 Aug. '75, Capt. 1 Nov., Brigade-Maj. of R.I. Troops on 19 Aug. '76, Maj. of Stanton's R.I. State Troops on 12 Dec. '76. (Heitman) Conceiving the idea of capturing Gen. Richard Prescott to exchange for Charles Lee, who at this time was considered to be an asset to the American cause, Barton carefully and secretly planned the daring raid that accomplished its mission the night of 9–10 July. With 40 volunteers of his regiment he landed on the western shore of R.I., moved a mile inland, silenced the guard on Prescott's billet, captured the general and his A.D.C., Maj. Wm. Barrington, and escaped with his prisoners. By the act of 25 July '77 he was commended by the Cont'l. Cong. and voted "an elegant sword." On 10 Nov. '77 he was promoted to Lt. Col. and on 24 Dec. '77 to Col. of Stanton's Regt. with the rank and pay of a Col. of the Cont'l. Army. (Heitman) In 1778 he was wounded in the British retreat from Warren, R.I.

Although his state declined to send delegates to the Federal convention of 1787, Barton joined others in sending the convention a letter pledging their support of the Constitution, and in 1790 he was a member of the state convention that adopted the Constitution. After refusing to pay a judgment of a piece of land he had bought or had been granted by Cong. in Vt. he was detained as a prisoner in the inn at Danville, Vt. On his visit of 1824–25 Lafayette heard of the old hero's plight, paid the claim, and Barton returned to R.I.

See Mrs. Catharine R. Williams, *Biographies of Rev. Heroes* (1839), and J. Lewis Dinman, *The Capture of Gen. Rich. Prescott....* (1877).

BASKING RIDGE, N.J., 13 Dec. '76. Charles Lee's capture. Having finally decided to comply with Washington's reiterated instructions to march south and join him, the afternoon of 12 Dec. Gen. Charles Lee established a bivouac a few miles south of Morristown. For reasons still unknown, Lee spent the night three miles from camp at the tavern of Widow White near Basking Ridge. He was accompanied by a guard of about 15 men and four other officers. Also on 12 Dec., Cornwallis sent a mounted patrol from his headquarters, which was 30 miles south of Lee at Pennington, N.J., to locate this rebel force in his rear. Lt. Col. Wm. Harcourt headed north with 25 men of his 16th Light Horse and four officers, including Cornet Banastre Tarleton. Early on the 13th, after a halt at Hillsborough, he headed for Morristown. Four or five miles from Basking Ridge a Tory gave them the location of Lee's main body, and within a mile of Lee's billet they captured two sentinels who, under threat, informed them that Lee was at the tavern with a small guard. Uncertain whether to credit this intelligence, Harcourt ordered Tarleton and two men to observe from a small hill; Tarleton soon sent back a prisoner who confirmed the other information.

The morning of Friday the 13th Lee had ordered his troops forward at about 8 o'clock but had delayed his own departure to do some paper work. He had scarcely finished his famous *"entre nous"* letter to Gates when, about 10 A.M., the British attacked from two sides. From an upstairs window Lee saw that his guard had been surprised and routed with a loss of two killed and two wounded. As fire poured into the house Lee paced the floor for about 15 minutes before sending his A.D.C., Maj. Wm. Bradford, to the door to capitulate. Lee came out to surrender to Harcourt, who had been his subordinate in Portugal, and was allowed to wait for a coat to be sent out. He then was carried off with one of his officers, the Sieur de Boisbertrand, who had received a sword wound on the head while trying to escape out the back door. Another French volunteer, Capt. de Virnejoux, and James Wilkinson, who had come with dispatches from Gates to Washington, and Bradford escaped because the British did not search the house. Although Sullivan sent out a rescue party, Harcourt got his prisoner safely to Brunswick.

The above account is based on Alden's *Lee* and generally follows the version given by Tarleton in his letter of Dec. '76 to Lord Vaughan. Alden believes that except for exaggeration of his own role Tarleton's account is the most reliable of the many that have been published. (See Freeman, *Washington,* IV, 290 *n.,* for a list of these.)

BASTION. A projection of a fortification that permits the defender to fire ENFILADE along the front of the main wall (or "curtain").

BATEAU. A flat-bottomed boat with tapering ends, it was adapted for American rivers. Most bateaux were built of plank and moved by oars, poles, or square sails. The decision to use this type of craft for Arnold's March to Quebec was a near-fatal blunder not only because it was too cumbersome for rapids and portages but also because the boats built for him were poorly constructed and were made of green lumber.

BATTALION. At the time of the Revolution the standard battalion in the British army was composed of 10 companies. The regiment was an administrative organization—as it is today in the British army—and it included two or more battalions. During the pe-

riod 1775–83, however, regiments consisted of only one battalion and the two terms were used synonymously. "Battalion companies" were the eight that remained when the two FLANK COMPANIES of grenadiers and light infantry were detached. The battalion or regiment was commanded in the British service by a Lt. Col. (the Col. having the post, often titular, of regimental commander); the Americans, who adopted the British organization, had to create the rank of "Lt. Col. Commandant" (i.e., commanding) for battalion or regimental commanders since EXCHANGE OF PRISONERS was on the basis of actual rank.

Authorized strength of the 8-company battalions (regiments) of the Cont'l. Army that Congress called for in late 1775 was about 780 men; the 88 battalions called for by the resolution of 16 Sept. '76 were to number 680 men each; this figure dropped to 522 for 1778–80, and was raised to 576 for 1781. As shown by the detailed tabulations in Upton, *Military Policy,* the battalions were seldom recruited to full strength, and replacements were rare. Many of the American and British regiments at Yorktown numbered around 200 rank and file, and few had more than 600. (See Johnston, *Yorktown,* 112–19.)

"BATTLE OF THE KEGS." After the British had won control of the Delaware (PHIL. CAMP'N.) and opened a water line of communications to captured Philadelphia, David Bushnell applied his inventive genius to destroying the British fleet by floating incendiary mines among them. The attempt failed (Jan. '78) but inspired Hopkinson's "Ballad of the Kegs."

Gallants, attend, and hear a friend
   Trill forth harmonious ditty.
Strange things I'll tell, which late befell
   In Philadelphia city.

'Twas early day, as poets say,
   Just when the sun was rising.
A soldier stood on a log of wood
   And saw a thing surprising.

As in amaze he stood to gaze—
   The truth can't be denied, sir—
He spied a score of kegs or more
   Come floating down the tide, sir.

A sailor, too, in jerkin blue,
   This strange appearance viewing,
First damned his eyes, in great surprise,
   Then said, "Some mischief's brewing.

"These kegs, I'm told, the rebels hold,
   Packed up like pickled herring,
And they're come down t'attack the
     town
   In this new way of ferrying."

In 11 more stanzas the author tells
how the alarm was spread among the
British forces and how "the cannons
roar from shore to shore, The small
arms make a rattle" until the menace
is eliminated. He concludes with:

An hundred men, with each a pen,
   Or more, upon my word, sir,
It is most true would be too few
   Their valor to record, sir.

Such feats did they perform that day
   Against those wicked kegs, sir,
That years to come, if they get home,
   They'll make their boasts and brags,
     sir.

(Quoted in C. & M., 635 *ff.*, from
Moore, ed., *Songs and Ballads,* 209 *ff.*)

BAYLOR, George. 1752–1784.
A.D.C. to Washington, Cont'l. officer.
Va. Coming from the upper layer of
Va. society, he was selected as A.D.C.
by Washington on 15 Aug. '75 and
commissioned Lt. Col. "Baylor was accepted primarily on Edmund Pendleton's recommendation, though Washington had known the young man's
father well and had a large acquaintance with the Baylor family," writes
Freeman. (*Washington,* III, 522) Commended by his chief in a letter of 27
Dec. '76 to President Hancock, he carried the news of Trenton and a captured flag to Congress, was thanked by
that body, and Hancock wrote Washington recommending that he be promoted and given a horse. The gift
horse came on 1 Jan. '77, the promotion
on the 9th, and with the latter he assumed command of the 3d Cont'l.
Dragoons. He was bayoneted through
the lungs and captured in the TAPPAN
MASSACRE, 28 Sept. '78. After being exchanged he returned to duty, assuming
command of the 1st Cont'l. Dragoons
on 9 Nov. '82 when the 3d was merged
with that unit. He was breveted B.G.
on 30 Sept. '83, and died the next
Mar. at Bridgetown, Barbados, where
he had gone in hopes of recovering
from the wound received at Tappan.

BAYONETS AND BAYONET AT-
TACKS. In the article on MUSKETS
AND MUSKETRY it is pointed out that
the standard infantry weapon was a
smoothbore musket with a rate of fire
averaging three or four rounds per minute and inaccurate at much over 50
yards. Defender and attacker delivered
about two volleys at each other and
closed for close combat with the bayonet—if they had them. But another
factor was involved:

"... in those days of flint-locks the
effect of very heavy rain was to put
military science four centuries back, by
reducing good musketeers to the condition of indifferent spearmen; and the
Americans were in worse case still, because some of their regiments were not
even provided with bayonets. British
soldiers prayed for rain so they could
attack with bayonets without fear of
enemy fire." (Trevelyan, *American Revolution,* VI, 285 and *n.*)

The American defeat at Bunker Hill has been attributed not only to ammunition shortage but also to their lack of bayonets. "The popular myth that the Revolution was fought between American troops who shot from behind trees and stone walls and British soldiers who were silly enough to stand in tight formations in the open is completely fallacious," comments Peterson. This happened a few times—LEXINGTON AND CONCORD, KINGS MOUNTAIN—but, continues the same author:

"American troops generally fought in the accepted European fashion as any tactical study of the battles of the Revolution quickly reveals. * * * Steuben . . . never taught 'backwoods' warfare and Washington in the climactic Yorktown campaign exhorted his men to place their principal reliance on the bayonet." (Peterson, *Colonial Arms,* 200)

In night attacks reliance usually was on the bayonet alone: this kept a soldier from sacrificing surprise by nervously firing prematurely, and in the dark it was too easy to shoot up friendly units by mistake. The trick was to load the piece but not permit the musket to be primed; then, if necessary, the commander could order his troops to complete this last step and open fire. Another technique was to put in the priming charge, close the firing pan, and remove the flint. Gen. Charles ("No-flint") Grey was accused of atrocities at PAOLI, Pa., 21 Sept. '77, and at TAPPAN, 28 Sept. '78, largely because his attacks succeeded.

BEAUFORT (Port Royal Island), S.C., 3 Feb. '79. When Prevost and Lincoln faced each other across the Savannah River at Purysburg, the British commander took advantage of his naval supremacy to direct a turning movement against Beaufort, 30 miles to Lincoln's rear and 60 miles south of Charleston. See "Lincoln's Campaigns" under SOUTHERN THEATER, Mil. Opns., for background.

Lincoln ordered Moultrie to turn out the militia to oppose this threat, and when Maj. Gardiner approached with 200 British troops, Moultrie was waiting at Beaufort with 300 Charleston militia, 20 Cont'ls., and three guns. The rebel militia performed well in a hot action that lasted three quarters of an hour. They had the disadvantage of fighting in the open while the enemy had some cover from woods, but Gardiner was handicapped by having his one cannon disabled early in the fight. Moultrie ordered a withdrawal when his ammunition ran out, but he then discovered that Gardiner was also withdrawing and ordered pursuit by his few mounted troops. The British escaped by boat to Savannah and Moultrie moved south to join Lincoln.

American losses were eight killed and 22 wounded. Although the numbers are not known, British losses were heavy. Lossing says almost all of Gardiner's officers were casualties (II, 759); a captured lieutenant was quoted as saying at least half the British force was lost, although this is highly improbable. (Ward, *W.O.R.,* 682)

This little action discouraged the British from any further operations into S.C. until Prevost moved against CHARLESTON, 11–12 May '79.

BEAUMARCHAIS AND THE AMERICAN REVOLUTION. See HORTALEZ & CIE.

BEAUSEJOUR, Nova Scotia. See FORT BEAUSEJOUR (for action in 1755) and FORT CUMBERLAND, Nov. '75.

BECKWITH, George. 1753–1823. British officer. Son of Maj. Gen. John Beckwith and elder brother of Lt. Gen. Sir Thomas Sydney Beckwith (1772–1831), he went to America as an ensign in 1771. He distinguished himself as a regimental officer in several engagements, leading the British advance into Elizabethtown and New Brunswick in 1776. (Appleton's) Promoted to Capt., he became Knyphausen's A.D.C. While the latter commanded British forces in the North, during Clinton's Charleston Expedition of 1780, Beckwith took over John André's business with the traitor Benedict Arnold. Beckwith continued to handle administrative details of Arnold's Treason and assisted Oliver De Lancey the younger in reorganizing the British intelligence service in early 1781. (Van Doren, *Secret History, passim*) He remained in the field of military intelligence until the end of the fighting in America. (Clinton, *Amer. Reb.,* 596, 598)

After the Peace of 1783 the British had refused to establish formal diplomatic relations with the new nation but had maintained a series of paid agents to supplement the reports of their consuls. Maj. Beckwith became the agent in 1787 and held the post until 1791. It has long been known that Alexander Hamilton, who became Sec. of the Treas. to Pres. Washington, was useful to Beckwith in reporting that a strong element of the American people favored a conciliatory policy toward Britain. (See Bemis, *Dipl. Hist.,* 89–90) But not until the publication of Prof. Julian P. Boyd's *Number 7* . . . in 1964 was it revealed that charges of double dealing and highly dishonorable conduct can now be supported against HAMILTON.

Beckwith became Gov. of Bermuda in 1797, of St. Vincent in 1804, and of Barbados in 1808. In 1809 he was knighted (K.B.) for taking Martinique, and the next year he drove the French from Guadeloupe. Promoted to full Gen. in 1814, the year he returned to England, he commanded the troops in Ireland from 1816 until 1820. Three years later he died in London.

BEDFORD–FAIR HAVEN RAID, Mass., 5–6 Sept. '78. With a relief force of almost 70 vessels and 5,000 troops, Sir Henry Clinton reached Newport on 1 Sept. He was 36 hours too late, and the Americans had escaped. (NEWPORT, 29 July . . .) The British sailed on to Boston, but saw no possibility of attacking the French fleet there and headed back for N.Y. Gen. Chas. ("No-flint") Grey was detached to raid the coast of Mass. Landing on Clark's Neck, at the mouth of the Acushnet River, between 6 P.M. on the 5th and noon the next day Grey destroyed an estimated $323,266 worth of property in Bedford and Fair Haven (across the river). He burned about 70 vessels (many of them privateers and their prizes), several vessels on the stocks, and many buildings. The raiders then sailed for MARTHA'S VINEYARD. (Lossing, II, 84 *n.*)

BEDFORD, Gunning. 1742–1797. Cont'l. officer, Gov. of Del. Often confused with his cousin and namesake (see next article), he was a deputy Q.M.G., became Lt. Col. of the DELAWARE CONT'LS., and was Muster Master Gen. in 1776–77. As a politician he held many offices, being in Congress 1783–85 and Gov. of Del. from Jan. '96 until his death in Sept. '97.

BEDFORD, Gunning. 1747–1812. Revolutionary statesman. Del. Calling himself Gunning Bedford, Jr., perhaps to minimize being confused with his cousin (see above), he was born in Philadelphia, where he studied law under Joseph Read and was admitted to the bar. He settled soon thereafter in Dover, Del., moved to Wilmington, and later in life lived on his farm on the Brandywine. The records do not support his daughter's claim that he was Washington's A.D.C. After holding a number of political offices in Del.—his career paralleling to a confusing degree that of his cousin—he was a delegate to Congress 1785–86, to the various conventions for ratification of the Constitution, and was Attorney General of his state 1784–89. In the latter year Washington appointed him a judge for the Del. district, an office he held until his death.

BELCHER, Jonathan. 1682–1757. Merchant, colonial Gov. of Mass. and N.J. Grandson of Andrew Belcher, who emigrated from England prior to 1654, and the son of the second Andrew (d. 1717), he was raised in a prosperous family that had important political and commercial connections. Jonathan's sister Elizabeth married Daniel Oliver, and their sons were Lt. Gov. Andrew Oliver and Chief Justice Peter Oliver. Another sister, Mary, was the wife of Lt. Gov. George Vaughan. Jonathan was born at Cambridge, Mass., where his grandfather kept a tavern from 1654 to 1673 and where his father was a prosperous merchant and member of the Mass. Council from 1702 to 1717. Jonathan graduated from Harvard in 1699 and traveled in Europe before becoming a wealthy merchant in Boston. In 1705 he married Mary Partridge, daughter of Lt. Gov. William Partridge.

After being elected to the Mass. Council eight times during the 12 years from 1718 to 1729 he happened to be in England when Gov. Burnet died, and he was able to secure this post for himself. On 10 Aug. '30 he landed in Boston with his commisson as Gov. of Mass. and N.H. His position was one that called for real genius, which Belcher lacked. Although reared with the advantages of wealth, culture, and education, he remained a narrow-minded and sanctimonious place holder who tried to walk the fence between royal and colonial interests. Controversies and conflicts with which he coped were in connection with the BROAD ARROW policy, which brought him into conflict with royal authority; the Land Bank, which found him on the side of the opponents of this unsound but popular scheme; and the Mass.–N.H. boundary dispute, in which he was unjustly accused of accepting a bribe. His enemies went so far as to forge signatures to charges against him, and on 7 May '41 he was dismissed.

In July '46, however, the British government had regained its faith in him and appointed him Gov. of N.J. He reached his new post in Aug. '47 and had a relatively tranquil tenure until his death on 31 Aug. '57. He took a great interest in the founding of Princeton and left the college his library of 374 volumes. When it was proposed that the main building be named "Belcher Hall" he—most fortunately—declined the honor and suggested the name of Nassau Hall, which it subsequently bore.

BELKNAP, Jeremy. 1744–1798. Clergyman and historian. Author of the *History of New Hampshire* (3 vols., 1784–92), he had the advantage of firsthand knowledge of many events and personalities of the Revolution. His work shows thorough research and considerable literary skill. Belknap had a leading part in establishment of the Mass. Hist. Soc. (The society first met 2 Jan. '91.)

BEMIS HEIGHTS, N.Y. Landmark of First and Second Battles of SARATOGA.

"BENNINGTON FLAG." See FLAG, American.

BENNINGTON RAID, 6–16 Aug. '77. (BURGOYNE'S OFFENSIVE) When Burgoyne's forces reached Ft. Edward and Ft. George on 29 July two defects in the British plan became apparent: supplies that came over their 185-mile L. of C. from Canadian bases would have to be supplemented by foraging; and the hoped-for Tory support was not going to materialize.

Riedesel proposed on 22 July that an expedition be sent by way of Castleton and Clarendon into the Connecticut Valley where horses were reported to be available. Although other supplies were important, horses were particularly needed not only to mount the 250 Brunswick dragoons but also for hauling wagons and artillery over the long lines of land communication to support a further advance south to Albany. On 31 July Burgoyne gave Riedesel preliminary instructions to plan the raid, but he ordered a much more ambitious expedition. Burgoyne's concept of the operation was based on the erroneous belief that Seth Warner had fallen back from Manchester to Bennington, and he wanted the raid to go farther south than Riedesel recommended so that it would end within closer supporting distance of the main body that would be moving toward Albany. Burgoyne's ease in taking Ticonderoga had increased his contempt for the rebels' ability to stop his regulars, but this feeling was not shared by Riedesel, who had experienced the fighting at HUBBARDTON, 7 July. The German general repeatedly protested that Burgoyne's plan was too dangerous, but the suave C. in C. was not to be convinced. (Nickerson, *Turning Point,* 235)

"The object of your expedition," read the final instructions, "is to try the affections of the country, to disconcert the councils of the enemy, to mount the Riedesel's dragoons, to compleat Peters's corps [of Tories], and to obtain large supplies of cattle, horses, and carriages." (*Ibid.*)

The expedition was to start from the Hudson opposite Saratoga (mouth of Batten Kill), move east to Arlington, follow the Batten Kill upstream to Manchester, and cross the mountains to Rockingham on the Conn. River. After remaining there "as long as necessary," the foragers were to descend the river to Brattleboro and march west to Albany. Burgoyne expected the operation to take about two weeks.

Lt. Col. Friedrich Baum, commander of the Brunswick dragoons who were the nucleus of the expedition, was to lead the raid. His combatant strength was about 800, of whom 374 were Germans. (All Brunswickers except for about 30 Hesse Hanau artillerymen.) The German strength can be further broken down as follows: 170 RANK AND FILE from the dragoons (70 were left behind); 100 infantrymen, most of them jägers and grenadiers of Breymann's Adv. Corps; the Hessian gunners with two little 3-pdrs. Just under 300 of the Germans were rank and file; the abnormally high proportion of officers, sergeants, musicians, and batmen accounts for the total of 374. The only British regulars were Capt. Fraser's company of about 50 marksmen. About 300 Tories, Canadians, and Indians were attached, and a few female camp followers went along. (One of these was killed by a stray shot during the battle.) The above figures are from Nickerson.

Burgoyne's planning was defective from start to finish. Baum could not "utter one word of English," which should have disqualified him from the command of an expedition that was supposed to rally English sympathizers along the way. By sending Philip Skene with him as a sort of public affairs advisor, Burgoyne admitted the error without correcting it. Baum's dragoons were particularly unsuited—literally—for a fast raid: heavy boots, cumbersome swords, and otherwise impractical uniforms made them slow on the roads and almost immobile in woods. The first false assumption, that the Americans would not fight and that large numbers of natives would be neutral if not friendly, led to all Burgoyne's errors, the biggest of which was assigning Baum too ambitious a mission.

AMERICAN DISPOSITIONS

The fall of Ticonderoga and the Jane McCrea atrocity had aroused New England and N.Y. Furthermore, the people of both areas realized that the British invasion could continue south along the Hudson, or could turn east to the Conn. Valley. Vermont was too thinly populated to raise enough militia for its own defense, and its Council of Safety called on· N.H. and Mass. for help. N.H. had similar problems; it had already taken steps to raise troops for its own defense but lacked the funds. According to an "old, if not true, story" (Ward, *W.O.R.*, 423), the wealthy John Langdon stepped forward to volunteer his personal fortune and his credit to fill the gap. Langdon also nominated "our friend Stark" to command the forces raised. John STARK was available, having resigned his Cont'l. commission in a huff, but accepted on the provision that his command remain independent of orders from Congress. The N.H. General Court (State Legislature) agreed readily (Nickerson, 227).

A week after his commission as B.G. was signed (17 July) Stark had raised 1,492 officers and men, which represented "10 per cent of all enrolled voters in the state, old and young." (Ward, 424) By the 30th, Stark started toward Manchester with his brigade, which was innocent of military uniforms and armed only with personal weapons. Seth Warner's Vermonters, in accordance with their last order at Hubbardton, "Scatter and meet me at Manchester," were at the latter place to greet the N.H. militia. (*Ibid.*) Also on hand was Maj. Gen. Lincoln, and a crisis arose.

STARK'S INSUBORDINATION

Lincoln was sent to command the American forces being raised by New England in this region, and he had orders from Schuyler that Stark's brigade should join the main army on the Hudson. Stark said no. The situation was not helped by the fact that Lincoln was one of the officers whose promotion over Stark's head (Mar. '77) had provoked this "rustic Achilles" to go sulk in his tent. But Lincoln handled the problem with remarkable skill. "The fat general from Massachusetts" (as Nickerson tags him) first pointed out the fearful responsibility Stark was taking by his attitude. Stark was ready with the answer that he took orders from the people who gave him his commission, not from Congress.

"Lincoln was wise enough not to give up Stark in disgust. It would take some time for Congress to overrule New Hampshire—if indeed they succeeded in doing so. Meanwhile, if Stark could not be commanded as a subordinate, some use might still be made of him and his independent brigade by treating him as an ally. Finding that Stark wished to cut in on Burgoyne's left rear, Lincoln therefore agreed to this plan, and agreed also to try to persuade Schuyler to support the move." (Nickerson, 232)

"Seldom has such rank insubordination produced such excellent results," comments Greene. "In this case it resulted in placing Stark, with superior force, at the very point where Baume [sic] was going...." (*Rev. War*, 112)

BAUM'S APPROACH

Although many accounts indicate that Bennington was Baum's objective from the beginning, it was last-minute intelligence that sent him there: a Tory officer reported an important rebel supply depot was located there with only 300 or 400 militia guards. "To Burgoyne such a windfall would be a Godsend. Could Baum return bringing with him any considerable stock of provisions, Burgoyne saw himself in Albany at once." (Nickerson, 240) The C. in C. clattered down the road to give him last-minute instructions personally.

Meanwhile, Fraser's Adv. Corps had moved eight miles from Ft. Edward to Ft. Miller on 9 Aug. to give Baum a more advanced jumping-off point. On 11 Aug., the day Burgoyne had modified his mission, Baum advanced from Ft. Miller to the mouth of the Batten Kill, a march of only four miles. (Nickerson, 240) He then waited until the 13th to resume his movement, and that day he marched 15 miles S.E. to camp at Cambridge. On this same day Burgoyne started crossing the Hudson with his main body and headed for the battlefields of SARATOGA.

As Baum advanced on the 13th he picked up some prisoners and supplies, but his undisciplined Indians engaged in a wanton destruction of property that brought him no supplies and that alerted the countryside. When Stark learned that Indians were in Cambridge he sent 200 men from Bennington, about 18 road miles away, to check them. By evening Stark learned that enemy regulars were approaching in strength behind the Indians, and he prepared to march toward them with his brigade the next morning, the 14th. Simultaneously he sent Warner word to move immediately from Manchester to Bennington, a distance of about 20 miles.

The militia were also ordered out. Baum, meanwhile, reported back that Bennington was occupied by 1,800 militia instead of 400, and he promised to advance cautiously.

THE BATTLE OF BENNINGTON

Contact was made about 9 A.M. on 14 Aug. at the mill known variously as Sancoick's, San or Saint Coick's, and Van Schaick's Mill. Here Col. Gregg's advance party fired one volley and retreated. Two miles S.E. the raiders were delayed more than an hour by a burned bridge (called St. Luke's Br.) across Little White Creek. They then moved another mile and three quarters to the bridge or ford on the Walloomsac River (about four miles from Bennington), where Stark was waiting with his brigade. When no attack materialized, Stark withdrew a mile toward Bennington and camped.

During the delay to repair the bridge (above) Baum sent his second message to Burgoyne. This merely confirmed the estimate of rebel strength, but added that they were not expected to offer much resistance. Later in the day, however, Baum requested reinforcements.

"At this point, on top of Burgoyne's original error in sending out such a force on such a mission, Baum now added three capital errors of his own, all three springing from a failure to realize his peril." (Nickerson, 243)

First, he asked only for the reinforcements needed to reach Bennington, which Burgoyne (reasonably) interpreted as good news (see below). Although outnumbered more than two to one, and 25 miles from friendly forces, Baum made no move to withdraw. Third, he deployed his command in a manner that invited defeat in detail.

Taking these errors in inverse order, let's look at the battlefield and consider certain features not apparent from the

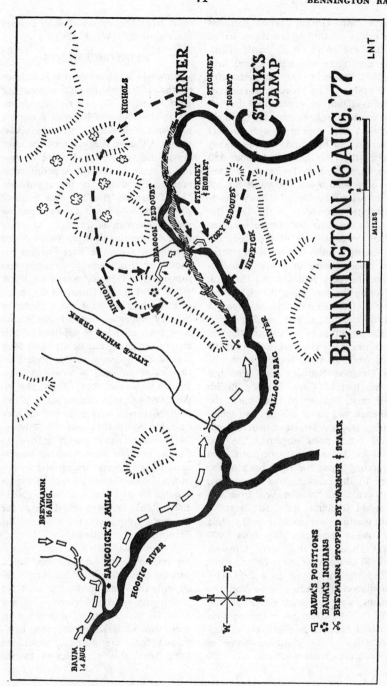

BENNINGTON, 16 AUG. '77

sketch map. Critical terrain included the bridge or ford where Baum halted on the eve of the main battle. (Lossing says there was only a ford here [I, 395], but most other accounts refer to a bridge.) This crossing was important to Baum in continuing the advance, and his dispositions for the night of 14–15 Aug. were made with this fact uppermost in his mind. On the enemy side of the river he posted about 150 men, most of them Tories; on a small rise of ground about 250 yards S.E. of the crossing they erected a hasty breastwork later referred to as the Tory Redoubt. Canadians and Tories occupied cabins on either side of the ford, and the German camp followers—for some odd reason—were in a log cabin between the Tory Redoubt and the ford. Covering the ford from the right bank were 50 German infantrymen, about 25 British marksmen, and one 3-pdr.

The major position was on the hill overlooking the river crossing from the right bank. In what became known as the Dragoon Redoubt were the dragoons, half of Capt. Fraser's British marksmen, and one of the 3-pdrs.; the 200 rank and file at this position represented Baum's largest cohesive unit. Three other posts supported the two redoubts. To keep the Americans from infiltrating along the right bank of the river to the crossing, and in an area that could not be observed from the Dragoon Redoubt, were 50 jägers. A fifth position was located back along the road to Sancoick's Mill, about 1,000 yards from the vital river crossing; here 50 German infantrymen and some Tories were deployed in a field with the mission of guarding to the rear. The Indians were grouped on a plateau N.W. of the dragoons. "Having thus scattered his men as effectively as possible all over the landscape—some of the little detachments more than a half-mile from the others—Baum awaited Stark's move." (Ward, 426)

REINFORCEMENTS

Burgoyne was awakened before dawn of the 15th with Baum's request for reinforcements. He saw nothing alarming in this and sent Riedesel a request to dispatch Breymann with the Adv. Corps. Although Riedesel took the most pessimistic view, he had given up trying to make his English superior comprehend the danger of the expedition. "Let Burgoyne give his own orders," he said to Sir Francis CLERKE, and he sent a German staff officer to relay these orders directly from Burgoyne to Breymann. Burgoyne later justified his choice of these heavily equipped and slow-moving German grenadiers for a relief mission that involved 25 miles of marching; he said it was a matter of military etiquette—the Germans would have been offended if deprived of this chance for glory. But he also said later that he did not want to risk good British troops on such a secondary mission. (Nickerson, 244) With two 6-pdrs. and 642 men (according to Ward, 429; Nickerson says 550, but he may be referring to rank and file only [p. 245]), Breymann's march started at 9 A.M., an hour after receiving his orders. It had begun raining, and by his own estimate the initial rate of march was hardly half a mile an hour (Nickerson, 246); he went into bivouac for the night having covered eight of the 25 miles to the battlefield.

Warner had gotten Stark's request for reinforcement on the 14th, but a considerable number of his men were off on patrol and he did not start for Bennington until the morning of the 15th. He had 350 men; although their speed was considerably better than Breymann's, and the distance about the same, they also were slowed by the rain. Warner joined Stark the evening of the 15th, and around midnight his troops camped about six miles (two hours' march) behind him. Neither Warner's nor Breymann's troops arrived in time to take part in the first phase of the battle of 16 Aug.

BAUM'S DEFEAT

The rain on Friday, 15 Aug., that slowed the advance of the reinforcements also kept Stark from attacking, since it would have neutralized his one tactical asset, musketry. But Stark did send out parties of skirmishers who gained a rough but sufficient knowledge of Baum's dispositions. They also picked off a few Indians, including two chiefs.

On the 16th Stark attacked, adopting the tactics dear to the heart of military amateurs, a double envelopment. Col. Moses Nichols led 200 N.H. men in the right arm of the pincers to march four miles through the wooded hills and hit the Dragoon Redoubt. He started his attack about 3 P.M. Shortly thereafter the other enveloping force, 300 strong (the Vt. rangers and Bennington militia), led by Col. Sam'l. Herrick, hit the enemy rear guard. A third column advanced down the road and pulled a miniature double envelopment against the Tory Redoubt; Col. David Hobart was on the left and Col. Thos. Stickney on the right; their strength was about 200. Another 100 demonstrated against Baum's front.

From his exceptionally fine observation post in the Dragoon Redoubt, the German commander had seen parties of Americans leave Stark's bivouac when the rain stopped around noon. But he had drawn the unfortunate conclusion that they were retreating. When small bodies of armed men later approached, he took them for Tories seeking protection to his rear or coming to him

for safety. The Americans realized Baum's error and capitalized on it to get into position.

The left bank Tories made a show of resistance, but were charged while reloading for a second volley and were routed. Undoubtedly demoralized by the sounds of battle on both flanks to their rear, Tories, Canadians, and Indians retreated. The other German positions also collapsed, but Baum held his ground in the Dragoon Redoubt for about two hours. When the firing started at 3 o'clock, Stark moved out of the bivouac area with 1,200 to 1,300 troops to make the main effort down the Bennington Road. At this time (according to Ward) or somewhat earlier (as implied by Nickerson) he shouted to his men, "We'll beat them before night, or Molly Stark will be a widow." (This particular wording of a quote generally repeated by historians is from Lossing, *op. cit.*, I, 397 *n*.)

Defenders of the Dragoon Redoubt, now including refugees from the other posts, were running low on ammunition when a wagon containing their reserve supply caught fire and blew up. The Americans closed in for the kill, but the dragoons rallied around their commander, drew their great swords, and started cutting their way out. The shirtsleeved farmers had no bayonets with which to oppose this movement, and the Brunswickers were making progress until Baum was dropped by a mortal wound in the abdomen. His men then gave up resistance; the time was about 5 P.M.

BREYMANN'S DEFEAT

The slow-moving German relief column reached Sancoick's Mill about 4:30 and found refugees from Baum's command who gave widely disparate accounts of the latter's situation. Although the Dragoon Redoubt was only four miles beeline from the mill, Breymann later reported that he heard no sound of firing; this was apparently a case of "acoustic shadow." Skene was now with Breymann, having left Baum earlier to bring up the relief column. The tired Germans resumed their march from the mill on the assumption that Baum was still holding out, and their flank patrols on the high ground left of the road drove off the small militia bands that attempted to stop their progress.

Stark's command was in a poor situation to meet this new threat: his men had scattered to chase fugitives, to loot, and had been detached to guard prisoners. Many of Stark's officers advocated retreat, and there is evidence that Seth Warner talked Stark into making a stand against Breymann. (Nickerson, 257; Ward, 430) The advance of Warner's men had been slowed by the need to draw ammunition on their way through Bennington, to drop packs at Stark's bivouac, to dry their weapons when the rain ceased about noon, to draw a rum ration, and to stop for water at the ford behind the Tory Redoubt. (Ibid.) They reached the latter crossing about the time Baum fell (Nickerson, 257), and after additional halts Warner's column (130 men led by Lt. Col. Sam'l. Safford, and 200 Vt. rangers) made contact with Breymann about a mile beyond the ford, near the present village of Walloomsac. (Ibid.) Because of faulty deployment on the low ground, the Americans had to drop back to a new position on high ground.

Although they might be called "fresh troops," in the sense that they had not yet done any serious fighting, the reinforcements of Breymann and Warner had experienced an exhausting march in oppressively hot, muggy weather. The Germans nevertheless attacked with vigor, attempting the same envelopment along high ground to their left

that had driven back earlier American attempts to delay them. The two 6-pdrs. went into action with good effect and a hot fight was soon in progress. Half of Warner's men stopped the envelopment of the American right after the Germans had made some progress, and the rest of the defenders extended their own line to threaten the German right with envelopment. The two lines then remained stationary, but a heavy fire continued. About sunset Breymann's ammunition was almost exhausted and he ordered a retreat. The Americans swarmed around them and panic began to break down the discipline of the regulars, many of whom surrendered. Breymann's drummers beat out the call for a parley to arrange a surrender, but the ignorant militia did not understand and kept on shooting. (Ward, 430) (Earlier, when Stark tried to turn Baum's captured guns on the enemy he found he was the only person who knew how to shoot them.)

Wounded in the leg and with five bullet holes in his clothes, Breymann personally commanded the rear guard action that permitted two thirds of his command to escape after dark. The ubiquitous Philip Skene also conducted himself bravely in this action. Stark wisely ordered his men to break contact and not attempt a pursuit after dark, when it would have been impossible to maintain any control and Americans would have been shooting each other. "Had day lasted an hour longer," Stark said, "we should have taken the whole body of them." (Ward, 430) He was probably right. Burgoyne may well have been correct also in his comment on the slow march of the German relief column: "Could Mr. Breyman have marched at the rate of two miles an hour, any given twelve hours out of the two and thirty, success would probably have ensued." (Ltr. of 20 Aug. to Germain, quoted by Ward, 475 *n*.)

NUMBERS AND LOSSES

Nickerson and Ward accept the figures of 30 Americans killed and 40 wounded out of 2,000 engaged. These CASUALTY FIGURES are so far from the normal ratio of three or four wounded for every battle death that they cannot be credited. Montross says a total of 40 killed and wounded is the generally accepted account. (*Rag, Tag,* 208) Stark reported 14 killed and 42 wounded. (Freeman, *Washington,* IV, 462 *n,* citing Stark's ltr. of 18 Aug. '77 in *Gates Papers,* N.Y.H.S.) These last figures appear to be as valid as will ever be obtained; the others, however, illustrate the disagreement among authorities.

The raiders left 207 dead on the field, and about 700 prisoners (including 32 officers and staff). The dragoons bore the brunt of the fighting: of 374 officers and men, only nine privates returned to Burgoyne. (Nickerson, 262) Their inept but brave commander, Baum, was buried on the road to Bennington. The Indians had taken off early in the action. Since Capt. Fraser escaped, it is likely that most of the British marksmen got away with him, although some are mentioned among the captives. The Tory prisoners were tied in pairs and paraded through Bennington in what Nickerson calls "a sort of Saturnalia ... a base show of rustic contempt." (pp. 262–63)

The haul of booty was rich: 12 drums, 250 broadswords, four ammunition wagons, several hundred muskets, a few rifles, and four brass cannon. (The latter were of French origin, captured by Wolfe at Quebec in 1759, surrendered by Hull at Detroit in 1812, and retaken at Niagara in 1813 [Fonblanque's *Burgoyne,* 273].)

COMMENT

The remarkable American victory at Bennington combined a sequence of chances that "can only be compared to the turning up of the double zero three or four times running at roulette," says Nickerson. "That Stark should reach Bennington unknown to Burgoyne and remain there just long enough to meet there a raid of which nothing whatsoever had been known in advance remains such an improbable stroke of luck that it would ruin the reputation of a writer of fiction." (*Ibid.,* 260) Lincoln's handling of the insubordinate John Stark, mentioned at the beginning of this article, also had much to do with making the fluky American victory possible. But all this good luck would not have been possible without the numerous mistakes of Burgoyne and the errors of his German subordinates (except for the sensible Riedesel). The errors may be partly explained by inability of Baum and Breymann to adapt their military thinking to the new military problems of fighting American irregulars—Breymann did not really have to stop his column and dress their ranks every 15 minutes during their approach march, for example. But almost all the errors may be traced to a single source: underestimating the enemy.

As for Stark's generalship, his plan of attack violated as many principles of war as did Baum's faulty dispositions for the defense. It was nothing more than luck that caused his two enveloping forces to get into position unmolested and to attack simultaneously. On the other hand, Stark's overwhelming numerical superiority reduced the risks of his tactics. As a commander of New England militia Stark had one rare and priceless quality: he knew the *limitations* of his men. They were innocent of military training, undisciplined, and unenthusiastic about getting shot. With these men he killed over 200 of Europe's vaunted regulars with a loss of 14 Americans killed. On 4 Oct. '77 Congress appointed him B.G. of the Cont'l. Army.

Bennington was a great boost to American morale at a time when it had been severely handled. More materially, however, it not only deprived Burgoyne of vital supplies but also weakened his combatant strength significantly. With the almost simultaneous failure of St. Leger's Expedition, Bennington helped set the stage for Saratoga.

BERM. Coming from a word meaning "brim," this was a term in fortification for the ledge between the ditch and the base of the parapet. If the defender had time he would FRAISE it. See FORT MERCER, 1777.

BERMUDA. See WEST INDIES IN THE REVOLUTION. Special studies are Wilfred Benton Kerr, *Bermuda and the American Revolution: 1760–1783* (Princeton, 1936), and Henry C. Wilkinson, *Bermuda in the Old Empire* (New York, 1950).

BERNARD, Sir Francis (burr' nurd). 1712–1779. Royal gov. of N.J. and Mass. After attending Westminster School he studied law and was admitted to the bar in 1737. In 1758 he became Gov. of N.J., and in 1760 he assumed this post in Mass. Although capable in many respects, he had the misfortune of serving during the Stamp Act crisis. He was unable to see what was happening in America and soon began to stumble under his burden. After a number of his letters to Hillsborough appeared in the public press his popularity reached such a low point that the Assembly was able to force his recall. Lt. Gov. Hutchinson took over temporarily and Bernard sailed on 1 Aug.

'69 for England. Four days later he was made a baronet. The charges were held to be "groundless, vexatious, and scandalous," but Sir Francis spent the last 10 years of his life in retirement.

BERTHIER, Louis Alexandre. 1753–1815. French Lt. in America, later Marshal of France and "chief of staff" (actually used more as an A.G.) to Napoleon. The son of an engineer officer, he was born at Versailles and entered the army at the age of 17. He had been instructed by his father, Louis XVI's chief of topographical engineers, and served successively in the staff, the *Corps de génie,* and in the dragoons. Going to America as a Lt. with Rochambeau, he is variously identified as A.D.C. to that officer (Chastellux, *Travels,* note by editor Rice on p. 580) and as Assist. Aide to the Q.M.G. (M. de Béville). The latter seems to have been his actual post (Heitman, 645); he is remembered in American history for his maps, the originals of which are with the Berthier Papers at Princeton, and for his *Journal de la Campagne d'Amérique, 10 Mai 1780– 26 Aôut 1781* (Gilbert Chinard, ed., Washington, 1951). The only English biography to my knowledge is *By Command of the Emperor,* by S. J. Watson (London, 1957).

BIDDLE, Nicholas. 1750–1778. Cont'l. naval officer. Pa. Of an old N.J. family, who originally were Quakers, Nicholas was born in Philadelphia shortly after his parents moved there. Bred to the sea, he made a voyage to Quebec at the age of 13 and continued to have a short but memorable career in the merchant service before deciding to enter the Royal Navy. Going to London with letters of recommendation from Thos. Willing, brother-in-law of Capt. (later Adm.) Sterling, Biddle was accepted as midshipman on Sterling's sloop-of-war *Portland* and served on a cruise that ended in the autumn of 1772. Having failed to get an assignment aboard a ship being sent out on polar explorations under Capt. Phipps (later Lord Mulgrave), he gave up his naval commission and joined the expedition as a seaman. On the subsequent exploration of the Arctic he made the acquaintance of Horatio Nelson, who also had sacrificed rank in the navy for this adventure.

Returning to America after this voyage, Biddle on 1 Aug. '75 took charge of the Pa. galley *Franklin* in the Delaware River defenses, but in Dec. he became one of the first four captains of the Cont'l. navy. Commanding the *Andrea Doria* (14), with a crew of 130, he took part in the NAVAL OPERATIONS led by Esek Hopkins in early 1776. After this he cruised in the North Atlantic, taking many supply ships whose cargoes were sent to Washington during the Boston Siege; off Newfoundland he captured two armed transports carrying 400 Highlanders to Boston. He returned to Philadelphia with only five of his original crewmen, all the rest having been detached to man prizes, their places filled by prisoner volunteers. (Cooper, *Navy*, I, 114, cited in *D.A.B.*) Rewarded with command of the recently launched *Randolph* (32), Biddle was sent to the West Indies, where his prizes included the *True Briton* (20) and her convoy of three merchantmen, which he took into Charleston. After being held in that port by the British blockade, in Feb. '78 he sailed out with four small warships fitted out by S.C. and attached to him for operations.

Sighting a sail at 3 P.M. on 7 Mar. '78, Biddle made for it. Unfortunately it turned out to be the two-decker *Yarmouth* (64), which destroyed the *Randolph* after a fierce, 20-minute action at close quarters. Biddle had been wounded and was directing the battle from a chair on the quarterdeck when his ship blew up with the loss of all but four of her 315 officers and men. Cooper wrote that the 27-year-old Biddle would unquestionably have risen to great prominence had he lived. "For so short a career, scarcely any other had been so brilliant." (*Op. cit.*, I, 148)

BILLETING ACTS. See QUARTERING ACTS, 1765–74.

BILLINGSPORT, N.J., 2 and 9 Oct. 1777. Located 12 miles below Cooper's Ferry (now Camden, N.J.), a double line of chevaux de frise, almost a mile long, stretched between Billingsport Island and the lightly held, unfinished redoubt at Billingsport. This barrier system was the first of the Delaware River forts the British had to reduce to open their water line of communications to Howe in Philadelphia. When Col. Stirling landed below the fort with his 42d Regt. and part of the 71st to attack it from the rear, the defenders spiked their guns, burned their barracks, and fled. Ward says this *attack* took place on 2 Oct.; Freeman says the British *occupied* it "two days before ... Brandywine," which would be the 9th; either Ward's date is wrong, or the Highlanders withdrew after routing the defenders and returned a week later to occupy the post. The British cut through the chevaux de frise, but did not advance immediately against Forts Mercer and Mifflin, five miles upstream. For subsequent events, see "Delaware River Forts" under PHIL. CAMP'N.

BIRD, Henry. British partisan leader. See KY. RAID.

BISSEL, Israel. Postrider who carried news of LEXINGTON AND CONCORD.

BLACK BOYS of Pa. See PAXTON BOYS.

BLACK MINGO CREEK, S.C., 29
Sept. 1780. To overawe rebels around
Williamsburg and serve as an advance
outpost for the recently completed British base at Georgetown, Col. John
Coming Ball and his 46 Tories took a
position near Shepherd's Ferry, about
20 miles N.N.W. of Georgetown. (This
spot is near where S.C. Hwy. 41 now
crosses Black Mingo Creek.) Learning
this, MARION led his partisans south
from PORT'S FERRY for a surprise attack. A Tory sentinel heard horses
crossing Willtown Bridge, a mile above
Shepherd's, about midnight, and Ball
deployed for action. Marion knew he
had lost surprise, but attacked with the
dismounted troops on the right (west)
under Maj. Hugh Horry, a small body
of supernumerary officers under Capt.
Thos. Waites in the center to assault
Dollard's Tavern (the "red house"),
and a small mounted detachment to
move east of Dollard's. He followed
with a small reserve.

Ball had formed in the field through
which Horry advanced, rather than fight
from the house as Marion expected,
and he calmly held his fire until the
rebels were within 30 yards. When his
men did open up they killed Capt.
George Logan, badly wounded Capt.
Henry Mouzon and Lt. John Scott,
and started a disorderly retreat among
Horry's troops. Capt. John James kept
his men under control, however, rallied
those of Mouzon, and started a cautious advance. When Waties skirted the
tavern and turned against the Tory right
flank, the defenders began to lose heart
and soon were routed. Although only
50 men were engaged on each side in
an action that lasted but 15 minutes,
the losses were heavy: two rebels killed
and eight wounded; three Tories left
dead on the field, 13 wounded and/or
captured, and several others mortally
wounded. Marion's booty included the

fine sorrel gelding of the enemy commander, a horse the Swamp Fox renamed Ball and rode the rest of the
war. (Bass, *Swamp Fox*, 62–67)

BLACK RIVER SETTLEMENT,
Oct. '82. See HONDURAS.

BLACKSTOCKS, S.C., 20 Nov. '80.
After the action at FISHDAM FORD, 9
Nov., Cornwallis called Tarleton back
from the lower Peedee and sent Maj.
McArthur to secure Brierly's Ford on
the Broad River with his 1st Bn. of the
71st Highlanders and the 80 remaining
men of Wemyss' 63d Regt. Seriously
worried about the safety of Ninety-Six,
the British commander wanted Tarleton to find and disperse the 1.000 rebels
reported now to be under Sumter's
command in the area. The British Legion reached Brierly's Ford by forced
marches the morning of 18 Nov. and
drew fire from a 150-man mounted
force when they went down to the river
to wash themselves and their horses.
Tarleton then forded the river and prepared to pursue with his Legion and the
63d.

Reinforced by the Ga. troops of
Cols. Clarke, Twiggs, and others, Sumter planned to attack the Tory post
commanded by Col. James Kirkland
on Little River about 15 miles from
Ninety-Six. But the evening of the 19th
a deserter from the 63d Regt. entered
Sumter's camp about midnight with the
information that Tarleton had returned
from the Peedee and was moving swiftly
toward the American camp. Sumter ordered a retreat, and the British pursued
vigorously the morning and early afternoon of the 20th. Before 10 A.M. Tarleton learned of Sumter's retreat. By
4 P.M. he realized that he could not
move swiftly enough with his entire
force to catch Sumter, so Tarleton
pushed ahead with 190 of his dragoons
and 80 mounted infantry of the 63d;
the foot troops and the crew of the

3-pdr. were ordered to follow at their own pace.

Within an hour the British advance guard closed up on the enemy rear guard. Sumter's main body had reached the Tyger River. The light was already failing, and it would be completely dark within less than an hour. But a woman of the neighborhood who had observed Tarleton's column from a hidden position rode into Sumter's command post to inform him that the British infantry and artillery were still to the rear. Encouraged by this information, knowing that it was sure death to be caught by Bloody Tarleton while astride a river, and being favored by good defensive terrain, Sumter decided to make a stand at Blackstocks Plantation.

Although the river was to his rear and right flank, on Sumter's left, as he faced the enemy, was a hill on which five log houses of the plantation were located in an open field. Col. Hampton and his riflemen were ordered to hold the houses, and the Ga. sharpshooters of Col. Twiggs were posted along a rail fence extending from the houses to the woods on the left flank. On the wooded hill that rose to his right from the main road he deployed the troops of Bratton, Hill, McCall, and Taylor. Col. Lacey's mounted infantry screened the right flank, and Col. Richard Winn was posted to the rear, along the Tyger, as a reserve.

When Tarleton closed up to this position with the Legion cavalry and infantry of the 63d Regt. he realized the position was too strong to attack until the rest of his force came up. He therefore dismounted the 63d and formed them on his right overlooking the creek that ran in front of Sumter's position. To the left of the road he formed his dragoons. Time now favored the British, but Sumter did not intend to stand idle with his 1,000 and wait until

the 190 dragoons and 80 enemy infantry were reinforced. Ordering Col. Elijah Clarke to turn the enemy right with 100 men and block the reinforcements that were coming from the rear, Sumter led 400 men in an attack on the 63d. The Americans crossed the creek and started up the hill against the British regulars, but they delivered their fire too early and were counterattacked and driven back through the houses of Blackstocks Plantation before they could be rallied. As these 80 regulars were engaged in this remarkable feat of routing a force five times their size, Sumter ordered Lacey to hit the left flank of the enemy dragoons.

The Legion cavalrymen were so intent on watching the infantry action on the east flank that Lacey was able to get within 75 yards and deliver a surprise fire that picked off 20 enemy troopers. (Bass, *Green Dragoon,* 119) But Lacey was then driven back; Sumter was riding back to the center of the line from the right flank when he was hit by a musket ball that penetrated his right shoulder, ripped along the shoulder blade, and chipped his backbone. (*Ibid.*) Twiggs assumed command, but the point is academic since the die was cast. Hampton's riflemen had stopped the advance of the British infantry, and the regulars were also being badly shot up by rebels on their flanks. Tarleton led a hazardous cavalry charge into the center to extricate his infantry, and he succeeded in so doing, although the price was high.

Darkness had now fallen and both sides withdrew. Both sides claimed the victory. "The only advantage actually gained by Tarleton was the temporary disablement of Sumter," says Ward. (*W.O.R.,* 747) Tarleton's biographer disagrees:

"Sumter had turned and provoked a battle. He had repulsed the British.

He had seized most of their dead and wounded. But even though Tarleton had been defeated in his tactics, he had succeeded in his strategy and achieved his objective. He had deflected the blow from Williams' house * and Ninety-Six. He had overtaken, battered, and dispersed the rebels. And he had sent their elected general from the field a speechless, helpless, bloody mass wrapped in a bull hide." (*Op. cit.*, 120)

The Gamecock was badly hurt, but within two and a half months he was back in the field (and lived to be 98, incidentally). Tarleton pursued for two days. He reached the Pacolet River, picking up rebel stragglers and collecting some British fugitives of Ferguson's defeat at Kings Mountain and Wemyss' defeat at Fishdam Ford; believing reports that Sumter was mortally wounded and that his force had dispersed (this being true), Tarleton returned to Brierly's Ford (about 1 Dec.). The next time he pushed a rebel force so hard that they turned at bay with their backs to a river was at COWPENS, 17 Jan. '81.

NUMBERS AND LOSSES

American losses out of 1,000 engaged were three killed and five wounded. (Lossing, II, 653)

Tarleton lost about 50 killed and wounded out of 270 engaged. (Bass, *op. cit.*, 121, 122)

BLAINE, Ephraim. d. 1804. Cont'l. commissary officer. Pa. According to Heitman, Blaine was commissary of the 8th Pa., 17 Oct. '76; Comm. of Supplies, Cont'l. Army, 1 Apr. '77; Dep. Comm.-Gen. of Purchases, 6 Aug. '77;

* The post commanded by Kirkland, mentioned earlier in this article, was located at the house of Col. James Williams.

Comm. Gen. of Purchases, 1 Jan. '80–24 July '82. Johnston's order of battle for the Yorktown Campaign shows *Col.* Blaine as Comm. Gen. (*Yorktown*, 112) Heitman shows no military rank.

BLAINVILLE. See CELORON de BLAINVILLE.

BLANCHARD, Claude. 1742–1802. Chief Commissary to Rochambeau. France. His *Journal* of three years' stay in America is an interesting and useful source. Wm. Duane's translation was published at Albany in 1876. The original text appeared in Paris five years later as *Guerrè d'Amérique, Journal de campagne de Claude Blanchard.*

BLAND, Theodorick. 1742–1790. Cont'l. officer. Va. Through his mother, the heiress of Drury Bolling, he was descended from Pocahontas. Schooled in England between 1753 and 1763, he graduated from the University of Edinburgh as an M.D. and practiced in Va. from 1764 until 1771, when bad health forced him to retire and become a planter. He was active in patriot politics and was one of the 24 who removed the arms from the governor's palace in Williamsburg to the powder magazine on 24 June '75. On 13 June '76 he became Capt. of the 1st Troop of Va. Cav. and on 4 Dec. he was promoted to Maj. of Light Dragoons. He subsequently became Col. of the 1st Cont'l. Dragoons; in one place Heitman says this appointment was dated 31 Mar. '77 and in another place he gives the date 25 Nov. '76 (Heitman, 28, 107); *D.A.B.*, on the other hand, says the commission was dated 31 Mar. '79. Almost certainly this last date is a typographical error and was meant to be 31 Mar. '77. Heitman's statement on p. 107 that Bland resigned as Col. of the 1st Cont'l. Dragoons on 10 Dec. '76 also appears to be a typographical error, since on p. 28 he shows him as com-

mander of that regiment until 10 Dec.
'79. (Note, however, in the footnote
below that Harry Lee calls him an officer of the *Virginia* horse, not of the
Cont'l. horse.)

In any event, Bland commanded
mounted troops in the N.J. Campaign
and in the Philadelphia Campaign. In
the battle of the Brandywine, 11 Sept.
'77, he commanded the few light cavalry troops at Washington's disposal
and was posted on the right (north)
flank. Since he failed to gain timely
knowledge of the enemy's main attack around this flank he is largely
to blame for the faulty intelligence
that caused the American defeat. "Light-
Horse Harry" Lee is wrong in putting
the entire blame on Bland, but he probably is justified in the judgment that
"Colonel Bland was noble, sensible,
honorable, and amiable; but never intended for the department of military
intelligence." *

* Lee says Washington promptly
learned that Howe had split his force
and had decided to take advantage of
this error and move his entire army
across the creek to crush Knyphausen's
wing. "In the very act of giving his
orders to this effect, Colonel Bland,
of the Virginia horse, brought him intelligence which very much obscured,
if it did not contradict, the previous
information; and the original judicious
decision was abandoned." (*Memoirs,*
88 *n.*) As explained in the article on
BRANDYWINE, Washington was quite
in the dark as to the enemy situation.
He was not preparing to strike the enemy across Chadd's Ford "with his
whole force" (*ibid.*), but merely to
counterattack with three divisions while
two others moved north to meet a
threat that Hazen had reported. Second, it was confusing and contradictory
information from Sullivan, not Bland,

On 5 Nov. '78 Washington gave
Bland the mission of escorting the Convention Army from Conn. to Va., and
on 1 May '79 Bland took command of
the guard detail at Charlottesville, Va.
In Nov. '79 he received permission to
leave this post, where he had earned
from Maj. Gen. Wm. Phillips the nickname "Alexander the Great." (Tharp,
Baroness, 327) Elected to the Cont'l.
Cong., he served for three years (1781–
83). He then retired to his plantation, Farmingdale or Kippax, in Prince
George co., which had been plundered
during his absence by British raiders.
In 1786 he was an unsuccessful candidate for governor against Edmund Randolph. He served in the House of
Delegates from 1786 to 1788, voted
against adoption of the federal Constitution in the Va. Conv. of 1788, and
in this same year was elected to the
first U.S. House of Representatives.
Here he served until his death on 1
June '90. He has been described as tall,
handsome, suave, strictly honest, and
of meager intellect.

See Charles Campbell (ed.), *The
Bland Papers* (2 vols., 1840).

BLOCK ISLAND, N.Y., 6 Apr. '76.
See ALFRED–GLASGOW ENCOUNTER.

"BLOODY BACKS." Derisive American term for British regulars, alluding

that caused Washington to call off this
counterattack. It was Bland who sent
confirmation of Squire Cheney's report
that Howe was turning Washington's
flank. The main criticism of Bland's
work was not so much that this last
information was several hours too late
but that he had not properly reconnoitered the creek on Washington's right
flank to inform the C. in C. that the
enemy could ford it to make a strategic envelopment. (Freeman, *Washington,* IV, 485)

to their severe discipline, which included lashing. Presumably the term lost its vogue after Washington got authority to increase lashing in the Cont'l. Army to 500 strokes.

"BLOODY BILL." See CUNNINGHAM, "Bloody Bill."

BLOODY POND (Lake George), N.Y., 8 Sept. '55. Wm. Johnson's victory over Dieskau in COLONIAL WARS.

"BLOODY TARLETON." Nickname of Banastre TARLETON, who also was called "Bloody Ban" or, by such as the "Old Wagoner," who was hazy about orthography, "Bloody Ben."

BLUE LICKS, Ky., 19 Aug. '82. A force of Indians and Tories threatened Wheeling in July and then tried to surprise Bryan's Station (about 5 mi. N. of Lexington) the evening of 15 Aug. The morning of the 18th they started a slow, deliberate withdrawal to the N.E. and frontiersmen converged a few hours later at Bryan's for pursuit. The next morning 182 pursuers caught up with the 240 raiders near the Lower Blue Lick Springs on the Middle Fork of Licking River. Daniel Boone and other leaders advised waiting for a large reinforcement under Gen. Benj. Logan, but Maj. Hugh McGary touched off a disorganized rush across the deep ford against the superior force. This is what Simon Girty hoped for and after a fierce fight lasting only a few minutes the Ky. force was routed with about 70 killed and captured. (Samuel M. Wilson in *D.A.H.*)

BLUE MOUNTAIN VALLEY, off Sandy Hook, N.J., 22–23 Jan. '76. When the Elizabethtown, N.J., Comm. of Safety learned that a British transport and provision ship was off the coast they ordered that an attempt be made to capture it. According to Lossing, the expedition was made up of volunteers under Elias Dayton and Wil-liam Alexander who moved in four small boats to where the British vessel was sighted about 40 miles from Sandy Hook. "The men in the boats were all concealed under hatches, except two in each, unarmed, who managed the oars. The enemy mistook them for fishing vessels, and allowed them to come along side." The Americans then poured through the hatches and captured the vessel by surprise. (I, 328–29)

Lossing and *D.A.B.* disagree with each other and contradict themselves on various details of this exploit. As for the date, it would appear that the expedition left Elizabethtown on 22 Jan. '76 and made their capture the next day. As for whether the *Blue Mountain Valley* was a transport or a supply ship, she probably was both. As for the number of Americans involved, it would appear that there were three shallops and a pilot boat, between 40 and 77 volunteers manning them. The *D.A.B.* article by W. L. Whittlesey on Elias Dayton says Alexander got the credit for Dayton's exploit; this writer cites *American Archives,* ser. 4, IV, 987–89.

BLUE SAVANNAH, S.C., 4 Sept. '80. After his successful coup at Great Savannah, 20 Aug., MARION led his 52 mounted men swiftly east to escape pursuit and camped 60 miles away, at PORT'S FERRY on the Peedee River. Although he now was safe from attack from the west, where the British forces were located, danger developed to northeast when Maj. Micajah Ganey called out his Tory militia and started down the Little Peedee early 4 Sept. Although seriously outnumbered —250 to 50, as it turned out—Marion marched to meet this threat. His advance guard under Maj. John James located and routed a 45-man advance guard under Ganey's personal leadership. When Marion saw the remaining

200 Tory militia under Capt. Jesse
Barefield formed for battle he retreated
to Blue Savannah, circled to set up an
ambuscade, and routed Barefield's men
by a sudden charge. The Tories delivered one volley, wounding three men
and killing two horses, before heading
for the swamps. This success broke the
spirit of the Tories east of the Peedee
and brought 60 volunteers in to double Marion's strength. (Bass, *Swamp
Fox,* 48–51)

Blue Savannah is about 60 miles
E.N.E. of Great Savannah, near modern Galivant's Ferry. (*Ibid.,* 252)

BOARD OF WAR. While the Cont'l.
Cong. waited for delegates of S.C. and
the Middle Colonies to get instructions
regarding the Decl. of Indep. they resolved on 12 June '76 "that a committee of Congress be appointed, by the
name of a board of war and ordnance,
to consist of five members...." The
Board was created the next day. (*A.A.,*
34) This, according to Professor Herbert L. Osgood, was "the earliest germ
of an executive department" in the U.S.
(*E.B.,* XXVII, 278) Members were
Chairman John Adams, Edward Rutledge, Roger Sherman, Benjamin Harrison, and James Wilson. Creation of
the board was prompted by Congressional dissatisfaction with the progress
of the war, particularly the failure of
the Canada Invasion. Although experience already had shown the faults of
the committee system, "throughout the
next critical year, the Board of War
and Ordnance can at least be credited
with becoming one of the busiest and
most energetic of the standing committees." (Montross, *Reluctant Rebels,*
147) One of their items of business, in
the hope of remedying the indiscipline
contributing to American military defeats, was to draw up the new articles
of war, which Congress adopted on 20
Sept. '76.

On 17 Oct. '77 the Cont'l. Cong.
approved reorganization of the Board
so that it would consist of three men
who were not members of Cong. Freeman's note on this reorganization is
as follows:

"Careless use of the term 'Board of
War' is apt to confuse the student. As
first designated, the 'new' Board was to
consist of three persons not members
of Congress... but this board was so
slow in organizing that Congress on
the 21st of November authorized two
members of the former congressional
Board of War to sit with the member
or members of the elected Board who
then were in York (9 *JCC.,* 946). Before this could be made effective, Congress changed its mind and decided
that the 'old' Board would act on its
own account until the 'new' Board was
prepared to begin its labors (*ibid.,*
953). Two days later the decision was
to increase the 'new' Board by two
members (*loc. cit.;* see also *Burnett,*
572–74). On the 24th of November, the
Board of non-members having still been
unable to organize, Congress amended
its previous resolve, and authorized the
'old' Board to act 'until such time as
a quorum of the commissioners of the
War Office shall attend.' (9 *JCC.,*
960)" (*Washington,* IV, 558 *n.*) All this
reorganization took place as the CON-
WAY CABAL was coming to light, and
while Washington was coping with the
problems of defending the Delaware
River forts while trying to recruit,
clothe, and feed his army. The reorganization was part of the movement
to exert closer Congressional control
over the army of Washington, if not
to replace him. "Washington doubtless
needed all his self control as he read
what some members of Congress favored: they wanted to put on the board,
Joseph Reed, Timothy Pickering, who
was Washington's Adjutant General,

and Robert H. Harrison, the indispensable headquarters Secretary, and they talked of electing General Conway—of all possible choices!—to be Pickering's successor...." (*Ibid.*, IV, 549) By 21 Nov., Pickering had agreed to take the new post and Harrison had declined. On 18 Nov., Thomas Mifflin had consented to serve on the Board; he was the most powerful member, the best informed, and the most persuasive. (*Ibid.*, IV, 558) To complete the membership, Congress elected Gates—to be president—Joseph Trumbull (27 Nov.), and Richard Peters. The latter had been secretary of the "old" Board. It was at this stage of the Conway Cabal that Conway submitted his resignation to Congress (14 Nov.), and the delegates referred it to the Board of War! (Purpose of the "cabal" was to replace Washington with Gates.) James WILKINSON was named secretary, but this was too much even for Gates.

The Board did not act on Conway's resignation one way or another, but some of the delegates about this time began to support the movement that led to Conway's appointment as I.G. Washington's masterful handling of the situation resulted in collapse of the Conway Cabal and the discrediting of Gates before the Board of War could do any damage to the American cause. Their "child of folly," the planned CANADA INVASION (1778), further proved that the Board was not the instrument to succeed Washington in over-all direction of military operations.

The Board was reorganized after a Congressional resolution of 29 Oct. '78 prescribed that three members not be members of Congress and that two be delegates (as before), and that three would constitute a quorum. Congress had a difficult time in getting delegates to fill the two posts, and failed to prevail on R. H. Harrison, William Grayson, and Henry Heath to serve.

BOISBERTRAND, René Etienne Henri de Vic Gayault de. 1746–?. French officer captured with Lee at BASKING RIDGE. Of a noble family that for a century had held the hereditary post of *Prévôt général des marechaussées de Berry,* he was born at Bourges and entered the Hainault Regt. on 10 July '63 as *sous-lieutenant.* Early "efficiency reports" characterize him as spirited but irresponsible. (*Etourdi,* which translates "giddy, thoughtless, heedless.") By 1766, however, he is considered *"bon officier."* In 1768 he inherited the family sinecure and left the regiment, but he apparently retained his military connections since the records show his promotion to Lt. Col. in 1772. When the first steps were being taken under Dr. Dubourg to send the Americans covert aid, Dubourg selected Boisbertrand to take important secret dispatches across the Atlantic. Two years' leave were granted without his request. (Lasseray, 481–85)

Seriously wounded and captured at Basking Ridge. 13 Dec. '76, the French volunteer received two years of deplorable treatment in a succession of British jails. Escaping at last, he reached France to find that his hereditary post had been given to another. He made two requests for reinstatement in the army but both were denied, presumably because of his poor physical condition. On 1 Mar. '91 he was retired as *maréchal de camp,* he was given a pension in 1793, and on 20 June 1820 he was admitted to the Invalides because of "incurable infirmities." (*Ibid.*) In 1788 he had been made Chevalier de Saint Louis.

Lasseray alphabetizes his name under V as De VIC GAYAULT DE BOISBERTRAND, etc. (*alias:* Gaiault).

BONHOMME RICHARD–SERAPIS ENGAGEMENT, 23 Sept. 1779. On the morning of this day John Paul Jones sighted two warships convoying 40 British merchantmen near the North Sea coast of York between Flamborough Head and Scarborough. His coastal pilot informed Jones that the warships were the *Serapis* (44) and the *Countess of Scarborough* (20). Although his converted merchantman, the *Bonhomme Richard*, was unseaworthy and mounted only 42 guns (*D.A.H.*), and his officers were inexperienced, Jones took up pursuit with his ship, the *Vengeance*, the *Pallas*, and the recently rejoined *Alliance*. About eight hours later, at around 8 P.M., Jones was within hailing distance of the *Serapis*, while the merchantmen had taken protection under shore batteries and the *Countess* was the quarry of Jones's other ships.

Fire opened almost simultaneously with an exchange of broadsides. Two of Jones's 18-pdrs. burst early in the action, and he was limited thereafter to the use of lighter pieces and musketry. After the initial exchange of broadsides the *Serapis* moved ahead of her adversary and on the leeward side. Not being able to gain enough distance for the maneuver intended (to cross in front of the *Bonhomme* and RAKE her), the *Serapis* lost headway in executing a turn and was rammed in the stern. During the few minutes that the ships remained in this position, which did not permit a single gun of the *Bonhomme* to be used, British Captain Pearson is alleged to have said, "Has your ship struck," and Captain Jones to have replied with his immortal, "I have not yet begun to fight." The ships separated, but when the *Serapis* came quickly around her jib-boom ran into the mizzen rigging of the *Bonhomme*, and Jones lashed on.

"A novelty in naval combats was now presented to many witnesses, but to few admirers," comments Lt. Richard Dale, who commanded a battery on the main deck of Jones's ship. (C. & M., 948) A desperate battle raged more than two hours longer, and Pearson finally struck his colors. During the action the *Bonhomme* had been shelled by the *Alliance*, commanded by the madman LANDAIS. During the action 500 British prisoners aboard the American ship had been released by Jones's "treacherous master-at-arms," as Jones called him in his 3 Oct. letter to Benj. Franklin (*ibid.*, 953), but the Americans used the prisoners to man the pumps of their sinking ship. Most of this terrible battle was fought in the moonlight; according to Jones the British surrendered at 10:30 P.M. (*Ibid.*) Jones had sustained about 50 per cent casualties among his 237-man crew. (*E.A.H.*, 102) The *Countess of Scarborough* surrendered to the *Pallas* about 10 minutes after the *Serapis*.

See also JONES and LANDAIS.

BONVOULOIR. See ACHARD DE BONVOULOIR.

BOONE, Daniel. 1734–1820. Frontiersman. Grandson of a weaver and small farmer who reached Philadelphia in 1717 from his former home near Exeter, England, the man who was to become America's most famous frontiersman was born about 11 miles from Reading, Pa. In 1750 he accompanied his family when they moved to Buffalo Lick, N.C., on the north fork of the Yadkin, where they settled in 1751 (having spent almost a year in the Shenandoah). Like Dan Morgan, he accompanied Braddock's expedition as a teamster; he escaped on one of his horses from the disaster of 9 July '55. (See COLONIAL WARS) On this expedition he met John Finley, a hunter whose stories of the Ky. wilderness fired him with a desire to visit this country. During the period 1769–71 he undertook an extensive exploration through Cumberland Gap, into what now is Estill co. From a camp at Station Camp Creek, Boone and five others —including a brother and a brother-in-law—roamed the Blue Grass. In 1775, as an agent of the Transylvania Company, he led about 30 men to the site of what became Boonesborough. Arriving 1 Apr., he immediately started construction of a fort, and in the fall he returned to N.C. to get his family and 20 more men. On this trip they blazed the Wilderness Road, the route subsequently used by thousands in the first great migration west. (It was known also as Boone's Trace, Virginia Road, Kentucky Road, and the "Road to Caintuck.")

This activity was in defiance of the PROCLAMATION OF 1763, and in their efforts to stop and drive back this invasion of settlers, the Cherokees and Shawnees started raids into what became known as the "dark and bloody ground." Boone was prominent in civic affairs, which at that time and place meant Indian fighting, surveying, and hunting. When Ky. became a county of Va. in the fall of 1776, Boone was made Capt. of the militia and later was promoted to Maj. (He is not listed in Heitman, however.) In Feb. '78 he was captured by Shawnees, taken to Detroit and then to CHILLICOTHE, from which place he escaped in June. (C.E.; D.A.B.) Apparently he returned with information that new Indian forays were being organized, intelligence that helped the settlers prepare for the successful defense of Boonesborough in Sept. '78. (Ibid.) The next month he went east for a stay that was to last a year, but in Oct. '79 he returned with a new party of settlers. The next spring

he started back east with $20,000 collected from settlers for the purchase of land warrants, since the state had repudiated land titles of the Transylvania Company, but he was robbed of the entire amount. (D.A.B.) He then moved to Boone's Station. The same year, 1780, Ky. was divided into three counties, and he was made Lt. Col. (sic) of Fayette co. After holding a number of public offices, in 1785 he had the first of a series of ejectment suits by which he was to lose his large land holdings. All his titles were improperly entered, and around 1798 he lost his last holding in the region he had done so much to develop. Meanwhile he had moved from Boone's Station to Maysville in 1786, to Point Pleasant (in modern W. Va.) in 1788, and to what now is Missouri in 1798 or 1799. His son Daniel had preceded him, and Boone was given a large Spanish land grant at the mouth of Femme Osage Creek. When the U.S. assumed title to this region Boone's titles were found to be defective, but after many delays Congress interceded to restore part of his holdings. Tradition has it that Boone went back to Ky. around 1810 to pay off his debts and returned home with fifty cents left. (D.A.B.)

After helping his father at weaving, blacksmithing, and stockraising, Boone had undertaken the life of a frontiersman with the benefit of little if any schooling. He was barely literate, but his career reveals strong native intelligence and good judgment in civic affairs (if not in land law). Exaggeration of his exploits by early historians and the seven stanzas that Lord Byron devoted to him in Don Juan (1823) helped create a legend that subsequent writers have had to destroy. He was not the discoverer of Ky., its first explorer, its first settler, nor its chief military protector, points out W. J. Ghent in

D.A.B. "Nor did his services to the community, meritorious though they were, equal in importance those of certain other men. He had, however, his own ample titles to fame and the regard of posterity." (*Ibid.*) Although physical descriptions run all the way from the statement of Audubon (who knew him) that he "appeared gigantic," to that of the Rev. J. E. Welch, "rather low," Daniel Bryant, a relative by marriage, says he was between 5 feet 8 inches and 5 feet 9. His head was large, his alert blue eyes were overshadowed by yellow eyebrows, and separated by a Roman nose. That he was brave, tough, and an outstanding woodsman goes without saying. He also is said to have been noted for his honesty; he was modest and well liked. One interesting quality on which Ghent comments is his remarkable "serenity of mind." He never showed excitement or irritation, and despite his many legitimate grievances in the matter of land rights, "he never harbored rancor." (*Ibid.*)

See John E. Bakeless, *Daniel Boone* (New York, 1939), Reuben G. Thwaites, *Daniel Boone* (1902), and Clarence W. Alvord's searching examination of "the Boone Myth" in the *Jour. of the Ill. State Hist. Soc.*, Apr.–July 1926.

BORDER WARFARE in New York.* With Canada and the Old Northwest in British hands at the start of the Revolution the Colonists had a long frontier that was vulnerable to invasion by regular troops and to Tory-Indian raids. After the failure of BURGOYNE'S OFFENSIVE, June–Oct. '77, and the supporting ST. LEGER'S OFFENSIVE, military operations were reduced to raids and punitive expeditions. Detroit was the British base for attacks against the

* See maps under COLONIAL WARS.

frontier settlements along the Ohio River and territory to the south, modern Ky. bearing the brunt. (See WESTERN OPNS. of Clark) Niagara and, to a lesser extent, Oswego were headquarters for British operations farther north. This article's purpose is to list and correlate the numerous operations against the N.Y. frontier.

"War out of Niagara" was directed toward TRYON COUNTY, N.Y., a vast territory whose western boundary was, in effect, the "Iroquois frontier." The spine of Tryon County was the Mohawk Valley, and it was against the settlements of this valley that the Tory exiles directed their efforts. Guy and Sir John JOHNSON, John and Walter BUTLER, and the Mohawk Joseph BRANT led the most terrible of the Tory-Indian raids against their former neighbors.

"The rout of St. Leger and the surrender of Burgoyne gave the North a false sense of security," points out Swiggett. (*Niagara,* 113) The French Alliance, which soon followed, furthered the illusion, as did the presence of Lafayette in Albany to organize a second patriot invasion of Canada. The Tryon County settlers, comprising a high percentage of "Palatine peasants," had never shown much of what Americans like to glorify as the frontier spirit—particularly after ORISKANY—and they believed the greatest sacrifice that remained to be made for the cause of freedom "had to do mainly with crops and cattle for Washington's army. . . ." (*Ibid.,* 112, 206) They learned the hard way.

The WYOMING "MASSACRE," Pa., 3–4 July '78, far south of the Mohawk, was the first thunderbolt from Niagara. Although Joseph Brant was long accused of participation in this operation, he was mobilizing an army of his own in the vicinity of Unadilla, an Indian town on the Susquehanna about 50 miles from the main settlements of the Mohawk Valley that would figure prominently in future operations. Despite the excellent intelligence furnished by James Deane, Schuyler's secret agent, the patriots were taken by surprise. (Swiggett, 114 ff.) Brant sacked AN-DRUSTOWN, 18 July, and returned to destroy GERMAN FLATS, 13 Sept. '78. The patriots retaliated by destroying UNADILLA, 6–8 Oct. These were relatively puny actions in which much property was lost with no casualties being inflicted, but they led to the serious patriot disaster at CHERRY VALLEY, 11 Nov.

SULLIVAN'S EXPEDITION, May–Nov. '79, was a savage American attempt to eliminate the Iroquois menace. After innumerable delays and having sacrificed all surprise, 4,000 Cont'l. troops crashed into the wilderness, routed a Tory-Indian force at NEWTOWN, 29 Aug., and burned 40 towns. (A preliminary was Brant's raid to MINISINK, 19–22 July.) Far from achieving its real purpose, however, this punitive expedition brought on a red whirlwind. The winter of 1779–80 was of record-breaking severity. Swiggett writes:

"No one could foresee the tragic link of the autumn's war and the winter's weather, but now it was plain that it was folly to have injured the Indians as Sullivan did, and then leave Niagara unscathed for them to refit, and strike back. To have injured them so dreadfully and not to have wiped them out was a colossal blunder." (*Op. cit.,* 204)

OPERATIONS IN 1780

Spring of the new year brought a number of ominous indications that the Indians were contemplating something quite different from "the overtures of peace which," in the words of Gov. Clinton, "we had some reason to expect from them." (*Ibid.,* 212) Hostile In-dians supported by British regulars and Tories attacked the Oneidas, destroyed their settlements, and forced them back into the Mohawk Valley. Most of them sought shelter around Schenectady, and they no longer served as a protective screen against attacks from Oswego and Niagara. Indians captured the militia garrison at Skenesboro in Mar. and burned a house in Tryon co. Brant raided HARPERSFIELD, 2 Apr., and would have attacked the Upper Fort of Schoharie Valley, 15 miles N.E., but for the false information of a prisoner (Capt. Alexander Harper) that this place was defended by 300 Cont'ls. With 19 prisoners, Brant's Indians and Tories moved south to raid MINISINK, *c.* 4 Apr. Seven Indian marauders attacked the blockhouse at Sacandaga, 3 Apr., but were all killed. Several whites were killed and captured when 79 Indians attacked Cherry Valley, 24 Apr.

These were raids by "small unorganized parties of starving men," comments Swiggett, and resistance "was itself desultory and unorganized." (*Ibid.*) Unfortunately for the patriots, however, their defenses were still unorganized when the enemy struck in force.

SIR JOHN JOHNSON'S FIRST RAID

With 400 Tories and 200 Indians Sir John Johnson entered the Johnstown settlements undetected the evening of 21 May. He had taken the Lake Champlain route to Crown Point and marched from there to the Sacandaga River. He detached Brant, who burned Caughnawaga, on the Mohawk River, at dawn of the 22d, and other detachments killed, burned, and took prisoners in the valley. On 23 May, Johnson burned Johnstown and withdrew slowly to Mayfield, about 8 miles to the N.E., with 40 prisoners. Having given the patriots every opportunity to attack him here, he withdrew on the 27th and continued slowly toward Crown Point with his booty, prisoners, and a number of "liberated" families of his Tory officers and men. Gov. Clinton made a feeble attempt to cut him off at Ticonderoga. (Neither of the Butlers is mentioned in the dispatches of either side, comments Swiggett, and they evidently were not along.)

Joseph Brant with 500 Tories and Indians sacked CANAJOHARIE, 1–2 Aug. '80, moved with amazing swiftness into another theater of operations for the coup known as LOCHRY'S DEFEAT, on the Ohio River, and returned to participate in Johnson's second raid into Tryon co.

This is the operation in which Sir John recovered the family silver and papers hidden at Johnson Hall, and the romantic myth has grown that the raid was organized for this purpose. But with the French army and fleet now at Newport and Cornwallis waging a major offensive in the South, the British high command in Canada had something less frivolous in mind. Haldimand thus explained the strategy in a letter of 17 Sept. to Germain:

"... to divide the strength that may be brought against Sir H. Clinton, or to favor any operations his present situation may induce him to carry on and to give His Majesty's loyal subjects an opportunity of retiring from the Province I have fitted out two parties of about 600 men each, besides Indians, to penetrate into the enemy's by the Mohawk River and Lake George...."
(Quoted by Swiggett, *op. cit.,* 222)

Remember that this was the time of the Benedict Arnold plot to surrender West Point, which gives a special meaning to Johnson's phrase of favoring operations Sir Henry might be induced to carry out. Note also that one mission was to evacuate Loyalist families,

the secondary purpose of almost all Tory raids into Tryon co.

Leaving Oswego in Sept., Johnson moved toward Unadilla, and picked up reinforcements under Brant and CORNPLANTER to bring his strength to between 800 and 1,500. He also had "artillery": two small mortars and a brass 3-pdr. ("GRASSHOPPER") Johnson's approach was undetected and he ravaged SCHOHARIE VALLEY, 15–17 Oct., destroyed all rebel property in the vicinity of FORT HUNTER, 17 Oct., started up the Mohawk the next day laying waste to everything on both sides of the river as far as Canajoharie (Ft. Plank or Ft. Plain), and camped that night near Palatine. The next morning he crossed the Mohawk at Keder's Rifts.

Gen. Robert Van Rensselaer assembled 400 to 500 militia in the lower Mohawk and started in pursuit, and Gov. George Clinton left Albany to catch up with him. While a detachment of 50 raiders headed for Fort Paris in Stone Arabia, Col. John Brown sallied forth from that place to attack Johnson's main body on orders from Van Rensselaer and with the promise that the latter would arrive in time to support him. Near ruined FORT KEYSER, 19 Oct., Brown and about 40 of his 130 men were killed and the rest routed after making a gallant attack against a vastly superior force. Stone Arabia was burned. Van Rensselaer was too late to prevent the annihilation of Brown's force but he was reinforced by 300 or 400 militia and 60 Oneidas under Col. Lewis DuBois and brought Johnson to bay at KLOCK'S FIELD, 19 Oct. The raiders made their escape via Lake Onondaga to Oswego.

Meanwhile, the raids from the north (called for in Johnson's 17 Sept. letter, quoted above) were taking place. A detachment of the 53d Regt. under an officer named Houghton struck the upper Conn. Valley and destroyed some houses at Royalton. Another force, under Maj. Carleton, moved through Ft. Anne, Ft. Edward, Ft. George, attacked Ballston (a mere 12 miles from Schenectady) and threatened other settlements north of Albany. Gov. Clinton wrote Washington on 30 Oct.:

"The losses we have sustained by these different incursions of the enemy will be most severely felt; they have destroyed, on a moderate computation, 200 dwellings and 150,000 bushels of wheat.... The enemy to the northward continue in the neighborhood of Crown Point, and the inhabitants, in consequence of their apprehensions of danger, are removing from the northern parts of the state...." (Clinton Papers, quoted in C. & M., 1031)

RAIDS OF 1781

The worst news Clinton had to report in this same letter was that Sir John, Brant, and Walter Butler escaped. In 1781 they returned. Brant, who had been wounded in the heel at Klock's Field, ranged the upper Mohawk Valley almost at will during the early months of the year. The Oneida were no longer in their settlements to furnish a screen of protection, or at least of warning, and militia resistance had collapsed. War parties revisited German Flats; Cherry Valley was attacked in Apr.; and two parties of the 2d N.Y. Cont'ls. were captured while trying to take supplies to Ft. Stanwix. The latter post was abandoned in May after being critically damaged by floods and fire. Despite all this, however, a visitor reported on 13 July that "there is a prospect of as plentiful crops as has been in the memory of man." It might be said that a housing shortage existed, but life in the valley went on, and spirits soared when Marinus Willett arrived late in June to assume command

of the scattered frontier posts. With 400 men Willett had the seemingly impossible mission of protecting some 5,000 settlers in an area of about 2,000 square miles—his posts at Ballston, Catskill, and Ft. Herkimer (German Flats) forming a triangle of roughly that area. His "main body," if it can be dignified by that term, comprised 120 men at Canajoharie, where he established his headquarters. The rest of his puny strength was parceled out among the far-flung settlements.

Willett did not have to wait much more than a week before the first challenge. About 350 Indians led by John Doxtader surprised CURRYTOWN, 9 July, and the remarkable Willett annihilated this force the next day at SHARON SPRINGS SWAMP. Donald McDonald was defeated (and killed) by the heroic stand of a single family at SHELL'S BUSH, 6 Aug. Capt. Wm. Caldwell struck south of Tryon co. and was driven off in the actions covered under WAWARSING, 22 Aug. On 7 Sept., Lt. Solomon Woodworth was killed near Ft. Plain when his party was ambushed.

FINAL OPERATIONS IN TRYON COUNTY

By this time the Northern Dept. had alarming and confusing reports that one enemy column was approaching along Lake Champlain and another along Lake Oneida from Oswego. Although Gen. Heath had only 2,500 men to guard the Highlands against the threat from Sir Henry Clinton's 17,000 in N.Y.C. while Washington and Rochambeau marched on Yorktown, "Our General" sent the N.H. Cont'ls. and some artillery north on 13 Oct. The threat from Lake Champlain resulted in widely conflicting intelligence reports, but this problem became academic on 24 Oct. when the smoke of burning buildings started rising in the Mohawk Valley. Maj. John Ross had left Oswego on the 16th with 700 men, only 130 of whom were Indians. He struck the valley near Warrenbush (now Florida) and burned a seven-mile stretch to come within 12 miles of Schenectady on the 25th. Although he had not met any real resistance, Ross then started withdrawing. "It seems apparent from this quick retreat . . . that a campaign had again broken down," says Swiggett. (*Op. cit.*, 240) "The phantom force in the North, said to be under Sir John Johnson, was probably to have joined hands with him," but Johnson apparently had been slow in his preparations. (*Ibid.*) Failure of the Indians to turn out in the numbers expected, muddy roads, and certainty that the militia was gathering all around him—these factors also figured in Ross's decision. Willett caught up with the raiders and attacked at JOHNSTOWN, 25 Oct. Darkness called a halt to the action that started late in the day. Ross claimed to have gotten the better of it, and Willett's failure to start pursuit until the 28th tends to support his contention. But the British leader lost most of his head start when his guides were slow in finding a trail north to the St. Lawrence, a route Ross had to choose because Willett might cut off a retreat to the boats left on Lake Oneida. After waiting for provisions, the rebels started pursuit the evening of the 28th, marched 20 miles in a snowstorm on the 29th, and caught up at 8 o'clock the next morning. Ross kept up a running fight as his tired and famished Tories, British regulars, and Indians headed for West Canada Creek, where they hoped to make a stand. Walter Butler's rear guard had just crossed this sizable stream when Willett's vanguard arrived at 2 P.M. The action at JERSEYFIELD, 30 Oct., was little more than a firefight across the ford, but

when the enemy resumed their retreat they left the dead body of the famous Walter Butler. After a pursuit of another 20 miles Willett called a halt. "The woods were strewed with the packs of the enemy," he explained, "provisions they had none.* * * In this situation to the compassion of a starving wilderness, we left them in a fair way of receiving a punishment better suited to their merit than a musquet ball, a tomahawk or captivity. . . ." (Quoted in C. & M., 1033)

This was the last Tory attempt in Tryon co. Indian raids continued in 1782 and a few prominent patriots were abducted by Tories, but the border warfare had ended.

See W. W. Campbell, *Annals of Tryon County; The Public Papers of George Clinton;* W. L. Stone, *Border Wars;* and Howard Swiggett, *War out of Niagara.*

BOSTON CAMPAIGN, 19 Apr. '75–17 Mar. '76. Military actions in Mass. from the day of LEXINGTON AND CONCORD, 19 Apr. '75, until evacuation of the BOSTON GARRISON on 17 Mar. '76 are sometimes grouped under the heading of the Boston Campaign. Operations during this period are covered under the cross references already mentioned, and under BOSTON SIEGE, 19 Apr. '75–17 Mar.' 76; the latter covering article refers to separate articles on BUNKER HILL, 17 June '75, KNOX'S "NOBLE TRAIN," and DORCHESTER HEIGHTS, 2–27 Mar. '76.

BOSTON GARRISON, 1 Oct. '68–17 Mar. '76. Increasing disorders in Boston, brought on by the Townshend Acts, caused the British government to instruct Gen. Gage to send at least one regiment to Boston. These instructions were dated 8 June '68 but were not received by Gage in N.Y.C. until late Aug. Meanwhile the LIBERTY AFFAIR,

10 June '68, impressed the London authorities with the need for more troops to back up their civil authorities in Boston, and the 64th and 65th Regts. were ordered there from the garrison in Ireland.

Before we describe the build-up of the Boston garrison that started with the above orders (the first troops did not land until Oct. '68) it should be mentioned that Gov. Bernard of Mass. had long wanted redcoats in Boston. He had hoped, however, that Gage, the *military* commander in America, would send them on his own initiative, thereby relieving the *civil* authorities of a decision that was certain to inflame further the already unruly Bostonians. Gen. Gage, on the other hand, felt he had no authority to send troops without a request from the governor. After the Liberty Affair the terrified customs commissioners had (15 June) asked Gage for troops and had also appealed to Col. Wm. Dalrymple at Halifax. Gage then ordered Dalrymple, C.O. of the Halifax garrison, to alert two regiments but to hold them until Gov. Bernard requested them. The latter still refused to accept the responsibility and asked Gage to send the troops on the pretext that this was a routine administrative movement to get better quarters for the regulars. Gage, quite properly, refused, and this was the situation when he received the 8 June instructions late in Aug. (Alden, *Gage,* 157–59)

Dalrymple sailed from Halifax on 19 Sept. '68 with the larger part of the 14th and 29th Regts. (*ibid.,* 163) and an artillery company of five guns (Fortescue, *British Army,* III, 34–35), a force numbering 800 men. (*Ibid.*) He was convoyed by an impressive naval escort of a ship-of-the-line, seven frigates, and two tenders, commanded by Commodore Samuel Hood. This armada reached the harbor on 28 Sept. It was a tense situation because the Boston radicals, directed by Samuel Adams and supported by the ever-ready city mob, were advocating armed resistance, but the influence of James OTIS prevented violence. On 1 Oct. the British landed under the guns of the fleet to establish a garrison that would be in Boston seven and a half years. "They were greeted with cold silence rather than hot lead," comments Alden. (*Op. cit.,* 163) The contingent from Ireland started arriving in mid-Nov., but a large portion of the 65th Regt., with its commander, Col. Alexander Mackay, was driven off the coast by a storm; after taking refuge on Nevis (in the W.I.) they reached Boston on 30 Apr. '69.

The British troops had trouble getting quarters and provisions in Boston, as was to be expected. Capt. John MONTRESOR had been sent by land from N.Y.C. to make an engineer reconnaissance and to repair Castle William. Dalrymple and Bernard wanted to billet the Halifax regiments in the town and keep the barracks of Castle William (in the harbor) available for the regiments expected from Ireland, but the Boston authorities refused to do anything about providing permanent troop housing in the city as long as the barracks on Castle Island were empty. They flatly refused to furnish provisions. All of this was in defiance of the QUARTERING ACT. Gage reached Boston on 15 Oct., and by 24 Nov., when he had to return to N.Y.C., makeshift quarters had been arranged for the regulars. Part of the troops were permitted to use Faneuil Hall temporarily, but the rest had to camp on the Common. Gage and Bernard got reluctant authority from the council to use the Manufactory Building, which belonged to the province, but this was frustrated by persons previously authorized to use this building. Gage then decided to rent property at the crown's expense. On 4 Oct. a Tory named James Murray made several buildings available. An adaptable patriot named Wm. Molineux rented the army several warehouses on Wheelwright's wharf (28 Oct.) and a week later rented them another building. (See Alden, *op. cit.,* 164 and *n.*) When the Irish contingent started arriving, part of them went to Castle Island and the rest were billeted in Boston.

Col. Dalrymple commanded the Boston garrison from its establishment (1 Oct. '68) until Col. John Pomeroy arrived in Nov. with his 64th Regt. Mackay, who had the local rank of Maj. Gen., succeeded to the command when he arrived on 30 Apr. '69 with the portion of his 65th Regt. from Nevis. Mackay left Boston on 18 Aug. '69 for leave in England (Pomeroy had gone on leave as soon as Mackay arrived), and Dalrymple resumed command of the garrison. (Alden, *Gage,* 164, 169, 170) Before the end of July the 64th and 65th were evacuated to Halifax, leaving only the 14th and 29th.

The BOSTON "MASSACRE," 5 Mar. '70, was the inevitable result of the agitation directed by the radical element of the city. The rabble rousers, led by Sam Adams, exploited the incident to force the British commander to accede to demands that the redcoats be withdrawn to Castle William. The 29th Regt. was ordered to N.J. in Apr. '70, leaving only Dalrymple's 14th Foot. Two years later the 14th was relieved by Lt. Col. Leslie's 64th Regt.

Gage returned to Boston on 17 May '74 to implement the British government's punitive policies against the city. What had heretofore been a "garrison" soon was built up to the largest British troop concentration in America. By early July '74 Gage had brought in four regiments from Great Britain, one from N.Y., and a few artillerymen. In Oct. the 10th and 52d arrived from Quebec, part of the 18th and the 47th arrived from N.Y., and two companies of the 65th came from Newfoundland. Excluding the 64th Regt. on Castle Island, this gave the British commander almost 3,000 men for operations. On 12 Dec. the warships *Asia* and *Boyne* arrived from England with about 400 Royal Marines that could be used in land action.

At the start of 1775 Gage had about 4,500 combat troops, including five artillery companies and 460 marines from ships that now included the *Scarborough* and *Somerset* plus frigates, sloops, and many transports. By the middle of June his strength in rank and file (not including officers) was between 6,340 and 6,716, according to the estimates of Murdock and French. No official list of units has been found, but it would appear that by the end of June '75 the following foot regiments were in Boston or on the way: 4th, 5th, 10th, 23d, 35th, 38th, 43d, 47th, 49th, 52d, 59th, 63d, 64th (at Castle William), and 67th. An "incorporated corps" consisted of 3 companies of the 18th Foot that had come from N.Y. in Oct. '74, and two companies of the 65th from Newfoundland this same date, plus four more companies of the 65th that arrived in the spring of 1774. The marine contingent had been increased to about 600. The 17th Light Dragoons, numbering fewer than 300 and counting on picking their horses up in America, reached Boston late in May. (Ward, *W.O.R.,* 59 and 438)

Leslie led his 64th Regt. in the expedition to SALEM, 26 Feb. '75. Elements of the units listed above took part in the fighting at LEXINGTON AND CON-

CORD, 19 Apr., and BUNKER HILL, 17 June '75. British reinforcements arrived during the remainder of the Boston Siege. When the British evacuated the city on 17 Mar. '76 their total strength in army and navy personnel was about 11,000.

In addition to the works of French and Frothingham see John Barker, *The British in Boston.* . . . (1924).

BOSTON "MASSACRE." 5 Mar. '70. Minor clashes between soldiers of the BOSTON GARRISON and citizens led to an inevitable climax on 5 Mar. '70. That afternoon an exchange of insults between citizens and an off-duty soldier seeking work at Grey's ropewalk led to a small riot, and bands of soldiers and civilians roamed the streets that evening looking for trouble. About 9 P.M. a sentry in King Street was so taunted and menaced by "an irresponsible mob of some 60 rioters" (R. W. G. Vail in *D.A.H.*) that he was reinforced by about 10 soldiers from the main guard. After continued provocation, the soldiers fired into the crowd, killing three and mortally wounding two others.

John Adams and Josiah Quincy, outstanding colonial lawyers, agreed to defend the soldiers in court. Capt. Thomas Preston, guard commander, and four soldiers were acquitted; two were convicted of manslaughter but released and discharged from military service after pleading their clergy (being branded on the hand). Meanwhile, popular pressure led to evacuation of all British troops to Castle William.

By means of biased and widely distributed propaganda (*ibid.*) the Patriots used this incident to stir up opposition to England. Paul Revere's engraving, grossly falsifying the event, was produced as "evidence" of British guilt. There is reason to suspect that Sam Adams provoked the entire incident— one of the victims made this accusation on his deathbed (Miller, *Sam Adams*) —to inflame the populace.

As for the moral problems involved, a modern American authority says the following analysis is so astute that it deserves repetition:

"There was futility in any argument either at the time or since, because if one held that the citizens were maddened by the soldiery, the answer was that the soldiers were nagged to desperation by the citizens. If against that rejoinder it was argued that the soldiers ought never to have been sent there, the reasonable reply was that the growing ascendancy of mob-law had made military force necessary. Following that chain one comes ultimately to ethical questions of right and wrong upon which none may speak with finality." (Van Tyne, *Causes*, 289, quoted by Alden, *Gage*, 184–85)

It is a striking example of historical distortion that some Americans still look on the Boston Massacre as the propagandists of 1770 wanted their contemporaries to see it. But for the American reader who still finds it hard to believe that his grade school history has deceived him, the following facts are offered:

"In 1887 the Massachusetts legislature, in conformance with the prevailing American opinion, voted a memorial to the victims. The Massachusetts Historical Society, however, formally protested and resolved that: 'While greatly applauding the sentiment which erects memorials to the heroes and martyrs of our annals, the members of the Society believe that nothing but a misapprehension of the event styled the "Boston massacre" can lead to classifying these persons with those entitled to grateful recognition at the public expense.'" (Alden, *Gage,* 184)

Leaving aside all consideration of contemporary morality and subsequent gullibility, the "massacre" was a milestone on the road to American independence, being "the first powerful influence in forming an outspoken anti-British public opinion," (Vail, *op. cit.*), which revolutionary leaders had almost despaired of achieving.

BOSTON PORT BILL (1774). One of the INTOLERABLE ACTS, it had the effect of rallying other colonies—notably Va.—to the support of Mass. and resulted indirectly in the call for the 1st Cont'l. Cong. to consider united measures of resistance.

BOSTON SIEGE. 19 Apr. '75–17 Mar. '76. The armed provincials who turned out at LEXINGTON AND CONCORD, 19 Apr. '75, drove the British back to Boston and invested the city. On 23 Apr. the MASS. PROVINCIAL CONGRESS reconvened and, among other actions, voted that 30,000 men be called to arms, 13,600 of them to be raised immediately in Mass. This body also appointed Artemas Ward C. in C. of Mass. troops and named the following major generals: John Thomas, Wm. Heath, John Whitcomb, and Dr. Joseph Warren. Rhode Island voted a brigade of three regiments, 1,500 men, with Nathanael Greene in command. New Hampshire set a quota of 2,000 with Nathaniel Folsom as commanding gen-

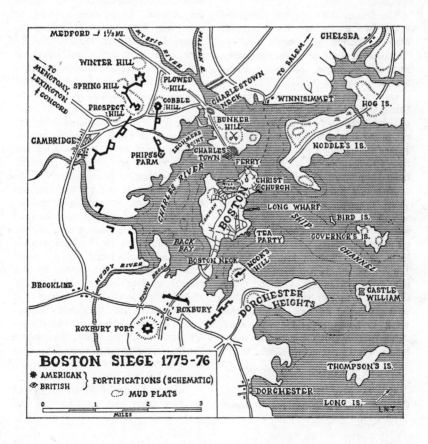

BOSTON SIEGE 1775-76
* AMERICAN } FORTIFICATIONS (SCHEMATIC)
◉ BRITISH
⌒ MUD FLATS
0   1   2   3
MILES

eral but actually led by Col. John Stark. Connecticut ordered 6,000 enlisted, naming David Wooster their major general, and Joseph Spencer and Israel Putnam brigadier generals. Although Conn. did not raise more than 3,000, and R.I. and N.H. both fell short of their quotas, by June there were about 15,000 provincials in the camps around Boston.

One third of these constituted the right wing, located at Roxbury, Dorchester, and Jamaica Plain, and commanded by Gen. Thomas. Troops included 4,000 from Mass., Greene's R.I. regiments, most of Spencer's Conn. troops, and three or four artillery companies.

The center, at Cambridge, comprised 9,000 men under Artemas Ward: 15 Mass. regiments, Maj. Sam'l. Gridley's battalion of four artillery companies, Putnam's regiment, and other Conn. troops.

On the left were three companies of Sam'l. Gerrish's Mass. regiment at Chelsea, John Stark's N.H. Regt. (the largest in the army) at Medford, and Col. James Reed's much smaller N.H. Regt. near Charlestown Neck. (These dispositions from Ward, *W.O.R.*, 54)

Although most men had their personal firearms, this improvised army was short of all other matériel, particularly gunpowder. Ward was in command of all Mass. troops, who constituted the bulk of the "Boston army," and the 1,000 N.H. militia had been directed to take orders from him. R.I. and Conn. contingents took orders only from their own officers at this time, although they seem to have cooperated with Ward. After Bunker Hill, Conn. put her troops under Ward's command. (*Ibid.*, 55)

THE BRITISH GARRISON

On 25 May '75, Gens. Burgoyne, Clinton, and Howe arrived in Boston with reinforcements, and by 15 June Gen. Gage had about 6,500 rank and file stationed in this city of 17,000 people. Under orders to proclaim martial law in Mass., and taken with the bizarre idea that he would simultaneously make a last effort to avoid war, Gage issued on 12 June a manifesto that Burgoyne had used his literary talents to write for him. Addressing "the infatuated multitude, who have long suffered themselves to be conducted by certain well known incendiaries and traitors," he offered the King's pardon to all except Sam Adams and John Hancock who should lay down their arms. The document was met with deserved derision on both sides of the Atlantic. Gage then decided to strengthen his defenses by taking unoccupied Dorchester Heights. On 13 June, five days before the operation was to take place, the Americans learned of it and ordered a countermove that resulted in the Battle of BUNKER HILL, 17 June '75.

On 15 June Washington was appointed C. in C. of the troops around Boston, which on 31 May had become the CONT'L ARMY. He took command at Cambridge on 2 July. By Nov. he had 17,000 men, all of them reasonably well fed, housed, and healthy. But, since the engagements of his men expired with the year—those of the Conn. militia on 10 Dec.—he was almost immediately faced with the problem of raising another army. In this critical period, as the politicians in Philadelphia debated how money was to be raised and the place hunters sought personal advantage from the reorganization of the army, Washington "had to struggle with himself to keep his patience and his faith." (Freeman, *Washington*, III, 570)

"Such a dearth of public spirit, and want of virtue, such stock-jobbing, and fertility in all the low arts to obtain advantages of one kind or another, in this great change of military arrangement, I never saw before, and pray God I may never be witness to again. What will be the ultimate end of these manoeuvres is beyond my scan. I tremble at the prospect. We have been till this time [28 Nov. '75] enlisting about three thousand five hundred men. To engage these I have been obliged to allow furloughs as far as fifty men a regiment, and the Officers I am persuaded indulge as many more. The Connecticut troops will not be prevailed upon to stay longer than their term (saving those who have enlisted for the next campaign, and mostly on furlough), and such a dirty, mercenary spirit pervades the whole, that I should not be at all surprised at any disaster that may happen.* * * Could I have foreseen what I have, and am likely to experience, no consideration upon earth should have induced me to accept this command." (Letter to Joseph Reed dated 28 Nov. '75, quoted in C. & M., 162)

Five weeks later he wrote Reed:

"Search the vast volumes of history through, and I much question whether a case similar to ours is to be found; to wit, to maintain a post against the flower of the British troops for six months together, without powder, and then to have one army disbanded and another to be raised within the same distance of a reinforced enemy.* * * The same desire of retiring into a chimney corner seized the troops of New Hampshire, Rhode Island, and Massachusetts, so soon as their time expired, as had wrought upon those of Connecticut.... We are now left with a good deal less than half-raised regiments and about 5,000 militia, who only stand engaged to the middle of this month, when, according to custom, they will depart, let the necessity of their stay

be ever so urgent. Thus for more than two months past I have scarcely emerged from one difficulty before I have been plunged into another." (Letter of 4 Jan. '76, as quoted by Upton, 10, from Sparks)

By 14 Jan., only 8,212 of the 20,370 authorized by Congress the preceding October had been enlisted, and only 5,582 were present and fit for duty. (Freeman, *Washington,* IV, 6) Meanwhile, the 5,000 militia called in from 10 Dec. would end their term of service on 15 Jan. Over 2,000 of Washington's men lacked muskets, the rest had no more than 10 rounds of ammunition each, and the Boston garrison, now commanded by Howe, was being reinforced. On 16 Jan., Washington prevailed on a council of war to accept his view that the British must be attacked before further reinforcement in the spring made this completely impossible. A call was then made for 13 militia regiments to serve during Feb. and Mar. to make such an operation possible. The next day Washington learned of the failure at Quebec, and Congress later detached three of the 13 new militia regiments for service in Schuyler's Northern Department.

On 16 Feb., before all the new militia units had arrived, Washington proposed to a council of war that advantage be taken of the ice on Back Bay to launch a surprise attack over the ice against Boston; he estimated that the enemy now numbered only 5,000 foot troops and believed his own 16,-000 militia and Continentals had a rare opportunity for success. (*Ibid.,* 20) His officers opposed this plan on various grounds—Washington had underestimated enemy strength and overestimated the offensive power of his own troops; no assault should be undertaken without an artillery preparation of several days. (Although KNOX's

"NOBLE TRAIN OF ARTILLERY" had begun arriving from Ft. Ticonderoga, powder was still short.) A less ambitious plan emerged from this meeting, however. The generals proposed that while an adequate supply of powder was being assembled they should, meanwhile, seize some position that would draw the British out of Boston and into an attack on an objective the Americans would have had time to fortify. (Such a plan is known in military jargon as a "strategic offensive—tactical defensive.") Although disappointed by the failure of his generals to see what he considered to be a golden opportunity (the ice lasted only a few days), Washington turned his attention to the plan they proposed. This led to the operations on DORCHESTER HEIGHTS, 2–27 Mar. '76.

THE BRITISH EVACUATE

Since the summer of 1775 the British had considered moving their forces from Boston to undertake the NEW YORK CAMPAIGN (which see for evolution of this strategy). After calling off an attack on American-held Dorchester Heights ordered for the night of 5–6 Mar., Howe decided on 7 Mar. to evacuate Boston. At 9 A.M., 17 Mar., the ships were loaded, and at 9 P.M. the 64th Regt. blew up Castle William when they departed. About 11,000 British army and navy personnel and nearly 1,000 Loyalists (including 100 civil officials) were taken from Boston. The convoy remained in Nantasket Roads, five miles south of the city, until 27 Mar., when it sailed for Halifax rather than New York, as the Americans expected. By tacit agreement, the British, in return for being allowed to depart unmolested, did not burn Boston. There was a great deal of looting by departing soldiers and Loyalists, however. A N.Y. Irish adventurer named Crean

Bush was authorized by Howe to seize clothing and other supplies that might benefit the Americans, but his loot-laden brigantine *Elizabeth* was recaptured. The Tories were given vessels but required to raise their own crews.

Gen. Ward entered Boston on 17 Mar. with 500 men. Washington visited the town the next day, and the American main body entered on 20 Mar. The British had left 69 cannon that could be salvaged for use by the American artillery, and 31 that were useless. Miscellaneous ordnance matériel, almost all the enemy's medical supplies, and—most surprising and welcome—3,000 blankets and much equipment were found on the wharves. (Freeman, *op. cit.,* 56) This windfall was due to Howe's lack of shipping and failure of subordinates to follow his orders as to destruction of matériel left behind. (Whitton, 122)

The eight-month siege had cost the Americans fewer than 20 men killed in action. Boston and the province of Mass. were free of British troops for the remainder of the war.

A number of patrol actions and raids took place during the siege, particularly at Boston and Charleston Necks, where the lines were in contact. The British sent foragers to nearby islands (Grape, Noddle's, and Hog), and to LECHMERE POINT, 9 Nov. '75. Gage sent three men of war and six transports from Boston on 25 July '75 to raid small islands in L.I. Sound (Block, Fisher's, Gardiner's, and Plumb); on 20 Aug. he reported their capture of 1,800 sheep and more than 100 oxen. (Freeman, *op. cit.,* III, 505–6 and *n.*) Majors Vose and Tupper led highly successful American raids to destroy the lighthouse on GREAT BREWSTER ISLAND, 21 and 31 July '75. Adm. Graves, who reached Boston on 1 July '75 to enforce the blockade, attacked FALMOUTH, Me., 16–17 Oct. '75.

Basic authorities on the Boston Siege are Allen French and Frothingham, whose works are identified in the main bibliography.

BOSTON TEA PARTY. 16 Dec. '73. When three TEA ACT ships reached Boston the colonists prevented their being unloaded, and Gov. Hutchinson would not issue the permit the ships needed to leave the harbor. Something had to be done by 17 Dec., when the prescribed 20-day waiting period expired and the cargo of the first ship to reach Boston became liable to seizure for failure to pay customs duties. The "Tea Party" was therefore organized by Sam Adams, who was interested in political agitation and who feared that the cheap East India Co. tea, if landed, would prove an "invincible temptation" to the people. He and the Boston Whigs were backed by certain men who had a large financial stake in smuggled tea. The evening of 16 Dec. a group of colonists, thinly disguised as Mohawk Indians, boarded the ships and threw overboard 342 tea chests valued at $90,000.

This episode "marked the beginning of violence in the dispute ... and put the most radical patriots in command throughout America." (Miller in *D.A.H.*) Boston's less radical element deplored the action and more than 100 merchants offered to pay the East India Co. damages. Benj. Franklin advised that this be done, but the radicals prevailed.

England retaliated with the INTOLERABLE ACTS, one of which closed the port of Boston. The Americans reacted by calling the first Cont'l. CONGRESS to consider united resistance.

BOTETOURT, Norborne Berkeley, Baron de. *c.* 1718–1770. Royal Gov. of Va. A kinsman of Sir William Berkeley, who had been Gov. of Va. (1642–77), he was appointed Gov. of that province in 1768. His tenure was notable for its ceremonial aspects, Botetourt arriving with a magnificent coach, a team of cream-white Hanoverian horses, a resplendent costume, and a determination to ape the methods and even the mannerisms of his royal master in representing the latter abroad. The local politicians went along with the pageantry but continued to oppose royal measures that they considered objectionable. Unequipped for these problems, he became despondent and died before he had time to become unpopular. Remembering him for the good features of his administration, the people of Va. erected in his honor a marble statue that still stands at the College of William and Mary.

BOUDINOT, Elias. 1740–1821. Jurist, Commissary General of Prisoners, Pres. of Cont'l. Cong., Director of U.S. Mint, Author. Pa. His great-grandfather came to the colonies after the 1685 revocation of the Edict of Nantes. After a classical education he became a prominent N.J. lawyer (hon. LL.D. Yale 1790). In his politics conservative, he supported the colonial cause mainly by opposing the N.J. gov't. He believed some ties to England necessary when, on 11 June '74, he became a member of the committee of correspondence, but in Mar. '75 he urged the state's approval of the first Cont'l. Congress. He was in the provincial congress in 1775 and sent gunpowder to Washington at Cambridge when his supplies ran low. On 6 June '77 he was named commissary-general of prisoners, with pay and rations of a Col., five deputies, and power to change even the directions of the Board of War. He personally contributed $30,000 and overcame great difficulties to organize the care of prisoners, becoming particularly close to Washington during this time. Boudinot regarded the general with reverence and aided him in a number of unofficial ways, such as reconciling Steuben with some other officers. On 20 Nov. '77 he was elected to the Cont'l. Congress but did not attend until 7 July '78. He was re-elected until 1784 and was named president 4 Nov. '82. In this capacity he signed the peace treaty with England, the alliance with France and a number of proclamations of cessation of hostilities, thanksgiving, and so forth. He was also Sec. of foreign affairs from 16 June '83. Under the new Constitution, he served in Congress 1789–95 as a strong Federalist, and in the last year succeeded David Rittenhouse as director of the U.S. mint. He resigned in July, 1805. In 1790, he had been the first counsellor named by the U.S. Supreme Court. An extremely rich man, he retired to study biblical literature and, as a trustee of Princeton (1772–1821), gave the school the cabinet of natural history. His sister married Richard Stockton, a Signer, who was father-in-law of Benjamin Rush. Elias married Stockton's sister Hannah. He was a tall and handsome man, "elegant, eloquent and emotional" (*D.A.B.*), who combined good sense with benevolence.

His *Journal; or Historical Recollections of American Events During the Revolutionary War, from his own original manuscript* was published in Philadelphia in 1894. His *Life, Public Services, Addresses, and Letters,* edited by J. J. Boudinot, 2 vols., was published in Boston in 1896.

BOUGAINVILLE, Louis Antoine de. 1729–1811. French explorer, Admiral. Born a Parisian, he studied law, published a book on integral calculus (1752), and while secretary of the French embassy in London was admitted to the Royal Society. During the Seven Years' War he was Montcalm's A.D.C. in Canada (1756–60) before being assigned to duty in Germany. He was cited for courage in the campaign on the Rhine the next year. After the peace of 1763 he entered the navy (which was common practice in France), established a colony in the Falkland Islands (1763–65), and made the famous, two-year voyage of discovery around the world (1767–69). It is thus that his name appears on the largest island in the Solomon group (which he rediscovered after visiting Tahiti and the Samoans); two straits in the S.W. Pacific, and the Buginvillaea [*sic*] vine are also named for him. His *Voyage autour du monde,* 2 vols., was published in 1771–72.

Almost 50 years old when France declared war against England, he commanded ships of the line in action in the West Indies. In the battle off Saints Passage, Apr. '82, aboard the *Auguste,* he rescued eight ships of his division but was accused by GRASSE of misconduct. In 1791 he was promoted to Vice-Adm., and the next year, after a narrow escape from the massacres in Paris, he retired to his estate in Normandy. (*E.B.*) He became a member of the Institut when it was formed. Napoleon honored him with an appointment as senator, the title of count, and named him for the Legion of Honor.

BOUND BROOK, N.J., 13 Apr. '77. While Washington's army was still in Morristown winter quarters and Howe's army was in N.Y.C., a British foraging expedition attempted to cut off the American outpost at Bound Brook. The latter place, seven miles up the Raritan from the estimated 8,000 British and Germans outposting Brunswick, was held by Maj. Gen. Benjamin Lincoln with the 8th Pa., part of the 4th Cont'l. Arty. with three 3-pdrs., and some militia; total American strength was about 500 men (Freeman, *Washington,* IV, 408). Cornwallis advanced with 2,000

men (Strait) across the Raritan, where
the militia outposts were negligent, and
tried to encircle Lincoln. Thanks largely
to the personal efforts of Lt. Simon
Spalding (Appleton's) Lincoln was able
to extricate most of his force, but
enemy light horse captured the artillery
detachment and its guns. Cornwallis
withdrew before Greene arrived with
reinforcements.

Knox estimated that the Americans
lost six killed and 20 or 30 captured.
(Freeman, *op. cit.*, IV, 409 *n.*) Strait
puts the losses at 60 in all, and Kemble
said 80 were captured. A neighborhood
farmer was suspected of having learned
the password and given it to the British,
but the primary blame for the surprise
was put on the militia who were supposed to be guarding the Raritan, which
was fordable at almost every point.
Lincoln and his men were considered
to have acquitted themselves well. The
incident did, however, cause Washington to reduce the number of his detached posts to prevent their being annihilated by other surprise attacks and
also to facilitate a rapid massing of
his forces when the British started
their anticipated spring offensive. (See
PHILADELPHIA CAMPAIGN for subsequent
operations.)

Strait has confused the above action
with that at SHORT HILLS, 26 June
'77, where the Americans also lost three
guns. The action of 13 Apr. at Bound
Brook is sometimes called Middle
Brook, which was a few miles away.

BOUNTIES (Commercial). As part
of MERCANTILISM the British government paid premiums (bounties) to
encourage certain industries or production. The Act of 1705, for example,
provided bounties on certain NAVAL
STORES that were listed as ENUMERATED
ARTICLES; continued until 1774, except
for hemp (which was allowed to lapse
during the period 1741–64), bounty

payments on naval stores totaled
£1,438,702. (*E.A.H.*, 484) Indigo
bounties, paid chiefly to planters of Ga.
and the Carolinas, amounted to more
than £185,000 up to the year 1776.
(*Ibid.*, 485)

BOUNTIES (Military). See PAY,
BOUNTIES, AND RATIONS.

BOUQUET, Henry. 1719–1765. British general. A Swiss who received careful schooling before entering a Dutch
regiment in 1736 as a cadet, he fought
with the Sardinians against the French
and Spanish. The Prince of Orange was
so impressed by his performance that in
1748 he was made captain commandant
with the rank of Lt. Col. in a new
Swiss Guards regiment formed at the
Hague to receive posts evacuated by the
French in the Low Countries. This duty
brought him into close and pleasant
contact with the British, and in 1754
he was appointed Lt. Col. of the Royal
American Regt., which was then being
raised in three battalions. His dealings
with the Americans won their respect
and admiration not only for his energy, military ability, integrity, firmness, and patience but also for a freedom from European closed-mindedness
when it came to dealing with the special political and military conditions in
America. In appearance the Swiss colonel was portly and undistinguished but
he was friendly and well-mannered.
Those who know the country of his
birth may attach significance to the fact
that he was Bernois. (People from
this canton have the reputation of being particularly slow in their physical and mental processes.) Colonial
officers, used to British arrogance and
superciliousness, were amazed by his
considerate treatment of themselves and
their troops. After recruiting in Pa.,
commanding briefly at Charleston when
a French attack was expected, he returned to Pa. and started studying new

tactics for use of regulars in Indian warfare.

"He was as careful as he was skillful and on matters he did not understand, such as dealings with the Indians, he sought the best council he could get. By temperament as by training, Bouquet probably was second only to Forbes among all the soldiers in America from whom Washington could learn." (Freeman, *Washington*, II, 313)

As second in command of Forbes's Expedition to Ft. Duquesne (later Pitt) in 1758 he was Washington's immediate superior. He erred badly in letting Maj. James Grant talk him into leading a detachment ahead of the main column against the French fort. Of this affair Freeman says, "Grant was foolish in proposing tactics when he had only the vaguest knowledge of the ground or of the strength of his adversary. Bouquet did not live up to his reputation when, in like ignorance, he gave explicit orders." (*Op. cit.*, II, 347)

During Pontiac's War Bouquet distinguished himself in a remarkable victory against the Indians at Bushy Run, 5–6 Aug. '63, and relieving Ft. Pitt (see PONTIAC'S WAR for an account of the battle), and in BOUQUET'S EXPEDITION OF 1764. In 1764 he was promoted to B.G. and made military commander in the southern colonies. The next autumn he died at Pensacola when an epidemic swept through his troops.

His letters and papers for the period 1757–65, 30 MS. volumes, are in the British Museum. Biographical sketches by S.M. Pargellis and T. F. Henderson are in *D.A.B.* (which includes an excellent bibliography) and *D.N.B.* See also Edward Hutton, *Henry Bouquet*.

BOUQUET'S EXPEDITION OF 1764. After relieving Ft. Pitt in 1763 (PONTIAC'S WAR), Bouquet's force of regulars was inadequate for the task of returning to the Old Northwest to finish subjugating the tribes and to free the numerous white prisoners. Not until 1764 did the Pa. Assy. vote an adequate force of militia for the expedition. Va. and Md. flatly refused to contribute. On 5 Aug. Bouquet reached Carlisle with the 1,000 Pa. troops and a detachment of regulars from the 43d and 60th. Within a week 200 provincials had deserted. On 17 Sept. he reached Ft. Pitt, having lost another 100 Pa. troops, but Va. had responded to his appeal and sent a body of woodsmen. (Fortescue, *British Army*, III, 21) After many delays he was able to leave Pittsburgh with 1,500 men in early Oct. His cautious advance west some 100 miles to the Muskingum River, into the heart of the Delaware and Shawnee country, was unopposed, and he was met by chiefs bringing 18 white captives and suing for peace. Demanding that all prisoners be surrendered, he took hostages and moved south to the forks of the Muskingum and waited until another 200 prisoners were brought in. Making peace, he directed the Indians to go to Sir Wm. Johnson to conclude treaty arrangements and returned to Pittsburgh with additional hostages to assure that the Indians delivered another 100 Shawnee captives and that they honored their obligation to make treaties with Johnson. The Indians did both, and their threat to the frontier was temporarily ended. Bouquet's success was in marked contrast to the failure of BRADSTREET'S EXPEDITION OF 1764. (Solon J. Buck in *D.A.H.*)

See *Bouquet's Expedition against the Ohio Indians* [in 1764], Philadelphia (1765 ?), London, 1766, and Cincinnati, 1868.

BOURG. See CROMOT DU BOURG.

BOWLER, Metcalf. 1726–1789. Chief justice of R.I. (1776), informer. A London-born merchant and speculator, he was a successful businessman during the years of Newport's commercial supremacy. As late as 1929 he was characterized in a scholarly work as a patriot. (*D.A.B.*) Subsequent research has, however, revealed that he was one of Gen. Henry Clinton's informers. (Van Doren, *Secret History*, 127–29, 235, 429) The woodwork and paneling from one room of his Providence house are in the Metropolitan Museum of N.Y.C.

BOYD, Thomas. d. 1779. Cont'l. officer. Pa. 1st Sgt. of Thompson's Pa. Rifles 25 June '75, he was captured at Quebec 31 Dec. '75 and exchanged in Nov. '77. Commissioned 1st Lt. of the 1st Pa. on 14 Jan., he was captured on 13 Sept. '79 while leading the advance guard of SULLIVAN'S EXPEDITION and tortured to death the next day. This atrocity is discussed in some detail under the cross reference.

BRADDOCK, Edward. 1695–1755. British general. In 1710 he became an ensign in the Coldstream Guards (of which his father, who retired as Maj. Gen. in 1715, was the Lt. Col.). In 1753 he left the regiment to become Col. of the 14th Foot at Gibraltar, and the next spring he was promoted to Maj. Gen. and named commander of military forces in America. Up until this time Braddock had seen little if any combat service, and had been outside the British Isles only three of his 45 years in uniform. Reaching Hampton Roads on 20 Feb. '55 he prepared to lead an expedition to drive the French from the Forks of the Ohio (Duquesne, subsequently Pittsburgh). In the action described under COLONIAL WARS he was mortally wounded on 9 July and died on the 13th near Great Meadows. His last words are said to have been: "We shall better know how to deal with them another time." (Freeman, *Washington*, II, 82, citing Franklin, *Auto-*

biography) Although modern historians have concluded that Braddock "was by no means incapable" (Alden, *Lee*, 11), there is little reason to believe that he would have done any better if the Indians had given him another chance. He epitomizes the closed military mind of all ages and the type during the Revolution who would not accept that the Americans might know something about fighting in America. "Beneath the show of strict conformity to military standards, and of blunt, open dealing on the part of the General," writes Freeman, "there was much slowness, inefficiency, stupidity, lack of resourcefulness and some laziness." (*Op. cit.*, II, 37) "To the failings common among military men of his day," comments H. Manners Chichester in *D.N.B.*, "he added . . . a hasty temper and a coarse, self-assertive manner. . . ." No portrait has been identified, but he has been described as short and fat. His one good quality was personal courage, which he exhibited on the day of his defeat.

George Washington, one of Braddock's A.D.C., took charge of burial arrangements and knowing that the French and Indians would try to find the body he had it interred in a short, deep trench in the road over which the retreating column would pass when it resumed its march on 14 July. In 1824 workmen repairing a nearby national highway discovered a skeleton which, from buttons and buckles, was believed to have been Braddock's. The bones were moved 100 yards and reinterred on a knoll overlooking the Old National Pike (U.S. Hwy. 40) and in 1913 a marker was erected there.

BRADSTREET'S CAPTURE OF FT. FRONTENAC, 27 Aug. '58. After the, disastrous British attack on Ticonderoga, 7 July '58, Lt. Col. John Bradstreet took command of 2,600 men secretly mobilized in the Mohawk Valley and led a swift raid through Oswego (24 Aug.) to capture Ft. Frontenac on 27 Aug. Located at the point where Lake Ontario flows into the St. Lawrence, the post controlled the French line of communications to their western posts, including Niagara (which fell in 1759) and Duquesne (Pittsburgh), which fell to the FORBES EXPEDITION on 25 Nov. '58. The site of Ft. Frontenac, then the village of Cataraqui, is now Kingston.

BRADSTREET'S EXPEDITION OF 1764. As part of the delayed punitive action directed by the British because of Pontiac's War, Col. John Bradstreet left Niagara with 1,200 troops in early Aug. with orders from Gen. Gage to attack the Shawnees and Delawares in conjunction with BOUQUET'S EXPEDITION from Ft. Pitt and to continue to Detroit. Near Presque Isle (Erie) Bradstreet was met by 10 Indians who claimed to be emissaries from the two tribes he was supposed to attack and they duped him into concluding a peace treaty (12 Aug.). He proceeded to Detroit, where he was only partially successful in his dealings with the Indians, and on his return to Niagara he failed to attack Scioto villages as instructed. "His reputation as a popular hero did not survive," comments Arthur Pound in *D.A.H.*, and it was left to BOUQUET'S EXPEDITION to restore white prestige.

BRANDYWINE, Pa., 11 Sept. '77. (PHILADELPHIA CAMPAIGN) Strategic uncertainties that plagued Washington during the first three months of the Philadelphia Campaign were removed when Howe landed at Head of Elk. Brandywine Creek then became the obvious place for the Americans to make their first real effort to stop the enemy advance toward Philadelphia.

"As a defensive barrier, the Brandywine had no particular value other than that it was of sufficient depth to re-

quire troops to use the fords," says Freeman, "but, unfortunately, the fords were so numerous that the King's men had a wide choice." (*Washington*, IV, 471)

Chadd's Ford was as good a place as any other for the Americans to center their concentration. (*Ibid.*) Greene's Div. and Wayne's Brig., supported by most of the artillery, were posted along the creek just south of Chadd's, and Maxwell's 800 light infantry were deployed on the enemy side of the creek to cover the ford. (The brigades of Wayne and Maxwell were in Lincoln's Div., but LINCOLN was absent.) Washington's left was guarded by Gen. Armstrong's Pa. militia at Pyle's Ford, less than half a mile downstream, where rough terrain ruled out the likelihood of any serious action. Sullivan's Div. had the mission of guarding all fords north of Chadd's. At some short distance east of the creek were the divisions of Alexander ("Stirling") on the right, with the mission of supporting either Sullivan or Greene, and of Stephen, with the mission of supporting the defense of Chadd's Ford.

Washington's right was screened by all available light cavalry, and mounted patrols operated a few miles west of the Brandywine. More about these later.

As for these initial dispositions, Freeman comments that Washington's letters do not tell where his divisions were on the eve of battle, and I have not dared go beyond Freeman's general description. Ward's map (*op. cit.*, 345, reproduced in C. & M., 612), and many others that resemble it, apparently errs in placing Sullivan too far to the right, and in showing the divisions of Stephen and Alexander still farther to the right.

HOWE'S MANEUVERS

The invaders advanced slowly, reconnoitering the country, bringing forward supplies from Head of Elk, and foraging. The weather was hot and rainy, the troops were still weak from their long confinement aboard ship, and the few horses that had survived the trip from N.Y. were not yet fit for active campaigning. Yet Howe's military intelligence was as good as Washington's was defective, and the British C. in C. planned a battle that was to bear an uncanny resemblance to his victory at LONG ISLAND.

After reaching Kennett Square, less than seven miles west of Chadd's Ford, Howe's force of about 12,500 rank and file (Ward, 468 *n.*) went into bivouac. His plan was for Knyphausen's "grand division" of 5,000 to make a secondary attack against Chadd's Ford while he and Cornwallis' grand division of 7,500 made a *turning* movement around Washington's right.

PHASE ONE: 5 TO 11 A.M.

The two British columns moved out at dawn, between 4:30 and 5 A.M., on 11 Sept. The weather was foggy until about 7 o'clock, after which a hot sun burned through.

Washington learned early in the morning that the enemy was advancing toward Chadd's Ford, and his troops were alerted. About 8 o'clock Maxwell's covering force was in contact, and two hours later they had withdrawn across the creek with exaggerated stories of their resistance and enemy casualties. (Freeman, 474) According to some accounts, Maxwell had started west before daybreak, halting his main body at the Kennett Meeting House and sending a mounted patrol a mile farther to Welch's Tavern. The patrol was surprised by the advance guard consisting of Maj. Patrick Ferguson's riflemen and Capt. Wemyss' Queen's Rangers, which pushed on through defiles and woods to the high

ground west of Chadd's Ford. (Baurmeister, 107) Here Knyphausen deployed his troops to drive back Maxwell and the Va. regiments of Porterfield and Waggoner that had crossed to support the covering force. (*Ibid.*, 107–8; Ward, 343) By 10:30 Knyphausen was in position along the creek and his activity was then limited to a relatively harmless exchange of cannon balls with Porter's American artillery on the left bank.

PHASE TWO: 11 A.M.–2 P.M.

When the enemy made no attempt to cross at Chadd's Ford, Washington and his officers suspected that Howe was making his main crossing elsewhere. (Freeman, 475) About 11 o'clock the American C. in C. began to get reports of Cornwallis' movement. Col. Moses HAZEN sent word from Jones's Ford, about two and a half miles above Chadd's, that an enemy column was marching to the forks of the Brandywine. (Some American officers confused this ford with others farther up the creek; this may account for Hazen's position being shown on Ward's map— mentioned above—at Buffington Ford, which was at the forks of the Brandywine.) Hazen's report was soon confirmed by Lt. Col. James Ross, who was patrolling the Great Valley Road with 70 men; in a message dated 11 A.M. he said about 5,000 men and 16 or 18 guns were moving up the road toward Taylor's and Jeffries Fords.

On receipt of Hazen's report, Washington sent a message to Col. Bland, who was with the cavalry screen on the right, to have an officer verify Hazen's information by reconnaissance. Then or shortly afterward, according to Freeman, he directed Alexander and Stephen to march their divisions to the Birmingham Meeting House, which was three and a half miles from Chadd's

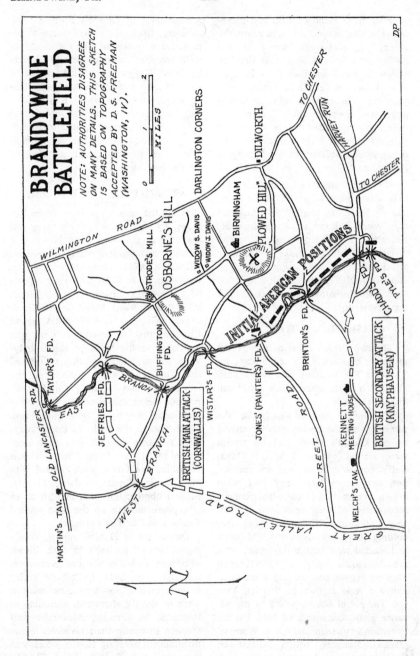

BRANDYWINE BATTLEFIELD

NOTE: AUTHORITIES DISAGREE ON MANY DETAILS. THIS SKETCH IS BASED ON TOPOGRAPHY ACCEPTED BY D. S. FREEMAN (WASHINGTON, IV).

MILES
0   1   2

TO CHESTER

HARVEY RUN

TO CHESTER

DARLINGTON CORNERS

DILWORTH

WILMINGTON ROAD

OSBORNE'S HILL

STRODE'S MILL

BIRMINGHAM

WIDOW S. DAVIS
WIDOW J. DAVIS

"PLOWED HILL"

INITIAL AMERICAN POSITIONS

CHADD'S FD.

PYLE'S FD.

BUFFINGTON FD.

WISTAR'S FD.

JONES' (PAINTER'S) FD.

BRINTON'S FD.

BRANCH

TAYLOR'S FD.

JEFFRIES FD.

EAST

BRANCH

KENNETT MEETING HOUSE

BRITISH MAIN ATTACK (CORNWALLIS)

MARTIN'S TAV.

OLD LANCASTER RD.

WEST BRANCH

STREET   ROAD

VALLEY ROAD

GREAT

WELCH'S TAV.

BRITISH SECONDARY ATTACK (KNYPHAUSEN)

N

DP

and on the road over which the enemy was most likely to move if he really were attempting a turning movement. But Washington did not overlook the tactical opportunity open to him if it were true that Howe had split his forces in this manner. If Howe had detached 5,000 men for such a maneuver this meant that Washington could counterattack with the divisions of Sullivan, Lincoln, and Greene to annihilate the enemy forces across Chadd's Ford. The operation had almost started when it had to be canceled because of this perplexing report from Sullivan:

"Since I sent you the message by Major Morris * I saw some of the Militia who came in this morning from a tavern called Martins on the forks of the Brandywine. The one who told me, said he had come from thence to Welches Tavern and heard nothing of the Enemy above the forks of the Brandywine and is Confident that [they ?] are not in that Quarters. So that Colonel Hazen's Information must be wrong.†"

* This may be a reference to Hazen's report. (Freeman, 475 n.)

† This version, quoted by Freeman, is from the L. of C. *Papers of Washington.* Comparing it with the version in Jared Sparks's *Writings of George Washington* presents an opportunity to show how Sparks has misled historians by his unfortunate editing of source materials as well as by carelessness. In addition to writing Maj. Spear's name into Sullivan's message (an accurate identification of Sullivan's source, but a falsification of the original document that might lead the unsuspecting historian to an erroneous conclusion as to the report's credibility when received by Washington), Sparks made two other unfortunate "corrections": a word is

No longer certain that the force opposite him had really been weakened, Washington not only canceled his counterattack but also halted the movement of Alexander and Stephen to Birmingham until the situation was clarified. He permitted Maxwell to cross the creek several times to probe the enemy position, but pulled the rest of his troops away from their forward locations to escape further damage from artillery. (Freeman, 477)

PHASE THREE: 2 TO 6:30 P.M.

Early in the afternoon an excited farmer clattered up to Benjamin Ring's house, below Chadd's Ford, where Washington had his C.P., and insisted on giving his message to Washington in person. Having talked his way past the staff officers, this swarthy, heavyset individual, whom tradition identifies as Squire Thomas Cheney, told Washington the British were about to surround him. Washington was incredulous, but thundering confirmation came almost immediately. In a message dated 1:15 P.M. (delivered at 2), Col. Bland, who was with the cavalry screen on the right, reported about two enemy brigades in the vicinity of Osborne Hill, two miles or so north of Sullivan's

changed so that Martin's Tavern is situated "at" and not "on" the forks of the Brandywine; another word is changed so that Sparks's version says no enemy are "about" these forks, whereas Sullivan wrote that none were "above" the forks. The slight changes turn out to have great historical significance, as will be explained more fully below. A fourth liberty that editor Sparks took with Sullivan's short text appears to be legitimate editing: changing the word "that" to "they." (These comments are based on Freeman, 476 n.)

flank. A message from Sullivan, dated 2 o'clock, relayed Bland's information and added, "He also says he saw a dust back in the country for above an hour." Not only had faulty intelligence robbed Washington of an opportunity, but it had perhaps gotten him into a trap. Yet the situation did not look entirely bleak. Washington ordered Sullivan to march immediately to meet the new threat. Alexander and Stephen were told to rush toward Birmingham, which was about two miles from the place where the previous counterorder had halted them. (Freeman, 476 n.) Washington would stay at Chadd's Ford with Greene's Div. and the brigades of Wayne and Maxwell since the situation was by no means clear and it could be that only two enemy brigades were to his rear.

About 4:30 there was the sound of cannons to Washington's rear. Then came the uneven volleys of the enemy regulars and the answering individual fire from the Americans. At the same time the enemy artillery fire quickened at Chadd's Ford to indicate that an attack might be starting there. Waiting perhaps 40 minutes longer, Washington finally started for Sullivan's front. A certain Joseph Brown was pressed reluctantly into service as a guide, and Washington started cross country with Greene's Div. following at a remarkably fast pace.

The enemy to Washington's rear had reached Trimble's Ford by about 11 A.M., Jeffries Ford before 2 o'clock and, after an hour's halt, had attacked in the vicinity of Birmingham about 4 P.M. (according to André, quoted in C. & M., 613) or perhaps half an hour earlier (according to Montresor, cited by Freeman, 487 n.). They had marched some 17 miles, and had been on the road about 11 hours.

ACTION ON THE PLOWED HILL

Alexander and Stephen had raced to occupy good defensive ground on a plowed hill S.W. of Birmingham. As the enemy advanced to make contact, these two units had almost completed their deployment when Sullivan arrived with his division and took over-all command. Sullivan was unfamiliar with the terrain, and as soon as he sized up the situation he realized his division was to the left and half a mile in front of Alexander and Stephen; furthermore, his advance guard was a mere 200 yards from an advancing enemy column. (Freeman, 481) He ordered the other two divisions to the right to give him room to deploy his own division; this forced Stephen's units to give up some good terrain, and it caused Sullivan's troops to be attacked while they were trying to get into position. Nevertheless, the Americans "formed quite a formidable front," in the words of a German opponent (Baurmeister, 110); the regiments of Hazen, Dayton, and Ogden on Sullivan's left, and the other divisions on his right held off the initial enemy attack. The American artillery also earned praise from both sides.

When Washington arrived, about 5:30, Sullivan's left was beginning to break under the attack of the British Guards, and the rest of the line was also sagging. When Weedon's Brig. started arriving about 6 o'clock, having covered almost four miles in 45 minutes, their deployment on the American right succeeded in stopping the enemy's pursuit on that flank. (Sullivan maintained that only this brigade of Greene's Div. was committed [Freeman, 482 n.].) In this sector, however, Col. Thomas Marshall's small regiment of 170 men had supported the guns of Woodford's Brig. (Stephen's

Div.) with great tenacity and dropped back only when ordered to do so to avoid being surrounded. Woodford was evacuated with a wound, but his guns kept up their fire until most officers and half the men were casualties. Weedon's troops opened ranks to let the fugitives through and then closed to check the enemy.

Washington let Sullivan continue to direct the action, but rode up and down the line with Lafayette and his aides to encourage the defenders and rally the fugitives. While so engaged, Lafayette was hit in the left thigh with a bullet. "So long as mounted officers shouted and threatened close to the front," says Freeman, "they were able to hold part of the line together." But Sullivan's wing was beaten, and was soon streaming back along the road to Chester.

Knyphausen had pushed across Chadd's Ford soon after Cornwallis attacked, as was the plan. Wayne and Maxwell withstood a heavy preparatory fire to meet the 1st Bn. of the 71st Highland Regt. as it spearheaded the attack across the ford and was followed by the riflemen and the Queen's Rangers. Knyphausen led the 4th British Regt. over next, and the rest of his command followed. The American left fell back first, and four guns were lost. "Our regiments . . . gained one height after another," wrote the German Baurmeister, in a description that shows the action was no pushover. "They withstood one more rather severe attack behind some houses and ditches in front of their left wing. Finally, we saw the entire enemy line and four guns, which fired frequently, drawn up on another height in front of a dense forest, their right wing resting on the Chester road." (*Op. cit.,* 109) Armstrong's militia withdrew from Pyle's Ford unmolested.

Knyphausen and Cornwallis made contact about dark (which would have been soon after 7 P.M.), and Howe established his Hq. at Dilworth. See PHIL. CAMP'N. for further comment on the American retreat.

NUMBERS AND LOSSES

Of some 11,000 RANK AND FILE present for duty (Ward, 465 *n.*), Gen. Greene estimated that Washington lost 1,200 to 1,300. About 400 of these were prisoners. The Americans lost 11 guns.

Of approximately 12,500 rank and file (*ibid.,* 468 *n.*), Howe lost 577 killed and wounded (Fortescue, 216) and six missing (Kemble, I, 135). All but 40 of the killed and wounded were British (Fortescue).

CRITIQUE

In a situation calling for good reconnaissance, the American defeat stemmed from "a most discreditable ignorance of the ground." (Freeman, 484) American officers not only were ignorant of what fords existed, but they did not know the correct names and locations of the ones of whose existence they were aware.

The ignorance of the terrain and the names of landmarks led to the apparent contradiction of Spear's intelligence with that of Hazen and Ross. When Spear said Martin's Tavern was "on the forks of the Brandywine," Washington and his officers assumed— as, apparently, did editor Jared Sparks —that he meant "at" the forks. If Washington had known the true location of Martin's and—quite another thing—if he had also asked *when* Spear had made his reconnaissance, he would have seen that Spear's report did not contradict the others. (*Ibid.,* 487)

After Long Island and Brandywine

it is not likely that Gen. Sullivan will ever be nominated as defensive end on anybody's All-American team. Since he was given the mission of guarding the fords above Chadd's, it would appear that Sullivan could be held responsible for the defeat of 11 Sept. But Washington acquitted him of all blame (Fisher, II, 27), and properly so. When given his mission late 10 Sept., Sullivan expected Howe would attack in his sector. He was told what fords to guard, but neither he nor the persons formulating his orders were familiar with the names or locations. "It is doubtful, indeed, if many of the responsible officers were aware of the existence of Jeffries Ford, over which the British crossed," says Freeman. (*Op. cit.*, 484–85) Sullivan understood that his sector extended only to Buffington Ford, and when he asked Washington whether there were any others farther upstream he was told there were none within 12 miles. (*Ibid.*, 487–88) When he took up his post at Brinton's Ford the evening of the 10th he had only four horsemen assigned, and was told all the rest of the American cavalry was reconnoitering his exposed flank. (See also BLAND)

"Washington conducted the Brandywine operation as if he had been in a daze," says his biographer. (Freeman, 488)

As for Howe's performance, this general was criticized for not following up his victory and annihilating the American army.

"Howe justified himself on the ground that his outflanking force had marched seventeen miles that day, fought a stubbornly contested action, and come up against fresh troops over whom a superiority was not established until after dark. Without doubt an endeavour to push the attack under such circumstances would have entailed consider-able risk and might possibly have led to losses so serious as to counterbalance the results of the victory." (Anderson, 287–88)

The above excuse is even more convincing when you take into consideration the PURSUIT PROBLEMS inherent to 18th-century British tactics.

Although Howe's battle plan succeeded, the military pedagogue can find fault in Knyphausen's secondary attack: it was premature, too large, and not executed with sufficient vigor to fix the bulk of Washington's force while the turning movement was executed. A competent opponent could have contained Cornwallis with minimum forces long enough to annihilate Knyphausen; a brilliant opponent could have gone on from there to use interior lines and defeat the other enemy wing.

BRANT, Joseph. 1742–1807. Mohawk war chief. Born in Ohio while his parents were there on a hunting expedition, Thayendanegea was the son of a full-blooded Mohawk of the Wolf clan. His mother apparently was not a Mohawk, but she was an Indian or at least a half-blood. (*D.A.B.*; *Handbook of American Indians*) His family home was at Canajoharie Castle, in the Mohawk Valley of N.Y. When his father died, his mother married an Indian known among the whites as Brant, hence the name by which Joseph is commonly known. (*Handbook; D.A.B.*, however, says his father probably was the Mohawk chief called Nickus Brant.)

When he was only 13, Brant joined the Indians under Sir Wm. Johnson at the battle of Lake George (1755). Johnson sent him, with two other Mohawks, to school in Lebanon, Conn., and after two years he left to become interpreter for a missionary (1763). Soon he joined the Iroquois contingent supporting the British in Pontiac's War, and in 1765 he married the daughter of an Oneida chief. An Anglican convert, Brant helped translate several religious works into his native tongue. When Guy Johnson succeeded his father-in-law, Sir William, as superintendent of Indian affairs in 1774, he made Brant his secretary. The Mohawk worked hard to bring the Iroquois into the British camp, but was unable to keep the missionary to the Oneidas, Sam'l. Kirkland, from converting most of that tribe and their political protégés, the Tuscaroras, to the American cause. After appearing as Mohawk spokesman at a conference with Carleton, Brant was given a captain's commission and sent to England in 1775. (His father's visit to London with four other Iroquois in 1710 had created quite a stir in the court of Queen Anne [Appleton's].) Brant was presented at court, entertained by notables including Boswell, and was painted in full regalia by Romney. He also was painted at this time by Benj. West as an ominous and shadowy figure standing at the shoulder of Guy Johnson, who also was visiting London. (Both portraits are in *Amer. Heritage Book of the Rev.*, 306, 317. C. W. Peale's portrait was hung in the State House in Philadelphia.)

After his return to America, Brant fought at the CEDARS. He then led the Indians on St. Leger's Expedition and with 400 savages supported by a few whites he set up the highly effective ambush at ORISKANY, 6 Aug. '77. (His sister Molly, whose situation as the mistress of Sir William had undoubtedly helped his career, had sent word to St. Leger that a column of patriot militia were moving toward Ft. Stanwix.) With the Butlers and the Johnsons he then undertook a series of raids in the BORDER WARFARE in N.Y. His name struck such terror among the patriots that for a long time he was falsely accused of having been responsible for the WYOMING VALLEY "MASSACRE." Brant and Walter Butler joined forces for the CHERRY VALLEY MASSACRE, and partisans of each leader blame the other for the atrocities there. Early in 1779 Germain wrote to Haldimand:

"The astounding activity of Joseph Brant's enterprises and the important consequences with which they have been attended gave him a claim to every mark of our regard and which you think will be most pleasing to him. What has occurred to me as most likely to gratify him has been done, and enclosed herewith you will receive a commission signed by H. M. [His Majesty] appointing him a Colonel of Indians and the brand [badge ?] of the 'Three Brothers.' * * * Major Butler and his son appear also to have done good service and you will acquaint them that their care to prevent the Indians from molesting the Inhabitants unarmed is much approved of by the King." (Clinton Papers, quoted in Swiggett, *Niagara*, 178–79)

Swiggett, whose views on Brant's character will be given later, adds this comment: "There is a certain irony in this making a colonel of an Indian, and then expressing the King's gratitude to a poor major and a lieutenant for their care in restraining the colonel's people." (*Ibid.*, 179)

After frustrating the efforts of Red Jacket to induce the Iroquois to negotiate a separate peace and after making his last raids (see MINISINK, July '79—one of his most brilliant actions—and BORDER WARFARE), Brant withdrew with his tribe west of the Niagara River. Failing to work out a settlement with the U.S., he obtained from Haldimand a grant of land six miles wide on each side of the Grand River, Ontario. In 1785 he revisited England and got some funds with which to indemnify the Iroquois for their war losses and with which to buy more land. As leader of the Mohawks and other Iroquois of the Grand River settlement, Brant devoted his remaining years to their welfare. He helped establish the Old Mohawk Church and translated religious works. "But his old age was saddened by the dissoluteness of his eldest son and the intrigues of his old enemy, Red Jacket," writes M. L. Bonham in *D.A.B.*

Howard Swiggett, who presents Walter Butler in such a favorable light, has this to say of Brant's character:

"Brant was in the action [at the CEDARS] and, as usual, when he was present, there was some killing of prisoners by his Indians. It is one of the mysteries of American history that this savage, who long after the war murdered his own son, and whose influence over his followers was never sufficient, if indeed it was ever exercised in that direction, to restrain them from atrocities, should be represented as a noble foe, almost, one historian says, 'a saint compared to Walter Butler.' (*Niagara*, 72. On page 155 this author repeats the charge of murdering his own son, which is not mentioned in Appleton's, *D.A.B.*, or *Handbook*) Appleton's says this: "As a warrior he was cautious, sagacious, and brave.... His humanity toward a captive or a fallen foe is too well established to admit of doubt, nor has the purity of his private morals ever been questioned."

Brantford, Ontario, is named in his honor. A monument, featuring a statue of heroic size, was dedicated there in 1886. A son, John (1794–1832), fought in the War of 1812 and was a member of the Canadian parliament in 1832. The last of his nine children (by three wives) died in 1867.

The standard biography is W. L. Stone, *Life of Joseph Brant* (2 vols., New York, 1838; new ed., Albany, 1865). According to *D.A.B.* this should be supplemented by L. A. Wood, *War Chief of the Six Nations* (1914). See also Edward Eggleston and Elizabeth E. Seelye, *Brant and Red Jacket* (New York, 1879).

BRANT, Molly. Indian mistress of Sir Wm. Johnson, she bore him eight children. Her position undoubtedly furthered the fortunes of her brother, Joseph BRANT, and her message to St. Leger of Herkimer's expedition to Ft. Stanwix made possible Brant's successful ambush at Oriskany, 6 Aug. '77.

BRAXTON, Carter. 1736–1797. Signer. Va. Son of a wealthy and well-born planter, George Braxton, he was the grandson of "King" Carter (see CARTER FAMILY). He graduated from William and Mary in 1755, and after the death of his first wife in Dec. '57 he spent the next three years in England. In May '61 he married Elizabeth Corbin and in the same year, when he was only 25, he started a 14-year tour as representative from William co. in the House of Burgesses (1761–75) that was interrupted only by a short period when he was county sheriff. In the controversies that led to the break with England he sided with the conservative aristocrats. He is credited with preventing bloodshed in the dispute between Gov. Dunmore and Patrick Henry's militia over the seizure of colonial powder in the spring of '75. (See VIRGINIA, Mil. Opns. in) He was a delegate to the Cont'l. Cong., succeeding Peyton Randolph, in 1776. He signed the Decl. of Indep., but there are few references to him in the *Journals of the Cont'l. Cong.* Probably because of his conservative and nondemocratic views expressed to the Va. Conv., he was not re-elected. Until shortly before his death he served in the Va. Assy.

BREED'S HILL. See BUNKER HILL, Mass., 17 June '75.

BREWSTER, Great, Island. See GREAT BREWSTER.

BRIAR CREEK, Ga., 3 Mar. '79. As recruits flocked to Lincoln's camp at Purysburg, S.C., the hefty major general from Mass. made preparations to recover Ga. For further background see SOUTHERN THEATER, Mil. Opns. Having already posted Gen. Andrew Williamson across the Savannah River from Augusta with 1,200 men, he ordered Gen. John Ashe to join him with his 1,400 N.C. militia and Col. Elbert's 100 Ga. Cont'ls. Ashe reached Williamson's post the evening of 13 Feb., and the British evacuated Augusta that night. Ashe crossed into Ga. on the 25th and descended the Savannah. At Briar Creek, the morning of Sat., 27 Feb., he found the bridge demolished; the creek in this area, close to its junction with the Savannah, ran through a deep swamp about three miles wide. (Lossing II, 713)

Ashe ordered the bridge rebuilt and also started work on a road to the Savannah so that Rutherford could reinforce him from Mathew's Bluff, S.C., about five miles to the east.

Col. Campbell had interrupted his retreat at Hudson's Ferry, a fortified British outpost 15 miles south of Briar Creek, but had then continued on to Savannah. Gen. Prevost ordered reinforcements to Hudson's Ferry, however, and issued orders for a counterstroke to check the rebel advance. The plan was for Maj. Macpherson's 1st Bn. of the 71st, with a reinforcement of militia and two guns, to occupy the south bank of Briar Creek as a diversion. His younger brother, Lt. Col. Mark Prevost, would execute a wide circuit westward and attack the American rear with his 2d Bn. of the 71st, Baird's

light infantry, three companies from the 60th Regt., a troop of mounted Tories (those of John COFFIN ?), and 150 militia infantry—about 900 in all.

The American force against whom this surprise attack was directed comprised the brigade of Gen. Bryan, the light infantry of Lt. Col. Lytle, Col. Elbert's Ga. Cont'ls., three small guns, and 200 mounted Ga. militia under Col. Marbury. The latter unit was on Briar Creek when Ashe's 1,500 troops arrived from the north.

In a remarkable 50-mile march, Col. Prevost crossed Briar Creek 15 miles above the enemy camp and was only eight miles to their rear when detected. Marbury's horsemen had picked up the enemy movement the afternoon of the 1st and the morning of the next day, but the messenger was intercepted before he reached the American commander. Backed up against the swamp and with the bridge not yet finished, Ashe was faced with annihilation; yet he took no steps to meet the attack other than to form his troops in column with the Cont'ls. out front. (Ward, W.O.R., 684)

The British deployed at a range of 150 yards. Elbert's regulars fired two or three volleys but then shifted left and masked the fire of the advancing New Bern Regt. The Edenton Regt. also got off course and moved right so that a gap was created in the N.C. militia line of battle. When the British capitalized on this and rushed into the gap, the Halifax Regt., on the left, broke without firing a shot, and panic quickly spread through the other militia units. The Cont'ls. held for some time but were finally routed; Elbert and many of his men were captured. Ashe tried to rally the fugitives, but they were too fast for him: they had already headed for the swamps and the

Savannah River; many were drowned, but large numbers escaped by swimming or on crowded rafts.

In a brilliant little operation that restored their hold on Ga., the British had only five killed and 11 wounded. The Americans lost between 150 and 200 killed or drowned and over 170 captured. "Of those who escaped not more than 450 rejoined the army; the rest returned to their homes." (Ward, *W.O.R.*, 684) Needless to say, the rebels lost all their bagagge, artillery, ammunition, and small arms.

The patriots howled for Ashe's hide, and he "appealed from the voice of public opinion to a court-martial." (Lossing, *op. cit.*, 714) The latter found that "he did not take all necessary precautions," as Lossing puts it in what may qualify as one of military history's greatest understatements. (*Ibid.*)

BRIGADE. A military formation of two or more regiments, generally temporary, and commanded by a brigadier in the British army or a brigadier general in the American army. (During the Revolution the terms "regiment" and "battalion" were virtually synonymous.)

BRISTOL, R.I. 7 Oct. '75. A small British fleet that had been operating in Newport harbor appeared off Bristol the afternoon of 7 Oct. and sent an officer ashore to state that if a delegation did not come out to Capt. Wallace's ship within an hour to hear his demands on the city he would open fire. Wm. Bradford told Wallace's emissary that it would be more fitting for Wallace to come ashore and make known his demands. About 8 P.M., in a pouring rain, the British started a bombardment that lasted an hour and a half and stopped only after Col. Potter had gone to Wallace's ship and asked that the town be given time to select a delegation to meet him. The British commander first asked for 200 sheep and 30 cattle, but finally settled for 40 sheep. Among the property destroyed by the bombardment was Gov. Bradford's house. (Lossing, II, 72)

BRITISH GUIANA. The Dutch West India Company established settlements at Essequibo, Demerara, and Berbice early in the 17th century. British privateers took the first two of these in 1781, and they were recovered the next year. Demerara is now Georgetown. Essequibo was located about 50 miles N.W., at the mouth of the Essequibo River.

BRITISH LEGION. Before Sir Henry Clinton left Philadelphia, in June '78, he started forming the VOLUNTEERS OF IRELAND. "The foundation of a legionary corps [see LEGION] was also at the same time laid, for the reception of such other Europeans as might choose to join it," writes Clinton in his memoirs, "the command of which I gave to a Scottish nobleman, Lord Cathcart, with the same views and expectations that had influenced me with respect to Lord Rawdon's." (*Amer. Reb.*, 111) While this implies that "Cathcart's Legion" was raised from scratch, the *D.N.B.* sketch of Tarleton says that a light infantry unit, raised and commanded by Capt. Wm. SUTHERLAND, was called the "Caledonian Volunteers"; Cathcart, according to this same source, took command of them toward the end of 1778 and formed them into a legion. Tarleton's American biographer has another version: "Three troops of dragoons, sometimes called the British Legion, usually operated as guides or scouts for the Queen's Rangers or the 16th and 17th Light Dragoons." These, continues the same writer, then became the British Legion of Cathcart, who was Capt. in the 17th Light Dragoons, and Tarleton subsequently took command. (Bass, *Green Dragoon*, 46–47) Tarleton was made Lt. Col. commandant of the British Legion toward the end of 1778. (*D.N.B.*, "Tarleton") This unit is still identified as "Cathcart's Legion" in the list of troops that sailed south with Clinton for the Charleston Campaign of 1780. Cathcart had been made acting Q.M.G. on the departure of Erskine in the summer of 1779, and it presumably is in this capacity that he accompanied Clinton to Charleston. He was nominally in command of the Legion until Apr. '80, when he was invalided back to N.Y. The subsequent history of the British Legion is the history of "Bloody Ban" TARLETON.

The British Legion was raised on the "American Establishment," which meant that they were "Provincials" and not entitled to the pay and retirement rights of the "Regular Establishment." The Legion subsequently was put on the Regular Establishment, presumably about 15 June '81, the date of Tarleton's commission as Lt. Col. in the regular army. Tarleton's men wore a distinctive green uniform similar to that of Lee's Legion. During some of their operations in the Carolinas the Legion had an attached troop of the 17th Light Dragoons, a fact that has caused some writers to confuse the two units. Fortescue points out, however, that the dragoons "seem to have held the irregulars in some contempt, since they refused to wear the green uniform of the Legion, but stuck to their own scarlet." (*British Army*, III, 309 *n.*)

It is interesting to note that the Legion performed poorly when Tarleton was not personally in command. (See WILLIAMSON'S PLANTATION, WAHAB'S PLANTATION, and CHARLOTTE, N.C., 26 Sept. '80) Somewhat spoiled by their successes as raiders, they also performed poorly at COWPENS, where Tarleton was in over-all command of the British side.

BROAD ARROW. A sign in the shape of an arrowhead with which royal property was marked. The "Broad Arrow Policy" in the Naval Stores Act of 1729 reserved white pines of 24 or more inches in diameter for the crown, unless they grew on lands granted before 7 Oct. 1692, at which time this restriction had been included in the Mass. charter. These trees, needed for naval masts, were marked with the broad arrow.

BROAD RIVER, S.C., 9 Nov. '80. Alternate name for action at FISHDAM FORD. The *A.A.*–Heitman list of battles includes an action on Broad River on 12 Nov. '80. Apparently this is a repetition of the error in Strait's *Alphabetical List of Battles*.

BRODHEAD, Daniel. 1736–1809. Cont'l. officer. Pa. Deputy Surveyor-Gen. of Pa. 1773–76, on 13 Mar. '76 he became Lt. Col. commanding the 2d Bn. of Miles's Pa. Rifle Bn. At LONG ISLAND, 27 Aug. '76, his unit escaped annihilation because Miles ordered him back to the Brooklyn defenses. Brodhead wrote what Freeman calls the best contemporary account of action in the center. (*Washington*, IV, 162 *n.*) Transferred to the 4th Pa. on 25 Oct. '76, he was given command of the 8th Pa. on 12 Mar. '77 with rank as Col. from 29 Sept. '76. Early in 1778 he was ordered to Pittsburgh (from Valley Forge) and the spring of '79 he succeeded Lachlan McIntosh there as commander of the Western Dept. BRODHEAD'S EXPED., 11 Aug.–14 Sept. '79, won him the thanks of Congress (27 Oct.). Although he showed more energy than his predecessors, Brodhead was considered a martinet and had a jealous, irascible temperament. His inability to cooperate with other commanders led Washington to remove him from his post at Pittsburgh. In the reorganization of 17 Jan. '81 Brodhead became commander of the 1st Pa. and retained this position until 3 Nov. '83. In 1781 he led one of the punitive expeditions against the Indians of the Old Northwest. He was breveted B.G. Cont'l. Army on 30 Sept. '83 and then served 11 years as Surveyor-Gen. of Pa.

BRODHEAD'S EXPEDITION, 11 Aug.–14 Sept. '79. In conjunction with SULLIVAN'S EXPEDITION, Col. Dan'l. Brodhead marched up the Allegheny valley from Pittsburgh with 600 men and ravaged Indian villages. According to Swiggett, he was supposed to join Sullivan at Genesee for an attack on Niagara, but for lack of adequate guides he turned back 50 miles short of that objective. (*Niagara*, 185) In a march of 400 miles he burned 10 villages (including Connewango, "at the falls," where Warren, Pa., is now located), destroyed crops, and returned to Pittsburgh "loaded with furs and booty and waited on by the Wyandot [Huron] warriors, for whom the spell of an Iroquois alliance was forever shattered." (Swiggett, *op. cit.*, 200) His only resistance was on 15 Aug., when his advance guard under Lt. Harding defeated a superior force of Indians. (C. & M., 1023–24)

BROOKLAND, BROOKLYN, BREUCKELEN, N.Y. A Dutch settlement on the western tip of Long Island, organized into a town in 1646, four years after the settlement had been known as The Ferry. Its name evolved from the Dutch word meaning marsh land (there were numerous variations of the Dutch spelling) and was perhaps adopted because its situation resembled that of Breuckelen, Holland. (*E.B.*) The present spelling, Brooklyn, was not

standardized until the end of the 18th century. There is disagreement as to whether "Brooklyn Heights" was the high ground close to the ferry or the line along which the Americans formed, the "Heights of Guian," for the battle of LONG ISLAND. The action at JAMAICA, 28 Aug. '76, is listed in *A.A.*–Heitman as "Jamaica (Brookland)," for no apparent good reason: the places were several miles apart.

"BROTHER JONATHAN." As early as Mar. '76 the British used this term to designate Americans. Gov. Jonathan Trumbull (the elder) of Conn. was a key man in the support of Washington's army and once when coping with a particularly tough problem Washington is alleged to have said, "We must consult Brother Jonathan." Legend has it that the expression spread as a generic term for Americans. There is, however, no historical evidence to connect the phrase with Gov. Trumbull. (*D.A.B.*, citing Albert Matthews, "Brother Jonathan," *Colonial Soc. of Mass. Pubs.*, vol. VII, 1905, pp. 95–125)

BROWN, John ("of Pittsfield"). 1744–1780. Patriot leader. Mass. Born and raised in Mass., he graduated from Yale in 1771 and was admitted to the bar in Tryon co., N.Y., the next year. In 1773 he settled in Pittsfield and became prominent in Whig politics. In Feb. '75 he volunteered for a mission to Montreal on behalf of the Boston Comm. of Corresp. with the dual purpose of evaluating Canadian sentiment toward the revolution and of setting up a network of informers. He is one of several credited with the rather obvious thought that the patriots should seize Ticonderoga, the strategic importance of the place—and, probably, its defenselessness at the time—having struck him when he crossed the N.H. Grants on this assignment. On 29 Mar. he reported to Adams and Warren in Boston, and he participated in the capture of TICONDEROGA, 10 May '75.

Commissioned a Maj. in Easton's Regt. on 6 July, he conducted a reconnaissance into Canada during the period 24 July–10 Aug., and reported his findings to Schuyler at Crown Point on the latter date. The degree to which Brown's scouting contributed 'to the advance of Montgomery's wing of the Canada Invasion is uncertain, but Brown figures prominently in all accounts of the operation. According to E. R. Dobson's sketch in *D.A.B.*, it was Brown's report that prompted Montgomery to start toward ST. JOHNS without waiting for Schuyler's approval. Operating deep within the enemy's lines, Brown's role in the abortive attack on MONTREAL, 25 Sept., contributes nothing to his reputation as a combat leader, but he did play a significant part in the capture of CHAMBLY, 18 Oct. Brown and Easton drove Allen McLean's Royal Highland Emigrants down the Sorel River to the St. Lawrence, and took over works they had started at this strategic spot. Here, on 19 Nov., "by audacity as much as by force they intimidated the British fleet coming down the river from Montreal, and caused it to surrender." (*D.A.B.*, citing *The Journal of Charles Carroll*. . . . This could not have been much of a "fleet"; McLean and Carleton were long gone on their way to Quebec. See CANADA INVASION.)

During the Quebec siege, Brown's insubordination to Arnold would have resulted in the former's removal from the scene if Montgomery had not intervened. The two clashed again, and this controversy is covered under AR- NOLD. Having been appointed Lt. Col. of Elmore's Conn. Regt. on 29 July '76, Brown resigned in Feb. '77. Dur-

ing Burgoyne's Offensive he returned to the field and took part in the TICON- DEROGA RAID, Sept. '77. Back to his law practice, he was elected to the General Court in 1778, and in Feb. '79 was commissioned judge of the county court of common pleas. The summer of 1780 he marched to the Mohawk Valley with the Mass. levies called out to oppose the Tory-Indian raids in the region, and he was killed in the action near FORT KEYSER, 19 Oct. '80.

BROWN, Thomas. Southern Tory partisan leader. As a young man he reached Ga. after 1773 to take up 5,000 acres near the confluence of the Broad and Savannah Rivers as an investment for his family of wealthy Yorkshire merchants. Rather than use black slaves, the Browns brought in about 85 indentured servants, most of them Orkney Islanders.

Naturally opposed to revolutionary agitation, young Brown made himself conspicuous by cleverly ridiculing the Whigs and their cause. For this he was tarred and feathered, publicly exposed on a cart, and forced to profess support of the Whigs. At the first opportunity he fled. In British E. Fla., Brown started partisan operations and raised a body known variously as the E. Fla. or King's Rangers. He took part in the capture of FT. MCINTOSH, Ga., in Feb. '77, and with the rank of Lt. Col. led his regiment on raids in Ga. In 1779 he was defeated by inferior forces near Waynesboro on two occasions. He took part in the defense of SAVANNAH, Oct. '79. In 1780 he established himself at Augusta, ran the Whigs out of town, sequestered their property, and successfully defended the strategic place against the abortive attack of Elijah Clarke and James McCall in Sept. '80. (See AUGUSTA, that date) The next year he repulsed a night attack by Col. Harden, but was forced to surrender after a heroic defense of AUGUSTA, 22 May–5 June '81.

Popular hatred of this successful Tory leader was so great that a special guard had to be assigned to guarantee his rights as a prisoner of war. That he was not hanged as an outlaw was probably the result of the British threat to retaliate by hanging six Whigs. (E. K. Alden in *D.A.B.*) After his release he was Col. of the Queen's S.C. Rangers and Supt. of Indian Affairs for the South. In the final defense of Savannah his attempted sortie was defeated by Wayne's night bayonet attack. (Mentioned in GA. EXPED. OF WAYNE)

Brown's forces then were dispersed, his S.C. and Ga. properties were confiscated, and he took refuge in the Bahamas. He was given a land grant on St. Vincent in 1809 and died there in 1825.

BROWN BESS. Selected by John Churchill, Duke of Marlborough, and introduced under his auspices into the British Army during the reign of Queen Anne (1702–14), this almost legendary flintlock MUSKET was a great improvement over its predecessors and, with only a few modifications, was the standard infantry arm for over a century until adoption of the military rifle. (Peterson, *Colonial Arms,* 165) Many authorities say its nickname comes from the artificial oxidation or acid pickling process that gave the barrel a brown color (*ibid.*), but the *Encyclopaedia Britannica* disagrees:

"The first part of the name derives from the colour of the wooden stock, for the name is found much earlier than the introduction of 'browning' the barrel of muskets; 'Bess' may be either a humorous feminine equivalent of the "brown-bill,' the old weapon of the British infantry, or a corruption of the 'buss,'

i.e. box, in 'blunderbuss,' " (*Op. cit.,* "Brown Bess")

The original weapon had a barrel 46 inches long; this was reduced, probably just before 1760, to 42 inches, and some time in the late 1770's it was further shortened to 39 inches. Around 1724 the iron ramrod was first introduced, but as late as 1757 some regiments were only partly equipped with them. (Peterson, *op. cit.,* 167) Without the one-pound, 14-inch bayonet the Brown Bess weighed 14 pounds. (Modern army rifles weigh about eight pounds without the bayonet.) The bullet was cal. 0.75 (its diameter in inches), and weighed about one ounce (14½ bullets to the pound).

See also MUSKETS AND MUSKETRY.

BROWNE, Montfort. Gov. of New Providence (1774–80), he was captured there on 3 Mar. '76 (see NASSAU) and six months later he and Maj. Cortlandt Skinner were exchanged for Gen. Alexander. He subsequently raised "Browne's Corps," which probably is the Provincial regiment known officially as the PRINCE OF WALES LOYAL AMERICAN VOLUNTEERS.

BRUNSWICK, N.J., 22 June '77. Washington's forces escaped from this place on 1 Dec. '76 with only minutes to spare and continued their retreat to the Delaware. (N.J. CAMP'N.) The town—also called New Brunswick —subsequently became the major British outpost in N.J., an estimated 7,800 British and Germans being reported by the American intelligence service in the vicinity the end of Mar. '77. At the start of the PHILADELPHIA CAMPAIGN, in the activities covered in that article under the heading of "Spring Maneuvers," Washington learned that the enemy was withdrawing from Brunswick. On 21 June he ordered an elaborate operation to harass their withdrawal to Amboy: Sullivan would make a feint toward Brunswick, Maxwell would take up a flanking position on the enemy's line of retreat. The next morning, the 22d, he modified these orders and sent Greene with his three brigades plus Wayne's Brig. and Morgan's rangers to attack the enemy's rear. But everything went wrong. Maxwell never got his instructions, and Sullivan got his too late. "The result of all these mishaps was a limping and ragged pursuit, during which Morgan's riflemen were the only American troops who got within range to inflict any damage," writes Freeman, "and they did much less than was indicated in first reports." (*Washington,* IV, 432) According to Ward, Morgan routed the Hessian outpost at the Brunswick bridge and pursued until he made contact with the British rear guard. "Greene and Wayne came up and charged upon the enemy, driving them through the town and across the bridge to their redoubts on the east side of the river. The Americans pushed them from these works and pursued them as far as Piscataway" (about two miles). Greene then broke off the pursuit because the other forces had not come up to support him. The British retreated to Amboy, setting fire to houses as they went. (Ward, *W.O.R.,* 326–27)

"In noting that Wayne's Brigade was the only one of Greene's Divisions that reached the front in time to be of service on the 22nd, Washington said Wayne's men 'behaved in a manner that does them great honor,' but he did not specify any particular service other than that of joining Morgan in advancing to the British redoubts on the left bank of the Raritan." (Freeman, *op. cit.,* IV, 432 *n.,* citing 8 *G.W.,* 282, 291)

"BUCK AND BALL." Three or more buckshot loaded behind a regular musket ball. See also "SWAN SHOT."

BULL, William (II). 1710–1791. Acting Royal Gov. of S.C. Second son of Lt. Gov. William Bull (1683–1755), and grandson of Stephen Bull, who had been prominent in the first settlement of S.C., he was the first native-born American to receive the Doctor of Medicine degree at the University of Leyden. On his return from Holland he turned to agriculture and politics. Becoming Lt. Gov. in 1759, he was acting Gov. a total of eight years during the periods 1760–61, 1764–66, 1768, 1769–71, and 1773–75. He particularly distinguished himself in Indian affairs (grandfather Stephen had been a trader), and Gov. Lyttleton's refusal to follow his counsel of moderation led to the Cherokee uprising in 1759. Bull was acting governor in 1761 and secured the outside support that led to the CHEROKEE EXPEDITION OF JAMES GRANT and subdued the Indians. During the critical years just before the Revolution he tried to perform his duties honestly; understanding the position of his fellow Carolinians, he nevertheless remained loyal to the government whose commission he held. In 1775 he was succeeded by Lord William Campbell, and although his extensive estates were not confiscated by the patriots—whose respect and affection he had retained— Bull left Charleston with the British troops in 1782 and spent the remaining nine years of his life in London. (*D.A.B.*) Alden says that in 1787 "Bull was given permission to return to his native country, though only after a warm dispute." (*South,* 327) Apparently he did not take advantage of this permission.

BULL'S FERRY, N.J., 20–21 July '80. On 20 July, Washington detached Wayne with his 1st and 2d Pa. Brig., four guns, and Moylan's dragoons to destroy a stockaded blockhouse erected at this place, about four miles N. of

Hoboken. According to Sir Henry Clinton, 70 Loyalists under Thos. Ward held "this trifling work" and used it as a base for woodcutting and for protection against "straggling parties of militia. . . ." (*Amer. Reb.*, 200) Wayne started shelling the blockhouse the morning of the 21st, but after an hour had been unable to do any appreciable damage with his field pieces. Meanwhile, his troops received a galling fire and the 1st and 2d Pa. Regt., "not withstanding the utmost efforts of the officers to restrain them [wrote Washington in his report], rushed through the abatis to the foot of the stockade with a view of forcing an entrance, which was found impracticable. This act of intemporate [*sic*] valor was the cause of the loss we sustained," which amounted to 15 men killed, three officers and 46 men wounded. (Quoted in *ibid.*, 446)

Clinton estimated Wayne's "select detachment" at "nearly 2,000 men." He says the bombardment inflicted 21 casualties and that the blockhouse was "perforated by at least 50 cannon shot." The episode inspired John André to compose a long, burlesque epic-ballad, "The Cow Chace," the last part of which appeared in Rivington's *Royal Gazette* the day André was captured. It starts:

To drive the kine one summer's morn,
  The tanner took his way,
The calf shall rue that is unborn
  The jumbling of that day.

and ends:

And now I've closed my epic strain,
  I tremble as I show it,
Lest this same warrio-drover, Wayne,
  Should ever catch the poet.
                    (Lossing, II, 878–80)

BUNKER HILL, Mass. 17 June '75. In the first months of the BOSTON SIEGE neither side had occupied Charlestown peninsula or Dorchester peninsula, both of which included hills whose possession would have given either side a marked advantage. On 13 June the Americans learned (probably through careless talk by Burgoyne) that the British intended to occupy Dorchester Heights five days later. To frustrate this plan the Committee of Safety on 15 June decided to occupy and defend Bunker Hill. At 6 o'clock the next evening the following units were paraded on Cambridge common for this operation: the Mass. regiments of Wm. Prescott, James Frye (under Lt. Col. James Brickett), and Ebenezer Bridge; a 200-man working party from Israel Putnam's Conn. regiment (under Capt. Thos. Knowlton); and Capt. Sam Gridley's artillery company of two guns and 49 Mass. men. The entire force of fewer than 1,200, under the command of Prescott, moved out at 9 P.M.

Putnam met the column at Charlestown Neck with wagons loaded with entrenching tools and fortification materials. After Capt. John Nutting's company (Prescott's Reg't.) and 10 of Knowlton's men moved forward to outpost deserted CHARLESTOWN, the main body climbed the gentle slope of Bunker Hill and moved a few hundred yards farther to the foot of what was later called Breed's Hill. Here Prescott assembled his officers and, for the first time, told them of his orders to fortify Bunker Hill. Called on for their recommendations as to where to locate the entrenchment, the officers had a two-hour discussion that resulted in the decision that the main fortification be erected on Breed's Hill and a secondary work then be built on Bunker Hill. This was a critical error. Whereas Bunker Hill could have been made almost impregnable, and with the captured cannon from Ft. Ticonderoga would

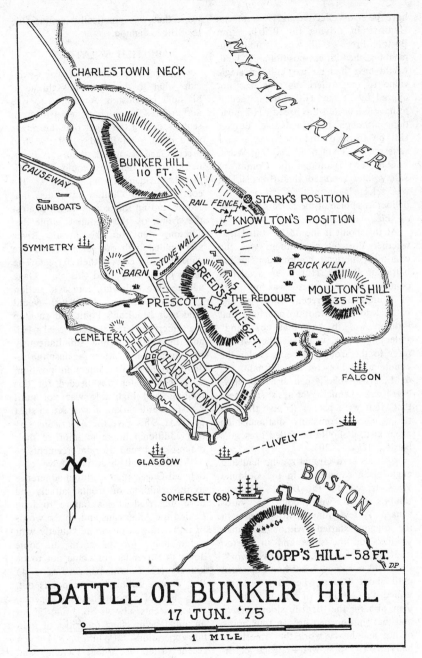

CHARLESTOWN NECK

MYSTIC RIVER

BUNKER HILL
110 FT.

CAUSEWAY

GUNBOATS

RAIL FENCE

STARK'S POSITION

KNOWLTON'S POSITION

SYMMETRY

STONE WALL

BARN

BRICK KILN

BREED'S HILL 62 FT.

PRESCOTT

THE REDOUBT

MOULTON'S HILL
35 FT.

CEMETERY

CHARLESTOWN

FALCON

N

LIVELY

GLASGOW

BOSTON

SOMERSET (68)

COPP'S HILL - 58 FT.

DP

BATTLE OF BUNKER HILL
17 JUN. '75

1 MILE

have been as effective as DORCHESTER HEIGHTS in driving the British from Boston, Breed's Hill was virtually untenable; the latter position, if held, would have had no particular strategic value to the Americans that was not offered by Bunker Hill. Putnam seems to have advocated the Breed's Hill position, although he urged that Bunker Hill be fortified first to cover a possible retreat. (Alden, *Gage*, 226; Ward, *W.O.R.*, 78) Although the Comm. of Safety later reported that Breed's Hill was selected by mistake, "it was the deliberate choice of the officers." (Ward, *op. cit.*, 440 *n.*)

At this point it should be stated that whether Prescott or Putnam was the over-all American commander at the battle of Bunker Hill is an academic controversy, since there was no unity of command. A recent study of the battle leads its author to conclude that Putnam was in "nominal command" (Fleming, 350), whereas other writers refer to the troops as being under the command of Prescott *and* Putnam. (C. & M., 116) Nobody can disagree, however, with Daniel Webster's statement that "if it were proper to give the battle a name, from any distinguishing agent in it, it should be called Prescott's battle." (*Ibid.*, 120)

Col. Richard GRIDLEY, who had had engineering experience in the Colonial Wars, traced out the Breed's Hill redoubt, which was about 45 yards square. A few minutes after midnight the digging started. Although British sentinels on the ships and in Boston itself heard this pick and shovel work, Gage did not know what had happened until about 4 A.M. when daybreak revealed the outlines of the redoubt to men aboard the British sloop *Lively* and that ship opened fire. In four hours of hot and heavy work the Americans had thrown up a well-designed earthwork that was practically invulnerable to British cannon.

BRITISH STRATEGY

Gage called a council of war to decide what to do about this threat to his hold on Boston. According to one authority, Clinton had learned from sentries during the night that the rebels were digging on Breed's Hill and had urged Gage to attack them at dawn, before their defenses could be completed. (Alden, *Gage*, 267) At the council of war Clinton advocated that Howe lead an immediate attack against the front of the redoubt while he, Clinton, went up the Mystic River and landed with 500 men behind the Americans to cut off their retreat. The other generals opposed this plan. Gage adopted the following course of action proposed by Howe: the British would land near Moulton's Point and envelop the American left between Breed's Hill and the Mystic while simultaneously making a frontal attack against the redoubt to fix its defenders in position. Since high water was needed for this landing, and high tide was not until 2 P.M., the debarkation was set to start at 1 P.M. This gave the Americans several additional hours to improve their defenses and send up reinforcements.

Practically all historians have condemned Gage's plan as stupid adherence to the tradition of frontal attack and have marveled at his failure to land behind the Americans and, in the words of one hallowed historian, "quietly wait a few hours for the enemy to come down to surrender, or come out to be killed." (C. F. Adams, *Studies*, 3–4) But, as one military writer points out, "the sight of a position upon a peninsula ... seems always to bring about an unbalancing effect on critics of military operations." (Whitton, 97) Such recent writers as Alden, Fleming, and

Ward have agreed with Whitton that, in view of the circumstances, Gage's decision was basically sound. Without digressing into a complete military critique, and bearing in mind the dangers of going too far in supporting a revisionist viewpoint, here are some points that tend to be overlooked by Gage's critics. A general must be judged in the light of what he knows or can reasonably be expected to know about the enemy situation at the time he makes his decision, not by what we now know. From Boston Gage could see that the rebels had thrown up a fortification on Breed's Hill in a very few hours and were manning it with militia. He could see that no earthworks extended toward the Mystic to guard that flank; he could not see whether Charlestown was well defended or whether the rebels were prepared to oppose landings along the Mystic or along the opposite side of the peninsula. Even today an amphibious operation is considered to be the most hazardous type a general can undertake; Gage's first and most critical problem was to establish a beachhead. Time was of the essence, and the tide would not wait. He could see that Moulton's Point was undefended, out of range of musket fire from the redoubt, and ideal for the covering fires of his supporting ships. Even so, the 1 o'clock landing at Moulton's Point was reported by Howe as being "just possible," even "with the greatest exertion." As for the possibility of an amphibious envelopment up the Mystic River, Howe wrote, "it would have met the ebb and, during its slow progress, the Americans would have had abundant time to take the necessary steps to hinder debarkation." (Howe to his brother, cited by Whitton, 338–39 n.) Gage has been accused of wasting six hours by adopting a plan that required him to wait for high tide; Flem-

ing points out that the records show that Howe had more than enough to do. The tactics prescribed by Gage and executed by Howe, which may loosely be called a frontal attack, would earn the British commanders high marks even by modern military standards. Considering that they were attacking irregulars, who were defending hastily constructed field works, the British had every reason to believe that the fastest, least costly way was to march right in as quickly as possible. Again, Gage and Howe must be judged in the light of what they could resonably be expected to know at the time; they could not have known that a few experienced American officers would be able to make their men hold their fire until the British regulars were almost within bayonet range; they would not have suspected, after the miserable demonstration of marksmanship in the retreat from LEXINGTON AND CONCORD, that this rabble in arms would be capable of the accurate, sustained fire they delivered at Bunker Hill.

Since the battle of 17 June is one of the few in the American Revolution that is of real military interest, I have felt justified in slowing the narrative of the action to present the above comments. In so doing it has been necessary to get somewhat ahead of our story.

THE BRITISH LANDING

Covered by a stepped-up bombardment, 28 barges moved out from Boston with 1,500 troops and 12 guns at 12 o'clock. Howe landed unopposed at about 1 P.M. and formed in three lines on Moulton's Hill. His artillery support consisted of the following: firing at the redoubt were the 68-gun ship of the line *Somerset,* two floating batteries, and the Copp's Hill (Boston) battery reinforced with three 24-pounders;

covering Charlestown Neck from the Charles River were the frigate *Glasgow,* the armed transport *Symmetry,* and two gunboats; in direct support of the landing beaches were the sloops *Lively* and *Falcon.* The *Lively* later moved to a position off Charlestown.

Since the American position had been strengthened (see below), Howe decided to delay his attack until the barges could return to Boston for additional troops. He pushed four light infantry companies forward of Moulton's Hill into a depression where they were protected from fire from the redoubt but where they could provide security for his beachhead. Brig. Gen. Pigot, his second in command, moved to the base of Breed's Hill with the "battalion companies" of the 38th and 43d Regiments (that is, with eight companies from each, since the light infantry and grenadier companies from each regiment were detached).

AMERICAN DISPOSITIONS

Meanwhile, the Americans had extended their defenses to cover the vulnerable east flank. The redoubt and the 100 yards of breastwork were manned by Prescott's regiment and parts of the regiments of Brewer, Nixon, Woodbridge, Little, and Doolittle (this last detachment being commanded by Maj. Wm. Moore). "The rail fence" was a stone structure surmounted by two wooden rails; as the map shows, it lay in the path of Howe's proposed envelopment of Breed's Hill. When Prescott saw the British landing he ordered Knowlton to take his exhausted working party and "oppose them." Seeing the madness of advancing against the beachhead, Putnam ordered Knowlton's men to take position behind this rail fence.

Despite repeated urgings of Pres-

cott and Putnam, Ward was reluctant to reinforce them, apparently believing the British intended to attack the American center and capture the precious stores at Cambridge and Watertown. He finally yielded to the extent of sending forward the N.H. regiments of John Stark and James Reed from Medford. At the Neck, Col. Stark found the way blocked by two other regiments that were afraid to cross through the barrage thrown by the *Symmetry* and her attendant gunboats. Asking that they stand aside to let him cross with his regiment and that of James Reed, Stark led the way at a very deliberate pace. When Capt. Henry DEARBORN of the leading company suggested speeding up to get out of the cross fire, Stark calmly commented that "one fresh man in action is worth ten fatigued men." (Ward, *W.O.R.,* 86, citing Dearborn's *Journals,* 17) From Bunker Hill, Stark saw that Knowlton's defenses at the rail fence were critically thin, and led the two N.H. regiments to reinforce him. Then, with the military quality known as *coup d'oeil,* he spotted another weak point and moved quickly to cover it: in the narrow strip of beach between the river and the end of the rail fence, where the ground dropped off to form an eight-foot bluff, Stark built a breastwork with stones from adjacent walls and posted three ranks of his best men. Stark remained to command this position and sent the rest of his regiment to reinforce Knowlton and Reed at the rail fence. (The latter was strengthened by dismantling another rail fence, placing it in front of the first, and filling the intervening space with newly cut grass that lay about in abundance; while this did but little to provide additional protection against musket fire, it did give the position a deceptively strong appearance.)

To cover the gap between the parallel lines of the breastwork and the rail fence, Col. Gridley had some Mass. men hastily throw together three small v-shaped outposts known as flèches. Three companies were located in Charlestown: Wheeler's (Doolittle's Regt.), Crosby's (Reed's Regt.), and one from Woodbridge's Regt. In a cartway to the right rear of the redoubt, and in the shelter of a barn and a stone wall, were Nutting's Co. (Prescott's Regt.), and a few other troops.

Back on Bunker Hill, Israel Putnam was constructing fortifications with the men who had trickled up from the Neck and those who had straggled back from Breed's Hill. Just before the first attack two famous patriots appeared as volunteers: 69-year old Seth POMEROY, and Dr. Joseph WARREN, President of the Mass. Provincial Congress.

Before the first group of reinforcements reached Howe, between 1 and 2 P.M., the British fired "hot shot" and CARCASS into Charlestown to set fire to the town and drive out the snipers who had been harassing the British left. Some writers say this was done to give Howe's troops a smoke screen through which to attack, but Fortescue speaks of the smoke, "borne by the wind straight into the eyes of the British," as a hindrance.

With the arrival of the 47th Regt., six more flank companies, and the 1st Marine Battalion (which landed between Moulton's Point and Charlestown, near where Brig. Gen. Pigot was already in position with the 43d and 38th Regts.), Howe was ready.

FIRST ATTACK

Pigot's left wing was to advance against the redoubt to hold its defenders in place while Howe's wing enveloped the American left. The grenadier companies, in the front rank, and the battalion companies of the 5th and 52d, in the second rank, were to attack the rail fence frontally. Along the very strip of narrow beach that had caught Stark's eye, 11 light infantry companies in column were to penetrate the American left and swing around to hit the defenders of the rail fence from the rear. Howe's entire wing would then envelop the redoubt.

In accordance with the tactics of the day, British 6-pounders were ordered ahead of the infantry to engage the entire American line. This part of Howe's plan failed dismally when the gunners discovered that all the extra ammunition sent over from Boston was for 12-pounders! Boggy ground kept the guns from getting close enough to fire grape shot effectively.

In the oppressive heat of early afternoon, the British light infantry advanced quickly, in a column of fours, along the unobstructed beach toward John Stark's line of nervous militiamen. The leading company (Royal Welch Fusiliers) had gotten to within 50 yards and had deployed for a bayonet charge when Stark finally gave the order to fire. The head of the British column was torn apart. Without hesitation the survivors of the leading company pressed forward and were cut down. The next two companies, the 4th (King's Own) and 10th (those of Lexington common) charged, in turn, with incredible valor and with the reasonable expectation that they could get to these farmers between volleys. But Stark had organized his men into three ranks, one of which was always ready to fire; there was no lull between volleys. Furthermore, Stark's N.H. troops, who were uncommonly good shots, had been warned to shoot low and to look

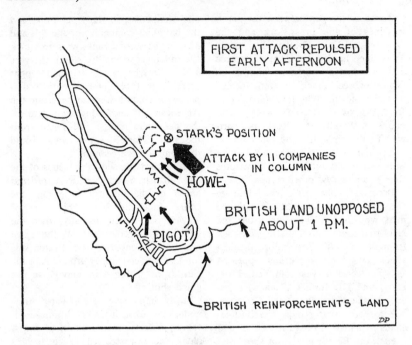

for the gorgets that marked the officers. The men of the 52d Regt. came forward, but their officers could not make them attack. When the light infantry was ordered to the rear they left 96 dead on the beach.

Despite failure of what was supposed to be the main effort, Howe carried on with his plan and personally led the frontal attack against the rail fence. The front rank of grenadiers came under heavy and accurate fire as they were getting through fences and walls to deploy for their bayonet charge. Again, the American irregulars held their fire until the enemy were within about 50 yards; here also they had been told to shoot low and to look for the officers. In violation of their instructions, the grenadiers paused to return the American fire. This not only was ineffective, but caused the second line to mingle with the first. As fire from the fence

continued to pour into the confused regulars, the latter finally dropped back to reorganize.

Pigot's "holding attack" on the British left was also stopped by effective musket fire.

Putnam had been at the rail fence during this first attack. He now rode back to Bunker Hill and to the Neck in a vain attempt to get volunteers to reinforce the front line. (When he later explained to Prescott, "I could not *drive* the dogs," Prescott is alleged to have retorted that he "might have led them up.")

SECOND ATTACK

Within 15 minutes Howe launched a second attack. This time he and Pigot moved toward the redoubt while the light infantry companies executed a secondary attack against the rail fence. Again the defenders held their fire until the British were a hundred feet away. The continuous fire from the redoubt, the breastwork, the three flèches, and the rail fence was even more murderous than before; the second attack failed as dismally as the first.

Although the Americans had suffered very few casualties, they were now critically short of ammunition. Putnam continued his efforts to get reinforcements forward to Prescott, Knowlton, and Stark. Although he personally had ridden across the Neck many times that day, many troops were afraid to cross through the naval fire. When Col. James Scammons was ordered from Lechmere Point to "the hill," he marched his regiment to Cobble Hill! Later he headed for Bunker Hill, but ordered a retreat before reaching the top. Col. Samuel Gerrish and his Conn. regiment refused to leave the safe side

of Bunker Hill, but Christian FEBIGER, his adjutant, did lead some volunteers of the regiment into the battle. (Gerrish was cashiered; Scammons was acquitted by a court-martial on the grounds that he had misunderstood his orders.)

American field artillery was particularly ineffective during the battle. From the confused accounts, Ward estimates that there were three companies led by Maj. Scarborough Gridley (son of the engineer) and Captains Samuel Trevett and John Callender; each had two guns. Both Callender and Gridley were dismissed from the service after the battle, although the former later redeemed himself as a volunteer in the ranks and had his commission restored. Trevett lost one gun on Bunker Hill but got the other forward to the fence; his was the only gun the British did not capture. (Ward, *op. cit.*, 96–97)

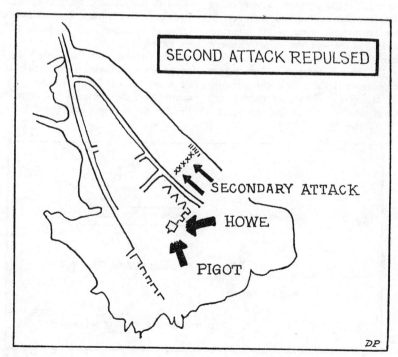

SECOND ATTACK REPULSED

SECONDARY ATTACK

HOWE

PIGOT

DP

FINAL ATTACK

Reinforced with 400 fresh troops, the 63d Regt. and the flank companies of the 2d Marine Battalion, Howe organized a third assault. He finally ordered his men to drop their knapsacks and other useless accoutrements; his men had made their first attacks with between 100 and 125 pounds, including three days' rations, a blanket, 15 pounds of musket and bayonet. Clinton had come across from Boston to rally two regiments he had seen milling on the beach without sufficient officers.

The plan this time was for little more than a demonstration against the rail fence while Howe, Pigot, and Clinton went for the redoubt. Field pieces (which now had the proper ammunition) were to move forward and enfilade the breastwork from the American left. The gunners accomplished their mission, routing the defenders of the breastwork; some of the latter retreated to the rear, but others withdrew into the redoubt.

The British infantry, advancing in column until they were close enough to deploy for a bayonet charge, suffered another devastating musket fire until they were within 10 yards of the redoubt. The marines on the extreme left (toward Charlestown) were again stopped by musket fire and, in violation of their instructions, stopped to shoot back. The 47th came up to steady the marines and resume the attack, but not before Maj. PITCAIRN was mortally wounded. The regulars then swarmed into the redoubt from two sides, and for a few moments there was desperate hand-to-hand combat. Having few bayonets, the Americans met their assailants with rocks and clubbed muskets. Adjutant Waller of the marines reported that the bayonet work of the regulars was "shocking"—which, considering the exhausted condition of the attackers, should be understandable to anybody who can imagine wielding a 14-inch bayonet on the end of a 14-pound musket. Only 30 Americans were killed in the redoubt, but among them was the patriot Warren. Prescott fought his way out, parrying bayonets with his sword.

"The retreat was no rout," Burgoyne reported, having watched the battle from Boston. Lord Rawdon, who commanded the grenadier company of the 5th Regt. after Capt. (later Lord)

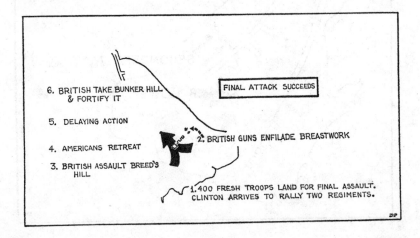

6. BRITISH TAKE BUNKER HILL & FORTIFY IT

5. DELAYING ACTION

4. AMERICANS RETREAT

3. BRITISH ASSAULT BREED'S HILL

2. BRITISH GUNS ENFILADE BREASTWORK

1. 400 FRESH TROOPS LAND FOR FINAL ASSAULT. CLINTON ARRIVES TO RALLY TWO REGIMENTS.

FINAL ATTACK SUCCEEDS

Harris was wounded, wrote home that the rebels "continued a running fight from one fence, or wall, to another, till we entirely drove them off the peninsula...." (C. & M., 130) As is normally the case, the defenders sustained most of their casualties in the retreat. The exhausted regulars pursued only to Bunker Hill, where they organized a defense.

NUMBERS AND LOSSES

American strength on the peninsula during the battle was probably somewhat in excess of 3,000. Not more than half of these were in action at any one time, and a third took no part in the fighting. Total casualties are estimated at 441, of whom 140 were killed and 301 wounded; 30 of the latter were captured.

British strength was about 2,500, including the 400 who took part in the final assault only. According to Fortescue, they lost at least 1,150—about 40 per cent. Reported casualties were 19 officers and 207 men killed, and 70 officers and 758 men wounded. Since the wounded of the 38th Regt. were omitted from the official list, and since this regiment had 25 killed (more than any other in the battle), an estimated 100 wounded have been included to arrive at the total figure of 1,150. (Fortescue, Br. Army, III, 159) Officer casualties were particularly heavy: of the British officer casualties in the 20 battles of the Revolution, one eighth were killed and about one sixth were wounded at Bunker Hill. (Channing, III, 169–70 n.)

SIGNIFICANCE

Bunker Hill rallied the colonies, spurred the Cont'l. Congress into action, and banished any real hope of conciliation. Although Americans first looked on the battle as unnecessary and discreditable, they saw that British regulars were not invincible. When the colonists later came to regard the battle with pride "the mistaken conviction seized the public mind that... patriotism was the sole qualification for a soldier's calling—a fallacy which paralyzed the military legislation of the Revolution." (Upton, 2) In this connection, the British historian, Fortescue, says, "Bunker's Hill was probably a greater misfortune, taken altogether, to the Americans than to the British." (op. cit., 160)

The secret of the defense of Breed's Hill, little realized even today, was the presence of American officers who had received military training in the French and Indian Wars. Gridley knew how to lay out and direct the construction of field fortifications. Prescott, Stark, Putnam, and Knowlton—to name them in approximate order of their importance in the battle—showed the highest of leadership traits: the ability to handle militia in battle. Putnam knew the psychological value of breastworks, however skimpy: Americans are afraid of being shot in the legs, he is supposed to have said, but don't worry about their heads; give them something to protect their legs and they will fight forever. Prescott at the redoubt, Knowlton at the rail fence, and Stark along the beach understood this. The calmness of the veteran officers kept them, first, from being routed by the ineffective British artillery fire, and then kept them in position as the champions of Europe's battlefields advanced to point blank range. Holding these irregulars in position through two attacks was a remarkable feat of leadership.

Bunker Hill showed the British Government they were in for a real fight. According to Fortescue, "It shook the nerve of Howe." (Ibid.) It was almost a year before the British resumed the offensive. Whereas it is easy to attach too much importance to their fear of "another Bunker Hill," British generals throughout the rest of the war never again reacted with the speed and aggressiveness they showed in Boston the morning of 17 June '75.

Standard authorities are Richard Frothingham's *History of the Siege of Boston* (4th ed., 1873) and Allen French's *First Year of the Amer. Rev.* (1934). A recent work is Thomas J. Fleming's *Now We Are Enemies* (1960).

BURGOYNE, John. 1722–1792. British general. Of an ancient Lancashire family, he received the education of a gentleman at Westminster School, became a cornet in the 13th Light Dragoons in 1740, and bought a lieutenant's commission the next year. While serving with his regiment at Preston he was a frequent visitor to the home of the tremendously powerful and wealthy Earl of Derby, whose son and heir had been a bosom friend of Burgoyne at Westminster. In 1743 the impecunious young officer of dragoons eloped with Derby's daughter, Lady Charlotte. Although the brother approved of the match, the great House of Stanley * did not, and the Earl's reaction was to give his daughter a small sum of money and make it clear that henceforth she and her dragoon were on their own. With this money Burgoyne purchased a captaincy in the 13th Dragoons and lived happily with his bride in London for three years before being forced

* The earls of Derby were of the Stanley family and the eldest son was generally called Lord Strange. Hence Burgoyne's wife is sometimes referred to as Lady Charlotte Strange (*D.N.B.*) and also as Lady Charlotte Stanley. Her father appears to have been the 11th earl. (*E.B.*)

to sell his commission and use the proceeds to set up housekeeping in France, where the pound went further. During this exile Burgoyne mastered .the French language and literature. Lord Derby having come around to accepting his son-in-law, he exerted the considerable influence needed to have him restored to active status in the army and Burgoyne returned from his seven years' absence to take up a commission as Capt. of the 11th Dragoons. The next year, in May '58, he exchanged this for one as Capt. and Lt. Col. of the Coldstream Guards.

He was 36 years old when his real military service began, but a combination of the Stanley influence and genuine ability caused him to rise rapidly. After taking part in the mismanaged expedition to the French coast—Cherbourg and St. Malo—in 1758–59, he showed the rare military quality of originality in bringing about the establishment of the first light horse units in the British Army. In Aug. '59 he was given command of one of the two regiments organized. Two years later he entered Parliament. In 1762 he took his regiment to Portugal, arriving in the Tagus River on 6 May, and it was his good fortune to serve under the remarkable Count la Lippe. After an initial period of outpost duty (for which his light horse was particularly suited), he led a 50-mile forced march and a dawn cavalry attack that captured Valencia d'Alcantara, cut a Spanish regiment to pieces, captured many prisoners and three flags, and brought a handsome contribution of money for sparing the city. Three months later Charles LEE of his command took the Spanish depot at Villa Velha, which ended the campaign. Lippe promoted him to temporary B.G., the King of Portugal gave him the captured flags and a diamond ring, the British people hailed him as a hero, and the army in which he had gotten such a late start recognized him as a gallant and effective combat soldier.

"Gentleman Johnny" was a nickname coined by Burgoyne's soldiers in tribute to his humanity in a day when soldiers were trained like dogs. In certain things Burgoyne was ahead of his times, points out Christopher Ward. "His treatise on the duties of officers urged that soldiers be treated like thinking human beings; they should not be subjected to frequent and brutal corporal punishment. . . ." (*W.O.R.*, 61) After this brilliant start in the military field, Burgoyne returned to Parliament with Derby's influence in 1768 and showed real ability as a politician. (H. Morse Stephens in *D.N.B.*) Belonging to fashionable clubs, he was a reckless gambler and also an amateur actor. A moderate Tory, his family influence and general support of the government led to sinecures that by the time he was commissioned Maj. Gen. in 1772 added up to £3,500 a year: he had been made Col. of the 16th Light Dragoons in 1763 and Gov. of Ft. William in Scotland in 1769. His literary career was launched with "Maid of the Oaks," played in 1774 and brought out the next year by Garrick at Drury Lane. ("Like Burgoyne's other efforts," comments Stephens in *D.N.B.*, "the play is rather tedious to read.")

On 25 May '75, meanwhile, Burgoyne reached Boston with the two other distinguished passengers of the frigate *Cerberus*, Maj. Gens. Wm. Howe and Henry Clinton, to help Gage get his army out of the Boston bottle. The junior of the three, Burgoyne was somebody Gage could very profitably have gone the rest of his life without. Even before landing at Boston Burgoyne had made himself the butt of Yankee humor when, after hearing that British regulars were shut up by only twice their number of Provincials, he is said to have remarked, "What! . . . Well, let *us* get in, and we'll soon find elbow-room." He promptly was dubbed "General Elbow-Room," probably among the redcoats as well as the rebels, if I know anything about soldier mentality. "The time was to come when Burgoyne, who usually enjoyed jests, especially his own, could not tolerate the expression." (Wallace, *Appeal*, 32) As Ward puts it: "Burgoyne, indeed, was of no help to Gage; he was, on the contrary, a menace. He began a voluminous correspondence with some of the home authorities in which he dilated upon Gage's errors and thus injured him in the judgment of the ministry." (*Op. cit.*, 61)

Under orders from London to proclaim martial law in Mass., Gage decided to make one last attempt to bring the colonists to reason, as the British saw it, but he made the mistake of calling on Burgoyne's literary talents to write a manifesto. Addressed to "the infatuated multitude," the document's "flamboyant, inflated, and verbose style widened the eyes of the simple New Englanders in sheer amazement. . . ." (*Ibid.*) (See also BOSTON SIEGE)

When Burgoyne was not stabbing his talented quill into the back of his C. in C. he found time to write a farce called "The Siege of Boston" to enliven the monotony of the strategic situation. This show was being presented at Charlestown, Mass., the evening of 8 Jan. '76 and a figure representing Washington had just shuffled onto the stage when a British sergeant appeared from the wings shouting, "The Yankees are attacking Bunker's Hill!" The audience had applauded before they realized that this was not one of Burgoyne's lines but that an enemy raid had struck. (It was led by Thos. KNOWLTON.)

Burgoyne had meanwhile returned to England in Nov. '75. In May '76 he reached Quebec with reinforcements for Carleton that drove the puny American forces from the vicinity of the city and pushed back the CANADA INVASION. He commanded the troops that repulsed the rebels at TROIS RIVIÈRES and took part in the pursuit that ended at Valcour Island on Lake Champlain in Oct. The prospect of winter quarters in Canada did not appeal to Gentleman Johnny, and he returned on leave to London.

BURGOYNE'S OFFENSIVE, his invasion of N.Y. in 1777 and surrender at Saratoga, 17 Oct. '77, climaxed his military career. An evaluation of his generalship will be found in that article and its cross references. While the subject remains highly controversial, I have subscribed to this verdict of Hoffman Nickerson: "Attractive though he was, he was certainly not great either as a soldier or as a man." (*Turning Point,* 424) An English scholar phrases it thus: "He was a gallant soldier; but he was vain, boastful, and superficial, and not a man to depend upon in a tight corner." (Egerton, *Causes,* 122) It should be pointed out that although he had held an army commission for many years and had been a Maj. Gen. since 1772, Burgoyne's combat service had been very limited up until the time he started his expedition from Canada. His strategic errors are therefore not too surprising.

After his surrender Burgoyne played into the hands of the Americans by giving Congress a much-wanted pretext for not honoring the "convention" made by Gates. (See CONVENTION ARMY) Allowed to return on parole to England, Burgoyne met a storm of disapprobation, only Charles Fox and the latter's immediate supporters siding with the general. On 26 May '78 a motion was made "to condemn the state and condition of the army which surrendered at Saratoga" and the question also was raised as to why Burgoyne had been allowed to come home on parole. Burgoyne defended himself in an able speech, which he published. A select committee was appointed by a large majority to investigate the defeat. In his *State of the Expedition from Canada, . . .* which Burgoyne published in 1780, he maintained that he was furnished only half the forces prescribed in his plan and that they were poorly supported; he also tried to shift the blame for his failure onto Howe and Clinton. These arguments have convinced many historians that Burgoyne's failure was not his own fault.

After acting as though he might accede to demands that Burgoyne be returned as a prisoner of war to America, the King restricted his retribution to depriving Burgoyne of his appointments as Col. of the 16th Dragoons and as Gov. of Ft. William, which left him only his pay as a general. The opposition leaders, Fox and Sheridan, used him as a champion in their attacks on the government, and in 1782 when the Whigs returned to power under Rockingham, Burgoyne was made C. in C. in Ireland (7 June), privy councilor in Ireland, and Col. of the 4th Regt. In Dec. '83 when the coalition ministry went out of power, Burgoyne went out with the supporters of Fox. After lending his pen to the attacks on Pitt's administration—Burgoyne wrote most of the vicious "Westminster Guide"—he turned more and more from politics toward the literary and social life. Practically his last political act was to manage the impeachment of Warren Hastings in 1787.

Meanwhile, in 1780 he had written the libretto for a comic opera, and in 1785 he translated one for "Richard

Coeur de Lion." In 1786 he scored his major success with his play, "The Heiress," which went through 10 editions in a year and was performed on the Continent. "The Heiress" was dedicated to the father-in-law who had refused to accept Burgoyne 37 years earlier and the old gentleman proceeded to marry the star of the show, Miss Farren. (*D.N.B.*) Lady Charlotte had died in June '76 and Lord Derby reared four illegitimate children born of Burgoyne's liaison with the singer Susan Caulfield between 1782 and 1788. Among Burgoyne's triumphs must certainly be listed that as a son-in-law!

He died suddenly on 4 June '92, having been in apparent good health the previous day. On 13 Aug. he was buried in Westminster Abbey. His eldest son by Miss Caulfield became Field Marshal Sir John Fox Burgoyne (1782–1871). As Lt. Col. and chief engineer, he took part in the Battle of New Orleans (1815).

Burgoyne's *State of the Expedition,* mentioned above, not only presents his version of the campaign but also includes a valuable collection of documents that make it a prime source. The standard work for many years was E. B. de Fonblanque's *Political and Military Episodes ... from the life and correspondence of ... Burgoyne.* ... (London, 1876). It was followed immediately by W. L. Stone's *Campaign of ... Burgoyne* (Albany, 1877), which Ward calls "the fullest story and perhaps the best." Hoffman Nickerson's *Turning Point of the Revolution, or Burgoyne in America* (Boston and N.Y., 1928) is considered by many historians to be the classic work on the subject; it suffers, however, from Nickerson's aversion to footnotes—it has no citations of authorities—and Troyer Anderson finds his "interpretation of the campaign" inaccurate. Dis-

agreements between these eminent scholars are pointed out under BURGOYNE'S OFFENSIVE. F. J. Hudleston's *Gentleman Johnny Burgoyne* (London, 1927) "makes a point of treating Burgoyne as an interesting and often amusing personality, but beneath it is found some good history," comments 'the historian Anderson. (*Howe Bros.,* 361) Burgoyne's *Dramatic and Poetical Works,* 2 vols., were published in 1808.

BURGOYNE'S OFFENSIVE, June–Oct. '77.* Although the idea of a British invasion from Canada along the traditional Champlain-Hudson route had been mentioned by Gage and Howe in 1775, and was actually being pursued by Carleton in 1776, the plan of 1777 was based on Burgoyne's "Thoughts for Conducting the War on the Side of Canada," which was submitted on 28 Feb. '77 at the request of Germain and the King and approved with few modifications. Both Burgoyne and Clinton had headed for London after the campaigns of 1776 with the ostensible purpose of warming their seats in Parliament, but actually to promote themselves into higher military position. Burgoyne got there first and had been named by the King to command the proposed operation before Clinton arrived. Clinton's political connections were so powerful, however, that the King reversed himself and on 20 Feb. gave Clinton the nod. The Cabinet made the final decision in Burgoyne's favor. (See CARLETON–GERMAIN feud for why Carleton was not given the command)

Instructions for the campaign were spelled out in a letter of 26 Mar. '77 from Germain to Carleton which the latter got on 6 May when Burgoyne

* See map with article on the CANADA INVASION.

reached Quebec. They called for Carleton to hold 3,770 troops in Canada while Burgoyne commanded a two-pronged offensive southward. The main effort by 7,173 men under Burgoyne's personal leadership would move up Lake Champlain, capture Ticonderoga, and advance to Albany. As a strategic diversion, ST. LEGER'S OFFENSIVE would be conducted along the line of the Mohawk River and link up with the other column at Albany; about 2,000 were allotted to this effort. At Albany a "junction" was to be made with Howe's forces from the south and Burgoyne would come under Howe's orders.

We should stop and look at this last provision because it brings up the most controversial point of this controversial campaign. What sort of "junction" was supposed to be made at Albany between Howe's 30,000 on the lower Hudson (including 3,000 in R.I. and 5,000 Tories) and the 8,000 from Canada? The basic authority on Burgoyne's campaign says that the "decisive blow at the Hudson . . . was marred by Howe's abandonment of the North [Hudson] River for the sake of attacking Philadelphia." (Nickerson, *The Turning Point of the Revolution,* 65) This judgment has been echoed by other historians. But another scholar concludes that "Howe certainly seemed somewhat indifferent to the need of reaching out from New York to join hands with Burgoyne" but "criticism of Howe on the ground that he did not make that the first feature of his plans for 1777 is without warrant." (Anderson, *Command of the Howe Brothers,* 271, 270)

It would be pretentious for me to attempt to resolve the disagreement between these two authorities, but it will be useful to point out the major bones of contention. First, there might be misunderstanding as to the British objective of securing control of the Hudson River line. Although you might assume that they planned to erect an impassable barrier, this was neither possible nor necessary. "What they were after was to prevent the movement across it of military supplies in considerable quantities and of armed bodies sufficient in numbers to menace the rear of British armies offensively engaged at some distance from the river line," explains Nickerson. (*Op. cit.*) "This could be easily done merely by controlling the navigation of the river." Second, neither Burgoyne, Howe nor the London authorities had any idea that Burgoyne would be unable to reach Albany without assistance from Howe; nor was it expected that Burgoyne would need immediate support at Albany. (Anderson, 248, 270) Furthermore, the purpose of Burgoyne's operation was *not* to bring reinforcements to Howe, since this could have been done better by naval transports from Quebec to the Atlantic coast.

"The decisive sentence of Germaine's order," writes Nickerson, contains these instructions to Burgoyne and St. Leger: " 'until they shall have received orders from Sir William Howe, it is his Majesty's pleasure that they act as exigencies may require. . . . [However,] in so doing, they must never lose view of their intended junctions with Sir William Howe as their principal objectives.' " (*Op. cit.,* 94–95) The only possible conclusion to be drawn, according to Nickerson, is that Germain intended Howe to stay on the Hudson (*ibid.,* 98) and that "the enormous initial blunder of sending no order to Howe" resulted in Burgoyne's expedition being left "to its fate." (*Ibid.,* 96) Germain's subordinates "allowed the all-important paper to be pigeon-holed or mislaid." (*Ibid.,* 98) This popular conjecture has sent uncounted archivists and historians grubbing through old pigeonholes, but let's see what Anderson says about this "all-important paper."

"There is not the slightest reason for believing that [orders from London] if sent, or if received and obeyed, would have directed Howe to move up the Hudson and rescue Burgoyne." (Anderson, 257) In his 26 Mar. letter (above) Germain said he would send Howe instructions "by the first packet." What Howe received by this packet was a copy of Burgoyne's instructions, the essential portions of which are quoted above. They reached him in July with an accompanying note from D'Oyley, one of Germain's secretaries; the note merely explained that the instructions were those given Burgoyne. (*Ibid.*, 256)

Germain had approved Howe's final plan for the PHILADELPHIA CAMPAIGN on 3 Mar., but wrote Howe on the 18th to urge that he complete it in time to "facilitate the junction with Burgoyne." (*Ibid.*, the words quoted are Anderson's). Howe received this last communication on 16 Aug., after he had heard of Burgoyne's easy capture of Ticonderoga (5 July) and had sailed for the Chesapeake (23 July) with no reason to worry about Burgoyne's future success, and certainly not about his safety. (*Ibid.*, 256–57) Burgoyne, incidentally, was in London until 27 Mar., and must have seen or known the contents of Germain's letters of the 3d and 18th to Howe. Before he left Canada he also saw Howe's letter of 5 Apr. to Carleton saying that Howe could give Burgoyne no help unless Washington marched against him. On 17 July Howe wrote Burgoyne that Clinton would remain in N.Y. during the Philadelphia Camp'n., but gave Burgoyne no reason to expect that

Clinton would give him any assistance. (See CLINTON'S EXPEDITION) Burgoyne indicated no surprise or concern about any of this news, which supports the theory that he considered his expedition strong enough to accomplish its mission unaided. Not until Burgoyne was well on his way to disaster did he (and Howe's critics) act as if reinforcement from Howe was a significant feature of his strategy. "After Saratoga Burgoyne developed another view of the purpose of his ill-fated expedition" and tried to shift blame onto Howe and Clinton. (Anderson, 247, 252–54, 261–62)

PREPARATIONS IN CANADA

Carleton's excellent preparations during the winter of 1776–77 and subsequent cooperation with his former subordinate enabled Burgoyne to start operations within six weeks of his arrival in Canada. The third week of June a "splendid regatta" moved south from St. Johns to Lake Champlain. The painted savages who led the way, the gaudy British and German regulars, the swarm of small boats and the sailing vessels presented a magnificent spectacle against the wilderness backdrop of water, hills, and forest. After assembling off Cumberland Head (now Plattsburgh, N.Y.) the expedition reached Crown Point on 27 June and approached Ft. Ticonderoga on the 30th.

Burgoyne had perhaps 10,500, of whom 1,000 were military noncombatants and authorized camp followers. His flotilla comprised nine ships (see CHAMPLAIN SQDNS.), 28 gunboats, and the bateaux needed to move troops and supplies. (Ward, *W.O.R.*, 402) He had at least 138 guns, 42 in the field train and the rest mounted in vessels or dropped off at various posts.

BRITISH ORDER OF BATTLE

Maj. Gen. Wm. Phillips commanded the Right Wing (3,700 RANK AND FILE), which was divided into three parts. B.G. Simon Fraser's Advance Corps was made up of the entire 24th Regt. and FLANK COMPANIES of the 29th, 31st, and 34th. B. G. Powell's 1st Brig. comprised the 9th, 47th, and 53d Regts. B. G. Hamilton's 2d Brig. was made up of the 20th, 21st, and 62d Regts.

The Left Wing was composed of 3,000 German rank and file under Maj. Gen. von Riedesel. Lt. Col. Breymann's Advance Corps included the Grenadier Bn. and a light infantry company of 40 jägers and 40 marksmen selected from different British regiments. The 1st Brig., under Brig. Specht, included his own regiment and those of Riedesel and Rhetz. Brig. Gall's 2d Brig. comprised the Prince Frederick and Hesse-Hanau Regts. Except for the latter unit, all Germans in Burgoyne's expedition were Brunswickers.

The guns were manned by 250 British artillery regulars, 150 British infantry recruits, and 100 Germans. Half the field guns were with each wing. Some 400 Indians (far short of the number Burgoyne had hoped to recruit) covered the German wing; according to Nickerson, the notorious ST. LUC and LANGLADE commanded these savages. The other wing was screened by 150 Canadians and 100 American Tories, numbers which had also fallen dissapointingly short of the quotas. Held in reserve, and used as headquarters guards, were 250 dismounted Brunswick dragoons. The expedition was badly lacking in land transport, there being not even enough horses to move all the field artillery.

"Here both Carleton and Burgoyne were at fault, [says Nickerson] for the former had done nothing during the winter to remedy the defect and the latter ... made no requisition for transport until June 7. ... Consequently the five hundred little Canadian two-wheeled carts which were hastily tacked together were made for the most part of unseasoned wood, and the whole transport service showed the weakness natural to hastily improvised organizations. It was a weakness that was to cost Burgoyne dear." (*Op. cit.,* 103)

Back in Canada, Carleton was left with 3,770 troops. (This is the figure in Germain's instructions of 26 Mar., just as 7,173 is the figure for Burgoyne's column and 675 is that prescribed for St. Leger's; the actual numbers were somewhat different.)

AMERICAN DISPOSITIONS

Schuyler had a meager 2,546 Cont'ls. under Maj. Gen. St. Clair at Ticonderoga; these were reinforced before the British attack by 900 fresh militia. Militia detachments were at Skenesboro, Ft. Anne, Ft. Edward, and Albany. A Cont'l. regiment was at Ft. Stanwix at the head of the Mohawk Valley (see ST. LEGER'S EXPEDITION) and the militia were being mobilized in this region.

INITIAL OPERATIONS

After BURGOYNE'S PROCLAMATION and Speech to His Indians, "Gentleman Johnny" moved south and captured TICONDEROGA, 2–5 July, with a speed and ease that shook American morale badly. Some went so far as to believe the SILVER BULLETS OF TICONDEROGA story. Actually, what had been called "The Gibraltar of America" could not have been defended by St. Clair's insufficient garrison and this general saved an army that otherwise would have been lost along with the overrated fortress. Bungling by Gen. Fermoy and drunken dereliction of duty by the bridge guard marred a well-conceived night withdrawal of the American forces and reduced the head start St. Clair needed to escape unmolested. There being no short road from Ticonderoga to Skenesboro, St. Clair led the largest part of his command on a 45-mile, roundabout route through Castleton. Failure of Seth Warner to obey orders, and tactical carelessness, led to defeat of the rearguard at HUBBARDTON, 7 July. The Americans who retreated in boats with the few guns and supplies that could be saved from Ticonderoga were vigorously pursued to SKENESBORO, 6 July; Col. Pierce Long was the bungler in this operation, with the result that St. Clair was forced to make a seven-day march around captured Skenesboro to reach Ft. Edward on 12 July. After a skirmish outside FT. ANNE, 7 July, Long burned the fort and retreated to Ft. Edward.

OTHER FRONTS

Howe delayed his departure from Staten Island until the news of Ticonderoga's capture assured him that Burgoyne's offensive was going well and would not need his assistance (Anderson, 274); on 23 July he sailed for Philadelphia, leaving Sir Henry Clinton in and around N.Y.C. with about 8,500 effectives. Depressed by the bad news from the Northern Dept. and bewildered as to where Howe would strike, Washington sent Schuyler what reinforcements he thought he could spare: Morgan's riflemen were detached from the main army (then near Ramapo, N.J.); the brigades of Nixon and Glover were sent from Putnam's command (around Peekskill, N.Y.); and the fiery Benedict Arnold was assigned (without troops) to Schuyler. At Washington's suggestion, Lincoln was ordered to the Vermont area to organize and

command New England militia being assembled there. Governors of the New England colonies and N.Y. were urged to fill their quotas of Cont'ls. and to turn out their militia.

ST. LEGER'S EXPEDITION is covered separately, but we can devote a few words here to this unsuccessful diversion. St. Leger left Oswego on 26 July, reached Ft. Stanwix with his main body on 3 Aug., repulsed a militia relief column at ORISKANY, 6 Aug.; Arnold led another relief column from Schuyler's army, routed St. Leger's Indians by a ruse, and the invaders started withdrawing on 22 Aug.

BURGOYNE'S FIRST MISTAKE

In his "Thoughts," Burgoyne had stated an assumption that the Americans would have a sizable flotilla on Lake George which might bar use of this "most expeditious and most commodious route to Albany." In the same paper he also foresaw that along the alternate route overland from Skenesboro "considerable difficulties may be expected, as the narrow parts of the river [Wood Creek] may be easily choked up and rendered impassable, and at best there will be necessity for a great deal of land carriage for the artillery, provisions, etc., which can only be supplied from Canada." Despite the inadequacy of his transport (mentioned earlier) and the lack of real naval opposition on Lake George, however, Burgoyne elected to take the alternate route, using Lake George only for the movement of supplies and heavy artillery. He later justified this decision on two grounds: since all his boats were needed to move supplies, he could not have reached Ft. Edward with his army any faster via Lake George than by the route along Wood Creek; and, he said, a rearward movement from Ft. Anne, Hubbardton, and Skenesboro (where his pursuit had stopped) might be construed as weakness by "enemies and friends." (Nickerson, 86; Ward, 417, 418; Fiske, *Struggle,* II, 65–66) These explanations discredit the story that Philip SKENE talked him into the shorter, land route with the personal motive of getting a road built between Skene's property and the Hudson.

The Americans went to work to improve the obstructions nature had placed in Burgoyne's path from Skenesboro to Ft. Edward (on the Hudson). Schuyler sent 1,000 axmen to fell trees across Wood Creek and across the trails. They dug ditches to create additional quagmires in a region that was boggy to start with; they rolled boulders into the creek to obstruct boats and to cause overflows. It took the British 20 days to cover the 22 miles. They had to bridge at least 40 deep ravines, and in one place constructed a two-mile causeway. On 29 July Burgoyne reached Ft. Edward and his supply column, commanded by Gen. Phillips, took Ft. George, 15 miles N.W., at the tip of Lake George. The murder of Jane McCRAE, 27 July, had taken place about this time and was to have an unexpectedly great effect on subsequent operations.

It now became apparent that "the fatal defect in Burgoyne's plan was the inability to supply his army." (Greene, *Rev. War,* 109) His 185-mile line of communications between Montreal and Ft. Edward entailed 23 miles of land transportation on the northern end, 147 miles along the lakes (broken by a difficult portage at Ticonderoga) and 15 miles of rough country between Fts. George and Edward. (*Ibid.*) The invaders were in a thinly settled region that provided slim pickings for foragers, and the rebels had stripped the area of subsistence. The BENNINGTON RAID, 6–

16 Aug., prompted by Burgoyne's need for supplies, was a disaster that hastened his doom.

GATES SUCCEEDS SCHUYLER

Despite his shortcomings as a commander, Schuyler had scored successes that left Burgoyne no sound alternative but retreat. The virus of sectional FACTIONALISM finally led to Schuyler's being relieved, however, and Gates arrived on 19 Aug. to command the Northern Dept. At this time the patriot forces numbered about 4,000. Most of the troops were at the junction of the Hudson and Mohawk rivers, but Arnold was marching away toward Ft. Stanwix, 110 miles west, and the victors of Bennington were sitting on their laurels 30 miles to the east. The militia were rising to arms rapidly. Burgoyne probably could have saved his army by a prompt retreat, but his orders to take Albany and the faint hope of support from Howe induced him to press on south. (Greene, 115) Since Albany was on the west side of the Hudson, and the farther he went the more of an obstacle the river would present, he decided to cross to Saratoga. This meant abandoning communications with the lakes, since he could not spare troops to guard the crossing site, so he had laboriously built up 30 days' supplies to take with him.

On 13 Sept., with 6,000 rank and file, he started crossing to Saratoga, and two days later he dismantled his bridge of boats. Since all but 50 of his Indians had deserted by now, Burgoyne was in the dark as to the enemy situation; Gates, on the other hand, was well informed. On 12 Sept. the Americans had advanced north a short distance from Stillwater to occupy strong defensive terrain at Bemis Heights, where Arnold and Kosciuszko had laid out the lines.

The First Battle of SARATOGA, 19 Sept. '77, was fought around Freeman's Farm.

"Burgoyne was of a mind to attack Gates in full force on the day after the Battle of Freeman's Farm. Had he done so, it is quite possible that he would have won. The ill organized American army was in confusion.* * * So were the British, . . . but there is greater resilience in the regular soldier than in the militiaman." (Ward, *W.O.R.*, 521)

But Fraser argued that his grenadiers and light infantrymen, who were to make the first move, would do better after a day's rest, and Burgoyne decided to wait. The British were ready to attack on the 21st when Burgoyne received Clinton's letter of 12 Sept. Burgoyne had been clamoring for .help from Clinton since he decided to continue the advance south from Ft. Miller, and this rather involved and controversial feature of his offensive is dealt with in the article on CLINTON'S EXPEDITION. However, this first communication from Clinton, offering to make a diversion against the Highlands, had an unfortunate result in that Burgoyne called off his attack to await the outcome of Clinton's move, "and by that decision he lost the last chance for success in his enterprise, the last chance even for a safe retreat." (Ward, 521) This same day, 21 Sept., the British heard sounds of rejoicing from the unseen American positions on Bemis Heights and a few days later they learned the noise was occasioned by news of John Brown's TICONDEROGA RAID.

BURGOYNE DIGS IN

The invaders now entrenched the positions they had taken up 20 Sept. in preparation for the canceled attack. Facing south along the plateau between the Hudson and the North Branch (of Mill Creek) were the Germans of Riedesel's column (on the east) and Hamilton's four regiments (the 9th, 20th, 21st, and 62d). Outposts were established a few hundred yards in front of these positions. Continuing west, the line was manned by units of Gen. Fraser's Advance Corps, the grenadiers, the 24th Regt., and the British light infantry, from east to west. The light infantry, under Balcarres, occupied the key terrain feature of Burgoyne's entire position: the salient at Freeman's Farm, where they built the fortification known as the Balcarres Redoubt. The German Advance Corps of Breymann was about 500 yards north of the latter position, and the intervening gap was screened by a few Canadians in stockaded cabins. Bateaux and stores were collected at the mouth of the Great Ravine (Wilbur's Basin) and a bridge of boats was constructed across the Hudson at this point. Three redoubts, one known as the Great Redoubt, were started on the high ground overlooking this area and about 600 yards west of the river's edge.

Burgoyne's strength had been reduced to about 5,000, and his desertions were mounting. The troops had been on a diet of salt pork and flour for some time, and on 3 Oct. their rations were reduced by one third Horses were starving to death. To add to the misery, the Americans harassed them continually. "I do not believe that either officer or soldier ever slept during that interval [20 Sept.–7 Oct.] without his cloaths, or that any general officer, or commander of a regiment, passed a single night without being upon his legs occasionally at different hours and constantly an hour before daylight," wrote Burgoyne. (Quoted in Ward, 525)

THE AMERICAN SITUATION

The only change in the defenses of Bemis Heights was the fortification of the high ground half a mile west of the Neilson House that Burgoyne had selected as his objective on 19 Sept. But Gates was reinforced heavily. All Lincoln's militia (from the Bennington region) had joined by 29 Sept., and other militia arrived from New England and N.Y. By 4 Oct. Gates had more than 7,000 troops and three days later he had 11,000; of this total, 2,700 were Cont'ls. Thanks to Schuyler, Gates's ammunition had been replenished. As mentioned above, the Americans were aggressively harassing the enemy in a situation ideally suited to militia operations, and patriot morale was high. The enemy was unable to probe through this swarm of skirmishers to gather essential information about the Bemis Heights positions.

BURGOYNE'S LAST EFFORT

On 4 Oct. Burgoyne proposed a turning movement around the American west flank while 800 men remained behind to guard the supplies. His generals talked him out of this foolhardy plan. Riedesel then proposed a retreat to the vicinity of Ft. Miller where they could re-establish communications with Canada and await help from Clinton, but Burgoyne insisted on making one more attempt to accomplish his mission. His reconnaissance in force led to the Battle of Bemis Heights or Second SARATOGA, 7 Oct.

After his defeat in this action and the loss of Breymann's Redoubt, Burgoyne's entrenched position was untenable and he withdrew, in good order, to the Great Redoubt and vicinity. The Americans occupied his former positions on the 8th, and Gates sent B.G. John Fellows with 1.300 Mass. militia

to get astride the enemy's line of retreat to Saratoga. Fellows moved up the east side of the Hudson, forded the river to Saratoga, and encamped west of that place. B.G. Jacob Bayley was already posted with 2,000 N.H. militia near Ft. Edward. Burgoyne was not hurried in his withdrawal, however, since the American supply system was so primitive that they had to pull troops back to Bemis Heights to draw and prepare rations; furthermore they would need all day of 9 Oct. for this purpose.

The evening of 8 Oct., leaving campfires burning to deceive the enemy, Burgoyne started north. Lt. Col. Sutherland had moved out earlier with the 9th and 47th Regts. to reconnoiter the route, and he reported back that Fellows' camp was unguarded. Burgoyne refused to let Sutherland attack it, and at 2 A.M. the main body of Burgoyne's army started going into bivouac within three miles of where "Fellows' farmer soldiers snored unmolested around their fires. . . ." (Nickerson, 375) After a march slowed by heavy rain and the need to keep abreast of the bateaux being rowed laboriously up the river, they did not reach Saratoga until late evening of the 9th. Their hospital had been left behind with more than 300 sick and wounded; tents and much baggage had been abandoned on the march when wagons could no longer be manhandled through the deepening mud; stragglers and many bateaux had been captured by bands of pursuers that hung on their flanks and rear.

The natural strength of Burgoyne's new position, in addition to the exhaustion of his troops and of himself, led him to succumb to "the fatal attraction of a fortress." When the little Baroness Riedesel expressed her astonishment to Gen. Phillips, he replied, "Completely wet through you still have the courage to go farther in this weather? Would that you were only our commanding general." (Quoted in Nickerson, 376)

Having given his opponent 36 hours' start, Gates finally got moving the afternoon of 10 Oct.; his forward elements approached the Fishkill between 2 P.M. (according to Riedesel) and 4 P.M. (according to Wilkinson). The British rear guard (Hamilton with the 20th, 21st, and 62d Regts.) withdrew across the creek, burning the Schuyler Mansion on Burgoyne's order. Gates suddenly became aggressive, and his troops were spared a bad mauling only because the strength of the enemy position was learned at the last minute. Sutherland had started for Ft. Edward from Saratoga on 10 Oct. with the two regiments mentioned earlier, some Canadians, and a party of artificers to build a bridge across the Hudson for Burgoyne's retreat. When this movement was reported to Gates, this general assumed that Sutherland's command was Burgoyne's main body. He was therefore heading blindly through a thick fog the morning of 11 Oct. to attack what he thought was merely a rear guard north of the Fishkill when John Glover picked up a British deserter who revealed the true situation. The attack was called off in the nick of time, and an almost certain defeat was avoided. (Ward, 534) On the 11th the Americans captured most of the enemy's bateaux, which deprived Burgoyne of his bridging equipment and increased Gates's capability for moving troops across the Hudson.

As Gates tightened the siege on 12 Oct., taking up positions on all sides but the north, Burgoyne presented a council of war with five proposals: (1) Stand fast and await events (he still hoped CLINTON'S EXPEDITION would help him); (2) Attack; (3) Fight northward to Ft. Edward, taking all guns

and baggage; (4) Abandon the latter and slip away under cover of darkness; or, (5) Should Gates shift more strength westward (perhaps to cut them off), to strike south for Albany. The British generals, Burgoyne, Phillips, and Hamilton, toyed with the fifth proposal, but Riedesel convinced them that only the fourth proposal made sense. The way north was still open when this plan was adopted, but when Riedesel notified headquarters at 10 P.M. that he was ready to move, word came back that the operation was canceled. It turned out that the gap had been closed on the north, and the man who had done it was Burgoyne's evil spirit, John Stark.

Gentleman Johnny is alleged to have turned to his "Civil Affairs Advisor," Philip SKENE, about this time and asked for his suggestion on how to get out of the trap. "Scatter your baggage, stores, and everything else that can be spared, at proper distances," said Skene, "and the militia will be so busy plundering them that you and the troops will get clean off." (Nickerson, 386) The more you ponder this proposal the less frivolous it becomes.

The SARATOGA SURRENDER, 17 Oct. '77, was inevitable.

SIGNIFICANCE

This campaign has been called the turning point of the Revolution because it led to the FRENCH ALLIANCE, without which the revolution would have failed. (Nickerson, 404) Saratoga bolstered American morale at a time when the PHILADELPHIA CAMPAIGN was giving it a beating. (It is interesting to speculate on the place of Saratoga in history if it had led to a successful CONWAY CABAL and Gates had succeeded Washington as C. in C.) The Americans captured matériel of vast importance to their cause, including 5,000 stand of small arms.

BURGOYNE'S PROCLAMATION
and Speech to his Indians, 23 June '77.* (BURGOYNE'S OFFENSIVE) While camped at Bouquet (or Bongrett) Ferry, 40 miles north of Ticonderoga, Burgoyne issued an "extraordinary document [that] shows Burgoyne at his worst." (Nickerson, *Turning Point,* 122) About the same time he gave his Indian allies a speech that was supposed to make them fight humanely. The two efforts at military rhetoric exposed him to ridicule from both sides of the Atlantic. (See below.)

After an introductory enumeration of his titles and a general comment on the justice of his cause, his political proclamation read:

"To the eyes and ears of the temperate part of the public, and to the breasts of the suffering thousands [of Loyalists] in the Provinces, be the melancholy appeal, whether the present unnatural Rebellion has not been made a foundation for the compleatest system of tyranny that ever God in his displeasure suffered for a time to be exercised over a froward [perverse] and stubborn generation.* * * Animated by these considerations, at the head of troops in the full power of health, discipline and valour, determined to strike when necessary, and anxious to spare when possible, I, by these presents, invite and exhort all persons, in all places where the progress of this army may point (and by the blessing of God I will extend it), to maintain such a con-

* Both on this date, according to C. & M., 544, 548. Nickerson quotes the proclamation in its entirety and shows 20 June as the date it was signed; he says the Indians were addressed the next day. (*Op. cit.,* 122, 123)

duct as may justify me in protecting their lands, habitations and families. The intention of this address is to hold forth security, not degradation. . . . The domestic, the industrious and even the timid inhabitants I am desirous to protect, provided they remain quietly in their houses. . . . [But, lest the others misjudge his mettle, he went on to say] I have but to give stretch to the Indian forces under my direction (and they amount to thousands [400, actually]) to overtake the hardened enemies of Great Britain and America."

Assembling his Indians in council, he started off with a why-we-fight dissertation "in his most animated House of Commons manner, his words being translated from time to time by an interpreter." (Nickerson, 123) He then said he would like to lay down a few simple rules:

"I positively forbid bloodshed, when you are not opposed in arms. Aged men, women, children and prisoners must be held sacred from the knife or hatchet, even in the time of actual conflict.* * * In conformity and indulgence of your customs, which have affixed an idea of honor to such badges of victory, you shall be allowed to take the scalps of the dead when killed by your fire and in fair opposition; but on no account . . . are they to be taken [otherwise]."

THE REACTIONS

After an initial flush of rage, Americans started laughing, and the more literate reached for their goose quills and foolscap. The most widely publicized of many satirical retorts—attributed to Francis ("BATTLE OF THE KEGS") HOPKINSON—included these lines:

By such important views there pres't to,
I issue this my manifesto.
I, the great knight of de la Mancha,
Without 'Squire Carleton, my Sancho,

Will tear you limb from limb asunder
With cannon, blunderbuss and thunder;
And spoil your feathering and your
    tarring;
And cagg you up for pickled herring.
(Quoted in C. & M., 549)

Another anonymous American commented, "General Burgoyne shone forth in all the tinsel splendour of enlightened absurdity." (Montross, *Rag, Tag,* 198) In England, Horace WALPOLE suggested that "the vaporing Burgoyne," whom he also referred to as "Pomposo," and "Hurlothrumbo," "might compose a good liturgy for the use of the King's friends, who ... have the same consciousness of Christianity, and ... like him can reconcile the scalping knife with the Gospel." In the House of Commons, Edmund BURKE evoked a picture of the keeper of the royal menagerie turning loose his charges with this Burgundian admonition: "My gentle lions, my humane bears, my sentimental wolves, my tender-hearted hyenas, go forth: but I exhort ye as ye are Christians and members of a civilized society, to take care not to hurt man, woman or child." (Montross, 198; a slightly different version is in C. & M., 544)

BURKE, Edmund. 1729–1797. British opposition statesman. Born in Dublin of a Protestant father and a Catholic mother, he graduated from Trinity College, Dublin, entered the Middle Temple, but abandoned the law to become a writer. His *Vindication of Natural Society* and *Philosophical Inquiry into the Origin of Our Ideas of the Sublime and Beautiful* established his reputation when they appeared in 1756. The next year he collaborated with another author, probably his cousin William Burke, on *An Account of the European Settlements in America.* From an historical point of view his most interesting writing was in the highly influential *Annual Register,* which he conceived in 1758 (*E.B.,* "Burke") and edited during the period 1759–97. A recent study has this to say about Burke's hidden influence on American history books:

"Few Englishmen had so profound a knowledge of colonial affairs as did Burke. His *Annual Register* articles were copious, acutely observant, and warmly sympathetic. Little wonder that the post-revolutionary writers naturally gravitated to them. Unfortunately, in that age when literary property was so little respected, practically every major American writer dealing with the era plagiarized shamelessly from the *Annual Register.* So it was with the most respected names—David Ramsay, John Marshall, William Gordon, and many more. The less pretentious popular historians merely borrowed the *Annual Register* at second-hand, via Ramsay, Marshall, Gordon, *et al.* These plagiarisms were uncovered a half-century ago by Professor Orin G. Libby and others, but Marshall's dereliction was found only in 1948.* * * Libby, who studied practically all of the histories of the American Revolution, finally concluded in disgust: 'Will it not be profitable, now that the last of the contemporary American historians yields his place of authority, to compile from the *Annual Register,* a history of the American Revolution which shall be known for what it is under its true colors?'" (Harvey Wish, *The American Historian.* New York, 1960)

Burke was private secretary to William Gerard ("Single-Speech") Hamilton, 1761–63, while this despicable politician was Irish Secretary. He then was Rockingham's private secretary, 1765–82. During the first year of this period Rockingham was prime minister. Entering Parliament for the rotten borough of Wendover as a Whig in 1766, he immediately made his presence felt by the force of his character and his brilliant oratory. It was Burke who did more than any one else to give to the Opposition, under the first half of the reign of George III, the stamp of elevation and grandeur." (*E.B.*) For the next 25 years he was a key figure in the revived Whig party. He protested against the coercive policies of the government against the colonies in a series of brilliant papers and speeches, several of which are studied today as models of English composition (of a certain sort). These memorable works include speeches on *American Taxation* (1774) and *Conciliation with America* (1775), and the *Letter to the Sheriffs of Bristol* (1777).

The opposition of the Opposition was too firmly entrenched, however, for Burke's influence to affect the course of events in London. After coercion had led to American independence and the war ministry had fallen, Burke was rewarded with the post of Paymaster of the Forces in the ministries of Rockingham and Portland (1782–83). He then became involved in drafting the famous East India Bill, and he reached new heights of oratory in his impeachment of Hastings (1785–94). With the acquittal of Hastings in 1794 Burke withdrew from Parliament and passed the torch to his only son, Richard. The latter appears from all contemporary evidence to have been completely devoid of ability in any form, but his premature death in the summer of 1794 was a crushing blow to the father. "The storm has gone over me," he said in a memorable speech. "They who should have been to me as posterity are in the place of ancestors." (See also LOGAN.)

A new edition of Burke's papers is T. W. Copeland (ed.), *The Correspondence of Edmund Burke* (Chicago, 1958–1963). Other volumes will follow the four that were issued by 1963.

BURKE, Thomas. *c.* 1747–1783. Congressman, Gov. of N.C. Ireland–Va.–N.C. After attending a university in Ireland he went to Va. and in 1771 moved to the vicinity of Hillsboro, N.C. He played a prominent part in the politics of his region and then served in the Cont'l. Cong. from Feb. '77 to June '81. As a delegate he championed civil rights whenever they appeared menaced by military power, and he was responsible for assuring that states be guaranteed any powers not specifically delegated by the Articles of Confederation to Cong. He is famous in the history of the Cont'l. Cong. for his performance in Apr. '78: disapproving of a proposed message to Washington and seeing that his presence was necessary to make a quorum, he simply walked out of the hall in which the delegates were meeting. It was 10 P.M., a motion to adjourn had failed, and when summoned to return Burke replied that "it was too late and too unreasonable." When Congress attempted the next day to discipline him Burke replied that he was responsible to his state and would not be tyrannized by a majority of Congress. Returning to N.C., he was exonerated and re-elected. He went back to Congress in Aug. The irony is that about the time he defied the authority of Congress he had been defeated in his state for re-election because he had favored the appointment of a Pa. officer over N.C. troops!

Burke returned to Hillsboro about the time the South became the major theater of operations. When the regulars under Kalb and Gates moved through N.C., Burke led resistance to what many people of his state considered to be unwarranted demands of Cont'l. officers for supplies. The well-fed N.C. militia of Maj. Gen. Richard Caswell therefore marched uselessly around the state and refused to join the regulars until just before the CAMDEN CAMPAIGN. In June '81 Burke was elected Gov. of N.C. and vigorously undertook to stiffen the spine of his people; Burke had won on the political point of civil authority versus military, but the British regulars, meanwhile, were chasing the ragged Cont'l. troops across his state and the performance of the N.C. militia had been sorry indeed. (Under SOUTHERN CAMPAIGNS OF GREENE see section headed "Opns. on the Yadkin.")

David Fanning captured Gov. Burke and his council in his HILLSBORO RAID, 12 Sept. '81. After being closely confined at Wilmington and then on Sullivan's Island in Charleston harbor, in Nov. Burke was paroled to James Island. When told that he was considered to be a hostage to guarantee the life of Fanning (should the latter be captured), lawyer Burke reasoned that his parole was no longer binding. He also claimed that he was fired on while at James Island. He escaped the night of 16 Jan. '82 (Appleton's), went to Greene's Hq., and on the latter's advice (D.A.B.) informed the British that he would return if they guaranteed the terms of his parole, or that he would arrange an exchange. Receiving no reply from Gen. Leslie, Burke returned to N.C. and completed his term as Gov. He refused to stand for re-election in the spring of 1782 and died the next year at his estate, "Tyaquin" (named for the family seat in County Galway). (Ibid.)

BURR, Aaron. 1756–1836. Cont'l. officer, 3d V.P., conspirator. N.J. Son of Aaron Burr (Sr.), 2d Pres. of Princeton, and grandson of Jonathan Edwards, "the greatest of New England divines" (D.A.B), young Aaron was a bright, attractive, unruly child. He grad-

uated with distinction from the College of N.J. (later Princeton) at the age of 16, studied theology until 1774, and then left this for the law.

THE SOLDIER

An "unattached volunteer" on ARNOLD'S MARCH TO QUEBEC, he survived the blast that killed Montgomery at Quebec and is credited with trying to evacuate his corpse. In his service with Arnold—the march, the attack, and the siege—he proved himself to be an outstanding soldier. In the spring of 1776 he was sent from Canada to N.Y.C., where he joined Washington's staff. After a few weeks he left headquarters, and during this time a mutual dislike and distrust had developed between the bright boy and his C. in C. On 22 June Burr became A.D.C. to Gen. Putnam, at which post he conducted himself admirably in the battle of Long Island and in the evacuation of N.Y.C. On 4 Jan. '77 he was commissioned Lt. Col. of MALCOLM'S REGT. Since this is the first regular rank that Heitman gives for him, presumably Burr was still in a volunteer category when he became Capt. on Arnold's staff in Canada, and Maj. on the staffs of Washington and Putnam. Stationed in Orange co., N.Y., the 21-year-old Burr was virtual commander of Malcolm's Regt., and he established a reputation for audacity and good discipline. (D.A.B.) After winter quarters at Valley Forge, where he barely missed getting involved in the "Conway Cabal," Burr commanded a brigade during the Monmouth campaign. Having suffered a repulse in the action of 28 June, he openly sided with Charles Lee in the controversy that followed. He then commanded his regiment in Westchester co., N.Y., where he maintained his reputation for discipline and alert soldiering in the field. On 3 Mar. '79 he resigned on grounds of ill health, and it was not until the fall of the next year that he was well enough to resume his study of law.

BURR AND HAMILTON

Burr became successful in this profession. In 1783 he moved to N.Y., and for six years he shared with Alexander Hamilton the pick of the practice. His attempts to enter politics were unsuccessful until Gov. Geo. Clinton made him his attorney general in Sept. '89. In 1791 he was elected U.S. senator, and during his six-year term he twice was mentioned for the governorship. Not re-elected to the Senate, he won a seat in the state legislature but lost it in Apr. '99. He then set about organizing the Democratic element of N.Y.C., and with a thoroughness not previously seen in local politics he used the St. Tammany's Society of mechanics and small householders to create a powerful political machine. When this resulted in the unexpected capture of the state legislature by the Democrats, which in turn meant that this pivotal state would insure the election of a Democratic president, the party decided to make Jefferson president and Burr V.P. Perhaps because of the newness of the party system, or perhaps because Burr contrived to have Republican Congressmen pledge him the same number of votes as Jefferson, these two men ended up with 73 electoral votes each. Choosing between two bitter political enemies, HAMILTON threw his weight behind the better man, and Jefferson was elected. As V.P., Burr presided over the Senate in a manner that won praise from both parties. His supporters nominated him for Gov. of N.Y. in 1804, but he was badly beaten by the regular Republican candidate, Morgan Lewis. Burr felt that for the third time he had been the victim of Hamilton's political enmity.

Hamilton and Burr met at 10 paces the morning of 11 July 1804 at Weehawken. Each man fired, and Hamilton fell mortally wounded. Burr retained his post in Jefferson's administration, presiding over the impeachment of Sam'l. CHASE. His most bitter critics praised his conduct of the trial, and on 2 Mar. 1805 he delivered a remarkable valedictory address.

THE CONSPIRATOR

War with Spain seemed inevitable to many Americans, and for some time Burr and Wilkinson had been making plans to capitalize on this eventuality. In commenting on Thomas P. Abernethy's *Burr Conspiracy* (New York, 1954), the L.O.C. *Guide* gives this summary:

"Burr envisioned himself as being at the head of an empire vaster than that which he had lost by a single vote in 1801. From 1804 Burr's major objective was the separation of the Western States from the Union, with New Orleans as the capital and the Alleghenies as the eastern boundary of the new political unit. Also involved were filibustering expeditions into the Floridas and Mexico, and the settlement of the Bastrop lands. Ever an opportunist, Burr presented to anyone who would listen to his scheme only such portions of it as would appeal to him as a prospective conspirator. The success of the conspiracy, which, Professor Abernethy asserts, next to the Confederate War 'posed the greatest threat of dismemberment which the American Union has ever faced,' depended upon disaffection in the West, the intrigues of certain Eastern Federalists, the adherence of various land speculators, soldiers of fortune, and office seekers, a war between the United States and Spain, and help from Great Britain. The basic patriotism and common sense of the frontiersmen, along with the defection of Burr's fellow conspirator, James Wilkinson, doomed Burr's plot, which ended in the farcical trial of 1807 at Richmond." (*Op. cit.,* 349)

Despite the personal influence of President Jefferson, on 1 Sept. 1807 the jury, basing its decision on "evidence submitted," acquitted Burr and his associates of treason. When Jefferson urged the district attorney to press the charge of misdemeanor, the jury again decided in Burr's favor. In June 1808 Burr sailed for England, where he tried to get official support of his plan for a revolution in Mexico. Ordered out of the country, he spent several months in Sweden, Denmark, and Germany before appearing in Paris (Feb. 1810), where he hoped to interest Napoleon in his schemes. Failing to secure any French support, he was reduced to direst poverty before he could secure a passport (July 1811) for America. The French ship on which he sailed was captured by the British, and after being detained in England he finally reached the U.S. in May 1812. For the rest of his life he pursued his law practice in N.Y.C.

HUSBAND AND FATHER

The 5 foot-6 inch Burr was notorious for his lurid love life which, if the tradition perpetuated in Kenneth Roberts' *Rabble in Arms* is to be credited, was sustained even on the march to Quebec. In July '82 he married Mrs. Theodosia Bartow Prevost, widow of a British officer. She was some 10 years his senior (he being 26), and a semi-invalid, but their 12 years of marriage (terminated by her death) were happy and intellectually stimulating to both. (*D.A.B.*) The one child of this union, Theodosia (1783–1813), grew up to be a woman of great charm and—thanks to the discipline of her devoted

but demanding father—a woman who could use her mind. She blindly adored her notorious father, and her loss at sea in 1813 was a crushing blow to him. In July 1833, the 77-year-old Burr married the widow of Stephen JUMEL. Seeing her hard-earned fortune about to be dissipated in land speculation, the aging adventuress and the aged adventurer were separated after four months, and in July 1834 she sued for divorce. This was granted on the day of his death, 14 Sept. 1836.

AUTHORITIES

According to I. J. Cox, whose *D.A.B.* sketch of Burr includes a good critical bibliography, the most important printed sources for Burr are M. L. Davis, *Memoirs of Aaron Burr* (2 vols., 1836–37) and *The Private Journal of Aaron Burr During His Residence in Europe* (2 vols., 1838, repr. 1903). James Parton, *The Life and Times of Aaron Burr* (1st ed., 1857; enlarged ed., 2 vols., 1858), a sympathetic account, probably remains the standard biography. More recent works, which Cox considers overly favorable on certain points, are Isaac Jenkinson, *Aaron Burr, His Personal and Political Relations with Thos. Jefferson and Alex. Hamilton* (1902) and S. H. Wandell and Meade Minnegerode, *Aaron Burr* (1925). A later work, sympathetic but relatively good, is Nathan Schachner, *Aaron Burr: A Biography* (N.Y., 1937). Abernethy, *The Burr Conspiracy,* has been cited above.

BUSHNELL, David. *c.* 1742–1824. Inventor of submarine. Conn. While a student at Yale, 1771–75, he demonstrated to skeptical instructors that gunpowder could be detonated under water, and he subsequently built a man-propelled submarine. His "American Turtle" was so called because the top-shaped craft of heavy oak beams was said to look like two turtle shells joined together with the tail end pointed downward. Unsuccessfully tried in the waters around Boston, N.Y.C., New London, and Philadelphia, 1776–78, the American Turtle proved that it could dive, travel under water, plant a large time-charge of powder against the hull of a ship, navigate under water, and surface, but primarily because no skillful operator was ever found, the submarine never sank a warship. (His operator was Sgt. Ezra Lee of the Conn. Line.) His attack on the *Eagle* (64) in N.Y. harbor failed in 1776. An attack on the *Cerberus* the next year off New London also failed, but a nearby schooner was blown up. Bushnell contrived various other devices to harry British shipping, and his unsuccessful attack in Jan. '78 inspired Hopkinson's "BATTLE OF THE KEGS."

Although the public guffawed at the failures of silly inventions that have since become standard weapons of naval warfare, Bushnell's technical qualifications were recognized by the army and on 2 Aug. '79 he was commissioned Capt.-Lt. of the newly organized Corps of Sappers and Miners. On 8 June '81 he was promoted to Capt. of Engrs., and on 4 June '83 he was given command of the Corps of Engrs. at West Point. When that body was disbanded he was mustered out in Nov. '83. He is believed to have lived in France for the next 10 or 12 years. In 1795 he appeared in Columbia co., Ga., under the assumed name of Dr. Bush. Through the assistance of Abraham Baldwin (1754–1807), a fellow veteran and the only man who knew his identity, "Dr. Bush" became head of a private school. Some time later, presumably after the death of Baldwin, he established a medical practice at Warrenton, Ga. (*D.A.B.*)

BUSHY RUN, Pa., 5–6 Aug. '63. This remarkable action, in which British troops under the Swiss officer, Col. Henry Bouquet, defeated the Indians in their own tactics of frontier warfare, is covered under PONTIAC'S WAR.

BUSKIRK, Abram Van. Lt. Col. in Tory Brig. of Cortlandt Skinner. Mentioned in article on PAULUS HOOK.

BUTE, Fort. Named for Lord Bute, it was at MANCHAC POST.

BUTE, John Stuart, 3d Earl of. 1713–1792. British prime minister. Known as "the Northern Thane," and characterized by an American historian as "the most hated man in the kingdom" (Miller, *O.A.R.*, 68), this Scottish peer had quietly pursued his interests in agriculture and botany until 1747. Having resided in England for the past two years (since "The '45"—see CULLODEN), he was summoned to make up a whist party with the Prince of Wales when a downpour of rain prevented the latter's departure from the Egham races. He immediately gained the favor of the prince and his sister, and soon was an important personage in the court. The public believed that he was the lover of the future George III's mother, but this almost certainly was not true. "The slander deeply distressed George III and made his attachment to Bute firmer," writes J. H. Plumb. (See GEORGE III)

When George III ascended the throne in 1760, the former pupil and his tutor went to work on their long projected strategy of concluding peace with France and destroying Whig control of power. On 25 Mar. '61 Bute became secretary of state for the northern department, and on 3 Nov. he appeared in the House of Lords as successor to the great Chatham, who had resigned the post of prime minister the preceding month. "His short administration was one of the most disgraceful and incompetent in English history," says the sketch in *E.B.* "Yet Bute had good principles and intentions . . . and his character remains untarnished by the grosser accusations raised by faction." He resigned on 8 Apr. '63, pleading ill health. "Fifty pounds a year and bread and water were luxury compared with what I suffer," he commented. For a short time Bute retained his influence over the king through Grenville, who had become P.M. on Bute's recommendation. When Grenville refused to be part of this arrangement, Bute tried to have him dismissed. This failed in Aug. '63 and the king agreed to Grenville's demand that Bute be removed from the court. In May '65 Grenville asked the king that he eliminate Bute from the political scene entirely, and George III complied. Muttering about ingratitude, Bute decided "to retire from the world before it retires from me."

BUTLER, Edward. Youngest of the five BUTLER BROTHERS of Pa., he became Capt. in Gibson's Regt. of Pa. levies in 1791 and was present at St. Clair's defeat. (See BUTLER BROTHERS) He became Wayne's A.G. in 1796, and was a Maj. in the permanent reorganization of 1802. He died at Ft. Wilkinson, Ga., 6 May 1803.

BUTLER, John. 1725–1796. Loyalist leader. N.Y. Born in New London, Conn., he moved with his parents to the Mohawk Valley, where his father, Capt. Walter Butler, had for many years commanded at Ft. Hunter and at Oswego. John served as a Capt. in Sir Wm. Johnson's expedition against Crown Point in 1755, under Abercromby at Ticonderoga, under Bradstreet in the expedition against Ft. Frontenac, and he was Johnson's second in command in the capture of Ft. Niagara. Forced to flee with his son Walter, Guy

Johnson, and Daniel Claus when Revolutionary sentiment reached the Mohawk, he managed Indian affairs in Canada as the deputy of Guy Johnson during the latter's long absence. As explained under Guy JOHNSON, Butler's policy was to keep the savages neutral, in accordance with instructions from Carleton. Butler took part in St. Leger's Expedition. After this unsuccessful operation he recruited his rangers from the refugee Loyalists at Niagara. He led these (with certain reinforcements) in the remarkable raid to WYOMING VALLEY. The patriots responded to this and other raids with SULLIVAN'S EXPEDITION, and in the only pitched battle of this campaign Butler was defeated at NEWTOWN, 29 Aug. '79. Early the next year Haldimand promoted him to Lt. Col. (Swiggett, *Niagara,* 207.) Despite contemporary opinion and historical statements to the contrary (e.g., *D.A.B.,* "John Butler"), evidently neither of the Butlers took part in Sir John Johnson's raid into the Schoharie and Mohawk valleys in the spring of 1780. (*Ibid.,* 214)

His property confiscated by the Act of Attainder of 22 Oct. '79, he was given land and a pension by the British. He was active in the establishment of a Tory settlement around Niagara, a project which he started in the summer of 1780. After the war he was commissioner of Indian affairs at Niagara, where he died on 14 May '96.

Father of Walter BUTLER.

BUTLER, Percival. 1760–1821. Cont'l. officer. Pa. Next to youngest of the BUTLER BROTHERS, he become 2d Lt., 3d Pa., on 1 Sept. '77, was promoted to 1st Lt. on 23 Nov. '77, and on 1 Jan. '83 transferred to the 2d Pa. He fought with Morgan at Saratoga, with Wayne against Simcoe at Spencer's Tavern, and took part in the siege of Yorktown. Serving to the end of the war, he moved to Ky. and was A.G. in the War of 1812.

BUTLER, Richard. 1743–1791. Cont'l. officer. Ireland–Pa. One of the BUTLER BROTHERS, Richard was an ensign on Bouquet's expedition of 1764 (see also PONTIAC'S WAR). With his brother William he was subsequently an Indian trader at CHILLICOTHE and Pittsburgh and led a Pa. company against the latter place in the Pa.-Va. dispute preceding DUNMORE'S WAR. In 1775 he was made an Indian agent but soon entered active military service: he was commissioned Capt., 2d Pa. Bn. on 5 Jan. '76 and promoted to Maj. of the 8th Pa. Cont'l. Regt. on 20 July. On 12 Mar. '77 he became Lt. Col, of this regt. with date of rank from 28 Sept. '76. (Heitman, 51, 137) He commanded the 8th Pa. at BOUND BROOK, N.J., 13 Apr. '77. (Freeman, *Washington*, IV, 409 *n.*) Joining Morgan's Riflemen in the spring, he took part in the battles around SARATOGA (Oct. '77). He is shown as commander of the 9th Pa. from 7 June '77 until 17 Jan. '81 (Heitman, 51) but led provisional units at various times during this period (e.g., Saratoga and Stony Point). During the British movements mentioned under TAPPAN MASSACRE, Butler's men (presumably the 8th Pa.) got the better of a skirmish above Kings Bridge (Manhattan) on 30 Sept. '78. (Freeman, *op. cit.*, V, 78) He led the 2d Regt. of Wayne's Lt. Inf. Brig. at STONY POINT, 16 July '79. During the MUTINY OF THE PA. LINE, Jan. '81, he and William Butler accompanied Wayne to Princeton to negotiate with the mutineers; since the latter refused to let any other officers deal with them, this can be construed as a mark of distinction. In the reorganization of 17 Jan. '81 Butler took command of the 5th Pa., which became part of WAYNE'S LIGHT INFAN-

TRY that joined Lafayette in June '81. He led the attack on Simcoe at SPENCER'S TAVERN, Va., 26 June, and took part in the engagement at GREEN SPRING, 6 July. In the siege of Yorktown he led the 2d Pa. Bn. of Wayne's Brig. in Steuben's Div. After the surrender of Cornwallis he marched with Wayne to the Carolinas and subsequently into Ga. Butler commanded the 3d Pa. from 1 July to 3 Nov. '83 and on 30 Sept. of that year was breveted B.G.

After the war Richard Butler became an Indian commissioner and took part in negotiating a series of important boundary treaties during the period 1784–86. In the latter year he was made Superintendent of Indian Affairs for the Northern District. (*D.A.B.* Heitman has the confusing statement that Butler was appointed Indian agent 17 May '78 "and lost rank in the army." Appleton's says he was agent for Indian affairs in Ohio in 1787, which indicates that Heitman's date is victim of a transposition.) In 1791 Butler was named Maj. Gen. of U.S. Levies, an appointment viewed with alarm by officers who were aware of his meager qualifications. Commanding the right wing of Arthur St. Clair's expedition against the Miami Indians, Butler was mortally wounded in the battle of 4 Nov. '91. (See BUTLER BROS., and Simon GIRTY.)

Richard Butler's "Journal of the Siege of Yorktown," *Historical Magazine,* VIII (Mar. 1864) is often cited by historians.

BUTLER, Thomas. 1754–1805. Cont'l. officer. Pa. One of the five BUTLER BROTHERS, he had been studying law with Judge Wilson in Philadelphia when he joined the Cont'l. army 5 Jan. '76 as a 1st Lt. in the 2d Pa. Bn. On 4 Oct. '76 he was promoted to Capt. in the 3d Pa. He fought in almost every major engagement of Washington's main army, being congratulated by the C. in C. for rallying retreating soldiers after Brandywine, and winning thanks from Wayne for covering the retreat of the regiment commanded by his brother Richard at Monmouth. Retiring from the army on 17 Jan. '81, he became a farmer in W. Pa. In 1791 he became a Maj. commanding the Carlisle Bn. of Gibson's Regt. and was twice wounded in the action of 4 Nov. (See BUTLER BROTHERS) A regular army Maj. on 11 Apr. '92, he was assigned to the 4th Sub Legion on 4 Sept. '92, became Lt. Col. on 1 July '94, was assigned to the 4th Inf. on 1 Nov. '96, and became Col. of the 2d Inf. on 1 Apr. 1802. During this time he took part in the operations of WAYNE. He died 7 Sept. 1805 in New Orleans.

BUTLER, Walter. 1752?-81. Tory leader. N.Y. In his *War out of Niagara: Walter Butler and the Tory Rangers*, which must be considered the definitive work on this man, author Harold Swiggett prefaces his study with these remarks:

"There is an absorbing mystery about his life and character. The date of his birth is unknown [but almost certainly is 1752, Swiggett says later]. There is a legend of his marriage to a daughter of Catharine Montour [see MONTOUR FAMILY], and another with a daughter of Sir William Johnson.* * * There is no physical description of him except in fiction. Letters about him in catalogues even of the Schuyler Papers, the Gates Papers, the Library of Congress, and many other papers, are mysteriously marked missing.* * * The histories have contented themselves with denouncing him as a bloody monster, but back of the histories in the primary material of the Revolution there is an amazing figure." (*Op. cit.*, 4-5)

A son of John BUTLER, he was raised in the Mohawk Valley. In 1768 he be-

came an ensign in the militia regiment of which his father was Lt. Col. (commissioned 18 Feb. '68), Guy Johnson was Col., and Jelles Fonda, Maj. In 1770 Walter, whom Swiggett calls "the most brilliant young man in the Valley," went to study law in the office of Peter Silvester in Albany. When news of Bunker Hill reached the Mohawk Valley, the Butlers, Guy Johnson, and Joseph Brant left for Oswego, where they arrived 17 July '75. (*Ibid.*, 62) Walter led a force of 30 Indians and rangers in an envelopment that defeated Ethan Allen at Montreal, 25 Sept. '75, and he took part in the action at the Cedars, in May '76. (*Ibid.*, 64-65, 71) As an ensign in the 8th ("King's") Regt. he accompanied St. Leger's Expedition and after taking part in the Oriskany ambush, he volunteered for "one of the bravest and most audacious enterprises of the war." (*Ibid.*, 90) With about 15 men he left the British camp around Ft. Stanwix on 10 or 11 Aug. and headed for German Flats with St. Leger's proclamation and the appeals of Sir John Johnson and John Butler for the inhabitants of the Mohawk Valley to join the loyal cause. He was holding a midnight meeting at Shoemaker's House when militia troops of Col. Weston, informed of his presence, surrounded the place and took him prisoner. On 21 Aug. he was convicted of espionage and sentenced to hang. Marinus Willett signed the minutes as J.A. and Benedict Arnold, who was on his way to relieve Ft. Stanwix, approved the sentence. (Swiggett, p. 92, gives 21 Aug. as the date of the trial and Arnold's arrival at German Flats, but the facsimile reproduced on the opposite page shows Willett's signature of the proceedings on 20 Aug.) Upon the intercession of various Cont'l. officers, including Schuyler, Butler was reprieved and imprisoned in Albany. On 21 Apr.

'78 he escaped from the house in which he apparently was living on parole. Down Lake Champlain to the St. Lawrence, Butler went first to Quebec and then to Niagara. His commission as Capt. had been signed 20 Dec., while he was imprisoned at Albany.

The CHERRY VALLEY MASSACRE, 11 Nov. '78, was Capt. Butler's most notorious operation. In Oct. '81 he accompanied Ross's raid to the Mohawk and was killed at JERSEYFIELD (Canada Creek), 30 Oct. '81. Swiggett comments on the various myths surrounding Butler's death. "There is a legend that Tories brought his body secretly to St. George's Church, Schenectady, and that he is buried there. It seems unlikely: wolves were closing in on the armies." (*Op. cit.*, 243) That Butler begged for quarter and that an Oneida shouted "Sherry Valley quarter" just before killing him with a tomahawk is shown by Swiggett to be "myth-making at its worst." (*Ibid.*, 251) Another fabrication, which even *D.A.B.* has perpetuated, was to give Butler a middle initial. He had no middle name, but Swiggett theorizes that "the infamous Walter N. Butler" sounded more villainous than "the infamous Walter Butler."

BUTLER, William. d. 1789. Cont'l. officer. Ireland–Pa. He and his brother Richard were born in Dublin before their father emigrated to Lancaster, Pa., where the other three BUTLER BROTHERS were born. (Appleton's; *D.A.B.*) After Bouquet's Expedition of 1764 the two elder brothers were partners at Chillicothe and Pittsburgh in the Indian trade. On 5 Jan. '76 William was made Capt. in the 2d Pa. Bn., and he advanced to Maj. on 7 Sept. '76, Lt. Col. of the 4th Pa. on 30 Sept. '76, and A.D.C. to Gen. Wm. Alexander on 7 May '78. Five months later he led the raid that wiped out Indian settlements around UNADILLA, N.Y., and he pub-

lished an account of that operation. When Sullivan's Expedition withdrew toward Wyoming, Butler was detached (20 Sept. '79) to destroy Indian villages east of Cayuga Lake; Zebulon Butler often is erroneously credited with leading this operation. (*D.A.B.*, III, 372, sets this straight. Lossing, I, 278, makes the mistake.) In the MUTINY OF THE PA. LINE he narrowly escaped death on 1 Jan. '81. On 17 Jan, in the reorganization that followed that mutiny, he became commander of the new 4th Pa., the regiment he had previously led as "Lt. Col. Commandant." According to Heitman he never was promoted to full Col. He retired 1 Jan '83 and died six years later. (Appleton's)

BUTLER, Zebulon, 1731–1795. Cont'l. officer. Conn. Grandson of Lt. Wm. Butler of Ipswich, Mass., and son of John and Hannah Perkins Butler, he was born at Ipswich but moved with his parents to their new home in Lyme, Conn., in 1736. After owning one or more sloops engaged in the West Indian trade, he saw service in the French and Indian War, rising from Ensign in 1757 to Capt. in 1760. He survived a shipwreck to arrive in time to participate in the siege of Havana in 1762. In 1796 he led the Conn. settlers to the Wyoming Valley and continued as their leader in the Pennamite Wars. (See WYOMING VALLEY "MASSACRE") In July '71 he forced the surrender of Pa. troops in Fort Wyoming, and on 20 Dec. '75 he drove back the Pa. troops under Col. Plunkett sent by Gov. Penn to establish a military government in the valley. Meanwhile he had served as director of the Susquehanna Company and represented Westmoreland in the Conn. Assy. (1774–76), and served (with Nathan Denison) as J.O.P.

When the war started he was commissioned Col. of militia and Denison became Lt. Col. On 1 Jan. '77 he became Lt. Col. of the 3d Conn. Cont'l. Regt. (Heitman; *D.A.B.* says he got this commission in 1776), and on 13 Mar. '78 he was promoted to Col. of the 2d Conn. Home on leave, he participated in the defense of the valley, but his part in what became known as the WYOMING VALLEY "MASSACRE" was not particularly creditable. He returned as commander in the valley and remained there during Sullivan's Expedition against the Iroquois in 1779. (Lt. Col. Wm. BUTLER, not Zebulon, as often stated, took part in the latter campaign.) At the request of the Cont'l. Cong., on 29 Dec. '80 Washington recalled Butler from Wyoming to reduce the friction there between the Conn. and Pa. elements. On 1 Jan. '81 he was transferred to the 4th Conn. Assigned to West Point, he became Col. of the 1st Conn. on 1 Jan. '83 and resigned on 3 June '83. He died at Wilkesbarre and was survived by his third wife.

BUTLER BROTHERS of Pa. The four eldest of five Butler brothers served together as Cont'l. officers in the Revolution, and three of the surviving four were together under St. Clair in the Indian expedition of 1791. Each is covered in a separate article, but certain common information can best be outlined here. The two elder sons of Thos. Butler, Wm. and Richard, were born in Dublin and went to America. The father followed sometime prior to 1754 (apparently without the mother of his first sons), and settled in Lancaster, Pa. Here Thos. (Jr.) was born in 1754, Percival in 1760, and then Edward. All but the latter, who presumably was too young, became officers in the Cont'l. army, and much of the time they were in the same unit or adjacent ones. At MONMOUTH, Thos. commanded a company whose rear guard action saved the regiment commanded by Richard. Wm. Butler died in 1789, but three of the four remaining brothers were together in the disastrous operations of St. Clair that led to the defeat of 4 Nov. '91. Richard, who commanded a wing of the army in which Thos. served as a Maj. and Edw. as a Capt., was mortally wounded and evacuated to the center of St. Clair's camp. Here Thos. was carried with two wounds, one of them being a broken leg. Before the retreat started, Edw. arrived to remove his brothers, but could take only one. Richard insisted that the other brother be saved, which Edw. did. The latter wrote to Percival, who had settled in Ky., "We left the worthiest of brothers . . . in the hands of the savages . . . nearly dead."

BUTLER–JOHNSON ENMITY. See under JOHNSON, Guy.

BUTLER'S RANGERS. Initially recruited in 1777 to a strength of eight companies by Tory Col. John BUTLER, they figured prominently in the BORDER WARFARE waged out of Canada. Their boldest operation resulted in the WYOMING VALLEY "MASSACRE," and the patriots retaliated with SULLIVAN'S EXPEDITION. They were disbanded in June '84. See works by E. A. Cruishank and Howard Swiggett.

BYNG, John. 1704–1757. British admiral. The son of George Byng, Viscount Torrington, a distinguished naval officer who became First Lord of the Admiralty (1727), John is famous in naval history for having been executed for failure to comply with the strict rules of tactics prescribed at the time. Sent to relieve the garrison on Minorca in 1756, he was defeated by the French fleet and withdrew without making a further effort. The French captured the island, Byng was acquitted of cowardice but was convicted of negligence and shot. His case loomed prominently in the minds of other British naval officers; it is referred to in connection with the sketch of Adm. George Brydges RODNEY and others.

BYRON, John ("Foul-weather Jack"). 1723–1786. British admiral. As a midshipman he sailed with Lord Anson for the Pacific and was shipwrecked 14 May '40 on the southern coast of Chile. His *Narrative* ..., published 1768, describes this experience and inspired the shipwreck scene in his grandson's *Don Juan*. During the period 1764–66 he conducted a secret exploration of the South Seas. These operations gained him his nickname and are reflected in Lord Byron's line, "He had no rest at sea, nor I on shore." ("Epistle to Augusta," quoted in Appleton's) Sir John Knox Laughton comments in *D.N.B.*, however, that although a "brave man, good seaman, and an esteemed officer," he lacked the qualities of an explorer and his journals include tall tales of giants who towered over his own six-foot frame. For three years starting Jan. '69 he was Gov. of Newfoundland. On 31 Mar. '75 he was promoted to Rear Adm. and on 29 Jan. '78 was Vice Adm. As successor to Adm. Howe he sailed from England on 9 June '78 with a "wretchedly equipped and badly manned" fleet. (*Ibid.*) Although he had the mission of intercepting d'Estaing, who had left Toulon with a large French fleet on 13 Apr., admiralty incompetence was responsible for this delay of five weeks. The first of the British ships did not reach Sandy Hook until 30 July, although this delay saved them from an encounter with d'Estaing, who had just sailed away. Storms had battered and scattered the British during the crossing and it was not until 18 Oct. that Byron could head to sea for operations. Struck almost immediately by another storm, his fleet was not again fit for action until 13 Dec. "Foul-weather Jack" then headed for the West Indies. Off Grenada, 6 July '79, he ordered his fleet of 21 ships to pursue and attack piecemeal a fleet under d'Estaing that he thought numbered only 16 ships. Even after counting 25 sails Byron did not cancel his orders. His leading ships were badly mauled and the two fleets were forming for a general action when the French unaccountably withdrew. "Only d'Estaing's incapacity saved him [Byron] from a thorough beating," comments the British authority previously cited. After some inconclusive maneuvering in the West Indies, Byron requested recall for bad health. On 10 Oct. '79 he sailed home, leaving Rear Adm. Parker in command. He was Vice Admiral of the White (see ADMIRALS, "Colored") when he died 10 Apr. '86.

C

"CABBAGE PLANTING EXPEDITION." Derisive name, possibly coined by Chas. Lee, for LOUDOUN's unsuccessful attempt against Louisburg in 1757. Loudoun ordered his men to plant cabbages at Halifax to provide themselves with fresh vegetables. (Alden, *Lee*, 11)

CADWALADER, John. 1742–1786. Militia general. Pa. Active in public affairs, he was a member of the Philadelphia Comm. of Safety, Capt. of the city's "silk stocking" militia company, C.O. of a city battalion and, in 1776, had become Col. of a Pa. militia regiment. His militia figured in Washington's plan for the attack on TRENTON, 26 Dec. '76, but were unable to cross the Delaware south of Trenton in sufficient strength to make any real contribution. His military intelligence materially contributed to Washington's success at PRINCETON. Although appointed Cont'l. B.G. on 21 Feb. '77, and although Washington then and later coveted his unusual abilities for the Continental cause (Freeman, *Washington,* IV, 536), he declined in order to serve as a B.G. of state militia from 5 Apr. '77 to the war's end. In the fall of 1777, at Washington's request, he organized militia on the eastern shore of Md. During this time he also served as a volunteer at Brandywine and Germantown, and was a volunteer at Monmouth, 28 June '78. On 4 July '78 he fought a duel with Thos. CONWAY and shot him in the mouth. On 10 Sept. '78 he was again offered a commission as Cont'l. B.G., this time with the post of Commander of the Cavalry, but he declined. After the war he moved from Philadelphia to Md. and became a state legislator. He died at the age of 43, leaving a large fortune.

He was the son of Dr. Thos. Cadwalader and first cousin of John and Philemon DICKINSON.

CALEDONIAN VOLUNTEERS. See BRITISH LEGION.

CALENDARS, "Old" and "New Style." The Julian ("Old Style") Calendar was used in Great Britain and her colonies until 1752, when the Gregorian ("New Style") finally was adopted. To adjust for overestimation of the solar year by 11 minutes 14 seconds, the Gregorian Calendar had added 10 days to each year from 1582 through 1699,

added 11 days to the succeeding years through 1751, and left 11 days out of 1752. Great Britain's decree made Sept. 14, 1752, follow Sept. 2. Under the "O.S."—which is the customary abbreviation—the year usually began 25 Mar. (vernal equinox). Washington's birthday is 22 Feb. '32 N.S. but 11 Feb. '31 O.S.; the latter year sometimes is expressed as 1731–32 or '31/'32. Unless otherwise stated, dates spanning the year 1752 are assumed to be "New Style." See Calendars, pages 156–157.

CALTROPS were known by the less sophisticated name of "CROWSFEET" during the Revolution.

CAMBRAY-DIGNY, Louis Antoine Jean Baptiste, Chevalier de. 1751–1822. Cont'l. officer. France. Born in Italy (presumably of French parents), he was an officer candidate (*aspirant*) in the French artillery in 1770 and discharged (*réformé*) four years later. In 1778 he went to America (Lasseray, 84), and on 13 June was commissioned Lt. Col. in Duportail's corps of engineers. During the Monmouth Campaign he served with the main army. On 20 Oct. '78 Congress ordered him to Charleston but then sent him on temporary duty to Pittsburgh where, as Lachlan McIntosh's chief engineer, he directed construction of Ft. McIntosh. (See Lossing, II, 500 *n.,* for an amusing letter he wrote in excellent, if picturesque, English during this tour of duty.) On 2 Feb. '79 Congress ordered him to Baltimore and thence to Edenton, N.C., with the mission of expediting troop movements to the South. He reported to Lincoln on these activities and then took part in the operations against Savannah and the defense of Charleston. Captured 12 May '80 with Lincoln's army, he was exchanged on 26 Nov. '82. (Lasseray, 140; Heitman, 140–41, says he was exchanged in 1781) On 30 Oct. '82 he was granted a year's leave in France

CALENDAR
FOR THE YEARS OF THE REVOLUTION.

1775

JANUARY
S	M	T	W	T	F	S
1	2	3	4	5	6	7
8	9	10	11	12	13	14
15	16	17	18	19	20	21
22	23	24	25	26	27	28
29	30	31				

FEBRUARY
S	M	T	W	T	F	S
			1	2	3	4
5	6	7	8	9	10	11
12	13	14	15	16	17	18
19	20	21	22	23	24	25
26	27	28				

MARCH
S	M	T	W	T	F	S
			1	2	3	4
5	6	7	8	9	10	11
12	13	14	15	16	17	18
19	20	21	22	23	24	25
26	27	28	29	30	31	

APRIL
S	M	T	W	T	F	S
						1
2	3	4	5	6	7	8
9	10	11	12	13	14	15
16	17	18	19	20	21	22
23	24	25	26	27	28	29
30						

MAY
S	M	T	W	T	F	S
	1	2	3	4	5	6
7	8	9	10	11	12	13
14	15	16	17	18	19	20
21	22	23	24	25	26	27
28	29	30	31			

JUNE
S	M	T	W	T	F	S
				1	2	3
4	5	6	7	8	9	10
11	12	13	14	15	16	17
18	19	20	21	22	23	24
25	26	27	28	29	30	

JULY
S	M	T	W	T	F	S
						1
2	3	4	5	6	7	8
9	10	11	12	13	14	15
16	17	18	19	20	21	22
23	24	25	26	27	28	29
30	31					

AUGUST
S	M	T	W	T	F	S
		1	2	3	4	5
6	7	8	9	10	11	12
13	14	15	16	17	18	19
20	21	22	23	24	25	26
27	28	29	30	31		

SEPTEMBER
S	M	T	W	T	F	S
					1	2
3	4	5	6	7	8	9
10	11	12	13	14	15	16
17	18	19	20	21	22	23
24	25	26	27	28	29	30

OCTOBER
S	M	T	W	T	F	S
1	2	3	4	5	6	7
8	9	10	11	12	13	14
15	16	17	18	19	20	21
22	23	24	25	26	27	28
29	30	31				

NOVEMBER
S	M	T	W	T	F	S
			1	2	3	4
5	6	7	8	9	10	11
12	13	14	15	16	17	18
19	20	21	22	23	24	25
26	27	28	29	30		

DECEMBER
S	M	T	W	T	F	S
					1	2
3	4	5	6	7	8	9
10	11	12	13	14	15	16
17	18	19	20	21	22	23
24	25	26	27	28	29	30
31						

1776

JANUARY
S	M	T	W	T	F	S
	1	2	3	4	5	6
7	8	9	10	11	12	13
14	15	16	17	18	19	20
21	22	23	24	25	26	27
28	29	30	31			

FEBRUARY
S	M	T	W	T	F	S
				1	2	3
4	5	6	7	8	9	10
11	12	13	14	15	16	17
18	19	20	21	22	23	24
25	26	27	28	29		

MARCH
S	M	T	W	T	F	S
					1	2
3	4	5	6	7	8	9
10	11	12	13	14	15	16
17	18	19	20	21	22	23
24	25	26	27	28	29	30
31						

APRIL
S	M	T	W	T	F	S
	1	2	3	4	5	6
7	8	9	10	11	12	13
14	15	16	17	18	19	20
21	22	23	24	25	26	27
28	29	30				

MAY
S	M	T	W	T	F	S
			1	2	3	4
5	6	7	8	9	10	11
12	13	14	15	16	17	18
19	20	21	22	23	24	25
26	27	28	29	30	31	

JUNE
S	M	T	W	T	F	S
						1
2	3	4	5	6	7	8
9	10	11	12	13	14	15
16	17	18	19	20	21	22
23	24	25	26	27	28	29
30						

JULY
S	M	T	W	T	F	S
	1	2	3	4	5	6
7	8	9	10	11	12	13
14	15	16	17	18	19	20
21	22	23	24	25	26	27
28	29	30	31			

AUGUST
S	M	T	W	T	F	S
				1	2	3
4	5	6	7	8	9	10
11	12	13	14	15	16	17
18	19	20	21	22	23	24
25	26	27	28	29	30	31

SEPTEMBER
S	M	T	W	T	F	S
1	2	3	4	5	6	7
8	9	10	11	12	13	14
15	16	17	18	19	20	21
22	23	24	25	26	27	28
29	30					

OCTOBER
S	M	T	W	T	F	S
		1	2	3	4	5
6	7	8	9	10	11	12
13	14	15	16	17	18	19
20	21	22	23	24	25	26
27	28	29	30	31		

NOVEMBER
S	M	T	W	T	F	S
					1	2
3	4	5	6	7	8	9
10	11	12	13	14	15	16
17	18	19	20	21	22	23
24	25	26	27	28	29	30

DECEMBER
S	M	T	W	T	F	S
1	2	3	4	5	6	7
8	9	10	11	12	13	14
15	16	17	18	19	20	21
22	23	24	25	26	27	28
29	30	31				

1777

JANUARY
S	M	T	W	T	F	S
			1	2	3	4
5	6	7	8	9	10	11
12	13	14	15	16	17	18
19	20	21	22	23	24	25
26	27	28	29	30	31	

FEBRUARY
S	M	T	W	T	F	S
						1
2	3	4	5	6	7	8
9	10	11	12	13	14	15
16	17	18	19	20	21	22
23	24	25	26	27	28	

MARCH
S	M	T	W	T	F	S
						1
2	3	4	5	6	7	8
9	10	11	12	13	14	15
16	17	18	19	20	21	22
23	24	25	26	27	28	29
30	31					

APRIL
S	M	T	W	T	F	S
		1	2	3	4	5
6	7	8	9	10	11	12
13	14	15	16	17	18	19
20	21	22	23	24	25	26
27	28	29	30			

MAY
S	M	T	W	T	F	S
				1	2	3
4	5	6	7	8	9	10
11	12	13	14	15	16	17
18	19	20	21	22	23	24
25	26	27	28	29	30	31

JUNE
S	M	T	W	T	F	S
1	2	3	4	5	6	7
8	9	10	11	12	13	14
15	16	17	18	19	20	21
22	23	24	25	26	27	28
29	30					

JULY
S	M	T	W	T	F	S
		1	2	3	4	5
6	7	8	9	10	11	12
13	14	15	16	17	18	19
20	21	22	23	24	25	26
27	28	29	30	31		

AUGUST
S	M	T	W	T	F	S
					1	2
3	4	5	6	7	8	9
10	11	12	13	14	15	16
17	18	19	20	21	22	23
24	25	26	27	28	29	30
31						

SEPTEMBER
S	M	T	W	T	F	S
	1	2	3	4	5	6
7	8	9	10	11	12	13
14	15	16	17	18	19	20
21	22	23	24	25	26	27
28	29	30				

OCTOBER
S	M	T	W	T	F	S
			1	2	3	4
5	6	7	8	9	10	11
12	13	14	15	16	17	18
19	20	21	22	23	24	25
26	27	28	29	30	31	

NOVEMBER
S	M	T	W	T	F	S
						1
2	3	4	5	6	7	8
9	10	11	12	13	14	15
16	17	18	19	20	21	22
23	24	25	26	27	28	29
30						

DECEMBER
S	M	T	W	T	F	S
	1	2	3	4	5	6
7	8	9	10	11	12	13
14	15	16	17	18	19	20
21	22	23	24	25	26	27
28	29	30	31			

1778

JANUARY
S	M	T	W	T	F	S
				1	2	3
4	5	6	7	8	9	10
11	12	13	14	15	16	17
18	19	20	21	22	23	24
25	26	27	28	29	30	31

FEBRUARY
S	M	T	W	T	F	S
1	2	3	4	5	6	7
8	9	10	11	12	13	14
15	16	17	18	19	20	21
22	23	24	25	26	27	28

MARCH
S	M	T	W	T	F	S
1	2	3	4	5	6	7
8	9	10	11	12	13	14
15	16	17	18	19	20	21
22	23	24	25	26	27	28
29	30	31				

APRIL
S	M	T	W	T	F	S
			1	2	3	4
5	6	7	8	9	10	11
12	13	14	15	16	17	18
19	20	21	22	23	24	25
26	27	28	29	30		

MAY
S	M	T	W	T	F	S
					1	2
3	4	5	6	7	8	9
10	11	12	13	14	15	16
17	18	19	20	21	22	23
24	25	26	27	28	29	30
31						

JUNE
S	M	T	W	T	F	S
	1	2	3	4	5	6
7	8	9	10	11	12	13
14	15	16	17	18	19	20
21	22	23	24	25	26	27
28	29	30				

JULY
S	M	T	W	T	F	S
			1	2	3	4
5	6	7	8	9	10	11
12	13	14	15	16	17	18
19	20	21	22	23	24	25
26	27	28	29	30	31	

AUGUST
S	M	T	W	T	F	S
						1
2	3	4	5	6	7	8
9	10	11	12	13	14	15
16	17	18	19	20	21	22
23	24	25	26	27	28	29
30	31					

SEPTEMBER
S	M	T	W	T	F	S
		1	2	3	4	5
6	7	8	9	10	11	12
13	14	15	16	17	18	19
20	21	22	23	24	25	26
27	28	29	30			

OCTOBER
S	M	T	W	T	F	S
				1	2	3
4	5	6	7	8	9	10
11	12	13	14	15	16	17
18	19	20	21	22	23	24
25	26	27	28	29	30	31

NOVEMBER
S	M	T	W	T	F	S
1	2	3	4	5	6	7
8	9	10	11	12	13	14
15	16	17	18	19	20	21
22	23	24	25	26	27	28
29	30					

DECEMBER
S	M	T	W	T	F	S
		1	2	3	4	5
6	7	8	9	10	11	12
13	14	15	16	17	18	19
20	21	22	23	24	25	26
27	28	29	30	31		

1779

JANUARY

S	M	T	W	T	F	S
					1	2
3	4	5	6	7	8	9
10	11	12	13	14	15	16
17	18	19	20	21	22	23
24	25	26	27	28	29	30
31						

FEBRUARY

S	M	T	W	T	F	S
	1	2	3	4	5	6
7	8	9	10	11	12	13
14	15	16	17	18	19	20
21	22	23	24	25	26	27
28						

MARCH

S	M	T	W	T	F	S
	1	2	3	4	5	6
7	8	9	10	11	12	13
14	15	16	17	18	19	20
21	22	23	24	25	26	27
28	29	30	31			

APRIL

S	M	T	W	T	F	S
				1	2	3
4	5	6	7	8	9	10
11	12	13	14	15	16	17
18	19	20	21	22	23	24
25	26	27	28	29	30	

MAY

S	M	T	W	T	F	S
						1
2	3	4	5	6	7	8
9	10	11	12	13	14	15
16	17	18	19	20	21	22
23	24	25	26	27	28	29
30	31					

JUNE

S	M	T	W	T	F	S
		1	2	3	4	5
6	7	8	9	10	11	12
13	14	15	16	17	18	19
20	21	22	23	24	25	26
27	28	29	30			

JULY

S	M	T	W	T	F	S
				1	2	3
4	5	6	7	8	9	10
11	12	13	14	15	16	17
18	19	20	21	22	23	24
25	26	27	28	29	30	31

AUGUST

S	M	T	W	T	F	S
1	2	3	4	5	6	7
8	9	10	11	12	13	14
15	16	17	18	19	20	21
22	23	24	25	26	27	28
29	30	31				

SEPTEMBER

S	M	T	W	T	F	S
			1	2	3	4
5	6	7	8	9	10	11
12	13	14	15	16	17	18
19	20	21	22	23	24	25
26	27	28	29	30		

OCTOBER

S	M	T	W	T	F	S
					1	2
3	4	5	6	7	8	9
10	11	12	13	14	15	16
17	18	19	20	21	22	23
24	25	26	27	28	29	30
31						

NOVEMBER

S	M	T	W	T	F	S
	1	2	3	4	5	6
7	8	9	10	11	12	13
14	15	16	17	18	19	20
21	22	23	24	25	26	27
28	29	30				

DECEMBER

S	M	T	W	T	F	S
			1	2	3	4
5	6	7	8	9	10	11
12	13	14	15	16	17	18
19	20	21	22	23	24	25
26	27	28	29	30	31	

1780

JANUARY

S	M	T	W	T	F	S
						1
2	3	4	5	6	7	8
9	10	11	12	13	14	15
16	17	18	19	20	21	22
23	24	25	26	27	28	29
30	31					

FEBRUARY

S	M	T	W	T	F	S
		1	2	3	4	5
6	7	8	9	10	11	12
13	14	15	16	17	18	19
20	21	22	23	24	25	26
27	28	29				

MARCH

S	M	T	W	T	F	S
			1	2	3	4
5	6	7	8	9	10	11
12	13	14	15	16	17	18
19	20	21	22	23	24	25
26	27	28	29	30	31	

APRIL

S	M	T	W	T	F	S
						1
2	3	4	5	6	7	8
9	10	11	12	13	14	15
16	17	18	19	20	21	22
23	24	25	26	27	28	29
30						

MAY

S	M	T	W	T	F	S
	1	2	3	4	5	6
7	8	9	10	11	12	13
14	15	16	17	18	19	20
21	22	23	24	25	26	27
28	29	30	31			

JUNE

S	M	T	W	T	F	S
				1	2	3
4	5	6	7	8	9	10
11	12	13	14	15	16	17
18	19	20	21	22	23	24
25	26	27	28	29	30	

JULY

S	M	T	W	T	F	S
						1
2	3	4	5	6	7	8
9	10	11	12	13	14	15
16	17	18	19	20	21	22
23	24	25	26	27	28	29
30	31					

AUGUST

S	M	T	W	T	F	S
		1	2	3	4	5
6	7	8	9	10	11	12
13	14	15	16	17	18	19
20	21	22	23	24	25	26
27	28	29	30	31		

SEPTEMBER

S	M	T	W	T	F	S
					1	2
3	4	5	6	7	8	9
10	11	12	13	14	15	16
17	18	19	20	21	22	23
24	25	26	27	28	29	30

OCTOBER

S	M	T	W	T	F	S
1	2	3	4	5	6	7
8	9	10	11	12	13	14
15	16	17	18	19	20	21
22	23	24	25	26	27	28
29	30	31				

NOVEMBER

S	M	T	W	T	F	S
			1	2	3	4
5	6	7	8	9	10	11
12	13	14	15	16	17	18
19	20	21	22	23	24	25
26	27	28	29	30		

DECEMBER

S	M	T	W	T	F	S
					1	2
3	4	5	6	7	8	9
10	11	12	13	14	15	16
17	18	19	20	21	22	23
24	25	26	27	28	29	30
31						

1781

JANUARY

S	M	T	W	T	F	S
	1	2	3	4	5	6
7	8	9	10	11	12	13
14	15	16	17	18	19	20
21	22	23	24	25	26	27
28	29	30	31			

FEBRUARY

S	M	T	W	T	F	S
				1	2	3
4	5	6	7	8	9	10
11	12	13	14	15	16	17
18	19	20	21	22	23	24
25	26	27	28			

MARCH

S	M	T	W	T	F	S
				1	2	3
4	5	6	7	8	9	10
11	12	13	14	15	16	17
18	19	20	21	22	23	24
25	26	27	28	29	30	31

APRIL

S	M	T	W	T	F	S
1	2	3	4	5	6	7
8	9	10	11	12	13	14
15	16	17	18	19	20	21
22	23	24	25	26	27	28
29	30					

MAY

S	M	T	W	T	F	S
		1	2	3	4	5
6	7	8	9	10	11	12
13	14	15	16	17	18	19
20	21	22	23	24	25	26
27	28	29	30	31		

JUNE

S	M	T	W	T	F	S
					1	2
3	4	5	6	7	8	9
10	11	12	13	14	15	16
17	18	19	20	21	22	23
24	25	26	27	28	29	30

JULY

S	M	T	W	T	F	S
1	2	3	4	5	6	7
8	9	10	11	12	13	14
15	16	17	18	19	20	21
22	23	24	25	26	27	28
29	30	31				

AUGUST

S	M	T	W	T	F	S
			1	2	3	4
5	6	7	8	9	10	11
12	13	14	15	16	17	18
19	20	21	22	23	24	25
26	27	28	29	30	31	

SEPTEMBER

S	M	T	W	T	F	S
						1
2	3	4	5	6	7	8
9	10	11	12	13	14	15
16	17	18	19	20	21	22
23	24	25	26	27	28	29
30						

OCTOBER

S	M	T	W	T	F	S
	1	2	3	4	5	6
7	8	9	10	11	12	13
14	15	16	17	18	19	20
21	22	23	24	25	26	27
28	29	30	31			

NOVEMBER

S	M	T	W	T	F	S
				1	2	3
4	5	6	7	8	9	10
11	12	13	14	15	16	17
18	19	20	21	22	23	24
25	26	27	28	29	30	

DECEMBER

S	M	T	W	T	F	S
						1
2	3	4	5	6	7	8
9	10	11	12	13	14	15
16	17	18	19	20	21	22
23	24	25	26	27	28	29
30	31					

1782

JANUARY

S	M	T	W	T	F	S
		1	2	3	4	5
6	7	8	9	10	11	12
13	14	15	16	17	18	19
20	21	22	23	24	25	26
27	28	29	30	31		

FEBRUARY

S	M	T	W	T	F	S
					1	2
3	4	5	6	7	8	9
10	11	12	13	14	15	16
17	18	19	20	21	22	23
24	25	26	27	28		

MARCH

S	M	T	W	T	F	S
					1	2
3	4	5	6	7	8	9
10	11	12	13	14	15	16
17	18	19	20	21	22	23
24	25	26	27	28	29	30
31						

APRIL

S	M	T	W	T	F	S
	1	2	3	4	5	6
7	8	9	10	11	12	13
14	15	16	17	18	19	20
21	22	23	24	25	26	27
28	29	30				

MAY

S	M	T	W	T	F	S
			1	2	3	4
5	6	7	8	9	10	11
12	13	14	15	16	17	18
19	20	21	22	23	24	25
26	27	28	29	30	31	

JUNE

S	M	T	W	T	F	S
						1
2	3	4	5	6	7	8
9	10	11	12	13	14	15
16	17	18	19	20	21	22
23	24	25	26	27	28	29
30						

JULY

S	M	T	W	T	F	S
	1	2	3	4	5	6
7	8	9	10	11	12	13
14	15	16	17	18	19	20
21	22	23	24	25	26	27
28	29	30	31			

AUGUST

S	M	T	W	T	F	S
				1	2	3
4	5	6	7	8	9	10
11	12	13	14	15	16	17
18	19	20	21	22	23	24
25	26	27	28	29	30	31

SEPTEMBER

S	M	T	W	T	F	S
1	2	3	4	5	6	7
8	9	10	11	12	13	14
15	16	17	18	19	20	21
22	23	24	25	26	27	28
29	30					

OCTOBER

S	M	T	W	T	F	S
		1	2	3	4	5
6	7	8	9	10	11	12
13	14	15	16	17	18	19
20	21	22	23	24	25	26
27	28	29	30	31		

NOVEMBER

S	M	T	W	T	F	S
					1	2
3	4	5	6	7	8	9
10	11	12	13	14	15	16
17	18	19	20	21	22	23
24	25	26	27	28	29	30

DECEMBER

S	M	T	W	T	F	S
1	2	3	4	5	6	7
8	9	10	11	12	13	14
15	16	17	18	19	20	21
22	23	24	25	26	27	28
29	30	31				

1783

JANUARY

S	M	T	W	T	F	S
			1	2	3	4
5	6	7	8	9	10	11
12	13	14	15	16	17	18
19	20	21	22	23	24	25
26	27	28	29	30	31	

FEBRUARY

S	M	T	W	T	F	S
						1
2	3	4	5	6	7	8
9	10	11	12	13	14	15
16	17	18	19	20	21	22
23	24	25	26	27	28	

MARCH

S	M	T	W	T	F	S
						1
2	3	4	5	6	7	8
9	10	11	12	13	14	15
16	17	18	19	20	21	22
23	24	25	26	27	28	29
30	31					

APRIL

S	M	T	W	T	F	S
		1	2	3	4	5
6	7	8	9	10	11	12
13	14	15	16	17	18	19
20	21	22	23	24	25	26
27	28	29	30			

MAY

S	M	T	W	T	F	S
				1	2	3
4	5	6	7	8	9	10
11	12	13	14	15	16	17
18	19	20	21	22	23	24
25	26	27	28	29	30	31

JUNE

S	M	T	W	T	F	S
1	2	3	4	5	6	7
8	9	10	11	12	13	14
15	16	17	18	19	20	21
22	23	24	25	26	27	28
29	30					

JULY

S	M	T	W	T	F	S
		1	2	3	4	5
6	7	8	9	10	11	12
13	14	15	16	17	18	19
20	21	22	23	24	25	26
27	28	29	30	31		

AUGUST

S	M	T	W	T	F	S
					1	2
3	4	5	6	7	8	9
10	11	12	13	14	15	16
17	18	19	20	21	22	23
24	25	26	27	28	29	30
31						

SEPTEMBER

S	M	T	W	T	F	S
	1	2	3	4	5	6
7	8	9	10	11	12	13
14	15	16	17	18	19	20
21	22	23	24	25	26	27
28	29	30				

OCTOBER

S	M	T	W	T	F	S
			1	2	3	4
5	6	7	8	9	10	11
12	13	14	15	16	17	18
19	20	21	22	23	24	25
26	27	28	29	30	31	

NOVEMBER

S	M	T	W	T	F	S
						1
2	3	4	5	6	7	8
9	10	11	12	13	14	15
16	17	18	19	20	21	22
23	24	25	26	27	28	29
30						

DECEMBER

S	M	T	W	T	F	S
	1	2	3	4	5	6
7	8	9	10	11	12	13
14	15	16	17	18	19	20
21	22	23	24	25	26	27
28	29	30	31			

(Heitman) and he reached Brest 11 June '83, exactly a month after sailing from America. (Lasseray) He was breveted Col. on 2 May '83 (Heitman, 141) and honorably discharged on 15 Nov. '83. (Lasseray; Heitman gives no date)

French military records are the basis of the following note on Cambray: "Cadet Corps of Engineers in 1770; was not made an officer, there being no vacancy; Lt. Col. in the service of the U.S. from 1778, date when he joined its army; merited this gracious but premature distinction for the gallant manner he served in South America [i.e., the Southern Theater]; name to be presented for a majority in the provincial troops." (Heitman, "List of French Officers . . . ," 647) Lasseray writes: "Certain information, difficult to verify, indicates that M. de Cambray-Digny received the grade of major in the provincial troops when he returned." (*Op. cit.*, 140) Since he already was a Lt. Col., these references to a commission as Maj. are difficult to understand; what is interesting about the two references is that Cambray apparently returned to America even though he did not—according to Lasseray—start his leave in France until June '83.

He took part in the French elections of 1789 and died 33 years later at his château in the Dept. of the Somme.

CAMBRIDGE, Mass., 1 Sept. '74. As patriot defiance of England became more ominous, Gen. Gage in Boston decided on a risky move. As early as Mar. '74 his secret agents had given him detailed information about cannon, powder, and other stores the patriots were collecting and hiding in Cambridge. (See French, *Gage's Informers*, 10 ff., for interesting details) Under his orders about 250 regulars embarked at the Long Wharf early in the morning with instructions to seize 250 half-barrels of powder from the provincial powder house and evacuate them to Boston. He ordered another detachment to march to Cambridge and confiscate two field guns recently procured by the town militia. Both British forces accomplished their mission efficiently and without violence, but the countryside was inflamed with reports that the redcoats had sallied forth in large numbers. As the news spread— by midnight it was known 40 miles away in Shrewsbury—the rumors embellished it: the citizens of Cambridge had resisted, the troops had fired, and six patriots were dead! The Boston Garrison was marching out in force! By the morning of 2 Sept., 4,000 armed patriots had crowded into Cambridge, and more were coming. Word reached Israel Putnam at Pomfret, Conn., on 3 Sept. that British ships had bombarded Boston and that as many as 30,000 militia were moving toward Cambridge! The Cont'l. Cong. was informed of the "dreadful catastrophe," and John Adams wrote his wife that "Every gentleman seems to regard the bombardment of Boston as the bombardment of the capital of his own province."

The excitement died down as the rumors were proved to be false, but the episode had been an impressive demonstration of how ready the patriots were to touch off the powder keg. On 5 Sept. Gage ordered the erection of defensive works on Boston Neck, an understandable military precaution but one that alarmed the patriots again and gave the PROPAGANDISTS more material to work with. The delegates to the Cont'l. Cong. began to worry less about their differences and more about the task ahead. (Alden, *Gage*, 213; Ward, *W.O.R.*, 18–19)

CAMDEN, S.C., 25 Apr. '81. See HOBKIRK'S HILL.

CAMDEN CAMPAIGN, July–Aug. '80. As explained in the article on military operations in the SOUTHERN THEATER, a force of about 2,000 Cont'ls. under Gen. Kalb was moving toward Charleston when that place surrendered (12 May '80). On 13 July Congress commissioned Gen. Horatio Gates to command the Southern Department. With the collapse of American military resistance in the South and with little prospect of assistance from the French Alliance, Congress hoped that the victor of Saratoga would rally militia to stop the British in the South as he was credited with having rallied them to defeat Burgoyne. Washington did not approve of Gates's appointment, and considered Greene better qualified, but Congress did not consult him on the matter. Charles Lee warned his friend Gates to "take care lest your Northern laurels turn to Southern willows."

When Gates reached Kalb's headquarters at Coxe's Mill, N.C., to take command on 25 July he found a half-starved force of about 1,200 regulars—the Del. and Md. Cont'ls. and three small artillery companies that had survived the march, and 120 survivors of Pulaski's Legion, now commanded by Armand, who had recently joined Kalb. Leaving the infantry under Kalb's command and designating the entire body of troops "the grand army," Gates ordered that they prepare to march on a moment's notice.

"The latter order was a matter of great astonishment to those who knew the real situation of the troops. But all difficulties were removed by the general's assurances that plentiful supplies of rum and rations were on the route. ..." (Narrative of Col. Otho Williams as quoted in C. & M., 1126)

A number of other American units were in the field and will be mentioned as they appear. Two that did not appear, however, were the cavalry units that Colonels Wm. Washington and Anthony White were trying to build around the survivors of LENUD'S FERRY and MONCK'S CORNER; when they asked Gates's support in recruiting horsemen and offered to join him, Gates not only refused to help but let it be known that he did not consider the Southern Theater good cavalry country.

Although British forces controlled Ga. and S.C., the situation of Cornwallis was far from rosy. Many of his 8,300 troops were sick, and he had 12 scattered posts to maintain in an area of about 10,000 square miles. He believed that an offensive into N.C. was the only alternative to abandoning all this territory and concentrating at Charleston. See map of Southern Theater, back end paper. (Fortescue, *British Army*, III, 136) To undertake this offensive he had a forward base at Camden with outposts at Hanging Rock, Rocky Mount, and Cheraw. But the necessary provisions had not yet been built up, and when Gates advanced there were 800 hospital cases in Camden: men who would have to be abandoned if the place were not defended.

Partisan General Thomas Sumter, who had been operating only a short time, sent Kalb a report of Cornwallis' scattered dispositions shortly before Gates arrived. "Probably on the strength of this letter, which set at seven hundred the total enemy strength in 'Camden and vicinity,' and encouraged by dreams of manna for his men and 'shoals of militia' gathering in North Carolina, Gates resolved to attack Camden." (S. & R., 405)

Subordinates who knew the country recommended that "the grand army" circle westward through Salisbury, Charlotte, and the Catawba region, a route that would take them through fertile country where the natives were sym-

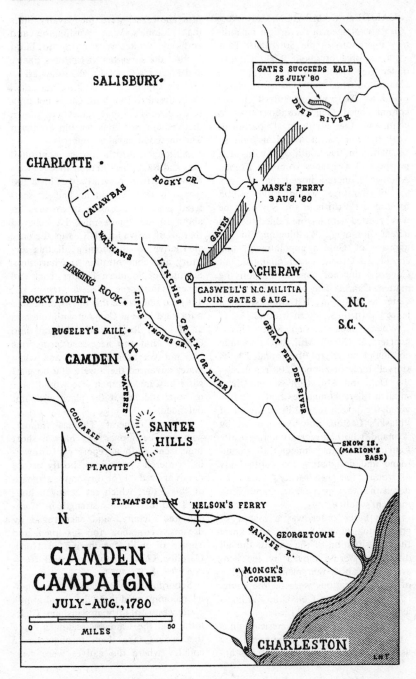

SALISBURY•

GATES SUCCEEDS KALB
25 JULY '80

DEEP RIVER

CHARLOTTE •

ROCKY CR.

MASK'S FERRY
3 AUG. '80

CATAWBAS

GATES

WAXHAWS

LYNCHES CREEK

CHERAW

HANGING ROCK

CASWELL'S N.C. MILITIA
JOIN GATES 6 AUG.

ROCKY MOUNT•

N.C.

S.C.

RUGELEY'S MILL•

LITTLE LYNCHES CR.

CAMDEN

LYNCHES CREEK (OR RIVER)

GREAT PEE DEE RIVER

WATEREE R.

CONGAREE R.

SANTEE
HILLS

SNOW IS.
(MARION'S
BASE)

N

FT. MOTTE

FT. WATSON

NELSON'S FERRY

SANTEE R.

GEORGETOWN •

CAMDEN
CAMPAIGN
JULY-AUG., 1780

MONCK'S
CORNER

0   MILES   50

CHARLESTON

L N T

pathetic. Gates insisted on taking a more direct route, 50 miles shorter but through an impoverished and Tory-infested region of pine barrens, sand hills, and swamps. The march started on 27 July, only two days after Gates's arrival. The sick and underfed troops took two weeks to cover 120 miles, although some days they marched 18 miles. When the promised rum and rations did not appear, Gates assured them they would find abundant corn on the Peedee River. He was right, but the corn was still green, and soldiers who had been getting sick on green peaches now got sick on green corn instead. They were so desperate that some tried using hair powder to thicken the stew they concocted from lean woods cattle and green corn. Ironically, their route took them through the area where the modern health resorts of Pinehurst and Southern Pines are located; Fisher comments that "the air ... is dry and invigorating, but the troops of Gates needed more than air to sustain them." (*Struggle,* II, 296)

After crossing the Peedee at Mask's Ferry on 3 Aug. the Cont'ls. were joined by 100 Va. militia whom Lt. Col. Chas. Porterfield had managed to keep in the field after the surrender of Charleston two and a half months earlier. Francis Marion also appeared with about 20 miserable-looking followers. As for these "men and boys, some white, some black," Col. Otho Williams says:

". . . their appearance was in fact so burlesque that it was with much difficulty the diversion of the regular soldiery was restrained by the officers; and the general himself was glad of an opportunity of detaching Colonel Marion, at his own instance, towards the interior of South Carolina, with orders to watch the motions of the enemy and furnish intelligence." (*Op. cit.,* 1128)

(For Marion's subsequent actions, see GREAT SAVANNAH, 25 Aug.)

One reason why Gates may have chosen his much criticized line of operations was to increase his opportunities for drawing militia reinforcements to him; the designation of his force as "the grand army" tends to support this supposition. In any event, former Gov. Richard Caswell was known to be hunting Tories with a body of 1,200 well-provisioned N.C. militia, whom he commanded as a Maj. Gen. Kalb had called on Caswell to join him—with the ulterior motive of alleviating his own problems of subsistence—but the militia leader "offered excuses and held aloof." (Ward, *op. cit.,* 715)

On 5 Aug., however, Gates received a message from Caswell that he was about to attack a British outpost on Lynches Creek, and the next day came Caswell's urgent appeal for help. Gates was already headed for Caswell's camp when the second message arrived, but the episode brought the N.C. militia into "the grand army." Although strength of these militia had been estimated originally as 1,200, they had now been reinforced to 2,100. (Ward, 913 *n.,* citing Dawson) The combined forces moved to Lynches Creek. (We shall see in a moment what had alarmed the Tory hunters.)

"What to do next might have puzzled an abler general than Horatio Gates. He could not stay where he was; there was no food there. If he turned to the left, Camden would be to his rear, cutting off any help from the north. If he turned to the right, to the flourishing settlements of the Waxhaws, a two or three days' march, he would seem to be retreating and the North Carolina militia would desert him. So, without any plan or purpose, he went blindly straight ahead." (Ward, *op. cit.,* 720–

21) He ordered his heavy baggage and camp followers back to Charlotte, but he lacked transportation to move the former, and the women and children refused to leave their "sponsors." Meanwhile, some edible corn and beef had been found to relieve temporarily the famine of his troops.

BRITISH REACTION

Young Lord Rawdon, who commanded at Camden, had sent a series of messages to Cornwallis in Charleston warning him that 7,000 Americans were approaching his advance base. Although Rawdon saw the necessity for concentrating at Camden, "he dared not remove the garrisons from Hanging Rock and Rocky Mountain, lest Sumter should slip past him and either cut his communications with Charleston, or move rapidly westward and overwhelm his posts on the Broad River." (Fortescue, *op. cit.,* 316) Sumter attacked ROCKY MOUNT, 1 Aug., and HANGING ROCK, 6 Aug., with precisely this strategy in mind (see below), and the British held the two outposts only after serious fighting.

About the time Gates's Cont'ls. crossed the Peedee, at a point some 25 miles north of the post held by the 71st Highlanders at Cheraw, Rawdon moved forward to delay the American advance. When Caswell's N.C. militia started acting as if they were going to attack his outpost on Lynches Creek, Rawdon threw them into disorder by feigning an attack, and withdrew.

On 11 Aug. Gates found Rawdon barring his advance across the bridge at Little Lynches Creek, 15 miles N.E. of Camden. Although the British were badly outnumbered, they had a strong position overlooking a broad marsh through which the enemy would have to attack. Tarleton commented that "by

a forced march up the creek, he could have passed Lord Rawdon's flank and reached Camden which would have been an easy conquest and a fatal blow to the British." (quoted in Ward, 913 *n.*) Kalb is said to have suggested this maneuver. (*Ibid.,* 721) According to Bass, "Gates wheeled his army to the right, forded the creek, and began a flanking movement" (*Green Dragoon,* 97); he may, therefore, have had a decisive action in mind, but he spoiled his chance by starting it in broad daylight and eliminating the essential element of surprise. Covered by Tarleton's dragoons, Rawdon withdrew to Camden.

The last British troops had now been pulled back from Hanging Rock and Rocky Mount. Sumter followed and seized all crossings across the Wateree as far down as Whitaker's Ferry, five miles below Camden.

"Trying to coordinate his movements with those of the main army, on August 12 he wrote General Gates. He suggested that a powerful corps be thrown behind Camden. For the second time he urged that a strong detachment be sent to the High Hills of Santee or to Nelson's Ferry to cut the British supply route and to prevent their expected retreat toward Charleston." (Bass, *op. cit.,* 97)

Although Gates consistently exhibited a complete immunity to *good* advice during this campaign, he acted on Sumter's suggestion. (The latter violates the principle of war known as "Economy of Force.") On 14 Aug., therefore, when his army had reached Rugeley's Mill (Clermont), Gates detached Lt. Col. Thos. Woolford with 100 Md. Cont'ls., a company of artillery with two guns, and 300 N.C. militia to reinforce Sumter. The latter scored a bright little success at WATEREE FERRY,

15 Aug., but contributed nothing to the campaign.

FROM BAD STRATEGY TO WORSE TACTICS

The American army at Rugeley's Mill was reinforced on 14 Aug. by 700 Va. militia who had come south under Gen. Edw. Stevens. With 900 rank and file of Kalb's Del. and Md. Cont'ls., 120 mounted and foot troops of Armand's Legion, Porterfield's 100 Va. light infantry, about 100 men and six guns in Col. Chas. Harrison's Va. artillery, the 1,800 N.C. militia, and about 70 volunteer horsemen, Gates now had about 4,100 rank and file. Cornwallis thought he had 7,000, an understandable error inasmuch as Gates himself was under the same misapprehension. When deputy A.G. Otho Williams showed Gates figures to prove that only 3,052 were present and fit for duty, the Hero of Saratoga waved this information aside with the comment that "there are enough for our purpose." The unit strengths given above are from Ward (p. 723) but are modified to correct his apparent failure to deduct the 300 N.C. militia sent to Sumter. Kalb's strength takes into account the detachment of 100 Md. Cont'l. troops. Six guns remained with Gates after two were sent to Sumter; the other 10 guns with which Harrison had started the march with Kalb had been left behind for want of horses. (Ward, 717)

Cornwallis reached Camden the night of 13 Aug. By this time Rawdon had been reinforced by four light infantry companies from Ninety-Six. According to Greene, the morning report showed 122 officers and 2,117 men fit for duty (*Rev. War,* 217) Most of his troops were well-seasoned regulars—three companies of the 23d (282 rank and file), the 33d (283 men), five companies of

the 71st (237 men)—or high quality Tory units brought from N.Y. with Clinton: the Volunteers of Ireland (287) and Tarleton's British Legion (289). There was a 17-man detachment of the Royal Artillery, a 26-man pioneer unit, and two N.C. Tory regiments with a total strength of over 550. (These figures from Ward, 722–23) Although Cornwallis still believed himself outnumbered more than three to one, he decided to fight; retreat would have meant abandonment of 800 sick, a quantity of stores, and the surrender of all of S.C. and Ga. but Charleston and Savannah. The decision reveals the element of greatness in Cornwallis.

In a meeting on 15 Aug., Gates announced that the army would make a night march to Saunders Creek, about five miles from Camden, and attack that place the next morning. His officers, who included eight generals, were too stunned by the prospect of maneuvering their columns of famished troops through the woods at night to voice their objections at this meeting; but the positive terms in which Gates read his orders to them clearly implied that he was not interested in their views. Col. Williams did point out later that Gates was more than 100 per cent wrong in his strength calculations, but we have seen the commander's reaction to this minor detail. When Armand learned that his mounted troops were to lead the column, and pointed out that cavalry is the wrong arm for such a mission, particularly through the woods and at night, Gates failed to comprehend the point.

"But Gates had seen the Green Horse wheeling around Rawdon's retreating column [on 11 Aug.] and he feared them. This fear he communicated to Colonel Armand in his order: 'In case of an attack by the enemy's cavalry,

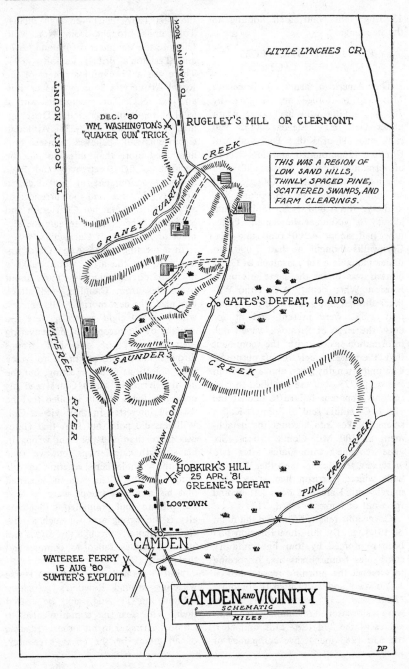

LITTLE LYNCHES CR.

TO HANGING ROCK

TO ROCKY MOUNT

DEC. '80
WM. WASHINGTON'S
"QUAKER GUN" TRICK

RUGELEY'S MILL   OR CLERMONT

CREEK

GRANEY QUARTER

THIS WAS A REGION OF
LOW SAND HILLS,
THINLY SPACED PINE,
SCATTERED SWAMPS, AND
FARM CLEARINGS.

GATES'S DEFEAT, 16 AUG '80

WATEREE RIVER

SAUNDERS   CREEK

WAXHAW ROAD

PINE TREE CREEK

HOBKIRK'S HILL
25 APR. '81
GREENE'S DEFEAT

LOGTOWN

CAMDEN

WATEREE FERRY
15 AUG '80
SUMTER'S EXPLOIT

CAMDEN AND VICINITY
SCHEMATIC
MILES

DP

in front, not only to support the shock of the enemy's horse, but to *rout* them. . . .' " (Bass, *op. cit.*, 98)

The true history of this battle has a touch that would be unacceptable in fiction. Some rations had been gathered to feed the troops a full meal before the attack, but there was still no rum. There was a supply of molasses, however, and Gates conceived the happy idea of issuing each man a gill of this delicacy as a substitute. The half-cooked meat, half-baked bread, followed by a mixture of molasses and corn meal mush had a gastrointestinal effect on the half-starved troops that would be funny if the tactical results had not been so serious. To spare the Rabelaisian details that abound in contemporary accounts, suffice it to say that men were "breaking the ranks all night and were certainly much debilitated before the action commenced in the morning." (Williams, quoted in Ward, 724)

The Americans started down the road from Rugeley's Mill toward Camden at 10 P.M. with Armand in the lead. The night was sultry and moonless, although the road showed up in the dark. Flanking Armand at a distance of 200 yards, Porterfield's Va. and John Armstrong's N.C. militia advanced through the dark woods and swamps in single file on each side of the cavalry "point." Back down the road came an infantry advance guard, followed by the Cont'ls., Caswell's N.C. militia, Stevens' Va. militia, and the baggage train under the escort of the volunteer horsemen.

By an uncanny coincidence, Cornwallis had left Camden at 10 P.M. and was marching along the same road toward Gates with a view to attacking *him* at Rugeley's Mill at daybreak. About 2:30 the morning of 16 Aug. the two forces met at a place called "Parker's Old Field" in Gum Swamp. The "point" of the British column, 20 mounted and 20 dismounted dragoons of the British Legion, charged and drove Armand's troops back in confusion, but the flank patrols closed in and drove back the British point. After a quarter of an hour the firing stopped on both sides.

THE BATTLE OF CAMDEN, 16 AUG. '80

Gates called his officers together for a council of war; this time he appeared anxious to have their recommendations.

"Gentlemen, you know our situation, what are your opinions?"

There was a painful silence from which it has been assumed that most of the officers favored a retreat but were unwilling to suggest it. It can reasonably be assumed also that Gates hoped the council would recommend this course of action.

Gen. Stevens broke the silence. "Gentlemen, is it not too late *now* to do anything but fight?" (Williams' Narrative, *op. cit.*)

There are other versions that put Stevens' comment in more positive terms, but all agree generally that he was the only subordinate to say anything at the meeting. So they got ready to fight.

The "meeting engagement" took place in a sandy area of widely spaced pines. Dense swamps narrowed the battlefield to about a mile at the point where the columns collided, but this defile widened toward the north. Gates was favored by slightly higher ground, but his flanks would be "in the air" if he had to withdraw from the narrowest part of the defile. Cornwallis had the disadvantage of being less than a mile forward of Saunders Creek, which Lossing describes as "a considerable stream, about two hundred feet wide." (II, 666) Despite the narrow front (which gave him no real opportunity for maneuver initially) and lack of depth to his position (which limited deployment of his reserves), believing himself to be outnumbered three to one, and knowing that the obstacle to his rear would make tactical defeat tantamount to annihilation, Cornwallis calmly prepared to attack at dawn.

The British deployed in a line perpendicular to the road. On the extreme right, against the swamp, the light infantry went into position. The three companies of the 23d (Royal Welch) and Lt. Col. James WEBSTER'S 33d Regt. extended this wing to the road. Webster commanded the entire wing. The Volunteers of Ireland were west of the road, then came the infantry of the British Legion, and the Royal N.C. Tories extended to the swamp. Col. Morgan Bryan's N.C. Tory volunteers were in echelon to the left rear of this flank. Lord Rawdon commanded the left wing. The two small battalions (totaling five companies) of the 71st Highlanders were to the rear, astride the road. Tarleton's cavalry was posted to the right of the road behind the Highlanders; the woods were so thick in this area that this cavalry reserve had to remain in column. (Bass, *op. cit.*, 99)

The American line was parallel to the enemy's. Unfortunately, Gates put his militia on his left, opposite the British regulars, and kept half his regulars in reserve. From east to west the American units were as follows: the Va. militia of Stevens on the flank, with Armand's Legion to their rear; Caswell's N.C. militia toward the center of the line; Gist's 2d Md. Brigade west of the road, constituting the right wing. (Gist's Brig. comprised the 2d, 4th, and 6th Md., and the Del. Regt. The latter was closest to the road, and the militia unit to its east was Col. Henry Dixon's N.C.) Kalb commanded the American right wing. Smallwood's 1st Md. Brig. was

astride the road to the rear as the reserve; the regiments of this brigade present were the 1st, 3d, and 7th Md.; Woolford's 5th Md. was the Cont'l. unit sent to reinforce Sumter. The six guns of the 1st Va. Arty. were posted in front of the American center, near the road (according to Williams, who, according to Ward, "ought to have known"; other accounts and maps indicate they were not massed in the center but dispersed along the front).

Although some skirmishing took place during the two hours between the time of contact and dawn, all this time must have been needed to form the opposing lines. Gates established his command post 600 yards behind the front and apparently had no plan other than to wait for Cornwallis to make the opening move. Col. Williams had apparently come from Stevens' Brig. toward the artillery in front of the center when the British were reported advancing in line of columns. Artillery Capt. Anthony Singleton told Williams he could see the British 200 yards away. Ordering Singleton to open fire, the A.G. rode back behind the reserve brigade to inform Gates. Cannon were now firing on both sides, and smoke settled over the battlefield in a heavy fog. Since Gates apparently intended to give no orders, Williams suggested that Stevens move forward and attempt to hit the enemy while they were deploying from column into line of battle. Since the Virginians were already formed, Williams pointed out that "the effect might be fortunate, and first impressions were important." Gates agreed, and this is evidently the last order he gave during the battle.

The enterprising A.G. hurried to the left flank and Stevens led his brigade forward, but it was too late to hit the enemy right wing before they deployed.

Williams then went ahead with 40 or 50 volunteers to disrupt the enemy's advance and weaken their impact on the Va. militia.

The desired effect of this expedient [says Williams] was not gained.

"General Stevens, observing the enemy to rush on, put his men in mind of their bayonets; but the impetuosity with which they advanced, *firing* and *huzzaing,* threw the whole body of the militia into such a panic that they generally threw down their *loaded* arms and fled in the utmost consternation. The unworthy example of the Virginians was almost instantly followed by the North Carolinians; only a small part of the brigade commanded by Brigadier General Gregory made a short pause. A part of Dixon's regiment of that brigade, next in the line of the Second Maryland Brigade, fired two or three rounds of cartridge. But a great majority of the militia (at least two thirds of the army) fled without firing a shot. The writer avers it of his own knowledge, having seen and observed every part of the army, from left to right, during the action.

"He who has never seen the effect of a panic upon a multitude can have but an imperfect idea of such a thing. The best disciplined troops have been enervated and made cowards by it. Armies have been routed by it, even where no enemy appeared to furnish an excuse. Like electricity, it operates instantaneously—like sympathy, it is irresistible where it touches. But, in the present instance, its action was not universal. The regular troops, who had the keen edge of sensibility rubbed off by strict discipline and hard service, saw the confusion with but little emotion. They engaged seriously in the affair; and, notwithstanding some irregularity, which was created by the militia breaking pell

mell through the second line, order was restored there—time enough to give the enemy a severe check, which abated the fury of their assault and obliged them to assume a more deliberate manner of acting." (Narrative of Col. Otho Williams, quoted in C. & M., 1131)

The attack of the British right had been commanded by Lt. Col. WEBSTER who, instead of pursuing the militia, had wheeled to roll up the exposed flank of the American right. Lord Rawdon had led the British left forward when Webster's wing advanced, but the Cont'ls. held their ground against repeated attacks. Fog, dust, and smoke hung over the battlefield from the start of this action; the reduced visibility undoubtedly contributed to the panic of the militia, and it isolated the American right from the knowledge that they were now standing alone against the entire enemy army. Kalb was sufficiently hard pressed, however, to call for the reserve when his flank came under attack. Although the 1st Md. Brig. had reformed after the militia passed through them, Gen. Smallwood had been swept away with the fugitives, so the omnipresent Otho Williams led the 1st Brig. forward. He tried to bring them up on the exposed flank of the 2d Brig., but the enemy held open a 300-yard gap between them. Cornwallis then turned Webster's regulars against the front of the reserve brigade; after being driven back twice and rallying twice, the Marylanders were driven from the field. Williams had meanwhile returned to the other brigade, where the British were closing in for hand-to-hand combat. Kalb had been unhorsed and was bleeding from several wounds, including a saber cut on the head, but the old Bavarian refused to quit or to retreat without orders from Gates. After leading a counterattack, which achieved a momentary success, the 58-year-old warrior fell mortally wounded. Maj. Geo. Hanger had led part of the Legion cavalry against the exposed flank of the American right, and Tarleton returned from his pursuit of the left wing to hit from the rear. The Battle of Camden was over and the pursuit began.

Maj. Archibald Anderson, Col. John Gunby, Lt. Col. John Howard, Capt. Henry Dobson, all of Md., and Capt. Robt. Kirkwood of Del. rallied about 60 men who retreated as a unit. Other survivors scattered individually or in small groups. Tarleton's cavalry met some resistance at Rugeley's Mill from Armand and a few other officers who were trying to save the baggage train from American looters and send it north to safety. The British pushed on to Hanging Rock before horses and men succumbed to exhaustion. Tarleton returned to Rugeley's late in the afternoon and left the next morning to destroy Sumter's command at FISHING CREEK, 18 Aug. See also PURSUIT PROBLEMS.

Gates, Caswell, and Smallwood were swept from the field with the first wave of fugitives. After abandoning hope of rallying at Rugeley's, Gates covered the remaining 60 miles to Charlotte, N.C., the day of his defeat. A few troops assembled at Charlotte—the remains of Armand's Legion (whose unit had done no fighting at Camden), Smallwood with a handful of men, and Gist with two or three. Believing Charlotte untenable, the wretched remnant of the army, accompanied by patriot refugees, 300 friendly Catawba Indians, and survivors of WAXHAWS started the arduous trek through Salisbury to Hillsboro. Gates arrived there on 19 Aug., having covered 200 miles in three and a half days. (See GATES'S FLIGHT)

NUMBERS AND LOSSES

Annihilation of Gates's army was so complete that no records of casualties exist and estimates vary tremendously. Of the 4,000 that had constituted "the grand army," only 700 reached Hillsboro. (Ward, 732)

There supposedly were 800 to 900 Americans killed and 1,000 captured at Camden (plus 150 killed and 300 captured at Fishing Creek two days later). These figures are given in the *Encyclopaedia Britannica* (11th ed.) and accepted by Richard B. Morris in his *Encyclopedia of American History*. Other estimates vary between Gates's report of 700 killed, wounded, and missing (he must have had his own definition of "missing"—perhaps his figures are for Cont'ls. only), and Cornwallis' claim of 1,000 killed and 800 captured. (Fisher, *op. cit.*, 298–99) The British historian Fortescue says about 1,000 Americans were killed and wounded and over 1,000 captured (*op. cit.*, 319); these figures indicate that he accepted Cornwallis' estimate of killed and wounded, but had some official basis for adding 200 prisoners. Ward says: "It has been estimated that 650 of the Continentals were killed or captured, [all of ?] the wounded falling into the hands of the enemy. About 100 of the North Carolina militia were killed or wounded, and [an additional?] 300 were captured. Only 3 of the Virginians were wounded [and none captured?]." (*op. cit.*, 732)

These figures of Ward are valuable primarily in showing which units did the fighting. Bear in mind that only 1,000 Cont'l. troops were on the field and that one battalion, Gist's 2d. Md., was far more heavily engaged than the other. Remember also that the Delawares on the east flank were under the heaviest pressure. Of the N.C. militia, Dixon's Regt., adjacent to the Delawares, was the only unit to put up any real resistance; most of the N.C. casualties must therefore have been in this unit.*

The British lost 324: two officers and 66 men killed, 18 officers and 238 men wounded, according to Fortescue. Most American writers accept the figures of Tarleton, which differ only in that he shows 11 fewer wounded and puts these 11 in the category of "missing"; Fortescue has "found" them, put them among the wounded; it all adds up to 324.

COMMENT

"Never was a victory more complete, or a defeat more total," wrote John Marshall; as late as 1900 it was called "the most disastrous defeat ever inflicted on an American army." (Marshall, I, 405; Fiske, II, 197) In England the victory appeared even greater because "Cornwallis had reported the disproportion [of opposing forces] as 5000 to 2000, and in Ross's edition of the Cornwallis correspondence, the dispro-

* If we interpret Ward's figures as meaning that total killed and wounded were 650 Cont'ls. and 100 N.C. militia, and if we apply the normal ratio of one killed to three wounded (see CASUALTY FIGURES), we arrive at an estimated 188 American dead. Considering the number of troops actually engaged on the field—the estimate of Williams (see above) that 2,000 of the 3,000 fled without firing a shot squares with the assumption that about 750 of the 1,000 Cont'ls. were seriously engaged, and perhaps 250 N.C. militia, for a total of 1,000—the above estimate of 188 killed is completely plausible. The fighting lasted less than an hour. Even if many fugitives were killed by Tarleton's cavalry and by Tory bands that hunted them in the swamps, it is hard to see how total American dead could number even half of the 1,000 so many historians accept.

portion is stated as 7000 to 2000." (Fisher, *op. cit.*, 298) Since Gates himself on the eve of battle thought he had 7,000, the errors of Cornwallis and his editor are excusable; they detract little from the magnitude of the triumph. In concept and execution the strategy and tactics of Cornwallis were first class. The performance of his troops and subordinate commanders, particularly Rawdon (before the battle), Webster (during the battle), and Tarleton (in the pursuit), was outstanding.

The unlovely Gates has been accused, with considerable justice, of making about every error possible. Since these have been pointed out in the course of this account, the following remarks will emphasize what has been said in his defense. Scheer and Rankin summarize it neatly:

"Civilians were quick to censure Gates, but few soldiers did; the harshest criticism leveled at him was not that he lost a battle but that he fought at all. Not many generals would have placed reliance on militia in the circumstances." (S. & R., 411)

Nathanael Greene, successor to Gates in the South, wrote him that after seeing the battlefield and reviewing Gates's dispositions, "I was more fully confirmed in my former sentiments that you was [*sic*] unfortunate but not blameable." (Quoted by Montross—a great Gates fan—from G. W. Greene, *Greene,* III, 54) The abandonment of Charlotte, however, Greene considered entirely unnecessary and, in his opinion, the thing that alienated the patriot public more than the defeat at Camden. (Fisher, *op. cit.,* 300) A committee of Congress fully exonerated Gates of misconduct. His famous, record-setting ride is covered separately under GATES'S FLIGHT FROM CAMDEN.

Following so closely after the American reverses at SAVANNAH, CHARLESTON, and WAXHAWS, Camden and Fishing Creek left the patriots in what Trevelyan calls "a morass of trouble which seemed to have neither shore nor bottom." (*Amer. Rev.*, V, 298) Cornwallis prepared for an invasion of N.C. that promised to meet no resistance. Congress let Washington pick the general to salvage what was left of the situation in the South after their selections, Lincoln and Gates, were eliminated. This led to the SOUTHERN CAMPAIGN of Greene, but even before this got under way the tide was turned at KINGS MOUNTAIN.

CAMDEN THANKS OF CONGRESS. As mentioned in the article above, the American defeat on 16 Aug. '80 has been described by eminent authorities as the most "total" or "disastrous" ever sustained by an American army. This did not deter the Cont'l. Cong. from their act of 14 Oct. '80 in which they:

"Resolved, that the thanks of Congress be given to Brigadier Generals Smallwood [who initially was in reserve, and subsequently was swept to the rear with the first wave of the retreat] and Gist and to the officers and soldiers in the Maryland and Delaware lines, the different corps of Artillery, Colonel Porterfield's and Major Armstrong's corps of Light Infantry and Colonel Armand's Cavalry, for their bravery and good conduct displayed in the action of the 16th of August last, near Camden, in the State of South Carolina." (Heitman, 249)

"CAMP FEVER." Any epidemic fever occurring in camps, chiefly typhus. (*O.U.D.*)

CAMPAIGN. "A connected series of military operations forming a distinct stage in a war; originally, the time during which an army kept the field [*campagne*]." (Webster's Unabridged) See MILITARY AFFAIRS for an index of campaigns covered in this book.

CAMPBELL, Archibald. 1739–1791. British officer. A military engineer in the West Indies during the Seven Years' War, this Archibald Campbell had no service in North America before the Revolution. (His sketch in *D.N.B.* is badly in error, I have been informed by a descendant, Mr. Colin Campbell of Belmont, Mass.) An M.P. for the Stirling boroughs (1774–1780), Archibald Campbell in 1775 became Lt. Col. of the 2d Bn., FRASER HIGHLANDERS. He was captured in mid-June '76 in Boston Harbor (see FRASER HIGHLANDERS).

Exchanged about two years later for Ethan ALLEN, having received some harsh treatment in retaliation for cruelties suffered by American prisoners, he led the expedition from New York that took SAVANNAH, 29 Dec. '78. Lt. Col. Campbell then marched virtually unopposed to occupy Augusta on 29 Jan. '79. After the subsequent maneuvers, covered under "Lincoln's Operations" on page 1034, Campbell commanded British forces occupying Georgia.

He had been given a provisional appointment as governor of that province and South Carolina, to be effective when subjugation was completed, but Campbell had little success in raising Loyalist militia and became discouraged about his prospects for a political future in the South. The most ardent Georgia Loyalists had already left to join the royal cause, and the conquest of South Carolina was beyond the capabilities of British troops in 1779. So in the spring of that year Campbell went home on leave and was promoted to Col. for his victory at Savannah. In July '82, he was appointed Gov. of Jamaica, where he distinguished himself in raising Negro militia for defense of the island and in rendering valuable service to the over-all war effort in America. On his return to England he was knighted (K.B.) on 30 Sept. '85.

Appointed Gov. and C. in C. at Madras, he reached his new post in Apr. '86. Cornwallis praised him for his treaty with the Nabob of Arcot and the settlement of the latter's debts, but he was plagued by criticism from the Nabob's creditors and the East India Company that his solution did not sufficiently protect their interests. Badgered and in bad health, he resigned in 1789 and came home. He was re-elected to Parliament but lived less than two years. He is buried in Westminster Abbey.

CAMPBELL, John. See John Campbell, 4th Earl of LOUDOUN.

CAMPBELL, John. 1753–1784. British officer. Second son of John Campbell of Stonefield, his mother was the sister of Lord Bute. In 1771 he entered the army as Ensign in the 37th Regt. and in 1774 he became a Lt. in the 7th Foot (Fusiliers). At the start of the Revolution this regiment and the 26th Foot, both of them under strength, were the only British regulars at the disposal of Carleton for the defense of Canada. (Fortescue, *British Army*, III, 153) According to *D.N.B.* he was captured early in the war, and this almost certainly took place at CHAMBLY, Canada, 18 Oct. '75. Soon exchanged, he was promoted to Capt. in the 71st Highlanders on 2 Dec. '75, and on 30 Dec. '77 he became Maj. in the 74th Highlanders. In 1780 he returned to England, and on 7 Feb. '81 he was promoted to Lt. Col. He distinguished himself in India, where he commanded the famous

defense of Mangalore, 19 May '83–23 Jan. '84, and surrendered his 856 survivors with the HONORS OF WAR. After taking his command to Bombay he left them on 9 Feb., exhausted by his experience, and on 23 Feb. '84 he died at that city. (H. Manners Chichester in *D.N.B.*)

He is confused with Gen. John CAMPBELL (d. 1806) by such eminent authorities as Fortescue. (*Op. cit.,* III, index)

CAMPBELL, John. d. 1806. British general. Entering the army in June '45 as Lt. in Loudoun's Highlanders, he served through the Second Jacobite Rebellion (see LOUDOUN and CULLODEN MOOR) and took part in the Flanders campaign in 1747. Promoted to Capt. on 1 Oct. of the latter year, he was appointed to the 42d Highlanders on 9 Apr. '56, and was wounded at Ticonderoga in 1758. (See COLONIAL WARS) On 11 July '59 he became Maj. of the 17th Foot, he was promoted to Lt. Col. in the army on 1 Feb. '62, and he commanded the regiment in the operations against Martinico and Havana in 1762. On 1 May '73 he became Lt. Col. of the 37th Foot, and in 1776 he went to America with this regiment. (The preceding information is from Appleton's. This Campbell is not in *D.N.B.*) During the Philadelphia Campaign he was part of Sir Henry Clinton's force left in N.Y. With the local rank of B.G. he apparently was commander on Staten Island in 1777 and 1778. (See STATEN ISLAND, Aug. '77) Starting the evening of 11 Sept. '77 he led a force that landed at Elizabethtown, N.J., with the dual mission of creating a diversion in favor of Gen. Howe's main army—which that day fought the battle of the Brandywine—and also of conducting a large-scale foraging operation through Newark and into the British position at Passaic. The raid netted some horses, about 400 head of cattle, the same number of sheep, and 20 milk cows, "which afforded a seasonable refreshment to the squadron and the army...." (Clinton, *Amer. Reb.*, 71)

Around the end of Nov. '78 Clinton detached two Campbells to the Southern theater, Lt. Col. Archibald Campbell to take Savannah, and Gen. John Campbell to take command in West Florida. The latter was sent, at the suggestion of Germain, with orders to capture New Orleans if Spain entered the war. (*Ibid.*, 133 *n.*, 154) Meanwhile he had been given the local rank of Maj. Gen. on 19 Feb. '79. (Appleton's) Far from being able to execute the ambitious strategy proposed by Germain, who neglected the detail of sending him adequate means (see Campbell's letter of 15 Dec. '79 to Clinton in *Amer. Reb.*, 437), Campbell was forced to surrender PENSACOLA, 9 May '81. He apparently was exchanged almost immediately and promoted, since he attended a council of war in N.Y.C. on 14 Sept. '81 and is identified with the rank of Lt. Gen. (*Ibid.*, 569)

After the war he was promoted to Lt. Gen. (regular, as opposed to "local rank in America") on 28 Sept. '87, and 10 years later he became a full general. (Appleton's)

CAMPBELL, Lord William. d. 1778. Royal Gov. of S.C. Fourth son of the 4th Duke of Argyll and of the Honorable Mary Bellenden, daughter of Lord Bellenden and maid of honor to Caroline, Princess of Wales, William was from what you might call a good family. He entered the navy and rose rapidly to the rank of Capt. (1762). In 1766 he resigned after two years in Parliament to accept appointment as Gov. of Nova Scotia. In 1773 he became Gov. of S.C., succeeding the able Lt. Gov. William BULL. Campbell had visited the province in 1763, when he commanded the *Nightingale*, and on 7 Apr. of that year had married Sarah, daughter of the

wealthy and influential Ralph Izard. He reached Charleston on 17 June '75 to find a situation that even a capable governor could not have salvaged for the Crown, and after attempting through secret negotiations to gain the support of the frontier element and the Indians (See John STUART) he was forced to take refuge on the British warship *Tamar* (on 15 Sept. '75) when the patriots started mobilizing. Although his secret negotiations had been discovered, the moderate faction of the province had prevented Campbell's seizure by the radicals, and even after his flight the Council of Safety invited him to return. Campbell refused, and threatened Charleston until the guns of recently captured Ft. Johnson drove the *Tamar* off. Having been joined by his Tory wife, the short-term governor withdrew to Jamaica (Appleton's). Aboard the new frigate *Syren* which had reached Cape Fear from England on 7 Jan. '76 and apparently had picked up Campbell near Charleston (Clinton, *American Rebellion*, 26 and *n.*), the exiled governor joined Gen. Henry Clinton for his expedition against Charleston. Serving as a volunteer he commanded the lower gun deck of the *Bristol* (Appleton's) in the attack of 28 June '76. "His Lordship received a contusion on his left side," reported Sir Peter Parker in his famous letter of 9 July '76 (published 24 Aug.), "but... it has not proved of much consequence." (Clinton, *American Rebellion*, 378) Returning to England, he died 5 Sept. '78 at Southampton, apparently as a result of this wound that Adm. Parker had reported as being inconsequential (Appleton's).

CAMPBELL, William. 1745–1781. Patriot leader at Kings Mountain. Va. Of a family that had settled in the Holston Valley at Aspenvale (near Abingdon), Va., after coming from

Argyll, Scotland, by way of Northern Ireland and Pa., William Campbell grew into a gigantic frontiersman of great strength and endurance. He married Elizabeth, sister of Patrick Henry. As a Capt. of militia he fought the Cherokees and took part in Dunmore's War of 1774. On 15 Dec. he became Capt. in the 1st Va., Patrick Henry's Regt., and after participating in the operations that drove Dunmore from the province, Campbell resigned his commission in Oct. '76. Thereafter he took part in the partisan warfare of the frontier, served as boundary commissioner in dealings with the Cherokees, rose to Col. in the militia, and was a delegate to the Va. legislature.

At the urging of Isaac Shelby, Campbell led 400 Virginia riflemen to join the forces being assembled to attack the column of Tories under Patrick Ferguson that was threatening to invade the country of the "Over Mountain Men." When the others could not agree upon a commander they elected Campbell "Officer of the Day," and as such he was nominal leader of the composite force that won the important victory at KINGS MOUNTAIN, S.C., 7 Oct. '80. Two months later he became B.G. of militia. (Heitman)

With a few riflemen he joined Greene for the battle of GUILFORD, N.C., 15 Mar. '81, and he later led a body of riflemen to reinforce Lafayette in Va. On 13 June he arrived with 600 men, and about 10 days later this force had grown to 780. (Johnston, *Yorktown*, 52, 55) The mountaineers did not, however, take part in the action at Green Spring, 6 July. Campbell fell sick shortly thereafter and died at Rocky Mills, Hanover co., on 22 Aug. '81.

CANADA, CONGRESSIONAL COMMITTEE TO. Mar.–June. '76. Realizing that the CANADA INVASION was failing politically as well as militarily,

Congress decided early in 1776 to send a special committee to do what they could to win over the people. Benjamin Franklin, Samuel Chase, and Charles Carroll (not then a member of the Congress) were selected. The latter was a Catholic, educated in France, and persuaded his brother, a priest, to go along. The group left Philadelphia on 25 Mar. and reached Montreal on 29 Apr., after a rigorous trip. For reasons mentioned under CANADA IN THE REVOLUTION, their task was foredoomed. They returned in early June with firsthand accounts of "shocking mismanagement" of military operations.

CANADA CREEK, N.Y., Action at. See JERSEYFIELD.

CANADA IN THE REVOLUTION. When British statesmen, under the domination of the new British king, GEORGE III, were negotiating the Treaty of Paris at the end of the Seven Years' (French and Indian) War in 1763, many advocated that the British take the small, sugar-rich island of Guadaloupe in the West Indies and leave the large territory of Canada in French hands. One of their considerations was that the continued presence of the traditional French and Indian enemies in Canada would make the 13 Colonies continue to look to England for protection. The British decided, however, to take Canada. Thanks largely, if not almost entirely, to the enlightenment of Guy CARLETON as viceroy of Canada after 1767, the new province remained loyal to George III, even though it was predominantly French in population. The QUEBEC ACT strengthened the ties between Canada and England, and struck the English colonies to the south as being another of the "intolerable acts." As patriot groups of the 13 Colonies began organizing their resistance they looked hopefully northward for a "14th colony" to join them. Having gotten no encouragement, the Americans launched the ill-fated CANADA INVASION and, when this had about collapsed, sent a congressional committee to Canada. (See CANADA, CONG. COMM. TO)

In his *Canada and the American Revolution,* George M. Wrong attributes American failure less to the acknowledged tactlessness of the provincial invaders than to the Canadians' ingrained respect for authority. The latter, he says, "derived less from loyalty to George III than from monarchical France and Catholic Rome."

Carleton discovered to his chagrin that Canadian loyalty to England was passive: it did not include a willingness to fight for George III against his southern subjects. Certain Anglo-Saxon Canadians sided with the Americans, and two CANADIAN REGTS. were formed to fight against England. A number of Canadians became prominent in the Cont'l. armies. (Moses HAZEN, for example.) The northern province became a refuge for many LOYALISTS; the latter article includes the comment of a Canadian historian that they "were makers of Canada."

According to Van Tyne, "The ablest analyses of this whole Canadian fiasco are in chapter vi of V. Coffin, *The Province of Quebec and the Early American Revolution,* and in R. Coupland, *The Quebec Act,* [pages] 160–73, and there are important differences of of opinion." He also cites J. H. Smith, *Our Struggle for the Fourteenth Colony* (2 vols., 1907) which Howard Peckham, writing in 1958, says is still the best account of the Montgomery-Arnold invasion (*War for Independence,* 212). Wrong's *Canada in the American Revolution* is, of course, a basic authority and Allen French deals with the subject in his *First Year of the American Revolution.* See also Joseph L. Rutledge, *Century of Conflict: the*

Struggle between the French and British in Colonial America, a recent book by a Canadian journalist, and Charles H. Metzger, *The Quebec Act.* Works pertaining to ARNOLD'S MARCH TO QUEBEC are listed at the end of that article.

CANADA INVASION, Aug. '75–Oct. '76. Although capture of Ticonderoga, 10 May '75, opened the way for an American advance into Canada, Congress resolved on 1 June that no such operation should be undertaken. On 27 June, however, they reversed themselves and directed Gen. Schuyler to invade, if practicable, what they hoped to make the "14th colony." After numerous delays resulting from Schuyler's preparations, his second in command, Gen. Richard Montgomery, started north on Lake Champlain with 1,200 troops and a small, heterogeneous fleet. The sick and despondent Schuyler joined Montgomery on 4 Sept., but was invalided to the rear on the 16th. Operations against strategic ST. JOHNS, 5 Sept.–2 Nov. '75, were started by Schuyler and finished by Montgomery. The stout British defense was overcome only after the fall of nearby CHAMBLY, 18 Oct. During this period Ethan Allen made his abortive attack on MONTREAL, 25 Sept. Although plagued with disciplinary problems, Montgomery pushed on to take Montreal, 13 Nov., without resistance.

Meanwhile, the start of ARNOLD'S MARCH TO QUEBEC on 13 Sept. unfolded the complete, misguided strategy of the campaign.

CARLETON WINS HIS SPURS

The humane and sensible Gen. Guy Carleton, governor of Canada since 1766 (three years after the Treaty of PARIS), had won the affection and respect of the 80,000 or so French Canadian "new subjects" to the extent that

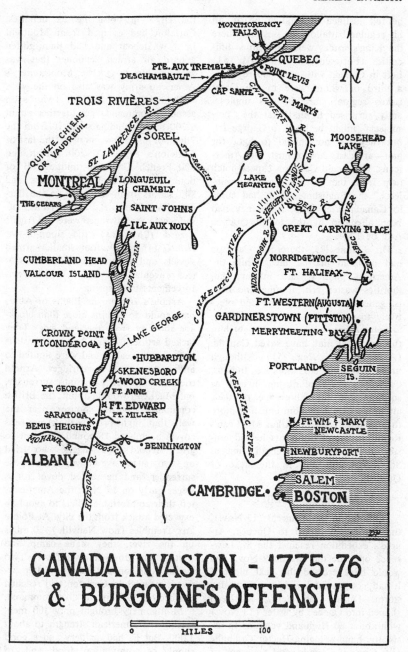

CANADA INVASION - 1775-76
& BURGOYNE'S OFFENSIVE

0 MILES 100

he felt justified in sending nearly all his regular battalions to Boston, where the King's forces were in serious difficulties. (Fortescue, *Br. Army,* III, 163) Left in Canada with only 800 regulars, a third of whom were in the Great Lakes region, Carleton was unpleasantly surprised to find that the "new subjects" might be loyal to George III, but they did not intend to fight for him—at least, not against the Americans. Nor could Carleton expect much help from the few hundred "old subjects," the Englishmen who had come to Canada after 1763, since they had been alienated by the recent QUEBEC ACT of 1774.

On 9 June '75, therefore, Carleton had declared martial law. While the American political and military authorities wasted critical time, the British general worked vigorously and effectively to scrape troops together. Then, at Saint Johns, his regulars bought him the time that may have saved Canada. (Alden, *Amer. Rev.,* 51) Although urged by Gage to mobilize Indians, Carleton's contempt of the savages as soldiers and his abhorrence of their atrocities kept him from enlisting more than a few. Lt. Col. Allan MacLean's Royal Highland Emigrants helped bolster British military strength, first at St. Johns and then in the siege of Quebec.

SIEGE OF QUEBEC

With the fall of Montreal (13 Nov.), the battlefield shifted to Quebec. Arnold's expedition reached the St. Lawrence opposite the city on 9 Nov., and would have crossed the next night if it had not been delayed by a three-day storm. During this delay, MacLean slipped into Quebec by water (13 Nov.) with about 80 Highland veterans to assist the hand-wringing Hector Cramahé (Lt. Gov. of Canada, and governor of

the city) in bolstering its defenses. Carleton had escaped from Montreal in a whaleboat and had then gotten aboard an armed schooner that was speeding him to Quebec. Montgomery's American army was also on the way.

Cramahé and MacLean (who soon assumed command) got together about 1,200 men, including some 70 from the 7th Foot and a few gunners (the last of Carleton's regulars), 200 British and 300 French Canadian militia (all of doubtful reliability), 37 marines and 345 sailors from the ships in the harbor. (Ward, *W.O.R.,* 183) In the half-mile-wide St. Lawrence were the frigate *Lizard* (26 guns), the sloop-of-war *Hunter* (16 guns), four smaller armed vessels, and two transports (*ibid.,* 182); ice prevented arrival of British reinforcements until spring.

Arnold's 700 on the Plains of Abraham could do nothing more than blockade the city from the land side. They lacked artillery, over a hundred muskets were unserviceable, and were limited to an average of five cartridges. Arnold tried to bluff MacLean into surrender, but MacLean wouldn't bluff; the British commander burned houses near the walls that might provide the Americans cover, he lobbed 18-pound shot out to greet Arnold's messengers who tried on two successive days to propose surrender, and he settled down for a siege. Early on 19 Nov. the Americans left their comfortable billets to avoid an expected attack from the city. At Pointe aux Trembles (now Neuville), 20 miles up the river, they made camp and waited for Montgomery's force. Two weeks later, on 2 Dec., the latter arrived; meanwhile, Carleton had reached Quebec on 19 Nov. to take command.

Montgomery brought only 300 men, raising the American strength to about 1,000. But he had artillery and a good supply of ammunition, food, and—of much more immediate interest to Arnold's threadbare survivors of the wilderness—a year's supply of clothing captured from the 7th and 26th British regiments.

On 5 Dec., the Americans were once more outside the gates of Quebec. Although the defenders outnumbered him more than two to one, and had the further advantage of fortifications, Montgomery planned to take Quebec by assault. This operation is covered under QUEBEC, 31 Dec. '75–1 Jan. '76, a brave but costly defeat in which Montgomery was killed and Arnold badly wounded.

THE RETREAT

With about 600 men—including Canadians and Indians who had joined, but soon reduced by 100 men whose time expired—Arnold remained outside the walls and called for a veteran general and fresh troops to renew the attack. Gen. David Wooster was holding Montreal, Chambly, and St. Johns with fewer than 600 men, and had no troops to spare. (A British regiment was still in the Great Lakes region, and the Indian threat was ever present.) Gen. Schuyler could offer no assistance from Albany, since he was occupied with Tory uprisings in the Mohawk Valley and Tryon county. Arnold's emissary, Edward Antil, continued on to Philadelphia, where Congress voted on 19 Jan. '76 to send reinforcements to Canada. Washington had learned two days earlier of the Quebec disaster. Despite his own problems of holding together enough troops for the BOSTON SIEGE, he proposed that a regiment of 728 men be raised for service in Canada, and that this total be deducted from the 13 militia regiments the Colonies had been asked to furnish for his own operations around Boston. (Freeman, *Washington*, IV, 11) Although Schuyler and Congress proposed that he detach trained

battalions, Washington steadfastly resisted this dilution of his meager military resources until April, when the British had evacuated Boston and he shifted his own operations to N.Y.C.; he then agreed to send four battalions to Canada. (*Ibid.*, 11, 12, 83)

Wooster joined Arnold at Quebec on 2 Apr. and took command of a force that now numbered 2,000. Arnold, who had been promoted to B.G. (10 Jan.), went to take command at Montreal; his wound had healed, but he had been injured subsequently by a fall from his horse. Maj. Gen. John Thomas reached Quebec on 1 May, and assumed command of an army that had been built up to 2,500, only to be reduced by death, discharges, and desertions to 1,900; the 1,000 of these carried on the rolls as "fit for duty" were further reduced by expiration of 300 enlistments, and 200 were under inoculation for smallpox. But more troops were on the way: the 2d N.J. and six companies of the 2d Pa. were starting, to reach Quebec in May; Brig. Gen. William Thompson had reached Ft. George with the four battalions from Washington (2,000 musketmen, a company of riflemen, and a company of artificers); Brig. Gen. Sullivan was moving from Albany with a brigade of 3,300 from N.Y. By May there were probably 7,000 Americans in Canada. (C. & M., 212) Among them was the special congressional committee composed of Benjamin Franklin, Charles Carroll, and Samuel Chase, who reached Montreal 29 Apr. (see CANADA, CONGRESSIONAL COMMITTEE TO).

Despite the apparent absurdity of their posture—500 effectives, on the end of a long line of communications, besieging a walled city of 5,000 inhabitants garrisoned by 1,600 armed men, who were supported by 148 cannon and several ships—the Americans waited outside the walls of Quebec. And when the ice started breaking up in the St. Lawrence, the inevitable happened: British sails and British reinforcements. On 2 May, Gen. Thomas learned that 15 ships had entered the mouth of the river. Carleton waited only to disembark 200 men, and on 6 May sallied forth with 900 troops and four guns to check a report that the Americans were preparing to retreat. Able to muster only 250 to oppose this reconnaissance in force, Thomas beat a disorderly retreat, leaving 200 sick, hundreds of muskets, their artillery, and the headquarters records. Carleton did not pursue, but waited to receive the reinforcements under Gen. John Burgoyne, which would bring his total strength to 13,000. (Fortescue, *op. cit.*, 178) Included in this force were 4,300 German mercenaries under Gen. Von Riedesel.

The American rout was halted at Deschambault, 40 miles up the St. Lawrence. Thomas led his men to Sorel, where they arrived on 17 May, having been harassed on the way by British marines. A group of men that had not heretofore been notably military, the Americans were now a demoralized, diseased mob. Smallpox had been prevalent among them for some time, but it now reached epidemic proportions. Thomas died of the disease on 2 June; when Congress learned of this four days later it immediately recalled the incompetent WOOSTER to prevent his normal succession to temporary command of the forces in Canada. On 1 June, Sullivan caught up with Thompson's column (mentioned above) at St. Johns, where it had been waiting two weeks.

Although the Americans had suffered another defeat at the CEDARS, arrival of fresh troops and adequate supplies raised hopes that something might be salvaged of the Canadian adventure. These hopes were rapidly extinguished at TROIS RIVIÈRES, 8 June.

CARLETON'S COUNTEROFFENSIVE

Sullivan had no alternative but to order a retreat to Lake Champlain. With the main portion of the army, about 2,500, Sullivan evacuated Sorel on 14 June; the British fleet reached that place within an hour after his last bateau left. With 300 men from Montreal, Arnold escaped across the river to Longueuil on 9 June and retreated toward St. Johns with the enemy on his heels. Arnold commanded the rear guard while crowded bateaux evacuated troops and matériel from St. Johns. On 19 June, the last of Sullivan's men reached Ile aux Noix. Here the 2,000 who were suffering from smallpox were joined within two days by another 1,500 or so who were victims of dysentery or malaria. During the first days of July the survivors straggled into Crown Point, 10 months after Montgomery had left that place to conquer Canada. They had left 5,000 casualties in Canada, 3,000 were hospital cases, and the remaining 5,000 "fit for duty" were such in the strictest administrative sense only. On 17 June, Congress ordered Gen. Horatio Gates to take command of the troops in Canada. Since Schuyler was still at his headquarters in Albany and Sullivan was with the troops at Crown Point, there was a question as to which of these officers Gates was succeeding. On 8 July, Congress clarified its instructions, and Gates became Schuyler's second in command; Gates accepted this with good grace, but Sullivan left the Northern Department with the intimation he would resign. Despite the objection of many subordinate officers, Schuyler, Gates, Sullivan, and Woedtke had decided in a council of war at Crown Point on 5 July to abandon Crown Point and concentrate their defense at Ticonderoga. Here the army was reinforced by militia and by three Cont'l. regiments.

Carleton stopped at St. Johns until 4 Oct., by which time he had been reinforced to 13,000 rank and file and had constructed a fleet. He planned to advance along the line of Lake Champlain and the Hudson to Albany, from which point he could cooperate with Howe, who would advance up the Hudson from N.Y.C. By 24 Aug., however, Arnold had constructed an American fleet that sailed north from Crown Point to challenge the British advance. In the battle of VALCOUR ISLAND, 11 Oct. '76, Arnold fought the British to a standstill. During the night he slipped away, and carried out a running fight on 13 Oct. The improvised American fleet was wiped out, but its existence—which forced Carleton to stop and build his own fleet—may well have saved the cause. (Van Tyne, *War of Indep.*, 373) Carleton reconsidered his plan of taking Ft. Ticonderoga, decided that even a short delay would prevent his pushing on through to Albany before winter endangered operations, and the British withdrew to St. Johns. "Had Ticonderoga been taken and held that coming winter, Burgoyne's campaign of 1777, starting from that point, would have almost certainly succeeded." (*Ibid.*)

COMMENTS

Time beat the Americans in Canada —Congress wasted weeks before authorizing it, Schuyler wasted weeks organizing it, and the British bought themselves more time by their admirable resistance at Ft. St. Johns. If any of these delays had been reduced by perhaps as little as two weeks, it is not likely that Carleton would have won knighthood for the defense of Quebec. On the other hand, what chance would the Americans have had of holding Canada against British naval supremacy?

It is interesting that American historians tend to consider the Canada Invasion as a useless frittering away of men, money, and supplies that could have been better used for defense. (Montross, *Reluctant Rebels,* 142, for example) Van Tyne says the American invasion of another province aroused the lethargic British ministry into preparations for war. "Minds too dull to be awakened by Lexington and the siege of Boston were stirred to action by this 'treason to the empire.'" (*Op. cit.,* 69) Channing points out that this strategic diversion, although a failure in itself, delayed Howe's NEW YORK CAMPAIGN, but an English historian goes much further:

"Indirectly [the American failure at Quebec] lured the British Government into a false plan of operations, and to a disaster [at SARATOGA] which, less for its strategic consequences than from its moral effect in Europe, virtually decided the issue of the war." (Fortescue, *op. cit.,* 165, 243)

See also CANADA IN THE REVOLUTION, where a list of authorities will be found.

CANADA INVASION (Planned). 1778. During the Conway Cabal, and apparently as part of it (Fisher, *Struggle,* I, 423), the new Board of War planned an invasion of Canada. Washington was not informed of this strategy until late Jan. '78 and referred to it as "the child of folly." (Freeman, *Washington,* IV, 598 *n.*) On 22 Jan., Congress had selected Lafayette to lead this operation. When the young Frenchman reached Albany to collect supplies and troops he found a lack of preparations that ultimately ruined what slim chance the plan might have had: quartermaster and commissary supplies were lacking; fewer than half of the expected 2,500 men were assembled; and Stark's militia, who were supposed to accompany him, had not even been called. Meanwhile the enemy made dispositions to oppose his line of operations down Lake Champlain and to Montreal. By mid-March Lafayette saw the operation was hopeless and Congress accepted his recommendation that it be abandoned. (Lafayette, *Memoirs,* quoted in C. & M., II, 707–8)

CANADIAN REGIMENT, 1st. Formed 20 Nov. '75 of refugees organized by James Livingston, it is considered by some authorities to have disbanded during the first few days of 1776, after the disastrous assault on QUEBEC. Yet Heitman shows James Livingston as its Col. from 20 Nov. '75 until his retirement on 1 Jan. '81. This same authority shows James Livingston's brother Richard as Lt. Col. of the regiment from 18 Dec. '76 [*sic*] to 2 Nov. '79 (when the latter resigned), and Maj. George C. Nicholson is shown as serving with the regiment from 1 Apr. '77 to 1 Jan. '81. Presumably the "Canadian Regt." that Livingston formed in late 1775 did disband the end of that year but this subsequent command drew Canadian refugees into its ranks and retained the nickname.

CANADIAN REGIMENT, 2d. Also called "Congress' Own" and "Hazen's Own," this unit was organized 22 Jan. '76 and commanded throughout the war by Col. Moses HAZEN.

CANAJOHARIE SETTLEMENTS, N.Y., 1–2 Aug. '80. (BORDER WARFARE) The principal fortification in this part of the Mohawk Valley was Ft. Plank, a three-story blockhouse of heavy timbers surrounded by earthworks and located on a plain overlooking the village that became Fort Plain. (Stone, *Border Wars,* I, 98) On 6 June Col. Peter Gansevoort occupied Ft. Plank with his regiment in preparation for escorting supplies from there to Ft. Stanwix (Schuyler). Joseph Brant, whose

presence in the area caused patriot authorities to prescribe special precautions, spread rumors that he intended not only to attack the convoy but also to attack Ft. Stanwix. This resulted in strength being drawn from the settlements and the fort to reinforce Stanwix and protect the westbound convoy. Brant then entered Canajoharie unopposed from the east and destroyed 53 dwellings, an equal number of barns, a church, and a mill; he killed 16 inhabitants who had not fled with the rest to Ft. Plank, Ft. Clyde, and other strong points, and he captured 50. An estimated 300 head of livestock were killed or carried away. Since his object was pillage and destruction—the harvest of SULLIVAN'S EXPEDITION—Brant did not waste his strength in attacking the forts. Stone comments that the Indians commited no atrocities (of the Cherry Valley, Wyoming variety), which he attributes to the fact that no Tories were along and to the fact that Brant was the single commander of this raid. (*Border Wars,* 99)

CANE CREEK, N.C., 12 Sept. '80. In the Tory invasion of western N.C. that preceded the battle of KINGS MOUNTAIN, Patrick Ferguson pushed some 22 miles north of Gilbert Town (now Rutherfordton), N.C. After a skirmish with rebel militia he started the withdrawal that led to his annihilation at Kings Mountain. The *A.A.–* Heitman List of Battles (see bibliography) includes an action on Cane Creek, N.C., occurring 12 Sept. '80, and the map from Avery's *History* that faces page 192 of F. V. Greene's *Revolutionary War* shows that the limit of Ferguson's advance was marked by a skirmish at Cane Creek, near Brindletown (about 22 miles N. of Gilbert Town) on 12 Sept. '80. Precisely where this action took place is uncertain, particularly since the spot shown in

Greene's work is actually on *Silver Creek*, according to the map of the Kings Mountain campaign in Scribner's *Atlas* (plate 75). By a strange coincidence another action took place exactly a year. later at another CANE CREEK, N.C., 12 Sept. '81.

CANE CREEK (Lindley's Mill), N.C., 12 Sept. '81. See HILLSBORO RAID.

CANISTER. An artillery projectile consisting of a can (canister) packed with small round shot that scatter—shotgun fashion—when the projectile leaves the muzzle. It was used at close range against personnel. It should not be confused with GRAPE or with shrapnel, a type of projectile in which the shot is scattered by a time fuze after the projectile leaves the gun.

CAPE VINCENT, Portugal, 16 Jan. '81. Naval victory of Adm. George B. RODNEY.

CARCASS. An incendiary projectile used for setting fire to buildings or ships. Of doubtful etymology.

CARLETON, Christopher. d. 1787. British officer. Nephew and brother-in-law of Sir Guy CARLETON and the latter's A.D.C., he has been described as "a man with an Indian as well as a white wife, who dressed like a savage, painted his face, and wore a ring in his nose" (Peckham, *War for Indep.*, 61). He was the second son of Sir Guy's elder brother William (*Collins's Peerage*). Becoming a Lt. in the 31st Foot on 29 July '63, around 1770 he married Anne, second daughter of Thomas, 2d Earl Effingham (1714–1763) (*Burke's Peerage*). It is said that in 1770 his uncle had proposed to this same lady while visiting the Earl's country house. Although much embarrassed to find that Christopher had been there before him, he subsequently married the third daughter, Mary, who was half his age.

Christopher Carleton was promoted to Capt.–Lt. on 25 Dec. '70, and to Capt. on 25 May '72. After leading the initial movement of Burgoyne's Offensive up Lake Champlain he was promoted to Maj. of the 29th Foot on 14 Sept. '77. The next year he was operating as a spy in the Mohawk Valley, as is revealed in this letter of 6 Mar. '78 from Col. (James?) Livingston to Col. Gansevoort: "Enclosed you have a letter from . . . Lafayette, relative to Col. Carleton, nephew to Gen. Carleton, who has for some time been in this part of the country as a spy. The general apprehends he has taken his route by the way of Oswego, and begs you'll send out such parties as you may judge necessary for apprehending him." The enclosed letter read:

"Sir,—As the taking of Col. Carleton is of the greatest importance, I wish you would try every means in your power to have him apprehended. I have desired Col. Livingston, who knows him, to let you have any intelligence he can give. . . . You may send as many parties as you please. . . . You may promise, in my name, fifty guineas, hard money, besides all money, &c. they can find [*sic*] about Carleton, to any party of soldiers or Indians who will bring him alive. As every one knows now what we send for, there is no inconvenience to scatter them in the country, which reward is promised in order to stimulate the Indians."

"Col. Carleton, it is believed, was not apprehended," concludes W. W. Campbell, from whose *Annals of Tryon County* (pp. 157–58) this is taken. Strangely, Swiggett does not mention this Carleton in his *War out of Niagara*. A Maj. Carleton, surely our man, reappears as leader of a raid that captured Ft. George on 11 Oct. '80 (date is from *A.A.*–Heitman list) and attacked Ballston, a mere 12 miles north of Albany; this was in connection with the phase of BORDER WARFARE covered in the section headed "Sir John Johnson's First Raid."

On 19 Feb. '83 he was promoted to Lt. Col. in the Army and he died at Quebec in 1787 (*Burke's Peerage*).

CARLETON, Guy. 1724–1808. British general, Gov. of Canada, C. in C. at N.Y.C. (May '82–Nov. '83). Of an old Irish family, he entered the army as an ensign on 21 May '42 and was a Lt. three years later. Transferring to the 1st Foot Guards on 22 July '51, six years later he became Capt.–Lt. and Lt. Col. of the regiment. In June and July '58 he served under Amherst in the capture of Louisburg and on 24 Aug. transferred to the 78th Foot. On 30 Dec. he received the "local rank" of Col. and became Q.M.G. to his friend James Wolfe. In the latter's capture of Quebec, 13 Sept. '59, Carleton was wounded while leading the grenadiers and was given the temporary rank of B.G. As an acting B.G. he took part in the siege of Belle Isle, off France, in 1761, was wounded at Port Andro, and promoted to Col. on 19 Feb. '62. He distinguished himself in the siege of Havana and was wounded there on 22 July. On 24 Sept. '66 he was appointed Lt. Gov. of Quebec and the next year took over the duties of Gov. when Gen. Murray left. In 1770 he left for England. On 2 Apr. '72 he became Col. of the 47th Foot and on 25 May was promoted to Maj. Gen. In the House of Commons in June '74 he argued for passage of the QUEBEC ACT, which he is said to have drafted. (G. F. Russell Barker in *D.N.B.*) Toward the end of this year he returned to Canada, where he already was popular and where he was warmly greeted by the clergy. On 10 Jan. '75 he was appointed Gov. of Quebec. He was subordinate to Gage until the latter's recall to England on 11

Oct. '75, and when Wm. Howe was formally named successor to Gage the next Apr. Carleton became an independent commander of the British forces in Canada.

Carleton badly misjudged the Canadians by believing that their recent loyalty to Great Britain (since 1763) meant they would fight for her against the 13 Colonies. As a result he sent many of his regulars to Boston. With only 800 regulars left, and with a third of these detached in the Great Lakes region, he declared martial law on 9 June '75. His remarkable attempt to defend his province is covered under the CANADA INVASION.

"In Canada everything was dominated by the personality of Guy Carleton. Since it is to this Irish gentleman ... that England owes the retention of all that the Revolution left of her empire in North America, it is strange that his name is not greater in her history. He was an extraordinary man. A soldier of long and honorable service, it is by his statesmanship in Canada that he most deserves remembrance. Although an Irish Protestant, and therefore belonging to a body more bitter against Rome than any in the world, he had the wisdom to see that Canada could be governed only by complete toleration.* * * Indeed, had it not been for his policy and personality the Canadians might very will have gone over to the rebels in a body." (Nickerson, *Turning Point,* 68–69)

His pursuit of the Americans having been slowed by the necessity to meet the threat of Benedict Arnold's *ad hoc* fleet (see VALCOUR ISLAND) and stopped by the approach of winter, Carleton left Crown Point on 3 Nov. '76 and withdrew to St. Johns. On 6 July, meanwhile, he had been nominated for knighthood (K.B.) and was given a special warrant to wear the insignia and use the title before being invested in the usual manner. (*D.N.B.*)

The CARLETON–GERMAIN FEUD, dissatisfaction in London over Carleton's failure to carry the war into N.Y., and the scheming of Burgoyne—who returned on leave to England and presented Carleton's Lake Champlain operations in an unfavorable light—ended Sir Guy's active battlefield service in America. Although he loyally supported BURGOYNE'S OFFENSIVE, he demanded that he be recalled to England. Meanwhile he continued to command in Canada and on 29 Aug. '77 was promoted to Lt. Gen. The next year he was appointed Gov. of Charlemont, Ireland, a sinecure he held the rest of his life. Before leaving Canada the end of July '78, to be succeeded by Haldimand, he dismissed Chief Justice Peter LIVIUS from his post without giving a reason, an act which further alienated him from the British authorities.

When the Rockingham ministry came to power almost the first act was to make Carleton C. in C. in the 13 Colonies. After describing the "robbery and extortion" that had become rampant in N.Y.C. among the civil and military administrators, Trevelyan says, "Lord Rockingham had an eye for an honest man, and he well knew that it needed something of a Hercules to clean out such a stable," and Carleton was the man he picked for the job. (*Amer. Rev.*, VI, 221) Appointed on 23 Feb. '82, he reached N.Y. on 5 May and immediately undertook to end hostilities while political arrangements for peace were worked out. On 25 Nov. '83 Carleton evacuated N.Y.C. and returned to England.

On 11 Apr. '86 he again was appointed Gov. of Quebec, and he arrived on 23 Oct. to receive a cordial welcome. On 21 Aug. of this year he had been created Baron Dorchester. In his second tour as Gov. he was effective and popular with the Canadians, but his agitation of the Western Indians helped precipitate the war crisis of 1794. (See JAY'S TREATY) Except for an absence of two years (17 Aug. '91–24 Sept. '93) he remained in Canada until succeeded by Maj. Gen. Prescott on 9 July '96. Surviving the shipwreck of the *Active* on Anticosti, he reached Portsmouth on 19 Sept. Thereafter he lived in retirement until his sudden death on 10 Nov. 1808.

Although never given an opoprtunity to prove himself fully, "Carleton was probably the ablest British general in America" (*C.E.;* Alden, *Lee,* 106, says essentially the same thing, substituting "possibly" for "probably"). He was tall, thin, and austere in appearance. "Put a black wig on him and a long black gown and he would be the image of the Abbé of Jérusalem," wrote Gen. Riedesel after meeting him in Quebec in June '76, referring to the tutor of the Hereditary Prince Charles William of Brunswick. "He has the same way of walking—the same tone of voice." (Tharp, *Baroness,* 41–42)

His papers for the period 1782–83 were held by Colonial Williamsburg, Inc., until Oct. 1957, when they were presented to Queen Elizabeth during her visit to America. Photostats are at Williamsburg and in the N.Y. Public Library. The papers were calendared by the Royal Hist. MSS. Comm.: *Report on Amer. MSS. in the Royal Inst. of Great Britain.* 4 vols., 1904–9.

Brother of Thomas CARLETON; uncle and brother-in-law of his A.D.C., Christopher CARLETON (!).

CARLETON, Thomas. 1736–1817. British officer. Twelve years younger than his famous brother, Sir Guy, he was an ensign in James Wolfe's regiment in 1755 and in Nov. '75 became Q.M.G. of the army commanded by his brother in Canada. He led the Indian advance guard up Lake Champlain in Sept. '76, by which time he had been promoted to Lt. Col. of the 19th Regt., and was wounded in action at Valcour Island. On 20 Nov. '82 he became Col. of the 19th Regt. He was appointed Lt. Gov. of New Brunswick when the province was organized in 1784. After 19 years in this post he returned to England. He was promoted to Maj. Gen. in 1793 and was made a full Gen. in 1803. (Appleton's) Guy Carleton's critics after 1776 accused him of favoring Thomas over other officers.

CARLETON–GERMAIN FEUD. The origin of the personal animosity between these two men is unknown but it had a significant effect on the outcome of the American Revolution in that it kept Carleton from being given opportunities commensurate with his ability. One theory is that the feud stemmed from Carleton's testimony against GERMAIN in connection with the Minden affair. It probably was heightened by the Scottish-English factionalism prevalent in British politics. Carleton's failure to take Ticonderoga in the fall of 1776 gave Germain his opportunity to kill whatever chances Carleton might have had for further advancement; this failure turned the King against Carleton, led to Burgoyne's appointment as commander of the expedition from Canada in 1777, and prompted Germain to go so far as to attribute the Trenton disaster to Carleton's "supineness" in not attacking Ticonderoga. (Nickerson, *Turning Point,* 94. Alden, *Gage,* 282 *n.,* mentions Carleton's refusal to comply with Germain's wish that Gabriel Christie, a Scot, be given a good post in Canada.)

CARLISLE PEACE COMMISSION, 1778. See PEACE COMMISSION OF CARLISLE.

"CAROLINA GAMECOCK." Nickname of Thos. SUMTER.

CARPENTER'S HOUSE, N.Y. See JAMAICA, 28 Aug. '76.

CARRINGTON, Edward, 1749–1810. Cont'l. officer, Greene's Q.M.G. Va. A man who deserves to be better remembered for his varied services in the Cont'l. Army, he was commissioned Lt. Col. of Col. Charles Harrison's 1st Cont'l. Arty. Regt. when this unit was activated on 30 Nov. '76. (Heitman, 14, 146) He distinguished himself at Monmouth, where his guns were posted with the left wing of Alexander. (Ward, *W.O.R.,* 582) In Mar. '80 he served with Gen. St. Clair and Alexander Hamilton as commissioner for the exchange of prisoners. (Editor Uhlendorf corrects the statement in Baurmeister's *Journals,* 336–37, that Harrison was the third commissioner.) Carrington commanded the three batteries that marched south with Kalb, and Appleton's is mistaken in saying he was captured at Charleston, 12 May '80, with other Va. artillery units sent earlier to reinforce Lincoln. When Col. Harrison unexpectedly joined Kalb in N.C. he superseded Carrington.

When Gates reached Kalb's headquarters (25 July '80), or soon thereafter, he gave Carrington the mission sometimes said to have been ordered by Greene. Here, in the words of Harry Lee's *Memoirs,* is the story:

"In consequence of a misunderstanding with his colonel [Harrison], Carrington retired, and was dispatched, upon Gates's arrival, to superintend the examination of the Roanoke River, to ascertain the readiest points of communication across it—not only for . . . expedition and celerity to his supplies coming from Virginia, but also with the view of insuring a safe retreat from North Carolina, should such a measure, then probable, become necessary. In this service Carrington was found by Greene, who pressed upon him the untried station of chief of the quartermaster's department, and dispatched him to hasten the execution of the various arrangements which he had formed as he passed through Richmond. Among those which, under this order, claimed the lieutenant-colonel's attention, was the examination of the Dan (the southern branch of the Roanoke), for the same purposes for which he had, by order of General Gates, explored the last-mentioned river; and with the further object of discovering whether the water of the Dan would admit of an inland navigation to be connected by a portage with the Yadkin; which mode of intercourse, in case of protracted war in the Carolinas, would be attended by the most beneficial consequences. Captain [John?] Smith of the [6th, later the 3d?] Maryland line, was appointed to this service with ... Carrington, and performed the duty with much intelligence.

"So engaged was Carrington in accomplishing the orders of the general, that he only joined the army two days before its concentration at Guilford Court-House [7 Feb. '81], where he assumed the direction of the trust assigned to him." (*Op. cit.,* 249–50) By this Lee means that he assumed his duties as Q.M.G., a post he apparently had not until then agreed to take, although Greene had, in the words of Lee quoted above, "pressed [the job] upon him" a month earlier. (In his letter of 9 Jan. '81 to Joseph Reed, Greene said, "I have got Colonel Carrington to accept ..., and am in hopes of getting a good man at the head of the commissaries, without which I foresee we must starve." [Quoted in C. & M., 1152] The "good man" turned out to be Wm. R. DAVIE.)

"In this most difficult crisis Carring-ton commenced his official duties; his subordinate officers habituated to expedients and strangers to system, his implements of every sort in a wretched condition, and without a single dollar in the military chest. Nevertheless, he contrived, by his method, his zeal, and his indefatigable industry, to give promptitude to our movements, as well as accuracy and punctuality...." (Lee, *op. cit.,* 250)

In the article on the SOUTHERN CAMPAIGNS of Greene is the account of how this advance planning enabled Carrington to propose a course of action that probably saved the Southern army. He later joined Williams' rear guard to play an active part in the delay of Cornwallis, and he personally supervised the crossing. (In SOUTHERN CAMP'NS. see section headed "Race to the Dan.")

Carrington brought forward the guns and some much-needed provisions just in time for the battle of Hobkirk's Hill, 25 Apr. '81. (The weapons, three 6-pdrs., and 40 Va. artillerymen were still commanded by Col. Harrison, which must have added to the Q.M.G.'s distaste for his job.)

When Greene's army withdrew into the High Hills of Santee in July '81 he granted Carrington's request to return to Washington's army to succeed Col. Thomas Proctor, who had resigned on 18 Apr. as commander of the 4th Cont'l. Arty. Regt. "Carrington was considered as entitled to the vacancy, and took command of the regiment on its arrival in Virginia," writes Lee. "But inasmuch as Congress had not established the mode of promotion in the cavalry and artillery, his continuance in the command of the regiment was uncertain; and therefore General Greene determined that, though absent, he should govern the [Q.M.] department through his deputy, for the purpose of securing his future services, should his expectation of promotion fail. On Captain [Richard?] Crump, of the Virginia [artillery?] line, second in the department, the important trust developed . . . , and he discharged its various duties with intelligence and effect." (*Op. cit.*, 562; Heitman has three Crumps from Va., all of them captains, but Abner was dismissed 19 Oct. '77, and Goodrich was cashiered the same day! The prosaic Richard's service is given simply as, "Captain Virginia Artillery, 1780 and 1781.")

As for this "regiment" of Carrington's, it appears in the order of battle for the Yorktown Campaign as a 25-man detachment, Capt. Whitehead Coleman's company of the 1st Cont'l. Arty. Regt. Three companies of the 4th Regt., those that had come to Va. with Wayne, are listed among "Detachments" but without any indication that Carrington exercised command over them (Johnston, *Yorktown,* 113 and *n.*), but Lossing says Carrington, Col. John Lamb, and Lt. Col. Ebenezer Stevens alternated as principal assistant to Knox. (II, 516 *n.*)

After the surrender of Cornwallis, Carrington reverted to his post of Q.M.G., not having been promoted in the artillery, and on Greene's instructions he went to Philadelphia to see Robert Morris about getting supplies for the Southern army. In this assignment he was successful, and Morris made funds available to Greene for the purchase of food and clothing. (Lee, *op. cit.,* 562. See also SUPPLY . . . for the role of Morris at this time.) Carrington rejoined Greene in the summer of 1782 (*ibid.*) and served until the end of the war.

From 1785 to 1787 he was a delegate to Congress from Va. When the prospect of war with France loomed in 1798 "the War Department, urged on by Washington and Hamilton, sought and

Congress authorized the appointment of a Quartermaster General with the rank, pay, and emoluments of a major general," writes Risch in her history of the Q.M. "Bearing in mind the qualifications needed in a wartime Quartermaster General, Hamilton wanted the appointment to go to Edward Carrington. . . ." The President, however, made no appointment at all. (See article on SUPPLY . . . for the original functions of a Q.M.G. and for citation of Risch's work. The quotes are from page 129.) Carrington was foreman of the jury that acquitted Aaron BURR of treason in 1807, and almost exactly three years later he died at the age of 61. Perhaps his epitaph should be the words of Greene: "No body ever heard of a quarter Master, in History."

Paul Carrington (1733–1818), Edward's brother, was a prominent lawyer and politician in Va. Heitman lists four other Va. Carringtons: Clement and George (Jr.) were junior officers in Lee's Dragoons; George (Sr.) was a militia Col., 1778–81; and Mayo was a Capt. when captured at Charleston (12 May '80), having been Q.M. of Woodford's Brig. from 16 July to 10 Dec. '79, and Dep. Q.M.G. of the Southern army from then until his capture.

CARROLL, Charles of Carrollton. 1737–1832. Signer. Md. His grandfather came to the colonies in 1689 and founded the family estate of Carrollton. Charles was sent to France in 1748 to be educated by the Jesuits. He spent six years at the Collège de St. Omer, one year at Reims, two years at the Collège de Louis-le-grand in Paris, and one year at Bourges studying law. In 1759 he entered London's Middle Temple and returned in 1765 to Maryland. He lived on his 10,000-acre estate Carrollton, his religion barring him by law from public life. *D.A.B.* says he had added "of Carrollton" to his signature as early as 1765 to distinguish himself from his father and cousins. His first disagreement with the Crown was over the general tax to support the Church of England and the laws that forbade Catholics their own schools and denied them the vote in Md. Carroll wrote a series of refutations of the government's stand on the Established Church between Jan. and July, 1773, becoming known and respected in the colony. In Dec. '74, he joined the committee of correspondence and in 1775 the committee of safety. He was in the Revolutionary convention at Annapolis 5 Dec. '75 and in Jan. '76 was one of the commissioners to Canada (see CANADA, CONG. COMM. to). He sat in the Md. convention in 1776 and on 4 July of that year he was sent to the Cont'l. Congress and signed the Decl. of Indep. 2 Aug. A member of the board of war, he continued in Congress until 1778. He was one of the writers of the Md. constitution and in Dec. '76 he was sent to the Md. senate. He was an ardent Federalist although he had not accepted election to the Constitutional Convention. He was elected first U.S. Senator under the new Constitution (1789–92) and later served in the state senate, resigning in 1800. He had between 70 and 80 thousand acres in Md., Pa., and N.J., and he was the wealthiest man in the U.S. when he died. He was one of the founding directors of the B. & O. railroad in 1827 and was the last surviving Signer.

CARS (Car's, Carr's), Ga. See KETTLE CREEK.

CARTER, John Champe. Cont'l. officer. Va. According to Heitman, this officer was Ensign of the 7th Va. from 18 Mar. '76 until he resigned on 13 Jan. '77. On 30 Oct. '77 he became Capt., 1st Cont'l. Arty., was taken prisoner at Charleston (12 May '80), remained a P.O.W. until the end of the war, and became Bvt. Maj. on 30 Sept. '83. A contemporary source writes of a Capt. Carter at WAXHAWS, S.C., 29 May '80, "who commanded the artillery and who . . . continued his march without bringing his guns into action; this conduct excited suspicions unfavorable to the character of Carter, and these were strengthened by his being paroled on the ground, and his whole company without insult or injury being made prisoners of war." (W. D. James, *Marion,* ltr. of Dr. Robt. Brownsfield to author, quoted in C. & M., 1112) Circumstantial evidence is that this Capt. Carter was John Champe Carter.

CARTER FAMILY OF VIRGINIA. D. S. Freeman writes: "The males of the Carter stock did not often aspire to public life or shine in it, but the women of the blood of 'King' Carter, when they married into other lines, became the mothers and grandmothers of a most extraordinary number of distinguished men.* * * It is hard to believe that pure chance should have made the five daughters of Carter the ancestors of three signers, three governors, and two Presidents." (*R. E. Lee,* I, 25, 26)

Freeman errs, however, in his count of governors: Edmund Randolph, whom he calls a grandson of Elizabeth Burwell ("King" Carter's grand-daughter), was actually the *husband* of a grand-daughter. (*D.A.B.,* "Robert Carter Nicholas," XIII, 486; this article on Nicholas, however, is mistaken in saying that he was son of Elizabeth Carter Burwell; he was son of the latter's daughter.)

CASTLE WILLIAM. Fortress on Castle Island in Boston harbor.

CASUALTY FIGURES. In land warfare of the 18th and 19th centuries the

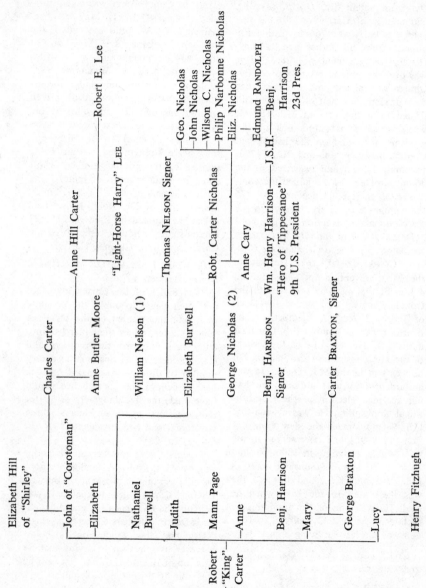

CARTER FAMILY OF VIRGINIA

ratio of wounded to killed in battle was about three or four to one. Figures that vary appreciably from this ratio are to be considered suspect: they stem either from deliberate falsification or from incomplete reporting. See BENNINGTON, STONY POINT, and MONMOUTH for examples. Among those classified as "wounded" in most battle reports of the Revolutionary War were men who subsequently died of their wounds. Those reported "missing" included prisoners, deserters, unrecovered dead, and men —wounded and otherwise—who subsequently rejoined their unit.

CASWELL, Richard. 1729–1789. Congressman, Gov. of N.C., militia general. N.C. Born in Md., he moved to Wake (which became Raleigh), N.C., when he was 17 and was in turn a surveyor and lawyer. Prior to the Revolution he held important political offices, commanded a wing of Tryon's army in the defeat of the Regulators at the Alamance River, 1771, and was speaker of the N.C. Assembly in 1770–71. He presided over the Prov. Cong., served on the committee that drafted the state constitution, and presided over the convention that prepared the latter. After being a delegate to the Cont'l. Cong., 1774–76, he became Col. of N.C. Partisan Rangers and took part in the patriot victory at MOORES CREEK BRIDGE. He was Gov. from 1776 to 1780. In 1780 he became Maj. Gen. of N.C. Militia and led them without political or military distinction at CAMDEN and in the SOUTHERN CAMPAIGNS OF GREENE. (See Thos. BURKE) In 1785 he was re-elected Gov., and he was speaker of the Assemby when he died.

CATAWBA FORD, S.C. Alternate name for FISHING CREEK, 18 Aug. '80.

CATHCART, Sir William Schaw. 1755–1843. British officer. Eldest son of the ninth Baron Cathcart,* he attended Eton from 1766 to 1771. Joining his father, who was ambassador at St. Petersburg, he remained in Russia until 1773, when he returned to Scotland. He studied law at the Universities of Dresden and Glasgow, and in 1776 was admitted as a member of the Faculty of Advocates. (D.N.B.) Having had no intention of practicing law, he bought a cornetcy in the 7th Dragoons the next June and then got leave to serve with the 16th Light Dragoons in America. He distinguished himself in the attack on Ft. Clinton, 6 Oct. '77 (see CLINTON'S EXPEDITION to the Highlands) and was rapidly promoted, becoming a Lt. in Nov. and a Capt. in the 17th Light Dragoons in Dec. '77. Joining the army of Howe in Philadelphia he surprised a rebel detachment on the Schuylkill in Jan. '78. Soldiering in America had its gayer social aspects for the young Scot: he courted Elizabeth Elliot, daughter of Andrew ELLIOT, and married her 10 Apr. '79; while in Philadelphia he had a prominent role in the MISCHIANZA, 18 May '78. He took part in the Battle of Monmouth, 28 June '78, apparently on Clinton's staff. Before leaving Philadelphia he was charged with raising a body of Scots known initially as the Caledonian Volunteers. Their organization completed in N.Y., they became Cathcart's BRITISH LEGION, which was subsequently led by Tarleton. (Rawdon raised the Volunteers of Ireland at the same time.) Having gotten the local rank of Maj.-commandant in connection with his last assignment, he was commissioned Maj. in the 38th Regt. on 13 Apr. '79. Soon

* William's mother was the sister of Lord Hamilton, whose ex-mistress and subsequent wife, Lady Hamilton, became the mistress of Lord Nelson. (D.N.B.)

thereafter he became a local Lt. Col. when he temporarily held the post of Q.M.G. on Erskine's departure and pending the arrival of Dalrymple. He commanded his legion on the Charleston Expedition until Apr. '80, when he was invalided back to N.Y. Given his choice between returning to his Legion or taking his post in the 38th Regt., he elected the latter and commanded the regiment in the Springfield Raid of Knyphausen in June '80. (*D.N.B.*) Still in bad health, in Oct. '80 he decided to return to England and received a cordial welcome from the King.

The 25-year-old baron—he succeeded to the title in 1776—was made Capt. and Lt. Col. in the Coldstream Guards, sat in the House of Lords, and in 1792 was appointed Col. of the 29th Foot. In 1793 he was commissioned B.G. and served in the Low Countries, 1793–95, having been promoted to Maj. Gen. in 1794. Advanced to Lt. Gen. on 1 Jan. 1801, he was C. in C. in Ireland, 1803–5, led the expedition to Hanover, commanded the forces in Scotland until 1807. He then headed the army in the Baltic and received the surrender of Copenhagen in 1807 after a bombardment that destroyed the university buildings and the principal church. Promoted to full Gen. on 1 Jan. 1812, he was sent to Russia a few months later. During the next eight years he served with distinction as ambassador; at the allied headquarters, 1812–14, he showed skill in maintaining harmony among the many nations represented and he entered Paris with the allies; he represented his country at the Congress of Vienna and signed the peace treaty. Made an earl in July 1814, he held the post of ambassador at St. Petersburg until 1820.

CATHCART'S LEGION. See BRITISH LEGION.

CAUCUS CLUB of Boston. A cabal that dominated Boston politics, it started meeting as early as 1724 and was led by Deacon John Adams, father of Samuel ADAMS. Composed of small shopkeepers, mechanics (tradesmen), and North End shipyard workers, its name *caucus* may be a corruption of *caulker*. Sam Adams in 1747 had helped found a group named the "Whipping Post Club" by its opponents, but at least as early as 1763 he had joined the Caucus Club and soon thereafter he had used it to make himself virtual dictator of Revolutionary Boston. (Miller, *Sam Adams*, 8) "The town meeting [in Faneuil Hall] was little more than a rubber stamp for the Caucus." (*Ibid.*, 39) The LOYALL NINE and the Boston SONS OF LIBERTY were offshoots of the Caucus Club. The Boston Caucus met at the Green Dragon Tavern in Union Street, Boston, a building that has been called "Headquarters of the Revolution." Transplanted to Philadelphia by the Mass. delegates to the Cont'l. Cong., in which George Wythe and Richard Henry Lee were front men while Sam Adams masterminded the radical strategy, the Caucus Club is credited with defeating the conservative followers of John Dickinson and expediting the movement toward independence.

CAUGHNAWAGA INDIANS of Canada. When the French found their advance into Canada frustrated by the Iroquois, the Jesuits hit upon the idea of winning over this confederacy by drawing converts from them and establishing them in a new mission village near the French settlements on the St. Lawrence. The French had some success in establishing this village at La Prairie, near Montreal, in 1668; they became known as the "French Praying Indians" or "French Mohawks," most of them being of the Oneida and Mohawk tribes, and a modified Mohawk becoming the common language. In 1676 the village was moved to Sault St. Louis, across the river from its former location (*Handbook of American Indians*). "The Iroquois made several unsuccessful efforts to induce the converts to return to the confederacy, and finally renounced them in 1684, from which time Caughnawaga [meaning "at the rapids"] became an important auxiliary of the French in their wars with the English and the Iroquois." (*Ibid.*) After the British took control of Canada (1763), many of them settled around Sandusky and Scioto, "where they numbered 200 at the outbreak of the American Revolution." (*Ibid.*) About 1755 the Caughnawaga Indians established a colony at St. Regis, farther up the St. Lawrence (i.e., farther westward), and they accompanied French hunters on their expeditions inland. (*Ibid.*) Ward quotes an unidentified source (apparently Smith, *Struggle*, I, 275) to the effect that the Caughnawaga chiefs were all "of English extraction captivated in their infancy" and although the tribe could muster only 200 braves in 1775 they were of such superior intelligence that despite their small numbers they were an important ally of the British in Canada. (*W.O.R.*, 142) They were among those whom ST. LUC tried to enlist.

Modern road maps show the town of Caughnawaga (pop. 2,200 in 1956) on the south bank of the St. Lawrence, opposite Lachine. According to Scribner's *Atlas* (plate 38), during the period 1690–1753 the village was located somewhat inland from the St. Lawrence and roughly 15 miles west of St. Johns.

CAUGHNAWAGA, N.Y., 22 May and 18 Oct. '80 (BORDER WARFARE) On the Mohawk River in the vicinity of modern Fonda, this settlement was surprised by Joseph Brant the morning of 22 May and burned to the ground. Sir John Johnson joined Brant there before withdrawing to Johnstown. On 18 Oct. Johnson passed through again and destroyed everything that had been built since the earlier visit.

CEDARS, The, Can., May '76 (retreat phase of CANADA INVASION). Col. Timothy Bedel was ordered to defend a small post called The Cedars, which was on the St. Lawrence, 30 miles west of Montreal. On 15 May, when he learned that about 600 enemy were approaching, Bedel left Maj. Isaac Butterfield in command and headed for Montreal. The report of a Congressional Committee said Bedel left to get reinforcements (C. & M., 213); Ward says he was suffering from smallpox (*W.O.R.*, 198). On 16 May, Maj. Henry Sherburne led a relief column from Montreal, and Benedict Arnold started assembling a larger one. Butterfield surrendered his entire garrison without any real attempt at resistance. The date of his capitulation is uncertain: Swiggett says it was 15 May (*Niagara*, 71); the Congressional Committee says it took place on 19 May, after two days' siege; Strait and the *D.A.H.* (I, 297) give the date as 16 May. Sherburne's force landed at Quinze Chiens, nine miles from The Cedars, on the 20th, and marched into an ambush about four miles from Butterfield's post. The relief column held out for 40 minutes, but the 100-man force was finally forced to surrender. Two prisoners were executed that evening, and four or five were later tortured and killed by the savages. On 26 May, the enemy (150 English and Canadians, 500 Indians, all commanded by a Capt. Forster) had moved to Quinze Chiens with their prisoners when they learned of Arnold's approach. In surrendering The Cedars, Butterfield had entered into a cartel with Forster that the post would be given up in return for protection of the prisoners from the Indians; Forster now sent Sherburne to tell Arnold that the prisoners would be turned over to the savages if Arnold disregarded the cartel and attacked. After an exchange of messages, Arnold agreed to take the American prisoners (for later exchange) and return to Montreal.

According to Swiggett, Joseph Brant led the Indians in this operation and Walter Butler was present as an ensign of the 8th Regt. (*Op. cit.,* 71)

CELORON DE BLAINVILLE, Paul Louis. 1753–? Canadian volunteer. Grandson of Jean Baptiste, who emigrated to Canada from Paris in 1684, and son of the celebrated French officer and explorer, Pierre Joseph (1693–1759), he was born at Detroit when his father commanded the garrison of Ft. Pontchartrain. (*D.A.B.*) Paul Louis became a gentleman cadet in the Rochefort Regt. on 3 May '74 and a *sous-lieutenant* in the Martinique Regt. the next year. (Lasseray, 147–49) On 16 Oct. '76 he volunteered for service in the American army, and on 18 Dec. became a Lt. in James Livingston's 1st Canadian Regt. At Schoharie, N.Y., until Burgoyne's Offensive started, he marched under Arnold to the relief of Ft. Stanwix and fought in Learned's Brig. at Saratoga. In the second battle, 7 Oct. '77, he received a bayonet wound in the leg and was hospitalized at Albany. Rejoining the regiment, he was with Varnum's Brig. at Valley Forge and as part of this command was at Monmouth and Newport. On 29 July '78 he became a Chevalier in the Order of Saint Louis.

Lasseray, who is the authority for the above information, says that de Blainville transferred into the 3d Bn., Pulaski Legion, in Feb. '79. Heitman's sketch starts with the statement that "Lewis Celeron" (whose state or country of origin this author did not know) became a Capt. in Pulaski's Legion on 1 Apr. '79. He was engaged at Charleston, 11 May '79, and at Savannah, receiving a bullet wound in the head during the latter action, 9 Oct. '79. On 12 May '80 he became a prisoner at Charleston and was exchanged 26 Nov. '82. Meanwhile, by a special Congressional action of 21 Jan. '82 he was retained in the American service, but according to Heitman he resigned 1 July '82. Lasseray, on the other hand, finds that he was honorably discharged 1 Jan. '83. Until the end of 1793 he served in the West Indies. Emigrating to Trinité Island, he became *sous-commissaire civil* of the National Guard of Abymes, Guadeloupe, on 20 June 1803, *commissaire commandant* two years later, and in 1807 was Capt. on the general staff at Guadeloupe. His subsequent history is not known. The French archives of Foreign Affairs note that an S. Seleron, a Canadian, was an officer in a colonial regiment and Capt. in Pulaski's Legin.

CERBERUS (32). Reaching Boston on 25 May '75, this British frigate was immortalized in the pasquinade posted soon thereafter in the town:

Behold the Cerberus the Atlantic plough,
Her precious cargo, Burgoyne, Clinton, Howe.
Bow, wow, wow! *

The three gentlemen, it might be noted, were members of Parliament in addition to being general officers. The *Cerberus* was destroyed at NEWPORT, 5 Aug. '78, in Suffren's attack. A year earlier it had been unsuccessfully attacked by the submarine of David BUSHNELL.

CHADD'S FORD, Pa. Landmark in the Battle of the BRANDYWINE, 11 Sept. '77.

* Cerberus was the dog that, in Greek mythology, guarded the gates of Hell.

CHAISE MARINE. A light, covered, two-wheeled wagon. During the critical shortage of transportation in 1776–77, Q.M.G. Mifflin proposed that these be manufactured to carry artillery and ammunition.

CHAMADE. A drum or trumpet signal by which one opponent requests a PARLEY.

CHAMBLY, Can., 18 Oct. '75. (CANADA INVASION) During the siege of ST. JOHNS, less than 10 miles south, Chambly was held by Maj. Stopford with 88 officers and men of the 7th Regt. Although the place was of great strategic importance, it was inadequately protected because Carleton did not think it could be taken so long as St. Johns held out. (Lossing, I, 170) The night of 17 Sept., 135 Americans under Maj. John Brown ambushed a supply train two miles north of Chambly. The British sallied forth the next day, but Col. Bedel arrived with 500 reinforcements to help Brown drive them back. The night of 17 Oct., two American bateaux slipped past the defenses of St. Johns with 9-pd. guns, and Chambly was surrounded by James Livingston's 300 Canadians, and 50 Americans under Brown and Bedel. After the guns put a few rounds through the impressive-looking but thin-walled stone fort, the British surrendered. Prisoners included 88 officers and men, 30 women, and 51 children. Matériel included six tons of gunpowder, 6,500 musket cartridges, three mortars, and 125 stand of British arms. (Freeman, *Washington*, III, 561) Large stocks of food were also taken: 80 barrels of flour, 134 barrels of pork, and a quantity of rice, butter, and peas. (Lossing, *op. cit.*, 171) The regimental colors, first such trophy of the war (*ibid.*), were sent to Congress; they are still to be seen on display at West Point.

Speaking of this as "a most discreditable surrender," Fortescue says, "This was the saving of Montgomery's campaign. The fall of Chambly gave him stores sufficient to renew the siege of St. Johns...." (*Br. Army,* III, 162)

CHAMPE, John. *c.* 1756–*c.* 1798.* Va. Cont'l. soldier who attempted to kidnap Arnold. On 20 Oct. '80 Washington directed Henry Lee to select volunteers from his legion to capture Benedict Arnold and also to check on intelligence that other high ranking American officers were dealing with the enemy. Lee picked Champe, Sgt. Maj. of his cavalry, whom he describes as of a "saturnine countenance, grave, thoughtful, and taciturn, of tried courage and inflexible perseverance." (*Memoirs,* 272.) Champe "deserted" about 11 P.M. the same day and on 23 Oct. was accepted by the British as a bona fide deserter. He then joined the legion of Tories and deserters being raised by Arnold and learned enough about the latter's habits to make a plan to capture him. Meanwhile he established communications with Lee, sent back word that he had found no evidence that other American officers were dealing with the enemy,** and informed Lee when the attempted abduction would take place. Champe had learned that every night

* Appleton's gives the dates 1752 to about 1798. Lee says he was 23 or 24 at the time of his exploit, which would make his birthdate about 1756. (*Memoirs,* 272)

** Although this may not really have been part of Champe's mission (Carl Van Doren does not mention it in his *Secret History*), Appleton's says the suspected officer was supposed to have been Gates (I, 568), and D. S. Freeman (who does not mention the Champe adventure) says groundless charges of double dealing were raised about this time against Robt. Howe. (*Washington,* V, 225, 226, and *n.*)

about midnight Arnold walked in the garden of his quarters, which were near the Hudson. (At No. 3 Broadway, next to Clinton's, says Lossing.) Having secretly loosened some palings between this garden and an alley, Champe and one accomplice were going to grab and gag Arnold and hustle him to the river, where a second confederate would be waiting with a boat that would take him to Hoboken. Before the attempt could be made, however, Champe was ordered to embark with Arnold's legion for operations in Va. (Van Doren, *Secret History*, 393), or Arnold changed quarters. Sgt. Champe was unable to escape safely from the legion until Arnold had completed his raids in Va., and he rejoined Henry Lee in the Carolinas. "When Lee wrote his spirited narrative of the undertaking long afterwards [pp. 270–87 of his *Memoirs*] he had forgotten so much—and remembered so much incorrectly—that he produced something close to historical fiction," says Van Doren. (*Ibid.*) This is pointed out because most accounts of the affair are based on Lee's *Memoirs*. Champe's comrades did not know until his return that his desertion to N.Y.C. had been faked. "His story was soon told," says Lossing, "and four-fold greater than before his desertion was the love and admiration of his corps for him." (II, 210) Although it was an entirely creditable performance, it probably grew fourfold in the retelling. Champe was rewarded and discharged from the service to protect him from British retaliation if he were captured. When Washington again became C. in C. in 1798 he proposed to commission Champe a captain, but he learned that Champe had recently died in Ky.

CHAMPLAIN, Lake. Stretching 125 miles from N. to S. and varying in width between 400 yards and 14 miles, Lake Champlain was a vital link in the strategic waterway between the Hudson and St. Lawrence river valleys. Ten miles of rapids in the Richelieu (or Sorel) River between St. Johns and Chambly bar navigation to the St. Lawrence, and five miles of swift, narrow channel bar navigation between Ticonderoga and Lake GEORGE. CROWN POINT and FORT TICONDEROGA were scenes of battle during the COLONIAL WARS and the Revolution. ST. JOHNS and CHAMBLY also were military objectives during the Revolution. VALCOUR ISLAND saw the important conflict between CHAMPLAIN SQUADRONS in 1776. Note that "up Lake Champlain" should be used in the sense of "upstream" or *south*.

CHAMPLAIN SQUADRONS, 1775–1776. Lake CHAMPLAIN presented a problem in improvisation since neither the Americans nor the British knew much about shallow-water sailing craft at this time. (Howard I. Chapelle, *The History of the American Sailing Navy* [New York, 1949], 112) One solution, the centerboard or drop keel, was proposed by a British officer on the lake in 1776, but this was too radical for his superiors to understand and was not adopted. Another problem was that navigation into the lake was blocked at both ends; the British had to build or reassemble their craft at St. Johns; the Americans had to build from standing timber. Most Lake Champlain craft were therefore of the small, rowing type, with sails that could be used only when wind was from the rear. A flotilla of these craft would be at the mercy of a single armed sailing vessel, which explains why the Americans were so worried about the incompleted *Royal Savage* at ST. JOHNS, 5 Sept. '75. On the other hand, narrowness of the lake put ships in danger of being bottled up and destroyed by attack from the shore.

THE AMERICAN FLOTILLA

During operations against FT. TICON-DEROGA, 10 May '75, Samuel Herrick led a raid that captured the schooner *Liberty* at Skenesboro. Arnold used this vessel to raid St. Johns, 17 May, where he captured the large sloop *Enterprise*. Montgomery used these two vessels (and a flotilla of small boats) to attack St. Johns, where the schooner *Royal Savage* was captured 2 Nov. '75. In the Canada Invasion the Americans lost their entire St. Lawrence squadron, but when they evacuated St. Johns on 18 June '76 they still had the three craft mentioned above. The schooner *Revenge* was being built at Ft. Ti, and from St. Johns they evacuated frame timber to build the cutter *Lee* at Skenesboro. Since the British were known to be assembling ships to continue their advance, Benedict Arnold, who knew something about sailing from his experience as a West Indies trader, undertook the seemingly impossible task of building a fleet to oppose them. Although difficulties seemed insurmountable, tools, craftsmen, and critical supplies eventually began to arrive. Starting with available tools, troops began felling trees. Abandoned sawmills at Ticonderoga, Crown Point, and near Skenesboro were put into operation and planks were produced. The improvised boatyard at Skenesboro was worked first by men from the ranks, but 30 craftsmen were then sent from Albany and another 200 started arriving from Mass., Conn., R.I., and Philadelphia. Being taken away from their lucrative business in support of PRIVATEERING, these patriots received exorbitant wages—up to $5, hard money, a day, free food, and a cow apiece, it was rumored and believed among the troops. (Kenneth Roberts, *Rabble in Arms,* 1953 ed., [New York, 1933], 224) Critical naval sup-

plies—spikes, nails, hawsers, anchors, canvas, paint, and caulking—came through; ironically, the British blockade of New York and Philadelphia helped divert supplies to Lake Champlain because it cut off the frigates being built at those cities. Brig. Gen. David Waterbury Jr. commanded the operations at Skenesboro; Arnold had over-all charge and provided the driving leadership that caused his fleet to be ready more than a month before the British.

To carry heavy enough armament to oppose ships the British were known to be constructing, Arnold ordered four galleys built: the *Washington, Congress, Trumbull,* and *Gates.* A novel and successful feature was that these were rigged like Spanish and Algerian coastal craft: "short masts; lanteen sails; a minimum of canvas and cordage to bother the landsmen that'll have to sail 'em," as Kenneth Roberts has Arnold explain, (*Op. cit.,* 250) The *Washington* was 72 feet 4 inches on deck, 20 feet beam, and 6 feet 2 inches in the hold, according to the Admiralty draught made after the British capture. (Chapelle, *op. cit.,* 106) The three other galleys probably were similar. (*Ibid.*) Carrying a complement of 80 men (Ward, *W.O.R.,* 388), the galleys had somewhat different armament. The *Washington* mounted two 18-pdrs., two 12-pdrs., two 9-pdrs., four 4-pdrs. in her broadside, with a 2-pdr. and eight swivel guns on the quarterdeck, according to Chapelle. Ward and Roberts say she mounted two heavy guns in the bow.

Eight or nine GUNDALOWS were built: the *Boston, Connecticut, New Haven, New Jersey, New York, Philadelphia, Providence, Spitfire,* and, possibly, the *Success.* The *Philadelphia* was recovered in 1935 by T. F. Hagglund, in a remarkably good state of preservation, and the following description has been assembled: an open boat measuring 53 feet 4 inches, 15 feet 6 inches beam, and 3 feet 10 inches depth amidships; flat-bottomed; and rigged with two square sails on a single mast. (Chapelle, *op. cit.,* 107 ff.) The gundalows were all armed with a 12-pdr. in the bow and two 9-pdrs. amidships (*ibid.,* 113); they carried 45 men, and were equipped with oars (as were the galleys). Having no outside keels, although this was called for in Arnold's specifications, the gundalows could not sail into the wind; however, "with their relatively powerful rig [they] were very fast off the wind," says Chapelle.

THE MYSTERY OF THE *SUCCESS*

As mentioned in the article on VALCOUR ISLAND, there is disagreement as to whether the *Success* took part in that battle. Chapelle says she did not, "and there is no record of what became of her." (*Op. cit.,* 112) Ward says she joined Arnold on 11 Sept. and fought at Valcour Island, making a total of 16 vessels there; Ward reinforces his opinion by noting that Riedesel listed 16 American vessels, but did not name them all. (*Op. cit.,* 472 n.) The problem apparently baffled Kenneth Roberts. In *Rabble in Arms* he mentions eight different gundalows by name (pp. 259, 291)—all except the *Success*. In the scene of Arnold's council of war (p. 291) just before the battle, there are seven gundalow captains present—all but those of the *Success* and *New Haven* (the latter having been mentioned on page 259 as one of the boats ready to sail). Yet, in speaking of vessels lost and those trying to escape to Crown Point, Roberts' characters allude to 16 vessels, implying that the *Success* (and *New Haven*) must have fought at Valcour Island, or that the 16th vessel joined during the retreat of 12–13 Oct. (pp. 323, 327, 329). Furthermore, having accounted for eight gundalows by name (all except the *Success*), and specifically mentioned that the *Gates* and *Liberty*—which were not at Valcour Island—had joined Wigglesworth in escaping toward Crown Point, Roberts has Arnold say, "[Wigglesworth] must have another gundelo with him." (P. 331) "Another" would have to be the ninth, which would have to be the *Success*. Since "one gundalow" is mentioned among the survivors of Arnold's fleet at Crown Point (e.g., Ward, 396), Roberts has apparently used his license as a novelist to avoid stating the total number of craft at Valcour Island, and to avoid specifying how Arnold suspected before catching up with Wigglesworth that the latter "must have another gundelo with him" when Arnold knew where the other eight were.

To return to preparations for the battle of Valcour Island, on 24 Aug. Arnold sailed from Crown Point with the 11 vessels that were ready. He was joined later by the galleys *Congress, Trumbull,* and *Washington,* and the gundalows *New Jersey* and *Philadelphia* as they were completed. The *Gates* was not completed in time for the battle.

THE BRITISH FLEET

At St. Johns the British built four sailing vessels and assembled a large number of boats. After trying to move the three-masted ship sloop *Inflexible* around the Richelieu River rapids on rollers, an otherwise feasible operation that was frustrated by soft ground, they took her apart and reassembled her at St. Johns. The schooners *Maria, Carleton,* and the large gundalow *Loyal Convert* were similarly moved. The most remarkable ship in Carleton's fleet was the 422-ton "radeau" or sailing scow built at St. Johns and named *Thunderer.* Carrying a 300-man complement and two large howitzers, six 24-pdrs., and six 12-pdrs. (manned during the battle of Valcour Island by the gunners of the Hanau Regt.), she was almost 92 feet long and over 33 feet in beam. The *Thunderer* had two masts but, being flat-bottomed, could not work to windward and did not participate in the battle.

The British also moved the following boats past the rapids from the St. Lawrence: 20 gunboats each having one gun, four long boats with a field gun each, and 24 provision boats or bateaux— many received in frame from England. (These figures are from Chapelle; Ward says the British had 30 long boats and 400 bateaux.) The *Maria,* with 14 6-pd. guns, the *Loyal Convert,* with seven 9-pdrs., and the *Thunderer,* did not get within effective range during the battle of Valcour Island. The *Inflexible* delivered a long-range fire with her 18 12-pdrs. initially, then was finally able to get within point-blank range and discharge five broadsides, which completely silenced Arnold's guns (Ward, *op. cit.,* 395), and probably did most of the damage suffered by the American flotilla. Cannon in the 15 to 20 gunboats that participated in the fight (Arnold estimated their number in those terms) varied in caliber from 9-pd. to 24-pd.

At the start of BURGOYNE'S OFFENSIVE in 1777 the British had the gunboats and sailing vessels of their 1776 squadron, the captured *Lee, New Jersey,* and *Washington,* and a newly built sailing vessel, the *Royal George.* They also had the necessary bateaux. (Ward, 402) At SKENESBORO, 6 July '77, the last of the American squadron was burned by the departing rebels (*Enterprise, Gates, Liberty*) or captured (*Trumbull* and *Revenge*). (*Ibid.,* 415)

CHANDELIER. A heavy timber frame filled with FASCINES and other materials to form a field fortification. Chandeliers are particularly useful in rocky, frozen, or boggy ground where digging is difficult. See DORCHESTER HEIGHTS, Mass., 2–27 Mar. '76.

CHARLES CITY C.H., Va., 8 Jan. '81. (VA. MIL. OPNS.) From Westover, where he had withdrawn after his raid on RICHMOND, 5–7 Jan., Arnold sent Simcoe on a reconnaissance toward Long Bridge on the Chickahominy. Simcoe learned from captured vedettes that Gen. Thos. Nelson was near Charles City C.H. with a body of militia. A Negro prisoner guided 40 mounted Rangers to the courthouse where they surprised 150 militia under Col. Dudley. Two Americans were killed and a number captured; the rest fled to Nelson's camp a few miles away, and some of the more sound-of-wind are credited with having continued on to Willamsburg. Simcoe returned to Westover before dawn with his prisoners and captured horses. (Lossing, II, 444)

CHARLESTON EXPEDITION of Clinton in 1776. During the summer of 1775, as the British situation in Mass. went from bad to worse, the London authorities conceived and started developing plans for a military expedition to the South. Although rebel elements in Va., N.C., S.C., and Ga. had showed sufficient virulence to drive out all four royal governors, these very officials convinced the home government that with the temporary assistance of a respectable force of regulars the Loyalists could restore and maintain royal authority. The planning started by Dartmouth and continued—although with less enthusiasm—by Germain coincided nicely with the stalemate that developed in the BOSTON SIEGE. Furthermore, the new C. in C., Howe, and his second in command, Henry Clinton, were already at odds, and detachment

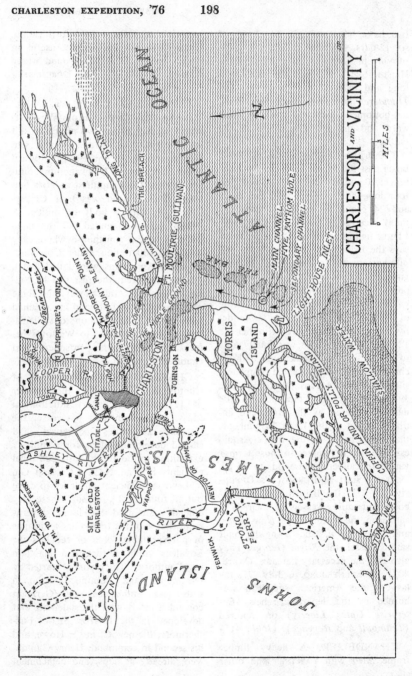

of ·Clinton to command operations in the South would neatly solve this personnel problem—at least for the moment.

Dartmouth's instructions of 22 Oct. '75 to Gen. Howe were passed to Clinton on 6 Jan. '76. The latter left Boston on the 20th with a force he has vaguely estimated at between 1,200 and 1,500: two light companies (from the 4th and 44th), and a few officers who were to raise a body of Highland emigrants in N.C. His ships included the frigate *Mercury*, two transports, and a supply vessel. A combined force of ships under Commodore Sir Peter Parker and troops under Gen. Cornwallis was supposed to set sail from Cork in Dec. '75 and rendezvous with Clinton in the mouth of the Cape Fear River, N.C. Clinton's orders were to restore the King's authority in the four southern colonies, turn their security over to the Loyalists, and rejoin Howe "as soon as the navigation of the northern coasts of North America became practicable." (Clinton, *American Rebellion*, 23–24) Told to move south rapidly, he had the contradictory instructions to call at ports along the way. (*Ibid.*, note by editor W. B. Willcox) Accordingly, Clinton put into N.Y. harbor on 4 Feb. and consulted with Gov. Tryon, who had taken refuge aboard ship. After being delayed by adverse winds, he left Sandy Hook on the 12th, and on the 17th visited Gov. Dunmore of Va., who was living aboard a British ship in Hampton Roads. After more delays because of bad weather, Clinton left on 27 Feb. and reached Cape Fear on 12 Mar. '76. He was soon joined by Gov. Wm. Campbell of S.C. and Gov. Josiah Martin of N.C.

Bad news came from all these refugee governors, whose optimistic reports to London, ironically, were responsible for Clinton's presence. A series of Loyalist defeats had eliminated any prospect of real assistance from "the well affected provincials" in the southern colonies. The most serious blow had just recently been struck at MOORES CREEK BRIDGE, N.C., 27 Feb. (See SOUTHERN THEATER, Mil. Opns. in, for the other actions.)

Most alarming, however, was the fact that the "Irish fleet" was not waiting for Clinton at Cape Fear. It was over a month before the first ships arrived (18 Apr.); most of the others were not there until 3 May, and the last straggler showed up on the 31st. Meanwhile, Clinton saw no possibility of accomplishing his original mission in time to rejoin Howe as ordered. Wanting to do something, however, he favored operations in the Chesapeake, where small, easily maintained outposts might serve as bases for raids and as havens for Loyalists. But when Parker arrived and made a naval reconnaissance toward Charleston, 16–26 May, he talked Clinton into a more ambitious plan: unfinished Ft. Sullivan, in Charleston harbor, was to be captured by a *coup de main* and garrisoned by a small force under the protection of a frigate or two; Clinton could then return north with the rest of the combined force. "Clinton surrendered his own scheme, apparently without protest, and fell in with this idea," comments Willcox. (*Ibid.*, xx)

AMERICAN PREPARATIONS

As early as 1 Jan. '76 Congress believed the British might attack Charleston, and they authorized S.C. to increase its allotment of Cont'l. regiments from 12 to 14. (Wallace, *Appeal*, 91) The colony had already raised six provincial regiments (1st, 2d, and 3d Foot, Roberts' Arty. Regt., and the 1st and 2d Rifle Regts.); these units took part in the coming action, but they were not yet part of the Cont'l. Army and took orders only from Gov. Rutledge. S.C. had also raised three volunteer artillery companies, 700 Charleston militia, and about 2,000 rural militia. Two Cont'l. regiments were ordered to the threatened city from N.C. and one from Va. Total strength available on the day of battle was more than 6,500 rank and file, although only a small percentage were actually engaged. (Ward, *W.O.R.,* 672)

Defenses had been constructed in Charleston itself, but the principal works were on the low, sandy islands that fringed the coast. The entrance to the harbor is between Sullivan's Island on the north and James Island on the south. This passage, six miles from the city, was covered by forts. Ft. Johnson, on James Island, captured by the rebels in Sept. '75, mounted 20 large guns; a 12-gun battery was on the same island, closer to Charleston.

Ft. Sullivan was planned in Jan. '76 and about half finished when the British attacked. It was laid out as a square redoubt with bastions on each corner. Although a proper seacoast fort of the period should have had stone walls to withstand heavy naval gunfire, Col. Wm. Moultrie built with the inferior materials at hand: parallel walls of palmetto logs were put up, and the 16-foot space between them was filled with sand. Only the south and east walls and the two southernmost bastions were finished in time. They held emplacements for 25 guns that ranged in caliber from 9- to 25-pd. The remaining half of the redoubt had been built to a height of only seven feet, so breastworks were erected and six 12-pdrs. emplaced to provide some protection to the rear. The northern tip of the island was three miles from the fort and separated from undefended Long Island (now Isle of Palms) by a narrow gap of water known as the Breach.

Charles Lee reached Charleston on 4 June to take command.* Although Moultrie spoke highly in his memoirs of the value of Lee's presence, it would appear that Lee concentrated his professional talent on attempting to ruin the work that had been accomplished prior to his arrival. Here is Moultrie's account:

"When he came to Sullivan's Island, he did not like that post at all; he said there was no way to retreat, that the garrison would be sacrificed: nay, he called it a 'slaughter pen,' and wished to withdraw the garrison and give up the post, but President Rutledge insisted it should not be given up." (Moultrie, *Memoirs,* I, 140–44, quoted in C. & M., 1064–65)

* When Washington learned on 8 Jan. '76 that the British were mounting a seaborne operation from Boston, he ordered Lee to N.Y.C., which was the enemy's most logical objective. Lee arrived 4 Feb., a few hours before Clinton's appearance in the harbor threw the city into panic. On 17 Feb. Congress ordered Lee to succeed Schuyler in the Northern Dept., but then changed its mind and sent him to command the Southern Dept. Lee left N.Y.C. on 7 Mar. and went to Williamsburg, Va., where he learned that Clinton had stopped off at Norfolk. An intercepted letter from Germain to Gov. Eden of Md., dated 23 Dec. '75, revealed that the British were sending naval forces and seven regiments across the Atlantic to N.C. with orders to strike S.C. or Va., as circumstances directed. From Wilmington, N.C., Lee reported on 1 June that the British fleet had appeared and then put back to sea. He personally felt they would reappear to the north, but was prevailed on to continue south; he reached Charleston three days after enemy sails were sighted outside the harbor

Lee then ordered construction of a floating bridge to permit the garrison's escape across the mile-wide Cove, but this improvised affair of planks and hogsheads would not support troops.

"For my part," [wrote Moultrie,] "I never was uneasy on not having a retreat because I never imagined that the enemy could force me to that necessity; I always considered myself as able to defend that post against the enemy. I had upwards of 300 riflemen, under Col. Thompson, of his regiment, Col. Clark, with 200 North-Carolina regulars, Col. Horry, with 200 South-Carolina, and the Racoon Company of riflemen, [plus] 50 militia at the point of the island behind the sand hills and myrtle bushes; I had also a small battery with one 18-pounder, and one brass field-piece, 6-pounder, at the same place, which entirely commanded the landing and could begin to fire upon them at 7 or 800 yards before they could attempt to land.* * * Col. Thompson had orders that if they could not stand the enemy they were to throw themselves into the fort, by which [time ?] I should have had upwards of 1000 men in a large strong fort, and Gen. Armstrong in my rear with 1500 men, not more than one mile and a half off, with a small arm of the sea between us, that he could have crossed a body of men in boats to my assistance. This was exactly my situation. I therefore felt myself perfectly easy because I never calculated upon Sir Henry Clinton's numbers to be more than 3000 men. As to the men-of-war, we should have taken very little notice of them if the army had attacked us.

"Gen. Lee one day on a visit to the fort, took me aside and said, 'Col. Moultrie, do you think you can maintain this post?'

"I answered him, 'Yes, I think I can.'

"That was all that passed on the subject between us." (*Ibid.*)

BRITISH PRELIMINARIES

Having left Cape Fear on 31 May, and reached the islands off Charleston the next day, the British frigates and most of the transports were prevented by adverse weather from crossing the bar to Five Fathom Hole until 7 June. Clinton then undertook a two-day reconnaissance in a small sloop and reached his fateful decision to land on Long Island (Isle of Palms) rather than Sullivan's Island to support Parker's naval assault on Ft. Sullivan. This decision was fatal, points out Willcox. "The reason behind Clinton's choice seems to have been the hope that by-passing Sullivan's Island would enable him to cut off and capture its entire garrison," says the same writer. (Clinton, 30 *n.*)

Clinton landed most of his troops on undefended Long Island 16 June to find that the Breach, which he had been told was fordable at low tide, to his "unspeakable mortification and disappointment" (*ibid.*, 31), was seven feet deep; or, to be more precise, his troops found when they tried to cross it that this peculiar stretch of water had 18-inch shoals that would ground a boat, but the bottom was pocked with seven-foot holes that would dunk the men who jumped overboard to pull the boat free. (Ward, 673) Since a secondary attack across the Breach to Sullivan's Island was out of the question, on 18 June Clinton sent Brig. Gen. Vaughan to inform Parker and to ask how else his troops might support Parker. British strength on Long Island was about 2,000 regulars and 500 to 600 seamen. (Lossing, II, 755) Vaughan returned on the 21st with an answer that Clinton said "seemed to imply that he [Parker] thought himself fully equal to the attempt with the ships alone, and only expected from the troops the best cooperation in their power when he made it." (*Ibid.*, 32) (Parker later implied, however, that he had been drawn into the attack against his better judgment. [*Ibid.*, editor's note])

Parker planned to attack on the 23d, but adverse winds made him delay until 28 June. During this period the Americans built up the strong defense on Sullivan's Island opposite Clinton that is detailed in the excerpt from Moultrie's memoirs quoted above. Since Clinton had only a few boats for an amphibious assault, even a feint across the Breach was now out of the question. He therefore proposed a diversionary effort from Long Island to the mainland (where he could hope to land unopposed) and then S.W. against Haddrel's Point; he told Parker he would need fire support from a few frigates from the S.W. of Sullivan's Island, and Parker answered that he was about to attack and would try to furnish this naval support.

THE ATTACK

On 28 June at 11 A.M. the British ships went into action. The bomb ketch *Thunder* opened fire at a range of a mile and a half with 10-inch mortars; she was covered by the 22-gun *Friendship*. The *Active*, *Bristol*, *Experiment*, and *Solebay* anchored 400 to 800 yards south of the fort (estimates of range vary) and opened fire. The *Actaeon*, *Sphynx*, and *Syren* then formed a second line and started blasting away. More than 100 enemy pieces converged on Moultrie's fort during the next hour. The ships of the second line then started into the harbor to get west of the fort and deliver an enfilade fire along its southern face and also to threaten its L. of C. But here the Americans had the lucky break that saved the day: all three ships ran onto

a shoal known as the Middle Ground. After several hours the *Syren* and *Sphynx* got free, but had to withdraw for repairs; the *Actaeon* could not be moved.

Moultrie had been visiting Thompson's position on the northern end of Sullivan's Island the morning of the 28th, and across the Breach he could see Clinton's force manning boats as if for an assault. But when he saw Parker's ships preparing to get under way he galloped the three miles back to Ft. Sullivan and "ordered the long roll to beat." The fort was now manned by 413 men of Moultrie's 2d S.C. and 22 men of the 4th Arty. (Ward, 672) Although the rebel gunners delivered their first shots "with a nervous rapidity that made alarming inroads on the supply of powder" (Wallace, 94), they settled down to a cool and, in the words of a British live target, "exceedingly well directed" fire. (C. & M., 1068) The defenders concentrated on the two 50-gun ships, particularly the *Bristol*, where Parker had his flag. On two occasions the *Bristol's* quarterdeck was swept clear of everybody except the Commodore, whose breeches were blown off by one blast; his flagship took 70 hits, and ended the action with 64 dead and 161 wounded. (Wallace, 95) Moultrie's only problem was lack of powder: "We had not more than 28 rounds, for 26 guns, 18- and 26-pounders, when we begun [*sic*] the action; and a little after, 500 pounds from town and 200 pounds from Captain Tufft's schooner lying at the back of the fort."

It turned out that the *ersatz* construction materials of Ft. Sullivan had certain surprisingly good qualities: the spongy palmetto logs did not shatter and splinter like ordinary wood, and the sandy earth of the walls further cushioned the impact of cannon balls. Most of the American casualties resulted from the few shots that came through the embrasures. Despite the punishment the British naval gunners were taking, however, they manned their pieces well. "At one time, 3 or 4 of the men-of-war's broadsides struck the fort at the same instant," wrote Moultrie, and the MERLONS were given "such a tremor that I was apprehensive that a few more such would tumble them down." Despite the long range, the *Thunder* "threw her shells in a very good direction; most of them fell within the fort, but we had a morass in the middle that swallowed them up instantly, and those that fell in the sand and in and about the fort were immediately buried so that very few of them bursted amongst us." (All the above comments by Moultrie are from his *Memoirs* as quoted in C. & M., 1068–69.)

Lee visited the fort during the action, pointed a few guns, and departed with the words, "Colonel, I see you are doing very well here. You have no occasion for me." (*Ibid.*) He later wrote:

"The behaviour of the garrison, both men and officers, with Colonel Moultrie at their head, I confess astonished me. It was brave to the last degree. I had no idea that so much coolness and intrepidity could be displayed by a collection of raw recruits." (Ward, 676)

When a shot struck the flagstaff and the flag fell outside the fort, Sgt. JASPER went out through an embrasure to retrieve it and put it back into view on an improvised staff. (This was more than bravado, since disappearance of the flag could have signaled to the enemy as well as to the thousands of American civilian and soldier spectators that the fort had surrendered.)

The firing slacked off at sunset, and at 9:30 it stopped. At 11 P.M. the enemy ships slipped their cables and drifted away with the tide—all but the marooned *Actaeon*, which was set on fire by her crew the next morning and abandoned.

As for Clinton's part in the action, he had ended up as a spectator, and with a rather poor seat at that. He had demonstrated toward the island and toward the mainland, but when the three frigates ran aground he had to abandon his planned diversion against Haddrel's Point. When he discovered the next morning what a beating the navy had taken, he could do nothing but make plans for a strategic retreat. His troops remained on Long Island three weeks before embarking (21 July) for N.Y. Only the *Solebay* accompanied the transports; Parker's other ships had to remain some time longer for repairs. Clinton's troops reached Sandy Hook on 31 July and joined Howe on Staten Island for the N.Y. CAMP'N.

LOSSES

Lee reported 10 Americans killed and 22 wounded in Ft. Sullivan; Ward's figures are 12 killed, 5 died of wounds, and 20 wounded.

British casualties totaled 225 (Lossing, II, 756 *n.;* Wallace, 95), most of whom were aboard the *Experiment* and *Bristol.* (Lossing and Ward agree on 111 casualties on the *Bristol,* and Lossing says 40 of these were killed, including her captain, John Morris; Lossing says 23 were killed and 76 wounded on the *Experiment,* but Ward's total for this ship is 20 less. Ward says 64 British were killed and 131 wounded in the entire engagement, or 30 fewer than Lossing's estimate.) Lord Wm. Campbell, the S.C. governor who had joined Clinton's expedition, had volunteered to man the *Bristol*'s guns; in the battle he received a wound of which he died two years later. Capt. Alexander Scott of the *Experiment* lost his right arm. Sir Peter Parker was slightly but painfully wounded.

COMMENT

The battle was a humiliating defeat to the British and a boost to rebel morale. The Southern colonies were to remain safely in rebel hands for three years before the British could send regulars again and by which time substantial Cont'l. forces would be free to move there from the north. During those three years it was downright dangerous to be a Loyalist in Va., N.C., S.C., or Ga.

Although the entire British operation was foredoomed because it depended on Loyalist military support, the King's military forces might have accomplished something if they had shown some speed. The relatively small force Clinton took from Boston was incapable of doing much alone, but in combination with the 2,500 troops of Cornwallis, and Parker's fleet, it should have been possible to accomplish part of Clinton's mission. The abortive Loyalist uprising that led to their defeat at MOORES CREEK BRIDGE deprived Clinton of some 1,600 American irregulars who could have played a significant part in regaining control of N.C.

As for the "Irish fleet," Fortescue says, "having consumed three months in crossing the Atlantic . . . it arrived just five months too late. . . ." (*British Army,* III, 180) Expected in Jan., it had not left Cork until 13 Feb.; five days out it had been scattered by gales and driven back to Cork and other ports. As already mentioned, the first vessels did not reach Cape Fear until 18 Apr., and another two weeks went by before most of Parker's fleet arrived.

Clinton erred in accepting Parker's strategy. The next mistake was in attacking Sullivan's Island instead of Charleston, "whose inhabitants, when the fleet arrived off the bar on June 1, were panicky, short of ammunition, and without confidence in their leaders," comments Willcox; "the British might have run past the two weak forts that guarded the harbor, and either stormed or surrounded the town." (*American Rebellion,* xx and note)

"Their second error was in trying to seize the island by a leisurely *coup de main,* which is a contradiction in terms. They spent weeks outside the harbor, discussing and reconnoitering, while General Lee arrived with American reinforcements and began to organize the defense." (*Ibid.*)

The next mistake, Clinton's landing on Long Island with the understanding that the Breach was fordable, has been mentioned. It is hard to understand how he could have been so stupid as to neglect reconnoitering this channel.

"Britain had worse defeats in the course of the war, but no more egregious fiasco," says Willcox.

Lord North, Germain, and the King found no fault with Clinton's conduct of the Charleston expedition, and gave him private assurances to this effect. A controversy developed, however, when Sir Peter Parker's public letter to the Admiralty charged Clinton wtih failure to support the naval attack. The published version of Clinton's letter to the Secretary of State was so abridged as to omit the portions that would have refuted Parker's contentions. The supersensitive Clinton was embittered by the government's unwillingness to make public their private assurances of his exoneration for the Charleston failure: in the autumn of '76 his friends in the House of Commons vigorously attacked the government on this matter; upon his return to England in the spring of '77 he was given the Order of the Bath to reestablish his prestige. (Willcox, *op. cit.*, 37 *n.* and 59 *n.*) See also CLINTON.

In view of this long list of British blunders there would appear to be little that the Americans might brag about in their victory. Certainly, S.C. had showed initiative and vigor in preparing for their own defense. "The stubborn insistence of Governor Rutledge and Colonel Moultrie upon holding the fort was responsible for the battle and the victory," writes Ward. (*Op. cit.*, 677–78) Paradoxically, Lee was entirely correct in urging that the fort be abandoned. "No one could possibly have foreseen the accident that enabled the Americans to win—the grounding of the *Actaeon*, the *Syren*, and the *Sphynx*," says Ward. "There was plenty of water between that shoal and the southern end of Sullivan's Island to permit the three vessels to come to anchor in the undefended rear of the fort and then to blast the garrison out of its defenses." (*Ibid.*) And who could have predicted that Clinton would bottle himself up on Long Island?

The courage of Ft. Sullivan's defenders has been mentioned, and no glory should be taken away from these brave men. It should be pointed out, however, that for every example of good conduct in open battle history offers hundreds of examples of men, women, and children fighting well from behind walls.

CHARLESTON EXPEDITION of Clinton in 1780. Ever since their failure at Charleston in 1776 the British had considered returning for another attempt. Howe planned such an operation for the winter of 1777–78, but disappointment with the results of his PHILADELPHIA CAMPAIGN led him to ask to be relieved as C. in C. and on 25 Mar. '78 Sir Henry Clinton succeeded him in

Philadelphia. (Anderson, *Howe Bros.*, 305–6) In the spring of '79, Germain urged Clinton to undertake a southern campaign, but Sir Henry had already decided to end the operations of that year with an attack on S.C. His preparations were well under way by Aug. and were interrupted only temporarily by the appearance of d'Estaing's fleet off the southern coasts. (Clinton, *American Rebellion*, note by editor Willcox, 151)

After the allied failure at SAVANNAH, 9 Oct. '79, prospects for successful British operations in the South looked particularly promising, yet there were serious problems. The optimist could point out that rebel morale and troop strength were at a particularly low ebb, whereas Loyalist morale and armed activity had picked up correspondingly; the shaky American economy had been further weakened by military disaster in the region on which they depended so heavily for foreign exchange and supplies; removal of the French fleet from American waters facilitated amphibious operations; to oppose Lincoln's weak garrison in Charleston, Clinton could spare an overpowering force from the 27,000 rank and file available between St. Augustine, Fla., and N.Y.; and he now had a base at Savannah to support his operations and rally Loyalists. "Altogether, Clinton's prospects were rosy," concludes Ward. (*W.O.R.*, 695–96)

British Army historian Fortescue takes quite an opposite view. Clinton would have to leave up to 15,000 troops to garrison N.Y.C. and its outposts, and also to keep Washington's army from undertaking a counteroffensive in the North (possibly against Canada) or reinforcing the South. Operations in the South could be profitable, but involved a long line of communications from N.Y.C. during a time when coastal shipping was menaced by winter storms, and the occupation of southern territory would require the immobilization of large forces to hold key positions and guard long lines of land communication. (This is what Clausewitz was later to term "strategic consumption.") Furthermore, a new major base would have to be established.

"The task set to Clinton was to make one army do the work of two, relying on the sea for communication between the different sections of the force. If the command of the sea were kept, the operations might be successful but could hardly be decisive; if the command of the sea were lost—and Clinton trembled night and day before the thought— they could hardly fail to be disastrous." (Fortescue, *British Army*, III, 307)

Although Sir Henry Clinton trembled easily over matters of grand strategy, as shown by his nervousness in N.Y.C. during the PHILADELPHIA CAMPAIGN, and his nerves were not steadied by recollections of joint operations with the British Navy against CHARLESTON in '76, still Fortescue's pessimism appears more warranted than Ward's rosy optimism.

THE EXPEDITION STARTS

Delayed until sure of d'Estaing's whereabouts, Clinton narrowly escaped being trapped in N.Y. harbor by ice. The reported presence of French ships wintering in Chesapeake Bay caused him to scrap his plan of dropping a force off in that area on his way south to safeguard against Washington's movement to oppose him in the Carolinas. He also had to talk Adm. Marriott Arbuthnot out of going after the French ships, since such an operation would further delay departure of the expedition.

Leaving Knyphausen behind with about 10,000, Clinton's force cleared

Sandy Hook on 26 Dec. '79. His 8,700 troops and Arbuthnot's 5,000 sailors and marines moved in 90 transports and 10 warships (530 guns); 396 horses, matériel, and supplies were aboard 18 of these transports. These figures are from the embarkation table sent by Baurmeister to von Jungkenn on 26 Mar. '80 and reproduced in facsimile in *The Siege of Charleston*, edited by Uhlendorf.

Major units of Clinton's army were the Light Infantry Corps, the 1st and 2d British Grenadier Bns., the 7th, 23d (Royal Welch), 33d, 63d, and 64th Foot, two jäger detachments (plus the chasseur company of Capt. George Hanger aboard the ill-fated ANNA), three Hessian grenadier battalions, and the regiment Huyn. CATHCART's Legion, FERGUSON's Rangers, 250 Hessian recruits for the regiments at Savannah, a 150-man detachment of the 71st Highlanders (also at Savannah), Turnbull's N.Y. Vols.,* and a detachment of guides and pioneers were also included. To plague historians—tripping up even the venerable Fortescue—the 42d (Black Watch) was scratched from the embarkation list at the last minute; it came to Charleston later with Rawdon (see below). (*Ibid.*)

The 38-day voyage was a real horror, which started with a storm when the convoy was only two days out of N.Y. Clinton commented that "scarcely a single day during the voyage passed without being marked by the foundering of some transport or other or the dispersion of the fleet...." (Clinton, 159) The *Anna*, a transport carrying about 200 Hessian troops, was blown

* Presumably these were replacements for Turnbull's Bn. of De Lancey's Vols., which (with Cruger's 1st Bn.) had been in the South since the capture of Savannah, 29 Dec. '78.

across the Atlantic. One particularly vexing hazard was that if the ships got too far from land to avoid being blown ashore they ran into the Gulf Stream, which not only slowed their movement south but also threatened to sweep them into mid-Atlantic. Almost all the horses, much of the artillery, and many valuable supplies were lost.

Although the North Edisto Inlet, just south of Charleston, was supposed to be their immediate destination (Uhlendorf, *Siege,* 23 *n.*), the convoy had to go to Savannah for repairs and reorganization. Most of the ships reached Tybee Island (in the Savannah River) by 30 Jan. '80, but many did not arrive until later.

SAVANNAH TO JAMES ISLAND

Clinton is known for his inability to get along with other commanders, and this trait played a significant part in the subsequent delays of his expedition. Before leaving N.Y. he had submitted a request to London that he be relieved and that Cornwallis succeed him. He therefore made no major decision without the latter's agreement. At Savannah, against his own judgment—he says —Clinton deferred to the recommendation of Cornwallis and a council of war to detach Maj. Gen. Paterson with 1,400 infantry and all the cavalry to make a strategic diversion in Ga. He was also overruled in his desire to avoid further hazards of the open sea by moving to Charleston by inland water routes. On a third point, however, he was saved by the professional support of Capt. ELPHINSTONE (of the Navy) on the matter of the landing site around Charleston; Arbuthnot wanted to make the landing at the Stono Inlet, but Elphinstone, who knew the area well, supported Clinton in the choice of the North Edisto Inlet. Clinton apparently favored the latter place because it involved less time at sea. As it turned out, if he had gone along with the admiral's recommendation the expedition would still have been in open water when a storm hit the night of 11–12 Feb. Arbuthnot resented the change in his plan, however, and this marked the beginning of hard feelings toward Clinton. It also marked the beginning of Clinton's warm regard for Elphinstone, who proved a tower of strength throughout the subsequent operations. (Clinton, 160, 161, and editor Willcox's notes on both pages) Having sent to St. Augustine, the West Indies, and the Bahamas for all the artillery and stores they could spare, Clinton left Savannah on 10 Feb. and started landing his troops the next afternoon on the S.W. tip of Simmons (now Seabrook) Island. His entire force was ashore the next day.

Slowed by lack of wagon horses and by delay of the galleys that were coming by "inland navigation" from Savannah, the British pushed forward to establish a beachhead on the mainland at Stono Ferry. During the next few days they took possession of James Island. Clinton then stopped to consolidate his position before moving against Charleston: he had to establish depots and, most important, to wait for Arbuthnot to get naval forces into the harbor to furnish heavy artillery for siege operations and also to furnish boats and seamen for crossing the Ashley River.

AMERICAN SITUATION

In the city of Charleston, the S.C. assembly was in session when the British armada appeared on 10 Feb., and they immediately gave Gov. Rutledge dictatorial powers. Years of peace, privateering, and relative prosperity had banked the fires of patriotism so conspicuous in '76, when Clinton had paid his first visit. Although such leaders as

Moultrie, Ramsay, Gadsden, and the Rutledge brothers were without peers, other South Carolinians put up a pretty poor show. So few S.C. militia turned out that state officials appealed to Washington for help. "Only about a third of the defenders of Charleston, chiefly militia and armed citizens, were recruited in South Carolina," points out Lynn Montross. (*Rag, Tag,* 356) Unwilling to fight, they certainly wouldn't work, and nothing was done to repair their dilapidated fortifications until the assembly authorized Rutledge to put 600 slaves to work.

Lincoln's garrison numbered about 3,600 when the enemy appeared. There were 800 S.C. Cont'ls., 400 Va. Cont'ls., about 380 survivors of Pulaski's Legion (now commanded by Maj. Vernier), Horry's dragoons, and about 2,000 militia of North and South Carolina. (Reinforcements of N.C. and Va. Cont'ls. started arriving in Mar.)

Charleston harbor was guarded by Forts Moultrie (formerly Sullivan) and Johnson, both of which were neglected ruins. Work was started to repair and rearm them, but Ft. Johnson was taken from the rear when the British occupied James Island. C. C. PINCKNEY was put in charge at Ft. Moultrie, but this position did little in the subsequent defense of the city. The small flotilla under Commodore Whipple was in no position to put up much resistance, and we can dispose of its efforts here. The eight vessels, several of which had been purchased from d'Estaing's fleet, withdrew into the Cooper River on 20 Mar. when the enemy fleet crossed the bar. Guns and crews of all but the 20-gun *Ranger* (John Paul Jones's raider, according to Fisher, II, 265) and the 28-gun *Queen of France* were sent ashore to defend the fortifications. Four frigates and several merchant ships were sunk to form the basis of a log and chain boom between Shute's Folly and Charleston. The other abandoned vessels were anchored north of the boom. Contemporary German diarists mention being attacked by two frigates, which have been identified as the *Ranger* and the *Queen* (Uhlendorf, *Siege,* 43), but Whipple's sailors made their main contribution to the Charleston defenses by manning guns ashore.

The line against which the British were to direct their main effort stretched about a mile and a half across the Charleston peninsula. The flanks were anchored on the Ashley and Charles rivers and further protected by marshes. What Clinton called a "broad canal" connected these marshes to form a sort of moat. Two lines of abatis were between this obstacle and a strong line of breastworks and redoubts that mounted 66 guns and a number of mortars. In the center of this line stood a masonry "horn work" of considerable strength known as the Citadel (not the site of the Military College of S.C.). On the southern tip of the town was a 16-gun redoubt. Six small forts of four to nine guns each were located along the Ashley River, and seven, mounting three to seven guns each, were along the Cooper.

CLINTON MOVES AGAIN

On 19 Mar., more than five weeks after debarking, Clinton received word from London that his resignation was not accepted. He immediately ordered Paterson to join him with the forces previously detached for operations in Ga. The next day Arbuthnot finally got some of his frigates over the bar and into Five Fathom Hole. Paterson arrived on 25 Mar. with 1,500 troops: the 1st Bn. of the 71st Highlanders, the light infantry, Tarleton's cavalry (still inadequately mounted), Ferguson's rangers, Turnbull's N.Y. Vols., Innes's S.C. Royalists, and Hamilton's N.C.

Royalists. (Uhlendorf, *Siege,* 220 *n.,* 221; Ward, 698)

Not knowing that the British had moved boats up for a river crossing operation, the Americans had concentrated their defenses opposite Ashley Ferry, where they expected Clinton to cross. The night of 28–29 Mar., however, 20 longboats and flatboats, manned by sailors and escorted by two armed boats, moved from their hiding place in Wappoo Creek and with muffled oars rowed undetected up the Ashley River to reach Drayton's House at dawn. Here, about three miles above Ashley Ferry, Cornwallis with the jägers, light infantry, and British grenadiers were waiting to cross. They embarked at 6 A.M., moved about a mile upstream to Benj. Fuller's house on the far shore, and landed unopposed at 7 o'clock. (This peculiar course—moving a mile upstream to cross a river only about 200 yards wide—was dictated by the need to embark from and debark on firm ground. A horseshoe bend helped conceal the troop movement.) Capt. Thos. Tonken, one of Arbuthnot's four agents for transports, had charge of the embarkation, and Elphinstone supervised the landing. By noon Clinton's main body had crossed in the 75 flatboats furnished by the navy. Some American dragoons withdrew when fired on by the 20 jägers who moved half a mile inland to cover the beachhead, but this was the only sign of American resistance. (The above details on the crossing are from the diary of Capt. Johann Ewald, who commanded the jäger outpost just mentioned, in *Siege,* 31 and 33.)

From his beachhead about 12 miles north of the city, Clinton moved south the next day (30 Mar.) and on Sunday, 1 Apr., broke ground within 800 yards of the Charleston defenses. (Clinton, 163) Lincoln had been outmaneuvered

and had lost his first and best line of defense, the river line.

The afternoon of 8 Apr. Arbuthnot ran past the guns of Ft. Moultrie with eight warships and about six transports loaded with supplies. Although the frigate *Richmond* (32) had her masts shot away, and the storeship *Aeolus* ran aground and had to be burned after her cargo was removed, the flotilla got into the harbor with only seven killed and 20 wounded. (*Siege,* 53)

On 3 Mar., 700 N.C. Cont'ls. under Gen. James Hogun had joined Lincoln after an arduous march of nearly three months through heavy snows and extreme cold, and at the same time an equal number of N.C. militia went home upon expiration of their enlistments. On 6 Apr., Gen. Wm. Woodford arrived with 750 Va. Cont'ls. after marching 500 miles in 28 days; the last lap of their trip was down the Cooper River, and Hessian Capt. Ewald comments that the 11 troop-laden schooners and sloops "would have paid dearly for their passage" if the bad roads on Charleston peninsula had been repaired soon enough to bring artillery up to a redoubt that was ready for them. (*Siege,* 49; Ewald says the vessels passed about 1 o'clock the afternoon of the 7th, not the 6th.)

On 10 Apr., when the first parallel was completed, Clinton and Arbuthnot sent Lincoln a summons to surrender. Lincoln declined, and work was started on the second parallel.

OPERATIONS AGAINST THE REBEL L. OF C.

With Charleston now cut off on three sides, a tenuous line of communications (L. of C.) was still open across the Cooper River and north to Biggins Bridge. A supply depot was located at nearby Monck's Corner (30 miles, in a straight line, north of Charleston) and another at Cainhoy (13 miles N.E. of the town). Gen. Huger was posted with about 500 mounted troops around Monck's Corner to defend these strategic points.

Although there would appear to be little basis for the theory that Clinton had taken his time closing in on Charleston so that the rebels would move troops there for him to bag, once his regular siege operations were under way he concentrated on completely isolating the defenders. He says in his memoirs that *"to secure the capture of all the rebel corps in Charleston* had been from the first a very principal object with me, as I saw the reduction of the rest of the province in great measure depended upon it." (*Op. cit.,* 164; emphasis in original.) The admiral volunteered to move some ships into the Cooper to cut the American L. of C., but Clinton expected little to come of this offer and organized a 1,400-man task force under Lt. Col. James Webster to undertake this mission.

Webster was to move north, cross the forks of the Cooper at Strawberry Ferry, and do as much damage as he could to supply lines, depots, and Huger. Clinton says he expected Webster to have a hard time of it and that "the inferiority of our light dragoons (both in numbers and quality of their horses) could not promise much success against [Huger's] three regiments of well appointed cavalry supported by a considerable body of militia." Webster started toward Dorchester on 12 Apr. with the 33d Foot and Tarleton's Legion; Ferguson took a parallel route on the right bank of the Ashley with his rangers. Tarleton and Ferguson joined forces about 10 miles north, on Goose Creek. The evening of the 13th, after Webster had caught up, Tarleton and Ferguson moved forward to check on reports that Col. Wm. Washington, whose cavalry

had been screening in this area, was withdrawing north. That night they had a stroke of luck that led to their bloody victory over Huger at MONCK'S CORNER, 14 Apr. The 64th Foot had followed Webster's leading regiment on the 13th, and the 23d left Charleston Neck the next day with the mission of covering the expedition's rear. On the 15th Webster reached Monck's Corner with the 33d and 64th regiments and within the next week had established control of the area east of the Cooper River to within six miles of Charleston.

On 18 Apr., Lord Rawdon arrived from N.Y. with reinforcements and supplies. Units were the 42d (Black Watch), Queen's Rangers, the Prince of Wales's Vols. ("Brown's Corps"), the Volunteers of Ireland, and the Hessian von Dittfurth Regt. The troops numbered 2,566 effective rank and file, of whom 1,863 were fit for duty (Clinton, 167 *n.*). Cornwallis was put in command of operations east of the Cooper, which was a good way for Clinton to get rid of him for a while. (*Ibid.*). The night of 23–24 Apr., the Earl crossed the Cooper at the Governor's House with the Volunteers of Ireland and the Carolina Tory units. He occupied the few remaining rebel positions, Lempriere's (Hobcaw) Point, Haddrel's Point (25 Apr.), and linked up with Webster at Cainhoy. Ft. Moultrie surrendered without a fight when sailors and marines landed on Sullivan's Is., 7 May; most of the garrison had been withdrawn, but 200 prisoners were taken. Tarleton scored another victory at LENUD'S FERRY, 6 May.

THE REGULAR APPROACHES

Meanwhile, the siege operations started 1 Apr. pushed toward the American lines under the direction of Maj. MONCRIEFF. A novel feature was his use of prefabricated mantelets shipped from N.Y. These are described by Capt. Ewald as being six feet high, 14 feet long, and standing on three feet. Needing 18 men to carry them, they were put in position to form the inner walls of a battery or redoubt. Workmen then had merely to pile dirt against the outer side, a task made particularly easy by the sandy soil of the peninsula. (*Siege,* 39)

By 19 Apr. Clinton's men had pushed their approaches to within 250 yards of the American lines despite the unbearable heat and the artillery fire directed against them. Convinced that capture of the town was inevitable, Lincoln called a council of war. Although the officers realized that the town could no longer be defended and were concerned with saving the troops for further military operations in the province, Lt. Gov. Gadsden had been allowed to sit in on the council and strongly opposed them. This clash of political and military led to adjournment, and Gadsden returned the next day with the Governor's Council to support his view. One of the latter went so far as to threaten that if the regular troops showed any sign of withdrawing and leaving the citizens to their fate they would side with the enemy and attack the Cont'ls. (Ward, 702; as quoted in C. & M., 1106. Moultrie says this threat was made at a council of war on 26 Apr.) Lincoln nevertheless proposed to Clinton on 21 Apr. that he be allowed to surrender with the HONORS OF WAR. Clinton immediately rejected the proposal.

At dawn on 24 Apr. Lt. Col. Henderson led about 200 Virginians and Carolinians in a sortie that overran the first line of works on the enemy right but was stopped by fire from the second; in this attack the Americans suffered only three casualties (including Capt. Thomas Moultrie, a brother of the general, killed) but the enemy lost about 50

killed and wounded (according to Capt. Hinrichs, *Siege,* 265) and 12 prisoners. The next night the British opened the third parallel, but sudden fire and cries of "*Avance, tue*" from the American abatis caused them to panic in fear of another counterattack. (The advanced work of the American left was occupied by Frenchmen [*Ibid.,* 235; 70 *n.*].) Although there is no evidence that the Americans left their lines (*ibid.,* 71 and *n.*), the besiegers had lost seven killed and 21 wounded by the time calm was restored around 2 A.M. (*Ibid.,* 263 *n.*)

Early on 26 Apr. Clinton had gained control of the first abatis and had reached the "wet ditch" at one point. Within the next few days work had progressed to the point that one 200-man shift could dig during the day. The same number worked at night, and the trenches were manned by 1,200 troops.

American fire continued to inflict casualties on the besiegers, intensifying as they came closer. On 2 May, Ewald commented that the defenders were loading their guns with scrap iron and glass. By the 6th of May the ditch had been drained to the point that it was dry in several places. The Americans were reduced to a week's supply of fresh provisions. On 8 May, Clinton started delivering a heavy volume of artillery and small arms fire, and at daylight sent Lincoln another summons to surrender unconditionally. Negotiations went on until 9 P.M. the next day, when they were broken off with mutual accusations of violating the intervening truce.

On 11 May came the beginning of the end. At 2 A.M., Gadsden, his Council, and a number of leading citizens asked Lincoln to accept the best terms he could get. (Lossing, II, 766) During the night the enemy had gained a lodgment 30 paces from the American works, and at 9 A.M. they started delivering hot shot, which set fire to several houses in the suburbs. At 2 P.M. Lincoln beat a parley, and the next day accepted Clinton's terms. The town was to be surrendered with all its troops, shipping, and military stores and installations. Cont'l. troops and sailors were to be held as prisoners until exchanged, but officers and their servants were allowed to retain their arms and baggage. The militia would be sent home on parole, and would be protected so long as they kept their parole. The French consul, French and Spanish residents of Charleston were to be considered prisoners of war, but would not be molested.

THE SURRENDER

At 11 o'clock the morning of 12 May the Cont'l. troops moved out of the lines, colors cased and (not permitted to play a British or American piece) beating The Turk's March; they grounded arms near the Citadel. The militia marched out later to do the same. Surprised at the small number, the British ordered that all weapons in the city be surrendered the next day. "I saw the column march out," wrote Moultrie, "and was surprised to see it so large; but many of them we had excused from age and infirmities; however, they would do to enrol on a conqueror's list." (*Memoirs,* quoted in C. & M.)

At 2 P.M. on the 12th there was a spectacular explosion caused by captured muskets being thrown into a storehouse where powder was deposited. "It was a terrible sight. Some were blown to bits, others thrown two hundred paces against walls and doors. . . . One hundred and fifty paces away was a magazine containing 180 barrels of powder. The muskets flew up into the air; ramrods and bayonets were blown onto the roofs of houses, and as much as six hours later some muskets went off. The fire was extinguished, but the

damage caused by this act of negligence was great indeed. . . . The entire siege did not cost us so many artillerymen. The loss of the muskets was an especially hard blow, for 4,000 had already been lost on the *Russia Merchant,* and now another 2,000 to 3,000 which were intended to arm the back-country people, all of whom are loyalists, or at least pretend to be." (*Siege,* 297, 298, diary of Capt. Hinrichs. See also RUSSIA MERCHANT.)

Moultrie estimated over 50 casualties, and comments that the British had been warned of the danger of their careless handling of captured muskets, many of which were loaded (C. & M.). The gruesome account of Capt. Ewald states that over 200 were killed and that the fire destroyed six houses, "including a brothel and a poorhouse"; he also attributes the accident to "the carelessness of the English," and voices the inevitable suspicion that "the powder was ignited maliciously by the rebels" (*Siege,* 89).

Official British returns of Maj. John André (then Deputy A.G.) list 5,466 officers and men (seven generals, 290 other Cont'l. officers), captured. The British also reported capture of 5,316 muskets, 15 regimental colors, over 33,000 rounds of small arms ammunition, about 8,400 round shot, 376 barrels of powder, and much other ordnance matériel. (Greene, *Rev. War,* 210)

Although most modern American histories accept the inflated British figure of about 5,500 troops captured, this total includes "the aged, the timid, the disaffected and the infirm, many of them who had never appeared during the whole siege." (Moultrie, quoted in C. & M., 1110) On 21 Aug. the Board of War finally reported the official total óf 245 [Cont'l.] officers and 2,326 N.C.O.s and privates captured (Freeman, *Washington,* V, 168 *n.,* citing 14 *J.C.C.,* 743); this is very close to the calculations of Edward McCrady that the Charleston garrison had 2,650 Cont'ls. (*Hist. of S.C. in the Rev., 1775–1780*, cited by Ward, 912 *n.*) Montross estimates that not more than 1,000 militia and armed civilians participated in the defense and that the total number of genuine prisoners probably did not exceed 3,300 (*Rag, Tag,* 362).

Whatever the total, this was the largest bag of American prisoners during the Revolution, and was not exceeded in American military history until the surrender of 10,700 Union troops to Stonewall Jackson at Harpers Ferry in 1862.

KILLED AND WOUNDED

Lincoln's losses are given as about 90 killed and about 140 wounded, an improbable ratio but one that American histories accept. (Lossing says 92 killed, 148 wounded [II, 767]; Ward says the *Cont'ls.* lost 89 k., 138 w., and the militia lost "not more than a dozen" [*Op. cit.,* 703]; Greene gives 92 k., 146 w. [*Op. cit.,* 211].)

Clinton reported 268 killed and wounded among "the King's troops"; Lossing says he had 76 killed and 189 wounded, and Fortescue says British losses did not exceed 265 killed and wounded. These figures presumably include German and Tory losses.

Clinton employed about 12,700 troops, including 450 seamen and marines; Arbuthnot had another 4,500 naval personnel. (*Siege,* note by editor Uhlendorf on pp. 106 and 107.)

COMMENT

Both Clinton and Lincoln have been severely criticized for their generalship in this campaign, the former for taking so long and the latter for permitting himself to be trapped. While neither commander ever showed more than

mediocre military talent, critics have ignored their problems in this operation.

We have seen Fortescue's argument that even though Clinton had impressive army and naval forces at his disposal the Charleston campaign was no pushover. Bear in mind also that the British commander in America had to husband his personnel resources: it took a long time for him to get replacements for battle casualties, if, indeed, the London authorities were inclined to furnish them at all. Bad weather, compounded by the ineptitude and uncooperativeness of Adm. Arbuthnot, slowed Clinton's sea movement from N.Y. Loss of horses and supplies delayed him still more. In deciding to capture Charleston by regular approaches, rather than assaulting the place as soon as possible after landing, Clinton says:

". . . I had not the smallest doubt of my becoming master of the town without much loss. This consideration alone would have been a sufficient incitement for me to prefer the mode of regular approaches to any other, less certain though more expeditious, which might have sacrificed a greater number of lives on both sides." (Clinton, 164)

There was nothing brilliant about Clinton's campaign, but he succeeded. He captured a place of major importance, he wiped out a huge rebel force (in terms of their total military resources), he opened the way for the conquest of the South, and the price was a mere 250 or so battle casualties. Clinton might well ask his critics, "What more do you want?"

Even in bush league warfare, to have a Cannae you need not only a Hannibal but also a Varro. Lincoln is commonly accused of making the disaster at Charleston possible by stupidly remaining with his army in a place where they were bound to be trapped, but this criticism ignores the political aspect of the decision.

"The greater part of his force was militia and armed citizens; his Continentals were from the Southern States, and disposed to render allegiance to State rather than Continental authority. The commanding general was the only Northern man in the army. If he had ordered a retreat his orders would not have been obeyed, and there would have been dissension on the part of the civil authorities which would have probably carried the State back to its British allegiance. The prudent course of Lincoln preserved its adhesion to the United States." (Greene, 211–12)

The next question is whether Lincoln would have been able to save his army if these political objections had not existed. Such an attempt could not have been justified prior to Clinton's debarkation on 12 Feb., nor could it have been delayed beyond 29 Mar., when the invaders crossed the Ashley River in force to the Charleston peninsula. During this period the Americans probably could have made better use of their small fleet in opposing Arbuthnot's movement across the bar and into the Five Fathom Hole. They might have able to do more in slowing the British occupation of the sea islands. With only reasonably good reconnaissance and with a minimum of risk, Lincoln should also have been able to move his regulars up to make better use of the Ashley River as an obstacle, thereby giving Clinton some opposition in his river crossing operation and also putting his troops in a better position either to escape north or to delay the enemy's advance to Charleston.

Once the enemy captured the sea islands and the harbor, Fisher thinks "it would probably have been better if Lincoln had evacuated [Charleston] as St. Clair evacuated Ticonderoga. He could still escape with his troops into the open country, ... save his troops, and might use them to prevent Clinton taking possession of the state" (*Struggle,* 266). Aside from this dubious (although popular) analogy between Ticonderoga in 1777 and Charleston in 1780, what real chance did Lincoln have of escaping? Zero, according to Greene.

"On strictly military grounds a retreat was out of the question [he says]. Clinton had 12,500 soldiers well equipped in every particular. Had Lincoln crossed the Cooper River with his 2,000 ill-equipped Continentals and attempted the long march—without transportation—to join Washington in New Jersey, he would probably have been overwhelmed and destroyed before he reached the Santee." (Greene, 212)

AFTERMATH

Tarleton's victory at WAXHAWS, 29 May, eliminated the last organized military force in the three southern provinces. Leaving Cornwallis in command, Clinton returned to N.Y. in June with about a third of his troops. For subsequent events, see SOUTHERN THEATER, Mil. Opns. in.

Bibliography. Clinton's *American Rebellion* and the Hessian diaries in *The Siege of Charleston* have been most valuable in the above account, particularly because of the notes of editors Willcox and Uhlendorf. A standard authority is Edward McCrady's two-volume *History of South Carolina in the Revolution.*

CHARLESTON RAID OF PREVOST, 11–12 May '79. When Lincoln undertook his counteroffensive toward Augusta, Prevost decided the best way to stop him was by the indirect strategy of threatening Charleston. But the British met so little resistance that they pushed on to the town and demanded its surrender. See "Lincoln's Campaigns" under SOUTHERN THEATER, Mil. Opns., for further background.

An advance guard of 900 British troops crossed the Ashley River on 11 May and moved south along Charleston peninsula. That morning Pulaski crossed the Cooper from his post at Haddrel's Point and was badly beaten when he sallied forth that afternoon. With 80 infantry and the cavalry of his legion, Pulaski had wanted to draw the enemy into an ambuscade, but his plan was spoiled when the men he posted behind earthworks rushed forward while the count was trying to bait the enemy into the trap. After the British closed up to the Charleston defenses and demanded surrender of the town, the rest of the day was spent in negotiations. The prosperous patriots of Charleston proposed a "deal": if the royal army would go away and leave them alone for the duration of the war they would pledge their neutrality and abide by the terms of the eventual winner of the conflict. Uhlendorf says they were led to this cowardly proposal because Congress was talking about arming Negroes. (*Siege*, 17) The British commander insisted that the armed garrison of Charleston be surrendered, and negotiations broke down. That night Gov. Rutledge, who shared with Gen. Moultrie the responsibility of defending the town, sent Maj. Benj. HUGER out to repair a gap in the abatis. He did not inform Moultrie of this, and when the front line troops saw movement in front of the lines they opened fire with small arms and artillery; Huger and 12 of his men were killed. (Lossing, II, 760 *n*.) Moultrie was then given over-all command, but the citizens were so terrified by the cannonade—thinking it meant they were about to be exposed to an all-out assault—that Moultrie was requested to renew their original surren-

der offer. The message went out at 3 A.M. and Prevost again refused.

The night of 12–13 May the British withdrew to James Island and then to Johns Island when they learned Lincoln was returning from Augusta. Evacuating the bulk of his command by boat to Savannah starting 16 June, Prevost left a rear guard that won the action at STONO FERRY, 20 June.

CHARLESTOWN, Mass., 17 June '75. Located on the peninsula opposite Boston, this town was settled in 1628 and at the start of the Revolution had a population of 2,700. According to Lossing, all but about 200 people had evacuated the place when the Boston Siege started. (I, 536) During the Battle of BUNKER HILL, 17 June '75, about 300 Americans in the town drew the first blood of that day's fighting when they fired on the British wing commanded by Pigot. When house-to-house fighting failed to dislodge the militia, Pigot asked Gen. Graves to set fire to the town. Hot shot from the ships and CARCASS from Copp's Hill (Boston) succeeded in doing this. The Americans rebuilt the place after the enemy evacuated Boston.

CHARLESTOWN, Mass., 8 Jan. '76. Successfully raided during Boston Siege by Thos. KNOWLTON during a performance of Burgoyne's play, "The Blockade of Boston."

CHARLESTOWN, S.C. The first English settlement in S.C. was established at Albemarle Point on the W. bank of the Ashley River in 1670 and named Charles Town, in honor of Charles II. The location proved to be undesirable, a new Charles Town was begun on the site of the present Charleston about 1672, and the seat of government was moved there in 1680. The name was changed to Charlestown about 1719 and Charleston in 1783. Hence the pedants are correct in calling this place "Charlestown" for the period of the American Revolution.

CHARLOTTE, N.C., 26 Sept. '80. Following the strategy outlined under KINGS MOUNTAIN, Cornwallis moved the largest of his three columns toward this village of 20 homes and a courthouse. Col. Wm. Davie was waiting to challenge him with 20 dragoons posted behind a stone wall near the courthouse and the rest of his command along Steel Creek road, which led to the stone wall. Maj. Geo. Davidson commanded two companies of riflemen, about 70 men, and Maj. Joseph Graham had a small body of Mecklenburg militia.

After being surprised by Davie at WAHAB'S, 21 Sept., Maj. Geo. Hanger now led the reinforced British Legion as an advance guard. When the rebel position was discovered at Charlotte, Hanger sent his infantry forward to clear the rebels from the fences along the road and he himself led the cavalry against the 20 dismounted dragoons. Both elements of this ill-conceived attack were stopped by fire and driven back. Hanger led a second charge against the stone wall and was repulsed. The British historian STEDMAN says, "The whole of the British army was actually kept at bay for some minutes by a few mounted Americans, not exceeding 20 in number." This sort of work was not to the liking of Tarleton's cavalry, and they were beginning to grumble when "Lord Cornwallis, feeling the absence of Tarleton, rode up and shouted: 'Legion! Remember you have everything to lose [in reputation], but nothing to gain.'" (Bass, *Green Dragoon,* 107)

This oratory probably impressed them less than the fact that the light infantry under Lt. Col. James Webster had forced the rebels to leave their fences along the road and fall back to the stone wall.

Hanger and Webster renewed the attack and Davie ordered a retreat when his right was turned. The Legion cavalry pursued vigorously for several miles, a task more to their taste.

American losses totaled 30 killed, wounded, and captured; the British lost 15. (Ward, *W.O.R.,* 739)

Bass says this action took place on 24 Sept.; the date 26 Sept. is that given in the *Army Almanac.* According to DeMond, Cornwallis' march from the Waxhaws was "constantly threatened by Colonel Davie, whose force of 150 men had been augmented by the arrival of 1,000 militia under Sumner and Davidson." (*Loyalists in N.C.,* 129) These forces chopped up British foraging parties, attacked convoys from Camden, and by intercepting messengers kept Cornwallis virtually without news of Ferguson's operations. Learning of the latter's defeat at Kings Mountain, Cornwallis abandoned his plans for a winter offensive into N.C. and left Charlotte the evening of 14 Oct. to start his retreat to Winnsboro.

CHARLOTTE RIVER, N.Y. Alternate name for East Branch of the Susquehanna. (Stone, *Border Wars,* II, 106)

CHARLOTTESVILLE RAID, Va., 4 June '81. (VA. MIL. OPNS.) Learning from a dispatch captured on 1 June that Gov. Jefferson and the legislature were meeting at this place, 60 miles west of Cornwallis' camp on the North Anna, Tarleton left before dawn on the 3d to scatter the legislators and capture the author of the Declaration of Independence. He took with him 180 troopers of his Legion and the 17th Light Dragoons plus a reinforcement of 70 mounted infantrymen from the 23d (Royal Welch Fusileers) under Capt. Champaigne. (The 2d Bn. of the 71st Highlanders had been designated for this supporting role, but their bitterness against Tarleton for sacrificing the 1st Bn. at COWPENS was such that Cornwallis accepted their request to accompany Simcoe's POINT OF FORK expedition instead.) Capt. John Jouett of the Va. militia spotted Tarleton's column the afternoon of the 3d and got ahead of the raiders that night to spread the alarm. Having reached Louisa C.H. at 11 P.M., Tarleton resumed his march at 2 A.M. on the 4th. Before dawn he captured and destroyed 12 wagons loaded with weapons and clothing for Greene's army. Six miles from his objective he split his force in two. One column rode to Belvoir, the home of John Walker, where Capt. David Kinlock captured his cousin, Congressman Francis Kinlock. Tarleton led the other column to Castle Hill, the home of Dr. Thos. Walker (John's brother), where he captured a number of prominent patriots; among these were Col. John Simms, a member of the legislature, and Gen. Thos. Nelson's two brothers, Robert and William. (Lossing, II, 549)

While Tarleton was at Castle Hill, where he let his men rest an hour and have breakfast, Jouett reached Monticello. Here Jefferson was entertaining the Speaker and other members of the Assembly. "The Speaker immediately convened and then adjourned the Legislature to Staunton," according to Burk's *Hist. of Va.* A detachment of dragoons under Capt. Kenneth McLeod was moving up the winding road to Jefferson's house when Mrs. Jefferson and her children left in a carriage. The Governor's horse was being shod at a shop some distance from the house at this moment; sending word for the smithy to hurry his work and send the horse to a certain gate, Jefferson walked to that point by a short cut, mounted, and joined his family. McLeod entered the house less than 10 minutes after Jeffer-

son left it. (Burk, as cited by Johnston, *Yorktown,* 44 n.) Monticello was not damaged, and the only property destroyed was some wine in the cellar, "drank [sic] and wasted by a few soldiers, without the knowledge of their commander." (Lossing, *op. cit.,* 549)

Meanwhile, the other raiders had routed a militia guard at the ford of the Rivanna and charged up the hill into Charlottesville. It would appear that the three or four members of the Legislature captured on this raid were those taken at Belvoir and Castle Hill, and that none were bagged in town. Bass says, "In spite of Jouett's warning, the British captured seven members of the Assembly. Brigadier-General Scott and several officers and men were killed, wounded, or taken." (*Green Dragoon,* 179) But Johnston points out that Tarleton could not have captured Scott, since the Cont'l. Gen. Scott was not then in Va., nor was any other by that name. (*Op. cit.,* 44 n.) Col. John Smith wrote two weeks later, "no money was taken by Tarleton, nor did our Types fall into his hands." (*Ibid.*) Tarleton destroyed 1,000 new muskets, 400 barrels of powder, some military clothing, and several hogsheads of tobacco before moving with his prisoners to join Cornwallis about 9 June at Elk Hill, some 30 miles S.E. of Charlottesville. Here the British engaged in a wanton destruction of a plantation belonging to Jefferson, slaughtering cattle, killing young horses, carrying off those of military value, burning barns and fences, and rounding up slaves. (Lossing, *op. cit.,* 550)

An amusing footnote to this raid is furnished by Lossing. When Col. Brooks led a small body of Va. militia into Staunton the morning of the 7th with a message from Steuben, "The members [of the Legislature], believing them to be a part of Tarleton's legion, took to their heels, and it was some time before they could be coaxed back to their duties." (*Op. cit.*, 549 *n.*)

CHASE, Samuel. 1741–1811. Signer. Md. Educated by his father, a Church of England clergyman, he studied law and was admitted to the bar in 1761. He became a prominent lawyer and sat in the colonial legislature (1764–84) where he had a reputation for extreme independence. He opposed the governor and at one point voted to regulate salaries of the clergy, which reduced his father's income by half. Chase resisted the Stamp Act and, as a member of the Sons of Liberty, publicly affirmed his own participation in the looting of public offices, destroying stamps and burning the collector in effigy. In the Continental Congress 1774–78, he was also a member of the committee of safety, the first Md. convention, and the committee of correspondence. He advocated total trade embargo with England, favored confederation, and supported George Washington in the face of Congressional intrigues. Chase was sent on the unsuccessful Canadian mission (see CANADA, Cong. Comm. to). In 1778 he attempted, with others, to corner the flour market, using Congressional information on the arrival of the French fleet. This cast a shadow over his reputation, and for two years he was not sent to Congress. However, he was sent to England in 1783 to recover from two fugitive Loyalists investments made by the state in the Bank of England before the war. In 1786 he moved from Annapolis to Baltimore and in 1788 became chief judge of the new criminal court. A member of the state convention that adopted the Federal Constitution in 1791, he opposed its ratification. After serving as chief of the Md. general court, he was named to the U.S. Supreme Court in 1796. In 1804, he was impeached but not convicted and, discharged in 1805, continued on the bench until his death.

CHASSEURS. Certain light infantry troops were known as JÄGERS in the German army and as chasseurs in the French and British army. Even the Germans, however, used the term chasseurs for those jägers who were part of a regiment, as opposed to those who were in von Wurmb's Jäger Corps.

CHASTELLUX, François-Jean de Beauvoir, Chevalier de. 1734–1788. French officer and writer. Of interest to us for his *Travels in North America in the Years 1780, 1781, and 1782,* Chastellux entered the army at the age of 13 as 2d Lt. in the Auvergne Regt. and was a Col. at 21. In May '55 he became the first Frenchman to be inoculated for smallpox. Although he continued his military career, fighting in Germany from 1756 to 1763, he distinguished himself as a writer in several fields, military, technical, the theater—he arranged *Romeo and Juliet* for the French stage—and philosophy.

Designated as one of the Maj. Gens. in Rochambeau's expeditionary force, he reached Newport on 11 July '80. He remained here until the start of the Yorktown Campaign, stayed in Va. until the summer of 1782, marched back with the French army to New England, relinquished his post as *maréchal de camp,* went to Philadelphia, and sailed from Annapolis early in Jan. '83. Speaking English and being number three in the hierarchy, Chastellux became what one writer called "the diplomat of Rochambeau's army." In his introduction to the 1963 edition of *Travels in North America* (2 vols., Chapel Hill, N.C.), editor Howard C. Rice Jr. writes: "He was equally at ease in staff conferences, in the drawing rooms of Philadelphia or Boston, and in roadside taverns." His book, therefore, is of historical value for its accounts of people, places, and events of the period 1780–82.

Early in 1784 he became the Marquis de Chastellux, entered the French Academy, and was made military Gov. of Gongwy and (later) inspector general. He married in 1787 and died suddenly the next year of a fever contracted during an inspection trip. He was 54.

CHATHAM, William Pitt, 1st Earl of. 1708–1778. English statesman. Grandson of Thos. Pitt (1653–1726), who had been Gov. of Madras and was known as "Diamond" Pitt after he sold the fabulous "Regency Diamond" to the regent Orleans, William was the younger son of a wealthy country squire. He attended Eton and Oxford. Elected to Parliament in 1735, he opposed the weak foreign policy of the Whig prime minister Robt. Walpole, supported the opposition party of the Prince of Wales against George II, and helped fell Walpole in 1742. For about four months starting in Dec. '56 he was a secretary of state and leader of the Commons. He then was forced to make an accommodation with his arch political foe the corrupt duke of Newcastle, and in June '57 the celebrated Pitt–Newcastle coalition ministry started its four-year tenure. Already known as "the Great Commoner," Pitt became virtual head of the government at a time when British fortunes in the Seven Years' War (1756–63) were at a low ebb, particularly in America, where the French and Indian War had started in 1755. "The Seven Years' War might well . . . have been another Thirty Years' War if Pitt had not furnished Frederick [the Great] with an annual subsidy of £700,000, and in addition relieved him of the task of defending western Germany against France." (*E.B.*, "Chatham") He also straightened out the mismanagement of military supplies, bolstered English morale, and reached down the list of seniority to advance such capable junior officers as Amherst and Wolfe for high command. The result was a crushing, humiliating defeat of the French in India and the capture of Canada. GEORGE III then forced Pitt out of the government and proceeded ineptly to throw away at the peace table the victories Pitt had won on the battlefield. Resigning in Oct. '61, he initially refrained from joining the opposition. In Feb. '63 he indignantly objected to the preliminary agreements for what was to become the Peace of Paris; already suffering severely from gout, he was carried to the House where he delivered a three-hour speech interrupted several times by paroxysms of pain. "The physical cause which rendered this effort so painful probably accounts for the infrequency of his appearances in parliament, as well as for much that is otherwise inexplicable in his subsequent conduct." (*Ibid.*)

In 1763 he spoke against a tax measure imposed by George Grenville, his brother-in-law; although his opposition had no effect in the House, it helped keep alive his tremendous popularity in England. In 1764 he entered the controversy over John WILKES to maintain the illegality of general warrants, thus identifying himself with the popular opposition to George III on the matter of Parliamentary privileges and freedom of the press. In 1766, having been incapacitated for a year, he argued for repeal of the Stamp Act. On three occasions Pitt had resisted appeals that he return to the government. When Rockingham's ministry fell in July '66, the King entrusted Pitt with forming a government. "The Great Commoner" astounded the people by making himself Lord Privy Seal, a sinecure office that removed him from the Commons. In Aug. '66 he became Earl of Chatham and Viscount Pitt. He had formed a cabinet of exceptionally capable individuals but that, for lack of leadership and diversity of political views, proved incapable of action. Shocked by his loss of popularity (for accepting a peerage) and suffering from physical and mental maladies, Chatham appeared indifferent to the momentous national problems that clamored for solution. And while he was in this condition the fateful TOWNSHEND ACTS of 1767 were put into effect. "It is probably the most singular thing in connexion with this singular administration, that its most pregnant measure should thus have been one directly opposed to the well-known principles of its head." (*Ibid.*)

Chatham resigned in Oct. '68 on the ground of bad health. Shortly thereafter a renewed attack of gout freed him from the mental condition bordering on insanity that had plagued him for almost two years. Returning to his seat in the House of Lords in 1770 he turned his still powerful eloquence against the government's coercive policy toward the colonies, but he now had virtually no following. On 7 Apr. '78 he spoke against a proposal by the Duke of Richmond that peace with America be concluded on any terms because of increasing evidence that France was preparing for *revanche*. The man who had humiliated this "natural enemy" and inspired this burning desire for revenge could not tolerate any thought that England's policy might be governed by fear of France. After Richmond had replied to his first protest, Chatham rose excitedly to speak. He then pressed his hand to his chest and collapsed. He died 11 May '78.

CHATTERTON'S HILL. Scene of decisive action in the Battle of WHITE PLAINS, N.Y., 28 Oct. '76.

CHEHAW POINT, 12 miles below COMBAHEE FERRY, should not be con-fused with Cheraw on the Peedee River, near the N.C.–S.C. border.

CHEMUNG, N.Y., 29 Aug. '79. Another name for action at NEWTOWN.

CHEROKEE EXPEDITION OF JAMES GRANT, 1761. In 1759 the militia were alerted for operations against the Cherokees but trouble was averted when Gov. Lyttleton made a treaty with them. The next year the Indians were defeated near modern Franklin, N.C., at Echoe (pronounced in three syllables), but heavy casualties were sustained from an ambush before Col. Archibald Montgomery's Highlanders and the S.C. militia won the day. In 1761 Amherst sent Lt. Col. James Grant to Charleston with 1,200 regulars for a punitive expedition, and he was supported by provincial troops raised by Thos. Middleton, Henry Laurens, and John Moultrie. Having arrived in Jan., Grant started up the Santee and Congaree rivers in mid-Mar., reached Ft. Prince John by 29 May, and on 6 June turned north. When an ambush was detected at the same place where Montgomery had been attacked, Grant picked Lt. Francis Marion of Capt. Wm. Moultrie's militia company to force the pass with a detachment of 30 men. Marion accomplished his difficult mission, leading his men forward despite 21 casualties, and the main body followed to take up an action that lasted until noon before the Indian army broke. Grant then burned Echoe and moved down the Tennessee and Tuakaseegee valleys to destroy more than 15 settlements and cut down growing corn. Chief Attakullakulla (also known as "Little Carpenter") threw in the towel. After spending 30 days in Cherokee territory Grant withdrew to Charleston. Other colonials on this expedition who became prominent in the Revolution were Andrew Williamson, Isaac Huger, and Andrew Pickens.

CHEROKEE FORD, S.C., 14 Feb. '79. Skirmish preceding the action at KETTLE CREEK, same date. Another Cherokee Ford, this one on the Broad River, figured in the KINGS MOUNTAIN CAMPAIGN.

CHEROKEE WAR OF 1776. The first Indian uprising of the Revolution was undertaken by the Cherokee at the instigation of the Shawnee and other northern tribes, and against the advice of British agents. They attacked the frontiers of Ga. and the Carolinas, making the main effort against the settlements in the Watauga and upper Holston valleys. These were beaten off and Congress aided S.C. in getting counteroffensives started from Ga., the Carolinas, and Va. Gen. Andrew Williamson in Aug. pushed into the Lower Cherokee villages (generally the area of what now is N.E. Ga.). Eventually collecting 1,800 troops and some Catawba scouts, he brushed aside Indian resistance, destroying villages and cornfields; refugees streamed toward Fla. Gen. Griffith joined Williamson in Sept. with 2,500 N.C. militia and the patriots drove through rugged Appalachian country to destroy the Middle Cherokee villages and drive the people west for safety among the Overhills, in what now is the western tip of N.C. But the third column, 2,000 Va. and N.C. militia under Col. William Christian, came down the Holston from the north (the country of the "OVER MOUNTAIN MEN") and passed among the Overhill Cherokee. Dispirited because the Creeks did not come up from the south to help them, and realizing that little assistance could be provided by the British, the Indians started suing for peace. In the treaties of Dewitt's Corner, S.C., signed 20 May '77 with S.C. and Ga., and of the Long Island of Holston, in modern Tenn., signed 20 July '77, the Cherokee ceded all their lands east of the Blue Ridge and dropped their claims to land north of the Nolachucky River. (Alden, *South*, 272–3) See INDIANS . . . for the story of the Cherokee who moved west to continue the struggle. A useful map is "Cherokee–Creek Country, 1760–1781" in Scribner's *Atlas* (plate 76).

CHERRY VALLEY MASSACRE, N.Y., 11 Nov. '78. In the spring of 1778 Maj. John Butler, who then directed Tory activities from Niagara, planned to "break up the back settlements" of Pa., N.J., and N.Y. as a strategic diversion to "distract the enemy . . . from his main purpose," which was "to effect joining Sir Harry Clinton" on the Hudson. In line with this over-all strategic plan—the quoted portions are from the 4 June '78 memorandum of his son, Walter Butler, to Carleton (Swiggett, *Niagara*, 118)—the elder Butler led an expedition that ended in the WYOMING VALLEY "MASSACRE," Pa., 3–4 July. Young Walter Butler then got authority to lead another Tory force from Niagara, join Joseph Brant, and attack Cherry Valley.

Tradition has it that Walter Butler's mission was prompted by a desire to get even with the Tryon county patriots for his recent treatment while a prisoner in their hands. (See Walter BUTLER) Swiggett, however, concludes that the Tory strategists had a sounder military motive. The Mohawk Valley settlements formed a salient that stretched toward Tory-held Ft. Oswego and along the northern boundary of Iroquois territory. (See map "Mohawk Valley," page 250.) Joseph Brant had established a patrol base around Unadilla and had raided settlements including GERMAN FLATS, 13 Sept. '78. Patriots retaliated by destroying UNADILLA, 8 Oct. If Butler could wipe out Cherry Valley this not only would relieve the pressure on Unadilla but would also set the stage for operations against the Schoharie Valley and Canajoharie. The Tories might then move against Ft. Stanwix (Schuyler) and regain the homes from which they had been forced to flee. (See TRYON COUNTY)

By the time Walter Butler and his Rangers reached the theater of operations, however, patriot forces had returned to ravaged Wyoming and moved up the Susquehana. In Oct., therefore, young Butler's headquarters was around Chemung, near Tioga, while he waited for this threat to subside. Meanwhile he was in contact with Brant and was making plans to join forces with him at Oquago (now Windsor). In his *War out of Niagara,* Howard Swiggett thus refutes earlier accounts that Butler met Brant near Genesee Castle, some 70 miles' march from Niagara, and there prevailed on Brant to return with him to raid Cherry Valley, a countermarch of over 200 miles. (Swiggett, *op. cit.,* 147–50) While it is not clear why Butler delayed his attack so long, knowing that the patriots would have more time to prepare their defenses, one reason might be that he had to make sure of his line of retreat through Tioga. Swiggett says:

"He may have waited to strike until the very lateness of the season convinced Alden [see below] and the townsmen that they were safe until spring. This, however, seems unlikely. Rains, cold, and hunger bore no more lightly on the Rangers than the Americans. It was a terrific march for 700 men down the Chemung [Tioga] River to the junction with the Susquehanna and up it to Otsego Lake and on to Cherry Valley, probably over 150 miles of heavy going. Such a force could not live entirely on the country, and ammunition and military baggage would have to be carried. It seems almost sure that unknown circumstances held Walter Butler at Chemung much later than was intended. Woodsmen, such as the Rangers were, would not purposely wait till mid-November to attack Cherry Valley with a march of 300 miles to Niagara, through snowy forests and winter rivers, to follow. The chance of defeat always existed and it meant death to scores of them, if not in action then in flight through the snow." (*Ibid.*)

HISTORY OF CHERRY VALLEY

In the summer of 1740 a John Lindsay had left N.Y.C. and established the first farm in the isolated valley to which he subsequently gave the name Cherry Valley. During the next 10 years not more than four families joined Lindsay, but cordial relations were established with the Mohawks and, since this tribe remained generally loyal to the British, the settlement survived the French and Indian wars. The inhabitants did, however, erect some crude fortifications, and they turned out to help defend other settlements of the Mohawk Valley. Early in 1775 they associated themselves with the patriot faction and the next summer raised a company of rangers under command of Capt. Robert M'Kean. When this unit was ordered away the Cherry Valley settlers started petitioning for troops. The N.Y. Provincial Congress responded to their appeal of 1 July '76 by sending a company of rangers under Capt. Winn. The house of Col. Samuel Campbell was fortified and enclosed to form a place where the inhabitants could gather for safety. Since Joseph Brant had assembled a considerable number of warriors around Oquago (60 mi. S.W.) and had appeared in Unadilla during the summer of 1777, military law was established in the Valley and most of the inhabitants gathered around Campbell's. They responded to Gen. Herkimer's call to meet St. Leger's Expedition, but only

Col. Campbell and one other joined him in time for the Battle of Oriskany. In the spring of 1778 Col. Campbell joined Lafayette at Johnstown, explained the exposed position of the Valley, and convinced him of the need for a fort there.

Meanwhile, the inhabitants of Cherry Valley returned to their stockade at Campbell's while waiting for the new fort to be built. Refugees came in from Unadilla and other settlements. Brant and his braves lurked in the vicinity, snapping up a few prisoners and forcing the inhabitants to form armed parties to work their farms. Col. Ichabod Alden arrived in July with his 7th Mass., numbering about 250 men, to take command. Alden is characterized by Swiggett as "a wretched officer," and his men were Easterners innocent of Indian warfare. It is ironical that Col. Peter Gansevoort sought the assignment of garrisoning Cherry Valley with his regiment, the defenders of Ft. Stanwix (ST. LEGER'S EXPED.), but Alden was given the post.

As mentioned at the beginning of the article on WYOMING VALLEY, James Deane, Schuyler's secret agent, had been sending in accurate intelligence of the Tory-Indian activities and intentions. It was hoped that a Seneca chief called Great Tree, who returned to his people after spending some time in Washington's headquarters, would prevail on the Iroquois to cancel their plans for war against the frontier, but Deane reported in Oct. that Great Tree had changed heart after hearing rumors of a planned invasion of Iroquois territory by patriot forces. On 6 Nov. a warning was sent to Alden from Stanwix: information had been received of a "great meeting of Indians and Tories" on the Chemung (Tioga) River, at which Walter Butler was present, and the decision had been made to attack Cherry Valley. (Perhaps

the "unknown circumstances [that] held Walter Butler at Chemung much later than was intended" were the powwows needed to mobilize the Indians.) On 8 Nov., Alden wrote back: "I am much obliged to you for your information. . . ." Swiggett comments:

"He adds in a postscript that General [Edw.] Hand was that day at Cherry Valley. If the blue-nosed Alden was not alarmed it is astonishing that General Hand, who was a rifleman, a former commander at Fort Pitt, and in a sense a frontiersman, should not have ordered the normal preparations made to receive an attack. He must have come out from Albany on an inspection trip, as he succeeded Stark in command at Albany as of that day, and it is strange that Major [Daniel] Whiting should have had to write him later of the lack of supplies at the fort." (*Op. cit.*, 147)

The settlers asked to move into the new fort, or at least to store their valuables there, but Alden refused on the ground that the intelligence was probably wrong and that the presence of their property in Ft. Alden would tempt his soldiers to pilfer it. The patriot commander did, however, send out reconnaissance parties. The one that scouted down the Susquehanna was captured the morning of 10 Nov. as they slept around their fire. Based on information from the prisoners that the rebel officers were billeted outside the fort, Butler and Brant planned their attack. The night of 10–11 Nov. several inches of snow fell and the next morning a thick haze and rain concealed the raiders' approach on the sleeping settlement.

The plan was first to hit the houses in which the officers were known to be billeted and then to attack the fort. At 11 A.M. the Tories and Indians were approaching their objective when a Mr. Hamble (or Hammell) rode by on his way to the fort. The Indians fired and wounded him but he escaped to spread the alarm. While the Rangers stopped to check their firearms, an advance party of Senecas raced ahead to attack the Wells house, 400 yards from the fort. Alden was billeted here with Lt. Col. Wm. Stacey, Whiting, and a headquarters company of 20 or 40 men. What happened is uncertain, although it is known that Alden was killed while running toward the fort, Stacey was captured, and several other officers and men were killed. The fort held out, and at 3:30 P.M. the raiders withdrew.

"No time is given for [the end of the] killings in the town [says Swiggett]. The details of the day are of confused horror. There were evidently 40 homes in Cherry Valley, and 31 or 32 noncombatants were slain during the day, 13 of them in the Wells house. In only six other houses of the 40 were people killed. This seems to be important in connection with Walter Butler's own responsibility for the massacre. While Lossing, Simms, and Campbell describe him as the instigator of it all, and while Dwight tells of his ordering babies killed, none of the four, in spite of their wealth of specific detail in other connections, ever gives the name of a family at whose murder he was present or a participant." (*Op. cit.*, 153. Lossing and W. W. Campbell have been frequently cited. Timothy Dwight is author of *Travels in New England and N.Y.*, 4 vols., New Haven, 1821. J. R. Simms wrote several books on the N.Y. frontier.)

In evaluating Swiggett's comments remember that his *War out of Niagara* is, in effect, a biography of Walter Butler, and one must be on guard. He himself underlines the pitfalls of biography when he says that although he has never found documentary evidence of Col. John Butler's allegation that Joseph

Brant "secretly incited the Indians in this massacre in order to stigmatize his son" (quoting Campbell, *Tryon*, 112), he (Swiggett) finds this accusation "in accord with the appearance of the facts." (*Op. cit.*, 155 n.) Stone, on the other hand, the biographer of Joseph Brant, says Brant "did all in his power to prevent the shedding of innocent blood" and pictures the Mohawk chief rushing about saving people from the Senecas. (*Border Wars*, I, 346)

Capt. McDonnell led a sortie from the fort that saved many settlers who had taken refuge in the woods. The raiders withdrew with 71 prisoners (*D.A.H.*), most of whom were released the next day. "No one seems to have been killed during the night," says Swiggett. The morning of the 12th, having camped near Cherry Valley, Butler started his long retreat to Niagara. Since his mother, aunt, and the wives of several Tory officers were prisoners in Albany, Butler kept two women and their seven children as hostages. (Col. Campbell's wife and four children; Mrs. James Moore and three daughters.) Gov. Clinton says Butler evacuated 33 prisoners, but most of these were Negro servants who probably went along voluntarily. (Swiggett, *op. cit.*, 156)

COMMENT

From a military viewpoint the Cherry Valley raid was a brilliant coup executed in the face of great difficulties. Its success was due largely to incompetent rebel leadership, which largely explains why American writers prefer to dwell on the horror aspects.

From the moral standpoint, Butler and the Indians justified the destruction of the settlement by pointing out that after the Wyoming Valley massacre Col. Denison violated his parole to join the punitive expedition up the Susquehanna. They also mentioned the destruction of Unadilla on 8 Oct.

The patriots retaliated by launching SULLIVAN'S EXPED. against the Iroquois, May—Nov. '79. This was supported by BRODHEAD'S EXPED., and Clark's WESTERN OPERATIONS were directed against Detroit.

CHESAPEAKE BAY, 16 Mar. '81. Naval action. As part of the strategy covered under VA. MIL. OPNS., Adm. Destouches led the French squadron from Newport, R.I., the evening of 8 Mar. and sailed for the Chesapeake to support Lafayette's expedition against Arnold. Adm. Arbuthnot detected this movement and started in pursuit from Gardiner's Bay, at the eastern end of Long Island, the morning of the 10th. Despite the handicap of 36 hours, the British were actually leading when the fleets came in sight of each other just off the capes of the Chesapeake. (Mahan says Arbuthnot was "favored either by diligence or luck," but mentions in a note that "The French ascribe this disadvantage to the fact that some of their ships were not coppered." Mahan, *Sea Power,* 386. The reputation of ARBUTHNOT being what it is, the French explanation is to be favored.)

Each admiral had eight ships, but the British had the advantage in the weight of metal they could throw. The French headed out to sea for a one-hour engagement in which Destouches had a slight advantage but which left both fleets badly damaged. Destouches, however, abandoned the expedition and returned to Newport, while Arbuthnot, in a gesture that goes far to explain why Britannia ruled the waves, moved into Chesapeake Bay and established contact with Arnold.

By making a strategic failure out of a tactical success the French admiral not only left his countryman, Lafayette, without the expected naval support to move against Arnold, but he left the

sea open for the British to send Gen. Phillips with sizable reinforcements to ravage Virginia.

CHESAPEAKE CAPES, 5 Sept. '81. (YORKTOWN CAMPAIGN) A British fleet of 19 ships (1,402 guns) under Adm. Thos. Graves reached the Chesapeake the morning of 5 Sept. to find that de Grasse had gotten there first. The section headed "Naval Operations" in the article on the YORKTOWN CAMPAIGN covers the British blunders and misfortunes leading up to this unpleasant surprise.

When the British appeared, the French fleet was inside Chesapeake Bay supporting the army: the West Indies troops were being landed, certain ships of the line were guarding the mouths of the James and York rivers to blockade the transports of Cornwallis, and the light vessels were preparing to move up the Chesapeake to embark the French and American troops waiting at Baltimore and Annapolis for movement to the Peninsula. Furthermore, de Grasse was expecting the convoy of Adm. de Barras that had left Newport on 25 Aug. with the French siege train and other vital equipment.

De Grasse issued prompt orders to the 24 ships-of-the-line (1,788 guns) that were immediately available for action and filed out of the bay at noon, when the tide favored the movement. He had formed his ships in order of swiftness, and although Graves could count them as they came forth, "the sense of numerical inferiority—19 to 24—did not deter the English admiral from attacking," comments Mahan. "The clumsiness of his method, however, betrayed his gallantry; many of his ships were roughly handled, without any advantage being gained." (*Sea Power,* 389)

Although this is all Mahan has to say about the tactics of this decisive naval engagement, here is a description of the main part of the battle as given by an anonymous French naval officer who took part:

"The issue of the expedition, the vacancy left by the crews employed in the debarkation [90 officers and 1,800 men], the fear of getting too far from the mouths of the York and James rivers, and the fear lest the English fleet, by its known superior sailing, should succeed in getting between these mouths and the French fleet, all obliged it to keep on the defensive. The enemy held the weather gage in excess. Their balls did not come near enough to the French to receive a reply. There was no appearance that the combat would become very warm, but the winds ordered otherwise; they shifted till they came to the northeast and forced the English to attack.

"The two vans having come so close as to be almost within pistol shot, the fire was long well sustained, and the affair seemed about to be decisive, when Admiral Hood made a signal to the English rear division, which he commanded, to bear down on the French rear. The admiral witnessed this movement with pleasure and prepared to tack his whole fleet together, bearing N.N.W., which would inevitably have thrown the English line into confusion, but Admiral Graves anticipated him and signaled his whole fleet to keep the wind. The heads of the two fleets gradually fell off in consequence . . . and the fire ceased at 6½, P.M." (Quoted in C. & M., 1220)

In this two-and-a-half-hour action, which was stopped by darkness, another French account points out that only the eight leading English ships and the first 15 French ships took a significant part in the battle.

For the next two days, 6–7 Sept., the two fleets held contact without renewing the action, but they drifted 100 miles southward to the vicinity of Cape Hatteras. On 8 Sept. the French turned north in an effort to get the weather gage and be in a position to protect Barras when he reached Chesapeake Bay. The morning of the 9th the French lost sight of Graves; then, they bore down in line of battle on a squadron whose flag they could not make out, but lost contact during the day. De Grasse then sailed for the Chesapeake and anchored there the 11th to find that Barras had arrived on the 10th; it was his squadron they had spotted on the 9th. (*Ibid.*, 1221) The British fleet left the Va. coast on 14 Sept. and returned to N.Y.

Cornwallis' days were numbered.

French losses on 5 Sept. were 220 killed and wounded among the 19,000 seamen aboard their 24 ships. As already mentioned, only 15 of these ships were engaged, so presumably only 12,000 men were in action. British losses were 90 killed and 246 wounded out of 13,000 seamen aboard their 19 ships; again, only eight ships were actively engaged, so these 336 casualties were sustained among about 5,500 men.

The *Terrible* (64 guns) was so badly damaged that the British had to destroy her the night of 9–10 Sept. Graves's flagship, the *London* (98), was so badly punished by de Grasse's *Ville de Paris* (110) that all her masts had to be replaced. The English frigates *Iris* and *Richmond* had left the fleet on the 6th to nip into the bay and were captured on the 11th when they emerged to rejoin Graves.

CHEVAL DE FRISE. A portable obstacle used to stop cavalry, form road blocks, close gaps in fortifications, etc., it was formed of large beams traversed by pointed spikes. A submarine version, whose invention was attributed to Benjamin Franklin and which differed considerably in design, consisted of a heavy timber frame bristling with iron-tipped spikes; sunk on the bottom of a river it could rip the hull of a vessel. Franklin's obstacles were used in the Delaware below Philadelphia and in the Hudson below West Point. Usually employed in the plural, *chevaux de frise,* the term means "horses of Friesland," the province in North Holland where they first were employed, apparently during the Dutch War for Independence, 1568–1648 (*E.B., O.U.D.*).

CHEVALIER. Many French volunteers came to America with this title, or were later awarded it, by virtue of being decorated with the Order of St. Louis. John Paul Jones was given the French cross of the Institution of Military Merit in 1781, which entitled its holder to be addressed as "Chevalier."

CHILLICOTHE, Ohio. This name was always given to the village occupied by the Chillicothe division of the Shawnee tribe, and the place was regarded as the chief town ("capital") of the tribe. Chillicothe on the Little Miami River is where Daniel Boone was held prisoner in 1778 and the place Clark destroyed on 6 Aug. '80. (*Handbook of American Indians;* C. & M., 1055) Chillicothe on the (Great) Miami River was destroyed by Clark on 10 Nov. '82. (This place was called Piqua when Clark burned it on 8 Aug. '80, and the modern city on that site was named Piqua in 1823. [*Ibid.;* E.B.]) In 1774, during DUNMORE'S WAR, a third Chillicothe, sometimes confused with the other two, was on Paint Creek near its junction with the Scioto River and close to the site of today's Chillicothe, Ohio; it was destroyed by Kentuckians in 1787.

CHOISEUL, Etienne François, Count of Stainville. 1719–1785. (Choiseul, pronounced shwa zearl) French statesman. Son of the marshal generally known as Plessis-Praslin, he entered the army and rose to the grade of Lt. Gen. Gaining the favor of Mme de Pompadour by getting her some letters the king had written to his cousin in the course of an intrigue, Choiseul entered the diplomatic service and rose rapidly through ability and the sponsorship of the royal mistress. In 1757 he started negotiations that led to the marriage of Marie Antoinette. As minister of foreign affairs, 1758–70, he brought about the "Family Compact." Although he came to power too late to save France humiliation in the Seven Years' War (1756–63), he developed colonies in the West Indies and added Corsica and Lorraine to the kingdom. He allowed the famous *Encyclopédie* to be published and brought about banishment of the Jesuits. In 1761, even before the Treaty of PARIS, he started rebuilding the army and navy. Foreseeing the American war for independence and the opportunity for France to profit from it to defeat England, after 1764 he sent secret agents (including KALB) to America and maintained a spy service in England. As the result of conflicting reports from his agents he had concluded by 1770 that the hoped-for rupture was not imminent. Spain also was undergoing a regeneration at this time and Choiseul therefore undertook to support this other Bourbon power in her quarrel with England over the Falkland Islands, hoping for a war in which France and Spain could defeat England. His failure to sell this policy to Louis XV and the other ministers helped bring about his political downfall, but he who had been elevated by one mistress was to be destroyed by another. Mme de Pompadour had died in 1764, and Mme Du Barry organized the opposition against him. In retirement at Chanteloupe from 1770 to 1774, he was greatly disappointed when Louis

XVI did not restore him to his former position but gave him a lesser post.

CHRISTOPHE, Henri, King of Haiti (1811–20), took part in the attack against Savannah, 9 Oct. '79, in the Negro legion commanded by FONTANGES. (Heitman, 655)

CHURCH, Benjamin. 1734–?1777. Informer. Mass. A grandson and namesake of the famous Indian fighter (1639–1718), he was born at Newport, reared in Boston (where his father was deacon of Mather Byles's church), educated at the Boston Latin School, and in 1754 he graduated from Harvard. After studying medicine under Dr. Joseph Pynchon he went to the London Medical College. He returned with an English wife. (Hannah Hill is the name given by *D.A.B.* French, *post,* notes that this is wrong or that Church had a second wife, "for the one who survived him, according to her petitions, was named Sarah." P. 148 *n.*)

A talented man who wrote and spoke well, he soon became prominent in Boston revolutionary politics. On 6 Mar. '70 he accompanied those who officially protested the Boston "Massacre," and the deposition he made after examining the body of Crispus Attucks was printed with other patriot propaganda. He was on the Boston Comm. of Corresp., he drafted several documents put out by this and other committees, and in 1773 he delivered orations in commemoration of the "Massacre." Meanwhile he is said to have contributed articles to the Loyalist paper, *The Censor.* Having already qualified himself soon after graduation from Harvard as a minor poet, he went on to establish a considerable literary reputation with elegies, satires, and his oration on the "Massacre" (which was printed).

Suspicion soon began to descend on Church, however. Paul Revere did not doubt that the high-living, adulterous, arty doctor had furnished Gov. Hutchinson with information gained at a secret meeting in 1774, but Church continued to be trusted by the top patriot leaders. (*D.A.B.*) He was a delegate to the Mass. Prov. Cong. in 1774. Shortly after the fighting at Lexington and Concord he went to Boston (22 Apr. '75) on the pretext of getting medicines and claimed to have been captured and taken before Gen. Gage. Still the busy patriot hierarchy suspected nothing, or did not suspect enough to make an investigation. On 25 July '75 Dr. Church was elected to the coveted medical post of chief physician at Cambridge. Meanwhile he had given Gage more than a month's advance notice that the Americans intended to fortify Bunker Hill, and he informed th British of business being conducted by the Prov. Cong. (Van Doren, *Secret History,* 20) Yet on 26 June this body had elected Church and Moses Gill as the two men to meet Washington when the new C. in C. arrived to take command at Boston (1 July), and on 16 May they had entrusted him with the letter to Congress begging that the delegates assume responsibility for the Boston army.

The treason of Church came to light late in Sept. '75 when Nathanael Greene brought Washington a coded letter that had been picked up from a woman of ill repute who apparently was trying to deliver it to the enemy. The woman was finally badgered into revealing that the letter had been given to her by Dr. Church. Washington sent for Church and ordered his papers seized, but the doctor claimed there was nothing incriminating in his cipher letter: that it was intended for his brother, Fleming, in Boston. Joseph Reed's search of his papers revealed nothing except that somebody—possibly Benj. THOMPSON (Van Doren, *Secret History,* 22)—had culled them just before Reed's arrival.

The mysterious letter (of 22 July) was deciphered by two amateur cryptologists working independently (the Rev. Mr. West and Col. Elisha Porter) and proved to be an intelligence report: Church told of his activities, described the strength and strategic plans of American forces, and mentioned the plan for commissioning privateers. After giving elaborate instructions for sending a reply, Church's letter ended: "Make use of every precaution or I perish."

A council of war held 3–4 Oct. concluded that Church was guilty of communicating with the enemy, but Washington and his generals found that the articles of war did not provide for any sentence more severe than cashiering, forfeiture of two months' pay, or 39 lashes. Church was confined at Cambridge while Washington awaited instructions from Congress. On 27 Oct. the Mass. authorities heard his case, in which he angrily and resentfully defended himself (ibid., 22), and on 2 Nov. the legislature expelled him. On the 22d he reached Lebanon, Conn., under guard. Congress had meanwhile resolved that Church be closely confined (7 Nov.) in some Conn. jail, and Gov. Trumbull selected the one in Norwich. Church petitioned Congress in Jan. '76 for mitigation of his close confinement, which had brought on severe asthma. The delegates directed Gov. Trumbull to move the prisoner to a more healthful place, but on 13 May they received another petition from the Norwich jail that showed he was still there and, according to the certificate of three doctors, in dangerously bad health. Since the British had by now evacuated Boston, Congress gave him permission to go to Mass. on parole. Apparently he was free until early June, but to protect him from mob violence he was put back in jail in Boston. Although Paul Revere says he left Boston in May

'76 (and this date is accepted by D.A.B.), Van Doren tells the end of his story as follows: "Church seems to have been kept in jail until the latter part of 1777, when he was allowed to leave—it is said for the West Indies—in a schooner which was never heard of again."

He had been so clever in his espionage that his guilt was not established until the 20th century when certain papers of the Gage MSS were brought to light. Allen French used this to write *General Gage's Informers; New Material Upon Lexington & Concord, Benjamin Thompson as Loyalist and the Treachery of Benjamin Church, Jr.* (Ann Arbor, Mich., 1932).

CINCINNATI, Society of the. In May '83, when the Cont'l. Army was about to be disbanded, Henry Knox got Washington's approval for a plan to form a society of officers. At a meeting of 10 May, with Steuben presiding, Knox, Edward Hand, Jed. Huntington, and Samuel Shaw were selected to draw up final plans for the organization, and three days later their constitution was adopted at a meeting held near Fishkill, N.Y., where Steuben's Hq. was located. "To perpetuate . . . as well the remembrance of this vast event [the Revolution], as the mutual friendships . . . formed," read the second paragraph, "the officers of the American army do hereby, in the most solemn manner, associate, constitute and combine themselves into one Society of Friends, to endure so long as they shall endure, or any of their eldest male posterity, and in failure thereof, the collateral branches, who may be judged worthy of becoming its supporters and members." Naval officers later were eligible. The founders named themselves after "that illustrious Roman, Lucius Quintius Cincinnatus," who twice was called from his farm to save Rome (458 and 439 B.C.) and who twice returned to his plow when the crisis was past. The society's stated purposes were "to preserve ... those exalted rights and liberties of human nature," to promote national unity and honor, to perpetuate the brotherhood of American officers, and to help those officers and their families who might need assistance. Other paragraphs of the constitution dealt with establishment of state societies, election of officers, and frequency of meetings, prescribed that each officer would contribute one month's pay for a fund whose interest would be used for the welfare mentioned earlier, and covered creation of a badge.

Washington had nothing to do with organization of the society, but on 19 June '83 he agreed to become its president. He was succeeded on his death by Alexander Hamilton, after whom the following original members held the office until their death: C. C. Pinckney, Thomas Pinckney, Aaron Ogden, Morgan Lewis, and William Popham. The latter was followed by Henry Alexander Scammell Dearborn, son of Henry Dearborn, and he served from 1848 until his death in 1851. Hamilton Fish, son of Nicholas Fish, was president from 1854 to 1893. About this time most of the state societies died out for lack of heirs, but the general organization was revived in 1902. In 1960 there were about 2,000 members in the U.S. and 150 in France.

The "order" of the Cincinnati was a bald eagle about the size of a silver dollar; this was suspended by a dark blue ribbon, two inches wide (and about twice that long) and edged with white to symbolize the alliance with France. L'Enfant designed this medal and the diploma of membership. (See Lossing, II, 128–29 for descriptions and illustrations.)

There was a good deal of opposition to the society's formation, particularly to the wearing of a distinctive badge. "Our General" Heath says that after deciding not to join the society he changed his mind only at the last minute when a senior officer pointed out his descendants might think he had not been accepted. (*Memoirs,* 398) Although the Cincinnati turned out to be nothing but an innocent club, John B. McMaster comments that "it would indeed have been a hard task to have brought to this mind the men who, in 1783, heard, with mingled feelings of alarm and disgust, that a military order had been established, that its honors had been made hereditary, that Frenchmen had been admitted to its ranks. ..." (*A Hist. of the People of the U.S. from the Rev. to the Civ. War,* I, 167) Benj. Franklin, John Adams, and Sam Adams attacked the society. R.I. disfranchised members in the state, and a committee of Mass. legislators investigated it. Supreme court judge Aedanus Burke of S.C. attacked the order in a pamphlet, which was translated and published by Count Mirabeau under his own name, twice translated from Mirabeau's French into English, and which then appeared in German. (*Ibid.,* 175 and *n.*) The Tammany societies of N.Y.C., Philadelphia, and other cities were founded partly in opposition to the Cincinnati. (*C.E.*)

The French branch was extremely vigorous, Mirabeau's pirated pamphlet in no way slowing the rush of army and naval applicants. Plaques on a Paris *hôtel particulier* at No. 40 rue du Cherche-Midi inform the modern antiques shopper that Rochambeau lived in this building when he was ordered to America in 1780 (having bought it the preceding year) and that here the French Cincinnati were organized in 1784. The eagle and blue ribbon are said to have been the only "foreign decoration" permitted to be worn by

French subjects in the court of Louis
XVI. When Camille Desmoulins proposed a cockade to his followers on 12
July '89 he is reported to have said,
"Shall it be green, the color of hope,
or shall it be blue, the color of the
Cincinnati?" And on this day when his
oratory marked the actual beginning of
the French Revolution (*C.E.*, "Desmoulins") the green may have been
chosen only because the chestnut trees
outside the Café de Foy furnished an
immediate source of supply. (McMaster,
op. cit., I, 176 and *n.*) But the French
Revolution brought a wave of republicanism and the French Cincinnati
were disbanded in 1792. Even today,
however, the American in France will
meet people who tell him with pride
that an ancestor was a member of the
Cincinnati, an experience he is not likely
to have in his own country.

See Asa Bird Gardiner, *The Order of
the Cincinnati in France. Its Origin and
History, with the Military or Naval
Records of the French Members,* R.I.
State Soc. of the Cincinnati, 1905.

CLAPP'S MILLS, N.C., 2 Mar. '81.
(SOUTHERN CAMP'NS. OF GREENE) During the period of maneuvering that preceded the Battle of Guilford C.H.,
forward elements of the opposing armies made contact for the first time
on the Haw River near Clapp's Mills.
Lee does not mention this brisk skirmish
in his *Memoirs,* but Greene reported
that on 2 Mar. "Lee, with a detachment
of [Col. Wm. Campbell's Va.] riflemen,
attacked the advance of the British army
under Tarleton, and killed and wounded,
by report, about thirty of them." Bass
says Lt. Col. James Webster's Brig.
routed the riflemen from thickets on
both sides of the road and that Tarleton's cavalry pursued. (*Green Dragoon,*
169) These forces met again at WET-
ZELL'S MILLS, 6 Mar.

CLARK. See also CLARKE.

CLARK, Abraham. 1726–1794.
Signer. N.J. After a general education
he became a surveyor and, informally,
a settler of land disputes. He was known
variously as "Congress Abraham" and
"The Poor Man's Counsellor." He was
high sheriff of Essex co. and clerk of
the colonial assembly under the Crown.
In Dec. '74 he was a member of the
committee of safety and sat in the
N.J. provincial congress, May '75, before going to the Cont'l. Congress 22
June '76. He signed the Decl. of Indep.
and was re-elected to the Congress continuously until 1783, with the exception
of 1779. He later served in it 1787–88.
In 1786 he attended the Annapolis convention, and in 1782–87 sat in the
N.J. legislature and was a delegate to
the Federal Constitution Convention in
1787, but poor health prevented his attendance. He opposed the Constitution
until the Bill of Rights was added. He
was a member of the 1789 commission
to settle the states' accounts with the
U.S. and sat in Congress from 1791
until his death in 1794 from sunstroke.
D.A.B. characterizes him as "a leader
of the dour, sensible, American middle class" and, sociopolitically, "a
seventeenth-century English 'Leveller.' "

CLARK, George Rogers. 1752–1818.
Conqueror of the Old Northwest. Born
near Charlottesville, Va., George had
little formal education when he started
studying surveying at the age of 19. He
had read history and geography, however, and his letters indicate a sharp
intellectual curiosity in matters of wood-
craft. He grew into a strong, red-haired
frontiersman with penetrating black
eyes. In June '72 he explored down the
Ohio from Pittsburgh to the mouth of
the Kanawha with a group of adventurers, and the next spring he went with
another group to the mouth of Fish
Creek, 130 miles below Pittsburgh. With
a single companion he then explored

170 miles farther down the Ohio; they then spent the winter on Fish Creek making preparations for a settlement. Clark took part in Dunmore's War in 1774 as a militia Capt. He then surveyed land on the Ky. River for the Ohio Co.

The WESTERN OPERATIONS OF CLARK describe his subsequent activities.

After the war Clark served for a number of years on the board that supervised allocation of the 150,000 acres north of the Ohio across from Louisville that Va. had granted for Clark's veterans. He also served with Richard Butler and S. H. Parsons on the commission that concluded the treaty at Ft. McIntosh, Jan. '86; in this the Indians acknowledged U.S. sovereignty over the western territory ceded by Great Britain. In 1786 he led a punitive expedition against the Wabash, but this failed because the Ky. troops mutinied. Clark did, however, establish a 100-man garrison at Vincennes and he seized the goods of three Spanish merchants of the city to supply them. Although this act was generally endorsed by American public opinion initially, it gave the scheming James WILKINSON an opportunity successfully to attack Clark's reputation.

"Public favor was never again accorded Clark by Virginia nor by the federal government. Thus, at thirty-five years of age, Clark was without means of support, although the State of Virginia was in his debt some twenty thousand dollars for his pay as an officer and for money he had advanced to secure supplies for his troops." (James A. James in *D.A.B.*)

His proposal to found a colony in La. opposite the mouth of the Ohio failed because the Spanish would not accept his demand for political and religious freedom. A planned expedition to take possession of disputed lands between the Yazoo River and Natchez was stopped by President Washington. More or less desperate, Clark accepted a commission as Gen. in the French army to attack Spanish territories west of the Mississippi. The U.S. demanded that he surrender this commission, and he was forced to take refuge in St. Louis. In 1803 he built a cabin at Clarksville, on the Indiana side of the Ohio near the falls. Here he ran a grist mill and served as chairman of the local commission for apportioning land to veterans of his Illinois regiment. A stroke of paralysis and amputation of his right leg resulted in his moving to his sister's home near Louisville in 1809. He died and was buried there nine years later.

There is no doubt that Clark's personality deteriorated rapidly after 1805, but J. A. James concludes that although he drank heavily in these later years he was by no means a sot. In 1791 he completed his *Memoir*, an important historical document, and about the same time he developed a theory on the origin of Indian mounds of the Ohio and Mississippi valleys that has now been universally accepted, although Clark's letter on the subject was not published until 1860. See WESTERN OPERATIONS for further evaluation of Clark.

James Alton James's edition of the *Clark Papers* (2 vols., Springfield, Ill., 1912–26), is the basis for his *Life of ...Clark* (Chicago, 1928), which the L.O.C. *Guide* calls "a somewhat impersonal narrative which emphasizes the background of international relations and intrigue." John E. Bakeless, *Background to Glory* (Philadelphia, 1957), also based on James's *Clark Papers,* is recommended by the L.O.C. *Guide.* Clark's 128-page *Memoir* is held by the Wis. Hist. Soc.

CLARK, Thomas. d. 25 Dec. '92. Cont'l. officer. N.C. Elected Maj. 1st

N.C. on 1 Sept. '75, he became Lt. Col. of the 1st N.C. Cont'l. Regt. on 10 Apr. '76 and commanded this unit on Sullivan's Island during the defense of CHARLESTON in 1776. He became Col. of the regiment on 5 Feb. '77. According to Heitman he was wounded at Stono Ferry, 20 June '79, and captured at Charleston, 12 May '80. On the other hand he is reported to have led the N.C. Cont'ls. at MONMOUTH, 28 June '78, and it is most likely that his regiment was part of the 700 N.C. Cont'ls. that marched with Gen. James Hogun from Washington's army to reinforce Lincoln at CHARLESTON, arriving 3 Mar. '80. A Lt. Col. Clark is also identified at KETTLE CREEK, Ga., 14 Feb. '79. Heitman lists two other N.C. officers named Thos. Clark, but neither appears likely to have been at Stono Ferry or Kettle Creek, nor does it seem probable that the Clark covered in this sketch could have been in these engagements. *D.A.B.* says the "Clark" at Kettle Creek was Elijah CLARKE. It is evident, therefore, that we are confronted with a composite N.C. Thos. Clark; two or more officers' records being confused by Heitman and other authorities. Our "composite Clark," to follow Heitman, was retired 1 Jan. '83 and died 25 Dec. '92. The Thos. Clark breveted B.G. on 30 Sept. '83 must be the Col. of the 1st N.C., although Heitman did not give him this Bvt. rank.

CLARKE. See also CLARK.

CLARKE, Alured. 1745?–1832. British officer. Probably the nephew of the Alured Clarke (1696–1742) who was Dean of Exeter and chaplain in ordinary to George I and II, he became an ensign in the 50th Foot in 1759. Little else is known of his background. (*D.N.B.*) In 1776 he went with Adm. Howe's reinforcements from Ireland to N.Y. as Lt. Col. of the 54th Foot. In Mar. '77 he took command of the 7th

Fusiliers, which had recently been sent to N.Y. from Canada, and held this commission until he succeeded Burgoyne as mustermaster general of the Hessian forces. Baurmeister does not mention him in this capacity, and little is known of his service in North America other than that he commanded the British garrison at Savannah until their withdrawal in July '82. Appleton's says "he gained the good will of the inhabitants by the strict discipline that he maintained, and by the uniform courtesy with which he treated the inhabitants and protected their property from pillage." Editor Uhlendorf says that Clarke was in command in Ga. and "judging from requisitions and correspondence (*Carleton Calendar*, II, 307), also responsible for East Florida." (Baurmeister, *Journals*, 440 *n*.)

Clarke was Lt. Gov. of Jamaica from 1782 until 1790. (*D.N.B.*) Having retained his commission in the 7th Fusiliers until then, he became Col. of the 1st Bn., 60th Foot, on 8 July '91. In 1795, as a Maj. Gen., he commanded a reinforcement being sent to India but had orders to rendezvous with Gen. James CRAIG to capture the Dutch colony at the Cape of Good Hope. After the Dutch surrender, 14 Sept., he continued on to Bengal. On 17 May '98 he succeeded Sir Robert Abercromby as C. in C., and on 21 July 1801 was back in England. In 1830 Clarke and Sir Samuel Hulse, the two oldest generals in the army, were made field marshals.

CLARKE, Elijah. 1733–1799. Patriot militia commander, adventurer. N.C.–Ga. Born in N.C., probably of Scottish-Irish stock, he moved to Wilkes co. ("Ceded Lands"), Ga., by 1774. Although uneducated, he possessed the native intelligence, bravery, and strength to become a partisan leader in the civil-war situation of the Southern frontier.

Modern authorities spell his name "Clark," the style in which he signed it, at least in later life; he is "Clarke" in traditional accounts. As such, he first appears in Heitman's *Historical Register* as a militia Col., no earlier service being mentioned. Wounded at Alligator Creek, Fla., 30 June '78 (see SOUTHERN THEATER for background), Clarke had his finest hour at KETTLE CREEK, Ga., 14 Feb. '79. After leading his troops in three skirmishes in S.C. in Aug. '80 (GREEN SPRING, Wofford's Iron Works [see under KINGS MTN.], and MUSGROVE'S MILL), being wounded in the last two, Elijah Clarke made his foolish attack on AUGUSTA, Ga., 14–18 Sept. '80. Some authorities (*D.N.B.*, for example) credit him with action at FISHDAM FORD. He was at BLACKSTOCKS, S.C., 20 Nov. '80, and back at AUGUSTA, 22 May–5 June '81.

In recognition of his war services Clarke was granted an estate by the county and state authorities of Ga. He then embarked on a tangled course of dubious adventure. After alternately negotiating with the Indians and fighting them, in 1787 he defeated them in an action at Jack's Creek, Walton co., Ga. In 1793 he entered the French service as a Maj. Gen. with a salary of $10,000 per year and was preparing to support the schemes of French minister Genêt against Spain when Genêt was recalled. The next year he led Ga. volunteers across the Oconee River into Creek territory and was establishing his "Trans-Oconee State" when Pres. Hamilton had Gov. George MATHEWS bring this freebooting to a halt by the use of Ga. troops. Blockaded along the Oconee, deserted by most of his followers, Clarke surrendered. He was later suspected of renewed designs on W. Fla. and was accused of involvement in the Yazoo Land Fraud, but died a popular hero in 1799.

CLARKE, Sir Francis Carr. See next entry.

CLERKE, Sir Francis Carr. 1748–1777. British officer. (Clerke, pronounced Clark.) The seventh baronet, he became an ensign in the 3d Foot Guards on 3 Jan. '70 and was promoted to Lt. and Capt. on 26 July '75. As Burgoyne's A.D.C. he was mortally wounded by Timothy MURPHY at Bemis Heights (see SARATOGA) on 7 Oct. '77 and died that night in the tent of Gen. Gates. James Wilkinson is responsible for the famous story that Gates undertook to convince Clerke of the merits of the American Revolution as the captured officer lay near death from his agonizing wound. Having been unsuccessful, Gates lost his temper and said to Wilkinson as they left the dying officer, "Did you ever hear so impudent a son of a bitch?" Ward comments that Wilkinson's account was written after he had become a bitter enemy of Gates, and that his memoirs are not to be trusted. (*W.O.R.*, 901 *n.*)

Burke's Peerage makes the double error of stating that Clerke died 15 Oct. '78. His death actually occurred the night of 7–8 Oct. '77. (*Ibid.*) Tripped up by the English pronunciation of Clerk(e), virtually all American accounts erroneously give this officer's name as Clarke.

CLEVELAND, Benjamin. 1738–1806. Patriot leader. N.C. Born near Bull Run, Va., he moved with relatives to the portion of the N.C. frontier that became Wilkes co. About 21 at this time, uneducated and with a fondness for gambling and horse racing, he developed into a frontiersman in the class with Davy Crockett and Daniel Boone. On 1 Sept. '75 he became Ensign in the 2d N.C. Line. The next summer he was a scout on the western frontier, and that fall he served under Gen. Griffith Rutherford in the CHEROKEE WAR OF 1776. He was promoted to Capt. after this campaign (23 Nov. '76) and saw the country where he was later to settle. In 1777 he served at Carter's Fort and the Long Island of Holston. The next year he retired from the 2d N.C. on 1 June and in Aug. was made Col. of militia; he also became justice of the Wilkes co. court when the county was organized, having been chairman of the Surry co. Comm. of Safety, and in 1778 he was elected to the House of Commons.

In 1780 he turned out to crush the Tories at RAMSEUR'S MILL, 20 June, but apparently was with the force led by his old commander, Gen. Rutherford, and therefore saw no actual fighting. Four months later, however, he led 350 men south to take part in the battle of KINGS MOUNTAIN, 7 Oct. '80. Cleveland is said to have been the man most responsible for the decision to hang nine prisoners after the battle. (*D.A.B.*)

"Cleveland's Bull Dogs" had a reputation along the Upper Yadkin for brutality and inhumanity as Tory hunters that was unmatched by David FANNING on the other side. As a "justice" he was a fast man with the rope. (*Ibid.*) In 1781 he was captured by Tories but soon rescued. (Appleton's)

After a title dispute Cleveland lost his plantation, so he moved to what is now Oconee co., the western tip of S.C. He became justice of the region. Gen. Andrew Pickens is among those who have testified that the uneducated, grossly fat patriot hero normally slept through the court proceedings—he became highly annoyed at legal arguments and technicalities. Having reached the incredible weight of 450 pounds (Appleton's), he died at the breakfast table when in his 69th year.

CLINTON, George. 1739–1812. First gov. of the state of N.Y.; Cont'l. gen-

eral. N.Y. As a subaltern in his father's regiment, and accompanied by his brother James CLINTON, George was with the expedition under John Bradstreet that took Ft. Frontenac on 27 Aug. '57. The next year he served for a short time on a privateer. After studying and practicing law, he sat in the N.Y. provincial assembly in 1768, where he became the rival of Philip Schuyler as a leader of the revolutionary minority. "His ostentatious defense of Alexander McDougall, who posed as the John Wilkes of America, augmented his reputation as a fiery young radical and defender of freedom of speech and of the press," writes Frank Monaghan in *D.A.B.* In 1775 he was sent to the second Cont'l. Cong. but lost the honor of signing because Washington ordered him to take charge of the defenses of the Hudson Highlands in July '76. After being commissioned B.G. of militia, on 25 Mar. '77 he was appointed B.G. of the Cont'l. Army. The British threat to the Highlands did not develop until Oct. '77, but in his failure to stop Sir Henry CLINTON'S EXPEDITION, George Clinton showed that despite personal courage and vigor he was cut out to be a politician and not a field commander. He himself had no illusions about his military limitations. Meanwhile, on 20 Apr. '77, he had become the first governor of N.Y. under the new state constitution, and although the loss of Forts Clinton and Montgomery (6 Oct.) and his failure to keep the enemy from burning KINGSTON (Esopus), 16 Oct., brought him criticism, he went on to serve six consecutive terms and to win the reputation of "a great war governor." (*Ibid.*) Fighting in his state was restricted to BORDER WARFARE during the rest of the war, but he was kept busy repelling the Tory-Indian raids from Canada. On 30

Sept. '83 he was given the brevet rank of Maj. Gen., Cont'l. Army.

The "father of his state" strongly opposed the Federal Constitution. John Fiske says he "preferred to remain the most powerful citizen of New York rather than occupy a subordinate place under a national government in which his own state was not foremost." (Quoted by Monaghan, *op. cit.*) He felt he and his state were giving up more than they stood to gain. Clinton's opinions were expressed in seven letters signed "Cato" that answered a series by Alexander Hamilton signed "Caesar." After serving six terms in a row, Clinton refused to run in 1795 because he recognized that his defeat was inevitable. But he allied himself with the Livingstons and Aaron Burr to win the governship in 1800. He was vice president of the U.S. for two successive terms, starting 1804 and 1808, to Jefferson and Madison. He died in office.

The *Public Papers of George Clinton,* 10 vols., were published by the state of N.Y. during the period 1899–1914, and the volumes dealing with the war years are a valuable source of information on Border Warfare. See E. W. Spaulding, *His Excellency George Clinton: Critic of the Constitution* (N.Y. 1938). This long overdue biography "leaves little if anything for other students to add" (*Amer. Hist. Rev.,* Oct. 1938).

CLINTON, Henry. 1730–1795. British C. in C. (1778–82). "In the familiar story of the War of the Revolution Sir Henry Clinton is inconspicuous," writes Professor Wm. B. Willcox in his introduction to Clinton's memoirs. "Yet Washington is the only general on either side who held a crucial position as long.... For that reason alone his obscurity is puzzling, and the puzzle is deepened by his achievements." (*Amer. Reb.,* ix) This is not to imply that the "smallish, paunchy, and colorless" general (Alden, *Amer. Rev.,* 35) has been underrated; it is more that he has been neglected. This is somehow symbolized by the fact that the manuscript of his three-volume apologia remained unnoticed among his other papers until an American collector bought them from his descendants in 1925, and another generation was to pass before this narrative was published. Magnificently edited by Wm. B. Willcox and supported by over 200 pages of letters, official reports, and other documents, Clinton's *Historical Detail,* retitled *The American Rebellion,* is a major work in this field of history. In his 43-page "Editor's Introduction" Willcox includes a brilliant evaluation not only of this complex commander and his subordinates—particularly Cornwallis—but also of British strategy during the last five years of the Revolution. I have drawn heavily on Professor Willcox's scholarship for the following sketch as well as for many other portions of this book.

Henry Clinton was the only son of Adm. George Clinton, who was Gov. of Newfoundland, 1732–41, and of N.Y., 1741–51. Henry's lineage was aristocratic: he was a cadet of the House of Lincoln, and was connected by marriage with the newer and greater dynasty of the Pelhams—the Earls of Newcastle. He grew up in N.Y. and became Capt.-Lt. of the local militia. Returning to England with his father, he was a Lt. in the Coldstream Guards on 1 Nov. '51, Capt. and Lt. Col. in the Grenadier Guards on 6 Apr. '58, and in 1760 saw his first active service. He distinguished himself in the brigade of guards under Prince Ferdinand of Brunswick (*D.N.B.*), was appointed A.D.C. to the latter, and on 24 June '62 was promoted to Col. At Johannisburg, 30 Aug. '62, he was wounded in action. With the termination of the

Seven Years' War he entered a period of military inactivity but formed political connections with the Dukes of Gloucester and Newcastle. In 1766 he became Col. of the 12th Regt., on 25 May '72 he was promoted to Maj. Gen., in July of this year, through the influence of his cousin, the Second Duke of Newcastle, he started a 12-year period as an M.P.

The death of his wife in Aug. '72 ended five years of an exceptionally happy marriage and proved to be a shattering experience. After virtually going out of his mind, he eventually regained control of himself. "But the episode suggests strong forces working under the surface," comments Willcox. (*Op. cit.*, xv) In May '75 he reached Boston on the *Cerberus* with Wm. Howe and Burgoyne to join Gates. Something of Clinton's personality is revealed in his comment to an unknown correspondent on his relations on shipboard with these two officers: "At first (for you know I am a shy bitch) I kept my distance, [and] seldom spoke till my two colleagues forced me out."

"Soon after landing he showed another side of his character," writes Willcox. "The discovery that the British were besieged in Boston led him to reconnoiter; he promptly worked out a plan for seizing Dorchester Heights, presented it to his commander in chief General Gage, and pressed it on him with more enthusiasm than tact. Gage did not adopt it. Clinton had his first indication, but not his last, that a superior officer might prefer muddling through on his own to accepting even the best ideas of a subordinate. A wholly different man would doubtless have absorbed this lesson and learned to keep his own counsel. But the 'shy bitch' was also aggressive, in planning and conduct; and his combination of diffidence and self-assertion was a trial

to his colleagues and himself." (*Ibid.*, xvii)

In the Battle of BUNKER HILL, 17 June '75, Clinton violated the letter of his instructions to lead a column in the final attack, an action that won him the highest praise for gallantry and contributed significantly to the British success. "But for months afterward he worried that he might be taken to task for disobedience," points out Willcox. "Both his courage and his worry are typical: he could defy orders, but could not really believe that success would justify defiance. . . ." (*Ibid.*)

In Sept. '75 Clinton received the "local rank" of Lt. Gen. and became second in command to Howe, who had succeeded Gage. Clinton and Howe were immediately at odds, but the problem was temporarily solved by Clinton's detachment to command the CHARLESTON EXPEDITION of 1776. His shortcomings are covered under the latter article. Meanwhile, in Jan. '76, he received the "local rank" of full Gen. Joining Howe on Staten Island, he distinguished himself in the Battle of LONG ISLAND, 27 Aug., "and claims (with apparent truth) to have planned that brilliant envelopment," says Willcox. (*Op. cit.*, ix) Throughout the N.Y. and N.J. Campaigns Clinton bombarded Howe with proposals for bold strategy, which Howe steadfastly rejected in favor of his own plans for occupying real estate instead of making Washington's army his objective. Howe got rid of his pesky subordinate by sending him off to capture Newport for use as a naval base. Clinton thoroughly disapproved of the mission, but departed with gratuitous advice that Howe not maintain an extended chain of outposts in N.J. He captured Newport in a well executed operation about the time Washington annihilated the Hessian outpost at Trenton. Disgusted with Howe's generalship and furious with

Germain for the latter's support of Sir Peter Parker in the controversy over the CHARLESTON fiasco, Clinton got leave to go home and was ready to quit the service. (*Ibid.,* xxiv)

"Germain had timely notice of Clinton's coming [writes Fisher], and not caring for either a quarrel or a duel, had one of his retainers wait for him at Portsmouth and deliver to him a letter full of approval and eulogy of his conduct in America and begging him to return there where his great abilities were so sorely needed.

"Clinton, however, was not to be put off in that way; and Germain hastily promised him the thanks of both houses of Parliament and the Order of the Bath for his valor in the conquest of Rhode Island. . . . Germain, Jones says, was so anxious to appease Clinton, that, the Order of the Bath being full, he used his influence to have an additional place constituted in order to let in the man he feared." (*Struggle,* II, 174, citing Jones, *N.Y. in the Rev.*)

Although Germain was not in quite the panic depicted above, he did welcome Clinton warmly and did get him a knighthood. Clinton was considered as commander of what became BURGOYNE'S OFFENSIVE from Canada, although he made no effort to advance himself as a contender at this time. His cordial reception in London stemmed from the fact that competent major commanders were in short supply, and he was prevailed upon to return as Howe's second. Now Lt. Gen. Sir Henry Clinton—the promotion was in the regular establishment; the knighthood has been said to have been for his valor at Long Island and as a consolation for not getting the command that went to Burgoyne, his junior—he returned to America with the thought that he might take over Burgoyne's command when the latter approached N.Y.C. (Willcox, *op. cit.,* xxiv)

Nor had he given up the thought of resigning, which he tried periodically the next four years. (*Ibid.,* xxiv, xxv)

Reaching N.Y.C. on 5 July '77 he was shocked to find that the army had not left winter quarters and, furthermore, that he was to have the mission of defending N.Y. while Howe moved by water against Philadelphia. Aside from disapproving of the strategy and apart from the fact that Howe and Burgoyne were to have a chance to win glory in the field while he conducted "a damned starved defensive," he was obsessed with the entirely reasonable fear that Washington would take advantage of this dispersion of British strength to launch an all-out attack against Manhattan. (For Clinton's scathing evaluation of his C. in C. see end of article on Wm. HOWE.)

In the article on CLINTON'S EXPEDITION to the Highlands, Oct. '77, there is a further discussion of the British strategy as well as the account of Clinton's capture of the Highlands.

On 7 Mar. '78 Germain signed orders naming Clinton as Howe's successor. On 21 Mar., after France allied herself openly with America, the King signed secret orders for Clinton to assume the defensive in the North, holding Newport but abandoning Philadelphia and, if necessary, N.Y.C.; he was to send an expedition to Georgia and also to supply 5,000 troops for an attack on St. Lucia in the West Indies. Clinton took over from Howe in Philadelphia in May '78. After an unsuccessful attempt to trap Lafayette at BARREN HILL, Pa., 20 May, Clinton executed a difficult retreat across N.J. in the operations covered under the MONMOUTH CAMPAIGN, June–July '78. Showing an unwonted stiffness of spine, Sir Henry had disregarded two details of his instructions: he had not evacuated by sea and he had refused to send reinforcements to the West

Indies. On 28 June he had turned to face Washington's army for a major engagement, and although this turned out to be indecisive, he had finished his retreat unmolested.

Clinton was calm in the face of the threat he found on his arrival at N.Y.— the large French fleet under d'Estaing acting as if it were going to enter the harbor. When the danger to N.Y. went away, Clinton moved promptly to reinforce the garrison at Newport, and the allies broke off their operations against this place as he approached. With the disappearance of the French fleet neither Washington nor Clinton made any significant move for almost a year. The British commander planned a campaign for 1779 that depended on the arrival of promised reinforcements. Meanwhile he restricted himself to a war of attrition. In May '79 the Mathews-Collier raid did an estimated £2,000,000 worth of damage in Va. (See VA. MIL. OPNS.) On 1 June Clinton captured Stony Point and Verplancks Point. He then launched the CONN. COAST RAID in July '79. His reinforcements still not having arrived, and being ordered to detach 2,000 men to Canada, he gave up hopes of striking the rebels a serious blow. When the reinforcements finally did appear, in Aug., his plans were jeopardized by intelligence of a large French naval force moving toward the West Indies, and when this threat was reported to be moving up toward the Atlantic coast Clinton was forced to take up a strategic defensive. Although the objective turned out to be SAVANNAH, where an allied attack was repulsed on 9 Oct., Clinton had evacuated Newport and had been forced to postpone the offensive he planned against the Carolinas.

During the summer of 1779 Cornwallis arrived to become Clinton's second in command and the cantankerous old Adm. Arbuthnot showed up as naval commander. The assignment of this naval mediocrity, when Clinton had been begging for a competent and cooperative admiral—he had gone so far as to name five—was a rebuff to the C. in C. The presence of the ambitious Cornwallis with his "dormant commission" as Clinton's successor was also considered intolerable, and Clinton immediately sent the King another request to retire. (See CORNWALLIS for Clinton's estimate of this officer's performance in the Princeton campaign and for a comment on the "dormant commission.") "Throughout the planning and execution of the attack on Charleston, consequently, the two men were in an anomalous relationship," comments Willcox, and Clinton and Arbuthnot were "eyeing each other askance. . . ." (*Op. cit.,* xxxii, xxxiii)

The CHARLESTON EXPEDITION of Clinton in 1780 has been characterized as "the one solid British triumph of the war." Although he had intended to move from Charleston to subjugate the South from Ga. to the Chesapeake, Clinton learned that another French expedition was headed for America and decided his proper post was back in N.Y. (Willcox, *op. cit.,* xxxiv)

How Cornwallis, who was left to command in the South, proceeded to take the war into his own hands is summarized in the articles on CORNWALLIS and the YORKTOWN CAMPAIGN. The latter article also outlines the errors that Clinton was able to make by himself and with the assistance of GERMAIN.

Carleton was appointed to succeed Clinton and reached N.Y. on 5 May '82. Whereas Cornwallis received a sympathetic welcome in England, Clinton found himself the scapegoat for the Yorktown defeat. He tried to get a parliamentary inquiry but was refused. In 1784 he quarreled with his cousin,

Newcastle, and failed to win re-election
as an M.P. from Newark, whence with
Newcastle's influence he had been returned since 1774. (*D.N.B.*) In 1790
he was re-elected to Parliament, in Oct.
'93 he was promoted to full Gen., in
July of the next year he became Gov.
of Gibraltar, and he died at this post
on 23 Dec. '95. Two sons rose to the
rank of full Gen. and were knighted.

Bad luck played a large part in Clinton's career, but in his case we have
an excellent illustration of what was in
the back of Napoleon's mind when in
evaluating a general he asked the
apparently frivolous question, "Is he
lucky?" Arbuthnot, Cornwallis, and Germain are three examples of bad luck
for which nobody can blame Clinton.
In the matter of political connections,
so vital to a British military career
during the Revolution, Clinton was unlucky in that the two Dukes who might
have helped him turned out to be failures: Gloucester, the King's brother,
lost favor with the court when he made
an unfortunate marriage; Newcastle was
"irascible, flighty, and far from intelligent—unfitted by nature and inclination
to carry on the Pelham tradition of
wire-pulling," writes Willcox. When
Clinton needed help "the Duke was a
broken reed." (*Op. cit.*, xiv) Turning
to the index of Fortescue's *History of
the British Army*, Vol. III, under "Clinton" one finds the subheading: "his ill-
luck, 397–404."

"... made the scapegoat for every
misfortune that occurred during his period of command [writes Fortescue], it
seems to me that no general was ever
worse treated. With fewer troops than
Howe, and with a French fleet constantly on the coast, he was expected
to do fully as much as his predecessor.
Had he been left to himself he might
have won better success, for his letters
show considerable insight into the real-

ities of the situation, and he had a
radical distrust of all operations based
on the support of loyalists. * * * His
views as to the conduct of the [South-
ern] campaign were always sane, and
he recognized, as Cornwallis did not,
that the naval operations far exceeded
the military in importance. Altogether
he was an unlucky man, unlucky above
all in the mistakes which were forced
upon him by the minister at home
[Germain]." (*Op. cit.*, III, 397)

Professor Willcox's appraisal starts
with the caveats that one must consider "Sir Henry's tortuous personality,"
the military doctrines of the period,
and the lack of complete data.

"He had, in summary, solid military
virtues, but his generalship did not last
the course. He was intelligent. He understood the map and the role of sea
power, and had a better than average
conception of the war's true character.* * * In his later campaigns he became so addicted to the bread of care-
fulness that he lost what taste he had
ever had for audacity, and at the same
time he was increasingly alienated from
the two men, Arbuthnot and Cornwallis, upon whom he chiefly depended for
implementing a slow, methodical strategy. Months before the final crisis burst
upon him in Virginia, his leadership
was bankrupt.

"The underlying causes of bankruptcy
were in him. He was utterly self-
centered, but the center was out of
focus; he never attained the integrated,
ruthless egoism that often makes a general great.* * * His nemesis was himself." (*Op. cit.*, l–li)

See Wm. B. Willcox, *Portrait of a
General, Sir Henry Clinton*... (New
York, 1964).

CLINTON, James. 1733–1812.
Cont'l. general. N.Y. As a militia Capt.
he served in the expedition of 1757
mentioned under the sketch of his

brother George CLINTON. A delegate to the N.Y. provincial congress of May '75, he was named Col. 3d N.Y. on 30 June, and accompanied Montgomery's column of the Canada Invasion to Quebec. On 8 Mar. '76 he was named Col. of the 2d N.Y. and on 9 Aug. was appointed B.G. in the Cont'l. Army. Serving under his brother in the Highlands, he escaped from Ft. Montgomery with a bayonet wound when this place and Ft. Clinton were captured by Sir Henry CLINTON'S EXPEDITION in Oct. '77. He led a major element of SULLIVAN'S EXPEDITION against the Iroquois, May–Nov. '79 (an operation often called the Sullivan-Clinton Expedition). The next year he became commander of the Northern Dept. with headquarters in Albany. In 1781 he marched his brigade to participate in the Yorktown Campaign. The D.A.B. article by Randolph G. Adams reiterates the story that "Clinton's brigade received the surrendered British colors at Yorktown." Lossing describes "this interesting ceremony" in detail and includes a full page etching. (II, 524–26) D. S. Freeman shatters the picture by saying, "No authentic details have been found of the surrender of the colors, from which fact it may be assumed that the cased flags were laid on the ground without incident. The absurd account in 2 Lossing, 524, does not deserve quotation." (Washington, V, 391)

James joined his prominent younger brother, George, in opposing the Federal Constitution, but James voted against it because it had no bill of rights. (D.A.B.) James was the father of De Witt Clinton (1769–1828).

CLINTON–CORNWALLIS CONTROVERSY. Whether Sir Henry Clinton, as C. in C., or Cornwallis, as commander of the British army in the South, was more responsible for the British defeat in America led to a controversy that is summarized under CORNWALLIS. The two-volume work with this title is identified at the end of this same article.

CLINTON'S EXPEDITION to the Highlands, 3–22 Oct. '77 (in support of BURGOYNE'S OFFENSIVE). Sir Henry Clinton was left to defend the N.Y.C. area with about 4,000 regulars and 3,000 Tories when Howe sailed south on 23 July (PHILADELPHIA CAMP'N.). Clinton objected strongly to Howe's strategy, arguing that "Mr. Washington would move with everything he could collect either against General Burgoyne or me, and crush the one or the other." (Anderson, Command of the Howe Brothers, 264, quoting Clinton, Historical Detail, 76–77) Howe did not specifically direct that Clinton do anything to assist Burgoyne, and his letter of 17 July to Burgoyne said merely that Clinton was in command around N.Y.C. and would "act as occurrences direct." Howe's letters to Clinton spoke vaguely about his "acting offensively," and on 30 July he wrote Clinton, "If you can make any diversion in favor of General Burgoyne's approaching Albany, I need not point out the utility of such a measure" (quoted by Ward, W.O.R., 513).

During Aug., Clinton was so engrossed with "excessive fear for his own position" (Anderson, 266) and Burgoyne was so confident of his own self-sufficiency that there was no question of military cooperation between them. In Sept., however, Burgoyne began calling on Clinton for help. By this time Clinton felt capable of giving some assistance, and on 12 Sept. he proposed making "a push at [Ft.] Montgomery in about ten days," by which time he would have gotten a sizable reinforcement of regulars from England. Burgoyne got this letter on the 21st, two days after the First Battle of SARATOGA, and it had the unfortunate result of causing him to delay an attack that might well have succeeded in opening the road to Albany. (Ward, 521) Burgoyne wrote Clinton that "an attack or even the menace of an attack upon Fort Montgomery must be of great use, as it will draw away great part of their force. . . . Do it, my dear friend, directly." (This letter, dated 23 Sept., reached Clinton on the 29th, according to Nickerson [p. 343]. According to Ward, however, Clinton got no answer to his 12 Sept. letter until 8 Oct., and made his diversion without waiting for it [*op. cit.*, 514]. Burgoyne sent Clinton another letter on 23 Sept., elaborating on the first one, and Nickerson presumes Clinton received it about the 29th [*op. cit.*, 343]. On the 28th, Burgoyne asked Clinton to instruct him whether to attack or retreat, and said he would not have given up his line of communications to the lakes had he not been counting on finding British forces in Albany [Anderson, 261]; Nickerson says Clinton received this message on 5 Oct. and the next day sent Burgoyne word that "Sir H. Clinton cannot presume to give any orders to General Burgoyne" [Nickerson, 344, 352; Anderson, 261—just to complicate matters, Anderson's note on p. 261 refers to "Burgoyne's message of September *18*" being received by Clinton on 5 Oct.; presumably this is a typographical error, and Anderson meant Sept. 28])

AMERICAN DISPOSITIONS

Maj. Gen. Israel Putnam had commanded since May '77 in the strategic region known as the Highlands of the Hudson River. (For its importance and for map, see HUDSON RIVER. . . .) His strength had been reduced by the detachment of troops to other fronts, and at the time of Clinton's offensive he had only 1,000 Cont'ls. and 400 militia around Peekskill; 100 of the latter were unarmed and, "what is worse," wrote Putnam on 16 Sept., "it would be damned unsafe to trust them" (quoted by Freeman, *Washington*, IV, 520). On the west shore of the Hudson, four miles N.W. as the crow flies, about 600 militia and a few Cont'ls. held the forts that were Clinton's objective.

"Fort Montgomery . . . was tolerably situated . . . to annoy shipping going up the river; and the works were pretty good on that side, but were not so, nor fully completed on the back side; and the right flank was commanded by higher ground on the south, and near the fort, on the other side of Pooplop's Creek, . . . [by] a strong redoubt, called Clinton. . . ." (Heath, *Memoirs*, 141)

Clinton was the stronger fort, although smaller, and had to be taken by an enemy that wished to hold Ft. Montgomery; the mouth of Popolopen Creek was about 120 feet below Clinton and the two forts were separated by its deep gorge. Approaches to the forts from the land side were through rugged defiles that could have been easily defended. Across the river between Anthony's Nose and Ft. Montgomery was a system of obstructions including so-called CHEVAUX DE FRISE that were strengthened by a log boom and a great iron chain. Upstream from the boom was a flotilla comprising the frigates *Congress* and *Montgomery*, a sloop, and two galleys. (Ward, 515) West Point, about five miles north, was not fortified at this time, and unfinished Ft. Constitution, opposite West Point, did not figure significantly in this operation (see below).

THE BRITISH STRATEGY

About 24 Sept., Clinton received reinforcements from England that brought his strength in regulars to 2,700 British and 4,200 Germans. On 3 Oct. he moved north with 3,000 troops organized into three divisions. The evening of the 5th he landed troops at Verplancks Point, on the east shore across the Hudson from Stony Point, and routed a small rebel outpost. Putnam hastily withdrew four miles into the hills and ordered reinforcements from Forts Montgomery and Clinton to join him, which was precisely what Sir Henry had intended to achieve by this initial diversion. Leaving 1,000 troops at Verplancks to deceive Putnam further, the British commander landed near Stony Point under cover of a thick fog the next morning. Despite cumbersome uniforms and equipment that weighed 60 pounds and more, the troops followed their Tory guide (one Brom Springster) quickly up a steep trail, through an 850-ft.-high pass called The Timp, and down to a trail junction at Doodletown, within two and a half miles of Ft. Clinton. Here, at about 10 A.M., they made contact with an American patrol and drove it back (see below). Sir Henry then sent 900 men around Bear Mountain to cross the creek and attack Ft. Montgomery from the rear (west); the rest waited to give the encircling column time to make their difficult seven-mile circuit before attacking Ft. Clinton from the south.

The forts were commanded by Gov. George Clinton, who hurried south from a meeting of the N.Y. Legislature at Esopus (now Kingston) when Putnam sent him word of the enemy's approach. He established his C.P. in Ft. Montgomery and his brother, Gen. James Clinton, commanded the other fort. Washington had recommended outposting The Timp, but others—including Greene and Knox—argued that rough terrain ruled out the possibility of an enemy's using this route; the strategic point was therefore undefended. Scouts

posted south of the Dunderberg informed Gov. Clinton of the British landing at Stony Point, and he dispatched the 30-man patrol the enemy met at Doodletown. A second delaying force was driven back from the same area, although the 50 Cont'ls. under Lt. Col. Jacobus Bruyn and 50 militia under Lt. Col. James McLarey conducted themselves creditably. Capt. John Fenno left Ft. Montgomery with 60 men to meet the column coming around Bear Mtn. Reinforced with a gun and 40 more men, he took up a strong delaying position along the rugged side of the creek, about a mile from the fort, and forced the enemy to deploy. When threatened with being outflanked, the Americans spiked their gun and dropped back to another gun that Capt. LAMB had run forward. Fenno was captured. When the second delaying position was threatened with envelopment the defenders spiked the second gun and retreated to the fort.

THE ASSAULT

After landing early and moving rapidly across difficult terrain, the British were not ready for a simultaneous attack by both columns until 4:30. After the customary summons to surrender and the heroic refusal, the action started. Opposite Ft. Montgomery was the advance guard of Lt. Col. Campbell that had led the advance from Stony Point and had then made a difficult seven-mile march to get into position. From left (north) to right were the 52d Regt., a group of N.Y. Vols., Col. Beverley Robinson's Loyal Americans (400 strong), Emmerich's Hessian jägers, and the 57th Regt. (The N.Y. Vols. are shown on the sketch map in Ward, p. 517, but not mentioned in the text.) Campbell was killed in the attack, and his men, enraged by his death, the rigors of their march, and the intense heat of the day, at first refused to give quarter. Some of the defenders were, however, spared, and others escaped north or east (across the river). Gov. Clinton was among the latter.

Ft. Clinton's main defenses were oriented southward to cover a 400-yard-wide strip of relatively flat ground between what is now called Hessian Lake and the drop-off to the river. An abatis and 10 cannon covered this approach. Since there was little opportunity to maneuver and no artillery support, the British commander committed the bulk of his forces in a frontal attack from the south. In the first wave were the flank companies of the 7th and 26th Regts., and a company of Anspach grenadiers. They were followed by the battalion companies of the 26th, a dismounted troop of the 17th Light Dragoons, and some Hessian chasseurs. The battalion companies of the 7th and a German battalion followed in support. (Nickerson, 350) The 63d Regt. circled west of Hessian Lake to attack from the N.W. In the best tradition of European regulars, Sir Henry's troops pushed forward through the abatis and the enemy's fire to claw their way into Ft. Clinton. Nickerson says over 300 of the attackers were killed or wounded in taking the two forts (*op. cit.,* 350); Fortescue says the British lost 18 officers and 169 men (*Br. Army,* III, 236), figures that may not include Germans and Tories (Ward, 519). Fortescue says Ft. Montgomery "was carried with little difficulty or loss" and that most of the garrison escaped. (*Op. cit.,* 235) American losses were heavy: out of the few Cont'ls. and 600 militia in the two forts, 250 were reported killed, wounded, or missing (Ward, 519, citing Marshall); 67 guns and a significant quantity of stores were also captured (*ibid.;* Fortescue, 236). The American flotilla

above the river obstructions could not escape north against the wind and was burned after dark.

On 7 Oct., the British broke through the boom and routed the small garrison from Ft. Constitution (see above). Although Sir Henry Clinton did not intend to go farther, he wrote Burgoyne:

> Fort Montgomery
> October 8th
>
> *Nous y voici* and nothing now between us and Gates; I sincerely hope this little success of ours may facilitate your operations. In answer to your letter of 28th September by Captain Campbell, I shall only say I cannot order or even advise for reasons obvious.
>
> I heartily wish you success.

(The "reasons obvious" were that only Howe could properly give orders to Burgoyne.)

The Second Battle of SARATOGA took place the day before Clinton wrote his *nous y voici* note, which, incidentally, was recovered in a SILVER BULLET from a spy's stomach. In response to repeated appeals from Burgoyne, Sir Henry sent Gen. John Vaughan with 1,700 men, supported by a flotilla under Sir James Wallace, with orders to "feel his way to General Burgoyne and do his utmost to assist his operations, or even to join him if required" (Clinton, *Amer. Rebellion,* quoted in C. & M., 589). Vaughan and Wallace picked their way through the so-called chevaux de frise on 15 Oct. and anchored that night near Esopus. The next day they burned the town (see KINGSTON [Esopus], N.Y., burned) and moved upstream to Livingston's Manor, about 45 miles from Albany. (*Ibid.*) According to Clinton, Vaughan reported that "he was unable to communicate with General Burgoyne, as Putnam with 5000 men had taken posts on his right and

Parsons with 1500 on his left." Clinton then got orders from Howe to abandon his gains in the Highlands and to send reinforcements to Pennsylvania. (*Ibid.*) On 22 Oct. Clinton wrote Vaughan to withdraw.

This operation of Clinton's, although skilfully conducted, was no threat to the Americans around Saratoga, yet it caused Gates considerable anxiety and raised Burgoyne's hopes. It explains the SARATOGA CONVENTION.

"CLUBBED MUSKET." Musket used as a club (in close fighting).

CLYMER, George. 1739–1813. Signer. Pa. Son of an English immigrant, he was orphaned in 1740 and reared by his uncle, a friend of Franklin, who left him his business and fortune. Through his wife's family, he met Washington many times as a young man. He was an early patriot and captain of a volunteer company in Cadwalader's brigade. In 1773 he was chairman of the "Philadelphia Tea Party," forcing the resignation of all merchants named by the British to sell tea. A member of the council of safety, he became one of the first Cont'l. treasurers (29 Jul. '75–6 Aug. '76), converting all his specie to Cont'l. currency and subscribing to a loan. On 20 Jul. '76, he was one of five Congressional delegates named by his state to replace those who would not sign the Decl. of Indep. On 26 Sept. '76, he was named to inspect the Northern Army at Ticonderoga and advocated increasing Washington's powers. He was re-elected 12 Mar. '77 but was not on 14 Sept. After the battle of Brandywine, his house at Chester City was sacked by the British. In 1777 he was named a commissioner to treat with the Indians near Ft. Pitt. In 1780 he was one of the founders of the Philadelphia bank formed to supply the army and was re-elected to the Cont'l. Congress (1780–82). Although a supporter of the Confederation, he was a member of the Federal Constitutional convention and in Nov. '88 was elected to the first Congress. He declined re-election in 1791 but served, at Washington's request, as collector of duty on spirits, and in 1796 helped negotiate a treaty with the Creeks and Cherokees. He was vice-president of the Pa. Agricultural Society and president of the Academy of Fine Arts and the Pa. Bank. He was ". . . noted by brevity, both in speech and in his writings." (Appleton's).

COCHRAN, John. 1730–1807. Last medical director of the Cont'l. Army. Pa. Son of Irish emigrants, he was born in Sadsbury, Pa., and received his early schooling under Dr. Francis Allison. He entered the British service as a surgeon's mate during the French and Indian War. After taking part in Bradstreet's capture of Ft. Frontenac (27 Aug. '58), during which campaign he became acquainted with Philip Schuyler, he settled at Albany and on 4 Dec. '60 married the widow of Peter Schuyler. Soon thereafter he moved to New Brunswick, N.J., helped found the N.J. Medical Society, and in 1769 became its president. When the war started he collaborated with William Shippen (see SHIPPEN FAMILY) in preparing the plans that were used to reorganize the army medical department after their submission on 14 Feb. '77. Washington was highly impressed by Cochran, who had served as a volunteer, and probably urged that he be given a regular appointment. On 11 Apr. '77 he was named Physician and Surgeon General of the Middle Department, and on 6 Oct. '80 he became Chief Physician and Surgeon of the Army. Following the triumvirate of Philadelphia doctors, Church, Morgan, and William Shippen, on 17 Jan. '81 he ascended to the top position in the Medical Department and served to the end of the war. In this position he was able to correct many of the inefficiencies he had so vehemently deplored. After the war he settled in N.Y.C. and in 1790 President Washington had him appointed commissioner of loans. After suffering a paralytic stroke he retired to Palatine, N.Y., where he died. His son, Walter Livingston, added a final *e* to the family name. The latter's son, John Cochrane (1813–1898), became a politician, was a B.G. in the Civil War, ran for vice president in 1864 with Fremont, and was Sachem of Tammany Hall in 1889.

COCK or COX HILL, N.Y. See Fort Cockhill.

COERCIVE ACTS. See Intolerable Acts.

COFFIN, Isaac. 1759–1839. British admiral. Mass. A descendant in the fifth generation from the founder of the Coffin Family, he entered the Royal Navy at the age of 14 and served under Lt. William Hunter aboard the new *Gaspée.* (This was not the vessel involved in the Gaspée Affair, but she is identified in that article.) In 1778 he was promoted to Lt. and placed in command of the cutter *Placentia,* fighting her in many engagements, including Rodney's victory off Saints Passage, Apr. '82 (see West Indies). In June '82 he took command of the *Shrewsbury* (74). He was court-martialed for disobedience and contempt after refusing to accept three young officers appointed by Rodney to his ship, but was acquitted. After having his naval rank suspended because of failure to comply with an obsolete technicality of naval regulations, he joined the Brabant patriots of Flanders in their fight against Austria. His naval rank then was restored, after an appeal, but he subsequently was retired after being in-capacitated by injuries. By 1814, however, he became full Adm., having been knighted in 1804. In 1818 he started a seven-year tour as M.P. With a deep interest in the country of his birth, he sent English race horses to improve the breed and imported plants and commercial fish (the turbot). In May 1827 he established the Coffin School at Nantucket.

COFFIN, John. 1756–1838. Loyalist officer. Mass. Elder brother of Sir Isaac (above), he went to sea as a small boy and at the age of 18 had been given command of a ship. On 15 June '75 he reached Boston with a shipload of British troops. Two days later he ferried these soldiers over for the battle of Bunker Hill, took part in the fighting on land, and for his gallant conduct was given a "battlefield commission." After serving successively as ensign and Lt., he was promised command of 400 Loyalists on the condition that he recruit them in N.Y. Going to N.Y.C. after the evacuation of Boston (15 Mar. '76), he raised and assumed command of the mounted rifle force known as the "Orange Rangers." He led them in the battle of Long Island. In 1778 he transferred into the N.Y. Volunteers. The same year he went to the South, where he raised a corps of mounted troops in Ga. According to Appleton's, Coffin took part in the action at St. Lucia (Dec. '78) and Briar Creek, 3 Mar. '79. *D.A.B.* says he distinguished himself in the action at Savannah (presumably in Oct. '79). He is also said to have been in the battle of Camden, 16 Aug. '80. (Appleton's) At Hobkirk's Hill, 25 Apr. '81, his gallant attempt to capture the American guns was beaten off, and he subsequently was routed by the cavalry of William Washington.

Capt. Coffin particularly distinguished himself at Eutaw Springs, 8 Sept. '81. The patriots are said to have offered a reward of $10,000 for his head (James Truslow Adams in *D.A.B.*). Whether or not the story is true, Coffin appears to have believed it: after the battle of 8 Sept. '81 he left the main British army, fought his way to Charleston. He subsequently served under Cornwallis at Yorktown (*ibid.*), but escaped the surrender there and returned to Charleston, the home of his fiancée, Ann Mathews of St. Johns Island. When the British evacuated Charleston he went to N.Y.C. On 25 Dec. '82 Carleton promoted him to Maj. in the King's American Regt., and about this time Cornwallis presented him with a sword for his services.

Before the British evacuation of N.Y.C. Maj. Coffin went to New Brunswick (Canada), where he was joined by his young wife and four slaves. Only 27, he started clearing his lands and eventually developed a valuable estate of 6,000 acres about 12 miles from St. John. He remained in the British Army on half pay, rose steadily in rank, and became a full Gen. on 12 Aug. 1819. When he died on 12 June 1838 he was the oldest Gen. in the British service. (*Ibid.*).

Another John Coffin, an uncle of the above, constructed the defenses that stopped Montgomery's column in the assault on QUEBEC, 31 Dec. '75. (Appleton's)

COFFIN FAMILY OF MASSA-CHUSETTS. The ancestor of all Americans bearing this name was Tristram Coffin (1605–1681), who came to America from Devonshire with his wife and a number of relatives in 1642. (Appleton's) Tristram founded the colony of Nantucket. His grand-daughter, Judith, daughter of Stephen, was the grandmother of Benjamin Franklin. Two other descendants, sons of Nathaniel, were the Loyalists John COFFIN and Sir Isaac COFFIN. The life of Tristram was published by Allen Coffin (Nantucket, 1881); that of Sir Isaac was published by Thomas Coffin Amory (Boston, 1886).

COLERAINE, 4th Baron. See George HANGER.

COLLIER, George. 1738–1795. British commodore. If Arbuthnot and Byron are examples of the incompetence of Lord Sandwich's navy, George Collier's career seems to indicate that the British Navy was blind to the talents of promising younger officers. Of undistinguished parentage—which may explain the mystery—he entered the navy in 1751 and served on the home station and in the East Indies. Given command of the frigate *Rainbow* in 1775, he performed some special mission off the American coast and, although the nature of his achievement does not appear to be known, he was knighted for it. (Appleton's, *D.N.B.*) He sailed back to America, leaving England on 20 May '76, and commanded the *Rainbow* off Denyse Point (in the Narrows) to cover the landing of Clinton and Cornwallis on LONG ISLAND. After the rebel army had been allowed, much to his disgust, to escape across East River, he was sent by Adm. Howe on 8 Sept. '76 to be senior officer at Halifax. (Collier, *Journal,* quoted in C. & M., 448; *D.N.B.*) On 8 July '77 he ended a long chase of Capt. Manly's newly commissioned frigate *Hancock* by capturing that ship, which joined the Royal Navy as the *Iris*. The next month he broke up a planned rebel expedition against Nova Scotia by destroying stores at Machias and 30 vessels that had been assembled along the coast. In Feb. '79 he was ordered to N.Y., and on 4 Apr. was promoted to commodore and temporary C. in C. to succeed Gambier. The next month he and Gen. Mathew conducted a raid in Va., "every object of which was fully attained even beyond my most sanguine expectations," wrote Sir Henry Clinton. (*American Rebellion,* 123) The "Mathew–Collier Raid," 5–29 May '79, is covered under VA. MIL. OPNS.

On 30 May, the day after returning from the raid, Collier led his squadron up the Hudson to support Clinton's capture of Stony Point and Verplancks. Sir Henry, who was notoriously incapable of getting along with his naval colleagues, writes that Collier's "zealous assistance contributed very much to our subsequent success." (*Ibid.,* 124) When Clinton sent out the CONN. COAST RAID, July '79, "Sir George Collier, who very cordially entered into all my views, was pleased to accompany this desultory expedition himself," writes Sir Henry. (*Ibid.,* 130) He then churned north to break up the PENOBSCOT EXPEDITION.

Back at N.Y. he found the new C. in C. on the American station had arrived. Although the 41-year-old commodore could hardly have aspired to the post himself, despite the brilliant four months he had just experienced, the appearance of the 68-year-old Arbuthnot as C. in C. was too much. (Clinton's reaction was to submit his resignation, which he did periodically.) On 29 Nov. Collier sailed home mad. In 1780 he commanded the *Canada* (74) in the Channel. The next spring he took part in Darby's expedition to resupply Gibraltar (Darby arrived 12 Apr. with almost 100 store ships on the day the Spanish opened a bombardment that would continue for 13 months) and on the return trip Collier captured the Spanish frigate *Leocadia* (44). He then resigned. Obviously the Royal Navy of Lord Sandwich was no place for a man of his qualifications.

After sitting in Parliament, he returned to the navy in 1790, was promoted to Rear Adm. in Feb. '93 and Vice Adm. of the Blue on 12 July '94.

(See ADMIRALS, "Colored.") In Jan. '95 he was given command at the Nore, an anchorage at the mouth of the Thames, but within a few weeks he had to resign because of bad health. He died on 6 Apr.

Collier adapted "Beauty and the Beast" to the stage and as "Selima and Azor" it was favorably received at Drury Lane in 1776. His *Journal on the Rainbow* was published in N.Y. in 1835, according to Appleton's, and the "Extract . . . from the Journal and Papers of Sir George Collier" was printed in the *Long Island Historical Society, Memoirs,* II, in 1869. The journal of his visit to Paris and Brussels in the summer of 1773 was published by his granddaughter, Mrs. Charles Tennant, as *France on the Eve of the Great Revolution* (1865).

COLOMB, Pierre. 1754–? French volunteer. Born at Nîmes, he entered the *gendarmes de la garde* on 8 Dec. '66 and served with them until they were disbanded 15 Dec. '75. He went to America and volunteered in the 1st Ga. Cont'ls. of James Scriven. (Lasseray) Heitman, who spells the name Colombe, notes that he was "allowed pay" as Lt., Cont'l. Army, from 1 Dec. '76, that he was promoted to Capt. on 15 Nov. '77, and until Oct. '79 served as A.D.C. to Lafayette and Kalb. Lasseray, on the other hand, finds evidence that in May '77 he served under Col. Sam'l. Elbert on the first expedition against E. Fla., went into the light dragoons of Col. Leonard Marbury, was captured 29 Dec. '78 in the defense of Savannah (Heitman says he was taken *at* Savannah), and paroled at Sunbury. It is more likely that he actually was captured at SUNBURY, 9 Jan. '79. (See also SOUTHERN THEATER. . . .)

In Nov. '79 he returned to France and resumed his army grade. (Lasseray) In 1781 he was a Capt. of Cavalry.

Although he was guilty of being surprised at Croix-aux-Bois, Sept. '92, in the first military campaign of the French Revolution, he was named B.G. on 7 Apr. '93, his appointment confirmed on 15 May '94, but at almost the same time he was retired for "service and infirmity." He was 40 years old, but had been wounded several times in America. In 1817 he was still alive at Lyon. (*Ibid.*)

COLONIAL WARS. *c.* 1560–1760. Many places, people, events, and issues of the colonial wars between England, France, and Spain reappear in the history of the American Revolution. It is, therefore, useful to summarize these conflicts in connection with the BACKGROUND AND ORIGINS OF THE REVOLUTION.

THE SPANISH IN FLORIDA

Spanish attempts to colonize Florida had been so unsuccessful that the King ordered them stopped in 1561. Three years later the French established Ft. Caroline, near the mouth of the St. Johns River, in a position from which they could threaten Spanish sea routes to the Caribbean. The Spanish therefore returned to the region and in 1565 built St. Augustine, wiped out the French post and its defenders, and renamed the place San Mateo. In 1586 Sir Francis Drake destroyed St. Augustine. By 1655, however, the Spanish had established about 40 missions and had made considerable progress in converting some 25,000 Indians. Ft. San Marcos was started in 1672.

THE FRENCH IN CANADA AND THE MISSISSIPPI VALLEY

In Canada the French established Quebec in 1608 and pushed exploration into the Great Lakes. Interested primarily in developing the fur trade, and

lacking the English genius for colonization (i.e., in establishing permanent settlements), the French excelled in exploration and in their relations with the Indians. (It should also be pointed out that the Frenchmen going to the New World were carefully screened by the government. They had to be financially solvent, politically reliable, and good Catholics. Hence they were not refugees, like so many of the Anglo-Saxon and European immigrants to the British colonies.) Only the powerful Iroquois remained hostile, but the friendly Algonquin, Montaignais, and Huron allied themselves with the French in pushing the Iroquois back.

In ACADIA the French established Port Royal in 1610 and two other stations. In 1613, however, an English force destroyed these three settlements, and in 1621 the region was granted to Sir William Alexander. Hostilities between England and France broke out in 1627. Richelieu immediately created the Company of One Hundred Associates (or of New France), giving them a monopoly of virtually all trade between Florida and the Arctic Circle, with the provision that they undertake colonization. England, meanwhile, gave Alexander a monopoly on fur trade in the St. Lawrence. Quebec was captured in 1629 by Alexander and Sir David Kirke. The treaty of 1632 restored Quebec and Acadia to France.

Competition in the fish and fur trade led to the capture of Acadia in 1654 by an expedition of New Englanders, who held the region until it was returned to France in 1670.

The St. Lawrence Valley was built up by the French under Champlain, and exploration pushed through the Great Lakes to Green Bay or farther. MONTREAL was established in 1611. French outposts were driven back by the Iroquois during 1642–53, but by 1666 the

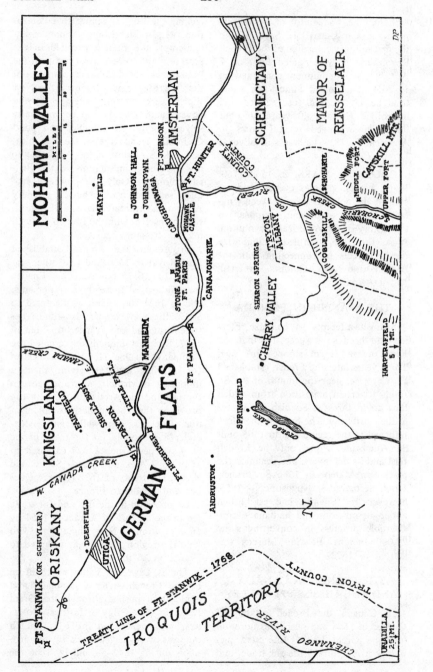

MOHAWK VALLEY

MILES
0 5 10 15 20 25

French had come back in sufficient strength to make them sue for peace. Exploration was then extended into the Mississippi Valley, culminating with a claim to the entire region, under the name of Louisiana, after La Salle reached the mouth of the Mississippi in 1683. La Salle's attempt to set up a French colony at the mouth of the Mississippi failed when he was unable to find the river from the Gulf of Mexico side.

THE ENGLISH IN CANADA

On Hudson Bay the English started establishing trading posts in 1668 to divert fur trade from the St. Lawrence. In 1686, Iberville captured the three James Bay posts, leaving the English with two at the mouths of the Severn and Hayes rivers. The French set up posts on Lakes Nipigon and Abitibi, checking operations of the Hudson's Bay Co. for the time. King William's War (1689–97) was America's phase of Europe's War of the League of Augsburg. Hostilities in America started on Hudson Bay and in the Mohawk Valley. In 1690 the French and their ABENAKI and CAUGHNAWAGA allies under the direction of Gov. Frontenac ruthlessly raided New England and New York border settlements and attacked the Iroquois on the western frontier. The continued French use of these savage allies in subsequent colonial wars caused a fierce enmity on the part of the Americans. Sir William Phips led a New England force in the capture of Port Royal and in an unsuccessful siege of Quebec. The French recaptured Port Royal and the remaining English posts on Hudson Bay; the English recaptured their James Bay posts. The Treaty of Ryswick (1697) restored all conquests.

In the interval preceding the next war, the French established the following posts in the Louisiana territory: Cahokia (near present East St. Louis), 1699; Kaskaskia, 1703; Mackinac, 1700; Detroit, 1701; Ft. Maurepas, on Biloxi Bay, 1699, moving this post to Ft. Louis on the Mobile River in 1702.

Queen Anne's War (1702–13) was the American phase of the War of the Spanish Succession (1701–14). France's Indian allies raided Maine and Massachusetts settlements. Col. Benjamin Church led a New England expedition that destroyed two French villages in Acadia. After two failures, New England colonists, with English support, captured Port Royal (1710). In Newfoundland the French and Indians took St. John (1708) and established control of the eastern coast. A British attack against Montreal and Quebec in 1711 was frustrated.

In the south a force of Carolinians and Indians sacked St. Augustine after failing to reduce the fort (1702). Another force destroyed all but one of the 14 Spanish missions in the Apalache country (1704), but was unable to get through the Choctaws to attack the French settlements along the Gulf of Mexico. The Treaty of Utrecht (1713) gave England the Hudson Bay area, Newfoundland, Acadia, St. Christopher (West Indies), and the Iroquois country. France retained Cape Breton Island and the islands of the St. Lawrence. The *asiento* sold the English South Sea Co. the exclusive right to import 4,800 Negro slaves a year into the Spanish colonies for 30 years and to send one trading ship a year to the Spanish colonies.

During the next interlude, 1713–39, the French expanded their hold in the Louisiana territory. Both sides constructed forts, many of which figured in the American Revolution. The French built the powerful fortress of Louisburg on Cape Breton Island (present Nova Scotia) in 1720, and Crown

Point on Lake Champlain in 1731; these two places guarded the sea and land approaches to the St. Lawrence. Forts Miamis, Ouiatenon (or Ouiataon), and Vincennes, in present-day Indiana, were built between 1715 and 1731 to cover the route from Lake Erie via the Maumee and Wabash rivers to the Mississippi. Ft. Niagara was built in 1726 to secure the Great Lakes route and serve as a base of operations against the Iroquois.

The English built Ft. Oswego on Lake Ontario in 1725 to oppose Niagara, which was about 125 miles due west. The New England colonists built frontier posts against the ABENAKIS.

On the Carolina frontier the Yamassee War was brought on by the expansion of South Carolina settlers along the coast; the Yamassee and Lower Creeks regained control of all area west of the Savannah River. In 1716 the Carolinians defeated the Yamassee with the aid of the Cherokee and virtually eliminated the Creek threat to their frontier. Forts were built at Port Royal and the present site of Columbia (Santee River) for protection against the Indians. Despite Spanish protest, other forts were built on the Altamaha, Savannah, and Santee rivers (1716–21).

A 13-month Anglo-Spanish War (1727–28) gave the Carolinians a pretext to invade Spanish Florida and destroy a Yamassee village near St. Augustine.

Georgia was founded by an English charter of 1732, with boundaries for settlement established on the Savannah and Altamaha rivers. One of the primary considerations in planting this colony was to serve as a buffer against the Spanish. Oglethorpe founded Savannah in 1733. To defend his southern frontier, by 1739 he had established forts on the islands of St. Simons, St. Andrew, Cumberland, and Amelia. He established Augusta and Ft. Okfuskee on the Talapoosa, in what is now Alabama.

War of Jenkins' Ear (1739–42).* British violations of the trade agreements with the Spanish in the Caribbean led to seizure of British ships and rough handling of her seamen. One Robert Jenkins claimed the Spanish had cut off his ear in 1731, and he publicly displayed the missing part to "prove" it. Admiral Edward Vernon, an M.P. who advocated armed aggression against the Spanish colonies, did much to force a reluctant government into declaring war against Spain. Vernon then attacked Spanish possessions in the Caribbean, winning wild acclaim at home for his capture of Puerto Bello, but was recalled after the failure of combined land-sea operations against Cartagena and Santiago de Cuba. George Washington's half-brother, Lawrence, was with the 3,600 colonials who attacked Cartagena, and named his estate "Mount Vernon" in the admiral's honor.

In North America, Oglethorpe with Virginia, Georgia, and Carolina troops invaded Florida in 1740. He captured two Spanish forts on the St. Johns River, besieged St. Augustine for more than a month, and withdrew when his rear was threatened. A Spanish invasion was crushed in the battle of Bloody Swamp (St. Simon's Island), Ga., in 1742. Oglethorpe failed in another attack on St. Augustine in 1743.

King George's War (1744–45) was the American phase of the War of the AUSTRIAN SUCCESSION (1740–48), in which England and Prussia were allied against France and Spain. This war

* This merged into King George's War (see below), and the peace treaty was signed in 1748. The dates given in parentheses are those during which actual fighting in America took place.

was not pressed vigorously in America. Since in America it overlapped dates of the War of Jenkins' Ear, it is sometimes considered part of that war rather than part of King George's War. French attacks on Annapolis (formerly Port Royal), Nova Scotia, failed in 1744. Maine villages were raided by French and Indians. William Pepperrell led an expedition of New Englanders, supported by an English fleet under Sir Peter Warren, in the capture of Louisburg (16 June '45). William Johnson instigated Iroquois attacks on the French, who retaliated by burning Saratoga and raiding Albany (1745). The Treaty of Aix-la-Chapelle (1748) restored all conquests including, to the embitterment of the colonials, Louisburg. The British maintained that the present New Brunswick was included in their claim to Acadia, and 2,500 settlers were sent out to found Halifax in 1749.

Creation of the OHIO COMPANY in 1748 and expansion of Pennsylvania traders the same year into the upper Ohio led the French to step up their efforts in the area. To woo the Iroquois from the English, the French established a mission on the St. Lawrence at the site of today's Ogdensburg, N.Y. To divert trade from Oswego, they established Ft. Rouillé (later York; now Toronto, Can.). Another post was built at the Niagara portage (where Ft. Niagara had been established in 1726), and Detroit was strengthened. All the above activity took place during 1748–49. In 1749 Céloron de Blainville (1693–1759) was sent with a force of about 215 Frenchmen and some Indians to secure the Ohio Valley.

In 1752 LANGLADE captured the trading post of Pickawillany on the Miami River (now Piqua, Ohio). All the defenders were killed. In 1753, Duquesne, the new governor of Canada, had forts built near the present city of Erie, Pa.

(Ft. Presque Isle), and at the present city of Waterford, Pa. (Ft. Le Boeuf). The English trading post of John Frazier at Venango (now Franklin, Pa.) was then taken and garrisoned.

The French had now established a line of operations from the Canada base into the Ohio Valley: a 15-mile portage from Ft. Presque Isle on Lake Erie to Ft. Le Boeuf on French Creek, thence by water into the Allegheny at Venango and on to the Ohio.

At this stage the 21-year-old George Washington was sent by Gov. Dinwiddie of Virginia to warn the French to withdraw from this area that was claimed by Great Britain as part of the Virginia colony. When he reached Ft. Le Boeuf (via the site of latter-day Pittsburgh, the Indian village of Logstown, and Venango), Washington was told politely but clearly that the French were in the area to stay.

In Jan. '54 Gov. Dinwiddie sent a militia company to build a fort at the Forks of the Ohio (present Pittsburgh). On 17 April a 500-man French force captured the half-completed fort, permitted the Virginians to withdraw, and then built Ft. Duquesne on the site. The Virginia assembly raised a small regiment of 300 frontiersmen. Washington, now a Lt. Col. and second in command to Col. Joshua Fry, led 60 men of this regiment into the wilderness with the mission of protecting the fort builders. He met them as they returned from their defeat. Asking for reinforcement, he pushed forward and on 7 May he reached a clearing on the Cumberland Road, about 10 miles east of Uniontown, known as Great Meadows. While camped here he learned that a small French force was hidden nearby. In a surprise attack the morning of 27 May he killed the enemy commander (Jumonville), nine others, and took 21 prisoners. Returning to camp, he built Ft.

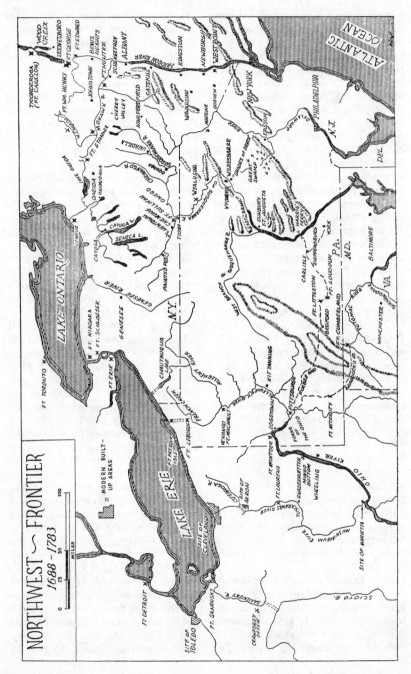

NORTHWEST FRONTIER
1688–1783

MILES
0   25   50   100

= MODERN BUILT-
UP AREAS

Necessity and waited for the rest of the expedition to come up. Washington assumed command on the death of Col. Fry, and in June he was joined by the rest of his regiment and Capt. James Mackay's Independent Company of S.C., a unit of about 100 regulars. On 3 July Ft. Necessity was attacked by about 500 French and 400 Indians. After a long-range exchange of musketry that caused few casualties on either side, Washington was forced to surrender his untenable position, but was allowed to withdraw (4 July) with the honors of war to the base at Wills Creek (now Cumberland), 50 miles away.

THE FRENCH AND INDIAN WAR (SEVEN YEARS' WAR, 1754–63)

After failure of the ALBANY CONVENTION (1754), Gen. Edward Braddock was sent to Virginia to command all British troops in America. His strategy called for expeditions against Duquesne, Niagara, Crown Point, and Beauséjour. For the principal effort, Braddock was to command a force of 1,400 British regulars (Halkett's 44th and Dunbar's 48th regiments) and 1,100 Virginia and Maryland colonials. Washington was appointed one of Braddock's three aides.

In the Battle of the Wilderness (Monongahela), about eight miles from Ft. Duquesne, on 9 July '55, the British were surrounded and defeated by a smaller force of 250 French and 650 Indians. The 400-man advance guard under Lt. Col. Thomas GAGE was driven back onto the main party. Braddock had five horses shot from under him before he fell mortally wounded. The British regulars were cut down as they tried to restore their formations and move forward into open country; bewildered by the unorthodox forest fighting, they shot down some of their colonial allies, who were fighting Indian fashion from the cover of trees. In the three-hour fight, 63 out of 86 British officers were killed or wounded, and 914 out of 1,373 soldiers were hit. The French lost only 43 in all. Horatio Gates was among the participants in this action.

Ft. Beauséjour, in ACADIA, had meanwhile been captured on 19 June '55 by Cols. Robert MONCKTON and John Winslow with a force of 2,000 New Englanders and a few British.

To capture Crown Point, the third element of British strategy for 1755, William JOHNSON led 3,500 colonials and 400 Indians to the southern tip of Lake George. Stopping here to construct Ft. William Henry, Johnson learned that a body of French and Indians were approaching. On 8 Sept. '55 the following actions, known as the Battle of Lake George, or Bloody Pond, took place. Dieskau's French and Indians ambushed and decimated a 1,000-man reconnaissance-in-force sent out by Johnson to make contact. Johnson then beat off fierce attacks on his hastily fortified camp. When several hundred French and Indians returned to the scene of the earlier ambush, they were surprised and routed by a scouting party from Ft. Edward (on the Hudson). Enemy dead were thrown into what was thereafter known as Bloody Pond. (A. C. Flick, *D.A.H.*) Because of dissension among his ill-disciplined troops, Johnson was unable to advance on Crown Point. The French fortified Ticonderoga (which they called Ft. Carillon).

The British formally declared war against the French on 15 May '56. Montcalm (1712–1759) reached Canada with reinforcements on 11 May to take command of the French forces, and LOUDOUN reached N.Y. 23 July to command the British and provincials. After collecting a force in Albany that could have crushed the French in Canada, the inept Loudoun disbanded his provincials and on 20 June '57 sailed to Halifax with a large force to attack Louisburg! What became known as his "CABBAGE PLANTING EXPEDITION" was abandoned when he learned that the French had gathered superior naval forces at Louisburg, and in Aug. he returned to N.Y. While Loudoun had thus diverted himself strategically, Montcalm took advantage of Quebec's temporary security and with 6,000 soldiers and 1,500 Indians he moved rapidly toward Albany, first capturing Ft. Oswego.

Although a move against Albany along the traditional Lake Champlain route had been anticipated, and Gen. Daniel Webb had 1,400 regulars and nearly 5,000 provincials to block it, "Webb, palsied physically and mentally, failed to maintain naval control of Lake George and to collect his troops at the critical spot, Fort William Henry at the south end of the lake." (Alden, *Gage*, 40–41) With most of the British and provincial forces a few miles away at Ft. Edward and points south, Lt. Col. George Munro and his garrison of about 2,200 men were besieged for a week and forced to surrender FORT WILLIAM HENRY, 9 Aug. '57. Montcalm destroyed the fort and withdrew into Canada.

In June '57 the Pitt-Newcastle coalition ministry came to power, and the great Pitt (see CHATHAM) started exerting the leadership that led to a steady series of victories that were to drive the French from North America. Pitt recalled Loudoun, and, against the objections of George III, selected Col. Jeffery Amherst—over the heads of mediocre superiors—to command an expedition against Louisburg. Amherst's 12,000 British and colonial soldiers, supported by a slightly larger naval force under Adm. Edward Boscawen, forced the strategic fortress to surrender on 26 July '58. Brig. Gen. James Wolfe distinguished himself in establishing a beachhead in the difficult amphibious operation that preceded the seven-week siege.

The inept James Abercromby, however, had shattered his 15,000-man expedition in a hopeless frontal attack against Ticonderoga (Ft. Carillon) on 8 July '58. Lord Howe, brother of William Howe, was killed.

CONQUEST OF CANADA

BRADSTREET'S CAPTURE OF FT. FRONTENAC, 27 Aug., contributed to the success of the FORBES EXPEDITION TO FT. DUQUESNE, 25 Nov. These were the only successful operations of Abercromby's forces, and he was recalled on 9 Nov. Amherst, now in supreme command, planned a three-pronged offensive against Canada. Wolfe was to take Quebec by moving up the St. Lawrence; Brigadier John Prideaux was to seal off French retreat by an advance through Niagara, Oswego, and LaGalette (now Ogdensburg, N.Y.); Amherst was personally to lead the most difficult operation, the capture of Ticonderoga and Crown Point.

With fewer than 7,000 men Amherst started up Lake George on 22 July '59. When he approached Ticonderoga the French withdrew their main body of 2,500 men; two days later, on 26 July, the 400-man holding garrison withdrew after blowing up the fort. Among the colonial commanders in this action were Israel PUTNAM, Ethan ALLEN, and Benedict ARNOLD. The French then destroyed Ft. Frederick at Crown Point before the British could reach it. Amherst spent Aug. reconstructing the works at Crown Point, establishing control of Lake Champlain, and putting through a road to the Connecticut River.

Meanwhile, Sir Wm. Johnson had temporarily succeeded Prideaux when the latter was killed in action. On 24 July Johnson received the surrender of

Niagara. GAGE then took command of this column of 2,000 British regulars and Johnson's 100 Indians; he was stopped at Oswego.

WOLFE TAKES QUEBEC

Wolfe's 9,000 soldiers, supported by Rear Adm. Charles Saunders' fleet, had started up the St. Lawrence 16 June '59. Six miles northeast of Quebec, at Montmorenci Falls, 31 July, Wolfe met a bloody repulse when he attempted to storm the French position frontally. As Saunders was worried about withdrawing his ships before winter set in, Wolfe moved his men upstream and pondered what to do next. He then discovered a small, undefended path leading onto the Plains of Abraham. Starting at dark on 12 Sept., Col. William HOWE led his light infantry (rangers) up the path. By dawn 4,500 British troops were on the plateau, overlooking the citadel of Quebec, and within a mile and a half of the French position. Without waiting for his 3,000 reinforcements in the Cap Rouge area, Montcalm sallied forth with 4,500. His gallant attack, unsupported by artillery, was repulsed with a loss of 200 French killed and 1,200 wounded; the British lost only 60 killed and 600 wounded. Both Wolfe and Montcalm were killed. Quebec surrendered 18 Sept. '59. A recent study is C. P. Stacey, *Quebec, 1759: The Siege and the Battle* (1959).

The conquest of Canada was completed in 1760. Amherst personally took command of Gage's 11,000-man force that had bogged down without taking Oswego. Col. William Haviland led 3,500 men who had the mission of reducing French defenses on Ile aux Noix and pushing into the St. Lawrence valley from the south. James Murray, Wolfe's successor, advanced up the St. Lawrence from Quebec, having narrowly escaped disaster when British reinforcements reached Quebec in April just in time to prevent the French from retaking that place. In a rare example of successful "strategic concentration," the three widely separated columns massed at Montreal almost simultaneously: Murray, with 2,500, arrived in late August; Haviland arrived the evening of 6 Sept.; and Amherst arrived the next morning!

Montreal was surrendered unconditionally on 8 Sept. '60. The village was crowded with refugees, the militia had deserted, and the 2,400 French regulars under Vaudreuil (Gov. of Canada) had no alternative. With his surrender all of Canada passed to the British.

Maj. Robert ROGERS took over Detroit and other Great Lakes posts of the French in 1760–61. (British control in this area, formerly controlled by the French, led to PONTIAC'S WAR.)

Spain entered the war belatedly, fearing that a British victory would jeopardize her New World possessions. Anticipating this move, Britain declared war 2 Jan. '62; after taking the French base of Martinique, she then captured St. Lucia, Grenada, Havana, and Manila. By the secret treaty of San Ildefonso, 1762, France compensated Spain for her losses by giving her all territory west of the Mississippi and the area of New Orleans ("Isle of Orleans").

The Treaty of PARIS, 10 Feb. '63, ended the last Colonial War.

Although Amherst's victories united the colonists with the mother country in common jubilation over elimination of the French threat in North America, they also brought the Revolution closer. Friction between the colonies and Great Britain had existed throughout the Colonial Wars. The colonies had not only proved themselves incapable of cooperation with each other (see, for example, ALBANY CONVENTION), but they had also failed to meet promptly or fully the British requests for men, money, and supplies; they had persisted in trading with the enemy. (*D.A.H.*, I, 425) "Had they made war upon the French with half the enthusiasm with which they sought to take the political scalps of their governors and cripple royal government in the provinces, the early part of the [French and Indian] war might have been less disastrous to British arms. Instead, they made the authority of the Crown one of the casualties of the war." (Miller, *O.A.R.*, 39) On the other hand, when colonial forces had reinforced British regulars the provincials had been offended by the supercilious attitude of the regular officers. Some particularly inept British commanders had badly mismanaged colonial volunteers, for example, at Quebec in 1711, Cartagena in 1742, Ft. Duquesne in 1755 (Braddock's defeat), Louisburg in 1757, and Ticonderoga in 1758.

The Colonial Wars, by Howard H. Peckham, was published in 1964. See also H. T. Wade, *A Brief History of the Colonial Wars.* . . . Other works are by Doddridge, Pargellis, Francis Parkman, Rutledge, Wood and Gabriel, and G. M. Wrong. Mr. Peckham has been kind enough to review the galley proofs of this article, and I would like to acknowledge his valuable assistance in correcting a number of errors derived from less reliable authorities.

COLUMN, COLUMN OF FILES. See FORMATIONS.

COMBAHEE FERRY, S.C., 27 Aug. '82. During the final stage of operations covered under SOUTHERN CAMPAIGNS OF GREENE, the light brigade of Gen. Mordecai Gist, which had been organized to oppose British attempts to forage for their besieged garrison of Charleston, was ordered from Stono Ferry to attack the enemy force on the south side of the Combahee (about 40 miles S.W. of Charleston). Around Combahee Ferry the British had about 18 sailing craft of various sizes, 300 regular troops, and 200 Tories. Gist emplaced a howitzer under Capt. Smith at Chehaw Point, 12 miles below the ferry, to cut off this expedition. When the Americans learned that the enemy was dropping down the river under cover of darkness, Col. John Laurens was ordered to march quickly to Chehaw Point with his infantry element of the light brigade (comprising Lee's infantry, the two remaining companies of Del. Cont'ls., 100 men from other Cont'l. units, and the dismounted dragoons of the 3d Va.). The enemy landed 300 men on the north bank above Chehaw Point and formed an ambuscade in the tall grass. Laurens was killed and a number of his men hit when they walked into this trap. The American advance guard fell back on the rest of Gist's advancing column, and the British followed. Gist was unable to drive the enemy from the line it then formed in the woods, since his cavalry could not operate in the rough, wooded terrain and the American infantry lacked the strength for a successful attack without cavalry support. (The cavalry element of Gist's light brigade, which was commanded by Col. Geo. Baylor, comprised Lee's Legion cavalry, and the cavalry of the 3d and 4th Va.) The enemy withdrew without loss and continued their foraging. Gist later attacked two armed galleys at Port Royal Ferry, capturing one and driving off the other. His corps then rejoined the main army.

American losses at Combahee Ferry were two killed, 19 wounded, and Capt. Smith was captured with his gun and crew. "These minor operations are noteworthy chiefly because they resulted in the death of . . . LAURENS," points out Ward. (*W.O.R.*, 842)

"COMMAND, ON." See "ON COMMAND."

COMMANDER-IN-CHIEF'S GUARD. See LIFE GUARD.

COMMISSARIES of the Cont'l. Army. See SUPPLY....

COMMITTEE OF SECRET CORRESPONDENCE. In anticipation of foreign contacts, if not alliances, on 29 Nov. '75 the Cont'l. Cong. appointed a five-man secret committee "for the sole purpose of Corresponding with our friends in Great Britain, Ireland and other parts of the world." Original members were John Dickinson, Franklin, Benjamin Harrison, John Jay, and Thomas Johnson. James Lovell later joined to become an influential and hardworking member, and on 30 Jan. '76 Robert Morris, chairman of the SECRET COMMITTEE, was made a member. "The official records of the diplomacy of the United States date back from the present day in practically unbroken series to the files of the first Secret Committee on [sic] Correspondence," writes Bemis. (*Diplomatic History of the U.S.,* 22)

Arthur LEE was the committee's first correspondent in Europe, and Charles Frederic William Dumas, a student of international law residing in The Hague, became a faithful correspondent. (*Ibid.*) After meetings with ACHARD DE BONVOULOIR the committee decided on 3 Mar. '76 to send an agent to France, in the guise of merchant, to investigate the possibilities of French aid and political support. The Secret Committee was involved in this matter. Silas DEANE was selected by the Cont'l. Cong. for the assignment, and the first of his accomplishments is covered under HORTALEZ & CIE.

A diplomatic commission consisting of Franklin, Deane, and Arthur Lee was appointed by Cong. in Sept. '76. Since the functions of the two congressional committees soon become entangled, the Committee of Secret Correspondence was renamed the Committee on Foreign Affairs (17 Apr. '77), and the Secret Committee became the Committee of Commerce (in July '77). Thomas Paine became paid secretary of the Committee on Foreign Affairs in Apr. '77, and this body thereafter directed American diplomacy. In the furor surrounding the recall of Deane and the investigation of Hortalez & Cie., Paine made use of confidential documents whose revelation embarrassed the French government and on 8 Jan. '79 he resigned under pressure. Soon thereafter James Lovell wrote Arthur Lee to complain about his crushing administrative load: "there really is no such Thing as a *Com'tee* of foreign affairs existing—no Secretary or Clerk—further than that I persevere to be the one and the other." On 27 Oct. '80 John Jay wrote from Europe about the paucity of information he was getting from the Committee: "One good private correspondent would be worth twenty standing committees, made up of the wisest heads in America, for the purpose of intelligence. What with clever wives, or pretty girls, or pleasant walks, or too tired, or you do it, very little is done, much postponed, and much more neglected."

James Duane, Lovell, and William C. Houston were appointed to investigate the problems of the committee. Their report was made in the summer of 1780 but not considered by Cong. until Dec., and on 6 Jan. '81 they agreed to replace the Committee on Foreign Affairs with an executive Secretary of Foreign Affairs. The first man to hold this office was Robert R. LIVINGSTON, who was elected 10 Aug. He was succeeded by John JAY, after the post had remained vacant over a year (Livingston resigned in June '83; Jay returned to America from Europe in July '84), and Thomas Jefferson took over the office on 22 Mar.

'90. The present Department of State was organized under the Constitution.

COMMITTEES OF CORRESPONDENCE. See SONS OF LIBERTY.

COMMON SENSE. See Thomas PAINE.

COMMUNICATION TIME. As covered under ATLANTIC CROSSING, one month was normal sailing time from America to England and two months was normal for the westward voyagè. News of the Boston Port Bill, which passed the Commons on 25 Mar. '74 and received royal assent on 31 Mar., reached Boston by a fast ship on 10 May. Paul Revere, with frequent changes of horses, rode 350 miles to Philadelphia in six days with the news. Six to nine days were required for a letter from Boston to reach N.Y.C. by ordinary postal service, and it took almost a month for a letter to go from N.H. to Ga. Gage's report on the affair of Lexington and Concord, 19 Apr. '75, was placed aboard ship (the *Sukey*) on 22 Apr. and reached London 10 June (50 days); the American propaganda version, on the other hand, left four days later and arrived 12 days earlier. "The Americans," writes Alden in his biography of Gage (p. 279), "had outwitted him by sending the *Quero* in ballast." In late 1781 Congress did not learn of the battle of Eutaw Springs for five weeks. During the YORKTOWN CAMPAIGN communications between Clinton in N.Y.C. and Cornwallis on the Peninsula—not much more than 300 miles airline—took eight days. As an example of the problems this presented, a letter from Germain in London dated 2 May reached Clinton in N.Y.C. with instructions that made it necessary for Clinton to countermand orders of his (Clinton's) that Cornwallis had received 26 June. Presumably, in a fast-moving strategic situation the British C. in C. in America might receive counterorders from London before he got their orders.

COMPO HILL. See DANBURY RAID, Conn., Apr. '77.

CONCORD, Mass., 19 Apr. '75. See LEXINGTON AND CONCORD.

CONFEDERATION. See ARTICLES OF CONFEDERATION.

CONGRESS. See the several articles on the CONTINENTAL CONGRESS for the activities, composition, and seats of the body generally known by that incorrect name. The Stamp Act Congress (Oct. '65) is covered under STAMP ACT.

CONGRESS–SAVAGE ENGAGEMENT, 6 Sept. '81. Cruising off Charleston the British naval sloop *Savage* (16) saw a ship that the captain, Charles Stirling, thought was a privateer carrying only 20 9-pdrs. Too late he discovered that she was the *Congress,* a Philadelphia privateer commanded by Capt. George Geddes and mounting 20 12-pdrs. on her main deck and four 6-pdrs. above. The *Savage* started a running fight but after a fierce action lasting over four hours the British ship was pounded into submission. "Our mizenmast being shot away by the board; our main mast tottering . . . ; the ship on fire dangerously; only forty men on duty to oppose the foe, who was attempting to board us in three places; . . . I was necessitated at a quarter before 3 P.M. to surrender," wrote the unhappy British captain to Adm. Thos. Graves. (C. & M., 977) The ubiquitous Allen McLANE commanded the marines aboard the *Congress.* The *Savage* was later recaptured by the British frigate *Solebay.*

CONNECTICUT COAST RAID, July '79. To punish Conn. for attacking British shipping in L.I. Sound and for supplying the rebel army, Sir Henry Clinton received approval from London to mount a large-scale punitive expedition. About 2,600 troops were assembled at Whitestone and transported up the Sound in 48 vessels. The amphibious force sailed up New Haven Bay the night of 4 July and started landing the next morning.

New Haven was the objective of the first division under Brig. Gen. Garth (54th Regt., a fusilier regt., flank cos. of the Guards, a jäger detachment, and four guns). A small body of volunteers, including some Yale students, delayed the invaders briefly, and about 150 patriots eventually turned out. Planks were removed from a bridge across West River and two guns were emplaced to cover this route, but Garth detoured along Milford Hill to the Derby Road. Although the British suffered some casualties—their adjutant, Maj. Campbell, was mortally wounded—they entered New Haven shortly after noon.

East Haven was the initial objective of the second division under Gen. (Gov.) Tryon, whose force comprised the Royal Welch Fusiliers (23d Regt.), the Landgrave's Regt. (Hessians), the King's Americans (Tories), and two guns. Tryon had to wait for the boats that landed Garth's division, but he met only token resistance and before dark had joined Garth in New Haven. Limiting themselves to plundering the town, the British embarked on the 6th with 45 prisoners.

Fairfield, some 20 miles S.W. of New Haven, was occupied on the 8th. The inhabitants had fled, and after taking a considerable quantity of plunder the British burned 83 homes, 54 barns, 47 storehouses, two schools, two churches, the jail, and the courthouse.

Green's Farms was then looted and burned (9 July). The tally here, according to most accounts, was about 30

buildings, but Lossing cites a document in the office of the Sec. of State of Conn. that puts the total at over 200. (I, 426 n.)

Norwalk was destroyed on 11 July. The invaders drove off 50 militia, who delayed them several hours, and then destroyed 130 homes, 87 barns, 22 stores, 17 shops, and took loot estimated at $150,000. (Ward, *W.O.R.*, 619)

See WESTERN RESERVE.

CONNECTICUT FARMS, N.J., 7 June '80. Burned during SPRINGFIELD RAID.

CONNOLLY, John. *c.*1750–?. Loyalist conspirator. Born in Lancaster co., Pa., about 1750 (Appleton's), he was a nephew of the famous Indian trader, agent, and land speculator, George Croghan. (Freeman, *Washington,* III, 261) Connolly became a doctor and settled in Pittsburgh. Meeting him there in Dec. '70, Washington found him "a very sensible, intelligent man." (*Ibid.*) Connolly had been granted land by Va. and with a view to making a fortune in land speculation he sided against his native province to become the agent of Lord Dunmore, royal Gov. of Va. In this capacity he had a large part in instigating DUNMORE'S WAR (1774). In Apr. '75 he was Capt. and commandant of the Va. militia at Pittsburgh, but at the outbreak of the Revolution, because of his unconcealed Loyalist convictions, he was forced by the local patriots to leave. In Aug. he joined Dunmore aboard a British warship off Portsmouth, Va. Two weeks later he carried Dunmore's dispatches to Gen. Gage in Boston, and after 10 days at the latter place he returned with Gage's approval of his plan for what Van Doren calls "The most grandiose conspiracy against the conspiring patriots. . . ." (*Secret History,* 23) Dr. Connolly's scheme was to return to the frontier, raise a regiment to be called the Queen's Royal Rangers, equip an expedition at Detroit, and launch an offensive that would capture Pittsburgh and Alexandria before joining Dunmore for the reconquest of Va. For this mission Connolly was made Lt. Col. on 5 Nov. With 18 sheets of instructions from Dunmore cleverly concealed in hollow sticks used to carry his baggage, Connolly and two fellow conspirators, Allan Cameron and J. F. D. Smyth, were taken prisoner in Frederick co., Md., after a servant had informed on them. The hidden papers were not found, but another document compromised part of their plan. To save themselves from mob justice they thereupon acknowledged their British commissions. Before they could be sent to Philadelphia, Smyth escaped from their Md. prison with letters from Connolly. He was recaptured and imprisoned in Philadelphia on 18 Jan. '76, 15 days after the other two had reached that city.

Too dangerois a man to be paroled or freed, Connolly was kept in prison in Philadelphia until the end of 1776, when he was moved to Baltimore. Finally exchanged in Oct. '80, he went to N.Y. and then returned to attempt to organize a Loyalist uprising around Pittsburgh. In June '81 Gen. Clinton sent him to serve under Cornwallis in Va. Three months later Connolly was recaptured, in Dec. he was imprisoned in Philadelphia, and in Mar. '82 he was released on the promise that he would go to England. (*Ibid.,* III, 23–26, 415)

According to Appleton's, Connolly held conferences at Detroit around 1798 on a plan for seizing New Orleans and gaining control of the Mississippi River, but Washington learned of the plan and prevented its execution.

CONSIDERATIONS ON THE AUTHORITY OF ... PARLIAMENT (1774). Originally attributed to Franklin and credited as late as 1889 (in Appleton's) to John Witherspoon, this important pamphlet was actually written by James WILSON.

CONSIDERATIONS ON THE PROPRIETY [of the Stamp Act].... Pamphlet by Daniel DULANY.

CONTINENTAL ARMY. "Continentals" were the "regulars" of the American Army, as distinguished from the state militia. The Cont'l. Army was created in June '75 when Congress raised companies of RIFLEMEN, made Washington C. in C., took over the "Boston Army," and started naming generals for Cont'l. commissions. (See CONT'L. CONG. for details.) When Washington assumed command at Boston on 3 July he found 17,000 militiamen whose enlistments would expire before the end of the year. A Congressional committee visited Boston, consulted Washington and the colonies of Mass., Conn., R.I., and N.H. on the best way of maintaining a regular army; they concluded that this force should number at least 20,370 men organized into 26 battalions of eight companies each, exclusive of artillery and riflemen. (Cavalry was out of the question.) Congress apportioned these battalions among the colonies as follows: Mass., 16; Conn., 5; R.I., 2; and N.H., 3. By mid-Nov. fewer than 1,000 had enlisted, and a month later there were only about 6,000. Washington therefore had to call for militia to serve from 10 Dec. to 15 Jan. '76. (See also BOSTON SIEGE for further detail and for Washington's exasperation at this period.)

During this first year Congress authorized the raising of Cont'l. troops in other colonies, and about 27,500 men were reported as being in her pay in 1775. An additional 10,000 militia were put in the field by Va., N.C., S.C., and Ga. (Upton, 9)

1776–78

On 1 Jan. '76, 27 Cont'l. regiments of infantry were raised for the year. The 1st Cont'l. Inf. was from Pa. (and was merely a reorganization, under the same commander, of THOMPSON'S PA. RIFLE BN.). The 2d, 5th, and 8th Cont'l. Inf. were from N.H. The 3d, 4th, 6th, 7th, 12th through 16th, 18th, 21st, and 23d through 27th were from Mass. The 9th and 11th were from R.I., and the 10th, 17th, 19th, 20th, and 22d Cont'l. Inf. were from Conn. It would be more precise to say these regiments were "designated" rather than "raised": they were militia units that had existed in 1775 but that were now given Cont'l. numbers; in almost all instances they retained the same organization and the same commander. (See Heitman, 20–24)

On 15 July Congress authorized Ga. to raise two infantry regiments and two artillery companies in Va., N.C., and S.C. to serve until the end of 1777.

On 16 Sept. the delegates resolved that 88 battalions (or regiments, if you prefer) be enlisted as soon as possible to serve "during the present war," and they asked states to furnish the following numbers of battalions: N.H., 3; Mass., 15; R.I., 2; Conn., 8; N.Y., 4; N.J., 4; Pa., 12; Del., 1; Md., 8; Va., 15; N.C., 9; S.C., 6; and Ga., 1. The Boston phase of the war had ended and the delegates were now faced with British threats against Charleston and N.Y. Furthermore, they had recently received a letter in which Washington gave his considered opinion that the MILITIA had done the cause more harm than good. Congress now was trying to raise a serious army to which states would contribute in accordance with their POPULATIONS. A $20 bounty was offered to every enlisted man who would engage for the duration, and land bounties varying from 500 acres for a Col. to 100 for an N.C.O. or Pvt. were offered. (See also PAY, BOUNTIES. . . .)

The 16 "ADDITIONAL CONT'L. REGTS." were authorized on 27 Dec. '76, on which date the delegates also resolved that 2,040 artillery (in three battalions) and 3,000 cavalry (or dragoons) be called for. Fewer than half the Cont'ls. actually were raised and the over-all strength of regulars and militia in 1777 was 68,720, a drop of 20,931 from the strength in 1776. In 1778 the Cont'l. figures dropped another 2,000 and the militia decreased 15,000 (due to lack of enemy activity).

1779–83

The reorganization of 29 Mar. '79 called for a regular force of 80 Cont'l. regiments, the 1776 quotas (see above) being changed as follows: N.Y. was to furnish 5, an increase of 1; N.J. to furnish 1, a decrease of 1: Pa. to furnish 11 (−1); Va., 11 (−4); and N.C. was to furnish 6 regiments, 3 fewer than before. All other states retained the same quota.

In the last years of the war, 1781–83, the authorized strength of the Cont'l. Army was reduced to 58 battalions. Mass. and Va. were assigned 11 each; Pa., 9; Conn., 6; Md., 5; N.C., 4; N.Y., 3; N.H., N.J., and S.C., 2 battalions each; and R.I., Del., and Ga., 1 each. These were supposed to be 576-man battalions, as compared with the 522-man battalions for the previous years, but fewer than half of the required 33,408 Cont'ls. actually showed up during these last years of the war.

TROOPS FURNISHED

Without allowance for the fact that many men served two, three, and even four terms in the American Army, and were therefore counted several times, the following figures are a basis for estimating how many men fought for

American independence. The numbers for the Cont'l. Army were estimated by Col. John Pierce of Conn., Paymaster General of the Cont'l. Army, and the Treasury accountants, in 1787; the numbers for the militia are those estimated by Heitman.

	Cont'l. Army	Militia	Total
N.H.	12,497	4,000	16,497
Mass.	67,907	20,000	87,907
R.I.	5,908	4,000	9,908
Conn.	31,939	9,000	40,939
N.Y.	17,781	10,000	27,781
N.J.	10,726	7,000	17,726
Pa.	25,678	10,000	35,678
Del.	2,386	1,000	3,386
Md.	13,912	9,000	22,912
Va.	26,678	30,000	56,678
N.C.	7,263	13,000	20,263
S.C.	6,417	20,000	26,417
Ga.	2,679	8,000	10,679
Totals	231,771	145,000	376,771

Heitman estimates that this total, 376,771, should be reduced to not more than 250,000 in view of the multiple enlistments (see above). (Heitman, 691)

The largest number of troops raised by Congress during any year of the war was 89,600 men in 1776; 42,700 of these were militia. (Upton, 65) The largest force Washington ever commanded in the field was under 17,000 regulars and militia, and in his finest campaign, that of Trenton and Princeton, he had only 4,000 regulars and militia. (*Ibid.*) The greatest strength of the Cont'l. Army, in Nov. '78, was about 35,000. (*A.A.,* 411 *n.*)

THE POSTWAR REGULAR ARMY

The British evacuated N.Y. on 17 Nov. '83, Washington resigned on 22 Dec. '83 as C. in C., and at the start of the next year the American nation of 4,000,000 people had an army of 700 rank and file. This was Col. Henry Jackson's Cont'l. or 1st American Regt. On 2 June '84 Congress abolished the Cont'l. Army except for 80 privates, "with a proportionable number of officers, no officers . . . above the grade of captain," to guard the stores at Ft. Pitt, West Point, and other magazines. What was left, under the command of Capt. John Doughty at West Point, was the vestige of Alexander Hamilton's Provincial Co. of N.Y. Arty. Hence only one organization of the modern American Army, the one whose lineage can be traced to Hamilton's Battery, dates from the American Revolution. See ARTILLERY . . . , HAMILTON.

On 3 June '84, the day after abolishing Jackson's Regt., Congress recreated a force of 700 rank and file. (See my *Military Customs and Traditions,* 70 *n.,* for an explanation of this curious procedure.) This force was successively increased and decreased as crises arose and were met: these included British refusal to abandon their military posts in the Old Northwest, Shays's Rebellion, Indian troubles with the Miamis (who whipped Josiah HARMAR and massacred Arthur ST. CLAIR before meeting their master in "Mad Anthony" WAYNE), and the Whiskey Rebellion of 1794.

See also MILITIA and NEGROES.

CONTINENTAL CONGRESS. One of the most serious weaknesses the colonists faced at the outset of their war with England was the lack of central government. Individual colonies (states) were fortunate in having a long tradition of local government and there was no lack of trained politicians, but the 13 colonies also had a long history of jealousy among themselves. One of the surprises of the Revolution was the Americans' ability to unite politically. The ALBANY CONVENTION of 1754 and the STAMP ACT Congress of 1765 gave the colonists some foretaste of "congressional" action.

As protest mounted against the Intolerable Acts of 1774 the first of many calls for an intercolonial congress came from Providence (17 May), Philadelphia (21 May), and N.Y.C. (23 May). (Morris, *E.A.H.*, 83) Boston had asked the other colonies to join in an immediate nonimportation agreement, but when she saw this hope was not to be achieved she fell in with the movement for a meeting. Boston framed a SOLEMN LEAGUE AND COVENANT, which was a form of nonimportation agreement, and 12 days later, on 17 June, the Mass. House of Representatives proposed that a congress be held in Philadelphia in Sept. By 25 Aug. all 13 colonies except Ga. had named delegates.

1ST CONT'L. CONGRESS

Fifty-six delegates from 12 colonies met for the first time at Carpenter's Hall, Philadelphia, on 5 Sept. Peyton Randolph (Va.) was elected president and Chas. Thomson (Pa.), although not a delegate, became secretary. The decision was made that each delegation would have one vote. The radical element succeeded in having the SUFFOLK RESOLVES endorsed by congress (17 Sept.) and defeated GALLOWAY'S PLAN OF UNION (28 Sept. '74). In a set of declarations the 1st Congress denounced the INTOLERABLE ACTS, the QUEBEC ACT, criticized the revenue measures imposed since 1763 (see BACKGROUND ...), the extension of ADMIRALTY COURTS, the dissolution of colonial assemblies, and the peacetime stationing of regular soldiers in colonial towns. (*Ibid.*, 84) Thirteen Parliamentary acts since 1763 were declared unconstitutional, and the delegates pledged to support economic sanctions until these acts were repealed. Ten resolutions set forth the rights of the colonists as they saw them. They signed the Cont'l. Association on 20 Oct. (Commager, *Documents*, 84), prepared addresses to the King and to the British and American people, agreed to reconvene on 10 May '75 if their grievances had not been set right, and on 26 Oct. they adjourned.

2D CONT'L. CONGRESS

On 10 May '75 the delegates met at the State House (later Independence Hall) in Philadelphia and re-elected the same president and secretary. On 24 May Randolph withdrew, however, and John Hancock was elected president of Congress. Still without an official representative from Ga., the delegates took the following action: resolved that the colonies be put in a state of military readiness (15 May), adopted an address to the Canadians asking them to join the revolution (29 May), resolved to raise companies of RIFLEMEN in Pa., Md., and Va. to support the Boston Army, named a committee to draft rules for administration of the Cont'l. Army (John Adams had previously proposed that Congress adopt the Boston Army as the Cont'l. Army), elected Washington C. in C. (15 June), adopted a general plan for the army, elected four Maj. Gens. (Ward, Chas. Lee, Schuyler and Israel Putnam), elected eight B.G.s (Pomeroy, Heath, Thomas, Wooster, Spencer, Sullivan, Montgomery, Greene), elected Gates to be A.G., and voted $2,000,000 in bills of credit to finance the Revolution. (See CONT'L. CURRENCY)

The Battle of Bunker Hill took place 17 June, and on 5 July Congress adopted the OLIVE BRANCH PETITION, one of several important papers drafted by the conservative John DICKINSON. On 6 July they adopted his "DECLARATION OF THE CAUSES. . . ." On the 15th the delegates voted to waive those provisions of the Cont'l. ASSOCIATION (see above) pertaining to war supplies, and on the 31st they rejected NORTH'S PLAN

FOR RECONCILIATION. They appointed commissioners to treat with the Indians for peace (19 July), and established a postal department (26 July) with Benj. Franklin as head. On 2 Aug. '75 the 2d Congress adjourned.

2D CONT'L. CONGRESS
(*continued*) *

On 12 Sept. '75 the 2d Cont'l. Congress reconvened, this time with a delegation from Ga. Learning on 9 Nov. that George III had on 23 Aug. proclaimed the colonies to be in revolt (rejecting the Olive Branch Petition), on 6 Dec. Congress replied with a statement of continued allegiance to the King but not to Parliament. The navy was authorized 13 Oct., and on 14 Dec. a Marine Committee was appointed. On 29 Nov. they appointed the COMMITTEE OF SECRET CORRESPONDENCE that evolved into the State Department. The movement toward independence having been spurred by Paine's "Common Sense" (10 Jan. '76), Congress voted the Declaration of INDEPENDENCE into existence on 2 July '76. Meanwhile, they sent a special committee to Canada; see CANADA, CONGRESSIONAL COMMITTEE TO. On 12 June the delegates appointed a Committee to Prepare

* Although its members changed (elections, deaths, etc.), it was the 2d Cont'l. Congress that sat from 10 May '75 until 2 Mar. '81, when the Articles of Confederation went into effect. The congress that never really had been "Continental," since such continental colonies as Canada, Nova Scotia, and the two Floridas did not join the rebellion, then became "The United States in Congress Assembled." One nevertheless finds statements that so-and-so was elected to the 3d Continental Congress, etc. Strictly speaking, there were only two *Continental* Congresses.

Treaties with European countries; on 17 Sept. they adopted the report of this committee, and on 23 Dec. they authorized its three commissioners (Deane, Franklin, and Arthur Lee) to borrow money for their operations. During 1776 Congress saw its armies triumph at CHARLESTON and BOSTON, fail in CANADA and at LONG ISLAND, saw N.Y.C. fall into British hands, received increasingly discouraging reports in connection with the NEW YORK CAMPAIGN, fought the overtures resulting from the PEACE COMMISSION OF THE HOWES, were cheered by the delay Arnold bought by his victory at VALCOUR ISLAND, and on 12 Dec. ran for the safety of Baltimore as the British success in the N.J. CAMPAIGN threatened Philadelphia. WASHINGTON'S "DICTATORIAL" POWERS were granted during this crisis, and 1777 was somewhat nervously joked about as promising to be the "Year of the HANGMAN."

At Baltimore the three-story brick house of Henry Fite was the meeting place of 20 to 25 members of congress who showed up for business. "In numbers the assembly had become a rump parliament," comments Montross, "fewer than half the members who decided the great issues of 1775 and 1776." (*Reluctant Rebels,* 198) Robt. Morris remained in Philadelphia, and on 21 Dec. '76 Congress formally appointed him, Geo. Clymer, and Geo. Walton as their "executive committee." While at Baltimore Congress resolved on 30 Dec. '76 to send commissioners to Austria, Prussia, Spain, and Tuscany. (Wm. Lee was assigned the first two posts on 9 May; Franklin covered the Spanish post—in addition to France—from 1 Jan. '77 until Arthur Lee was named to succeed him at Madrid on 1 May; Izard was assigned to Tuscany on 7 May.)

Back at Philadelphia on 4 Mar. '77,

Congress reconstituted the Comm. of Secret Correspondence as the Committee on Foreign Affairs (17 Apr. '77), passed the Flag Resolution creating the Stars and Stripes (see Francis HOPKINSON), and on 19 Sept. fled the city again. Howe's threat to Philadelphia was real this time (see PHIL. CAMPN.); Congress went first to Lancaster and then to York (30 Sept.). The so-called CONWAY CABAL, problems of the CONVENTION ARMY, and Lafayette's abortive "irruption into Canada" (see CANADA INVASION . . . 1778) occupied the talents of Congress in the military field during the winter of Valley Forge. They also sent a committee to confer with Washington on army reorganization.

The ARTICLES OF CONFEDERATION, adopted 15 Nov. '77, were the third great document of the Revolutionary assembly. (Montross, op. cit., 11; the first two being the Articles of Association and the Decl. of Indep.) The FRENCH ALLIANCE became a reality 8 Jan. '78, and Congress ratified the implementing treaties on 4 May. The PEACE COMMISSION OF CARLISLE furnished an interlude in the drama of ratification.

For the next years of the war Congress coped with problems of CONT'L. CURRENCY, military disasters in the South until they let Washington pick an American general to command that theater, British raids in Va., Arnold's Treason, the Mutiny of the Pa. Line, ratification of the Articles of Confederation (1 Mar. '81), and PEACE NEGOTIATIONS.

On 24 June '83 Congress again demonstrated its strategic mobility by fleeing to Princeton when some 300 veterans marched in to demand their rights. Remaining at Princeton until 3 Nov., it reconvened at Annapolis on the 26th under a plan calling for alternate sessions there and at Trenton. (Morris, op. cit., 110)

It is interesting that whereas civilian historians are harsh in their criticism of Congress' interference with Washington's leadership—which won the Revolution—the eminent military historian Lynn Montross (War Through the Ages, etc., etc.) has the most charitable judgments about this body of politicians. As for their personal sacrifices, quite apart from the fact that their acts made them all gallows bait if the patriot cause had failed, Montross says: "Before the war ended, more than half of the members were fated to have their property looted or destroyed. Others were to be imprisoned or driven into hiding by man hunts, and even their families would not escape persecution." (Reluctant Rebels, 131) With reference to their periodic flights from Philadelphia and their granting of Washington's "dictatorial" powers, the same author makes this comment:

"It would scarcely be a cynicism to add that one of the foremost functions of any parliament is its usefulness as a scapegoat in time of disaster. The Continental Congress of this crisis [Dec. '76, when they left for Baltimore] has been handled roughly not only by historians of the nineteenth century but also some debunkers of the twentieth.* * * Congress, as the collective villain, is cast as a group of scared civilians fleeing to Baltimore to save their own skins. In their panic the delegates leave the whole burden to Washington. . . . * * * The question of withdrawing from the imperiled city was of course decided by broader considerations than those of personal safety. But if the courage of the delegates is to be questioned, the statistics of the Continental Congress show a record of military service which has probably never been bettered by any other parliament of history. Of the 342 men elected during the fifteen years, 134 bore arms in either the militia or the Continental army. One was killed in action, twelve seriously wounded, and twenty-three taken prisoners in combat. When it is recalled that a majority of the delegates had passed the age of 40, the valor of Congress needs no apologies." (*Ibid.*, 190–91) Turning to a civilian historian and an earlier publication date, here are the observations of Van Tyne:

"One of the greatest handicaps . . . from which Washington had suffered had been Congressional interference.* * * Often he had two masters, Congress and the State Governments. At times they quarreled with each other, and Washington was uncertain which to obey. They countermanded each other's orders and his own, even entering into ruinous rivalry in the matter of the bounties which they offered to recruits. There was discord intense over the choice of the higher officers, and the Commander pleaded in vain for a decision.* * * He actually had to plead with Congress to inform him of the dispositions they made of troops, and the orders they gave to officers, since ignorance of these involved him in difficulties. They went so far as to discharge troops of which he had need, and they ordered him to do futile things like building fire-rafts on the Hudson quite against his better judgment. Only in the hysteria of flight did they finally give him full power, which they partially withdrew when they felt safe again. But they had lost a bit of their self-assurance, and talked thereafter of not wishing to 'counteract the judgment of your Excellency.'" (*War of Indep.*, 267–68) John Richard Alden points out the achievements of a body that, in his opinion, has not received just recognition from many other historians:

"The Congress declared the independ-ence of the United States; appointed the commander in chief and higher officers of the Continental army; established the American navy and the marine corps; formed a diplomatic service; negotiated treaties with European nations and Indian tribes; organized a postal service; issued currency; and borrowed money. It even gave advice to the colony-states with respect to the making of their constitutions; and it drew up the Articles of Confederation.* * * After the close of 1776 the greatest stars in the Revolutionary galaxy were not to be found among them, but shone in military camps, in European drawing rooms, and even at the state capitals.* * * After 1776 talent, integrity, and energy were not lacking in the Congress; genius was.* * * Members faltered in their tasks. . . . There was self-seeking among them.* * *

"Too much has been said, perhaps, regarding the failings of the Congress. It was created in emergency, endowed with uncertain authority, and plagued by rapid changes in personnel. Hence it exhibited obvious defects lacking or less conspicuous in long- and well-established legislatures.* * * Not until 1781 was the burden of clerical and routine duties in great part lifted . . . by the creation of four executive departments.* * * But their record, when the difficulties to be faced are taken into account, is splendid rather than dismal.* * * If the deeds of the Continental officers and men have not been excessively praised, too little credit has usually been given to the faithful in the Congress who struggled in adversity." (*Amer. Rev.*, 166–69)

AUTHORITIES

The basic source is the 34-vol. *Journals,* the 34th and last volume of which did not appear until 1937. Burnett used his 8-vol. *Letters* as the basis for his

Cont'l. Cong., which is considered the standard reference. A popular and more recent work is *Reluctant Rebels* by Montross. Nevins' *American States* includes a study of the relation of the states to Congress. Special studies are cited in the articles cross referenced from this one.

CONTINENTAL CONGRESS, Members of.

CONNECTICUT

Andrew Adams, '78–82
Josiah P. Cooke, '84–85, '87–88
Silas Deane, '74–76
Eliphalet Dyer, '74–79, '82–83
Pierrepont Edwards, '88
Oliver Ellsworth, '78–83
Titus Hosmer, '78
Benj. Huntington, '80, '82–83, '88
Sam'l Huntington, '76, '78–81, '83
Wm. S. Johnson, '85–87

Richard Law, '81–82
Stephen M. Mitchell, '85–88
Jesse Root, '78–82
Roger Sherman, '74–82, '84
Joseph Spencer, '79
Jonathan Sturges, '86
James Wadsworth, '84
Jeremiah Wadsworth, '88
Wm. Williams, '76–77
Oliver Wolcott, '76–78, '81–83.

Elected from Conn. but did not serve: Joseph Trumbull, Erastus Wolcott, Jed. Strong, John Treadwell, Wm. Pitkin, Wm. Hillhouse, John Canfield, Chas. Church Chandler, John Chester.

DELAWARE

Gunning Bedford, Jr., '83–85
John Dickinson, '79
Philemon Dickinson, '82–83
Dyre Kearny, '87–88
Eleazer McComb, '83–84
Thos. McKean, '74–76, '78–82
Nathaniel Mitchell, '87–88
John Patten, '86

Wm. Peery, '86
Geo. Read, '74–77
Caesar Rodney, '74–76
Thos. Rodney, '81–82, '86
James Tilton, '83–84
Nicholas Van Dyke, '77–81
John Vining, '84–85
Sam'l. Wharton, '82–83

Elected from Del. but did not serve: John Evans, James Sykes, Henry Latimer, John McKinly, Sam'l. Patterson, Isaac Grantham.

GEORGIA

Abraham Baldwin, '85, '87–88
Nathan Brownson, '77
Archibald Bulloch, '75
Wm. Few, '80–82, '86–87
Wm. Gibbons, '84
Button Gwinnett, '76
John Habersham, '85
Lyman Hall, '75–77
John Houstoun, '75
Wm. Houstoun, '84–86

Richard Howley, '81
Noble Wymberly Jones, '81–82
Edw. Langworthy, '77–79
Wm. Pierce, '87
Edw. Telfair, '78, '80–82
Geo. Walton, '76–77, '80–81
John Walton, '77
Joseph Wood, '77–78
John J. Zubly, '75

Elected from Ga. but did not serve: Joseph Clay, Benj. Andrew, Sam'l. Stirk, Lachlan McIntosh.

MARYLAND

Robert Alexander, '76
Wm. Carmichael, '78–79
Chas. Carroll of Carrollton, '76–78
Dan'l. Carroll, '81–83
Jeremiah T. Chase, '83–84
Sam'l. Chase, '74–78
Benj. Contee, '88
James Forbes, '78–80
Uriah Forrest, '87
Robt. Goldsborough, '74–76
John Hall, '75
John Hanson, '80–82
Wm. Harrison, '86
Wm. Hemsley, '82–83
John Henry, '78–80, '85–86
Wm. Hindman, '85–86
John E. Howard, '88
Daniel of St. Thomas Jenifer, '79–81

Thos. Johnson, '74–76
Thos. Sim Lee, '83
Edw. Lloyd, '83–84
James McHenry, '83–85
Luther Martin, '85
Wm. Paca, '74–79
Geo. Plater, '78–80
Richard Potts, '81
Nathaniel Ramsey, '86–87
John Rogers, '75–76
David Ross, '87–89
Benj. Rumsey, '77
Joshua Seney, '88
Wm. Smith, '77
Thos. Stone, '75–78, '84
Matthew Tilghman, '74–76
Turbutt Wright, '82

Elected but did not serve: Richard Ridgely, Gustavus Scott, Edward Giles.

MASSACHUSETTS

John Adams, '74–78
Sam'l. Adams, '74–82
Thos. Cushing, '74–76
Francis Dana, '77–78, '83–84
Nathan Dane, '85–88
Elbridge Gerry, '76–80, '83–85
Nathaniel Gorham, '83, '86–88
John Hancock, '75–78
Stephen Higginson, '83
Sam'l. Holten, '78–80, '83–85, '87
Jonathan Jackson, '81–82

Rufus King, '84–87
James Lovell, '77–82
John Lowell, '82
Sam'l. Osgood, '81–84
Sam'l. A. Otis, '87–89
Robt. Treat Paine, '74–76
Geo. Partridge, '79–82, '87
Theodore Sedgwick, '85–86, '88
Geo. Thatcher, '88–89
Artemas Ward, '81

Elected from Mass. but did not serve: James Sullivan, James Bowdoin, Timothy Edwards, Caleb Strong, Timothy Danielson, Tristram Dalton.

NEW HAMPSHIRE

Josiah Bartlett, '75–78
Jonathan Blanchard, '83–84
Nathaniel Folsom, '74, '77–80
Abiel Foster, '83–85
Geo. Frost, '77–79
John Taylor Gilman, '82–83
Nicholas Gilman, '87–89
John Langdon, '75–76, '86–87
Woodbury Langdon, '79–80

Sam'l. Livermore, '80–83, '85–86
Pierse Long, '84–86
Nathaniel Peabody, '79–80
John Sullivan, '74–75, '80–81
Matthew Thornton, '76–77
John Wentworth, Jr., '77
Wm. Whipple, '76–79
Phillips White, '82–83
Paine Wingate, '88–89

Elected from N.H. but did not serve: Ebenezer Thompson, Timothy Walker, Jr., Joshua Wentworth, Geo. Adkinson, Benj. Bellows, Moses Dow, Elisha Payne.

NEW JERSEY

John Beatty, '83–85
Elias Boudinot, '78, '81–83
Wm. Burnet, '80–81
Lambert Cadwalader, '84–87
Abraham Clark, '76–78, '80–83, '86–88
Silas Condict, '81–83
Stephen Crane, '74–76
Jonathan Dayton, '87–88
John De Hart, '74–76
Sam'l. Dick, '83–85
Jonathan Elmer, '77–78, '81–83, '87–88
John Fell, '77–80
Frederick Frelinghuysen, '79, '83
John Hart, '76

Francis Hopkinson, '76
Josiah Hornblower, '85–86
Wm. C. Houston, '79–81, '84–85
James Kinsey, '74–75
Wm. Livingston, '74–76
James Schureman, '86–87
Nathaniel Scudder, '78–79, '81
Jonathan D. Sergeant, '76–77
Richard Smith, '74–76
John Stevens, '84
Chas. Stewart, '84–85
Richard Stockton, '76
John C. Symmes, '85–86
John Witherspoon, '76–82

Elected from N.J. but did not serve: John Cooper, John Neilson, Wm. Paterson.

NEW YORK

John Alsop, '74–76
Egbert Benson, '84, '87–88
Simon Boerum, '74–75
Geo. Clinton, '75–76
Chas. De Witt, '84
James Duane, '74–79, '81–83
Wm. Duer, '77–78
Wm. Floyd, '74–76, '79–83
Leonard Gansevoort, '88
David Gelston, '89
Alexander Hamilton, '82–83, '88
John Haring, '74, '85–87
John Jay, '74–79, '84
John Lansing, Jr., '85
John Lawrance, '85–87
Francis Lewis, '75–79, '81–83
Ezra L'Hommedieu, '79–83, '88

Philip Livingston, '75–78
Robt. R. Livingston, '75–76, '79–81, '85
Walter Livingston, '84–85
Isaac Low, '74
Gouverneur Morris, '78–79
Lewis Morris, '75–77
Alexander McDougall, '81
Ephraim Paine, '84
Philip Pell, '89
Zephaniah Platt, '85–86
Philip Schuyler, '75, '77, '79–80
John Morin Scott, '80–82
Melancton Smith, '85–87
Henry Wisner, '75–76
Abraham Yates, '87–88
Peter W. Yates, '86

Elected from N.Y. but did not serve: none.

NORTH CAROLINA

John B. Ashe, '87
Timothy Bloodworth, '86
Wm. Blount, '83, '86–87
Thos. Burke, '77–81
Robt. Burton, '87
Richard Caswell, '74–75
Wm. Cumming, '85
Cornelius Harnett, '77–79

Benj. Hawkins, '82–83, '87
Joseph Hewes, '74–77, '79
Whitmill Hill, '78–80
Wm. Hooper, '74–77
Sam'l. Johnston, '80–82
Allen Jones, '79–80
Willie Jones, '80–81
Abner Nash, '82–83

NORTH CAROLINA

John Penn, '75–80
Wm. Sharpe, '79–81
John Sitgreaves, '84–85
Richard D. Spaight, '83–85

John Swann, '87–88
James White, '86–88
John Williams, '77–79
Hugh Williamson, '82–85, '87–88

Elected from N.C. but did not serve: Ephraim Brevard, Adlai Osborn, Thos. Person, Chas. Johnson, Joseph McDowell, Nathaniel Macon, Alexander Martin, Thos. Polk, Benj. Smith, John Stokes.

PENNSYLVANIA

Andrew Allen, '75–76
John Armstrong, '79–80, '87–88
Sam'l. J. Atlee, '78–82
John B. Bayard, '85–86
Edw. Biddle, '75
Wm. Bingham, '86–88
Wm. Clingan, '77–79
Geo. Clymer, '76–78, '80
Tench Coxe, '88–89
John Dickinson, '74–76
Thos. FitzSimons, '82–83
Benj. Franklin, '75–76
Joseph Galloway, '74
Joseph Gardner, '84–85
Edw. Hand, '84–85
Wm. Henry, '84–85
Chas. Humphreys, '74–76
Jared Ingersoll, '80
Wm. Irvine, '87–88
David Jackson, '85
James McClene, '79–80
Timothy Matlack, '81
Sam'l. Meredith, '86–88
Thos. Mifflin, '74–75, '83–84

John Montgomery, '82–84
Joseph Montgomery, '81–82
Cadwalader Morris, '83–84
Robt. Morris, '76–78
John Morton, '74–76
Frederick Muhlenberg, '78–80
Richard Peters, '82–83
Chas. Pettit, '85–87
Joseph Reed, '78
James R. Reid, '87–89
Sam'l Rhoads, '74
Daniel Roberdeau, '77–79
Geo. Ross, '74–77
Benj. Rush, '76–77
Arthur St. Clair, '86–87
James Searle, '78–80
Wm. Shippen, '79–80
James Smith, '76–78
Jonathan B. Smith, '77–78
Thos. Smith, '81–82
Geo. Taylor, '76
Thos. Willing, '75–76
James Wilson, '75–77, '83, '85–87
Henry Wynkoop, '79–82

Elected from Pa. but did not serve: Matthew Clarkson, Wm. Montgomery.

RHODE ISLAND

Jonathan Arnold, '82–84
Peleg Arnold, '87–89
John Collins, '78–83
Ezekiel Cornell, '80–82
Wm. Ellery, '76–85
John Gardiner, '88–89
Jonathan J. Hazard, '88
Stephen Hopkins, '74–77

David Howell, '82–85
James Manning, '85–86
Henry Marchant, '77–79
Nathan Miller, '85–86
Daniel Mowry, Jr., '81
James M. Varnum, '81, '87
Sam'l Ward, '74–76

Elected from R.I. but did not serve: none.

SOUTH CAROLINA

Robt. Barnwell, '88–89
Thos. Bee, '80–82
Richard Beresford, '83–84
John Bull, '84–87
Pierce Butler, '87–88
Wm. H. Drayton, '78–79
Nicholas Eveleigh, '81–82
Christopher Gadsden, '74–76
John L. Gervais, '82–83
Thos. Heyward, Jr., '76–78
Dan'l Huger, '86–88
Richard Hutson, '78–79
Ralph Izard, '82–83
John Kean, '85–87
Francis Kinloch, '80

Henry Laurens, '77–80
Thos. Lynch, Sr., '74–76
Thos. Lynch, Jr., '76
John Mathews, '78–82
Arthur Middleton, '76–77, '81–82
Henry Middleton, '74–76
Isaac Motte, '80–82
John Parker, '86–88
Chas. Pinckney, '84–87
David Ramsay, '82–83, '85–86
Jacob Read, '83–85
Edw. Rutledge, '74–76
John Rutledge, '74–75, '82–83
Thos. T. Tucker, '87–88

Elected from S.C. but did not serve: Paul Trapier, Rawlins Lowndes, Alexander Gillon, Wm. Moultrie, Thos. Sumter.

VIRGINIA

Thos. Adams, '78–79
John Banister, '78
Richard Bland, '74–75
Theodorick Bland, '81–83
Carter Braxton, '76
John Brown, '87–88
Edw. Carrington, '85–87
John Dawson, '88
Wm. Fitzhugh, '79
Wm. Fleming, '79–80
Wm. Grayson, '85–87
Cyrus Griffin, '78–80, '87–88
Sam'l. Hardy, '83–85
Benj. Harrison, '74–77
John Harvie, '77–79
James Henry, '80–81
Patrick Henry, '74–75
Thos. Jefferson, '75–76, '83–84

Joseph Jones, '80–83
Arthur Lee, '82–84
Francis Lightfoot Lee, '75–79
Henry Lee, '86–88
Richard Henry Lee, '74–80, '84–87
James Madison, '80–83, '87–88
James Mercer, '79–80
John F. Mercer, '83–84
James Monroe, '83–86
Thos. Nelson, Jr., '75–77, '79
Mann Page, '77
Edmund Pendleton, '74–75
Edmund Randolph, '79, '81–82
Peyton Randolph, '74–75
Meriwether Smith, '78–81
John Walker, '80
Geo. Washington, '74–75
Geo. Wythe, '75–76

Elected from Va. but did not serve: Gabriel Jones, John Blair.

This roster of the 342 delegates who actually served in the Congresses that sat between 5 Sept. '74 and 2 Mar. '89 is from an appendix to Lynn Montross' *Reluctant Rebels*. This author states that "Burnett's *Letters* have been the guide for the years of actual attendance (often varying widely from the periods of election)...." (*Op. cit.*, 435) It should be noted that the second and last so-called *Continental Congress* ceased to exist on 2 Mar. '81; many of the men listed above were not, strictly speaking, members of the Continental Congress, but Montross has not seen fit to split this historical hair. I have included all 342 men because even those who served only in 1788–89 were part of the Revolutionary era.

CONTINENTAL CONGRESS, Presidents of.

	elected		elected
Peyton Randolph of Va.	5 Sept. '74	Elias Boudinot of N.J.	4 Nov. '82
Henry Middleton of S.C.	22 Oct. '74	Thos. Mifflin of Pa.	3 Nov. '83
Peyton Randolph of Va.	10 May '75	Richard Henry Lee of Va.	30 Nov. '84
John Hancock of Mass.	24 May '75	John Hancock of Mass.	23 Nov. '85
Henry Laurens of S.C.	1 Nov. '77		(did not serve)
John Jay of N.Y.	10 Dec. '78	Nathaniel Gorham of Mass.	6 June '86
Sam'l. Huntington of Conn.	28 Sept. '79	Arthur St. Clair of Pa.	2 Feb. '87
Thos. McKean of Del.	10 July '81	Cyrus Griffin of Va.	22 Jan. '88
John Hanson of Md.	5 Nov. '81		

As noted in the article on the Seats of the Cont'l. Congress, the so-called *Continental* Congress ceased to exist on 2 Mar. '81, at which time it became "The United States in Congress Assembled."

CONTINENTAL CONGRESS, Seats of.

Philadelphia	5 Sept.–26 Oct. '74	1st Cont'l. Congress
	10 May '75–12 Dec. '76	2d Cont'l. Congress
Baltimore	20 Dec. '76–4 Mar. '77	End of N.J. Campaign
Philadelphia	5 Mar.–18 Sept. '77	
Lancaster, Pa.	27 Sept. '77	} British occupy Philadel-
York, Pa.	30 Sept. '77–27 June '78	phia
Philadelphia	2 July '78–21 June '83	

Strictly speaking, the 2d Cont'l. Congress ceased to exist on 2 Mar. '81. (See article on CONT'L. CONG.) Seats of Congress after the Revolution were Princeton (30 June–4 Nov. '83), Annapolis (26 Nov. '83–3 June '84), Trenton (1 Nov.–24 Dec. '84), and N.Y.C. (11 Jan. '85–2 Mar. '89). The 1st U.S. Congress was called on 4 Mar. '89 in N.Y.C. and began regular sessions on 6 Apr. On 17 Nov. 1800 the new federal city of Washington was first used as the seat of Congress when the second session of the sixth U.S. Congress met there.

CONTINENTAL CURRENCY. On 22 June '75 the Cont'l. Cong. voted the issue of $2,000,000 in bills of credit to finance the Revolution. By 29 Nov. '77 they had authorized issue of $241,-552,780, the states had issued bills in the amount of $209,524,776, and a certain amount of unauthorized currency probably was in circulation. (*Concise D.A.H.*). Since Congress had no source of revenue from taxation, the money had little or no real backing; all Congress could do was to recommend that the states provide the means for redeeming their currency. State paper money had some backing, but not nearly enough. The result, inevitably, was depreciation in value of the paper money: in Jan. '77 its value in relation to specie (hard money) was down 33 per cent, in Jan. '78 it was down 75 per cent, and in Jan. '79 it had dropped to 90 per cent below face value. Then it went down "like a collapsed balloon," writes Trevelyan.

"In June of that year $50 were paid in Philadelphia for two pairs of shoes, and $60 for two silk handkerchiefs. Fish-hooks, in that piscatorial city, cost half a dollar apiece. In October 1780 beef sold in Boston for $10 a pound, and butter for $12. * * * Samuel Adams, who was not a dressy man, paid $2,000 for a hat and a suit of clothes." (*American Revolution,* V, 299–300, with dollar figures in Arabic numerals.)

Despite partial redemption and retirement after 1779, and despite efforts to enforce laws on the acceptance of the currency at par value, Cont'l. currency collapsed in May '81; two months later only hard money was used in the market. The phrase "not worth a Continental" was created. Fisher points out, however, that Cont'l. currency, "though steadily depreciating, had dragged the patriot cause through six years of war, a fact which must be remembered . . . in spite of the ruin and poverty it caused." (*Struggle,* II, 472–73) Under the funding act of 1790 the old Cont'l. issues were accepted at the rate of 100 to 1 in U.S. bonds.

The index of wholesale prices varied as follows, using 1850–59 as a base of 100:

1776	108	1781	5,086
1777	330	1782	140
1778	598	1783	119
1779	2,969	1784	113
1780	10,544	1786	105

(Source: U.S. Dept. of Commerce, *Historical Statistics. . . ,* 772)

See also FINANCES . . . , MONEY . . . , ROBERT MORRIS.

CONTINENTAL VILLAGE. About three miles north of Peekskill, N.Y., and at the main entrance to the Highlands on the E. bank of the Hudson, the rebels in 1777 constructed a camp for 2,000 men and established a supply center. On 9 Oct. '77 Gov. Tryon with Emerick's chasseurs, other German troops, and a 3-pdr. routed the small guard detachment commanded by a Maj. Campbell and destroyed the settlement. A few days later Gen. S. H. Parsons marched south from Fishkill with 2,000 men and occupied Peekskill. "From that time it was the scene of no stirring military events, other than those incident to the brief encampment of regiments or divisions of the American army," writes Lossing. (II, 174)

"CONTINGENT MEN." Like "WARRANT MEN," each British foot regiment had several "noneffectives" whose subsistence was paid to the Col. for repair of regimental weapons and other contingent expenses.

CONVENTION ARMY. The SARATOGA SURRENDER, 17 Oct. '77, was by "convention," and the prisoners became known as the Convention troops or army. According to Wilkinson's return, they totaled 4,991 (2,139 British, 2,022 Germans, and 830 Canadians). The agreement was that they would lay down their arms, march to Boston, and be returned to Britain with the promise to serve no more in America during the revolution. Almost immediately a controversy broke out that kept the convention from being honored, and both sides have been charged until this day with perfidy. Congress wanted to evade Gates's terms because, although the prisoners were shipped back to Europe, they would free an equal number from other duties for service in America.

The prisoners were marched under armed escort to Cambridge, where the first delay was caused by Howe's attempt to have them shipped home from a port in British hands: Newport or New York. The Americans seized this as evidence that Howe intended to keep them to reinforce his own army. While waiting for the transports Burgoyne gave Congress additional ammunition: complaining in a letter to Gates that his troops had not been furnished with the quarters they had a right to expect, he used the unfortunate phrase, "the public faith is broke." (Heath, *Memoirs,* 156)

Congress had appointed a committee that started furnishing technical reasons to justify delay in ratifying the convention. The first technicality was that since Burgoyne's 5,000 troops had turned in only 648 cartridge boxes, they had not surrendered all their arms. Now, if Burgoyne charged "the public faith is broke" he might be building up a case for invalidating the convention. Congress therefore suspended the embarkation until it got "a distinct and explicit ratification of the convention . . . by the court of Great Britain." (*Journals of Cong.,* X, 29–34, quoted by Ward, *W.O.R.,* 541) The British transports arrived off Boston late in Dec. '77, but were not permitted to enter. Finally, when the King sent orders to Clinton (Howe's successor as C. in C.) to ratify the convention, Congress took the position that the orders might be a forgery; they wanted a witness to swear he had seen the King sign them!

Burgoyne and two of his staff were permitted to leave for England (5 Apr. '78), but the rest of the Convention troops finished the war as prisoners. After a year in Mass., first in the towns around Boston and then at Rutland, in Jan. and Feb. '79 they were marched through Conn., N.Y., N.J., Pa., and Md. to Charlottesville, Va. Baroness Riedesel has told the story of this 12-week trek with her three daughters in the dead of

winter and on starvation rations. Most of the Hessians disappeared as the column passed through Pa., "which was just what the Americans wanted." (C. & M., 866) After another year they were moved to Winchester, Va., and then to Frederick, Md. In the summer of 1781 they were moved north on the approach of Cornwallis to prevent their rescue by Tarleton and Simcoe; some went to Easton, Pa., and others back to Rutland. By the end of the war their numbers had been reduced by death, desertion, paroles, and exchange to about half the original 5,000. Although the majority returned home, a few stayed in America. (*D.A.H.*)

American historians generally agree that Congress handled this matter of the convention with "refuge in subterfuges not creditable to their honor" (C. & M., 866) and "reflected great discredit upon the nation." (Ward, 542) On the other hand, "research within the past quarter century has pretty well established the fact that the real perfidy was Sir William Howe's," writes Wallace. Among the Clinton Papers, which were not generally available to historians until the 1930's, is a letter of 16 Nov. '77 in which "Howe revealed his intention of diverting to New York the homeward-bound transports and exchanging the Convention troops for American prisoners." (Wallace, *Appeal,* 168)

CONWAY, Thomas. 1733–1800? Cont'l. general. Born an Irish Catholic, taken to France at the age of six and educated there, he became *lieutenant en second* in the Regt. of Clare 16 Dec. '47. (Lasseray, 160. *D.A.B.* says he entered the army in 1749.) In 1754 he was deprived of his commission for having joined the *Mestre-de-camp-général-dragons,* but on 1 Aug. '56 was reinstated. In 1772 he was promoted to Col., and on 26 Apr. '75 became Maj. in the Anjou Regt.

After getting authority to go to America he embarked 14 Dec. '76 with a letter of introduction from Silas Deane and reached Morristown on 8 May '77. Washington was favorably impressed and sent Conway to Congress with an unusually commendatory letter. On 13 May he was elected B.G., was assigned to Sullivan's Div., and in the operations from the Brandywine to Germantown ended by creating in Sullivan's mind "a respect that amounted almost to awe." (Freeman, *Washington,* IV, 421, 547) He then launched into activities that are covered in detail under the entry CONWAY CABAL. On 13 Dec. '77 he was promoted over the heads of 23 other brigadiers to Maj. Gen. and I.G. After the "cabal" collapsed, Lafayette refused to accept Conway as second in command for his projected expedition into Canada. The adventurer nevertheless joined Lafayette in a subordinate position to Kalb, who had been appointed Lafayette's second in command, and continued his intrigues to get a separate command. (Randolph G. Adams in *D.A.B.*) On 23 Mar. '78 Conway was directed to put himself under McDougall's orders at Peekskill. On 22 Apr. he wrote Congress a reproachful letter about their failure to give him a command and he again raised the threat of resignation. His friends in Congress had by this time turned against him and, much to his surprise and chagrin, his resignation was promptly accepted (28 Apr.).

The trouble-making Irish-Frenchman got into an altercation with John Cadwalader that resulted in a duel. Tradition has it that Cadwalader "called out" Conway because of the latter's insolent attitude toward Washington. Freeman comments that there seems to be no basis for this popular story but "it is

entirely possible some criticism of the Commander-in-Chief provoked the remark that led Conway to send a challenge." (*Op. cit.,* V, 39 *n.*) Note that Conway, not Cadwalader, sent the challenge. Perhaps it was a sense of patriotism that prompted Cadwalader to set 4 July as the date, and perhaps it was poetic justice that his bullet hit Conway in the mouth. Although there was little real reason to hope the wound was mortal (*ibid.*), romanticists would have us believe Conway thought he was on his death bed when he wrote this to Washington on 23 July:

"I find myself just able to hold the pen during a few minutes, and take this opportunity of expressing my sincere grief for having done, written, or said anything disagreeable to your Excellency. My career will soon be over; therefore justice and truth prompt me to declare my last sentiments. You are in my eyes the great and good man. May you long enjoy the love, veneration, and esteem of these States, whose liberties you have asserted by your virtues."

Remembering the correspondence during the Conway Cabal and the foreigner's talent for persiflage, "Washington decided that prudence and experience both forbade an answer...." (*Ibid.,* 56) Conway returned to the French Army and on 1 July '79 was named *Aide-major-général* of the Army in Flanders. On 1 Mar. '80 he was promoted to B.G., a year later he became Col. of the Pondichéry Regt., and on 1 Jan. '84 was named *Maréchal de camp.* Gov. Gen. of French forces in India as of 9 Mar. '87, he was elevated to Gov. Gen. of all French forces beyond Cape of Good Hope on 14 Apr. '89. On 26 Aug. '90 he was relieved, presumably by a man of more reliable republican lineage. In 1793 he was back in France, but because of his royalist affiliations he had to flee the country. He died in exile about 1800.

CONWAY CABAL, Winter 1777–'78. The name of Maj. Gen. Thos. Conway has improperly been given to a secret movement by which the New England faction of Congress was trying to regain their lost leadership of the Revolution. According to John C. Fitzpatrick, "Fastening Conway's name to the cabal has improperly stigmatized the least of its factors, and long diverted attention from the real purpose of the scheme." (*D.A.H.*) The disasters suffered by the army under George Washington left many patriots with reason to suspect that the Virginian was not up to the task assigned him, particularly when his failures were contrasted with the success of Maj. Gen. Horatio Gates at Saratoga. Although there were many individual expressions of dissatisfaction, certain politicians apparently got together to organize what could properly be called a cabal. The best-known leaders of this shadowy movement were Samuel Adams, Richard Henry Lee, Thos. Mifflin, and Dr. Benjamin Rush. (Fisher, *Struggle,* II, 128) Their cautious approach was to drop hints and suggestions in influential circles and to circulate an anonymous paper called "Thoughts of a Freeman." The latter was not only a formal attack on Washington's ability but also on his popularity. "The people of America have been guilty of idolatry in making a man their God," it said, borrowing a phrase from a letter of John Adams and showing the latter's spiritual alliance with the schemers. But the leaders of the cabal wanted to find out how deeply rooted this popularity of Washington really was before they made a serious move to effect his ouster.

Into this situation rushed Thos. Conway with all the impetuosity of his Irish-French background. The most junior of 24 brigadier generals in the American service at this time, Conway had made himself a pest to Congress by virtually demanding promotion to major general. His letters as well as his conduct reflected "ambitious pretentions and incredible self-esteem"; as for Washington, he wrote Congress, the Virginian was a fine gentleman but "his talents for the command of an Army . . . were miserable indeed." (Freeman, *Washington,* IV, 588, 547) After Burgoyne's surrender the importunate Conway began to appear to some congressmen as an instrument they might use.

The sequence of events culminating in "Conway's cabal" may be said to have started the night of 28 Oct. when James Wilkinson, A.D.C. to Gen. Gates, passed on to Maj. Wm. McWilliams, A.D.C. to Gen. Alexander ("Stirling"), a certain tidbit of headquarters gossip. Wilkinson had stopped for the night at Reading, Pa., en route to York with Gates's report to Congress on the Saratoga surrender. On 3 Nov., Alexander concluded a letter to Washington with the remark that he was enclosing a statement made by Wilkinson to McWilliams that showed "such wicked duplicity of conduct" he felt it his duty to report it. The enclosure read:

"In a letter from Genl. Conway to Genl. Gates he says—'Heaven has been determined to save your country; or a weak General and bad Councellors would have ruined it.' "

What shocked Washington most was not the disparaging remark but the evidence that two of his subordinates were in collusion to discredit him. Washington's only action was to send Conway a brief note starting, "Sir: A Letter which I received last Night, contained the following paragraph" and concluding with a verbatim repetition of the above enclosure. Washington thought Wilkinson might have leaked this information on instructions from Gates to warn him against "a dangerous incendiary" (Washington's letter to Gates dated 4 Jan. '78), and his note to Conway, which would become known within Washington's headquarters, would inform Conway that his comment had been reported. (*Ibid.*, 550–51)

Conway immediately * wrote back to protest that there was nothing improper in his conduct: apparently sensing Washington's suspicion of collusion, he said he had written Gates on 9 or 10 Oct. to congratulate him on his Saratoga victory; he admitted that his previously voiced criticisms of American military methods may have been in this letter, but denied using the expression "weak general" and said: "I defy the most keen and penetrating detractor to make it appear that I leveled at your bravery, honesty, patriotism or judgment, of which I have the highest sense." Conway added he was willing that his original letter be shown to Washington.

The affair might have ended on 14 Nov., when Conway sent Congress his resignation. As reasons he mentioned the criticism he had received in requesting promotion, but he particularly cited the promotion to major general of Kalb, who was Conway's junior in the French Army. Congress did not act on the resignation but sent it to the Board of War. The latter was in the process of reorganization, but Thos. Mifflin was already its most powerful member and Gates soon became its president. During the delay to act on Conway's resignation some congressmen began to support a proposal that an Inspector General

* Washington's note was dated 9 Nov. Conway's reply was misdated 5 Nov., but Freeman says it must have been written about the 9th or 10th. (*Ibid.*, 551, 557 *n.*)

be appointed for the Army. On 13 Dec. Congress adopted this proposal and shortly thereafter Conway was given the post with the grade of major general. Washington viewed this development with disgust and he knew that Conway's promotion would be strongly resented by the 23 brigadier generals who had been senior to him. (Conway's promotion, incidentally, was "on the staff," so he had no command authority over the brigadiers who held their rank "in the line," but this mollified the latter little if at all.) The new I.G. visited Valley Forge winter quarters and was received with "flawless, cold courtesy, the 'ceremonious civility,' which Washington had described two years previously as tantamount to incivility." (*Ibid.*, 588) When Washington sent an officer to ask Conway how he intended to go about his new duties the latter answered on 29 Dec. with a general outline of his plans and then volunteered the statement that "if my appointment is productive of any inconvenience or anyways disagreeable to your excellency, ... I am very ready to return to France where I have pressing business. ..." An interchange of letters followed in which the C. in C. calmly and formally informed Conway that although the brigadiers were determined to protest his promotion—"By consulting your own feelings upon the appointment of ... Kalb you may judge what must be the sensations of those Brigadiers"—he (Washington) would always respect the decisions of Congress. The French officer then proceeded to impale himself on his own pen.

"The general and universal merit which you wish every promoted officer might be endowed with is a rare gift [wrote Conway]. We know but the great Frederick in Europe and the great Washington in this continent. I certainly never was so rash as to pretend to such a prodigious height. *** However, sir, by the complexion of your letter and by the reception you have honored me with since my arrival, I perceive that I have not the happiness of being agreeable to your Excellency and that I can expect no support in fulfilling the laborious duty of an Inspector General."

Quite apart from his anger at the Frenchman's hypocrisy in pretending a sincere parallel between him and Frederick, Washington was infuriated by Conway's accusation that Washington would not support him in the execution of his I.G. duties and by Conway's charge that he had not been properly received. On 2 Jan. Washington forwarded this correspondence to Congress with a straightforward statement of his position:

"If General Conway means, by cool receptions . . . that I did not receive him in the language of a warm and cordial friend, I readily confess the charge. . . . my feelings will not permit me to make professions of friendship to a man I deem my enemy. . . . At the same time, Truth authorizes me to say that he was received and treated with proper respect to his official character, and that he has had no cause to justify the assertion that he could not expect any support for fulfilling the duties of his appointment."

Meanwhile there were developments resulting from Wilkinson's report of Conway's remark about "a weak General." Conway had seen Wilkinson and gotten a denial that the aide had uttered the exact words relayed to Washington. When Conway reported the occurrence to Mifflin the latter was aghast at this breach of secrecy and wrote Gates to be more careful about his papers. Gates, in turn, was much disturbed, but he thought he saw a way of capitalizing on the blunder: he decided that Alexander Hamilton, Washington's aide, had

taken advantage of being left alone in Gates's room during a recent visit and had secretly copied a letter; Gates believed he could use this to disgrace Washington and Hamilton. (Wilkinson, *Memoirs*, I, 373) On 8 Dec., therefore, Gates wrote the C. in C. in feigned alarm: Conway's letters to him had been "stealingly copied"; having no reason to suspect any member of his own headquarters he thought Washington could render "a very important service, by detecting a wretch who may betray me, and capitally injure the very operations" that Washington himself was directing. Since he did not know whether Washington's note to Conway was based on information from an army source or from a congressman, Gates said he was reporting the matter to Washington and Congress simultaneously.

Gates had hoisted himself on his own petard. He learned from Washington that the information had come from Gates's own aide, and he got this news in a letter sent through Congress! Wilkinson had succeeded up to this point in shifting suspicion to Lt. Col. Robert Troup, another aide to Gates and the officer who had carried the trouble-making letter from Conway. When Gates learned the truth about the leak and dressed Wilkinson down, Wilkinson challenged his commander to a duel, but the two men were reconciled before it took place.

Congressmen who had championed Conway or Gates as possible successor to Washington were now faced with the two sets of correspondence Washington had sent them to review; this evidence clearly showed their candidates as pygmies coping with a giant. Other forces came to bear against Washington's enemies. Nine brigadiers joined in a "memorial" to Congress protesting the promotion of Conway, and the colonels were preparing a similar paper objecting to Wilkinson's brevet promotion to brigadier for bringing Congress the news of Saratoga. Congress also became increasingly aware of Conway's military mediocrity and of how thoroughly he was disliked, if not actually distrusted, by other officers.

On 19 Jan. Gates reached York with the original of the famous letter and Conway thought his position has been strengthened by this proof that he had not written the sentence Alexander had sent Washington. Conway put up a show of wanting to have the letter published, yet neither he nor Gates offered to let Washington see it. President Henry Laurens was not offered a look either, but after reading a copy secured from another source he wrote a friend that, although Wilkinson's quote was not verbatim, Conway's original was "ten times worse in every way." Both Gates and Conway maintained in subsequent correspondence with Washington that the letter was harmless, but neither offered to send him a copy.

The attack on Washington had failed completely. Congress sent Gates, Conway, and Mifflin back to the army, and those rival authorities, the Board of War and the office of I.G., ceased to represent any significant threat to Washington's position as C. in C. Washington was able to establish a harmonious working relationship with Gates. MIFFLIN and CONWAY soon were taken completely off his hands.

COMMENTS

Historians disagree as to whether any real cabal actually existed. Dr. Fitzpatrick's views at the beginning of this article, coming from the scholar whose work includes editing 39 volumes of Washington's writings, deserve respect. Edmund C. Burnett, who wrote the authoritative *Continental Congress* and who edited the eight-volume *Letters of*

Members of the Continental Congress, expresses the traditional view that there was a "plot" against Washington. (See Chapter 15 of the first work cited.) On the other hand Bernhard Knollenberg in *Washington and the Revolution* ". . . points out in a cool and closely reasoned essay that evidence of a 'Cabal' is almost completely lacking," writes John Richard Alden. L. H. Butterfield in his edition of the *Letters of Benjamin Rush* (2 vols., Princeton, 1951) reaches the same conclusion.

Much of this controversy must hinge on the question of when the normal opposition to any leader reaches the state of organization necessary to qualify it as a "cabal." It should be borne in mind, however, that Washington undoubtedly *thought* there was a "cabal," regardless of what subsequent scholarship has concluded, and his reactions must be judged accordingly. One thing certain—and ironic—is that Thomas Conway's main contribution to the affair remembered as "Conway's Cabal" was to wreck it!

CONYNGHAM, Gustavus. 1747–1819. "The Dunkirk Pirate." American naval officer. Ireland. In 1763 he emigrated to Philadelphia and entered the service of his cousin, Redmond Conyngham, who had founded a shipping house there in 1745. The family belonged to the landed gentry of County Donegal. In Sept. '75 Gustavus sailed for Europe as master of the brig *Charming Peggy.* His was a "powder cruise": picking up a cargo of flax seed at Londonderry, along with Irish registration, he intended to return with a load of war supplies critically needed in the American colonies. At Dunkirk he had taken on a load of powder and, having been warned by French friends, had unloaded it just in time to frustrate a search demanded by the local British consul, Andrew Frazer. He managed to pick up war supplies off the Texel, Holland, but Frazer got word of this through a deserter while Conyngham was becalmed in Nieuport Canal, and the British got permission from the Dutch to put a guard aboard the *Charming Nancy*. When a wind came up, Conyngham slapped the guard in irons, headed for open water, and almost immediately was becalmed again! He and his crew took to the boats and headed for Dunkirk. His ship was plundered by Nieuport fishermen, the Dutch officials were corrupt, and Conyngham was stranded in Europe after selling his ship and what remained of a valuable cargo for almost nothing. (Augur, *Secret War,* 81–84)

It was Apr. '76 when he had reached the Texel, and for a year he remained at Dunkirk trying to find something to do. On 1 Mar. '77 the American commissioners in Paris appointed him to command the lugger *Surprise,* which was owned partly by Congress and partly by Wm. Hodge, and on 3 May he captured the British packet *Prince of Orange.* Bringing her back to Dunkirk rather than continue his cruise into the North Sea (since she had a tremendous quantity of mail aboard), he snapped up the brig *Joseph* and her valuable cargo of wine, lemons, and oranges. The British ambassador in Paris, Lord Stormont, raised an uproar over this raid by an American ship fitted out in a French port, and the red-faced Vergennes had no alternative but to order the arrest of Conyngham and his crew. Soon released, Conyngham was commissioned Capt. in the Cont'l. navy, given command of the *Revenge,* and on 16 July '77 he sailed on the first of the cruises into British waters that were to make him dreaded as "The Dunkirk Pirate." In a period of two months he raided the North Sea, the Baltic, circumnavigated the British Isles, and went safely into the Spanish port

at Cap Ferrol. In this audacious venture into British home waters he took many prizes, terrified the coast towns, and sent maritime insurance rates soaring. (Capt. Lambert WICKES had meanwhile penetrated the Irish Sea on another famous raid.) Of Conyngham's two-month cruise, Deane wrote Morris this report on 23 Aug. '77:

"Our last accounts are, that they had taken and destroyed about twenty sail, and had appeared off the town of Lynn, and threatened to burn it unless ransomed; but the wind proving unfavorable, they could not put their threats into execution. In a word, Cunningham [as most contemporary accounts misspelled his name], by his first and second bold expeditions, is become the terror of all the eastern coast of England and Scotland, and is more dreaded than [the French corsair] Thurot was in the last war [Seven Years' War]." (Quoted in Augur, *op. cit.,* 188)

In 1778 he used Spanish ports with great success until British pressure caused the Spanish to become less hospitable. Conyngham moved to the West Indies, took two valuable British privateers off St. Eustatius, and reached Philadelphia on 21 Feb. '79 with a cargo of military supplies. (*D.A.B.*) In 18 months he had taken 60 prizes. (*Ibid.,* citing Neeser, *post,* xlvi) On 27 Apr. '79 he was captured off N.Y.C. by the British naval vessel *Galatea* while sailing as a privateer aboard the *Revenge,* which had been bought by some Philadelphia merchants and converted to this new role. In view of his odious reputation, the British subjected him to unusually severe treatment, first in Pendennis Castle, Falmouth, and later in Mill Prison, Plymouth. On his third attempt he escaped, 3 Nov. '79, by digging out. He reached Texel while John Paul Jones was there (after his fight with the *Serapis*), and embarked on the *Alliance.*

Returning to America on the *Experiment*, he was recaptured on 17 Mar. '80, and sent back to Mill Prison. Here he remained a year until exchanged.

After the war Conyngham returned to the merchant service. He failed in efforts to re-enter the Navy and to get compensation from the government for his war services. Augur gives this description: "The smoldering, reckless, unpredictable Conyngham had all the devil-may-care brilliance in action of [John Paul] Jones, but not his knack of making his feats known far and wide. Conyngham was inarticulate and modest, and he worked in a period of secrecy." (*Op. cit.*, 178)

The best reference, according to C. O. Paullin in *D.A.B.*, is R. W. Neeser's "Letters and Papers relating to the Cruises of Gustavus Conyngham," *Naval Hist. Soc. Pubs.*, 1915. The *D.A.B.* sketch cites a number of other sources. In her *Secret War* Helen Augur devotes considerable space to "The Dunkirk Pirate" and appears to use sources not known to Paullin.

COOCH'S BRIDGE (Iron Hill), Del., 3 Sept. '77. (PHILADELPHIA CAMPAIGN) To harass the advance of Howe from Head of Elk, MAXWELL'S LIGHT INFANTRY took up a position near Cooch's Bridge (Iron Hill, as it is called in Beveridge, *Marshall*, I, 93–94). This place was on Christiana Creek about five miles N.E. of Elkton, Md. On 2 Sept. Washington warned Maxwell that the enemy would move in his direction the next day. About 9 o'clock the morning of the 3d the advance guard of Cornwallis' "grand division" was fired on by Maxwell. Lt. Col. von Wurmb, commanding the leading element of jägers, brought his AMUSETTES into action and then drove the Americans back by an envelopment and bayonet attack against their right. (Baur-

meister *Journals*, 102; Ward *W.O.R.*, 339) Maxwell was forced out of several delaying positions. The British light infantry came forward to support the Germans, and although the Americans delivered several close, well-directed fires, the running fight soon degenerated into a running flight back to Washington's main body on White Clay Creek, some four miles north of Cooch's Bridge.

Baurmeister says the Americans left 30 dead, including five officers, but evacuated their wounded (*op. cit.*, 102); Ward accepts this figure, but mentions Montresor's figure of 20 American dead left on the field, and Marshall's estimate of 40 American killed and wounded (*op. cit.*, 466 *n.*). Enemy losses were three killed and 20 wounded, according to Montresor, or 30 killed and wounded, according to Robertson.

The recently adopted Stars and Stripes is said to have made one of its earliest appearances in this battle. (Quaife *et al.*, *U.S. Flag*, 50)

See Edward W. Cooch, *The Battle of Cooch's Bridge.* . . . (1940).

COPLEY, John Singleton (kop-lee). 1738–1815. American painter. Mass. Of an Irish father who died about the time John was born and an Irish mother of English origins, he presumably was born in Boston. The widow Copley married Peter Pelham in 1748. The latter was an excellent engraver and painter; he is credited with giving his step-son an early training in art. Long before he became of age, Copley had established himself as a professional portrait painter and pastellist. Exhibition of his "Boy with the Squirrel" in England in 1766 made him known in that country and started a long correspondence with Benj. West. Copley seems to have been in sympathy with the patriot cause but was too engrossed in his art to let it be diverted by politics. His father-in-law,

Richard Clarke (1711–1795), was the merchant to whom was consigned the merchandise that figured in the Boston Tea Party, and Copley's in-laws all happened to be Loyalists, so in June '74 the artist yielded to a long-standing desire to further his training in Europe. Leaving his mother, wife, and children temporarily in the care of his half-brother, Henry Pelham (the boy with the squirrel), he went to England. Here he met Sir Joshua Reynolds, visited the Royal Academy, was dined by Gov. Hutchinson and other Bostonians-in-exile, and then undertook a tour through Italy. On his return to London he was joined by his wife and children, and they soon established what was to be their permanent home on Hanover Square.

"As an English painter Copley began in 1775 a career promising at the outset and destined from personal and political causes to end in gloom and adversity," writes F. W. Coburn in *D.A.B.* In the fashion of the times he painted historical scenes as well as portraits, and his "Death of Lord Chatham" was his most successful venture into that field. He did portraits of John Adams, John Quincy Adams, and other Bostonians when they visited London after the war. But few of the "English Copley's" matched the works of his youth. Although he continued to paint, during the last 15 years of his life he was plagued by physical, mental, and financial troubles.

His son and namesake, who became Lord Lyndhurst (1772–1863), had a brilliant career as a lawyer.

CORAM, L.I., N.Y. See FORT GEORGE.

CORBIN, Margaret Cochran. 1751–1800. American heroine. Pa. When she was four years old her father, a Scottish-Irish pioneer of W. Pa., was killed by Indians and her mother taken into captivity. Margaret, who had been away from home at the time, was reared by an uncle. In 1772 she married John Corbin, a Virginian who enlisted in the 1st Co. of Pa. Arty. (organized under Capt. Thos. Proctor on 27 Oct. '75). When he was mortally wounded at Ft. Washington, 16 Nov. '76, Margaret stepped forward to take over his duties as matross on a small cannon near the ridge later named Ft. Tryon. After helping keep the gun in action she was severely wounded, one arm nearly severed and a breast mangled by grape-shot. With other casualties she was moved to Philadelphia, where she was paroled and later assigned to the Invalid Corps. On 29 June '79 the Executive Council granted her $30 for immediate needs. On 6 July '79 Congress voted her half-pay for life and "one complete suit of cloaths." (*Journals*, XIV, 805) Mustered out in Apr. '83 she settled in Westchester co., N.Y., where she died a hard-drinking, impoverished veteran at the age of barely 48 years. In 1926 her body was moved from an obscure grave to the West Point cemetery.

Called "Captain Molly" after the war, she is confused with Margaret HAYS of the MOLLY PITCHER LEGEND. (From *D.A.B.* and a MS article by Fairfax Downey for *Blue Book*)

CORNPLANTER. Born between 1732 and '40, died in 1836. Seneca chief. N.Y. According to Cyrus Thomas in the *Handbook of American Indians,* this Seneca chief, also known as John O'Bail and as Garganwahgah, Koeentwahka, etc. ("by what one plants"), was born at Conewaugus on the Genesee River between the dates given above. His father was an English or Dutch trader, John O'Bail, O'Beel, or Abeel; his mother was a full-blooded Seneca. He may have been present at Braddock's defeat in 1755, but Thomas says he was not old enough to have been a warrior in that battle, as is sometimes stated. He visited his father in Albany at the outbreak of the Revolution (*ibid.*), and in the BORDER WARFARE that followed he fought with the Indian and Tory raiders. (Appleton's. Thomas does not mention this.) His participation in Indian treaties between 1784 and 1802, in which large areas were conveyed to the U.S., made him so unpopular with his tribe that for a time his life was in danger. In 1790 he visited Gen. Washington to present Indian grievances, and in 1816 he was living on a 1,300-acre farm that he owned on the banks of the Allegheny, just inside Pa. and seven miles below the mouth of the Conewango. The state of Pa. had given him 640 acres of this tract for his services and in 1866 erected a monument to him on this land; during part of his old age he received $250 a year from the U.S. He and Red Jacket for many years were leaders of their people, and Cornplanter is said to have been the first temperance lecturer in the country. (Appleton's)

CORNSTALK. *c.* 1720–1777. Shawnee chief. Commanded Indians at Point Pleasant in DUNMORE'S WAR, 1774. In 1777 he went to the latter place to warn settlers that he might be forced to accede to the demands of his tribe and renew hostilities. While being held hostage, he and his son were killed in retribution for the death of a white settler. This touched off a wave of warfare by the Shawnee that was not broken until 1794. (*Handbook of American Indians*)

CORNWALLIS, Charles. 1738–1805. British general. Born into an old and distinguished English family, he developed into what Trevelyan has described as "an English aristocrat of the finest type ... enlightened, tolerant and humane; contemptuous of money and indifferent to the outward badges of hon-our ... a living and most attractive example of antique and singleminded patriotism." (Quoted in Ward, *W.O.R.,* 282–83) One modern American historian has said that had James Wolfe held the supreme British command in the early years of the war "the patriots might have been beaten down by swift and daring strokes" and that "Cornwallis might have performed almost as brilliantly. . . ." (Alden, *Amer. Rev.,* 71) Yet other historians argue that his poor strategic judgment in the Carolinas, his insubordination to Clinton, and his errors in Virginia, culminating in his being trapped at Yorktown, cost the British the war. After the Revolution he went on to win the reputation of being one of the greatest generals of British history. With this forewarning that we are dealing with a controversial leader, here is a sketch of his career.

Schooled at Eton, where a sports injury inflicted by a future bishop of Durham left him with a permanent cast in one eye, he became an ensign in the Grenadier Guards shortly before his 18th birthday. After traveling in Europe with a Prussian officer, he was attending a military academy in Turin when he learned that his regiment was ordered to Europe as part of the British contingent to make up the allied army under Prince Ferdinand. Reaching the headquarters ahead of his unit, he subsequently served more than a year on the staff of Granby, the British second in command to Sackville (Germain), and he was present at the battle of Minden, 1 Aug. '59. This same month he was promoted to Capt. in the 85th Regt. and went to join his new regiment in England. Elected to Parliament in Jan. '60, he was promoted to Lt. Col. of the 12th Regt. on 1 May and the next month he assumed command of the unit. His regiment was heavily engaged at Vellinghausen (Kirch Donkern), Germany, 15 July '61, and in many minor engagements before going into winter quarters. In 1762 he saw more action before taking his seat in the House of Lords in Nov., having become the second Earl Cornwallis on the death of his father in June.

Although a Whig and an opponent of Bute's policies, he maintained sufficient court favor to be appointed a lord of the bedchamber in July '65, A.D.C. to the King in Aug. '65, and Col. of the 33d Foot in Mar. '66. When his friend Shelburne left office he declined further service in the government, and in 1769 he gave up his appointment as lord of the bedchamber to become joint vice treasurer of Ireland. The next year, however, he became constable of the Tower of London and in 1775 he was promoted to Maj. Gen. "George III no doubt felt that he could depend on the loyalty of Cornwallis, who did not refuse to take a command in the war ... though he had systematically opposed the measures which caused the insurrection," comments H. Morse Stephens in *D.N.B.*

In Feb. '76 Cornwallis sailed for America as commander of the 2,500 troops convoyed by Adm. Peter Parker's fleet to join Clinton off Cape Fear for operations in the South. Having had no opportunity to do anything in the fiasco that followed (CHARLESTON EXPEDITION OF CLINTON in 1776), he joined the main British army on Staten Island. He and Clinton led the 4,000-man force that landed on Long Island the morning of 22 Aug. In the Battle of LONG ISLAND, 27 Aug. '76, Cornwallis commanded the "reserve" that followed Clinton's vanguard in the turning movement through Jamaica Pass, and in the final stage of the battle he held off the heroic efforts of the American right wing to fight their way back to Brooklyn Heights. He commanded troops in the assault division at KIP'S BAY, 15 Sept. In the operations against FORT WASHINGTON, 14–15 Nov., he commanded the 3,000-man force that crossed the Harlem River to attack Laurel Hill. Leading 4,000 British and German troops across the Hudson, he narrowly missed trapping the rebel army at FORT LEE, 18 Nov.

Howe's plan now was to drive the American army far enough south to secure control of N.J. for winter quarters. In the N.J. CAMPAIGN Cornwallis failed to carry out his boast of "bagging the fox" and was preparing to return for a winter of politics in London when the news of Washington's Trenton victory, 26 Dec. '76, brought him back into the field. The "fox" gave him a sound drubbing in the maneuvers covered under PRINCETON, 3 Jan. '77. Clinton's comments were scathing. Convinced that Washington had escaped annihilation in the second Battle of Trenton only through the negligence of Cornwallis, who had been duped by an elementary and, according to Clinton, awkwardly executed ruse, he felt Cornwallis was guilty of "the most consummate ignorance I ever heard of [in] any officer above a corporal." (Clinton, *Amer. Reb.*, 60 *n.*) Editor Willcox says, "In British military circles in America the Earl's blunder was notorious." (*Ibid.*)

Delayed in his return to London, Cornwallis missed his opportunity to compete with Burgoyne and Clinton for command of what evolved into BURGOYNE'S OFFENSIVE from Canada. He returned to America on 5 June '77 and took part in the maneuvers in N.J., having a prominent role in the unsuccessful attempt to annihilate the large American detachment under Gen. Alexander ("Stirling") at SHORT HILLS, 26 June. He defended Gen. Howe's decision not to take the field earlier against Washington and with Gen.

Grant and Adm. Howe was among the minority that favored Gen. Howe's plan for thế Philadelphia Campaign. In the latter operation Cornwallis and Knyphausen commanded the two divisions of the British army; he made the main effort in the Battle of the BRANDYWINE, 11 Sept., occupied Philadelphia, 26 Sept., and led three fresh battalions to reinforce Howe at Germantown, 4 Oct. After von Donop's bloody repulse at Ft. Mercer, 21 Nov., Cornwallis moved against the fort with 2,000 men but the Americans evacuated the position before he arrived.

He skirmished with the vanguard of Washington's army at MATSON'S FORD, 11 Dec.

In Jan. '78 he returned to England, was promoted to Lt. Gen., and on 21 Apr. sailed back to be second in command to Sir Henry Clinton, who in May succeeded Howe as C. in C. With him he carried a "dormant commission" that would make him Clinton's successor should anything happen to incapacitate the latter. "The importance of this ... has sometimes been exaggerated," points out Alden. "The commission merely made certain that the American command would be held by the senior British officer" and would not be claimed by a German senior to Cornwallis. (*Amer. Rev.*, 241 *n.*, citing Ross (ed.), *Cornwallis*) In the retreat across N.J. following the evacuation of Philadelphia, Cornwallis followed Knyphausen's division and it was his element of Clinton's army that was attacked by Charles Lee at MONMOUTH, 28 June; in the subsequent action Cornwallis personally led the attack by the elite of Clinton's force against Greene, on the American right, in the final stages of the battle.

In Dec. '78 Cornwallis again left for England, this time because his wife was dying. (Appleton's) When he returned to America, almost a year later, Clin-

ton was pressing the government to accept his resignation and Cornwallis' prospects for getting the C. in C. post were very bright. When Clinton moved south for his CHARLESTON EXPEDITION of 1780 he made quite a point of consulting Cornwallis before making any major decisions. During the course of this operation, however, Clinton learned that he was to retain the American command.

Cornwallis was left to hold the South after the surrender of Charleston, 12 May '80, and subsequent actions had destroyed all organized American military resistance in Ga. and the Carolinas. The military history of Cornwallis in America and the evaluation of his controversial generalship will be found in the article on the SOUTHERN THEATER and its cross references. The following summary may, however, satisfy the reader who does not want to eat an entire cow to find out how beef tastes. The aggressive, ambitious, and very capable Cornwallis did not subscribe to Clinton's passive strategy. His instructions authorized him to undertake offensive operations so long as he did not jeopardize his primary mission of holding the large region of Ga. and S.C. left more or less in British control when Clinton returned to N.Y. Cornwallis believed the best defense of his large area was an offensive into N.C., the only place where some armed resistance could still be mustered south of Va., and he wanted then to carry the war into the Old Dominion and be joined there by reinforcements Clinton would send from N.Y. With the excellent pretext that Clinton in N.Y. was too far away to direct his operations, Cornwallis got authority to communicate direct with London. Clinton, who had a strong persecution complex anyhow (see Henry CLINTON) and whose enthusiasm for his job was low, acquiesced in this arrangement and Cornwallis soon convinced the London authorities that his strategy was right and Clinton's wrong.

Cornwallis was struggling with the logistical problems of building up a base for the invasion of N.C. when Horatio Gates marched against him and was thoroughly beaten in the CAMDEN CAMPAIGN, July–Aug. '80. Cornwallis' conduct of this action was brilliant, thanks largely to the initial actions of Lord Rawdon; * another large American force had been annihilated, and the prospect of successfully marching through N.C. and into Va. appeared even brighter. The N.C. Tories should rise in strength to support the 4,000 men of the British field army and the equal number holding the scattered posts in S.C. and Ga. The British disaster at KINGS MOUNTAIN, S.C., 7 Oct. '80, and the other "friction of war" evident at this time should have showed the energetic Earl that his strategic appetite was larger than his ample stomach. But even the catastrophe of the COWPENS, S.C., 17 Jan. '81, did not deter him; instead of restoring his reason it had quite the opposite effect. Although Cornwallis had no way of knowing it, another element had been introduced into his war: a general named Nathanael Greene, who had enough natural ability and who had acquired enough professional training to know how to capitalize on the errors Cornwallis was persisting in making. The SOUTHERN CAM-

* From his reading of Rawdon's letters to Cornwallis that are filed in the British Public Records Office, Professor Hugh F. Rankin concludes that "Rawdon did little but run from one place to another, wring his hands, and cry for help. . . ." To this comment on my manuscript Professor Rankin adds, "Frankly, I feel that Camden belongs to Cornwallis."

PAIGNS of Greene opened with a strategy that led Cornwallis to defeat himself; Cowpens, the Race to the Dan, and GUILFORD constituted a pyramid of errors.

But no matter how serious his most recent defeat was, he had the quality of going on to a greater one. In an astounding disregard for Clinton's orders, he marched to Virginia. Here he failed in his attempts to trap and annihilate the American forces under Lafayette. After first having proposed that Clinton abandon N.Y. in order to send him the necessary reinforcements in Va., which he considered the decisive theater of operations, he then suggested that he return with his troops to Charleston! Clinton in N.Y. was now getting pressure from the allied forces of Washington and Rochambeau and called for reinforcements from Cornwallis. The latter felt this would leave him without sufficient strength to hold a position on the Peninsula, as he had intended, and he started a withdrawal. At GREEN SPRING, 6 July, he created an excellent opportunity to deliver a crushing blow against Lafayette, but then muffed his chance.

The YORKTOWN CAMPAIGN, closing with the surrender of Cornwallis on 19 Oct. '81, virtually ended the American Revolution. See this article for the generalship of Cornwallis and for his personal conduct at the surrender.

"Neither the government nor the English people blamed Cornwallis," points out H. Morse Stephens in *D.N.B.* The statement is astounding but true. "His schemes had been admirable in a political as well as in a military aspect, and had it not been for the arrival of the French troops they might have succeeded," concludes this same British author. The Clinton-Cornwallis controversy continues to rage, but I find it impossible to arrive at any other conclusion than that Cornwallis was a superior tactician but a very bad strategist. Under strong superiors—let's say with James Wolfe as C. in C. in America and Wm. Pitt directing the war from London—Cornwallis would have been a terrible opponent; with a pair like Clinton and Germain over him Cornwallis speeded the winning of American independence by many months.

Shortly before his exchange for Henry Laurens was arranged, in May '82, Cornwallis was asked to take the post of Gov.-Gen. in India, but his parole made him ineligible. In Feb. '83 he resigned as constable of the Tower, the sinecure passing to Lennox, but in Nov. he took over the strictly *military* duties of constable of the Tower. On 23 Feb. '86 he accepted the post in India and as Warren Hastings' successor he won a great reputation in defeating Tippoo Sultan and as a civil administrator. He was made the 1st Marquess Cornwallis in 1793 and returned to England in Feb. '94. On 11 Feb. '97 he was sworn in as Gov.-Gen. and C. in C. of Ireland. In 1805 he returned to India and succeeded Lord Wellesley, whose policy was not approved by the East India Company. A sick man when he arrived, he died on 5 Oct. 1805.

He has been described as "short and thick-set, his hair somewhat gray, his face well formed and agreeable, his manners remarkably easy and affable." (J. F. Watson, *Annals*, II, 287, quoted in Lossing, II, 309 *n.*)

See W. S. Seton-Karr, *The Marquis Cornwallis*, 1890. Benjamin F. Stevens (ed.), *Clinton-Cornwallis Controversy*, 2 vols., 1888; Ross (ed.), *Correspondence of . . . Cornwallis*, 3 vols., 1859; Wm. B. Willcox, "The British Road to Yorktown: A Study in Divided Command," *Amer. Hist Review*, 52, Oct., 1946, and the introduction of editor Willcox to Clinton's *American Rebellion.*

CORNY, Dominique-Louis Ethis de. 1736–1790. French commissary officer. As *commissaire des guerres* he was given a paltry fund of 50,000 livres and sent to America with Lafayette, when the latter returned in the spring of 1780. His assignment was to make advance preparations for Rochambeau's expeditionary force. A Canadian-born patriot, James Price, loaned him another 200,000 livres, according to Chastellux. (*Travels,* 174) Commissary Blanchard did not think highly of M. de Corny, and the latter returned to France in Feb. '81, supposedly because of bad health. (Editor Price's notes in *ibid.,* 258) Congress gave him the brevet rank of Lt. Col. of Cav. 5 June '80. He and his second wife knew Thos. Jefferson after the latter became minister in Paris, and Mme de Corny corresponded with Jefferson for many years afterward. (*Ibid.*)

CORPS OF INVALIDS. The Board of War on 21 Apr. '77 reported in favor of an eight-company Corps of Invalids with a view to making use of veterans who were unfit for further field duty but still capable of limited service. Congress approved on 16 July and named Col. Lewis Nicola commander. One mission assigned the Corps was to provide a "school for young gentlemen previous to their being appointed to the marching regiments," but apparently this role was never actually performed. Another mission was recruiting and the training of these new men, but the records give no indication that this role was accomplished either. The Corps's main duty was guard. States retained partial control over their men in the Corps, and this limited its effectiveness. (Lerwill, 24–25)

COUDRAY. See TRONSON DE COUDRAY.

COUNCIL OF WAR   **290**

COUNCIL OF WAR. A formal assembly of senior subordinates called to advise a commander, usually in an emergency. The members voted on several proposed courses of action, which normally were written out. In theory the commander was obliged to accept the majority vote, but in practice he could disregard it. See, for example, SARATOGA SURRENDER. By the same token a commander was at liberty to issue orders without calling a council of war. But the fact that he did call one was not considered evidence of indecision on his part. In some instances the commander might be accused of contempt for the judgment of his subordinate commanders if he did not make them party to major decisions. The council of war also had the quality inherent in modern "committee solutions": it diluted the leader's responsibility for incorrect decisions. When a council of war met to consider whether the column commanded by Col. Roger Enos in Arnold's March to Quebec should turn back, Enos is said to have covered his own reputation by voting against the retreat after first assuring himself that the majority would vote the other way.

For an interesting council of war, under NEW YORK CAMPAIGN see the section headed "Battle for Manhattan." Another one is covered near the end of the article on BURGOYNE'S OFFENSIVE.

COUP DE MAIN. A sudden attack that captures a position. See STONY POINT and PAULUS HOOK.

COWAN'S FORD, N.C., 1 Feb. '81. Operations leading up to this action are covered in detail under SOUTHERN CAMPAIGNS OF GREENE. Cowan's was a private ford a few miles downstream from Beattie's. The swollen Catawba was almost 500 yards wide at this point and the current swift. About midstream the

ford split, the wagon ford continuing straight ahead, but the shallower horse ford turned south at a 45-degree angle, passed over the corner of a small island, and hit the shore several hundred yards below the exit from the wagon ford. Gen. Wm. L. Davidson posted the largest portion of his 300 militia to cover the exit of the horse ford, he put a small outpost at the wagon ford, and stationed his mounted troops on a small hill a few hundred yards behind the river.

Robt. Henry gives an excellent eye-witness account of the preparations for the battle as well as the action at the wagon ford, where he was posted. "When about to start," wrote this schoolboy veteran of Kings Mountain, "I gave . . . a hundred-dollar Continental bill for a half pint of whiskey. My brother gave another . . . for half a bushel of potatoes. We dispatched the whiskey. Being thus equipped, we went to the Ford, which was about a mile and a half." (Quoted in S. & R., 436)

A Tory guide named Dick Beal led the British into midstream and then deserted without telling them about the two exits. The Guards pushed bravely forward, although they were under fire and men were being swept away by the current. Gens. O'Hara and Leslie were thrown into the water when their horses fell; Cornwallis' horse was hit, but did not collapse until reaching the shore. But the error turned out to be fortunate for the British because they had established a firm bridgehead before Davidson could bring reinforcements from the position downstream. Davidson withdrew his men from the bank and was trying to stop the oncoming enemy when he was killed. His militia scattered, and the action ended.

Tarleton pushed on to rout other militia forces that were assembling at TARRANT'S TAVERN, 1 Feb.

COWBOYS AND SKINNERS. Names given to marauders operating in the "NEUTRAL GROUND" of N.Y. from 1778 until the end of the war. Their main occupation was stealing cattle and selling them to the British in N.Y.C. While the names undoubtedly were loosely applied to all lawless bands and individuals, including those of no political affiliation, the cowboys were generally considered to be Tories and the skinners "patriots." (Lossing, II, 185 *n.*, citing Sparks's *Arnold*) According to B. Irvine Haines, however, the cowboys were from Col. James de Lancey's Westchester Light Horse Bn., and the skinners from Gen. Courtlandt Skinner's Brig. of N.J. Vols.; the former was a Tory unit but the latter shifted allegiance. (*D.A.H.*)

COWPENS, S.C., 17 Jan. '81. When Earl Cornwallis learned in late Dec. '81 that Brig. Gen. Dan Morgan was operating deep in his rear with a force of dragoons and light infantry he reacted violently. Morgan had gained a certain reputation at Quebec and Saratoga for his ability with light troops, and Cornwallis' plans for a winter offensive into N.C. could not be implemented until this annoying new threat was eliminated. But the British commander also knew that the rest of the rebel Southern Army, under Greene, was 120 miles away from Morgan's raiders. With a numerical superiority of two to one, and located in between the forces of Greene and Morgan, Cornwallis realized he had an opportunity to trap and destroy Morgan. It was Ban Tarleton who proposed the strategy: he would take off through the rough country between Ninety-Six and Kings Mountain with his Legion and a reinforcement of supporting troops to destroy Morgan or drive him toward Kings Mountain; Cornwallis would move with his main body from Winnsboro to trap

the rebel fugitives, if Tarleton should catch Morgan and defeat him, or to cut off Morgan's line of retreat if he escaped Tarleton. Further details are covered under SOUTHERN CAMPAIGNS OF GREENE.

Early 16 Jan. Morgan was retreating north with Tarleton's scouts a mere five miles behind him. "There was no question about it," says Kenneth Roberts, "Morgan and his army were running for dear life, and the one certain thing that Morgan couldn't risk was having Tarleton's cavalry catch him in the act of running." (*Cowpens,* 65) * A number of things were bothering the Old Wagoner. First, he was confident in the fighting ability of his 600 or so Cont'ls. and veteran Va. riflemen, but he had no faith in the 300 militia who had joined him. Additional militia were on their way, but did not know where to make contact with his troops. Furthermore, Morgan was so hard up for forage he had written Greene several days before the British started out to get him that he would have to move down into Ga. or retreat. (See SOUTHERN CAMP'NS.)

Morgan had with him some officers who knew this country, and they told him about a place called "the cowpens." Not far off their route, this was a piece of relatively high, rolling ground where a couple of men used to winter cattle for owners who lived in Camden. (Lossing, II, 63 *n.*) Its name came from the fact that a wealthy Tory named Hiram Saunders had owned extensive cattle enclosures there. The place, also called "Hannah's Cowpens," was known to

* Two historical works by Kenneth Roberts are listed in the main bibliography. *Cowpens* contains many glaring errors, but I have felt justified in quoting it where the quoted passages are supported by more reliable sources.

every guide in the Carolinas, since the patriots had used it as a final assembly area before the Battle of Kings Mountain, some 30 miles due east.

By midafternoon, when he was 10 miles from the Broad River and five miles from the Cowpens, Morgan made up his mind to head there and make a stand. Many explanations have been given for this decision, and these will be mentioned later; but the Cowpens had the obvious advantages of forage and being easy for the militia reinforcements to find. Morgan sent word back to Andrew Pickens and other militia leaders to meet him there, and he rode forward to look over the ground.

THE BATTLEFIELD

Approaching the position from the direction the enemy would follow, Morgan rode out of the woods to see a tree-dotted meadow that rose gradually for about 400 yards to a "military crest" and another 300 yards to a geographical (or true) crest some 70 feet in total elevation. About 600 yards behind this, across a grassy swale, was another crest approximately the same height. The ground then dropped off into a grassy plain that stretched five miles to Broad River. The people who recommended this area were probably thinking of it as a camp site, and his officers were appalled when Morgan announced it was just the place to fight. They must have pointed out that the flanks of a position astride this mole hill were "in the air," and that the enemy would have every opportunity to surround, cut off, and annihilate him. But Morgan had also inquired thoroughly into Tarleton's methods of operations and he had an unorthodox deployment in mind for this unconventional battlefield.

The troops with which Morgan had left Charlotte were Howard's and Wm.

Washington's 600 light infantry and dragoons; about 300 of these were Md. and Del. Cont'ls. who had survived Camden, and 200 were Va. riflemen who, for the most part, had completed an enlistment as Cont'ls. and rejoined as volunteer militia. Washington's dragoons were survivors of MONCK'S CORNER and LENUD'S FERRY. About 500 militia joined Morgan before the battle; most of them, according to Col. Howard, arrived with Andrew Pickens after Morgan bivouacked at Cowpens, and Howard adds that Morgan did not decide to fight the next day until Pickens arrived (Lee, *Memoirs*, 222 *n.* and 226 *n.*). Although Howard should know, most historians disagree: Ward says Pickens arrived with only 70 men on the eve of battle and that almost 400 N.C., S.C., and Ga. militia had already joined, most of them while Morgan was in camp along the Pacolet (Ward, *W.O.R.*, 755); Kenneth Roberts says Pickens came in with 150 mounted riflemen early the night of the 16th, "and small detachments followed him noisily at intervals...." (*Cowpens*, 74) *

In their noisy camp on the grassy swale the night of 16–17 Jan., fires were lit, rations were distributed from wagons, food was cooked for supper and for breakfast, militia groups straggled in, and mounted patrols moved in

---

* In the absence of military records it is useless to attempt to estimate Morgan's exact strength. He himself reported having 800 in the battle. (Fisher, *Struggle*, 385 and *n.*, citing Myers, *Cowpens Papers*, 26) Ward goes into considerable detail as to the composition and strength of Morgan's command; his figures are not consistent, but they add up to about 1,050. (*Op. cit.*, 751, 752, 755, 757) He gives a detailed list of sources in the notes on p. 916.

and out. Amidst all this confusion Morgan hobbled among the campfires, half crippled by sciatica and rheumatism though he was, to make sure each detachment knew what it was to do the next day.

A forward line of 150 picked militia riflemen—Georgians commanded by Maj. John Cunningham and North Carolinians under Maj. Charles McDowell—would be concealed in the grass and behind trees. Their job was to fire twice and run. Now this was what militia usually did, but Dan Morgan wanted them to do it a special way. They were selected because they knew how to shoot. He wanted them to let the enemy get within 50 paces before they opened fire, and he wanted them to get two hits. Then they were to move straight back to the second line, firing at will as they withdrew. (American *riflemen,* to the astonishment of European soldiers, could reload and fire while running.)

The second line, commanded by Pickens, would be along the military crest, 150 yards behind the first. Here the bulk of the militia, 300 N.C. and S.C. troops, would wait for the 150 riflemen to drop back and reinforce them. They also were told to fire and fall back, but in a way the Old Wagoner had figured it out to fox Ben Tarleton (as Morgan called him). First, he wanted them also to get some hits before they pulled out. Hold your fire until they're within killing distance, he told them, then pick out the officers and sergeants. The militia were also warned about the tendency to shoot too high. When the enemy got within range for a bayonet charge and it was time to leave, everybody in the second line was to head around the left flank of the third line. Here they could reassemble in defilade and under the protection of the third line and the reserve.

The third and main battle line was 150 yards forward of the geographical crest, and 150 yards uphill from the second line. Commanded by Maj. John Howard, about 450 men would hold a front of approximately 400 yards. The Del. and Md. Cont'ls. were in the center, the Va. riflemen of Capts. Triplett and Tate were on their left and right, and Capt. Beale's small company of Ga. militia would be on the extreme right, next to Tate.

The reserve, consisting of Washington's 80 dragoons and Lt. Col. James McCall's 45 mounted Ga. infantry, would initially be posted half a mile behind the main battle position. (McCall's men were armed with sabers to fight from horseback.)

Many stories are told about Morgan's performance the night before the battle. In a sort of backwoods eve of Austerlitz, he apparently didn't overlook a trick. He'd heard a lot of talk about Carolinians being able to outshoot everyone else, he told the riflemen who would occupy the forward line— here was their chance to prove it, with all the rest of the army watching from up the hill. Morgan knew his men were scared of Tarleton, but they had also heard about what his Virginians had done at Saratoga, and the Old Wagoner had a way of talking to troops that made them like and trust him. Being an unsophisticated individual, he thought hate was a pretty good military motivation. He reminded his men of what the British and Tories had done to their property and their kinfolk. He probably *did* pull up his shirt to show the scars of the famous flogging he had taken from them years ago (see MORGAN).

Less dramatic, but probably more important, Morgan sent his men into battle fed and rested. In plenty of time before the enemy had completed his exhausting four-hour march to the battlefield the Americans were in position and waiting.

TARLETON'S APPROACH

Giving his men little sleep, Tarleton beat reveille at 2 A.M. He broke camp at 3 A.M., leaving the wagons behind, under guard, with orders to follow at daybreak, and led out with three light infantry companies. Behind them, and spaced out in the approved tactical manner, came the Legion infantry, 7th Regt., 71st Regt., a Royal Artillery detachment with two little, horse-carried 3-pd. cannon (GRASSHOPPERS), 50 troopers of the 17th Light Dragoons, and the Legion cavalry. A body of Tories is believed to have been present, but since they are not mentioned in the battle they may all have been guides. Total strength was about 1,100. The 250 infantry and 300 dragoons of his BRITISH LEGION, the 50 men of the 17th Dragoons, his gunners, and the 200 Highlanders of the 71st Regt. (1st Bn.) were seasoned troops. The 200 men of the 7th Regt. were recruits originally destined to garrison Ninety-Six. Although Ward comments that "in trained regulars Tarleton outnumbered him [Morgan] more than three to one," the British historian Fortescue sees it differently:

"The numerical superiority was slightly on Tarleton's side, but the quality inclined to the side of Morgan, whose militia were veterans in partisan warfare as well as practised marksmen. . . ." (*British Army*, III, 362–63)

After feeling their way cautiously for about two hours the advance guard reached Thicketty Creek an hour before dawn. (Dawn was shortly after 6 o'clock and sunrise an hour later.) Tarleton sent forward a cavalry patrol which soon made contact with an American patrol commanded by Capt. Inman, which clattered back to tell Morgan the news. (Heitman identifies a Joshua Inman as Capt. of Ga. Rangers, 1779–80; he may be the one.) Learning that Morgan's camp was five miles away, Tarleton sent Capt. Ogilvie forward with two troops—50 sabers—of the Legion to reinforce the advance guard and feel out the American position. About 6:45 Ogilvie rode out of the woods in full sight of the waiting but only dimly seen lines in the meadow. Sniffing suspiciously at the situation, he sent out a few horsemen for a closer look. Scattered shots from hidden marksmen sent the troopers scampering back into the woods with the information Tarleton wanted: Morgan had made a stand.

Although his troops had marched four miles over difficult terrain, most of it in darkness, Tarleton wasted no time getting ready to attack. Tory guides were able to brief him accurately on this well-known spot. He moved his troops out of the woods and into line about 400 yards in front of the first American position. Then, with orders to drive in the skirmishers—the standard opening move—Ogilvie's dragoons trotted out, spread into a thin line, and charged. The unseen riflemen picked their targets, aligned their sights, held their breaths, and fired. Even a horse cavalryman should have realized when the dragoons came back with 15 empty saddles out of 50 that something unorthodox had happened and might keep on happening, but Tarleton had to learn the hard way. He prepared to make a frontal assault.

From left to right he formed the 7th, the Legion infantry, and the three light infantry companies. A grasshopper went into action on each flank of the Legion infantry to hurry the withdrawal of the skirmishers, who dropped slowly back to Pickens' line, firing as they moved. (Bass, 156; Ward, 758) On

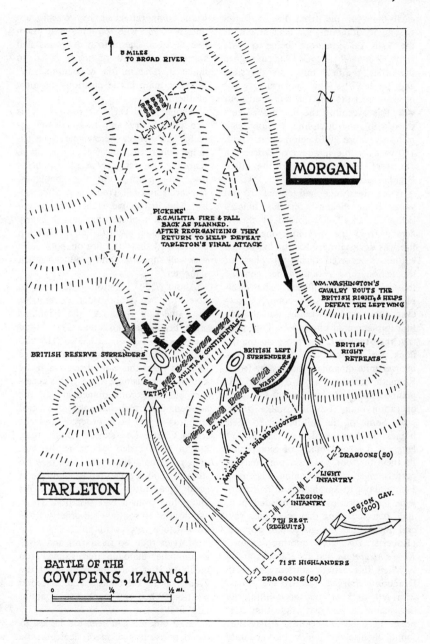

5 MILES
TO BROAD RIVER

MORGAN

PICKENS'
S.C. MILITIA FIRE & FALL
BACK AS PLANNED.
AFTER REORGANIZING THEY
RETURN TO HELP DEFEAT
TARLETON'S FINAL ATTACK

WM. WASHINGTON'S
CAVALRY ROUTS THE
BRITISH RIGHT, & HELPS
DEFEAT THE LEFT WING

BRITISH RESERVE SURRENDERS

BRITISH LEFT
SURRENDERS

BRITISH
RIGHT
RETREATS

VETERAN MILITIA & CONTINENTALS

WASHINGTON

S.C. MILITIA

AMERICAN SHARPSHOOTERS

DRAGOONS (50)

TARLETON

LIGHT
INFANTRY

LEGION
INFANTRY

LEGION CAV.
(200)

7TH REGT.
(RECRUITS)

BATTLE OF THE
COWPENS, 17 JAN '81

71 ST. HIGHLANDERS

DRAGOONS (50)

0   ¼   ½ MI.

each flank of the front line Tarleton posted 50 dragoons, the detachment of the 17th Lt. Dragoons being on the right. About 7 o'clock Tarleton gave the order, the field music set the step, and he led the line forward. A few nervous recruits on the left fired, but with this exception the line moved forward with good discipline. Waiting back in reserve were 200 Legion cavalry and, 150 yards to the left rear of where the 7th Regt. had started, were the kilted Highlanders.

When the range had closed to 100 yards from Pickens' line his officers bellowed "Fire!" Reinforced by the riflemen from the first line, the militia fire was devastating. Most of the British casualties occurred during this phase of the action, and about 40 per cent of those killed were officers. The disciplined British line kept coming, however, their bayonets ready, and the militia implemented phase two. That is to say, they took off. For those on the far flank, this involved an uphill run of a quarter mile diagonally across the front. Kenneth Roberts points out that this planned stampede was not the smooth operation many accounts make it appear. Some of the militia got to their horses and vanished. Lt. (Joseph ?) Hughes, a strong man "of remarkable fleetness on foot," put on the amazing performance of outrunning his men, facing about to harangue and flail them with his sword as they pounded past, and then repeating this procedure several times until he got them stopped. (Roberts, *op. cit.,* quoting Draper, *King's Mountain and Its Heroes*)

When this retreat started, the 17th Dragoons charged toward the American left to hack up the militia, but they came in for two unpleasant surprises in quick succession. First, they found themselves under the accurate fire of Triplett's Va. riflemen; then, they

were counterattacked by Washington and McCall, who outnumbered them five to two. The British dragoons fled for safety, but 10 of them failed to make it. The militia reassembled behind the main battle position—or most of them did.

About 7:15 Tarleton re-formed his line of infantry and resumed the attack. The British were cheering in triumph when the first volley hit them. Kneeling for greater accuracy, firing low, and picking out the epaulettes, Howard's line delivered volley after volley. The British were checked but not stopped. In a phase that lasted nearly half an hour (Ward, 760), Tarleton commented that "the fire on both sides was well supported and produced much slaughter."

About 7:30 Tarleton rode back to give Maj. McArthur orders to envelop the American right. As the Highland pipes began to skirl and 200 kilted veterans started forward, Maj. Howard ordered his right company to change front to meet this new threat—a tactic known as "refusing a flank." This necessary but dangerous maneuver led the adjacent units to believe that a general withdrawal had been ordered, and the entire Cont'l. line started to the rear, but in good order. To make the best of a movement that could not now be stopped, and seeing that it might be a good idea, after all, to extricate his entire line from a bad situation, Howard decided to continue an orderly withdrawal to a new position.

Morgan rode up in alarm, and after a dramatic dialogue that sounds too much as if it were made up after the event, said: "I'll choose you a second position. When you reach it, face about and fire!"

"Had not Morgan been too honest to claim praise for a mere accident, he might have credited himself with one of the most daring stratagems ever practiced in war," says Fortescue. (*Op. cit.*, 363) The British line rushed forward for the kill. From his position on the flank, where he had halted after his pursuit of the dragoons, Washington sent word to Morgan:

"They're coming on like a mob. Give them one fire, and I'll charge them."

Morgan got this message just as his line reached its new position, and he ordered Howard to face about and fire. The British were racing down the reverse slope, not 50 yards away, when the rebels turned, fired from the hip, and charged with the bayonet. About the same time, Washington and McCall hit their right flank and rear. It was just too much for troops who had tramped four hours through the wilderness, attacked a good half mile, continued despite heavy casualties to "rout" three lines of enemy marksmen —and now this.... The recruits of Maj. Timothy Newmarsh's 7th Regt. threw down their weapons and cried "Quarter!" The American officers acted fast enough to keep their men from making this "Tarleton's quarter," and they shouted to the other surrounded enemy, "Throw down your arms and we'll give you good quarter."

The veterans on the British right, although hit harder than the recruits, tried to escape to the rear, but were rounded up by the American cavalry before they covered 200 yards. The Highlanders and the dragoons of the left flank would not quit, however. About the time the troops of Howard's line were free to turn their entire strength against them, Pickens appeared on their flank with some of the militia, who had made almost a complete tour of the battlefield. As Maj. McArthur tried to fight his way out, Col. James Jackson led his Georgians into the center of the embattled Scots. Only when surrounded, locked in hand-to-hand combat, and after nine of their 16 officers were killed or wounded, did the Highlanders give up. McArthur handed his sword to Pickens, who had earned a sword that day.

Tarleton, meanwhile, had not quit either. When his horse collapsed, Dr. Robt. JACKSON insisted that the commander take his. Tarleton then rode back to his cavalry reserve—his own Legion cavalry—to lead them in a counterattack which he thought might save the day. The Americans were disorganized, and the 200 troopers were fresh. All 200 rode off and left him! "The dragoons of the Legion, ill disciplined at the best of times, and spoiled by the easy successes which Tarleton's energy had gained for them, were not the men to face so desperate a venture," explains Fortescue. (*Op. cit.*, 362) The handful of British artillerymen were still hurling round after round at the enemy, however. Some 40 men of the 17th Dragoons and 14 officers rallied around Tarleton, and he rushed to save the guns. Capts. (Richard?) Anderson and Kirkwood charged the guns and took them before Tarleton could intervene (Bass, 159); "they never did surrender," says Ward, "almost to a man they were struck down at their posts." (*Op. cit.*, 761)

Tarleton and his small force now retreated, but Washington followed in hot pursuit. He was leading the pack by about 30 yards when Tarleton turned back with two officers for a dramatic finale. Washington slashed at the officer on Tarleton's right and broke his saber off near the handguard. His intended victim was about to come down on Washington when a 14-year old bugler (or orderly) dropped the British's sword arm with a pistol shot in the shoulder. Sgt. Maj. Perry then saved his chief by deflecting the saber of the other British officer and wounding him. Tarleton charged Washington, who parried successfully with the broken saber. "Reining his charger in a circle, Tarleton snatched his pistol and fired. The ball missed Washington but wounded his horse. Having fired the last shot at Cowpens, Banastre galloped after his fleeting Green Horse." (Bass, *op. cit.,* 159) (Wm. Ranney's painting of this episode is in *Amer. Heritage Book of the Revolution,* 320.)

Tarleton's party arrived in the rear to find that the guards had cut loose the horses, abandoned the baggage, and fled. The Tory guides were looting the wagons. The dragoons chopped up or ran off these vultures, burned what they could, and rode for the main British camp. After rounding up his 200 dragoons, Tarleton crossed the Broad and entered the British camp on the 18th.

Morgan wasted no time gloating over his triumph. Leaving Pickens behind with some militia to take care of the dead, wounded, and captured, and gathering up what booty he could use, Morgan left the battlefield about noon, moved six miles toward the east and camped on the other side of Broad River. Pickens set up tents for the wounded (who were paroled), left them in care of the surgeons under a white flag, and caught up with Morgan on the 18th. Subsequent operations are covered under SOUTHERN CAMP'NS. OF GREENE.

NUMBERS AND LOSSES

The hour's fighting had cost the British 100 killed and 229 wounded. All the latter were captured, and an additional 600 were captured unwounded. Officer casualties (included in the above totals) were 66, of whom 39 were deader than herrings. Sixty Negro batmen were also captured, an interesting commentary on lightning warfare of the period. The booty included 100 dragoon horses, 800 muskets, 35 wagons, the colors of the 7th Regt., one traveling forge, and all the enemy's musical instruments. The two captured guns have an interesting history, which is covered under GRASSHOPPERS OF SARATOGA.

American losses were 12 killed and 60 wounded.

As for numbers engaged, a preceding footnote points out that American strength has been estimated at between 800 (Morgan's report) and about 1,050. In his final summary of Morgan's dispositions, Ward gives figures totaling 1,025. (*Op. cit.,* 757) This number is generally accepted.

As stated above under "Tarleton's Approach," the British strength is generally given as 1,100, including an unspecified number of gunners and Tories whose total is assumed to be 100. Only 600 infantrymen can be found in his order of battle (200 each in the 7th, 71st, and Legion), however, and it is a puzzle where the additional 200 captured muskets came from, unless Tarleton was carrying them in his baggage to supply Tory recruits.

COMMENTS AND CONTROVERSIES

Although the Battle of Cowpens saved half of Greene's army and destroyed a large part of Cornwallis'—depriving him of light troops when he needed them most—its farther-reaching effects were to raise patriot morale when it badly needed raising: Southern militia started turning out in greater numbers, and the North started sending the support that the South so badly needed. The substantial but not fatal British tactical reverse at Cowpens led Cornwallis into strategic errors that *were* fatal to the British at Yorktown.

For only the second time since Bunker Hill, Cowpens showed "what can be done with militia provided they are good marksmen and are commanded by competent officers who understand them." (F. V. Greene, *Rev. War,* 230)

The contention that the battle "proved a death-blow to Tarleton's reputation" (Trevelyan, *Amer. Rev.,* VI, 153) is not sound. It destroyed his "reputation" among older British officers in the South, who said the Cowpens disaster "was the consequence of trusting such a command to a boy like Tarleton" (*ibid.*), but Cornwallis is to blame for this. Tarleton's boyish "reputation" was well founded on his leadership of the British Legion in hit-and-run tactics; if this reputation was undeserved the fact was lost on the large body of N.C. militia he routed a mere two weeks later at TARRANT'S TAVERN, 1 Feb. It was not noticed at GUILFORD C.H., 15 Mar., where he operated not as an independent raider but in a stand-up-and-knock-down major engagement. As for his one and only action as commander of a combined force of infantry, cavalry, and artillery, Fortescue says:

". . . Morgan's situation with an impassable river in his rear certainly invited attack, and the flanking movement whereby Tarleton strove to snatch the victory was well and boldly conceived. . . . It seems to me, therefore, that Tarleton deserves no blame, for the fortune of war was his chief enemy; though, looking to the behaviour of the dragoons of the Legion, there can be little doubt but that the best men won the day." (*British Army,* III, 363)

Cornwallis acquitted Tarleton of all blame, as he had acquitted Ferguson for Kings Mountain (*ibid.,* 364), but Bass says, "There was never again between them that free, spontaneous, almost father-son relationship." (*Op. cit.* 160) When a full report reached London of what Bass calls "the worst British defeat since the surrender of Burgoyne at Saratoga," the *London Chronicle* of 29 Mar. said: "By all accounts Col. Tarleton was never more distinguished for spirit and gallantry than on this occasion." (*Ibid.,* 160, 162) It takes more than spirit and gallantry to make a great commander of combined arms, but these qualities were the basis of this "reputation" that was supposed to have been destroyed. Trevelyan's statement, echoed by subsequent writers, is therefore misleading. Tarleton took a hell of a beating at Cowpens and there is nobody the Americans would have rather seen it happen to, but one more thought should be considered What if Cornwallis had been at Kings Mountain where Tarleton's plan called for him to be? Is it not possible that Tarleton's defeat would have resulted in giving Cornwallis time to destroy Morgan as he retreated? Is it not likely Greene could then have been defeated in detail? Whose "reputation" would then be where?

Morgan's victory must rank as a classic, any way you look at it. By magnificent personal leadership of precisely the sort needed for the occasion, and with a few outstanding subordinates (Pickens, Wm. Washington, Howard), he achieved a superior victory with "inferior" troops, weapons, and terrain. The inferior troops, militia, usually ran in battle, but he shaped his tactics so they would first do some good and then run the right way. The inferior weapons, *rifles,* well known in Europe as a sporting arm but spurned by professional soldiers because of their slow rate of fire, were used at Cowpens with devastating effect by the militia marksmen. The terrain was "inferior" because Morgan's flanks were in the air, a river was at his back, and a tactical defeat would have meant annihilation; yet without these "defects" the militia probably would not have fought. Eliminate any one of these elements—leadership, militia, rifles, terrain—and the Cowpens would have been the scene of another slaughter by Tarleton; Morgan combined them for just the opposite effect.

Exactly *when* Morgan decided to fight at Cowpens and exactly *why* will never be known. The above account follows the more or less accepted view that he chose the battlefield deliberately and planned the action some 12 hours before it started. At the other extreme is the view that Morgan was surprised in camp the morning of the battle, not having suspected that Tarleton would make a night march to attack at dawn.

As for *why* Morgan fought at Cowpens, it is logical and fair to start with his own explanation, which was given, however, with the benefit of hindsight: "I would not have had a swamp in view of my militia on any consideration; they would have made for it, and nothing would have detained them from it. And, as to covering my wings, I knew my adversary, and was perfectly sure I should have nothing but downright fighting. As to retreat, it was the very thing I wished to cut off all hope of. I would have thanked Tarleton had he surrounded me with his cavalry. It would have been better than placing my own men in the rear to shoot down those who broke from the ranks. When men are forced to fight they will sell their lives dearly and I knew that the dread of Tarleton's cavalry would give due weight to the protection of my bayonets and keep my troops from breaking as Buford's regiment did [at WAXHAWS]. Had I crossed the river, one half of my militia would immediately have abandoned me." (Quoted in Ward, 756, from Wm. Johnson, *Greene,* I, 576)

In apparent contradiction to the self-confidence that marks this after-the-fact explanation are Morgan's letters of 4 and 15 Jan. to Greene expressing his determination to retreat, and his later opposition to Greene's bold strategy in continuing the retreat toward the lower Dan River rather than heading for the western hills for safety. (Under SOUTHERN CAMP'NS. OF GREENE, see sections headed "Cornwallis Reacts" and "Hare and Hounds.")

Ward says Greene's explanation "seems labored, to excuse an unmilitary decision. The truth seems to be that Morgan, a fighter by nature, was irked by being obliged to retreat before Tarleton, and turned on his foe because he wanted to give battle, disregarding the weakness of his position." (*Ibid.*) Yet this determination to fight must have come over the Old Wagoner after he wrote Greene on the 15th, and after Tarleton had maneuvered him out of his defensive position on the Pacolet later that same day. It is possible that when Morgan saw the Cowpens he suddenly realized the possibilities for his "dream battle," as Napoleon did when he saw the field of Austerlitz. I am more inclined to agree with Kenneth Roberts that after spending the day of the 16th "running for dear life" (see above) Morgan realized he could not get away. Henry Lee thinks Morgan could have gotten across the Broad River to a much better battlefield, but ". . . sat down at the Cowpens to give refreshment to his troops, with a resolution no longer to avoid action, should his enemy persist in pressing it. Being apprised at the dawn of day of Tarleton's advance, he instantly prepared for battle. This decision grew out of irritation of temper, which appears to have overruled the suggestions of his sound and discriminating judgment." (Lee, *Memoirs,* 226)

Light-Horse Harry was not there, so his opinion that Morgan could have safely continued his retreat is questionable—as is his opinion that Morgan's decision to fight was made only when

Tarleton approached—but his views are quoted because they have influenced subsequent writers. Morgan's military reputation, record, and rheumatism would, however, support Lee's view that he fought out of exasperation, if not desperation, at Cowpens.

"The disposition for battle was masterly," however, says Lee; this was after all the important thing. *When* and *why* he decided to fight at Cowpens are academic questions whose answers cannot dim the laurels he won there.

COX HILL, N.Y. See FORT COCKHILL.

CRAIG, James Henry. 1748–1812. British officer. Son of Hew Craig, who for many years was civilian and military judge at Gibraltar, James was gazetted ensign in the 30th Regt. when he was 15 but got leave of absence to attend military schools in Europe before taking up his military duties. Having then served as A.D.C. to the Lt. Gov. of Gibraltar (Robert Boyd) and advanced to Capt. of the 47th Regt. on 14 Mar. '71, he accompanied his regiment to America in 1774. He was seriously wounded at Bunker Hill, led his company in the action at Trois Rivières, Can., and served with the advance guard in Carleton's subsequent advance to Crown Point in 1776. In Burgoyne's Offensive he was present at the capture of Ticonderoga, was wounded at Hubbardton, and fought in the First Battle of Saratoga. His performance had been so outstanding that he was sent home with Burgoyne's dispatches (*D.N.B.*) and in Dec. '77, shortly after reaching England, was rewarded by a majority (without purchase) in the newly raised 82d Regt. of Col. Francis MacLean. Returning almost immediately to America, he served in Nova Scotia and took part in MacLean's Penobscot Expedition of July–Aug. '79.

Maj. Craig commanded the remnants of the two flank companies and two other companies of the 82d to accompany Leslie's force that left N.Y. on 16 Oct. '80 for operations in the Chesapeake. Diverted by subsequent developments in the SOUTHERN THEATER, they reached Charleston exactly two months later. (Clinton, *Amer. Reb.*, 148, 214, 231, 419)

As commandant at WILMINGTON, N.C., 1 Feb.–18 Nov. '81, Craig performed the services for which he is famous in the Revolution. He evacuated the town in time to escape capture and took up a new position within the Charleston defenses. (See JOHNS ISLAND, 28–29 Dec. '81)

Referred to as Maj. Craig in official correspondence from Charleston as late as 30 Nov. '81 (Clinton, *op. cit.*, 588), he was promoted before he left America. (*D.N.B.*) He became Lt. Col. of the 16th Regt. in Ireland, was promoted to Col. in 1790, and took advantage of his peacetime leisure to study his profession. He traveled on the Continent and observed Prussian tactics. After a correspondence with David Dundas he became the first regimental commander to adopt the latter's new system of drill. In the war with France he fought in the Netherlands and on 3 Oct. '94 was promoted to Maj. Gen.

When an expedition was organized to capture the Dutch colony at the Cape of Good Hope, Craig took command of a force escorted by Adm. ELPHINSTONE's squadron to South Africa. They were to rendezvous with another force under Gen. Alured CLARKE, but not finding the latter on their arrival, Craig and Elphinstone established a beachhead at Simon's Bay on 14 Aug. '95 and the troops pushed toward Capetown. Boer militia turned out to oppose the British, and Craig was being pressed hard when Clarke arrived on 3 Sept. to save the day. The Dutch surrendered on 14 Sept.

Craig remained as Mil. Gov. until 1797, when he was knighted (K.B.) and ordered back to England. Immediately sent to take command of the division in Bengal, he saw no fighting in India but by sound, if not universally popular, leadership prevented a mutiny. He was picked to command an expedition to Manila, but the operation was canceled. (*D.N.B.*) Promoted to Lt. Gen. on 1 Jan. 1801, he returned to England in 1802 and commanded forces in the eastern district. In Mar. 1805, although in bad health, he was appointed a "local (full) Gen." and sent with 7,000 troops to the Kingdom of Naples, where he was supposed to act in conjunction with the Russians and Neapolitans against French forces in northern Italy. Learning of Napoleon's victories at Ulm and Austerlitz, Craig had the good strategic sense to ignore the local political uproar and pull back to a defensible position in Sicily. In Mar. 1806, because of bad health, he turned his command over to Gen. John Stuart. In Aug. 1807 he was appointed Gov. Gen. of Canada. This duty was marked by antagonism from French Canadians and from Americans, whose resentment of British naval policies was leading toward war. Despite his lack of political qualifications, Sir James emerged from this unpleasant duty respected if not beloved. He resigned his post in Oct. 1811. On 1 Jan. of the next year he was promoted to full Gen. and 11 days later he died.

Sir Henry Bunbury's *Narrative,* which deals with Craig's service in the Mediterranean, describes this remarkable soldier as "very short, broad, and muscular, a pocket Hercules, but with sharp, neat features, as if chiselled in ivory. Not popular, for he was hot, peremptory, and pompous ... [he was] clever, generous to a fault, and a warm and unflinching friend to those he liked." (Quoted in *D.N.B.*)

CRAIK, James. 1730–1814. Chief physician and surgeon of the Cont'l. army. Scotland. Son of the Scottish squire whose gardener was the father of John Paul Jones, Craik studied medicine at Edinburgh. In 1750 he emigrated to America, practicing medicine in the West Indies, Norfolk, Va., and Winchester, Va. He was physician at the fort of Winchester, and on 7 Mar. '54 became surgeon of Col. Fry's Regt. The next year he was with Washington at Great Meadows, tended the mortally wounded Braddock after the latter's defeat, and became Washington's chief medical officer when the latter became C. in C. of Va. forces on 14 Aug. '55. Thereafter he was closely associated with Washington, accompanying him on a trip to the interior in 1770 and becoming senior medical officer in 1777 of the military district bounded by the Hudson and Potomac rivers. He organized the hospitals for Rochambeau's expeditionary force, became Chief Hospital Physician of the Cont'l. Army on 6 Oct. '80, and Chief Physician and Surgeon of the Army on 3 Mar. '81. (Heitman) He warned Washington of the "Conway Cabal," naming Mifflin as a conspirator. (A. C. Malloch in *D.A.B.*) Serving in the army until 23 Dec. '83, he returned to be Physician General on 19 July '98 and was honorably discharged 15 June 1800. He attended WASHINGTON in the latter's final illness and left an account of his treatment.

CRANE, John. 1744–1805. Cont'l. officer. Mass. At 15 he served in the French and Indian War. He became a housewright and was one of the Boston Sons of Liberty. At his shop (modern Tremont St. near Hollis) some of the "Indians" dressed for the Boston Tea Party. A tea chest fell on Crane as he was working in the hold, knocking him unconscious and leading his companions to believe he was dead. The next year, 1774, he moved to Providence because business in Boston was at a standstill. As a Capt. in Gridley's regt. of Mass. Arty. (3 May '75) he took part in the Boston Siege and on 10 Dec. was promoted to Maj. in Knox's regt. Meanwhile, he had been active in skirmishes at the Neck and on 8 July had led a successful attack against an advance post. He was wounded in the foot on 14 Sept. '76 while shelling a man of war from Corlear's Hook (E. River), N.Y. On 1 Jan. '77 he was named Col., 3d Arty. After raising this regiment he was mentioned for his service in Sullivan's operations at Newport, under Gates in the Saratoga battles, and in the defense of Ft. Mifflin (Red Bank), N.J. On 17 June '83 he transferred to the Corps of Arty., and on 30 Sept. he was breveted B.G. Resigning on 3 Nov. '83, he went into the lumber business. Failing in this, he occupied a 200-acre grant at Whiting, Me., which he had received for war service. In 1790 he became a judge in the court of common pleas. (*D.A.B.*)

CRAWFORD, William. 1732–1782. Frontiersman, Cont'l. officer. Va.–Pa. Born in what became Berkeley co., in the northern part of the Shenandoah Valley, his long association with Washington started when the latter came to the frontier in 1749 to survey the vast holdings of Lord Fairfax. The two men, who were the same age, about the same size, and similar in temperament, were together on the expeditions of Braddock (1775) and Forbes (1758). (See COLO-NIAL WARS) In the latter operation, the expedition to Ft. Duquesne, Crawford commanded a company. After taking part in Pontiac's War (1763) and becoming familiar with the rich region S.E. of Pittsburgh then claimed by Va. and Pa., Crawford built a cabin in 1765 on Braddock's Road at Stewart's Cross-

ing. (Anderson, *post.*, 3) In the "howling wilderness" where modern Connellsville is located, about 35 miles S.E. of Pittsburgh, he spent two years clearing 376 acres, probably with the help of slave labor (*ibid.*), and developed the best known and most hospitable place west of the mountains. Joined by his wife and three children in the spring of 1766, Crawford established himself as an Indian trader, surveyor, and farmer.

In 1770 Washington again visited Crawford (13 Oct.–25 Nov.) and the two men traveled extensively through the Ohio Valley. They shared an interest in land speculation, and selected and surveyed vast tracts for Washington, for Washington's brothers Samuel and John, and for their cousin Lund Washington. George Washington referred to his lands—over 40,000 acres—as "the first choice of" and "the cream of the country." On 21 Sept. '67 Washington had written Crawford from Mt. Vernon: "If you will be at the trouble of seeking out the lands, I will take upon me the part of securing them as soon as there is a possibility of doing it, and will moreover be at the cost and charges of surveying and patenting the same. You shall then have such a reasonable proportion of the whole as we may fix upon at our first meeting." (Sparks, *Writings of Washington,* II, 348, quoted in Anderson, *post.*) Lord Dunmore visited Crawford in 1773, and only the death of Washington's step-daughter kept him from making the trip also.

In Dunmore's War Crawford was commissioned Capt. (May '74). On 8 May '74 he wrote Washington that he was starting for Ft. Pitt with 100 men, and on 20 Sept., having meanwhile been promoted to Maj. and given command of 500 men, he wrote Washington that he was leaving that day from Ft. Pitt with the first division of Va. troops for a rendezvous with Dunmore's second division near the mouth of the Hocking River, where he had previously selected some fine bottom land for Washington. "I am ... to erect a post on your Bottom." (Anderson, *post.*, 7, quoting Butterfield, *Letters,* 52) During the operations that followed, Crawford destroyed two of the three Mingo villages near the site of Steubenville, he built Ft. Fincastle at WHEELING, rescued several white captives, and took 14 Indians prisoner.

In 1770 Crawford had been appointed justice for what then was Cumberland co., Va., where his home was located. When Gov. Penn designated this region part of Bedford co., Pa. (9 Mar. '71), Crawford and Arthur ST. CLAIR were among the local leaders appointed justices of the peace (11 Mar.). And when a further reorganization on 26 Feb. '73 took land from Bedford to make Westmoreland co., Pa., Crawford became a justice and the president judge of the courts. Arthur St. Clair wrote Gov. Penn on 22 July '74: "Captain Crawford, the president of our court, seems to be the most active Virginia officer in their service. He is now down the river at the head of a number of men, which is his second expedition. How is it possible for a man to serve two colonies in direct antagonism to each other at the same time?" (Anderson, *post.*, 6, citing *Washington–Irvine Corresp.,* 114) Continuing to support Va. in the boundary dispute renewed in 1775, Crawford was "superceded" from his Pa. office in Westmoreland co. and lost popularity with some of his neighbors. Colonial boundary disagreements were temporarily put aside on the eve of the Revolution, however, and Crawford became a prominent member of the committee of defense organized at Pittsburgh after a meeting on 16 May '75. When Crawford offered his services to the Council

of Safety in Philadelphia they were not accepted, but Va. authorities welcomed his offer. He was appointed Lt. Col. of the 5th Va. on 12 Jan. '76, according to the *Washington–Irvine Corresp.* (p. 116), or on 13 Feb., according to Heitman. He quickly recruited a regiment, and on 11 Oct. '76 the Cont'l. Cong. appointed him Col. of the 7th Va., backdating this commission to 14 Aug. '76.

Col. Crawford, now in his mid-40's, led his regiment in the battles of Long Island, Trenton, and Princeton. His exact status during the Philadelphia Campaign is uncertain. According to Heitman he resigned on 22 Mar. '77; Alexander McClanachan took command of the 7th Va. on this date and the regiment was led by Maj. John Cropper at Brandywine. The mystery is somewhat clarified by the following passage from Anderson: "In August [1777] Crawford was with Washington near Philadelphia, using all his powers ... to keep the British out of that city; and his services later on, at the head of a detachment of 300 light armed men acting as scouts, were of the highest value, and so regarded by Washington. 'He rendered efficient service,' and 'took an active and prominent part' in the Battle of Brandywine, where he 'came near being captured;' and afterwards fought with his usual bravery at Germantown. Washington received a letter from General [Joseph] Reed, saying that Crawford, then with him, was 'a very good officer.' " (*Op. cit.,* 9–10, citing *Washington–Crawford Letters,* p. x)

In Nov. '77 the Cont'l. Cong. asked that Washington send Crawford to serve under Gen. Hand at Pittsburgh as commander of regulars and militia in the Western Dept. Crawford visited York briefly to get instructions from Cong., and returned to the frontier. In the spring of 1778 he built Ft. Crawford (so named by Gen. Hand), and in May he took command of the new Va. regiment that Gen. McIntosh had raised. McIntosh succeeded Hand in Aug. '78 and the next month Crawford's command included the troops at Ft. Pitt, the militia raised on the frontier, and those from other parts of Va.

Meanwhile Crawford had an important part in the establishment of FORTS MCINTOSH and LAURENS, and he commanded Ft. Crawford. George Rogers Clark invited him to take part in his WESTERN OPERATIONS of 1778, but Crawford did not feel he could leave his other duties and declined. When Forts Laurens and McIntosh were abandoned in Aug. '79 the Indians pushed their raids deeper into the white settlements of the Ohio country and Crawford led a number of small punitive expeditions in retaliation. In 1779 he also took part in Brodhead's Expedition. The next year he visited Cong. and succeeded in getting badly needed increases in appropriations for western operations.

Crawford had long advocated an offensive against the Sandusky region, but it was not until 1782, when he was looking forward to the pursuit of personal affairs and the "art of being Grandfather" (as the French say), that renewed Tory-Indian depredations stirred the settlers and the central government into organizing such an expedition. Now 50 years old and the veteran of many a narrow escape from the Indians, Crawford resisted the movement to give him command of this enterprise, but Gen. William Irvine—Regular Army commander of the Western Dept.—and others finally prevailed on him to accept. The will he made on 16 May '82, two days before leaving home, shows the extent of his estate: in addition to other property, he left his original 376 acres and three slaves to his wife; another slave and 500 acres to John, his only son; and 400 acres to each of his three grandchildren.

After CRAWFORD'S DEFEAT, 4–5 June '82, the Americans started a disorganized retreat. Not seeing his son John, his son-in-law William Harrison, his nephew William Crawford, nor his aide, Lt. Rose, Crawford had fallen some distance to the rear when he met the expedition's surgeon, Dr. Knight. With two other stragglers they finally started following the retreating column and later fell in with Capt. Biggs and Lt. Ashley. On 7 June, about 2 P.M., the party was surprised by a body of Delawares. Crawford, for some reason, ordered his party not to fire. (Anderson, op. cit., 26) The others escaped, but Crawford and Knight were captured and taken about half a mile to the Indian camp, where they found John McKinley, formerly an officer of the 13th Va., and eight other prisoners. On 10 June the captives and their 17 guards started marching toward the Half King's town, on the Upper Sandusky, 33 miles away. Here they met the renegade Simon Girty, who allegedly promised to use his influence in getting them freed; Girty may well have been sincere, but it is doubtful whether he could have prevented the ensuing atrocities even if he had tried. The morning of 11 June Capt. William Caldwell, who had commanded in the action of 4–5 June (see CRAWFORD'S DEFEAT), reached Half King's Town with the Delaware chiefs Capt. Pipe and Wingenund. Capt. Pipe, who knew Crawford well, personally painted the prisoners black (Indian sign of doom), and they then started walking toward the village of the Wyandots. Four of the nine prisoners soon were tomahawked and scalped. When the party reached the place where Upper Sandusky now stands, their route was changed toward the Delaware village on the Tymochtee Creek. During a break in the march the prisoners were seated on the ground and a number of squaws and boys proceeded to tomahawk all of them but Crawford and Knight.

CRAWFORD'S DEATH

About 4 o'clock on the afternoon of Tuesday, 11 June '82, the torture of Crawford started at a spot about seven miles N.W. of Upper Sandusky, between modern Carey and Crawford. The place was on a low piece of bottom land on the east bank of the Tymochtee Creek. (Anderson, *op. cit.*, 31 and *n.*) The details of Crawford's death are particularly horrible, but in the interests of historical accuracy they must be given. The *Narrative* of Dr. Knight, an eyewitness who expected to share Crawford's fate, is the basis for the following account.

Six or seven yards from a 15-foot post a fire of long hickory poles had been built so that the poles were burned through the middle. "Distinguished guests" present for the occasion were the two Delaware chiefs (Capt. Pipe and Wingenund), some Wyandots, the notorious renegades Simon Girty and Mathew Elliott, and possibly another white officer. Around them were about 35 braves and twice that number of squaws and boys. Crawford was stripped and the two prisoners were beaten with sticks and fists. The colonel's hands were bound behind him and a rope was run from his wrists to the foot of the post, leaving enough slack for him to circle the post once or twice and return. Dr. Knight was bound and held a few yards away.

Capt. Pipe then made an inflammatory speech, probably with many a reference to the GNADENHUETTEN MASSACRE, after which the braves fired at least 70 charges of powder into the naked prisoner's body. They then closed in on him and apparently cut off his ears, since Knight saw blood running down both sides of Crawford's head after the Indians cleared away. Three or four Indians at a time then ringed the post and prodded the captive with the burning ends of the hickory poles, forcing him to move back and forth at the end of his rope. The squaws then entered the game, scooping up live coals and throwing them in Crawford's path until the post was ringed with embers and bits of burning wood. At this point Crawford begged Girty to shoot him, but the renegade called back that he had no gun and turned to laugh with his Indian associates over the joke. Knight estimated that this phase of the torture lasted almost two hours before the victim fell face down in the embers. The savages then scalped him and repeatedly tossed the gory mop into the doctor's face shouting "He is your great captain." When an old squaw threw live coals and ashes onto Crawford's head and back, the prisoner rose again to walk around the post while the savages prodded him with burning sticks. At this point Knight was dragged away, but the end of the story is supplied by Capt. Caldwell in his letter of 13 June to his superior in Detroit: "Crawford died like a hero; never changed his countenance, tho' they scalped him alive, and then laid hot ashes upon his head; after which they roasted him by a slow fire." (Butterfield, *Girtys,* 183)

Knight escaped the morning of 13 June and after wandering through the wilderness for three weeks he reached Ft. Pitt at 7 o'clock the morning of 4 July.

Authorities. A long biographical sketch of Crawford by James H. Anderson is in *Ohio Archaeological and Historical Pubs.,* VI (1898), 1–34; the article is illustrated with pictures of

Crawford, Dunmore, Irvine, "Battle Island—Crawford's Battle Ground," Maj. A. S. DePeyster (commandant at Detroit), Simon Girty (a caricature of little value), Baron de Rosenthal (Lt. Rose), and "The Burning of Crawford at the Stake." An article by W. H. Hunter, "The Pathfinders of Jefferson County," in the same volume has an account of Crawford's expedition and his death. (*Pp.* 149–58) Both of these authors draw heavily from the works of Consul W. Butterfield: *History of the Girtys, Crawford's Sandusky Expedition, Washington–Crawford Letters,* and *Washington–Irvine Correspondence.* The last work includes reports and correspondence of British (Tory) leaders in Crawford's Defeat. Narratives of Crawford's expedition were left by the guide John Slover, by John Leith, by Lt. Francis Dunlevy (or Dunlavey), and— the best known—by Dr. John Knight. A sketch of Crawford by Edmund K. Alden is in *D.A.B.*

CRAWFORD'S DEFEAT (Battles of Sandusky and Olentangy), Ohio, 4–5 June '82. As mentioned in the article on William CRAWFORD, this frontier leader and close friend of Washington had long advocated an expedition to the Upper Sandusky region, where Tories and Indians rallied for their raids against the Pa.–Va. frontier. (See also FT. MCINTOSH.) After reluctantly agreeing to accept the leadership of this expedition—which he felt was about three years too late insofar as his personal participation was concerned—Col. Crawford left his home on 18 May, rode to Ft. Pitt for final instructions from Gen. William Irvine, and went on to Mingo Bottom. Here, about three miles below modern Steubenville, the forces were assembling. In the election of officers Crawford received 235 votes to become commander of the 480 volunteers. A close second was Maj.

David Williamson, with 230 votes, who became the second in command. Other "Field Majors," in order of rank, were Thomas Gaddis, John McClelland, and a Maj. Brinton. Brig. Maj. was Daniel Leet. Guides were Thomas Nicholson, John Slover, and Jonathan Zane. Two men had been assigned by Gen. Irvine after Crawford requested additional officers: one was Dr. John Knight, surgeon, who left the valuable narrative of the expedition, and the other was Irvine's A.D.C., known in the American army as Lt. Rose. This remarkable individual, the only Russian to fight with the Americans during the War of Independence, is covered under his real name, Baron de ROSENTHAL. Other volunteers were John Crawford, the colonel's only son; Maj. William Harrison of the famous Va. family, who was the colonel's son-in-law; and William Crawford, his nephew.

In *Crawford's Sandusky Expedition,* Consul W. Butterfield says, "The project was as carefully considered, and as authoritatively planned as any military enterprise in the west during the Revolution" (quoted by Anderson, *post.,* 18), but the enemy knew all about the expedition long before it got started. "It is said that Indians were on the hill back of Mingo, watching every movement made by the small patriot army; they knew the plans of the commander as they were talked over in the councils of war, and therefore the Indian forces at Sandusky were prepared for the onslaught." (Hunter, *post.,* 151)

The 150-mile approach march, except for 30 miles through almost unbroken forest, followed the straightest possible line toward the objective. The entire force was well mounted, and in the first four days they covered 60 miles to the abandoned Moravian settlements where the GNADENHUETTEN MASSACRE had taken place less than a month earlier. On 3 June they camped near the site of modern Wyandot, nine miles S.W. of Bucyrus. The next day they reached Sandusky Old Town, about three miles S.E. of modern Upper Sandusky, and the Indian village was deserted. About three and a half miles N.E. of Upper Sandusky, in a grove situated on high ground rising from the Sandusky Plain—a place later called Battle Island—the American scouts made contact with a sizable enemy force.

The latter was commanded by Capt. William Caldwell of Butler's Rangers, who had about 100 Rangers from Detroit and 200 Indians initially. Indian leaders were Capt. Pipe and Wingenund of the Delawares, the Wyandot chief Zhaus-sho-toh, and the renegades Simon GIRTY, Alexander McKee, and Mathew Elliott.

A two-day skirmish took place, both sides keeping their distance and firing at long range. Crawford lost five killed and 19 wounded the first day, and the patriots claimed the advantage. Caldwell reported one Ranger, an interpreter (Le Vellier), and four Indians killed; and three Rangers (including himself, shot through both legs) and eight Indians wounded in the two-day action. The afternoon of the second day the Americans realized, to their consternation, why they had had the advantage thus far: Caldwell had been waiting for reinforcements. John Leith's narrative says, "we heard a cannon fire at Upper Sandusky." (Quoted in Anderson, *post.,* 23 *n.*) A detachment of Rangers had arrived from Detroit with two field pieces (probably GRASSHOPPERS) and a mortar (coehorn?). About 140 Shawnees and some more "lake Indians" had also arrived and were working around the flanks and rear of the patriots. About 9 P.M. the latter started withdrawing but this movement turned into

a panic as small arms and artillery fire cut into them. Most of the Americans got through the encircling Indians, but some were cut off and annihilated. Maj. McClelland, leading the advance guard, was fatally wounded.

About 2 P.M. the next day, 6 June, Crawford turned and made a stand about five miles from the site of Bucyrus near Olentangy Creek. Lt. Rose reported a loss of three Americans killed and eight wounded in a one-hour action. Maj. Williamson led most of the volunteers safely to Mingo Bottom, where they arrived 13 June. Crawford's capture and horrible death are covered in his biographical sketch, above. Maj. William Harrison and young William Crawford were captured and tortured to death; John Slover escaped and reported seeing their bodies at Wapatomica.

Authorities are cited at the end of the article on CRAWFORD.

See map "Northwest Frontier" on page 254.

CRESAP, Michael. 1742–1775. Border leader and Cont'l. officer. Md. The son of a famous pioneer, Thomas Cresap (*c.* 1702–*c.* 1790), Michael was born in Md. but settled near Wheeling. When hostile Indians made it impossible for him to continue clearing land he took the field against them and was blamed by LOGAN for a massacre that led to DUNMORE'S (OR CRESAP'S) WAR, 1774. Although Logan's accusation has been discredited it has given Cresap a place in history. ("When Gibson reported Logan's speech, the charge against Cresap was laughed at as ridiculous; and George Rogers Clarke, who was standing by, said, 'He must be a very great man, as the Indians palmed every thing that happened upon his shoulders.' " [Lossing, II, 490 *n.*])

A Capt. during the war sometimes known by his name, Cresap was appointed Capt., 1st Co. Md. Rifles, on 21 June, and accepted this Md. commission to raise a company of riflemen from Ohio and western Md. Although plagued by sickness since 1774, to the extent that he had been unable to resume his land clearing around Wheeling (*D.A.B.*), he marched his company 550 miles in 22 days to become the first southern unit to join Washington around Boston. Two months later (about 15 Oct.) he was forced by illness to give up his command, and on 17 Oct. '75 he died in N.Y.C. at the age of 33. He was buried in Trinity churchyard.

CRESAP'S WAR. Alternate name for DUNMORE'S WAR, 1774.

"CRITICAL TERRAIN." An esoteric term used by modern students of tactics and strategy, it is applied to any natural or man-made feature whose control would give either opponent a "marked advantage." In many instances "critical terrain" is immediately apparent: see KINGS BRIDGE, N.Y. Less obvious features, however, were DORCHESTER HEIGHTS (Boston), Mount Defiance at TICONDEROGA, July '77, and the ford (or bridge) at BENNINGTON.

CROMOT DU BOURG, Baron de. French officer. According to Heitman this officer entered the French Army in 1768, was promoted to 2d Lt. 18 Mar. '70, to Capt. on 24 Feb. '74, and was a Capt. of Dragoons on half pay in 1776. (Heitman, 649) He was Rochambeau's aide from 26 Mar. to 18 Nov. '81, and left a valuable journal. Part of this was published in Balch, *The French in America*, and still more in *Mag. Am. Hist.* (vols. 4 and 7) under the title "Diary of a French Officer (Presumed to be that of Baron Cromot du Bourg, aid to Rochambeau)." (Freeman, *Washington*, V, 520–21, 530)

CROMPO HILL. See COMPO HILL.

CROOKED BILLET, Pa., 1 May '78. When the British occupied winter quarters in Philadelphia, about 450 Pa. militia were posted at Crooked Billet, 15 miles N.N.E., to interfere with the enemy's supply activities. By the end of Apr. this force, commanded by Brig. Gen. John Lacey, had been reduced by expiration of enlistments to fewer than 60 fit for duty. The morning of 1 May, Lacey suddenly found himself virtually surrounded by a large force: Lt. Col. Robert Abercromby was to his front with 400 light infantry and a detachment of light horse; Maj. Simcoe had gotten behind him with 300 of his Rangers. Lacey withdrew into a wood where he was able to hold off the enemy temporarily. After a two-mile retreat he executed a sudden change of direction that extricated his command. He had been forced to abandon his baggage, and he reported 26 killed and eight or 10 seriously wounded. The British lost nine men wounded. (Ward, *W.O.R.*, 555)

CROSSWICKS, N.J. Eight miles S.E. of Trenton and three and a half miles E. of Bordentown, this place figured in the TRENTON raid and the Monmouth campaign. Although the *A.A.*–Heitman list of actions does not include Crosswicks, Elias DAYTON of the 3d N.J. is widely reported (*D.A.B.*, Appleton's, Lossing) to have had his horse killed there. The action may have taken place about 23 June '78 at a point on Crosswicks Creek, four miles from Trenton, where the British encountered difficulty in rebuilding a drawbridge. (Freeman, *Washington*, V, 15)

CROTON RIVER, N.Y., 14 May '81. Advancing under cover of darkness, De Lancey's Tories crossed the Croton and surprised the outpost commanded by Col. Christopher Greene. Maj. Ebenezer Flagg fell mortally wounded after emptying his pistols at the Tories. According to Henry Lee:

"... the ruffians (unworthy the appellation of soldiers), [then] burst open the door of Greene's apartment [in a farm house]. Here the gallant veteran singly received them with his drawn sword. Several fell beneath the arm accustomed to conquer, till at length, overpowered by numbers, and faint from the loss of blood streaming from his wounds, barbarity triumphed over valor." (*Memoirs,* 590)

Apparently his body was mutilated after he fell: Lee quotes an unidentified source as saying that Greene had seven severe sword and bayonet wounds in the arms and abdomen in addition to "several sword-cuts on the head, and many in different parts of the body." Oliver De Lancey did not lead his Tories on this occasion. (*Ibid.*)

CROWN POINT, N.Y. About 10 miles N. of Ticonderoga on the W. shore of Lake Champlain, Crown Point was the scene of a battle between Champlain and the Iroquois in 1609 that started the long enmity between the French and that Indian confederation. Dutch and English traders later established a trading post there. In 1731 the French built Ft. Frédéric to mark the beginning of Crown Point's history as a military site. Colonial and English expeditions failed in 1755 and 1756 to capture the place. Amherst occupied it after taking Ticonderoga in 1759, the garrison blowing up the fort on his approach. That winter Amherst started building a large fort a few hundred yards from the site of Ft. Frédéric; it was garrisoned but never completed, and its ruins remain. (*E.B.*)

On 12 May '75 Ethan Allen sent an expedition under Seth Warner, his second in command, to take Crown Point. This disabled British post fell without resistance, yielding some cannon, nine enlisted men, and 10 women and children. (See TICONDEROGA, 10 May '75 for background.)

During the period 14 Oct.–3 Nov. '76 Carleton occupied Crown Point after repulsing the CANADA INVASION.

In June '77 the forces of BURGOYNE'S OFFENSIVE took Crown Point. The *A.A.*–Heitman list of battles gives 16 June as the date of an action there; this would have been about the time Fraser's Advance Corps could have reached this place, and this body is known to have left 26 June to continue the advance. Crown Point was abandoned by the British when they were forced to withdraw their L.O.C. troops after Burgoyne's surrender at Saratoga in Oct. '77.

"CROWSFEET." Properly known as caltrops, these are small devices with four points forming a tetrahedron. Dropped at random, they will always have one point straight up. In ancient warfare they were scattered in the path of cavalry; in Korea they were dropped at night by American planes along Chinese supply routes to puncture tires. When the British evacuated Boston by sea in 1776 they sprinkled the last mile of the road into the city with them to harass the American advance.

CRUGER, John Harris. 1738–1807. Tory officer. N.Y. Scion of the CRUGER FAMILY, according to Appleton's he "succeeded his father as a member of the New York city council, was its mayor in 1764 [?], and at the beginning of the Revolution was its chamberlain." A son-in-law of Oliver De Lancey (the elder), he was given command of one of the Loyalist battalions raised by him and went south with the expedition of Lt. Col. Archibald Campbell that captured SAVANNAH, 29 Dec. '78. According to Appleton's, it was the 1st Bn. that Cruger commanded. Posted at Ft. Sunbury, he was recalled to take part in the defense of SAVANNAH, 9 Oct. '79, where he held a redoubt on the southern side of the perimeter against the poorly managed secondary attack of Gen. Isaac Huger. He is mentioned several times in this article on Savannah and is quoted on the low caliber of American troops engaged. Captured at Belfast, Ga., in June '80, he was soon exchanged for John ("Come and Take It") McIntosh. (Appleton's) He then succeeded Nisbet Balfour around mid-Aug. as commander of the Tory stronghold at Ninety-Six, and led the relief column from this place that relieved the siege of AUGUSTA, 14–18 Sept. '80.

He then distinguished himself in commanding the defense of NINETY-SIX, 22 May–19 June '81, the operation for which he was justly praised for his "vigilance and gallantry" by Clinton. (*Amer. Reb.,* 315) Joining the main British army in the South, he was commended for his "conduct and gallantry" at EUTAW SPRINGS, 8 Sept. '81. (*Ibid.,* 569) Speaking of the defenses of Charleston as organized the end of 1781, Baurmeister reported that "Colonel Cruger and 350 men are posted at the Stono; Colonel Stewart is in command of six battalions of British and provincials posted . . . across the narrowest part of the Neck. . . ." (*Journals,* 485) This assignment of Cruger, a Provincial officer, to one of the two defensive sectors is evidence of the high regard the British commander had for him and his troops.

Cruger's property having been confiscated, he went to England after the war and died in London.

CRUGER FAMILY OF NEW YORK. John Cruger, who probably was of German origin, went to N.Y.C. from Bristol, England, in 1698; he became a prominent shipper, was alderman for 22 years, and mayor from 1739 until his death in 1744. The third son of his marriage to Maria Cuyler was John Cruger (1710–1791), mayor of N.Y.C. (1756–65), president of the city's first chamber of commerce (elected 1769), speaker of the last colonial assembly (1775); although opposed to British policies that led to the Revolution, his strong sense of responsibility as a public official and his close ties with certain active Tories led him to be suspected of "disloyalty" by the patriot chiefs. He retired to Kinderhook (20 mi. south of Albany) during the British occupation of N.Y.C., returned there after 1783 to live with his nephew, Nicholas, and died unmarried on 27 Dec. '91.

Henry Cruger (1702–1780), brother of John the younger (just sketched) and father of the British politician, Henry (1739–1827), and the outstanding Tory soldier, John Harris CRUGER (1738–1807), moved to Bristol in 1775. According to Appleton's, the elder Henry was mayor of Bristol at the time of his death (1780).

Henry the younger left King's College (Columbia) in 1757 to join his English cousins in Bristol, where he became a successful merchant and exceptionally popular citizen. Feeling strongly that the British policy with regard to America was wrong, in 1774 he stood for Parliament with the slogan, "[Edmund] Burke, Cruger, and Liberty." Entering Parliament in the session that began 29 Nov. '74, he made his first speech on 16 Dec. and with an eloquence that brought praise from the Irish orator Flood ("he speaks more eloquently than any man I have yet heard in the House"), but with admirable restraint, Cruger deplored the Parliamentary measures that "widened the breach instead of closing it" and argued for a program that would "secure the colonists in their liberties, while it maintains the just supremacy of Parliament." (Quoted in *D.A.B.,* "Henry Cruger"). Failing re-election to Parliament in 1780, he was a successful candidate again in 1784. Meanwhile he was elected mayor of Bristol in 1781 (*ibid.*), succeeding his father. (Appleton's) In 1790 he returned to N.Y.C., and in Apr. '92 was elected to the state Senate. (See Henry C. Van Schaack, *Henry Cruger: the Colleague of Edmund Burke in ... Parliament* [1859].)

Henry's brother, John Harris CRUGER, is covered separately.

CULLODEN MOOR, Scotland, 16 Apr. '46. In a bloody defeat at the hands of William, Duke of Cumberland, the forces of the Young Pretender (Charles Edward) were destroyed. This ended The '45, or the Second Jacobite Rebellion. Hundreds of Highlanders sought refuge in N.C., and many established themselves around Cross Creek (later Fayetteville). There is reason to believe that the oath to the Crown taken after Culloden is what kept so many of these refugees loyal during the American Revolution. Culloden was repeated on a minor scale at MOORES CREEK BRIDGE, N.C., 27 Feb. '76, and at KETTLE CREEK, Ga., 14 Feb. '79.

CUNNINGHAM, "Bloody Bill." d. 1787. Tory partisan. Notorious leader of a band known as the "Bloody Scout," he operated in Ga. and the Carolinas. One authority credits him with training David FANNING. Commenting on the remarkable leniency of Southern patriots after the Revolution, Alden notes, "It is a striking fact that William Cunningham, a well-known Tory partisan leader, died in Charleston early in 1787." (*South,* 328 *n.*)

CUNNINGHAM, Gustavus. See CONYNGHAM, Gustavus.

CUNNINGHAM, Robert. *c.* 1739–1813. Tory leader. Ireland. Settling around Ninety-Six in 1769, he became a judge. He opposed the revolutionary movement in Ga. and in 1775 was imprisoned in Charleston. After his release he raised Tory militia and joined the British forces in 1780. In a letter of 3 Dec. '80 Cornwallis informed Clinton that after the action at Blackstocks, Tarleton "assembled some militia under Mr. Cunningham, whom I appointed Brig. General of the Militia of that district, and who has by far the greatest influence in that country...." (N.C. State Records, XV, 303–6, quoted in C. & M., 1150) Cunningham is mentioned in connection with the HAMMOND'S STORE RAID. Refused permission to remain in S.C. after the war, he settled at Nassau and was given a generous British allowance for his losses. (Appleton's)

CUNNINGHAM, William. *c.* 1717–1791. British provost marshal. Ireland. Not to be confused with another notorious enemy of the patriots, "Bloody Bill" CUNNINGHAM, the subject of this sketch reached N.Y.C. in 1774 and for a while was engaged in breaking horses and giving riding lessons. Forced to take refuge in Boston, he was made provost marshal by Gage. (Appleton's) In 1778 he had charge of the prisons in Philadelphia, and later those in N.Y.C. Lossing refers to him as "that infamously cruel scoundrel, Captain Cunningham, a burly, ill-natured Irishman of sixty years, whose conduct as provost marshal ... has connected his name with all that is detestable." (II, 306–7) Appleton's says he starved 2,000 prisoners to death and hanged more than 250 without a trial. Tradition has it that he was hanged at Newgate in London (*ibid.*) on the charge of having forged a draft (Appleton's), but Lossing points out that the records of the prison do not support this story.

CURRENCY. See CONT'L. CURRENCY, CURRENCY ACT, and MONEY OF THE 18TH CENTURY.

CURRENCY ACT. 1764. Primarily to prevent the colonies from paying debts in England with depreciated currency, Grenville's Cont'l. Currency Act prohibited issue of legal tender currency in all the colonies and extension of recall dates on outstanding issues. The act created a money shortage in the colonies at a time when Grenville's Sugar Act had cut off the specie formerly acquired from the West Indies trade.

CURRYTOWN, N.Y., 9 July '81. (BORDER WARFARE) About noon several hundred Tories and Indians under John Doxtader surprised this small settlement near Canajoharie. Most of the inhabitants were in the fields at the time, and they fled to the woods or into their "fort." The raiders burned the 12 dwellings (leaving only the fort and one Tory house) and killed and captured a number of people. Willett reacted promptly and defeated Doxtader the next day at SHARON SPRINGS SWAMP.

CUSTOMS COMMISSIONERS were established in America by the NAVIGATION ACT of 1673 with jurisdiction over collectors, searchers, and surveyors of customs. They were under the jurisdiction of the Treasury Board (see TRADE, Board of). Not until Townshend's Acts of 1767, however, was the customs system organized efficiently in America. Prior to this an estimated £700,000 worth of goods a year was smuggled into the colonies; it had cost more than £8,000 a year to collect about £2,000. The chief customs commissioners held their posts as sinecures, living in England and delegating their duties to poorly paid agents in America, who were "bought out" by colonial merchants. Townshend's reorganization resulted in greatly improved efficiency, which is why the colonists were so alarmed by it; between 1768 and 1774

the American customs brought in an average of £30,000 a year at an annual cost of £13,000. A five-man American Board of Commissioners of the Customs at Boston was directly responsible to the British Treasury Board, but had authority to rule without consulting it.

Professor Edmund S. Morgan writes: "The full extent of Townshend's mischief did not become apparent until the customs commissioners set to work at Boston. Professor O. M. Dickerson, the first historian to scrutinize carefully the records of the commission, has called the act establishing it 'England's most fateful decision,' because most of the events that goaded Americans into independence may be attributed directly or indirectly to it.* * * Unfortunately the commissioners who descended on Boston in November, 1767, . . . were a rapacious band of bureaucrats who brought to their task an irrepressible greed and a vindictive malice that could not fail to aggravate the antagonism not only against themselves but also against the Parliament that sent them.* * * Professor Dickerson calls their activities "customs racketeering," and they richly deserve the epithet. In the complicated provisions of the Sugar Act it was easy to find technicalities on the basis of which a ship could be seized. The commissioners used these technicalities in a deliberately capricious manner to trap colonial merchants. Their favorite method was to follow a lax procedure for a time and then, suddenly shifting to a strict one, seize all vessels that were following the practice hitherto allowed. By playing fast and loose with the law in this way they could catch the merchants unawares and bring in fabulous sums. [The offending vessel and cargo were sold. One third of the proceeds went to the British treasury, a third to the governor of the colony, and a third to the customs officers responsible for the seizure.] (*The Birth of the Republic,* 37, 38)

The customs commissioners brought on the LIBERTY AFFAIR, they drew the crowd that provoked the BOSTON "MASSACRE," and one of the warships sent to support them was involved in the GASPÉE AFFAIR.

See Oliver M. Dickerson, *The Navigation Acts and the American Revolution* (1951).

"CXIII." To reduce what he called "embezzlement of the public tools," Washington ordered the Q.M.G. to have entrenching tools branded with this mark, meaning the Continent and the 13 colonies. After the Decl. of Indep. the mark was changed to the "U.S." with which government issue (G.I.) property still is marked.

D

DALLING, John. d. 1798. British general and Gov. of Jamaica. A Maj. of infantry under Loudoun in 1757, he fought at Louisburg in 1758, and commanded a body of light infantry in Wolfe's assault of Quebec in 1759. In 1760 he became Lt. Col. of the 43d Foot, and he commanded the regiment at Havana in 1762. In 1767 he was appointed Lt. Gov. of Jamaica, and a year or so after the start of the Revolution he succeeded Keith as Gov., presumably in 1777, when he was promoted to Maj. Gen. (Appleton's) Directing British operations from JAMAICA, where Sir Peter Parker was military commander (1779–81), he sent expeditions to HONDURAS and NICARAGUA. "While Dalling, faithful to the example set by Germaine, was thus frittering away the lives of his men," writes Fortescue, the Spanish gobbled up the posts of Mobile and Pensacola, whose defense was Dalling's responsibility. (*British Army,* III, 340–41) With regard to the later failures, however, it must be pointed out that Dalling lacked the naval means to accomplish the latter mission. (See also WEST INDIES for his strategic prob-

lems.) He was promoted to Lt. Gen. in 1782, and became a baronet the next year. (Appleton's)

DALRYMPLE, John. 1749–1821. British officer. Eldest son of the 5th Earl of Stair, he became a Capt. in the 87th Regt., which was raised in July '79. (*D.N.B.;* Fortescue, *British Army,* 290 *n.*) Since the 87th served in the West Indies, he presumably is the Maj. Dalrymple who in Oct. '79 led a mixed force of 150 seamen, mariners, and soldiers in a daring capture of Omoa, key Spanish fortification in the Bay of Honduras. (Fortescue, *op. cit.,* III, 302–3) It is also assumed that his father (*d.* 1789) is the Sir John Dalrymple who in Mar. '78 proposed that the Peace Commission of Carlisle be empowered to offer Washington a dukedom in return for his assistance in working out peace terms. (See C. & M., 694) After distinguishing himself in the New London Raid, 6 Sept. '81, young John Dalrymple was sent home with the dispatches. On 5 Jan. '82 he was appointed minister plenipotentiary to Poland. During the period 5 Aug. '85 to 1788 he held the same post in Berlin.

In 1789 he succeeded his father to the peerage. He appears to be confused by historians (and indexers) with William DALRYMPLE.

DALRYMPLE, William. d. 1807. British general. With the "local rank" of Col. (or Lt. Col.) he was stationed at Halifax with his regiment, the 14th Foot, and was garrison commander in 1768 when Gen. Gage ordered troops from Halifax to Boston. Dalrymple landed at Boston on 1 Oct. '68 with most of the 14th and 29th Regts. He was commander of the BOSTON GARRISON until the summer of 1772, when his regiment was relieved by Lt. Col. Alexander Leslie's 64th Regt. Meanwhile he had lived through the trying period climaxed by the Boston "massacre" in Mar. '70. As a Lt. Col. he was left in command of the fortified camp on Staten Island when Gen. Howe undertook his N.Y. Campaign in 1776. (Baurmeister, *Journals,* 34) In mid-Dec. '76 he embarked on the ship that was to take Cornwallis back to England, the remnants of his regiment having been distributed among other units of Howe's army. (*Ibid.,* 76)

He is apparently the Col. Dalrymple who took command of the 79th Regt. ("Liverpool Blues") raised in the spring of 1778 and sent to Jamaica. Fortescue says "detachments of the 60th, Liverpool Regiment (79th), and of Dalrymple's Jamaica Corps" operated in Central America starting early in 1780. (*British Army,* III, 338 and *n.*) The "Jamaica Corps" is probably that of John DALRYMPLE, not William. If the latter accompanied the 79th to Jamaica he obviously had returned to England before the end of 1779 because he is known to have reached Charleston with dispatches from Germain to Clinton on 10 May '80. (Clinton, *Amer. Reb.,* 171 *n.*) He was a B.G. on the latter date (whether this was regular or "local"

rank is not known) and was appointed Clinton's Q.M.G. (succeeding Erskine in a post temporarily held by Lord CATHCART) with the "local rank" of Maj. Gen. Early in the fall he was Clinton's emissary to Germain with the oral request that the uncooperative Adm. Arbuthnot be recalled or that Clinton's resignation be accepted. (*Ibid.,* 205 and *n.*) He rejoined Clinton in 1781, bearing an ambiguous answer from Germain, and took part in the indecisive councils of war held in N.Y. during the Yorktown Campaign. In Nov. '82 he became a Maj. Gen., and he was eventually promoted to full Gen.

DANBURY RAID, Conn., 23–28 Apr. '77. After the successful PEEKSKILL RAID, N.Y., 23 Mar. '77, Gen. Howe sent Gov. Wm. Tryon of N.Y. to destroy the important rebel depot at Danbury. The 2,000-man force was composed of Brown's Prov. Regt. (300 men), and 250 from each of the following regular units: the 4th, 5th, 23d, 27th, 44th, and 64th. Dragoons and artillery were attached, and Gens. Agnew and Erskine accompanied Tryon. Escorted by two frigates, the expedition left N.Y. on 23 Apr. and landed near Fairfield, Conn., the evening of the 25th. The next day they marched 23 miles unopposed and started burning Danbury at 3 P.M. The 150 Cont'ls. stationed in the area had removed a small quantity of stores, but by the next morning the British destroyed 19 dwellings, 22 barns and storehouses, together with provisions, clothing, and almost 1,700 tents.

Militia were meanwhile rallying under Gens. Arnold and Wooster, who had recently returned from Canada. By 2 A.M. on the 27th there were 100 Cont'ls. and 500 militia at Bethel, some four miles S.E. of Danbury. Wisely observing the principle of returning by a different route, the British withdrew through Ridgefield, about 15 miles south of Danbury. Arnold therefore moved with 400 men to block them at that place, and Wooster followed them with the other 200. Wooster snapped up about 40 prisoners before falling mortally wounded. Arnold and Gen. Silliman, meanwhile, had established a blocking position at Ridgefield astride the narrow road. While 200 men defended a hasty barricade of carts, logs, stones, and earth on the road, the others were posted on a rock ledge on the left and around a house and barn on the other flank. Another 100 militia joined Arnold to hold this position.

Tryon approached in mid-afternoon (having left Danbury at 10 A.M.). When his column drew fire he sent detachments out to envelop both enemy flanks, and Agnew brought enfilade fire to bear on the barricade from the American left. Arnold ordered a withdrawal and he himself was fired on at a range of 30 yards by an enemy platoon that cut the road behind him. When his horse was killed under him, Arnold managed to escape after shooting a Tory who rushed forward demanding his surrender.

The British camped a mile from the scene of this action. Arnold set up another position to block their retreat to the ships, but the next morning a Tory guided Tryon's column to Compo Hill, behind Arnold's position and near the point of debarkation. As the Americans prepared to attack Compo Hill, Erskine led 400 in a successful "spoiling attack" that enabled the raiders to get away safely.

Although the Conn. militia failed miserably in the defense of their country, the Americans made a good show of attempting to annihilate the raiders after the damage to Danbury had been done. The British leaders deserve credit for keeping this from turning into an-

other Lexington and Concord by their choice of return route, their promptness in retreating before more militia could turn out, and their vigorous action at Ridgefield and Compo Hill. Arnold and Wooster showed splendid leadership, as did Col. John Lamb, whose three guns made a valiant attempt to break up Erskine's bayonet attack. Congress finally recognized Arnold's service and made him a major general within a week (later predating his commission to give him seniority over the five officers promoted over his head; see ARNOLD); on 20 May they gave him a horse, "properly caparisoned . . . as a token of their approbation of his gallant conduct . . . in which General Arnold had one horse killed under him and another wounded." (Resolution quoted in Heitman)

American casualties were about 20 killed and 80 wounded. The British lost 154 killed and wounded. (Freeman, *Washington,* IV, 410. Howe reported a loss of only 60 killed and wounded; other estimates reached the absurd figure of 600.)

"DARK AND BLOODY GROUND." The region that became the states of Ky., W. Va., and Ohio was known by this lugubrious name even before the Indians started trying to fight back the encroachment of white settlers. Called "dark" probably because of its heavy forests, which extended hundreds of miles with hardly a clearing, it had been virtually uninhabited by the savages. Strange as it might seem, the Ohio River had no villages of any significance—Logstown, within 20 miles of Pittsburgh, was the only one worth noting. (See Scribner's *Atlas,* 47, 56, 57, and 77) The Delawares, Shawnees, Hurons, and Miamis had tribal territories in the region that became Ohio and Indiana, but the southern portion of the Ohio Valley was not claimed by any tribe; it was a hunting ground and a battle ground—a "bloody ground." As outlined in the article on WESTERN OPERATIONS, this dark region became even more bloody when Indian raiders tried desperately to drive back the American pioneers.

DARTMOUTH, William Legge, 2d Earl of. 1731–1801. British statesman. A step-brother of Lord North, he was Pres. of the Board of Trade and Plantations for a few months in 1765 and 1766. In 1772 he returned to that office during the Hillsborough administration and also was Secretary for the Colonies, becoming known as a friend of the colonists despite his firm convictions of Parliamentary supremacy. He was succeeded in the latter post by Germain (10 Nov. '75). A gentle, pious man, whose association with the early Methodists earned him the nickname of "Psalm singer," he was president of a fund-raising campaign in Britain for Moor's Indian Charity School. The latter had been founded at Lebanon, N.H., by Eleazer Wheelock (1711–1779) about 1750, and five years later it was named in honor of Joshua Moor, who gave it lands and buildings. A famous alumnus was Joseph BRANT. In 1769 it was gratefully renamed for Lord Dartmouth.

DATES BEFORE 1752. See CALENDARS, "Old" and "New Style."

DAVIDSON, George. Cont'l. and militia officer. N.C. A Capt. in the 1st N.C. Regt. on 1 Sept. '75, he resigned 5 Feb. '77. Presumably this is the Maj. Davidson at WAHAB'S PLANTATION.

DAVIDSON, William Lee. 1746–1781. Militia general. N.C. Four years after his birth in Lancaster co., Pa., he settled with his parents in the part of Rowan co., N.C., that later became Iredell co. He married Mary, sister of Dr. Ephraim Brevard, reputed au-thor of the Mecklenburg Declaration of 20 May '75. (*D.A.B.*) After serving on the county Comm. of Safety he was appointed Maj. of the 4th N.C. on 15 Apr. '76 and went north under Col. Francis Nash to take part in the N.J. Camp'n. For gallant conduct in the battle of Germantown, 4 Oct. '77, he was promoted to Lt. Col. of the 5th N.C., his commission dating from the battle. On 1 June '78 he was transferred to the 3d N.C., and on 9 June '79 to the 1st N.C. (Heitman) In Nov. '79 the N.C. Cont'ls. were sent to the Southern Theater, which then was becoming the major theater of operations. Having stopped to visit his family, he arrived too late to join his regiment in the Charleston defenses.

He commanded a battalion of 300 light infantry in the patriot force rallied by Gov. (Gen.) Rutherford for the operation that ended with the Tory defeat at RAMSEUR'S MILL, N.C., 20 June '80. (Ward, *W.O.R.*, 707) In the summer of 1780 he was severely wounded in an engagement with Tories near Coulson's (or Calson's) Mill, on the Yadkin; a musket ball passed through his body and he was out of action for eight weeks. (Appleton's) He then was promoted to B.G. of state troops and had command of the Salisbury district.

Two weeks after arriving to take command of the Southern Theater, Greene ordered Dan Morgan to march south from Charlotte and join the N.C. militia of Davidson for operations between the Broad and Pacolet rivers. Around 25 Dec. '80, Davidson joined Morgan in his camp on the Pacolet, bringing with him 150 men. Although he was with Morgan shortly before the battle of Cowpens, he was off recruiting and did not see action at Cowpens. Two weeks later (31 Jan. '81) he was directed by Greene to rally the unenthusiastic N.C. militia for service in guarding the fords of the Catawba after the withdrawal of the main army. Davidson was killed at COWAN'S FORD, 1 Feb. '81, while engaged on this mission, and with him died Greene's hope of militia assistance. (In addition to Cowan's Ford, under SOUTHERN CAMPAIGNS OF GREENE see section headed "Action on the Catawba.")

The Cont'l. Cong. voted in 1781 for a monument to his memory; money was appropriated in 1903 (sic), and the monument later was erected on the battlefield of Guilford. Davidson College and Davidson counties in N.C. and Tenn. are named for him.

DAVIE, William Richardson. 1756–1820. Patriot officer, Greene's Comm. Gen., Gov. of N.C. Born in England, he went to the wild Waxhaw settlement of S.C. with his father in 1763 and was adopted by his maternal uncle, William Richardson, a Presbyterian clergyman. In 1776 he graduated from Princeton with first honors, having left school briefly to see some military service in N.Y. Returning to Salisbury, N.C., he started studying law but soon left his books to become a partisan fighter. He served for three months under Gen. Allen JONES in 1777–78 and rose to the militia grade of Maj. Meanwhile he had helped raise a troop of cavalry. Joining Pulaski's division, he was seriously wounded at Stono Ferry, S.C., 20 June '79. Early the next year, after a slow recovery, he raised another troop of cavalry and operated north of Waxhaw Creek, sometimes with Sumter, in the bloody partisan warfare that followed the surrender of Charleston. He particularly distinguished himself at HANGING ROCK, 6 Aug. '80. After the patriot disaster at Camden he is credited with using his little command, in contradiction to the orders of Gates, to save valuable supplies. Now a Col.,

he scored a bold success at WAHAB'S, 21 Sept., and then with only 20 men brought Cornwallis and his entire army to a halt, temporarily, at CHARLOTTE, N.C., 26 Sept. '80. When the British withdrew into S.C., Davie harassed their flanks and rear.

Having proved himself to be an exceptional commander, Davie was bitterly disappointed when Greene singled him out to be his commissary general, a fate to which the new C. in C. of the Southern Theater had once been subjected himself. When Davie protested that he knew nothing of money and accounts, Greene said, "Don't concern yourself. There is no money and hence no accounts." Despite overwhelming difficulties and an acute distaste for the work, Davie measured up to Greene's expectations. In 1782 he settled at Halifax, N.C., and married Sarah Jones, wealthy daughter of his former commander and niece of Willie JONES. He had been licensed to practice law in 1780, and became prominent on the circuits of his state in "all the important civil cases, and for the defense in every capital case." (C. C. Pearson in D.A.B.) "Tall, elegant, and commanding, he had a mellow and flexible voice and a 'lofty and flowing' style which . . . 'astounded and enraptured' his audiences." (Ibid.) He represented Halifax in the legislature almost continuously from 1786 to 1798, had a prominent role in important state and national issues, and was largely responsible for the establishment and organization of the Univ. of N.C. He became commander of state troops in 1797 and B.G. in the U.S. Army during the crisis of 1798–1800. He became Gov. of N.C. in 1798, and was peace commissioner to France the next year.

In national politics he swung his delegation to the "Conn. Compromise," fought for ratification of the Constitu-

tion, denounced the Va. and Ky. resolutions, advised against Federalist support of Aaron Burr, and spurned overtures from "that man" Jefferson.

"His political attitude seems to have
been grounded originally on contempt
for the war boards, the judges, and the
legislators whom democracy thrust up.
. . . Refusing either to modify his aristocratic habits or to solicit votes personally, he was eliminated from politics
by the Jefferson-Macon * machine in
the important congressional election of
1803. Disgusted with politics and saddened by the loss of his wife, he retired in 1805 to his plantation, 'Tivoli,'
in Lancaster County, S.C., where he
could enjoy farming, friends, horses,
and books, and give an occasional bit
of advice to his university or make a
biting remark about North Carolina
politicians." (*Ibid.*) He declined appointment by Madison as Maj. Gen.
in 1813.

DAWES, William. A fellow courier
of Paul Revere, he had no Longfellow
to immortalize him. Under LEXINGTON
AND CONCORD see section headed "Paul
Revere's Ride."

DAYTON, Elias. 1737–1807. Cont'l.
general. N.J. A native of Elizabethtown,
apprenticed as a mechanic, he joined
the "Jersey Blues," became a Lt. on 19
Mar. '56, and fought with them at Quebec (1759). As a Capt. (19 Mar. '60)
he led his company against the Indians
and fought around Detroit during Pontiac's War (1763). Back in Elizabethtown he established a general store, became a member of the comm. of safety
(6 Dec. '74) and was named one of
four Essex co. mustermasters on 26
Oct. '75. In Jan. '76 (*D.A.B.* says the
10th; Heitman says 18 Jan.) he became

* Nathaniel Macon (1757–1837) of
N.C., who was speaker of the House of
Representatives from 1801 to 1806.

Col. of 3d N.J. Cont'ls., and that month
he took part in the capture of the
BLUE MOUNTAIN VALLEY. Leading his
regiment to Albany in May '76, he
rebuilt FT. STANWIX and constructed
Ft. Dayton at Herkimer. He saw some
action against the Indians before rejoining the main army at Morristown in
Mar. '77. He took part in the skirmishes at Bound Brook and Staten Island (presumably those of 13 Apr. and
22 Aug.) before engaging in the Battles of BRANDYWINE (11 Sept.) and
Germantown (4 Oct. '77). After spending the winter at Valley Forge (Maxwell's Brig.) he led his regiment in the
Monmouth Campaign (June '78) and
then performed outpost duty in N.J. He
joined SULLIVAN'S EXPEDITION against
the Iroquois in 1779 and is specifically
credited (*D.A.B.*) with the destruction
of Runonvea, near Big Flats, on 31
Aug. '79. (*Handbook of American Indian,* II, 397) Dayton and his son Jonathan (see below) refused to sign the
semipolitical indorsement that SULLIVAN
secured from his officers. (*D.A.B.*)

Back in his home state to rejoin the
main army under Washington, Dayton figured prominently in delaying
and stopping Knyphausen's SPRINGFIELD
RAID, 7–23 June '80. During this and
previous operations he was serving close
to his home, Elizabethtown, and, in
marked contrast to such patriots as
John CADWALADER and Philemon DICK-
INSON, he not only remained with the
Cont'l. Army rather than resign to become a militia general but also declined
election to Congress. During the MU-
TINY OF THE N.J. LINE, Jan. '81, Dayton showed skill in handling the portion
of the brigade under his command. In
the reorganization of 1 Jan. '81, Dayton
left the 3d N.J. to become commander
of the 2d N.J. (however, see Israel
SHREVE). Although nominally the commander of the latter regiment, Col. Day-

ton led a brigade of 1,300 men in the YORKTOWN Campaign. On Washington's insistence he was appointed B.G. on 7 Jan. '83.

After returning to his business in Elizabethtown he became a leading citizen, state legislator, Maj. Gen. of militia, and was in the Congress of 1787–88. A personal friend of Washington, he is said to have borne him a physical resemblance.

Father of Jonathan DAYTON.

DAYTON, Jonathan. 1760–1824. Cont'l. officer. N.J. The son of Elias DAYTON, he graduated from the college at Princeton in 1776 (Appleton's), joined his father's regiment, the 3d N.J., as an ensign on 7 Feb., became regimental paymaster on 26 Aug., and Lt. on 1 Jan. '77. Capt-Lt. on 7 Apr. '79, he became A.D.C. to Sullivan on 1 May (during SULLIVAN'S EXPED.), and Capt. on 30 Mar. '80. Captured at Elizabethtown (his home) on 5 Oct., he was exchanged (at an unknown date), and in the reorganization of 1 Jan. '81 became a member of his father's 2d N.J. (Heitman) During this time he presumably saw action in the engagements mentioned in the sketch of Elias DAYTON. Although Appleton's says he served under Lafayette at Yorktown, his regiment was in his father's brigade of Lincoln's Div. Leaving the Cont'l. Army on 3 Nov. '83, he was a N.J. legislator and Speaker of the N.J. House in 1790, delegate to the Federal constitutional convention in 1787, a U.S. Representative for three terms ending 3 Mar. '99, and a U.S. Senator from then until 1805. He was arrested on charges of being involved in the Conspiracy of Aaron BURR (1805) but not brought to trial. (Appleton's)

DEANE, Silas. 1737–1789. Cont'l. congressman, first American diplomat abroad. Conn. The son of a blacksmith,

he graduated from Yale in 1758, was admitted to the bar in 1761, and the next year started a rapid rise to comparative wealth, social prestige, and political prominence. He was greatly assisted in the process by having married a well-endowed widow, Mehitabel Webb, in 1763, and, after her death in 1767, by marrying the granddaughter of former Gov. Saltonstall. A leader in the Revolutionary movement of his colony, he was sent to the first Cont'l. Cong. in 1774 and reappointed the next year. D.A.B. places him in the legion of patriots credited with sending out the force that captured TICONDEROGA, in May '75. In the first session of the 2d Cont'l. Cong. Deane served on committees appointed to organize the navy.

The visit of ACHARD DE BONVOULOIR to Philadelphia late in 1775 led the Secret Committee to decide that an agent should be sent to France to explore the possibilities of military assistance. Since Deane had fallen from grace in Conn. politics and was not reelected to Cong., he was selected for this European mission.

Until recent years the consensus of historians has been that Deane was a dedicated patriot who fell victim to bad luck and intrigue. Prof. Julian P. Boyd has drastically revised that verdict in a series of articles entitled "Silas Deane: Death by a Kindly Teacher of Treason?" in *The William and Mary Quarterly*, XVI (1959).

Prof. Boyd pictures Deane as an intensely enterprising, ambitious man "with a capacity for penetrating analysis in matters of commerce . . . and endowed with an ardent cupidity." (*Ibid.*, 166) As luck would have it, Cong. had instructed him to arrange a meeting in Paris, as soon as he arrived there, with his old friend Edward Bancroft. Deane did this, passing American and French secrets to Bancroft with a view to making their fortune in trade, purchasing supplies for Cong., land speculation, and all forms of profiteering and double dealing. (*Ibid.*, 187) What Deane did not know, and what the world did not learn until 60 years after Bancroft's death, was that Bancroft was a double agent!

Deane sailed for Europe in Apr. '76 with instructions from two separate committees of Cong., both of them secret. For the Commercial Committee he was one of five merchants authorized to buy American produce with Congressional funds, to ship this abroad, and to bring back supplies needed by the colonies; Deane was the European agent for this traffic. The Secret Committee instructed Deane to buy clothing and equipment for 25,000 men, and to purchase artillery and munitions; he was to do this on credit, if possible. He also was to explore the possibilities of French recognition and alliance. (Ralph V. Harlow in *D.A.B.*)

HORTALEZ & CIE. was the first fruit of Deane's efforts. Although details of this secret operation were passed promptly to Lord Stormont in Paris and to British authorities in London, Deane and Bancroft withheld critical information about shipments in which they had a stake; hence vital supplies continued to flow to America. Congress had directed Deane to take Arthur Lee into his confidence, but Deane did not do so. As explained under HORTALEZ & CIE., this made Lee a bitter enemy of Deane's. The suspicion of the Lees, Ralph Izard, and others that Deane was engaged in dishonest dealings was not based on specific evidence—they "suspected almost everyone." (Boyd, *op. cit.*, 328)

The matter of foreigners in the American army brings up the name of Silas Deane most frequently in the pages of military history. As early as 2 Dec. '75

Congress had asked the Secret Committee to find four "able and skillful engineers" for the Cont'l. army, but Deane went far beyond his authority in making contracts with foreign officers who wanted Cont'l. commissions. He had no qualifications for sorting out the real soldiers from the mere opportunists. Henry Laurens was to write later that Deane apparently "would not say nay to any Frenchman who called himself Count or Chevalier" and solicited a high commission in the American army. (Freeman, *Washington,* IV, 421, quoting ltr. of 12 Aug. '77)

In Sept. '76 Congress appointed Franklin and Arthur Lee to form a committee with Deane to continue the mission originally entrusted to Deane alone. This led to the French Alliance, which Congress ratified 4 May '78, and ended Deane's diplomatic mission. Recalled ostensibly to report to Congress on affairs in Europe, but actually—as he himself suspected (*D.A.B.*)—to answer charges raised by Arthur Lee, he stirred up a lively controversy that is part of the story of HORTALEZ & CIE. Deane also was attacked at this time for showing poor judgment in letting so many foreign adventurers come to America.

After two years in America he returned as a private citizen to Europe to pursue his nefarious affairs with Bancroft. In 1781, he wrote to friends in America of his failing confidence in the cause of Independence and advocated an accommodation with Britain. He sent these through Bancroft, who showed them to the British authorities. With a view to giving these letters more credence, and helping their own cause, the British pretended they had been intercepted and Deane's letters were published in Rivington's *Gazette* about the time Cornwallis surrendered. Now accused of treason in addition to the older charges of profiteering, dishonest financial methods, and incompetence, he became an exile. Bankrupt, sick in spirit and in body, he lived a short time in Ghent and for a few years in England. He died at the start of a voyage to Canada, 23 Sept. '89. His reputation was cleared to some degree when Congress voted his heirs $37,000 in 1842 as partial restitution for his war expenses. At this time the audit of his accounts that had been made under Arthur Lee's direction was called "a gross injustice to Silas Deane." Prof. Boyd's article, mentioned above, makes it evident that although Deane was not a traitor of the same type as his close personal friend Benedict Arnold, and although he did not know that Bancroft was a British agent, Deane was guilty of most charges raised by his enemies; but the proof was lacking at the time.

The best biography is G. L. Clark, *Silas Deane* (1913); this is so characterized by *D.A.B.* in 1930, and is the only biography listed by the *Harvard Guide* (whose cutoff date is 31 Dec. 1950). The Silas Deane Papers, edited by Charles Isham, are in the N.Y. Hist. Soc. *Collections,* XIX–XXIII (New York, 1887–91). Previous judgments on Deane must be reevaluated in the light of Prof. Boyd's article of 1959, cited above.

DEARBORN, Henry. 1751–1829. Cont'l. officer, later Sec. of War. N.H. Descended from a native of Exeter, England, who came to America in 1639, Henry had studied medicine and started practicing (1772) before he organized and was elected Capt. of a militia company. After learning of the fighting at Lexington and Concord he led 60 of his men to Cambridge, where his company became part of Col. John Stark's Regt. Dearborn distinguished himself as part of the latter's command at BUNKER HILL. Commanding a company of mus-

ketmen in Arnold's March to Quebec, he became sick and had to be left behind on the Chaudière River but rejoined in time to be captured at Quebec, 31 Dec. '75. Held for a while in the city, he was paroled in May '76 but not exchanged until 10 Mar. '77. On 19 Mar. he was appointed Maj. of Scammell's 3d N.H. Regt. (with rank from 8 Nov. '76), and he fought at Ticonderoga and the 1st battle of Saratoga, 19 Sept. '77. On the latter date he was promoted to Lt. Col.*

After spending the winter of 1777–78 at Valley Forge (in Enoch Poor's Brig. [Heitman, 11]), Dearborn took part in SULLIVAN'S EXPEDITION against the Iroquois. On 19 June '81 the Q.M.G., Timothy Pickering, requested that Washington appoint Dearborn his assistant, and this was granted. While serving in this capacity during the Yorktown campaign he had the sad duty of writing home that his former commander, Col. Scammell, had been killed. (Johnston, *Yorktown,* 112 n., 175; Heit-

* In his *D.A.B.* sketch J. W. Pratt says that in Sept. '77 he was transferred to Cilley's 1st N.H.—there is no mention of a promotion—and that he fought against Burgoyne. Heitman, on the other hand, shows in his summary of Dearborn's record, in his rosters of regimental officers, and in his roster of troops at Valley Forge that he was a Lt. Col. after 19 Sept., and that he remained with the 3d N.H. until 1781. (Pp. 190, 41, 11) In one place, however, Heitman gives 1 Apr. '81 as the date of his transfer to the 1st N.H. (p. 190) and in another he shows him as Lt. Col. of this regiment from 1 Jan. '81 to 1 Mar. '82. (P. 41) As mentioned later in the present sketch, Dearborn was on the army staff during the Yorktown campaign, although he probably continued to be carried on the regimental rolls.

man, 190, does not indicate that Dearborn ever was appointed Assist. Q.M.G.)

Serving in the Cont'l. Army until 21 Mar. '83, he settled in Kennebec co., in the Maine district of Mass., where he rose to Maj. Gen. of militia and, in 1790, U.S. Marshal for the district. He was a Republican congressman, 1793–97. He was Sec. of War during Jefferson's eight years in office, 1801–9. On 27 Jan. 1812 Pres. Madison made him the senior Maj. Gen. with command of what was expected to be the critical theater, the sector between the Niagara River and the New England coast.

According to J. R. Jacobs, *The Beginning of the U.S. Army, 1783–1812,* Dearborn and his successor, Wm. Eustis, had been incompetent secretaries of war. As a field commander Dearborn was more conspicuously incompetent, and the American defeats of 1812 and 1813 were largely due to his lack of strategic sense and his lack of vigor. Morgan LEWIS succeeded him in the summer of 1813 as field commander, but further evidence of Dearborn's incompetence being revealed by subsequent American defeats, he was relieved of command on 6 July '13. His request for a court of inquiry being unheeded—they were too busy trying to salvage the mess he had created—Dearborn was given command of N.Y.C., and, as such things happen, he was later made president of the court-martial that tried and condemned Gen. Wm. HULL, for his defeat at Detroit. It was the inept strategy of Dearborn that had enabled the British to concentrate their entire force against Hull at Detroit.

In Mar. '15 James Madison nominated Dearborn for Sec. of War! In the ensuing uproar Madison withdrew his name, but not before the Senate had time to reject it. He was honorably discharged from the army on 15 June '15, three days before the battle of Waterloo. *D.A.B.* comments that "Dearborn, like William Hull [*q.v.*], had exhibited excellent military qualities as a young officer in the Revolution, but, as with Hull, those qualities appeared to have evaporated with age and long disuse." It might be mentioned, as being more to the point, that the qualities that make an officer a good Lt. Col. and second in command of a regiment do not necessarily make him a competent theater commander.

During Monroe's administration Dearborn was minister to Portugal two years, 1822–24; he returned at his own request and retired to Roxbury, where he died five years later.

His *Revolutionary War Journals ... 1775–1783,* edited by L. A. Brown and H. H. Peckham, was published in 1939.

DE BORRE. See PREUDHOMME DE BORRE.

"DECKHARD" RIFLE. See DICKERT RIFLE.

DECLARATION OF INDEPENDENCE. See INDEPENDENCE, DECL. OF.

"DECLARATION OF RIGHTS AND GRIEVANCES." 19 Oct. '65. See STAMP ACT.

DECLARATION OF THE CAUSES AND NECESSITIES OF TAKING UP ARMS, 6 July '75. Drawn up by a committee comprising Franklin, Jay, William Livingston, and Thomas Johnson as an address for Washington to read to his troops, the first product was rejected by Congress, which called on John Dickinson and Jefferson to prepare a document for a wider audience. The final draft, except for a few paragraphs by Jefferson, is the work of Dickinson. (Montross, *Reluctant Rebels,* 80) The heart of the document is in these lines:

"We are reduced to the alternative of chusing an unconditional submission to the tyranny of irritated ministers, or resistance by force.—The latter is our choice.—We have counted the cost of this contest, and find nothing so dreadful as voluntary slavery.* * * Our cause is just. Our union is perfect. Our internal resources are great, and, if necessary, foreign assistance is undoubtedly attainable.* * * With hearts fortified with these animating reflections, we most solemnly, before God and the world, declare, that, exerting the utmost energy of those powers, which our beneficient Creator hath graciously bestowed upon us, the arms we have been compelled by our enemies to assume, we will, in defiance of every hazard, with unabating firmness and perseverance, employ them for the preservation of our liberties; being with one mind resolved to die freemen rather than to live slaves.* * *" (Commager, *Docs.*, 95.)

The delegates adopted the resolution on 6 July, the day after accepting another product of Dickinson's pen, the Olive Branch Petition.

DECLARATORY ACT. 18 Mar. '66. The day it repealed the Stamp Act Parliament asserted its authority to make laws binding the American colonies "in all cases whatsoever," using the same general terms as in the Irish Declaratory Act of 1719. One of the greatest forces in bringing about repeal of the Stamp Act had been the masterful performance of Benjamin Franklin in his testimony before the House of Commons on 13 Feb. '66, the thrust of which had been that Americans objected only to "internal" taxes, not to taxes on trade. An authority on the Stamp Act Crisis, Professor Edmund S. Morgan, gives this explanation of how the Declaratory Act evolved:

"Franklin's testimony was a dangerous piece of deception with unfortunate aftereffects, but it did help to secure the immediate end in view.

"Even with Franklin's assistance Rockingham could not bring about repeal until he had first arranged for a 'Declaratory Act,' affirming Parliament's authority. Here too it was necessary to exercise a certain amount of deception. Pitt was the first to suggest such an act. In denying Parliament's right to tax America and demanding repeal of the Stamp Act, he had also proposed that Parliament assert its sovereignty over the colonies in 'every point of legislation whatsoever.' When Rockingham drafted such an assertion in the form of an act, some of his advisers suggested that it be made to state specifically Parliament's right to tax. But Rockingham preferred to leave this point comfortably vague by merely affirming Parliament's right to make laws and statutes binding the colonists 'in all cases whatsoever.' By this general phraseology he hoped to pacify the majority of members, who thought the power to legislate included the right to tax anyhow, and yet not offend Pitt and his followers who took the opposite view. As it turned out, the majority were satisfied, but not Pitt. Since he knew that other members of Parliament interpreted the phrase 'in all cases whatsoever' to include taxes, he argued for its deletion, and when he could not prevail, he and his friends voted against the declaration which he himself had suggested in almost identical wording.

"Repeal of the Stamp Act was thus secured by persuading Parliament that the Americans objected only to internal taxes; and repeal was accompanied by a declaration of Parliament's authority which the members interpreted to include the right to tax but which did not specifically state such a right.

"The Americans were overjoyed at repeal, for it seemed to mean the restoration of their old freedom, but they were puzzled by the accompanying

Declaratory Act.* * * In Boston John Adams wondered 'whether they will lay a tax in consequence of that resolution.' He did not have to wonder long." (*The Birth of the Republic, 1763–89*, 31–32)

John Adams read his answer in the TOWNSHEND REVENUE ACT.

DE COUDRAY. See TRONSON DE COUDRAY.

DEFEAT IN DETAIL. In the correct military sense—today as well as in the 18th century—this term means "the defeat in turn of the separated parts of a force." To avoid "defeat in detail" a commander keeps all his units within "supporting distance" of each other.

DE FERMOY. See FERMOY.

DEFILADE. A person or thing protected by a natural or man-made barrier—a rise in the ground, or mounded earth—is said to be in defilade. In modern military parlance, this is "cover," as opposed to "concealment."

DE HAAS, John Philip. c. 1735–1786. Cont'l. general. Pa. Born in Holland, he came to America with his parents around 1737 and settled in Lancaster, Pa. His family was an illustrious and ancient one, first prominent in Prussia and later moving to Alsace before going to Holland. John was an ensign in the Provincial Bn. of Pa. in Dec. '57 and was stationed on the Susquehanna. He accompanied Forbes's expedition to Ft. Duquesne the next year, served throughout the rest of the French and Indian War, and during Pontiac's War took part in Bouquet's victory at Bushy Run, Aug. '63. During the period 1765–79 he was a local magistrate and engaged in the iron industry of Lancaster co. In 1775 he raised a militia company on his own responsibility, was named Maj. of Pa. Provincials, and on 25 Oct. '76 was appointed Col., 1st Pa. Bn. He led this unit to Canada and is cred-

ited with saving Benedict Arnold from possible capture at Lachine by arriving with four companies to drive off an enemy column. (*D.A.B.*) During the retreat from Canada he operated between Montreal and Sorel during the month of June '76, and then moved with the backwash of the CANADA INVASION to Ticonderoga.

His 1st Pa. Bn. formed the nucleus of the 2d Pa. Cont'ls., of which he was named Col. on 25 Oct. '76 with rank from 22 Jan. He was appointed B.G. on 21 Feb. '77 but was "so slow acknowledging his appointment . . . that Washington wrote [15 June] to inquire whether he still considered himself an officer of the Army." (Freeman, *Washington,* IV, 395 and *n.*) For reasons that are still unexplained he suddenly resigned. (*D.A.B.*) The official record shows that he *retired* on 3 Nov. '83 (Heitman), and that he was breveted Maj. Gen. on 30 Sept. '80, so his actual status from 1777 to the end of the war is a mystery. According to *D.A.B.* he offered his services to the board of war in 1778 to lead an expedition to revenge the Wyoming Valley "Massacre" (July '78); he led some local militia to the valley but the arrival of regulars under Col. Thos. Hartley made his presence superfluous. In 1779 he moved to Philadelphia (*D.A.B.*), where he "rendered no subsequent service." (Heitman)

DE LA BALME. See MOTTIN DE LA BALME.

DE LANCEY, Oliver (the elder). 1718–1785. Senior Loyalist officer in America. N.Y. Youngest son of Stephen, who came to N.Y. in 1686 after revocation of the Edict of Nantes, and of Anne van Cortlandt, Oliver and his brother James (1703–1760) built the family party into a position of power in N.Y. provincial politics. "It was Oliver De Lancey's fate to . . . survive his brother into a period of entirely new conditions in contest with which the family 'interest' was utterly wrecked...," writes C. W. Spencer in *D.A.B.* Lacking the political leadership qualities of his brother, "His contribution was made by vigor in action and in exploiting the prestige and formidable power of the family interest." Oliver had raised troops and commanded a provincial contingent in the Ticonderoga campaign of 1758. A highly successful merchant and holder of many offices, he had become Col. in chief of the Southern Mil. District in 1773. Meanwhile the De Lancey faction of N.Y. politics became identified with the Loyalist cause while their enemies, the Livingstons, were leaders of the Whigs. Oliver's greatest contribution was in raising a brigade of 1,500 "for the defense of Long Island and for other exigencies." Of the three battalions known variously as "De Lancey's N.Y. Volunteers" or "Refugees," two served in the South with distinction and the third remained throughout the war in Queens co., N.Y., as did B.G. De Lancey himself. He was included in the N.Y. Act of Attainder of 1779, and his property was confiscated. Two years earlier his mansion in Bloomingdale was sacked by the "patriots." Leaving N.Y.C. with the British in 1783, he died two years later in England. The crown awarded him $125,000 on a claim of $390,000 war losses.

DE LANCEY, Oliver (the younger). 1749–1822. British officer, Clinton's A.G. N.Y. Of the powerful N.Y. family led by his father (see preceding entry), young Oliver was born in N.Y.C., educated in England, and in 1766 he entered the British army as Cornet of the 14th Dragoons. In May '73 he became Capt. in the 17th Dragoons, in which he remained for 49 years and succeeded the first Duke of Newcastle

as its Col. in 1795. Preceding his regiment to America in 1774 to secure remounts and arrange accommodations, he joined them on their arrival in Boston on 24 May '75. His mounted detachment led the British turning movement at Long Island and assured its success by capturing the American patrol at Jamaica Pass. (Appleton's) He took part in the action at JAMAICA, L. I., 28 Aug. '76, and in an affidavit of Lt. Robt. Troup, not made public until 1846, was accused of striking the wounded B.G. Nathaniel Woodhull after his surrender. (The N.Y. militia general, who Heitman says was "wounded after capture," died 20 Sept. '76.) More valid testimony indicates that De Lancey saved the general—who was a kinsman—after a trooper had inflicted the wounds from which he eventually died. (*Ibid.*) After serving with his regiment in Pa. and N.J., on 3 June '78 De Lancey was promoted to Maj. and given the post of Deputy Q.M.G. in the Charleston Expedition of Clinton. He succeeded John André as Clinton's A.G. in 1780 and, in this capacity, reorganized the secret service in the North. During the Mutiny of the Pa. Line, in Jan. '81, he initiated various schemes to exploit the situation, but he had no success. (See Van Doren, *Secret History,* 409–11, 414, and *Mutiny,* 243–49. The latter is De Lancey's journal of the Pa. mutiny.) In May '81 he became the A.G. of the British army in America and was promoted to Lt. Col. (*Mutiny,* 243) After the fighting ended he was head of a commission to settle accounts of the war.

De Lancey became barrackmaster general of the British Army, an office he held for 10 years. In 1794 he was promoted to Maj. Gen., and in 1812 he became a full Gen. For many years he represented Maidstone in Parliament. He died a bachelor at the home of his sister Charlotte, who had married Sir David Dundas, C. in C. of the British Army after the Duke of York.

DELAPLACE, William. British officer who surrendered TICONDEROGA, 10 May '75.

DELAWARE CONTINENTALS. Organized 19 Jan. '76 under Col. John Haslet, this was the only regiment furnished by Del. during the war (see POPULATIONS. ...) Called "the best uniformed and equipped in the army of 1776" (Lefferts, 26; see UNIFORMS), its men had blue coats faced and lined with red, white waistcoats, buckskin breeches, white woolen stockings, and black gaiters. Their peaked black hats were smaller versions of the British grenadier hats. Armed with "lately imported" English muskets, they were among the few continental troops to have BAYONETS.

Their first action was at LONG ISLAND, 27 Aug. '76; Maj. Thomas McDonough led them in the absence of Haslet and never rejoined after being wounded there. HASLET led them until killed at PRINCETON, 3 Jan. '77. Col. David Hall, who succeeded Haslet, was invalided for wounds received at Germantown, 4 Oct. '77. Gunning Bedford became Lt. Col. of the Delawares on 19 Jan. '76, was wounded at White Plains, 28 Oct. '76, and left the regiment in Jan. '77. Lt. Col. Charles Pope was wounded at Mamaroneck, 21 Oct. '76, and resigned 13 Dec. '79. Lt. Col. Joseph Vaughan and Maj. John Patten were captured at Camden, 16 Aug. '80, and were prisoners on parole to the end of the war.

This reduced the regiment to two 96-man companies. One of these distinguished itself during the rest of the war in the South under the remarkable Capt. Robert KIRKWOOD. The other, under Capt. Peter JAQUETT, served with distinction with the 1st Md. Regt. Capt. Enoch Anderson, 2d Lt. of the regiment on 13 Jan. '76, who was wounded at Long Island, promoted to Capt. on 3 Dec. '76, and resigned 1 Mar. '79, wrote the lively and valuable *Personal Recollections.* ... (Wilmington, 1896).

The Delaware Continentals, 1776–1783 (Wilmington, 1941) was published by Christopher Ward for the Hist. Soc. of Del. "Much more than the story of one of the best units in the Continental army ..., put forth in a limited edition ... which deserved a much wider circulation," it was expanded into the posthumous *War of the Revolution* (2 vols., New York, 1952). The comments quoted above are from editor John Richard Alden's preface to that work.

DELAWARE RIVER FORTS. See PHILADELPHIA CAMPAIGN, 1777.

DEMILUNE. Meaning "half moon," this was a standard fortification term for a crescent-shaped outwork.

DEMONT, William. American traitor. Pa. Commissioned Ensign, 5th Pa. Bn., 6 Jan. '76, he became Regt'l. Adj. on 29 Sept., and deserted the night of 2–3 Nov. '76 to the camp of Earl Percy at McGown's Pass, Manhattan. "I sacrificed all I was worth in the world," he later said, "and brought with [me] the plans for Fort Washington by which plans that fortress was taken by his Majesty's troops the 16th instant. ... At the same time I may with justice affirm, from my knowledge of the works I saved the lives of many of his Majesty's subjects." (Quoted in Van Doren, *Secret History,* 17) Heitman spells his name Dement.

DENISON, Nathan. c. 1740–1809. Militia officer. Conn. A native of New London, he was a well-educated man who became one of the early Conn. settlers of the Wyoming Valley and was active in its affairs. In 1774 he and Zebulon Butler became justices of the peace of the newly established town of Westmoreland. In 1777 Denison was made Lt. Col. of Conn. militia, and later in the year he was promoted to Col., a grade he held until 1780. (Heit-.nan) He commanded troops in the WYOMING VALLEY "MASSACRE" in July '78 and figured prominently in that action. After the war he held several important posts under the authority of Pa. He died 25 Jan. 1809 at the age of 68. (Lossing, I, 348, 361 *n.*)

DENTAL RECORDS, as a means of identifying a corpse, were used probably for the first time on record by Paul Revere in identifying the body of Joseph WARREN.

DE PEYSTER, Abraham. 1753–*c.* 1799. Loyalist officer. N.Y. A lineal descendant of Johannes De Peyster, whose French forebears had taken refuge in Holland to escape persecution as Huguenots, Abraham was of an illustrious and wealthy N.Y. family. He entered the British service and rose to be Capt. in the 4th ("King's") American Regt., also called the King's American Rangers. He had the "local rank" of Lt. Col. When Ferguson was killed in the battle of Kings Mountain, S.C., 7 Oct. '80, De Peyster succeeded as commander and was forced by the helplessness of the situation to surrender his force. According to Appleton's, he had been paid the morning of the battle and his life was saved when a bullet was stopped by a doubloon among the coins in his vest pocket. Wounded and taken prisoner, he apparently saw no further action. In 1783 he was retired at half pay as a Capt. and settled at St. Johns, New Brunswick, where he became treasurer of the province.

His brothers Frederick and James also were Loyalist officers. The former distinguished himself during CLINTON'S EXPEDITION TO THE HIGHLANDS in the attack on Fort Montgomery; he left a famous son, Frederick (1796–1882), and grandson, John Watts De Peyster (1821–1907).

Nephew of Arent Schuyler DE PEYSTER.

DE PEYSTER, Arent Schuyler. 1736–1832. Loyalist officer. N.Y. Entering the 8th Foot in 1755, he served in the French and Indian War under his uncle Peter Schuyler (1710–1762). During the Revolution he commanded Detroit (see Wm. CRAWFORD), Mackinac, and other Canadian posts, where "his tact and . . . conciliatory measures" kept the Indians loyal. (Appleton's) A Maj. in 1782, he eventually became Col. of the 8th Foot. Retiring to Dumfries, Scotland, he enlisted and drilled the 1st Regt. of Dumfries during the French Revolution. An original member of his command was Robert Burns, who dedicated a poem ("Life") to De Peyster and later became involved in a political controversy with him in the local newspaper.

Uncle of Abraham DE PEYSTER.

DESPARD, Edward Marcus. 1751–1803. British naval officer, governor in Central America, conspirator. Confused by indexers with his eldest brother, John DESPARD, he was born in Ireland and entered the navy in 1766. Promoted to Lt. in 1772 and stationed at Jamaica, "he soon proved himself to have considerable engineering talent" (*E.B.*). After taking part in the San Juan expedition (1779) and the operations in NICARAGUA—with the man who became Lord Nelson—he was promoted to Capt. and made Gov. of the Mosquito Shore and the Bay of Honduras. He took part in the capture of the Black River Settlements in Oct. '82 (see HONDURAS);

Baurmeister calls him a colonel, and the indexer of the *Journals* erroneously identifies him as John Despard. (*Op. cit.,* 537; *E.B.*)

In 1784 Edward took over the administration of Yucatan. "Upon frivolous charges he was suspended by Lord Grenville, and recalled to England." (*E.B.*) The charges were held over him from 1790 until 1792 before being dismissed, but no compensation was awarded and he made himself so offensive in his demands for justice that he was arrested in 1798. Imprisoned until 1800, except for a short interval, and by that time desperate, he laid a plot to seize the Tower of London, the Bank of England, and to assassinate George III. Found guilty of high treason, he and six fellow conspirators were sentenced in 1803 to be hanged, drawn, and quartered. "These were the last men to be so sentenced in England," comments *E.B.,* and Despard was executed 21 Feb. 1803.

DESPARD, John. 1745–1829. British officer. Entering the army as an ensign of the 12th Foot in 1760 and promoted to Lt. in 1762, he served in Germany before going to Quebec with the 7th ("Royal Fusiliers") in Mar. '73. He was surrendered at SAINT JOHNS, 2 Nov. '75, exchanged in Dec. '76, and promoted to Capt. in Mar. '77. He took part in CLINTON'S EXPEDITION to the Highlands, in which operation his regiment assaulted Ft. Clinton, 6 Oct. '77. The next June he became Maj. in Lord Rawdon's Volunteers of Ireland, and in Dec. '79 was appointed Dep. A.G. He took part in the Charleston Expedition of Clinton in 1780 and the subsequent operations of Cornwallis, including the Yorktown Campaign.

Promoted to Col. in Aug. '95 and Maj. Gen. in 1798, he was Gov. of Cape Breton from 1800 to 1807, and in 1814 was made a full Gen. He had been in 24 engagements, most of them during the Revolution (*E.B.*), and was shipwrecked three times (Appleton's).

See also Edward DESPARD.

DESTOUCHES, Charles-René-Dominique Gochet, Chevalier. French admiral. Succeeding Adm. Ternay (d. 15 Dec. 1780) as commander of the French squadron at Newport, he sailed south to support Lafayette in Va. but withdrew after the action off CHESAPEAKE BAY, 16 Mar. '81. He was succeeded in May '81 by Adm. Barras.

DE WOEDTKE. See WOEDTKE.

DIAMOND ISLAND (Lake George), N.Y., 24 Sept. '77. See TICONDEROGA RAID, Sept. '77.

DICKERT RIFLE. Many misguided writers have referred to a famous "Deckhard rifle" carried by "OVER MOUNTAIN MEN" at Kings Mountain. The weapon was a long rifle made by Jacob Dickert of Lancaster, Pa., and I am informed by an expert that one was sold in recent years for the price of a fine automobile. Carl Pippert of Bladensburg, Md., an authority on Jacob Dickert, owns and fires a Dickert. One is in the museum at Ft. Wayne, Ind. Another was used by a defender of the Alamo in 1836 and is displayed there. (For being set straight on this matter I am indebted to Mr. La Dow Johnston of Toledo, Ohio, past president of the Ky. Rifle Assoc.)

To add to the confusion, there is reference in a gun book to a rifle "with C. Gumpf on the barrel and Deckert on the lock." (C. P. Russell, *Guns on the Early Frontiers....* [1957 and 1962]. See discussion of Golcher rifle under Timothy MURPHY.) Many weapons are mistakenly identified by the name of the *lockmaker*—this is particularly true of the name Golcher or Goulcher (*ibid.,* 133). So the non-existent "Deckhard" may be a phonetic rendering of "Dickert" or "Deckert."

DICKINSON, John. 1732–1808. American political theorist. Born in Md., reared on the family estate near Dover, Del., a B.G. of Pa. militia, and an elected representative from Del. and Pa. as well as being president of each state at various times, it is difficult to say what state can claim John Dickinson or his brother, Philemon (see below). His strongest associations, however, were with Pa., as will be shown. Taught by tutors until 1750, he studied law under John Moland for the next three years before going to London for another three years at the Temple (1753–57). Admitted to the bar, he practiced in Philadelphia and within five years had become a prominent lawyer. In Oct. '60 he was elected to the Assembly of the Lower Counties of Del., became speaker of that body, and in 1762 was elected representative from Philadelphia to the Pa. legislature. Here his intensely conservative views threw him into the role of leading the unpopular patriots, and the opposing leader at this time was Benjamin Franklin. "In the great debate of 1764," writes James Truslow Adams in *D.A.B.*, "he admitted all the evils of the proprietary system but feared that any change might bring worse, and that any royal government granted by a British ministry of that day would be still more dangerous. As a result, he lost his seat in the Assembly and was not re-elected until 1770." A vigorous opponent of the Stamp Act, he attended the congress of 1765 and is credited with doing most of the work on the "Declaration of Rights and Grievances." (See STAMP ACT) In "The Late Regulations Respecting the British Colonies . . . Considered," also published in 1765, he advocated enlisting the aid of British merchants to secure repeal of the Sugar and Stamp

acts. His FARMER'S LETTERS had a serious impact on political thought in England as well as America.

Re-elected to the Assembly, he drew up the first "Petition to the King" (1771), which won unanimous acceptance, but he lost more popular strength by opposing the use of force against the mother country and by condemning the approach of the New England radicals. In 1774 he would not approve of any more positive assistance to Boston than sending an expression of sympathy. He epitomized the conservative viewpoint in his "Essay on the Constitutional Power of Great Britain over the Colonies in America." Elected (from Pa.) to the 1st Cont'l. Congress, Dickinson withdrew after the first week in Oct. '74, "believing he had been excluded up to that time by Galloway's influence." (*D.A.B.;* GALLOWAY'S PLAN OF UNION was presented 28 Sept.) Congress nevertheless called on him to draft their "Petition to the King" after rejecting the efforts of Richard Henry Lee and Patrick Henry, and then called on him to write the "Address to the Inhabitants of Quebec."

Made chairman of a committee of safety and defense on 23 June '75, he held this position a year. He also became Col. of the first battalion raised in Philadelphia. In the 2d Congress he continued to advocate peaceful methods. He wrote the "Olive Branch Petition," adopted 5 July '75 despite the furious objections of New England delegates. He wrote much, if not all, of the "Declaration of the Causes of taking up Arms" (*D.A.B.*). He voted against the Declaration of Independence, not willing to accept that a peaceful settlement was not yet possible and believing that the colonies lacked the central government and the support of allies needed for war. When war came, however, he and Thos. McKean were the only Congressmen who immediately turned out to fight. Dickinson led his regiment to Elizabethtown, took command of a militia brigade, but soon resigned his commission when he lost his seat in Congress. (*D.A.B.*) Meanwhile, he had headed the committee that drafted the ARTICLES OF CONFEDERATION. In Nov. '76 he was elected to Congress from Del. but declined and withdrew to his estate in Del. During the Philadelphia Campaign he appears to have served as a private in a special Del. force during the Battle of the Brandywine (*D.A.B.*), and in Oct. '77 he was a militia B.G. While he saw no combat, Dickinson's actions in 1777 supported the words he wrote the first time he took the field (mentioned above): "... I can form no idea of a more noble fate than ... to resign my life, if Divine Providence should please so to dispose of me, for the defence and happiness of those unkind countrymen whom I cannot forbear to esteem as fellow-citizens amidst their fury against me."

Again elected to Congress from Del., he accepted in 1779 but resigned in the fall. In 1781 he became president of the Supreme Executive Council of Del., and when he returned to live in Philadelphia he held the same office in Pa. during 1782–85. During the first two months of 1783 the *Freeman's Journal* carried his "Vindication," which he wrote in answer to a series of scurrilous letters attacking him. During this year he helped found and endow Dickinson College. In 1787 he was a delegate from Del. to the convention that framed the Federal Constitution, and the next year he published nine letters signed "Fabius" urging its adoption. During his last 17 years he held no public office but in 1797 he published 14 letters advocating friendship with France. In 1801 he published two volumes of his writing, which were republished in 1814, after his death.

Philemon DICKINSON was a brother, and John CADWALADER was a first cousin. The standard biography is C. J. Stillé's *Life and Times of John Dickinson* (1891).

DICKINSON, Philemon. 1739–1809. Militia general. Born probably in Md. but perhaps in Del. (*D.A.B.*); appointed from N.J. When the Revolution began he was living in comfortable circumstances in his estate on the Delaware River just west of Trenton. In July '75 he was named Col. of the Hunterdon County Bn. and on 19 Oct. became B.G. of N.J. militia. In 1776 he was elected to the N.J. provincial congress. While Washington occupied winter quarters at Morristown, Dickinson led one of the raids that seriously jeopardized British attempts to get provisions: during the period 20–22 Jan. '77 he marched 400 untrained troops through a waist-deep river to surprise and defeat a large foraging party near Somerset C.H. (Millstone), N.J. He took 40 wagons, about 100 draft horses, and some prisoners. On 15 Feb. '77 he resigned his commission as militia B.G., but on 6 June he was named Maj. Gen. and C. in C. of the N.J. militia, a post he retained until the end of the war. During the Philadelphia Campaign (June–Dec. '77) he and David Forman were in the field with militia detachments, but Washington was unable to draw Dickinson's command to the main army for the Battle of Germantown (4 Oct.). (Freeman, *Washington*, IV, 496) On 27 Nov. he took part in an attack on Staten Island. During the MONMOUTH CAMPAIGN (June–July '78) Dickinson's militia performed usefully in destroying roads and bridges to retard the British retreat across N.J.; although they did not do any significant fighting in the Battle of Monmouth, they were in contact with the British army as

Washington's army arrived and were the source of important intelligence. (See MONMOUTH.) On 4 July '78 he stood as second for his cousin John Cadwalader in the latter's duel with Thos. CONWAY. For a short time (*D.A.B.*) in 1778–79 Dickinson served as chief signal officer of the Middle Dept. When Knyphausen undertook the SPRINGFIELD RAID, 7–23 June '80, Dickinson and his militia performed valuable service as a delaying force and actually did some fighting.

Dickinson's home, "The Hermitage," was the place where Sullivan made contact with the enemy in his advance to TRENTON, 26 Dec. '76, and this property had been destroyed by the enemy. In this same month the patriot leaders were outraged when it became known that Philemon had written his brother John DICKINSON advising him to receive no more Cont'l. money on his bonds and mortgages. Dickinson was in Congress 1782–83 as a representative from Del., where he also owned property, and in 1783–84 (two terms) he was vice-pres. of the N.J. State Council. In 1785 he, Robt. Morris, and Schuyler constituted a commission to select the site for the national capital. During the war he ran for governor and was defeated by Wm. Livingston in 1778, '79, and '80. He was defeated by Wm. Paterson as a candidate for U.S. senator, but served the unexpired term, 1790–93, when Paterson succeeded Livingston as governor.

Philemon Dickinson was a brother of John DICKINSON and a cousin of John CADWALADER. He had married the latter's sister, Mary, in 1767, and married another sister, Rebecca, when Mary died.

DIGBY, Robert. 1732–1814. British admiral. Having commanded the *Dunkirk* (60) during the period 1756–63, taking part in the actions off Rochefort in 1757 and at Quiberon Bay in 1759, he was appointed to command the *Ramillies* (74) in 1778 and was in battle off Ushant, 27 July '78. Meanwhile he had been an M.P. from 1757 to 1761. In Mar. '79 he became Rear Adm. and had his flag aboard the *Prince George*. During the next two years he was second-in-command of the Channel Fleet and in the expeditions of Adm. George Rodney and Adm. Darby to relieve Gibraltar. In Aug. '81 he was sent to America as C. in C. to succeed Graves, but arriving just as the latter was about to sail for the Chesapeake he courteously deferred his assumption of command. He then moved his flag to a smaller ship and let Adm. Samuel Hood take the *Prince George* and most of his other ships to the West Indies. The war being virtually over, Digby had no opportunity for significant naval operations. He returned to England and, although he had no further appointments, was promoted to Vice Adm. in 1787 and Adm. in 1794. In 1779 he had been made governor of Prince William Henry, who began his naval career in the *Prince George*. In 1784 Digby had married the daughter of Andrew Elliot.

DIPLOMACY OF THE AMERICAN REVOLUTION. European exploration and colonization of the New World led to the COLONIAL WARS, and the political settlements that followed these conflicts must be considered as the background of the diplomacy during and after the American Revolution. In simplest terms, British diplomacy *during* the Revolution amounted to little more than the attempt to maintain European neutrality while the "revolting colonists" were brought back into line. The Americans, on the other hand, needed European support to win. France and Spain, the major powers on the Continent, looked on England's misfortune in America as their opportunity to settle scores in Europe and in the colonies.

The purpose of this summary is to identify the main articles dealing with diplomacy and to tie them together in a logical sequence insofar as is possible. The article serves also as a heading for a classified bibliography.

The Colonial Wars had no sooner ended than the remarkable French minister CHOISEUL and his successor, VERGENNES, were anticipating the American Revolution and planning to exploit it. The SECRET COMMITTEE OF CONGRESS was created 18 Sept. '75, just 10 days before ACHARD DE BONVOULOIR sailed from Europe on his mission. Although Vergennes was somewhat alarmed at the extent to which this emissary might have committed France, he nevertheless went ahead with his concurrent plans for furnishing secret aid to the Americans, which was done through Beaumarchais' HORTALEZ & CIE. The Cont'l. Cong., meanwhile, created their COMMITTEE OF SECRET CORRESPONDENCE on 29 Nov. '75, and the history of American diplomacy started being written. The two "secret committees" combined their efforts and objectives to send Silas DEANE to France. In Sept. '76 the Cont'l. Cong. appointed FRANKLIN and ARTHUR LEE to join Deane as a committee to perform the mission originally entrusted to Deane alone. This led to the FRENCH ALLIANCE in the spring of 1778. PEACE NEGOTIATIONS then occupied the diplomats, but in the process of accomplishing this business the marplots Ralph IZARD, Arthur Lee, and William LEE had to be recalled to America. Major participants on behalf of the colonists in these peace negotiations were FRANKLIN, JAY, ADAMS, and (in the final phase only) Henry LAURENS. In these names you have the roster of American diplomats of the Revolution. The next business had to do with the PEACE TREATY of 3 Sept. '83, which ended the war but left problems that had to

be settled later by JAY'S TREATY (1794) and Thomas Pinckney's Treaty (1795). British diplomats involved in various matters mentioned above were Lord STORMONT, Richard OSWALD and Henry Strachey. VERGENNES, of course, remained a major actor throughout.

SPANISH PARTICIPATION was a negative but important factor of diplomacy during and after the Revolution. DUTCH PARTICIPATION is covered in a separate article, and the role of Prussia is sketched in the entry on FREDERICK THE GREAT AND THE AMERICAN REVOLUTION. See also ARMED NEUTRALITY and GERMAN MERCENARIES.

The standard authority on American diplomacy is Samuel Flagg Bemis, whose many works are identified in the main bibliography. Specialized works, also identified in the latter place but whose shortened titles are shown here for convenience, are Brown, *Empire or Independence;* Corwin, *French Policy;* Doniol, *Histoire;* Graham, *British Policy and Canada;* Lokke, *France and the Colonial Question;* Richard B. Morris, *The Peacemakers;* Perkins, *France in the American Revolution;* Phillips, *The West in the Diplomacy of the American Revolution;* Spector, *The American Department of the British Government, 1768–82;* Sullivan, *Maryland and France;* and Wharton (ed.), *Diplomatic Correspondence of the U.S.* Short, general histories of the Revolution in which diplomacy is covered in particularly lucid fashion are Alden, *American Revolution,* and Edmund S. Morgan, *Birth of the Republic, 1763–89.*

Other works are cited in the articles cross referenced from this one, particularly the biographical sketches. See also those listed under WESTERN OPERATIONS.

DIRECTION. When a military writer speaks of going down a body of water he means *in the direction of flow.* Burgoyne's Offensive, for example, advanced *up* Lake Champlain from Canada to N.Y. No difficulty is encountered in the case of streams that run from north to south, as does the Hudson, but frequent errors are made as a result of thinking that *north* always means *up*, as it does on the conventional map. The left bank of a stream is the one on an observer's left as he faces downstream. The left flank of a formation is the left side as its members face the enemy; unless the enemy is retreating, *his* left flank is on the side of *your* right flank.

DISALLOWANCE. Colonial ROYAL GOVERNMENT was set up so that the popularly elected assemblies initiated laws. The Board of TRADE then reviewed all legislation that had not been vetoed by the Royal Governor; they recommended "allowance" of the legislation if in their opinion it did not deviate from imperial policy, and recommended "disallowance" in other cases. The Privy Council submitted final recommendations to the king. According to E. B. Russell, 469 out of 8,563 acts were disallowed, not including those from Pa. before 1700 or those from Md. during 1691–1715. Colonial assemblies evaded disallowance by passing temporary acts.

DISPLAY. The modern tactical term is "deploy," which *O.U.D.* dates from 1796. See also WORDS, Archaic.

DOBBS FERRY (Hudson River), N.Y. About 15 miles below Kings Ferry and less than 10 miles north of Kings Bridge, this was an important crossing site on the Hudson. During most of the war this ferry was too close to the British defenses of N.Y.C. for the Americans to use, so Kings Ferry—covered by Stony Point and the works at Verplancks Point—became the crossing that both sides sought to control.

DOLLAR, Spanish milled. See MONEY. . . .

DONOP, Carl Emil Kurt von. *c.* 1740–1777. Hessian officer. At Long Island he commanded the body of Hessian grenadiers and jägers engaged in the center of the line, under Heister. After the pursuit of Washington's army to the Delaware, Col. von Donop was relieved by Col. Rall as commander of the Trenton garrison on 14 Dec. '76 and was given over-all responsibility for the chain of outposts along the Delaware. (Baurmeister, *Journals,* 75, 76) He does not appear to have had the contempt for Washington's army that was held by most of his German associates, comments Alfred H. Bill in his study of this campaign, and he was overruled by Gen. Howe when he advocated a concentration of his forces at Trenton; Howe directed him to occupy Bordentown and Burlington to protect Loyalists of the region, but he withdrew from the latter place when its mayor informed him it would be shelled by American naval vessels from the river if the Hessians remained. (*Princeton,* 35–36) He stationed the 42d Foot ("Black Watch") and one of his grenadier battalions at Black Horse (now Columbus), and moved the rest of his command to the vicinity of Bordentown.

After the annihilation of Rall's force at TRENTON, 26 Dec., Donop wisely withdrew to Princeton, where he ordered the construction of two small redoubts to cover the approach from Stony Brook.

He was mortally wounded in the attack on FORT MERCER (Red Bank), N.J., 22 Oct. '77, and died three days later. He is alleged to have said to a brother officer: "It is finishing a noble career early; but I die a victim of my ambition, and of the avarice of my sovereign" (Appleton's). This sounds more like the work of American propagandists than the dying sentiments of a soldier; needless to say, it is not mentioned in Baurmeister's report (*Journals,* 127).

DORCHESTER, Baron. Title of Guy CARLETON after Aug. '86.

DORCHESTER, S.C., 1 Dec. '81. After recuperating from the hard-fought Battle of Eutaw Springs, 8 Sept., Greene left the High Hills on 8 Nov. Maj. John Doyle, in temporary command of British forces while Alexander Stewart recovered from a wound, had resumed operations, and a Tory uprising had been inspired by Fanning's daring HILLSBORO RAID, 13 Sept. Doyle withdrew to Goose Creek Bridge as Greene approached. Greene then decided to try to cut off the post of Dorchester on the Ashley River 15 miles N.W. of Charleston. This place was held by 850 men, and Greene moved against them with 200 Md. and Va. Cont'ls. and 200 cavalry from the commands of Lee, Washington, and Sumter. The rest of the American army, under Col. Otho Williams, marched to Round O, but when the enemy identified Greene in the column approaching Dorchester they assumed that his entire army was following. There were cavalry skirmishes, and a clash between the American advance guard and a reconnaissance force from Dorchester, but the enemy did not attempt to defend the post. Destroying their stores and throwing the guns into the river, they withdrew to within five miles of Charleston. Stewart returned to take command, and Charleston was so concerned about the possibility of attack that Negroes were enlisted and armed. The Americans went into camp at Round O.

DORCHESTER HEIGHTS, Mass., 2–27 Mar. '76. (BOSTON SIEGE) The plan to occupy Dorchester Heights evolved from the council of war held 16 Feb. '76 (see BOSTON SIEGE). Agreeing with Washington that some offensive action should be taken before arrival of British reinforcements in the spring, but believing that they lacked the strength to attack Boston, Washington's generals proposed seizure of some position and forcing the enemy to attack. Unoccupied Dorchester Heights, the only ones in the Boston area not held by one side or the other (Heath, *Memoirs,* 47) was the obvious choice. As finally worked out, the plan was for this high ground to be fortified in the course of a single night, as had been done at Bunker Hill. One problem, however, was that the frozen ground made quick pick-and-shovel work impossible, but Rufus Putnam came up with the suggestion that the fortifications be constructed above ground by the use of prefabricated parts. Heavy timber frames (chandeliers) were assembled, and gabions, fascines, and bales of hay were made up to fit into them. Another novel feature was adopted: the works would be surrounded by barrels of earth, which would give an appearance of strengthening the fortification but whose main purpose would be to roll down the steep, bare slopes into the ranks of attacking forces. (*Ibid.,* 49) Abatis would be constructed from orchards adjoining the heights.

A secondary attack across Back Bay to turn the defenses of Boston Neck was also set to go if the British attacked the Dorchester Heights works. For this operation Putnam would lead the division of Sullivan and Greene: 4,000 men in 45 bateaux, supported by two floating batteries. As a diversion, American guns would start a heavy bombardment on 2 Mar. and continue nightly through 4–5 Mar., when the fortifications were to be built. (The whole plan, needless to say, was made possible by KNOX'S "NOBLE TRAIN OF ARTILLERY" from Ft. Ticonderoga, and by the assembly of sufficient gunpowder in the early months of 1776.)

The main operation was commanded by Gen. John Thomas, who moved out the night of 4 Mar. with a work detail of 1,200 men, a covering force of 800, and a train of 360 ox carts to move the heavy fortification materials. The weather was ideal; the air was mild, a bright moon gave light to work by, and a ground haze obstructed enemy observation from Boston and Castle William. Although the artillery drowned out much of the noise of shovels, picks, and axes on the hill, a British officer detected the work at 10 P.M. and reported it to Gen. Francis Smith. That venerable regular officer, who had shown himself to be mentally and physically slow at LEXINGTON AND CONCORD and whose record was not spoiled by promotion to brigadier general, did nothing. By daylight the Americans had completed their work unmolested; a fresh fatigue party had reported at 3 A.M., the ox carts had made two trips, and reinforcements—including five rifle companies—had arrived to man the two small forts.

"The rebels have done more in one night than my whole army could do in months," Howe is said to have remarked when the works became visible. He reported to London that at least 12,000 men must have been employed; a British engineer estimated that up to 20,000 were involved.

British cannon could not elevate sufficiently to hit the new works. The naval commander said he would have to pull his ships out of the harbor if the positions were not eliminated. Howe therefore planned a night attack with 2,200 men under Brig. Gen. Jones to take Dorchester Heights with the bayonet and push on into the American lines at Roxbury, if possible. At a council of war around 7 P.M., shortly before Jones's troops were to move out, Howe and his generals agreed that the attack should be called off. A few hours later (the night of 5–6 Mar.) a severe storm struck, and Howe informed his troops in general orders that this was why the operation was canceled. (Ward, *W.O.R.*, 129)

The Americans attempted to extend their Dorchester Heights position by occupying and fortifying Nook's Hill the night of 9 Mar., but were driven off with the loss of five dead by artillery. Howe realized, however, that occupation of Dorchester Heights made Boston untenable, and on 7 Mar. he had decided to evacuate the city. (See BOSTON SIEGE for the end of the story.)

"DORMANT COMMISSION." One that became effective in a certain contingency. Since German generals in America were senior to the second ranking British generals and one would have become C. in C. if anything had incapacitated Gen. Howe or his successor, Clinton, in the spring of 1776 Clinton was given a "dormant commission" as a full general in America to take effect if Howe could no longer command (thus blocking Heister); when Clinton succeeded Howe, Cornwallis was given a "dormant commission" that would make him senior to Knyphausen if Clinton were incapacitated. When Clinton sent Benedict Arnold to conduct his Va. raid (Dec. '80) he secretly furnished Dundas and Simcoe with "dormant commissions" authorizing one of these trusted British officers to take command "in case of the death or incapacity" of Arnold. See Van Doren, *Secret History*, 419; Willcox (ed.), *American Rebellion*, 61 *n.*, 241 *n.*

DRAGOON. A mounted infantryman who, strictly speaking, rode his horse into battle but dismounted to fight, as opposed to a cavalryman, who was supposed to fight on horseback. He got this name from the primitive firearm, called a "dragon" because flame came from its mouth, with which the original dragoons were armed. Since dragoons could fight on horseback and cavalry could fight dismounted, the two names generally were used synonymously.

DUANE, James (dew ane) 1733–1797. Patriot statesman, jurist. N.Y. He was the son of a prosperous N.Y.C. merchant who had come to America from Ireland soon after 1700. James studied under the father of William ALEXANDER, was admitted to the bar in Aug. '54, and soon had a large, highly successful practice. In revolutionary politics he was conservative, and after his election to the Cont'l. Cong. (4 July '74) he became a leader of the conservative party. John Adams noted: "Mr. Duane has a sly, surveying eye . . . a little squint-eyed . . . very sensible, I think, and very artful." As a member of the committee to draft a statement of the rights of Americans he did much to moderate its tone. He seconded Galloway's Plan of Union on the grounds that Parliament did have the right to regulate colonial trade, but he signed the nonimportation agreement (20 Oct. '74) even though he felt it went too far. Reelected to the Cont'l. Cong., he was one of the strongest opponents of the movement toward INDEPENDENCE. "Why all this haste?" he argued.

Serving as a delegate from 1774 to 1779 and again from 1781 to 1783, Duane was on a large number of committees, and his most important work was done in the fields of finance and Indian affairs. He assisted in making the final draft of the Articles of Confederation (adopted 15 Nov. '77 by the delegates). Inevitably, his loyalty to the Revolution was challenged, and in the summer of 1781 the press raised charges of which he was cleared only after John Jay, Alexander McDougall, William

Floyd, Philip Livingston, and other influential colleagues had stepped forth to defend him. When N.Y.C. was evacuated by the British, Duane entered the city as a member of Gov. Clinton's council. On 4 Feb. '84 he was appointed mayor, an office he held until Sept. '89, when Washington appointed him the first federal judge of the N.Y. district. In Mar. '94 he retired from public life because of bad health but continued to be active in land development. As a lawyer he had represented New Yorkers in private suits involving the boundary dispute with Vermont. Prior to 1765 he had carried out colonizing projects on his large Mohawk Valley holdings, and his interest in this undertaking continued. The township of Duanesburg, created in 1765, was owned almost entirely by him, and portions remain in the possession of descendants. Other lifelong interests were centered around Trinity Church and Columbia College. By his wife, the daughter of Robert Livingston Jr. (third "Lord of the Manor"), he had five children who grew to maturity.

DUBUYSSON DES HAYS, Charles-François, Vicomte. 1752–1786. Cont'l. officer. France. Of noble birth, he became an artillery officer candidate (*aspirant*) on 7 Aug. '68 and was discharged (*reformé*) in 1776. He accompanied Lafayette to America and left a picturesque account of the trip from Charleston to Philadelphia. (Lasseray, 191–94) On 4 Oct. '77 he was made Maj. in the Cont'l. Army and assigned as A.D.C. to Kalb. On 11 Feb. '78 he was promoted to Lt. Col. (Heitman) In a futile attempt to save the life of his chief at Camden, 16 Aug. '80, he suffered four serious wounds and was captured; both of his arms were broken, and he was spitting blood from a chest wound. (Lasseray) Heitman says he was a prisoner on parole when the war ended, but Lasseray says that on 4 Sept. '81 Congress authorized his return to France on grounds of bad health, that he was honorably discharged on 1 Jan. '82 (citing Gardiner), and that N.C. had meanwhile made him B.G. of state militia. He died of wounds on 27 Mar. '86.

DUCHE, Jacob (doo shay). 1738–1798. Chaplain of Cong., turncoat. Pa. Son and namesake of a former mayor of Philadelphia, he graduated from the first class of the College of Philadelphia in 1757, spent the next year at Cambridge, and returned with the orders of an Anglican deacon. After a trip to England for ordination in 1762, he developed into a popular preacher. In 1759 he had married Elizabeth, sister of his friend and classmate Francis Hopkinson. The year the war started he was made rector of the united parishes and on 6 July '76 he was appointed chaplain of Cong. He officiated every morning at 9 o'clock until mid-Oct., when he resigned and asked that his $150 salary be used for the relief of widows and children of Pa. officers. Although he prayed for the royal family the first Sunday after the British occupied Philadelphia, he was arrested while leaving church and jailed because of his former affiliation with Cong. Apparently Duché had begun to lose his patriotic fervor when the Decl. of Indep. was announced, but he now turned Loyalist. Arrested on 28 Sept., and released after only a day in prison, he wrote Washington a long letter on 8 Oct. urging him to give up the hopeless struggle and urge Cong. to recall the Decl. of Indep. Washington promptly forwarded the astounding letter to the delegates at York, who were even more painfully shocked than they had been by the revelation of Church's treason in 1775. Nothing is known about what prompted Duché to write this letter. In it he said

it was done without any British prompting, but Washington doubted this. Lord Howe wrote Dartmouth that Duché had done "a great deal of harm. He is thought to be a tolerable sample of American confidence." Of this remark Van Doren says the "duplicity" may refer only to Duché's loss of faith in Cong. after being appointed chaplain of that body for what the delegates had called his "uniform and zealous attachment to the rights of America." On the other hand, comments Van Doren, this remark of Howe's "may hint at calculated double-dealing." (See *Secret History*, 39–43 for Van Doren's account and analysis of the Duché affair.)

The letter, which damned not only the Cont'l. Cong. but also the army as collections of "Bankrupts, attorneys, men of desperate fortunes" (delegates John and Sam Adams, Oliver Ellsworth, and Roger Sherman) and "undisciplined men and officers, many of whom have been taken from the lowest of the people, without principle, without courage"—this letter was distributed throughout the colonies and on 29 Nov. was printed in Rivington's *Royal Gazette*. Duché seems to have thought that Washington would consider the letter confidential, says Van Doren, but he found himself cursed by Americans as a traitor and held in contempt by the British as a blundering fool. He sailed for England in Dec. '77 and was rewarded for his return to the fold by being made secretary and chaplain of the Asylum for Female Orphans in Lambeth Parish. Who says the British don't have a sense of humour? The state of Pa. confiscated his property but left his family enough money to join him. Duché's conversion to the teachings of Swedenborg and certain eccentricities of later life caused some to question his sanity more than his patriotism, and hence to be more lenient in their judgment of what they once considered to be simple treason. (*D.A.B.*) After writing Washington and other prominent men begging to come home, in May '92 he finally returned to America. He already had suffered a paralytic stroke, but lived until 3 Jan. '98.

DU COUDRAY. See TRONSON DE COUDRAY.

DUER, William (dew er). 1749–1799. Congressman, speculator, militia officer. England–N.Y. Born in Devonshire, he was the third son of a wealthy owner of large plantations in Antigua and Dominica. He was educated at Eton, commissioned in the army, and went to India as A.D.C. to Lord Clive in 1764. Unable to stand the climate, he returned to England, and in 1768 visited N.Y. to buy timber on contract for the navy. In this connection he met Philip Schuyler and on the latter's advice bought large timber tracts above Saratoga. In 1773 he settled his affairs in England and established himself in N.Y., where he quickly became a leader in the patriot party. A delegate to the Cont'l. Cong., 1777–78, he was active, eloquent, and a member of seven committees. When his state was deprived of its vote because of Duer's serious illness he defied the orders of his doctor and was preparing to return to enable his delegation to block the nomination of a committee to remove Washington from command when, according to *D.A.B.*, "the faction, hearing of his intent, abandoned the project." This was during the Conway Cabal, at which time Duer was serving on the Board of War.

In 1779 he married "Lady Kitty" (Catherine), daughter of William Alexander ("Lord Stirling"), and Washington gave the bride away. He became wealthy from varied financial and commercial ventures. In Mar. '86 he was appointed secretary to the Board of the Treasury. The next year he was the principal organizer of the Scioto Company, which became connected with the OHIO COMPANY OF ASSOCIATES; he planned to sell lands chiefly to European capitalists. In Sept. '89 Duer became assistant secretary of the new Treasury Dept. under his friend Hamilton, but six months later he resigned. After engaging in large-scale speculations in New England lands and in other business ventures, he was losing control of his finances when suit was brought against him by the government for irregularities in his Treasury accounts. On 23 Mar. '92 he was arrested for debt and imprisoned, which "caused the first financial panic in the history of New York." (*D.A.B.*) Except for a short period in 1797 he remained in jail until his death on 7 May '99.

DULANY, Daniel. 1722–1797. Lawyer, political leader. Md. Son of Daniel (1685–1753), who had reached Md. about 1703 and had become a prominent lawyer and political leader, young Daniel was schooled at Eton, Cambridge, Middle Temple, and in 1747 was admitted to the Md. bar. On the eve of the Revolution he was recognized by his political enemy, Charles Carroll, as "indisputably the best lawyer on this continent." He had become a member of the Council in 1757, was commissary general from 1759 to 1761, and secretary of the province from 1761 to 1774. After passage of the Stamp Act he wrote a pamphlet entitled *Considerations on the Propriety of Imposing Taxes in the British Colonies, for the Purpose of raising a Revenue, by Act of Parliament.* (1765) The gist of his argument was that the theory of virtual representation did not apply to the colonies because Members of Parliament were not affected by measures that might hurt America; since the colonies were not represented and could not be, they could not be taxed. This· was more subtle than the mere charge that TAX-ATION WITHOUT REPRESENTATION IS TYRANNY. He also advocated that the colonists do their own manufacturing as a means of achieving economic independence and, with this, of ending England's attempts at exploiting the Americans. "His forceful arguments ranked foremost among the political writings of the period and were freely drawn upon by William Pitt when speaking for repeal." (*D.A.B.*) Dulany was no radical, however, and at the outbreak of the Revolution he retired to Hunting Ridge, near Baltimore, an avowed Loyalist. Nearly all his property was confiscated in 1781 while he was on a brief visit to England. He lived the rest of his life in Baltimore.

DUNDAS, Thomas. 1750–1794. British officer. Son of the M.P. for Orkney and Shetland, he was appointed a cornet in the King's Dragoon Guards in 1766, obtained a company in the 63d Foot three years later, and on 20 Jan. '76 bought a majority in the 65th. After serving in America and the West Indies with this regiment he returned to Scotland and on 17 Dec. '77 was made Lt. Col. of the 80th Foot, a regiment raised by the city of Edinburgh. On 25 Aug. '79 he reached N.Y. with reinforcements escorted by Adm. Arbuthnot and almost died shortly after of the JAIL FEVER that had reached epidemic proportions during the crossing. (Clinton, *Amer. Reb.,* 140, 141 and note. Clinton comments on the fine example set by Dundas during the crossing in performing menial tasks when his ship was shorthanded.) When Arnold was sent with an expedition to Va., Dundas and Simcoe accompanied him with their troops and were given "dormant commissions" by Clinton, unknown to Arnold, that authorized them to take command should Arnold be killed or incapacitated. (Van Doren, *Secret History,* 419) Clinton

also instructed Arnold to consult with these two officers before "undertaking any operation of consequence." (Clinton, *op. cit.,* 483) (See also, SIMCOE) After taking part in Arnold's raids (see VA. MIL. OPNS.), Dundas came under the command of Cornwallis. At Green Spring, Va., 6 July '81, he commanded a brigade (43d, 76th, and 80th Regts.) on the British left to drive back the Pa. regiments of Anthony Wayne. During the Yorktown Siege he commanded the detachment at Gloucester and was one of two British commissioners to arrange terms of surrender.

On 20 Nov. '82 he was breveted Col. and after his regiment was disbanded the next year he was retired on half pay. When the war with France broke out he was commissioned Maj. Gen. and he commanded the light infantry brigade in the expeditionary force of Gen. Charles ("No-flint") Grey in the capture of Martinique, St. Lucia, and Guadaloupe. In May he became Col. of the 68th Foot, and on 3 June '94 he died of fever at Guadaloupe. When the French retook the island the French republican deputy, Victor Hughes, issued a proclamation "that the body of Thomas Dundas . . . be dug up and given a prey to the birds of the air; and that upon the spot shall be erected . . . a monument having . . . the following inscription: 'This ground restored to liberty and valor of the Republicans, was polluted by the body of Thomas Dundas, major-general and governor of Guadaloupe for the bloody King George the Third.'" (H. Manners Chichester in *D.N.B.*)

"DUNKIRK PIRATE." British epithet for CONYNGHAM.

DUNMORE, John Murray, 4th Earl of. 1732–1809. Royal governor of Va. A nobleman descended from the Stuarts, in 1761 he was elected one of 16 Scottish peers to sit in Parliament. In 1770,

Hillsborough named him Gov. of N.Y. Arriving 19 Oct. '70 with his family, he was well accepted by the provincial aristocracy, but about 11 months later he was promoted to the post of Gov. of Va. to succeed Gov. Botetourt (d. 15 Oct. 1770). Here he also was popular initially: his newborn daughter was named Virginia and adopted by the province; the new counties of Dunmore and Fincastle (another of his titles) were named in his honor. The first discordant note was struck in 1773, when Dunmore's reaction to rising patriot sentiment was to dissolve the House of Burgesses after they proposed forming a committee of correspondence. He did the same thing the next year when the Burgesses set a day of mourning over the Boston Port Bill.

DUNMORE'S WAR, 1774, may have been inspired by his desire to divert the minds of Virginians from revolutionary politics, but the Gov. had previously shown a real interest in affairs of the frontier and he may have had an honest desire to cope with the Indian menace. His subsequent career in America, outlined under Military Operations in VIRGINIA, shows that this singleminded Scot lacked the finesse his situation called for. "Had he lived in quiet times, he might have been one of Virginia's popular and successful governors," writes L. P. Kellogg in *D.A.B.* "Personally brave, he showed weakness in the crisis, and by rash measures brought about his own downfall" (*ibid.*), not to mention that of royal authority in his colony.

After being driven from his last foothold (GWYNN ISLAND, July '76), Dunmore conducted a raid up the Potomac (see Mil. Opns. in VA.) before returning by way of N.Y. to England. He again sat as a Scottish peer in Parliament before being named Gov. of the Bahamas (1787–96).

Thwaites and Kellogg, *Doc. Hist. of*

Dunmore's War (1905), includes a biographical sketch of Dunmore. In her *D.A.B.* article, already cited, Kellogg comments that Eckenrode's *Rev. in Va.* (1916) "is prejudiced and presents the Governor's activities as they appeared to his enemies."

DUNMORE'S (OR CRESAP'S) WAR, 1774. Early in 1774, Dr. John Connolly, the unprincipled agent of Va. Gov. Dunmore, took Ft. Pitt and started retaliating against the Indians of the region for their recent outbreak of attacks against settlers. He seemed to welcome hostilities between whites and Indians as a diversion from the long-standing conflict between Pa. and Va. interests in this disputed territory. Trouble had already started when it was aggravated by a series of white atrocities. Near the junction of Yellow Creek and the Ohio at "Logan's Camp" or Baker's Cabin (35 mi. W. of Pittsburgh), Capt. Michael CRESAP'S party killed one Indian and captured another in a fair fight on 27 Apr. Three days later, however, Daniel Greathouse lured a group of Indians into an "entertainment" and then murdered six of them. The half-breed LOGAN, heretofore a great friend of the whites, lost a brother and a sister in the "Baker's Cabin Massacre" and took 13 white scalps in retaliation. Although this satisfied him, the Shawnees went to war.

On 10 June, Dunmore called out the militia of S.W. Va. and the Royal Governor established headquarters at Pittsburgh. Early in Aug., Maj. Angus McDonald raided Shawnee villages on the Muskingum River (100 mi. from Pittsburgh). The next month Dunmore started down the Ohio with almost 2,000 militia and ordered Col. Andrew Lewis to lead another column of over 1,000 down the Kanawha River to join forces with him deep in Indian territory. The Shawnee chief CORNSTALK mobilized

1,000 Shawnee, Miami, Wyandots (Hurons), and Ottawas to attack Lewis before Dunmore was within supporting distance. The Indians were defeated in a major engagement on 10 Oct. at the mouth of the Kanawha near Point Pleasant. Resistance collapsed, and the two columns linked up near the site of modern CHILLICOTHE, Ohio. Despite the famous refusal of LOGAN to join in the peace talk, Cornstalk met with Dunmore and hostilities ended.

Many Revolutionary War leaders, on both sides, were veterans of "Dunmore's War."

The above version of this controversial vignette of American history is based on James's *Clark* and Louise P. Kellogg's short article in *D.A.H.* Other accounts vary considerably in detail and on essential facts and dates. (See, for example, Stone's *Border Wars*, I, 46 ff., which gives 24 May as the date of Greathouse's atrocity and indicates that Cresap's "land-jobbers" perpetrated earlier outrages.) See main bibliography for special studies by Kellogg (in collaboration with Thwaites) and Downes.

DUPORTAIL. See LE BÈGUE ... DUPORTAIL.

DURHAM BOATS. Developed to carry iron ore, grain, whiskey, and other bulk freight between Philadelphia and the northern counties of N.J., they ranged between 40 and 60 feet in length, were eight feet wide, and drew only 20 inches of water when fully loaded. The largest could carry 15 tons. They could be sailed or poled. (Bill, *Princeton,* 28–29) Another writer describes them as being "like large canoes, ... usually painted black, pointed at each end, and manned by four or five men." (Stryker, *Trenton and Princeton,* 129) Washington used them in his attack on TRENTON, 26 Dec. '76.

DU SIMITIÈRE. See SIMITIÈRE.

DUTCH PARTICIPATION IN THE AMERICAN REVOLUTION. By the time the American Revolution started, the Dutch, who had once been a race of tough fighters, had become the bankers and traders of continental Europe. Their representatives in N.Y. had passed under English domination with the Treaty of Westminster, 19 Feb. 1674. Dutch possessions in the West Indies comprised only the small islands of Aruba, Caraçao, and Bonaire off the coast of Venezuela, and Saba, St. Eustatius, and (shared with France) St. Martin in the Leeward Islands. They had no sentimental or diplomatic interest in the American Revolution; their only interest was to profit by the breakdown of the British NAVIGATION ACTS to restore their domination of continental shipping and to sell supplies to belligerent countries (Bemis, *Diplomatic Hist. of the U.S.,* 35). "Their prosperity depended on their neutrality." (*Ibid.*)

Although Britain was able to require that neutral Portugal and Holland prohibit the shipment of goods direct to the American colonies, vast quantities went there via France as contraband. ST. EUSTATIUS became a bustling center of contraband trade. When France entered the war (May '78) the neutrality of Holland was put in jeopardy for the first time when Britain contended that naval stores and timber could no longer be shipped to France under the protection of a neutral flag. There followed a period of diplomatic skirmishing, with the British applying increasing pressure. Too late to be effective the States General on 24 Apr. '80 voted to increase their naval power so as to fight off threatening British interference with their convoys. Britain then invoked the Anglo-Dutch alliance of 1678, which required either ally to assist the other in case of war and which, therefore, precluded the Dutch from trading with the enemy. The

Dutch were lying over this barrel when the concept of ARMED NEUTRALITY was proclaimed by Russia, and on 4 Jan. '81 the Netherlands desperately but foolishly joined the League formed by Russia, Denmark, and Sweden.

Prior to this England had on 20 Dec. '80 used a curious excuse to declare war on Holland. This is covered in the biographical sketch of William LEE. Adm. Rodney promptly captured ST. EUSTATIUS, and the Royal Navy swept the seas of Dutch commerce.

Although the Dutch no longer could hurt Britain by their profitable contraband traffic, and this source of supply was cut off from the Americans, Dutch bankers supplied four loans between 1782 and 1788 that kept American finances alive during that crucial period. (*Ibid.*, 43)

The first American minister to Holland was Henry LAURENS, whose capture en route furnished the British with their excuse to declare war on the Dutch Republic. Laurens was succeeded by John Adams, who secured Dutch recognition of the U.S. on 19 Apr. '82, arranged for a loan of 5,000,000 guilders with bankers on the basis of popular subscription (first of the four loans mentioned above), and in Oct. '82 arranged a treaty of amity and commerce. "Since 1782 relations between the United States and the Netherlands have been cordial, friendly and unbroken," points out Bemis. (*Op. cit.*, 43–44)

E

EAST HAVEN, Conn., 5 July '79. See CONN. COAST RAID.

EASTON, Treaty of. Oct. '58. Pa. agreed with the Western Indians to make no settlements west of the Alleghenies. See PROCL. OF 1763.

EDEN, Robert. 1741–1784. Royal Gov. of Md. Of the same family as Charles Eden, Gov. of N.C. from 1714 to 1722, he married the sister of Lord Baltimore in 1765 and two years later was commissioned Gov. of Md. With his wife and two sons he reached Annapolis on 5 June '69 and immediately proved himself to be admirably suited for his difficult post. His first important official act was to prorogue the General Assembly before it could protest passage of the Townshend Acts. He skillfully attempted to steer a middle course between the demands of the colonists and the coercive policies of his masters. Although his reports went to great pains to explain the viewpoint of the colonists, in Apr. '76 a letter from Eden to Germain was intercepted and interpreted to mean that the governor was an enemy of the people. The Md. Council of Safety considered the charges groundless and refused to act on a resolution of the Cont'l. Cong. that Eden be arrested. The next month, however, he was asked to leave the province when it was learned that the government had ordered him to support the British armed forces in America. He left Annapolis on 26 June '76 aboard a warship, was delayed some weeks in the Chesapeake, and returned to England. On 10 Sept. '76 he was made a baronet for his service. When the war ended he returned to Md. to recover some property and died at Annapolis a few months later.

His brother was William EDEN. His grandson, Sir Frederick, became an officer in the British Army and was killed in the battle of New Orleans, 24 Dec. 1814. (Appleton's)

EDEN, William. 1744–1814. British politician. After his schooling at Eton, where he was an intimate friend of Lord Carlisle, he pursued a brilliant academic career through Oxford (Christ Church) and got his M.A. in 1768. In 1772, the year he published *Principles of Penal Law,* he became Under Secretary of State. Two years later he was seated in Parliament. In 1776 he was appointed to the Board of Trade and Plantations, and the same year he strengthened his political ties by marrying the only sister of Sir Gilbert Elliot (later Earl of Minto). As part of his official duties he managed the secret service on the Continent. In 1778 he organized and went to America with the PEACE COMMISSION OF CARLISLE. Two years later he became Carlisle's secretary when the latter was named Viceroy of Ireland. Alert and ambitious, he went on to become famous as a statesman and diplomat. In 1793 he was created Lord Auckland in the peerage of Great Britain.

EGG HARBOR, N.J. See LITTLE EGG HARBOR.

EGLESTON, Joseph. 1754–1811. Cont'l. officer. Va. Soon after graduating from William and Mary he joined the Cont'l. Army (Appleton's), becoming paymaster in the Cont'l. Dragoons in Mar. '77, and resigning this post 18 Nov. '77. On 21 Apr. '78 he became Lt. and paymaster of Lee's Dragoons, and on 5 Sept. '79 he advanced to Capt. Captured at Elizabethtown, N.J., on 25 Jan. '80, (Heitman), he was exchanged and joined Lee's Legion for operations

in the South. According to Appleton's he excelled as a cavalry commander in rear guard actions, particularly against Tarleton. His performance was outstanding at Guilford, AUGUSTA (May–June '81), and EUTAW SPRINGS. Having been promoted to Maj. in 1781, he served in this grade until the end of the war. He then was a member of the Va. legislature for several years and a congressman from 3 Dec. '98 to 3 Mar. 1801.

ELBERT, Samuel. 1743–1788. Cont'l. general. S.C.–Ga. Son of a Baptist clergyman and orphaned as a young child, he moved to Ga. and became a very prosperous merchant and West Indies trader. In July '74 he was elected Capt. of a Savannah grenadier company. Having been a Son of Liberty and member of the first local council of safety (June '75), he was commissioned Lt. Col. of the 1st Ga. Cont'ls. on 7 Jan. '76. After serving under Lachlin McIntosh, he was made Col. of the 2d Ga. on 5 July '76 and the next May commanded the Cont'l. troops on the abortive expedition against E. Fla. that Button Gwinnett had planned. He made a successful landing on Amelia Island, but the heat, lack of supplies, and loss of surprise led him to abandon plans to attack the mainland. Gov. Tonyn of E. Fla. was so alarmed by Elbert's threat, however, that he undertook to organize an Indian invasion of S.C. or Ga. Elbert withdrew to Savannah, where he succeeded McIntosh as commander of Cont'l. troops in Ga. After Gen. Robt. Howe arrived to take command in Ga. and undertook an invasion of E. Fla. (see SOUTHERN THEATER), Elbert led 300 men and three galleys to capture Ft. Oglethorpe in Frederica, near the mouth of the Altamaha River. Recalled for the defense of SAVANNAH, Dec. '78, he unsuccessfully urged that the main defense be made on Brewton's

Hill. At BRIAR CREEK, Ga., 3 Mar. '79, his 100 regulars put up about the only real resistance before the American force was routed. Elbert was wounded and captured. Exchanged in June '81,* he commanded a brigade at Yorktown. He was breveted B.G., Cont'l. Army, 3 Nov. '83. After the war he became Gov. and a militia Maj. Gen. (*D.A.B.* sketch is by Frank Edward Ross.)

ELIZABETHTOWN, N.J. On 6 Jan. '77 this place was recaptured by the Americans at the end of the NEW JERSEY CAMP'N. According to the *A.A.*-Heitman list of actions, there was fighting here on 25 Jan. and 6 June '80.

ELIZABETHTOWN–NEWARK–PASSAIC RAID, 11 Sept. '77. See CAMPBELL, John (*d.* 1806).

ELLERY, William. 1727–1820. Signer. R.I. After graduating from Harvard in 1747, he entered his father's business, served as a state naval officer and clerk of the General Assembly, and then practiced law. An early advocate of colonial rights, he was sent to the Cont'l. Congress in May, 1776. Ellery sat in Congress continuously until 1786, with the exceptions of 1780 and 1782. He served on many committees and specialized in naval and commercial matters. During the British occupation of R.I. his house was burned and his property sacked. He was named chief justice of the R.I. superior court but never took his seat, feeling himself more valuable in Congress. He was commissioner of the Cont'l. Loan office for R.I. (18 Apr. '86–1 Jan. '90) and, from 1790 until his death, collector of the port of Newport. Appleton's describes him as of "... moderate stature, with a large head and impressive features."

* Heitman incorrectly states that he was wounded and captured a second time at Charleston, 12 May '80.

He was a wealthy and widely read man. Two of his grandsons were Richard Henry Dana and William Ellery Channing.

ELLIOT, John. *d.* 1808. British naval officer. As a commodore commanding the *Trident* he entered the stage of the American Revolution unhappily in Apr. '78 when he sailed for the New World with the PEACE COMMISSION OF CARLISLE. Arriving early in June, he served during the next two months as second-in-command to Adm. Howe, and he was one of the naval officers later named by Gen. Clinton as an acceptable successor to Adm. Howe. (Clinton, *Amer. Reb.*, 142) Returning to England and given command of the *Edgar* (74), he sailed with Adm. George Rodney on 29 Dec. '79 for the relief of Gibraltar and had a distinguished part in the action off Cape Vincent, 16 Jan. '80. The next two years he commanded the *Edgar* in the Channel Fleet. During the period 1786–89 he was Gov. of Newfoundland. On 16 Apr. '95 he was promoted to Adm., but because of health had no further naval service. He had been in Parliament for a year starting in 1767.

He was an uncle of Gilbert Elliot, 1st Earl Minto, whose only sister married Wm. EDEN. He was related by marriage to Lord CATHCART and Adm. DIGBY, both of whom married daughters of his brother Andrew Elliot.

ELLIS, Welbore. 1713–1802. British statesman. Son of the noted Bishop of Meath, he attended Westminster School, went to Oxford in 1732, and received his B.A. in 1736. In Dec. '41 he entered Parliament. He was appointed a lord of the Admiralty in 1747 and served until 1755. On 17 Dec. '62 he succeeded Charles Townshend as Sec. at War, and resigned in 1765. On 11 Feb. '82 he succeeded Germain as Sec. of State, but the next month he resigned when the Rockingham ministry came in. He was created 1st Baron Mendip on 13 Aug. '94.

ELMIRA, N.Y. Modern name of NEWTOWN or Chemung.

ELPHINSTONE, George Keith. 1746–1823. British naval officer. Scotland. In 1761 he followed three brothers into the Royal Navy. In 1767 he sailed to China aboard an East India Co. ship commanded by his brother William and, with money borrowed from his granduncle, is said to have laid "the foundation of a pecuniary independence." (*D.N.B.*) Promoted to Lt. in 1770, in July '76 he was aboard the frigate *Perseus* as part of a convoy to America. In the following years he was active in operations against American privateers and blockade runners, and in cooperating with British land operations. He was particularly valuable to Sir Henry Clinton in the latter's operations against CHARLESTON in 1780 and returned to England when Capt. Sir Andrew Hamond took back the dispatches. In Sept. '80 he was returned to parliament for Dumbartonshire. Having taken command of the *Warwick* (50), on 5 Jan. '81 he distinguished himself by capturing the Dutch ship *Rotterdam* (50). On 27 Mar. '81 he sailed with a convoy from Cork and spent the rest of the war in American waters. On 15 Sept. '82, supported by the *Lion, Vestal,* and *Bonetta* sloop, he captured the frigate *Aigle* (50) and two smaller craft at the mouth of the Delaware and forced the *Gloire* into the safety of shallow water. In bad health when the war ended, he was inactive for the next 10 years but returned to pursue a long and distinguished naval career, becoming Vice Adm. and in 1814 becoming the first Viscount Keith. As commander of the Channel fleet, he became intermediary between the government and Napoleon when the latter sought refuge on the *Bellerophon. D.N.B.* devotes five and a half pages to his life.

ENFILADE. A fire from small arms or artillery that sweeps a line of men or defensive works from end to end, as opposed to "frontal fire." RAKE is the naval equivalent.

ENGINEERS. Military engineering preceded civil engineering, and in America the latter profession did not develop until about the time of the Civil War. Chief Engineers of the Cont'l. Army were (dates of appointment in parentheses): Col. Richard GRIDLEY (17 June '75), Col. Rufus PUTNAM (5 Aug. '76), and Maj. Gen. Duportail (22 July '77). Gridley had had some professional training, but was too old to be really effective. As for Putnam, Trevelyan comments that his citadels were death traps for their garrisons. (*American Revolution,* II, 214) When he resigned, "Washington was in no hurry to replace him either by a native amateur, or by one of those numerous foreigners who, to hear them talk, were as good as anything that had appeared since Archimedes; but whose only ascertained qualifications were that they could not speak English, and stood in urgent need of a salary." (*Ibid.*)

Help came from France in the form of four French engineers sent by Franklin at the request of Congress: Duportail (see LE BÈGUE...DU PORTAIL, which is his real name), La Radière, de GOUVION, and de LAUMOY. Duportail became chief of engineers on 22 July '77 and continued in this post until 10 Oct. '83. Another foreigner whose engineering ability contributed greatly to American victory was KOSCIUSZKO, who had been trained at the French school of artillery and military engineering at Mézières.

Engineering and artillery often were

combined in a common arm of the service until recent times, the *Ingeniator* of 1066 becoming the *Atillator* around 1300, and a separate artillery arm not emerging until three centuries later. (See also ARTILLERY. . . .) Cols. Jeduthan BALDWIN and GRIDLEY had combined artillery-engineer functions early in the American Revolution, and between 1794 and 1802 the new nation had a "Corps of Artillerists and Engineers." Topography was a separate function in the Cont'l. Army, and Robert ERSKINE was its first map-maker.

Famous British engineers were MONCRIEF and MONTRESOR.

"ENGLAND" AND "ENGLISH." Strictly speaking, England is that part of the British Isles excluding Wales, Scotland, and Ireland, and inhabitants of the latter parts cannot properly be called "Englishmen." (Furthermore, there are no Scotch in Scotland, only Scots or the Scottish people.) Reassured by the blast that Fowler takes at this pedantry in his *Modern English* [*sic*] *Usage,* I have occasionally used the words *England* and *English* where *Great Britain* and *Great British* might have been more precise. Nit pickers will also note that writers often speak of the British doing something in the Revolution when they really mean the British, Tories, Indians, and GERMAN MERCENARIES ("Hessians").

For comment on the usage of *American,* see "UNITED STATES. . . ."

ENOS, Roger. 1729–1808. Cont'l. officer. Conn. Born in Simsbury, Conn., he served with colonial troops in 1759 and in 1764 had become a Capt. in Israel Putnam's regiment. He took part in the Havana campaign of 1762 and 10 years later went on the commission sent by Conn. to look at land in the Mississippi Valley granted to veterans. (See Israel PUTNAM) Maj. of the 2d

Conn. Regt. on 1 May '75, he was promoted to Lt. Col. on 1 July. He commanded a battalion in ARNOLD'S MARCH TO QUEBEC and on 1 Dec. was court-martialed for "quitting without leave." Although honorably acquitted, he left the Cont'l. service on 10 Dec. '75. He subsequently became Col. of the 16th Conn. militia, resigned 18 Jan. '76, but was Col. of another regiment in 1777 through 1779. (Appleton's) In Mar. '81 he settled in Enosburg, Vt., and that year he was appointed B.G. in command of all Vt. militia. He was promoted to state Maj. Gen. in 1787 and held this post until his resignation in 1791. Meanwhile he had been active in political affairs and according to Appleton's, between 1779 and 1792 he was one of the most prominent and honored figures in the history of Vt.

ENUMERATED ARTICLES. As part of British MERCANTILISM reflected in the NAVIGATION ACTS and Trade Acts, certain colonial products that were allowed to be exported from the place of origin only to England or one of her colonies were "enumerated." The Act of 1660 put sugar, tobacco, indigo, cotton, ginger, and certain dyewoods on the list. In 1705 the list was expanded to include rice, molasses, and NAVAL STORES; furthermore, the colonists were given bounties for production of these articles. In 1721 the enumerated list included beaver skins, furs, and copper. The Sugar Act of 1764 enumerated hides and skins, pot and pearl ashes, iron, lumber, whale fins, and raw silk. In 1767 it was decreed that all non-enumerated goods destined for any part of Europe north of Cape Finisterre be shipped through England, but only a small percentage of colonial exports were affected.

ENVELOPMENT. An attack directed against the enemy's flank—or flanks, in the case of a double envelopment. It should not be confused with the TURNING MOVEMENT, although the latter is commonly known also as a "strategic envelopment."

EPAULEMENT. Coming from the French word for "shoulder" (*épaule*), this was the shoulder of a BASTION or, in another sense, an outwork for flank protection.

EPINE or DES EPINIERS. See L'EPINE.

ERSKINE, Robert. 1735–1780. Mapmaker of the Cont'l. Army. Scotland–N.J. After studying at the University of Edinburgh, he went to London where the treachery of a business partner got him seriously in debt. Escaping a jail sentence only because of his excellent character and innocence in the affair, he continued his studies and for his work in the field of hydraulic engineering became a fellow of the Royal Society in 1771. He reached N.Y.C. on 5 June '71 as representative of a British capitalist who had invested in the American Iron Company, which was mining and manufacturing in what is now the upper part of Passaic co., N.J. He soon became a supporter of the patriot cause and in the summer of 1775 organized his employees into a military company. Erskine was made a Capt. in the Bergen co. militia, and his men were exempted from compulsory service in other units.

On 27 July '77 Erskine was commissioned "Geographer and Surveyor to the Army of the United States," as Heitman gives the title. *D.A.B.* says Washington met Erskine early in the war and, learning that this able engineer and F.R.S. was well acquainted with the region west of the Hudson, offered him the position of "geographer and surveyor-general to the Continental Army." Although Freeman's biography

of Washington includes several sketches based on Erskine's maps, he mentions no personal connections between the men; one wonders why Erskine was not given the post until the second year of the war if Washington had met him at least eight months earlier.

In three years of zealous work, Erskine produced maps that contributed significantly to Washington's operations, despite their numerous inconsistencies in scale and errors in distance and orientation. (Freeman, *Washington,* IV, 259, 277) Among the prized possessions of the Pierpont Morgan Library in N.Y.C. is an engraved copy with annotations believed to be in Washington's hand of "A Map of part of the States of New-York and New-Jersey: Laid down, chiefly from Actual Surveys, received from the Right Honble Ld Stirling and others, and Deliniated for the use of His Excely Genl. Washington, by Robt. Erskine F.R.S. 1777." (*Ibid.,* 303 *n.*)

Erskine died 2 Oct. '80 of an illness contracted during his field work. (*D.A.B.*) In his *Military Journal* entry for 25 Jan. '81, Dr. Thacher, who was accompanyng Gen. Robert Howe's force from the Hudson Highlands to put down the MUTINY OF THE N.J. LINE, speaks of the excellent accommodations given to Howe and his field officers in Pompton "at the house of Mrs. Erskine, the amiable widow of the late respectable geographer of our army." Robert and Margaret (Simson) had known lean years during his struggle for success (*D.A.B.*), and it is comforting to hear Thacher report: "Mrs. Erskine is a sensible and accomplished woman, lives in a style of affluence and fashion; every thing indicates wealth, taste and splendor; and she takes pleasure in entertaining the friends of her late husband with generous hospitality." (*Op. cit.,* 251)

See A. H. Heusser, *The Forgotten*

General [sic], *Robert Erskine, Geographer* (Paterson, N.J., 1928). His papers are held by the N.J. Hist. Soc. Records of the Q.M.G. contain numerous references to Erskine and his works. (*D.A.B.*) His original maps are in the possession of the N.Y. Hist. Soc. Library.

ERSKINE, William. 1728–1795. British general. Entering the Scots Greys in 1743, he became a cornet at Fontenoy (1745), a Maj. in the 15th Light Dragoons in Mar. '59, and served with great credit in Germany. In 1762 he became a Lt. Col. and the next year, after presenting George III with 16 stands of colors captured by his regiment at Emsdorf, "he was raised to the dignity of knight banneret, but as the ceremony was not performed on the field of battle, the creation was considered irregular, and his possession of the rank was not generally recognized." (*E.B.*, "Flag," X, 457 *b*) As a B.G. he commanded a brigade in the battle of Long Island, 27 Aug. '76, and the next night surprised an American detachment at JAMAICA. In Apr. '77 he was Tryon's second in command during the CONN. COAST RAID. Sir Henry Clinton made Erskine his Q.M.G., in which capacity he also led troops during the Monmouth Campaign, and during the winter of 1778–79 he commanded the eastern district of Long Island. When Clinton moved up the Hudson in the winter of 1778 in an attempt to intercept the Convention Army, which was reported to be moving to Va. (late Nov. '78), Erskine commanded five infantry battalions and a cavalry squadron, but the expedition returned to N.Y.C. after getting as far as Kings Ferry. In the summer of 1779 he turned over his duties as Q.M.G. to Maj. Duncan Drummond and sailed for London. "The army will miss in him an experienced and very well-liked man," wrote Baurmeister,

"but he followed the sincere advice of his warmest friends, who urged him to retire from this important position which demanded his constant attention all day and always made him late for supper." (*Journals,* 276)

He had been made Col. of the 80th Regt. in 1777, was promoted to Maj. Gen. in 1779, Lt. Gen. in 1787, and became a baronet in June '91. During the Flanders campaign of 1793–95 he was second in command to the Duke of York.

ESOPUS, N.Y., 13 or 16 Oct. '77. See KINGSTON.

ESSEX JUNTO (1803–04). See under Timothy PICKERING.

ESTABLISHMENT. See REGULAR ESTABLISHMENT.

ESTAING, Charles Hector Théodat, Comte d'. 1729–1794. French admiral. Born in the château of Ruvel, in Auvergne, he was Col. of a regiment at the age of 16 and a brigadier at 27. The next year, in 1757, he went to the East Indies. In 1759 he was captured at the siege of Madras and paroled. Before his exchange was ratified he led naval operations against the British, and in 1760, having returned to France, he was again captured. Charged with violation of parole, he was imprisoned at Portsmouth. Released because the charge could not be substantiated, he emerged from his brief confinement with an even greater hatred of England than that shared by most Frenchmen. This was probably intensified by the statement of Adm. Boscawen, C. in C. in India, that if he ever caught Estaing again he would "chain him upon the quarter-deck and treat him like a baboon."

In 1763 he was named Lt. Gen. in the Navy [sic], in 1777 he became Vice Adm., and in 1778 he took command of the fleet organized to fight the British in America. (*E.B.*) "The navy did not credit him with natural ability when the war broke out, and it is safe to say that its opinion was justified by his conduct during it," comments Chevalier in his *Histoire de la Marine Française* (quoted in Mahan, *Sea Power,* 371). He sailed from Toulon on 13 Apr. '78 and after an incredibly slow crossing of 87 days missed an opportunity to bottle up an English fleet in the Chesapeake. At NEW YORK, 11–22 July, and NEWPORT, 29 July–31 Aug. '78, he went on to successively greater failures. On 4 Nov. he sailed for the West Indies, after abandoning plans for an amphibious Franco-American expedition against Halifax and Newfoundland. Adm. Barrington frustrated d'Estaing's feeble attempt to retake Santa Lucia, but the French admiral succeeded in capturing St. Vincent and Grenada. He also forced Adm. Byron to withdraw from an effort to relieve Grenada. On 6 July '79 d'Estaing and Byron fought a drawn battle but when the latter retired to St. Christopher the Frenchman would not use his superior forces to attack him in the roadstead.

At SAVANNAH, 9 Oct. '79, he capped an inept career and brought American disenchantment with French military assistance to a demoralized low. D'Estaing was brave—he was severely wounded while trying to make a success of the Savannah assault—but his lack of naval experience combined with army origins to create lack of cooperation from his naval subordinates. The French military historian Guérin is quoted by Mahan as follows: "Brave as his sword, D'Estaing was always the idol of the soldier, the idol of the seaman; but moral authority over his officers failed him on several occasions, notwithstanding the marked protection extended to him by the King." (*Ibid.*) An

American writer disagrees on the matter of his popularity: "Comparatively young, handsome, and energetic, he was brusque and autocratic in manner and not liked by his officers and men." (Lewis, *De Grasse,* 71)

Early in 1780 he returned to France where his advice, seconding that of Lafayette, influenced the government in sending out Rochambeau's expeditionary force. The biggest problem the latter had to contend with, however, was the memory of d'Estaing's military failures. In 1783 d'Estaing was at Cadiz commanding the combined fleet being assembled there for renewed operations in the West Indies, but the war ended before he and Lafayette had finished their preparations.

Turning to politics, he was elected to the Assembly of Notables in 1787, became commandant of the National Guard in 1789, and was named admiral by the National Assembly in 1792. Although in favor of national reforms he remained loyal to the royal family. He testified on behalf of Marie Antoinette and exchanged friendly letters with her. This led to his ultimately being brought to trial, and on 28 Apr. '94 he was executed.

EUTAW SPRINGS, S.C., 8 Sept. '81. (SOUTHERN CAMPAIGNS OF GREENE) When Greene was sufficiently reinforced to resume the offensive he took a roundabout route and surprised the British army under Lt. Col. Alexander Stewart near Nelson's Ferry on the Santee River at the place called Eutaw Springs. "Notwithstanding every exertion having been made to gain intelligence of the enemy's situation," complains Stewart in his after-action report to Cornwallis, "they rendered it impossible by waylaying the by-paths and passes through the different swamps." (Lee, *Memoirs,* 604–5).

Breaking camp at 4 A.M. on the 8th,

Greene started a cautious approach march from Burdall's Plantation toward Eutaw Springs, seven miles away. Lt. Col. John Henderson led the column with his 73 S.C. state infantry (units of which were commanded by Lt. Cols. Ezekiel Polk and Hugh Middleton) and Light-Horse Harry Lee's Legion. Francis Marion, who had just joined Greene after a 400-mile march (see PARKER'S FERRY, 30 Aug.), followed with his partisans, the N.C. militia of Malmedy, and the S.C. militia of Andrew Pickens. Next came Jethro Sumner with his N.C. Cont'ls. (battalions of Lt. Col. J. B. Ashe and Majs. John Armstrong and Reading Blount), the Va. Cont'ls. of Lt. Col. Richard Campbell (the latter's battalion and that of Maj. Smith Snead), and Col. Otho Williams' Md. Cont'ls. (Lt. Col. John Howard and Maj. Henry Hardman). Wm. Washington's horsemen and the durable Robt. Kirkwood's Del. Cont'ls. brought up the rear. Two "grasshoppers" (3-pdrs.) under Capt.-Lt. (*sic*) Wm. Gaines and two 6-pdrs. commanded by a Capt. Browne (probably Wm. Brown of Md.) were in the column.

Although Ward refers to S.C. militia "under Sumter and Pickens" (*W.O.R.*, 826), Sumter was absent on sick leave; his infantry and cavalry partisans were led in this battle by John Henderson and Wade Hampton, respectively. Greene's total strength was about 2,200 in this advancing column.

Stewart had between 1,800 and 2,000 effectives, the lesser figure being Fortescue's estimate. Flank companies of the 3d, 19th, and 30th Regts. constituted Maj. John Marjoribanks' "flank battalion"; its strength was 300 men. The eight battalion companies of the 3d Foot ("Irish Buffs") were present, as were the understrength 63d and 64th Foot, Cruger's Tories, and Coffin's S.C. horse.

His artillery included two 6-pdrs., one 4-pdr., a 3-pdr., and at least one swivel gun; Ward mentions only the first three pieces, but Stewart's report mentions losing one 3-pdr., and one swivel gun figured in the action (see below).

THE PRELIMINARY BOUTS

To make up for a shortage of bread, Stewart had been sending foraging parties out each morning around dawn to dig sweet potatoes. The day of the battle the detail was drawn from Marjoribanks' Bn. and the Buffs; unarmed and with a small guard, the yam diggers left camp about 5 A.M. An hour later two N.C. deserters were brought to Stewart with the story that Greene was approaching with 4,000 men. The British commander says in his official report that Maj. Coffin was already reconnoitering in the direction from which Greene would approach, but other accounts say Stewart sent him out after receiving the information from the deserters. Ward subscribes to the popular theory that Stewart refused to believe the deserters and had them confined. In any event, around 8 A.M. Coffin made contact about four miles from Stewart's camp. Maj. John Armstrong, leading the rebel column with a party of N.C. horse, reported Coffin's approach in time for Henderson to set an ambuscade. When the Boston Tory raced down the road in pursuit of Armstrong he came under small arms fire from both flanks and was enveloped by the Legion cavalry under Maj. Joseph Egleston. (He had charged into the same sort of trap after HOBKIRK'S HILL.) Coffin escaped with his cavalry to warn Stewart, but four or five of his infantry were killed and about 40, including their captain, were captured. Lee says the 200 to 300 yam diggers in the area escaped (*Memoirs.*

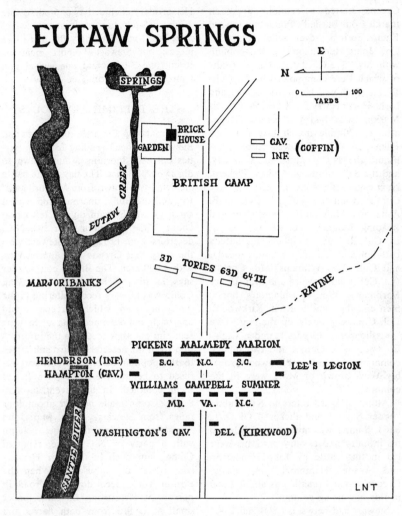

EUTAW SPRINGS

466 and *n*.). Ward says 400 of them rushed to the scene of action (which, since they were unarmed, is hard to believe) and were all captured. Other accounts say there were only 100 foragers and that all were taken. (Ward, *op. cit.*, 828, 921 *n*.) Since they came from the strongest part of Stewart's line (as later organized) it would be interesting to know the actual losses; the account of Lee, who was present, seems the most plausible.

Sending out a force to delay Greene, Stewart deployed forward of his camp. Marjoribanks was posted in a blackjack thicket some distance from the British right flank. Coffin's horse and foot troops were held in reserve to the rear. The others were deployed in a line that extended across the River, or Roche's

Plantation, Road. Greene had organized his column with a view to his intended deployment, and he formed his lines several miles from the enemy camp, after the initial contact with Coffin. Dispositions as the two armies came into contact are shown schematically on the opposite page.

The British flank battalion (Marjoribanks) was in a dense blackjack thicket that made them virtually invulnerable to cavalry, in which arm Greene had a marked superiority. Maj. Sheridan of Cruger's Tory corps had orders to occupy the brick house "to check the enemy, should they attempt to pass it" (Stewart's report). Coffin's 100 or so remaining infantry and 50 horse were initially in reserve. Bear in mind that Greene and Stewart had approximately equal numbers. Because of Greene's deployment and the large number of units in his army, many maps of the battle give the false impression that his force was much bigger than Stewart's.

PHASE I:
GREENE'S MILITIA ATTACK

A little past 9 A.M., the Americans moved through the woods. The British delaying force was encountered between two and three miles from the enemy camp and driven back as the rebels struggled to preserve their formation in the woods. (Greene's report, Lee, *op. cit.*, 600–3) It was not long before "a most tremendous fire began on both sides from right to left, and the Legion and State troops were closely engaged." (*Ibid.*) Gaines's "grasshoppers" were put out of action by the three enemy guns after an exchange that silenced one of the latter. The militia performed admirably, firing 17 volleys before showing any signs of weakening. Lee tried to turn the enemy left but was fought off by the 63d Foot.

PHASE II:
BRITISH COUNTERATTACK ROUTS THE MILITIA

Worried about the enemy cavalry on both flanks, and noting that Greene's initial attack was made by militia, Stewart was content to hold his ground rather than advance and expose his flanks. But by what Stewart calls "an unknown mistake," the troops on his left advanced and others followed. Malmedy's N.C. militia broke first, then the S.C. militia on their flanks. Lee stood fast on the right against the 63d, and the S.C. troops on the other flank held back the 3d Regt.

Greene responded adroitly to the new situation by ordering Jethro Sumner's N.C. Cont'ls. forward to plug the gap left by the militia's withdrawal.

Although they were green troops with less than a month's training, Sumner's men not only regained the lost ground but drove the enemy back to their original positions.

PHASE III:
SUMNER IS DRIVEN BACK

Stewart now brought up his reserve: Coffin's cavalry taking position to protect the left flank against the threat of Lee's horse, and Coffin's infantry reinforcing the faltering front line. Heavy fighting continued on both flanks while the opposing commanders were occupied with restoring their centers: the American left faltered momentarily when Henderson was wounded, but Hampton rallied them to push back the Buffs and take 100 prisoners. Lee's Legion held on the right, and Greene's best troops had not yet been committed.

Having done so well in their baptism of fire, Sumner's N.C. Cont'ls. were finally broken by the renewed British advance in the center. But as the King's troops surged forward to exploit this second breakthrough, Greene put in his first team to shatter their visions of victory. The Md. and Va. Cont'ls. of Otho Williams and Richard Campbell moved forward to deliver their first volley at 40 yards and follow through with a bayonet charge. Almost simultaneously, Capt. Rudolph led the Legion infantry into an attack against the vulnerable British left flank. Stewart's left and center were routed and they retreated in confusion through their tents. The Buffs held for a while against Howard's Md. Brig. "Such was the obstinacy with which the contest was maintained, that a number of the soldiers fell transfixed by each other's bayonets," writes Lee (*Op. cit.*, 467 *n.*, 469). But the Buffs finally retreated with the rest of the line.

PHASE IV:
STEWART'S STRONGPOINTS HOLD

Several things now happened to deprive Greene of what appeared to be a hard-fought victory. First, Marjoribanks' flank battalion held fast in their blackjack thicket. When Greene sent Washington's cavalry against them, half of the command was wiped out as they rode across the front of Marjoribanks' position in an attempt to reach an open space to his rear. Col. Washington was bayoneted and captured after his horse was shot out from under him. Wade Hampton charged with his S.C. horse and the survivors of Washington's, but he also was repulsed, and with heavy losses. The second misfortune was that most of Greene's army fell apart when they got among the enemy's tents and started finding food and liquor. Gorging and swilling themselves were not only the militia of Pickens, Malmedy, and Marion, but also the Cont'l. regiments—with the exception of Howard's—that had originally constituted the second

line. Greene, occupied on the left, was "strangely unaware of the disorder in the camp." (Ward, *op. cit.*, 833)

Coffin's cavalry was still in the field, and Greene's loss of control was apparent from the unsuccessful attempts made to run him off. While Greene personally directed the battle on the left, Lee had commanded the operations of his Legion infantry on the right. Lee realized that the rout of Coffin's cavalry would eliminate the force that was most valuable to Stewart in his attempts to rally, and he believed that an attack by the Legion cavalry against the British left would not only destroy Coffin but would also lead to the final rout of the entire enemy army. But when Lee sent for Egleston and made preparations to lead the Legion cavalry in an attack that promised to be completely successful he found that Egleston had already been committed on the other flank and had been defeated. Ward says Greene had ordered Egleston to attack Coffin from the American left (*op. cit.*, 833), but Lee says these orders were "officiously communicated . . . as from the general, when in truth he never issued such orders." (*Op. cit.*, 473) Lee considers that the errors in connection with employing Egleston against Coffin were the principal cause of Greene's defeat in this battle.

Wade Hampton attacked Coffin after Egleston's repulse and drove the Tory horse back after a closely fought action, but in pursuing him Hampton was exposed to a close fire from Marjoribanks' second position that badly chopped up the S.C. horsemen.

PHASE V:
MARJORIBANKS COUNTER-ATTACKS

The race for the brick house had been close, Kirkwood's men and some

of the Legion infantry having literally
gotten a foot in the door before Sheridan's Tories could shut and bar it. "By
so doing," writes Lossing, "several of
their own number were shut out. . . .
Those of the legion who had followed
to the door seized each a prisoner, and
interposing him as a shield, retreated
back beyond the fire from the windows."
(II, 703) Capt. Manning, who commanded Lee's infantry, grabbed as his
shield a British officer who protested
by solemnly reciting his titles: "I am
Sir Henry Barré," he is alleged to have
said, "deputy adjutant general of the
British army, captain of the 52d regiment, secretary of the commandant at
Charleston. . . ." "Are you, indeed?" interrupted Manning; "you are my prisoner now, and the very man I was
looking for; come along with me." And
using this brother of the famous Col.
BARRÉ to protect himself from the
enemy's fire, Manning made good his
retreat. (Ibid.)

Two 6-pdrs. were brought forward to
batter Sheridan's citadel, but they were
driven back by fire of muskets and a
swivel gun in the house. British troops
began to rally to reinforce Sheridan's
strong point, some entering the house
and others forming around the edge of
the palisaded garden. The flank battalion had drawn back to the garden, and
Marjoribanks led them in a gallant sortie that captured the rebel guns. He
then came forth again in a counterattack that won the day for the British.
John Howard with Oldham's Md. Co.
was wounded in an attempt to stop this
attempt, but Marjoribanks drove on to
rout the rabble among the British tents
and drive them into the woods. The
gallant Marjoribanks was mortally
wounded in this action, but other British
troops reinforced his flankers and the
battle was soon over.

NUMBERS AND LOSSES

Of approximately 2,200 Americans
engaged, over 500 were casualties. Congress published the following figures:
139 killed, 375 wounded, and 8 missing,
for a total of 522. Officer casualties
(included in the above totals) were 17
killed and 43 wounded. Four of the six
Cont'l. officers commanding regiments
were hit, Henry Lee and Otho Williams
being the two who emerged unscathed.
Richard Campbell was among the dead.
Militia leaders Pickens and Henderson
were wounded.

The British suffered the highest percentage of losses sustained by any force
during the war. Starting with between
1,800 effectives (according to Fortescue) and 2,000 (the figure favored by
American writers), they lost 693, according to official returns. Stewart reported that 85 of these were killed, 351
wounded, and 257 missing. There is
considerable disparity in the reports of
British prisoners taken: Greene says he
took 500, including over 70 wounded.
Stewart's report may not include the
yam gatherers captured in the opening
skirmish, but we have seen that this
figure is highly uncertain. The historian
F. V. Greene accepts Stewart's figures
of 85 killed and 351 wounded, but puts
his missing at 430, for a total of 866.
(Rev. War, 256–57) Fortescue says with
considerable justice that since the greater
part of Greene's army "was dispersed
among the British tents, plundering and
drinking," it is hard to believe that they
had only 8 missing.

As for detailed estimates of numbers,
Ward says Greene had 1,256 Cont'ls.,
73 infantry and 72 cavalry of S.C. state
troops (these, apparently, were Sumter's
partisans, commanded by Henderson
and Wade Hampton), 150 N.C. militia,
307 S.C. militia, Francis Marion's 40
horse and 200 foot, and about 300

cavalry under Lee and Washington. Of these 2,400, about 200 were detached as baggage guards at Howell's Ferry on the Congaree. (*Op. cit.*, 826) Component strengths of the British force have already been mentioned. Note that most of Stewart's troops were British regulars; Cruger's Tories, the defenders of NINETY-SIX, were veterans and of the caliber of regulars. Only the mounted troops of Coffin were relatively inexperienced militia.

COMMENTS

Eutaw Springs, the last major engagement in the South, was one of the hardest-fought actions of the Revolution. Troops on both sides fought exceptionally well, and there is little fault to be found with the tactical performance of either commander. Greene scored a fine strategic surprise and followed through well to exploit it. But Stewart recovered promptly and made an excellent deployment, particularly in placing the flank battalion and in his preparations to defend the brick house. The British simply outfought the Americans in the confused action that followed, and in a day marked by gallantry on both sides John Marjoribanks towers above the rest. As for the ill discipline that snatched victory from Greene when it seemed assured, looting has ruined the plans of greater commanders: Stonewall Jackson and Napoleon, to cite but two.*

* During Jackson's Valley Campaign, May 1862, the escape of Banks from Strasburg was faciliated because the crack Louisiana Zouaves and Turner Ashby's cavalry stopped to loot a Union supply train. Napoleon's brilliant strategic penetration at the start of his First Italian Campaign was almost spoiled when his troops started looting in cap-

For the fourth time Greene failed to win a battle, but he had again won a campaign: the British army was so weakened by losses at Eutaw Springs that they had to withdraw to the vicinity of Charleston. Liberation of the South was virtually assured.

EVACUATION DAY, 25 Nov. '83. British departure from N.Y.C. on this date was followed immediately by what Freeman calls the "last and greatest march" of the Cont'l. Army, which by then had dropped to a strength of about 800 men. (See Henry JACKSON) Although Boston, Philadelphia, Savannah, Charleston, and other occupied cities must have been happy to see the enemy army leave, the term "Evacuation Day" is associated with N.Y.C. See Henry P. Johnston, "Evacuation of New York by the British, 1783," *Harper's Magazine,* Nov. 1883, and James Riker, *Evacuation Day, 1783,* both cited by Freeman (*Washington,* V, 460 *n.*). The lithograph by E. P. & L. Restein from the Lib. of Cong. entitled "Evacuation Day" is reproduced in Alden, *The American Revolution,* and is featured on the dust jacket of that work.

EWALD, Johann von. 1744–1813. Hessian officer. Entering the army at the age of 16, he took part in the closing campaigns of the Seven Years' War. He lost his left eye in a duel in 1770. Having studied military engineering in Cassel, he published a book on military tactics in 1774 and was made Capt. of the Leibjäger. As commander of the 2d Co. (jägers) he reached New Rochelle on 22 Oct. '76, was in action the next day against a force of American riflemen. For his action with the advance guard at the Brandywine he

tured Dego and were driven from that place.

and Capt. von Wreden were awarded a medal that until that time had not previously been presented to officers of such low rank. Sir Wm. Howe wrote him a letter of appreciation before returning to England in 1778. He was conspicuous in the Charleston Expedition of Clinton in 1780 and left a valuable record of this operation. (See under JUNGKENN) Surrendered at Yorktown, he almost died of dysentery while on parole on Long Island. He returned to Cassel in May '84, waited four years in vain for promotion, and then became a Lt. Col. commanding a jäger corps in Denmark. He reorganized the corps, was elevated to the Danish nobility, and was a Maj. Gen. in 1802. Commanding forces in Holstein, he skirmished with French under Murat and Soult in maintaining the neutrality of Denmark against Napoleon. He was made a Lt. Gen. in 1807 after taking part in the assault on Stralsund. He died six years later after a brief illness. (Uhlendorf, *Charleston*, 6–7)

A prolific military author, his best-known work, which Uhlendorf calls "a veritable source book for American Revolutionary history," is *Belehrungen über den Krieg . . .*, which appeared in three parts between 1798 and 1803.

EXCHANGE OF PRISONERS. At the time of the Revolution (and for another century) it was normal to PAROLE prisoners of war and then arrange for their exchange. As a rule only officers could be exchanged. Exchange of "other ranks" was not favored by American civil or military authorities because the emaciated American prisoner often did not live long after his release from a British jail; this meant that the enemy stood to gain from the practice. Little is known about how many prisoners were taken during the war and even less about how many were exchanged, but the following "tariff" was worked out in Dec. '79 on the basis of how many privates were equivalent to various ranks: a Sgt. could be exchanged for two privates; a Second Sgt. or Ensign, 4; a 1st Lt., 6; Capt., 16; Maj., 28; Lt. Col., 72; Col., 100 (see also REGIMENT); B.G., 200; Maj. Gen., 372; Lt. Gen., 1,044. (Lossing, II, 852 *n.*)

F

FACTIONALISM in America during the Revolution. The colonists were split into hostile factions on the grounds of race, religion, social and economic interests, and politics. In many instances "factionalism" amounted to "regionalism"—the New Englanders being opposed to New Yorkers, Northerners being incompatible with Southerners, tidewater settlers being against those living inland. "The upper class had almost everywhere entrenched itself so firmly in power that aristocracy rather than democracy seemed likely to be the coming order in America." (Miller, *O.A.R.*, 55) Boundary disputes were at the base of animosities between colonies, particularly N.Y. and N.H. (hence most of New England) over the region that became Vermont; the Wyoming

Valley was the scene of bloody conflict before and after the Revolution, and Pa. struggled against Va. for control of what is now Ohio and western Pa. (particularly Pittsburgh). "New Englanders hated the citizens of Albany because they sold guns and ammunition to the Indians, who used them against the New England frontier." (*Ibid.*, 61)

The population of the colonies was predominantly Anglo-Saxon, many New England families having fourth, fifth, and sixth generations participating in the Revolution. These older elements were hostile to the Scotch-Irish, German, and Huguenot * immigrants who followed, and the newcomers gravitated toward the western frontier where they soon had economic as well as racial and religious differences with the older settlements. The Quaker oligarchy of Pa. denied the western counties proportionate representation and failed to give them the protection they wanted against the Indians. Money was another bone of contention: certain farmers and town artisans favored inflated currency (such schemes as the Land Bank), but in Mass. were frustrated by the wealthy oligarchs who wanted hard money. Regulator troubles rent the deep South. Although these factions might be expected to unite to destroy a common foe they were looking beyond the victory over Great Britain: there was the problem of how small states might secure an adequate voice in the government; there was the problem of the "three-sided states" whose western boundaries had not been defined.

While most of these problems had to be worked out after the war against Britain had been won, and are beyond the scope of this book, others are at

* Professor Rankin points out, however, that Huguenots were scarce on the frontier.

the root of trouble that plagued colonial leaders during the war. The New England leaders who dominated the period 1763–75, and this group can virtually be limited to the Mass. element, realized that they needed the support of other colonies, particularly Va., if the Revolution were to succeed. Hence they went to considerable effort to avoid the impression they wanted to dominate the early Congresses. Selection of the commander in chief of the Cont'l. army, which could have been a stumbling block if Mass. had insisted that this be one of their generals, turned out to be very easy. The New Englanders actually feared that a successful Eastern general at the head of a victorious army would be a danger to the country once the British were defeated. (Van Tyne, *War of Indep.*, 62–63) Furthermore, Mass. realized that the best way of assuring the full support of the powerful colony of Va. was for one of her generals to be given the supreme command. The fortuitous result was Washington's selection.

Although the necessity of appointing other generals with an eye to equitable state representation resulted in the elevation of many incompetents to positions of military leadership, these were soon pushed into assignments where they could not do too much harm to the cause. Only in the Northern Dept. did factionalism seriously jeopardize military operations. Here the New England–N.Y. antagonisms soon became evident. As C. in C. of this department Schuyler did not receive the whole-hearted support of the New England colonies during the Canada Invasion. He encountered lack of cooperation that verged on treason in his opposition to BURGOYNE'S OFFENSIVE, and it was pressure from the New England delegates in Congress that led to his relief by Gates. Regionalism loomed large in the American effort against the BENNINGTON RAID. It also figured in the so-called CONWAY CABAL.

In his *Articles of Confederation* (see bibliography) Jensen has concluded that while the conflicts arising out of the concrete issues during the Revolution centered on group interests, social cleavages, and state interests, the basic disagreement was between radical and conservative elements. Paradoxically, this split the patriots *within* regions and states but unified them *among* the regions and states. (Lib. of Cong., *Guide,* 344)

Professor Edmund S. Morgan gives an interesting analysis in his *Birth of the Republic, 1763–89,* of the factors that pulled Americans apart and that held them together so that they ended by uniting them to form a government "that has had a longer continuous existence than that of any Western country except England." (Under the index heading "Americans, unity of," are many references.)

See also MERCHANTS IN THE REVOLUTION and POPULAR SUPPORT OF THE REVOLUTION. . . .

FAIRFIELD, Conn. Occupied and burned by the British on 8 July '79 during the CONN. COAST RAID. See also WESTERN RESERVE.

FAIR LAWN, S.C., 27 Nov. '81. A strong British post at this place, near Monck's Corner, was captured by forces under the joint command of Isaac Shelby and Col. Hezekiah Maham of the Carolina dragoons.

FAIR LAWN, S.C., 29 Aug. '82. See Francis MARION.

FALMOUTH (now Portland), Me., destroyed by British, 18 Oct. '75. Adm. Graves's frustration from inability to stop American privateers on the high seas, and his irritation at criticism in Boston that he was doing nothing to support the British garrison (see C. &

M., 168–69 for Burgoyne's eloquent summation of his inactivity), caused Graves to plan a series of punitive expeditions against American coastal towns. BRISTOL, R.I., was the objective of an inglorious raid on 7 Oct. '75. The Falmouth expedition under Capt. Henry Mowat left Boston on 6 Oct., stopped for a look at Gloucester, Mass. (whose houses were considered too scattered to destroy effectively by naval gunfire), and anchored off Falmouth on 16 Oct. "After much bluster, warning, futile negotiations and demand for cannon and hostages" (Freeman, *Washington,* III, 559), his two warships, *Canceau* (8 guns) and *Halifax* (6 guns), shelled the town with solid shot and incendiary carcass from 9 A.M., 18 Oct., until about 6 P.M. Landing parties came ashore to set fires (Mowat's task force included 100 soldiers). Patriot groups from Falmouth and neighboring towns put up an unorganzied resistance since they were, unfortunately, "under the direction of a committee [that] did not, and we suppose could not, get together in the hurry of affairs, and therefore could give no authoritative directions." (Report by the Selectmen of Falmouth, quoted in C. & M., *op. cit.,* 172–73) British casualties were two men wounded.

Since the inhabitants had been warned by Mowat on 16 Oct. of the shelling, most of them had left town, and no lives were lost. The greater portion of the prosperous town was, however, destroyed: 139 dwellings and 278 other structures (Freeman and Strait both accept these figures); 11 vessels were burned and four captured. (Ward, *W.O.R.,* 134)

The British did not carry out their threat to visit this same destruction on other coastal towns, but Washington did see fit to send Gen. Sullivan and a small body of riflemen from the BOSTON

SIEGE to support Portsmouth, N.H., where the British were expected to hit next. The Americans were outraged by the Falmouth raid and cited it as an example of British ruthlessness against defenseless citizens.

FANNING, David. *c.* 1755–1825. Tory partisan. Va.–S.C. Although details of his origin are obscure, James T. Adams in his *D.A.B.* sketch says David Fanning was born at Beech Swamp, Amelia co., Va., and was the son of David Fanning. Having run away from a harsh master to whom he was apprenticed, he was an Indian trader among the Catawba (in S.C.) in the years just before the Revolution. Although he says he was only 19 years old in 1775, he also claims to have owned 1,000 acres in Va. and two slaves. Another detail of his prewar life that may have influenced his character was a disfiguring scalp disease known as scald head: this was so offensive during his childhood that he was not allowed to eat with other people, and when he outgrew this childhood disease it left his scalp so disfigured that he always wore a silk cap. Adams thinks this may in part account for "his extreme cruelty."(*Ibid.*) In the early stages of the split with England he sided with the patriots but changed sides, according to Adams, when he was robbed of his Indian trade and a considerable quantity of goods by a gang that called themselves Whigs. "He received his training in cruelty and courage under 'Bloody Bill' CUNNINGHAM, and not, as has usually been stated, under McGirth." (*Ibid.*)

A sympathetic picture of Fanning is presented by DeMond in his *Loyalists of N.C.* According to this author, Fanning was a native of S.C. when the war started and was a Sgt. in the same militia company as Thos. BROWN when this organization was split into Whig and Tory factions in May '75. Having signed a paper in favor of the King at that time, he returned to his home on Reburn Creek and for the next six years—during which time he apparently received his "training" under Cunningham—he was in and out of patriot prisons. Captured and paroled in Jan. '76, recaptured and imprisoned on 25 June, he escaped, was recaptured, tried for treason, and acquitted but charged £300 for court expenses. This life continued, according to his own account (see below), for another five years. The place of his confinement usually was Ninety-Six. (Fisher, *Struggle,* II, 419)

On 5 July '81 he was commissioned Col. by Maj. CRAIG, British commandant at Wilmington, N.C., and for the next 10 months he led his guerrillas in a number of remarkable actions. It is of this brief and final phase of his career that DeMond writes: "Probably no friend of the [British] government during the entire war accomplished more for the British, and certainly none received less credit." (*Op. cit.,* 140) While Col. Benj. Cleveland, one of the KINGS MOUNTAIN heroes, led his patriot bands along the Upper Yadkin, where he was "his own vigilance committee, judge and hangman" (Fisher, *op. cit.,* 418), Fanning undertook the same role on Deep River, some 30 miles N.E. His most impressive operation was the HILLSBORO RAID, 12 Sept. '81. Bloody retaliatory warfare continued after regular military operations ended in the South; Fanning apparently outclassed his opposition, but when he met rebel peace overtures with the request that his followers not be required to oppose the King during the remainder of the war, the civil authorities became arrogant. "There is no resting place for a Tory's foot upon the earth," quoth a certain Col. Balfour. Fanning sacked Balfour's plantation and killed him. (DeMond, *op. cit.*) The Tory leader got the upper hand in the region and continued to raid, but also continued efforts to arrange an armistice. He was married in the spring of '82, and on 7 May entered a truce area on the lower Peedee. He settled in E. Fla. when Charleston was evacuated, and went to Halifax in Sept. '84, after Spain was ceded E. Fla. He was elected to the provincial parliament of New Brunswick and served from 1791 until Jan. 1801, when he was expelled for some unknown crime. For the latter he was condemned to death but pardoned. Fanning moved to Digby, Nova Scotia, and became Col. of militia. (*D.A.B.*) He died at Digby in 1825. His tombstone says he was 70 at that time, a figure that does not square with his own statement that he was 19 years old in 1775; *D.A.B.* has accepted the later statement in fixing his year of birth at around 1755 rather than 1751.

In requesting compensation from the Crown, Fanning claimed to have led 36 skirmishes in N.C. and four in S.C., commanding bands that varied in strength between 100 and 950 men. He was allowed £60! Colonel Fanning's *Narrative* was written in 1790, first published (in Richmond, with an introduction by J. H. Wheeler) in 1861. The 50-page manuscript was twice reprinted prior to 1908, when a new edition was published in Toronto with an introduction by A. W. Savary. DeMond, who calls this *Narrative* "the best contemporary account of the Loyalists for the latter period of the war" (*op. cit.,* 141), gives 1906 as the date of Savary's edition; *D.A.B.* gives 1908.

FANNING, Edmund. Tory leader. N.Y.–N.C. 1739–1818. Great-grandson of Edmund Fanning who settled at New London in 1653, he was born on Long Island, graduated with honors from Yale in 1757, moved to Hillsboro, N.C., and was admitted to the local bar in 1762.

He became a favorite of Gov. Tryon and was the storm center of the subsequent REGULATOR movement. Of the notorious reputation he gained at this time, one writer says his "crime seems to have been only that he was Tryon's friend." (Bridenbaugh, *Myths and Realities,* 162, quoted in Alden, *South,* 154) In his *D.A.B.* sketch, James T. Adams says:

"Some of the charges of extortion made against him break down completely on examination and it is not unlikely that they were used to cloak the real objections to him, which were his relations with the governor and his immoral private life."

Holder of many offices, "He was a grasping young man 'on the make,' and may be described as an 'honest grafter,' " concludes Alden. (*South,* 155)

On 8 Apr. '68 the REGULATORS fired shots into Fanning's house. In May he arrested two of their leaders, but prudently released them when the mob threatened to raid the jail. A show of force by Tryon restored order temporarily, but violence again flared up and in the election of 1769 Fanning lost his seat in the assembly. Tryon then created the borough of Hillsboro to give him a seat in the assembly and Fanning was elected to it. On 24 Sept. '70 a mob of Regulators broke up the session of the superior court at Hillsboro, dragged Fanning from the courthouse and whipped him. The next day they ran him out of town and destroyed the fine house they maintained he had built from money extorted in official fees.

Fanning followed Tryon to his new post as Gov. of N.Y. in 1771 and became his private secretary. (He was not, as Appleton's and others say, Tryon's son-in-law.) Although unable to get compensation from the N.C. legislature for the loss of his property, Fanning received many lucrative offices in N.Y. before the war, among them the post of surveyor-general in 1774. An ardent Loyalist when the Revolution broke out, he raised "FANNING'S REGT." in 1776 and was wounded twice during the war. His N.C. property having been confiscated in 1779, he moved to Nova Scotia at the end of the war. In Sept. '83 he became councillor and Lt. Gov. of that province, and in 1785 he married. The next year he became Lt. Col. of Prince Edward Island. Charges of tyranny were brought against him by the people, but after investigation by the Privy Council in England were dismissed in Aug. '92. Meanwhile he had been made Col. in the British Army in Dec. '82, and in Apr. 1808 he was promoted to full general. His resignation as Lt. Gov. was effective in July 1805, and in 1813 he moved to England.

His nephew and namesake (1769–1841) became known as the "Pathfinder of the Pacific." The latter's brother was Nathaniel FANNING (1755–1805).

FANNING, Nathaniel. 1755–1805. American privateersman. A nephew of Edmund FANNING and brother of the famous explorer, Nathaniel went to sea at an early age. In 1778 he was on his third voyage with the *Angelica* privateer when he was captured and held 13 months in Forton Prison near Portsmouth. After being exchanged he became midshipman and private secretary to Jones on the *Bonhomme Richard*. Highly commended by Jones for promotion, he served with him on the *Ariel* until Dec. '80, when he and most of the ship's other officers refused to remain under Jones's command. In 1781 he was captured aboard a French privateer and spent six weeks in prison. Early the next year he became a French citizen, commanded French privateers, was twice held prisoner by the British for short periods, accepted a commission in the French navy, but gave this up and

returned to America at the war's end. Having married in 1784, he apparently was a merchant seaman until he accepted a lieutenant's commission in the U.S. Navy on 5 Dec. 1804. Ten months later he died of yellow fever while commanding the station at Charleston.

His *Narrative* gives an excellent account of the *Bonhomme Richard–Serapis* engagement, in which he commanded the maintop. (See C. & M., 950–53 for an extract) It "also shows how closely French and American interests were mixed in privateering," comments R. G. Albion in *D.A.B.*, and throws an unfavorable light on John Paul Jones, whom he considered brutal, unfair, and immoral. (*Ibid.*) A man of little education, Fanning was stocky, roundfaced, boastful, and a dapper dresser.

FANNING'S REGIMENT. Raised in N.Y. by Edmund FANNING in 1776, the unit was officially known as the Associated Refugees or the King's American Regiment of Foot. (*D.A.B.*, "Fanning.") Like all other successful Tory troops, they had a bad reputation for cruelty. The regiment went south with Gen. Leslie in 1780, reached Charleston on 16 Dec., and was sent to Georgetown, S.C.

"FARMER GEORGE." Nickname of King George III, stemming from his interest in agriculture.

FARMER'S LETTERS. Constitutional objections to the Townshend Acts were presented in 14 essays by John DICKINSON that appeared 5 Nov. '67–Jan. '68 in the *Pa. Chronicle*. They were entitled "Letters From a Farmer in Pennsylvania to Inhabitants of the British Colonies." Dickinson argued that Parliament had no right to tax the colonies solely for revenue, but had authority only to regulate trade, even if this resulted incidentally in revenue. He also called suspension of the NEW

YORK ASSEMBLY a blow to colonial liberties. In pamphlet form the letters circulated widely in England and America.

FASCINE. A long bundle of brushwood firmly bound together and used to fill ditches (in the assault of a fortified position) or in other military engineering tasks. See also GABION.

FEBIGER, Christian ("Old Denmark"). 1746–1796. Cont'l. officer. Denmark–Va. After a military education he joined the staff of his uncle, Gov. of Santa Cruz. In 1772 he visited the American colonies from Cape Fear to the Penobscot and the next year entered the lumber, fish, and horse business in the East. (Frank Edward Ross in *D.A.B.*) Having settled in Mass., he joined Gerrish's Mass. Regt. on 28 Apr. '75, became Adj. on 19 May, and rendered valuable service at BUNKER HILL, 17 June '75. He was Brig. Maj. during ARNOLD'S MARCH TO QUEBEC, Sept.–Nov. '75, and was captured in the attack on QUEBEC, 31 Dec.–1 Jan. In Sept. '76 he went to N.Y. with the other prisoners and was exchanged in Jan. '77. (*D.A.B.*; Heitman says he was exchanged in Nov. '76)

Meanwhile he had been named Lt. Col. of Daniel Morgan's 11th Va. on 13 Nov. '76 and fought at the Brandywine, 11 Sept. '77. On 26 Sept. he was promoted to Col., was on Greene's right at Germantown, 4 Oct., and on 9 Oct. '77 took command of the 2d Va. After the winter at Valley Forge he fought at Monmouth and as part of Wayne's light infantry brigade took part in the storming of Stony Point, 16 July '79. He wrote the next morning to his American bride:

"My Dear Girl: I have just borrowed pen, ink and paper to inform you that . . . at 12 o'clock last night we stormed this confounded place. . . . A musket ball scraped my nose. No other

damage to 'Old Denmark.' God bless you. Farewell—FEBIGER." (*Mag. Amer. Hist.*, VI, 194, quoted in Montross, *Rag, Tag,* 324)

His fighting days were over, however. In Aug. '80 he was stationed in Philadelphia with the mission of forwarding arms and supplies to the South, a duty in which he proved highly effective. (*D.A.B.*) He went to Va. the next spring, assisted Wayne in quelling a Loyalist uprising in Hampshire co., served as a recruiting officer, commanded a body of newly raised Va. Cont'ls. under Lafayette, and in the fall described himself in a letter to Washington as "Superintending officer of the Virginia line." (See VA. MIL. Opns. for events during the period. The Loyalist uprising occurred during May and June of 1781, and Wayne did not join Lafayette until 10 June.) He retired 1 Jan. '83, was breveted B.G. on 30 Sept. '83, settled in Philadelphia, went into business, and was Treas. of Pa. 1789–96.

A remarkable and unmelancholy Dane, his papers, orderly books, and correspondence have been microfilmed for the Va. State Lib., and presumably for others. They include an informal will he made the eve of Stony Point and that starts: "As there is . . . some danger of my taking a place among the deceased heroes of America. . . ."

FEDERALIST PARTY. Evolving from the group who had led the constitutional movement of 1787, the Federalists became the party of Alexander Hamilton and supported his controversial financial system, his belief in a strong central government and a strong national judiciary, his aristocratic views that the country should be governed by "the wise and good and rich," and the feeling that the United States should maintain a strict neutrality in international affairs. The opposition was organized by Thomas Jefferson as the REPUBLICAN PARTY. The first real weakening of Federalist strength came with ratification of JAY'S TREATY, which lost supporters in the South. But the popularity of Pinckney's Treaty (covered under SPANISH PARTICIPATION) and the warlike attitude of the Federalist Party toward France in 1798 revived enthusiasm of the people for the Federalists. After Jefferson became President in 1801, however, the Federalists ceased to be a significant challenge to the REPUBLICAN PARTY, and soon thereafter they disappeared into the American past.

FELTMAN, William. Cont'l. officer, diarist. Pa. Of interest for his diary (below), which Freeman calls a "most useful source," he became an ensign in the 10th Pa. on 4 Dec. '76 and on 13 Jan. '77 was promoted to 2d Lt. of Capt. Jacob Weaver's Independent Co. guarding prisoners at Lancaster. On 30 Oct. '77 he advanced to 1st Lt. Weaver's Co. was transferred to the 10th Pa. on 17 Jan. '77 and to the 1st Pa. on 1 Jan. '81. Feltman was captured at Green Spring, Va., 6 July '81, and resigned 21 Apr. '81. (Heitman, "Feltman," and "Weaver, Jacob [of Pa.]") His "Military Journal, May, 1781–April, 1782," is in the *Collections of the Hist. Soc. of Pa.*, II, and *Pa. Archives* (2), XI (Freeman, *Washington*, V, 330 n., 530, 533).

"FENCIBLES." Short for "defensibles," the term was applied to regular troops enlisted for service in Great Britain only, with special exemption from being drafted. (Fortescue, *British Army*, III, 288; *O.U.D.*) There were "fencible infantry" as well as land-, river-, and sea-fencibles in 1796 (*O.U.D.*) and perhaps earlier.

FERGUSON, Patrick. 1744–1780. British officer. Of an illustrious Scottish family, he studied in a London military academy and at the age of 14 (12 July '59) was appointed a cornet in the Scots Greys (Royal North British Dragoons). Poor health kept him out of military service during the period 1762–68. (*Ibid.*) On 1 Sept. '68 he was bought a captaincy in the 70th Foot and served with them in Tobago (W.I.) putting down a slave uprising. Inspired by the "boasted skill of the American marksmen" (*D.N.B.*) that impressed the British in the early stages of the Revolution, he invented the first breechloading rifle used in the British Army (*ibid.*), securing a patent on 2 Dec. '76. The weapon not only was highly accurate and had a high rate of fire, but it was dependable in wet weather when the standard flintlocks were not. With authority to raise a body of riflemen he joined his regiment at Halifax. He led this ranger detachment ahead of Knyphausen's column in its approach to the BRANDYWINE, 11 Sept. '77. Before this action he had an opportunity to pick off George Washington but did not fire at the unsuspecting father of his country because it was unprofessional to kill enemy officers. Professor Rankin writes me that Ferguson's manuscript letter in Edinburgh explains, "it was not pleasant to fire at the back of an unoffending individual who was acquitting himself very cooly [*sic*] of his duty, so I let him alone."

At Brandywine he received a wound that shattered his right elbow and permanently crippled his arm. While he was convalescing his corps was disbanded by Gen. Howe, who is alleged to have been irritated not only because some junior officer had invented a better military weapon—almost 100 years later American officers were resisting the introduction of breechloading rifles into the Federal army—but because Ferguson's corps had been formed before he was given an opportunity to disapprove.

(*D.N.B.*, with editorial slant by the present author.) The rifles were put into storage, and it is not known how many were subsequently reissued or where they were used.

The next mention of Ferguson is in connection with his successful raid to LITTLE EGG HARBOR, N.J., 4–5 Oct. '78. His high standing in the eyes of the British C. in C. is shown in Clinton's *American Rebellion* when, in connection with a planned raid toward Middletown, N.J., in the summer of 1779 he writes that his confidence in Guards Col. Hyde, who would lead the expedition, and in "the partisan abilities of Capt. Ferguson of the 70th Regt., who accompanied him, made me almost certain of success." (P. 123. A change of weather ruined the British plan.)

On 26 Oct. '79 Ferguson was appointed Maj. in one of the battalions of the 71st Highlanders, and he accompanied the CHARLESTON EXPEDITION of Clinton in 1780. As shown in that article, the embarkation table indicates that he went to Charleston with his rangers—150 in number—and that another 150 men of the 71st Highlanders were in the convoy. Ferguson and his rangers were part of Gen. Paterson's task force until it rejoined Clinton on 25 Mar. '80 outside Charleston.* He was then detached to operate against the American line of communications (see section of

---

* Although assigned to the 71st, the 1st Bn. of which was also with Paterson and the 2d Bn. of which had sailed from Savannah to join Clinton at Charleston on 3 Mar. (Uhlendorff, *Charleston,* 220 *n.,* 221), Ferguson apparently remained on detached service as commander of his rangers. He was subsequently promoted to the temporary grade of Lt. Col., but word of this did not reach America until after his death.

article on CHARLESTON EXPED. with this heading). After cooperating with Tarleton in the bloody success at MONCK'S CORNER, S.C., 14 Apr. '80, Ferguson was happy to go his own way and discontinue his association with "Bloody Ban," of whose methods he did not approve. He operated on the north bank of the Cooper River during the remainder of the siege and took part in the bloodless capture of Ft. Moultrie, 7 May.

The article on KINGS MOUNTAIN continues and ends the story of Patrick Ferguson. "The British answer to Dan Morgan," as Howard Peckham calls him, had been a professional soldier 21 years when he died on 7 Oct. '80 at the age of only 36. He has been described as slender, of medium height and rather grave countenance. His operations during the Kings Mountain campaign, in which his Tory troops plundered and burned rebel homes, made him the object of particular abhorrence (Peckham, *War for Indep.,* 148), yet he appears to have destroyed because this was his military duty and not because he was bloodthirsty or cruel by nature.

No full-fledged biography has been written. His kinsman Dr. Adam Ferguson wrote an article for the first edition of *E.B.* which the editors considered too long and which was not published in the encyclopedia because he refused to abridge it; this was later printed as "Sketch or Memoir of . . . Ferguson" (London, 1817) and is scarce. He is one of James Ferguson's *Two Scottish Soldiers. . . .* (Aberdeen, 1888). His military exploits figure in the *Cornwallis Correspondence,* edited by Chas. Ross (London, 1859, 3 vols.), Lyman Draper's *King's Mountain* (Cincinnati, 1881; N.Y., 1929), and other works.

FERGUSON RIFLE. See FERGUSON, Patrick.

FERMOY, Matthias Alexis de Roche.* Cont'l. general. Born in Martinique about 1737, he reached America in 1776 claiming to be a French Col. of engineers and wearing the Croix de St. Louis. (Hence the title of Chevalier.) Commissioned B.G. on 5 Nov. '76, he commanded a brigade in the attack on Trenton, 26 Dec. '76. Starting out at the head of Sullivan's Div. as part of the right wing, he subsequently was moved behind Greene's Div. and sent with Adam Stephen to block the enemy's retreat toward Princeton. He and Stephen met the Hessians with small arms fire while other American forces completed the encirclement and forced the enemy surrender.

In the next phase of the N.J. CAMPAIGN he unaccountably left his post as commander of a large force whose mission was to delay the expected enemy advance on Trenton from Princeton. It is interesting to speculate on what chance Washington would have had to score his brilliant maneuver to PRINCETON, 3 Jan. '77, if the incompetent Fermoy had commanded this delaying force on 2 Jan. in the place of Edw. Hand. Sent north in Mar. '77 to oppose Burgoyne's Offensive, the Martinique volunteer disgraced himself at TICONDEROGA, 2–5 July. (See section headed "Ticonderoga Abandoned") James Wilkinson, who had been in a position to observe Fermoy's performance at Trenton and Ticonderoga, wrote in his memoirs, "This man, like De Woedtke, turned out to be a worthless drunkard. . . ."

* His family name was Rochedefermoy or de Rochefermoy, and his signature was written derochefermoj.

After persistent efforts to win promotion from Congress he resigned on 31 Jan. '78 and was awarded $800 by that grateful body to get himself back to the West Indies. (According to Appleton's, Congress refused his last request for promotion on 31 Jan. and accepted his resignation on 16 Feb. '78. Heitman gives 31 Jan. as the date of his *resignation*.)

FERSEN, Hans Axel, Count von. 1755–1810. Swedish nobleman; French officer in America. Son of a famous Swedish politician, the handsome and engaging young Fersen appeared at Versailles in 1774 and quickly became a favorite. Friendship with Marie Antoinette led to his being given a regiment and a large pension. In 1779, amid persistent but unfounded rumors that he had become the queen's lover, *le beau Fersen* went to America as senior aide-de-camp to Rochambeau. He was cited for gallantry at Yorktown. Returning to Versailles in 1783, he was recalled after a few months to a position of close association with his own sovereign, Gustavus III. When the French Revolution started, Fersen was sent back to Versailles with the mission of attempting to save the royal family. After heroic but futile efforts to do this, he went home and was killed by a mob in the Swedish revolution of 1809.

FEU DE JOIE. Literally, a "fire of joy"—Heath spells it "feu-de-joy" (*Memoirs*, 364)—this was a form of public, military celebration in which musket fire was timed so as to progress from one man to another, producing a continuous roar. According to *O.U.D.* this was the sense of the term in 1801, but as early as 1771 "feu de joie" meant a bonfire in the literal as well as the figurative sense.

FEVER. See CAMP FEVER, JAIL FEVER, SWAMP FEVER.

FIELD OFFICER. Dating back as far as 1656 in English, the term was defined in that year as "An officer above the rank of captain, and under that of general" (*O.U.D.*).

"FIELDS," Meeting in the, 6 July '74. Presided over by Alexander McDougall, a mass meeting of patriots heard Alexander Hamilton speak against British measures and ended by deciding to send N.Y. delegates to the 1st Cont'l. Cong. The site now is City Hall Park, N.Y.C. The meeting is variously referred to as being "in 'the Fields' " and "in the 'Fields' " (*D.A.B.*, "Hamilton," "McDougall").

FILE. See FORMATIONS.

FINANCES OF THE REVOLUTION. Since taxation was one of the main reasons for the Revolution, Congress was in no position to tax the independent states to finance that revolution. Yet the Revolution cost at least $170,000,000, two thirds of which was disbursed by Congress. Right after Bunker Hill Congress resorted to the method inherited from the Colonial Wars and authorized the issue of CONTINENTAL CURRENCY, which quickly depreciated and eventually became worthless. State paper money also was issued, but it too became worth little more than the paper it was printed on. Counterfeiting by the British as well as by Americans also cheapened the currency. Requisitioning, which the Americans had insisted was good enough for the mother country in the colonial era, proved as big a failure for Congress as it had for the Crown. "The revolution was therefore never financed," states Professor Herbert L. Osgood. "It early became necessary to resort to loans and that chiefly from foreign sources." The latter, primarily from the French and Spanish govern-

ments and from private Dutch bankers, amounted to about $7,830,000. (*E.B.*, XXVII, 679) By May '81 Cont'l. finances had collapsed. Foreseeing this earlier in the year, Congress knew that a financial dictator was needed, and on 20 Feb. '81 they gave this job to Robt. MORRIS. The rest of the story is his.

In addition to the biographical works cited under MORRIS, see Davis Rich Dewey, *Financial Hist. of the U.S.*, 12th ed. (New York: Longmans, Green, 1934), and Paul Studenski and Herman E. Krooss, *Financial Hist. of the U.S.* (New York: McGraw-Hill, 1952). An older work, presumably superseded by the above, is *Finances of the U.S., 1775–89, with Especial Reference to the Budget,* by Charles Jesse Bullock (U. of Wisc. Bull., Vol. I, No. 2, Madison, 1895).

FINCASTLE. One of the titles of Lord DUNMORE, the name of the fort at WHEELING, and the name of a village on the James River that previously had been called Botetourt C.H. Fincastle co. included what is now the southern part of W. Va. and the adjacent portion of Va.

FIRE CAKE. Flour and water baked in thin cakes on hot stones.

FISHDAM Ford, S.C., 9 Nov. '80. Hearing that Sumter with 300 men was camped at Moore's Mill, only 30 miles N.W. of the main British army at Winnsboro, Cornwallis gave Maj. James Wemyss authority to go after him with his 100 mounted infantry of the 63d Regt. and 40 horsemen of Tarleton's British Legion. The plan was to surprise Sumter at dawn of the 9th at Moore's Mill, but the Gamecock had unexpectedly moved five miles south, and Wemyss blundered into his outposts about 1 A.M. The surprise was mutual, but the rebel picket fired five rounds before withdrawing, and Wemyss fell from the saddle with a broken arm and a wounded knee. Not knowing that Cornwallis had given Wemyss specific instructions not to misuse Tarleton's cavalry by employing them at night, young Lt. John Stark led a mounted charge down the road and into Sumter's bivouac, where they were silhouetted against the campfires and badly shot up. The 63d Regt. then went into action dismounted, but after a short period of heavy fighting both sides withdrew. Meanwhile, five dragoons who had been given the mission of getting Sumter dead or alive were led to Sumter's tent by a Tory named Sealy. As two men entered the front of his tent Sumter slipped out the back and spent the night hiding under a bank of nearby Broad River. Stark left Wemyss and the other wounded under a flag of truce and returned to Winnsboro. When Sumter ventured back to his camp about noon— the British sergeant in charge of the wounded said no rebels were seen until two hours after sunrise—he took the paroles of the wounded. Maj. Wemyss had in his pocket a list of the men he had hanged and the houses he had burned in the punitive raid up the Peedee to Cheraw, an operation which Bass says made him "the second most hated man in the British army" (*Green Dragoon,* 105), but Sumter threw the list in the fire after glancing at it. (*Ibid.,* 116)

NUMBERS AND LOSSES

Although Cornwallis says Sumter had about 300 militia and "banditti" (that is to say, noble partisans) at Moore's Mill, it is not likely that that number were at Fishdam Ford. The only unit commanders specifically mentioned in the action are Col. Thos. Taylor, who commanded the advance guard with which the enemy first made contact (Lossing, II, 651), and Col. Richard

Winn, whose marksmen shot up Stark's cavalry charge. (Bass, 116) British strength probably was close to the figure of 140 mentioned above. Cornwallis reported that 23 of his wounded were left on the field (Willcox [ed.], *Amer. Reb.,* 478); about five British probably were killed, if we use normal CASUALTY FIGURES as a guide. Lossing says 23 British were killed in the initial outpost action, and he implies that many more were later hit (*op. cit.,* 652); this is improbable, particularly if we accept the statement of Bass that only five shots were fired and two of these hit Wemyss. The claim of Cornwallis that the 63d Regt. killed and wounded about 70 rebels is, of course, absurd. American losses are not known; considering the nature of the action, they probably would not total more than five; considering the action of their leader, and the report that no rebel reappeared on the battlefield until seven hours after the last shot was fired, it is quite likely that there were no battle casualties.

"The enemy on this event cried victory," reported Cornwallis, "and the whole country came in fast to Sumter." Alarmed for the safety of Ninety-Six, the British commander recalled Tarleton and sent Maj. Archibald McArthur with his 1st Bn. of the 71st Highlanders and the 63d Regt. to guard Brierly's Ford on the Broad River. Tarleton reached this place on 18 Nov. and his efforts to trap Sumter led to the action at BLACKSTOCKS, 20 Nov. '80.

FISHING CREEK (Catawba Ford), N.C., 18 Aug. '80. After the defeat of Gates at Camden, 16 Aug., Capt. Nathaniel Martin and two dragoons rode to warn Sumter of the disaster and to appoint a rendezvous near Charlotte. Loaded down with the booty and prisoners taken around WATEREE FERRY, 15 Aug., Sumter and Woolford's detachment marched day and night in an effort to escape. Cornwallis, meanwhile, had moved with his main body to Rugeley's Mill (Clermont). When Tarleton returned to this place late on the 16th from his pursuit to Hanging Rock, Cornwallis had picked up information of Sumter's location and ordered Tarleton to pursue him the next morning.

With 350 men and one cannon Tarleton started up the east side of the Wateree early 17 Aug. By late afternoon he learned that his quarry was across the river on a parallel course. Reaching the ferry at Rocky Mount around dusk, Tarleton saw enemy campfires about a mile west of the river and he bivouacked without fires in the hope that Sumter intended to cross the river and could be attacked while in this vulnerable position. When his scouts reported the next morning that the Americans were continuing up the west side, Tarleton crossed the Wateree and followed Sumter, undetected, to Fishing Creek. Reaching this point, some 40 miles from Camden, about noon, Tarleton's foot troops said they were unable to continue. Tarleton pushed forward with 100 dragoons and 60 infantry, the latter riding double with the horsemen. After another five miles two of Sumter's scouts were cut down after they had fired and killed one man of the enemy advance guard. When the advance guard continued forward they reached a hill from which they could see Sumter's troops resting in complete innocence of their danger. Tarleton must have had to pinch himself to make sure he was not dreaming: with their arms stacked, some of the Americans were sleeping, some were cooking, and others were bathing in the creek! Tarleton made a hasty deployment and charged. When Sumter woke up in the scene of general confusion he indulged in no false heroics but saved his own skin by leaping coatless astride an unsaddled horse; two days later he rode into Maj.

Davie's camp. Some of his men rallied to defend themselves from behind the wagons, and in this action they killed Capt. Chas. Campbell, who had burned Sumter's house and launched the Gamecock on his career.

With a loss of 16 killed and wounded, Tarleton killed 150 Americans, captured 300, released 100 British prisoners, and recaptured 44 wagons full of supplies. (Ward, *W.O.R.,* 734) Reports of the coup made Tarleton a national hero. (Bass, *Green Dragoon,* 101–3, is the principal source of this account and authority for the last statement.)

FLAG, American. Up until the outbreak of the Revolution, Americans used the British Union Flag, which was proclaimed by King James I in 1606 and was superseded by the present Union Jack in 1801. On 14 June '77 Cong. passed the Flag Resolution, which specified that there be 13 stripes, red and white alternately, and that the union be 13 white stars in a blue field, "representing a new constellation." This left considerable latitude to flag makers as to the type of stars, their arrangement, and the arrangement of the stripes.

The "Bennington Flag" is believed by many authorities to be the first Stars and Stripes flown by ground forces. Said to have been carried or present at the battle of BENNINGTON, Vt., Aug. '77, its field—nine stripes wide—has an arch of 11 seven-pointed stars over the numerals "76" and has two more stars in the top corners of the field. Top and bottom stripes are white, rather than red.

After an exhaustive study of the claim that the Stars and Stripes were flown over Ft. Stanwix (Schuyler) in Aug. '77 when it held out against St. Leger's Expedition, one top authority concludes that this "was not the Stars and Stripes, but a flag of the same design as that raised by Washington at

Cambridge on taking command of the Continental Army [3 July '75], having thirteen alternating red and white stripes and the united crosses of St. George and St. Andrew in the canton" (John Spargo, *The Stars and Stripes in 1777...*, 29–30). This "Cambridge Flag," just described, was the Great or Grand Union Banner, which was nothing more than the British Meteor Flag modified by having six horizontal white stripes imposed on its red field, thereby forming 13 alternate red and white stripes (Quaife, *post,* 26, 49). "While Congress never formally adopted it, this banner soon became known as the 'Union Flag,' the 'Grand Union Flag,' the 'Congress Flag,' and the 'Colours of the United Colonies." (*Ibid.,* 27) One of the earliest Stars and Stripes may have been in evidence at COOCH'S BRIDGE, Del., 3 Sept. '77.

Other famous American flags that preceded the Stars and Stripes are: The traditional Bunker Hill flag, the Gadsden or S.C. Rattlesnake flag ("Don't Tread on Me"), the New England Pine Tree Flag ("An Appeal to Heaven"), and the Crescent Flag of S.C. (see also Wm. JASPER). The famous story about the first Stars and Stripes being made by Betsy Ross (1752–1836) at the request of George Washington, Robert Morris, and George Ross (1730–1779) is based on a family tradition first made public by her grandson, Wm. Canby, in Mar. 1870. Although Betsy is known to have made flags, the one with 13 five-pointed white stars in a circle within the blue union and with seven red and six white stripes, popularly called the Betsy Ross flag, is not among the many that historians consider seriously as a contender for the honor of being "the first Stars and Stripes." (*Ibid.,* 53; *D.A.B.,* "Betsy Ross") Nor did Francis HOPKINSON qualify.

See Milo M. Quaife, Melvin J. Weig, and Roy E. Appleman, *The History of the United States Flag....* (1961).

FLAG OF S.C. "As there was no national flag at the time [Sept. '75]," wrote Wm. Moultrie in his *Memoirs,* "I was desired by the [Charleston] Council of Safety to have one made, upon which, as the state troops were clothed in blue, and the fort [Ft. Johnson on James Island] was garrisoned by the first and second regiments, who wore a silver crescent on the front of their caps, I had a large blue flag made, with a crescent in the dexter corner.... This was the first American flag displayed in the South." (*Op. cit.,* I, 90, quoted in Lossing, II, 751 *n.*)

FLANK COMPANIES. Each battalion of the British Army included a light infantry company and a grenadier company; they were known as "flank companies" and were made up of the best soldiers in the battalion. During field operations they normally were pooled to form special corps of light infantry and grenadiers. The remaining eight companies were called the "battalion companies." The American Army never formed grenadier companies but did have LIGHT INFANTRY.

FLANKING POSITION. A form of defense in which the defender takes up a position so located that the enemy will expose his flanks or line of communications if he continues his advance. Rarely found in combat, a good flanking position must have these characteristics: strong defensive terrain; protection for one's own line of communication; the possibility of sallying forth to attack the enemy if he does try to ignore the position and continue his advance. The defender also must have sufficient strength so that the attacker cannot contain him with part of his force and continue on to his original objective.

FLECHE. A small earthwork shaped like an arrowhead or **V**, and open to the rear.

FLEURY. See TEISSÈDRE DE FLEURY.

FLORIDAS, The. See map next page.

FLOWER, Benjamin. 1748–1781. Cont'l. officer, Pa. Commissary of Military Stores for the FLYING CAMP, 16 July–Dec. '76, he was directed by Washington on 16 Jan. '77 to raise the unit that became known as the Regiment of Artillery ARTIFICERS. He died young (28 Apr. '81) and is buried at Philadelphia's Christ Church. A portrait, believed to be by Charles Willson Peale, is in the Star-Spangled Banner House in Baltimore.

FLOWER, Samuel. Cont'l. officer. Mass. Commissioned 2d Lt. of Danielson's Mass. Regt. in May '75 to Dec. '75, became Capt. in 3d Mass. on 1 Jan. '77, resigned 9 Feb. '80, and was Maj. of Mass. militia in 1782. (Heitman)

FLOYD, William. 1734–1821. Signer. N.Y. He had little formal education, although from a wealthy family, and led the life of the landed gentry on Long Island. He soon became a civic and military leader and was militia Maj. Gen. by the outbreak of the war. He was sent to the Cont'l. Congress in Philadelphia in 1774. The next year he sat in the N.Y. provincial congress and was returned to the Cont'l. Congress until 1783. In 1777–83, he was N.Y. state senator by appointment rather than election, for his district was occupied by the British. He and his family had fled before the British in 1776, and his lands were ruined by the enemy. His farm was seized as rebel property and throughout the war he had only his congressional pay to live on. He was elected to the same office 1784–88 and in 1787 and 1789 was a member of the council of appointment. He sat in the first U.S. Congress (1789–91),

and in 1792, 1800, and 1804 he was a presidential elector. In 1801 he attended the N.Y. constitutional convention. During the war, he was briefly a militia captain and after the war was Maj. Gen. of the Long Island militia. He was described as being practical, firm, unpolished, and a hard worker.

FLYING CAMP, July–Nov. '76. When the British evacuated Boston in Mar. '76 the Americans were faced with the need for defending widely scattered areas where the enemy might strike next. Part of their solution was the establishment of a "flying camp," the term being a literal translation of *camp volant,* and in the military doctrine of the day meaning a mobile, strategic reserve. Washington met with Congress and with specially appointed committees during the period 24 May–4 June '76 to discuss plans for future military action. One decision was that Del., Md., and Pa. would furnish until Dec. '76 a total of 10,000 militia to constitute a "flying camp." Formal authorization came on 3 June, Hugh Mercer was designated commander, and the newly appointed B.G. reported to N.Y.C. on 3 July to assume his duties with much energy. (Freeman, *Washington,* IV, 147 and *n.*) Men arrived slowly, however, and they were of poor military quality. When Washington called for 2,000 to assist in the fortification of N.Y.C., Mercer was hard put to find this number of reliable soldiers. Units of the Flying Camp were piecemealed from Amboy to Long Island before and after the British attacked there on 27 Aug. '76. "From the list of officers taken prisoner at Fort Washington [16 Nov.]," says Freeman, "it is possible to identify four Battalions that had been part of the Flying Camp—Michael Swope's, Frederick Watts's, William Montgomery's and Baxter's." (*Op. cit.,* 248 *n.;* "Baxter" is not further identified here or in

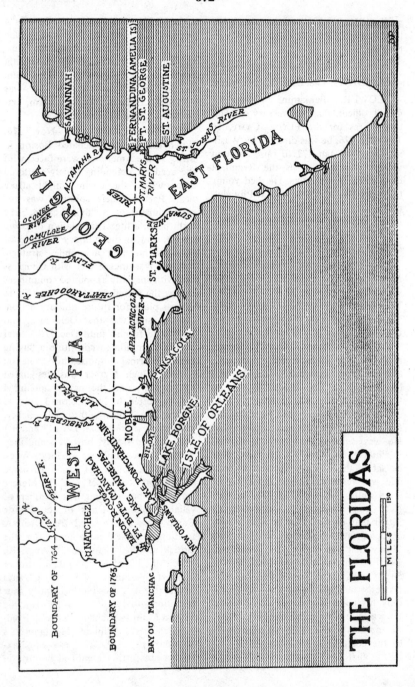

THE FLORIDAS

Heitman, but the latter says he was killed on 16 Nov.) Most of the 2,000 to 3,000 men who followed Washington and Greene out of FT. LEE, 18 Nov., were from the Flying Camp. On 30 Nov. the organization ceased its inglorious existence when 2,000 enlistments expired. Washington was disappointed by the small number of militia that had reported to Mercer's camp at Amboy, but the organization had been of some use as a source of reinforcements. (*Ibid.*, 254, 278)

FLYING SAP. See SAP.

FONTANGES, Vicomte de. 1740–1822. French Maj. Gen. A Lt. on 1 Jan. '56, he fought in Germany as a Capt. and remained in this grade until 1775, when he was detailed in the navy as Maj. In Sept. '75 he reached the West Indies, was made Chevalier of Saint Louis in 1777, and Lt. Col. in 1778. In July '79 he was named Maj. Gen. of the troops of debarkation of the Naval Army of d'Estaing. According to Heitman, who is the source of this sketch—Lasseray mentions Fontanges but does not give a biographical notice—he was seriously wounded at Savannah on 7 Oct. '79, although the assault took place two days later. Heitman also says Fontanges "commanded . . . a legion composed of mulattos and free negroes of St. Domingo [which] . . . saved the army at Savannah by bravely covering its retreat." Henri CHRISTOPHE served in this unit. (Heitman, 655)

FONTENOY, Battle of. 11 May '45. A decisive action in the War of the AUSTRIAN SUCCESSION, this battle is famous for the episode mentioned in connection with MUSKETS AND MUSKETRY. Among those who saw action at Fontenoy are Gage, Germain (who distinguished himself as a regimental commander), James Grant, Robert Monckton, and Philip Skene, all of whom figured in the American Revolution.

"FOOL, KNAVE, AND HONEST, OBSTINATE MAN." Alexander McDougall's characterization of Joseph Spencer, Geo. Clinton, and Wm. Heath in connection with their recommendation that N.Y.C. be defended during the NEW YORK CAMPAIGN.

FORBES EXPEDITION TO FT. DUQUESNE (Pittsburgh), 1758. A major operation of the French and Indian War in which the French were once and for all driven from the strategic place that became Pittsburgh, it is of interest in this book primarily because of the many later-famous American officers who participated. As part of the strategy covered under COLONIAL WARS, a force of over 6,500 British regulars and colonials under the command of Gen. John Forbes was gathered to eliminate the growing threat from Ft. Duquesne. Pa. militia were commanded by Cols. John Armstrong, James Burd, and Hugh Mercer. Va. troops were under Cols. George Washington and James Byrd. Md. forces were led by Col. George Dagworthy. British regulars of Lt. Col. Henry Bouquet's Royal American Regt. and of the newly raised 77th (Montgomery) Highlanders completed the expedition.

Upon the illness of Forbes in Apr. '58, the capable Bouquet took charge of preparations for the expedition and led it forward, along the route thereafter known as Forbes Road. The advance party was defeated on 21 Sept. and its commander, Maj. James GRANT, captured along with 19 other officers including Andrew LEWIS. The main body, meanwhile, had moved from assembly areas at Carlisle and Winchester in July to link up for the final advance at Loyal Hannon or Ligonier. Here they fought off a furious attack by French and Indians on 12 Oct., and difficulties in constructing the road, supply deficiencies, and faulty intelligence (which overestimated the enemy strength) combined with bad weather to bring the expedition to a halt. On 12 Nov., however, Bouquet learned from three prisoners that the French garrison was in desperate straits—Bradstreet's capture of Ft. Frontenac had isolated Duquesne, the Indians were deserting—so the advance was resumed shortly after a decision had almost been reached to spend the winter at Ligonier. The French destroyed Ft. Duquesne and Bouquet took possession on 25 Nov. '58.

Forbes Road, constructed at tremendous effort between Bedford and Pittsburgh for this expedition, was used for the next 30 years not only as a military line of communications but for a stream of settlers. U.S. Route 30 now follows roughly the same trace.

FORLORN HOPE. A small body of picked troops that precedes the main body in an attack. Dutch in origin, the term originally meant "lost troop," but both words became corrupted in English to give the sense of "suicide mission."

FORMAN'S REGT. was one of 16 "ADDITIONAL CONT'L. REGTS."

FORMATIONS. When soldiers stand shoulder to shoulder facing the front they are formed in a rank or a *line*; when they stand one behind the other they constitute a *file*. Two or more files make a *column;* two or more ranks (or single lines) are also called a *line.** "Linear tactics"—as opposed to the massed formations of the Greek Phalanx of ancient times and the Spanish

* The term *column* is most commonly used in the sense just defined, although men can also be in a "column of (single) files" or "Indian file."

Square that was doomed by the field ARTILLERY—evolved with the advent of effective MUSKETS. A "line of columns," as was used in the Franco-American attack on SAVANNAH, 9 Oct. '79, can be shown graphically as follows:

```
XXXXXXXXXXXXX
XXXXXXXXXXXXX

XXXXXXXXXXXXX    direction of
XXXXXXXXXXXXX    advance ⟶

XXXXXXXXXXXXX
XXXXXXXXXXXXX
```

FORT ANDERSON, S.C. Also called THICKETTY FORT.

FORT ANNE, N.Y. 8 July '77. (BURGOYNE'S OFFENSIVE) Although Burgoyne captured SKENESBORO, 6 July, he failed to trap the defenders. On 7 July, Lt. Col. Hill pursued along the 12 miles of rugged wilderness road to Ft. Anne and camped a mile from the fort. He failed to catch Col. Pierce Long's 150-man rear guard, but he did capture several boats full of invalids, camp followers, and other baggage that were trying to escape up Wood Creek. Early on the 8th an American who claimed to be a deserter appeared in Hill's camp with the story that 1,000 rebel troops were in Ft. Anne but were demoralized by fear of attack. Since Hill had but 190 officers and men, and did not feel he could either attack or safely retreat in the face of such odds, he decided to stand fast and call for reinforcement. The "deserter" then escaped to Ft. Anne and reported how weak the British detachment was.

Col. Henry van Rensselaer had, in fact, reached the fort with 400 N.Y. militia, and at 10:30 he sallied forth with Long to annihilate Hill. The enemy detachment was camped in a narrow, heavily wooded area between Wood Creek and a steep, 500-foot ridge. Hill and his men scrambled for this high ground and fought off their adversaries for two hours. When their ammunition was running low, and they were being attacked from all sides, an Indian war whoop was heard from the north. This meant that Burgoyne's reinforcements were arriving from Skenesboro, and the Americans—who also were low on ammunition—broke off the engagement, burned Ft. Anne, and retreated to Ft. Edward. It turned out that the "reinforcements" was one Capt. Money; when his Indians had refused to follow him into the action he had advanced alone with a borrowed war whoop.

FORT BEAUSEJOUR, Acadia (later Nova Scotia). During the COLONIAL WARS this French fort was captured on 19 June '55. See also FORT CUMBERLAND, Nov. '75.

FORT BLAIR was erected on the site of the battle of Point Pleasant (10 Oct. '74).

FORT BUTE, La. Fort at MANCHAC named for Lord Bute.

FORT CARS (Car's, Carr's), Ga. See KETTLE CREEK.

FORT CLINTON, N.Y., 6 Oct. '77. Captured along with Ft. Montgomery by CLINTON'S EXPEDITION. . . .

FORT COCKHILL, N.Y., 16 Nov. '76. At the mouth of SPUYTEN DUYVIL, the little fort at Cock or Cox Hill was an outpost of Ft. Tryon, which was in turn an outpost of FORT WASHINGTON.

FORT CORNWALLIS (Augusta), Ga. See AUGUSTA.

FORT CUMBERLAND (Beauséjour), Nova Scotia, 7–29 Nov. '76. With 14,000 to 15,000 New Englanders present in Nova Scotia (or ACADIA) it was inevitable that an attempt at insurrection would be made, although the British garrison at Halifax and the presence of warships served as deter-

rents. Early in 1776 a Scot named John Allen and an emigrant from Mass. named Jonathan Eddy (a veteran of the French and Indian War) led a movement to secure control of the province from the British. Other men prominent in the attempt were Sam Rogers, Zebulon Rowe, and Obadiah Ayers, all of New England origin. Although Washington and Congress could not promise support, Mass. agreed to supply whatever force the rebels could muster. Allen visited Mass. to make plans for the insurrection and returned to Sackville with a small body of men, including Indians, gathered at Machias, along the St. John River, and Memramcook. En route he captured the small outpost at Shepody. Although only 180 men were finally assembled, the rebel leaders decided to attempt the capture of Ft. Cumberland (formerly Beauséjour and near modern Amherst). On 7 Nov. they got possession of a sloop anchored near the fort, gaining much-needed supplies, and on the 10th Eddy sent the enemy commander a summons to surrender.

Ft. Cumberland was held by Col. Joseph Goreham with a unit called the Royal Fencible Americans. Including local inhabitants and deducting the 48 men lost at Shepody and on the sloop, his garrison numbered about 200. The besiegers realized that Goreham could expect prompt support from Halifax and that their time was limited. The summons having been refused, Eddy launched attacks on 13 and 22 Nov., but both failed. Enemy reinforcements then arrived from Halifax—a company of the Royal Highland Emigrants and two companies of marines. A sortie on 29 Nov. broke the siege, but bad weather and lack of proper clothing forced Goreham to cancel a planned pursuit. Having shown a lack of military vigor, the British commander then announced a conditional pardon to the rebels. More than 100 came in to surrender their weapons and express their regret for having participated in the operation. Thus ended the Acadian adventure with little glory for winner or loser. Although Eddy and Allen continued their efforts, the British later established a base (Ft. Howe) at the mouth of the St. John that checked further rebel action in what is now New Brunswick. (G. F. G. Stanley, *Canada's Soldiers* [Toronto, 1954], 117–20)

FORT DAYTON (Herkimer), N.Y. located in GERMAN FLATS about two miles west of "Fort Herkimer Church," the site of Fort Dayton, built in 1776 by Col. Elias DAYTON, is marked in the present village of Herkimer. Presumably on the site of the "dilapidated block-house" left from the Colonial Wars, the fortified stone house was the point of departure for the ill-fated march to ORISKANY in Aug. '77. Fort Dayton figured in the action at nearby SHELL'S BUSH exactly four years later. The site is marked by a heroic bronze statue in Myers Park depicting the desperate defense of his position at Oriskany.

FORT DREADNOUGHT, S.C. See FORT GALPHIN.

FORT FINCASTLE, Va. See WHEELING.

FORT GAGE. Located in Kaskaskia and captured 4 July '78 in the WESTERN OPNS. OF CLARK. During the Colonial Wars, the British built a small earthwork near the site of FORT WILLIAM HENRY called Fort Gage. (In my *Landmarks of the American Revolution* see the entry "Lake George Village and Vicinity")

FORT GALPHIN (Dreadnought), S.C., 21 May '81. When Henry Lee moved from FT. GRANBY to link up with the militia forces of Pickens besieging AUGUSTA he learned that a quantity of supplies were temporarily stored at Ft. Galphin, a small, stockaded place 12 miles below Augusta that was the home of George Galphin, the deputy superintendent of Indian affairs. These supplies were the annual King's present to his loyal Indians. Mounting his Legion infantry double behind his cavalrymen, Lee made a forced march and reached his objective the morning of the 21st and was joined by some Ga. and S.C. militia. Lee had part of his force make a feint against the position from one direction and when the defenders sallied forth Capt. Rudolph rushed in from the other side with a detachment of Legion infantry to capture the fort and its supplies. The latter included blankets, clothing, small arms, ammunition, medical stores, and provisions, all of which the rebels needed. Having lost only one man in this *coup de main* against a strong point defended by two Tory companies, Lee withdrew.

FORT GEORGE, Fla. See PENSACOLA.

FORT GEORGE (on Lake George), N.Y. See FORT WILLIAM HENRY.

FORT GEORGE, L.I., N.Y., 21–23 Nov. '80. With 80 dismounted troopers of the 2d Cont'l. Dragoons, Maj. Benj. Tallmadge left Fairfield, Conn., in the afternoon and landed on L.I. at 9 A.M. His objective was "Ft. George," on the south shore, where Tory refugees from R.I. had converted the manor house of Gen. John Smith into a base for woodcutting operations and also a depot. Bad weather forced Tallmadge to delay 24 hours, but he surprised and captured Ft. George at dawn on the 23d. Recrossing the island he led a 12-man detachment to destroy 300 tons of hay collected at Coram for the British army. Early the evening of the same day he returned to Fairfield with his prisoners and with the loss of only one man wounded. Seven Tories were killed or wounded, 54 officers and men were captured, and another 150—"presumably noncombatants" (Ward, *W.O.R.*, 624) also were taken. (Lossing, II, 834) Tallmadge's coup was officially recognized by Washington and by Congress.

Secondary accounts are confusing as to the location of Tallmadge's objective. The site is preserved in a 127-acre public park, all that remains of the Manor of St. George, which was patented by Col. Wm. ("Tangier") Smith in 1693. It is near Mastic Beach, just north of Smith's Point Bridge (Wm. Floyd Parkway).

FORT GEORGE (Manhattan), N.Y. The position defended by Col. Baxter on Laurel Hill consisted merely of field fortifications in the battle for FORT WASHINGTON, 17 Nov. '76. In this vicinity the British subsequently built Ft. George as part of the Ft. Knyphausen (formerly Ft. Washington) defenses. Lossing identifies Rawlings' position as Ft. George in one mention of the Ft. Washington defenses but as FORT TRYON in two other places on the same page. (II, 826)

FORT GEORGE (N.Y.C.), N.Y. On the site of Ft. Amsterdam, this was the principal fortification in N.Y.C. on the eve of the Revolution and was not garrisoned at the start of the Stamp Act Crises. Ft. George and the nearby Grand Battery were located near what is now known in N.Y.C. as "The Battery." (Lossing, II, 799 *n*.)

FORT GRANBY, S.C., 15 May '81. (SOUTHERN CAMPAIGNS OF GREENE) This British post, near modern Columbia, was held by 352 men under a Md. Tory, Maj. Andrew Maxwell. The garrison included 60 German mercenaries; the rest were Tories, presumably of Maxwell's Prince of Wales Regt. Although this was a strong post, Henry Lee knew that Maxwell was not noted either for courage or military proficiency and that he had devoted most of his energies to collecting plunder. Lee left Ft. Motte on 13 May and the next night emplaced a 6-pd. gun within 600 yards of the fortified frame building known as "Fort Granby." When the fog cleared the next morning, Lee fired the cannon and his Legion infantry moved forward to deliver a musket fire on Maxwell's pickets. When summoned to surrender, Maxwell agreed to do so if he and his men could keep their plunder, and if the garrison (including Tories) could withdraw to Charleston as prisoners of war until exchanged. Knowing that Rawdon might arrive at any minute to save the fort, Lee agreed with the condition that all horses fit for public service be surrendered. Maxwell's mercenaries, who were mounted, objected, and negotiations were suspended. When Lee received word from Capt. Armstrong, who had been screening in the direction of Camden with a small cavalry force, that Rawdon was across the Santee at Nelson's Ferry and was approaching Ft. Motte, Lee agreed to Maxwell's terms. The capitulation was signed before noon of the 15th, and Maxwell moved off with two wagons full of his personal plunder. Without the loss of a man—on either side—the rebels gained possession of an important post along with a considerable supply of ammunition, some salt and liquor, two cannon, and the garrison's weapons.

Lee's good sense in handling this situation is expressed in Napoleon's Maxim 46: "The keys of a fortress are well worth the freedom of the garrison. . . ."

FORT GRIERSON, Ga. See AUGUSTA (1780 and 1781).

FORT GRISWOLD, Conn., 6 Sept. '81. Major action of Arnold's NEW LONDON RAID.

FORT HENRY (Wheeling), Va. See WHEELING.

FORT HUNTER, N.Y. In the Mohawk Valley at the mouth of Schoharie Creek, the old Ft. Hunter of the French and Indian War was torn down at the start of the Revolution but rebuilt and often garrisoned.

FORT INDEPENDENCE FIASCO, N.Y., 17–25 Jan. '77. On 5 Jan., immediately following the rebel victories at Trenton and Princeton, Washington wrote to Wm. Heath in the Hudson Highlands:

"The enemy are in great consternation; and as the present affords us a favourable opportunity to drive them out of the Jerseys ... you should move down towards New York with a considerable force, as if you had a design upon the city; that [place] being an object of great importance, the enemy will be reduced to the necessity of withdrawing a considerable part of their force from the Jerseys, if not the whole, to secure the city." (Quoted in Heath, *Memoirs*, 117)

The night of 17–18 Jan. Heath started three divisions toward Kings Bridge so as to converge simultaneously on the enemy's outposts at dawn. Lincoln's command moved from Tarrytown on the Albany road; the forces of Wooster and Parsons advanced from New Rochelle and East Chester; and the center column comprised the militia of John Scott, who marched from a point below White Plains. Initially the plan worked smoothly, all columns arriving on schedule, and Heath's troops overran the outposts at Valentine's Hill, Van Courtland's, Williams', and the Negro Fort. The rebels closed up to Fort Independence (in the Valentine's Hill area just north of Spuyten Duyvil) and Heath summoned the German commander to surrender. The enemy commander not only failed to respond in the proper spirit of cooperation but started shooting back with artillery Heath did not suspect he possessed. (*Ibid.*, 120) Instead of driving in to take the fort, Heath undertook an ineffective cannonade and started maneuvering. On the 19th he ordered an envelopment across the frozen creek to cut off the battalion at Kings Bridge, but on the 20th, the day set for the attempt, he canceled it because the weather turned warmer and the ice was not considered safe. After several days of inconclusive skirmishing, the British sallied forth early on the 25th in the direction of Delancey's Mills and routed the rebel force in that sector. "Emboldened by this success," writes "Our General," they then attacked toward Valentine's, cleared the Americans from the house and the Negro Fort, and pushed on "with great impetuosity" to scatter rebels before them. (*Ibid.*, 122–23) On 29 Jan. the signs of an approaching blizzard convinced Heath and his generals that they should withdraw.

The British had a good laugh over what D. S. Freeman calls "this seriocomical affair." (*Washington*, IV, 384 n.) See the article on Wm. HEATH for Washington's views.

FORT JOHNSON, S.C. Located on James Island, it guarded the entrance to Charleston harbor. It was captured by the rebels in Sept. '75, and its 20 large guns were ineffectually employed in the action of 1776. Allowed to fall into ruin, it was retaken (from the land side) by the British in their CHARLESTON EXPEDITION of 1780.

FORT JOHNSTON, N.C. Guarding the mouth of the Cape Fear River and located some 10 miles below Brunswick, it figured in the Stamp Act Crisis, when British naval Capt. Jacob Lobb spiked its guns to keep them from being used by the aroused patriots. Gov. Tryon was unable to prevent the citizens from

occupying the fort in Feb. '66, after
Lobb had refused to give him armed
support. Gov. Josiah Martin fled to the
safety of Ft. Johnston on 2 June '75,
and on 18 July he escaped to a British
warship when the patriots occupied the
fort in an attempt to capture him. The
fort was burned at this time.

FORT KEYSER, N.Y., 19 Oct. '80.
(BORDER WARFARE) Col. John BROWN
held Ft. Paris in Stone Arabia with 130
militia when Sir John Johnson approached. On news of the destruction
of SCHOHARIE, 15–17 Oct., Gen. Robert
Van Rensselaer had assembled militia
and was moving up the Mohawk Valley
behind Johnson. In obedience to Van
Rensselaer's order and with the assurance that the latter would arrive in time
to strike the enemy's rear, Brown sallied
forth to attack a force 10 times his
size. Near the ruins of Ft. Keyser he
was killed with a third of his men and
the rest were routed before the promised
support arrived. Johnson destroyed
Stone Arabia before being brought to
bay at KLOCK'S FIELD late in the afternoon of the 19th.

FORT KNYPHAUSEN, N.Y. The
former FORT WASHINGTON.

FORT LAFAYETTE, N.Y. Located
at Verplancks Point, it was captured by
the British on 1 June '79 in the operations described under STONY POINT, 16
July '79. Principal British leaders in
the attack were Generals James PATTI-
SON and James PATERSON.

FORT LAURENS, Ohio, Nov. '78–
Aug. '79. Located near today's Bolivar
and now a state historical site, this was
the first fort established in what became
the state of Ohio. (Hunter, post., 186)
Work was started after the 1,200-man
expedition under Lachlan McINTOSH
reached the spot on 21 Nov. Having
been slowed by their horses and cattle
in the march from Ft. Pitt through the
heavy forest, and having learned that
supplies had not reached Ft. McIntosh,
70 miles to the east, the expedition's
leaders agreed that they could not continue the proposed invasion of Indian
territory in the direction of Detroit.
(Butterfield, post., 393–94) The alternative was to establish this isolated
post, hold it with a small garrison
throughout the winter, and use it as a
jumping-off place for an offensive in the
spring of 1779, or at least as an outpost
to hold down Indian depredations.
(McIntosh gave Washington the latter
reason in his letter of 27 Apr. '79, after
he had been accused of having established a "slaughter pen, impossible to
maintain. . . ." Quoted by Butterfield,
394 n.)

As slow as McIntosh's advance had
been, it found the site on the Tuscarawas River uncontested and a fort was
built on the west bank before the
Indians realized it. Work was planned
by a Regular Army engineer—possibly
CAMBRAY-DIGNY—and garrisoned by
150 men of the 13th Va. under John
GIBSON. The main army withdrew on
9 Dec. before work was completed, and
it was not until late Dec. that Gibson
was able to report his post was tenable.
Meanwhile, however, he was so short
of provisions that he opened negotiations with friendly Delawares at Coshocton to buy cattle. One man was killed
and another wounded seriously when a
detachment under Samuel Sample, an
assistant Q.M., went to Coshocton for
supplies. A week or so later, toward
the end of Jan. '79, Capt. John Clark
of the 8th Pa. was returning from Ft.
Laurens to Ft. McIntosh with a Sgt.
and 14 men when they were attacked
three miles from Ft. Laurens; with a
loss of two killed, four wounded, and
one man captured, Clark fought his way
back to Ft. Laurens. The attack had
been made by 17 Indians, chiefly

Mingoes, led by the renegade Simon GIRTY, who captured valuable dispatches in this action. (Butterfield, 397) Further attempts to resupply the garrison were unsuccessful, and by the middle of Feb. the food situation was critical. Lurking savages massacred 18 guards and a wagoner who went out from the fort on 23 Feb. to cut wood; two were made prisoners, but the rest were killed and scalped within sight of Gibson's garrison.

Shortly thereafter the fort was besieged by a force composed primarily of Wyandots and Mingoes. Their numbers were variously reported as being from 180 to almost 300, but the Indians are said to have tricked the defenders so that they counted 847 from the fort. (*Ibid.*) John Gibson, however, beat them at their own game: when his garrison had been reduced to a quarter of a pound of sour flour and an equal amount of spoiled meat a day, the Indians, who also were suffering for lack of food, proposed to lift the siege if he would give them a barrel of flour and some meat. Assuring the Indians that he had rations to spare, Gibson promptly agreed, and the siege was soon lifted. (Hunter, 187) In his *History of the Girtys* Butterfield writes: "The siege (though a failure), considering that the fort was a regularly built fortification, planned by an engineer of the regular army of the United States, and garrisoned by regular troops, and considering, also, the persistency of the besiegers, nearly all of whom were savages, and who closely invested the post for 25 days, was the most notable of any in the West during the Revolution." (*Op. cit.*, 95. See comments on authorities, below.) Note that Butterfield implies that some whites, probably renegades and Tories, were involved.

On 3 Mar. '79 Gen. McIntosh received a message from Gibson inform-

ing him of the situation. On 19 Mar. a force of some 200 militia and over 300 Cont'ls. from Forts Pitt and McIntosh left the latter post and covered the 70 miles to Ft. Laurens in four days to find the siege lifted. A *feu de joie* fired by the garrison stampeded the pack train, causing the loss of some horses and supplies, to end the epic on a note of comic opera. The defenders had been living for almost a week on raw hides and such roots as they could find in the area. A council of war decided against McIntosh's plan for continuing the advance toward the Sandusky region. (McIntosh had left Brodhead in command at Ft. Pitt to lead this expedition.) Maj. Frederick Vernon was left to hold Ft. Laurens with 106 rank and file of the 8th Pa. and was given less than 60 days' supply of food. On 28 Mar. '79, soon after departure of McIntosh's column, Indians reappeared and attacked a 40-man wood-cutting party; Ensign John Clark and another man were killed. By the middle of May most of the garrison had to be sent away for lack of provisions, and 10 days later Capt. Robert Beall of the 9th Va. reached Ft. Laurens with supplies when its 25-man garrison was on the verge of starvation. Lt. Col. Campbell reinforced the garrison with 75 well-supplied men some time after 15 June and assumed command. (Vernon returned to Ft. Pitt but his men remained.)

Col. Daniel Brodhead succeeded McIntosh as commander of the Western Dept. in Mar. '79. He soon realized that Ft. Laurens was untenable, and on 16 July he informed Campbell that the post would be abandoned as soon as horses could be sent to evacuate the stores. After another serious threat to the fort it was abandoned early in Aug. '79, but not before two more Americans had been killed in the immediate vicinity. With the idea that the place might be reoccupied it was not destroyed, and Ft. Laurens remained intact until demolished after the war.

Authorities. *Ohio Archaeological and Historical Society Publications,* VI, has a nine-page "History of Fort Laurens" written by C. W. Butterfield in 1881, and this author points out that his *History of the Girtys,* written 10 years later, contains "much additional information" and "a few corrections." Butterfield's article is included in a section of the *Ohio Arch. and Hist. Soc. Pubs.* called "Addenda to the Pathfinders of Jefferson County" (pp. 384–406); the basic article (pp. 95–313) is by W. H. Hunter.

FORT LEE (Constitution), N.J. 20 Nov. '76. Captured by British. Ft. Lee (originally Ft. Constitution) and Ft. Washington were built to cover a line of obstructions across the Hudson River to bar the movement of British ships. When the British captured FT. WASHINGTON, N.Y., 16 Nov. '76, Ft. Lee was no longer worth defending. Actually, the British had run their ships up the Hudson on several occasions and proved that even when manned by American troops these forts were useless.

Moving with unwonted celerity, Gen. Howe sent Cornwallis across the Hudson the morning of 20 Nov. with between 4,000 and 6,000 troops to take Ft. Lee. Crossing in the rain, the British landed at modern Alpine six miles (by road) above Ft. Lee and marched south to capture that place and its garrison. Warned of this movement, the Americans evacuated their troops but left a considerable amount of valuable equipment. The British found 200 or 300 tents still standing and patriotic pots still boiling. Twelve drunken Americans were captured in the fort, and about 150 other prisoners were taken in the vicinity. Although the Americans had

managed to evacuate stocks of gunpowder, they left behind 1,000 barrels of flour, all their entrenching tools, about 50 cannon, and their baggage.

By sacrificing this matériel, however, Washington had led 2,000 troops from the fort to safety before the British could seize the one bridge across the Hackensack River. Greene had returned to the fort about two hours after the main body's departure and had rounded up several hundred stragglers, many of whom were drunk on abandoned sutler's stocks.

(NOTE: Accounts of the Ft. Lee affair vary widely on several salient points. Many give 18 Nov. as the date; I have accepted the opinion of Freeman, Ward, and C. & M. that 20 Nov. is correct. Strength of Cornwallis' command varies between 4,000 and 6,000: Ward says 4,000; Fortescue says 4,500; and most modern American writers favor the figure 6,000. Surprise and the opportunity to bag the garrison of Ft. Lee were lost when news of the British landing at Closter was brought to the Americans by: a deserter, according to Fortescue; a countryman, according to Freeman, who cites hearsay evidence of British Ensign Thos. Glyn [MS in Princeton Univ. Lib.]; or by "an American officer on patrol," according to Ward.)

It was not known until 1963 who had led Cornwallis up the hazardous trail at Closter, N.J., in his attempt to trap the Americans. Professor Richard P. McCormick of Rutgers University has found a memorandum in the British Public Records Office stating that Maj. John Aldington was the man. (*N.Y. Times,* 21 Nov. 1963)

FORT McINTOSH, Ga., 2–4 Feb. '77. As the rebels got the upper hand in Ga., Tory refugees gathered in East Florida where Gov. Tonyn was actively organizing militia and fitting out privateers. Here Thos. BROWN assembled his Florida Rangers and led them on raids from a base on the St. Marys River (the boundary between Fla. and Ga.). The rebels organized an expedition against St. Augustine from Savannah, led by Brig. Gen. Robt. Howe, but it got no farther than Sunbury before disintegrating because of disease and lack of adequate equipment. The Tories then attacked Ft. McIntosh, a small bastioned stockade about 100 feet square on the left bank of the Satilla River in S.E. Georgia. The garrison of Capt. Richard Winn surrendered after two days, and all of them were paroled except two officers taken to St. Augustine as hostages. Lossing, on whom this account is based, says the attack started 7 Feb. (II, 728) The *A.A.*–Heitman list of battles gives 2–4 Feb. as the dates of the action.

FORT McINTOSH, Pa. On the Ohio River at the mouth of Beaver Creek, about 30 miles N.W. of Pittsburgh, this fort and FORT LAURENS, 70 miles farther west, were built in Nov. '78 during the abortive expedition of Lachlan MCINTOSH toward Detroit. Col. William Crawford was involved in the erection of both forts, and the engineering work at Ft. McIntosh was directed by CAMBRAY-DIGNY. Both forts proved to be untenable and were abandoned in Aug. '79. Ft. McIntosh was reoccupied later in the war, and its commandant, Col. James Marshal, wrote to his commander, Gen. William Irvine at Ft. Pitt, the following warnings in early Apr. '82: "This is most certain that unless an expedition be carried against some of the principal Indian towns early this summer, this country must unavoidably suffer," and "The people in general on the frontiers are waiting with anxious expectations to know whether an expedition can be carried against Upper Sandusky early this spring or not." (Letters of 2 and 4 Apr. '82 quo-

ted in *Ohio Arch. and Hist. Soc. Pubs.*, 15 *n.*, from *Washington–Irvine Corresp.*, 285, 286. See William CRAWFORD for further identification of these sources.) Col. Marshal's warnings are part of the background of the expedition covered under the heading of CRAWFORD'S DEFEAT, 4–5 June '82.

FORT MERCER (Red Bank, Gloucester co.) N.J., 22 Oct.–21 Nov. '77. As part of the system of Delaware River forts (see this section under PHILADELPHIA CAMPAIGN), a triple row of chevaux de frise extended between FORT MIFFLIN, Pa., and Fort Mercer, N.J. Ft. Mercer was a large earthwork mounting 14 cannon and was protected on the land side by a ditch and abatis. Col. Christopher Greene commanded a garrison of about 400 R.I. rank and file from his own regiment and from the regiment of Col. Israel Angell. N.J. militia were supposed to reinforce the garrison, but did not answer the call. When du Plessis arrived to help Greene organize the defense, he directed one significant change: seeing that the fort was too extensive for the size of the garrison, he had a new, interior wall built to cut off the northern wing.

On 21 Oct. '77 Col. von Donop was detached from Howe's army with 2,000 Hessians to capture the fort. His command was made up of the Hessian jäger corps (four companies), the Hessian grenadiers (three battalions), the Regiment von Mirbach, and was supported by two guns. (Baurmeister, 125) After camping at Haddonfield, N.J., they started 3 o'clock the morning of the 22d, approached the fort at noon, and at 4:30 sent an officer to demand surrender. The threat of "no quarter" was also made. His challenge accepted, the leisurely German commander attacked around 9 P.M., according to Baurmeister (P. 126).

Von Donop posted von Lengerke's Bn. and the jägers to protect his flank and rear, and attacked in two columns: two grenadier battalions and the von Mirbach from the north, the rest from the west. The northern column stormed the breastworks shouting "Vittoria!" and found themselves unexpectedly confronted with du Plessis' new wall. Simultaneously, von Donop led the other attack through the abatis and across the ditch to find himself stopped at the berm for lack of scaling ladders with which to assault the parapet. It had all gone nicely until this point, and the defenders had not yet fired a shot.

Then Greene gave the order, and a sustained hail of grape and aimed musket fire started pouring mercilessly and at point blank range into the bunched ranks. It was butchery. The conspicuous von Donop went down with a leg wound that was to be fatal. His troops withdrew, reformed, and their officers led them forward again, this time against the south side of the redoubt. This time they were stopped not only by fire from the fort but also from the American rowing galleys in the river. Nothing about this German performance was very bright tactically, but they showed discipline and guts.

Freeman says the cost to the assailants was "intense humiliation and about 400 casualties" among the 1,200 engaged. (*Washington,* IV, 528) Baurmeister says the two grenadier battalions and the Mirbach Regt. lost 377 killed and wounded, including about 100 wounded who were captured. (*Op. cit.,* 126) Twenty more were captured uninjured on the berm. (Ward, *W.O.R.,* 376)

American losses have been estimated as 14 killed and 23 wounded (*ibid.*), an unlikely ratio but a credible total. (See CASUALTY FIGURES)

EVACUATION

The defenders of FT. MIFFLIN were forced to abandon their post the night of 15–16 Nov., which made Ft. Mercer no longer tenable. As Cornwallis approached with 2,000 for another assault, Greene pulled out of Ft. Mercer the night of 20–21 Nov. The Delaware was now open to the British up to Philadelphia.

FORT MIFFLIN, Pa., 10 Oct.–15 Nov. '77. (Under PHIL. CAMP'N., see "Delaware River Forts" for background.) Located opposite Ft. Mercer (Red Bank, Gloucester co., N.J.) on Port Island, between Mud and Hog Islands, Ft. Mifflin covered one end of a band of obstructions across the Delaware. (Freeman notes that, "Port Island often was confused in reports with Mud Island. . . ." See his *Washington,* IV, 527 for map.) The fort was garrisoned by 450 men, who were reinforced by small detachments during the siege. Bombardment started from Province Island against the weak, land side of the poorly engineered fort on 10 Oct. On 23 Oct., the day after von Donop's unsuccessful attack on Ft. Mercer, the guns of Ft. Mifflin and supporting river craft inflicted severe damage on six enemy men of war that approached through a gap the British had made in the chevaux de frise. The 64-gun British ship *Augusta* and the 16-gun frigate (or sloop) *Merlin* ran aground and were destroyed. The date of this action is erroneously given as 22 Oct. in many accounts; Freeman, p. 528 *n.,* and Baurmeister, p. 127, say it took place 23 Oct.

On 10 Nov. the British started a severe bombardment with five batteries from Province Is. and a floating battery of 22 large guns (24-pdrs.) that moved within 40 yards of the fort. The defenders fired back as best they could, but their four blockhouses (four guns each) and their 10-gun battery of 18-pdrs. were severely damaged. Lt. Col. Samuel Smith was evacuated for injuries and Maj. Simeon Thayer succeeded to command of Ft. Mifflin. On the 15th the British fleet brought its guns and small arms to bear on the defenders, who now had only two guns left in action. The ships came so close that marines were firing into the fort from the rigging. By nightfall the fort was virtually destroyed, and Thayer evacuated the survivors to Ft. Mercer. Showing remarkable tenacity, the Americans had stuck to their guns despite 250 casualties. (Ward, *W.O.R.*, 377) See PHIL. CAMP'N. for further details.

FORT MONTAGU, Bahamas. See NASSAU, 3–4 Mar. '76, and NASSAU RAID OF RATHBUN, 1777.

FORT MONTGOMERY, N.Y., 6 Oct. '77. Captured along with Ft. Clinton by CLINTON'S EXPEDITION....

FORT MORRIS, Ga. See SUNBURY.

FORT MOTTE, S.C., 12 May '81. (SOUTHERN CAMPAIGNS OF GREENE) Strategically located where the Congaree and Wateree join to form the Santee River, this post was the principal depot on the British line of communications between Charleston and the interior. The large mansion of the widow Mrs. Rebecca Brewton Motte had been strongly fortified by a stockade, ditch, and abatis, and was held by British Lt. McPherson with 150 infantry and a small detachment of dragoons. (The latter had been carrying dispatches to Camden from Charleston when the rebels approached the place.) After their maneuvers against Watson (see SOUTHERN CAMP'NS. ...), Lee and Marion reached Ft. Motte on 8 May and started regular approaches. A surrender summons sent on the 10th was refused. That evening the rebels received

information that Rawdon was retreating toward Ft. Motte from Camden; beacon fires the morning and evening of the 11th encouraged the defenders and told the attackers they would have to take the place quickly or abandon the operation. Lee conceived the idea of setting fire to the Motte mansion by firing flaming arrows onto the shingle roof, which was dry after a period of sunny weather. When Mrs. Motte was informed that this decision had reluctantly been made, she not only accepted the fact but produced a fine East Indian bow and bundle of arrows. (Mrs. Motte had been living at a nearby farmhouse from which Lee and Marion directed the siege.) The morning of the 12th, Dr. Irvine of Lee's cavalry advanced with a flag to inform McPherson that Rawdon was not yet across the Santee and to request his surrender. The British commander again refused. By noon the rebel trench was within range and Pvt. Nathan Savage of Marion's Brig. dropped two "AFRICAN ARROWS" onto the roof. When enemy soldiers went to the attic to knock off the burning shingles they were driven away by artillery. A white flag appeared, the fire was extinguished, and the garrison surrendered at 1 P.M.

"By invitation of Mrs. Motte," says Lossing happily, "both the victorious and the captive officers partook of a sumptuous dinner from her table...." Greene arrived the day of the surrender, having been worried about completing this operation before Rawdon could intervene; he returned to his camp after ordering Lee to take FT. GRANBY and Marion to take GEORGETOWN.

Marion lost two men in the siege, Lt. Cruger and Sgt. McDonald; there were no other men killed on either side. The prisoners were paroled, and the officers joined Rawdon at Nelson's Ferry on the Santee.

FORT MOULTRIE, S.C., 28 June '76. For Col. Moultrie's successful defense of this place, then known as Fort Sullivan, against the fleet of Sir Peter Parker, see CHARLESTON EXPED. of Clinton in 1776.

FORT MOULTRIE, S.C., 7 May '80. During the CHARLESTON EXPED. of Clinton in 1780 the fort surrendered without a fight; although most of the garrison had been evacuated, British sailors and marines took 200 prisoners.

FORT NELSON (Norfolk), Va., 9 May '79. The Matthews-Collier raid (see VA. MIL. OPNS.) started with an attack on Ft. Nelson, which had been built to protect Portsmouth, Norfolk, and the navy yard at Gosport. When the British approached, Maj. Thos. Matthews and his 100-man garrison struck out for the Dismal Swamp so fast that they left the American flag flying from the ramparts.

FORT PARIS (Stone Arabia), N.Y. Col. John Brown marched from this place to his defeat at FT. KEYSER, 19 Oct. '80.

FORT PLEASANT, S.C. Located at HADDREL'S POINT.

FORT SACKVILLE (Vincennes), Ind., 25 Feb. '79. Surrendered to George Rogers Clark during WESTERN OPERATIONS.

FORT SAINT GEORGE, L.I., N.Y. See FORT GEORGE.

FORT SAINT JOHNS. See SAINT JOHNS.

FORT ST. JOSEPH (Mich.), Jan. '81. In a counterexpedition to the British offensive that was stopped at ST. LOUIS, 26 May '80, the Spanish sent a force against Detroit. With about 60 militia and 60 Indians, Capt. Eugenio Pourré surprised Fort St. Joseph in Jan. '81 and the British garrison surrendered immediately. Holding the place

only 24 hours, the Spaniards subsequently claimed the valleys of the St. Joseph and Illinois Rivers "by right of conquest"! (Ward, *W.O.R.*, 862, citing articles on this operation by F. J. Teggart and Lawrence Kinnaird in the *Miss. Valley Hist. Rev.*, 1918 and 1932)

FORT SCHUYLER, N.Y. See FORT STANWIX.

FORT SLONGO, N.Y. See TREADWELL'S NECK.

FORT STANWIX (Schuyler), N.Y. Located at the head of navigation of the Mohawk, and at the portage between that river and Wood Creek, which led to Oswego, this place was astride the main avenue of approach from Canada through the Iroquois country and into the Mohawk Valley. Here, on the site of modern Rome, the French had built a fort to protect their trade with the Indians. The British had built Ft. Stanwix in the same area in 1758 at a cost of $266,000. This fell into disrepair after 1763, but in June '76 a detachment of Con'tl. troops under Elias DAYTON started rebuilding it. For a time it was called Ft. Schuyler, in honor of Gen. Philip Schuyler. "It has been confounded by some with [another] Fort Schuyler, which was built in the French wars, near where Utica now stands, and named in honor of Col. Schuyler, the uncle of Gen. [Philip] Schuyler." (Campbell, *Tryon County*, 60) The new Fort Stanwix–Schuyler figured prominently in ST. LEGER'S EXPED.

FORT STANWIX, Treaty of. 1768. After a council with the Iroquois, presided over by Sir Wm. Johnson, the Indians gave up claims to lands southeast of a line running from Ft. Stanwix to Ft. Pitt, and thence along the southern bank of the Ohio to the mouth of the Tenn. (Cherokee) River. (Scribner's *Atlas*, 60) This opened vast tracts along the frontiers of N.Y., Pa., and Va. for settlement. Pressure of white settlers and fraudulent methods practiced by many of them had led to the PROCLAMATION OF 1763.

FORT SULLIVAN, S.C., 28 June '76. For Col. Moultrie's successful defense of this place, subsequently known as Fort Moultrie, see CHARLESTON EXPED. of Clinton in 1776.

FORT TRYON, N.Y. Here, on the highest ground in Manhattan, the British improved rebel earthworks captured in the operation against FORT WASHINGTON and renamed their fort in honor of GOV. TRYON.

FORT WASHINGTON, N.Y. Captured by British 16 Nov. '76. (N.Y. CAMPAIGN) Howe's maneuvers forced Washington up the Hudson, leaving the 1,200-man garrison of Col. Robt. Magaw isolated at Ft. Washington. At White Plains Howe stopped his pursuit of the main American army and turned south to capture Ft. Washington. (Under N.Y. CAMPAIGN see "The Fort Washington Trap.") Howe's decision may have been affected by the treachery of Wm. DEMONT.

In 1776 the northern tip of Manhattan Island was a densely wooded plateau commanded by Mount Washington (now called Washington Heights —generally within modern Fort Tryon Park). This hill was 230 feet high and a mile long; almost vertical cliffs rose a hundred feet from the Hudson and Harlem Rivers to the plateau.

Ft. Washington (at today's West 184th St.) had been laid out by Rufus Putnam and was erected in July '76 by the 3d and 5th Pa. Regts. of Cols. John Shee and Robt. Magaw. As the eastern end of an ineffective line of obstructions across the Hudson to Ft. Lee, Ft. Washington was a crude, pentagonal earthwork that lacked most of the features needed to resist siege or attack. Although an extremely strong fortress could have been built on this site, particularly by doing a considerable amount of blasting into the underlying rock, Ft. Washington had no ditch, no casements, no palisade, no barracks, and weak outworks. It lacked water, food, and fuel. (Freeman, *Washington*, IV, 243; Ward, *W.O.R.*, 269) These weaknesses, however, were not fully known by either the American or the British. Putnam considered it impregnable; Magaw, the commandant, said he could hold it until the end of December, and could evacuate the garrison and stores across the Hudson to N.J. should this become necessary. Washington had lost direct communication with the place about 22 Oct., being forced to leave its defense to subordinates, and knew little about true conditions there; when he later urged that it be abandoned, Greene advanced five specific reasons for its retention and reiterated that the garrison could be evacuated if necessary. (Freeman, *op. cit.,* 245, 247) As evidence of how deceptive this position was, a British officer who saw the fort after its capture said he would have undertaken to defend it with 800 men against 10,000 (Miller, *Triumph*, 138); Fortescue, well over a century later (1902), wrote, "The position was in fact exceedingly strong. . . ." (*British Army*, III, 191)

About three quarters of a mile north of Ft. Washington was the site of FORT TRYON. Here Col. Moses Rawlings was posted with his regiment of 250 Md. and Va. riflemen, supported by three cannon. Paths leading to his position were obstructed by deep abatis, and an outpost was located at Cock or Cox Hill (Ft. Cockhill), a short distance north of Ft. Tryon. On the Harlem River side of Ft. Washington and about half a mile to the east was

Laurel Hill (later FORT GEORGE), where Col. Wm. Baxter of the FLYING CAMP was posted in a couple of FLECHES with his Pennsylvania militia from Bucks County. A mile and a half south of Ft. Washington, in the old HARLEM HEIGHTS defenses, were about 800 troops under Lt. Col. Lambert Cadwalader; these comprised Magaw's and Shee's Pa. troops, part of Miles's Regt., the Rangers, and others. An outpost was located at Harlem Cove (Manhattanville) to detect and delay the enemy's advance against Cadwalader's main position. Ft. Washington was occupied by a small garrison under the personal command of Magaw. Total American strength in the rectangle of two miles by one mile was about 2,800.*

THE ATTACK

The night of 14–15 Nov., the British moved 30 flatboats up the Hudson past Ft. Washington, into SPUYTEN DUYVIL Creek and down the Harlem to an assembly area from which an attack would be launched westward. This movement was unobserved by the Americans. On 15 Nov., a British officer approached the fort with a demand for surrender, which Magaw refused. The next morning Howe attacked from three directions.

From the north, Gen. Knyphausen with 3,000 Germans made the main effort, attacking in two columns since the narrow front and other considerations ruled out the normal linear formation. He crossed Kings Bridge at 7 A.M., made contact with Rawlings' riflemen and gunners about 10 o'clock,

* In the A.A.–Heitman list, all the following are given as individual actions on 16 Nov.: Ft. Washington, Ft. Tryon, Ft. George, Harlem Cove (Manhattanville), and Cock-Hill Fort.

but had to delay until the British crossed the Harlem. (This was to be coordinated by signal cannon.)

Lord Percy advanced against Cadwalader from McGown's Pass, where he had been stationed while Howe chased Washington toward White Plains. His column of 2,000 men—one Hessian brigade and nine British battalions—made contact, but it also had to halt until the delayed attack across the Harlem got under way.

Gen. Mathews finally crossed the Harlem at noon with two light infantry battalions and established a foothold along the lower reaches of the cliffs below Baxter's position on Laurel Hill. (This landing was in a cove or creek at about 200th St., according to Lossing, II, 826 n.) Cornwallis followed with two guards battalions, two grenadier battalions, and the 33d Foot. Col. Stirling's 42d Highlanders ("Black Watch") had the mission of feigning a landing farther south, but when Percy resumed his attack and met substantial resistance in a second line of defense, Cornwallis reinforced Stirling with two battalions to hit the flank of this line. Stirling dropped down an estuary of the river and landed near the foot of today's 152d St. in the face of small arms fire and an 18-pdr. Cadwalader detected the British envelopment and sent 150 men of the 3d Pa. to oppose it; Magaw sent an additional 100 from the fort. In a spirited action, Stirling lost 90 men but captured Baxter's position and 170 prisoners.

Washington reached Ft. Lee and the day of the attack he crossed to Ft. Washington with Putnam, Greene, and Mercer for a personal reconnaissance. They reached the fort about the time Percy's column was attacking Cadwalader's second defensive position. Since there was nothing the four generals could do to assist Magaw at this stage of developments, they returned to Ft. Lee.

Forced by collapse of his flank and heavy frontal pressure to retreat, Cadwalader turned at bay to check the converging forces of Stirling and Percy near Trinity Cemetery (present 155th St.); having inflicted heavy casualties on the Hessian brigade (Lossing, *op. cit.,* 827), he retreated into Ft. Washington.

Meanwhile, Knyphausen's column pressed south through difficult terrain and against effective resistance from the riflemen and gunners of Rawlings' command. In the left (eastern) column, the Wutginau Regt., which followed a 100-man vanguard, was particularly hard hit by small arms and fire from the most advanced gun battery. (Baurmeister, *Journals,* 70) The right column moved along a route that was in defilade from the second gun battery, which was therefore abandoned upon their approach. (*Ibid.*) Rawlings' men put up the longest and most effective resistance of the day. (Ward, *op. cit.,* 273) Col. Rall, whose regiment was with the right column of Knyphausen's force, led his troops up to Ft. Washington and demanded its surrender.

Accounts vary considerably, but surrender was at 3 P.M., and the Americans started marching out of the fort an hour later. (Freeman, *op. cit.,* 252 and *n.*) The Hessian regiments of Rall and Lossberg were formed to receive the American colors. Ironically, Rall was selected primarily because of his outstanding performance at Ft. Washington to command the post of danger at TRENTON; here, a mere six weeks later, his inefficiency and overconfidence cost Rall his life, and caused the surrender of the Rall and Lossberg regiments.

NUMBERS AND LOSSES

Magaw's original garrison of almost 1,200 was reinforced by nearly 1,700 in the few days preceding the attack. Howe reported 2,818 American officers and men captured, and 53 dead; these figures are accepted by Freeman. (*Op. cit.,* 252) The 8,000 troops engaged in the brief attack had 458 killed and wounded. Of these, 330 (or 72 per cent) were Hessians. Half the British casualties were sustained by Stirling's 42d Highlanders. (Fortescue, *op. cit.,* 193) The number of Americans wounded in the action is unknown; the generally quoted figure of 96 (Ward, *op. cit.,* 274) being in complete variance with the normal CASUALTY FIGURES. The Hessians lost 272 wounded and 58 killed; the British had 102 wounded and 20 killed. Using this ratio of 374 wounded to 78 killed among the enemy troops, the Americans should have had about 250 wounded, if the figure of 53 killed is correct. All the wounded were presumably captured.

SIGNIFICANCE

Aside from its damage to American morale, the loss of trained military manpower was a serious blow. A large amount of valuable matériel was also lost at Ft. Washington and four days later at FT. LEE, N.J.: 146 cannon, 12,000 shot and shell, 2,800 muskets, 400,000 cartridges, in addition to tents, entrenching tools, and other equipment. (Ward, *op. cit.,* 274) Howe had demonstrated again his capacity for bringing off "a pretty little action, neatly designed and very neatly executed...." (Fortescue, *op. cit.,* 193) Washington had again shown vacillation and indecision. Greene, who was to emerge from the war as a military leader second in ability only to Washington, had shown remarkably bad judgment.

FORT WATSON, S.C., 28 Feb. '81. A mismanaged attack by Thomas SUMTER was repulsed.

FORT WATSON, S.C., 15–23 Apr. '81. (SOUTHERN CAMPAIGNS OF GREENE) When Greene turned from his pursuit of Cornwallis to march toward Camden he detached Lee to screen against a possible movement of Cornwallis in that direction from Wilmington and, if this threat did not materialize, to join forces with Marion and capture Ft. Watson. With his Legion, Capt. Oldham's company of Md. regulars, and one gun, Lee joined Marion on 14 Apr. The next evening they invested Ft. Watson.

This post was a link in the British line of communications from Charleston, 60 miles S.E. It was named after Col. John WATSON, who was in the area with a large Tory force. Ft. Watson was a small but strong stockade, surrounded by three rings of abatis, that perched on an Indian mound. This tumulus was on the edge of Scott's Lake, part of the Santee River, and provided a piece of commanding terrain in the bare, level plain. It was between 30 and 50 feet high. (Ward, W.O.R., 799, gives the first figure; Lossing, II, 706, gives the second.) British Lt. McKay commanded its garrison of 80 regulars and 40 Tories.

After the customary demand for surrender and the refusal, the rebels seized the water supply point on the lake. The defenders dug a well and ran a trench that filled it from the lake. The score was then even, but without siege artillery and with the danger that Col. Watson might come to McKay's relief, the situation looked bad for the attackers. Col. Hezekiah Maham then suggested building a type of tower that was thereafter known by his name and used in other sieges. This was a prefabricated log crib, rectangular in plan, on which a protected platform was built for riflemen to deliver plunging fire into the fort. It took five days to cut, trim, and

notch the logs; on the dark night of the 22d they were carried to within range of the fort and by dawn a company of riflemen started delivering a deadly drizzle of aimed shots into the stockade. At the same time two assault parties attacked the abatis, one composed of militia under Ensign Johnson and another of Legion infantry. Unable to defend the stockade without exposing themselves to fire from the Maham Tower, the garrison had to surrender. Rebel losses were two killed and six wounded.

FORT WILLIAM AND MARY, Portsmouth Harbor, N.H., was captured in Dec. '74 by patriots under the leadership of John Langdon and John Sullivan.

FORT WILLIAM HENRY (Ft. George), N.Y., 1755–80. At the southern tip of Lake George, William JOHNSON started construction of Ft. William Henry after his victory of 8 Sept. '55. Montcalm besieged the place on 4 Aug. '57, and on the 9th its garrison of about 2,200 men was surrendered by Lt. Col. George Munro. The Indians got out of hand and started murdering prisoners, and Munro reached Ft. Edward with 1,400 survivors. (Alden, Gage, 41; Morris, E. A. H., 68) This atrocity was blamed on ST. LUC; the half-breed LANGLADE also was present. For the over-all strategic situation at this time, see COLONIAL WARS.

Fort George was built about a mile S.E. of the ruins of Ft. William Henry (which Montcalm destroyed), and it was the northern link of the overland route to Ft. Edward on the Hudson, a straight-line distance of 10 miles. In "a very declining condition" according to a letter from Carleton to Gage on 15 Feb. '67 (Whitton, 30), it became an important British base during Burgoyne's Offensive. Gen. Phillips occupied the place on 29 July '77, and the

British abandoned it after the Saratoga surrender. It was recaptured 11 Oct. '80 but not held (see BORDER WARFARE).

FORTY FORT, Pa. See WYOMING VALLEY "MASSACRE."

FOSTER'S HILL. Alternate name for Nook's Hill, which figured in final phase of BOSTON SIEGE.

FOUQUET. According to Heitman, Mark Fouquet Sr. and Mark Jr. received Cont'l. Army brevets on 17 Nov. '77 as Capt. and Lt. Lasseray says the father and son—he gives no first names —went to America with Coudray. The father called himself "the best powder maker (*poudrier*) in France," and the two were engaged by Silas Deane. Since Beaumarchais would have wanted a monopoly on powder manufacture, Deane signed up the Fouquets as artillerymen (*bombardiers*). In the French records they are identified as "engineers employed early in 1778 as *poudriers* and to examine powder magazines on the continent." (Lasseray, 218–19)

FOUR CORNERS, N.Y. See YOUNG'S HOUSE, 3 Feb. '80.

FOURTEENTH COLONY. Term hopefully applied to Canada by the American patriots early in the Revolution.

FOX, Charles James. 1749–1806. British opposition politician. Third son of the 1st Lord Holland and of Lady Caroline, eldest daughter of Charles Lennox, 2d Duke of Richmond, he was reared as a wealthy aristocrat. His father not only was indulgent with respect to his children, but he took Charles on a tour of the Continent in 1763 and saw to it that he had every opportunity to meet and cavort with the most immoral society of the times. "That he learnt anything [at Eton and Oxford], and that he grew up an ami-

able and magnanimous man, were solely due to his natural worth. . . ." (*E.B.*) The "precocious rake" grew into a charming, brilliant, notoriously dissipated man with three dominant passions: women, gambling, and politics. In 1768 his father bought him a pocket borough and Fox started his career in Parliament and London society. True to his class, he initially supported the court. He attracted the eye of Lord North, and in 1770, when only 21, he became a junior lord of the admiralty. During the violent controversy centering around John WILKES over the Middlesex election, Fox took the unpopular side and argued the right of Parliament to exclude Wilkes. In 1772 he and North were attacked by a pro-Wilkes mob and rolled in the mud. This was a peculiar beginning for a man who was to become a notorious opposition leader. The transformation started with the King's dislike of Fox as a gambling libertine and a person incapable of blind conformity with his party line. In Feb. '72 Fox resigned his government post to oppose the Royal Marriage Act. In Dec. he returned to office as junior lord of the treasury, but his insubordination and growing sympathy with the American cause (*E.B.*) led to dismissal in Feb. '74. His father's death the following July removed one remaining tie with the King's party, and his friendship with Burke drew him toward the camp of the Rockingham Whigs.

Other personal events caused a marked change in Fox in 1774 as he stood on the threshold of his great political career. Not only his father, but also his mother and elder brother died within six months. One of Lord Holland's last acts had been to raise £ 140,-000 to cover the gambling debts of the sons he had taught to gamble. According to Trevelyan, Fox was struck with "a penitance which was sincere and lasting." (*American Revolution,* V, 43) The timing was fortunate in that he was in a perfect position to make political capital of a new political development. In the words of Trevelyan:

"In his salad days, when he was green in judgment, he had never uttered a word about America,—good, bad, or indifferent,—which remained on record. And therefore when Lord North, throwing open the casket of Pandora, invited Parliament to wreck the prosperity of Boston and extinguish the freedom of Massachusetts, Fox, to the astonishment and amusement of the House of Commons, presented himself in the very unusual attitude of a cold and cautious neutrality." (*Ibid.*)

He did not maintain that attitude long, but launched into a career that was unique among British statesmen of the first rank in that it was passed almost wholly in opposition. The full scope of his oratory was first displayed on 2 Feb. '75. The text is lost, but Gibbon, who was present, told a friend that Fox, "taking the vast compass of the question before us, discovered powers for regular debate which neither his friends hoped nor enemies dreaded." (*E.B.*) Becoming undisputed leader of the Opposition in the Commons, "He spoke on every important occasion with increased acceptance, and immense authority," according to Trevelyan. "Intent on convincing, he reiterated the substance of his case in fresh forms, and with new illustrations, until the stupidest of his hearers had caught his full meaning; while the cleverest, and the most fastidious, never complained that Charles Fox spoke too long, or repeated himself too often." The bitterly hostile Joseph GALLOWAY, often present in the House, had to admire his

oratory: "He does not leave his hearers to follow. He drives them before him." (From Trevelyan, *op. cit.,* V, 44, 45) Horace Walpole went to hear him speak and wrote in a letter of 9 Apr. '72 (even before Gibbon was to comment on his maiden speech for the Opposition, see above):

"The object answered: Fox's abilities are amazing at so very early a period, especially under the circumstances of such a dissolute life. He has just arrived from Newmarket, had sat up drinking all night, and had not been in bed. How such talents make one laugh at Tully's rules for an orator. His laboured orations are puerile in comparison with this boy's manly reason." (From Mumby, *George III,* 302)

During his eight years of negative brilliance he is credited with one positive contribution to British politics: "He planted the seed of the modern Liberal party as opposed to the pure Whigs." (*E.B.*)

When the North ministry was about to be discarded, and the King applied to the Whigs—through Shelburne—to form a government, Fox erred badly in persuading Rockingham not to deal directly with the King in this matter. This resulted in a cabinet "partly of Whigs who wished to restrain the King, and partly of the King's friends, represented by Lord Shelburne, whose real function was to baffle the Whigs." (*Ibid.*) As the two secretaries of state in the Rockingham ministry, Fox and Shelburne were at cross purposes. On Rockingham's death, 1 July '82, Shelburne was offered the premiership by the king, and Fox resigned. On 14 Feb. '83 he formed a coalition with the man he had been denouncing for years, Lord North! The public saw this as a desperate move to gain power at any price, but the coalition was sufficiently strong to drive Shelburne from office in ten days. After all possible resistance, on 2 Apr. the King had to accept the Duke of Portland as P.M. with Fox and North as his secretaries of state. Objection to the new ministry crossed party lines, and Fox increased his own unpopularity by consenting, against the desires of most of his colleagues, that the Prince of Wales be granted the staggering sum of £100,000. (In the Hanoverian family tradition, the king and his son were enemies.) Fox fell when his East India Bill, introduced in Nov. '83, was defeated on 17 Dec. The next day the Portland ministry was dismissed.

Returning to the ranks of the Opposition for which he appears to have been born, Fox now was committed as a political enemy of Pitt the Younger. On the latter's death in 1806, Fox was so conspicuously the top man in public life that the king could not hope to exclude him from office. In the "Ministry of All the Talents" of Lord Grenville, Fox was foreign minister. He was in bad health, however, and did not live out the year.

In appearance he was strikingly unattractive: short, swarthy, unkempt, unpleasant looking, and with a voice that was naturally harsh and shrill. (He overcame the latter defect.) Since the derogatory aspects of his controversial character have received the most stress, his biographers may tend to minimize them. His morals were very much those of his class and time. Nobody has questioned his towering ability as an orator.

"Fox made many mistakes, due in some cases to vehemence of temperament, and in others only to be ascribed to want of sagacity. That he fought unpopular causes is a very insufficient explanation of his failure as a practical statesman. He could have profited by the reaction which followed popular excitement but for his bad reputation and his want of discretion." (*E.B.*)

FOX'S MILLS, N.Y. Alternate name for the action at KLOCK'S FIELD, 19 Oct. '80.

FRAISE. A palisade around a fortification between the main wall and the ditch (i.e., the "berm"); its timbers were pointed horizontally toward the direction of attack, or were slanted either up or down. The fraising normally was pointed, and its purpose was to hinder an enemy in his final assault without giving him the protection that an ABATIS might offer.

FRANCISCO, Peter. *c.* 1760–1836. War hero. Portugal?–Va. Put ashore from a strange ship and abandoned near the present Hopewell, Va., when he was about four years old, Peter was reared by Judge Anthony Winston, an uncle of Patrick Henry. The boy's true name and origin are not known, but one theory is that he had been kidnaped to save his life after his noble Portuguese family was ordered to witness his execution for some political offense of theirs. He grew into a 6-foot 6-inch giant weighing 260 pounds and joined the 10th Va. Regt. at the age of 15. He was wounded at the Brandywine (Sept. '77) and met Lafayette when they were both receiving treatment. After fighting at Germantown and Ft. Mifflin, he re-enlisted and was seriously wounded by a musket ball at Monmouth (28 June '78). He was one of the 20-man forlorn hope led by Lt. James Gibbons at Stony Point (16 July '79) and one of the four who reached the final objective. In this action he first used the huge, 5-foot broadsword Washington had ordered made for him and that is now owned by the Va. Hist. Soc. Despite a nine-inch bayonet slash across the abdomen received in this action, he took part in the assault on

Paulus Hook, slightly more than a month later, and is credited with splitting the skulls of two grenadiers. At the expiration of his second enlistment he joined the militia regiment of Col. Wm. Mayo. In the rout at Camden, S.C., 16 Aug. '80, he is said to have carried off a 1,000-pound cannon to prevent its capture and to have rescued Col. Mayo after he was taken prisoner. He then joined the mounted troop of Capt. (Thos.?) Watkins and took part in the subsequent guerrilla operations of Col. Wm. Washington's dragoons. At Guilford, N.C., 15 Mar. '81, he received a bayonet wound while charging at the head of Washington's counterattack, and in returning to the attack his thigh was laid open by a bayonet. Historians repeat the tradition that he killed 11 British this day.

Found lying among the dead, Francisco was rescued by a Quaker. He recovered and volunteered as a scout in the operations against British raiders in Va. At a place called Ward's Tavern he was surrounded by nine of Tarleton's dragoons, but managed by ruse and by single combat to fight his way out, leaving at least two of the enemy dead. He took part in the siege of Yorktown.

After the war he opened a combination store-tavern-smithy and launched into a program of adult self-education. In 1785 he married, acquired property as part of the dowry, and became a country squire of fastidious dress and avid reading habits. After producing four sons and two daughters by wives who died in 1790 and 1821, he remarried in 1823, moved to Richmond, and became Sgt. at Arms in the House of Delegates. In 1824 he accompanied Lafayette on a tour of the state. He died at the age of about 71 of an intestinal ailment, possibly appendicitis. (Fred J. Cook, *What Manner of Men,*

Chapter V. See also *American Heritage,* Vol. X, No. 6, for an adaptation of this chapter.)

FRANKLIN, Benjamin. 1706–1790. American statesman. Signer. Mass.–Pa. At the start of the Revolution Franklin was almost 70 years old. He had an international reputation as a scientist, inventor, writer, and editor, to mention but some of his achievements. British army historian Sir John Fortescue goes so far as to characterize him as being "the strongest intellect to be found at that time [1764] in the whole Anglo-Saxon race." (*British Army,* III, 25) The story of his life and remarkable achievements is to be found in varying detail in so many other places that I will restrict this sketch to his role in the political events just before and during the Revolution.

Born in Boston, he attended school only a short time before going to work first in his father's tallow shop and then in his brother's printing shop. In 1723 he reached Philadelphia with one Dutch dollar and a copper shilling, but six years later he was part owner of the *Pennsylvania Gazette,* and the next year, in 1730, he was sole owner at the age of 24. On 1 Sept. of this year he "took to wife" an illiterate but devoted woman named Deborah Read, the daughter of his first landlady. Out of this common law union (Deborah had been deserted by a husband named Rogers, who was never heard of), there were two "legitimate" children and two others. William FRANKLIN, the prominent Tory, is generally believed to have been one of the latter, although there is a question as to whether Deborah was his mother.

Poor Richard's Almanack began appearing in 1732 and was edited by Franklin until 1757. He edited the *Gazette* until 1748. The Junto, a debating club he founded in 1727, became the American Philosophical Society in 1743. He established a circulating library (1731), Philadelphia's first fire company (1736), an academy (1751) that was nucleus of the U. of Pa. In 1747 he and 23 other citizens had formed an association that established this academy and that also recognized the militia organization known as the "Philadelphia Associators." See ASSOCIATORS for their history. In the scientific field—which gained him fame abroad—he invented his stove (1742) and suggested methods by which the identity of lightning and electricity were demonstrated in France in 1752 and later confirmed by him in his kite experiment this same year.

Clerk of the Pa. Assembly (1736–51), he was a member of that body (1751–64), deputy postmaster at Philadelphia (1737–53), and with Wm. Hunter was postmaster general of the colonies from 1753 to 1774. He attended the ALBANY CONVENTION of 1754 and submitted his famous plan of union. In 1757 he went to England on behalf of the Pa. Assembly; he became agent for Pa. in 1764, for Ga. after 1768, and for Mass. starting in 1770. Preceded by his scientific reputation, he was accepted in England and on the Continent. He was accompanied to London by his son William; the latter's appointment in 1763 to be Gov. of N.J. may have been made with the ulterior motive of attaching the father more closely to the mother country. Ben Franklin was instrumental in securing repeal of the Stamp Act (1766). (See DECLARATORY ACT for his role.) He was publicly censured in 1774 for his part in the HUTCHINSON LETTERS AFFAIR.

On 5 May '75 Franklin returned to Philadelphia, and the next day he was chosen as a member of the 2d Cont'l. Cong. He was the first Postmaster General (1775–76), and was one of the three men sent to Canada by Congress in 1776. (See CANADA, Cong. Comm. to) He helped draft the Decl. of Indep. and was a signer. He was one of three appointed by Congress (26 Sept. '76) as commissioners to go to Paris to negotiate a treaty. He left Philadelphia on 26 Oct. and reached France 4 Dec. '76. Already known for his scientific works, as well as for his previous visits in 1767 and 1769, he was lionized by the public and in society, although the government could not openly receive him as an official American representative. Vergennes singled Franklin out as the only one of the three with whom he would deal, so the chief burden of negotiations with the French government fell on him. His popularity did much to expedite secret aid (see HORTALEZ & CIE.) and to bring about the FRENCH ALLIANCE. Meanwhile he suffered the "magisterial snubbings and rebukes" of the psychotic Arthur Lee but got along with the third commissioner, Arthur Deane. On 14 Sept. '78 he was appointed by Congress as sole plenipotentiary. On 8 June '81 he was named one of three American commissioners for PEACE NEGOTIATIONS, in which he played the major role.

On 26 Dec. '83 Franklin reminded Congress of their promise to recall him after the peace was made (the treaty had been signed 3 Sept.), but he did not get his authority until 2 May '85. Leaving Passy on 12 July, he reached Philadelphia on 14 Sept. '85. Soon chosen Pres. of the Pa. Exec. Council, he served until 1788. He was a member of the Constitutional Convention which met in May '87, and although none of his cardinal ideas was adopted—he favored a single chamber, an executive board, and opposed payment of salaries to executive officials—he made a considerable contribution in bringing about the necessary compromises among the delegates. He did not like the way the Constitution was finally worded, but urged its unanimous adoption. "The older I grow, the more apt I am to doubt my own judgment," he said with the whimsy that had ironed out other controversies of the convention. He asked the others to join him in doubting a little of their own infallibility and "to make manifest our unanimity, put his name to the instrument."

His one book, the *Autobiography*, was never completed and covers his life only to 1757. It has been published under various titles. Recent works include Verner W. Crane, *Benjamin Franklin and a Rising People* (Boston, 1954), I. Bernard Cohen, *Benjamin Franklin: His Contribution to the American Tradition* (Indianapolis, 1953), and Carl Van Doren, *Benjamin Franklin* (New York, 1938). Of the many editions of his studies the chief is that edited by his grandson, William Temple Franklin: *Memoirs of the Life and Writings of Benjamin Franklin* (6 vols., 1818). The 10-vol. edition by A. H. Smyth has been favored by historians. A new collection of Franklin papers, edited by Leonard W. Labaree, started appearing in 1959; dealing with Franklin's life up to March 1758, the seventh volume of these *Franklin Papers* was published in 1963. Labaree and others brought out *The Autobiography of Benjamin Franklin* in 1964; Max Savelle calls this "one of those rarest of historiographical achievements: a publication of the original text of a historical and literary classic in which the bookmaker's art and the historian's best technical editorial skills are combined to produce a work that is both a dependable scholar's source, a reader's delight, and a thing of beauty." (*Am. Hist. Review*, April 1965)

FRANKLIN, William. 1731–1813. Royal governor of N.J., Tory leader. Pa–N.J. Illegitimate son of Benj. Franklin, probably by his common-law wife, Deborah Read (*D.A.B.*), he had joined the company of Va. troops raised by Beverley ROBINSON in 1746 for the expedition against Canada (Van Doren, *Secret History*, 4) and at the age of about 15 had risen to the grade of Capt. (*D.A.B.*) For almost 30 years after this he was closely associated with his father, first as comptroller of the Gen. Post Office (1754–56), clerk of the Pa. Prov. Assembly, and in 1757 as his father's companion when Ben Franklin went to England as agent for Pa. and N.J. Will, as his father called him, was "a tall proper Youth, and much of a Beau." He studied at the Middle Temple, was admitted to the bar, traveled with his father, and aided him with his scientific investigations. Having become acquainted with the Earl of Bute, in 1763 he was appointed Gov. of N.J. through the latter's influence. This unsolicited honor may have been given with a view to winning Benj. Franklin over to the British side. (*Ibid.*)

Wm. Franklin's tenure as last royal governor of N.J. started successfully. His adherence to the royal cause at the start of the Revolution appears to have been prompted by nothing more complicated than a sense of duty to the government that appointed him. In this he was estranged from his father, who after failing in all arguments to win him over characterized William as "a thorough government man." On 15 June '76 the Prov. Cong. of N.J. declared him an enemy and ordered his arrest. After severe treatment as a prisoner at East Windsor, Conn., he returned to N.Y.C. in Oct. '78 after being exchanged for John McKinley, American Pres. of Del. (Van Doren, *Secret History*, 114) Franklin became Pres.

of the ASSOCIATED LOYALISTS, who were deprived by Clinton of their powers after the HUDDY–ASGILL AFFAIR in 1782. After Capt. Lippincott was acquitted, "responsibility for the killing of Huddy was shifted to Gov. William Franklin and certain fellow-directors of the 'Associated Loyalists.' . . ." (Freeman, *Washington*, V, 425) Franklin left for England in Aug. '82. He was allowed a relatively paltry £1,800 for the loss of his estate and was given a life pension of £800 a year. His first wife, whom he had married in England in 1762, died while he was a prisoner in Conn. and was never allowed to visit him there. In the family tradition, William sired a natural son, William Temple Franklin, who became his grandfather's secretary in Paris and later edited the works of the great man. (See under Benj. FRANKLIN)

FRANKS, David Solebury. Maj. and A.D.C. to Arnold. Canada–Pa. A native of Montreal, he broke with his Loyalist father while the Americans occupied that place in 1776 and became a volunteer on Benedict Arnold's staff. In May '78, when Arnold became military commander of Philadelphia, Franks was commissioned Maj. A.D.C. (Heitman), a position he apparently had held unofficially for more than two years. He testified at Arnold's court-martial in Philadelphia in Dec. '78 and accompanied the general when he took command of the Hudson Highlands. In the tense situation that developed at Robinson's House shortly before Arnold's treason was exposed, Franks had decided that he would leave the position he had held for three years: the money he had brought from Canada was depreciating in value, and for some months Arnold had subjected Franks to what the latter called "repeated insults and ill treatment. . . ." Through Hamilton he tried to get transferred to the staff of

Rochambeau or some other French general in R.I. He also considered going to Spain, where his friend Henry Brockholst Livingston was private secretary to John Jay. (Van Doren, *Secret History*, 295, 319) Franks was an innocent participant in the denouement of ARNOLD'S TREASON. Cleared of complicity, he remained on the army rolls as Maj. and A.D.C. until retired on 1 Jan. '83 (Heitman), but in July '81 he was sent by Robert Morris as a confidential courier to Jay in Madrid and Franklin in Paris. In 1784 Cong. sent him to Paris with the ratification of the peace treaty, and the next year he acted for a short time as vice consul at Marseilles before returning to the U.S. In 1789 he failed in an attempt to be made consul general in France. Apparently he then went into business, and in 1791 he was assistant cashier of the Bank of North America. (Van Doren, *op. cit.*, 428–29, citing *Pubs. of the Jewish Amer. Hist. Soc.*, I, 76–86; IV, 18–87; X, 101–8)

FRASER, Simon. 1726–1782. Col. of FRASER HIGHLANDERS. Eldest son of the 12th Baron Lovat, a "notorious Jacobite intriguer" executed in 1747 for high treason (*D.N.B.*), he gave up his studies at the University of St. Andrews in 1745 when his father called him to head the clan. He was active in the Second Jacobite Rebellion (1745–46) but was not at Culloden and in 1750 was given a full and free pardon. After practicing law in London and declining command of a regiment in the French service, in 1757 he raised 800 recruits to form the first regiment known as Fraser's Highlanders (78th Regt.). Commissioned Col. on 5 Jan. '57, he led the regiment with distinction in America until about 1761, fighting in 1758 at Louisburg and Cape Breton, in 1759 at Montmorenci during Wolfe's advance on Quebec (being wounded in this action of 31 July), and at Sillery (in the defense of Quebec, on 28 Apr. '60). He commanded a brigade in the advance on Montreal.

In 1762 Fraser was with the British expedition to Portugal and was commissioned Maj. Gen. in the Portuguese Army. The next year he was put on half pay when his regiment was disbanded, and in 1771 was made a Maj. Gen. In 1775 he raised two battalions that became famous in the Revolution as the 71st Regt., better known as the Fraser Highlanders, but he did not accompany them to America.

FRASER, Simon. 1729–1777. British general killed at Saratoga. Youngest son of Hugh Fraser of Balnain, Scotland, he appears to have entered the Dutch service and to have been wounded in 1748. (*D.N.B.*) On 31 Jan. '55 he was appointed Lt. in the 62d Royal Americans and two years later he became Capt.-Lt. in the Fraser Highlanders. On 22 Apr. '59 he was promoted to Capt. During the French and Indian War he fought at Louisburg, Cape Breton, and Quebec. He is said to have served subsequently as a staff officer in Germany, and on 8 Feb. '62 he was promoted to Maj. in the 24th Foot. Going with the 24th to Gibraltar and, several years later, to Ireland, where he became Lt. Col. in 1768, he accompanied the regiment to Canada in 1776. Arriving 28 May with the reinforcements under Burgoyne, he was given command of a brigade on the south side of the St. Lawrence River; it comprised his own regiment (the 24th) and the grenadiers and light infantry of Carleton's army. Two days after his successful defense of TROIS RIVIÈRES, 8 June, he was given the "local rank" of B.G. (Appleton's) The next year Fraser commanded one of the Advance Corps in Burgoyne's Offensive and particularly distinguished himself at HUBBARDTON, Vt., 7 July '77. In the First Battle of SARATOGA, 19 Sept., he led a wide envelopment on the British right and arrived after the action ended. In the Second Battle of SARATOGA, 7 Oct., his fearless leadership marked him as a target for Timothy MURPHY, and he was mortally wounded.

Nursed through the night by Baroness Riedesel, he died at 8 A.M. on the 8th, and in accordance with his request was buried on the field at sunset. The funeral service, witnessed only by members of Fraser's personal staff, at first drew artillery fire but, if the romantic accounts are to be accepted, the Americans stopped their shelling as soon as they realized what was taking place in the Great Redoubt and saluted "the noble Fraser" with minute guns. (Lossing, I, 66) The grave is still there. His death is described in the memoirs of Mme. Riedesel and his burial is the subject of a painting by John Graham.

FRASER, Simon. 1738–1813. British officer. The senior of many subalterns of this name in Fraser's Highlanders (78th Regt.) during the French and Indian War, he was wounded at Sillery, 28 Apr. '60. Retired as a Lt. on half pay in 1763, he raised a company for the second Fraser Highlanders (71st) and served in America as a Maj. Retired on half pay in 1783, he raised the third Fraser Highlanders (133d) in 1793. In 1795 he was promoted to Maj. Gen., and during the period 1797–1800 commanded a body of British troops in Portugal. In 1802 he became a Lt. Gen. and for several years was second in command of forces in North Britain. According to editor Willcox, he is the Maj. Fraser named with six other commanders for outstanding leadership at Hobkirk's Hill. (Clinton, *Amer. Reb.*, 515 and index)

FRASER HIGHLANDERS. Two regiments known by this name and both raised by Simon Fraser (*d.* 1782) were conspicuous in America during the French and Indian War and during the Revolution. The first was raised in 1757 and designated the 78th Regt. (See FRASER for its battle credits.) It was disbanded in 1763. In 1775, following the British slaughter at Bunker Hill, this same Fraser raised a regiment of two battalions. Officially the 71st Highlanders, the regiment was commonly known as the Fraser (or Fraser's) Highlanders. They sailed from Scotland for Boston at the end of April 1776, not knowing that Boston had fallen into patriot hands (17 Mar. '76). Two transports were captured at sea, one of them carrying a company of the 71st and the other with a company of the "Black Watch." Four more were captured off the Massachusetts coast in mid-June. Among the prisoners was Lt. Col. Archibald CAMPBELL, whose transport was taken in Boston Harbor. Many writers have erred in saying that both battalions of the 71st and a battalion of the "Black Watch" (42d) were captured; only six companies actually were made prisoner at sea. (See *New Eng. Hist. & Geneal. Register*, CXII [July 1958], 200–201)

Companies of the 71st took part in the Battle of Long Island, 27 Aug. '76, being the first ashore on the 24th and being with the force that cut off Alexander's retreat in the final phase of the battle.

The 3d Bn. of the 71st was created in May '77. This unit stayed in the north when the other two went south under Archibald Campbell. The 1st Bn. (under John MAITLAND) and the 2d (Campbell's) captured SAVANNAH, 29 Dec. '78, and fought at BRIAR CREEK, Ga., 3 Mar. '81. After joining Clinton's CHARLESTON EXPEDITION (re-

ceiving 150 replacements), the Fraser Highlanders took part in the final siege operations against Charleston. Under Maj. Archibald McArthur, the 1st Bn. distinguished itself before being captured at COWPENS, 17 Jan. '81; the 2d Bn. was with Cornwallis until the final surrender at Yorktown.

Another Simon FRASER (*d.* 1813), who raised a company for the above regiment in 1775, organized a Scottish unit in 1793 that was designated the 133d Regt. and also known as Fraser's Highlanders. It was soon broken up, however, and used to bring other regiments up to strength.

FRAUNCES' TAVERN, N.Y.C. Washington's farewell to his officers, 4 Dec. '83.

Preserved in the restored Fraunces' Tavern at Pearl and Broad Sts. is the historic Long Room that was the scene of Washington's farewell to his officers on Thursday, 4 Dec. '83, the day the British fleet sailed from N.Y. harbor. Soon after noon he arrived to find the small group of officers who had entered the city on 25 Nov. and all others who had been assembled on short notice for the occasion. "With a heart full of love and gratitude, I now take leave of you," Washington said. "I most devotedly wish that your later days may be as prosperous and happy as your former ones have been glorious and honorable." Gripped with an emotion that threatened to overwhelm the small assemblage, they mumbled a confused answer and drank their wine before Washington, blind with tears, continued: "I cannot come to each of you, but shall feel obliged if each of you will come and take me by the hand." Henry Knox stepped forward as the senior officer present. Impulsively, Washington put his arms around his Chief of Artillery and, now weeping openly, kissed him. "Once done," writes Freeman in describing this scene as reported by Benjamin TALLMADGE, "this had of course to be done with all, from Steuben to the youngest officer. With streaming eyes, they came up to him, received the same embrace and passed on. Even the most talkative was awed. Not a man had the bad taste to attempt any expression of thanks or of admiration.* * * Washington could not endure it longer. When the last weeping officer had received his embrace, the General walked across the room, raised his arm in an all-inclusive, silent farewell and passed through the door, out of the tavern, between the open ranks of a guard of honor, and then along the street to Whitehall." (*Washington*, V, 468) The wharf was crowded as Washington approached, climbed into a barge, and headed for Paulus Hook. From there he proceeded by way of Philadelphia to Annapolis to surrender his commission to Cong. (23 Dec. '83).

FREDERICK THE GREAT AND THE AMERICAN REVOLUTION. One historian has summed up this subject as follows:

"Frederick had no desire for war with England [which had given him an annual subsidy in the last conflict; see CHATHAM], but his wish to injure her led to the curious idea that he had a sentimental friendship for the Americans. An amusing myth grew up that he sent Washington a sword inscribed 'From the Oldest General to the Greatest,' yet in truth he was a severe critic of Washington's military fitness. * * * He refused his ports to German mercenaries on the way to fight America, but that was because he wanted to hire them for his own wars. * * * On the whole, his love of America was wholly platonic, but he did make trouble for England, and that was useful." (Van Tyne, *England and America*, 178–79)

This same writer says Frederick was so busy with Bohemia and Saxony that, in Frederick's own words, he "hardly so much as remembered that there were Americans in the world." (*Ibid.*) Other writers disagree. Speaking of how Arthur Lee "only reaped disaster from his mission to Prussia" in the summer of 1777, Helen Augur says: "A clever negotiator could have done much there, for Frederick despised the British and the little German states that sold them mercenaries; he took a lively interest in the progress of the American war, and was ready to expand Prussia's trade with the Americans, which so far had been *sub rosa*." (*Secret War*, 214–15) After being repeatedly frustrated in his attempts to get beyond Minister Schulenberg to see Frederick, Lee wrote the monarch a preposterous letter telling him how to run Prussia. "That about concluded Prussian-American relations for the whole course of the war, except for 800 fusils Lee ordered in Berlin, which proved to be defective." (*Ibid.*, 216).

Frederick came into the league of ARMED NEUTRALITY on 19 May '82, but on 10 Apr. '81 he had proclaimed his own code.

Other authorities support the contention that Frederick "called Washington's achievements [at Trenton and Princeton] the most brilliant of any recorded in the annals of military history." (This quotation is from *Lexington to Fallen Timbers* [p. 12]. An editor of the latter work, Howard H. Peckham, makes substantially the same statement in his *War for Indep.* [p. 57].)

Prussia's great contribution to American independence, although Frederick had no direct part in making it available, was STEUBEN.

FREEMAN'S FARM, N.Y. Landmark of First and Second Battles of SARATOGA.

FREEMASONS. See MASONRY IN AMERICA.

FRENCH ALLIANCE. (Ratified by Congress 4 May '78) The greatest and probably the oldest nation in Europe, with a population of about 25,000,000 in comparison with one third of that number in Great Britain and less than one tenth of that number in the 13 colonies, France was the object of colonial hatred and suspicion in the years preceding the Revolution. The French and Indian Wars, a term sometimes applied to all the Colonial Wars in which Canada was involved, these wars were remembered for the outrages against frontier settlements of the English colonies. "The repugnance of Puritan New England to Catholic Canada waxed rather than waned with the decades," writes Van Tyne. "All American leaders believed that Bourbon despotism far exceeded anything ever attributed to a British ruler by the most violent colonial demagogue." (*War of Indep.*, 455) The British decision in 1763 to take Canada from France (rather than the sugar-rich island of Guadaloupe) was considered by many to be a mistake, since this would decrease colonial dependence on the mother country by eliminating the military threat from Canada; farsighted French statesmen realized that the American Revolution was merely a matter of time, and they saw that England's misfortune would be their opportunity for *revanche*.

When the fighting started in America the French could not risk open alliance with the colonists until they were sure the latter were really seeking INDEPEND-ENCE and were capable of a sustained fight to win it. Otherwise the French might find themselves at war with a Britain no longer engaged in America. The advisers of young Louis XVI believed that he would do best by letting England wear herself down in a transatlantic war; meanwhile they would keep themselves informed of the situation in the colonies (see KALB and ACHARD DE BONVOULOIR) and would send the rebels secret aid. In Mar. '76 Silas Deane was sent as an American agent to Paris, and two months later HORTALEZ & CIE. was in business. "Washington's victory at Trenton and Princeton was, perhaps, made possible by the supplies furnished by the French or through their instigation," writes Van Tyne, and although Saratoga was the decisive event that brought France into open alliance, "nine tenths of the military supplies that made the victory at Saratoga possible came from France or through foreign merchants whom she secretly encouraged." (*Op. cit.*, 476, 439–40)

On 17 Dec. '77, having learned of the Saratoga victory, and impressed by the spirit shown by Washington at GERMANTOWN, French authorities told American envoys in Paris that France had decided to recognize American independence. On 8 Jan. '78 Vergennes informed the envoys that France was ready to make an alliance. On 4 May Congress ratified two treaties: a treaty of amity and commerce (recognizing independence), and a treaty of alliance to become effective in the event of war between France and England. On 13 Mar. the French ambassador at London informed the British of these treaties, and the British ambassador was immediately recalled from Paris. Spain offered to mediate, but the war started on 17 June when Adm. Keppel, leading 20 ships on a cruise out of Portsmouth, fell in with two French frigates and fired his guns to bring them to. (Mahan, *Sea Power,* 350)

The PEACE COMMISSION OF CARLISLE was prompted by an urgent desire on the part of the British to settle the dispute in America before France could throw her tremendous potential into the conflict. ("Potential" seems a more appropriate word than "power.") French entry into the war, followed by the Spanish Alliance a year later, meant that the decisive theater now was the sea. For years the French had considered a direct attack against the British Isles, which in 1778 could muster only about 10,000 trained troops. De Broglie put detailed plans into the hands of Louis XVI. Nickerson gives this summary of failure:

"The mere occupation of the Isle of Wight would have bottled up Portsmouth, the chief British naval dockyard. ... Nor was superiority at sea lacking. In '79 and again two years later overwhelming Franco-Spanish fleets were masters of the Channel. In '79 fifty thousand French troops were ready to embark. On both occasions, however, time was allowed to slip by and nothing was done. Instead of concentrating all efforts against South England, the French spent most of their energy upon campaigns west of the Atlantic. Toward the end a squadron was even sent [under SUFFREN] to the Indian Ocean. * * * For three years after Saratoga the contrast is striking between the absence of results shown by France with her immense resources —not to speak of Spain—and the steady, definite gains previously established by Washington and his handful of men." (*Turning Point,* 416)

A negative effect of the French Alliance in the beginning was the overconfidence it inspired in America. A large fleet under Adm. d'Estaing left Toulon on 13 Apr. '78, and made an incredibly slow crossing of 87 days which enabled the British fleet to withdraw from the Chesapeake (MONMOUTH CAMPAIGN). D'Estaing failed successively at NEW YORK, 11–22 July, and NEWPORT, 29 July–31 Aug. '78, abandoned plans for an amphibious offensive against Halifax and Newfoundland, and headed for the West Indies. The Franco-American fiasco at SAVANNAH, 9 Oct. '79, was the final disservice of this mediocre General-Admiral to the alliance. Early in 1780 the French government warned the Americans that they must do more for themselves and in Apr. Congress responded by ordering Kalb south with a small force of regulars around whom, it was hoped, the militia would rally. This led indirectly to the disaster at Camden, 16 Aug. '80.

The arrival of Rochambeau's expeditionary force at Newport, 11 July '80, however, marked the beginning of a new and decisive phase of Franco-American military cooperation. A series of British strategic blunders, the decision of Adm. de Grasse to move his large French fleet north from the West Indies to support the allied armies of Rochambeau and Washington, and—to a lesser extent—the skillful operations of Lafayette in Va., all these contributed to the victorious YORKTOWN CAMPAIGN and the end of British military power in America.

The 1778 treaty of alliance had given the U.S. a free hand to conquer Canada and Bermuda; France was at liberty to take the British West Indies. Both countries agreed to respect the other's territorial gains in these areas, and neither was to conclude a treaty with Britain without the other's consent. France's motive in the war, therefore, **was** abasement of England by helping America win independence; she was not in the war for any significant increase of her overseas possessions. Mahan speculates that the failure of d'Estaing to attack the British fleet in N.Y. harbor in July '78 might have been because "France had nothing to gain by the fall of New York, which might have led to peace between America and England, and left the latter free to turn all her power against his own country." (*Sea Power,* 361) Nickerson points out that France "failed to see the war as a whole and consequently achieved results disproportionately small in comparison with the effort made." (*Op. cit.,* 415)

In his *Diplomatic Hist.,* Bemis devotes a 31-page chapter to the French Alliance and particularly recommends the special studies by E. S. Corwin and Bernard Faÿ. A more extended treatment is in Bemis, *Foundations . . . The Revolution.* Alden's chapter, "The Bourbons Enter the War," in his *Amer. Rev.* traces the evolution of the alliance and covers the secret negotiations; he draws attention to the special study by Carl L. Lokke. A standard work is Doniol's *Histoire de la participation de la France. . . .* Lasseray covers the participation of individual French volunteers. Miller, *Treaties . . . ,* is considered to have the best texts. See also Perkins, *France in the American Revolution.*

FRENCH AND INDIAN WAR(S). Although used literally to mean all the conflicts between the English and French colonists in North America, the term applies more precisely to the last of the COLONIAL WARS, the one called the Seven Years' War (1756–63) in Europe.

FRENCH SECRET AID. See HORTALEZ & CIE.

FRENEAU, Philip Morin. 1752–1832. Poet, mariner, journalist. N.J. The first American poet of outstanding ability, he was of Huguenot descent. Philip was born at Freehold, N.J., and graduated from Princeton in 1771. A classmate and perhaps his roommate was James Madison (*D.A.B.*). Wealthy and cultured, Freneau was in no hurry to enter a profession. Even as a college undergraduate he had had visions of a poetic career, and in collaboration with classmate H. H. Brackenridge had written the remarkable "Rising Glory of America." At the outbreak of the Revolution he penned no fewer than eight political satires within a period of a few months, among them *General Gage's Soliloquy* and *General Gage's Confession.* After teaching school, studying law, and some excursions into journalism he became secretary to a prominent planter of Santa Cruz in the West Indies. During the next three years he wrote what have been called his most significant poems, "Santa Cruz," "The Jamaica Funeral," and "The House of Night." These placed Freneau among the pioneers of the romantic movement that was about to open in Europe.

Returning to America during the Revolution, he built and commanded the privateer *Aurora* in 1780. After several escapes from British cruisers on the run between N.Y. and the Azores he was captured on 25 May and imprisoned aboard the *Scorpion.* Because of ill treatment his health became critical and he was transferred to the hospital ship *Hunter.* His experiences inspired two poems, "The Hessian Doctor" and "The British Prison-Ship: A Poem, in Four Cantos." During the three years after his release in 1781 he was employed in the Philadelphia Post Office, where he had the leisure to turn out a steady stream of poetry: he blasted the Loyalists, satirized the British, and glorified the patriots.

In 1784 he entered another phase of his maritime career, surviving shipwrecks and hurricanes, and writing magnificent poems about these experiences. "No other American poet has known the ocean as he knew it or has pictured it more graphically." (*D.A.B.*) In 1789 he married and spent the next seven or eight years as an editor, first of the N.Y.C. *Daily Advertiser* and, starting 31 Oct. '91, of the *National Gazette* in Philadelphia. In both efforts he was highly successful; his passionately democratic journalism was lauded by Jefferson, who credited him with saving the country from monarchy, but bitterly criticized by Washington, who called him "that rascal Freneau." On 26 Oct. '93 the *National Gazette* was suspended for lack of funds and because of a yellow fever epidemic. Freneau then edited the *Jersey Chronicle* and the N.Y.C. *Time-Piece* before retiring from journalism. He went to sea several more times and spent the intervening periods on his N.J. farm. On 19 Dec. 1832 he died in a snowstorm while trying to find his way home from the country store.

Among his published works is *Poems Written and Published During the American Revolutionary War . . .* (3d ed., 2 vols., Philadelphia, 1809). Biographical studies include Mary S. Austin, *Philip Freneau, The Poet of the Revolution* (1901).

FRONTAL ATTACK. Although often used in the literal sense of an attack on the enemy's front (as opposed to an ENVELOPMENT or TURNING MOVEMENT), in the precise meaning used by military writers it is an attack wherein the available forces are equally distributed and strike the enemy all along his front.

FRYE, Joseph. 1712–1794. Colonial Wars veteran, Cont'l. general. Mass. (Me.) Born 19 Mar. 1712 (N.S.) in a family long prominent in Andover, Mass., he was a 63-year-old veteran of the Colonial Wars when the Revolu-

tion started. As an ensign in Hale's 5th Mass. he had taken part in the capture of Louisburg in Feb. '45, was a Lt. Col. in Winslow's Kennebec expedition in 1754, and the next year had the unpleasant duty of burning houses in ACADIA. In 1757 he was commissioned to raise 1,800 men to reinforce Gen. Webb for the attack on Crown Point. He served under Lt. Col. Munroe when this officer was surrounded near Ft. William Henry and forced to surrender on 9 Aug. '57 to Montcalm. When the Indians got out of hand, Frye escaped after killing his red captor and made his way to Ft. Edward after enduring incredible hardships. Under the terms of the capitulation he was on parole for 18 months. After this, from Mar. '59 to the end of 1760, he was commander at Ft. Cumberland (near modern Amherst, Nova Scotia).

On 3 Mar. '62, in response to his petitioning, he was granted a township in Me. and in 1770 he moved there and opened a store. In Jan. '77 the place was incorporated as Fryeburg, a name it has retained. On 21 June '75 he was named Maj. Gen. of Mass. militia and served in this capacity about three months before being appointed B.G. of the Cont'l. Army on 10 Jan. '76. On 23 Apr. of that year he resigned for ill health, to use the popular euphemism. In fact, the aged warrior was useless to Washington, who had recently written to Joseph Reed that Frye "has not, and I doubt will not, do much service to the cause; at present he keeps his room and talks learnedly of emetics, cathartics, &c. For my own part, I see nothing but a declining life that matters [to?] him." (Quoted in Freeman, *Washington,* IV, 41)

FUSILS AND FUSILIERS. During the 17th century a light flintlock musket or *fusil* was developed for artillery guards, and a special type of light infantry called fusiliers was created. Like the GRENADIERS, they continued to exist as elite units after their original mission had disappeared. Until a few years before the American Revolution the SPONTOON was carried by infantry officers; it then was replaced by the fusil, although some were carried during the Revolution (e.g., at Trenton).

G

GABION. A wicker basket of cylindrical form, usually open at both ends, and filled with earth. It was used for field fortifications and other works of military engineering. See DORCHESTER HEIGHTS, Mar. '76, and SAP.

GADSDEN, Christopher. 1724–1805. Merchant, Revolutionary statesman, Cont'l. general. S.C. A successful Charleston merchant and an aristocrat, he was influential in the provincial assembly and as an opponent of the Stamp Act in his province. He became the acknowledged leader of the S.C. radicals and was an early advocate of revolution, but despite a fiery temper he represented the respectable, responsible element in S.C. that opposed royal rule. He sat in the 1st Cont'l. Cong. (1774), became Col. of the 1st S.C. Regt. on 17 June '75, and took his seat in the 2d Cont'l. Cong. He left that body in Jan. '76 to command S.C. troops in the defense of Charleston. In Feb. he startled friend and foe by proposing to the provincial congress that they move for independence. Commanding Ft. Johnson in June, he had a good view of the British attack on Moultrie's palmetto fort but was not otherwise engaged in defeating the Charleston Expedition of Clinton in 1776. He was promoted to B.G. on 16 Sept. '76.

In the absence of significant military operations in the South for the next three years he had no opportunity to show his qualifications, if any, as a general. On the political scene, however, he reached the climax of his career (D.A.B.) in 1778 while engaged in creation of the state constitution, which was adopted in Mar. With Wm. Henry Drayton, he stood for disestablishment of the church and the election of senators by popular vote. John Rutledge led the conservatives in a political counterattack that eliminated Gadsden's influence in the assembly by having him elected V.P. of that body. Dispute over the command of Cont'l. troops in the province led Gadsden to resign his commission and resulted in a duel with Robt. HOWE.

Surrendered at Charleston on 12 May '80, he was first paroled but then evacuated to St. Augustine. When he refused to give another parole he was closely confined for 10 months before being exchanged. Elected Gov. in 1782, he declined on grounds of age and ill health, but sat two years in the assembly. Here he was one of the few who opposed the confiscation of Tory property. His later years were marked by increased conservatism. In 1790 he voted to ratify the Constitution and opposed the rise of republicanism. His grandson, James Gadsden (1788–1858), gave his name to the Gadsden Purchase.

GAGE, Thomas. 1719?–1787. British C. in C. in America (1763–75). Despite his vital role in the events leading up to the Revolution and in the first year of the fighting, Gage has remained relatively unknown until the 20th century. The reason for this is that many of his official papers did not become available to historians until they were found and brought to America by W. L. Clements in 1930. John R. Alden's *General Gage in America,* published in 1948 on the basis of the Clements Collection, is the first accurate portrayal of the man who was a villain in America for doing his job too well and a villain in England for not doing it well enough.

Descendants of a French nobleman named de Gaugi who went to England with William the Conqueror, the Gages of Firle in Sussex had a long history of defending the wrong cause in their new homeland. They remained Catholics for 150 years after the establishment of the Church of England "and frequently suffered for it in those days when loyalty to Rome was considered by the majority of the English to be an admission of treason." (Alden, *op. cit.,* 3) They sided with King John, Bloody Queen Mary, Charles I, and James II, but "were consistently able to avoid the scaffold. . . ." (*Ibid.*)

The father of the Gage we are concerned with here, who also was named Thomas, joined the Anglican Church in 1715, probably to qualify for the House of Commons. Seven years later he was elected, and in 1720 was created a viscount in the Irish peerage. Characterized as "a petulant, silly, busy, meddling, profligate fellow," he had a wife whose reputation led a notorious debtor to declare that he would settle up when "Lady Gage grows chaste." (*Ibid.,* 6–7)

Their second son, the subject of this sketch, was born late in 1719 or early the next year. In 1728 he and his brother entered Westminster School, where Thomás knew Francis Bernard (later Gov. of Mass.), Burgoyne, Dartmouth, George and Richard Howe, the Keppel brothers, and George Sackville. Sometime between his departure from Westminster in 1736 and 1740 he was commissioned ensign. He was promoted to Capt. in Jan. '43. As A.D.C. to Albemarle, father of the Keppels, he saw action in 1745 at Fontenoy and Culloden. After taking part in the campaigns of 1747–48 in the Low Countries he transferred to the 55th Regt. of Col. John Lee, which was soon renumbered the 44th, and remained with it for almost 10 years. He purchased a majority in 1748 and was promoted to Lt. Col. on 2 Mar. '51.

"Honest Tom" was a popular officer at this period of his career despite his relatively sober nature. Charles Lee, son of the regimental commander, became a lifelong friend. Another friend was James Wolfe. "As a young man of the world Gage was extremely popular with the ladies as well as with the men," Alden points out. "Slender and moderately tall, with regular features, large eyes, and a long, aristocratic nose, he must have been very handsome in his youth." (*Ibid.,* 16) What appears to have been a common-law marriage with an English lady of rank and fortune ended, after a short period of happiness, with the lady's death. He made an unsuccessful foray into politics shortly before his regiment was ordered to America in the fall of 1754.

As part of Braddock's expeditionary force Gage commanded the advance guard on 9 July '55, the day of the disaster in the wilderness. Although Capt. Orme, Braddock's too-influential A.D.C., accused Gage's force of falling back too precipitously and disorganizing the main body, the charge appears to be unfounded. Gage showed great personal courage. "With his fellow officers and men falling all about him under the fire of an invisible foe—Gage actually saw only one enemy during the whole conflict—he stubbornly continued to carry on the unequal struggle until the French and Indians ceased their pursuit." (*Ibid.*, 27) He was slightly wounded. Washington and Gage got to know each other during this expedition and corresponded for at least three years, but long before they faced each other at Boston the friendship had cooled, "probably for lack of association, since the two men did not meet more than once between 1755 and 1773." (*Ibid.*, 29)

Gage took command of the 44th on the death of Col. Peter Halkett in the Battle of the Monongahela but despite his own appeals and the efforts of influential friends the colonelcy was denied him. During winter quarters at Albany he visited N.Y.C. and had an obscure part in the intrigue by which Wm. Shirley was removed as C. in C. and succeeded by Loudoun. He was second in command of an unsuccessful expedition up the Mohawk in Aug. '56, and spent a second winter in Albany. In 1757 he accompanied Loudoun on his "cabbage planting expedition" to Halifax. The last month of that year Gage got authority from Loudoun to organize a special body of provincial troops that became "the first definitely light-armed regiment in the British army." (Pargellis, *Loudoun,* quoted by Alden, *op. cit.,* 42) It was designated the 80th Regt. and qualified Gage for promotion to Col. In the operations of 1758 Gage was slightly wounded while leading part of Abercromby's advance guard in the unsuccessful attempt to capture Ticonderoga. After the army set up winter quarters he went

to N.Y.C. where, in Nov., he met his old acquaintance, Amherst, newly designated C. in C. He also learned that the devoted efforts of his brother had gotten him a temporary promotion to B.G. On 8 Dec. '58 he married Margaret, daughter of Peter KEMBLE of Brunswick, N.J., whom he had courted the preceding winter while recruiting his 80th Regt. In mid-Jan. he reached Albany with his bride and assumed command of this place and its neighboring posts. He served on Amherst's staff in the initial operations of 1759 but in July was named to succeed Prideaux (killed in action) as commander of the column operating on Lake Ontario. Amherst directed Gage to move down the lake, seize and secure Fort La Galette, and if at all possible to push on down the St. Lawrence and take Montreal. Reaching Niagara in mid-Aug., Gage made an estimate of the situation and concluded that he lacked the means to carry out Amherst's orders and that his most realistic course of action was to strengthen Niagara and Oswego while Amherst continued his advance from Crown Point down Lake Champlain to Montreal and Wolfe carried on with the primary strategic mission of taking Quebec. Amherst was infuriated by this cautiousness and in a sharp letter expressed his disapproval and disappointment. But he was not one to sack a valued subordinate for an honest error of judgment, a generosity he might not have been able to afford if the gallant Wolfe had not captured Quebec in the face of almost overwhelming difficulties. Gage was again put in command of Albany for the winter and he commanded Amherst's rear guard in the advance from Oswego to Montreal the next year.

After the French surrender in Canada, 6 Sept. '60, Gage started a three-year assignment as military governor of some 25,000 civilians in Montreal and in a district extending south to Crown Point and southwest to Lake Ontario. (James Murray commanded at Quebec and Ralph Burton in the Trois Rivières region, midway between Montreal and Quebec.) Despite his ancestry Gage disliked Catholics in general and detested their clergy. He despised Indians. His duties called for him to preside over the supreme court in his district and litigious French Canadians subjected him to many tedious hours in court. Yet he proved to be a successful governor in this trying assignment, his tenure being in marked contrast to that of Murray in Quebec. "His strong sense of justice and fair play, his caution, and his good humor won public acclaim," writes Alden, "and his intimate association in private life with aristocratic French families helped to make the most influential laymen less hostile to British rule." (*Ibid.*, 58) He may well have set the stage for the even more successful governorship of Carleton.

Fortune smiled on the outpost commander, however. In 1761 he was promoted to Maj. Gen., in 1762 he received a valuable sinecure as Col. of the 22d Regt., and on Amherst's departure Gage was named acting C. in C. of the British army in America. On 16 Nov. '63 he reached N.Y.C. to take up his new duties, and exactly a year later he was confirmed as Amherst's successor. In PONTIAC'S WAR Gage had inherited the problems created by Amherst's inept Indian policies, but this insurrection was stamped out in 1764. Despite the mounting political tensions Gage's life in N.Y.C. for the next nine years was pleasant from the personal as well as the professional point of view. He was popular in society and among his officers. "Some, perhaps because of his diffidence, doubted the capacity of his intellect," writes Alden, "but none denied the qualities of his heart. It was a matter of general repute that Gage was a decent sort." (*Op. cit.*, 66) His marriage was known throughout the colonies for "conjugal felicity." The tall, slender, and strangely beautiful Margaret—in whose veins ran equal parts of French, Greek, Dutch, and English blood—was somewhat less popular than her husband. She was accused of being overly proud, of using her husband's position to secure favors for her relatives, and of trying to dominate N.Y. society. "Half of the years between 1761 and 1777 were marked by new arrivals in the Gage family," observes Alden, so society had long periods of relief from whatever domination she tended to exert. (*Ibid.*, 59–60, 66)

The British army in America at the start of the Stamp Act crisis in 1765 comprised 15 regiments of infantry and one of artillery. Although this was a "paper strength" of 8,000 men, only about 5,000 were actually present, and many of these were not fit for duty at any given time. As political disorders increased, Gage pulled in troops from the western posts and concentrated them along the seaboard towns, principally in N.Y.C. When Boston became the focus of rebellion he gradually built up the BOSTON GARRISON, starting in Oct. '68. Gage reached that place by land on 15 Oct. to deal with the difficult problems presented by the arrival of redcoats in the hostile town, but on 24 Nov. the pressure of other business demanded his return to his N.Y. headquarters. Although the problems in America at this time were more within the domain of the royal governors than the military commander—who was responsible only for furnishing them what they called for in the way of troop support to maintain order—Gage seems to have evaluated the political situation more realistically than did the British politicians on either side of the Atlantic. After the furor resulting from the Boston "massacre" (Mar. '70) died down, however, three years of relative tranquility began and in Oct. '72, after more than 17 years in America, Gage asked for a leave of absence in England to take care of family affairs. On 8 June '73 the Gages sailed with three of their children (three others were at school in England, another was born two months later). While the general was home the government passed the Boston Port Bill. Since Gov. Hutchinson was about to take leave, since Lt. Gov. Andrew Oliver was believed to be dying, and since the immediate return of Gage was considered essential, "Somebody had a bright thought: why not send Gage back ... as both governor of Massachusetts and commander in chief?" (Ibid., 212) This appointment, immediately approved, was announced on 2 Apr. and signed five days later. On 13 May Gage reached Boston harbor and on the 17th he landed. (See Robert ROGERS)

Events led swiftly to LEXINGTON AND CONCORD, 19 Apr. '75, the BOSTON SIEGE, and BUNKER HILL, 17 June '75. Even before London learned of these reverses the feeling was prevalent that Gage was not the man for the job in America. The day the British were fighting at Bunker Hill, or the preceding day, Germain was already laying the groundwork for his recall on the grounds that Gage lacked the necessary vigor and initiative. Alden develops the thesis that his disgrace was due less to his ineptitude than to a clique of Scottish politicians in London led by Alexander Wedderburn and Lord Mansfield. (Ibid., 281)

On 26 Sept. '75 Gage received orders to return home, ostensibly to help plan operations for the next year, although this pretext deceived nobody. On 10 Oct. he surrendered command to Wm. Howe, and on 14 Nov. he reached London. Not until 18 Apr. '76 was he informed by Germain that his appointment as C. in C. was revoked. Retaining his sinecure as Gov. of Mass. and his military rank, but cut off from the other sources of government income that had made him a relatively wealthy man, Gage was forced to live on a reduced economic scale in order to rear and educate his large family. After virtual military retirement while Germain remained in authority, Gage was appointed to the staff of Amherst in Apr. '81 and given the short-lived mission of organizing militia in Kent against a possible attack from France. Fall of the wartime ministry permitted his promotion to full Gen. on 20 Nov. '82. For some time now he had suffered from "an inflammation of the bowels," and his health declined steadily. After a protracted and painful illness he died at his home in Portland on 2 Apr. '87. His widow survived him almost 37 years and died at the age of 90.

The record indicates that Gage was not a great field commander, but it would be difficult to prove that his successors, Howe and Clinton, were any better. "If he was not a master of the arts of battle," concludes Alden, "neither was he guilty of truly major blunders." (Ibid., 295) He was an honorable man in a day when this quality was not common; he was more than competent as a military administrator. "On the whole, Gage exhibited greater talents as a politician than he did as a general." (Ibid.) As proconsul and C. in C. in America he lacked the spark of greatness; although he correctly saw the situation in 1775 as being beyond the means at his disposal, there is little reason to believe he would have been able to manage if the government had given him adequate support.

Alden's *Gage* is cited above.

GAIAULT or **GAYAULT.** See BOISBERTRAND.

GALLOWAY, Joseph. *c.* 1731–1803. Prominent Loyalist. Md. A leading Philadelphia lawyer and vice-president of the American Philosophical Society (1769–75), he was a close friend of Franklin, who left his papers and letterbooks with him for protection when he went to England in 1764. Galloway sat in the Pa. assembly 1757–74 and was speaker 1766–74. He was an able colonial politician, and he never failed to advance the interests of his province and his class, that of the aristocratic merchants. He was in favor of changing the state government from proprietary to royal form and was an active Tory in the early part of the war. In the 1774 Cont'l. Congress, he wrote GALLOWAY'S PLAN OF UNION. This was first accepted and later rejected, and Galloway refused to be a delegate for the second Congress. He then wrote "A Candid Examination of the Mutual Claims of Great Britain and the Colonies: with a Plan of Accommodation on Constitutional Principles," castigating the Cont'l. Congress. His essentially conservative stand coupled with a rather cold and unsympathetic nature made him extremely unpopular and, fearful of the Philadelphia mob, he retired to his country home where Franklin tried to change his Loyalist views. Galloway joined Howe in the advance through N.J. in Dec. '75 and was in charge of the Philadelphia civil government during the British occupation. He withdrew with the British and the next year went to England where he remained for the rest of his life. In 1779 he was examined by the House of Commons on the British conduct of the war, and he charged Lord Howe with incompetence and also published pamphlets on this subject. He continued to explore the possibilities of a reconciliation of the colonies with the Crown, based on a written constitution, and believed that America would benefit more by a continued connection with the mother country. The Pa. Assembly in 1788 charged Galloway with high treason and ordered the sale of his estates. His petition to return in 1793 was rejected. He wrote a number of books and pamphlets, among them "Historical and Political Reflections on the American Rebellion," "Letters to a Nobleman on the Conduct of the War in the Middle Colonies, 1779," and "Cool Thoughts on the Consequences to Great Britain of American Independence."

GALLOWAY'S PLAN OF UNION. 28 Sept. '74 (1st Cont'l. Cong.) Defeated by a single vote, although favorably received at first, the plan of Joseph GALLOWAY proposed solving the problem of home rule by giving the American colonies something approaching dominion status. The plan drew the support of the conservatives who saw in it a means of offsetting Congressional endorsement of the SUFFOLK RESOLVES. Galloway proposed that a royally appointed president-general serve at the king's pleasure with authority to veto acts of a grand council, whose members would be chosen by each province for three-year terms. (*E.A.H.*) See Commager, *Documents*. An especially important feature of Galloway's plan was that the colonial government, while inferior to that of Great Britain, would nevertheless have authority to regulate commercial, civil, criminal, and police affairs when more than a single colony was involved, and the colonial government was to have veto power over all Parliamentary legislation affecting the colonies. (Gipson, *Coming of the Rev.*, 228, 230)

GALVAN, William (?) de. French volunteer. Having come to America on business, he applied for a commission on 30 Nov. '79 and, despite the objection of the Board of War, was granted it on 12 Jan. '80. (Lasseray, 646. Heitman has no entry on him.) He was backed by Steuben and became a Maj. in Lafayette's command. On 19 May '80 he was designated by Lafayette to wait for Ternay's fleet at Cape Henry, Va. (Lasseray, 225) As commander of a light infantry battalion he won Lafayette's praise for a gallant attempt to capture a British gun in the opening phase of the action at GREEN SPRING, Va., 6 July '81. Maj. Galvan was Steuben's division inspector at Yorktown.

GALVEZ, Bernardo de. 1746–1786. Gov. of La. and Fla. Born into a family of ancient lineage that distinguished itself during his lifetime in the colonial service, he had military service in Portugal (1762) and in New Spain against the Apaches before being stationed in Algiers and attending the military school at Avila. He then was ordered to La. as Col. of the fixed regiment. On 10 July '76 he was appointed governor and intendant of the Spanish province and on 1 Feb. '77 he took over these duties. During the next two years, before Spain's entry into the war, the young Gov. did everything within his power to weaken the British in his area. His most notable contribution to the American cause was his support of the patriot supply agent Oliver POLLOCK. He also was energetic in seizing British ships that had been engaged in a profitable contraband trade. When Spain entered the war Gálvez proved himself to be even more capable in the field of overt action than he had been in covert operations. In 1779 he took the British river posts of Manchac, Baton Rouge, and Natchez. He took Mobile in 1780, and forced the surrender of PENSACOLA,

9 May '81. "In three campaigns he reduced every British post in West Florida, thus making it possible for Spain to obtain both Floridas in the peace settlement of 1783 and to control the mouth of the Mississippi and the Gulf of Mexico." (A. P. Whitaker in *D.A.B.*)

He was in Spain in 1783–84 to give advice on future Spanish policy in the Floridas and the Louisiana territory. Promoted to Maj. Gen., given his Castilian title of nobility (Count de Gálvez and Viscount de Galveztown), and appointed Capt.-Gen. of Louisiana and the Floridas, he returned to America and had a prominent part in subsequent diplomatic negotiations with the U.S. He became Capt.-Gen. of Cuba, and in 1785 succeeded his father as Viceroy of New Spain, but he retained his previous posts. Only a few months after his 40th birthday he died in Mexico.

GAMBIER, James. 1723–1789. British admiral. An uncle of the namesake dealt with below, he was the grandson of a Norman Huguenot who came to England after the Edict of Nantes was revoked (1685). He became a Lt. in the navy in 1743. As commander of the *Burford* he took part in the operations at Louisburg in 1758, and Guadeloupe, Martinique, and Quiberon Bay in 1759. During the period 1770–73 he was C. in C. on the American station, being succeeded by Samuel Graves. After his promotion to Rear Adm. on 23 Jan. '78 he was second in command to Lord Howe and Byron, temporarily serving as C. in C. when each of these left the American station. He left N.Y. on 5 Apr. '79. Promoted to Vice Adm. on 26 Sept. '80, he was C. in C. at Jamaica, 1783–84, but his health became so bad that he had to give up his assignment. He died 8 Jan. '89.

GAMBIER, James (Baron Gambier). 1756–1833. British naval officer. Born at New Providence (now Nassau), where his father was Lt. Gov. of the Bahamas, he was entered on the books of his uncle's guard ship, *Yarmouth,* at Chatham, when he was 11 years old. On 12 Feb. '77 he was a Lt. on the American station. The next year he commanded the *Thunder* bomb, was captured by d'Estaing, but was exchanged promptly and on 9 Oct. '78 was posted to the frigate *Raleigh.* In May '79 he took part in the expedition to relieve Jersey and exactly a year later participated in the capture of Charleston. This ended his Revolutionary War career, but he went on to become Adm. of the fleet in 1830.

Nephew of the James GAMBIER whose biographical sketch is above.

"GAMECOCK." Nickname of Thos. SUMTER.

GANSEVOORT, Peter. 1749–1812. Cont'l. officer. N.Y. Coming from a prominent family of Albany, he became Maj. of the 2d N.Y. Regt. on 30 June '75 and was with Montgomery's wing of the Canada Invasion. On 19 Mar. '76 he was promoted to Lt. Col. and placed in command of Ft. George. He became Col. of the 3d N.Y. on 21 Nov. '76 (see also RITZEMA) and subsequently distinguished himself in the defense of Ft. Stanwix (or Ft. Schuyler) against ST. LEGER'S EXPEDITION, June–Sept. '77. For this he not only received the thanks of Congress but most thoroughly deserved them.

Only 28 years old at this time, the young Col. was temporarily in command at Albany (Oct. '77). Early the next year he married Catherina Van Schaick * and until Nov. '78 Gansevoort commanded again at Ft. Stanwix,

---

* Gose VAN SCHAICK had been his C.O. in the 2d N.Y. The kinship of Catherina is not mentioned in Appleton's or *D.A.B.*

where there was no enemy activity. Seeing that Cherry Valley "was obviously a post of danger and difficulty . . . the splendid Gansevoort, the defender of Stanwix, sought the honor of its command," writes Swiggett. "Through stupidity in Albany [where Lafayette was preparing for another CANADA INVASION] . . . Gansevoort was refused the post. There is no question that had he been in command the attack in November [the CHERRY VALLEY MASSACRE] would have been beaten off." (*War out of Niagara,* 138)

Some authorities credit him with the famous raid of Apr. '79 against the Onondagas that actually was led by Van Schaick. He was the commander of the Saratoga garrison in 1780. The next year he was at Albany during some of the worst of the Mohawk Valley raids, and on 26 Mar. '81 he was appointed B.G. of militia. The next year he became Maj. Gen. of militia, and on 15 Feb. 1809 he was commissioned B.G. in the U.S. Army. The standard authorities are mute as to why he was given this appointment or what the 58-year old B.G. did in the army, if anything. Apparently he held the commission until his death on 2 July 1812 at the age of 61. His brother, Leonard (1751–1810), was a patriot politician, lawyer, and judge.

GARTH, George. d. 1819. British general. The son of an M.P., he entered the 1st Regt. of Footguards in Sept. '55 and was made Col. in Feb. '79. (Appleton's) As a "local" B.G. he commanded a division in the CONNECTICUT COAST RAID, July '79 and was second-in-command to Gov. Tryon. Sailing from N.Y. to take command in Ga., he was captured by the French. (See SAVANNAH, 9 Oct. '79) After being exchanged he served as a Maj. Gen. in the West Indies. He became a full Gen. in 1801.

GASPEE AFFAIR, 9 June '72. The armed revenue schooner stationed in Narragansett Bay, R.I., was attacked and burned the night of 9 June '72 after having run aground on what is now called Gaspée Point, seven miles below Providence, while chasing another vessel. Despite a £500 reward offered for information, the British were never able to uncover sufficient evidence to try the culprits. The 64 attackers had been organized by John Brown and led by Abraham Whipple (Lossing, II, 62). See also CUSTOMS COMMISSIONERS.

Another British vessel named the *Gaspée* (which Ward spells *Gaspé*) was an armed brigantine. Isaac COFFIN served aboard her, under Lt. William Hunter, in 1773. An ensign and 12 marines of her complement took part in the unsuccessful defense of ST. JOHNS, Sept.–Nov. '75, and became prisoners there, and she was captured after the fall of MONTREAL, 13 Nov. '75.

GATES, Horatio. 1728–1806. Cont'l. general. Eng.–Va. Son of the Duke of Leeds's housekeeper, whose friendship with Horace Walpole's mother's waiting-maid resulted in his being a godson of the 11-year old Walpole, much of Horatio Gates's offensive personality has been attributed to a resentment over his failure to rise above his servant-class social background. Nickerson characterizes him as a "little ruddy-faced Englishman, peering through his thick spectacles," "a snob of the first water" who had "an unctuously pious way with him," and who had such a "repellent personality" that "he still [1928] awaits his biographer." (*Turning Point*, 282, 278) While this is the commonly accepted picture of the unlovely and unlovable Gates, he had a number of good qualities that will be pointed out below.

Gates entered the English Army at an early age and was promoted rapidly.

(*E.B.*) He took part in Braddock's Defeat, the defense of Ft. Herkimer (Mohawk Valley), and served under Monkton at Martinique. In 1765 he retired on half pay as a Maj. (60th Regt.) and with the help of George Washington he settled in Va. in 1772. Freeman speaks of him as "a cherished neighbor of Washington's brother, Samuel" and (at this time) "Washington's long-time friend." (*Washington*, III, 416) As war approached, Gates sided with the colonists, perhaps more from hatred of the English social system than from ideals of "liberty" and probably because he saw personal advancement in supporting a cause that would desperately need professionally trained officers. After Washington was made C. in C., Gates was selected on 17 June '75 to be his A.G. with the rank of B.G. Gates was "almost certainly" nominated for this post by Washington, who "had formed a good opinion of Gates during the years they had served together and ... had confirmed that judgment by what he had seen of Gates after the Major had moved to Virginia." (*Ibid.*, 441)

During the following months Gates proved a valuable officer and on 16 May '76 he was promoted and sent to the Northern Dept. The strategic situation at this time and the command crisis caused by the vague instructions of Congress are covered under CANADA INVASION. Although Gates had hoped that he might succeed Schuyler as overall commander of the Northern Dept., he accepted his position as Schuyler's subordinate and performed useful service as commander of the field army. He left the department at the head of the N.J. and Pa. regiments that had been ordered south to support Washington in the critical N.J. CAMPAIGN. Gates reached Peekskill on 8 Dec. '76 and joined Washington on the 20th. When

Charles Lee was captured, just a week earlier, Gates's courier barely escaped with the letter in which Lee had said to him: *"entre nous,* a certain great man is damnably deficient...." Although Washington desperately needed experienced officers at this moment, he reluctantly granted Gates permission to visit Congress with the ostensible aim of soliciting greater support for his forces in the North. (*Ibid.,* 309 *n.;* 367)

In the spring of 1777 the New England faction of Congress found a flimsy pretext to undermine the authority of SCHUYLER by sending Gates north to command the army at Ticonderoga. In May, two months later, they reversed themselves, restored Schuyler to command of a redefined Northern Dept., and instructed Gates either to remain as second in command or resume his duties as Washington's A.G. This time Gates did not accept the disappointment as he had the previous July (see CANADA INVASION) but raced south to protest his treatment. On 18 June '77 he made a spectacle of himself by gaining the floor of Congress on the plea that he had important information to divulge and by then launching into an assault on his critics and a defense of his own conduct. When Congress finally found time, on 8 July, to consider what to do with "a man who manifestly had lost his head" they passed the problem on to Washington. Since Gates did not want to resume his A.G. post, Washington was about to give him temporary command of Lincoln's Div. when news was received of Ticonderoga's fall. Schuyler's enemies and Gates's partisans succeeded this time in getting Congress to name Gates as new commander of the Northern Dept. on 4 Aug. On the 19th Gates reached Stillwater to direct the operations that concluded BURGOYNE'S OFFENSIVE. See this entry and its cross references for an evaluation of Gates's leadership. For a partisan viewpoint in the GATES–SCHUYLER controversy see Henry Brockholst LIVINGSTON.

The victory at Saratoga was in stunning contrast to Washington's lack of success during 1777, and there was a strong movement to name Gates C. in C. The events surrounding this are covered under CONWAY CABAL. During this period Congress attempted to dilute Washington's authority by establishing the new Board of War (17 Oct. '77) and by naming Gates president. On 19 Jan. '78 Gates reached York (where Congress was temporarily located) to find that his inept efforts to discredit Washington had already backfired. (See CONWAY CABAL) He managed to patch up a harmonious working relationship with Washington, but on 15 Apr. '78 Congress directed him to resume command of the Northern Dept. The next winter and summer he was in Boston as commander of the Eastern Dept.

By this time the war had moved south and the patriots were taking a beating. Congress thought Gates, the Victor of Saratoga, was the man to save the situation and, without consulting Washington—who was known to oppose their selection—on 13 July they commissioned him commander of the Southern Dept. Their mistake is covered under CAMDEN CAMPAIGN, July–Aug. '80. See also GATES'S FLIGHT.

Retiring to his farm, he spent the next two years pressing for a Congressional inquiry. In 1782 he was cleared of all stigma of misconduct and he rejoined the army at Newburgh for the final days of the war. According to Randolph G. Adams in *D.A.B.,* Gates loyally and effectively supported the successful efforts of Washington to quell the discontent among Cont'l. officers that led to the NEWBURGH ADDRESSES, Mar. '83, but it should be noted that he accepted leadership of the clique that precipitated the crisis.

Retiring to his home in Va., he was made president of the state society of the Cincinnati. His son had died in 1780, when Gates was further burdened with the stigma of his defeat at Camden. In 1784, shortly after the death of his wife, Gates proposed marriage to Janet Livingston Montgomery, the young widow of the general killed at Quebec; to the credit of womanhood, she declined his suit. In 1786 he married Mary Vallance, who brought him a fortune of several hundred thousand dollars. Four years later, "his old doubts as to social inequality besetting him" (*D.A.B.*), he freed his slaves and moved to N.Y.C. Most of his wife's fortune was used for the relief of veterans. He served in the N.Y. legislature for one term, 1800–1, and died five years later.

The portrait done by Charles Willson Peale during the war, when Gates was about 49, bears little resemblance to the better-known portrait painted by Gilbert Stuart about 1794, when the general was 67. In the Stuart picture one can see why a soldier called Gates "an old, granny-looking fellow." In fairness it must be pointed out that the sly, peering expression rendered by Stuart must be attributed largely to the fact that the general had removed his thick spectacles. During the early months of the war Gates gave Washington valuable service in his capacity as A.G., points out D. S. Freeman. "Whether Gates actually hoped to supersede Washington is doubtful," concludes this authority, "but naturally he was willing to make the most of what appeared [after his Saratoga victory] to be a rising tide of favor." (*Washington*, III, 473 B) Of the two Englishmen who held high rank in the American army, Gates and Lee, the British historian Fortescue writes, "both were a discredit to the country alike of their birth and of their adoption." (*British Army*, III, 161) This is the consensus of historians. By strange coincidence both Lee and Gates became known as enemies of Washington, which in itself was a sure way of going down in the American history books as unmitigated scoundrels. Lynn Montross in his *Rag, Tag and Bobtail* presents a revisionist approach to Gates.

"In a month from the day he took over the command [writes Montross of the Saratoga campaign], Gates had transformed a beaten army into an instrument capable of fighting regulars to a finish in the open field." (P. 217)

Writing of the period between the two battles of Saratoga, Montross says:

"Arnold not only stayed with the army but devoted his energies to open insubordination. . . . He found eager disciples in two New York officers, Colonel Henry B. Livingston and Colonel Richard Varick, both of whom had served in Schuyler's official family.* * *

"The New York general [Schuyler] could hardly be created into a combat hero, but Arnold loomed as the ideal candidate. . . . The new hagiology is shown in process of evolution by a letter from Schuyler to Varick: 'I wonder at Gates' policy. He will probably be indebted to him [Arnold] for the glory he may acquire by a victory. . . .'

"Thus was fired one of the opening guns in a campaign of character assassination that has few parallels in American history. From that time onward, Gates would be attacked at every opportunity, by fair means or foul, until few rags remained of his military reputation. The story of Schuyler's silver bullets at Ticonderoga (see SILVER BULLETS. . . .) is no more preposterous than slanders about his rival that the New York faction propagated. But if facts rather than legends are to be accepted, Gates's generalship at Saratoga leaves little room for censure." (Pp. 221, 223)

Moving to the period of the so-called Conway Cabal, Montross says that while Lafayette was in the Northern Dept. preparing for the abortive "irruption into Canada" that was to take place in early 1778, he visited the home of Gen. Schuyler and "emerged as the most vociferous opponent of Gates in the Continental Army." (*Ibid.*, 266) Montross continues:

"Only a few months before, Colonel Alexander Hamilton had also been a guest at the Schuyler home while bearing dispatches. There he met Elizabeth Schuyler, whom he was to marry a few years later. This encounter did not seem so interesting to him at the time as the persuasion that Gates had played a small part at Saratoga in comparison to Schuyler and Arnold. From that moment, Hamilton became one of the leaders of the New York faction along with Duane, Jay, Duer, Robert R. Livingston and Gouverneur Morris." (*Ibid.*)

The premature death of Montross may have removed from the historical scene a writer who could have done for the reputation of Horatio Gates what J. R. Alden did for his countryman in *General Charles Lee, Traitor or Patriot?* (1951).

The Gates Papers, which cover almost his entire life, were kept intact by his widow, who survived him by four years, and most of them are now in the N.Y. Hist. Soc. Other pertinent papers are in the Lib. of Cong. and the Univ. of Mich. (*D.A.B.*) Thirteen years after Hoffman Nickerson wrote that "he still awaits his biographer," Samuel W. Patterson published *Horatio Gates* (1941), which Peckham says

"casts the most favorable light on the general." (*War for Indep.*, 213 *n.*)

See also McCREA ATROCITY for the "Tickler upon Scalping" he wrote to Burgoyne.

GATES'S FLIGHT FROM CAMDEN, 16–19 Aug. '80 After retreating to Rugeley's Mill with the routed militia of his left wing from Camden, Gates covered 60 miles on a horse famous for its speed and reached Charlotte the day of the battle (16 Aug.) During the next two days, mounted on a relay of horses, he covered 120 miles to reach Hillsboro, N.C., on 19 Aug. Alexander Hamilton, whom Montross calls "the leading character assassin" of Gates, commented: "Was there ever an instance of a general running away as Gates has done from his whole army? And was there ever so precipitous a flight? One hundred and eighty miles in three days and a half! It does admirable credit to the activity of a man at his time of life. But it disgraces the general and the soldier." (Quoted from 6 Sept. ltr. to James DUANE in Montross, *Rag, Tag*, 380)

Gates explained in a letter of 22 Aug. to Gov. Caswell his reasons for going so precipitously to Hillsboro:

"I therefore resolved to proceed directly thither, to give orders for assembling the Continental Troops on the March from Virginia, to direct the Three Corps of Horse at C[ross] Creek to cover the stores ... and to urge the Resources of Virginia to be drawn forth for our support." (*Ibid.*)

Henry LEE praises Gates for seeing that Hillsboro was the best place to rebuild his army and for going immediately there despite "the calumny with which he was sure to be assailed." (*Ibid.*, 381)

I have turned to Lynn Montross for testimony in Gates's behalf, knowing that if there is anything good to be said Montross will say it. "Gates had never been a good tactician, but few generals have ever equalled his resolution after such an appalling disaster," he says. "Hillsborough, far in the rear, was the logical base . . . , and Gates was at his best as an organizer. . . . it probably did not occur to him that his political foes would insinuate cowardice." Draw your own conclusions, but it appears to me that the more Montross excuses Gates the more he accuses.

GATES–SCHUYLER CONTROVERSY. As part of the FACTIONALISM that prevailed among Americans, the antipathy between New Englanders and New Yorkers forced these two generals into the roles of contending champions. It was not that either had any particular animosity toward the other, but the New Englanders felt their interests would be served if Gates commanded the Northern Dept. and the New Yorkers wanted Schuyler to hold this position. In Mar. '77 the New England faction prevailed in Congress and Gates succeeded Schuyler. The latter managed to have himself reinstated the next month. On 4 Aug. '77 Congress, dissatisfied with failure of Schuyler to stop Burgoyne's Offensive, ordered him superseded by Gates. The Northern Army remained split into partisans of the two generals; the Schuyler supporters could not make a hero out of their general during the Revolution, but they conducted a successful postwar campaign to make a villain out of Gates. What Lynn Montross calls "a campaign of character assassination that has few parallels in American history" is covered in the article on GATES. For another partisan viewpoint see Henry Brockholst LIVINGSTON.

See also Freeman, *Washington*, IV, 130, 416, 464, and Montross, *Rag, Tag*, *passim*.

GAYAULT. See BOISBERTRAND.

"GENTLEMAN JOHNNY." Nickname of BURGOYNE.

"GENTLE SHEPHERD." Nickname of GRENVILLE.

GEORGE III. 1738–1820. King of Great Britain and Ireland (1760–1811). George William Frederick, grandson of George II, was not a promising child. "Had he been born in different circumstances it is unlikely that he could have earned a living except as an unskilled laborer," writes J. H. Plumb, a British scholar who is identified below. "He was eleven before he could read. . . . He was lethargic, apathetic, childish, a clod of a boy whom no one could teach." His mother and her favorite counsellor, Lord Bute, for whom George had a pathetic devotion, nevertheless made the effort. Ears ringing with his mother's reiterated "George, be King!" and his dull mind steeped in Bolingbroke's *Patriot King,** he ascended the throne at the age of 22. † He immediately saw that his first task was to break the power of the great Whig families that had ruled England since 1714. The ouster of William Pitt proved to be relatively easy, and the young King imposed his own ideas in the Treaty of PARIS, 1763, that ended the Seven Years' War and ushered in the era of the American Revolution. His next task was to gain control of Parliament, and although this turned out to be a struggle, he used a technique that caught his opponents off guard. "They were prepared to fight the Crown upon the ancient battlefield of the prerogatives," writes Miller, "but George III gave them no opportunity to take their stand upon this familiar ground." (*Origins*, 66)

---

* The truth of this oft-repeated statement is generally accepted, although it has not been proved.

† George II died 25 Oct. 1760. George III was born 4 June 1738.

Patronage was his weapon. With an annual income of £800,000 he had a surplus with which to buy parliamentary seats at an average price of £5,000 each. He had royal gifts, honors, and sinecures for the right people. When he took the throne there were 174 peers; he conferred 388 more titles. (Montross, *Rag, Tag,* 64, citing Taswell-Langmead, *Eng. Const. Hist.,* 713)

Although he was able to gather a body known as the King's friends, who voted the way he told them, there were 10 years of political chaos before he could impose on Parliament a ministry of his own selection. Lord BUTE, the King's first choice as Prime Minister after Pitt's resignation in 1761, was forced to resign early in 1763; Newcastle and Hardwicke, two political veterans, saw to that, and maintained such effective pressure that the King could not even keep him as an adviser. GRENVILLE was in office until 1765, ROCKINGHAM until 1766, and when the King was driven to recalling Pitt (now Earl of Chatham), the latter was almost immediately forced by mental illness to retire. The King waited two critical years for the Great Commoner's recovery, while the ministry drifted along without a leader, but CHATHAM returned only to retire and become an ardent supporter of the Opposition.

In 1770 the King found a P.M. who was to be as loyal as a dog, but fortunately for America he was no more qualified for the office. This was, of course, Lord NORTH. Although George III's English birth and wholesome family life made him reasonably popular with a people who had never accepted his German predecessors, he needed a great national issue on which to rally a political following. Parliament's right to tax the colonies emerged as the issue he needed, and he hastened to exploit it. The British people, crushed

by the debts of the Seven Years' War, could comprehend the idea that America should share the tax burden. They could not really comprehend the arguments of the Opposition that their constitution was being cast aside, nor did they understand all this American prattle about "the rights of Englishmen."

Under BACKGROUND AND ORIGINS the path of George III toward the American Revolution is traced. When the King appointed Lord North prime minister in 1770 "the object of his ambition was achieved with the concurrence of a large body of politicians who had nothing in common with the servile band of the king's friends." (*E.B.*) The opposition of Edmund BURKE, of Pitt (Chatham), and of John WILKES on the grounds of constitutionality gained no popular strength. With a sincere conviction of his own right and with an inflexible tenacity of purpose, George III pursued his policy of coercion while remaining deaf to advice that he lacked the means of carrying it through in the face of armed American resistance. He was now surrounded with his handpicked ministers, and in North, GERMAIN, and SANDWICH he had a remarkable collection of ineptitude. George III had become a king, there was no doubt about that, but he was not the man to replace the leadership he had destroyed.

Although the people responded to the news of Burgoyne's defeat in 1777 with subscriptions of money to raise new regiments and build new warships, British statesmen saw the handwriting on the wall. Early in 1778 when the French Alliance was announced, Lord North begged the King to accept his resignation and to call the great Pitt back as prime minister, but the King would hear nothing of it. Before the end of 1779 two leading members of the Cabinet, Lords Gower and Weymouth, resigned rather than continue following the King's ruinous policy. News of the Yorktown surrender reached London on 25 Nov. '81, and on 20 Mar. '82 the King finally accepted North's resignation. George III admitted defeat, brought in the Whig ministry of Rockingham, and authorized them to begin the final PEACE NEGOTIATIONS. The death of Rockingham on 1 July '82 brought on another crisis. The King selected Lord SHELBURNE, leader of the Pitt element of the Opposition, as prime minister. Fox and the Rockingham faction insisted that the Duke of Portland have the post. The outcome was that a coalition of Fox and North defeated Shelburne and on 2 Apr. they took office as secretaries of state with Portland as P.M. On 3 Sept. '83 the final treaties with the U.S., France, and Spain were signed, although provisional treaties had been concluded much earlier. With all his stubbornness George III had always shown a readiness to give way when further resistance was hopeless. (*E.B.*) When John Adams, whose family name "had been a stench in the nostrils of George III for almost twenty years," presented his credentials as the first U.S. minister, the King answered graciously that he was happy Adams had been selected for the post. " 'I will be very frank with you,' the King continued slowly, rather haltingly, searching out his words. 'I was the last to consent to the separation; but the separation having been made, and having become inevitable, I have always said, as I say now, that I would be the first to meet the friendship of the United States as an independent power.' " (Page Smith, *John Adams,* 629)

In his personal life George had shown a moral character unusual for the time. Sheltered from the world by his mother and BUTE, he had sacrificed his own passion for the toothsome Lady Sarah

Lennox to marry the drab Princess Charlotte of Mecklenburg-Strelitz, the choice of Bute and the Princess Dowager. (When somebody commented that Queen Charlotte's looks were improving with age, her Chamberlain replied, "Yes, I do think the *bloom* of her ugliness is going off!" [Mumby, *George III,* 23])

After the peace treaty had been signed the coalition ministry overplayed their hand by attempting to modify the East India Company's charter, seize control of India, and thereby gain a source of patronage they needed to keep power. The King, who had driven them to this desperate move by withholding all royal favors and honors, brought in the 24-year old Wm. Pitt (the Younger) as prime minister (Dec. '83). "At last George III's long search was over," comments J. H. Plumb. "He had found a Prime Minister whom he and the nation could safely trust." The rest is English history and outside the scope of the present work.

Returning to George III as a man, symptoms of insanity had first appeared in 1765, but were concealed from the public. In Oct. '88 he became ill and early the next month he obviously was mad. The Prince of Wales, who loathed his father (in the Hanoverian tradition), waited fully dressed for two days and nights for the news that he was George IV, but the King lived and recovered his sanity. Furthermore, with the government now in Pitt's firm hands and the country worried about the revolution in France, he found himself popular. In 1811, however, his mind broke completely after the death of Princess Amelia, his favorite child. The Prince of Wales, whose conduct had done much to bring on the father's insanity, became regent. George III had moments of lucidity during the next nine years but most of his time was spent "wandering through the rooms of his palace, addressing imaginary parliaments, reviewing fancied troops, holding ghostly courts," as Thackeray describes it in *The Four Georges*. Blindness fell and deafness closed in before he died on 29 Jan. 1820.

Having pictured George III as most historians see him, let me present another viewpoint. J. H. Plumb, Fellow of Christ's College, Cambridge, and author of scholarly works that include *The First Four Georges,* writes:

"Poor George III still gets a bad press.* * * Since Jefferson's great philippic in the Declaration of Independence, few historians, English or American, have had many good words to say for him. True, he has been excused direct responsibility for many items of the catalogue of enormities that Jefferson went on to lay at his door, but to the ordinary man he remains one of England's disastrous kings, like John or the two Jameses.

"Actually . . . toward the end of his life and immediately after it his reputation improved, and even the writings of American school textbooks did not at first hold him personally responsible for the disasters that led to independence. They held his ministers responsible. It was after the publication of Horace Walpole's *Memoirs* in 1845 that George III began to be blamed. Walpole's gossip appeared to give substance to Burke's allegations that the King deliberately attempted to subvert the British constitution by packing ministries and Parliament with his personal party —the King's friends—a collection of corrupt politicians bought with place and with pensions.

"Later historians held that these Tory incompetents, bent on personal government for their master, pursued a ruinous policy that ended only with the breakup of the first British Empire and

a return of the Whigs to power. Historians reminded themselves not only of the disasters in America, but the failure of parliamentary reform in England, of the oppression of the Irish, the Catholics, the Dissenters; they remembered the treatment of radicals at the time of the French Revolution; they recalled the merciless suppression of trade unions; the violent opposition to the abolition of slavery. It all added up to a huge indictment of George III and a magnificent justification for Whig doctrine. Here and there a scholar urged caution, but was little heeded. What the great historians formulated, the textbook writers cribbed. When English historians found so much to condemn, why should Americans lag behind?

***

"These views, however, are no longer fashionable. The greatest living historian of the eighteenth century, Sir Lewis Namier [d. 1960], has hammered at them for thirty years. His friend, Romney Sedgwick, with a more caustic pen and no less scholarship, has subjected them to ridicule. . . . Professor Herbert Butterfield has not only traced the origins of the myths of George III's tyranny but has also shown how the now-fashionable view of George III was held by historians and textbook writers long, long ago in the early nineteenth century. So the wheel has come full circle. Will it turn again? Or will blame and justification give way simply to understanding? Shall we at last have a balanced portrait of America's last king?" ("Our Last King," *American Heritage,* June 1960, p. 6)

The Correspondence of King George the Third from 1760 to December, 1783 was published by Sir John Fortescue in six volumes (London, 1927–28); "incomplete and not too carefully edited" by Fortescue, comments

J. R. Alden, "but nevertheless valuable." Other works are W. W. Massey's *History of England During the Reign of George III* (4 vols., 1855–63), J. H. Jesse's *Memoirs of the Life and Reign of George III* (3 vols., 1867), Horace Walpole's *Memoirs of the Reign of George III* (1894), Lewis Melville's *Farmer George* (1907), B. Willson's *George III as Man, Monarch, and Statesman* (1907), and Frank A. Mumby's *George III and the American Revolution: The Beginnings* (1923).

GEORGE, Lake, N.Y. About 35 miles long and varying in width between one and three miles, Lake George is connected with Lake CHAMPLAIN by a swift, narrow channel at Ticonderoga. Since the smaller lake is about 240 feet higher than Lake Champlain this five-mile channel is not navigable; a portage of about three miles, on the N.E. tip of Lake George, was used. (Scribner, *Atlas,* 45) Burgoyne has been criticized for not using this route. (See BURGOYNE'S OFFENSIVE) Diamond Island was the scene of action in the TICONDEROGA RAID, Sept. '77.

GEORGETOWN, S.C., 15 Nov. '80. Acting on information that this small coastal town off the mouth of the Peedee was garrisoned by only 50 regulars, Marion moved to capture it. The regulars, however, were subsequently reinforced by Tory militia under Capts. Jesse Barefield and James ("Otterskin") Lewis. At dawn of the 15th, Col. Peter Horry's mounted militia collided with Lewis at White's plantation and in a short skirmish Lewis was killed and four rebels were captured. Capt. John Melton led another mounted force that collided with Barefield's troops in a dense swamp near The Pens, Col. Alston's plantation. Barefield was hit in the face and shoulders with buckshot but survived. Marion's nephew Gabriel was unhorsed and subsequently murdered. His ammunition supply reduced to six rounds per man, Marion withdrew after two days in the neighborhood of the port. (Bass, *Swamp Fox,* 88–89)

GEORGETOWN, S.C., 24 Jan. '81. (SOUTHERN CAMPAIGNS OF GREENE) Soon after Lee joined Marion the two commanders raided Georgetown, which at that time was held by 200 British troops under Col. Campbell. The night of 22–23 Jan. the infantry of Lee's Legion dropped down the Peedee and hid on an island near the town. The next night this group landed undetected on the undefended waterfront; Capt. Carnes led one party to seize Campbell in his quarters near the parade ground, and Capt. Rudolph led another party into positions from which they could cut off the garrison as they moved into their defenses or to rescue their commander. Lee's cavalry and Marion's partisans charged through the light defenses on the land side to link up with the Legion infantry. Everything had worked perfectly, but the rebels then were astounded to find nobody to fight! "Not a British soldier appeared; not one attempted either to gain the fort, or repair to the commandant," says Lee (*Memoirs,* 224). Lacking the necessary means (battering rams, scaling ladders, artillery) to force the garrison out into the open, and not wanting to take casualties in assaulting the enemy positions, Lee and Marion paroled Campbell and withdrew.

GEORGETOWN, S.C., 25 July and 2 Aug. '81. After Loyalists had been plundered by the irregulars of Thomas SUMTER, the British retaliated by virtually destroying the town. This resulted in the prohibition of further operations in accordance with "Sumter's law," and ended the military career of the "Carolina Gamecock."

GEORGIA EXPEDITION OF WAYNE, Jan.–July '82. On 12 Jan., Gen. Anthony Wayne crossed the Savannah River with 100 of Moylan's dragoons (commanded by Col. Anthony White) and a detachment of artillery, with the mission of restoring American authority in Ga. "as far as might be possible." He was soon joined by 300 of Sumter's mounted infantry under Col. Wade Hampton, and 170 Ga. militia under Col. James Jackson and McCoy (not further identified). Although Savannah was too strong to be taken with the means at his disposal, Wayne drove the enemy's outposts back into the town, suppressed Tory bands, and cut off supplies. Brig. Gen. Alured Clarke had ordered a scorched earth policy, and his withdrawing outposts burned what he could not carry back into Savannah. He also called for reinforcements from the Cherokee and Creeks, but these Indians were still disorganized after PICKENS' PUNITIVE EXPEDITION. A British force sent out to open the way for the Indian reinforcements was attacked by Jackson. Col. Brown was sent from Savannah to reinforce the first force, but in a severe skirmish Wayne drove him back into the British camp. The night of 22–23 Jan. 300 Creeks approached Wayne's bivouac with the intention of attacking the pickets, but they accidentally fell upon the main body at 3 o'clock the morning of the 23d. In a fierce action the Indians were driven off with the loss of their leader (Guristersigo) and 17 others killed (including some white guides). Wayne's pursuit netted another 12, who were executed at sunrise. According to Lossing's account, 117 pack horses were also captured "loaded with peltry." (II, 740–41)

The Americans entered Savannah 11 July when the enemy garrison left for Charleston. Col. Posey led the main body of troops north a few days later, and Wayne soon followed with the rest to rejoin Greene in S.C.

GERARD, Conrad Alexandre. 1729–1790.* 1st French Minister to U.S. During the period July '78–Oct. '79 Gérard was ambassador to the U.S. in Philadelphia. His *Despatches,* edited by John J. Meng, contain "a wealth of information that may be sought for in vain in the *Journals of the Cont'l. Congress,*" comments Meng. The latter includes an 88-page historical introduction that gives biographical data about Gérard.

"GERM WARFARE." At the outbreak of Pontiac's War Amherst wrote Bouquet in July '63: "Could it not be contrived to send the small pox among the disaffected tribes of Indians?" Bouquet answered that he would try to do this by means of infected blankets. (Quoted in Peckham, *Pontiac,* 226–27) For fear that the epidemic might boomerang among the whites, the experiment was never tried.

GERMAIN, George Sackville. 1716–1785. British Sec. of State for American Colonies (1775–82). Known as Lord George Sackville from 1720 until 1770, and as Lord Germain from then until he became Viscount Sackville on 11 Feb. '82, his name is sometimes spelled Germaine. (*D.N.B.* is inconsistent on this but favors *Germain.*) Entering his key Cabinet position on 10 Nov. '75, and remaining there throughout the war, Germain is charged with most of the British errors of strategy during the Revolution. Although this haughty

* This date of death is from Appleton's, where no date of birth is given and where the common mistake is made of confusing this Gérard with J. M. Gérard de Rayneval. Meng gives 12 Dec. '29 as C. A. Gérard's birth date.

aristocrat had many contemptible traits of character as well as shortcomings in the field of colonial politics and grand strategy, an impartial re-examination of the evidence shows that he has been overdamned. (See the works of Gerald S. Brown cited below.)

Son of the 1st Duke of Dorset, who was a friend of George II and Lord Lt. of Ireland during the periods 1731–37 and 1751–56, George Sackville attended Westminster School and got his M.A. from Trinity College, Dublin, in 1734. In July '37 he was appointed Capt. in the 7th Horse (Lord Cathcart's) of the Irish Establishment and three years later he became Lt. Col. of the 28th Foot. Next year, 1741, he became an M.P. He commanded his regiment in the Low Countries and distinguished himself for bravery at Fontenoy, 11 May '45, where his attack penetrated so deep that he ended up in the tent of the French king when he was wounded. He took command of the 20th Foot just after Culloden, having been made its Col. on 9 Apr. '46. In Nov. '49 he became Col. of the 12th Dragoons and the next year was promoted to Col. of the 7th Horse, his original regiment. During his father's second tenure in Ireland, 1751–56, he was his principal secretary and Secretary of War.

Promoted to Maj. Gen. in 1755, Sackville took part in the abortive expedition of 13,000 guards and line soldiers and 6,000 marines against Cancale and St. Malo on the Channel coast of France. As Marlborough's second in command he accompanied this expedition to Hanover to constitute the British element of the allied army under Prince Ferdinand. Soon after their arrival in Sept. '58, Sackville became senior British commander on the death of Marlborough. Granby became second in command. Because of an offensive personality and an "exacting temper" he soon was on bad terms with Ferdinand and Granby, a situation that undoubtedly led to his famous misconduct at Minden, 1 Aug. '59. On this day Sackville had taken his post with the British cavalry, which was in general reserve some distance from where the allied infantry successfully beat back four French cavalry attacks and a supporting infantry brigade. (The father of Lafayette was killed leading an infantry regiment.) When Ferdinand sent Sackville orders to go into action and clinch the victory by a pursuit, the British commander did not consider his orders sufficiently precise. He halted an advance started by Granby and went to confer with the C. in C. The British horse finally moved, but it was too late. "The King [of England], it was said, wanted him to be court-martialed and shot for cowardice," writes Fisher, "but family influence saved his life, and the court found him guilty only of disobedience of orders." (*Struggle*, I, 426) Actually, when Sackville returned on leave to London around 21 Aug. he was merely informed (10 Sept.) that the King no longer needed his services. For various reasons Sackville's request for court-martial was delayed seven months. On 5 Apr. '60 the court found him guilty of disobeying orders and expressed the opinion that he was "unfit to serve ... in any military capacity whatever." (Quoted by H. Manners Chichester in *D.N.B.*) In a remarkably vindictive action, however, George II directed that this "sentence" be entered in the order book of every British regiment at home and abroad. Sackville also was stricken from the list of Privy Councillors.

Whitton points out that Sackville "was not 'broke' nor 'cashiered,' and he was not accused of 'cowardice.'" (This author cites his own *Service Trials and Tragedies.*) Sackville's treatment was considered unjustified in the eyes of the public and it was not long before he made a successful entry into politics and became a supporter of Lord North. His conduct in a duel in Dec. '70, resulting from a slur from "a noisy politician" named Capt. George JOHNSTONE, brought him praise from his opponent and approbation of the public. (*D.N.B.*)

This same year, 1770, he assumed the name Germain on inheriting property from Lady Betty Germain, whose will had included this stipulation.

On 10 Nov. '75 he succeeded Dartmouth as Secretary of State for Colonies, a position he held until 11 Feb. '82. (At the same time he became Lord Commissioner of Trade and Plantations, a title he held until 1779.) "A firm believer in coercion, he infused new energy into the Cabinet and ably supported North from the Treasury bench," points out Alden. "Exhibiting great energy, he hurried across the ocean regiment after regiment, well equipped and commonly well trained." (*Amer. Rev.,* 68) The historian of the British Army has this to say:

"There can be no question but that he was a man of more than ordinary ability, though, owing to the persistent English mistake of confounding a certain dexterity in Parliamentary management with genuine administrative power, his capacity has been rated more highly than it deserves. In any case it was a disgraceful thing that one who had been publicly degraded for misconduct and struck off the list of the Privy Council should have been restored to high office; still more that he should have been appointed to a department which gave him control of the Army abroad, from which he had been expelled as unworthy to hold a commission. It was asking very much from the loyalty of brave officers that they should

receive their orders from one whose name they could never hear without shame; and the evil of the appointment was not diminished by the fact that Germaine nourished an old grudge against Carleton, and was not too well disposed toward Howe. The only excuse for the selection of such a man to direct the operations in America would have been exceptional ability as a minister of war; and this talent Germaine most assuredly did not possess." (Fortescue, *British Army,* III, 174–75)

Personality conflicts with Howe, Carleton, and Clinton, his favoring of Burgoyne and Cornwallis in their independent operations, and his misguided attempts to control the war from London—all these things contributed in large measure to the ultimate British defeat. The CARLETON–GERMAIN FEUD is covered separately. His tampering with Clinton's letter in connection with the CHARLESTON EXPEDITION of 1776 almost led to a duel (see CLINTON), but Germain got a sort of revenge by supporting the strategic concepts of Cornwallis in the South in 1780. (See comment of Fortescue in article on YORKTOWN CAMPAIGN.)

During the YORKTOWN CAMPAIGN, in the further conflict in strategy between Cornwallis and Clinton, Germain was guilty of an "ill-timed interference... in every respect fatal," points out Fortescue. (*Ibid.,* 391) On 11 Feb. '82 his resignation was announced and on the same day, despite two motions in the House of Lords that the Minden incident made him unfit for a peerage, he became Viscount Sackville. Already in declining health, he retired to his country home in Sussex and died 18 months later (26 Aug. '85).

His papers are in the Historical MSS. Comm., *Report on the Manuscripts of Mrs. Stopford-Sackville...,* 2 vols., London, 1904–10, and in the Clements

Collection, Ann Arbor, Mich. A new and relatively favorable evaluation is presented by Gerald S. Brown in *The Colonial Policy of Lord George Germain, 1775–1778* (Ann Arbor, Mich., 1963). The dubious story of the pigeonholed order is covered under BURGOYNE'S OFFENSIVE.

GERMAN FLATS (now Herkimer), N.Y. 13 Sept. '78 (BORDER WARFARE) Originally called Burnet's Field, from the man who in 1720 was granted a patent for a 10-mile stretch of the Mohawk Valley extending west from the mouth of West Canada Creek, this settlement comprised about 70 houses on both sides of the river when the Revolution started. Its name derives from the fact that the first settlers were Germans. Gen. Herkimer's mansion was built in 1764; stockaded in accordance with frontier custom, it was also known as "Fort Herkimer." Two miles westward was Ft. Dayton, a relic of the French and Indian Wars and "little better than a dilapidated block-house" (Lossing, I, 255) when the Revolution started. The house of Rudolph Shoemaker, a famous Tory, was about two miles down the river from the village.

Joseph Brant raided the settlement on 13 Sept. '78 with 150 Indians and 300 Tories commanded by Capt. Wm. Caldwell. According to Lossing, the raiders approached their objective the night before, hid in a ravine near Shoemaker's, and attacked before dawn. (*Ibid.*) But the patriots had suspected an attack and one of the four scouts sent toward Unadilla escaped to spread the alarm, while the settlers clustered for safety in the two forts and the church (Ward, *W.O.R.*, 633).

"The enemy burned 63 Dwelling houses, 57 barns, with grain and fodder, 3 grist mills, 1 saw mill, and took away 235 horses, 229 horned cattle, 269 sheep, killed and destroyed hogs and burned many outhouses. Two white men, 1 negro killed. No crimes yet reported against women and children." (Swiggett, *Niagara*, 143, quoting letter of 19 Sept. from Col. Peter Bellinger to Gen. Stark's headquarters in Albany.)

On 29 Oct. '80 Sir John Johnson passed through German Flats after raiding Schoharie Valley. In early 1781 Indians appeared in small parties and destroyed property. (See BORDER WARFARE) The notorious Walter BUTLER was captured at Shoemaker's house.

GERMAN MERCENARIES. Almost 30,000 Germans fought against the Americans as mercenary units, taking part in every major campaign north of the Floridas. Many other individuals were recruited in British regiments. Perhaps one of the reasons why they incorrectly were known as "Hessians" is the fact that their three successive C. in C.'s were Hessian: von Heister, von Knyphausen, and von Lossberg. Riedesel, who led the German contingent in BURGOYNE'S OFFENSIVE, started his career as a Hessian officer but came to America as head of the Brunswick contingent.

The German mercenaries won no laurels in America. Well disciplined and drilled in the tradition of Frederick the Great (who laughed at admirers who thought his Potsdam parade ground exhibitions showed his formula for strategic success), they at first were respected by the British and feared by the Americans. Toward the end of the Philadelphia Campaign Howe's civilian secretary, Ambrose Serle, commented that the "Hessians are more infamous and cruel than any. It is a misfortune we ever had such a dirty, cowardly set of contemptible miscreants." This is exaggerated and supercilious, but the Germans were noted in their early campaigns for unwonted cruelty. They became a subject of ridicule and "after the first few years, judging by diaries, the Hessians [*sic*] were not hated as bitterly as the loyalists and redcoats." (Montross, *Rag, Tag,* 458)

"Only about 60 per cent of the German mercenaries ever returned to their homeland. . . . Of the 29,867 who reached these shores, some 5,000 deserted and 7,754 found a grave in America, including deaths from disease as well as battle. [Lowell, *Hessians,* 300] A large proportion of the 17,313 survivors had been wounded or captured without the consolation of winning a single fight in which Hessians exclusively were pitted against Americans. Far from learning any tactical lessons in the New World, the mercenaries departed with an unshaken faith in the outworn methods of Frederick the Great." (*Ibid.*)

The most famous German defeats were at TRENTON and BENNINGTON. Another operation that was primarily German was the SPRINGFIELD, N.J., RAID of Knyphausen, and this too was a failure.

As for the morality of Britain's hiring mercenaries (which stemmed from their failure in RECRUITING), the Whig opposition in England and the propagandists in America were certainly justified in raising a roar of righteous indignation. If a mercenary is defined as one who fights for money and not for love of country, however, the charge could be made that without large bonuses and promises of veteran's benefits Washington would never have reached his peak strength of 10,000 soldiers in a country that had an estimated 60,000 white patriots. (See RESOURCES. . . .) There was nothing new in the hiring of mercenaries in Europe, and it was proposed in America by Charles Carroll. German mercenaries had fought in England. (Channing, III, 215)

The Duke of Brunswick was the first German prince to conclude a treaty to supply troops. The British were to provide the mercenaries the same pay, food, hospital care, and medical evacuation to Europe as they provided their own troops (which was not much). The Duke would receive £7 4s 4½d for each of the original 4,300 Brunswickers and for each replacement needed to maintain this strength. If an entire unit should be lost at sea, in battle, or in an epidemic, the British agreed to bear all the costs of recruiting a new unit and also to pay the original "levy money" of £7 4s 4½d. (Channing, III, 214. According to Tharp this amounted to 30 thalers or about $22.50. *Baroness,* 13) For each man wounded the Duke would get one half this last amount, and for each one maimed he collected one third. He had to replace at his own expense all who died of sickness or deserted. The British paid, in addition, an annual subsidy of £11,517 17s 1½d starting 9 Jan. '76, when the treaty was signed, and would pay twice that amount each year for the next two years after the mercenaries returned to Europe. "This sounds like a stiff bargain," writes Tharp, "but the Landgrave of Hesse-Cassel got more than twice as much per man. Hesse-Hanau, also, stood out for more money." (*Op. cit.,* 13)

On the next page is a tabulation of the numbers sent to America and the amount voted by Parliament.

The manpower figures are agreed to by the two standard sources, Eelking and Lowell (*post.*). The cost figures are Eelking's, but Van Tyne warns: "The exact profits cannot be computed, even the details of payment were kept secret by the British Ministry. . . ."

German deserters entered the American melting pot, many of them coming from the CONVENTION ARMY. Others received permission at the end of the

	Number	Amount voted	Years of service
Brunswick	5,723	£750,000	8
Hesse-Cassel	16,992	2,959,800	8
Hesse-Hanau	2,422	343,130	8
Anspach-Bayreuth	2,353	282,400	7
Waldeck	1,225	140,000	8
Anhalt-Zerbst	1,160	109,120	7
Totals:	29,875	£4,584,450	

war to remain in America. (Uhlendorf, *Charleston,* 3)

Writings of German officers are among the most valuable documents for historians of the Revolution. The Baurmeister Journals and Letters and the works of Baron and Baroness Riedesel are pre-eminent. Uhlendorf has edited German source material of the recently available Clements Collection. Standard secondary works are by Eelking and Lowell, identified in the main bibliography.

GERMAN REGT. or Bn. was raised in Md. and Pa. under the Congressional resolution of 25 May '76. Col. Nicholas Haussegger was in command 17 July '76–19 Mar. '77, and Col. (Baron) De Arendt from the latter date to 1 Jan. '81. In 1777 it became one of the 16 "ADDITIONAL CONT'L. REGTS." The unit disgraced itself at Trenton, 2 Jan. '77, during the NEW JERSEY CAMPAIGN and HAUSSEGGER surrendered or defected to the enemy.

Another "German Regt." was the 8th Va., raised by Peter MUHLENBERG and subsequently commanded by Abraham Bowman (22 Mar.–10 Dec. '77), John Neville (to 14 Sept. '78), and James Wood (to 1 Jan. '83).

GERMANTOWN, Pa., Battle of, 4 Oct. '77 (PHILADELPHIA CAMPAIGN). See map. Washington had suffered a humiliating series of defeats, crowned by the loss of Philadelphia (26 Sept.), but his situation was not entirely black. The Delaware River forts blocked British supply ships, and forced Howe to detach considerable strength not only for their reduction but also to escort supplies from Head of Elk. Washington's intelligence agents informed him that 3,000 enemy troops were on this last mission. He also knew that Howe's forces were split into two parts: the garrison under Cornwallis in Philadelphia, and the main body five miles to the north at Germantown. The American army had been reinforced to 8,000 Cont'ls. and 3,000 militia, so plans were made for an attack on the 9,000 British estimated to be in and around Germantown. On 29 Sept. Washington moved five miles from Pennypacker's Mill to the Shippack road, and on 2 Oct. he moved three miles down that road to Centre Point, 15 miles from Germantown and as close as he could get in daylight without giving away his attack.

The plan finally adopted by Washington was for Greene to lead a wide envelopment through Lucken's Mill against the British right, which was believed to be their stronger flank. Sullivan would advance along the Shippack road, and Alexander ("Stirling") would follow in reserve. The sketch on page 427 shows the divisions making up these three commands; Greene's three divisions, being larger than the others,

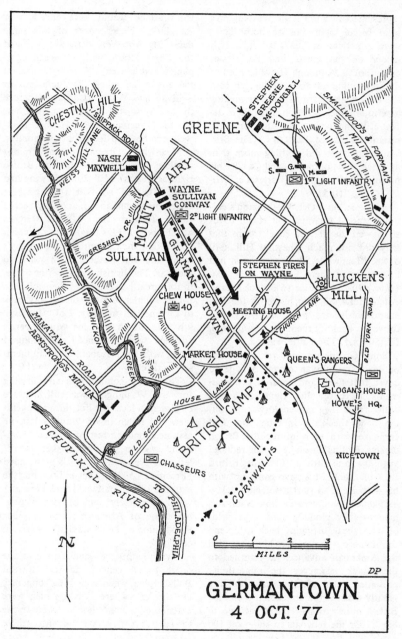

GERMANTOWN
4 OCT. '77

represented two thirds of Washington's total force. Operating on both flanks were American militia: Md. and N.J. troops on the north, and Pa. troops on the south. Although Howe learned of the impending advance, he had no idea the Americans were capable of making a serious attack so soon after their defeat at Brandywine. (The situation much resembled that of TRENTON.) The British commander did nothing more than advance his outposts and warn his patrols to be vigilant (Fortescue, *British Army*, III, 219).

At 7 P.M. on 3 Oct. Washington's columns started forward, but rough roads so slowed the ill-shod rebel troops that they did not reach Chestnut Hill until dawn. Meanwhile, British outposts had first reported their advance at 3 A.M. (*Ibid.*) Just at sunrise (6 o'clock) Capt. Allen McLane's light horse hit the first enemy resistance near Mt. Airy and drove it back (Freeman, *Washington*, IV, 506 *n.*). The battle was on.

Since Greene was not yet in position on his left, Sullivan moved Wayne to cover that flank and ordered two regiments to cover the right. Sullivan's entire force then moved forward, pushing back the light infantry that had come forward to reinforce the British pickets. By this time a heavy fog reduced visibility to as little as 30 yards. British Lt. Col. Thos. Musgrave came up with his 40th Regt. to start a splendid delaying action; counterattacking Sullivan's men as they plodded across the fields of buckwheat, dropping back to defend the numerous fence lines that impeded the American advance, he returned to the attack whenever the opportunity presented itself. At this stage the fog greatly assisted the attackers by limiting British observation. "Had it been possible ... for the redcoats to stand off 100 yards and fire at the Continentals on top the fences," says Freeman, "Sullivan's attack would have ended in a slaughter." Under cover of this same dense fog, however, Musgrave occupied the Chew House with six weak companies and posted 120 men to fire on the advancing rebels. The divisions of Sullivan and Wayne had passed before the enemy started firing from the Chew House (Freeman, 513–14), but Maxwell was held up for about 30 minutes.

Meanwhile, Greene's column, minus Stephen, pushed on to hit the British right at Luken's Mill. But this wing had been extended so that the attackers risked being outflanked, and they veered south toward the Market House. Muhlenberg led his brigade in a bayonet attack that then penetrated the enemy's front line and pushed 1,000 yards to the rear. The British had superior forces in this area, however, and their advance forced Muhlenberg to fight his way back to Greene's main body. Col. Mathews' 9th Va., which had led Muhlenberg's advance, was surrounded and captured along with 100 prisoners they had themselves taken.

The center column was now driving forward. Washington was still unaware of Greene's location, but since Stephen's men had fallen in on Wayne's left, he assumed that the rest of Greene's command was in position farther to the left and prepared to attack as planned (Freeman, 509). The militia on the extreme left (Smallwood and Forman) were completely out of the picture, but those of Armstrong on the other flank, along the Schuylkill, were in contact.

"Washington was about to give the order for a general advance toward Philadelphia, when something happened. On the left, where Wayne's men were extending Sullivan's line and were trying to keep up with the advance, there was confused firing. Shouts were heard and were answered from a greater distance. On Sullivan's front a loud volley shook the ground but provoked an uneven answer. The clatter of musketry soon was nearer and more nervous. Out of the fog men came back on the run, some frantic with fear, some able to gasp a few words—that the enemy was in the rear, that the flank had been turned, that friends had been mistaken for foes, that orders to retreat had been shouted. Every man had a different tale, but none paused long to tell it. Nor could they be halted, even to snatch up the booty of the British camps they had overrun. Presently the artillery galloped past and took the road to the rear. Officers from the front, swinging their swords and swearing or pleading, tried to stop what in the course of a few minutes became a mad panic. Washington, his staff and several mounted Colonels joined in the attempt to rally the troops. It was as if they had been shouting to the fog to dissipate itself. Hundreds ran as if the Devil himself were lunging at them; the line was a mob; the road was jammed; the fields were crowded with fugitives. By 10 o'clock, incredibly, the action was over." (Freeman, 510–11)

Within a few minutes the worst of the panic had ended, but Washington could do no more than order a general retreat. The British did not pursue vigorously. Cornwallis came onto the field with three fresh battalions from Philadelphia and followed Greene's command for five miles, but made no effort to do more.

CASUALTIES

American losses were reported as 152 killed, 521 wounded, and over 400 captured. "The disastrous siege of the Chew House laid 53 Americans dead on its lawn," says Ward. (*Op. cit.,* 371) Gen. Nash was mortally wounded. British losses were 537 killed and wounded,

and 14 captured. These figures include one German officer and 23 men wounded. (Fortescue, 220) Gen. Agnew and Col. Bird were among the four British officers killed.

COMMENTS

Most accounts say the panic was caused when the troops of Stephen and Wayne collided in the fog, mistook each other for the enemy, fired, and ran. (Ward, 368) Resistance from the Chew House is also credited with ultimately causing the disaster. "Not only did Sullivan's advance lose its momentum, but the pause ruined the timing of the other assaults, throwing the whole machine out of gear," writes Montross, expressing a view held by many other historians. (*Rag, Tag,* 231) Ward says musketry "blasting away at the Chew House, convinced Wayne that his comrade in arms, Sullivan, was in trouble back there. He wheeled about, started to the rescue, and met Stephen's division coming down to the main battle." (*Op. cit.,* 368) Washington thought the delay caused by his following Knox's recommendation that the Chew House be reduced, on the principle that it was militarily unsound to leave "a castle to our rear," had been responsible in whole or in part for the American failure. (Freeman, 513) Freeman concludes that the Chew House had little if any effect on the outcome (*ibid.,* 514); he finds nothing to corroborate Sullivan's statement that Wayne turned back toward the strong point for fear that the enemy might be attacking there; the only effect of the half-hour delay of Maxwell might have been that his earlier arrival at the front might have prevented the panic. (*Ibid.*)

Greene's failure to get in position to attack at the prescribed time was a major factor in the American defeat, but this was due to Washington's defective plan (see below). Furthermore, his guide lost his way and delayed the column half an hour. Stephen peeled off without authority and headed toward the firing around the Chew House, with the unfortunate results already mentioned. He was accused of giving the order to retreat that contributed to the general panic; Stephen denied this and said the panic started when Wayne's flank guards shot at a group of enemy troops coming forward to surrender. In any event, he was tried and dismissed from the service (see STEPHEN, Adam).

The fog has also been blamed for the American failure, but although it undoubtedly contributed to the ultimate rout it favored the Americans in their initial advance (see above). Without the fog the Americans would probably not have gotten close enough to Howe's main body to have been routed.

While historians have thoroughly investigated all the above points with a view to finding the basic cause of Washington's failure at Germantown, the real explanation for the student of military operations lies in the American plan of attack. Washington with 11,000 amateur soldiers and officers divided into four columns (the flanks being seven miles apart) was attempting a concentric advance at night over comparatively unfamiliar roads for a simultaneous attack against 9,000 professionals who were deployed on a three-mile front with the advantage of defending on relatively good terrain. It is not being pedantic to question how so fundamentally unsound a concept of operations *could* have succeeded. The wonder is that Washington's troops were able to follow the plan as well as they did.

The American C. in C., his troops, and many historians subscribe to the view that the attack almost did succeed. This is epitomized by Christopher Ward,

who says, "For all the misadventures it was a near thing, a very near thing." (*Op. cit.,* 371) Freeman says, "The American commander shared, also, the general belief that the advance halted and the panic began when Howe was about to retreat across the Schuylkill, and perhaps even to Chester—a belief for which there is not a shadow of justification in Howe's report to his government." (*Op. cit.,* 517) Of course, you would not expect Howe's report to admit this last matter even if true, but there was nothing about the situation as Howe saw it—or as we now see it— to suggest that the British should have considered retreating.

As for the effect of the battle on Washington's army, however, there can be no disputing the paradoxical fact that this failure boosted their morale and self confidence. *They* thought they had almost won. "They are now in high spirits and appear to wish ardently for another engagement," wrote an unidentified officer. (*Ibid.,* 519) Washington was not criticized for poor tactics but was applauded—by soldier and civilian, in America and abroad—for his audacity. "The French government, in making up its mind on the question whether the Americans would prove to be efficient allies, was influenced almost as much by the battle of Germantown as by the surrender of Burgoyne," wrote Trevelyan. (Quoted by Ward, 371)

GERRY, Elbridge (pronounced with a hard G). 1744–1814. Signer. Mass. Son of a Marblehead man who had come from England, he graduated from Harvard in 1762 and joined the family shipping business. He had first spoken out against colonial injustices in a college paper. As a merchant and businessman, he soon became wealthy and entered public life in 1772 in the general court of the Mass. Bay Colony. He met and came under the influence of Sam

Adams at this time, and also became a member of the committee of correspondence. In 1774, he was a member of the Mass. general assembly when this body evolved into the MASS. PROV. CONG. Gerry was active in the committee of safety and in gathering militia supplies, particularly when enforcement of the Boston Port Bill made Marblehead a leading port of entry for colonial supplies. He was chairman of the committee of supply until 25 Jan. '76, when he was sent to the Cont'l. Congress. There he sat on the financial and militia supply committees. He was an early advocate of independence and an eager signer of the Decl. and of the Articles of Confederation. Alarmed by the continuing inflation, he proposed means to halt the currency depreciation and served with Morris on a committee to examine Washington's plans for the 1777–78 winter campaign. Their report showed dissatisfaction with the commander's vigor, and Gerry was an avowed supporter of Conway. (See CONWAY CABAL.) Gerry was not in favor of the French alliance and supported Arthur Lee, believing that Franklin had been corrupted by his stay in France. (Samuel Eliot Morison in *D.A.B.*) In 1780, as chairman of the treasury committee, he antagonized Benedict Arnold by examining his financial accounts. In Feb. of that year, he quarreled with Congress and resigned, charging that personal privilege and states' rights had been infringed upon. He then spent his time in trade and privateering and was called to the state senate twice as joint representative but accepted a seat in the lower house only. He returned to Congress and was active in the peace negotiations with Great Britain. After the war, he worked to abolish the standing army and the Order of the Cincinnati and pursued his interests in the Northwest Territory.

His congressional term expired in Nov. '85, and he then entered the Mass. legislature. Although he had been opposed to a strong Federal government, he reversed himself in 1786 and refused to attend the Annapolis Convention, saying that it was too restricted in scope. He sat in the Federal Constitutional Convention and followed an erratic course, proposing and opposing almost at will. He refused to sign the Constitution and resumed his anti-Federalist mantle but retired from public life for several years. In 1797–98 he was used by Talleyrand to forestall a break with France in the "X.Y.Z. Mission." After several defeats for governor, he was elected in 1810 on the RE-PUBLICAN ticket, and he was re-elected in 1811. This term brought about the "Gerrymander Bill" of 1812. This redistricted the state in such a way as to create Republican senators in excess of the party's voting strength and it created one district that had a dragon-like shape on the map. Gilbert Stuart or Elkanah Tisdale sketched in facial features and wings and called it a salamander. Another wit—editor Benj. Russell, according to John Fiske's citation in Webster's unabridged (2d ed.)—said the monster should be called a "Gerrymander." Webster's says this division of districts was wrongly attributed to Gerry, and Morison points out that the method was not new, but a new word entered the American language. Although the act worked with spectacular success to elect 29 Republican senators and only 11 Federalists despite a vote of about 50,000 for the Republican candidates and about 52,000 for their opponents, Gerry himself was defeated for the governorship (Apr. 1812). A few months later he was elected vice-president to Madison, and on 23 Nov. 1814 he died suddenly in office.

"GERTRUDE OF WYOMING." Poem about the WYOMING VALLEY "MASSACRE."

GIBAULT, Pierre. 1737–1804. Catholic missionary. Born in Quebec, the great-grandson of a Frenchman who had emigrated from Poitiers around 1650, he was educated at the Seminary of Quebec and served for a short time at the cathedral. In 1768 he was sent to the Illinois country by Bishop Briand of Quebec, and with his mother and sister he set up his residence at Kaskaskia. The next year he became vicar-general of the territory; in this capacity he got to know Vincennes.

Grateful to George Rogers Clark for his tolerant religious attitude, Father Gibault made himself extremely useful to the Americans in their WESTERN OPERATIONS. He later denied doing anything more than attempting to avoid bloodshed, but this position appears to have been adopted in 1780 to avoid British charges of treason (J. A. James in *D.A.B.*). In 1785 he moved to Vincennes, and four years later established his residence in Cahokia. In 1790 he petitioned Gen. St. Clair for a grant of Seminary land to compensate for his losses in the war, and when this was blocked by Bishop Carroll of Baltimore —who objected to alienation of church land to an individual clergyman—Father Gibault moved across the Mississippi to become parish priest in the Spanish settlement at New Madrid. He died there early in 1804. (*Ibid.*)

GIBSON, George. 1747–1791. Cont'l. officer. Pa. After an apprenticeship with a merchant and West Indies trader he joined his brother, John GIBSON, at Pittsburgh but returned to eastern Pa. after failing as operator of a trading post. He returned to the West to take part in Dunmore's War (1774). Commissioned Capt. of the 1st Va. on 2 Feb. '76, he organized a rowdy company of frontiersmen and took them to join Mercer's Brig. at Williamsburg, Va. "He commanded the company and played the fife," writes Thomas Denton McCormick in *D.A.B.*, and in the absence of redcoats in Va. at this time his men became notorious camp brawlers. (*Ibid.*) Appointed agent to deal with Oliver POLLOCK in New Orleans, he left Ft. Pitt on 19 July '76 with about 25 men disguised as traders, traveled down the rivers to reach the Spanish city in mid-Aug., and returned with close to 10,000 pounds of powder. A Maj., 4th Va., on 4 Jan. '77, he then served in the 1777–78 military operations in N.Y. and N.J., being promoted to Col. of the 1st Va. State Regt. on 5 June '77. In 1779 he was put in charge of prisoners at York, Pa., and held this position until Jan. '82. (*D.A.B.;* Heitman)

He returned to his farm at Carlisle, Pa. In 1791 he was commissioned Col. of the Pa. and N.J. Levies to take part in St. Clair's ill-fated expedition against the Indians. Twice wounded at Black Swamp, near Ft. Recovery, on 4 Nov., he was evacuated about 30 miles to Ft. Jefferson and died there on 14 Dec. '91.

Brother of John GIBSON, he was the father of jurist John Bannister Gibson.

GIBSON, John. 1740–1822. Cont'l. officer. Pa.–Va. Having been reared on the Pa. frontier (around Carlisle ?), he went on the Forbes expedition when he was 18 and then settled at Ft. Pitt to become an Indian trader. He was captured at the start of Pontiac's War and released in 1764 after a year's captivity. During this period he was rescued, Pocahontas-fashion, and may have taken an Indian wife, who possibly was a sister or sister-in-law of Logan. (Thos. Denton McCormick in *D.A.B.*) After resuming his trading from Ft. Pitt, he took part in Dunmore's War and relayed the controversial speech of LOGAN.

In 1775 he was an agent of Va. to the Indians and, being an excellent linguist by this time and well known among the savages, he did much to keep them pacified. On 12 Nov. '76 he was commissioned Lt. Col. of the 13th Va. and on 25 Oct. '77 was made Col. of the 6th Va. (Heitman) He took part in operations in N.Y., N.J., and Pa. (*D.A.B.*) before transferring west to take part in the inept expedition of McIntosh in 1778. He was left as commander of the newly established Fort Laurens, when McIntosh returned in the late summer or early fall to Ft. Pitt, and remained there throughout the winter. (C. & M., 1022) Meanwhile, in the reorganization of the Va. line he was given command of the 9th Va. on 14 Sept. '78, which probably was a "paper transfer." His position back in the East is indicated by his letter of 22 Jan. '80 to Gates commenting on Alexander's "slaying [sleighing] frolic" to Staten Island. Soon after this he apparently returned to the Western Dept. He was named second in command to George Rogers Clark for a proposed expedition toward Detroit but Brodhead refused to make his regiment available for this operation. Gibson got his revenge by helping oust Brodhead as commander of the Western Dept. toward the end of the year. He became commander of the 7th Va. on 12 Feb. '81 and was in command at Ft. Pitt for a while before Gen. Wm. Irvine was ordered there on 8 Mar. '82. On 1 Jan. '83 he retired from the army (Heitman) and on 30 Sept. '83 was breveted B.G.

Settling in Allegheny co. (W. Pa.), he became judge of the court of common pleas and a Maj. Gen. of militia. With Richard Butler he negotiated the purchase of the "Erie triangle" in 1789. During the Whiskey Rebellion (1794) he made serious enemies among his neighbors and within his own family

by siding with federal authorities. He was Sec. of the Indian Territory, 1800–16, served as Gov. while the territory was being organized, and took part in the War of 1812.

His son, John Jr., joined his regiment as an ensign on 11 Oct. '80, transferred with him to the 7th Va., and retired with him. His brother was George Gibson (1747–1791).

GIMAT, Jean-Joseph Sourbader de. b. 1743 or 1747. Cont'l. officer, A.D.C. to Lafayette. France. Son of an officer, he was born in Gascony and on 10 Apr. '61 became an ensign in the Regt. of Guyenne. The following "remarks" appear in his record: 1764: "young, promising"; 1767: "good, suited for the general staff"; 1768–70: "fine (*joli*) officer, highly intelligent, suited for the general staff." (Lasseray, 420) On 8 June '76 he was promoted 1st Lt. He and De la Colombe went to America with Lafayette as members of his staff (*ibid.*, 32, 38); in the agreement signed 7 Dec. '76 by Deane, Lafayette, and Kalb, de Gimat was to have the rank of Maj. and with pay as of 1 Dec. '76. Reaching Philadelphia in July '77 with Lafayette, Gimat was given a commission as Maj. in the Cont'l. Army with retroactive pay and date of rank as agreed to by Deane. (Heitman, 249) He served as Lafayette's aide until Jan. '79, when he returned to France on a leave of absence that had been granted by Congress the preceding 5 Nov. In 1780 he went back to America with Lafayette. On 17 Feb. '81 Washington named Gimat commander of a light infantry regiment formed from the light infantry companies of the 9th and 10th Mass., the five Conn. regiments, and the R.I. Regt. (Lasseray, 419) Leaving Peekskill on 22 Feb. '81 (*ibid.*), Gimat marched south with Lafayette and led his regiment in the subsequent operations in Va. He had a prominent part in Lafayette's actions at Green Spring (Jamestown Ford), 6 July. Lafayette selected him to lead the attack on Redoubt 10 during the operations against Yorktown, but Hamilton claimed the honor on the ground of seniority and Washington settled the matter in Hamilton's favor. Gimat's regiment followed the 40-man forlorn hope in the night attack of 14–15 Oct. Wounded in the foot during the assault (Gottschalk, *Lafayette and the Close of the Amer. Rev.*, 322; Heitman, 249; Lasseray, 420, concludes that since Lafayette did not mention this wound in his report of the action to Washington Gimat must have received the wound later in the siege), Gimat was commended for his brilliant and distinguished conduct.

On 4 Jan. '82 he left Philadelphia for France on indefinite leave and with a letter to Lafayette from Washington. His discharge from the Cont'l. Army was dated 3 Nov. '83. On 25 Aug. '82 he was promoted to Col. in the French Army and put in command of the colonial regiment of Martinique. He was Gov. of St. Lucia from 21 June '89 to 3 June '92.

GIRTY, Simon. 1741–1818. Renegade white terror of the Old Northwest. The son of an Irish immigrant to Pa., in 1756 Simon and his three brothers were captured by Indians. After living with the Senecas he was an interpreter around Ft. Pitt in 1759, served in 1774 as a scout under Simon KENTON, and was an interpreter for the Americans until he deserted to the British in 1778. In his *History of the Girtys,* Consul W. Butterfield presents a large amount of evidence to show that none of the brothers took part in the attack on WHEELING, 1 Sept. '77, as many other writers have maintained. (This same authority points out that James Girty, not Simon, was with the

besiegers of Wheeling in 1782.) Simon did, however, figure prominently in the WESTERN OPERATIONS, but like Joseph Brant and Walter Butler he had such an evil reputation that many writers have erroneously named him as the leader of actions in which he had no part. After operating against FORT LAURENS early in 1779, on 4 Oct. of this year he ambushed Col. David Rogers on the Ohio River, killing 57 out of 70 men and capturing 600,000 Spanish dollars in addition to much needed blankets and other supplies being transported from New Orleans to Ft. Pitt. (Swiggett, *Niagara,* 201) George Girty, not Simon, served under Brant in LOCHRY'S DEFEAT, 24 or 25 Aug. '81, Simon being engaged at this time in a futile attempt to intercept George Rogers Clark on the Ohio River near the site of Louisville. When Brant later boasted of his own success, Simon Girty called Brant a liar, whereupon Brant inflicted a sword wound that increased the natural ugliness of Girty's face. "Girty often boasted of the scar as having been received in many conflicts with the Americans." (W. H. Hunter, *Ohio Arch. and Hist. Soc. Pubs.,* VI, 384–85) Although neither Simon nor James Girty was in any way involved in the evacuation of the "Moravian Indians" (Butterfield, *op. cit.,* 132 *n.*), Simon had an important part in CRAWFORD'S DEFEAT in June '82 and witnessed his being tortured to death. A strange string of circumstance links these events: Lochry's Defeat is considered by many to have been one provocation for slaughter of the "Moravian Indians" in the GNADENHUETTEN MASSACRE, and the terrible torture of William CRAWFORD is believed to have been inspired by a desire on the part of the Indians to get even for the latter massacre—Simon Girty was on the fringe of all these events, yet not personally involved in any one of them.

After taking part in the raid that led to the slaughter of pursuers at BLUE LICKS, Ky., 19 Aug. '82, Simon Girty continued to lead Indian raids. He took part in the defeat of Arthur St. Clair on 4 Nov. '91, where he is charged with having a warrior tomahawk the wounded Gen. Richard Butler and chop up his heart for distribution among the tribes (*ibid.*); and he is also supposed to have been at the Battle of Fallen Timbers, 20 Aug. '94. When Detroit was surrendered to the U.S. in 1796, Girty married a white captive, moved into Canada, and lived on a British pension.

His brothers James (1743–1817) and George (1745–*c.* 1812) lived among the Shawnees and Delawares, respectively; both fought against the Americans and were Indian traders. Modern Saint Marys, Ohio, is on the site of (James) Girty's Town. (*E.B.*) A fourth brother, Thomas (1739–1820), was closely associated with the Indians but did not take part in their wars.

The Girty boys, like the MONTOUR FAMILY, are frequently confused by writers. Lossing says Simon was killed in the Battle of the Thames in 1813 (II, 499 *n.*); since George died "*c.* 1812" (*E.B.*), this may explain the error. The *Handbook of American Indians* says "Girty's Town" was the site of a trading station established by Simon, not James.

See W. Butterfield, *History of the Girtys* (Cincinnati, 1890) and Thos. Boyd, *Simon Girty* (New York, 1928).

GIST, Christopher. *c.* 1706–1759. Colonial explorer and scout. Md. (See GIST GENEALOGY) Joining Washington on the frontier, he accompanied the 21-year-old Va. militia Col. on his mission into the Ohio country in 1753 and is credited with twice saving his life.

(W. J. Ghent in *D.A.B.*) He was with Washington in the operations that led to the surrender at Ft. Necessity in 1754. The next year he served as Braddock's guide and with two sons fought in the defeat on the Monongahela. (See COLONIAL WARS) Prior to this time he had established a reputation as an explorer and mapper of the central and southern frontier, living near Daniel Boone on the Yadkin in northern N.C. in 1750, and preceding Boone by 18 years in the exploration of southern Ohio and northeastern Ky. (*Ibid.*) His reports and maps indicate that the rugged frontiersman was well educated, although little is known of his early life and schooling. He died of smallpox either in S.C. or Ga. (1759), having gone there a few years earlier in an unsuccessful attempt to enlist Cherokee of E. Tenn. for military service. As mentioned under GIST GENEALOGY, he was the uncle of Gen. Mordecai GIST and may be the father of Col. Nathaniel GIST.

See W. M. Darlington, *Christopher Gist's Journals.* . . . (1893).

GIST, Mordecai. 1743–1792. Cont'l. general. Md. Great-grandson of Christopher Guest (d. 1691) and nephew of the famous colonial scout (see GIST GENEALOGY), he received an elementary education and somewhat later entered business in Baltimore. (Curtis W. Garrison in *D.A.B.*) In Dec. '74 he was elected Capt. of the Baltimore Indep. Co. (*ibid.;* Heitman's date is July '75) and on 14 Jan. '76 was commissioned second Maj. of the 1st Md., the famous regiment raised by SMALLWOOD. He commanded this unit at LONG ISLAND, 27 Aug., where he and his men distinguished themselves in heavy fighting in the open against European professionals. Smallwood commanded the Marylanders at White Plains, but was wounded there and Gist led them in their role as rear guard during the retreat through N.J. He was promoted to Col. on 10 Dec. '76 and commanded the 3d Md. at Germantown. After this he was engaged in minor skirmishes in his home state. On 9 Jan. '79 he was appointed B.G. and assumed command of the 2d Md. Brig. In Apr. '80 he started south with Kalb's column. At CAMDEN, 16 Aug., he won the praise of Kalb and on 14 Oct. '80 was included in the CAMDEN THANKS OF CONGRESS. Thereafter he was engaged in recruiting and gathering supplies for Greene's army. He fought at COMBAHEE FERRY, 27 Aug. '82. Retiring on 3 Nov. '83, he bought a plantation near Charleston and settled there with his third wife. He carried his preoccupation with American politics so far as to name one son Independence (born 8 Jan. '79) and another States Rights (1787). A grandson, B.G. States Rights Gist, was killed in action at Franklin, Tenn., 30 Nov. 1864, while leading his Confederate brigade.

Some Gist Papers are in the Md. Hist. Soc. Archives. Much material is included in the Cont'l. Congress and the Washington Papers in the Library of Congress. K. W. Blakeslee, *Mordecai Gist and His American Progenitors* (1923), "though laudatory, seems to be accurate as to details," says Garrison in *D.A.B.*

GIST, Nathaniel. d. 1796. Cont'l. officer. Va. Possibly the son of the famous colonial scout (see GIST GENEALOGY), which would make him a first cousin of Gen. Mordecai GIST, he took command of one of the 16 "ADDITIONAL CONT'L. REGTS." on 11 Jan. '77. The only information that Heitman can add is that he was taken prisoner at Charleston, 12 May '80, retired 1 Jan. '83, and died in 1796. His only appearance in the history books is as "the head of the Wrongheads," so dubbed by Geo. WEE-

DON (who qualifies as a good judge in such matters) after Gist preferred charges against "Light-Horse" Harry Lee for his conduct of the PAULUS HOOK raid, 19 Aug. '79. (Freeman, *Washington*, V, 131 *n.*)

GIST GENEALOGY. Christopher Guest immigrated to America from England about 1682, settled in Baltimore co., Md., and died there in 1691. His son, Richard, married in 1705, was a surveyor of the western shore of Md., was one of the commissioners who plotted Baltimore; he reared two sons who are of interest to us: Christopher GIST (d. 1759), and Thos. Gist. The latter played a minor role in the Revolution as a training officer, but his son became famous as Gen. Mordecai GIST (1742–1792), and his grandson, B.G. States Rights Gist was killed in action as a Confederate brigade commander. The second Christopher GIST (d. 1759) had a son named Nathaniel, who may be the Col. Nathaniel GIST (d. 1796) of Va., whose son was killed at Kings Mountain, 7 Oct. '80. (*D.A.B.*, VII, 323–25)

GIST'S LIGHT BRIGADE. A task force commanded by Gen. Mordecai Gist. See COMBAHEE FERRY, S.C., 27 Aug. '82.

GIST'S REGT. One of the 16 "ADDITIONAL CONT'L. REGTS.," it was commanded by Col. Nathaniel Gist.

GLACIS. A bank sloping away from a fortification in such a way as to expose the attacker to fire from the defenders. Since a considerable amount of labor is usually involved in clearing timber and grading the soil to form a glacis, it normally was found only around permanent fortifications.

GLOUCESTER, Cape Ann, Mass., 9 Aug. '75. Capt. John Linzee of the sloop of war *Falcon* chased two American schooners in Mass. Bay as they returned to Salem from the West Indies. Capturing one, he pursued the other into Gloucester harbor, where his boarding party was fired on from shore by infuriated citizens of the town. Linzee opened fire on the settlement, but lost both schooners and two barges before being driven off on 10 Aug. According to an account in the *Pa. Packet* of 28 Aug. Linzee lost 35 men, including one who died of wounds. (C. & M., 931–33)

GLOUCESTER, N.J., 25 Nov. '77. (PHIL. CAMP'N.) Leading a reconnaissance in force against Cornwallis' command, LAFAYETTE with 300 men from Greene's Div. got the better of a skirmish with a more numerous body of Hessians.

GLOUCESTER, Va., 3 Oct. '81. The buildup of opposing forces around Gloucester Point is covered in the article on the YORKTOWN CAMPAIGN. Dundas was returning to camp the morning of the 3d after leading the largest portion of his garrison on a foraging expedition when the allied force under Gen. de Choisy pushed forward to invest his position on the Point. Lauzun's dragoons, about 35 of whom were armed with lances, formed the allied vanguard, and the cavalry of Tarleton's Legion covered the British rear. Here is Lauzun's account of what happened:

"[When enemy dragoons were reported, he says,] I went forward to learn what I could. I saw a very pretty woman . . . [who] . . . told me that Colonel Tarleton had left her house a moment before; that he was very eager to shake hands with the French Duke. I assured her that I had come on purpose to gratify him. She seemed very sorry for me, judging from experience, I suppose, that Tarleton was irresistible. . . .

"I was not a hundred steps from the house when I heard pistol shots from my advance guard. I hurried forward at full speed to find a piece of ground where I could form a line of battle. As I arrived I saw the English cavalry in force three times my own; I charged it without halting; we met hand to hand. Tarleton saw me and rode towards me with pistol raised. We were about to fight single-handed between the two troops when his horse was thrown by one of his own dragoons pursued by one of my lancers. I rode up to him to capture him [as he lay pinned under his horse]; a troop of English dragoons rode in between us and covered his retreat; he left his horse with me. He charged me twice without breaking my line; I charged the third time, overthrew a part of his cavalry and drove him within the entrenchment of Gloucester." (Quoted in C. & M., 1227)

The action took place along a road that ran between enclosed fields about four miles from Gloucester. This lane debouched into an area where there were woods on Lauzun's left and an open field on the right; half a mile farther along the road was a small redoubt. (Lee, *Memoirs,* 497) After the last charge mentioned above by Lauzun, Tarleton reassembled his cavalry behind the infantry company of Capt. Champaigne (23d Fusiliers), which then advanced through the woods with other infantry and drove the French hussars back. While the French withdrew "slowly, and in good order," says Henry Lee, the select battalion of Va. militia under the experienced John Mercer came forward to form an unyielding line. Tarleton, meanwhile, formed on the left of the British infantry. But Mercer's men "received the onslaught with a steadiness that surprised Choisy as much as it did the enemy," comments Freeman. (*Op. cit.,* 355). Tarleton sounded the retreat, and the fighting days of the famous British dragoon were over. Within about half an hour the rest of Choisy's force was on the field and he pushed forward to lay siege to Gloucester.

French casualties were three killed and 16 wounded. Mercer's losses, if any, are not known. A British infantry officer, Lt. Moir, was killed within a few paces of the militia line, and Tarleton lost 12 men. (Johnston, *Yorktown,* 129)

GLOVER, John 1732–1797. Cont'l. general. Mass. Born in Salem, he moved to nearby Marblehead as a boy and progressed from cordwainer (shoemaker) to shipowner and merchant to become a wealthy fisherman. A short, heavy-set redhead, he was too wrapped up in other matters to take much part in revolutionary politics until a few years before the shooting started, although he was a militia ensign in 1759 and by 1773 was a Capt. commanding a company in the regiment of John Gallison. He probably devoted more energy at this time to the smallpox hospital he and Elbridge Gerry were trying to establish with the radical idea of inoculation. The public first succeeded in having official support withdrawn from this project; raised such a clatter when the hospital nevertheless opened on 16 Oct. '73 that it was closed; not content with this triumph of ignorance, they burned the building on 26 Jan. '74. (*D.A.B.*) Glover's talents now began to be channeled toward the Revolution. He was a member of the Marblehead committee of correspondence. On 19 May '75 he became Col., 21st Mass., and raised a body of 1,000 blue-jacketed fishermen stationed initially at Marblehead but around Boston in June.

Col. Glover was charged with equipping and manning armed vessels to attack British supply ships in Mass. Bay, and some of his men took part in the NANCY CAPTURE. Glover's regiment was then ordered off to meet a threat against Marblehead and then to protect Beverly. His regiment redesignated the 14th Cont'l. at the end of the year, Glover led them south on 20 July '76 for the defense of N.Y. His unit did not take part in the Battle of Long Island, 27 Aug., but reached Long Island early on the 28th and were in the Brooklyn lines until late that night. Glover then was put in charge of manning the boats assembled for the LONG ISLAND EVACUATION, 29–30 Aug., a remarkable operation in which his regiment and the 27th Mass. safely ferried men and equipment across East River. At Kip's Bay, 15 Sept., his Marbleheaders were rushed up to contain the British beachhead while Sullivan's Brig. and Knox's guns made good their escape from N.Y.C. Commanding a brigade at PELL'S POINT, 18 Oct., Glover fought a well-managed independent action. At White Plains, 28 Oct., his regiment gave a good account of itself. (*D.A.B.*).

Washington's famous crossing of the Delaware was made possible by the skilful work of Glover's Marbleheaders under extremely adverse weather conditions and with equipment—DURHAM BOATS—foreign to them. Putting the last man of Washington's main body across at 3 A.M., they participated with Sullivan's Div. in the attack on Trenton, 26 Dec., playing a key role in bottling up the enemy's last escape route, and then ferried more than 900 Hessian prisoners back across the Delaware! It was an almost incredible achievement: in 36 hours, in subzero weather, operating much of the time in a storm of wind, hail, rain, and snow, Glover's men had put 2,400 rebel troops, 18 cannon, and horses across the river without a loss, marched nine miles to Trenton, fought a battle, marched nine miles back to McKonkey's Ferry with prisoners and captured matériel, and recrossed the river.

The amphibious regiment ended its famous career with 1776, their enlistments up and the call of the privateer in their frostbitten ears. Glover went home with them to see a sick wife and tend to neglected business affairs. He declined the appointment of B.G. when it was offered on 21 Feb. '77, but in June returned to the army in that grade and with that date of rank. It had taken a personal letter from Washington to make Glover change his mind. (George A. Billias, "Soldier in a Longboat," *Amer. Heritage*, XI, 2 [Feb. 1960] p. 94; Heitman)

Glover served under Gates in stopping Burgoyne's Offensive and escorted the Convention Army to Cambridge, Mass. He commanded one of the two veteran brigades that Washington sent under Lafayette's command to support Sullivan's militia in the Franco-American attack against Newport, R.I., in 1778. In the spring of 1779 he succeeded Sullivan as commander at Providence, but joined the main army on the Hudson in June and remained in the Highlands during the Yorktown Campaign. Early in 1782 he went to Mass. to muster recruits, but bad health led to his retirement on half pay on 22 July '82. He was breveted Maj. Gen. on 30 Sept. '83.

See George A. Billias, *General John Glover and His Marblehead Mariners* (1960).

GNADENHUETTEN MASSACRE, Ohio, 7–8 Mar. '82. In 1773 the Moravian Brethren established the settlements of Gnadenhuetten (huts of mercy), Salem, and Schoenbrunn in what is now N.E. Ohio (Tuscarawas co.). In these places they gathered the Delaware, Mahican, and Munsee Indians—chiefly the latter—whom they had started Christianizing in N.Y. in 1740 and

whom they had moved to Pa. six years later. In 1781 the Hurons evacuated these Moravian Indians to northern Ohio either to prevent their assisting the rebels or to protect them from the frontiersmen. When 140 of the peaceful Indians visited their settlements the next spring to gather corn they were surrounded by rebel militia and 90 to 100 men, women, and children were massacred in cold blood. One explanation for this barbarity is that Col. David Williamson's militia were incensed when they saw a squaw wearing a dress identified as coming from a settlement recently raided by the Indians. (S. J. Buck in *D.A.H.*) On 8 Mar., after the massacre at Gnadenhuetten, some more Indians were brought to this place from nearby Salem and also murdered. The towns and crops were destroyed. This massacre touched off a vicious wave of Indian raids. (See WESTERN OPNS. of Clark)

GOLDEN HILL, "Battle" of, 19 Jan. '70. Opposition to the QUARTERING ACTS led to events covered under NEW YORK ASSEMBLY SUSPENDED. When a new assembly finally supported the acts with appropriations, Alexander MC-DOUGALL, a leader of the N.Y. Sons of Liberty, published a broadside "To the Betrayed Inhabitants. . . ." Clashes between troops and citizens finally led to a riot on Golden Hill; 30 or 40 soldiers used bayonets against citizens armed with swords and clubs, seriously wounding several of the latter.

GONDOLA. See GUNDALOW.

GORDON, William. 1728–1807. Historian, clergyman. England–Mass. Known as the American historian of the Revolution, he was born in England and in 1752 began his ministry in an Independent Church in Ipswich. Twelve years later he left after a quarrel with a leading member of the church over the latter's use of workmen on Sunday. He then became minister in Southwark. In 1770, having become sympathetic to the colonial cause, he emigrated to Mass. He became pastor of the Third Congregational Church in Roxbury (6 July '72), published a pamphlet advocating old age pensions, and in 1775 was made chaplain of both houses of the Prov. Cong. assembled at Watertown. Before moving from England he had corresponded with colonial leaders. After reaching America he became an ardent supporter of the patriot movement. Soon he appointed himself to the task of writing a history of the Revolution. In his *D.A.B.* sketch Frank Monaghan gives this summary:

"He conducted a vast correspondence, interviewed generals and statesmen, consulted manuscript collections, borrowed letters and memoranda, and in his wide travels became a familiar figure in council and camp. But he was rash and devoid of restraint; he was 'somewhat vain, and not accurate nor judicious; very zealous in the cause, and a well-meaning man, but incautious.'" (C. F. Adams, *Works of John Adams,* II, 1850, 424)

In 1786 Gordon returned to England thinking that he would find it easier to publish his book in that country. This proved not to be the case, and his manuscript had to be revised by several hands to eliminate statements that were believed to be too favorable to the Americans and subject to English libel laws. Emasculated and with a considerable amount of original material deleted, the four-volume *History of the Rise, Progress, and Establishment of the Independence of the United States of America* was published in 1788. A three-volume American edition was published in N.Y.C. the next year, and a second American edition appeared in 1794. After being considered a prime author-

ity for more than a century, the work was discredited and shown to be largely a plagiarism from the *Annual Register.* (See Edmund BURKE) The book is nevertheless valuable because Gordon used letters borrowed from participants (and seldom returned) and corresponded with generals to secure missing details. In 1789 Gordon secured a congregation at St. Neots in Huntingdonshire. Returning to Ipswich in 1802 he lived the last five years of his life in great poverty, having realized only £300 from the sale of his *History*.

GORDON RIOTS, 2–9 June '80. In violent objection to removal of restrictions against Catholics (Savile's Roman Catholic Relief Act) the eccentric Lord George Gordon (1751–1793) headed a Protestant Association in the presentation of a petition to Parliament on 2 June. That night the mob took control of London and it was a week before regular troops could restore order. This domestic disturbance temporarily brought the public back to support George III at a time when his popularity was at a low ebb because of bad news from America, and word of British military successes at Charleston and Camden further strengthened the monarch's position. Locally, however, the Gordon Riots destroyed the reliance of politicians on the London mob. Several of the agitators were executed, but Gordon escaped justice on a plea of insanity. The riots are described in Dickens' *Barnaby Rudge.*

GORHAM, Nathaniel. 1738–1796. Cont'l. Cong. Pres. Mass. After a common-school education and an apprenticeship to a New London merchant, he became a leading businessman in Charlestown, prosperous and highly regarded. He sat in the colonial legislature 1771–75, in the provincial congress 1774–75, on the board of war 1778–81, and in the state constitutional convention 1779–80. He was in the state senate 1780 and the state house 1781–87, being speaker in 1781, 1782, and 1785. Sent to the Cont'l. Congress 1782–83 and 1785–87, he was elected president 6 June '86. He presided over the 1787 Federal Constitutional convention for three months and was influential in his state's ratification of the Constitution the next year. After the war, he and a partner were involved in the development of six million acres ceded by N.Y. to Mass. in settlement of a border dispute. Complications over rising prices and Indian claims, however, wiped him out financially, and he died of apoplexy.

GORNELL, George. See MUTINY OF GORNELL.

GOULD, Paston. d. 1783. British commander in the South. A Capt. in the 23d Foot on 16 Oct. '55, he became Maj. of the 68th Foot on 1 Mar. '62 and Lt. Col. of the 30th Foot on 28 Mar. '64. On 29 Aug. '77 he was promoted to Col. in the Army. Col. Gould reached Charleston on 3 June '81 with the reinforcements from Ireland. From that time until the arrival of Lt. Gen. Leslie on 8 Nov. '81 he was the senior British officer in the South. Apparently he was given the local rank of B.G. by Clinton when he reached America, and by the time he led reinforcements to join Col. Alexander Stewart at Monck's Corner on 12 Sept. he had been given the local rank of Maj. Gen. (Clinton, *American Rebellion,* 354 *n.,* 356). Stewart was in command of British forces at Eutaw Springs, 8 Sept., despite the statement in his regimental history that Gould was in command and that this action took place 17–18 Mar. (N. Bannatyne, *History of the XXX Regiment* [1923]). Gould was invalided in 1782 and died the next year (*Army Lists*).

GOUVION, Jean Baptiste [Obrey dè].* 1747–1792. French volunteer. One of the four French military engineers sent to America on the request of Congress (others were Duportail, La Radière, and de Laumoy), Gouvion was from Toul and was the son of a *conseiller du roi.* On 1 Jan. '69 he became 2d Lt. and student at the engineering school of Mézières, and 10 years later he was an engineer *capitaine en second.* On 25 Jan. '77 he was given leave of absence to go to America, and on 8 July entered the Cont'l. Army as Maj. of Engrs. with rank from 13 Feb. On 17 Nov. '77 he advanced to the grade of Lt. Col. In his entries of 21 and 22 Nov. '80, Chastellux comments that the West Point fortifications were planned and executed by Duportail and "M. de Gouvion," and that the latter built the redoubt at Verplancks Point. It is also known that he took part in the Yorktown Campaign. On 16 Nov. '81 he was breveted Col. and granted six months' leave to France. (Heitman; Lasseray) On 10 Oct. '83 he retired from the Cont'l. Army (Heitman) and, presumably, resumed his military career in France. He was killed in action at Maubeuge, 11 June '92. (Lasseray) Although he is said to have "served brilliantly" in America (Editor Rice, *Chastellux,* 270), little is known of his specific activities.

GOZNALL, George. See MUTINY OF GORNELL.

GRAFTON, Augustus Henry Fitzroy, 3d Duke of. 1735–1811. British politician and acting P.M. Known in public life as an opponent of Lord Bute, he

* Heitman, who is not usually accurate in the names of French officers, adds these two given names; they are not mentioned by Lasseray or the editor of Chastellux.

became a secretary of state under Rockingham in 1765. His resignation led to the fall of Rockingham's ministry in July '66. In Chatham's second ministry, which was then formed, he was first lord of the treasury and nominal P.M. Chatham's incapacity at the end of 1767 made him the effective leader of an ineffective administration (see CHATHAM and GEORGE III). Because of political differences and attacks by JUNIUS he resigned in Jan. '70. He became lord privy seal in North's ministry in 1771 but resigned in 1775 because of disagreement with the policy of coercion. He held the same post in the short-lived ministry of Rockingham, Mar.–1 July '82.

GRAHAM, Joseph. 1759–1836. American officer. Pa.–N.C. Son of James, a Scots-Irishman who settled in Pa. in 1733, he moved to the vicinity of Spartanburg, S.C., with his widowed mother in 1763, and about five years later to Mecklenburg co., N.C. Having been educated at Queen's Museum in Charlotte (*D.A.B.*), in Sept. '78 he was commissioned as a Lt. in the N.C. Rangers, according to Heitman, and later was promoted to Capt. *D.A.B.* says he enlisted in the 4th N.C. Cont'ls. in 1778 and served a year as Q.M. Sgt. After completing this duty he again volunteered in 1780, was appointed Adj. of a militia regiment, and later became Capt. of a mounted infantry company. He distinguished himself at CHARLOTTE, 26 Sept. '80, receiving nine severe wounds. Two months after his recovery he returned to his regiment and remained until Mar. '81. In Aug. he organized a dragoon company and soon thereafter was promoted to Maj. (*D.A.B.;* Heitman shows him as a Maj. in 1780) For about two months he served near Wilmington, and in Nov. '81 resigned his commission.

After the war he became a successful businessman, acquiring a considerable fortune. In 1814 he was appointed commander of a brigade for duty in the Creek War, but delays in equipping his force resulted in its arrival too late to see action. In 1820 he started writing letters and articles for Archibald D. Murphey's projected history of N.C. "His account, based on memory, of the adoption of the much disputed MECKLENBURG DECLARATION OF INDEPENDENCE is one of the chief reliances of the proponents of the authenticity of the Declaration." (*Ibid.*) His accounts of fighting in western N.C. and in S.C. are, however, valuable.

See Wm. A. Graham, *Gen. Jos. Graham and his Papers....* (1904); G. W. Graham, *The Mecklenburg Decl. of Indep.* (1905); Wm. H. Hoyt (ed.), *Papers of Archibald D. Murphey* (1914)

GRANT, James. British officer killed at Long Island. Not to be confused with Gen. James GRANT, this officer became an Ensign in the 77th ("Montgomery") Highlanders in 1756, and saw much service with this regiment in North America and the West Indies. Capt. in the 40th Foot, 17 Aug. '62, Maj. in 1769, and Lt. Col. on 11 Dec. '75, he was badly wounded early in the battle of LONG ISLAND, 27 Aug. '76, while leading his regiment in a counterattack against the exposed east flank of the American right. His Adj., Lt. John Doyle—later Gen. Sir John Doyle— saw that his commander was in danger of being trampled to death in the fighting that continued around his prostrate body and rushed forward with a few men to evacuate him to safety, but by the time Doyle reached Grant the latter was dead.

GRANT, James. 1720–1806. British general. After studying law he was commissioned Capt. of the 1st Bn., Royal Scots, on 24 Oct. '44 and fought with them at Fontenoy and Culloden. In

Feb. '57 he became Maj. of the new 77th (Montgomery) Highlanders and accompanied them to America. Leading an 800-man advance detachment of Forbes's expedition toward Ft. Duquesne, he split his forces to draw the enemy into an ambuscade and was badly defeated on 21 Sept. '58 with the loss of about one third killed, wounded, and missing. He and 19 other officers, including Andrew LEWIS, were taken to Montreal as prisoners. (Lossing, II, 480. See also Freeman, *Washington,* II, 346) Despite this inept performance he was promoted to Lt. Col. in 1760 and led the successful CHEROKEE EXPEDITION of 1761. When the Floridas passed into British possession in 1763, Grant was appointed Gov. and held this post from 1764 until he went home sick in 1771. In *The South in the Revolution,* Alden says, "he was sensible, able, industrious, relatively good-humored, and hospitable" in this civil capacity. "He invested money of his own . . . , and he encouraged the ventures of others." (P. 122) His temporary successor was William MOULTRIE.

During his first American sojourn, however, Grant developed a "vehemently anti-American" attitude that grew progressively worse. (Freeman, *op. cit.,* 377) After commanding the 40th Foot in Ireland in 1772 he entered Parliament the next year. An American named William Alexander ("Stirling") allegedly was present in the House of Commons on 2 Feb. '75 when Grant proclaimed "that the Americans could not fight, and that he would undertake to march from one end of the continent to the other with 5000 men." (Quoted in *ibid.* See, however, ALEXANDER.) He was appointed Col. of the 55th Foot in Dec. '75 and as a B.G. in 1776 reached Boston with Gen. Howe. At LONG ISLAND, 27 Aug. '76, an American named William Alexander

happened to be commanding the forces opposite Grant, and the Scot had occasion for second thoughts about his boasted transcontinental march. Some writers have improved this story by confusing him with the Lt. Col. James Grant who was killed in this battle.

Grant's military education entered its next phase when he succeeded Cornwallis as commander of the outposts the British left in N.J. when they withdrew the bulk of their forces to N.Y. at the end of 1776. "You may be assured," Grant wrote to the German commander Rall, who shared his contempt for the American soldier, "that the rebel army in Pennsylvania . . . have neither shoes nor stockings, are in fact almost naked, dying of cold, without blankets and very ill supplied. . . ." Five days later Rall was annihilated at TRENTON and Washington followed through with his success at Princeton, 3 Feb. '77. American good fortune in these actions can be attributed largely to Grant, who was now a Maj. Gen. and was "probably of all British officers of high rank the one who had the most vindictive contempt for his foes." (Freeman, *op. cit.,* IV, 377)

During the Philadelphia campaign he commanded the 1st and 2d Brigades at the Brandywine and Germantown. He led the unsuccessful attempt to cut off Lafayette at BARREN HILL, 20 May '78. In Clinton's memoirs the British C. in C. comments on Grant's "very reprehensible inattention" during the Monmouth campaign when Grant failed to obey written orders on 28 June to send troops back to meet the threat that suddenly developed to Clinton's rear and brought on the Battle of MONMOUTH. This failure of Grant did not turn out to be crucial and Clinton did not make an official issue of it (*Amer. Reb.,* 93 n.), but it may explain why Grant was selected to lead the 5,800-man detachment from Clinton's army to the West Indies in Dec. '78. He reached ST. LUCIA on 12 Dec., captured the island, and gallantly defended it against d'Estaing (18–28 Dec.). (*D.N.B.;* Fortescue, *British Army,* III, 265) After showing strategic ability as army commander in the WEST INDIES, he sailed on 1 Aug. '79 for England.

Grant had been a B.G. in 1776, a Maj. Gen. in 1777, and in 1782 he was promoted to Lt. Gen. In 1796 he advanced to Gen. He was a member of Parliament in 1787, '90, '96, and 1801. Noted for his love of good living, he became "immensely corpulent" before his death at the age of 86. (Appleton's; *D.N.B.*)

GRAPE or GRAPESHOT. Iron balls, held together in a rack or bag, that scatter when discharged from a cannon. Differing from CANISTER only in that the balls are much larger, hence less effective against personnel, grape was designed for fire against enemy gun batteries, ships, light fortifications, but could be effective against massed formations.

GRASSE, François Joseph Paul, Comte de. 1722–1788. French admiral. At the age of 11 he attended the naval school at Toulon and the next year became a page to the Grand Master of the Knights of Saint John at Malta. In 1740 he returned to the French Navy during the War of Jenkins' Ear. On 3 May '47 he was captured while serving as an ensign in the battle off Finisterre and was a prisoner in England for three months, "long enough . . . to make some good English friends and secure definite information concerning the English Navy which was to be of great use. . . ." (Charles Lee Lewis, *Admiral De Grasse and American Independence.* Annapolis: U.S.N.I., 1945) An aristocrat of one of France's oldest families, 6 feet 2 inches tall, and considered one

of the handsomest men of the period, he rose steadily in his profession, serving in Indian waters, the West Indies, in the expedition against the corsairs of Morocco, and in the Mediterranean before taking command of the Marine Brigade at Saint Malo in 1773.

On 5 June '75 he sailed for Haiti as commander of the 26-gun frigate *Amphitrite.* Back in France the next year he took command of the 74-gun ship of the line *Intrépide,* and on 1 June '78 became a commodore (*Chef d'escadre*). The Franco-American alliance having been signed four months earlier, the revitalized French Navy was now ready to settle some scores with the British. He commanded a division in the indecisive battle off Ushant, 27 July '78, before returning to American waters. He commanded a squadron under d'Estaing in the battle against Adm. Byron off Grenada and in the operation against Savannah. After temporarily commanding the French fleet in the West Indies, he led a squadron in De Guichen's engagement with Rodney off Martinique. Now in bad health, he sailed home with Guichen, reaching Cadiz on 23 Oct. '80 and Brest on 3 Jan. Although his health had not recovered and he was almost 60 years old, on 22 Mar. '81 he was promoted to Rear Admiral and the same day he sailed from Brest with a fleet of 20 ships of the line, three frigates, and a convoy of 150 ships for the West Indies.

With discretionary orders to give Rochambeau and Washington whatever support was possible, De Grasse played a decisive role in the YORKTOWN CAMPAIGN and, consequently, in the winning of American independence.

He started back for the West Indies on 4 Nov. '81, and after capturing St. Kitts (12 Feb. '82), despite efforts of Hood to relieve the 1,100-man garrison, was defeated and captured aboard the battered *Ville de Paris* on 12 Apr. in the battle off Saints Passage (9–12 Apr.). While in London as a royally entertained prisoner during the period 2–12 Aug. '82 he had several conversations with Lord SHELBURNE, who spoke to him of terms under which the new ministry would consider negotiating peace. The day after he returned to Paris on parole, De Grasse sent his nephew to see Vergennes and give an oral report, and on this same day (17 Aug.) Vergennes used this information to draft his "Preliminary Articles of Peace." De Grasse then served as an intermediary between Shelburne and his government in this important preliminary phase of the peace negotiations. Although the official attitude toward his defeat in the West Indies was favorable at this time, De Grasse found himself the popular scapegoat for this French disaster. The admiral had bluntly reported to the Minister of Marine, de Castries, that most of his fleet had abandoned him on 12 Apr. '81. In a flood of letters and memoirs he spelled out his accusations against his subordinates, particularly BOUGAINVILLE. The subordinates went to de Castries with their counteraccusations and "a veritable cabal" developed. (*Ibid.*, 289) During four months a tribunal heard 222 witnesses and on 21 May '84 announced its findings. Bougainville was officially reprimanded for misconduct on the afternoon of the 12th—which amounted to a slap on the wrist. One ship's captain was condemned to *prison perpetuelle,* one was suspended for three months, and the others were completely exonerated or merely reprimanded. No official action was brought against De Grasse, but when he appealed to the King to pass judgment he found the latter was displeased not by the naval defeat but by De Grasse's attempts to clear his own name at the expense of

his subordinates and the French Navy. He was informed of this in a blunt letter from de Castries and advised to retire to his country home. Within two years he was back in the King's favor, but he had little time to live. On the eve of the French Revolution (14 Jan. '88) he died suddenly at his town house in Paris. His beloved Château de Tilly, some 50 miles west of Paris, was destroyed by the rabble and the four captured cannon from Yorktown which Congress had sent him in 1884 were dragged off to be melted into revolutionary coin. De Grasse's four daughters escaped to America, reaching Salem, Mass., on 7 July '94, and a year later they joined their brother in Charleston. (All children of the first of De Grasse's three marriages, the son was about 29 at this time, and the girls' ages were between 21 and 26.) In Feb. '95 Congress granted the daughters $1,000 each, and in Jan. '98 granted each $400 a year for the next five years. In 1799 Amélie and Mélanie died in Charleston of yellow fever. Adelaide and Silvie married and left descendants in the country whose liberty their father had played a decisive role in establishing.

GRASSHOPPER. Soldier name for the small, 3-pdr. field gun. Mounted on legs instead of wheels, the weapon jumped when fired, hence the nickname. It could be carried on horseback, so was frequently the only artillery accompanying a unit that had to travel light.

GRASSHOPPERS OF SARATOGA. Two GRASSHOPPERS captured from the British at Saratoga were recaptured at Camden, taken back by the Americans at Cowpens, and recaptured by the British at Guilford Courthouse. (Lossing, II, 642 *n.*)

GRAVES, Samuel. 1713–1787. British admiral. A naval Lt. in 1739, he took part in the Cartagena expedition of 1741 aboard the Norfolk, which was commanded by his uncle, Capt. Thos. Graves (*d.* 1755). The latter's son, Thos. GRAVES, served aboard the same ship. Samuel commanded the *Duke* in the battle of Quiberon Bay, France, 20 Nov. '59, and remained in command of this ship until his promotion to Rear Adm. in Oct. '72. In 1774 he was a Vice Adm. and in July he reached Boston as C. in C. on the American station. Without precise instructions from the government and without adequate naval means, his task is described in *D.N.B.* as "perhaps the most ungracious duty that has ever fallen to the lot of a naval officer...." On 27 Jan. '76 he was superseded by Adm. Howe. Although no charges of inefficiency were brought against him, he was not offered any subsequent active service. He angrily declined the command at Plymouth when it was offered him. In Jan. '78 he became Adm. of the Blue and four years later was made Adm. of the White. (See ADMIRALS, "Colored.")

Cousin of Adm. Thos. GRAVES.

GRAVES, Thomas. 1725?–1802. British admiral. Entering the navy young, he served aboard his father's ship at Cartagena in 1741. After duty in the Mediterranean and the Channel, he was court-martialed for failure to attack a large French ship the night of 26–27 Dec. '56 off the French coast. He and the officers of his 20-gun frigate thought they were opposed by an enemy ship-of-the-line, but the Admiralty believed he had muffed an opportunity to take a homeward-bound East Indiaman. On 27 Jan. '57, the day Adm. Byng was condemned to death by another court-martial, Graves was sentenced to public reprimand for "error in judgment." (*D.N.B.*) After advancing to flag rank in early 1779, in 1780 he was sent with six ships-of-the-line to join Arbuthnot

in N.Y. He arrived 13 July, three days after a French squadron under de Ternay appeared with Rochambeau's expeditionary force off Newport, R.I. Serving as second in command to the inept Arbuthnot, Graves commanded the blockading squadron in Gardiner's Bay when the other admiral was absent at the British headquarters in N.Y.C. He took part in the Battle off CHESAPEAKE BAY, 16 Mar. '81, and in July became temporary commander on the American station when Arbuthnot returned to England. Although Graves and Clinton worked together amicably, their various plans were postponed repeatedly until they evaporated. When the crisis of the YORKTOWN CAMPAIGN arrived, Graves tried to reach Cornwallis, fought the action off the CHESAPEAKE CAPES, 5 Sept.' 81, and returned to N.Y. to refit. "He and Clinton resumed their discussions, this time on ways and means of rescue, and held frequent councils of war," writes editor Willcox in his introduction to Clinton's *American Rebellion.* (p. xlii)

Adm. Digby had joined Graves on 24 Sept. with three ships and with orders that Graves take the *London* to Jamaica. Two more ships arrived from Jamaica on 11 Oct., and by the time Graves finally headed back toward the Chesapeake he had 25 ships of the line, two of 50 guns, and eight frigates. The day he sailed from N.Y., however, Cornwallis surrendered. After sailing around the entrance to Chesapeake Bay, which he reached on 27 Oct., Graves headed back to N.Y. (Under YORKTOWN CAMPAIGN see sections headed "Naval Operations" and "Sequel.") On 10 Nov. Graves turned over command to Digby and sailed toward Jamaica on the *London.* On 25 July '82 he started for England with a squadron consisting largely of prizes captured by Rodney. The convoy was badly damaged by storms, the flagship *Ramillies* (74) had to be blown up, and Graves reached Cork aboard a merchant ship on 10 Oct.

Although he had lost one of the decisive naval campaigns of history—being criticized primarily for failure to reach the Chesapeake ahead of De Grasse in Aug. and to keep the French fleet out—Graves was not held officially responsible for the Yorktown disaster. His defenders could argue that by protecting Yorktown he would have left N.Y. vulnerable to attack by de Grasse. Promoted to Vice Adm. in Sept. '87, he became C. in C. at Plymouth the next year, and in 1793 was named second in command to Lord Howe in the Channel fleet. On 12 Apr. '94 he was advanced to the grade of Adm. With his flag on the *Royal Sovereign* he distinguished himself in the Battle of the First of June (1794). His right arm was badly wounded and he had to resign, but he was made Baron Graves of the Irish peerage and given a pension of £1,000 a year.

Cousin of Adm. Samuel GRAVES.

GRAVIER, Charles. See VERGENNES.

GRAYSON'S REGT. was one of 16 "ADDITIONAL CONT'L. REGTS."

GREAT BREWSTER ISLAND, Mass. American raids of 21 and 31 July '75. (BOSTON SIEGE) Also called Light House Island, a mile offshore from Nantasket Point, it was successfully raided on 21 July by Maj. Joseph Vose. "The detachment under his command, brought off 1,000 bushels of barley, all the hay, &c. [from Nantasket]—went to Light-House Island; took away the lamps, oil, some gunpowder, the boats, &c. and burnt the wooden parts of the light-house. An armed schooner and several boats, with men, engaged the detachment; of the Americans, two were wounded." (Heath,

Memoirs, 33) The night of 30–31 July, Maj. Benj. Tupper led a force of 300 men in whaleboats to stop repair work on the lighthouse and capture the British guard and workmen. Tupper's excellent leadership resulted in the killing or capture of the entire enemy detachment, which numbered 32 marines, a subaltern, and 10 carpenters. Although Tupper's escape was delayed by missing one tide, he evacuated all the enemy wounded and sustained only two casualties. (For sources, see Freeman, *Washington,* III, 508 *n.*)

GREAT BRIDGE, Va., 9 Dec. '75. As the result of events outlined under VA. MIL. OPNS., Col. Wm. Woodford led a patriot force against Norfolk and Gov. Dunmore picked Great Bridge as the place to meet them. Here he fortified one end of a long causeway the rebels would have to cross on their way to Norfolk, about nine miles away (Lossing, II, 533); surrounded by tidal swamps and covering a defile, the British position was almost impregnable.

Woodford built a redoubt at the other end of the causeway, posted a Lt. Travis there with about 90 men (*ibid.,* 535) and encamped the rest of his force on a hill about 400 yards to the rear. John Marshall, later Chief Justice, was a lieutenant in Woodford's command, and his father, Maj. Thos. Marshall, was also there. Legend has it that the senior Marshall's clever servant went to the enemy pretending to be a deserter and told them there were no more than 300 "shirt-men" (militia riflemen) at the bridge. (Beveridge, *John Marshall,* I, 76) This "strategem" is traditionally credited with causing Dunmore to order an assault on the rebel breastworks, but it is difficult to see the point inasmuch as his men would have to cross the bridge, which was about 40 yards long, and advance along the causeway; 300 riflemen protected by a redoubt would present an impressive opposition under such circumstances, and the attack actually was stopped by 90. The story is mentioned here only because it is part of the American Legend, and is included in Woodford's report. (C. & M., 112) True American strength is not known beyond the statements that Woodford had one Va. Cont'l. regiment, some N.C. troops, and 200 "shirt-men," but he could not have had many more than the number reported by the "clever servant."

Whatever prompted his unfortunate decision, Gov. Dunmore ordered Capt. Fordyce to spearhead a frontal attack down the causeway with his 60 grenadiers and another 140 or so available regulars; Capt. Samuel Leslie was to follow up with a reserve of 230 of Dunmore's "Ethiopians" and "Loyal Virginians." Fordyce crossed the bridge before dawn, but his first advance was driven back. Having brought forward two cannon to support his second attempt, the gallant grenadier captain led his men down the causeway. Lt. Travis had his men hold their fire until the enemy was 50 yards away. "Believing the redoubt to be deserted, Fordyce waved his hat over his head, shouted 'The day is our own!' and rushed forward toward the breast-work." (Lossing, *op. cit.*, 535) The story that Fordyce fell with 14 bullets in him is hard to believe (see MARKSMANSHIP) unless the Americans were using "BUCK AND BALL" or "swan shot," but he was killed close to the redoubt and his men retreated in the face of Travis' surprise fire. Woodford says in his report that Capt. Leslie's "blacks, etc." did not advance beyond the bridge. An envelopment led by Col. Edw. Stevens drove them back to their redoubt.

The Virginians captured the two guns and 16 wounded, including Lt. Batut, who brought Woodford the story about Marshall's servant. They buried Capt. Fordyce and 12 others. Additional British casualties, according to Gordon, brought the total to 62. The only rebel casualty was one man slightly wounded in the hand. The action lasted less than 25 minutes.

This was the first fight between British soldiers and colonists since Bunker Hill, and the first Revolutionary War battle in Va. It was followed by the rebel occupation of and the subsequent destruction of NORFOLK, 1 Jan. '76.

"GREAT JEHOVAH AND THE CONTINENTAL CONGRESS." Four years after the capture of TICONDEROGA, N.Y., 10 May '75, Ethan Allen recorded that he had demanded the surprised commandant to surrender "in the name of the Great Jehovah and the Continental Congress." (*Narrative*, 1779 [Burlington edition, 1849, p. 98]) Van Tyne observes wryly that, "in truth, he had no commission from either of those high authorities, and other witnesses reported something about a challenge to a 'd—d old rat' to come out." (*War of Indep.*, 55) Allen French analyzes the incident in *First Year of the Amer. Rev.*, 733–34.

GREAT SAVANNAH (Nelson's Ferry), S.C., 20 Aug. '80. When the Whigs of the Williamsburg district (30 mi. up the Peedee from Georgetown) asked that Francis Marion come take command of their militia, Horatio Gates was happy to oblige. As shown by the quotation from Otho Williams in the article on the CAMDEN CAMPAIGN, the regulars were unimpressed by the military potential of the little partisan band that had joined them. But Gov. Rutledge was with Gates's camp and was unhandicapped by a military mind: when the man who was to win immortality as The Swamp Fox left Rugeley's Mill on 14 Aug. he went as a newly commissioned brigadier of S.C. State

Troops. He also left with instructions from the fatuous Gates to destroy boats along the Santee, to assist in trapping and destroying whatever portion of the British army might escape the defeat Gates expected to inflict around Camden.

By the time Gates had led his army to annihilation at Camden (16 Aug.), Marion had completed his first task as a brigadier: organizing a brigade. On the 17th he sent Col. Peter Horry with four new dragoon companies to operate against Georgetown, and with the rest of his command Marion started a march of about 60 miles toward the Santee. On the 19th he learned of Gates's defeat, but he continued his advance without telling his men. That night he received information that a large group of prisoners from Camden had camped with a strong guard on Sumter's abandoned plantation at Great Savannah, six miles above Nelson's Ferry on the Santee. Although greatly outnumbered, he prepared a surprise attack at dawn. Just before daylight he sent Col. Hugh Horry with 16 picked men to block the main road where it crossed a wide swamp at Horse Creek pass, and with the rest of his command Marion circled around to strike the enemy from the rear. Reporting the action to Peter Horry, he wrote:

"On the 20th instant, I attacked a guard of the 63d and Prince of Wales's regiment, with a number of Tories . . . ; killed and took 22 regulars and two Tories prisoners, and retook 150 Cont'ls. of the Md. line . . . ; one captain and a subaltern were also captured. Our loss is one killed; and Capt. Benson is slightly wounded on the head." *
(Quoted in Lossing, II, 706)

* The date 20 Aug. is accepted by most historians, although Bass says the action took place on the 25th (*Green*

After this coup Marion wasted no time high-tailing it back to the swamps and Cornwallis also was prompt in sending troops to clear the guerrillas from his line of communications with Charleston. On 28 Aug. Cornwallis ordered Maj. James Wemyss to march the 63d Regt. from the High Hills of Santee to Cheraw on the upper Peedee, and on 5 Sept. Wemyss started a raid that left a 15-mile-wide swath of destruction between these two places.

GREATON, John. 1741–1783. Cont'l. general. Mass. Son of a trader and the last landlord of the famous Greyhound Tavern in Roxbury, John also became a trader (*D.A.B.*) and innkeeper (Appleton's). He became a militia Lt. on 18 Nov. '74, took part in the pursuit of the British from Lexington and Concord, and on 19 May '75 was appointed Lt. Col. of Heath's Mass. Regt. Promoted to Col. of that unit on 1 July, he led raids on British depots during the Boston Siege. The most famous of these operations was against LONG ISLAND (Boston Harbor), 12 July '75. In the reorganization of 1 Jan. '76 he was named commander of the 24th Mass. and on 15 Apr. was ordered to Canada.

Dragoon, 104). The only British regulars involved were those of the 63d; the PRINCE OF WALES REGT. was a Tory unit. Ward's account differs in several respects from Bass's: he says "Marion and 16 of his daredevils" accomplished this "gallant exploit" in which *160* prisoners were liberated. (*W.O.R.*, 733) Bass says Capt. Roberts and *38* escorts were captured. As for the prisoners, Lossing says only three consented to join Marion's command, and he implies that all the rest went home. Ward says fewer than half returned to the army. These were the regulars who didn't think Marion and his men were up to their standards.

After an arduous and demoralizing service in the north he took command of the 36th Mass. in Oct. and the 3d Mass. on 1 Nov. In Dec. '76 he joined Washington's army at Morristown and took part in the battles of Trenton and Princeton. He served in Nixon's Brig. in opposing Burgoyne's Offensive, then became senior officer at Albany and for a time commanded the Northern Dept. "His further promotion was bound up in the jealousies and diplomacies of the Continental Congress," writes Viola F. Barnes in *D.A.B.* He was among those who memorialized Congress in Dec. '82 on the dissatisfactions within the army. He was appointed B.G. on 7 Jan. '83, well after the cessation of hostilities in the North. He retired 3 Nov. and died 16 Dec. '83.

GREEN, John. d. 1793. Cont'l. officer. Va. According to Heitman, John Green was Capt. 1st Va. on 6 Sept. '75, Maj. 13 Aug. '76, wounded at Mamaroneck 21 Oct. '76, Lt. Col. 22 Mar. '77, Col. 10th Va. 26 Jan. '78, and transferred to the 6th Va. on 14 Sept. '78. (Heitman, 58, 260) Ward mentions that Green joined Greene's army with 400 militia in mid-Jan. '81, before the battle of Cowpens, and that he commanded the 4th Va. Cont'ls. at GUILFORD, where his regiment was held out of the main line to cover the withdrawal of the main body. "Under heavy fire Green's regiment stood firm until all the rest of the American [army] had left the field; then it too retired." (*W.O.R.*, 753, 784, 792) Harry Lee tells this story:

"Colonel Green was much dissatisfied with the general's selection of his regiment for this service....

"When it was announced upon the first of the retreat, that the British were close advancing, he became better humored; but soon the pursuit was discontinued, and his sourness returned.

His friends would often console him by stating his selection as an evidence of the confidence reposed in him as a soldier. This would not satisfy the colonel, who never failed to reply that he did not like such sort of distinction; and he hoped the general would, upon the next occasion, attach to some other regiment the honor of covering his retreat. [The general] took the first opportunity of telling the colonel, whom he much esteemed and respected, that he heard he did not relish the post assigned to his regiment the other day. 'No, that I did not,' replied the old colonel. 'Well,' rejoined Greene, 'be patient: you shall have the first blow the next time.' This delighted him, and he always reckoned upon the promised boon with pleasure." (*Memoirs*, 282 n.)

Apparently the old soldier never received his "promised boon." The 4th Va. was commanded by Lt. Col. Richard Campbell at Hobkirk's Hill, the next battle, and Col. John Green is not mentioned again, although Heitman shows him as retaining command of the 6th Va. until 1 Jan. '83, when he retired. (*Op. cit.*, 58, 260)

GREEN DRAGON TAVERN, Boston, Mass. The meeting place of the CAUCUS CLUB and Sons of Liberty, it has been called "Headquarters of the American Revolution."

GREEN MOUNTAIN BOYS. Under the leadership of Ethan ALLEN, whose most famous lieutenants were Ira Allen, Seth WARNER, and Remember Baker, the Green Mountain Boys were organized to defend the claims of settlers in the region that became VERMONT. They figured prominently in the capture of TICONDEROGA, 10 May '75, and during the Revolution were useful in guarding passes through their home country.

GREEN (or Greene's) SPRING, S.C., 1 Aug. '80. A body of 210 mounted Tories under Capt. Dunlap preceded Patrick Ferguson's main column in the advance toward Gilbert Town during the movements that eventually led to the Battle of KINGS MOUNTAIN. Warned of Dunlap's approach, Col. Elijah Clarke's 196 rebels were waiting when the enemy attacked before dawn and in a sharp, 15-minute skirmish the Tories were driven back. Losses were about 15 per cent on each side.

GREEN SPRING (Jamestown Ford), Va., 6 July '81. (VA. MIL. OPNS.) Having failed to catch and destroy Lafayette and being ordered by Clinton to detach reinforcements to N.Y., Cornwallis abandoned his plan of holding Williamsburg and prepared to cross the James River. Lafayette followed cautiously and on 6 July started getting indications that he might catch Cornwallis astride the river.

"Cornwallis had shrewdly conjectured that Lafayette would take the occasion to attack his rear, and when he learned of his approach he did everything to confirm his antagonist in the belief that at that time, the afternoon of the 6th, only his rear remained to cross. Simcoe's Rangers and the baggage alone had passed over." (H. P. Johnston, *Yorktown*, 61)

Anthony Wayne led a 500-man advance guard to keep contact and feel out the situation. When Lafayette joined Wayne about 1 P.M. there were contradictory reports as to whether the British main body was still on the Peninsula or whether only a rear guard remained. Under these circumstances Lafayette ordered the remaining Pa. Cont'ls. and all the light infantry to close upon Wayne's command at Green Spring Plantation. The militia remained 12 miles to the rear. (*Ibid.*, 61)

While waiting for these reinforcements to advance the six miles from Norrell's Mills, Wayne spent most of the afternoon skirmishing with the enemy. Against the delaying tactics of Tarleton's outposts the Va. riflemen of Majs. Richard Call and John Willis (about 200 men), supported by John Mercer, Galvan, and McPherson with their dragoons and light infantry, gained ground steadily. Walter Stewart's Pa. Cont'l. Bn. followed in reserve. From Green Spring Plantation (whose mansion had belonged to Gov. Sir Wm. Berkeley) the Americans had to cross 400 yards of marshy ground to the main Williamsburg-Jamestown road. About a mile along this road the enemy camp, hidden behind some woods, was on the river bank opposite the north end of Jamestown Island. Although the American light forces performed splendidly, shooting down three rear guard commanders in succession, "The striking feature of this preliminary skirmishing was the art practiced by Cornwallis in attempting to draw Wayne and Lafayette to destruction." (*Ibid.*)

By the time the reinforcements reached Green Spring, about 5 P.M., Wayne was close to the main British army, although he apparently thought he had nothing but a rear guard on his hands. Lafayette, however, seems to have suspected that things were not as they appeared, and he held in reserve at Green Spring the veteran light infantry battalions of Francis Barber and Joseph Vose. Across the swamp to support Wayne went the light infantry battalion of Maj. John P. Wyllys and the two remaining Pa. Bns., those of Richard Butler and Richard Humpton. Supported by three guns, these reinforcements brought Wayne's total strength up to about 900 men. (*Ibid.*, 64) When Lafayette rode to a tongue of land on the river bank for a personal reconnaissance to see, if possible, whether the main body of enemy troops was still on his side of the James, he discovered the alarming truth and rushed back to keep Wayne from getting drawn into a general engagement. But it was too late.

Cornwallis could have attacked as early as 4 P.M. and crushed Wayne's advance guard, but he waited until he was sure that enough of Lafayette's corps were on the field to make his blow decisive. While the young Marquis was making his reconnaissance, Maj. Galvan was ordered to lead his 50 or 60 light infantry in an attempt to capture an exposed enemy gun; after a spirited effort he had to fall back on the American left flank. Assured either by this attack or by other evidence that Lafayette's main body was now on the field, Cornwallis sprung the trap. Lt. Col. Yorke's light infantry formed the British right, and the 43d, 76th, and 80th formed the left under Lt. Col. Dundas.

When Wayne suddenly found himself attacked by Cornwallis' entire force he reacted with courage and also with good tactical sense: *he* attacked. In what he called "a choice of difficulties," he realized that under the circumstances an attempted retreat might turn into a panic. An attempted stand against such odds would be disastrous, particularly since the enemy line overlapped both his flanks. Wayne's solution also had the feature of surprise, and it showed an understanding—probably instinctive —of the human factor. There is a chapter of battlefield leadership in this decision.*

"The movement was successful, though costly," says Johnston. Wayne's men charged through grapeshot and musket fire to within 70 yards of the enemy and stopped them in their tracks for 15 minutes. Lafayette took a prominent part in salvaging the situation he had not quite been able to prevent. Retreating rapidly but in good order to the reserve line at Green Spring, the Americans remained there a few hours and then withdrew during the night to Chickahominy Church. Since Cornwallis did not attack until "near sunset," as he reported to Clinton, this left him only an hour of daylight for the entire action, and there was no pursuit.

NUMBERS AND LOSSES

Out of 900 engaged, Wayne lost 28 killed, 99 wounded, and 12 missing. Two guns were lost, one of them a piece captured at Bennington. British losses were 75 killed and wounded. As for numbers, about 7,000 British were on the field, since only Simcoe's Rangers and the baggage had crossed the James, but the Guards, 23d, 33d, and Hessians were in reserve when Cornwallis launched his counterattack and participated little, if at all.

COMMENT

Although clearly defeated, Lafayette handled the action well. "The criticism that he exposed his army to destruction, when so much depended upon keeping it intact, is hardly supported by the

---

* The classic work on "why men fight," or "moral force," which Foch called "the most powerful element in the strength of armies," is *Battle Studies,* by Col. Ardant du Picq (New York: The Macmillan Co., 1921). See also, S. L. A. Marshall, *Men Against Fire* (New York and Washington; Combat Forces Press and William Morrow & Co., 1947)

facts," says Johnston. His dispositions were such that not more than a third of his regulars could have been destroyed even under the worst possible turn of events. As for Earl Cornwallis, after all his skill in luring "the boy" into position for a knockout, he swung just a little bit too late. "One hour more of daylight must have produced the most disastrous conclusions," said Light-Horse Harry Lee. Cornwallis himself said another 30 minutes of daylight would have enabled him to destroy most of Lafayette's force. His military reputation would fare better in India where he was not opposed to such boys as Lafayette and such generals as Mad Anthony Wayne.

GREENE, Christopher. 1737–1781. Cont'l. officer. R.I. A distant kinsman of Nathanael Greene,* he was elected Lt. by the same Kentish Guards who rejected the limping Nathanael. Prior to this time Christopher had been a businessman engaged with his relatives in the operation of forges, anchor works, dams, and sawmills on the south branch of the Pawtuxet River. He also had represented Warwick in the R.I. legislature in 1771 and 1772. He marched with the Kentish Guards on the day of Lexington and Concord. The next month, 3 May '75, he was appointed Maj. of Varnum's R.I. Regt., and shortly thereafter he moved with them to the Boston Siege.

Volunteering for Arnold's March to Quebec (Sept.–Nov. '75), he was commissioned Lt. Col. (date unknown, according to Heitman) and given command of the first battalion. (*D.A.B.*) He was captured during the assault of Quebec, 31 Dec. '75–1 Jan. '76, and

* Both were descended from the founder of the family in America, John Greene, who came to Boston from Salisbury, England, in 1635.

held prisoner until Aug. '77. His promotion to Col., 1st R.I., was dated 27 Feb. '77, but he was given seniority from 1 Jan. '77.

Soon after being given command of strategic Fort Mercer on the Delaware near Philadelphia, he conducted the defense of this place and then supervised its evacuation when it was no longer tenable. (See FORT MERCER [Red Bank, Gloucester co.], N.J., 22 Oct. and 21 Nov. '77.) Congress voted him a sword for his performance. Commanding a newly raised regiment of Negro troops, recruited from slaves freed to serve in the army (*D.A.B.*), he had a prominent and highly commended part in the battle of Rhode Island, 29 Aug. '78. (See this heading in article on NEWPORT, July–Aug. '78.) In both the Fort Mercer and Newport operations he was under the command of his famous kinsman, Gen. Greene. After continuing to serve with Washington's main army, in the spring of 1781 Greene took command of the lines in Westchester co., N.Y. He was killed at CROTON RIVER, 14 May '81, an event that much distressed Washington and the army as they prepared for the Yorktown Campaign. (Freeman, *Washington,* V, 286 n.)

Henry Lee points out that "Greene was murdered in the meridian of life," being only 44. The same author describes him as about 5 feet 10 inches in height, "stout and strong," of a manly but pleasant countenance, and mild in nature. (*Memoirs,* 591)

Writing in 1931, *D.A.B.* says the best life is M. S. Raymond, "Col. Christopher Greene," *Mag. of Hist. with Notes and Queries,* Sept.–Oct. 1916. See also G. S. Greene and Louise B. Clarke, *The Greenes of R.I.* (1903).

GREENE, Nathanael. 1742–1786. Cont'l. general. R.I. The American who emerged from the Revolution with a military reputation second only to Washington's was descended from English immigrants who reached Mass. in 1635 but soon moved to R.I. to escape religious persecution. Greene was a good student, particularly in mathematics. His reading was guided by Ezra Stiles (later president of Yale) and possibly by a Boston book dealer named Henry Knox. After working in his father's iron foundry at Potowomut (Warwick) until 1770, he took charge of the family forge at Coventry. From that year until 1772 and again in 1775 he was a deputy to the Gen. Assy. of R.I. His military career may be considered to date from 30 Sept. '73, the day he was "put from under the care of the [Quaker] meeting" for attending a military parade. (Quoted by Randolph G. Adams in *D.A.B.*) In Oct. '74 he helped raise a militia company called the Kentish Guards, but his fellow soldiers considered his stiff knee a disqualification as an officer. Although touchy about this infirmity, which had been with him since childhood, Greene joined the unit as a private. When the state raised three regiments the next year they considered this hobbling private the best qualified man to lead them, and in May '75 he became a B.G. of militia. On 3 June he reached Long Island at the head of these state troops and his brigade was augmented by several other regiments. On 22 June, shortly before his 34th birthday, he was appointed B.G. of the Cont'l. Army, the "youngest of the first crop of brigadiers." (Peckham, *War for Indep.*, 45–46)

During the Boston Siege the new general showed a talent not only for assembling supplies but also for working harmoniously within an atmosphere of intercolonial jealousy. On 1 Apr. he led his brigades to N.Y. but, unfortunately for the patriot cause, was incapacitated by a fever and relieved as commander on Long Island a week before the Battle of LONG ISLAND, 27 Aug. '76. He was out of action three weeks, but his commission as Maj. Gen. was dated 9 Aug. and on his return to duty he was given command of all patriot forces in N.J. He attacked Staten Island on 12 Oct. but withdrew when he learned that the British had landed the same day at Throg's Neck.

The disaster at FORT WASHINGTON, 16 Nov. '76, was largely his fault. His errors are discussed under that entry.

After the evacuation of Fort Lee, 20 Nov., and the retreat to the Delaware, Greene proved himself a worthy commander in the action at TRENTON, 26 Dec. Following the winter at Morristown, Washington sent him to confer with Congress when that body indicated a growing dissatisfaction with the performance of the army. This and other evidence of Washington's confidence in Greene's judgment led to criticism that Greene was dominating the C. in C. After the preliminary moves of the British in early 1777 (see PHILADELPHIA CAMPAIGN) Greene and Knox were sent to study the terrain of the Highlands when it appeared that the British might launch an offensive in that direction. In connection with the DU COUDRAY affair, Greene joined Knox and Sullivan in a threat to resign if Congress appointed this foreigner over their heads. The politicians resented this "dictation" by army officers, and John Adams advised Greene to apologize. Greene did not take the advice, and Congress worked out a solution acceptable to the generals.

Greene's division made a forced march from Chad's (Chadd's) Ford to help stop the enemy turning movement at BRANDYWINE, 11 Sept. '77. At GERMANTOWN, 4 Oct., he led the largest column. The next month he was ordered to do whatever was possible to hold the Delaware River forts, but the situation was beyond saving. (See PHILADELPHIA CAMPAIGN)

While the army was in winter quarters at Valley Forge it promptly became apparent that Thos. Mifflin had failed miserably as Q.M.G. On 25 Feb. '78 Greene reluctantly accepted the post and on 2 Mar. his appointment was confirmed by Congress. Having insisted that he still be permitted to claim command in the field, he led the right column in the Battle of MONMOUTH, 28 June, and fought at NEWPORT, particularly distinguishing himself in the heavy engagement on 29 Aug. After going to Boston with the delicate mission of helping stop what promised to be a disastrous rupture of Franco-American relations (see NEWPORT, July–Aug. '78), by Oct. he was back in R.I. in his capacity as Q.M.G.

The effects of Greene's good administration were dramatically apparent during the Morristown Winter Quarters, when weather conditions were much worse than they had been at Valley Forge. Operations in the summer of 1780 also showed that Greene's system of field depots and his improvement of the transportation system had greatly increased the army's mobility. (*D.A.B.*) He had an enemy in the man who had failed so miserably at the job, however, and on 27 Mar. '80 Thos. Mifflin and Timothy Pickering presented a plan for reorganizing his department. His methods, if not his results, had given Congress grounds for criticism, and the reorganization plan gathered support. Incensed, Greene demanded a vote of confidence but was refused it by Congress. After they adopted the new plan, on 15 July, Greene announced he would no longer serve as Q.M.G. Con-

gress considered this a second challenge of their authority and after accepting his resignation on 3 Aug., some delegates made an unsuccessful attempt to have him expelled from the army. Greene succeeded Arnold as commander in the Hudson Highlands.

Meanwhile, another bit of Congressional military business had come to grief and Washington was asked to name a commander to salvage the situation in the South. Without hesitation Washington nominated the man some of the delegates had so recently advocated dismissing. On 14 Oct. '80 Washington gave Greene his new appointment and, drawing on his logistical experience, Greene went first to Congress to get from them as much support as they might be capable of furnishing him in his new enterprise.

The SOUTHERN CAMPAIGNS of Greene, Dec. '80–Dec. '81, capped the career of the man who had not qualified to be an officer in the Kentish Guards. Sir George Otto Trevelyan comments that as author of the monumental *History of the British Army* Fortescue "is singularly qualified to form a true estimate of a general's relative rank among generals," and he quotes that writer:

"Greene's reputation stands firmly on his campaign in the Carolinas. . . . His keen insight into the heart of Cornwallis's blunders and his skilfull use of his guerilla troops are the most notable features of his work, and stamp him as a general of patience, resolution, and profound common sense, qualities which go far towards making a great commander. One gift he seems to have lacked, namely, the faculty of [battlefield?] leadership, to which, as well as to bad luck, must be ascribed the fact that he was never victorious in a general [tactical] action. [Yet he never lost a strategic action in the South.]" (Fortescue, *op. cit.,* 403. Trevelyan, *op cit.,* VI, 188 *n.*) *

Turning to a modern American military historian we find this evaluation of Greene by D. S. Freeman:

"Ability and a sense of military values were credited to Greene by all except a few who were enviously irreconcilable; his defects were of his own making—a haste in decision, an overconfidence in his judgment, an insistence that his integrity be acknowledged formally whenever any act of his was criticized." (*Washington,* IV, 367 A.)

We must pause with this reference to Greene's integrity to point out that sufficient suspicion exists as to his wartime speculation for Freeman to present with evident reluctance but as "a historical duty" a four-and-a-half-page appendix on the subject. The complete details are lacking, and Freeman can do no more than conclude by expressing "the hope that a refining of all the facts will show Greene guiltless as an individual of selling himself as Quartermaster General, except, perhaps, in instances that were trivial or, from the

---

* Trevelyan has somewhat distorted Fortescue's evaluation of Greene by omitting the latter's comments on whether being a gentleman—in the older sense of the word—is a military asset. Eliminating the two sentences that express this undemocratic philosophy, Trevelyan picks up the next sentence of Fortescue: "Failing this one small matter Greene, who was a very noble character, seems to me to stand little, if at all, lower than Washington as a general in the field." Fortescue's "one small matter" was that Greene was not a "gentleman" and Washington was, but Trevelyan's editing has made it appear that the "one small matter" was Greene's failure ever to win a battle.

nature of the business, unescapable." (*Ibid.,* V. 509)

Greene left Charleston in Aug. '83 and made a triumphal return to R.I. He went home with serious financial troubles, however. In order to support his army he had pledged much of his personal fortune to indorse the paper of a contractor, John Banks. The latter then went bankrupt, and during the next two years Greene traveled between R.I. and Ga. getting his business straightened out. Having had to sell his property in the North, in 1785 he established a new home on the confiscated estate of Loyalist Lt. Gov. Graham that the state of Ga. had given him near Savannah. The next year, at the age of only 44, he died of sunstroke.

The Greene Papers, not available until after World War I, are in the Clements Collection at the University of Michigan. Other Greene papers are in the Library of Congress, Duke University, the Pa. Hist. Soc., the Huntington Library, Marietta College, the R.I. Hist. Soc., and the American Philosophical Society. The standard biography is George W. Greene's *Life of Nathanael Greene,* 2 vols., New York, 1867–1871. It supersedes those by W. G. Simms (1849) and Wm. Johnson (1822). An older and very inaccurate work is Charles Caldwell, *Memoirs of ... Greene* (1819). Incomplete but nevertheless valuable for its military analysis is F. V. Greene, *General Greene* (1893); I have cited this author's *Revolutionary War* (1911) frequently (see main bibliography). Important essays are by Fletcher Pratt in his *Eleven Generals* (1949) and Theodore Thayer in G. A. Billias (ed.), *Washington's Generals* (1964). The most recent study is Thayer, *Nathanael Greene: Strategist of the Revolution* (1960).

GREEN'S FARMS, Conn., 9 July '79. Looted and burned during CONN. COAST RAID.

GRENADIERS. One of the FLANK COMPANIES of each British regiment was composed of grenadiers. Originally they had been large, powerful men selected from the battalion (regiment) to throw the "hand bombs" introduced during the Thirty Years' War (1618–48). Later they were formed into special companies, and long after their grenade-throwing function had ceased to exist the grenadiers were retained as elite troops. In some cases they were formed into permanent regiments, like the "Grenadier Guards." Grenadier and light infantry companies were usually detached from their regiments for special, particularly important or hazardous, combat missions. While the American army copied the British to the extent of having flank companies in each regiment, they had two light infantry companies but no grenadier companies.

GRENVILLE, George. 1712–1770. British premier. Educated at Eton and Oxford, and called to the bar in 1735, he entered Parliament in 1741. A member of the "Boy Patriot" party that brought about the fall of Robt. Walpole, in Dec. '44 he became a lord of the admiralty. Teaming up with his brother Richard and with his brother-in-law Pitt (later CHATHAM), he pushed himself up the political ladder by rebelling against the authority of Henry Pelham (the P.M.). Under successive PRIME MINISTERS, in June '47 he became a lord of the treasury and in 1754 he became treasurer of the navy and privy councillor. He was in office until Lord BUTE succeeded Pitt in 1761, when Bute entrusted him with leadership in the Commons. In May '62 he became secretary of state, in Oct. he became 1st lord of the admiralty, and in Apr. '63 he rose to 1st lord of the treasury and chancellor of the exchequer. A master of finance and of administration, he also had exceptional knowledge of parliamentary procedures, but "his tact in dealing with men and with affairs was so defective that there is perhaps no one who has been at the head of an English administration to whom a lower place can be assigned as a statesman." (*E.B.*, "Grenville") His administration is remembered for his persecution of John WILKES and for the GRENVILLE ACTS. The latter did much to hasten the American Revolution. Lord BUTE tried to keep his hands on the reins of power by using Grenville as his agent with George III. When Rockingham agreed to accept office Grenville was dismissed in July '65. He died five years later without again holding office. He got his nickname of "gentle shepherd" during the debate on the Cider Bill of 1763; asking Commons over and over "where" he could lay the new tax if not on cider, Pitt brought down the House by whistling the tune "Gentle Shepherd, tell me where." (*Ibid.*)

GRENVILLE ACTS. Under the premiership of George GRENVILLE, who came to power as a master of finance at a time when a statesman was needed, the British passed a number of acts that "led to the first symptoms of alienation between America and the mother country" (*E.B.*, "Grenville"). The principal of these was the STAMP ACT. Others were the CURRENCY ACT and the American Revenue (or Sugar) Act (see under NAVIGATION ACTS). All indicated termination of SALUTARY NEGLECT. Not strictly part of the Grenville program but generally blamed on him was the QUARTERING ACT; this was requested by Gen. Gage.

GREY, Charles ("No-flint"). 1729–1807. British general. An ensign at the age of 19, he became Lt. of the 6th Regt. on 23 Dec. '52 and served with them at Gibraltar. Later promoted to Capt., he raised an independent company which in 1755 became part of the 20th Foot. In the battle of Minden, 1 Aug. '59, he was wounded while serving as A.D.C. to Prince Ferdinand. The next year he was wounded while leading a light company at Campen, 14 Oct. On 21 Jan. '61 be became Lt. Col. commanding the newly raised 98th Foot, which he led in the siege of Belle Isle that year and at the siege of Havana the next year. Retired on half pay in 1763, he became Col. and A.D.C. to the King in 1772. With the "local rank" of Maj. Gen. he went to America with Gen. Howe in 1776. He won his nickname at PAOLI, 21 Sept. '77, in what D.N.B. blandly calls "a success bitterly resented by the Americans," and in a night action the Americans called a massacre. He gave a repeat performance at TAPPAN, 28 Sept. '78. Meanwhile he had led the 3d Brig. at Germantown and conducted raids to BEDFORD, 6 Sept., and MARTHA'S VINEYARD, c. 8 Sept. '78. In this year he was appointed Maj. Gen. and made Col. of the 28th Foot.

He returned to England and in 1782 was promoted to Lt. Gen. Named C. in C. of British forces in America, he did not have time to take up this duty before hostilities ceased, and Carleton took the post. In the war against France he led the expedition to relieve Nieuport in 1793 and then fought in the West Indies. In Nov. '94 he returned to England, became a full general, and was made privy councillor. He retired after commanding the Southern Dist. (Kent, Sussex, Surrey) 1798–99. On 23 May 1801 he became Baron Grey de Howick and in 1806 was advanced to Viscount Howick and Earl Grey. (H. Manners Chichester in D.N.B.)

As for the charges of inhumanity against Grey for his actions at Paoli and Tappan, with the perspective of two centuries it is possible for an American to see through the propaganda and acknowledge that the only legitimate complaint is that Grey was too good when it came to leading a surprise attack.

GRIBEAUVAL, Jean Baptiste de. 1715–1789. French artillery general. A great name in the history of artillery development, Gribeauval figures in the American Revolution because the adoption of his superior system by the French army in 1776 put his country in the position of having vast stocks of perfectly good but outdated matériel to liquidate. TRONSON DE COUDRAY was selected to screen the arsenals for supplies that could be given to Beaumarchais for secret shipment to America.

GRIDLEY, Richard. 1710–1796. 1st American Chief of Engineers. (A.A., 98) Mass. A 4th-generation Bostonian, he was apprenticed to a merchant but developed his talent for mathematics and became a surveyor and civil engineer. He studied under John Henry Bastide, a British military engineer who was planning the fortifications of Boston and vicinity. In 1745 he was commissioned Lt. Col. and Capt. (sic) of the artillery train in the expedition to Louisburg, became chief bombardier during the siege, and supervised the erection of batteries. His "Plan of the City and Fortress of Louisburg . . ." was published in Boston (1746) and London (1758). After more artillery and engineering service during the colonial wars—he built Fort Western (Augusta), Fort Halifax, Fort William Henry, and served under Wolfe at Quebec—he was retired on half pay and granted the

Magdalen Islands in the Gulf of St. Lawrence (with a cod and seal fishery) and was also given 3,000 acres in N.H. He lived for several years on his islands. In 1772 he and Edmund Quincy began smelting iron ore in Sharon, Mass.

When the Revolutionary War started, this distinguished veteran had passed his 65th birthday. In Apr. '75 he was commissioned chief engineer by the Mass. Prov. Cong. and the next month he became Col. of Arty. and Maj. Gen. of state troops. He directed the engineering work at BUNKER HILL and was wounded in the battle. The Cont'l. Cong. commissioned him Col. and Chief of Cont'l. Arty. on 20 Sept., but because of his advanced age he was replaced 17 Nov. '75 by Henry Knox. He remained chief engineer, in the grade of Col., until succeeded 5 Aug. '76 by Rufus Putnam, and thereafter served as "Col. and Engineer" until his retirement from the Cont'l. Army on 1 Jan. '81. (Heitman) His specific assignment from 1 Jan. '77 to 31 Dec. '80 was engineer general of the eastern department, and during 1776 and 1777 he manufactured mortars and howitzers in his furnace at Sharon. (*D.A.B.*) While many officers had a low opinion of his ability, and on 28 Apr. '76—after the main army had left Boston—Washington had written him a strong reprimand about "shameful neglect" of duty, Col. Gridley deserves much credit for successful artillery and engineering work in the Boston Siege. (F. V. Greene, *Rev. War*, 5–7, 18)

His brother Jeremiah (1702–1767) became a lawyer, was appointed attorney general of Mass., and in defending the writs of assistance (1761) became an opponent of a former pupil, James Otis.

GRIFFIN, Cyrus. 1748–1810. Pres. of Cont'l. Cong. Va. He studied law in England and Scotland, and in 1770 eloped with the eldest daughter of the Earl of Traquair. They went to Va. in 1774 where he practiced law. He was not an advocate of rebellion, believing that settlement of the differences between Crown and colonies could be peacefully accomplished. While in London again on business, he sent a "Plan of reconciliation between Great Britain and her Colonies" to the Earl of Dartmouth on 30 Dec. '75. He sat in the Va. Legislature 1777–78 and was sent to the Cont'l. Congress 1778–80. However, the factions in Congress that led to delay and procrastination were distasteful to him, and he welcomed the appointment 28 Apr. '80 as Judge of the Court of Appeals in Cases of Capture. This was, in a modest way, a forerunner of the U.S. Supreme Court and, its business done in 1787, was abolished with provision made for a more comprehensive federal judiciary. He was highly commended by Congress for his work in this and returned to the legislature 1786–87. Sent back to the Cont'l. Congress, he was elected its last president 22 Jan. '88 and served for a year. Griffin returned to the bench, after having been commissioner to the Creek Nation in 1789, and served as Judge of the U.S. District Court of Va. from Dec. '89 until his death 21 years later.

GROTON HEIGHTS, Conn. Site of Ft. Griswold. See NEW LONDON RAID.

GUICHEN, Luc Urbain de Bouëxic, Comte de. 1712–1790. French admiral. Rising slowly in rank after his entry into naval service in 1730, he took command of the frigate *Terpsichore*. (A volunteer aboard was the man later known as Philippe Egalité.) As a Rear Adm. he took part in the battle off Ushant, 27 July '79. In Mar. '80 he led a strong squadron to the West Indies, where he escaped disaster at the hands of Adm. George Rodney off Martinique, 17 Apr., only because the

British admiral's ships were clumsily handled by his captains. Although Guichen scored no victories, he showed skill in handling his fleet against a powerful enemy and kept the British from doing any harm to French island possessions. (David Hannay in *E.B.*) Reaching Brest in Sept. '80, Guichen was selected the next year to convoy supplies and reinforcements back to the West Indies. British Adm. Kempenfelt, sent with an inadequate force to intercept this convoy, struck the transports in the Bay of Biscay, 12 Sept., at a moment when the fog cleared temporarily and showed that the French warships were to leeward. Twenty transports were captured, the rest driven in panic-stricken flight, and Guichen's mission was a complete failure. "As a tactician he had no superior in the French navy," says the American historian Lewis. (*De Grasse,* 83) British historian Hannay says: "The comte de Guichen was, by the testimony of his contemporaries, a most accomplished and high-minded gentleman. It is probable that he had more scientific knowledge than any of his English contemporaries." (*Op. cit.*) But in the tradition of the French navy of his day, he lacked the combative instinct that characterized the most mediocre British admiral.

He was present when Adm. Richard Howe relieved Gibraltar for the final time (1782) and died in 1790 without having another opportunity to show his ability.

GUIDES AND PIONEERS. A Provincial regiment with this designation appears on the Return of Provincial Forces dated 15 Aug. '79. (Van Doren, *Secret History,* 124, citing Clinton Papers) There is reference to 30 men of this organization accompanying Arnold to Va. from N.Y.C. in Dec. '80. (*Ibid.,* 419) Regimental commander was Beverley ROBINSON, who also had raised

and was Col. of the LOYAL AMERICANS. A "corps of guides and pioneers" was normally to be found in all armies of the 18th century and it usually was recruited from local citizens who knew the country in which the army was operating. Writing of his difficulties in filling up Provincial organizations, Clinton says "I was reduced to the necessity of reforming some of these nominal battalions and placing their officers either upon half pay or in a corps of guides and pioneers, which I had instituted principally with a view of affording a maintenance to the most needy." (*Amer-Reb.,* 110. Clinton was speaking of the period of about mid-1778.)

GUILFORD, 2d Earl of. See NORTH, Frederick.

GUILFORD COURTHOUSE, N.C., 15 Mar. '81. The SOUTHERN CAMPAIGNS OF GREENE opened with an unorthodox splitting of American forces; then came Morgan's victory at Cowpens and the race to the Dan. For the ambitious Earl Cornwallis this had been a provocation, a slap in the face, and a frustrated pursuit. When the British dropped back from the Dan, Greene followed to chop up their Tory reinforcements, dance around their flanks, and harass their foraging parties. After three weeks of avoiding a major engagement, Greene took up a position around Guilford C. H. and virtually defied Cornwallis to attack him. The Earl was more than ready, even though badly outnumbered, and the morning of the 15th he started a 12-mile march to the battlefield.

Greene had received reinforcements on 11 Mar. that brought his strength up to 4,300, although about 85 per cent of his troops had never been in action. Cornwallis knew of these reinforcements, and actually thought the American army now numbered up to 10,000 (Cornwallis' report, quoted in Moore, *Diary,* II, 403), but although his own force numbered only 1,900 his men were all veterans, and he did not hesitate. (Further details are given below under "Numbers and Losses.")

AMERICAN DISPOSITIONS

Greene had carefully studied the area six weeks before the battle when he considered making a stand there during his retreat to the Dan. Now he knew exactly what he wanted to do.

The isolated courthouse stood in an extensive clearing on high ground. To the south the ground dropped off for about half a mile into a heavily wooded valley. About a mile south of the courthouse the Salisbury Road emerged from the woods and crossed a cleared area that apparently had been planted in corn the preceding summer. The road continued to cross a small, marshy stream and leave the valley through a defile. (Lee, *Memoirs,* 275, map facing 276; Lossing, II, 607)

Greene set up three lines, as shown in the sketch. The first was manned by the two N.C. militia brigades of Brig.

Gens. John Butler and Pinketham Eaton, which numbered about 500 men each. These were rated the least reliable of Greene's troops. But they were posted behind a zigzag rail fence with a clear, 500-yard field of fire, and if they would only deliver two well-aimed volleys as the enemy advanced they would have made a significant contribution. Capt. Anthony Singleton was in the center of the militia line with two of Greene's four 6-pd. guns. The flanks were strengthened by good infantry troops echeloned forward to deliver enfilade fire across the front, and cavalry units were posted behind each flank. Col. Wm. Washington's Legion was on the west; it comprised his 86 seasoned dragoons, Capt. Robt. Kirkwood's 110 veteran Del. Cont'ls., and Col. Chas. Lynch's 200 Va. riflemen. On the opposite flank, after they completed their delaying action, would be Lee's Legion of 75 horse and 82 infantry, and Col. William Campbell's 200 Va. riflemen. Schematically, it looked like this:

Washington	Butler	Eaton	Lee
(86 Cav.)	(500)	(500)	(75 Cav.)
	XXXXXXX	XXXXXXX	
Lynch (200) X		X (200) Campbell	
Kirkwood (110) X	(FRONT)	X (82) Legion Inf.	

The second line was some 300 yards behind the first, astride the road, and completely in the woods. It was manned by the Va. militia brigades of Brig. Gens. Edw. Stevens and Robt. Lawson, which numbered about 600 each. Although there is disagreement, the best evidence indicates that Stevens was on the right (west) of the line.

The third line was on high ground 550 yards to the right rear of the second. Capt. Samuel Finley's two 6-pdrs. were in the middle, and the brigades of Otho Williams and Isaac Huger were thus:

	HUGER	x	WILLIAMS	
	(778)		(630)	
Green	Hawes		Gunby	Ford
4 Va.	5 Va.		1 Md.*	5 Md.
XXXXX	XXXXX		XXXXX	XXXXX

(FRONT)

Although this deployment bore a superficial resemblance to that employed

*Capt. Peter Jacquett's Del. Co. was part of 1 Md.

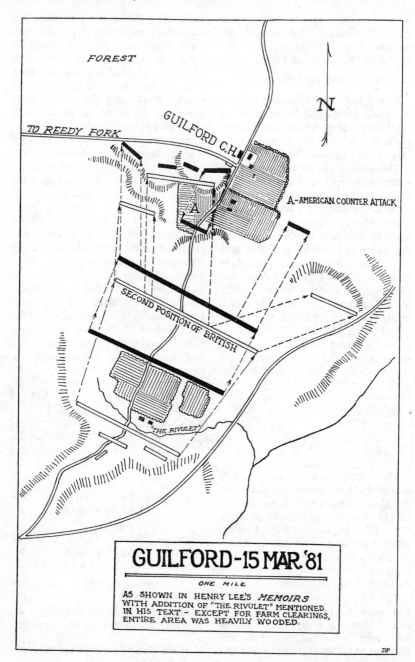

FOREST

TO REEDY FORK

GUILFORD C.H.

A—AMERICAN COUNTER ATTACK

A

SECOND POSITION OF BRITISH

"THE RIVULET"

N

GUILFORD—15 MAR. '81

ONE MILE

AS SHOWN IN HENRY LEE'S *MEMOIRS*
WITH ADDITION OF "THE RIVULET" MENTIONED
IN HIS TEXT – EXCEPT FOR FARM CLEARINGS,
ENTIRE AREA WAS HEAVILY WOODED.

DP

at Cowpens by Morgan (who wrote Greene a letter suggesting the same deployment), the differences were more significant: Greene had no reserve; his three lines were not within supporting distance of each other; and from his command post near the courthouse or from his main battle position Greene could not see the two front lines. On the other hand these weaknesses were pretty much dictated by the terrain —the high ground being the logical place for the main line, the big clearing to the south the logical place for the first line, and the dense woods in between being a good place for the Va. militia. It would appear that he should have been able, however, to set himself up a general reserve, either from the flanking units of his first line, or by eliminating the second line and using these flanking units as a delaying force between the first and last lines.

CORNWALLIS ADVANCES

The clear and chilly dawn of 15 Mar. saw the troops of Cornwallis break camp without breakfast and (about 5 o'clock) start the 12-mile march north from New Garden Meeting House toward Guilford. About an hour after sunrise (about 7:15) Tarleton's advance guard clashed with Lee's Legion and Campbell's Va. riflemen four miles south of Guilford (Lee, *Memoirs,* 274 and *n.*). Both sides claimed the better of this engagement, and Tarleton received the wound that was to cost him two fingers. (Bass, *Green Dragoon,* 170) About noon the British debouched onto the battlefield and started deploying. They knew they had reached the battlefield because Capt. Singleton's 6-pdrs. gave them a salute. Lt. Macleod of the Royal Artillery replied to the honors with the two little 3-pdrs. he was to employ so admirably during the next few hours, and Cornwallis made immediate preparations to attack.

The British commander knew nothing about the terrain; his guides "were extremely inaccurate in their description," and the prisoners taken that morning, "having been several days with the advanced corps, could give me no account of the enemy's order or position." (Cornwallis' report, quoted in Moore, *Diary,* II, 403–4) He was told that the woods on both sides of the clearing were impracticable for cannon, and he could see that the woods to his right (east) were the more open, so he deployed with a view to making his main effort against that side of the American line waiting on the far edge of the clearing. (*Ibid.*) The assault wave was deployed as shown below.

The rest of his forces were in reserve. The 1st Bn. of Guards was behind Leslie and the 2d Bn. of Guards and Grenadiers, all under Brig. Gen. Chas. O'Hara, were behind Webster's wing.*

* The Guards were drawn from the 23d, 33d, and 71st Regts. For this ac-

(FRONT)			
XXXXX	XXXXX	XXXXX	XXXXX
33d Regt.	23d Regt.	71st Regt.	Bose Regt.
	Lt. Col. Webster x	Maj. Gen. Leslie	

A small body of jägers and British light infantry and Tarleton's 155 dragoons were also in reserve.

THE BATTLE

The movement of the 10 British units against three successive lines can be made to look immensely complicated if you try to depict the battle on a single map. But if you consider the battle by the phases into which it can be divided, you will find it relatively easy to follow.

PHASE I: THE N.C. MILITIA FIRES AND GOES HOME

After an ineffectual 20-minute artillery exchange the four regiments of Webster and Leslie started across the 500 yards of open ground. The N.C. militia waited until they were 150 yards away and delivered their first volley. The British came on, stopped to fire one volley, and charged with the bayonet. But they came to a momentary halt when they got about 40 yards from the fence, and Sgt. Lamb of the 23d (Royal Welch Fusileers) tells why:

". . . their whole force had their arms presented and resting on a rail fence. . . . They were taking aim with the nicest precision. . . . At this awful period a general pause took place; both parties surveyed each other for the moment with the most anxious suspense. . . . Colonel Webster rode forward in front of the 23d Regiment and said with more than even his usual commanding voice (which was well known to his brigade), 'Come on, my brave Fuzileers!'

―――――――

tion they were "sorted into two mixed battalions" plus a grenadier and a light infantry company; combined strength of all these units at the start of the action was 481 officers and men (Fortescue, *British Army*, III, 369 *n*., 374 *n*.) The two battalions will hereafter be identified as 1/Gds. and 2/Gds.

This operated like an inspiring voice; they rushed forward amidst the enemy's fire; dreadful was the havoc on both sides. At last the Americans gave way. . . ." (*Journal*, quoted in C. & M., 1164–65)

The flank units held their ground when the militia fled, and Cornwallis had to commit all his infantry reserves to continue the advance to the second line, but we will come to that in a moment. Although there is some debate, recent authorities state that Greene had asked the militia to deliver three rounds before they ran; he gave them permission to leave the field, although some of them did so without firing their three shots. One thing is undebatable: they did not stop to reinforce the second line—"most of them were not again heard of," says F. V. Greene (*Rev. War,* 239). Ward says the militia ran because they had no bayonets with which to meet the attack and that, "After all, they had done everything they had been asked to do, and they had Greene's permission to leave the field." (*Op. cit.,* 788, 919 *n.*) "Light-Horse Harry" Lee had rejoined the main army after being detached for several days and it is obvious from his comments that he did not know Greene had authorized the militia to "desert."

"To our infinite distress and mortification [he says], the North Carolina militia took to flight, a few only of Eaton's brigade excepted [Capt. Forbes's Co.], who clung to the militia under Campbell; which, with the Legion, manfully maintained their ground. Every effort was made by the Generals Butler and Eaton, assisted by Colonel Davie, commissary general, with many of the officers of every grade, to stop this unaccountable panic; for not a man of the corps had been killed, or even wounded. Lieutenant-Colonel Lee joined in the attempt to rally the fugitives, threatening to fall upon them with his cavalry. All was vain; so thoroughly confounded were these unhappy men, that, throwing away arms, knapsacks, and even canteens, they rushed like a torrent headlong through the woods. In the mean time the British right became so injured by the keen and advantageous contest still upheld by Campbell and the Legion, as to render it necessary for Leslie to order into line the support under Lieutenant-Colonel Norton [1/Gds.], a decided proof of the difficult condition to which he must have been soon reduced, had the North Carolina militia done their duty. The chasm in our order of battle, produced by this base desertion, was extremely detrimental in its consequences; for, being seized by Leslie, it threw the corps of Lee out of combination with the army, and also exposed it to destruction." (*Op. cit.*, 277–78)

When the N.C. militia stampeded to the rear the British could not move against the second American line of defense until they dealt with the enemy on their flanks. The Bose regiment therefore wheeled against Lee and Campbell, and the 33d executed a corresponding maneuver on the opposite flank. The Lt. Inf. and jägers also moved onto Webster's left flank. The Grenadiers and the two Guards Bns. advanced to extend the original line and to fill the gaps. The deployment was now as follows:

(O'Hara's Brig. moved into line so as to split Webster's wing; Webster continued the attack initially with the 23d and then, as we shall see, moved over to command the Lt. Inf., and 33d.)

PHASE II: THE VA. MILITIA ARE HAMMERED BACK

Plunging on through woods that Cornwallis says were so thick as to render bayonets useless (Moore, *op. cit.*, 405), the British hit the second line; at the same time their two right flank regiments drove a wedge between this line and the troops of Lee and Campbell. Washington's flank forces, however, fell back to extend the Va. militia line. The second American line was no pushover; the brigades of Stevens and Lawson fought well. But the right brigade was slowly driven back, partly because they were opposed by Lt. Inf. and jägers—who were Cornwallis' best woods fighters. They also came under attack first. Washington's forces counterattacked to relieve pressure, but this brigade was finally split, the flank elements being driven to the rear and the other half of the brigade being bent back almost at a right angle with the other brigade. As mentioned above, accounts disagree as to which brigade was on the west side of the line, but the best evidence seems to be that it was Edward Stevens' (the maps in Ward, C. & M., and F. V. Greene all show Stevens on the west; Lee's *Mem-*

XXX	XXX	XXX	XXX	XXX	XXX
33d	Gren.	2/Gds.	23d	71st	1/Gds.
	(O'HARA)		(LESLIE)		

XXX					XXX
Jägers					Bose
	(WEBSTER)				

XXX					
Lt. Inf.					

oirs, on the other hand, says Lawson was on the west and that his brigade broke first). Stevens had seen the Va. militia run at CAMDEN, and in the interim he had formulated some thoughts on holding them to their duty on this day. Lee says he placed a line of sentinels to their rear "with orders to shoot every man that flinched"; his brigade held until he himself was hit in the thigh with an (enemy) musket ball and he was evacuated. (Lee, *op. cit.,* 277, 278) The rest of the second line fought on, and the two regiments on the British right continued to be occupied with Lee and Campbell, but all these American forces were now being pushed off to the N.E. Only the flankers of Washington's Legion (that is, his dragoons, Kirkwood, and Lynch) fell back to reinforce the third line, and the enemy flankers were on their heels.

PHASE III: WEBSTER ATTACKS THE CONT'L. LINE

Lt. Col. James Webster must have decided that things were getting dull on the front of his "brave Fuzileers" because about the time the three British flank units found that no enemy was left between them and the main American battle position, Webster arrived to lead them against it. As luck would have it, however, they picked the toughest part of Greene's line to hit first—the part defended by the 1st Md., which Fortescue calls "the finest battalion in the American Army." (*Op. cit.,* 371–72). Waiting with this unit was Kirkwood's Del. Co. of whom Ward says, "none could be superior." (*Op. cit.,* 794) And beside them were Finley's guns and Hawes's 5th Va. The Americans watched from good defensive terrain as the gallant Webster formed 200 yards to their front. They waited until he had charged to within 100 feet. Then they delivered a murderous fire and fol-

lowed up with a bayonet attack. Although severely wounded and his command badly chopped up and disorganized, Webster pulled back and got ready to have another go at it.

"Now was the critical moment of the battle," says Ward. Webster's command was stunned and temporarily out of action. The Bose and 1/Gds. were still tied up on Cornwallis' other flank. The four center regiments had not yet finished with the Va. militia. If Greene had counterattacked at this moment with the troops of his third line, using Washington to screen against Webster, he might well have routed the British center. It would have been Cowpens on a grander scale. But Greene had previously decided never to risk destruction of his army, and he used good judgment in letting this tantalizing opportunity pass by. If he had had a general reserve, and if he had been able to observe the entire battlefield and realize the plight of Cornwallis at this moment, the story might have ended differently.

PHASE IV: CORNWALLIS MASSES AGAINST THE THIRD LINE

As resistance slackened in the center, the British started shifting their main effort against the Cont'l line. O'Hara moved over with the 2/Gds. and Grenadiers. Leslie soon detached the 23d and 71st in the same direction. The enterprising Lt. Macleod moved his busy little 3-pdrs. up the road to an elevation from which he could pepper the American left. The situation is indicated schematically on the opposite page.

As the 2/Gds. prepared to attack without waiting for the three other regiments to arrive, Otho Williams, "charmed with the late demeanor of the first regiment [1 Md.], hastened toward the second [5th Md.], expecting a

```
            Huger    x    Williams

         4 Va.   5 Va. │ 1 Md.   5 Md.
         XXXX    XXXX  │ XXXX    XXXX


                                    XXXX
              Lt. Inf. X            2/Gds.
          (WEBSTER)    Jäg. X                ↖ (O'HARA)
          (Reorganizing)      33d X         Gren.

                                      ↖
                                     23d    ↖
                                            71st


                              1/Gds. XX Lawson
                    (LESLIE)         XX Campbell
                              Bose XX Lee
```

similar display. . . ." (Lee, *op. cit.,* 279) Finley had moved his two guns into the threatened wing. But the 5th Md. was virtually a new regiment. "The sight of the scarlet and steel was too much for their nerves," says Ward. "Without firing a shot, they turned and ran." (*Op. cit.,* 791) Lt. Col. Stuart led his Guards into the gap, taking Finley's guns as he went, and was pushing forward when he was hit by two vicious counterattacks: Wm. Washington's dragoons were the first to pass among his startled Guardsmen; then came the 1st Md. and Kirkwood. Stuart was killed, but his men fought valiantly to avoid annihilation. Cornwallis then resorted to the desperate measure of ordering his artillery to fire into the melee. Macleod naturally directed his shots so as to spare his own troops as much as possible, but the normal dispersion of grape shot made it inevitable that the fire would inflict casualties on both sides. Despite protests of the wounded O'Hara, Cornwallis persisted in his decision. The Americans were driven back, but the Guards suffered heavy casualties from the fire. There was a short lull as Cornwallis prepared for his final assault.

Before going on to the final phase I would like to point out a number of details on which accounts of this third phase disagree. Cornwallis makes it clear that only the Guards took part in the attack against Ford's 5th Md. "The 2d battalion of the guards first gained the clear ground," says he in connection with the movement of his regiments from the front of the Va. militia toward the third line. "Glowing with impatience to signalize themselves, they instantly attacked and defeated them, taking two six-pounders, but pursuing into the wood with too much ardor, where thrown into confusion by a heavy fire, and immediately charged and driven back into the field, by Colonel Washington's dragoons. . . ." (Quoted in Moore, *op. cit.,* 405; also in Lee, *Memoirs,* 599) The 2/Gds. later renewed the attack, supported this time by the Grenadiers, which probably is why many accounts make it sound as if the Grenadiers participated in the initial assault. According to Ward, Lt. Col. Howard was leading the 1st Md. and Kirkwood's Del. Co. back to their defensive positions when Stuart's attack took place, and Ward says Howard was therefore forward of the Cont'l. line when he and Kirkwood counterattacked Stuart. (Gunby had been "unhorsed," so Howard had succeeded him for this action.) Lee, on the other hand, disagrees on two points: both the 1st Md. and Kirkwood were back in the line before the counterattack was launched, and Kirkwood did not participate. Since Lee was not present on this portion of the field I have rejected his version of the action in favor of Ward's. Lee also says Webster launched his second attack simultaneously with Stuart's, and that Kirkwood supported Hawes's 5th Va. in repulsing it. This contradicts other accounts, which say Webster attacked later, and I have rejected Lee's version for the same reason as just stated. (There is some question as to what Lee was doing during the battle, and from his actions it appears that he himself did not know.) Cornwallis speaks of Macleod's guns being directed against Washington's dragoons only, and he makes no mention of the infantry counterattack against Stuart; we can assume that this is because the dragoons were the most conspicuous targets, but that the Cont'l. infantry were still in contact with the Guards when the British artillery drove the Americans back into their lines.

FINAL PHASE: CORNWALLIS RENEWS ATTACK—GREENE RETREATS

The final phase of the battle is succinctly reported by Cornwallis as follows:

"The enemy's cavalry was soon re-pulsed by a well-directed fire from two three-pounders just brought up by Lt. McLeod, and by the appearance of the grenadiers of the guards, and of the 71st regiment, which, having been impeded by some deep ravines, were now coming out of the wood on the right of the guards, opposite to the Court House. By the spirited exertions of Brig. Gen. O'Hara, though wounded, the 2d battalion of guards was soon rallied, and, supported by the grenadiers, returned to the charge with the greatest alacrity. The 23d regiment arriving at that instant from our left, and Lt. Col. Tarleton having advanced with part of the cavalry, the enemy were soon put to flight, and the two six-pounders once more fell into our hands; two ammunition wagons, and two other six-pounders.... About this time the 33d regiment and light infantry of the guards [no mention of the jägers!], after overcoming many difficulties, completely routed the corps which was opposed to them, and put an end to the action in this quarter. The 23d and 71st regiments, with part of the cavalry, were ordered to pursue; the remainder of the cavalry was detached with Lt. Col. Tarleton to our right, where a heavy fire still continued, and where his appearance and spirited attack contributed much to a speedy termination of the action. The militia, with which our right had been engaged, dispersed in the woods; the Continentals went off by the Reedy Fork [Road], beyond which it was not in my power to follow them, as their cavalry had suffered but little. Our troops were excessively fatigued by an action which lasted an hour and a half; and our numerous wounded, dispersed over an extensive space of country, required immediate attention." (As quoted in Moore, op. cit., with style retained except for abbreviation of ranks.)

A few comments on this account of

Cornwallis are in order. I have retrogressed slightly to quote Cornwallis' comments on the end of the preceding phase of the action in order to repeat his version of the timing. Some accounts speak of *three* British guns; Cornwallis says two. As for the American artillery, the implication of the above account is that Capt. Singleton had withdrawn his guns safely to the third line; all four were abandoned because their horses had been killed and Greene did not want to risk lives in "drawing them off by hand." (Lee, *op. cit.,* 282) Note also the British commander's comment that the enemy cavalry had "suffered but little," and that the entire action lasted only an hour and a half. As for Webster's "routing" on one flank, and the "heavy fire" on the other flank, we shall see another version in a moment.

After cavalierly dismissing so much of Light-Horse Harry Lee's evidence on events on the front of the Va. and Md. Cont'ls. during the preceding phase of the battle, we can now turn to him for the actions in which he personally participated and on which his facts can be accepted.

"Having seen the flight of the second regiment of Maryland,* preceded by that of the North Carolina militia, the corps of Lee severed from the army, and considering it, if not destroyed, at least thrown out of battle by Leslie's judicious seizure of the interval produced by the panic of the North Carolina militia ... Greene, immutable in the resolution never to risk annihilation of his force, and adverting to his scanty supply of ammunition, ... determined ... to provide for retreat. Colonel Green, one of the bravest of brave sol-

* That is to say, Ford's 5th Md. Some historians, including Fortescue, are tricked by this statement into calling this regiment the 2d Md.

diers, with his [4th] regiment of Virginia, was drawn off without having tasted of battle [which partly explains why Webster's command "completely routed the corps which was opposed to them," as Cornwallis put it], and ordered to a given point in the rear for the security of this movement. [See GREEN, John, for anecdote.]" (Lee, *op. cit.,* 281–82)

As for the action on Henry Lee's front, Light-Horse Harry presents a picture that differs from other accounts:

"At length Lt. Col. Norton, with his battalion of guards [1/Gds.], believing the regiment of Bose adequate to the contest, and close to the great road to which he had been constantly inclining, pressed forward to join the 71st. Relieved from this portion of the enemy, Lt. Col. Lee dispensed with his cavalry, heretofore held in the rear to cover retreat in case of disaster, ordering it to close with the left of the Continental line, and here to act until it should receive further orders. Upon Bose the rifle and the Legion infantry now turned with increased animation, and with confidence of success. Maj. De Buy, of the regiment of Bose, continued to defend himself with obstinacy; but pressed as he was by superior force, he at length gave ground, and fell back into the rear of Norton. Still annoying him with the rifle corps under Campbell, Lee hastened with his [Legion] infantry to rejoin his cavalry upon the flank of the Continentals, the point so long and vainly contended for. In his route, he found the battalion of guards under Norton in possession of the height first occupied by Lawson's brigade of Virginia militia. With this corps, again the Legion infantry renewed action; and supported by the van company of the riflemen, its rear still waiting upon Maj. De Buy, drove it back upon the regiment of Bose. Every obstacle now removed, Lee pressed forward, followed by Campbell, and joined his horse close by Guilford Court-House." (*Ibid.*, 281)

By the time Tarleton arrived to charge the Americans on this flank he "found only a few resolute marksmen in the rear of Campbell," who was moving toward the courthouse, according to Lee. (*Ibid.*, 283) Tarleton's account makes it look as if his attack broke up an organized line rather than running off a rear guard. As soon as he reported to Leslie, says Tarleton, "the Guards and the Hessians were directed to fire a volley upon the largest party of the militia, and, under the cover of the smoke [he] doubled round the right flank of the guards, and charged the Americans with considerable effect." (Quoted in Bass, *Green Dragoon,* 170) Although Tarleton's role at Guilford after his morning clash with Lee's delaying force appears negligible, Cornwallis in his order of the day went out of his way to praise him for "the conduct of the Cavalry, which so greatly contributed to the final success of the glorious day." Aside from the fact that he led the last charge despite a badly wounded right hand (much of which had to be amputated later) and was again wounded, it is hard to find anything remarkable about his performance; this is no reflection on the man: Guilford C. H. was simply not cavalry country, and Cornwallis had held him back. The orderliness of Greene's retreat ruled out successful cavalry pursuit.

THE RETREAT

Greene had made his decision at 3:30 P.M. to retreat. (Ward, *op. cit.,* 792) Moving west, he halted three miles from Guilford to collect stragglers and then marched all night to reach his former camp at the Speedwell Iron Works on Troublesome Creek. Cornwallis camped on the hard-won battle-field until the 18th, when he started his retreat to Wilmington.

NUMBERS AND LOSSES

A few days before the battle, according to Lee, Greene's army numbered 4,449 (rank and file, infantry, dragoons, and artillery) of whom 1,670 were Cont'ls. and the rest militia. Lee says the Cont'ls. lost 14 officers and 312 men killed, wounded, and missing; he has no figures on the number of militia missing, but their killed and wounded amounted to 17 officers and 77 men. (*Op. cit.,* 283 n., 285) Ward puts American losses at 78 killed and 183 wounded, and has no figure on the missing (*op. cit.,* 793).

Cornwallis' numbers are generally put at 1,900 rank and file engaged. Fortescue accepts this figure but points out that Charles STEDMAN quotes the A.G. return as giving 1,445 men exclusive of the cavalry, or 1,600 in all (*op. cit.,* 368 n.). The British lost 532 officers and men, of whom 93 were killed in action; another 50 died of wounds within a few hours. The Guards lost 11 out of 19 officers and 206 out of 462 men; 41 of these officers and men were killed or died of wounds. Among the Guards officers, Webster died of wounds, Stuart was killed, and O'Hara was long disabled. O'Hara's son, an artillery lieutenant, was killed.

COMMENTS

Battle honors for Guilford go to the British. Having been on short rations during their race to the Dan and during the three weeks of vigorous maneuvering that preceded this engagement, they fought the battle of Guilford after a 12-mile approach march on an empty stomach. However unsound Cornwallis' other assumptions, his faith in the superior quality of his troops was certainly borne out by their performance on this day. The historian of the British Army says: "Never perhaps has the prowess of the British soldier been seen to greater advantage than in this obstinate and bloody combat." (*Op. cit.*, 373)

Taken in context with his SOUTHERN CAMPAIGNS since the opening move, Nathanael Greene had now proved himself to be the master of Earl Cornwallis as a general. In doing so he made Cornwallis beat himself with his own strength: the Earl's fine professional background, his aggressiveness, his magnificent subordinate leaders, and his splendid troops. In evaluating Greene's generalship it is only fair to keep this opponent in mind; against another opponent Greene might not have used jujitsu. Comparisons between Cowpens and Guilford keep suggesting themselves. We have already pointed out that Greene can hardly be blamed for failing to take the offensive and destroy the enemy as Morgan did Tarleton (see above). And in discussing COWPENS Fortescue defends Tarleton's impetuosity. With respect to Cornwallis at Guilford this same British military author says this:

"... it is impossible not to admire the nerve of a man who would thus enter the lists, as it were blindfolded, against an enemy of twice his numbers, trusting to his own skill and to the discipline of his troops to tear the bandage from his eyes in sufficient time." (*Op. cit.*, 369)

I might admire his nerve, but I would not want him as an independent theater commander defending any part of my empire. Especially against Nathanael Greene.

"GULPH, The." Now West Conshohocken, Pa., near MATSON'S FORD.

GUN. This word should be restricted to cannon, but in the 18th century as in the 20th it also was used to mean a musket or rifle.

GUNBY, John. Cont'l. officer. Md. Capt. of a Md. Independent Co. on 14 Jan. '76, he became Lt. Col. of the 7th Md. on 10 Dec. and Col. on 17 Apr. '77. Serving in Smallwood's 1st Md. Brig. at Camden, he was not committed in the action. On 1 Jan. '81 he took command of the 1st Md. Cont'ls., which Fortescue calls "the finest battalion in the American Army," and he led them with distinction at GUILFORD, 15 Mar. '81. (Under this entry see "Phase III. ..." and "Phase IV. ...") At HOBKIRK'S HILL, 25 Apr. '81, he commanded the 1st Md. in an unfortunate action that resulted in his being made the scapegoat for Greene's defeat. He served the rest of the war. According to Heitman he commanded the 2d Md. from 1 Jan. '81 to 1 Jan. '83, when he was transferred to the 1st Md., although this does not account for his leading the 1st Md. at Guilford and Hobkirk's Hill. On 30 Sept. '83 he was breveted B.G., and on 15 Dec. '83 he left the army. (*Ibid.*)

GUNDALOW. Sometimes spelled *gundalo* (properly, *gondola*), this was a boat pointed at both ends, usually flat bottomed, and normally rigged with two square sails on a single mast. (Chapelle, 101 ff.) Although very fast in a favoring wind, they were essentially rowboats. Gundalows figured prominently in the CHAMPLAIN SQUADRONS.

GUSTAVUS. Pseudonym used by Arnold in ARNOLD'S TREASON.

GWINNETT, Button. *c.* 1735–1777. Signer. Eng. Well educated, he was a Bristol merchant before emigrating first to Charleston and then to Savannah. He became a general trader in 1756 and bought St. Catherine Island. The island was opposite Sunbury, Ga., which was largely settled by New Englanders, and his contacts there drew him into politics. He held several minor public offices and by 1775 had become a vociferous patriot. As a member of the Ga. council of safety, he was sent on 20 Jan. '76 to the Cont'l. Congress. He arrived in May, signed the Decl. of Indep., and returned to Ga. in Aug. While in Congress, he was proposed as B.G., but the Cont'l. brigade in question was given to Lachlan McINTOSH. Gwinnett, much embittered, then tried fruitlessly for a militia generalship in Ga. He was elected Speaker of the Assembly in Oct. '76 and re-elected to the Cont'l. Cong. During this time he is credited with blocking S.C. efforts to absorb Ga. and with drafting the first state constitution. In March '77, upon the death of the governor, he was appointed to serve out the term as Gov. and C. in C. of Ga. forces. In May '77 he failed to be re-elected. About this time, his plantation was destroyed by the British. In his short term as Gov., he had followed the extreme views of the Sunbury group, thus antagonizing the conservatives. McIntosh was of the latter faction. Gwinnett had arrested McIntosh's brother on suspicion of treason, and the two men had often clashed over the limits of military and civil authority and state control of Cont'l. troops. After the Ga. expedition against British posts in Fla. in the spring of 1777 (see SOUTHERN THEATER), the Assembly investigated its failure and decided that McIntosh, rather than Gwinnett, was to blame. The general then denounced him as a "scoundrel and a lying rascal" before the Assembly. Gwinnett called him out, both men were wounded, and Gwinnett died three days later on 16 May. '77. (Other accounts say the duel took place on this date.)

Of this shadowy figure *D.A.B.* says: "He died insolvent, and it is not known where he was buried; his descendants are apparently extinct; there is no trustworthy portrait of him; but of his thirty-six autographs, one, in 1924, was sold at public auction for $14,000." In 1965 an autograph dealer said the signature would bring $50,000.

GWYNN ISLAND, Va. (Chesapeake Bay), 8–10 July '76. Dunmore's last stand. (VA. MIL. OPNS.) After setting fire to NORFOLK, 1 Jan., the royal governor established a base on Gwynn Island, just south of the mouth of the Rappahannock. The island of 2,000 acres, located about 500 yards from the mainland, was "remarkable for its fertility and beauty" (Lossing, II, 537). With his little fleet and some 500 Tory troops—black and white—Dunmore hoped to maintain a foothold in his province and establish a base from which to raid the neighboring plantations. On 8 July, Gen. Andrew Lewis arrived with a brigade of Va. troops to eliminate this last vestige of royal authority. At 8 A.M. of the 9th, Lewis opened fire at a range of 500 yards with an 18-pd. gun and put three shots into the *Dunmore,* wounding her namesake. The other 18-pdr. and a second battery of lighter guns then bombarded the enemy fleet, camp, and fortifications for an hour. Most of the governor's vessels slipped their cables and tried to escape; some ran aground and were burned by their crews. The guns that did fire back were quickly silenced. When no sign of surrender came from the island the rebel guns resumed their cannonade at noon. Col. McClanahan crossed the next morning with 200 men in boats collected in the neighborhood, and he found a horrible scene that explained why so little resistance had been shown the preceding day. The enemy camp had been ravaged by smallpox: graves dotted the island, and the dead and dying were scattered about in various directions. The rest had fled with Dunmore. (See VA. MIL. OPNS. for their subsequent raid up the Potomac toward Mount Vernon.) The only patriot casualty was Capt.

Dohickey Arundell, who was killed "by the bursting of a mortar of his own invention." (Lossing, *op. cit.,* 538) Loyalist losses are not known but must have been sizable.

H

HABERSHAM, James. 1712–1775. Merchant, planter, colonial official. Ga. At the age of 25 he emigrated from Yorkshire to the newly established (1732) colony of Ga. Arriving with his friend George Whitefield, the evangelist, Habersham opened a school for destitute children, later cooperated with Whitefield in establishing the Bethesda Orphanage (one of the first in America), and was in charge of that institution from 1741 to 1744. In the latter year he resigned and organized Harris & Habersham, the first commercial enterprise in Ga. and for many years the most important. He then developed large farming interests, and took the lead in getting the trustees to consent to the importation of slaves (1749). This saved the economy of the colony, converting its agriculture from grapes and silkworms—for which the climate and soil had proved to be unsuited—and permitting the profitable cultivation of rice and cotton.

Having become the leading merchant, trader, and one of the largest planters, Habersham was prominent in public life. In 1767 he had become president of the Council. A close personal friend and political supporter of royal Gov. James WRIGHT, he helped the latter maintain British authority in the province during the Stamp Act crisis and was acting governor during Wright's

absence in England, 1771–73. Overburdened with work and mentally distressed by the revolutionary trend in Ga., he then went north for a change of climate and died 28 Aug. '75 in New Brunswick, N.J.

Three surviving sons were educated at Princeton. Two of them, John and Joseph, became prominent patriot leaders (see below), and the other was also a patriot. Their mother was Mary Bolton, whose marriage ceremony on 26 Dec. '40 had been performed by Whitefield.

HABERSHAM, John. 1754–1799. Cont'l. officer. Ga. Third surviving son of James HABERSHAM, like his brother Joseph (below) he was educated at Princeton and in England before entering business. (Appleton's) On 7 Jan. '76 he became 1st Lt. in the 1st Ga. Cont'l. Regt., was promoted to Capt. on 8 May '76, became Brig. Maj. to Gen. Robert Howe on 25 Dec. '77, Maj. of the 1st Ga. on 1 Apr. '78, was captured at Savannah, 29 Dec. '78, and was again a prisoner after the battle of Briar Creek, 3 Mar. '79. Exchanged both times, he served to the end of the war. (Heitman) In 1785 he was a delegate to the Cont'l. Cong. (Appleton's; Montross, *Reluctant Rebels,* 426. The latter reference shows only John as a congressman, and *D.A.B.* presumably is incorrect in saying that Joseph was a delegate in 1785–86.) John was respected by the Indians, and Washington appointed him Indian agent. During the 10 years before his early death in 1799 he was collecter of the customs at Savannah.

HABERSHAM, Joseph. 1751–1815. Patriot leader, U.S. Postmaster General (1795–1801). Ga. Second son of the prominent James HABERSHAM, he went to New Jersey at the age of nine to be educated, attended Princeton, but in 1768—partly because of bad health and partly because his father was dissatisfied with his schooling—he was sent to England. After three years with a mercantile firm he returned to Ga. and was set up in business by his father, first with his elder brother James and in 1773 with his kinsman, Joseph Clay.

Although their father was president of the Council and a close friend and supporter of Gov. James Wright, the Habersham boys—all educated at Princeton—were caught up in the revolutionary movement. Joseph emerged as the patriot leader who threw over royal authority in Ga., and it was he who led the expulsion of Gov. WRIGHT. This action is covered under HUTCHINSON'S ISLAND, 7 Mar. '76.

Maj. of the 1st Ga. on 7 Jan. '76, he became Lt. Col. on 5 July and Col. on 17 Sept. '76. He resigned his military commission in the Cont'l. Army on 31 Mar. '78. (Heitman, 29, 265) When the British captured Savannah, 29 Dec. '78, he moved his family to Va., but he himself took part in the disastrous Franco-American attack on Savannah, 9 Oct. '79 (Appleton's).

After the war he was twice speaker of the Gen. Assy. of Ga., and in 1788 was a member of the convention that ratified the Federal Constitution in Ga. Washington appointed him Postmaster General in Feb. '95. He held the post during Washington's second term, and during John Adams' administration. When Jefferson invited him to become Treasurer of the U.S. he considered this as a request for his resignation.as Postmaster, and he left this post in Nov. 1801. Returning to Savannah he resumed his commercial career. "He is said to have raised and exported the first cotton shipped from America." (*D.A.B.*)

The statement that he served in the Cont'l. Cong. (*ibid.*) appears to be incorrect, although his brother John HABERSHAM was a delegate after the war.

HADDREL'S POINT (Charleston Harbor), S.C. Fortified by the rebels prior to the unsuccessful British attack against Charleston in 1776, it was occupied by the British on 25 Apr. '80. It was later used as a camp for prisoners of the American army surrendered by Lincoln on 12 May. It was the site of Ft. Pleasant during the Revolution and is the site of modern Mt. Pleasant.

HALDIMAND, Sir Frederick. 1718–1791. British general. A Swiss who (like Bouquet) may have served in the Sardinian army against the Spanish in Italy, he was Lt. Col. in the Regt. of Swiss Guards in the Dutch service after 1 July 1750. On 4 Jan. '56 he was appointed Lt. Col. of the 62d Royal Americans then being raised in the colonies. He went to America in 1758, distinguished himself at Ticonderoga (8 July '58) and the next year defended Oswego against 4,000 French and Indians. After taking part in Amherst's expedition against Montreal in 1760, he was commandant at Three Rivers until 1766 and British commander in Fla. until 1778. Meanwhile, as a Maj. Gen., he was second-in-command to Gen. Gage and commanded in N.Y. during the latter's temporary absence (1773–75). In Aug. '75 he was called to England allegedly to give information on the state of affairs in the colonies but actually because the London authorities did not want a Swiss officer to succeed Gage in the command of British forces against the Americans. (Alden, *Gage,* 262; *D.N.B.*) On 27 June '78 he was appointed to succeed Carleton as Gov. and C. in C. in Canada, a post he retained until he returned to England in Nov. '84.

In marked contrast to his predecessor, Haldiman's tenure appears to have been harsh and arbitrary. More than one charge of false imprisonment was sustained against him after his recall. Although he never spoke or wrote English well, the Swiss soldier of fortune was an exceptionally good commander in the Colonial Wars preceding the Revolution and in Pontiac's War. It is perhaps fortunate for the Americans that the British relegated him to a minor role after 1775.

HALE, Nathan. 1755–1776. "Martyr Spy," Cont'l. officer. Conn. Son of a successful farmer and patriot, six of whose nine sons took part in the Revolution, Nathan graduated from Yale in 1773. He has been described by a friend as a little above average height, plump, exceptionally agile—there are many stories about his athletic prowess —blue eyed, pious, and "his voice rather sharp or piercing." (*D.A.B.*) After teaching school with great success, he was commissioned Lt. in the 7th Conn. militia on 6 July '75, Capt. on 1 Sept., and on 1 Jan. '76 he became Capt. in the 19th Cont'l. Regt. (Heitman; *D.A.B.* gives 1 July '75 for the date of his first commission.) During this time he had started his service with two months of recruiting duty before taking part in the Boston Siege. Moving with the army to N.Y.C., where he arrived 30 Apr., sometime before 15 May he led a group of seamen from his company in an exploit that captured a supply sloop from

under the guns of the man-of-war *Asia.* Thos. Knowlton selected him to command a company of his rangers. When Washington asked for a Capt. to volunteer from Knowlton's Rangers for an intelligence mission within the enemy lines shortly before the battle of Harlem Heights, Hale stepped forward after the first appeal had brought no volunteers. "I wish to be useful, and every kind of service, necessary to the public good, becomes honorable by being necessary," he explained to a friend who tried to dissuade him. In the guise of a schoolteacher he left the camp at Harlem Heights about 12 Sept., moved to Long Island by a roundabout route, gathered the desired information about enemy dispositions, and was captured the night of 21 Sept. as he approached his own lines. At Howe's headquarters, then located at the Beekman mansion, he allegedly was betrayed by his Tory cousin, Sam'l. Hale, Howe's Deputy Commissioner of Prisoners. Since incriminating papers were found on his person and he was not in uniform, there was no question about his being guilty of spying and, without the formality of a trial, Howe ordered him hanged. While awaiting execution on Sunday, 22 Sept., he occupied the tent of Capt. John Montresor, chief engineer of the British army in America, who treated him with cordiality. Here he wrote to his brother Enoch, and to Knowlton, not knowing that the latter had been killed six days earlier. At the gallows he made a statement that closed with, "I only regret that I have but one life to lose for my country." The phrase undoubtedly was inspired by the lines of Joseph Addison (1672–1719): "What a pity is it/ That we can die but once to save our country!" (*Cato.* Act IV, Scene 4, quoted in Bartlett's). See John ANDRÉ.

HALE, Nathan. d. 1780. Cont'l. officer. N.H. A Capt. of N.H. Minutemen
on 19 Apr. '75, he was a Maj., 3d N.H.,
on 23 Apr. and remained with that unit
when it was redesignated the 2d Cont'l.
Inf. on 1 Jan. '76. On 8 Nov. '76 he
was promoted to Lt. Col. of the 2d
N.H. Line and was made Col. on 2
Apr. '77. He and about 70 of his men
were captured while fleeing from the
battlefield of HUBBARDTON, Vt., 7 July
'77, and Hale died on 23 Sept. '80 while
a prisoner.

HALFWAY SWAMP – SINGLE-
TON'S, S.C., 12–13 Dec. '80. When
Marion learned that the easy-going
Maj. Robert McLeroth with his 64th
Regt. was escorting some 200 recruits
of the 7th Foot from Charleston toward
Winnsboro he assembled 700 mounted
men and moved to intercept this force.
Some 20 miles N.W. of Nelson's Ferry
(Santee R.), just above Halfway
Swamp, Marion made contact. The
British pickets were driven in, their rear
guard attacked, and McLeroth took up
a defensive position. His path now
blocked, McLeroth sent a flag to protest the shooting of pickets and daring
Marion to meet him in the open. The
Swamp Fox replied that so long as the
British burned houses and continued
their raids he would continue to pick
off pickets. As for the fair fight in the
open, Marion sent word that "if Major
McLeroth wishes to see mortal combat
between teams of twenty men picked
by each side, I will gratify him." This
archaic challenge was accepted, a field
was selected, and the fascinating contest was organized. Marion named Maj.
John Vanderhorst team captain and
carefully picked 20 men. The rebels
decided to hold their fire until they
were within 50 yards, one man was
designated to notify Vanderhorst when

the range was right, and Marion's
men, each one eyeing his target, moved
forward. The deadly game was not
played out, however: on orders from
their officers the British team marched
off the field, and it became apparent
that McLeroth had merely been stalling for time.

Capt. James Coffin was moving with
140 mounted men to join McLeroth,
but when he got word of Marion's
presence he declined to come forward
to attack. Around midnight McLeroth
slipped away from his burning campfires and headed toward Singleton's.
Learning of this maneuver, Maj. John
James beat the British to this place,
took position on Singleton's Hill, delivered one volley at the approaching
redcoats and then, to the amazement of
the latter, fled. The rebels had just discovered that the Singleton family was
down with smallpox. Marion withdrew
toward Nelson's Ferry. Coffin joined
McLeroth near Singleton's and on 16
Dec. the British column reached Winnsboro. (Bass, *Swamp Fox*, 107 ff.)

HALIFAX RESOLVES, 12 Apr. '76.
Soon after the patriot victory at MOORES
CREEK BRIDGE on 27 Feb. '76 the 4th
Provincial Congress of North Carolina
met at Halifax and quickly adopted
the set of "resolves" that gave them the
distinction of being the first colony to
come out officially for INDEPENDENCE.

HALL, Lyman. 1724–1790. Signer.
Conn. He graduated from Yale in 1747
and was ordained a minister in 1749 in
Fairfield, Conn. Never popular with his
congregation, he was dismissed two
years later on proved charges of immoral conduct. However his repentance
was accepted as sincere, and for the
next two years he filled vacant pulpits
in the area. Soon, however, he took up
medicine and, abandoning the ministry,
set up practice in Wallingford. Around

1752 he moved to S.C. to join a colony of New England Congregationalists who had settled in the South more than 50 years before. This group then moved, between 1752 and 1756, to Sunbury, St. John's Parish, Ga., and Hall soon became a leader in the area. Georgia was predominantly loyalist and opposed to rebellion. Only the New Englanders were interested in joining with the other colonies in the revolutionary movement, and St. John's Parish held a convention, which failed to produce sympathetic reactions in the other Ga. parishes. Nothing daunted, St. John's elected Hall in March '75 as its delegate to the Cont'l. Cong. He took part in debates but did not vote. When Ga. did join the colonies he was officially sent as state delegate and signed the Decl. of Indep. In 1778 the British swept the Ga. coast, destroying his plantation and Savannah home. He moved his family north, returning at the end of the war to practice medicine in Savannah. Elected Gov. in 1783, he proposed that the state give a grant of land to support an "institution of higher learning," and this led to the chartering of Franklin College, which later became the U. of Ga. After a term in office, Hall moved to Burke co., Ga., where he had a plantation, and died a few months later.

HAMILTON, Alexander. 1757–1804. Cont'l. officer, statesman, economist. B.W.I.–N.Y. Son of a Scottish merchant of St. Christopher, his mother was Rachel Fawcett (Faucette), daughter of a Huguenot physician and planter of Nevis (Leeward Is.). Rachel had been married young to a Danish proprietor on St. Croix and although a divorce was procured in 1759 the court prohibited her remarriage. (*E.B.*) Her union with James Hamilton was socially accepted on Nevis, and Alexander was one of two sons born to

them. Although the legally irregular *ménage* was on an "irreproachable moral foundation," as Allan Nevins puts it (*D.A.B.*), the economic underpinning soon collapsed. Rachel was living apart from Alexander's father and dependent on relatives on St. Croix for support when she died in 1768. His father lived until 1799, but the boy was virtually an orphan at the age of 11. By this time he had received some schooling from his mother, who was well educated, and from a Presbyterian clergyman at St. Croix. He also had learned to speak French fluently. At the age of 12 he went to work as a clerk in the general store of Nicholas Cruger. in Christiansted (St. Croix), and soon showed exceptional intelligence not only in his mercantile duties but also as a writer. He burned for a college education, and in 1772 his aunts raised the money to send him to N.Y.

After some preliminary schooling at Elizabethtown, N.J., he entered King's College (now Columbia) in 1773. "Little weight need be attached to his statement that he temporarily inclined toward the royal side," says Nevins. He attended the mass meeting presided over by Alexander McDOUGALL in the "Fields," and spoke against the British coercion. In a series of anonymous pamphlets he "showed such grasp of the issues, so much knowledge of British and American government" that their authorship was attributed to John Jay. At this time he was only 17, but in his writing and in his conduct he showed moderation and maturity. (*D.A.B.*)

Casting aside his ambitions for formal education, he formed a volunteer company in 1775. After application and examination he was commissioned Capt. of the Provincial Co. of N.Y. Arty. on 14 Mar. '76. (Heitman) The skill with which he commanded his 93 gunners won praise from Greene, who is said to have introduced Hamilton to Washington. Declining an opportunity to join the staff of Gen. Alexander ("Stirling"), he commanded his guns in the Battles of Long Island, helped fortify Harlem Heights, and employed two pieces effectively at WHITE PLAINS. He led his company throughout the N.J. Campaign and saw action at Trenton and Princeton.

On 1 Mar. '77 he became secretary and A.D.C. to Washington, who undoubtedly had been impressed by his reputation as a writer and who badly needed aides with this qualification to assist him with military business that went far beyond the command of his little field army. Having been promoted to Lt. Col. on assuming his new post, Hamilton attained a rank he hardly could have reached as an artillery commander; he was only a few months past his 20th birthday. Although it was hard work at a desk for a man anxious to win military glory in the field, Hamilton was military secretary for almost four and a half years. Allan Nevins writes:

"As secretary and aide, Hamilton held a position of great responsibility, and his duties were by no means confined to giving literary assistance to Washington. He became a trusted adviser.* * * Before he had been at the headquarters a year he had drafted the first of a series of important reports on the defects of the military system and the best mode of improving it. * * *. Meanwhile, he was giving attention not only to the management of the army but to the problem of invigorating the whole government, and in facing this his *flair* for bold political theorizing again awakened." (*D.A.B.*)

Gates tried, with disastrous results to himself, to incriminate Hamilton during the CONWAY CABAL episode. On 14 Dec. '80 Hamilton married Elizabeth Schuyler, thereby connecting himself with one of the wealthiest and most powerful families in N.Y. and, lest his intentions in this matter be considered mercenary, finding great happiness in the match. They had eight children. On 16 Feb. '81 an unpleasant incident occurred that revealed an ugly side of Hamilton's character, although it gave him a pretext to get the field command he had long wanted. During the anxious days when Washington was preparing the Yorktown Campaign he passed Hamilton on the stairs as he was going up and the aide was hurrying down to deliver a paper to Tench Tilghman. The General asked Hamilton to come to his office, and Hamilton answered he would be there as soon as he had seen Tilghman. Either Hamilton was detained or Washington was particularly edgy, but this dialogue ensued:

"Colonel Hamilton, you have kept me waiting at the head of the stairs these ten minutes. I must tell you, sir, you treat me with disrespect."

"I am not conscious of it, sir; but since you have thought it necessary to tell me so, we part."

"Very well, sir," Washington replied —or words to this effect—"if it be your choice."

According to Freeman, from whose account the above is taken, Washington's attempt to reconcile this unpleasantness, through Tilghman, was met with Hamilton's statement that he would continue his duties until a replacement was found. (*Washington,* V, 260) A vacancy did not become available for several months. When the "brilliant and somewhat spoiled aide" angrily turned in his commission Washington and Tilghman prevailed on him to wait until he could be given the command he wanted. (*Ibid.,* V, 284, 310 *n.*) Expansion of the light infantry corps finally made this possible, and on 31

July '81 Hamilton took command of a battalion in Moses Hazen's Brig. of Lafayette's Div. When an attack on the two redoubts at Yorktown was planned, Hamilton claimed the right to lead one of the columns and acquitted himself with great credit. (Under YORKTOWN CAMPAIGN see section headed "Assault of Redoubts 9 and 10.") He was breveted Col. on 30 Sept. '83 and left the service 23 Dec. '83. (Heitman)

After a year in Congress (1782–83) he practiced law in N.Y. In the Annapolis Conv. of 1786 he drafted the report that led to the Constitutional Conv. in 1787, where he became the advocate of strong central government. Working hard for ratification of the Constitution, he wrote more than half of the *Federalist* papers and overcame strong opposition in the N.Y. convention. As 1st Sec. of the Treas., 1789–95, he was the key member of Washington's cabinet, since finances were the most critical problem facing the new nation. In establishing the "Hamiltonian system" he became leader of the Federalists, who advocated strong central (Federal) government. Their opponents, led by Thos. Jefferson, with chief strength in the South and West, took the name Democrat-Republicans, but were more commonly known as REPUBLICANS.

Recent scholarship has shown that in his dealings with Maj. George BECKWITH, Hamilton was guilty of revealing Cabinet secrets, of "gross misrepresentations" in reporting his meetings with Beckwith to Washington and the cabinet, of fabricating stories to discredit the performance of Gouverneur Morris in London, and by "calculated and continuing use of deception" of bringing about the eventual triumph of his own policies while foredooming those of Jefferson to failure. These conclusions are presented by Prof. Julian P. Boyd of Princeton in his *Number 7: Alexander Hamilton's Secret Attempts to Control American Foreign Policy* (1964); they were revealed during the author's preparation of Vol. 17 of his new edition of Jefferson's Papers and are presented in this 166-page monograph. Involved in the dishonorable dealings with Beckwith were Hamilton's father-in-law, Peter Schuyler, and Sen. Wm. Samuel Johnson of Conn. "Number 7" was the code word by which Beckwith identified Hamilton in his reports to Whitehall. There now is more reason than ever to believe that JAY'S TREATY should be called Hamilton's Treaty.

Resigning on 31 Jan. '95, mainly because he could not live on his salary of $3,500 a year, Hamilton resumed his law practice. "Until his death, Hamilton remained out of civil office," writes Allan Nevins. "His best work had all been done; his cruellest errors remained to be committed." (*D.A.B.*) He defended JAY'S TREATY, an unpopular settlement that had been drafted in accordance with the "Hamiltonian system" and perhaps with British collusion. (See above.) Before long, Hamilton was earning $12,000 a year from his law practice, mainly in cases involving commerce and insurance. He continued to advise Washington, and helped write the famous Farewell Address. Southern hostility precluded his considering the presidency for himself, but he was leader of the Federalists in the elections of 1796. In the latter contest he alienated John Adams permanently by urging Federalist electors to cast a unanimous vote for Thos. Pinckney as V.P. Hoping by this strategy that Pinckney would actually end up as Pres. and John Adams as V.P., Hamilton was responsible for excluding Pinckney from either post and having Jefferson elected V.P. Hamilton then attempted to maintain an influence over Timothy Pickering and Oliver Wolcott, secretaries of State and Treasury, and he succeeded until John Adams found out about the strings and angrily reorganized his cabinet. When the war with France threatened to break out in 1798 Hamilton was commissioned Maj. Gen. on 25 July with the post of I.G.; he served until 15 June 1800. In this year his feud with John Adams came to a head, and in what Nevins calls "so palpable a surrender to personal irritation that it was without excuse" Hamilton published an attack on Adams' presidency. Attempting to manipulate the election of 1800 he brought about the defeat of both Federalist candidates, John Adams and C. C. Pinckney. Although he disliked Jefferson more than Adams, he rose above petty motives he had shown thus far and threw his influence in Jefferson's favor when Burr and the latter tied for the presidency. In 1804 he brilliantly fought and defeated the movement to elect Burr Gov. of N.Y.

Although Burr and Hamilton had had friendly personal relations, Hamilton considered Burr a "dangerous man and one who ought not to be trusted with the reins of government." For 15 years Hamilton had opposed Burr's campaigns for election to the U.S. Senate, the presidency, and the governorship of N.Y. Burr now was thirsting for revenge. His excuse came when Dr. C. D. Cooper published a statement that included the reflection on Burr quoted above. After an unsatisfactory exchange of correspondence Burr challenged Hamilton to a duel. On the morning of 11 July 1804 Hamilton was mortally wounded, and the next afternoon he died after excruciating suffering. He was only 47 years old.

Hamilton was 5 feet 7 inches tall, erect, and of slender build. Characteristically Scottish in appearance, he had reddish brown hair, a ruddy complexion, and deep blue eyes. A prodigious worker with great power of concentration, he was an invaluable member of Washington's staff. The greatest portion of the above sketch has been devoted to his performance during the Revolution, although his mark as a founding father was made during his tenure of office in Washington's cabinet.

BIBLIOGRAPHY

Modern biographies are Nathan Schachner, *Alexander Hamilton,* 1946, and Broadus Mitchell, *Alexander Hamilton* (2 vols., 1957, 1962). "Mr. Schachner's biography is well proportioned and solidly researched, using manuscripts to supplement printed sources," comments the Lib. of Cong. *Guide.* "It takes a middle-of-the-road position, and certainly does not gloss over its protagonist's errors of judgment or temper. Professor Mitchell is more enthusiastic. . . ." (p. 353) Another recent study, published too late for inclusion in the Lib. of Cong. *Guide,* is John C. Miller, *Alexander Hamilton* (1959). Strongly partisan biographies were written by Lodge (1882), J. T. Morse (1876), and F. S. Oliver (1906). More impartial ones are by W. G. Sumner (1890), James Schouler (1901), and H. J. Ford (1920). *The Federalist; . . . a collection of essays written in support of the Constitution . . . from the original text of Alexander Hamilton, John Jay [and] James Madison. . . .* was published in the Modern Library series, 1941. The 6-vol. *History of the Republic . . . as Traced in the Writings of Alexander Hamilton* (1857–60), by his son, John Church Hamilton, "is a documentary life on an excessively grand scale." The son also published a 7-vol. edition of the *Works* (1850–51), which is supplemented by 9- and 12-vol. editions by Henry Cabot Lodge in 1885–88 and 1904. Grandson Allan McLane Hamilton's *Intimate Life of Alexander Hamilton,* 1910, contains valuable material not found elsewhere. (*Guide,* 353) The last two volumes of a 9-vol. edition of Hamilton's writings, *The Papers of Alexander Hamilton* edited by Harold C. Syrett, are to be published in 1965. The first seven volumes cover Hamilton's life to 1791. The recent and startling revelations by Prof. Julian P. Boyd in his *Number 7: Alexander Hamilton's Secret Attempts to Control American Foreign Policy,* 1964, are covered above.

HAMILTON, Henry (The "Hair Buyer"). d. 1796. British officer who had served under Amherst at Louisburg, under Wolf at Quebec, and in the West Indies as a Lt. Col., he was Lt. Gov. of Canada and Commandant at Detroit 1775–79. With only a few regulars of the 8th Regt. under his command, Hamilton exploited Indian hostility toward the encroaching American settlers and cultivated such white renegades as Simon GIRTY, Elliott, and McKee. Detroit became headquarters and supply base for the Old Northwest. In June '77 Hamilton received instructions from Germain (through Gov. Carleton) to send Indian raiders under white leaders to attack frontier settlements. Although an attack was made on WHEELING, 1 Sept. '77, Burgoyne's Offensive drew off his Indians, and he was not able to organize these forays until early 1778, when Daniel BOONE was a prize catch. Clark's WESTERN OPERATIONS then disrupted Hamilton's plans, and after leading a remarkable march to retake Vincennes, Hamilton was captured 25 Feb. '79 when Clark surprised him by an even more audacious move. After being kept under close guard for several months in Williamsburg, Va., he was subsequently paroled and sent to N.Y.

Valid doubt exists as to whether Hamilton offered rewards for scalps, but like American, French, and other British authorities before and after him he probably paid for these grim trophies when the savages brought them in. (Ward, *W.O.R.,* 856, 922 *n.;* Wallace, *Appeal,* 201; etc.) Hamilton showed exceptional ability in his difficult assignment at Detroit: he knew how to handle the Indians, and his march to Vincennes would do credit to any military leader. His misfortune was in having Clark as an opponent; the latter was just as good an Indian diplomat and perhaps better in leading men through the ardors of wilderness warfare. What perhaps tipped the balance was Clark's success in winning support of the politically lukewarm French settlers of the Illinois country: whereas Clark gained the support—or, at least, the neutrality —of the *habitants,* Hamilton "alienated the local French by failing to conceal his British contempt for them as a people." (Peckham, *War for Indep.,* 108)

After the war Hamilton was Lt. Gov. of Quebec, 1784–85, and Gov. of Bermuda, 1790–94, and Dominica, 1794–95. Excerpts of his interesting journal are in C. & M. See J. D. Barnhart, *Henry Hamilton and George Rogers Clark* (1951).

HAMMOND'S STORE RAID of Wm. Washington, 27–31 Dec. '80. For lack of a better name, operations from Morgan's camp near Grindall's Shoals on the Pacolet River by Washington's dragoons and mounted militia before the Battle of Cowpens will be sketched under this heading. On 27 Dec. Morgan detached Washington with his 80 dragoons and 200 mounted militia to attack a party of 250 Tories who were ravaging the country along Fairfort Creek (or Fair Forest Creek, between the Pacolet and Enoree). Riding 40 miles on the second day, they found the

Tories near Hammond's Store (around modern Oakland Mill) and, without a loss to themselves, brutally killed or wounded 150 and captured 40. The next day, 29 Dec., Col. Joseph Hayes rode west with 40 dragoons toward Williamson's Plantation, where the Tories held a little stockaded log house called Fort Williams. Late the afternoon of 1 Jan., Cornwallis got the following message from Maj. Archibald McArthur, whose 71st Highlanders were posted at Brierly's Ferry on the Broad River: "General [Robert] Cunningham & his people quitted the fort on Saturday night & mounted for 96 & the Rebels took possession of it ye Sunday morning at eight o'clock" (quoted in Bass, *Green Dragoon*, 142). Sunday was 31 Dec. Ninety-six was only 15 miles S.S.W. of Ft. Williams, and, as Bass says, "There was consternation at British headquarters [at Winnsboro]. . . . McArthur's report crushed all hope for an effective Loyalist militia" (*ibid.*), and Cornwallis could not start his planned winter offensive into N.C. until this threat to his rear was eliminated. He therefore sent Tarleton out to "get Morgan," and this led to the Battle of COWPENS.

HAMPTON, Va., 24–25 Oct. '75. (VA. MIL. OPNS.) The conflict between Gov. Dunmore and the rebels reached the shooting stage when the frustrated royal governor sent naval forces to destroy Norfolk. Capt. Squire brought six tenders into Hampton Creek on 24 Oct., started bombarding the town, and sent landing parties in to apply the torch. Riflemen drove the boats off and killed several seamen. At dawn of the 25th, Col. Wm. Woodford arrived with 100 Culpeper militiamen and deployed to repel an expected renewal of the effort. British ships moved in at sunrise, sprung their cables, and opened fire. Woodford's marksmen then gave the Royal Navy a taste of what Va. squirrels

could have warned them about: Squire's gunners and crewmen started dropping to the decks, and when he ordered a withdrawal his tars were shot out of the rigging and helmsmen driven from their posts. Two sloops got out of control and were captured when they drifted ashore; five vessels were sunk; and one boat was captured with seven sailors aboard. There were no rebel casualties.

HAMPTON, Wade. 1751 or 1752–1835. Planter, politician, soldier. S.C. Born in Va., he probably was descended from a clergyman, Thomas Hampton, who was living in Jamestown in 1630. Wade had been raised on the frontier of the Old Dominion, and when the Revolution started he was living on the Middle Fork of Tyger River (modern Spartanburg co., S.C.). In 1776 he was a Lt. and paymaster of the 1st S.C. Regt., and was promoted to Capt. in 1777 (Heitman). On 21 Sept. '80 he declared himself to be a loyal British subject, but some time prior to 2 Apr. '81 he renounced this allegiance and joined Gen. Thomas Sumter (*D.A.B.*). Commissioned Col. at this time or shortly thereafter, he became one of the Gamecock's most valuable subordinates. He particularly distinguished himself at EUTAW SPRINGS.

After the war he held a number of important political posts, and during the periods 1795–97, 1803–5 served in the House of Representatives. He opposed the Federal Constitution. Although the record indicates that he followed an independent course in politics, he was normally a Republican. On 10 Oct. 1808 he was commissioned Col. of Light Dragoons, and on 15 Feb. 1809 he became a B.G. In the fall of that year he succeeded James Wilkinson as commander in New Orleans. In 1812 he took command at Norfolk, Va., on 2 Mar. '13 he was promoted to Maj. Gen., and in July he was made commander of the forces on Lake Champlain. Wilkinson, for whom Hampton had nothing but contempt, soon became Hampton's senior officer in Mil. Dist. No. 9 and subsequently blamed him for failure of the campaign against Montreal in the fall of 1813. Hampton resigned 16 Mar. '14 but was exonerated by the general public. In accepting his resignation, the War Dept. likewise held him blameless. (*D.A.B.*)

Meanwhile he had laid the foundations of a great fortune. After 1811 he extended his S.C. holdings into the lower Mississippi, where he also was involved in the Yazoo land speculations. When he died in 1835 he was reputed to be the wealthiest planter in America (U. B. Phillips, *Life and Labor in the Old South* [1929], 98–99, cited in *D.A.B.*). His grandson and namesake was the famous Gen. Wade Hampton (1818–1902) of the Civil War.

HANCOCK, John. 1737–1793. Millionaire patriot, Signer. Mass. Son of a minister of Braintree, he was orphaned early in life and adopted by his uncle, Thos. Hancock, the richest merchant in Boston. "He went, of course, to the Boston Latin School and Harvard, graduating in 1754," writes J. T. Adams in an unsympathetic sketch in *D.A.B.* In 1764 he inherited his uncle's business at the age of 27. Four years later the LIBERTY AFFAIR rocketed Hancock into prominence. In 1769 he was elected to the General Court, and the next year he was head of the town committee to investigate—perhaps "exploit" is a better word—the Boston "Massacre." Although he had shown little genius as a merchant (*ibid.*) and was not by nature a leader in any field (*E.B.*), he was recognized by the agitator Sam Adams as a valuable asset, and Adams soon became a determining influence on his life (*D.A.B.*). What Hancock had was money, and he became "immensely

popular with those who did not work with him so closely as to perceive that his mind was of mediocre quality." (*Ibid.*)

He was elected president of the Mass. Prov. Cong. and also was chairman of a committee of safety that had authority to call out the militia. He and Sam Adams were specifically excluded from the 12 June '75 amnesty offer, their offenses, according to this document, being "of too flagitious a nature...." Hancock was a member of the Cont'l. Cong. from 1775 to 1780, and was president from 24 May '75 until 29 Oct. '77. He expected to be named C. in C., and when the delegates quickly killed this hope "he never forgave what he considered this slight to his ability and pretentions." As president of Congress he was the first to sign the Decl. of Indep. After resigning the presidency he soon came to spend much of his time in Boston. In 1778, as Maj. Gen. of militia, he commanded 6,000 Mass. troops in the operations around NEWPORT; his role was minor, as was the quality of his performance. (*Ibid.*)

On 1 Sept. '80 he became the first governor of Mass. At the approach of Shays's Rebellion, in 1785, he resigned after an attack of gout, but he returned to the governorship in 1787 and continued to win re-election until his death. On 23 Nov. '85 Congress had elected Hancock president of that body although he had not appeared as a delegate. He accepted but still did not show up in N.Y.C., where Congress was then sitting, and as a stop-gap measure David Ramsay of S.C. was named "Chairman of Congress." In May or June '86 Hancock resigned—on grounds of ill health—without having served a day of this term. (Montross, *Reluctant Rebels,* 383, 425 *n.*) As president of the state convention to ratify the Federal Constitution in 1788, Hancock withdrew with an attack of gout. When a group of Federalists worked out amendments to break a deadlock in the convention and suggested to Hancock that he present these as his own, Hancock snapped up the proposal, presented the amendments, and gained more local prestige. (*D.A.B.*) Re-elected governor, he was serving his ninth term when he died at the age of 56.

While vain, of mediocre mental capacity, and not a real leader, Hancock had great influence because of his wealth and social position. He was liberal, public spirited, and popular. (*E.B.*)

See Herbert L. Allen, *John Hancock, Patriot in Purple* (1948).

HANCOCK, The. See TRUMBULL–IRIS ENGAGEMENT.

HANCOCK'S BRIDGE, N.J., 21 Mar. '78. After the action at QUINTAIN'S BRIDGE Col. Chas. Mawhood returned to Salem, N.J., and planned an attack on Hancock's Bridge, five miles away, where 200 militia were reported. Simcoe descended the Del. R. with his Rangers in flatboats and the N.J. Vols. and moved up Alloway Cr. to land within striking distance of their objective. The 27th Regt. approached overland. During the stormy night of 20–21 Mar. Simcoe led his men across two miles of marsh to a final assembly area. The operation should have been a great success, but as luck would have it all but 20 of the militia had been withdrawn. After bayoneting two sentries, the attackers charged through the front and back doors of Hancock's house to kill everybody including old Judge Hancock, the owner, and his brother, both of whom were known Loyalists. A seven-man patrol was surprised along the creek and all but one killed. Simcoe plundered the neighborhood, returned to the mouth of Alloway Cr., and sailed to Philadelphia. "The affair," says Lossing, "was unmitigated murder.* * *

The chief perpetrators were unprincipled Tories—the blood-hounds of the Revolution." (II, 346)

HAND, Edward. 1744–1802. Cont'l. general. Ireland–Pa. As surgeon's mate of the 18th Royal Irish Regt. he came to Philadelphia in 1767. Made an ensign in 1772, he went to Ft. Pitt with the regiment, returned to Philadelphia with the unit in 1774, and then resigned to practice medicine. (James H. Peeling in *D.A.B.*) During the Boston Siege he served as Lt. Col. (25 June '75) in Wm. Thompson's Pa. Rifle Bn. Later active in organizing and drilling the Lancaster co. Associators, on 1 Jan. '76 he was assigned to the 1st Cont'l. Inf. On 7 Mar. he was made Col., and on 1 Jan. '77 he assumed command of the 1st Pa. Regt. (Hand actually remained in the same unit as its designation was changed from Thompson's Bn. to 1st Cont'l. to 1st Pa. [Heitman, 48].) On Long Island he was Washington's principal source of information as the British built up strength on Staten Island. His regiment performed well in the events immediately preceding the Battle of LONG ISLAND and was engaged at White Plains. He and his men executed a skillful and well-disciplined delaying action without which Washington's victory at PRINCETON, 3 Jan. '77, would not have been possible. Impressed by the consistently fine conduct of his tough, deadeyed Pa. riflemen, Washington prevailed on Congress to appoint Hand B.G. (1 Apr. '77). Gen. Hand then went to Ft. Pitt with orders to mobilize the militia of western Pa., push into the Indian country, and destroy the British base at Detroit. (Alden, *South,* 281) Unable to get started until Feb. '78, Hand moved with 500 militia toward Sandusky, but snow, rain, and swollen streams stopped him short of his objective. He returned to Salt Lick, in modern Mahoning co.

of eastern Ohio, where he killed and captured a few squaws. His operation was dubbed the "Squaw Campaign." (*Ohio Arch. and Hist. Soc. Pubs.*, VI [1898], 133) Hand did, however, furnish George Rogers Clark "with every necessity I wanted" when Clark left Red Stone in May '78 for his successful WESTERN OPERATION. Criticized for his own failure, Hand resigned in disgust, was succeeded at Ft. Pitt by Lachlan McIntosh, and on 8 Nov. '78 he took over from John Stark as commander at Albany. He arrived just in time for the CHERRY VALLEY MASSACRE and subsequently played a major role in SULLIVAN'S EXPEDITION against the Iroquois, May–Nov. '79. During the SPRINGFIELD, N.J., RAID of Knyphausen in June '80, Gen. Hand led a task force of 500 men, and in Aug. he was given command of a new brigade of light infantry. When Alexander Scammell resigned as Washington's A.G. (16 Nov. '80), Washington selected Hand to succeed him. Although this change was arranged by 23 Jan. '81, Hand did not actually assume his duties until almost two months later. (Freeman, *op. cit.,* 251 *n.;* Heitman gives 8 Jan. as the date Hand became A.G. Cont'l. Army.)

Breveted Maj. Gen. on 30 Sept. '83, he served until 3 Nov. '83 and then returned to his medical practice. Active also in political and civic affairs, he was a congressman in 1748–85, and in 1790 signed the Pa. constitution. He was inspector of revenue 1791–1801. A staunch Federalist, he started having trouble with his accounts early in the Republican administration, and in 1802 a petition was brought into court to sell his lands. He died of an apoplectic stroke in the midst of this trouble. (*D.A.B.*)

"HANG TOGETHER OR HANG SEPARATELY." Slogan coined by Benj. Franklin when he presented his plan of union to the ALBANY CONVENTION (1754). (Somervell, 27)

HANGER, George. 1751?–1824. British officer. Third son of Gabriel, Lord Coleraine, he was a noted hellion at Eton before attending the University of Göttingen. Having learned German, he joined the Prussian Army and "learned cavalry tactics under the eye of the famed General von Luckner." (Bass, *Green Dragoon,* 85–88) On 31 Jan. '71 he was gazetted ensign in the 1st Regt. of Footguards. Five years later he resigned in disgust when a junior officer was promoted over his head. During these years he had found little time for his military duties, having married a gypsy who deserted him for "a bandy-legged tinker," and having fought three duels before his 21st birthday. (*Ibid.*) He bought a captaincy in the Hessian Jäger Corps—being appointed in Feb. '76—and sailed with Knyphausen to America. Named commander of a detachment formed for the Charleston Campaign of 1780, he escaped their fate aboard the ANNA, and as part of Gen. Paterson's column marched from Savannah to Charleston as commander of a Hessian battalion. He personally reconnoitered the defenses of this city and advised Clinton on his plan of attack. (*Ibid.*) Clinton made him A.D.C. and before returning to N.Y. named him second in command to Patrick Ferguson with the mission of raising militia. This duty had little appeal to Hanger, who was now a Bvt. Maj. of militia, and on 6 Aug. '80 he was named commander of Tarleton's cavalry. "Bloody Ban" and George Hanger were dyed in the same vat, and Tarleton had gone to considerable effort to effect this transfer. The garrison brawler temporarily succeeded to command of the British Legion when Tarleton was ill with fever and immediately found the Southern rebels a lot smarter and somewhat tougher than expected. He was surprised at WAHAB'S PLANTATION, N.C., 21 Sept. '80, and won no laurels at CHARLOTTE, N.C., 26 Sept. '80. He was wounded in the latter action. (*D.N.B.*) On 25 Dec. '82 he was appointed Maj. in the regular establishment and the next year was retired on half pay.

"Owing to the embarrassment of his affairs," as *D.N.B.* puts it, he was in the King's Bench prison from 2 June '98 until the next Apr. In 1800 he went into business as a coal merchant. The next year his *Life, Adventures, and Opinions* was published. The barony of Coleraine descended to him in Dec. 1814, but he refused to assume the title. He and Tarleton continued the close friendship started in America, and both of them were boon companions of the profligate Prince of Wales. Hanger's writings included *An Address to the Army in reply to the strictures by Roderick McKenzie . . . on Tarleton's History. . . .* (1789), *The Lives and Adventures and Sharping Tricks of Eminent Gamesters* (1804), and *General Hanger to all Sportsmen. . . .* (1806 and 1814).

HANGING ROCK, S.C., 6 Aug. '80. (CAMDEN CAMPAIGN) For the reasons mentioned under ROCKY MOUNT, 1 Aug., Sumter undertook operations against these two British outposts north of Camden. The enemy force at Hanging Rock * comprised Maj. John Carden's detachment of the Prince of Wales Loyal American Vols., part of the British Legion infantry, Col. Morgan Bryan's N.C. Prov. Regt., and part of Col. Thos. Brown's S.C. Rangers. Although some accounts state that Brit-

---

* The name comes from a huge boulder, 20 or 30 feet in diameter, located on the 100-foot east bank of a creek. The British post was on the west bank. (Lossing, II, 662)

---

ish regulars were in the garrison, all these troops had been withdrawn to Camden, which is one of the reasons Sumter had for attacking the post. (Bass, *Green Dragoon,* 96)

Maj. Davie led a column against Hanging Rock when Sumter attacked Rocky Mount. With his cavalry and some Mecklenburg militia under Col. Higgins, Davie learned during his approach march that three companies of Bryan's Tories had camped in a farmhouse after returning from a foraging expedition; the latter were attacked from two sides and virtually annihilated. Davie captured 60 horses, 100 rifles and muskets, and alerted Carden's main body. (Lossing, *op. cit.,* 662) During the night of 5–6 Aug., Sumter's mounted partisans made a rapid march from Rocky Mount, hitched their horses, and approached the enemy camp in three columns at dawn of the 6th. Because of errors of their guides, all three rebel columns arrived opposite the enemy left, which was defended by Bryan's Tories. The latter were routed by an attack from front and flank and fell back on the Legion infantry and Brown's Rangers, who held the center of the line. While heavy fighting took place in the center, Carden led his regiment from the British right and hit the left flank of the rebel force just as the Legionaries and Rangers retreated. Sumter's men faced this new threat with astonishing steadfastness and delivered a deadly fire that practically annihilated the Prince of Wales Regt. "At that point," says Bass, "Major Carden lost his nerve. He resigned the command of the British to Captain Rousselet," who was the senior captain of the Legion infantry after the death of Capt. Kenneth McCulloch in the fighting that had just taken place. (*Green Dragoon,* 96)

Accounts vary as to the timing of subsequent events. According to Bass,

Capts. Charles Stewart and McDonald appeared unexpectedly on the field at this moment with 40 mounted infantry of the Legion who had been moving toward Camden from Rocky Mount. These reinforcements charged into the thick of the fight and were gaining ground when Maj. Davie's dragoons attacked and drove them to the protection of the Legion infantry. (*Ibid.*) According to Ward, Sumter's men rushed into the abandoned enemy camp after destroying the counterattack by the Prince of Wales Regt. and were plundering the commissary stores when Carden "saw a chance to retrieve his fortunes. A number of his Tories were got together near the center and formed into a hollow square. A larger body was collected in the woods." (*Op. cit.,* 710) Sumter and his officers could rally only about 200 men to join Davie's dragoons and renew the battle, says Ward, and although Davie routed the force in the woods, the hollow square—which was supported by two guns—could not be broken. At this point, according to Ward's account, the Legion dragoons appeared and were driven off by Davie.

Sumter broke off the action about noon. His troops were loaded with plunder and Jamaica rum, but Davie's dragoons herded the stragglers toward the rear of the column and Sumter retreated toward the Waxhaw.

The four-hour action was one of the most hotly contested of the war. The rebels lost 12 killed and 41 wounded. (Lossing, *op. cit.,* 663) The British admitted a loss of 192. (Montross, *op. cit.,* 373)

"HANGMAN, Year of the." To superstitious patriots, particularly in the Cont'l. Cong., the last three digits of 1777 suggested gibbets awaiting them should their cause fail. (Montross, *Reluctant Rebels,* 205)

HANSON, John. 1721–1783. Cont'l. Congress President. Md. He was a member of the Md. House of Delegates almost every year from 1757 to 1779, and was extremely active in events leading to the war. He was a member of the legislative committee that drafted instructions for the Md. delegates to the 1765 Stamp Act Congress. He also signed the nonimportation agreement that Md. adopted 22 June '69 in protest to the Townshend Acts and the Association of Md. in June '74 that approved armed resistance to British troops. Serving as treasurer of Frederick co. in 1775, he was chairman of the committee of observation and was commissioned, about that same time, by the Md. convention to start a gun-lock factory at Frederick. He entered the Cont'l. Congress 14 June '80 and started working immediately for ratification of the Articles of Confed. This was completed 1 March '81, and Hanson was elected President of the Congress of the Confed. 5 Nov. '81, serving a one-year term. He then retired from public life, dying 22 Nov. '83.

HARADEN, Jonathan. 1744–1803. State naval officer and privateer. Mass. Born in Gloucester, he went to Salem as a boy, and in July '76 started his sea service as Lt. on the Mass. navy sloop *Tyrannicide* commanded by John Fiske. After two successful cruises that year, he took command of the vessel in 1777, when she was converted into a brigantine. With Capt. Fiske's *Massachusetts* Haraden's *Tyrannicide* took 25 prizes off France and Spain, including a transport loaded with Hessian troops. Back to Boston in Aug. '77, Haraden sailed again in the fall and was in the West Indies during the winter. In the summer of 1778 he started his career as a privateersman, commanding the *General Pickering* (16). Distinguishing himself as a commerce raider, he was famous for fighting against heavy odds and winning. Off Sandy Hook in Oct. '79 he captured three enemy privateers of 14, 10, and 8 guns in a 90-minute action, and took them all into port. In June '80 he fought the much more powerful British privateer *Achilles* at close range for nearly three hours in the Bay of Biscay; the *Achilles* broke off the engagement and the *Pickering* recaptured her prize, a 22-gun schooner that had been taken a few days before this action. When Rodney captured St. Eustatius, 3 Feb. '81, he set a trap that caught Haraden with all his vessels and prizes. After being released he commanded the *Julius Caesar* (14), another Salem privateer, which started operations in 1782. In June he fought a British ship of 18 guns and 16-gun brig for two and a half hours and escaped. (G. W. Allen in *D.A.B.*) Appleton's says he took nearly 1,000 guns from the British during the war.

He married in 1767, 1782, and 1797, and had two daughters. After the war his health failed and he was reduced to straitened financial circumstances. A few days after his 59th birthday he died at Salem after a long illness. See Allen's *Naval Hist.* and *Mass. Privateers*.

"HARD MONEY." Coin or specie, as opposed to paper money. See CONT'L. CURRENCY and MONEY OF THE 18TH CENTURY.

HARLEM COVE (Manhattanville), N.Y., 16 Nov. '76. In the British attack on FORT WASHINGTON, this date, the column of Lord Percy drove in the American pickets at Harlem Cove before attacking the forces under Lt. Col. Lambert Cadwalader in the old Harlem Heights defenses.

HARLEM HEIGHTS, N.Y. 16 Sept. '76. (N.Y. CAMPAIGN) After KIP'S BAY, 15 Sept., the British established a line from Horn's Hook (East River at mod-

ern 90th St.) across the Bloomingdale district to the Hudson. By evening, Howe's advance posts extended from MCGOWN'S PASS (near N.E. corner of Central Park) southwest to the Hudson in the vicinity of modern 105th St., and—in the opposite direction—a Hessian brigade started south along the Post Road toward N.Y.C. at about 5 P.M. A small detachment landed from the fleet on the southern tip of Manhattan. (Freeman, *Washington,* IV, 194 *n.* and 198 *n.;* Bliven, *Manhattan,* 61) The Americans retreated to the strong natural defensive terrain of Harlem Heights, where work had been started on a three-line defense in depth.

Washington disposed his troops initially as follows: Greene's 3,300 (brigades of Nixon, Sargent, and Beall) were along the southern edge of the plateau, generally between modern Manhattan Ave. and the Hudson, overlooking what is now West 125th St.; Putnam's 2,500 (brigades of James Clinton, Heard, and Douglas) were half a mile to the rear; and Spencer's 4,200 (Fellows, Silliman, Wadsworth, Mifflin) were another half mile to the rear in the first of three fortified lines. This first line contained three small redoubts, and work on a line of connecting trenches was expedited. A second fortified line, about three quarters of a mile to the rear, was to include four redoubts. Still farther north was Ft. Washington. At strategic Kings Bridge, 5,000 American troops were posted.

The morning of 16 Sept. Washington ordered a reconnaissance toward the British lines, about two miles south of his own forward positions. Lt. Col. Thos. Knowlton moved out before dawn on this mission with 150 of his Conn. rangers, crossing a depression known as the Hollow Way (roughly south of today's W. 125th St.) and moving up the densely wooded slopes

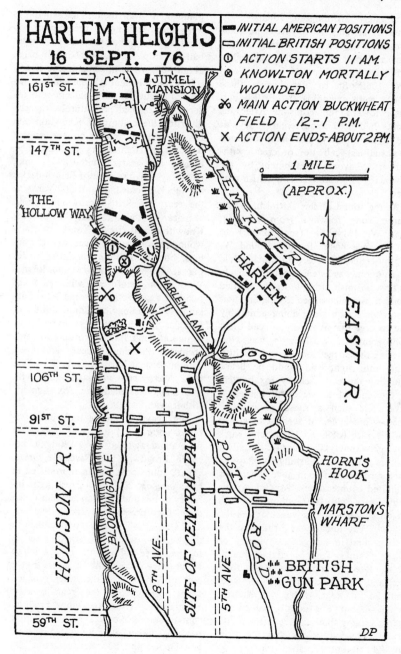

HARLEM HEIGHTS
16 SEPT. '76

▬ INITIAL AMERICAN POSITIONS
▭ INITIAL BRITISH POSITIONS
① ACTION STARTS 11 AM.
⊗ KNOWLTON MORTALLY WOUNDED
✂ MAIN ACTION BUCKWHEAT FIELD 12-1 P.M.
X ACTION ENDS-ABOUT 2 P.M.

0   1 MILE
(APPROX.)

N

161ST ST.

JUMEL MANSION

147TH ST.

THE "HOLLOW WAY"

HARLEM RIVER

HARLEM

EAST R.

HARLEM LANE

106TH ST.

91ST ST.

HUDSON R.

BLOOMINGDALE

8TH AVE.

SITE OF CENTRAL PARK

POST ROAD

5TH AVE.

HORN'S HOOK

MARSTON'S WHARF

BRITISH GUN PARK

59TH ST.

DP

of modern Morningside (then Vande-water's) Heights. At daybreak he made contact with two light infantry battalions and part of the 42d Highlanders ("Black Watch") near Jones's Farm (W. 106th St. at Broadway); these troops were extending the British outposts toward the Hudson. After his scouts had fired about eight volleys at the light infantry and had sustained 10 casualties, Knowlton ordered a withdrawal to avoid envelopment by the advancing Highlanders. The British pursued.

At the sound of this skirmish, Washington rode forward from his Hq. near W. 161st St. (see JUMEL) to the advance posts, located around W. 135th St. Shortly before 9 o'clock, while Washington was listening apprehensively to this skirmish, Joseph Reed returned from a reconnaissance to report that Knowlton's men were doing admirably and to urge that Washington send them reinforcements. Washington was considering this suggestion when the British came into sight and could be heard sounding the call used by fox hunters at the end of a successful chase. "I never felt such a sensation before," Reed wrote later, "it seemed to crown our disgrace [of Long Island and Kip's Bay, presumably]." Although the effect of this taunt on Washington may be only surmised, he soon gave orders for a limited counterattack. Lt. Col. Archibald Crary with 150 volunteers from Nixon's Brig. would advance across the Hollow Way toward the British on the high ground in the general vicinity of where Grant's Tomb is today. Meanwhile, Reed would guide Knowlton's men and three rifle companies of Weedon's 3d Va. Regt., under Maj. Andrew Leitch—about 230 in all—behind the enemy's right flank and cut them off. Crary advanced boldly and the British light infantry rushed forward, as

planned, to meet them. The two forces were soon exchanging fire, but at too great a range to be effective. To further bait the trap, the rest of Nixon's Brig., about 800, was sent to reinforce Crary.

The encirclement started well but was spoiled by unidentified officers who ordered fire opened prematurely, thereby diverting the column of Knowlton and Leitch into an attack on the enemy flank. The Highlanders realized their danger and started withdrawing and, encouraged by the sight of British backs, the rebels pursued. About 200 yards to the rear, the British reformed behind a fence. In the fire fight that ensued, Knowlton and Leitch were mortally wounded within the space of 10 minutes, but the fighting continued under the leadership of their subordinates. Washington reinforced with parts of two Md. regiments and some New Englanders, including the Conn. militia of Douglas who had been so ingloriously routed at Kip's Bay. According to some accounts, Putnam, Greene, and Geo. Clinton rushed into the fray. Two field guns were run forward and with two shots hastened the fox hunters' withdrawal.

The heaviest fighting took place between noon and 1 P.M. in a buckwheat field about at today's W. 120th St. between Broadway and Riverside Drive. (H. P. Johnston's sketch, reproduced in Freeman, *op. cit.*, 199) Fresh light infantry troops and Highlanders reinforced their hard-pressed advance elements, and Gen. Leslie—who commanded in this sector—called for British reserves located three miles to the rear. First to arrive were a company of jägers and a pair of 3-pounders, the latter dragged three miles from the rear by the Highlanders. These two guns fired 60 rounds before shortage of ammunition forced another withdrawal; however, von Donop and Baurmeister credit this reinforcement with saving the light troops from annihilation. (Ward, *op. cit.,* 458 *n.;* Baurmeister, *op. cit.,* 50) Hotly pursued, the British turned for a brief skirmish in an orchard around today's W. 111th St. and made their final stand near Jones's Farm, where the day's action had started. British and Hessian grenadiers and the 33d Foot had now arrived to swell the defenders' ranks to 5,000. Not wanting to bring on a general engagement, Washington sent Tench Tilghman with orders for withdrawal. The action ended about 2 P.M.

This small affair is summarized in Fortescue's 13-volume *History of the British Army* as "sharp skirmishing between the detached parties of the two armies, but with no result. . . ." He goes on to say, however, that Howe spent the next four weeks erecting strong fortifications to cover New York City from the north. (*Op. cit.,* 188–89) Howe's reputation for slowness being what it is, Fortescue can hardly be accused of belittling American achievement by not considering this delay a *result* of the skirmish at Harlem Heights. The Americans did not attempt to elevate their achievement above the level of a successful skirmish, but from private soldier to C. in C. they saw its significance: "This little advantage has inspired our troops prodigiously," wrote Washington, "they find that it only requires resolution and good officers to make an enemy (that they stood in too much dread of) give way" (Letter of 20 Sept. '76 to Schuyler, cited by Freeman, *op. cit.,* 203 *n.*). Some modern historians go so far as to regard Harlem Heights as "a turning point in the uphill progress of their national military efficiency" (Ward, *op. cit.,* 458 *n.,* quoting Trevelyan).

American losses were probably about 30 killed and 100 wounded and missing.

The loss of KNOWLTON and Leitch (who died of wounds) deprived the patriots of two outstanding leaders. Howe reported 92 British casualties (Fortescue, *op. cit.,* 188 *n.*), but the final count—presumably adding German losses—was 14 killed and 154 wounded.

Sources: The above account is from Freeman and Ward, with many supplementary details from Bliven; all three have relied primarily on H. P. Johnston's *Harlem Heights,* which is the basic authority. See main bibliography, and "Notes on Authorities" at the end of N.Y. CAMPAIGN.

HARMAR, Josiah. 1753–1813. Cont'l. officer, Lt. Col. commandant of the U.S. Army, 1784–91. Pa. Born in Philadelphia, he was educated at the Quaker school of Robert Proud. Commissioned Capt. 1st Pa. Bn. on 27 Oct. '75, he was Maj. 3d Pa. 1 Oct. '76, Lt. Col. 6th Pa. 6 June '77, Lt. Col. commanding the 7th Pa. after 9 Aug. '80, transferred to the 3d Pa. in the reorganization of the Pa. Line 17 Jan. '81, Harmar was second in command to Wayne in the Yorktown Campaign. Transferred to the 1st Pa. on 1 Jan. '83, he was promoted to Col. on 30 Sept. '83 and served until 3 Nov.

After abolition and reconstitution of the CONT'L. ARMY, Harmar was recalled and given the title of "Lt.-Col. Commandant of the United States Infantry Regt. and also Commander of the Army." (Heitman) He held this post from 12 Aug. '84 to 29 Sept. '89. The second part of this title was extended for the period 29 Sept. '89 to 4 Mar. '91, and he resigned 1 Jan. '92. Meanwhile he had been breveted B.G. on 31 July '87.

This is the strange "service record" as given by Heitman's *Historical Register.* The "commander of the U.S. Army" during this period had been struggling, meanwhile, with a task for which he had neither the means nor the aptitude, expulsion of intruding Indians from the Ohio territory. "He was brave, but not suited for a commander against Indians, and was not in sympathetic touch with the frontiersmen," says E. K. Alden in *D.A.B.* In 1790 he pushed the Shawnees along the Scioto River and later in the year he left Ft. Washington (Cincinnati) to attack the Indians in the Maumee Valley. "His army, composed of Kentucky and Pennsylvania troops, 1,400 to 1,500 in number, was of poor material, and imperfectly equipped; all but 320 were militia. Bad discipline prevailed, and although the expedition returned to its base, it was in its general results a failure." (*Ibid.*) A court of inquiry cleared Harmar in 1791, and Gen. ST. CLAIR took over to suffer even greater failure against the Indians. From 1793 to 1799 Harmar was state Adj. Gen.

HARPERSFIELD, N.Y., 2 Apr. '80. (BORDER WARFARE) This exposed settlement, 20 miles south of Cherry Valley and 15 miles S.W. of the Lower Fort of Schoharie Valley, was destroyed by Tories and Indians under Brant. Most of the inhabitants had left, but several were killed and Capt. Alexander was captured with 18 others. After overhearing the Indians say they planned to attack Lower Fort if this place was not too strongly held, Harper gave Brant the false information that it was defended by 300 Cont'ls. The raiders therefore called off their planned action in this direction and struck toward Minisink before withdrawing. (Campbell, *Tryon,* 151; Swiggett, *Niagara,* 212)

HARRISON, Benjamin. 1726?–1791. Signer. Va. The fifth of the name in direct line, he came of a wealthy and powerful Va. family. He attended the College of William and Mary before taking charge of the family estate "Berkeley" upon his father's death. He served in the House of Burgesses (1749–75), frequently as speaker. Although strongly in favor of colonial rights in 1764, he did oppose Patrick Henry's 1765 Stamp Act Resolutions as impolitic. However, by 1773 he was a member of the committee of correspondence and completely in favor of rebellion. He was appointed to the first Cont'l. Congress and four times reelected. He was active in all forms of politics that supported the Revolution, signed the Decl. in 1776, and sat on the committees concerned with foreign affairs, war and ordnance, and the navy. Returning to state politics in 1777, he served in the House of Delegates and was speaker 1778–81. He was then Gov. for three years. Going back to the House of Delegates until his death, he was opposed to the Federal Constitution at the 1788 convention but supported it when it had passed that body. Appleton's describes him as being large, fleshy, gouty, and good humored with abundant judgment, honor, and cheerfulness. His youngest son, William Henry, and his great-grandson, Benjamin, were Presidents of the U.S.

HART, John. 1711?–1779. Signer. Conn. His parents moved to Hopewell, N.J., about a year after he was born, and Appleton's says that his father commanded the New Jersey Blues, a volunteer company, in the French-Indian Wars. John became a farmer and the leading man in the community, and served several years (1761–71) in the provincial legislature, where he successfully sponsored road and school improvements. The 1765 Stamp Act aroused his indignation at colonial oppression, and he became active in the events leading to the Revolution. He was judge of the court of common pleas when, 8 Jul. '74, he was sent to the first provincial congress. He served in that body until June '76, when he was sent to the Cont'l. Congress, where he signed the Decl. of Indep. He was on the committee of correspondence and in 1777–78 was chairman of the N.J. council of safety. In Aug. '76 he was elected to the first state assembly and was unanimously chosen speaker. When the British invaded the state they destroyed his farm and livestock. His family fled, and he, aged about 70, hid in the woods for several months to avoid capture. His wife, who also had to hide out, died as a result of this experience. After the battles of Trenton and Princeton he was able to return to his farm. But his health was undermined, and retiring from public life in 1778, he died 11 May '79.

HART, Nancy Morgan. Patriot heroine. Born about 1735 on the frontier of Pa. or N.C., Nancy grew to be about 6 feet tall, very muscular, cross-eyed, vulgar, and illiterate. She married Benj. Hart, a prominent citizen by whom she had eight children. The couple settled first in S.C., about 1771, and then moved to Ga. Half a century after the Revolution her exploits were written up in a Milledgeville paper, but all copies were lost. In the 1830's the legend was recorded again by Elizabeth Ellet, whose sources were old-timers with first- or second-hand knowledge. She was credited with performing several scouting trips and with entering Augusta as a "crazy man" to get information about the enemy. The episode of the six Tories is the best. Correctly assuming that she had aided the escape of a patriot they were pursuing, six Tories from Augusta entered her house and ordered a meal. While they sat drinking she had her 12-year-old daughter, Sukey, run off to warn her husband. Nancy then managed to slip two of

their muskets through a hole in the wall before they saw her with the third one in hand. With this weapon she killed a Tory who rushed her. Sukey returned to pass her mother a second musket, with which she wounded another Tory. While she covered the rest of the party with the third weapon her husband arrived with a posse of neighbors, and the surviving Tories were hanged. E. Merton Coulter, history professor at the Univ. of Ga., suspicious of the myth, found that a railroad excavation through the site of Nancy's cabin years after the Revolution had uncovered six skeletons. (Cook, *W.M.O.M.*, 238–44)

HARTLEY'S REGT. was one of 16 "ADDITIONAL CONT'L. REGTS."

HARVEY, Edward. Acting C. in C. of British Army. When the Marquess of Granby resigned in 1770 the office of C. in C. was not filled. As the highest ranking officer left, Adjutant General Harvey was, in effect, the acting C. in C. Having had little influence with the Cabinet, he is remembered only for his pungent professional comments on their mismanagement. "To attempt to conquer it [America] internally by our land force is as wild an idea as ever controverted common sense," he wrote to Gen. Irwin on 30 June '75, before receiving news of Bunker Hill. The same day he wrote to Gen. Howe, "Unless a settled plan of operations be agreed upon for next spring our army will be destroyed by damned driblets. . . ." Eight days later he wrote to Lt. Col. (Francis?) Smith: "America is an ugly job . . a damned affair indeed." (*C. in C.'s Letter Books,* quoted in Fortescue, *British Army,* III, 167, 169.)

HASLET, John. Cont'l. officer. Del. Born in Ireland, he studied theology before turning to medicine and at the outbreak of the war he was a successful doctor in Kent and Sussex counties,

Del. He also served repeatedly in the state assembly and was Col. of the militia. On 19 Jan. '76 Haslet became Col. of the Del. Regt. This outfit, which was to become one of the best in the army, distinguished itself at LONG ISLAND under Maj. Thos. McDonough. Haslet was absent on court-martial duty, but he led the raid to MAMARONECK and rejoined Washington's main body in time for the battle at WHITE PLAINS, 28 Oct. '76, where the Delawares fought like regulars. Haslet was killed in action at PRINCETON, 3 Jan. '77.

HAUSSEGGER, Nicholas. Cont'l. officer and turncoat. Pa. On 4 Jan. '76 he became a Maj. in the 4th Pa. Bn., and on 17 July was named Col. of the GERMAN REGT. This unit was routed near Trenton on 2 Jan. '77 and Haussegger "surrendered under somewhat suspicious circumstances." (Freeman, *Washington*, IV, 343) (Heitman erroneously gives 4 Jan. as the date of his capture.) He was paroled to his home in Lancaster co. and Washington, who suspected him, had him watched. On 19 Mar. '77 he was "superseded, ... having joined the enemy," according to Heitman. Van Doren, on the other hand, says the British ordered him to return to captivity in Jan. '79. "As Haussegger later joined the British," says this authority, "he may already have offered them his services as a secret assistant to RANKIN. But his mysterious career has left so few records that it seems impossible to do more than make guesses about him." (*Secret History*, 232 and 506 n.) Heitman says he died in July 1786.

HAW RIVER (PYLE'S DEFEAT),* N.C., 25 Feb. '81. (SOUTHERN CAMPAIGNS OF GREENE) Pickens and Henry Lee crossed the Dan on 18 Feb., ahead of Greene's main body, with the mission of breaking up the Tory uprising Cornwallis had called for. After a frustrating failure to surprise Tarleton, and learning that several hundred mounted militia were marching to join the British in Hillsboro, the rebels decided to try a trick. The uniform of Lee's Legion was so similar to that of Tarleton's Legion that Lee would pretend his men were a reinforcement sent to join Tarleton. Two captured officers of the latter's command were placed with Lee's cavalry "to give currency to the deception." (Lee, *Memoirs*, 256) This stratagem started working immediately. Two of Col. John Pyle's 300-or-so Tories rode up, were gulled into thinking Lee was Tarleton, and one was sent back with two rebel dragoons to ask that Pyle pull his troops off to the side of the road so "Tarleton" could lead his "much fatigued troops ... without delay to their night positions." (*Ibid.*, 257) Meanwhile, Pickens' militia, who could be identified by the green twigs in their hats ("insignia" of the Southern militia), were hidden in the woods. Lee says his plan was to get his cavalry among the unsuspecting enemy troops and then give them the alternatives of disbanding or "uniting with the defenders of their common country against the common foe."

Fortunately for Lee's plan, Pyle's mounted men had formed on the right side of the road so that Lee would lead his troopers the length of their front to meet Pyle. Furthermore, they had their rifles and fowling pieces on their shoulders, so the rebel cavalry, with drawn sabers and close to the heads of the enemy's horses, could do a lot of damage before the Tories could recover from their surprise and defend themselves. Here, in the words of Light-Horse Harry Lee, is what happened:

"Lee passed along the line at the head of the column with a smiling

* See ALTAMAHAW FORD.

countenance, dropping, occasionally, expressions complimentary to the good looks and commendable conduct of his loyal friends. At length he reached Colonel Pyle, when the customary civilities were promptly interchanged. Grasping Pyle by the hand, Lee was in the act of consummating his plan, when the enemy's left, discovering Pickens' militia, not sufficiently concealed, began to fire upon the rear of the cavalry commanded by Captain Eggleston. This officer instantly turned upon the foe, as the whole column did immediately afterward. The conflict was quickly decided, and bloody on one side only. Ninety of the royalists were killed, and most of the survivors wounded. Dispersing in every direction, not being pursued, they escaped. During this sudden recounter, in some parts of the line the cry of mercy was heard, coupled with assurance of being our best friends; but no expostulation could be admitted in a conjuncture so critical. Humanity even forbade it, as its first injunction is to take care of your own safety, and our safety was not compatible with that of the supplicants, until disabled to offend. Pyle, falling under many wounds, was left on the field as dying, and yet he survived. We lost not a man, and only one horse." (*Ibid.*, 258)

Lee rebuts Stedman's charge that 200 to 300 Tories were "inhumanely butchered while in the act of begging for mercy" and that it was a "foul massacre." Aside from the fact that Stedman's figures are exaggerated, Lee says the close and instantaneous nature of the conflict made it impossible to kill fewer than 90. "Had the officer or the corps been capable of massacre," says Lee, "it was only necessary to have ordered pursuit, and not a man of the enemy would have escaped." (*Ibid.*, 259 *n.*). Ward comments that Lee's explanation "has too much the air of an

afterthought to palliate a piece of strategy fully matured and intentionally executed, whose outcome shocked its author.* * * The bloody results of the attack are, in themselves, sufficient proof of its relentless ferocity." (*W.O.R.*, 918 *n.*)

Cornwallis fought the battle of Guilford C. H. on 15 Mar. without any Tory troops in his ranks, and the action at Haw River is the main reason why.

HAYNE, Isaac. 1745–1781. Militia officer executed by British. S.C. Remembered primarily as the victim of British injustice, Hayne was a planter and breeder of fine horses before the war. He and William Hill also owned the iron works in York District, S.C., that manufactured ammunition for the Cont'l. forces before their destruction by British and Tory raiders led by Capt. Huck. After serving as a Capt. in the Colleton militia he resigned and reenlisted as a Pvt. when a junior officer was put in command over him. He was captured at Charleston, 12 May '80, having served in the outposts, and was paroled to his farm. Ordered in 1781 to join the British army, he considered his parole invalidated and took the field as a militia Col. In July he captured the turncoat Gen. Andrew Williamson, but he himself was taken in the action that rescued WILLIAMSON. Without a trial, he was condemned to death by a court of inquiry on charges of espionage and treason and was hanged in Charleston, 4 Aug. '81.

The patriot uproar over this act really has not died down yet. There can be no denying that Hayne was condemned without a fair trial, but it has been inaccurately stated or implied that the main charge against him was violation of his parole. British officers blamed for the execution were Lord Rawdon-Hastings and Lt. Col. Nisbet Balfour, commandant in Charleston, whose troops had captured Hayne. Bancroft has charged Rawdon, with attempting to shift blame for the deed on Balfour after the latter's death. (Bancroft, *History*, V, 503) In a letter dated 24 June 1813, which Rawdon wrote to Henry Lee after the latter had sent him a copy of his *Memoirs*, and which is published as an appendix to the later edition of Lee's work, Rawdon includes this statement:

"Shortly after we had withdrawn from Ninety-six and the upper country, Lieutenant-Colonel Balfour wrote to apprise me, that an insurrection had taken place in the rear of my army, but had luckily been crushed. He stated the imperious necessity of repressing the disposition to similar acts of treachery, by making an example of the individual who had planned, as well as headed the revolt, and who had fallen into Lieutenant-Colonel Balfour's hands. He solicited my concurrence ... for the public policy of the measure. On the justice of it, there was not then a conception, that in possibility a question could be raised. I replied that there could be no doubt as to the necessity for making the example, to which I would readily give the sanction of my name.

"Collateral circumstances were then unknown to me. Immediately on my arrival at Charleston, application was made to me by a number of ladies (principally of your party) to save Hayne from the impending infliction. Ignorant of the complicated nature and extent of the crime, I incautiously promised to use my endeavors toward inducing ... Balfour to lenity.* * * As a mode of gaining time, I had solicited ... Balfour to have the particulars of the case ascertained by a court of inquiry for my satisfaction, alleging the chance ... that circumstances might have been distorted by the animosity of Hayne's neighbors. This step, although a court of inquiry was the same form of investigation as had been used in the case of Major André [*touché!*], was an indiscretion on my part; because it afforded a color for perversion, by seeming to imply that there might be a doubt as to the amount of guilt; whereas by all the recognized laws of war, nothing was requisite in the case of Hayne, but to identify his person previous to hanging him on the next tree. * * * He was, from his correspondence with the enemy, while within our posts, a spy in the strictest sense of the word; and to that guilt was added the further crime of his having debauched a portion of our enrolled militia, at the head of which he menaced with death all persons of the vicinage ... and actually devastated the property of those who fled from participation in the revolt." (*Op. cit.,* 616–17)

This is merely a portion of the British side of this controversy (Rawdon's letter runs to almost eight pages of small print), and this portion can be attacked at several obvious points. On the other hand, it refutes a number of charges commonly made against Rawdon and Balfour, including that of Bancroft mentioned above.

The American side of the argument is well represented in the passage of Lee's *Memoirs* that, having painted Hayne as a noble patriot leading a daring militia raid, gives the following summary:

"The proceedings in this case exhibit a prevarication and precipitance, no less disreputable to the authors, than repugnant to the feelings of humanity.* * * Had the discovery of truth and execution of justice been the sole objects in view, those who well knew English law, liberty, and practice, could not have erred. Colonel Hayne was certainly either a prisoner of war, or a

British subject. If the latter, he was amenable to the law, and indisputably entitled to the formalities and the aids of trial; but if the former, he was not responsible to the British government, or its military commander, for his lawful conduct in the exercise of arms. Unhappily for this virtuous man, the royal power was fast declining in the South. The inhabitants were eager to cast off the temporary allegiance of conquest; it was deemed necessary to awe them into submission by some distinguished severity, and Hayne was the selected victim!" (*Op. cit.,* 456–57)

Before cutting poor Col. Hayne down from the gibbet and giving this subject a decent burial, three more points should be mentioned. First, RAWDON was not Balfour's superior; he makes this clear in his letter to Lee. (*Ibid.,* 615) Second, Rawdon was an exhausted, sick man when he got involved in this affair; he was invalided home on 20 July '81, two weeks before Hayne was hanged. Historians tend to ignore such human factors when evaluating the decisions of commanders. Third, by their handling of this case the British authorities made a martyr out of Hayne instead of an "example," thereby defeating the purpose that such a severe act might have accomplished. Greene marched his army out of the High Hills of Santee after issuing a proclamation that "reprisals for all such inhuman insults" would be against "officers of the [British] regular forces, and not the deluded Americans who had joined the royal army." Far from "repressing" the sort of "insurrection" that Hayne had been accused of starting, Balfour had sent Carolinians flocking to the American colors. (*Ibid.,* 458)

HAYS, Mary Ludwig. 1754–1832. Heroine of the MOLLY PITCHER LEGEND. Pa. A stocky, ruddy-faced girl of Palatine German descent, she worked on her father's dairy farm before becoming a servant in Carlisle, Pa. At 16 she married a barber named John Caspar Hays. Five years later she accompanied her husband's regiment, the 1st Pa. Arty., when it marched off to join Washington. During the Monmouth campaign her husband served initially in the infantry, and in the record-breaking heat of 28 June '78 "Molly" brought water to the troops. In the final phase of the action Hays was ordered back to the guns. When he fell wounded she stepped up with a rammer staff to take his place in the crew and keep the gun in action. Hays died shortly after the war, but he left a son by Molly who was an infantry sergeant in the War of 1812.

She married George McCauley, a comrade in arms of her former husband, but a man whom she subsequently left because of his shiftlessness. She supported herself as a laundress and nursemaid, receiving some grants of money but apparently never being able to collect a military pension. In other respects, however, she was an old soldier, smoking a pipe, chewing tobacco, drinking, and cussing like a female trooper.

HAZEN, Moses. 1733–1803. Cont'l. officer. Mass.–Canada. As Lt. of a ranger company he fought at Crown Point (1750), Louisburg (1758), Quebec (1759), and Sillery (1760). During this service he became company commander and won a commendation from Wolfe. In 1771 he was commissioned Lt. in the 44th Foot, and two years later he retired on half pay at St. Johns, Quebec.* Having become engaged in many successful commercial enterprises, he was a wealthy man when the Revolution started. He also found

* He also had a share in his brother's land grants around St. John, New Brunswick.

himself regarded with suspicion by both sides, apparently with good reason: he took Carleton news of Arnold's capture of St. Johns, 17 May '75, but he was imprisoned and his property confiscated by Canadian authorities as well as by Gen. Robt. Montgomery. He then made himself useful to the Americans during their Canada Invasion and joined Montgomery's forces for the operations around Quebec and Montreal. During the retreat he clashed with Benedict Arnold and was charged with insubordination, but a court-martial acquitted him. Congress recompensed him for property destroyed by the British and on 22 Jan. '76 commissioned him Col. of the 2d Canadian Regt. This unit, known as "Congress's Own" and also as "Hazen's Own," was recruited from Albany and composed of Canadians, including refugees. The regiment fought at Long Island, Brandywine, and Germantown.

An advocate of further operations into Canada, Hazen was engaged in planning and gathering supplies for the proposed Canada Invasion of 1778. After this misguided scheme was abandoned Hazen proposed that a military road be constructed to the Canadian border, and in the summer of 1779 he was back in the North working on this project. Recalled to N.J., he tried unsuccessfully to have Congress pay his regiment; the answer was simply "no funds." He also ran afoul of Steuben's regulations, was arrested by the I.G. for halting on a march (Freeman, *Washington,* V, 185 *n.*), but again was acquitted by a court-martial (*D.A.B.*). On 29 June '81 he was breveted B.G. and on 27 Sept. took command of a brigade in Lafayette's Lt. Inf. Div. just before the allied armies closed in on Yorktown. Edward Antill succeeded to command of "Hazen's Own," which was part of Hazen's new brigade. (In the

fall of 1778 this regiment had absorbed fragments of the 16 "Additional Regiments" and of the German Regt. [Freeman, *op. cit.,* 230 *n.*].) Having charge of prisoners at Lancaster, Pa., in 1782, he precipitated an embarrassing dilemma for Washington in the Huddy–Asgill Affair.

Retiring 1 Jan. 83, Hazen settled on land he had bought in Vt. during the war.

HEATH, William. 1737–1814. Cont'l. general. From Roxbury (near Boston), in the fifth generation of his family to occupy land settled in 1636, Heath was a farmer, militiaman, and politician before the Revolution. He represented Roxbury in the Mass. Gen. Court in 1761 and again from 1771 until its dissolution by Gen. Gage in '74. Then he became a member of the Prov. Cong. of Mass. and of the Comm. of Safety. (Heath, *Memoirs,* 15) He describes himself candidly as "of middling stature, light complexion, very corpulent, and bald-headed. . . ." (*Ibid.*) Interested in soldiering from an early age, he read every military work he could get his hands on. During the French and Indian War he was in a militia company but saw no action. He joined Boston's Ancient and Honorable Artillery Company in 1765, became Capt. of a Suffolk co. company, and as war approached he was active in arousing the militia. On 9 Feb. '75 he was appointed B.G. by the Mass. Prov. Cong. The first American general on the scene as the British retreated to Boston from Lexington and Concord, he ordered the initial dispositions for what became the Boston Siege. Promoted to Maj. Gen. of Mass. troops on 20 June, he was appointed Cont'l. B.G. two days later. On 13 Mar. '76 he led the first detachment of troops from the Boston lines to N.Y., and became Putnam's second in command when the latter arrived on 3 Apr. "Our General," as Heath calls himself in his *Memoirs,* was elevated to two-star rank on 9 Aug. '76 and a month later was one of the three who voted to defend N.Y.C. (See Joseph SPENCER) Washington was quick to recognize Heath's limitations and during the N.Y. and N.J. Campaigns posted him at places where no major threat was expected. (Freeman, *Washington,* III, 489; IV, 216, 367) (See also SPENCER for an evaluation of both generals.) On 12 Nov. Heath was placed in command of troops defending the Hudson Highlands. His one chance for distinction as a field commander resulted in the mismanaged diversion against FORT INDEPENDENCE, N.Y., 17–18 Jan. '77. Of this fiasco Timothy Pickering wrote, "[Heath] has, in the estimation of every discerning man, acquired nought but disgrace." Washington wrote him, "your conduct is censured . . . as being fraught with too much caution by which the Army has been disappointed, and in some degree disgraced." (Quoted in Freeman, *op. cit.,* IV, 384 *n.*)

On 11 Feb. '77 Heath left Peekskill for a short leave. He reached Roxbury on the 19th and on 14 Mar. had started back toward his headquarters when he received orders to succeed Artemas Ward as commander of the Eastern Dept. (Heath, *op. cit.,* 126) Highlight of this tour of duty was his temporary custody of Burgoyne and the Convention Army. He remained in Boston until 11 June '79, when he left to join the main army on the Hudson. On the 23d he took command of troops on the east side of the river, the advance posts of which were then at Peekskill. He remained in the Highlands the rest of the war except for the period 16 June–1 Oct. '80 when he was in Providence to handle the reception of Rochambeau's expedition.

On 1 July '83 he returned to his farm at Roxbury and the pursuit of occupations for which he was better suited than war. He was on the state convention that ratified the Constitution in 1791, and the next year became state senator and probate judge. In 1806 he was elected Lt. Gov. but declined. (*D.A.B.*) William Heath was the last surviving Maj. Gen. of the Revolution when he died in the house where he had been born.*

HEISTER, Leopold Philip von (or de). 1707–1777. Hessian C. in C. Described as "a crippled veteran of many campaigns when he was selected to command the Hessian troops" (Appleton's), he led the first contingent of German mercenaries to America. With 7,800 mercenaries and 1,000 British Guards he sailed from Spithead in late May '76, touched at Halifax to find that Howe had left for N.Y., and early in July he joined the British on Staten Island. Heister commanded the center of the British line in the battle of LONG ISLAND, personally receiving the sword of Gen. Alexander ("Lord Stirling"). He led the Germans in the action at WHITE PLAINS, N.Y., 28 Oct. '76. Disagreements with Gen. Howe and the German defeat at Trenton, 26 Dec. '76, led to Heister's recall in 1777; he was succeeded by Knyphausen. On 19 Nov. '77 he died "of grief and disappointment" because of Trenton. (Quoted in Tharpe, *Baroness,* 403) See "DORMANT COMMISSION."

HENDERSON, Gustavus. See ROSENTHAL.

HENLEY'S REGT. was one of 16 "ADDITIONAL CONT'L. REGTS."

---

* The house was destroyed in 1843. An editor's note to the 1904 edition of Heath's *Memoirs* says the site is at the E. corner of Heath St. and Bickford Ave.

HENRY, John Joseph. 1758–1811. Jurist, author. Pa. See bibliography.

HENRY, Patrick. 1736–1799. Revolutionary orator and statesman. Va. Born in the frontier region of Hanover co. a few years after his father had emigrated there from Aberdeen, Scotland, Patrick was reared in a home noted for culture and social grace, despite its distance from the tidewater aristocrats. From his father, a sturdy Scot of good character, good education, and moderate finances, Patrick learned enough Latin to read with ease the great classics. With his mother, a woman of marked abilities and social charm, he often listened to the magnificent sermons of Sam'l. Davis; this famous preacher undoubtedly aroused the orator in young Henry. At the age of 15 he became a clerk in a crossroads store, at 16 he and his brother William opened their own store, at 18 he married and started farming, at 21 he lost his house and furniture in a fire and returned to store-keeping, at 23 he was hopelessly in debt and faced with ruin. With three or four children to feed, Henry now turned to law. In the spring of 1760 he obtained a license, and during the next three years he won most of his 1,185 suits.

His sparkling performance in the PARSON'S CAUSE, 1763, established his reputation throughout Va. Two years later he became a member of the House of Burgesses and emerged as champion of the frontier and backwater elements. In reaction to the Stamp Act he proposed seven resolutions, the last of which claimed that Va. enjoyed complete legislative autonomy. He pressed his resolutions in a speech closing with the famous lines: "Caesar had his Brutus—Charles the first, his Cromwell—and George the third—may profit by their example. . . . If *this* be treason, make the most of it." All Henry's resolutions were enthusiastically passed by the committee of the whole house, but the next day (30 May '65) the older leaders succeeded in defeating two of them in the full house. Henry's entire list was, however, rushed off in its unrevised form to other colonies, "and became the basis of violent agitation from Boston to Charleston," writes W. E. Dodd in *D.A.B.* Not yet 30, Henry had become a major political figure in the colonies, and for the next five years he dominated public life of the Old Dominion.

Under his leadership the legislators met at Raleigh Tavern on 27 May '74 after Dunmore dissolved the Assembly. On 23 Mar. '75 he urged armed resistance in a speech that declared: "Give me liberty, or give me death!" He had been a delegate to the 1st Cont'l. Cong. and was preparing to attend the second when he learned that Dunmore had seized the ammunition in the arsenal at Williamsburg. On 2 May '75 Henry marched on Williamsburg with the militia of Hanover County, and two days later Dunmore reimbursed the colony for the powder. On 6 May Dunmore outlawed "a certain Patrick Henry" for disturbing the peace. On 18 May the outlaw took his seat in Congress, but early in Aug. he returned to Va. to assist in military preparations against Dunmore. He was appointed Col. of the first regiment formed in Va., which made him C. in C. of all state militia, but Henry's political enemies chose a committee of public safety and put it under control of Edmund Pendleton. The latter was Henry's most resolute political opponent and made sure that he had no chance to win military laurels. Wm. WOODFORD was given command of the force that ran Dunmore out of the colony. Henry was infuriated by this cavalier treatment and he also resented the attitude of the military committee of the Cont'l. Cong., so on 28 Feb. '76 he resigned his commission and went home.

He promptly came back into the political arena when he was elected to the third revolutionary convention. In May he had a decisive part in drafting the Va. constitution and on 29 June he was elected Gov. In this post he authorized the Western Operations of George Rogers Clark. One biographer, W. W. Henry, credits him with being the first to send Washington evidence that led to defeat of the Conway Cabal. (Reference is presumably to the anonymous letter of Benj. RUSH.) Shortly before the end of his tenure in the summer of 1779, Va. was hit by the first of the raids against which it was to show itself virtually helpless. In this initial operation Adm. Collier and Gen. Edw. Mathew did an estimated £2,000,000 worth of damage without losing a man.

Succeeded by Jefferson, his close friend and political lieutenant, Patrick Henry retired to a huge tract of land in Henry co., on the eastern slopes of the Blue Ridge, 200 miles S.W. of Richmond. In 1781 he joined those who demanded an investigation of Jefferson's conduct as Gov., and this led to a feud ended only by death. With sharply changed political views he returned to state politics and was again Gov. (1784–86). He opposed the Constitution on the grounds of states rights, led the movement for the Bill of Rights, and wrote the Va. appeal to the 1st Cong. for amendments to the Constitution. "Henry was probably more responsible than any or all others for the adoption of the first ten amendments to the federal Constitution." (*D.A.B.*)

Although in bad health when he ended his last term as Gov. in 1786 at the age of only 50, during the next 13 years of his life he remained active in law and politics. In 1795 he caused a sensation by making a public statement of admiration for Pres. Washington after declining the positions of Sec. of State and Chief Justice. In Jan. '99 he consented to Washington's request that he campaign for election as a Federalist to the Va. House of Delegates. This put him in opposition to nearly all his former political associates, particularly Jefferson and John Marshall, and it has never been made clear why Henry changed political sides. He defeated young John Randolph in this last campaign, but died on 6 June '99 before he could take his seat.

Recommended biographies are by M. C. Tyler and R. D. Meade. (See main bibliography) Wm. Wirt, *Sketches of the Life and Character of Patrick Henry* (1817) and Wm. Wirt Henry, *Patrick Henry: Life, Correspondence and Speeches* (3 vols., 1891), are cited in the *D.A.B.* sketch by W. E. Dodd.

HERKIMER, Nicholas. 1728–1777. N.Y. militia general. Of a family that emigrated from the Rhenish Palatinate to the Mohawk Valley of N.Y., his German name was written Herchheimer or Erghemer. Nicholas was born near the present town of Herkimer within a few years after his parents' arrival in America. When the Revolution began he was moderately wealthy and influential among the Palatines of the valley. Active in patriot affairs in politically divided TRYON COUNTY, he succeeded Christopher P. Yates as chairman of the committee of safety and was promoted from Col. of militia to B.G. In July '77 he led 380 militia to Unadilla for a conference with Joseph Brant, who had 130 warriors with him. Herkimer hoped to work out some arrangement to keep Brant's Mohawks neutral, but the conference did not accomplish this purpose and only the militia general's cool-headedness kept this meeting from turning into a battle. (Campbell,

Tryon County, 53–54) After learning that St. Leger's Expedition was approaching and after getting little response from the militia when efforts were made to turn out 200 men for the defense of Ft. Schuyler (Stanwix), on 17 July Herkimer published a proclamation that "it shall be ordered by me as soon as the enemy approaches, that every male person, being in health, from 16 to 60 years of age, in this county, shall, as in duty bound, repair immediately, with arms and accouterments, to the place to be appointed...." (*Ibid.,* 61) On 30 July a friendly Indian told Herkimer that the enemy was getting close, and on 4 Aug. the old German started the march that ended in the tragic ORISKANY ambush, 6 Aug. About 10 days later his leg was unskillfully amputated by a French surgeon of Arnold's command, who could not stop the bleeding. As described by Henry R. Schoolcraft, the dying Herkimer "called for his family Bible, and having gathered his domestic circle around him, he read aloud, in a clear voice, the thirty-ninth psalm." (*Proceedings of the N.Y. Hist. Soc.,* quoted in Campbell, *op. cit.,* 75 *n.*) Although twice married, he left no children.

HESSIANS. See GERMAN MERCENARIES.

HEWES, Joseph. 1730–1779. Signer. N.C. The son of Conn. farmers who escaped from the Indians in 1728 and settled near Kingston, N.J., he received a common school education there. He was in business in Philadelphia and had moved to Edenton, N.C., by 1763. Reared a Quaker, he had left the sect by the beginning of the Revolution. He was elected to the colonial assembly in 1766 and in 1773 became a member of the committee of correspondence. He went to all the provincial congresses and in 1774 was elected to the Cont'l. Congress. Active on several committees,

he signed the Decl. of Indep. He was not re-elected in 1777, sat in the state House of Commons in 1778, and returned to the Congress in 1779, where he died 10 Nov. He sat on numerous committees and was particularly effective in naval affairs. He appointed John Paul Jones, whom he had known in N.C., to the navy and gave him a ship.

HEWETT, Capt. Detrick. Killed in WYOMING VALLEY "MASSACRE."

HEYWARD, Thomas Jr. 1746–1809. Signer. S.C. He was from a wealthy family and studied in the Middle Temple before becoming a S.C. lawyer in 1771. In 1772 he sat in the provincial assembly and in 1774 and 1775 went to the conventions in Charleston. He was a member of the council of safety and continued in the provincial congresses of 1775 and 1776, helping to write the state constitution as well. Sent to the second Cont'l. Congress, he signed the Decl. of Indep. and served in that group until 1778. He was a S.C. circuit judge and capt. of a militia arty. bn. in Charleston. On 4 Feb. '79 he was wounded on Port Royal Island, and he was captured at Charleston and paroled the same day, 12 May '80. This was, however, recalled, and he was held prisoner in St. Augustine until exchanged in July '81. He sat in the state legislature 1782–84 and served as circuit judge until 1789, when he retired from public life. He was one of the founders and the first president of the S.C. Agricultural Society in 1785.

HICKEY, Thomas. See MUTINY OF HICKEY.

HILLSBORO RAID, N.C. 12 Sept. '81. After a number of preliminary successes, on 6 Sept. '81 Tory Col. David FANNING felt sufficiently powerful to call for volunteers. Within a short time he had 950 men under his command

and he undertook a long-cherished scheme of capturing rebel Gov. Burke of N.C. Reaching Hillsboro the morning of 12 Sept., having marched all day and all night, he got possession of that place after a skirmish in which he lost only one man (wounded) but killed 15 patriots, wounded 20, and captured more than 200. Among his prisoners were Burke, the council, several Cont'l. officers, and 71 Cont'l. soldiers. He also liberated a number of Loyalist and British soldiers. Leaving Hillsboro at noon (12 Sept.) the Tory raiders had covered 18 miles when they were attacked at Cane Creek (Lindley's Mill) by 400 Cont'l. soldiers under the command of Col. Maybin and Gen. John Butler. Although Col. Hector McNeil had jeopardized the Tory command by careless security precautions, Fanning's skilful handling of the situation saved his expedition and left him in possession of the prisoners. McNeil and seven other Tories were killed. To secure his retreat, Fanning then launched an attack. In a four-hour fight the rebels were finally routed with a loss of 25 killed, 90 wounded, and 10 captured, but FANNING was badly wounded, 27 of his men were killed, and 90 were wounded. While Fanning and 60 other wounded had to be left behind, Lt. Cols. Archibald McDugald and Archibald McKay, and Maj. John Ranes succeeded in eluding pursuit with the rest of the expedition until it linked up four days later with the relief column led by Col. J. H. CRAIG from Wilmington.

Fanning's coup has been called "without doubt the most brilliant exploit of any group of Loyalists in any state throughout the Revolution" (DeMond, *Loyalists in N.C.*, 147). DeMond, on whose account the above is based, says the two actions at Hillsboro and Cane Creek took place on 12 Sept., whereas other sources give 13 Sept.

HINRICHS, Johann. d. 1834. Hessian officer. Arriving with the first contingent of Hessians to America, he served as a jäger Lt. until promoted to Capt. in early 1778. He received a severe chest wound after the British occupied N.Y.C., and was wounded several other times. In the Charleston operations of 1780 he was actively engaged and left an important historical record. (See under JUNGKENN) Although schooled as an engineer and distinguished during the Revolution as a jäger, he transferred to the infantry in 1784. Soon thereafter he entered the Prussian service, was raised to the nobility, and died in 1834 as a Lt. Gen. Little else is known of his life, but his writings (mentioned above) indicate that he was well educated and had a keen and intelligent interest in a wide variety of subjects from fighting to music.

HOAGLANDT'S FARM. Located where Riverside Drive crosses W. 115th St., this was the end of the Bloomingdale Road in 1776. The action of HARLEM HEIGHTS is sometimes called "Hoadlandt's Hill" (e.g., Baurmeister, 50, who spells it Hogeland).

HOBKIRK'S HILL (Camden), S.C., 25 Apr. '81. When Cornwallis retreated to Wilmington, N.C., after the Battle of Guilford C. H., he left the defense of S.C. in the hands of young Lord RAWDON. The latter's principal post was at Camden. As is more fully outlined under SOUTHERN CAMPAIGNS of Greene, Lee's Legion was detached to operate initially with Marion to the east when Greene moved against Camden with his main body. Rawdon had previously detached Col. John WATSON with almost half the British field army to wipe out Marion's partisans in the Peedee swamps. Both Greene and Rawdon expected these detached forces to rejoin them around Camden. Greene also expected Sumter to meet him for the attack on Camden, but "The Gamecock" declined to subordinate himself. Further details will be found under SOUTHERN CAMPAIGNS. See map "Camden and Vicinity," page 164, for Greene's advance to Hobkirk's Hill and the subsequent battle.

After a march of 140 miles in 14 days, three of them spent collecting boats on the Peedee, Greene approached Camden. Although he had hoped to surprise Rawdon, the latter expected the movement and was kept informed of it by Tory agents. On 20 Apr., Wm. Washington's dragoons probed the British positions. When Greene learned that Rawdon was too strong to be attacked he camped on Hobkirk's Hill, about a mile and a half from Rawdon, to await reinforcements and supplies. On 21 Apr. the American commander was alarmed to learn that Col. Watson's 500 men were moving from the east to rejoin Rawdon; meanwhile, Sumter had not arrived, Lee and Marion— who were supposed to be preventing Watson's return to Camden—were still detached, and Greene was badly in need of supplies and provisions. Greene therefore left Hobkirk's Hill and moved east of Pine Tree Creek so as to interpose his force between Rawdon and Watson; since the terrain did not permit the artillery to participate in this shift in position, the guns were ordered north to Lynches Creek, a distance of 20 miles, where they would be safe. As it turned out, Lee and Marion had successfully blocked Watson's route, and Greene returned to Hobkirk's Hill on 24 Apr.

Rawdon had become an expert on defending Camden, since this was the second time he had found himself sit-ting in this advanced and vulnerable outpost while the Americans moved against him from N.C. (See CAMDEN CAMPAIGN for the other occasion.) With many other isolated outposts to worry about, with his forces scattered, short on supplies and provisions, Lord Rawdon handled his strategic problem with a skill and courage that would have done credit to a veteran commander. He had been kept informed of Greene's arrival at Hobkirk's Hill on 19 Apr., his movement east on 22–24 Apr., and his return to the hill on the latter date. The night of the 24th–25th he learned from an American deserter that Greene's artillery had been evacuated, that Sumter had not arrived, and that the enemy was short of supplies.* This deserter also informed the enemy of Greene's troop dispositions. Rawdon therefore scraped together every man who could carry a weapon, including a group of convalescents, and prepared to attack on the 25th.

Hobkirk's Hill was a sandy ridge in the typical pine woods of the region. Bisected by the Great Road from Camden to Waxhaws, its west flank was protected by the Wateree and its left by the swampy bottom of the good-sized stream called Pine Tree Creek. (The old name of Camden was Pine Tree.) The long axis of the hill ran east and west. Toward the south the ground sloped about 100 yards to a bushy plain

---

* The deserter was a drummer named Jones from the Md. line who claimed to have been captured by the British and to have enlisted with the enemy as a means of later escaping to rejoin his regiment. Recaptured by Lee and Marion at FT. WATSON, 23 Apr., he reached Greene's camp the next day, was welcomed back by his regiment and thereby was able to learn Greene's situation before defecting to the enemy.

that extended less than a mile to the clearing around Logtown, a few hundred yards north of Camden. The terrain was such that an enemy approach from the south could not be seen from Hobkirk's Hill until the enemy was almost within assaulting distance.

Greene disposed his troops skilfully to conform to the terrain. To the S.E., which was the main avenue of approach, he posted the crack troops of Kirkwood's Del. Co. with two strong outposts to their front; the latter were commanded by Capts. Perry Benson and Simon Morgan. Patrols covered the S. and W. approaches. The main body was camped on the hill so as to take up positions as shown schematically below.

The Cont'l. line numbered 1,174, and the Great Road separated the Va. and Md. brigades. The dragoons and N.C. militia were in reserve. Chas. Harrison's 40 Va. artillerymen arrived with their three 6-pdrs. in time for the battle (which was an unpleasant surprise for Rawdon) and took up a concealed position on the road. The outposts of Benson and Morgan apparently were located to the W. of Kirkwood, in front of the Md. Brig., since this is the point where initial contact was made. (Lossing, *op. cit.,* sketch on p. 679 from Stedman) Greene's total strength (adding the figures given above) was 1,551. (Ward, *op. cit.,* 803)

With about 800 combatants scraped together from his 900-man garrison (Fortescue, *British Army,* III, 379, gives first figure; Ward, *op. cit.,* 800, the second), Rawdon moved out of Camden on the clear, warm morning of 25 Apr. and took a route that led him toward the relatively gradual S.E. slopes of Hobkirk's Hill. This same morning Greene's army received a welcomed supply of provisions brought forward by Edw. Carrington (the Q.M.). The guns also returned. American writers say Greene was not guilty of being surprised (Lee, *Memoirs,* 337 *n.,* for example); if so they are not using the word in the precise military sense of the principles of war, or they are using it rather loosely. It is true that the defenders were able to turn out in time to meet the attack. but this is only because the enemy came from the di-

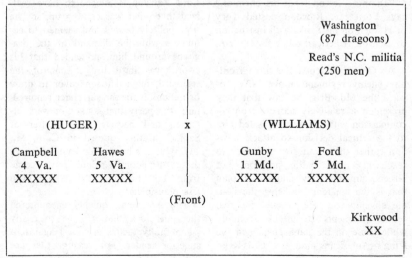

rection expected and that Kirkwood did a fine job of delaying. Yet the dragoons, whom one might expect to have found patrolling toward Camden, did not have their horses saddled! The troops were cooking their recently issued rations, or some of those who had finished this were washing in the spring N.E. of the position. Gen. Greene was sitting down to breakfast with some of his officers in the same area when the first shots were fired. Fortunately, or through good tactics, the Americans were encamped roughly in battle formation.

When Rawdon made contact, about 10 A.M., he deployed in the following manner:

(Front)

King's Americans	N.Y. Vols.	63d Regt.
Convalescents		Vols. of Ireland
N.Y. Drags.	S.C. Tories	

"Taking a lesson from his enemies," says Fortescue, Rawdon posted Tory marksmen on his flanks with instruction to pick off American officers. (*Op. cit.,* 380)

As Greene watched the three front-line enemy regiments move N.W. toward the Md. Brig. he saw that they presented a relatively narrow front in comparison with his own. This led him to the critical decision to attack Rawdon rather than wait for the latter to reach his main battle position, but Greene unfortunately adopted a plan that is the amateur's delight: the double envelopment. He ordered the two center regiments to attack frontally while those on the flank enveloped the King's Americans and the 63d Regt.

Compounding this faulty tactical plan, he ordered Washington to make a wide sweep down the road and hit the enemy rear. (This violates the principle of war called "Mass"; as Henry Lee points out, it would have been better to hold the dragoons in reserve [*Op. cit.,* 340–41].)

The operation started auspiciously. The enemy was surprised and momentarily checked when three American guns opened on them with grape and cannister at short range. As soon as Greene's infantry started forward, however, Rawdon turned the tables on him by moving his second-line regiments up to extend the front line; the British now overlapped the Americans, who found themselves advancing into the same sort of trap they had expected to be springing on the enemy. Things continued to go well for a few minutes, however. Huger's Va. Brig. was gaining ground against the British left. There is the picturesque story of Rawdon's being cut off and surrounded by the forward elements of Gunby's 1st Md. just before the latter retreated under circumstances to be explained in a moment. Lord Rawdon is alleged to have realized that relief was coming up, so "he very politely bowed and seemed to acquiesce with the demand of the dragoons around him, pretended that his sword was hard to get out of the scabbard, feigned to endeavor to draw or unhook it for the surrender required, until the party that took him were attacked and had to fly." (Letter of Samuel Mathis, quoted in C. & M., 1177–78; it is hard to understand where these "dragoons" would have come from, but the other details are even less plausible.)

The Americans quickly encountered the hard luck that can be so costly when faulty tactics are used against a superior leader. For reasons that are not clear, Gunby's crack 1st Md. fell apart; the regimental commander then compounded the misfortune by ordering a short withdrawal to reorganize, but the enemy quickly exploited this error by a charge that routed the unit. (Gunby claimed, and Greene supported him in this, that he had halted to let the wings catch up. This would not explain his withdrawal, but Gunby was later exonerated and restored to command.) The 5th Md. then broke, and the 4th Va. followed suit. Hawes's 5th Va. was the only Cont'l. regiment that remained unbroken, and they probably saved Greene's army from annihilation; they held fast to check the enemy pursuit and withdrew only on orders from Greene to avoid encirclement. The other three regiments could not be rallied, and Greene had no choice but to order a general retreat.

There was a gallant fight to save the three guns. When the matrosses started abandoning the gunners, Greene sent Capt. James Smith with a company of 45 young Irishmen of the Md. line to the rescue. The regulars dropped their tow ropes twice to beat off the attacks of Capt. Coffin's "handsome corps" of 60 N.Y. Provincial dragoons. Enemy infantry fire had shot down Smith and all but 14 of his men when Coffin came back to kill or capture these survivors. Greene returned with some matrosses and personally assisted in towing the guns.

The American dragoons, meanwhile, had been off on a misguided operation. Having hit deep in the enemy rear, Washington made the mistake of stopping to round up 200 noncombatants instead of moving through them to attack the British line from the rear. When he learned of the retreat, he hastily paroled the enemy officers he could not evacuate, and rode back encumbered with 50 prisoners. He arrived just in time to save the guns by hitching them to his horses.

Greene retreated two or three miles in good order while an effective rear guard checked pursuit. About 4 P.M. he sent Washington and Kirkwood back to collect the wounded and round up stragglers. All the enemy except Coffin's dragoons had returned to Camden, and Washington set up an ambush that drove the enemy horse off the field in disorder. The Americans camped near the old Camden battlefield at Saunders Creek and moved back to Rugeley's Mill the next day.

What had caused the panic? Accounts generally agree that it started in Gunby's 1st Md. and spread to the 2d Md. and 4th Va. They also agree that Gunby made the mistake of attempting to withdraw his regiment some 60 yards to the base of the hill and reform them to continue the attack. It is also evident that the loss of American officers figured prominently in the panic. (Rawdon had learned his lessons well.) But there are several conflicting versions of what caused the veteran 1st Md. to break.

Henry Lee says that when Gunby's troops fell in for battle Capt. Armstrong moved out ahead of the regiment with two sections. Instead of using Armstrong as a base on which to bring forward the rest of his regiment, Gunby ordered Armstrong back. "The enemy was not yet in strength in this point," says Lee, and if Gunby had moved forward instead of recalling Armstrong, it is probable "that the fate of the day would have been favorable to our arms. This Greene always declared as his opinion, and Gunby as uniformly denied." The falling back to reorganize, then, stemmed from this incident, according to Lee's version. (*Memoirs*, 338 *n.*)

Another version is that the right

flank company of Capt. Wm. Beatty, Jr., faltered and fell back when he was killed. The adjacent company then fell back also, at which point Gunby ordered his entire regiment back to re-organize. (Lossing, 680 *n.*, citing Marshall, II, 6; without source citation, the same version is in Ward, 806)

Samuel Mathis of Camden recorded the story of the battle after talking to witnesses. The battle was going well when "only *one* word, a *single word* ... turned the fate of the day," says he. Gunby's regiment was advancing well with orders not to fire. When within a few paces of the enemy, Gunby ordered his men to charge with the bayonet.

"Those near him, hearing the word first, rushed forward, whereby the regiment was moving forward in the form of a bow. Colonel Gunby ordered a 'halt' until the wings should become straight. This turned the fate of the day. Previously being ordered not to fire and now ordered to 'halt,' while the British were coming up with charged bayonets, before the colonel could be understood and repeat the charge. the enemy were in among them and made them give way...." (Mathis ltr. of 26 June 1819, *Amer. Hist. Record,* II, 106–9, quoted in S. & R. 456–57, and C. & M., 1177–78).

A court of inquiry, called at Gunby's request, found that his "improper and unmilitary" order for his regiment to retire was "in all probability, the only cause why we did not obtain a complete victory." Although the court found no criticism with his personal "spirit and activity," Gunby was made the official scapegoat for Greene's incompetent tactical plan. The latter has tarnished his record of over-all military competence by leaving these words in a letter to Joseph Reed: "Gunby was the sole cause of the defeat."

Losses were about equal on both sides. Greene reported 266 casualties, of whom 18 were killed; Rawdon reported a total of 258 lost, 38 of them killed. Greene successfully evacuated his artillery and supply train. Not having destroyed the American army, Rawdon gained nothing from his tactical victory and was forced to retreat toward Charleston.

See also VOLUNTEERS OF IRELAND, where a portion of Rawdon's account of the battle is quoted.

HOGUN, James. ?–1781. Cont'l general. Ireland–N.C. About 1751 James Hogun came from Ireland and settled in Halifax co., N.C. In 1774 he was in the Halifax Safety Committee and represented his county in various provincial congresses. On 22 Apr. '76 the Prov. Cong. elected him the first Maj. of the Halifax militia, and on 26 Nov. he became Col. of the 7th N.C. Cont'ls. Joining Washington's army in July '77, he fought at Brandywine and Germantown (11 Sept. and 4 Oct. '77). When Congress called for new Cont'l. regiments he was ordered home to help raise and organize the four from N.C. In Aug. '78 he reached White Plains, N.Y., with the first of these regiments. During the last two months of the year he was involved with fortification work at West Point and then went to Philadelphia. Although his state's delegation to Congress followed their instructions to nominate Jethro Sumner and Thos. Clark to fill N.C. vacancies for promotion, Congress appointed Sumner and Hogun to B.G. on 9 Jan. '79. In so doing they noted not only that Hogun was senior to Clark but also that he had performed well at Germantown. After briefly commanding the N.C. Brig. of Washington's army, on 19 Mar. the new B.G. succeeded Benedict Arnold as commander in Philadelphia and retained that position until 22 Nov.

'79. He then led his brigade to the defense of Charleston, arriving 3 Mar. with 700 men after an arduous march of nearly three months through snow and extreme cold. Taken prisoner when Lincoln surrendered the city on 12 May '80, he later refused parole in order to stay with his men, who were being subjected to British pressure to serve in Jamaica as royal militia. He died in captivity at HADDREL'S POINT on 4 Jan. '81.

HOLKER, Jean. 1745–1822. French merchant, Consul to U.S. Son of Chevalier John Holker, 1719–1786, who escaped to France after taking part in the Jacobite rebellion of 1745 and who got his title for teaching his adopted country the manufacturing techniques of his native Manchester, young Holker went to America with Gérard in 1778. (Editors' notes to Chastellux, *Travels,* 330–33) He had been at Dunkirk waiting to sail on a secret mission to America to gather information on the possibilities of French aid when the news of Saratoga eliminated the need for this task. (Lasseray) Holker used his position as consul in Philadelphia to grow wealthy as a speculator. He resigned early in 1781 when the French government prohibited further commercial enterprise by their representatives. After the war he returned to France, having been detained by the need to unsnarl some accounts with Robert Morris, who had been a partner in his war profiteering.

HOLTZENDORFF, Louis-Casimir, Baron de. 1728–? Cont'l. officer. Germany–France. Son of a councillor to the King of Prussia, he had served on the latter's general staff and was living in Paris in 1775. He took advantage of close personal relations with the French court to obtain a commission as Maj. in Nov. '76 and then paid his own way to America. Silas Deane wrote that Holtzendorff was recom-

mended by persons "of the first order." As author of *Elements of Tactics . . . ,* he was highly regarded by Saint-Germain and de Broglie, although his work has been called "minutiae treated in the style of higher mathematics." (Bardin, *Dictionnaire,* quoted by Lasseray) On 20 Nov. '76 Holtzendorff was commissioned Lt. Col. in the Cont'l Army. He was at Brandywine and Germantown before resigning on 31 Jan. '78. (Heitman) Breveted Col. for service in America, he returned to France and on 3 June '78 was made Capt. of Inf. to perform three months' duty per year in the Anhalt (later Salm-Salm) Regt. On 17 June '85 he entered the service of Holland but continued to draw a French pension. (Lasseray, 241–42)

HONDURAS. (See WEST INDIES for map.) In Sept. '79 the Spanish governor of Honduras took the British settlement at St. George's Key, a small island in the harbor of Belize, capturing many woodcutters and expelling the rest. Prior to this, however, three ships and a handful of troops from Jamaica had started for this area and on 16 Oct. the British recaptured St. George's Key. Maj. (John ?) DALRYMPLE then stormed Omoa, although the defenders outnumbered him two to one and were behind 18-foot walls. With the loss of 365 prisoners and only two men wounded, the Spanish surrendered gold, ships, and cargoes valued at $3,000,000 without inflicting a single casualty on the British.

Dalrymple left a garrison at Omoa and sailed off to take a place Fortescue calls "Rattan," which presumably was the Bay Island now called Roatán; presumably the attack was successful. Gov. Dalling of Jamaica meanwhile had conceived his unfortunate plan for operations in NICARAGUA and had written Dalrymple orders to destroy and evacuate Omoa. These instructions were not received in time, and on 28 Dec. '79 the Omoa garrison, "hopelessly reduced by fever and disease," abandoned the post "at the mere menace of a Spanish attack." (Fortescue, *British Army*, III, 303)

On 26 Aug. '82 the new Gov.-Gen. of Jamaica, Maj. Gen. Archibald Campbell, learned that the Spaniards were planning an expedition against Cape Gracias á Dios, the northernmost tip of Nicaragua. He sent Col. Edward DESPARD with Maj. William Odell and 80 of the latter's Loyal American Rangers to launch a "spoiling attack" against the Black River Settlement, about 130 miles N.W. of the cape and some 200 miles east of the British post at Omoa. Covered by the fleet of Commodore (Francis ?) Parry—the 50-gun ship *Preston* and five or six frigates—the American rangers landed in Oct. '82 and were immediately joined by 500 Negroes and 600 Mosquito Indians, who were eager to get even with the Spaniards. The governor immediately surrendered the garrison, which comprised some 740 men of the Guatemala Regt. The prisoners were sent to Omoa, and their surrendered blockhouse yielded a large sum of money in addition to quantities of artillery, small arms, and ammunition. (These details are from Baurmeister, *Journals*, 537. Editor Uhlendorf cites an account of the expedition in the *Royal Gazette*, 13 Nov. '82.) Fortescue covers this final operation in the West Indies with these words: "in October a motley band of American rangers, British logwoodcutters, and Indians, under British officers ... regained for New England [*sic*] her possessions in the Gulf of Honduras." (*Op. cit.*, III, 409)

HONORS OF WAR. A military force is said to be accorded "the honors of war" when the terms of its capitulation include the right to march away with colors flying, bands playing, bayonets fixed, and in possession of weapons and equipment. Conditions may vary somewhat in accordance with the agreement worked out between the opposing commanders. Originally, the honors of war probably were reserved for defenders who had distinguished themselves by a particularly heroic resistance. In practice, however, it is good strategy to gain time and save casualties by convincing the defenders of a strong position to surrender their fortress or terrain in return for being allowed to go free and with honor. Troops accorded the honors of war normally are required to proceed to a specified place before they are free to resume hostilities.

See FORT GRANBY.

HOOD, Samuel Hood, 1st Viscount. 1724–1816. British admiral. He entered the navy in 1741, served part of his time as midshipman with Rodney, and saw action in the North Sea. As commander of the *Jamaica* sloop he was in North American waters in 1753–56. During the Seven Years' War he remained in the English Channel, and in 1759 was engaged with Rodney in breaking up concentrations of French ships destined for the invasion of England. In 1778 he became commissioner of the dockyard at Portsmouth and governor of the Naval Academy. This ordinarily would have meant the end of active service, but with the miserable Lord Sandwich in control of the Royal Navy nothing was normal. Hence Hood was made a baronet, promoted to Rear Adm. (26 Sept. '80), and sent to the West Indies as second in command to Rodney. He arrived in Jan. '81 and immediately proved himself to be an outstanding commander, but with Rodney's inept direction of strategy in 1781 Hood was unable to keep De Grasse from raising the blockade of

Martinique, 29 Apr. When Rodney sailed for England in July, Hood was sent north with 14 ships to support Adm. Graves. Again in a subordinate position, Hood shares none of the blame for the British naval failures in the YORKTOWN CAMPAIGN. Returning to the West Indies ahead of Rodney he was temporarily in command and conducted a brilliant operation against odds in his unsuccessful attempt to relieve ST. KITTS, Jan.–Feb. '82. For his part in the defeat of De Grasse off Saints Passage, Apr. '82, he was made an Irish peer. (See WEST INDIES IN THE REV. for Hood's operations.)

He entered Parliament in 1784, was promoted to Vice Adm. in 1787, and in July '88 was appointed to the Board of Admiralty. When war against France broke out he became C. in C. in the Mediterranean. In the operation that brought an obscure Corsican into prominence, his allied fleet was driven out of Toulon. He then took and occupied Corsica (at the invitation of Paoli). In June '94 he tried to draw the French fleet into action. "The plan which he laid ... may possibly have served to some extent as an inspiration, if not as a model, to Nelson for the battle of the Nile, but the wind was unfavourable, and the attack could not be carried out." (David Hannay in *E.B.*) Having been promoted to full Adm. in Apr., he was recalled to England in Oct. '94 for a reason that has never been fully explained. (*Ibid.*) He held no further command at sea but was Gov. of Greenwich Hospital from 1796 until his death.

HOOD'S POINT (James River), 3 Jan. '81. (VA. MIL. OPNS.) An American battery fired at Arnold's expedition when it anchored near Jamestown late in the evening. Simcoe landed with 130 of the Queen's Rangers reinforced by the flank companies of the 80th Regt., moved about a mile to the fort, and found the garrison had abandoned it.

HOOPER, William. 1742–1790. Signer. N.C. After attending the Boston Latin School and graduating from Harvard in 1760, he studied law under James Otis. It was apparently this association that turned him toward the patriotic cause, in spite of his family's Loyalist stand. He moved to Wilmington, N.C., in 1764, where he was active in the law and politics. In 1770, as deputy attorney-general, he took the royal government's part against the insurgents ("REGULATORS"), and in 1771 marched with Gov. Tryon against them. In the 1773 general assembly he opposed the Crown's arbitrary measures. Upon the overthrow of the government he became a member of the committee of correspondence, and he presided at the meeting that called the provincial congress, to which he was duly elected. Sent to the Cont'l. Congress in 1774–77, he signed the Decl. of Indep. Active on committees and in debate, he compared favorably as an orator with R. H. Lee and Patrick Henry, according to John Adams. He resigned 29 Apr. '77, to practice law and restore his ruined fortune, living in the country and sitting in the House of Commons 1777–82. However, the British invasion caused him to leave his family in Wilmington while he escaped, and much of his property was then destroyed. After the war, he was again in the House of Commons, where he advocated leniency to the Tories, curbing the masses, and ratification of the Federal Constitution. He retired in 1787 and declined rapidly in health. *D.A.B.* characterizes him as "... essentially an aristocrat, cultivated, fearless, aloof. ... Lacking somewhat in strength of character. ..."

HOPKINS, Esek. 1718–1802. First C. in C. of Cont'l. Navy. R.I. Born and reared on a farm near Providence on the site of modern Scituate, R.I., he went to sea shortly after his father's death in 1738 and retired to his farm in 1772. In the interim he had been a successful sea captain and privateer (in the Seven Years' War). In his prime he was "a strong, tall, fine-looking man, energetic, dominant, out-spoken, and aggressive" (Edith R. Blanchard in *D.A.B.*). Having taken a keen interest in local politics and being the brother of the most prominent figure in R.I., Stephen Hopkins, Esek became state B.G. on 4 Oct. '75 and was put in command of the militia. Stephen, meanwhile, was a delegate to Congress and an influential member of the Marine Committee. When the Cont'l. navy was organized it came to pass that Esek was C. in C. (confirmed 22 Dec. '75), and the latter's son, John B. HOPKINS, was appointed captain.

After the expedition to Nassau outlined under NAVAL OPERATIONS, particularly the humiliating failure to destroy the British ship *Alfred* in Long Island Sound on the return voyage, Hopkins' fleet began to fall apart. Personnel melted away because of sickness, the lure of privateering, failure of Congress to pay them, and bad morale. The latter must be attributed in large part to Hopkins' inadequate leadership. "To whip the infant navy into effective shape would have required the genius of a Washington, but though Hopkins was a capable seaman, he had no such genius," comments Blanchard in *D.A.B.* (One wonders whether the lesser genius of Benedict Arnold, John Paul Jones, Jonathan Haraden or a number of others might not have been equal to this lesser task.)

Despite the support of John Adams, Hopkins received a formal vote of censure from Congress for failure to carry out his (impossible) instructions. (See NAVAL OPNS.) Although Nicholas BIDDLE, JONES, and Whipple (with the *Columbus*) got out to sea for successful operations, the rest of Hopkins' fleet remained idle, and in Dec. '76 it was blockaded in Narragansett Bay. When Congress learned from disgruntled officers that the C. in C.'s incompetence was combined with insubordination to his political masters, they suspended him from command on 26 Mar. '77. Formal dismissal came on 2 Jan. '78.

See Edward Field, *Esek Hopkins . . . ,* Providence, 1898.

HOPKINS, John Burroughs. 1742–1796. Cont'l. naval officer. R.I. Eldest of Esek HOPKINS' 10 children and nephew of Stephen HOPKINS, he followed family tradition in going to sea early. He took part in the GASPÉE AFFAIR, 9 June '72. On 22 Dec. '75 he became the junior of the first four captains appointed in the new Cont'l. navy and took command of the *Cabot* (14). He took part in the expedition to Nassau led by his father, and in the *Alfred-Glasgow* Encounter, 6 Apr. '76, his ship, being in the lead, bore the brunt of the action. Named commander of the frigate *Warren* in 1777, he slipped through the British blockade of Narragansett Bay early in Mar. '78, took two prizes, and put into Boston. In 1779, with the *Warren, Queen of France,* and *Ranger,* he led a six-week cruise off the Virginia capes that captured the N.Y. privateer schooner *Hibernia,* the *Jason* (20), and six other ships. Although highly pleased at this triumph initially, the Marine Committee learned that Hopkins had not strictly followed instructions and ordered an investigation. Young Hopkins ended by being suspended, and (understandably) he never returned to the regular navy.

Commanding the Mass. privateer

Tracy (16) he took some prizes before being captured. The next year he was captain of the R.I. privateer sloop *Success.* Retiring to private life after the war, he died at the age of 54.

HOPKINS, Stephen. 1707–1785. Signer. R.I. Descended from an associate of Roger Williams, he became a farmer and surveyor before starting a political career that eventually made him the most prominent figure in R.I. (*D.A.B.* article on Esek [*sic*] Hopkins by Edith R. Blanchard) He was town clerk and councilman in Scituate, sat in the general assembly all but four of the years from 1732 to 1752, and held several other public offices before moving to Providence in 1742 to join his brother Esek in business. On the superior court 1747–49, he became chief justice in 1751. In 1755 he became governor and held this office until 1768 with the exception of three years when he was defeated by Sam'l. Ward of Newport. Hopkins and Ward were leaders in a feud that raged between Providence and Newport, but in 1768 both men withdrew in favor of a coalition candidate, Josias Lyndon. An early champion of colonial rights and union, Stephen was sent to the general congresses of 1754, 1755, and 1757. At the first one, the Albany Convention, he became a close friend of Benj. Franklin. In 1764 he wrote "The Grievances of the American Colonies Candidly Examined," in which he argued against the Stamp and Sugar Acts and foreshadowed John Dickinson's theory of colonial home rule. As chief justice of the superior court he frustrated the crown authorities in the GASPÉE AFFAIR (1772). He was a delegate to the 1st and 2d Cont'l congresses, signed the Decl. of Indep., and was a member of the committee to organize the navy. In this capacity he would appear to have done his country a disservice in supporting the selection of his brother Esek as naval C. in C. Presumably he was not an innocent bystander when the latter's son, John B. Hopkins, was appointed to one of the four captains' positions in the new navy. After serving on the committee for preparing the articles of confederation, he returned home for ill health in Sept. '76.

Although a man of little formal education, he gained great knowledge by his insatiable reading habits. Born with political instincts, he acquired literary and scientific tastes. In 1762 he helped establish the *Providence Gazette,* and for years was a contributor. He was first chancellor of what now is Brown University.

HOPKINSON, Francis. 1737–1791. Signer, writer, artist. Pa. His father, an English lawyer, immigrated to Philadelphia in 1731 and became a member of the governor's council as well as numerous civic and social organizations. Francis was the first graduate (1757) of the Coll. of Philadelphia (later the U. of Pa.). He studied law under Benj. Chew, was admitted to the bar in 1761, but for the next 12 years tried a variety of careers. In 1763 he was named customs collector in Salem, N.J. In 1766–67 he made an unsuccessful trip to England for political preferment. After becoming a shopkeeper, he was named customs collector at New Castle, Del. (about 40 miles below Philadelphia). Returning to the law, he set up practice at Bordentown, N.J., and was an immediate success. In 1774 he was named to the governor's council, but in this same year he published a political satire, *A Pretty Story,* in which he showed his ardent Whig convictions. Another work, called *A Prophecy,* anticipated the Decl. of Indep. Elected to Congress from N.J. in June '76, he was one of the Signers. A few months after adoption of the Flag Resolution of 14 June '77 he was appointed one of three Commissioners of the Cont'l. Navy Board. As chairman and secretary he served capably for almost two years before Congress elected him Treasurer of Loans. A year later, while still holding the latter post, he became Judge of the Pa. Admiralty Court. Ten years later the court was dissolved (1789) and Hopkinson was judge of the U.S. district court of eastern Pa. the last two years of his short but memorable life.

Hopkinson designed, or had a part in designing, seals of the American Philosophical Society, the State of N.J., and what is now the U. of Pa. On 25 May '80 he wrote the Board of Admiralty that he was pleased they liked his design for their seal; he also requested recognition for this work and a number of other "devices." At the top of the list he claimed to have created the Stars and Stripes, and he later valued this work at £9 cash or £540 paper money. Congress eventually decided (23 Aug. '81) that too many others had worked on design of the flag for Hopkinson to deserve credit for being its originator. (Quaife *et al.*, *U.S. Flag*, 39–40) Meanwhile, a serious quarrel had resulted in his resignation as Treasurer of Loans.

Among his wartime writings were *A Letter to Lord Howe, A Letter Written by a Foreigner,* and *An Answer to General Burgoyne* (all in 1777). The latter work is quoted, in part, under BURGOYNE'S PROCLAMATION. *A Letter to Joseph Galloway* and his famous "BATTLE OF THE KEGS" appeared in 1778. In 1781 he wrote words and music of a cantata, *The Temple of Minerva,* celebrating the French alliance. In his later years he invented a ship's log, a shaded candlestick, and other things. He continued to write, producing Federalist essays, general social criticism, satire,

and verse. His son Joseph followed in his footsteps as politician, jurist, and composer: he wrote "Hail Columbia."

See Geo. E. Hastings, *The Life of Francis Hopkinson.* (Chicago: 1926).

HORRY, Daniel Huger. American officer, S.C. After taking part in the defense of Charleston as a company commander (2d S.C.) in 1776 and as a Col. in 1780, Horry (pronounced O'Ree; see also HUGER BROTHERS) swore allegiance to the crown after the surrender of Charleston (12 May '80). His estate consequently was spared, and Hampton Plantation House has evolved into one of America's most stately homes.

HORRY, Hugh. American officer. S.C. A brother of Peter HORRY, who commanded the mounted troops of MARION'S BRIGADE, Hugh was acting commander of the foot element at one time. He is reported by Heitman to have been a Maj. and Lt. Col. of a S.C. Regt. in 1779–81. See GREAT SAVANNAH.

HORRY, Peter. American officer, S.C. A Capt. in the 2d S.C. Regt. on 17 June '75, he was promoted to Maj. on 16 Sept. '76, and subsequently served in MARION'S BRIGADE. Heitman notes that he was reported to have been a Col. of S.C. militia in 1779–81, but Appleton's says he was a B.G. under Marion. At Eutaw Springs, 8 Sept. '81, he was wounded in action. He is remembered mainly for his unhappy collaboration with Parson Weems on the biography of MARION. See also GEORGETOWN, S.C., 15 Nov. '80.

HORSENECK LANDING (West Greenwich), Conn., 26 Feb. '79. Gov. Tryon with a body of about 600 light troops left the vicinity of Kings Bridge to raid this place. A 30-man American patrol made contact at New Rochelle and dropped back the next morning to Horseneck, where Gen. Israel Putnam attempted to make a stand with a pair of old iron cannon and 150 militia. With the loss of only two killed and 20 captured, Tryon destroyed the salt works, three small vessels, a store, plundered the settlement, and carried off about 200 head of cattle and horses. (Heath, *Memoirs,* 214–15) Putnam escaped capture by a daring ride down a steep, rocky hill where enemy dragoons were afraid to follow. (Lossing, I, 412) The date of this action is from the *A.A.*–Heitman list.

HORTALEZ & CIE. In May '76 the French foreign policies under the direction of VERGENNES had evolved to the point of considering secret aid to the Americans. At this time Vergennes asked Beaumarchais to submit a plan. Although remembered almost entirely for his literary works, Pierre Augustin Caron (1732–1799), who assumed the name de Beaumarchais in 1756, had distinguished himself in his father's trade of watchmaking, had become accepted at court, had shown himself to have a remarkable business talent, and had successfully accomplished a secret mission in London for Louis XV and Mme Du Barry in 1774. Beaumarchais proposed that the French immediately subsidize the colonists to the extent of a million livres ($200,000); half of this was to bolster their sagging currency and half was to buy European war supplies through a fictitious firm he proposed to call Roderigue Hortalez & Cie. Although the government accepted the creation of this firm it rejected the other features of the plan: it was not willing to risk direct dealings with the rebels, and it did not want to part with its scarce cash, particularly when the new GRIBEAUVAL system of artillery resulted in its arsenals being full of obsolete war matériel. Hortalez and Co. was, therefore, directed to operate under Beaumarchais as follows: as an independent commercial house it would

get a million livre *loan* from the French government, Spain would lend the same amount, and Beaumarchais would raise a third million among his business connections. He would be allowed to draw certain military supplies from French arsenals and depots, either paying for them or replacing certain stock with approved articles. The Americans would pay for supplies in products such as rice and tobacco, which the French government would help Beaumarchais sell in France. Hortalez & Cie. was to be self-supporting; Beaumarchais was expected to bear any losses of the firm and was entitled to any profit.

On 5 June '76 Vergennes gave the Treasury orders to pay Beaumarchais a million livres, and he received this amount in gold coin on 10 June. On 11 Aug. he got the Spanish contribution, and about the same time he raised the third million from French merchants. Establishing his home and business in a large building once used as the Dutch Embassy, and now known as the Hôtel des Ambassadeurs de Hollande (47 Rue Vieille du Temple), he got in touch with Silas Deane on 18 July '76 and the same month contracted to ship supplies to America. Actual shipment was, however, hindered by several complications (although France had already contrived to send the Americans muskets, gunpowder, and other supplies that summer from French and Dutch West Indies ports). Shortly before the French government approached Beaumarchais in May '76 they had selected Dr. Barbeu Dubourg, a botanist who knew Franklin, to serve as their intermediary on the matter of secret aid. While in London on an earlier official mission, Beaumarchais had been approached by Arthur Lee on the matter of French aid. When the government suddenly decided to attempt the Hortalez venture both Dubourg and

Lee were antagonized and undertook to hamper Beaumarchais. Furthermore, British ambassador to France Stormont learned of Beaumarchais' undertaking and forced the French to issue ordinances against the smuggling of war supplies. Although Beaumarchais' operations were supposed to be overlooked, a few minor French officials failed to cooperate.

Further harm was done by that prince of troublemakers, TRONSON DE COUDRAY. When the latter was selected to accompany the other artillery instructors who were to go with a shipment of 200 guns to America in late 1776, de Coudray persuaded Deane to commission him Maj. Gen. in the name of Congress. Then, while waiting for favorable winds at Le Havre he talked openly about the illegal shipment of arms. Then he suddenly left for Versailles to see the Minister of War, Vergennes, whom he knew personally, to arrange that he be put directly under the latter's orders. Beaumarchais had de Coudray ordered back, went himself to Le Havre to prevent any further hitch, but was identified by British agents when he appeared for a dress rehearsal of his *Barber of Seville*. When Stormont learned all about the shipment and lodged an official protest, Vergennes had to order the ships not to sail. One of them, *L'Amphitrite*, got away, and de Coudray was aboard.

Despite this setback, in 1777 Beaumarchais had more than 12 vessels operating out of Le Havre, Nantes, Bordeaux, and Marseilles. Eventually he had about 40. From Martinique or San Domingo, often earlier, they would swing north. Portsmouth, N.H., was port of entry for most of them; they usually stopped at Charleston on the return trip in hopes of picking up rice or tobacco, but usually they returned empty. The first Hortalez convoy reached Portsmouth in early 1777 with three million livres' worth of goods: 200 field guns, thousands of muskets, a large supply of powder, blankets, clothes, and shoes—enough for 25,000 men. (Lemaitre, *Beaumarchais,* 220) "Nine tenths of the military supplies that made the victory at Saratoga possible came from France or through foreign merchants whom she secretly encouraged," writes Van Tyne. (*War of Indep.,* 439–40) "Washington's victory at Trenton and Princeton was, perhaps, made possible by the supplies furnished by the French or through their instigation." (*Ibid.,* 476)

By Sept. '77 Beaumarchais had sent five million livres' worth of supplies to America. His return was zero: not a cargo nor any money from Congress. The Americans could not have paid anything at this time if they had wanted to, but Congress had not been informed by the Committee of Secret Correspondence of Deane's contract with Beaumarchais (see above). The reason was that Tory delegates in Congress would have told the British. During the summer of 1777 Vergennes came to Beaumarchais' relief with three large loans totaling over a million livres. The financier-playwright sent Jean-Baptiste Theveneau de Francy to find why Congress was ignoring his existence. Arthur Lee and Coudray, meanwhile, had been busy spreading the word that the Hortalez firm was a blind for dishonorable business. Two months before de Francy's arrival in America, Arthur Lee mendaciously wrote the Committee on Foreign Affairs: "The Minister [Vergennes] has repeatedly assured us [Franklin, Deane, and Lee], and in the most explicit terms, that no return is expected for these subsidies." (Ltr. of 6 Oct. '77, quoted by Lemaitre, *op. cit.,* 230) After the Committee of Commerce examined the evidence brought by Francy, however, they signed a contract (16 Apr. '78, four and a half months after the envoy's arrival) in which they assured payment for past shipments and arranged for new ones. Rival factions in Congress then started a long haggle over whether France should be paid for military aid. It was convenient for those in opposition to argue that Beaumarchais and France were acting in self-interest; they capitalized on the fact that France, officially neutral, could not publicly admit the arrangements under which Beaumarchais operated. The latter's supporter, Deane, reached America in July '78 after his recall from Paris and fell into an acrimonious controversy with the Congressional faction that opposed payment of Beaumarchais. The Va. Lees and Mass. Adamses led this opposition. "Arthur Lee's brothers and friends whispered that Deane was a grafter and an unscrupulous rascal who stood by Beaumarchais because the two had made huge war profits together." (*Ibid.*, 245) Deane's supporters finally succeeded in getting an official statement from Vergennes that Hortalez & Cie. was a private, commercial firm and that some of its stocks had come from French arsenals with the understanding that these stocks be replaced by the firm. Before this critical information reached Philadelphia, however, Deane had blown the entire affair into a public scandal by publishing a letter (5 Dec. '78) that denounced Arthur Lee's machinations and accused Congress of neglect and appalling ignorance of foreign affairs. Congress split into Pro- and Anti-Deanites. Henry Laurens, a member of the latter element, was forced to resign as President of Congress; he was succeeded by John Jay, a friend of Deane. Thos. Paine, then secretary of the Committee of Foreign Affairs, entered the lists as a supporter of Arthur Lee and on 2 Jan. '79 claimed publicly that he had written evidence that France had promised the supplies as a gift before Deane ever reached Paris. The French minister issued an official denial, followed up with a formal protest against Paine's indiscretion in revealing "classified" information, and on 9 Jan. Paine resigned under pressure. On 15 Jan. Beaumarchais was given a written apology from Congress and a pledge of payment.

The Franco-American alliance had meanwhile been consummated and the covert operations of Hortalez & Cie. were dwarfed by the open shipment of supplies under the protection of the French navy. Seriously in the red, Beaumarchais rose to the occasion with the business genius that characterized his entire life: while continuing to send the Americans war supplies on credit, he now brought his ships back from Martinique and San Domingo with sugar and other products which he sold at tremendous profit. Between 1776 and 1783, when his company was dissolved, he engaged in business that involved over 42,000,000 livres, and despite the U.S. debt he showed a profit of slightly more than two tenths of one per cent, says Lemaitre. (*Op. cit.*, 250–51) On 6 Apr. '81 Deane submitted an official document showing that, based on his own records, Congress owed Beaumarchais 3,600,000 livres. But Beaumarchais' case was hurt by the scandal that wrecked DEANE, and settlement was postponed. When Beaumarchais renewed his claims, in 1787 Congress appointed Arthur Lee to examine the Hortalez accounts! Lee concluded that Beaumarchais owed Congress 1,800,000 livres. It was not until 1835, when the Frenchman had been in his grave 36 years, that Congress acknowledged its debt: after protracted negotiations his heirs settled for 800,000 francs.

Beaumarchais is immortal for his literary works, but one emerges from a study of his financial and commercial activities with the feeling that his writing was almost in the category of a hobby. During his directorship of Hortalez & Cie. he produced his two famous comedies. *The Barber of Seville* was staged in 1775, after being prohibited for two years, and was a failure; revised for a second presentation, it was a complete success. His *Marriage of Figaro* was completed in 1778, but Louis XVI, "who alone saw its dangerous [republican] tendencies," held up its public staging until 1784. Napoleon called the play the "'revolution already in action." (*E.B.*, "Beaumarchais.")

In the above account of the Beaumarchais operations I have drawn most heavily on the biography by Georges Lemaitre. While most convincing, the work is not that of a professional historian and in its sympathetic treatment of its subject is at variance with the conventional evaluation. John Richard Alden summarizes the latter: "it is not certain even today whether the subsidies which he handled were entirely gifts, although they were so in the main. * * * The validity of the [heirs'] claim may well be questioned, especially since the firm of Roderigue Hortalez and Company closed its activities with a small net profit." (*American Rev.*, 183) The latter comment appears to underestimate Beaumarchais' commercial genius. (Lemaitre, *op. cit., passim*)

Lemaitre cites French biographical works of Gudin de La Brenellerie (188), Lafon (1928), Latzarus, (1930), Lescure (1887), and the two standard authorities, Loménie, *Beaumarchais et son temps* (1880) and Marsan, *Beaumarchais et les affaires d'Amérique* (1919). The 6-vol. *Histoire de la participation de la France à l'établissement des E.U.* by Doniol is,

of course, valuable as is *The Diplomacy of the American Revolution* by Bemis. The standard American work is Elizabeth S. Kite, *Beaumarchais and the War of Independence,* in two vols. (1918). Alden cites Stillé, "Beaumarchais and the Lost Million," *Pa. Mag. of Hist. and Biog.,* XI (1887); Kite, "French 'Secret Aid' Precursor to the French American Alliance 1776-1777," *French American Review,* I (1948); Van Tyne, "French Aid before the Alliance of 1778," *Amer. Hist. Rev.,* XXXI (1925); and Meng, "A Foot-note to Secret Aid in the Amer. Rev.," *Amer. Hist. Rev.*

HOTHAM, William. 1736–1813. British naval officer. After attending Westminster School, he entered the Royal Naval Academy in 1748. As a commodore on the *Preston* (50) he joined Adm. Howe in 1776 for service in America. He supported the landing at Kip's Bay, N.Y., 15 Sept. '76. During the Philadelphia Campaign he remained in N.Y. as senior officer and gave the naval support for Clinton's Expedition to the Highlands, Oct. '77, although he was skeptical about capturing forts that were not to be held. (Clinton, *Amer. Reb.,* 72 *n.*) In the operations against the French off Newport in Aug. '78, he boldly engaged the crippled but stronger *Tonnant* (80) until forced by the approach of other enemy ships to withdraw. (Under NEWPORT, July–Aug. '78, see section headed "Naval Action....") Commanding the reinforcements for Barrington in the West Indies, Hotham had a creditable part in the 15 Dec. '78 battle at St. Lucia. The next summer he was stationed at Barbados. Early in 1780 he took command of the *Vengeance* (74) and fought under Adm. George Rodney in the meeting engagements of 17 Apr., 15 May, and 19 May. When Rodney sailed north to N.Y., Commodore Hotham was senior officer in the Leeward Islands. The hurricane of 10–12 Oct. damaged the *Vengeance* so badly that the next spring he sailed her back to England and had no further part in the Revolution. Although Hotham was one of the officers suggested by Clinton as commander on the American station, he is considered to be the least distinguished on the list that included Roddam, Barrington, John Elliot, and John Jervis. (*Ibid.,* 143 *n.*) "A good officer and a man of undaunted courage, he had on several occasions done admirably in a subordinate rank; but he was wanting in the energy, force of character, and decision requisite in a commander-in-chief." (Sir John Knox Laughton in *D.N.B.*)

HOUDIN, Michel-Gabriel. d. 1802. Cont'l. officer. France. Possibly related to the Michel Houdin (b. 1705) who guided Wolfe toward Quebec and who died a Protestant pastor in New Rochelle, N.Y., in 1766, the subject of this sketch became 1st Lt., 15th Mass., on 1 Jan. '77. After serving against Burgoyne, at Valley Forge, in the Monmouth Campaign, and at Newport, he was promoted to Capt. on 28 June '79 and transferred to Rufus Putnam's 5th Mass. on 1 Jan. '81. On 12 June '83 he joined Sproat's 2d Mass. Honorably discharged 1 Jan. '84, he was breveted Maj. on 6 Feb. '84, and returned to France. Settling in America a few years later, he died on 4 Feb. 1802 at Albany. Lasseray, whose work is the basis of this sketch, says Houdin became Capt. and Deputy Q.M.G. of the army in 1791 and Store-Keeper (*garde-magazin*) of the army in 1801. Heitman, who identifies him as being from Mass., does not credit Houdin with holding the latter postwar positions.

HOUK, Christian. See HUCK.

HOWARD, John Eager. 1752–1827. Cont'l. officer. Md. The well-educated son of a Md. planter, he became a Capt.

in the 2d Md. Bn. of the Flying Camp in July '76 and fought at White Plains. On 22 Feb. '77 he was commissioned Maj. of the 4th Md. and saw action at Germantown. Promoted to Lt. Col. of the 5th Md. on 11 Mar. '78, he fought in the Monmouth Campaign. On 22 Oct. '79 he was transferred to the 2d Md. and distinguished himself at Camden and COWPENS, 17 Jan. '81. For his part in the latter victory he received the thanks of Congress and one of the eight MEDALS awarded by that body. He figured prominently in the battles of Guilford, Hobkirk's Hill, and Eutaw Springs, being wounded in the last action.

Simple participation in the actions listed above would make an officer exceptional, but in truly distinguishing himself in most of these engagements as leader of one of the army's finest regiments Col. Howard emerges as one of the truly remarkable officers of American history. "Light-Horse Harry" Lee writes:

"This officer was one of the five lieutenant-colonels on whom Greene rested throughout the hazardous operations to which he was necessarily exposed by his grand determination to recover the South, or die in the attempt. We have seen him at the battle of Cowpens seize the critical moment and turn the fortune of the day;—alike conspicuous, though not alike successful, at Guilford and the Eutaws; and at all times, and all occasions, eminently useful. He was justly ranked among the chosen sons of the South.

"Trained to infantry service, he was invariably employed in that line, and was always to be found where the battle raged, pressing into close' action to wrestle with fixed bayonet. Placid in temper and reserved in deportment, he never lessened his martial fame by arrogance or ostentation, nor clouded it with garrulity or self-conceit.

"General Greene, whose discriminating mind graduated with nice exactitude the merit of all under him, thus speaks of this officer in a private letter to his friend in Maryland, dated the 14th of November, 1781:—

'This will be handed to you by Colonel Howard, as good an officer as the world affords. * * * My own obligations to him are great—the public's still more so. He deserves a statue of gold no less than the Roman and Grecian heroes.' " (*Memoirs,* 592)

After the war Howard was a delegate to the Cont'l. Congress (1788), Governor of Md. (1788–91), and U.S. Senator (1796–1803). In 1795 he declined the position of Sec. of War. He was a leader of the Federalists and a candidate for Vice. Pres. in their last unsuccessful campaign in 1816. On 18 May '87 he married Peggy Oswald Chew, daughter of Chief Justice Benjamin Chew of Pa. Their son, Benjamin Chew Howard (1791–1872), became a distinguished lawyer and politician. It is nice to know that Col. Howard was tremendously rich, owning much of the land now covered by Baltimore. He is mentioned in "Maryland, my Maryland."

One wonders what it takes to attract a biographer when no life of Howard can be found. *D.A.B.* cites only the *Memoir* that appeared in the Baltimore *Gazette* of 15 Oct. 1827, three days after his death, and a memoir by Elizabeth Read in the *Mag. of Amer. Hist.,* Oct. 1881.

HOWE, George Augustus. 1724–1758. British general. Eldest brother of William Howe, he entered the army at an early age and came to America as Col. of the 60th Regt. in July '57. In Sept. he assumed command of the 55th Regt. and was promoted to Brig Gen. in Dec. '57. A man who scorned the luxurious habits of other British officers while in the field, who liked the colonists and made an effort to learn their methods of frontier warfare, he was tremendously popular in America. He was killed 6 July '58 while leading his men in Abercromby's inept attack on Ticonderoga. The province of Mass. appropriated £250 to place a monument to his memory in Westminster Abbey.

HOWE, Richard, 1726–1799. British admiral and C. in C. on American Station (1776–78). Although Adm. Howe is more prominent in British history than his brother William, the latter played a more conspicuous role in the American Revolution; for this reason, and since they shared a joint politico-military command, much of Adm. Howe's career is covered under Wm. Howe.

Richard started his naval service young, going aboard the *Severn* at the age of 14 for the around-the-world voyage of Anson. His ship got only a short distance beyond Cape Horn before being forced back by storm damage. In 1742 he served in the West Indies and was made acting Lt., this rank being confirmed in 1744. By 7 Dec. '75 he had risen to the grade of Vice Adm. Although he earned a reputation as an able naval officer, his career was aided by his royal connections.

On the death of his elder brother at Ticonderoga, 6 July '58, he succeeded to the Irish title as Viscount Howe. In 1762 he entered Parliament as a representative for Dartmouth. During 1763 and 1765 he served on the Admiralty board, and he was treasurer of the navy from 1765 to 1770. (David Hannay in *E.B.*) In Feb. '76 Adm. Howe was given the naval command in America (*D.N.B.*), where his brother William had been acting C. in C. of the army for several months. Before leaving, however, he insisted that he and his brother be given the authority outlined under PEACE COMMISSION OF THE HOWE BROTHERS, and soon after his arrival off Mass. Bay in June '76 Lord Howe started exercising his limited power in this political field.

After taking army reinforcements to Staten Island, Adm. Howe furnished naval support of the N.Y. CAMPAIGN and continued the fruitless effort covered under PEACE COMMISSION. ... Sharing his brother's dissatisfaction with the backing they were getting from London, and offended by the government's action in sending the Peace Commission of Carlisle to America in 1778, Adm. Howe sent in his resignation. It was reluctantly accepted by Lord Sandwich, but when the entry of France into the war resulted in the approach of a large French fleet under d'Estaing, the Admiral remained long enough to defend N.Y. harbor and to break up the Franco-American operation against NEWPORT in Aug. '78. On the arrival of Adm. Byron's naval reinforcement from England, he returned home. The subsequent investigation by Parliament and an evaluation of the command of the Howe brothers in America is to be found under William HOWE. Richard refused to continue in service while Sandwich retained office.

When the Rockingham ministry took over in Mar. '82, Adm. Howe assumed command of naval forces in the Channel, and in the autumn he brilliantly achieved the complex and difficult mission of relieving Gibraltar. He was First Lord of the Admiralty from 28 Jan. '83 until Aug. '88, except for the period 16 Apr.–Dec. '83. When the war with France started in 1793 he again took command in the Channel. "His services in 1794 form the most glorious period of his life," writes Hannay. (*Op. cit.*) "Though Howe was now nearly seventy, and had been trained in the old school, he displayed an originality not usual

with veterans, and not excelled by any of his successors in the war, not even by Nelson. ..." Although he continued in nominal command, he saw no active service after 1794. Three years later he was called on to put down the mutiny at Spithead, an unpleasant task facilitated by his great popularity and respect among the seamen.

Having received the U.K. title of Viscount in 1782, he became Baron and Earl Howe in 1788. (His Irish title passed to William on the death of Richard.) "Black Dick," so called for his swarthy complexion, died in 1799.

The standard biography, which includes letters and notes from his journal, is John Barrow's *Life. ...* (1838). *The Command of the Howe Brothers During the American Revolution,* by Troyer Anderson (1936) is an original and provocative work; it includes an exhaustive bibliography. Lord Howe's defense of his performance in America, published in 1780, is entitled *Narrative of the Transactions of the Fleet.* Many of his official papers are held in the Admiralty; other papers unfortunately were destroyed with those of Wm. HOWE.

HOWE, Robert. 1732–1796. Cont'l. general. N.C. Son of a wealthy planter on the Cape Fear River, he was educated in Europe and had acquired his own fortune as a planter before the war started. He was Capt. of Ft. Johnston in 1766–67 and 1769–73. On Gov. Tryon's expedition against the Regulators he was an artillery Col. An ardent Whig, he served in the N.C. Assembly in 1772–73 and was a delegate to the colonial congress at New Bern in Aug. '74. Gov. Martin denounced him (8 Aug. '75) for his radical politics and also for his activity in forming and training rebel militia. On 1 Sept. '75 he became Col. of the 2d N.C. Regt. and three months later he marched north to assist the Virginians in the action covered under NORFOLK, 1 Jan. '76. Widely acclaimed for his success in this affair, he was appointed a Cont'l. B.G. on 1 Mar. '76. Returning to the South, he received a hero's welcome in N.C. and continued on to S.C., where a British attack against Charleston was expected. His plantation (at Brunswick) was ravaged by Cornwallis on 12 May. (See MOORES CREEK BRIDGE)

Howe took command of the Southern Dept. and was promoted to Maj. Gen. on 20 Oct. '77. The presence of this N.C. man at Charleston was resented by S.C. and Ga. authorities, and Howe's expedition against the British in Fla. was a fiasco. (See SOUTHERN THEATER, Military Operations in) Criticism of Howe was led by Christopher Gadsden, and when the latter refused to deny or retract certain statements the two met in a duel on 13 Aug. '78. Howe's shot grazed Gadsden's ear; Gadsden fired in the air; John André wrote a funny poem about the affair; and Howe and Gadsden ended up being close friends. Benjamin Lincoln succeeded Robert Howe as department commander in Sept. '78, but Howe continued to command in Ga. The British capture of SAVANNAH, 29 Dec. '78, led to such public outcry against the unfortunate Howe that it was necessary for the Cont'l. authorities to order him north in Apr. '79, even though a court-martial had acquitted him "with highest honor" of any misconduct at Savannah. Washington selected him as president of the court-martial resulting from Benedict Arnold's troubles as commander of Philadelphia. (See ARNOLD) Howe then went to the Hudson Highlands and led the unsuccessful operation against Verplancks that was ordered after Wayne's capture of STONY POINT in July. When Wm. Heath went home on leave, 21 Feb. '80, Howe succeeded him as commander of West Point and the support-

ing posts in the Highlands. He was succeeded by Benedict Arnold about 5 Aug., having carefully shown the traitor around West Point in mid-June, innocently pointing out its numerous weaknesses. On 29 Sept. he sat with the board of officers that recommended the hanging of John André. He commanded troops from the Highlands that successfully stopped the MUTINY OF THE N.J. LINE, 20–25 Jan. '81. In 1783 he dispersed the Philadelphia mob that had driven Congress out of town. (*D.A.B.*)

Resuming the life of a rice planter in 1783, he was appointed by Congress in May '85 to work on boundary negotiations with the Western Indians. The next year he returned to N.C. and was elected to the state legislature, but he died before he could take his seat. Robert Howe was not a man to attract biographers. Contemporary comments run the gamut from Josiah Quincy's appraisal that he was "a happy compound of the man of sense and sentiment with the man of the world," to the acid comment of the Royalist Janet Schaw, who found him "the worst character you ever heard through the whole province...." (Quoted in *D.A.B.*)

HOWE, William. 1729–1814. British C. in C. (1775–78). "It is safe to say that the war of the American Revolution was won and lost during the first three years," comments Troyer Anderson in the introduction to his provocative and highly respected work, *The Command of the Howe Brothers During the American Revolution* (New York, 1936). "Except for the first few months... the commander of the British army in America during the first period of the war was Sir William Howe. With the beginning of the summer of 1776 his older brother, Lord Richard Howe, held the naval command. Any explanation of British failure during these years thus becomes a verdict upon the conduct of the two brothers." Historians continue to be perplexed by the failure of Gen. Howe, who had a brilliant record at the start of the war and who was still young for his rank—not yet 50—when he succeeded Gage as C. in C. of the British army in Boston. Steele speaks for most historians when he writes that "his inactivity, his sloth, his apparent timidity, his lack of persistence, make one marvel for an explanation." (*American Campaigns,* 18) It has even been conjectured that the Howes did not want to win.

William Howe was an aristocrat whose grandmother had been the mistress of George I, a liaison which made him and his two brothers illegitimate uncles of George III. After attending Eton, William became a cornet in the Duke of Cumberland's Light Dragoons on 18 Sept. '46. Promoted to Lt. the next year, he entered the famous 20th Foot on 2 Jan. '50, became Capt. on 1 June, and was a friend of James Wolfe, then Maj. of the regiment. On 4 Jan. '56 Howe became Maj. of the new 60th Regt. (redesignated the 58th Foot a year later) and on 17 Dec. '59 he was commissioned Lt. Col. The next year he commanded the unit in Amherst's successful operation against Louisburg. Wolfe, who distinguished himself in the siege, commented on Howe's personal performance and referred to the 58th as "the best trained battalion in all America." As commander of a light infantry battalion Howe gained fame by leading Wolfe's force onto the Heights of Abraham (13 Sept. '59) for their epic victory at Quebec. After returning to his regiment for the defense of Quebec that winter, he led a "brigade of detachments" under Murray in the capture of Montreal by Amherst in 1760. The next year he

commanded a brigade in the siege of Belle Isle, off Brittany, and in 1762 he was A.G. of the army that captured Havana. "When the war was over no officer had a more brilliant record of service than Howe," comments H. Manners Chichester in *D.N.B.* "Sir William Howe was a fine figure, full six feet high, and well proportioned, not unlike in appearance to General Washington. His manners were graceful, and he was much beloved by his officers and soldiers for his generosity and affability." (J. F. Watson, *Annals,* II, 287, quoted in Lossing, II, 309 *n.*)

His eldest brother, George HOWE, had been killed in 1758 at Ticonderoga and at the instigation of their mother, William succeeded him as of that year in Parliament as the Whig representative from Nottingham, an office he held until 1780. In 1764 he became Col. of the 46th Foot in Ireland, in 1768 he was made Lt. Gov. of the Isle of Wight, and in 1772 he was promoted to Maj. Gen. Two years later he took charge of training selected line companies in a new system of light infantry drill.

In the field of politics the Whig representative from Nottingham condemned the government's coercive policy toward the American colonies. Aside from party affiliations, Howe's sympathies toward the colonists were increased by the honor paid to the memory of his brother. (See George HOWE) When word got around that he was being considered for an important assignment in America, a Mr. Kirk, to whom Howe had written that he would never accept a position of command against the colonists, reminded Howe of this promise. On 21 Feb. '75, after he had gotten his orders, Howe offered this explanation to his constituents in a letter to Kirk: "My going thither was not of my seeking. I was ordered, and could not refuse, without incurring the odious name of backwardness to serve my country in distress. . . ."

One of the famous passengers on the CERBERUS, he reached Boston on 25 May, proposed the tactics for the Battle of BUNKER HILL, 17 June, and commanded the operation with tremendous valor. On 10 Oct. '75 he assumed command of the Boston army in what supposedly was to be the temporary absence of Gage, and at the same time he was given the "local rank" of full Gen. In Apr. '76 Howe was formally named C. in C. of the British army in the 13 Colonies, Carleton being given command in Canada at the same time.

For a rebuttal of Troyer Anderson's thesis (see above), see Ira D. Gruber, "Lord Howe and Lord Germain: British Politics and the Winning of American Independence," *William and Mary Quarterly,* Series 3, Vol. XXII, No. 2 (April, 1965), 225–243. Gruber concludes that at the beginning of the American rebellion was primarily a political problem but it soon became a military one, and attempts by such men as North and the Howes to achieve a political settlement only hampered the efforts of the majority who had determined on a military victory.

Gen. Howe's subsequent career in America is covered under the N.Y. CAMPAIGN, the PEACE COMMISSION OF THE HOWE BROTHERS, the N.J. CAMPAIGN, and the PHILADELPHIA CAMPAIGN. (A summary of his generalship and an attempt at evaluation follows below.) Even before the Delaware River forts had been cleared, Howe wrote on 22 Oct. to ask that he be relieved. His reasons were the failure of the government to send him the reinforcements he wished for in 1777, the diversion of an appreciable number of his reinforcements for BURGOYNE'S OFFENSIVE, and the failure of his final campaign to achieve what he had hoped.

(Anderson, *op. cit.,* 305) His letter was received by Germain in early Dec. '77, and on 14 Apr. '78 he learned from Germain that his resignation was accepted but that he would have to wait for his replacement. (As an interesting comment on the problem of trans-Atlantic communications, this last letter had been sent by Germain on 18 Feb.)

After Clinton's arrival at Philadelphia but before he took over command, Howe's officers staged the extravagant MISCHIANZA to protest the loss of a general who was tremendously popular. Two days later an unsuccessful attempt was made to trap Lafayette's large detachment at BARREN HILL, 20 May. Five days later Howe sailed for England.

Adm. Howe remained a few months longer and distinguished himself by running d'Estaing's large French fleet out of North American waters. Although the British government had remained satisfied with Gen. Howe's prosecution of the war—Germain took credit for having him knighted in the autumn of 1776 —news of Burgoyne's surrender led to "a rapidly growing volume of criticism of the Howes . . . together with some directed against the ministry." (Anderson, *op. cit.,* 322) Germain himself became increasingly hostile toward the brothers. In Jan. '78 Fox, leader of the Opposition, started agitating in Parliament for an investigation. A pamphlet war was inaugurated against the Howes by Israel Mauduit. Burgoyne reached London in May, Sir William Howe arrived in July, Lord Richard Howe appeared in Oct., and the Opposition sharpened their bayonets. Burgoyne, whose return to England had been met by popular and official approbation, tried to blame his defeat on Gen. Howe and Clinton. Sir William proposed that his correspondence with Germain be examined by Parliament, but the government resisted until "Germain, in answering an attack by Burgoyne, assailed the Howes and thus made it impossible to deny an inquiry." (*Ibid.*, 323)

The latter started in May '79 and ended inconclusively with the adjournment of Parliament on 29 June. "The pamphlet war continued several months longer and was as inconclusive as the inquiry, except that it has left a suspicion that has survived ever since that there was something sinister in the Howes' lack of success." (*Ibid.*) In 1780 Howe published his *Narrative*.

"There appears to have been some idea of reappointing Howe to the American command," writes H. Manners Chichester in *D.N.B.* Although he had serious grievances against the government, particularly against Germain and his supporters, Sir William announced on his return from America that he had no intention of joining the Opposition, and he held to this position. In 1782 he was appointed Lt. Gen. of the ordnance. On 23 Oct. '93 he was promoted to full Gen. and when the armies of Napoleon threatened England he held various large commands in the island. In 1799 he succeeded to the Irish title as 5th Viscount Howe when his brother died. In 1803 he resigned his ordnance post because of bad health and in 1814 he died after a long, painful illness. (*D.N.B.*) He had no children.

Sir William Howe has been described as a man "of coarse mould" (*D.N.B.*), about six feet tall, and with the swarthy complexion that gave his brother the nickname "Black Dick." He had one physical trait in common with Washington: exceptionally bad teeth. William and his brother Richard were also known for being "so reserved and taciturn that any accurate estimate of their characters was extremely difficult." (Anderson, *op. cit.*, 43) Writing of the general, Horace Walpole said: "Howe was one of those brave, silent brothers, and was reckoned sensible, though so silent that nobody knew whether he was or not." (*Last Journals*, I, 432, quoted in Anderson, *op. cit.*, 45)

Although Burgoyne and Clinton also had mistresses in America, Howe's liaison with Mrs. Loring and his high living in N.Y.C. and Philadelphia were notorious. Some have attributed his inertia and British military failures to his personal shortcomings. In the spring of 1777 an English wag penned the lines:

> Awake, arouse, Sir Billy,
> There's forage in the plain.
> Leave your little filly,
> And open the campaign.

The eccentric and outspoken Charles Lee, who may have known Howe during the French and Indian War and who as a prisoner in N.Y.C. had occasion to learn something of his conduct, had this to say:

"From my first acquaintance with Mr. Howe I liked him.* * * He is ... [however] the most indolent of mortals.* * * I believe he scarcely ever read the letters he signed.... You will say I am drawing my friend Howe in more ridiculous colours than he has been represented in: but that is his real character. He is naturally good humoured, complaisant, but illiterate and indolent to the last degree, unless as an executive soldier [meaning, presumably, as a tactical commander], in which capacity he is all fire and activity, brave and cool as Julius Caesar. His understanding is ... rather good than otherwise, but was totally confounded and stupefied by the immensity of the task imposed upon him. He shut his eyes, fought his battles, drank his bottle, had his little whore, advised with his counsellors [whom Lee identifies elsewhere as McKensey, Balfour, and Galloway], received his orders from North and Germain (one more absurd than the other), took Galloway's opinion, shut his eyes, fought again, and is now, I suppose, to be called to account for acting according to instructions." (Ltr. of 4 June '78 to Rush. The first sentence is quoted from Nickerson, *Turning Point,* 63; the rest from Anderson, *op. cit.,* 319–320. The latter author comments that "There was a kernel of truth in everything Lee alleged" but that this "rank caricature" cannot be accepted as a true picture.)

Anderson concludes that there is absolutely no foundation for the charges that the Howes did not want to win, that they made no real effort to do so, and that they carried on a "flirtation with treason because of their tenderness toward the Americans and their dislike of the ministerial party." (*Ibid.,* 337) He submits that Gen. Howe's personal vices probably "were the consequence of his ill success and discouragement rather than the cause." (*Ibid.*)

Sir Henry Clinton, who served as second in command to Howe and then succeeded him, gives this harsh evaluation:

"Had Sir William Howe fortified the hills around Boston, he could not have been disgracefully driven from it: Had he pursued his victory at Long Island, he had ended the Rebellion: Had he landed above the lines at New York, not a man could have escaped him: Had he fought the Americans at Brunswick he was sure of victory: Had he cooperated with the Northern Army, he had saved it, or had he gone to Philadelphia by land, he had ruined Mr. Washington and his forces; But, as he did none of these things, had he gone to the D—l, before he was sent to America, it had been a saving of infamy to himself and indelible dishonor to this Country." (Clinton Papers, quoted in Van Tyne, *War of*

Indep., 432, with a few changes in capitalization.)

In the preface of the work so heavily relied on in this sketch, Anderson gives this succinct statement: "It is my belief that the failure of the Howes is a mystery only because the conventional division between military and political history had diverted attention away from the points that serve best to explain the conduct of British operations in America." He concludes that if one allows for the fact that the brothers "had to be politicians and military men at the same time," perhaps the most important single reason for their failure is that they did not "adjust their methods to the support that the government was willing to provide." (*Op. cit.,* V, 341)

The private papers of the Howe family and the British headquarters papers for the period Sir William was C. in C. are said to have been destroyed by a fire in Ireland. In addition to the work of Anderson, see Bellamy Partridge, *Sir Billy Howe* (1932).

HOWITZER. A short cannon for high-angle fire of heavy projectiles at low velocity. In trajectory it is between a mortar and a rifle.

HUBBARDTON, Vt., 7 July '77. (BURGOYNE'S OFFENSIVE) Defeat of American rear guard. After the fall of TICONDEROGA, 2–5 July, St. Clair led the largest part of his command, about 2,500, on the roundabout route through Castleton; from here he intended to join Col. Long's force at Skenesboro (see SKENESBORO, 6 July). Along the primitive trail, over numerous hills and in oppressive heat, they marched to the two-house settlement of Hubbardton, which is now East Hubbardton, Vt. St. Clair then led most of his troops another six miles to Castleton, where they camped for the night. Seth Warner was left behind with orders to wait with his 150 men for the rear guard regiments to arrive, and then to join the main body at Castleton. Warner failed to comply with these specific orders and remained in Hubbardton for the night. His command comprised his own Vermonters, Col. Turbott Francis' Mass. Regt., and Col. Nathan Hale's N.H. Regt. (This is not the famous Hale.) Including stragglers, they numbered about 1,000. Warner's worst error, however, was in failing to post adequate security detachments.

The enemy pursued vigorously. Fraser's Adv. Corps left Mt. Independence on 6 July at 4 A.M.; Riedesel followed with his own regiment and Breymann's Adv. Corps. (See Order of Battle under BURGOYNE'S OFFENSIVE.) About 1 P.M. Riedesel with a body of jägers and grenadiers caught up with Fraser. They agreed that Fraser would go on another three miles and that both would resume the advance the next morning at 3 o'clock. Fraser bivouacked about three miles from Warner's camp, at the place now called Hubbardton. During the night his Indians discovered Warner's camp, which Fraser then made plans to surprise at dawn.

Led by the Tories of Jessup and Peters, the British moved at dawn. At 4:40 they surprised and routed

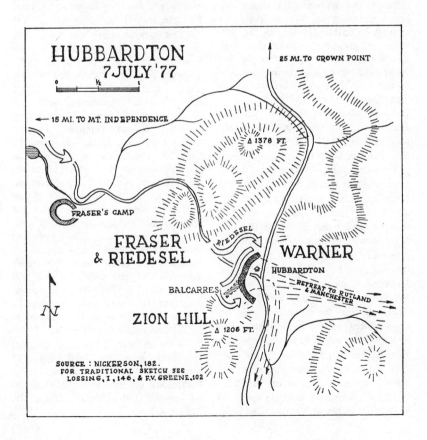

HUBBARDTON
7 JULY '77

0   ½   1

← 15 MI. TO MT. INDEPENDENCE

↑ 25 MI. TO CROWN POINT

Δ 1378 FT.

FRASER'S CAMP

FRASER
& RIEDESEL

RIEDESEL

WARNER

HUBBARDTON

RETREAT TO RUTLAND
& MANCHESTER

BALCARRES

ZION HILL

Δ 1205 FT.

N

SOURCE : NICKERSON, 182.
FOR TRADITIONAL SKETCH SEE
LOSSING, I , 146, & F.V. GREENE, 102

Hale's regiment at breakfast near what is now called Sucker Brook. Fraser's 750 pushed on to attack the regiments of Warner and Francis. Although the latter had little time to form, they dropped 21 Britishers with their first volley, killing Maj. Grant of the 24th and wounding Balcarres. (The latter, who commanded the flank companies of Fraser's Adv. Corps, came out of the battle only slightly wounded, but with the marks of 30 bullets in his clothes.) A 1,000-yard line of battle formed in the woods. The American left flank was on the slopes of 1,200-foot Zion Hill (its modern name); Fraser must have instinctively seen that this was "critical terrain," and he started thinning out his forces on the left to build up strength to envelop by way of this hill. When his grenadiers clawed their way up the steep, rocky, wooded slopes, the Americans curved this end of their line to the rear in a maneuver known as "refusing the flank" and kept up their fire. On the other end of the line Francis started pushing back the weakened British left. The British were getting the worst of it, being unaccustomed to forest fighting and taking heavy losses from accurate American fire, when the Germans rushed up to save them. Riedesel had moved that morning as planned, and when he heard the firefight start he hurried forward with the jägers and grenadiers who had caught up with Fraser the day before. Riedesel launched a piecemeal attack, sending his jägers straight against the American right, starting the grenadiers on an envelopment of the same flank, and ordering his main body to come up quickly. Further, the chubby little German major general sent his men forward singing to the music of their band, a nice psychological touch to bolster the spirits of his own men while dramatizing the arrival of reinforcements and exaggerating their size.

The Mass. Regt. held their ground against the jägers for 10 minutes, however, and pulled back only after Col. Francis was killed and they were threatened with envelopment. About this time the Vt. Regt. was hit with a bayonet attack. With the other two regiments driven from the field and his own threatened with annihilation, Warner's last order was as sensible as it was unorthodox: "Scatter and meet me at Manchester." St. Clair sent no support to Hubbardton "principally, it is said, because the two militia regiments that were nearest would not obey his orders and the rest were too far away." (Fiske, *Struggle*, II, 64)

The two-hour action was "as bloody as Waterloo" in proportion to the numbers engaged. (Ward, *W.O.R.*, 414) Casualty figures show considerable disagreement. Nickerson says Francis and 40 other Americans were left dead on the field, and 274—including 40 wounded—were captured. (*Turning Point*, 159) Col. HALE was captured with 70 of his men in their retreat; since other modern writers put American prisoners at around 320 (Montross, *Rag, Tag*, 202), Nickerson's figure of 274 prisoners apparently does not include Hale and his men. Ward says, "The American casualties, including those captured, were 12 officers and 312 men, out of a force which after Hale's defection did not much exceed 600 fighting men" (*op. cit.*, 414); Ward implies that Hale's men are to be added to get the final number of Americans captured. The rebels lost 12 guns.

Nickerson says British and German casualties were 35 killed and 148 wounded, figures that come close to Fortescue's estimate that the total did not exceed 140. (*British Army*, III, 225)

HUCK, Christian. Loyalist officer. Described by American writers as "a profane, unprincipled man" who "hated Presbyterians bitterly, and made them suffer when he could," he is also said to have been fond of stating that "God Almighty was turned rebel; but that if there were twenty Gods on their side, they should all be conquered." (Lossing, II, 659) As British and Tory raiders ravaged S.C. after the surrender of Charleston, Huck commanded a body of cavalry in the outposts around Camden. Presumably he was an officer of Tarleton's British Legion. Not long after destroying the iron works of William Hill and Isaac HAYNE he led a raid that resulted in his death at WILLIAMSON'S PLANTATION, S.C., 12 July '80. His name has also been spelled Hucke and Huyck. (*Ibid.*) In Sabine's *American Loyalists* his name is spelled Huck, and he is identified as a Capt. on 7 June '78.

HUDDY–ASGILL AFFAIR, Apr.–Oct. '82. Artillery Capt. Joshua Huddy of the N.J. militia was captured 24 Mar. '82 in a surprise attack by Tory irregulars at Toms River, N.J., and was eventually confined on a prison ship near N.Y.C. The ASSOCIATED LOYALISTS got permission from Sir Henry Clinton's headquarters to take Huddy and two others "ostensibly for the purpose of being exchanged for three Associators [who were] prisoners with the enemy," according to Clinton's memoirs. (*Amer. Reb.*, 360) According to D. S. Freeman's account, he had been demanded by the Associated Loyalists on a charge that he had slain one of their partisans, Philip White. (*Washington*, V, 413) Van Doren says the British released the prisoners in good faith that they were to be traded, but that the board of the Associated Loyalists had issued "discreet verbal orders" that Huddy be hanged for White. (*Secret History*, 430)

In any event, Capt. Richard Lippincott escorted Huddy under guard to the heights of Middletown in Monmouth co., and on 12 Apr. hanged him to a tree with the following placard pinned to his breast:

"We, the Refugees, having long with grief beheld the cruel murders of our brethren . . . therefore determined not to suffer without taking vengeance . . . ; and thus begin, having made use of Captain Huddy as the first object to present to your view; and we further determine to hang man for man while there is a Refugee existing." Below this was written "Up Goes Huddy for Phillip White."

On 18 Apr. David Forman brought Washington a dispatch from Knox and Gouverneur Morris, exchange commissioners, in which this episode was reported. Forman had many supplemental details including five affidavits and the proceedings of a meeting of 14 patriots who recommended an eye for an eye. On the 24th Washington wrote Clinton demanding the delivery of the guilty officer, who was believed to be Lippincott. Clinton "judged it right, out of delicacy" to address himself first to the Tory authorities on the circumstances of Huddy's death, as he wrote later. "For I could not conceive it possible that those gentlemen would have authorized such an act of barbarity or wished to screen the offenders." (*Amer. Reb.*, 360) Receiving evasive answers, he had Lippincott arrested and courtmartialed, but the latter was acquitted on grounds that he had only obeyed orders.

Washington, meanwhile, received an unsatisfactory reply in which Clinton denied countenancing the cruel treatment of any prisoner, and on 3 May he directed Moses Hazen to select "by lot . . . a British Captain, who [was] an unconditional prisoner." If he had no qualified captain he was to pick a lieutenant. This officer was to be executed in retaliation, a course of action recommended almost unanimously by a council of war. Hazen made the embarrassing mistake of allowing the choice to fall on Capt. ASGILL.

See Katherine Mayo, *General Washington's Dilemma* (1938), for a full account of the episode and an extensive bibliography.

HUDSON RIVER and the Highlands. The estuary known as the Hudson River, where tides are felt 150 miles upstream at Albany and which could be navigated by the largest warships to within 46 miles of that city, was a vital avenue of strategic movement between Canada and the Thirteen Colonies during the Colonial Wars and during the Revolution. Another feature that attracted the British was the fact that the Hudson Valley was inhabited predominantly by Dutch, with a considerable number of Germans, and with groups of English, Scots, Scots-Irish, Huguenots, and Swedes. "Nowhere in the colonies was toryism stronger," comments Nickerson. (*Turning Point,* 54)

The Hudson Highlands are a topographical curiosity of the valley in that they cross this strategic avenue a mere 45 miles north of N.Y.C. to constitute a natural barrier of easily defensible terrain; rising above the 500-foot contour, they are the highest ground along the Hudson, Mohawk, Lake Champlain system of waterways. Early in the war, on 25 May '75, the Cont'l. Cong. therefore resolved to fortify the Highlands, and a few months later work was started opposite West Point at Martelaer's Rock (now Constitution Island). Early the next year this effort was abandoned, but Forts Clinton and Montgomery were built astride Popolopen Creek.

CLINTON'S EXPEDITION TO THE HIGHLANDS in Oct. '77 made short work of these defenses, but for strategic reasons the British were forced to abandon their gains. The Americans took another look at this critical terrain and decided that the main fortification should be at WEST POINT. Planned for the most part by the French engineer de La Radière, the construction was started 20 Jan. '78 by Samuel H. Parsons' brigade. Fort Arnold, later called Ft. Clinton, was situated on the tip of the 40-acre plateau that dominated the double right-angle bend of the river at West Point. From Mar. '78 until June '80 the Polish engineer Kosciuszko was in charge, and an elaborate system of redoubts and water batteries was constructed. In Apr. '78 a great 60-ton chain was stretched across the river to Constitution Island, and the land approaches to West Point from the west were barred by Forts Putnam, Webb, and Wyllys. These were in turn protected by four redoubts.

Despite British efforts covered under STONY POINT and ARNOLD'S TREASON, the Hudson Highlands remained in American hands for the rest of the war. Visiting West Point in Nov. '80, Chastellux was overwhelmed by the engineering wonders accomplished here "by a people, who six years before had scarcely ever seen a cannon...." (*Travels,* II, 91)

"Sometimes an analogy is drawn between the Richelieu-Lake Champlain-Hudson route in 1777 and the Mississippi in 1863," writes the British military historian Whitton, "but a very brief consideration will show that no real comparison is possible." His argument is basically that Union control of the Mississippi meant that the main Confederate army was enclosed within a definite area by Union forces on land, sea, and river; British control of

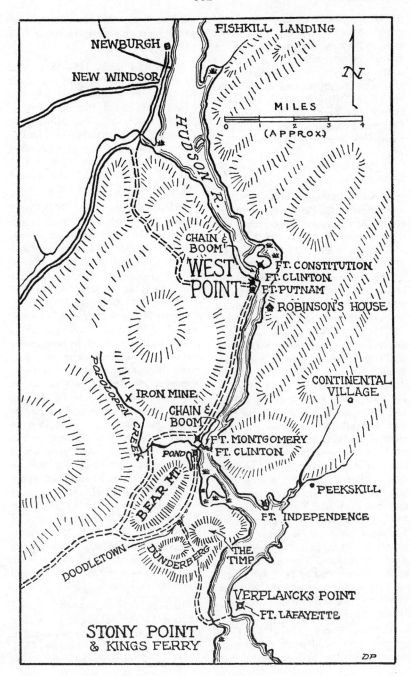

the Hudson, however, might have "enclosed" New England but Washington's main American army would have remained outside with the capability of continued operations. "Other points will also occur to the student—such as the use of the Mississippi as a base—but enough has been said to expose the fallacy of a comparison too often made." (*American War of Independence,* 178–79)

See also BURGOYNE'S OFFENSIVE and WEST POINT.

HUGER, Benjamin. 1746–1779. Militia officer. S.C. Fourth eldest of the HUGER BROTHERS, he was a member of the assembly and the Prov. Cong. (1775). On 17 June '75 he became Lt. of the 4th S.C. Arty., and on 16 Sept. '76 he was promoted to Maj. of his brother Isaac's 5th S.C. Rifles. (Heitman, 55, 306) When Lafayette landed near Georgetown, S.C., from France (1777) his ship was piloted to Huger's plantation by Negro slaves; Lafayette and Huger became close friends. Benjamin was accidentally killed by friendly troops at CHARLESTON on 11 May '79. His son Francis Kinloch Huger (1773–1855) was educated as a doctor in England and in 1794 was briefly on the medical staff of the British army in Flanders. Learning that Lafayette was imprisoned at Olmutz, Francis and Dr. J. E. Bollman succeeded in liberating him temporarily. Both were captured and put in prison for eight months. Lafayette was retaken on the Austrian frontier. (*D.A.B.,* "F. K. Huger") Francis got his M.D. in 1797, married the daughter of Thos. Pinckney in 1802, and during the War of 1812 was Pinckney's A.G. His son was the undistinguished Confederate Maj. Gen. Benj. Huger (1805–1877).

HUGER, Daniel. 1741–1799. Congressman. S.C. Eldest of the famous HUGER BROTHERS, he was a delegate to the Cont'l. Cong. from 1786 to 1788 and a representative in Congress from 1789 to 1793.

HUGER, Francis. 1751–1811. Militia officer. S.C. Youngest of the HUGER BROTHERS, he became Capt. in the 2d S.C. Cont'ls. when this unit was organized under Col. Wm. Moultrie on 17 June '75. He served under Moultrie in the famous defense of Charleston, 28 June '76. In 1777 he was named Lt. Col. and Q.M.G. of the Southern Dept. He resigned in 1778. (Heitman)

HUGER, Isaac. 1743–1797. Cont'l. general. S.C. One of the HUGER BROTHERS, he was educated in Europe and served as a Lt. against the Cherokee in 1760. He was made Lt. Col. 1st S.C. Regt. on 17 June '75, Col. 5th S.C. Cont'ls. on 16 Sept. '76, and B.G. on 9 Jan. '79. At STONO FERRY, S.C., 20 June '79, he was severely wounded while leading the left wing. In the fiasco at SAVANNAH, 9 Oct. '79, he commanded the Ga. and S.C. militia in an unsuccessful diversion. During the Charleston campaign of 1780 he was routed by Tarleton at MONCK'S CORNER, 14 Apr. In the Southern campaigns of Greene he led one wing of the army in a remarkable march from Cheraw to link up with Morgan's wing at Guilford C. H. (under SOUTHERN OPERATIONS OF GREENE see section headed "Operations on the Yadkin"). He was seriously wounded at GUILFORD, N.C., 15 Mar. '81, but commanded Greene's right wing at HOBKIRK'S HILL, S.C., 25 Apr. '81. His brigade in both of these actions was composed of the 4th and 5th Va. Cont'ls. He was in the S.C. General Assembly in 1782.

HUGER, John. 1744–1804. Patriot leader. S.C. Third eldest of the HUGER BROTHERS, he probably was educated in England. He and his brother Isaac served as junior officers in the CHER-

OKEE EXPEDITION OF 1761 and the operations of the preceding year. In the early phases of the Revolution he was prominent in patriot politics, and according to Heitman was a militia Capt. in 1776 and 1777. Under the new state constitution he became the first Sec. of State. His first wife (m. 1767) was Charlotte Motte, whose father had been Treas. of S.C. (He was undoubtedly kin to the husband of Rebecca, heroine of FT. MOTTE.) His second wife (m. 1785) was Mrs. Anne Broun Cusack. One son was Alfred Huger (1788–1872), who was prominent in the Nullification Controversy of 1830–33 and was postmaster at Charleston for 25 years; in 1835 he raised a national issue by requesting authority to bar anti-slavery literature from the mails. (A bill to this effect was defeated in the Senate the next year.)

HUGER BROTHERS OF S.C. Five brothers of this name (pronounced u'-gee) served during the Revolution. Their grandfather, Daniel, was a Huguenot merchant who settled on the Santee River, S.C., in 1685 and laid the foundations of a wealth that was sustained through several subsequent generations. Their father, also named Daniel, married Mary Cordes, raised the boys at the plantation called "Limerick," and gave them liberal educations. In chronological order the brothers were Daniel (the third), Isaac, John, Benjamin, and Francis. Each is sketched separately.

HULL, William. 1753–1825. Cont'l. officer, B.G. in War of 1812. Conn.–Mich. A fifth-generation American of English ancestry, he was born in Derby, Conn., graduated from Yale when he was 19, studied law at Litchfield, and was admitted to the bar in 1775. Becoming Capt.-Lt. of the 7th Conn. on 6 July of this year and Capt. on 9 Oct., he served with his militia company in the Boston lines. On 1 Jan. '76 he became Capt. of the 19th Cont'l. Inf. (Conn.). Rising steadily in grade—Maj., 8th Mass., 1 Jan. '77; Lt. Col. 3d Mass., 12 Aug. '79—"he saw active and almost continuous service, taking part in the battles of White Plains, Trenton, Princeton, Saratoga, Monmouth, and Stony Point, and commanding, for three successive winters, the American advanced lines just above New York City," writes J. W. Pratt in *D.A.B.* He led the bold raid to MORRISANIA, 22–23 Jan. '81. He was brave and energetic, and won commendations from Washington and Congress. (*Ibid.*) Retained in Jackson's Cont'l. Regt., 3 Nov. '83, he served to 20 June '84.

After leaving the army he returned to the law, became active as a Jeffersonian politician, and helped suppress Shays's Rebellion. On 22 Mar. 1805 Pres. Jefferson appointed Hull Gov. of the newly organized Mich. Territory. On 8 Apr. 1812 he was appointed B.G. Having reluctantly accepted this commission and command of an army to defend his territory (*ibid.*), he suffered a series of defeats at the hands of the British—including surrender of Detroit on 16 Aug. '12—and was cashiered after a court-martial presided over by Henry DEARBORN. (Three days after he surrendered Detroit, his nephew Capt. Isaac Hull, whom he had adopted, won his famous victory over the *Guerrière* in Chesapeake Bay.) William Hull spent his remaining years with his family at Newton, Mass., where he had established a home after the Revolution.

See *Revolutionary Services and Civil Life of Gen. Wm. Hull Prepared from His Manuscripts, by His Daughter, Mrs. Maria Campbell: together with the Hist. of the Campaign of 1812, and Surrender of the Post of Detroit, by His Grandson, James Freeman Clarke* (1814). Hull published his *Defense* . . .

in 1814 and *Memoirs of the Campaign of the North Western Army* in 1824. See also bibliography in *D.A.B.*

HUMPTON, Richard. c. 1733–1804. Cont'l. officer. England–Pa. As a British Capt. he took part in the siege of St. Malo * and resigned while in the West Indies. He later settled on an upper branch of the Susquehanna. Named Lt. Col. of the FLYING CAMP on 16 July '76, he became Col. of the 11th Pa. on 25 Oct. As Washington retreated across N.J., Humpton was assigned the task of removing boats from the mid stretches of the Delaware River; his success on this mission helped stop the British pursuit and made possible Washington's counterstroke at Trenton, 26 Dec. '76. He fought at Brandywine and was "the most vigorous accusant" of Wayne for failing to avoid the Paoli "massacre." (Freeman, *Washington*, IV, 495 and *n.*) He took command of the 10th Pa. on 1 July '78, assumed command of the 6th Pa. in the reorganization of 17 Jan. '81, and led the 2d Pa. from 1 Jan. '83 until the Cont'l. Army was disbanded on 3 Nov. '83. He was breveted B.G. on 30 Sept. '83. After the war he returned to his farm and was A.G. of the militia. (Appleton's; Heitman.)

HUNTINGTON, Jabez. 1719–1786. Patriot, militia general. Conn. A wealthy West Indies trader of great social and political prominence when the Revolution started, he was one of two Maj. Gens. commissioned by Conn. in Dec. '76. He became a member of the council of safety in May '75 and was active in it the next four years. In Apr. '77 he succeeded David WOOSTER as commander of all state militia. In Feb. '79 he was incapacitated by a nervous

* The British attacked this French port in 1758 and '59. (*E.B.*)

disease brought on by overwork. The war took a heavy toll of his shipping. Of four famous sons, the most prominent was Jedediah HUNTINGTON.

HUNTINGTON, Jedediah. 1743–1818. Cont'l. general. Conn. Reared amid wealth and great social prominence, he graduated from Harvard in 1763 and joined the business of his father, Jabez HUNTINGTON. He became an active Son of Liberty, was made ensign of the first Norwich company in 1769, and was a Lt. in '71. In 1774 he rose from Capt. in May to Col. of the 20th Regt. of colonial militia in Oct. On 26 Apr. '75 he reached Cambridge with his regiment to join the Boston Siege. He was Col. of the 8th Conn. Cont'ls. from 6 July to 10 Dec. '75, and commanded the 17th Cont'l. Inf. (Conn.) during 1776. Although *D.A.B.* says he fought at Long Island, in subsequent skirmishes of the N.Y. Campaign, and at DANBURY in Apr. '77, D. S. Freeman says he was absent sick during the first battle (*Washington*, IV, 163), he was not engaged in any significant fighting during the remainder of the N.Y. Campaign, nor is he mentioned in the accounts of the Danbury Raid. As a matter of fact, Jed. Huntington's military career is remarkably free of any mention of combat, although he was an able officer (*ibid.*) and was in the field throughout most of the war. He commanded the 1st Conn. Cont'ls. from 1 Jan. '77 until he was promoted B.G. on 12 May '77. According to *D.A.B.* he joined Putnam at Peekskill in July, went to the main army near Philadelphia in the fall, and then served at various posts along the Hudson. He was on Chas. Lee's court-martial (July '78) and a member of the board that investigated John André. Breveted Maj. Gen. on 30 Sept. '83, he resumed his commercial affairs after 3 Nov. President Washington, a personal friend, appointed him collector of customs at New London in 1789, a post he held 26 years.

HUNTINGTON, Samuel. 1731–1796. Signer. Conn. He was descended from Simon Huntington, who died on the trip to the colonies and left his widow to settle in Boston in 1633. He shared this ancestor with Gen. Jedediah Huntington. At 16 he was apprenticed to a cooper. Later he worked on his father's farm and in his shop, and, although he had little education, studied Latin and the law by himself. Admitted to the Bar in 1758, he settled in Norwich and was sent to the general assembly in May '65, becoming King's Attorney the same year. In 1765–75 he was also J.O.P., and in 1773 was named superior court judge. He sat in the upper house of the assembly in 1775–84, and in May '75 he was named to the committee for the colony's defense. He was elected to the Cont'l. Congress 1775–84. He signed the Decl. of Indep. and was elected president, to succeed John Jay, on 29 Sept. '79. Serving until 6 Jul. '81, he resigned for poor health and took a leave of absence from the Congress, returning in 1783 for another year. He was elected Lt. Gov. in 1785 and became Gov. 1786–96. He was a strong supporter of the Federal Constitution and helped get it ratified in his state.

HUTCHINSON, Thomas. 1711–1780. Royal Gov. of Mass. Great-great-grandson of the famous Anne (Marbury) Hutchinson (1591–1643) who emigrated from England with her husband and children in 1634 and was banished from the Mass. Bay Colony for her religious beliefs, Thomas was a leader of the conservatives in the colony before the American Revolution. He entered Harvard at the age of 13, graduated in 1727, and three years later

received his M.A. Wealthy, able, and socially part of what he called the "better sort," his first big step in alienating the "common sort" came in 1749, when his leadership succeeded in establishing "hard money" as the medium of exchange in the colony. He did this by his plan to call in the major portion of the inflated bills of credit, which the government had been issuing since 1690 without adequate backing, and paying these off at the rate of 11 to 1 by using the £183,650 that England had sent to reimburse Mass. for their expenses in the Louisburg expedition. This measure, like the abolishment of the Land Bank (1740–41), was to the benefit of persons living on fixed incomes and of creditors—who, naturally, were of the "better sort"—and was tremendously unpopular with debtors. He attended the ALBANY CONVENTION of 1754 and probably had a hand in drafting the famous Plan of Union with which Franklin's name is primarily associated. In 1758 he became Lt. Gov., and in 1760 he became chief justice, a position to which the father of James OTIS had aspired. Hutchinson opposed the Sugar Act and the Stamp Act, but only because of their adverse effect on British as well as on colonial trade. Loyal to the authority that had commissioned him, however, he made every effort to enforce the unpopular acts.

Hutchinson had given the popular leaders of Boston several reasons to believe he had a personal interest in enforcing the British measures they found so objectionable. Already a wealthy man, he appropriated more than his fair share of offices and salaries, which brought him perhaps £300 a year in days when an ordinary family could live comfortably on £40 a year. His brother-in-law, Andrew Oliver, was a stamp distributor. So the night of 26–

27 Aug. '65 his home was sacked by the Boston mob. In the absence of Bernard he was acting governor during the period 1769–71. In the latter year he became governor and served until 1774. Hutchinson weathered the resistance to the Townshend Acts, but during the subsequent lull in agitation he proved his congenital inaptitude for the post he held. "A wise governor would have made the most of so favorable a situation; in fact Hutchinson was the chief ally of [Sam] Adams in reviving the waning controversy," observes Carl L. Becker in *D.A.B.* The HUTCHINSON LETTERS AFFAIR in 1773 was his final undoing. Then, having unwisely used his influence for the personal profit of himself and his sons, Thomas and Elisha, in the matter of the East India Company tea being sent to America, and in his refusal to make it easy for this tea to be removed, Hutchinson played into the hands of the rabble rousers and brought on the BOSTON TEA PARTY, 16 Dec. '73. "This, the last important executive act of Hutchinson, contributed to bring about the very crisis which he wished to avert." (*Ibid.*)

Although he did not know it at the time, he was through. On 29 June '74 he reached England, and a few days later he spent two hours reporting to George III on the situation in his province. Gen. Gage had meanwhile taken over as governor, but the understanding was that Hutchinson would return to that post when the crisis was over. Hutchinson had no idea that he would have more than a few months to wait, and he urged on the London authorities a policy of conciliation that he had not followed when he was in a position to do so in Boston. So it was that those of the "common sort" rose as leaders of the American Revolution and Hutchinson never realized his hope of laying his "bones in New England."

"Thomas Hutchinson was a man of character and ability, one of the finest representatives of colonial America, with the virtues and limitations of those to the manner born. Honorable and gracious to his equals, benevolent and kindly to his inferiors, he had to an unusual degree the instinct that founds and perpetuates families, and the love of property that often goes with it. Scrupulously honest in the performance of all obligations, both private and public, Hutchinson was unfortunate in that, like so many eighteenth-century aristocrats [allusion is to the French Revolution], he was compelled by circumstances to pay the penalty of a divided allegiance." (Becker in *D.A.B.*)

He was an historian of note, publishing the first volume of his *History of the Colony of Massachusetts Bay* in 1764 and writing the third while exiled in England (it was published in 1828). The work is still useful "for its accuracy, judgment, and quoted documents not now elsewhere available" (*ibid.*). He also wrote a pamphlet that ably attacked the *Present State of the Bills of Credit* (1736), *The Witchcraft Delusion of 1692* (1780, the year of his death), and many other works of a political and historical nature.

See P. O. Hutchinson, *The Diary and Letters of Thos. Hutchinson* (2 vols., 1883–86) and J. K. Hosmer, *The Life of Thos. Hutchinson* (1896).

HUTCHINSON LETTERS AFFAIR. 1773. Letters to English friends from Thos. Hutchinson and Andrew Oliver, written 1767–69 when they were Chief Justice and Province Secretary of Mass., fell into the hands of Benj. Franklin in late 1772, when Franklin was a colonial agent in London. The letters urged a tougher policy with the colonies and were given to Franklin to show him the type of advice from America that was influencing Parliament. Franklin sent the six Hutchinson and four Oliver letters to Thos. Cushing, Speaker of the Mass. House of Representatives, with the warning that they should be shown to influential patriots for their information only, and should not be copied or published. Sam Adams read them before a secret session in the House in June '73 and later had them published. In the resulting scandal, the House petitioned the King to remove Hutchinson and Oliver, a duel was fought between two prominent Englishmen over the alleged theft of the letters. Franklin then came forward to announce (25 Dec. '73) that he alone was responsible. The British government disciplined Franklin by taking away his position as Deputy Postmaster General for America. Hutchinson prorogued the Mass. Assembly on 30 Mar. '74 before it could institute impeachment proceedings against him.

HUTCHINSON'S ISLAND (Savannah), Ga., 7 Mar. '76. The Ga. patriots take control. News of Lexington and Concord created a public opinion that rallied the province to the support of the other colonies. On 11 May '75 the "Liberty Boys" seized 500 pounds of powder from a provincial magazine. When an armed schooner appeared on 2 June a mob expressed the town's defiance by spiking a battery in Savannah. Three days later they erected the colony's first liberty pole and paraded under arms. On 13 June they called for a provincial congress to meet on 4 July, and later in the month helped a S.C. force drive Indian Superintendent John Stuart to E. Fla. After more powder had been seized, Gov. Sir James Wright gave up hope of keeping the revolution out of his province and appealed to Gen. Gage and Adm. Graves for armed support. Although the rebels assumed control of the colony when the Provincial Congress met, the royal governor remained unmolested in Savannah until Jan. '77. When two warships and a loaded transport arrived in belated response to his request, the council of safety decided to arrest Wright and other officials to prevent their rallying Ga. Loyalists. Joseph Habersham, who had risen as leader of the patriots, led a group that captured the governor on 18 Jan. and placed him under house arrest. He escaped the night of 11 Feb. and took refuge aboard the *Scarborough*.

After the Assembly refused to answer his conciliatory letter of 13 Feb., Wright resorted to force. The warships moved up the river on 6 Mar. and took 11 rice-laden merchant vessels; troops under Majs. Maitland and Grant landed on Hutchinson's Island, opposite the town. After their warnings to the British to withdraw were ignored, on 7 Mar. the rebels set fire to two merchant ships. These drifted toward the troop transport and caused a panic. Col. Bull arrived about this time with 400 Carolinians, and the British abandoned their plan for attacking the town. Only two of the rice ships escaped.

This action drove Gov. WRIGHT from the province, and it was three years before he could make his next attempt to rally Loyalists in Ga. (Alden, *South,* 192–93; Lossing, II, 726–27)

HYLER, Adam. Whaleboat guerrilla. N.J. In cooperation with Wm. MARRINER he figured in a number of daring exploits in the coastal waters between Egg Harbor and Staten Island, where every Tory fisherman was compelled to pay them enormous tribute. (Lossing, II, 851) Their boats were destroyed by the British in the summer of 1777, but they built new ones and undertook a systematic harassment of the enemy. Hyler captured several small British vessels, and with two armed boats seized a corvette off Coney Island. He captured a Hessian major in Gowanus one night, surprised and carried off a sergeant's guard from Canarsie, and was the terror of prominent Tories. An attempt to capture Lippin-

cott, the man charged with murdering HUDDY, was foiled only by the absence of his quarry from his home in Broad Street, N.Y.C. (*Ibid.*) See MARRINER for reference to Cook's work.

I

ILE AUX NOIX, Canada. A low, flat, brush-covered island dotted with insect-infested swamps, it was located in a bend of the Richelieu (Sorel) River between the outlet of Lake Champlain and St. Johns. The island was about a mile long and 400 yards wide. A solitary farm occupied a slight elevation in the middle. The French organized defenses on this unwholesome spot in 1759 after they had been forced by Amherst's advance to abandon their works at Ticonderoga and Crown Point. During the Revolution the island was an intermediate objective of American and British forces in their advances and retreats along the Lake Champlain route. Some 8,000 Americans camped on the island in June '76 as survivors of the CANADA INVASION retreated into N.Y. Thousands of them fell victim to smallpox, malaria, and dysentery. It subsequently was garrisoned by the British.

"ILLUMINATION." As early as 1702 one definition of *illuminate* was: "To decorate profusely with lights, as a sign of festivity or rejoicing" (*O.U.D.*). Col. Tench Tilghman reached Philadelphia at 3 A.M. on 22 Oct. '81 with news of the Yorktown surrender and on the 24th a Committee of Safety handbill, headed "Illumination," announced that "those Citizens who chuse to ILLUMINATE on the GLORIOUS OCCASION, will

do it this evening at Six, and extinguish their lights at Nine o'clock. Decorum and harmony are earnestly recommended...." (*Amer. Herit. Book of the Rev.*, 374)

Soon after Gen. Riedesel reached Quebec he reported this curious episode (as recounted in a recent biography):

"The next day [4 June '76] was the birthday of George III. The city of Quebec was 'illuminated' in the evening by means of lighted candles set in every window. It was well known that a good many French people living in Quebec had hoped that the Americans would win. Yet it seemed that in all of Quebec's fifteen hundred houses, everyone was joyously burning candles in honor of the King of England. The reason for this was soon apparent, however. Soldiers were going about heaving rocks through any unlighted windows." (Tharp, *Baroness*, 42–43)

INDEPENDENCE. Although there apparently was no general or conscious drift of the colonies toward the idea of independence until near the close of 1775, many Englishmen suspected that the colonists had it in mind. As early as 1701 the Board of Trade wrote that the American thirst for independence was notorious, says Van Tyne in his *War of Indep.* "One wonders at times whether the reiteration of the accusation . . . was not a factor in creating the desire...." (Pp. 359-60) However, an unidentified French spy traveling through the colonies at the height of the Stamp Act crisis reported, "No nation was better calculated for independence, the people were disposed to it, and there was nothing they talked of more." (*Ibid.,* citing *Amer. Hist. Review,* xxvii, 84) In 1768 KALB allegedly found "the spirit of independence everywhere" in the colonies. (*Ibid.,* 452-53)

In a pamphlet published by Franklin in London around 1763 he asserted that the Americans were never likely to claim independence. Knollenberg in his *Origin of the Amer. Rev.* also supports the contention that independence was not desired by Americans before 1763, but that many in England suspected the contrary, and he gives a number of quotations that bear out the latter belief. (Pp. 8-10) In 1768 Samuel Adams was probably the only patriot leader who believed in independence as a political objective. (Van Tyne, *Loyalists,* 93) The idea certainly began to grow in the five years preceding the war, but R.I. regiments reporting for the siege of Boston spoke of themselves as being "in his Majesty's service," and Congress in its declaration of war, 6 July '75, said: "We have not raised armies with the ambitious design of separating from Great Britain and establishing independent states." (Quoted in Muzzey, *Hist.,* 101)

Late in 1775 the idea was so radical that Congress delicately approached the problem of how they could "lead the public mind" toward an acceptance of independence. "But while the publicists of Congress were lighting a candle in the hearts of their countrymen, an unknown Philadelphia scribbler touched off a bonfire," writes Lynn Montross. (*Reluctant Rebels,* 112) The scribbler was Thos. Paine, whose COMMON SENSE is credited with starting the fire. The

first colony to give official sanction of independence was N.C., which on 12 Apr. '76 authorized its delegates to join others in Congress who might advocate such a movement. The first colony to instruct its delegates to take the initiative on this matter was Va. (15 May '76), and on 7 June Richard Henry Lee moved a resolution "that these United Colonies are, and of right ought to be, free and independent States." John Adams seconded the motion. These two subsequently led the movement that ended with adoption of the Decl. of Indep.

Opponents of the document included such conservatives as John Dickinson, James Wilson,* Edward Rutledge,* and Robert R. Livingston. "Their resistance was based largely on the premise that these decisions were being crammed down the throats of an unready and unwilling people," comments Montross. (*Op. cit.,* 130)

"Other delegates of proved courage and patriotism, among them Robert Morris,* John Jay, George Read,* James Duane, and Benjamin Harrison,* also believed that independence was being advocated prematurely at America's peril," says this same writer. "They agreed with Carter Braxton,* who wrote ... on April 14th that independence 'is in truth a delusive Bait which men inconsiderably catch at, without knowing the hook to which it is affixed.' " (*Ibid.*)

See also, INDEPENDENCE, Declaration of (below).

INDEPENDENCE, Declaration of. 4 July '76. Having come around belatedly to the idea of INDEPENDENCE (see above), on 11 June '76 Congress elected Jefferson, John Adams, Frank-

* These men, nevertheless, became SIGNERS. This encyclopedia contains a separate biographical sketch of each Signer.

lin, Roger Sherman, and Robt. R. Livingston to draw up a declaration. Although only 33 years old, Jefferson already had a reputation for political writing that marked him to be the author of this document. It should be mentioned at this point that the document about which so much historical fuss has been made was probably regarded as nothing more than routine work at the time. "It actually seems to have been forgotten for fifty years," writes Van Tyne (*War of Indep.*, 362 *n.*), and few of the subsequent Signers mentioned it in their letters. (Montross, *Reluctant Rebels,* 164)

Some changes were made by the committee, and others by Congress, but "this most famous American political document belongs indisputably to Jefferson," as Dumas Malone says in his *D.A.B.* article on Jefferson. This authority summarizes the paper as follows:

"The philosophical portion strikingly resembles the first three sections of George Mason's Declaration of Rights. ... Jefferson probably availed himself of this, but he improved upon it. The doctrines are essentially those of John Locke.* * * The charges against the King, who is singled out because all claims of parliamentary authority are implicitly denied, are in general an improved version of those that had already been drawn up by Jefferson and adopted as the preamble of the Virginia constitution of 1776. Relentless in their reiteration, they constitute a statement of the specific grievances of the revolting party, powerfully and persuasively presented at the bar of public opinion. The Declaration is notable both for its clarity and subtlety of expression, and it abounds in the felicities that are characteristic of Jefferson's unlabored prose." (*Ibid.,* citing Carl Becker, *The Decl. of Indep.,* 1922)

The document can be criticized on points of historical fact, logic, and originality. On the latter point Madison commented, "The object was to assert, not to discover truths." John Adams, who had little part in writing the document, led the difficult battle for its adoption by Congress, which took place on 4 July by a vote of 12 states. The decisive act, however, occurred on 2 July, when the deferred resolution of 7 June (see INDEPENDENCE) was adopted.

The night of 4–5 July the Declaration was printed for distribution to the army and the state assemblies. This was headed, "In Congress, July 4, 1776. A Declaration by the representatives of the United States of America in General Congress assembled." The legend that the Declaration was *signed* on 4 July, which it was not, has been supported by a number of authoritative errors. John Trumbull's famous painting, "The Signing of the Declaration of Independence," in the national Capitol, has played a part. The *Journals* of the Cont'l. Cong. give the text of the Declaration under the date of 4 July with the statement that "The foregoing declaration was, by order of Congress, engrossed, and signed. ..." John Adams and Jefferson both insisted many years later that the document had been signed on the 4th. (Montross, *Reluctant Rebels,* 164) The facts appear to be, however, that the rough draft was not ordered engrossed until 19 July, and that nobody signed until 2 Aug. (*Ibid.;* Van Tyne, *War of Indep.,* 362) On that day the document was signed by all the delegates present. At least six names were added later. (See also SIGNERS)

The significance of this document, which merely gave official notice of the course Congress had already set, was to destroy any lingering thought of conciliation and to make it possible for foreign powers to ally themselves with the colonies.

See works by J. P. Boyd, Dumbauld, and Latham.

INDIANA, Va. A tract in what became W. Va., between the Little Kanawha River and the boundary of Pa., and extending from the Ohio River on the west to the Monongahela on the east, was known as "Indiana." By the Treaty of Sycamore Shoals, 1775, this became part of Vandalia. See Scribner's *Atlas*, 60.

INDIANS IN THE COLONIAL WARS AND IN THE REVOLUTION. When the white man came to America the Indian population north of Mexico is calculated to have been 1,150,000. An estimated 220,000 of these inhabited British America. (*Handbook of American Indians*, "Population.") In the period of a little less than three centuries between the arrival of Columbus and the end of the Revolution "the aboriginal population had been subjected to ... destructive influences, which had already wiped out many tribes entirely and reduced many others to mere remnants." (*Ibid.*) In order of importance, the chief causes of this decimation were smallpox and other epidemics, tuberculosis, sexual diseases, and whiskey. (*Ibid.*)

The role of the red man in the Colonial Wars is epitomized in the term "French and Indian Wars," which often is applied to the whole series of conflicts between the French and British in America. As discussed more fully under COLONIAL WARS, the French were considerably more successful than the British in winning Indians to their side, but in the process the French alienated the powerful IROQUOIS. The latter turned to the British for support and continued to side with them when the Revolution broke out. Tribes of the Old Northwest and of the Southeast also were hostile to the American patriots, and therefore cooperative with the British, primarily because they resented the westward migration of British settlers. Among the more important tribes involved were the Cherokee, Creek, and Seminole in the Southeast, and the Chippewa or Ojibwa, Delaware, Iroquois (comprising Mohawk, Oneidas, Tuscaroras, Onondagas, Cayugas, and Senecas of the "Six Nations"), Miami ("of Ohio"), Pequot, Sauk and Fox, and Shawnee. (*Concise D.A.H.*, "Indian")

It is interesting to note how few warriors there were. See IROQUOIS.

It may also be a surprise to find that the patriots, not the British, were the first to use Indians in the Revolution. In Mar. '75 the Mass. Prov. Cong. accepted the offer of the Stockbridge Indians to form a company of minutemen. Although this body was not retained for long (Stone, *Border Wars*, I, 65 *n.*), overtures were made to the Iroquois, Penobscot, and St. Francis Indians. In May '75 Congress instructed its Indian commissioners to try to keep the savages neutral, otherwise to enlist them. A few months later three departments were created to administer Indian affairs: one for the Six Nations; one in the South, to pay particular attention to the Cherokees; and a middle department. An appropriation of almost $17,000 was voted for rum and gifts. An address to the Iroquois was drawn up: "Brothers and friends! ... This is a family quarrel between us and Old England. You Indians are not concerned in it. ..." Montross makes this observation:

"In urging a policy of neutrality, Congress undoubtedly hoped to spare the frontier the horrors of warfare waged with tomahawk and scalping knife. But it is also worth noting that after a century of border warfare, Americans had acquired a low opinion of the Indian as a fighting man—a lesson which the British would learn at a heavy cost in both money and prestige." (*Reluctant Rebels,* 83–84) Not all British officials were wrong; Carleton, for one, opposed Burgoyne's use of Indians in 1777. Nor were the Americans quite so right as Montross indicates. In his *War out of Niagara,* Howard Swiggett presents the picture in a different light:

"...a gang of reckless, ambitious, and enormously capable men were pushing west, hungry for Indian lands, eager for a general Indian war in which they might exterminate the Indians and own their rich lands in western New York, Pennsylvania, Ohio, and Kentucky. These American frontiersmen formed parties for the purpose of killing Indians, whether on a winter's hunt, or bound to a friendly council. Cresap's war was a small beginning of it.

"In May, 1776, Congress passed a resolution that it was highly expedient to engage Indians in the service of the colonies.* * * The next year Schuyler, as American Superintendent, won three hundred Oneidas and Tuscaroras [of the Iroquois League] to the American cause. In 1776 New Hampshire offered £70 for each scalp of a hostile male Indian, £37–10–0 for each scalp of a woman or child twelve years of age." (*Op. cit.,* 45)

British authorities (Lord Dartmouth, to be specific) had officially sanctioned the use of Indians in July '75, but Guy Johnson had long since been at work on this matter, and it was this same month that his plans were successfully culminated by the Council at Oswego. The Canada Invasion cut off British supplies from the Iroquois, hence these savages could not immediately join the British, but in 1776, when the Americans were retreating back to N.Y., the British started winning over the tribes.

Meanwhile the inability of Congress to furnish the promised financial support to its agents, particularly George Morgan at Pittsburgh, and the pressure of western expansion combined to defeat the American policy of keeping the Indians neutral. (*D.A.H.*)

The Cherokee War of 1776 was the first Indian uprising of the Revolution; it was crushed, and the Indians paid a heavy forfeiture in land titles. The main body of this tribe remained peaceful throughout the rest of the Revolution (largely because of the efforts of the N.C. Indian agent, James Robertson, who resided at their capital, Echota), but a disgruntled element moved west and established new towns on Chickamauga Creek, where British agents had their headquarters. Aided by certain Creek towns, the Chickamauga raided frontier settlements throughout the war. In 1779 they allied themselves with northern tribes to oppose the Western Operations of Clark and to support "The Hair Buyer," Henry Hamilton. In 1779 the colonists conducted two successful punitive expeditions against the Chickamauga. When Robertson left Echota in the fall of that year for a new settlement on the Cumberland the heretofore peaceful body of Cherokees rose up in arms, and joined the Chickamauga and Creeks. After Kings Mountain, the N.C. and Va. militia again passed among the Indians and again devastated their country. The Chickamauga continued their hostilities despite constant operations against them by John Sevier in 1781 and 1782. Andrew Pickens' Punitive Expeditions and the defeat of 300 Creeks during the Georgia Expedition of Wayne were the only other Indian actions of note in the South.

Along the western frontier, which had already seen Pontiac's and Dunmore's Wars in 1763–64 and 1774, the

Mingo raided the Ky. settlements in 1776. Often led by such white renegades as Simon Girty, Indians in this region were a serious menace throughout the Revolution; main actions are covered under WESTERN OPERATIONS of Clark and its cross references. The unsuccessful raid on WHEELING in Sept. '82 may qualify as being the last battle of the Revolution.

BORDER WARFARE IN N.Y. is the heading under which the much more serious Indian troubles of the northern frontier are outlined. This "war out of Niagara," where the Tory–British base of operations and supply was located, started with Indian support of ST. LEGER'S EXPEDITION (which featured the ORISKANY ambush, and in which "the military worthlessness of Indians was established, if it was not already known" [Swiggett, *Niagara,* 97]) and their support of BURGOYNE'S OFFENSIVE (which featured BURGOYNE'S PROCLAMATION and an Indian atrocity, the murder of Jane McCRAE, which did much to inspire the *levée en masse* that resulted in the Saratoga Surrender).

Tory–Indian raids to WYOMING and CHERRY VALLEY prompted SULLIVAN'S EXPEDITION against the IROQUOIS in 1779. They struck back in a series of bloody raids led by Joseph Brant, Sir John Johnson, and Walter Butler. (See BORDER WARFARE) The outstanding patriot military commander in the Mohawk Valley for the last two years of the war was Marinus WILLETT.

In summary, the Indians were much more of a menace to the Americans in the North than in the South. IROQUOIS, in a word, was the difference, but other factors were the closer proximity to British bases (primarily Niagara), outstanding Tory leadership and the genius of the Mohawk Brant, and—let us face it—the inferiority of the Northern frontiersmen and settlers in comparison with the Southern frontiersman. There were no "OVER MOUNTAIN MEN" in the Adirondacks. As sympathetic as he is to his subject, the author of *War out of Niagara* writes:

"But the irony of it all is that the Indians as fighters were worthless and the British high command were early sick of them. Time and again ... their fighting qualities proved lower than the most worthless militia.* * * The problem of feeding them was terrific. They poured into the northwestern posts from Oswego to beyond Detroit, cold and hungry, and the £17,000 spent on them by Sir William Johnson in thirteen months was to be quintupled in a few months, and all for naught. They brought disgrace on the British arms and confusion to the management of the war." (*Op. cit.,* 48)

See W. W. Campbell, *Tryon County;* F. W. Hodge, *Handbook;* Hunt, *Wars of the Iroquois;* Lewis Morgan, *League of the Iroquois;* Parkman, *Pontiac;* Peckham, *Pontiac;* Stone, *Border Wars;* Swanton, *Indians of the Southeast;* and Swiggett, *Niagara.*

INTERIOR LINES. A term used in tactics and strategy to indicate a situation in which one commander has an advantage in being able to employ his forces against the enemy faster than the enemy can counter his moves. A commander may possess interior lines by virtue of a central position with respect to his opponent. This is so self-evident that one is led into error in assuming that there is nothing more to the concept of interior lines. But a commander may possess interior lines by virtue of having *superior lateral communications.* Consider Washington's dilemma at the start of the Philadelphia Campaign: he was located in N.J.; the British were in N.Y.C. and Burgoyne's Offensive was moving south along the Lake Champlain–Hudson River line. Washington had a "central position" from which, in theory, he could move the bulk of his forces to meet Burgoyne's threat in the north or any of three threats from Gen. Howe in N.Y.C.: up the Hudson to join Burgoyne, overland through N.J. to Philadelphia, or by sea to the Delaware and against Philadelphia. Yet by virtue of their superior *lateral communications*—which in this instance were by water—the British actually had "interior lines."

An understanding of interior lines and a correct use of the concept has been a hallmark of successful tacticians and strategists through the ages; the concept has been misunderstood by other military men and by most writers for the same period. The main purpose of this article is to put the reader on guard: it is beyond the scope of the present work to attempt a complete explanation of what interior lines *are,* but it is possible to point out what they *are not.*

Before leaving the subject, however, it should be noted that a commander who does not possess the advantage of interior lines at the start of a campaign may often *create* the situation by a "strategic penetration." The campaigns of Napoleon offer many examples.

INTOLERABLE (or Coercive) ACTS. 1774. Colonial resistance to the Tea Act, culminating in the Boston Tea Party, led an exasperated British ministry to passage of punitive measures.

The Boston Port Bill, effective 1 June '74, prohibited loading or unloading of ships in Boston harbor until damages had been paid for tea destroyed in the "Tea Party." As an exception, military stores, food, and fuel could be brought in if cleared by a customs official in Salem, to which place the customs office was moved from Boston.

The Administration of Justice Act, 20 May '74, protected royal officials by providing that those accused of a capital crime committed in aiding the government would not be tried by the provincial court where the official was located, but would be tried in another colony or in England.

The Massachusetts Government Act, 20 May '74, virtually annulled the colony's charter, and gave the governor control over the town meeting.

Extension of the Quartering Act and the Quebec Act were not an integral part of the coercive program, but were so considered by the colonists.

The Intolerable Acts "rallied the other twelve colonies to the side of Massachusetts, produced the first Continental Congress, and led to the Declaration of Independence." (Pollard, *Factors in Amer. Hist.,* 1)

INVALID. Disabled soldier assigned to limited military service (garrison duty, P.O.W. guard, etc.) See CORPS OF INVALIDS. . . .

IRISH VOLUNTEERS. See VOLUNTEERS OF IRELAND.

IRON HILL, Del., 3 Sept. '77. Another name for the battle of COOCH'S BRIDGE.

IROQUOIS LEAGUE. Five related tribes in upper N.Y. formed a confederation known in history as the Five Nations until around 1712, when the Tuscaroras from N.C. joined to make them the Six Nations. Although the date of the original union is not known, there is evidence that it took place about 1570. (J. N. B. Hewett, *Handbook of American Indians,* I, 618) The tribes (listed below) spoke distinct dialects but were capable of understanding each other. (There were tribes of the Iroquoian linguistic stock who were not in the league; the best remembered were the Hurons, hereditary enemies of the other Iroquois tribes and virtually exterminated by them in the war of 1648–50.) Hewett says this of the Iroquois League:

"The northern Iroquoian tribes, especially the Five Nations so called, were second to no other Indian people N. of Mexico in political organization, statecraft, and military prowess. Their leaders were astute diplomats, as the wily French and English statesmen with whom they treated soon discovered. In war they practised ferocious cruelty toward their prisoners, burning even their unadopted women and infant prisoners; but far from being a race of rude and savage warriors, they were a kindly and affectionate people, full of keen sympathy for kin and friends in distress, kind and deferential to their women, exceedingly fond of their children, anxiously striving for peace and good will among men, and profoundly imbued with a just reverence for the constitution of their commonwealth and for its founders. Their wars were waged primarily to secure and perpetuate their political life and independence." (*Op. cit.*, I, 616) Having reached their greatest numerical strength of 16,000 around the year 1650, by 1774 they had been reduced by war and desertions to Canada to about 10,000, according to Hewett. (*Ibid.*, I, 619) Two estimates of their strength in warriors are given below; one column shows the results of Sir Wm. Johnson's census of 1763, and the other gives a British agent's estimate of the numbers who were in the British service during the Revolution:

	1763	1775–83
Mohawk	160	300
Oneida	250	150
Tuscarora	140	200
Onondaga	150	300
Cayuga	200	230
Seneca	1,050	400
	1,950	1,580

Since the arms-bearing element of a "civilized" nation is generally considered to be about 10 per cent, these totals are reasonable. Disparity between the figures for each tribe may result from confusing the Mohawk, Onondaga, and Seneca. (Figures are from Stone, *Border Wars*, I, 81 *n.*) One certain conclusion is that a mere handful of Iroquois caused a heap of trouble.

In the COLONIAL WARS the Iroquois became allies of the British against the French for reasons explained under the cross reference. When the Revolution started, most of the Tuscaroras, who had only recently moved north after a series of defeats in their wars against the settlers of N.C., followed the example of their political sponsors, the Oneidas, in remaining faithful to the American cause. (*Handbook of American Indians* says "major portions" of both tribes sided with the rebels. *Op. cit.*, II, 848) The other tribes invaded Tuscarora country,* scattered the people, and destroyed their possessions. The Oneidas, whose villages were located around the head of the Mohawk Valley, constituted a valuable protective screen for the patriots of that valley until the Iroquois passed among them early in 1781.

For operations of the Iroquois and bibliography see INDIANS IN THE COLONIAL WARS AND IN THE REVOLUTION.

IRVINE, William. 1741–1804. Cont'l. general. Ireland–Pa. Having graduated from Dublin University, he studied medicine and was a naval surgeon during the Seven Years' War (1756–63). Shortly before the war ended he resigned and in 1764 settled at Carlisle as

---

* Many settled originally in and around OQUAGA. The Oneidas later assigned them land bounded by the UNADILLA, Chenango, and Susquehanna rivers. (*Ibid.*)

a doctor. Siding with the patriots, he attended the provincial congress of 1774 in Philadelphia. On 9 Jan. '76 (Heitman) he was commissioned Col., 6th Pa., and ordered to raise that unit and lead them on the Canada Invasion. Captured at TROIS RIVIÈRES, Can., 8 June, he was paroled on 3 Aug. but not exchanged until 6 May '78, almost three years later. In July '78 he sat on the court-martial of Chas. Lee. Meanwhile, his 6th Pa. Bn. having been redesignated the 7th Pa. in Oct. '76, he had been named Col. of the 7th in Jan. '77. (Heitman, 50, 314) On 12 May '79 he was appointed B.G. and given command of the 2d Brig. of Wayne's Pa. Line. He took part in the unsuccessful operations against Staten Island, 14–15 Jan., and Bull's Ferry, N.J., 21–22 July '80. After unsuccessful attempts to raise new troops, including cavalry, in Pa., on 8 Mar. '82 he was ordered to take command at Ft. Pitt. (Appleton's) By this time the garrison of regulars at Ft. Pitt was reduced to about 200, too few to take the field. (Ltr. of 6 July '82 quoted in C. & M., 1058) Gen. Irvine called for volunteers, however, and their disastrous expedition into hostile territory resulted in Crawford's Defeat, 4–5 June '82. Leaving Ft. Pitt on 1 Oct. '83, Irvine resigned from the army on 3 Nov. In 1785 he was appointed agent to purchase lands for distribution to Pa. veterans. He recommended purchase of the "triangle" that gave Pa. an outlet on Lake Erie. He was a congressman in 1786–88 and 1793–95. He was involved in the Whiskey Rebellion, first as a commissioner and then as commander of the state militia. In the emergency of 1798 he again commanded Pa. troops. He moved from Carlisle to Philadelphia and on 13 Mar. 1800 (according to Heitman; Appleton's says Mar. 1801) was appointed superintendent of military stores there.

One brother, Andrew (d. 1789), accompanied him in the Canada Invasion as a Lt., was wounded at Paoli, and became Capt. on 25 Sept. '77. Another brother, Matthew (d. 1827), was a surgeon's mate in Thompson's Pa. Rifle Bn. until Dec. '75, and surgeon of Harry Lee's dragoons from 20 July '78 to the end of the war. Three sons became Army officers.

IZARD, Ralph (rhymes with lizard). 1742–1804. American diplomat, U.S. senator. S.C. Grandson of the Ralph Izard who went from England to S.C. in 1682 and became one of the colony's founders, he was the son of the wealthy indigo and rice planter, Henry Izard. His mother was Margaret Johnson, daughter of Robert, who had been Gov. under the proprietors and the first Gov. under the crown. The only surviving son of this wealthy and honored line, Ralph was sent to school in England when he was 12, five years after the death of his father. He returned to S.C. in 1764, took over the management of his inherited estates, and in 1767 married Alice De Lancey, daughter of Peter and niece of Oliver DE LANCEY the elder. (Peter was the second son of Etienne, or Stephen, founder of the De Lancey family in America.)

In 1771 Ralph went to London with the intention of remaining. Cultured, wealthy, tall, and exceptionally handsome—the sketch in Appleton's is that of a *beau garçon*—Izard could have been very happy in London if it had not been for the American Revolution. He became what Helen Augur calls "an anomaly in patriot ranks, by temperament and family sympathies he belonged in the Tory aristocracy" (*Secret War,* 266), yet he was an American who, according to his daughter, declined to be presented in Court because he could not "bow the knee...to mortal man" (Anne Izard Deas, *Correspond-*

ence ..., vi, 1844), and who found it impossible to remain in England once that country was at war with his own. In the fall of 1776 he moved his family to Paris with the intention of returning to America.

On 7 May '77, however, he was elected by Congress as commissioner to Tuscany. The only problem was that the latter state had no intention of receiving the representative of a would-be state they had not recognized. Unable to do anything constructive in the diplomatic field, Izard teamed up with his good friends Arthur and William LEE in attempting to mar the work of Benjamin Franklin.

"He considered that as a diplomatic representative of the United States he had a right to take part in the consultations between the French court and the ministers commissioned to that court, but this right was not recognized by Benjamin Franklin, toward whom Izard developed a bitter antagonism. The latter also contended that his goods should be exempt from duties, and that out of funds collected in France his salary as minister to Tuscany should be paid. These claims, also rejected by Franklin, led to further alienation." (*D.A.B.*)

Helen Augur casts a more personal light on the antagonism: "His violent temper and arrogance were matched only by that of the Lees, and he adopted toward Franklin the air of a feudal lord toward a tallow chandler—which Ben Franklin had been as a boy." (*Op. cit.*, 266) Although he was supported to a degree by John Adams and was in alliance with the politically powerful Lees, the gouty young Southern aristocrat had tangled with the wrong man. He and the Lees not only failed in their subversive efforts to have "Poor Richard" recalled but were themselves dismissed. Izard was recalled in June '79, but on 9 Aug. '80, the month he reached Philadelphia, Congress passed a resolution approving his conduct.

In 1782 he was elected to the Cont'l. Cong., and he served until 1783. He declined to run for Gov. of S.C. but served in the legislature and in 1789 was elected U.S. senator. He was president *pro tempore* in the Third Congress. In 1795 he retired from public life. Two years later he was invalided by a stroke of paralysis, and six years later he died. One of his 14 children, George Izard (1776–1828), was a Maj. Gen. in the War of 1812 and was territorial governor of Arkansas the last three years of his life.

J

JACKSON, Henry. 1747–1809. Cont'l. officer. Mass. Commissioned Col. of one of the 16 ADDITIONAL CONT'L. REGTS. on 12 Jan. '77, he commanded it after it was designated the 16th Mass. on 1 Jan. '81, and took part in the operations at NEWPORT, 1778, and the SPRINGFIELD RAID, N.J., 1780. On 1 Jan. '83 he assumed command of the 4th Mass. On Evacuation Day, 25 Nov. '83, he was "senior infantry officer present" and in this capacity commanded the 800-man column that marched into N.Y.C. (Freeman, *Washington*, V, 460 *n.*) He had been breveted B.G. on 30 Sept., and on 3 Nov. '83 had become Col. of the 1st American Regt., the only infantry regiment remaining in the army. He held this position until 20 June '84, at which time the American standing army had been reduced to 80 men. During the period 1772–96 he was Maj. Gen. of the Mass. militia.

JACKSON, Michael. 1734–1801. Cont'l. officer. Mass. During the French and Indian War he served as a Lt. As Capt. of a Minute Man company in 1775 he arrived to take part in the pursuit of the British from Lexington and Concord. On 3 June he was promoted to Maj. in Gardner's Mass. Regt. and was wounded at Bunker Hill. (Appleton's; Heitman) He became Lt. Col. of the 16th Cont'l. Inf. on 1 Jan. '76 and was wounded 23 or 24 Sept. in the attack on MONTRESOR'S ISLAND, N.Y. On 1 Jan. '77 he was commissioned Col. of the 8th Mass. After recruiting this regiment he left 6 July '77 to join Gates for the Saratoga campaign. He transferred to the 3d Mass. on 12 June '83, was breveted B.G. on 30 Sept., and on 3 Nov. '83 left the army. Five brothers and five of his sons were in the Cont'l. Army. (Appleton's)

JACKSON, Robert. 1750–1827. British medical officer. This interesting, if not important, individual was the son of a small farmer on the River Clyde, Scotland. After a good schooling, he spent some time as a doctor's apprentice at Biggar before joining the medical classes at Edinburgh in 1768. He financed this education by two voyages as surgeon on whaling ships. Finishing his studies without graduating, he was assistant to a doctor in Jamaica during the period 1774–80. Traveling to N.Y. with the idea of joining a militia unit, he was accepted into the 71st Highlanders as an ensign and surgeon's mate. "After various adventures he arrived at Greenock in 1782 and traveled to London on foot," says Charles Creighton in *D.N.B.*, and dismisses his Revolutionary War service at that. One of these "adventures" took place at Cowpens, 17 Jan. '81, and is worth relating.

When Tarleton's horse collapsed toward the end of this action, Jackson insisted that Tarleton take his own mount and escape. "Your safety is of the highest importance to the army," said the doctor, and whipping out his handkerchief, fastening it on his cane, he strolled casually toward the American positions. When he was challenged he answered, "I am assistant surgeon to the 71st Regiment. Many of the men are wounded and in your hands. I therefore come to offer my services to attend them." Morgan accepted Jackson's proposal that the British wounded be paroled, since the Americans could not properly take care of them. "But so great was American admiration for the jaunty doctor that Morgan released Jackson without his parole." (Bass, *Green Dragoon,* 158, 164)

A muscular, ruddy-faced, blue-eyed Scot of middle height and "pleasing expression," (*D.N.B.*) he passed his medical examinations at Leyden in 1786, soon after marrying a lady whose money made this schooling possible. In 1793 he launched a violent personal crusade to reform the corrupt medical service of the British Army. After adventures that included six months in jail for caning the surgeon general, he broke the monopoly of the College of Physicians over medical appointments in the army and opened the way for qualified men to advance in the army medical service. (*Ibid.*)

JACKSON'S REGT. Henry Jackson commanded one of the 16 "ADDITIONAL CONT'L. REGTS." He also was Col. of the last infantry regiment of the Cont'l. army (see Henry JACKSON).

JACQUETT. See JAQUETT.

JÄGERS (jaegers). After encountering a great deal of trouble from a species of guerrilla troops known as the Austrian Light Infantry, Frederick the Great formed his own light infantry, recruiting them from foresters and gamekeepers. These units he called *Jäger* (literally "huntsmen"). The French followed suit in 1759 and formed a Corps of *Chasseurs* (literally "huntsmen"). One jäger company went to America with von Heister in Aug. '76 and a second went with Knyphausen in Oct. '76. They proved to be so useful in America that by a special treaty in Dec. '77, Hesse-Cassel raised its jäger establishment from 260 to 1,067; it is not likely that more than 700 effectives actually were raised. (Uhlendorf, *Charleston,* 13) In the summer of 1777 the entire force of Hesse-Cassel, Hesse-Hanau, and Anspach jägers, about 600 men, were put under the command of Lt. Col. Ludwig von Wurmb to form the Jäger Corps. They seldom operated as a corps, but generally were detached for such special missions as reconnaissance, headquarters security, advance guards, and to occupy the front trenches at sieges to snipe at the American defenses.

The term "chasseurs" generally was applied to those jägers who served as part of German regiments, as opposed to those of the Jäger Corps of von Wurmb. But 120 to 200 regimental chasseurs were formed into a company under Capt. George Hanger for the Charleston Campaign of 1780. They were the unlucky passengers on board the ANNA, which was blown across the Atlantic to England.

Because of their uniforms the jägers and chasseurs were called "greencoats," and green remains the traditional uniform color of modern regiments of European (including British) armies

who trace their lineage to a light infantry organization of the 18th century. Jägers were expert marksmen, armed with rifles, and some of them were mounted.

"JAIL FEVER." A virulent type of typhus fever that developed when men were confined to close quarters, such as jails or troop transports. (*O.U.D.*–1753)

JAMAICA. As explained in more detail under WEST INDIES, Jamaica was 1,000 miles to windward of the principal British and French possessions in the Caribbean and was virtually a separate division of the British possessions in the West Indies. *E.B.* comments, "The only prominent event in the history of the island during the later years of the 18th century, was the threatened invasion by the French and Spanish in 1782." (See WEST INDIES) Jamaica had the posts of Pensacola and Mobile attached for defense, and it was the base for the operations against HONDURAS and NICARAGUA. In 1775 the Assembly had shown a disloyal spirit when Keith was governor, and Fortescue has this to say of the situation in 1781, when Dalling was governor:

"The safety of Jamaica was seriously endangered by the behaviour of the Assembly, which, although always clamouring for military stores, refused to make any provision for housing them, and would not vote a penny even for repair of the fortifications. Herein there was treachery as well as faction, with greed of gain, as usual, at the root of both. Again, most of the merchants had ventures in privateers, American as well as British, and spared no pains to seduce sailors from the Royal Navy to man them.* * * In fact, in Jamaica, as in the rest of the islands, the military measure which was most sorely needed was the hanging of half a dozen members of the Assembly." (*British Army,* III, 350)

Between 1 Aug. and 31 Dec. '80 the seven and a half battalions at Jamaica had 1,100 men die, and half of the remaining 3,000 were sick. This was largely because the civil authorities would not bear the expense of moving barracks from low and unhealthful ground. "Considered only as an article of commerce," wrote Dalling, alluding to the transportation costs, "these eleven hundred men have cost £22,000, a sum which if laid out above ground might have saved half their lives." (*Ibid.*, 341–42) Dalling applied to Cornwallis for Tory militia from the Carolinas, and even sent an officer to enlist American prisoners for service against the Spanish. Fortescue writes that "the whole of the Continental troops captured at Camden, after a little hesitation, took service under the flag of the brutal oppressor, and became part of the garrison of a British Colony." (*Ibid.*, 351, citing ltrs. of 10 Aug. and 10 Oct. '81 from Dalling to Germain.) This is an exaggeration, but some prisoners did volunteer. Alden says "hundreds of the defenders of Charleston afterward fought for Britain in the West Indies, though not against their own people." (*South*, 242.)

In Feb. '80 Dalling embarked a regiment of American Tories with the plan of reinforcing Pensacola and, possibly, of attacking New Orleans to relieve once and for all the threat to British Fla. Unable to get a naval escort, he had to abandon this operation, and the next month the Spanish undertook the capture of PENSACOLA; it held out for two months, but MOBILE fell with little resistance.

JAMAICA (Brookland), N.Y., 28 Aug. '76. The American defeat at Long Island, 27 Aug., resulted in the isolation of a militia force of barely 100 men under B.G. Nathaniel Woodhull who had been posted on the eastern end of the island with the mission of protecting the inhabitants and driving cattle out of the enemy's reach. Woodhull moved to his headquarters at Jamaica and awaited orders and reinforcements. (*D.A.B.*, "Woodhull") The night of the 28th Sir Wm. Erskine led elements of the 17th Light Dragoons and the 71st Highlanders—about 700 men, according to Appleton's—in an operation that surprised Woodhull and many of his men at Carpenter's House, Jamaica. WOODHULL died as a result of ill treatment in captivity, according to *D.A.B.*, "which raised him to the rank of hero and martyr." Another version is mentioned under Oliver DE LANCEY the younger.

JAMAICA PASS. In the battle of Long Island, 27 Aug. '76, the British moved through this place to envelop the American lines.

JAMESTOWN, VA. Here, the abandoned site of the first English settlement in America, Adm. de Grasse disembarked his troops from the West Indies to take part in the YORKTOWN CAMPAIGN.

JAMESTOWN FORD, Va., 6 July '81. See GREEN SPRING.

JAQUETT, Peter. d. 1834. Cont'l. officer. Del. According to Heitman, Jaquett was Ensign of the Del. Regt. on 17 Jan. '76, 2d Lt., 27 Nov. '76; 1st Lt. 1 Dec. '76; Capt., 5 Apr. '77; captured at Camden, 16 Aug. '80; Bvt. Maj., 30 Sept. '83; served to the end of the war, and died 13 Sept. 1834. Ward, on the other hand, mentions nothing about his being captured and states that in the reorganization after Camden, Jaquett was given one of the remaining companies of Del. troops when KIRKWOOD was given the other. This same authority says that Jaquett was with Kalb at Camden when the latter's head was laid open by a saber slash. "Captain Peter Jaquett, adjutant of the Delawares, fighting by his side, hastily bandaged the wound and begged him to retire." (*W.O.R.*, 729, 733) Other writers indicate that only Kirkwood commanded the Del. troops during the Southern campaigns of Greene, but Ward identifies Jaquett's Del. Co. in the battle of Guilford, where it was part of the 1st Md. Regt. Presumably Jaquett remained with the Md. Regt. throughout the rest of the war.

JASPER, William. *c.* 1750–1779. Rev. hero. S.C. Of obscure parentage, but apparently from the vicinity of Georgetown, S.C., he enlisted on 7 July '75 in Francis Marion's Co. for service in Wm. Moultrie's Regt. During the defense of Charleston in 1776 he braved enemy artillery to replace the flag that had been shot from the parapet of Ft. Sullivan (later Ft. Moultrie). Given a sword by Gov. Rutledge, he declined a commission on the ground of being ignorant. As a roving scout under Moultrie, Marion, and Lincoln, successively, he gathered valuable information of British activities. He was killed while planting the colors of the 2d S.C. on the Spring Hill redoubt in the assault on SAVANNAH, 9 Oct. '79. An impressive monument has been erected at Savannah in his honor, and one of the redoubts at Ft. Moultrie was named "Jasper Battery." (James W. Patton in *D.A.B.*)

JAY, John. 1745–1829. Statesman, diplomat. N.Y. Grandson of a Huguenot who settled in N.Y. about 1686, son of a prominent merchant, and related through his mother to the Van Cortlandts, John was carefully reared as a provincial patrician. Studious, grave, and self-confident, he graduated from King's College (now Columbia) in 1764, was admitted four years later to the bar, and became a successful N.Y.C. lawyer. Marriage in 1774 to Sarah,

youngest daughter of Wm. Livingston of N.J., further extended his family connections. When the Revolution started he was a wholehearted supporter of the patriot cause but as a wealthy, intelligent aristocrat without any burning personal ambition he had a conservative political outlook. In 1773 he had been secretary of the N.Y.–N.J. boundary commission. He became a member of the N.Y.C. committee of correspondence and served in the Cont'l. Cong. Although opposed to independence in the beginning, he nevertheless supported the movement once it gained momentum and in 1776 worked for ratification of the Decl. of Indep., which Cong. had passed while he was absent on political business in N.Y. He guided the formulation of the state constitution and served as Chief Justice of N.Y. until 1779. Re-elected to Cong. in Dec. '78, he became Pres. of that body on the 10th and held this post until named minister to Spain on 27 Sept. '79. Meanwhile, he had been elected Col. of state militia in 1775, but had no military service in the field.

Spain's attitude toward the American Revolution was such that Jay had no chance of getting that country's recognition of the U.S.—which was one of his missions. Arriving at Cadiz with his wife on 22 Jan. '80 and remaining in the country two years, Jay could accomplish no more than raising a $170,000 loan from Floridablanca and getting the Spanish to keep up their secret assistance in war supplies. On 23 June '82 Jay reached Paris to take part in the PEACE NEGOTIATIONS. He shared John Adams' suspicion of Vergennes and helped him convince Franklin to sign preliminary articles of peace with the British without awaiting French concurrence.

On 24 July '84 Jay reached N.Y., having declined the post of minister to

London, and he found he had been drafted for Sec. of Foreign Affairs. Although he never had any ambitions for high public office and had hoped to resume the law practice abandoned 10 years earlier, Jay held this post until relieved by Thos. Jefferson on 22 Mar. '90. His most vexatious problems during this period stemmed from British and Spanish refusal to withdraw their garrisons from territory claimed by the U.S. The impotence of the Confederation weakened Jay's hand, and he became one of the strongest advocates of a strong Federal government. He wrote five of the Federalist Papers, a weak personal constitution keeping him from contributing more to the support of the Federal Constitution.

Becoming 1st Chief Justice of the U.S. on 4 Mar. '89 (but serving as *ad interim* Sec. of State until Jefferson arrived to be sworn in on 22 Mar. '90), he sat during the first five years during which the Supreme Court procedures were formed. While Chief Justice he was sent in the summer of 1794 to arrange a peaceful settlement of controversies with Great Britain that threatened war. "Jay's Treaty was the price paid by the Federalists for the maintenance of peace and financial stability at a time when both were vitally necessary for the establishment of American nationality under the new Constitution," comments Samuel Flagg Bemis in *D.A.B.*; "history has justified it as a sort of necessary evil." See also JAY's TREATY.

Jay had been defeated by George Clinton in 1792 for the governorship of his state. He returned from England in 1795 to find himself elected, and he served six years (two terms); his administration was conservative and upright, but no great issues arose to challenge it. (*Ibid.*) Near the end of his tenure he forthrightly refused to go along with Hamilton's slippery suggestion to strengthen the party cause in the 1800 election: since the newly elected Republican legislature was certain to choose Jeffersonian electors, Hamilton urged that Jay call a special session of the outgoing Federalist legislators to select Federalist electors.

Republican strength assured Jay's defeat for Gov. in 1800 and he declined to run for re-election. His mind set on retirement, he also refused to be considered for renomination as Chief Justice. (Fortunately for the stature of that office, the great John Marshall took it.) Jay spent his last 28 years in complete retirement on his 800-acre property at Bedford, Westchester co., N.Y.

"Jay was a very able man but not a genius," writes Bemis. He performed all his public duties with consistent intellectual and physical vigor. In personal character "he was second to none of the [founding] 'Fathers.' . . ." (*Ibid.*) Physically, he was tall, slender, long of nose and chin, and refined looking. Although fairly wiry and robust, he does not appear to have been particularly addicted to outdoor pursuits. "His was a townman's life." (*Ibid.*)

Frank Monaghan's *John Jay . . .* (1935) has been called, "A sympathetic narrative rich in the detail of the life and character of an aristocratic New Yorker who prided himself on the rectitude of his motives and his devotion to public duty. The author seeks to restore Jay . . . to public esteem, a task not facilitated by the fact that Jay, ever conscious of his dignity, wrote with the feeling that posterity was peering over his shoulder." (Lib. of Cong., *Guide*, 357) See also Samuel Flagg Bemis (ed.), *The American Secretaries of State and their Diplomacy*, vol. 1 (1927). In his *D.A.B.* sketch, published in 1933 (and before publication of Monaghan's *Jay*), Bemis says the best biography is

George Pellew's *John Jay* (1890), the work of a descendant and based on family papers. The son, William Jay, wrote *The Life of John Jay* (2 vols., 1833). Bemis considers Wm. Whitelock's *Life and Times* ... (1887) "not adequate." H. P. Johnston (ed.) used a selected part of the letters in Pellew's *Jay* for his *Corresp. and Public Papers of John Jay* (4 vols., 1890–93). Some of Jay's papers are being edited by R. B. Morris for publication in two volumes in 1966.

JAY'S TREATY, 19 Nov. '94. Justifying their actions on the allegations that the U.S. had not complied with articles four and five of the PEACE TREATY of 1783 (payment of pre-Revolutionary War debts to British merchants, and reimbursement to Loyalists for property confiscated by the states), Britain refused to honor those articles calling for withdrawal of troops from posts in the Northwest. The two countries came to the brink of war after the British Orders in Council of 8 June and 6 Nov. '93 resulted in seizure of American ships and crews. John Jay, chief justice of the U.S., negotiated the treaty signed on 19 Nov. '94 and remembered as Jay's Treaty. By it the British agreed to withdraw their posts by 1 June '96. The debts were to be referred to joint commissions (British claims of $2,664,000 were settled 8 Jan. 1802), as were the problems of the northeast boundary and compensation for illegal seizures ($10,345,200 paid by 1802). Various trade agreements were made, but no mention was made of Loyalist claims, the slaves "stolen" by the British during the war, impressment of American sailors under the Orders in Council, or the Indian problem (see Guy CARLETON).

Although Jay had triumphed in getting important concessions and had restored amicable relations that permitted resumption of trade that was essential for the success of Hamilton's fiscal system, his treaty aroused a popular uproar from many elements whose own interests had been violated or ignored. Southern planters wanted compensation for their lost slaves, and Va. owed most of the debt that joint commissions were to settle; Southern Federalists howled. Northern shipping and commercial interests were antagonized by the treaty's limitations on their trade with the West Indies. After suspending the article dealing with the latter, the Senate finally ratified the treaty on 24 June '95, but only after long and bitter debate. Although Washington had considered the treaty unsatisfactory he established an important precedent by asserting executive prerogative and refusing the House of Representatives' request of 24 Mar. '96 for Jay's papers relating to the treaty. After attempting to block the treaty by denying appropriations, on 30 Apr. '96 the House approved them. (*E.A.H.*) It did so only after what Commager calls "one of the greatest political debates in American history," in which memorable speeches were made by Albert Gallatin and Fisher Ames. (*Docs.*, 165)

See also John JAY.

JEALOUSY. This word in the 18th century had evolved from the sense of "anger, wrath, indignation" (1649) to "suspicion, apprehension, or knowledge of rivalry" (hence its modern meaning). (*O.U.D.*) See also, WORDS, Archaic.

JEFFERSON, Thomas. 1743–1826. Founding father. Va. Statesman, diplomat, author of the Decl. of Indep., 3d U.S. Pres., scientist, architect, "apostle of freedom and enlightenment" (*D.A.B.*), Jefferson was great in so many fields during America's emergence as a nation that "founding father" is perhaps the best tag to put on him at the beginning of this sketch. And at the outset it is well to point out what he was *not:* "He was not a man of arms, dreaded the duties of a soldier, had no stomach for physical combat." (Beveridge, *Marshall,* I, 129)

Family tradition was that the first Jefferson in Va. was Welsh. Whether or not this is true, a Thos. Jefferson was living in Henrico co. in 1677. Three generations later the Thos. Jefferson in whom we are interested was born on the edge of western settlement, in a plain frame house close to where he would later build "Monticello." The family had been neither aristocratic nor wealthy, but through his mother, Jane Randolph, Thomas was connected with one of the Old Dominion's most distinguished families. (Dumas Malone in *D.A.B.*) Thomas' father, Peter (1708–1757), was a surveyor who made the first accurate map of Va., became burgess and county lieutenant, and left Thomas 2,750 acres. Peter also gave his son an established position in the community, a love of the frontier, and may have passed on his fondness for science.

Jefferson studied the classics, graduated from the College of William and Mary in 1762, and five years later was admitted to the bar. Having been trained by George Wythe (1726–1806), he was highly successful in his practice even though a weak voice and lack of oratorical ability kept him from being a good courtroom lawyer. Although he gave up his practice in 1774, his legal training strongly influenced his subsequent political career. After serving as justice of the peace and parish vestryman, he was elected to the House of Burgesses in 1769. He served in every succeeding assembly and convention of his province until he was elected to the Cont'l. Cong. in 1775. Never an effective speaker and hating the "morbid rage of debate" (for which he was quite unsuited), he soon became known as a literary draftsman. His *Summary*

View of the Rights of America, a pamphlet printed in 1774, was widely read. This direct attack on the Crown was regarded by the majority as being too radical at the time, but it placed him among the leaders of the Revolution and earned him the honor of drafting the Decl. of Indep. In England his pamphlet was somewhat modified, probably by Edmund Burke, and widely circulated by the Opposition. Cutting at the common root of allegiance, emigration, and colonization—shunning the indirect approach of blaming the ministry for the King's errors—this paper maintained that "the relation between Great Britain and these colonies was exactly the same as that of England and Scotland after the accession of James and until the Union [1707]; and that our emigration to this country gave England no more rights over us than the emigration of the Danes and Saxons gave to the present authorities of their mother country over England." (Quoted in *E.B.*) The pamphlet ignored the protection the mother country gave the colonies during the Colonial Wars and maintained that since the earlier support had been only with a view to commercial return it could be repaid in trade privileges. "Throughout his career as a Revolutionary patriot he emphasized 'rights as derived from the laws of nature,' not a king; and here, as elsewhere, he strove for the 'revindication of Saxon liberties,' " comments Malone.

Taking his seat in the Cont'l. Cong. in June '75, Jefferson drafted several other papers that were rejected as being too anti-British at a time when hope of conciliation still lived. After being absent from 28 Dec. until 14 May '76, called home for personal reasons and for state duties—he was appointed commander of Albemarle militia on 26 Sept.—Jefferson was elected on 11 June to a committee to draft the declaration of independence. Although changes were made by John Adams and Benj. Franklin, who with Roger Sherman and Robert R. Livingston were the other committee members, and some changes were made by Congress, "this most famous American political document as a composition belongs indisputably to Jefferson." (Malone, citing Becker and Fitzpatrick)

Re-elected to Congress, Jefferson felt that his presence was more valuable in Va., where he wanted to take part in revising the laws. He surrendered his seat, declined election as a commissioner to serve in Paris with Franklin and Silas Deane, and entered the House of Delegates on 7 Oct. '76. The four corners of Jefferson's frame for "a government truly republican" were: abolition of land-holding in fee-tail (inheritance limited to a particular class of heirs); abolition of primogeniture; separation of church and state; and a system of general education. His objective was to eliminate "every trace . . . of ancient or future aristocracy" and develop a natural aristocracy based on ability rather than birth and wealth. Elected to the board of five men to revise the laws of Va., Jefferson, Wythe, and Edmund Pendleton were the only ones to serve to the end. On 18 June '78 they submitted 126 bills, at least 100 of which were ultimately enacted in substance. Jefferson's educational bills failed almost entirely, but by 1786 his other three ideals had been achieved.

On 1 June '79 he succeeded Patrick Henry as Gov. "The philosophical qualities that made him so conspicuous as a planner and prophet were of little avail to him, however, as an executive," points out Malone. "Resourceful in counsel, he was ever hesitant and reluctant in the exercise of authority, the very necessity of which he deplored." (*D.A.B.*) He got by the first year, but

when the British were able to make a serious military effort in Va. in 1781 Jefferson's miserable failure as a leader was a vivid illustration of what happens to a society guided by a philosopher when it needs a "man on horseback." Unwilling to use means of doubtful legality even in times of crisis, and maintaining his confidence in militia, he became a pathetic spectacle of ineptitude. When British occupation of Richmond forced the legislature to Charlottesville, where they were called to meet on 24 May '81, Jefferson proceeded to nearby "Monticello" and last exercised his functions as Gov. on 3 June. Then, interpreting his term to have expired, even though a successor had not been elected, he in effect abdicated. The next day he narrowly escaped capture when Tarleton made his CHARLOTTESVILLE RAID, 4 June. Thos. Nelson Jr. was elected Gov. on 12 June by the legislators who met at Staunton, and an investigation into Jefferson's conduct was ordered. Jefferson, meanwhile, after evacuating his family, had been disabled by a fall from his horse. (No writer of fiction would dare use such symbolism.)

Allegations of personal cowardice were later made by political enemies, but the official charges had to do with lack of military preparations and leadership. "After the crisis actually arose, Jefferson seems to have done everything possible and with as great speed as could have been expected," writes Malone. On 12 Dec. '81 the investigating committee reported they could find no grounds for censure, and a week later the House of Delegates adopted resolutions of thanks to Jefferson. Nevertheless it took many years for him to recover his prestige in Va. The fall from public esteem coinciding with the fall from his horse, Jefferson, who had not yet reached his 39th birthday (13

Apr.), was able to enjoy leisure with his beloved books and family. During this time he worked on his *Notes on the State of Virginia,* which he arranged in the order of questions submitted in 1781 by Barbé de Marbois, secretary of the French legation, from careful research he had made and recorded over a period of many years. Printed while he was in France a few years later, and including in the edition of 1786 another proposed constitution for his state, *Notes* "laid the foundations of Jefferson's high contemporary reputation as a universal scholar and of his present fame as a pioneer American scientist." (*Ibid.*)

The death on 6 Sept. '82 of his beloved wife, Martha Wayles, who was the 24-year-old widow of Bathurst Skelton when he married her on 1 Jan. '72, brought Jefferson out of his retirement. (Only three of their six children survived Martha, and only two, Martha and Mary, reached maturity.) On 12 Nov. '82 he was appointed peace commissioner, but PEACE NEGOTIATIONS progressed so that his presence was unnecessary before he could sail for France, and the appointment was withdrawn. Elected to Cong. in June '83, he was a member of almost every important committee. Among the 30 or more state papers he drafted, Americans should be particularly grateful for his Notes on the Establishment of a Money Unit, which spared the New World the absurdity of English pounds, shillings, and pence. In his report of 22 Mar. '84, second only to the Decl. of Indep. among his state papers (*D.A.B.*), Jefferson set down practically all the features of the epoch-making Ordinance of 1787. "Certainly he was a major architect of American expansion," says Malone, and if this report had not been changed by Congress slavery would have been prohibited after 1800 in the western territories.

On 6 Aug. '84 Jefferson reached Paris to assist Franklin and John Adams in drawing up treaties of commerce, instructions on which he had himself drafted. In 1785 he succeeded Franklin as minister to France. With the assistance of LAFAYETTE he achieved some commercial concessions. He negotiated a commercial treaty with Prussia in 1785. Early the next year he joined Adams in London to negotiate a similar treaty, but their efforts failed. His scientific curiosity led him to a study of English mechanical devices. In 1787 he visited the Po Valley to see rice-cleaning machinery and smuggled rice seed out for experiments in S.C. and Ga. In Oct. '89 he sailed for America on leave of absence to settle private business and to take home his two daughters. With some reluctance he accepted Washington's appointment as Sec. of State, being sworn in on 22 Mar. '90.

Much of his fame rests on his subsequent achievements—he was only 47 when he became the 1st Sec. of State under the Constitution—but these accomplishments are beyond the scope of the American Revolution, and only the highlights can be given here. Although he first tried to work in harmony with Hamilton, who although almost 14 years his junior dominated national politics as Sec. of Treas., cooperation soon became impossible.

"The schools of thought for which they stood have since contended for mastery in American politics: Hamilton's gradually strengthened by the necessities of stronger administration, as time gave widening amplitude and increasing weight to the specific powers—and so to Hamilton's great doctrine of the "implied powers"—of the general government of a growing country; Jefferson's rooted in colonial life, and buttressed by the hopes and convictions of democracy." (Francis S. Philbrick in *E.B.*)

Jefferson came to feel that Hamilton's system "flowed from principles adverse to liberty, and was calculated to undermine and demolish the republic, by creating an influence of his department over the members of the legislature." Hamilton resented the challenge to his power and the opposition to his specific projects by a man he considered a quibbling theorist. (*D.A.B.*) Two opposing political parties grew up around the secretaries—the Democrat-Republicans rallying to Jefferson and the Federalists to Hamilton. Washington was reluctant to accept the existence of political parties and patiently used the genius of his two great secretaries, following the policies of neither exclusively, but Jefferson refused to serve beyond 31 Dec. '93.

Although leader of his party in retirement at "Monticello," Jefferson hoped to stay out of public life and pursue his many other interests in the country. In 1796, however, he was elected vice president under John Adams. In 1800 he tied with Aaron Burr and, with the support of HAMILTON, was chosen president by the house of representatives. His administration was marked by a reduction of the army, navy, diplomatic service, and by some reduction of the civil service. He has been charged with innovating the "spoils system" because he appointed so many Democrat-Republicans to office, yet it should be pointed out that the Federalists had heretofore maintained an absolute one-party monopoly. The Louisiana Purchase (1803) was the greatest achievement of his presidency, although it required Jefferson to compromise many of his most cherished political principles. Other highlights of the two terms of Pres. Jefferson were the Lewis and

Clark Expedition, the Pike Expedition, successful war against the Barbary pirates (1801–5), the Burr treason trial, and the Embargo Act (adopted in 1807 to preserve U.S. neutrality rights and repealed in 1809).

He was the first president inaugurated in Washington, and he had much to do in the transformation of that wilderness village into a monumental city. As part of a premeditated system he practiced a democratic simplicity in dress and personal conduct. A minister who appeared in gold lace and dress sword to pay his initial, official call found the American president in lounging clothes and slippers. Hostile observers looked on all this as an affectation; admirers found it the natural conduct of a great man who had the courage to be himself. As a young man Jefferson has been described as tall, loose-jointed, sandy-haired, and somewhat rustic in appearance. He was a skilled horseman, an expert violinist, a good singer and dancer, and had been a gay companion in the society of colonial Va. The sober side of his nature soon became predominant, however, and it is said that he never gambled, played cards, smoked, or let himself be drawn into personal quarrels. Soon after coming of age he concluded that the Bible did not stand up under historical examination and although he never lost faith in conventional morality he turned from organized religion to the works of great classical writers for personal inspiration.

Declining a third term as president, although the legislatures of five states asked him to run, he continued to have a tremendous influence on national politics. Madison and Monroe, his immediate successors, had been neighbors and were disciples of the "Jeffersonian system," which they continued for another 16 years. During the last 17 years of his life he never ventured more than a few miles from "Monticello." He readdressed himself to the problem of education and after many frustrations succeeded in having the Univ. of Va. chartered (1819). Thereafter he was the dominant figure in the establishment of its curriculum as well as its architecture. The Embargo of 1807, which Malone calls his most original and daring measure of statesmanship and his greatest practical failure, financially ruined Jefferson (and many other Va. planters). Sale of his 10,000-volume library to the government for a low price in 1815 relieved his financial burden for a few years. (This collection was the nucleus of the Lib. of Cong.) In 1819 he was ruined by the failure of a friend, Wilson Cary Nicholas, to cover a $20,000 note Jefferson had endorsed. After trying unsuccessfully to find a buyer for his lands—some 10,000 acres acquired by inheritance, marriage, and purchase—he got legislative permission in the last year of his life to dispose of his holdings by the then-common method of a lottery. The public responded with voluntary contributions of $16,500 and the lottery was called off, but "Monticello" did not remain long in the possession of his heirs.

Thomas Jefferson died on the 50th anniversary of the Decl. of Indep., a few hours before John ADAMS. He wrote his own epitaph in which he asked to be remembered for only three things: the Decl. of Indep., the Va. statute for religious freedom, and the Univ. of Va.

Of the man Malone calls "this most enigmatical and probably the most versatile of great Americans" Henry Adams said:

"Almost every other American statesman might be described in a parenthesis. A few broad strokes of the brush would paint the portraits of all the early Presidents with this exception, . . . but Jefferson could be painted only touch by touch, with a fine pencil, and the perfection of the likeness depended upon the shifting and uncertain flicker of its semi-transparent shadows." (*History*, quoted in *D.A.B.*)

"Among the Founding Fathers, only Franklin was his peer in universality of mind, and his writings of every description, but particularly the voluminous correspondence which he maintained until a few weeks before his death, constitute an incomparable mirror of the general and especially the intellectual history of his age." (Lib. of Cong., *Guide*, 354) *The Papers of Thos. Jefferson*, planned and initiated by Julian P. Boyd of Princeton, will supersede all previous editions. Between 1950 and 1965, 17 vols. have appeared. The best of the older editions is P. L. Ford, *Writings* (10 vols., 1892–99), which Malone says should be supplemented by the more extensive Memorial Edition (20 vols., 1903–4) and the edition of H. A. Washington (9 vols., 1853–54).

Still in preparation is *Jefferson and His Time,* by Dr. Dumas Malone, whose *D.A.B.* sketch I have relied on heavily in this article. The third volume was issued in 1962. Older biographies that are still valuable (*ibid.,* D.A.B.) are the 3-vol. work of H. S. Randall (1858) and the shorter one by A. J. Nock (1926). Numerous other works on Jefferson may be located through the bibliographies of Malone's *Jefferson,* his *D.A.B.* article, and in many other places.

JENKINS' EAR, The War of (1739–42). One of the COLONIAL WARS.

JERSEYFIELD, N.Y., 30 Oct. '81. (BORDER WARFARE) After the action at JOHNSTOWN, 25 Oct., Col. Marinus Willett started his pursuit the evening of the 28th and caught up with the tail of Maj. John Ross's column at 8 A.M. on the 30th. With Walter Butler commanding the rear guard, the mixed force of British, Germans, Tories, and

Indians were across West Canada Creek by 2 P.M. Several men on each side were hit during the firefight that took place across this deep and fairly wide stream. The enemy fire then stopped, and when the rebels splashed across they found Walter Butler mortally wounded near the bank. The famous Tory leader was scalped and robbed by an Oneida. (See Walter BUTLER for various myths associated with his death and burial.) The sequel is covered under BORDER WARFARE.

The battlefield is between modern Ohio City and Russia, N.Y., probably at the ford known as Hess's Rift. (Swiggett, *Niagara*, 242–46)

JERSEY PRISON SHIP. See PRISONS AND PRISON SHIPS.

JOHNS ISLAND, S.C., 28–29 Dec. '81. When Maj. Craig evacuated Wilmington (Nov. '81) he was posted with some additional infantry and cavalry on Johns Island, near Charleston. The main American army was now located at Pompon on the Stono River, opposite Craig's position. Lee conceived an intricate plan of attacking Johns Island, which was to take advantage of the fact that on one or two nights of the month the tide was low enough for troops to ford the Wapoo River, which separated the island from the mainland. The project was assigned to Col. John Laurens and Lee. Detachments of Cont'l. troops reinforced Lee's Legion to about 700. Lee's column crossed according to plan but had to be recalled and the operation abandoned when a second column, under Maj. James Hamilton, got lost and arrived too late to ford the river. (Lee, *Memoirs*, 528 *n.*, 531 ff.)

JOHNS ISLAND, S.C., 4 Nov. '82. In leading a successful attack against a British foraging party in the vicinity of this island, Capt. William Wilmot of the 2d Md. Cont'ls. was killed. According to Heitman and Strait, "The blood of Captain Wilmot was the last spilled in the war. . . ." The former authority gives 4 Nov. '82 as the date of the action, whereas the latter (who says Wilmot attacked and defeated the party of British, whereas Heitman merely says Wilmot was "killed . . . by a British foraging party") gives the date as Aug. '82, and identifies the location as James Island. It is clear, however, that both Heitman and Strait refer to the action in which Wilmot was killed. As for the "last battle of the war," see also WHEELING.

JOHNSON, Guy. *c.* 1740–1788. Loyalist leader, Indian Supt. Born in Ireland, he may have been a nephew of Sir William Johnson, whom he followed to the Mohawk Valley some time prior to 1756 and whose secretary he became. In the campaign of 1759–60 he commanded a ranger company under Amherst. In 1762 he became Sir William's deputy for Indian affairs, and he gained the confidence of his superior as well as that of the Indians. In 1763 he married the boss's daughter, Mary, and established Guy Hall, near Amsterdam. During the period 1773–75 he was in the N.Y. Assembly, and in 1774 he succeeded Sir William as Supt. of Indian Affairs. (On the death of the latter, Gage directed Guy to take over the post. The appointment was later confirmed from England.) Anticipating an order from London, Guy worked to win the Indians to the British side in the conflict that appeared imminent, and in the Council of Oswego, July '75, he signed up all but two tribes of the IROQUOIS. He went on to Montreal the same month, accompanied by some Indians and 220 rangers, and offered his services to Carleton. He helped for a time in the defense of St. Johns. Visiting England in the winter of 1775–76 with Joseph BRANT, he reached Staten

Island on 29 July '76 and stayed in N.Y. until Sept. '78. His alleged purpose was to coordinate operations of the main British army with those of the Indians and Tories in Canada, but he accomplished little. One suspects that he found London and N.Y.C. more pleasant than the Northern frontier.

The Mohawk Valley refugees had split into two factions: one including the Johnsons, Daniel Claus (Guy's brother-in-law), and Joseph Brant; and the other comprising John Butler and his son, Walter. According to Howard Swiggett, whose story of the Butlers (*War out of Niagara*) is naturally favorable to them, Guy Johnson and Claus asked for leave to England after they had been denied permission to lead a large Indian raid against N.Y. in 1775.

"The matter is not clear [writes Swiggett] but it decidedly appears that Johnson and Claus, who were now to begin their intrigue against the Butlers, father and son, shared with Joseph Brant an idea of war repugnant both to Guy Carleton and to the Butlers, and that Carleton had far more trust in John Butler than in them.* * *

"When they [Johnson and Claus] were gone Carleton sent John Butler to Niagara, thereafter to be his headquarters. He was instructed by Carleton to retain the Indians in an attitude of absolute neutrality. The bitterly hostile Claus letter to Knox at the War Office . . . leaves no doubt either that these were his instructions or that he faithfully carried them out." (*Op. cit.,* 65–66. The "Claus letter," 6 Nov. '77, complains that Claus's expenses for 15 years "during which time I had a two years Indian war to manage . . . did not amount to ¼ the sum of what I hear Mr. Butler's expenses do within the two years and that expended merely to

keep the Indians inactive contrary to their inclinations." *Ibid.,* 103–4)

Having been obliged to spend the winter at Halifax, Guy Johnson did not reach Quebec until July '79. W. E. Stevens in his *D.A.B.* sketch says Guy Johnson "was with the British and Indians at the battle near Newtown," but Swiggett (*op. cit.,* 197) shows that "the typical non-combatant" was actually headed for Niagara on the eve of the battle directed many wilderness miles away by the Butlers. (See NEW-TOWN, 29 Aug. '79) For the next two years Johnson, as senior officer responsible for Indian affairs, directed raids from his headquarters at Niagara. But he appears never to have taken the field in person; in the final phase of the BORDER WARFARE the apparent failure of Sir John and Guy Johnson to push an advance along the Lake Champlain–Lake George route to the Mohawk Valley may have caused the failure of the Ross Expedition. (See end of BORDER WARFARE) "Guy Johnson . . . apparently made no effort to get his levies up," writes the hostile Howard Swiggett (*op. cit.,* 240).

He was succeeded as Indian Supt. by Sir John Johnson (whose commission was dated 14 Mar. '82). He went to England after the war and died in London in 1788. W. L. Stone describes him as "a short, pursy ["short winded" is one definition; "corpulent" and "purse-proud" are others] man, of stern countenance and haughty demeanor. . . ." (*Brant,* II, 67, quoted in *D.A.B.*)

JOHNSON, Henry. 1748–1835. British officer. Commissioned an ensign in the 28th Foot on 19 Feb. '61, he was a Capt. in 1763 and is said to have served with his regiment, probably in the West Indies, during that time. (*D.N.B.*) In 1775 he went to America with the 28th as a Maj. and was assigned to one of the provisional battalions of light infantry during the next three years. On 8 Oct. '78 he was appointed Lt. Col. of the 17th Foot and was captured with his garrison at STONY POINT, N.Y., 16 July '79. He was court-martialed for this defeat, but records of the trial have not been found. Apparently he was acquitted, since he is said to have commanded the 17th Regt. in subsequent operations in Va. and the Carolinas. (*D.N.B.*) After the war he was posted in Nova Scotia and Newfoundland, still as C.O. of the 17th. From 1793 until 1798 he was I.G. of recruiting for the English establishment in Ireland. On 5 June '98 he was given command of 3,000 troops for the defense of New Ross, and in successfully accomplishing his mission he is credited with fighting the hardest action of the rebellion. (*Ibid.*) Made Col. of the 81st Regt. in 1798, Lt. Gen. the next year, and Gov. of Ross Castle in 1801, he was promoted to full Gen. in 1809 and created baronet on 1 Dec. '18.

JOHNSON, Sir John. 1742–1830. Loyalist leader. N.Y. The son of Sir Wm. JOHNSON by a German servant named Catherine Weisenberg, he turned into a dull young man despite his better-than-average educational opportunities. He served as Capt. in the militia, fought in Pontiac's War, and while visiting England in 1765 was knighted. On the death of his father in 1774 he inherited his title and the greater part of his estates, including Johnson Hall. In Nov. he succeeded also to his father's post as Maj. Gen. of militia. When news of Bunker Hill sent other prominent Mohawk Valley Tories flying north into Canada, Sir John was forced to remain behind because his wife was expecting a child. He entered into correspondence with Gov. Tryon in regard to the possibility of organizing the settlers of the valley for the Loyalist cause. In Jan. '76 the Cont'l. Cong., having learned that munitions were pouring into Johnson Hall, ordered Schuyler to stop the warlike preparations of Sir John. He had mustered some 200 Highlanders and, during the winter, had started fortifying Johnson Hall. "The number of armed dependents which he retained around him, gave credit to a report that, when the fortification should be completed, it would be garrisoned by 300 Indians in addition to his own men, and that from thence they would sally out and ravage the surrounding country." (Campbell, *Tryon County*, 50) On 13 Jan. Schuyler wrote Johnson, "If Lady Johnson is at Johnson Hall I wish she would retire (and therefore enclose a passport) as I shall march my troops to that place without delay." On the 17th Johnson came to terms which involved disarming his supporters and giving his parole to hold himself at the orders of Congress. In May he broke the parole and fled with a large number of his tenants to Canada. Lady Johnson, again pregnant, was taken to Albany as a hostage, and it is probable that the wife and young children of John Butler were taken to Albany at this same time. (Swiggett, *Niagara*, 68)

On reaching Montreal Sir John was commissioned Lt. Col. and authorized to raise the body of rangers that became known as the "Royal Greens." He participated without personal distinction in ST. LEGER'S EXPEDITION. Contrary to statements in such authoritative works as *D.A.B.*, he was not at ORISKANY with the Butlers, but "characteristically, remained at Headquarters [around Ft. Stanwix] with St. Leger." (Swiggett, *op. cit.*, 85) He and his Greens were routed by a sortie made from Ft. Stanwix during the action at Oriskany, six miles away. Returning to Canada, he devoted his energies to taking care of Loyalist refugees who were arriving in large numbers. In 1778 and

1780 he led raids into Tryon co. that are covered under BORDER WARFARE. In the autumn of 1779 he was at Niagara and Oswego, engaged in Indian affairs. In Sept. '81 he commanded a column that was supposed to advance up Lake Champlain to the Hudson while another advanced from Oswego, but this offensive petered out around Lake George. (See BORDER WARFARE)

Sir John then went to England and returned with a commission dated 14 Mar. '82 as successor to his brother-in-law, Guy Johnson, as Indian Supt. This was reissued in 1791. He also was made Col. in the British Army. His American holdings having been confiscated (Act of Attainder of 22 Oct. '79), he received a large sum of money and a large tract of land in Canada, where he continued to be active in Indian affairs and in relief measures on behalf of Tory refugees.

JOHNSON, Sir William. 1715–1774. Supt. of Indian Affairs, Colonial baron. Born in Ireland, he reached the Mohawk Valley about 1738. By the time of his death, on the eve of the Revolution, he had become a gigantic figure in Colonial affairs. "His influence among the Indians was paramount past the Ohio and almost to Florida," writes Swiggett. "The Crown's commanders in chief needed his support. He acquired a vast estate in the Valley and with his clansmen, Guy Johnson and Claus, and his son, and his brother-in-law, Joseph Brant, and his scores of bastards, and his forts and highland regiments, and his vast knowledge of men and affairs at home and abroad, dominated the American scene beyond the royal governors or the army commanders." (*Niagara*, 8)

Soon after his arrival in America he laid the foundation of a huge fortune and grew very friendly with the Iroquois, particularly the Mohawks who lived nearby. He also got on intimate terms with the daughter of a settler, Catharine Weisenberg, "whose contract service Sir William is said to have bought." (*Ibid.*, 17) W. E. Stevens puts it more delicately in his *D.A.B.* sketch: "Though it has been a matter for dispute, it would seem that about 1739 he married a German girl of the neighborhood, named Catharine Weisenberg, for he refers to her in his will as 'my beloved wife' (Stone, II, 492). By her he had a son [Sir John in 1742] and two daughters."

He first became known in King George's War, when his influence with the Iroquois kept them in the British camp. At the Albany Convention of 1754 he helped formulate Indian policy and, at the request of the Indians, he was appointed their agent. A commission from Braddock dated 15 Apr. '55 gave him "sole Management & direction of the Affairs of the Six Nations of Indians & their Allies." Named to lead a colonial force comprising troops from N.Y., Mass., N.H., Conn., and R.I. against Crown Point—about 2,000 militia and more than 200 Indians—Johnson was commissioned Maj. Gen. Attacked by a French and Indian force under Dieskau at Lake George on 8 Sept. '55, he won a decisive victory in which the French commander was captured. Although he was too weak to press on and capture Crown Point, he had saved the northern colonies from the menace of this enemy force, an achievement the more conspicuous because the other offensives against Niagara and Ft. Duquesne had failed. For accomplishing his mission he was knighted (27 Nov. '55) and made Supt. of Indian Affairs north of the Ohio (17 Feb. '56).

After his defeat of Dieskau, Johnson had built Ft. Wm. Henry at the south end of Lake George. For the next three years he was concerned primarily with the defense of the northern frontiers. Succeeding Prideaux, he commanded the column that captured Niagara on 25 July '59. He then led the force that took Montreal. (See COLONIAL WARS) In 1761 he visited Detroit and apparently succeeded in winning the allegiance of the tribes formerly under French domination, and when Pontiac's War proved that his mission had not been a success he organized Iroquois cooperation in putting down the rebellion. In 1768 he presided over the Council at FT. STANWIX.

Sir William led a strenuous life, making long trips to hold Indian councils, striving to protect the frontier settlements, to civilize the savages, and to develop his vast personal holdings. In 1742 or 1743 he established a residence north of the Mohawk called Mount Johnson. In 1749 he built a stone house that came to be known as Fort Johnson in this same area. In 1762 he moved to Johnson Hall, a baronial hall just north of the settlement that became Johnstown. This house has been preserved. After the death of Catharine he had two "Indian wives": Caroline, niece of the Mohawk chief Hendrick, bore him three children, and Joseph Brant's sister, Molly, who succeeded her, produced eight more.

He was commissioned Maj. Gen. of militia in 1772. Two years later he had to exert himself to keep his Iroquois from becoming involved in Dunmore's War. He had long suffered from an intestinal ailment and was desperately sick when he called a council to hear the complaints of his Indians that the Treaty of Ft. Stanwix was being violated. On the fourth day, after telling his wards that the crimes were the work of individuals whom the King would punish, he died suddenly.

The best biographies are W. L. Stone Jr., *The Life and Times of Sir William Johnson, Bart.* (2 vols., 1865) and Arthur Pound and Richard E. Day, *Johnson of the Mohawks* (New York, 1930). Others are A. C. Buell, *Sir William Johnson* (1903) and W. E. Griffis, *Sir William Johnson and the Six Nations* (1891). The largest body of manuscripts, although badly damaged by fire, is listed in Richard E. Day, *Calendar of the Sir William Johnson MSS. in the N.Y. State Library* (1909).

JOHNSTONE, George. 1730–1787. British naval officer. Fourth son of a Scottish baronet, he entered the navy around 1746 and in Feb. '50 passed his examination for a commission as Lt. He was actually promoted to this rank in 1755. Of proved physical courage in combat, he is described by John Knox Laughton in *D.N.B.* as being "without self-restraint, temper, or knowledge." In 1757 he was convicted of "insubordination and disobedience," but in view of his former gallant conduct received only a reprimand. Prior to this he had killed a captain's clerk in a duel. On 20 Nov. '63 he was formally appointed Gov. of W. Fla. In 1767 he returned to England, was elected to Parliament the next year, and "at once distinguished himself by his shameless and scurrilous utterances." (*Ibid.*) A gross public insult to GERMAIN resulted in a bloodless duel in Dec. '70. His conduct as member of the PEACE COMMISSION OF CARLISLE in 1778 led Congress to resolve on 11 Aug. that they could not honorably deal further with him, and he resigned on the 26th.

Despite his lack of professional qualification for high command in the navy, on 6 May '79 Lord Sandwich rewarded him for his political support by giving him command of a small squadron for service off the Portuguese coast. In 1781, after operating off the Cape of Good Hope and scoring some successes, he retired on half pay and returned to Parliament. Having been violent in his attacks on Lord Howe in 1779, he now turned on Lord Clive and the conduct of affairs in India. In 1783 he became a director of the East India Company. About two years later he became an invalid and passed unlamented from the public scene.

Although often called "a noted duellist," the record shows only three encounters; one of these was bloodless (see above) and another may not actually have occurred. (*D.N.B.*) Knox, author of most naval biographies in *D.N.B.*, says it cannot be denied that he was a commodore but has this comment on his other "titles": "He used to be commonly styled 'Governor Johnstone,' though with very little reason; he is, even now [1908], sometimes described as a politician, with less."

JOHNSTOWN, N.Y., 25 Oct. '81. (BORDER WARFARE) In his retreat up the Mohawk Valley after leading 700 Tories and Indians to within 12 miles of Schenectady, Maj. John Ross brushed aside some militia and entered Johnstown about 2 P.M. (Swiggett, *Niagara*, 240) Col. Marinus Willett had marched all the preceding night and during the day of the 25th to bring his 400 men into action against the raiders, and close to dark he made contact. The weather had been wet for several days, the roads deep in mud, and both forces were tired and wretched. (*Ibid.*) But Willett sent Col. Aaron Rowley to envelop the enemy with a force of state troops and militia while his main body attacked them frontally. In the dismal, rainy October twilight, fighting into the woods, Willett believed he had the advantage until the enemy captured his one gun and stripped its ammunition cart before he could retake it. (Willett's report, C. & M., 1031) When the situation was stabilized on this left flank the militia panicked on the right. Ross claimed he had Willett almost surrounded and that only darkness saved the rebels from being annihilated. (Swiggett, *op. cit.*, 240) Ross retreated six miles and Willett did not pursue for 72 hours, an indication that Ross was correct in claiming the advantage in the engagement.

Willett reported finding the bodies of seven enemy and three of his own men on the field. He estimated that 30 or 40 were wounded on each side and that he took 30 prisoners. The next action was at JERSEYFIELD, 30 Oct.

JOHNSTOWN, N.Y., 21–23 May '80. See BORDER WARFARE.

JONES, Allen. 1739–1807. Militia general and politician. N.C. Elder brother of the more famous Willie JONES, he was the great-grandson of a Welshman who settled in Va. around 1650. His father, Robert or Robin ap Jones, went to N.C. as attorney and agent for Lord Granville. He and Willie spent some years at Eton. Back in N.C. he became prominent in politics and in 1771 assisted Gov. Tryon in operations against the Regulators. "His chief distinction was gained in the Revolution by able, devoted, and continuous labor in camp and council for the patriot cause," writes A. R. Newsome in *D.A.B.* In 1776 he was appointed B.G. for militia of the Halifax district, and in 1778 he protested on legal grounds the sending of N.C. militia to S.C. In 1779–80 he was a delegate to the Cont'l. Cong. Unlike his brother, he favored ratification of the Constitution.

A large property holder, owning 177 slaves in 1790, he was politically conservative and opposed the confiscation of Loyalists' property after the war. His home, "Mount Gallant," across the Roanoke River from "The Grove" of his brother, extended hospitality to the man who became famous under the adopted name of John Paul JONES.

JONES, John Paul. 1747–1792. American naval hero. Scotland. Born in Kirkcudbrightshire, which is bounded on the south by Solway Firth, he was the son of John Paul. The latter was gardener for a Scottish squire whose son was Dr. James CRAIK. Young John Paul crossed the Solway at the age of 12 to become apprentice to a shipowner in Whitehaven, and on his first voyage he visited his elder brother, William, who was established as a tailor at Fredericksburg, Va. The young mariner was released early from his apprenticeship because his employer went bankrupt, and he shipped aboard a slave ship. Trading between the Guinea coast and Jamaica, he became first mate on another slaver at the age of 19. He later sold out and booked passage for England, having become dissatisfied with this livelihood. On the way home he took command when both the captain and the mate died of fever, and for bringing the ship in safely the owners gave him and the crew 10 per cent of the cargo. Furthermore, they signed him as captain of one of their merchantmen, *John* of Dumfries, and he made two voyages to the West Indies in 1760–70. During the second voyage he flogged the ship's carpenter for neglect of duty, and a few weeks later this man died at sea. John Paul was charged with murder by the man's father, was imprisoned at Kirkcudbright, released on bail, and subsequently cleared of the charge. Back in the West Indies in 1773 as master of the *Betsy* of London, he killed the ringleader of his mutinous crew. Although the victim apparently impaled himself by rushing into John Paul's sword, the latter now had a bad reputation in Tobago, where both these

incidents took place; on the advice of friends he secretly left for America with the idea of staying away until a court-martial could be assembled to try the case rather than a civil court.

When the Revolution started he was living in America without employment and reduced to the charity of friends. Meanwhile he had assumed the name of Jones; apparently the name was chosen for no more complicated reason than its obvious merit in concealing his identity. The story that the name was selected in gratification for hospitality at the homes of Allen and Willie JONES is supported by nothing more substantial than the traditions of the latter family. (*D.A.B.*, X, 184, 210) John Paul Jones went to Philadelphia and was employed in fitting out the *Alfred,* the first naval ship bought by Congress. He also became friendly with two influential delegates who were prominent in organizing the Cont'l. navy: Robt. Morris of Pa., and Joseph Hewes of N.C.

Jones got into the navy very much the same way a certain equally unprepossessing and politically unimportant individual named U.S. Grant got into the Union army almost a century later: both had congressmen who felt obliged to see that their constituencies received a share of the military commissions being given out. Delegate Hewes of N.C. insisted that one of the naval lieutenancies go to a Southerner, and thanks to him the little Scot, who technically was a Virginian but who also had N.C. connections, was commissioned on 7 Dec. '75 as the senior first lieutenant. Aboard the *Alfred,* commanded by Dudley Saltonstall, Lt. Jones had no opportunity to distinguish himself, but when given command of the *Providence* later in 1776 he started earning a reputation for success that was to have no equal in the Cont'l. navy. A small fleet soon was placed under his command, he was promoted to Capt., and in one cruise of the *Providence* he took 16 prizes.

When Congress established the rank of naval captains on 10 Oct. '76, however, they placed him 18th. Already unpopular with many of the unremembered Yankee captains senior to him on this list, Jones did not suffer this political slight in silence. Congress had recognized his professional abilities, however, and on 14 June '77 this body gave him the choice appointment as commander of the sloop *Ranger*. Ordered to France, where he was to take command of the *Indien*, building at Amsterdam for Congress, Jones arrived in Dec. '77 to find that the frigate was being given to France by the American commissioners in Paris.

On 10 Apr. '78 he sailed from Brest in the *Ranger* with a crew of about 140 men and armed with 18 six-pounders and six swivel guns. (C. & M., 943) Heading for the home waters of his youth, he raided WHITEHAVEN, 27–28 Apr., and then made an unsuccessful attempt to kidnap the Earl of Selkirk as a hostage to assure the proper treatment of American prisoners. The earl was away from home and thus escaped capture. Crossing the Irish Sea to Carrickfergus, Jones captured the British sloop *Drake* in a brilliant one-hour action in which Jones lost eight killed and wounded to the enemy's 40 or more. (*Ibid.,* 946) On 8 May he regained Brest with seven prizes and numerous prisoners to show for his 28-day absence. His cruise had spread consternation along a considerable portion of the English coast and it marked the start of his international fame.

The French, whose war with England was about to start, hailed Jones as a hero and the authorities called him to Paris in June for consultation on ways

of employing naval forces against England. On 4 Feb. '79 he was informed that the old East Indiaman *Duras* (40) was placed under his command for joint (army-navy) operations against enemy ports. The plans were abandoned (Lafayette was to command the army element; Jones the naval), but by the end of the summer the French had fitted out a small fleet of five naval vessels and two privateers for Jones. Franklin's *Poor Richard's Almanac* was enjoying a vogue in France at the time Jones was refitting the *Duras,* and since he was greatly indebted to Franklin for support he renamed his flagship the *Bonhomme Richard.*

DEFEAT OF THE *SERAPIS*

With the American flag flying over a makeshift flotilla financed by France and with most of the ships commanded by French officers resentful of his authority, Jones put to sea from L'Orient on 14 Aug. '79. Sailing clockwise around the British Isles, up the west coast of Ireland, around Scotland, and to the coast of Yorkshire, Jones captured 17 ships and made an unsuccessful attempt to lay Leith under contribution. He then won the BONHOMME RICHARD–SERAPIS engagement, 23 Sept. '79. In this demonstration of superior seamanship and indomitable fighting spirit John Paul Jones became a great naval hero. On 3 Oct. he reached the Texel, Holland, having left the crippled *Richard* at sea. (She sank on 25 Sept.) The British ambassador, in compliance with orders from George III, demanded that the Dutch seize the ships and crews captured by the "pirate, Paul Jones, of Scotland, who is a rebel subject and a criminal of the state." (Quoted from Sherburne, 135, in *D.A.B.*) After many difficulties arising from Holland's neutrality, Jones had to turn everything but the *Alliance* over to the French government. He sailed aboard the *Alliance* in Dec., evaded the British fleet, and reached L'Orient on 10 Feb. '80 after cruising in the Channel and searching for prizes as far south as Corunna, Spain.

Now occupied primarily with refitting the *Alliance* for his return to America, Jones visited Paris in Apr. '79 to raise the prize money needed to pay his disgruntled crew. While he was absent from L'Orient, however, he lost his last chance to command a fighting vessel when the mad LANDAIS succeeded in resuming command of the *Alliance*. In Dec. '80 he sailed for America as captain of the *Ariel*, which the French loaned for the transportation of military supplies. The crossing was enlivened by his capture of the British ship *Triumph*, "which however escaped by a discreditable ruse," and by his suppression of a conspiracy among the English members of his crew. (Charles O. Paullin in *D.A.B.*)

After being abroad for more than three years, he reached Philadelphia on 18 Feb. '81. Older officers blocked a resolution of Congress to make him a rear admiral, but on 26 June Congress was able to give him command of the largest ship of the Cont'l. Navy, the *America* (76), which was then under construction at Portsmouth, N.H. After more than a year's frustration in constructing this vessel, Jones saw the *America* turned over to the French. The best he was able to do thereafter was to get permission to sail aboard the fleet of Vaudreuil, and he left with them from Boston for a four-month cruise in the West Indies. After the Cont'l. Navy was disbanded, Jones got authority to return to Europe as agent to collect prize money due the U.S. as the result of his operations. His mission was successful, although payment was slow. Jones returned to the U.S. for the

last time in the summer and fall of 1787, and on 16 Oct. Congress voted him the only gold medal awarded to an officer of the Cont'l. Navy. Early the next year he accepted an offer from Catharine the Great to serve in the Russian Navy against the Turks. On 26 May '88 he raised his flag on a squadron in the Black Sea, but although he had an important part in several successful operations his position in the Russian service was undermined by a jealous French adventurer, Prince Nassau-Siegen. Relegated to a position of idleness, he was then victim of a malicious rumor that he had violated a girl. In Sept. '89 he left St. Petersburg with nothing but bitterness and the Order of St. Anne to show for his Russian experience.

Although only a few months past his 45th birthday at this time, his health was bad. He spent his last two years in Paris, where he was no longer a popular hero but where he had a few good friends and comfortable accommodations. In 1845 a movement was started to bring Jones's body back to the U.S., but his relatives in Scotland blocked it a few years later. In 1899 Gen. Horace Porter, Ambassador in Paris, started a systematic search of the site of the old St. Louis cemetery for foreign Protestants (which had been covered by houses), and after six years he wired that the body of Jones had been found. In 1905 the remains were escorted to America by a naval squadron, and in 1913 they were placed in a $75,000 tomb in the crypt of the naval academy at Annapolis. "Porter's proof of identification, while not absolute, appears to have carried conviction to most minds," says Paullin of a controversy that still rages.

Superficially, John Paul Jones was a Scottish adventurer, an ex-slaver turned pirate (in the eyes of the British), who used the American Revolution as an opportunity to get a job. He himself said his motivation was "glory"—nothing about the defeat of Tyranny, although before accepting his commission in the Russian Navy he wrote to Jefferson that he could "never renounce the glorious title of *a citizen of the United States.*" On the other hand, having accepted a commission in the Cont'l. Navy he performed his duties with complete political loyalty to the American cause, despite personal disappointments and lack of opportunity to give his remarkable leadership abilities a full test. Paullin writes:

"Few servants of the Republic have deserved better of it.... Jones's excellences are apparent from his achievements.... His defects, both of taste and character, sprang from his indifferent breeding and education. These he never completely overcame.... His principal fault was vanity. Often obsequious to those above him, he sometimes forgot what was due to those below him and to his own character as an officer."

The American Navy that hails this bachelor as its father would call him a "mustang," and would be happy to have more of his type around in wartime. Archetype of the combat leader, Jones did not look the part: he was short (under 5 feet 7 inches), thin, and homely. Midshipman Nathaniel Fanning, Jones's secretary, described him as being "rather round shouldered, with a visage fierce and warlike, and wore the appearance of great application to study, which he was fond of." ("Fanning's Narrative," *Pubs. of the Naval Hist. Soc.,* 1912, quoted in *D.A.B.,* "Jones.") The naval hero is the subject of one of Houdon's finest statues (1780). If this work and Jones's combat record did not assure him of immortality, one of the sayings attributed to him would do so: "I've just begun to fight." Although this stirring remark is mentioned in only

one participant's account of the BON-HOMME RICHARD–SERAPIS action (C. & M., 946, 948), it characterizes the man's combat record.

Until the recent publication of S. E. Morison's *John Paul Jones: A Sailor's Biography* (1959) the best study was Anna F. (Mrs. Reginald) de Koven's *Life and Letters ...* (2 vols., N.Y.C., 1913). Of the earlier works the best is John Henry Sherburne's *Life and Character of Chevalier John Paul Jones* (London and Washington, 1825), which is chiefly a collection of his correspondence. (*E.B.,* "Jones.") (See CHEVALIER) His memoirs were published in 1830.

JONES, Thomas. 1731–1792. Loyalist historian. N.Y. Author of the only history of the Revolution from the standpoint of a Loyalist (see bibliography), he was born into a prominent N.Y.C. family. His marriage in 1762 to Anne, daughter of Chief Justice James De Lancey, brought him more wealth and influence. Meanwhile, he had graduated from Yale (1750), probably studied law with his father and Joseph Murray, and held a number of public offices. Three years after his marriage he built "Mount Pitt" on about two acres of land between the Bowery and the East River (the land was a gift to Anne from her brother James); one of the finest residences and estates on Manhattan, it was the site of Jones's Hill Fort when Charles Lee organized the defenses of N.Y.C.

In 1773 he succeeded his father, David (1699–1775), as a judge of the Supreme Court. As a loyal crown official and wealthy man he was a natural enemy of the patriots. On 27 June '76 he was arrested at his home. The N.Y. Prov. Cong. released him on parole to reappear before them on reasonable notice. On 11 Aug. that same body voided the parole and Jones was again arrested. Charged with disaffection, he was a prisoner in Conn. until paroled in Dec. '76 by Gov. Trumbull. During the next three years he quietly compiled the history that was published just over a century later.

On 6 Nov. '79 his house was suddenly entered and robbed by a patriotic force under Capt. Daniel Hawley of Conn. (Appleton's) The Conn. heroes had captured Jones with a view to exchanging him for Gen. Gold Selleck Silliman, a Yale classmate and friend who had been captured in his home six months earlier. The exchange was effected in April '80. The next year Jones and his family went to Bath, England, where Jones recovered from injuries received in a sleigh accident in Conn. Named in the Act of ATTAINDER, he remained in England. He had no children, but his adopted niece, Anne Charlotte De Lancey, became the second wife of road-builder John L. McAdam.

JONES, Willie (pronounced Wylie). c. 1741–1801. Patriot leader. N.C. Younger brother of Allen Jones, he studied and traveled in Europe before returning in 1760 to become a socially prominent and popular Carolinian. His handsome house in Halifax, "The Grove," was a center of high life and patriot politics, and its guests included a refugee who adopted the name John Paul JONES. Willie was an aide to Gov. Tryon in the Alamance operations against the Regulators. He rose to the position of leader of the democratic element in his state and shaped the N.C. constitution if he did not actually write it. In 1780 he was elected to the Cont'l. Cong. and served a year. Fundamentally opposed to the Constitution, he led the movement against it in his state and withdrew from public life in 1789 rather than alter his political position. An aristocrat with a genuine de-sire for political democracy, "he was a man of superior ability and was a political organizer of genius." (D.A.B.)

JUMEL, Stephen. c. 1754–1832. Wine merchant. France. From a family of Bordeaux merchants, he appeared in N.Y.C. in 1795, having been driven from his coffee plantation in Haiti by an insurrection. A "handsome, graceful giant" and accomplished profiteer, he amassed a fortune in the wine business. In 1804 he married Betsey Bowen, a beautiful blonde who had been his mistress for several years. In 1810 he bought her the Roger Morris house, which was Washington's headquarters during the action at HARLEM HEIGHTS, and which is better known in history as the Jumel Mansion. It is now a museum. Unable to crash Betsey into N.Y. society, he had more luck in Paris, where they arrived in 1815. Jumel is said to have offered to bring Napoleon to America after Waterloo. (D.A.B.) Betsey (she was also known as Eliza) returned to N.Y. in 1826 with a power of attorney that she used to take over her husband's fortune. He returned in 1828 and died in 1832 after falling from a wagon. On 1 July 1833, when she was about 55, she married Aaron BURR.

JUNGKENN, Friedrich Christian Arnold, Baron von, Münzer von Mohrenstamm. 1732–1806. Minister of State for Hesse-Cassel, 1780–89. Born into a very old family of the lesser German nobility, he entered a Prussian infantry regt. commanded by a cousin and was an ensign at the age of 21. After a brilliant military career in the Prussian and Hessian services, he reached the rank of Maj. Gen. and in 1779 was a member of the council of the Landgrave of Hesse-Cassel, who for some time had been bargaining with the British on the matter of furnishing mercenaries. In 1780 he succeeded Baron

Martin Ernst von Schlieffen as minister of state (which included the duties of minister of war). The next year he was commissioned Lt. Gen. The von Jungkenn Papers, acquired by the Clements Library in 1932, include letters and reports to him from Hessian officers in America. *The Siege of Charleston,* edited by Bernhard A. Uhlendorf (Ann Arbor, Mich., 1938), contains parallel German and English texts of letters and diaries of Capt. Johann EWALD, Capt. Johann HINRICHS, Gen. von Huyn, and a Maj. Wm. von Wilmowsky.

JUNIUS. Pen name of an unknown British political writer who attacked Grafton, Bedford, and George III. He defended the cause of John Wilkes. His most notable series appeared in the London *Public Advertiser* between Jan. '69 and Jan. '72. The writer has never been identified, but he obviously was a Whig of the Chatham-Grenville faction and he had access to secret government matters. There is evidence—handwriting and political outlook—that Junius was Sir Philip Francis (1740–1818), first clerk in the War Office when the series started. The chief biographer of POWNALL has claimed authorship of the papers for his subject, but there is little support from other investigators of the mystery. As a sample of his style, here is how Junius starts his letter of 19 Dec. '69 to George III: "Sir, It is the misfortune of your life... that you should never have been acquainted with the language of truth, until you heard it in the complaints of your people. It is not, however, too late to correct the error of your education." (From Mumby, *George III,* 268)

K

KACHLEIN (or Kichlein), Andrew. American officer. Pa. A 1st Lt. in the 2d Pa. Bn. 5 Jan.–21 June '76, he became a Col. of militia (Heitman) and commanded a force of Berks co. riflemen at LONG ISLAND, 27 Aug. '76, as part of Alexander's right wing. (Ward, *W.O.R.,* 214–24 *passim*)

KACHLEIN (or Kichlein), Peter. d. 1789. Militia officer. Pa. A 2d Lt. in Baxter's Pa. Bn. of the FLYING CAMP, he was wounded and captured at Ft. Washington, 16 Nov. '76. He was exchanged in 1778 and died 11 years later. (Heitman)

KALB, Johann. 1721–1780. Cont'l. general. Son of Bavarian peasants, the man who was to be known in America as "Baron de Kalb" left home at the age of 16 and six years later appeared as a Lt. (1 Sept. '43) in a French infantry regiment under the name of Jean de Kalb. He subsequently fought in the army of the great Marshal Saxe, served through the War of the Austrian Succession (1740–48), was promoted to Maj. in 1756, and distinguished himself in the Seven Years' War (1756–63). Meanwhile he had become an assiduous student of languages and mathematics in addition to strictly military subjects. In 1764 he married a wealthy heiress whose fortune enabled him to retire from the army on 5 Jan. '65 (Lasseray) and settle near Paris. During the first four months of 1768 he traveled in America as a secret agent for Choiseul to report on the colonists' feelings toward Great Britain. "His numerous and detailed reports were the observations of a shrewd and impartial investigator," writes Frank Monaghan in *D.A.B.*, but he made the mistake of reporting the truth rather than what Choiseul wanted to hear, comments Van Tyne. "Choiseul rewarded his faithful endeavor by tiring of the reporter and turning his noble back." (Van Tyne, *War of Indep.*, 453)

The accession of Louis XVI brought the Comte de Broglie back into influence and Kalb, who had served in the latter's corps, returned to the army. He served under Broglie in the Metz garrison and on 6 Nov. '76 was commissioned B.G. By this time he had decided to seek his military fortune in America and received permission to go as a volunteer. Silas Deane drew up one of his contracts and Kalb sailed on 20 Apr. '77 with LAFAYETTE. Although Congress made satisfactory arrangements for the wealthy and influential young marquis, they saw no way of accommodating the bogus baron. Kalb threatened a civil suit for breach of contract and was about to return to France when on 15 Sept. he was voted a commission as Maj. Gen. After some hesitation about accepting it he joined Washington early in Nov. and spent the winter at Valley Forge. In the spring of 1778 he was named as Lafayette's second in command for the proposed CANADA INVASION (Planned).

Not until two years later did Kalb finally receive an assignment commensurate with his rank. On 3 Apr. '80 he was ordered to the relief of Charleston with the Md. and Del. Cont'ls. His remarkable march is covered under "American Regulars Move South" in the article on Military Operations in the SOUTHERN THEATER. On 25 July he surrendered command to Gates but remained with the Southern army at the head of his division. Gates ignored .the professionally sound advice of Kalb, to lead the army to annihilation in the Camden Campaign. In the battle of 16 Aug. Kalb fell bleeding from 11 wounds. He died at Camden three days later. (See CAMDEN CAMPAIGN for his activities in the campaign and the battle.)

Kalb was a remarkable soldier. Over six feet tall, with a strong, handsome, intelligent face that showed "an expression of good nature mixed with shrewdness" (Ward, *W.O.R.*, 713), he was a man of temperate personal habits and tremendous endurance. An avowed soldier of fortune when he reached America in 1777, he was "transformed into a sincere, selfless patriot." (*Amer. Heritage Book of the Rev.*, 324) His misfortune as a European officer was to have been born a peasant; his misfortune as an officer in America was in being a European without political influence, with the result that he could not be given high command in the Cont'l. Army.

The standard biography is Friedrich Kapp's *Leben* ... (Stuttgart, 1862), translated as *The Life of John Kalb* (New York, 1884).

KASKASKIA, Ill., 4 July '78. British post on the Mississippi seized in the WESTERN OPERATIONS OF GEORGE ROGERS CLARK.

KEGS, Battle of the. See "BATTLE OF THE KEGS."

KEMBLE, Peter. 1704–1789. N.J. Loyalist. Born in Smyrna of an English father who was a merchant in Turkey and a Greek mother, he was well educated in England before settling in N.J. around 1730 to become a prosperous, respected, and politically prominent citizen. He was connected by marriage to the Schuylers, De Lanceys, and Van Cortlandts, and the seven children of this union included Stephen KEMBLE and Margaret. The latter married GAGE. Kemble's home in Brunswick was a stopping place for distinguished travelers between Philadelphia and N.Y. About 1765 he built the manor near Morristown that was used by Washington's army during the winter quarters of 1779–80 and 1780–81. During this time the old Tory was treated with the utmost respect by Washington, who had known him before the war. (Alden, *Gage*, 43 *n.;* N.P.S., *Morristown, passim.*)

KEMBLE, Stephen. *c.* 1730–1822. British officer and Loyalist. N.J. Son of Peter KEMBLE, he was one of the first students of what developed into the U. of Pa. In May '57 he was commissioned ensign in the regiment being raised by Thos. Gage, and in Dec. '58 he became that officer's brother-in-law. After taking part in the siege of Havana in 1762 he went to Montreal as A.D.C. to Gage, and was promoted to Capt. in 1765. In 1772, through the influence of his brother-in-law, he became deputy A.G. and a Maj. He was put in charge of the intelligence service. In 1773–74 Stephen was in England with the Gages. After Gage's recall in 1775 he remained as deputy A.G. to Howe and Clinton, but neither valued his services highly. (Alden, *Gage*, 209) When ARNOLD'S TREASON got under way Clinton was anxious to have John André take over the duties of Kemble (the secret service was an A.G. function), and he did this by arranging a deal whereby André became deputy A.G., received thereby an automatic promotion to Maj., and out of this increased salary André paid Kemble £300 a year for vacating the post. (*Ibid.*, 290; as part of this "deal" Lord RAWDON resigned as A.G.) Kemble's resignation was dated 16 Sept. '79. (Van Doren, *Secret History*, 233) Meanwhile the ex-

ertions of Gage and the latter's family connections had resulted in getting Kemble an appointment as Lt. Col. in the 60th Regt. in 1778 and he was ordered from N.Y. to join his unit. He served in the West Indies and Nicaragua, was promoted to Col. in 1782, and in 1793 became deputy judge advocate, but "his military career really ended with the close of the war, since his brother-in-law was unable to help him further." (Alden, *op. cit.*, 290–91) He returned to N.J. in 1805 and died there on 20 Dec. 1822. Alden characterizes him as "a man of respectable but not major talents" and points out that his criticism of Clinton may have been a factor in the "deal" of 1779. (*Ibid.*, 74, 209 *n.*)

The Kemble Papers were printed in the *Collection of the N.Y. Historical Society for the Year 1883, . . . 1884*, 2 vols., 1884–85. They include his journals and are of considerable historical value.

KENTON, Simon. 1755–1836. Frontiersman. Va. At the age of 16 he fled across the Allegheny Mtns. when he believed he had killed another boy in a fist fight. Under the assumed name of Samuel Butler he hunted, explored, and fought Indians along the Ohio. As a secret agent in Dunmore's War and as a scout he got to know Simon Girty and Daniel Boone. He joined George Rogers Clark and took part in the capture of Kaskaskia and Vincennes. He accompanied three expeditions against CHILLICOTHE: Boone's in 1779 and Clark's in 1780 and 1782. After the first of these he was captured by Indians, sentenced to death, saved by Girty, again condemned, saved through the efforts of LOGAN, and sent to Detroit as a prisoner. He escaped in July '79. Learning that his boyhood "victim" was alive, he returned to Va. (as Kenton) and brought his family back to settle in 1784 around modern Maysville, Kentucky, where his old campsite (Limestone) had been. In subsequent wars he rose to the rank of militia B.G. and acquired large land holdings, but through ignorance of the law he ended up destitute in his last years. Saved from poverty by a pension from Ky. in 1824, he also regained some of his land. (Appleton's)

See Edna Kenton, *Simon Kenton* (1930).

KENTUCKY RAID of Bird, Apr.–June '80. (Ruddle's and Martin's Stations) Capt. Henry Bird, an exceptionally capable British partisan leader, left Detroit in Apr. with about 600 Indians and whites to raid Ky. His expedition is remarkable in that six guns were taken on this long-range operation. Moving along the Maumee–(Great) Miami River route to the Ohio and up the Licking River to its fork near modern Falmouth, Ky., Bird started overland to strike the settlements between the Licking and Kentucky rivers in June. Meanwhile, despite a "quarrelsome delay" (Peckham, *War for Indep.*, 116), his ranks had been swelled to about 1,200. Unable to resist Bird's cannon, Capt. Ruddle surrendered after being assured that the refugees in his stockaded post would not become prisoners of the Indians. Bird was unable to carry out this promise, but he did persuade the chiefs that all future prisoners must come under his control. Martin's Station, about five miles farther south, next fell, and there was no resistance. Although the Indians had been encouraged by their successes to propose that the offensive be continued against Bryan's Station and Lexington, Bird managed to talk them into withdrawing. The expedition retraced its route, taking 350 prisoners and much plunder. Bird's daring raid was one of the operations in 1780 that altered plans in the WESTERN OPERATIONS of Clark,

limiting him to punitive action against the Indians and delaying his proposed offensive against Detroit.

KETTLE CREEK, Ga., 14 Feb. '79. Tory defeat. Encouraged by Campbell's capture of Savannah (29 Dec. '78) and his advance on Augusta, Col. Boyd raised a force of Tories in Anson County, N.C.—near the S.C. border—and marched to join Lt. Col. John Hamilton in Ga. Hamilton was a N.C. Tory of high social position and a veteran of CULLODEN, respected by Whigs as well as his own people, who had organized a regiment in Fla. and whom Campbell sent with his 200 mounted partisans to rally Loyalists in the back country of Ga. (DeMond, *Loyalists of N.C.*, 105; Ward, *W.O.R.*, 682) As Boyd crossed S.C. he was joined by other Loyalists who swelled his ranks to about 700. Writing from the Tory point of view, DeMond mentions that they "lived off the land as they pursued their march." (*Ibid.*) Putting the same fact in somewhat different language, Lossing says: "Like plundering banditti, they appropriated every species of property to their own use, abused the inhabitants, and wantonly butchered several who opposed their rapacious demands." (II, 711).

Campbell took Augusta on 29 Jan. and, leaving a Tory garrison under Thos. Brown, started establishing posts in western Ga. There were skirmishes about 30 miles up the Savannah River from Augusta between Patriot Col. John Dooley and 300 Tories under Col. McGirth and Hamilton. Dooley had crossed the river and then been driven back into S.C. by Hamilton when Andrew Pickens joined him with reinforcements that brought their total strength up to about 350. Pickens assumed command of the combined forces and on 10 Feb. crossed the Savannah at Cowen's Ferry to attack Hamilton. The latter was besieged at Carr's Fort (or Ft. Cars) and in bad straits when Pickens learned of Boyd's approach. The rebels considered Boyd bigger game than Hamilton and started after him. Pickens recrossed the Savannah near Ft. Charlotte (close to the junction of the Broad and Savannah rivers). Learning of his approach, Boyd, who was moving due west toward the Savannah from Ninety-Six, headed for the crossing of the river at Cherokee Ford, 10 miles north of Ft. Charlotte. Here he was stopped by eight men with two swivel guns in a redoubt, but he moved five miles upstream, crossed on rafts, and continued toward Augusta.

There is disagreement as to what happened around Cherokee Ford. Lossing, whose account I have followed in connection with Boyd's crossing of the river, says he was attacked about 12 Feb. by Capt. Anderson, losing 100 men while Anderson lost 16 killed and 16 captured. (*Op. cit.*, 712) Ward, on the other hand, says that Anderson was driven back after failing to keep Boyd from crossing at Cherokee Ford, and he says nothing of an action in which so many casualties were sustained. (*Op. cit.*, 683)

Pickens, meanwhile, made a complete circle, moving upstream on the S.C. side to cross the Savannah behind Boyd and follow him down the Ga. side. (Avery's map facing p. 192 in F. V. Greene, *Rev. War*) Oblivious that he was being followed, Boyd crossed the Broad near its junction with the Savannah the morning of the 13th and camped that night on the north side of Kettle Creek. Here he was surprised on the 14th while his horses were turned out to graze and his men were slaughtering cattle. The rebels attacked in a line of battle whose right was commanded by Dooley, the center by Pickens, and the left by Col. Elijah Clarke.*

The Tory pickets fired and fell back into camp. Although his troops were in the greatest disorder, Boyd pulled them together and put up a fight that lasted nearly an hour, according to Ward, and nearly two hours, according to Lossing. The Tories were finally routed with a loss of 40 killed (according to most authorities; Lossing says 70) and 70 captured. Boyd died of wounds that night. The attackers lost nine killed and 23 wounded; according to Lossing the latter were mortally wounded. The Tory prisoners were all convicted of high treason ("war crimes" is the more sophisticated modern counterpart). Five were hanged, the remainder were pardoned.

Boyd's strength in this action is generally given as 700; Ward says 300 of these reached Augusta to join Campbell. Pickens' strength is generally given as about 300. His victory prevented any serious rallying of Tories in the South for a long time and it also encouraged patriot militia to flock into Lincoln's camp at Purysburg, leading the latter to undertake his counteroffensive to liberate Ga. The victory opened up the back country and was a factor in Campbell's evacuation of Augusta. (See "Lincoln's Campaigns" under SOUTHERN THEATER, Mil. Opns.)

As for the conflicting accounts of Lossing and Ward mentioned earlier, it is most likely that Lossing's sources confused this action of Anderson with the Battle of Kettle Creek; otherwise, it is hard to explain why other accounts fail to mention an engagement in which the losses were as high as at Kettle Creek. This theory is supported by the fact that Heitman's list of battles shows both Cherokee Ford, S.C., and Kettle

* Some writers have stated erroneously that this was not Elijah Clarke but Thomas CLARK.

Creek, Ga., on 14 Feb. (Heitman, 681; *A.A.*, 414). Strait's list of battles shows: "Cherokee Ford, or Kettle Creek, S.C." [*sic*]. Carr's Fort, 10 Feb., is the only other action listed by Heitman (and *A.A.*) during the period 10–14 Feb. in this area.

KICHLEIN. See KACHLEIN.

KING GEORGE'S WAR, 1744–45. Mentioned under COLONIAL WARS, this was the American phase of the War of the AUSTRIAN SUCCESSION (1740–48).

KING WILLIAM'S WAR (1689–97). See COLONIAL WARS.

KING'S AMERICAN REGIMENT OF FOOT. See FANNING'S REGT.

KINGS BRIDGE, N.Y. The point at which the Post Road crossed Spuyten Duyvil Creek—which separates Manhattan from the Bronx—Kings Bridge was strategically important in the N.Y. Campaign and subsequently in the British defense of N.Y.C. It was an objective of American forces under Maj. Gen. Lincoln in the Operations against Manhattan at the start of the YORKTOWN CAMPAIGN, in July '81. The name is also variously spelled King's Bridge and Kingsbridge.

KINGS FERRY, N.Y. About 25 miles N. of N.Y.C. and half that distance S. of West Point, this Hudson River crossing was between Stony Point (on the W. bank) and Verplancks Point. It was strategically important as the southernmost crossing site that the Americans could safely use while the British held N.Y.C.

KINGS MOUNTAIN, S.C., 7 Oct. '80. After the fall of Charleston (12 May '80) Sir Henry Clinton appointed Maj. Patrick Ferguson of the 71st Highlanders Inspector of Militia in the Southern Provinces. Assisted by Maj. Geo. Hanger (until 6 Aug., when the latter took command of Tarleton's cavalry),

Ferguson raised about 4,000 Loyalist militia in the vicinity of Ninety-Six. As early as July Ferguson started pushing north to extend his operations. Meanwhile, the Tory leaders Morgan Bryan and John Moore had raised about 1,500 men in the Catawba District. About the same time Thomas ("Gamecock") Sumter was starting his partisan operations, and Col. Chas. McDowell, who commanded N.C. rebel militia, was calling for assistance from the "OVER MOUNTAIN MEN" across the Blue Ridge Mountains. Between 20 June and the Battle of Kings Mountain, 7 Oct., a number of raids and skirmishes took place in the region between the Catawba and Ninety-Six. The principal ones are mentioned under Mil. Opns. in the SOUTHERN THEATER, and only those connected with activities leading to the Battle of Kings Mountain will be mentioned here.

Chas. McDowell was what the historian Fisher calls "a rather inactive partisan leader," but he was joined by a couple of the other kind. Col. Isaac Shelby arrived with some 600 "over mountain men," and Col. Elijah Clarke was in the area with a force of Ga. and Carolina militia. Shelby captured THICKETTY FORT, S.C., 30 July. In two minor engagements around Wofford's Iron Works (Cedar Springs), 8 Aug. (also referred to as Old Iron Works), Clarke and Shelby gained no advantage, but they gave the Tories a good licking at MUSGROVE'S MILL, 18 Aug. They were considering an attack against Ninety-Six, about 30 miles away, when news of Gates's defeat at Camden, 16 Aug., prompted them to beat a hasty retreat. Ferguson got as close as 30 minutes behind them as they headed for Gilbert Town, but he was stopped by a message calling him to Camden. At British headquarters Ferguson was told by Cornwallis of the forthcoming invasion of N.C.

Cornwallis planned to lead the main portion of his field army from Camden north to Charlotte and Salisbury, an axis along which the strongest rebel resistance was expected. Around Cross Creek (now Fayetteville) on the Cape Fear River, over 100 miles east of Charlotte, strong Loyalist concentrations were located. West of the Catawba, in what was then Tryon county, N.C., there also were strong Loyalist elements. By this strategic penetration with his main force Cornwallis expected to link up the two Loyalist sections and then establish control over the rest of N.C. (Fisher, *Struggle,* II, 346, citing Stedman).

Ferguson had previously penetrated as far as Gilbert Town and maintained that he had sufficient Loyalist support in this region to control it. Cornwallis therefore authorized him to move with an independent force into this area, but he had misgivings which he expressed as follows in a letter to Clinton:

"Ferguson is to move into Tryon County with some militia, whom he says he is sure he can depend upon for doing their duty; but I am sorry to say that his own experience, as well as that of every other officer, is totally against him."

On 8 Sept. Cornwallis marched north with his main body east of the Wateree, and with Tarleton's Legion, reinforced by one gun and a body of light infantry on the other side. At WAHAB'S PLANTATION, N.C., 21 Sept., Col. Wm. Davie surprised and defeated this flanking force and then dropped back to contest Cornwallis' capture of CHARLOTTE, 26 Sept. The army then stopped to wait for Ferguson to join them from the west.

On 7 Sept. Ferguson entered N.C. and marched to Gilbert Town. Many of the local people came in to take the British oath of allegiance, although large numbers did this only as a temporary expedient to protect their property. On the 10th, Ferguson withdrew south to rejoin his main body in an attempt to intercept Clarke, who was leading an expedition against AUGUSTA, Ga., 14–18 Sept., and who was expected to withdraw into N.C. On 23 Sept. Ferguson was back in Gilbert Town, having meanwhile moved about 22 miles N.W. of the town to Old Fort, near the source of the Catawba in the Blue Ridge Mountains.

Ferguson now boldly announced that the rebellion was finished in his area. "He visited patriot families in person, treating them with the most kindly consideration and advising them to recall their husbands or sons who were 'out liers.'" says Fisher. (See "OUT LIERS") But trouble was brewing. Before he had withdrawn on the 10th, he paroled Samuel Phillips and sent him across the Blue Ridge with a warning to the militia commander, Shelby. If they did not "desist from their opposition to the British arms, and take protection under his standard," said Ferguson, "he would march his army over the mountains, hang their leaders, and lay their country waste with fire and sword." The "over mountain men" had already decided they had better go get Ferguson before he came after them, and this message served to accelerate their efforts. When Clarke and Shelby reached N.C. after the action of 18 Aug. their men were suffering from exhaustion and malnutrition, and their forces as well as McDowell's had scattered. This is why Ferguson had so far met no resistance. But the rebel leaders had also decided at this time that a large force should be raised from both sides of the mountain to stop the invaders, and the call for volunteers had gone out. Shelby now met with Col. John Sevier, another "over mountain" leader, to make final preparations. The two patriots pledged themselves to cover the money taken from the public treasury to finance their *posse comitatus*. They sent out a final call for men, and appealed to Col. Arthur Campbell in Va., and Cols. Chas. McDowell and Benj. Cleveland along the N.C. border. Rendezvous was set for 25 Sept. at Sycamore Shoals, on the Watauga near modern Elizabethton, Tenn.

More than 1,000 men showed up, most of them mounted and carrying the long hunting rifle of the American frontier. Arthur Campbell's giant brother-in-law, Col. Wm. Campbell, came with 400 Virginians.

Sevier and Shelby each arrived with 240 "over mountain men." They were a hardy little band of frontiersmen who gathered that day, many of whom brought friends and relatives to see them off. Some of those who rallied at Sycamore Shoals were left behind to defend the settlement from Indians.

"The over-mountain men, it will be observed, were considerably less than half and this statement is necessary because there is a general impression that the expedition was principally made up of the romantic hunters from the Tennessee. A week or so later they were joined by several hundred South Carolinians,* so that the proportion of over-mountain men became still smaller. The little army would be properly described as composed of patriot riflemen of the farmer, hunter, and Indian fight-

* As will be mentioned later, N.C. and S.C. reinforcements raised the total strength to a figure estimated as high as 1,800. This statement of Fisher is based on the assumption that Cleveland joined the expedition at Sycamore Shoals, but the Tenn. mountaineers would still number "considerably less than half" of the force listed above.

ing class from the frontiers of the two Carolinas and Virginia." (Fisher, *op. cit.*, 352)

The Rev. Samuel Doak told the gathering the story of Gideon's uprising against the Midianites and, although it turned out to be a bit long for the occasion, suggested as a battle cry, "The sword of the Lord and of Gideon."

On 26 Sept. this impromptu army left Sycamore Shoals, the next day they plowed through deep snow on the crest of the mountains, and on the 30th they reached McDowell's plantation at Quaker Meadow (near modern Morgantown, N.C.), where Charles McDowell's 160 Burke Co. militia were assembling. While taking a day's rest after this 90-mile march they were joined by Col. Benj. Cleveland and Maj. Joseph Winston, who brought 350 N.C. militia from the upper Yadkin (Wilkes and Surry counties of N.C.). They also learned that Col. James Williams was raising forces to join them farther south. As they continued toward Gilbert Town, where Ferguson was reported still to be located, on 1 Oct. the expedition leaders sent Chas. McDowell to ask Gates in Hillsboro that Daniel Morgan or Wm. Davidson be assigned to command them. Meanwhile, having gotten their senior militia officer off the scene, on 2 Oct. they elected Wm. Campbell temporary commander of the combined forces. Maj. Joseph McDowell assumed command of his brother's regiment.

FERGUSON RETREATS

On 27 Sept. Ferguson started withdrawing south, having learned through agents of the rebels' approach and also having received a message two days earlier from Lt. Col. John Cruger, British commander at Ninety-Six, that Elijah Clarke's forces might be heading north from Augusta to reinforce the other rebel expedition. On Green River, 30 Sept., Ferguson was joined by James Crawford and Samuel Chambers, who had deserted the patriots on the 27th; from them he got further information about the expedition, and he sent urgent requests to Cornwallis and Cruger for reinforcements. On 1 Oct. the British turned east toward Charlotte with a view to deceiving the rebels, who would expect them to continue south toward Ninety-Six. From Tate's Plantation on Buffalo Creek, 10 miles west of Kings Mountain, Ferguson wrote Cornwallis on 5 Oct.:

"I am on my march towards you, by a road leading from Cherokee Ford, north of Kings Mountain. Three or four hundred good soldiers, part dragoons, would finish this business. [Something] must be done soon. This is their last push in this quarter and they are extremely desolate and [c]owed."

Ferguson obviously was not particularly worried, because he had marched only four miles on 2 Oct., having decided there was no chance of cutting off Clarke. On the 6th, he wrote Cornwallis that he had stopped his retreat and was making a stand. "I arrived to day at Kings Mountain," his message said, "& have taken a post where I do not think I can be forced by a stronger enemy than that against us." What he did not know when he made this decision was that the British could send him no support. Cruger had written that he did not have enough men to garrison Ninety-Six properly, much less to send him reinforcements. Tarleton had been desperately ill with malaria the past two weeks; after leading the Legion into Charlotte, his second in command, Hanger, succumbed to the same disease; and now Cornwallis was incapacitated by a "feverish cold." On 6 Oct., therefore, Cornwallis answered Ferguson's message of the preceding day: "Tarleton shall pass at some of the upper Fords, and clear the Country; for the present both he and his Corps want a few days rest."

The patriot army entered Gilbert Town on 3 Oct. and, fooled by Ferguson's change of direction, they lost his trail at Denard's Ford on the Broad River. The night of the 4th they camped at this place, where the enemy had been three nights before. On the 5th the rebels camped 12 miles farther south, at Alexander's Ford on Green River, where Ferguson had stopped five nights earlier. The next day they picked up the scent, however, and marched 21 miles to the Cowpens. (See COW-PENS for description of place and origin of name.) Col. James Williams had started raising militia from both the Carolinas about 23 Sept., and he joined the expedition at Cowpens with about 400 men; his subordinate leaders were Wm. Hill, Edw. Lacey, James Hawthorne, Fred. Hambright, Wm. Chronicle, and Wm. Graham. Fisher says one reason Ferguson's change of route deceived the rebels was because "some of the South Carolina patriots under Williams ... wanted Campbell's army to keep on southward, abandon their enterprise against Ferguson and attack Ninety-Six so as to help the patriots in that region protect their property from the loyalists." (*Struggle*, II, 352)

When a spy named Joseph Kerr confirmed previous reports of the enemy's location, 900 of "the best horsemen" started forward at 8 P.M., 6 Oct., leaving "the weak horse and footmen to follow as fast as possible." (Report of Campbell, Cleveland, and Shelby quoted in Moore, *Diary*, II, 338 ff.; hereafter cited as "Official Report.")

Ferguson's decision to make a stand is a mystery, since he undoubtedly could have retreated to the safety of the main army at Charlotte. Aside from the fact that he did not know Cornwallis was unable to send him any appreciable amount of assistance—he did order out one detachment—the best explanation probably is that Ferguson thought he had found a position where he could win distinction by defeating a large rebel force in battle. The spót was a rocky, relatively treeless ridge with steep, heavily wooded and boulder-strewn slopes. It was shaped roughly like a human footprint that pointed to the N.E. Rising 60 feet above the surrounding country, it varied in width between 120 and 60 yards. The slopes were so rugged that Ferguson was content to rely on nature's gifts and failed to improve his position by field fortifications; while he made preparations to defend the entire perimeter of the ridge, he established his camp in parade ground fashion on the broad, N.E. portion. With about 200 men absent foraging the morning of the battle, his available strength on Kings Mountain was 800 militia and 100 picked men from the King's American Rangers, the Queen's Rangers, and the N.J. Vols. The only man on either side during the battle who was not American was Patrick Ferguson, himself, which makes it amusing to see writers refer to the subsequent action as a battle between "the British" and "the Americans."

Having marched all night and all the next morning through rough country—not to mention the preceding movement to the Cowpens—the attackers began to lose the fine edge of their enthusiasm by noon of the 7th. It had rained during the night, and a light drizzle kept up after daylight. About noon Shelby had to veto the proposal that the expedition halt for a rest. Interest quickened, however, when they captured two enemy scouts and a messenger. The prisoners confirmed Ferguson's position and furnished an interesting detail that was dis-

seminated through the ranks: the enemy leader could be identified by a checkered shirt worn over his uniform; the rebels already knew that Ferguson could also be spotted by a crippled right arm, the elbow having been shattered by a musket ball at Brandywine.

The rebels had followed Ferguson's route to the vicinity of Tate's Plantation near Buffalo Creek. Expecting to find enemy outposts to detect or contest their crossing of the Broad River, they detoured south to Cherokee Ford about two and a half miles below Tate's. They then followed the Ridge Road past present-day Antioch Church, thence north to a point on the modern state boundary some four miles W.N.W. of Kings Mountain, and then toward their objective. (N.P.S., *Kings Mtn.*, 18–19) About a mile away they halted, hitched their horses, broke up into four columns, and moved toward the assigned positions around the ridge. The approach was so skilfully conducted, and Ferguson's security measures so lax, that Shelby's command was within a quarter of a mile of the ridge when the first shots were fired by the Tories. Ferguson was completely surprised.

Shelby did not let his men return the enemy's fire until they had worked their way well up the slope. Campbell, meanwhile, was closing in from the opposite side, and the other forces were also moving, Indian fashion, into position. (See map) The weakness of Ferguson's planning now became apparent: the trees, boulders, and ravines on the slopes did not constitute an obstacle to the attackers but furnished ideal terrain for their infiltration tactics. But the man who had devoted so much effort to introducing the rifle into the British Army—who had invented the first true military rifle, and who was possibly the best marksman in the Army —this man, Ferguson, made another

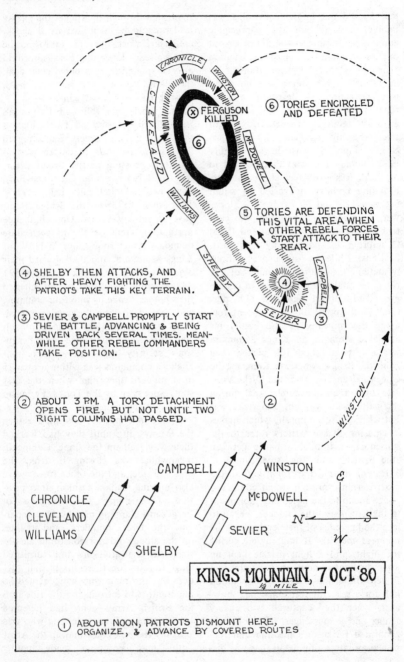

CHRONICLE

WINSTON

CLEVELAND

Ⓧ FERGUSON KILLED

Ⓖ TORIES ENCIRCLED AND DEFEATED

MCDOWELL

Ⓖ

WILLIAMS

⑤ TORIES ARE DEFENDING THIS VITAL AREA WHEN OTHER REBEL FORCES START ATTACK TO THEIR REAR.

④ SHELBY THEN ATTACKS, AND AFTER HEAVY FIGHTING THE PATRIOTS TAKE THIS KEY TERRAIN.

SHELBY

CAMPBELL

④

SEVIER

③

③ SEVIER & CAMPBELL PROMPTLY START THE BATTLE, ADVANCING & BEING DRIVEN BACK SEVERAL TIMES. MEANWHILE OTHER REBEL COMMANDERS TAKE POSITION.

② ABOUT 3 P.M. A TORY DETACHMENT OPENS FIRE, BUT NOT UNTIL TWO RIGHT COLUMNS HAD PASSED.

②

WINSTON

CAMPBELL

WINSTON

CHRONICLE
CLEVELAND
WILLIAMS

MCDOWELL

SHELBY

SEVIER

Ⓔ
N —— S
W

KINGS MOUNTAIN, 7 OCT '80
¼ MILE

① ABOUT NOON, PATRIOTS DISMOUNT HERE, ORGANIZE, & ADVANCE BY COVERED ROUTES strange error: he decided to defend Kings Mountain with the bayonet! First he sent his men in a bayonet charge against Shelby, who gave ground but whose over-mountain men thinned the Tory ranks as they fell back. Meanwhile, Campbell's Virginians made their way up the opposite side of the ridge and attacked. "Here they are, boys!" shouted their rugged giant of a leader. "Shout like hell and fight like devils." The air was shattered by human sounds that may well have been ancestor to the Confederate Yell (Fisher, *op. cit.*, 354); and it was also shattered by the inhuman sounds from hunting rifles with such pet names as "Sweet Lips" (see below). The Tories charged the Virginians, but they too dropped back, firing, and Sevier's men reached the crest. Soon the Tories were being pushed back from the "heel" and across the "arch" by the combined forces of Shelby, Campbell, and Sevier; and they were being pushed back toward the other rebel forces. Ferguson galloped from one threatened point to the next, signaling with his silver whistle, rallying his beleaguered Tories, and cutting down white flags that started to appear. By the time the defenders had been driven back to their camp area, where Ferguson hoped to make a successful stand, they found themselves in the open and surrounded by riflemen who were almost within pistol range. When Ferguson suddenly tried to break through the rebel lines with a few officers he was shot from the saddle. A certain Robert Young claimed that his "Sweet Lips" killed Ferguson, but there were seven other bullets in the dying chieftain.

Capt. Abraham DE PEYSTER took command of the hopeless situation. From the disorganized mass huddled around the wagons there came shots from those who tried to fight back and white flags from those who tried to surrender. De Peyster finally put up a flag, and with great difficulty Shelby and Campbell stopped the rebel firing.

As in other "massacres" (HAW RIVER, PAOLI, and WAXHAWS, for example), it is hard to determine where the battle ended and the butchery began. The "Official Report" says demurely that after de Peyster's flag went up, "Our fire immediately ceased, and the enemy laid down their arms, the greatest part of them loaded. . . ." (*Op. cit.*) Fisher says that either the surrendered men or some returning foragers fired a shot that mortally wounded Col. James Williams, and that Campbell then ordered the riflemen around him to shoot into the prisoners; a young officer is quoted as saying, "We killed near a hundred of them and hardly could be restrained from killing the whole." (*Op. cit.*, 357) Unquestionably, atrocities were committed by the rebels, but the most balanced version, between the two extremes mentioned above, appears to be the following explanation by Shelby:

"It was some time before a complete cessation of the firing on our part could be effected. Our men who had been scattered in the battle were continually coming up and continued to fire, without comprehending in the heat of the moment what had happened; and some who had heard that at Buford's defeat [WAXHAWS], the British had refused quarters . . . were willing to follow that bad example." (Quoted in S. & R., 419)

The action had lasted about an hour. On Sunday, 8 Oct., the victors left their camp on the battlefield and headed for Gilbert Town. Here 30 prisoners were convicted by a sort of early-day war crimes court, 12 were condemned to death, and nine were actually hanged. The other prisoners were entrusted to Cleveland's command and marched to

Hillsboro. The rest of the militia army broke up and went home.

NUMBERS AND LOSSES

The rebels lost 28 killed and 64 wounded among the 900 who participated in the battle. The "British" lost 157 killed, 163 who were too badly wounded to be evacuated, and another 698 who were marched off as prisoners. (Because of inadequate facilities for handling them, all but 60 of these escaped from Hillsboro within a few months.) The casualty figures for Ferguson's command add up to 1,018; if accurate, these indicate that the 200 foragers are included. Clinton says the rebels captured 14,000 stand of arms (*Amer. Reb.*, 227); this must be a typographical error; Ward says 1,500 were taken.

Strength of the rebel force that assembled at the Cowpens the day before the battle is estimated at between 1,400 and 1,790. (Ward, 741; N.P.S., 16) According to the figures given throughout the above account, which are confirmed by the "Official Report," the total was 1,790.

COMMENT

Fisher comments that, "taken in all its details [the battle] is a most striking evidence of the military incapacity of both Cornwallis and Ferguson." (*Op. cit.*, 358) The C. in C. permitted Ferguson to undertake an expedition about which he had the mental reservations expressed in the letter to Clinton (above); that he then "should have failed to send him any reinforcements and allowed him to remain with less than a thousand men seventy miles away for nearly a month, seems like very gross carelessness" (*Ibid.*) Ferguson's errors were political, strategic, and tactical, which is about as wrong as a soldier can get: he overestimated the Tory support and underestimated the patriot resistance in his area of responsibility; he failed to retreat when faced with defeat in detail; he failed to outpost Kings Mountain, failed to fortify it for frontier-style fighting, and failed to see that his position was "more assailable by the rifle than defensible with the bayonet," as Henry Lee expressed it. (*Memoirs*, 200)

For the Southern militia Kings Mountain was their greatest hour, just as Bennington was for the Northern militia. A large number of small units rallied quickly, achieved unity of command, and destroyed their enemy in a remarkably businesslike manner. One common denominator of militia victories was in evidence in this action: a considerable number of outstanding leaders; and the remarkable thing is how successfully they worked together. Ferguson's tactical situation was ideally suited to the methods of these frontiersmen, whose concentric attack eliminated problems of coordination that would have been present in a more conventional battle plan, yet it is remarkable that all the attacking units were able to get into their assigned positions and attack almost simultaneously—this achievement is a triubte to the militia leaders. Bravery is another quality exhibited by the patriots, who sustained about 10 per cent casualties; considering the Indian-fighting, open-order nature of this action, this is a very respectable casualty figure and indicates that they worked for their victory.

Results of Kings Mountain were far-reaching. Sir Henry Clinton called it "the first link of a chain of evils that followed each other in regular succession until they at last ended in the total loss of America." The battle was the turning point of the war in the South: it tipped the balance of Whig-Tory armed support in favor of the rebel cause; it made Cornwallis withdraw into S.C. (Winnsboro) and delayed his offensive three months (see comment on RAMSEUR'S MILL); it enabled Nathanael Greene, immediately upon assuming command of the Southern Army (3 Dec. '80) to seize the initiative and keep it until the successful conclusion of his SOUTHERN CAMPAIGNS.

Bibliography. The standard authority is Lyman C. Draper, *King's Mountain And Its Heroes* (Cincinnati, 1881; New York, 1929). The National Park Service historical handbook, *Kings Mountain* (Washington, 1955), by Geo. C. Mackenzie and Rogers W. Young, is a brief but complete coverage that presents a number of facts and interpretations at variance with the standard accounts of the operation.

KINGSTON (Esopus), N.Y. Burned by British on 16 Oct. '77 in a sequel to CLINTON'S EXPED. Although Gordon, Stedman, and many other writers give 13 Oct. for the date that Vaughan and Wallace burned the town on the Hudson then known as Esopus, Nickerson believes the correct date is the 16th. (*Turning Point*, 480)

KIP'S BAY, N.Y. 15 Sept. '76. The faulty troop dispositions on Manhattan Island and the events leading up to the American rout at Kip's Bay are described under N.Y. CAMPAIGN.

As dawn broke on Sunday, 15 Sept., the Conn. militia troops under Col. Wm. Douglas at Kip's Bay (where today's 34th St. reaches the East River) could see five British warships lying 200 yards off shore. They had heard these arrive before dawn; when American sentinels had relayed the prescribed cry of "All is well," British sailors had shouted back, "We'll alter your tune before tomorrow night." (Narrative of a Cont'l. private, now identified as Joseph Plumb Martin, cited by C. & M., 463)

Crouched behind their inadequate entrenchment, which this same soldier called "nothing more than a ditch dug along on the bank of the river with the dirt thrown out towards the water," the Americans could also see the six British transports that had anchored near the mouth of Newtown Creek, opposite Kip's Bay, on Long Island. About 10 A.M. 84 flatboats pulled out of this creek and moved with 4,000 British and Hessian troops to take cover behind the transports. Shortly before 11 o'clock the warships started a heavy bombardment of the American positions while the landing craft, aided by wind and tide and concealed by the heavy gunsmoke, came up abreast of the warships. More than 70 large cannon plus swivels and small arms from the ships delivered a bombardment for more than an hour. "So terrible and so incessant a roar of guns few even in the [British] army and navy had ever heard before," wrote Ambrose Serle, secretary to Adm. Howe. Witnesses along the shore were even more impressed.

About 1 P.M. the firing ceased, the smoke began to clear, and British and Hessian troops began to land on both sides of Kip's Bay. Although the attackers were faced with difficult tide conditions, an unfavorable beach for amphibious operations, and a rocky shore line over which to scramble, the naval preparation had been so effective that the defenders fled without firing a shot. (Freeman, *Washington*, IV, 193) American units along the shore south of Douglas, five Conn. militia regiments under James Wadsworth, abandoned their positions and retreated north. The supporting units, the brigades of Fellows and Parsons, "did not venture within less than half a mile of the shore." (Freeman, *op. cit.*, 192)

"The dastardly behaviour of the Rebels ... sinks below remark," wrote Serle.

(cited by C. & M., 465) This remark by a British observer pretty well sums up Washington's sentiments on the day of the rout. Tradition pictures him hurling his hat to the ground in rage and shouting, "Good God, have I got such troops as these?" or, "Are these the men with which I am to defend America?" (Geo. Weedon Papers and Heath *Memoirs,* cited by Freeman, *op. cit.,* 194 *n.;* see C. & M., 467, for pertinent excerpt of former.) Other accounts have Washington misfiring his pistols at fugitives, cane-whipping privates, colonels, and brigadier generals with democratic indiscrimination. Freeman dismisses these traditions of Washington's behavior as "repeated camp gossip" of an "improbable or unverifiable" nature.

Putnam was probably with Washington, Parsons, and Fellows in trying to rally the troops retreating from the shore of the East River. But, seeing that it was going to be impossible to contain the British in their beachhead, Putnam galloped south to rescue Sullivan's Brig., Knox's artillery, and other troops in N.Y.C. before all lines of retreat were cut. Having assembled these troops, he started leading them north along the Post Road (now Lexington Ave.), which was the only route he knew. Since the British were already astride this route, Putnam would have led his troops into a trap, but Aaron BURR, his aide de camp, was able to guide him to safety by way of the Bloomingdale road on the Hudson River side of Manhattan. At one time the retreating Americans were separated from the advancing redcoats by no greater distance than the width of today's Central Park. (Ward, *op. cit.,* 243–44) See HARLEM HEIGHTS map.

Gen. Howe had ordered the first division of about 4,000 men, under Gen. Henry Clinton, to land at Kip's Bay and then to seize and hold Murray Hill until the 9,000 men of the second division could be landed and brought into action. Murray Hill, then called Inclenberg, is a mile northwest of Kip's Bay; in terms of modern N.Y.C. streets it is bounded by 35th and 38th Streets between Lexington and 5th Avenues. (Lossing, II, 817; Bliven, 33). When the first division landed, Leslie swung north about half a mile with his three light infantry battalions, von Donop turned south about a mile with his three Hessian grenadier battalions, while Clinton, Cornwallis, Vaughan, and Mathew moved with the other troops—four battalions of British grenadiers, one brigade of Guards, and the Hessian jägers—to Murray Hill. (Ward, *op. cit.,* 243) There they were joined about 2 P.M. by Gen. Howe. (*Ibid.,* 939)

Much has been made of Howe's failure to move his forces immediately across Manhattan to cut off the American troops in N.Y.C. Among the explanations is that the British generals could not resist an invitation of Mrs. Murray to stop for refreshments; this specious theory is covered under the entry MURRAY HILL MYTH.

It was not until 5 P.M. that Howe's entire force was ashore. One brigade then moved south, while the remainder pushed west to the Hudson and northwest toward Harlem Heights. Howe had captured N.Y.C. intact, but had failed to destroy Washington's army. The NEW YORK CITY FIRE, 20–21 Sept., deprived the British of much of this first prize; their repulse at HARLEM HEIGHTS, N.Y., 16 Sept., did much to restore the morale of Washington's army.

KIRKWOOD, Robert (H.). 1730–1791. Cont'l. officer. Del. Born in New Castle co., Del., he was educated at Newark Academy and became a farmer. When the Del. Regt. was formed he was commissioned Lt. on 17 Jan. '76 and fought with them at Long Island, Trenton, and Princeton. Promoted to Capt. on 1 Dec. '76, according to Heitman (early in 1777, according to Appleton's), he led his company in all the important actions of the next three campaigns. In 1780 he went south with Gates. The Del. Regt. lost its two senior officers and eight others in the battle of Camden, and the unit was reorganized into two 96-man companies commanded by the senior remaining captains, Kirkwood and Peter Jaquett. (Ward, *W.O.R.*, 733) Of the subsequent operations a biographer of Greene says that the Del. Cont'ls. were "the admiration of the army and their leader, Kirkwood, was the American Diomed. Like the Marylanders, they had enlisted for the war and, like the veterans of that brigade, were not excelled by any troops in America, perhaps in the world." (Johnson, *Greene*, I, 443, quoted in Ward, *op. cit.*, 779–80. Diomedes, or Tydides, was a legendary Greek hero in the siege of Troy.)

Kirkwood distinguished himself at COWPENS, GUILFORD, HOBKIRK'S HILL, and EUTAW SPRINGS, to mention only the major battles of Greene's Southern campaigns. Since there was only one regiment from his state "and that regiment was reduced to a captain's command, Kirkwood never could be promoted in regular routine," wrote "Light-Horse Harry" Lee in his eulogy of "the gallant Kirkwood." (*Memoirs*, 185 *n.*) On 30 Sept. '83 he was breveted Maj.

Moving to Ohio after the war, he settled at a point almost opposite Wheeling. (Appleton's) In the subsequent Indian troubles he was commissioned Capt., 2d U.S. Infantry, on 4 Mar. '91, and was killed in action on 4 Nov. (See ST. CLAIR'S defeat.) "It was the thirty-third time he had risked his life for his country," writes Harry Lee, "and he died as he had lived, the brave, mer-

itorious, unrewarded, Kirkwood." (*Op. cit.*, 185 *n.*)

His *Journal and Order Book* was published in 1910 in the *Papers of the Hist. Soc. of Del.* (No. XVI). See also Ward, *The Delaware Continentals . . .* (1941).

KLOCK'S FIELD, N.Y., 19 Oct. '80. (BORDER WARFARE) In pursuit of the raiders who had ravaged SCHOHARIE VALLEY, 15–17 Oct., and defeated John Brown at FORT KEYSER, 19 Oct., Gen. Robert Van Rensselaer caught up with the enemy the evening of the 19th. Sir John Johnson's booty-laden column of 800 to 1,500 men was moving along the north bank of the Mohawk, however, and the rebels were on the south. While his subordinates looked for a way to cross over and close with the enemy, Van Rensselaer left them to dine at Fort Plain with Gov. Clinton. When he came back to his army the rebels had improvised a bridge by driving baggage wagons into the river, and Sir John turned to do battle.

Behind a hasty breastwork at Klock's Field (or Fox's Mills), the Tory leader deployed his company of British regulars, the three companies of his Royal Greens, the 200 Butler Rangers, and his artillery (a 3-pdr. and two small mortars). In a growth of scrub oaks on his left he concealed Brant's Indians and the jäger company. Col. Morgan Lewis led the attack, and the main battle line to his rear was commanded on the left by Col. Abraham Cuyler and on the right by Col. Lewis DuBois. Part of the right wing was made up of Robert McKean's volunteers and 60 or so Oneidas under Louis. (Geo. Clinton's report, C. & M., 1030; Lossing, I, 281; Ward, *W.O.R.*, 649) The rebel force, according to Gov. Clinton, numbered about 850.

Attacking about sunset, the right flank units (Louis and McKean) routed the jägers and Indians on Johnson's flank, but the Tories and regulars held their ground. Van Rensselaer's officers were eager to assault the breastwork, but the commander refused to authorize this or to permit a pursuit of the jägers and hostile Indians. Louis and McKean took up the chase the next morning and the main body followed as far as German Flats, but on 21 Oct. he turned back.

"It seems to be certain that only his [Van Rensselaer's] irresolution stood in the way for a complete victory, either in the battle or in the retreat," comments Ward. (*Op. cit.,* 650)

KNOWLTON, Thomas. 1740–1776. Cont'l. officer. Conn. Enlisting as a boy of about 15, he rose to the grade of Lt. in the French and Indian War and took part in the siege of Havana (1762). As Capt. of a militia company, 1 May–10 Dec. '75, he distinguished himself at BUNKER HILL. Promoted to Maj., 20th Cont'l. Inf., on 1 Jan. '76, he led a daring raid into Charlestown on the 8th, burning enemy quarters and taking off five prisoners. On 12 Aug. he was promoted to Lt. Col., reached Long Island the day before the battle, and was posted with 100 of his regulars at Flatbush Pass. After this action he organized a body of Conn. rangers and was killed leading them at HARLEM HEIGHTS, 16 Sept. '76.

KNOX, Henry. 1750–1806. Cont'l. general and chief of artillery. Mass. Having an early interest in the army, Knox joined the militia at 18 and read extensively on military matters. In about 1771 he lost the third and fourth fingers of his left hand when a fowling piece burst during a hunting trip. He witnessed the Boston "massacre" (1770) and tried to restrain the British guard commander from firing into the mob. (*D.A.B.*) In 1775 he was a beefy young man with a maimed hand earn-ing a good living as proprietor of "The London Book-Store" in Boston. He served Gen. Ward as a volunteer during the Battle of Bunker Hill and the start of the Boston Siege. Washington was favorably impressed by Knox from the time they met on 5 July '75. On 17 Nov. the 25-year-old military amateur was appointed Col. of the (virtually nonexistent) Cont'l. Regt. of Artillery and he undertook the epic exploit covered under KNOX'S "NOBLE TRAIN OF ARTILLERY." This achievement led directly to the British evacuation of Boston. After laying out the defenses of vulnerable points in Conn. and R.I., Knox joined Washington in N.Y. He and his gunners rendered valuable service in the Battle of Long Island, in the subsequent retreat through N.Y. and N.J., and at Trenton and Princeton. On 27 Dec. '76 Knox was appointed B.G. While the main army was in winter quarters at Morristown, he established the Springfield arsenal in Mass. The arrival of TRONSON DE COUDRAY in May '77 threatened Knox's position as chief of artillery, but Congress found an interim solution until the arrogant foreigner managed to drown himself.

By the spring of 1778 the Cont'l. field artillery had developed from a make-shift organization of inadequate weapons and inexperienced men into a combat arm that very nearly met Washington's needs. Of Knox's achievement, D. S. Freeman writes:

"... as late as 1777, he seemed to at least one French professional neither to know how to take cannon into action nor how to withdraw them; but if he acquired slowly the fine points of the employment of artillery, he quickly developed high skill in dealing with men. His administration of his arm of the service was quiet and was marred by few jealousies on the part of his subordinates." (*Washington,* IV, 131B)

The guns performed well at Brandywine and Germantown, although Knox personally contributed to the American failure at the latter place. (Under GERMANTOWN, see "Comments.")

During the CONWAY CABAL Knox showed "unwavering loyalty to his chief," a quality Freeman considers as admirable as his efficient administration. (*Ibid.*) After continuing to merit Washington's high opinion throughout the rest of the war, performing particularly well at Monmouth and Yorktown, Knox was appointed Maj. Gen. on 22 Mar. '82 with rank from 15 Nov. '81. He took command of West Point on 29 Aug. '82 and succeeded Washington as C. in C. during the period 23 Dec. '83–20 June '84. (Heitman, 336) Returning for a short time to private life in Boston, he became Sec. of War under the Confederation on 8 Mar. '85 and retained this post under Washington until 28 Dec. '94. (Officially, Knox became the first U.S. Sec. of War on 12 Sept. '89 and held the post until 31 Dec. '94. [*A.A.*, 48.]) During the emergency of 1789 he was reappointed Maj. Gen. but was nettled at being listed after Alexander Hamilton and C. C. Pinckney.

Knox possessed administrative abilities, a loyalty to his chief and the cause, and a sanguine outlook that made him a major figure in the winning of American independence. But he was a very human hero with human shortcomings and faults. He could storm and threaten resignation like any other B.G. when Congress promoted such persons as Conway, de Coudray, and Smallwood over his head. He was "forceful, often profane" and was criticized for a "pompous, self-complacent walk." (*D.A.B.*) The latter may perhaps be attributed partially to his weight of nearly 300 pounds by 1783, his contented married life with the "lively and meddlesome but amiable" Mrs. Knox, who bore him 12 children, in addition to a certain deserved pride in his public achievements. He was accused, with Greene, of "dominating" Washington; even if the charge were true it could hardly be considered a reflection on Knox. His luxurious habits and extravagant entertaining earned him the title, "Philadelphia nabob," and along with some unfortunate land speculations starting as early as 1791 in Me. with Wm. Duer also brought him money problems.

This Gargantuan hero of American Independence passed prematurely to his eternal rest at the age of 56 when a chicken bone lodged in his intestines! There is no portrait of Knox as he appeared during the war. Of the several later painted, the most beautiful is by Gilbert Stuart (original in Boston Museum of Fine Arts; color reproduction in *Amer. Herit. Bk. of Rev.*, 116). One by Edward Savage, probably the earliest, is at Philipse Manor Hall, Yonkers, N.Y. (black and white reproduction in Freeman, *Washington,* IV, 131B). Another is in the Independence Hall Historical Park Collection (see Billias, *op. cit.*, 108C).

The Knox Papers are held by the New Eng. Hist. Geneal. Soc. in Boston. The most recent study is *Henry Knox: General Washington's General* (1958), by North Callahan of N.Y.U. In his essay on Knox in G. A. Billias (ed.), *George Washington's Generals* (1964), Callahan includes a bibliography and comments that the older work, *Henry Knox: A Soldier of the Revolution* (1900), is still valuable for some of the letters it quotes. Another standard work, valuable for its letters, is Francis S. Drake, *Life and Correspondence of Henry Knox* (1873).

KNOX'S "NOBLE TRAIN OF ARTILLERY." Lack of heavy (siege) artillery was a critical American problem during the Boston Siege and a principal reason for the capture of Ft. Ticonderoga and other northern posts. The next problem was how to move the guns over 300 miles of indifferent roads to the Boston lines. Beefy young Henry Knox proposed a plan which, on 16 Nov. '75, Washington ordered him to carry out. Leaving Cambridge a few days later with a small escort, Knox reached Ft. Ti on 5 Dec. He selected 50 or 60 cannon and mortars, had 42 sledges built, and secured 80 yoke of oxen. It took until 7 Jan. '76 to get the weapons to the southern end of Lake George, but the remaining 300 miles of difficult terrain were covered with a speed that surprised even the impatient and ambitious Knox (Freeman, *Washington,* IV, 17 *n.*). From Ft. Edward through Saratoga, Albany, Kinderhook, and Claverack, the weapons were then dragged east through the steep grades and heavy snows of the Berkshires to Framingham, 20 miles from Cambridge. According to some accounts the first guns reached Cambridge on 24 Jan. (E. P. Alexander, "Ft. Ticonderoga," in *D.A.H.*), but others say they reached Framingham on 25 Jan. (C. & M., 174), where they were parked temporarily, and where John Adams inventoried them on the 25th. (Freeman, *op. cit.*) Knox himself reached Cambridge on 18 Jan. (Heath, *Memoirs,* 45–46) The exact number of weapons involved is also disputed: Freeman says Knox reached Framingham with 52 cannon, nine large mortars, and five coehorns; Alexander says he left Ft. Ti with 59 weapons (14 mortars and coehorns, two howitzers, and 43 cannon). Three of the large siege mortars (13-in.), including "Old Sow," weighed a ton each. Total weight of the guns and mortars was 119,900 pounds (Alexander, *op. cit.*), and the convoy included 2,300 pounds of lead and a barrel of flints (Lossing, II, 9).

The Americans were able to end the BOSTON SIEGE successfully by the emplacement of heavy guns on DORCHESTER HEIGHTS, a move that would not have been possible without the weapons from Ft. Ti. Knox himself termed these "a noble train of artillery." (Ward, *W.O.R.,* 124)

KNYPHAUSEN, Wilhelm, Baron von. (knip, rhymes with ship, houzun) 1716–1800. German C. in C. after Heister. Son of the Col. of a German regiment that had served under Marlborough, he entered the Prussian army in 1734 and became a general in 1775. His grade in the German service was Lt. Gen., but this corresponded to B.G. in the American army. Sailing from Bremen, he reached N.Y. harbor on 18 Oct. '76 with the second grand division of German mercenaries, 3,997 Hessians, 670 Waldeckers, and a company of jägers. In the same convoy, which numbered 120 sail, were 3,400 British recruits. (Ward, *W.O.R.,* 261) The Germans were sent on by water to New Rochelle, and with this base thus secured behind him Howe continued his pursuit of Washington north toward White Plains. Gen. von Heister, the senior German officer in America, led the Hessians at White Plains, 28 Oct., but thereafter it was Knyphausen who commanded the bulk of the mercenaries in British operations. His baptism of fire in America was at FORT WASHINGTON, 16 Nov. '76, where the Germans claimed the honor of making the main attack and where they sustained 330 casualties in heavy fighting while the British lost 122.*

* The "Regiment Knyphausen" was engaged at White Plains, which has led many writers to assume that the general was there also. Knyphausen reached

Disagreements between Gen. Howe and the elderly von Heister, aggravated by the German disaster at Trenton, 26 Dec. '76 (where the black uniformed "Regiment Knyphausen" was captured with two others), led to von Heister's recall in 1777. Knyphausen remained as C. in C. of German troops in America for the remainder of the war, and since his seniority made him the successor of the British C. in C. for the post of over-all British commander in America, special precautions in the form of "DORMANT COMMISSIONS" were issued by the London authorities to preclude this. During the Philadelphia Campaign Knyphausen commanded one of the two grand divisions of Howe's army. He led this force at BRANDYWINE, where his mission was to make Washington believe the main attack was against Chadd's Ford while Cornwallis led the other grand division in a strategic envelopment. His forces were not engaged to any significant degree at Germantown. In the Monmouth Campaign he commanded the column that escorted Clinton's baggage train across N.J., and only a body of his grenadiers saw any action on 28 June. Germans deserted in large numbers while the invading army was in Pa. and N.J.; 440 of them were lost during the Monmouth Campaign. (Ward, *W.O.R.*, 585) Three months later Knyphausen led 3,000 men up the east side of the Hudson in the large-scale forage that led to the "Tap-

New Rochelle with his command on 23 Oct. and did not leave there until the 29th, when he went to Kings Bridge. He was to attack Fort Washington on the 31st while Howe was to continue the attack at White Plains, but a heavy storm forced Howe to cancel these orders. On 12 Nov. Howe's entire army was concentrated around Kings Bridge. (Baurmeister, *Journals,* 61–69)

pan Massacre," but his forces were not involved in that affair. For the remainder of the war he was based in N.Y., where he commanded during Clinton's absence in the Charleston Campaign of 1780. He led the SPRINGFIELD RAID into N.J. in June '80. In May '81 Knyphausen's "precarious state of health" was a factor in keeping Clinton from joining Cornwallis in Va. (This was during the preliminaries leading to British disaster in the Yorktown Campaign.) Appleton's states that "Bodily infirmity and the loss of an eye" led to Knyphausen's retirement in 1782. Before his death in 1800 he was military governor of Cassel.

"General Knyphausen was much of the German in his appearance," says J. F. Watson in his *Annals of Philadelphia* (2 vols., 1857); "not tall, but slender and straight. His features were sharp; in manners he was very polite. He was gentle, and much esteemed. He spread his butter upon his bread with his thumb!" This last statement, which certainly is contradicted by the rest of Watson's description, is included only because the slander was perpetuated— or *created*—by the contemporary American cartoonist whose sketch of a fat, pigtailed Knyphausen using his thumb for a butter spreader is reproduced (among other places) in the *Amer. Herit. Book of the Rev.* (p. 211). He has been characterized as "a grim and silent man" (Ward, *op. cit.,* 274) "who understood the temper of his troops, and rarely entered on hazardous expeditions." (Appleton's) The *Columbia Encyclopedia* comments that "He handled his somewhat unreliable troops with skill."

KOSCIUSZKO, Thaddeus. (Tadeusz Andrzej Bonawentura) 1746–1817. Cont'l. officer. Poland (Lithuania). Son of an impoverished member of the small gentry (*D.A.B.*), he was orphaned as a young boy. In 1771 he graduated from the Royal School at Warsaw and, as a Capt., was sent to the school of artillery and military engineering at Mézières, France. Returning to Poland in 1774, he found little opportunity for advancing his career, and after an unfortunate love affair he returned to France. His contact with French philosophy aroused an interest in the concept of liberty. He borrowed money to pay his passage to America, reached Philadelphia in Aug. '76, and in due course the Pa. Comm. of Defense employed him, with Payne and De Lisle, to plan the Delaware River forts. (See PHILADELPHIA CAMPAIGN) This initial assignment gained him a commission from Congress as Col. of engineers on 18 Oct. '76. He joined Gates at Ticonderoga and played an important role in stopping Burgoyne's Offensive; although his advice to fortify Mt. Defiance at Ticonderoga was probably unrealistic in that it would have overextended the inadequate American garrison, his selection and fortification of the Saratoga battlefield made possible the American victory that marked the turning point of the war. From Mar. '78 until June '80 Kosciuszko was engaged in planning and building the defenses of West Point, a place of utmost strategic importance. He and Gates had become close friends. Invited to become the chief engineer of the Southern Dept., he arrived after Gates's defeat at Camden but remained to serve under Greene. He was assigned the mission of exploring the Catawba and was in charge of transportation during Greene's dramatic race to the Dan. (See SOUTHERN CAMPAIGNS OF GREENE) In the Siege of NINETY-SIX,

S.C., 22 May–19 June '81, Kosciuszko got a costly lesson in the art of practical military engineering, making two mistakes that may well have caused this operation to fail. During the remainder of his service in the South there was more opportunity for him to show his ability as a cavalry leader than as an engineer. In the spring of 1783 he went north with Greene and in Oct. was breveted B.G. In July '84 he left N.Y. and returned through Paris to Poland. After four years in rural retirement he became a Maj. Gen. in Oct. '89. In the spring of 1792 he fought a gallant but futile campaign against the Russian invaders before his king ended Polish resistance. He and other Polish generals emigrated to Leipzig, and Kosciuszko later went to Paris to enlist support of the French revolutionary government. Although the Jacobins withheld French assistance, he returned to his homeland to lead a noble but unsuccessful uprising. Defeated and captured in Oct. '94, he was freed after two years as a prisoner, and in Aug. '97 reached Philadelphia. He was given more than $15,000 owed him by the American government and was granted 500 acres in Ohio. In May '98 he left America and went to Paris, where Napoleon earnestly sought his cooperation but not on Kosciusko's terms: the promise that Napoleon would support the restoration of Poland. The rest of his life he strove for the latter goal, but without success. Before his death he emancipated his serfs. Money from the sale of his Ohio land was used to establish the Colored School at Newark, N.J.

Biographies by Haiman are listed in the main bibliography.

L

LA BALME. See MOTTIN DE LA BALME.

LA CORNE. See ST. LUC DE LA CORNE.

LAFAYETTE, Marquis de.* 1757–1834. Cont'l general. Before his second birthday he lost his father, a Col. of grenadiers killed at Minden. His mother died before he was 13, and Lafayette was a wealthy orphan when his grandfather died a few weeks later. When he was 16 he married Marie Adrienne Françoise de Noailles and thus became allied with one of the most powerful families of France. A shy, awkward boy, he had entered the Royal Army on 9 Apr. '71, three years before this marriage, and until the outbreak of the American Revolution had had little real military experience.

The spark was struck on 8 Aug. '75 when Capt. de Lafayette attended a dinner at which the Duke of Gloucester expressed some candid and sympathetic views on the course being pursued by the American insurgents. Mo-

* Marie Joseph Paul Yves Roch Gilbert du Motier, Marquis de Lafayette, to be precise. From his signature it is impossible to determine whether he used a large or small f, but his immediate ancestors spelled the name Lafayette. Such modern French authorities as the *Larousse du XXe Siècle* use the form La Fayette; the *D.A.B.* and Professor Gottschalk (see sources at the end of this article) spell it Lafayette. "La Fayette" was an estate of the Motier family in Aix, Auvergne, in the 13th century. (*E.B.*; Freeman, *Washington,* IV, 450 *n.*)

tivated by romantic ideas of the American revolt, sharing the French desire for *revanche* against the British, and thirsting for *la gloire,* he made plans to join the Americans. Knowing that his family and the King would disapprove of his action, he confided in the Comte de Broglie, who, after trying to discourage him, introduced Lafayette to Johann KALB. The latter, already seeking service in America, became a sort of guardian, and after many delays the two sailed for America with written agreements from Silas Deane that they would be commissioned major generals. With a party of other adventurers they landed near Georgetown, S.C., on 13 June '77, and were in Philadelphia six weeks later. Their reception by Congress was chilly, but after Lafayette offered to serve at his own expense and start as a volunteer, Congress on 31 July commissioned him a Maj. Gen. without command. The next day he met Washington, and the American cause acquired a valuable, if enigmatic, asset.

Washington took an immediate liking to the wealthy young nobleman, who responded in a manner that was "appreciative and almost embarrassingly affectionate." (Freeman, *op. cit.,* IV, 616) It was another thing, however, to figure out what to do with this boy volunteer —he was not yet 20—who hungered to lead American troops against the British but who spoke only a few words of English and had never heard a shot fired in anger. At the BRANDYWINE, 11 Sept., '77, the ardent volunteer helped check the enemy's advance and was slightly wounded in the left thigh. "Kalb called this an excellent bit of good fortune, for it established Lafayette in the eyes of his American comrades." (Frank Monaghan in *D.A.B.*) After two months of recuperation at Bethlehem, Pa., he rejoined the army at White Marsh (after the Battle of Germantown). On 25 Nov. he led a reconnaissance force of Greene's division against the position of Cornwallis at Gloucester, N.J., and with 300 men got the better of a skirmish with a superior force of Hessians. (Appleton's; *D.A.B.*) On 1 Nov. Washington wrote to Congress:

"The marquis de La Fayette is extremely solicitous of having a command equal to his rank. I do not know in what light Congress will view the matter, but it appears to me, from a consideration of his illustrious and important connexions, the attachment which he has manifested for our cause, and the consequences which his return in disgust might produce, that it will be advisable to gratify his wishes, and the more so as several gentlemen from France who came over under some assurances have gone back disappointed in their expectations. His conduct with respect to them stands in a favourable point of view—having interested himself to remove their uneasiness and urged the impropriety of their making any unfavourable representations upon their arrival at home. Besides, he is sensible, discreet in his manners, has made great proficiency in our language, and from the dispositions he discovered at the battle of Brandywine possesses a large share of bravery and military ardor." (Quoted in *E.B.*)

This excerpt explains more about Lafayette's true role in the Revolution than first meets the eye. On 1 Dec. '77 Congress voted him command of the division of Va. light troops that had been commanded by Adam Stephen (who was dismissed on 20 Nov. for

misconduct). After sharing the hardships of Valley Forge and proving himself one of Washington's most stalwart supporters in the so-called Conway Cabal, he went to Albany to lead the proposed CANADA INVASION of 1778. Returning to Valley Forge in Apr. '78 after this frustrating experience he was involved in the action at BARREN HILL, Pa., 20 May. He then figured prominently in the MONMOUTH CAMPAIGN. Washington gave him command of the two veteran brigades engaged at NEWPORT, July–Aug. '78, where he had a prominent part in salvaging the wreck of the first Franco-American venture. Activities of the PEACE COMMISSION OF CARLISLE led Lafayette to a theatrical gesture that created a sensation but left the Anglo-Saxon with the last laugh. (Freeman, *op. cit.*, V, 80 *n.*)

At the same time (Oct. '78) he requested permission to visit France "and survey the opportunities of service there and in Canada," as Freeman puts it. "Congress poured on the unction of formal thanks and yielded, slowly and reluctantly, to his persistent and scarcely modest application for the reward and compensation of his aides," as well as for approximately $4,000 to cover his own travel expenses. (*Op. cit.*, V, 80 and *n.*) He sailed on 11 Jan. '79 (his departure having been delayed by a fever), reached Paris a month later, and after a week of "political quarantine" to purge himself of disobedience in defying the royal will in leaving France he was given a hero's welcome. He was received with favor at court, appointed Col. of dragoons, and in presenting an accurate picture of affairs in America he won the confidence of Vergennes. Although he failed to get approval of many schemes he advocated—an invasion of England, Ireland, or Canada; hiring part of the Swedish navy for service in America;

floating a large loan in Holland—he did lay the groundwork for sending a French expeditionary force to serve under Washington.

On 28 Apr. '80 he landed at Boston. Rochambeau reached Newport in July, and although he did not achieve quite the role to which he aspired, Lafayette was a valuable intermediary in working out plans for allied cooperation. (See ROCHAMBEAU for an explanation of the veiled allusion.) When Benedict Arnold's raid in Va. forced Washington to send regulars there, he selected Lafayette as commander of this detachment. In his VIRGINIA MILITARY OPERATIONS Lafayette proved himself a competent strategist in eluding efforts of Cornwallis to "trap the boy," and at GREEN SPRING, 6 July '81, he showed ability as a tactician. When Rochambeau and Washington moved south for the YORKTOWN CAMPAIGN Lafayette was given command of the light division for the final action against Cornwallis.

He sailed for home in Dec. '81 and reached France "with a renewed enthusiasm and a new vision," writes Monaghan. (*D.N.B.*) Unfortunately, he lacked the qualities to become a national leader either in the French Revolution or its aftermath. While the details are beyond the scope of the present work, the highlights can be given. He was assembling an army of 24,000 French and Spanish troops at Cadiz for operations against the British when the war ended. In the last half of 1784 he revisited America at Washington's invitation. During the next five years he was of great assistance to Thos. Jefferson, U.S. minister to France, on various important economic and political matters. In 1787 he was a member of the Assembly of Notables, in 1789 he represented the nobility of Auvergne in the States General. On 26 July '89 he was named commander of the newly es-

tablished National Guard and in Oct. saved the royal family from the Paris mob. In 1790 he was the most popular man in France (*D.A.B.*). The next year he was promoted to Lt. Gen., on 8 Oct. he left his post with the National Guard, and when war against Austria was declared in the spring of 1792 he took command of the 52,000-man Army of the Center. The rise of Jacobin influence led to his being replaced on 19 Aug., and soon thereafter he fled to Belgium. Taken by the Austrians and turned over to the Prussians, he was imprisoned for a year at Magdeburg and for the next four years in a dungeon at Olmutz. On 23 Sept. '97 he was freed by Napoleon and in Mar. 1800 he returned to France to find his fortune destroyed. He acknowledged Napoleon but declined his offers of a senatorship, the Legion of Honor, and the post of minister to the U.S. He also declined President Jefferson's offer in 1805 to become Gov. of La. (Appleton's) During this period and until 1818 he kept out of politics, cultivating his lands at La Grange, 43 miles from Paris. He then sat in the Chamber of Deputies until 1824, and in this year accepted the invitation of President Monroe to visit the U.S. Reaching Staten Island on 15 Aug., he started a tour of the country and was met by "demonstrations of frenzied enthusiasm without precedent or parallel in American history," writes Monaghan. "This was one of the happiest years of his life, for he had never lost his one great foible, as Jefferson had described it, 'a canine appetite for popularity and fame.'" (*D.A.B.*) He sailed back for France on 8 Sept. '25 and re-entered politics, but lack of decisiveness lost him the opportunity in the July Revolution of 1830 to establish the republic of which he had dreamed. (*Ibid.*)

"A trick of history, a perverse trick,

has denied Lafayette the place he deserves among the eminent men of his generation: Posterity has been more mindful of what he did not achieve in the French Revolution than of what he contributed to the success of the earlier Revolution in America.* * * He deserves better estimation." (Freeman, *op. cit.*, IV, 461B)

He spent an estimated $200,000 of his personal fortune in support of the American Revolution and never sought repayment. In 1794 Congress voted him some $24,500 to cover the salary he had declined during the Revolution, and in 1803 they granted him 11,520 acres. These lands eventually were located in La., says Monaghan, but brought him no income until about 1815. (*D.A.B.*)

The biography by Tower (1895) was the standard English work until the publication of the four volumes by Gottschalk (1935–50). See main bibliography. The *Mémoires...du général La Fayette*... were published in six volumes in Paris, 1837–38; three volumes of these were published in London in 1837, and one volume was published the same year in America. Monaghan (*op. cit.*) calls these the most valuable source for his life; writing before the appearance of Gottschalk's works, Monaghan says the best biography, although not translated into English, is *Le général Lafayette*...by Etienne Charavay (Paris, 1898). A critical bibliography by Gottschalk is in the *Journal of Modern History* for June 1930. See LAFAYETTE MYTH, below.

LAFAYETTE MYTH. In its comments on the works of Louis R. Gottschalk (see bibliography), the Lib. of Cong. *Guide* gives this summary. "The Lafayette myth has been scrutinized by Mr. Gottschalk, and his results indicate that Lafayette came to America in 1777 motivated less by liberal idealism

than by a sense of frustration and dissatisfaction with affairs at home, by a desire for glory, and by the traditional French hatred of the English adversary. The symbol of Lafayette, the French noble enamored of American ideals of liberty, was the product of others who sought advantage [as propaganda and for French military aid] in having Lafayette accepted as such, but once Lafayette became the symbol, he lived the role to such an extent that the symbol became the reality, and in later years, Lafayette deserved the symbol of being the outstanding liberal of his day." (*Op. cit.*, 343)

LAKE GEORGE, N.Y., 8 Sept. '55. Victory of Wm. JOHNSON over Dieskau during COLONIAL WARS. Montross calls this "the first pitched battle fought by Americans on the soil of the present United States" (*War Through the Ages*, 409).

LAKE GEORGE, N.Y., 18 Sept. '77. See TICONDEROGA RAID.

LA LUZERNE, Chevalier de. See LUZERNE.

LA MARQUISIE, Capt. See MAUSSAC.

LAMB, John. 1735–1800. Cont'l. Arty. Col. N.Y. Son of a man who had been deported to America and had subsequently become a respectable and prosperous citizen of N.Y.C.,* John

* Andrew, the father, was apprenticed to a maker of mathematical instruments when he became an accomplice in July '74 of John Sheppard (1702–1724), a famous burglar and escape artist. (See *E.B.*) Sheppard was hanged on 16 Nov. '24, so Andrew's association was short; as a first offender he received a "favourable prosecution" and was "sentenced to be transported to the American colonies." (*D.A.B.*) After serving his time in Va. he moved

started in his father's businesses. He was a good writer and fluent speaker (Lossing, *op. cit.*), and with the troubles stemming from the Stamp Act (1765) he launched on a 10-year career as an "irrepressible agitator" in N.Y. (*D.A.B.*). In 1769 he publicly denounced the N.Y. ASSEMBLY, and on learning of the events of Lexington and Concord he and Isaac SEARS seized the customs house and prevented vessels from leaving N.Y. harbor. (*Ibid.*) On 30 July '75 (*ibid.*) he was commissioned Capt. of the Independent Co. of N.Y. Arty. (Heitman says 30 *June*). At the head of these regulars he joined Montgomery's column of the Canada Invasion. During the operations against Saint Johns, Lamb aroused the displeasure of Montgomery, who wrote Schuyler on 24 Nov. '75 that although the artillery captain was brave, active, and intelligent, he was pursuing his vocation as a rabble-rouser and troublemaker. (*D.A.B.*) He accompanied Arnold's column in the attack on QUEBEC, 31 Dec. '75, was wounded and captured. (Heitman says he lost an eye.) Paroled a few days later, he was named A.G. and Commandant of Arty. in the Northern Dept. on 9 Jan. (with rank from the 1st), but was inactive because of his parole. Exchanged in Jan. '77, his commission as Col., 2d Cont'l. Arty. Regt., was dated 1 Jan. During the DANBURY RAID, Apr. '77, he was wounded at Campo Hill (28 Apr.) in a gallant but unsuccessful attempt with three guns to break up an enemy bayonet attack.

In the reorganization of the Cont'l. Army in early 1778, Lamb joined in the

to N.Y.C., married a "Dutch lady" (*ibid.*), became an optician and instrument maker, and in 1760 started to prosper as a wine merchant (*ibid.; Los-*sing, II, 791 *n.*)

general protestation over adjustment of seniority. Although Eleazer Oswald, another famous artillerist, resigned over this matter, Lamb "fumed but stuck to his guns." (Freeman, *Washington,* V, 78) In 1779 and 1780 he was artillery commander at West Point, and he commanded the post at the time of Arnold's treason. Early the evening of Arnold's desertion (25 Sept. '80) Washington sent Lamb to take command at Kings Ferry while he assured himself that the regular commander, Col. James Livingston, was loyal.

Col. Lamb led his 2d Regt. south as part of Knox's Brig. for the Yorktown Campaign. He and his Lt. Col., Ebenezer Stevens, won particular praise from Knox for their performance during the siege. Lamb was breveted B.G. on 30 Sept. '83. (Montross, *Rag, Tag,* 472 [Heitman's list as corrected by Simon Gratz])

In 1784 he was appointed customs collector in N.Y. He became an active opponent of the proposed federal constitution, to the extent that his house was threatened by a Federalist mob. Lamb promptly fortified his home. After ratification, Washington appointed him to the collectorship at N.Y. A few years later a large shortage was found in his accounts, and although his deputy was supposed to be guilty, Lamb was held responsible. He sold his lands to cover the loss, resigned his post (1797), and died in poverty. (*D.A.B.*) The Lamb Papers are held by the N.Y. Hist. Soc. The standard biography is Isaac Q. Leake, *Memoir of the Life and Times of General John Lamb.* Albany, 1857.

LAMB, Sgt. Roger. British soldier and author. See p. 464 and bibliography.

LANDAIS, Pierre (de). 1734–? . French naval officer. Of a noble but impoverished Normand family, he entered the navy as a volunteer in 1745. In 1762 he was wounded in action and for a short time was a British prisoner. During a 29-month period starting in Nov. '66 he accompanied Bougainville on his voyage of discovery around the world. In 1777 he was discharged from the service after an undistinguished career and at the relatively young age of 44. Early in 1779 he was named captain of the *Alliance* and ordered to join the squadron of John Paul Jones. Landais and Jones appear to have taken a dislike to each other from the start. During the BONHOMME RICHARD–SERAPIS engagement, 23 Sept. '79, Landais unaccountably attacked Jones's ship and continued to fire into it with considerable effect until the battle ended. "Such is the American account [of Jones]," writes Lasseray; "one would like to find—if Landais ever wrote it—the French account." (*Les Français sous les treize étoiles,* 259–60 and *n.*) In May '80 Jones and Landais—the latter no longer under Jones's command—were at L'Orient where both of them claimed command of the *Alliance,* which was preparing to sail to America with Rochambeau. During this period Landais met Jones on the street, challenged him, and pursued him with a drawn sword. In his *Memoirs,* Moré de Pontgibaud, awaiting passage aboard the *Alliance,* tells of Jones's precipitation into his room for safety. Landais did not appear, and the American naval hero left soon thereafter for a triumphal visit to Paris. In the absence of Jones from L'Orient, Arthur Lee, who was returning to America aboard the *Alliance,* took it upon himself to name Landais captain of the ship so that the voyage could get underway. "We had suspected that he [Landais] had something wrong in the head," wrote Pontgibaud, "but we soon knew for sure." The captain of the frigate was carving a turkey for dinner when Lee, seated by his side, helped himself to the liver.

Landais flew into a rage, threatened Lee with the carving knife, and roared that as captain he was entitled to this choice morsel. The crew was called in to overpower the madman, and command of the ship was turned over to his first lieutenant.

According to Pontgibaud, on whose account the turkey incident is based, the career of Landais was ended. The French archives show, however, that he remained in the American service until 1792 and on his return to France was given command of a warship at Brest (1 July '92). In Revolutionary France the veteran of the American Revolution was so warmly received that a naval division was put under his command. On 5 Sept. he sailed with four vessels to join the squadron off Toulon. On 1 Jan. '93 he was promoted to Vice Adm., and during that month took part in operations against Cagliari, Sardinia. The next spring he operated off the coast of Brittany (around Belle Isle). Mutinies among the crews of Morard de Galles's fleet forced Landais to put into Brest. His commission was revoked on 26 Oct. '93. He is known to have been living on retired pay in Paris in 1802. (Lasseray, *op. cit.,* 263–64) The official records do not give the date of his death. Balch, who erroneously supports the belief of Pontgibaud that Landais' active service ended with his insanity in 1780, is probably wrong in stating that he died impoverished and forgotten in N.Y. in 1820.

LANGDON, John. 1741–1819. Patriot merchant and politician. N.H. Born at Portsmouth, N.H., he had become a wealthy merchant when the Revolution started. In 1774 he took part in the raid that seized munitions from the fort in his town. During the war he held a number of important political offices, being speaker of the state legislature in 1775 and for four years starting 1777. He served in the Cont'l. Cong. (1775–76, 1786–87). On 25 June '76 he became agent for prizes in N.H. and actively performed this duty throughout the war. He quickly saw the possibilities of naval operations against British shipping, built several vessels for the government, and made money on private ventures. During the preparations for what became the BEN-NINGTON RAID, Aug. '77, he not only organized Stark's force, having named Stark for the command, but also is said to have pledged his silver and to have sold 70 hogsheads of Tobago rum to raise the necessary funds. He led a body of militia in Stark's subsequent triumph, was present at Saratoga, and commanded N.H. troops in the New-port operations of Aug. '78.

Originally a Federalist, he gradually moved toward the opposition. He served in the U.S. Senate from 1789 to 1801. In the latter year he declined Jefferson's offer of the post of Navy Sec., and in 1812 he declined nomination as Re-publican candidate for V.P. In 1805 he had become Gov. of N.H. and was re-elected every year until 1811 except 1809. (*D.A.B.*)

Brother of Woodbury LANGDON.

LANGDON, Woodbury. 1738–39–1805. Patriot merchant, congressman. N.H. Elder brother of John LANGDON, he also acquired wealth before the Rev-olution but took the conservative side. In 1769 he was influential in keep-ing Portsmouth out of the nonimpor-tation agreement. The town nevertheless elected him to represent them in various Revolutionary assemblies until 1775. When war broke out Langdon went to England to take care of his financial interests. He returned in the summer of 1777. Landing at N.Y.C. he became a prisoner but escaped in Dec. '77. He served in Cong. from 1779 to 1780 but declined to take his seat when elected

in 1780, 1781, and 1785. Instead, he held offices in N.H. In 1790 he was impeached for neglecting his duty as a justice of the superior court. He ran unsuccessfully as a Republican candi-date for Congress in 1796 and 1797. Woodbury and his brother, John, mar-ried daughters of Henry Sherburne, a local merchant.

LANGLADE, Charles Michel de. 1729–c. 1801. Indian leader. Canada. Son of a French nobleman, Augustin Mouet de Langlade, and an Ottawa woman, he was educated by Jesuits at Mackinac. As a boy of 10 he accom-panied his Indian uncles on a war party down the Mississippi. By 1750 he was a cadet in the French colonial troops, and in 1760 he had risen to the grade of Lt. Leading his first expedition, in June '52 he drove the Miami Indians and five British traders from Pick-awillany (near modern Piqua, Ohio). During the French and Indian War he was an active leader of Indian auxil-iaries. He has been credited with setting up the ambush in which Braddock was killed (1755), with defeating Rogers' Rangers on Lake Champlain in 1757, with participating in the attack on Ft. William Henry, and with taking part in the Quebec campaign of 1759. In 1760 he left Montreal before its capture by the British and returned to Mackinac. As second in command of this post he surrendered it when the commandant deserted the garrison, and Langlade transferred his allegiance to the British.

After supporting the British effec-tively in Pontiac's War, the half-breed established a new home at Green Bay, where he and his father had long had a trading post. From this point he sup-ported British operations of Carleton and Burgoyne, and he opposed the American and Spanish advances into the Old Northwest. His personal par-ticipation is not known. Swiggett makes two references to a Capt. Langland (as Walter Butler spelled it) or Langlade as a rather mysterious being about whose identity he is uncertain. (*Niagara*, 78, 82, and index) Nickerson says that Langlade and St. Luc led the Indians of Burgoyne's Offensive, and Ward cites Burgoyne to the same effect (*Turning Point*, 179; *W.O.R.*, 402, 473 n.), but *D.A.B.* implies that he was not himself present with the Indians he sent to support Burgoyne.

After the war Langlade was granted lands in Canada for his services. As one of the first settlers in the region, he has been called the "Father of Wisconsin." He lived in lordly fashion at Green Bay and left many descendants. Akewaugeketauso was his name among the Western tribes, but he is not mentioned in *Handbook of American Indians* under any name.

The Langlade Papers are in the *Wisconsin Hist. Soc. Colls.* (1879). His life, as narrated by his grandson, appeared in the same publication (1857).

LANNEAU'S FERRY (Santee R.), S.C. See LENUD'S FERRY.

LA ROUERIE. See TUFFIN.

LAST AMERICAN GENERAL OF THE REVOLUTION. When Thomas ("Carolina Gamecock") SUMTER died in 1832 at the age of 98 he was the oldest surviving general of the Revolution.

LAST AMERICAN SOLDIER OF THE REVOLUTION? The Annual Report of the Commissioner of Pensions for 1874 notes that "With the death of Daniel T. Bakeman, of Freedom, Cattaraugus County, N.Y., April 5, 1869, the last of the pensioned soldiers of the Revolution passed away." (Heitman, 61)

LAST MILITARY ACTIONS OF THE REVOLUTION? See WHEELING (10–11 Sept. '82) for what has been called the last battle, and JOHNS ISLAND, S.C., 4 Nov. '82, for what has been called "the last blood shed" (Strait).

LAUMOY, Jean Baptiste Joseph, chevalier de. 1750–1832. Cont'l. officer. France. The son of an infantry captain who had been made a chevalier in the order of Saint Louis, Jean Baptiste entered the school of military engineering in 1760, became a 2d Lt. on 31 Mar. '68, and on 1 Jan. '70 was appointed Engineer and 1st Lt. On 18 Jan. '77 he became a Maj., and soon thereafter was ordered to America. See ENGINEERS. He arrived in the early autumn of 1777 and on 17 Nov. was commissioned Col. of Engineers. His first action was with Lafayette at Gloucester, N.J., 25 Nov., after which he went to Valley Forge. Ordered south on 8 Feb. '79, he was wounded at Stono Ferry, 20 June, and taken prisoner at Charleston, 12 May '80. He was exchanged on 26 Nov. '82, breveted B.G. on 30 Sept. '83, and honorably discharged 10 days later.

Meanwhile he had been promoted to Lt. Col. in the French army on 13 June '83, and on 13 Dec. of that year was back home. On 1 July '85 he was *Aide maréchal général des logis* at San Domingo, and after his return to France was *Mestre de camp* on 2 Dec. '87. Six months later he was serving on the army general staff. On 14 Feb. '89 he was second in command at Martinique, where he put down several Negro uprisings. Summarizing this part of his career, when the French Revolution reached the West Indies, he said: "He would have liked to *follow* it [the Revolutionary movement], but not being in a position to permit its being *gotten ahead* of [*ne pouvant permettre de la devancer*], he and his chief soon were the object of hate ... and were finally obliged to ... return to France [on 14 May '90]."

In Revolutionary France he held a number of high administrative posts in the army before being forced to flee with Lafayette on 19 Aug. '92. He lived in Holland until Napoleon invaded the country. Escaping to America, he lived around Philadelphia until he was removed "by the justice of the First Council" from the émigré list. (Laumoy's words) He arrived in France in the summer of 1801 (Thermidor, year IX). Ten years later he retired, and on 19 Jan 1832 he died a bachelor. On 4 July 1784 he had been made a chevalier de Saint Louis. (Lasseray, 269–71)

LAURANCE, John. 1750–1810. Judge Advocate General of Cont'l. Army. N.Y. Born near Falmouth, England, he moved to N.Y. in 1767, was admitted to the bar in 1772, and about two years later married Elizabeth, daughter of Alexander McDOUGALL. When the province started raising Cont'l. regiments he became a 2d Lt. in the 4th N.Y. on 1 Aug. '75 and took part in the Canada Invasion. On the promotion of his father-in-law, Laurance became his A.D.C. but was carried on the rolls as paymaster of the 1st N.Y. after 15 Aug. '76 (D.A.B.; Heitman). On 11 Apr. '77 he succeeded William Tudor as J.A.G. on Washington's staff, holding this post until he resigned from the army on 3 June '82. In his capacity of J.A.G. he prosecuted the cases of Benedict ARNOLD and John ANDRÉ, winning commendation from the Cont'l. Cong. for his "great uprightness, diligence and ability" (Journals, 9 Nov. '80, quoted in D.A.B.).

After the war he acquired an excellent reputation for legal learning and was active in public life. He was a delegate to the Cong. of the Confed. (1785–87), served in the state Senate (1788–90), enthusiastically supported the Federalists, and on ratification of the federal Constitution he became the first congressman from N.Y.C. Remaining in the House of Representatives from 1789 to 1793, he was judge of the U.S. district court for the next two years. On 8 Nov. '96 he succeeded his friend Rufus King in the U.S. Senate, resigning this post in Aug. 1800. "The whole of his successful career in national politics is thus coincident with the period of Federalist dominance" (D.A.B.).

Less than a year after the death of his first wife in 1790 he married Elizabeth Lawrence, widow of James Allen of Philadelphia, and to the children of these marriages he left a substantial fortune. His name in Appleton's and Heitman is incorrectly spelled Lawrence.

LAURENS, Henry. 1724–1792. Cont'l. Congress President. S.C. Of Huguenot ancestry, he was clerk first in a Charleston counting house and then in London. Returning to S.C., he became a wealthy man, "probably the leading merchant of Charleston" (D.A.B.), an avid although not radical agitator, and a pamphlet writer against the Crown. Retiring from business, he returned to England in 1771, after the death of his wife, to supervise his sons' education and to travel. In 1774 he was one of 38 Americans in England signing a petition to Parliament against the British Port Bill (Appleton's), and he returned to America the same year. Sent to the Provincial Congress in 1775, he was president of the council of safety and in 1776 was vice-president of S.C. He was active in the defense of Charleston in June, 1776, and helped prevent active civil war in the Carolinas. In 1777, he was sent to the Cont'l. Congress and was elected President 1 Nov. '77, succeeding John Hancock. During his term, Congress was split by bitterness and factions, and Laurens did not always stay above partisanship, siding occasionally with the Adams-Lee group. He helped suspend the Saratoga Convention (see CONVENTION ARMY) on 8 Jan. '78 and exposed part of the so-called CONWAY CABAL, strongly supporting George Washington. In the Lee-Deane dispute, he was extremely unfair toward Silas DEANE, which lead to the failure of his motion to suspend hearings until Congress could hold an investigation. Laurens felt that this showed lack of faith in himself and resigned the presidency 9 Dec. '78. In 1779 he was elected to negotiate a treaty of friendship and commerce with Holland and to arrange for a $10,000,000 loan. Unable to sail from Charleston because of the threatened British attack, it was not until nine months after his resignation and departure from Congress (9 Nov. '79) that he finally left Philadelphia (13 Aug. '80) on the brig *Mercury*. The vessel was captured by the British off Newfoundland 3 Sept. Laurens threw his official papers overboard but the British recovered them. As explained in the sketch of William LEE, one of the captured documents was used by the British as a pretext for declaring war on the Dutch.

After being examined by the Privy Council, Laurens was confined in the Tower of London on 6 Oct. "on suspicion of high treason." Held almost 15 months, under conditions so severe at times that his health was seriously impaired, he twice refused pardon offered him in return for serving the British. In two petitions to British authorities, however, he justified his own role in the American Revolution in terms that some patriots considered unduly subservient. On 31 Dec. '81 he was finally released on heavy bail (put up by Richard OSWALD), thanks to the efforts of Franklin and Burke, and about four months later his exchange for Cornwallis was arranged. On 14 June '81 Laurens had been named one of the

commissioners to handle PEACE NEGOTIATIONS (Morris, *E.A.H.*, 105; *D.A.B.* gives May '82 as the date of appointment [XI, 35]). Efforts had meanwhile been made by Madison to annul his diplomatic commission because of the petitions mentioned earlier, but on 20 Sept. '82 Congress refused to recall him. They did not send him definite instructions until about this time, however, and he reached Paris only two days before the preliminary peace articles were signed. Between this time and his release from the Tower he had gone to Bath for his health, had held conferences with Shelburne on the matter of ending the war, and had made a trip to The Hague to get the views of John Adams for the British.

Despite his 11th-hour arrival, Laurens was useful to the peace commissioners on several points of the treaty. "For the next year and a half he acted as a sort of unofficial minister to England, frequently crossing the Channel to confer with the ministry on commercial and other matters" (*D.A.B.*). On 3 Aug. '84 he was back in N.Y., and shortly thereafter he reported to Congress on his mission. His final years in public life had not been happy, his health had been broken, his son had been killed in action in the closing phase of the war (see below), and his property losses—according to his own estimate—amounted to 40,000 guineas. (Then about $187,000. See MONEY. . . .) Although mentioned for another term as president of the Cont'l. Cong., he left Philadelphia for his home in S.C., reaching Charleston early in 1785, and retired to his plantation, "Mepkin," on the Cooper River some 30 miles above the city. He died seven years later after a long illness. As stipulated in his will, Laurens was cremated; this is one of the first instances of this practice in America.

LAURENS, John, *c.* 1754–1782. Cont'l. officer. S.C. The son of Henry LAURENS, he was educated in England and Geneva and returned to the colonies in 1777. He was Washington's volunteer A.D.C., serving often as secretary and translator. He fought at Brandywine, 11 Sept. '77, and was wounded at Germantown, 4 Oct. '77, and at Monmouth, 28 June '78. On 23 Dec. '78 he shot Gen. Charles LEE in a duel. He was named Lt. Col. and A.D.C. to Washington 29 March '79 after having declined a similar commission voted him by Congress on 5 Nov. '78. In 1779 he was elected to the S.C. Assembly but withdrew from it when the British invaded the state. Joining Gen. Moultrie's militia, he fought at Charleston against Prevost and was wounded at Coosashatchie Pass. (Appleton's) At Savannah he led the light infantry. He was at Charleston during Clinton's siege and was captured, paroled, and exchanged. Congress sent him to France in the spring of 1781, when he was 26, to help Franklin arrange for more money and supplies. He received the Thanks of Congress for his success in this and then returned to the field. At Yorktown, he captured a redoubt and, with the Viscount de Noailles, negotiated the surrender with Cornwallis. (The latter was Constable of the Tower of London where the elder Laurens was imprisoned and was exchanged for him.) Young Laurens returned to the South and was killed at COMBAHEE FERRY, S.C., 27 Aug. '82.

LAUZUN, Armand Louis de Gontaut, Comte de Biron and Duc de. French officer. Inheriting the title of his famous uncle (1632–1723), the Duc de Lauzun of the American and French Revolutions proved to be almost as romantic a character as the controversial courtier whose name he perpetuated. Handsome, witty, brave, and wealthy,

he was very popular in America as commander of the 600-man LEGION bearing his name. Frequently cited by historians of the American Revolution are his "Memoirs" (*Mag. of Am. Hist.,* VI [1881]) and *Memoirs of the Duc de Lauzun* (Am. ed., 1912). Becoming Citizen Biron in the French Revolution, he was executed in 1793 for lack of initiative in suppressing the Vendée counterrevolution.

LAWRANCE, John. See LAURANCE.

LAWSON, Robert. American officer. Va. After serving as Maj. in the 4th Va. from 13 Feb. '76, Lt. Col. after 13 Aug. '76, and Col. after 19 Aug. '77, he resigned 17 Dec. '77 and subsequently saw action at GUILFORD and in the YORKTOWN CAMPAIGN as a B.G. of Va. militia.

LEAGUE OF NEUTRALS. See ARMED NEUTRALITY.

LEARNED, Ebenezer. 1728–1801. Cont'l. general. Mass. A native of Oxford, Mass., he commanded a militia company in Col. Ruggles' Regt. and led the revolutionary movement in his town. In 1774 and '75 he was a delegate to the provincial congresses at Concord and Cambridge. He led his minutemen to the latter place on 19 Apr. '75 and two days later was assigned to the right wing of the Boston army. During the battle of Bunker Hill his men were under fire at Roxbury. Commissioned Col. of a Mass. regiment on 19 Apr. '75, he became Col. of the 3d Cont'l. Regt. on 1 Jan. As intermediary between Howe and Washington he negotiated the British evacuation of Boston. About 11 A.M. on Sunday, 17 Mar., he unbarred the gates on the main road with his own hands and marched in. (Freeman, *Washington,* IV, 42, 44, 51, 53; *D.A.B.*) His men then were assigned the mission of operating from whaleboats to watch the British fleet in the harbor before they sailed away.

In May '76 he resigned because of bad health, but on 2 Apr. '77 he was appointed B.G. and returned to duty. Assigned to the Northern Dept., he collected militia at Fts. Edward and Anne, and assisted in the evacuation of stores from Ticonderoga before its occupation by Burgoyne (July '77). He accompanied Arnold in the move to Ft. Stanwix that ended St. Leger's Expedition (Sept. '77). His brigade took part in the battles of Saratoga but (D.A.B. to the contrary) contributed nothing to the first battle, for which (says D.A.B.) it was "publicly thanked by Gates for its valiant behavior." Benedict Arnold took command of the brigade to attack some enemy outposts, which also was a relatively insignificant operation. (See First and Second Battles of Saratoga)

On 24 Mar. '78 he again resigned for physical disability. In 1783 he was a member of the state legislature. In 1786 he supported the authorities against Daniel Shays's Rebellion, although this brought him into conflict with his family and neighbors and exposed him to serious personal danger.

LE BEGUE DE PRESLE DUPORTAIL, Louis. 1743–1802. Cont'l. general and chief engineer. France. The man known in American history as Gen. Duportail was the son of a nobleman, J.-G. Le Bègue de Presle, *avocat,* King's Councillor, and former Master of Streams and Forests. The son was born at Pithiviers, became a Lt. and student at the engineers' school of Mézières on 1 Jan. '62, and three years later was accepted as *ingénieur ordinaire.* In Aug. '73 he was promoted to Capt. and on 25 Jan. '77 he was given leave of absence with the grade of Lt. Col. in order to "take care of personal business" (*vaquer à ses affaires particulières*). He was one of the four officers chosen by the French court in response to Franklin's request that trained military Engineers be made available to the colonists.

Duportail joined the Cont'l. Army on 13 Feb. '77 and on 8 July was appointed Col. of Engrs. with his commission backdated to 13 Feb. '77. (Lasseray, citing Gardiner) On 22 July Congress gave him seniority over all engineers previously appointed, and on 17 Nov. '77 he was named B.G. and Chief of Engrs. (*Ibid.*) Having joined the main army at Morristown, he took part in the Philadelphia Campaign. One of his first major assignments was to work on the Delaware River Forts (see Phil. Camp'n.), and this brought him into conflict with the ambitious Coudray. He remained with Washington at Valley Forge and during the Monmouth Campaign. On 29 June '78 he was sent to work on the defenses of Philadelphia, and in 1779 he served in the Hudson Highlands. (Lasseray) In Mar. '80 he was put under Lincoln's orders but arrived at Charleston too late to play any significant role in the defense of that city. (See Charleston ... 1780) Becoming a prisoner on 12 May '80, he had been exchanged by 25 Oct. '80 (*ibid.*) and rejoined Washington in time to play a vital part in the Yorktown Campaign.

On 11 May '79 his title had been changed to Commandant of the Corps of Engineers and Sappers and Miners. On 16 Nov. '81 he was promoted to Maj. Gen., and on 10 Oct. '83 he resigned from the American service. Meanwhile, in the French service, he had been made Lt. Col. attached to the infantry, and on 13 June '83 he became a French B.G. of infantry. Four years later he was authorized to go to Naples to instruct the army of that kingdom. Apparently he remained in France, since he was appointed *Aide-maréchal général des logis* at army headquarters on 29 June '87. Three years later, on 16

Nov. '90, Duportail became Minister and Secretary of State for War, but in early Dec. '91 he was relieved of this post. (Apparently the order was dated 5 Dec., but he actually ceased to function in this capacity on the 2d. Lasseray.) On 13 Jan. '92 he was promoted to Lt. Gen. and given command of the 21st region (*division militaire*) at Moulins. His politics were suspected, however, and Duportail did not take over this post. (He was a supporter of LAFAYETTE, who also was having political difficulties about this time.) After spending two years in hiding, having learned that serious political charges had been brought against him, Duportail escaped to America and settled on a small farm near Philadelphia. On 18 June '97 Mathieu Dumas got his name removed from the proscribed list. In 1802 he died on a ship bound for France and was buried at sea. (Lasseray)

Two important mss. of his are in the *Archives historiques de la Guerre;* they are: *Mémoire sur la défense de Westpoint,* dated 20 Aug. '79 (21 pages), and *Mémoire sur la campagne 1780 en Amérique . . .* (17 pages).

While the services of this noble French volunteer were not spectacular they were invaluable to the American cause. He was one of the few foreign officers whom Washington considered useful, and D. S. Freeman ranks him with Lafayette and Steuben. (*Washington,* IV, 540, 567)

LECHMERE POINT (now East Cambridge), Mass., 9 Nov. '75. (BOSTON SIEGE) Nine companies of British light infantry and 100 grenadiers landed at this place, which at high tide was surrounded by water, to seize cattle needed for the Boston garrison. Thinking that this might be more than a foraging raid, the Americans ordered Col. Wm. Thompson to counterattack with his Pa. riflemen, and Col. Benj. Woodbridge to support Thompson with part of his regiment and part of Col. John Paterson's. Despite two feet of icy water the Americans advanced resolutely and the British withdrew with 10 cows. Although Washington commended the action in G.O. of 10 Nov., he later concluded that reports of it had been colored; his troops had merely driven off some foragers—and this by musket fire from a safe range. Only two Americans were wounded. (Freeman, *Washington,* III, 570 *n.*)

LEE, Arthur. 1740–1792. American diplomat, troublemaker. Va. Youngest of the four famous sons of Thomas Lee and last of his 11 children (see LEE FAMILY), Arthur was about 10 years old when he came under the guardianship of his eldest brother, Philip Ludwell, on the death of their father. Young Arthur was sent to Eton, went on to the University of Edinburgh, studied science, literature, and medicine, got his M.D. degree in 1764, traveled a few months in Europe, and returned to Va. He started practicing medicine in Williamsburg in 1766, but after two years returned to London to study law, and his brother William went along to set up business in London. In 1775 he was admitted to the bar. (E. C. Burnett in *D.A.B.*) Meanwhile, in 1766 (while in Va.), he had been made a fellow of the Royal Society. Arthur and William became deeply involved in English politics and were followers of the flamboyant John WILKES. Arthur had a fling at political writing prior to his return to England in 1768, turning out 10 "Monitor's Letters" with the purpose of supplementing the "FARMER'S LETTERS" of John Dickinson. Although such leaders as Jefferson were unimpressed by these, others thought highly of them; one of these was Sam Adams, and it was his influence that led to Arthur's being chosen in 1770 as London agent of Mass. (*Ibid.*) The diatribes of JUNIUS inspired Lee to emulation, and he produced a series of letters signed "Junius Americanus."

The Lee brothers were deeply involved in the Middlesex elections that made WILKES a national idol, and Arthur "procured the insertion in the famous Middlesex Petition of a resolution protesting against the obnoxious American measures, and the chief burden of much that he wrote was that the cause of Middlesex was the cause of Englishmen everywhere." (*Ibid.*) In 1774 he published the anonymous *Appeal to the Justice and Interests of the People of Great Britain,* followed by a *Second Appeal* in 1775, and signed "By an Old Member of Parliament." Burnett comments that during this period he nourished hopes that he might himself be elected to Parliament.

At the house of Wilkes in 1775 Arthur Lee met Beaumarchais. "Arthur Lee was ambitious, impetuous, witty, talkative, and fond of scheming and intriguing," comments a biographer of the remarkable Frenchman. "In short, he possessed all the good qualities and defects that would please a man like Beaumarchais." (Lemaitre, *Beaumarchais,* 177–78) The two were soon holding long, confidential conversations, and the seed of secret French aid was sowed. The fruit was Beaumarchais' HORTALEZ & CIE. Arthur Lee was furious at being left out of something he had helped start and his reaction was to accuse everybody concerned of being dishonest. He did not exclude Benjamin Franklin. "I am more and more satisfied that the old doctor is concerned in the plunder," he wrote his brother Richard Henry Lee on 12 Sept. '78, "and that in time we shall collect the proofs." Burnett comments, "This was character-istic: accusations following close upon the heels of suspicion; proofs to be collected in time." (*Ibid.*)

It is primarily in connection with the Deane–Lee controversy that Arthur is remembered, but for his full record as a marplot it is necessary to go back to the year 1775. In Nov. '75 he was asked by the Secret Committee of Congress to be its correspondent in London. In Oct. '76 he was appointed to join Deane and Franklin in Paris to bring about the French Alliance. (He took the place of Jefferson, who had declined.) Reaching Paris the end of Dec., he was prevailed on by the two other commissioners to see what might be done in Spain. Going there in Feb. '77, he was able to get substantial aid from the government through the intermediary of a commercial concern, but was not allowed to enter Madrid. A journey to Berlin, May–July, was fruitless. Returning to Paris, where there was nothing constructive for him to do, he nosed further into the secret aid business—which Franklin was letting Deane handle by himself—and on 4 Oct. '77 Lee wrote Samuel Adams and brother Richard Henry that he should be made sole minister to France.

In what Burnett calls "militia diplomacy," Congress in May '77 appointed brother William commissioner to Berlin and Austria and Ralph Izard to the court of Tuscany. They ended by spending most of their time in Paris, however, where they joined Arthur in "what might well be called guerrilla or sniping diplomacy" (*ibid.*) against Franklin and Deane. The French Alliance nevertheless came about. Deane then was recalled on the basis of Lee's charges and was ruined. (See DEANE) The sordid controversy did, however, make Lee *persona non grata* with Vergennes, and Congress recalled him 27

Sept. '79. William Lee and Izard had been dismissed in June, leaving "the old doctor" the sole commissioner in Paris. Returning to America in Sept. '80, Lee was elected to the Va. House of Delegates in 1781 and to the Cont'l. Cong. for the next three years (1782–84). Here he was useless: incapable of constructive effort, he apparently could not even cause trouble. He wrote Sam Adams (21 Apr. '82) that he could only lament what he could not prevent. (*Ibid.*) Congress made him Northwest Indian Commissioner and he was one of those who negotiated the treaties of Ft. Stanwix, 22 Oct. '84, and Ft. Mc-Intosh, 21 Jan. '85. In July '85 Congress appointed him to the unsuccessful treasury board, a post he held until the new government was inaugurated. The last thing he found to be against (other than women—he never married) was the Constitution, and he lived his last few years on his estate, "Lansdowne."

One could wear out the books of abnormal psychology and synonyms trying to characterize this morbidly suspicious, cantankerous scion of the distinguished Lee Family of Va. Franklin had one word for him: insane.

Most of the works on Lee are by Lees. Burnett calls the *Life of Arthur Lee* by R. H. Lee (2 vols., 1829) "eulogistic and inaccurate." He cites C. H. Lee, *A Vindication of Arthur Lee* (1894) and E. J. Lee, *Lee of Va., 1642–1892* (1895) without comment.

LEE, Charles. 1731–1782. Cont'l. general, soldier of fortune. Eng.–Va. After attending school in England and Switzerland, he entered his father's regiment as an ensign in 1747 and on 2 May '51 became a Lt. in the 44th Foot. He was on Braddock's expedition (1755) and then went to the Mohawk Valley where he purchased a commission as Capt. Adopted by the Mohawks, he "married" the daughter of a Seneca chief. During Abercromby's attack on Ticonderoga (7 July '58) he was badly wounded, but he rejoined his regiment for the capture of Niagara and Montreal. The winter of 1760–61 he spent in England. On 10 Aug. '61 he was appointed Maj. of the 103d Regt. and the next year served with real distinction under Burgoyne in Portugal, advancing to Maj. He was retired on half pay in Nov. '63 when his regiment was disbanded. (Randolph G. Adams in *D.A.B.*) In 1765 Lee became a soldier of fortune in the Polish Army, where he got to be on intimate terms with King Stanislaus Poniatowski. He was promoted to Maj. Gen. in 1767. The next two years he spent in England, where he devoted his time to horses and criticism of the government. He returned to Poland in 1769, fought against the Turks, and was invalided home the next year. In 1773 he went to America, where he immediately aligned himself with the revolutionary element. Scenting great possibilities for personal advancement, he urged patriot leaders to raise an army, and in May '74 he started buying an estate in Berkeley co. (West) Va., "with the specific motive of recommending himself, as a landowner, to the Continental Congress." (G. H. Moore, *Treason of Lee,* quoted by Carl Van Doren, *Secret History,* 30)

The half-pay British Lt. Col. (promoted in 1772) not only had military experience but was a good pamphleteer and an articulate speaker. Many influential Americans came to look on him as a valuable acquisition, and when Congress appointed him Maj. Gen. on 17 June '75 he was subordinate only to Washington and Ward. Since acceptance of this commission would lead to confiscation of his English estates and his property in Va. was not paid for, Lee waited until Congress promised compensation for his property losses before he wrote British authorities about discontinuing his half pay.

After serving in the Boston siege, where "his dirty habits and obscenity gave offense" but where he was "endured for what he was supposed to know" (Freeman, *Washington*, III, 373B), Lee was detached in Jan. '76 and directed to raise volunteers in Conn. for the defense of N.Y.C. He reached the city on 4 Feb., having been delayed by a bout with the gout. On the 17th he was ordered by Congress to succeed Schuyler in the Northern Dept., but on 1 Mar. a counterorder sent him to command the Southern Dept. His activities during this period are covered under N.Y. CAMPAIGN and the CHARLESTON EXPEDITION of 1776.

On 7 Oct. '76 he was back in Philadelphia. He had received the thanks of Congress on 20 July for his service at Charleston and on his return to the city Congress advanced him $30,000 to pay for his Va. property. He reached Washington's army in time for the Battle of White Plains, N.Y., 28 Oct., and was left at Peekskill with some of the best American troops when the main army went south for the N.J. Campaign. When Washington called for him to rejoin the main army on the retreat to the Delaware, Lee reacted in such a way as to raise suspicion that he hoped for Washington's defeat so that he could be appointed to succeed him. This is covered under N.J. CAMPAIGN. On 24 Nov. '76 Lee wrote a letter to Joseph REED that Washington innocently opened by mistake. Although Washington's reaction insofar as Reed was concerned was one of personal hurt rather than official outrage, he realized he would have to be on guard against the "fickle" Englishman. On 9

Dec. Lee wrote Heath that in his opinion Washington really did not need his support on the Delaware and went on to say: "I am in the hopes here [at Morristown] to reconquer (if I may so express myself) the Jerseys." He had just penned and dispatched to Gates the famous letter that said, *"entre nous* a certain great man is damnably deficient. . . ."* when he was captured at BASKING RIDGE, 13 Dec. '76.

Germain ordered Lee returned to England for trial as a deserter, but Howe thought Lee had resigned his half pay before joining the enemy and did not comply. As a prisoner in N.Y., Lee conducted himself in such a way as to be accused of treason when the facts were generally known, more than 70 years after his death. On 29 Mar. '77 he submitted his plan for ending the rebellion by an offensive that would "unhinge the organization of the American resistance" by gaining control of the middle colonies—Md., Pa., and Va. (Anderson, *Howe Brothers*, 221–22) The British apparently paid little attention to the strategic advice of this former Lt. Col. (*Ibid.*, 224)

Exchanged in Apr. '78, Lee complained to Congress about the promotion of others while he was a prisoner, and on 20 May was greeted at Valley Forge by officers still innocent of his double-dealing. In the MONMOUTH CAMPAIGN he had his first test as a field commander and in the opinion of most observers he failed it miserably. The LEE COURT MARTIAL was brought on not by his performance in the battle but by his conduct afterward. During his trial he cast aspersions that nearly led to a duel with STEUBEN. After his "Vindication" appeared in the *Pa. Packet* of 3 Dec. '78 he was called out and slightly wounded by Col. John Laurens, but the wound was enough to keep him from accepting a challenge from Wayne. By July '79 he was back at his estate in the Shenandoah, where he "bred horses, enjoyed the company of his dogs, and attempted farming," writes Fisher. (Fisher, *Struggle,* II, 194) When his year of suspension from command expired, Lee heard a rumor that Congress intended to dismiss him. The letter he wrote them on this matter was so offensive that on 10 Jan. '80 Congress did dismiss him from the service. Two days later he left his home and moved to Philadelphia, where he died in 1782.

"An enigma Lee was—and still is," wrote Freeman in 1951, but this same year John R. Alden published *General Charles Lee, Traitor or Patriot?,* a study that completely revises the image of this strange but able and much maligned man. Further light is cast by John W. Shy of Princeton in his remarkable essay on Lee in Billias (ed.), *Washington's Generals* (New York, 1964). The Lee Papers were published in four volumes by the N.Y. Hist. Soc. in 1871–74.

LEE, Charles. 1758–1815. Officer in Va. navy. Va. Younger brother of "Light-Horse Harry" (see LEE FAMILY), he entered the College of N.J. (Princeton) in 1770 and received his A.B. degree in 1775. He was commended for "application and genius." During the entire period 1777–89 he appears to have served as "naval officer of the South Potomac," after which he became customs collector at Alexandria. A close friend of Washington—despite 26 years' difference in age—he supported the president's policies against Jefferson and was rewarded in Nov. '95 with the post of U.S. Atty. Gen. Losing this office in 1801, he was named judge of one of the new circuit courts by Pres. Adams and served as one of the so-called "midnight judges" until Congress in 1802 repealed the Ju-

diciary Act under which he was appointed. With the fall of the Federalists his political life ended, and he went into private law practice. (He had been admitted to the bar in June '94.) A friend of John Marshall, he frequently appeared before the Supreme Court, and took part in the *Marbury vs. Madison* case. He was a defense lawyer in the impeachment of Judge Chase (1805) and in the trial of Aaron Burr (1807).

LEE, Francis Lightfoot. 1734–1797. Congressman, Signer. Va. One of the famous four brothers of the LEE FAMILY, he was educated by tutors at "Stratford" and then left the family home to settle on an estate in Loudoun co. inherited from his father. For 10 years starting in 1758 he represented that county in the House of Burgesses. In 1769 he married Rebecca Tayloe and settled on a plantation named "Menokin" in Richmond co., where his wife's family was influential. He represented that county in the Burgesses from 1769 to 1776, taking a bold and effective part in every measure of defiance to the mother country. Elected to the Con'l. Cong. to fill the place of Patrick Henry, he served from 1775 to 1779, when the call of country life prevailed over his limited political ambitions. "Lee was an influential and useful member of Congress," writes H. J. Eckenrode in *D.A.B.* "He would have ranked as one of the leaders of the American Revolution if he had been a good speaker and had been self-seeking. But he was shy and inarticulate in public bodies and his excellent committee work remained unknown to the general public." (*Ibid.*) See LEE FAMILY for bibliography.

LEE, Henry ("Light-Horse Harry"). 1756–1818. Cont'l. cavalry leader. (See LEE FAMILY) Va. Graduating from Princeton at the age of 17, he was admitted to the Middle Temple and about to leave for England when the war changed his plans. On 18 June '76 Patrick Henry's nomination got him a commission as Capt. in Bland's Regt. of Va. cavalry. On 31 Mar. his company was attached to the 1st Cont'l. Dragoons (Heitman), and in Apr. '77 they joined Washington's main army. At this time Washington was engaged in the perplexing "Spring Maneuvers" preceding the PHILADELPHIA CAMPAIGN and badly needed cavalry for reconnaissance. Although only 21 years old at the time, Capt. Lee favorably impressed the C. in C. with his soldierly qualities and they continued to be close friends in later years. Lee's fine defense of the Spread Eagle Tavern (5 mi. S. and slightly E. of Valley Forge) on 20 Jan. '78 was the immediate cause of the following resolution of Congress on 7 Apr.:

"Resolved, whereas Captain Henry Lee, of the Light Dragoons, by the whole tenor of his conduct during the last campaign, has proved himself a brave and prudent officer, rendering essential service to his country, and acquired to himself and the corps he commanded, distinguished honor, and, it being the determination of Congress to reward merit, Resolved, that Captain H. Lee be promoted to the rank of Major-Commandant; that he be empowered to augment his present corps by enlistment of two troops of horse to act as a separate corps." (From Heitman, "Lee"; authority that the 20 Jan. action was the "immediate cause" is Freeman, *Washington*, IV, 627 and *n.*)

The addition of three infantry companies resulted in the creation of LEE'S LEGION, one of the elite units of the war.

PAULUS HOOK, N.J., 19 Aug. '79, won the ambitious boy-commander the thanks of Congress and one of the eight MEDALS voted by Congress during the war. On 21 Oct. '80 his battalion (as Heitman terms it) was designated "Lee's Partisan Corps," and on 6 Nov. he was promoted to Lt. Col. He had not yet reached his 24th birthday (29 Jan. '56). Major operations in the North had long since ceased, but Nathanael Greene had taken command of the Southern Theater and was desperately in need of cavalry. Ordered there, Lee joined Greene in S.C. on 13 Jan. '81.

"His subsequent story is the history of the Southern campaign," writes H. J. Eckenrode in his *D.A.B.* sketch of Lee. It can be traced starting with the section of SOUTHERN CAMPAIGNS OF NATHANAEL GREENE headed "Operations on the Yadkin." Just prior to this he had been detached to support Marion, and the two had attacked GEORGETOWN, S.C., 24 Jan. '81. To summarize his activities, after performing brilliantly against Tarleton's cavalry in covering Greene's nip-and-tuck retreat to the Dan, Lee recrossed to shatter a Tory force at HAW RIVER, N.C., 25 Feb. '81. At GUILFORD, 15 Mar., the infantry and cavalry of Lee's Legion fought gallantly and effectively, but Eckenrode criticizes Lee for failure "to keep Greene informed of his position." (*D.A.B.*) Again detached from Greene's main army, Lee took part in the actions at FT. WATSON, S.C., 15–23 Apr., FT. MOTTE, 12 May, FT. GRANBY, 15 May, AUGUSTA and NINETY-SIX in May–June '81. In the last major battle of the Southern campaign, EUTAW SPRINGS, 8 Sept. '81, his infantry and cavalry distinguished themselves in separate parts of the battlefield.

Lee then paid a short visit to Washington's army around Yorktown. He evidently was present during the action at GLOUCESTER, Va., 3 Oct. '81 (the excellent account in his *Memoirs*, 497–98, does not make this clear); Freeman says "it is entirely possible that the fine handling of Mercer's men was due in large part to the presence of "Light-Horse Harry" Lee, whom Greene had permitted to go to the Peninsula of Virginia, ostensibly to carry dispatches but actually, it would appear, to be 'in' at the 'kill.' " (*op. cit.,* V, 355 *n.*). Lee returned to his command in the South. Joining Greene in the High Hills of Santee, he participated in the operation against DORCHESTER, S.C., 1 Dec., before conceiving the attack on JOHNS ISLAND, 28–29 Dec. '81.

Around the middle of Feb. '82 Lee left the army on leave of absence and never returned, being honorably discharged at the end of the war. Greene had written to him on 27 Jan. '82: "I have beheld with extreme anxiety, for some time past a growing discontent in your mind, and have not been without my apprehensions that your complaints originated more in distress than in the ruin of your constitution. Whatever may be the source of your wounds, I wish it was in my power to heal them." Robert E. Lee in the introduction to his father's *Memoirs* quotes this letter and says "Colonel Lee left the army at the close of the campaign, in sickness and sorrow." He and Greene remained the closest of friends but it is apparent that "Light-Horse Harry" was in a depressed mental state that probably can be attributed to true battle fatigue. (*Memoirs,* 38–39) Soon after reaching Va. he married his cousin Matilda Lee, heiress of "Stratford." He entered politics as a Federalist and supporter of Washington. In Congress from 1785 to 1788, he also was active in state affairs and gained a reputation as an orator. After the death of his wife in 1790 he considered entering the military service in France, but he gave up this plan and served as Gov. of Va. from 1792 to 1795. The summer of 1794 Washington gave him command of 15,000 troops raised to quell the Whiskey Rebellion in Pa., a mission Lee accomplished without loss of life and with increase of his military reputation. He had remarried in 1793, and in 1799 he returned to Congress. It is he who called Washington "first in war, first in peace, and first in the hearts of his countrymen."

Lee's life at this point started on a downward path. Living far beyond his means and having no head for business, he got heavily involved in unsuccessful land speculation and was imprisoned for debt. During this period, 1808–9, he wrote his *Memoirs.* He left "Stratford," the legacy of his first wife, to live in Alexandria, where the family lived on the means of his second wife, the former Anne Hill Carter of "Shirley." It was into this sad situation that their famous son, Robert E. Lee, was born in 1807. In 1812 Henry Lee was badly injured by a mob in Baltimore—he had been attempting to help his friend Alexander C. Hanson defend his press—and the next year he went to the West Indies for convalescence. Slander had it that he really was fleeing his creditors. After several years in the Caribbean it became evident that Lee was dying, and he set sail for home. His strength failing enroute, he was put ashore in Ga., where he was nursed by the daughter of Nathanael Greene. He died at Cumberland Island, Ga., and was buried there. His remains were transferred in 1913 to Washington and Lee University.

His *Memoirs of the War in the Southern Department of the United States* were published in two volumes in 1812, republished by his eldest son (by his first wife) in 1827, and again published, with a biographical sketch, by his son Robert E. Lee in 1869. Written by a magnificent soldier who also was "a learned and accomplished man of letters" (*D.A.B.*), Lee's *Memoirs* are not only an essential historical document for any study of war in the South, but they are also one of the finest military memoirs in the language. See also Thos. H. Boyd, *Light-Horse Harry Lee* (1931), and C. B. Hartley, *Life . . .* (1859).

LEE, Richard Bland. 1761–1827. Statesman. This member of the famous LEE FAMILY OF VA. was too young to play any part in the Revolutionary war and showed no particular ability when he later entered politics. Yet "it was his destiny to be one of the determining factors in an event of importance to the country," writes H. J. Eckenrode in *D.A.B.* By changing his stand as an opponent to Hamilton's plan for "ASSUMPTION," Lee (and Alexander White) got Hamilton's consent to establishing the national capital on the Potomac.

LEE, Richard Henry. 1732–1794. Congressman, Signer. Va. Eldest of the four famous sons of Thomas Lee (see LEE FAMILY), he studied in England after being tutored at home, returned about 1752, and five years later started his political career. J.O.P. in his home county of Westmoreland in 1757, the next year he followed the path of his ancestors to the House of Burgesses. After a slow start, apparently because of his deference to the older leaders, he became prominent in the patriot politics that led to the break with England. He became an ally of Patrick Henry, and for the rest of his life he was a political supporter and close personal friend of Henry. During the lull in agitation between 1768 and 1773 he kept up his political activity but also was engaged in the profitable business of shipping tobacco to his brother William in London.

In the Cont'l. Cong. from 1774 to 1780 he quickly formed a lasting friendship with John and Sam Adams; he believed in strong measures in dealing with the mother country, and was one of the first to advocate a direct attack on the king, rather than the ministry, as the oppressor of the colonies. He saw independence primarily as a prerequisite to the essential winning of foreign support, and he had an important part in getting his state to send Congress resolutions in behalf of independence, foreign alliances, and confederation. It is thus that Richard Henry Lee touched off the movement toward INDEPENDENCE, and having done so he left Philadelphia on 13 June '76 without taking any part in the subsequent drafting of the Decl. of Indep. (E. C. Burnett in *D.A.B.*) He subsequently became a Signer, however.

He took a leading part in convincing fellow Virginians that their sacrifice of claims to western lands was necessary if a confederation were to be achieved. With his brother Arthur he became deeply involved in the controversy with Silas DEANE. In May '79 he was forced by ill health, resulting from arduous work, to resign from Congress, but he came back in 1784 and was elected president of that body. He sat again in 1787 (Montross, *Reluctant Rebels,* 431). Meanwhile, despite bad health, he had sat in the state House of Delegates. He led opposition to adoption of the Constitution, feeling that the lack of a bill of rights and other features gave the central government powers that could be abused. Patrick Henry, who shared Lee's objections, was instrumental in getting him elected to the new U.S. Senate, where Lee worked toward amending the Constitution. His principal propositions found their place in the first 10 amendments. (*Ibid.*)

In Oct. '92 he again resigned on grounds of health, and a little more than two years later he died at "Chantilly," the home he had established around 1757 near the family seat, "Stratford." Burnett calls the two-volume *Memoir of . . . Lee* (1825) by his grandson and namesake unsatisfactory. This authority (see main bibliography) has drawn for his *D.A.B.* sketch from J. C. Ballagh (ed.), *Letters of R. H. Lee* (2 vols., 1911–14), the *Journals of the House of Burgesses,* the *Journals of the Cont'l. Cong.,* and Lee's *Lee of Va.* (see LEE FAMILY).

LEE, William. 1739–1795. American merchant, diplomat, troublemaker. Va. Only 16 months older than his brother Arthur (see LEE FAMILY), William was closely associated with him in Europe after 1768. Little is known of William's prior life. Soon after reaching London he married his wealthy cousin (7 Mar. '69), Hannah Phillippa Ludwell of "Green Spring." The next year he was in partnership with Stephen Sayre and the Dennys De Berdts (father and son). With Sayre and Arthur LEE he got deeply involved in British politics as a supporter of John Wilkes. Sayre and Arthur became sheriffs of London, and two years later, in 1775, Arthur became the only American ever to hold the office of alderman of the City of London. (E. C. Burnett in *D.A.B.*) He cherished his British citizenship and alderman's gown until 1780. (Augur, *Secret War,* 175)

Early in 1777 William's brother Richard Henry Lee had used his newly acquired power on the Commercial Comm. of Cong. to have William appointed as joint commercial agent with Thomas Morris in France. He reached Paris with his family in June, and with brother Arthur started the cabal that was to end with the recall of Silas Deane. In May '77 he was selected by Congress to be commissioner to Prussia and Austria, but neither power had any idea of recognizing the U.S. at this time and William was not permitted to visit either capital. William's formal appointment as commercial agent had been sent by Robert MORRIS to his brother Thomas, but the latter was making such a killing in prizes at Nantes that he withheld the document. (Lambert WICKES had just completed his sweep through the Irish Sea.)

The Lee brothers and Ralph Izard had been rebuffed in their diplomatic assignments, so they stayed in Paris and tried to justify their existence. All three were born troublemakers and the outlet for their energies was to undermine Deane and Franklin. The resulting controversy is covered under DEANE, and one consequence was elimination of William Lee and Izard from their posts in June '79, and the recall of Arthur Lee three months later.

Meanwhile, however, he had taken a step that led to war between England and Holland. Unable to gain entrée to the Prussian and Austrian courts, William Lee took it on himself to see what he could do in Holland. With a minor Dutch official, John De Neufville, he framed a draft treaty of commerce, and although the Dutch gave no indication of interest Lee proudly sent his draft to Congress. When Henry Laurens was sent to the Netherlands in the summer of 1780 to get a treaty and a loan, the Lees gave him William's "treaty" as a model. Laurens was captured at sea. "Whitehall believed, or chose to believe, William Lee's . . . treaty genuine, and immediately declared war on Holland." (Augur, *op. cit.,* 322)

William lived in Brussels for four years after losing his official status. In Sept. '83 he retired to "Green Spring" and died in 1795 after several years of almost total blindness.

The *Letters of Wm. Lee* (3 vols., 1891) were edited by W. C. Ford. See bibliography under LEE FAMILY.

LEE COURT MARTIAL, 4 July–12 Aug. '78. Although Washington apparently had no intention of making an official issue of Chas. Lee's poor performance at MONMOUTH, 28 June '78, Lee sent Washington a letter on 30 June (misdated 1 July) that complained about the "very singular expressions" the C. in C. had addressed to him on the field, accused Washington of "cruel injustice" based on misinformation, and affirmed the right to "demand some reparation for the injury committed." Washington flared up at these personal reflections and promised Lee an official hearing. But Lee would not let it go at that and became even more reckless in two more letters written the same day (the first of these misdated 28 June). In response to Lee's request for an immediate court martial, Washington informed him the same day that he was under arrest and that charges were forthcoming. Gen. Alexander ("Stirling") was named president of a court appointed on 1 July to sit the next day at Brunswick. The charges were: I. Disobedience of orders, in not attacking the enemy on 28 June, as instructed; II. Misbehavior before the enemy on the same day by making an unnecessary, disorderly, and shameful retreat; and III. Disrespect to the C. in C., in two letters, those Lee had misdated 1 July and 28 June.

The trial is of interest in revealing Lee's conduct at Monmouth. The proceedings establish that Lee did not follow orders in moving to make contact (testimony of John Laurens and Alexander Hamilton) and that he had no control over the action that developed (testimony of Maxwell, Chas. Scott, and Anthony Wayne). Numerous witnesses testified that Lee had shown personal, physical courage. Lee conducted his own defense but showed little skill and did nothing in cross-examination to discredit the evidence submitted against him. The court, which had moved with the army to Paramus, ended its hearing on 9 Aug. and three days later found Lee guilty of all charges. They sentenced him to suspension from command for 12 months. On 16 Aug., Washington forwarded the case to Congress without comment for their review, but that body did not start their discussions until 23 Oct. Lee, meanwhile, remained with the army until Sept., when he went to Philadelphia. More than five months after the trial had started, Congress voted on 5 Dec. that the sentence be executed.

Fisher has this to say about the trial: "Gordon, whose statements as a contemporary are certainly entitled to weight, says that many were of the opinion that Lee should have been found guilty only on the last charge ... [but] there were people who believed that the court regarded the two letters to Washington as so grossly insubordinate and disrespectful, that they found Lee guilty on the other two charges because of the greatness of his offence in the last one. The sentence ... was supposed also to indicate that the court were inclined to think him innocent on the first two charges; for, as both Harry Lee and Gordon pointed out, if he had really been guilty of disobedience and an unnecessary and shameful retreat on such an occasion, a year's suspension was a very trifling punishment." (*Struggle,* II, 190–91)

Lee's foolish pen brought on the trial and ruined his excellent chances of having Congress disapprove the sentence of the court. In Philadelphia "Lee spoiled all his chances by ... writing and talking too much and too cleverly, and abusing Washington," comments Fisher. "In short, his indiscretion seems to have put the Congress in such a position that a vote to help him would have been a vote of want of confidence in Washington." (*Ibid.*)

LEE FAMILY OF VIRGINIA. Founder of the family in America was a well-born Englishman named Richard who came to Va. about 1642, became a large-scale tobacco planter, held public offices, and died about 1664. By his wife Ann, whose last name is not known, he left eight children. Their son Richard (II), 1647–1714, married Letitia Corbin (or Lettice Corbyn); they had five sons and a daughter. The eldest, Richard (III), became a London merchant, but his three children returned to Va. Philip went to Md. and left many descendants there. Francis died a bachelor. The daughter married Wm. H. Fitzhugh of "Ravenwood," and her descendants married back into the Lee family. (Hence Fitzhugh Lee, 1835–1905, nephew of Robert E. Lee.)

But the branches of the Lee family most famous in history are those established by Thomas and Henry, the 4th and 5th sons (according to Wm. Lee [*q. v.,* and his *Letters*], 3d and 5th, according to Appleton's). The genealogical table shows, in abbreviated form, the relationships of the various Lees who figured in the Revolution. You can see how "Light-Horse Harry" Lee's marriage to his cousin Matilda Lee, heiress of "Stratford," connected the two branches of the family. Ironically, once the "Leesylvania" branch inherited the home of the "Stratford" branch they proceeded to lose it through the poor business sense of "Light-Horse Harry": his failure to manage the estate properly, plus his unfortunate land speculations, led to abandonment of "Stratford" in 1811—a few years after Robert E. Lee was born there—and its sale in 1828 for a paltry $11,000. (Freeman, *Lee,* I, 97)

The two branches of the Lee family were also connected through the Ludwells of "Green Spring." A family of German origin that had settled in England, the Ludwells had been established for three generations in America before the third Philip Ludwell died in 1767 and the male line became extinct. The first Philip in America was governor of the Carolinas 1691–93; he later settled in Va. and married the widow of Gov. Sir Wm. Berkeley (d. 1677). Their son Philip (II) inherited the plantation where the battle of GREEN SPRING was fought between Lafayette and Cornwallis in July '81. Philip (III) married a Grimes and so did his sister Lucy. The third child of Philip (II), Hannah Ludwell, married Thomas Lee of "Stratford." Now things begin to get more complicated because the Lucy mentioned a moment ago had a daughter named Lucy Grymes who married Henry Lee (II) of "Leesylvania." Hence the mothers of the two branches were aunt and niece. Another link through the Ludwells was even more involved: William Lee of the "Stratford" branch married the daughter and co-heiress of Philip Ludwell III, Hannah Phillippa Ludwell (his mother's niece), and inherited "Green Spring"!

This same William Lee worked out the family pedigree in 1771 and Robert E. Lee used this material for his biographical sketch of "Light-Horse Harry" in his edition of the latter's *Memoirs.* With corrections from *D.A.B.* and Freeman's *R. E. Lee* I have used William Lee's genealogical information for this article and the accompanying diagram. The Lees were connected through the CARTER FAMILY and the RANDOLPH FAMILY with many other distinguished Americans.

E. J. Lee, *Lee of Virginia, 1642–1892,* published in 1895, was for many years the standard work. A recent book, listed in the L.O.C. *Guide,* is *The Lees of Virginia; a Biography of a Family* by B. J. Hendrick (Boston, 1935).

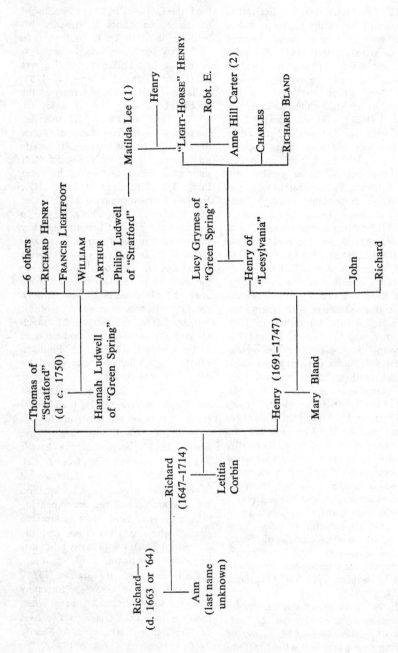

LEE'S LEGION was created 30 Nov. '80 when "Light-Horse Harry" LEE was promoted to Lt. Col. and his corps of three mounted troops augmented by three infantry companies. (Lee, *Memoirs*, 17, 29) Officers and men were carefully selected from other units of the army, "the officers with reference only to their talents . . . , and the men by a proportionable selection from the troops of each State enlisted for three years or for the war." (From Greene's *Greene*, I, 344, quoted in *Memoirs, op. cit.*) When they reported to Greene on 13 Jan. '81 the Legion numbered 100 horse and 180 foot.

"The men . . . were worth far more to Greene than their numbers would seem to indicate. They were 'the most thoroughly disciplined and best equipped scouts and raiders in the Revolution' and one of the few corps of American troops that were maintained in uniform. Their short, green coats closely resembled those of Tarleton's men. Lee was 'horse-proud,' and the mounts of his horsemen were 'powerful, well bred and kept in high condition.' On the march, the horsemen frequently took up the foot soldiers behind them [as the Romans also had done] and thus expedited their progress." (Ward, *W.O.R.*, 753)

For their battle credits see LEE.

LEE'S REGT. Col. Wm. R. Lee commanded one of the 16 "ADDITIONAL CONT'L. REGTS."

LEGION. In the 18th century (and later) a "legion" was a unit composed of infantry and mounted troops. See Henry LEE'S LEGION and Tarleton's BRITISH LEGION. Other legions of the American army were led by PULASKI and TUFFIN (Armand) in succession, and by William WASHINGTON. Benedict Arnold's Tory organization was called the "American Legion," and this name was applied also to the legions of Armand-Tuffin, Pulaski, and Henry Lee.

L'ENFANT, Pierre Charles. 1754–1825. Cont'l. officer, architect. France. Son of an artist, he was born in Paris and had held a commission as Lt. of colonial troops before signing a contract with Silas Deane that guaranteed him the rank of engineer Lt. in the American army with rank from 1 Dec. '76. At this time he was not yet 23 years old but was six feet tall, well built, and of a dignified bearing that made him stand out in the crowd. (*D.A.B.*) Going to America with Coudray in 1777, his contract with Deane was honored by Congress and he spent the winter at Valley Forge. On 18 Feb. '78 he was promoted to Capt. of Engineers and attached to the staff of Steuben. Since stagnation of the war in the North left little prospect of action he arranged a transfer to the South, where he served under John Laurens. (*Ibid.*) Now acting as an infantry officer, he received a serious gunshot wound while leading the advance of the American column against Savannah on 9 Oct. '79. Left on the field, he was recovered by friendly forces and taken to Charleston for a slow recuperation. He was bedridden as late as Jan. '80 and at the time of the British landing was still using a crutch. Replacing an American major who was more severely wounded than he, L'Enfant took an active part in the defense of the city. (Lasseray) He became a prisoner when the garrison surrendered on 12 May '80 and was not released until Jan. '82, when Rochambeau intervened to have him exchanged for Capt. Van Eyden. (*Ibid.*) He returned to Philadelphia and on 2 May '83 was breveted Maj. A few weeks later he received a French pension of 300 livres and was named for promotion to Capt. in the

French provincial forces. During July and Aug. he accompanied STEUBEN on his unsuccessful mission to Canada.

Although he had had little if any formal artistic or architectural training, L'Enfant showed great talent even before he doffed his Cont'l uniform. He did several portraits of Washington, designed pavilions and other trappings for military and civic pageants, designed the insignia and diploma of the Cincinnati, and converted the old N.Y. City Hall into Federal Hall when the government was temporarily established in that city. In 1791 he submitted the basic concept for what survives as the city of Washington. Completely irresponsible in matters of funding his grandiose architectural schemes, intolerant of suggestions by public officials, L'Enfant was dismissed from his post of supervising the execution of his plans in the federal capital after little more than six months on the job, but he was not removed from the scene before he had given the city its fundamental character. In 1792 he was engaged to lay out the manufacturing city of Paterson, N.J., but the next year he was dismissed because of his visionary plans—100 years ahead of his time—and his high-handed manners. In 1794 the federal government gave him the job of rebuilding Fort Mifflin, below Philadelphia, but apparently he again submitted plans far beyond the financial means available and little work was done under his supervision.

"After 1800 he appears chiefly as a claimant against the federal government; haunting the halls of Congress," writes Fiske Kimball in *D.A.B.* "His compensation for the work at Washington had not been fixed in advance. His claims for services ultimately rose to the fantastic amount of $95,500, as against the sum of $2.500 to $3,000 which Washington and the Commissioners had thought he would consider liberal."

Although Congress voted him two grants of money and offered him the post of engineering professor at West Point, L'Enfant nursed his grievances, refused the teaching job, and led a threadbare existence as a "guest" of Thos. Digges near Fort Washington. He died in 1825 leaving personal effects valued at $45 and was buried at the foot of tree on the estate of Wm. Digges. In 1909 his body was moved from its unmarked grave and reburied at Arlington.

See J. J. Jusserand, *With Americans of Past and Present Days* (1916), which is reprinted (insofar as the work pertains to L'Enfant) in Elizabeth S. Kite's "L'Enfant and Washington," *Hist. Docs.: Inst. Français de Washington,* cahier III (1929).

LENUD'S (or Lanneau's) **FERRY, S.C.,*** 6 May '80. (CHARLESTON EXPED.) After the American defeat at MONCK'S CORNER, 14 Apr., the survivors of this action and some fresh cavalry troops from the North gathered at several places on the Santee River. On 5 May Col. Anthony White crossed the river at Dupui's Ferry and the next morning captured an officer and 17 light infantrymen of Tarleton's command who were foraging at Wambaw, the plantation of Col. Elias Ball, near Strawberry. Circling S.E., White then headed for Lenud's Ferry on the Santee where Col. Abraham Buford was located with 350 men of his 3d Va. Cont'l. Regt. and a small body of Col. Wm. Washington's horse. Buford had reached this point in his march to reinforce Charleston, 40 miles away, when he learned of the town's surrender and was ordered by

* Located near where U.S. Hwy. 17 now crosses the Santee, and often spelled Lenew or Laneau, this Huguenot name is pronounced Le-noo. (Bass, *Swamp Fox,* 252)

Huger to withdraw to Hillsboro, N.C. As Tarleton moved north with 150 dragoons he picked up a Tory who had witnessed the action at Ball's plantation and who gave him accurate information about the composition of the rebel force and their line of march toward Lenud's. About 3 P.M. Tarleton attacked White as he was about to join Buford. There was no contest: White's troopers were surprised by the sudden charge, and Buford's men were standing around the ferry unprepared for action. Tarleton reported five American officers and 36 men killed or wounded, seven officers and 60 dragoons captured, the British prisoners liberated just as they were about to be ferried across the Santee, and he claims to have taken all the rebel horses. There is no mention of British casualties, and there probably were none. Cols. White, Washington, and John Jamieson joined those who escaped by swimming the river; a number were drowned in the attempt. (Bass, *Green Dragoon,* 76–77, is the primary source of the above account. Buford's strength—350—is from Ward, *W.O.R.,* 705; Bass says 200 men of the 3d Va.)

Buford met Tarleton next at WAXHAWS, 29 May.

L'EPINE. French volunteer. A nephew of Beaumarchais, he apparently went to America in 1777 and served under Sullivan. According to the *Mémoires secrets* he traveled with an officer's commission and a stock of his uncle's works for sale in America. The French archives show that as a Maj. he was A.D.C. to Kalb and then to Steuben. Thos. Conway is quoted to the effect that Epine fought "like a little hero" at Brandywine. Unsuccessful in his commercial mission, he returned to France to meet the displeasure of his uncle and the scorn of friends. A letter from Steuben to Benj. Walker on 23 Feb. '80 says: "I received a particularly

stupid letter from M. des Epiniers. He has not left for France. He asks my advice as to whether he should come back as my aide or take care of his uncle's business. You may be sure I recommended the latter." An entry of 8 Feb. '82 in the *Mémoires secrets* tells how after several inept attempts at suicide Epine accidentally set fire to his house and died of the effects. (Lasseray)

LESLIE, Alexander. *c.* 1740–1794. British general. A descendant of the famous Earl of Leven (*d.* 1661), Leslie was Lt. Col. of the 64th Regt. at Halifax prior to commencement of hostilities in America and was later ordered to Boston. He commanded the expedition to SALEM, Mass., 26 Feb. '75, which came close to starting the shooting phase of the Revolution. At the beginning of the N.Y. Campaign he was a B.G. in command of the light infantry (Appleton's), which he had led in the Battle of Long Island and at Kip's Bay. He figured prominently in the Battle of HARLEM HEIGHTS, 16 Sept. '76, being in command of the outposts attacked by Lt. Col. Thos. Knowlton. At WHITE PLAINS, 28 Oct. '76, he led two regiments in a foolhardy attack that was repulsed with heavy losses. When Cornwallis marched toward Trenton after Washington's victory of 26 Dec., Leslie's brigade of about 1,200 men was dropped off at Maidenhead (now Lawrence), where they slept soundly the night Washington's army marched past at a distance of about three miles to score their triumph at PRINCETON, 3 Jan. '77. By 1780 he was a Maj. Gen., and that summer he was picked by Clinton to lead an expedition into the Chesapeake as a strategic diversion to support the operations of Cornwallis in the Carolinas. (Clinton, *Amer Reb.,* 210) In the section of Military Operations in the SOUTHERN THEATER headed "Operations after Camden" the composition and movements of Leslie's expedition of 2,500 men to join Cornwallis are described. With orders initially to defend Camden while the main army of Cornwallis was at Winnsboro and while Tarleton went looking for Morgan, on 9 Jan. '81 he received orders to join Cornwallis for an invasion of N.C. On the 18th, Leslie reached the camp of Cornwallis just as Tarleton rode in with the survivors of his defeat at the Cowpens. (See SOUTHERN CAMPAIGNS OF GREENE, sections headed "Cornwallis Reacts," and "Hare and Hounds.")

At Cowan's Ford, N.C., 1 Feb. '81, Leslie and Gen. O'Hara were swept into the flooded Catawba when their horses lost their footing. At GUILFORD C. H., 15 Mar., Leslie commanded the British right in the opening phases of the attack and then joined O'Hara for the final assault. In late July Cornwallis sent Leslie to Charleston, apparently for reasons of health, and Clinton ordered him back to N.Y. Reaching N.Y. around mid-Aug., he was supposed to sail for Charleston on 28 Aug. but Clinton rescinded this order and held him at headquarters another two months. During this time Leslie took part in the councils of war that Clinton held during the Yorktown Campaign. In late Oct. Leslie sailed to Charleston as Cornwallis' successor in the Southern Theater. (Clinton, *op. cit.,* 354 and editor's note, 562–80 *passim*) Reaching Charleston on 8 Nov., two months after the Battle of Eutaw Springs, Leslie saw there was nothing the British army could do but try to hold Charleston. Clinton authorized withdrawal of the Savannah garrison at Leslie's discretion, and the city was evacuated by sea on 11 July '82. He withdrew from Charleston on 14 Dec. '82. (See SOUTHERN CAMPAIGNS OF GREENE for military operations during Leslie's tenure.)

Clinton apparently promoted Leslie to the "local rank" of Lt. Gen. during the later's sojourn in N.Y. after the Battle of Guilford C. H., since he refers to him by this grade as early as 14 Sept. '81. (*Ibid.,* 569) In a letter dated 3 Jan. '81, however, Germain refers to him as a B.G., which apparently was his rank in the regular establishment. (*Ibid.,* 484) Leslie's performance during the Revolution was not distinguished for much other than personal courage—he was guilty of poor security in the Princeton Campaign and his slow movement to join Cornwallis during the Cowpens Campaign contributed indirectly to the British failure. On the other hand it is strange that more has not been written about him merely on the basis of his long service and his high rank at the end of the war; Appleton's includes a brief sketch, but he is not included in *D.N.B.* or *E.B.*

LEWIS, Andrew. 1720–1781. Cont'l. general. Ireland–Va. Son of a man who fled to America after killing his Irish landlord in self-defense, settling near Staunton, Va., in 1732 and becoming one of the leading men on that frontier, Andrew settled near modern Salem, Va. He became county Lt. of Augusta, justice of the peace, and built up a considerable fortune. In 1754 he served with Washington and surrendered at Ft. Necessity. The next year he was part of Braddock's expedition but was not present at the latter's defeat. He then commanded the Sandy Creek expedition against the Indians (1756). As part of Forbes's expedition to Ft. Duquesne in 1758 he was captured about 21 Sept. '58 with Maj. (later Maj. Gen.) Grant and sent to Montreal. After his release, Lewis participated in important negotiations with the Indians, including the Treaty of Ft. Stanwix, 1768.

An impressive-looking man, over six feet tall and of an agile but exceptionally strong physique, Lewis commanded 1,000 men in DUNMORE'S WAR, 1774, and won the decisive victory at Point Pleasant on 10 Oct. His brother Charles was killed in this battle. Despite this impressive background, Lewis was not appointed B.G. of the Cont'l. Army until 1 Mar. '76. He took command of the forces at Williamsburg, Va., and at GWYNN ISLAND, 8–10 July, he commanded the action that drove royal Gov. Dunmore out of the Old Dominion. When the promotion list of 19 Feb. '77 was announced, Lewis thought he deserved an appointment as Maj. Gen., and "Washington had to spend hours smoothing down" his old comrade in arms. (Freeman, *Washington,* IV, 394–95) Lewis resigned on 15 Apr. '77, allegedly for ill health, but continued to serve in the Va. militia and on Jefferson's executive council until his death over four years later.

His brother Thomas (1718–1790) was in the House of Burgesses and in the state conventions that ratified the Federal Constitution. Another brother, William (1724–1811) served with him in the Colonial Wars, rose from Lt., 1st Va. (2 Oct. '75) to Maj., 10th Va. (12 May '79), was captured 12 May '80 at Charleston, and was a prisoner when the war ended. The third brother, Charles, was killed under Andrew's command in 1774 (above).

LEWIS, Francis. 1713–1802. Signer. Wales–N.Y. An orphan, he was reared by relatives in Wales and attended Westminster School before going into business in London. In 1738 he came to America and established mercantile houses in New York and Philadelphia. He made several trading voyages to Russia, Europe, and Africa, was twice shipwrecked, and saw his affairs prosper. In 1752 when he was Gen. Mercer's volunteer A.D.C. and clothing contractor for the troops at Oswego, he was captured

by the Indians. Sent to Montreal and then to France, he was exchanged and received as compensation a land grant from Great Britain. In 1765, a rich man, he retired to Long Island. In 1771, he returned briefly to New York and London to establish his son in business and then went back to Long Island to devote himself to public affairs. He became increasingly involved with Revolutionary activities and in 1774 was sent to the Provincial congress. In the Cont'l. Congress May '75–Nov. '79, he signed the Decl. of Indep. In the fall of 1776, the British destroyed his Long Island house and imprisoned his wife. She was finally exchanged on the personal order of Washington, but her health was ruined, and she died in 1779. In Congress, Lewis was active on the Marine, Commercial, and Secret committees. From 1779 to 1881, he was one of the Board of Admiralty commissioners. Father of Morgan Lewis.

LEWIS, Morgan. 1754–1844. Cont'l. officer. N.Y. Second son of Francis Lewis, he graduated from Princeton in 1773, studied law, and joined the army the summer of 1775. He was Capt. in the N.Y. militia at Cambridge and in N.Y.C. He was promoted to Maj. when his unit became the 2d N.Y. Cont'ls. in early 1776, and later that year, he was named Col. and deputy Q.M.G. of the Northern Army. *D.A.B.* puts this date at June '76, while Heitman gives 12 Sept. He was Gates's chief of staff at Ticonderoga and SARATOGA (19 Sept. '77) and in 1778 was named Col. He led the advance at KLOCK'S FIELD, 19 Oct. '80. In 1783 he returned to the law, passing the bar and, in 1789, entering public life as assemblyman. His marriage in 1779 to Robert R. Livingston's daughter allied him with the anti-Federalist and Republican parties, and he had a successful political career that led to his being elected N.Y. Gov. in

1804. Unable to cope with N.Y. power politics, he was soundly defeated by his former supporters in 1807. In 1812 he declined the offer to be Madison's Sec. of War (Appleton's). But he became B.G. and Q.M.G. of the U.S. Army 3 Apr. 1812. He was promoted to Maj. Gen. 2 March 1813 and served on the Niagara frontier. In 1813–15 he commanded the N.Y.C. area.

LEXINGTON AND CONCORD. 19 Apr. '75. Disorders in Boston led to the INTOLERABLE ACTS and appointment of Gen. GAGE (Br. C. in C. in America) as Gov. of the Province of Mass. to enforce these acts, particularly the Boston Port Act. After reaching Boston in May '74 Gage moved to Salem, where he had been instructed to establish the new capital. Within three months, however, patriot opposition made him move back to Boston and abandon attempts to enforce the Intolerable Acts outside that city itself. The First Cont'l. Cong. met in Philadelphia on 5 Sept., and the MASS. PROVINCIAL CONGRESS established itself in Concord as a revolutionary government. During the winter of 1774–75 the patriots raised and drilled militia units, accumulated military stores at Concord and Worcester, seized military stores in R.I. (Fort Island and New Castle), in Boston, and at Charlestown; they terrorized Loyalists and coordinated among colonies by Committeees of Correspondence.

Gage increased his BOSTON GARRISON to about 3,500 men, fortified Boston Neck, raided militia depots at Charlestown and CAMBRIDGE (1 Sept. '74), sent the abortive expedition to SALEM, Mass. (26 Feb. '75), and vigorously enforced the Port Act. Although assistance from other colonies kept Boston supplied, normal business had been at a standstill since 1 June '74, when the Port Act had gone into effect.

The British government intensified its determination to bring Boston and the rest of the province to heel. They voted to increase the garrison to 10,000, and passed more coercive acts. Furthermore, the home country refused to believe they faced a serious rebellion in America. When Gage reported it would take 20,000 men to reconquer New England, Dartmouth answered (27 Jan. '75), "I am unwilling to think that matters have come to such a pass yet." It was being noised around London that Gage lacked the qualities to deal with the situation.

On 14 Apr. '75 Gage got instructions to take some decisive action. It was suggested that he arrest leaders of the Mass. Prov. Cong., but their adjournment the next day ruled this out. Gage did decide to send an expedition to seize the supplies at Concord. A well-organized system of informers had told him where the supplies were, and he had been planning such a raid for several weeks.

On 15 Apr., a Saturday, the "flank companies" (grenadiers and light infantry) of eight regiments were ordered relieved from normal duties. About midnight (15–16 Apr.) boats taken earlier from naval vessels in the harbor for repair on shore were returned to the vessels. These activities were reported by various bands of townsmen who had been organized to patrol the city and watch for suspicious troop activity.

Sunday, 16 Apr., Dr. Joseph Warren sent Paul Revere to warn John Hancock and Sam Adams in Lexington that Gage might be sending troops to arrest them. Returning from this mission, Revere arranged with Col. Conant and others in Charlestown to flash the "one if by land, two if by sea" signal. Gage took extraordinary precautions to keep his plan secret. Lt. Col. Smith, who was to command the expedition, was not told until the last minute that his objective was Concord (French, *Concord,* 74, quoting Stedman). The order of 15 Apr. stated that the grenadiers and light infantry were being detached to learn new drill formations; the troops were not told where they were going; and elaborate measures were prescribed to assemble them after dark on the 18th.

Considering the delicate nature of the operation, there is mystery as to why Gage named fat, slow Smith to lead a detachment of elite troops in its execution. Old Col. Smith's one claim to this distinction was that he was the senior field grade officer in Boston. There has also been considerable speculation as to why Marine Maj. John Pitcairn was named second-in-command; most likely it was because the "portly, comfortably middle-aged, devout Scotsman" (S. & R., 27), "a seasoned veteran and general favorite, popular with Whigs as well as Tories" (French, *op. cit.,* 71), was the type of man Gage wanted with Smith on a mission that might call for good judgment. The best authorities find no basis for the plausible story that Pitcairn was picked because he knew the roads to Concord and had studied the village in disguise (*ibid.*), but this disregards some evidence mentioned in the sketch of PITCAIRN. Hugh, Earl Percy, was informed by Gage shortly before Smith's departure that he would lead any reserves that might be sent to Smith's assistance.

Gage's written order to Smith—the paper that started the war—read as follows:

"Sir, A Quantity of Ammunition and Provision together as Number of Cannon and small Arms having been collected at Concord for the avowed Purpose of asserting a Rebellion against His Majesty's Government, You will march with the Corps of Grenadiers

and Light Infantry put under your Command with the utmost expedition and secrecy to Concord, where you will seize and destroy all the Artillery and Ammunition, provisions, Tents & all other military stores you can find. . . ." (*Lexington to Fallen Timbers,* pp. 1, 2)

Smith's force probably numbered about 700 (French, *op. cit.,* 73), although the British Army historian, Fortescue, says 400, and 800 is generally favored by American historians (Ward, *W.O.R.,* 435 *n.*). The flank companies of the 5th, 10th, 18th, 23d, 38th, 43d, 52d, and 59th regiments accompanied Smith; that is, eight light infantry and eight grenadier companies (Fortescue). Since regimental strengths averaged about 292 rank and file, the above companies contained only about 30 men.

By the evening of 18 Apr. Boston had further indications of the British move. A soldier told the townsman with whom he was billeted that the troops were about to march. Another was left word to fall out at 8 P.M. on the Common with a day's provisions and 36 rounds. Several people saw another soldier in field dress in a store. After dark on the 18th, just after being told of the expedition by Gage, Lord Percy overheard loiterers on the Common talking about a suspected British attempt to seize the stores at Concord. Gage was shocked when Percy reported this information back to him a few minutes later, since he claimed to have told only one person other than Percy that Smith's objective was Concord. (Stedman, *Hist.,* I, 134, cited by French) (Gordon, *Hist.* I, 309, is apparently responsible for the conjecture that Gage's American wife betrayed the British plan. Alden summarizes the evidence and discredits the story in his *Gage. . . .,* pages 247–50.) Although Gage knew his plan was compromised, he believed it was too late to revoke Smith's orders.

PAUL REVERE'S RIDE

Dr. Warren sent for William Dawes and Paul Revere at about 10 P.M. to take the alarm to Concord. Dawes, about whom little is known other than that Warren had found him a resourceful courier, was dispatched by way of Boston Neck before Revere reached Warren's house. When Revere got his orders he arranged with a friend, probably John Pulling, to show the lantern signal from "North Church," which is probably the present Christ Church. (French, *op. cit.*, 79) Revere crossed to Charlestown just as the moon was rising, checked in with Conant, secured a horse, and pounded across Charlestown Neck at about 11. It was now bright moonlight. He had been warned in Charlestown that British officers were on the roads ahead; perhaps as early as noon Gage had sent about 10 armed officers to stop just such couriers as Dawes and Revere.

Turning west off the Medford (Mystic R.) road to take the most direct route, Revere saw two mounted men, whom he quickly made out to be British officers. He turned as they started toward him and raced through Medford and Menotomy. After alerting the captain of the minutemen in Medford, he "alarmed almost every house until he got to Lexington" (French, *op. cit.*, 89) about midnight. Hancock and Adams had been guests of Rev. Jonas Clark for almost a month while the Mass. Prov. Cong. met in Concord. Revere was surprised to find the house guarded. Earlier in the evening, Solomon Brown had returned to Lexington from Boston and told William Munroe, orderly sergeant of the Lexington minutemen, of seeing nine armed British officers on the road. Munroe turned

out eight of his men to stand guard on Clark's house, and Hancock sent Brown with two others to alert Concord.

Dawes reached Lexington about half an hour later than Revere, having covered a route almost four miles longer. Between 1 and 2 A.M. Revere and Dawes were halfway between Lexington and Concord when they ran into a British patrol. Revere was captured after attempting to get away. Dawes escaped back to Lexington. Dr. Samuel Prescott, who had joined them as they left Lexington, escaped to alert Concord. Solomon Brown, his two men, and a fourth individual who turned out to be an innocent peddler, had previously been captured by this patrol. Revere told the British he had alerted the countryside and that 500 militia would soon be in Lexington; he also fabricated the story that Smith's column had been delayed. Maj. Mitchel, who commanded the patrol of about eight officers and several men, was apparently taken in by Revere's yarn. All other prisoners were released, but Revere was held until the patrol neared Lexington and heard the alarm guns.

Mitchel's patrol had questioned the Lexington prisoners about Hancock and Adams, and may have had discretionary orders to capture them. If so, they abandoned the plan when they realized the countryside was alerted and that Smith's column was delayed. (French, *op. cit.* 93) The British released Revere, after taking his horse, and moved to make contact with Smith. When Hancock and Adams got Revere's first warning, Hancock had insisted he would fall out with the Lexington militia and fight, but when Revere returned to Clark's house with news of the British patrol, Hancock was finally persuaded to escape. Revere accompanied the two Patriot leaders a few miles on the road toward Philadelphia (where the Second

Cont'l. Cong. was to meet in May), and got back to Lexington at sunrise to witness the shooting.

Capt. John Parker had turned out some 130 of his minutemen at about midnight. Since there was no further evidence of the British approach, and since the night was cold, Parker dismissed his men after about an hour with orders to reassemble at the beating of a drum. "Tradition says that as many as three messengers [scouts] were sent down the Boston road, none of whom returned. Instead of regarding this as suspicious, it was taken as confirming the idea that there had been a false alarm." (French, *op. cit.*, 97)

SMITH'S ADVANCE

The grenadier and light infantry companies had formed on Boston Common at dusk. In the pitch darkness before moonrise they marched with utmost caution to a spot French identifies as being near the west side of modern Park Square. Here they were met by the boats and rowed, with muffled oars, to Lechmere's Point. The distance by water—the "sea" of Longfellow's poem about Paul Revere's Ride—was at least a mile and a quarter (French). Revolutionary landmarks of Boston's Back Bay have been obliterated by filling and construction. The place where the British landed was then Phips's Farm, later Lechmere Farm and Point, now East Cambridge. Between 11 o'clock and midnight the troops waded ashore to wait, cold and miserable, for about two hours while extra provisions were landed and distributed. Since they were carrying rations, most of the troops threw away those they had been delayed two vital hours to receive. It was between 1 and 2 A.M. that Smith finally got his column marching, starting them off through a waist-deep ford to avoid the noise of crossing a plank bridge.

By the time he reached Menotomy, about 3 A.M., Smith had ample evidence that his advance was expected. According to Gage's report, Smith called his officers together during a halt and issued orders not to fire unless fired on. Soon thereafter, apparently dissatisfied with the speed of his column, Smith ordered Pitcairn ahead with six light companies to secure the bridges at Concord. Then, having additional evidence that the countryside was alarmed, he reported this back to Gage and requested reinforcements. (As it turned out, this was the soundest tactical decision Smith made all day.)

Leading Pitcairn's advance guard was a smaller body known in modern military parlance as a "point." These men moved as stealthily as possible, keeping to the sides of the road, and taking cover when they spotted anything suspicious. In this manner they soon scooped up the scouts sent out from Lexington to bring word of their approach. They were waiting in the shadows to grab the fourth, Thaddeus Brown, when Brown's horse detected them and refused to be ridden into the trap. Brown finally read his horse's warning, turned, and clattered into Lexington at about 4:30 to tell Parker the British were half a mile away. Pitcairn, meanwhile, had made contact with Mitchel's patrol and had been told Revere's yarn about the entire countryside being alerted and the presence of 500 militia in Lexington. Apparently taken in by Revere's deception, Pitcairn slowed his advance to let Smith's column close up on him a little more.

LEXINGTON

Since not all who assembled for Parker's second call had ammunition, fewer than 70 armed men formed on the green. Others went off to the meetinghouse, where the town's supply was kept. Whereas most historians believe Parker's group numbered 60 to 70 men on Lexington green (Ward, *W.O.R.*, 37, citing Coburn and French), and that they were formed in two lines rather than the customary three, others accept the figure of about 40. The latter evidence comes from the 1826 deposition of a participant, Sylvanus Wood, who says Parker formed a *single* line of exactly 38—Wood says he walked from one end to the other and counted them. (S. &. R., 29)

Pitcairn's advance guard came in sight of Parker's little band of brave men at about 5 o'clock, just as the sun was beginning to rise. The marine major ordered his troops from march column into battle line, an "evolution" that called for men in the rear to run forward to form three parallel lines. Just as a modern football team rushes into formation with accompanying "chatter," the regulars were trained to shout and huzza as they ran into position. We may suppose that on this brisk morning, after a miserable night march, the British regulars may have put a little more zest than usual into this shouting and huzza-ing; in any event, it is much commented on in American accounts of the day.

Parker ordered his men to stand fast, but some of them started drifting away (Ward, *W.O.R.*, 37). "Don't fire unless fired upon!" he is alleged to have commanded, "But if they want a war, let it begin here!" (This is magnificent, but it is not John Parker!)

Pitcairn with two other officers galloped around the meetinghouse (which was behind his lines) and took a position on the left (west) flank of the two platoons of the 10th Infantry that had formed battle line. "Full of confidence in his light infantry, and scornful, perhaps, of the little force against him, his thought appears to have been to disarm the provincials. Several of the contemporary accounts agree that Pitcairn ordered the minutemen to lay down their arms." (French, *op. cit.*, 108)

"And what was Parker's thought now?" writes French. "Steadier than his own men, who were still hurriedly assembling, watching the oncoming regulars spread out to a front of two platoons, hearing their already triumphant shouts, and seeing that that triumph was sure because of very numbers —he must have seen at last the danger to his men, felt his responsibility for their lives, realized how futile would be any resistance. There was only one thing to do, and he did it. He gave the order to disperse and not to fire." (*Ibid.*, 109)

The Americans were disbanding when there was a single shot, followed by two or three others. A British officer ordered "Fire!" Each platoon of regulars delivered a volley at Parker's dispersing men—who were at a range of about 40 yards—and closed in with the bayonet. Probably not more than eight Americans shot back. (French, *op. cit.* 119, citing Coburn) The so-called battle was over in a matter of minutes, leaving eight Americans dead and 10 wounded. Among the dead were Park-

er's cousin, Jonas, who stood his ground after being wounded and was bayoneted while trying to reload. Jonathan Harrington, mortally wounded on the common, died at his own doorstep. One redcoat received a slight leg wound, and Pitcairn's horse had two light wounds.

WHO FIRED FIRST?

"With quick foresight," the Mass. Prov. Cong. on 22 April appointed a committee to take depositions from all participants and spectators they could find. Elbridge Gerry was chairman, and Col. James Barrett of Concord (see below) was a member. The whole purpose of the Lexington depositions was to establish only two things: that Parker's men were dispersing; that the British fired first. "Each separate deposition covers these two points and then stops." (French, *op. cit.*, 115) For some reason "the politicians who managed this matter" (*ibid.*) apparently wanted to conceal that there was any return fire from the Americans in Lexington; as a result, Concord claimed the honor of making "the first forcible resistance"—of firing "the shot heard 'round the world." This led to a second round of depositions, those of 1825, to establish that the men of Lexington had fired back. (The feud between Lexington and Concord was carried to the extreme that they refused to celebrate the centennial jointly.)

"It is impossible to say which side fired first and it is a question to-day of no historical importance," wrote James T. Adams in 1923. Without challenging either of these points, Allen French devotes 33 pages of his *Day of Concord and Lexington* to presenting and evaluating the evidence. He finds no real evidence that the British fired first, although he leans toward the theory that the first shot was from a pistol; since this weapon would have been carried by only the mounted British officers, the implication is clear. French then presents this argument. "If the first shot came from some young or reckless or irresponsible man [which seems most probable], it seems right to believe that he was not among the Americans, who for months had been told, even by their ministers, that they were not to fire first. But among the British there were hotheaded young officers, there were men who hated and despised the Yankees exceedingly, there were green and nervous men who had never seen a fight." (*Op. cit.*, 111) To rebut this astounding line of reasoning, one has only to imagine an Englishman's reaction to it; it would be belaboring the obvious to spell out that reaction here.

Bancroft says Pitcairn ordered his men to fire the first shots. Fiske goes so far as to say that when the militia refused to disperse, Pitcairn ordered his troops to fire, which they refused to do until he set the example by firing his own pistol. There is no evidence to support Bancroft's contention. As for Fiske's, Fortescue says merely, "the proved good discipline of the British makes [this theory] absolutely incredible...." (*Br. Army*, III, 150 *n.*). As epitomized in the incident at FONTENOY in 1745, the problem of leaders in this period of linear tactics was to make their men *hold* their fire until ordered to shoot; the "proved good discipline of the British" enabled them to slaughter the French guard at Fontenoy and should be considered, also, in connection with the theory of Allen French, mentioned above, that a "green and nervous" British regular, rather than an American irregular, probably fired first.

Maj. Pitcairn's account of the affair at Lexington has come down through Ezra Stiles. A John Brown talked to Pitcairn about the matter while Brown was a prisoner in Boston awaiting exchange. Brown passed Pitcairn's account on to Deputy Gov. Sessions of R.I., who relayed it to Stiles.

Pitcairn *"does not say that he saw the Colonists fire first,"* wrote Stiles in his *Literary Diary* (F. B. Dexter, ed., N.Y., 1901. vol. I, 604–5). *"He expressly says he did not see who fired first;* and yet believed the Peasants began. His account is this—that riding up to them he ordered them to disperse; which they not doing instantly, he turned about to order his Troops so to draw out as to surround and disarm them. As he turned he *saw* a Gun in a Peasant's hand from behind a Wall, *flash in the pan without going off;* and instantly or very soon 2 or 3 Guns went off by which he *found his horse wounded* & also a man *near him wounded. These Guns he did not see*, but believing they could not come from his own people, *doubted not* & so asserted that they came from our people; & that thus they began the Attack. The Impetuosity of the King's Troops were such that a promiscuous, uncommanded but general Fire took place, which Pitcairn could not prevent; tho' he struck his staff or Sword downwards with all Earnestness as the signal to forbear or cease firing." (Quoted from French, *op. cit.;* some abbreviations are altered, but *italics* are in the original version.)

Stiles concluded that although Pitcairn was innocent of firing the first shot himself and innocent of ordering his men to fire, he was deceived as to the origin of the first shots. (Ward, *W.O.R.,* 38) Pitcairn's official report, unknown to historians until the 20th century, said specifically that the firing started when a minuteman's musket flashed in the pan, and shots followed from other minutemen not on the Common. Since the American leaders who rushed to assemble depositions from spectators and participants apparently presumed that proof that a redcoat fired the first shot would establish that the British had *started the war*, it is interesting to consider the "historical doubts" raised by Harold Murdock in 1925. Murdock points out that Capt. Parker, although "a soldier of experience," formed his Lexington minutemen in a most peculiar tactical position. He did not post them where they could fire from behind cover, but stood them in broad daylight within a hundred yards of the road the British would have to take to Concord.

"Has it ever occurred to you that Parker acted under orders: that the post he took was not of his choosing? [Wrote Murdock.] Samuel Adams, the great agitator, had been a guest at Parson Clark's for days, and he was the dynamo that kept the revolutionary machinery in motion. The blood shed by Preston's men [BOSTON MASSACRE] had been ably used by Adams to solidify the popular cause; and now did he feel that the time had come to draw once more the British fire."

Commenting in 1959, Tourtellot says, "There was more to Mr. Murdock's wild surmise . . . than he supposed. Later study of the papers of the Reverend Jonas Clark . . . reveals that Clark was the undisputed political leader of Lexington. Examination of the papers of General Thomas Gage, brought to the United States in 1930, gives further forceful circumstantial evidence to support Mr. Murdock's theory. In the Gage papers . . . are the traitorous letters of Dr. Benjamin Church, a member of the Provincial Congress, to General Gage, not only reporting details of the sessions but diagnosing with thoroughness and accuracy the moods of the members and the basic problems facing the patriots. The thrust of the

Church documents is that the patriot cause was slipping, that support for it was weak, and that Sam Adams needed a new crop of martyrs—an episode like the splendidly exploited Boston Massacre.

"Now, add to this the further information that Captain Parker first put the problem to his minutemen at midnight and that they concluded not to be discovered, nor meddle or make with said regular troops. But the company did exactly the opposite three hours later— after Hancock, Adams, and probably Clark had consulted with Captain Parker." (Comment by A. B. Tourtellot to Harold Murdock's "The Nineteenth of April 1775," *American Heritage*, Vol. X, No. 5 [Aug. 1959], 64)

Hearing the British volleys two miles away (French, *op. cit.*, 141), Sam Adams said to Hancock as they continued their escape, "What a glorious morning this is!" Apparently thinking Hancock mistook this for a weather reading, Adams added, "I mean for America." (C. & M., 69)

Consider, also, Pitcairn's statement that after the first few scattered shots went off *"he found his Horse wounded* and also a man *near him wounded."* These were the only British casualties reported in the entire affair, and they appear to have been inflicted by the first scattered shots that preceded the British volleys. The American depositions establish that Parker's men did not fire until fired upon. Although not impossible, it is improbable that the regulars would fire into Pitcairn's small group off on their left flank. The finger of suspicion must therefore start moving among the American spectators around Lexington green.

For a denial of these accusations see Professor Knollenberg's article, "Did Samuel Adams Provoke the Boston Tea Party and the Clash at Lexington?",

Proceedings of the American Antiquarian Society, LXX (1960), 493–503.

CONCORD

By the time the skirmish had ended at Lexington, the remainder of Smith's force had closed up on Pitcairn's advance guard and the entire force soon started for Concord, six miles away.

Samuel Prescott had, meanwhile, brought the alarm to Concord between 1 and 2 A.M. The town's three companies of minutemen and the alarm company of old men and boys were soon reinforced by a company from Lincoln, bringing to about 150 the strength of the colonists who turned out under arms. While a patrol went toward Lexington to verify Prescott's report that the British were coming, the others busied themselves concealing or evacuating the military supplies that had not already been removed the preceding day.

The British column approached Concord about 7 A.M. Militiamen who had taken position on a ridge outside the village were flushed by Pitcairn's flank patrols without a shot's being fired on either side. Col. James Barrett, the 65-year-old local militia commander, returned to Concord at this time from overseeing removal or concealment of supplies that had been stored on his place a few miles beyond Concord. Barrett ordered his men to withdraw across North Bridge to a ridge overlooking that spot and to await reinforcements.

One light infantry company was sent to secure South Bridge, and six were sent toward North Bridge. Three of the latter were left at or near the bridge while Capt. Lawrence Parsons led the others to search Barrett's Farm, where they had been correctly informed most of the rebel supplies were kept. The Grenadiers, meanwhile, searched Concord. The raiders found little at Barrett's Farm or in Concord, since most of the supplies had been recently evacuated or hidden. The regulars conducted themselves properly at both places.

American forces on the high ground above North Bridge had, meanwhile, grown to 300 or 400 men as reinforcements arrived. They could see smoke

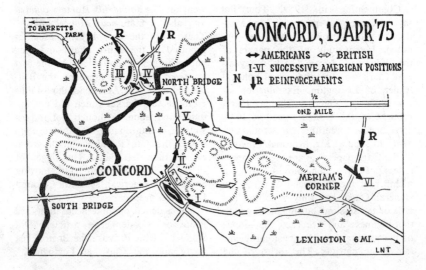

CONCORD, 19 APR '75

←→ AMERICANS ⇔ BRITISH
I-VI SUCCESSIVE AMERICAN POSITIONS
N ↓R REINFORCEMENTS
ONE MILE

TO BARRETTS FARM — NORTH BRIDGE — CONCORD — SOUTH BRIDGE — MERIAM'S CORNER — LEXINGTON 6 MI.

LNT

rising from the village and, although the British had themselves put out fires they had started in the courthouse and in a blacksmith shop, the patriots suspected the regulars were burning the town. On orders from Barrett and with instructions not to fire first, they started moving toward the bridge.

Capt. Walter Laurie's Light Company of the 43d Regt., numbering about 35 men, had been apprehensively watching the militia body increase in size. As the Americans advanced to the tune of fifes and drums, the 4th and 10th Light Companies dropped back from more advanced positions to join Laurie at the bridge. Laurie sent back to Concord for reinforcement. The Americans halted momentarily on the last rise overlooking the "rude bridge that arched the flood"—then Maj. John Buttrick led his irregulars forward against "the flower of the King's army," as the flank companies were known.

Having already been blooded at Lexington—about which fight the Concord militia knew nothing at this time—the British did not hesitate to fire first. The three British companies, however, were so formed that only one of them could bring its muskets to bear. Return fire from the minutemen drove the regulars back in disorder. In this three-minute exchange the British had three killed and eight wounded; the Americans lost two killed (Isaac Davis, captain of the Acton company, and one of his men) and three wounded. British reinforcements were late because fat old Col. Smith insisted on leading them personally.

Smith made no attempt to retake the bridge to cover Parsons' return from Barrett's Farm. But, since the Americans made no attempt to pursue or to cut Parsons off, the latter was back in Concord at 11 A.M., an hour after Smith's return. Col. Smith delayed his departure from Concord until noon, possibly because he hoped the reinforcements from Boston would arrive.

When Parsons' three light companies had recrossed North Bridge, unopposed, they passed a wounded British soldier who appeared to have been mutilated. This was the basis of reports that the Americans had been guilty of atrocities; Gage reported that this soldier had been "scalped, his Head much mangled, and his ears cut off" while still alive. Parsons' men brought the story back to the rest of Smith's command, and the latter passed it on, improved, to Lord Percy's men; the story may help account for the ruthlessness of the redcoats during the retreat.

Apparently a teen-age boy who crossed the bridge alone after the skirmish had, for some reason, struck a seriously wounded British soldier in the head with an ax or hatchet. Although some writers have tried to explain this senseless act by assuming the boy was half-witted, French says "it was not so."

MERIAM'S CORNER
TO LEXINGTON

The British covered the first mile from Concord without difficulty, but at Meriam's corner they started running the gauntlet—16 miles of it. The minutemen who had fought at North Bridge had cut around north to this point, where reinforcements from other villages were also converging. As the regulars crowded across a narrow bridge they came under fire from a range of less than 150 yards. The Americans fought Indian fashion, sniping from the cover of walls, hedges, trees, and buildings. Light infantry flank patrols moved to keep the militia out of point-blank range, killing a good many snipers who were careless about their rear, trapping and annihilating small bodies of Americans—but the tired regulars, low on ammunition, were in serious trouble. At Fiske Hill, where they tried unsuccessfully to rally, Pitcairn's horse policed its rider and charged into the American lines with the prize trophies of the war: PITCAIRN'S PISTOLS. Col. Smith was wounded in this action.

LORD PERCY TO THE RESCUE

The evening of the 18th, Gage had alerted 33-year-old Lord Percy for a possible mission to reinforce Smith. Before Gage went to bed the night of 18–19 April he had sent orders for Percy's 1st Brigade to be ready to move at 4 A.M. But the brigade major was not in his quarters when this order was delivered, and his servant forgot to give it to him when he did get home. At 5 A.M., with Percy's men snug in their bunks, Smith's request for reinforcement arrived. By 6 o'clock most of Percy's brigade had been paraded. At 7 there were inquiries as to why the marines had not shown up, and it was discovered that their orders had been delivered to Maj. Pitcairn's quarters! After having lost five hours, Percy finally moved out at 9 A.M.

Percy's force numbered about 1,400 men and included two 6-pound cannon. Units involved were the 4th, 23d, and 47th Regiments, each lacking its flank companies, and 460 marines organized into 10 companies. Crossing Boston Neck, they marched through Roxbury and toward Cambridge. The countryside was ominously deserted. At the Charles River bridge they were slowed briefly because the rebels had removed the planks, but since these were neatly stacked on the opposite shore the foot soldiers simply crossed on the stringers and replaced enough of the planking for all but the supply train to continue the march. (The two supply wagons and their 12-man guard were ambushed

and captured before they could catch up.) Moving through deserted Cambridge, the relief expedition was unable to get any news of Smith's detachment until they reached Menotomy. Soon they could hear the firing. Reaching Lexington at about 2:30 P.M., Percy deployed to cover the arrival of Smith's force.

A few minutes later the light infantrymen and grenadiers staggered exhausted into Percy's ranks. The two 6-pounders opened fire and scattered the provincials who had been following just out of musket range to capture stragglers and wounded redcoats. Rebels who took shelter in the meetinghouse, which happened to be the nearest cover, were routed by a cannon shot through that edifice. Some regulars took off in pursuit, but were stopped by the swampy ground northwest of the common, behind which the militia had withdrawn. About 3:15 Percy got Smith's tired troops back on their feet and resumed the retreat.

Although "Our General" Heath was now on the scene, lack of leadership and absence of tactical cohesion kept the American irregulars from executing the maneuver that could have annihilated the British force. (The "school solution" in a pursuit is for one portion of your command to keep maximum pressure on the rear of the enemy column while another circles ahead to cut their route of retreat.) It is interesting to speculate on whether, at this stage of the Revolution, it would have been good from a political point of view for the Americans to have annihilated these 1,800 British regulars.

The running fight from Lexington followed the same pattern as before: the Americans sniped from behind cover, the light infantry patrolled the flanks, and the British column struggled along the road. Close fighting in Menotomy resulted in 40 casualties on each side. The regulars, enraged by the "cowardly" rebel tactics of firing from cover, broke into houses along the road, killed all males they could find, looted, and burned.

Approaching Cambridge, where the Americans had gathered to cut him off (Alden, *Gage* ... , 246), Percy executed a skilful feint to indicate a return to Boston by the route he had left that morning. Moving instead for Charlestown, he was twice more brought to bay: at what is now Somerville and again at Prospect Hill. Dusk was falling when his exhausted troops crossed Charlestown Neck and reached the protection of their naval guns. The Americans could not pursue, but they fanned out to start the BOSTON SIEGE.

NUMBERS AND LOSSES

Although estimates run as high as 20,000, "it has been computed that 3,763 Americans were engaged in the day's fighting at one time or another, though perhaps not more than half that number at any one time." (Ward, *W.O.R.*, 50) New militia units were continually arriving, but others were dropping out after exhausting their 36 or 40 rounds of ammunition. American losses were 49 killed, 39 to 41 wounded, and 5 missing. Although most authorities agree to these figures, the ratio of killed to wounded—normally about 1 to 3 in land battles—is highly suspicious. British losses were 19 officers and 250 men killed and wounded, out of 1,800 involved, according to Fortescue. (*Br. Army*, III, 151) Alden says British casualties seem to have been 73 killed and 174 wounded (*Gage* ... , 246). Channing adds 26 missing to these same figures. (*Hist.*, III, 158 *n.*) As a commentary on the low quality of American tactics and MARKSMANSHIP,

Ward calculates that "only one [American] bullet out of 300 found its mark ... only one man out of 15 hit anybody." (Ward, *op. cit.*, 50).

SIGNIFICANCE

"The Day of Lexington and Concord" marked the transition from intellectual to armed rebellion. (S. & R., 40) The British were unpleasantly surprised by "the efficiency, for short and sudden effort, of the levies of the New England townships." (Fortescue, *op. cit.*, 152) Despite the general uselessness of MILITIA, they were to be even more unpleasantly surprised by this phenomenon at Saratoga.

Politically, the day furnished just what the American agitators needed to mobilize popular support of the colonists against England. An insignificant and inept military victory was skilfully used by patriot propagandists at home and abroad. Fast couriers delivered a colored account to other colonies. Israel Bissel left Watertown, six miles west of Boston, at 10 o'clock the morning of the 19th with a message from the comm. of safety to "All Friends of American Liberty" telling of the Lexington affair and of the march of Percy's column. By 23 April he was in New York, having spread the word across Conn., and he continued across N.J. to carry his message to Philadelphia. A fuller dispatch reached New York the 25th, and was relayed by night and day express riders to Baltimore (evening of the 27th), Annapolis (morning of the 28th), Edentown, N.C., on 4 May, and Charlestown, S.C., on 10 May.

England got the American version of the day's events, complete with the depositions mentioned above, 12 days before Gage's report (which arrived 10 June). The latter had been dispatched four days ahead of the American letter to "The Inhabitants of Great Britain," but a faster American ship did the trick.

Bibliography. French, *Concord*,* is the basis of this article, which has drawn heavily on Alden,* Ward,* and Fortescue * as well. Frank W. Coburn, *The Battle of April 19, 1775* (Lexington, Mass., 1912), is cited by Ward-Alden as an exhaustive and copiously annotated study of both original and secondary materials, but by a "blindly patriotic" author (Ward, *W.O.R.*, 435, 436). The revisionist work of Murdock has won the respect of historians; this article has drawn heavily on the portion of his *Nineteenth of April, 1775* (Boston, 1925) reprinted with comments by A. B. Tourtellot in *American Heritage*, Vol. X, No. 5 (Aug. 1959). New light has been shed on Lexington and Concord since the Clements Collection * became available to historians, which was after French and Murdock did their studies. Excerpts from selected contemporary letters and journals, together with valuable commentary, are to be found in the recent works cited as S. & R. * and C. & M. * A recently published book that may well supersede those of Coburn, French, and Murdock as the definitive study of Lexington and Concord is Arthur B. Tourtellot's *William Diamond's Drum . . .*, New York, 1959.

"LEXINGTON OF THE SEA." See MACHIAS, Me., May '75.

LIBERTY AFFAIR, 10 June '68. The customs officials in Boston had a long-standing grudge against John Hancock, a prosperous merchant who displayed an open contempt toward them but whose careful observance of the laws gave them no opportunity to pros-

---

ecute him. When two minor customs officers had gone below decks on one of his ships, where they had no right to be, he had ejected them by force,* and the Attorney General of the colony ruled that he was within his rights. His sloop *Liberty* reached Boston from Madeira with 25 casks of wine on 9 May '68, paid the duty, and started taking on a cargo of tar and whale oil. The law required that Hancock give bond for the new cargo before loading it, but the customs commissioners had sanctioned the practice of delaying the bond until a ship cleared the port. Seeing their chance to get even with Hancock, the commissioners ordered the vessel seized. On 10 June the *Liberty*, with a wharf official held prisoner in its cabin, was towed alongside the 50-gun frigate *Romney*. The Boston mob then turned out, assaulted customs officials on the dock, and demonstrated around their homes in such a manner that the officials fled for safety to Castle William. The officials were not actually attacked, but they reported to London that the province was in a state of insurrection, and the incident led the British authorities to a step they had tried to avoid. On 1 Oct. two regiments of regulars arrived, and the stage was set for the BOSTON "MASSACRE." (This interpretation of the *Liberty* affair, which is at some variance with the standard account that Hancock was charged with failure to pay duty on the wine [*e.g.*, Morris, *E.A.H.*, 77], is from Morgan, *Birth of the Republic*, 39–40.)

See also CUSTOMS COMMISSIONERS.

LIBERTY BELL. Not given this name until 1839 (in connection with

---

* See main bibliography at end of this book for complete identification.

* H. L. Allen, biographer of HANCOCK, says one official was nailed inside a cabin while the ship was unloaded and the other had gone home drunk.

the antislavery movement), it was originally ordered by the Provincial Council in 1751 for the Golden Jubilee of Pa.'s 1701 Charter of Privileges. Cracked in testing upon arrival, it was recast in Philadelphia. It first proclaimed American Independence when rung from the State House in Philadelphia after the Decl. of Indep. was read there 8 July '76. Hidden in Allentown, 1777–78, it was frequently rung to mark various celebrations. It was strained in tolling the obsequies of Chief Justice Marshall in 1835 and the final damage, which silenced it, occurred in 1846 when it was rung on Washington's birthday. Weighing over 2,080 pounds and costing £60, it is inscribed: "Proclaim Liberty throughout all the land unto all the inhabitants thereof." (Julian P. Boyd in *D.A.H.*) See J. B. Stoudt, *The Liberty Bells of Pennsylvania*.

LIBERTY STREET JAIL. See PRISONS. . .

LIBERTY TREES and poles. At dawn on 14 Aug. '65 two effigies were discovered in the largest of a group of elms in an enclosure where Orange and Essex Streets of old Boston converged. (Now Washington and Essex) One effigy was Andrew Oliver; the other was the Devil peeking from a huge boot, in dishonor of Lord Bute, whom Bostoners blamed for the Stamp Act. This elm, already some 120 years old, had thus made its professional debut as the original Liberty Tree, and others rapidly appeared throughout the colonies. (Forbes, *Revere*, 97) The Boston tree was cut down by British soldiers in 1775 and yielded 14 cords of firewood. (Lloyd C. M. Hare in *D.A.H.*) A Liberty Pole was later erected on the spot.

The best-known Liberty Pole, according to Hare (*op. cit.*) was erected in N.Y.C. in 1766, with approval of the royal governor, to celebrate repeal of the Stamp Act. Such trees and poles became the symbols before which Sons of Liberty met to stir up opposition to the crown. The affair of the MASS. CIRCULAR LETTER and the famous Issue No. 45 of John WILKES's magazine inspired a numerology: a Liberty Tree would have 92 branches and the stubs of 17 others; a 45-foot Liberty Pole would be raised by 92 Sons of Liberty. (Hare, *op. cit.*)

LIFE GUARD of Washington. Officially The Commander-in-Chief's Guard but commonly called The Life Guard, it was organized in 1776 at the beginning of the N.Y. Campaign. With a strength of 180 men, it was first commanded by Capt. Caleb Gibbs of R.I., whose appointment to this post was 12 Mar. '76. (Heitman, source of this date, says Gibbs commanded "a Company of Washington's Guards." Lossing says Gibbs commanded the entire unit.) Other officers of the bodyguard were Henry P. Livingston, Wm. Colfax (who succeeded Gibbs as C.O. toward the end of 1779, according to Lossing), and Benj. Goymes. During the winter of 1779–80 the strength of the unit was increased to 250, the next spring it dropped back to 180, and in 1783 it numbered 64 enlisted men. Despite its impressive unit designation and its important mission, "Washington's Life Guard" appears to have been nothing more than what today would be called a headquarters security detachment. D. S. Freeman has only a few passing references to Gibbs and his Guard but cites *The Commander-in-Chief's Guard, Revolutionary War* by Carlos E. Godfrey (Washington, 1904). Lossing has some material on the unit in II, 120–21.

LIGHT-HOUSE ISLAND (near Boston), Mass. See GREAT BREWSTER.

LIGHT-HOUSE ISLAND, N.Y. Another name for Governor's Island, in N.Y. harbor.

LIGHT-HOUSE ISLAND, S.C. Opposite the main ship channel into Charleston harbor, this island was the middle portion of a feature known collectively as Morris Island (Scribner's *Atlas*, 69). The southern of the three islands making up this feature was called Coffin Land (map facing p. 158 of Clinton's *American Rebellion*).

LIGHT INFANTRY had become standard in European armies shortly before the Revolution and were in one of the two FLANK COMPANIES in British regiments. So called because they were "light" in equipment and armament to give them maximum mobility for their primary role as skirmishers, the first light infantry of the American army were the companies of RIFLEMEN organized in 1775. Later, when Washington was struggling with the problems presented by the shortage of trained military manpower, it was decided that each Cont'l. regiment would form a light infantry company and keep it up to strength regardless of how understrength the rest of the regiment became. On 28 Aug. '77, with the detachment of Morgan's newly formed "Corps of Rangers" north to oppose Burgoyne, Washington ordered the formation of what became known as MAXWELL'S LIGHT INFANTRY.

Thereafter the American light infantry was a corps of select troops drawn from line regiments for short periods of time and returned to these units. Washington used them as an elite corps for specific missions. Based on his recommendations to a committee that visited Valley Forge the winter of 1777–78, on 27 May '78 Congress decreed that each infantry battalion (regiment) would have nine companies, one of which would be light infantry; the lat-

ter company was to be kept up to strength and would be detached during operations to form a Corps of Light Infantry. Dan Morgan returned from Saratoga with his rifle corps (18 Nov. '77), and during the summer of 1778 he commanded the Light Infantry Corps. (Lerwill, 27) He did little with them since major operations ended with Monmouth, 28 June, and about 1 Dec. the men were returned to their parent regiments. (*Ibid.*)

The organization formed in 1779, and that distinguished itself at Stony Point, was WAYNE'S LIGHT INFANTRY. (The temperamental Dan MORGAN resigned when he learned he was not to have the command.) This force was disbanded by 15 Dec. '79.

The Light Infantry Corps for the campaign of 1780 was ordered into existence on 16 July. Initially commanded by St. Clair, it was led by Lafayette from 8 Aug. '80 until disbanded on 26 Nov. '80. The two-brigade division had little opportunity to distinguish itself during this year of relative inactivity in the North.

On 1 Feb. '81 the new corps was formed. The situation was desperate in the South, which was why the corps was formed so early this year, and Lafayette led them in the VIRGINIA MILITARY OPERATIONS of 1781, including the YORKTOWN CAMPAIGN. They particularly distinguished themselves under Hamilton in the assault on Redoubt No. 10. (Composition of Lafayette's Force is detailed under the two cross references.)

Since the experience of Frederick the Great against the Austrians had led him to adopt their use of fast-moving, lightly armed marksmen in regular warfare, making him really the modern innovator of light infantry—he even adopted the Austrian term of *jäger*, hunter—the German mercenaries came to America with JÄGER companies. Thos. GAGE is credited with pioneering the idea in the British Army, and from the very beginning of the Revolution the British used light infantry with great effect. Cornwallis distinguished himself in the early campaigns as commander of the light infantry corps. Another outstanding British leader of light infantry was Robert ABERCROMBY.

LILLINGTON, Alexander. Name by which John Alexander LILLINGTON was known.

LILLINGTON, John. Militia officer. N.C. Son of Gen. John Alexander LILLINGTON, he came home from college in Philadelphia to fight in the Revolution. Commissioned Lt. of the 1st N.C. on 1 Sept. '75, he resigned in May '76, and was Col. of militia from 1779 to 1782.

LILLINGTON, John Alexander. d. 1786. Militia officer. N.C. The son of Col. George Lillington, a British officer who fought in the West Indies, settled on Barbados and became a member of the Royal Council in 1698, John Alexander emigrated to N.C. On the N.E. branch of the Cape Fear River, about 30 miles above Wilmington, he built "Lillington Hall" in 1734. Apparently he was a wealthy and elderly man when the Revolution started, but he sided from the first with the patriot party, served on the Wilmington council of safety, became Col. of militia, and led a force of 150 minutemen from Wilmington in the important victory over the Highlanders at MOORES CREEK BRIDGE, N.C., 27 Feb. '76. On 15 Apr. '76 he was commissioned Col. of the 6th N.C., but on 16 May '76 he resigned and served throughout the rest of the war as a militia B.G. He and his son, Col. John Lillington, took part in Gen. Gates's ill-fated CAMDEN CAMPAIGN, probably as part of the fleet-footed N.C. militia force commanded

by Lillington's friend and neighbor Richard Caswell.

A man of great size and strength, he lived to "a good old age." He and his son are buried near "Lillington Hall," which is said to have been saved from the Tory torch by the interposition of Tory neighbors who appreciated his kindness. Although his tomb is inscribed "John Alexander Lillington" and he is so listed in Heitman's *Historical Register,* he signed his name "Alex Lillington." His autograph, a reproduction of his crescent cap badge with the initials "A * L," and a drawing of "Lillington Hall" made in 1852 are in Lossing, along with a biographical sketch based on information supplied to Lossing by a descendant. (II, 585 n.–587 n.)

LINCOLN, Benjamin. 1733–1810. Cont'l. general. Mass. Coming from a long-established (1632) but undistinguished family in Mass., Lincoln had only a common school education, although his wartime dispatches subsequently showed a good command of the written word. (James Truslow Adams in *D.A.B.*) His father was a maltster, farmer, and a representative from Hingham in the General Court. Benjamin was chosen town clerk in 1757, justice of the peace in 1762, and became a moderately prosperous farmer. Meanwhile he had worked up in the militia hierarchy from Adj. of Suffolk county's 3d Regt. in July '55 to Lt. Col. in Jan. '72. He served in the colonial legislature, the local committee of correspondence, and the provincial congress.

Lincoln's wartime career during the first year and a half varied markedly from the norm. When he met Washington at Cambridge on 2 July '75, Lincoln was only a Lt. Col. of militia. For another year and a half he remained a state militia officer, although he rose in that service from B.G. in Feb. '76 to Maj. Gen. in May '76. On 2 Aug.

'76 he was given command of Mass. troops around Boston and in Sept. he commanded the militia regiments raised to reinforce the defenses of N.Y. During this time he became known to Washington, who apparently saw he was "an abler and more industrious man than his great bulk and his loose jowl would indicate." (Freeman, *Washington*, V, 385B) The C. in C. "paid him an odd compliment," as Freeman puts it (*ibid.*), by forgetting that Lincoln did not have a Cont'l. commission (*ibid.*, IV, 394 and *n.*) and (in early 1777) by naming him in a postscript of a letter to Congress as "an excellent officer, and worthy of your notice in the Continental Line." Congress reacted promptly and Lincoln was one of the five officers appointed Maj. Gen. on the list of 19 Feb. '77. So Lincoln moved from a late-blooming militia general, whose main assignment had been training state troops, to No. 16 on the list of Cont'l. Maj. Gens.*

As a militia general Lincoln had commanded troops in Heath's mismanaged diversion against FT. INDEPENDENCE, N.Y., Jan. '77. Soon thereafter he joined Washington at Morristown with militia reinforcements. At BOUND BROOK, N.J., 13 Apr. '77, his advance detachment was surprised, but Lincoln extricated his command without serious loss. On 24 Apr. his division and Stephen's were ordered south toward the Delaware when Washington saw that the British were probably moving from N.Y. by water to attack Philadelphia. But Washington also had to watch the progress of Burgoyne's Offensive, and on 24 July he ordered

---

* ARNOLD, among others, was infuriated at being passed over, and his commission as Maj. Gen. was later backdated to place him ahead of the five promoted 19 Feb. '77.

Lincoln to join Schuyler and assume command of the New England militia forming east of the Hudson. This mission presented Lincoln with a real test when he arrived to find the militia being commanded by John Stark, who refused to recognize the authority of Congress. Lincoln's masterly handling of this situation is covered under the BENNINGTON RAID, Aug. '77. After directing the fruitful TICONDEROGA RAID against Burgoyne's supply line, Lincoln moved his militia to reinforce Gates in the defensive position on Bemis Heights. By 29 Sept., after the First Battle of Saratoga (19 Sept.), all his troops had arrived. During the Second Battle of Saratoga, 7 Oct., Lincoln commanded the American defenses (hence saw no action). Leading a small force forward the next day, he received a severe leg wound. For the next 10 months he convalesced at Hingham, and he was left permanently lame. (Appleton's)

Rejoining Washington in Aug. '78, he offered to resign during the controversy Benedict ARNOLD had created over promotions, but he was prevailed on to remain in the service. On 25 Sept. Congress appointed him commander of the Southern Dept., a decision on which Washington was not consulted but of which he approved.

Detained 10 days in Philadelphia by Congress, he reached Charleston on 4 Dec. '78. Too late to play any part in preventing the British capture of Savannah, 29 Dec., his subsequent actions are covered in the section headed "Lincoln's Operations" in the article on the SOUTHERN THEATER.

After surrendering Charleston on 12 May '80 he was paroled but his arrival in Philadelphia was delayed for various reasons until July. He asked for a court of inquiry, but none was appointed and no charges were made against him.

(See CHARLESTON EXPED. OF . . . '80, SOUTHERN THEATER, and their cross references for an evaluation of his generalship during this period.) Back to the farm at Hingham, Lincoln waited until Nov. to be exchanged for Gens. Phillips and Riedesel. (The exchange was approved 13 Oct.) That winter he raised recruits and gathered supplies in his home state, and the next summer he commanded troops in the vicinity of N.Y.C. He was the Maj. Gen. picked to lead the American element of the allied army that marched south for the Yorktown Campaign. Freeman points out that while "Washington did not select Lincoln because of special regard for the skill of the Massachusetts General, he had not the least reason to regret that, after McDougall declined, Lincoln was the officer next in seniority." Freeman goes on to give this capsule evaluation of the general's military career: "Brilliant? No. A great strategist? No. An administrator of parts? Yes, and better than he was credited with being. The word that best fitted him was *solid.*" (*Op. cit.,* V, 385B)

Various myths in connection with Lincoln's role in the final surrender are covered toward the end of the article on the YORKTOWN CAMPAIGN. In brief, Lincoln was not selected to receive the surrender in compensation for his surrender at Charleston, nor was he handed the sword of Cornwallis. On 30 Oct. '81 Lincoln was appointed Sec. of War, a post he held two years, until the peace treaty was signed.

He returned to Hingham and was almost ruined by speculating in land in Maine. About 1 Jan. '87 he was appointed to lead troops against Shays's Rebellion, and after a famous night march (2–3 Feb.) he captured the 150 survivors of Shays's band. In 1788 he was a member of the convention to consider ratification of the federal Constitution and he worked effectively for its ratification. This same year he became Lt. Gov., but was defeated for this office in 1789. His appointment as collector of the port of Boston helped him out of straitened circumstances (*D.A.B.*). In 1789 and 1793 he was a federal commissioner to negotiate boundary treaties with the Indians.

Harvard gave Lincoln an M.A. degree in 1780. He became a member of the American Academy of Arts and Sciences and of the Mass. Hist. Soc. He wrote papers on such diverse topics as the migration of fish, the soil and climate of Maine, "The Religious State of the Eastern Counties," and "Indian Tribes, the Causes of their Decrease, etc." On 1 Mar. 1809 he retired from his post at Boston and died at Hingham on 9 May '10. His biography, by Francis Bowen, appeared in 1847.

LINDLEY'S MILL (Cane Creek), N.C., 12 Sept. '81. See HILLSBORO RAID.

LINE. In the sense of a FORMATION, a line is a row or rank of soldiers or ships, as distinguished from a column. By extension, this came to mean the combatant elements of an army or navy, and it further had the significance of "regulars," as distinguished from MILITIA. In the British Army, whence the Americans got the term, "the line" meant "the regular and numbered troops as distinguished from the guards and the auxiliary forces" (*O.U.D.*); hence certain units that were "regular" in the sense of being in the permanent, professional service, were not "of the line" —the Guards, for example (*ibid.*). In the American Army of the Revolution the terms "Cont'l. Line" and "CONT'L. ARMY" may be considered synonymous. A "line officer" belongs to the combatant branch of the Army (*Dict. of U.S. Army Terms,* Aug. 1950), and there is a further connotation of "command," as distinguished from "staff." (See Con-way Cabal and Tronson de Coudray for examples of promotions "on the staff" rather than "in the line.")

A "ship of the line [of battle]" was one large enough to take part in the main action, and in the 18th century this meant one of 74 guns or more.

You will note that throughout this discussion there is an almost mystical connotation in the word "line." This can be explained by reminding the reader that the 18th century was the period of "linear tactics" that had evolved with the use of firearms, as opposed to the phalanx concept that was more effective in the day of the spear and sword. In order to deliver the most effective firepower from muskets (or naval guns), which were slow to load, the commander formed a "line of battle"—quite literally. In naval tactics this line could be maneuvered, the commander's dream being to "cross the T," but in land warfare it took hours to form the line and, once formed, it advanced to victory or defeat—it simply could not be maneuvered. (The maneuvering was done by the infantry and cavalry "auxiliaries." See Light Infantry.) "The line" therefore won the day or lost it by disciplined, nerveless delivery of sustained fire, as explained in the article on Muskets and Musketry.

See my *Military Customs and Traditions* for a simplified explanation of the evolution of weapons and tactics, and for a bibliography of standard works in this field.

LINE OF COMMUNICATIONS. A route by land or water that connects an operating military force with its base and along which move supplies and reinforcements as well as messages.

LINSTOCK. Device for holding the slow match with which cannon were fired.

LIPPINCOTT, Richard. Tory officer in Huddy–Asgill Affair.

LITTLE EGG HARBOR, N.J., 4–5 Oct. '78. To raid this privateers' nest, a few miles north of modern Atlantic City, Capt. Patrick Ferguson marched with 300 men of the 70th Regt. and the 3d N.J. (Tory) Regt., while a sizable naval force approached from the opposite direction to support him. Pulaski's Legion was sent to oppose the British, but the latter destroyed 10 large vessels (most of them prizes) and moved 20 miles up the Mullica River destroying storehouses, shipyards, and houses of prominent patriots. When Ferguson returned to the mouth of the river he learned that Pulaski was camped a few miles away and that his security measures were lax. Capt. Gustav Juliet has been accused of deserting to the enemy and revealing this information. (Appleton's, "Pulaski") Ferguson embarked 250 men in small boats and rowed 10 miles under cover of darkness to surprise the infantry of Pulaski's Legion at Mincock Island. About 4 A.M. on 5 Oct. the British regulars and Tories charged into three houses and killed 50 officers and men with the bayonet. Col. de Boze, commander of the Legion infantry, was killed. Pulaski arrived with the dragoons, rallied the infantry survivors, and drove Ferguson back to his boats in some confusion and with the loss of several men captured.

The Americans raised the charge of massacre, and the victors of this coup offered the usual denials. Authorities disagree on the date of the action. It is mentioned in Heath's *Memoirs* under the date of 5 Oct., and Fisher speaks of its taking place about a week after the 28 Sept. massacre at Tappan. (*Struggle*, II, 221) Heitman says Boze was killed 15 Oct. and other writers give this as the date of the action. (*E.g.*, Ward, *W.O.R.*, 617)

LIVINGSTON, Abraham. Cont'l. officer. Canada. A brother of Richard and James,* he became Capt. in the latter's regiment 18 Dec. '76 (according to Heitman; this date almost certainly should read '75), retired 1 Jan. '81, and served subsequently as Capt. of N.Y. Levies. (Heitman, 353) See also CANADIAN REGT., 1st.

LIVINGSTON, Brockholst. See LIVINGSTON, Henry Brockholst.

LIVINGSTON, Henry Beekman. 1750–1831. Cont'l. officer. N.Y. Son of Robert R., he raised a company and was named Capt. 4th N.Y. 28 June '75. He went with his brother-in-law Gen. Richard Montgomery to Quebec and acted as his A.D.C. July to Dec. '75. For his part in the capture of Chambly, he was given a sword of honor by the Cont'l. Congress 12 Dec. '75. In Feb. '76 he became A.D.C. to Schuyler and on 21 Nov. of that year he was made Col. of the 4th N.Y. He played a decisive part in the battle of MONMOUTH, 28 June '78. (See section headed "Final Phase. . . .") In the battle of R.I., 29 Aug. '78 (see NEWPORT), he and Col. John Laurens commanded the two columns of light troops that first attacked the oncoming British force. Greene commended him for his performance in the battle. (See Henry Brockholst LIVINGSTON) He resigned from the army on 13 Jan. '79.

See also LIVINGSTON FAMILY.

LIVINGSTON, Henry Brockholst. 1757–1823. Cont'l. officer. N.Y. After graduating from Princeton in 1774, this son of William Livingston entered the army in 1775 as Capt. and A.D.C. to Schuyler. In Dec. '75 he was named Maj. 3d N.Y. and then became Lt. Col. and A.D.C. to St. Clair on 8 Mar. '76. He was in the Ticonderoga campaign and on Arnold's staff. After the first

* See LIVINGSTON FAMILY.

battle of Saratoga he wrote to Schuyler (23 Sept. '77):

"I am much distressed at Gen. Arnold's determination to retire from the army at this important crisis. His presence was never more necessary. He is the life and soul of the troops. Believe me, Sir, to him and to him alone is due the honor of our late victory.* * * The difference between him and Mr. Gates has arisen to too great a height to admit of a compromise. [After summarizing the strained relations between Arnold and Gates, and informing Schuyler that Arnold was leaving the next day for Albany, Livingston concludes his letter.] The reason of the present disagreement between two old cronies is simply this—*Arnold* is your friend. I shall attend the general down. Chagrinning as it may be for me to leave the army at a time when an opportunity is offering for every young fellow to distinguish himself, I can no longer submit to the command of a man whom I abhor from my very soul.* * * A cloud is gathering and may ere long burst on his head." (C. & M., 583–84, from Schuyler Papers, N.Y.P.L.)

In his report to Washington on the battle of NEWPORT, 29 Aug. '78, Greene wrote: "Lieutenant-colonel [Henry Brockholst] Livingston, Colonel Jackson and Colonel Henry B. [Beekman] Livingston did themselves great honor in the transactions of the day" (C. & M., 720). In 1779 he took a 12-month leave of absence to serve as private secretary to his brother-in-law John Jay during Jay's mission to Spain and was captured on his return trip in 1782 by the British. Jailed in N.Y.C., he was freed almost immediately on the order of Sir Guy Carleton and sent home on parole. Enforcedly a noncombatant, he then went to Albany to study law and was admitted to the bar in 1783. At this point he dropped his

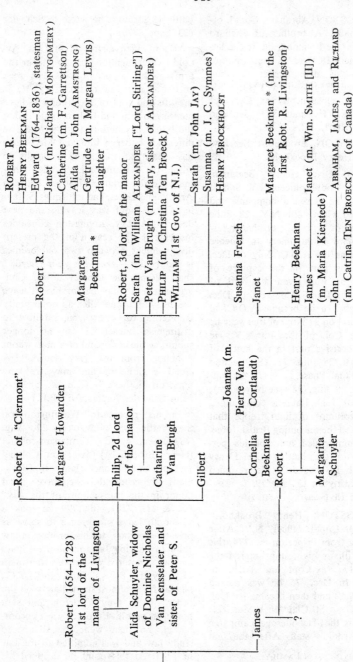

LIVINGSTON FAMILY OF NEW YORK

* Note that Margaret Beekman married Robert R. Livingston, the grandson of her father's brother.

first name and was thereafter known as Brockholst Livingston. He became a highly successful lawyer and an anti-Federalist. In 1802 he was named to the state supreme court, and in 1807 he became associate justice of the U.S. Supreme Court. He was a founder of the N.Y. Historical Society in 1805 and in 1808 helped organize the state's public school system. See LIVINGSTON FAMILY.

LIVINGSTON, James. 1747–1832. Cont'l. officer. Canada. He was distantly related to the N.Y. Livingstons through his father, John, who was the grand-nephew of Robert Livingston, "first lord of the manor." His mother was Catryna, daughter of Gen. Abraham Ten Broeck and Elizabeth van Rensselaer, and James probably was born in Montreal. Having settled in the latter place shortly after their marriage, James's parents returned to N.Y. when the Revolution started, but James and his brothers Richard and Abraham joined the column of the Canada Invasion that was led by their kinsman, Gen. Richard Montgomery. (See LIVINGSTON FAMILY) James raised a body of refugees and led them in the operations around CHAMBLY, 18 Oct. '75. On 20 Nov. this unit was designated the 1st Canadian Regt., and he was named its Col. After the disastrous attack on QUEBEC he found himself without a command, according to Katharine E. Crane in *D.A.B.*, but a week later, on 8 Jan. '76, Congress commissioned him Col., and shortly thereafter he was given "an additional battalion of the New York line." (*Ibid.*) Heitman, on the other hand, shows him as Col. of the 1st Canadian Regt. until his retirement 1 Jan. '81 (pp. 16, 354). Livingston served under Arnold in the relief of Ft. Stanwix and fought in the two battles of Saratoga.

As commander of the garrisons around Kings Ferry he figured prominently in the events surrounding ARNOLD'S TREASON. (See his firing on the *Vulture,* which indirectly resulted in Arnold's exposure, his visit from "John Anderson," and Washington's suspicion of Livingston's loyalty.)

In 1786, 1787, and 1789–91 he was in the state assembly. He was the grandfather of Gerrit Smith and Elizabeth Cady Stanton, reformers and abolitionists.

LIVINGSTON, Philip. 1716–1778. Signer. N.Y. Fifth son of Philip, second lord of the manor, he graduated from Yale in 1737 and became an importer in N.Y.C. He grew wealthy from trade and privateering during the French wars and entered enthusiastically into the civic life of N.Y.C. He contributed to the establishment of Columbia (then King's College) and gave a chair of divinity at Yale. He helped organize the N.Y. Society Library in 1754, the St. Andrew's Society, the N.Y. Chamber of Commerce, and N.Y. Hospital. He was elected a city alderman 1754–63. He was also elected to the provincial assembly 1758–69, terminating with its dissolution. An early partisan of independence, he corresponded with Edmund Burke and was a delegate to the Stamp Act Congress in 1765, although he disapproved of the rioting of the Sons of Liberty. He opposed the Intolerable Acts and sat in the Cont'l. Congress from Sept. '74 until his death 12 June '78. John Adams describes him as a conservative, saying ". . . [he] is a great, rough rapid mortal. There is no holding any conversation with him. He blusters away; says if England should turn us adrift, we should instantly go to civil wars among ourselves." John A. Krout, in *D.A.B.*, says that he and his cousin Robert R. "apparently had an arrangement whereby one would be in New York [attending to provincial affairs] while the other was attending sessions in Philadelphia." Neither Livingston was in Philadelphia when the Decl. of Indep. was voted upon, but Philip signed it in Aug. '76. "Dignified" is the word most often used to describe him, and his austerity blocked close friendships, but he gave generously of his energies and money, underwriting the Cont'l. Cong. as well as many philanthropies. See LIVINGSTON FAMILY.

LIVINGSTON, Richard. Cont'l officer. Canada. A brother of James LIVINGSTON, he was Lt. Col. of the latter's CANADIAN REGT. from 18 Dec. '76 until 2 Nov. '79, according to Heitman. (Pp. 16, 354) Since Abraham and Richard are known to have joined Montgomery's column of the Canada Invasion about the same time as did their brother James, it is likely that their commissions in the 1st Canadian Regt. were dated 1775, not 1776. Richard was captured at Ft. Montgomery, 6 Oct. '77. He resigned 2 Nov. '79, and according to Heitman he died in 1786.

LIVINGSTON, Robert R.* 1746–1813. Statesman, diplomat. N.Y. Scion of the distinguished LIVINGSTON FAMILY, he was to become one of its most outstanding members. After graduating from King's College (Columbia) in 1765 he studied law, was admitted in 1770 to the bar, and for a short time was in practice together with his college classmate and relative by marriage, John Jay. In 1773 Gov. Tryon named him Recorder of the City of N.Y., but two years later he lost this post because

* This is not an initial in the sense of standing for a middle name. His father was called Robert R. to distinguish him as Robert son of Robert from the other Roberts in the family. This was standard practice among N.Y. families at that time. (*D.A.B.*, "Robt. R. Livingston [Sr.]")

of his revolutionary leanings. He immediately was elected to the Cont'l. Cong. and was a delegate during the periods 1775–76, 1779–81, and 1784–85. He was on the committee that drafted the Decl. of Indep., but although he felt that independence was both desirable and inevitable he did not think that the time had yet come. Accordingly, Livingston was one of the principal advocates of postponing the issue; he did not vote for the Decl. of Indep. and when the time for signing came he was absent. It should be pointed out, however, that N.Y. did not decide until 9 July that its delegates should vote for independence, and Livingston had left for N.Y. on the 15th to sit in the newly elected state convention.

In the Cont'l. Cong. Livingston worked hard and ably on many important committees. "Few other members were more indefatigable or more in demand as committee members, and probably no one else showed a greater versatility in the variety of work in which he engaged," writes Robert C. Hayes in *D.A.B.* Yet it was after the Revolution had been won that Livingston most distinguished himself.

After Cong. established a department of foreign affairs on 10 Jan. '81 they rejected various candidates to elect Livingston secretary of this department on 10 Aug. In this capacity he had a key role in the Peace Negotiations and in establishing diplomatic precedents. In June '83 he resigned, after twice being prevailed on to remain at his post. He had pointed out that his salary was $3,000 less than his expenses, but the real reason for his resignation may have been due to the vacillating and improper actions of Cong. (*Ibid.*)

In state politics he was a member of the N.Y. congress and committee of safety of 1776. The next year he was on the council of safety and on the committee to write the state constitution. Chancellor of the state from 1777 to 1801, he administered the oath of office to President Washington in 1789. In 1788, meanwhile, he had chaired the N.Y. convention that ratified the Constitution, and as head of the Livingston faction he was second only to Hamilton as a Federalist leader. When the new government failed to recognize his services with appropriate patronage he changed sides and took his relatives with him into the Republican camp around 1791. He helped Aaron Burr take away the U.S. Senate seat of Philip Schuyler and disagreed with Hamilton's financial plans, particularly the matter of "ASSUMPTION." A leading opponent of Jay's Treaty, in 1795 he published, under the name of "Cato," his *Examination of the Treaty*.... In 1801 he accepted Jefferson's nomination as minister to France, having previously declined to become Sec. of the Navy. In negotiating the La. Purchase he accomplished what Henry Adams has called "the greatest diplomatic success recorded in American history" (*Hist. of U.S.*, II, 48, quoted in *D.A.B.*). Resigning his ministerial post in the autumn of 1804, he again retired to "Clermont," the family estate he had left in 1781 to take his previous public office.

Experimenting in agriculture and corresponding with learned men, he also pursued an earlier interest in steam navigation. While in Paris he had given technical and financial aid that made the experiments of Robert Fulton possible. Transferring their experiments from the Seine to the Hudson, by 1807 they had produced the *Clermont,* the first practical steamboat. Livingston used his political influence to get a monopoly for steam navigation on the Hudson, but plowed his earnings back into the development of the steamboat.

Livingston founded the American Academy of Fine Arts. "As a versatile intellectual luminary, a jurist, and a political leader," writes R. C. Hayes in *D.A.B.,* "he occupied a higher place in the esteem of his contemporaries than it has been his lot to retain in the memory of his countrymen."

See E. B. Livingston, *The Livingstons of Livingston Manor* (1927). In *The American Secretaries of State and their Diplomacy* (10 vols., 1927–29), Samuel F. Bemis (ed.) deals in vol. 1 with Livingston's and John Jay's tenures as secretaries for foreign affairs. Articles on Livingston's role in the La. Purchase have been published in the June 1904 issue of the *Columbia Univ. Quarterly* and the 1906 *Proceedings of the N.Y. State Hist. Association.*

LIVINGSTON, William. 1723–1790. Congressman, Gov. of N.Y. Reared by his maternal grandmother in Albany, he was the son of Philip, the second lord of the manor, and brother of Philip, the Signer. He spent his fourteenth year as a missionary among the Mohawks and the next year entered Yale, graduating in 1741 at the head of his class. He then studied law under James Alexander, father of William Alexander (alias "Lord Stirling"). It was then that his liberal philosophy began to take shape, and his political views were further influenced by a group of friends, mostly Calvinist, who disputed the dominance of the Anglican gentry. This is particularly interesting, for Livingston, while not Anglican, was most certainly gentry and, further, kin by blood and marriage to almost every important Hudson River family. He was admitted to the bar in 1745 and became "a leader among those of assured position who like to be known as supporters of the popular cause.

Petulant and impatient of restraint, he . . . aroused . . . resentment . . . by his sweeping criticism of established institutions." (John A. Krout in *D.A.B.*) He continued to oppose the Anglican projects, among them King's College, and this brought him into dispute with the De Lanceys, thereby causing the formation of the Livingston and De Lancey factions in provincial politics. In 1758 his party had driven the other family from control of the assembly, and he became the acknowledged leader in the pre-Revolutionary resistance to Crown interference in provincial affairs and, ultimately, the Stamp Act. When his patrician companions became alarmed at the riots inspired by the Sons of Liberty, Livingston tried to reconcile the Sons and their more radical allies to a temporizing position. This was completely unsuccessful, and by 1769 the De Lanceys regained control of the assembly. At this point, dispirited by his political defeats, he moved in May '72 to his country house "Liberty Hall" near Elizabethtown, N.J. He quickly became a member of the local committee of correspondence and was sent by N.J. to the first Cont'l. Congress, serving until 5 June '76. On that date, he took command of the state's militia as B.G. and resigned 31 Aug. '76 upon election as the first governor. He held this post for fourteen trying years and used his "boundless energy" to lead his state through the war and to face the problems of the young country. He helped draft the federal Constitution and was influential in its ratification in his state.

William Livingston had been an associate of William SMITH (II) in law and had collaborated with him on the *Laws of N.Y....* (1752, 1762) and on *Military Operations in North America ...* (1757).

See also LIVINGSTON FAMILY.

LIVINGSTON FAMILY OF N.Y.

The founder of the family in America was the son of a vigorous Scottish minister, John, who took his family to Rotterdam in 1663. Here young Robert became as fluent in Dutch as he was in English, and when he appeared in Albany in 1674, the year the colony of N.Y. passed from Dutch to English control, he quickly became a success in that hybrid society. His marriage in 1679 to Alida Schuyler, widow of Nicholas Van Rensselaer and sister of Peter Schuyler, brought him social connections with two of the most important families in the province. (See SCHUYLER FAMILY and VAN RENSSELAER FAMILY) He established the 160,000-acre manor of Livingston on the east side of the Hudson below Albany (in the present counties of Dutchess and Columbia), and left it to his son Philip. His younger son, Robert, received 13,000 acres at "Clermont." These two sons and their descendants built on the fame and fortune of their father to become a dominant force in N.Y. and beyond. Those whose names are given in CAPITALS in the chart on p. 640 are covered in individual articles.

See T. S. Clarkson, *A Biographical History of Clermont* (1869) and E. B. Livingston, *The Livingstons of Livingston Manor* (1910).

LIVIUS, Peter. 1729–1795. Canadian jurist. Born in England, he settled in N.H., was given an honorary M.A. degree by Harvard in 1767, was a member of the royal council, and moved to Canada in the early stages of the Revolution. On 31 May '77 he was appointed chief justice of Canada. A year later Carleton dismissed him without giving a reason, declined to appear before the privy council to justify this act, and Livius was restored by an order dated 25 Mar. '79. (*D.N.B.*) He retained the post until 1786, when he returned to

England. In 1778, after leaving N.H. for Canada, he was proscribed as a Loyalist. (Appleton's)

LLOYD'S NECK, L.I., N.Y. 5 Sept. '79. With 150 dismounted dragoons Maj. Benj. Tallmadge left Shippan Point, near Stamford, Conn., and surprised 500 Tories at this place (due south of Stamford). He returned before dawn on the 6th with most of the garrison as prisoners and without having lost a man.

LOCHRY'S DEFEAT, Ohio River, 24 or 25 Aug. '81. Sending eight men ahead with a message to George Rogers Clark, Col. Archibald Lochry followed down the Ohio River with about 100 men of his picked company of Pa. volunteers to join Clark's expedition to Kaskaskia. (See WESTERN OPERATIONS) The famous Joseph Brant had moved into the Ohio Valley and shortly thereafter he captured five of Lochry's eight-man advance party, taking from them a letter telling of Lochry's movement to join Clark. (Swiggett, *Niagara,* 221) The Americans landed about 10 miles below the mouth of the Big Miami River at 10 A.M. on 24 or 25 Aug. Almost immediately they were surprised by Brant and annihilated. The Americans had five officers and 36 privates killed, 48 privates and 12 officers captured. (Hunter, *post,* 384–92) Although several of the prisoners, including Lochry, were killed (James, *Clark,* 243), more than half of them eventually returned to Pa. (Hunter, 142) Capt. Robert Orr and Lt. Isaac Anderson wrote firsthand accounts of the expedition; the latter kept a journal, and his date for the battle, 24 Aug., is probably more reliable than that given by Orr, 25 Aug. Heitman gives 24 Aug. as the date Lochry was killed. Swiggett, on the other hand, implies that both the capture of the messengers and the defeat of Lochry's main party took place on the 16th. (*Op. cit.,* 221) See also Simon GIRTY.

Principal source for the above sketch is the article by W. H. Hunter and his addenda to the same article, "The Pathfinders of Jefferson County," in the *Ohio Arch. and Hist. Soc. Pubs.,* VI (1898), 140–42 and 384–92. Hunter says this was the first recorded conflict between Indians and whites in Indiana.

LOCKE AND THE AMERICAN REVOLUTION. John Locke (1632–1704), the English philosopher, was educated at Christ Church, Oxford, and later studied medicine. He held several minor diplomatic and civil posts and had much to do with drafting the Fundamental Constitutions for the Carolinas in 1669–70. This plan for an artificially conceived aristocracy based on land was never accepted by the colonists. He also served as secretary to the Board of Trade, but after the fall of his patron, the Earl of Shaftesbury, he came under suspicion of the government, took exile in Holland, and remained there until the revolution of 1688 made his return possible. Starting to write on political philosophy, he justified this revolution, was rewarded with official posts under William and Mary, and was a member of the Board of Trade from 1696 until failing health caused his resignation four years later.

"Locke became a philosopher late in life and his formal learning was meager. The consequence was that his ideas, though no less profound, are much more simply expressed than is usual with philosophers; there is a strong reliance upon 'common sense' and practicality. Locke has had a wide audience, won by the clarity and simplicity of his writing." (*C.E.*)

Following the lead of Sir Edward Coke, who declared that the Common Law in many cases controlled acts of Parliament, and Thomas Edwards, whose *Gangraena* (1646) advanced the Puritan tenet that by "naturall birth all men are equally and alike born to like propriety, liberty, and freedom," in his *Two Treatises on Government* (London, 1689) Locke justified England's recent "Glorious Revolution"; he contended that the purpose of government was to insure men their rights to life, liberty, and property; when the government acted in such a way as to oppose the general good it ceased to be a legitimate government. "Not only Otis and the other leaders of the American Revolution were greatly indebted to Locke for his clear statement of political theory, but Rousseau, whose *Contrat social* was published in Amsterdam in 1762, also drew largely from the same source, as may be seen from a comparison of their writings." (Channing, *Hist. of the U.S.*, III, 10 *n*.) Locke's other works dealing with the principles of government, all published during the period of the "Glorious Revolution" of 1688–89, were "An Essay concerning Human Understanding" (London, 1690) and "Letters on Toleration" (London, 1692).

"If any one man can be said to have dominated the political philosophy of the American Revolution, it is John Locke," writes John C. Miller. "Indeed, it is not too much to say that during the era of the American Revolution the 'party line' was John Locke." (*Origins of the American Revolution,* 170) "The American mind seemed to have an affinity for the writings of Locke," comments Van Tyne, "it was unable to resist them. His arguments were not always clear; many a colonial mind could not have followed them; but his conclusions fitted colonial needs perfectly." (*War of Independence,* 354)

LOGAN. *c.* 1725–1780. Indian leader in British service. Son of a French captive who became a Cayuga chief, Logan presumably was named after James Logan, secretary to Wm. Penn and acting Pa. Gov. 1736–38. Logan turned against the whites during DUNMORE'S WAR, 1774, when some of his relatives were treacherously murdered by a party he believed to be under Michael CRESAP. He claimed that all his relatives were killed, and he took 13 scalps in retribution. This apparently satisfied his vengeance, but he sent Dunmore a famous note of defiance when invited to the peace talk. Here is one version of the speech allegedly dictated to Col. John Gibson and repeated to Dunmore:

"I appeal to any white man to say if ever he entered Logan's cabin hungry, and he gave him not meat; if he ever came cold and naked and he clothed him not. During the last long and bloody war [Dunmore's], Logan remained quiet in his cabin, an advocate for peace. Such was my love for the whites, that my countrymen as they passed, said 'Logan is the friend of white men.' I had even thought to live with you, but for the injuries of one man, Colonel Cresap, who the last spring, in cold blood and unprovoked, murdered all the relations of Logan, not sparing even my women and children. There runs not a drop of my blood in the veins of any living creature. This called on me for revenge. I have sought it; I have killed many; I have fully glutted my vengeance. For my country, I rejoice at the beams of peace. But do not harbor a thought that mine is the joy of fear. Logan never felt fear. He will not turn on his heel to save his life. Who is there to mourn for Logan? Not one!" (This version is from James, *Clark,* 18–19)

Although the sentiment is undoubtedly Logan's, the syntax must be credited to somebody else. Perhaps the most startling indictment of its authenticity is another Indian speech delivered by one

Lonan (!) to the Gov. of Va. in 1754. Picked up by a French traveler named Robin and translated into English, Lonan's speech is almost identical to the one attributed to Logan, even its final, magnificent lines: "I will die content if my country is once more at peace. But when Lonan shall be no more, who, alas! will drop a tear to the memory of Lonan?" (Quoted in Stone, *Border Wars,* 55 *n.*)

When the Revolution started, Logan was 50 years old and already a victim of liquor (Appleton's); he soon became "an abandoned sot" (*Handbook of American Indians*). He sided with the British but his role in the war is limited to his part in saving the life of Simon KENTON: he managed this by prevailing on Druyer, a Canadian trader, to ransom the condemned frontiersman and turn him over to the British at Detroit. A year later Logan was killed by a nephew, "apparently in a quarrel." (*Ibid.*)

"LONDON TRADING." When the British were firmly established in the N.Y.C. area "they tempted the Americans with the gains to be derived from bartering soil [agricultural] products for the finery of European looms and workshops. A brisk business was soon established on this basis, and 'London trading,' as the operation was called, assumed a dangerous form, for it became a vehicle for the supply of the British army and navy.... From almost every inlet from New London to Shrewsbury, light boats, freighted with provisions, darted across to the islands [Staten and Long Islands], or to British vessels anchored in the channels." (Lossing, II, 851)

This led to the "whaleboat warfare" in which Adam HYLER starred.

LONG ISLAND OF HOLSTON (in modern Tenn.) Located actually in the South Branch near where this river and the North Branch join to form the Holston River, this "Long Island" figures in the earliest maps of the "over mountain" settlements. (See "OVER MOUNTAIN MEN") It gave its name to the treaty ending the CHEROKEE WAR OF 1776. Another Long Island, this one located in the Tenn. River, was a village of the Middle Cherokee, in the N.E. corner of what now is Ala.

LONG ISLAND (Boston Harbor), Mass., 12 July '75. The entry for 11 July '75 in Heath's *Memoirs* gives this account of raids during the Boston Siege:

"In the morning, a party of Americans drove back the British advance guard, and burnt Brown's store. The same night a detachment went on to Long Island, and brought off the stock, &c. The next day [12 July] in the forenoon, Col. Greaton with 136 men, went on to Long Island, and burnt the barns; the flames communicated to the house, and all were consumed. An armed schooner, and several barges put off after the Americans, and some of the ships of war near the island cannonaded them. The detachment made their way for the shore, and narrowly escaped being taken. One man on the shore who came to the assistance of the detachment, was killed: It was supposed that several of the British were killed and wounded." (*Op. cit.,* 32)

LONG ISLAND, N.Y., Battle of. 27 Aug. '76. (NEW YORK CAMPAIGN) At dawn, 22 Aug., Col. Edw. Hand's outpost on Long Is. near Denyse Point (later Ft. Hamilton, Brooklyn) sent word that the British were preparing to cross to Long Island from Staten Island. Three frigates (*Phoenix, Rose,* and *Greyhound*) and two bomb ketches (*Carcass* and *Thunder*) were in Gravesend Bay, and the frigate *Rainbow* was anchored in The Narrows. At 8 A.M., a mixed force of 4,000 under Clinton and Cornwallis, and including von Donop's corps of jägers and grenadiers, started crossing to Denyse Point, covered by guns of the *Rainbow.* Hand's 200 men of the 1st Pa. Cont'ls. withdrew to Prospect Hill, burning and destroying property and supplies that the enemy might use. The British boats returned to Staten Island and rowed back with over 5,000 more troops, which landed in Gravesend Bay under protection of the ships. By noon, almost 15,000 men, at least 40 cannon, and the horses of the dragoons had been put ashore in a smoothly conducted operation. Three days later Gen-von Heister crossed with two brigades of German grenadiers and landed to the right (S.E.) of the preceding waves. Against scattered American resistance, the invaders pushed four miles inland to Flatbush, where Cornwallis' 10 light

infantry battalions and von Donop's jägers and grenadiers encamped. There was a brisk skirmish in front of Flatbush Pass and against Bedford Pass on the 23d. In the latter action Hand's Pennsylvanians advanced and drove von Donop's men from some houses before being forced back onto high ground by a German counterattack. The British expanded their beachhead to include the villages of New Utrecht, Gravesend, and Flatlands. Although Washington was not yet convinced that Howe's main effort would be made on Long Island, he sent reinforcements there from New York City.

THE BATTLEFIELD

Between the plain on which Howe's troops were encamped and the Brooklyn lines was a low, densely wooded ridge known as the Heights of Guian or Guan. Although this ridge is often

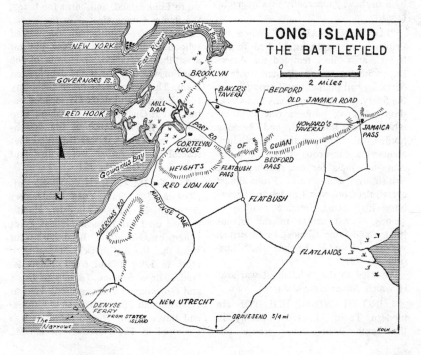

LONG ISLAND
THE BATTLEFIELD

0   1   2
2 Miles

referred to as Brooklyn Heights, the latter name is more correctly applied to the hills around the village of Brooklyn, along which the principal American works were situated.

Guian Heights presented an abrupt face to the British, and varied in elevation between 40 and 80 feet, whereas the northern side sloped gradually. So covered by woods and dense thickets as to be virtually impenetrable to troops in formation or to horse-drawn equipment, this terrain was "as if designed by the Almighty to protect the defenders of Brooklyn Heights," writes D. S. Freeman. "The strength of this natural position was all the greater because it overlooked a wide and open plain that extended eastward and northeastward from Gravesend Bay." (Freeman, *Washington*, IV, 158) The barrier was, however, pierced by four roads. (See map opposite and those on pp. 650–53.)

INITIAL DISPOSITIONS

Greene had been incapacitated by fever and was succeeded by Sullivan on 20 Aug. "This change was unfortunate, because Greene, a much abler general officer, had a thorough knowledge of the Long Island terrain, while Sullivan knew little of the lay of the land. Still more unfortunate was another change, made on the 24th, by which Major General Israel Putnam superseded Sullivan in general command on Long Island, Sullivan being retained there as a subordinate. Putnam, who knew practically nothing of the topography of the island, was for other reasons totally unfit for the controlling position into which he had been put." (Ward, *W.O.R.*, 213)

The evening before the battle the American forces were distributed as follows: on the Gowanus road were 200 men of Hand's 1st Pa. Regt., half of Col. Sam J. Atlee's Pa. musketry bn.,

part of Lutz's Pa. troops, and certain detachments of N.Y. troops; their total strength was about 550. Over a mile and a half to their left, at the Flatbush Pass, were about 1,000 troops with four artillery pieces behind a hasty fortification of felled trees; units involved here were Dan'l. Hitchcock's R.I. and Moses Little's Mass. Cont'l. Regts., commanded by their lieutenant colonels, Elias Cornell and Wm. Henshaw; and Thos. Knowlton's 100 Conn. Cont'ls. At Bedford Pass, a mile to the east, were Sam. Wyllys' Conn. Cont'ls., and John Chester's Conn. State Regt. (actually commanded by Lt. Col. Solomon Wills); this force numbered about 800 and had three guns; they had built a hasty defense of felled trees. A short distance farther east was Sam. Miles with about 400 Pa. riflemen (from Alexander's Brig.); Miles had orders to patrol toward Jamaica Pass.

THE ACTION OPENS

Shortly before midnight, 26–27 Aug., Hand's men fired on a couple of British soldiers who were foraging a watermelon patch near the Red Lion Inn. Hand's troops, exhausted after four days of patrolling, were then relieved by Maj. Edward Burd's Pa. Bn. of the FLYING CAMP. Soon after midnight the latter were hit by 200 to 300 men, the advance guard of Grant's 5,000-man column which was advancing along the Gowanus Road with the mission of drawing American attention away from Howe's main attacking force. Burd and several men were captured, but the rest withdrew safely to high ground. Back in the Brooklyn defenses, Putnam was notified of this action at about 3 A.M. and he immediately ordered Alexander ("Stirling") to move out with the two regiments nearest at hand to repulse the enemy. About 40 minutes later, in the ominous red dawn of a chilly day,

Alexander started forward with Smallwood's Md. Bn. and Haslet's Del. Bn. (Since the colonels and seconds in command of both these units were absent on court-martial duty in N.Y.C., they were being led by their majors, Mordecai Gist and Thos. McDonough.) About half a mile short of the Red Lion, Alexander found Col. Atlee with 120 men of his Pa. Musketry Bn. and Lt. Col. Joel Clark, commanding Huntington's Conn. Cont'l. Regt. Sam'l. Parsons had taken charge of all these troops. Atlee was ordered forward to delay the enemy until an American line could be organized. Considering their lack of military experience and the presence of an overwhelming force to their front, Alexander's men performed admirably. Atlee held his ground against the advance of light infantry skirmishers, not dropping back until ordered. Meanwhile, by about 8 o'clock Alexander had established his troops in open order, colors flying; with their flank anchored on a small patch of trees at the top of the hill to their left, they stood firm for four hours while artillery plowed into their ranks and light infantry moved to within 150 yards.

Sullivan had probably reached the sector of the American line opposite Flatbush about the time Alexander arrived at the right flank. Learning that the Hessians on this front had done no more than shell the American positions, Sullivan detached a battalion to reinforce Alexander. Washington reached Long Island about 8 o'clock, having previously dispatched reinforcements there.

Howe's plan was working perfectly. Grant's secondary attack had drawn American reserves to the west flank, while the main effort—10,000 men under Howe's personal command—was turning the exposed flank. Alexander's battle against Grant, although secondary in the over-all scheme, merits examination in some detail. After Alexander had formed his men he took the occasion to remind them that Grant, while an M.P., had delivered his famous boast to the House of Commons (2 Feb. '75) that Americans would not fight and that with 5,000 men he could march from one end of the American continent to the other. (See ALEXANDER and CRUGER FAMILY for the story of this speech.) Because of the peculiar lay of the land on the American right, the troops there were deployed in an odd man-

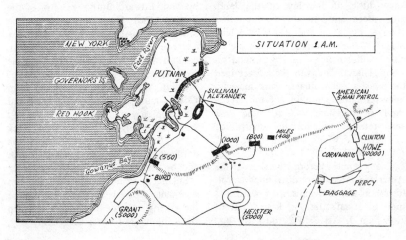

SITUATION 1 A.M.

ner. The Marylanders were across the Gowanus Road with their right flank on the marsh and their left in the small group of trees at the top of the ridge overlooking the road. Forming a V with the Marylanders, the Delawares extended back toward the rear so that troops at the ends of the V were closer to each other than they were to the flanks of their own regiments at the tip of the V. A few hundred yards along the ridge, east of the point of the V, Parsons had command over a mixed group: Huntington's Regt. (temporarily led by Joel Clark, as mentioned above); the elements of Atlee's Pa. Bn. that had originally been in action, plus units of the same battalion that joined later; and a portion of Kachlein's Pa. riflemen, who were among the reinforcements sent by Sullivan to Alexander. (Another portion of Kachlein's riflemen were posted in front of Alexander's right flank.) Another remarkable thing about Alexander's dispositions was that he formed his troops in the open, European style, rather than behind cover.

By the time all reinforcements arrived, Alexander's command numbered about 1,600; Grant's original 5,000 were augmented to 7,000 when he was joined by the 42d (Highlanders)—who had been with Heister—and two Loyalist companies. Grant formed his numerically superior forces as if for an immediate attack, massing with two lines on his left (west) and extending his right so as to threaten to overlap Alexander's position. Alexander countered this last threat by ordering Parsons to extend to the east, a move that left Alexander with a mere 1,000 to oppose the bulk of Grant's forces on the west. For the next two hours, however, action on Alexander's front was limited to an exchange of artillery and the movement of British light infantry to within 150 yards of the defenders.

The Americans were much concerned by the efforts of six British warships to get up the East River and attack their flank and rear. Fortunately, a strong wind frustrated this attempt; the *Roebuck* was able to get as far north as Red Hook and exchange a few shots with Ft. Defiance, but all ships had to withdraw when the tide began to ebb.

Atlee's troops (Parsons' command) got into a hot and creditable little skirmish when they moved east to extend Alexander's line. Approaching a small hill, they were surprised by fire from what turned out to be the British 23d, 44th, and part of the 17th. There was some confusion and a certain amount of retreating (by Del. troops, not by his Pa. troops, according to Atlee) before Atlee led a well-disciplined advance that took the hill. The regulars left 12 dead and five wounded. Atlee's men then repulsed a counterattack and stood fast in the face of a threatened second counterattack. (British Lt. Col, James GRANT, sometimes confused with *General* James Grant, was killed.)

HOWE SPRINGS THE TRAP

The head of the British column reached Bedford, directly behind the American left (Sullivan's command), at 8:30. They had marched nine miles in five or six hours without their column of 10,000 men and 28 guns being detected. When Cornwallis' "reserve" closed up on Clinton's advance guard, and without waiting for Lord Percy's main body, Howe ordered two signal cannon fired. This happened at 9 o'clock. The Germans heard the guns and immediately attacked Sullivan's front, while the British moved against his rear. Grant heard the signal but, perhaps being short of ammunition, did not attack immediately. Alexander apparently did not hear the signal guns and was not aware of the threat to his rear until 11 o'clock.

How had the enemy gotten behind the Americans in such force without being detected? The Germans had moved from Flatbush at 6 A.M. and, although they did not attack until three hours later, they had been cannonading Sullivan. Col. Samuel Miles, whose Pa. riflemen were on the American flank, reported that he started moving toward Bedford Pass at 7 A.M., as soon as he heard the Americans firing in that area. Col. Wyllys stopped him and said he was supposed to be defending Old Jamaica Road. So Miles started back in that direction and, after a two-mile march through the woods, came in view of the road and saw British troops. The time was now about 8 A.M., and what Miles discovered was the tail of Howe's column: the baggage train. Miles sent word back to Lt. Col. Brodhead's second battalion, which was somewhat behind him, to escape to the Brooklyn defenses; most of them succeeded, entering the lines by the mill dam. With his remaining 230 men, Miles launched a vain attack against the light infantry baggage guard and then tried to fight his way to safety. Miles

and 159 men were captured, but a few got back to give Putnam the first word of the turning movement. (The signal cannon had not yet been fired.)

At Bedford Pass the troops of Wyllys and Wills had already been alarmed by firing to their left (Miles's skirmishes) when, an hour later, they heard the cannon to their rear and saw the Germans advancing to their front. They headed for Brooklyn. (Ward, op. cit., 223)

At Flatbush Pass, the troops realized their hopeless predicament and most of them (Freeman, op. cit.) fled to Brooklyn along the Port Road, which was still open. Sullivan and some of the remaining men tried to fight their way to the rear; they brought three guns into action against a light infantry battalion that tried to bar their withdrawal, and were giving the battalion trouble until it was saved by reinforcements from the Guards. (Fortescue, Br. Army, III, 184) The blocking force then attacked, taking heavy casualties (Baurmeister, 37), but capturing the guns and driving Sullivan's troops back into the bayonets of Donop's oncoming jägers.

"Through the woods, down the slopes,

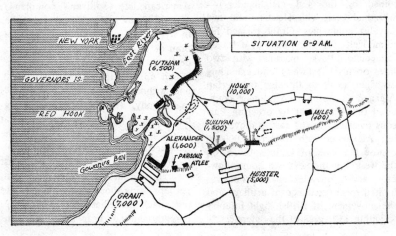

across the fields, singly, in groups, in companies, they fled. Meeting here and there light infantry, dragoons, and grenadiers who fired at them, they ran for the fortified camp. Many of them reached it, but many others were killed and many captured.... It was in these ragged encounters that most of the American casualties occurred." (Ward, *op. cit.,* 223)

The heaviest fighting took place near Baker's Tavern, close to the intersection of modern Fulton St. and Flatbush Ave.; Sullivan and most of the others were captured here. (Lossing, II, 806, 810 *n.*)

Rolling up the shattered east flank, the Germans next hit Parsons' command; the troops of Atlee, Huntington (Joel Clark), and Kachlein's riflemen retreated in broken groups only to find their way blocked by grenadiers. Atlee was trapped and forced to surrender. By 11 o'clock, Howe was formed within two miles of the Brooklyn lines, having swept Guian Ridge clean of all but the two regiments opposite Grant.

ALEXANDER'S ANNIHILATION

The Maryland and Delaware Regts. were under attack by Germans moving along the ridge from the east, and (although they did not yet know it) Cornwallis was to their rear, when Grant attacked and penetrated at the point where their lines joined to form the V. Grant's already overwhelming numbers had been further reinforced by 2,000 marines. (Ward, *op. cit.,* 224) The Americans did remarkably well against these odds. When a reserve force of Delawares counterattacked the 2d Br. Grenadiers their uniforms were mistaken for Hessian and they captured Marine Lt. Wragg and a 22-man patrol sent forward to tell the "Hessians" to stop firing on their own troops.

With Cornwallis and the 71st Regt. ("Fraser Highlanders") astride their natural line of retreat, the Americans started across Gowanus Creek—80 yards of water, a swift ebb tide, broad salt marshes on both banks, and enemy musket and artillery fire cutting among them. To relieve pressure on the fugitives, Alexander detached Maj. Gist and about 250 Marylanders for a diversion that he personally led against Cornwallis. After five attempts to force the roadblock, Alexander's sixth attack was stopped only when British reinforcements were brought up. (The Cortelyou House, center of this fighting, is west of modern Brooklyn's Fifth Ave. in the

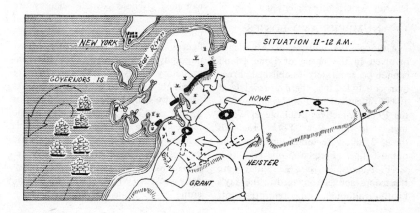

area of 3d and 8th Streets.) Breaking up into small groups to attempt escape, only Gist and nine men succeeded. Alexander tried it alone but was finally surrounded; he handed his sword to Heister.

The retreating Marylanders and Delawares, under McDonough, fought their way to the creek. Fortunately, Smallwood had come over from N.Y.C. and, anticipating developments, had put a small body of troops and two field pieces in position to cover the retreat across the mouth of the creek. Fire from Smallwood's command silenced the guns that were firing on the fugitives, all but 12 of whom waded and swam to safety. (Ward, *op. cit.,* 226) Others had crossed earlier at Brower's Mill Dam, the "Yellow Mill," and in between. Smallwood charged that premature destruction of a bridge near Brower's Mill closed an escape route to many, including Alexander's troops; Heath went so far as to attribute the defeat to this blunder. Subsequent historians have found no support for these charges; apparently the bridge was destroyed only when enemy troops were about to use it to trap more Americans. (Freeman, *op. cit.,* 166 *n.,* citing H. P. Johnston) All fighting ended before 2 P.M. (C. F. Adams, *Studies,* 34) (See LONG ISLAND, American evacuation.)

NUMBERS AND LOSSES

Although the number of Americans involved in the battle of Long Island cannot be accurately established, Freeman concludes that there were at least 10,000 effectives *on Long Island* out of the 19,000 effectives available to Washington *in the New York area.* Of these, 3,500 were along the three-mile outpost line (Freeman, *op. cit.,* 162; C. F. Adams, *op. cit.,* 33); they were the troops actively engaged in the day's fighting, although some reinforcements

joined them from the Brooklyn defenses. Estimates of American casualties vary from Washington's figure of 800 to Howe's figure of 3,300, and as high as 6,000 (Clinton's estimate). Freeman estimates 1,407 total American losses (wounded, captured, and missing); of these, about 312 were killed. As for prisoners, Freeman finds no reason to question the official British report: 89 American officers and 1,097 others. (See Freeman, *op. cit.,* 157 *n.,* 162, 167 *n.*) Among the prisoners were Alexander, Sullivan, Atlee, and Miles. Baurmeister, a German participant, says, "This day [of the battle] we took eleven hundred prisoners, and on the 28th picked up another 426." (*Journals,* 38–39) Christopher Ward points out that the American strength returns of 8 Oct. showed 1,012 casualties. (*Op. cit.,* 226) As a final footnote to confusion it should be pointed out that Washington never received strength and casualty reports of some temporary units of the FLYING CAMP or of other militia units. (Freeman, *op. cit.,* 167 *n.*)

Of 22,000 British and Germans on Long Island, the total loss was 377: the British lost five officers and 56 men killed, 13 officers and 275 men wounded and missing; the Germans had two men killed, three officers and 23 men wounded. (These casualty figures are from Fortescue, *op. cit.,* 184 *n.* Ward puts total casualties at 392. Freeman's figures reflect an error either of typography or arithmetic, but his contradictory totals of 359 and 367 are reasonably close to other estimates. As for Howe's total strength, the figure of 22,000 on Long Island the day of the battle is open to little controversy; his "effectives fit for duty" on Long Island *and* Staten Island were officially reported as 24,464 out of 31,625 physically present [Whitton, *op. cit.,* 344 *n.,* citing H. P. Johnston].)

CRITIQUE

In this first pitched battle of the Revolution, American leadership was remarkably inept. Howe's performance was masterful, although marred by his characteristic inability to clinch a victory. Even though Washington was faced with an almost impossible strategic problem in New York, his solution bears out Van Tyne's judgment that he had "little genius and not much natural aptitude for war." (*War of Indep.*, 251) "In plain words, the redcoats had outclassed the Continentals," writes Freeman. (*Op. cit.*, 178)

One cause of British blundering at Bunker Hill resulted from their failure to reconnoiter Charlestown peninsula during the long months they occupied Boston before the battle; the Americans were guilty of the same failure at New York: apparently no American general other than Greene knew the terrain well enough to recognize the importance of Jamaica Pass. Supposedly in home territory, the patriots did not have anything resembling an intelligence service (which had been well organized around Boston); the movement of Cornwallis' troops from Flatbush to Flatlands the afternoon before the battle should have "telegraphed" Howe's punch.

Much has been made of Washington's failure to use cavalry; he refused the services of several hundred Conn. mounted volunteers who reported in early July. Any armchair strategist can see how differently things might have turned out if a few of these horsemen had been patrolling the road toward Jamaica Pass.

Freeman summarizes the considerations around which the battle has been analyzed: (1) Much of the disaster stemmed from the unavoidable removal of Greene from the scene and the substi-tution of Sullivan; (2) Putnam's arrival at the last moment led to confusion and divided authority; (3) Washington erred in splitting his forces between N.Y.C. and Brooklyn; (4) Sullivan did not see the danger of Jamaica Pass, and did not cover this avenue of approach; (5) the Americans were fooled by Grant's secondary attack; (6) the American leaders were generally unaware until the last minute of what Howe was doing. (*Op. cit.*, 178 *n.*)

On the British side, Howe's turning movement was well conceived and magnificently executed: a textbook example of this type of military maneuver. Grant's and Heister's secondary missions succeeded perfectly. Grant has been blamed for allowing so many to escape across the mill dam, but Fortescue says it is impossible to decide on the justice of this criticism. (*Op. cit.*, 185) Howe's failure to storm the Brooklyn defenses is difficult to justify. Although it is too pat to attribute it all to "fear of another Bunker Hill," the earthworks must have looked impressive. Howe justified his action on the grounds that since the Americans were trapped by naval forces in East River it would have been "inconsiderate and even criminal" to make a costly frontal attack. With a line of communications 3,000 miles long, Howe felt he must husband his resources. (Miller, *Triumph*, 125)

The most complete story of the battle and subsequent retreat (next article) is in Henry P. Johnston, *The Campaign of 1776* ... (1878). Another full account is in T. W. Field, *The Battle of Long Island* (1869). Both books are publications of the L.I. Hist. Soc., being volumes III and II, respectively. Ward points out that "Force, Fitzpatrick, Kemble, Serle, Read, Reed, Robertson, Gordon, Ramsay, and the original documents printed in Johnston, Field, and Dawson form the major part of the contemporary or near-contemporary authorities. They are supplemented by Carrington, Dawson, Johnston, Bancroft, Trevelyan-Anderson, and other writers." (*W.O.R.*, 453) Other authorities have been cited throughout the above article.

LONG ISLAND, N.Y. American evacuation 29–30 Aug. '76. After the battle of LONG ISLAND, 27 Aug., the British started formal siege operations against Brooklyn Heights. The north wind that had kept their ships out of the East River the day of the battle continued to blow, and Washington brought reinforcements over from N.Y.C. The afternoon of the 28th a cold rain began to fall on the ground that was already watersoaked, and the demoralized, ill-equipped American troops suffered severely.

Although appearance of a redoubt within 600 yards of the American left confirmed Washington's earlier suspicion that Howe was taking his time and did not intend to make an immediate assault on the Brooklyn defenses, Washington still had to cope with the enemy capability of attacking N.Y.C. with fresh troops from Staten Island as well as the possibility that Howe might execute a strategic envelopment from Flushing Bay to Kings Bridge. After a council of war the afternoon of 29 Aug., with unanimous support from his generals, Washington decided to abandon Long Island and regroup his forces on Manhattan Island.

That morning he had ordered Gen. Heath and his Asst. Q.M.G., Hughes, to assemble all available boats and move them to the East River by dark. These reached Brooklyn Ferry at dusk to supplement the much larger number of boats that the Americans had been using for weeks to move men and supplies across the river. (Some accounts imply that only the miraculous assembly of

boats by Heath and Hughes made the evacuation possible. C. F. Adams points out that Washington was not such an "utter military simpleton" as to "put himself and his army into a most dangerous position depending wholly, or in chief, on some suddenly improvised means of extrication. * * * The mass of what [transportation] was required had already long before been provided." (*Studies,* 42)

To withdraw secretly from Brooklyn Heights and move 10,000 or 12,000 inexperienced and demoralized troops across East River was a military operation to try the skill and courage of veterans. Yet it was achieved with the loss of only three stragglers (who had stayed behind to plunder) and five heavy cannon (which could not be manhandled through the hub-deep mud); all other men, artillery, supplies, and horses were safe in N.Y.C. by 7 A.M., having been evacuated in six hours.

The only hitch that took place is dismissed by Freeman with the bland statement that some troops reached the waterfront before their turn to embark and had to be marched back to their posts. (Freeman, *Washington,* IV, 175) There was something more to this episode, which might have been fatal. About 2 A.M. Maj. SCAMMELL, then acting as Washington's A.D.C., reported with orders to Gen. Mifflin, who was commanding the covering force on Brooklyn Heights. (This force comprised the troops of Haslet's Delawares, the remnants of Smallwood's Marylanders, Shee's and Magaw's Pennsylvanians, and Chester's Conn. Bn.) Scammell told Mifflin that his boats were waiting and that Washington wanted him to move immediately to the ferry. Thinking this order premature, Mifflin told Scammell he must be mistaken. Scammell maintained that he was repeating his instructions and that, furthermore, he had already passed them on to other elements of the covering force, which were then executing them. Mifflin therefore called in the outposts and started moving his troops to the rear. When well on their way to the ferry they met Washington, who accused them of deserting their posts.

"Good God! General Mifflin," he is reported to have said, "I am afraid you have ruined us by so unseasonably withdrawing. . . ."

"I did it by your order," said Mifflin with some warmth.

When it became apparent that Scammell had made a bad mistake, the covering force moved back to their positions, which had been abandoned nearly an hour. The terrors of Europe's battlefields were peacefully ignorant of these nocturnal activities. At about 4 A.M. a small British patrol peered into the abandoned forward positions, and half an hour later these were occupied by Howe's troops. The American rear guard was still at Brooklyn Ferry, but a dense fog settled to cover their withdrawal. Among the last to leave was Washington.

There is disagreement among historians as to the weather during this operation. After reviewing the contradictions, C. F. Adams arrives at the following conclusions. The day of the 29th was cold and foggy, with a light breeze from the northeast. "Later the night was still, the water quiet, the atmosphere luminous; a fog settled on the bay towards morning; every atmospheric condition aided the patriots, and, at the proper stage of the tide the boats passed to and fro, favored by a light west breeze, and loaded to the gunwale." (*Studies,* 47) There was a full moon, which occurred at about 3:15 A.M. (*Ibid.*) Twilight would have ended at about 7:30 the evening of the

29th, and would have begun about 4:30 the next morning.

Glover's and Hutchinson's regiments of Mass. fishermen and sailors distinguished themselves in handling the boats that shuttled across the river; not an instance is known of collision, swamping, or upset—not a life was lost. (C. F. Adams, *op. cit.*)

"Both Howe's attack [of 27 Aug.] and Washington's retreat were masterpieces of planning and execution, and each was successful because of the mistakes of the other principal." (Ward, *W.O.R.,* 236) There probably is no other conclusion on which historians are in such complete agreement as this one.

LONG ISLAND, N.Y., Aug. '77. In conjunction with Sullivan's raid to STATEN ISLAND, 22 Aug. '77, Gen. Samuel H. Parsons attacked Setauket, which was defended by 150 Tories of De Lancey's Regt. under the command of Lt. Col. Richard Hewlett. The attack was repulsed "after a brisk cannonade and five hours' perseverance," notes Sir Henry Clinton. (*American Rebellion,* 68 *n.*)

LONG ISLAND, N.Y., 10 Dec. '77. An American raid against Long Island was broken up by British ships and Col. S. B. Webb was captured with his regiment. Although several writers refer to Samuel H. Parsons' "unfortunate raid to Long Island" and Webb's capture, details of the action are lacking.

LONG ISLAND (Charleston), S.C. See CHARLESTON.

LONG ISLAND SOUND. Almost landlocked by Long Island and Conn., this inland sea—100 miles by 20—figured not only in such regular military operations as Tryon's DANBURY RAID, the CONN. COAST RAID, and Arnold's NEW LONDON RAID, but also in "WHALEBOAT WARFARE."

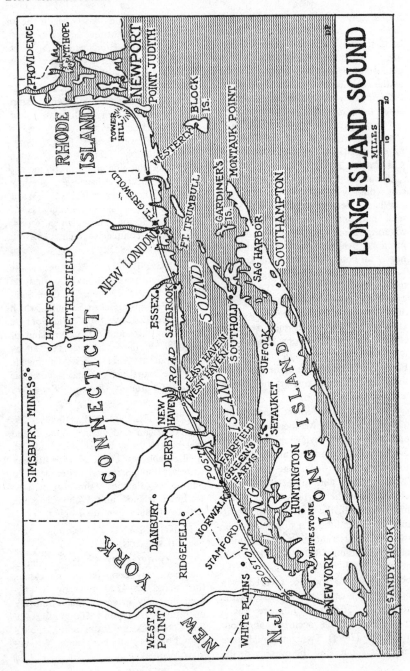

LONG ISLAND SOUND

LONGUEUIL, Canada. Located on the south bank of the St. Lawrence opposite Montreal, this place and La Prairie, 10 miles south, were the two main approaches to Montreal from the south. Ethan Allen and John Brown reached these two places during Montgomery's siege of St. Johns and subsequently launched their abortive attack on MONTREAL, 25 Sept. '75. The main action at Longueuil was on 30 Oct. '75 when Carleton assembled a force of nearly 800 and attempted to relieve St. Johns. The British expedition comprised some of Allan MacLean's newly raised Royal Highland Emigrants, 60 men of the Royal Fusiliers, and a large contingent of Caughnawaga Indians. Part of the latter were led by the notorious ST. LUC. The river crossing was contested by Seth Warner with his Green Mountain Boys and the 2d N.Y., supported by a 4-pdr. Artillery and musket fire drove back the main attacking force. MacLean tried to make a secondary crossing upstream but turned back when he found the site well defended. (Ward, *W.O.R.*, 160, citing Force)

When Benedict Arnold led the American garrison out of Montreal after the collapse of the Canada Invasion in the summer of 1776, he crossed with his 300 men to Longueuil, hotly pursued, and retreated to St. Johns.

LORING, Joshua. 1744–1789. Loyalist, commissary of prisoners. Mass. Best known as the husband of Gen. Howe's mistress, "a brilliant and unprincipled woman," he was detested by the patriots for his alleged mistreatment of prisoners. He had served in the British Army, retiring in 1768 as a Lt. and receiving a grant of 20,000 acres in N.H. The next year he was appointed permanent high sheriff of Mass. and married Elizabeth Lloyd of Boston. One of the "PROTESTERS," he subsequently left Boston with the British and early in 1777 was made Howe's commissary of prisoners. This remunerative office was undoubtedly obtained through the influence of his unfaithful wife. He died in England. His father, Joshua (1716–1781), had been a privateer, British naval officer, and one of Gage's "MANDAMUS COUNCILLORS."

LOUDOUN, John Campbell, 4th Earl of. 1705–1782. British C. in C. in America (1756–57). Grandson of the famous John Campbell, 1st Earl of Loudoun (1598–1633), he entered the army in 1727, succeeded to the title in 1731, and fought against the Jacobites in 1745. In 1755 he became Col. in Chief of the 60th Foot ("Royal Americans"). On 17 Feb. '56 he was appointed Capt.-Gen. and Gov. in Chief of Va., although Robert Dinwiddie continued to administer the province. (*D.N.B.;* Appleton's) On 20 Mar. '56 he was appointed C. in C. of British forces in America, and on 23 July he reached N.Y. to take over these duties. His leadership at the outset of the French and Indian War was inept militarily and offensive to the colonists politically. After collecting a force in Albany that could have crushed the French, he disbanded the provincials and illegally billeted his officers in N.Y.C. and Philadelphia. He further alienated the colonists by imposing an embargo on commerce; the purpose of this, as it was later learned, was to preserve the secrecy of his proposed expedition against Louisburg—his "CABBAGE PLANTING EXPEDITION." How Loudoun's strategy failed to take Louisburg and led to the bloody defeat of other British and provincial forces in northern N.Y. is covered under COLONIAL WARS and FORT WILLIAM HENRY (Aug. '57).

Recalled by Pitt and succeeded by Amherst in America, Loudoun in 1762 was second in command of troops sent to Portugal. With powerful political connections, he received many military sinecures prior to his death 20 years later. Of his performance in America, Benjamin Franklin quoted a wag as saying, "He is like St. George on the signs, always on horseback, but never rides on."

LOUIS XVI in the American Revolution. Only 21 and in the first year of his reign in 1775, he was patriotic, conscientious and, in the words of Nickerson, had "a good working knowledge of the dynastic diplomacy of Europe. Where neither military affairs nor insight into individual character was concerned, his leisurely judgment was not to be despised." (*Turning Point,* 22) As eager as any other Frenchman for revenge against England, he was, however, forced to be cautious. His comptroller-general of finances Turgot (1727–81) was a restraining influence on the more aggressive plans of foreign minister VERGENNES, but he agreed, with strong mental reservations, to secret aid to the colonies during the first three years of the war. Turgot's dismissal, engineered by Marie Antoinette and minister of state Maurepas (1701–1781), and British failures in America, finally created a situation that convinced the king to accept Vergennes' recommendation that France cast aside neutrality. Louis therefore deserves credit for assisting the American cause in permitting the secret aid under which HORTALEZ & CIE. functioned and for approving the FRENCH ALLIANCE; it is doubtful whether the colonists could have won without either. Unlike the Spanish authorities, who saw the American Revolution as a threat to their own governments, Louis did not foresee that in helping the colonists in America he was hastening his own doom.

LOUISBURG, Canada. Erected at enormous expense by the French in 1720, this powerful fortress on Cape Breton Island at the mouth of the St. Lawrence was second only to Quebec in importance during the French regime. It guarded the approaches to Canada and was the center of the cod fisheries. Captured in 1745 by American colonists with the support of the British fleet, it was returned to France by the treaty of 1748, to the intense resentment of Americans. The British recaptured it in 1758. (See COLONIAL WARS) The English spelling is Louisburg, but some writers favour Louisbourg, the French spelling.

LOVELL, James. 1737–1814. Cont'l. Congressman. Mass. Graduating from Harvard in 1756, and an accomplished linguist and mathematician, he became an instructor under his father (John LOVELL) in the South Grammar (now Boston Latin) School. His life was uneventful for 18 years, and he was chosen to deliver the first commemorative speech on the Boston Massacre more, apparently, for his oratorical skill and his standing as a respectable citizen of Boston than for any publicly expressed patriotic views. However, this speech on 2 Apr. '71 put him firmly on the rebel side. The school was closed by the British 19 Apr. '75, and when the British and the Loyalists evacuated Boston in Mar. '76, Lovell was arrested for spying and taken to Halifax with them. His father was one of the fleeing Tories. Young Lovell was exchanged for Col. Philip Skene in Nov. '76 (Appleton's) and returned to a welcoming Boston. A few days later, he was sent to the Cont'l. Congress, taking his seat 4 Feb. '77 and serving until Apr. '82. Overzealous and fanatical, he earnestly mixed in practically all the controversies of the Congress. He became a fervid admirer of Gates, and, by consequence, a sarcastic critic of Washington. He had taken Gates's side in his quarrel with

Schuyler, and encouraged Gates to deal with Congress over Washington's head. He was involved in the "Conway Cabal," and even wrote Washington threatening letters. (Appleton's) He was a member of the committee of foreign applications and, speaking French, served as interpreter for the French volunteers seeking commissions from Congress. Montross says, "As . . . interpreter [for Congress, he] combined a cold perfection in speaking the language with a distaste for the people and customs . . . in a first interview he dismissed the Marquis de Lafayette and his companions, as one of them complained, 'like a set of imposters.' " From these experiences came much of the distrust, and later the hostility, toward Silas Deane, who was responsible for many of the French officers being in America. Also, Lovell, as a member of the committee of foreign affairs, had many dealings with Arthur LEE and became entangled in that contentious gentleman's many feuds. Edmund C. Burnett, in *D.A.B.*, says that Lovell was overdiligent in his Congressional duties, often being the only member of the foreign affairs committee remaining in Congress and "never once in five years so much as visiting his wife and children." He plotted and planned and schemed, mainly for Franklin's job in France, but nothing came of it, and he resigned in 1782 to return to Boston as receiver of continental taxes. He became customs collector for the state in 1788 and in 1789 was appointed naval officer for Boston and Charlestown. His son was James LOVELL, Cont'l. officer; his grandson, Joseph Lovell, was surgeon-general of the U.S.; his great-grandson, Mansfield Lovell, was a Confederate general.

LOVELL, James (Jr.) 1758–1850. Cont'l. officer. Mass. Son of James LOVELL, he graduated from Harvard in 1776 and became an ensign in Lee's

Cont'l. Regt. 25 May '77. Named Regt'l. Adj. 10 May '78, he transferred to Henry Jackson's Mass. Regt. 22 Apr. '79 as Adj. Appleton's says that he fought in many battles and was severely wounded, but Heitman does not substantiate this. In Mar. '80 he transferred to Lee's Bn. of Light Dragoons and was Adj. until the end of the war.

LOVELL, John. 1710–1778. Loyalist. Mass. He graduated from Harvard in 1728 and became an usher of the South Grammar (now Boston Latin) School the next year. In 1734 he was named headmaster and continued in this until the siege of Boston, when the British military authorities dispersed the school 19 Apr. '75. According to Lawrence S. Mayo in *D.A.B.*, Lovell taught, among others, Samuel Adams, Samuel Langdon, James Bowdoin, Robert Treat Paine, Andrew Oliver, John Lowell, John Hancock, Thomas Brattle, Jeremy Belknap, Francis Dana, Henry Knox, William Phillips, William Eustic, Christopher Gore, and Harrison Gray Otis. He was severe in the schoolroom but genial and witty as a companion. Considered a sound classicist and critic, he was an entertaining writer and orator. When the British withdrew to Nova Scotia in March '76, he chose loyalty to the Crown and followed them to Halifax where he died two years later. His son JAMES, who chose the other side, was held prisoner there briefly by the British in 1776. A portrait of John by his former pupil Nathaniel Smybert is at Harvard. See James LOVELL for genealogy.

LOYALISTS. Generations of American school children were taught that if anything during the American Revolution was lower than a British regular or a Hessian it was a Tory or Loyalist. What good could possibly be said about a native-born American who sided with the British? With the publication of Van

Tyne's *Loyalists in the American Revolution* in 1902 a revisionist trend got under way, and there was a tendency to glorify Loyalists as honorable people victimized by a diabolical mob. This is epitomized in the works of Kenneth Roberts, particularly in *Oliver Wiswell* (1940). The truth lies somewhere in between; just where I will not presume to impose an opinion, but in the following comments I will attempt to outline the views of authorities.

Here, for a starter, is the statement of a Canadian historian:

"It is but truth to say the loyalists . . . were the makers of Canada. They were an army of leaders. The most influential judges, the most distinguished lawyers, the most capable and prominent physicians, the most highly educated clergy, the members of the council of various colonies, the crown officials, the people of culture and social distinction—these . . . were the loyalists. Canada owes deep gratitude to her southern kinsmen, who thus, from Maine to Georgia, picked out their choicest spirits, and sent them forth to people our northern wilds." (Henry Smith Williams [ed.], *Historian's History of the World* [1907], quoted in Steele, *American Campaigns* [1909], 12. Page reference is to 1951 edition of Steele's classic.)

Van Tyne gives an interesting breakdown of the categories of Tories before the arrival of Gage in Boston:

Office holders, whose income was at stake.

"Those gregarious persons whose friends were among the official class."

Anglican clergymen, many of whom had motives similar to those of the crown officials.

"Conservative people of all classes, who glided easily in the old channels."

"Dynastic" Tories, who believed in kings.

"Legality" Tories, who thought Parliament had a right to tax.

"Religious" Tories, whose dogma was "Fear God and honor the King."

"Factional" Tories, whose action was determined by family friends and old political animosities. De Lanceys in N.Y. became Loyalists because Livingstons were Whigs. Sower in Pa. embraced the opposition primarily because the patriot leadership of his region represented the critics of his family and religious sect. The antipathy of the Otises (see James Otis) toward British authority stemmed from a personal animosity toward Gov. Bernard. (*Op. cit.,* 25–26)

Yet the Loyalists showed a peculiar inability to organize.

"It is not far wrong to say that a genuine Loyalist party did not exist in the colonies until the commercial war failed and the real war began. * * * Instead of taking part in the colonial politics, they withdrew, in many cases, and looked frowningly on while rebellion advanced by leaps and bounds." (Van Tyne, *War of Indep.,* 22 n.; *Loyalists,* 87)

Surprisingly, the greatest Loyalist strength appears to have been in the frontier regions. (Egerton, *Causes,* 169) Col. Wm. Rankin headed a movement in Pa. and adjacent areas. The Border Warfare in N.Y. and the civil war that raged in the Southern Theater are illustrations. Organized Tory resistance was promptly squelched in Va. when the fighting started; farther south the rebels also got the upper hand initially, but subsequent Tory uprisings were serious. (See Southern Theater)

In the North the Loyalists first acted as associated bands but then enlisted by thousands in the British army. Egerton writes:

"New York alone furnished about

15,000 to the British Army and over 8,000 Loyalist militia. All of the other colonies furnished about as many more, so that we may safely say that 50,000 soldiers, either regular or militia, were drawn into the service of Great Britain from her American sympathizers. Tories formed no inconsiderable part of Burgoyne's army. Even when they did not join, their known presence in large numbers among the inhabitants of the region prevented the Americans from leaving their homes to join the American army. [See WYOMING and CHERRY VALLEY] The British forces were also greatly helped in the matter of supplies by the Tory inhabitants." (*Op. cit.*, 178)

"New York supplied more recruits to George III than to George Washington," says Brinton. "It has been estimated that perhaps only one third of the colonists actively backed the Revolution." (*Modern Civ.*, 317) The Tories may be correct in claiming to have had more long-term troops in service than the rebels after 1778, says Montross. This was because the British could equip them. Although no fewer than 69 Loyalist regiments were organized to the extent of seeking volunteers, at least 21 of these actually took the field with an average strength of several hundred men each. (*Rag, Tag,* 384)

The Loyalists had an interesting effect on British strategic planners, who tended to count on finding stronger support in some new region of America where they had not yet tried to operate. When Tory support failed to materialize in New England the British expected to find it in N.Y. and shifted military operations there. Simultaneously, they got drawn into the CHARLESTON EXPEDITION of Clinton in 1776. The hope of Loyalist assistance had a part in luring them into the unfortunate BENNINGTON RAID. Ferguson's defeat at KINGS MOUNTAIN

also stemmed from this fallacy. Another effect of the Loyalists was in restricting British strategic movement when they became burdened with Loyalists who had to be evacuated or protected. One reason why Howe went from Boston to Halifax rather than direct to N.Y. was because he had Tories to evacuate from Boston. One reason why Howe permitted himself to get overextended in the winter of 1776 was because he had to outpost Trenton, Bordentown, Princeton, and Brunswick to protect the Tories of N.J. The isolated post of Ninety-Six, S.C., had to be garrisoned (by a Northern Tory unit) for the protection of loyal inhabitants of the region. It is interesting to note that the two most brilliant American victories, TRENTON and COWPENS, can be traced indirectly to this requirement for the British to overextend themselves to protect the Loyalists.

Persecution of the Loyalists started with mob action by the Sons of Liberty and continued throughout the Revolution. ". . . while liberty-loving pamphleteers were writing about the 'rights of man,' thousands of our patriotic ancestors were subjecting innocent, but loyal, persons to every sort of indignity and torture. * * * There was absolutely no freedom of the press or tongue, save for those that expressed opinions against the government." (Steele, *op. cit.*, 12) TEST LAWS and statutes confiscating Tory property were passed. Perhaps 40,-000 Loyalists were expelled from the states. (*D.A.H.*, I, 299) N.Y. made $3,600,000 from the sale of confiscated property, and Md. collected over $2,000,000. When the British evacuated N.Y.C. in 1783 they took out 7,000 Tories, and the estimated total of those who left America during the Revolution is almost 100,000. In July '83 the British government established a commission that examined 4,118 claims before it finished in 1790, having allotted almost £3,300,000 to compensate loyal Americans for their losses.

In 1974 Prof. Pauline Maier commented, "The Loyalists lost the Revolution, but they seem to be winning the Bicentennial. Within a year at least three books on the Loyalists . . . have been published. All are 'sympathetic' accounts. And there are more to come." The books mentioned are Robert Calhoon, *The Loyalists in Revolutionary America, 1760–1781*; Mary Beth Norton, *The British-Americans*; and Catherine S. Crary, *The Price of Loyalty: Tory Writings from the Revolutionary Era*. The pioneer work is *The Loyalists in the American Revolution* by Claude H. Van Tyne (1929). Still valuable is the *Biographical Sketches of Loyalists* by Lorenzo Sabine (1864, 1966). Of many popular histories probably most solid is *The Good Americans* by Wallace Brown (1970). Revisionists will swarm around the Loyalists during the bicentennial years, so readers will have to consult the latest bibliographies to keep up. Presumably the Library of Congress will update their 1968 pamphlet, *The American Revolution: A Selected Reading List*, which covers "The Loyalists." An excellent summary to about 1970 is the essay on pp. 488–489 of Don Higginbotham, *The War of American Independence* (1971).*

LOYAL AMERICAN RANGERS. Raised in Jamaica in late 1780 by William ODELL, this Tory regiment was in N.J. and N.Y. before returning to the West Indies. See MUTINY OF THE PA. LINE and HONDURAS.

---

* Scholars now estimate the number of Tories in the 13 colonies at 500,000 (or 20 percent), of whom about 80,000 went into exile.

LOYAL AMERICANS. A Provincial regiment raised by Beverley ROBINSON in N.Y.C. in early 1777, "chiefly among his tenants and neighbors in the country" (Van Doren, *Secret History,* 4), it went to Va. with Arnold in Dec. '80 but returned with him to N.Y. in June '81 "because the men [of this unit as well as those of Arnold's American Legion] had deserted so fast in Virginia they could no longer be trusted there." (*Ibid.,* 420) Meanwhile they had taken part in CLINTON'S EXPEDITION to the Highlands, where Robinson led them with distinction in the capture of Ft. Montgomery, 6 Oct. '77, and a detachment of the Loyal Americans was part of the garrison surprised and captured at STONY POINT, 16 July '79.

"Robinson's Corps" may apply also to the regiment of loyal GUIDES AND PIONEERS, which he also commanded. Another Provincial regiment, commanded by Maj. Wm. F. Odell, was called the Loyal American Rangers, not to be confused with Robinson's Loyal Americans.

"LOYALL NINE." An offshoot of the CAUCUS CLUB and leaders of the SONS OF LIBERTY, these men and Sam Adams (who was not a member) operated behind the scenes to keep agitation alive in Boston. The nine were: John Avery (secretary), John Smith, Thos. Crafts, Benj. Edes (printer of the *Boston Gazette*), Stephen Cleverly, Thos. Chase, Joseph Field, Geo. Trott, and Henry Bass (a cousin of Sam Adams). (Miller, *Sam Adams,* 53)

LUC DE CHAPT DE LA CORNE SAINT-LUC. See ST. LUC.

LUZERNE, Chevalier Anne-César de La. Second French Minister to U.S. As successor to Gérard, he reached Philadelphia with his secretary, Marbois (see BARBÉ-MARBOIS), after a leisurely overland trip from Boston in the fall of 1779. La Luzerne presented his credentials on 4 Nov. About 36 years old, friendly, tolerant, and worldly wise, but speaking little or no English when he arrived, he soon "wielded so much influence that he may almost be considered one of the heads of the American government," writes Montross. (*Reluctant Rebels*, 314-15) When ratification of the Articles of Confederation continued to be blocked by Md., La Luzerne brought this state into line by suggesting that the French naval forces they were requesting in the Chesapeake for protection against the British would not be possible unless Md. ratified the Articles. In this matter he exceeded his diplomatic authority, but it worked: Md. ratified in Feb. '81. The Ambassador remained in America until the summer of 1784. A town in the Wyoming Valley and the surrounding county of Pa. are named for him. His correct family name is La Luzerne, not Luzerne, and he is so indexed in such works as Chastellux's *Travels*.

LYNCH, Charles, 1736–1796. Militia officer, "founder of Lynch law." Va. Son of an Irish indentured servant who married his Quaker boss's daughter, he was born on his father's plantation near modern Lynchburg. He was elected J.O.P. in 1766 and expelled the next year by the Quakers for having taken this oath of office. Entering the House of Burgesses in 1769, he retained his seat until the Revolution. As he gained wealth and influence he became an increasingly powerful supporter of the patriot cause: he signed the Williamsburg Protests against taxation in 1769 and '74, attended the state constitutional convention in 1776, sat in the House of Delegates until 1778, and raised troops. On 24 Feb. '78 he was made Col. of militia. In the spring of 1781 he led a regiment of 200 Va. riflemen south to reinforce Greene. Many of his men were ex-Cont'ls. whose enlistments had ex-

pired. With the elite Del. Cont'ls. of Capt. Kirkwood his volunteers formed the infantry of Wm. Washington's new legion. At GUILFORD, 15 Mar. '81, Lynch and Kirkwood held the right flank of Greene's first line, and Lynch's volunteers proved themselves worthy companions in arms of the Delawares in the battle. Lynch's men were not bound to any specific term of service (Ward, *W.O.R.*, 785), but they remained with Greene in the Carolinas until Cornwallis surrendered at Yorktown. (*D.A.B.*) Lynch came home to resume his duties as J.O.P. and later served inconspicuously in the state senate between May '84 and Dec. '89.

As for "Lynch's law," Webster's unabridged dictionary says it probably was named for him as a result of his "extralegal methods of trial and punishment against Tories" for which he was "indemnified . . . by an act of the Virginia Assembly in 1782." Citing several special studies on the origin of the term, John C. Wylie supports this theory in his *D.A.B.* article on Lynch. Apparently Lynch's court did not hand down sentences any more severe than whippings (*ibid.*, E.B.); during the Reconstruction Period of U.S. history "Lynch law" came to mean capital punishment.

Lynchburg, Va., was named for John, a younger brother of Charles. The latter's son, also named Charles (d. 1853) was Gov. of Miss., 1835–37. (Appleton's)

LYNCH, Thomas. 1727–1776. Cont'l. Congressman. S.C. Grandson of an early Irish immigrant and son of one of the first Carolina rice planters, he inherited large land holdings and considerable wealth. He sat in the provincial assembly (1751–57, 1761–63, 1765, 1768, 1772) and was an early advocate of colonial independence. A delegate to the Stamp Act congress of 1765, he was sent to the first Cont'l. Congress in 1774. There he opposed importation of British goods and was strongly opposed, in turn, by the colonial merchants. He was re-elected but a stroke in early 1776 cut short his political career. His only son, THOMAS JR., was sent to Congress to aid him, and together they started home, but a second stroke in Annapolis killed him in Dec. '76. Silas Deane described him as he appeared in Congress: "He wears the manufacture of this country, is plain, sensible, above ceremony, and carries with him more force in his very appearance than most powdered folks in their conversation. He wears his hair strait, his clothes in the plainest order, and is highly esteemed." His widow later married B.G. William Moultrie, and one of his daughters was the mother of James Hamilton, S.C. Gov. and nullification champion.

LYNCH, Thomas, Jr. 1749–1779. Signer. S.C. Sent at 12 to England, he studied at Eton, Cambridge, and in the Middle Temple, returning home in 1772. He decided not to practice law, and his father, THOMAS SR., concurred, having himself decided that his son should enter public life. Young Lynch, the only son of a wealthy and important man, had no trouble acquiring elected offices. While running his North Santee plantation, a gift from his father, he soon became influential in patriotic circles. In 1774–76, he sat in the provincial congress and, also in 1776, was on the state constitutional committee and in the first gen'l. assembly. On 12 June '75 he was named Capt. in the 1st S.C., which he accepted against the advice of his father, who had offered to get him higher rank. He caught a bilious fever while recruiting his company, was left in permanently poor health, and there is no record that he ever commanded the company. On 23 Mar. '76, he was sent by the gen'l. assembly to the Cont'l. Congress as an additional delegate to assist and care for his ailing father, who had suffered a paralytic stroke a few weeks earlier. However, his own health was too feeble to allow him to participate actively in the Congress, although he voted for and signed the Decl. of Indep. When, in the fall of 1776, his father's health had recovered slightly, ailing father and son started south, but the elder died in Maryland, and the younger reached home seriously ill. In late 1779, in hopes of finding a better climate, he sailed, with his wife, for the West Indies, where they would take passage for the south of France. Their ship was never heard of and is presumed to have been lost at sea with all hands.

M

MAC. Note on spelling and alphabetizing of Gaelic names. In this book I have adopted the spelling most commonly found in American reference works and have alphabetized in the letter-by-letter manner (rather than listing all names beginning with "Mc" or "M" as though the full form "Mac" were used).

"Gaelic speakers resist the abbreviation 'Mc' for 'Mac,' and do not like to use a capital letter after 'Mac' unless it prefixes their father's Christian name," I am informed by Dr. James N. M. Maclean, official historian of the Clan Maclean. "Donald MacDonald Macdonald would be Donald, son of Donald of the Clan Donald."

MACHIAS, Me., 12 June '75. The British schooner *Margaretta* (4) entered the port of Machias, in the province of Maine on 2 June '75 with two sloops (*Polly* and *Unity*) and the schooner *Margaretta* (4 guns) to get lumber for the British garrison in Boston. Determined to prevent the British from accomplishing their mission, local patriots conceived a plan to capture the enemy officers while they were in church on 11 June. But Midshipman James Moore, commander of the *Margaretta*, and some of his officers escaped through the windows of the church and regained their ship.

A hastily organized pursuit by about 40 volunteers under Jeremiah O'Brien and Joseph Wheaton resulted in capture of the *Unity* on Sunday and of the *Margaretta* the next day (12 June). A considerable chase had ended with a brisk skirmish in which seven men were killed or wounded on each side. Midshipman Moore was among the dead.

O'BRIEN became the first naval hero on the patriot side, and the action is generally considered to be the first naval engagement of the war. Many authorities erroneously give 12 May as the date of the action.

O'Brien was given command of the *Unity*, which was armed with guns from the captured schooner and renamed the *Machias Liberty*. A few weeks later he captured the British naval schooner *Diligent* and her tender off Machias without a shot, and, under his command, the two schooners became the first ships of the Mass. navy.

MacLEAN, ALLAN. 1725–1797. British officer. Born at Torloisk, Scotland, he was a Lt. in the Jacobite Army (1745), fought at CULLODEN the next year, took refuge in Holland, and was commissioned in the Scots Brigade of the Dutch Army. He and Francis MacLEAN were captured in 1747 during the siege of Bergen-op-Zoom, both being commended by the enemy general for valor. Exchanged in 1748 and returned

to Britain two years later under amnesty, MacLean eventually was commissioned Lt. in the 60th ("Royal American") Regt. (8 Jan. '56). Wounded at Ticonderoga in 1758, promoted to Capt. in the 60th (16 Jan. '59), he took part in Wolfe's victory at Quebec before being transferred to command a N.Y. Independent Co. of Infantry. In the operations against Niagara he was seriously wounded. Returning to Britain in 1761 he was empowered to raise the 114th Regt. of Royal Highland Vols. (MacLean's Highlanders) and as Major Commandant he left with this unit for America on 18 Oct. '61.

In 1763 this regiment was disbanded, some of the veterans settling on grants in St. John (now Prince Edward) Island, Canada. Allan was put on half pay as a Maj. Large grants were later made to him, his nephew Lachlan (later a Lt. Gen.), Francis MacLEAN, and to the notorious political adventurer Col. Lauchlin MacLeane.

Restored to full pay as Lt. Col. on 25 May '72, MacLean was given a warrant (12 June '75) to raise two battalions to form the 84th Regt. ("Royal Highland Emigrants"). Officers, predominantly Macleans, were from Mull and Morvern; the troops came from among the settlers on Prince Edward Is. With about 70 men he reinforced the beleaguered garrison of St. Johns and in the final stages of the siege made an unsuccessful attempt to bring in a relief column. (See ST. JOHNS, 5 Sept–2 Nov. '75)

Learning of Benedict Arnold's arrival at Point Levis, opposite Quebec, on 9 Nov. '75, MacLean made a forced march from Sorel and reached Quebec on the 13th with about 80 Highlanders. These were reinforced a few days later by more recruits for his regiment. The Scots officer stiffened the spine of the

Quebec garrison, insuring their defiance of Arnold's threats until Carleton arrived to take over from the weak Lt. Gov. Hector Cramahé. (See CANADA INVASION)

As a reward for his service at Quebec Allan was promoted to brigadier general on 6 June '77 and put in command of Montreal as its military governor. His Highland Emigrants served here and at Niagara, remaining in Canada and not participating in operations into New York. (Burgoyne recommended leaving the Highlanders behind "because I very much apprehend desertions from such parts of it as are composed of Americans, should they come near the enemy.")

Allan MacLean retired from the army in 1784, took up residence in London and died there without issue on 18 Feb. '97.

Allan MacLean being a common Scottish name, there is considerable confusion among writers and indexers. For the above facts I am indebted to the official historian of the Clan Maclean, Dr. James N. M. Maclean of the University of Edinburgh, who is compiling a four-volume history of the Macleans. (He expects to complete this by 1978.) From this authority I learn that the subject of this sketch always spelled his name "Maclean," but I have preserved the other spelling (MacLean) because this is, right or wrong, more common in English and American works about the American Revolution.

See also the following entry and Allan McLANE (formerly Maclean).

MacLEAN, Francis, 1718–1781. British officer. Francis was the third son of Capt. Charles Maclean of Blaich, the latter being a veteran of Marlborough's campaigns and his wife Mary being daughter of Sir Francis Kinloch. Commissioned Ensign in the Cameronians in 1738, promoted in 1742, he resigned in 1745 to join the Clan Maclean Bn.

of the Jacobite army as a lieutenant. With Allan (above), he was a fugitive after CULLODEN. Resigning his Dutch commission in 1750, he rejoined the British Army and purchased a lieutenancy in the 42d ("Black Watch") two years later. As a Capt. of this regiment he fought in Canada and the West Indies before taking part in the capture of Belle Isle, off Brittany, in 1761.

Having distinguished himself in Portugal, 1762–78, he was ordered back to England, promoted to Brig. Gen., and sent to Canada as Gov. of Halifax. After routing the patriots in the campaign described under PENOBSCOT EXPEDITION, July–Aug. '79, he returned to Halifax, died there (a bachelor) 4 May '81, and was buried in the vault of St. Paul's Church in Halifax.

MacLEAN'S CORPS. Royal Highland Emigrants raised and commanded by Lt. Col. Allan MacLEAN in Canada.

"MAD ANTHONY." Nickname of Anthony WAYNE.

MAD DOG ANECDOTE. See James WOLFE.

MADISON, Dolly. See James MADISON.

MADISON, James. 1751–1836. Cont'l. congressman, 4th U.S. President. Va. Of a family that can be traced with certainty to John Madison, a ship carpenter who received large grants of Va. land in 1653, James Madison received his B.A. degree from Princeton in 1771 and remained another year for further study. After showing signs of wanting to enter the ministry he threw himself into politics. Elected to the Orange co. committee of safety in 1775, he wrote its response to Patrick Henry's call for arming the militia. The spring of the next year he was chosen as a delegate to the Va. convention and was on the committee that framed the constitution and bill of rights. He proposed an amendment declaring that "all men are equally entitled to the full and free exercise" of religion; this would have disestablished the Anglican Church in Va., and it was rejected for a similar but less radical proposal made by George MASON. A member of the first Assembly under the new constitution, he was not re-elected in 1777; historians give some credence to the tradition that he refused to canvass or buy drinks for votes. In Nov. '77, however, the Assembly elected him to the governor's council, and two years later they elected him to the Cont'l. Cong. Taking his seat on 20 Mar. '80, he served until Dec. '83. He favored duties on imports for 25 years to raise federal revenue. He drafted the instructions of 17 Oct. '80 to John Jay in Madrid that gave him arguments for free navigation of the Mississippi. Seeing the impotence of Congress, he advocated strengthening the central government.

During the period 4 Nov. '82–21 June '83 Madison kept notes on the debates of Congress that are of considerable value in supplementing the official *Journals*. He played a significant part in solving two problems that threatened to bar agreement on a federal government: he worked out the compromise of Sept. '83 on the cession of Va. claims to the Northwest territory in such a way that it was acceptable to his own state; he broke a deadlock on the basis of state contribution to the central government by suggesting that three free persons be considered the equivalent of five slaves. (See POPULATION for disproportionate number of slaves in Va.)

Highlights of his subsequent career are his authorship of 29 of the *Federalist* papers and the Bill of Rights. He was Jefferson's Sec. of State (1801–9). Defeating C. C. Pinckney (1808) and De Witt Clinton (1812), he was Presi-

dent from 1809 to 1817. The disgraceful performance of an unprepared and disunited country in the War of 1812— "Mr. Madison's War"—cost him popularity. At the end of his second term, 4 Mar. '17, he retired to his magnificent country home, "Montpelier" (then spelled with two l's). Except for controversial writing, some minor public service, and participation in the Va. constitutional convention of 1829, the rest of his life was spent in gracious living as a country gentleman. His famous hospitality put him in straitened circumstances and he ultimately had to reduce his scale of living and sell some of his land. Dying childless in his 87th year, he was buried at "Montpelier." (J. W. Pratt in *D.A.B.*) A new edition of the Madison papers is W. T. Hutchinson and W. M. E. Rachel (eds.), *Madison Papers* (1962–1965). Other volumes will follow these four, which deal with his life up to July 31, 1782.

"Dolly" (Dorothea?) Payne Madison, his widow, had lost her first husband, John Todd Jr., in 1793. She was introduced to Madison by Aaron Burr, and they were married in 1794. Although almost 20 years younger than her husband, Dolly made him a good wife. Her reputation as a Washington hostess dates from 1801, when Madison became Sec. of State. Pres. Jefferson was a widower, and Dolly was, in effect, "first lady" for him as well as for Madison—16 years. Friendly, tactful, and with a remarkable memory, she was extremely popular. She was no meddler in politics, however, and is said to have been "brilliant in the things she did not say and do." (Goodwin, *Dolly Madison*, 101, quoted in *D.A.B.*, "Dolly Madison") Fleeing before the British invaders of Washington in Aug. 1814, she saved many state papers and a portrait of George Washington. After her husband's death she moved from

"Montpelier" to a house on the N.E. corner of Lafayette Square, opposite the White House. Financial difficulties, complicated by the waywardness of her son by her first marriage, forced her to sell "Montpelier" and saddened her last years. She died 12 July 1849 in Washington at the age of 81, and her grave was ultimately moved to "Montpelier." "Her reign as a queen of official society may have been benign rather than brilliant, but in length and popular acclaim it has had no parallel in American history," writes Dumas Malone in *D.A.B.* (1933).

MAHAM, Hezekiah. 1739–1789. Militia officer. S.C. Born in St. Stephen's Parish, he was active in patriot politics and had been a member of the 1st S.C. Prov. Cong. before becoming a Capt. in Isaac Huger's 1st S.C. Rifle Regt. in 1776. He took part in the unsuccessful defense of Savannah, 29 Dec. '78, and the action at Stono Ferry, 29 June '79, before becoming a Maj. of State Dragoons. In 1780 he was promoted to Lt. Col., and the next year he became Col. of an independent dragoon regiment. The tower known by his name was first used in the capture of FORT WATSON, Apr. '81. Maham took part in the actions at Quinby Bridge, 17 July '81, and FAIR LAWN, 27 Nov. '81, in addition to many smaller, independent operations (Appleton's). While home on sick leave he was captured in Aug. '82 and paroled; he saw no further combat. Although he frequently served with Marion he was not part of MARION'S BRIGADE when it was organized and, despite statements of some writers (e.g., Appleton's), does not appear ever to have been part of the latter command.

MAITLAND, John. d. 1779. British officer. Eighth son of the Earl of Lauderdale, he had been a Lt. Col. of Marines and M.P. for Haddington before becoming Lt. Col. of the 1st Bn. of 71st Highlanders, on 14 Oct. '78. Going south as part of Archibald Campbell's force, he led his battalion in the capture of SAVANNAH, 29 Dec. '78, distinguished himself at STONO FERRY, 20 June '79, and commanded the detachment left behind at Beaufort when Prevost withdrew to Savannah. In the defense of SAVANNAH, Sept.–Oct. '79, he contributed immeasurably to the British success by making a remarkable march from Beaufort to reinforce the garrison. Ill before he started this movement, he died of malaria a few days after the battle of 9 Oct. '79. He was a bachelor.

MAJORIBANKS. See MARJORIBANKS.

MALCOLM'S REGT. Col. Wm. Malcolm commanded one of the 16 "ADDITIONAL CONT'L. REGTS."

MALMADY, Marquis de. Cont'l. officer. As a 2d Lt. of Cavalry in the French Army he reached America the end of 1775, was breveted Maj. in the Cont'l. Army on 19 Sept. '76 and in Dec. '76, on the recommendation of Gen. Chas. Lee, was made B.G. of R.I. state troops. (Heitman, Lasseray) During the operations of 1776 he was employed as an engineer officer in the field. On 10 May '77, two months after expiration of his state commission (Heitman), he was given the Cont'l. commission of Col. In the fashion of foreign volunteers he wrote to Washington complaining that this rank was beneath his merit and his former grade. In a blistering reply Washington expressed his astonishment that the ex-Lt. did not feel Congress had recognized his service in commissioning him a colonel. The C. in C. went on to state his astonishment that the marquis had not grasped the distinction between state and Cont'l. commissions, and concluded his letter with the request that the French veteran of seven months in America cease his importunities. (Lasseray, 298–300, quoting Washington's letter of 16 May '77.) Heitman states that Malmady served to Apr. '80 as a Col. in the regular army. He commanded a light infantry company on one flank of the American force at Stono Ferry, S.C., 20 June '79 (Ward, *W.O.R.*, 686). In his letter of 10 Apr. '81 to Clinton, Cornwallis wrote from Wilmington, N.C., that "Colonel Malmedy, with about twenty of the gang of plunderers that are attached to him, galloped in among the sentries [at Ramsey's Mill on Deep River] and carried off three Jägers." (Clinton, *Amer. Reb.*, 509) At EUTAW SPRINGS, 8 Sept. '81, Malmady commanded the N.C. militia.

Malmady, Malmedy, and Malmédy are variations of the name given by Lasseray's sources. The first form is favored by this French authority; the second is used in almost all American and British works.

MAMARONECK, N.Y., Raid of 22 Oct. '76. (N.Y. CAMPAIGN) During the American withdrawal from PELL'S POINT and Harlem Heights to White Plains, the village of Mamaroneck was abandoned by the Americans (unjustifiably, in Washington's view [Freeman, *Washington*, IV, 224]). The place was then occupied by Maj. Robt. ROGERS and his notorious "Queen's Rangers" as a detached camp of about 500 men near the British right wing at New Rochelle. Col. John Haslet was selected to lead his Del. Regt., reinforced by certain Va. and Md. companies to a total strength of 750, in a raid against Mamaroneck. With accurate information about Rogers' dispositions, Haslet started from near White Plains, marched some five miles, slipped undetected past the British flank, and silenced the single sentinel who covered the approach to Rogers' bivouac. During the day, however, Rogers had realized the possibilities of surprise along this route and had posted Capt. Eagles with 60 men between the lone sentinel and his main camp. Haslet's advance guard stumbled

on this unsuspected force, and a melee ensued. The enemy added to the confusion by echoing the cry, "Surrender, you Tory dogs! Surrender!" The Americans managed to capture 36 prisoners, 60 muskets, 60 highly prized blankets, and a pair of colors, all of which they evacuated safely. Eagles escaped with the rest of his command, and Rogers' main camp forced the raiders to withdraw after an exchange of fire. American casualties were three killed and 12 wounded; there is no record of enemy losses.

(Ward, *W.O.R.*, 258–59, on which the above is based, and Freeman, *op. cit.*, 224 and 224 *n.*, give the principal sources for this affair.)

MANCHAC POST (Ft. Bute). Bayou Manchac or the Iberville River was the northern boundary of the Isle of (New) Orleans and provided a water route from the Mississippi east into the Amite River and through Lakes Maurepas, Ponchartrain, and Borgne into the Gulf of Mexico. (This route was used by Pierre Le Moyne, Sieur d'Iberville, when he returned in 1699 from his exploration up the Mississippi to the mouth of the Red River.) Since the Treaty of Paris in 1763 left the Isle of Orleans in Spanish hands (ceded by France in 1762), this route was of vital importance as an outlet for British navigation from the upper Mississippi. (Scribners' *Atlas*, 49) At the mouth of the Manchac–Iberville stream, on the Mississippi, the British established Ft. Bute or Manchac Post in 1763. From then until its capture by GALVEZ on 7 Sept. '79 it was an important military and trading post. (See map on p. 372)

"MANDAMUS COUNCILLORS." The Mass. Govt. Act of 20 May '74, one of the Intolerable Acts, prescribed that effective 1 Aug. the Mass. Council would no longer be elected by the House of Representatives but be appointed by the Gov. on a "royal writ of

Mandamus." The 36 appointed by Gage became marked men, their names being published by the Whig press along with the "ADDRESSERS" and "PROTESTERS." The councillors soon felt the rage of the rabble. Van Tyne writes:

"Old and infirm Israel Williams ... was 'smoked to a Whig' when the doors and chimney of his house were closed by a mob. Thomas Oliver was besieged by three or four thousand armed men and compelled to recant. Later, he and Mr. Hallowell and Deacon Edson, all councillors, fled into Boston. Some like Colonel Saltonstall met the ... [rabble] with splendid courage, but all sooner or later became refugees. Gentle Samuel Curwen ... became an outcast...." (*War of Indep.*, 23–24)

MANHATTAN ISLAND, N.Y. At the time of the Revolution this was also called City Island, New York Island, and York Island. At its northern tip was strategically important KINGS BRIDGE.

MANLEY, John. *c.* 1734–1793. American naval officer. Mass. A Bostonian, he was selected by Washington to command one of the vessels in the "navy" being organized in the fall of 1775 to operate against British supply vessels. As captain of the armed schooner *Lee,* he left Plymouth on 4 Nov. '75 and recaptured a schooner laden with wood that the British were taking to Boston as a prize. Toward the end of the month he made the first important capture of the war when he took the *Nancy* in the entrance to Boston harbor, within sight of her escort. The next month he took several other prizes and was hailed as a naval hero. In Jan. '76 Washington named him commander of his "navy." With his flag aboard the *Hancock* he made several successful cruises. Originally commissioned a Capt. in the army (Paullin in

D.A.B.; Heitman does not confirm this detail), on 17 Apr. '76 he was commissioned Capt. in the new Cont'l. Navy, and in the list of 10 Oct. he was ranked third in seniority. On 22 Aug. he took command of the new frigate *Hancock* (32), then building at Boston, and on 21 May '77 he sailed in company with the frigate *Boston* and a small fleet of privateers. On 7 June he captured the frigate *Fox* (28), but on 8 July he and his prize were taken off Halifax by the *Rainbow* (44), which was commanded by Sir George Collier. (See *Hancock*) After being confined on a prison ship in N.Y. Harbor, Manley was exchanged in Mar. '78. A court-martial acquitted him of losing his ship (*D.A.B.*), but Capt. Hector McNeill of the *Boston* was suspended (or dismissed) from the navy for failure to support Manley in the action of 8 July.

There being no suitable new command for him in the navy, Manley went to sea as a privateer and in the fall of 1778 made a successful cruise in the *Marlborough*. Early in 1779, as captain of the *Cumberland,* he was captured by the *Pomona* near Barbados. Escaping from prison at the latter place (Appleton's) he was recaptured while making his second cruise in the *Jason,* and he spent two years in Old Mill Prison, England, before being exchanged. In Sept. '82 he took command of the *Hague,* one of two frigates remaining in the Cont'l. Navy. (The other was Barry's *Alliance.*) His last cruise, in the West Indies, was marked by a brilliant escape from a British ship of the line (74 guns) and by his capture of the *Baille* in Jan. '83. Thus having the distinction of closing the regular maritime operations of the U.S. in the Revolution, the man who took the first important prize of the war also took the last one captured by a Cont'l. ship.

See I. J. Greenwood, *Captain John Manley* (1915).

MANTELET. A movable shelter to protect men attacking a fortified place. British engineer Moncrieff used them in the CHARLESTON EXPED. of 1780. (See section headed "The Regular Approaches.")

MANUFACTURING IN AMERICA. As outlined in the article on SUPPLY . . . , few of the shortcomings in manufactured goods were made up by American industry during the Revolution. Manufacturing had been discouraged by the policy of MERCANTILISM; furthermore, the colonists had sought other endeavors for their risk capital and labor was so high that imported nails, for example, were cheaper than ones made in America. A notable exception was the shipbuilding industry: by 1760 a third of all British tonnage was American-built, and in the 10 years up to 1775, 25,000 tons a year were turned out; costs were 20 to 50 per cent lower than in Europe, thanks largely to availability of NAVAL STORES. Iron manufacturing also advanced rapidly, despite restrictions in 1750 and 1757 under the NAVIGATION ACTS. In 1775 the colonies produced over 14 per cent of the world's iron, but the same legislation that encouraged this output had prohibited the development of plants needed to make finished products. By 1775, nevertheless, the foundries of Philadelphia were casting cannon of bronze and iron, and that winter more than 4,000 stand of arms were made in Pa. Technical knowledge was undeveloped, however, and the homemade products were inferior. The arsenal at Springfield, Mass., in 1777 was so poorly managed that in 1780 the Board of War recommended its abandonment. (The modern Springfield Arsenal dates from 1794.)

American gunsmiths were probably the finest in the world, but they did not develop the mass production techniques needed to meet the demand for small arms during the Revolution. A shortage of saltpeter and lack of knowledge frustrated local efforts to produce gunpowder. Perhaps with the assistance of FOUQUET and son, Pa. produced several thousand pounds of powder a week from six mills, but American powder was considered to be inferior.

"Everywhere, the shortage of labor blighted American enterprise," writes Miller in his excellent chapter on supply during the Revolution. (*Triumph,* 108) Sudbury Furnace, Conn., started casting cannon in 1775 but had almost ceased to operate by 1778; the Philadelphia foundry for casting brass cannon did not exist long; the lead mines of Va. were abandoned early in the war. (*Ibid.*)

Textiles were another critical shortage. Women made linen at home, but the colonies had little wool for winter clothing and blankets. Canvas for tents and sails was needed. Peter was robbed to pay Paul: "not only in 1775 but later, awnings and ships' sails were utilized to provide tents," and after the large loss of tentage during the evacuation of N.Y.C. a committee of Congress reported " 'we have now a parcell of fine vessells lying here useless at a time they might have been most advantageously employed.' " (Risch, *Q.M. Support,* 17.) The NONIMPORTATION policy had given an impetus to weaving, but the industry had not developed enough to supply an army. The same policy had gotten the shoe industry going, and during the war the patriots had struggled with the problem of turning the hides of cattle slaughtered for the army into shoes. A Commissary of Hides was appointed in 1777 for this task, but results were unsatisfactory. (See SUPPLY. . . .)

Flour mills existed throughout the colonies, and in the vicinity of N.Y.C. and Philadelphia there was production for export. The latter city was the center of what little manufacturing was done in colonial America; in addition to the items mentioned above it produced hats, shoes, stockings, earthenware, cordage, and soap.

MARINE COMMITTEE. A body of 13 members of the Cont'l. Cong., one from each colony, that directed NAVAL OPERATIONS after the Cont'l. Navy was organized by the NAVAL COMMITTEE in 1775 and until it was replaced in Dec. '79 by an American Board of Admiralty.

MARINES. One theory as to the origin of "marines" as a distinct category of troops stems from the requirement in the early 18th century to protect British officers on shipboard from their "pressed" crews. They were a species of seaborne military police. But there also was a requirement for crack troops who could constitute landing parties, boarding parties, and deliver musketry from the rigging in close sea fights. British marines made up a considerable portion of the BOSTON GARRISON. Although they did not accompany the British column to Lexington and Concord, 19 Apr. '75, a marine officer, Maj. John Pitcairn, was second-in-command of this force and figured prominently in the day's historic events. Two battalions of British marines took part in the assault on BUNKER HILL (see section headed "Final Attack"), where Pitcairn was mortally wounded. British and French marines figured in subsequent land operations in America and in practically all sea battles. The rule of thumb was one marine assigned aboard a ship for each gun.

American marines can be traced to The War of Jenkins' Ear, when a regiment was raised in 1740. Commanded by Col. Gooch of Va. and officially identified as the 43d Foot, "Gooch's Marines" were raised in N.Y. and fought creditably in the West Indies. American marines served aboard privateers during the French and Indian War (1754–63), and were sometimes known as "gentlemen sailors."

A force known in the history of the U.S.M.C. as the "Original Eight" took part in the capture of Ticonderoga, 10 May '75. They were from Conn. Several of the state navies made provisions for marines when they were organized at the start of the Revolution. On 10 Nov. '75 the Cont'l. Cong. resolved that two battalions be raised, and 200 Cont'l. marines spearheaded the assault on NASSAU, 3–4 Mar. '76. They hit the same objective in the NASSAU RAID OF RATHBUN, 27 Jan. '78. The first Cont'l. Marine detachment on record, however, was the 17-man group under Lt. James Watson serving aboard the *Enterprise* from 3 May '75. Although from Mass., on 10 June they came under control of the Cont'l. Cong. when the delegates voted themselves control of all forces on Lake Champlain; they took part in the battle of Valcour Island, 11–13 Oct. '76. Cont'l. Marines landed from the *Hancock* on 12 Dec. '76, took part in the decisive actions at Trenton and Princeton, and were withdrawn on 20 Feb. '77. They participated in the defense of Fort Mifflin in Oct. and Nov. '77 (PHILADELPHIA CAMPAIGN).

A company of marines under Capt. James Willing left Fort Pitt on 10 Jan. '78 in the armed boat *Rattletrap* for an expedition to New Orleans, and on 3 Feb. they took part in the capture of two French trading vessels near Kaskaskia. The company reached New

Orleans, where Willing remained, but they returned to Kaskaskia prior to 16 Mar. '79 and, the 40 of them now commanded by Capt. Robert George, took part in Clark's operations against the Indians.* George's Marines apparently were disbanded 3 June '79 and distributed among Clark's other forces, but a payroll dated 12 Aug. '83 for the period 9 Mar.–9 Sept. '82 shows a marine company under Capt. Jacob Pyatt serving with Clark against the Indians. (U.S.M.C. *Chronology*)

Marines had meanwhile taken part in the action under Benjamin Tupper at TAPPAN SEA (now Tappan Zee), 3 Aug. '76, in the PENOBSCOT EXPEDITION, and the unsuccessful defense of Charleston in 1780. On the high seas they were in practically every battle involving privateers, ships of the state navies, and those in which ships of the Cont'l. Navy were engaged. American marines served under John Paul Jones in his WHITE-HAVEN RAID, and French marines were with him in the *Bonhomme Richard–Serapis* Engagement, 23 Sept. '79.

One authority has written:

"At no period of the naval history of the world is it probable that Marines were more important than during the War of the Revolution. In many instances they preserved the vessels to the country by suppressing the turbulence of ill-assorted crews [in accordance with what was mentioned at the beginning of this article as their original purpose], and the effect of their fire . . . has been

---

* U.S.M.C. *Chronology,* citing Mc-Clellan, Mason, and English. Heitman identifies a Capt. James Willing of unknown state and regiment as "a prisoner in August, 1778; when and where taken not stated." He identifies Robert George as Capt. of Clark's Ill. Regt., 1779 to 1782, and has no further details on either officer.

singularly creditable to their steadiness and discipline." (Collum, *post,* 41)

The U.S. Navy and the Marine Corps ceased to exist in 1785 and were not revived until 1794, when troubles started with the Barbary Corsairs. By the spring of 1798 there were marines aboard the ships that had been completed for this emergency. On 11 July '98 the U.S.M.C. became an individual service within the Navy.

This article is based on two mimeographed pamphlets in the U.S.M.C. Hist. Ref. Series: *A Chronology of the U.S.M.C., American Marines in the Revolution* (No. 27, revised 1962), and *A Brief History of the U.S.M.C.* (No. 1, 1961). Among the authorities cited in the first pamphlet are G. W. Allen, W. B. Clark, R. S. Collum, W. H. English, E. S. Maclay, E. N. McClellan, and C. O. Paullin. See bibliography of NAVAL OPERATIONS for their works. The standard reference is Clyde H. Metcalf, *A History of the U.S.M.C.* (1939).

MARION, Francis. ("Swamp Fox.") *c.* 1732–1795. Southern partisan leader. S. C. The grandson of Huguenots who came to S.C. in 1690, Marion was "small enough at birth to be put into a quart mug" and he was a frail child with badly formed knees and ankles (Bass, *Marion,* 6 and 41, citing Peter Horry and Wm. D. James, who are identified below). When he was about six years old his family moved from St. John's Parish (modern Berkeley co., astride the Cooper R.) to the vicinity of Georgetown. He was reared under modest circumstances and received a country school education. After surviving a shipwreck at the age of 16 he gave up ideas of becoming a sailor and settled down to the life of a farmer on the family property. In 1761 he was a Lt. in the militia company of Capt. Wm. MOULTRIE that took part in the CHER-OKEE EXPEDITION of Grant. In his first experience under fire he was selected to lead an attack to clear an Indian force from a critical defile, and despite sustaining 21 casualties in his party of 30 men he pushed on to accomplish the mission. His performance having been witnessed by important S.C. men (see CHEROKEE EXPED.), he rose to a position of respect in his community. In 1773 he was able to buy a plantation on the Santee four miles below EUTAW SPRINGS. In 1775 he was a delegate to the S.C. Prov. Cong. and on 17 June of this year was named Capt. in Moultrie's 2d S.C. Regt. (Heitman) He took part in the bloodless operations that drove the royal governor from S.C. and established rebel supremacy over the Loyalists, and on 10 Feb. '76 he was at Charleston, ready to take part in the fortification of the harbor. On 22 Feb. he was promoted to Maj. (Bass, *op. cit.*, 15; Heitman's date is 14 Nov. '75)

In the defense of Charleston, 28 June '76, Maj. Marion commanded the left side of Ft. Sullivan (later Ft. Moultrie) and received Moultrie's permission to fire the last shot of the engagement. On 23 Nov. he became Lt. Col. and on 23 Sept. '78 took command of the regiment. Owing to a new Congressional policy of keeping regimental commanders in the grade of Lt. Col. (to simplify the matter of prisoner exchange, which was done on a grade-for-grade basis), his title was Lt. Col., Commandant of the 2d S.C. Regt. Military operations in the SOUTHERN THEATER had been limited up until this time, but monotony increased the problems of commanders. Marion, however, established high standards of discipline. At SAVANNAH, 9 Oct. '79, he led his regiment in a gallant but unsuccessful assault. When Lincoln returned to Charleston, Marion commanded the three regiments left in the vicinity of Sheldon, S.C. On 19 Mar. '80 he re-

sumed command of his own regiment at Charleston. Lossing gives this account of the lucky break that saved him from capture when the city was surrendered on 12 May. Soon after his arrival in the city, the austere little Huguenot attended a dinner party given by Moultrie's A.G., Capt. Alexander McQueen. "... the host, determined that all of his guests should drink his wine freely, locked the door to prevent their departure. Marion would not submit to this act of social tyranny, and leaped from a second story window to the ground. His ankle was broken, and before communication ... toward the Santee was closed he was carried to his residence, in St. John's parish, on a litter." (Lossing, II, 769 *n.*)

With all organized resistance in the South soon destroyed, Marion started his career as a guerrilla. About 3 Aug. he made contact with the American force moving south under Gates; his unenthusiastic reception by the regulars is described under CAMDEN CAMPAIGN. After the action at GREAT SAVANNAH, 20 Aug., Marion then led his 52 men in an audacious attack that scatttered 250 militia under Maj. Ganey who were gathering around BLUE SAVANNAH, 4 Sept., routed the Tory outpost of Col. Ball at BLACK MINGO, 29 Sept., and broke up a Tory uprising under Col. Tynes at TEARCOAT SWAMP, 26 Oct. '80. After the British disaster at Kings Mountain (7 Oct.), Marion's operations were of such concern to Cornwallis that he gave Tarleton permission to take most of his legion off in an attempt to eliminate this guerrilla menace. While Tarleton was gone, Sumter's operations were so successful (Fishdam Ford, 9 Nov.) that Cornwallis sent an urgent order for Tarleton's return to the vicinity of Winnsboro. "Come, my boys! Let us go back, and we will find the Gamecock," Tarleton is reported to have said after trailing Marion for seven hours through 26 miles of swamp. "But as for this damned old fox, the devil himself could not catch him!" (Quoted by Bass, *Marion,* 82) Unsuccessful in an attack on GEORGETOWN, 15 Nov., he shot up a column of replacements at HALFWAY SWAMP, 12–13 Dec. '80, and then established a camp on Snow's Island. This "island" was a low ridge five miles long and two miles wide that was protected by the Peedee on the east, Lynches River on the north, Clark's Creek on the south and west. Further protected by swamps and a lake to the west, it became the Swamp Fox's favorite base. (*Ibid.,* 104) He now organized MARION'S BRIGADE.* The SOUTHERN CAMPAIGNS OF GREENE were now under way, but after teaming up briefly with Lee's Legion for the raid against GEORGETOWN, 24 Jan. '81, Marion was left to his own devices for another three months. In Feb. '81, Thomas Sumter started an expedition into Marion's district and called on the Swamp Fox to join him. The two partisan leaders did not succeed in uniting (see SUMTER), and as Sumter withdrew the British undertook a serious campaign to wipe out Marion's guerrillas.

As mentioned in the article on Lt. Col. 'John W. T. WATSON, this officer was detached with a force of 500 Tories "for the purpose of dispersing the plunderers that infested the eastern frontier." Since Watson was Lt. Col. of the 3d

---

* Although Marion was named B.G. of militia by Gov. Rutledge before he left Gates's headquarters on 14 Aug., and Heitman gives "Aug. '80" as the date of this appointment, Bass implies that he did not start acting in this capacity until Gov. Rutledge wrote on 30 Dec. '80 to the S.C. delegation in Congress notifying them of this appointment. (*Op. cit.,* 126. 257)

Foot Guards some writers have assumed that he led this crack regiment (Bass, *op. cit.,* 117, 143 ff.), but although Clinton refers to Watson's command as including "a considerable part of his [Rawdon's] best troops," these were predominantly if not entirely Tories of Maj. John Harrison's Regt. Whether it was against regulars or Tories, however, Marion checked Watson at Wiboo Swamp, blocked his drive toward Kingstree at Lower Bridge, and caught him astride the Sampit River as he headed for the British base at Georgetown. In the last action, which drove the British out of Marion's district, Watson's horse and about 20 of his men were killed. "I have never seen such shooting before in my life," said Watson, but he complained that Marion "would not fight like a gentleman or a Christian."

While Marion was scoring this remarkable success, however, the enemy achieved one that was equally brilliant: Col. Welbore Doyle found and destroyed Marion's base at Snow's Island. Hugh Horry led the pursuit of Doyle's N.Y. Vols., and Marion followed with the rest of his command. After Horry had shot down nine and captured 16, and two casualties were inflicted on the enemy rear guard at Witherspoon's Ferry (Lynches R.), Col. Doyle destroyed his baggage and rushed to Camden. It was not Marion's pursuit that prompted this sudden speed, but a message from Rawdon that Greene's army was again approaching Camden! Marion made contact with Henry Lee's Legion at Black River on 14 Apr., but only 80 partisans now remained with him. The rest had gone home.

The section of the SOUTHERN CAMPAIGNS OF GREENE headed "Greene versus Rawdon" will show how Marion's and Lee's operations against FT. WATSON, 23 Apr., and FT. MOTTE, 12 May, were related to the over-all American strategy. Marion occupied Georgetown, 28 May, and then moved farther south to support the attacks on Augusta and Ninety-Six. Lt. Col. Alexander Stewart cleverly eluded Marion's attempt to block his move from Charleston to reinforce Rawdon at Orangeburg.

While Greene's main body was recuperating in the Santee Hills, Marion came under the orders of Sumter and took part in the unfortunate action at QUINBY BRIDGE, 17 July. The fears that previously had led Marion to avoid service under the Gamecock (Bass, *op. cit.*, 141, 201) were realized in this poorly managed and costly skirmish. He then raced off to win a skirmish at PARKER'S FERRY, 13 Aug., and after covering 400 miles rejoined Greene to command the militia forces of N.C. and S.C., including his own brigade, at EUTAW SPRINGS, 8 Sept. "At the peak of his career, in his greatest battle, commanding the largest contingent of troops in his life, he had seen the men he had trained fight like professionals," writes Bass. (*Op. cit.*, 217) It was due largely to Marion's personal influence on the field that Greene could tell Congress, "the militia gained much honor by their firmness," and could write Steuben, "such conduct would have graced the veterans of the Great King of Prussia." (*Ibid.*)

Elected to the state senate, Marion was at Jacksonboro for the Gen. Assy. starting 8 Jan. '82, but his brigade was given the mission of protecting the area. On 10 Jan. he wrote Col. Peter Horry to assume command, but on the 24th he had to take leave from his urgent political duties and rush back to take over. Because of jealousy between Horry and Col. Hezekiah Maham, who commanded the dragoons of the brigade, both of these officers had found one pretext or another to turn their responsibilities over to subordinates. At this critical moment Col. Benj. Thompson led a 700-man expedition from the Charleston defenses, crossed the Cooper (23 Feb.) and scattered Marion's divided forces. He rallied the remnants and directed a counterattack, but poor execution on the part of some of his untrained horsemen led to another reverse around Wambaw Bridge. (This place is about 40 mi. N.E. of Charleston, near the Santee.) He withdrew to his old camp at Cantey's Plantation (near Murray's Fy.) much demoralized by this sorry performance of his subordinates at a time when all should have been making the final effort to win the war. (Bass, *op. cit.*, 231) The next summer Marion was again assigned the mission of patrolling east of the Cooper River. At Fair Lawn, 29 Aug., he ambuscaded a force of 200 dragoons under Maj. Thos. Fraser sent from Charleston to surprise him. Capt. Gavin Witherspoon's reconnaissance party led the enemy into a trap that cost Fraser 20 men. The British captured an ammunition wagon, however, and Marion was forced to retreat for lack of powder. He had fought his last action.

When the war ended, Marion was appointed commandant of Ft. Johnson, a sinecure that brought £ 500 a year and compensated somewhat for losing virtually all his personal property during the Revolution. He was re-elected to the state senate in 1782 and '84, and sat in the state's constitutional convention in 1790. The latter year he left his post at Ft. Johnson, and in 1791 he was elected to fill an unexpired term in the state senate. Meanwhile, in 1786, he married Mary Esther Videau, a wealthy spinster cousin about his own age. He died on 27 Feb. '95 at the age of about 63.

The "Marion Legend" has long obscured the history of his life, and the principal villain is Parson Weems, who invented much of the "Washington Legend" and who, unfortunately, rewrote a manuscript on Marion's life that Peter Horry had drafted. After reading the Weems book, Horry wrote him in despair: "Most certainly 'tis not my history, but your romance." William James, who joined Marion at the age of 15, wrote a simple biographical sketch of his idol, and Wm. Gilmore Simms fashioned this into another fantasy. The Swamp Fox emerged as an American Bayard, and Wm. Cullen Bryant started his "Song of Marion's Men" with: "Our band is few, but true and tried,/ Our leader frank and bold;/ The British soldier trembles/ When Marion's name is told." Robert D. Bass gives this summary:

"He was neither a Robin Hood nor a Chevalier Bayard. He was a moody, introverted, semiliterate genius who rose from private to Brigadier General * through an intuitive grasp of strategy and tactics, personal bravery, devotion to duty, and worship of liberty.

"By nature Marion was gentle, kind, and humane. Yet his orders, orderly books, battle reports, and personal letters reveal another side of his character. He shot pickets, retaliated from ambush, failed to honor flags of truce, and knowingly violated international law. He could forgive the Tories, and yet he could court-martial his closest friend." (*Op. cit.*, 4)

Unlike Thos. Sumter, he could subordinate himself to higher military au-

---

* Of militia. His highest rank in the Cont'l. Army, not attained until 30 Sept. '83, was Col., 2d S.C. This is an interesting commentary on the value attached to Marion's service by Congress, who appointed 26 Bvt. B.G.'s on this same date.

thority and fit his partisan operations into the over-all strategy of Greene. While most famous as a guerrilla, he had the military standards of a regular. "The personal as well as the soldierly qualities of the plain little man endeared him to his contemporaries," says Robt. L. Meriwether in *D.A.B.* Uncounted babies, some 29 towns, and 17 counties were named after him. (Bass, *op. cit.*, 4)

The definitive biography is Robt. D. Bass, *Swamp Fox* (1959).

MARION'S BRIGADE. After being named B.G. of S.C. State troops late in 1780, Marion appointed officers and started recruiting his brigade. Col. Peter Horry's mounted element comprised troops under Maj. Lemuel Benson and Capts. John Baxter, John Postell, Daniel Conyers, and James McCauley. Lt. Col. Hugh Horry (Peter's brother) commanded the foot regiment while Col. Adam McDonald was on parole; companies were headed by Maj. John James and Capts. John James, James Postell, and James Witherspoon. (James was a popular name!) Col. Hugh Ervin was Marion's second in command; A.D.C. were Capts. John Milton, Lewis Ogier, and Thos. Elliott, the latter handling the semiliterate commander's correspondence with Gov. Rutledge and Gen. Greene. An estimated 2,500 men served at one time or another in the brigade. (Bass, *Swamp Fox,* 127)

MARJORIBANKS, John. d. 1781. British officer, hero of Eutaw Springs. Commissioned Ensign 24 May '49, he became Lt. in the Scotch-Dutch Brigade on 21 Oct. '49, Lt. 19th Foot on 22 Sept. '57, and was wounded in the siege of Belle Isle (Belle-Ile en Mer, 1759 ?). On 26 Sept. '61 he became Adj., and the 22d of the next month he was promoted to Capt. of the 108th Foot. On 2 Apr. '62 he returned to the

19th Foot as Capt.-Lt., was advanced to Capt. on 15 June '63, Bvt.-Maj. 29 Aug. '77, and Maj. on 17 Nov. '80. From Dec. '79 to June '80 he commanded a light infantry company at Kilkenny, Ireland. He presumably accompanied his regiment when it crossed the Atlantic to reinforce Clinton in the South, arriving at Charleston 4 June '81, and marched with Rawdon to the relief of Ninety-Six. As commander of the flank battalion he was mortally wounded at EUTAW SPRINGS, 8 Sept., and died 23 Oct. '81. His name is officially spelled Marjoribanks (pronounced Marshbanks), although many modern American writers omit the first r.

MARKSMANSHIP. A lot about tactics and courage is explained by the little-realized fact that American marksmanship during the Revolution was very bad and British marksmanship was almost nonexistent, except in the special units of RIFLEMEN organized by both armies and by the Germans. At Lexington and Concord "only one American bullet out of 300 found its mark," writes Ward, "only one man out of 15 hit anybody." (*W.O.R.*, 50) At WETZELL'S MILLS, six years later, 25 expert *riflemen*, all of them veterans of Kings Mountain, fired from relatively close range at the gallant British Lt. Col. James Webster as he led his troops on horseback across a ford they were covering—eight or nine of these riflemen fired twice—and Webster was not hit once. (*Ibid.*, 782, citing many sources) See also TICONDEROGA, 2–5 July '77.

As for the British regulars, they were not even taught to aim. An American captured at Ft. Washington said that not fewer than 10 pieces were fired at his group within a range of 40 to 50 yards, some at within 20 yards, and he was alive to give this critique: "I observed that they took no aim, and the moment [movement ?] of presenting and

firing was the same." (Curtis, *Org. of Br. Army*, 19) In wet weather only about one shot out of four went off. Whereas a good American flint could be used for 60 rounds without resharpening, a British flint was good for only six. (*Ibid.*, 19, 21) Defective American cartridge boxes, on the other hand, rendered Washington's army virtually defenseless at WARREN TAVERN.

As shown in the article on MUSKETS AND MUSKETRY, marksmanship was satisfactory for the linear tactics of the 18th century, and RIFLEMEN were of little value in battle. Outstanding sharpshooter of the Revolution was Timothy MURPHY.

MARQUE AND REPRISAL, Letters of. Paper authorizing the operations of PRIVATEERS. The ship itself was often referred to as a *letter of marque*.

MARQUISIE. See MAUSSAC DE LA MARQUISIE.

MARRINER, William. Whaleboat guerrilla. N.J. Natives of New Brunswick, he and Adam Hyler operated in small boats between Egg Harbor (near modern Atlantic City, N.J.) and Staten Island to prey on British and Tory vessels. Marriner was a prisoner on Long Island and after being exchanged he returned to capture his captor, a Maj. Sherbrook. He also captured the Tory Simon Cortelyou from his house near what later was Ft. Hamilton, L.I. See main bibliography for Cook, *What Manner of Men*.

MARSHALL, John. 1755–1835. Cont'l. officer, Chief Justice. Va. Remembered as the "principal founder of judicial review and of the American system of constitutional law" (E. S. Corwin in *D.A.B.*), John Marshall won this reputation long after the period of American history with which we are primarily concerned in this book. He first saw action in the military operations that drove Dunmore from his state, serving at Great Bridge, 9 Dec. '75, and Norfolk, 1 Jan. '76. Leaving the Culpeper Minute Men, on 30 July he became a 1st Lt. in the 3d Va. Cont'ls. He became Capt.-Lt. of the 15th Va. in Dec., with rank retroactive to 31 July '76. On 20 Nov. '77 he became Deputy J.A., and on 1 July '78 he was promoted to Capt. On 14 Sept. '78 he transferred to the 7th Va., and on 12 Feb. '81 he retired from the army. (Heitman) During this time he fought at the Brandywine, Germantown, Monmouth, and Stony Point.

On 28 Aug. '80 he was admitted to the bar, and in 1783 he moved to Richmond from the frontier region where he had been reared. He quickly became successful as a lawyer and entered the political arena. A number of the Va. assembly (1782–91 and 1795–97), delegate to the state convention that ratified the Constitution (1788), he declined the post of Attorney General (1795) and of Minister to France (1796) offered by Washington, but served on the "X.Y.Z." mission to France (1797–98). He was a Federalist congressman from 1799 to 1800, and then succeeded Pickering as Sec. of State, being appointed 12 May 1800 but not accepting the post for another two weeks. In an unpopular and unilateral move, Pres. John Adams then nominated Marshall to succeed Chief Justice Ellsworth, a position that Marshall accepted 4 Feb. 1801.

During the next 34 years he established the prestige of the Supreme Court. Major opinions include *Marbury v. Madison* (1803), *Fletcher v. Peck* (1810), the *Dartmouth College Case* (1819), a dissenting opinion in *Ogden v. Saunders* (1827), *McCulloch v. Maryland* (1819) (with its doctrine of implied powers), and *Gibbons v.*

Ogden (1824). Summing up Marshall's personal role, one authority writes:

"Of a total of 1,215 cases during that period [1801–35], in 94, no opinions were filed; in 15, the decision was by the Court; and in the remaining 1,106 cases, Marshall delivered the opinion in 519 [of which 36 involved constitutional questions and 80 involved questions of international law or kindred questions]." (*D.A.B.*, quoting Warren, *Supreme Court in U.S. Hist.* [3 vols., 1922].)

His 5-vol. *Life of Washington* was republished in two volumes in 1930.

MARTHA'S VINEYARD RAID, *c.* 8 Sept. '78. After his BEDFORD–FAIR HAVEN RAID, Mass., 6 Sept., Gen. Chas. Grey descended on Martha's Vineyard and force-requisitioned a large number of sheep and cattle. He landed at Holmes's Hole (Vineyard Haven) and did damage that seriously crippled the island's whale-fishing industry. (*E.B.*) According to Freeman, the episode "cost the British far more in ill-will than they gained for their commissary." (*Washington,* V, 77) Lossing says they destroyed several vessels, and that the defenseless inhabitants lost 300 oxen, 10,000 sheep, the militia arms, and "the public money." (II, 84 *n.*)

MARTIN, Josiah. 1737–1786. Royal Gov. of N.C., British officer. One of 23 children, and son of a British Col. of Antigua, West Indies, he entered the army in 1757. In 1761 he married his cousin, Elizabeth Martin of "Rockhall" on Long Island. Because of bad health he sold his commission as Lt. Col. in 1769. Early in 1771 he was commissioned royal Gov. of N.C.—succeeding Tryon—and, going there from N.Y., he took office at New Bern on 12 Aug. (A. R. Newsome in *D.A.B.*) "Governor Josiah Martin was a soldier, but a sensible one," points out Alden. (*South,* 195) Furthermore, and the military marvels mount, he was preceded to N.C. by "reports of his amiable character" (*D.A.B.*). He soon started a losing battle on matters of taxation, the "foreign attachment issue," and other local matters. Since he could not reconcile the demands of the assembly with the instruction from the Crown, Gov. Martin saw the colony's juridical system collapse even before he was faced with the local patriot movement that started in 1774. He had the unfortunate impression that he could muster sufficient Loyalist strength to hold his province, and in Mar. '75 he urged Gen. Gage to send him arms and ammunition. As the patriot militia gathered around him Martin sent his family off to N.Y. and on 31 May '75 he himself fled to the safety of Ft. Johnston, on Cape Fear. (*Ibid.*, 196) He reached the fort two days later. (*D.A.B.*) On 18 July he boarded H.M.S. *Cruizer,* just a jump ahead of capture.

His incorrect evaluation of the local situation, and that of other royal governors-in-exile, led the British to send the ill-fated Charleston Expedition of Clinton in 1776 and helped bring about the abortive Loyalist uprising that was crushed at MOORES CREEK BRIDGE, 27 Feb. '76.

After watching the Charleston fiasco in June, he went to his wife's home on Long Island. In 1779 he returned to Charleston with Clinton and served usefully and creditably as a volunteer under Cornwallis in the Carolinas in 1780–81. (*D.A.B.*). Again bothered by bad health, he left Cornwallis at Wilmington in Apr. '81, and after a visit to Long Island he sailed to London. He drew his salary as Gov. until Oct. '83 and was compensated for the loss of his property in N.C. Shortly thereafter he died in London.

Martin also had been involved with the REGULATORS.

MARTIN'S STATION, Ky. Since Ky. was part of Va. during the Revolution, it may be said that two places existed in the Old Dominion called Martin's Station. The more famous was on the Wilderness Road in the western tip of modern Va. and within 20 miles of Cumberland Gap. The other Martin's Station was captured in the KY. RAID OF BIRD in June '80.

MASON, George. 1725–1792. American statesman, constitutionalist. Va. The master of "Gunston Hall" (built between 1755 and 1758) and its large plantation on the Potomac below Alexandria, George Mason was a tidewater aristocrat who, through his connection with the Ohio Company, also knew the frontier. For several reasons his important role in the years preceding the Revolution were played off stage: he was running a large estate, he suffered from chronic ill health, his wife died early in 1773, and he had nine children. Another reason was his low opinion of committee efforts. (Helen Hill in *D.A.B.*)

He served with Washington in the House of Burgesses in 1759 and succeeded the newly elected C. in C. in the July '75 convention. During these years the two collaborated closely. Mason also had a relationship with George Rogers Clark that was as close as father to son. (*Ibid.*)

To hit the highlights of George Mason's role in the American Revolution, in 1765 he contrived a way of circumventing the Stamp Act in a certain legal procedure without the use of stamped paper. He drafted the VIRGINIA RESOLVES, May '69, and the Fairfax Resolves of 18 July '74. His statement of the colonies' constitutional position in the latter paper was successively adopted by the county, the state, and by the Cont'l. Cong. In 1775 he emerged from political retirement to attend the

July convention (mentioned above), and he was on the committee of safety that took over the powers vacated by DUN-MORE. As a member of the May '76 convention he framed the Va. Bill of Rights and Constitution. The former piece of writing had wide influence: Jefferson drew on it in drafting the first part of the Decl. of Indep., it was copied by many states, it was the basis for the first 10 amendments to the U.S. Constitution, and it even had influence in the French Revolution. Mason's state constitution was also a remarkably successful pioneering effort. He was involved with the revision of state laws and with disestablishment. He was on the committee that authorized the Western Operations of Clark, and he received Clark's full report. In connection with the problem of western lands, Mason was in some measure responsible for establishing the boundary of 1783 at the Great Lakes rather than at the Ohio, and he outlined the plan for his state's cession of western lands to the central government.

A believer in states' rights, Mason was one of three of the 42 delegates to the Constitutional Convention of 1787 in Philadelphia who refused to sign the final draft. (The others were Gerry and Edmund Randolph.) His views were expressed in *Objections to the Proposed Federal Constitution*, one of his finest pieces of political writing. Mason's principal reasons for failing to sign—a decision he did not make until the final two weeks of the "Great Debate"—were that the Constitution compromised on Northern and Southern positions with respect to the tariff and slavery. "His opposition to the institution of slavery was perhaps the most consistent feature of his public career." (*Ibid.*) He objected also to the omission of a bill of rights from the Constitution. History bore him out.

See Helen Day (Hill) Miller, *George Mason, Constitutionalist* (Cambridge, 1938).

MASONRY IN AMERICA. Early in the 17th century a society of London stone workers started admitting honorary members as "accepted masons" and initiating them into their secret signs and legendary history. In 1717 four of these London societies or lodges united to form a grand lodge with the object of mutual assistance and the promotion of brotherhood. Thirteen years prior to this the American Jonathan BELCHER became a Freemason during a visit to England but on his return to Boston he is said to have been the only member of the society in that city. In 1733, lodges were installed in Boston and Philadelphia. The latter lasted only five years but was revived in 1749 by Benjamin Franklin. In Boston, however, the original lodge flourished and another was organized in 1756. They included such men as James Otis and Paul Revere, a carefully selected group based entirely on character rather than wealth and prestige but whose belief in the brotherhood of man happened to coincide with the spirit of the American Revolution. (Forbes, *Revere*, 59) Many prominent Revolutionaries therefore happened to be Masons, and the secret nature of their meetings lent itself to patriot politics. Washington was initiated in Fredericksburg, Va., in 1752, took the oath of office as President on his Masonic bible, and used a Masonic trowel to lay the cornerstone of the Capitol at Washington. Joseph Warren was a Grand Master, and in 1824 Lafayette, a French Mason, laid the cornerstone of the Bunker Hill Monument that had been donated in his honor by the Order. It is said that every Maj. Gen. of the American Army except Benedict Arnold was a Master Mason. (Lossing, II, 437 *n.*) There are several stories of men being spared during the Revolution because the enemy recognized their Masonic sign. (See, for example, Lossing, II, 386 *n.*)

Anti-Masonic sentiment reached a peak in 1826 after William Morgan of Batavia, N.Y., was kidnapped and allegedly murdered for revealing secrets of the Order. The investigation of this event and trials revealed that almost all officeholders of N.Y. State were Masons. This led to creation of the Anti-Masonic Party in N.Y. to oppose the re-election of Andrew Jackson (a Mason); this was the country's first third party. Half a century was to pass before popular feeling against the Masons and other secret societies disappeared.

MASSACHUSETTS CIRCULAR LETTER. 11 Feb. '68. To inform the other 12 colonies of steps taken by the Mass. General Court to oppose the Townshend Acts, this letter, drafted by James Otis and Sam Adams, was approved 11 Feb. '68. It denounced the acts as TAXATION WITHOUT REPRESENTATION, reasserted that Americans could never be represented in Parliament, attacked British moves to make colonial governors and judges independent of colonial assemblies, and invited proposals for concerted resistance. See also TAXATION, external and internal.

Gov. Bernard dissolved the Mass. Gen. Court on 4 March on the grounds that the Circular Letter was seditious. Before other colonial governors received a message from Hillsborough dated 21 Apr. to prevent their assemblies from endorsing the letter, N.H., N.J., Conn., and Va. had rallied to support the letter. The Sam Adams–Joseph Hawley–Otis triumvirate led the majority in the Mass. House of Representatives that on 30 June '68 voted 92 to 17 against rescinding the letter. "This spirited defiance did more to unite the colonies than any measure since the

Stamp Act," writes Samuel Eliot Morison in his *D.A.B.* article on Otis. "The Massachusetts '92' became another such talisman as No. 45 of the *North Briton.*" (See John WILKES) Gov. Bernard dissolved the new General Court on 1 July. The 17 "Rescinders" came under heavy attack by the Sons of Liberty and seven lost their seats in the election of May '69. (*E.A.H.*)

MASSACHUSETTS PROVINCIAL CONGRESS, 1774. The Mass. Gov't. Act, 20 May '74, in addition to virtually annulling the Mass. Charter, prescribed that effective 1 Aug. members of the Council would be appointed by the King and hold office at his pleasure. Previously they had been elected by the House of Representatives. In accordance with the King's orders, Gage established the capital at Salem, where on 17 June the General Assembly met under protest against the removal of their seat from Boston. Locking the door against Gage's order to dissolve, the Assembly proposed that a Cont'l. congress be called, and they elected five delegates from Mass.

A few weeks later Gage appointed 36 members to the Governor's Council. Eleven immediately declined to serve, and the others came under such public pressure that no more than 16 remained. The latter then were forced to take refuge in Boston. In Sept., Gage called for the Council and Assembly (together comprising the General Court) to meet at Salem on 5 Oct., but he then withdrew the summons because he realized his 16 fugitive councilmen would not be permitted to attend. Assuming that Gage had no right to cancel his call, the patriots elected delegates to the Assembly and this lower house was seated at Salem on the announced date, 5 Oct. When Gage failed to appear after two days —the neglect was intentional—the delegates adjourned to Concord and organized themselves into a Provincial Congress. With John Hancock as president this completely illegal body thereafter operated as the government of all Mass. outside British-controlled Boston. (Alden, *Gage,* 216; Ward, *W.O.R.,* 16–17)

MASSACRES AND "MASSACRES." See BOSTON "MASSACRE," CHERRY VALLEY, GNADENHUETTEN, HAW RIVER, LITTLE EGG HARBOR, LOGAN, PAOLI, PAXTON BOYS, TAPPAN, WAXHAWS, and WYOMING VALLEY.

MATHEW, Edward. 1729–1805. British general. Starting his military career as an ensign in the Coldstream Guards in 1746, in 1775 he became Col. and A.D.C. to the King, and the next year he reached America as a B.G. commanding a brigade of Guards. He landed with Clinton's first wave at Kip's Bay, 15 Sept., took part in the capture of Ft. Washington, 16 Nov. '76, and collaborated with Adm. Collier in the highly successful raid to Va. in May '79. (See VA. MIL. OPNS.) As a volunteer with Knyphausen's SPRINGFIELD, N.J., RAID in June '80, he led the turning movement across Vauxhall Bridge. Promoted to Maj. Gen. in 1779 (having apparently gotten this "local rank" in the spring of 1778), he returned to England in 1780. In Nov. '82 he was appointed C. in C. in the West Indies, and in 1797 was promoted to full Gen. His name often is misspelled *Matthews.*

MATHEWS, George. 1739–1812. Cont'l. officer, postwar Gov. of Ga. Va.–Ga. Son of a recent Irish immigrant, he led a volunteer company against the Indians when he was 22, and took part in the battle at Point Pleasant, 10 Oct. '74 (DUNMORE'S WAR). Lt. Col. of the 9th Va. on 4 Mar. '76, he was promoted to Col. on 10 Feb. '77, fought at the Brandywine,

and led the regiment in a deep penetration at GERMANTOWN, 4 Oct. '77, where he and most of the 9th Va. were finally surrounded and captured. Mathews is said to have received nine bayonet wounds. (Heitman) After spending several months on a prison ship in N.Y. harbor, he was exchanged on 5 Dec. '81, joined Greene's army in the South as Col. of Va. troops. (He was "attached" to the 3d Va., says Heitman. Abraham Buford remained in command of the regiment. [*op. cit.,* 56, 384].) He was breveted B.G. on 30 Sept.

In 1785 Mathews moved with his family to Ga., became a B.G. of militia, was elected Gov. in 1787, represented the state in Congress 1789–91, and again served as Gov. 1793–96. During the latter period he opposed the trans-Oconee adventures of Elijah CLARKE and signed the notorious Yazoo Act. In 1798 President Adams nominated him to be the first Gov. of the Miss. Territory, but within a month his name was withdrawn because of dubious land speculations and for suspected complicity in the Blount Conspiracy. He then became involved in highly questionable activities whose aim was to draw East and West Florida into the U.S. His technique was ahead of the times: he sought first to stir up an insurrection of the English-speaking element, support them with recruits from Ga., and finally to bring in "volunteers" from U.S. regular army units. Although the local military commander scotched the last feature, the "insurgents" rose up and on 17 Mar. 1812 declared independence of Spain. With the insurgents and Ga. volunteers Mathews took formal possession of Fernandina on 18 Mar. in the name of the U.S. and by June was within sight of St. Augustine. Sec. Monroe finally stepped in to repudiate Mathews and bring his adventure to a halt. Mathews was on his way to avenge himself on the federal government when he died at Augusta. Isaac J. Cox says in his *D.A.B.* article that Mathews "carried to the grave much evidence that might explain his de‚ batable conduct."

MATROSS. A soldier who assists artillery gunners in loading, firing, sponging, and moving the guns.

MATSON'S FORD, Pa., 11 Dec. '77. After Howe's sortie toward WHITE MARSH, 5–8 Dec., Cornwallis was sent from Philadelphia with 3,500 men and almost all the dragoons and mounted jägers to forage along the south bank of the Schuylkill. He left the night of 10–11 Dec.—at 3 A.M., according to André. By coincidence, Washington started from White Marsh toward Valley Forge winter quarters on the 11th, and his leading elements clashed with the foragers at "fhe Gulph," near Matson's Ford (modern W. Conshohocken, Pa.) just after crossing the Schuylkill. The American vanguard withdrew, destroying their makeshift bridge of wagons and planks. The raiders returned to Philadelphia the evening of the 12th with 2,000 sheep and cattle. (Baurmeister, *Journals,* 139) Washington's army stayed on the north bank through the 13th, remained in the vicinity of the Gulph until the 19th, and then moved to Valley Forge. (Freeman, *Washington,* IV, 564 *n.*)

MAUSSAC DE LA MARQUISIE, Bernard. French volunteer. Heitman has no notice of this officer, under any of the five possible forms of his name (de Marquisie, La Marquisie, Marquisie, Maussac, or the alias given by Lasseray, Moissac). Lasseray gives only these facts: as a Capt. he is mentioned in a letter of 31 July '76 from Washington to Congress; he became Maj. in the 4th N.Y. Regt.; he distinguished himself under the command of Wash-

ington, St. Clair, and Wayne; in a letter to the deputies of the Gironde in 1791 he mentioned his American service and the praise they had evoked from his commanders; he was from Bordeaux.

Nickerson, who unfortunately cites no sources, makes these references to a French engineer sent to repair Ft. Stanwix. "As late as May 19, '77, Capt. La Marquisie had written to Gates that it had become so dilapidated that it could not be repaired, but must be built over again, for 'all is destroyed.' " Nickerson says the Frenchman "was certainly incompetent and probably a rascal"; Gansevoort and Willett "sent him to Albany under arrest." (*Turning Point,* 197, 198)

MAWHOOD, Charles. d. 1780. British officer. Cornet in the 1st Dragoons 13 Aug. '52 and Lt. 8 Nov. '56, he became Capt.-Lt. in the 15th Light Dragoons on 20 Mar. '59, Capt. in the 18th Light Dragoons on 6 Dec. '59, Maj. in the 3d Foot ("Buffs") on 17 May '63, and Lt. Col. of the 19th Foot on 17 June '67. On 26 Oct. '75 he became Lt. Col. of the 17th Foot, a unit that had been sent to America prior to Aug. of that year. (Fortescue, *British Army,* III, 173 *n.*) He led British forces at PRINCETON, 3 Jan. '77, QUINTAIN'S BRIDGE, 18 Mar. '78, and HANCOCK'S BRIDGE, 21 Mar. '78. Having been appointed Col. of the 72d Regt. ("Manchester Volunteers") on 16 Dec. '77, he died on 29 Aug. '80, shortly after joining his regiment at Gibraltar.

MAXWELL, William. *c.* 1733–1796. Cont'l. general. Ireland–N.J. Coming to America with his Scotch-Irish parents around 1747, he received a very ordinary education as a farm boy in what is now Warren co. At the age of 21 he joined a British regiment and was on Braddock's unfortunate expedition of

1755. He then became an ensign in Col. John Johnston's N.J. Regt. and subsequently a Lt. in the N.J. Regt. of Col. Peter Schuyler. During the final years of the French and Indian War he took part in Abercromby's disastrous attack on Ticonderoga and is believed to have been with Wolfe at Quebec. As a Col. he was subsequently on duty with the British commissary department at Mackinac. In 1774 he went home as a veteran of 20 years' military service to take an active part in the revolutionary movement in N.J.

"Scotch Willie" was a tall, ruddy-faced, stalwart man who spoke with a burr (*D.A.B.*) and who probably had already acquired a weakness for liquor. He was a member of the N.J. Prov. Cong. of May and Oct., '75, and in Aug. of that year became chairman of the county committee of safety. On 8 Nov. he was commissioned Col. and raised the 2d N.J. In Feb. '76 he marched north with five full companies as part of the column Gen. John Sullivan led to support the ill-starred CANADA INVASION. Maxwell commanded his troops in the disaster at TROIS RIVIÈRES, 8 June, and was one of those who, the next month, opposed abandonment of Crown Point. He complained to Congress when Arthur St. Clair was promoted ahead of him (9 Aug.). On 23 Oct. he was appointed B.G. and returned to his home state about the time the British turned to chase Washington's army across it to the Delaware. (N.J. CAMPAIGN) Initially in command of four new regiments of N.J. Cont'ls., on 21 Dec. Maxwell was sent by Washington to take charge of the militia at Morristown. A few days later, after the American success at Trenton, Maxwell got Washington's appeal for a diversionary effort against the British flank to speed their withdrawal from N.J., but he was not

able to accomplish anything worthwhile. (Freeman, *Washington*, IV, 295 *n.*, 330)

During the preliminary maneuvers of the PHILADELPHIA CAMPAIGN, Maxwell failed to arrive for the action at BRUNS-WICK, N.J., 22 June '77, because the order was not delivered to him. MAX-WELL'S LIGHT INFANTRY then was organized and opposed the enemy for the first time at COOCH'S BRIDGE, Del., 3 Sept., before taking a prominent—if not terribly important—part in the Battle of the BRANDYWINE, 11 Sept. '77. By this time a definite movement was afoot to have Maxwell dismissed from the army. His principal critic evidently was Maj. Wm. Heth, a veteran of Morgan's Rifles, who wrote his former commander on 2 Oct.:

"... since the enemy's landing at Head of Elk Maxwell's corps 'twas expected would do great things—we had opportunities and anybody but an old woman would [*sic*] availed themselves of them—He is to be sure a damned bitch of a General...." (Quoted in *ibid.*, 535 *n.*)

But administration had to wait for a halt in field operations, and "Scotch Willie" was not brought to trial until after he had taken part in the Battle of GERMANTOWN, 4 Oct. Charged generally with misconduct and excessive drinking, on 4 Nov. he was given what Freeman calls "something of a Scotch verdict" (*ibid.*): he was not exonerated, but the charges were not proved. During the Valley Forge Winter Quarters Maxwell's Brig. comprised the 1st, 2d, 3d, and 4th N.J.

On 7 May '78 he was ordered to Mount Holly, N.J., as Washington coped with the complex strategic problems preceding the MONMOUTH CAMPAIGN. Maxwell figured prominently in the maneuvers that followed and in the Battle of MONMOUTH, 28 June. He testified at LEE'S COURT-MARTIAL that the accused was so out of touch with the tactical situation in the initial phase of the battle that he did not know on which wing Maxwell's Brig. was located.

In July '78 Maxwell was guarding the N.J. coast opposite Staten Island, and he continued with this mission until the next year, when he led his brigade in SULLIVAN'S EXPEDITION against the Iroquois. He returned to N.J. and opposed Knyphausen's SPRINGFIELD RAID, 7–23 June '80. Dissatisfied with his lot, Maxwell submitted his resignation and then tried to withdraw it, but Congress accepted it on 25 July '80. This undistinguished old soldier was elected to the N.J. Assembly in 1783. After this he seems to have faded quietly away. He had never married.

MAXWELL'S LIGHT INFANTRY. On 28 Aug. '77 Washington directed that each of his six brigades contribute nine officers and 109 enlisted men to form a LIGHT INFANTRY corps. Placed under command of Brig. Gen. Wm. Maxwell, they fought their first action at COOCH'S BRIDGE, Pa., 3 Sept. '77. As part of Lincoln's Div. and reinforced to about 800 officers and men, Maxwell's corps was posted on the enemy side of the Brandywine initially and then defended Chadd's Ford. (See BRANDYWINE, 11 Sept. '77.) They followed the main body of Washington's army during the retreat, collecting stragglers and wounded. The corps was in reserve during the battle of Germantown, 4 Oct. '77, and was disbanded shortly thereafter. See MAXWELL for Heth's comment.

McALLISTER, Archibald. d. 1781. Cont'l. officer. Md. A Lt. in the Md. Bn. of the FLYING CAMP in July '76, he became an ensign in the 2d Md. Cont'ls.

on 10 Dec., was promoted to 2d Lt. of the 1st Md. on 17 Apr. '77 and became 1st Lt. on 27 May '78. With Michael RUDOLPH he was breveted Capt. on 24 Sept. '79 for their "military caution so happily combined with daring activity" at PAULUS HOOK. (The quote is from the Congressional resolution.) He died 16 Jan. '81. (Heitman) In Heitman the name is spelled McCallister.

McARTHUR, Archibald. British officer. Promoted to Capt. of the 54th Foot on 1 Sept. '71 and to Maj. of the 71st Foot on 16 Nov . '77, he was captured at COWPENS, 17 Jan. '81. On 24 Apr. '81 he was made Lt. Col. of the 3d Bn. of the 60th ("Royal Americans"). (*Army Lists*)

McCOWAN'S FORD, N.C. See COWAN'S FORD.

McCREA ATROCITY. Daughter of a Presbyterian minister of N.J., Jane McCrea left her father's house after her mother died and he remarried. She went to live with a brother who had settled along the Hudson River about halfway between Saratoga and Ft. Edward. She was engaged to David Jones, a Tory who was with Burgoyne's invading army in 1777, and when her brother moved to Albany Jane went to Ft. Edward with the hope of meeting her fiancé when the invaders arrived. She was taken in as a guest by the elderly Mrs. McNeil, a cousin of British Gen. Fraser (1729–1777). On 27 July '77 a band of Burgoyne's Indians reached abandoned Ft. Edward, two days ahead of the main body. Taking the two women, they started back to Ft. Ann, where the army had its headquarters at the time. They arrived with one woman, and a scalp that was promptly identified by Lt. David Jones as that of his fiancée, Jenny McCrea.

The most generally accepted version of her death is that she had been shot, scalped, and stripped of her clothing after her drunken captors had gotten into an altercation as to which should be her guard. Another version, which Lossing got from the granddaughter of Mrs. McNeil, is that she was accidentally shot by a member of an American pursuing party. She was 23 years old but at this point the authorities pursue their own ways on the matter of physical description. Either a beauty with long, raven tresses (Nickerson, *Turning Point,* 183; Lossing, I, 99 *n.*), or "a country girl . . . without either beauty or accomplishment" according to James Wilkinson, who probably saw her (Ward, *W.O.R.,* 497, citing Wilkinson, I, 231), she is also said to have had "clustering curls of soft blonde hair" (*ibid.,* citing Hudleston, *Burgoyne,* 166)—or it might have been "of extraordinary length and beauty, measuring a yard and a quarter . . . darker than a raven's wing" (Lossing). On the other hand, she might not have been 23—a British diarist says she was "about 18"—but she was a female and she was scalped and her hair was recognized in the British camp.

The culprit apparently was identified as a noble savage yclept the Wyandot Panther, but Burgoyne's hands were tied, since he could not discipline the Panther without losing his Indian allies. Recognizing that they had a rare opportunity for using this atrocity to whip up popular indignation against the invaders, the Americans skilfully exploited it. Horatio Gates, who had recently assumed command in the north and to whom Burgoyne had written a complaint about the treatment of prisoners taken at Bennington, sent back what he proudly called this "Tickler upon Scalping":

"* * * That the savages of America should in their warfare mangle and scalp the unhappy prisoners who fall into their hands, is neither new nor extraordinary; but that the famous Lieutenant General Burgoyne, in whom the fine Gentleman is united with the Soldier and the Scholar, should hire the savages of America to scalp Europeans and the descendants of Europeans, nay more, that he should pay a price for each scalp so barbarously taken, is more than will be believed in Europe, untill authenticated facts shall, in every Gazette, convince mankind of the truth of the horrid fate.* * * The miserable fate of Miss McCrea was particularly aggravated by her being dressed to receive her promised husband, but met her murderer employed by you.* * *" (C. & M., 560, from Gates Papers)

When Lincoln and Wilkinson commented that this was rather personal, Gates said, "By God I don't believe either of you can mend it." Burgoyne wrote back that Jenny's fate "wanted not of the tragic display you have labored to give it to make it as sincerely abhorred and lamented by me as it can by the tenderest of her friends." Gentleman Johnnie went on to say that from his considerable insight into the Indian mentality he was convinced, beyond the possibility of a doubt, that "a pardon, under the forms which I prescribed and they accepted, would be more efficacious than an execution to prevent similar mischiefs."

This exchange of correspondence took place the first week in Sept. '77, a month after word of the atrocity had started to spread. Propaganda had borne its first fruit at Bennington, where an unexpectedly large and effective body of militia had turned up and annihilated a detachment from Burgoyne's army. Militia continued to gather, and they were a major factor in the ultimate defeat of Burgoyne. The story of Jenny McCrea's murder, as improved by American PROPAGANDISTS, played a large part in mustering this mushroom army.

See Nickerson, *Turning Point*, 470–72, for what Ward calls an elaborate discussion of the incident. Ward has a good summary of the various versions (*W.O.R.*, 496–97, 898 notes).

"McCULLOCH'S LEAP." After bringing reinforcements to WHEELING, Sept. '77, Maj. Samuel McCulloch (or McColloch) was separated from his men and pursued by Indians. He escaped by riding his horse down an almost vertical, 150-foot precipice to the bank of Wheeling Creek, and across the stream to safety. (Lossing, II, 499 *n.*) How much of this descent was "free fall" and how much of it was a perilous slide is uncertain. Although Lossing speaks of a "momentous leap," he calls the cliff *"almost* perpendicular" (italics added) and says the horse and rider "reached the foot of the bluff" and then "dashed through the creek. . . ."

McDONALD, Donald. This elderly British officer who figured prominently in the Tory defeat at MOORES CREEK BRIDGE, 27 Feb. '76, was paroled and later exchanged in Philadelphia. Continuing to serve until the end of the Revolution, he died shortly thereafter in London. American accounts generally spell his name as given above, but he himself signed as Mac-Donald.

McDONALD, Flora. 1722–1790. Jacobite and Tory heroine. As a schoolgirl she helped the Young Pretender escape to the Isle of Skye in June '46, after CULLODEN. Imprisoned in the Tower, she was released when the story of her exploit aroused national admiration. She even was presented in court,

and when George II asked why she had helped an enemy of the crown and the kingdom she replied, "It was no more than I would have done for your majesty, had you been in like situation." This simple answer epitomized the "defense" that won her life and freedom. Four years later, on 6 Nov. '50, she married Allan McDonald. In Aug. '74 she went with him and their children to join the colony of Highlanders in N.C. (*D.N.B.*) Here she did much to rally the Scots to the standard of Donald McDonald. Her husband, who had become a Tory B.G., was captured at Moores Creek Bridge (27 Feb. '76) and sent to Halifax, Va. On his advice she returned to Scotland in 1779, and he followed later. Two of their sons were lost with the *Ville de Paris*, 12 Apr. '82, when GRASSE surrendered her. Flora is buried on the Isle of Skye. (Lossing, II, 584 *n.*) The *D.N.B.* spells her name Macdonald.

McDOUGALL, Alexander. 1732–1786. Cont'l. general. Scotland–N.Y. Born at Islay, Inner Hebrides, he came to America at the age of six when his father was with a party that planned to establish a settlement near Ft. Edward, south of Lake George, N.Y. When this enterprise failed, the father was reduced to laboring as a milkman in N.Y.C. At the age of 24, young McDougall was commanding a privateer in the French and Indian War, sailing the *Barrington* and *Tiger* between the years 1756 and 1763. Having accumulated sufficient capital, he set up a store in N.Y.C., became a successful merchant, and undertook to educate himself. With the background of privateer and merchant (in addition to being a Scot) he naturally became an opponent of Britain's measures to end their policy of "salutary neglect." One of the most prominent radical leaders of the colony, he was suspected of having written the anonymous pamphlet, *A Son of Liberty to the Betrayed Inhabitants of the City and Colony of New York,* which was published 16 Dec. '69. The document was declared libelous and he was arrested on 8 Feb. '70 on testimony of the printer. Refusing to give bail, he was thrown into prison and soon became famous as "the first martyr in the patriot cause" (Appleton's) and "the John WILKES of America." Writing in *D.A.B.,* Daniel C. Haskell says, "So numerous were visits of his partisans that he was obliged to appoint visiting hours." His case was dramatized by the death of the principal witness, which meant there could be no trial, but when he refused to answer the summons of the General Assembly for questioning he was held in contempt and kept in jail until Mar. '71—a confinement of over a year. He presided over the meeting in the "FIELDS," 6 July '74. Commissioned Col. 1st N.Y. on 30 June '76, he was appointed B.G. on 9 Aug., just before the start of the N.Y. Campaign. He took part in the battles of WHITE PLAINS (28 Oct. '76) and Germantown (4 Oct. '77), but rendered his most important service in the Hudson Highlands, where he was the commanding general during much of the war. (*D.A.B.*) (On 16 Mar. '78 he was named to succeed the incompetent Israel PUTNAM.) Having been appointed Cont'l. Maj. Gen. on 20 Oct. '77, he succeeded Arnold as commander at West Point in 1780, represented N.Y. in the Cont'l. Cong. of 1781–82, declined appointment as minister of marine in 1781, was court-martialed in 1782 for insubordination to Heath (*D.A.B.*), and during the winter of 1782–83 headed the delegation of officers to discuss pay problems with Congress.

"Washington rated him high for sound sense, energy and military judg-ment [writes D. S. Freeman]. A slight impediment of speech did not interfere greatly with McDougall's public utterance. If his letters were too numerous and too long, they never were lacking in reason or staunchness. Had the health of McDougall been better, his place among American commanders might have been near the top." (*Washington,* IV, 617B)

He retired from the Cont'l. Army on 3 Nov. '83, served as state senator 1783–86, and was in the Congress of 1784–85. The man who had roused rabbles in his youth grew conservative with age. One indication of this change, points out *D.A.B.,* is that he helped organize the Bank of N.Y. and became its first president.

His son, John, died near St. Johns in 1775 (Appleton's). A daughter, Elizabeth, married John LAURANCE. A cousin, John, was killed 7 Mar. '78, when the *Randolph* (32) blew up while in action against the *Yarmouth* (64). (*Ibid.*)

McGOWN'S PASS (Manhattan), N.Y. A defile at the N.E. corner of modern Central Park, where the (Boston) Post Road ran between two steep hills before winding down a steep grade to Harlem Plains, this terrain feature was one of Howe's objectives after landing at KIP'S BAY, 15 Sept. '76. It was held by Lord Percy when the main British force moved toward White Plains. Here the traitor William DE-MONT entered the British lines, and it was from this position that Percy started his attack on FT. WASHINGTON, 16 Nov. '76. Preferred spelling seems to be McGown (Bliven, *Manhattan, passim;* Freeman, *Washington,* III, 470 *n.,* and IV, 198 *n.,* although the latter work *indexes* the name as McGowan).

McINTOSH, John. 1755–1826. Cont'l. officer. Ga. A nephew of Lachlan McIntosh and born in McIntosh co., Ga., he was an officer of the Ga. Line in 1775 and on 7 Jan. '76 became a Capt. in the 1st Ga. On 1 Apr. '78 he was promoted to Lt. Col. Commandant of the 3d Ga. Heitman identifies him by the nickname "Come and take it," a phrase included in his reply of 25 Nov. '78 to the demand of Col. L⁚ V. Fuser that McIntosh surrender Ft. Morris (Sunbury) with the honors of war. (The exchange of notes is in C. & M., 1075–76.) He was not present at the British capture of SUNBURY, 9 Jan. '79, but was taken prisoner at Briar Creek, 3 Mar. '79, and exchanged in the fall of 1780 for John Harris CRUGER. (Heitman gives no date, but Cruger was captured in June '80, exchanged for McIntosh soon thereafter, and was on duty at Ninety-Six prior to mid-Sept. '80.) According to Heitman, he served to the end of the war.

Moving to Fla. after the war, he settled on St. Johns River. There he was suddenly arrested by Spanish troops and imprisoned at St. Augustine on suspicion of illegal activities against the government. He then was held for a year in Morro Castle, Havana, and after his release is said to have "aided in destroying a fort on the St. John's river opposite Jacksonville and done the Spanish government other injuries." (Appleton's) During the last months of the War of 1812 he was a Maj. Gen. of militia at Mobile (*ibid.;* Heitman does not confirm this).

John's son, James Simmons McIntosh (1787–1847), was wounded as a Lt. in the War of 1812, remained in the Regular Army, and was mortally wounded while leading a brigade at Molino del Rey, Mexico. Two sons of James Simmons McIntosh fought on opposing sides in the Civil War: James McQueen McIntosh (1828–1862) graduated last in the 43-man West Point class of 1849,

joined the cavalry, and was a B.G. in the Confederate army when he was killed in action at Pea Ridge, Ark.; John Baillie McIntosh (1829–1888) entered the navy in 1848, resigned two years later, was commissioned 2d Lt. of cavalry in 1861, lost a leg at Winchester, 16 Sept. '64, where he commanded a cavalry brigade, and retired in 1870 as a B.G.

McINTOSH, Lachlan. 1725–1806. Cont'l. general. Scotland–Ga. Born at Inverness, he came to Ga. with his parents in 1736, shortly after Oglethorpe established that colony, and settled at the place later named Darien. In 1748 he went to Charleston, where he is said to have become a friend of Henry Laurens, lived in his home, and to have become a clerk in his counting house. Little is known of his life until July '75, when he appeared in Savannah as a member of the provincial congress. Lossing says his father was taken as a prisoner to St. Augustine when Lachlan was 13, and that he became a surveyor after returning home from Charleston. (II, 728 *n.*) About this time "he was considered the handsomest man in Georgia." (*Ibid.*).

On 7 Jan. '76 he became Col. of a Ga. Bn. that later was augmented and incorporated into the Cont'l. Army. On 16 Sept. '76 he was promoted to B.G. As a result of the conflict between state and federal authorities over control of Cont'l. troops in Ga., efforts of civil authorities to blame Cont'l. officers for the abortive military efforts toward Fla. (see SOUTHERN THEATER), and personal differences, including Button Gwinnett's arrest of McIntosh's brother on suspicion of treachery, McIntosh mortally wounded GWINNETT in a duel (May '77). McIntosh was himself wounded. Although acquitted in the trial that followed, he met with such hostility from Gwinnett's supporters that he had himself transferred to the North. In May '78, after commanding the N.C. Brig. during winter quarters at Valley Forge, he was ordered to head the Western Dept.

Here he showed a combination of incompetence and inability to handle subordinates. Ordered to suppress the Tory-Indian forays that were ravaging the frontier, he did little more than to establish a fort some 30 miles down the Ohio from Ft. Pitt at the mouth of Beaver Creek (FT. MCINTOSH) and another (FT. LAURENS) on the Tuscarawas River roughly 100 miles west of Ft. Pitt. It then being too late in the year for further operations, he left John Gibson with a 150-man garrison at Ft. Laurens and with the rest of his 1,000-man force "returned to Fort Pitt barren of the honors of an Indian fight." (Lossing, II, 500) Daniel Brodhead and George Morgan complained of McIntosh's conduct of this expedition and Gouverneur Morris wrote Washington that he was "one of those who excel in the Regularity of still Life from the Possession of an indolent uniformity of soul." (*D.A.B.*, citing Kellogg)

On 5 Mar. '79 Washington directed McIntosh to turn over command to Brodhead, and on the 18th Congress ordered him back to the South. There he had a prominent part in the allied attack on SAVANNAH, 9 Oct., leading Lincoln's march from Charleston to make contact with d'Estaing, urging the latter to attack promptly (which he did not do), and commanding the 1st and 5th S.C. with some Ga. militia in the second echelon of the attack. He became a prisoner of war on 12 May '80 when Lincoln surrendered Charleston. He was exchanged for Gen. O'Hara by an agreement dated 9 Feb. '82. According to Lossing, he took his family to Va. after his release—presumably he

was paroled soon after capture.* George Walton, delegate to Congress from Ga., induced Congress to suspend McIntosh from active service in a resolve of 15 Feb. '80. This was repealed 16 July '81, McIntosh was breveted Maj. Gen. on 24 Feb. '84, and a Congressional committee that included James Monroe "quoted with approval a resolution of the Georgia Assembly charging Walton with forgery, and praised McIntosh for his Revolutionary services." (*D.A.B.*)

He had returned to Ga. in 1783, "incredibly poor," as he put it, and took little part in public life. On 23 Feb. '84 he was elected to Congress but apparently did not serve. He was on commissions to adjust the Ga.-S.C. boundary, to treat with the Southern Indians (1785–86), and was a member of the committee to welcome Washington to Savannah in 1791. He died in comparative poverty.

Uncle of John MCINTOSH.

MCKEAN, Thomas. 1734–1817. Signer. Del.–Pa. His father, grandson of an Argyleshire Scot who emigrated to Londonderry, came to Pa. as a child and married into a well-connected and wealthy Scotch-Irish family. Thomas had a classical education and studied law in Del. before becoming a prothonotary's clerk and, in 1752, a deputy prothonotary and recorder of wills. His family connections were invaluable in insuring a successful career, and he soon had a prosperous practice in Pa., Del., and N.J. He was deputy attorney-general in 1756; clerk of the assembly in 1757–59; and assembly member 1762–79. In 1762 he also helped Caesar Rodney revise the state assembly laws. The next year he mar-

---

* Heitman incorrectly says he was *exchanged* in Dec. '80 and served to the end of the war; he probably was *paroled* in Dec.

ried Mary, daughter of Joseph Porden of Bordentown, N.J. This made him brother-in-law of Francis Hopkinson, the Signer. Becoming increasingly outspoken against British rule, McKean was one of the more radical members of the Stamp Act congress of 1765. As justice of the court of common pleas and quarter sessions he ordered the use of unstamped paper. As speaker of the assembly he led the movement in Dec. '72 for a colonial congress.

After the death of his wife in 1773 he remarried the next year and moved to Philadelphia. In the 1st Cont'l. Congress he was a delegate from Del. In the 2d Cont'l. Congress he advocated reconciliation with England until early 1776, then started working for independence. Although still a member of the Del. delegation, he was influential in swaying opinion in Pa. toward independence. When his vote for the resolution for independence was tied with that of fellow delegate George Reed, McKean's initiative brought Caesar RODNEY, the third Del. representative, racing back to cast the decisive vote. Exactly when he became a SIGNER is uncertain, but shortly after 2 Aug. '76 he led a battalion of Philadelphia Associators to Perth Amboy to reinforce Washington's hard-pressed little army. Returning then to Dover, he helped frame the first constitution of Del. Failing re-election to Congress— he did not sit during the period Dec. '76–Jan. '78—McKean became speaker of the assembly of Del., and for two months of 1777 he was acting president of the state. During the period 1777–79 he also was chief justice of Pa., but he remained politically active in Del. and was re-elected to Congress from the latter state. On 10 July '81 he was elected president of Congress, and he served until 5 Nov. of that year. In 1787 he sat in the Pa. Constitutional ratification convention as a Federalist. He drew many protests in Pa. from those who felt he should not hold so many important and conflicting political jobs. In Congress, he was an advocate of extending the judiciary to include a federal court of appeals and he supported the Articles of Confederation. In 1792 the Federalist foreign policy drove him to the other party, and in 1799 he was elected Gov. of Pa. as a Jeffersonian. He served two tumultuous terms, being much accused of nepotism, constitutional violation, and other abuses of the office.

Although impeachment proceedings were begun in the state legislature, the charges were dropped, and he ended his second term peacefully. J. H. Peeling in *D.A.B.* describes him as "Cold in manner, energetic, independent, proud and vain ... [yet with] ability, candor and honesty."

McKINLY, John. 1721–1796. Pres. of Del. Ireland–Del. Moving to Wilmington, Del., from the north of Ireland, he practiced as a doctor and rose rapidly in local civil and militia affairs. He served as sheriff (1757–59) and was 12 times elected chief burgess of the borough of Wilmington between 1759 and 1776. In Oct. '71 he was elected to the colonial Assembly, two years later he became a member of the Assembly's five-man standing Comm. of Corresp., and he had a part in the major events leading to his state's joining the Association (28 Nov. '74), calling up their militia (the next month), sending delegates to the Cont'l. Cong. (Mar. '75). In county affairs he also was active. In Feb. '77 McKinly was chosen Pres. and C. in C. of Del. for a term of three years. When the British occupied Wilmington the night of 12–13 Sept. '77, shortly after the battle of Brandywine (11 Sept.), they took McKinly prisoner and evacuated him to

Philadelphia after the capture of that city. When the British left Philadelphia they took him to N.Y.C., where he was paroled in Aug. '78. Having gone to Philadelphia to get agreement of the Cont'l. Cong., he was exchanged for Wm. Franklin, former Royal Gov. of N.J., and in Sept. he was free to resume his medical practice in Wilmington. McKinly took no further part in public life. (*D.A.B.*) He was elected to the Cont'l. Cong. but did not serve. (Montross, *Reluctant Rebels*, 426)

McLANE, Allan. 1746–1829. Cont'l. officer. Pa.–Del. Born in Philadelphia, the son of Allan McLean or Maclean, who had come to America in 1738 from the Isle of Coll (Scotland), young Allan had an aristocratic upbringing. In 1767–1769 he toured Europe and visited cousins in Scotland. Allan's father was a merchant, first in Philadelphia and later in Wilmington, Del., and in 1774 the son settled near the site of Smyrna to start a trading business. In July 1775 he changed his name to McLane "to avoid confusion with that renegade Scot serving the Hanoverian King," as he wrote. He was referring to Allan MacLEAN, who had just reached Canada to recruit his Royal Highland Emigrants. (James N. M. Maclean, *post.*)

McLane's father died about this time, leaving Allan property worth more than $15,000. After fighting as a volunteer at Great Bridge, Va., 9 Dec. '75, and at Norfolk, 1 Jan. '76, McLane served with Washington's army in New York as Lt. and Adj. of Caesar Rodney's militia regt. His commission was dated 11 Sept. '75 (*ibid.*). At LONG ISLAND, 27 Aug. '76, he captured a British patrol. After fighting at White

Plains, 28 Oct., he was with the rear guard in the retreat across N.J., took part in the attack on Trenton, and was promoted for gallantry at Princeton, 3 Jan. '77. Three days later, on the 6th (*ibid.*), Capt. McLane joined Col. John Patton's command, one of the so-called "ADDITIONAL CONT'L. REGTS." After seeing action at Cooch's Bridge and the Brandywine, 3 and 11 Sept. '77, McLane was detached to raise his own company in Del. Within a few weeks he dedicated his entire personal fortune to equipping and paying his force of about 100 men (Montross, *Rag, Tag,* 279).

After serving as advance guard of Washington's main column at GERMANTOWN, 4 Oct. '77, on 7 Nov. McLane was given the mission of screening the army as it prepared to take up winter quarters· at Valley Forge. On 3 Dec. he warned Washington of a large-scale sortie from Philadelphia, this intelligence contributing to the successful patriot defense of their concentration around WHITE MARSH a few days later.

During the winter of Valley Forge, McLane's troops harassed enemy convoys and foraging parties so successfully they earned the nickname "market stoppers." During Jan. and Feb. '78 they gathered livestock in Del. and the eastern shore of Md. to supply Valley Forge and Smallwood's command at Wilmington. Rejoining the main army with 100 to 150 mounted men, who were reinforced on certain occasions by 50 Oneidas, he resumed his reconnaissance mission. As the MISCHIANZA was breaking up in Philadelphia, around dawn of 19 May, his company, supported by a company of dragoons, brought many a red-eyed redcoat running to repel an "attack" he simulated by galloping along the enemy's outpost line dropping iron pots full of gunpowder and scrap metal. The next night his scouts detected the movement to surprise Lafayette at BARREN HILL, a piece of good outpost work that may have saved a large portion of the army from annihilation. On 8 June he narrowly escaped an ambush. He may well have been the first American to reenter Philadelphia when the British evacuated the city 10 days later.

McLane apparently had an instinctive dislike of Benedict Arnold; soon after the latter took command in Philadelphia, McLane went to Washington to expose Arnold's profiteering and, according to Cook, to "outline his darker suspicions of Arnold's treachery." (*What Manner of Men*) If the latter is true, McLane was premature by almost a year (ARNOLD'S TREASON did not really start until May '80). For his pains he received a stinging rebuke from Washington.

During the Monmouth Campaign, June–July '78, McLane's company operated with Dickinson's militia, and he claims to have lost only four men killed in taking more than 300 stragglers. In the reorganization that followed, McLane's partisan command was made part of the Del. Regt. on 16 Dec. and on 13 July '79 was attached to Henry Lee's new "Partisan Corps." (These dates from Heitman. Cook, *op. cit.*, says he was "reattached" to the Del. Regt. on 1 June '79 and attached to Lee on 9 June.) Under Lee's command he had a dramatic role in the events leading up to Wayne's capture of STONY POINT, 16 July, and he figured prominently in Lee's raid on PAULUS HOOK, 19 Aug. '79. Animosity developed between Lee and McLane, however, and Washington solved the problem by sending McLane to reinforce Lincoln at Charleston. Fortunate

in not reaching the city in time to be captured, he came under Steuben's command and was promoted to Maj.

Early in June '81 he left Philadelphia to accompany the messages urging de Grasse to come from the West Indies to support Washington and Rochambeau. Although some writers credit McLane with persuading de Grasse to abandon a proposed attack on Jamaica and sail north, the written communications apparently were enough to convince the French admiral. (Under YORKTOWN CAMP'N. see "Naval Operations.") On the return voyage McLane commanded the marine company of the privateer *Congress* (24) during its capture of the sloop of war *Savage* (16). During the Yorktown Campaign he scouted N.Y.C. from Long Island to keep Washington informed on the essential point of whether the British were detaching strength to reinforce Cornwallis.

He left the army on 31 Dec. '81, according to Cook, and had attained the rank of Col., according to Appleton's. Heitman has no record of his promotion above the grade of Capt. in the Cont'l. Army, however, and shows that he retired on 9 Nov. '82. His personal fortune gone, he entered a mercantile venture with Robt. Morris. In 1789 he was appointed a marshal of Del., and in 1797 became collector for the port of Wilmington, a post he retained the last 33 years of his life. He held many public posts in his state. At the age of 68 he commanded the defenses of Wilmington (War of 1812), observed the British capture of Washington, and in a damning memorandum commented that with the 300 men he had led at Paulus Hook he could have saved the capital.

Described as a handsome man of medium height, he shows in what Cook calls his "disconnected writings" a spirit of self-pity and a resentment at the failure of authorities to appreciate his service. Much of the McLane legend comes from Alexander Garden's *Anecdotes of the Revolutionary War*. Fred J. Cook has a long chapter on McLane in his *What Manner of Men*. His manuscript *Papers and Journals* and a signed portrait are owned by the N.Y.H.S. For elusive facts about Allan McLane I am indebted to Dr. James N. M. Maclean of Edinburgh (see the "other" Allan MACLEAN).

Only three of Allan McLane's 14 children survived infancy. The elder son, Louis McLane (1784–1857), and a grandson, Robt. Milligan (1815–98), were prominent in government service.

MECKLENBURG DECLARATION OF INDEPENDENCE. On 31 May '75 a committee met at Charlotte, Mecklenburg co., N.C., and drew up 20 resolutions for the N.C. delegation to present to the Cont'l. Cong. They stated— among other things—that all laws and commissions derived from royal or Parliamentary authority were suspended and that all legislative or executive power henceforth should come from the Prov. Cong. of each colony under the Cont'l. Cong. Although adopted, the resolutions never were presented to Cong. In 1819 the *Raleigh Register* printed what was claimed to be a document that the Charlotte committeemen had adopted on 20 May '75 in which they declared themselves "a free and independent people" and which contained other phrases later made famous in *the* Decl. of Indep.

For many years it was believed that the Mecklenburg document had inspired the real Decl. of Indep., although no written copy of the former was found until 1847, when a copy of a Charleston newspaper of 16 June '75 revealed the full text of the 20 resolutions adopted 31 May '75. The word "independence" was not mentioned. The explanation appears to be this: the records of the 31 May proceedings were destroyed by a fire in 1800; the version printed in 1819 was from memory— see Joseph GRAHAM, whose memory was involved—and was embellished with phrases taken from the real Decl. of Indep. The difference in dates—20 and 31 May—can be explained in terms of old and new style calendars. "Although the date May 20, 1775, is on the state seal and the state flag, most historians agree that the Mecklenburg Declaration of Independence is a 'spurious document,'" as Thomas Jefferson had called it long before the evidence of 1847 was produced (*Concise D.A.H.*).

The *resolutions*, which are quite genuine, are in Commager, *Docs*. See G. W. Graham, *The Mecklenburg Decl. of Indep.* (1905), the work of the same title by Wm. H. Hoyt (1907), and A. S. Salley Jr., "Mecklenburg Declaration," *Am. Hist. Rev.* (1908).

MEDALS voted by Congress during the war numbered only eight: to Washington in 1776 for taking Boston; to Gates in 1777 for Burgoyne's capture; to Wayne, Stewart, and Teissèdre de Fleury* in 1779 for STONY

---

* Voted a *silver* medal, he was sent a *gold* medal four years later by Franklin. Lasseray says Congress had directed Franklin to have this medal made in France. Did the alchemy of Congressional conscience over the delay turn silver into gold, or is Lasseray's information wrong as to the color of the metal? The latter seems unlikely, since he sites Franklin's letter of 15 Aug. '83 forwarding a medal made by Benj. Duvivier.

Point, and to Henry Lee for Paulus Hook; and to Morgan and Howard in 1780 for Cowpens.

MEDICAL PRACTICE DURING THE REVOLUTION. As late as the Spanish-American War of 1898 the battlefield was safer than the military camp or the army hospital. During the Revolution John Adams wrote: "Disease has destroyed ten men for us where the sword of the enemy has killed one." Benjamin Rush said that "hospitals are the sinks of human life in an army. They robbed the United States of more citizens than the sword." (C. & M., 815) The greatest scourge was smallpox, which probably did more to defeat the Canada Invasion than anything else. Inoculation was known, but under camp conditions—administered to soldiers weakened by hunger, fatigue, and exposure—it probably killed more men than it saved. In any event "More died from wounds by bacilli than from lead," writes Ganoe (*Hist. of U.S. Army*, 45). "In spite of the general's specific orders to the contrary, surgeons so persisted in their pernicious scratchings that they had to be tried by court-martial." (*Ibid.*) Other diseases swept through the army camps, typhus being one of the most dangerous and mumps being prevalent. (Lossing, II, 879 *n*.) Diphtheria, dysentery, malaria, measles, and even scurvy took their toll. Surgery was medieval: those who survived the shock and the bleeding were likely to be infected by the knife or by unsanitary conditions under which they were supposed to recover. Yet men survived. In one of his few passages dealing with his own profession Dr. Thacher comments on his duties at the Albany general hospital following the battles of Saratoga:

"*October 24, 1777.*—This hospital is now crowded with officers and soldiers from the field of battle; . . . The foreigners are under the care and management of their own surgeons. I have been present at some of their capital operations, and remarked that the English surgeons perform with skill and dexterity, but the Germans, with a few exceptions, do no credit to their profession; some of them are the most uncouth and clumsy operators I ever witnessed, and appear to be destitute of all sympathy and tenderness towards the suffering patient. Not less than one thousand wounded and sick are now in this city. . . . We have about thirty surgeons and mates; and all are constantly employed. I am obliged to devote the whole of my time, from eight o'clock in the morning to a late hour in the evening, to the care of our patients.

"Here is a fine field for professional improvement. Amputating limbs, trepanning fractured skulls, and dressing the most formidable wounds, have familiarized my mind to scenes of woe.* * * If I turn from beholding mutilated bodies . . . a spectacle no less revolting is presented, of miserable objects languishing under afflicting disease of every description. . . ." (*Military Journal*, 112–13)

It is not likely that German doctors of the period were any worse than the British, but Thacher's comment points to the problem of the American army: that of getting the proper caliber of military surgeons and of properly organizing the medical service. "American surgeons at the beginning of the war were as good as any in existence" (Mitchell, *World's Military History*, 423) but they were few in number, the country had almost no medical facilities and less experience in the problems of military medicine, and there was a desperate lack of drugs, surgical instruments, and other supplies. The Cont'l. Cong., furthermore, failed to provide an adequate portion of its limited funds to establish a decent medical service. (C. & M., 815) The delegates also were unfortunate in their choices of men to head the medical department of the army: their first appointment went to Benjamin CHURCH, most of whose energies were devoted to spying for Gage and whose treason was exposed late in Sept. '75. He was succeeded by John MORGAN, a good doctor and administrator but a man who made so many enemies he had to be relieved. William Shippen (see SHIPPEN FAMILY), his successor, also was capable but he too fell victim to back-stabbing from his professional colleagues, "notably the third member of the Philadelphia fraternity" (ibid., 816), Dr. Benjamin RUSH. Congress had had enough of Philadelphia doctors and their next selection, Dr. John COCHRAN of N.J., appointed 17 Jan. '81, survived the few remaining months of combat and served to the formal end of the war. "His experience in British service enabled him to make great improvements," comments D.A.B. Another senior doctor of the Cont'l. Army was James CRAIK. John WARREN served with the army both as surgeon and common soldier. It should be noted that the title "Chief Physician and Surgeon of the Army" did not signify the top position in the Medical Dept., as might be assumed: Church's title was "Director and Chief Physician," Morgan was called "Director General and Chief Physician," William Shippen was given the title "Director General of all Hospitals," and Cochran was called "Director General of Military Hospitals," according to Heitman.

See Louis C. Duncan, *Medical Men in the American Revolution, 1775–1783* (Carlisle, Pa., 1931), and James Edgar Gibson, *Dr. Bodo Otto and the Medical Background of the American Revolution* (Baltimore, 1937). Chapter 20 of C. & M. (pp. 815–42) is devoted to "Health, Hospitals and Medicine."

MEETING ENGAGEMENT. A battle that takes place before either side can execute a planned attack or defense. PRINCETON and MONMOUTH are classic examples in the Revolution, and the decisive battle of Gettysburg in the Civil War is another.

MEIGS, Return Jonathan. 1740–1823. Cont'l. officer, pioneer. Conn. Son of a hatter, he became Lt. in the 6th Conn. Regt. in 1772 and two years later was promoted to Capt. He led his company to the Boston lines after the action at Lexington and Concord, was commissioned Maj., and as second in command to Lt. Col. Enos he took part in Arnold's March to Quebec. His *Journal* of the expedition, written with ink made by mixing powder and water in his palm, was published in the *Mass. Hist. Soc. Colls.* in 1814 and privately printed in 1864 (*D.A.B.*). After scaling the walls of Quebec, 31 Dec. '75, he was captured, paroled, and exchanged 10 Jan. '77 (Heitman). On 22 Feb. he became Lt. Col. of SHERBURNE'S REGT.

Meigs is famous for his brilliant SAG HARBOR RAID, N.Y., 23 May '77, for which Cong. voted him one of their "elegant swords." On 10 Sept. he was made Col. of the 6th Conn. ("Leather Cap") Regt. and during the summer and fall he led them in the principal actions along the Hudson. He led a regiment of Conn. troops at STONY POINT, 16 July '79. Washington sent him a personal note of thanks for his part in stopping the MUTINY OF THE CONNECTICUT LINE, 25 May '80, and his regiment was one of the first sent to reinforce the Hudson Highlands when Arnold's Treason was discovered in Sept. '80. He retired 1 Jan. '81 when the Conn. regiments were reorganized.

Becoming interested in the Ohio Company, he was appointed one of its surveyors and in Apr. '88 landed at the mouth of the Muskingum with a small party of settlers. In 1801 he became agent to the Cherokee, and in 1808 was authorized to negotiate a convention between that tribe and Tenn. He died at the age of 82, having caught pneumonia when he gave his quarters to an elderly Indian guest and moved into a tent. His second wife, the former Grace Starr, had died in Tenn. in 1807.

"The origin of his name is of peculiar interest," says Appleton's, which goes on to explain that his father was riding away after having his suit repeatedly rejected by a Quaker lady when the damsel repented and called out, "Return, Jonathan!" He gave these happy words to his son for a name. Actually, our Return Jonathan Meigs was the son of Return and Elizabeth Hamlin Meigs, but the story may only be a generation off.

Two namesakes of Return Jonathan Meigs became prominent. The first, a son by his first wife (Joanna Winborn, who died in 1773), was Gov. of Ohio, senator, and postmaster general; he died in 1824, only 14 months after his father. Another Return Jonathan Meigs (1801–1891) was a prominent lawyer; he was the grandson of the first R. J. and nephew of the second. All three are sketched in *D.A.B.*, as is Josiah Meigs, brother of the Revolutionary War hero; Josiah (1757–1822) is identified as a "lawyer, editor, and public official." (*Ibid.*)

MERCANTILISM is a system of public economy that developed in Europe when feudalism was giving way to nationalism. A form of economic nationalism, it advocated governmental regulation of trade and commerce, favorable balance of trade, development of agriculture and manufacture, development of a strong merchant marine, establishment of colonies for the enrichment of the mother country, foreign trade monopolies, and accumulation of gold and silver (on the premise that money alone is wealth).

Colonies existed under the mercantile philosophy only to furnish the mother country with gold, silver, raw materials, and markets. The NAVIGATION ACTS represented mercantilism translated into statute law (Miller, *O.A.R.,* 4). One historian points out that there never was such a thing as a formally defined mercantile system and, in attacking the school of economic determinism, says "it is a gross historical blunder to start with the premises that British colonial policy and mercantilism were at any time convertible terms or that the colonists were ever seriously hampered by the restrictions placed upon their desire to manufacture." (Andrews, *Policy,* 427) On the other hand, mercantilism loomed large in the BACKGROUND AND ORIGINS OF THE REVOLUTION and does much to explain British acts which the colonists considered "tyrannical."

MERCER, Hugh. *c.* 1725–1777. Cont'l. general. Scotland–Pa.–Va. The son of a Scots minister, he was educated as a doctor at the University of Aberdeen (1740–44) and was in the surgeons' corps of the Young Pretender. After Culloden he emigrated to America, reached Philadelphia in 1746 or 1747, and soon settled near what is now Mercersburg, Pa. Here he practiced medicine and became a respected member of the community. In the troubles leading to the French and Indian War he became Capt. in the Pa. Regt. (1755). According to Appleton's he was at Braddock's defeat and was wounded in the shoulder; other authorities express some doubt about this. He took part in the expedition against Kittanning (Sept. '56). As a Lt. Col. of militia he was on Forbes's expedition to Duquesne (1758), was promoted to

Col. of the 3d Bn. on 23 Apr. '59, and was made commandant of Ft. Pitt. During these frontier operations he met Washington, and it may have been at his suggestion that Mercer moved to Fredericksburg, Va. (Edward E. Curtis in *D.A.B.*) Here he opened an apothecary shop, practiced his profession, joined Washington's Masonic lodge, and became prominent in local affairs. On 12 Sept. '75 he was elected Col. of minutemen in four counties. Having narrowly lost out to Patrick Henry for command of the 1st Va., the 50-year-old doctor was commissioned Col. of the 3d Va. on 13 Feb. '76. (Heitman) Appointed B.G. of the Cont'l. Army on 5 June, he was put in command of the FLYING CAMP. He led a column at TRENTON, and is one of several officers credited in contemporary accounts with suggesting the strategy leading to the triumph at PRINCETON, 3 Jan. '77. Mortally wounded in this action, he died on 11 Jan. Freeman believes that Mercer might have been the peer and possibly the superior of Greene as a Cont'l. officer. (*Washington*, IV, 368)

See J. T. Goolrick, *The Life of . . . Mercer* (1906).

MERCHANTS IN THE REVOLUTION. In his *Colonial Merchants and the American Revolution, 1763–1766* (New York, 1918 and 1939), Arthur Meier Schlesinger's argument is summarized as follows in the Lib. of Cong. *Guide:* "Seeking a relaxation of commercial restrictions imposed by the parliamentary legislation of 1764–65 [See BACKGROUND], the merchants of the North American commercial provinces . . . were the instigators of the first discontents in the Colonies. The events of the years 1767–70 brought the mercantile interests to an even sharper realization than before of the growing power of the radical elements of colonial society; however, their withdrawal

to conservatism was delayed while they allied themselves with the radicals to defeat the purposes of the East India Company. The outcome convinced the merchants, as a class, that their future welfare depended upon the maintenance of British authority. Some of them, hoping to control the situation from within, remained within the radical movement. With the meeting of the First Continental Congress, others threw aside the cloak of radicalism, and some of these became active Loyalists. With the outbreak of hostilities, economic interest caused many merchants to follow the line of least resistance and profess adherence to the colonial cause; others, anticipating a British victory, openly cast their lot with Great Britain. Following the Revolution, however, the mercantile interests once more closed their ranks and became a potent factor in the conservative counter-revolution which led to the adoption of the Constitution." (*Op. cit.*, 346)

NONIMPORTATION affected the merchants of Britain as well as America. The former were among the most dedicated opponents in England of the king's coercive policy toward the colonies.

See also Robert A. East, *Business Enterprise in the American Revolutionary Era* (New York, 1938). In this meticulous treatment the author examines the transactions of Robert Morris and Jeremiah Wadsworth, to mention but the most famous merchants.

MERLON. Part of a fortification wall, or of the battlements on top of the wall, between two embrasures (openings).

METUCHEN MEETING HOUSE, N.J., 26 June '77. See SHORT HILLS. . . .

M'FINGAL. Comic epic by John (the poet) TRUMBULL. Some lines are quoted under SALEM, Mass., 26 Feb. '75.

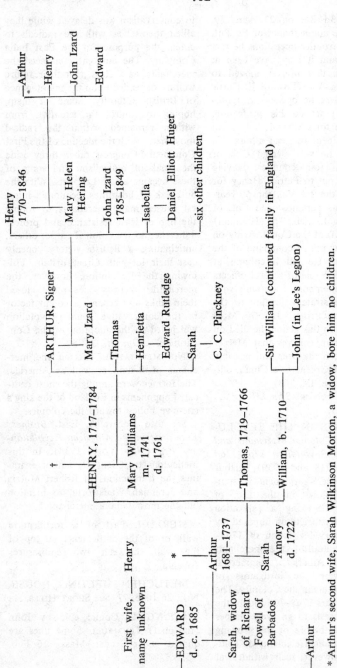

702

MIDDLETON FAMILY OF SOUTH CAROLINA

First wife, —— Henry
name unknown

EDWARD
d. c. 1685

Sarah, widow
of Richard
Fowell of
Barbados

Arthur

Arthur
1681–1737

Sarah
Amory
d. 1722

*

†

HENRY, 1717–1784

Mary Williams
m. 1741
d. 1761

Thomas, 1719–1766

William, b. 1710

Henry
1770–1846

Mary Helen
Hering

John Izard
1785–1849

Isabella

Daniel Elliott Huger

six other children

ARTHUR, Signer

Mary Izard

Thomas

Henrietta

Edward Rutledge

Sarah

C. C. Pinckney

Sir William (continued family in England)

John (in Lee's Legion)

Arthur

Henry

John Izard

Edward

* Arthur's second wife, Sarah Wilkinson Morton, a widow, bore him no children.
† Henry had five sons and seven daughters by his first wife, Mary Williams. Subsequent wives, by whom he had no children were
Maria Henrietta, daughter of Lt. Gov. William Bull (m. 1762), and Lady Mary Mackenzie, widow of John Ainslie and daughter of
George, third earl of Cromartie (m. 1776).

MIDDLE BROOK, N.J., 13 Apr. '77. See BOUND BROOK.

MIDDLE FORT (now Middleburg), N.Y. With Upper and Lower Forts, Middle Fort was built to defend the SCHOHARIE VALLEY.

MIDDLETON, Arthur, 1742–1787. Signer. S.C. Eldest son of the wealthy Henry MIDDLETON, like so many of his class in the South he was educated in England. After two years of travel on the Continent he returned to S.C. in 1763 and married the daughter of Walter Izard. In 1765 he was elected to the state House of Representatives, where he sat for many years. After a visit to England, 1768–71, he became a patriot leader in S.C., attending the Prov. Cong. of 1775, and being a member of the committee of safety. He took his father's seat in the Cont'l. Cong. in 1776, signed the Decl. of Indep., and was a delegate again in 1777. In 1778 he declined the governorship. After taking an active part in the defense of Charleston, he became a prisoner on 12 May '80 and was sent to St. Augustine. Exchanged in July '81, he returned to Cong. and sat also in 1782. Middleton had been elected to Cong. for the intervening years, 1778–80, but either declined the election or failed to attend each time. "He left little imprint on the records of that body," comments D.A.B. After the war he returned to "Middleton Place," the estate on the Ashley River near Charleston, inherited from his mother in 1771 and partially destroyed by the British in 1780.

The most famous of Arthur's nine children by his wife Mary was Henry (1771–1846), who was Gov. of S.C. from 1810 to 1812, Congressman from 1815 to 1819, minister to Russia until 1830, and then a prominent Unionist. He was survived by eight of his 12 children, the most prominent of whom was Henry (1797–1876), who wrote

important works on political and economic subjects. Three other sons— grandsons of Arthur and brothers of the Henry just noted—were Arthur (1795–1853), who was secretary of the legation in Spain for eight years; John Izard (1800–1877), author and secessionist who was ruined by the Civil War; and Edward (1810–1883), who was appointed to Annapolis in 1828 and became a Rear Admiral.

Another son of Arthur and Mary was John Izard Middleton (1785–1849), who distinguished himself as an archaeologist and artist in Italy. John's sister Isabella married Daniel Elliott Huger (1779–1854), S.C. judge and Unionist, and son of Daniel HUGER.

For other family connections see below.

MIDDLETON, Henry, 1717–1784. 2d Pres. Cont'l. Cong. S.C. One of the greatest landowners in S.C. and from one of the dozen families that dominated the province prior to the Revolution (Alden, South, 91), he was elected to the state assembly as a young man and was speaker in 1747 and 1754. Little else is known of his early life. In 1755 he became commissioner of Indian affairs and sat on the state council until he resigned in 1770 to become leader of the opposition. Sent to the 1st Cont'l. Cong., he succeeded Peyton Randolph as president on 22 Oct. '74 and held this office until the re-election of Randolph on 10 May '75. He also was president of the S.C. Prov. Cong. in 1775–76. When the radicals gained control of the Cont'l. Cong. he resigned his seat in 1776 and was succeeded by his son Arthur. Although a member of the council of safety after 16 Nov. '75 and active in state affairs until Clinton's invasion of the South in the spring of 1780, he then felt that the patriot cause was hopeless. (Alden, South, 237 n.) For this reason he took the protection of the British, but did not suffer property loss as a consequence.

In 1741 Henry Middleton had married Mary Williams, whose father, John, was member of the S.C. House of Commons from St. George's. They had five sons and seven daughters. Of the latter, Henrietta married Edward Rutledge and Sarah married C. C. Pinckney, connecting the Middletons with two of the other ruling families of S.C. Henry's eldest son and heir, Arthur MIDDLETON, married into the Izard family and left a number of sons and grandsons who became famous. Another son, Thomas, "became a Revolutionary patriot and generous public servant." (*D.A.B.*, "Henry Middleton.")

Henry's eldest brother, William (b. 1710), had several sons: the eldest, Sir William, headed the English side of the family; the youngest, John, was a Lt. in Lee's Legion from 1780 to 1782. (Heitman) The latter's widow, Frances Motte, married Thomas PINCKNEY in 1797.

Henry's younger brother, Thomas (1719–1766), was a member of the S.C. House of Commons for many years. "In 1759 he commanded the gentlemen volunteers in an expedition into the mountains of the Cherokee country," notes Appleton's. (IV, 316) The next year, according to the same source, he commanded the S.C. militia regiment in the battle of Echoe and in a subsequent controversy over rank he fought a duel with James Grant. "Colonel Middleton's conduct in this matter was highly approved by public opinion, and his popularity rose to a great height." (*Ibid.*) See also CHEROKEE EXPEDITION OF JAMES GRANT, 1761. The only son of this Thomas was William, who was a member of the legislature.

See also MIDDLETON FAMILY.

MIDDLETON FAMILY OF S.C. The two members who figured prom-

inently in the American Revolution are Henry MIDDLETON (1717–1784) and his eldest son, Arthur MIDDLETON (1742–1787). The articles on these two men include information on other members of the family, including those by marriage. In order to clarify the Middleton genealogy a chart is provided on p. 702.

MIFFLIN, Thomas. 1744–1800. Cont'l. general, politician. Pa. Born in Philadelphia of Quaker parents, he graduated from the College of Philadelphia in 1760 and was a business partner of his brother before entering politics. He was in the Prov. Assy. in 1772 and '73, one of the most radical members of the Cont'l. Cong. in '74, and an ardent Whig in the Pa. house of representatives until '75. In the early stages of the war he was active in recruiting and training troops (despite his Quaker heritage) and was elected Maj. On 4 July he became one of Washington's A.D.C., and on 14 Aug. he became Q.M.G. He was promoted to Col. on 22 Dec., Brig. Gen. on 16 May '76, and Maj. Gen. 19 Feb. '77. Until this time Mifflin had been exceptionally valuable as a soldier-politician, particularly "in the gloomy winter of 1776 by rallying the drooping courage of the militia of his native State.... His influence was much promoted by an elegant person, an animated countenance, and popular manners. Had he fallen in battle, or died in the year 1778, he would have ranked with Warren and the first patriots of the Revolution," said Benj. Rush. (Quoted in Freeman, *Washington,* IV, between pp. 21 and 22.) A puzzling degeneration in Mifflin's standards seems to date from early summer of 1777 when he was alienated by Washington's refusal to disregard the possibility of a British attack from N.Y.C. and to divert all military resources to defend Philadelphia. (*Ibid., 559*) He had been succeeded as Q.M.G. by Stephen Moylan on 5 June '76, but had resumed the office on 1 Oct. when Moylan proved incompetent. But Mifflin was notoriously negligent during the Philadelphia Campaign and instead of replacing him or ordering him to do his duties, "Washington's amiability had led him to hope against hope for some betterment until, in this respect, he was unjust to his own troops." (*Ibid.*, 573) Mifflin is therefore largely to blame for the sufferings during the VALLEY FORGE WINTER QUARTERS. See also SUPPLY....

The so-called CONWAY CABAL is believed to have been strongly supported, if not organized and led, by Mifflin, whose motives may have been jealousy of Washington's fame and a hope for his own advancement by supporting Gates as the new C. in C. In justice to Mifflin it must be pointed out that many honest and intelligent patriots had grounds for believing that Washington was incompetent. Mifflin had resigned as Q.M.G. on 7 Nov. '77 and became a member of the new Board of War the same day, retaining his grade of Maj. Gen., but without pay. Mifflin huffily left his post on the Board when false accusations were aired about his personal desire to succeed Washington, but to the latter's "scarcely concealed disgust" he subsequently reappeared as a division commander, apparently entertaining some hope that he could serve with Gates. (*Ibid.*, 585; V, 4–5 and *n.*) However, he was quickly (June '78) summoned by Congress to face an injury into his accounts as Q.M.G. But before the investigation had proceeded far, Congress granted him $1,000,000 to settle all claims against his office. (*E.B.*) On 25 Feb. '79 he resigned from the army.

Mifflin was a delegate to Cong. in 1782–84 and as president of that body during the 12 months starting 3 Nov.

'83 he received Washington's resignation. Continuing an active career in state and national politics, he was the first Gov. of Pa. (1790–99) and personally commanded the militia during the Whiskey Insurrection. Speaking of his election in 1790, Rush, who has already been quoted, said: "His popularity was acquired by the basest acts of familiarity with the meanest of people."

MILE SQUARE, N.Y. Now in Yonkers, this place got its name when a tract of land one mile square was sold in 1676. It was the scene of skirmishes after the British landing at PELL'S POINT and in their movement to WHITE PLAINS in Oct. '76.

MILITARY AFFAIRS in this book are covered under the general headings listed in the chart on the following page (page 706). The purpose of this listing is to provide an index to "covering articles," some of whose titles are arbitrary. These articles will direct the reader to such major topics as ARNOLD'S MARCH TO QUEBEC (an operation of the CANADA INVASION), CLINTON'S EXPEDITION to the Highlands, the BENNINGTON RAID, and ST. LEGER'S EXPEDITION (all having to do with BURGOYNE'S OFFENSIVE). Certain major operations that are not part of a larger campaign are not listed below if their headings are such as to present no trouble; examples are PAULUS HOOK and STONY POINT. Although the reader would need no guidance in finding such subjects as the massacres of CHERRY VALLEY and WYOMING, these articles also are cross references from BORDER WARFARE. See chart on next page.

MILITIA IN THE AMERICAN REVOLUTION. Standing armies are a relatively recent institution in the history of warfare. The Colonial Wars in America were fought by British regulars

CHART TO ACCOMPANY ARTICLE ON MILITARY AFFAIRS, p. 705.

COLONIAL WARS
PONTIAC'S WAR

LEXINGTON AND CONCORD
BOSTON SIEGE
CANADA INVASION

CHARLESTON, 1776

NEW YORK CAMPAIGN
NEW JERSEY CAMPAIGN
PHILADELPHIA CAMPAIGN
BURGOYNE'S OFFENSIVE
MONMOUTH CAMPAIGN
NEWPORT

WESTERN OPERATIONS, 1774–82

WEST INDIES IN THE REVOLUTION

SAVANNAH, 1778
SAVANNAH, 1779

SULLIVAN'S EXPEDITION

CHARLESTON, 1780
CAMDEN
KINGS MOUNTAIN
SOUTHERN CAMPAIGNS OF GREENE

YORKTOWN CAMPAIGN, 1781

See also: BORDER WARFARE, SOUTHERN THEATER, Military operations in (before Greene), VIRGINIA, Military operations in, and NAVAL OPERATIONS.

---

reinforced by American militia, whom they called "Provincials." British battles of the Revolution were fought by their regulars, German mercenaries, and Tory militia (whom they again called "Provincials"). American militia units that rallied for the battle of Lexington and Concord, undertook the Boston Siege, and fought at Bunker Hill were the nucleus of the Cont'l. Army, the American "regulars" of the Revolution. But "state troops" or militia continued to be used.

Being part-time soldiers, subject only to state authority, militia troops generally were unreliable. Of the 8,000 men in 13 Conn. militia regiments serving under Washington on Long Island in Aug. '76, only 2,000 were still present after the battle. Writing of this defection Washington told Cong. in his letter of 24 Sept. '76: "if I were called upon to declare upon oath, whether the militia had been most serviceable or hurtful upon the whole, I should subscribe to the latter." Just before the second battle of Saratoga, the turning point of the Revolution, Stark's militia joined Gates in the morning and left before noon because their term of service had expired. "Few events in the war so proved the utter failure of the militia system," comments Van Tyne (*War of Indep.*, 115).

This same author contradicts himself, however, in a statement that well explains the inherent contradiction of the subject:

"Fortunately for America's success, its army was not merely the armed and disciplined force, obedient throughout the years of war to its patriot leaders, but the ill-trained farmers, citizens, shopkeepers, ready to leave their work, and fight when the enemy approached, and forming at all times a potential force far beyond the army in being. It was a nebulous, incalculable, yet occasionally, as at Bennington, a mighty force." (Van Tyne, *England and America*, 153. It should be pointed out, in reference to the earlier quote, that Stark had come from BENNINGTON.)

In the above statement Van Tyne is paraphrasing the comment made a quarter-century earlier by the historian of the British Army: "there was always that incalculable factor, the American militia, a factor which could never be counted on by its friends, but equally could never be ignored by its enemies." (*British Army*, III, 306)

This "militia phenomenon," as it might be called, beat the British at Lexington and Concord, Bennington, Saratoga, and Kings Mountain. It gave them a bad mauling at Bunker Hill, if it did not beat them. Southern militia probably did as much to defeat the British as did the American regulars, once the

latter had to be ordered into the theater. At Bunker Hill, Cowpens, and Guilford the militia showed that *if commanded by experienced officers who understood their inherent weakness* they could fight like regular soldiers. Failure to comprehend this one vital qualification, however, led to the "militia complex" that cost the American people so dear in subsequent wars.

As for the Tory "Provincials," they were unlike the rebel militia in that many units attained the virtual status and competence of regulars: Tarleton's BRITISH LEGION actually became recognized as part of the "regular establishment" (although politics were involved here); the De Lancey battalion commanded by John Harris Cruger was more reliable than most regular outfits; and the VOLUNTEERS OF IRELAND were in the same category.

See Robert C. Pugh, "The Revolutionary Militia in the Southern Campaign," *William and Mary Quarterly*, Series 3, XIV, No. 2 (April, 1957), 154–175. The author attacks the idea that the militia was totally useless, pointing out its several contributions, particularly in the South.

MILLSTONE, N.J., 22 Jan. and 17 June '77. See SOMERSET C. H.

MINCOCK ISLAND "MASSACRE." See LITTLE EGG HARBOR, N.J.

MINDEN, Battle of. 1 Aug. '59. A decisive action in the Seven Years' War, it is of interest in this work because of the alleged misconduct of GERMAIN and because many other veterans of the battle subsequently were involved in the American Revolution. Among those who distinguished themselves there are William PHILLIPS, Riedesel, Charles Grey (wounded), and Hugh Percy (who led a regiment). In this French defeat the father of Lafayette was killed leading the Touraine Regt., which subsequently took part in the Yorktown Campaign.

MINISINK, N.Y., 19–22 July '79. While the patriots were slowly preparing for SULLIVAN'S EXPEDITION, Joseph Brant led a force of Indians and Tories down the Delaware from Oquaga. Leaving his main body at Grassy Brook (on the E. bank of the Del., about two miles above the mouth of Lackawaxen Cr.) the Mohawk moved on with 60 Indians and 27 Tories to surprise the village of Minisink the night of 19–20 July.

This village was about 25 miles E. of Grassy Brook and 10 miles N.W. of Goshen. (Lossing, II, 101 *n*.) * Brant entered the sleeping village and had several fires started before the inhabitants awoke to their danger. Making no effort to man their "paltry stockade-fort," they took to the hills. The raiders were bent on booty and destruction, not scalps; Brant reported taking only four scalps and three prisoners. (Swiggett, *Niagara*, 194) After looting and burning what they could, and knowing that pursuit would not be long in coming, the raiders retraced their route toward Grassy Brook. They took off a considerable number of cattle, a large amount

* Another village of Minisink is located near Port Jervis, and Minisink Ford is near the site of the subsequent battle of Minisink. I have accepted Lossing's location of the village raided by Brant and also his statement as to where the battle took place. Other accounts and maps disagree, confusing the three Minisinks, but Lossing was on home ground and his locations square with accounts of the rebel pursuit from the raided village. According to *Handbook of American Indians,* the Minisink "are said to have had three villages in 1663"; this may account for the confusion.

of booty, a few prisoners, and left the village in flames.*

The morning of 21 July, 149 militia answered the call of Lt. Col. (Dr.) Benj. Tusten to meet him at Minisink. Most of the men were from the vicinity of Goshen, where refugees had arrived with word of the disaster, but Maj. Sam'l. Meeker—whom we shall hear from in a moment—is listed by Heitman as a N.J. militia officer. The assembled patriots debated whether it was wise to pursue the renowned Mohawk chief, but the advocates of action had already begun to prevail when Maj. Meeker struck the spark: "Let the *brave* men follow me," he is alleged to have shouted, "the *cowards* may stay behind." (Lossing, *op. cit.,* 102) The entire group apparently moved forward, and they followed Brant's trail for 17 miles before camping for the night.

The morning of the 22d, Col. John Hathorn joined them with a few men of his Warwick regiment and, being senior to Tusten, he assumed command. They covered only a few miles before they came upon the recently occupied camp of the enemy. Another town meeting took place. The number of still-smoking watch-fires in the camp-site indicated a larger force than the patriot militia might prudently challenge. Over the objections of Hathorn and Tusten, however, the hotter heads again won out. Capt. Bezaleel Tyler started forward with an advance party and the rest followed.

Since Brant had started with a good day's lead and now was only a few miles ahead, we may safely assume that he had called up most of his main

* Lossing says they burned the fort, a mill, and 12 houses and barns. (*Op. cit.,* 101) Stone says they burned *two* mills, 10 houses, *and* 12 barns. (*Border Warfare,* I, 376)

body to help evacuate the cattle and other loot.

When an unseen marksman dropped Capt. Tyler dead there was only a moment's hesitation before the rest of his patrol pushed on. About 9 A.M. they reached the top of a hill and saw the enemy column marching toward a fort of the Delaware near the mouth of the Lackawaxen. The main forces must have been about a mile apart when Hathorn started a maneuver designed to catch Brant astride the ford. But the latter had already gotten his impedimenta across, and as soon as the two forces were hidden from each other by intervening woods and high ground, the Mohawk circled to Hathorn's rear and set up an ambuscade along the route he would use for withdrawal. Surprised and disappointed at finding no enemy around the ford, the militiamen were starting for home when they ran into Indians.

BATTLE OF MINISINK, 22 JULY '79

After a few shots had been exchanged, Brant claims to have walked forward to tell his enemy they were cut off and to offer quarter. His answer was a shot that hit his belt and that, but for this good luck, might well have been fatal. Early in the hard-fought contest, Brant executed a skilful maneuver that cut off a third of the militia force. The rest took up a strong position on high ground and held it for several hours against great odds. Around dusk, when the defenders were low on ammunition, Brant noticed that a rebel who held one corner of the position had been taken out of action. His attack penetrated this weak spot, organized resistance collapsed, and a massacre started. Tusten was killed with 17 wounded he had been tending. Several men were shot as they tried to swim

the Delaware. At least 45 were killed, this being the number of names on the monument erected in Goshen. Hathorn was on hand to lay the cornerstone of the latter in 1822, and 29 others survived.

COMMENTS

It is generally assumed that Brant's raid was supposed to be a strategic diversion to draw rebel forces away from Clinton and Sullivan and stop or delay preparations for SULLIVAN'S EXPEDITION. Swiggett questions this, his main argument being that:

". . . there is no mention of it in any of the Butler letters until August 4 when John Butler writes, 'Dear Walter, a couple of Indians came in this evening from Joseph. He has been down to Minisink and I believe has met with a disappointment.' " (*Op. cit.,* 193–94)

This last statement has been used as evidence that Brant's disappointment was due to his failure to draw regular troops away from Clinton and Sullivan. Swiggett does not advance any other explanation, but he does make it clear elsewhere that John Butler's preparations for meeting Sullivan's offensive were hamstrung by inadequate provisions. Joseph Brant's raid probably was a "commissary offensive," undertaken on his own initiative.

MINISINK, N.Y., *c.* 4 Apr. '80. (BORDER WARFARE) This place was revisited by Brant after his destruction of HARPERSFIELD, 2 Apr.

MINUTEMEN. The term was used as early as 1756, but the type of militia with whom the name is generally associated appeared in Mass. the year before the American Revolution started. As a device for eliminating Tories from the old militia organizations, in Sept. '74 the resignations of all officers in the three regiments of Worcester co., Mass., were called for; these regiments then were broken up to form seven new ones, and new officers were elected. The new officers were instructed to elect one third of the men in each new regiment to be ready to assemble under arms on a minute's notice, and on 21 Sept. '74 they were specifically referred to as "minutemen." The Mass. Prov. Cong., meeting in Oct., found that the militia of other counties had adopted the same system and the delegates directed (26 Oct.) that the reorganization be completed. The process was slow and never was completed, but there was in Mass. a dual system of militia and minutemen companies and regiments. The true minutemen stood on Lexington green the morning of 19 Apr. '75 and led the attack on Concord bridge. (See LEXINGTON AND CONCORD) The ordinary militia also turned out and took part in the day's operations. With the subsequent formation of Washington's Eight Months Army, which drew from both the minutemen and militia organizations, the minutemen ceased to exist in Mass.

On 18 July '75 the Cont'l. Cong. recommended that other colonies organize units of minutemen for short terms of service. Md., N.C., N.H., and Conn. are known to have complied, and minutemen turned out to repulse the Danbury Raid. (Allen French in *D.A.H.*)

MISCHIANZA, Philadelphia, 18 May '78. An extravaganza organized and directed by Capt. John André and Capt. Oliver De Lancey to mark Gen. Howe's departure as C. in C. of the British army in America. It featured a grand regatta of decorated barges, gun salutes, a mock tournament between the knights of the Blended Roses and the Burning Mountain, a banquet, fireworks, and a concluding exhibition in which an allegorical Fame saluted Howe with the words, "Thy laurels shall never fade." Tory girls graced the event, and soldiers participated as silk-clad pages. According to Julian P. Boyd, 750 invitations were sent, 330 covers were laid, the affair lasted from 4 P.M. to 4 A.M., and a London firm is said to have sold £ 12,000 worth of silk, laces, and other fine materials. (*D.A.H.*) At dawn of 19 May, Allen McLANE pulled one of his more imaginative stunts and the next day saved Lafayette at BARREN HILL.

MOBILE, 14 Mar. '80. Captured by Spanish. Satellited for defense on JAMAICA, the unhealthful British post at Mobile was garrisoned by 300 men. It was captured by Gálvez with a small force supported by a single armed vessel. PENSACOLA was saved by the intervention of a British squadron but fell the next year. (Fortescue, *British Army,* III, 341)

MOHAWK VALLEY, N.Y. A strategic avenue of approach into the American colonies from Canada and situated in TRYON COUNTY, it was the objective of ST. LEGER'S OFFENSIVE in 1777 and a cockpit of BORDER WARFARE. See map on p. 250.

MOLLY PITCHER LEGEND. "The name Molly Pitcher, applied to several different heroines of Revolutionary legend, was long accepted without question," writes Montross. "But there is much to support the theory that this generic term was given to various women who carried pitchers of water for thirsty soldiers on duty." (*Rag, Tag,* 143) The name is generally associated with Mary Ludwig HAYS, who manned a gun at Monmouth, but is also applied to "Captain Molly" (Margaret) CORBIN of Ft. Washington fame. Van Tyne could have been referring to either of them when he wrote: "as all historians know, that good woman's reputation was so tarnished that a society of patriotic women in Philadelphia gave up the idea of a monument to her, and thanked their lucky stars when certain contemporary testimony was brought to their attention." (*England & America*, 21)

MONCK'S CORNER, S.C., 14 Apr. '80. After the preparations outlined under "Opns. against the Rebel L. of C." during the CHARLESTON CAMP'N. of 1780, Tarleton moved with his Legion and Ferguson's Rangers toward Monck's Corner the evening of 13 Apr. A captured Negro messenger revealed complete information about Huger's dispositions and served as guide. About 3 A.M. the British made contact, routed the Cont'l. cavalry posted in front of Biggins Bridge, and then scattered the militia guarding the bridge. Lt. Col. Webster arrived on the 15th with two regiments to consolidate Tarleton's gains, and the rebel line of communications to Charleston was cut. Tarleton commented that his surprise was made easier by Huger's faulty tactical dispositions: not only had he failed to send out patrols to detect and delay an enemy's approach, but he had used mounted troops to screen the bridgehead instead of employing foot troops on this mission.

Huger's command consisted of militia and 300 to 500 Cont'l. cavalry. The latter comprised remnants of the regiments of Baylor, Bland, Horry, and Moylan, plus what was left of Pulaski's Legion (under Maj. VERNIER, who was mortally wounded) and Wm. Washington's horse. (Ward, *W.O.R.,* 698)

American losses, according to Ward, were 20 killed or wounded, 67 captured, and 42 loaded wagons, 102 wagon horses, and 83 dragoon horses. (*Op. cit.,* 702) Tarleton says he took 400 badly needed dragoon (and officers') mounts, about 100 officers and men, and 50 wagons. (Quoted in C. & M., 1104) According to Lossing, Huger's

300 cavalry lost 25 men killed and had almost 300 horses captured (II, 765).

Tarleton says one officer and two of his men were wounded, and five horses were killed and wounded.

MONCK'S CORNER, S.C., 16 Oct. '81. According to Strait, a Col. Malone (not identified in Heitman) attacked the British camp and took 80 prisoners.

MONCKTON, Henry. 1740–1778. British officer. Fourth son of the 1st Viscount Galway, he commanded the 45th Foot from 25 July '71 until sometime in 1772. Presumably he remained with this regiment, the "Sherwood Foresters," and led them as part of Clinton's right wing in the battle of Long Island. As commander of the 2d Bn. of grenadiers he was mortally wounded and captured at MONMOUTH, 28 June '78. Clinton does not mention his death, but the German Baurmeister notes in his *Journals* (p. 187): "Colonel Monckton of the British Grenadiers was killed, a great loss indeed."

Brother of Robert MONCKTON.

MONCKTON, Robert. 1726–1782. British officer. Second son of the 1st Viscount Galway (created in 1727) and of Lady Elizabeth Manners, daughter of the 2d Duke of Rutland, he entered the 3d Foot Guards in 1741, became Capt. in the 34th Regt. in 1744, and Maj. in 1747. He served at Dettingen and Fontenoy, and in 1751 became Lt. Col. of the 47th Regt. After succeeding his father as M.P. for Pontefract, he joined his regiment in Nova Scotia in 1752 and was commander at Ft. Lawrence during the period Aug.–June '53. He led 270 regulars and about 2,000 New England militia in the capture of Ft. Beauséjour, 19 June '55, and then had the unpleasant duty of collecting 1,100 French settlers for evacuation from ACADIA. In Dec. '57 he became Col. of the 2d Bn. of the Royal

American Regt. The next year he was acting Gov. of Nova Scotia in the absence of Charles Lawrence, having been made Lt. Gov. in 1755. Appointed temporary B.G., he was second-in-command to James Wolfe in 1759, having been requested by Wolfe for this post. He was wounded in the lungs at Quebec, 13 Sept. '59.

Monckton was commander in Canada until forced by ill health to move south. Appointed Col. of the 17th Foot in Oct. '59, he became commander of the southern district under Amherst in 1760 and the next year was named Gov. of N.Y., Maj. Gen., and C. in C. of the expedition against Martinique. He sailed in Nov. '61, joined forces with Adm. Rodney, and received the capitulation of the French island on 5 Feb. '62. Four months later he resumed his post in N.Y., and in June '63 he left for England. In 1770 he became a Lt. Gen. Three years later he failed in an attempt to become Warren Hastings' second-in-command in India. According to Pargellis (*post*), "he was offered instead the chief command in North America, which he refused," and authority for this statement is cited as Fortescue, *Corresp. of George III*, II, 494–503. The biographer of Gage, on the other hand, says: "The leading aspirant for the command was probably the gallant and generous-spirited Robert Monckton. The fur trader, intriguer, and Indian agent, George Croghan, Sir William Johnson's deputy, who was in London in February, 1764, reported to his superior that Monckton could then have had the post merely for the asking; that Monckton's friends, however, were out of power; and that he would not ask for it, although he desired it." (Alden, *Gage*, 62) The *D.A.B.* sketch by S. M. Pargellis, on which the above article is based, includes an extensive bibliography.

MONCRIEFF, James. 1744–1793. British engineer officer. A Scot, he entered Woolwich on 11 Mar. '59 and on 28 Jan. '62 was appointed "practitioner engineer and ensign." In June of that year he landed in Cuba and took part in the arduous siege operations that resulted in the capture of Havana. He was appointed ensign of the 100th Foot during this operation (10 July) and sustained a serious wound. For the next few years he served in the West Indies, E. Fla., and other parts of North America, ending up at N.Y.C. on the eve of the revolution. "As he was related by marriage to Gov. William Livingston and other Americans of high station, it was hoped that he would espouse their cause," says Appleton's, "but he adhered to the crown, and in 1776 was with Lord Percy on Staten Island." On 10 June of this year he became "engineer extraordinary and captain-lieutenant." (*D.N.B.*) The only mention of his activities in the North is that he guided the 4th Regt. across a ford in the Battle of the Brandywine, that he built a bridge across the Raritan of sufficient military interest for a model to be preserved at Woolwich, and that he was captured at Flatbush (L.I.) in 1778 "by a party that went from the N.J. shore ... expressly to seize him and other persons of note." (*D.N.B.*; Appleton's)

It was in the South that he gained his fame as an extraordinary military engineer. He was at Stono Ferry, S.C., 20 June '79, where he assisted Maitland in his splendid rear guard action and in the pursuit "captured an ammunition wagon with his own hand." (*D.N.B.*) He distinguished himself in planning and building the fortifications that enabled Prevost to hold SAVANNAH, 9 Oct. '79. Promoted to brevet Maj. on 27 Dec. for this outstanding achievement (a niggardly recognition, comments *D.N.B.*), he had a leading role during the CHARLESTON EXPEDITION of 1780 and when the city surrendered on 12 May he remained there in charge of its defenses. Although praised by his superiors for this campaign, recognition from the crown again being limited to brevet promotion (Lt. Col. on 27 Sept. '80), the Hessian Capt. Johann Ewald found the highly touted British engineer negligent in some aspects of his planning. (Uhlendorf, *Charleston*, 37–41)

The British evacuated some 800 slaves from Charleston to the West Indies when they left the city 14 Dec. '82. He has been accused not only of directing this larceny but also of benefiting personally. (Appleton's) He is known to have owned property in the West Indies of considerable value, and there is circumstantial evidence of his war profiteering, but few officers on either side—given the opportunity—were innocent of this. Back in England he rose to the position of deputy Q.M.G. and when a British expeditionary force went to Holland in 1793 he accompanied it as Q.M. He actually assumed the duties of chief engineer, however, and directed the Duke of York's siege operations against Dunkirk. He was mortally wounded on 6 Sept. when the French made a powerful sally; he died the next day and was buried at Ostend. He had never married and his considerable estate was willed to his sisters.

Moncrieff is the spelling of his name in *D.N.B.* and in most accounts. Appleton's, however, adds an e, and editor Uhlendorf says it should be spelled with only one f. (Baurmeister, 352 *n*.)

MONEY OF THE 18TH CENTURY. When the Cont'l. Cong. resolved on 22 June '75 to finance the war with CONT'L. CURRENCY it announced that these bills of credit would be backed by the "Spanish milled dollar." In so doing they adopted a monetary system long known in the New World, and this Spanish dollar later was the model for U.S. currency. (For this reason it is convenient, if not historically precise, to use the $ and ¢ symbols.)

A chronic shortage of currency existed in America before and after 1775. England not only had failed to face the problem during the colonial period, coining virtually no silver or copper money between 1760 and 1816 (*E.B.*, "Numismatics"), but they also discouraged any American efforts to do so. (England's problem was that she could not stabilize the value of silver in relation to gold.) Desperate for currency, Mass. established a mint in 1651 and the next year started turning out crude silver pieces. The best known of these was the Pine Tree Shilling, about the size of a modern quarter. Thirty years later the mint shut down, but the date 1652 on the coins was not changed during this period. (Oak Tree and Willow Tree money was also minted, the coins being so called because they bore these symbols.) In 1690 the same colony printed 20-shilling bills of credit, the first paper money produced in British America.* Other colonies also

---

* Out of desperation the Canadian Intendant, Jacques de Meulles, five years earlier had used the blank backs of playing cards to make handwritten notes. At first denounced vehemently by authorities in France, the method was officially sanctioned during the years 1729–60; specially prepared cards were supplied at certain periods, but playing cards were again used when nothing else was available. Economist Richard A. Lester suggests that the success of this Canadian experiment led Mass. to start issuing paper money in 1690. (*Monetary Experiments* [1939], 41. See Phares O. Sigler, "Canadian Card Money," in *Selections from The Numismatist: Modern Foreign Currency*, post.)

printed bills, and the value of the shilling subsequently varied from one part of the country to another in accordance with the depreciation of each colony's bills of credit. (See below) Each colony therefore established its own currency laws and also used certain commodities as substitutes for money. (See PARSON'S CAUSE)

Coins from England, Spain, France, Portugal and Holland were legal tender in America, and others appeared also. Spanish coins (most of which were minted in the New World) eventually predominated, but accounts continued to be kept in English pounds, shillings, and pence. The latter had the same relative values as today: 12 pence made a shilling, and 20 shillings made a pound. The latter was "money of account," which is to say there was no corresponding coin; but there was a guinea gold piece (21s.). The English pound and the Spanish dollar had the same relative values that prevailed until recent years: £1 made $5, which made the shilling worth 25¢.

The Spanish milled dollar, *peso duro*, hard dollar, or piece of eight (reals), was a silver coin about the size of a modern dollar. Authorities have shattered the appealing myth that ingenious American colonists solved a small change problem by cutting Spanish dollars into four "two-bit" pieces: no such pieces dating to before 1798 have been reported; after 1798 such cut dollars were made (by machinery) in Spain and in the West Indies. They subsequently appeared in North America. The silver quadrants or "sharpshins" were worth two reals (four being cut from a "piece of eight") and became known as "two-bit" pieces. In the South and in the West Indies the real was therefore known as a bit. In Pa.,

Md., Del., and certain other middle colonies, the real circulated at its geometrical value of one-eighth of a dollar (or 12½¢, to use modern parlance). Farther north the same coin was called a shilling. (Webster's, "Real")

To get an idea of how much the shilling varied in value, here are the rates of exchange in 1784, when the newly established Bank of N.Y. considered a London pound to be worth $4.44 or the shilling worth 22.22¢: in New England and Va., the shilling was worth 16.66¢ (six to the dollar); in N.Y. and N.C., 12½¢ (8 to the dollar); in N.J., Pa., Del., and Md., 13.35¢; in Ga., 20¢; and in S.C., 3¢ (32½ shillings to the dollar!).

Various copper coins circulated in America. What was generally meant by a "copper" was the *value* of a British penny, although this *coin* was not first struck until 1797. At the time when a dollar was valued in N.Y. at 8s. or 96 pence ("coppers"), one found the guinea quoted at $4 64/96, the *louis d'or* at $4 52/96, etc.

OTHER SPANISH COINS

The silver pistareen was marked as two reals and should have been worth one-fourth of a dollar; because of low silver content, however, some assayed as low as 16.8¢. The gold escudo was worth $2, and the pistole or doblon was a gold coin equivalent to two gold escudos, or $4.

Whereas the name *pistole* was given to this last gold coin by the French in jest, there being no such meaning for the Spanish and Italian words *pistola*, the English and Americans gave the name *doubloon* to the Spanish gold 8-escudo piece. This famous coin was therefore worth about $16. (See Schilke and Solomon, post., passim)

FRENCH MONEY

The livre tournois ("of Tours") was worth about 19¢ or 9.4d when replaced in 1795 by the franc. It had about this value during the American Revolution. In round figures, five livres made a Spanish dollar, and 25 livres made a British pound. The livre was divided into 20 sous of 12 deniers each. The silver *écu* was about equal to three livres, or 55¢. The *louis d'or,* known in America as the French Guinea, was worth 12¢ less than the British Guinea in N.Y.C. in 1784.

OTHER MONEY IN AMERICA

The Portuguese johannes or joannes, named after John V (d. 1750) and always called a joe, was a gold coin issued between 1722 and 1835. The half-joe, worth about $8, was so much more common that it was generally referred to as a joe and the $16 coin then became known as the dobra or double johannes. (Webster's)

The Portuguese moidore was a gold coin worth over $6.

The carlin was a small silver coin first struck in Italy and worth about 19¢. The carolin, a gold coin of Bavaria and Wurtemburg, was worth $4.75 in N.Y.C. in 1784. A gold ducat circulated in the Carolinas at about $2.25. The gold Italian chequin or sequin (*O.U.D.*) was worth $1.67. "The German piece," valued at $5.18, circulated in the South but seldom in the North.

The thaler, or German dollar, of the 18th century was worth about 75¢. (Tharp, *Baroness,* 13) The florin known in Northern Europe about this time was valued at approximately 40¢. (Lossing, II, 852 *n.*)

In speaking of the value of all these coins, reference is, of course, to their *intrinsic* value—their fineness and their weight, the latter being affected by wear and sometimes by clipping or other forms of mutilation.

PURCHASING POWER

It is difficult, and downright dangerous, to attempt to estimate the value of money today in comparison with that of any other period. The Bureau of Labor Statistics has constructed a wholesale commodity price index that gives an approximate idea of how the dollar has changed in value since pre-Revolutionary times. Using the 1926 dollar as being equal to $1.00, the dollar of 1775 was worth $1.96. During most of 1779–80 it was at a low of 67¢. Thereafter it rose to $1.67 and remained fairly stable until the War of 1812, falling to 76¢ in Dec. 1814. (*D.A.H.,* "Money, Purchasing Power of.") The U.S. Dept. of Commerce's *Historical Statistics . . . ,* has a chapter on Prices and Price Indexes and cites Arthur H. Cole, *Wholesale Commodity Prices in the United States, 1700–1861* (Cambridge, 1938) as a particularly valuable source. Another is *Wholesale Prices in Philadelphia, 1784–1861,* by Anne Bezanson and associates (Philadelphia, 1936).

In his *D.A.B.* sketch of Thos. Hutchinson, Carl L. Becker says a common family could live comfortably in Boston on £40 a year in 1763. Gottschalk and R. R. Palmer equate the French livre to a 1940 dollar in terms of purchasing power. (*Close,* 38; *Twelve Who Ruled,* 17). Based on the Metropolitan Life Insurance Company's Statistical Bulletin of Jan. 1944, which gives the cost of children at various dates, Morton M. Hunt in his *Natural History of Love* (New York, 1959) says £100 in 1776 would in terms of 1959 money have been at least $1,000 and possibly three times that much.

One of the problems facing the new

nation after the American Revolution was to unscramble this monetary mess. The first U.S. dollar coins, modeled on the Spanish dollar, were issued in 1794.

See Oscar G. Schilke and Raphael E. Solomon, *America's Foreign Coins ...* (New York, 1964), which contains an excellent bibliography. I am grateful to James C. Risk for bringing this book to my attention and for giving me his expert comment on this article. John B. McMaster in the first volume of his *History ...* (New York, 1883) has an interesting and detailed account of the currency situation in America after the Revolution. See also *Selections from the Numismatist: Modern Foreign Currency* (Racine, Wis., 1961).

MONMOUTH, N.J., Campaign (16 June–5 July '78) and Battle (28 June). British strategy for 1778 included Clinton's evacuation of Philadelphia and movement of the garrison to N.Y. Since Clinton lacked shipping to do this without shuttling, and since danger of French naval interference made the latter too dangerous, he was forced to march with some 10,000 troops and much impedimenta through N.J. By late May '78 Washington knew the British in Philadelphia were preparing for some operation, and he knew that a march through the Jerseys might be undertaken, but a council of war on 17 June acquiesced in his judgment that the army should remain at Valley Forge until there was some definite indication of enemy intentions. (Freeman, *Washington,* V, 10) This council of war is frequently confused with that of 24 June, covered below.

Before dawn of 16 June Clinton removed artillery from his redoubts and during the day several regiments crossed the Delaware into N.J. By the 18th he had successfully accomplished the dangerous task of evacuating his entire force from the city, moving his troops and supply train to Haddonfield, and shipping his heavy equipment, invalids, and 3,000 Tories down the river. Receiving word of this evacuation almost immediately, Washington started his army north toward Coryell's Ferry.

STRATEGY OF THE CAMPAIGN

A limited net of poor roads presented the British commander with the danger of being attacked while in column. Clinton was encumbered with 1,500 wagons, artillery, and slowed by destroyed bridges and obstructed roads. Once he reached Bordentown he had two possible routes. He could move through Trenton, Princeton, and cross the Raritan at Brunswick; from here he could march east to Amboy, with his flank protected by the Raritan, and ferry his troops to Staten Island. Or he could move N.E. from Bordentown to Raritan Bay, where points of embarkation were provided between South Amboy and Sandy Hook. The latter route was longer by at least a day's march. Much would depend on Washington's movements.

The speed with which the Americans started north is testimony to the transformation brought about at VALLEY FORGE by Steuben, Greene, and Jeremiah Wadsworth. Washington reported a strength of 13,503 officers and men in his official returns of 12 June. Of these, Maxwell's Brig. of about 1,300 was at Mount Holly. Another 800 N.J. militia under Philemon Dickinson were also in the Jerseys. The first division to leave Valley Forge was that of Charles Lee, which had the brigades of Hunterdon, Poor, and Varnum. Wayne followed a few hours later, at 3 P.M., with Mifflin's Div., which comprised Conway's Brig. and the 1st and 2d Pa. Brigs. The divisions of Lafayette, De Kalb, and Alexander ("Stirling") left early 19 June.

When Washington reached Coryell's

Ferry on 21 June he still lacked sufficient information to tell whether Clinton was in fact heading north or
whether he was moving south along the
Delaware, but he proceeded on the
former assumption. (Freeman, 12) Intelligence the next day began to indicate that Washington's guess was right,
and he ordered the militia to keep up
their activity in obstructing the routes
over which the enemy would have to
move. He also reinforced Morgan's riflemen and sent them with Moylan's
mounted troops to reinforce Dickinson
on Clinton's east flank. Arnold (who
had taken command in Philadelphia)
was urged to have Cadwalader's Pa. militia and Cont'ls. nip at Clinton's heels,
and about 300 men went out on this
mission. All units were urged to harass
the British and, above all, to send in
reports of their movement.

On 23 June Washington established
his headquarters at Hopewell (7 miles
N.W. of Princeton) where he learned
that the enemy was just south of Bordentown and acting in such a way as to
indicate they might follow either of the
two possible routes mentioned earlier.

"Now commenced in earnest a guess-
ing game the like of which Washington
had not seen since he had worn out his
men and their shoes chasing Howe's
fleet in the summer of 1777 [PHIL.
CAMP'N.]. The task of the American
commander was simply stated but was
difficult to execute: He must use his
outposts . . . in such a manner that he
would have a force on almost every
road the British might use, and, at the
same time, he must not so scatter his
troops that he would be unable to concentrate quickly when his adversary's
plan was disclosed." (Freeman, 15–16)

Most accounts ignore the strategic
problems faced by Clinton in selecting
his route and Washington's problems in
learning of his enemy's intentions. An-

other point that may not be apparent is
that the Monmouth campaign could have
had a decisive effect on the Revolution's
outcome: Washington could have destroyed Clinton's entire army which, on
the heels of the Saratoga surrender,
would have won the war (Freeman,
14); on the other hand "he could not
forget there also was the possibility of
a defeat that would ruin the American
cause." (Ibid.)

On 24 June Washington called a
council of war to recommend whether
the army should adopt an active or
passive strategy. Charles Lee, whose
professional competence was still held
in awe by most of the other generals,
dominated the discussion and argued
that it would be "criminal" to risk a
general engagement with Washington's
amateurs against Clinton's professionals.
Since the new French Alliance assured
American success in the war, he reasoned, they not only should let Clinton
get away but would be justified in building a "bridge of gold" to facilitate his
change of base. (Lafayette, Memoirs,
quoted in C. & M., 710) Alexander and
Knox subscribed to Lee's views. Greene,
Wayne, Steuben, Duportail, and Lafayette favored varying degrees of major
offensive action, but the council's final
recommendation was to avoid a general
engagement while sending a force of
1,500 to "act as occasion may serve, on
the enemy's left flank and rear." All
signed this paper except Wayne, who
wrote a letter of protest, as did Lafayette and Greene. Alexander Hamilton
commented that the recommendation
"would have done honor to the most
honorable body of midwives and to
them only."

Col. Charles Scott was put in command of the 1,500 who were to harass
the enemy's left flank. For the moment
Washington complied with the midwives' strategy, his only modification

being to send Daniel Morgan's small command of riflemen to work against the other flank. Almost immediately, however, new intelligence established that the enemy was moving from Allentown toward Monmouth Court House, and this called for a revision of Washington's plans. Scott's force would have to be strengthened, and somebody of higher grade would have to command it. Lafayette was the logical candidate, but Lee was senior and therefore entitled to the post.

"Washington undertook to meet this in the most direct manner by a personal appeal to Lee, who proved compliant, almost condescending, in fact. The proposed task, said Lee, more properly could be discharged by a 'young, volunteering General,' than by the second in command of the entire Army." (Freeman, 18–19)

But when Lee saw that the task force was going to number more than 4,000 he changed his mind, saying that ceding its command "would have an odd appearance." The C. in C. then conceived a peculiar compromise solution: since Lafayette had already left (Freeman, 19), he would be allowed to make the first move against the enemy and to carry it out if the action were taking place before Lee joined him. "After that, and earlier if Lafayette was not committed to action, Lee would have the usual authority of senior Major General." (Freeman, 19)

This controversial matter is covered in some detail because it can be distorted by oversimplification. Ward says, for example, "This shift in command from Lafayette to Lee was the fundamental error of the campaign," since Lee was known to oppose the tactics Washington wanted pursued. (Ward, 575) But Freeman makes clear the realities of command that Washington could not ignore; Washington almost solved the problem of sidelining Lee but was then forced to compromise.

Clinton reached Monmouth the afternoon of 26 June after an exhausting 19-mile march over a road deep with sand. The humid heat, which reached 100 degrees in the sun, was fatal to many of his heavily-burdened troops. Washington's main body had started toward Cranbury soon after it became known that Clinton was heading for Monmouth, and the Americans made the march the night of 25–26 June.

The morning of 27 June the British were disposed around Monmouth in such a manner that they were capable of attack, defense, or continuing their retreat. Washington's intelligence service had temporarily broken down, his forces were scattered, and the supply wagons had been unable to keep up. It looked as if Clinton would escape before a decisive blow could be struck against him, but later in the day Washington started moving the main body to within three miles of Englishtown so as to be able to support the advance force at that place. Lafayette had been ordered to Englishtown the afternoon of the 26th, and on the 27th Lee was ordered to go there and take command of the detachment that had now been reinforced to 5,000. Lee's orders were to attack as soon as the British left Monmouth, but Lee soon sent back word that *he expected the enemy to attack him!*

On the eve of battle the situation was, therefore, as follows: Clinton occupied a strong defensive position around Monmouth and intended to resume his retreat at 4 A.M. on the 28th. Washington's main army was eight miles to the west, and Lee's strong advance element was a mere five miles away. Dickinson's 1,000 N.J. militia were close to Clinton's west flank and observing the enemy camp. Morgan's 600 riflemen were on the opposite flank, but out of contact with Washington. Moylan's mounted troops—now reduced to 30—were screening the roads the British would have to travel, but lacked the strength to make any real contribution to American operations. "Small contingents of New Jersey militia were wandering about aimlessly . . . Brig. Gen. William Winds had 800 of these men at Brunswick but showed no disposition to bestir himself." (Freeman, 20 *n.*)

BATTLE OF MONMOUTH, 28 JUNE '78

At 4 o'clock the morning of 28 June, Knyphausen started north toward Middletown with his portion of the army and the baggage train. Dickinson observed this movement and his report was in Washington's hands at about 5 A.M. Lee, however, had done nothing during the night to reconnoiter, and it was not until 6 A.M. that he complied with the order he had received at 1 A.M. to send out a force to observe the enemy. Col. William Grayson then left Englishtown (at 6 A.M.) with his own Va. Regt., Scott's Brig., part of Varnum's Brig., and four guns: a total of 600 men. Lee had informed his officers in a meeting the afternoon of the 27th that in the absence of adequate intelligence he would prescribe no plan of attack for the next day but intended to move forward cautiously and play it by ear; he started about 7 A.M.

Meanwhile, Dickinson's militia had retreated across the swamp of the West Ravine when an enemy patrol advanced against them. Grayson's force then arrived and the Americans pushed back to their original position. When Lee reached the Meeting House he received conflicting reports as to whether Clinton had really started retreating. This led to an altercation between Lee and

Dickinson, who soon met, as to the veracity of the latter's report to Washington. The explanation was simply that when Knyphausen started north Clinton had remained behind with Cornwallis' command to give the others a head start. Wayne was ordered forward to command Grayson's advance guard. Another enemy security element was driven back and Lee's command advanced to a position between the East Ravine and the enemy's line of retreat.

By this time Cornwallis' division had evacuated Monmouth, leaving a sizable rear guard at that place. With a view to cutting off this enemy detachment, Lee launched what he intended to be an attack. There followed a confused series of orders and counterorders, marches and countermarches, advances and withdrawals. "The one fact that emerges clearly from that welter of maneuvers is that Lee had no plan of attack," says Ward. All Lee accomplished was to alert Clinton to the fact that elements of Washington's main body were now in contact and that he had more to contend with than the forces that had previously harassed his flanks. The British commander therefore sent for a brigade of British foot and the 17th Light Dragoons from Knyphausen's division to cover his northern flank and headed back toward Monmouth to face Lee.

Most accounts of the extremely confused series of actions that followed are content to limit themselves to broad generalization: Lee's 5,000 men and 12 cannon retreated in confusion some three miles until they met Washington, who took personal command of the situation and formed a line behind West Ravine that checked the enemy's further advance. Perhaps it would be best to leave it at that, not only because the action was so complicated that it cannot be explained in a few pages, but

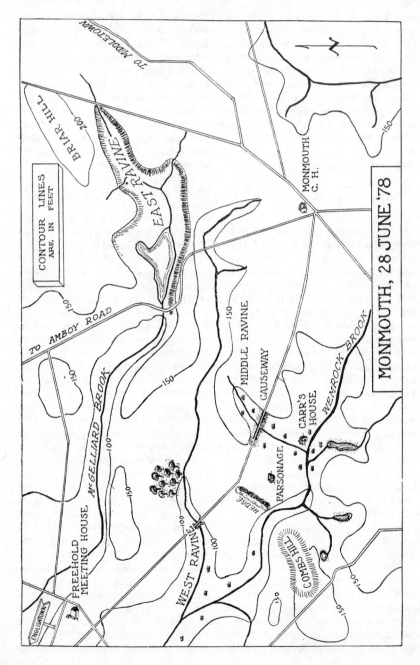

MONMOUTH, 28 JUNE '78

because there is so much contradiction among contemporary accounts that it probably will never be possible to piece together an accurate picture. With these reservations in mind I will, however, present what most modern military historians submit as being the main facts of the action.

The portion of Clinton's army that left Monmouth at 4 A.M. comprised 10 battalions, the 17th Light Dragoons, and the 1,500 wagons. (Fortescue, *British Army,* III, 253) Knyphausen, who commanded this "division," was subsequently ordered to send back a foot brigade and the 17th Dragoons. Since the rest of Knyphausen's command continued their retreat and the units detached from him were used as flank security only, we can forget about them.

The second "division" of Clinton's army, commanded by Cornwallis and accompanied by Clinton, comprised 14 battalions and the 16th Light Dragoons (Fortescue, 253–54); units were the 3d, 4th, and 5th British infantry brigades, the 1st and 2d British grenadier battalions, all the German grenadiers, the British Guards, the 1st and 2d British light infantry battalions, Simcoe's Tory Queen's Rangers, and the 16th Dragoons (Ward, 577).

Cornwallis' troops had started leaving their bivouac to follow Knyphausen at 8 A.M., and Lee's abortive attempt to cut off the rear guard started at 10 o'clock. (Fortescue, 254) This rear guard, between 1,500 and 2,000 men (Freeman, 25), was composed of the 16th Dragoons, the light infantry, and the British and German grenadiers. When other of Cornwallis' units turned to meet Lee's threat they formed a line composed of the Guards and three infantry brigades.

As for American forces in contact during this initial phase, Grayson's 600-man advance guard has already been mentioned, as has the 1,000-man militia force of Dickinson. The rest of Lee's command had left Englishtown in the following order of march: Col. Richard Butler led with 200 men, Col. Henry Jackson followed with the same number, then came part of Woodford's Brig. and Varnum's Brig. (each having 600 men and two guns), next was Wayne with 1,000 men and four guns, Scott with 1,400 and four guns, and Maxwell with 1,000 men and two guns —a total of 5,000 troops and 12 cannon. (Ward, 578; Freeman, 25)

When Lee saw he had lost his opportunity to annihilate the British rear guard he ordered Lafayette to lead three regiments of Wayne's command and some artillery against the enemy's left (south) flank. The young Frenchman got into position to attack but then decided that this position was unsuitable and was maneuvering to another line of departure when this was mistaken by other commanders for a withdrawal. Scott and Maxwell dropped back, then Grayson and Jackson, according to Ward's account. (Ward, 580) According to other accounts, however, Scott and Maxwell were *ordered* back when Lee discovered they were under heavy pressure, and that Lafayette was at this time moving to block a British penetration on the American right. (Wallace, *Appeal,* 187–88, citing *Lee Papers* and Stryker's *Monmouth*.) Whatever started it, there followed a general and confused retreat, some units in good order and others completely disorganized. According to certain versions of the battle, a second position was formed along the Amboy road, but this line was not defended.

WASHINGTON TAKES CHARGE

About noon Washington heard cannon fire from Monmouth C. H., but there was no sound of small arms.

Alexander Hamilton rode up to report that Lee was about to attack. Henry Knox then arrived to say that Lee's troops were in disorder and that precautions should be taken against a possible reverse. (Freeman, 26) When a local civilian and a fugitive soldier, a musician, arrived to report that Lee was retreating, Washington refused to believe this unexpected news. He ordered the soldier put under guard and threatened to have him whipped if he repeated his incredible story, but Washington soon saw the retreat with his own eyes.

Pushing on to the ridge overlooking the swamp of West Ravine, the C. in C. saw that "the yellow road in front of him, a merciless furnace [in the 100-degree heat], was crowded with armed men. They were moving toward him, not in wild disorder but manifestly in retreat, staggering, exhausted. . . ." (Freeman, 27) The Cont'l. regiments of Grayson and Patton were the first to appear, and others followed along the road and in the fields. They said they were retiring on orders. Washington rode forward to encounter Lee about 400 yards east of the bridge across West Ravine. (Lossing, II, map on p. 356; Greene, *Rev. War,* map facing p. 146) Washington unceremoniously demanded an explanation of the retreat.

"Sir, sir?" Lee is reported to have asked, apparently not understanding the question. Then,

"Lee answered, in manifest embarrassment, that contradictory intelligence had caused confusion, that he did not choose to meet the British when he was in that condition. . . . Besides, the attack had been made contrary to his opinion.

"Washington retorted hotly that whatever Lee's opinions, he expected his orders to be obeyed. If Lee had not believed in the operation, he should not have undertaken it. With perhaps one other exchange, Washington hurried off. . . ." (Freeman, 28–29)

Lafayette is responsible for the story that Washington called Lee "a damned poltroon" and ordered him to the rear, but since Lafayette was not a witness and produced this much-quoted account many years later it cannot be accepted as true. Gen. Scott related that Washington "swore that day till the leaves shook on the trees. Charming! Delightful! Never have I enjoyed such swearing before or since." In view of the fact that Lee charged Scott with precipitating the retreat by abandoning a favorable position, accusations Scott hotly denied, and since he does not appear to have witnessed the encounter between Washington and Lee, I subscribe to Ward's judgment that this "most thoroughly satisfying" version is "probably apocryphal." (Ward, 581) Freeman's version, quoted above, is based on the statements of five witnesses, including Lee himself.

FINAL PHASE OF THE BATTLE

Although Clinton had at first been reluctant, he had soon decided to bring on a general engagement. He regrouped his forces in two lines, the British grenadiers, Guards, and light infantry from left to right; the 4th Brig., 3d Brig., and Hessian grenadiers behind them. His initial maneuver was to attack with the light infantry against Lee's left— the operation that led to Lee's retreat from the first position. The British then pushed west on the dusty heels of the American advance detachment.

The "Third Position" of the Americans checked Clinton's advance until Washington organized the final defense overlooking West Ravine. Authorities disagree as to the location of the Third Position, most of them believing it to have been on the ridge between the Middle and West ravines. An important feature of this delaying position was a hedgerow behind which Henry Beekman Livingston, on his own initiative, started rallying his men. Washington quickly saw the importance of this feature and collected other regiments to form a line, which soon included—from right to left—the troops of Livingston, Varnum, Stewart, and Ramsay. Now, Freeman says this hedge was "on the eastward gradient" of the ridge where the final stand was made (*op. cit.,* 29), but other accounts and maps place it on the enemy side of West Ravine and about 1,000 yards in front of the final American defenses. (Lossing, II, 356; Greene, 146 *n.* and map; Ward, 581 and map on p. 583; and the Harper & Row map common to Wallace, C. & M., and Alden.) The contemporary map of the action which Freeman reproduces (between pages 29 and 30 of *Washington,* V) shows at "Point 13" the delaying position depicted by the other authorities just cited, yet he does not accept that the delaying position was actually located there. The only comment Freeman has on this disputed point is that the map, which may have been Lafayette's, if accepted as accurate "supplies some information not given in reports or brought out by witnesses at the court-martial [of Charles Lee]; if it is an approximation, filled in with surmise, it adds confusion to the field." Nobody can disagree with the last point.

Out of this historical confusion we can be reasonably sure that Washington did organize the regiments of Livingston, Varnum, Stewart, and Ramsay into a line that delayed the British until the main defense could be established behind West Ravine. Col. Eleazer Oswald brought four guns into action to support this forward line, and Knox subsequently reinforced Oswald with guns from the rear. (Free-

man, 30 and *n.*) Greene put four guns in position on Comb's Hill where they delivered an effective enfilade fire on the enemy's left and center; Woodford's Brig. provided local security for these pieces. The forward position was finally driven back, Ramsay and Stewart not being able to hold off a mounted attack on the northern flank and Varnum and Livingston then being pushed back by dragoons and grenadiers.

Washington was fortunate in having an officer available who knew the local topography and could tell him how to make the best use of the favorable terrain where he was improvising a hasty defense. This officer, Lt. Col. David Rhea of the 4th N.J., pointed out that the swamp east of the ridge would present a serious obstacle to the enemy, that there was high ground on the American left that was suited for defense, that woods behind the ridge would provide concealment for reserves, and it was he who showed Greene the important artillery location on Comb's Hill. While Wayne posted his five regiments forward of the American center, where the enemy could be expected to hit first, Alexander took the high ground on the American left and Greene occupied the right. Lafayette commanded the troops between and somewhat to the rear of Alexander and Greene.

Alexander's wing was the first to come under attack. For nearly an hour a detachment of British light infantry, the 42d Regt. ("Black Watch"), and a number of field guns worked to penetrate or envelop the American left, but Washington, Steuben, and Alexander were there to exert their personal leadership, and the rebels held. Heavy fire from the guns of Lt. Col. Edward Carrington's 1st Cont'l. Arty. answered the British guns in a smart artillery duel, and volley after volley of musketry poured from each side. After watching American regiments maneuver under the eye of their drillmaster, Steuben, Alexander Hamilton later commented that this showed him for the first time the value of military discipline. A counterattack by the 1st and 3d N.H. and the 1st Va. through heavy woods on the American left (east flank) against the British right drove back the enemy and relieved the threat to Alexander's wing.

Clinton then hit Greene's (right) wing with a massive attack that Cornwallis personally directed. Units in this attack were the Coldstream Guards, another guards battalion, the English and Hessian Grenadiers, another light infantry detachment, and the 37th and 44th Foot, all of them elite troops. This attack also was brought to a bloody halt and driven back, largely by flanking fire from Comb's Hill.

Wayne's position in the center was hit by a series of frontal attacks that started while Greene's wing was being attacked. The first, by light infantry, dragoons, and grenadiers, was shattered by well-controlled fire that was held until they were at close range and then delivered in a sustained series of volleys. A second charge met the identical fate. The third effort, led an hour later by Lt. Col. Henry MONCKTON, was formed not more than 500 feet away. "Forward to the charge, my brave grenadiers," commanded Monckton, who led them from the right flank as they rushed forward. American discipline continued to hold as Wayne commanded, "Steady, steady! Wait for the word, then pick out the king-birds!" When the word came the British ranks went down in the hail of lead. Monckton fell mortally wounded so close to the hedge that Wayne's men captured his body and the colors of his battalion. Clinton's account of this confused

battle is hard to reconcile with the above narrative; the latter is based on Ward's study of W. S. Stryker's *Monmouth,* which Ward calls "an exhaustive monograph." The heat was killing, quite literally (see below), and Clinton's idea now was merely to extricate those of his troops still in contact with the enemy. In the biographical sketch of the remarkable James WEBSTER is Clinton's account of the final attack that made this possible. With both of his flanks now threatened, Wayne withdrew in good order from his forward position, and the main battle line— the forces of Alexander, Lafayette, and Greene—stood ready to withstand an attack that the British were incapable of delivering.

Although 16 British cannon continued to pound the American positions, soon after 5 o'clock the infantry actions and dragoon attacks were discontinued. The sun was still up, but now it was thirst more than heat that tortured the exhausted troops on both sides. Yet Washington ordered a counterattack and sent word to Steuben, who had been collecting stragglers on the Englishtown road, to bring reinforcements forward in preparation for a pursuit! Woodford led his brigade out from its position on Comb's Hill, and on the other flank Poor moved forward with his regiments and the N.C. Brig. of Thomas Clark. But before either of these columns could get within range of the enemy they were stopped by heat, fatigue, and failing light; they collapsed on their arms within a few hundred yards of their points of departure. Clinton withdrew about half a mile east of Middle Ravine and rested his troops. He then slipped away undetected at midnight, caught up with Knyphausen at daybreak, and was in Middletown by 10 A.M. of the 29th. The next day his entire force was at Sandy Hook, and by 5 July in New York (Ward, 585).

CASUALTIES

The Americans lost 356, of whom 72 were killed, 161 wounded, and 132 missing; many of the latter had dropped of heat exhaustion and soon rejoined their units, but at least 37 of them are believed to have died of sunstroke. (Ward, 585, citing Stryker) Freeman accepts these casualty figures (*op. cit., 43 n.*), but it must be pointed out that the ratio of a little over two wounded for each fatality is not realistic. (See CASUALTY FIGURES)

Clinton's losses in killed and wounded were 358, according to Fortescue (*op. cit.,* 254), who says that no fewer than 60 died of sunstroke. Baurmeister speaks of 286 *British* casualties (112 killed and 174 wounded) and mentions that 62 died of heat; he implies that there were no German casualties (Baurmeister, 187). The Americans buried at least 217 enemy dead, however, and Washington put this figure at over 249; Freeman estimates Clinton's total losses were over 1,200; in addition, more than 600 deserters—440 of them Germans—came into Philadelphia by 6 July. (Freeman, 43 *n.;* Ward, 585)

COMMENT

This was the last important engagement in the North, and was the longest action of the war (Ward, 586). Tactically it was a draw. Freeman calls it "the best the Army yet had fought. . . . Action at Trenton and at Princeton had been with detachments: This time all of Clinton's troops had been near enough to have participated if their commander had wished to have a full engagement." (*Op. cit.,* 44) Presumably by "the Army" Freeman means the forces under Washington's personal command.

Troops of both sides showed astounding vigor and courage considering the heat not only on the day of battle but during the preceding days. Freeman quotes one source as saying the temperature reached 92 degrees on 28 June (*op. cit.,* 25 *n.*); other writers say it was 100 in the sun. Trevelyan says the battle was fought on "the most scorching summer day ever known in America." (*American Revolution,* V, 290)

One valuable achievement of the battle was to eliminate Charles Lee from the American service; this is covered under LEE COURT-MARTIAL. The MOLLY PITCHER LEGEND is associated with the battle.

MONROE, James. 1758–1831. Cont'l. officer and fifth U.S. President. Va. Son of a prosperous family, he attended William and Mary College but soon left with a contingent from the college to join the Cont'l. Army. He entered the 3d Va. under Col. Hugh Mercer as 2d Lt. 28 Sept. '75. At HARLEM HEIGHTS, he volunteered to accompany Knowlton in the encirclement. He also fought at White Plains and at TRENTON, where he was wounded. On 20 Nov. '77, he was named Maj. and A.D.C. to William Alexander. He fought at Brandywine, Germantown, and Monmouth before resigning 20 Nov. '78. In 1780 he became a law student under Thomas Jefferson, then Gov. of Va., staying with him until 1783. Appleton's says that he was sent, as a Lt. Col., by Jefferson as a military commissioner to ascertain conditions and prospects of the Southern army. In 1782 he was elected to the Va. assembly and also sat in the Congresses of the Confederation from 1783 until 1786. He was a member of the Va. convention that ratified the Federal Constitution and became a prominent anti-Federalist. Briefly, his public offices were: U.S. Senator 1790–94; envoy to France 1794–96; Gov. of Va. 1799–1802 and 1811; negotiator in France and Spain for the La. Purchase and in England 1801–6; Sec. of State 1811–17; Sec. of War 1814–15; and President of the U.S. 1816–25. During his two terms he strengthened the Atlantic seaboard defenses, accomplished numerous internal improvements, launched the first Seminole War, saw the acquisition of Fla. as a state, and the passage of the Missouri Compromise. He is perhaps best known for the Monroe Doctrine (2 Dec. '23). In 1786 he married Elizabeth Kortwright, daughter of a N.Y.C. merchant who was a Loyalist officer. While he was minister to France she was instrumental in having Mme de Lafayette released from La Force Prison. (Appleton's)

MONTGOMERY, Richard. 1738–1775. Cont'l. general. Ireland–N.Y. Son of an Irish M.P., he was educated at St. Andrews and Trinity College, Dublin, decided on a military career, and at 18 became an ensign in the 17th Foot. Going to Canada the next year (1757), he took part in the siege of Louisburg (1758), was promoted to Lt., and served under Amherst in the successful operations against Ticonderoga, Crown Point, and Montreal. Meanwhile he became Regt'l. Adj. in 1760. In the West Indies he was at the capture of Martinique and Havana (1762), becoming a Capt. Returning to Great Britain, he became well known by Burke and Fox and was greatly influenced by their liberal views. "For some reason, never fully determined," says James Truslow Adams in *D.A.B.*, "he appears to have felt that he had no future in England and that his friends either could not or would not help him." He sold his commission on 6 Apr. '72, went to America, and on 24 July '73 settled on a 67-acre farm he had bought at Kings Bridge, N.Y. Having developed a sudden, but real and lasting, passion for farming, and having married the daugh-

ter (Janet) of Robert R. Livingston, he accepted a commission as Cont'l. B.G. on 22 June '75 with personal regret. Although in the colonies only three years, in May he had been made a delegate to the first provincial congress in N.Y.

Leaving his young wife and their new home near Rhinebeck (her estate), Montgomery went north to become second in command to Schuyler in the CANADA INVASION. With Schuyler soon evacuated for illness, Montgomery showed real military ability in leading an offensive into Canada despite the poor quality of troops and subordinate leaders at his disposition and the logistical problems he faced. After taking ST. JOHNS, 5 Sept.–2 Nov. '75, and Montreal, he pushed on to make the unsuccessful attack on QUEBEC, 31 Dec.–1 Jan. '76. He was killed in the latter action. The British recognized his body and ordered it "decently buried." In 1818 the body was moved to St. Paul's Church, N.Y.C. Much of his highest praise came from London, from his former friends as well as his political foes. In Parliament Burke contrasted the disgrace of the large army shut up in Boston with "the movements of the hero who in one campaign had conquered two thirds of Canada." (Appleton's) To this Lord North replied: "He was brave, he was able, he was humane, he was generous; but still he was only a brave, able, humane, and generous rebel." Fox retorted: "The term of rebel is no certain mark of disgrace. The great asserters of liberty, the saviors of their country, the benefactors of mankind in all ages have been called rebels." (North and Fox as quoted in Appleton's)

He has been described as being "tall, of fine military presence, of graceful address, with a bright, magnetic face, winning manners. . . ." (Quoted in *Ibid.*) *D.A.B.* cautions that early histories have confused him with an elder brother, "the notorious and cruel Capt. Alexander Montgomery." A good biography is in *D.N.B.* John Armstrong's *Life of Richard Montgomery* in Jared Sparks's *Library of American Biography,* vol. I, 1834, is less accurate. (J. T. Adams, *op. cit.*)

MONTMORENCI FALLS, Canada, 31 July '59. See COLONIAL WARS.

MONTOUR FAMILY. "Madam Montour," daughter of a French nobleman who settled in Canada about 1665, was captured by Indians when she was about 10 and spent the rest of her life among the Iroquois. Those who met Madam Montour when she visited Albany (1711) and Philadelphia (1727) as an official interpreter for her adopted people, and white travelers who later visited her in the Iroquois settlements, picture her as a lady of refinement and education, accepted in the best white society. In his long article on the Montours in the *Handbook of American Indians,* J. N. B. Hewett comments that these stories are undoubtedly exaggerated. The loyalty of Madam Montour to the proprietary government of Pa., however, was so valuable to the colony that at least two of her sons received large land grants. Montoursville, Pa., is now located on land belonging to Andrew. About 1729 Madam Montour's first husband, a Seneca, was killed fighting the Catawba (in S.C.). Although she remarried, her four or five children were by her first husband. She became blind prior to 1745, but continued to be vigorous. Hewett discredits the story that she was the daughter of a French governor of Canada and also doubts that she was alive during the Revolution. This same authority, incidentally, says it seems almost certain that Madam Montour was a French Canadian "without any admixture of Indian blood," but he mentions that her mother might have been a Huron.*

"French Margaret," one of Madam Montour's daughters, married an Indian and had daughters named Catherine and Esther. Many writers have merged three of these women into a single personality. This error is epitomized in Lossing's statement: "Queen Esther ... was the celebrated Catherine Montour ... and her father was one of the French governors, probably Frontenac." (I, 357 *n.*) The belief that Madam Montour was alive during the Revolution may stem from her being confused with the granddaughter who gave her name to Catherinetown. (Destroyed in 1779 by SULLIVAN'S EXPEDITION.)

"THE WITCH OF WYOMING"

Esther Montour married a ruling chief and lived near Tioga. Hewett says categorically that she and several other Montours took part in the WYOMING VALLEY "MASSACRE," and that she murdered prisoners in the following manner:

"Placed around a huge rock and held by stout Indians, 16 men were killed one by one by the knife or tomahawk in the hands of 'Queen Esther.' In a similar circle 9 others were killed. . . ." †

---

* Hewett's article is contradictory and ambiguous on several points. Part of this is bad editing, but much of it is due to inaccurate and incomplete source material.

† Lossing describes "Queen Esther's Rock," which he visited and sketched in 1848, as "a sort of conglomerate, a large proportion of which is quartz. Some of it is of a reddish color, which the credulous believe to be stains of blood still remaining. The rock projects only about eighteen inches above the ground. . . ." His sketch shows it to be roughly flat and about six feet across. (*Op. cit.,* 357 and *n.*)

Lebbeus Hammond and Joseph Elliot managed to break away and escape in a hail of bullets and tomahawks. Presumably it is they to whom posterity is indebted for this description of Queen Esther's performance.

MONTREAL. The strongly palisaded Iroquois village of Hochelaga ("at the place of the beaver dam"), on an island 30 miles long by 12 miles wide in the St. Lawrence, almost 1,000 miles inland, was visited by Jacques Cartier in 1535 and by Champlain in 1603. Cartier named it Mount Royal because of the 900-foot extinct volcano rising above the site, and Champlain built a fort at Montreal in 1611. Maisonneuve arrived in 1642 to establish a mission, and this date is generally given for the establishment of the town.

Missionaries, fur traders, and the military garrison constituted a heterogeneous population. The place was periodically attacked by Iroquois, and in 1725 a stone fort was added to the other defenses. The British threatened the place in 1711, and it was the objective of Amherst's unsuccessful expedition of 1759. As covered in the article on the COLONIAL WARS, Montreal surrendered on 8 Sept. '60. Subsequent military events are dealt with below.

MONTREAL, 25 Sept. '75. Ethan Allen's abortive attack. (CANADA INVASION) When Montgomery started his final investment of St. Johns (now St. Jean) he sent Ethan Allen ahead to recruit Canadians for the American army. John BROWN had gone toward La Prairie with the same purpose. Allen had such success along the Richelieu River in gathering volunteers that he decided to invest Montreal, which was virtually undefended. But most of his new recruits drifted away before he could make the attempt. Moving back toward St. Johns, Allen then linked up with Brown, who had about 200 men,

and the two conceived a plan of capturing Montreal: Allen would cross the St. Lawrence with his 110 men below the town and Brown would cross above it; the two forces would then attack simultaneously from opposite sides.

Allen got across the night of 24–25 Sept. but Brown did not. Since a shortage of canoes required Allen to make three shuttles and there was not enough time to withdraw his entire force safely before daybreak, he took up a defensive position a few miles from the town. Carleton sallied forth with about 35 soldiers and some 200 volunteers. After some brisk skirmishing, Allen's recruits scattered for the woods and Allen was captured with about 40 men. Walter BUTLER had a decisive part in this action.

This irresponsible adventure harmed the American cause by swaying Canadian sympathy toward the British, or it, at least, killed what slim hopes the Americans might have had of getting Canadian support. It also assisted the British in gaining support of the Indians, who wanted to side with the winners.

See Ethan ALLEN for his treatment in captivity.

MONTREAL, 13 Nov. '75. Occupied by Americans. (CANADA INVASION) The fall of ST. JOHNS, 2 Nov., left Montreal open to capture. The advance from the former place started on 5 Nov., and the first of Montgomery's men landed above Montreal on the 11th. Having but 150 regulars and a few militia to oppose Montgomery, Carleton sailed away the same day with these troops and the most valuable military stores. American shore batteries, adverse winds, and some bluffing by John BROWN led to surrender of the briganteen *Gaspée*, two other armed vessels, eight smaller craft, the stores. and all personnel except Carleton and one or two of his officers.

The latter escaped from the *Gaspée* in civilian disguise to a point opposite Sorel, and made their way to QUEBEC. Montgomery accepted the surrender of Montreal on the 13th.

MONTRESOR, James Gabriel. 1702–1776. Military engineer in Colonial Wars. Son of a naturalized Normand, J. G. Le Tresor, who was Lt. Gov. of Ft. William (Scotland) and a Maj. in the Royal Scots Fusileers, Montresor entered the Royal Artillery at Minorca in 1727. In 1754 he went to America as Braddock's chief engineer, was wounded at the Monongahela, was promoted to Lt. Col. and director of engineers in 1758, and served until the end of 1759 in N.Y. Thoroughly competent but unimaginative and physically weak, he was given the mission of building small fortifications and camps, and he had a hand in the construction or repair of most forts in upstate N.Y. Injured in 1759, he returned on leave to England in 1760. For his American service he was granted 10,000 acres to the east of Lake Champlain. John MONTRESOR was a son of his first marriage. His second wife (m. Aug. '66) was the daughter of novelist Henry Fielding.

MONTRESOR, John. 1736–1799. British military engineer. Born at Gibraltar, he went to America with his father in 1754 and was appointed an additional engineer by Braddock. He and his father were wounded at the Monongahela. The son served in upper N.Y., took part in Loudoun's "Cabbage Planting Expedition," was present at Amherst's capture of Louisburg and Wolfe's siege of Quebec, and served under Murray in the final operations of 1760. During most of this time he had specialized in scouting missions and dispatch carrying. In 1761 he explored the route later used in ARNOLD'S MARCH TO QUEBEC. At the end of the French and Indian War he was a Lt. in the regular establishment.

In Pontiac's War Lt. Montresor was sent from N.Y.C. with letters for the commander at Detroit. Delayed at Niagara for almost a month awaiting passage, he sailed on 26 Aug. '63 with provisions and a 17-man detachment of the 17th Regt. commanded by Capt. Edward Hope. Shipwrecked two days later, Montresor fortified the temporary camp and enabled the survivors, and a 100-man reinforcement that arrived on 2 Sept., to beat off Indian attacks that lasted from dawn to dusk on 3 Sept. Finally reaching Detroit, he stayed there until 20 Nov. '63, when he left with Robert Rogers (the famous ranger) and a large detachment to return to Niagara. The next year he fortified the portage at the latter place and went with Bradstreet to Detroit, where he improved the defenses.

He returned from England in 1766 as Capt.-Lt. and barrackmaster. During the next few years he worked on fortifications or barracks in N.Y.C., Boston, Philadelphia, and the Bahamas. He surveyed the N.Y.–N.J. boundary. In 1772 he bought what now is called Randall's Island (see MONTRESOR'S ISLAND), and lived there with his wife (m. Mar. '64) and family.

In 1775 he was commissioned chief engineer in America with the grade of Capt., but the British did not see fit to make use of his considerable experience in the colonies. Perhaps it was because he, even more than his father (see above), lacked formal engineer training and was not considered qualified to direct a siege or a defense; he had been trained, "on the job," in frontier warfare and exploration. In any event, Montresor was present at Lexington, Bunker Hill, Long Island, and the attack on the Delaware River forts (he had built the defenses on Mud Island).

He acted as chief engineer at the Brandywine. Having incurred the displeasure of Clinton (who calls MON-CRIEFF "an engineer *who understood his business,"* and doesn't mention Montresor once in his *American Rebellion*), Montresor returned to England in 1778. He soon retired from the army.

He is remembered for his *Journals.* Edited by G. D. Skull, they were published by the N.Y. Hist. Soc. in 1882.

MONTRESOR'S ISLAND (now Randall's), N.Y. Owned by John MON-TRESOR from 1772 until the British evacuation of N.Y. in Nov. '83, this island at the mouth of Harlem River was occupied by the British on 10 Sept. '76. "From that well-chosen advance post," comments Freeman, "they could land either on the plains of Harlem, South of Kings Bridge, or on the Morrisania estate, whence they could flank the position at Kings Bridge by a march of six or seven miles." (*Washington,* IV, 187) Up until this time it had been used by the Americans as an isolation area for troops inoculated with small-pox. (Heath, *Memoirs,* 55) Learning from two deserters that the island was lightly held, Heath got Washington's authority to retake it. Lt. Col. Michael Jackson of the 16th Cont'l. (Mass.) Inf. led 240 men in an attempt to surprise the outpost at dawn of 23 Sept. An American sentinel near the mouth of Harlem Creek had not been informed of this operation and fired at the friendly force as it passed on the way to Montresor's. Jackson landed about dawn with three field officers and men from the first boat. When the British guard attacked, the men in the other two boats pulled away instead of landing to join their leaders. In the withdrawal about 14 Americans were killed, wounded, and captured. Maj. Thos. Henly, Gen. Heath's A.D.C., who had insisted on accompanying the attack,

was killed as he re-entered the boat. Jackson was wounded by a musket ball in the leg. "The delinquents in the other boats were arrested, and tried by court-martial, and one of the Captains cashiered." (*Ibid.,* 73–76) The Heitman-*A.A.* list of battles gives 24 Sept. as the date of this action.

MOORE, Alfred. 1755–1810. Cont'l. officer, jurist. N.C. Son of Judge Maurice MOORE, he was educated in Boston and returned to N.C. to study law under his father. He was licensed to practice in 1775, and on 1 Sept. '75 became Capt. in the 1st N.C. Regt. commanded by his uncle, James MOORE. He took part in the Moores Creek Bridge campaign in Feb. '76 and the defense of Charleston in June. On 8 Mar. '77 he resigned his commission but served as a Col. of militia. In this capacity he was active in harassing the British based at WILMINGTON, 1 Feb.–18 Nov. '81. His plantation in Brunswick co. was plundered and his fortune impaired, but by 1790 he owned 48 slaves. (A. R. Newsome in *D.A.B.*)

Elected attorney general of N.C. on 3 May '82 he served almost nine years with distinction and then went on to become a brilliant criminal lawyer. President Adams appointed him an associate justice of the U.S. Supreme Court in Dec. '99. In 1804 he had to resign because of poor health.

MOORE, James. 1737–1777. Cont'l. general. N.C. Son of a founder of Brunswick, he served in the French and Indian War as a Capt. For a year he was commandant of Ft. Johnston (below Brunswick, at the mouth of the Cape Fear River). In provincial politics he sat in the House of Commons from 1764 to 1771 and in 1773; he actively opposed enforcement of the Stamp Act in 1776, and became a Son of Liberty. During the troubles with the Regulators he sided with the eastern oligarchy and the established government, serving as an artillery Col. in Gov. Tryon's expedition of 1758 and in the Battle of Alamance, 16 May '71.

He played a prominent role in driving Gov. Martin from the province, being the first to sign the circular letter calling for the first Revolutionary Prov. Cong. held in New Bern, Aug. '74. He represented his county (New Hanover) at the Third Prov. Cong. which met 20 Aug. '75 at Hillsboro. On 1 Sept. he was selected by this body to command the 1st N.C. Cont'ls. In this capacity he directed the campaign that ended with the important victory at MOORES CREEK BRIDGE, 27 Feb. '76.

Appointed B.G. by Congress on 1 Mar. '76, he was made C. in C. of patriot forces in N.C. During the defense of Charleston that year, Moore had the relatively inactive role of observing a small British fleet in the Cape Fear River. On 29 Nov. he was ordered to Charleston, where he remained until Feb. '77. On 5 Feb. he was ordered north to join Washington. About two months later he died at Wilmington, N.C., where his command had been delayed by lack of money for supplies. Although there is some question as to the exact date of death, *D.A.B.* accepts Heitman's date of 9 Apr. and cites *State Records of N.C.* that the cause was "a fit of Gout in his stomach." Only 40, he was a leader of great promise.

Brother of Maurice MOORE and of Rebecca, who married John ASHE.

MOORE, Maurice. 1735–1777. N.C. jurist and patriot. Son of a pioneer settler and founder of Brunswick, N.C., he was educated in New England. He became a prominent politician in his home province, where his support of the royal government led to his appointment to Gov. Tryon's council in 1760 (he served a year) and to an associate judgeship. His pamphlet attacking the Stamp Act on the grounds of no American representation in Parliament led to his suspension as judge, but he was reinstated in 1768 and served until the court ceased to function in 1773. Although he first sympathized with the Regulators, he served as a Col. in Tryon's expedition against them in 1768 and was a judge in the trials of 1768 and 1771 (after the Battle of Alamance). Having become bitterly hated by the Regulators, he then became their champion. In the Revolutionary politics that led to war with Great Britain he served on important committees of the Third Prov. Cong. in 1775 but was too conservative to become a leader. His brother's victory over the Tories at Moores Creek Bridge destroyed all chances for the course he advocated: reconciliation on the basis of political conditions in 1763. (A. R. Newsome in *D.A.B.*) Although elected to the Fifth Prov. Cong. of Nov. '76, he did not attend. He died some time before 20 Apr. '77. A man of ability and ambition, his political conduct had been "fickle and undecided." (*Ibid.*) He was brother of Gen. James MOORE, brother-in-law of Gen. John ASHE, and father of Alfred MOORE. Another Maurice Moore was commissioned ensign of the 1st N.C. on 1 Sept., promoted to 2d Lt. on 4 Jan. '76, and killed 18 Jan. (Heitman) The place of his death and his kinship are not known.

MOORES CREEK BRIDGE, N.C., 27 Feb. '76. Reports of Lexington and Concord so fanned the flames of Revolution in N.C. that within a few months the royal governor, Josiah MARTIN, had fled, the so-called MECKLENBURG DECL. OF INDEP. allegedly was adopted, a provincial congress had been organized, and the N.C. patriots were preparing for war.

N.C. contained a strong Loyalist element as well as a large number of people who advocated neutrality. Alden says:

"Royal officials, many merchants, some of the wealthy Tidewater planters, Scottish Highlanders in the Cross Creek country, and some of the quondam Regulators on the Piedmont were vigorously pro-British; and other old Regulators, Quakers, and Germans of the Piedmont sought to remain aloof. Perhaps no more than half the Tarheel population was firmly patriot." (*South,* 196–97)

Although the Provincial Congress had little or no success in winning over these factions, the latter were slow to unite for action. This enabled the rebels not only to send assistance to Va. and S.C. (see NORFOLK, 1 Jan. '76, and REEDY RIVER, 22 Nov. '75) but also to be ready when the Loyalists finally made their first move.

The CHARLESTON EXPEDITION of Clinton in 1776 was prompted largely by Martin's assurance—supported by other refugee governors—that the South could be won back if only a force of redcoats and royal tars were sent to show the flag. Dartmouth approved this strategic diversion just before leaving office, and Germain endorsed it over the protests of Gens. Harvey and Howe. When Martin learned that forces would leave Ireland on 1 Dec. '75 to link up with an expedition under Clinton from N.Y. off Cape Fear, he made plans for a coordinated uprising of Loyalists. Gen. Gage sent the elderly Donald McDonald and Donald McLeod to lead the enterprise. These two, Allan McDonald, and "half a dozen McLeods, McLeans, Stewarts, Campbells, McArthurs, and sundry others not bearing Celtic names" called for a rendezvous 15 Feb. at Brunswick, near Cape Fear. (Ward, *W.O.R.,* 663)

Donald McDonald raised the royal standard at Cross Creek (now Fayetteville) and on 5 Feb. '76 called for an assembly of armed supporters. Because of his own reputation as a veteran of CULLODEN and the work of others including the legendary Flora McDONALD, 1,000 Highland Scots gathered by 18 Feb. They came with bagpipes, broadswords, dirks, drums, and many wore kilts and tartans. Most of them were recent immigrants and were motivated not so much by loyalty to George III (from whom they held their land) as by their dislike for the Lowlanders and Ulstermen so prominent in the rebel camp. (Montross, *Reluctant Rebels,* 134) Another 500, some of them REGULATORS, also joined McDonald.

In the absence of Col. Robt. Howe's regiment at NORFOLK, Va., Col. James Moore's 1st N.C. Cont'ls., about 650 men and five guns, formed the nucleus of the force that marched from Wilmington and on 15 Feb. camped about 12 miles south of Cross Creek at Rockfish Creek. On the 18th he was joined by Cols. Alex. Lillington's 150 Wilmington minutemen, James Kenan's 200 Duplin co. militia, and John Ashe's 100 Vol. Indep. Rangers.

McDonald then sent Moore a copy of Gov. Martin's proclamation and "a friendly but firm letter . . . urging him to prevent bloodshed by joining the royal standard." (Lossing, II, 584) After stalling to send an express message to Col. Richard Caswell, who was approaching from New Bern with 800 Partisan Rangers, Moore sent McDonald a copy of the TEST OATH with the suggestion that bloodshed be avoided by his bringing the Loyalists into the rebel camp. "Neither accepted the other's invitation," comments Ward. (*Op. cit.*)

By this time McDonald knew the enemy was gathering strength around him; he decided to avoid a general engagement and march to the coast. His route was generally east across the Cape Fear and South rivers, thence S.E. toward Wilmington. Moore had the problem of withdrawing along the Cape Fear River and intercepting this march. When Caswell reported that he was between Black River and Moores Creek, and that the enemy had crossed the former, Moore sent word that he would attempt to stop the Tories at Moores Creek Bridge, about eighteen miles above Wilmington. He asked Caswell to meet him there if possible, otherwise to follow the enemy toward that place. (Moore's report, C. & M., 115)

Lillington and Ashe reached Moores Creek on the 25th. Caswell arrived the next day, set up earthworks on the enemy (or west) side of the narrow but deep stream, but then abandoned the works to join Lillington and Ashe on the far bank. After removing some of the bridge flooring, leaving a gap where the enemy could cross only on the log stringers, the 1,000 rebel troops deployed to cover the bridge. If subsequent Tory accounts are to be believed, the rebels got the bright idea of greasing the stringers. Through the chilly night of 26–27 Feb. they rested on their arms. Lillington seems to deserve most of the credit for the preparations at the bridge and for the subsequent action (Alden, op. cit., 198), and Moore, having been at Elizabethtown blocking the route to Cape Fear, did not arrive until after the battle.

The Tories had been advancing three days through rough terrain, and late on 26th Feb. they camped six miles from the bridge. After scouts reported that the rebels were located on the near bank of Moores Creek (see above), the Highlanders resumed their advance at 1 A.M., approaching the creek at dawn.

McDonald had become ill during this night of 26–27 Feb., and command passed to Col. Donald McLeod. Capt. John Campbell * led the advance guard of 80 picked Scots armed only with claymores; 1,400 men made up the main body; and 300 riflemen brought up the rear. The terrible skirl of bagpipes alerted the waiting rebels.

The abandoned earthworks on the near bank led the enemy to believe that their crossing would be unchallenged. Campbell's advance guard, accompanied by a few others including McLeod, charged onto the bridge shouting "King George and Broadswords!" Rebel infantry and two artillery pieces opened fire at a range of 30 yards from behind breastworks, and the Tory attack was shattered in a matter of minutes. McLeod and Campbell were killed with several of their men within a few paces of their objective. Others were hit on the bridge or merely lost their balance and fell into the deep stream, where a good many drowned.

The rebels then counterattacked. Some rushed forward to replace planks on the bridge and pursue the panic-stricken Tories. (Ward, op. cit., 664) Lt. (Ezekiel?) Slocum forded the creek with a small detachment, pushed through the swamp on the west bank, and hit the enemy rear. (Lossing, op. cit., 588; Heitman lists only one Slocum who fits this occasion.)

Moore had directed the 2d and 4th N.C., under Lt. Cols. Alex. Martin

---

* Often identified as *Farquard* Campbell. Prof. Rankin tells me that the latter was "a man of wavering allegiance, having been a member of N.C.'s 1st Prov. Cong.," who finally came into the Tory camp, suggested the march to the coast, but did not accompany the expedition.

and James Thackston, to occupy Cross Creek, and this undoubtedly accounts for the large haul of prisoners made on the 28th. Gen McDonald, several other officers, and 850 men were taken prisoner. The booty included £15,000 in specie, 13 wagons, 1,500 rifles, 350 muskets, and 150 swords and dirks. (Ward, *op. cit.*, 664. This haul came not only from prisoners but also from known and suspected Tories in the region.)

About 30 Tories were killed or wounded in the brief action at the bridge. Moore estimates total enemy casualties in killed, wounded, or drowned as about 50; Lossing says about 70. Only two of the defenders were hit; and one of these died on 2 Mar. (Moore's report, *op. cit.*)

COMMENT

Although the rebel military leaders, Moore, Lillington, and Caswell deserve praise (Alden, *op. cit.*, 198), as do the N.C. political leaders responsible for the readiness of their armed forces, the King's representatives failed him at all levels of planning and execution. Gov. Martin was overoptimistic about Loyalist support and premature in calling it out.

The CHARLESTON EXPEDITION, already delayed by late arrival of the fleet from Ireland, was now doomed to failure. In the words of Fisher, McDonald "had conducted a most ill-judged movement long before there was any force on the coast to help him." (*Struggle*, I, 449) McLeod's tactics at the bridge gave the patriots their final lucky break. (The action closely resembles that at GREAT BRIDGE, Va.)

One popular historian, Lynn Montross, says the vanquished Highlanders were treated with such remarkable consideration by the Provincial and Continental Congresses that "Moore's Creek became a memorable victory of persuasion as well as arms" (*op. cit.*, 135). Just the opposite conclusion is reached by Professor Duane Meyer, author of *The Highland Scots of North Carolina, 1732–1776* (Chapel Hill, 1961). The patriots threw their prisoners in common jails, pillaged and burned the unprotected Tory farms, and forced many Highlanders to flee the province.

The HALIFAX RESOLVES were adopted on 12 Apr. '76 by the Provincial Congress, and exactly a month later Sir Henry Clinton declared N.C. to be in a state of rebellion. Lord Cornwallis landed from Clinton's frustrated invasion fleet off Brunswick and ravaged the area with 900 troops. The plantation of Robt. Howe was virtually destroyed. Brunswick was irretrievably destroyed, but North Carolina was spared further British military operations for almost five more years.

MORAVIAN SETTLEMENTS. Count Nicolaus Ludwig Zinzendorf (1700–1760) revived the evangelical sect of Protestants called Moravians on his Saxon estate of Herrnhut and looked to the New World as a place to escape persecution and exercise their missionary zeal. Bishop Augustus Gottlieb Spangenberg (1704–1792) reached Ga. in 1735 with a few Swiss colonists and during the next five years was followed by some 30 other Moravians including David ZEISBERGER. The War of Jenkins' Ear broke out four years after Spangenberg landed at Savannah, and he went north to look for new land. In 1741 the Moravians from Ga. established Nazareth and Bethlehem, Pa., as a communistic society. On 2 Dec. '41 Count Zinzendorf arrived in America with hopes of uniting all German

Protestants in Pa. This plan was quickly frustrated by a paper war waged by Christopher SOWER "and everyone else who could afford to print a pamphlet" (*D.A.B.*, "Zinzendorf"), but during his 13-months in the colonies Zinzendorf exerted an important influence in ecclesiastical affairs and made three trips among the Indians.

Spangenberg was succeeded by Bishop John Nitschmann as overseer of Bethlehem in 1750, and within two years his "General Economy" had started to fail because of mismanagement and laziness. After spending some time in London, he returned to America and led a party of Bethlehem Moravians south to find a new home. In Aug. '53 they purchased 100,000 acres from Lord Granville in N.C.; within a few months 12 Moravians from Bethlehem founded Betharaba (Dutch Fort), and a few years later the nearby villages of Bethania and Salem were founded. The latter is now part of Winston-Salem. Spangenberg's new settlements were organized under a plan of family life, as opposed to communistic labor, and became the Moravian center of the South.

The Moravians of Pa. were swelled by immigration to 2,500 people by 1775. They were more active than any other religious body in conducting missionary work among the Indians, and their converts were given special protection by the government of Pa. during the last of the Colonial Wars. See also GNADENHUETTEN MASSACRE and ZEISBERGER.

MORGAN, Daniel. 1736–1802. Frontiersman, Cont'l. general. N.J.?–Pa.–Va. Grandson of a Welsh immigrant to Pa. and a first cousin of Daniel Boone, Daniel may have been born in Bucks co., Pa., where his father was ironmaster at the Durham Works, but more probably he was born just across the river in Hunterdon co., N.J. (Daniel C. Haskell in *D.A.B.*.) After quarreling with his father, Dan left home at the age of 17, moved into the Shenandoah, worked as a farm laborer and teamster, and at the age of 19 joined Braddock's expedition as a teamster. After Braddock's defeat (1755) he rendered good service in evacuating the wounded and got to know Washington. He then hauled supplies to frontier posts. In 1756 he hit back at a British officer who had slapped him with the flat of his sword. According to Haskell (*op. cit.*), Morgan was sentenced to receive 500 lashes. In later years the six-foot, 200-pound "Old Wagoner" liked to say he owed the British one stripe because the drummer miscounted. In 1758 Morgan became an ensign and while carrying dispatches to Winchester he lost all the teeth on one side when an Indian bullet passed through his neck and mouth. In 1762 he took possession of a small grant near Winchester and married. The next year he served as a Lt. in Pontiac's War, and he took part in Dunmore's War (1774). Meanwhile he prospered as a farmer.

Commissioned Capt. of one of the two Va. rifle companies on 22 June '75, he enlisted the prescribed 96 men in the next 10 days and in the following 21 days rode 600 miles to the Boston lines without having lost a man. Morgan's company led ARNOLD'S MARCH TO QUEBEC, Sept.–Nov. '75, their position in the van being initially a post of honor but subsequently a means of keeping them honest! (See ARNOLD'S MARCH....) In the disastrous assault on QUEBEC, 31 Dec., Morgan took command from the wounded Arnold and drove on with magnificent *élan* until subordinates prevailed on him to make a decision that probably was fatal to the enterprise. (See QUEBEC) A prisoner in Quebec until the next summer, he returned on parole and was exchanged in the fall. He was commissioned Col., 11th Va., on 12 Nov. '76. In Apr. '77 he joined Washington's main army and raised a body of 500 sharpshooters who served in the N.J. operations preceding the Philadelphia Campaign. On 13 June, in sending instructions to Morgan, the C. in C. spoke of his organization as "the Corps of Rangers, newly formed."

When Burgoyne's Offensive reached the point that Washington had to reinforce the Northern army, Morgan was detached to join Gates. Morgan and his riflemen played a decisive role in winning the two battles of SARATOGA, 19 Sept. and 7 Oct. '77. Their performance is fully covered under these two entries. Morgan and Gates were temporarily estranged when the Old Wagoner refused to join in the intrigues against Washington, and on 18 Nov. Morgan's corps had rejoined the main army outside Philadelphia at White Marsh. While in winter quarters at Valley Forge, Morgan's 11th Va. was brigaded with the 7th Va. under the command of B.G. Wm. Woodford. He was not engaged in the Battle of Monmouth, 28 June '78, but he did conduct a vigorous pursuit after that action.

Morgan's resignation on 18 July '79 was allegedly for ill health but actually because he thought he should have been given command of the troops that became WAYNE'S LT. INF. BRIG. (Freeman, *Washington,* V, 111) Congress ordered him in June '80 to report to Gates in the Southern Theater, but since that body apparently did not value his services highly enough to accompany this call with the suggestion that they would restore his relative rank, much less make him a general, he declined to comply. When Morgan learned of the disaster at Camden, however, "he put aside his personal grievances and hastened to join Gates at Hillsboro, arriving late in September." (Ward, *W.O.R.,* 735) On 2 Oct. he was given command of a corps of light troops Gates had organized. On 13 Oct. Congress appointed him B.G., and when Greene succeeded Gates he confirmed the assignment of Morgan as commander of the elite corps. The composition of this force and Morgan's unorthodox mission are covered under SOUTHERN CAMPAIGNS OF GREENE.

At COWPENS, S.C., 17 Jan. '81, the Old Wagoner stopped running before the vigorous pursuit of "Bloody Ban" Tarleton and turned to win a little battle that is considered a classic. He then, and wisely, started running again. Soon after linking up with the main body under Greene, Morgan again resigned with a very convincing plea of ill health (10 Feb. '81), but his real reason seems to have been that he disapproved of Greene's bold stragey and wanted no part of the responsibility for the disaster that he—quite incorrectly—predicted. (See SOUTHERN CAMPAIGNS. . . .)

He was deaf at first to appeals to support Lafayette in halting British raids in Va., although he did arrive after the real danger was over. (See TARLETON'S VA. RAID, 9–24 July '81)

Back on the frontier the old warrior's aches and pains—arthritis, rheumatism, and sciatica, according to different accounts—did not prevent an active life in diverse enterprises. He commanded militia troops during the Whiskey Insurrection of 1794, ran unsuccessfully for Congress in 1795, but was elected in 1797. By 1796 he owned more than 250,000 acres. (*D.A.B.*) He also became a devout member of the Presbyterian Church. (*Ibid.*)

The Morgan Papers are in the NYPL. James Graham's *Life of Daniel Morgan* (1856) and T. B. Myers' *Cowpens Papers* (1881) are basic references and contain many of the Morgan papers. A study that has appeared since my article was written is Don Higginbotham, *Daniel Morgan: Revolutionary Rifleman* (1961), and this same L.S.U. professor has an essay on Morgan in Billias (ed.) *Washington's Generals* (1964). Another new work is North Callahan, *Daniel Morgan: Ranger of the Revolution* (1961).

See also RIFLEMEN.

MORGAN, John. 1735–1789. Medical director of the Cont'l Army. Pa. Graduating with the first class of the College of Philadelphia (now U. of Pa.) in 1757, he had started a medical apprenticeship under Dr. John Redman about 1750. For several years he was Lt. and surgeon of provincial troops during the French and Indian War. In 1760 he undertook a period of study abroad and returned five years later with proposals that led to establishment of a medical school at his alma mater. He was appointed professor and at the Commencement in 1765 he delivered "A Discourse upon the Institution of Medical Schools in America."

On 17 Oct. '75 the Cont'l. Cong. elected Morgan director-general of hospitals and physician-in-chief of the American army. Joining the army at Cambridge and accompanying it later to N.Y., he worked skilfully to achieve an efficient organization of his service but, in so doing, made so many enemies that he first was reduced to the position of directing hospitals east of the Hudson only (9 Oct. '76) and then, on 9 Jan. '77, he was removed from the latter post without explanation. On 11 Apr. '77 William Shippen (see SHIPPEN FAMILY) was given the office originally held by Morgan at the start of the war. The real reason for Morgan's removal apparently was because his methods led to so many antagonisms within the medical service (*D.A.B.*). Crushed and embittered, he published *A Vindication . . .* in 1777, making the inevitable charges of Congressional meddling and the plotting of *"a mean and invidious* set of men" to remove him. Although he was cleared of any misconduct he considered himself disgraced and withdrew from public life. His remaining few years were spent in private practice and as professor and physician at the Pennsylvania Hospital.

MORNINGSIDE HEIGHTS (Manhattan), N.Y. Modern name of Vandewater's Heights, which figured in the battle of HARLEM HEIGHTS, 16 Sept. '76.

MORRIS, Gouverneur (goo vurnoor). 1752–1816. American statesman. N.Y. Born in the manor house at Morrisania established by his grandfather Lewis Morris (1671–1746), he was reared as a cultured provincial aristocrat. His mother, Sarah Gouverneur, was of Huguenot descent and he attended school in the Huguenot settlement of New Rochelle. David S. Muzzey says:

". . it was doubtless the French strain in Morris' blood that lent to his conversation and his writings the charming combination of graceful manner, pervasive humor, and cynical philosophical detachment which contrasts so noticeably with the rather ponderous and prosaic rectitude of most of his revolutionary associates." (*D.A.B.*)

He graduated from King's College (now Columbia) in 1768, studied under William Smith (historian and later chief justice of N.Y.), was admitted to the bar at the age of 19 (in 1771), and soon built up a successful practice in N.Y.C. As a member of the landed aristocracy he naturally had misgivings about revolution. Although his half-brothers Lewis and Richard were patriots, his mother was a Loyalist and his half-brother Staats Morris was a general in the Brit-

738

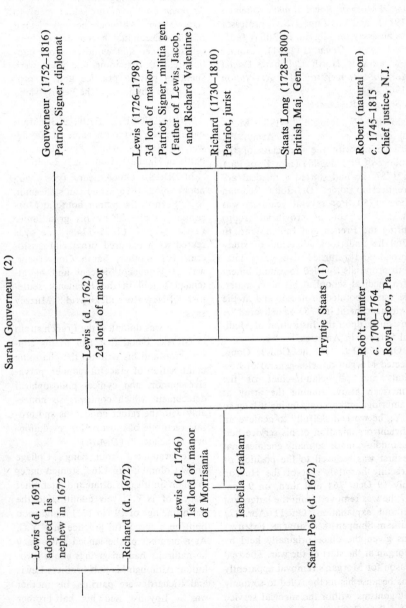

MORRIS FAMILY OF NEW YORK

Sarah Gouverneur (2)

Gouverneur (1752–1816)
Patriot, Signer, diplomat

Lewis (d. 1762)
2d lord of manor

Lewis (1726–1798)
3d lord of manor
Patriot, Signer, militia gen.
(Father of Lewis, Jacob,
and Richard Valentine)

Richard (1730–1810)
Patriot, jurist

Staats Long (1728–1800)
British Maj. Gen.

Tryntje Staats (1)

Rob't. Hunter
c. 1700–1764
Royal Gov, Pa.

Robert (natural son)
c. 1745–1815
Chief justice, N.J.

Lewis (d. 1691)
adopted his
nephew in 1672

Richard (d. 1672)

Lewis (d. 1746)
1st lord of manor
of Morrisania

Isabella Graham

Sarah Pole (d. 1672)

ish army.* Gouverneur Morris nevertheless adhered wholeheartedly to the patriot cause when it appeared that war was inevitable, despite fears expressed in 1774 that this would bring "the domination of a riotous mob." In the provincial congress of 1776–77 he was a leader in holding the balance between the wild-eyed radicals and the Tory element. From the beginning he supported the position of the Cont'l. Cong. as a necessary instrument of central control.

With John Jay and Robert L. Livingston he drafted the constitution under which N.Y. was governed for the next 50 years. He strongly supported Gen. Schuyler and with Jay attempted to prevent his being superseded by Horatio Gates. Elected to Cong. for the years 1778–79, the youthful Morris was interested primarily in financial, military, and diplomatic matters. He drafted many important documents, including the diplomatic instructions for Franklin and, later, for the peace commissioners. He visited Valley Forge early in 1778 and returned to Philadelphia a life-long admirer and supporter of Washington.

Defeated for re-election to Cong., because he refused to enlist congressional support for the claims of N.Y. in the dispute over Vermont, he transferred his citizenship to Pa. and set up his home and law practice in Philadelphia. Pursuing an early interest in currency and credit, however, he contributed a brilliant series of financial articles to the *Pa. Packet,* Feb.–Apr. '80, under the pen name "An American." This brought him an invitation from Robert Morris (no kin) in 1781 to serve as his assistant. Holding this post while the "Financier of the Revolution" (Robt. MORRIS)

performed his most remarkable feats and remaining until 1785, he worked out a decimal system of coinage later perfected by Jefferson and Hamilton that has spared America the miserable pounds, shillings, and pence of the mother country.

Although opposed to "democracy"— "Give the votes to the people who have no property and they will sell them to the rich," he said—and against many of the ideals later incorporated into the American system of government, Morris "loyally accepted the bundle of compromises which compose the Constitution, and used his incomparable skill in putting the document into its final literary form," writes Muzzey. He had meanwhile disqualified himself as a representative of "the people," and there was no future in American politics for him. Now only 35, he returned to Morrisania (which he had bought from his elder half-brother) but soon went to Europe (1789) as agent (more or less) for Robert Morris. A famous American, wealthy, well-born, affable, and speaking the language fluently, he became the most influential American in Paris when Jefferson left at the end of 1789.

In 1790–91 Morris was Washington's executive agent in London with the mission of making preliminary efforts to establish diplomatic relations between Britain and her former colony. His attempts were undermined by HAMILTON to an extent that had not been fully realized until publication of Prof. Julian P. Boyd's *Number 7* in 1964.

Early in 1792 he became minister to France, but with less stomach for a "riotous mob" of tricolored Frenchmen than he had shown for their American-grown counterpart, he probably did not regret being recalled, at the request of the French government of the moment, in the late summer of 1794. (This was in retaliation for the dismissal of "Cit-

* All these half-brothers are covered in the article on Lewis MORRIS (1726–1798), the Signer. See also MORRIS FAMILY OF N.Y.

izen" Genet.) Highlights of his six years in Paris were his pressing of a claim against the Farmers General arising from a monopoly Robert Morris had gotten in 1785 in the tobacco trade, his involvement in a plot to get Louis XVI out of Paris, and his distinction of being the only foreign minister to remain in Paris during the reign of terror. A voluminous diary kept in France is cited by a French historian, Hippolyte Taine (1828–93), as one of the prime sources on the French Revolution.

Now 42 years old, Morris traveled in Europe for four years before returning to America in 1798, after an absence of almost a decade. In Apr. 1800 he had what he called in his diary "the misfortune" to be elected a Federalist senator (to fill an unexpired term). With Aaron BURR in control of N.Y. politics, Morris was not re-elected; in Mar. '02 he left Congress and retired (again) to Morrisania. Rebuilding the estate that had been wrecked during the Revolution, he spent the last 13 years of his life there. On 25 Dec. '09 he married the sister of Thomas Mann Randolph of Va. He was among the first to propose plans for the Erie Canal and was chairman of the board of canal commissioners, 1810–16. In his declining years he became such a bitter critic of national politics that, in the words of Theodore Roosevelt, one of his biographers, "he lost all loyalty to the nation." Muzzey warns that this should not be taken literally, but says Morris died in 1816 "with his faith in the future of his own country unrevived."

Morris was an impressive-looking man, although somewhat rotund in his later years. In May '80 a fall from his carriage in Philadelphia resulted in loss of a leg. When a Paris mob closed in on his carriage with taunts of "Aristocrat," Morris shook his wooden leg back at them and in his excellent French

shouted: "An aristocrat! Yes, one who lost his limb in the cause of American liberty!" (Appleton's) Morris is said to have so closely resembled Washington that Houdon used him as a model for his bust of Washington. (*Ibid.*)

A. C. Morris (ed.), *The Diary and Letters....* (2 vols., New York, 1888), covers the years 1789–1816. B. C. Davenport (ed.), *A Diary of the French Revolution* (2 vols., Boston, 1939), covers the years 1789–1793. Commenting somewhat gratuitously that the first of these is the more comprehensive, the Harvard *Guide* says the other is more accurate. Daniel Walther, *Gouverneur Morris, Witness of Two Revolutions* (New York, 1934) is the translation of a 1932 French work; *D.A.B.* comments on the "extensive bibliography and list of manuscript sources." Older biographies are by Jared Sparks (3 vols., 1832) and Theodore Roosevelt (1888). An article by H. C. Lodge, "Gouverneur Morris," was printed in the *Atlantic Monthly* in Apr. 1886 and reprinted in *Hist. and Pol. Essays* in 1892.

MORRIS, Lewis. 1726–1798. Signer, militia general. N.Y. Third lord of the manor of Morrisania, his relationship to other famous members of the MORRIS FAMILY OF N.Y. is explained and diagrammed in the latter article.* He completed work for his A.B. degree at Yale in 1746, the year his grandfather died, and for the next 16 years he contentedly assisted his father in the management of the extensive family estates. On the death of his father in 1762 he became the third and last lord of the manor. For the first time he now showed an interest in politics. After a single term in the provincial assembly

* Sketches of his two brothers, Richard and Staats Long Morris, and of his three sons are included in this article.

in 1769, and finding that few of his Westchester co. constituents endorsed his anti-British sentiments, he succeeded in organizing that minority. Despite opposition from the De Lanceys, Pells, and Philipses, he succeeded in having a meeting called on 28 Mar. '75 to select the county's deputies to the provincial convention in N.Y.C. Morris was named chairman of the eight-man delegation elected by his faction. At the convention Morris was elected a delegate to the Cont'l. Cong., an honor he had enthusiastically sought.

Taking his seat on 15 May '75 and remaining a delegate for two years, Morris performed administrative assignments of a type not recorded in the history books. First placed on a committee to decide what posts should be defended in N.Y., he later served on a committee to supply military stores and ammunition, and then he was on the permanent committee on Indian affairs. On 7 June '76 he was appointed B.G. of Westchester co. militia, and was on leave of absence from Congress when the Decl. of Indep. was signed. Later in 1776 he returned to Philadelphia and became a "Signer." He took part in the N.Y. Campaign of 1776, when Howe chased Washington right through the family manor and the rest of Westchester. For the remainder of the war he retained his militia rank but his services appear to have been valued by the state more in the civil domain; he was county judge in Westchester, 8 May '77–17 Feb. '78, and was intermittently in the upper house of the state legislature between 1777 and 1790.

At the end of the war he retired as a Maj. Gen. of militia and restored Morrisania, which had been the scene of skirmishes on 5 Aug. '79, 22 Jan. '81, and 4 Mar. '82, according to the *A.A.*-Heitman list. The estate—no longer a manor—was bought by his half-brother,

Gouverneur MORRIS, in 1789, the year Lewis died.

Lewis' son, listed in Heitman as Lewis Jr., became Brig. Maj. of N.Y. Militia on 7 June '76 (when his father was made B.G.), was Sullivan's A.D.C., 14 Aug. '76–12 June '79, and A.D.C. to Nathanael Greene from the latter date to the end of the war. He was breveted Lt. Col. by Congress on 9 Sept. '78 for bringing that body "the account of the repulse of the British forces on Rhode Island on the 29th of August last" and for "great spirit and good conduct" on several occasions. (Heitman)

Richard Valentine Morris (1768–1815), youngest son of Lewis the Signer, was commissioned Capt. of the Navy in 1798, and later commanded a squadron sent to subdue the Tripoli pirates. Ignoring the difficulties he faced in the operations of 1802–3, a court of inquiry held that he had not shown the requisite naval genius and revoked his commission 14 May '04 (Appleton's, "Lewis Morris," *D.A.B.*, "R. V. Morris"). His elaborate and convincing pamphlet, *A Defense....* (1804), is an important source for the study of U.S. relations with the Barbary Powers. He returned to Morrisania.

Another son of Lewis the Signer, Jacob Morris (1755–1844), served during the Revolution. According to Heitman, he was Maj., N.Y. Militia, 1775; A.D.C. to Charles Lee, Oct. '76–Oct. '78 (being wounded at Monmouth); and A.D.C. to Greene from May '81 to 1782. (His brother Lewis also was Green's A.D.C.) He served in the N.Y. legislature after the war, and in 1787 moved to Butternuts, Otsego co., N.Y., where he died 57 years later. (Appleton's, "Lewis Morris")

Lewis' brother Staats Long Morris (1728–1800) entered the British Army and became Capt. in the 36th Foot in May '56. As Lt. Col. of the 89th High-

landers he served in the siege of Pondichéry, India, in 1761, and was promoted
to B.G. two years later. A Maj. Gen. in
1777 and full Gen. in 1796, he sat in
Parliament and married the Duchess of
Gordon. In 1797 he became Gov. of
Quebec. He died three years later. (Appleton's)

His other brother, Richard (1730–
1810), graduated from Yale in 1748,
was admitted to the bar in 1752, and—
in the family tradition—became a good
lawyer. His father made him his deputy
judge of the court of vice admiralty and
authorized him to hold court in N.J. In
1762 he was given jurisdiction over
N.J., N.Y., and Conn., a position his
father and grandfather had held before
him. In the autumn of 1775 he resigned,
but his association with this unpopular
royal office, his aristocratic temperament, and his failure to make noises
like a patriot led to his citation in June
'76 as a person of "equivocal neutrality." (*D.A.B.*, "Richard Morris")

He nevertheless was elected to fill an
unexpired term in the state senate in
1778, and in 1779 he was appointed to
succeed John Jay as chief justice of the
state supreme court. He became a
staunch Federalist, but had nothing
original to offer in advancing party
politics in N.Y. In 1789 his name was
mentioned as a possible candidate for
Gov., but the nomination went to Robert Yates. He retired from public life in
1790 and spent his last 20 years at the
country estate he had bought during the
Revolution at Scarsdale.

MORRIS, Robert. 1734–1806. "Financier of the Revolution." Pa. At the
age of 13 he came to America with his
father from Liverpool, England, and
went to work in a Philadelphia counting house. In 1754 he had become a
partner. For the next 39 years the firm
of Willing, Morris & Co. and its successors under other names held the

leading position in colonial trade. In his
first appearance in public affairs Morris
signed the nonimportation agreement of
1765. He held a number of offices and
went to the 1st Cont'l. Cong. in 1774,
but as a busy merchant he had not yet
thrown himself in with the patriot politicians. When the shooting started in
Apr. '75, however, unlike many other
MERCHANTS IN THE REVOLUTION, Morris became a leading figure of the
patriot cause. On 30 June '75 the Assembly made him a member of the
council of safety, and later they reappointed him to serve during 1776. His
commercial talents were immediately
put to use, and when Franklin was absent Morris ran the Council. Re-elected
to Cong., he succeeded his partner,
Willing, on the Secret Committee. He
drew up the instructions to Silas DEANE
in Feb. '76, and personally arranged for
Cong. the procurement of vessels (Nov.
'75), munitions, and naval armament.
In these matters he continued to tend
the commercial affairs of Willing &
Morris, a firm that owned ships for
the foreign trade and that conducted
general exchange and banking business. In performing his valuable official
services he remained a businessman,
collecting his broker's commission and
overlooking no opportunity to make a
profit; while he made great profits,
largely because of his ability, he also
took huge risks in accomplishing the
financial missions assigned by Congress
and Pa. authorities. This was understood and accepted by his colleagues.
The austere John Adams wrote this to
Horatio Gates when asked about the
activities of Morris: "I think he has a
masterly Understanding, an open Temper and an honest Heart. . . . He has
vast designs in the mercantile way. And
no doubt pursues mercantile ends, which
are always gain; but he is an excellent
Member of our Body."

Morris thought the movement toward Independence in 1776 was premature. He voted against the Decl. of Indep. in July, but when he saw it was the will of the majority he signed it in Aug. '76. Returned to Cong. in this year, he became the first Pres. of the Pa. Assembly under the new constitution in Nov. When Cong. fled to Baltimore in Dec. '76, Morris remained in Philadelphia to carry out the work of his Secret Committee and later was designated by Cong. with Geo. Clymer and Geo. Walton as their "executive committee" (21 Dec. '76). As Washington prepared the desperate strategy that was to end with his brilliant riposte at Trenton and Princeton, it was Morris who furnished him the necessary backing as civil authority of the country. Meanwhile looking after the commercial interests of his firm—which may have been an important reason why he did not flee to Baltimore with the other delegates—Morris carried a tremendous personal load at this critical period of American history, and he carried it without a stumble.

In Mar. '78 Morris signed the Articles of Confederation. From Aug. to 1 Nov. '78, the expiration of his term in Cong., he was chairman of the Cong. Comm. on Finance. Ineligible for re-election to Cong. (because of the new state constitution), Morris was immediately re-elected to the Pa. Assembly and on 6 Nov. he took his seat.

The life of Morris now began to turn. During the winter of 1777–78 a temporary misunderstanding between Morris and the commissioners Deane and Franklin in Paris had been precipitated by the misconduct of Thomas Morris, a younger half-brother for whom Robert had secured appointment as commercial agent in France. The controversy that followed the recall of Silas DEANE involved Morris, although he stayed out

of it until Jan. '79. At this time Thos. Paine attacked Morris and Deane in the press, and Henry Laurens, then Pres. of Cong., officially charged Willing & Morris with fraud. All this had to do with the mysterious operations of HORTALEZ & CIE. (where the controversy is covered in a little more detail). Both Laurens and Paine lost their posts as a result of their attacks on Morris and Deane, and an investigation exonerated the firms of Hortalez & Co. and Willing & Morris. But public opinion began to turn against Morris, led by political opponents who resented his success, and he was defeated at the polls in Nov. '79. A year later he was again elected to the Pa. Assembly, where he served until June '81.

Meanwhile, FINANCES OF THE REVOLUTION had collapsed. Over the objection of many, and with the nomination of Hamilton, Morris was appointed on 20 Feb. '81 as Supt. of Finances, a unique office established to salvage what appeared to be a total loss. Insisting first that Cong. permit him to continue his personal business, and that he be allowed to control the personnel of his department, Morris accepted the post on 14 May. For a long time he had opposed the carefree and financially irresponsible procedures that had led to the collapse of Cont'l. Currency—price control and legal pressure to make people accept the worthless paper at par value. "It would be difficult to find in history a more remarkable instance of such a thorough-going hard money man in the midst of circumstances so overwhelmingly against him," comments Fisher. (*Struggle*, II 474) This authority goes on to summarize:

"But Morris went on in his jovial, confident way to put the cause on a specie basis at the moment of its greatest depression. The principal feature of his undertaking was the establishment of the Bank of North America..., which was to be the financial institution of the patriot cause, lend money to the government and carry on its business on a hard money basis. This was all very well in theory; but where was the hard money to be obtained at this most hopeless period of the war?

"Morris had three sources for obtaining it: First, he intended making the bank a place of deposit and concentration of what little specie there was in the country, and for this purpose asked all the prominent men in the whole patriot party to subscribe any specie they happened to have. But this source, as was naturally to be expected, produced very little. Second, in the absence of money some of the states had been paying the trifling amounts they furnished the patriot cause in flour, provisions and any goods they could obtain; these Morris with his knowledge of trade tried to sell in the West Indies or other foreign ports for cash; but this also amounted to very little. Third, was the great loan of specie from France, which Colonel [John] Laurens had been sent to bring over; and this alone saved Morris's plan from utter failure." (*Op. cit.*, 474–75)

A French fleet brought over $200,000 in specie, and the Bank of North America opened its doors in Jan. '82. Strengthening the bank by his personal credit, Morris also was one of its heaviest subscribers. By various economies in purchasing and administration, by the use of notes that circulated only on the basis of his personal credit, by risky financial sleight-of-hand, and to the tune of personal criticism and abuse, he financed the Yorktown Campaign, which ended organized British military power in the colonies. Meanwhile, however, he contracted as many debts during his two years in office as there had been before his advent. The states still refused to accept their obligations and furnish the revenue needed for a viable economy. Congress remained impotent. In despair and disgust Morris submitted his resignation 24 Jan. '83. Again an uproar from the people and abuse from the press. Nobody stepped forth to take over the job, however, and in May he was prevailed on to retain office until the army was paid and demobilized. A Dutch loan secured by John Adams saved the day, and in Sept. '84 Morris "extricated himself from the affairs of the states with his personal fortune unimpaired and the public credit as high as it could be placed under the circumstances." (Ellis P. Oberholtzer in *D.A.B.*).

Convinced of the need for a strong central government, he actively supported the the Federalists in postwar politics. He declined the office of Sec. of the Treas. in Washington's first cabinet, but served in the new U.S. Senate, 1789–95. His financial downfall came after he had overextended himself in land speculation—western lands and partnership in a large tract of the wilderness that was to become the site of Washington, D.C. Having heretofore succeeded in an incredible series of financial gambles, he did not foresee the Napoleonic wars and the collapse of an economy founded on credit. He was "land poor" because nobody had the money to buy from him when he needed money for taxes and interest on loans.

His financial empire collapsed as L'Enfant was building him a palace in Philadelphia, and he retreated to a country estate. There in Feb. '98 he was arrested on the charges of a small creditor and hauled off for over three and a half years in debtors' prison. Released on 26 Aug. 1801 under the federal bankruptcy law, he lived his last five years in a small house in Philadelphia. His business associate, Gouverneur

Morris (no kin, however), secured for his wife an annuity that was the only support for the "financier of the Revolution." He died at the age of 73, "a nearly forgotten and much pitied man" (*D.A.B.*).

See E. P. Oberholtzer, *Robert Morris, Patriot and Financier* (New York, 1903) and W. G. Sumner, *The Financier and Finances of the American Revolution* (2 vols., 1891), which is condensed as *Robert Morris* (1892). The transactions of Morris (and Jeremiah Wadsworth) are noteworthy among the many covered in Robert A. East, *Business Enterprise in the American Revolutionary Era* (New York, 1938). A more recent work, published by the U. of Pa., is Clarence L. Ver Steeg, *Robert Morris: Revolutionary Financier* (1954).

MORRIS, Robert. c. 1745–1815. Jurist. Natural son of Robert Hunter Morris—where his career is sketched —and grandson of the 1st lord of the manor of Morrisania (see Morris Family).

MORRIS, Robert Hunter, c. 1700–1764. Chief justice of N.J., Gov. of Pa. A member of the Morris Family, he was the second son of Lewis, 1st lord of the manor of Morrisania. When his father became Gov. of N.J. in 1738, Robert was named chief justice by his father. In this capacity he belligerently defended the royal prerogative. (*D.A.B.*) In 1754 he was offered the governorship of Pa. by Thos. Penn and accepted. An unruly legislature, led by Benj. Franklin, kept Morris from performing the duties expected from him by the proprietors, and in 1756 he resigned. Meanwhile his resignation as chief justice in N.J. had not been accepted and in 1760, after a visit to England, he resumed his duties in N.J. He never married but had at least three children. One of these, Robert Morris

(*c.* 1745–1815), inherited most of his large estate. He became chief justice of the newly created supreme court of N.J. in Feb. '77 and held the position until his resignation in June '79. Although he had never before presided over a court and was assisted only by what he called "but reputable farmers, doctors and shopkeepers," he is credited with setting up a workable system of state courts under the new plan. (*D.A.B.*) Having been admitted to the bar in Sept. '70, he established a practice in New Brunswick and in 12 years accumulated large land holdings. When the U.S. district courts were organized under the Act of 1789 he was named by Washington to be judge in the N.J. district, a position he filled for 25 years. (*D.A.B.*, "Robert Morris.") He was no kin to his namesake, the financier Robert Morris.

MORRIS FAMILY OF N.Y. Founder of the family in America was Richard (d. 1672), a veteran of Cromwell's army, who became a merchant in Barbados and married the wealthy Sarah Pole. With his brother Lewis he bought 500 acres in N.Y. just north of the Harlem River, then known as Bronck's land (now the Bronx). Richard and Sarah died there in 1672, only two years after the purchase, and their infant son was adopted by Uncle Lewis. The latter built the Bronx estate to almost 2,000 acres and also acquired 3,500 acres in Monmouth co., N.J., all of which he passed on to his ward in 1691. In May 1697 the N.Y. estate became the manor of Morrisania. Richard's son Lewis (1671–1746) then became first lord of the manor, a title that passed through his son to his grandson, Lewis Morris (Jr.), the Signer. The genealogical table shows the relationships of descendants of Richard Morris who became famous. The most prominent of these, Gouverneur Morris, is covered in a separate sketch. Under Lewis MORRIS, Signer and 3d lord of the manor, will be found mention of Richard and Staats Long Morris, his (full) brothers, and of his three sons. Under Robert Hunter MORRIS will be found a mention of his illegitimate son Robert (he had several others, hence no comma). The "Financier of the Revolution," another Robert MORRIS, was no kin, but he and Gouverneur MORRIS became close associates in 1781.

See Appleton's, *D.A.B.,* and E. M. W. Lefferts, *Descendants of Lewis Morris of Morrisania* (1907)

MORRISANIA, N.Y., Actions at. Located in what now is the Bronx, "Morrisania" was the ancestral home of the MORRIS FAMILY. It was very much in the way of the war, being on the British route of advance to White Plains during the N.Y. Campaign and subsequently lying within the British lines. The *A.A.*–Heitman list of actions identifies three skirmishes: on 5 Aug. '79, 22 Jan. '81, and 4 Mar. '82. Only the second of these is mentioned in most accounts of the war. In a bold raid that pushed more than three miles within the British lines, Lt. Col. Wm. Hull of Parsons' Conn. Brig. attacked the quarters of Lt. Col. James De Lancey's Tory Bn. in Westchester co. by way of Horse Neck and Williams' bridge, "to range as far as Morrisania," wrote Baurmeister. (*Journals,* 411) He burned barracks and the ponton bridge over the Harlem River, destroyed a great store of forage, and at the price of 25 casualties withdrew with 52 prisoners, some horses, and some cattle. (Freeman, *Washington,* V, 251–52, 246) "At daybreak [23 Jan.] Lieutenant Colonel James De Lancey collected the scattered Refugees and made the rebels' retreat very uncomfortable. But he could follow them no farther than Williams' bridge, for on the far side of the bridge

the greater part of the rebels had taken post under cover of two fieldpieces, in order to give firm support to their returning comrades. Hence, the Refugees fell back, buried sixteen killed, picked up twice as many wounded, and then rebuilt their burned huts. Seventeen men were taken prisoners. General Parsons lost but few or none." (Baurmeister, *op. cit.,* 411) I have deliberately left these conflicting casualty figures as evidence of the disagreement among "primary sources." For the statement that Hull lost 25 men, Freeman cites the *Heath Papers,* III, 168. For the figures on British losses he cites these and a number of others. (*op. cit.,* V, 252 *n.*)

In the maneuvers of July '81 preceding the YORKTOWN CAMPAIGN, Lauzun's proposed attack on De Lancey's Bn. at Morrisania did not achieve the intended surprise, and the plan was canceled (Ward, *W.O.R.,* 880–81).

MORRISTOWN WINTER QUARTERS, N.J., 6 Jan.–28 May '77. After his operations at TRENTON and PRINCETON, Washington established winter quarters at Morristown. Although he first considered this to be merely a temporary location, the merits of the place became more apparent as circumstances required him to prolong his stay. Several ranges of hills protected his army from the enemy, whose winter quarters were around N.Y.C. Morristown was centrally located with respect to the British main outposts at Newark, Perth Amboy, and Brunswick, and it constituted a sort of flanking position from which Washington could threaten an enemy move up the Hudson or through N.J. toward Philadelphia. Morristown was in the center of an important agricultural region, which not only gave Washington access to these resources but also denied them to the enemy, and the place was close to the forges and furnaces of Hibernia, Mt. Hope, Ringwood, and Charlottenburg. (N.P.S., *Morristown*, 4)

While coping with the eternal problems of recruiting, reorganization, and logistics, Washington undertook a bold medical program of inoculating his troops and the neighborhood civilians against smallpox. He also kept up a vigorous patrol activity against the enemy in N.J. Anderson cites the following letter from N.Y.C. as evidence of how seriously this activity annoyed the British:

"For these two months, or nearly, [says this letter of mid-Feb. '77] have we been boxed about in Jersey, as if we had no feelings. [After all, *proper* military commanders should know enough to let their troops rest during the cold winter months!] Our cantonments have been beaten up; our foraging parties attacked, sometimes defeated [!], and the forage carried off from us; all travelling between the posts hazardous; and, in short, the troops harassed beyond measure by continual duty." (*Howe Bros.*, 236)

By this activity Washington not only kept up the fighting spirit of his troops, but also foraged for his own army. By the time Gen. Howe bestirred himself and resumed operations (see PHILADELPHIA CAMPAIGN) Washington's army had been built up to over 8,000 effectives and was reasonably well supplied.

MORRISTOWN WINTER QUARTERS, N.J., 1 Dec. '79–22 June '80. After another year closed without major military operations in the North, and after d'Estaing failed to appear off Sandy Hook with his powerful French force, Washington informed Nathanael Greene on 30 Nov. that the main army would go into winter quarters at Morristown. The weather already had turned cold and most units were faced with a hard march to reach this place. Units started arriving the first week in Dec. and the last arrived at the end of that month. Four Mass. brigades were left in the Highlands; Poor's Brig. and most of the cavalry units were sent to Danbury, Conn., with the mission of guarding the coastal towns on L.I. Sound; the N.C. Brig. and Pawley's N.Y. State troops were posted with Lee's dragoons around Suffern, N.Y.

The merits of Washington's main campsite are covered under MORRISTOWN . . . '77. But the winter quarters of 1779–80 became an ordeal of almost unbelievable suffering because of the record-breaking cold. The commissariat again broke down and the 10,000 to 12,000 troops at Morristown faced death from cold and starvation. At least the army had the experience of previous winter encampments to draw on, and they built an extensive "log-house city" that eventually numbered more than 1,000 buildings. About 600 acres of woodland were consumed. Soldier huts had a standard floor plan of about 14 by 15 feet and accommodated 12 men; they were about six and a half feet high at the eaves, with wooden bunks, a fireplace at one end and a door at the other. Construction was of notched logs and chinks of clay sealed the walls. Windows apparently were not cut until spring. The soldier huts were in rows of eight, three or four rows to a regiment. Officers' cabins were larger, more elaborate, and less crowded. Parade grounds and company streets were laid out at regular intervals. (N.P.S., *Morristown*, 15) Most of the men were able to move into huts before the end of Dec., but it was another six weeks before all the officers were accommodated. (Thacher, *Journal*, 190)

Jockey Hollow was the name of the site about three miles S.W. of Morristown where most of the army was camped—here were eight infantry brigades: Hand's, N.Y., 1st and 2d Md., 1st and 2d Conn., and 1st and 2d Pa. Stark's Brig. and the N.J. Brig. occupied separate camps within a mile of Jockey Hollow. Knox's Arty. Brig. and the gun park were about a mile W. of Morristown. "On the Lines" were detachments at Princeton, Brunswick, Perth Amboy, Rahway, Westfield, Springfield, Paramus, and other outposts. These detachments, totaling from 200 to 2,000 at different times, were periodically relieved. (N.P.S., *op. cit.*, 12, 19)

Severity of the winter limited military operations during the first months of the year, but it also made possible the remarkable (although unsuccessful) STATEN ISLAND EXPEDITION of Alexander, 14–15 Jan. The action at YOUNG'S HOUSE, N.Y., 3 Feb., was a British attempt to annihilate a unit "on the Lines." The British operations around SPRINGFIELD, N.J., 7–23 June, heralded the start of the 1780 campaign in the North.

MORTAR. So named because of its resemblance to pharmacist's mortar, a military mortar is a short gun used for firing projectiles at a high angle. It is most suitable for lobbing projectiles over walls of fortifications, over high ground that would mask the target from weapons having a flatter trajectory, or for firing from and into heavy woods. There were gigantic siege mortars and diminutive coehorns or royals.

MORTON, John. *c.* 1724–1777. Signer. Pa. Great-grandson of Morten Mortenson, who sailed to America in 1654, he was educated as a surveyor by his step-father, an Englishman named John Sketchley. He was elected to the Prov. Assy. in 1756, re-elected for 10 consecutive years and, after failing in 1767 to win a seat, he served seven more terms starting in 1769. After 15 Mar. '75 he was speaker. Meanwhile he had been J.O.P. of Chester (now Delaware) co., and judge of several courts. He attended the Stamp Act Cong., and was in the Cont'l. Cong. from 1774 to early in 1777. A believer in independence, he joined with Franklin and James Wilson to give the Pa. delegation a majority of one in voting for indorsement of the Decl. of Indep., and he became a Signer. He was chairman of the committee of the whole that adopted the Articles of Confed., which were ratified after his death. A Swedish-American museum in Philadelphia has been named for him.

MOTTIN DE LA BALME, Augustin. 1736–1780. French volunteer. Of middle class (*bourgeois*) origins, he entered the Gendarmerie in 1757, took part in the Seven Years' War, and was employed in cavalry training. On 18 June '63 he received an appointment in the French Army, and the next year he became inspector of the academies at Lyon (near his birthplace of St. Antoine in Dauphine) and Riom. He rose to the grade of Maj. on 23 Feb. '66 and in 1773 retired with a pension. With two of his books accepted as basic authorities on cavalry training and tactics, de La Balme sought to improve his military fortune by service in America. His attempt to get a passport through normal channels resulted in a note from Vergennes to the local police saying that the request was disapproved (29 Jan. '77) on the ground that France still was officially neutral. Masquerading as a doctor, he embarked at Bordeaux with two other officers on 15 Feb. '77. With him he carried a letter of 20 Jan. '77 from Franklin to John Hancock introducing de La Balme as a man of excellent character who had been recommended as an able cavalry officer and one who might be valuable in forming this branch of the American army.

On 26 May '77 the officer whom Vergennes had identified as a former *sous-aide-major de la gendarmerie* was commissioned Lt. Col. of Horse in the Cont'l. Army. On 8 July he was made Col. and I.G. of Cavalry. (Heitman, 84; Lasseray, 331, gives the date as 18 July) The tall, 41-year-old cavalry expert submitted his resignation in a letter of 3 Oct. to Congress. He had not come to America to train cavalry that would be led into battle by another person who had less experience, less real zeal, no more courage, and certainly less knowledge of cavalry service than he, wrote de La Balme in reference to Pulaski's appointment as chief of cavalry. On 13 Feb. '78 Congress accepted the resignation as I.G., leaving de La Balme with his commission of Col. but without command, assignment, or pay. "He continued to importune Congress for months," notes Freeman, although he had been paid $910 for his claims and told that Congress had no further requirement for his service. (*Washington,* IV, 539) The French historian, Lasseray, comments that de La Balme still burned with the desire to serve the cause of Liberty despite these discouragements. "Henceforth his predominant thought would be to extend the insurrection and find supporters for it in Canada." (Lasseray, 333)

With the latter purpose in mind he received authority from Gates in 1778 to take part in the operations around Albany. (See CANADA INVASION, Planned) Waiving rank and pay, says Lasseray, he offered his services to Washington to train men and horses. He organized a bureau 28 miles from Philadelphia and issued manifestoes in French, English, and German calling for volunteers to join the cause of Liberty. (*Ibid.*)

On 13 May '79 he left Boston with a Col. Allen (or Allan), the Abbé La Motte, and another officer to see what they could do to rally support for the colonists in the frontier settlement of Machias, Me. Arriving on the 19th, he established contact with Indians who traded at the village and was warmly received by the former subjects of the French King. Because of events described in connection with the PENOBSCOT EXPEDITION, de La Balme's timing was unfortunate. He and Allen organized a body of Indians and marched toward the British, but their force was crushed by superior numbers. La Balme was captured, but escaped or was exchanged.

On 27 June '80 he was at Pittsburgh, and for the next three months he conducted recruiting operations in the direction of Vincennes, Cahokia, and Kaskaskia. With about 100 French and American volunteers he started, on his own initiative and to the displeasure of local authorities, an advance through Kaskaskia toward Detroit. In the vicinity of modern Ft. Wayne, Ind., some 75 miles S.W. of Detroit, de La Balme was killed on 5 Nov. '80 by Indians under the orders of Little Turtle. His bivouac near Ft. Miami was surprised, and about 40 of his men died in the massacre. The papers of the unfortunate volunteer found their way to Quebec and later to the British Museum. They cover the Detroit expedition in detail.

Usage notes. Lasseray, whose style I have accepted in alphabetizing this man, refers to him variously as M. de La Balme, de La Balme, and La Balme. Heitman and other American authorities look on Mottin as a given name.

MOULTRIE, John. 1729–1798. Loyalist Lt. Gov. of E. Fla. S.C.–Fla. Eldest son of Dr. John Moultrie of Charleston and a brother of Wm. MOULTRIE, he graduated as M.D. from Edinburgh, came home in 1753, and became a prominent and wealthy doctor, plantation owner, and citizen. He was on the CHEROKEE EXPEDITION OF GRANT in 1761 and when Grant established the government of E. Fla. became a member of the council. Moultrie took up almost 20,000 acres in land grants, built a mansion near St. Augustine, and when he succeeded Grant as acting Lt. Gov. in 1771 (Grant was invalided home) he sold his S.C. properties and moved his slaves to Fla. He retained his post of Lt. Gov. when Col. Patrick Tonyn arrived 1 Mar. '74 as Gov. In July '84 he sailed to England and three years later was awarded about £4,500 for his war losses, slightly more than half of his claim. Three brothers, Alexander, Thomas, and William, were patriot soldiers. (Wilbur H. Siebert in *D.A.B.*)

MOULTRIE, William. 1730–1805. Cont'l. general. S.C. Son of a prominent physician who came to Charleston from England about 1728 (R. L. Meriwether in *D.A.B.*), the well-to-do young Moultrie spent eight inconspicuous years in the community before the Cherokee expedition of 1761 gave him an opportunity to find his role. After serving as a militia Capt. in the operation commanded by Lt. Col. James GRANT, "he became a recognized leader in the military affairs of the province." (*Ibid.*) He was elected to the 1st Cont'l. Cong., but did not serve. (Montross, *Reluctant Rebels,* 431) On 17 June '75 he became Col. of the 2d S.C. Colonial Regt. Against the CHARLESTON EXPEDITION of Clinton in 1776 he became a national hero in his defense of the palmetto and sand fort that was renamed in his honor. But in his preparations for this action he "offered some ground for the criticism that he was too easy going and neglected his opportunities, a criticism that followed later

incidents in his career." (*D.A.B.*) He was appointed a Cont'l. B.G. on 16 Sept. '77 but had no opportunity for significant field operations until after the British capture of Savannah, 29 Dec. '78. During Lincoln's operations in the SOUTHERN THEATER Moultrie was employed in a semi-independent role. He commanded the successful action at BEAUFORT, S.C., 3 Feb. '79. When Gen. Prevost pushed through his screening force and threatened CHARLESTON, 11–12 May, Moultrie helped organize the defenses of the city. His part in the American defeat at STONO FERRY, 20 June '79, is uncertain. Re-elected to Congress, he again declined to serve. (Montross, *op. cit.,* 431) The CHARLESTON EXPEDITION of 1780 made him a prisoner of war (12 May) for almost two years. He was exchanged in Feb. '82 and on 15 Oct. he became a Cont'l. Maj. Gen.—the last officer appointed to that grade—but the fighting was over. (Heitman says he was on parole to Nov. '81, but he apparently did not leave Haddrel's Point.) In 1783 he sat in the S.C. House of Reps., and the next year was Lt. Gov. He served two successful two-year tours as Gov. starting in 1785 and '94. Moultrie's two-vol. *Memoirs of the American Revolution* (1802), composed largely of his correspondence, is of great value for the history of military operations in S.C. and Ga. during the war.

His brother John MOULTRIE was a Loyalist. Another brother, Thomas, was a Capt. of the Cont'l. Army killed in the sortie of 24 Apr. '80 from CHARLESTON. A third brother, Alexander, is identified in Heitman as a militia Capt. in 1776.

MOUNT PLEASANT, N.Y. See YOUNG'S HOUSE, 3 Feb. '80.

MOUNT PLEASANT, S.C. See HADDREL'S POINT.

MOUNT WASHINGTON (Washington Heights), N.Y. Site of FORT WASHINGTON, which was renamed Fort Knyphausen after its capture by the British on 8 Nov. '76.

MOYLAN, Stephen. 1737–1811. Cont'l. officer. Ireland–Pa. Born in Cork, the son of a prosperous Catholic merchant, he was educated in Paris and spent three years in the shipping business in Lisbon before reaching Philadelphia in 1768. He quickly achieved wealth and social standing. On the recommendation of his friend John Dickinson he became muster-master general of the Cont'l. Army on 11 Aug. '75. Joining Washington at Cambridge, his duties included the fitting out of privateers. An early advocate of complete independence, he had hopes early in 1776 of being appointed ambassador to Spain. (Frank Monaghan in D.A.B.) On 5 Mar. '76 he became secretary to Washington, on 5 June Congress elected him Q.M.G. to succeed Thos. Mifflin, and on 7 June Moylan left Washington's headquarters to take up his new assignment. He was given the grade of Col.

He was not successful as Q.M.G., although it must be pointed out that his difficulties were virtually insurmountable. Washington wrote brother Samuel on 5 Oct. '76 that Long Island and N.Y.C. would have been evacuated of all matériel "but for a defect in the department of the Quarter Master General's not providing teams enough." (Quoted in Freeman, Washington, IV, 196) Failing also in the business of procuring other equipment for the army, he resigned as Q.M.G. on 28 Sept. '76 and Mifflin was reappointed to the post. "Moylan acted wisely and honorably in resigning," wrote John Jay to Edmund Rutledge. (Ibid., IV, 211 n.) He remained on Washington's staff as a volunteer, and about 12 Dec.

he left the Delaware to hurry the movement of Lee and Gates south to join Washington's main army. (Ibid., 283 n.) A snowstorm prevented his rejoining in time for the action at Trenton, but he served with distinction in the victory at Princeton, 3 Jan. '77. (D.A.B.) He had responded to Washington's request to raise a mounted regiment, which started as a Pa. volunteer unit (1st Pa. Regt. of Cav.) but became the 4th Cont'l. Dragoons. Moylan was commissioned its Col. on 5 Jan., an assignment he held for the rest of the war. Pulaski's appointment as over-all cavalry commander on 21 Sept. '77 raised problems of cooperation that came to a head the next month. Acquitted of court-martial charges pressed by PULASKI in Oct., he became temporary commander of the four mounted regiments when Pulaski resigned this post in Mar. '78. Meanwhile he had spent the winter at Valley Forge.

An adequate cavalry arm would have been invaluable to Washington in the Monmouth Campaign. Despite inadequate numbers and poor equipment Moylan struggled manfully to do the job with the 30 troopers left in service by 25 June. (Ibid., 19 n.) Moving ahead of the rebel army from Englishtown, N.J., on that date, he got in front of the enemy the day before the Battle of Monmouth and furnished Washington with some useful intelligence. For the next three years he served on the Hudson and in Conn. He took part in Wayne's expedition to BULL'S FERRY, N.J., July '80.

"Moylan's Virginia regiments of horse" are referred to as taking part in the Charleston campaign of 1780 (Ward, W.O.R., 701). Presumably "Moylan" is used in the sense of his being chief of all American cavalry, and it is also possible that detachments of his 4th Cont'l. Dragoons were in the

Carolinas, but Moylan himself was not there. In May '81 he was sent to join Lafayette in Va., according to *D.A.B.*, but he played no part in Lafayette's independent operations against Cornwallis. Presumably he did not arrive until the allied army of Washington and Rochambeau undertook the closing operations of the Yorktown Campaign. Order of Battle for the latter indicates that he was present with 60 dragoons. (Johnston, *Yorktown*, 113; this is the only place Moylan is mentioned in this basic reference for Lafayette's independent operations and the Siege of Yorktown.) After Cornwallis' surrender Moylan's health forced him to return to Philadelphia. He was breveted B.G. on 3 Nov. '83, the date he left the army.

Col. Moylan was a jovial Irishman who cut quite a figure in what Monaghan describes as "his very remarkable uniform, consisting of a red waistcoat, buckskin breeches, bright green coat and bearskin hat." (*D.A.B.*) Washington appointed him commissioner of loans in Philadelphia in 1793. In 1771 he was the first president of the Friendly Sons of St. Patrick, and in 1796 he was re-elected to this post. One of his brothers was Bishop of Cork, another, Jasper, was a lawyer in Philadelphia, and a third, John, was a Philadelphia merchant and Clothier General of the army.

A biography by M. J. Griffin, *Stephen Moylan,* was published in 1909. Frank Monaghan, on whose *D.A.B.* sketch this article is primarily based (with some missing details from Appleton's), wrote "Stephen Moylan in the American Revolution" for *Studies: an Irish Quarterly Review* (Dublin), Sept. 1930.

MUHLENBERG, John Peter Gabriel. 1746–1807. Lutheran clergyman, Cont'l. general, politician. Pa.–Va. Son of a Lutheran missionary who came to America in 1742 from Germany, he was sent back to Germany at the age of 16 with two brothers to be educated at Waisenhaus or, at the discretion of the director, to be apprenticed. The bright, high-spirited youngster impressed the director as being better suited for the latter and was bound for six years to a grocer in Lübeck. Peter (as he was called) absconded to join the 60th Foot ("Royal Americans") and as secretary to one of its officers, who happened to be a family friend, reached Philadelphia and was discharged early in 1767. He studied theology and became an assistant to his father at Bedminster and New Germantown, N.J. In 1772 he moved to Woodstock, Va. (in the Shenandoah Valley) to be pastor of the large colony of German immigrants. "To secure the privileges of a clergyman of the Established Church," as George Harvey Genzmer expresses it in *D.A.B.*, or to "enforce the payment of tithes," as Appleton's more bluntly says, he went to England and on 23 Apr. '72 was ordained by the bishop of London. Apparently never ordained as a Lutheran, "his status as a Luthero-Episcopalian is of considerable interest," comments Genzmer. (*Op. cit.*) Back in the Shenandoah he soon was a leader of his community and in 1774 was elected to the House of Burgesses. He became associated with Revolutionary leaders and was made chairman of the Dunmore co. committee on public safety. In 1775 he became a militia Col. at the invitation of Washington and soon thereafter preached his final sermon. "There is a time for all things," he said, taking his text from Ecclesiastes 3:1, "—a time to preach and a time to pray; but there is also a time to fight, and that time has now come." Tossing aside his robes to reveal his militia uniform, he walked to the church door, ordered the drums to beat for recruits, and enlisted almost 300 of his congregation. They became the 8th Va., better known as the "German Regt.," and his Cont'l. commission as Col. of the unit was dated 1 Mar. '76. Marching south, he was on hand to help repel the Charleston Expedition of Clinton in 1776, but his troops were among the large percentage of the defending force not engaged. There was no further military activity of significance in the SOUTHERN THEATER prior to the time Muhlenberg was appointed B.G., 21 Feb. '77, and ordered north.

In the Battle of the BRANDYWINE, 11 Sept. '77, his brigade and Weedon's (who with Nash's constituted Greene's Div.) followed Washington to support Sullivan on the Plowed Hill when the enemy's main attack developed. Although Sullivan maintained that only Weedon's Brig. was subsequently engaged, other authorities give Muhlenberg credit for helping stop the British and permitting the army's escape. (See Freeman, *Washington,* IV, 482 *n.*) At GERMANTOWN, 4 Oct. '77, the Parson-General led his brigade in a deep penetration of the enemy's line and then fought his way back as superior enemy forces tried to cut him off.

The list of troops at Valley Forge Winter Quarters shows Muhlenberg's Brig. as composed of the 1st, 5th, 6th, 9th, and 13th Va., and the other "GERMAN REGT." (Heitman, 11–12) In the spring of 1778, Muhlenberg, Wm. Woodford, and Geo. Weedon, "jealous and ambitious men," were engaged in the patriot pastime of "quarreling over their relative rank." (Freeman, IV, 613 *n.*) At MONMOUTH, 28 June '78, he commanded the second line of Greene's right wing, which was not engaged until the final phase of the battle. Later in 1778 Muhlenberg was assigned to Putnam's Div. on the Hudson and he commanded the division during the winter while Putnam was absent. After

winter quarters at Middlebrook, he commanded a 300-man reserve during Wayne's assault of Stony Point, 16 July '79. In Dec. he was sent by Washington to take command in Va., but it was Mar. '80 before he reached Richmond. During this delay, caused by snows of the exceptional winter, Steuben was assigned chief command in the Old Dominion, and Muhlenberg became his second. He was involved in the unsuccessful attempt to keep Phillips and Arnold from destroying stores in PETERSBURG, 25 Apr. '81. He and Weedon then worked to assemble Va. militia units (see "Lafayette *vs.* Cornwallis" phase of VA. MIL. OPNS. and continued to command troops on the south bank of the James. In the final operations against Cornwallis, Muhlenberg commanded a brigade in the Lt. Inf. Div. of Lafayette. Gimat's Bn. of his brigade was in the assault on Redoubt No. 10. (Under YORKTOWN CAMP'N. see "Order of Battle" and "Assault of Redoubts 9 and 10.")

Breveted Maj. Gen. on 30 Sept. '83, he retired on 3 Nov., settled his affairs at Woodstock, and moved to Philadelphia. Among the Pa. Germans he now was a hero second only to Washington (*D.A.B.*) and a political career lay before him. In 1784 he was elected to the Supreme Executive Council of Pa. and during the period 1785–88 was V.P. of the state under Benjamin Franklin. He was influential in the early adoption of the Constitution in the state. Although heretofore a Federalist, he and his brother Frederick were nominated by the Republicans for congressman-at-large and were both elected. He served in the 1st, 3d, 6th Congresses. On 18 Feb. 1801 he was elected Senator, but resigned a month later to become supervisor of revenue in Philadelphia. From 1802 until his death five years later he was collector of customs in the city.

A truly outstanding man from a remarkable family, Peter Muhlenberg looked the part of a national hero: tall, strikingly handsome, and courtly. His statues are in City Hall Plaza, Philadelphia, and in Statuary Hall in Washington, D.C. *The Life of Major-Gen. Peter Muhlenberg,* by H. A. Muhlenberg (a grand-nephew), was published in 1849.

MURPHY, Timothy. 1751–1818. War hero. Pa. Legendary Cont'l. rifleman, perhaps the most famous marksman of the Revolution, Tim was born near the Del. Water Gap of Irish immigrant parents. When he was about eight the family moved west to what is now Sunbury, Pa. (then Shamokin Flats). Later he was apprenticed to the Van Campen family and moved with them to the frontier region of WYOMING, Pa. On 29 June '75, when he was 24, he and his brother John were mustered into Capt. John Lowdon's company of Northumberland County riflemen. Fortunately for us a companion named Aaron Wright kept a diary that records their adventures.

Murphy served in the Boston Siege, at Long Island, and in the N.J. Campaign. In the summer of 1777 he was one of 500 picked riflemen sent north under Morgan to oppose Burgoyne. He and his constant companion, David Elerson, specialized in chopping up British foraging parties. One night they captured a sentinel, learned the password, and Murphy entered the enemy camp to carry off a British officer.

Tradition credits Murphy with picking off Sir Francis CLERKE and Gen. Simon FRASER in the Second Battle of SARATOGA, 7 Oct. '77, although no contemporary accounts mention him as being the sharpshooter. Firing from a perch in a tree, he is said to have hit Clerke with the second shot at a range

of 300 yards and to have hit Fraser with the third round. That his weapon was a double-barreled Golcher (or Goulcher) rifle, as is sometimes stated, should be taken with much skepticism: expert Carl Pippert writes me "I have seen many double rifles but never have I seen one of Revolutionary period." John Golcher of Easton, Pa., became famous *after* the war for his over-and-under revolving rifles; Murphy probably had one of these when interviewed in the early 1800's about his exploits, and it was erroneously stated that he used this weapon during the Revolution. (The remarkable Goulcher or Golcher family is covered in C. P. Russell, *Guns on the Early Frontiers . . .* [1957 and paperback reprint in 1962].)

Murphy was at Valley Forge. He did not take part in the Battle of Monmouth but the next day, 29 June '78, he and Elerson pursued with two other riflemen and captured the elaborate coach of a British general. Moving north with three companies of Morgan's Riflemen to protect the ravaged Mohawk Valley and adjacent settlements from Tory–Indian raids, Murphy tracked down and killed the notorious Christopher Service. He took part in the action at Unadilla in Oct. '78, in the pursuit of the raiders who had retaliated by sacking Cherry Valley, and then went on Sullivan's Expedition. When his enlistment with Morgan's Riflemen expired (late 1779), Murphy returned to Schoharie and enrolled in Capt. Jacob Hager's Co. of Peter Vrooman's Albany County militia (15th Regt.). Scouting with militia Capt. Alexander Harper in the Del. County Forest during the spring of 1780, he was captured by Indians and taken toward Oquago. During the night the two white men freed each other's bonds while the 11 Indians slept; they then collected and hid their captors' firearms, started methodically knifing the sleeping braves, and killed all but one before escaping.

During the action at SCHOHARIE VALLEY, 15–19 Oct. '80, Murphy accomplished his most remarkable feat. Early in 1781 he re-enlisted in the Cont'l. Army and served in the Pa. Line under Wayne. He was present at Yorktown. Twice married, he had five sons and four daughters by his first wife (Peggy Feeck, d. 1807), and four sons by Mary Robertson. Although he never learned to read or write, he acquired a number of farms, a grist mill, and became a local political power before his death at 67 of cancer of the neck.

He was relatively short (estimates vary between 5 feet 6 inches and 5 feet 9 inches), powerful, fleet of foot, dark in coloring, and determined looking. (Cook, *What Manner of Men*, Chapter III; Lossing, I, 62 *n*.)

MURRAY, David. See Lord STORMONT.

MURRAY HILL MYTH. Historians have contended that after his landing at KIP'S BAY, 15 Sept. '76, Clinton could have moved promptly across the island of Manhattan, a mere 3,000 yards, and captured a large portion of the American army. The story of Mrs. Robert Murray first appeared in Thacher's *Military Journal* (p. 58) and seemed so plausible that other writers picked it up, or got their version from the same source as did Thacher. In an appendix entitled "General Howe and Mrs. Murray," Ward says:

"The legend presents Mrs. Murray, a middle-aged Quaker lady, the mother of twelve children, in the light of a siren, a veritable Circe, 'with feminine delaying wiles' (Frothingham, 145) beguiling 'the gallant Britons ... with smiles and pleasant conversation, and a profusion of cakes and wine' (Lossing,

II, 611) while they 'lingered over their wine, quaffing and laughing, and bantering their patriotic hostess about the ludicrous panic and discomfiture of her countrymen' (Irving, II, 355). It has been accepted as a historic fact, by Irving, Lossing, Johnston, Gordon, Fortescue, Frothingham, Bancroft, Winsor, Trevelyan, Fiske, Bryant, and the *Dictionary of American Biography* [article by Richard E. Day on Robert Murray, 1721–1786], not only that the 'subtile' hostess served her guests cakes and wines, but that she actually held up the whole British force for those two critical hours. . . .

"With such a wealth of authority behind it, who shall deny the lady her heaped-up honors? Yet one must." (*W.O.R.* 937–38)

Ward goes on to say that since Murray Hill was the objective of the first wave, the Quaker lady may well have invited the British generals into her parlor "to enjoy her old Madeira," as Gen. G. W. Cullum puts it in Winsor's *Narrative History* (VI, 284). But that this stopped the entire army is not probable in terms of the personalities of the British officers involved nor does it square with the tactical situation. (See KIP'S BAY) In a note to Clinton's memoirs, editor Willcox says "Clinton's account [of why he did not push on from Murray Hill] ... is only part of the evidence that disproves that pleasant legend [of Mrs. Murphy's delaying action]." (*American Rebellion*, 47 *n*.)

MUSGRAVE, Thomas. 1737–1812. British officer. Sixth son of Sir Richard Musgrave, a baronet of Cumberland, he entered the army in 1754 as ensign in the 3d ("Buffs") Regt. After serving in the 64th, and being breveted Maj. in 1772, he joined the 40th Foot in Dec. '75 and came to America with the regiment in 1776. He succeeded James Grant as Lt. Col. when the latter was killed at Long Island. Commanding the 40th in the Philadelphia Campaign, he distinguished himself in the defense of the Chew House at GERMANTOWN, 4 Oct. '77. The next year he accompanied Gen. Grant's expedition to St. Lucia as Q.M.G. Invalided home, he was made Col. and A.D.C. to the King in 1782 and in this same year returned to America as a B.G. to serve as the last British commandant of N.Y.C. He then went to India, was Maj. Gen. in 1790, Lt. Gen. in 1797, and full Gen. in 1802.

MUSGROVE'S MILL, S.C., 18 Aug. '80. In the skirmishing that preceded the Battle of KINGS MOUNTAIN, Cols. Elijah Clarke and Isaac Shelby made an attempt against the Loyalists to the rear of Patrick Ferguson's main force. After failing to surprise the enemy at Musgrove's Mill on the Enoree River, they took up a defensive position and repulsed an attack in which they killed 63 Loyalists, wounded 90, and captured 70 with a loss of only four rebels killed and eight wounded. (Fisher, *Struggle*, II, 344)

MUSKETS AND MUSKETRY. The principal army weapon of the 18th century was the flintlock musket, a smoothbore weapon that threw a large lead ball with reasonable accuracy and a satisfactory rate of fire. The most common musket, and prototype of most others of the period, was the famous BROWN BESS. Much has been made of the inaccuracy of the musket in comparison with the rifle, but this is because infantry tactics of the day are not understood. With the development of firearms "linear tactics" were adopted. The line of battle consisted of two or three ranks drawn up shoulder to shoulder and with minimum depth; another rank of "file closers" might follow at about six paces, the role of men in this line being to replace casualties. With fixed bayonets the attackers moved forward, keeping their alignment, knowing that until within 100 yards they were relatively safe from enemy musketry. Their officers tried to achieve a discipline whereby they could make men hold their fire until within about 50 yards. Nickerson points out that "it became the *ne plus ultra* of the art to take, not to give, the first fire; to stand the losses and to put in your own volley so close that every shot went home." (*Turning Point*, 13–14) When the opposing commanders at Fontenoy (1745) invited the other to fire first, they were being smart, not gallant; French discipline broke first, and the British methodically annihilated them with coolly delivered volley fire. Peterson explains:

"Volley-firing from a line of battle was a very formal practice. All loading and firing was done by command, or, as a modern soldier would say, 'by the numbers.' There was little or no aiming as it is understood today. The volley was delivered directly ahead or to the right or left oblique as commanded. The theory was to lay down a pattern or field of fire, and consequntly rapidity of fire was prized much more highly than accuracy.* * * [Soldiers were drilled to deliver] a sustained fire of one shot every fifteen seconds, a rate which would assure at least two volleys at an approaching enemy in any average charge. * * * It should be remembered also that this attacking force was ... a compact and solid mass of men, a perfect target for fire from another compact body of men at point blank range. Accuracy would have been superfluous in this type of warfare. Speed was everything. Speed for the defending force to pour as many bullets into the attacking force as possible; speed for the attacking force to close with its adversary before it had been too severely decimated to have sufficient strength to carry the position [with the bayonet]." Harold L. Peterson, *Arms and Armor in Colonial America, 1526–1783* (Harrisburg, Pa., 1956), 160, 162.

Another authority explains:

"Twelve separate motions were prescribed in the manual of arms for the Brown Bess, which meant that an indifferent soldier could fire two rounds, while a good man could get off five and Frederick the Great's troops allegedly fired six rounds per minute. One of the reasons why the first volley was more effective was because the first round could be loaded in a relatively leisurely fashion and properly rammed before the bayonet was fixed; the 14-inch bayonet made it more difficult to ram subsequent rounds." (Curtis, *Org. of the Br. Army*, 16 and *n*.)

As for accuracy, George HANGER is quoted:

"A soldier's musket, if not exceedingly ill-bored (as many of them are), will strike the figure of a man at eighty yards; it may even at 100; but a soldier must be very unfortunate indeed who shall be wounded by a common musket at 150 yards, provided his antagonist aims at him. . . . I do maintain and will prove, whenever called on, that no man was ever killed at 200 yards, by a common soldier's musket, by the person who aimed at him." (Hanger, *Sportsmen* [1814 ed.], 205, quoted in Peterson, *op. cit.*, 163)

Caliber of most muskets was .75—three quarters of an inch in diameter—and the lead ball weighed about an ounce; this put quite a hole in a man, and up to 300 yards the ball had enough velocity to be effective.

RIFLEMEN were superior to musketmen on certain special missions, but were no match in a real battle. This was mainly because of their slow rate of fire and because a bayonet for the rifle had not been developed. Another

thing was that MARKSMANSHIP of riflemen was less remarkable than is popularly assumed.

In addition to the Brown Bess, many models of musket were used in the Revolution, but they were generally similar. By the end of the war the Americans had begun to favor the French musket, of which 15 successive models—between 1717 and 1777—are described by Peterson. (*Op. cit.*, 171–76) Changes were so slight, however, that many are hard to detect.

The "Committee of Safety musket" was one made by a private gunsmith under specific contract to a committee or council of safety, and the term does not include domestic and foreign weapons purchased and issued by those bodies. (*Ibid.*, 180) Since state governments soon were created and took over procurement, "the period of the true Committee of Safety musket lasted only two or three years . . . and . . . the number of guns . . . was remarkably small." (*Ibid.*, 182)

See also BAYONETS AND BAYONET ATTACKS and LINE.

MUTINY ACT OF 1765. See under QUARTERING ACTS.

MUTINY OF THE CONNECTICUT LINE, 25 May '80. While in MORRISTOWN WINTER QUARTERS, N.J., two Conn. regiments turned out about dusk on 25 May and prepared to march away without orders. These men had been without pay for five months and had been on short rations, or worse, for several weeks. Order was restored only after Col. R. J. Meigs, acting brigade commander, had been hit by one of the men and after a unit of the Pa. Line had been brought in to seize the leaders. Most of the men then went back to their huts but a few of the more determined ones were arrested and confined. "The whole affair was soon over and afterwards disregarded." (Van Doren, *Mutiny,* 22–23)

MUTINY OF 1st N.Y. REGT., June '80. Early in June '80, 31 men of the 1st N.Y. deserted from Ft. Stanwix (Schuyler) and were believed to be headed for the enemy camp. Lt. Abraham Hardenbergh pursued with some Oneidas, caught them astride a river, and shot 13 of those who had not yet crossed. "This is perhaps the only time in the history of the American Army when an officer used Indians to kill white soldiers," comments Van Doren. (*Mutiny,* 20)

MUTINY OF GORNELL, Apr. '82. Inadequate supplies and other administrative grievances, combined with lack of military activity, had brought some of Greene's army to the edge of mutiny in Oct. '81 (see SOUTHERN CAMPAIGNS OF GREENE). These same conditions returned in the spring of '82, but this time the Southern army had among it some Northern troops who had experience in mutinying and, as had happened in the North, the British sent agents into the American camp to help organize things properly. The plot this time included the abduction of Greene. (Lee, *Memoirs,* 547) A day before it was scheduled to take place the mutiny was discovered and crushed. The ringleader, a Sgt. Gornell of the Pa. Cont'ls., was executed and four of his known conspirators were confined. Carl Van Doren identifies this man as George Goznall of the 2d Pa. (*Mutiny,* 236)

MUTINY OF GRIFFIN, Oct. '81. See under SOUTHERN CAMPAIGNS OF GREENE.

MUTINY OF HICKEY, June '76. On 15 June '76, when Washington was in N.Y.C. and Gov. Tryon was a refugee aboard a British ship in the harbor, Thomas Hickey and another Cont'l. soldier were brought before the provincial congress on the charge of passing counterfeit currency. Hickey was a member of Washington's LIFE GUARD. The two prisoners bragged openly about being part of a conspiracy to turn against the Americans as soon as the British army arrived. Hickey was tried by a court-martial on the 26th, convicted of mutiny and sedition, and two days later was hanged near Bowery Lane in the presence of 20,000 spectators. The real extent of the conspiracy was so magnified and propagandized that the facts never were known. It seems to have been established at Hickey's trial that Gov. Tryon had been sending money to Gilbert Forbes, a gunsmith on Broadway, to recruit men for the King. The money was passed by Mayor David Mathews of N.Y.C., who had authority to visit Tryon and who claimed innocence of what real purpose the money was for. There was no proof that Tryon was counterfeiting money on shipboard or that he had offered land bounties to stimulate recruiting. Nor could it be proved that as many as 700 men had signed up, much less that the plans included assassination of Washington and other leaders. John Jay headed the committee that investigated the affair for N.Y. authorities. Only Hickey was tried, but 13 others, including Forbes and Mathews, were imprisoned in Conn.; they all escaped or were sent back to N.Y. before they could be given a hearing. The main result of the affair was to blacken further the name of "Loyalist." (Van Doren, *Secret History,* 13–15)

MUTINY OF THE MASSACHUSETTS LINE, 1 Jan. '80. "Early in the morning about 100 soldiers belonging to the Massachusetts regiments [of the West Point garrison] ... marched off with intent to go home: they were pursued and brought back: some of them were punished; the greater part of them pardoned." This is the succinct summary in Gen. Heath's *Memoirs*. These men had enlisted at various times after Jan. '77 for three years and maintained—not all of them, obviously, with accuracy—that their time was up.

MUTINY OF THE NEW JERSEY LINE, 20–27 Jan. '81. The 500 men of the reorganized N.J. Brig. were in winter quarters at Pompton, N.J., with a small detachment at Suffern, N.Y., when the MUTINY OF THE PA. LINE started on 1 Jan. Wayne ordered part of the brigade south and they eventually camped at Chatham under the command of the able Elias Dayton. The portion of the brigade remaining at Pompton was commanded by Col. Israel SHREVE, a fat, loyal, but incompetent officer. Having the same complaints as the Pa. regulars, men of the Jersey Brig. followed developments of the Pa. mutiny with avid attention. Even after the latter had been settled and the Jersey troops were granted some of the benefits won by the Pa. mutineers, on 20 Jan. a mutiny broke out at Pompton. In a small-scale repetition of the recently concluded performance, some 200 men marched from their camp at Pompton and headed for Chatham. Shreve puffed along behind them. Dayton managed to disperse much of his detachment before the Pompton mutineers arrived on the 21st and only a few recruits were acquired at Chatham. After two disorderly days the Pompton group was prevailed on to follow Shreve back to their camp and the men were promised pardon if they subsequently behaved.

Washington, meanwhile, learned of the new disorder the evening of the 21st and ordered Heath to make 500 or 600 good troops available to stamp it out. Robt. Howe was put in command of the operation and told to enforce unconditional submission. After a hard march through deep snow the troops from around West Point reached Ringwood, N.J., on the 25th. Here they were joined by other troops of the expedition and by three guns that followed from the Highlands. Washington arrived at midnight of the 26th and Howe led his command forward an hour later.

The troops at Pompton, eight miles away, had become disorderly soon after their return from Chatham. They would obey some officers but not others. They once turned out when ordered but then became insubordinate when dismissed. Sergeants George Grant, Jonathan Nichols, and John Minthorn had been the nominal leaders of the original uprising (although they apparently were forced by their men into assuming leadership and may well have done so in collusion with Shreve when it was apparent that the mutiny could not be stopped); Sgt. David Gilmore (or Gilmour) and John Tuttle were the most conspicuous agitators of the later disorders.

With some well-founded doubts about whether his Mass., Conn., and N.H. troops would do their duty, Howe surrounded the Pompton encampment before daylight of the 27th. With three cannon in plain view of the huts, Howe sent in word for the mutineers to assemble without arms. After some hesitation they complied.

Officers of the N.J. Brig. submitted the names of the worst offenders and from these candidates selected one from each regiment. Grant, Gilmore, and Tuttle were named, tried on the spot, and sentenced to be shot immediately. The latter two were executed by a firing party formed by 12 other mutineers who had been named as prominent offenders. Grant was reprieved at the last minute; Van Doren comments that "it is tempting to guess that he may have been privately told by Shreve not to worry over the trial and sentence." (*Mutiny,* 223) Dr. Thacher, who saw the trials and executions, gives no indication of suspecting that Grant's case was rigged. (*Journal,* 252)

MUTINY OF THE PENNSYLVANIA LINE, 1–10 Jan. '81. Inactivity of winter quarters plus accumulated grievances about food, clothing, quarters, pay, bounties, and terms of enlistment finally led the Pa. Cont'ls. to mutiny on 1 Jan. '81. Many of these troops had enlisted "for three years or during the war"; they contended that the phrase "whichever comes first" was implied and that their contracts were terminated. Almost nothing is known about how this mutiny was organized; the mutineers kept no written records and none of them wrote of the event afterward. The names of only two leaders are known for sure: Wm. Bowzar, secretary of the 12-man Board of Sergeants that represented the mutineers, and Daniel Connell, who signed the Board's last communication (see below). A man named Williams—probably John Williams—was president of the Board of Sergeants, but does not appear to have been the real leader or organizer of the revolt. (Van Doren, *Mutiny,* 58)

The 10 infantry regiments and the artillery regiment of Gen. Anthony Wayne's Pa. Line were near Morristown, N.J., where they occupied huts built the previous winter at Jockey Hollow (also known as Mount Kemble). Total strength in officers and men was about 2,500. The mutiny started about 10 o'clock the evening of 1 Jan. when soldiers emerged from their huts under arms, with field equipment, captured the guns and ammunition, and assembled to march away. Fewer than half the men fell out initially, and probably not more than 1,500 eventually joined the march. During a confused hour before

they left camp the mutineers resisted the efforts and the eloquence of Wayne and about 100 officers to stop them. They did this with a remarkable lack of violence and with the simple argument that the officers could do nothing to settle their grievances—they intended to present these directly to Congress in Philadelphia. Lt. Francis White and Capt. Samuel Tolbert were shot (not fatally) while trying to keep their men from moving to the assembly area. Capt. Adam Bettin was mortally wounded by a soldier who was chasing Lt. Col. Wm. Butler (4th Pa.) and who mistook Bettin for Butler. One man was killed accidentally by a fellow mutineer who, unknown to the other, had replaced the regular guard on the captured magazine. These are the only identified casualties, although it is hard to believe that there were not others. When Wayne rode onto the scene with several field officers he was unable to restore order but the men stated "it was not their intention to hurt or disturb an officer of the Line, two or three individuals excepted." (Account of Lt. Enos Reeves, quoted by Van Doren, *op. cit.,* 46) The majority of the troops were reluctant to join the mutiny. The 2d Regt. of Col. Walter Stewart was forced at bayonet point to go along. Capt. Thos. Campbell turned out part of the 4th Regt. and attempted to recapture the artillery, but his men would not carry through with the attack. The 5th (Col. Francis Johnston) and 9th (Col. Richard Butler) occupied huts some distance from the others and joined only after being threatened with the cannon. Other men hid as mutineers ran from hut to hut gathering supporters. At 11 P.M. the column marched away to camp at Vealtown (Bernardsville), four miles distant, to await stragglers before resuming their advance toward Philadelphia the next morning.

Wayne had long feared a mutiny and had urged higher authority to do something about the legitimate grievances of his troops, but he was surprised by the events that had just taken place. Powerless to stop the marchers, and not a bit sure they did not intend to go over to the enemy—or that the British would not strike at this critical time—Wayne prepared to follow his men and try to restore order. He was accompanied by Cols. Walter Stewart and Richard Butler. Before dawn of the 2d, however, Wayne wrote out "what he called an order but what was a request and a promise," as Van Doren puts it:

"Agreeably [sic] to the proposition of a very large proportion of the worthy soldiery last evening, General Wayne hereby desires the noncommissioned officers and privates to appoint one man from each regiment, to represent their grievances to the General, who on the sacred honor of a gentleman and a soldier does hereby solemnly promise to exert every power to obtain immediate redress of those grievances; and he further plights that honor that no man shall receive the least injury on account of the part they have taken on the occasion." (Ibid., 49)

The mutineers entered Princeton in the late afternoon or evening of 3 Jan., took control of this village of some 70 houses, and prepared to wait there until Congress responded to the appeals they had sent forward to Philadelphia. The Board of Sergeants established themselves in the ruins of Nassau Hall and the men pitched tents south of the College. The sergeants had sent back a delegation to confer with Wayne, who was following at a safe distance, but they would not halt their advance on Princeton to let him address the troops. The sergeants had also furnished Wayne with a personal guard, and when the general and his colonels took up quar-

ters in a tavern near Nassau Hall on 3 Jan. they had some doubts as to whether this guard was a mark of respect or whether it indicated they were hostages.

During Thursday, 4 Jan., Wayne and the colonels negotiated with the Board, and later in the day Wayne sent word to the state authorities—the Council of Pa.—that somebody should come and consult with the mutineers. Congress and the Pa., Council, both sitting in what is now Independence Hall, had learned on 3 Jan. of the alarming developments at Morristown. That afternoon Congress appointed a committee to deal with the Pa. Council on the mutiny. When the Council received Wayne's letter on Friday they got together with the committee of Congress and decided to send Joseph Reed, President of the Pa. Council and therefore of the state, and Gen. James Potter, a militia officer and Council member. The three original members of the Congressional committee, Gen. John Sullivan, the Rev. John Witherspoon, and John Mathews, were now augmented by Samuel John Atlee and Theodorick Bland. Reed and Potter left Philadelphia late Friday afternoon with an escort of 20 light horsemen from the famous city troop, and entered Trenton by noon the next day (6 Jan.). Sullivan's committee (less Mathews, who stayed in Philadelphia) reached Trenton after dark on the 6th and stayed there during the negotiations. Capt. Samuel Morris with the rest of his Philadelphia Light Horse accompanied them.

Meanwhile, the Board of Sergeants had had a number of visitors in Princeton on 4 Jan. Gen. Arthur St. Clair, senior officer of the Pa. Line, Lafayette, and Col. John Laurens were in Philadelphia on 3 Jan. when the newly created Congressional committee decided that some officers should go see what could be done about the mutiny. These three were received by the Board of Sergeants and talked to Wayne, but the Board then told them to leave—the sergeants preferred to continue their negotiations through Wayne, Butler, and Stewart. This same day Col. Thos. Craig approached with 80 armed officers from Morristown and sent word to Wayne of his coming; the officers were not allowed to enter Princeton and they sat out the subsequent negotiations at Pennington, nine miles away. Some members of the N.J. legislature also showed up on the 4th from Trenton but were not allowed to enter Princeton.

Washington got his first news of the mutiny about noon on 3 Jan. Located at New Windsor with the main portion of the army, he was too far away to exert much influence on subsequent events, and as it turned out Wayne on his own initiative was following almost precisely the course advocated by the C. in C. Washington's letter of 3 Jan., received by Wayne on the 7th, recommended that Wayne stay with his troops, that he not attempt force, and that he try to have them move south of the Delaware. Washington disagreed with Wayne's proposal that Congress leave Philadelphia to keep away from the mutineers, but this point turned out to be academic since Congress had decided to stay. Washington had made preparations to ride south but changed his mind at 7 A.M. on the 4th when he realized he could not arrive in time and that he had the more important task of keeping the mutiny from spreading through the rest of the army. (*Ibid.*, 66) Sympathy of the troops was with the mutineers, particularly since the latter showed such good discipline in pressing their demands and showed no disposition to deal with the enemy, but civil and military authorities went ahead with plans

to surround Princeton with militia and regulars.

British headquarters in N.Y.C. learned of the mutiny before Washington, and Sir Henry Clinton promptly sought means of exploiting the situation. He alerted troops for a possible march into N.J. and started looking for emissaries to offer the mutineers pardon, payment of the money owed them by Congress, and the privilege of declining military service if they would come over to the British.

REED BEGINS NEGOTIATIONS

Many agencies were concerned with the mutiny, but Joseph Reed promptly assumed the key role. Although Gen. Potter stayed by his side he contributed nothing but an occasional signature. The Congressional committee (Sullivan *et al.*) may be regarded as a rubber stamp that waited in Trenton to approve Reed's solution. Washington was virtually out of the picture. St. Clair sat at Morristown, in command of the troops who had not joined the mutiny, and muttered about using force. So, probably, did the 80 officers who had left government bed and board to live at their own expense at Pennington.

Reed did not go straight to Princeton, where for all he knew Wayne and the colonels were prisoners and where his own safety was uncertain; he undertook a line of action designed to remind the anonymous sergeants of his personal dignity and their lack of status. (*Ibid.*, 120–21) Reed started a correspondence with Wayne, but wrote with a view to these letters being read by the sergeants. When he received a letter from Sgt. Bowzar assuring him safe conduct —for several days the Board was not convinced that President Reed had really been sent to deal with them— Reed played dumb and wrote Wayne:

"I have received a letter from Mr. Bowzar, who signs as secretary but does not say to whom." Reed very well knew "to whom" Bowzar was secretary, but he wanted to avoid tacit recognition of the Board and to stress that Wayne was still their lawful commander.

Reed and Potter had ridden on to Maidenhead (now Lawrenceville, four miles S.W. of Princeton) Saturday evening and proposed that Wayne meet them there. After the sergeants were made to understand that Reed's reluctance to enter Princeton was due to their inhospitality toward St. Clair, Wayne sent word he would meet Reed at Maidenhead Sunday morning. Reed returned to Trenton, where the Committee (which arrived that evening) gave him final guidance.

A significant development took place during the night. Clinton's emissaries—John Mason and a guide named James Ogden—got into Princeton and presented the enemy's proposals to Sgt. Williams. The latter promptly slapped them under guard and delivered them to Wayne at 4 A.M. Reed was riding to Maidenhead Sunday morning when he met the prisoners being escorted to Trenton. Any suspicion that the mutineers were flirting with the enemy was now dispelled. Taking the prisoners with him, Reed rode on to Maidenhead, met Wayne, and accepted the latter's recommendation that they proceed to Princeton.

Just as Wayne, Reed, and their parties were leaving Maidenhead a message came from the Board of Sergeants asking that the captive emissaries be returned to their custody. Apparently the mutineers had figured, on second thought, that they would be in a better bargaining position if they held these two men.

The mutineers were formed along the post road to honor Reed's arrival about 3 P.M. In this unreal situation Reed took the salutes of sergeants, who stood before their men in the positions normally occupied by officers, and he returned the salutes ("though much against my inclination"). The artillery was drawn up to fire a salute, but Reed or Wayne managed to stop this rendering of honors on the ground that it might alarm the countryside.

The first order of business in Princeton Sunday afternoon was what to do with Mason and Ogden. "Reed and the officers were plainly much afraid that the British would land and the mutineers either join them, or refuse to fight, or try to drive some bargain before they fought." (*Ibid.*, 127) Most of the sergeants favored Wayne's proposal that the men be promptly executed as spies, but Williams, who was a British deserter, and another sergeant of the same antecedence blocked this solution. Williams had the novel idea of sending the men back to Clinton "with a taunting message." Reed objected to this pointless suggestion and proposed a compromise that was adopted: the sergeants would hold the prisoners subject to Reed's call, and their disposition would be decided later. Meanwhile there was fresh intelligence of an enemy move from Staten Island into N.J. and there was no time to waste in settling the mutiny.

A good deal of preliminary work had already been done between Wayne and the sergeants. The Committee of Congress had instructed Reed to honor Wayne's promise of total amnesty and they agreed that the men should not be considered traitors, unless they were considering deserting to the enemy or refused to compromise on terms for settling the mutiny. It had also been decided in Trenton that men enlisted for three years or for the war should be discharged if they had served three years and had not re-enlisted. Men who had voluntarily enlisted or re-enlisted for the war were not, however, to be released. (*Ibid.*, 108)

At the Sunday night conference in Princeton the sergeants advanced a single proposal which embodied the wishes of the men who had the longest service and who represented the strongest of several parties in their camp. This proposal was:

"That all and every such men as was enlisted in the years 1776 and 1777 and received the bounty of twenty dollars, shall be without any delay discharged and all the arrears of pay and clothing to be paid unto them immediately when discharged; with respect to the depreciation of pay the State to give them sufficient certificates and security for such sums as they shall become due."

Reed could not agree to this since it would permit the release of men specifically precluded by his guidance from the Committee of Congress. Although this proposal was undoubtedly phrased to release some men not honestly entitled to discharge, the sergeants proceeded to open the eyes of the President of Pa.—and, to a lesser extent, those of their commanding officer of the Line —to certain sharp and dishonest practices that military officers had employed in enlisting them. In short, "the enlistment papers did not tell all the truth of what had happened." (*Ibid.*, 128)

The sergeants showed much difference of opinion among themselves, they were incapable of drafting a new set of compromise proposals, they had doubts about getting the men to accept such proposals if drafted, and Sgt. Williams was not the man to unify their demands. In order to have some basis for working out a solution Reed undertook to write up a document which "promised as much as he thought he could perform and as little as he thought the men would accept." (*Ibid.*, 130) After some minor alterations by Wayne, Reed's proposals were generally as follows: no man would be held beyond the time for which he freely and voluntarily enlisted; a commission would decide on disputed terms of enlistment; if enlistment papers were not promptly produced by official custodians the soldier's oath on the matter would be accepted; back pay, adjustment for depreciation, and clothing shortages would be taken care of as soon as possible.

On Monday, 8 Jan., the mutineers announced their general acceptance of Reed's proposals and the next morning they marched to Trenton for final negotiations. That evening the Board of Sergeants had a long conference with the Committee of Congress. The morning of the 10th Reed informed the sergeants that since they had accepted his proposals and these would now go into effect he would like the spies surrendered as evidence of the mutineers' willingness to abide by their agreement. The Board countered with a demand that the mutineers remain together under arms until final arrangements were completed. Reed refused to accept this condition and asked for a final answer within two hours. Within the time limit the Board agreed to give up the prisoners and to turn in their weapons. This communication came "Signed by the Board in the absence of the President, [by] Daniel Connell, Member." Van Doren comments that Williams and Bowzar may actually have been absent, or they may have been unwilling to sign this paper. (*Ibid.*, 153)

John Mason and James Ogden, Clinton's emissaries, were convicted on 10 Jan. of spying and were hanged the next morning. Mason was a hard character with a long record as a criminal Loyalist. Ogden is known in history only as Mason's guide.

Putting the settlement into effect involved a number of knotty problems and took several weeks. On 29 Jan., however, Wayne wrote Washington that the task was completed. About 1,250 infantrymen and 67 artillerymen were discharged; nearly 1,150 remained. Enlistment papers had been gathered quickly and most of them clearly committed the men for the duration of the war, but the commissioners had discharged men of the first five infantry regiments and most of the artillery by 21 Jan. without waiting for the papers and many men got away on false oath. There was talk of bringing action against the perjured soldiers, but the State decided against this because it was finding it impossible to raise the money to fulfill its part of the bargain. A high percentage of the discharged men subsequently re-enlisted, and all the Pa. Line—mutineers and others—were furloughed until 15 Mar. with instructions to rendezvous at various places in accordance with a reorganization plan originally scheduled for 1 Jan.* Only recruiting sergeants and musicians were not given furloughs. (*Ibid.,* 202, 232–33)

Other soldiers with the same grievances as the Pa. Line had followed developments with keen interest. The MU-

* This plan, delayed until 17 Jan., eliminated the 7th through the 11th Regts. and deployed the others as follows: 1st and 2d, under Daniel Brodhead and Walter Stewart, at Philadelphia; 3d, under Thos. Craig, at Reading; 4th, under Wm. Butler, at Carlisle; 5th, under Richard Butler, at York; and the 6th, under Richard Humpton, at Lancaster.

TINY OF THE N.J. LINE, 20–25 Jan., was the most significant result. Wayne was preparing to lead the 2d, 5th, and 6th Pa. to join Lafayette (see VA. MIL. OPNS.) when a small-scale mutiny flared up in York; six men were convicted and four of them executed on 22 May. See also MUTINY OF GORNELL.

MUTINY ON PROSPECT HILL (Cambridge), Mass., 10 Sept. '75. Ill-disciplined RIFLEMEN in the Boston Siege were a constant cause of concern to those responsible for military law and order. The climax came after the Adj. of Thompson's Bn., which included all the Pa. riflemen, arrested and confined a sergeant. Since the "shirtmen" threatened to follow their tradition of breaking into the jail to release a comrade, the culprit was removed to the main guardhouse in Cambridge. Some men of James Ross's Pa. company swore to release him and, joined by men of other companies, headed for the jail with loaded weapons. The guard detail was strengthened to 500 men and several regiments were turned out under arms for what promisd to be the best brawl of the Boston Siege, and the rioters were corralled on Prospect Hill. According to one report, Washington, Charles Lee, and Greene had to intervene and order the mutineers to ground their arms, and another Pa. regiment surrounded the subdued riflemen and marched them back to camp.

In a court-martial of which Col. John Nixon was president, 33 men were convicted of disobedient and mutinous behavior; each was fined 20 shillings. The ringleader, John Seaman, got the additional punishment of six days' confinement. The "shirtmen" did not threaten to spring him, but they continued to be a disciplinary problem throughout the siege. (Freeman, *Washington,* III, 525–26; Ward, *W.O.R.,* 107–8)

MYTHS, MOOT POINTS, AND MISCONCEPTIONS. The articles on PROPAGANDA and TRUTH VERSUS TRADITION point out why the written record of the American Revolution has been distorted in some instances. Separate articles cover the ARNOLD LEGEND, FREDERICK THE GREAT AND THE AMERICAN REVOLUTION, the question of whether Ethan Allen really demanded surrender of Ticonderoga in the name of the "GREAT JEHOVAH AND THE CONTINENTAL CONGRESS," MARKSMANSHIP, the MECKLENBURG DECLARATION OF INDEPENDENCE, the MOLLY PITCHER LEGEND, the MURRAY HILL MYTH, origin of the American FLAG, and the SILVER BULLETS OF TICONDEROGA. Washington's alleged temper tantrums at KIP'S BAY and MONMOUTH are covered under those articles. Revisionist viewpoints on David FANNING, Charles LEE, and Horatio GATES are presented, as is the matter of whether Arnold or Gates deserves credit for the victory over Burgoyne at Second SARATOGA. The performance of GERMAIN at Minden, the "lost order" of BURGOYNE'S OFFENSIVE, the dying words of Joseph WARREN, the quote attributed to Samuel Prescott at LEXINGTON AND CONCORD ("But if they want war, let it begin here!"), that Washington almost won at GERMANTOWN, that the Declaration of INDEPENDENCE was signed on the 4th of July, Peggy Shippen Arnold's role in ARNOLD'S TREASON, and the bogus titles of William ALEXANDER ("Lord Stirling"), "Baron von" STEUBEN, and "Baron de" KALB—all these are discussed or touched on in the articles indicated.

Walter BUTLER and Simon GIRTY were accused of atrocities at places where they were not present. The nonexistent "Deckhard rifle" is identified under DICKERT RIFLE. The conflicting descriptions of Jenny McCrae are given under McCRAE ATROCITY. The "double barreled Golcher" is discussed under Tim MURPHY, where doubt is also cast on whether he was the man who shot the two important British officers at Second SARATOGA. Under MILITIA and RIFLEMEN are attempts to evaluate their actual importance in the war.

See Sydney George Fisher, *The Legendary and Myth-Making Process in Histories of the American Revolution.* Philadelphia, 1912.

N

NANCY CAPTURE. *c.* 27 Nov. '75. Possibly from information sent by Arthur Lee, the Americans learned that two British ordnance brigantines were headed for Boston late in 1775. On 27 Nov., Washington was informed that Capt. John Manley had sighted both of them off the Mass. coast and although one escaped, the *Nancy* was captured. (see also John GLOVER.) This was the first important prize taken by the Americans, and they unloaded her at Cape Ann. (This point forms the northern side of Boston harbor.) "As the men went about this hurried task, every lift from the hold of the *Nancy* seemed to bring a military treasure into daylight," writes D. S. Freeman. "When he saw her papers, Horatio Gates exclaimed that he could not have made out a better invoice if he had tried." (*Washington*, III, 567) She yielded 2,000 muskets, 100,000 flints, 30,000 round shot, 30 tons of musket shot, and a 13-inch brass mortar weighing over 2,700 pounds. The latter was entered into the American service and dubbed "Congress" by Col. Mifflin. It has been observed that 18 months would have been needed to manufacture in America the matériel taken from the *Nancy*.

While this event is not mentioned in many general accounts of the Revolution, Freeman says: "The report of the committee of Congress, recommending the effort to capture the ordnance ships, is a major document in the history of the beginnings of the American Navy." (*Op. cit., 566 n.*)

NANTASKET POINT, Mass. See GREAT BREWSTER ISLAND.

NANTASKET ROAD, Mass., 17 and 19 May '76. Capt. James Mugford of Marblehead with a 21-man crew on the schooner *Franklin* captured a British transport from Cork that was heading into Boston, unaware that the British had evacuated this place. Two days later, on 19 May, the *Franklin* and *Lady Washington* were heading toward the bay when the British sent boats to capture them in a night action. The *Franklin* was grounded, but about 12 British boats carrying 200 men were repulsed after a half-hour fight in which the only American casualty was Mugford, who was killed.

NASH, Abner. *c.* 1740–1786. War governor of N.C. Va.–N.C. Born of parents who had come to Va. from Wales about 1730, he moved to Halifax, N.C., in 1762 and from there to New Bern about 10 years later. He married the young widow of Gov. Arthur Dobbs and in 1774, after the death of this wife, made another advantageous match. Genial, suave, and epicurean,

he was also an energetic lawyer and politician. Supporting the conservative eastern interests in the Regulator disturbances, he was rewarded by an appointment as major of brigade in 1768. As the South began to follow the North's lead toward revolution, however, he became an ardent patriot, taking a lead in the movements that drove Royal Gov. Martin out of N.C. Martin later called him one of the four "foremost . . . patrons of revolt." (A. R. Newsome in *D.A.B.*)

In the spring of 1780, as his state became a theater of active military operations, Abner Nash was elected Gov. While he was energetic, he chafed under the constitutional weaknesses of his office and then objected to what he considered to be unconstitutional acts by the Assembly in appointing Richard Caswell as commander of the militia, in establishing a board of war and, subsequently, a council extraordinary whose powers undermined his own. He therefore declined to serve a second term. Soon back in politics, however, he represented Jones co. in 1782, '84, and '85. He declined election to Congress in 1778, but accepted in 1782, '83, and '85. He died the next year.

Brother of Gen. Francis NASH.

NASH, Francis. *c.* 1742–1777. Cont'l. general. Va.–N.C. The son of a Welsh immigrant, he was born in Va. and moved at an early age to Hillsboro (then Childsburg), N.C. "Of superior training, handsome in person, affable, and industrious," writes A. R. Newsome in *D.A.B.*, "he rose quickly to local prominence as merchant and attorney." In 1763 he became clerk of the court of pleas and quarter sessions. He was representative from Orange co. to the House of Commons in 1764, '65, and '71, and for Hillsboro in 1773–75. By the nature of his duties he was objectionable to the Regulators, being one of those officials charged with taking excessive fees, and as a Capt. in the royal militia he won a reputation for courage and military ability in defeating them at the Alamance, 16 May '71. (His brother Abner NASH also participated on the same side in this intramural affair.) As the Revolution approached he identified himself with the Whigs, was elected to the second and third provisional congresses of N.C. in Apr. and Aug. '75, and on 1 Sept. was named Lt. Col 1st N.C. Cont'ls., one of two regular regiments being formed at that time. He was promoted to Col. on 10 Apr. '76, became B.G. on 5 Feb. '77, was ordered to raise troops in western N.C., and joined Washington for the Philadelphia campaign. He commanded a brigade in Greene's Div. at the Brandywine, 11 Sept., but did not reach Plowed Hill in time to see action. (Freeman, *Washington,* IV, 482 *n.*) At GERMANTOWN, 4 Oct. '77, his thigh was broken by a cannon ball as he led his N.C. brigade into action from the reserve, and he died 7 Oct. Freeman refers to him as "a promising young" B.G. (*Ibid.,* IV, 535)

Brother of Abner NASH.

NASSAU (then Providence or New Providence), Bahamas, 3–4 Mar. '76. In the first and virtually the only planned major operation of the Cont'l. Navy, Esek Hopkins put to sea in Feb. '76. Acting on intelligence that the British were assembling vast quantities of stores in the West Indies, he sailed for the Bahamas · and attacked the island of New Providence or Providence, now called Nassau. Capt. Samuel Nicholas, senior Marine officer of the American Revolution, led the first action in which American MARINES ever participated as an organized unit, and on 3–4 Mar. he captured Ft. Montagu. This netted over 100 cannon and mortars and a large quantity of stores that Washington's army found invaluable. (See also NAVAL OPERATIONS)

Gov. Montfort BROWNE was captured in this raid.

NASSAU RAID OF RATHBUN, 27 Jan. '78. Marines and seamen from Capt. John Peck RATHBUN's sloop *Providence* landed and seized the forts. "This was the first time the Stars and Stripes appeared over a foreign stronghold." (U.S.M.C. Chronology, citing McClellan, *Hist. of U.S.M.C.,* I, Chapt. VI, p. 1)

NATURAL LAW, also called Fundamental Law and Natural Rights. This doctrine, which figured prominently in the BACKGROUND of the American Revolution, can be traced back to Sophocles; it was developed as a political philosophy in the 17th and 18th centuries by John Milton, John Locke, Jean Jacques Rousseau, and Sir William Blackstone. They contended that an individual was entitled to certain intrinsic rights that no government could take away. As modified by Sam Adams, Thos. Jefferson, James OTIS, and Thos. Paine, natural rights included the right of revolution, popular sovereignty, democracy, liberty, and the pursuit of happiness. This political philosophy formed the American "party line" in arguments against English authority. (Miller, *Origins,* 170) OTIS probably deserves credit for first advocating natural law in Revolutionary politics. See Charles F. Mullett, *Fundamental Law and the Amer. Rev.* (1933) and B. F. Wright, *Amer. Interpretations of Natural Law* (1931).

NAVAL COMMITTEE. Appointed by the Cont'l. Cong. on 30 Oct. '75, it was composed of John Adams (who had been the principal force in creating the Cont'l. Navy), Deane, John Langdon, Christopher Gadsden, Gov. Stephen Hopkins of R.I., Joseph Hewes, and

Richard Henry Lee. Meeting each evening at six in a rented room in the Tun Tavern on the Philadelphia waterfront—selecting this after-duty hour "in order to dispatch this business with all possible celerity"—they accomplished an amazing amount of work in a matter of weeks. For this and for the subsequent organizations that controlled marine business, see NAVAL OPERATIONS.

NAVAL OPERATIONS. In theory, the British should have been able to crush the American Revolution with the Royal Navy and a few marines. They had the most powerful navy in the history of the world; the American colonies were so disposed along the coast and so divided by estuaries and navigable rivers as to make all regions accessible to sea power; and the rebels obviously were incapable of raising a navy to win a maritime war. Yet the Royal Navy did not win the war for King George, and even before France in 1778 sent her ships to support the colonies the British failed to exploit an advantage that should have been decisive. As a result, the naval battles of the Revolution were secondary in strategic importance to the land operations; the British were, of course, entirely dependent on their navy for logistical support, yet they had lost the war before the French fleets appeared. No real American navy ever appeared. PRIVATEERING was developed fully by the colonists, but although this may be considered an aspect of "naval operations" it will be covered under its own heading.

In 1775 the British had 131 ships of the line and 139 craft of other classes. By 1783 this total of 270 had been swelled to 468, of which about 100 —mainly frigates and lighter vessels— were committed in America. In quality, however, the British Navy was in an incredibly bad state: the ships had been reduced by neglect to floating coffins, officers and men were substandard, and the Admiralty was headed by Lord Sandwich, an evil and incompetent politician. One cause of the trouble was the economy wave instituted by Lord North, and Professor Rankin points out that the war caught the country without a supply of seasoned timber for ship construction. Furthermore, the British were faced with a tremendously long line of communications.

"WASHINGTON'S NAVY"

The action off MACHIAS, May '75, has been called the first naval engagement of the war, although this is stretching the point somewhat.

A few months later, during the Boston Siege, Washington organized a flotilla of six schooners and a brigantine to prey on enemy supply ships. He had the double purpose of depriving the enemy of cargoes and of getting critically needed supplies for his own forces. On 2 Sept. '75 he commissioned the *Hannah,* which has been called America's first war vessel. (The *Machias Liberty,* rechristened after the action of May '75 mentioned above, could probably be called the first war vessel in the service of an American *state.*) Washington's little navy took 35 prizes with cargoes valued at over $600,000 before it was disbanded in 1777, when the British evacuation of Boston ended its usefulness. Capt. John Manley made the most important capture when he took the NANCY, *c.* 27 Aug. '75.

THE CONTINENTAL NAVY

"What think you of an American Fleet?" asked John Adams in a letter of 19 Oct. '75 to James Warren. "I don't mean 100 ships of the Line," he went on to say, but the colonists should be able to create a small force that could do *something*. The idea was popular with the New England delegates and opposed by others, but by the end of the month Congress had authorized four armed vessels and (30 Oct.) appointed John Adams and six others a NAVAL COMMITTEE. On 10 Nov. the MARINES were born, on the 23d Congress considered John Adams' draft of "rules for the government of the American navy" (based on those of the British), and on the 25th Congress passed the resolutions that established the American Navy.

Naval affairs were controlled thereafter by various bodies designated by Congress. Until Dec. '79 a Marine Committee of 13 members, one from each colony, was responsible. A Board of Admiralty was then established to comprise three private citizens and two members of Congress. After 1781 the administration was handled as an additional duty by Robert Morris, Director of Finance. Subordinate boards in Boston and Philadelphia were also established. (See Burnett, *Letters;* Paullin, *Navy*)

Esek HOPKINS was appointed C. in C. of this fleet of eight vessels purchased and assembled at Philadelphia by the end of the year. The largest were the merchant vessels *Alfred* and *Columbus,* converted into frigates of 24 and 20 guns. Others were the brigs *Andrea Doria* and *Cabot* with 14 6-pdrs. each and the *Providence* (12), *Hornet* (10), *Wasp* (8), and *Fly* (8). The captains, in order of seniority, were Dudley Saltonstall, Abraham Whipple, Nicholas Biddle, and John B. Hopkins. Heading the list of lieutenants was John Paul Jones.

Ice-bound in the Delaware for several weeks after all other preparations were completed, the American Navy put to sea on 17 Feb. '76. Congress had given Esek Hopkins orders to clear the Chesapeake of Dunmore's fleet (see VA. MIL. OPNS.), drive the British from the Carolina coasts, and then run the Royal Navy away from R.I.! This was quite an assignment for eight ships mounting 110 guns; the British then had 78 ships with over 2,000 guns in American waters. But Hopkins took advantage of a discretionary clause in his orders that authorized him to use his judgment in adopting whatever other course of action appeared to be more promising, and he captured NASSAU, 3–4 Mar. Heading for the coast, he took a British armed schooner and a brig before the unfortunate ALFRED–GLASGOW ENCOUNTER, 6 Apr. The American ships put into New London and then went to Providence, R.I. Esek HOPKINS was through as America's first admiral. A court-martial convicted Capt. Hazard of cowardice and John Paul Jones succeeded him as commander of the *Providence*. Although he was placed behind 17 other captains on the seniority list established by Congress in Oct. '76, JONES promptly established himself as the top American naval commander: during the last six months of 1776 he captured or destroyed five transports, two ships, six schooners, seven brigantines, a sloop, and a 16-gun privateer.

During the first two years of the war Lake Champlain was the scene of naval operations that are covered under CHAMPLAIN SQUADRONS and VALCOUR ISLAND, Oct. '76.

Naval supremacy was the cornerstone of British strategy in America during the years 1776–77. It enabled them to evacuate Boston in Mar. '76, to mass a large army on Staten Island for the N.Y. Campaign after dispatching the Charleston Expedition of Clinton; this superiority made the Hudson River a line of operations while confronting Washington with the problems of defending against an amphibious attack toward Philadelphia and such Southern ports as Charleston and Savannah.

FRENCH FLEET FAILURES

Although the French Alliance of early 1778 theoretically ended British naval supremacy, French naval operations off North America were inconclusive until 1781. British and French fleets clashed in European waters off Ushant, 27 July '78, but the results were inconclusive. D'Estaing led a large French fleet to America for a heart-breaking series of failures: he arrived too late to bottle up the British fleet in the Chesapeake (see MONMOUTH CAMP'N.), he failed to attack them at NEW YORK, 11–22 July, he failed at NEWPORT, 29 July–31 Aug., he abandoned a proposed attack on Newfoundland, he sailed for the West Indies where he did some damage to the British but failed to gain any real advantage (see WEST INDIES, Mil. Opns.), and then conducted the fiasco at SAVANNAH, 9 Oct. '79. The French fleet had failed to prevent the British capture of SAVANNAH, 29 Dec. '78, and failed to recapture it in Oct. '79, and failed to stop the CHARLESTON EXPEDITION OF CLINTON IN 1780. The decisive American victory of the war, however, was made possible by the actions of the French fleet of de Grasse in the YORKTOWN CAMPAIGN of 1781.

AMERICAN NAVAL BATTLES

On the high seas, meanwhile, John Paul Jones conducted a remarkable raid in the *Ranger* that is covered under JONES and WHITEHAVEN, Apr. '78. His greatest triumph was in the BONHOMME RICHARD–SERAPIS ENGAGEMENT, 23 Sept. '79. Capt. James Nicholson's TRUMBULL–WATT ENGAGEMENT, 2 June '80, was second in severity. In the TRUMBULL–IRIS ENGAGEMENT, 8 Aug. '81, Nicholson was forced to strike his colors.

A frigate of the Mass. navy won a memorable victory in the PROTECTOR–DUFF ENGAGEMENT, 9 June '80. As captain of the *Alliance* John BARRY proved himself to be an outstanding American commander. The ALLIANCE–SYBILLE ENGAGEMENT, Jan. '83, was the last real naval fight of the war (excepting some privateering exploits). The American naval commander who took the first important prize of the war (the *Nancy*), closed the regular maritime operations of the U.S. by brilliantly eluding pursuit in the West Indies, and his capture of the *Baille* in Jan. '83 netted the last valuable prize taken by a Cont'l. ship; the commander was John MANLEY.

In summary, the raid on Nassau, Mar. '76, was virtually the only planned major operation of the Cont'l. Navy. A total of 53 ships served in the Cont'l. Navy; of the 13 original frigates, only four were at sea by 1777, and only two Cont'l. ships (Barry's *Alliance* and Manley's *Hague*) were in action in 1783. Lack of resources kept the rebels from building anything larger than a frigate, and PRIVATEERING proved to be a more formidable enemy than the British Navy.

Whereas the Cont'l. and state navies did not commission more than 100 ships during the war, the British increased theirs from 270 to 468 ships, 174 of which carried 60 or more guns. The American frigates nevertheless sank or captured almost 200 British warships. Privateers cost the British another 600 ships. The Royal Navy performed miserably under a succession of incompetent admirals and an inept ministry. A haughty reluctance to support army forces in America further reduced their contribution to the war effort. In 1783, however, the British Navy rebounded from adversity, and its successes in the West Indies, European waters, and India enabled Britain to stiffen its terms of peace with America and to convince France and Spain that the war should end. (C. & M., 913)

FRENCH AND SPANISH NAVIES

The French Navy, which had lost 93 ships carrying 3,880 cannon in the Seven Years' War, had only 40 ships of the line and 10 frigates remaining in 1763. Rejuvenated by the Duc de Choiseul and Gabriel de Sartine, successive ministers of marine, the French Navy turned out beautifully designed and efficiently built ships, but her naval commanders seemed reluctant to jeopardize these vessels in action. "French naval philosophy was quite different from the victory-at-any-cost English tradition. The fine ships were not to be risked in all-out decisive action, but preserved to fight another day." (*American Heritage Book of the Revolution*, 278) Only SUFFREN rose above the mediocrity of other French admirals, and he had little chance for distinction in American waters.

The Spanish Navy made a pathetic showing. A French officer is quoted as saying that their ships sailed so badly that "they can neither overtake an enemy nor escape from one." (*Ibid.*) A projected Franco-Spanish invasion of England in 1779 never got far enough for the badly outnumbered British channel fleet to drive it away. (See FRENCH ALLIANCE) Off Cape St. Vincent, Portugal, 16 Jan. '81, in what has been called "one of the few decisive naval actions of the war" (*ibid.*, 282), a Spanish fleet was defeated by the aged George RODNEY.

BIBLIOGRAPHY

G. W. Allen's *Naval History of the American Revolution* uses primary American and British sources to produce a very full narrative of all operations of Cont'l. Navy ships. "Within its sphere it is very nearly definitive, but it has only incidental treatment of the State navies, the privateers..., and of marine administration, which last receives thorough analysis in Charles O. Paullin's *The Navy of the American Revolution*.... Nor does it enter into the fateful large-scale operations of the French, Spanish, and British navies from 1779, which may be followed in Sir William M. James' *The British Navy in Adversity*...." (Lib. of Cong., *Guide*, 446)

As for PRIVATEERING, in his *Massachusetts Privateers of the Revolution* Allen covers the largest portion of that field, since Mass. commissioned 600 commerce raiders. E. S. Maclay's *History of American Privateers* "deserves a back shelf," according to Helen Augur (see below), but she considers Middlebrook's *History of Maritime Connecticut during the American Revolution* (vol. 2) as being "a first-class account of Connecticut privateers...." She also cites Asa E. Martin, "American Privateers and the West Indies Trade, 1776–1777," *Amer. Hist. Rev.,* July 1934.

Helen Augur's *Secret War of Independence,* dealing with the neglected "commercial-maritime-diplomatic complex," is devoted largely to America's war on the seas against British commerce and is valuable for its source citations.

Other important American works are by William B. Clark (*Washington's Navy, Barry*), James Fenimore Cooper (*Lives, History*), Dudley W. Knox (*History, Naval Genius of Washington*), Charles Lee Lewis (*Grasse*), C. H. Lincoln (*Naval Records*), Alfred Thayer Mahan (*Influence of Sea Power, Major Operations*), and H. H. and Margaret Sprout (*Rise of American*

Naval Power). The works of Chapelle present U.S. naval history from the standpoint of marine architecture but skillfully integrate national affairs, naval policy, and naval administration. A basic French work is Louis E. Chevalier, *Histoire de la Marine Française pendant la Guerre de l'Indépendence Américaine* . . . (Paris, 1877). Comprehensive bibliographies are in G. E. Manwaring (*British Naval History*), Pargellis and Medley (*British History*), and Neeser (*Statistical and Chronological History,* vol. I).

U.S. Marine Corps histories have been written by Collum, McClellan, and—now the basic work—Clyde H. Metcalf (1939). William H. English, *Conquest of the Northwest* (1896), includes marine participation.

NAVAL STORES. The term now applies to such pine products as resin, tar, pitch, turpentine, and most of the world's supply comes from the American Southeast. Originally the term included masts and cordage, and before the establishment of the American colonies the main source was the Baltic region. In 1705 naval stores became ENUMERATED ARTICLES.

NAVIGATION ACTS. In accordance with the doctrine of MERCAN-TILISM, Parliament passed a series of "Acts of Trade and Navigation" between 1645 and 1767. There had been earlier acts for the regulation of trade, but the original colonial charters exempted Americans wholly or for a term of years. Although a distinction can be made between navigation and trade acts, they are all known commonly as "navigation acts." (O. M. Dickerson in the *D.A.H.* article with this heading points out that the trade acts were, for the most part, enacted after 1700; the purely navigation acts were those of 1649 and 1651, consoli-dated and modified in 1660, and revised into the final act of 1696.)

NAVIGATION ACTS, 1645, 1649, 1651

Dutch commercial rivalry brought on the Navigation Acts. Starting in the Far East early in the 17th century, Dutch superiority over the English had spread into the Baltic and to the American colonies. By 1650 "the Dutch were exhibiting so many points of superiority over the English, particularly in the naval, mercantile, and commercial fields, that there seemed little chance of English success on the basis of ability alone." (Andrews, *Policy,* 23) The ordinance of 1645 prescribed that products of the whale fisheries could enter England only in English ships manned by English seamen. (MacDonald, *Doc. Source Book,* 55) An ordinance of 1656 restricted foreign trade of the English colonies to English ships. An act of 1649 prohibited importation of French wines, wool, and silk into England, Ireland, and the colonies. In 1650, when opposition to Puritanism in Virginia and the West Indies had led the Commonwealth to declare those colonies in rebellion, foreign ships were required to have a license to trade wtih the colonies. The Act of 1651 prescribed that no goods grown in Asia, Africa, or America could be carried to England, Ireland, or the English colonies except in English, Irish, or colonial ships whose owner, master, and most of whose sailors were British; goods entering England, Ireland, and the colonies had to be transported on ships of the country producing the goods. This was an act of pure coercion against the Dutch carrying trade. Although the Acts of 1645, 1649, and 1651 have each been called "the first Navigation Act," the one mentioned below is more generally accorded that title (MacDonald).

NAVIGATION ACTS OF 1660–1696

Navigation Act of 1660. Known as the Magna Carta of English Commerce (Miller, *O.A.R.*, 5), this is considered by many American historians as the "First Navigation Act." It modified, consolidated, and re-enacted the acts of 1649 and 1651. (Dickerson, *op. cit.*) In addition to prohibiting foreign ships from carrying goods to or from England, and excluding foreign merchants from the colonies, it established a list of ENUMERATED ARTICLES.

Navigation (or Staple) Act of 1663. This prescribed that all but a few commodities must come to the colonies from the British Isles and on British ships. This meant that goods of Continental origin, for example, reached the American market after having their prices augmented by British duties, transportation and handling charges, and middleman's fees. A naval officer, appointed in England, generally enforced this a;t for the Royal Governor in each colony. This act completed the structure of English mercantilism. (Miller, *O.A.R.*, 6) The navigation acts that followed were extensions of those of 1651, 1660, and 1663, and attempts to enforce them.

Navigation Act of 1672. By prescribing that customs be assessed at ports of clearance when ENUMERATED ARTICLES were shipped from one colony to another, this act was designed to stop colonial shippers from evading English duties by shipping to Europe by way of another colonial port. The act was directed primarily at the illicit trade in tobacco. (Note: some authorities give 1673 as the date of this act; I have accepted McDonald's date of 1672.) CUSTOMS COMMISSIONERS were appointed to collect duties.

Navigation Act of 1696. This revised the preceding acts and added provisions for plugging loopholes. It restricted all colonial trade to English-built ships; gave provincial customs officers the same powers, including forcible entry, assigned those in England; expanded enforcement responsibilities of the naval officer established by the act of 1663. This one has been called the last of the purely navigational acts (Channing).

ACTS OF TRADE

The Wool Act of 1699 forbade export of wool products from the American colonies. This act, which also restricted woolen manufacture in Ireland, was passed to protect English producers from Irish and American competition; it illustrates one feature of MERCANTILISM.

In 1705 and 1721 the list of ENUMERATED ARTICLES was expanded, and in 1767 it was decreed that all non-enumerated articles destined for any part of Europe had to be shipped through England.

Naval Stores Acts of various types were passed between 1709 and 1774. In 1729 the cutting of white pines, which were valuable for ships' masts, was restricted to those on private property and cutting of those of 24 or more inches in diameter was restricted to lands granted before 1692.

The Hat Act of 1732 prohibited export of hats from one colony to another and imposed other restrictions on the growing colonial hat industry for the benefit of English manufacturers. A curious feature of the act was the barring of Negro apprentices.

The Molasses Act of 1733, enacted on a plea from planters in the British West Indies, who were being outproduced and undersold by the French and Dutch West Indies after 1715, put prohibitive duties on sugar and molasses imported into the colonies from the

French and Dutch islands. If enforced, the act would have destroyed the New England rum industry and the profitable TRIANGULAR TRADE. The act also deprived the colonies, particularly New England, of a good market and cut off an important source of specie ("hard money"). Evasion of the act by widespread smuggling led England to order use of WRITS OF ASSISTANCE in 1755 and passage of the Sugar Act in 1764 (below).

Iron Acts of 1750 and 1757 were designed to restrict American iron production to England and, at the same time, to stop expansion of iron finishing in the colonies. While prohibiting further construction of rolling mills, steel furnaces, and other finishing plants in the colonies, it admitted colonial pig and bar iron into England without duty.

The Sugar Act of 1764 (Grenville's American Revenue Act) was Parliament's first law for the specific purpose of raising money in the colonies; it was a sequel to the French and Indian (Seven Years') War. Specifically, it perpetuated the Molasses Act of 1733, but reduced duty on foreign molasses by 50 per cent, continued the old duty on raw sugar, and increased the duty on foreign refined sugar; it prescribed new or higher duties on non-British textiles, coffee, and indigo, and on Madeira and Canary wines imported direct; it doubled the duties on foreign goods reshipped from England to the colonies; it added iron, hides, whale fins, raw silk, potash, and pearl ash to the list of enumerated articles; and banned foreign rum and French wines from the colonies. (Morris, *E.A.H.*, 72–73)

Since all the above acts had generally been ignored by the colonies or had been circumvented by smuggling, Grenville took steps in 1764 to end the policy of SALUTARY NEGLECT.

He revitalized the customs system (see CUSTOMS COMMISSIONERS), established a new Vice-ADMIRALTY COURT at Halifax and put through the CURRENCY ACT.

See O. M. Dickerson, *The Nav. Acts and the Amer. Rev.* (1951), L. A. Harper, *The Eng. Nav. Laws; a 17th century experiment in social engineering* (1939), and G. E. Howard, *Prelims. of the Rev., 1763–1775* (1905).

NEGRO APPRENTICES. Under NAV. ACTS see "Hat Act of 1732."

NEGROES IN THE AMERICAN REVOLUTION. In 1775 the 13 colonies had a population of about 2,256,-000, excluding Indians and including 506,000 Negro slaves. (See POPULATIONS for their distribution.) There also were a good many free Negroes. One of the three men killed in the Boston "Massacre," Crispus ATTUCKS, probably was of Negro blood. At the outset of the Revolution Negroes served in the patriot ranks, and the percentage increased as the years went by. The substitute system, which permitted a man to send his slave into the ranks, naturally accounted for the presence of many Negroes in the American armies, but many colored soldiers were free men who had volunteered. Washington's army is said to have averaged about 50 Negroes per BATTALION, and at least 700 were among the 13,500 troops in the Monmouth Campaign. (Miller, *Triumph,* 509; this writer says this many were actually in the *battle.*)

According to a special return of the A.G. dated 24 Aug. '78, the Cont'l. Army included 755 Negroes on that date; 148, or almost 20 per cent, were in the brigade of S. H. Parsons, and 162 were in the three Va. brigades. (Freeman, *Washington,* V, 99 *n.*) A newly raised Negro regiment from R.I. distinguished itself on 29 Aug. '78 when the Americans withdrew from NEW-PORT. This unit and a regiment from Mass. appear to be the only two in which Negro soldiers were "segregated." (Officers of both regiments were white.)

Southerners opposed the use of Negro troops, although all colonies sanctioned slavery and Northern slave traders supported Southerners—Congressional delegates from Ga. and S.C., to be specific —in removing from Jefferson's original draft of the Decl. of Indep. an indictment of George III for protecting the slave trade. (Miller, 508) In 1775 a S.C. delegate moved, unsuccessfully, that Negroes be discharged from the Cont'l. Army; the next year Congress approved their *re-enlistment*. (Note that the CONT'L. ARMY included only regular soldiers, not the militia.) Although Americans and British frequently used Negroes as service troops—to build defenses, and to work on the lines of communications—and occasionally armed them during sieges (at Savannah in 1779, at NINETY-SIX and Dorchester, S.C., in 1781, to mention a few examples)—Southern patriots continued to oppose the enlistment of Negro soldiers until late in the war. In 1779 Congress sent John LAURENS south to enlist 3,000 slaves, whose owners would be compensated at the rate of $1,000 per man, but the planters of S.C. and Ga. refused to sanction the plan. A counter-proposal was made in the legislatures of S.C. and Va. to offer slaves as bounties to stimulate enlistment of whites. (See Miller, 510–11)

Meanwhile the British ran rough-shod over Ga., the Carolinas, and Va., with the white militia doing a remarkably inept job of stopping them. In 1781 Md. raised 750 Negro soldiers to serve in white regiments, and Va. freed all slaves who had served honorably, but the crisis was over before Americans were forced by military ne-cessity to make more use of their Negro manpower. "So ventures which might have given a powerful impulse toward gradual destruction of slavery failed," writes Alden (*South*, 226); slavery survived in the South (and in N.Y.) when the Revolution ended,* but every colony prohibited the *slave trade* during the war.

The British had seen the political, economic, and military advantages of bringing American slaves into their camp. Lord Dunmore of Va., when pushed to the wall by the vigorous patriot movement in 1775, had threatened to cause a slave uprising and then had raised "Dunmore's Ethiopians." (See VA. MIL. OPNS. and GREAT BRIDGE) The British promised freedom to all slaves who served them, hoping thereby to acquire a labor force while ruining the patriot owners. But slaves became booty, and were seized for resale in other British colonies, particularly in the West Indies. Dunmore took almost 1,000 from Va. When Rawdon withdrew before Greene's offensive he left Camden with more than 400 slaves, policed up more on his way back to Charleston, and when the British evacuated that place at the end of the war they took more than 5,000 slaves with them. Considering that Congress had offered to pay owners $1,000 for each slave contributed for military service (see above), one can get a rough idea of what a tremendous property loss this represented, and the South made a great international issue of it. (See JAY'S

* Vt., Mass., and N.H. had abolished slavery by the end of the American Revolution; Pa., R.I., and Conn. had made plans for gradual emancipation, a step which N.Y. did not undertake until 1799. In the Civil War, Lincoln did not authorize the enlistment of Negroes until 25 Aug. 1862.

TREATY, 1794) More pathetic, however, was the fact that the men who had been offered freedom ended up suffering even greater slavery elsewhere. Many British officers made a fortune out of their service in the South. (See MONCRIEFF)

Miller has a good survey of Negro participation in the Revolution and patriot attitudes toward their use as soldiers. See also, George Livermore, "An Historical Research Respecting the Opinions of the Founders of the Republic on Negroes as Slaves, as Citizens, and as Soldiers," a work of over 200 pages in which the author contended in 1862 that the Founders had considered Negroes capable of being citizens and bearing arms and that the Union should adopt the same attitude during the Civil War. The essay was read before the Mass. Hist. Soc. (14 Aug. 1862), printed in their *Proceedings* (Ser. I, Vol. I), and issued separately in four other editions. Lincoln was influenced by the work and gave Livermore the pen with which he signed the Emancipation Proclamation.

See also Benjamin A. Quarles, *The Negro in the American Revolution* (Chapel Hill, N.C., 1961).

NELSON, Horatio. 1758–1805. British naval hero. Appointed in 1770 to a ship commanded by his uncle, Nelson passed his examination as Lt. on 9 Apr. '77, several months before his 19th birthday. He went to the West Indies, served aboard the flagship of Sir Peter Parker, and rose rapidly to command first of the brig *Badger,* then the frigate *Hinchinbrook.* His first active service was in the expedition to NICARAGUA. In Mar. '83 his second combat experience came when he was repulsed in an attempt to retake Turk's Island in the Bahamas from the French.

NELSON, Robert. 1743–1818. Patriot. Va. Born at the Yorktown home of the NELSON FAMILY, he graduated from William and Mary in 1769 and was professor of law there from 1813 to 1818. He served in the army during the Revolution, presumably in the state militia that so ineffectively opposed the British raiders. He was captured with his brother William NELSON by Tarleton in June '81. (Appleton's.)

NELSON, Thomas (Jr.). 1739–1789. Patriot, Signer, militia general, Gov. of Va. Grandson of the founder of the NELSON FAMILY OF VA. and son of the wealthy merchant, planter, and council member known as "President (William) Nelson," Thomas was educated in England. After three years at Cambridge he returned to Yorktown in 1761 and immediately entered the House of Burgesses. In 1764 he took his place on the King's Council. Although in patriot politics he was a conservative, he ardently supported all measures proposed to prepare for war, particularly those urged by Patrick HENRY in Mar. '75. When state regiments were organized shortly thereafter, Nelson became Col. of the 2d Va. in July. He resigned this commission later in the year when elected to fill the vacant seat of Washington in the Cont'l. Cong. Nelson and his fellow-Virginian Benj. Harrison have been described as the "two jovial fat men" of Cong. (Montross, *Reluctant Rebels,* 93) James Adams remarked on Nelson's physique but noted: "He is a speaker, and alert and lively for his weight." (*D.A.B.*) The new Va. delegate played a leading role in getting his state to support independence, and he signed the Decl. of Indep. In May '77 a sudden and serious illness forced his resignation from Congress. In 1779 he was re-elected but after a few months again had to resign. His problem was asthma, which was to lead to his early death 10 years later.

Meanwhile Thomas Nelson had been

appointed B.G. and commander of state forces in Aug. '77. When Cong. called for volunteer units he raised a cavalry troop largely at his own expense and led them to Philadelphia, but they were disbanded when Cong. decided they could not be supported. (According to Heitman, Nelson was commissioned Capt., 1st Va., on 22 Feb. '76 and resigned 7 Aug. '77, presumably when he received the state B.G. commission.) In 1779 the British started a series of devastating raids in Va., and in May of this year Nelson took the leading part in organizing militia resistance. (See VIRGINIA, MIL. OPNS. IN) On 12 June '81 he was elected to succeed the militarily inept Thos. Jefferson and given emergency powers by the frightened refugees of the CHARLOTTESVILLE RAID.

During the six months of his governorship Nelson was virtually a military dictator, which was precisely what the state needed at this period. He struggled to raise the men and supplies to support Lafayette's Expedition (see VIRGINIA, MIL. OPNS. IN), and when Washington and Rochambeau marched south the governor-general was in the field to join them for the kill. The story of how he directed artillery fire against his own house is told in the article on the YORKTOWN CAMPAIGN. In Nov. '81 he resigned, again because of bad health.

"With the victory of the American cause Nelson reaped the ruin of his personal fortune," says D.A.B. In helping to raise the loan of 1780 he had been met with the remark that "We will not lend the government a shilling, but we will lend you, Thomas Nelson, all we possibly can." (Appleton's) This amounted to $2,000,000, and having spent large sums also in equipping and feeding troops Nelson was left a poor man with a wife and 11 children. He moved to a small estate, "Offley," in

barren country not far from Hanover Courthouse. Writing of his visit to this place on 10 Apr. '82 (Gov. Nelson was away but "five or six Nelsons had gathered to receive me"), CHASTELLUX has this to say about Thomas Nelson:

"At the time when the English armies were carrying desolation into the heart of his country, and when our troops arrived unexpectedly to succor and avenge it, he had been obliged to use all means and all possible resources, either to assist Monsieur de La Fayette... or to furnish General Washington with the horses, wagons, and provisions which he needed most urgently. It does no honor to Virginia to add that the only recompense he earned by all his labors was the hatred of a great part of his fellow citizens, and that... he experienced neither the satisfaction of being freed from servitude, nor that emulation which success generally inspires; but instead... he found great dissatisfaction arising from the fact that their horses, wagons, and forage had frequently been 'pressed.' Those laws and customs which would have been wiped out had the state been conquered were now invoked against the defender...." (Travels, 382)

Eight years after his resignation as Gov. and a few days after his 51st birthday he died of asthma. (D.A.B.) According to family tradition (see my dedication in the front of this book) he was buried in an unmarked grave to keep creditors from finding his body and holding it as collateral. D.A.B. says he was buried in the Yorktown cemetery, but does not specify when. The Nelson family tombs may be seen today at Yorktown, where the Nelson house still stands.

NELSON, William (Jr.). 1760?–1813. Cont'l. officer. Va. Of the NELSON FAMILY, he graduated from William and Mary in 1776 and returned to be professor of law from 1803 until his death 10 years later. According to Heitman, he was a militia Pvt. in 1775 and on 29 Feb. '76 became a Maj. in the 7th Va. Cont'ls. If Nelson was born in 1760 as Appleton's says, he would have received his military majority at 15 or 16! Heitman shows him promoted to Lt. Col. on 7 Oct. '76, at which time the commander of the 7th Va. was Wm. CRAWFORD. He resigned on 25 Oct. '77. (Heitman, 58, 411) He and his brother Robert were captured by Tarleton in June '81 (Appleton's); this would have been during the CHARLOTTESVILLE RAID.

NELSON FAMILY OF VIRGINIA. "Scotch Tom" Nelson (1677–1745) came to Va. from Penrith, a town on the English side of the Scottish border that then was part of Scotland. Around 1700 he settled at Yorktown and became a wealthy merchant and landholder. His son Thomas (*c.* 1716–1782), was defeated by Patrick Henry in the first election for Gov. under the new constitution of Va. (29 June '76) He is known as "Secretary Nelson," being secretary of the governor's council for 30 years. "Scotch Tom" had other sons, but the most famous was "President" William Nelson (1711–1772), who was in the Va. Council from 1744 until his death, president of that body for many years, and *ex officio* acting Gov. from the death of Botetourt to the arrival of Dunmore (Oct. '70–Aug. '71). William's eldest son, Thos. NELSON (Jr.), was prominent in the Revolution. Two others, Robert and William NELSON, also achieved some eminence.

"NEUTRAL GROUND" OF N.Y., 1778–1783. The territory east of the Hudson between British positions around N.Y.C. and American positions in the Highlands. Extending roughly 30 miles north and south, it included most of Westchester co. (P. C. Brooks in *D.A.H.*)

NEUVILLE. Two French brothers incorrectly identified in American works as Chevalier de la Neuville and Noirmont de la Neuville, Jr., (!) should properly be known by the family name of PENOT LOMBART. (Lasseray) While indexing them both under PENOT LOMBART, Lasseray uses the following forms of their names: L.-P. Penot Lombart de La Neuville, Lombart de La Neuville, and M. de La Neuville (the elder brother); René-Hippolyte Penot Lombart de Noirmont, and Lombart de Noirmont.

NEVILLE, John. 1731–1803. Cont'l. officer. Va. Son of George Neville, who had acquired large holdings around the headwaters of the Occoquan River in Va. (*D.A.B.*), John took part in Braddock's Expedition of 1755 and then settled near Winchester, where he became sheriff. He later bought large tracts of land near Pittsburgh and became joint holder of an additional 1,000 acres as a reward for his military service. The Va. faction in this disputed region elected Neville a delegate to the Va. convention of 1774, but illness prevented his attending. In Aug. '75 the Va. comm. of safety ordered him to occupy Ft. Pitt, and during the first two years of the Revolution he was commandant of that frontier post. (*Ibid.*) Meanwhile, on 12 Nov. '76, he was commissioned Lt. Col. of the 12th Va. He fought with Washington's army at Trenton, Princeton, and Germantown. On 11 Dec. '77 he became Col. of the 8th Va. and led them in the Monmouth Campaign. Transferred to the 4th Va. on 14 Sept. '78, he was breveted B.G. on 30 Sept. '83.

His land becoming part of Pa. after the war, he held a number of elected posts and became a prominent figure in the Whiskey Rebellion of 1794. After several abortive attempts the mob burned his house and drove him into temporary exile, but he returned with the federal force that put down the rebellion. He died at his estate on Montour's Island, near Pittsburgh. Among his descendants who were important in the region for the next 50 years was his son, Presley NEVILLE.

NEVILLE, Presley. 1756–1818. Cont'l. officer. Son of John NEVILLE, he was born in Pittsburgh (Pa./Va.) and graduated from the College of Philadelphia in 1775. On 9 Nov. '76 he became a Lt. in the 12th Va. (of which his father was Lt. Col.), and transferred to the 8th Va. on 14 Sept. '78. In 1778 he was A.D.C. to Lafayette with the temporary grade of Maj. On 21 Oct. '78 he became Bvt. Lt. Col., on 10 May '79 he was given the regular rank of Capt., and on 12 May. '80 was captured at Charleston. Exactly a year later he was exchanged. After this he became brigade inspector and was elected to the state assembly. He married a daughter of Daniel Morgan, and from 1792 until his death was a merchant in Pittsburgh. His son Morgan Neville (1786–1839) edited the *Pittsburgh Gazette* before moving to Cincinnati about 1824. "He was a pioneer of literature in the west, a skilful musician, and a patron of art." (Appleton's)

NEW BERN, N.C., Aug. '81. On 1 Aug. Maj. James Craig led 250 regulars and 80 Tories north from WILMINGTON on a punitive expedition. Reinforced en route by another 300 Tories, he destroyed rebel plantations along his 75-mile march to New Bern, entered this place on 19 Aug., destroyed property, and returned to Wilmington burning additional Whig plantations.

NEW BRUNSWICK, N.J., was generally known as BRUNSWICK during the Revolution, although both names were used (Freeman, *Washington,* IV, 256 n.; Baurmeister *Journals,* 73 n.). The original settlement was called Inian's [*sic*] Ferry (Scribner's *Atlas,* 23).

NEWBURGH ADDRESSES, 10 and 12 Mar. '83. These were the culmination of officer grievances about arrears in pay, unsettled food and clothing accounts, and the failure of Cong. to make provisions for the life pension of half pay starting 21 Oct. '80, the date they had been promised discharge. The movement, also called the "Newburgh Conspiracy," was what Hatch calls "a carefully laid plot which had friends in Philadelphia and in the government itself" (*Admin. of Amer. Rev. Army,* 159). Early in Jan. '83 a delegation of officers sent Cong. a "memorial" regarding the problems listed above. Maj. Gen. Alexander McDougall headed the committee of senior officers that formulated this document, and it was he who took it to Philadelphia. Organizer of the movement, however, was Col. Walter Stewart, who informed the officers of the army about plans of the Cont'l. Cong. to dissolve the army without acting on their demands (rejected 25 Jan.). He argued that the officers should act in concert to insist that Cong. promptly pay all that had been promised them. "Stewart spread this view everywhere he went in camp . . . , and when he became satisfied that Washington would not take the lead in making demands on Congress he turned to Gates . . . , who proved sympathetic." (Freeman, *Washington,* V, 437 n.) Washington was aware of the discontent among his officers but suspected nothing ominous until 10 Mar., when he was handed a written call for a meeting of general and field officers the

781   NEWBURGH ADDRESSES

next day, and was also given a copy of the fiery and rhetorical appeal subsequently known as the first Newburgh address. The anonymous document proposed that the officers inform Congress that unless their demands were met they would refuse to disband when the war ended, and that if the war should continue they would "retire to some unsettled country" and leave Congress without an army. In General Orders of 11 Mar. Washington denounced the "irregular invitation" and the "disorderly proceedings"; he directed that representatives of all regiments meet on the 15th, presided over by the senior officer present, to decide how "to attain the just and important object in view." Surprised, shocked, and deeply worried (*ibid.*, V, 431–32), the C. in C. reported the developments to Congress. The second address appeared on 12 Mar., expressing the crafty view that the language of Washington's G.O. made him party to the complaints. Washington realized that he would have to step forward at the meeting of the 15th and do all within his power to keep them from going further with their movement.

Visibly agitated (*ibid.*, V, 434), Washington appeared before a tense group of officers on 15 Mar. and read them a statement he had prepared, probably with the help of Jonathan Trumbull, Jr. Commenting that the anonymous addresses showed a good literary style, he criticized them for the implication that the civil authorities were guilty of "premeditated injustice." He denounced the alternatives proposed in the first address. He entreated the officers not to take "any measures which, viewed in the calm light of reason, will lessen the dignity and sully the glory you have hitherto maintained. . . ." Climaxing his appeal with what Freeman calls "the finest phrase with which he ever had exhorted disgruntled, sul-

len or resentful men," Washington said, ". . . you will, by the dignity of your conduct, afford occasion for posterity to say, when speaking of the glorious example you have exhibited to mankind, 'had this day been wanting, the world had never seen the last state of perfection to which human nature is capable of attaining.' " (*Ibid.*, V, 434–35)

Not quite sure that he had convinced his officers that Congress meant well toward them, Washington took from his pocket a letter of Va. delegate Joseph Jones, who had written of the financial problems with which Congress had to cope before it could meet the just claims of the officers. After stumbling over the closely written letter, Washington stopped to get out his glasses and said, in effect, "Gentlemen, you must pardon me. I have grown gray in your service and now find myself growing blind." When Washington left the meeting a few minutes later a few of his most trusted officers took charge and the conspiracy was dead. Against mild opposition from Timothy Pickering, Washington was given a vote of thanks. Then, without dissent the officers expressed their confidence in the justice of Congress and repudiated the "infamous propositions . . . in a late anonymous address."

Washington never knew the entire history of these addresses, but they were the work of Gates's A.D.C., Major John Armstrong, Jr. They were copied by Gates's friend, Capt. Christopher Richmond, and distributed by Maj. William Barber. As previously mentioned, Walter Stewart had fomented the trouble. Armstrong and others considered reviving the movement in Apr., but then abandoned their plans when Armstrong thought they had been revealed to Washington. (*Ibid.*, V, 432, 433 *n.*, 437 *n.*) Horatio GATES either had a change of heart during the "conspiracy" or else lost his nerve.

In his handling of this incident Washington not only spared the young nation a disgrace of the type common in the histories of other peoples, but he also gave evidence of his tremendous personal leadership. "On other occasions, he had been supported by the exertions of an Army and the countenance of his friends," wrote Samuel SHAW, "but in this he stood single and alone."

NEWCASTLE, Thomas Pelham Holles, Duke of. 1693–1768. English statesman. Privy councillor in 1717 and secretary of state under Robt. Walpole in 1724, he held the latter post 30 years. "He was a peculiarly muddleheaded man, and unhappy if he had not more than he could possibly manage, but at the same time he was a consummate master of parliamentary tactics. . . ." (*E.B.*) Despite his mismanagement of foreign affairs and his incompetence in domestic matters, his great wealth and powerful Whig connections, combined with energy and a real skill in debate, kept him in power. In 1754 he succeeded his younger brother, Henry Pelham, as premier on the latter's death. The people, long accustomed to him in his former role, could not accept his incompetence as prime minister. Success of the French expedition against Minorca led to his resignation in 1756. (This was the failure for which Adm. John Byng was shot for neglect of duty.) In July '57 he again became P.M. when he formed the famous coalition with CHATHAM; this was a political expedient whereby Chatham was permitted to handle the matters of state while Newcastle took care of party politics. "Mr. Pitt does everything, the duke gives everything," as Horace Walpole sized it up. Succeeded by Bute in May '62, Newcastle became a strong member of the opposition to George III. He was lord privy seal for a few months in 1765, but his health was failing and he died in Nov. '68.

NEW HAVEN, Conn., 5–6 July '79. Plundered during CONN. COAST RAID.

NEW JERSEY CAMPAIGN, Nov. '76–Jan. '77. After the fall of FT. LEE, N.J., 18 Nov. '76, Washington retreated to Newark. His 16,400 troops were at this time distributed as follows:

At Newark, 4,400 men, including those that had been at Hackensack, Ft. Lee, and in the FLYING CAMP;

At Brunswick and Rahway, to guard against amphibious operations, Gen. Alexander ("Stirling") had 1,000;

At White Plains, N.Y., under Chas. Lee, were more than 7,000, including some of the best troops (Lee's division and those of Sullivan and Spencer);

At Peekskill, N.Y., were 4,000 men under Heath to guard the Highlands of the Hudson.

As early as 10 Nov., after the battle of White Plains and before loss of the Hudson River forts, Washington had writtten Lee: "If the enemy should remove the whole, or the greatest part of their force, to the west side of Hudson river, I have no doubt of your following with all possible dispatch, leaving the militia and invalids to cover the frontiers of Connecticut &c in case of need." On 20 Nov., Washington suggested that Lee cross the river and there await further orders. The next day Washington reiterated that Lee should make this move, unless "some new event should occur, or some more cogent reason present itself. . . ." Having received no specific order, Lee clung to his contention that his force could best be used east of the Hudson to guard against any move Howe might attempt toward New England. On 21 Nov., the supercilious Lee wrote to Adj. Gen. Reed that, since he had no means of crossing the Hudson at Dobbs Ferry with his own forces in time to give Washington any assistance, he had ordered Heath to send Washington 2,000 men by way of Kings Ferry, which was closer to Heath's position than to Lee's. At a time when reinforcement by Lee "was in reality a matter of life and death" (Freeman, *Washington,* IV, 261), this action raises the suspicion that Lee's ambition to succeed Washington as C. in C. was being carried so far as to include deliberately jeopardizing the American cause by allowing the British to defeat the forces under Washington's personal command.

Howe, meanwhile, continued to exhibit a talent for missing strategic opportunities: he did not elect to move against Heath and clear the line of the lower Hudson for operation in conjunction with British forces from Canada; he did not choose to capitalize on the possibilities of subduing New Enggland by way of Conn.; nor did he see fit to move in the direction of Philadelphia with his entire force, an operation that would have captured the rebel capital and—more important—that might well have destroyed Washington's army. Instead, he got ready to bed down for the winter. As a preliminary to operations against New England in the spring, Clinton sailed from N.Y.C. with 6,000 men to take NEWPORT, R.I. To gain space for part of the British forces to winter in N.J., Cornwallis was to pursue Washington beyond Brunswick. Boasting that he would catch Washington as a hunter bags a fox, Cornwallis approached Newark on 29 Nov. Washington retreated to Brunswick, and from there his paltry 3,400 effectives escaped across the Raritan with so little time to spare that they could only partially destroy the bridge before the arrival of jäger advance guards. After this final march of 20 miles in a single day through heavy rain and over poor roads, Cornwallis was forced to stop and rest his troops.

Leaving Alexander at Princeton as a delaying force, Washington reached Trenton on 3 Dec. with the rest of his troops. Here he was distressed to learn that Lee was still several days away. Having already assembled boats to ferry his troops across the Delaware, and having evacuated all supplies and equipment not needed for operations, Washington crossed his troops into Pennsylvania on 7 Dec. and deployed them on an overextended 25-mile front. His right front was opposite Burlington, N.J., and his center was in the vicinity of McKonkey's Ferry (now Taylorsville), N.J. The Americans seized or destroyed all boats they could find along a 75-mile stretch of the lower Delaware to hamper British efforts at further pursuit.

Having missed his fox, Cornwallis got permission to stop at the Delaware. There is evidence that Howe's failure to employ his entire strength in this pursuit was because he had instructions not to end the war by military action if some peaceable method remained. (Fuller, *Battles,* 21, citing Belcher) His offer of amnesty, announced in Nov., brought Loyalists to his camp in large numbers. The N.J. militia had failed to muster, desertions further weakened the already dispirited patriot force, and there was no reason to expect that Pennsylvania, "a state not hitherto distinguished by its exertions in the cause of American independence" (Miller, *Triumph,* 153), would give Washington much support. On 13 Dec., therefore (the day Lee was captured at BASKING RIDGE), Howe announced he was through campaigning for the season. The preceding day Congress had resolved to move from Philadelphia to Baltimore.

Howe was inclined to pull back to a line between Brunswick and Newark, a plan supported by Clinton. However, Cornwallis prevailed on him to deploy farther forward; principal posts were therefore established at Bordentown, Pennington, and Trenton, with a base 25 miles to the rear at Brunswick. Although this forward strategy exposed these posts to defeat in detail and made for vulnerable lines of communications, the dispositions were justified on the grounds that the Americans were too contemptible a military threat to justify the normal strategic precautions. Furthermore, withdrawal would have indicated British weakness and would also have deprived a great many N.J. Loyalists of military protection. Although Howe's proffer of pardons won a great many Americans over to the King, the misconduct and brutality of his troops —particularly the Hessians—had made bitter enemies and staunch rebels out of a greater number. "Residents may have expected to lose their horses and livestock to the enemy," writes Peckham, "but the pillaging advanced to the robbery of food, silver plate, jewelry, bric-a-brac, and blankets. Officers helped themselves to wine, books, and furniture. The camp followers, like harpies, even stole clothing for themselves and their children." (Peckham, *War for Indep.*, 46–47)

WASHINGTON STRIKES BACK

The American cause had reached a critical point, but as often happens when professionals are up against amateurs, an upset was in the making. Thomas Paine's first number of *The Crisis* helped set the stage. Gen. Thos. MIFFLIN was sent on a whirlwind tour of Pa. to whip up support, accomplishing what "was probably one of the most important missions of the war." (Miller, *Triumph.* 153) By 5

Dec., Washington had started getting reinforcements. On the 20th, Sullivan joined with 2,000 bedraggled troops, the remnants of 5,000 Lee had belatedly brought to Washington's support. Gates arrived with 500 ragged and ill-equipped men from Schuyler's Northern command. Col. John Cadwalader appeared with 1,000 Philadelphia ASSOCIATORS, and Col. Nicholas Haussegger brought his regiment (or battalion) of Md. and Pa. Germans. (Advance elements of both units had joined Washington on 5 Dec.)

By Christmas, Washington had about 6,000 men listed, somewhat imprecisely, as fit for duty. Since the British could resume their offensive when the Delaware froze hard enough to support troops, and since Washington's force would be reduced to about 1,400 with the expiration of enlistments on 31 Dec., Washington issued orders for a blow against the scattered British garrisons.

As every schoolboy knows, Washington crossed the ice-choked Delaware on Christmas night and defeated the Hessians at TRENTON, N.J., 26 Dec. '76.

When he returned to the south bank of the Delaware on 27 Dec., Washington found himself in "a tight hair shirt of time" (Freeman's phrase). The British were still capable of resuming their offensive by crossing the Delaware as soon as it iced over sufficiently to support the movement of troops; despite Howe's announcement, Washington did not believe that the British were really through for the winter. Washington's one hope, therefore, was to launch a spoiling attack, but he had only four days—until 31 Dec.—before most of his army would dissolve upon expiration of enlistments. Furthermore, since adequate rations to prepare his men for an operation were not expected until 29 or 30 Dec., he could count on only one day for his offensive.

Although Cadwalader had not been able to accomplish his mission of crossing the Delaware and attacking the German garrison at Bordentown on 26 Dec., this resolute general did get across the morning of the 27th. When he learned of Washington's withdrawal, Cadwalader decided to remain on the left bank, and he took advantage of the enemy's withdrawal (caused by the news of the Trenton raid) to occupy Burlington. He then proposed that Washington lead a portion of the main army to Crosswicks, about four miles east of Bordentown, to trap the German garrison of the latter place while he attacked it from Burlington. Hard as Washington tried to find some way of executing this aggressive and promising plan, he was unable to get his troops rested and resupplied in time. Another tantalizing opportunity developed when Gen. Mifflin moved from Philadelphia toward Burlington with 500 fresh troops and with more to follow. (Mifflin's recruiting efforts had succeeded only in Philadelphia itself.)

START OF PRINCETON CAMPAIGN

On 30 Dec., Washington started back across the Delaware, although at the time he could not see how a sustained operation might be conducted. In cruelly cold weather, forcing their way through ice that was thick enough to obstruct boats but too thin to allow passage by foot, marching through snow that drifted six inches deep in places, the Americans returned to abandoned Trenton. "Then, coldly but apparently with a certain confidence, Washington played his last card, the one that pessimists might have considered decisive, one way or the other, in the gamble of American independence." (Freeman, *Washington,* IV, 331) Having earlier decided on the necessity of offering a special—and

completely unauthorized—$10 bounty to all who would extend their term of service six weeks beyond the end of 1776, on 30 Dec. Washington succeeded in exhorting many of his New Englanders into standing by the Va. Continentals a few more weeks. The next day Mifflin's skilful address to Hitchcock's Brig. at Crosswicks (Cadwalader's command) got a high percentage of these troops to remain a while longer with the colors. The evening of 31 Dec., copies of the Congressional resolutions that granted WASHINGTON'S "DICTATORIAL" POWERS arrived at Trenton.

Washington started 1777 with not more than 1,600 troops, about 1,100 of whom were the volunteers who had extended their enlistments, and the remainder were Va. Continentals. In addition, a few N.J. and Pa. militia were available for subsidiary tasks. From the sketchy information available, Washington knew that as many as 6,000 enemy troops were located in N.J., most of them at Brunswick and Princeton. Another 1,000 were reported on the move from Amboy. In striking contrast to his errors in scattering his forces for the defense of New York City, Washington now ordered a concentration of troops at Trenton. Muddy roads would make this movement slow, so while Cadwalader's militia marched from Allentown and Crosswicks, and Mifflin's moved from Bordentown, a strong covering force was sent out to delay the expected enemy approach from Princeton.

This outpost was made up of Fermoy's Brig., Hand's, Haussegger's ("German"), and Scott's (Va.) regiments, reinforced with a detachment with two cannon of Forrest's Btry. On 1 Jan. they were in position along Five Mile Run, and on the next day, while Cadwalader's units were still arriving at Trenton, the British appeared on the road from Princeton. Fermoy inexplicably left the advanced position for Trenton, but Edw. Hand commanded the delaying action with great skill. After forcing the enemy to deploy for a coordinated attack, which cost them more than two hours, Hand dropped back in good order and with few casualties. Half a mile north of Trenton the Americans took advantage of a ravine to make the British deploy once more. The covering force then continued their delaying action through the town (about 4 P.M.) and finally reached the main battle position south of Assumpink Creek. About sunset, which would have been around 4:45 P.M., the Americans easily repulsed what Stryker calls "a feeble and unsupported effort" to storm the bridge. Washington had achieved his vitally important purpose of delaying a coordinated attack on his main position during daylight, an attack that could hardly have failed to destroy him. All American units conducted themselves well, except the German Bn., which had been swiftly routed and whose commander, HAUSSEGGER, "surrendered under somewhat suspicious circumstances." (Freeman, *Washington,* IV, 343)

However, the Americans were in a bad spot: they could not expect to resist an attack on 3 Jan., and they were vulnerable to envelopment; they lacked boats for an escape across the Delaware, even if this operation had been otherwise possible; retreat south along the left bank would have only postponed disaster. Another course of action was open, however, and it caught Cornwallis flatfooted: leaving his camp fires burning, Washington slipped out of his positions during the night to execute the brilliant strategic envelopment that led to the battle of PRINCETON, 3 Jan. (See p. 286 for British criticism.)

The American army then went into winter quarters at MORRISTOWN, N.J.

On 6 Jan., other American contingents captured Hackensack and Elizabethtown.

CRITIQUE

In a campaign that Peckham calls "The Nine Days' Wonder," Washington had driven Howe from all his posts in N.J. except Amboy and Brunswick. Although 5,000 British remained in each of the latter places, they presented no strategic threat.

"This considerable feat had been accomplished by an army of fewer than 5,000 ragged, shoeless, ill fed, poorly equipped, often defeated amateur soldiers, mostly militia, operating against twice that number of veteran professionals, abundantly supplied with all martial equipment, and within a space of eleven days in the depth of winter." (Ward, *War of Indep.,* 318)

Howe's failures in this campaign have been discussed above, and Col. Rall's contribution to Washington's success at Trenton is covered under the article on that battle. Cornwallis, an aggressive commander, ignored the advice of his quartermaster general, Sir Wm. Erskine, to attack the night of 2–3 Jan. But the British Army historian, Fortescue, in justifying Mawhood's fight at Princeton (when he might better have escaped with his entire force), points out that it would have been difficult for any man "to divine that Washington, who was credited with the glaring blunders of the past campaign, could be capable of movements so brilliant and so audacious." (Fortescue, *Br. Army,* III, 201)

Bibliography. The standard reference is Wm. S. Stryker, *The Battles of Trenton and Princeton,* Boston, 1898. T. J. Wertenbaker's article, "The Battle of Princeton" in *The Princeton Battle Monument* (1922), is commended by Freeman as "the work of a trained historian ... based on a careful study of the ground...." More recent works are: Leonard Ludin, *Cockpit of the Revolution: The War for Independence in New Jersey,* Princeton, 1940; and Alfred H. Bill, *The Campaign of Princeton ...,* Princeton, 1948.

NEW LONDON RAID, Conn., 6 Sept. '81. As a diversion to draw strength from the allied army marching south for the Yorktown Campaign, Benedict Arnold proposed an amphibious expedition into Conn. New London was picked as an objective because it contained important rebel stores, was close to N.Y.C. (135 miles), and was in an area well known to the traitor Arnold, who was born and reared in the vicinity. The town was on the west bank of the Thames River and about three miles from its mouth. A mile below New London and on the same side of the river was a small work called Ft. Trumbull; oriented for protection of the harbor and virtually defenseless from the land side, it was occupied by 24 state troops under Capt. Adam Shapley. Across the river was Ft. Griswold (on Groton Heights), a square fortification with stone walls 12 feet high, surrounded by a FRAISED ditch, having outworks, and held by 140 militia under Lt. Col. Wm. Ledyard.

Arnold planned a night attack, but the north wind held him off the mouth of the river until 9 A.M. on 6 Sept. He landed at 10 o'clock on the west bank with the 38th Regt., two Tory regiments (the Loyal Americans and the American Legion), a detachment of jägers, and some guns. Lt. Col. Eyre landed on the other side of the river with the 40th and 54th Regts., the 3d Bn. of N.J. Vols., a jäger detachment, and artillery. Capt. Millett was detached from Arnold's column with four companies of the 38th (subsequently joined by Capt. Frink's Tory company) to take Ft. Trumbull. Capt. Shapley delivered one volley of grape and musketry, spiked his eight guns, and crossed to reinforce Ledyard at Ft. Griswold. Arnold, meanwhile, pushed on to New London after encountering some resistance from a body of townsmen at "Fort Nonsense" and being fired on by an old, iron 6-pdr. as he got closer to his objective. In New London his mission of destruction was aided by Loyalists. A committee appointed after the war estimated his damage at $485,980. (See WESTERN RESERVE) Lossing says 143 buildings were burned, including 65 dwellings that left 97 families homeless. (II, 43 *n.*) About 12 ships were destroyed, but 15 escaped up the river with personal effects of the townspeople. (*Ibid.*) Arnold was accused of viewing the scene "with the apparent satisfaction of a Nero" (*ibid.,* 44), but he claimed his men made every effort to put out the fires that started accidentally.

Ft. Griswold, meanwhile, resisted fiercely for 40 minutes against repeated attacks. Eyre was mortally wounded in the first assault, and Maj. Montgomery was killed as he mounted the parapet. (Ward says Shapley bayoneted Montgomery; Lossing says a Negro got him with a spear.) Ledyard was stabbed with his own sword after surrendering it to Lt. Col. Van Buskirk of the N.J. Vols. and then bayoneted to death. (Lossing, however, says Maj. Bromfield, another Tory, was the murderer. *Op. cit.,* 44) "It is also asserted," says Heath, "that upon the foregoing taking place, an American officer, who stood near to Col. Ledyard, instantly stabbed the British [Tory] officer who stabbed the colonel; on which the British [including the Tories and Germans] indiscriminately bayoneted a great number of Americans." (*Memoirs,* 321)

American losses at Ft. Griswold were reported by Gov. Trumbull as 70 to 80 killed, all but three of them after the surrender. (*Ibid.*) Arnold reported that 85 were found dead in the fort, and 60 wounded, most of them mortally. (Quoted in C. & M., 731) Total American losses (including those on the west bank) were about 240 (Ward, *W.O.R.,* 628); Arnold says 70 of these were captured, "besides the wounded, who were left paroled."

Arnold lost 48 killed and 145 wounded (*ibid.*), which testifies to the stubborn defense of Ft. Griswold.

This was the last action in the North during the Revolution. It contributed nothing to the British war effort, and it further blackened Arnold's name. While it is strange that Arnold would deny his guilt in destroying New London and nearby Groton if he were really guilty, and we must remember the record of American PROPAGANDISTS, there is evidence that the atrocity was deliberate. (See, for example, Ward, *op. cit.,* 908 *n.*)

NEW ORLEANS as a source of Spanish military aid. When the British naval blockade cut off normal routes of American supply from Europe the colonists turned to Spanish New Orleans. Although the Spanish were careful to avoid war with Great Britain they had selfish reasons for furnishing supplies to the rebels. Oliver POLLOCK was invaluable as the intermediary between American agents and the Spanish authorities starting in 1776, and the rebels were able to purchase weapons, ammunition, blankets, and such critical medical supplies as quinine. These supplies were moved up the Mississippi under the Spanish flag, which got them safely past British posts above New Orleans. Under the governorship of Gálvez, who succeeded Unzaga in 1777, the support became even more signifi-

cant. (See POLLOCK) French entry into the war opened the Atlantic routes of supply in 1778 and the Spanish alliance in 1779 eliminated the need for secrecy in the river trade, which by then had lost most of its importance. (*Concise D.A.H.,* 889)

NEWPORT, R.I., Sept. '77. An amphibious operation from Tiverton against Rhode Island was cancelled at the last minute when Joseph SPENCER learned that his plan had been compromised.

NEWPORT, R.I., 29 July–31 Aug. '78. Franco-American failure. In Dec. '76 Sir Henry Clinton was sent with 6,000 troops and a large supporting fleet to occupy Newport, and in the summer of 1778 Gen. Robt. Pigot held the place with a garrison of 3,000. Gen. John Sullivan commanded 1,000 American regulars at Providence. When it became apparent that the recently arrived French fleet under d'Estaing could not attack the British ships inside Sandy Hook (see NEW YORK, 11–22 July '78), Congress proposed an attack on Pigot at Newport.

In preparation for this combined operation—which looked like a sure thing —Washington called for 5,000 New England militia. He also sent Lafayette with the veteran brigades of Varnum and Glover to support Sullivan, and he sent Nathanael Greene, a native of R.I. Although the militia did not complete their concentration until about 10 days after the French fleet arrived, 6,000 of them showed up with John Hancock at their head. This gave Sullivan an army of 10,000. In accordance with Washington's instructions, he organized it into two divisions, one under Greene and the other under Lafayette. D'Estaing had an impressive fleet and several thousand men he could detach for land operations.

The French fleet reached R.I. (Point

Judith) on 29 July and established contact with the American army. Despite the tone of exaggerated compliment to Sullivan in d'Estaing's early communications,* there was friction between the two allied leaders from the start. (Freeman, *Washington,* V, 65) "Where Washington or Greene would deferentially have suggested cooperation," says Freeman, "Sullivan had written in plain, direct words, 'I wish ... your Excellency would make a show of landing your troops ... ' and again, 'you will move your ships ...' " (*Ibid.*) Furthermore, the general-turned-admiral was unimpressed by Sullivan's preparations: "we found that the troops were still at home," d'Estaing wrote in his report of 5 Nov. Lafayette was supposed to be bringing soldiers; "he appeared with nothing but militia," said the Old World warrior about the two crack Cont'l. brigades of Varnum and Glover. Water and provisions were not supplied as expected.

D'Estaing, nevertheless, agreed to Sullivan's plan of operations. On 8 Aug. he would enter the Middle Passage, running the British defenses. The night of 9–10 Aug. Sullivan would move his troops from Tiverton to the N.E. tip of Rhode Island and prepare to attack south. Early the next morning the French were to land as many men as possible on the west side of the island, opposite the Americans, bombard the enemy fortifications from the water,

* On 3 Aug., for example, d'Estaing wrote Sullivan: "I fear that you left on my table a plan, which I have had the presumption to keep, because anything made by yourself is too precious a keepsake.... I beg you, Sir, to be kind enough to accept some pineapples and two barrels of fresh lemons...." (Quoted in Montross, *Rag, Tag,* 293–94)

and the ground forces would assault. As a preliminary, on 5 Aug. the remarkable Adm. SUFFREN led two frigates up the Sakonnet (East) Passage and caused such panic that the British destroyed their fleet, one way or another: the 32-gun frigates CERBERUS, *Juno, Orpheus, Lark,* the 16-gun *Kingfisher,* and *Pigot* galley all ran aground and were destroyed by their captains; the *Flora* (32), *Falcon* (18), and several transports were scuttled to bar the French from Newport harbor. (Ward, *W.O.R.,* 589–90) On the 8th the French moved up the Middle Passage according to plan.

Then the trouble started. Early 9 Aug., learning that the British had evacuated their works on the northern end of the island, Sullivan crossed to occupy them before the enemy returned. Tradition has it that d'Estaing was offended by this breach of military etiquette—the Americans landing ahead of the French, and without prior notification. The point is academic, however, since French eyes were straining seaward even before d'Estaing received Sullivan's message requesting that the French land contingent come ashore. About noon the British fleet was seen appearing off Newport.

"Lord Howe's fleet from New York had arrived at the worst conceivable time—when the French warships were high up the Middle Channel and d'Estaing's sick were on Conanicut, and Sullivan's troops had been landed where they might be cut off and destroyed in event of a decisive British naval victory." (Freeman, *op. cit.,* 62. Freeman points out that, contrary to some reports, the landing of French sailors on Conanicut Island was not part of the plan of attack but a measure of relief for scurvy victims.)

For the student of military history— or the armchair strategist, to be less pedantic about it—the situation presents an interesting problem: should d'Estaing continue to be guided by the original plan of action, or would it be strategically more sound to sail forth to meet this new threat? At mid-20th century this matter of military doctrine is still being disputed, with army adherents saying they should not be abandoned under such circumstances, and with the navy and air force partisans saying the army is best served by their destroying the strategic threat.

NAVAL ACTION OFF NEWPORT, 10–12 AUG. '78

Adm. John Byron had reached N.Y. with four ships after d'Estaing's departure, and with this reinforcement Adm. Richard Howe headed to the support of the British garrison of Newport on 1 Aug. Unfavoring winds delayed his arrival until the 9th, by which time the enemy fleet was inside the bay. On that day the wind continued from the south, compelling the French to keep their position, but during the night it shifted to the north and about 11 o'clock the morning of 10 Aug. d'Estaing started out to do battle with a fleet two thirds his strength. (Mahan, *Sea Power,* 362) Here is Mahan's account of what happened:

"Howe, though surprised by this unlooked-for act,—for he had not felt himself strong enough to attack,—also made sail to keep the weather-gage. [See WEATHER GAGE] The next 24 hours passed in maneuvering for the advantage; but on the night of the 11th of August a violent gale of wind dispersed the fleets. Great injury was done to the vessels of both, and among others the French flag-ship 'Languedoc,' of 90 guns, lost all her masts and her rudder. Immediately after the gale [14th Aug.] two different English 50-gun ships, in fighting order, fell in

the one [*Renown*] with the 'Languedoc,' the other [*Preston*] with the 'Tonnant,' of 80 guns, having only one mast standing. Under such conditions both English ships attacked; but night coming on, they ceased action." (*Op. cit.,* 362)

Ward says the *Marseilles* (80) and the *Preston* (50) fought until darkness, without decisive result, and that the *César* (74) was worsted by the *Isis* (50), but not put out of action. (*Op. cit.,* 591) The British intended to renew the action on the 14th, but most of their ships were unseaworthy and other French ships appeared, so Howe withdrew to N.Y. and d'Estaing returned to Newport. "Scarcely a shot had been exchanged between the two fleets," comments Mahan, "yet the weaker had thoroughly outgeneralled the stronger." (*Op. cit.,* 363)

THE AMERICANS CARRY ON

The 48-hour storm punished the American troops severely, but on 15 Aug. they pushed toward Pigot's lines. Still expecting assistance from the French, Sullivan started regular approaches on the eastern side of the line, apparently leaving the other side for the French. When d'Estaing reappeared on the 20th, however, no entreaties could prevail on him to debark the men he had taken back on board his ships the 9th. At midnight of the 21st he sailed off to Boston for repairs. (Lafayette rode to Boston in an unsuccessful effort to talk d'Estaing into returning. Trying not to miss the battle he felt was shaping up, he rode the 70 miles in slightly over seven hours and returned in six and a half. He got back only in time to take part in the withdrawal from the island. [Lossing, II, 84])

Despite the punishment they had taken from what was long known around Newport as "the great storm," the American militia remained with Sul-

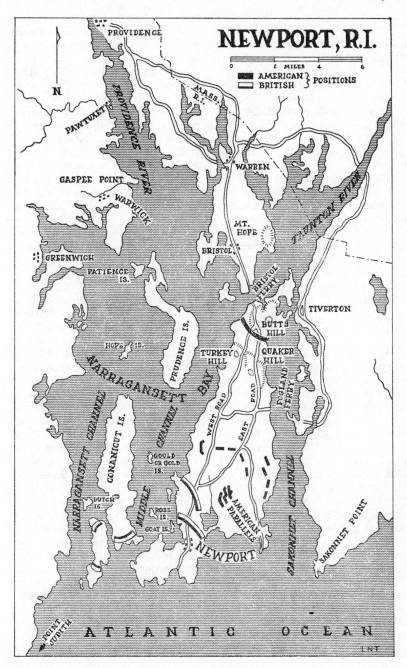

NEWPORT, R.I.

livan and apparently were full of fight —particularly since Pigot's annihilation looked like a sure thing. News of the French withdrawal, however, led to wholesale desertions. Meanwhile, Sullivan's siege operations showed little promise of success against works recently strengthened by the British; now the little American army was in trouble. "To evacuate the island is death," wrote Greene on the 22d; "to stay may be ruin."

After issuing general orders on the 24th that intemperately commented on "the sudden and unexpected departure of the French fleet," Sullivan reassured his men that the enemy was still so inferior in strength that "nothing can tempt them to an Action" and ordered siege operations continued. The eveing of the 28th, however, he started withdrawing.

BATTLE OF RHODE ISLAND, 29 AUG.

Pigot was on his heels, and the light infantry covering forces of Col. Henry Beekman Livingston on the east road and Col. John Laurens on the west road had to be reinforced before they could stop the British pursuit temporarily. Pigot had pushed three columns forward and he now prepared to attack. On the American left (east), Gen. Prescott had been advancing with the battalion companies of the 38th and 54th Regts. Gen. Francis Smith had advanced up the east road with the flank companies of these two regiments and with the 22d and 43d Regts. Pigot reinforced him with the battalion companies of the 54th and with Brown's Provincial Regt. Gen. von Lossberg had been advancing up the west road (against Laurens) with a body of Hessians led by jägers under Capt. von der Malsburg. Two Ansbach Regts., the Hessian Regt. Huyn, and Fanning's

Provincial Regt. moved forward to complete Lossberg's command after contact was made with the American delaying force.

Sullivan's forces had fortified Butts's Hill, on the N.W. end of the island near the Bristol Ferry. Here, about 12 miles from Newport, the Americans made a stand when they learned of Pigot's pursuit, and between 7 and 9 A.M. on the 29th their covering forces were driven back to that position. Greene had advocated counterattacking to wipe out Lossberg's jägers and Ansbachers while they were still unsupported by Huyn and Fanning, but he was overruled in a dawn council of war and the enemy were allowed to form on Turkey and Quaker Hill, about two miles to the south. (Lossing, II, 80 [map], 83)

The British right wing attacked but were stopped by forces under Nathanael Greene. Here the brigades of Varnum and Glover were located, and the latter drove the enemy back to Quaker Hill in confusion. British ships, meanwhile, moved up the Middle Channel and delivered enfilade fire against the American right, and Malsburg took positions from which field guns could be brought to bear on this flank. (Baurmeister, 210) With this advantage, and supported by four vessels, the British shifted their main effort to envelop Sullivan's right, but Sullivan reinforced this wing and held off three assaults. Between 2 and 3 P.M. the final enemy attempt was repulsed by effective American fire—artillery and musketry—and they retreated in disorder to Turkey Hill, leaving many dead and wounded. A newly raised R.I. regiment of Negroes under Col. Christopher Greene is mentioned as having shown "desperate valor" in repelling three "furious assaults" by Hessian regulars. (Amory, *Sullivan,* quoted by Ward, *op. cit.,* 592)

Both forces kept up a heavy artillery fire for another hour, and desultory musket fire continued until dark.

Pigot sent back to Newport for additional artillery, and Sullivan made a show of preparing to receive his attack. The night of 30–31 Aug., however, the Americans successfully executed the dangerous operation of evacuating the island. Glover's Marbleheaders again performed their specialty and ferried most of the troops to Tiverton. A smaller number of troops crossed to Bristol, where the heavy baggage and stores had been sent earlier. It was a clean getaway, and it did not happen a day too soon—Clinton reached Newport the morning of 1 Sept. with 5,000 troops!

American losses were 30 killed, 137 wounded, and 44 missing out of an estimated 1,500 who were engaged on 29 Aug. The British (including Tories and Germans) lost 38 killed, 210 wounded, and 12 missing. (Greene, *Rev. War*, 154, citing official reports) The heavy engagement took place on a hot, sultry day, and a number of fatalities were due to heat stroke. (Lossing, *op. cit.*, 83)

Sullivan's army was now reduced by departure of the militia to 1,200 regulars. With these he moved back to Providence. Adm. Howe sailed with Clinton's troops to Boston, but withdrew without attacking d'Estaing's fleet. On the way back to N.Y. Clinton detached Gen. Chas. Grey for operations covered under BEDFORD–FAIR HAVEN RAID, Mass., 6 Sept., and MARTHA'S VINEYARD, *c.* 8 Sept. '78.

COMMENT

As is usual after a military disappointment, uninformed public opinion clamored for a scapegoat and the French were the obvious choice, thanks largely to Sullivan's poor judgment. The day the fleet sailed for Boston, Sullivan and his generals signed a letter of protest saying that d'Estaing's peremptory departure and other actions, "stain the honor of France, are contrary to the interests of His Most Christian Majesty, are most pernicious to the prosperity of the United States, and an outrageous offense upon the alliance between the two nations." * Later, "—his ambition balked and his utter defeat not improbable—Sullivan lost his head," says Freeman, and on 24 Aug. he said this in general orders:

"The General cannot help lamenting the sudden and unexpected departure of the French fleet.... He yet hopes the event will prove America is able to procure with her own arms that [which?] her Allies refused to assist her in obtaining.* * * " (Quoted in Freeman, *op. cit.*, 70 *n.*)

Although Lafayette was as opposed to d'Estaing's departure as were the others, and did all he could to prevent it, he hotly defended d'Estaing when the Americans spoke of his "desertion." On 25 Aug. he wrote Washington: "I am more upon a warlike footing in the American lines than when I came near the British lines at Newport."

Getting news piecemeal of these undiplomatic developments, Washington tried to repair the damage. On 2 Sept. he wrote Lafayette as the first step toward restoring harmony. When he had "curbed the tongues of his own lieutenants," as Freeman puts it, he wrote d'Estaing a letter of "balanced caution and confidence." (*Op. cit.*, 75)

---

* This quotation is from Bonsal, *French*, 46, citing French Naval Archives. In Freeman, *op. cit.*, 68, the wording is slightly different; it would appear that Bonsal re-translated into English a French translation of Sullivan's original.

John Hancock, Gates, Greene, and others did what they could. In a resolution of 19 Sept., Congress thanked Sullivan and his subordinates for their performance (on the battlefield, not at the writing table), and specially mentioned Lafayette's personal sacrifice in riding to Boston and his gallantry during the evacuation.

Popular feeling against the French meanwhile had reached the point that there might be trouble in Boston about getting their ships repaired; it was suggested that Newport had excellent facilities. On 5 Sept. the young Chevalier de Saint Sauveur was mortally wounded when he tried to stop a Boston mob from pilfering a bakery established by the fleet in the town. Three or four French sailors were killed at Charleston when a riot was directed against the French. D'Estaing was able to conceal his ire, and the Mass. House of Delegates resolved to erect a monument over Saint Sauveur's grave.*

Preceded by the failure outside NEW YORK, 11–22 July '78, and followed by the fiasco at SAVANNAH, 9 Oct. '79, d'Estaing's performance at Newport did not ease the task of his successor, Rochambeau. The latter reached Newport on 10 July '80 to find that his first enemy was the memory of d'Estaing.

NEWTOWN, N.Y., 29 Aug. '79. (SULLIVAN'S EXPEDITION) Leaving Tioga on 26 Aug. with 4,000 troops, Sullivan advanced slowly up the left (east) bank of the Chemung River. Maj. John Butler, who had been watching Sullivan's build-up from Genesee, had by this time joined his son Walter 14 miles from Tioga, and they moved with their 250 Rangers and 15 men of the British 8th Regt. to combine forces with the

* Not so promptly, on 24 May 1917 (sic) to be exact, the resolve was carried out. Bonsal, op. cit., 48.

800 Indians and Tories under Joseph Brant around the destroyed village of Chemung. Against John Butler's judgment—the Indians insisted on making a stand—an ambuscade was prepared near Newtown, about six miles S.E. of modern Elmira. A log breastwork was built along a ridge parallel to the river, the left anchored against a steep hill and the right protected by a defile. (Swiggett, Niagara, 198) Having carefully camouflaged this position, their plan was to throw the rebel column into confusion by a surprise fire from the flank and then to sally forth from both ends of their line and rout Sullivan's army. Brant and Capt. John McDonnell (a Loyalist who had been with Brant at Cherry Valley) commanded the Indians and Tories on the right, which was the least vulnerable sector. The Rangers and regulars formed the left, under Walter Butler, and the center, under John Butler.

About 11 A.M. the advance guard of Sullivan's column approached the ambuscade and, fortunately, the Va. riflemen who constituted this forward element were better soldiers than the Indian scouts who had led Herkimer into a similar trap at Oriskany. The column halted and organized an attack. The three companies of Morgan's riflemen who made up the advance guard under Maj. James Parr were attached to Enoch Poor's Brig., and Poor was directed to envelop the enemy left. James Clinton's Div. was to follow in support. The guns were to take positions on a height from which they could enfilade the enemy line. (For Order of Battle details, see SULLIVAN'S EXPEDITION.)

In a well-managed maneuver through difficult terrain and against sporadic musket fire, Poor led his column onto the steep hill the Butlers had expected to protect their flank. The New Englanders charged with the bayonet and the artillery opened up about the same time. According to John Butler, "the shells bursting beyond us made the Indians imagine the enemy had got their artillery around us and so startled and confused them that great part of them ran off. . . ." (Quoted in Swiggett, *op. cit.*, 198)

Brant held many of his Indians with him, however, and the defenders fought like wildcats to stop the force of Cont'l. veterans that outnumbered them at least five to one. Col. John Reid's 2d N.H., on the right of Poor's Brig., was hit on three sides by a savage counterattack and would have been wiped out if help had not arrived promptly. Col. Henry Dearborn turned back with his 3d N.H., and two of Clinton's N.Y. regiments came forward to support Reid. Meanwhile, the brigades of Hand and Maxwell worked their way along the river and got on the enemy's right flank. The defenders, now faced with annihilation, managed to break contact and retreat safely to Nanticoke, five miles away. Some of Sullivan's troops pursued less than half that distance, but the patriots failed to exploit their advantage. "They move with the greatest caution," commented John Butler.

Rebel losses were only three killed. Dearborn says 33 were wounded and other estimates run as high as 50 wounded. One cannot credit such CASUALTY FIGURES. Butler admitted the loss of five killed or captured and three wounded, which is another peculiar set of figures. Stone says 11 dead Indians were found on the field, eight more were killed during the pursuit, and 14 bodies were found hidden under leaves. (*Border Warfare*, II, 23)

Lt. Wm. Barton of the 1st N.J. wrote in his journal of skinning two dead Indians "from their hips down for boot legs; one pair for the Major and the other for myself."

COMMENT

Newtown could have been an important victory if the rebel forces had been commanded by a less mediocre general than John Sullivan. He should have been able to capitalize on enemy blunders (that is, electing to fight at Newtown and failing to withdraw as soon as it became apparent that the ambuscade had failed); with a superiority of four to one, Sullivan should have annihilated Brant and the Butlers. Richard Cartwright, military secretary to John Butler, says a major error was in allowing the artillery to open fire and scare off the Indians before Poor completed his envelopment. This, however, is the military judgment of a quill driver, with the advantage of hindsight. Sullivan's sin was the eternal one of failure to pursue.

NEW YORK, 11–22 July '78. D'Estaing at the bar. On 8 July d'Estaing reached the Delaware Capes after taking 87 days to get there from Toulon. Three days earlier the British fleet completed ferrying Clinton's army from the vicinity of Sandy Hook (heights of Navesink), where they had marched after evacuating Philadelphia. (See MONMOUTH) Although the incredibly slow passage of the French fleet across the Atlantic had saved the British fleet from being trapped in the Delaware, Adm. Richard Howe's problem now was "to defend a practicable pass . . . against nearly double his own force." (Mahan, *Sea Power*, 360) D'Estaing's problem, on the other hand, was to get ships drawing 27 feet across a bar where there was no more than 21 feet of water at low tide.

D'Estaing wasted no time off the Delaware when he saw there was no enemy fleet to engage and no promise of making contact with Washington. After 87 days at sea he had many sick aboard and was low on water and provisions, so on the 9th he sailed north to reach Sandy Hook on the 11th. Here the American pilot who had come aboard off the Delaware reneged on his promise to take the fleet inside the Hook. It was not until 16 July that John LAURENS reached the fleet to establish liaison between d'Estaing and Washington, but he brought no plan of action since this depended on whether the French ships could cross the bar.

After days at anchor off the treacherous coast while the best available pilots were consulted, d'Estaing was told they could take his ships in only "when a northeast wind coincided with a strong spring tide." (Quoted in Bonsal, *French*, 45) According to Mahan these conditions existed on the 22d and after getting into position for the attempt, "D'Estaing's heart failed him under the discouragement of the pilots." (*Op. cit.*, 360–61) Actually, the admiral had decided on the 20th to leave N.Y. and was heading for Newport the morning of the 22d. "A gust of wind, just as we were sailing, all but forced us over the bar, and at the instant when we had no desire to cross," he says wryly in his report. (Quoted in Freeman, *Washington*, V, 51 and *n.*)

Many writers have echoed Mahan's verdict that abandonment of the enterprise indicates d'Estaing's inferiority as a naval commander. Whereas a Nelson or a Farragut might or might not have been able to damn the difficulties and charge in to win the Revolution at N.Y., d'Estaing certainly made every reasonable effort. The American authorities must have thought so at the time, because on 17 July Washington received a letter from Congress proposing the operation against NEWPORT. (Freeman, *op. cit.*, 50) Independently and almost simultaneously the French commander had the same thought.

The FRENCH ALLIANCE was off to a bad start, however, and until d'Estaing left to be succeeded by Rochambeau it would get worse.

NEW YORK ASSEMBLY SUSPENDED. 1767–69. On 13 Dec. '65 Gen. Gage asked Gov. Moore to request that the N.Y. Assembly make provisions for complying with the QUARTERING ACTS. The Assembly refused full compliance (Jan. '66), contending that their colony, being Gage's Hq., would be unfairly burdened by the act. On 13 June '66, Moore again informed the Assembly that provisions should be made for quartering troops expected in N.Y.C. On the 19th, the Assembly again refused full compliance, pleading insufficient financial resources. A period of mounting tension led to a clash between soldiers and citizens on 11 Aug. On 19 Dec. '66, the Governor ended the session of ("prorogued") the Assembly, which had again (15 Dec.) refused to support the Quartering Act. On 15 June '67 royal assent was given Townshend's act suspending legislative powers of the N.Y. Assembly, effective from 1 Oct. until it should comply with the Quartering Act. About the same time, the Assembly had finally voted some funds for troop support, and the Governor used this as a basis for not carrying out the suspension. But when the Board of Trade reviewed the matter in May '68 it ruled that Assembly acts after 1 Oct '67 were invalid. After a new assembly was dissolved for failure to cooperate, a third one, elected in Jan. '69, made the required provisions for quartering when it voted an appropriation of £2,000 in Dec. '69. The patriots considered this a betrayal by the Assembly, and the ensuing friction between soldiers and citizens culminated in the Battle of GOLDEN HILL, 19 Jan. '70.

NEW YORK CAMPAIGN. 1776. Even before being forced from Boston, the British C. in C., Gen. Gage, started looking to New York as a new base. He wrote Dartmouth to this effect on 12 June '75—five days before Bunker Hill—and as early as Aug. '75 started secret preparations. Howe succeeded Gage a month later, and adopted Gage's plan of remaining in Boston during the winter. This appeared to be sound strategy, since the Boston garrison was in no apparent danger and reinforcements were being sent from England.

Washington's seizure of DORCHESTER HEIGHTS in Mar. '76, however, upset Howe's timetable by making Boston suddenly untenable. He did not yet have the strength he thought necessary for an offensive in New York; furthermore, he had hundreds of Loyalists to evacuate. So Howe moved from Boston to Halifax. The CANADA INVASION of Montgomery and Arnold put Howe further behind schedule: diversion of troops to the St. Lawrence delayed his departure from Halifax until June '76; diversion of field equipment to Quebec forced him to wait on Staten Island until Aug., when other equipment arrived from England. (Whitton, 126)

AMERICAN DEFENSES AROUND N.Y.C.

Chas. Lee had been detached from the Boston army in Jan. '76 to raise volunteers in Conn. (since Washington could spare no troops) for the defense of N.Y.C. When he finally reached the city, 4 Feb., Lee soon saw that the strategic problem practically defied solution. "What to do with the city, I own, puzzles me," he wrote on 19 Feb. "It is so encircled with deep navigable waters that whoever commands the sea must command the town."

Manhattan Island is bounded on the west by the Hudson, or North, River, a broad, deep estuary that offered the British navy almost unlimited strategic license; on the other hand, the river would prevent any significant American troop movement to or from New Jersey. The East River is a crooked waterway, with many hazards to navigation, that winds some eight or ten miles from New York's Upper Bay to Long Island Sound, presenting the British with numerous possibilities for amphibious operations. Lee's scheme of defense called for 4,000 to 5,000 troops on Long Island with primary emphasis on the fortification and defense of strategic Brooklyn Heights, which dominated N.Y.C. Another piece of critical terrain was Kings Bridge, which connected the northern tip of Manhattan Island with the mainland; with their naval superiority the British could land troops to attack this point from the Hudson or from Long Island Sound and, if successful, cut off all American forces on Manhattan Island.

It should also be pointed out that the British had a fine anchorage at Narragansett Bay, R.I., about 135 miles from N.Y.C. Closer to the city they had anchorages off Sandy Hook and in the Lower Bay. LONG ISLAND SOUND (see map accompanying that article) provided Adm. Howe's warships and transports with a line of operations that presented many amphibious possibilities: a strategic penetration to seize the line of the Hudson; landings along the Conn. shore; or landings on Long Island.

Charles Lee reasoned that although N.Y.C. could not be made a tenable fortress it could be "made a most advantageous field of battle, so advantageous, indeed, that if our people behave with common spirit, and the commanders are men of discretion, it might cost the enemy many thousands of men to get possession of it."

When Washington arrived in N.Y.C.,

13 Apr., to establish his headquarters in the city, he hurried construction on the fortifications that Lee had planned but on which little work had been done. Lee had been in N.Y. only a month before Congress sent him to CHARLESTON. From his departure, 7 Mar., until Washington's arrival five weeks later, the troops around N.Y.C. had been commanded by Wm. ALEXANDER ("Lord Stirling") and then—when the brigades of Heath, Sullivan, Greene, and Spencer arrived from Boston—by Putnam. (These brigades had started moving to N.Y. on 18 Mar., the day after Howe evacuated Boston.)

The Americans dug like prairie dogs, throwing up numerous fortifications in and around N.Y.C. during the five months that Howe's offensive was delayed. By the time the British arrived Washington had 19,000 troops present and fit for duty, although his authorized strength was 28,500 officers and men. He had little artillery, no cavalry, and no naval support. Most of his troops were green Continentals and untried militia, poorly armed, badly equipped, and led by amateurs.

STATEN ISLAND

On 25 June Howe arrived off Sandy Hook with three ships, the vanguard of his force from Halifax. Five days later he had 130 ships in New York's Lower Bay, and on 2 July he landed unopposed on Staten Island. His 9,300 troops from Halifax were joined on 12 July by Adm. Lord Howe, the general's elder brother, with 150 more ships and reinforcements from England. These were followed by German mercenaries and more British troops from England. When the battered expedition from CHARLESTON arrived 12 Aug., Gen. Howe mustered 31,625 of all ranks, 24,464 of whom were effectives fit for duty on 27 Aug. (Whitton, 344 n., cit-

ing H. F. Johnston) Adm. Howe supported his brother with 10 ships of the line, 20 frigates (totaling 1,200 guns), numerous transports, and 10,000 seamen. These were professional soldiers and sailors, well armed and abundantly supplied, the largest expeditionary force England had ever sent overseas. (This last statement, although supported by Christopher Ward and J. F. C. Fuller, may be disputable.)

AMERICAN DISPOSITIONS

To meet the bewildering variety of strategic combinations that Howe might employ against him, Washington had dispersed his meager forces. Nathanael Greene had 4,000 troops on Long Island with the primary mission of holding Brooklyn Heights; the rest of Greene's Div., Smallwood's Md. and Haslet's Del. Continentals, his best troops, were on Governor's Island. The divisions of Putnam, Spencer, and Sullivan, plus some Conn. militia, were in and around N.Y.C. Of Heath's Div., Mifflin's Brig. of 2,400 was at Ft. Washington, and Geo. Clinton's 1,800 troops were at KINGS BRIDGE. (For troop dispositions after Howe started his offensive, see LONG ISLAND, 27 Aug. '76.) The recently created Pa. FLYING CAMP, under Hugh Mercer, was at Amboy, N.J. Back in Boston, too far away to figure in the campaign, was the garrison commanded by Artemas Ward.

OPERATIONS BEGIN

A small British naval force passed the American batteries in the Hudson and anchored in TAPPAN SEA (now Tappan Zee), 12–18 July.

On LONG ISLAND, 27 Aug., the Americans were soundly beaten in a well conceived and professionally executed tactical operation. Howe's failure to follow through, and Washington's greatness in the face of disaster, led to the masterful American evacuation from LONG ISLAND, 29–30 Aug.

A fruitless PEACE CONFERENCE ON STATEN ISLAND, 11 Sept. '76, took place during the two and a half weeks before the British resumed the offensive.

BATTLE FOR MANHATTAN

As Washington coped with strategic problems that would have staggered a better general, he continued to struggle with the continual problem of holding enough patriots together to constitute an army. The militia were going home in masses, Connecticut's contingent dwindling from 8,000 to 2,000 in a few days. Morale of the troops that remained was rock bottom; natural dejection following their defeat on Long Island was compounded by disorganization, lack of supplies, fatigue, bad weather, and—perhaps most serious—by a justifiable lack of confidence in their leaders.

Washington reorganized his forces into three "grand divisions." Putnam's Div. comprised Parsons' Brig. of Conn. and Mass. regiments, James Clinton's and Fellows' brigades from Mass., Scott's N.Y. Brig., and Silliman's Conn. Brig. Greene's Div. (commanded by Spencer until Greene returned 5 Sept. from convalescence) included Nixon's Brig. (Hand's Pa. riflemen); Varnum's and Hitchcock's R.I. brigades; and Prescott's, Little's, and "Late Nixon's" brigades from Mass. The third division, commanded by Heath, consisted of Geo. Clinton's N.Y. Brig. and Mifflin's brigades (Magaw's and Shee's Pa. troops; Hutchinson's, Sargent's, and Andrew Ward's Conn. troops; Haslet's Delawares; and the remnants of Smallwood's Md. Regt.). (Source: Ward, *W.O.R.*, 239, citing Fitzpatrick and H. P. Johnston.) Washington estimated his strength at 20,000 effectives, of whom one fourth were sick (Freeman, *Washington*, IV, 182).

Whether to abandon N.Y.C. was the big question at this time. Greene's arguments that the town should be burned and abandoned were endorsed by Joseph Reed, Putnam, and John Jay (who was a large N.Y.C. property-holder). Congress resolved on 3 Sept., however, that the town not be damaged; this group based its decision on the belief that if N.Y.C. were lost it could be recaptured, whereas Greene had argued that this would be impossible without naval superiority. After a council of war on 7 Sept., the day after learning of the resolution, Washington decided to leave Putnam's Div. of 5,000 men in the town, to post Heath's 9,000 to defend the area between Harlem and Kings Bridge, and to deploy Greene with five brigades, mostly militia, to repel landings along East River.

"Such a disposition was of course fatuous," as Fortescue says. (*Br. Army.*, III, 187) Washington had spread his forces over 16 miles, with the weakest part in the middle.

When Washington wrote Congress on 8 Sept. that these dispositions were due largely to a belief among those attending the council of war that Congress wanted N.Y.C. defended, he was promptly informed that he could not put that particular monkey on the back of Congress. On 14 Sept. Washington received Congress' resolution of the 10th that they had never expected him to "remain in that city a moment longer than he shall think it proper. . . ." Meanwhile, Greene and five other officers had persuaded Washington to hold another council of war to reconsider his "fatuous" decision; on 12 Sept. it was voted 10 to three that the entire area on Manhattan south of Ft. Washington be evacuated as soon as supplies could be withdrawn. (The three dissenters were Joseph Spencer, Geo. Clinton, and Wm. Heath. Alex. McDougall, at whose headquarters the second council of war was conducted, later characterized these three as "a fool, a knave, and an honest, obstinate man." [*McDougall Papers*, N.Y.H.S., cited by Freeman])

It was too late, however; lacking adequate transportation, Washington was still trying to evacuate supplies when the British attacked—his "fatuous" troop dispositions had not been corrected.

The tides now being favorable for amphibious operations, Howe resumed the offensive. Clinton urged a bold course of action to seize Kings Bridge, thereby cutting off and destroying most of the American army. Howe favored a less ambitious plan. He did not want to make a direct assault against the city because this would damage houses needed for winter quarters (Miller, *Triumph*, 133). Although anticipating American withdrawal from the city, he still thought that a landing at Kip's Bay, believed to be lightly defended, could trap a sizable part of the rebel army (C. & M., 461); he also hoped to draw Washington into a general engagement. (Miller, *op. cit.*, 134)

In a series of preliminary moves, the *Rose* towed 30 flatboats into Wallabout Bay (L.I.) on 3 Sept., but was forced by American batteries on Manhattan to drop back, with considerable damage, to Newtown Creek. On 10 Sept. the British occupied strategic MONTRESOR'S ISLAND. Four other frigates moved up the East River on 13 Sept. and were joined the next day by another warship and six transports. On the other side of Manhattan, three warships and an armed schooner ran the Hudson River batteries on 15 Sept. and anchored above the American works, not only cutting off further evacuation of supplies from N.Y.C. by water but also presenting the threat of a landing.

At this same moment Howe's troops undertook their successful landing at KIP'S BAY, 15 Sept. '76.

For a second time Washington had disposed his troops in such a way that they could be annihilated; for a second time Howe had failed to follow up an excellent tactical move and capitalize on Washington's error. While Howe and the first wave waited at Murray Hill for the second wave to reinforce them, Washington reformed his army on strong defensive terrain at Harlem Heights. (See MURRAY HILL MYTH)

After the repulse of his impetuous advance guard at HARLEM HEIGHTS, 16 Sept., Howe did not resume the offensive for a full month. Meanwhile, the NEW YORK CITY FIRE, 20–21 Sept., destroyed a large portion of the city.

THE FT. WASHINGTON TRAP

During the month's respite accorded by the British, Washington grappled with a new strategic dilemma: whether to hold Ft. Washington or abandon it. So long as he held the strongly entrenched position on Harlem Heights there was no problem. But when Howe executed his strategic envelopment by way of THROG'S POINT, 12–18 Oct., and PELL'S POINT, 18 Oct., Washington was forced to abandon his Harlem Heights position to avoid being trapped by a British move against Kings Bridge. Ft. Washington was then isolated.

Although the British had previously run ships through the line of obstructions that stretched across the Hudson between Forts Washington and Lee (Constitution), there was reason to believe that this barrier might be sufficiently strengthened to become a serious obstacle. Furthermore, Congress had expressed its desire that the river be closed to British ships, if this could be done. Washington finally accepted the advice of a council of war that Ft. Washington be held as long as possible;

Greene, the commander on the ground, was to be responsible for exercising the judgment as to how long was "possible." This decision was made shortly before the British landing at Pell's Point (18 Oct.); subsequently Washington was too occupied with the advance of Howe's main body toward White Plains to concern himself with Greene's situation at Ft. Washington. On 27 Oct., the day before the action at White Plains, two British frigates moved close to Ft. Washington while a land force started maneuvering in front of the fort's southern outworks. "The whole undertaking was a quick failure," writes Freeman. "One of the frigates was mauled remorselessly; the British infantry did not attempt to assault even an isolated redoubt. The comment at White Plains doubtless was that this affair vindicated the judgment of those officers who had insisted that the North River could be made impassable and Fort Washington impregnable...." (*Washington*, IV, 226–27)

At WHITE PLAINS, N.Y., 28 Oct., the main forces again clashed. Using his preferred tactics, envelopment, Howe took Chatterton's Hill on the American right flank. That night Washington withdrew five miles to North Castle, where better defensive terrain was located. Howe had missed another chance to destroy the American army. After scouting thoroughly in the direction of the new defensive position, he halted his offensive against the main American army and turned south to capture bypassed FT. WASHINGTON, 16 Nov. This operation netted him almost 3,000 prisoners and a large quantity of matériel. Although this was a staggering blow to the patriot cause, it is interesting to speculate on whether that cause did not benefit from it in the long run. Howe had sufficient land and naval strength to "contain" this fort while concentrat-

ing on the pursuit and destruction of Washington's army, which would have ended the war. If he failed to catch and destroy Washington—a most likely assumption, to judge from his past performance—Howe should still have been able to capture the fort.

FT. LEE, N.J., was taken by the British on 20 Nov.; although more matériel was captured, the garrison escaped. Since the battle of Long Island the Americans had lost some hundreds of lives, much precious equipment, and more than 4,400 prisoners. Howe had captured N.Y.C. for a new base of operations, and he had opened the line of the Hudson. But he had failed to destroy the American army; that is to say, he had failed to destroy the American Revolution.

For subsequent events, see NEW JERSEY CAMPAIGN.

(Notes on authorities. The works of H. P. Johnston, the basic authority on the battle of Long Island and the subsequent retreat [Ward, *op. cit.,* 453] are listed in the main bibliography. Documents he collected to be appended to John Jay's "Centennial Oration" make the latter "the standard authority" [Freeman, *op. cit.,* 200 *n.*]. Although Freeman speaks highly of Thomas W. Field, Ward finds that Field's "fervor, excitability, and one-sidedness... disqualify him as a reliable historian" [*op. cit.,* 453]. Bliven's *Manhattan* covers the Kip's Bay and Harlem Heights actions in detail, building on the research of Johnston and others to relate the 1776 geography of Manhattan to modern N.Y.C.)

NEW YORK CITY FIRE, 20–21 Sept. '76. Shortly after midnight 20–21 Sept. a fire broke out in a wooden house near Whitehall Slip and spread rapidly north with a stiff breeze. A shift of wind at about 2 A.M. confined the fire to an area between Broadway and the North (Hudson) River, but 493 houses were destroyed before British troops and citizens of the city could put out the flames. (C. & M., 471) The British accused the Americans of setting the fire, but the N.Y. Historical Society has been unable to find any proof of this. The fire caused the British army great inconvenience, since they had counted on billeting troops in the city. Washington commented, "Providence, or some good honest fellow, has done more for us than we were disposed to do for ourselves." (Congress had prohibited destruction of the city to deny the enemy its use.)

NEW YORK VOLUNTEERS. Three Provincial battalions raised by Oliver DE LANCEY (the elder) fought with the British. One of them, under James De Lancey, remained in the North. The others, commanded by John Harris CRUGER and George TURNBULL served in the South, going there in Dec. '79 for the capture of SAVANNAH. One is identified by Ward as taking part in the capture of Ft. Montgomery, N.Y., Oct. '77. (W.O.R., map on p. 517)

NICARAGUA. On the assumption that he could count on support not only of the local Indians but also of the Spanish settlers, Gov. Dalling of Jamaica proposed an expedition to move up the San Juan River into the Lake of Nicaragua to Grenada and Leon; thereby establishing a chain of posts across Central America, the ambitious Dalling proposed to cut Spanish America in half. On 3 Feb. '80 a force of 400 regulars under Capt. Polson sailed from Jamaica. They were escorted by Capt. Horatio Nelson of H.M.S. *Hinchinbrook,* who was to continue with the expedition up the river to the lake. After spending three weeks at Cape Gracias á Dios, where they were joined by a small flotilla from the Black River Settlement and a contin-

gent of local Indians, the expedition made its way slowly to the mouth of the river that was to be their axis of advance. Various delays were encountered, but on 1 Apr. the flotilla started up the river. Sweltering heat and a rapid current slowed them to only five to ten miles a day. Ft. San Juan surrendered on 29 Apr. after a six-day siege. By the middle of May the expedition had been stopped by sickness before they could reach the lake, and Col. Kemble, who had assumed command, left a garrison at the fort and withdrew to the sea. Dalling had planned to send only 400 reinforcements to complete his operation once the Lake of Nicaragua had been reached. He ended by sending an estimated 1,400 in all to Nicaragua; by the end of Sept. only 320 were left alive, and not a half were fit for duty. On 8 Nov. '80, Dalling ordered Ft. San Juan demolished and the expedition abandoned.

The man who was to become Lord Nelson distinguished himself by his impetuous energy during the advance up the river. In the siege of Ft. San Juan the British strength was so reduced by sickness and exhaustion that "almost every gun was laid either by Nelson or by Lieutenant [Edward] Despard, the chief engineer." Fortescue comments that the disastrous expedition "is remembered chiefly by the fact that Nelson took part in it and came out alive. Judging by the medical certificate upon which he was invalided, it was almost a miracle that Nelson recovered." (*British Army,* III, 303, 339–40 and *n.*)

NICHOLAS, Samuel. Senior Cont'l. Marine officer. A native of Philadelphia, he was appointed Capt. of Marines on 28 Nov. '75, and his commission was confirmed prior to that of any other officer of the Cont'l. naval service. He led the storming of Fort Montagu, NASSAU, 3–4 Mar. '76, and on 25 June was promoted to Maj. He commanded the Marine Bn. that reinforced Washington's army at Trenton and Princeton, 2–3 Jan. '77.

NICOLA, Lewis. 1717–1807. Cont'l. officer. France–Ireland–Pa. In discussing the problems with which Washington coped during the summer of 1782, after the Yorktown victory and before the peace treaty, D. S. Freeman writes this:

"Worst if briefest of these exasperations was the preposterous and plundering suggestion of Col. Lewis Nicola ... that America become a monarchy with the Commander-in-Chief as king. 'Be assured, sir,' Washington wrote in reply, 'no occurrence in the course of the war has given me more sensations ... I must view [this] with abhorrence and reprehend with severity'—a statement that led Nicola to expostulate, though with some dignity."

Of this man who appears only once in Freeman's seven-volume biography, he adds the footnote: "Nicola is sketched in *DAB*. He was a considerable figure." (*Washington,* V, 416 and *n.*)

All Heitman has to say about him is that he was from Pa., served as Col. of the Invalid Regt. from 20 June '77 to the end of the war, and was made Bvt. B.G. on 30 Sept. '83.

This remarkable man whose bid to change the course of American history got such short shrift was of Huguenot stock. According to Louise B. Dunbar's article in *D.A.B.*, which is the basis of the following sketch, he "appears to have been born in France ... and to have been educated in Ireland." He came to Philadelphia from Dublin about 1766, at which time he already had 26 years' service as an army officer. By 1770 he was a Philadelphia merchant, editor of *The American Magazine ...*, operator of a circulating library, and as member of one of the city's two scientific organizations he had negotiated the merger that formed the American Philosophical Society. In 1774 he became a justice in Northampton co. and established a home there. "He was," as Freeman says, "a considerable figure."

Approaching 60 years of age when the Revolution started, Nicola apparently had no ambitions for military duty in the field, but he "frequently displayed his aptitude for framing ingenious projects for public service." (*D.A.B.*) Early in 1776 he became barrack master of Philadelphia and from Dec. '76 until Feb. '82 was town major in command of the "home guards." In June '77 Congress put him in command of the Invalid Regiment, and among the useful duties he found for these incapacitated veterans was the instruction of recruits. Meanwhile he had been active as a recruiting officer and had published three military manuals: *A Treatise of Military Exercise* (1776), *L'Ingénieur de Campagne: or Field Engineer* (1776), and *A Treatise, on the Military Service, of Light Horse and Light Infantry* (1777), the last two being translated from French. For about two years starting in the summer of 1781 Nicola was with the main encampment of the army around Newburgh. His letter to Washington proposing that a monarchy be established was written in May '82. This solution to the problems stemming from weak central government by Congress and the Confederation was by no means original with Nicola; "similar sentiments were held by numerous persons," comments *D.A.B.*, "but Nicola was not their spokesman." Needless to say, Congress did not know about his proposal that they be put out of business and they innocently included him among the 26 officers breveted B.G. in their resolution of 30 Sept. '83.

He held various offices in Philadelphia until 1798, when he moved to

Alexandria, Va. His name is sometimes given as Nichola (the form preferred by Appleton's), and he may be the Ludwick Nichola of Berks co. who was naturalized in Philadelphia on 18 Nov. '69. (*D.A.B.*) A few years before he moved to Alexandria his name appeared officially as Nicolas. (*Ibid.*) Louise B. Dunbar sums up his remarkable life by saying:

"Nicola frankly regarded public appointments as a means of livelihood where 'private advantage' should 'coincide with the public utility.' He discharged his public trusts with much diligence." (*D.A.B.*)

NINETY-SIX, S.C. Before the Revolution this was a stockaded village on the "Charleston Path" into Cherokee territory. Its name came from the erroneous belief that it was 96 miles from Ft. Prince George, the frontier post. The straight-line distance actually was less than 65 miles. (Scribner's *Atlas*, 56) It was the center of conflict between Tories and patriots of the region in 1775 (see next article). When the British conquered Ga. and the Carolinas they established an important post at Ninety-Six: in addition to being a healthful site, already fortified to a degree, it was so located as to maintain contact with the Indians, to provide a base for the strong Tory element in the region, and to threaten the "Over Mountain" settlements. One reason why Cornwallis reacted so promptly to Morgan's movements before the battle of COWPENS was because he thought Morgan's objective was Ninety-Six. The most important action took place at NINETY-SIX, 22 May–19 June '81 (see below).

NINETY-SIX, S.C., 19 Nov. '75. As tension mounted between patriots and Tories, the S.C. Council of Safety sent Wm. H. Drayton and the Rev. Wm. Tennent inland during the month of Aug. '75 to organize patriot forces. Tory leaders Thos. Fletchall, Moses Kirkland, Robt. and Patrick Cunningham, and Thos. Brown reacted by taking the field with a body of armed supporters. In Sept., 1,000 patriot militia under Drayton were confronted near Ninety-Six by a larger force under Fletchall. Drayton persuaded the Tories to disperse, but they were later encouraged by his inability to rally militia and took the field again. On 19 Nov. about 600 patriots under Maj. Andrew Williamson were driven into Ninety-Six by 1,800 Tories. After two days and a little bloodshed a truce was arranged and the forces again separated. (Alden, *South,* 200) The sequel is covered under REEDY RIVER.

NINETY-SIX, S.C., 22 May–19 June '81. (SOUTHERN CAMPAIGNS OF GREENE) Being the most important interior post after Camden, Ninety-Six was Greene's major objective when the British abandoned Camden. Rawdon ordered Ninety-Six evacuated, but his message was intercepted. At the time of Greene's approach this strategic post had been considerably strengthened by Lt. Haldane, a British army engineer. On the east end of the stockaded village was a strong, star-shaped redoubt encircled by a ditch and abatis; it was known as the Star Redoubt. Connected by a covered way to the west end of the village was a stockaded outpost called Fort Holmes whose purpose was to protect parties going for water from the little stream across which ran the covered way. Niney-Six was garrisoned by 550 Tories under the command of Col. John CRUGER. Provincial units were the 3d Bn. of De Lancey's N.Y. (150 men), the 2d Bn. of N.J. Vols. (200 men), and Col. Andrew Devaux's S.C. militia (200 men). The Northern troops were veterans who had started their operations on Long Island and who had been seasoned not only by the partisan warfare of the South but also by service with British regulars at Savannah, Charleston, and around Camden; they were dedicated Loyalists who believed that loss of their fort would mean the massacre of Tories in the region. Provisions were adequate, but their artillery was limited to three 3-pdrs.

The rebel army under Greene reached Ninety-Six on 22 May. With Lee's Legion detached to support Pickens' militia in the siege of Augusta (22 May–5 June), Sumter still off fighting his own war and refusing to conform to Greene's strategy, and with Marion dogging Rawdon's heels from Camden to the vicinity of Charleston (Monck's Corner) and then patrolling the lower Santee (after taking GEORGETOWN, S.C., 29 May)— with all these detachments, Greene had fewer than 1,000 regulars at Ninety-Six. He hoped to be reinforced by Lee and Pickens when they captured Augusta, and he hoped that Marion and Sumter could help by blocking British forces that might march against him from Charleston, but he had to start operations against a strong position with the forces immediately available. Aside from an unknown and unreliable number of untrained militia, Greene had the following troops: 427 Md. and Del. Cont'ls., 431 men of the Va. Brig., Kirkwood's 60 Del. light infantry, and 66 N.C. militia. These are rank and file present and fit for duty. Lacking heavy artillery, Greene had no choice but to undertake formal siege operations by regular approaches.

On the recommendations of his engineer, Kosciuszko, Greene—who was inexperienced in this type of operation —made two errors right at the beginning: he directed his main effort against the strongest point of Cruger's defenses, the Star Redoubt, instead of against his water supply; and he started his works too close to the enemy's lines.

Cruger had seen Greene's scouts appear on 21 May and the main army arrive the next day to make camp at four points around his post. The morning of the 22d a rebel trench was seen a mere 70 yards away from the abatis that surrounded the Star. At 11 A.M. Cruger had completed construction of a gun platform on which his men had been working for several days. Covered by a surprise artillery fire from this platform, and by small arms fire, Lt. John Roney sallied forth to wipe out the rebel work party. He was followed by militia and Negro laborers who filled in the trench and withdrew with the enemy's tools before Greene could react. It was a brilliant little coup, although Roney was mortally wounded.

The night of 23–24 May Greene started his approaches at the respectable distance of 400 yards. The defenders sent out raiding parties at night to interrupt this work, but by 3 June the second leg of the three-leg approach had been completed and the rebels were at about the point where Roney had scored his victory. Greene now went through the formality of summoning the garrison to surrender. In return for the discourtesy of sending this message by his A.G. (Otho Williams) and not addressing it to Cruger by name (Greene knowing perfectly well who commanded the fort), Cruger returned an oral refusal by way of the Officer of the Day, Lt. Edw. Stelle. (Kenneth Roberts, *Oliver Wiswell,* 691–93. Although this is a work of historical fiction, I will cite or quote it on points that are supported by original sources or sound secondary works. Several chapters of *Oliver Wiswell* are devoted to this operation and, with the latitude permitted the novelist, Roberts presents a picture of this siege, from the Loyalist viewpoint, that is better "history" than most histories.)

While artillery raked the Star and the village from the completed portion of the approaches, work on the third and last leg of Kosciuszko's parallels went on night and day. Cruger ordered trenches dug for the protection of the refugees. "Men, women and children crawled down into the trenches and went to living in holes like woodchucks, or lay huddled against the inside of the stockades," writes Roberts. "The town ... lay scorched and motionless in the quivering heat like a dying town in which there was neither strength nor resistance." (*Ibid., 694*).

Yet there were both. When the attackers erected a MAHAM TOWER within 35 yards of the abatis, the defenders raised the parapets with sandbags for protection against the plunging fire from the 40-foot tower. When the attackers tried to set fire to the buildings with AFRICAN ARROWS, Cruger had the shingle roofs stripped off. When enemy artillery made the gun platform in the Star untenable during daylight, the defenders took down the guns and used them only at night. (Roderick Mackenzie, quoted in C. & M., 1181–85) Cruger tried to set fire to the tower with hot shot, but failed because adequate furnaces could not be improvised.

The morning of 8 June "Light-Horse Harry" Lee arrived from Augusta with his Legion to reinforce Greene. As the defenders watched this troop movement —having hoped momentarily it was Rawdon coming to their rescue—part of Lee's force marched within artillery range of the fort with the Tory prisoners from Ft. Cornwallis (Augusta). The garrison of Ninety-Six took this to be a deliberate attempt to humiliate and demoralize them, but it served only to convince them that "death was preferable to captivity with such an enemy." (Mackenzie, *op. cit.*) The garrison of Ninety-Six believed that the rebels were using their prisoners to shield themselves from retaliatory fire during this bravado. Henry Lee presents a different picture, saying that the officer commanding this detachment took the wrong road and was "very severely reprimanded by Lt. Col. Lee, for the danger to which his inadvertence had exposed the corps." (*Memoirs, 371*)

Lee started siege operations from the north against Ft. Holmes with a view to cutting off the enemy's water supply. Although Lee says that Kosciuszko's "blunders lost us Ninety-Six," and comments on his failure to attack the water supply, Lee does not claim credit for proposing that his troops be assigned this mission (*ibid., 371*); Ward, on the other hand, says Lee "immediately suggested" the plan (*W.O.R.*, 818) and other writers echo this opinion. (I suspect this is one of those logical assumptions that just happen to be wrong. False modesty was not one of Lee's character defects.)

The night of 9–10 June the defenders sent two raiding parties out to check on their "apprehension that something extraordinary was carrying on in the enemy's works." One party overran a four-gun battery, which, for lack of spikes and hammers, they could not spike, but they discovered the mouth of the mine that had been started north of the Star. Kosciuszko was on the scene and, according to Mackenzie, was ingloriously wounded in "the seat of honour." (*Op. cit.*) The other group of Tories attacked the covering party in Lee's sector, bayoneted several of them, and captured the officer in command.

On 11 June, Greene got a message from Sumter saying that British reinforcements had reached Charleston (3 June) and were marching to the relief of Ninety-Six. To join Sumter in blocking this movement, Greene sent Pickens and Wm. Washington, with all his cavalry, and called on Marion to participate in the same mission. The besiegers redoubled their efforts to reduce the little fortress. At 11 A.M. on the 12th, covered by "a dark, violent storm ... from the west, without rain," (Lee, *op. cit.*, 373), a sergeant and nine privates of the Legion infantry crawled toward Ft. Holmes in an attempt to set fire to the stockade; they were discovered in the act of starting the fire and the sergeant and five men were killed. By the 17th, Lee's troops had pushed so close as to force the defenders to withdraw their guards from the vicinity of their water supply, but naked Negroes went out during the night and got water, "their bodies not being distinguishable in the night from the fallen trees with which the place abounded" (Mackenzie, *op. cit.*).

This same day, however, the Tories got the news for which they had been praying: an unsuspected countryman rode unchallenged along the rebel lines to the south and then wheeled suddenly to charge toward the fort waving a paper. The gate was flung open for him, and he rode in unscathed with the message that Rawdon was not more than 30 miles away. "The incorrigible and truculent Sumter violated Greene's orders to keep in Rawdon's front" (C. & M., 1179); as had been the case before Hobkirk's Hill, the Carolina Gamecock had a better idea of his own and, assuming Rawdon would march against Ft. Granby, had faked himself out of position by moving to that place. (Fisher, *Struggle*, II, 434)

Greene had three alternatives: give up the entire operation and retreat; move against Rawdon; or take the fort by storm before Rawdon could arrive. Having only half Rawdon's strength in regulars, Greene rejected the second alternative and adopted the third. According to Lee, Greene probably would have retreated, but "his soldiers, with one voice, entreated to be led against the fort." In a scene that would ruin Kenneth Roberts' reputation as a writer of historical fiction (to borrow a phrase from Hoffman Nickerson), "Light-Horse Harry" presents the following challenge to our credulity:

"The American army having witnessed the unconquerable spirit which actuated their general ... recollected, with pain and remorse, that by the misbehavior of one regiment at the battle of Guilford, and of another at Hobkirk's Hill, their beloved general had been deprived of his merited laurels; and they supplicated their officers to entreat their commander to give them now an opportunity of obliterating their former disgrace. This generous ardor could not be resisted by Greene." (*Memoirs*, 375)

THE ASSAULT

A coordinated attack by Lee and Col. Richard Campbell was to be made against Ft. Holmes and the Star Redoubt. "Forlorn hopes" were commanded by Capt. Rudolph on Lee's front and by Lts. Isaac Duval and Samuel Seldon on Campbell's. The latter two parties were equipped with iron hooks on long poles to pull down the sandbags, and carried fascines to bridge the ditch around the Star. On the firing of a prearranged cannon signal at noon of the 18th, Rudolph fought his way into Fort Holmes, which was now lightly held; the rest of the Legion infantry and Kirkwood's Co. followed. Lee then awaited the outcome of Campbell's attack and prepared to attack across the stream.

Campbell's 1st Va. with a reinforcement of Md. and Va. Cont'ls. moved into the trenches at 11 A.M. and sharpshooters manned the tower. The assault groups of Duval and Seldon "entered the trenches, manifesting delight in the expectation of carrying by their courage the great prize in view." (Lee, *op. cit.,* 376) When the second gun was fired at noon the forlorn hopes moved out. Axmen cut gaps through the abatis at two points, fascines were thrown into the ditch, the hooks went to work pulling down sandbags, and Campbell's main body waited until gaps had been made through which they could charge over the enemy parapet. Riflemen picked off every Tory soldier who showed his head, the Va. and Md. Cont'ls. fired by platoons from their trenches, and the artillery roared. (Cruger massed the fire of his three puny guns first against Lee and then against Campbell; one of these 3-pdrs. delivered a particularly effective fire against the latter, according to the accounts both of Lee and Mackenzie.)

The Star was defended by Maj. Green and 150 N.Y. Tories. Seeing that passive measures would lead inevitably to defeat, he struck back by sending out two groups to attack the rebels in the ditch (who were in defilade and could not be shot at from the fort). Capts. Thos. French and Peter Campbell each led 30 men out a sally port behind the Star, circled in opposite directions to the front, and in desperate fighting succeeded in defeating the rebels under Duval and Seldon. Both of the latter were disabled by wounds, and their men retreated with heavy losses. French was wounded. (Roberts, *op. cit.,* 723)

Greene had been beaten again; although his men performed as well as any commander could ask, he, Kosciuszko, and Sumter had made too many blunders against enemy officers and men who were too good for them. Lee's forces were withdrawn from Ft. Holmes after dark, and preparations were made for a general retreat to es-

cape Rawdon. Greene left on the 19th, was joined on the Saluda River by the cavalry that had been detached to Sumter, and continued his retreat in the direction of Charlotte. Rawdon reached Ninety-Six the morning of the 21st, having marched almost 200 miles under a blazing sun through desolated country with 2,000 troops, three regiments of whom (3d, 19th, and 30th Foot) had just completed the arduous crossing from England. After a dramatic welcome by Cruger and his garrison, Rawdon undertook to pursue Greene, but when he reached the Enoree River (about 30 miles N.E.) he received intelligence that convinced him he was too far behind. The British commander returned to Ninety-Six, made preparations to evacuate that post, and started back toward Charleston. (As evidence of the hardships endured, 50 of Rawdon's men died of sunstroke on this retreat. [Fortescue, *British Army,* III, 383].)

LOSSES

During the 28-day siege the rebels lost 185 killed and wounded, according to Lee (*op. cit.,* 377); Ward says they lost 147: 57 killed, 70 wounded, and 20 missing. Cruger lost 27 killed and 58 wounded. Only one officer was killed on each side, Roney and Capt. Geo. Armstrong (1st Md.).

NIXON, John.* 1727–1815. Cont'l. general. Mass. Son of a man who also spelled his name Nickson, he was born at Framingham, Mass. At 18 he enlisted in Sir Wm. Pepperrell's Regt. and took part in the attack on Louisburg. In 1755 he again enlisted, became a Capt. six months later (8 Sept.), and fought at Crown Point. The

* Note that there is another John Nixon.

next year he was in the force organized to capture Ticonderoga and, becoming a Capt. in Col. Ruggles' Regt., in 1758 had considerable military service in the last years of the French and Indian War. On 19 Apr. '75 he reached Concord with one of the militia companies from Sudbury, and on the 24th was appointed Col. to raise a regiment. Some of his men manned the redoubt and breastworks at Bunker Hill, 17 June, and he was wounded in action. He took part in the Boston Siege and the defense of N.Y.C., rising to Col. 4th Cont'ls. on 1 Jan. '76 and B.G. on 9 Aug. '76. His brigade assigned to Greene's Div., he did not take part in the battle of Long Island but figured prominently at HARLEM HEIGHTS, 16 Sept. '76. He remained in the Hudson Highlands at the start of the N.J. Campaign, but moved south with the column led by Chas. Lee. During the Trenton campaign his brigade of three R.I. and two Mass. regiments was down the river with the forces led by John Cadwalader and saw no action.

Ordered to reinforce the Northern army against the invasion of Burgoyne, he reached Ft. Edward on 13 July. Schuyler complained that he had taken four days to cover 46 miles with his brigade of only 575 rank and file fit for duty. In the two battles of SARATOGA his brigade had a passive role defending the works on the extreme right overlooking the Hudson. His brigade led the tardy pursuit, however, and was halted at the Fishkill on 11 Oct. after drawing fire from what Gates suddenly learned was not the enemy's rear guard but his main force. (See BURGOYNE'S OFFENSIVE) After escorting the Saratoga prisoners to Cambridge, Nixon spent several months on sick leave, married the widow of a comrade killed at Harlem Heights (Micajah Gleason), sat on the court-martial of Schuyler (Oct. '78),

and on 12 Sept. '80 resigned for ill health.

An eye and an ear permanently damaged when a cannon ball passed close to his head during the Saratoga fighting, he apparently took no part in public life after the war. About seven years before his death he moved from Sudbury to Middlebury, Vt. (Appleton's; Edward E. Curtis in *D.A.B.*)

NIXON, John.* 1733–1808. Patriot merchant, financier. Pa. Grandson of Irish immigrants, he had little schooling before inheriting his father's shipping business and wharf in Philadelphia when he was about 16. He was soon a leading figure in public affairs of the city and province. He became a Lt. of the Dock Ward Company in 1756, signed the nonimportation agreement in that year, was one of the signers of Pa. paper money in 1767, helped organize and became Lt. Col. of the "Silk Stockings" (3d Bn. of Associators), and in late 1775 acted as president of the provincial committee of safety when Benj. Franklin and Robt. Morris were absent. In 1776 he had a particularly active year: after commanding the defense of Fort Island in the Delaware in May, he took command of the Philadelphia city guard, served on the Cont'l. navy board, on 8 July gave the first public reading of the Decl. of Indep. in Philadelphia, marched a short time later with his battalion to the defense of Amboy, returned to Philadelphia six weeks later, and returned to the field for the Trenton and Princeton campaign. Succeeding John Cadwalader as Col., he remained in the field until late Jan. '77. (John H. Frederick in *D.A.B.*)

In 1779 he was an auditor of public accounts and was involved in settling

* Note that there is another John Nixon.

and adjusting the depreciated Cont'l. currency. The next spring he helped organize the Bank of Pa. to supply the army, contributed £5,000, and was appointed one of its two directors. In 1784 he became a director of the Bank of North America; in 1792 he became its second president and held this post until his death. Meanwhile he was city alderman 1789–96. His son, Henry, married a daughter of Robt. Morris and was the bank's fourth president.

"NO-FLINT." Nickname of Charles GREY.

NONIMPORTATION. A form of economic sanction (boycott) by which the colonies successfully sought repeal of offensive economic measures of the British government. Nonimportation first sprang up in 1764 when, in protest to the GRENVILLE ACTS, a Boston town meeting (24 May) denounced taxation without representation and proposed that the colonies unite in opposition. By the end of the year other colonies, notably N.Y., had agreed to nonimportation. The STAMP ACT (1765) gave new impetus to the program, but repeal of the act (news of which was received in N.Y. on 26 Apr. '66) led to abandonment of nonimportation.

The TOWNSHEND REVENUE ACT of 1767 revived the measures, and by the end of 1769 only N.H. had not joined. Colonial ASSOCIATIONS resulted in widespread nonimportation agreements and reduced the value of British imports by almost 40 per cent between 1768 and 1769. When the Townshend duties were limited to tea alone (this received the King's approval on 12 Apr. '70) the opposition of merchants and others led to the abandonment of nonimportation, despite efforts of Boston radicals. The movement started in Albany, Providence, and Newport in May '70, spread to N.Y.C. in July, and by the end of the year Philadelphia (12 Sept.), Bos-

ton (12 Oct.), and S.C. (13 Dec.) withdrew from the nonimportation associations. Va., which had organized the first ASSOCIATION, finally bowed in July '71. (*E.A.H.,* 79)

Whereas the mercantile aristocracy originally advocated nonimportation, from which they stood to gain, it was they who took the initiative in ending it. They were horrified to find that nonimportation was passing from their control into the hands of the politicians and the mob, who were leading the colonies toward anarchy or, worse for the merchants, war with Britain. The ending of nonimportation was a severe setback to AGITATION. Miller, whose *Origins* should be consulted on this subject (nonimportation), writes:

"For three years after the collapse of the boycott, the patriot leaders were compelled to struggle against widespread indifference and 'political Lethargy' among the people. They lamented that 'the Spirit of Patriotism seems expiring in America in general,' and many of them gave up the fight as lost and began to make their peace with the Tory oligarchs." (*Op. cit.,* 315)

Nonimportation was revived by Congress in 1774. See ASSOCIATION.

NOOK'S HILL, Mass., 9 Mar. '76. See DORCHESTER HEIGHTS.

NORFOLK, Va., 1 Jan. '76. Burned by Dunmore. After defeating Dunmore's forces at GREAT BRIDGE, 9 Dec. '75, Col. Wm. Woodford entered Norfolk on the 13th. Col. Robt. Howe arrived the next day with a N.C. regiment and took command. Dunmore had taken refuge on British ships in the harbor where he and his Tory recruits suffered from cramped accommodations and lack of provisions. The rebels not only refused his royal demands for the latter but also refused to let him send foraging parties ashore. John Marshall tells of seeing the light-hearted Va. riflemen amuse themselves by shooting at the vessels. When Col. Howe refused to stop the firing and refused to supply provisions, Dunmore announced the morning of 31 Dec. that he was going to bombard the town. At 4 A.M. of the New Year he put his threat into effect. While the naval guns shot into the town, landing parties set fire to warehouses near the waterfront. The rebels retaliated by burning homes of prominent Tories, and a wind helped spread the flames through the prosperous town of 6,000 inhabitants. Although many had left—most of them taking refuge in Suffolk—about three noncombatants were killed and seven wounded. Col. Stevens was conspicuous in fighting off the landing parties.

Montross says that "as Virginia's largest town went up in flames the loyalist cause perished with it" (*Reluctant Rebels,* 134). The portion of the town that had not been destroyed in the 50-hour fire (Lossing, II, 537) was razed to prevent its use by the enemy when Col. Stevens withdrew his troops in Feb. "It is significant that of the Tory property confiscated by Virginians during the Revolutionary War, one third belonged to the hated Scotch merchants of Norfolk," writes Miller. (*Origins,* 17) Dunmore then landed and built barracks with a view to maintaining a beachhead, but Howe's troops, from their camps at Kemp's Landing, Great Bridge, and Suffolk, made it impossible for the enemy to get provisions from the countryside. With his miserable collection of refugees and Loyalist militia Dunmore returned to his ships and eventually established a new base on GWYNN ISLAND.

NORTH, Sir Frederick. 1732–1792. British Prime Minister. Although best known by his courtesy title of Lord North, which he used until the death of his father in 1790, on the latter date he became the 2d Earl of Guilford by inheritance. Educated at Eton and Oxford, he entered Parliament at the age of 22 and for nearly 40 years, until his death at 60, sat for the town of Banbury. In 1759 the Duke of Newcastle made him a lord of the treasury, and he held this office under Bute and Grenville until 1765. Because of his ability and unruffled good humor he rose steadily in the government, entering the privy council and becoming paymaster general under Grafton in 1766 and chancellor of the exchequer on Townshend's death in Dec. '67. In Mar. '70 he succeeded Grafton as P.M., and GEORGE III finally had just the man he had been seeking.

Lord North remained in this post for 12 of the most eventful years in English history, and these years left him with few admirers on either side of the Atlantic. The *E.B.* has this to say of his tenure:

"How a man of undoubted ability such as Lord North was could allow himself to be thus used as a mere instrument cannot be explained; but the confidential tone of the king's letters seems to show that there was an unusual intimacy between them, which may account for North's compliance. [!] The path of the minister in parliament was a hard one; he had to defend measures which he had not designed, and of which he had not approved, and this too in a House of Commons in which all the oratorical ability of Burke and Fox was against him, and when he had only the purchased help of Thurlow and Wedderburne to aid him. The most important events of his ministry were those of the American War of Independence. He cannot be accused of causing it, but one of his first acts was the retention of the tea-duty, and he it was also who introduced the Boston

Port Bill in 1774. When the war had broken out he earnestly counselled peace, and it was only the earnest solicitations of the king not to leave his sovereign again at the mercy of the Whigs that induced him to defend a war which from 1779 he knew to be both hopeless and impolitic. At last, in March 1782, he insisted on resigning after the news of Cornwallis's surrender at Yorktown, and no man left office more blithely." (*Op. cit.,* "Guilford")

In Apr. '83 he formed the famous coalition with his former subordinate and opponent, Charles J. Fox, and became Sec. of State with him under the nominal premiership of the Duke of Portland, but this ministry collapsed in Dec. '83 on the rejection of Fox's East India Bill. Lord North already was losing his sight and he began to drop out of public life. In 1789, however, although completely blind, he played an important part in the Regency Bill.

NORTHERN CONFEDERACY. See under Timothy PICKERING.

NORTH'S PLAN FOR RECONCILIATION, 1775. With the grudging consent of George III, Lord North presented a plan for reconciliation that was received by the House of Lords on 20 Feb. '75, endorsed by Commons on 27 Feb., and rejected by the Cont'l. Cong. on 31 July '75. (The plan prescribed that the British would deal with individual colonies, and thereby avoided tacit recognition of the Cont'l. Cong.) By its terms Parliament had royal approval to "forbear" to lay any but regulatory ("external") taxes on any American colony whose own assembly passed "internal" taxes to support the civil government and judiciary and to provide for the common defense. "This was merely a repetition of the gesture that Grenville had made in advance of the stamp act, and it was still as vague and undefined, still as unacceptable, as it had been then," comments Morgan (*Birth of the Republic,* 69).

NORTHUMBERLAND. Title of Hugh PERCY after 1786.

NORWALK, Conn., 11 July '79. Plundered and destroyed during CONN. COAST RAID.

NOVA SCOTIA. See ACADIA.

N.S. See CALENDARS, "Old" and "New Style."

O

O'BRIEN, Jeremiah. 1744–1818. American naval officer. Me. Eldest son of an immigrant tailor, he was born in Kittery (then in the province of Mass.), and in 1765 he moved with his family to Machias. He became the first naval hero of the Revolution in the action off MACHIAS, May '75. Commanding a small fleet of the Mass. navy, he took a few prizes before his ships were put out of commission in the fall of 1776. As a privateersman he was captain of the *Resolution* in 1777 and captured the *Scarborough.* His *Hannibal* was captured in 1780, and he was imprisoned first in the *Jersey* prison ship at New York and then in Mill Prison, England. After suffering considerable hardship, he escaped and commanded the *Hibernia* and then the *Tiger.* For the last

813

seven years of his life he was collector of customs at Machias. (C. O. Paullin in *D.A.B.*)

ODELL, Jonathan. 1737–1818. Loyalist secret agent, satirist. N.J. Descended from William Odell, who settled in Concord, Mass., around 1639, and grandson of Rev. Jonathan Dickinson, first Pres. of Princeton, he graduated from the latter college in 1759, was educated as a doctor, and became a surgeon in the British Army. After serving in the West Indies he left the army, studied in England for the ministry, and in Jan. '67 was ordained. In July '67 he became a missionary in Burlington, N.J., under the Society for the Propagation of the Gospel, and in 1771 he also took up the practice of medicine. While studying in England he had shown a talent for poetry and in the early stages of the Revolution he so antagonized the patriots with his Loyalist verses that on 20 July '76 the Prov. Cong. ordered that he be placed on parole whereby his movements were limited to within a short distance of Burlington. On 18 Dec. he escaped to the British.

Becoming a secret agent, he joined Joseph STANSBURY in handling the correspondence between Arnold and André during ARNOLD'S TREASON. (See Van Doren, *Secret History, passim*) He published essays and verses in Rivington's *Gazette* and other papers that lampooned patriots of N.J. "These stinging verses engaged much attention on both sides, and were among the most influential published during the period," writes A. Van Doren Honeyman in *D.A.B.* Many of them are in Winthrop Sargent (ed.), *The Loyal Verses of Joseph Stansbury and Doctor Jonathan Odell* (Albany, 1860). The versatile Odell was chaplain of a regiment of Pa. Tories, translated French and Spanish papers, was Assist. Sec. to the Board

of Directors of Assoc. Loyalists, and on 1 July '83 became Assist. Sec. to Carleton, who then was British C. in C. in America. He went to England with Carleton after the war, taking his wife and three children, but in 1784 he returned to the Loyalist settlement in New Brunswick, Canada. Throughout his years in N.J. and N.Y. he had been closely associated with Gov. Wm. Franklin, who was the godfather of his only son. The latter, Wm. Franklin Odell (1774–1844), is confused with the Tory leader, Wm. ODELL.

ODELL, William. Tory officer who raised and commanded the LOYAL AMERICAN RANGERS. He is confused, particularly by indexers, with the only son of Jonathan ODELL, William Franklin Odell, who was born in 1774 and would have been a little young to command troops in the American Revolution. Since Jonathan's first American ancestor was William Odell, the Tory leader could well have been a brother or cousin.

OGDEN, Aaron. 1756–1839. Cont'l. officer, Gov. of N.J., steamboat pioneer. N.J. Brother of Matthias OGDEN, he graduated from Princeton in 1773 with "Light Horse Harry" Lee and a year behind Aaron Burr, who was a childhood companion. After teaching school for three years he became paymaster of a militia regiment on 8 Dec. '75, and his first military exploit was to assist in the capture of the BLUE MOUNTAIN VALLEY in Jan. '76. On 26 Nov. '76 he was commissioned 1st Lt. in the 1st N.J. Cont'l. Regt. (This was his brother's unit.) He became Regt'l. Paymaster on 1 Feb. '77, fought at the Brandywine, was made Brig. Maj. of Maxwell's Brig. on 7 Mar. '78, and in the Monmouth Camp'n. served in the advance element of Charles Lee. During this campaign he also served as Assist. A.D.C. to Gen. Alexander. The next year he was Maxwell's A.D.C. during Sullivan's Expedition against the Iroquois, and in 1780 he took part in the delaying action of Maxwell's Brig. against the Springfield, N.J., Raid of Knyphausen. When Maxwell resigned, Ogden joined the light infantry corps of Lafayette. He had been promoted to Capt. of the 1st N.J. on 2 Feb. '79. In the fruitless exchange of correspondence between Sir Henry Clinton and Washington that preceded John André's execution, Capt. Ogden served as courier between British and American headquarters. His part in the dubious matter of proposing the exchange of André for Arnold seems to have been nothing more than the delivery of the letter written in a disguised hand by Alexander Hamilton. (See Van Doren, *Secret History*, 363, 366–68, 370, and facsimile facing p. 376. Ogden claimed to have broached this proposal unofficially and orally to British authorities at Paulus Hook, and that Clinton's headquarters replied, "a deserter was never given up." Freeman adds "There is no reason to believe that this was reported by Ogden to Washington." [*Washington*, V, 219 *n.*].)

In the Yorktown Campaign Ogden was wounded 14 Oct. '81 in the storming of Redoubt 10. After the war he studied law with his brother Robert and became one of the leading lawyers in his state (*D.A.B.*). When war with France was threatened he became Lt. Col. of the 11th U.S. Infantry on 8 Jan. '99 (Heitman) and Deputy Q.M.G. of the army (*D.A.B.*). He was discharged on 15 June 1800. In 1812 he was elected Gov. of N.J. on a peace ticket but defeated the next year. Madison nominated him Maj. Gen. in 1813, apparently with the intention of giving him a command in Canada, but Ogden declined to retain command of the state militia.

During the War of 1812 Ogden turned from the law to a steamboat venture that was his undoing. Having built the *Sea Horse* in 1811, he proposed to operate a line between Elizabethown Point and N.Y.C., but in 1813 the monopoly of James Fulton and Robert R. LIVINGSTON was upheld and his boat was barred from N.Y. waters. He then got into a long, expensive monopoly fight with another line, that of Thomas Gibbons. Ogden won his case in the N.Y. courts but lost the Supreme Court appeal in 1824. This gave occasion for one of the famous opinions of John Marshall. In 1829 Congress created the post of customs collector at Jersey City for Ogden. Despite this assistance the impoverished Ogden was soon imprisoned for debt, but the N.Y. legislature— apparently at the instigation of Burr— released him by passing a quick bill prohibiting the imprisonment of Revolutionary War veterans for debt.

"He was a man of powerful physique and massive features, with an expression fully as truculent as that of his antagonist Gibbons" (*D.A.B.*). His brief *Autobiography* (1893), written for his two daughters and five sons by Elizabeth Chetwood (m. 1787), deals primarily with his military experiences.

OGDEN, Matthias. 1754–1791. Cont'l. officer. N.J. John Ogden emigrated from Hampshire, England, to Long Island about 1640. In 1664 he established himself at Elizabethtown, N.J. His descendants were prominent in the province. Robert (1716–1787), father of Matthias, was a member of the King's council, speaker of the legislature in 1763, delegate to the Stamp Act Congress (N.Y.C., 1765), and chairman of the Elizabethtown committee of safety in 1776.

Matthias and Aaron Burr left the college at Princeton after the Battle of

Bunker Hill, joined the Boston army, and as unattached volunteers accompanied Arnold's March to Quebec. Ogden made the first attempt to present Arnold's surrender summons at Quebec and "retreated in quick time" after an 18-pd. shot hit the ground near him. (Ogden, *Journal,* quoted in Ward, *W.O.R.,* 184) He was wounded in the attack that started 31 Dec. '75. Having served as Brig. Maj. in this expedition (Heitman), he became Lt. Col. of the 1st N.J. Cont'ls. on 7 Mar. '76 and assumed command of the regiment on 1 Jan. '77. As part of Alexander's Div. his regiment performed well in slowing the British advance on "the plowed hill" in the Battle of the BRANDYWINE, 11 Sept. '77. During the Valley Forge winter quarters he was in the brigade of Wm. Maxwell. In the Battle of Monmouth, 28 June '78, he took part in the initial action under Lee. At the latter's court-martial Lt. Col. Richard Harrison testified that in attempting to find out why Lee was retreating he came on Ogden's regiment, which was near the rear of the column. "He appeared to be exceedingly exasperated," Harrison testified, "and said, 'By God! they are flying from a shadow.' " (C. & M., 712) He was captured at Elizabethtown on 5 Oct. '80 and exchanged in Apr. '81, according to Heitman. (Appleton's says he was taken prisoner in Nov. '80.)

Col. Ogden proposed a plan for the capture of Prince William Henry, the future William IV, when the latter was in N.Y.C. According to Heath, the rebels learned on 30 Sept. '81 that the prince had arrived five days earlier with Adm. DIGBY and was lodged in the mansion of Gerardus Beekman in Hanover Square. Washington approved Ogden's plan of leading 40 officers and men into the city on a rainy night to land near the mansion and kidnap

Digby and William. The plan was compromised and had to be abandoned. (*Memoirs,* 326, 418)

On 21 Apr. '83 he was granted leave to visit Europe and did not return to the army. Louis XVI honored him with "le droit du tabouret," which permitted him to sit in the royal presence. Congress breveted him B.G. on 30 Sept. '83.

The *Journal of Maj. Matthias Ogden* was printed in the *N.J. Hist. Soc. Proc.* for Jan. 1928.

Brother of Aaron OGDEN. Father of Francis Barber Ogden (1783–1857), whose varied career included service as A.D.C. to Jackson at New Orleans (1815), consul at Liverpool (1830–57), and sponsorship of naval inventor John Ericsson.

OGHKWAGA. Variant of OQUAGA.

O'HARA, Charles. 1740?–1802. British guards general. Illegitimate son of James O'Hara, second Lord Trawley and Col. of the Coldstream Guards, Charles was educated at Westminster School, appointed cornet of the 3d Dragoons on 23 Dec. '52, and on 14 Jan. '56 entered his father's regiment with the grade of "lieutenant and captain." (H. Manners Chichester in *D.N.B.*) At this time he would have been about 16 years old. After service in Germany and Portugal, on 25 July '66 he was appointed commandant at Goree, Senegal, with the rank of Lt. Col.–commandant of the Africa corps. This was a unit composed of military offenders who were pardoned for life service in Africa. Maintaining his seniority in the Coldstream, he was named Capt. and Lt. Col. (*sic*) of that regiment in 1769 and was brevet Col. in 1779.

Meanwhile he had come to America and in July '78, when the newly arrived French fleet under d'Estaing was threatening N.Y.C., and commanded the forces at Sandy Hook. Clinton gave him this assignment because he was considered a good engineer and was well known to Adm. Howe, says Sir Henry in a loose note. "But I soon found he was the last man I should have sent with a detached corps—plans upon plans for defense; never easy, satisfied, or safe; a great, nay plausible, talker." (*Amer. Reb.*, 100 *n.*) The dark and ruddy-faced Irishman, whose ready tongue lay behind teeth of magnificent whiteness, distinguished himself as an aggressive commander of his guards brigade in the Southern operations of Cornwallis. He spearheaded the latter's frustrating pursuit of Greene across N.C. to the Dan River, leading the gallant attack at COWAN'S FORD, 1 Feb. '81.

Commanding the 2d Bn. of Gds. at GUILFORD, 15 Mar. '81, he rallied his troops after receiving one dangerous wound and led them forward again to deliver the final blow that broke the resistance of Greene's army. He was wounded a second time. Moving to Va. with Cornwallis, O'Hara represented the Earl in the Yorktown Surrender and dined that night with Washington. When he was exchanged on 9 Feb. '82 he returned to England as a newly appointed Maj. Gen. and with the highest praise from Cornwallis.

In 1792 he finally was appointed Lt. Gov. of Gibraltar, a post he had long coveted, and the next year was promoted to Lt. Gen. He was captured on 23 Nov. '93 at Ft. Mulgrove, Toulon, in the operations that brought an obscure French officer named Napoleon to the attention of his military superiors. Imprisoned in the Luxembourg, he was exchanged for Rochambeau in Aug. '95, named Gov. of Gibraltar, promoted to full Gen. in 1798, and proved himself an efficient commander of that stronghold at this critical time. After much suffering from his wounds he died at Gibraltar in 1802. Gen.

O'Hara had managed to accumulate a considerable fortune and left £70,000 to two local ladies for their support and for the support of his illegitimate children.

OHIO COMPANY OF ASSOCIATES (1787). Under the leadership of Rufus Putnam and Benjamin Tupper, two Revolutionary War generals, officers and soldiers formed an association for the settlement of western lands. On 1 Mar. '86 their delegates met in Boston to organize a company for the purchase of land around what now is Marietta, Ohio. After Gen. Samuel Parsons had proved unsatisfactory in the role, the Rev. Manasseh Cutler became the company's representative before Congress and, jointly with a group of N.Y. speculators led by William Duer, he eventually made arrangements to purchase 1,781,760 acres; the terms were $500,000 down and the same amount when the survey was completed, but this could be paid in government securities worth about 12 cents on the dollar. The Scioto Company of Duer was authorized to buy nearly 500,000 acres.

The Ohio Associates were unable to complete their payments, but Congress granted title to 750,000 acres, granted 100,000 acres free to actual settlers, and authorized that 214,285 acres be bought with army warrants. Rufus PUTNAM established what now is Marietta, which *Concise D.A.H.* calls "the great achievement of the company."

OHIO COMPANY OF VIRGINIA, 1747–73. Early in 1749 the Gov. of Va. was directed to grant this company 500,000 acres in the upper Ohio Valley. After explorations by Christopher Gist in 1750 and 1751, Gist and a number of others settled in what now is Fayette co., Pa. Prior to this a storehouse had been built on the Potomac opposite the mouth of Wills Creek, in

1753 another was built on the Monongahela at the site of Brownsville, and early the next year Ft. Prince George was started at the Forks of the Ohio (later Pittsburgh). French capture of this place led to the last of the COLONIAL WARS, which also caused withdrawal of settlers. WASHINGTON was involved in these matters, as was BRADDOCK. The company that had been started for land speculation and Indian trading—but blessed by George II as an aid in pushing English territorial claims—had turned into "the lever which upset the political balance, first between French and British forces in the New World, and then, after the Peace of Paris [1763], between Crown and Colony across the Alleghanies. ..." (*D.A.B.,* "George Mason." MASON became a member of the company in 1752 and served as its treasurer until its rights were transferred in 1773.) Elimination of French claim to the Ohio region was offset by the PROCLAMATION OF 1763, and in 1773 the Crown regranted the area to the Grand Ohio (or Walpole) Company.

The Ohio Company had included two brothers of George Washington, Lawrence (who became its manager on the death of Thomas Lee in 1750) and Augustine. A wealthy London merchant, John Hanbury, was one of its organizers.

OLIVE BRANCH PETITION, 5 July '75. After the first armed clashes of the Revolution (Lexington and Concord, Bunker Hill) the patriots made one more attempt to settle their grievances with Great Britain by means short of war. Written by John Dickinson, adopted on 5 July by the delegates (who, however, signed as individuals and not as members of the Cont'l. Cong.), and carried to London by Richard Penn (a staunch Loyalist and descendant of William Penn), the petition reiterated the grievances of the colonists but professed their attachment to the King, expressed the desire for a restoration of harmony, and begged the King to prevent further hostile action until a reconciliation could be worked out. Penn reached London on 14 Aug. '75. On 9 Nov. '75 the Cont'l. Cong. learned that George III had refused to see Penn or receive his petition.

OMOA. See HONDURAS.

"ON COMMAND" in 18th-century military parlance meant "on detached service."

"ON THE LINES." Outposted towns or other locations were referred to as being "on the lines" when the bulk of the army was in winter quarters or otherwise disposed in garrison.

ONONDAGA CASTLE, Apr. '79. Destroyed in raid by Gose VAN SCHAICK. Peter GANSEVOORT is sometimes credited with this operation.

OQUAGA (now Ouaquaga), N.Y. Iroquois village on E. Branch of the Susquehanna about 20 miles S.W. of UNADILLA. In 1765 it had about 750 inhabitants, most of them Mohawks. It was Joseph Brant's headquarters during ST. LEGER'S EXPEDITION and in much of the subsequent BORDER WARFARE. Its name is Mohawk for "place of wild grapes," and the *Handbook of American Indians* gives over 50 spelling variations ranging from Anaquago through Oghkwaga to Skawaghkee.

ORANGEBURG, S.C., 11 May '81. (SOUTHERN CAMPAIGNS OF GREENE) Refusing to join Greene for the attack on Camden (HOBKIRK'S HILL), Thomas Sumter led his partisans first against Fort Granby but, finding it too strong, decided to take Orangeburg on the N. Edisto River, 50 miles south. Rawdon had ordered this post abandoned, but the message was not received. After Sumter invested them the garrison surrendered. Ward says the garrison consisted of 15 British regulars and 70 militia (*W.O.R.,* 812); F. V. Greene says it numbered 350. (*Amer. Rev.,* 249) There were no rebel casualties.

ORANGE RANGERS. Loyalist force raised by John COFFIN.

ORANGETOWN, N.Y. Another name for Tappan.

ORISKANY (N.Y.) Ambush, 6 Aug. '77. ST. LEGER'S EXPEDITION was a few days' march from Ft. Stanwix when (on 30 July) a friendly Oneida reported its advance to HERKIMER. Despite considerable reluctance of the settlers to muster for their own defense (Swiggett, *Niagara,* 84; Lossing, I, 241), Herkimer managed to raise 800 men and boys. On 4 Aug. they left Ft. Dayton and although encumbered with 400 ox carts they were within about 10 miles of Stanwix when they camped the next night. Runners were sent ahead to tell Col. Gansevoort of their approach and to ask that a sortie be made from the fort as they arrived.

The next morning, 6 Aug., the cautious old Dutchman wanted to await Gansevoort's cannon signal indicating start of the sortie, but his impetuous subordinates insisted on an immediate advance. Herkimer refused to be budged. His regimental commanders—Ebenezer Cox, Isaac Paris, Richard Visscher (or Fisher), and Peter Bellinger—allegedly won their way by accusing him of cowardice and Tory sympathies. Against his better judgment he authorized the advance and even allowed himself to be talked out of providing adequate advance and flank guards. (Swiggett, 85) The militia general rode at the head of the main body, presumably a display of physical courage to make up for failure to show the necessary moral courage with his subordinates. (In repeating this famous story of the council of war, Swiggett gives it as hearsay.

Lossing says only Cox and Paris went so far as to impugn Herkimer's courage and honor [I, 243]. The general's position was not helped by having a brother with St. Leger.)

When St. Leger learned the evening of the 5th that the militia was approaching, he sent Joseph Brant with 400 savages and a few white auxiliaries to ambush them at a place now known as Battle Brook, six miles from the fort. Here a ravine 200 yards wide could be crossed only on a corduroy causeway, and the surrounding woods provided concealment. John Butler's Tory Rangers and part of John Johnson's Royal Greens were deployed so as to hit the head of the column, and the Indians took up positions from which to attack the flanks and rear.

The 60 Oneida scouts somehow failed to detect signs of the ambush and Herkimer's column, which was almost a mile long (Nickerson, *Turning Point,* 204), plunged blindly into the trap.

"No one of course knows just what happened. Evidently Herkimer had come down the ravine, across the bridge, and was going up the western bank; and the wagons were evidently on the bridge itself. Visscher's regiment [200 men, serving as rear guard] jammed together in the rear.... There was probably a long piercing shriek from a Ranger whistle, a war-whoop, a blaze of firing in a great circle around the whole column.

"The officers went down in the first burst of fire like clay birds in a riflerange—Herkimer; Cox [killed]...; Thomas Spencer...; Eisenlord; Klepsattle; and a dozen others. * * * Visscher's regiment ran at the first whistle, but the Canajoharie men somehow held together in the murderous hand-to-hand fighting." (Swiggett, 86–87)

According to other versions the rear guard was attacked before the entire column had entered the trap. Although Visscher's men apparently panicked—skeletons were later found two miles from the battlefield (Nickerson, 206)—the others reacted with a courage and tactical instinct seldom shown by veterans: instead of bunching on the road they rushed their hidden assailants and took up positions on high ground. Herkimer had the saddle taken from his dead horse, placed on the ground among his men, and he sat on it to direct the fight; although bleeding from a leg wound and presenting a conspicuous target, he is said to have calmly smoked his pipe and refused all urging to take cover. The Americans had formed first in small groups, which made them vulnerable from all directions. They then organized themselves into a single perimeter. Nickerson points out that the Indians' reluctance to follow up their initial surprise fire by closing in immediately for the kill probably saved the militia from annihilation.

Swiggett says the action started at 6 A.M.; most other accounts say 10 o'clock. After three quarters of an hour the vicious fighting was stopped temporarily by a heavy rain that silenced all firearms for an hour. During this enforced armistice Herkimer ordered another change in tactics. Individual defenders had been strung along their perimeter, and the Indians would wait until a man fired and then rush in to dispatch him with a tomahawk before he could reload. So the militia started operating in mutually supporting pairs: while one reloaded, the other held his fire to pick off any enemy who charged him.

John Butler heard firing from Ft. Stanwix after the storm and guessed that the Americans were making a sortie. (See ST. LEGER'S EXPED.) When Maj. Stephen Watts arrived with a reinforcement of Royal Greens, Butler had them turn their coats inside out and approach the beleaguered Americans in the guise of a friendly sortie from Ft. Stanwix. A sharp-eyed Palatine recognized a turncoat neighbor just in time, and a terrific hand-to-hand fight ensued. (Ward, W.O.R., 488) By this time the Indians were ready to quit, and their retreat forced the Tories to withdraw also. Contemporary writers mention the improbable story that the redskins suddenly got the idea that Herkimer and the Tories had arranged the battle just to destroy them.

"Thus, after a conflict of six hours, ended the battle of Oriskany, the bloodiest encounter, in proportion to the numbers engaged, that occurred during the war," says Lossing. (Op. cit., 247) American losses were 160 killed, according to Thacher. (Military Journal, 88) Fewer than 400 of the 600-man main body left Oriskany on their feet (Swiggett, 87), and they carried away about 50 wounded (Ward, 488). Bellinger and Maj. John Frey were captured, Cox and Paris were killed, and HERKIMER died later. St. Leger claimed to have taken 200 prisoners, but since he also reported "above 400 [patriots] lay dead on the field" (11 Aug. ltr. to Burgoyne) his figures must be rejected. Likewise, the figure of 160 Americans killed is improbable in the light of the fact that only 50 were wounded in the 600-man main body; although Visscher's 200 might well have sustained more fatalities than those who stood and fought, it is unlikely that these would bring the total to 160 killed.

Swiggett says the Indians lost over 100 (op. cit., 98), and others say 70—the implication is that all these were killed. Again, these figures simply don't square with known battle statistics: if Brant's Indians fought until they sustained 25 per cent casualties (100 out of 400), then their reputation as warriors has been slandered, for Swiggett says a result of the Oriskany-Stanwix Campaign was that "the military worthlessness of Indians was established, if it was not already known." (*Op. cit.*, 97)

O.S. See CALENDARS, "Old" and "New Style."

OSBORNE'S (James R.), Va., 27 Apr. '81. (VA. MIL. OP'NS.) Hearing of a rebel flotilla and some supplies located at this place, Arnold marched from Petersburg the morning of the 27th. Although the American commander refused to surrender when the enemy unexpectedly appeared on the right bank, British field guns drove the supporting militia from the opposite bank and quickly silenced the fire of the only vessel that answered their fire. Arnold captured two ships, 10 smaller craft, and more than 2,000 hogsheads of tobacco. Four ships, five brigs, and a number of smaller vessels were destroyed. When the traitor Arnold asked what the Americans would do if they captured him, an imaginative prisoner is alleged to have said: "They would bury with military honors the leg which was wounded at Saratoga, and hang the remainder of you on a gibbet." (Lossing, II, 545)

OSWALD, Eleazer. *c.* 1755-1795. Cont'l. artillery officer, journalist. England–Conn. A kinsman of Richard OSWALD, he became sympathetic to the patriot cause and emigrated to America about 1770. He served as a Pvt. in the Lexington Alarm, took part in the capture of Ticonderoga, and volunteered for Arnold's March to Quebec. In the latter operations he became Arnold's secretary, commanded the forlorn hope at Quebec, where he was wounded and captured 31 Dec. '75. Exchanged 10 Jan. '77, he was commissioned Lt. Col. of John LAMB's 2d Cont'l. Arty. as of 1 Jan. '77 and became famous as an artil-

lerist. He particularly distinguished himself at Compo Hill during the DANBURY RAID, Apr. '77. After the battle of Monmouth, 28 June '78, he was praised in official orders for his performance. As a result of his failure to be credited with the seniority he felt he deserved, Oswald resigned from the army on 28 June '78. (See also John LAMB)

Oswald then joined Wm. Goddard in publication of the *Maryland Journal*, and his printing of Gen. Charles Lee's criticisms of Gen. Washington led to a popular demonstration against him. In Apr. '82 he started publishing the violently partisan *Independent Gazetteer, or the Chronicle of Freedom* in Philadelphia. The next year he reopened Bradford's London Coffee House and started publishing the monthly *Price Current*, "the earliest commercial paper in the United States." (Appleton's) Between 1782 and 1787 he published the *Independent Gazette, or New York Journal Revived* in N.Y.C., a paper that had previously been printed by his wife's kinsman, John Holt. He attacked the policies of Hamilton and challenged him to a duel, but friends adjusted the matter before a meeting took place. In 1792 Oswald went to England and then to France, where he was commissioned Col. of artillery and regimental commander in the Republican army. He fought at Jemappes. Sent on a secret mission in connection with a contemplated French invasion of Ireland, he reached that country, submitted his report, and not receiving any further instructions from Vergennes he returned to the U.S. Shortly after reaching N.Y.C. he died of yellow fever.

OSWALD, Richard. 1705-1784. British diplomat. Scotland. Married to Mary Ramsay, whom Robert Burns celebrated in one of his poems, he was related to the famous Cont'l. artillery officer, Eleazer OSWALD. Richard spent many years in America and when the Revolution started he was a merchant in London. In 1781 he put up £50,000 to bail Henry Laurens out of the Tower. In Apr. '82 the Shelburne ministry selected Oswald to conduct the final PEACE NEGOTIATIONS. (Appleton's)

OTIS, James. 1725–1783. Patriot politician, publicist, and orator. Mass. Descended in the fifth generation (Appleton's) from an English yeoman who settled in Mass. about 1631 (*D.A.B.*), his grandfather, John Otis (1657–1727), had moved to Barnstable and had become commander of the county militia, judge, and councillor of the province. The latter's son, James (1702–1778), generally called Col. Otis, was a self-educated lawyer who married a descendant of the Pilgrims. Their son James, the subject of this sketch and first of their 13 children, graduated from Harvard in 1743, studied general literature the next two years, studied law under Jeremiah Gridley, was admitted to the bar of Plymouth co. in 1748, and in 1750 established his practice in Boston. Ten years later, at the age of 35, he was perhaps the foremost lawyer in the province, an expert in common, civil, and admiralty law in addition to being a scholar whose *Rudiments of Latin Prosody* ... (1760) became a Harvard text. In 1761 he resigned his lucrative office as King's advocate general of the vice admiralty court at Boston rather than argue for the WRITS OF ASSISTANCE. He then took the side of the Boston merchants in opposing the writs, which the royal customs collectors were seeking in order to find evidence that the Sugar Act of 1733 was being violated.

In his famous speech of 24 Feb. '61 against the writs he gave one of the earliest statements of the doctrine that a law against NATURAL LAW is void. No formal record of his argument exists, but young John Adams took notes (see Commager, *Documents,* 45–47), and 60 years later he wrote this recollection: "Otis was a flame of fire! ... He burned everything before him. American independence was then and there born. ..." Adams said this oration gave the Revolution its slogan: "Taxation without representation is tyranny." (The memory of Adams was notoriously inaccurate. Knollenberg in his *Origin* says the "flame of fire" metaphor is a gross exaggeration [p. 69], and Samuel Eliot Morison in his *D.A.B.* article on Otis points out that the "taxation without representation ..." phrase was not germane to the case and appears only in the final expansion Adams made in his notes.) "The significance of Otis' speech," points out Morison, "lies in his harking back to the constitutional doctrines of Coke and Sir Matthew Hale, invoking a fundamental law embodying the principles of natural law, and superior to acts of Parliament; a doctrine upon which colonial publicists leant during the next twenty-five years, which was embodied in the federal and state constitutions, and which in its final form became the American doctrine of judicial supremacy." (*D.A.B.*) This was his major contribution to the Revolution, and although he participated vigorously in the developments of the next few years he had shot his bolt.

Otis had quit his royal post in 1760 and became an ardent opponent of the crown authorities under circumstances that have cast doubt on his motives. Gov. Shirley had promised to appoint Col. Otis to the superior court and asked his successor, Francis Bernard, to honor this commitment. Bernard became Gov. in Aug. '60, Chief Justice Sewall died the next month, and Col. Otis, assuming Sewall's post would be filled from the court, asked Lt. Gov. Hutchinson to use his influence in getting him appointed junior associate justice. When Hutchinson was appointed chief justice (13 Nov. '60) James Otis (the son) is alleged to have been so infuriated by what he considered to be a double-cross by Bernard and Hutchinson that he declared he would "set the province in flames, if he perished by the fire." Young James Otis denied this story and the implication that his subsequent actions were motivated by a desire to avenge frustrated family ambitions, and modern historians have also rejected this pat explanation of his conduct after 1760. (*D.A.B.*)

In May '61, two months after his famous speech against the writs, Otis became one of Boston's four representatives to the provincial legislature. His father, Col. Otis, was re-elected speaker of the House and the two formed a popular bloc of Boston and rural interests to oppose the crown officials. In 1762 he wrote his first pamphlet, *A Vindication of the Conduct of the House of Representatives,* and in 1764 he wrote *The Rights of the British Colonies Asserted and Proved.* In these he developed the principles stated in his famous speech, and from 1761 to 1769 he was the acknowledged political leader of his province. (*Ibid.*) Already, however, signs of insanity began to appear. "Level-headed John Adams thought Otis 'fiery and feverous' and given to unseemly outbursts of passion," writes Miller. "He was either very gay or very despondent. . . . Otis's love for the British Empire was constantly tormenting him with doubts. . . . Whenever Otis took a step forward on the slippery path to rebellion he was immediately conscience-stricken." (*Sam Adams,* 96)

Meanwhile, however, Otis was made head of the Mass. Comm. of Corresp. in 1764, and the next year he made a proposal that resulted in the Stamp Act

Congress. He considered the Va. resolves of Patrick Henry treasonable, and on 26 Nov. '65 wrote that he preferred "dutiful and loyal Addresses to his Majesty and his Parliament, who alone under God can extricate the Colonies from the painful Scenes of Tumult, Confusion, & Distress." For the next three years Otis played a key role in the swiftly moving political developments in Mass. Elected to the General Court in the spring of 1766, he formed a triumvirate with Sam Adams and Joseph Hawley that led the legislative attack against the embattled royal Gov., Bernard, and his deputy, Hutchinson. Otis presided over the town meeting that revived the nonimportation movement (28 Oct. '67). He and Sam Adams produced the MASS. CIRCULAR LETTER and led the majority that voted not to rescind it. Throughout these activities, which caused British authorities to threaten Adams and Otis with trial for treason, Otis viewed the idea of independence with abhorrence and repeatedly opposed mob violence. "Neither in theory nor in tastes was Otis a democrat," comments Morison; "his often vituperative language arose from his own hot passions, not from any catering to popularity." (*D.A.B.*) Although his confederates worried about the violence of Otis' tongue, it was he who time and again stopped them from *actions* that would have provoked a crisis. He organized and moderated the town meeting of 12–13 Sept. '68 that quashed efforts of Sam Adams to use armed resistance against the British regulars coming to establish the BOSTON GARRISON.

His sudden turn to oblivion apparently was caused by his violent reaction to charges by crown officials—revealed in intercepted letters to England—that Otis had been been guilty of provoking disloyalty. The evening of 5 Sept. '69 he charged into the British Coffee House and loudly demanded an apology from some officials seated there. In a brawl that followed, John Robinson laid Otis' head open with a sword. The blow drove him over the brink of madness, and although his reason returned from time to time he was finished as a public figure. He sued Robinson, was awarded damages of £2,000, and then refused all this amount except legal and medical costs. In 1771 he seemed so completely restored that he returned to the General Court, but in Dec. was declared legally insane. With a borrowed musket he rushed into the Battle of Bunker Hill, 17 June '75, and emerged unscathed. (*Ibid.*, citing *Proceedings Mass. Hist. Soc.*, XII, 1873, p. 69) Early in 1778 he was able, during one of his periodic lucid intervals, to argue a case in Boston, but he found the physical exertion too much and the darkness redescended. Although he sometimes became violent and had to be tied down, during most of his final years he was harmless. A "great Leviathan" of a man, always moody, irritable, and subject to violent outbursts, he became an alcoholic as his reason dimmed. His marriage in 1755 to Ruth Cunningham, a wealthy, beautiful, and prosaic lady of high Tory convictions, was unhappy; it may well have contributed to the breakdown of a mind that struggled with revolutionary politics. The end came dramatically to this man who could have been the protagonist of a classical tragedy: while calmly watching a summer storm he was struck by lightning!

Although the spirit of James Otis is preserved in many documents, he has been strangely neglected by historians. According to Morison, a major American writer who, fortunately, was selected to contribute the sketch on Otis in *D.A.B.*, the only biography and the only article worth mentioning are: Wm. Tudor, *The Life of James Otis* (1823) and J. H. Ellis, "James Otis," *American Law Review,* July 1869. His pamphlets are reprinted, with an introduction by C. F. Mullett, in *The Univ. of Mo. Studies,* July, Oct. 1929. The best discussion of their doctrine, according to Morison, is in the work of B. F. Wright, Jr., which is cited in the article on NATURAL LAW. Otis destroyed all his papers before he died. He did not write many letters and few are in existence; some of these are in the Mass. Hist. Soc., where his father's law papers are held.

OTTO, Bodo. 1711–1787. Cont'l. Army surgeon. Pa. Born in Hanover, he received an excellent education in preparation for becoming a doctor, was apprenticed in Harzburg and Hamburg, interned at the latter place, and served as surgeon in the Duke of Celle's Dragoons. In 1755 he emigrated to America with his second wife and their children. Until 1760 he practiced in Philadelphia, moving then to N.J. and returning to Philadelphia in 1766. In 1773 he settled in Reading, Pa., where he achieved great influence among the German element. At the start of the Revolution he was a leader in the patriot cause, held several elected offices before being appointed senior surgeon of the Middle Division. On 17 Feb. '77 he was ordered by the Cont'l. Cong. to establish a smallpox hospital at Trenton, where he remained until Sept. Then assigned to a hospital at Bethlehem, Pa., he served until the spring of 1778, when he took charge of the hospitals at Yellow Springs near Valley Forge. During this period he was holding the commission of Col. in the N.J. militia, according to Heitman. When the medical department was reorganized, Otto was one of 15 physicians selected for the hospital department (*D.A.B.*), being given the title of Hospital Physician and Surgeon on 6 Oct. '80 (Heitman). He retired 1 Feb. '82, reopened his Philadelphia office, but soon returned to Reading. Three of his sons assisted him during his Revolutionary War service.

A descendant, James Edgar Gibson, wrote *Dr. Bodo Otto and the Medical Background of the American Revolution* (Baltimore, 1937).

"OUT LIERS." Patriots, particularly in the Carolinas, who left their families at home and hid out to avoid taking the oath of allegiance to the King. The term also was applied to patriots or Tories escaping the vengeance of their political enemies.

"OVER MOUNTAIN MEN." Although this term is loosely applied to other groups of American colonists beyond the Blue Ridge Mountains, it is more accurately restricted to those living in what later became Tenn. Also known as Back Water men, "apparently because they lived beyond the sources of the eastern rivers, and on the waters which flowed into the Mississippi," says Fisher (*Struggle,* II, 350 *n.*), their principal settlements were along the Watauga, Nolachucky (now Nolichucky), and Holston rivers. Principal leaders were John Sevier and Isaac Shelby. Although they are often referred to as "mountain men," Fisher points out that "very few people lived in the

mountains at the time of the Revolution, and the Back Water men were merely North Carolinians, mostly of Scotch-Irish stock, who had crossed the mountains to enjoy the level and fertile lands of Tennessee, in the same way that the Virginians who followed Boone crossed the mountains into Kentucky." (*Op. cit.,* 351 *n.*) Another misconception is that the Battle of KINGS MOUNTAIN was won by the over mountain men; although their leaders, Shelby and Sevier, deserve credit for this *levee en masse,* their manpower contribution was only 480 out of the 1,800 or so who eventually arrived on the eve of the battle.

Aside from their part in the skirmishes leading up to this battle and in the battle itself, the over mountain men did little fighting. Sevier and Shelby showed up with some men after the Battle of Eutaw Springs (8 Sept. '81), but they faded back into the mountains when Greene asked them to reinforce Marion during the subsequent operations leading up to the advance on Dorchester, S.C., 1 Dec. '81. (Ward, *W.O.R.,* 838) Wm. Campbell's Va. mountain riflemen, who figured prominently at KINGS MOUNTAIN and appeared in the final phases of Lafayette's maneuvering against Cornwallis in the VIRGINIA MILITARY OPERATIONS, were not "over mountain men" in the strict sense of the term.

P

PACA, William (pah kuh). 1740–1799. Signer, Gov. of Md., jurist. Md. Son of a wealthy Eastern Shore planter who may have been Italian in origin, he graduated from Philadelphia College in 1759, entered the Middle Temple in 1762, and was admitted to the bar of the provincial court two years later. For the rest of his life he was identified with all important political movements of his state (*D.A.B.*). In 1765 he opposed the Stamp Act. He was in the legislature from 1771 to 1774, when he became a member of the Comm. of Corresp. and a delegate to the 1st Cont'l. Cong. After his state removed restrictions from its delegates in June '76, Paca voted for independence and became a Signer. Although he remained a delegate to the Cont'l. Cong. until 1779, sitting throughout most of this five-year period and serving on many important committees, he helped frame the Md. constitution in Aug. '76, was state senator from 1777 to 1779, and in 1778 became chief judge of the Md. Gen. Court. Two years later Cong. made him chief justice of the court of appeals in admiralty and prize cases. In Nov. '82 he was elected Gov.; twice re-elected, he served until 26 Nov. '85. During this period he took a particular interest in veterans' affairs. He finally voted for the Constitution as submitted to the Md. Conv. of 1788, although he was far from satisfied with the document and had proposed 28 amendments. Washington appointed Paca federal district judge in 1789, and he held this post until his death on 13 Oct. '99.

PAINE, Robert Treat. 1731–1814. Signer, jurist. Mass. A direct descendant of Maj. Robert Treat (*c.* 1622–1710), who had been Gov. of Conn., he also had a signer of the Mayflower Compact and other notables of early New England among his ancestors. He was born in Boston, christened in Old South Church, and was headed for the ministry before he turned to law. Meanwhile, however, he had graduated from Harvard in 1749, served as chaplain on the Crown Point Expedition of 1755, and taken a long sea voyage to Carolina, Europe, and Greenland (as a whaler). Admitted to the bar in 1759, he practiced first in Boston but in 1761 moved his office to Taunton. His iden-

tification with the nascent patriot movement led to selection as associate prosecuting attorney in the trial resulting from the Boston "Massacre," and his prosecution of Capt. Preston, although unsuccessful, gave him widespread publicity as an advocate of colonial rights. He represented Taunton in the Prov. Assy. during the periods 1773–75, 1777–78. He was delegate to the 1st Cont'l. Cong. and served in the 2d Cong. until the end of 1776. He was elected for the next session, but remained in Mass. to serve as speaker in the assembly. In Cong. he gained the distinction of being one of the few to sign both the Olive Branch Petition and the Decl. of Indep. He also had been chairman of the committee to provide gunpowder, and after leaving Cong. he continued to experiment with its manufacture. In 1775 he had declined appointment to the Mass. supreme court, but in 1777 he became the first Atty. Gen. of the state. Paine declined a Mass. supreme court appointment in 1783 on financial grounds but finally accepted in 1790. After 14 years in this post he was forced by increasing deafness to retire from the bench. His second son and namesake (1773–1811) became famous as a poet. A great-grandson and namesake (1835–1910) was a Boston philanthropist. The latter's eldest brother, Charles Jackson Paine (1833–1916), was a general in the Civil War, a railroad tycoon, and a yachtsman who successfully defended the America's Cup three times in succession.

PAINE, Thomas. 1737–1809. Revolutionary writer. England–N.Y./N.J. Son of a small farmer and corset maker, who was a Quaker, he had an impoverished and unhappy childhood. At 13 he was apprenticed in his father's trade, at 19 he left home for a year aboard the privateer *King of Prussia,* and for the next 17 years he led a life of ugly, monotonous poverty while failing in the occupations of exciseman, corset maker, school teacher, tobacconist, grocer, and husband. During this time, however, he educated himself by serious reading in the natural and political sciences. In 1772 he was chosen by his fellow excisemen as their agent in the cause of getting higher salaries from Parliament, and although this resulted in his dismissal and bankruptcy it brought him into contact with Benjamin Franklin in London. On 30 Nov. '74 the frustrated, 37-year-old, self-educated failure reached Philadelphia with Franklin's letters of introduction as an "ingenious, worthy young man." For a year he supported himself as a free-lance journalist on a variety of subjects including recent inventions. Dr. Benj. Rush was introduced to him by Mr. Aitken in the latter's bookstore, and after several conversations on politics suggested that Paine write a pamphlet urging the colonists to commit themselves to independence. Rush had intended to write such a paper but was afraid of the personal consequences to himself. "I suggested to him [Paine]," said Rush in his autobiography, "that he had nothing to fear from the popular odium . . . for he could live anywhere, but that my profession and connections . . . forbade me to come forward as a pioneer in that important controversy."

Common Sense appeared in Philadelphia on 10 Jan. '76 as an anonymous two-shilling pamphlet of 47 pages. It contained no original political thinking, but it put into words what a great many patriots had been forming in their own minds. Unlike the works of James Otis and John Dickinson, the best known American pamphleteers to this time, *Common Sense* was not written by a lawyer for men of education but was in the language of the people. It started with this paragraph:

"Some writers have so confounded society with government as to leave little or no distinction between them; whereas they are not only different, but have different origins. Society is produced by our wants and government by our wickedness; the former promotes our happiness *positively* by uniting our affections, the latter *negatively* by restraining our vices. The one encourages intercourse, the other creates distinctions. The first is a patron, the last a punisher."

After further elaboration on this theme and arguing the superiority of natural law over political codes, he boldly attacked an institution that most Americans still considered sacred: the monarchy.

"In the early ages of the world, according to the Scripture chronology there were no kings; the consequence of which was there were no wars; it is the pride of kings which throws mankind into confusion. Holland without a king hath enjoyed more peace for this last century than any of the monarchical governments in Europe.* * * One of the strongest natural proofs of the folly of hereditary right in kings, is that nature disapproves it, otherwise she would not so frequently turn it into ridicule by giving mankind an *ass for a lion.*"

The time has come for America to declare its independence, wrote Paine. "Everything that is right or reasonable pleads for separation. The blood of the slain, the weeping voice of nature cries, *'Tis time to part.*" America has a moral obligation to the whole world, he contended, and *Common Sense* ended with this paragraph:

"O ye that love mankind! Ye that dare oppose not only the tyranny but the tyrant, stand forth! Every spot of the old world is overrun with oppression.

Freedom hath been hunted round the globe. Asia and Africa have long expelled her. Europe regards her like a stranger, and England hath given her warning to depart. O receive the fugitive, and prepare in time an asylum for mankind!" (C. & M., 285–91)

In less than three months 120,000 copies of the pamphlet were sold, and according to the best estimate 500,000 copies eventually were sold. "Paine was the first publicist to discover America's mission," comments Crane Brinton in *D.A.B.* Congress had been gingerly working toward preparing the people for the idea of independence, but Paine did the job for them.

When the war turned against the Americans in 1776, Paine enlisted in time to join Washington's army in N.J. and while a volunteer aide to Nathanael Greene (*E.B.*) he started work on the first of a series of tracts called *The Crisis*. The first of these was published in the *Pa. Journal* on 19 Dec. and in pamphlet form on the 23d. Familiar as they are, the words of the opening paragraph still have a ring:

"These are the times that try men's souls. The summer soldier and the sunshine patriot will, in this crisis, shrink from the service of their country; but he that stands it *now,* deserves the love and thanks of man and woman. Tyranny, like hell, is not easily conquered; yet we have this consolation with us, that the harder the conflict, the more glorious the triumph."

One of Paine's most hostile biographers concedes that "the number was read in the camp, to every corporal's guard, and in the army and out of it had more than the intended effect." (Cheetham, *Life,* 56) To reward the impecunious pamphleteer and give him some regular means of support, Congress in Apr. '77 appointed him secretary to the committee on foreign affairs.

On 8 Jan. '79, under pressure from the French minister, Gérard, Paine was forced to resign; becoming involved in the claims of Beaumarchais' HORTALEZ & CIE., he had published a reply to Silas Deane in the newspapers that referred to confidential documents and that embarrassed the French government. In Nov. '79 he was appointed clerk to the Pa. Assy. In 1780 he published *Public Good,* an expansion of *Common Sense.* He continued his *Crisis,* bringing out 11 numbers in addition to the one quoted above, and four supernumerary ones during the Revolution. (*D.A.B.*) In 1781 he accompanied John Laurens on a successful trip to France for money and supplies.

"The successful peace found him honored but poor," writes Brinton. Never capable of managing his meager funds, he had contributed $500 in 1780 to a subscription for the relief of the army; he had given up his job to accompany Laurens in 1781 and had received nothing but his expenses. N.Y. gave him a confiscated Loyalist estate in New Rochelle after the war, Pa. gave him £500. "For Paine's modest needs this was enough, and until 1787 he lived in Bordentown, N.J., and in New York, mildly lionized, writing, and working on his most cherished invention, an iron bridge." (*Ibid.*)

In 1787 he went to Europe, where the chances of getting his bridge built were better, and for the next two years he basked happily in the light of the political reputation he had won in America. He traveled between London and Paris, drew large crowds with the model of his iron bridge, succeeded in having the bridge built—an engineering triumph but, characteristically, a financial failure—and established himself as a missionary of world revolution. (*D.A.B.*) Burke's *Reflections on the Revolution in France* (1790) provided the springboard for *The Rights of Man* (Mar '91 and Feb. '92) in which Paine defended the revolution. The British suppressed the work and in May '92 indicted the author for treason and outlawed him *in absentia* the following Dec. Meanwhile, on 26 Aug. '92, the Assembly elected him a French citizen (along with Washington, Hamilton, and Madison), and in Sept. Paine was elected to the Convention from four departments. *The Rights of Man* is said to have sold 200,000 copies by 1793.

Not speaking French, the new citizen did not cut much of a figure in the Convention. When the Gironde party, to which he had attached himself, fell from power in June '93, he withdrew from politics and lived quietly in the suburbs of Paris (Faubourg St. Denis). The Convention deprived him of his citizenship and on 28 Dec. '93 imprisoned him in the Luxembourg as an English alien! The following Nov., U.S. minister Monroe secured his release. While being held in confinement he started *The Age of Reason,* which was to become "the atheist's bible." Its two parts were published in 1794 and 1796, and the work "represents the deism of the 18th century in the hands of a rough, ready, passionate controversialist." (*E.B.*) Although this attack on organized religion aroused indignation in America, what really made him a pariah was the long *Letter to George Washington* which Paine published in 1796. With inexcusable bitterness (*E.B.*) he criticized the military reputation and presidential policy of this national idol. Brinton explains it as "the outburst of a disappointed man not wholly free from delusions of persecution. . . ." (*D.A.B.*)

Returning to America in 1802, Paine's last seven years were a return to the poverty of his early life but with the complications of waning health and ostracism. What sort of a man was Thomas Paine? His writings speak for themselves—magnificent political journalism. As for his character, the sympathetic sketch by Crane Brinton refutes the common charges of sexual and financial irregularities; "he was incapable of financial dishonesty," says this writer, and "all the evidence makes him out a singularly chaste man." This, it should be pointed out, at a time when national heroes on both sides of the Atlantic were not paragons of virtue by today's standards. He was a deist, he was no gentleman—either in speech or the cleanliness of his linen—and, even by the standards of the day, he was a heavy drinker. "Any attempt at a calm appraisal of Paine's character runs the risk of shading hostile black and friendly white into a neutral gray. Men always described him in superlatives, and in anything less than superlatives he seems unreal." (*Ibid.*)

Hostile biographies are the *Life* published by George Chalmers in 1791 and the one by James Cheetham in 1809. The standard work, although done by "an uncritical admirer" (*D.A.B.*), is the two-volume *Life* by M. D. Conway published in 1892. The same author brought out *The Writings of Thomas Paine,* 4 vols., 1894–96. The 10-volume *Life and Works* edited by W. M. Van der Weyde (1925) "adds nothing of importance." (*Ibid.*)

PALATINE, N.Y., 19 Oct. '80. See FORT KEYSER.

PAOLI, Pa., 21 Sept. '77. (PHILADELPHIA CAMPAIGN) When Washington withdrew across Parker's Ford on 19 Sept. he left Wayne's Div. (1,500 men, four guns) south of the Schuylkill to harass Howe's advance. Wayne secretly occupied a position two miles S.W. of Paoli Tavern (in a neighborhood where he had lived as a boy); his plan was to strike the enemy flank or their baggage train as they pursued Washington north. (Smallwood's Brig. was also left behind to cooperate with Wayne, but it did not take part in the action that followed.)

British intelligence learned not only of Wayne's mission but also of his location, and Maj. Gen. Grey was sent to make a night attack against him. Grey marched at 10 P.M., 20 Sept., with the 2d Light Infantry Bn., and the 42d ("Black Watch") and 44th Regts. He was followed an hour later by two other regiments under Col. Musgrave, but these did not figure in the operation. Since night attacks are particularly difficult to control, it is interesting to see Maj. André's account of the special instructions that earned Grey the nickname "No-flint":

"No soldier of either [Musgrave's or Grey's column] was suffered to load; those who could not draw [unload] their pieces took out the flints. We knew nearly the spot where the Rebel corps lay, but nothing of the disposition of their camp. It was represented to the men that firing discovered us to the enemy, hid them from us, killed our friends and produced a confusion favorable to the escape of the Rebels. . . . On the other hand, by not firing we knew the foe to be wherever fire appeared and a charge ensured his destruction. . . ." (André, *Journal,* quoted in C. & M., 622)

Shortly after midnight, having made a fast and skilful approach, the British hit Wayne's bivouac. Four sentries fired and ran, Wayne's men turned out to defend themselves, and a short but decisive action took place.

"Those Continentals who thoughtlessly ran in front of the camp-fire were shot down; many who sought the shadows were bayonetted. Wayne succeeded, somewhat surprisingly, in getting his cannon beyond the reach of the enemy

and he collected his survivors after daylight, but he had lost at least 150 killed, captured or wounded" (Freeman, *Washington,* IV, 495)

Estimates of Wayne's losses run as high as 500 (Howe's claim), but 150 appears to be the true figure. (*Ibid.*) The British withdrew with 71 prisoners but left 40 of the badly wounded ones in houses along their route. Residents of the area reported finding 53 "mangled dead" on the scene of what was promptly dubbed the "Paoli Massacre." Howe reported the loss of six killed and about 22 wounded.

COMMENT

Wayne was acquitted by a court-martial "with the highest honors" of charges that he had failed to heed "timely notice" of the attack.

American propagandists succeeded in whipping up anti-British sentiment with false accusations that Grey's men had refused quarter and massacred defenseless patriots who tried to surrender. Gen. Heath's comment is simply that, "the bayonet was chiefly made use of, and it proved but too efficacious. . . ." (*Memoirs,* 138) The "no quarter" charge is refuted by the fact that the British took 71 prisoners. The "mangled dead" is explained by the fact that the bayonet is a messy weapon. (See Ward, *W.O.R.,* 469 *n.,* for some amusing comments on the massacre myth.)

PARALLELS. See REGULAR APPROACHES.

PARIS, Treaty of, 10 Feb. '63. Signed by Britain, France, and Spain, this ended the French and Indian War in America and the Seven Years' War in Europe. (Actually, the German phase of the war ended with another treaty signed 15 Feb.) France ceded to Britain all claims to Canada, Acadia, Cape Breton, and the islands in the St. Lawrence, but was given the islands of St.

Pierre and Miquelon—to the annoyance of school children, who have to memorize such details—and retained fishing rights off Newfoundland. France gave England her territories east of the Mississippi, except the Isle of Orleans; to compensate Spain for her losses as France's ally, by the secret Treaty of San Ildefonso (3 Nov. '62) France ceded Spain the Isle of Orleans and all her territory west of the Mississippi. Of the West Indies Islands captured during the war, Martinique and Guadeloupe were restored to France; St. Vincent, Dominica, and Tobago were restored to Britain. Britain restored Cuba to Spain in return for the Floridas. Spain acknowledged Britain's rights to maintain log-cutting settlements in Central America. (See SPANISH PARTICIPATION) France agreed to evacuate her position in Hanover and to restore Minorca to the British; the *status quo* in India was restored.

The Treaty of Paris eliminated France from America and left only Spain and England. GEORGE III has been criticized for failure to capitalize on the strong position in which the genius of Pitt had placed England at the end of the Seven Years' War; in his eagerness to present his people with a victorious peace, the new king settled for less than he could have gotten. John Wilkes quipped that the Peace of Paris was "the peace of God, for it surpasseth all understanding." France was shattered, exhausted, and humiliated, but she was not permanently crippled and was already beginning to mutter *revanche!* The man who was to direct the latter, Vergennes, is reported to have said of the treaty, "When I heard its conditions I told several friends [in Constantinople] that England would ere long have reason to repent of having removed the only check that could keep her colonies in awe." He was referring to the French in Canada, and some Englishmen argued that instead of Canada the British should have taken the sugar-rich island of Guadeloupe.

America gained everything: elimination of the French threat from Canada and opportunity for westward expansion. The Treaty of Paris opened the era of the American Revolution.

PARIS, Treaty of, 3 Sept. '83. See PEACE TREATY OF 3 Sept. '83.

PARKER, Sir Hyde. 1714–1782. British admiral. After service in the merchant marine he entered the Royal Navy at the age of 24. During the later part of the Seven Years' War he saw action at Pondichéry and Manila. In 1778 he was promoted to rear admiral and went to North America as second in command; for a short time before Rodney's arrival he commanded naval forces in the West Indies. On 23 Mar. '80 De Guichen, who had just assumed command of French naval forces, sailed to attack St. Lucia, "but a crusty, hard-fighting old admiral of the traditional English type, Sir Hyde Parker, had so settled himself at the anchorage, with sixteen ships, that Guichen with his twenty-two would not attack." (Mahan, *Sea Power*, 376–77) Rodney arrived 27 Mar. to take over-all command. In 1781, having returned to England and been promoted to Rear Adm., he resigned after a fiercely contested but indecisive action with a better-equipped Dutch fleet on 5 Aug. near the Dogger Bank. (*E.B.*) In 1782 he accepted the East Indies command, although he had just succeeded to the family baronetcy, but on the outward voyage his flagship, the *Cato* (60), was lost with all aboard.

He was called "Old Vinegar," not for his dietary ideas on how to prevent scurvy among his crews but because of his forbidding manner and speech. (Lewis, *De Grasse*, 80)

PARKER, Sir Hyde (Jr.). 1739–1807. British admiral. Second son of "Old Vinegar" (above), he served aboard his father's ships before becoming a Lt. in 1758. Starting in 1766 he spent many years in the West Indies and in North American waters. As captain of the *Phoenix* (40) he led the raid to TAPPAN SEA (now Tappan Zee), 12–18 July '76, and in 1779 was knighted for this performance. (*E.B.*) His ship was in action during the battle of LONG ISLAND, 27 Aug. '76, and he convoyed the expedition that captured SAVANNAH, 29 Dec. '78. The next year he was shipwrecked on Cuba, where he was forced to dig in to ward off hostile forces until rescued. (*Ibid.*) He served with his father in the action of 5 Aug. '81, with Howe in the two operations around Gibraltar, and with Hood at Toulon and in Corsica in 1793. In the latter year he was promoted to Vice Adm. of the White. After ably commanding at the Jamaica station, 1796–1800, he took command of the fleet sent into the Baltic in 1801. His second in command, Horatio Nelson, took Copenhagen on 2 Apr. with little support from Parker. He was severely criticized for his hesitation in exploiting this victory by an advance up the Baltic, and shortly thereafter he was recalled and succeeded by Nelson. His eldest son became First Sea Lord in 1853 (dying the next year), and that son's son was killed in action as a naval captain in the Black Sea in 1854.

PARKER, John. 1729–1775. Hero of Lexington, Mass. A native of Lexington, Mass., he served in the French and Indian War, fighting at Louisburg and Quebec and probably as one of Robert Roger's rangers for a time. When the Revolution started he had been married 20 years, had seven children, was a farmer and mechanic, and held various town offices. As Capt. of the local company of minutemen he figured prominently in the action covered under LEXINGTON AND CONCORD, 19 Apr. '75. It is not like him to have said the famous words carved on the stone at Lexington: "Stand your ground. Don't fire unless fired upon. But if they mean to have a war, let it begin here." This is, however, what he *should* have said. Parker assembled as many militia as possible after the action on the green and marched toward Concord to harry the British there and on their retreat to Boston. He then led a small force to Cambridge but was too ill to take part in subsequent actions. He died 17 Sept. '75

PARKER, Sir Peter. 1721–1811. British admiral. A post captain in 1747, he left England in 1775 with a force that was to cooperate in the CHARLESTON EXPEDITION OF CLINTON (1776). He distinguished himself in this affair only insofar as his personal bravery was concerned; after losing his pants, figuratively and literally, he proved that his pen was mightier than the sword—or, at least, his pen was faster than that of CLINTON. He supported the N.Y. Campaign and commanded the squadron that convoyed Clinton to Newport in Dec. '76. As military commander at Jamaica, 1779–81, under Gov. DALLING, he was repeatedly urged by Clinton to send naval support to protect Mobile and Pensacola, but to no avail. In 1782 he was knighted for bravery at Charleston (in 1776), and he eventually succeeded Lord Howe as Adm. of the Fleet. His grandson and namesake served under Sir George Cockburn in the Chesapeake during the War of 1812 and was mortally wounded the night of 30–31 Aug. 1814 when he led a party ashore for "a frolic with the Yankees" (as he put it) near Chestertown, Md. Lord Byron, his first cousin, wrote a poetic eulogy. (Appleton's)

PARKER'S FERRY, S.C., 13 Aug. '81. Col. Wm. Harden commanded a body of rebel troops near this place, some 30 miles W.N.W. of Charleston, when Maj. Thos. Fraser was sent with 200 dragoons to support an uprising of some 450 Tories. Harden called for help and Greene wrote Marion from the Santee Hills, "You know the Colonel's force, your own and the enemy's, and will do as you think proper." In a remarkable march of about 100 miles with 200 picked men, moving only at night and undetected by the enemy, Marion joined Harden on 13 Aug. He then set up an ambuscade on the causeway leading to Parker's Ferry and sent a party of his fastest horsemen to lure Fraser into the trap. Fraser took the bait, charged in to take a surprise fire of buckshot at 50 yards range; courageously he rallied his men, launched another attack in the face of a second volley, and was hit by a third when his horsemen again came parallel to the hidden partisans. Marion counted 27 dead horses and estimated that his sharpshooters had killed or wounded 100 dragoons. Although he had not lost a man, Marion's ammunition was almost exhausted and he could not exploit this success by pursuing. After covering a total of 400 miles (Lossing, II, 699, 775) he rejoined Greene in time for the major engagement at Eutaw Springs. (Bass, *Swamp Fox,* 214) The dates 30 and 31 Aug. are sometimes given for this action at Parker's Ferry, but 13 Aug. appears to be the correct one.

PARLEY. As early as the 16th century this term was used to mean an informal conference between military opponents to treat or discuss terms. A parley usually was requested to discuss surrender, but it also was called to arrange a truce to care for wounded men lying between the lines. It often was a means of gaining time. See also CHAMADE. A parley with the Indians was known in America as a POWOW.

PAROLE. Derived from the French *parole d'honneur* (word of honor), a parole is a pledge or oath under which a prisoner of war is released with the understanding that he will not again bear arms until exchanged. Sometimes the parole included geographical restrictions. The victor often is happy to parole prisoners because this relieves him of the administrative burden of caring for them; sometimes he does not have the transportation or guards to evacuate prisoners, particularly the wounded. Another sense of "parole" is a "watch-word differing from the countersign in that it is only communicated to officers of the guard, while the countersign is given to all members." (Thomas Wilhelm, *Military Dictionary,* rev. ed., 1881)

PARSON'S CAUSE (1763). When droughts of the 1750's brought on several crop failures and shot up the price of tobacco, the Va. Assy. in 1755 and '58 passed the Two Penny Acts, which made it legal to pay debts formerly callable in tobacco at the rate of 2d. a pound. This was considerably below the free market price and the Anglican clergy, entitled to an annual salary of 17,000 lbs. of tobacco a year, made an issue. The Privy Council exercised its right of disallowing the Act of 1758, and the clergy brought suit. Rev. James Maury presented the suit in Hanover Court in 1763, and the judges had to declare the act null and void. But when a jury was called to determine how much "the parson" would collect, young Patrick Henry's brilliant defense resulted in Maury's being awarded only 1d. The case marked the beginning of Henry's political career.

PARSONS, Samuel Holden. 1737–1789. Cont'l. general. Conn. Son of a clergyman whose adherence to the theology of George Whitefield made him so unpopular that he moved from Lyme, Conn., to Newburyport, Mass., in 1746, Samuel returned to Lyme after graduating from Harvard in 1756. His mother, Phebe Griswold, had important family connections and he studied law under one of them, his uncle, Gov. Matthew Griswold. Getting a master's degree from Harvard, he was admitted to the bar in 1759, and settled in Lyme to become a prominent figure in patriot politics. Serving 18 consecutive terms in the assembly, in 1773 he became King's attorney and also a member of the standing committee of inquiry with the sister colonies. He was one of the first to suggest holding a colonial congress (*D.A.B.*) and is said to have originated the plan for the first one, held in N.Y.C. Around 1774 he moved to New London. A Maj. of the 14th militia regiment since 1770, he became Col. in Apr. '75 and, given this same grade in the Cont'l. Army on 1 May, took command of the 6th Regt. He figured prominently in the plan to capture TICONDEROGA, 10 May. After taking part in the Boston siege he accompanied the reinforcements sent to N.Y., was promoted to B.G. on 9 Aug. '76, and was heavily engaged in the fighting on the American right (Alexander's wing) at LONG ISLAND, 27 Aug. D. S. Freeman comments that his 8 Oct. '76 letter to John Adams provides the best available description of the battlefield and is "a model of lucid and simple explanation...." (*Washington*, IV, 158; see C. & M., 432–33) At KIP'S BAY, 15 Sept., his brigade of regulars proved they could run as well as militia (*ibid.*, 194), but he himself joined the C. in C. in trying to stop the rout. After the N.Y. Campaign Parsons had a relatively obscure role in command of troops on the Hudson or along the Conn. shore; "skirmishing and foraging were his lot," writes Jane Clark in *D.A.B.*, "with little opportunity for brilliance."

After the battle of Harlem Heights he was posted in the Highlands until Dec. '76, when he was detached to reinforce Washington's troops in N.J. The winter of 1776–77 he recruited in N.Y. and N.J. In late Sept. he warned Israel Putnam that 3,000 British reinforcements had reached N.Y.C. (These were employed in CLINTON'S EXPEDITION... Oct. '77.) The winter of 1778–79 he was in charge of construction at West Point and in July '79 attacked British raiders at Norwalk, Conn. (*D.A.B.*) In Dec. '79 he succeeded Israel Putnam as commander of the Conn. division, "having been the virtual head for over a year" (*ibid.*), and on 23 Oct. '80 he was promoted to Maj. Gen. He was thanked by Congress for his successful raid against MORRISANIA, 22–23 Jan. '81.

As early as Dec. '77 Parsons had been alarmed by the depreciation of Cont'l. currency, which was wiping out the small fortune he had invested in government securities when he entered the army. A year later he is mentioned as being on leave and impatient to be released from military service (Freeman, *op. cit.*, V, 99 n.), but Congress would not approve his resignation until hostilities ceased. During this time the double agent Wm. Heron, who had dealt with Parsons on espionage matters, marked the discontented general as a good prospect for winning over to the British cause. Carl Van Doren traces the efforts in this direction and concludes that "Parsons, often disgruntled and resentful, never showed himself disloyal or treacherous." (*Secret History*, 400)

Retiring from the army on 22 July

'82, Parsons practiced law in Middletown, Conn., and was elected several times to the legislature. He was quick to see the advantages of getting government land in exchange for his pay-certificates and undertook to get an appointment that would enable him to look over the western lands. This opportunity came when Congress named him an Indian commissioner on 22 Sept. '85. He then became a promoter of the Ohio Co. and on 8 Mar. '87 was chosen one of its three directors. In Oct. he was named the first judge of the Northwest Territory and in Apr. '88 moved to Adelphia (now Marietta, Ohio). At the age of 51 he embarked on the life of a frontiersman and undertook to recoup his fortune. There is justifiable suspicion that he engaged in some dishonest practices in his eagerness for profit. (*D.A.B.*) He drowned on 17 Nov. '89 when his canoe capsized in the rapids of the Big Beaver River while he was returning from a visit to the Western Reserve, where he also had an interest. (*Ibid.*)

Much of his correspondence has recently come to historical light in the Clinton Papers, which are in the Clements Library of the U. of Mich. Other manuscript materials are in the Conn. State Library. C. S. Hall published the *Life and Letters of . . .* in 1905.

PATERSON, James. British general. Appointed Adj. Gen. in America on 11 July '76, he held this office until he was sent home with dispatches after the battle of Monmouth, 28 June '78. With the "local rank" of B.G. he commanded three infantry battalions and a jäger detachment in the capture of Stony Point, 1 June '79, and B.G. James Pattison managed to get guns and mortars onto this rocky position to support the capture of Verplancks Point, across the Hudson. (See also STONY POINT, 16 July '79) Taking part in the CHARLESTON EXPEDITION of Clinton in 1780, Paterson initially was put in command of a force that was to make a diversion toward Augusta, Ga., but subsequently was called back to support the siege of Charleston. He returned to N.Y.C., presumably with Clinton in June '80. (Clinton, *Amer. Reb., passim*) In the spring of 1781 he commanded the defenses of Staten Island and in Oct. of that year was preparing to take part in the expedition to relieve the siege of Yorktown when news was received of Cornwallis' surrender. (Baurmeister, *Journals,* 431, 470)

His name is commonly misspelled Patterson (Anderson, *Howe Bros.;* Freeman, *Washington,* IV); it is spelled with one t in such works as C. & M., Clinton's *American Rebellion,* and Baurmeister's *Journals.*

PATERSON, John. 1744–1808. Cont'l. general. Conn.–Mass. Grandson of a Scot who came to New England prior to 1704, and son of a militia officer who had served in the Colonial Wars, he graduated from Yale in 1762, taught school for several years in his home town of WETHERSFIELD, Conn., and then started practicing law. In 1774 he moved to Lenox, Mass., and became prominent in the Revolutionary politics of Berkshire co. He sat in the Mass. Prov. Cong. in 1774 and 1775 and raised a militia regiment. An impressive-looking man, over six feet tall and vigorous until late in life, he had long shown a taste for military life. (Edward E. Curtis in *D.A.B.*) When news of Lexington and Concord reached Lenox he marched within 18 hours for Boston with a unit that was armed and almost completely in uniform. On 27 May '75 he was commissioned Col. of the regiment known at that time by his name; reorganized and reinforced, it be-

came the 15th Cont'l. Regt. on 1 Jan.
'76. During the Boston Siege he was
posted near Prospect Hill, where he
built and garrisoned Fort No. 3. He
was held in reserve during the Battle
of Bunker Hill. On 9 Nov. '75 he was
involved in driving off an enemy foraging raid on LECHMERE POINT. In Mar.
'76 he accompanied the army to N.Y.
and was then sent with Gen. Wm.
Thompson to Canada. Maj. Henry Sherburne led 100 men of the regiment to
relieve the force under attack at The
CEDARS, May '76, and 79 of these (according to Appleton's) were captured.

Col. Paterson retreated with Benedict
Arnold's column. After working on the
defenses of Mt. Independence, opposite
Ticonderoga, from July until Nov. '76,
he moved south to join Washington's
army on the Delaware. He took part in
the battles of Trenton and Princeton,
and on 21 Feb. '77 was promoted to
B.G. He returned to the Northern Dept.
and was one of the undistinguished general officers (with Fermoy and Enoch
Poor) who commanded troops under
Arthur St. Clair in the operations at
TICONDEROGA, 2–5 July. His brigade
had an inactive part in the two battles of Saratoga, although Paterson's
horse was shot out from under him by
a cannon ball during this campaign.
(D.A.B.) The list of troops at Valley
Forge shows his brigade as consisting
of the 10th, 11th, 12th, and 14th Mass.
Cont'ls. After participating in the Monmouth Campaign, June–July '78, without seeing any action, he spent the rest
of the war in the Hudson Highlands.
On 30 Sept. '83 he was breveted Maj.
Gen., and on 3 Nov. he left the army.

Resuming his law practice at Lenox
and holding many public offices, he
helped organize the Ohio Company and
as commander of the Berkshire militia
took part in suppressing Shays's Rebel-

lion (1786). Meanwhile he became a
proprietor of the Boston Purchase (10
townships in Broome and Tioga cos.)
and in 1791 he moved there with his
family. In N.Y. he was elected to the
legislature (1792–93), the constitutional
convention of 1801, and to Congress
(1803–5). In 1798 he was appointed
to the bench and was judge of the two
counties. (D.A.B.)

Thos. Egleston published *The Life of
John Paterson* in 1898.

PATTISON, James. 1724–1805. British general. An artillery officer, he was
promoted to Col. on 25 Apr. '77 and
reached N.Y. on 24 Sept. '77 with the
"local rank" of B.G. Clinton promoted
him to Maj. Gen. on 19 Feb. '79.
After assisting Gen. James PATERSON
in the operations against Stony Point
and Verplancks Point on 1 June '79, he
won the praise of Clinton for his work
in organizing a local militia for the defense of N.Y.C. (Clinton, *Amer. Reb.,*
190, 455, 456) Although he served as
commandant of N.Y.C. during most if
not all of his time in America, he also
commanded a brigade in the field operations during June '79. (Baurmeister,
Journals, 280, 289) On 4 Sept. '80
he sailed from N.Y. to England with
the fleet that took Gov. Tryon home.
(*Ibid.,* 367)

PATTON'S REGT. Col. John Patton
commanded one of the 16 "ADDITIONAL
CONT'L. REGTS."

PAULDING, John. 1758–1818. Captor of John André. N.Y. According to
Appleton's, "He served throughout the
war of the Revolution, and was three
times taken prisoner by the British."
A few days after escaping from his
second imprisonment, Paulding, Isaac
Van Wart, and David Williams captured André under circumstances described in the article on ARNOLD'S

TREASON. This article also goes into the matter of their motives and rewards.

He was descended from Joost Pauldinck, who came to N.Y. from Holland prior to 1683. John's seventh child, Hiram Paulding (1797–1878), became a naval hero. (*D.A.B.*, "Hiram Paulding")

PAULUS HOOK, N.J., 19 Aug. '79. Henry Lee's Raid. After Wayne's brilliant coup at Stony Point, 16 July, Washington's strategic and administrative problems still were such that he could do little more than concentrate on strengthening the defenses of West Point. However, he and his subordinates did look around for some limited operation that might be within their means. Washington concluded that Paulus (or Powles) Hook might be raided; it was an isolated British post, and there were reports that the garrison was second-rate. After Henry Lee had reconnoitered the place, however, Washington decided the risks outweighed the possible advantages. But Lee studied the situation some more and finally got Washington's qualified approval to make an attack.

"Stony Point had piqued his [Lee's] emulation," wrote Washington Irving. Freeman discredits the traditional belief that Lee conceived the operation, however. (*Washington*, V, 125 *n.*)

Paulus Hook, now in Jersey City near Washington and Grand Streets, was a low point of sand protruding into the Hudson. Its northern face and about half of its western face could be approached through a salt marsh, but a creek and a tidal moat ran across this front. From a contemporary British map,* it would appear that an attacker

* Reproduced in Freeman, *op. cit.*, from the original in the Clinton Papers; this is the basis for my sketch. It should be noted, however, that the original is

would have to cross 500 yards of marsh to reach the abatis and defensive perimeter. At almost the geometric center of the camp was a circular redoubt located on a slight rise in the ground. Blockhouses, an oval fortification, barracks, and earthworks had been constructed. The 200-man garrison under Maj. Wm. Sutherland included part of the 64th Foot, the light infantry company of Capt. Dundas, 41 Hessians under Capt. von Schaller, a body of Invalids, and some Tories of Skinner's N.J. Vols. Lt. Col. Abram Van Buskirk had left camp with about 150 men of the latter unit on a foraging expedition, and the troops of Dundas and Schaller arrived the night before the attack to take their place.† A number of artificers and camp followers were also in camp.

Lee had 400 men for the attack: 200 attached Virginians, Capt. Allen McLane's partisans (dismounted), and Lt. Levin Handy's two Md. companies.

At 10:30 the morning of 18 Aug., Lee started from Paramus with Handy's two companies and a number of wagons, to give the impression he was off on a foraging expedition. At New Bridge, about four miles away, he was joined by the rest of the troops, and around 4:30 he started south toward Bergen. Allen McLane had reconnoitered the approaches to Paulus Hook and had gotten precise information about its garrison from a deserter. To

dated 24 July '78, and does not necessarily show the man-made features of the British camp as they existed in July '79.

† This is according to Ward, *W.O.R.*, 605. The *N.Y. Gazette* of 23 Aug. reported that one light infantry company of the Guards, under Dundas, joined Sutherland at 8:30 A.M. on the 19th, and started in pursuit of Lee. (Quoted in C. & M., 727)

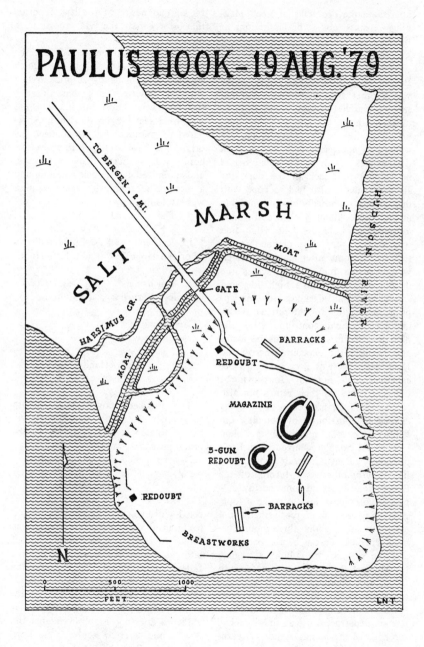

PAULUS HOOK—19 AUG. '79

appreciate the problems of Lee's planning we must look at his limitations of time, space, tide, and light. For "strategic map" see front endpaper.

The distance from New Bridge to Bergen was 16 miles, and the objective was another two miles away. Normal rate of march for foot troops is three miles an hour, so Lee had to count on about five hours of marching. He wanted to approach the objective area during darkness to avoid detection and he wanted to attack in the dark for surprise, but he also had to cope with ditches that supposedly were unfordable at high tide. About 4 o'clock the next morning it would be light. High tide was about 2 A.M. Lee planned to attack half an hour after midnight, which would enable him to get across the ditches and back before high tide, and would give him darkness for his approach as well as for the retreat. Washington's personal contribution to the plan was to insist that boats be available to ferry the expedition across the Hackensack west of Bergen—below Secaucus Island—not only to provide a different route for their return but also to give them the protection of the river against the possibility of pursuit from Paulus Hook. So much for the plan.

The first trouble occurred when Lee's principal guide misdirected him (deliberately or otherwise); turning off the Bergen road to avoid some enemy outposts, the column had to make a long, exhausting detour to reach their final assembly area, about three hours behind schedule. Troops began to mutter, and the rear of the column straggled. Lt. Michael Rudolph was sent forward to find out whether there still was time to get across the ditch, and the rest of the force moved cautiously toward their line of departure. Just as they reached the edge of the marsh, some 500 yards from their objective, Lee got another

bit of bad news: Maj. Clark reported that nearly half the Va. troops were missing! *

Washington had prescribed that the operation be called off if the attack could not be made by surprise. When Rudolph reported back that although the ditch was almost full it could still be forded near the drawbridge, Lee prepared to continue. But he changed his original plan of attacking in three columns with a fourth body in reserve, and organized two attack columns and a reserve. Schematically, the new plan was as follows:

↑	↑
Lt. Rudolph	Lt. McAllister
(Forlorn Hope)	(Forlorn Hope)
Lt. Armstrong	Major Clark
(Advance Party)	(Main Body)
Capt. Forsyth	
(Main Body)	

Capt. Handy
(Reserve)

The attackers moved slowly across the marsh. To insure that no trigger-happy soldier fired prematurely, elaborate measures were prescribed: muskets were loaded, but not primed; they were carried at the shoulder; each

* Ward says Clark had already quarreled with Lee about being subordinated to him on this operation (Clark was senior to Lee), and this author speculates that the Va. troops may have fallen out because this dispute as well as the mismanaged march undermined their confidence in their leaders. (*W.O.R.*, 606) Freeman warns that evidence does not establish whether the Va. troops deserted Lee or were honestly lost. (*Op. cit.*, 126 & *n.*)

man was to hold his hat in his right hand and as close as possible to the thigh until he passed the ditch; officers had instructions to kill any man who tried to fire without orders. Suspense mounted as the rebels struggled forward. McAllister reached the tidal moat first and halted. Then Rudolph reached the spot he had previously picked as being the best place for fording the ditch. The enemy camp was still silent, and the thought must have been in everybody's mind that this might mean surprise had been achieved, or it could mean that the enemy merely were holding their fire to butcher them as they waded the ditch.

Rudolph whispered a command and his men plunged into the water with no further effort at silence. McAllister's party advanced a moment later. There was a shout from the enemy camp, a few shots, and the sounding of the general alarm. The Americans capitalized on their hard-won surprise to overrun the position in a few minutes. McAllister was first through the abatis, and Clark was hard on his heels with the rest of the right column. They found an opening in the main work—left by the British to facilitate communication with the countryside—and charged in to capture a redoubt. Bayonets stabbed into those who offered resistance and scores of sleepy-eyed British soldiers raised their hands in surrender. Forsyth and McLane overran another blockhouse. As the reserve arrived, "Handy was dealing out the men . . . to right and to left, as the sound of the firing indicated need." (Freeman, *op. cit.,* 128) Many British and Hessians had been captured and a number killed, but pockets of resistance remained. Capt. Schaller held the round redoubt with about 25 of his men (Baurmeister, *Journals,* 296) and refused to surrender it. Lee's men discov-

ered that all their powder had been ruined when they forded the ditch, and they did not have the means of knocking down the door of the British magazine. The situation suddenly became precarious: alarm guns were sounding in N.Y.C., a mere mile and a half across the Hudson; dawn was fast approaching, and with it would come the danger of being raked with grape shot from the six heavy guns in the round redoubt. (Ward, *op. cit.,* 605) Lee therefore ordered a rapid withdrawal. He had intended to burn the barracks, but was forced to abandon this plan when prisoners told him they held women, children, and bedridden soldiers. He had more than 150 prisoners, including a man who claimed to be the British commander, so he could not burden himself further by trying to carry off the captured cannon—he was not even able to spike them.

It is difficult to estimate the time that Lee left Paulus Hook. The action had taken only a few minutes—less than 30, according to Handy—but whereas the latter says the attack started after 4 o'clock, the enemy reported the time as being an hour or an hour and a half earlier. (C. & M., 726–27)

Everything went well until the expedition reached the Hackensack to find that no boats were in sight. Capt. Henry Peyton of Lee's Dragoons had been there but had taken the boats back to Newark when the expected time of rendezvous had long passed and no word had been received from Lee; Peyton assumed the operation had been called off. Messengers from Lee had failed to reach Peyton. So instead of a safe water movement of five miles or so to Newark, Lee's men were now faced with a long, dangerous retreat over the route by which they had approached Bergen, with the hazard of meeting Van Buskirk's foragers and/or pursuit from Paulus Hook. And there was not a charge of dry powder in Lee's command.

Near Weehawken (or Wihack) the bone-tired raiders met Capt. Thos. Catlett of the 2d Va. with 50 men. (Ward says these were stragglers from the original expedition. Freeman says this *probably* is so, although Lee's report does not say so.) Now, at least, there was enough dry powder for one or two rounds if they had to fight. As the column cleared the fork of the road to Ft. Lee, Lt. Col. Burgess Ball of the 1st Va. arrived with a relief column that Alexander had sent as soon as he received Lee's request from the boat rendezvous. It was not a bit too soon, for Van Buskirk attacked Lee's right flank in the vicinity of Liberty Pole Tavern (now Englewood), not three miles north of the point at which Ball joined Lee. "These redcoats opened on the American rear," says Freeman; "but Lee had observed these assailants, also, and he did not wait for his rescuers to deal with them. Perhaps pridefully, Lee sent out two small parties under officers [Rudolph being one of them] whose adroit maneuvers and bold resolution quickly discouraged the enemy." (*Op. cit.,* 130) At 1 P.M. the American force was safe at New Bridge.

NUMBERS AND LOSSES

Of the 400 who started with Lee, about 300 took part in the assault. Two were killed and three wounded, according to Ward, who has a tendency to accept improbable CASUALTY FIGURES. Baurmeister says Van Buskirk brought in seven prisoners. (*Journals,* 296)

Of the 250 or so combatants at Paulus Hook, Handy says about 50 were "put to the bayonet" (C. & M., 727), and we must assume that some of these were wounded and captured. Lee returned with 158 prisoners, seven

of them officers. To his special disgust, however, the man who claimed to be Sutherland turned out to be a private; it is not known whether this impersonation was the soldier's own idea or whether he acted on orders. (Freeman, *op. cit.,* 130 and *n.*) The British commandant had taken refuge in the round redoubt with Schaller.

COMMENT

Maj. Lee had conducted a successful raid despite difficulties, bad breaks, and his own mistakes. He and his men showed great courage and resolution. This should not be passed over lightly in going on to make an academic analysis of the operation's strategic significance and errors made by the 23-year-old leader. Congress thanked Lee for his exploit and gave him a gold medal to match the one Wayne got for Stony Point. Washington praised him and was grateful for the morale boost the operation gave his army; he did not point out the errors that might have caused disaster: "Failure to keep his column closed, to issue sufficient rations, to assure dry ammunition and to make certain the boats were at Secaucus...." (Freeman, *op. cit.,* 130)

Washington was powerless to head off the demands of jealous Va. and Md. officers that a court-martial investigate whether Lee properly took precedence over officers of the expedition who were senior, even though he did this on Washington's orders. Maj. Jonathan Clark, who had the most solid ground for complaint, supported Lee, but charges were preferred by Col. Nathaniel Gist. At first merely amused by all this (Geo. Weedon later dubbed Gist "that head of the Wrongheads" for his action), Lee decided "to give Gist blow for blow, and, in the end, he had complete vindication and high praise by the court." (Freeman, *op. cit.,* 131)

The British commander at Paulus Hook had fallen into the eternal error of neglecting security measures because he felt safe behind a terrain barrier. "Major Sutherland was courtmartialed," writes Baurmeister; presumably he was convicted. According to the Hessian A. G., Clinton warmly thanked the Hessians for their role in the affair: one of their posts had been overrun, but five of the 15 escaped; Schaller and Ensign Kress with the remaining 25 or so Germans refused to surrender their redoubt.* (*Journals,* 296)

PAXTON BOYS, 1763–65. As a result of the Indian depredations on the Pa. frontier that culminated in PONTIAC'S WAR, the Scots-Irish and German settlers had violent sentiments toward the savages (all of whom they thought should be exterminated) and the Quaker-dominated government of the colony (whom they thought should do more to protect the frontier). Led by Lazarus Stewart, some 57 rangers from Paxton and Donegal senselessly massacred the defenseless settlement of Conestoga Indians living near Lancaster, killing 20 of them on 14 Dec. '63. Five of these were women and eight were children. Gov. Penn ordered the culprits brought to trial, but sympathetic justices and juries made this impossible. The "Boys" then undertook a political campaign to win their demands, and in Jan. '64 some 600 of them marched under arms on Philadelphia. Largely through the efforts of Franklin the Paxton Boys were

* Despite the excellent British map mentioned earlier, Freeman points out that defenses at the time of Lee's raid are not known exactly. He says it was the round redoubt that held out, although Ward says McAllister entered this work and "struck the colors." (Freeman, *op. cit.,* 128 *n.,* 130 *n.;* Ward, *op. cit.,* 608)

stopped before they could massacre any Quakers, and as a result of their formal protest they were given more representation in the legislature. "The Paxton massacre marked the close of Quaker supremacy and the beginning of the predominance of the Scotch-Irish pioneers," says one authority. (*E.B.,* "Pennsylvania," XXI, 112) Although the turning point was about this time, it would be hard to support the theory that these border ruffians deserve the credit. In his *Origins of the American Revolution,* Miller goes so far as to say, "The Paxton or Black Boys failed to get support." (P. 62) Whether it was the same band or another with similar political views and lack of morality, "ruffians in Cumberland County, known as the Black Boys" (Peckham, *Pontiac,* 279) disguised themselves as Indians and at Sideling Hill, in May '65, and destroyed a convoy of gifts and trade goods being sent to Ft. Pitt for the Indians at the end of Pontiac's War.

Lazarus Stewart, disgusted with the proprietary government and threatened with prosecution, moved with his followers to the Wyoming Valley in 1769 and was granted a township by the Conn. authorities. He figured in the Pennamite Wars and was killed in the Wyoming Valley "Massacre," 3–4 July '78. (*D.A.H.*)

PAY, BOUNTIES, AND RATIONS. The three subjects are related and must therefore be considered together. With respect to the first, pay, it was inadequate in both the American and the British armies; but, what is more to the point, even this inadequate amount seldom actually got into the hands of the troops. In the case of the Americans, the authorities rarely had the money; then there was the matter of inflation, which is covered under CONT'L CURRENCY. Rates also varied tremendously: privates of the Mass. militia were entitled to $36 per lunar month in 1775, whereas their counterparts in the Cont'l. Army were supposed to draw $6.67 or 40 shillings per calendar month. (Privates in the artillery, cavalry, and military police were entitled to $8.33.) Early in the war the pay scale was $10 per month for ensigns, $13.33 for Lts., and $20 for Capts., but late in 1776 these rates were raised about 30 per cent. A British Capt. drew about twice as much as an American Capt., but a more significant difference was that he could buy almost anything he needed at moderate rates. (Hatch, 78) Inequities of pay scales between the Cont'l. Army and the militia, arrears in pay, and inflation plagued American commanders, including Washington, throughout the war and created serious morale problems. In the British Army the situation became so bad after the Revolution that "the only alternatives open to the private soldier were to desert or to starve...." (Fortescue, III, 521)

Authorities disagree so radically on actual figures pertaining to military pay that I have deliberately avoided an attempt to give them here, particularly since the value of these salaries in terms of modern purchasing power can hardly be established. (Ganoe equated $36 in 1775 to $150 in 1924. [p. 13], but what is this in 1970?)

BOUNTIES

Not having authority to draft men for military service, Congress and the states used bounties to induce voluntary enlistment. The states started using this device early in the war, and Washington soon realized that the bounty system was a necessary evil. "When the Army was first raised at Cambridge," he wrote Congress on 24 Sept. '76, "I am persuaded the men might have been got without a bounty for the war. After this they began to see that the contest was

not likely to end so speedily as was imagined, and to feel their consequence by remarking that, to get in their militia in the course of the last year, many towns were induced to give them a bounty." He then recommended that recruits be offered "a good bounty" and at least 100 or 150 acres of land, a suit of clothes, and a blanket for enlisting. (Sparks, *Writings of Washington,* IV, 112) On 19 Jan. '76 Congress advised the states to offer a bounty of $6.66 to all men who would enlist with a good firearm, a bayonet, and other accouterments, and to offer $4 to those who enlisted without these items. On 26 June the delegates resolved to offer $10 to all men who would enlist for three years. A few weeks later they extended this offer to all regulars who would continue their service in the Cont'l. Army for three years after expiration of their current tour. On 16 Sept., when they voted the army of 88 battalions, Congress increased the bounty to $20 plus 100 acres to all enlisted men who would agree to serve "during the war." Two days later they extended this offer to all "who are enlisted or shall enlist for during the war," which took care of the regulars of the Cont'l. Army. Any of the latter who already had received a Cont'l. bounty of $10 for a former enlistment would, however, receive only $10 more under the new offer. On 8 Oct. Congress agreed to give a $20 suit of clothes each year (or this amount in cash if the man's Capt. would certify that he had procured such a suit himself) to all men enlisted for the duration. Officers were authorized recruiting expenses at the rate of $1.33 per new man.

But the states, also faced with the problem of raising men, undertook to compete for recruits by increasing their bounties. Early in 1777 some of the New England states agreed to offer $33.33 in addition to the $20 set by Congress;

Mass. then doubled this ante, offering $86.66; other states fell in line and some went higher. This stopped re-enlistments in the Cont'l. regiments, and it also led men to desert these units to enlist fraudulently in state regiments for the larger bounty. "Bounty jumpers" would enlist, collect their bounty, desert, re-enlist, and collect another.

The bounty battle continued to rage. On 23 Jan. '79 Congress authorized Washington to grant up to $200 to each able-bodied man who would enlist or re-enlist for the war. On 9 Mar. the delegates resolved to pay this bounty out of the Cont'l. treasury to men recruited by the states or, if the state was giving this amount or more, to credit the state with $200 for each man enlisted against its quota. On 29 Mar. Congress recommended that Va. and N.C. raise as many regular battalions as possible, and to give these men the $200 bounty *for a single year's service in Va., the Carolinas, or Ga.*

Again the states outdid the central government. N.J. added $250 to the Congressional bounty of $200, land, and clothing. On 3 May '79 Va. offered $750, a suit a year, and 100 acres to men who signed up for the duration; from this the state retained the cash and clothing offered by Congress. In 1780 N.J. increased its bounty to $1,000 more than all Cont'l. offers. Much of this increase was due to depreciation of the CONT'L. CURRENCY, which hit the officers particularly hard, and on 21 Oct. '80 Congress finally adopted Washington's urgent recommendation that to keep officers in service until the end of the war they be granted half pay for life.

"The bounty system was a child of the Revolution, called into being when the colonies denied Congress the power of compelling enlistments," comments Upton (p. 21). The child grew into a man who did not die until after the Civil War, and recruiting bounties were expressly forbidden by the Selective Service Act of 1917. One American military historian has written: "It is curious fact that these very patriots who resented so thoroughly the mercenary troops sent against them from England were themselves but highly paid hirelings of their own government." (Ganoe, 14)

RATIONS

Integrated with the system of pay and bounties was the matter of rations, insofar as officers were concerned. Whereas the soldier was entitled to a single ration (three meals), officers were authorized extra rations. The scale prescribed by Congress on 22 Apr. '82 was five rations for a Maj. Gen., four for a B.G., two for a Lt. Col., one and a half for a Maj. or Capt., and one for a subaltern. (Ganoe, 80 *n.*)

The ration, like pay, was prescribed but not necessarily handed out. While Jonathan Trumbull was Q.M.G. and the army was in the Boston area, drawing on resources of the rich Connecticut River Valley, and with the assistance of his father, Gov. TRUMBULL of Conn., the troops actually were issued more than the prescribed ration. Problems of SUPPLY later reduced the army to starvation. The Cont'l. Cong. prescribed the army's ration on 12 Sept. '75, and on 4 Nov. '75 it modified this somewhat to the following: "Resolved, That a ration consist of the following kind and quantity of provisions: 1 lb. beef, or ¾ lb. pork or 1 lb. salt fish, per day; 1 lb. bread or flour, per day; 3 pints of peas or beans per week, or vegetables equivalent, at one dollar per bushel for peas or beans; 1 pint of milk, per man per day, or at the rate of 1-72 of a dollar; 1 half pint of rice, or one pint of Indian meal, per man per week; 1 quart of spruce beer or cider per man per day, or nine gallons of mollasses, per company of 100 men per week; 3 lbs. candles to 100 men per week, for guards; 24 lbs. soft, or 8 lbs. hard soap, for 100 men per week." Rum and whiskey were later authorized but seldom issued.

SPRUCE BEER was not available in the Boston area, and "mollasses" was substituted without the disastrous results this had on Gates's army just before the battle of Camden. (See section of the article on the CAMDEN CAMPAIGN, headed "From Bad Strategy to Worse Tactics.") See also FIRE CAKE.

The British ration varied in accordance with what was locally available, but in a representative contract of 1778–79 it provided 1 lb. of flour per day; 1 lb. of beef per day or slightly more than 9 oz. of pork; 3 pints of peas per week; ½ lb. of oatmeal a week, and either 6 oz. of butter or 8 oz. of cheese per week. (E. E. Curtis, "Provisioning of the British Army in the Revolution," *Mag. of Hist.*, XVIII, 234, cited in Risch, *Q.M. Support . . .*, 9 and *n*. The latter work is fully identified at the end of the article on SUPPLY. . . .)

Although the Q.M. issued firewood and cooking utensils when possible, soldiers prepared their meals individually or formed small groups in which men took turns cooking. Since flour and beef were the only items usually issued, food preparation was an all-too-simple task and "an unrelieved diet of half-cooked meat and hard bread was responsible for much of the sickness that reduced the strength of the Army when it frequently was most needed." (Risch, *op. cit.*, 10)

PEACE COMMISSION OF CARLISLE. 1778. As one of the measures to block American ratification of the French Alliance a peace commission was sent from England with powers to negotiate with Congress and suspend, if necessary, all acts passed since 1763. Frederick Howard, 5th Earl of Carlisle, a young man not yet 30 but of prestige and great wealth and a close friend of Opposition leader Charles Fox (which was expected to please the Americans), was appointed on 22 Feb. '78 to head the commission. In addition to the Howe brothers, already in America, the following members were commissioned on 12 Apr.: Wm. Eden, a close friend of Carlisle since Eton, member of the Board of Trade, and a man who had been "as energetic in the matter of conciliation . . . as he had been in the secret service before the Franco-American treaty" (Van Doren, *Secret History,* 66); and George Johnstone, a Scot who had been Gov. of W. Fla. and "was known in Parliament as a partisan for America." (*Ibid.,* 68) (He is the "noisy politician" who fought a duel with GERMAIN in Dec. '70.) Eden's wife, four months pregnant, went along for the trip aboard the man-of-war *Trident* (64), as did a third Etonian, Anthony Morris Storer, "known as the best dancer and skater in London." A particular friend of Johnstone, Adam Ferguson, renowned professor of moral philosophy at Edinburgh, served as acting secretary of the commission. On board, also, was Cornwallis, returning to become Clinton's second in command. Commodore John Elliot, Capt. of the *Trident* and uncle of Mrs. Eden, "hoped he would never again have such a service assigned to him: 'for the servants and baggage is past all belief.' " (*Ibid.,* 84) The excursion ship left Portsmouth on 16 Apr. and reached Philadelphia on 6 June.

Carlisle immediately encountered almost insurmountable obstacles: Congress had resolved on 22 Apr. that any man or group that came to terms with the commission was an enemy of the U.S.; furthermore, Clinton was preparing to evacuate Philadelphia. When Carlisle on 9 June requested a conference, Congress replied on the 17th that the only negotiable points were British withdrawal and recognition of independence. Before leaving Philadelphia, Johnstone attempted to bribe Congressmen Joseph Reed, Robert Morris, and Francis Dana; this led to his resignation on 26 Aug. Funds for covert activities had been given to the commission, and Sir John Temple and John Berkenhout followed Carlisle from England to join him in N.Y.C. as secret agents early in Aug. The last week of Aug. Berkenhout left N.Y.C. with a pass from Clinton, managed to pick up a pass from Gen. Wm. Maxwell at Elizabeth, proceeded with his American credentials to Trenton and from there by sloop to reach Philadelphia on 27 Aug. Introducing himself to Richard Henry Lee as a friend of Arthur Lee—he had known the latter in London—the agent tried to represent himself as a man looking for a new home in the land of liberty. But Maxwell had become suspicious and had written to warn Richard Lee, and Congress learned from a London newspaper quoted in Philadelphia that Berkenhout and Temple were on some sort of ministerial errand. Berkenhout was questioned by the Council of Pa. on 3 Sept., jailed, paroled on the 14th, and on 19 Sept. was back in N.Y.C., his mission having done no good and having further prejudiced Congress against dealing with the commission.

In Oct. Lafayette challenged Carlisle to a duel on the grounds that he was personally responsible for the commission's attacks on France in letters to Congress; on the 11th Carlisle informed the offended Frenchman that he was answerable only to his country for his "public conduct and language," and Lafayette ended in looking somewhat ridiculous. On 3 Oct. Carlisle and Eden made a fruitless attempt to appeal direct to the people, offering general pardon for past disloyalty of Americans at large and full pardon to all military or civil office holders who would ask for it within the next 40 days. (Excepting only those who might be responsible for "putting to death any of his Majesty's subjects" after the date of their proclamation.)

Conceding failure, the commissioners boarded the *Roebuck* 27 Nov. and reached Plymouth on 20 Dec. '78 after an exceptionally fast crossing. Temple stayed behind, tried to pose as a refugee looking for a new home, succeeded to the extent of meeting with Samuel Adams and Henry Laurens on 1 Dec. and dining with Congress that night, but making a sudden departure on the 20th when Gérard hinted to Congress that they might be dealing with an enemy emissary.

Alden cites Van Doren, *Secret History,* 63–116, as "the best account of the Carlisle commission" and also recommends Weldon A. Brown, *Empire or Independence* . . . (Baton Rouge, 1941), 205–90.

PEACE COMMISSION OF THE HOWES. 1776–78. By the end of 1774 the British government got the idea of sending commissioners to attempt to settle the dispute brewing in America, although George III at this time felt that the colonists might greet this step as an indication of British weakness. (Anderson, *Howe Bros.,* 43) In Mar. '76, when Lord Richard Howe was working out with the ministry the conditions under which he would assume the naval command in America, he informed Germain that he would not accept a commission that limited his brother and him to the use of armed force. (*Ibid.,* 149) Lord Howe's final instructions of 6 May '76 authorized the two brothers, as special commissioners, to do little more than offer pardons. "They could grant the King's peace and remove the restrictions upon trade," writes Anderson, "but before doing so they were to exact reasonable assurance that there would be no revival of the revolution." These "reasonable assurances" included the dissolution of all rebel political and military bodies, surrender of all forts and posts, and restoration of the King's officials.

On 7 June '76, soon after reaching the shores of Mass. with a large naval force and with army reinforcements for his brother, Lord Howe issued a declaration announcing his role as commissioner, stating his authority to grant pardons, but not mentioning the rest of what Sir William later characterized as "our very limited commission and instructions." On 14 July the Howes issued a joint declaration and sent a copy under a flag of truce addressed to "George Washington, Esq. etc. etc." Cols. Reed and Knox, on instructions from Gen. Washington, informed the British emissary that they knew of no such person in the American army as the gentleman to whom the envelope was addressed. When Lt. Col. James Paterson, Gen. Howe's A.G., finally got to Washington with a lame explanation about the "etc. etc." and informed the rebel commander of the Howes' authority and desire for negotiations, Washington replied that he had no authority as the military commander to work out any accommodation, but commented that the Howes appeared to offer nothing but pardon, which the Americans did not need.

The next overture led to the PEACE CONFERENCE ON STATEN ISLAND, 11 Sept. '76, which led nowhere. These political activities are sometimes credited with slowing up British military movements during the N.Y. Campaign, but Anderson believes the efforts in July had little effect (*ibid.*, 155), and since Gen. Howe did not excuse himself from his military duties to attend the conference on 11 Sept. it is hard to see how it might have

slowed his operations. On 19 Sept. the Howes issued a proclamation that appealed direct to the people; this offered nothing more than had been rejected on the 11th and there is no evidence that it had any effect. (*Ibid.*, 161)

On 30 Nov., when rebel military fortunes were at a particularly low ebb (see N.J. CAMP'N.), the Howes offered absolute pardon to all who within 60 days would subscribe to a declaration of allegiance. For a few days it appeared that this offer, in combination with the British advance, would bring all of N.J. into submission, but several things combined to turn this effort sour. First, misconduct of British troops alienated the people of N.J. Second, Washington issued a proclamation that anybody who had received a pardon had the choice of surrendering it and swearing allegiance to the American cause or moving lock, stock, and barrel within the British lines. Furthermore, Germain took exception to this wholesale offer of pardons and although he gave his formal approval to the idea of offering a general pardon he warned the Howes in a letter of 18 May '77 not to be too soft-hearted. By this time, however, the commissioners had about given up hope. During the winter of 1776–77 they attempted through Charles Lee, who was their prisoner in N.Y.C., to have Congress send two or three members to visit him. "The Howes offered to provide safe conducts and Lee promised very salutary results from the visit, although he did not specify what they were to be." (*Ibid.*, 166) Although Washington thought the offer should be accepted, Congress decided against it. Anderson expresses some uncertainty as to whether the Lee proposal was another effort by the Howes to open peace negotiations but points out that in view of the "difficult, if not quite desperate situation of the Americans . . . one cannot but wonder what might have been the effect had the commissioners possessed something really attractive" to offer. (*Ibid.*, 165–67) The Howes made no significant further steps in the field of political settlement, but one of the things that led to their resignation was the PEACE COMMISSION OF CARLISLE, which reached America early in 1778. In summary, "In placing a hope in conciliation, the Howes had in mind measures very different from those intended by Germain and the British government. They undertook a task for whose successful accomplishment their instructions allowed them insufficient latitude." (*Ibid.*, 168)

Lord Howe's arrival so shortly before the Declaration of Independence also restricted the opportunities remaining for peaceful settlement under the limited commission he held. (As a matter of incidental interest, the Howes drew what Trevelyan has called "exorbitant" salaries as peace commissioners.)

PEACE CONFERENCE ON STATEN ISLAND, 11 Sept. '76. Gen John Sullivan, who was captured in the Battle of Long Island, 27 Aug., got the impression from discussions with Lord Howe that the Howes had greater powers under their peace commissions than the Americans realized. He thereupon got Lord Howe's permission to visit Congress and persuaded that body to take steps to find out the exact extent of the Howe brothers' authority. On 5 Sept. Congress resolved to send a committee to find out whether Lord Howe could treat with representatives of Congress and, if so, what proposals he had for negotiations. Although Lord Howe was disappointed to learn on Sullivan's return, 9 Sept., that the committee was coming not to treat but merely to secure information, he and his brother decided to go ahead with the conference. "The Howes thought it important to dispel the idea that their powers were limited

to granting pardons after unconditional surrender, since the continuance of such an impression would only make the Americans desperate and destroy any possibility of negotiation." (Anderson, *Howe Bros.*, 158)

On 7 Sept. Benjamin Franklin, John Adams, and Edward Rutledge were elected for this mission, and on the 11th they met with Lord Howe on Staten Island opposite Amboy. Gen. Howe excused himself because of military duties. The Americans confirmed their previous understanding that the Howes had no real power and that anything he agreed to would have to be referred back to London. Although Lord Howe painted the rosiest possible picture of what he hoped to do for the Americans, he was honest. In his report to Germain he said he had informed the committee members that "for very obvious reasons, we could not enter into any treaty with their Congress, and much less proceed in any conference of negociation upon the inadmissible ground of independency. . . ." This left no basis for further discussion and after expressions of personal good will the three went back to Philadelphia and reported to Congress on the 17th.

PEACE NEGOTIATIONS, 1780–84. Military operations in America virtually ceased when Cornwallis surrendered on 19 Oct. '81. The British proclaimed a cessation of hostilities on 4 Feb. '83, and Congress issued a similar proclamation on 11 Apr. '83. Here is a chronology of steps leading to the uneasy peace.

On 15 Feb. '80 a Cong. Comm. completed a report on minimum peace demands: independence, certain boundaries, British withdrawal from all U.S. territory, certain fishing rights, and free navigation of the Miss. R. This report was submitted to Cong. on 23 Feb. Only the last two points were controversial, and on 14 Aug. Cong. accepted all points but the one having to do with fish. John Adams was selected by Cong. on 27 Sept. '79 to negotiate peace with England and also to draw up a commercial treaty. On the same day John Jay was named minister to Spain to draw up the peace treaty with that country. As explained under ADAMS and JAY, each man found that his mission was premature.

On 11 June '81 Congress decided to have the peace with Britain negotiated by a committee, instead of by Adams alone. Jay was named to this committee on the 13th; Franklin, Henry Laurens, and Jefferson were appointed on the 14th. The next day Congress limited essential peace demands to independence and sovereignty, giving the committee discretion on the other points. Furthermore, in deference to the nation without whose help victory would have been impossible, Congress instructed the commissioners to act only with the "knowledge and concurrence" of the French ministry and to "ultimately govern yourselves by their advice and opinion." Jefferson never left America, and Laurens had been captured at sea by the British (3 Sept. '80).

On 12 Apr. '82 Richard Oswald reached Paris as representative of the Rockingham ministry and started talks with Franklin, the only American commissioner on the scene. Laurens was released and sent to sound out John Adams, who remained at The Hague to secure Dutch recognition of the U.S. (19 Apr.), arrange a loan, and bring about a treaty of amity and commerce (Oct. '82). Laurens returned to London and did not reach Paris until Nov. '82.

On 19 Sept. the new Shelburne ministry authorized Oswald to treat with the commissioners of the "13 United States." This tacit recognition of independence started formal negotiations

between Oswald, Franklin, and Jay. On 5 Oct. Jay gave Oswald the draft of a preliminary treaty. Henry Strachey joined Oswald on 28 Oct. and by about 1 Nov. Jay and Adams (who reached Paris on 26 Oct.) prevailed on Franklin to exclude France from preliminary treaty negotiations. On 5 Nov. a new set of articles was agreed to by the U.S. and British commissioners. With a few last-minute modifications these became the preliminary treaty, and with no further changes they became the final PEACE TREATY of 3 Sept. '83. Vergennes, meanwhile, voiced his objections to the unilateral action of the commission but he was impressed by the favorable results they had achieved. Franklin's tactful reply to the French minister on 17 Dec. '82 and the latter's desire for a speedy settlement prevented serious discord. Of the course adopted by Franklin on the recommendation of Adams and Jay, Samuel Flagg Bemis, the diplomatic historian, has this to say in his D.A.B. article on Jay:

". . . they certainly violated their own instructions to negotiate only with the full confidence of the French ministry. They did not violate the Franco-American treaty of alliance, for the peace was not to go into effect until preliminaries of peace should also have been ratified between Great Britain and France. France could not make peace till Spain was ready. Undoubtedly the American preliminaries, together with the relief of Gibraltar, opened the way for Vergennes to bring Spain into line."

On 20 Jan. '83 Great Britain signed preliminary articles with France and Spain. Peace preliminaries then were complete and hostilities were officially ended. On 4 Feb. the British proclaimed the cessation of hostilities. Congress received the text of the provisional treaty on 13 Mar. and on 11 Apr. proclaimed hostilities ended. After considerable criticism of the commissioners for not consulting France, Congress ratified the provisional treaty on 15 Apr. On 3 Sept. the treaty was signed in Paris, on 14 Jan. '84 it was ratified by Congress, and on 12 May ratifications were exchanged to complete the peace negotiations.

Both Spain and Great Britain found reasons for not honoring all the terms of the treaty; see JAY'S TREATY and PINCKNEY'S TREATY.

See Richard B. Morris, *The Peacemakers: The Great Powers and American Independence* (1965), for an authoritative account of the negotiations and for fascinating portraits of the diplomats involved.

PEACE OF PARIS. See PARIS, Treaty of, 1763.

PEACE TREATY of 3 Sept. '83. After the PEACE NEGOTIATIONS that started in 1780 the treaty was signed in Paris on 3 Sept. The nine articles may be summarized as follows: (1) U.S. independence was recognized by Great Britain; (2) the following boundaries were established: the St. Croix River between Maine and Nova Scotia, the St. Lawrence–Atlantic watershed, the 45th parallel, a line through the Great Lakes westward to the Mississippi, down that river to the 31st parallel, eastward along that parallel and the Apalachicola and St. Marys rivers to the Atlantic; (3) the U.S. had the "right" to fish off Newfoundland and Nova Scotia, and the "liberty" to cure their fish on unsettled beaches of Labrador, the Magdalen Islands, and Nova Scotia; (4) creditors of each country were to be paid by citizens of the other; (5) Congress would "earnestly recommend" that states fully restore the rights and property of Loyalists; (6) no future action would be taken against any person for his actions during the war just ended; (7) hostilities were to end and all British forces were to be evacuated "with all conven-

ient speed" (8) navigation of the Mississippi "from its source to the ocean shall forever remain free" to U.S. and British citizens; and (9) conquests made by either country from the other before the arrival of the peace terms would be restored. (Commager, *Docs.*, 117–19; *E.A.H.*)

The treaty was ratified by Cong. on 14 Jan. '84, and on 12 May ratifications were exchanged to complete the action.

JAY'S TREATY, 19 Nov. '94, and Pinckney's Treaty, 27 Oct. '95 (see under SPANISH PARTICIPATION . . .) ended U.S. difficulties with Britain and Spain that arose from the treaty.

PEALE, Charles Willson. 1741–1827. Portrait painter, naturalist, patriot. Md. The son of a schoolmaster, Charles became a saddler. His success as an amateur portrait painter encouraged him to seek instruction in art, and in 1767 he was accepted as a student of Benj. West in London. Three years later he returned to Md. and soon was established as a portrait painter in the middle provinces. He had met John Singleton Copley in 1765, and with the latter's departure for England in 1774, Peale's activities extended farther northward. (*D.A.B.*) Early in 1776 he moved to Philadelphia, where many prominent patriots subsequently sat for him.

The artist had joined the Sons of Freedom in 1764, and after settling in Philadelphia he enlisted in the city militia. (*Ibid.*) He later was elected Lt., took part in the Trenton-Princeton campaign, and in 1777 was promoted to Capt. of the 4th Pa. Regt. of Foot. Until the British evacuation of Philadelphia, Capt. Peale served with the army, and while in uniform he did many miniatures of American officers. He also held a number of public offices, being chairman of the Constitutional Society and a representative in the Gen. Assy. of Pa.

During the post-war depression he started engraving mezzotints of his portraits, and at this time he also developed an interest in natural history after recovering and ˙making drawings of two skeletons of mammoths. His art gallery became the repository of natural curiosities and evolved into the Philadelphia Museum. The Pa. Academy of the Fine Arts owed its establishment in 1805 largely to Peale's efforts.

A sincere and trained craftsman, although not a master, he did for Pa., Md., and Va. what Copley did for Mass. in portraying colonial Americans. (*Ibid.*) He is best known for his many pictures of Washington; seven of these are from life, and about 60 portraits in all were done of him by Peale. His full-length portrait of Washington in uniform, left hand on a cannon, painted in 1779, "represents Washington of the Revolution more truthfully than do later portraits. . . ." (*Ibid.*)

By his first two wives Peale had 12 children who survived infancy. Sons Raphael and Rembrandt were painters; Titian, Rubens, Franklin, and Titian Ramsay were best known as naturalists. Charles's brother James (1749–1831) was also a portrait painter.

PEEKSKILL RAID, N.Y., 23 Mar. '77. About 500 British troops and four light guns landed from a frigate and several transports to destroy American magazines and storehouses. The garrison of Brig. Gen. Alexander McDougall was too small to do anything but burn some of the stores and withdraw, and the landing party under Col. Bird had no men killed. Lt. Col. Marinus Willett led a patriot force from Ft. Constitution to attack the raiders on the 24th. This enemy action was alarming to Washington inasmuch as it might herald the beginning of operations to seize the forts and passes of the Hudson, which might be fatal to the American cause and

would certainly necessitate the evacuation of Ticonderoga. (Freeman, *Washington,* IV, 398) Heath was therefore directed to send eight of his newly recruited Mass. Cont'l. regiments to Peekskill and seven to Ticonderoga. (Heath, *Memoirs,* 127) The British then undertook the DANBURY RAID, 23–28 Apr.

PELHAM. See NEWCASTLE.

PELL'S POINT, N.Y. 18 Oct. '76. (N.Y. CAMPAIGN) Frustrated at THROG'S POINT, Gen. Howe shifted his line of operations to Pell's Point, three miles north. Meanwhile, Washington had decided that his positions on HARLEM HEIGHTS were untenable, and he started withdrawing north. In the Pell's Point area was a small brigade commanded by Col. John Glover; it comprised about 750 men from four Mass. regiments: his own Marbleheaders, Joseph Read's, Wm. Shepard's, and Laommi Baldwin's. They were supported by three guns. From his position near Eastchester (about a mile from Pell's Point), Glover looked out over Eastchester Bay early on 18 Oct. and saw that British ships had come in during the night. He ordered a captain and 40 men forward as a delaying force and formed the rest of his brigade to bar the road along which the British would have to come. Read's regiment was on the left, Shepard's next, and Baldwin's on the right; Glover's regiment was in reserve. The American delaying force exchanged fire with the British advance party and fell back in good order. Read's regiment, which was the first to come within range (the other two being echeloned to his right rear) let the British get within 100 feet before rising from behind a stone wall to deliver a fire that drove the enemy back. It was an hour and a half before the British main body organized an attack, which was supported by seven guns. Read's men fired seven volleys before withdrawing behind Shepard's regiment. The latter poured forth 17 volleys, forcing the British to make several attacks before they could advance. Glover then ordered a withdrawal to a new position, which the enemy did not attack. The two forces exchanged artillery fire until after dark, when Glover withdrew another three miles and pitched camp.

American losses were eight killed and 13 wounded; among the latter was Shepard. Howe reported three killed and 20 wounded; his figures may not have included the Hessians, who comprised most of the attacking force, but Baurmeister (Adj. Gen. of the Hessian Forces) passes over the action without any mention of German casualties. (*Journals,* 60)

On 21 Oct. the British occupied New Rochelle without resistance. The same day, Washington's forces were hurrying to WHITE PLAINS, which they expected to be Howe's next objective. Haslet raided the detached camp of the Tory Robt. ROGERS at MAMARONECK, 22 Oct.

See William Abbatt, *The Battle of Pell's Point* (1901).

PENN, John. 1740–1788. Signer. Va.–N.C. Although from a well-to-do family, he was provided no formal education other than what was offered by the local country school. After the death of his father, however, Penn used the fine library of his kinsman Edmund Pendleton to such advantage that he was licensed to practice law at the age of 21. After 12 successful years as a lawyer in Va. he moved to Williamsboro, N.C., in 1774. He had many relatives in this area (Granville co.) and after establishing himself as a local leader he was elected to the Cont'l. Cong. Here he served at considerable personal sacrifice, remaining for the period 1775–80. His duties included a heavy burden of state business in the fields of purchasing, transportation of

supplies to N.C., and financing. During the Deane-Lee controversy (see Silas DEANE) Penn became such a violent defender of Robert Morris against the accusations of Henry Laurens in Jan. '79 that he finally was challenged by the latter to a duel. Setting out after breakfast at the boarding house that they shared, Penn found himself assisting his elderly opponent across an almost impassable street and the absurdity of the situation became apparent. Penn suggested that they call it off, and President Laurens agreed. (*D.A.B.*)

Returning to his state, Penn became a member of the N.C. board of war in 1780. Cornwallis was moving north, the state authorities were clashing with the Cont'l. officers being sent to defend the South, and Penn had to wage an administrative battle against all three. His post was abolished when Burke became Gov. in 1781. In July he declined on the grounds of health to serve on the council of state. Appointed receiver of taxes by Morris in 1784, he served only a few weeks. All that is known of his last few years is that he resumed his law practice and died a wealthy man.

PENOBSCOT EXPEDITION, Maine, July–Aug. '79. In June '79 Col. Francis MacLean with about 800 British troops from Halifax started building a base near modern Castine, Me., to get timber for the Halifax shipyards, to block patriot advances toward Nova Scotia, and to send out marauding parties. Without consulting Cont'l. political or military authorities, Mass. launched an expedition to eliminate this threat. Gens. Solomon Lovell and Peleg Wadsworth commanded the 1,000 militia and Capt. Dudley Saltonstall of the Cont'l. Navy commanded the naval element. The latter comprised three ships of the Cont'l. Navy, three brigantines, 13 privateers, and 20 transports from

Mass., and one N.H. vessel; the 20 armed vessels carried 2,000 men.

The Americans reached their objective on 25 July. MacLean was not surprised and, although his position had not been completed and could have been taken by a determined assault, he held off the attackers. Saltonstall favored aggressive action but Lovell undertook elaborate preparations that delayed operations until Sir George Collier arrived on 12 Aug. from Sandy Hook with 10 vessels, including a 64-gun ship, and 1,600 men. The Americans were bottled up, and after making only a token resistance they fled up the river, grounded their ships, and started an arduous retreat through the wilderness. The Americans lost 474 men and the British 13. All the ships of the expedition were lost, including several fine frigates and almost the entire fleet of trading vessels Mass. had used as transports and warships. The British maintained a strong post at Penobscot for the rest of the war.

Several American officers were court-martialed for misconduct. Paul Revere, who commanded the artillery, was acquitted. Lovell and Wadsworth were praised by the Mass. authorities. Perhaps with the motive of establishing a claim on Congress for part of the $7,000,000 their fiasco cost, the state authorities blamed Saltonstall. On 7 Oct. '79 he was dismissed from the service and in May '80 the state of Mass. received an order from Congress for $2,000,000.

PENOT LOMBART, Chevalier de La Neuville, Louis-Pierre. (See NEUVILLE) 1744–c. 1800. French volunteer. Before reaching the age of six (25 Feb. '50) he appears on the rolls of a Paris militia battalion as a Lt., and in Sept. '59, within two weeks of his 15th birthday, he was listed as Capt. of the same unit. (Lasseray) M. de La Neu-

ville then served in Germany during the Seven Years' War. In 1766 he was made Capt. *aide-major* in the Regt. of recruits of the colonies, and two years later took a 200-man detachment to Martinique. (*Ibid.*) Discharged (*réformé*) in 1773, on 31 Jan. '74 he was commissioned Maj. of the Provincial Regt. of Laon. Three years later (5 Mar. '77) the court granted him leave of absence for the alleged purpose of tending to business in San Domingo but actually to enable him (and his brother) to fight the British in North America.

Arriving in America with glowing letters of recommendation and accompanied by his younger brother, the Chevalier de la Neuville (who had been granted this honor in the Order of St. Louis on 16 Sept. '76) was appointed Col. with rank as of 21 Mar. '77. On 14 May he was named I.G. of the Northern Army (under Gates) with the promise that he would be promoted at the end of three months in accordance with his merit. A year later he was still waiting for advancement. In May '78 he was recommended to Congress for promotion to B.G., and on 28 June Gen. Parsons signed a eulogistic letter about his service. Congress breveted him B.G. on 4 Oct. '78, with date of rank of 14 Aug., and on 4 Dec. accepted his request for retirement. On 11 Jan. '79 he sailed with Lafayette for France. Two years later he asked for permission to return to America but Ségur refused the necessary authority. In early 1783 he was in command of a battalion of colonial auxiliaries at Cadiz preparing to accompany the proposed expedition to the West Indies, but the peace treaty stopped this operation. Lafayette, who was to lead the army element of this expedition, wrote in 1787 that "M. de La Neuville has always shown much intelligence and zeal. He conducted himself perfectly in America." (Quoted in Lasseray, 356) He was in N.Y. in 1790 on business. Despite repeated attempts, he failed to secure a regular appointment in the French Army.

Elder brother of PENOT LOMBART de NOIRMONT.

PENOT LOMBART de NOIRMONT, René-Hippolyte. (See NEUVILLE) 1750–1792. French volunteer. A *sous-lieutenant* attached to the dragoons on 18 June '68, he became Lt. in the Royal Comtois (infantry) five years later. In 1777 he received leave of absence to accompany his elder brother to America. (See preceding entry.) On 13 Dec. '77 he entered the American army as a volunteer and from that date to 28 Apr. '78 was Thos. Conway's A.D.C. On 14 May '78 he became Assist. I.G. of infantry in the Northern Army, where his brother had been acting as I.G. for the preceding year. He was rewarded for good service in this post on 29 July by being appointed Maj. with date of rank of 13 Dec. '77. Then assigned as A.D.C. to Lafayette, he held this position until the latter returned to France in Jan. '79. Lombart de Noirmont was ordered by Congress on 1 Apr. '79 to join Lincoln in the Southern Dept. In the operations around Savannah he served as a Lt. of infantry. On 18 Nov. '79 Congress breveted him Lt. Col. in recognition of his services. According to Heitman, who identifies this officer as Neuville . . . Jr., he was "permitted to retire" at this time; Lasseray says he was granted leave to France and was honorably discharged on 1 Jan. '81. On the latter date de Noirmont was ordered to the West Indies and there was assigned to the chasseur company of the 2d Bn., Royal Comtois. Returning to France in 1784, he rose to become Lt. Col. in his reorganized regiment in July '91 and four months later he was discharged (*dé-missioné*). Three weeks later (30 Nov.) he became Capt. in the Garde Constitutionnelle, and on 2 or 3 Sept. '92 he was killed in the Abbaye Massacre. Pontgibaud, who has confused the two brothers, says that the victim on this date "escaped by running his sword through his body"; Lasseray, who quotes this passage, says he was massacred after attempting suicide. (Lasseray, 354)

PENSACOLA, 9 May '81. Captured by Spanish. The unhealthful British outpost and seat of the British government of W. Fla. was threatened by Gálvez in 1780, when MOBILE was captured. Gov. Dalling in JAMAICA wanted to reinforce Pensacola early in 1781 with a regiment of American Loyalists but was unable to get the necessary naval escort. Fortescue tells the subsequent story:

"His [Dalling's] apprehension proved to be well founded, for on the 9th of March a Spanish squadron appeared before Pensacola, and on the following day a Spanish army began to disembark. Then, proceeding in their own leisurely fashion, the Spanish forces by land and sea increased, until at last from eight to ten thousand men were encamped around the forlorn British post. The British garrison, under command of Brigadier [John] Campbell, numbered no more than 900 men, but defended itself so stoutly, that on the 28th of April the Spaniards actually broke ground in form [*i.e.*, "regular approaches"], and a few days later opened fire. For a week afterwards the siege made little progress, until the Spanish gunners, guided by a deserter from one of Campbell's American regiments, succeeded in dropping a shell into the principal magazine. The explosion [on 8 May] killed or disabled over 100 men, and utterly demolished one of the principal redoubts; whereupon the Spaniards at once advanced to the assault. The garrison met them gallantly and repelled the first attack; but the enemy, despite all their efforts, succeeded in establishing themselves in the ruined fortifications, whence they could shoot down any man who attempted to work the British guns. With his defenses thus paralysed, and his garrison reduced to 650 men, Campbell capitulated; and Florida passed once more into the hands of Spain." (*British Army,* III, 351–52)

The garrison that Campbell had found when he took command at Pensacola at the end of 1778, and presumably the one he surrendered, is thus described by Fortescue: "seven companies of the 16th Foot, chiefly worn-out veterans, and eight companies of the [3d and 4th Bns. of the] 60th, composed principally of Germans, condemned criminals, and 'other species of gaol-birds.'" Campbell brought with him from Clinton's army "a battalion of Waldeckers, unfit in dress, equipment, and discipline for service in the wilds, and two battalions of Provincial Infantry, raised in Maryland and Pennsylvania from Irish vagabonds who had deserted from the American army, and were quite ready to desert from the British." (*Ibid.,* 301–2) Thus does a British historian evaluate the triumph for which GÁLVEZ was ennobled.

According to Peckham, Campbell withdrew to Ft. George in an agreement with Gálvez to spare the town. This same writer says the explosion of the magazine *killed* 105 redcoats; 300 of the garrison having escaped to Ga. and 56 having deserted, 1,113 were surrendered. "The capitulation later cost England both West and East Florida in treaty negotiations with Spain." (*War for Independence,* 185)

PEPPERRELL, Sir William. 1696–1759. Colonial merchant, militia officer, first native American baronet. Rising from poverty to become one of the

most prosperous merchants of New England, he also became a Col. in command of all Maine militia at the age of 30 and held a number of important political offices. In 1730 he was appointed chief justice, although he had no formal education and knew nothing of law. Gov. SHIRLEY gave Pepperrell command of the militia forces raised for the expedition against Louisburg. For his success in this operation he was commissioned Col. in the British Army (1 Sept. '45) and the next month he became the first native American ever to be created baronet. From the capture of the French fortress (17 June '45) until late in the spring of 1746 Pepperrell shared with Commodore Sir Peter Warren the governorship of the conquered territory. Promoted to Maj. Gen. in 1755, he commanded on the eastern frontier during the unfortunate military events of that year. (See COLONIAL WARS) A proposed expedition under his leadership against Crown Point was canceled early in the year by Gov. Shirley. For about six months between the death of the Lt. Gov. and Pownall's arrival in Aug. '57, Pepperrell was *de facto* Gov. of Mass. by virtue of being President of the Council. After raising troops for the defense of Mass. he was commissioned Lt. Gen. in the British Army on 20 Feb. '59 but was prevented by failing health from taking part in operations of the French and Indian War. He died 6 July '59.

Pepperrell's only son died unmarried but his grandson, William Pepperrell Sparhawk, inherited the bulk of his estate after accepting the stipulation of the will that he change his name to Pepperrell. In 1774 this grandson also was created baronet; a Loyalist, he fled to England shortly thereafter and lost his entire estate by confiscation.

See Usher Parsons, *The Life of Sir William Pepperrell, Bart.* (rev. ed.,

1856), and J. F. Sprague, *Three Men from Maine* (1924).

PERCY, Hugh. 1742–1817. British general. Known by the courtesy title of Earl Percy after the death of his mother in 1776, he had been gazetted ensign of the 24th Foot in 1759 and three months later became Capt. of the 85th. In 1762 he distinguished himself as a Lt. Col. commanding the 111th Regt. in the battles of Bergen and Minden, and this same year he entered the Grenadier Guards. He became an M.P., married Lord Bute's daughter, became one of the "King's friends," and was promoted in Oct. '64 to Col. and A.D.C. to George III. Disapproving of the King's policies, he nevertheless offered to command troops in America and went to Boston in the spring of 1774 as a B.G. On the day of LEXINGTON AND CONCORD he led the relief column that saved Francis Smith's command from probable annihilation. His 5th Fusiliers, of which he had become Col. in 1763, took part in the battle of Bunker Hill and were badly shot up, but Percy was not in the action. Appleton's says he pleaded illness; *D.N.B.* says his absence was probably due to disagreement with Gen. Howe. Given the "local rank" of Maj. Gen. on 11 July '75, he received this regular rank on 29 Sept. '75, and after getting "local rank" of full Gen. on 26 Mar. '76, he was promoted to regular Lt. Gen. on 29 Aug. '77.

Meanwhile he had commanded a division in the Battle of Long Island, 27 Aug. '76, and in the attack on Ft. Washington, 16 Nov. '76. In the latter action he is said to have been the first to enter the enemy lines. He served with Clinton in the capture of Rhode Island in Dec. '76 and assumed command of that post when Clinton went on leave to England. (Clinton, *Amer. Reb.,* 58) After many disagreements with Gen. Howe, Percy returned to England in June '77. Described by Horace Walpole as "totally devoid of ostentation, most simple and retiring in his habits," he embodied the ideal of noblesse oblige: widows of his men killed at Bunker Hill were sent home at his expense and given additional funds when they reached England; succeeding his father as Duke of Northumberland in 1786, he became famous for his benevolence as a landlord.

Despite his family connections and his influence in politics he was not cut out to be an officeholder. He supported Pitt initially, but feeling that his war services had not been properly rewarded he joined the Opposition. In 1779 he divorced Bute's daughter and remarried. In 1793 he was promoted to full Gen. but gained no further distinction either in the military or political field.

PERTH AMBOY, N.J. See AMBOY.

PETERSBURG, Va., 25 Apr. '81. (VA. MIL. OPNS.) The combined forces of Arnold and Phillips landed at City Point on 24 Apr. and advanced toward Petersburg, where Muhlenberg and about 1,000 militia were guarding an important depot of military supplies and tobacco. About noon the British, advancing along the road on the south bank of the Appomattox River, came in sight of the rebel position near Blandford, a village about a mile east of Petersburg. Although the British had about 2,500 high-quality troops, the 1,000 militia occupied good defensive terrain and Phillips did not want to pay the price of a frontal attack. Instead, he first sent his jägers by a defiladed route to hit the flank of the enemy outpost line and drive them back on their main battle position. He then had Simcoe's Rangers and Capt. Boyd's light infantry execute a turning movement to the south while Lt. Col. Robert Abercromby, supported by artillery, led the main body against the enemy's front. The Americans put up a good defense for a while, their artillery firing grape into Abercromby's column with good effect. But the British finally got four of their own guns into position on the American right (PHILLIPS was a gunner general), and the turning movement was also detected, so the defenders started an orderly withdrawal. It was now between 3 and 4 P.M., and it took the British two hours to advance about a mile to the height near Blandford Church. By this time the Americans had emplaced their artillery on a hill across the river to fire on the British and cover the American retreat. Muhlenberg withdrew across the Appomattox, destroyed the bridge, and after camping briefly on Baker's Hill, withdrew 10 miles to Chesterfield C. H.

In this creditable little action the Americans lost 60 or 70 killed and wounded; British losses were probably about the same.

Phillips burned 4,000 hogsheads of tobacco and several small vessels, but did not destroy the buildings. The main body went on to destroy barracks and stores at Chesterfield C. H., 27 Apr., while Arnold led a column to surprise and destroy a rebel force at OSBORNE'S, 27 Apr.

PEYSTER, Abraham de. See DE PEYSTER.

PHILADELPHIA. Located about 100 miles up the Delaware from the Atlantic (accessible even today to ocean steamers), the city was established in 1682 by Wm. Penn as a Quaker colony. Its name means "City of Brotherly Love." The site was first occupied by Indians and the Swedes established a settlement there not later than 1643. The first truly American city in layout, it had parallel streets that were numbered and cross streets that were named

after trees. As early as 1751 the city had illuminated its streets and organized a body of paid constables to replace the traditional nightwatchmen. In 1768, when London and Paris still contended with medieval filth, Philadelphia contracted for garbage collection and street cleaning. After a lusty growth in the decade preceding the Revolution, by 1775 Philadelphia's population of 34,-000 to 38,000 was second in the British realm only to London. The latter had 750,000, but Bristol and Dublin, the next largest in the British Isles, were smaller than the Quaker City. (Montross, *Reluctant Rebels,* 32–33) It was the center of MANUFACTURING IN AMERICA. The 1st Cont'l. Congress met at Philadelphia in 1774, and Congress sat there during most of the war. When the British occupied this capital on 26 Sept. '77 nearly 600 houses were unoccupied, over 200 shops were closed, and fewer than 5,500 males of military age (18 to 60 years) were in town. Most of the latter were Quakers and many, of course, were Tories. "The capture and occupation of Philadelphia ... had no important effect on the war," comments Steele (*Amer. Campaigns,* 18); Congress moved to York, and the place proved a poor base for the British. (*Ibid.*) On 18 June '78 the Americans reoccupied Philadelphia when the enemy completed its evacuation. (See MONMOUTH CAMP'N.)

In his descriptions of Philadelphia at the time of the Revolution and the surviving landmarks a century later Lossing (II, 247 ff.) draws heavily from J. F. Watson's *Annals of Philadelphia and Pennsylvania, in the Olden Time* (2 vols., 1857).

PHILADELPHIA   CAMPAIGN, June–Dec. '77. After the N.J. CAMPAIGN Howe abandoned all major outposts in N.J. except Brunswick and

Amboy and wintered the main part of his army in N.Y.C. Washington's winter quarters were at MORRISTOWN, N.J., where he was considerably reinforced. During the first months of 1777 Washington sent out numerous raids to harass the British and to build up the morale of his own men; the raids accomplished both purposes. Although Howe has been criticized for inactivity during this period, he followed accepted military doctrine by resting his troops in winter quarters; furthermore, a winter offensive against Washington's strong position at Morristown would not have been worth the risks and hardships involved. (Anderson, *Howe Bros.*, 237)

JUNE MANEUVERS IN JERSEY

Since the British could be expected to resume operations as soon as weather permitted, Washington decided in late May to occupy a position closer to the enemy that would permit faster reaction to any move they might undertake. He selected the well-protected area at Middle Brook, on the left bank of the Raritan and near the passes of the Watchung Mountains; this put him a mere seven miles from the British outpost at Brunswick. Sullivan commanded the post at Princeton. (See NEW JERSEY map, front endpaper.)

Although Howe might logically be expected to resume his overland offensive through the Jerseys, he had already decided to move against Philadelphia by water (Anderson, 238); Washington had no way of knowing what Howe's objective would be, but he did have reason to believe that the British would move by water (Freeman, *Washington*, IV, 424). These points are mentioned because many accounts of the maneuvers about to be discussed are written from the viewpoint that Washington expected Howe to march toward

Philadelphia in a continuation of his 1776 campaign.

Washington established his Hq. at Middle Brook the evening of 28 May, and the greater part of his army followed on the 31st. (Freeman, 425) On 10 June there was much British naval activity reported off N.Y., and on the 12th a large column of troops marched from Amboy toward Brunswick. The 18,000 enemy troops then moved west to form a nine-mile front between Somerset Court House (Millstone) and Brunswick, a position from which Howe could move north against Washington or south to the Delaware. Washington had meanwhile pulled Sullivan back to Flemington (15 miles N. W. of Princeton), where he was on Howe's flank and removed from the danger of being cut off.

Since Washington had refused to be lured out of his strong position, Howe was now in an embarrassing situation. He remained there from 14 to 19 June, and his men worked busily on erecting redoubts around Somerset and Middlebush (four miles E.). Then he tried a second maneuver: having sent his baggage trains back to Brunswick on the 17th—which could mean that he was stripping down for a rapid advance on Philadelphia—two days later he feigned a precipitous retreat through Brunswick to Amboy. Washington did not take the bait immediately (Freeman, 431), but contented himself with following and harassing the enemy. On 21 June he learned that the British were evacuating Brunswick and heading for Amboy, and that night he issued orders for sizable forces to disrupt this move. Owing to various errors of staff work, however, no effective pursuit was carried out and the British took up a strong defensive position around Amboy. Washington had serious misgivings as to his ability to hold the ground being occupied, but he nevertheless moved forward on 24 June. Alexander's division and some other regiments were put into position around Metuchen. The rest of the army was located around Quibble Town.

Having thus lured Washington out of his strong positions, Howe undertook his third maneuver. He sallied forth from Amboy at 1 A.M. on 26 June with the intention first of annihilating Alexander's isolated force, moving then to block Washington's retreat by seizing the passes near Middle Brook, and then forcing the American main body to stand and fight in the open. He came close to accomplishing the first part of his operation in an action known as SHORT HILLS, N.J., 26 June, but Alexander withdrew successfully and Washington's army returned to the position around Middle Brook. Howe then gave up his attempts to draw Washington into a general engagement and moved his army to Staten Island in preparation for the amphibious operation to the south. He fell back to Spanktown on the 27th, Amboy on the 28th, and by 30 June had completely evacuated the Jerseys.

Although Howe has been criticized for not attacking Washington at Middle Brook, he has also been praised for his caution. Cornwallis testified that the British C. in C. took great pains to gather intelligence about this position and had no reason to believe it might be successfully attacked.

"But that perhaps is not the real question. Howe had already decided to make an attack upon Philadelphia by sea, his main effort of the year. His manoeuvres in New Jersey were to be pushed only as far as compatible with that larger purpose. He had no intention of staking everything upon some risky procedure during this subordinate phase of his operations." (Anderson, 240)

STATEN ISLAND TO HEAD OF ELK

On 23 July, after a delay of over three weeks on Staten Island, Howe sailed with 15,000 troops (officers and men) and 260 ships. Since Burgoyne's Offensive was well under way (Ticonderoga fell 5 July), Washington had to worry about which of four likely courses of action Howe might take: a move up the Hudson, a return to Boston, an operation against Philadelphia, or another attack on Charleston. When he learned that Howe's armada had sailed into the Atlantic, Washington started his troops toward Philadelphia, but when he himself reached the Delaware on 29 July, after Howe had been at sea six days, Washington found to his bewilderment that the British had not yet been spotted off the Delaware Capes. Perhaps Howe's movement into the Atlantic had been made only to fake him into moving south, and Howe was sailing up the Hudson after all! The American C. in C. halted his troops in N.J. to await further information. The morning of 31 July he learned that Howe had been sighted off the Delaware Capes the preceding day. Washington started his army once more in the direction of Philadelphia. But the British invasion fleet disappeared from sight of land the afternoon of 2 Aug., and as late as the 21st Washington had received no further news of its whereabouts. The next day, however, it reappeared—in the Chesapeake! Now Washington knew the objective was Philadelphia and he moved accordingly. On Sunday, 24 Aug., he marched his army through Philadelphia, making quite a show of this to impress Congress and the citizens. After a personal reconnaissance on 26 Aug., Washington moved his force of about 11,000 rank and file into position around Wilmington.

The British disembarked at Head of Elk (near modern Elkton, Md.). Although the landing in this area had been expected for several days, the four militia companies posted to oppose it scattered without firing a shot. On the 28th the invaders started moving slowly northward after a delay caused by storms and the need for rehabilitation of their sea-weary forces. Washington continued to be uncertain as to Howe's exact intentions, but on 9 Sept. he started shifting his troops from the general vicinity of Wilmington to positions along the creek that gives its name to the battle of BRANDYWINE, 11 Sept. '77.

HOWE OUTMANEUVERS WASHINGTON

Turned out of his defenses along the Brandywine in an operation that was the mirror image of the Battle of Long Island, Washington started rallying his disorganized force at Chester Bridge, 12 miles east of the battlefield. "And yet, though they had been as badly beaten as any army could be without being entirely destroyed, there had been no panic; there was no suggestion of despair," comments Ward. (*W.O.R.*, 354) Fortunately for the rebels, Howe did not order a vigorous pursuit and did not resume the offensive until 16 Sept. Washington, meanwhile, left Chester on the 12th, moved to Germantown to be between the enemy and Philadelphia. Then, to avoid the danger of being trapped against the Schuylkill and Delaware rivers as well as to contest Howe's use of Swede's Ford in advancing on Philadelphia, on 14 Sept. Washington moved west to the vicinity of Warren and White Horse taverns.

(The latter place is today's village of White Horse. Swede's Ford was where modern Norristown is located.)

While his army camped on the battlefield of Brandywine, Howe sent Maj. Gen. Grant to Chester Bridge on 12 Sept. with the Queen's Rangers, the 1st and 2d Light Infantry Brigs., and three troops of dragoons to re-establish contact with Washington's army. Grant found Sullivan posted behind Chester Creek and did not attempt to force a crossing. The baggage train reached Dilworth from Head of Elk the evening of the 12th, and the 71st Regt. (Fraser Highlanders), which had escorted them, was sent to occupy Wilmington. On 14 Sept. the sick and wounded were sent to Wilmington, where the British fleet was expected to arrive soon from the Chesapeake to establish a shorter L. of C. (Because of the Delaware River forts —see below—this was not possible until several weeks later.)

On 16 Sept. Howe's army started north again. Cornwallis joined Grant near Chester on the 14th with the British grenadiers and light infantry; he marched N.W. to link up with the rest of Howe's force in the vicinity of Warren and White Horse taverns.

A major engagement at WARREN TAVERN, 16 Sept., was prevented by a sudden deluge. Three days later Washington was forced to retreat behind the Schuylkill by way of Parker's Ford, having been skilfully maneuvered back by Howe. Almost without food, lacking tents, at least 1,000 men barefooted, hundreds of soldiers shivering through cold, wet nights without blankets (abandoned on the Brandywine), the American columns marched and countermarched as Washington danced to Howe's strategic tune. The gloom was darkened when Wayne's Div., which had been left south of the Schuylkill to harass the enemy advance, was surprised and routed with sizable losses in the night attack at PAOLI, 21 Sept.

Congressmen had been routed out of bed on 13 Sept. for a 6 o'clock meeting at which they were informed of Washington's defeat on the Brandywine. Meeting again at 10 A.M. they had decided to call reinforcements to Pa.: Cont'ls. from the Hudson Highlands and militia from Md., N.J., and Va. On the 19th, Congress left for Lancaster, Pa., and then moved to York, Pa., where they remained until June '78. Meanwhile, expecting Philadelphia to fall, they had ordered the most important military stores evacuated 50 miles W.N.W. to Reading (then known also as Warwick). This shift of the government and the major supply base explains why Washington initially maneuvered west after the 16 Sept. clash at Warren Tavern; he had gone by way of Yellow Springs (now Chester Springs) to Reading for resupply. After crossing the Schuylkill at Parker's Ford he had marched down the left bank to a point about three miles north of Valley Forge. The day before he crossed the river, Cornwallis and Knyphausen captured a sizable supply depot at VALLEY FORGE, 18 Sept.

Now what would Howe do?

The morning of 21 Sept. the British pushed north from Valley Forge to the Schuylkill. This perplexed Washington, since it would have been more likely for the enemy to move in the opposite direction and head for the lower crossings of the Schuylkill to capture Philadelphia. But when Howe then started up the right (south) bank of the river—*away from Philadelphia*—Washington thought he understood: the enemy was undertaking a turning movement by way of Reading, which not only would take that irreplaceable new base of supplies but would also turn the exposed American flank. The Brandywine strategy again!

Posting Sullivan to watch the fords, Washington led the rest of his army up the creek before dawn of 22 Sept. to counter what he thought was the real threat. This was exactly what Howe wanted, and during the same darkness that concealed the Americans on the left bank, the British were marching the opposite direction, on the other bank, to secure the fords at Flatland and Gordon's. Pushing aside puny militia resistance, they crossed at Flatland Ford the night of 22–23 Sept. Cornwallis led a column into Philadelphia on 26 Sept., and Howe moved the rest of his command into camp at nearby Germantown.

"The American commander was out maneuvered so easily that the sole immediate question became that of where he should place and how he should employ his troops now that he had lost the largest American city, in a manner more humiliating, if possible, than that of his forced abandonment of New York in September, 1776." (Freeman, 498)

During the 11 days from the Brandywine to 22 Sept. Washington's troops had marched 140 miles under miserable weather conditions and with pitifully inadequate food and supplies. His strength had dwindled to about 6,000, or a loss of 50 per cent. (*Ibid.*, 459 n.)

But the reinforcements called for earlier started to come in, and Washington successfully resisted the efforts of Congress to weaken his army by sending detachments to strengthen the Delaware River forts. Washington called on Putnam to send him 2,500 men from the Hudson Highlands, including McDougall's Brig. He also called for the Jersey militia of Dickinson and Forman, as well as for 1,000 Va. militia. He sent for the Cont'l. regiments under Heath in Mass., and he recalled Morgan's riflemen from the Northern Dept. When all these arrived Washington told Congress he had 8,000 Cont'ls. and 3,000 militia.

Washington attacked GERMANTOWN, 4 Oct. '77, and was repulsed. It was a strange defeat, however. Morale of the patriot army was boosted because they felt they had come close to winning this hard-fought engagement (they hadn't, but that was beside the point); furthermore, Germantown raised world opinion of Washington's men, who had shown the capacity for recovering so quickly from a series of defeats and disappointments to attack so vigorously. (See Trevelyan's comment at end of article on GERMANTOWN.)

THE DELAWARE RIVER FORTS

But the Philadelphia Campaign did not end with the fall of the American capital.

Lord Howe, the general's brother and commander of the supporting fleet, had commented as early as 23 Dec. '76 that the Americans were known to be building obstructions and forts in the Delaware to protect Philadelphia. Capt. Hammond, who commanded the British fleet observing the Delaware, had led a naval reconnaissance in force up the river in May '77 and had been driven back by American rowing galleys. (Anderson, 278) Although there has been considerable controversy as to the role of these river forts in shaping Howe's strategy for capturing Philadelphia, a matter that will be discussed below, now that he had taken the city he had to clear the river without further delay.

Three bands of underwater obstacles, somewhat inaccurately known during the Revolution as chevaux de frise, blocked the Delaware between Billingsport, N.J., and the Ft. Mercer–Ft. Mifflin line; the former place was 12 miles below Philadelphia, and the latter line was seven miles downstream from the city. (Freeman, 526 n.) Although Washington was charged with manning the *forts*, defense of the *river* was in the hands of officers who answered to the Navy Board and who worked in cooperation with a flotilla controlled by Commodore John Hazelwood. (*Ibid.*, 526) Thus there was no unity of command. Washington has been criticized for attacking Germantown when his forces might have been used more effectively in strengthening the river defenses, thereby making Philadelphia untenable by the British (if this indirect strategy had succeeded). Gen. Howe, on the other hand, abandoned Germantown after the attack of 4 Oct., and on 18–19 Oct. started shifting strength from that place to clear the river defenses.

Despite American efforts to prevent it, the British got siege artillery onto Province Island, a swampy region at the mouth of the Schuylkill (now the U.S. Naval Depot), and on 10 Oct. they started bombarding Ft. Mifflin from the upstream side; since the fort had been constructed to challenge vessels on the river, this heavy artillery fire was directed against its rear, where its "unskillfully constructed" defenses were weakest. Meanwhile, British ships had started up the Delaware in early Oct. The Americans abandoned BILLINGSPORT, 2 Oct., and the British occupied this place on the 9th. (Freeman, 526) A Hessian attack on FORT MERCER (Red Bank, Gloucester co.), N.J. 22 Oct., was repulsed with heavy enemy losses. A naval action against FORT MIFFLIN the next day was frustrated by American land and naval gunfire.

Washington did everything possible to hold Mifflin and Mercer, but the task was virtually hopeless. (Freeman, 551) Not only did he lack unity of command (mentioned above) but the CONWAY CABAL came to light about this time to throw more political sand into the military machinery. A plan for Wayne and Morgan to conduct a raid to silence the Province Island batteries could not be undertaken in time. Greene was detached to reinforce Ft. Mercer, but the approach of Cornwallis forced his retreat. After bravely enduring a terrible beating, the survivors of FORT MIFFLIN withdrew to Ft. Mercer the night of 15–16 Nov., and the latter post had to be abandoned the night of 20–21 Nov. '77. Hazelwood's flotilla, which had done nothing for a month, had to be abandoned and burned.

This delay of almost two months in clearing the river had been a serious logistical embarrassment to the British in Philadelphia, forcing them to maintain their vulerable overland L. of C. to Head of Elk. Although BURGOYNE'S OFFENSIVE had failed by mid-Sept., long before Howe was far enough with his leisurely Philadelphia campaign to help Burgoyne, it is ironic that Howe felt obliged to reinforce himself in Pa. with troops from CLINTON'S EXPEDITION, which was supposed to be helping poor old Johnny Burgoyne at Saratoga.

Howe led a sortie against Washington's camp at WHITEMARSH, 5–8 Dec., but withdrew without bringing on a major engagement. Washington's movement to VALLEY FORGE WINTER QUARTERS started on 11 Dec., but a chance encounter with a foraging expedition under Cornwallis at MATSON'S FORD the same day delayed the operation a week. Congress, meanwhile, had been meeting in York, Pa., since 30 Sept.

CONTROVERSIES AND COMMENTS

The Philadelphia campaign has caused wide disagreement among authorities as to the generalship of the opposing commanders. C. F. Adams' conclusion is epitomized by a remark he quotes from "an English contemporary" dated 1778: ". . . any other General in the world than General Howe would have beaten General Washington; and any other General in the world than General Washington would have beaten General Howe." (*Studies*, 115)

The criticism of Washington as a military commander draws much unfavorable evidence from this period of his career. Soon after the Paoli disaster Pickering said to Greene, "Before I came to the Army, I entertained an exalted opinion of General Washington's military talents, but I have since seen nothing to enhance it." Greene replied, "Why, the General does want some decision. . . ." On 24 Sept., the newly joined Gen. Kalb wrote, "Washington is the most amiable, kind-hearted and upright of men; but as a General he is too slow, too indolent and far too weak; besides, he has a tinge of vanity in his composition, and he overestimates himself." (Freeman, 496)

An outstanding general in Washington's position on 30 July, when Howe was reported at the mouth of the Delaware, might have marched north to join Schuyler, crushed Burgoyne within a week, and returned the first part of Sept. to face Howe with equal numbers, and with an army "flushed with success and full of confidence in itself and its leader" in addition to being "rich in the spoils [arms, equipment, and artillery] of Burgoyne." In outlining this strategy, Adams, who is quoted above (pp. 135–36), shows it would have been completely feasible insofar as time, space, and numbers are concerned; the political detail of how Congress would have reacted to leaving Philadelphia defenseless does not enter into Adams' calculations. This indifference to political considerations, incidentally, is the fallacy in many historical evaluations; it makes Adams' flight of strategic fancy just plain silly.

Troyer Anderson presents the provocative thesis that "... failure of the Howes is a mystery only because the conventional division between military and political history has diverted attention away from the points that serve best to explain the conduct of British operations in America." (*Howe Bros.,* v.)

For every criticism of Gen. Howe's conduct of the campaign, Anderson has a convincing and documented explanation. And although these explanations do not profess to be justifications of Howe's actions, Professor Anderson leaves you with the feeling that Howe's critics were not in possession of all essential facts.

There is little to add to comments that have already been made about Washington's performance in this campaign other than that he was out-maneuvered and defeated time and again, but his army was not destroyed and neither was Washington's will to keep fighting. Whatever his military or other limitations, he kept the Revolution alive.

As for Howe's performance, the matter is more complicated and we should take a brief look at the main points of criticism.

HOWE'S INACTIVITY

Sir William Howe has been criticized principally for lethargy in starting this campaign and for subsequent slowness in its execution. Whereas his greatest admirer could not say he was an exponent of lightning war, critics ignore many *reasons* for Howe's alleged lethargy. He put his army into winter quarters at the end of the N.J. Campaign not only because this was approved military doctrine of the time, specifically approved—more than that, *urged*—by GERMAIN in this instance, but also because there was nothing in particular to gain by attacking Washington's strong Morristown position. (Anderson, 230, 236) Howe did not take the field with the first robin because he had plenty of time to achieve what he considered to be his primary mission for the year, the capture of Philadelphia. (*Ibid.,* 276) He did not race up the Hudson to clasp hands with Burgoyne at Albany because he had no orders to do this unless Burgoyne got into unexpected trouble. (*Ibid.,* 269–70) This is discussed further under BURGOYNE'S OFFENSIVE. One reason for Howe's three-week delay on Staten Island (1–23 July) was to receive Burgoyne's assurance that he was getting along well; another reason was to wait arrival of Clinton from England to take command in N.Y.; still another reason was to await arrival of camp equipage, on the recommendation of Germain. (*Ibid.,* 274–76) Unfavorable winds account for the slow sailing time from N.Y. south. Bad weather and the need to rehabilitate an army that had been at sea 40 days (some of his men had been loaded into the sweltering ships 16 days before sailing) delayed the British march from Head of Elk.

WHY THE CHESAPEAKE AND NOT THE DELAWARE?

Howe's apparent consideration of a landing in the Delaware and subsequent movement to the Chesapeake has been cited as another example of his incompetence, but closer examination does not bear out this condemnation. It is a gross oversimplification to say the decision resulted from Howe's information on reaching the Delaware that the river obstructions were found to be too formidable, a view supported by many contemporary British accounts. As mentioned earlier, the British had known about the river forts since Dec. '76. Furthermore, these obstructions did not preclude their landing at New Castle or Chester, both of which presented better debarkation areas than Head of Elk in addition to being closer to Philadelphia and to their supply base in N.Y. But the Chesapeake was still their preferred line of operations, provided Washington elected to defend Pa. and did not move toward Clinton in N.Y. or Burgoyne. (*Ibid.*, 277–80) The determining factor, therefore, was Washington's movements, not naval problems in the Delaware. The reasons the Howes nipped into the Delaware was not to get a progress report on the river obstructions but for a last-minute report on Washington's movements; he was not showing any inclination to move north, so that question mark was eliminated.

But there was another enemy course of action that could have presented a problem to the British: Washington could move south to the line of the Susquehanna (which flows into the Chesapeake near Head of Elk). Gen. Howe wrote Clinton on 30 July, when the armada was still off the Delaware, that he might have landed in the Delaware if he had arrived "in time to have got between the Susquehanna and Mr. Washington's army," but there was no longer "the slightest prospect" of this. (Quoted in Anderson, 279) Now Howe wanted to operate along a line that not only would permit his capture of Philadelphia, but that would also keep Washington's army to his front where it could be contained or destroyed; this could best be done by landing in the Chesapeake. If the British landed along the shores of the Delaware, as advocated by so many of Howe's critics, Washington could escape west of the Susquehanna where "he could not easily be followed, yet he might strike eastward at will" against the British flank, rear, or their L. of C. (*Ibid.*)

Charles Lee claimed to have hoodwinked Howe into adopting the Chesapeake Bay line of operations (Alden, 118; Wallace, 135), but there is no real evidence that Lee significantly influenced the British plan. (*Ibid.*, and Anderson, 224)

THE OBJECTIVE

Any military fool now knows that the proper objective is the enemy's armed force and not his real estate, so Howe's capture of Philadelphia, while allowing Washington's army to escape annihilation, was, on purely military grounds, a failure. But this raises Anderson's point that the Howe brothers "had to be politicians and military men at the same time" (*op. cit.*, v); destruction of a rebel army was not necessarily their proper objective. (*Ibid.*, 10 ff.)

Capture of Philadelphia did little to damage the American cause, as Washington and his generals realized, to their surprise, shortly after it fell. (Freeman, 499–500) Congress and essential property had been evacuated, so the political and economic base of the Revolution had not been materially reduced. Washington's army was still intact; as a matter of fact it was growing stronger both in numbers and quality. Psychologically, fall of the American capital and principal city had long been expected on both sides of the Atlantic, so the fact created little impression. Some have advanced the dubious theory that occupation of the Quaker City softened Howe's army just as "the delights of Capua" had taken the zip out of Hannibal's.

When informed (in Paris) that Howe had taken Philadelphia, Benjamin Franklin replied, "No, Philadelphia has captured Howe!"

Authorities. Ward comments that Anderson's *Howe Bros.* is the most useful account of Howe's maneuvers in this campaign. "Anderson is always helpful on the plans and thought of the Howes. He is perhaps too gentle in his treatment of them." (*W.O.R.,* 464) One who follows Anderson's reasoning with an open mind is not likely to share this last conclusion. In Freeman's *Washington* will be found the American side of the "plans and thought" that Anderson presents from the British side.

PHILLIPS, William. 1731?–1781. British general. Appointed a gentleman cadet at Woolwich in 1746, he became a "lieutenant fireworker" the next year. During the period Apr. '50–May '56 he was Q.M. of the Royal Regt. of Arty. Promoted to Capt. in 1758, he took command of a British artillery "brigade" of three companies and led them with distinction in Germany. He was praised for the "superlative practice" of his guns at Minden (1 Aug. '59), and at Warburg (30 July '60) he brought his guns into action at the gallop, which to that time had been considered impossible. Phillips, who is somewhat of a hero in the Royal Artillery, also established the first artillery band of that corps. (*D.N.B.*) His brilliant service in Germany was rewarded by promotion to Lt. Col. in Aug. '60 over the heads of many seniors. He was made Col. in May '72 and in 1776 was given the "local rank" of Maj. Gen. in America. He reached Quebec with Burgoyne in May '76, commanded at St. Johns from July until Dec., and then went to Montreal as Burgoyne's second in command.

He retained this appointment during Burgoyne's Offensive in 1777. The aggressive employment of his guns resulted in the capture of TICONDEROGA, 2–5 July. His commission as Maj. Gen. was dated 29 Aug. He accompanied Riedesel's column on the left in the first Battle of SARATOGA, 19 Sept., where his guns were employed with great aggressiveness and effect and where he personally distinguished himself for gallantry. As senior officer of the Convention Army he gained a reputation among the Americans for blustering arrogance, particularly in connection with what he called the "murder" of Lt. Richard Brown. This officer had been shot and killed by a sentinel on 17 June '78 when he passed through the line of guards and failed to respond to the repeated challenges of the sentinel. Phillips became so offensive that Gen. Heath placed him under arrest. (Heath, *Memoirs,* 188) In Nov. '79 the gunner general was allowed to go on parole to N.Y. and on 13 Oct. '80 his exchange and that of Riedesel for Lincoln was finally agreed to. (*Ibid.,* 276; Tharp, *Baroness,* 353; Heitman, "Lincoln." *D.N.B.* errs in saying this exchange was in early 1781.)

In Mar. '81 Phillips was sent to R.I. to attempt to prevent Rochambeau's army from marching to join Washington. (*D.N.B.*) On 20 Mar. he sailed from Sandy Hook with 2,000 troops to join Arnold and take command in Va. His subsequent raids are covered under VA. MIL. OPNS. He died in Petersburg on 13 May '81 of typhoid fever and is buried there. Capt. Duncan in his *History of the Royal Artillery* calls Phillips "a model for artillerymen to imitate in gallantry, ability, and progress." (Quoted in Appleton's) In his introduction to Clinton's *American Rebellion* editor Willcox writes that Phillips, "almost the only man to whom Clinton could open his heart, . . . was reputedly fat and easygoing, and his military gifts were not outstanding." (*Op. cit.,* xiv–xv)

PHIPP'S FARM (Point), Mass., 9 Nov. '75. Alternate name for LECHMERE POINT.

PICKENS, Andrew. 1739–1817. Militia general. S.C. Born near Paxtang, Pa., he moved south with his parents and other Scotch-Irish families through the Shenandoah (where they lived for a while) to an 800-acre holding on Waxhaw Creek, S.C. Two years after taking part in James Grant's CHEROKEE EXPEDITION OF 1761, he and his brother sold their inheritance and obtained lands on Long Cane Creek in S.C. (*D.A.B.*) At the outbreak of the Revolution he was a farmer and justice of the peace. As a Capt. of militia he took part in the conflict at NINETY-SIX, 19 Nov. '75. His services in the civil-war activities of the next two years brought him promotion to Col., and he won the battle of KETTLE CREEK, Ga., 14 Feb. '79. After the surrender of Charleston in May '80 and subsequent conquest of the now-undefended South by the British, Pickens surrendered a fort in the Ninety-Six District and with 300 of his men went home on parole. When his plantation was plundered, however, he gave notice that his parole was no longer valid and took the field again. With Marion and Sumter he was one of the most prominent partisan leaders in the subsequent guerrilla warfare of the region.

For his part in the victory at COWPENS, 17 Jan. '81, he was given a sword by Congress and a commission as B.G. from his state. In Apr. he raised a regiment of "state regulars" who were to be paid in plunder taken from Loyalists. (Under SUMTER see "Sumter's Law.") With these he had an active part in the capture of AUGUSTA and the unsuccessful siege of NINETY-SIX, May–June '81, and in the last pitched battle in the South, EUTAW SPRINGS, 8 Sept. '81. He was wounded in the latter action. He

contributed to the final operations in the South with PICKENS' PUNITIVE EXPEDITIONS against the Indians.

Elected to represent the Ninety-Six District in the Jacksonboro Assembly in 1782, he remained in the state legislature until sent to Congress for the 1793–95 session. He became a state Maj. Gen., and for many years was engaged in dealing with the Indians on boundary matters. After living for a number of years at "Hopewell," his plantation in Oconee, Ga., he settled in the Pendleton District of S.C. In 1765 he had married an aunt of John C. Calhoun; their son, Andrew Pickens (1779–1838) was Gov. of S.C. in 1816–18. Andrew Pickens Sr. was an austere Presbyterian who seldom smiled, never laughed, and who talked so guardedly that "he would first take the words out of his mouth, between his fingers, and examine them before he uttered them." (Quoted in *D.A.B.*) In physique he was lean, of medium height, and robust.

See A. L. Pickens, *Skyagunsta, the Border Wizard Owl, Major-General Andrew Pickens* (Greenville, S.C., 1934). According to *D.A.B.*, this is a revision and extension of *The Wizard Owl of the Southern Highlands* (1933).

PICKENS' PUNITIVE EXPEDITIONS. During the final stages of military operations in the South the Cherokees started an uprising. Andrew Pickens led a campaign of less than three weeks in which he killed 40 Cherokees, burned 13 towns, and took many prisoners while sustaining a loss of only two wounded. In his *Memoirs* (p. 527) Harry Lee comments on Pickens' effective use of mounted troops, against which the Indians proved to be surprisingly vulnerable. About nine months later, in Sept. '82, Pickens and Elijah Clarke again moved among the Indians and forced them to surrender claim to all land south of the

Savannah River and east of the Chatta-hoochie to Ga. (Lossing, II, 740–41) See also GA. EXPED. OF WAYNE.

PICKERING, Timothy. 1745–1829. Cont'l. colonel, A.G., Q.M.G. Mass. Born into a family that had been prominent in Salem since 1637, he graduated from Harvard in 1763 and was employed in Salem in the office of the register of deeds until the eve of the war. Meanwhile he studied law and in 1768 was admitted to the bar. Two years prior to this he became Lt. in the Essex co. militia and started a serious study of military history and tactics. He became register of deeds in Oct. '74. Four months later he was made Col. of the 1st Regt. of the Essex militia. His *Easy Plan of Discipline for a Militia*, published in 1775, was adopted by Mass. the next year and was widely used in the American army until replaced by the famous manual of Steuben.

He took part in the Lexington Alert of Apr. '75 and in the N.Y. and N.J. Campaigns (1776–77). This service brought him to Washington's attention and he served thereafter in top staff positions. When Horatio GATES found the post of adjutant general too small for him, Pickering eventually was prevailed on to resign as register of deeds and accept it. (See Freeman, *Washington*, IV, 392) Despite his lack of professional background, he performed his exacting and tedious duties with competence. An A.G. in those days was more than a paper man, and at Germantown, 4 Oct. '77, Pickering showed a good grasp of strategy and tactics: he urged bypassing the strong point at the Chew House, and he saw the dangers of Washington's strategic plan for the battle. (*Ibid.,* 508–9, 516)

When the new Board of War was organized during the CONWAY CABAL episode, Pickering was pulled out of Washington's headquarters to be a member; he was elected to the board on 7 Nov. '77, but since nobody qualified to take over as A.G. was immediately available he did not leave this post until 13 Jan. '78. (Heitman) Pickering succeeded Nathanael Greene as quartermaster general in the summer of 1780. He was named to this post on 5 Aug. and on the 11th he wrote the C. in C. that since the appointment was altogether unexpected it would be some time before he could wind up his affairs in Philadelphia. Freeman comments that the new Q.M.G. "was not an enthusiastic admirer" of Washington. When Pickering had not arrived by 15 Sept., Washington sent him orders to report. (Freeman, *op. cit.,* V, 185–86 and *n.*) Holding this vital post until 25 July '85 (Heitman), he showed "indefatigable industry and iron determination." (*D.A.B.*) A man refreshingly devoid of illusions, on 6 Mar. '78 he wrote: "If we should fail at last, the Americans can blame only their own negligence, avarice, and want of almost every public virtue."

After going into business in Philadelphia he moved to the Wyoming Valley in early 1787 and was involved in the dispute between Pa. authorities and the Conn. settlers. He became "land poor" and to improve his finances he decided to seek a post in the new federal government. After a successful mission to keep the Senecas out of a war being waged by the western tribes, he was appointed postmaster general on 12 Aug. '91. On 2 Jan. '95 he became secretary of war. After the resignation of Edmund Randolph in Aug. '95 as secretary of state, Pickering held that post until 10 May 1800. He was abruptly dismissed after intriguing with Hamilton and other Federalists against Pres. Adams.

He returned to Wyoming, but his Federalist friends arranged for the purchase of his lands and his return to Mass., where they hoped he might come to the aid of the party. He was U.S. Senator from 4 Mar. 1803 to 3 Mar. '11, and became a formidable debater. His term was marred by leadership of the Essex Junto in an abortive scheme (1803–04) to form a Northern Confederacy comprising N.Y., N.J., and the five New England states. (Morris, *E.A.H.*, 133) Defeated for the Senate, he was elected to the House and served from 4 Mar. '13 to 3 Mar. '17.

The Life of Timothy Pickering (4 vols., 1867–73) was started by his son, Octavius, who completed the first volume, and finished by C. W. Upham.

PIECEMEAL is the military term for committing portions of a command into action as they become available on the battlefield. It is good tactics provided you can build up a preponderant force (superior combat power) faster than the enemy, and it is common in a MEETING ENGAGEMENT.

PIGOT, Robert. 1720–1796. British general. In the 31st Foot he fought at Fontenoy (1745) and served with his regiment on Minorca and in Scotland during the period 1749–52. On 1 Oct. '64 he became Lt. Col. of the 38th, and in 1774 went with his regiment to America. His two flank companies fought at Lexington and Concord but Pigot probably was not on the expedition. He distinguished himself at BUNKER HILL, 17 June '75, where he led his regiment and the 43d against the redoubt. For this action he was promoted on 11 Dec. '75 to Col. As commander of Rhode Island, 1777–79, he successfully defended NEWPORT, 29 July–31 Aug. '78. Meanwhile he had been gazetted Maj. Gen. on 29 Aug. '77, succeeded his brother George (1719–1777) to become 2d baronet, and on 20 Nov. '82 was promoted to Lt. Gen.

Lord George Pigot had been Gov. of Madras since 1775. Another brother, Hugh (1721?–1792), was an admiral but did not serve in North American waters during the Revolution.

PINCKNEY, Charles. 1757–1824. Militia officer, S.C. Gov., statesman, diplomat. S.C. Second cousin of C. C. and Thos. PINCKNEY, he was the son of Col. Charles Pinckney (1731–1782). The latter, a wealthy planter, initially opposed the Revolutionary movement, then supported it actively, but returned his allegiance to the crown when Charleston was captured in 1780. Young Charles was educated in S.C. and became a lawyer. He was a militia Lt. at Savannah in Oct. '79 and was captured at Charleston. Refusing to follow his father's example, he remained a prisoner from 12 May '80 until June '81. Not even mentioned in Heitman, he is remembered in history for his subsequent political and diplomatic career. In Congress from 1 Nov. '84 until 21 Feb. '87, he is most famous for his draft of the Constitution, an estimated 30 or more of his provisions being eventually adopted. After working hard to achieve ratification in S.C., he was Gov. from Jan. '89 to Dec. '92. His alienation from the Federalists may have started when his cousin Thomas was given the post of minister to Great Britain that he wanted. He denounced Jay's treaty in 1795, defeated his brother-in-law Henry to win a third term as Gov. in 1796, and in 1798 was elected to the U.S. Senate with the same back-country Republican support that enabled him to beat Laurens. He led Republican senators against the administration and later managed Jefferson's campaign in S.C., which led to his estrangement from his strongly Federalist cousins, C. C. and Thos. Pinckney. His effective support of Jefferson, who became president in 1801, won him appointment that year as minister to Spain. In that post he failed to work out a satisfactory solution to the complex diplomatic problems involving the U.S. with Spain and France, but most of the fault lay with the administration. (J. Harold Easterby in *D.A.B.*)

Returning to Charleston in Jan. 1806, he resumed an active role in state and national politics. In marked contrast to his two cousins, he has been criticized for dissoluteness in his private life and for shady politics, but he possessed a political genius that they lacked. "He honestly believed that he had virtually written the federal Constitution, and this, together with other extravagant claims that he made for himself, has raised doubts in the minds of historians which have obscured his real achievements." (*Ibid.*)

PINCKNEY, Charles Cotesworth. 1746–1825. Bvt. B.G. Cont'l. Army, statesman, diplomat. S.C. He and his brother Thos. PINCKNEY went to London with their parents in 1753 when the father became agent for S.C. When he returned late in 1769 he had been educated at Westminster School, Oxford, Middle Temple, had studied botany and chemistry in France and attended the royal military academy at Caen, and on 27 Jan. '69 had been admitted to the English bar. Although not a brilliant lawyer, he built up an immense practice in S.C. throughout the years. Genial, impressive in appearance, a cultured aristocrat without being a snob, and a sound judge of men and movements, he became prominent in public affairs. (J. G. deR. Hamilton in *D.A.B.*) In 1773 he extended his already impressive family connections by marrying Sarah, the sister of Arthur MIDDLETON.

At the outbreak of the Revolution he became senior Capt. of the 1st Regt. of S.C. troops on 17 June '75. Promoted almost immediately, he served under Moultrie in the defense of Fort Sullivan (later Moultrie) on 28 June. (CHARLESTON EXPEDITION . . .'76) Promoted to Col. on 16 Sept. '76, he took leave from his regiment and served as Washington's A.D.C. at Brandywine and Germantown in the fall of 1777. He then led his regiment in the abortive expedition against Fla. in 1778 (see SOUTHERN THEATER).

Meanwhile he had continued his political advance. Starting as member of the provincial Assembly the year he returned to S.C. from his European upbringing, he progressed through the normal sequence of Revolutionary promotion to become president of the S.C. Senate in Jan. '79. He was involved in the military alarms and excursions occasioned by Prevost's appearance before CHARLESTON, 11–12 May '79. During the Charleston operations the next year he commanded Fort Moultrie, where there was little action, and was taken prisoner when Lincoln surrendered on 12 May '80. (Brother Thomas, who had been at Fort Moultrie for two years after the attack in 1776, and who had been with the Charleston garrison in 1780, escaped capture because he had been sent from the city to speed the arrival of reinforcements. Cousin Charles became a prisoner on 12 May.) He was sent on parole to Philadelphia, exchanged in Feb. '82. Appleton's and Lossing (II, 763) say he was confined during this period; *D.A.B.* says Thos. and C. C. were sent to Philadelphia and paroled. Lossing says C. C. "suffered much from sickness and cruel treatment"; *D.A.B.* says, "As a prisoner he was treated with great courtesy. . . ." Rejoining the army, he served until 3 Nov. '83, on which date he was breveted B.G.

In 1782 he had been elected to the S.C. legislature, and after the war he resumed his law practice and his participation in public life. Although a zealous

Anglican, he strongly advocated disestablishment and opposed the imposition of any religious test for political office. He was a Federalist of the conservative states'-rights wing. (*D.A.B.*) After taking a prominent part in the Federal Convention (1787), the state convention that ratified the Constitution (1788), and the constitutional convention of 1790, he established some sort of a record in declining presidential appointments. In 1791 he declined command of the army. (St. Clair took the post.) He and his brother-in-law, Edward Rutledge, turned down Washington's urgent request that one of them become associate justice of the Supreme Court. Twice he refused the post of Sec. of War, and in Aug. '95 he declined to become Sec. of State.

Finally accepting an offer from Washington, he reached Paris in Dec. '96 as Monroe's successor. The Directory refused to accept his credentials, he subsequently was threatened with arrest, and in Feb. '97 he stormed off to Holland. In Oct. he was back in Paris on the special mission that resulted in the X.Y.Z. Affair. When X. made his proposal to Pinckney and pressed for an answer, Pinckney replied, "It is No! No! Not a sixpence!" The more dramatic "Millions for defense but not one cent for tribute" is attributed to Robert Goodloe Harper. (*D.A.B.*) When the U.S. prepared to fight France, Pinckney was commissioned Maj. Gen. on 19 July '98; he commanded the forces and installations in Va., Ky., and to the south. Serving until 15 June 1800, he was Federalist nominee for Vice Pres. in this year and presidential candidate in 1804 and 1808.

Brother of Thos. PINCKNEY. Second cousin of Charles PINCKNEY.

PINCKNEY, Thomas. 1750–1828. Cont'l. officer, S.C. Gov., diplomat. S.C. Sharing a European education with his elder brother, Charles C. PINCKNEY, he came home in 1774 and was admitted to the bar. Early the next year he became a Lt. of rangers and—like his brother—Capt. in the 1st S.C. Regt. (17 June '75). He performed highly successful service as a recruiting and training officer before assuming the duties of a military engineer at Fort Johnson, Charleston Harbor. After having an orchestra seat while his brother and Col. Moultrie defended Fort Sullivan, Thomas was assigned to that post in Aug. '76. Except for a few months' absence recruiting in Md., Va., and N.C., he stayed two years at what was now called Fort Moultrie. On 17 May '78 he was promoted to Maj., again helped organize and train new troops, and then took part in the bootless expedition against Fla. (See SOUTHERN THEATER) As A.D.C. to Lincoln he was at Stono Ferry and as A.D.C. to d'Estaing participated in the attack on SAVANNAH, 9 Oct. '79.

Meanwhile, he served in the legislature of 1778, kept up his law practice, and married Elizabeth Motte (22 July '79). In 1780 he took part in the defense of Charleston, but he was sent from the city before the final stages of the siege and escaped capture. After making his way to Washington's headquarters, he returned to the South, became A.D.C. to Gates on 3 Aug. '80, and at Camden was seriously wounded (16 Aug.) and taken prisoner. He recuperated at the home of his mother-in-law (née Rebecca Brewton), but his wound gave him trouble for years to come. He went to Philadelphia with his brother, C. C. Pinckney, who had been captured at Charleston 12 May, and they were paroled in the Quaker City. In Dec. '80 Thomas was exchanged. In Sept. '81 he was recruiting in Va., where he met Lafayette and served under the latter's command. The two became good friends. Pinckney also was a partisan of Gates, and on his return to S.C. after the surrender at Yorktown he published a defense of Gates.

Establishing a new home in Charleston—his plantation, "Auckland," having been destroyed by Prevost in 1779—he was a successful lawyer and served as Gov. for two one-year terms starting 20 Feb. '87. In Jan. '92 his nomination by Washington as minister to Great Britain was confirmed. Although well received in the country where he had been reared and educated, "his ministry, viewed in the large, was not highly successful." (J. G. deR. Hamilton in *D.A.B.*) He was offended by John Jay's appointment to negotiate a treaty, and in Apr. '95 accepted a special mission to work out a treaty with Spain. With a combination of the bold persistence (which had not worked in London) and unfailing tact, his efforts resulted in "Pinckney's Treaty" of 27 Oct. '95, which is covered under SPANISH PARTICIPATION. (His cousin Charles had aspired to Thomas' post in London in 1792, denounced Jay's treaty of 1795, and had an unsuccessful diplomatic mission to Spain in 1801–6.) Back in London, Thomas worked unsuccessfully to win LAFAYETTE'S release from prison. In Sept. '96, almost a year after asking for recall, he returned home.

The Federalists nominated him for V.P., but the efforts of Hamilton to have him elected president in order to defeat John Adams resulted in Pinckney's getting neither post. (His brother lost out in a similar manner in the next election, and his cousin was building his own political career in the opposite camp.) His first wife had died in England in 1794. On 19 Oct. '97 he married her sister, Frances, the widow of John Middleton. In Congress from Nov. '97 until his voluntary retirement in Mar. 1801, he loyally supported the administration despite strong states'-rights convictions and opposition to the elaborate preparations in 1798 for war against France. During the War of 1812 he was appointed Maj. Gen. on 27 Mar. '12 but as commander of the region from N.C. to the Mississippi he had no active service. He succeeded Jackson after the Creek War, and negotiated the peace treaty.

Establishing plantations on the Santee, Thomas Pinckney engaged in scientific agriculture. With the technical assistance of an imported Dutch engineer he reclaimed vast areas of tidal marsh and produced highly successful rice crops. On an experimental farm he did fruitful work on diversification of crops and published articles in the *Southern Agriculturist*. He also imported improved breeds of cattle. Sharing with his brother a reputation as the highest type of Southern aristocrat, he has been described physically as tall, lean, and poised. Some found a resemblance to Washington. He died in Charleston on 2 Nov. '28 after a long, painful illness. A son by his first marriage, Charles Cotesworth, was the only child to produce sons through whom his name was perpetuated.

This son, C. C. Pinckney, wrote the *Life of General Thomas Pinckney*, which was published in 1895. His papers and those of his brother are owned by descendants and are also in the S.C. Hist. Soc. and the State Dept. Archives.

PINCKNEY FAMILY OF S.C. In his *South in the Revolution*, Alden writes: "A few dozen families, including the Pinckneys, Rutledges, Manigaults, Middletons, and Lowndeses, directed the Commons House and through it spoke for South Carolina. They also composed the upper house, or council, until after the Seven Years' War, when natives of Britain and British officeholders increasingly found their way into that body."

(P. 91) The Pinckneys further strengthened their ties by marrying into the Laurens family and the MIDDLETON FAMILY. The first Charles (d. 1758) was Atty. Gen. (1733), Chief Justice (1752–53), and agent in England (1753–58) for S.C. His nephew, the second Charles (1731–1782), father of the (third) Charles, whose life is sketched in a separate article above, was a wealthy lawyer and planter who was first president of the first S.C. Prov. Cong. (Jan.–June '75). He went over to the British in 1780 and two years later suffered the amercement of his estate.

PINCKNEY'S TREATY, 27 Oct. '95. Negotiated by Thomas Pinckney, this is covered under SPANISH PARTICIPATION.

PISCATAWAY, N.J., 10 May '77. In an attempt to surprise the 42d Highlanders (Black Watch) who were camped at this place, which was between Brunswick and Amboy, approximately where Greensand is now located (Freeman, *Washington,* IV, 417 *n.*), Maj. Gen. Adam Stephen ordered an attack. Although the Americans killed eight or nine of the enemy and wounded 19, they were driven off and pursued almost three miles to their camp near Metuchen, leaving 27 dead and between 38 and 73 prisoners, according to British accounts. (*Ibid.,* 418 *n.*) Stephen, however, reported "a certain and considerable advantage gained over the enemy's best troops. . . ." He estimated that the enemy lost at least 200 killed and wounded. With suspicion based on long association with the man, Washington investigated the affair and wrote STEPHEN a strong letter. *A.A.* gives 8 May as the date of the action.

PITCAIRN, John. 1722–1775. British officer. Born in Scotland, the son of a minister, he was commissioned Capt. in the Royal Marines on 8 June '56 and Maj. on 19 Apr. '71. He went with the marines sent to garrison Boston in 1774, and he was "perhaps the only British officer . . . who commanded the trust and liking of the inhabitants" (*D.A.B.*). He also was well liked by his men. As second in command of the expedition to LEXINGTON AND CONCORD, 19 Apr. '75, he had a prominent and controversial part in the fateful events of that day. In the battle of Bunker Hill, 17 June '75, he led the final assault on the redoubt with the cry of, "Now for the glory of the marines." In what was probably the final volley from the redoubt, his chest was crushed by a bullet said to have been fired by a Negro, Peter Salem, who is so depicted in Trumbull's painting. He was carried to a boat by his son, a marine Lt., but despite the efforts of Dr. Thomas Kast to stop the flow of blood he soon died. (Forbes, *Revere,* 443) He left 11 children; two became famous, David as a physician and Robert as a naval officer; both are in *D.N.B.*

Pitcairn's role in the events of 19 Apr. '75 is fully discussed in the article on LEXINGTON AND CONCORD. Chastellux is authority for the statement, discredited by modern authorities, that Pitcairn covered the country around Concord, "usually in disguise," to get information for Gage; and the editor of a recent edition of Chastellux's *Travels* comments that this evidence has been overlooked by two prominent authorities, French and Tourtellot (*Travels,* 481, 618, notes by editor Howard C. Rice, Jr.).

A miniature of Pitcairn in the possession of the Lexington Historical Society shows a young man whose looks can be described only as pretty. (See *American Heritage Book of the Revolution,* 107)

PITCAIRN'S PISTOLS. Carried into the American lines after Pitcairn's horse threw him during the action at Fiske

873

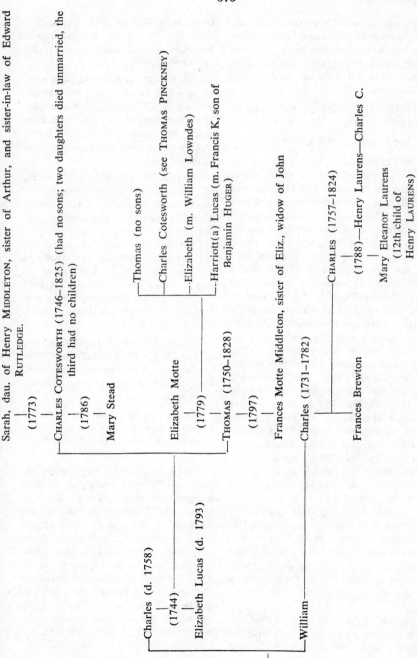

PINCKNEY FAMILY OF SOUTH CAROLINA

Hill near Concord, they were used during the war by Gen. Israel Putnam. Now in the Lexington Historical Museum, they are of interest in that one may have fired the shot that started the American Revolution.

PITCHER, Molly. See MOLLY PITCHER LEGEND.

PITT, William. See CHATHAM.

PITTSBURGH.* (Fort Pitt) Located west of the Alleghenies at the point where the Allegheny and Monongahela rivers join to form the Ohio, the "Forks of the Ohio"—as the place was first known—was of key strategic importance as soon as white men started pushing into the Ohio Valley. In 1731 a few Frenchmen tried to establish a settlement but were soon driven off by the Indians. In 1748 the colonies of Pa. and Va., both of which claimed the area, started activities that brought them into conflict with the French and led to the last of the COLONIAL WARS. This entry, starting with section headed "King George's War," tells of military operations around this critical site. Briefly, in Apr. '54 a French force started construction of Ft. Duquesne and subsequently defeated expeditions under Washington and Braddock to drive them out. The FORBES EXPEDITION forced the French to destroy Ft. Duquesne, and Bouquet occupied the site on 25 Nov. '58.

In Oct. '72 Gen. Gage ordered Ft. Pitt abandoned, and it was partially dismantled. In Jan. '74, Dr. John CONNOLLY occupied the place with an armed body of Va. men to defy the Pa. claim to the disputed region. Events took a different turn, however, and led to

---

* This is the official spelling of the charter and seal. The "h" was dropped by the U.S. Geographical Board, but the older form is still favored.

DUNMORE'S WAR in 1774. During and after the Revolution, Pittsburgh was American army headquarters for WESTERN OPERATIONS.

PLAINS OF ABRAHAM (Quebec), 13 Sept. '59. By occupying this plateau overlooking Quebec, James Wolfe drew Montcalm into an abortive attack in which both commanders were killed. Quebec surrendered five days later. See COLONIAL WARS.

PLAINS OF ABRAHAM (Quebec), 15 Nov. '75. After completing his famous march to Quebec, Arnold moved with 700 men onto this position and unsuccessfully tried to bluff the Quebec garrison into surrender. (See CANADA INVASION) Although he landed in the cove where Wolfe had landed 16 years earlier (see above), Arnold climbed onto the plateau by a road that had replaced Wolfe's goat trail. (Ward, *W.O.R.,* 183)

PLAINS OF ABRAHAM (Quebec), 6 May '76. Carleton sallied forth from Quebec with 900 men and four guns to rout 250 troops of John Thomas. See CANADA INVASION.

POINT. Modern technical term for a patrol or reconnaissance party that precedes an advance guard or follows a rear guard.

POINT OF FORK, Va., 5 June '81. (VA. MIL. OPNS.) With the Queen's Rangers and the 2d Bn. of the 71st (which had refused to accompany Tarleton on the raid to CHARLOTTESVILLE, 4 June), Simcoe moved from Cornwallis' camp on the North Anna to raid Steuben's main supply depot at Point of Fork. This place was where the Fluvanna and Rivanna joined to form the James River, about 45 miles above Richmond. Steuben was located there with about 500 of his Cont'l. recruits. Learning of Simcoe's approach, the Cont'ls. evacuated the supplies across the Fluvanna and lost only a 30-man rear guard when Simcoe entered Point of Fork with his 100 cavalry and 300 infantry troops, Unable to pursue, since he lacked boats, Simcoe then outsmarted his Prussian adversary: he deployed his troops along the river and lighted camp-fires to exaggerate his strength and make it appear that he was the advance of the entire British army. Steuben abandoned the stores to save his troops from annihilation, and Simcoe sent men across in canoes to destroy the supplies. (Ward. *W.O.R.,* 873–74)

POLLOCK, Oliver. *c.* 1737–1823. Patriot supply agent. Ireland–Pa.–New Orleans. At 23 he came from Ireland with his father and brother, settled at Carlisle, and eventually became a West Indies trader. In 1768 he moved to New Orleans, became a prosperous trader, planter, and financier, and established good relations with the Spanish authorities. When Capt. Geo. GIBSON arrived on his mission, Pollock got the covert assistance of Gov. Unzaga in sending Gibson back to Ft. Pitt with almost 10,000 pounds of powder. Despite efforts of the British to stop him, Pollock furnished vital supplies for the WESTERN OPERATIONS OF CLARK. By the end of 1777 he had sent $70,000 worth of supplies on his own credit, and when this was exhausted in July '79 he mortgaged personal property to raise $100,000 and borrow another $200,000. "This amount surpasses the contribution of any other person to the direct cause of the Revolution," writes J. A. James in *D.A\H.* Early in 1778 he had become commercial agent for Congress and procured goods from Spanish creditors for Washington's army. In 1779 he accompanied Gálvez in the capture of Manchac, Baton Rouge, and Natchez.

Although his postwar commercial ventures were highly successful, Con-gress and Va. were slow in reimbursing him and he spent 18 months in custody for failure to satisfy his creditors. U.S. and state authorities eventually paid his claims and he returned to settle on an estate in Cumberland co., Pa.

See James A. James, *Oliver Pollock . . . an Unknown Patriot* (1937).

POMEROY, Seth, 1706–1777. Cont'l. general. Mass. Great-grandson of a man who came to America in 1630, Seth took up the trade of gunsmith, which had brought his family prosperity and prominence in Northampton, Mass. He was a militia ensign in 1743, accompanied the 4th Mass. Regt. to Louis-burg in 1745 as a Maj., and performed valuable service in repairing captured French cannon for use against the defenders. As Lt. Col. of troops raised in western Mass. for Sir Wm. Johnson's attack on Crown Point in 1755, Pomeroy led the heaviest fighting in the Battle of Lake George, N.Y., 8 Sept. '55, and captured Dieskau, the French commander. Apparently not interested in local politics, but considered "very high in Liberty" (quoted in *D.A.B.*), in 1774 he sat in the Northampton comm. of safety, represented the town at the 1st and 2d Prov. Cong., and was elected B.G. of militia in Oct. '74. With Artemas Ward and Jedidiah Preble he was appointed to start military preparations in the province. "His greatest contribution to the American cause was the raising and drilling of troops in western Massachusetts in 1775 and 1776." (*D.A.B.*) He took part in the council of war that preceded the Battle of Bunker Hill, 17 June '75, and seconded Putnam's proposal that the hill be fortified. The 69-year-old veteran, carrying the musket he himself had made and had used at Louisburg 30 years earlier, had ridden to Charles-town Neck on a borrowed horse, turned it over to a sentry so as not to expose it to the heavy fire there, and "trudged all the way to the rail fence, where he took his place with the others amid an enthusiastic welcome." (Ward, *W.O.R.,* 88) In the heavy action that followed, Pomeroy fought as a volunteer private until the forces of Knowlton and Stark had to withdraw. "Old Seth Pomeroy, grasping his veteran musket, its stock shattered by a bullet, walked away backward, still facing the foe," writes Christopher Ward. (*Ibid.,* 95)

Thus ended his role in the Revolution. On 22 June '75, five days after this battle, Congress named him B.G., but on 19 July he declined the appointment and was superseded by John THOMAS. He became a Maj. Gen. of Mass. militia on 20 June '75. On 19 Feb. '77, while on his way to join the army in N.J., he died of pleurisy at Peekskill. Little is known about the man whom the legend describes as a tall, lean, and intrepid soldier; "he remains a shadowy figure whose qualities can be little more than surmised." (*D.A.B.*) *The Journals and Papers of Seth Pomeroy,* edited by L. E. de Forest, were published in 1926.

PONTCHARTRAIN. French fort at Detroit and lake in La., they were named for the minister of the navy of Louis XIV.

PONTIAC'S WAR. 1763–64. The surrender of Canada to Amherst (8 Sept. '60) gave the British title to the French posts in the Old Northwest. Maj. Robert Rogers led a party to take possession of Detroit on 29 Nov. '60 and other scattered forts were subsequently garrisoned by small detachments of regulars, most of them from the 60th ("Royal American") Regt. Amherst immediately showed incompetence in dealing with the Indians of this vast region and his policies, in sharp contrast to those of the French,

led the Indians to rise in arms against their new masters. Not only did the savages resent the arrogance of the newcomers but since the British were settlers rather than hunters and traders like the French, they saw a new and more sinister white threat to their hereditary lands. Furthermore, Amherst abruptly cut off the flow of clothing, arms and ammunition, food, and trinkets with which the French had kept the Indians supplied. In his righteous ignorance of the wild children with whom he was dealing, and despite the advice of the experienced Sir Wm. Johnson, he adopted the attitude of a stern parent who believed in punishment for bad behavior, not bribery for good.

Capt. Donald Campbell, commandant at Detroit, and Johnson managed for some time to keep the peace, but during 1762 the Indians gradually realized the bleak future in store for them under the policies of Amherst. The considerable number of French in the area fomented this spirit of rebellion and spread rumors that an expedition was coming to recapture Quebec and Montreal. (Peckham, *Pontiac,* 92–93) In this situation emerged a remarkable Indian leader, Pontiac (*c.* 1720–1769), an Ottawa chief. Another influence in rallying the various tribes—Indians being notoriously weak when it came to working as allies—was a visionary called the Delaware Prophet, who preached that the Indians should seek regeneration by eliminating the corrupting influence of the white man and his accompanying vices. This doctrine gained great currency among the scattered tribes, and Pontiac capitalized on it to unite them in a common war effort. (*Ibid.,* 101)

Pontiac's primary role in the war that followed was to command the three villages surrounding Ft. Detroit, and he had some tenuous leadership over the other tribes (Chippewas, Hurons, and Potawatomies) who reinforced him here. Howard Peckham finds no authority for Francis Parkman's thesis that Pontiac planned, organized, and directed the simultaneous uprising against the scattered British posts. (*Op. cit.*, 108 *n.*)

Maj. Henry Gladwin reached Detroit on 23 Aug. '62 to assume command and Campbell, although originally named to move on to command another post, remained. When hostilities started the garrison numbered about 120 military personnel and perhaps 20 English traders who would reinforce them. Gladwin sensed that the situation was reaching the kindling point and in May '63 he frustrated several attempts by Pontiac to take the fort by treachery. On 9 May the Indians started murdering isolated settlers outside Ft. Detroit and laid siege to the garrison. Within a few weeks other war parties took every fort west of Niagara except Detroit and Pitt. Sandusky fell 16 May; Ft. St. Joseph, 25 May; Ft. Miami, 27 May; Ft. Ouiatenon, 1 June, Ft. Michilimackinac, 2 June; Ft. Edward Augustus, abandoned in June; Ft. Venango, *c.* 16 June; Ft. Le Boeuf, 18 June; and Ft. Presque Isle (Erie), 20 June. Most of these were taken by treachery and the entire garrisons slaughtered. Forts Ligonier and Bedford, along the Forbes Road between Ft. Pitt and the East, repelled Indian attacks.

The year 1763 is commonly taken as the start of the Revolutionary era and the following acid comments of British military historian Sir John Fortescue provide an interesting insight into the British viewpoint of the situation at this time:

"The first violence of the storm had spent itself, and the British had gained a little breathing-time. Amherst, at first

incredulous of the extent of the mischief, and unduly contemptuous of his enemy, had already set himself to arrange for the despatch of a relieving force; but despite the urgency of the danger, he was cruelly hampered by want of men. Though the posts between Pennsylvania and the Ohio still held out, the whole of the country between them was laid waste; while the forts themselves were crowded with refugees, who waited only for rumour to revive fresh panic in them before they fled away in wild terror to eastward. Fort Ligonier was held by but twelve soldiers, yet not one of the flying settlers would remain to stand by them. Amherst early decided that his relieving column must move along the line of these forts ... but in the dearth of regular troops he was fain to apply to Pennsylvania for local levies. It is hardly credible, but it is a fact, that even in the face of the deadly peril upon its borders the province refused to provide a man." (*British Army*, III, 15)

SIEGE OF DETROIT

Lt. Abraham Cuyler of the Queen's Rangers had left Niagara on 13 May with 96 men and 139 barrels of provisions in 10 bateaux for Detroit. Unaware that hostilities had broken out, he landed at Point Pelee, about 25 miles from Detroit, after dark on the 28th. Here he was surprised and all but 40 of his men were killed or captured. On 30 June he reached Detroit aboard the sloop *Michigan* with a reinforcement of 55 men and a quantity of supplies. On 29 July Capt. James Dalyell reached Detroit with a convoy of 22 boats carrying a reinforcement of 260 men. Dalyell, the younger son of a baronet, was Amherst's A.D.C. and had been sent from headquarters in N.Y.C. via Albany and Niagara to collect reinforcements for Gladwin's garrison. Robert Rogers and 21 N.Y. militia joined him at Albany, and he reached Niagara on 6 July with 200 men from the 55th and 60th Regts. Picking up 40 men of the 80th Regt. at that place, he loaded his force in bateaux and made the hazardous voyage to Detroit.

Against his better judgment, Gladwin acceded to the ambitious young aide's insistent demand that he be permitted to lead a sortie. Pontiac expected this and was waiting in ambush at the point where a narrow timber bridge crossed a creek two miles from the fort. At 2:30 the morning of 31 July 247 officers and men moved out. By 8 o'clock the survivors got back, owing largely to the rear guard action of Rogers and the sound leadership of Capt. James Grant. Dalyell and 19 men were killed, three men were mortally wounded, three officers and 31 men were wounded, and an undertermined number were captured. The scene of Pontiac's victory has since been known as Bloody Run.

Pontiac's situation had been impossible from the start. Without supplies and matériel for siege operations, and at the head of a race notorious for their lack of military stamina, he was opposed by a breed of man, the British, famous for their bulldog tenacity against impossible odds. Furthermore, Detroit was not really besieged inasmuch as its line of communications by water to Niagara was not cut. Pontiac's allies began to melt away, the rumored French expedition obviously was not coming, winter was approaching, and, finally, word arrived that the Peace of Paris had been signed. On 31 Oct. '63 Pontiac wrote Gladwin a note of farewell and faded from the scene.

FORT PITT HOLDS OUT

Whereas Gladwin had exhibited the Anglo-Saxon qualities of which the race is so proud, Capt. Simeon Ecuyer and Col. Henry Bouquet, two Swiss in the service of Great Britain, provided the leadership that held Ft. Pitt. With a garrison of 250 regulars and militia, 16 cannon, and a well-fortified position, Ecuyer was not alarmed about the security of his post. By the end of June Bouquet had assembled a relief column of 460 regulars at Carlisle—214 men of the 42d ("Black Watch"), 133 of the 77th Highlanders, a battalion of the 60th ("Royal Americans"), and a party of rangers—but his departure was delayed until 18 July because the settlers were too terrified to accompany him as wagoners. When he got to Fort Bedford (25 July) he had to delay another three days. On 2 Aug. he had gotten to Fort Ligonier, having been forced to drop off regulars along the way to protect the panic-stricken settlers, and he then pushed forward without his wagons toward the fort from which no news had been heard for over a month. After a parley with the Delaware and Shawnee chiefs on 26 July, in which Ecuyer refused to leave Ft. Pitt, the Indians launched an attack on the 27th but then abruptly lifted their siege on 1 Aug. Ecuyer, who had been wounded by an arrow, knew that they were going to attack Bouquet, and the obvious question at this point was: Would Bouquet meet the fate of Bradstreet?

At 1 P.M. on 5 Aug. '63 Bouquet's advance guard was suddenly attacked at Edge Hill, 26 miles east of Fort Pitt. The regulars, who had already marched 17 miles that day, attacked with the bayonet to relieve the advance guard, but the Delawares, Shawnees, Mingoes, and Hurons worked their way around Bouquet and kept up a galling fire until dark (around 8 P.M.). Bouquet's column included 340 horses loaded with flour, and the Swiss colonel moved onto a little hill to form a perimeter defense for the night. Flour bags were used to form a central strong point, outposts were pushed forward, and the regulars probably thought of Braddock as they waited for dawn. Several officers and about 60 men had already been killed or wounded, the troops were tired from the long march and the seven-hour battle, and they suffered severely from lack of water.

The savages renewed their attack at first light, but since victory was almost inevitable they confined their efforts to sniping. The regulars could hold their position, but time was against them. At 10 A.M. the British began to weaken from sheer exhaustion, the Indians saw men start withdrawing from a portion of the perimeter, and they rushed toward this gap. Then they found they were fighting a Bouquet, not a Braddock. The Swiss colonel had resorted to a desperate stratagem. He had pulled two companies from the west side of the line and sent them on a compass course around to a point from which they could counterattack the south flank of the expected penetration. (Fortescue, *British Army,* III, plate I) The Indians met this surprise fire bravely but retreated when the regulars charged with the bayonet. The lesson, however, was not over. Bouquet had advanced two more companies on this side of the circle, and these gave the Indians a destructive fire. All four companies then pursued, and the Indians on the other sides of the circle fled before the defenders could attack them.

"Around the ring lay the corpses of some 60 dead warriors, but Bouquet's loss was little less severe, amounting to eight officers and 96 men, or fully a fourth of his force, killed and wounded. ... The action was one of the fiercest ever fought with Indians; and had any man of less experience in such warfare than Bouquet been in command, its

issue might well have been disastrous. Nothing but perfect confidence in him, added to the dread of being roasted alive, could have kept the exhausted troops to their work. ... Long though the combat has been forgotten in England, the history of the Army can show few finer performances on its own scale than this victory of a handful of English, Highlanders, and Germans under the leadership of a Swiss colonel." (Fortescue, *British Army,* III, 18)

Peckham says Bouquet had 50 killed, 60 wounded, and five missing. (See, however, CASUALTY FIGURES) The relief column moved a mile to Bushy Run, by which name the action is known, and reached Pittsburgh on 10 Aug.

Before he was recalled to England Amherst had planned the reconquest of the Old Northwest by two expeditions, one from Niagara to Detroit and then south from Lake Erie against the Delawares and Shawnees in what now is central Ohio; the other to penetrate into this same area from Pittsburgh. The first of these, BRADSTREET'S EXPEDITION OF 1764, was badly mismanaged, but the other, BOUQUET'S EXPEDITION OF 1764, was a complete success. Pontiac finally submitted to Sir Wm. Johnson at Oswego on 24 July '66 and was thereafter loyal to the British. On 20 Apr. '69 he was assassinated by a Peoria Indian in Cahokia, Ill. It is generally believed that this deed was instigated by white traders, who feared Pontiac might again cause trouble, but there is nothing certain about this plausible theory.

Pontiac was "a warrior of heroic proportions who set in motion the most formidable Indian resistance the English-speaking people had yet faced, or ever would face, on this continent," concludes Peckham. He stands out above other leaders of his race for having succeeded in getting a concerted effort out of the tribes in the Old Northwest, although, as has been mentioned, his achievement was less than Francis Parkman would have us believe. Had Pontiac succeeded in bringing the southern Indians into his "conspiracy" the British would have been faced with a tremendous problem. (Alden, *Gage,* 92)

Pontiac's War shows the problems faced by the mother country that was expected to maintain regulars for the defense of its colonies—the latter not only being incapable of turning out militia for their own defense but also resenting having to help pay to support the regulars. (They thought the King owed them protection in return for allegiance.)

The above account is based primarily on Peckham's *Pontiac and the Indian Uprising* (Princeton, 1947), which makes use of new source material and supersedes Parkman's *Conspiracy of Pontiac . . . ,* 2 vols. (Boston, 1851 [1st ed.] and 1915 [10th ed.]) Mr. Peckham was kind enough to review this article and make valuable corrections.

See also PROCLAMATION OF 1763.

POOR, Enoch. 1736–1780. Cont'l. general. Mass.–N.H. Great-grandson of an English immigrant who had settled at Newbury, Mass., he was reared on the family farm, had little education, and was apprenticed to a cabinetmaker. In 1755 he took part in Col. John Winslow's expedition to Acadia. Around 1760 he moved from Andover to Exeter, N.H., and became a trader and ship builder. After holding various public offices and being elected to sit in two provincial congresses of N.H., on 24 May '75 he was named Col. of the 2d N.H. Regt. His regiment's first mission was to build fire rafts to protect Exeter and work on coastal defenses. Poor then led them to the Boston lines, moved to N.Y.C. in the spring of 1776,

and was later sent to strengthen the forces withdrawing up Lake Champlain. In the council of war on 5 July '76 he argued against the abandonment of Crown Point and organized a protest by 21 field grade officers (including John Stark and Wm. Maxwell) to Washington when Schuyler wisely decided the place was untenable. (See CANADA INVASION) He was president of the court-martial that acquitted Moses Hazen and ordered the arrest of Benedict ARNOLD. In Dec. '76 he went south to join Washington's army for operations at Trenton and Princeton (*D.A.B.*), and on 21 Feb. '77 he was promoted to B.G. Although his record had been as good as many others promoted to general officer rank, he owed his advancement partly to a factional dispute. (*Ibid.*)

After the perplexing British movements that preceded the Philadelphia Campaign his brigade and Varnum's were detached to Peekskill. Poor subsequently took part in the operations at TICONDEROGA, 2–5 July '77. His brigade of 800 men moved forward on the American right to open the Second Battle of SARATOGA, 7 Oct. '77, and performed well. He then rejoined Washington for winter quarters at Valley Forge and had a prominent part in the action at BARREN HILL, 20 May '78. As part of Chas. Lee's command he marched with the first troops to leave Valley Forge for the MONMOUTH CAMPAIGN and he led one of the final movements of the battle of 28 June.

During the winter of 1779–80 his brigade was posted at Danbury, Conn. Ordered to join Sullivan's Expedition against the Iroquois, he won the battle at NEWTOWN, N.Y., 29 Aug. '79, which was the only major action of the campaign. In 1780 his brigade was incorporated in Lafayette's Light Inf.

Div. He died 8 Sept. '80 at Paramus, N.J. of typhus ("putrid fever"), according to Dr. Thacher. (*Journal*, 212) Edward E. Curtis in his *D.A.B.* article, on which this sketch is largely based, mentions that Poor may have been killed (or mortally wounded) in a duel with a junior officer, but it is difficult to understand how Thacher could be wrong on this point.

See S. C. Beane, *Gen. Enoch Poor* (1899).

POPULAR SUPPORT OF THE REVOLUTION in America and England. On this subject we get into the problem of TRUTH VERSUS TRADITION, particularly insofar as popular American support goes. Perhaps the most balanced statement is the following by Van Tyne:

"Patriotism of the kind shown in the Civil War ... of that even higher variety manifested in the Great War (1917–1918), was very rare. The 'Spirit of '76' meant in the main enthusiasm for Independence, loyalty to a great commander, hate of George III, but not love of country, or of a great ideal, or a cause worth more than life itself. Washington rose to that, as did a few others who had the nobility and the vision, but in the masses loyalty to county, province, or section was the ruling motive." (*War of Indep.*, 271)

Another American historian, John Fiske, offers this blustery rebuttal:

"... the preposterous theory has been suggested that the American Revolution was the work of an unscrupulous minority, which, through intrigue mingled with violence, succeeded in forcing the reluctant majority to sanction its measures. Such a misconception has its root in an utter failure to comprehend the peculiar character of American political life." (*Amer. Rev.*, I, 195.)

British Army historian Sir John Fortescue presents this view:

"... it is, I think, unquestionable that the American Revolution was, as is generally the case, the work of a small but energetic and well organized minority, towards which the attitude of the mass of the people, where not directly hostile, was mainly indifferent." (*British Army*, III, 168)

Another British historian, D. C. Somervell, who must command respect for having condensed Toynbee's *Study of History,* delivers this judgment in his short *History of the U.S.:*

"Of course, if the movement for American independence had been one of the flamingly heroic national movements of history Washington would have secured ... an army sufficient to sweep the small British forces with their inefficient commanders off the face of America in a few months." (*Op. cit.,* 51)

"There is a hundred times more enthusiasm for the revolution in any Paris café than in the whole of the United States put together," wrote Le Bègue Duportail to the Comte de St. Germain on 12 Nov. '77. (Quoted in Fortescue, *op. cit.,* 257 *n.*)

Negative views have been gathered above to help balance the more common image of a colonial past in which "all the brothers were brave and all the sisters virtuous." But having reminded ourselves that the 18th century American colonists were human, let us also remind ourselves that they did create a form of government that has had longer continuous existence than any other except the British government from which it won independence. For positive aspects of American unity during the Revolutionary era see E. S. Morgan, *The Birth of the Republic ...* (indexed under "Americans, unity of").

BRITISH POPULAR SUPPORT

"Few things are more certain in the history of the American Revolution than that England as well as America was a house divided against itself," says Van Tyne in the work quoted earlier. (P. 162) The major political parties, Old Whigs, Pitt's Party, Bedford's "Bloomsbury Gang," and George III's Party, contended among themselves. The commercial elements of the "nation of shopkeepers" followed with considerable material and selfish interest the government's steps toward coercion of the American colonies, and petitions were submitted by merchants to protest certain acts that reflected in their balance sheets, but "Among the middle classes and poorer folk the war never became genuinely popular." (Alden, *Amer. Rev.,* 17) This—and Irish prosperity at the period—had much to do with the failure of RECRUITING IN GREAT BRITAIN. The effective Whig opposition, under talented leadership, turned a large element of the British population against their government. The King had no great national issue on which to rally support until about 1770, when he seized on Parliament's right to tax the colonies. When it came to shooting, however, the King not only failed to rally volunteers into the army and navy but had trouble with his senior military commanders. "Lord Amherst, the former commander-in-chief in America, Lord Effingham, and Admiral Keppel did resign, and the elder Pitt took his son out of the army rather than have him serve in such a war," writes Nickerson. (*Turning Point,* 63) Gen. Wm. HOWE told his parliamentary constituents he would never lead British troops against Americans. Burgoyne's defeat in Oct. '77 aroused the people and spurred RECRUITING, particularly when their old enemy France joined America. Ironically, the same events that rallied popular support in Britain convinced their more sensible statesmen that the cause was hopeless. (See GEORGE III)

POPULATIONS of Great Britain and America. In 1775 the British had 8,000,-000 people; 2,350,000 of these could be considered military manpower. Complaining of his difficulties in mobilizing an army for the Revolutionary war, Lord Shelburne commented that whereas 300,000 Englishmen entered the armies in the Seven Years' War, only 30,000 men, including German mercenaries, could be raised to put down the American rebellion.

In 1775 the 13 colonies had about 2,256,000, excluding INDIANS and counting 506,000 slaves. Using the experience factor of 10 per cent as the arms-bearing population and excluding slaves, the colonies had 175,000 men.

The "traditional calculation" that Americans were divided approximately equally into Whigs, Tories, and Neutrals has fallen into ill repute. It stems from an estimate made by John Adams, and recent research shows that actually he was referring to the French Revolution.

Approximate populations of major American cities in 1776 were: Philadelphia, 34,000; N.Y.C., 22,000; Boston, 15,000; Charleston, 12,000. Although London's population of 750,000 dwarfed Philadelphia's, the Quaker City outranked Bristol and Dublin as the second largest city of the British empire. (Montross, *Reluctant Rebels,* 32)

See Evarts B. Greene and Virginia D. Harrington, *American Population before the Federal Census of 1790* (New York, 1943).

PORTAIL. See LE BÈGUE ... DU-PORTAIL.

ESTIMATED AMERICAN POPULATION *

WHITE AND NEGRO	1780	1770	1760
Total	2,780,369	2,148,076	1,593,625
Maine (counties)	49,133	31,257	——
New Hampshire	87,802	62,396	39,093
Vermont	47,620	10,000	——
Massachusetts	268,627	235,308	222,600
Rhode Island	52,946	58,196	45,471
Connecticut	206,701	183,881	142,470
New York	210,541	162,920	117,138
New Jersey	139,627	117,431	93,813
Pennsylvania	327,305	240,057	183,703
Delaware	45,385	35,496	33,250
Maryland	245,474	202,599	162,267
Virginia	538,004	447,016	339,726
North Carolina	270,133	197,200	110,442
South Carolina	180,000	124,244	94,074
Georgia	56,071	23,375	9,578
Kentucky	45,000	15,700	——
Tennessee	10,000	1,000	——

NEGRO			
Total	575,420	459,822	325,806
Maine (counties)	458	475	——
New Hampshire	541	654	600
Vermont	50	25	——
Massachusetts	4,822	4,754	4,866
Rhode Island	2,671 †	3,761	3,468
Connecticut	5,885 †	5,698	3,783
New York	21,054	19,112	16,340
New Jersey	10,460	8,220	6,567
Pennsylvania	7,855	5,761	4,409
Delaware	2,996	1,836	1,733
Maryland	80,515	63,818	49,004
Virginia	220,582	187,605	140,570
North Carolina	91,000	69,600	33,554
South Carolina	97,000	75,178	57,334
Georgia	20,831	10,625	3,578
Kentucky	7,200	2,500	——
Tennessee	1,500	200	——

* *Historical Statistics of the United States* (Bureau of the Census, Washington, 1960).

† Includes some Indians.

PORT ROYAL ISLAND, S.C., 3 Feb. '79. See BEAUFORT.

PORT'S FERRY, Peedee R., S.C., which figured in the operations of Francis Marion, was located about five miles below the bridge of modern U.S. Hwy. 378. "Traces of the landing, road, and Marion's fort still exist [in 1959]." (Bass, *Swamp Fox*, 252)

POUNDRIDGE (now Pound Ridge), N.Y., 2 July '79. Tarleton moved with 360 men toward this place, 20 miles N.E. of White Plains, with the dual mission of capturing Maj. Ebenezer Lockwood, an active patriot, and defeating Col. Elisha Sheldon's 2d Cont'l. Dragoons. The latter unit, about 90 strong, had been supporting militia of Westchester co. Tarleton's command included 70 troopers of the 17th Lt. Dragoons, Simcoe's Rangers, and part of his own Legion. His advance was reported in time for Lockwood to escape, but Tarleton pushed Sheldon back two miles from the village before the militia started gathering and he had to withdraw. The raiders burned the church, several buildings (including Lockwood's), and carried away the colors of Sheldon's regiment. The rebel dragoons had 10 wounded and eight missing in action; Tarleton lost one man killed and one wounded. The raid was a failure, but Tarleton gloated over the captured flag, which had been found with some officers' baggage in a house.

POWLES HOOK, N.J. See PAULUS HOOK.

POWNALL, Thomas (pou'nl). 1722–1805. Colonial Gov. Educated at Lincoln and Trinity College (Cambridge), he entered the office of the Board of Trade soon after 1743. His brother John was secretary of the board. When the president of the board, Lord Halifax, secured the governorship of N.Y. for his own brother-in-law, Sir Danvers Osborn, Thomas Pownall became Osborn's secretary. Soon after reaching the colony in Oct. '53 the new governor, melancholy over the recent death of his wife, committed suicide. Instead of returning to England, Pownall "seized the opportunity to become a sort of free-lance observer for Halifax and the Board of Trade," writes Leonard W. Labaree in *D.A.B.* In May '55 he was appointed Lt. Gov. of N.J., but so long as the aged and infirm Gov. Jonathan Belcher remained alive Pownall was at liberty to continue his study of colonial administration and military affairs. He became a lifelong friend of Benjamin Franklin and, attending the Albany Conference as an observer, he presented a memorandum pointing out the strategic importance of the Great Lakes to British control of the continent. The following spring (1755) he assisted Gov. William Shirley in getting support from N.Y. and Pa. for the forthcoming military operations, and in Apr. '55 he attended the council of governors held in Alexandria by Gen. Braddock. He also came into intimate contact with such important colonial leaders as James De Lancey (1703–1760) and Sir William Johnson.

Early in 1756 he returned to England, where he presented a paper stressing the need for UNITY OF COMMAND in America and urging that immediate steps be taken to gain control of Lake Ontario. Although offered the governorship of Pa. he elected instead to accompany Lord Loudoun, the newly appointed C. in C., to America as secretary. After remaining in the colonies only a few months this time, he returned to London in Oct. '56 to present Loudoun's case against Shirley. It so happened that his arrival coincided with the rise of Pitt (CHATHAM) to control of the waning British fortunes in the Seven Years' War. Pitt was looking for new talent and was impressed by the young, vigorous, knowledgeable student of colonial affairs, and Pitt appointed him to succeed the discredited Shirley as Gov. of Mass. "It is not necessary to assume, as Shirley's supporters believed, that Pownall, De Lancey, and Johnson had plotted Shirley's downfall," points out Labaree. (*Ibid.*)

The 35-year-old Gov. reached Boston on 3 Aug. '57. Reacting promptly to a desperate call from Gen. Webb on the Hudson, he sent militia to his assistance without wasting time in getting the prescribed authority of his Assembly, but it was too late to prevent the disaster at FORT WILLIAM HENRY, which surrendered 9 Aug. When Gov. Belcher of N.J. died, 31 Aug., Pownall (who still was Lt. Gov.) hurried to N.J., put the senior councillor in charge, and returned immediately to Boston. For the three years of his administration he successfully achieved the effective participation of Mass. in the French and Indian War, but in so doing he alienated the friends of Shirley, antagonized such strong crown supporters as Thomas Hutchinson, and clashed with his old friend Loudoun over the war powers claimed by the military authorities. As much as he desired to command forces in the field, his only military exploit was the leadership of an expedition to build a fort on the Penobscot in May '59.

"Pownall was an able governor—too able and too independent from the point of view of a military commander like Loudoun, who sought unified leadership of all the governors in prosecuting the war and who called Pownall 'the greatest Man I have yet met, and from whom I foresee more trouble to whoever commands in this Country than from all the People on the Continent.'" (*Ibid.*)

The Board of Trade recalled him late in 1759, feeling that they could better use him elsewhere now that the war had ended. In Nov. '59 he was ordered to S.C. as Gov. but given leave to visit England first. On reaching England he was offered the governorship of Jamaica but declined it, and he also resigned the S.C. post without assuming office. In the summer of 1761 he became commissary general to the British-Hanoverian army on the Rhine with the rank of Col., and he held this post until the end of the war. The next year he published his famous *Administration of the Colonies,* which ran into five subsequent editions, the last being published in 1777. Urging that colonial administration be reorganized, he also argued for closer union, better centralization of colonial administration, and more precise definition of powers of governmental branches in England and abroad.

In 1767 he became an M.P., first as a Whig but then as a supporter of Lord North. He opposed Burke's bill for conciliation, but introduced a peace bill on 24 May '80 when he realized that the war was lost. This was defeated 113 to 50. In the summer of 1781 he declined to run again for Parliament and spent the rest of his life in travel and writing. Failure to gain an office commensurate with his abilities was a source of bitterness for this vain and ambitious man, but he continued in retirement to pursue his studies on a great variety of subjects and to write. An unconvincing attempt has been made to identify him as JUNIUS.

See C. A. W. Pownall, *Thomas Pownall, M.P., F.R.S., Governor of Massachusetts Bay, Author of the Letters of Junius* (1908); Labaree calls this the only full-length biography but comments that it is "uncritical and too laudatory" (*D.A.B.*). All his writings are listed in this work and in the

D.N.B. sketch. See *D.A.B.* for other works bearing on various aspects of Pownall's career.

POWOW. Derived from Indian words for a priest, wizard, magician, powow came to have the following meanings: (1) a medicine man, (2) his conjuring over a patient, (3) noisy festivities preceding a council, expedition, or hunt, (4) a council or PARLEY. (*Handbook of American Indians,* "Powow.") *O.U.D.* traces the history of the word, which it spells powwow, to 1642 in the first meanings given above; this same authority gives 1780 as the date when it was first used in the sense of a conference or PARLEY. It almost certainly was used earlier in the latter sense, but since "minutes" of such meetings were not normally made or filed, *O.U.D.* probably has not found earlier documentation on which to fix a date.

PRESCOTT, Oliver. 1731–1804. Physician and militia general. Mass. Younger brother of William ("Bunker Hill") PRESCOTT, son of Benjamin and Abigail Oliver Prescott, and grandson of John Prescott, who had reached New England in 1640, he graduated from Harvard in 1750 and built up a successful medical practice in Groton, his birthplace. He was a militia officer before the Revolution, became a B.G. of Middlesex co., Mass., militia when the war started, and became a Maj. Gen. of militia in 1778. During the Boston Siege he was charged with setting up check points to stop communication between the British garrison and Loyalists. During Shays's Rebellion he was active in recruiting and the dispatch of intelligence to the state authorities. Aside from these military activities he held a number of important civil posts, helping enforce the Association of 1774, serving on the supreme executive council from 1777 to 1780, holding the post

of J.O.P. and judge of probate for Middlesex co. from 1779 until his death, and having a vital role in the establishment and operation of Groton Academy. In the medical field he was active in the establishment of several societies. Over six feet tall, inclined to fatness, deaf in his later years, courtly in manner, he was a kindly and popular man.

See William Prescott (1788–1875), *The Prescott Memorial, or a Geneal. Memoir of the Prescott Families in America* (1870).

PRESCOTT, Richard. 1725–1788. British general. A Maj. in the 33d Foot on 20 Dec. '56, he became Lt. Col. of the 50th Foot in May '62 and served in Germany during the Seven Years' War. In 1773 he was breveted Col. of the 7th Foot and ordered to Canada, where his abuse of the captured Ethan ALLEN was followed by his own capture on 17 Nov. '75 when he failed in an attempt to escape from Montreal to Quebec. At this time he had the local rank of B.G., and about 25 Sept. '76 he was exchanged for John Sullivan. In Nov. '76 Prescott became Col. of his regiment and the next month he was third in command of the British expedition that occupied Newport. Remaining there as commander of the garrison, the insolent, ill-tempered, and supercilious Prescott made himself an object of American hatred. The night of 9–10 July '77 he was captured by Maj. William Barton (1748–1831) and 40 men in a daring raid that had left Tiverton in boats the night of 4 July. Exchanged 6 May '78 for Charles Lee—this had been Barton's purpose in capturing Prescott (*D.A.B.,* "Barton")—he briefly resumed his command in Newport before being superseded by Gen. Robert Pigot.

Although lampooned and criticized in the British press for his humiliating capture (*ibid.*), he had been promoted to Maj. Gen. on 29 Aug. '77. (Appleton's) Apparently remaining at Newport, he commanded a brigade in the Battle of R.I., 29 Aug., during the operations covered under NEWPORT, ... '78. About a year later he succeeded Pigot and in Oct. '79 complied with the orders of Clinton to destroy the works and evacuate his garrison of slightly more than 4,000 effectives to N.Y. (Clinton, *Amer. Reb.*, 146–47) On 26 Nov. '82, six years before his death in England, he was promoted to Lt. Gen.

PRESCOTT, Robert. 1725–1816. British general. In 1755 he was gazetted Capt., 15th Foot, and saw action with them at Rochefort in 1757 and Amherst's capture of Louisburg in 1758. The next year he was A.D.C. to this general before joining the command of James Wolfe. In Mar. '61 he became Maj. of the 95th Foot and took part in Robert Monckton's expedition against Martinique. In Nov. '62 he advanced to the grade of Lt. Col. On 8 Sept. '75 he became Lt. Col. of the 28th Regt. and took part in the N.Y. Campaign (Long Island, Westchester co., and the capture of Ft. Washington). He took part in the Philadelphia Campaign and saw action at the Brandywine in 1777. The next year he was named first brigadier in James Grant's expedition against St. Lucia. On 6 July '79 he was promoted to Col. and on 19 Oct. '81 he became a Maj. Gen. Advanced to Lt. Gen. on 12 Oct. '93, he received orders to take command at Barbados. The next Feb. he sailed for Martinique, landed unopposed, and on 22 Mar. received the surrender of the island. He is credited with a judicious military government that prevented a native uprising. Receiving sick leave, he reached England on 10 Feb. '95. In 10 Apr. '96 he was sent to succeed Carleton as Gov. of Canada, and on 1 Jan. '98 he was promoted to full Gen. He was recalled in 1799, when Sir Robert Milnes became Gov., and settled in Sussex.

PRESCOTT, Samuel. 1751–c. 1777. Physician. Mass. Son of Dr. Abel and Abigail Brigham Prescott, grandson of Dr. Jonathan Prescott, and a descendant of John Prescott, who settled in New England in 1640, he is remembered for carrying to Concord the warning of the British advance after Paul Revere and William Dawes were stopped outside Lexington. (See LEXINGTON AND CONCORD, 19 Apr. '75) According to Heitman he was a volunteer surgeon at Lexington, 19 Apr. '75. He then served at Ticonderoga in 1776. About a year later he was captured on board a privateer and died while imprisoned in Halifax. (*D.A.B.*)

PRESCOTT, William. 1726–1795. Militia officer, hero of Bunker Hill. Mass. Brother of Oliver PRESCOTT, he served in the last two Colonial Wars and settled in Pepperell, Mass., where he married Abigail Hale (1758) and became a prosperous farmer. Col. of a Mass. Regt., he arrived too late for the action at Concord, 19 Apr. '75, but marched on to Cambridge, where he later became a member of the council of war. He figured prominently in the battle of BUNKER HILL, 17 June '75, and there has been much debate over whether he or Israel Putnam was the actual American commander. Certainly he deserves credit for directing the action at the most prominent portion of the field, the redoubt on Breed's Hill. Col. Prescott took part in the evacuation of Long Island, the action at Kip's Bay, and the defeat of Burgoyne's Offensive. During the entire year 1776 he had held the commission of Col., 7th Cont'l. Inf. (Heitman) The elderly warrior, who was further handicapped physically by an injury sustained in farm work, retired to his home in 1777.

Over six feet tall, well-built, and possessing strong, clean-cut features, he had a way of inspiring respect and obedience as a militia leader. "His customary movements were unhurried, and his coolness and self-possession in moments of danger were notable," writes Ward. (*W.O.R.*, 76) Bunker Hill was his kind of battle, and the opportunity never again presented itself for him to repeat his performance.

His grandson was the famous historian, William Hickling Prescott (1796–1859).

PRETTY. "Conventionally applied to soldiers," says *O.U.D.*, its archaic meaning is "Brave, gallant, stout (chiefly *Sc.* [Scottish])."

PREUDHOMME DE BORRE, Philippe Hubert, Chevalier de. 1717–? Cont'l. general. France. Entered as a volunteer on the rolls of the Regt. de Champagne on 1 May '40, he became *sous lieutenant* on 26 July '41, Lt. on 20 Apr. '42, and Capt. of a cavalry regiment (Bretagne, later Bourgoyne) on 6 Aug. '44. During the War of the Austrian Succession (1740–48) he took part in the campaigns on the Rhine, and in Bavaria, Bohemia, and the Low Countries. During the crossing of the Rhine in June '45 he received four saber strokes on the head and one on the wrist; one hand was disabled permanently. Promoted to Lt. Col., he organized a regiment from Liége (his birthplace) in 1757. When this unit was reorganized, 1 Jan. '62, de Borre was reassigned in grade to the Metz garrison on 1 Mar. He apparently saw no active field service during the Seven Years' War (1757–63). Between 1764 and 1767 he had the duty of restraining desertion from the Liége area toward Russia. (Lasseray, 367) Meanwhile he had been made a chevalier in the order of St. Louis on 20 June '57.

With the temporary rank of B.G. and official authority to go to America, de Borre sailed from Le Havre on 14 Dec. '76 with de Coudray and a large French contingent aboard the *Amphitrite*. When the *Amphitrite* turned back, de Borre changed to the *Mercure* and reached Portsmouth, N.H., on 17 Mar. Reporting to Washington's headquarters at Morristown on 17 May, he was given a commission as B.G. with date of rank from 1 Dec. '76. (Heitman) His brigade of Sullivan's Div. comprised Hazen's 2d Canadian ("Congress' Own"), and the 2d, 4th, and 6th Md. Cont'l. Regts. Lasseray is being figurative when he writes that de Borre's Brig. had its baptism of fire on 26 June '77 (*op. cit.*, 368); while Alexander was fighting at SHORT HILLS on that day, Sullivan's Div. was maneuvering far to the west. (See PHIL. CAMP'N.) He commanded his brigade in the Staten Island raid of Sullivan, 22 Aug., and at the Brandywine, 11 Sept. '77. In the latter action he is said to have claimed the position of honor—the right of the line—and to have tried to take it even after Sullivan refused his request; this resulted in a delay of Sullivan's deployment at a critical moment. (Appleton's) De Borre's Brig. then was the first to collapse under the British attack. Charged with "mismanagement or worse," as Freeman puts it (*Washington*, IV, 535), de Borre tendered his resignation on 14 Sept. when he learned that a court of inquiry was to be called. (*Ibid.*) Congress gladly accepted it. De Borre later maintained he had been condemned without a hearing and that he deserved promotion to Maj. Gen. (*Ibid.*, 539)

Of this matter Lasseray gives the following version:

"...man of experience and of method,—[De Borre] was intolerant of the defeat [of Washington's army on the Brandywine] that a little preparation and *sang froid* might have prevented.

He recommended that the entire army be withdrawn into Philadelphia, that it fortify itself there, and await the enemy, whose rear could be harassed by the 50,000 militia of the country. He was not listened to. 'Seeing all the bad dispositions and commanding nothing but bad troops,' he noted on 15 September, 'I sent my commission back to Congress so as not to be in a position to be dishonored.' " (Lasseray, 368)

In attempting to excuse his compatriot, Commandant Lasseray has used de Borre's own words to accuse him. Considering the war record of the regiments in his brigade, one can understand the statement in Appleton's that "He was unpopular . . . and totally unfit to command American troops."

Sailing from Charleston on 20 Jan. '79, the chevalier carried dispatches to d'Estaing at Cap François (Haiti). He re-embarked on the *Andromaque* on 15 May, witnessed the fight in which this ship sank the British privateer *Tartar,* and reached Brest on 5 July. The grade of B.G. in the Royal Army was not given to de Borre until 1 Mar. '80. As early as 5 Apr. action was initiated to retire him for physical disability.

Several studies by de Borre are in the *Archives historiques de la Guerre.* His manuscript *Journal* on the American campaigns of 1777 and 1778 is also located there.

PREVOST, Augustine. 1723–1786. British general. Born in Geneva, the son of "an officer in the English army," according to Appleton's, it would appear almost certain that he was the son of the Swiss officer who raised the ROYAL AMERICAN REGIMENT (60th Foot). Butler's *Annals of the King's Royal Rifle Corps* ("ROYAL AMERICAN"), on the other hand, does not confirm this last detail and gives 22 Aug. '23 as Augustine's date of birth. He joined the 60th Foot as a Maj.

on 9 Jan. '56 and was dangerously wounded while serving under Wolfe around Quebec in 1759. (*ibid.*) On 20 Mar. '61 Prevost was advanced to the rank of Lt. Col. and on 18 Sept. '75 he became a full Col.

At the start of the Revolution he commanded British forces in E. Fla. Moving north to cooperate in the attack on SAVANNAH, 29 Dec. '78, he had orders to assume over-all command of British forces in the South. On 19 Feb. '79 he was promoted to (local?) Maj. Gen. (*ibid.*) and he undertook the operations outlined in the article on SOUTHERN THEATER Military Operations. Highlights of his outstanding performance were his victory at BRIAR CREEK, Ga., 3 Mar. '79 (where his younger brother, Lt. Col. Marc Prevost, distinguished himself) and his defense of SAVANNAH, 9 Oct. '79. Shortly thereafter he returned to England, having served for 22 years in North America and the West Indies. He died in 1786.

In 1765 he had married the daughter of a Swiss gentleman named Grand. Three sons and two daughters survived Gen. Prevost. The eldest, Sir George, born in N.Y. in 1767, served in the 60th Foot, distinguished himself in the West Indies, was promoted to Lt. Gen. in 1811, and at this time succeeded Sir James CRAIG as Gov.-Gen. of Canada; his invasion of N.Y. was stopped by Gen. Macomb at Plattsburg, 11 Sept. 1814. (See *D.N.B.*)

In July '82 Aaron BURR married Theodosia Bartow Prevost, the widow of a British officer (*D.A.B.,* "Burr"), but this was not the widow of Augustine Prevost, as has been stated by Appleton's and others.

PRIME MINISTERS of Britain. The first statesman in English history who properly deserved the name of prime minister—although this term was not then used—was Robert Walpole, 1st

Earl of Orford (1676–1745), who, according to *E.B.*, held this post during the period 1721–42. His successors were: Henry Pelham, 1743–6 Mar. '54 (died); his brother, the Duke of NEWCASTLE, 1754–56; the coalition of Newcastle and CHATHAM (William Pitt the elder), 1757–61; Lord BUTE, to 8 Apr. '63; GRENVILLE, to July '65; ROCKINGHAM, to July '66; Chatham again to Oct. '68. GRAFTON was nominal P.M. in Chatham's ministry, and effective P.M. after the latter's incapacity in late 1767; he resigned in Jan. '70. For the next 12 years Lord NORTH held the post (Mar. '70–Mar. '82). Rockingham returned as P.M. but died 1 July. On 2 Apr. '83 a coalition ministry took office with the Duke of Portland as P.M.; this collapsed in Dec. '83, after the peace treaty ending the Revolutionary War had been signed. (See also GEORGE III)

PRINCE OF WALES LOYAL AMERICAN VOLUNTEERS. Also identified as "Brown's" or "Browne's Corps," this Tory regiment went to Charleston with Rawdon in the spring of 1780 and subsequently served in the South. A detachment was virtually annihilated at HANGING ROCK, S.C., 6 Aug. '80; they are not to be confused with Col. Thomas Brown's S.C. Rangers, who also took part in that action. Another detachment of the Prince of Wales Regt. was annihilated by Marion at GREAT SAVANNAH, 20 Aug. '80. Tory Maj. Andrew Maxwell (of Md.), who surrendered FT. GRANBY, 15 May '81, was an officer of this same regiment, and presumably the garrison included men of the unit.

Gov. Montfort Browne (who held this office from 1774 to 1780) had been captured in the raid on NASSAU, 3–4 Mar. '76; he and Maj. Cortlandt Skinner were exchanged in Sept. '76 for Gen. Alexander ("Lord Stirling").

(Baurmeister, *Journals,* 54, 55 and *n.*) Identified at this time as a Maj. (*ibid.*), he subsequently raised a Tory unit known as "Browne's Corps." In Aug. '77 it numbered 450 men and was stationed at Kings Bridge, N.Y.; Gov. Tryon commanded the force of several Tory regiments in which it was included. (*Ibid.,* 92 and *n.*) A year later it is identified among the troops located on Staten Island. Baurmeister says they served under Prevost before and during the defense of Savannah in 1779 (*ibid.,* 294), but it is apparent that he has them confused with the command of Thomas BROWN (whose S.C. or "King's" Rangers are mentioned above). It seems safe to assume that Gov. Browne's Tories did not go south until 1780.

A regular British regiment, also called the Prince of Wales's, was formed from nine companies raised in Wales in 1778 but did not serve in America (Curtis, *Organization of the British Army,* 70 *n.,* 72).

PRINCETON, N.J. 3 Jan. '77. (NEW JERSEY CAMPAIGN) Although his covering forces under Edw. HAND delayed Cornwallis' approach to Trenton on 2 Jan. so that the British did not hit the main American battle position along Assumpink Creek until dark, Washington knew that he could not stand up against the superior British forces when they resumed their attack the next day. Cornwallis was so sure of victory that he scoffed at advice from his officers to attack immediately.

Freeman says Washington probably selected the position along Assumpink Creek with the thought of maneuvering in the direction of Princeton before he could be trapped. (*Op. cit.,* IV, 345 *n.* and 374–75) On the other hand, Gen. St. Clair says that in the council of war held the evening of 2 Jan. it was he—St. Clair—who suggested a maneuver around the British left flank, and some writers subscribe to the opinion of the impeachable James WILKINSON that only blind luck and St. Clair's eleventh-hour suggestion saved the army. Whoever deserves credit for its conception, the plan was for the Americans to slip out of their bivouac during the night and march secretly by way of Quaker Bridge to strike Princeton and then Brunswick. American patrols had reported the roads clear of British as far as the bridge. As another piece of good fortune, the weather turned cold enough during the night to freeze the roads, eliminating the mud that would otherwise have slowed the march.

Leaving 400 men around burning campfires to simulate presence of the army, and evacuating the baggage and heavy guns south to Burlington, the rest of Washington's command started marching at 1 A.M. (3 Jan.) Every precaution was taken to ensure secrecy: only the generals knew where the expedition was headed; orders were given in whispers; wheels of gun carriages were wrapped with rags to muffle their sound on the frozen ground. The march was a nightmare for the exhausted and ill-fed veterans as well as for the inexperienced militia. A considerable number of the latter were routed when the noise got through their ranks that they were surrounded by Hessians. By 3 A.M., however, the column was crossing Stony Brook, a mere two miles from Princeton. Back at Trenton, Cornwallis slept soundly, without a dream that the fox had once more escaped; on the Princeton-Trenton road, at Maidenhead, Gen. Leslie's brigade of about 1,200 men was unaware that Washington's force had passed within an hour's march of them.

Princeton had been left with about 1,200 British troops under Lt. Col. Chas. Mawhood as a rear guard when Cornwallis marched for Trenton on 1 Jan. At dawn the next day, unaware of Washington's approach, Mawhood left Princeton with the 17th and 55th Foot to join Leslie at Maidenhead and then move on to Trenton. The 40th Foot stayed in Princeton to guard supplies. Mawhood was crossing Stony Brook Bridge with the 17th, part of the 55th, and a troop of the 16th Light Dragoons when he saw armed men approaching in his direction. In the morning fog Mawhood first mistook these men for Hessians (the same error that led to the capture of 23 British at LONG ISLAND by Haslet's Delawares, whose uniform resembled that of the Hessians); then he thought they were Americans retreating from a defeat at Trenton and he faced his troops about to cut off and capture them.

THE BATTLE

Using the rough sketch of the approaches to Princeton and of British dispositions in the town that Cadwalader had made from a spy's observations on 30 Dec., Washington had formed a simple plan of attack: Mercer was to take 350 men and destroy Stony Brook Bridge, sealing the Post Road against reinforcement from Trenton and cutting off escape from Princeton; the main body of American troops was to enter Princeton by the "Back Road." When Mercer's men were sighted, shortly before 8 o'clock, Washington was near the fork of Quaker Road and the back road, the main body—under Sullivan —were ahead on the way to Princeton, and Hitchcock's Brig. was behind him on Quaker Road.

As Mawhood withdrew to take up a defensive position, Mercer's men moved in such a direction that the two forces clashed in Clark's Orchard. The traditional version is that both forces were

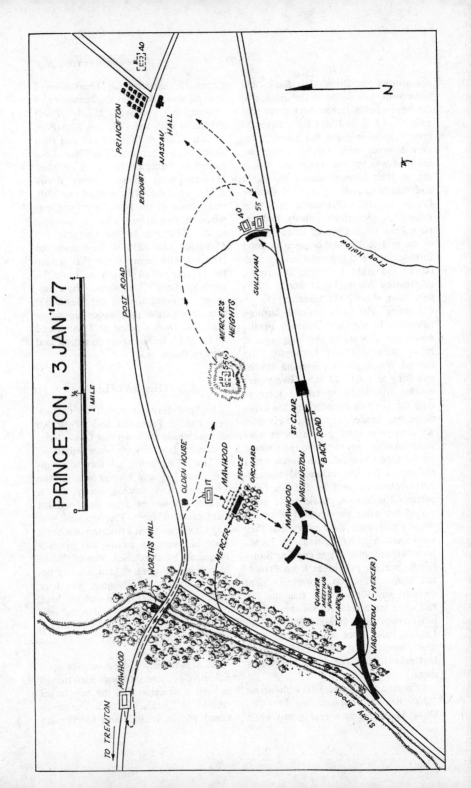

PRINCETON, 3 JAN '77

1 MILE

N

TO TRENTON

MAWHOOD

WORTH'S MILL

Stony Brook

OLDEN HOUSE

MAWHOOD

FENCE

ORCHARD

MAWHOOD

MERCER

QUAKER MEETING HOUSE

T. CLARK

WASHINGTON

WASHINGTON (-MERCER)

"BACK ROAD"

ST. CLAIR

MERCER'S HEIGHTS

POST ROAD

PRINCETON

REDOUBT

NASSAU HALL

SULLIVAN

Frog Hollow

40

55

40

racing for the orchard, but Freeman subscribes to the theory of T. J. Wertenbaker that the British were heading for the high ground later known as Mercer's Heights. "There was no point," Wertenbaker maintained, "in a race for the orchard of William Clark, because the ground there was not commanding." (Quoted in *Washington*, IV, 350 *n.*) Mercer probably intended first to head off Mawhood, but when he saw this was impossible was moving cross country to join Sullivan on the back road when an accidental encounter took place in the orchard. (*Ibid.*, 351 *n.*)

As Mercer's men passed through the orchard they were fired on by troops of the 17th Foot, who were located behind a fence on their left. The Americans changed front and drove the British from this position. Both forces then formed battle lines and each brought two field guns into play. The 17th launched an attack that drove the Americans back, leaving Mercer mortally wounded and Haslet dead. Washington rushed forward with Cadwalader's militia too late to prevent the collapse of Mercer's force, but two guns under command of Capt. Joseph Moulder went into action and stopped the British pursuit in time to prevent a complete rout. Washington, Greene, and Cadwalader rode among the bewildered troops to rally them, while Hitchcock's New England Brig. of Cont'ls. hurried forward. Then, with the Pa. militia on the left, Hitchcock's Brig. on their right, Hand's riflemen beyond Hitchcock's flank, Washington led his men against an unflinching British line. At 30 yards he reined his horse and gave the order to fire. The thin red line returned the volley and then broke and fled, the 17th fighting their way south to Cornwallis and the others retreating to Princeton. (Since the 40th was still in Princeton and part of the 55th was on Mercer Heights, the 17th Foot represented most of the enemy troops engaged in the "battle" we have been describing. They lost 66 killed and wounded, and 35 captured. "Since the battalion [or regiment] could not have taken more than two to three hundred men into action, this feat was rightly judged to be one of the most gallant exploits of the war." (Fortescue, *Br. Army,* III, 201)

Sullivan's force had remained inactive on the back road during this fight because enemy troops were visible on Mercer Heights. When Mawhood's command was driven off the field the enemy on Mercer Heights (which turned out to be a portion of the 55th Foot) retreated to Princeton, where the 40th Foot had remained. The British then made a show of defending a ravine south of the town (today's Frog Hollow) but soon retreated northward. When the Americans entered Princeton some enemy troops occupied the college building. Their ideas of putting up a defense here were altered when Capt. Alexander Hamilton rolled up a gun and fired a round into the building; 194 prisoners were then collected. The other British troops escaped north.

Having heard the fight start at Princeton, Cornwallis rushed reinforcements up from Trenton. The last Americans were leaving the college town when the first enemy troops entered from the south. Although he had a great opportunity to continue his raid to Brunswick, Washington's tired troops were not equal to the task. He later wrote that 600 or 800 fresh troops on 3 Jan. could have destroyed British supplies in that town, captured the £70,000 war chest and "put an end to the war." The Americans marched through Kingston and made camp at Somerset Court House, arriving between dusk and 8 P.M. They then moved to Morristown, reaching there on 5 and 6 Jan., and went into winter quarters.

NUMBERS AND LOSSES

In the 45-minute battle near Princeton the Americans lost 40 killed or wounded. British losses were about 28 killed, 58 wounded, and 187 missing. (Ward, *op. cit.*, 316, from Howe's official return.) Fortescue says the three regiments did not exceed 700 men in total strength (*op. cit.*, 201 *n.*), and probably not more than half that number were actually engaged.

See N.J. CAMPAIGN for bibliography.

PRISONS AND PRISON SHIPS. The lot of the Revolutionary War prisoner was hard, not so much because of deliberate policy as because neither the British nor the Americans were prepared in 1775 to take care of those they caught. Normal jail facilities soon were filled with political prisoners: Whigs and Tories. Then came the large hauls: some 4,000 rebels taken around N.Y.C. in 1776; approximately 5,000 British, Germans, and Canadians marched off from Saratoga as the CONVENTION ARMY and 1,000 Germans taken earlier at Trenton; over 5,000 Americans surrendered in May '80 at Charleston; and perhaps 8,000 British taken captive at Yorktown, Oct. '81. Naval prisoners continued to be taken throughout this period—fishermen, privateers, officers and men of the regular navies, and such special diplomatic prizes as Henry LAURENS.

While the written record abounds with stories of hardships, atrocities, and escapes, precise facts and accurate figures about prisoners during the Revolution are lacking. We do not know how many were taken, although there is some reason to believe that the numbers for each side were about even. Since the Americans lacked—even more than the British—the means of securing

prisoners, captured British and Germans tended to drift away from American camps after relatively short confinements; the Germans, in particular, were allowed to "escape" in the knowledge that they tended to end up as American farm hands and not to return to their British masters. (C. & M., 844, 873) American military prisoners, however, were packed into improvised jails and prison ships to suffer and die in large numbers. British political prisoners—Loyalists—were subjected to equal horrors in such places as the abandoned Simsbury copper mines in Conn., although their numbers were relatively few. Problems in connection with the EXCHANGE OF PRISONERS prolonged the misery of captives and ran up the death rate. Elias BOUDINOT was the American commissary general of prisoners during the most important years; his British counterpart was the corrupt Joshua Loring, whose wife was the famous mistress of Gen. Howe. Other British commissaries of prisoners were men named Sproat and Lennox.

Infamous British prisons in N.Y.C. were Van Cortlandt's Sugar House (N.W. corner of Trinity churchyard), Rhinelander's (corner of William and Duane Streets), the Liberty Street Sugar House (Nos. 34 and 36 Liberty Street), and the Provost Jail. The latter had been constructed in the "FIELDS" in 1758 and was known as the "New Jail"; it was administered by the notorious William CUNNINGHAM. The Provost and Liberty jails, in that order, were the most dreaded by patriots. Other places in N.Y.C. were used as prisons: some of the Dissenter churches, the hospital, King's College (Columbia), and one or more other sugar houses.

The prison ships were probably more horrible than the land jails. Originally used for naval captives, they subsequently were filled with soldiers. The

British started using them not only to solve their problems of space in N.Y.C. —particularly after the fire of Sept. '76—but because they promised to be more secure and more healthful than conventional jails. Both assumptions proved wrong: any prisoner who could swim could escape from a ship more easily than from a land jail; improper administration of the prison ships— overcrowding, poor sanitation, inadequate food—turned them into death traps. "In the end the British prison ships probably killed more American soldiers than British rifles: the total estimate runs to 7,000 or 8,000." (C. & M., 854) When the bones of those buried around the shores of Wallabout Bay were collected for reinterment in 1808 it was estimated that more than 11,000 bodies were represented; Lossing points out that many British and Hessian bones are doubtless included (II, 867 n.), but reputable modern authorities estimate that as many as 11,-500 prisoners died aboard the N.Y.C. prison ships (Concise D.A.H., 767).

Most notorious was the Jersey, a 64-gun ship that had been dismantled in 1776 as unfit for service and that held 1,000 or more prisoners. Other ships in Wallabout Bay were the Hunter and the Stromboli. The hospital ship Scorpion was moored off Paulus Hook; one of its guests was Philip Freneau, who wrote a dramatic poem about the horrors and hopelessness of life aboard a prison ship. At least 13 different ships were used around N.Y.C. during the war. Others were, of course, used elsewhere. The Sandwich—although not a prison ship—was used to take political prisoners to St. Augustine from Charleston.

Other Americans were jailed at Halifax, and those taken on the high seas or in European waters saw the inside of such famous English prisons as Dartmoor, Old Mill Prison at Plymouth, Forton Prison at Portsmouth, and the Tower of London. Cont'l. Army prisoners taken at Charleston, 12 May '80, were caged for 13 months at nearby Haddrel's Point, where they suffered great hardships. Some elected to join the British Army or to serve in units formed to fight in the West Indies.

In his Struggle for American Independence Fisher writes:

"The cruel treatment which the British inflicted on their prisoners in Philadelphia was one of the stock horrors of the Revolution, like the suffering at Libby and Andersonville in the Civil War of 1861. Among the starving prisoners in Philadelphia rats were a luxury. Dr. Waldo said, that some of the prisoners, in their last agonies of hunger, scraped mortar and rotten wood from the walls and greedily ate it for the temporary sensation of nourishment which it gave. Such scenes of cruelty in the midst of the extravagance, luxury and gaiety which the loyalists and British officers enjoyed that winter, very naturally stimulated the hatred of the patriots for everything English, and inspired them with more desperate determination in the contest.

"The condition of the prisoners was the result of the system by which army officials were permitted to make fortunes.

* * *

"The Americans who were taken to prisons in England had also their tales of horror; but mitigated to a great extent by philanthropic efforts of the English Whigs. . . . Franklin also raised money for them in France. And the most remarkable contrast to the prisons in Philadelphia and New York was the conduct of General Carleton in Canada, who in all his campaigns was so kind and humane to prisoners . . . that these men on their return were kept away from the starving and ragged patriotic forces, whose devotion to the cause might, it was feared, be weakened by the relation of Carleton's kindness.

* * *

"During the last three years of the war under Clinton the British were apparently much more humane in their treatment of prisoners. There is very little evidence of American cruelty to prisoners, except in the case of imprisoned loyalists, who often endured much suffering, and some letters on the subject will be found scattered through the volumes of the *American Archives*. In New York many loyalists were imprisoned under the Court House at Kingston, in which the patriot Provincial convention held its sessions. These prisoners were kept in such a state of crowding and filth, that the stench rose up into the room of the convention; and a curious resolution was passed on motion of Gouverneur Morris, describing the 'nauseous and disagreeable effluvia' in which the members were compelled to sit, and allowing them to smoke 'for the preservation of their health.' * * * The crowding . . . at last became so intolerable . . . that many of the loyalists were removed and confined in the prison ships at Esopus on the Hudson. When Clinton took the Hudson Highlands . . . these prison ships were run up Esopus Creek and burnt, and Judge Jones says that one hundred and fifty of the loyalists were burnt in them. But this . . . lacks confirmation from other sources. . . ." (*Op. cit.*, II, 132–36. Thomas Jones and Albigence Waldo are covered by biographical sketches in Fisher's book.)

In addition to the authorities cited above see also the W. C. Ford edition of *The Writings of Washington* (14 vols., 1889–93), in which "Prisoners" is indexed. The writings of Elias BOUDINOT are pertinent and Bolton's *Pri-*

vate Soldier Under Washington includes details of prison life and death. See also Onderdonk's *Revolutionary Incidents*. A long chapter in C. & M. is devoted to "Prisons and Escapes" (pp. 844–91); Lossing includes sketches and other valuable information (II, 864–67, *passim*).

PRIVATEERING. The word *privateer* apparently comes from *private man of war*, in which sense it is traced back to 1664. (*O.U.D.*) A privateer is an armed vessel belonging to a private owner and commissioned by a government under a *letter of marque* to carry on operations of war. The American colonists had a long tradition in this field, starting with King William's War, 1689–97.

"In King George's War (1744–48) privateering began to assume the proportions of a major maritime business; and it is said that during the French and Indian War (1754–63) 11,000 Americans were engaged in private-armed operations." (*Concise D.A.H.*)

The big incentive of privateering was, of course, PRIZES, and for this reason privateering had more appeal to individuals than the regular navy. It is a moot point whether American privateers during the Revolution did the patriot cause more harm than good: while they destroyed a much greater number of British ships than did the Cont'l. Navy (see below), they drained off resources of manpower and materials that prevented the regular American Navy from developing into a significant element of the patriots' armed forces. A privateer's mission was where the prize money lay, not where he could take part in NAVAL OPERATIONS. Many of the actions covered under the latter heading, however, were of a privateering nature, even though they involved naval ships. (See CONYNGHAM, Nathaniel FANNING, John Paul JONES, and WICKES.)

At the start of the Revolution, most

of the colonies issued letters of marque and reprisal. Three months before the Decl. of Indep., on 23 Mar. '76, Congress resolved: "That the inhabitants of these Colonies be permitted to fit out armed vessels, to cruise on the enemies of these United Colonies." Since privateers sometimes operated only for a single voyage it is not too meaningful to state the number commissioned. One authority says 1,151 American privateers went to sea (*Concise D.A.H.*), whereas another puts the total at about 2,000, some 1,700 being commissioned by Congress and 600 by Mass. (C. & M., 964) The ships varied between less than 100 to 500 tons, carried up to 20 guns, and had crews averaging 100 men. (*Ibid.*) Under the more conservative estimate of ships given above, over 11,000 seamen would have been engaged in this business. "Some estimates place the number . . . at upwards of 60,000, but these figures doubtless involve a good deal of duplication," conclude C. & M. (*Ibid.*)

American privateers took about 600 British vessels during the years 1775–83, including 16 men of war; prize money is estimated at $18,000,000. A record high was reached in 1781, when 449 American privateers carrying 6,735 guns were at sea. The Cont'l. Navy, which had only three ships in commission in 1781 and only two in 1783, took 196 ships amounting to $6,000,000 in prize money during the war. Most authorities accept these figures of British losses (in specie dollars, incidentally). One writer, however, says that only 792 American privateers, carrying more than 13,000 guns and swivels, were engaged. (See Maclay [p. viii] in bibliography of article NAVAL OPERATIONS) One privateer, the *Rattlesnake,* took $1,000,-000 in prizes in one Baltic cruise.

While the privateers were little more than licensed pirates who contributed little to the American cause—since

prizes were sold to the highest bidder, often in Europe, the privateersmen pocketed the money, and the cargoes often were bought back by the British—still the privateers incurred great risks and figured in some heroic fights. See CONGRESS–SAVAGE, 6 Sept. '81, TRUMBULL–WATT, 2 June '80, and YANKEE HERO–MELFORD, 7 June '76, for examples. A former state naval officer turned privateer was Jonathan HARADEN.

Bermuda and the West Indies, particularly JAMAICA, built many privateers and furnished support to those of both sides, British and American.

See NAVAL OPERATIONS for bibliography.

PRIZES and Prize Money. Although associated primarily with operations at sea, prize money also was awarded to officers and men who captured enemy property on land. The value of the capture was computed and prize money was awarded in accordance with a scale based on rank. In his *American Rebellion,* Sir Henry Clinton says this about the dispute that developed after the surrender of Charleston, 12 May '80:

"But, when upon Charleston surrendering [,] an equitable division of those [prizes] now taken was proposed to the navy (who alone, *it seems, are authorized by law to share prize money*), the Admiral was not inclined to admit the army to any proportionate share; and the captains of the King's ships thought the navy had a right to at least half, although their proportion in numbers did not amount to a third. The matter was therefore referred . . . to the decision of the King in council. But in the meantime . . . the navy . . . divided among themselves three-fourths—while the poor soldier, who from the nature of services at a siege bore . . . the principal burden of fatigue and danger, got nothing. For the insignificant remaining fourth (£10,000), which the troops had themselves taken and lodged with their agents until His Majesty's pleasure should be known, continues to this hour in the agents' hands, as they have refused to part with the money and the troops have, unfortunately, no legal power to compel them." (*Op. cit.*, 180. The *italics* are in the original. According to the note of editor Willcox, the troops apparently never did get any of the Charleston prize money.)

As for naval prizes and prize money, under maritime law, private property of an enemy power captured at sea under certain legal circumstances was a "prize," and proceeds of its sale were normally adjudicated by a "prize court." Prize money usually went in its entirety to privateersmen, but if the prize were taken by a warship only half of its value, prorated in accordance with the normal pay scale, went to the officers and men. A "prize master" and crew took the captured ship into the port of a belligerent or allied power for condemnation in accordance with prize law. If the capture were illegal, *i.e.* inside neutral waters and by a ship not bearing letters of marque and reprisal, the prize court would release the ship and award damages. Since an estimated $18,000,000 worth of prizes were taken by 600 American privateers whose crews averaged 100 men, privateering during the Revolution had a greater appeal than the Cont'l. Navy.

PROCLAMATION OF 1763. To reduce Indian unrest stemming from colonial land frauds and westward expansion, the British and colonists had taken steps in 1755 to limit migration. Elimination of the French and Indian threat by the expulsion of the French from Canada in 1763 and disregard of the Treaty of FORT STANWIX, however, intensified the problem. At the very time PONTIAC'S WAR was about to break out, Lord Shelburne—head of the Board of Trade—had drafted a plan that was put in final form by his successor, the Earl of Hillsborough, and rushed to the King for his signature on 7 Oct. '63. Under this Proclamation of 1763 the territories recently won from France were organized into four distinct and separate governments: the provinces of Quebec, East and West Florida, and "Grenada." (The latter comprised the island of Grenada, the Grenadines, Dominica, St. Vincent, and Tobago.) The Proclamation established a line along the watershed of the Alleghenies as the temporary western limit of British settlement and—in modification of Shelburne's draft—ordered withdrawal of colonists already west of this line, which meant those in the upper Ohio valley. Trade with the Indians was to be under royal control. Quebec was put under English law, a provision that alarmed the Catholic, French inhabitants. The boundary of Georgia was extended from the Altamaha to the St. Marys River. The act specifically mentioned colonial land frauds and other offenses against the Indians, and went into great detail on how these were to be prevented in the future.

The colonists strongly opposed this Proclamation, which withdrew lands promised to veterans of the French and Indian War, curtailed trade with the Indians, and cut into the claims of the "THREE SIDED" colonies. Land speculators and frontiersmen objected to the restrictions on western migration. Canadians resented the imposition of English law, fearing it would be anti-Catholic and would disrupt the law they had known under France. An interesting effect of the Proclamation was that it confined Americans to the seaboard, where they could be more easily controlled by the mother country, where debtors to Britain could not escape over the Alleghenies, and where Americans could not start their own manufactures and evade dependence on British manufacturers and merchants. (Miller, *O.A.R.*, 75)

(See Commager, *Documents*, 47–50, for verbatim text of the proclamation, and Scribner, *Atlas*, plate 60, for the Proclamation Line of 1763.)

PROPAGANDA IN (AND AFTER) THE AMERICAN REVOLUTION. The patriots realized early in their dispute with the mother country that for purposes of AGITATION at home and friendship abroad they should tell their own side of every story quickly and effectively. They became pioneers and masters of propaganda. They were so good, in fact, that for many years propaganda was passed down as history, and some writings of American scholars were enough to make Sam Adams grin in his grave at their gullibility. One amusing backblast of Yankee propaganda occurred in connection with LEXINGTON AND CONCORD: patriots of the former village did such a thorough job of proving they did not fire the first shot that they had to go to work half a century later to prove that any of their heroes fired at all! For other examples of propaganda see BOSTON "MASSACRE," the Jane McCREA ATROCITY, the "massacres" at PAOLI, TAPPAN, and WYOMING, the biographical sketches of Sam ADAMS (whom a recent biographer has called "Pioneer in Propaganda"), David FANNING, "Bloody Ban" TARLETON, Joseph BRANT, and Walter BUTLER. See also TRUTH VERSUS TRADITION in the American Revolution, and TAXATION WITHOUT REPRESENTATION.

PROSPECT HILL. This is an obvious name to give to any hill from which there is a good view. One was located near Cambridge, Mass. (see MUTINY OF PROSPECT HILL), and another was the place to which the American outposts withdrew in the preliminary maneuvers leading to the battle of LONG ISLAND.

PROTECTOR–DUFF ENGAGEMENT, 9 June '80. Off the banks of Newfoundland the frigate *Protector* (26) of the Mass. navy sank the *Admiral Duff* (32) in a fierce action recorded by Midshipman Luther Little of the Mass. ship. According to him the marksmanship of 60 American marines was decisive. Opposing captains were John Foster Williams of Mass. and Richard Stranger. (See C. & M., 959–60)

"PROTESTERS." Name applied by Whig radicals to the Boston merchants who objected to the SOLEMN LEAGUE AND COVENANT.

PROVINCIAL MILITARY ORGANIZATIONS. Loyalist units formed in America by the British during the Colonial Wars and the Revolution were officially designated "Provincials," to distinguish them legally from the units of the "Regular (British) Establishment." As is mentioned in the article on LOYALISTS, no fewer than 69 Provincial regiments were organized at least to the extent of seeking recruits, and at least 21 took the field with an average strength of several hundred men. (For comments on recruiting problems see GUIDES AND PIONEERS and VOLUNTEERS OF IRELAND.) The most famous Tory units were BUTLER'S RANGERS, the BRITISH LEGION of Tarleton, Robinson's LOYAL AMERICANS, De Lancey's NEW YORK VOLUNTEERS, Simcoe's QUEEN'S RANGERS, Sir John Johnson's ROYAL GREENS, SKINNER'S BRIGADE, and the VOLUNTEERS OF IRELAND. Most of these would stand in battle against regulars, whereas the others were suited only for ambushes, bushwhacking, and raiding.

Other Provincial regiments of interest for one reason or another are the As-

SOCIATED LOYALISTS, the King's American Regiment of Foot (see FANNING'S), the Queen's Royal Rangers, which Dr. John CONNOLLY proposed to form, the LOYAL AMERICAN RANGERS, and the Royal Highland Emigrants organized in Canada by Allan MACLEAN.

PROVOST JAIL. See PRISONS AND PRISON SHIPS.

PRUSSIA AND THE AMERICAN REVOLUTION. See FREDERICK THE GREAT . . . .

PULASKI, Casimir. *c.* 1748–1779. Cont'l. dragoon leader. Poland. A well-educated nobleman, he entered military service in 1767 and the next year started fighting the Russians in his father's Confederation of Bar. In 1772 he fled to Turkey when the First Partition of Poland occurred, and in late 1775 he was in Paris. Here it was suggested that he serve against the British in America. With a letter from Benj. Franklin to Washington and with funds advanced by Silas Deane, young Count Pulaski reached Boston in July '77 and served as volunteer A.D.C. to Washington at the Brandywine, 11 Sept. Meanwhile Pulaski had spoken to the C. in C. of his cavalry experience in Poland, and Washington decided he might be the man to command the four regiments of dragoons recently authorized in the army. Washington proposed this to Congress in a letter dated 27 Aug.; Congress created the post of "Commander of the Horse" on 15 Sept., appointed him B.G., and elected him to this position.

In the tradition of other foreign adventurers Pulaski had already created considerable prejudice against himself by demanding rank subordinate only to that of Washington and Lafayette. (Freeman, *Washington,* IV, 498) Speaking no English, unable to understand the Americans (*ibid.,* IV, 615), unwill-

ing to take orders from Washington but reporting direct to Congress (*ibid.,* V, 80; *D.A.B.*), he was in trouble almost from the start. After taking an insignificant part in the Battle of Germantown, 4 Oct. '77, he performed outpost duty at Trenton and Flemington while the army was in winter quarters at Valley Forge, and acted with Wayne on foraging expeditions. As evidence of his problems, however, he preferred court-martial charges against Stephen Moylan, one of his regimental commanders, for "disobedience to the orders of General Pulaski, a cowardly and ungentlemanly action in striking Mr. Zielinski, a gentleman and officer in the Polish service, when disarmed . . . and giving irritating language to General Pulaski." Moylan was acquitted, but became an even more ardent enemy than before. (Freeman, *op. cit.,* IV, 537 *n.*)

In Mar. '78 Pulaski resigned his post as chief of cavalry, and to add to his grievances, Moylan was temporarily elevated to fill it. Congress granted Pulaski's request to raise an independent body of mounted troops and approved his proposal to include prisoners and deserters if Washington had no objection. Although Washington had no intention of approving this last policy, Pulaski started recruiting prisoners anyway. On 17 Sept. the Pole appeared before Congress to complain that he was being given no opportunity for action. (The last major engagement in the North was at Monmouth, three months earlier, and the Revolutionary War was moving south.) Less than a fortnight later he got his chance, but it came in the form of a surprise attack by Ferguson on his poorly disciplined and carelessly deployed legion near LITTLE EGG HARBOR, 4–5 Oct. '78. When the Cherry Valley Massacre, N.Y., 11 Nov., brought cries for the protection of frontier settlements, his legion was posted on the Delaware River at one of the villages called MINISINK. From here he wrote Congress plaintively on 26 Nov. that he could find "nothing but bears to fight."

With the British capture of Savannah, Ga., 29 Dec. '78, and the desperate need for American cavalry in the South, on 2 Feb. '79 Pulaski was ordered to march into that theater. He arrived just in time to oppose an enemy advance into S.C. and was badly beaten in an action covered under CHARLESTON, 11–12 May. Now under Lincoln's command, he wrote Congress on 19 Aug. to complain of disappointments in a service "which ill treatment makes me begin to abhor," but expressing hopes that he might still have a chance to prove his devotion to the American cause. (D.A.B.) He did. Mortally wounded in a gallant but foolhardy cavalry charge at SAVANNAH, 9 Oct. '79, he died aboard the U.S. brig *Wasp*, probably on the 11th, after a surgeon had been unable to extract a grapeshot from his loin. It has never been established whether he was buried at sea, on St. Helena's (about 50 mi. from Savannah), or in Greenwich, Ga. (D.A.B.)

"His American career was tragic," comments Frank Monaghan in the D.A.B. article on which most of the present sketch is based, "for it was a chronicle of disaster and embittered disappointment. He was fortunate in his last days, for his gallant death served to ennoble even his mistakes in the eyes of posterity."

No adequate biography exists. The most satisfactory one, says Monaghan, is *Kuzimierz Pulaski w Ameryce* (Warsaw, 1930). This may well be so.

PUNISHMENTS in military forces of the 18th century were incredibly severe by modern standards; many left the soldier or sailor maimed for life if they did not kill him. "Keelhauling" consisted of lowering a man on one side of a ship and hauling him across to the other side, or, in the case of small vessels, of hauling him from bow to stern; aside from the fact that the victim risked drowning, he could be virtually flayed alive by barnacles. Flogging was the most common punishment, 1,000 lashes with the cat-o'-nine tails being not uncommon in the British Army or Navy and with 300 frequently being awarded for a mere misdemeanor. (Whitton, 75) Dan MORGAN was sentenced to receive 500 lashes for assaulting an officer. Americans derided the "BLOODY BACKS" until their own officers started awarding comparable punishment, and flogging was not abolished in the U.S. until 1861. Other punishments were "riding the wooden horse" and running the gauntlet, the former surviving through the Civil War and the latter dating from the earliest military organizations. "Minor punishments were clubbing, bottling, cobbing, booting, and—perhaps most terrible of all— 'Removal to the Navy.' " (*Ibid.*, 76)

Perhaps the most startling thing to the modern reader is the attitude of the men toward these punishments: instead of agitating for reforms, they rather enjoyed watching a fellow soldier or sailor suffer for his crime. "General Washington . . . is determined that discipline and subordination in camp shall be rigidly enforced and maintained," writes Dr. Thacher in his *Journal* for 1 Jan. '80. After describing how floggings were administered and how the gauntlet was run, he concludes with the observation that although "corporeal punishment may be made sufficiently severe as a commutation for the punishment of death in ordinary cases, *** it remains to be decided, which is the most eligible for the purpose of maintaining that subordination so indispensable in all armies." (*Op. cit.,* 187)

PURSUIT PROBLEMS inherent to 18th-century British tactics and organization are likely to be overlooked today as they were by critics of British generalship during the Revolution. Although the British had experimented with breaking away from the rigid tradition of linear tactics, they did not succeed until Napoleon forced the change on them in the 1800's.

"The cumbersomeness of the British tactics was made more serious in America by the rough and broken character of much of the countryside. Cornwallis and others testified to the importance of this factor. Under such conditions it was not easy to manage the regular formations required by orthodox tactics and effective pursuit was very difficult without radical departure from the usual discipline. Against an enemy adept in escape, and possessing an organization so loose that it could be broken and reformed a few days later without disastrous results, it was very hard to strike a decisive blow. Another factor that militated against effective pursuit was the dependence of the British army upon its baggage trains. For some curious reason British troops never developed much of a knack of living off the country. Where a French army would manage to support itself comfortably, the British would be in distress if anything delayed their supply trains. Both Generals Grey and Robertson testified to the influence of this dependence upon British operations in America." (Anderson, *Howe Bros.,* 21 and *n.*)

The *Morning Post,* newspaper of the British ministry, commented on 22 Oct. '80 that the only British victory in America that had been followed by a proper pursuit was CAMDEN, 16 Aug. '80. (Trevelyan, *Amer. Rev.,* V, 296)

PUTNAM, Israel. 1718–1790. Cont'l. general. Conn. "Old Put" was already an American hero when the Revolution started. The great-grandson of an English immigrant who had reached Salem (now Danvers), Mass., in 1634, he had moved from that place around 1740 and settled on a farm in the present townships of Pomfret and Brooklyn, Conn. One of the earliest legends associated with him is that in the winter of 1742–43 he killed a large wolf in her den, and if you don't believe it you can go to Pomfret and see the den. (*E.B.*) If he didn't really kill the wolf he probably could have because, although only about 5 feet 6 inches tall, he was powerfully built, square-jawed, and in the only surviving sketch done from life (by John Trumbull), bears a marked resemblance to Sir Winston Churchill. He had practically no education, and James Truslow Adams comments in *D.A.B.* that "his writing remained illiterate to a degree unusual even in his time." By 1755, however, he had become a prosperous farmer. He entered the French and Indian War as a 2d Lt. of Conn. volunteers (*D.A.B.*), became one of Robert Rogers' Rangers, was promoted to Maj., was captured in Aug. '58 and rescued just as the Indians were about to burn him at the stake, was exchanged and promoted to Lt. Col. in 1759, and the next year led his regiment in Amherst's march from Oswego to Montreal. He went on the ill-fated expedition to Havana in 1762 and was among the few survivors of a shipwreck off Cuba. Starting as a Maj. in Pontiac's War, he was promoted to Lt. Col. in May '64 and commanded five companies of Conn. troops in Bradstreet's march to Detroit. In 1772–74 he and Gen. Phineas Lyman went up the Mississippi as far as Natchez to look at land granted to Conn. veterans of the Havana expedition (Appleton's) and to see what possibilities existed for land speculation (Freeman, *Washington*, III, 473A).

Back in Conn. he became a prominent member of the Sons of Liberty and a second marriage in 1767 to a well-to-do widow helped him move into higher social strata. About this time he opened a tavern, "The General Wolfe," which widened his political horizons. (*E.B.*) "In every phase of the trouble with Britain after his return home, Putnam had a part," says Freeman, and his part was dramatic. When the port of Boston was closed and her people hungry, Putnam drove a herd of 125 sheep into the town (Aug. '74). When news of Lexington reached him as he was plowing on his farm at Pomfret, he is supposed to have left the plow in the furrow, unhitched one of the horses, left word for the militia to follow, and ridden 100 miles in 18 hours to Cambridge. In the council of war that preceded the battle of Bunker Hill he is alleged to have offered the sage advice that made that victory possible: "The Americans are not at all afraid of their heads, though very much afraid of their legs; if you cover these, they will fight forever." During the battle he is alleged to have given the order (also attributed, probably with more accuracy, to Col. Wm. Prescott): "Don't fire until you see the whites of their eyes." Later in the war, on 26 Feb. '79, he is alleged to have escaped capture by riding his horse in a headlong gallop down a flight of rocky steps near Stamford, Conn., where a granite monument was later erected to commemorate the feat. (*E.B.;* Ward, *W.O.R.*, 75) These stories are repeated here not as history but as part of the American legend and as an indication of Putnam's reputation. The Cincinnatus-like departure from Pomfret has been disproved (Tarbox, *Putnam*), the quotations are

apocryphal, the horsemanship attributed to him at the age of 61 is improbable, and few modern writers care to repeat the yarn about the wolf.

Returning from the legendary Putnam to the record, he was made Col. 3d Conn. on 1 May '75 and was a militia B.G. of Conn. troops the next month at BUNKER HILL. Freeman speaks of him as "a rock and a rallying-post" in that battle, and perhaps this is the most diplomatic way of putting it. (See BUNKER HILL, 17 June '76) Two days later he was appointed Maj. Gen. of the Cont'l. Army, and during the Boston Siege he commanded the American center. At the start of the N.Y. CAMPAIGN he was in over-all command for a short period before Washington arrived. On 24 Aug. he superseded Sullivan to command the forces defeated in the Battle of LONG ISLAND, 27 Aug. '76. During the remainder of the N.Y. Campaign and Washington's withdrawal to the Delaware, Putnam played no significant part. He was put in command of Philadelphia toward the end of the year, and when the British withdrew after Washington's victories at Trenton and Princeton, Putnam commanded the American wing posted in the latter place (Jan.–mid-May, '77).

By this time it was sadly apparent to Washington that the old hero lacked the qualities of a field commander. "In the eyes of young soldiers," says Freeman, "Putnam stood even lower, as the exemplar of an outdated type of warfare." (*Washington,* IV, 367–68) In May '77 he was made commander of the Hudson Highlands and in Oct. Forts Clinton and Montgomery were captured by the enemy and the town of Kingston burned. (CLINTON'S EXPEDITION to the Highlands) Freeman writes:

"A great name had lost its resonance...; the frail nag, reputation, no longer would carry an obese rider. On the 16th of March [1778], Alexander McDougall was named to relieve 'Old Put,' whose standing as a commander was alleged to have been destroyed by indolence, ignorance and patent incompetence. The veteran of Bunker Hill was given the task, more important than honorific, of hurrying forward the recruits from New England, an assignment that made him agitate for more active duty. Meantime he posted himself, so to say, on the list of the dissatisfied higher elements in the Army...." (*Op. cit.*, IV, 613)

This is perhaps too severe a condemnation of the old gentleman. As pointed out under CLINTON'S EXPEDITION in the section headed "American Dispositions," there were mitigating circumstances. A court of inquiry cleared Putnam of "any fault, misconduct or negligence" (quoted in *E.B.*). Fortunately for the Americans, the British abandoned the captured forts.

The winter of 1778–79 Putnam commanded the forces quartered around Redding, Conn. In May he was in command of troops on the west side of the Hudson until a paralytic stroke in Dec. '79 forced his retirement. Ward gives this over-all evaluation:

"He was courageous, enterprising, energetic, active, and persevering. As colonel of a fighting regiment, he would have been admirably placed; he would have led his men against the enemy, and they would have followed him with a cheer. Of the conduct and care of an army, of strategy in major operations, [etc., etc.] he knew nothing and should not have been expected to know anything. *Colonel* Israel Putnam he should have remained throughout the war." (*W.O.R.*, 76)

He was a cousin of Rufus PUTNAM and a granduncle of the founder of the G. P. Putnam's Sons publishing house.

Biographies are David Humphreys, *Life of . . . Israel Putnam* (1810, 1818, 1847),* John Fellows, *The Veil Removed; or, Reflections on David Humphreys' . . . Life of Israel Putnam* (1843); Increase N. Tarbox [*sic*], *Life of . . .* (1876), and W. F. Livingstone, *Israel Putnam* (1901).

See Beverley ROBINSON for the latter's attempt to win Putnam over to the British side in 1777.

PUTNAM, Rufus. 1738–1824. Cont'l. general and engineer. Mass. His father, a fourth-generation New Englander, died when Rufus was seven; after his mother remarried, the boy was reared by relatives. In 1754 he was apprenticed to a millwright. Three years later he enlisted in the militia. He lacked formal schooling but his efforts at self-education supplemented his practical training to make him useful in the construction of defensive works around Lake Champlain. Back in Braintree after the last Colonial War, he farmed, worked as a surveyor, and built mills. In 1773 he helped survey bounty lands along the Mississippi River.

When he became Lt. Col. of Brewer's Mass. Regt. on 19 May '75, Putnam had just passed his 37th birthday. A sturdy six-footer, he had "a peculiar oblique expression" caused by a childhood eye injury. (Beverley W. Bond, Jr. in *D.A.B.*) He naturally became involved in military engineering during the Boston siege and made the valuable suggestion that chandeliers be used to solve the problem of erecting fortifications on frozen ground. This technique contributed much to the rebel success on DORCHESTER HEIGHTS, Mar. '76. Meanwhile, he was commissioned Lt. Col. of the 22d Conn. on 1 Jan. '76, and after working on the defenses of

* These are the dates given by *D.A.B.*, Appleton's, and Ward.

N.Y.C. was promoted to Col. on 5 Apr. and named acting Chief Engineer. He resigned the latter appointment when Congress would not establish a corps of engineers and in Nov. assumed command of the 5th Mass. He served under Gates in halting Burgoyne's Offensive, but saw no important action. After this interlude of field duty, during which he commanded the 4th and 5th Regts. in Nixon's Brig. (Appleton's), he served under his cousin, Israel Putnam, in working on the defenses of West Point and its supporting posts. In Feb.–July '82 he was one of the claims commissioners in N.Y.C. On 7 Jan. '83 he was appointed B.G. and on 3 Nov. '83 he left the army.

Rufus Putnam had been prominent in presenting officer grievances to the state and federal authorities. He had some success in getting relief from the Mass. Gen. Assy., but Congress did not act on the Newburgh Petition of June '83, which he framed as chairman of a board of officers. This asked that some definite provision be made to give land bounties in the Ohio territory. Putnam then undertook to survey Maine lands for Mass. and to administer their sale.

As a legislator he was involved in putting down Shays's Rebellion in 1787. Today he is best remembered for his role in establishing a 1,500,000-acre colony on the north bank of the Ohio River. On 7 Apr. '88 he reached Adelphia (now Marietta, Ohio) as Supt. of the Ohio Co., which was composed largely of veterans who had contracted for this land. Washington appointed him a judge of the Northwest Territory in Mar. '90, and as a regular army B.G. (4 May '92) he took part in negotiating Indian treaties and in the operations of Anthony WAYNE. He became the first surveyor general of the U.S. and held this post from 1 Oct. '96 until 1803.

"As a soldier he was brave and resourceful," writes Bond, "but he was neither a great strategist nor an eminent military engineer." (*D.A.B.*) In the latter field as in his surveying in civil life he was limited by his lack of education, particularly in mathematics. (*Ibid.*) Rowena Buell edited *The Memoirs of Rufus Putnam* (1903), which includes much of his correspondence.

"PUTRID FEVER." Typhus.

Q

QUAKER GUN. See RUGELEY'S MILLS, 4 Dec. '80.

QUAKER HILL, R.I., 29 Aug. '78. Under NEWPORT, see section headed "Battle of Rhode Island."

QUARTER. As a noun the word means the promise not to kill an enemy soldier if he surrenders: a soldier may offer quarter to an enemy who appears to be losing the fight, or the latter may "cry quarter"—ask for quarter. After the battle of the WAXHAWS, N.C., 29 May '80, in which patriots were said to have been killed after demanding quarter, the expression "Tarleton's Quarter" arose to mean "no quarter." See MASSACRES. . . .

As a verb, "to quarter" means to put soldiers into "quarters" (billets, barracks, or other form of lodging). See next entry.

QUARTERING ACTS. 1765–74.
The Mutiny Act of 1765 was passed to
improve discipline of the British Army
throughout the world, and included a
provision for quartering troops in private houses. Alarmed by the latter
provision, Americans adopted the evasion of refusing to recognize any clause
of the act that did not refer specifically
to overseas British possessions. (Fortescue, *Brit. Army,* III, 30) A supplementary act, generally known as the
Quartering Act, was therefore passed—
at the specific request of Gen. GAGE
(Commager, *Doc.*, 61)—that required
colonial authorities to furnish barracks and supplies to British troops in
America. (Hence, it is not strictly correct to 'consider the Quartering and
Mutiny Acts as being the same thing.)
This Quartering Act was to take effect
24 Mar. '65 and to be in force two
years; it eliminated the provision for
billeting troops in private houses. Colonial assemblies not only were reluctant
to vote money for such a purpose but
they also realized that compliance with
this act would be evidence that they
acknowledged the right of Parliament
to tax them without their consent. They
therefore were careful not to meet fully
the requirements for supplies or else
they furnished them as a gift. "When
word of this new defiance got back to
England in the summer of 1766," writes
Morgan, "the Americans lost many of
the friends who had stood by them in
the Stamp Act crisis." (*Birth of the
Republic,* 33) In 1766 a second act
authorized the use of public houses
and unoccupied houses for billets. On
2 June '74 the act was applied to all
the colonies and extended to include
occupied dwellings.

See NEW YORK ASSEMBLY SUS-
PENDED, 1767–69.

QUARTERMASTERS of the Cont'l.
Army. See SUPPLY. . . .

QUEBEC. Site of an Indian village
(Stadacona) when first visited by Jacques
Cartier in 1535, it was founded (and
named) by Champlain in 1608. When
captured by the British in 1629 the
village had only two permanently settled
families, but there was "a shifting population of monks, officials, and fur
traders." (*E.B.*) Returned to France in
1632, the place was unsuccessfully
besieged by Sir Wm. Phips in 1690, and
a large British expedition under Sir
Hovenden Walker was shipwrecked in
the Gulf of St. Lawrence in 1711 as it
advanced on Quebec. Notre Dame des
Victoires, erected in 1688 and named
in 1711, commemorates these British
failures. The settlement became the
capital of Canada in 1763. Some 1,500
houses had been built in the Upper and
Lower Town by 1775. (The present
citadel was not started on top of 333-
foot Cape Diamond until 1823, but the
place was well fortified.) The British
under Gen. James Wolfe captured
Quebec in 1759. (See COLONIAL WARS)

The QUEBEC ACT and the military
actions of 1775–76 are covered below.

QUEBEC, 31 Dec. '75–1 Jan. '76.
(CANADA INVASION) Unsuccessful American assault by Montgomery and Arnold. Lacking siege artillery, faced with
expiring enlistments, and unable to
bluff the defenders into surrender, Gen.
Montgomery's only chance of capturing the fortified city of Quebec was by
assault. Further, this operation would
have to be undertaken at night and under cover of a snowstorm to permit getting close enough for the assault to have
some hope for success. The western
walls, facing the Plains of Abraham,
being too strong to attack, the final plan
called for feints in this area while Arnold and Montgomery converged on
the lower town from opposite sides. The
latter forces were to link up at Mountain Street, force Prescott Gate, and

push up into the upper town. British Gen. Guy Carleton had, unfortunately for the Americans, seen that the attack would probably be directed against the lower town, and he had organized his defenses accordingly. The Sault au Matelot, a narrow, winding street that Arnold's column would have to follow to reach the heart of the lower town from the north, was well defended. Astride the route Montgomery would have to follow to enter the lower town from the other direction, the defenders had erected a two-story block house from which they could deliver cannon and musket fire along the narrow avenue of approach at Cape Diamond.

On 29 and 30 Dec. '75, the weather was fair, but signs of bad weather became apparent on the 31st. The sky clouded over during the afternoon, the wind rose, and whiffs of fine snow appeared. Soon after dark a fierce snowstorm was in progress. The time had come. Troops were ordered to their billets by midnight and told to get ready. They assembled at 2 A.M., and two hours later were moving out. The feints fizzled out quickly without deceiving Carleton in the least; Col. James Livingston's small force of Canadians approached St. John's Gate but then broke and ran; 100 Massachusetts men under Capt. Jacob Brown (brother of the more famous John BROWN) delivered a sustained fire against the Cape Diamond bastion, but without any significant effect.

MONTGOMERY'S COLUMN

From his position on the Plains of Abraham, Montgomery led 300 men of the 1st N.Y. through the howling blizzard, down a mile of narrow, twisting, snow-choked trail to Wolfe's Cove. From this point they struggled another two miles along the river's edge with their cumbersome scaling ladders. Because of shoal ice, which the tides had pushed up from the river into their path, they were forced at several points to climb onto the slate slopes on the land side to get past. When they had gotten to Point Diamond, Montgomery halted his advance guard of about 50 men within 50 yards of a fortified position that the faint dawn revealed astride their path. When Montgomery and a small group of four officers and 13 men rushed forward, the defenders, who had craftily held their fire until the Americans were within a few paces, cut loose with a hail of cannon and musket fire. Montgomery was killed instantly with two of his officers, Capt. Macpherson, his A.D.C., and Capt. Cheeseman. Only Aaron Burr and Edw. Antil and one or two men escaped unhurt. The unheroic Col. Donald Campbell took command and led the New Yorkers to the rear. (According to some accounts, Montgomery's party was shot up when assaulting a fortified dwelling house, and after passing the blockhouse and another barrier unopposed [Ward, *W.O.R.,* 195, relying, apparently, on Dearborn's *Journal*]. According to another version, the British defense was made by a mixed group of 50 men with four small [3-pdr.] cannon from the blockhouse [Lossing, I, 198 *n.,* relying on the report of "Judge Henry," who visited the scene soon after the action; presumably Lossing is citing John J. Henry's *Accurate and Interesting Account of Arnold's Campaign Against Quebec . . . ,* Lancaster, Pa. 1812.])

ARNOLD'S COLUMN

With the vanguard of 25 men led by Arnold and Eleazer Oswald, the other attacking column moved parallel to the northern wall of Quebec and within 50 yards of its defenders, through the suburb of St. Roque, and toward the Sault au Matelot's northern end. Capt.

John Lamb followed with a 6-pdr. on a sled, and with 40 artillerymen. In single file came the rest of Arnold's command: Virginia riflemen under Capt. Dan Morgan, Pennsylvania riflemen under Lt. Archibald Steele (in the absence of Capt. Matthew Smith) and Capt. Wm. Hendricks. With the exception of Capt. Henry Dearborn's company, which was late assembling, the New Englanders with some 40 Canadians and Indians brought up the rear. Total strength was about 600.

Arnold's advance guard had passed a two-gun battery undetected and was beyond the Palace Gate when the enemy opened fire from the wall. The Americans sustained several casualties as they pushed on another few hundred yards and came up against the first barrier outside the lower town. Lamb's cannon was supposed to be used to batter this down, but it had overturned and subsequently had been abandoned during the march. Although the weather had rendered most of their muskets useless, the Americans assaulted. Arnold was taken out of action by a leg wound, but Morgan assumed command and carried the first barrier, cutting off and capturing about 50 of its defenders. In this action, Morgan had been blasted from the top of the first scaling ladder and knocked back into the snow with bullets through his cap, his beard, and his face pocked with grains of burned powder; he had roared back to his feet, up the ladder, and over the barrier at the head of his men. The advance guard charged into the Sault au Matelot to the next barrier, some 300 yards away. The British defenders were thrown into confusion, and Morgan was burdened down with more prisoners than he had men to guard them. Although the barrier was virtually undefended, Morgan's subordinates convinced him that it should not

be attacked immediately: they argued that the prisoners constituted too great a burden and a potential threat; with the majority of their troops still strung out to the rear, they lacked sufficient strength to carry the second barrier, and Montgomery might arrive at any moment. "To these arguments I sacrificed my own opinion and lost the town," Morgan wrote later. (S. & R., 126) Around dawn, when the Americans had gathered enough troops to assault the 12-foot walls of the second barrier, the enemy had organized its defense. In fierce fighting at close quarters, all attempts to escalade or envelop the barricade were repulsed. About the time the Americans had decided to retreat, they were attacked from the rear by a force of 200 men and two cannon that sallied forth from the Palace Gate. Dearborn's company, which had caught up with Morgan's column, was surprised just outside the gate and overwhelmed. Although some Americans escaped across two miles of treacherous ice on the St. Lawrence, the bulk of them were trapped and surrendered at about 9 A.M.

Of the 1,800 men under Carleton's command in Quebec, five were killed and 13 wounded in this action. The Americans had employed about 800; of these, 426 were captured and another 60 were killed or wounded. The loss of Montgomery was a particularly hard blow to the cause, since he was a general of exceptional promise.

CRITIQUE

Although this attack on Quebec verged on the foolhardy, one must admire the audacity that prompted the attempt and the courage that carried it as far as it went. For the student of warfare, the battle offers one more example of the danger of attempting a "concentration on the battlefield"—a strategy that looks good on the map but presents so many hazards that even Napoleon did not attempt it. On the other hand, it is difficult to see what other plan Montgomery could have used. The question, "What would Napoleon have done in this situation?" must be answered with the quip, "He would never have gotten into it." Even if the Americans had taken Quebec, they could not have held it against British naval superiority and the reinforcements that were on the way.

QUEBEC, 6 May '76. A sortie by Gen. Carleton routed Gen. Thomas' force of American besiegers. See CANADA INVASION.

QUEBEC ACT, 20 May '74. Although not one of the INTOLERABLE ACTS, it alarmed the colonies as much as did some of the latter. By extending Canada's boundaries to the Ohio River, it cut into territories claimed by Conn., Mass., and Va. It granted the French Canadians free use of their Catholic religion. This last feature, together with recognition by England of civil laws and land tenure in the former French possession, "has always been regarded [by Canadians] as their Magna Carta, and it kept them surprisingly loyal during America's Revolution and its subsequent wars with Great Britain." (Pollard, *Factors in Amer. Hist.,* 1) Van Tyne, on the other hand, writes: "Some have thought that the Quebec Act kept the mass of the Canadians loyal, but in some cases the effect of that most unfortunate of well-meant laws ... was alienation, especially when misrepresented and misunderstood." He goes on to say that although "the simple-minded Canadian peasants" appreciated their religious freedom and continuance of their old ways, they were not *loyal* to Britain so much as *neutral.* "Only the clergy, and the French *noblesse,* much favored by the English government, and en-couraged to hope for a renewal of their old privileges, were faithful to the British rule at this crisis [of 1775-76]." (*War of Independence,* 69-71) See also CANADA IN THE REVOLUTION, where two works on the Quebec Act are identified.

QUEEN ANNE'S WAR (1702-13). See COLONIAL WARS.

QUEEN'S RANGERS. This Tory regiment was organized in 1776 by the dissipated and ineffective former hero of the Colonial Wars, Maj. Robert ROGERS. Presumably it is the same unit that was commanded by Capt. James WEMYSS at the BRANDYWINE, 11 Sept. '77. A little over a month later the exceptionally capable John Graves SIM-COE was named commander, and its subsequent history is outlined in the sketch of that British officer.

QUEEN'S ROYAL RANGERS. Proposed Provincial regiment that was to be formed by Dr. John CONNOLLY.

QUINBY BRIDGE, S.C., 17 July '81. While Greene's army was resting in the Santee Hills, Thos. Sumter got authority to employ the forces of Henry Lee and Marion with his own to attack the outpost at Monck's Corner. The latter position was commanded by Lt. Col. John Coates, who had his unseasoned 19th Reg. and some mounted S.C. rangers. (Balfour's report in Clinton, *Amer. Reb.,* 551) When Sumter attempted a turning movement Coates withdrew on 14 July (*ibid.*) to a virtually unassailable position around Biggin Church. But about 3 o'clock the morning of the 17th he set fire to the church and withdrew another 18 miles down the Cooper River toward Charleston to Quinby Bridge, and that afternoon he held a strong position along the creek. To frustrate the cavalry pursuit he had loosened the flooring of the bridge, but was waiting for his rear guard and baggage to cross before removing the planks. Unknown to Coates, Lee had gobbled up his rear guard and Capt. Armstrong charged across the bridge, closely followed by the second section of cavalry under Lt. Carrington, to surprise the British and drive off all but their commander and a few men who stood by him. Capt. O'Neal's third section was stopped at the bridge because the preceding ones in their passage had dislodged the planks and created an impassable gap and the creek was unfordable because of its muddy banks. The British infantry rallied to their hard-pressed commander, Armstrong and Carrington were forced to withdraw, and the advance guard action had to be broken off. (Lee, *Memoirs,* 390–91)

Marion arrived to reconnoiter with Lee and they decided the enemy position was now too strong to attack, but when Sumter and his infantry came on the scene about 5 P.M. the Gamecock overruled them. The British had formed a hollow square with a howitzer covering their front and their flanks protected by outbuildings and rail fences of Capt. Thos. Shubrick's plantation. Sumter formed Marion's infantry on the left, Col. Thos. Taylor's veteran militia regiment and his own troops in the center, and Col. Horry's cavalry (of Marion's Brig.) on the right flank. Taylor charged across an open field, took position along a fence, but was counterattacked and driven back. Marion's infantry diagonaled over to reoccupy the fence line but had to withdraw after sustaining 50 casualties and almost exhausting their ammunition supply. Sumter's men, meanwhile, had been firing from the protection of buildings, and he had failed to bring forward his artillery. Furious at this useless sacrifice and Sumter's failure to support the attack properly, Taylor walked up to the Gamecock and informed him he would

no longer serve under him. Marion and Lee, disgusted by Sumter's mismanagement of the approach march (Lee, *op. cit.,* 392) and by the abortive attack (in which Lee had not participated), retreated 15 miles with their dead and wounded. The next morning they both left Sumter. (Bass, *Swamp Fox,* 205–9) Meanwhile, British reinforcements numbering about 700 men were on the way to join Coates, and Sumter's position was no longer tenable. (Clinton, *op. cit.,* 551)

QUINTON'S BRIDGE, N.J., 18 Mar. '78. Col. Chas Mawhood crossed the Del. R. on 12 Mar. with a mixed force of British regulars and Simcoe's Rangers to forage and to counteract the foraging activities of Anthony Wayne. At Salem the British were joined by Tories who told them that Col. Asher Holmes was about three miles S.E. with 300 militia. Holmes had taken a position to cover Quinton's Br. on Alloway Cr. while his foragers operated in the area. Before dawn on the 18th, Mawhood concealed several detachments on the side of the creek opposite the rebels: 70 men of the 17th Regt. and three separate bodies of Simcoe's Rangers were posted in a brick house (Wetherby's tavern), behind a fence to its rear, and in a wood. The Americans knew of the enemy's presence in the vicinity and had removed planks from the bridge as an additional security precaution. But they were completely taken in by Mawhood's stratagem: when the detachment of the 17th Regt. was seen moving to the rear from the tavern a Capt. Smith had the planks replaced on the bridge and crossed in pursuit. Leaving 100 men on high ground by the creek, but without reconnoitering the tavern or surrounding area, Smith led 200 troops down the road until they made contact with the enemy force posted behind the fence. Capt. Saunders then emerged from the house to their rear, cutting off retreat to the bridge, and drove the rebels in confusion toward another crossing of the creek. They were pursued by Saunders, who was soon joined by 30 mounted Rangers and later by Mawhood's entire command. Col. (Elijah ?) Hand arrived with his Cumberland militia and two guns in time to occupy the original position abandoned by the Americans and stop the enemy from crossing the bridge and completely annihilating Holmes's command. The rebels lost 30 to 40 men, most of whom were drowned, and the cry of MASSACRE was raised. The enemy had one man mortally wounded. Irritated at his failure to score a complete success here, Mawhood tried again at HANCOCK'S BRIDGE, 21 Mar. (The preceding account is from Ward, *W.O.R.*, 547, and Lossing, II, 344.)

R

RAID. In the strict strategic or tactical sense, a raid differs from other offensive operations in that the attacker does not intend to *hold* the objective once he has taken it. Raids can be on a small (tactical) scale, to capture prisoners, knock out gun positions, or disrupt an enemy attack before it starts ("spoiling attack"). Examples are the operations against GREAT BREWSTER ISLAND, Mass., during the Boston Siege, and Abercromby's sortie during the Yorktown siege (under YORKTOWN CAMPAIGN see section with his heading). Strategic raids were those to LEXINGTON AND CONCORD, BENNINGTON, and PAULUS HOOK. The attack on STONY POINT, 16 July '79, was not planned as a raid, but Washington subsequently decided that the captured position could not be held, so it turned out to be a raid after all.

RAKE. To fire down the length of a vessel's deck. This is the sailor's equivalent of the soldier's ENFILADE.

RALL, Johann Gottlieb. *c.* 1720–1776. Hessian Col. at Trenton. Born in Hesse-Cassel, he was a veteran of the Seven Years' War and was proud of having subsequently fought the Turks in the army of Russian Gen. Alexis Orloff. He was an elderly 55 or so years old when he came to America, but he led his regiment with vigor and distinction at WHITE PLAINS and FT. WASHINGTON. Ignorant of English, looking with military contempt on the raw American soldiers and their unimpressive officers, the arrogant German soldier was not considered by Howe to be qualified to command the large, isolated outpost at Trenton, but Rall had done such outstanding work so far that he could not be denied this critical and dangerous command. He was mortally wounded in Washington's attack on TRENTON, 26 Dec. '76, and died the next day. An English officer characterized him as "noisy, but not sullen, unacquainted with the language, and a drunkard." (Bill, *Princeton,* 41)

RAMSAY, David. 1749–1815. Historian, physician, politician. Pa.–S.C. Born in Lancaster co., Pa., he graduated from Princeton in 1765, studied medicine, got his degree from the Coll. of Pa. in 1772, practiced for a year in Md., and then went to Charleston. Although successful as a doctor from the start—Dr. Benj. Rush gave him a letter stating he was "far superior to any person we ever graduated at our college"—he soon became absorbed in local politics and represented Charleston in the legislature from 1776 to the end of the war. In Aug. '80 he was exiled with 32 other eminent Charlestonians to St. Augustine and kept there a year. Although returned to the legislature of S.C., he was a delegate to the Cont'l. Cong. in 1782–83 and 1785–86. While John HANCOCK dallied over the acceptance of office as Pres. of Cong. the delegates in N.Y.C. created the post, "Chairman of Cong.," and elected Ramsay to fill it. He held this title until Nathaniel Gorham was elected Pres. of Cong. on 6 June '86. As a delegate he supported moves to strengthen the central government. From 1784 to 1790 he was again in the S.C. House of Representatives. In 1792, 1794, and 1796 he was in the state Senate, and each time was president of that body. A moderate Federalist and representative of the tidewater class, he opposed issue of paper money, easing of obligations of debtors, and importation of slaves. Although able, honest, and influential in public affairs, he was inept in matters of personal finance and by 1798 had bankrupted himself by unwise and disorderly speculation and investment. As a doctor he subscribed to the unfortunate "system" of his friend RUSH, but nevertheless he made important contributions to medical knowledge.

Despite his distinction in these fields, Ramsay is best remembered as a historian. With a facile pen and a copious memory, he turned out a number of works. His *Hist. of the Rev. of S.C.* (2 vols., 1785) and *Hist of the Amer. Rev.* (2 vols., 1789) contain much original material but were largely plagiarized from the British *Annual Register,* whose principal author on American affairs was Edmund BURKE. However, the second volume of his *Hist. of S.C.* (2 vols., 1809) is still of value to historians (R. L. Meriwether in *D.A.B.*). His *Life of George Washington* (1807) achieved great popularity. *Universal History Americanized,* an ambitious work in nine volumes, appeared posthumously (1816–17, 1819). He died 8 May 1815, two days after being shot by a maniac (*D.A.B.*), against whose sanity he had testified (Appleton's).

Ramsay's second wife was Frances, daughter of John Witherspoon, a Signer. Each of his first two wives lived only a year after marriage. In 1787 he married Martha, daughter of Henry Laurens; she died in 1811, and the next year he published *Memoirs of the Life of Martha Laurens Ramsay.*

Brother of Nathaniel RAMSAY.

RAMSAY, Nathaniel. 1741–1817. Cont'l. officer, politician. Md. Elder brother of David RAMSAY and son of an immigrant from the north of Ireland to Lancaster co., Pa., he graduated from Princeton in 1767 (two years later than the brother who was eight years his junior), studied law, and settled in Cecil co., Md., to practice and acquire an estate. In 1775 he was a delegate to the Md. Conv. and to the Cont'l. Cong. On 14 Jan. '76 he was chosen Capt. in Smallwood's Md. Regt. The next July that unit became part of the Cont'l. Army, and on 10 Dec. '76 he was commissioned its Lt. Col. when the regiment was redesignated the 3d Md. (Heitman, 30) "Smallwood's Regt." had distinguished itself at Long Island in Aug. '76. Ramsay is particularly famous for his role in checking the retreat of the American army at Monmouth, 28 June '78, where he was wounded, left for dead, and captured. On parole until his exchange on 14

Dec. '80 (Heitman, 457), he retired from the army on 1 Jan. '81. He is credited with giving Washington time to rally his army at Monmouth and is commemorated on the monument erected on the battlefield.

Returning to Cong. for the period 1785–87, where his brother David also was serving, he became U.S. Marshal for the district of Md. in 1790. Four years later he became naval officer of the Baltimore district, a position he held until his death 13 years later. In 1771 he married Margaret Jane, sister of Charles Willson Peale. She died in 1788 and four years later he married Charlotte Hall, whose son and two daughters survived him. His portrait is in Independence Hall, Philadelphia.

Although Appleton's and *D.A.B.* make no mention of the fact, Montross points out that Nathaniel spelled his name *Ramsey*. (*Reluctant Rebels*, 383) Heitman gives his name as Ramsay in his section of field officers of the Cont'l. Line (p. 30) and as Ramsey in his alphabetical list of officers (p. 457).

RAMSEUR'S (also **RAMSAUER'S** and **RAMSOUR'S**) **MILL, N.C.,** 20 June '80. The surrender of Charleston, 12 May '80, and the establishment of British posts at Camden, Cheraw, and Ninety-Six made it apparent that the Revolutionary War was about to move into N.C. During the four preceding years there had been only one military engagement in the state, the Battle of MOORES CREEK BRIDGE, 27 Feb. '76, and this humiliating Tory defeat had left the patriots more or less in control of the state. But in the summer of '80 the N.C. Loyalists believed the time had come to rise up and even some scores. Although Cornwallis expressed the desire that the North State Loyalists delay their military activities until the wheat crop was harvested, thereby avoiding another premature uprising

and also assuring provisions for his invading army, the Tories could not wait. Col. John Moore, returning to Ramseur's Mill in June after serving under Cornwallis in S.C., called a meeting of the Tories on 10 June at his father's house. Before the 40 men left this meeting, at which Moore revealed Cornwallis' plan for pushing north into the state, they learned that Maj. McDowell was approaching with a company of rebel militia. The Tories made an unsuccessful attempt to surprise and defeat McDowell. Moore then issued instructions for Loyalists to assemble at Ramseur's Mill on the 13th. By the 20th he had 1,300 men, although a fourth were unarmed.

The patriots, meanwhile, had responded to Gen. Rutherford's call for militia. While 800 gathered near Charlotte, Col. Francis Locke assembled another 400 at Mountain Creek, near Moore's camp, and on 19 June moved out to surprise the Tories. His column was led by three small groups of mounted men; the rest of his force followed in a double file—"an unorganized crowd of inexperienced, undisciplined, armed civilians." (Ward, *W.O.R.*, 707)

Moore's men were camped on a hill about 300 yards from the mill and half a mile north of the present village of Lincolnton. (DeMond, *Loyalists in N.C.*, 126) At the approach of the rebel horsemen a 12-man outpost fired and fled 600 yards to the Tory camp, which they threw into confusion. When the horsemen pursued up the hill they were driven back. The unarmed Tories fled, but the others formed at the base of the hill and withdrew over the top and reformed on the reverse slope only after Locke's men started forward in a sort of battle line. The defenders fired from their reverse slope position, advanced, and then withdrew when rebels worked around each flank. The attackers then got behind the enemy position and a hot encounter took place at close quarters. Neither side had bayonets; lack of uniforms or insignia made it difficult to tell friend from foe and many a skull was cracked by a "friendly" musket butt. "Neighbor fought against neighbor, kindred against kindred," points out DeMond. "Old personal and political enemies sometimes met, and then the fighting was doubly ferocious." (*Ibid.*) Tory Capt. Warlick rallied his men time and again to counterattack, but Wm. Shays, seeing this, worked his way stealthily forward until he was in position to drop Warlick with a bullet. The Tory resistance then collapsed, but they rallied behind a creek at the base of the hill. (*Ibid.;* Ward, *op. cit.*, 707)

Locke could re-form only 110 of his original 400 on the hill for the expected counterattack, and he sent an urgent message to Rutherford to hurry forward with the column from Charlotte. But the Tories had had enough. Moore joined Cornwallis at Camden with only 30 men.

Not more than 250 of Locke's 400 were actually engaged, but over 150 were killed and wounded; Tory losses were about the same, and they had approximately 700 engaged. (Ward, *op. cit.*, 708) DeMond says more than 20 officers and men were killed on each side. (This authority calls the place Ramsauer's Mill.)

COMMENT

Moore's abortive action was a disaster for the British cause, and Cornwallis threatened to court-martial him for violating instructions. DeMond points out that if Moore had waited for Patrick Ferguson's approach (see KINGS MOUNTAIN) there might have been 2,000 Tory militia to support Ferguson; but when Cornwallis finally did get into N.C. the Loyalists were afraid to support him and the British lost more by desertion than they gained in recruits. (*Ibid.*, 126–27)

RANDOLPH, Edmund (Jenings). 1753–1813. Statesman, U.S. Atty. Gen. and Sec. of State. Va. In the tradition of the RANDOLPH FAMILY, he attended William and Mary, and studied law. When the war started he was practicing in Williamsburg, but when Washington was elected C. in C. young Edmund went to Cambridge with letters of recommendation from prominent Virginians and on 15 Aug. '75, five days after his 22d birthday, was named A.D.C. His father, meanwhile, had left Va. with Lord Dunmore and Edmund had been taken into the family of his uncle, Peyton RANDOLPH. On the latter's sudden death, 22 Oct. '75, Edmund returned to Williamsburg. The next year he sat in the Va. Conv. that adopted the constitution and he became the state's first Atty. Gen. Retaining this office, he went to the Cont'l. Cong. in 1779, but soon resigned. On 7 Nov. '86 he defeated Richard Henry Lee and Theodoric Bland to become Gov., but he resigned in 1788 to enter the state legislature and take part in revising the Va. legal code. Meanwhile he had attended the Annapolis Conv. and the Federal Conv. in 1787. He joined George Mason in refusing to sign the completed Constitution, believing that it was not sufficiently republican, but when time came for Va. to ratify the document he changed his position.

Edmund was 1st Atty. Gen. of the U.S. (1789), and Jefferson's successor as Sec. of State (1794–95). After serving creditably through the storms of "Citizen" Genet's and Gouverneur Morris' recalls, and the negotiations that led to Jay's Treaty, Randolph resigned on 19 Aug. '95. He had been charged by French Minister Fauchet, Genet's successor, with improper conduct in negotiating the treaty; the charges, contained in a letter from Fauchet to his government that had been intercepted and revealed by the British, were subsequently found to be false. Returning to law practice, he became prominent as senior defense counsel in the treason trial of Aaron Burr. During the last years of his life he was paralyzed, and he died a little more than a month after his 60th birthday. His grandson, Edmund Randolph (1819–1861), was a famous and fiery lawyer in Calif. whose activities included advising William Walker on the organization of the Nicaraguan government (winter of 1855–56).

RANDOLPH, Peyton. c. 1721–1775. Crown official, 1st Pres. of Cont'l. Cong. Va. Son of Sir John of "Tazewell" (see RANDOLPH FAMILY) and a brother-in-law of Benj. Harrison, he has been characterized as "the most popular leader in Virginia in the decade before the Revolution." (*D.A.B.*) He went from William and Mary to the Middle Temple in 1739 and was admitted to the bar in 1744. Establishing his practice in Williamsburg, he was appointed King's Attorney in 1748 and the same year entered the House of Burgesses. In 1755 he organized a company of 100 lawyers and other gentlemen who, at their own expense, moved out to support the survivors of Braddock's defeat. Peyton Randolph represented the old, conservative element of Va. that the fiery young Patrick Henry had to challenge for leadership. Although Randolph deplored the trend that developed and retained a cautious, conservative view, he nevertheless retained authority in the patriot party. "He was made the presiding officer of every important revolutionary assemblage in Virginia." (*D.A.B.*) He topped the list of delegates to the 1st Cont.'l.

Cong. and became the first president of that body (5 Sept.–21 Oct. '74). "Our President seems designed by nature for the business," wrote Silas Deane of this honorary office. "Of an affable, open and majestic deportment—large in size, though not out of proportion, he commands respect and esteem by his very aspect, independent of the high character he sustains." (Quoted in Montross, *Reluctant Rebels*, 36–37) In bad health, Randolph was succeeded by Henry Middleton on 22 Oct. '74, but was reelected on 10 May '75. Two weeks later he had to give up this office, and five months later he died suddenly of apoplexy. He was only 54. There being no children, Peyton Randolph's large estate was left to his wife and passed on her death to his nephew and ward, Edmund RANDOLPH.

RANDOLPH FAMILY OF VIRGINIA. The first William Randolph (*c.* 1651–1711), an English gentleman, came to Va. from Warwickshire around 1673 and in 1684 bought lands on the south bank of the James River that had been known from earliest colonial times as "Turkey Island." By 1705 he owned 10,000 acres in Henrico co. alone, and he willed a plantation to each of his seven sons (see chart). Meanwhile he had held a number of official appointments, including that of King's Attorney (an office subsequently held by his son John and the latter's two sons) and in 1699 he had been appointed Lt. Col. of militia. Sometime prior to 1681 he married into the Isham family of "Bermuda Hundred," and the descendants of Col. William and Mary Isham Randolph included not only those who retained the family name but also Thos. Jefferson, John Marshall, "Light-Horse Harry" Lee, and the latter's son, Robert E. Lee. "Perhaps no other couple in American history is so remarkable for the number of distinguished descendants," writes the biographer of John Marshall. (Beveridge, *Marshall,* I, 10) Col. Randolph was among the founders and trustees of the College of William and Mary (founded 1693, the second oldest college in America [after Harvard, 1636], and named not for the Randolphs but for the king and queen who ascended the English throne in 1689). Six of the seven sons of Willam and Mary Randolph attended the college, as did their descendants Jefferson and Marshall.

NOTE. Only two Randolphs, Peyton and his nephew Edmund Jenings, are of sufficient interest to warrant separate biographical sketches in this book. Notice, however, that Thomas JEFFERSON and John MARSHALL are Randolph descendants. Robert E. Lee was another, although I have not attempted to show the connection. (See E. J. Lee, *Lee of Va.,* 82, 89)

RANK AND FILE. In both the American and British armies the term meant enlisted men present in the line of battle with weapons in their hands, including corporals and privates but not sergeants and drummers. Nickerson points out that if the effective rank and file strength of a British unit is known, 17.5 per cent should be added to get the total effective combatant strength; American overhead being higher even in those days, 28 per cent must be added to get the corresponding figure. Conversely, from a known total strength of infantry effectives, to get the number of rank and file one should subtract 14.8 per cent from the British figures and 21.8 per cent from the American. (*Turning Point,* 436)

RANKIN, William (alias Mr. Alexander). Tory leader. Pa. Until he learned that the objectives of Congress included independence, this influential landowner and officeholder in York, Pa., had been a Whig. Then, "With the approbation and at the request of the friends of government," he wrote later, "he continued in the command of his regiment of militia, because he might thereby not only have an opportunity of favouring the loyalists but also of rendering essential services to the government." (Van Doren, *Secret History,* 134, quoting "Loyalist Transcripts.") When ordered in 1776 to capture certain Loyalists of York co. and destroy their estates he contrived to assist them while giving the appearance of obeying his instructions. (*Ibid.*) In 1778 he started organizing the Loyalists of Lancaster, York, and eventually of adjacent regions of Md. and Del. until he claimed that 6,000 would answer his call for an uprising. He got in contact with Gen. Clinton, dealing with John André through Christopher SOWER. When Sullivan's Expedition of 1779 against the Iroquois was being planned, Rankin and other Tory leaders tried unsuccessfully to have one of their supporters put in command of the Pa. militia that was to accompany the regulars. "If this can be obtained, of which they have the fairest prospects," Sower informed Clinton, "Colonel [John] BUTLER will have little to fear." (*Ibid.,* 131) Sower also told Clinton that if he would direct that Butler make a raid on Carlisle, where the principal rebel supply depot was located, Rankin and his supporters could not only assist in this operation but could also arm themselves for future action. After André's death Rankin and his associates in Pa., Del., and Md. sent an address to the King through Simcoe, who had been André's friend and in whom they apparently had more confidence than Clinton, proposing that Simcoe lead an operation into the Chesapeake Bay area to rally the local Loyalists. Simcoe forwarded this com-

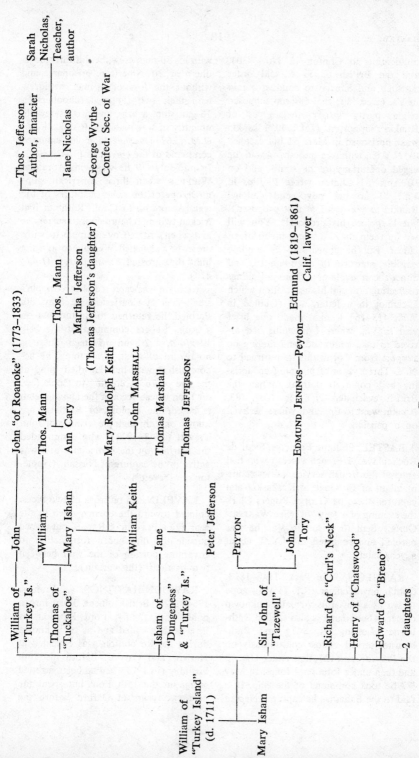

RANDOLPH FAMILY OF VIRGINIA

munication to Clinton (2 Nov. '80), and the British C. in C. did order ARNOLD and Simcoe to conduct a raid in Va. (Dec. '80) that Clinton supposed might partly satisfy the hopes of Rankin's supporters. (*Ibid.*, 405) Rankin was imprisoned in Mar. '81 but escaped to N.Y.C. within a month. Again he urged operations to the south, and on 30 Apr. '81 Clinton wrote Phillips in Va.: "I do not now send Colonel Rankin to you (as I at first proposed), but I enclose his proposals. You will see by them that he is not much of an officer. But he appears to be a plain sensible man worth attending to, and Simcoe can explain a thousand things respecting him and his association which I cannot in a letter...." (Quoted in *ibid.*, 415–16) Rankin made one brief visit to Va., where Cornwallis had arrived to take command, and finding no support from Cornwallis he returned to N.Y. Three years of planning an uprising had come to nothing. When the British evacuated N.Y. in Nov. '83, Rankin went to England, where he lived on a pension.

RASTEL, Philippe François, Sieur de Rocheblave. A French veteran who had entered the British service, he was commandant of Ft. Gage at Kaskaskia and captured there by George Rogers Clark the evening of 4 July '78. (See WESTERN OPNS.) Sent to prison in Va., he was paroled and returned to N.Y.C. about a year later.

RATHBUN, John Peck. 1746–1823. Cont'l. naval officer. R.I. Having gone to sea as a boy, this virtually unknown officer, whose name is also spelled Rathburne (Lossing, II, 847) and Rathbourne, served almost continuously on the *Providence* (12), first under Hazard and then under John Paul Jones. In May '77 he took command of the ship. In a raid to the Bahamas he captured Nassau

with his 50-man crew, held it three days, liberated 30 American prisoners, and without the loss of a man withdrew with their two captured schooners, a 16-gun ship, a brig, and a considerable quantity of war matériel. (Cook, *W.M.-O.M.*, 267) A year later he assumed command of the *Queen of France* (28). In mid-July '79 he was with Abraham WHIPPLE when three American ships made one of the richest captures of the war. According to Cook, Rathbun had tricked two merchantmen into surrender and when ordered by Whipple to withdraw, he persuaded Whipple to join the hunt that grossed 11 fat prizes. (*Ibid.*, 270)

Rathbun was captured with Whipple's small fleet at Charleston, 12 May '80. Paroled, he returned to Boston and on 4 Aug. '81 got command of the brig *Wexford*, a 20-gun privateer. There is no record of what, if anything, he accomplished with her. He died blind at the age of 76. According to Cook (*op. cit.*), on whose account the above sketch is based, the exploits of Rathbun are known only through the writings of John Trevett (1747–1823), who commanded the marines on the *Providence* and was active in the capture of Nassau. (Appleton's, "Trevett")

RAVELIN. An outwork of two faces, pointed toward the enemy, open to the rear like a FLÈCHE or REDAN, but placed outside the ditch of a fortification to cover the portion of the wall between two bastions (the curtain).

RAWDON-HASTINGS, Francis. **1754–1826.** British officer. Born into a noble Irish family, Lord Rawdon, as he was then called and as he is known during the Revolution, was educated at Harrow and Oxford. Before his 16th birthday (in 1771) he had been gazetted ensign in the 15th Foot but spent the next two years at Oxford before the outbreak of hostilities prematurely ended his schooling. In July '74 he went to America with the 5th Foot and distinguished himself in his baptism of fire at Bunker Hill, where he took command of the company after his captain was hit and led it forward with conspicuous gallantry. As A.D.C. to Clinton and later on the staff of Cornwallis he took part in the N.Y., N.J., and Philadelphia Campaigns, being mentioned in connection with the battles of Long Island, White Plains, and Ft. Washington.

The youthful Rawdon was tall, dark, strong, vigorous, and had a fine bearing, but he had "a curious reputation as the 'ugliest man in England.'" (Peckham, *War for Indep.*, 136) In America he acquired a certain reputation for ruthlessness in his last act before leaving the country (July '80) of ordering the execution of Col. Isaac HAYNE. Early in his American career he included this oft-quoted paragraph in a letter from Staten Island in Aug. '76:

"The fair nymphs of this isle are in wonderful tribulation, as the fresh meat our men have got here has made them as riotous as satyrs. A girl cannot step into the bushes to pluck a rose without running the most imminent risk of being ravished, and they are so little accustomed to these vigorous methods that they don't bear them with the proper resignation, and of consequence we have most entertaining courts-martial every day." (Quoted in C. & M., 424)

This, it should be pointed out, is more a comment on Anglo-Saxon morality (and humor) of the time than on the personal code of the young Irish lord. In June '78 he was promoted to Lt. Col. and A.G. About this time Clinton selected Rawdon to raise a provincial regiment called the VOLUNTEERS OF IRELAND. After taking part in the Battle of Monmouth, 28 June '78, Rawdon remained in the North until the spring of

1780, when he was ordered to join Clinton for the final phase of the CHARLESTON EXPEDITION. He reached S.C. three weeks before the surrender with a body of reinforcements, including his Vols. of Ireland. Prior to this time, on 3 Sept. '79, he had resigned his post as A.G., informing Clinton he had "no longer the honour of being upon those terms of mutual confidence in a station whose duties are most irksome to me." (Quoted by Van Doren, *Secret History*, 233. John André succeeded Rawdon as A.G. on 23 Oct.)

Clinton did not like Rawdon (*ibid.*) and the latter found himself under the command of Cornwallis in the offensive into S.C. In the CAMDEN CAMPAIGN Rawdon distinguished himself, and his calm leadership in a position of great danger did much to make possible Cornwallis' destruction of the American army under Gates. Rawdon took part in the subsequent advance to Charlotte, N.C., and the withdrawal to Winnsboro, S.C., after the British disaster at Kings Mountain, 7 Oct. '80. When Cornwallis resumed his plans for an offensive into N.C., after Tarleton's defeat at the Cowpens, 17 Jan. '81, Rawdon was left behind to hold S.C. and Ga. with 8,000 troops. After the Pyrrhic victory of Cornwallis at Guilford, then the subsequent withdrawal to Wilmington, Cornwallis marched north to Va. and left Rawdon to defend the scattered British posts.

As Greene marched against him at Camden the 26-year-old British commander showed outstanding generalship. The subsequent operations are covered under the SOUTHERN CAMPAIGNS OF GREENE, but can be quickly summarized here. Instead of remaining on the defensive, Rawdon scraped together every able-bodied man and attacked Greene at HOBKIRK'S HILL, 25 Apr. '81, where his audacity and skill, and the good performance of his own Vols. of Ireland, were rewarded by victory. Furthermore he had the good strategic sense and the moral courage to order the evacuation of the most exposed posts. Unfortunately, his orders were not all received in time, and as posts fell he realized that Camden was untenable. By 24 May he had withdrawn from there to Monck's Corner, and a few days later he marched with reinforcements from England to reinforce the only post that had not been captured. Eluding the rebel cavalry screen that Greene had ordered to intercept him, Rawdon relieved the siege of NINETY-SIX, pursued Greene a short distance despite the killing heat, ordered the evacuation of Ninety-Six, and withdrew to hold the area between the Santee and Edisto rivers while Greene rested his army in the Santee Hills. Summer weather and a shortage of rations prohibited further operations.

Incapacitated by fatigue and failing health, Rawdon turned over command to Col. Paston Gould and on 20 July '81 sailed for England. He was captured by a French privateer and held a prisoner at Brest until exchanged the next year, after hostilities had ended in America. For his war service he was promoted to Col. and appointed A.D.C. to the King. A young and inexperienced officer, only 27 when he left S.C., he had "stood up to and worsted in battle the able Greene, the most competent of all American leaders after Washington, and caused him to pay so dearly in time and casualties for his ultimate strategic success in the South," comments Maj. E. W. Sheppard of the British Army. (*The Army Quarterly*, Apr. 1962, 73) Commenting on the outstanding British officers of the war, Fortescue writes that "the ablest of all was Lord Rawdon, who received his baptism of fire at twenty-one ... and at twenty-six contrived with great skill to save the position abandoned by Cornwallis." (*British Army*, III, 404)

It is worth noting that Rawdon was not the senior British officer in the Carolinas during this campaign against Greene. As he himself explains it in his letter to Henry about the Isaac HAYNE affair:

"When Lord Cornwallis suddenly marched into South Carolina, he wrote to me ... to assign to me the very unexpected charge of maintaining that post [of Camden], and the frontier beyond the rivers. In the same letter he entreated me, as a proof of friendship to himself, that I would act cordially with Lieutenant-Colonel Balfour, between whom and me his lordship knew there had been some estrangement. [Rawdon then goes on to say how he got involved in the case of HAYNE.] * * * You mistake entirely in supposing [along with subsequent historians] that the province of South Carolina was under my command. Lieutenant-Colonel Balfour was my senior in the army list; and my provincial rank of Colonel, held for the purpose of connection with the regiment raised by me, did not alter that relation, as the colonels on the provincial establishment were subordinate to the youngest lieutenant-colonels of the line. Sir Henry Clinton, in order to give me the management of affairs in South Carolina, subsequently promoted me, as a brigadier of provincials; but we had no intimation of this till the commission arrived, after I had actually embarked for England [20 July '81]. ..." (Lee, *Memoirs*, 615, 616)

He was elevated to the English peerage as Baron Rawdon in Mar. '83. In 1789 his mother succeeded to the barony of Hastings, and Rawdon added the surname of Hastings to his own. (*E.B.*, "Hastings, Francis Rawdon-Hastings.") In 1793 he succeeded his father as Earl

of Moira, and in Oct. of this year he was
a Maj. Gen. in the war against Napoleon. He was moving with 10,000 men
to support the Vendée insurgents when
the French victory at Fleurus caused
this plan to be canceled and his force
was diverted to Belgium. Landing at
Ostend, he was faced with the problem
of getting past the French army at
Bruges to join the allies at Amsterdam.
He deceived the French as to his strength
by ordering rations for 25,000 men and
managed by a remarkable march to
reach Amsterdam, but years later his
widow was forced to repay the government for the 15,000 unauthorized rations! (Sheppard, *op. cit.*, 73) This ended
his active army service.

Promoted to Lt. Gen. in 1798, full
Gen. in 1803, and C. in C. in Scotland
in 1804 (*ibid.*), he married Flora Mure
Campbell, Countess of Loudoun in her
own right. On his return from the American war he had entered the House of
Commons—having been elected in his
absence—and sided with the Opposition.
When Fox and Grenville came to power
in 1806 he was made Constable of the
Tower. He earned respect as a statesman and his long-standing intimacy with
the Prince of Wales brought him social
status but was "a running financial sore
from which his pocket never recovered."
(*Ibid.*) In 1813 he became Gov.-Gen.
and C. in C. in India, where until 1826
he distinguished himself by his handling
of political as well as military problems.
He directed the war against the Gurkhas
(1816), the Pindaris and Mahrattas
(1817), and by mid-1818 was able to
devote his energies to reconstruction.

He was rewarded for his services by
being created the 1st Marquess of Hastings in Feb. 1817. (During the period
1793–1817 this man of many names and
titles was known as Lord Moira.) His
career is remarkable in that he started

as a "boy wonder" in America and at
the age of 60, after years of military
inactivity, directed a campaign that has
been called "a masterpiece both of conception and of execution . . . [which]
could have emanated only from a military mind of the first order." (*Ibid.*, 79)

Too honest to line his own pocket in
India and reduced to serious financial
straits not only by his own extravagance
and unbounded generosity—he had
boarded refugee Bourbons, giving them
each a book of blank checks—but also
by the sponging Prince of Wales,
Hastings now asked for the post of
Gov. and C. in C. at Malta. He held
this position the last two years of his
life. Before being buried on the ramparts at Malta, his right hand was cut
off with his express wish that it be buried
with his wife.

His papers are in the *Report on the
Manuscripts of the Late Reginald Raw-
don Hastings*, 4 vols., Gr. Brit. Hist.
Mss. Comm., 1930–47, several extracts
of which appear in C. & M. and S. & R.
The Private Journal of . . . Hastings, 2
vols., edited by his daughter, the Mar-
chioness of Bute, was published in 1858.
A biography by Ross-of-Bladensburg,
The Marquess of Hastings, is in the
"Rulers of India" series (1893).

RAWLINGS' REGT. Col. Moses
Rawlings commanded one of the 16
"ADDITIONAL CONT'L. REGTS."

READ, Charles. 1715–*c*.1780. American deserter. N.J. A militia Col. who
went over to the British in Dec. '76, he
is referred to in Count Donop's diary
as being protected by the British prior
to this time. Confusing him with Joseph
Reed led the historian Bancroft to
impugn the latter's loyalty. See end of
article on Joseph READ (1741–1785).

READ, George. 1733–1798. Lawyer,
Signer, Acting Pres. of Del. Born in Md.
of an Irish father and Welsh mother of

good ancestry, he moved with his parents to New Castle, Del., and was educated as a lawyer. In 1763, 10 years
after being admitted to the bar, he was
elected Atty. Gen. for the Lower Counties and he held this post until his resignation on 15 Oct. '74 in protest to the
Stamp Act. His political convictions
were those of a moderate Whig, like
his close friend John Dickinson. In the
Cont'l. Cong. from 1774 until Sept. '77,
he opposed independence but became a
Signer and enthusiastic supporter of the
Decl. of Indep. once it was adopted. He
played a prominent part in shaping the
state constitution and in 1776 became
Vice Pres. of Del. When Pres. John
McKinly was captured by the British
at Wilmington in Sept. '77, Read left
Philadelphia to take over his duties and
performed them until being relieved, at
his own request, on 31 Mar. '78. He is
credited with getting the maximum possible support of the war effort out of a
lukewarm people and an inexperienced,
incompletely organized legislature.

Continuing as a member of the Del.
Council, he played a prominent part in
postwar politics. As an upholder of the
rights of small states and sharing the
ideas of Hamilton for the strongest possible central government, he nevertheless
accepted the compromises of the Constitution and is largely responsible for
his state's being the first to ratify it. One
of the first U.S. Senators, he was re-
elected in 1790. He supported the Federalist party line on assumption, the national bank, and the excise law. On 18
Sept. '93 Read resigned from the Senate
to become Chief Justice of Del., a post
he held until his death five years later.

A tall, slender, handsome gentleman,
he had three distinguished descendants
(see READ BROTHERS).

*The Life and Correspondence of
George Read* was published in 1870 by
Wm. T. Read.

READ, James. 1743–1822. Militia
officer, naval commissioner. Del. One
of the READ BROTHERS, he is identified
by Heitman as "Major Pennsylvania
Militia in 1777. (Died 1822.)" Appleton's—which makes no distinction between militia and regular officers—says
he was promoted from 1st Lt. to Col.
for gallant services at Trenton, Princeton, Brandywine, and Germantown. On
4 Nov. '78 he was appointed one of
three naval commissioners for the middle states, and on 11 Jan. '81 was invested with sole power to conduct the
navy board. "When his friend, Robert
Morris, became agent he was elected
secretary, and was the virtual head of
the marine department while Morris
managed the finances of the American
confederacy." (*Ibid.*) Another amphibious brother, Thos. READ, fought with
him on Assumpink Creek.

READ, Thomas. 1740?–1788. American naval officer. Del. Fourth of the
READ BROTHERS, he was master of vessels in the West Indies and Atlantic
trade prior to being commissioned Capt.
of the Pa. Navy on 23 Oct. '75. Commodore of 13 rowing galleys initially,
he took command of the newly purchased *Montgomery* in Mar. '76 and was
stationed at Fort Island to guard the
chevaux de frise. On 5 June he became
eighth ranking Capt. in the Cont'l. Navy
and was assigned to command the frigate *George Washington*. This vessel not
being completed when the British pushed
Washington back to the Delaware, Read
marched on 5 Dec. with a naval battery
to join the army and took part in the
defense of Assumpink Creek, near Trenton, the afternoon of 2 Jan. '77. (See
PRINCETON, 3 Jan. '77) When the British captured Philadelphia, Read and his
superior, John Barry, dismantled and
scuttled their ships (*Washington* and
Effingham) just below Bordentown in
Dec. '77, and on 7 May '78 they were

destroyed by the British. During the rest of the war Read saw little sea duty. In Apr. '78 he was in Baltimore fitting out the fast brigantine *Baltimore* and he apparently made one voyage in her that year. In Feb. '79 he was ordered to take station in the Chesapeake. Later in the year he was put in command of the frigate *Bourbon* being built in Conn., but the vessel was never completed. In 1780 he took out the privateer *Patty* of Philadelphia, and he was at sea in 1782. As Capt. of the *Alliance* frigate, purchased by his friend Robert Morris, Read made a remarkably fast, "out-of-season" trip to China by a new route east of the Dutch Indies. He left Philadelphia on 7 June '87, reached Canton on 22 Dec., was back at Philadelphia on 17 Sept. '88, with a tea cargo valued at $500,000. He died five weeks later.

READ BROTHERS OF DELAWARE. Their father, John (1688–1756), a descendant of Sir Thos. Read of Berkshire, went to America from Ireland and became a large landholder in Md. and Del. With six associates he established Charlestown at the head of Chesapeake Bay as a trade rival to Baltimore, which had been begun 12 years earlier (Appleton's). Soon after 1734 he moved to nearby New Castle, Del. Mother of his three distinguished sons, George (b. 1733), Thomas (b. 1740?), and James (b. 1743), was Mary Howell, "a Welsh lady" whose father was a planter (*D.A.B.*). Another son, William, was in business in Havana. George's son, John (1769–1854), became a prominent lawyer and banker. John's son, John Meredith Read (1797–1874), and grandson of the same name (1837–1896), were famous as jurist and diplomat. The Read brothers were closely associated with Robert Morris during and after the Revolution.

RECRUITING IN GREAT BRITAIN. At the time of the American Revolution the British Army was recruited in the following, traditional manner: the crown contracted with a distinguished officer or civilian to raise a regiment, giving him a "beating order" that made his enlisting legal. (A drum was beat, not a soldier.) The "contractor" was given bounty money for each recruit, or in lieu thereof he might be authorized to nominate all or some of the regimental officers, and he could pay recruiting expenses by selling commissions; this created the purchase system of promotion. The colonel was paid by the crown, which also gave him an annual sum for payment of the troops, for their clothing, and for enlisting replacements. Since general officers of the British Army were not paid as such until the end of the 18th century they remained as nominal colonels of their regiments.

Enlistments generally were for life, but the term of service was a matter of contract between the soldier and the colonel. Under exceptional circumstances men were enlisted for several years or for the duration of a war.

Military service was so unpopular at the outbreak of the Revolution that only 20,000 English soldiers were available in 1776. Ireland, normally a good recruiting area, was enjoying rare prosperity. Soldier pay was a miserable eight pence a day for a private, most of this being deducted for expenses. The brutality of noncoms, miserable living conditions, and the horrors of life aboard a transport were enough to keep all but the desperately poor out of the service. Even after releasing debtors and criminals from jail, impressing paupers and vagrants, and offering bounties the British had to resort to hiring GERMAN MERCENARIES.

Burgoyne's surrender and the entry of France into the war were a spur to voluntary mobilization in Britain. Noblemen and towns raised regiments (FRASER

HIGHLANDERS, Royal Edinburgh, Royal Liverpool, Royal Manchester, for example) and donated warships. An estimated 31 regiments of foot were formed between 1778 and 1781. Recruits for British regiments serving in America also were enlisted locally, and many American deserters took the King's shilling. (Approximately 250 of these were evacuated from Yorktown on the *Bonetta* before Cornwallis' surrender.)

See Edward P. Curtis, *The Organization of the British Army in the Revolution* (New Haven, Conn., 1926).

REDAN. A field work of two sides, pointing toward the enemy and open to the rear. It is virtually the same thing as a FLÈCHE or RAVELIN.

RED BANK, N.J. See FT. MERCER.

REDOUBT. A relatively small, independent outwork, completely enclosed. Fortresses are surrounded by redoubts covering the main avenues of enemy approach.

REED, James. 1723–1807. Cont'l. general. Mass.–N.H. His great-grandfather and grandfather emigrated (together) from England in 1635 and settled a few years later in Woburn, Mass., where James was born. After an elementary education he became a tailor. By 1748 he was a tavern keeper in Lunenburg and a selectman. During the French and Indian War he served almost continuously as a Capt., taking part in the expedition to Crown Point in 1755, Abercromby's mismanaged operations of 1758 (including Ticonderoga), and the final campaigns under Amherst. About 1765 he moved to the place known after 1773 as Fitzwilliam, N.H. Here he also kept a tavern, maintained his militia affiliation, and as one of the original proprietors was a large landowner. (Katharine Elizabeth Crane in *D.A.B.*)

When the Revolutionary War started.

he raised a unit and on 28 Apr. '75 was commissioned Col. of the 3d N.H. As the rebel army was deployed for the Boston Siege, Reed's relatively small regiment was posted near Charlestown Neck on 14 June. When Prescott and Putnam sent back repeated requests to Ward for reinforcements the morning before the British attack on BUNKER HILL, 17 June, Ward finally agreed to let John Stark lead his own 1st N.H. and Reed's regiment to the battlefield. (Under BUNKER HILL, see section headed "American Dispositions" for Stark's famous approach march.) It was this body of N.H. troops that Gen. Howe observed moving from the true Bunker Hill to reinforce the redoubt on Breed's Hill and that caused him to delay his attack until more British troops landed. One of Reed's companies (Crosby's) was detached to outpost Charlestown. He moved with the rest of his command to take up a position with Thos. Knowlton along the "rail fence." Here he distinguished himself in keeping his green troops in position, although his leadership was obscured by that of Prescott, Stark, Putnam, and Knowlton. In the reorganization of 1 Jan. '76 his regiment became the 2d Cont'l. Inf.

Ordered to the Northern Dept. to reinforce the army that had retreated from Canada, Col. Reed commanded the 2d Brig. at Ticonderoga in July '76. A short time later he suffered an illness that left him blind and partially deaf. (*D.A.B.*; Appleton's says he had gotten smallpox after joining the disease-ridden Northern army and before retreating with it to Ticonderoga.) Appointed B.G. on 9 Aug., he accepted the commission in the hope that he would recover, but in Sept. '76 he resigned. Despite his physical impairment he lived another 30 years and remarried after the death of his first wife in 1791.

His son, Sylvanus (*d.* 1798), was commissioned ensign in his regiment on 1 Jan. '76, and was Adj. to Gen. John Sullivan during the operations at NEW-PORT, 1778. (Appleton's)

REED, Joseph. 1741–1785. Patriot statesman and soldier. N.J.–Pa. Great-grandson of an immigrant from Northern Ireland and son of a wealthy Trenton merchant, he was well educated in America and London. After practicing law in Trenton and developing an extensive business that brought him into contact with important leaders in other colonies, he established his law practice in Philadelphia in 1770. In Nov. '74 he became a member of the committee of correspondence, and the following Jan. he was president of the 2d Prov. Cong. Cosmopolitan, intellectual, and of a courteous nature, he reluctantly abandoned the cause of conciliation, but before and after the war he was accused of lacking the enthusiasm of the radicals and of a cautious attitude toward military affairs. (Richard B. Morris in *D.A.B.*)

At the outbreak of hostilities the 34-year-old Reed was appointed Lt. Col. of militia, and on 19 June he agreed to join Washington as a temporary staff officer. With the rank of Lt. Col. in the Cont'l. Army, he is shown in the records as Washintgon's military secretary during the period 4 July '75–16 May '76. (Heitman, 13) But on 29 Oct. '75 he left the headquarters to take care of certain cases pending in his law practice. Despite the urgings of Washington he appeared to be in no hurry to return. (Freeman, *Washington,* IV, 18.) He sat in the Cont'l. Cong. during this absence and served briefly with a militia regiment sent to N.Y. In Mar. '76 Washington was able to offer him the post of A.G., but Reed accepted only after considerable urging. His appointment, which carried the rank of Col. and gave him the equivalent of £700 a year, was dated 5 June '76. The income apparently was an important consideration in his acceptance. (*Ibid.,* IV, 106)

The shift of military operations from Boston to N.Y. presented difficult problems that made Washington particularly anxious to regain the services of Reed, whose character, exceptional intelligence, legal experience, and skill as a writer he valued highly. Reed played an important role in the military and political features of the N.Y. Campaign. (See PEACE COMMISSION OF THE HOWES for his part in this delicate matter.) He advocated that N.Y.C. be abandoned and destroyed to keep the British from using it for a base. He also advocated that Fort Washington be abandoned. When subsequent events bore out his judgment he wrote to Charles Lee criticizing Washington's direction of the campaign. A letter from Lee to Reed arrived during the latter's absence from headquarters and Washington, assuming it was an official communication, opened it to see this:

"Camp, Nov'r the 24th, 1776
"My Dr. Reed:

"I received your most obliging, flattering letter—lament with you that fatal indecision of mind which in war is a much greater disqualification than stupidity or even want of personal courage. Accident may put a decisive blunderer in the right, but eternal defeat and miscarriage must attend the man of the best parts if cursed with indecision.* * * " (Quoted in *ibid.,* IV, 269)

The character of the two men and their admiration for each other enabled their friendship to survive this nasty episode. (*Ibid.,* IV, 21A; *D.A.B.*) Sharing the view of the C. in C. that a counteroffensive should be launched from the Delaware into N.J., Reed was a key figure in the Trenton-Princeton operations. As a former resident of Trenton and student at Princeton, he furnished valuable advice for the surprise attack on Trenton (*D.A.B.*), but he was particularly useful in gathering information for the bolder moves that followed. The night of 28–29 Dec. '76 he had hidden in a house in Bordentown and received reports of Donop's movements that led him to recommend the further advance of Washington into N.J. On the 29th he reported to Washington on the situation he found in Trenton, and this reinforced Washington's decision to recross the Delaware that day. With a dozen light horsemen he pushed up to the outposts of Princeton on 2 Jan., and sent back the report that British reserves were moving toward that place. (A. H. Bill, *Princeton, 76–92 passim*)

Reed resigned from the army on 22 Jan. '77. Named B.G. and offered command of the cavalry on 12 May, he declined the appointment on 9 June '77, but as a volunteer A.D.C. without pay he gave Washington valuable service at Brandywine, Germantown, and Monmouth. In 1777 he also declined the position of chief justice under the new constitution of Pa., but he accepted election to Congress and in 1778 was on many important committees. A member of the PEACE COMMISSION OF CARLISLE in 1778 attempted to bribe him, and he exposed the matter. From Dec. '78 until 1781 he was president of the Supreme Executive Council of Pa. In this capacity he led the state's attack on Benedict ARNOLD and had the key role in settling the MUTINY OF THE PA. LINE in Jan. '81.

He resumed his law practice in 1781 and visited England in 1784. Elected to Congress on his return, his health prevented him from serving and he died the next year at the age of 44.

Joseph Reed's loyalty to the patriot cause in 1776–77 has been suspected. In 1778 he was accused by Arthur Lee of correspondence with the enemy, but neither he nor anybody else took this seriously. His military record was attacked in an article of the *Independent Gazetteer* of 7 Sept. '82 signed "Brutus"; Benj. Rush was generally believed to have been the author, but Reed unfortunately suspected his former comrade, Gen. John Cadwalader, and exchanged a bitter correspondence with him for several years. Historians picked up an attack that Reed's contemporaries abandoned. George Bancroft's *History of the United States* (vol. IX, 1866) established Reed's guilt, but in *The Reed Controversy* (1876) Wm. S. Stryker established that Bancroft had confused Joseph Reed with Col. Charles Read, who deserted to the British in Dec. '76. The great historian withdrew his definite charge in the 1876 edition of his *History* but did not revise his judgment that Reed was "a trimmer of the most pronounced type." (*E.B.* A trimmer is one who changes his political loyalty to suit his personal interests.) J. R. Alden concludes that Reed's fidelity to the patriot cause seems well established in John F. Roche's article, "Was Joseph Reed Disloyal?" in the *Wm. and Mary Quarterly*, Third Series, VIII (1951).

The Reed Papers are held by the *N.Y. Hist. Soc.* His grandson, W. B. Reed, published *Life and Corresp. of ...Reed*, 2 vols., in 1847.

REED, Sylvanus. Son of James REED (1723–1807).

REEDY RIVER (Cane Brake), S.C., 22 Dec. '75. After the truce that resulted from the actions at NINETY-SIX, 19 Nov., a force of S.C. militia and newly raised regulars under Cols. Richard Richardson and Wm. Thompson moved into the region between the Broad and Saluda rivers to break up Loyalists assembling there. They were reinforced by 700 N.C. militia under

Cols. Thos. Polk and Griffith Rutherford, and 220 regulars under Col. Alex. Martin; by Dec. the patriot army totaled more than 4,000. Loyalist resistance collapsed in the face of this strength, and Richardson captured leaders including Thos. Fletchall. The only Tory unit that refused to disband was easily routed by part of Richardson's command. Alden says this action took place at Reedy River on 22 Nov.; however the *A.A.*–Heitman list of battles shows an action at Cane Brake, S.C., *22 Dec.;* it is likely that these are the same, but that an error in date has been made. (Alden, *South,* 200)

REGIMENT. The British regiment, after which the American regiment was modeled, was an *administrative* organization, not a tactical one. The nominal ("administrative") head of a British regiment was a Col., but the unit was normally led in battle by its Lt. Col. For all practical purposes the words *regiment* and *battalion* at the time of the Revolution can be considered to be synonymous. The normal British regiment/battalion had 10 companies, eight of which were called "battalion companies" and two of which were FLANK COMPANIES. (See also RECRUITING. . . .) in Nov. '75 the Cont'l. Cong. prescribed that the Cont'l. regiment have eight companies whose strength was set at 91 officers and men each, or a total of 728. The states (as they soon became) had regiments of various sizes: those from Mass., N.H., and R.I., for example, were supposed to number 590 *enlisted men* at one time, while those from Conn. varied from 1,000 to 600. These prescribed strengths were academic, however. At Lexington and Concord the American regiments averaged 292 RANK AND FILE. Average strength of the regiments/battalions under Washington at Long Island, Aug. '76, was about 350 officers, noncommissioned officers, and privates *fit for duty.*

American regiments originally were commanded by a Col., but since British regiments were commanded by a Lt. Col. and this made for a disparity in the matter of prisoner EXCHANGE, the Cont'l. Cong. created the rank of "Lt. Col., Commandant of the——Regt."

REGULAR APPROACHES. One meaning of "approaches" is "entrenchments, etc., by which the besiegers draw closer to the besieged" (*O.U.D.*). When one reads that the attacker "undertook regular approaches" it means that he declined to attempt capturing a place by immediate assault (which often is less costly in the end) and elected the time-consuming and laborious process of formal siege operations. The basic technique was to dig a first "parallel" just outside the defender's artillery range, to run forward a zigzag trench or SAP, and then dig a second parallel. This process is continued, successive parallels enabling the besieger to move forward his work parties and artillery, until the enemy surrenders or until a final assault can be made against his weakened fortifications. See CHARLESTON, 1780; PENSACOLA, 9 May '81; ST. LEGER'S EXPEDITION; and SAVANNAH, 1779.

REGULAR ESTABLISHMENT. The British Army was said to have a wartime and peacetime establishment. and these were, in turn, broken down into what might be called "geographical" establishments. After the Peace of Paris in 1763 "the establishment for Great Britain" was fixed at 17,500 men, "that for the Colonies" at 10,000, that for Minorca and Gibraltar at something over 4,000, "which, with 1,800 artillery, and the invariable 12,000 men on the Irish establishment, made up a total of rather more than 45,000 men in all." (Fortescue, *British Army,* III, 10–

11) As used in accounts of the American Revolution, the "regular establishment" of the British Army was what is now called the Regular Army in the U.S.: its personnel were administered in accordance with laws and regulations that governed pay, promotion, retirement, etc. Units and individuals of the "Irish Establishment" were subject to similar controls. Units and individuals serving the British in America—*i.e.*, Loyalists—were said to be on the "Provincial Establishment," so that by commissioning a Col. of a Tory regiment the British were not committed to giving him the same retirement benefits he would have as a "regular."

REGULATORS. The *O.U.D.* traces the word back to 1655 in England but gives it the following definition in U.S. usage in 1767: "A member of one of the bands formed at various times in wild parts of the country, with the professed object of supplying the want of the regular administration of justice." Regulation or regulator movements existed before the Revolution in the Carolinas. They represented one of the several varieties of FACTIONALISM in the colonies, and this particular type may be further described as east—west, low country—upcountry, or tidewater—piedmont sectionalism. In a chapter of his *South in the Revolution* headed "Sectional Clash," Alden summarizes the conflict between these elements and cites several special studies.

The N.C. Regulators were active as an organized group after 1768, when Herman Husbands (1724–1795) led them in a protest against lack of representation in the provincial assembly and other grievances including embezzlement of public funds by crown officials. Their demands ignored, the N.C. Regulators became bolder in their opposition to authority and more vig-

orous leaders took control. On 8 Apr. '68, 70 armed Regulators rode into Hillsboro, freed a horse that had been taken by the authorities when its owner refused to pay taxes, and put a few bullet holes in the house of crown official Edmund Fanning. The latter called out the militia, asked Gov. Tryon for aid, and in May arrested Husbands and another leader, Wm. Butler. When 700 Regulators headed for the jail, Fanning released his prisoners. Tryon appeared in Hillsboro with more than 1,400 men in Sept. to see that the local court was not molested, and a band of 3,700 Regulators dispersed rather than challenge this authority. Troubles continued to brew, however, and the cauldron boiled over after Fanning was whipped, run out of town, and his fine house destroyed. On 15 Jan. '71 the assembly passed the "Bloody Act" that made rioters guilty of treason, and in April Tryon (who was an army officer) took the field to restore order by force. This led to the Regulator defeat at the ALAMANCE, 16 May '71. One insurgent leader, James Few, was executed the next day on the battlefield; 12 others were convicted of treason, six of these were publicly hanged on 19 June at Hillsboro. The other six and some 6,500 settlers were obliged to swear allegiance to the government. (*E.A.H.*, 80) Many Regulators migrated to the trans-Allegheny region, and one group formed the Watauga settlement. (See "OVER MOUNTAIN MEN") Tryon and Fanning soon left for their new posts in N.Y. and the new governor, Josiah Martin, adopted a conciliatory policy toward the Regulators in the misguided hope that he could thereby win them to the loyal cause. Although it once was believed that the Regulators tended to side with the crown in the Revolution, of 883 whose record is known, 289 were patriots and only 34 were Loyalists; 560 cannot be classified. (Alden, *op. cit.*, 162, citing Lefler and Newsome, *North Carolina,* 178)

The Regulator movement in S.C. was older than the movement in N.C., but owing largely to the prudence of Lt. Gov. Wm. Bull there was no pitched battle, and from 1769 until the Revolution the interior settlements were quiet. Richard Maxwell Brown in *The South Carolina Regulators* (Cambridge: Harvard University Press, 1963) maintains that in S.C. there was no conflict between east and west but that the Regulator movement stemmed from a need to correct the lawlessness following the Indian troubles covered under CHEROKEE EXPEDITION OF . . . 1763.

REIDESEL. See RIEDESEL.

REPUBLICAN PARTY. In opposition to the FEDERALIST PARTY of Alexander Hamilton the Republican Party was formed under the leadership of Thomas Jefferson. They professed to be the party of the common man, hence the title "Republican," and established "Democratic Clubs" throughout the country. When Jefferson became president (1801) the Republican Party drove the Federalists off the national scene but within a generation they themselves had split into elements: the National Republicans, who soon changed their name to Whigs, and their opposition, under Andrew Jackson, who first called themselves Democratic Republicans and then merely Democrats. The modern Republican Party—which adopted the name in 1854—drew about a third of its original strength from the old Democratic Republicans who had formed the Free Soil Party, and the rest from the old National Republicans who had become the Whig Party.

RESCINDERS. See MASS. CIRCULAR LETTER.

RESOURCES OF AMERICA AND GREAT BRITAIN COMPARED. In general terms, Great Britain had five times the military manpower of the colonists (see POPULATIONS), much of this existing as a trained army and navy, whereas the Americans had no armed forces and no real military cadre to train its men. (See MILITIA) "Staff, command, army, equipment, supplies— all these had to be created from nothing!" writes D. S. Freeman. (*Washington,* III, 443) In 1774 the British had an effective army of about 17,500 and a navy of 16,000, but in 1775 Parliament voted 55,000 soldiers and 28,-000 seamen. "Her fighting marine could muster 100 ships to America's one (the British Navy had 270 ships in 1775, 468 in 1783, despite the loss of 200 [C. & M., 912])," says Van Tyne, but her financial resources were 1,000 times those of the 13 colonies. (*Eng. and America,* 119–20) In comparison with an American revenue of perhaps £75,-000 per year, the British had a "sinking fund" of two or three million pounds a year. During its last war the British had spent £17,000,000 in a single 12-month period, and before the start of the American Revolution their national debt exceeded £130,000,000. (Van Tyne, *War of Indep.,* 95)

On the other hand, Britain had not only the threat of traditional enemies but also had staggering logistical and command problems in fighting a transatlantic war. Despite her naval supremacy during the first years of the war, only one British supply ship passed safely from England to Boston between Aug. and Nov. '75.

Americans had the advantage of fighting on their own ground, where they were familiar with the type of terrain and climate that upset the methods of European trained regulars. While there was an almost complete lack of military engineers and artillerymen in America, and an absence of men with experience in army organization, administration, and training, there were many officers with tactical experience in the COLONIAL WARS. While the colonies had a large percentage of city dwellers who knew no more about firearms than modern Americans, they did have frontiersmen who were effective as RIFLEMEN, and American musketry was superior to that of the British and Germans. The presence of a high percentage of LOYALISTS was not really a handicap to the Americans—the patriot elements achieved and maintained superiority in most areas; on the other hand, the British suffered from a disinclination to mobilize the Loyalists and their tendency to base strategy on the assumption that Loyalist support could be counted on in some region where they had not yet tried to operate. In the field of leadership, the British military and civil authorities proved to be inept, particularly in their transatlantic cooperation; Washington lacked military genius but had other qualities that made him emerge as "the man" of the Revolution.

On the material side, the quantity of colonial shipping is not known, but it was vastly inferior to Britain's. Manufacturing in the colonies was primitive; building an "armaments industry" was out of the question and supplies would have to come from abroad—on credit. See MANUFACTURING. . . .

A questionnaire from Lord Dartmouth to all colonial governors in 1773 revealed the following state of military preparedness at that time: "Not one fort now," answered Va. and N.J. A "quite ruinous" stone castle was reported by N.H., and Pa. had a half-finished fort in the Delaware to ward off pirates. Boston's Castle William was in ill repair, and only a few batteries at other Mass. ports were in existence. Ga. had four forts. New York had a fort and batteries at the mouth of the Hudson, forts at Albany and Schenectady, but none was properly equipped with cannon or adequately supplied.

POPULAR SUPPORT proved to be a deficiency on both sides.

REVERE, Paul. 1735–1818. Patriot, craftsman, courier. Known to every American schoolboy for his midnight ride, immortalized somewhat inaccurately in the poem of Henry Wadsworth Longfellow (1863), Paul Revere was a relatively unknown figure in American history until the appearance of that work.

"Silver made by Revere grew rapidly in value, until a good piece fetched $5,000; it was rumored that the late J. P. Morgan offered Mrs. Marston Perry $100,000 for Revere's famous 'Sons of Liberty' punch bowl. His engravings and caricatures were cherished. The folk mind, upon learning that Paul Revere made false teeth and that George Washington wore false teeth, invented the well-known statement that Revere made a set of dentures for the master of Mt. Vernon." (Dixon Wecter, *Hero in America* [1941], quoted in Forbes, *Revere,* 472)

Yet Paul Revere deserves an important place in American history, not particularly for his dramatic ride to warn the patriots of the British advance on LEXINGTON AND CONCORD, 19 Apr. '75, but for his Revolutionary War activities as leader of the Boston "mechanics," as an effective political cartoonist, and for several other important rides before and after he became the official courier between the Mass. Prov. Assy. and the Cont'l. Cong. He also is important as one of the country's finest silversmiths and for significant developments in metallurgy and founding. In her *Paul Revere & The World He*

Lived In (Boston, 1942), Esther Forbes does full justice to the man, and she does so in a particularly delightful style.

Revere was the son of a Huguenot, Apollos Rivoire (*ibid.*) or De Revoire (*D.A.B.*), who came to Boston from the isle of Guernsey at the age of 13 to serve three years as apprentice to the silversmith John Coney (1655–1722). He Anglicized his name for the same reason many non-Anglo-Saxons have continued to do so: "that the Bumpkins should pronounce it easier" (*D.A.B.*, quoting Taylor, *Paul Revere*, 14). Young Paul, the third of 13 children—his mother was Deborah Hichborn (*D.A.B.*) or Hitchbourn, whose family owned the wharf of that name—learned his father's trade, and took part in the Crown Point expedition of 1756. There being a superabundance of silversmiths in Boston, Revere branched into other crafts, engraving portraits, a songbook, political cartoons, seals, bookplates, coats-of-arms, and the manufacture of dental devices. He álso became the leader of the mechanic class of Boston (see WORDS, Archaic), which brought him into close contact with Hancock, Sam Adams, and Joseph Warren. He helped organized the Boston Tea Party and became one of its "Indians." He then made the long ride, in mid-winter, to inform the N.Y.C. Sons of Liberty of the event. The next spring he rode to N.Y.C. and Philadelphia with word of the Boston Port Bill and with an appeal for help. He carried the Suffolk Resolves to Philadelphia. Becoming official courier of the Mass. Prov. Cong. to the Cont'l. Cong., he got to be so well known that his name was mentioned in London newspapers. When the patriots learned that Gage had ordered seizure of valuable military supplies at FORT WILLIAM AND MARY, Revere galloped to Durham to warn Gen. Sullivan and then alerted the patriots of Portsmouth. Two days before making his most famous ride he rode to warn the patriots to move their military stores from Concord. This and the subsequent mission are covered under LEXINGTON AND CONCORD.

Although he wanted a military commission Revere was kept busy with such tasks as printing the first issue of Cont'l. currency, learning the process of manufacturing gunpowder, and supervising the process at Canton, Mass. He made the first official seal for the colonies and the one that Mass. still uses (*D.A.B.*). On 29 Mar. '76 he became a member of the Comm. of Corresp. In 1778–79 he commanded at Castle William. Opportunity for field duty came finally, and he was ordered "to hold himself and one hundred of the Matrosses under his command, including proper officers, in readiness at one hours notice to embark for the Defence of this State, and attack the Enemy at Penobscot." (Quoted in Forbes, *Revere,* 340) Revere had been commissioned a Maj. of militia on 10 Apr. '76, was promoted to Lt. Col. in the fall, and toward the end of 1778 he was put in charge of the three artillery companies that remained in Boston. The expression "put in charge" is used advisedly, since Revere really had little "command" over his men and was having trouble with two disgruntled captains, Winthrop Gray and William Todd. (*Ibid.*, 331) The PENOBSCOT EXPEDITION, July–Aug. '79, was a fiasco, and in the epidemic of recrimination that ensued, Revere was accused by Capt. Thomas Carnes, who commanded the marines aboard the PUTNAM, of disobedience, unsoldierly conduct, and cowardice. Gen. Wadsworth also criticized his performance. On 6 Sept. '79 Revere was relieved of command at Castle Island and placed in house arrest. After many delays a court-martial convened in Feb. '82 and rendered the following findings:

"The Court finds the first charge ... to be supported (to wit) his refusing to deliver a certain Boat to the Order of General Wadsworth when upon the Retreat up Penobscot River from Major Bagwaduce: but the Court taking into consideration the suddenness of the refusal, and more especially that the same Boat was in fact employed by Lieu't Colo Paul Revere to effect the Purpose ordered by the General ..., are of the Opinion that ... Revere be acquitted of this Charge.

"On the second charge, ['For his leaving Penobscot River without Orders from his Commanding Officer'], the Court considers that the whole army was in great Confusion and so scattered and dispersed, that no regular Orders were or could be given, are of the Opinion, that Lieu't Colo Paul Revere, be acquitted with equal Honor as the other Officers in the same Expedition." (*Ibid.*, 350–51)

Revere, meanwhile, had gone on with his trade, and biographer Forbes comments that "It is doubtful if he took the affair too hard." (*Ibid.*, 351) He was active in civic affairs, especially in working for ratification of the federal Constitution. His reputation as a silversmith was established and he turned to the casting of bells and cannon. His foundry supplied the bolts, spikes, pumps, and copper accessories for *Old Ironsides,* and in 1808–9 he used his recently discovered process for rolling sheet copper to make boilers for a steam ferry boat being built by Robert Fulton. "The quaint figure of the aged silversmith, who persisted in wearing the costumes of Revolutionary days throughout his life, was long a familiar one on the streets of Boston." (*D.A.B.*) By his first wife, Sarah Orne, whom he

married 17 Aug. '57, he had eight children. By his second, Rachel Walker, whom he married 10 Oct. '73, shortly after Sarah's death, he had eight more. His last years were saddened by the loss of his second wife and eldest son, and he died three years later at the age of 83.

The biography by Esther Forbes, already identified, includes a lengthy bibliography. Older works are E. H. Goss, *The Life of ... Revere* (2 vols. 1891), C. F. Gettemy, *The True Story of Paul Revere* (1905), Emerson Taylor, *Paul Revere* (1930), A. H. Nichols, *Bells of Paul and Joseph Warren Revere* [his son] (1911), Richard Frothingham, *Life and Times of Joseph Warren* (1865), and the works on early American silver by F. H. Bigelow, C. L. Avery, and Hollis French.

Revere was a close friend of Joseph WARREN.

RHODE ISLAND, Battle of. 29 Aug. '78. See NEWPORT.

RICHMOND, Va., 5–7 Jan. '81. (VA. MIL. OPNS.) Although an insignificant village of 1,800 people, half of them slaves, Richmond offered a secure place for supplies and a safer place than Williamsburg for the legislature, so in May '79 it was made the seat of the rebel government in Va. (Earlier attempts had been made to move the capital to Richmond.) When Arnold approached (5 Jan.), Gov. Thos. Jefferson had been able to turn out only 200 men to defend the town, although most of the military supplies had been evacuated. Simcoe's Rangers drove the defenders from Richmond Hill, and the rest of Arnold's command entered the village at 1 P.M. Jefferson watched helplessly from Manchester, across the James. When the governor refused Arnold's offer to spare the village if British vessels were allowed to come up and evacuate tobacco from the warehouses, Arnold burned the warehouses and a number of private and public buildings. He withdrew on the 7th.

RIDGEFIELD, Conn., 27 Apr. '77. Scene of main action during DANBURY RAID.

RIEDESEL (ree' day zel), Baron Friedrich Adolphus. 1738–1800. German general. His father was government assessor at Eisenach, and his maternal grandfather was Baron von Borke, a Prussian Lt. Gen. (B.G. equivalent in the American Army) and Gov. of Stettin. Riedesel was attending the law school at Marburg when he was commissioned ensign in the Hessian battalion on duty in the city. At the age of 18 he went to England with a German regiment in the service of George II. The next year he returned to the Continent to serve in the Seven Years' War, became A.D.C. to Duke Ferdinand of Brunswick, although he remained on the rolls as a Capt. under the Landgrave of Hesse. He performed with credit in a position of responsibility in the battle of Minden, but feeling that he was not advancing rapidly enough in the Hessian service he entered that of the Duke of Brunswick, where he could capitalize on the friendship of Ferdinand, "hero of Minden." It was Duke Ferdinand who gave the splendid military wedding for his ex-aide and the charming Frederica, second daughter of Commissary General von Massow.

As a 37-year-old Col. of carabineers Riedesel was commanding the garrison at Wolfenbuttel when the Duke of Brunswick contracted with George III to furnish a body of 3,936 infantrymen and 336 dismounted dragoons for service in America. The next day, 10 Jan. '76, Riedesel was named commander of the first contingent of 2,282, and on 4 Apr. he sailed from Dover for America.

On 1 June '76 the convoy reached Quebec, bringing Carleton the reinforcements that restored British control of Canada. After spending a year in Canada, where he was joined by his wife and three daughters—who reached Quebec on 4 June '77—Riedesel took part in Burgoyne's Offensive. He particularly distinguished himself at HUBBARDTON, 7 July '77, strongly objected to the disastrous BENNINGTON RAID, and showed particularly vigorous leadership in the first battle of SARATOGA (see section headed "Phase Three"). Surrendered with Burgoyne's army, 17 Oct. '77, he and Gen. William Phillips were exchanged for Lincoln on 13 Oct. '80. (Tharp, *Baroness,* 353) (William THOMPSON appears also to have been involved in this exchange.)

After being given the local rank of Lt. Gen. "with the corresponding English allowance" and named commander on Long Island, in the summer of 1781 Riedesel was ordered back to Canada. He went with a plan proposed by Clinton to Haldimand for an offensive from the North, but since it was not until 25 Sept. '81 that he submitted these *"idées du Général . . . Clinton d'une diversion de Canada. . . ."* (as his memorandum is titled) it is obvious that Clinton did not expect this assistance until the campaign of 1782. (Comment of editor Willcox, Clinton, *American Rebellion,* 292 *n.*)

In mid-Aug. '83 the Riedesels sailed from Quebec, reached England a month later, were cordially received by the royal family, and after a stay in London they returned to Brunswick. Of the 4,000 troops who had followed Riedesel to Canada, only 2,800 returned. On 8 Oct. '83 he led these in a grand review for the new Duke of Brunswick. It was Riedesel's good fortune to be received as a hero, and not like the unfortunate old Hessian, von HEISTER. In 1787 he was promoted to Lt. Gen.—again, this corresponds to B.G., or "one star" general—and sent as commander of the Brunswick troops to support the "Stadtholder" or Gov. in the southern provinces of Holland. After six years on this assignment he had recently retired to his ancestral castle of Lauterbach when he was recalled to become Commandant of the city of Brunswick, an office he was holding when he died in his sleep, the night of 6–7 Jan. 1800.

Although Riedesel was an outstanding soldier on the few occasions in America when opportunity presented itself, he probably is remembered more as the husband of the remarkable Baroness who followed him to Canada with three daughters under the age of five, stayed as close to him as possible during six years in America, and left the famous memoirs of that experience. Its formidable title was *Extracts from the Letters and Papers of General, Baron de Riedesel and His Wife, née Massow, Concerning Their Common Voyage to America and Their Sojourn in That Country*. A Berlin publisher got out a public edition of initial work, which had been "Printed as a Manuscript for the family," according to the title page, and this was called *The Voyage of Duty to America. . . .* (1800). A "defective English translation" was printed in N.Y. in 1827, and a complete one was made by W. L. Stone Jr.: *Letters and Journals relating to the War of the American Revolution* (Albany, 1867). A recent dual biography is *The Baroness and the General* (1962) by Louise Hall Tharp. The general's *Memoirs, Letters, and Military Journals* (2 vols., Albany, 1868) are a translation by W. L. Stone Jr. of the German *Life of General Riedesel* by Capt. Max von Eelking.

RIFLEMEN. Although the rifle was well known in Europe at the time of the Revolution as a hunting weapon it was not considered to be an effective military firearm because of the time needed for reloading and because it was not equipped with a bayonet. German immigrants brought the skills of rifle construction to America (whence the "Kentucky" rifle) and the frontiersmen became formidable LIGHT INFANTRY troops. Indian fighting and the Colonial Wars had led to a merger of sporting and military application; to the amazement of European regulars, the American frontiersman not only could deliver a reasonably high rate of fire but also could reload on the run.

"The first important military decision of the Continental Congress, even before appointing Washington to command, had been the resolution 'that six companies of expert riflemen, be immediately raised in Pennsylvania, two in Maryland, and two in Virginia.'" (Montross, *Rag, Tag,* 49) The response in Pa. was so great that Congress subsequently (22 June '75) raised this state's authorization to eight companies. These were organized as William THOMPSON'S PA. RIFLE BN. The company raised by Dan MORGAN, 96 men, completed a (mounted) march of 600 miles to Boston in 21 days without losing a man from fatigue or illness. This amounts to 28½ miles per day average rate, and Washington was so moved by this feat of his fellow Virginians that he "went along the company front shaking hands with each man . . . [as] tears . . . streamed down his cheeks." (Nickerson, *Turning Point,* 286) Although Morgan's march got the best publicity, Michael CRESAP and other rifle company commanders performed comparable ones.

The rifled gun was unknown in New England at this time, and the riflemen were as much of a curiosity around Boston as they would have been around London in 1775. John Adams, for example, wrote his wife about "a peculiar kind of musket, called a rifle." (Ward, *W.O.R.,* 31, 434–35) The frontiersmen dazzled the rest of the Boston Army with their marksmanship, but they were otherwise quite useless "except to pick off an occasional regular who incautiously showed himself. . . ." (Fisher, *Struggle,* I, 364) Soon they were a disciplinary problem because of their rowdy, frontier ways. The "shirtmen," as the Va. riflemen were called, precipitated the MUTINY ON PROSPECT HILL, 30 Sept. '75.

After that the main achievements of American riflemen were led by Dan MORGAN. (See his biographical sketch for a summary and for appropriate cross references.) KINGS MOUNTAIN, S.C., 7 Oct. '80, was another triumph of another body of American riflemen, and its is ironical that it was at the expense of Britain's foremost exponent of that weapon, Patrick Ferguson. Organization of the LIGHT INFANTRY corps gave Washington another elite body of troops who, although not riflemen, took over the missions formerly performed by them. (Riflemen were light infantry, but light infantry were not necessarily riflemen.)

Before the end of the war every British battalion in America had organized a rifle company. (Curtis, 19) Prior to this time each battalion had had one or two marksmen armed with this weapon (*ibid.*), but despite the efforts of FERGUSON the British were slow to accept the need for rifle *units.* The German jägers were armed with rifles.

It should be noted that despite all his special qualities the rifleman remained of little military value except for special operations—scouting, skirmishing, sharpshooting, etc. The man with the MUSKET—capable of putting out a higher volume of fire, accurate enough for the tactics of the day, and armed with a BAYONET—was the man who won or lost battles. "When Maryland proposed to send a rifle company to Philadelphia for the Continental Army, the Secretary of the Board of War replied [26 Oct. '76] that they would be delighted to have the men, but—

" 'If muskets were given them instead of rifles the service would be more benefitted, as there is a superabundance of riflemen in the Army. Were it in the power of Congress to supply musketts they would speedily reduce the number of rifles and replace them with the former, as they are more easily kept in order, can be fired oftener and have the advantage of Bayonetts.' " (Peterson, *Colonial Arms,* 200)

This same authority, after quoting Simcoe as saying that American riflemen "were by no means the most formidable of the rebel troops; their not being armed with bayonets," gives these excerpts from *General Hanger to all Sportsmen:*

"Riflemen as riflemen only, are a very feeble foe and not to be trusted alone any distance from camp; and at the outposts they must ever be supported by regulars, or they will constantly be beaten in, and compelled to retire. [Speaking of how he would deal with] meeting a corps of . . . *riflemen only,* I would treat them the same as my friend Colonel Abercrombie [see Robert ABERCROMBY], . . . treated Morgan's riflemen. When Morgan's riflemen came down to Pennsylvania from Canada, flushed with success gained over Burgoyne's army, they marched to attack our light infantry, under Colonel Abercrombie. The moment they appeared before him he ordered his troops to charge them with the bayonet; not one man out of four, had time to fire, and those that did had no time given them to load again; the light infantry not only dispersed them instantly but drove them for miles over the country. They never attacked, or even looked at, our light infantry again, without a regular force to support them." (*Op. cit.,* 201, 202, citing Hanger, *op. cit.,* 199, 200 Morgan had rejoined Washington's main army at Whitemarsh on 18 Nov. '77. Presumably the action mentioned above was in connection with the skirmishes at WHITEMARSH, 5–8 Dec., or MATSON'S FORD, 11 Dec. '77, although 170 of Morgan's riflemen—only this number had shoes stout enough for marching —were ordered to support Gen. Greene when he attempted to reinforce Ft. Mercer [under PHILADELPHIA CAMPAIGN see section headed "The Delaware River Forts"].)

RITZEMA, Rudolph(us). Cont'l. officer, turncoat. Son of Johannes (1710–1795), Dutch clergyman and original trustee of Kings College (later Columbia), Rudolph graduated from the latter in 1758. (Appleton's) On 30 June '75 he became Lt. Col. of the 1st N.Y. Promoted to Col. of the regiment on 28 Nov. '75, he assumed command of the 3d N.Y. on 28 Mar. '76. Eight months later, Nov. '76, he left the American army and "subsequently joined the British army." (Heitman) There is disagreement as to which units Ritzema actually commanded. Ward speaks of his reaching Ticonderoga on 22 Aug. '75 with four companies of his 4th N.Y., and leading Montgomery's wing of the CANADA INVASION down Lake Champlain to the operations around ST. JOHNS, Sept.–Nov. '75. The same writer speaks of Ritzema's excellent performance as commander of the 3d N.Y. at WHITE PLAINS, 28 Oct. '76. (*W.O.R.,* 147, 153, 262–65) Appleton's says the defection of Ritzema resulted in the promotion of Philip VAN CORTLANDT to be Col. of the 2d N.Y. Cont'l. Regt.: from Heitman's rosters of regimental officers it is apparent that when

Ritzema left the 3d N.Y. he was succeeded by Lt. Col. Peter Gansevoort, who left the 2d N.Y. on 3 Nov. and was promoted to Col. (3d N.Y.) on 21 Nov. '75; Gansevoort had been acting C.O. of the 2d N.Y. since the departure of Col. James Clinton on 29 Aug. '76, and Van Cortlandt was promoted into the vacancy. (Heitman, 43–44)

RIVINGTON, James. 1724–1802. Bookseller, journalist, printer. Best remembered as a loyalist ʼpublisher, he is also credited with establishing what was virtually the first daily newspaper in America (1778–83). He was born in London, where he and his brother John (1720–1792) continued their father's publishing business until Mar. '56 and then went into partnership with the firm of James Fletcher Jr. After a smashing success with Smollett's *History of England* and other works, James indulged in a period of high living and neglect of business that ended his publishing career in England. Liquidating his business obligations in full and still having a good working capital left, he went to America in 1760 and founded a successful chain of book stores in Philadelphia and N.Y.C. (1760), and in Boston (1762). About 1765 he concentrated his book business in N.Y.C., but the next year he lived at Annapolis until his "Maryland Lottery," a land scheme, led to bankruptcy. Again he recovered quickly from business failure. In Nov. '68 the firm of J. Rivington & Company moved from Hanover Square to the lower end of Wall Street. He published the poetic works of Charles Churchill (1768), married into the influential family of Elizabeth Van Horne (1769), and in 1773 expanded his business to include job printing.

On 18 Mar. '73 he published a preliminary, free issue of what was to be *Rivington's New-York Gazetteer; or the Connecticut, New Jersey, Hudson's*

River, and Quebec Weekly Advertiser.
Unlike other American newspapers, this
one proposed to appeal to all interests,
to be nonpartisan, and to give good
coverage to the international news so
conspicuously lacking even in many
modern American papers. Well edited
and excellent in typography and layout,
it was a success. Within little more than
a year its circulation reached 3,600
copies; considering the POPULATIONS of
N.Y.C. and neighboring regions, this
was impressive.

But freedom of the press did not fit
in with the views of the Sons of Liberty.
They didn't want both sides of a controversy to be printed. Several Whig meetings condemned Rivington's policy and,
although he signed their Association
after being arrested, his plant was
attacked and destroyed on 27 Nov. '75
by a mob whose leaders included Isaac
Sears, one of the patriots who particularly resented the "press" Rivington had
given him. The Prov. Cong. and then
the Cont'l. Cong. investigated the loyalty
of Rivington and the latter made his
official peace with the patriots. But he
still was vulnerable to mob action, and
in Jan. '76 he sailed for England.
Appointed King's Printer in N.Y.C., he
returned to start publication on 4 Oct.
'77 of a strictly Loyalist paper. *Rivington's New York Loyal Gazette* changed
its title on 13 Dec. '77 to *The Royal
Gazette.* During the period May '78–
July '83 Rivington set up a mutual
arrangement with other N.Y. papers
whereby they produced what was virtually a daily newspaper for the first
time in America.

It has recently been proved that
Rivington started sending secret information to the patriots in 1781. (See
"The Tory and the Spy: The Double
Life of James Rivington," by Catherine
Snell Cary, *William and Mary Quarterly,* XVI [Jan. 1959], 61–72.) Benjamin TALLMADGE was sent into N.Y.C.
before the British evacuation to protect
him, and Rivington was allowed to remain in the city after the Americans reoccupied it. He removed the royal arms
from his paper, changed its name to
*Rivington's New York Gazette and Uni-
versal Advertiser,* and continued publication, despite a sharp drop in circulation, until 31 Dec. '83. On this day,
according to the *D.A.B.* sketch on Isaac
Sears, "With Alexander McDougall and
Marinus Willett, he [Sears] waited upon
Rivington . . . and silenced his paper forever." The man characterized as "the
long-nosed, competent, and jolly printer"
(Alden, *Lee,* 50), tried unsuccessfully
to stay in business as a bookseller and
stationer, but he died poor. Gilbert
Stuart's portrait (N.Y. Hist. Soc.) shows
a fine if somewhat worried face. A
street in N.Y.C. has been named for
him. The N.Y. Hist. Soc. has a complete
file of his newspapers.

ROBINSON, Beverley. 1721–1792.
Tory leader. Va.–N.Y. Born into a
prominent Va. family—his father was
acting Gov. at his death in 1749—
Beverley (which was his mother's family
name) raised a company in 1746 for a
proposed expedition against Canada.
While in N.Y. he married the wealthy
Susanna Philipse. When the Revolution
started he had increased his wife's fortune by good management and had retired as one of the state's wealthiest
landowners. On 20 Feb. '77, after John
Jay had told him he would have to get
with the Revolution or get out (Van
Doren, *Secret History,* 4), Robinson
refused to take the oath of allegiance.
Leaving his fine house, which was just
across the Hudson from West Point and
which subsequently was used variously
as American headquarters for the Highlands district and as a hospital, Robinson took refuge in N.Y.C. Here he
raised the Loyal American Regt. Made

Col. of this unit, he later was Col. and director of the loyal Guides and Pioneers as well. (*D.A.B.*) He led his troops with distinction on several occasions, particularly in the storming of Ft. Montgomery, 6 Oct. '77, during CLINTON'S EXPEDITION to the Highlands.

His main service, however, was in the secret service, "for which his knowledge of the country, his wide acquaintance, and a certain shrewdness in his nature admirably fitted him." (Jane Clark in *D.A.B.*) In the guise of returning to check on his property, while the Robinson House was headquarters for Gen. Israel Putnam, he visited his home under a flag of truce and informed Mrs. Putnam that he would willingly discuss with the general the means by which the latter might honorably return his allegiance to the "legal government." The invalid Mrs. Putnam died a few days later; Robinson never knew whether she relayed his message, nor have historians been able to find out. Putnam agreed to a meeting with Robinson on 14 Nov. '77, but it is not known whether this took place. "If there was a meeting, of course nothing came of it such as Robinson had in mind," comments Van Doren. (*Op. cit.*, 6) Nor is there any evidence that Putnam knew Robinson's purpose.

Robinson figured in ARNOLD'S TREASON, but merely in the arrangements for the André–Arnold meeting. In Oct. '79 he was banished by N.Y. state and his property confiscated. His wife and eldest son were attainted with him for no other reason than that part of the estate belonged to her and the son was their heir. "I acted from upright and conscientious principles," Robinson wrote to Clinton on 8 Aug. '82 when he was leaving his native land, "and was it to do over again I should take the same part. . . ." He was appointed to the first council of New Brunswick but went to England without taking his seat. Living near Bath, he was granted £17,000 for the loss of his estate. One of his sons became a Lt. Gen. in the British Army, another became commissary general, and both were knighted. Two others settled in New Brunswick to found families still notable in Canada. (Van Doren, *op. cit.*, 429)

ROCHAMBEAU (fils), Donatien Marie Joseph de Vimeur, Viscount de. 1750–1813. French officer, son of the Comte de ROCHAMBEAU. Becoming a Lt. in the Bourbonnais Regt. in 1767, he had risen to the grade of Col. in 1779. The next year he accompanied his father to America as Assist. A.G. On 28 Oct. '80 he returned to France with dispatches, and in May '81 he was back in America. (Appleton's) Remaining with his father until the end of hostilities (*Chastellux*, note by editor Rice, 572), he was promoted to Maj. Gen. in 1791 and Lt. Gen. on 9 July '92. The next month he was appointed Gov. Gen. of the Leeward Islands. After pacifying Santo Domingo (Haiti) and forcing his royalist predecessor, the Count de Behagues, to abandon Martinique, he surrendered this place with the honors of war on 22 Mar. '94 to a greatly superior French force and its supporting British fleet. His subsequent career—reappointment as Gov. Gen. of Haiti, recall and imprisonment by the Directory, return to and conquest of Haiti, surrender to the British in 1803, imprisonment in Jamaica and England until exchanged in 1811—is beyond the scope of this work. As a division commander in the corps of Lauriston in 1813 he took part in the battles of Lutzen, Bautzen, and Leipzig. He was killed in the closing actions of the last battle, on 18 Oct. 1813. (Appleton's)

ROCHAMBEAU, Jean Baptiste Donatien de Vimeur, Comte de. 1725–1807. Commander of French army in

America. Born at Vendôme of an ancient and honorable family, he was being schooled for the church (the traditional career for a third son) when his elder brother died. At the outbreak of the War of the Austrian Succession (1740–48) he was commissioned in the cavalry regiment of Saint-Simon. In July '43 he took command of a cavalry troop (company), having served in Bohemia, Bavaria, and on the Rhine. In 1747 he was promoted to Col. (at the age of 22), and the next year he was appointed A.D.C. to the Duke of Orleans. He took part in the siege of Maestricht (1748), became governor of Vendôme (1749), distinguished himself in the capture of Port Mahon, Minorca, from the British in 1756, and then fought in Germany. He distinguished himself at Crefeld, June '58, took command of the Auvergne Regt. in Mar. '59, and saved the French army from a surprise attack at Clostercamp, Oct. '60. Wounded several times in the latter action, he was commended for personal bravery and fine tactics. Early in 1761 he was promoted to B.G. and named inspector of cavalry. In this post he improved the tactics of this arm and, while strengthening discipline, showed exceptional concern for improving the welfare of the troops. In 1776 he was made governor of Villefranche-en-Roussillon.

In 1780 he was given command of the expeditionary force sent to America to start a new and decisive phase of the FRENCH ALLIANCE. Promoted to Lt. Gen. for this assignment, Rochambeau took command of some 7,600 soldiers assembled at Brest. He sailed on 1 May '80 with the 5,500 for whom there were transport accommodations, and with the escort of Adm. TERNAY's fleet he arrived off Newport on 10 July.

Rochambeau faced a difficult task. Up until his arrival in America the FRENCH ALLIANCE had been a frustrat-

ing disappointment to the patriots, owing largely to the failures of his predecessor, ESTAING. The British fleet promptly bottled up TERNAY. Young Lafayette was "deliberately, if cautiously" rejected by Rochambeau as liaison officer between himself and Washington (Freeman, *Washington*, V, 275D) and had to be put in his place when he persisted in advocating the unsound strategy of attacking N.Y.C. before naval superiority was achieved. But with characteristic delicacy Rochambeau wrote the influential young marquis that in rejecting his proposed plan "it is always the old father Rochambeau who talks to his dear son whom he loves...." (The phrase loses something in translation: *le vieux père* and *son cher fils* have a somewhat more subtle connotation in the original. The quote is from Doniol, *Histoire*, IV, 380.) The other problem was the inefficiency of the French war and naval departments in failing to send shipping for the full expeditionary force across the Atlantic in the spring of 1780; this was aggravated by lack of SPANISH PARTICIPATION (Frank Monaghan in *D.A.B.*). Rochambeau's son, the Vicomte de Rochambeau, reached Boston early in May '81 with Adm. BARRAS and the bad news that the "follow up" contingent of French forces would not come; the good news, however, was that Adm. de GRASSE was headed for the West Indies and had instructions to cooperate in North America.

This led ultimately to the YORKTOWN CAMPAIGN.

Rochambeau sailed from the Chesapeake on 14 Jan. '83 and reached Brest in Mar. Lafayette had monopolized the public enthusiasm for welcoming French heroes of the American Revolution, but Louis XVI recognized his achievement with official commendation and royal favors. Early in 1784 he was made

Gov. of Picardy. Rochambeau took part in the second Assembly of Notables. Given command of the important Alsace district in 1789, he was forced by ill health to retire in Dec. '89. In Sept. '90 he was put in command of the Army of the North, and in Dec. '91 he became a Marshal of France. During the Terror he was arrested and escaped the guillotine only because the death of Robespierre brought a halt to the slaughter.

Freeman has this evaluation:

"Why he was selected . . . the records do not disclose. He possessed proven ability, but he spoke no English and had no previous acquaintance with American life. *** After he reached Newport and saw the gaunt and ragged Continentals, he might have concluded that he had been assigned to encourage a riot, rather than to support a revolution. Fortunately for America he was both careful in his words and appreciative in his judgment of men. He had been told to regard Washington as his superior officer; in doing so, he did not cavil. For some months he insisted that his orders forbade the separation of his army from the fleet; but when he thought the situation called for his presence on the Hudson, he advocated that move, and from the hour junction was formed, he was flawless in his cooperation." (*Op. cit.*, V, 275D)

Frank Monaghan writes:

"Rochambeau's administrative skill and his unceasing application did something to counteract the characteristic inefficiency of the French war department [at the start of his expedition]. . . . The admirable conduct of the French soldiers, together with the tact, courtesy, and charm of the officers, removed many old American prejudices against the French and prepared the way for effective cooperation and mutual good-will." (*D.A.B.*)

His *Memoires militaires, historiques et politiques* (2 vols., Paris, 1809) were dictated to Luce de Lancival and published by the latter. Extracts were translated by M. W. E. Wright and published in Paris in 1838 as *Memoirs of . . . Rochambeau relative to the War of Independence in the United States.* Almost 300 pages of his documents concerning the American Revolution are printed in Doniol (*op. cit.*, V) from French archives. Writing in 1935, Monaghan says that the only satisfactory biography is J. E. Weelen, *Rochambeau* (Paris, 1934), but that this work fails to use the large collection of Rochambeau papers in the Lib. of Cong. The works and sources pertaining to LAFAYETTE in the American Revolution must also be consulted to complete the story of Rochambeau's role.

ROCHE FERMOY. See FERMOY.

ROCHEBLAVE, Chevalier de. See RASTEL.

ROCKINGHAM, Charles Watson-Wentworth, 2d Marquess of. (Rockingham is pronounced with the "ha" silent: rok′ ing-m.) 1730–1782. British prime minister on two occasions. Taking his seat in the House of Lords on the death of his father in 1750, he became a leading Whig and opponent of the King's Friends (formed by GEORGE III). In 1765 he succeeded Grenville as P.M. and headed an administration remembered for its repeal of the Stamp Act—see DECLARATORY ACT—and its attempts at reconciliation with the American colonies. Resignation of Grafton from his cabinet led to the fall of Rockingham's ministry in July '66. He continued to oppose the coercive policies of the King and was friendly toward the American cause. Resignation of Lord North in Mar. '82 led to Rockingham's return as P.M. with authority to pursue peace negotiations. After having some success in curbing the power of the crown and having conceded the legislative independence of Ireland, this ministry, which included Fox and Shelburne, was ended by Rockingham's sudden death on 1 July '82.

ROCKY MOUNT, S.C., 1 Aug. '80. (CAMDEN CAMPAIGN) Encouraged by the rebel success at Williamson's Plantation, 12 July, patriots of the Catawba District flocked to Sumter's standard, and he soon had sufficient strength to undertake offensive operations in support of Kalb's—later Gates's—advance from the North. As mentioned in the article on the CAMDEN CAMPAIGN, Sumter wrote Kalb on 17 July to propose operations against the British line of communications from Charleston to Camden and other interior posts. On 30 July Sumter moved against Rocky Mount with about 600 men, while Maj. Wm. Davie moved against HANGING ROCK. These two places were outposted by Loyalist troops and served to protect the vital British base at Camden, about 25 miles south.

At Rocky Mount, Lt. Col. Geo. Turnbull held a strong natural position with 150 men of his N.Y. Vols. and some S.C. militia. Three log cabins had been loopholed and encircled by a ditch and abatis to form a little fortress. Early on 1 Aug. Sumter appeared opposite this position and summoned Turnbull to surrender. Having been warned of the enemy's approach, the Tories were ready and told Sumter that if he wanted the post to "come and take it." (Quoted in Bass, *Green Dragoon,* 95–96)

The rebels had no artillery, so there was no alternative but to assault the place. In a hotly contested series of charges Lt. Col. Thos. Neal succeeded in pushing through the abatis and forcing the defenders into their cabins, but he and five others were killed. (Ward, *W.O.R.,* 709) Sumter tried un-

successfully to set fire to the houses by having burning fagots thrown against them. He then rolled a burning wagon against the buildings, and the defenders put up a white flag. Just at this moment, however, a sudden deluge extinguished the flames and the enemy renewed their resistance. (Lossing, II, 660) Sumter gave up and withdrew to Land's Ford on the Catawba.

In an action that lasted about eight hours, both sides lost approximately a dozen killed and wounded. (Ward, *ibid.;* F. V. Greene, *Rev. War,* 214) Ward says Sumter's strength is unknown, but Greene and Lossing say he had about 600. Patriot units were the S.C. militia of Col. Wm. Hill and Capt. Edw. Lacey Jr., and Col. John Irwin's Mecklenburgers. Sumter's next move was against HANGING ROCK, 6 Aug.

RODNEY, Caesar. 1728–1784. Signer. Del. His grandfather emigrated from England to Philadelphia shortly after William Penn, and the family later moved to Del., where Caesar inherited a large estate from his father. In 1755–58 he was high sheriff, J.O.P., and county judge. In 1756 he was named militia captain and held other important public offices, including delegate to and speaker of the colonial legislature. He was an active delegate to the 1765 Stamp Act Cong. in N.Y.C. An early supporter of the colonies' position, he was chairman of the Del. committee of safety and was sent to the Cont'l. Congress in 1774 and 1775. He was named Col. in the Del. militia in May '75 and promoted to B.G. in Sept. During 1776 he sat in the Cont'l. Cong. and was influential in suppressing the Loyalists in Del. His hasty return to Cong. on 2 July '76 enabled the Del. delegation to vote two to one for R. H. Lee's resolution for independence and for the adoption of the Decl. of Indep. This made the document unanimous with the colonies. The state "royalists" then defeated him for the state constitutional convention, the new legislature, and for the next Cont'l. Cong. Rodney turned to military affairs and was active on the councils of safety and inspection, and collecting supplies and recruiting for Washington's army, and in raising militia companies. Alexander made him post commandant at Trenton for a few weeks, and he then served at Morristown, but with Washington's permission returned home in Feb. '77. He declined an appointment to the state Supreme Court at the same time, but was named Judge of Admiralty 5 June '77. During the British advance into his state he commanded 'the militia and in Sept. '77 was named state Maj. Gen. In Dec. '77, he was again elected to the Cont'l. Cong. but did not take his seat, having also been elected President of Del. He held this post until Nov. '81. Chosen for Cong. that year and in 1783, again he did not take his seat. The next year he died from cancer of the face, a condition from which he had suffered about 10 years. John Adams described Rodney at the first Cont'l. Cong. as "... the oddest looking man in the world; he is tall, thin and slender as a reed, pale; his face is not bigger than a large apple, yet there is sense and fire, spirit, wit, and humor in his countenance."

Brother of Thomas Rodney.

RODNEY, George Brydges. 1719–1792. British admiral. Of an old military family with close court ties, he went to Harrow and entered the navy at the age of 13 as a "King's letter boy." He won his first laurels for gallantry as commander of the *Eagle* (60) in the victory over the French off Ushant, 14 Oct. '47. The next year he took command of the *Rainbow* (40). In May '49 he was appointed Gov. and C. in C. of Newfoundland with the rank of commodore. He took part in the capture of Louis-burg in 1758. In May '59 he became Rear Adm. and soon after this promotion was given a small squadron whose mission was to break up a concentration of barges and store ships at Le Havre intended for an invasion of England. He accomplished this by a two-day bombardment (5–6 July) that destroyed a large quantity of enemy equipment and supplies, and a year later he conducted a raid along the Channel coast to destroy more invasion craft. In Oct. '61 he became C. in C. on the Leeward Islands station. He captured Martinique in Feb. '62 and within the next two months took St. Lucia, Grenada, and St. Vincent. These successes were rewarded by promotion to Vice Adm. (21 Oct. '62) and he returned to England in Aug. '63. On 24 Jan. '64 he was created a baronet. In Nov. '65 he started what was to be a five-year tour as Gov. of Greenwich Hospital.

Having reached this peak in his professional career and his personal fortunes, Rodney entered a period of frustration and disappointment. He had been elected to Parliament in 1751 and in 1761. In 1768 he had to finance his own re-election, and this is said to have cost him £30,000. Not wealthy to start with and having a taste for high life, this expense was ruinous. His appointment in 1771 to command on the Jamaica station, which promised to lead to the governorship of Jamaica, raised a hope that he could recoup his finances. But Lord Sandwich refused to let him hold the sinecure as Gov. of Greenwich Hospital, he was not made Gov. of Jamaica, and although nominated for Rear Adm. he was not, for some reason, given the pay. (*D.N.B.*) In the summer of 1774 he returned to England in such bad financial straits that early the next year he had to move to Paris to escape his creditors. But his extravagant habits during his four years in

France led to further debt, and it was only after his friend Marshal Biron loaned him 1,000 louis that he was able to take his family back to England in May '78. The story that he was offered a command in the French service has been discredited. (*E.B.; D.N.B.*)

On 29 Jan '78 he had been promoted to full Adm. and after reaching England he got his arrears in pay and was able to get out of debt. It was not until the end of 1779, however, that he was given a command. His enemy Sandwich was forced to offer him the post of C. in C. on the Leeward Islands station because no other qualified admiral would accept it. Rodney took the post with the understanding that the King had proposed it. (*D.N.B.*)

At this time the admiral was almost 61 years old, in bad health (gout), prematurely old, and long past his professional prime. On 29 Dec. '80 he left Plymouth with 21 sail of the line, the normal complement of frigates, some 300 store ships, and a fleet of transports. With this armada he was to relieve the siege of Gibraltar, which was blockaded by the Spanish, before going on to the West Indies. In the engagement off Cape St. Vincent, 16 Jan. '81, he hurled his fleet into action against a smaller Spanish force despite the fact that night was falling and a storm was raging. His audacity paid off. Two of Adm. de Langara's ships were already out of sight when the action started and two others escaped, but Rodney captured or destroyed the other seven. Again a national hero, he was made an "extra knight of the Bath." (*D.N.B.*) With four sail of the line he continued on to the West Indies, reaching St. Lucia on 22 Mar.

French Adm. De Guichen had taken command of the French fleet in the West Indies about this time. Rodney informed his captains that when he fought De Guichen he intended to violate the iron-clad instructions of the Admiralty that prescribed tactics under certain circumstances. The Admiralty order was that a British fleet windward of an enemy in line of battle should engage van to van, and so on down the whole length of the line. In other words, they would attack piecemeal. (Adm. Byng was shot in 1757 for not giving effect to this order, points out Sir John Knox Laughton in *D.N.B.*, Adm. Thos. Mathews was cashiered in 1746, and by attempting to follow the instructions Graves was defeated "and the American colonies lost" in the action off the CHESAPEAKE CAPES, 5 Sept. '81.) While Rodney is to be admired for his courage in violating Admiralty orders when, in his opinion, the circumstances warranted, he failed to make his new instructions clear to his subordinates. In the battle off Martinique, 17 Apr. '80, therefore, he failed to achieve decisive results. Although he was personally to blame for failure to issue proper instructions, his report to the Admiralty accused several of his captains, especially Carkett, of misconduct. Subsequent maneuvers against De Guichen were inconclusive. The French admiral headed into the Atlantic and Rodney, thinking that he perhaps was sailing north, reached Sandy Hook with 10 sail of the line on 13 Sept. De Guichen had returned to France, however, and on 16 Nov. Rodney left the American station after achieving nothing. (Clinton, *Amer. Reb.*, 213, 234 *n.*) The expedition did, however, precipitate a controversy with Adm. ARBUTHNOT.

Adm. Samuel Hood reached Rodney's station the end of Dec. '80 with a large reinforcement and on 27 Jan. '81 Rodney received word that Holland had entered the war against Great Britain. Acting under instructions from London that coincided with his own ideas, he captured the Dutch possession of St. Eustatius on 3 Feb. '81. Having taken booty worth several million pounds sterling at this center of the contraband trade, Rodney seems to have lost his mental balance. Under the rules of 18th-century warfare he stood to make a personal fortune out of the affair, but he overlooked the fact that much of the merchandise belonged to English merchants. Confiscating everything, he sold a good deal at auction and sent much of it back to England. Adm. Lamotte-Piquet intercepted this convoy (commanded by Wm. Hotham) as it entered European waters and captured a large portion of it. De Bouillé recaptured the island. Rodney's dream of wealth was shattered, and subsequent law suits took much of his remaining gains. (*D.N.B.*)

Meanwhile he had ignored reports of a large French fleet approaching the West Indies and failed to take his proper post with Hood, who was blockading Fort Royal off Martinique. Hood was driven off and rejoined Rodney at Antigua. "Rodney's ill health was doubtless largely responsible for his blunder," comments *D.N.B.*, but his selfish preoccupation with St. Eustatius also figured prominently in his failure, and the unfavorable outcome of this business certainly did nothing to improve his health. On 1 Aug. '81 he sailed for England, leaving Hood in command. Despite his poor performance in the West Indies he was promoted on 6 Nov. to Vice Adm. and on 16 Jan. '82 he sailed back. He rejoined Hood on 19 Feb. and resumed command.

Adm. de GRASSE had returned to the West Indies after his decisive role in the Yorktown Campaign. In the battle off Saints Passage, 9–12 Apr. '82, Rodney defeated the French and captured de Grasse aboard the magnificent *Ville*

de Paris. To the horrified astonishment of Hood, however, Rodney called off the chase at a time when the former believed that 20 French ships could have been taken. Hood, who was now a bitter critic, attributes Rodney's failure to a childish preoccupation with the possession of the French admiral and his great ship.

As soon as the Rockingham ministry came to power (22 Mar.) they sent Adm. Hugh Pigot to succeed the admiral whose performance in the West Indies had been so unimpressive. They were much embarrassed, therefore, to learn of Rodney's victory; it was too late to rescind Pigot's orders—he reached the West Indies on 10 July—but the government outdid themselves in heaping honors on Rodney. On 19 June he was created Baron Rodney, and eight days later the House of Commons voted him a yearly pension of £2,000. The committee of inquiry on the St. Eustatius affair was discharged. Rodney reached England in Sept. '82 to find himself a wealthy hero. For the next 10 years before his death he lived quietly in the country.

Adm. Sir George Rodney has been described as being so delicate in appearance as to be almost effeminate. He was vain, selfish, and unscrupulous not only in seeking prize money but also in blaming subordinates for his own failures. "Despite his brilliant personal courage and professional skill, which in the matter of tactics was far in advance of his contemporaries in England," writes Mahan, "Rodney, as a commander-in-chief, belongs rather to the wary, cautious school of the French tacticians than to the impetuous, unbounded eagerness of Nelson." (*Sea Power*, 377–78)

His portrait was painted by Sir Joshua Reynolds. His son-in-law, Gen. Godfrey Basil Mundy, published the

Life and Correspondence of ... Rodney (2 vols., 1830). See also David Hannay's *Life of Rodney*.

RODNEY, Thomas. 1744–1811. Cont'l. Congressman. Del. Named J.O.P. in 1770 and reappointed in 1774, the next year he became a member of the state assembly, the council of safety, the committee of observations, and a captain in the state militia. During Washington's retreat across N.J. in 1776, Rodney and his company joined Cadwalader at Bristol, Pa., on Christmas; they fought in the second battle of Trenton and at Princeton. In 1777, when the British invaded Del., he joined his brother Caesar as adjutant. He was Del. Judge of Admiralty 1778–85 and in 1781–88 was sent to the Cont'l. Congress five times. In 1786 and 1787 he was also in the state assembly and served as Speaker in 1787. In 1803 he was named U.S. judge for the Missouri territory. The town of Rodney, Jefferson co., Missouri, where he owned a great deal of land, was named for him.

ROGERS, Robert. 1732–1795. Ranger hero of Colonial Wars, Tory. N.H. Born on the frontier of Mass., reared on his father's farm near what is now Concord, N.H., he developed into a typical frontiersman but one with exceptional talents for recruiting. In 1755 he entered the N.H. Regt. to escape prosecution for counterfeiting. After showing skill as a leader of raids and scouting expeditions, in Mar. '56 he became Capt. of an independent ranger company supported by British funds, and in 1758 Abercromby made him the Maj. of nine such companies to be used for reconnaissance. After serving with Loudoun at Halifax (1757), with Abercromby at Ticonderoga (1758), with Amherst at Crown Point (1759)— during which campaign he destroyed the St. Francis Indians in an audacious raid—in 1760 he took part in the final operations against Montreal and then went west to receive the surrender of Detroit and down the Scioto River to Sonioto (Shawneetown) on the Ohio. Lieutenants in "Rogers' Rangers" were John STARK, Israel PUTNAM, and James Dalyell (killed at Detroit in PONTIAC'S WAR).

In 1761 he married the daughter of the Rev. Arthur Browne and the same year he led an independent company in the operations covered under CHEROKEE EXPEDITION. . . . During PONTIAC'S WAR he commanded an independent N.Y. company and took part in the relief and defense of Detroit. In 1765 he went to England to seek the advancement that no responsible authority in America would give him: starting one jump ahead of prosecution for counterfeiting, he had proved himself a brave and rugged wilderness leader but one incapable of maintaining discipline or following orders himself; he also had shown himself to be unprincipled in commercial dealings with the Indians, incapable of handling his own money without getting deeply in debt, and unable to cope with the most rudimentary forms of administration. In London, however, he got the appointment as commander of Ft. Michilimackinac. Rogers probably was the only person in London who could pronounce this, much less seek the appointment as commandant. During this visit to England the ranger hero published his *Journals,* his *Concise Account of North America* (both in 1765), and *Ponteach: or the Savages of America. A Tragedy.* The latter, which came out anonymously in 1766, is "one of the first dramas written by a native New Englander." (*D.A.B.*)

Rogers and his wife Elizabeth lived for two years at his post. After repeated violations of his instructions he was charged by Gage with embezzlement of public property and with treasonable dealings with the French but acquitted for lack of evidence. Returning to England in 1769, he was unable to get another appointment. "With typical ingenuity," writes Alden, "Rogers opened a suit for damages against Gage in 1774 in England, just as the general was leaving for America. However, the suit was soon dropped by Rogers upon the advice of Grey Cooper, a treasury official and a friend of Gage." (*Gage*, 77 *n.*) Having run up debts totaling £13,000, Rogers was thrown in prison and released only after his brother James pacified his major creditors. In 1775 he was allowed to return to America to visit his family, and from N.Y.C. he wrote Gage (30 Sept.) begging forgiveness and asking the general to withdraw his opposition in London to his preferment. (*Ibid.*, 78 *n.*) "Gage's reply has not been found," notes Alden (*ibid.*), but S. M. Pargellis states that after his return to America Rogers "for a time courted both the Americans and British." (*D.A.B.*)

Under suspicion of being a spy, despite his note to Washington that "I love America . . . and I intend to spend the evening of my days in it" (quoted in Appleton's), Washington had him imprisoned in 1776. During the subsequent investigation, Rogers claimed to have business with the Cont'l. Cong., was escorted there, and then turned over to the authorities of N.H. for disposition of his case. Escaping to the British (*D.A.B.*; Appleton's says he violated his parole), he was commissioned to raise the Queen's American Rangers. According to Pargellis, Rogers "was utterly defeated in a skirmish near White Plains and deprived of his command." (*D.A.B.*) Reference must be to the action at MAMARONECK, but although Rogers was almost surprised he hardly was "utterly defeated." More than a month later Chas. Lee is writing of his plans for the elimination of "Rogers and Co." (This is in his famous letter of 24 Nov. '76 to Joseph Reed. See N.J. CAMPAIGN.)

The dissipated ex-hero did not remain long in command of the Queen's Rangers (taken over later by SIMCOE), and he proved useless even as a recruiter. After 1776 nothing more is heard of his military activities. In 1778 his wife was granted a divorce and the custody of their one child. In 1780 Rogers fled to England, and 15 years later he died in a cheap London boarding house.

See John R. Cuneo, *Robert Rogers of the Rangers* (New York, 1959).

ROSE, John. See ROSENTHAL.

ROSENTHAL, Gustave Henri. 1753–1829. Cont'l. Officer. A baron of the Russian empire, born in Livonia (later Latvia), he fled to America after killing another nobleman in a duel and studied medicine in Baltimore before joining the Cont'l. Army as Lt. Rose (Heitman, 474), becoming "the only Russian on the American side" (Anderson, *post*, 26). On 12 June '77 (Heitman) he was made surgeon of Wm. Irvine's 7th Pa. and was at Valley Forge (Higginbotham, *War of Am. Indep.*, 224 *n.* 26). Relieved for incompetence, transferred to the general hospital as surgeon's mate under the name of Gustavus Henderson, according to Heitman he was later captured while serving as surgeon of the *Revenge* (see CONYNGHAM).

Rosenthal became Lt. in the 4th Pa. on 1 Apr. '81, at which time this unit would have been stationed at Carlisle and while Gen. Irvine was trying unsuccessfully to raise new troops in Pa. Presumably, "Lt. Rose" joined his former commander as A.D.C. and went with him when he was ordered on 8 Mar. '82 to take command at Ft. Pitt. The rest of the story is told in the article on CRAWFORD'S DEFEAT.

Transferred to the 3d Pa. on 1 Jan. '83, "Lt. Rose" was honorably discharged in June '83. (*Ibid.*) He was pardoned by Emperor Alexander and left Philadelphia in Apr. '84 for home, where he married an early love, became grand marshal of Livonia, and raised a large family. He corresponded with Gen. Irvine until the latter's death in 1804, and afterward with one of his sons. The federal government granted Rosenthal bounty land in Ohio, and Pa. gave him two tracts in the N.W. part of the state. Apparently without ever returning to America, he died on his estate in Rival on 26 June 1829. The article by J. H. Anderson in *Ohio Arch. and Hist. Soc. Pubs.*, VI (1898), 1–34, my source for many of the above details, includes a picture of Rosenthal.

His "Journal of a Volunteer Expedition . . ." is in the *Pa. Mag. of Hist. and Biog.*, XVIII (1894). Higginbotham, in the work cited above, spells the name "Rozenthal" and notes that considerable information about this interesting minor character has been found by David Griffiths in the Estonian State Archives.

ROSS, Betsy. See FLAG, American.

ROSS, George. 1730–1779. Signer, jurist. Del.–Pa. His father graduated from Edinburgh, prepared for the Presbyterian ministry, switched to the Church of England, and came to America as a missionary. George (Jr.) was born at New Castle, Del., became a lawyer in 1750, and established a successful practice at Lancaster, Pa. Elected to the Prov. Assy. in 1768, he was also elected to the provincial conference at Philadelphia and subsequently to the 1st Cont'l. Cong. in 1774. At this time he was considered a Tory, but in 1775 he swung over to the patriot cause and became an effective and energetic Whig in the Assy., the Pa. Comm. of Safety,

and in the 2d Cont'l. Cong. He also served briefly as Col. of Associators. Early in his career he had been a protector of the Indians (Appleton's), and in 1776 he helped negotiate a treaty with the tribes of N.W. Pa. He was re-elected to the Cong. but was forced by bad health to withdraw in Jan. '77.

As judge of the Pa. admiralty court he sat on the famous case of the British-owned sloop *Active*. This vessel had left Jamaica in Aug. '78 for N.Y. Four American crewmen, including Gideon Olmsted of Conn., took over the ship the night of 6 Sept. and were headed from Long Island to Egg Harbor when the Pa. brigantine *Convention* and the privateer *Gerard* fell in as escorts. Both of the latter ships claimed a share of the prize, and Olmsted claimed all of it for himself and his companions. Although Judge Ross sympathized with Olmsted, he felt bound to confirm the jury's verdict that the Conn. captors receive only one fourth. On 15 Dec. a committee of Cong. annulled the verdict and gave the entire prize to Olmsted and his three cohorts. Ross started a controversy that raged between Cong. and that state of Pa. for more than 30 years when he contended that under the state's law the verdict of a jury was conclusive upon the facts without an appeal. (*D.A.B.*) See ACTIVE CASE for more on this story.

On 14 July '79 Ross died suddenly of gout only two months after his 49th birthday.

ROYAL. A small mortar. A royal sail and mast were above the topgallant sail and mast.

ROYAL AMERICAN REGIMENT. Officially the 60th Foot, this unit is not to be confused with the Provincial regiments formed by Tories during the American Revolution. Still in existence in the British Army as The King's

Royal Rifle Corps, the Royal Americans were formed after Braddock's defeat when the War Ministry appointed a Swiss officer, Jacques Prevost, to raise a four-battalion regiment in America.* With 40 German officers Prevost reached America on 15 June '56 and started recruiting, mainly among the Pa. Germans. (Lerwill, 3, citing Fuller, *British Light Infantry in the 18th Century*, 99). Authorized strength was 4,000, and the date usually given for the regiment's origin is 25 Dec. '55 (Whitton, 74), although the appointment of Henry BOUQUET as Lt. Col. in the unit is said to have dated from 1754. Robert MONCKTON was named C.O. of the 2d Bn. in Dec. '57, and Robert ROGERS led 200 men of the 1st Bn. west to receive the surrender of French posts in 1760.

Men of the Royal American Regt. were garrisoning the lonely western posts in 1763 when PONTIAC'S WAR broke out. They took part in the relief expedition of Bouquet that scored the frontier victory at Bushy Run, 5–6 Aug. '63 (see PONTIAC'S WAR), and they took part in BOUQUET'S EXPEDITION OF 1764. The 3d and 4th Bns. then were disbanded, and the 1st and 2d were sent to the West Indies. (*Ibid.*) When the American Revolution started, the

* Although named the "Royal American" at the beginning, the regiment appears initially to have been numbered the 62d. The *D.N.B.* articles by H. Manners Chichester on William HOWE and HALDIMAND indicate that in Jan. '57 the 62d ("Royal American") was redesignated the 60th ("Royal American"), and the former 60th Regt. was redesignated the 58th Regt. The first Col. of the unit was Loudoun (1755), succeeded by Lord George HOWE (1757), and Jeffery AMHERST. These were the titular colonels.

3d and 4th Bns. were re-formed in Europe of Hanoverians and British. (*Ibid.*, 334 *n.*) Three grenadier companies of these battalions fought at BRIAR CREEK, Ga., 3 Mar. '79; the grenadier companies held one of the gun batteries and with the marines sallied forth from the Spring Hill Redoubt to clinch the British victory at SAVANNAH, 9 Oct. '79. One battalion of the Royal Americans is mentioned as having been added to the defending force of the Spring Hill Redoubt when it was learned that the main effort of the Franco-American attack was to be made there. (Ward, *W.O.R.*, 684–94, *passim*) Operations of the 3d and 4th Bns. were limited to the South. Eight companies were surrendered with the garrison of PENSACOLA, 9 May '81. Disbanded in 1783, these two battalions were reconstituted in the army expansion of 1787. (Fortescue, *British Army*, III, 517)

The 1st and 2d Bns. remained in the West Indies during the Revolution. At St. Vincent, 16 June '79, the sickly garrison of 400 Royal Americans surrendered to d'Estaing. Men of the regiment were also stationed at Antigua. They took part in the operations in NICARAGUA in 1780, Capt. Polson being an officer of the 60th Foot.

See Lewis Butler, *Annals of the King's Royal Rifle Corps,* vol. 1 (London, 1913).

ROYAL DISALLOWANCE. See DISALLOWANCE.

ROYAL GOVERNMENT IN AMERICA. England gradually supplanted charter and proprietary governments in the American colonies until 1763, when only Pa. and Md. remained proprietary, and Conn. and R.I. were chartered colonies with elected governors. Eight of the 13 were royal colonies. Mass. remained in a peculiar situation, "dually constituted, with a restless, dissatisfied, protesting Puritan soul encased within a royal body...." (Andrews, *Policy*, 401)

The eight royal colonies had a governor and council appointed by the Crown, and an assembly elected by the people. The governor, as executive head of the colonial legislature and the king's chief representative, was expected to execute *instructions,* which came usually from the Board of TRADE. The council served not only as the upper house of the legislature and the governor's advisory board but also as the colony's highest court of appeal. (Miller, *Origins of the American Revolution,* 32, 34) Both the home government and the colonial assemblies progressively weakened the governor's authority. Soon after 1763 the Secretary of State began appointing an increasing number of colonial officials, including the naval officer responsible for enforcing the Navigation Acts. The colonial assemblies had taken it upon themselves to appoint certain administrative officials, despite protests from the governor.

After 1680 the assemblies had authority to initiate all colonial laws. The governor either vetoed these or sent them to the Privy Council, where they met with "allowance" (approval) or DISALLOWANCE. The assemblies had also gained the all-important right to make financial appropriations and supervise actual expenditures. Thus they got the whip hand on the governor and the provincial judges by controlling their salaries. The Crown tried in vain to make the assemblies establish fixed annual salaries. The assemblies also fought off all efforts of the Crown to establish a fixed civil list in the colonies, which would have given the governor a powerful patronage weapon, (See TOWNSHEND REVENUE ACT, 1767) The Crown did, however, succeed after 1761 in establishing the governor's right to appoint judges "during the pleasure of the Crown," whereas the assemblies had fought to permit them to retain office "during good behavior." Resentment over this point is reflected in the Decl. of Indep.

Success of colonial assemblies over royal authority—particularly marked during the French and Indian War— can be attributed largely to the low caliber of men appointed to be royal governors. Miller characterizes them as "dull, commonplace Englishmen who badly needed a job but who ought to have been given a clerkship instead of a governorship." (*Op. cit.,* 33) It was looked on as a post for political hacks or for influential men who had to be "kicked upstairs."

When the Revolution started, the only colonial governor who remained on the patriot side was Jonathan TRUMBULL (1710–1785). Gov. Thomas HUTCHINSON of Mass. figured prominently in the events leading to the Revolution. William TRYON served as royal governor in N.C. and N.Y., after which he returned to his former calling as an army officer and fought against the Americans. Josiah MARTIN succeeded Tryon in N.C.; he also was a former army officer and reverted to this role. In addition to Martin, Governors Sir William CAMPBELL of S.C., Sir James WRIGHT of Ga., and Lord DUNMORE of Va. were forced early in the war to flee for safety; their overly optimistic reports of potential Loyalist support in the South led the British to undertake the ill-fated Charleston Expedition of Clinton in 1776. In any roster of royal governors a prominent place should be reserved for John Murray, 4th Earl of DUNMORE. The last royal governor of N.J. was William FRANKLIN, son of Benjamin Franklin. See Leonard W. Labaree, *Royal Gov-*

ernment in America (1930), and Evarts Boutell Greene, *The Provincial Governor in the English Colonies of North America* (1898).

ROYAL GREENS. A Provincial corps that figured prominently in the BORDER WARFARE waged out of Canada, they were raised by Sir John Johnson about the same time John Butler started recruiting BUTLER'S RANGERS. Although their leaders were hostile to each other, the Royal Greens and Butler's Rangers generally took part in the same operations. Johnson's commission as Col. was given to him in Montreal after he fled from the Mohawk Valley in May '77. He was authorized to raise two battalions, "entitled the Royal Greens from the color of their coats, which conformed to the customary uniforms of the Loyalist troops attached to the British army." (Ward, *W.O.R.,* 481) Accompanying ST. LEGER'S EXPEDITION against Ft. Stanwix with 133 men, the Royal Greens furnished 62 men for the advance guard and detachments took part in the ambush at ORISKANY, 6 Aug. '77. Characteristically, Sir John remained to the rear while the operations of the Greens and Butler's Rangers in this action were directed by John Butler. (See ORISKANY for story of the "turned coats.")

The Greens served under John Butler in the remarkable raid to the WYOMING VALLEY, held the center of the Tory line in the brief battle that took place, and subsequently performed well in a futile attempt to stop Sullivan's Expedition at NEWTOWN, N.Y., 29 Aug. '79. They took part (together with Butler's Rangers) in Sir John Johnson's first raid into the Mohawk Valley in the summer of 1780, fighting at KLOCK'S FIELD, 19 Oct. Four companies were with Walter Butler when he raided the Mohawk Valley in 1781, and they took part in the final action, at JERSEY-FIELD, 30 Oct. '81, when Walter Butler was killed.

ROYAL HIGHLAND EMIGRANTS. See Allan MacLEAN.

ROZENTHAL, Gustav. See ROSENTHAL.

RUDOLPH, John. *d.* 1782. Cont'l. officer. Md. Joining Lee's Legion as a Lt. of light dragoons on 20 Apr. '78, he was promoted to Capt. on 1 Oct. '78, to Maj. in 1781, and died 8 Dec. '82. (Heitman) Brother of Michael RUDOLPH.

RUDOLPH, Michael. Cont'l. officer of Lee's Legion. Md. Born about 1754, Michael and his brother John RUDOLPH joined LEE'S LEGION in Apr. '78, at which time Michael became Sgt.-Maj. (7 Apr.). A year later (1 Apr. '79) he was made Regt'l. Q.M., and three months later he was promoted to Lt., and in a resolution of the Cont'l. Cong. (24 Sept. '79) he and McALLISTER were breveted Capt. for their performances in leading the forlorn hopes at PAULUS HOOK, N.J., 19 Aug. (Heitman) On 1 Nov. '79 he received the actual rank of Capt. In the Southern Campaigns of Greene, Capt. Rudolph performed gallantly and effectively (there is a distinction) with the infantry of Lee's Legion, being mentioned particularly in connection with the actions at Guilford, Ninety-Six, and Eutaw Springs.

Serving to the end of the war (Heitman), he subsequently settled at Savannah and then became a farmer and collector of taxes at Sunbury, Ga. (Appleton's) He was commissioned Capt. of the 1st U.S. Inf. on 3 June '90, Maj. of Light Dragoons on 5 Mar. '92, and on 22 Feb. '93 he was named Adj. and Inspector of the Army. Resigning on 17 July of this year (Heitman) he entered the West Indies trade.

According to Appleton's, he "subsequently embarked for France to enter its military service, after which nothing more was heard of him." Heitman has information that he was drowned in 1795, presumably at sea.

RUDDLE'S STATION, Ky. See KY. RAID OF BIRD.

RUGELEY, Col. Henry. Tory officer. "In commission of the crown after the capitulation of Charleston," according to Sabine, Bass says he was "a Loyalist with a foot in each camp," and that when Gov. Rutledge and party were staying at his house he warned them in time to escape the pursuit of Tarleton that ended at WAXHAWS. (*Green Dragoon,* 79) Located 12 miles north of Camden on the road between that strategic place and Charlotte, N.C., his home—Clermont or Rugeley's Mill(s)—figured prominently in the war. His military career came to a humiliating end in the action known as RUGELEY'S MILLS, 4 Dec. '80, which prompted Cornwallis to write Tarleton: "Rugeley will not be made a brigadier." Lossing, who quotes this statement from Tarleton's *Memoirs,* says, "Poor Rugeley never appeared in arms afterward" (II, 666).

RUGELEY'S MILLS (Clermont), S.C., 4 Dec. '80. As part of Morgan's newly organized light corps, Col. Wm. Washington rode with his dragoons to investigate a report that Col. Henry Rugeley was there with a body of Tories. Washington found the enemy in a fortified log barn surrounded by a ditch and abatis. Unable to make any impression with small arms and lacking artillery, he tried the Quaker gun trick —making a fake cannon out of a pine log, moving it into view, and summoning the Tories to surrender or be blown to bits. It worked. Out came Col. Rugeley, a major, and a number of privates

variously reported at 107 to 112. These were marched back to the American camp, and the military career of RUGELEY was ended.

RUMFORD, Count. See Benjamin THOMPSON.

RUSH, Benjamin. 1746–1813. Physician, Signer. Pa. Six years after graduating from Princeton he entered the Univ. of Edinburgh to complete his medical studies. In June '68 he received his M.D. and went to London for intern training. At Edinburgh and London he showed a lively interest in what today is called social science. Young Dr. Rush returned to Philadelphia in 1769 and soon was appointed Prof. of chemistry at the Coll. of Philadelphia, the first such chair established in America. (*D.A.B.*) He also built up a successful medical practice and found time to associate with such patriot leaders as Thos. Paine, John Adams, and Thos. Jefferson. In London he had been on friendly terms with Benj. Franklin. In June '76 he took a leading part in the movement toward independence and the next month he became a delegate to the Cont'l. Cong. Thus he became a Signer.

Rush had volunteered in 1775 for service in the army, and on 11 Apr. '77 he became Surg. Gen. of the Middle Dept. (*D.A.B.* According to Heitman he had been "Surgeon in May, 1775– 1776.") His military career was brief. Not finding the administration of the medical service to his liking, he charged Dr. Wm. Shippen with inefficiency, but a Congressional investigation upheld Shippen. Dr. Rush then concluded that Washington's handling of military matters was unsatisfactory. After helping start what became known as the Conway Cabal, Rush wrote Patrick Henry anonymously from Yorktown on 12 Jan. '78 to recommend that Washington be replaced by Gates or Conway. Gov. Henry forwarded the letter to Washington, the latter recognized Rush's excellent penmanship and confronted him with this evidence of personal disloyalty. Rush resigned on 30 Apr. '78. (Heitman)

Returning to his practice, Rush soon started pioneering a number of social reforms: he established the first free dispensary in America (1786), became Pres. of the country's first antislavery society, demanded penal reforms, became what might facetiously be called "father of the W.C.T.U.," and was responsible for the establishment of Dickinson College (1783). In the political arena he urged acceptance of the federal Constitution and was rewarded by Pres. Adams with the post of Treas. of the U.S. Mint (1797–1813). In the field of medicine he developed a revolutionary "system" that, in simplest terms, was built around the hypothesis that all diseases resulted from too much or too little nervous stimulation and all could be treated the same way: by drastic bleeding (up to four fifths of the blood drained) and purging. This was soon condemned as idiotic and it is fortunate that Rush lacked either the time or the inclination to test his hypothesis.

Rush is credited with pioneering in a number of medical fields: experimental physiology, dental decay, veterinary training, and psychiatry. "He was, finally, the first medical man in the country to achieve a general literary reputation," writes R. H. Shryock in his fine *D.A.B.* article on this versatile and complex American. "Rush, therefore, was probably the best-known American physician of his day, though his reputation as a scientist was exaggerated because of his popularity as a teacher."

See N. G. Goodman, *Benj. Rush, Physician and Citizen, 1746–1813* (1934).

RUSSELL, William, Jr. 1758–1825. Militia officer. Va. Accompanying his family to the frontier as a child, he went on an expedition with Daniel Boone when he was 15. (Appleton's) During the Revolution he served as a militia Lt. and was at Kings Mountain, S.C., Oct. '80. (Heitman) As a militia Capt. he fought the Cherokees. According to Appleton's he also saw action at Wetzell's Mills and Guilford, N.C., in Mar. '81. (This would indicate that he served in the Va. militia under Wm. CAMPBELL.) Moving to Ky. after the war, he "bore an active part in almost every general expedition against the Indians until the settlement of the country, commanding the advance under Gen. John Hardin, Gen. Charles Scott, and Gen. James Wilkinson." (Appleton's) He led a regiment of Ky. volunteers in the final operations of Anthony Wayne. Active in the movement for statehood, he then was elected annually to the legislature until 1808, when President Madison appointed him Col. of the 7th U.S. Inf. Succeeding Gen. Wm. H. Harrison as commander of the Indiana–Illinois–Missouri frontier in 1811, he planned and led the expedition the next year against the Peoria Indians. (*Ibid.*)

RUSSELL, William (Sr.). d. 1793. Cont'l. officer. Va. Moving from Culpeper co. to the Va. frontier about 10 years before the Revolution, he became Col. of the 13th Va. on 19 Dec. '76 and transferred to the 5th Va. on 14 Sept. '78. He was taken prisoner at Charleston, 12 May '80, exchanged six months later, and served until 3 Nov. '83. On the latter date he was breveted B.G. (Heitman). Father of Wm. RUSSELL, Jr.

RUSSIA MERCHANT. This 243-ton British transport, carrying 200 artillery personnel (Embarkation Table in Uhlendorf, *Siege,* facing p. 108) foundered with valuable supplies needed for Clinton's CHARLESTON EXPED. of

1780. All personnel were apparently saved, but the ship sank with 4,000 muskets shipped for the use of Ga. Tories, which deprived the British of many armed irregulars. (Uhlendorf, *Siege*, 221, 299) The loss also made Clinton more dependent upon his naval commander, Arbuthnot, from whom he had to borrow guns, shot, and powder. (Clinton, 438, 439) Some of the artillerymen from the ship reached the Charleston lines on 6 Apr. '80 from the Bermudas. (*Siege*, 239)

RUTHERFORD, Griffith. c.1731–c.1800. Southern patriot. N.C. Born in Ireland, he settled west of Salisbury. In 1775 he sat in the Prov. Cong., and on 22 June '76 this body elected him B.G. of state troops. In the CHEROKEE WAR OF 1776 he led 2,400 troops into the rugged Indian country in Sept. '76. He took part in the unsuccessful efforts to keep the British from overrunning Ga. in the winter of 1778–79, leading 800 men to reinforce Lincoln; his command was posted at Mathew's Bluff, S.C., when the patriots were defeated, five miles away, at BRIAR CREEK, 3 Mar. '79. Returning to N.C., he called out the militia to inflict a decisive defeat on the Tories at RAMSEUR'S MILL, 20 June '80, although he himself did not arrive in time to take part in the battle. He commanded a brigade at Camden, 16 Aug. '80, was wounded there (Heitman), and was captured by Tarleton in the pursuit that followed the battle. (Ward, 731)

Held prisoner first at Charleston and then at St. Augustine, he was exchanged 22 June '81 and returned to the field. He took command of Wilmington after its evacuation on 18 Nov. '81. Off and on until 1786 he served in the N.C. senate. During the period of reconstruction he was identified with the Democrats or Radicals who demanded majority rule, social equality, and destruction of privileges. He advocated harshness toward ex-Tories, whom he called "imps of hell." (Alden, *South*, 311, 326)

He moved into what became the state of Tenn. and after Sept. '94, when this became a separate territory, was president of the legislative council. (Appleton's)

Counties and colleges in N.C. and Tenn. are named for him, as is Rutherfordton (formerly Gilbert Town), N.C.

RUTLEDGE, Edward (Ned). 1749–1800. Congressman, Signer, Gov. of S.C. Seventh and youngest child of Dr. John Rutledge, he was 10 years younger than the brother whose path he followed through life. Edward entered the Middle Temple in 1767, was admitted to the English bar in 1772, returned to Charleston in Jan. '73, and a few months later represented the printer Thos. Powell in a famous case before Assist. Justice Rawlins Lowndes (who preceded his brother as Gov. of S.C. in 1778–79). Elected with brother John to the 1st Cont'l. Cong., the youthful Edward was characterized by acid John Adams as "a perfect Bob-o-Lincoln —a swallow, a sparrow, . . . jejune, inane and puerile." On another occasion he commented, "Rutledge is a very uncouth and ungraceful speaker; he shrugs his shoulders, distorts his body, nods and wriggles with his head, and looks about with his eyes from side to side, and speaks through his nose, as the Yankees sing. His brother John dodges his head too, rather disagreeably, and both of them spout out their language in a rough and rapid torrent, without much force or effect." (John Adams, *Works* [1850–56], II, 401, 422) What most irritated the New England Yankees, with what Rutledge called their "low Cunning, and those levelling Principles" (29 June '76 ltr. to John Jay), was *what* the undemocratic brothers had to say in Congress more than how they said it. "Our claims, I think, are well founded on the British constitution," said Edward Rutledge to the delegates of the 1st Cont'l. Cong., "and not on the law of nature." Taking over leadership of the delegation after the departure of his brother and Gadsden, in 1776 Edward delayed action on the resolution for independence almost a month before finally influencing his delegation to vote for it on 2 July. He felt that confederation should have preceded independence, but he was afraid of a strong central government. In all this he represented the views of the planter oligarchy of his state.

After accompanying John Adams and Benjamin Franklin to the PEACE CONFERENCE ON STATEN ISLAND, 11 Sept. '76 in Nov. '76 Rutledge returned to S.C. "The state gained a captain of artillery but lost a delegate in Congress whose service in the critical years to come would have been of greatest assistance," comments R. L. Meriwether in *D.A.B.* After taking part in the action at Beaufort (Port Royal), 3 Feb. '79, he became a prisoner when Charleston surrendered on 12 May '80. (Alden, *South,* 241; *D.A.B.;* Heitman. Appleton's says Lincoln sent him out of the city in May to speed the arrival of reinforcements and he was captured while on this mission.) Meanwhile he had been re-elected in 1779 to Congress but did not attend. (Appleton's says sickness prevented his going.) Imprisoned at St. Augustine from Sept. '80 to July '81, he lived in Philadelphia until most of the South had been liberated by Greene. He returned in time to sit in the Jacksonboro Assembly that his brother called to convene in Jan. '82.

After the war he prospered in private and public life. He retained his aristocratic outlook while representing Charleston in the House of Representatives, 1782–96, and in the state conventions of 1788 and 1790. He was an influential Federalist. In 1796 and 1798 he was state senator, and in the latter year was elected Gov. Already in bad health, he died six months before his elder brother and nearly a year before the end of his term.

Edward's first wife was Henrietta, daughter of Henry Middleton, whom he married in 1774. C. C. Pinckney was a brother-in-law by marriage to Henrietta's sister Sarah. Edward's brother Hugh (*c.* 1741–1811), jurist and politician, was imprisoned with him at St. Augustine; their elder brother, Gov. John RUTLEDGE, left Charleston a month before its surrender.

RUTLEDGE, John. 1739–1800. Congressman, Gov. of S.C. Eldest son of Dr. John and Sarah Hext Rutledge, he was born shortly after his mother's 15th birthday. He became a brilliant lawyer in Charleston after studying in the Middle Temple and being admitted to the English bar in 1760. Because of his ability, his personal qualities, and his identification with the interests of the ruling planter element of S.C., John Rutledge progressed inexorably from representative of Christ Church Parish (near Charleston) in the Commons House (1761) to delegate to the Cont'l. Cong. (1774–75), and Pres. of the S.C. Gen. Assembly (1776–78). He resigned in Mar. '78 after opposing a liberalization of the state constitution, but in the desperate situation that was presented by the British invasion of the South (see SAVANNAH, 29 Dec. '78), Rutledge was elected Gov. in Jan. '79, being the first patriot to hold that post. (His predecessor, Rawlins Lowndes, had been the last to use the title of Pres. of S.C.) When Gen. Prevost menaced CHARLESTON, 11–12 May '79, the new Gov. favored the proposal by his council that the state should promise the

British to remain neutral if Prevost would withdraw. The historian Ramsay thinks this was a ruse to buy time, but *D.A.B.* says "Rutledge's purposes in the affair are obscure, and the whole matter is involved in contradictions." The honor of S.C. was saved by opposition to this deal from Gadsden, John Laurens, and Moultrie, and Lincoln arrived by forced marches to make Prevost withdraw.

When Clinton closed in on Charleston in Mar. '80 the Assembly adjourned after giving Rutledge virtual carte blanche. A month before Charleston's surrender, Rutledge slipped out of the doomed city to rally state resources in the interior. Tarleton was trying to capture him when the warning of Col. Henry RUGELEY saved him. Rutledge withdrew across the N.C. border and joined the army of Gates in its move toward Camden. He commissioned Thos. Sumter, Francis Marion, and other militia officers to conduct partisan operations. He wrote to the Cont'l. Cong. and Washington and he visited Philadelphia to urge that American regulars be sent to liberate the South.

Returning to his state in Aug. '81, he skilfully tackled the tremendous economic, legal, and military problems left in the wake of Greene's successful campaign. On 20 Nov. he called for election of members of a legislature to meet at Jacksonboro on 8 Jan. '82. After receiving a glowing tribute for his services, on 29 Jan. he vacated the office in which he could not succeed himself and a few days later took his seat as member from St. Andrew's Parish. He returned to Congress to sit from May '82 to Sept. '83, and the next year he started his judicial career after being elected to the state chancery court. In Feb. '91 he was elected chief justice of S.C. after accepting an appointment as senior associate justice of the U.S. Supreme Court and resigning it for the state position. In response to Rutledge's request in June '95 to succeed John Jay as Chief Justice, Washington immediately nominated him. At the same time, however, Jay's Treaty was published and Rutledge killed his chances of Senate confirmation by leading a bitter attack on the treaty. Since the death of his wife, Elizabeth Grimké, in 1792, Rutledge had showed signs of insanity. About the time the Senate rejected his nomination, Dec. '95, he was forced by his derangement to withdraw from public life.

"The most gifted and devoted leader of the ruling group of eighteenth-century South Carolina, John Rutledge embodied, perhaps, more perfectly than any other man, the ideas of his class," concludes R. L. Meriwether in his *D.A.B.* sketch.

Elder brother of Edward RUTLEDGE.

S

SACKVILLE, George. See GERMAIN.

SAG HARBOR RAID, N.Y. 23–24 May '77. In retaliation for Tryon's Danbury Raid, Col. Meigs planned an attack against a British foraging party that had gone from N.Y.C. to Sag Harbor, near the eastern end of Long Island. The British force comprised 12 vessels, an armed schooner of 12 guns that carried 40 men, and a 70-man company of Stephen De Lancey's Bn. Leaving Guilford, Conn., with 170 men in 13 whaleboats and escorted by two armed sloops, Meigs moved under cover of darkness through the British cruisers in the Sound, landed on Long Island, and surprised the Tories before dawn. After killing six, capturing the rest, burning all the vessels except the schooner, and destroying the stores, Meigs withdrew without the loss of a man. He was back at Guilford by noon, having covered almost 100 miles in 18 hours. (*D.A.B.*, "Meigs, R. J."; Ward, *W.O.R.*, 323–24). Although most authorities give 23 May as the date of this exploit, Heitman says Return Jonathan MEIGS was promoted 10 Sept. '77 to rank from 12 May '77; this latter date, if correct, would indicate that the raid took place on 12 May.

ST. CLAIR (pronounced sinclair), Arthur. 1737–1818. Cont'l. general. Scotland–Mass.–Pa. Probably the son of Wm. Sinclair, according to Randolph C. Downes in *D.A.B.*, and a great-grandson of the second Laird of Assery, not of the Earl or Baron of Roslyn, as is sometimes stated. (*Ibid.*) "It is said that he enjoyed the advantages of an incomplete term at the University of Edinburgh and an unsuccessful apprenticeship under William Hunter, the celebrated anatomist of London," comments Downes. (*Op. cit.*) After getting a considerable inheritance from his mother, Arthur bought an ensign's commission in the 60th Foot ("Royal Americans") on 13 May '57. In America he took part in Amherst's capture of Louisburg, Wolfe's attack on Quebec, was promoted to Lt. on 17 Apr. '59, resigned on 16 Apr. '62, and settled in Boston. After his Mass. wife inherited £14,000 he moved to the Pa. frontier where he used this money and his own military service claims to buy some 4,000 acres in the Ligonier Valley. This made him

the largest resident landowner "beyond the mountains," and he soon attained considerable influence. He was involved in the ugly land disputes between Pa. and Va., but the latter province had gained the upper hand and St. Clair was able to do little. In July '75 he became Col. of a militia regiment, and in the fall be played a minor role in negotiations with Indians at Ft. Pitt. On 3 Jan. '76 he became Col. 2d Pa. Bn., led them north, and took part in the disaster at TROIS RIVIÈRES, Can., 8 June. On 9 Aug. he was appointed B.G. and in Nov. joined Washington's army. Authorized by the C. in C. to raise N.J. militia, he was at TRENTON and Princeton. On 19 Feb. '77 he was promoted to Maj. Gen. and returned to the Northern Dept. to succeed Gates as commander on Lake Champlain.

His abandonment of TICONDEROGA, 2–5 July '77, climaxed his career as a field commander. As discussed under that article, although St. Clair was not of Maj. Gen. caliber, he used sound military judgment in not risking his command in the defense of this untenable position and showed rare moral courage in ordering the withdrawal. Furthermore, his plans for this difficult operation were excellent; they were ruined by incompetent subordinates. A court-martial in 1778 cleared him, but in their search for a scapegoat many people suspected St. Clair of disloyalty. His foreign birth made this suspicion seem even more plausible, and when Arnold's treason in 1780 brought rumors that another high-ranking American officer was involved in dealings with the enemy St. Clair's name was again mentioned. (See CHAMPE)

The discredited general served Washington as a volunteer A.D.C. at Brandywine, assisted Sullivan in mounting his expedition against the Indians, was a commissioner to arrange a cartel with the British at Amboy on 9 Mar. '80, served on the board that investigated André's conduct, and commanded West Point in Oct. '80. He had a minor part in settling the Mutiny of the Pa. Line, helped raise troops for the Yorktown Campaign, and joined Washington a few days before Cornwallis surrendered. Soon thereafter he led 2,000 regulars south to reinforce Greene, joining him near Charleston on 4 Jan. '82. On 3 Nov. '83 he retired from the Cont'l. Army.

The fact that St. Clair had no important military assignment during the last four years of the war would imply that Washington questioned his loyalty as well as his competence. "The truth was undramatic; St. Clair was so busy with his own affairs and, during part of 1781, was so concerned over the illness of his wife, that he did not feel he could take the field," says Freeman. "His record was clean; the minds of some of his critics were not." (Freeman, *Washington*, V, 169B)

St. Clair was in Congress from 2 Nov. '85 to 28 Nov. '87, and ended as president of that body. He became the first governor of the Northwest Territory, 1789–1802. On 4 Mar. '91 he was named Maj. Gen. and commander of the U.S. Army. Badly defeated by the Miami Indians under Little Turtle on 4 Nov., he was refused a court of inquiry and on 5 Mar. '92 resigned his military commission. A Congressional investigation cleared him of responsibility for the disaster. Jefferson removed him as Gov. in 1802 because St. Clair opposed statehood for Ohio. In 1812 he published a defense of his Indian campaign, and six years later died in poverty. (Appleton's)

See Wm. H. Smith, *The Life and Public Services of Arthur St. Clair* (Cincinnati, 1882), which includes his letters and other papers.

ST. EUSTATIUS. Taken by the Dutch in 1632, this island of about 8 square miles in size, located 8 miles N.W. of St. Kitts, had become one of the leading centers of West Indies trade in the 18th century. At the beginning of the Revolution it became established as a center of contraband trade between Europe and America, even British merchants being involved. Gov. Johannes de Graaf was recalled as a result of British diplomatic pressure, but although evidently guilty of encouraging trade with the rebels he was exonerated and sent back to his post. When Adm. George Rodney learned that Holland had entered the war he moved almost immediately against the Dutch island and captured it 3 Feb. '81. (See George RODNEY) The French recaptured the island on 25 Nov. '81. See John Franklin Jameson, "St. Eustatius in the American Revolution," *Amer. Hist. Rev.*, VIII (1903).

ST. FRANCIS INDIANS. See ABENAKI.

ST. JOHN (Acadia), Quebec. This place, now in New Brunswick, Canada, is likely to be confused with ST. JOHNS on the Richelieu River, now called St. Jean, in Quebec Province, Canada. (See, for example, Moses HAZEN) St. John's (written with apostrophe) is in Newfoundland.

ST. JOHNS, Canada (now called St. Jean), 14–18 May '75. As part of the operation against TICONDEROGA, 10 May, the Americans had sent a detachment to capture Skenesboro. The afternoon of 14 May (Dawson, *Battles*, I, 36) this party reported to Arnold with a captured schooner, and Arnold immediately headed for St. Johns with 50 of his men in the vessel. Allen followed in bateaux with about 60 men. Early on the 17th Arnold surprised the 15-man British garrison; captured the 70-ton sloop *George III* (16 guns); destroyed five bateaux; evacuated the prisoners, some stores, and four bateaux; and headed back for Ticonderoga. About 15 miles away he encountered Allen, who —despite Arnold's advice—decided he would occupy and hold St. Johns. Allen landed just before dark and made dispositions to ambush the British relief column advancing from Chambly, 12 miles away. He then was prevailed on to withdraw his undisciplined, tired, and hungry men. Having recrossed the river, he was attacked before dawn by 200 men and six guns. Allen retreated with the loss of three men captured. (*Ibid.;* Ward, *W.O.R.,* 69–70)

USAGE NOTE. This place is called Saint John on some early maps and in some correspondence, writes Freeman, but "Americans nearly always spoke of it as Saint John's." (*Washington,* III, 561 *n.*) It is now commonly called St. Johns in the U.S., St. Jean-Iberville in Canada. Since it consisted of little more than the fort, the settlement would more properly be called Fort St. Johns. See next article for strategic importance of this place.

ST. JOHNS, Canada, 5 Sept.–2 Nov. '75. (CANADA INVASION) Twenty miles S.E. of Montreal and near the head of navigation from Lake Champlain down the Richelieu (or Sorel) River to the St. Lawrence, St. Johns occupied a critical position along a historic invasion route. Military works established there by Montcalm in 1758 were enlarged and strengthened by Carleton in 1775. The settlement comprised a barracks, some brick buildings, and a stone house; around these had been constructed two redoubts. When the Americans approached on 5 Sept., the place was defended by 200 regulars, several cannon, a small Indian contingent, and the British were building two 60-foot, 12-

gun vessels. Maj. Chas. Preston was in command of the post.

On 17 Aug., Schuyler left Montgomery in temporary command on Lake Champlain and went to Albany for a meeting. When Montgomery learned shortly thereafter that the two ships at St. Johns were nearing completion (threatening to seize control of Lake Champlain), he decided to move against this threat without waiting for Schuyler's approval. On 28 Aug., he started toward Ile aux Noix, a swampy island in the Richelieu, 20 miles south of St. Johns; here he intended to set up defenses that would bar passage of the two newly constructed ships into the lake.

Montgomery's command comprised about 1,200 men and a few cannon; their advance was made in a small fleet of two sailing vessels (the sloop *Enterprise* and schooner *Liberty*), gondolas, bateaux, rowing galleys, piraguas, and canoes. (Ward, *W.O.R.,* 150) Troops involved were most of Waterbury's Conn. Regt., four companies of Ritzema's 4th N.Y., and Mott's small artillery section. (*Ibid.*)

Schuyler caught up with his aggressive subordinate the morning of 4 Sept., (surprisingly) approved his action, and that night the invaders were at Ile aux Noix. Although the expected Canadian allies did not appear to reinforce them, Schuyler stripped his men of baggage and pushed toward St. Johns. Landing a mile and a half away, the Americans were advancing through the swamps to attack when a flank patrol was ambushed by 100 Indians under the command of a N.Y. Tory (Capt. Tice). A skirmish developed in the dense underbrush; the Indians were driven off, but the Americans lost 16 men and did not pursue. That night a man who was apparently sympathetic to the American cause visited Schuyler's entrenched camp and convinced him that St. Johns was too strongly held for him to capture.

Back on Ile aux Noix, Schuyler was soon reinforced to 1,700 men. (Ironically, this was more than twice the entire strength of British regulars in Canada.) The ailing Schuyler organized a second attack, which was undertaken the night of 10 Sept. Ritzema's 500 New Yorkers landed and started through the heavy woods with the mission of investing St. Johns from the north. Colliding in the dark with part of Gen. Montgomery's covering force, which had moved into position near the camp abandoned on 6 Sept., the skittish New Yorkers thought they were ambushed. Most of them stampeded back to the boats, but Montgomery rallied some of these heroes and sent them forward again. A second rout occurred when a few rounds of British artillery shook the trees around them, but Ritzema managed to hold together some 50 troops and continue the advance. Ritzema was halted by fire from a small house and, although reinforcements came forward, he stopped the action at about 3 A.M. and withdrew to the beachhead. Another advance had been organized the next morning when the men were panicked by a report that the *Royal Savage,* one of the new ships, was near their boats and ready to go into action.

Back on Ile aux Noix, Montgomery assumed command on 16 Sept. when Schuyler was invalided to the rear. Despite a sick list of 600, and all the makings of a mutiny among his demoralized, ill-disciplined troops, Montgomery was able to resume the offensive. He had received additional reinforcements: 170 GREEN MOUNTAIN BOYS under Seth Warner, 100 N.H. Rangers under Timothy Bedel, and an Independent Company of Volunteers

that included some Dartmouth students. Others were on the way.

THE BRITISH DEFENSE

Rather than pull in his outposts and concentrate his meager forces around Montreal and Quebec, Gen. Guy Carleton adopted a "forward strategy": he reinforced St. Johns to a total of 500 regulars from the 7th ("Royal Fusiliers") and 26th ("Cameronians"). Another 90 officers and men of the 7th Regt. were posted at nearby Chambly. Preston was further reinforced by 225 men scraped together from all the sources at Carleton's disposal: an ensign and 12 sailors from the *Gaspée,* 100 Canadian militia, and 70 of Allan MacLean's newly recruited Royal Highland Emigrants.

As for what Freeman calls Montgomery's "soldierly advance and investment" (*Washington,* III, 561), the Americans, suffering from cold weather, struggling to construct their lines and batteries in the swampy ground, beset by illness, and short on supplies, were having a bad go of it. Although an effective artillery fire could be delivered into the British camp, this has never been sufficient to make good soldiers quit, and the Americans were incapable of taking the place by assault. The forces under Montgomery were an undisciplined, untrained group over whom the officers had little control. "The men had to be coddled," writes Ward, "their permission obtained before this or that could be done. At one time, when Montgomery wanted to erect a battery in a certain position, his field officers absolutely refused to do so." (*W.O.R.,* 158)

With the surrender of CHAMBLY, 18 Oct., however, the Americans obtained supplies that permitted successful conclusion of the siege. Carleton's attempt to rescue Preston was stopped at LONGUEUIL, 30 Oct., when American forces kept the British from crossing the St. Lawrence; another detachment kept MacLean from crossing farther up the river. After having delayed the American invasion almost two months, and with only three days' supplies left, Preston surrendered St. Johns on 2 Nov. '75. Among the prisoners was John ANDRÉ. Although Carleton lost almost all his regular troops at St. Johns and Chambly, they forced the Americans to fight a winter campaign, and in so doing had bought him time that may have saved Canada for the British. (Alden, *Amer. Rev.*, 51)

ST. KITTS CAPTURED BY FRENCH, 11 Jan.–12 Feb. '82.

After his decisive part in the Yorktown Campaign, De Grasse returned to Martinique with his fleet on 26 Nov. '81. Bad weather frustrated his attack on Barbados. He then undertook an operation against St. Kitts (or St. Christopher). On 11 Jan. '82 he reached the British island with a powerful fleet and 6,000 troops. Landing unopposed the same day, he captured Basseterre and drove the 600 or 700 British regulars and local militia back to the famous Brimstone Hill, nine miles from the city. Since the position was too strong for assault, the French started siege operations. Adm. Samuel Hood, learning of the situation, sailed from Barbados on 14 Jan., stopped at Antigua for the 700 men who could be spared, and on the 24th appeared off St. Kitts. During the next three weeks Hood with 22 ships against 29 conducted what Mahan calls "the most brilliant military effort of the whole war." (*Sea Power*, 470) In a few words, Hood drew the French from their anchorage, took up their former position, and then held it against the odds already stated. These operations of the 25th and 26th also enabled British troops to land, on the 28th. Gen. Robert Prescott, who commanded the landing

force, easily defeated the French effort to eliminate his beachhead and then sent two officers to make contact with the defenders of Brimstone Hill commanded by Gen. Fraser. Since Hood had destroyed the French ammunition ships, which made it impossible for them to conduct a siege, Fraser sent word to Prescott that he needed no help. But guns and ammunition sent to Fraser by the governor of the island fell into enemy hands, and the picture changed. By 12 Feb. the 600 or 700 defenders had lost more than 150 men killed and wounded; many were sick and exhausted, and the militia that did not desert petitioned Fraser to surrender. The garrison capitulated on this day. Hood slipped away at 11 o'clock the evening of the 14th. (See WEST INDIES for subsequent operations.)

ST. LEGER, Barry. 1737–1789.

British officer. Of Huguenot descent—the pronunciation of his name is given variously as sill' in-ger and saint leg' er— he was a nephew of the 4th Viscount Doneraile and a fellow of St. Peter's college, Cambridge. On 27 Apr. '56 he entered the army as an Ensign of the 28th Foot and during the French and Indian War he became known as a good leader in frontier warfare. His experience in this war included service under Abercromby in 1757, the siege of Louisburg, and the capture of Quebec by Wolfe in 1759. In July '60 he became Brig.-Maj., in which capacity he participated in the campaign that captured Montreal. On 16 Aug. '62 he was promoted to Maj. of the 95th Foot.

As a Lt. Col. he led ST. LEGER'S EXPEDITION, June–8 Sept. '77, the operation for which he is generally remembered. During the remainder of the Revolution he commanded a body of rangers in operations based on Montreal, being promoted to Col. in 1780. In 1781 he led two unsuccessful expeditions, one whose mission was to capture Philip Schuyler and another to meet commissioners from Vermont at Ticonderoga to bring that region back under crown control. His name disappears from the Army List after 1785, and he served until this time in Canada. *St. Leger's Journal of Occurrences in America* was published in London in 1780.

ST. LEGER'S EXPEDITION, June–Sept. '77. (BURGOYNE'S OFFENSIVE) In his "Thoughts for Conducting the War on the Side of Canada," Burgoyne had recommended a small diversionary effort under Lt. Col. Barry St. Leger to move down the Mohawk Valley and link up with the main effort at Albany. Although this would have some military value, the main purpose was political. See TRYON COUNTY, N.Y. St. Leger, appointed a temporary B.G., left Montreal on 23 June '77, reached Oswego on 25 July, and started his offensive the next day. (At this time Burgoyne was almost to the Hudson.) St. Leger had about 2,000 officers and men. Half of these were Indians, a third were Tory and Canadian auxiliaries, and 340 were regulars. The latter were from the British 8th and 34th Regts. and the Hesse-Hanau jägers—about 100 from each unit; 40 were artillerymen. His white auxiliaries, about 360 rank and file, included Johnson's Royal Greens, Butler's Tory Rangers, and some Canadian militia. Two 6-pdrs., two 3-pdrs., and four small mortars comprised his artillery support; these guns were too few and too light to be effective in reducing fortifications that might be encountered, and inadequate provision had been made for ammunition supply.

The invaders advanced at the creditable rate of 10 miles a day through the wilderness and the vanguard reached Ft. Stanwix on 2 Aug., just too late to prevent 200 American reinforcements from entering the fort. The next day the main body arrived to invest the American garrison of 750. British intelligence had seriously underestimated the size of the garrison and the condition of the old fort. St. Leger tried to bluff the defenders into capitulation by staging a review within their sight, but the presence of his Indians convinced the garrison that neither they nor the settlements they protected could expect any quarter from these savages. Lacking the means for an immediate assault, St. Leger laid siege.

THE AMERICAN DEFENSES

Strategic FT. STANWIX had been reoccupied by Col. Peter Gansevoort's 3d N.Y. Cont'ls. in Apr. '77. He had 550 men and an exceptionally capable second in command, Marinus Willett. By the time the British arrived they had gotten the abandoned and dilapidated old fort in a state of defense. St. Leger's three main positions formed a triangle about a mile on each side. His principal post, occupied by the regulars, was somewhat more than a quarter of a mile N.E. of the fort and on slightly higher ground. At a place called the Lower Landing, on the right (west) bank of the Mohawk and half a mile from the fort, most of the Tories and Indians were located. At the other point of the triangle, half a mile from the fort, a Tory post was established on Wood Creek. A cordon of Indians stretched along the edge of a wooded swamp S.W. of the fort and between the last two main positions. Indians were posted also on the left (east) bank of the Mohawk opposite the Lower Landing. (Nickerson, *Turning Point*, 210; Ward, *W.O.R.*, 484) The British commander lacked the numbers to make this a tight investment, particularly since he had to detach large work parties to clear Wood Creek and to cut 16 miles of supply track through the woods.

While Indian marksmen and jägers sniped at the fort on 4 and 5 Aug., fewer than 250 regulars were held in camp, and most of the other white troops were detached on work details. The evening of the 5th, St. Leger got word from Molly BRANT that an American relief column was 10 miles away. Although his forces were already dispersed, the British commander accepted the danger of splitting them further.

ORISKANY, 6 Aug., was a tactical draw but, since it turned back Herkimer's relief column, it was a strategic victory for the invaders, at least temporarily. In the long run, however, it caused St. Leger's failure. First, the Indians, who had been encouraged to accompany the expedition with the promise of much looting and little serious fighting, had borne the brunt of this first battle—they felt St. Leger had not kept his word. Then, they returned to find that an American raid on their camp had left them to finish the campaign with nothing more than their battle dress, a breech clout, between them and the night air. Messengers sent ahead of Herkimer's relief column had reached Ft. Stanwix between 10 and 11 A.M., after the militia had blundered into the trap. They had been sent to inform Gansevoort of Herkimer's approach and to ask that a sortie be made as a diversion. Unfortunately, they were delayed. St. Leger's men had seen the messengers arrive and, since they were now outnumbered three to one (white troops) around the fort they expected the worst. However, Gansevoort missed his opportunity and limited his counterstroke to an attack on the Tory and Indian camps. After waiting for the end of the same shower that caused the lull at Oriskany, Willett sallied forth with 250 men and one cannon, scattered the few enemy in his way, and methodically looted the abandoned camps. Sir John Johnson fled in his shirt sleeves, leaving everything including his personal papers. The Americans withdrew before St. Leger could intervene with the regulars. In what Nickerson calls "a pretty little action," they had not lost a man.

ARNOLD RELIEVES STANWIX

When news of Oriskany reached Schuyler at Stillwater, that embattled commander was faced with a nasty situation. Burgoyne's 7,000 were at Ft. Edward, a mere 24 miles away. Although Schuyler correctly figured that Burgoyne would allow him time to detach troops for the relief of Ft. Stanwix, the New England faction of his command all but openly accused him of neglecting the safety of their own region by favoring the protection of his own. Controlling his rage at implications of treachery from his own subordinates, Schuyler announced he would personally accept responsibility for sending relief to Ft. Stanwix. When he called for a brigadier general to command the expedition, Maj. Gen. Benedict Arnold claimed the post.

At Ft. Stanwix, however, the sands were running out. The evening of the Oriskany ambush Gansevoort received a letter from two American prisoners, Col. Peter Bellinger and Maj. Frey, presumably under duress, "which contained many misrepresentations and a recommendation to cease resistance." (In quoting this passage from Lossing [I, 248], Howard Swiggett implies that no coercion was involved [*War out of Niagara*, 88].) When Gansevoort told John BUTLER he would talk only to St. Leger, Butler returned the next day with British Maj. Ancrom and another officer to inform the American commander of the enemy's terms: the Indians had reluctantly agreed to spare American lives and personal property if the garrison would surrender; otherwise, St. Leger would probably be powerless to prevent the savages from massacring the inhabitants of the valley. "Colonel Gansevort nobly replied in the negative," reports Thacher. (*Mil. Journal,* 89) A more dramatic version is that Willett blasted Ancrom with words ending, "the message you have brought is a degrading one for a British officer to send and by no means reputable for a British officer to carry." (Ward, who with Nickerson apparently credits this last version, comments that the conference is fully reported in Willett's *Narrative,* 55–58; this source citation leads one to suspect that the mighty sword of Marinus Willett had close competition from his pen. Swiggett does not mention this alleged reply of Willett's, but quotes the "grand letter" of Gansevoort to St. Leger that night stating his determination to hold the fort "at every hazard, to the last extremity, in behalf of the United American States who have placed me here to defend it against all their enemies." Swiggett quotes the letter without identifying his source; C. & M., 566 *n.,* cites W. W. Campbell, *Annals of Tryon County,* 80.)

Gansevoort agreed to St. Leger's proposal for a three-day armistice. Willett and another officer (Lt. Stockwell) slipped away at 1 A.M. on 9 Aug., waited several hours in the cedar swamp until getting their bearings from the morning star, and reached Schuyler at Stillwater. (Swiggett, 89) Arnold left the next night with 800 men—Livingston's 1st N.Y. and some of Learned's Mass. (*Ibid.*) (Nickerson says he had no fewer than 950 Cont'ls., and that Arnold met Willett before the latter reached Schuyler [271, 272]). Slowed by "abominal roads" (*ibid.*), Arnold reached Ft. Dayton on 21 Aug. and accepted the decision of a council of war not to advance further until reinforced. The Tryon County militia had lost enthusiasm after Oriskany and had

turned out only 100 men to support him. The next day, however, Arnold learned that the enemy had pushed REGULAR APPROACHES to within 150 yards of Ft. Stanwix's N.W. bastion, so he pushed forward. After covering 10 miles from Ft. Dayton on 23 Aug. Arnold got a message from Gansevoort: St. Leger was retreating. They had been routed by an idiot, but a foxy one.

HON YOST'S RUSE

A halfwit called Hon Yost SCHUYLER had been condemned to death for association with a Tory plot. Lt. Col. John Brooks of Arnold's advance guard is credited by Thacher with suggesting a stratagem which Arnold readily approved. Hon Yost had lived among the Indians and, "like all mental defectives, he was looked upon by the savages with awe and reverence." (Nickerson, 273) In return for a reprieve he was to go among St. Leger's Indians and tell exaggerated stories of Arnold's strength to make them desert. Meanwhile, his brother would be held hostage. Hon Yost played the role with enthusiasm, skill, and cunning, enlisting the support of other Indians to follow him into the British camp and corroborate his story. The stratagem worked, and the Indians not only started deserting but turned against their former ally, massacring stragglers and plundering. On 23 Aug. Hon Yost met Arnold's advancing column to report his mission accomplished.*

Arnold reached Ft. Stanwix the eve-

* Although historians generally accept the story of Hon Yost's trick, it was probably not decisive in routing St. Leger inasmuch as the Indians had already lost interest in the operation. Those who had not already deserted St. Leger would probably have done so before Arnold reached Ft. Stanwix.

ning of the 23d and the next day sent a pursuing force after St. Leger, and a handful of the more persistent reached Lake Oneida just in time to see the last enemy boats pull out of range. Leaving about 700 at Ft. Stanwix, Arnold started to the rear with 1,200 men and rejoined the main army the first week of Sept. as it moved to the battlefield near SARATOGA.

ST. LOUIS (Mo.), 26 May '80. A British expedition sent out by Lt. Gov. Patrick Sinclair from Michilimackinac was repulsed by Capt. Don Fernando de Leyba, Spanish commandant of San Luis de Ylinoises (modern St. Louis, Mo.). Sinclair had hoped that with the support of the "very noted Chief Machiquawish and his band of Indians," and under the leadership of "Mr. Hesse, a trader and a man of character (formerly in the 60th Regiment)," this expedition could reduce the Spanish post and ultimately push on to Natchez. (C. & M., 1052) The Spanish reported that Hesse (whom they called "Esse") had 300 regulars and 900 Indians, obviously an exaggeration. Defenders numbered 29 "veteran soldiers" and 281 "countrymen," according to the same source. (*Ibid.*, 1053) A Spanish counteroffensive, against Detroit, took FT. ST. JOSEPH, Jan. '81.

ST. LUC DE LA CORNE, Pierre (or Louis). French Canadian soldier. Known by many variations of this name (see below), according to Appleton's he was a French Canadian who was with Sieur Joncaire on a mission to the Indians of Niagara in 1720, took part with M. de St. Pierre in the defeat of the Indians at Lachine Rapids in 1747, went with De Ramezay to Acadia and succeeded that officer as commander when he was wounded at Grand Pré, and with Father La Loutre tried unsuccessfully in 1749 to induce the Acadians to leave British territory and move north of the Bay of

Fundy. (Appleton's, "La Corne, Pierre") Prominent in military events in Canada that followed, he was wounded at the Rapids, Lake Ontario, in 1759 as a commander of French colonial troops, and was again wounded when Wolfe took Quebec that same year. (*Ibid.*)

When Canada passed into British hands St. Luc started a long and effective career in organizing and leading Indian auxiliaries. Peckham has found evidence that he was attempting (unsuccessfully) to get the Indians around the mouth of the St. Lawrence to take the warpath against the British in the uprising that became known as Pontiac's War (1763). (*Pontiac,* 106) At the start of the Revolution St. Luc worked to organize Indians of the "Seven Nations," who were allies of the Iroquois ("Six Nations") and included the savage ABENAKIS and the CAUGHNAWAGAS. Although St. Luc bought the allegiance of some younger Caughnawaga braves, the older men made them return the money. (Ward, *W.O.R.,* 142) During the siege of Saint Johns by Montgomery in Sept.–Nov. '75, St. Luc sent over some Caughnawagas to propose an "accommodation." Distrusting the Frenchman who was notorious as a "fiend incarnate" and held responsible for the massacre of prisoners at Ft. William Henry in 1757 (*ibid.,* 142), Montgomery nevertheless investigated the proposal. "He is a great villain and as cunning as the devil," he wrote at the time, "but I have sent a *New Englander* to negotiate with him." The conference between the "devil" and the *"New Englander,"* John BROWN, came to nothing. (*Ibid.,* 159–60) St. Luc and Carleton were repulsed at LONGUEUIL, 30 Oct. '75, when they attempted to relieve Saint Johns. With Langlade—who had served with him against Ft. William Henry in 1757—St. Luc led the Indians of Burgoyne's Offensive and is said to have advised the British commander not to punish the culprit charged with the McCREA ATROCITY. (*Ibid.*, 496 *n.*) In the BENNINGTON RAID the Indians were led by St. Luc and the Canadians by his son-in-law, Charles de Lanaudière. (*Ibid.*, 428)

Described as "the white-haired French noble, a courtier off the trail and a savage on it," he was largely responsible for the British use of Indians as an instrument of terror in Burgoyne's Offensive. "*Il faut brutaliser les affaires,*" was his Gallic way of putting it. (*Amer. Herit. Book of the Rev.*, 239) He is said to have been at least 65 years old when the Revolution started (Ward, *op. cit.*, 473), but Appleton's information that he was treating with the Indians of Niagara in 1720 (see above) would, if true, mean that he was close to 70 years old when the Revolution started.

He had been Supt. of the Canadian Indians under the French regime and was succeeded when the British took over by his son-in-law, a Maj. Campbell. Ward gives the French leader's name as Luc de Chapt de la Corne Saint-Luc, and says he was commonly called La Corne St. Luc or even La Corne or St. Luc. (*Op. cit.*, 473 *n.*) This same author indexes him under L as "de La Corne, Louis St. Luc." Appleton's lists him as "La Corne, Pierre, Chevalier de."

ST. LUCIA CAPTURED BY BRITISH, 12–28 Dec. '78.

Adm. Hotham reached Barbados with 5,800 army troops under Gen. James Grant from N.Y. on 10 Dec., just a day before d'Estaing reached Martinique from Boston. Adm. Barrington took command of the British forces and immediately moved against St. Lucia. (See WEST INDIES for further background.) The afternoon of 12 Dec. Grant's two brigades landed, and with the loss of only a few men they captured the fortified French naval base not an hour before d'Estaing arrived on 13 Dec. with a superior fleet and 9,000 troops he had picked up at Martinique. The British army troops were divided into three detachments, one on the Vigie peninsula that formed the north side of the harbor, one on the mountain called the Morne Fortuné that commands the south side of Castries Bay, and the other at Cul de Sac. Even with an advantage of three ships to one, the French admiral could not break Barrington's skilfully deployed defense of Cul de Sac Bay. On 18 Dec. d'Estaing landed his troops in the Anse de Choc to force the British defenses at Vigie Point, thereby opening the harbor to his fleet. D'Estaing got an expensive lesson in New World tactics when he threw two battalions against an isolated detachment of light infantry deployed on two wooded hills forward of the main British position. Veterans of the fighting in America, "the five light companies made utter havoc of his two battalions, and withdrew through a belt of brushwood to the isthmus before he could cut them off," writes Fortescue. (*British Army*, III, 265) Two successive attacks were repulsed with heavy losses by the main battle position. In the three hours' action the French lost 1,200 wounded and left 400 dead on the field. The British force of 1,300 men of the 5th Foot, Grenadiers, Light Infantry, and four guns, commanded by Col. Medows, had 13 killed and 158 wounded. After doing nothing for 10 days, the shattered French forces withdrew to Martinique, the original garrison of St. Lucia surrendered, and the British owned St. Lucia.

"A more brilliant series of little operations by both army and navy, under the favour of fortune, it would be difficult to find. Had Barrington waited for a day longer at Barbados, his squadron and transports must have fallen a prey to d'Estaing's superior fleet. Had Grant delayed for an hour in landing and attacking the French posts, the French militia might have held their own till d'Estaing came to their relief. But for Barrington's very bold and skilful dispositions in Cul de Sac Bay, his squadron must have been dispersed, if not destroyed, and Grant's army cut off. But for Grant's equally skilful defense of his posts on Vigie, the French could have brought up guns to force Barrington's squadron from Cul de Sac Bay into the jaws of a superior fleet." (*Ibid., 265–66*)

Fortescue cites two sources of further detail: *Lives of the Lindsays,* III, 331 ff., and "St. Lucia, 1778," *Macmillan's Magazine,* Apr. 1902.

SAINT-SIMON, Claude Henri, Comte de. 1760–1825. French officer, social philosopher. Distantly related to Gen. SAINT-SIMON and to the celebrated writer of memoirs (Louis de Saint-Simon, 1675–1755), he entered the army in 1777, commanded a company in the West Indies operations of the Marquis de Bouillé starting two years later, and took part in the Yorktown Campaign of 1781. On 12 Apr. '82 he was captured in the action off Saints Passage (WEST INDIES) and taken to Jamaica. In 1790 he surrendered his title to become a supporter of the French Revolution, but he played no important part, and during the Terror he was imprisoned for 11 months as an aristocrat. To finance his project of reorganizing society he had made a small fortune in land speculation during the French Revolution, but he lost this and spent most of his remaining years in poverty. He nevertheless produced writings that, although "entirely deficient in system, clearness and consecutive strength," resulted in his being "the founder of French socialism."

(*E.B.*) In his ambitious youth Saint-Simon had been awakened each morning by his valet with the words, "Remember, monsieur le comte, that you have great things to do." (*Ibid.*)

SAINT - SIMON MONTBLERN, Claude Anne, Marquis de. French general. Often identified as Claude Anne de Rouvroy, and confused with other members of the various branches of this famous family, he was commander of the French troops that reached Yorktown with Adm. De Grasse.

SAINTS PASSAGE, 9–12 Apr. '82. See WEST INDIES. . . .

SALEM, Mass., 26 Feb. '75. On orders from Gen. Gage, Col. Alex. Leslie sailed with his 64th Foot Regt. from Castle William (in Boston harbor) at midnight, 25 Feb., to destroy an ordnance depot reported to be at Salem. The raiders dropped anchor about 12 hours later in Marblehead Bay, and about 2 P.M. started the five-mile march to Salem. Maj. John Pedrick, an American whom Leslie knew and believed to be loyal, managed to pass through the 240-man column of redcoats on horseback and race ahead to alert the citizens of Salem, who were attending church. Col. Timothy Pickering, the militia commander, sent 40 minutemen to Capt. Robt. Foster's forge near the North River Bridge to remove 19 brass cannon that were there to be fitted with carriages. When the King's men arrived, the cannon had been removed, the draw of the bridge leading to the forge had been opened, and a large crowd had joined the militia on the opposite bank. Some redcoats barely failed to capture the last available boat in the area, but the patriot Joseph Wicher stove in its bottom and then, in a grandstand gesture, bared his breast—literally—to the enemy. A British soldier obliged him with a bayonet thrust that inflicted a slight but bloody wound. When the British threatened to fire, the Loyalist minister, Thos. Barnard, and Capt. John Felt, countered with a face-saving offer to let them cross unmolested, if they would then withdraw peacefully. Leslie accepted, marched his troops some 30 rods (165 yds.) to the agreed limiting point, faced about, and headed back to Marblehead. Despite its comic-opera nature, this affair came close to setting off the "shot heard round the world"; a company of Danvers militia arrived just as the British were leaving, and other armed citizens were gathering. Salem can claim the distinction of seeing the first American blood shed; it also generated a Barbara-Fritchie-type heroine in Sarah Tarrant, who after taunting the redcoats from an open window and being threatened by one of them, is alleged to have said, "Fire if you have the courage, but I doubt it." (C. & M., 65) Leslie is said to have retreated to the tune of "THE WORLD TURNED UPSIDE DOWN." (*Ibid.*) The poet John Trumbull commemorated the affair in these lines in his *M'Fingal:*

Through Salem straight, without delay,
The bold battalion took its way;
Marched o'er a bridge, in open sight
Of several Yankees armed for fight;
Then, without loss of time or men,
Veered round for Boston back again,
And found so well their projects thrive
That every soul got home alive.

(This account is drawn largely from the article by Eric W. Barnes in *Amer. Heritage,* Oct. 1960. Trumbull's lines are quoted from C. & M.)

SALEM, Ohio Terr. See GNADEN-HUETTEN. . . .

SALLY, SALLY PORT. A sally or sortie is a going forth, particularly by

besieged against besiegers. A sally port is an opening in a fortification to permit this operation.

SALT was vital to the American economy since it was needed to preserve meat and fish. While salt-making was one of the earliest industries attempted in the 13 colonies, the commodity was not produced in sufficient quantity and had to be imported. Turks Island in the West Indies was the principal source, and the British Navy was able to cut off this supply to all but smugglers and privateers. The great Onondaga salt deposits were known in the 17th century but were not worked until after the Revolution (see Lossing, I, 230 *n.*), nor were the large deposits of rock salt that later supplied the country. When the shortage became critical the Americans set up salt factories along the coast from Cape Cod to Ga.; bounties were offered and state works established, but the shortage was never alleviated. Salt works were prime objectives of British raiders, and many were destroyed by the coastal storms for which the North Atlantic seaboard is noted. The colonists persisted, however. Benj. Franklin turned his talents to drawing up instructions, and in Aug. '77 John Adams wrote: "all the old women and children are gone down to the Jersey shore to make salt. Salt water is boiling all around the coast." (Miller, *Triumph,* 110) Profiteers did a thriving business, mobs rioted for salt, and the British Navy carried salt as ballast and traded it for fresh provisions. (*Ibid.*)

SALTONSTALL, Dudley. 1738–1796. Cont'l. naval officer. Conn. A direct descendant of Richard Saltonstall (d. 1694), who settled in Mass. in 1630, he was born at New London, Conn. Before the Revolution he had been a privateersman and merchant captain. Early in 1775 he commanded the fort at New London, and when the Cont'l. Navy was established he became (22 Dec. '75) the senior officer after Esek Hopkins and commander of the latter's flagship *Alfred*. Taking part in the first of the war's NAVAL OPERATIONS, he was exonerated after an investigation of the ALFRED–GLASGOW ENCOUNTER, 6 Apr. '76. On 10 Oct. '76 he was ranked fourth on the list of captains. The next year he was named to command the new frigate *Trumbull*. Although this vessel did not get to sea for two years, "in some manner unexplained, he sailed in another ship of the same name and reported the capture of two British transports." (G. W. Allen in *D.A.B.*) He succeeded the more capable John B. Hopkins as captain of the *Warren* (32). After the PENOBSCOT EXPEDITION, he was dismissed from the navy (7 Oct. '79). He later was successful as a privateersman and after the war returned to the merchant service. He died of yellow fever in Haiti.

SALUTARY NEGLECT. For various reasons the NAVIGATION ·ACTS were not enforced in America; colonial charters in many instances prescribed exemptions and often it was of mutual benefit to British and American businessmen for the government not to observe the letter of the law. "Salutary neglect" was instituted as a policy by Sir Robert Walpole, who was in power 1721– 42. He believed that unrestricted trade would bring more gold into England than taxes would. The policy began to be changed in 1763 when the British government, badly in debt as a result of the Seven Years' War, began looking for ways to get revenue from the colonies.

SAMPSON, Deborah. 1760–1827. Cont'l. heroine. Mass. Of old colonial stock, Deborah was reared by friends and relatives until she was 10, was an indentured servant the next eight years, but by the time she was 20 had educated herself to the degree of qualifying as a part-time teacher. She was a heavy-boned young woman of about 5 feet 8 inches in height and rather horse-faced. Early in 1782 she masqueraded as a man, enlisted in the army, but was exposed after joining the boys for a few rounds in a tavern. In May '82 she enlisted as Robert Shurtleff in Capt. Geo. Webb's Co., 4th Mass. Regt. She seems to have been motivated by nothing more complicated than the realization that soldiering was easier and more interesting than farm work and substitute teaching. Having learned the hard way of the first pitfall, roistering, she fell into another: issued the usual ill-fitting army clothing, she altered the garments to fit. Thinking fast, she explained to suspicious comrades in arms that she had learned to sew as a boy because there were no girls in her family. Nicknamed "Smock face" and "Molly" because of her whiskerless features, Robert marched off to West Point with her outfit. In a skirmish with Tories at Tappan Sea (Tappan Zee) she gave a good account of herself and received a saber wound across the left side of the head. A family friend visited camp in an effort to find her, but failed. She was wounded while part of a detachment ambushed by Tories at East Chester and carried to the aid station with a serious musket wound in the thigh. Knowing that she again faced exposure, she escaped from the medics and suffered agonies until the wound healed itself, but it bothered her the rest of her life. In Nov. '82 she went with her company to Ft. Ticonderoga, where she saw some service against the Indians. She then was transferred to Philadelphia where she was orderly to

Gen. Patterson. (Presumably this was Sam'l. Patterson of the Del. militia.) Another unexpected hazard presented itself here: having come down with a fever, she was treated by a Dr. Binney, who discovered her secret but concealed it; but Binney's niece then became infatuated with her uncle's patient. This led to her exposure as a fraudulent enlistee, Washington was informed, and Robert Shurtleff was honorably discharged.

She married Benj. Gannett, a farmer of Sharon, Mass., whom she bore three children. The war wound continued to cause her trouble, and she could not do much farm work. After Mass. awarded her a bonus, Congress in 1805 gave her a pension of $4 a month as an invalided soldier, and in 1818 this was doubled. In 1802, however, she began capitalizing on her fame and started giving lectures in Mass., R.I., and N.Y. As perhaps the first female lecturer in the country, she delivered a set speech about her experiences and normally concluded by appearing in military costume to do the manual of arms. A narrative of her life was published by her as *The Female Review* (Dedham, Mass., 1797). Rev. John A. Vinton published a new edition, with introduction and notes, in Boston in 1866. (Appleton's; Cook, *What Manner of Men,* 217–28; Fairfax Downey MS article for *Blue Book*)

SANDERS CREEK, S.C., 16 Aug. '80. Alternate name for battle of Camden (see CAMDEN CAMPAIGN).

SANDUSKY, Ohio. 4–5 June '82. Site of CRAWFORD'S DEFEAT.

SANDWICH, John Montagu, 4th Earl of. 1718–1792. 1st Lord of Admiralty. Characterized by Fortescue as "a politician of evil reputation and an inveterate jobber" (*British Army,* III, 170), Sandwich is generally held responsible for the miserable condition of British naval vessels and personnel at the outbreak of the American Revolution. (Professor Rankin believes the poor condition of the fleet was due more to Lord North's economy policies.) His ancestor, the 1st earl (1625–1672), was a famous admiral whose secretary was Samuel Pepys. John Montagu, the subject of this sketch, entered the House of Lords as a follower of the Duke of Bedford in 1739 after being educated at Eton and Cambridge. In Feb. '48 he became 1st lord of the admiralty, a post he held until dismissed by the King in June '51. In Aug. '53 he became one of the principal secretaries of state and took a leading part in the persecution of one of his former associates in the infamous fraternity of Medmenham, John WILKES. He was postmaster general in 1768, secretary of state in 1770, and in 1771 he returned to his post as 1st lord of the admiralty. "For corruption and incapacity Sandwich's administration is unique in the history of the British navy," says *E.B.* "Offices were bought, stores were stolen and, worst of all, ships, unseaworthy and inadequately equipped, were sent to fight the battles of their country." He retired in Mar. '82 and died 10 years later.

Capt. Cook named the Sandwich Islands for him. (These are now the Hawaiian Islands.) The article of diet with which his name is associated entered the language in 1762, according to *O.U.D.* "Named after John Montagu, 4th Earl of Sandwich," says this authority, "who once spent twenty-four hours at the gaming-table without other food than beef sandwiches."

SAN ILDEFONSO, Treaty of, 3 Nov. '62. See PARIS, Treaty of, 10 Feb. '63.

SAP. Underground gallery dug to get beneath fortifications, usually for the

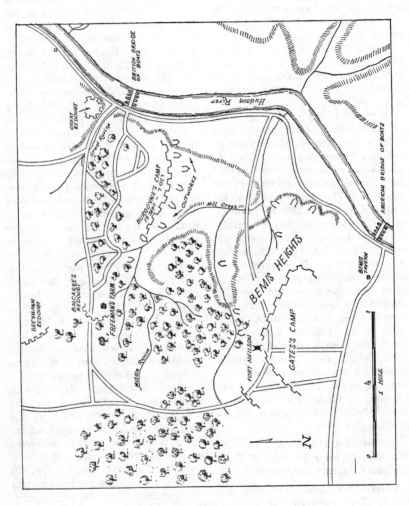

SARATOGA BATTLEFIELD

purpose of blowing a mine. It is also a trench pushed toward the enemy by digging at the *saphead* (head of the sap) while using the trench for defilade. If the earth is thrown to one side for additional protection it is known as a full or single sap; if dirt is thrown to form parapets on both sides it becomes a double sap. A flying sap is one constructed under fire by using two GABIONS for cover and pushing them forward, side by side, as the work progresses. A sap roller is a gabion rolled forward to protect the sappers as they work. A sapper is a military engineer trained not only for this type of siege work but also for other varieties of field fortification.

SARATOGA BATTLES, Alternate names. The actions which for strictly alphabetical reasons I have referred to as the First and Second Battles of Saratoga are known by many alternate names. The first battle, on 19 Sept., is generally called Freeman's Farm by modern historians, and the second action, on 7 Oct., is usually called Bemis Heights. They are sometimes called by the name STILLWATER.

SARATOGA, First Battle of, 19 Sept. '77. BURGOYNE'S OFFENSIVE moved across the Hudson on 13 Sept. and pushed slowly down the west bank. Having been deserted by all but about 50 of his Indians, the British commander lacked the scouts that had kept him informed of the enemy's location; when he heard the reveille drums of the American camp on 16 Sept. he made camp and spent the day trying to reconnoiter the rebel position. The next day he advanced three miles and deployed his troops on a line extending about a mile and a half west from Sword's House. On 18 Sept., he planned a reconnaissance in force to develop the situation.

The Americans had observed Bur-goyne's river crossing, and their patrols harassed his advance. Gates's army now numbered 7,000 in all, and since 12 Sept. had been disposed in well-entrenched positions on Bemis Heights; the American commander was content to wait for Burgoyne's attack.

BURGOYNE'S PLAN

Three columns were formed to execute the operation that followed. Gen. Simon Fraser was to lead 2,200 men on the right in a wide sweep to the vicinity of the clearing known as Freeman's Farm; his command comprised a corps of British and German light infantry and grenadiers, the battalion companies of the 24th Regt., and the Canadian, Indian, and Tory auxiliaries. The center column of about 1,100 men was to move south and then turn west to make contact with Fraser. Although Hamilton commanded this element, Burgoyne accompanied the center column and was, therefore, its actual commander. The left (east) column, 1,100 men commanded by Riedesel and accompanied by Phillips, was to move south along the river road. "What was next to be done—if the Americans did not come out and attack one or more of the advancing columns—we do not know," says Nickerson. (*Turning Point,* 305) Since Burgoyne's troops were moving in broken, wooded terrain, without the means of coordinating the three columns, the plan invited DEFEAT IN DETAIL.

The day of the battle dawned cold and foggy, but turned bright and clear by 11 A.M. A signal gun then set the columns in motion, and an American patrol on the east bank of the Hudson watched this activity and reported it to Gates. By 12:30 the advance guard of the center column had occupied the cabin of Freeman's Farm, and Burgoyne halted the column to await word

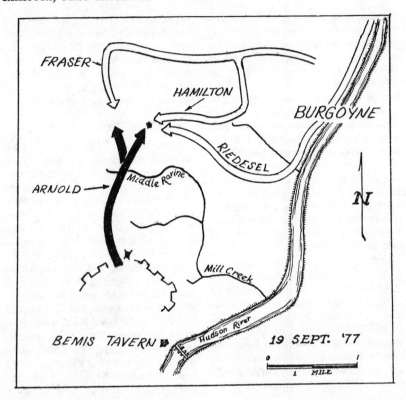

FRASER

HAMILTON

BURGOYNE

RIEDESEL

ARNOLD →

Middle Ravine

N

Mill Creek

Hudson River

BEMIS TAVERN

19 SEPT. '77

0 1

1 MILE

of Fraser's location. Riedesel, slowed by the need to repair bridges, had gotten to a point on the river road due east of Freeman's Farm and about a mile and a half away.

The uninspired Gates, meanwhile, sat with superior forces in his entrenchments and ignored the opportunities his opponent had extended. Only at the vehement urging of Arnold did he finally send Morgan's riflemen and Dearborn's light infantry out from his left to make contact. Arnold's division, on this flank, was alerted to support them.

THE ACTION BEGINS

About 12:45 Morgan's men delivered a surprise fire that picked off every officer in the advance guard around Freeman's cabin. An impressive number of others were knocked out of action by this fire and the rest stampeded to the rear. Morgan's Virginians followed with an enthusiastic but unorganized charge that collided with Hamilton's main body, bounced off, and dispersed into the brush. Morgan was afraid his elite corps had been destroyed, but at the sound of his turkey call they materialized from their scattered cover and reassembled.

Panic-stricken refugees of this turkey shoot so unnerved the other regulars toward whom they ran for safety that some of the latter fired without orders, inflicting casualties among their own troops. Burgoyne decided to wait no longer for word from Fraser and fired the prearranged gun signal to tell the other two columns he was moving out. The center column reached the clearing of Freeman's Farm without opposition, and by 1 o'clock had formed along its northern edge. With the 9th Regt. in reserve, the 20th, 62d, and 21st were arranged in that order from left to right. (Only the eight battalion companies of these four regiments were involved; their flank companies were with Fraser.)

PHASE TWO OF THE BATTLE

Morgan and Dearborn took positions along the southern edge of the clearing, and seven other regiments were sent from Bemis Heights to support them. The 1st and 2d N.H. Cont'ls., under Cilley and Scammell, were the first to reinforce the riflemen, and they formed to the left; others extended in this direction as they arrived. The best evidence indicates that Arnold was on the scene; in an appendix on this controversy, Ward says:

"One must conclude that John Marshall, Washington Irving, Botta, Lossing, Fiske, Woodrow Wilson, F. V. Green, Fonblanque, S. G. Fisher, Hall, Trevelyan, Nickerson, Fortescue, Dawson, and Carrington are right in rejecting the statements of Wilkinson and Gordon and giving Arnold the honor of active participation in the battle as the directing head of the American troops." (*W.O.R.*, 942)

The fight in the clearing continued three or four hours. (Nickerson, 310) American fire would cut into the ranks of the three British regiments that attempted to stand shoulder to shoulder, European style, in the clearing; the regulars would then be driven back into the shelter of the woods; but when the Americans charged into the clearing to pursue, the regulars would drive them back to their line of departure. The rebels had the advantage of numbers and marksmanship; the British had discipline and artillery. The Americans were winning on points, but a battle is not scored by this system.

PHASE THREE

Riedesel had heard the firefight start, and about 2 P.M. an officer arrived from the center column to inform him that a general engagement appeared imminent. On his own initiative, of which the German general appeared to have plenty, Riedesel sent four guns to support the center column and also sent an aide as liaison offcer. The latter returned about 5 o'clock with orders from Burgoyne: Riedesel was to leave a force to defend his position along the river road and was to bring reinforcements to attack the American east flank and take pressure off the center column. Arrival of additional American regiments had forced the three regiments at Freeman's Farm to thin out to prevent being overlapped on their right. This left the British 62d in a salient raked by fire from front and flanks; the unit not only took its punishment but went forward with the other two in several bayonet attacks, all of which were driven back. On one occasion the 62d pushed beyond support of the other two regiments, lost 25 men cut off and captured, and escaped annihilation only because Gen. Phillips personally led the 20th in an attack east of the clearing to permit it to withdraw. So the center column was in a desperate situation when the Germans came to their support.

Riedesel, on the other hand, risked annihilation of his force on the river as well as loss of the vital bateaux and supply train he was protecting on that flank. But he accepted this risk and moved out with about 500 infantry rank and file and two guns (his own regiment, two companies of the Rhetz, and 6-pdrs. from the Hesse Hanau Arty.). With the same vigor he had shown at Hubbardton in rescuing Fraser, the fat major general led the two Rhetz companies west along a road that he had previously reconnoitered. Puffing to the top of a hill he saw the desperate situation of the British and committed the two companies PIECEMEAL; as at Hubbardton, he ordered them to advance cheering and beating their drums.

The American right flank rested on the North Branch Ravine, which prevented their extending in this direction as fresh regiments came up to reinforce. Furthermore, they had not screened this flank with patrols, so the sound of volley fire from this quarter led them to suspect the worst. With proper tactical leadership the Americans could have won this last phase of the battle, since they still outnumbered the enemy about two to one and Hamilton's troops were almost fought out. (Nickerson, 316) Unfortunately, Arnold was with Gates at Bemis Heights when the Germans arrived on the battlefield; he had ridden back to get more troops, and when he started to return to the battle he was called back by Gates at the suggestion of Col. Morgan Lewis. (*Ibid.*, 315) Learned's Brig. was, however, ordered forward, but without the leadership that Arnold would undoubtedly have furnished, this unit blundered off toward Fraser's wing and contributed nothing to the battle at Freeman's Farm.

Burgoyne launched a counterattack when Riedesel's reinforcements were available. The Americans held their ground at first, but then started drawing back. Darkness was falling and they lacked unity of command.

Fraser had been off in the wilderness while Burgoyne and the center column fought for their lives. Late in the day his forward elements exchanged fire with those of Learned, but that was the extent of the action in this area.

Burgoyne could claim the victory, since he camped on the battlefield. As mentioned in the article on BURGOYNE'S OFFENSIVE, he probably could have beaten Gates if he had continued his attack during the next day or two.

Gates's performance in the battle was entirely passive. Perhaps it is unfortunate that Schuyler was no longer in command: although no great commander, his personal relationships with Arnold were such that he probably would have given Arnold the support with which the battle could have been won. There is reason to suspect, on the other hand, that the personality conflict between Gates and Arnold played a large part in Gates's reluctance to give Arnold freer rein. It is difficult to excuse Gates for not annihilating what was left of Reidesel's column during phase three of the battle. Gates had at least 4,000 on the height overlooking the 800 or 900 enemy troops left to guard Burgoyne's supplies. "A swift descent by half of these could hardly have failed to capture and destroy all the British bateaux and land carriages with all their contents, leaving Burgoyne . . . to surrender or starve," comments Ward. (*Op. cit.*, 512)

Burgoyne lost about 600. Of the 800 effectives in the three British regiments that bore the brunt, 350 (44 per cent) were killed, wounded, or captured; the 62d Regt. was reduced from 350 to 60 men, a loss of 83 per cent! While the American must look on these figures as a testimony of rebel marksmanship, he must also see in them a badge of British courage.

American losses totaled 319: eight officers and 57 men killed, 21 officers and 197 wounded, 36 reported missing.

This account of the Battle of Freeman's Farm, which I have called First Saratoga for alphabetical reasons, is based on Nickerson and Ward. Other versions vary in essential features such as Burgoyne's objective, strength and composition of his three columns, Fraser's participation, Arnold's presence, and Gates's competence.

SARATOGA, Second Battle of, 7 Oct. '77 (BURGOYNE'S OFFENSIVE) Still unable to get reconnaissance parties close enough to Gates's Bemis Heights position to determine his chances of forcing them, Burgoyne planned another reconnaissance in force, very similar to the one that resulted in the First Battle of Saratoga, 19 Sept. The article on BURGOYNE'S OFFENSIVE deals with the significant developments during the interval between these two battles. For the second engagement Burgoyne planned to use his 600 auxiliaries and 1,500 of his remaining 5,000 regulars. They would advance in three main columns, while Capt. Fraser with the 600 auxiliaries and his company of rangers were to screen their right by making a wide circuit to the west.

"Should the reconnaissance show the rebel left to be approachable, then Burgoyne proposed on Wednesday the 8th to attack in force [says Nickerson]. Should an attack seem unwise, he would retreat to the Battenkill on Saturday, October 11. There was some talk of dislodging the enemy to facilitate a retreat. The whole thing was vague." (Nickerson, *Turning Point*, 357)

THE BATTLE: PHASE ONE

Between 10 and 11 A.M. the three British columns advanced slowly for some two thirds of a mile S.W. from their entrenchments on the field of the First Battle of Saratoga. Capt. Fraser's force moved off into the wooded hills on their right, out of contact. The main body then formed a line 1,000 yards long on a gentle rise north of Mill Creek. While officers tried unsuccessfully to make out the rebel positions through their spyglasses, batmen and camp followers foraged in the wheat field in front of the line. (This may have been part of Burgoyne's plan, since the animals were critically short of green forage. [Nickerson, 358].) Balcarres was on the right (west) flank of the line with his light infantry; Riedesel was in the center with a composite group of Brunswickers and with the 24th Regt.; on the left were the British grenadiers under Maj. John Acland. By European standards it was a good position (although 1,000 yards of front overextended the 1,500 troops): it provided excellent observation and fields of fire for the 10 cannon—to the front, at least. But the untutored Americans didn't like to charge across open fields into the mouths of cannon and drawn ranks of disciplined regulars; they were good in the woods, and there were good woods through which to approach against both flanks of Burgoyne's line.

When Wilkinson returned from checking outpost reports that the enemy was forming along Mill Creek, Gates—who apparently had learned something from the last battle—accepted Morgan's suggestion that his riflemen attack the British west flank. "Order on Morgan to begin the game," is the theatrical quote attributed to Gates. While Morgan worked around the high ground to turn Burgoyne's west flank, Poor was to lead his brigade in a simultaneous attack against the opposite flank.

The game was actually opened by Poor's 800 men. By 2:30 P.M. they had deployed coolly, despite losses from enemy artillery, at the base of the elevated position occupied by the grenadiers. American units, many of them

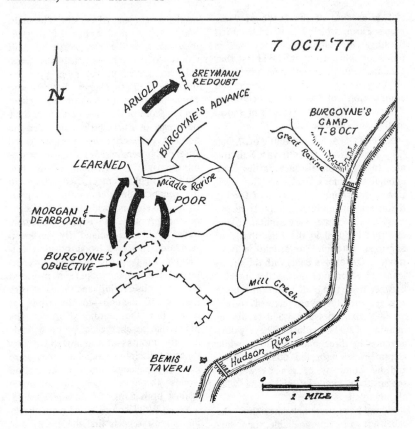

7 OCT. '77

BREYMANN REDOUBT

ARNOLD

BURGOYNE'S ADVANCE

BURGOYNE'S CAMP 7-8 OCT

Great Ravine

LEARNED

Middle Ravine

MORGAN & DEARBORN

POOR

BURGOYNE'S OBJECTIVE

Mill Creek

BEMIS TAVERN

Hudson River

0   1

1 MILE

N

veterans, were the N.H. Cont'l. regiments of Cilley, Hale, and Scammell; Van Cortlandt's and Livingston's N.Y. militia; and the Conn. militia of Cook and Lattimer. The grenadiers, outnumbered two or three to one, opened fire with cannon and muskets; as is generally the case when troops fire down hill, most of the British fire was too high. When the redcoats rose to Acland's order, "Fix bayonets and charge the damned rebels," one of the latter, Col. Cilley, called out a heroic command in defiance, his men delivered a murderous volley that stopped the enemy's charge, and swept over the grenadiers' position.

Among the many British casualties was their commander, ACLAND, who was captured as he lay helpless with bullet holes through both legs.

Morgan had meanwhile gone into action. First routing Capt. Fraser's flank security in the woods, and having turned the enemy line of battle, he hit Balcarres in flank and rear. As the British light infantry were changing front to meet this threat, Dearborn's light infantry arrived to deliver an effective small arms fire that routed them. Balcarres rallied his men a short distance to the rear, but was unable to hold.

Sir Francis Clerke was coming forward with Burgoyne's order for a general withdrawal when mortally wounded and captured. The Germans, now with both flanks uncovered, fought on, not knowing of the order to retreat. Learned's Brig. was advancing against them frontally when Arnold clattered up to lead them. Arnold had rowed with Gates after First Saratoga and had been relieved of command; he had stayed with the army at the insistence of those officers of the Schuyler faction, and rushed into this action with no authority whatsoever. Maj. Armstrong had the unhappy assignment of galloping after him with orders from Gates to return to camp. Reinforced by detachments from the Rhetz and Hesse Hanau Regts., Col. Specht drove off the first frontal attack. As overwhelming American strength built up on three sides they were ordered back into the Balcarres Redoubt.

Gen. Simon Fraser had been conspicuous throughout the action. Now, with the 24th Regt., which had seen little action so far, he tried to establish a delaying position with the light infantry survivors. With the same sentiments that "Stonewall" Jackson was later to voice on the need for eliminating brave enemy officers, Arnold said to Morgan, "That man on the gray horse is a host in himself and must be disposed of." Tim MURPHY got him with the third shot, and the British delaying position collapsed. Ten Broeck's Brig. of N.Y. militia arrived on the field but was not needed. The battle had lasted 52 minutes. (Nickerson, 364)

PHASE TWO

Had it not been for Arnold the battle would have ended, but "with true military instinct," says the British military historian Fortescue, he "seized the opportunity for a general attack upon the British entrenchments." His assault on the Balcarres Redoubt got through the abatis but was stopped by the light infantry and other survivors of the initial action who had taken refuge here. Seeing little to be gained here, Arnold galloped recklessly between the front lines to see what could be done on the American left. Finding Learned's Brig. arriving on the field, and at the suggestion of Wilkinson, Arnold led an attack that cleared the stockaded cabins between the Balcarres and the Breymann redoubts. Having thus exposed this flank of Breymann's position, Arnold raced to the other flank to lead four regiments in an impetuous assault that captured Breymann's Redoubt. (The regiments were those of Wesson, Livingston, and Morgan—which had already encircled the redoubt—and the newly arrived Mass. regiment of Brooks.) Defense of the Breymann Redoubt had been reduced to 200 men since the 300 detached to participate in the earlier advance had retreated along with Capt. Fraser's rangers and the Canadians to the Balcarres Redoubt. The brave but brutal Breymann was shot dead by one of his own men after having sabered four others "to keep them to their work." (Nickerson, 367) Arnold was wounded in his Quebec leg.

COMMENT

General Gates, whose name would be associated with this decisive battle of world history, had never gotten close enough to the fighting to smell gunpowder. His detractors claim he was more interested in discussing the merits of the American Revolution with the mortally wounded Sir Francis CLERKE.

As for the real significance of Arnold's participation in the battle, opinions are strongly colored even today by the GATES–SCHUYLER CONTROVERSY: the Schuyler partisans tend to exaggerate the role of Arnold (who was on Schuyler's side), and the Gates men go to the other extreme. Lynn Montross, for example, says, "The British army had been beaten when Benedict Arnold made his appearance.* * * Here at the end of the day occurred the worst rebel losses without adding anything to a victory already gained.* * * There can be no doubt that after two weeks of open insubordination Arnold took a brave part in the action of October 7th. It is also clear from contemporary accounts that the victory had been gained by Morgan, Poor and Learned before he made his dramatic appearance." (Montross, *Rag, Tag,* 223, 227)

In his enthusiasm for doing justice to the much maligned "Granny" Gates, this distinguished author of *War Through the Ages* (Montross) appears to lose sight of the fact that Burgoyne was far from beaten when Poor, Morgan, and Learned drove his reconnaissance force back into their entrenchments. Arnold's contribution was in following up on this initial success and, by the capture of the Breymann Redoubt, making Burgoyne's entire position untenable. We now know there was no real danger of Clinton's force coming up the Hudson to reinforce Burgoyne. But nobody on the Saratoga battlefield knew this at the time, and Arnold's costly assaults on Burgoyne's entrenchments must be considered with this in mind. Where would Gates's militia have been if Burgoyne were still in his fortifications and they were exposed to attack—real or rumored —from the rear?

Burgoyne credited his defeat to Arnold (ltr. to Clinton 25 Oct. cited by Wallace, 167, 290 *n.*), and this undoubtedly influenced Fortescue's judgment that "It was he and no other who beat Burgoyne at Saratoga." (*Br. Army,* III, 404)

Alden points out, as does Montross, that many of the writers who credit

Arnold and Schuyler for Burgoyne's defeat "have placed faith in the statements of enemies of Gates." Channing concludes that "*Prima facie* the verdict is for Gates; the burden of proof is on the other side." (Alden, *Amer. Rev.,* 148 *n.,* quoting the analysis of Channing, III, 276–78)

American losses were about 150 in all. The British lost four times as many, and lost all 10 cannon that were taken forward the morning of the battle. Gen. Fraser was mortally wounded and Breymann killed.

SARATOGA SURRENDER, 17 Oct. '77. (BURGOYNE'S OFFENSIVE) On 13 Oct. Burgoyne's officers unanimously agreed he should treat for surrender on honorable terms, and Burgoyne sent an officer to Gates proposing a meeting with one of his officers "to negotiate matters of high importance to both armies." (Ward, *W.O.R.,* 536, quoting Riedesel) Gates consented, and the next day Maj. Kingston, Burgoyne's A.G., was led blindfolded to the former's Hq. To the amazement of the British emissary (as well as Gates's aide, Wilkinson), Gates immediately produced from his pocket a paper saying that only unconditional surrender would be considered. This was Gates's first blunder. Uncertainty as to the status of CLINTON'S EXPEDITION as well as inability of the Americans to assault the strong British defenses without heavy losses put Gates in no position for such a dramatic demand. Burgoyne called Gates's bluff: in addition to the HONORS OF WAR, he now proposed that his command be PAROLED "upon condition of not serving again in North America during the present contest." When this was presented on the 15th, Gates consented, provided the capitulation be finished by 2 P.M. and that the enemy leave its positions by 5 P.M. Gates had blundered again, since Burgoyne divined from the urgency of this time schedule that his adversary was worried about the arrival of British forces from the south. So Burgoyne agreed "in principle," but insisted on more time to work out details. Both commanders then appointed representatives with full powers to negotiate for them; Wilkinson and a militia B.G. named Whipple were the Americans, Lt. Col. Sutherland and a Capt. Craig were their counterparts. They met between the lines and drew up articles of capitulation that all four signed at 8 P.M. (Nickerson, *Turning Point,* 389) At 11 o'clock that night Wilkinson was given a letter from Craig saying Burgoyne would sign the agreement if it were termed a *convention* rather than a *capitulation.* Gates promptly sent his consent, feeling there was no material distinction between the words. (*Ibid.*)

This same evening of the 15th, however, Burgoyne was told by a Tory messenger that Clinton's forces had taken the Highlands, reached Esopus, and had probably gotten to Albany. Gentleman Johnny called a council of war to consider this development. They voted 14 to 8 that he could not honorably withdraw from a treaty he had promised to sign and, by the same majority, that the favorable terms should not be thrown away on the strength of the Tory's dubious report. (See CLINTON'S EXPED.) Burgoyne refused to be bound by these votes and, to stall for time, on 16 Oct. he informed Gates he had learned that Gates had detached a considerable force, which meant that the Americans might no longer have the numerical superiority that had persuaded him to start negotiations; Burgoyne therefore wanted to verify the remaining American strength. The detachment to which Burgoyne alluded was a body of several hundred N.Y. militia departing because their term of service was up. Gates sent Wilkinson to

have Burgoyne state his intention to fight or give up. Only with considerable difficulty and after further delays did Burgoyne's officers prevail on him to sign the convention.

THE CEREMONIES

The son of a Duke's housekeeper was "determined to show his good manners by playing the magnanimous victor," and Burgoyne appeared determined to "play Gates off the latter's own stage." (Nickerson, 399) Riding forward on 17 Oct. in a splendid uniform, Burgoyne was introduced by Wilkinson to a small, plainly clad American general who peered at him through thick spectacles. "The fortune of war, General Gates, has made me your prisoner," said the Englishman. "I shall always be ready to testify that it has not been through any fault of your Excellency," replied Gates. The senior officers of both sides then went to dinner while Burgoyne's men laid down their arms. Gates did not permit his troops to observe this humiliating scene, and there is doubt whether even the two American officers designated as witnesses were present. (Nickerson, 400) The CONVENTION ARMY then forded the Fishkill and marched south along a road lined by American soldiers standing silent, in obedience to their orders. With instructions to play a selection that might enlighten the solemn occasion, the American musicians gave forth with YANKEE DOODLE. As the marching column passed a tent pitched along their route, Burgoyne and Gates emerged to watch the scene for a moment. Then, by prearrangement, Burgoyne handed Gates his sword and Gates returned it to Burgoyne.

When the captives cleared the silent ranks of American troops, they began to curse their misfortune and their captors; American camp followers and country folk through whom they now passed replied in kind. The handful of captured Indian braves and their squaws had to be protected from farmers who were ready to massacre them. Some of the New Englanders thought it might be more fitting for Gentleman Johnny to continue his trip in a suit of tar and feathers, and Gates had to furnish him a dragoon escort for his own protection. (Nickerson, 403) See CONVENTION ARMY for subsequent experiences of the Saratoga captives.

SAUCISSON. A large FASCINE.

SAUNDERS CREEK, S.C., 16 Aug. '80. Another name for the (first) Battle of Camden. See this heading under CAMDEN CAMPAIGN.

SAVANNAH, Ga., 7 Mar. '76. The Ga. patriots took control in the action covered under HUTCHINSON'S ISLAND.

SAVANNAH, Ga., 29 Dec. '78. British capture. On 27 Nov. '78 Lt. Col. Archibald Campbell left Sandy Hook with 3,500 troops escorted by a squadron under Commodore Hyde Parker, and on 23 Dec. the expedition anchored off Tybee Island at the mouth of the Savannah River. The rebel Southern army at this time was commanded by Gen. Robt. Howe and was located at Sunbury, about 30 miles south of Savannah; it numbered 900 Cont'ls. and 150 militia. Gen. Prevost, commander of British forces in East Florida, was at St. Augustine and had orders to move north to cooperate with Campbell in the capture of Savannah. (See SOUTHERN THEATER, Mil. Opns. for over-all British strategy and for preceding events in the South.)

Lacking information on which to plan his actions, Campbell sent Grenadier Capt. Sir James Baird ashore the night of 25–26 Dec. with a light infantry company; Baird picked up two men who furnished what Campbell

called "the most satisfactory intelligence concerning the state of matters at Savannah." (Campbell's report, quoted in C. & M., 1076–79) Their information convinced the British commander that he and Parker could capture the town without waiting for Prevost. The closest high ground for a landing between Tybee and Savannah was at Girardeau's Plantation, about two miles below the town. (It is now a handsome suburban estate.) Parker's ships reached the area about 4 o'clock the afternoon of the 28th, drove off two rebel galleys, but could not put the troops ashore because the tide had turned, the light was failing, and several transports had grounded downstream. About daybreak of the 29th, Lt. Col. Maitland went ashore with the light infantry, the 1st Bn. of the 71st, and the N.Y. Vols. From the levee on which they landed a narrow causeway led 600 yards across flooded ricelands to high ground where Capt. J. C. Smith was posted with 50 S.C. Cont'ls. (This apparently was Brewton's Hill, although some accounts make it appear that this hill was closer to Savannah.) After rebel fire had killed Capt. Cameron and two men of the light infantry and wounded five, the Highlanders drove Smith's outpost back and secured the beachhead.

Howe reached Savannah about Christmas day with 700 Cont'ls. and 150 militia, having left Maj. Lane with 200 Cont'ls. at Sunbury. The old fortifications of the town were untenable, having been allowed to fall into disrepair, so Howe established his main line of defense half a mile S.E. of the town to cover the road that led from the enemy landing site. This road crossed a marshy stream by a causeway and was flanked on the river side by the rice swamps of Gov. Wright's Plantation and by wooded swamps on the other side. The American left, extending from the road to the rice swamps, consisted of Ga. militia under Col. Sam'l. Elbert. Col. Isaac Huger commanded the S.C. Cont'ls. on the right: his own 1st Rifles and Lt. Col. Wm. Thompson's 3d Rangers. Col. Geo. Walton was posted on Huger's right in some buildings ("the new barracks") with 100 Ga. militia riflemen and a cannon. Another gun was on the left flank and two were in the center of the main line, on the road. This line was 200 yards behind the stream mentioned earlier; the bridge at that point was destroyed and halfway between this stream and the American line a trench was dug at what Campbell called "a critical spot between [the] two swamps." Although outnumbered four to one, the Americans appeared to be in a good position that left the enemy no choice but to make a costly frontal assault.

About 3 P.M. on the day of battle the light infantry advance guard halted and formed on the river side of the road 800 yards from the American line. The main body of the British force halted on open ground 200 yards to the rear. "I could discover from the movements of the enemy that they wished and expected an attack upon their left," says Campbell in his report, "and I was desirous of cherishing the opinion." (*Op. cit.*) But he had accidentally picked up an old Negro named Quamino Dolly who told of an obscure path through the swamps and around the American right. Col. Walton is alleged to have warned Howe of this danger, but Howe did not think the enemy would find or use this route and he left it unguarded. (Lossing, II, 732)

Campbell skilfully used the ground and took advantage of Howe's preconceptions to achieve surprise: he sent the 1st Bn. of the 71st up to join the light infantry and convey the impression that he was strengthening this wing for an attack on the American left. Then, using a "happy fall of ground" (Campbell, *op. cit.*), he had Baird's light infantry slip to the rear and circle around to execute the turning movement. Turnbull's N.Y. Vols. fell in behind the light infantry to reinforce their maneuver.

Innocent of the real danger, Howe cannonaded Campbell's line. Baird reached the White Bluff road undetected and pressed on to wipe out Walton's Ga. unit by an attack from their flank and rear. (Lossing, *op. cit.*, 732) At the sound of this action, Campbell had his guns run forward from concealed positions to open on the American line, and his infantry charged. Howe ordered a general retreat across the Musgrove Swamp causeway, west of the town, but his men had to fight their way through enemy forces that got there first. The American right and center got across with difficulty, saving all their artillery except the piece captured with Walton, but Elbert's Ga. militia were cut off from the causeway and had to retreat through flooded Musgrove Swamp—many were drowned and others were captured. The British did not pursue, and Howe camped for the night at Cherokee Hill, eight miles away. He then retreated to Benj. Lincoln's camp at Purysburg on the S.C. side of the Savannah River.

NUMBERS AND LOSSES

The Americans lost 83 killed or drowned and 453 (including 38 officers) captured. The British had three killed and 10 wounded; their losses in the main attack amounted to only five wounded, and the other casualties were sustained in Cameron's attack to secure the beachhead (see above). (Campbell, *op. cit.*) In Savannah the enemy took three ships, three brigs, eight smaller craft, 48 cannon, 23 mortars, and large quantities of supplies.

As for numbers involved, Campbell's strength of 3,500 is accepted but is somewhat academic since Baird's light infantry and the Highlanders did almost all the fighting. Ward says Howe had 700 Cont'ls. and 150 militia in the action, but Lynn Montross' figure of 1,200 appears more plausible. (*Rag, Tag,* 315) This point is also academic since only the 50 S.C. Cont'ls. of Capt. Smith and the 50 Ga. riflemen of Col. Walton did any fighting.

COMMENT

Although a court of inquiry cleared Robt. Howe of blame for the defeat, his career as a field commander was over. Strategically, he was blamed for atttempting a stand with untrained troops against superior numbers when he could have retreated to join Lincoln, after which a strengthened American army could have returned to take Savannah. Tactically, he was criticized for failing to oppose Campbell's landing at Girardeau's and for failing to guard the route by which he was turned. Campbell, on the other hand, deserves the highest praise for his strategy and tactics; as a result of his success Savannah and most of Ga. remained under British control until almost the end of the Revolution.

SAVANNAH, Ga., 9 Oct. '79. Franco-American fiasco. After the British capture of SAVANNAH, 29 Dec., '78, and the subsequent actions outlined under SOUTHERN THEATER, both sides suspended operations during the intensely hot and unhealthful summer months. Charleston was still in American hands, but the British held Savannah and several outposts. Sir James Wright returned from England on 20 July to resume his post as royal governor in Savannah, where Gen. Prevost, military commander in the South, also had his headquarters. The town was garrisoned by about 2,400 troops, a large percentage of whom were Loyalists.

Admiral-General Count Charles-Hector Théodat d'Estaing (whom we'll call d'Estaing from here on) had sailed to the West Indies after the disappointing allied effort against Newport in Aug. '78. He had discretionary orders to aid the rebels if circumstances permitted, and had promised to return in May '79. British and American commanders in North America were therefore anxiously anticipating his reappearance. From Charleston, Gen. Lincoln and the French council appealed for his assistance, and although Washington had plans for combined operations in the North, the independent Frenchman decided to strike the British in the South.

Sending five ships ahead to notify Charleston of his coming, d'Estaing followed with 33 warships (totaling more than 2,000 guns) and transports bearing over 4,000 troops. His appearance off the Georgia coast was so unexpected that he easily captured the 50-gun *Experiment,* the frigate *Ariel,* and two store ships; booty included Brig. Gen. Garth, on his way to succeed Prevost, and a £30,000 payroll for the Savannah garrison. (Clinton, *American Rebellion,* 149) This took place the first part of Sept. '79—the journal of a French officer says the fleet reached the mouth of the Savannah River on 8 Sept. (C. & M., 1091); Lossing says 3 Sept. (II, 734) A privateer reached N.Y.C. on 8 Oct. with news of d'Estaing's return (Clinton, 149), and there was much consternation as to where the French would strike. Cornwallis was just about to leave with 4,000 men for the defense of Jamaica. His departure was stopped, and Clinton evacuated the British garrison from Rhode Island to N.Y. (Fortescue, *Brit-*

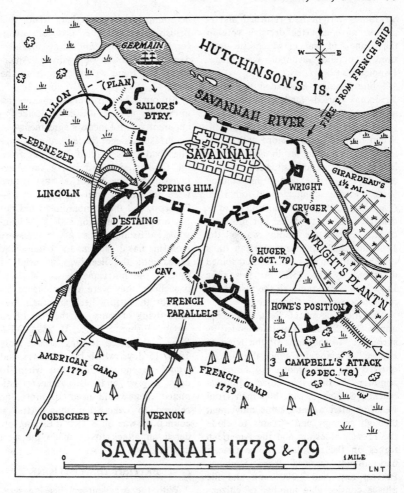

SAVANNAH 1778 & 79

ish Army, III, 285) While Clinton waited and worried about Georgia, Washington was hoping for reports of French sails off Sandy Hook. (Clinton, 149 *n.;* Freeman, *Washington,* V, 136)

When the French fleet disappeared the evening of 4 Sept. (using Lossing's dates), Prevost hoped he was safe from attack. He sent his "commanding engineer," Capt. MONCRIEFF, with 100 infantry to reinforce the outpost on Tybee Island, in the mouth of the Savannah River. But the enemy reappeared on the 6th, and three days later started landing troops on the south side of the island. Moncrieff spiked his guns and withdrew. British ships moved into the river, and six of them were sunk to bar the channel. Lt. Col. John CRUGER was ordered to bring his battalion back to Savannah from Ft. Sunbury, and Lt. Col. John Maitland was ordered to bring his large detachment back from Beaufort (Port Royal). Gov.

Sir James Wright had returned and is said to have cast the decisive vote in the council of war in which the decision to defend Savannah was made. (Appleton's)

While his fleet blockaded the coast, d'Estaing started landing troops the night of 11–12 Sept. at Beaulieu, a point some 14 miles south of Savannah. When he had gotten ashore with 1,500 men, bad weather set in and he was left in this vulnerable situation for several days until the rest of his landing force and the supplies could join him. (C. & M., 1092) Here again, there is disagreement as to dates, but most accounts say that the landing was on the 12th and that advance American units under McIntosh and Pulaski had joined d'Estaing by the 15th. At this time Lincoln was moving with the rest of the rebel troops from Charleston.

The morning of 16 Sept., d'Estaing approached Savannah and demanded its surrender "to the arms of the King of France." Playing for time, Prevost requested and was granted 24 hours to consider. During this truce Maitland reached Savannah with 800 men from Beaufort after a remarkable movement through swamps and streams to elude the French blockade and the American forces on the mainland. Since Cruger had already arrived from Sunbury, Prevost now had 3,200 rank and file plus a considerable number of citizens and slaves who would be useful in the defense. Prevost sent word he would fight.

Lincoln joined d'Estaing the evening of 16 Sept. to swell the American ranks to 1,500 (600 Cont'ls., Pulaski's 200 cavalry, and 750 militia). Contemporary accounts emphasize the lack of cordial relations between the allies. Cruger wrote that Lincoln's command was "so much despised by the french as not to be allowed to go into their Camp,

no communication together." While this British observation is probably exaggerated, d'Estaing's unilateral surrender demand did not sit well with the Americans, and there was friction from the start.

Although Moultrie urged making an immediate assault, d'Estaing decided— apparently with Lincoln's agreement—to undertake a siege. Since guns and supplies had to be hauled 14 miles from the landing site, and heavy rains delayed operations, REGULAR APPROACHES were not started until the night of 23– 24 Sept., and the bombardment did not begin until the night of 3–4 Oct. Meanwhile, d'Estaing was under pressure from his naval captains to abandon the expedition: the fleet was in need of repairs, the hurricane season was approaching, they were vulnerable to attack by the British fleet, and their men were dying of scurvy at the rate of 35 a day. (Fisher, *Struggle,* II, 259) D'Estaing had agreed to stay ashore only 10 or 15 days, which his engineers said would be enough time. But when 10 days elapsed and his engineers estimated they would need 10 more, he refused to delay that long. After a council of war on 8 Oct. d'Estaing ordered an attack to be made the next day at dawn.

BRITISH DISPOSITIONS

With the excellent engineering services of Moncrieff, Prevost had constructed a line of field fortifications in a rough half circle to cover the land approaches to Savannah. The five-day bombardment had damaged many of the 430 houses in the town and had inflicted casualties among noncombatants, but the earthworks were virtually unscathed. Prevost realized that the right half of his line was the most vulnerable and organized his defenses accordingly. The wooded marshes to the west (Yamacraw Swamp) would give an enemy concealment to within 50 yards of his fortifications in this area, and to cover this threat the Sailors' Battery (see sketch) was located; the position was manned by sailors with 9-pd. cannon. The armed brig *Germain* was stationed in the river to deliver ENFILADE fire along this N.W. flank.

The broad finger of flat ground leading toward Spring Hill from the S.W. was recognized as being terrain over which "regular troops would choose to act," as Prevost says in his after-action report. (Clinton, *American Rebellion*, 433) A strong redoubt was therefore built on Spring Hill; it was manned initially by dismounted dragoons and supported by a S.C. Tory regiment. Along the quarter-mile that separated Spring Hill from the Sailors' Battery were two more redoubts and a second battery. Smaller fortifications and outposts covered the gaps, and a strong line of earthworks protected the right flank of the Spring Hill (or Ebenezer Road) redoubt.

Continuing counterclockwise around Prevost's perimeter, a fourth redoubt, commanded by Cruger, covered the road leading to Savannah from the south; a fifth redoubt, commanded by Maj. James Wright, son and heir of Gov. WRIGHT, was situated on the N.E. end of the line. Lesser works were located along the entire line, and a ditch and abatis were out front. The regular regiments and the better Tory units were deployed to the rear. (For fuller details, see Lossing, II, 736, or Stedman for map drawn under Moncrieff's direction.)

THE ATTACK

The allies planned their main attack just where Prevost says he expected it —against Spring Hill. A secondary attack by Gen. Dillon's battalion (French)

was to move secretly from the N.W. and follow a defiladed route that would enable them to turn the enemy's right near the Sailors' Battery. Gen. Isaac Huger prepared to lead 500 militia from the south toward Cruger's redoubt; his mission was to make a feint that would draw the enemy's attention away from the main effort, and to break through the defenses if this appeared possible.

American histories repeat the story that Sgt. Maj. James Curry of the Charleston militia deserted and told Prevost where the main attack would hit. Tales of treachery are so commonly produced to justify defeats that this one must be viewed with suspicion; Prevost may well have gotten such intelligence from Curry, but since he makes no mention of it in his report (and from other statements in that report) (Clinton, 432) it would appear that he did not take advantage of this information, if, indeed, he ever received it. (Military commanders learn early that information from deserters is among the most unreliable gathered by their intelligence service.)

We can dispose of operations on the flanks by saying that they failed. Dillon's column lost its way in the swamp, emerged in plain view of the enemy's lines, and was driven back by fire. Huger's command was also forced to withdraw without getting close enough to threaten the British left.

The attack on Spring Hill was supposed to be made by three French and two American columns. To get into position, the French had to march about half a mile west to the American camp and then move north to the line of departure (L.D.). Here they would deploy along the edge of a woods in a "line of columns" (see FORMATIONS) and be prepared on signal to attack N.E. across about 500 yards of open ground toward Spring Hill. Two American columns were to form on their left and attack Spring Hill from the west. These preliminary movements were supposed to take place so that a coordinated attack could be made at dawn, which was about 5 A.M.

The French were late, and it was 4 A.M. before the entire allied army of about 4,500 troops started marching in one long column from the vicinity of the American camp toward the L.D. (Account of Thos. PINCKNEY from Hough, *Siege of Savannah,* quoted in C. & M., 1097 ff.) When the first French column reached its position on the right flank of the L.D. around dawn, d'Estaing led it forward without waiting for the others to file off to the left. This column was badly shot up by grape as they moved across the open space and by musket fire when they reached the abatis.

"... in spite of the effort of the officers, the column got into confusion and broke away to their left toward the wood in that direction; the second and third French columns shared successively the same fate, having the additional discouragement of seeing, as they marched to the attack, the repulse and loss of their comrades who had preceded them." (Pinckney, *op. cit.*)

In the American zone, Pulaski's 200 horse were to lead the approach march, pull off to the left, wait for the abatis to be breached, and charge through the gap. Col. John Laurens would lead the 2d S.C. Cont'ls. and the 1st Bn. of Charleston militia against the Spring Hill redoubt. Gen. McIntosh would bring up the rear with the 1st and 5th S.C. Cont'ls. and some Ga. regulars. Francis MARION'S 2d S.C. Cont'ls. spearheaded the attack through heavy frontal and enfilade fire of an enemy that was now thoroughly alerted. They crossed the open area, swarmed over the ditch,

hacked their way through the abatis, and planted the Crescent Flag of the 2d S.C. and the French flag on the parapet of the Spring Hill redoubt. But this marked the high tide of their attack, and the S.C. troops were unable to continue on. Lieutenants Bush and Hume (or Homes) fell mortally wounded beside the American standard, and the French standard bearer, one of d'Estaing's aides, also went down. (Lossing, 738 *n.*) After a third American officer, Lt. Gray, had replaced the flags, he was hit. Sgt. JASPER, of Ft. Sullivan fame, was mortally wounded putting the flags up for a third time.

As Laurens' men were starting to retreat, the British counterattacked with the grenadiers of the 60th Regt. and a small company of marines. Maj. Beamsley Glazier led this sortie and in fierce, hand-to-hand fighting drove back the French and Americans who had clung to their forward positions. "In an instant the ditches of the [Spring Hill] redoubt and of a battery to its right and rear were cleared," reported Prevost. (Clinton, 433) Other British troops apparently advanced to support Glazier's counterattack, and Ward says "the fight at that point raged with unremitting fury for nearly an hour; but the crowded and confused allies were at last driven back, and retreated to their camp, leaving 80 dead in the ditch and 93 between it and the abatis." (*Op. cit.,* 694)

While this fight was going on, Pulaski was trying to force his way between the Spring Hill and the works to its west. Cavalry is unsuited for an attack against organized defenses, and the infantry had not carried out the plan of breaching the abatis for him. The gallant Polish volunteer nevertheless led his troopers forward. They were caught in the abatis and badly shot up by well-organized enemy fire that covered this obstacle. When Pulaski was carried mortally wounded from the field, Col. Daniel Horry took command and tried to continue the attack, but the cavalry had started a retreat and could not be stopped.

McIntosh arrived to meet a scene of bloody confusion. The retreating cavalry had swept away part of Laurens' command as they moved into Yamacraw Swamp, and Laurens had lost effective control of his scattered and disorganized units. The wounded d'Estaing was trying to rally French troops, and when McIntosh asked him for instructions he was told to circle left so as not to interfere with the French reorganization. The fresh American column was consequently diverted into Yamacraw Swamp, where its left flank came under fire from the *Germain,* and was still floundering there when the sounds of battle died down. Pinckney went forward on reconnaissance and returned to report that not an allied soldier was left standing in front of Spring Hill. McIntosh therefore ordered his column to withdraw. (Pinckney, *op. cit.*) (As for light conditions on the day of battle, "dawn"—or, to be precise, the beginning of morning nautical twilight [B.M.N.T.]—would have been at about 5 o'clock and sunrise at 6. Because of the heavy fog, however, visibility was poor even after B.M.N.T. Prevost says it was still dark when firing started to his flanks and center, and that by the time the allies withdrew the fog was still too thick to permit his making "a respectable sortie to take advantage of the confusion of the enemy. . . ." [from Clinton, 433].)

NUMBERS AND LOSSES

The allies lost over 800, of whom about 650 were French. Ward points out that this was 20 per cent of the total engaged, and may have repre-sented 50 per cent of those in action against Spring Hill. Prevost says he buried 203 allied dead around Spring Hill, 28 on his left, and delivered 116 wounded prisoners (many of whom were mortally wounded). Prevost's estimate of 1,000 to 1,200 allied killed and wounded is very close to the American estimate of 1,094 given by Lossing (*op. cit.,* 739 *n.*). One modern American historian puts the total at 172 killed and 580 wounded (Peckham, *War for Indep.,* 125); this is about 10 per cent lower than the "traditional" figure of 828 (16 officers and 228 men killed, 63 officers and 521 men wounded)— these are given by Greene, *Rev. War,* 204–5 (although he arrives at an incorrect total of 837) and Ward, *W.O.R.,* 694. Bonsal puts French casualties at 642, which is very close to the "traditional" figure of 637. This same authority points out that "A very large percentage of the wounded died, and the total loss was three times that later sustained in the successful siege of Yorktown." (*Cause of Liberty,* 61)

About 3,500 French and 1,500 American troops took part in the attack; these figures include the forces under Dillon and Huger. (These are the figures from Ward, 692–93. "According to the most accurate calculations," says editor Uhlendorf in a note on p. 167 of *The Siege of Charleston,* "d'Estaing's force . . . consisted of no more than about 4,500, while the Americans numbered some 2,000." He cites Jones's *Siege of Savannah,* 39. The extra 1,000 French and 500 Americans may have had passive missions in the unfinished siege works, at the Beaulieu landing site, and elsewhere.)

British losses, according to Clinton, did not exceed 16 killed and 39 wounded. (*Op. cit.,* 150; 433) Lossing says they lost at least 120; Greene and Ward accept the figures of 40 killed,

63 wounded, and 52 missing (an improbable ratio in any type of land action, and particularly unlikely in a defensive situation; see CASUALTY FIGURES); this total of 155 appears in many modern American histories. It is quite likely that Clinton's total of 55 casualties among "the King's troops" does not include losses in the Tory, Hessian, and other units in Prevost's command.

On 16 Sept., when d'Estaing submitted his summons to surrender, Prevost had not more than 10 guns in position, "and his garrison, including the armed inhabitants and sailors, did not consist of more than four thousand, of which not above twenty-four hundred were regimented troops." (Clinton, 150) The first 400 arrived from Beaufort with Maitland by noon of the 16th, and "by the same time next day we had all the rest fit for duty except the Hessian artillery, which by some strange neglect was left behind." (*Ibid.,* Prevost's report, 432) This brought the strength of the regulars up to 3,200. (MAITLAND, incidentally, had malaria when he led his detachment on their remarkable march to Savannah and died a few days after the battle.)

THE END OF THE AFFAIR

Although Lincoln urged d'Estaing to continue the siege, the French returned to their ships on 20 Oct., and Lincoln was then obliged to retreat to Charleston. Bearing out the aphorism, *Jamais deux sans trois,* d'Estaing had now failed the Americans at New York, Newport, and Savannah. The Americans were bitter about the impotency of the FRENCH ALLIANCE. Discouragement naturally was strongest in the South, and the militia which had been gathering at Charleston started melting home.

Having "remained in cruel suspense as to the fate of Georgia until the middle of November" (Fortescue, *op. cit.,* 285). Clinton greeted news of d'Estaing's failure as "the greatest event that has happened in the whole war." (Letter quoted by editor Willcox in Clinton, 149 *n.*) He was now free to undertake his long-considered return to Charleston.

See Lawrence, *Storm over Savannah . . . ,* Athens, Ga., 1951.

SAVANNAH, Ga., 29 Dec. '78–11 July '82. British occupation.

SCAMMELL, Alexander. 1747–1781. Cont'l. officer. Mass. His parents settled in Mendon (now Milford), Mass., about 1737, having come from Portsmouth, England. Alexander's father was a prominent and well-to-do doctor who died when the boy was six. Graduating from Harvard in 1769, Alexander taught, was a surveyor, and then started studying law in the office of John SULLIVAN in Durham, N.H. He became Maj. of N.H. militia in Apr. '75, Brig. Maj. of Sullivan's Brig. on 21 Sept. '75, serving in the Boston Siege and in Canada. He returned to N.Y.C. with SULLIVAN, was appointed his A.D.C. on 14 Aug. '76, and as acting A.D.C. to Washington made a mistake that might have lost the War of Independence for the Americans; this is covered in the article on the evacuation of LONG ISLAND, 29–30 Aug. '76. This did not slow his military advancement; on 29 Oct. he became Brig. Maj. in Charles Lee's Div., and on 8 Nov. '76 he was made Col. of the 3d N.H. Regt. Returning to the Northern Dept., he was present when St. Clair evacuated Ticonderoga, 5 July '77, and led his regiment in the two battles of Saratoga; in one of the latter actions he was slightly wounded.

On 5 Jan. '78 he succeeded Timothy Pickering as Washington's A.G., in which capacity it was his duty to arrest Charles Lee (LEE COURT MARTIAL) and, curiously, to execute his British counterpart, John André. On 16 Nov. '80 Scammell submitted his resignation as A.G. to take command of the 1st N.H., but it was not until 1 Jan. '81 that he actually left Washington's staff. (This is the date implied by Heitman, who says he resigned on this day. See the sketch of Edward HAND, who succeeded Scammell as A.G., for further details.) "I shall very reluctantly part with Colonel Scammell," wrote the C. in C., "as he has constantly performed his duty to my entire approbation and to the satisfaction of the Army...." (quoted in Freeman, *Washington*, V, 229 *n.*) In the Yorktown Campaign he commanded 400 light infantry in the preliminary operations against Manhattan in July '81. After describing the movement of Washington's army to start the siege of Yorktown, Johnston writes:

"This favorable prospect was clouded only by the fall, early on the 30th [of Sept. '81], of the brave and much-loved Colonel Alexander Scammell.... When the pickets reported the evacuation of the enemy's outer position he went forward, with a small [mounted] party, as field-officer of the day, to reconnoitre the deserted works. Proceeding along a short distance toward Yorktown, he was suddenly surprised by some troopers of Tarleton's Legion, under Lieutenant Cameron, and mortally wounded the moment after his surrender. [In a footnote the author comments] That Scammell was shot after his surrender is well established—an accident, perhaps, in the haste of the surprise." (*Yorktown*, 123 and *n.*)

Other writers are not convinced that he was shot after surrendering. "Contemporary reports of his death are not agreed in making such a charge, and it is not clear by what channels the report of any eye-witness could have found its

way back to the American lines," points out *D.A.B.* There can be no doubt, however, as to his popularity; the fact that so many contemporary diarists and letter-writers commented on the sad event "is one indication of the Army's grief over this hurt to one of the most admired of American field officers." (Freeman, *op. cit.,* V, 351 *n.*) Paroled and evacuated into the American lines, he died in Williamsburg on 6 Oct. of the gunshot wound, variously described as having been in the side or back.

SCHAFFNER, George. Cont'l officer. Pa. According to Lasseray, this man was from Lancaster and in Mar. '76 enrolled as a private in Abraham de Huff's Co. of Atlee's Pa. Musket Bn. of militia. Promoted to Sgt., he went with his unit to Philadelphia, reached Amboy on 21 July, and N.Y.C. on 11 Aug. Eight days later he was promoted to Ensign, and on 25 Aug. fought with Alexander's right wing at Long Island. Remnants of his unit were incorporated into Sam'l. Miles's Regt. for the march to Fort Lee and to the Delaware. Then as part of Hand's Brig. they fought at Trenton and Princeton. On 4 Feb. '77 Schaffner became a 2d Lt. in John Paul Schott's Co. of Ottendorf's three-company battalion. The latter unit was soon incorporated into the 1st Bn., Cont'l. Partisan Legion, of Col. Armand-Tuffin.

Heitman, who spells the name Shaffner, says he was a 2d Lt. in the "German Regt." on 12 July '76, but his other dates and facts are in accord with Lasseray's. Schaffner fought at Short Hills (see TUFFIN), Brandywine, and Germantown. On 8 Feb. '78 he was promoted to Capt., on 1 Dec. he was made Maj., and on 25 Nov. '83 he was honorably discharged.

Having become an intimate friend of the remarkable Armand-Tuffin, he accompanied the latter to France. A letter of 23 May '86 from Chastellux says that Armand-Tuffin was visiting Germany, "probably with M. Schafner [*sic*], a young and excellent officer who was a major in his legion." (Quoted in Lasseray, 151) He supported TUFFIN in Brittany, was arrested on 24 Aug. '92, but released a few days later. From Dec. '92 to Jan. '93 he visited London as Tuffin's liaison officer to the *émigrés*. On 31 Jan. he signed the *procès-verbal* of Tuffin's burial and took refuge outside France. Learning that friends of his were being executed (incriminating documents are said to have been found when Tuffin's body was located and exhumed [Lossing, II, 466 *n.*]), Schaffner returned, joined the Vendée counterrevolutionaries, and his trace disappears. According to Lenôtre (see TUFFIN) he was captured in an action on the Loire and died in the *noyades* (judicial drownings).

Of an obscure and poor family, George Schaffner, known in France as Chafner, was considered a worthy companion of the dashing and capable Armand-Tuffin. He was known for his wit, but a Frenchwoman, who was not among his admirers, pointed out that the Pennsylvania "Dutchman" never learned French well and suggested that his interpreter was the one who showed *"beaucoup d'esprit."*

SCHOENBRUNN, Ohio Terr. See GNADENHUETTEN. . . .

SCHOHARIE VALLEY, N.Y., 15–19 Oct. '80. Under the circumstances outlined under BORDER WARFARE, Sir John Johnson led a force of between 800 and 1,500 Tories, British regulars, and Indians into the Schoharie Valley from the S.W. on 15 Oct. (See KLOCK'S FIELD for composition of his expedition.) That night he bypassed the Upper Fort and, burning farms as he went, approached the Middle Fort early 16 Oct.

The American commander of this place, Maj. Melancthon Woolsey, sent out a 40-man reconnaissance force which withdrew before the invader. The garrison of 150 "three-months men" and 50 militia found themselves besieged by a vastly superior enemy who had the further advantage of possessing artillery.

Maj. Woolsey was ready to discuss surrender, but a certain militia soldier took matters into his own hands. When a flag started forward it was fired on. Woolsey and his officers were outraged at this breach of etiquette and discipline, but Timothy MURPHY and his famous long rifle were unrepentant. Twice more they repeated the performance, and by the time Woolsey and some of his officers were ready to arrest Murphy the latter had gathered the support of enough militia buddies and of a few officers to protect him. When Woolsey ordered a white flag raised, Murphy threatened to kill the man who moved to comply. Meanwhile, Johnson found that his artillery was too light to make any impression on the fort and, not knowing what had been going on among the defenders, he decided they were too tough for him to handle. In between flags the raiders had dispersed to pillage and burn, and the defenders had made a few sorties. They finally abandoned the siege and continued down the Schoharie, made a feeble attack on the Lower Fort, crossed the Mohawk, and started up the valley. Patriot forces under Gen. Robert Van Rensselaer were gathering to meet them. (See BORDER WARFARE)

Schoharie Valley had been an important source of provisions; Washington wrote that it had furnished 80,000 bushels of grain for public use. A strong west wind fanned the fires started by the raiders (Swiggett, *Niagara*, 222), and by the time Johnson's column cleared the Lower Fort, at 4 P.M. on the 17th (C. & M., 1028) the prosperous valley was in flames. Tory houses left by the invaders were destroyed by the patriots. During the next two years, however, the valley was spared the raids that continued to scourge the Mohawk Valley. (Campbell, *Tryon,* 147)

SCHUYLER, Hon Yost. Mentally defective nephew of Gen. Herkimer whom the Americans used to panic the Indians around Ft. Stanwix and end ST. LEGER'S EXPEDITION.

SCHUYLER, Philip John. 1733–1804. Cont'l. general. N.Y. Scion of one of N.Y.'s most ancient, honorable, and well-heeled Dutch families, Philip Schuyler was connected by marriage to just about all the others. He was born into the fourth generation of the SCHUYLER FAMILY in America. After an excellent education, mathematics and French being his particular fortes, he was commissioned Capt. at the beginning of the French and Indian War, fought at Lake George on 8 Sept. '55, and almost immediately thereafter showed the military inclinations that were to characterize his Revolutionary War career—he became a logistician. Even before 1755 he had had his first attack of rheumatic gout, a hereditary disease that occurred throughout the rest of his life and that may well have inclined him toward army administration rather than troop leading. After the action of 8 Sept. '55 he was detailed to escort the French prisoners of war to Albany. Without wasting a day he married Catherine Van Rensselaer on 17 Sept. before rejoining the forces in the field. He established a military depot at Ft. Edward, and the next spring served under Bradstreet in carrying provisions to Oswego. Resigning his commission in 1757, he kept up his commissary interests and derived a substantial income from provisioning the army.

(John A. Krout in *D.A.B.*) In 1758 he returned to military service as deputy commissary and in the grade of Maj. took part in the unsuccessful attack on Ticonderoga and the capture of Ft. Frontenac. During 1759–60 he operated from Albany—his birthplace, incidentally—in provisioning Amherst's forces. He had become a close friend of Bradstreet and in Feb. '61 sailed to England with him to settle his War Office accounts. At the end of the last Colonial War he was therefore a man with rich experience in provisioning field forces.

It so happened that the year the Peace of Paris was signed—1763—the final settlement of his father's estate, including a third of his grandfather's lands, brought him thousands of acres in the valleys of the Mohawk and the Hudson. In addition he received from his Uncle Philip the old Schuyler homestead near West Troy and, his favorite heritage, lands in the Saratoga Patent. (*D.A.B.*) He became an efficient manager of his birthright and a happy family man.

Elected to the state assembly in 1768, he proved to be an ardent patriot but an opponent of the radical Sons of Liberty and the advocates of mob action. As a commissioner in the boundary dispute with Mass. and N.H. over the region that later became Vermont he had already become disliked in New England for his support of the N.Y. claims. When the Cont'l. Cong. started naming generals, however, one of the top ones had to be from N.Y. and on 15 June '75 Schuyler became Maj. Gen. and commander of the Northern Dept. Of Washington's generals only Artemas Ward and Charles Lee ranked above Schuyler.

In preparations for his part of the CANADA INVASION the austere Dutch patrician immediately showed his good and bad qualities as a senior commander: knowing the importance of logistics, he was slow getting started; with only the half-hearted support of the New Englanders to start with, he further alienated these republicans by his personal manner and by his insistence on discipline; and when he finally took the field to lead his troops down Lake Champlain into Canada he almost immediately was prostrated by rheumatic gout. As is more thoroughly covered in the article on the CANADA INVASION, Richard Montgomery took command of the field army and Schuyler directed the forwarding of supplies from Albany.

The events leading to Schuyler's downfall at the hands of Congress started on 9 Jan. '77 when the delegates voted to dismiss Dr. Samuel Stringer, Director of Hospitals in the Northern Dept. Schuyler's protest at this interference in his business without being consulted revealed what Fisher calls "the somewhat arrogant trait which caused his unpopularity among the New Englanders" (*Struggle*, II, 56); this element in Congress seized this as a flimsy pretext to reprimand Schuyler in terms that were almost insulting and to order Horatio Gates north as commander of the American forces then (Mar. '77) at Ticonderoga. (*D.A.B.*; Freeman, *Washington*, IV, 389, 401) Schuyler visited Washington's headquarters early in Apr. and then went to Philadelphia and won this first round with Congress, which clarified Gates's status as being subordinate to Schuyler. Given the alternative of accepting this position or resuming his post of A.G., Gates left the Northern Dept. and rushed to Congress. (See GATES)

Schuyler returned to find his army "weak in numbers, dispirited, naked, in a manner, destitute of provisions ... with little ammunition, and not a single

piece of cannon." (Quoted in *D.A.B.*) Except for his indecisiveness in connection with the defense of Ticonderoga, Schuyler's generalship in the initial stages of BURGOYNE'S OFFENSIVE was sound. But the loss of Ticonderoga was enough to rally support to his enemies in Congress. On 4 Aug. '77 the delegates ordered Gates to relieve him. It was more than a year before Schuyler had the satisfaction of being acquitted by a court-martial (in Oct. '78) of charges of incompetence. On 19 Apr. '79 he resigned his commission.

Although out of the army under humiliating circumstances, Schuyler had continued to make himself useful in the operations against Burgoyne and deserved much of the credit for the British defeat. (*C.E.*) After his resignation he remained on the Board of Commissioners for Indian Affairs and performed valuable service in reducing the ravages of the Border Warfare that continued along the Iroquois frontier. Having already served in the Second Cont'l. Congress (1775) and again in 1777, Schuyler returned as a delegate from N.Y. in 1779–80. He participated in the sessions of Nov.–Dec. and Feb.–Apr. during this last period and prepared a report on depreciated currency and the issue of new bills of credit that was adopted with only slight modifications. (*D.A.B.*) From 13 Apr. until 11 Aug. '80 he was chairman of a committee at Washington's headquarters to assist the latter in reorganizing the army's staff departments and to work out a scheme for effective cooperation with the French expeditionary forces. (*Ibid.*) From 1780 until 1798 he held public office continuously.

Of this complex personality, whom he calls "one of the most interesting figures of the Revolution," Freeman has these comments:

"... he was not unlike a considerable number of successful eighteenth-century Americans, who found to their surprise that war called for rarer qualities than business and commerce demanded.* * * While he never was facile in dispositions for actual combat, he had sound strategical judgment, Washington thought, and he would work patiently, through any maze of detail, when he thought the duty aided the cause and became a gentleman.* * * Any criticism of his acts was a challenge of his integrity. . . . He could be ingratiating and he could be lofty, too. New Englanders resented his air of superiority; he returned disfavor with contempt—but all the while, in his own fortune as in his daily comfort, no man was readier to sacrifice for American freedom." (*Op. cit.,* IV, 367B)

The Schuyler Papers are in the N.Y. Public Library. His Letters are in the Lloyd W. Smith Coll., Morristown Nat'l. Park. The standard biography is B. J. Lossing, *The Life and Times of Philip Schuyler* (2 vols., 1860–73). See also G. W. Schuyler, *Colonial New York: Philip Schuyler and his Family* (2 vols., 1885).

Alexander Hamilton was Schuyler's son-in-law. The relationship of G. W. Schuyler, the author cited above, is shown in the diagram accompanying the article on the SCHUYLER FAMILY.

SCHUYLER FAMILY OF N.Y. (pronounced sky-ler) Philip Pieterse Schuyler emigrated from Amsterdam and appears first in the records of Albany on the occasion of his marriage in 1650 to the daughter of the resident director of Rensselaerswyck. He was a merchant and held offices under both the Dutch and English governments of the colony. His second son, Peter, married the daughter of Jeremias Van Rensselaer; the latter was a son of the first patroon of Rensselaerswyck. Pe-

ter's daughter by his first marriage was Margarita, who married the nephew of the first Robert Livingston. Her sons were the soldiers in the Canada branch of the LIVINGSTON FAMILY, and her grand-daughter tightened the Schuyler-Livingston bonds by marrying the first Robert R. Livingston; this led to ties with other prominent families (see LIVINGSTON FAMILY). Peter's son Philip married his cousin Margarita in 1720; this remarkable woman (see sketch in *D.A.B.*) helped rear her nephew Philip John Schuyler, the famous Revolutionary War general.

SCHUYLER – GATES CONTROVERSY. See GATES–SCHUYLER. . . .

"SCOTCH WILLIE." Wm. MAXWELL.

SCOTT, Charles. c. 1739–1813. Cont'l. general. Va. Characterized by Appleton's as having "strong natural powers, but rough and eccentric in manner and somewhat illiterate," he is more euphemistically described by *D.A.B.* as rich in practical wisdom, frank and direct in speech. After receiving only an elementary education he served as an N.C.O. under Washington in Braddock's expedition. At the start of the Revolution he raised the first volunteer troops south of the James River in Va. and commanded a company at Williamsburg in July '75. On 13 Feb. '76 he was commissioned Lt. Col. 2d Va., on 7 May he became Col. of the 5th Va., and on 12 Aug. '76 he took command of the 3d Va. He led this regiment well at Trenton and as part of the covering force that so effectively delayed the British advance on that place before Washington scored his victory at PRINCETON, 3 Jan. '77. Promoted to B.G. on 2 Apr. at Washington's urging (Freeman, *Washington,* IV, 395), he and the brigade of Wm. Woodford constituted the division of Adam Stephen in the Philadelphia and Monmouth campaigns. He

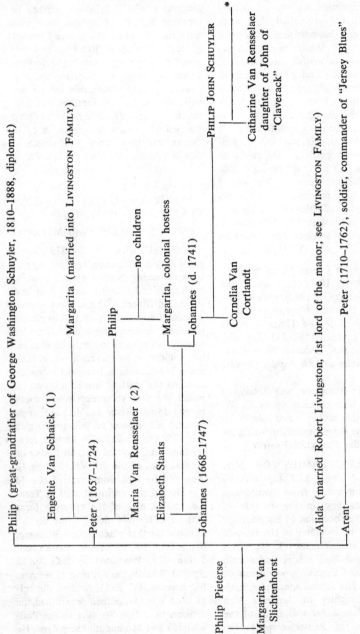

SCHUYLER FAMILY OF NEW YORK

* One daughter, Elizabeth, married Alexander Hamilton; another, Margaret, married Stephen Van Rensselaer (1764–1839), eighth patroon of Rensselaerswyck. There were nine other children. Their grandson, George Lee Schuyler, married successively two granddaughters of Alexander Hamilton.

was heavily engaged at the BRANDYWINE, facing the British turning column before Washington reinforced that flank. As part of Greene's column he saw action at Germantown, where his performance was severely criticized in a letter from Stephen to Washington on 7 Oct. '77. (*Ibid.*, IV, 512 *n.*) After spending the winter at Valley Forge he had a prominent role in the MONMOUTH CAMPAIGN, first as commander of a large detachment and finally as part of Charles Lee's command in the battle of 28 June. He is responsible for the dubious but beloved story of how the father of his country cursed out Lee (see MONMOUTH), and he testified effectively against the latter at the Lee court-martial.

Scott had been one of the nine B.G.'s to memorialize Congress when they were considering the promotion of Thos. Conway. A year later, around the end of 1778, the man whom Freeman characterizes as "a useful Brigadier" was talking of retirement. (*Ibid.*, V, 79) Although Scott is said to have taken part in Wayne's capture of Stony Point, 16 July '79 (Appleton's, *D.A.B.*), he played no significant role. Ordered south to reinforce Lincoln, he was captured at Charleston, 12 May '80, paroled, but not exchanged until the war ended. He was breveted Maj. Gen. on 30 Sept. '83.

In 1785 he moved to Ky. He was representative to the Va. Assy. from Woodford co. in 1789 and 1790. In Apr. '90 he took part in Harmar's unsuccessful expedition. The next year he was B.G. of Ky. levies and, with Col. James Wilkinson as second-in-command, led them against the Indians on the Wabash River (23 May–4 June) before taking part in St. Clair's defeat on 4 Nov. '91. In Oct. '93 he joined Anthony Wayne for an expedition against the Indians, but this was abandoned. On 20 Aug. '94 he led about 1,500 mounted volunteers in Wayne's victory at Fallen Timbers. (Samuel M. Wilson in *D.A.B.*) The old soldier became Gov. of Ky. in Aug. 1808 and served four one-year terms.

A brother, Joseph Scott Sr., was Muhlenburg's Brig.-Maj. and was wounded at Germantown. Joseph Scott Jr. became a Capt. on 12 May '80 and served throughout the war in the 1st Va.

SCOTTISH LEGION. See BRITISH LEGION.

SEARS, Isaac. 1730–1786. Privateer, N.Y.C. mob leader. Born in Mass. and reared in Norwich, Conn., he became a seaman and during the French and Indian War established a reputation as a privateer that made him a recognized leader of the sailors and shopkeepers of the N.Y.C. waterfront. As a Son of Liberty, "King" Sears was with the leaders of nearly every mob action in N.Y.C. for 10 years. He was wounded 11 Aug. '66 in the events covered in the article headed NEW YORK ASSEMBLY SUSPENDED. In 1774 he led the Sons of Liberty in turning back the first tea ship and dumping the cargo of the second into the water. Having worked with John Lamb and Joseph Allicocke in 1765 to propose that the Sons of Liberty be organized into a continental military union, he worked with Alexander McDougall in 1774 in proposing to the Boston Comm. of Corresp. that a meeting be held of delegates from the principal towns. This led indirectly to the 1st Cont'l. Cong., and shows the considerable scope of Sears as a revolutionary leader on paper as well as on the streets and waterfront. Arrested on 15 Apr. '75, he was rescued at the prison door by his supporters. When news of Lexington and Concord reached the city, 23 Apr., he and John Lamb led 360 men in scattering the Tory leaders and officials, seizing arms from the arsenal, taking over the customs house and preventing vessels from leaving, and starting the regular military training of the mob. Until the arrival of Washington's army the city was virtually under the martial law of Sears and his comrades. (*D.A.B.*) In Nov. '75 he returned from a short absence in New Haven to burn a naval supply ship, capture prominent Tories, and wreck the Tory press of James Rivington. He was commissioned by Chas. Lee in Jan. '76 to administer the oath of allegiance to Loyalists on Long Island, to raise volunteers in Conn., and to capture British supplies for the army. From 1777 to 1783 he operated privateers out of Boston. Returning to N.Y.C. to resume his general merchandise business, he and other prominent Revolutionary leaders undertook to terminate the publishing career of James RIVINGTON. Sears died of fever while on a business trip to Canton, China, and was buried there.

SECONDARY ATTACK. A commander normally groups his forces so as to provide for a main attack, secondary attack, and reserve. The secondary attack is allocated minimum essential combat power and has the missions of deceiving the enemy as to the location of the main attack, of forcing him to commit his reserve prematurely and at the wrong place, and of fixing enemy troops in position so they cannot be shifted to oppose the main attack. By the use of his reserve or by other means the commander may convert his secondary attack into a main attack.

SECRET COMMITTEE OF CONGRESS. Not to be confused with the COMMITTEE OF SECRET CORRESPONDENCE (which Bemis, for example, also calls the "Secret Committee"), this standing committee was created 18 Sept.

'75 to put the procurement of war supplies on a methodical basis. Given wide powers, large sums of money, and authorized to keep its proceedings secret —it destroyed many of its records—the Secret Committee was effective largely because its first chairman was Thomas Willing, who was succeeded in Dec. '75 by his partner, Robert Morris. (On 30 Jan. '76 the latter was appointed also to the other Secret Committee.) Other original members were Franklin, Deane, Robert R. Livingston, John Alsop, John Dickinson, Thomas McKean, John Langdon, and Samuel Ward. These men and their successors were practical men experienced in foreign trade. As a matter of fact, since the biggest contracts went to the firm of Willing & Morris, to relatives and friend. of Deane, and to firms connected with Alsop, Livingston, and Francis Lewis (who subsequently joined the committee), there was criticism of the committee's activities. The Adamses and Lees led the outcries against Willing & Morris.

Authority of the Secret Committee soon was extended to include supplies other than guns and ammunition. In Jan. '76 it was asked to import medicines, surgical instruments, blankets, cotton goods, and various metals. Soon it virtually controlled all foreign trade. "There was profit making and profiteering, but the sinews of war were supplied." (Augur, *Secret War*, 70) One of the most questionable operations of the committee started in Jan. '76 when Cong. voted it £40,000 for the importation of Indian presents; contracting merchants were allowed a commission of 5 per cent and the government insured their vessels against British seizures. Three of the four contracting merchants were members of the Secret Committee: Morris, Alsop, and Lewis; the other was Philip Livingston, a cousin of Robert R.! In Apr. the Secret Committee was empowered to arm and man vessels in foreign countries for the work of Cong., hence it became involved in PRIVATEERING.

The body launched itself boldly into the field of foreign affairs when, in conjunction with the Committee of Secret Correspondence, it sent former-member Silas Deane to France. The results are covered under DEANE and HORTALEZ & CIE. Affairs of the two secret committees became hopelessly scrambled early in 1777 when Franklin, Deane, and Arthur Lee started their duties as peace commissioners. The name of the Secret Committee was therefore changed in July '77 to the Committee of Commerce, which later evolved into the Dept. of Commerce; and the Committee of Secret Correspondence became the Committee on Foreign Affairs (17 Apr. '77).

SELORON. See CÉLORON DE BLAIN-VILLE.

SENTER, Isaac. 1755–1799. Army physician, diarist. N.H.–R.I. Born in N.H., he went to Newport early in life and studied medicine under Dr. Thos. Moffat. At the age of 20 he joined the Boston army as a surgeon and volunteered for ARNOLD'S MARCH TO QUEBEC. His journal of the expedition, which C. & M. calls "probably the best" of the many produced (*op. cit.,* 192), was first published in the *Bulletin of the Hist. Soc. of Pa.* and recently as "The Journal of Isaac Senter, M.D., on a Secret Expedition against Quebec, 1775" in *The Mag. of Hist.* . . . , Extra No. 42, 1915. Extracts are in C. & M. (pp. 196–201, 215–16) and in S. & R. (117–21, 123, 127).

In Nov. '75 he became surgeon of the 3d R.I., a position he held until Mar. '76. Subsequently he was Hospital Surg., 20 July '76 to Apr. '79, and Surg. Gen. of R.I. Militia, 1779–81. (Heit-

man) Establishing private practice in Pawtucket, he later moved to Newport and became one of the most eminent surgeons and practitioners in R.I. An honorary member of the medical societies of London, Edinburgh, and Mass., he was Pres. of the R.I. Soc. of the Cincinnati for many years. (Appleton's)

SERLE, Ambrose. Civilian secretary to Lord Richard Howe. *The American Journal of Ambrose Serle, Secretary to Lord Howe, 1776–1778,* edited by Edward H. Tatum, Jr., was published by The Huntington Library (San Marino, Calif.) in 1940. With a light pen, a position at the top, and an ear for gossip, Serle produced a work that has been valuable to historians since its recent appearance in print. Many excerpts are in C. & M. and S. & R.

SEVEN YEARS' WAR (1756–63). Known in America (where it started and spread to Europe) as the French and Indian War (1754–63), it is covered under COLONIAL WARS.

SEVIER, John (suh-veer'). 1745–1815. Pioneer, militia officer, 1st Gov. of Tenn. Grandson of a French emigrant to England, and eldest son of Valentine Sevier, who had emigrated from London to Baltimore to the Shenandoah Valley, John was born near the site of New Market. His mother, Joanna Goade, was a native of the Valley. Sevier also married a local girl, Sarah Hawkins (m. 1761). After early experience that included farming, trading, surveying—he laid off the town that became New Market—and service as a militia officer, Sevier was ready to move southward along the mountain valleys to a newer frontier. In Dec. '73 he reached the Holston settlements with his wife, their six or seven children, and all their possessions.

Sevier had the background, the personal courage, and the natural leadership that made for a big man on the frontier. In 1776 he signed a petition requesting that N.C. extend jurisdiction over the Watauga and Holston settlements, and when this request was granted he became first a representative to the Prov. Cong. and then Lt. Col. of militia. (*D.A.B.*) In 1777 he was promoted to Col. (Heitman) Until 1780, however, Sevier took no active part in military operations and it was not until his chief political rival, James Robertson, moved on to middle Tenn. that he rose above the level of a minor local office holder. At the head of 240 "OVER MOUNTAIN MEN" Sevier became one of the heroes of KINGS MOUNTAIN, S.C., 7 Oct. '80. Immediately after his return from that victory he started his career as leader of punitive expeditions against the Cherokees, or, to be more specific, against the Chickamauga element of that tribe. (See INDIANS. . . .) In 1781 he again moved eastward across the mountains, this time with 200 men, to support American regulars and militia against the British. "Greene had sent them to Marion to help in holding back Doyle, but he got word on the march that the freeborn mountaineers had gone home," points out Ward. (*W.O.R.*, 838) Although it is commonly stated that Sevier rendered some real assistance against the British in 1781 (*D.A.B., E.B.*), this is debatable.

When the war ended, Sevier entered into a project to establish a colony at Muscle Shoals and he was so engaged when his Holston and Watauga neighbors started a movement to become a separate state. "Finding the movement irresistible, he put himself at the head of it, was elected governor of the state of Franklin, and tried to convert the new state into an instrument for promoting his Muscle Shoals enterprise." (*D.A.B.*) Three years later Sevier's career and the "State of Franklin" had

been blasted: no longer hailed as a hero of Indian warfare, he now was denounced as a disturber of peace, and his "state" was condemned by the N.C. authorities as illegal. Taking refuge on the far frontier, "he sank to the level of a bushwhacker, defied the efforts of Congress to control Indian affairs, and entered into a dubious correspondence with Spanish agents who were seeking to disrupt the Union." (*Ibid.*)

In this decisive year of 1788, which saw the collapse of his position as a leader on the old frontier, a turn in national politics presented the opportunity for a new career: N.C. refused to ratify the Constitution, but it was apparent that the new national government would be successful and Sevier came forth as a Federalist. The next year he was elected to the state senate, was fully pardoned, and was elected to Congress. When Tenn. was admitted as a new state he became its first governor, 1796–1801, and held this post again from 1803 to 1809. Two years later he was re-elected to Congress and served until his death.

See J. R. Gillmore, *The Rear-Guard of the Revolution* (1886), and *John Sevier as a Commonwealth Builder* (1887). Errors in these works are pointed out in Theodore Roosevelt's *Winning of the West* (see main bibliography). A critical analysis of Sevier's career is in the *D.A.B.* sketch by Arthur P. Whitaker. A modern biography is Carl S. Driver's *John Sevier: Pioneer of the Old Southwest* (1932).

SHAFFNER, George. See SCHAFFNER.

SHARON SPRINGS SWAMP, N.Y., 10 July '81. (BORDER WARFARE) Col. Marinus Willett was at Ft. Plank (Canajoharie) the afternoon of 9 July when he saw smoke rising from CURRYTOWN, about four miles south. At the same time he received a report from Capt. Gross, who was patrolling in the direction of New Dorlach with about 35 men, that the enemy had established a camp in Sharon Springs Swamp (as it was subsequently called). Capt. Robert McKean was sent immediately to Currytown with 16 militiamen and Willett soon headed south with about 100 men. His guide was unable to lead Willett through the dense cedar swamp to surprise the camp that night, and when contact was made at 6 A.M. the 300 Tories and Indians under John Doxtader were on more advantageous ground, ready to defend themselves.

Having been rejoined by Gross and McKean (with some volunteers from Currytown), Willett now had about 150 men, but he was determined to fight. Not being able to outnumber the enemy, he outsmarted them. The dense vegetation enabled him to form a crescent with the tips pointing toward the enemy. Lt. Jacob Scammons then advanced with orders to fire, fall back, and draw Doxtader into the trap. It worked, and the raiders were met by a devastating fire. McKean was either in reserve (Lossing, I, 294) or on Willett's left flank (Campbell, *Tryon,* 172); he hit the enemy flank, and Willett led the rest of his command forward "with bullet and bayonet." (*Ibid.*) Doxtader put up some resistance but soon broke and fled, leaving 40 dead and abandoning the camp and its plunder. The rebels lost five killed and nine wounded or missing. McKean died of wounds a few days after the battle.

SHAW, Samuel. 1754–1794. Cont'l. officer. Mass. As a Lt. of Arty. he served in the Boston Siege, the N.Y. Camp'n. (being for a while at Ft. Washington), and took part in the battles of Trenton, Princeton, Brandywine, Germantown, and Monmouth. (*D.A.B.*) He became a 1st Lt. in the 3d Cont'l. Arty. on 1 Jan. '77 and was promoted to Capt. on 12 Apr. '80. During the period June

'82–Nov. '83 he was A.D.C. to Knox, being transferred to the Corps of Arty. on 17 June '83. His *Journals* are a particularly valuable source of information on the conspiracy covered under NEWBURGH ADDRESSES. He was present when Washington reoccupied N.Y.C. and assisted in the disbandment of the Cont'l. Army. Washington commended him for his intelligence, energy, and courage. In 1784 he started establishing commercial relations with the Orient, in 1785 Knox appointed him to a position in the War Dept., and in 1786 he became the first U.S. consul in China. After serving three years he returned to the U.S., was reappointed (by Washington), and returned to China aboard the *Massachusetts,* whose construction he had directed. After another visit to the U.S., during which time he was married (21 Aug. '92), he returned to the Orient in 1793. He died near the Cape of Good Hope, 30 May '94, of a liver disease picked up on a visit to Bombay.

See *The Journals of* [Brevet?] *Major Samuel Shaw, with a Life of the Author,* by Josiah Quincy (1847).

SHAYS, Daniel. 1747?–1825. Cont'l. officer, insurrectionist. Mass. A 2d Lt. in Woodbridge's Mass. Regt. from May to Dec. '75, he became Capt. in the 5th Mass. Cont'l on 1 Jan. '77. He resigned 14 Oct. '80 for "reasons quite problematical." (Quoted in Appleton's without attribution.) He had served 11 days during the Lexington alarm, was promoted for gallantry at Bunker Hill, and served at Ticonderoga, Saratoga, and Stony Point. A brave and efficient officer, he was considerate of his subordinates and popular with his men. (*D.A.B.*) Lafayette presented him with a sword, which Shays later had to sell because of poverty. (*Ibid.*) He is remembered for SHAYS'S REBELLION, although others were as active in this uprising as he. After being pardoned he moved to Schoharie co., N.Y., and then to Sparta, N.Y., where he died. A man of humble origin and little real ability, he was a brave and honest leader. (*Ibid.*)

SHAYS'S REBELLION, 31 Aug. '86–4 Feb. '87. As the newly independent American colonies coped with the problems of establishing a viable economy despite the post-war depression, the collapse of currency, and the colonial aversion to taxation, Capt. Daniel Shays (1747?–1825) became leader of an armed revolt in western and central Mass. against constituted authority. Those who so recently had united in revolt against English authcrity were now divided in opinion as to whether the "right of revolution" could be exercised any time citizens objected to governmental authority. Malcontents under Shays objected to a Mass. decree that debts be paid in specie; they objected to the mounting number of farm and home foreclosures; and many of them lacked property qualifications for voting. The central government, under the Articles of Confederation, was powerless to suppress the revolt, and the outcome depended on "loyalty" and effectiveness of the state militia. Mob actions started on 31 Aug. '86, when armed men prevented the court from sitting at Northampton. Similar events took place at Worcester, Concord, and Great Barrington, whereupon Gov. James Bowdoin sent Gen. Wm. Shepherd with 600 militiamen to protect the Supreme Court at Springfield. Shays confronted the militia with 500 men on 26 Sept. and obliged the Court to adjourn. Since this was the site of a federal arsenal, Congress on 20 Oct. authorized that 1,340 federal troops be raised, mostly in Mass. and Conn., ostensibly for service against the Indians. Toward the end of the year the insurrection collapsed in other parts of the state, but Shays marched on Springfield the day after Christmas with some 1,200 men to reinforce those under Luke Day. Shepherd's small militia force guarded the arsenal. Gov. Bowdoin met this new menace by calling for 4,400 men, and Gen. Benj. Lincoln was named their commander. When official funds were not forthcoming, Lincoln raised $20,000 from private sources. On 25 Jan. '87 the militia of Shepherd held the arsenal against a mismanaged attack by the Shaysites. Lincoln arrived two days later, dispersed the force under Day, and pursued Shays toward Petersham through a blizzard. Early on 4 Feb. Lincoln completed a vigorous night march to surprise the insurgents, capturing 150 and scattering the rest. By the end of Feb. the uprising had been completely crushed.

Mass. offered to pardon all but Shays, Day, and two others, and Shays was finally pardoned on 13 June '88. While some looked on the revolt as evidence that republican government was not feasible, the majority interpreted the experience to mean that a stronger central government would have to be established, not only to crush such uprisings but, better still, to prevent them by improving economic conditions. Thus Shays helped speed the movement toward adoption of the Federal Constitution. On the other hand, the rebellion brought relief to those on whose part it had been undertaken: the Mass. legislature postponed imposition of a direct tax and limited the liability of debtors, exempting tools and certain personal effects. (*D.A.H., E.A.H.*)

SHELBURNE, William Petty Fitzmaurice, Earl of. 1737–1805. British statesman. Born in Dublin of a noble family, he graduated from Oxford and served in Wolfe's regiment during the Seven Years' War. Having distinguished himself at Minden and Kloster-Kampen, he was promoted to Col. and made A.D.C. to the King (1760). He joined the Grenville ministry in 1763 as Pres. of the Bd. of Trade but resigned after a few months. During his brief tenure, however, he had drafted the portentous PROCLAMATION OF 1763. His support of Pitt made him unpopular with George III, and he retired to his estate. In 1761 he had succeeded his father as Earl of Shelburne in the Irish peerage and Baron Wycombe in the British peerage. He became Pitt's secretary of state in 1766, but with the incapacity of Pitt (see CHATHAM) his conciliatory policy toward America was frustrated, and in 1768 he was dismissed. In 1782 he consented to join the Rockingham ministry on condition that the King would recognize the U.S., and when Rockingham died (1 July '82) Shelburne became P.M. For reasons stated in the sketch on Fox, the ministry was doomed to failure and was succeeded on 24 Feb. '83 by the coalition of Fox and Lord North. When Pitt the younger came to office in 1784 Shelburne was not offered a place in the cabinet but was created 1st Marquess of Lansdowne.

Although he was an unscrupulous politician when it came to his own advancement, "no statesman of his time possessed more enlightened political views...." (*E.B.*, "Lansdowne, Wm. P. F.")

SHELBY, Isaac. 1750–1826. Militia leader, 1st Gov. of Ky. Son of the soldier and frontiersman Evan Shelby, Jr. (1719–1794), Isaac was reared on the frontier of Md. About 1773 he moved with his family to the Holston settlements and in 1774 he served in his father's Fincastle (County) Company as a Lt. He distinguished himself in the battle of Point Pleasant, 10 Oct. '74 (DUNMORE'S WAR), and his account of that action is considered to be one

of the best. Until July '75 he was second in command of the garrison at Point Pleasant. After surveying lands in Ky. for the Transylvania Company and, later, for himself, he was appointed Capt. of a company of Va. minutemen in July '76. For the next three years he was engaged in providing supplies for various frontier garrisons and for the expeditions of Lachlan McIntosh (1778) and George Rogers Clark (1779). He also was involved in important dealings with the Indians and in surveying lands in Ky. Early in 1780 he was appointed Col. of militia in Sullivan co., N.C.

In response to an urgent call from Col. Charles McDowell, in July '80 he joined the latter at Cherokee Ford, S.C., with about 600 "OVER MOUNTAIN MEN" and captured THICKETTY FORT. He combined forces with Elijah Clarke to repulse the attack of a Tory detachment at Cedar Springs, 8 Aug., and to win the engagement at MUSGROVE'S MILL ten days later.

Shelby figured prominently in the victory at KINGS MOUNTAIN, 7 Oct. '80, and he also "has been accorded credit for the scheme of attack...." (*D.A.B.*) Local Indian problems kept the frontiersmen close to home until a treaty was negotiated on 20 July '81. With 200 men Shelby joined Col. Hezekiah Maham to capture a British post at Fair Lawn, near Monck's Corner, S.C., 27 Nov. '81. While engaged in this expedition he was elected to the N.C. legislature. He attended its sessions in Dec. '81 and, re-elected, he sat in the sessions held at Hillsboro in Apr. '82.

The next year he moved to Ky., where he was a member of the conventions of 1787–89 that prepared the way for statehood. On 4 June '92 he took office as the first Gov., but four years later he declined re-election and devoted the next 15 years to his private affairs. In Aug. 1812 he again became Gov., and the next year he led 4,000 volunteers north to take part in the victory over the British at the Thames, 5 Oct. 1813. In Mar. 1817 he declined the portfolio of Sec. of War to Pres. Monroe, maintaining that he was too old. A rugged frontiersman and a good military commander, Shelby was also a remarkably able statesman. Throughout the various movements organized by land speculators and political opportunists "Shelby pursued a wise and moderate course which baffled the plots of all conspirators and held Kentucky firmly to her federal moorings." (*D.A.B.*) During the war crisis that brought him back into public office in 1812 he proved himself "an active, resourceful, and patriotic leader." (*Ibid.*) Confederate Gen. Joseph Orville ("Jo.") Shelby (1830–1897) was a kinsman but not a direct descendant.

His manuscript autobiography is in the Durrett Collections, University of Chicago, and a few other papers are in the Lib. of Cong. His account of the battle of Point Pleasant is in Kellogg and Thwaites, *Dunmore's War,* and in Roosevelt's *Winning of the West* (I, 341–44).

SHELDON, Elisha. Col. of 2d Dragoons. Conn. After commanding a battalion of Conn. light horse from June '76, he was commissioned Col. on 12 Dec. '76 and commanded the 2d Dragoons from then until the end of the war. He was breveted B.G. on 30 Sept. '80. In the Philadelphia Campaign of 1777 he performed the normal cavalry tasks of reconnoitering the enemy's movements. Thereafter he served on the east side of the Hudson. Tarleton made an unsuccessful attempt to defeat him at POUNDRIDGE, 2 July '79. As part of his preparations to give West Point to the British, Benedict Arnold had to hoodwink Sheldon into permitting "John Anderson" (John André) to enter the

American lines if he should make the attempt. Sheldon had been temporarily succeeded by his Lt. Col., John Jameson, when "John Anderson" arrived. (See ARNOLD'S TREASON) In the operations against Manhattan preceding the YORKTOWN CAMPAIGN, Sheldon took part in the unsuccessful attempt on 3 July '81 to surprise De Lancey near Morrisania. When the allies marched to Va. he remained under Heath in the Highlands. At the end of the war his unit was called a "Legionary Corps." The last official paper issued by Washington before leaving West Point to reoccupy N.Y.C. had to do with the discharge of the three-year men in Sheldon's unit.

SHELL'S BUSH, N.Y., 6 Aug. '81. (BORDER WARFARE) Donald McDonald with 60 Indians and Tories surprised this settlement while its inhabitants were working in the fields. Most of the patriots ran for Ft. Dayton, five miles to the south, but John Christian Shell, a wealthy German whose real name probably was Schell, made a stand in his blockhouse. Two sons who were with him in the fields were captured, but Shell, his wife, and six other sons made it to the blockhouse. While Frau Schell reloaded muskets the male members of the family kept up a fire that held off the enemy. Attempts to set the place on fire were not successful, and McDonald was wounded and dragged inside after trying to force the door with a crowbar. The enemy finally withdrew. McDonald died the next day after his leg was amputated. Eleven assailants were killed, six wounded, and the captured boys said another nine died of wounds before reaching Canada. The defenders suffered no casualties. John Shell was mortally wounded and one of his sons killed a short time later while in their fields. (Lossing, I, 299–300, citing Stone's *Brant.*)

SHEPARD. Of the various possible spellings of this name, Heitman's *Register* includes 10 Shepards, one Shephard, and seven Shepherds.

SHEPARD, William. 1737–1817. Cont'l. officer. Mass. Grandson of an English immigrant and son of a tanner and deacon of the Congregational Church, he enlisted at the age of 17 and ended the French and Indian War as a Capt. with six years of valuable military experience. A farmer, selectman, and member of the Westfield Comm. of Corresp. prior to the Revolution, he was elected Lt. Col. of Timothy Danielson's Mass. Regt. in May '75 and joined the Boston army. On 1 Jan. '76 he was commissioned Lt. Col. of the 3d Cont'l. Inf., was wounded in the Battle of Long Island, 27 Aug., and promoted to Col. on 2 Oct. with seniority from 4 May. (Heitman) He performed well at PELL'S POINT, N.Y., 18 Oct. '76, and was wounded in this action. On 1 Jan. '77 he took command of the 4th Mass. and led them in the battles around Saratoga. After spending the winter at Valley Forge (John Glover's Brig.) he was on recruiting duty around Springfield, Mass.

Breveted B.G. on 30 Sept. '83, after having retired from military service on 1 Jan., he farmed at Westfield. As a Maj. Gen. of Hampshire co. in 1786 he defended the federal court at Springfield during Shays's Rebellion and starting on 25 Jan. '78 held off Shays's attack on the arsenal until LINCOLN arrived. He was never fully reimbursed for public expenditures from his own pocket, and he had personal property destroyed by Shays's sympathizers. In addition to other public offices, he served in the House of Representatives for three two-year terms starting 4 Mar. '97. The veteran of six years' military service before the Rebellion and of 22 Revolutionary War engagements (Appleton's) spent his last 15 years quietly on his farm. (Katherine Elizabeth Crane in *D.A.B.*)

SHERBURNE'S REGT., commanded by Col. Henry Sherburne, was one of the 16 "ADDITIONAL CONT'L. REGTS." Lt. Col. Return J. Meigs served with it 22 Feb.–22 May '77, and Maj. Wm. Bradford served 12 Jan. '77–1 Jan. '81. (Heitman, 26)

SHERMAN, Roger. 1722–1793. Quadruple Signer, statesman. Mass.–Conn. With the distinction of being the only man to sign four of the great documents of the Cont'l. Cong., the Articles of Association of 1774, the Decl. of Indep., the Articles of Confederation, and the Constitution, Roger Sherman epitomizes the self-made man. Educated in country schools near his father's farm at Stoughton, just south of Boston, he had a natural thirst for knowledge and a methodical approach to self-education. He read widely in history, law, politics, mathematics, and theology. Apprenticed as a cobbler, he is said to have worked with an open book always before him. In 1743, after the death of his father, he moved to New Milford, Conn., where his elder brother had settled, and the tradition is that he walked the entire distance—some 170 miles by road—with his cobbler's tools on his back. When the final break came with England, Sherman was a conservative Whig in New Haven, where he had moved in 1760. He had been county surveyor, 1745–58, had been admitted to the bar in 1754, had held a large number of public offices, and had made a good deal of money not only as a multiple officeholder but also as a merchant. He was elected treasurer of Yale in 1765 and held, the post until 1776. As evidence of his tremendous energy and versatility, in 1752 he published *A Caveat Against Injustice, or an Enquiry into the Evil Consequences of a Fluctuating Medium of Exchange,* and between 1750 and 1761 he published a series of almanacs based on his own astronomical calculations. In 1775 and during the period 1758–61 he was elected to the legislature. He also had served as commissary for Conn. troops during the French and Indian War.

Roger Sherman was therefore well qualified to represent his province in the Cont'l. Cong. and he served as a delegate from 1774 to 1781, and again in 1783–84. Although not the hero of any particular act of that body, perhaps because of his undramatic personality and lack of oratorical ability, the stern old Puritan, "honest as an angel and as firm in the cause of American independence as Mount Atlas" (John Adams speaking), ended with more legislative experience than any other delegate. (J. P. Boyd in *D.A.B.*) He was on the committee to draft the Decl. of Indep., on various ways and means committees, on the board of war and ordnance, on the treasury board, and on the committee on Indian affairs. With Yankee standards of economics, and based on his considerable fiscal experience before and during the war, Roger Sherman defied popular opinion to argue for sound currency, minimum government borrowing, and high taxes. He also disregarded the vested interests of friends and former business associates to advocate Connecticut's cession of western land claims.

In addition to his burdensome Congressional duties he had important state business. He was on the Conn. council of safety (1777–79, 1782), and in 1783 he and Richard Law worked five months to revise the statutory law of Conn. In the federal convention of 1787 he introduced and took the leading part in having adopted the essential Connecticut Compromise, giving Congress its dual system of state representation.

SHIP OF THE LINE. One of 74 guns or more. See LINE.

SHIPPEN FAMILY of Philadelphia. Edward Shippen (1639–1712) emigrated from Yorkshire to Boston in 1668, became wealthy as a merchant and landowner, joined the Quakers around 1671, and some 23 years later moved to Philadelphia because of religious persecution. He was elected in 1695 to the provincial assembly, became its speaker, was president of the council for 10 years starting in 1702, was acting governor from Apr. '03 to Feb. '04, mayor from Oct. '01 to Oct. '03, city treasurer from 1705 until 1712, and an associate justice of the supreme court from 1699 to 1703. Married three times, he had 11 children, of whom Joseph became the grandfather of Edward (1729–1806) and William (1736–1808).

Edward Shippen, just mentioned, became chief justice of Pa. after the Revolution even though he had been a moderate Loyalist and his daughter Margaret ("Peggy") married Benedict Arnold.

William Shippen (1736–1808), Edward's cousin, was a physician and pioneer teacher of anatomy and midwifery. About 1760 he married Alice Lee, a daughter of Thomas of "Stratford" and the sister of Richard Henry, Francis Lightfoot, William, and Arthur Lee. (See LEE FAMILY OF VIRGINIA) After studying under William Hunter in London, Shippen started teaching anatomy in Philadelphia on 16 Nov. '62. Although there was violent popular objection to his use of human bodies—a method taught by Hunter—he rapidly gained recognition. In 1765 he became professor of surgery and anatomy in the newly established medical school of the College of Philadelphia, and prior to this time he started teaching midwifery not only to medical students but also to women who intended to become midwives.

In 1776 he was appointed chief physician and director general of the Cont'l. Army hospital in N.J., and in Oct. became director general of all hospitals on the west side of the Hudson, according to *D.A.B.;* Heitman says he was "Chief Physician of the Flying Camp, 15th July to 1st December, 1776." On 11 Apr. '77 he succeeded John Morgan as chief physician and director general of the Cont'l. Army hospitals. His appointment undoubtedly was earned to a large extent by the plan for reorganization of the medical service that he submitted to the Cont'l. Cong. in Mar. '77 and that was adopted almost in its entirety. (His father, William, also a prominent doctor, was later a delegate to the Cong., 1779–80.) Morgan accused Shippen of engineering his discharge and Benjamin RUSH charged him with inefficiency. Shippen later was acquitted by a court-martial of financial irregularities in his department. On 3 Jan. '81 he resigned from the army and continued his career as teacher and practitioner, although the death of his only son, a young man of great promise, in 1798, marked the beginning of a decline in his health and his interest in life (*D.A.B.*).

SHIRLEY, William. 1694–1771. Colonial governor of Mass. Son of a London merchant, who died when William was only seven, he grew up amidst aristocratic connections but without the financial means for the life to which he aspired. He graduated from Cambridge, was admitted to the bar in 1720, and for 11 years practiced law in London. During this time he increased his circle of influential connections but not his financial status. Deciding to emigrate to America, he reached Boston in 1731 with a letter of introduction to Gov. Belcher from Newcastle, who was Shir-

ley's kinsman and lifelong patron. A long period of place-hunting was marked by his appointment as judge of admiralty in 1733 and, soon thereafter, as advocate general. In his search for higher office Shirley undertook to undermine the already unstable reputation of BELCHER and on 25 May '41 succeeded him as governor of Mass.

Faced with the problem of the land bank, which made the finances of the colony unstable, and with the need to strengthen military defenses as war with France appeared to be inevitable, Gov. Shirley proved himself an able and tactful administrator. He overcame British and American resistance to gain approval for an expedition to capture Louisburg, the French fortress that threatened New England fisheries, and on 17 June '45 this place surrendered to an expeditionary force of New Englanders under William Pepperrell and the supporting British fleet under Commodore Peter Warren. The hard money allowed by Parliament in 1748 to reimburse Mass. for her expenses in the Louisburg operation was used to reestablish finances of the province on a firm basis. (See also Thomas HUTCHINSON) Shirley was absent during the period 1749–53 as a commissioner in Paris to establish the boundary between New England and French Canada. On his return he worked to prepare for the expected renewal of hostilities in America.

In 1755 Shirley was appointed Maj. Gen. and led the unsuccessful expedition against Niagara. One of his sons, a Capt., died of fever on this operation, and his eldest son was killed while serving as Braddock's secretary. Shirley became C. in C. after Braddocks' death but was succeeded by James Abercromby when the home authorities became dissatisfied with his conduct of military affairs. When Loudoun became

C. in C. he developed an intense dislike for Shirley, and the latter finally was recalled to England in 1756 to face charges not only of mismanagement of military strategy and organization but also of irregularities in his financial accounts. It was his misfortune to arrive just as the tenure of Newcastle was ending, but in the fall of 1757 the War Office was forced to drop its court-martial charges for lack of evidence. Thomas POWNALL meanwhile took office as Gov. of Mass. Promoted to Lt. Gen., Shirley became Gov. of the Bahamas in 1761 after having been finally denied the promised post of Gov. of Jamaica. In 1767 he relinquished the governorship to his only surviving son, Thomas, and two years later he returned to his home at Roxbury, Mass., where he died in Mar. '71.

See C. H. Lincoln (ed.), *Correspondence of William Shirley . . . 1731–1760* (2 vols., 1912); the works of Thomas HUTCHINSON, Osgood (*American Colonies,* Vols. III and IV), and Pargellis (*Loudoun*). G. A. Wood, *William Shirley* (1920), deals with his administration during the years 1731–49.

SHIRTMEN. A term for American riflemen, it appears to have been coined by the British and applied originally to to the Va. riflemen. (Lossing, II, 535 n.) In his entry of 20 July '75 Thacher speaks of the arrival of Pa. and Md. riflemen in the Boston lines: "They are dressed in white frocks, or rifle-shirts, and round hats." (*Military Journal,* 31)

See also GREAT BRIDGE, MUTINY ON PROSPECT HILL, and RIFLEMEN.

SHOEMAKER'S HOUSE. See Walter BUTLER (who was captured there) and GERMAN FLATS, N.Y.

SHORT HILLS (Metuchen), N.J., 26 June '77. During the "June Maneuvers" of the PHILADELPHIA CAMPAIGN, Alexander ("Stirling") camped with his division and some other regiments near Metuchen Meeting House, about five miles N.W. of Amboy, to which place Howe had hastily withdrawn his army. The rest of Washington's army was at Quibble Town (modern New Market) between Alexander's strong detachment and Middle Brook. At 1 o'clock the morning of 26 June, Howe marched out of Amboy in two columns with the intention of first annihilating Alexander, seizing the passes back to Middle Brook, and then defeating Washington in a pitched battle. Washington learned of Howe's sortie, however, realized the enemy's intentions (Freeman, *Washington,* IV, 433), and ordered a retreat. Although Washington referred to Alexander's position as being on "low and disadvantageous" ground, Trevelyan said, "Stirling, who was still something of a military pedant, neglected the rare advantages which the locality presented, and drew up his command in parade-ground order; while Cornwallis made no mistakes and gave full play to the indignant valour of his followers," almost cutting off the American outpost (Freeman, IV, 433; Ward, 464 n., 327). Casualties were not heavy, but Alexander's rear guard lost three valuable French field guns. The British pursued Alexander some five miles N.W. toward Westfield.

The name of this action in the *A. A.–* Heitman list of battles is "Short Hills," and I have retained this designation although it might more logically be called the Affair at Metuchen Meeting House. The other name is confusing because the Short Hills Meeting House was near Springfield, more than 12 miles away. (See SPRINGFIELD, N.J., RAID. . . .)

SHORT HILLS (Springfield), N.J., 7–23 June '80. See SPRINGFIELD RAID.

SHREVE, Israel. d. 1799. Cont'l. officer. N.J. Lt. Col. of the 2d N.J. on

31 Oct. '75, he was Col. on 28 Nov. '76 and served until his retirement in Jan. '81. According to Heitman, he retired on 1 Jan., when the reorganization of the N.J. Line took effect, but Col. Shreve was present during the MUTINY OF THE N.J. LINE, 20–27 Jan. '81. When Washington wrote Shreve for an explanation of his failure to put in an appearance on 27 Jan., Shreve mentioned nothing about being out of the service but said, "[I] thought it best to not go to camp until the matter was over, as those who suffered might look up to me for to intercede for their pardon." Washington did not learn until 7 Feb. that Shreve had left the service when the N.J. Brig. was reorganized as of 1 Jan. '81. (Freeman, *Washington*, V, 250 *n.*) Although Elias DAYTON theoretically moved from command of the 3d N.J. to succeed Shreve as commander of the 2d N.J. on 1 Jan. '81, this change apparently did not actually occur until the end of Jan.

A loyal patriot who had been impoverished by his long war service, the immensely fat Shreve was an incompetent officer whose slim prospects for promotion to B.G. were killed by Washington's statement in Dec. '80 that "here I drop the curtain." (Quoted in Van Doren, *Mutiny*, 209)

SHURTLEFF, Robert. Alias under which Deborah SAMPSON enlisted in the Cont'l. Army.

SIGN MANUAL. In one sense this meant the signature of the sovereign on a document to signify royal authentication. It also meant the regulations governing naval tactics, perhaps because these were authenticated by the sovereign but also because they involved a manual (small book) of signals (signs) flown from the flagship to direct an engagement.

SIGNERS. In American history a "Signer" is one of the 56 members of the Cont'l. Cong. who signed the Declaration of INDEPENDENCE. "At this historical distance it is hard for citizens of the world's most powerful republic to realize that the founding fathers actually were committing an act of treason when they scrawled their names," wrote Montross in 1950 (*Reluctant Rebels,* 165). Considering the bleak outlook for the American cause in 1776, the Signers are particularly to be admired for the act that in a more sophisticated age would have made them "war criminals" had the war turned out otherwise. The danger to the Signers was so great that their names were held secret until 18 Jan. '77, when the victories at Trenton and Princeton prompted Cong. to take the bold step of ordering an authenticated copy of the Decl. of Indep. and the names of the Signers to be sent to each state. Francis LEWIS and Richard STOCKTON each suffered a particularly hard fate at the hands of the British for having signed the famous document. The lot of Thos. Hart was almost as cruel. Elbridge GERRY and Thos. JEFFERSON escaped capture by minutes, and another six were fortunate enough to avoid being taken by enemy forces sent in their pursuit. Homes of 15 of the Signers were destroyed. (*Ibid.,* 165)

Among the famous men in the Cont'l. Cong. who refused to sign the document after its approval are John DICKINSON, James DUANE, Robt. R. LIVINGSTON, and John JAY. Opponents of the document who nevertheless signed it were Carter Braxton, Robt. Morris, Geo. Read, and Edmund Rutledge. Outstanding members of the Cont'l. Cong. who did not have a chance to sign were Washington, Sullivan, and Geo. Clinton (all of whom were in the field); Gadsden and Patrick Henry (occupied in their home states); and "youthful patriots born a few years too late, such as Madison, Hamilton and Monroe." (*Ibid.,* 164) As opposed to these "famous non-Signers," one might list as a non-famous Signer the man who joined the Cont'l. Cong. on 4 Nov. '76: Matthew Thornton.

Thomas McKean apparently was the first to challenge what later was the popular impression that the Decl. of Indep. was *signed* on 4 July, points out J. H. Peeling in *D.A.B.* "Finding that his name did not appear as a signer in the early printed journals of the Congress, he asserted in a letter [of 26 Sept. '96]... what the corrected Journals and contemporary letters have since substantiated, that no one signed on July 4. The exact date of his signing is not known. Although he later insisted it was in 1776, it is almost certain that it was after Jan. 18, 1777. That it was as late as 1781, as some writers aver, is doubtful." (*Ibid.*) See INDEPENDENCE, Decl. of, for more on actual date of signing.

An alphabetical list of the Signers, all of whom are sketched individually, is below. Standard works are William Brotherhead, *Book of the Signers* (1860, and new edition in 1875), and John and James Sanderson, *Biographies of the Signers...,* (7 vols., 1823–27). Editorship of the latter work was taken over about 1820 by Robert Waln, Jr., who brought out vols. III–VI. (*D.A.B.,* "Waln")

SILLIMAN, Gold Selleck. 1732–1790. Militia general. Conn. Son of Ebenezer (1707–1775), who had been judge of the Conn. superior court 1743–66, Gold graduated from Yale in 1752. Active in the militia, he was Col. of the Conn. Regt. 20 June–25 Dec. '76 and subsequently was B.G. of militia. (Heitman) During the N.Y. Camp'n. he had commanded his regiment at Long Island and White Plains. In 1777 he saw action in the DANBURY RAID. Captured by the Loyalists, he was paroled on Long Island and exchanged a year later for his Yale classmate Thomas JONES.

THE 56 SIGNERS

Adams, John (Mass.)	Hooper, William (N.C.)	Read, George (Del.)
Adams, Samuel (Mass.)	Hopkins, Stephen (R.I.)	Rodney, Caesar (Del.)
Bartlett, Josiah (N.H.)	Hopkinson, Francis (N.J.)	Ross, George (Pa.)
Braxton, Carter (Va.)	Huntington, Samuel (Conn.)	Rush, Benjamin (Pa.)
Carroll, Charles (Md.)	Jefferson, Thomas (Va.)	Rutledge, Edward (S.C.)
Chase, Samuel (Md.)	Lee, Francis Lightfoot (Va.)	Sherman, Roger (Conn.)
Clark, Abraham (N.J.)	Lee, Richard Henry (Va.)	Smith, James (Pa.)
Clymer, George (Pa.)	Lewis, Francis (N.Y.)	Stockton, Richard (N.J.)
Ellery, William (R.I.)	Livingston, Philip (N.Y.)	Stone, Thomas (Md.)
Floyd, William (N.Y.)	Lynch, Thomas, Jr. (S.C.)	Taylor, George (Pa.)
Franklin, Benjamin (Pa.)	McKean, Thomas (Del.)	Thornton, Matthew (N.H.)
Gerry, Elbridge (Mass.)	Middleton, Arthur (S.C.)	Walton, George (Ga.)
Gwinnett, Button (Ga.)	Morris, Lewis (N.Y.)	Whipple, William (N.H.)
Hall, Lyman (Ga.)	Morris, Robert (Pa.)	Williams, William (Conn.)
Hancock, John (Mass.)	Morton, John (Pa.)	Wilson, James (Pa.)
Harrison, Benjamin (Va.)	Nelson, Thomas, Jr. (Va.)	Witherspoon, John (N.J.)
Hart, John (N.J.)	Paca, William (Md.)	Wolcott, Oliver (Conn.)
Hewes, Joseph (N.C.)	Paine, Robert Treat (Mass.)	Wythe, George (Va.)
Heyward, Thomas (S.C.)	Penn, John (N.C.)	

His sons and grandsons became famous as scientists and lawyers.

SILVER BULLET TRICK. Messengers or spies would sometimes carry a message in a hollow, silver bullet that could be swallowed to prevent incrimination if they were captured. In his entry of 14 Oct. '77, Dr. Thacher wrote: "After the capture of Fort Montgomery, Sir Henry Clinton despatched a messenger by the name of Daniel Taylor to Burgoyne with the intelligence; fortunately he was taken on his way as a spy, and finding himself in danger, he was seen to turn aside and take something from his pocket and swallow it. General George Clinton, into whose hands he had fallen, ordered a severe dose of emetic tartar to be administered. This produced the happiest effect as respects the prescriber; but it proved fatal to the patient. He discharged a small silver bullet, which being unscrewed, was found to enclose a letter from Sir Henry Clinton to Burgoyne." (*Military Journal*, 106. See CLINTON'S EXPEDITION for contents of the message. The spy was tried, convicted, and executed.)

SILVER BULLETS OF TICONDEROGA. The sudden and bloodless British capture of TICONDEROGA, 2–5 July '77, led to camp stories that Burgoyne had bought his victory by firing into this "Gibraltar of America" silver balls that St. Clair had gathered up and sent down to Schuyler in Albany. "Absurd as the story was," writes Ward, "the New Englanders, in their dislike of Schuyler as a New York aristocrat, seem to have believed it, or at least affected to do so." (*W.O.R.*, 420) Even John Adams took some notice of it and reported the rumor to his wife, Abigail.

SIMCOE, John Graves. 1752–1806. British commander of QUEEN'S RANG-

ERS. Son of a Royal Navy Capt. killed at Quebec in 1759 (*E.B.; D.N.B.*), he was schooled at Exeter, Eton, and Oxford before becoming an ensign of the 35th Foot in 1771. He accompanied the regiment to America as Adj. and saw active service around Boston in 1775. Promoted to Capt. of the 40th Foot in that year, he was severely wounded at the Brandywine, 11 Sept. '77, and on 15 Oct. was promoted and named commander of the QUEEN'S RANGERS. He led this unit of Tory horse and foot troops in the skirmishes at QUINTAN'S and HANCOCK'S BRIDGES, N.J., Mar. '78, and in the action at CROOKED BILLET, Pa., 1 May, before taking part in the Monmouth Campaign and winning promotion to temporary ("local rank") Lt. Col. in June. He took part in the foraging expedition that led to the TAPPAN MASSACRE, N.Y., 28 Sept. '78, but was not engaged in the latter action. On 1 June '79 his Rangers took part in the capture of STONY POINT and Verplancks Point, and they raided POUNDRIDGE, N.Y., 2 July '79. He narrowly escaped death when he was ambushed, wounded, and captured with four of his men on 17 Oct. after a successful raid from Amboy to Somerset C. H., N.J.; he was exchanged on 31 Dec. '79 (*D.N.B.*).

When the traitor Arnold was sent to raid Va. a year later, Clinton included these instructions in a directive to Arnold on 14 Dec.: "Having sent Lieutenant Colonels Dundas and Simcoe (officers of great experience and much in my confidence) with you, I am to desire that you will always consult those gentlemen previous to your undertaking any operation of consequence." (Quoted in Clinton, *Amer. Reb.*, 482–83) Highlights of Simcoe's operations in Va. were his rout of the militia defenders of RICHMOND, 5 Jan. '81, his surprise and rout of another militia concentration by a night raid to CHARLES CITY C. H., 8 Jan., his part in the attack at PETERSBURG, 25 Apr., his raid to scatter Steuben's command at POINT OF FORK, 5 June, and his battle at SPENCER'S TAVERN, 26 June. During the Yorktown siege he was posted on the north bank of the York River at Gloucester, and surrendered there with the rest of Cornwallis' army on 20 Oct. '81.

Promoted to full Col. of the British Army on 19 Dec. '81 and invalided home this same month, he married in 1782 and until 1790 divided his time between London and his family estate in Devon. He then entered parliament. On the division of Canada in 1791 he was appointed the first Lt. Gov. of upper Canada. In July '92 he arrived to take up his new duties (under Carleton) and selected Niagara (then called Newark) as his capital. The next year he started moving to Toronto. Simcoe's administration, according to *D.N.B.*, "has been generally commended, despite his displays of prejudice toward the United States." The *E.B.*, on the other hand, says that although he showed the most disinterested devotion to his task, he had "military and aristocratic conceptions quite unsuited to the pioneer conditions," and that his administration was "rendered ineffective by the impracticable character of his projects and the friction which developed between himself and ... the governor-general."

On 3 Oct. '94 Simcoe was appointed commander of recently captured San Domingo and given the rank of Maj. Gen. In July '97 he returned to England, and on 3 Oct. '98 was promoted to Lt. Gen. In 1801 he commanded at Plymouth when Napoleon's invasion was expected. In 1806 he was named C. in C. in India but, his health broken, he took sick on the way out, returned home, and died on 26 Oct. 1806.

Simcoe's Military Journal ... A History of ... the Queen's Rangers ... (1844) is a valuable source book, particularly for the minor actions in which he participated. Most of its 10 useful battle sketches are reproduced in Lossing's *Field Book*. See also D. C. Scott, *John Graves Simcoe* (1905; rev. ed., 1926).

SIMITIERE, Pierre-Eugène du. 1736–1784. Artist. Switz. Born in Geneva, he went to the West Indies when he was about 14, and after almost 15 years there went to N.Y. before settling in Philadelphia in 1766. (Appleton's) Around 1779 he drew the portraits of Washington, Steuben, Silas Deane, Joseph Reed, Gouverneur Morris, Gates, John Jay, Wm. H. Drayton, Henry Laurens, Charles Thompson, Sam'l. Huntingdon, John Dickinson, and Benedict Arnold. (See first portion of article on ARNOLD.) Engraved in Paris, published there in 1781, pirated in England (1783), and reprinted many times, "These engravings did much to establish the iconography of the 'famous men' therein represented." (Note of editor Rice in Chastellux, *Travels,* 309) The Swiss was an avid collector of natural curiosities, books, and pamphlets. In 1782 he opened his celebrated collection to the public as the "American Museum." Sold in 1785, his papers and printed materials are preserved in the Library Company of Philadelphia and the Lib. of Cong., Washington. He died a bachelor.

SIMSBURY MINES, Conn. Abandoned copper mines, 10 miles N.W. of Hartford, where Loyalist prisoners were incarcerated.

SKENE, Philip. 1725–1810. Loyalist. Born in England, he entered the 1st Royal Regt. in 1736 and was in the battles of Cartagena, Porto Bello, Dettingen, Fontenoy, and Culloden. In

1750, having risen to Brig. Maj. of the 10th Foot, he married an Irish heiress who was related to Sir Wm. Johnson. He served under Lord Howe in the attack on Ticonderoga in 1758, under Amherst in the capture of that place and Crown Point the next year, and in the subsequent operations against Martinique and Havana. In 1759 he received a large grant of 34,000 acres on Lake Champlain which he expanded by purchase to 60,000 acres. He founded Skenesboro (now Whitehall), N.Y., a place that figured prominently in subsequent military operations on Lake Champlain. (Appleton's) Part of his domain lay in the Hampshire Grants (later Vt.), and in the controversy between N.Y. and N.H. over claims to this region, Skene sided with N.Y. In this matter he shared cause with Philip Schuyler, whom he had known during the campaigns of 1758. Skene became postmaster of Skenesboro in 1771, visited England, and in Jan. '75 was appointed Lt. Gov. of Ticonderoga and Crown Point. Meanwhile he had developed a flourishing little wilderness empire with sawmills, foundries, and shipyards. He was also the principal official in a new government the British hoped to establish on Lake Champlain to end the N.Y.–N.H. claims conflicts. This explains why Skenesboro was one of the objectives of the New England expedition that captured TICONDEROGA, 10 May '75. His son and daughters were taken, and when Skene himself went to Philadelphia in June he was arrested and sent to internment in Conn. He was released in Oct. '76, served a short time under Gen. Howe in N.Y., and then joined Burgoyne's Offensive on Lake Champlain. Although he expected to assume his duties as Gov. of the region, he became Burgoyne's principal Loyalist advisor and in this capacity—much resented by the other

Loyalists—he took part in subsequent military operations. He has been accused, without apparent justice, of recommending the overland line of operations from Skenesboro to the Hudson. (Under BURGOYNE'S OFFENSIVE see section headed "Burgoyne's First Mistake.") He accompanied the BENNINGTON RAID in Aug. '77 and showed personal courage in the portion of that operation covered under "Breymann's Defeat." Just before Burgoyne was forced to surrender he turned to Skene for advice and got the suggestion quoted toward the end of the article on BURGOYNE'S OFFENSIVE.

Skene was paroled after spending some time as a prisoner. Property of his that had not been destroyed during the British advance was burned on orders from Haldimand to deny its use to the Americans. His land was confiscated after the war and he was unsuccessful in recovering it from the state of N.Y. The British eventually allowed him £20,350 for his property losses and paid him his salary as Gov. retroactively from his appointment to the year the peace treaty was signed. This enabled him to buy an estate in England.

Appleton's points out that this Skene is confused with two namesakes, one who was Col. of the 69th Foot and who died in 1788, and another who died as Lt. of the 72d Foot in 1774. His only son, Andrew (1753–1826), entered the 5th Dragoons in 1763, graduated from King's (now Columbia) College in 1772, served with his father in 1777, and later was a paymaster in the British Army. Andrew's two sons entered the British military service: the elder, Philip O. (c. 1790–1837), became a prominent writer and pioneer in the field of language training; the other, Andrew Motz (d. 1849), entered the Navy, accompanied Napoleon to St.

Helena, explored the Arctic with Sir John Ross in 1818 and Sir Wm. E. Parry in 1819 (hence Skene Islands in Baffin Bay, and Skene Bay).

Philip Skene is not in *E.B.*, *D.A.B.*, or *D.N.B.* The above sketch is from Appleton's, supplemented materially from Van Doren, *Secret History.*

SKENESBORO (now Whitehall), N.Y., 6 July '77. (BURGOYNE'S OFFENSIVE) After the British capture of TICONDEROGA, 2–5 July, St. Clair led the main body of American troops overland to Castleton with the plan of moving then to Skenesboro. Col. Pierce Long was put in command of a force that was to retreat by water to Skenesboro. With five vessels and 220 boats that remained of the CHAMPLAIN SQUADRON, Long's 450 effectives were to escort the invalids and all stores and artillery that could be saved. Leaving Ticonderoga shortly after midnight, he made two tactical errors that jeopardized his operation: (1) assuming that the boom and bridge between Ticonderoga and Mt. Independence would delay pursuit, he took his time sailing up the lake; (2) he made no attempt to set up positions along the winding watercourse to check the enemy's advance (Nickerson, *Turning Point,* 154).

Burgoyne needed less than half an hour to shoot his way through the undefended obstacle, and by 3 P.M. was three miles from Skenesboro, where Long had landed two hours earlier. In a piecemeal commitment, Burgoyne put three regiments (9th, 20th, and 21st) ashore in South Bay with orders to move overland and cut off Long's retreat south from Skenesboro; he then continued with the rest of his force by water to attack Skenesboro from the north by way of Wood Creek. But since he did not give his enveloping force time to complete their march, Long was able to escape the trap. Setting fire to everything that would burn, Long hurried south toward Ft. Anne with the 150 men who were still at Skenesboro when Burgoyne approached. The British captured the *Trumbull* and *Revenge,* but the *Enterprise, Liberty,* and *Gates* went down in flames.

Early 7 July, Lt. Col. Hill pursued with his 9th Regt., which led to their near annihilation at FT. ANNE, 8 July.

Long's poor management of his part of the evacuation from Ticonderoga deprived the Americans of time they should have been able to gain in delaying Burgoyne's offensive, and it forced St. Clair to make a seven-day detour with the main body to bypass captured Skenesboro.

SKINNER, Cortlandt. 1728–1799. Tory officer. N.J. Related to prominent families of N.J. and N.Y., he received a good education and showed great ability and integrity as Atty. Gen. of N.J. in 1775. As a Maj. of Loyalist troops he was captured and in Sept. '76 he and Gov. Montfort Browne were exchanged for Gen. William Alexander ("Lord Stirling"). He then was authorized to raise a body of Loyalists. These were organized into the several battalions of Skinner's Brig. (one commanded by Lt. Col. Abram Van Buskirk), and Skinner was appointed B.G. of Provincials. After the war he was put on half pay as a B.G. for life. One of his daughters married Sir. Wm. Robinson, Comm. Gen., and another married Field Marshal Sir Geo. Nugent. His son, Philip Kearny Skinner, was a British Lt. Gen. in 1825, the year before his death.

See also COWBOYS AND SKINNERS.

SKINNER'S BRIGADE or West Jersey Volunteers. A Provincial force raised by Cortlandt SKINNER. It usually consisted of three battalions, but a 4th Brig. is identified among the troops on Staten Island in Nov. '78. (Baurmeister,

Journals, 356 *n.,* 229) Two battalions took part in Knyphausen's SPRINGFIELD, N.J., Raid, June '80, and some of Skinner's troops were located around PAULUS HOOK, Aug. '79. Two battalions were ordered to Long Island in Sept. '82 but almost immediately called back to reinforce the N.Y.C. garrison when the local citizens refused to furnish Gen. Carleton with more than 180 militia for local guard duty. (*Ibid.,* 526–27)

See also COWBOYS AND SKINNERS.

SKINNERS. See COWBOYS AND SKINNERS.

SMALLPOX. See MEDICAL PRACTICE ... and "GERM WARFARE."

SMALLWOOD, William. 1732–1792. Cont'l. general. Md. Descended from a man who had settled in Md. in 1664 and become a prosperous planter and politician, William is said to have attended school in England. (*D.A.B.*) He was a soldier in the French and Indian War, and in 1761 was a delegate from Charles co. to the Md. assembly, where he was a liberal leader. On 14 Jan. '76 he was commissioned Col. and raised the unit that was to become famous as Smallwood's Maryland Bn. (or Regt.). Composed of "men of honor, family and fortune," according to their Major, Mordecai Gist, they left Annapolis on 10 July '76 and marched to join Washington's army in N.Y. They distinguished themselves in the Battle of LONG ISLAND, 27 Aug., fighting under Alexander ("Stirling") on the American right. Smallwood was absent on court-martial duty in N.Y.C. during this action that established the reputation of his regiment (which was commanded by Gist) but he was wounded while leading them at WHITE PLAINS, 28 Oct., where they again distinguished themselves in several phases of that battle. Promoted B.G. on 23 Oct., Smallwood's wounds had not recovered in time for him to take part in the N.J. Campaign, and in Dec. he was sent to raise new levies in Md. and Del. (Bill, *Princeton,* 12) His brigade was left south of the Schuylkill in Sept. '77 with orders to cooperate with Wayne's Brig. in retarding the British advance on Philadelphia, but Wayne's disaster at Paoli, 21 Sept., ended this strategy before it could start. In the Battle of GERMANTOWN, 4 Oct., Smallwood commanded a militia force that never reached the battlefield. When the army went into winter quarters at Valley Forge, Smallwood was given command of Sullivan's Div. and ordered to Wilmington, Del., with the mission of protecting supplies at Head of Elk, observing British movements in the Chesapeake, and (later) of suppressing a Tory uprising on the eastern shore of Md. In Apr. '80 he marched with Kalb's command to take part in operations in the SOUTHERN THEATER. (See this entry for composition of his brigade.) In reserve at the start of the disastrous Battle of CAMDEN, 16 Aug. '80, he was separated from his brigade and swept to the rear by the flood of fugitives. Although he did nothing in that battle, he was included in a blanket "thanks of Congress" that named all troops and commanders except the militia and Gates. He succeeded Kalb (who was mortally wounded at Camden) as division commander, and was appointed Maj. Gen. on 15 Sept., but when Gates left and Smallwood—whom some proposed as the successor to Gates—became subordinate to Steuben he objected to serving under this foreigner and threatened to resign. Washington expressed his displeasure and Congress was adamant, but Greene solved the problem by sending him to Md. to raise troops and assemble supplies. He remained in the service until 15 Nov. '83, declined to accept when elected a delegate to Congress on 4 Dec. '84, but was elected governor the next year and served three consecutive one-year terms. He never married.

Writing in *D.A.B.*, Newton D. Mereness comments that Smallwood's forte was as a military administrator and drill master. White Plains was his only real combat, and his name is remembered for the performance of his troops under the command of Mordecai Gist. While he is not on record as expressing concern over the staggering losses suffered by his men, he was highly articulate in complaining about his own lack of promotion, about foreign officers, and of the inadequate recognition of his state's contribution to the war. Charles Willson Peale's portrait of Smallwood as a Maj. Gen. shows a coarse, heavy-jawed man peering complacently out of small, hard eyes.

SMITH, Francis, 1723–1791. British officer. Commissioned Lt. in the Royal Fusiliers on 25 Apr. '41, he became Capt. in the 10th Foot on 23 June '47 and on 16 Jan. '62 became Bvt. Lt. Col. of the regiment. The next month he was promoted to Lt. Col. and in 1767 he took the regiment to America. On 8 Sept. '75 the fat, slow-thinking old soldier was promoted to Bvt. Col., just a few weeks before his 52d birthday, and his seniority in the Boston Garrison seems to have been his only qualification for selection to command the expedition to LEXINGTON AND CONCORD, 19 Apr. '75. Tourtellot points out also that he had served at least 12 years in the colonies and had had a long association with Gage (*Drum*, 105). Having received a serious leg wound in the action at Fiske Hill, outside Concord, on 19 Apr., he applied for retirement in Aug. (*ibid.*), but he was retained in the service and promoted. Before the end of the year he became Col. and A.D.C. to the King (Appleton's). As a local

B.G. he showed himself as mentally slow at DORCHESTER HEIGHTS, Mar. '76, as he had been as a colonel at Concord. He commanded a brigade at Long Island, Aug. '76, and at Quaker Hill, NEWPORT, in Aug. '78. Before the end of the year his regiment returned to England to recruit and reform. He was promoted to Maj. Gen. in 1779 and Lt. Gen. in 1787. The unanswered question is, "Why?"

Sources of this sketch other than those mentioned above are *Army Lists* and the *History of the 10th Foot*, by Albert Lee (1911).

SMITH, James. *c.* 1719–1806. Signer. Ireland–Pa. Around 1729 he went to Pa. with his family to join the brothers of his father, who had previously settled in Chester co. James was schooled in Philadelphia, admitted to the bar in 1745, and soon thereafter he became a lawyer and surveyor on the frontier near Shippensburg. Four or five years later he returned to York, near which place he had been reared, and this remained his home for the rest of his life. Although the only lawyer in town until 1769, he found little legal business and in 1771 he launched into an unsuccessful iron manufacturing business that cost him £5,000 before he sold out in 1778. Meanwhile he had become a leader of the back-country element, whose cause he continued to champion as he rose in politics. In July '74 he read his "Essay on the Constitutional Power of Great Britain over the Colonies in America" to the provincial conference. He also urged non-importation and advocated that a general congress of the colonies be called. Returning to York full of revolutionary zeal, in Dec. '74 he raised a volunteer company, was elected its Capt., expanded this unit into a battalion, and accepted the honorary title of Col. Being about 55 years old at this time, he did not take command of this unit but continued to be active in provincial politics. He was a delegate to the provincial congresses of Jan. '75, June '76, and in the constitutional convention of 1776 he was on the committee to draft a state constitution. On 20 July, before the state convention had been in session a week, he was elected to the Cont'l. Cong. and thus became a Signer. Not returned to Cong. for the next session, he was re-elected on 10 Dec. '77 and sat as a delegate the next year. He declined re-election, but thanks to the efforts of Gen. Howe the Cont'l. Cong. came to him, and while that body met in York the board of war held its meetings in Smith's office.

He held a number of political posts after the war, was B.G. of militia in 1782, and was counselor for his state in the Wyoming Valley controversy. Between 1781 and his retirement in 1801 he acquired a substantial estate through the practice of law. Sharp-witted, eccentric, and possessed of an exceptional memory, he was a prominent and popular man of the Pa. frontier. Practically all his papers were destroyed by fire in 1805, and *D.A.B.* notes that an adequate appraisal of his life has not been written (1935).

SMITH, Joshua Hett. 1736–1818. Lawyer. N.Y. A son of William SMITH (I) and his first wife, Mary Het (*sic*),* he was a successful lawyer in the tradition of his father and elder brother, Chief Justice William SMITH (II). Although his father and brother were suspected of having Loyalist sympathies, Joshua was an active Whig, a member of the N.Y. Prov. Cong., and had been active in the patriot militia. His wife was from S.C., and he had met Gen.

* Both Appleton's and *D.A.B.* give the mother's maiden name as Het and the son's middle name as Hett.

Robert Howe in Charleston in 1778. When the latter assumed command at West Point, Smith directed Howe's secret service. Arnold also had met Smith, in Philadelphia in 1778, and asked Smith to continue for him the secret services he had performed for Howe. (Van Doren, *Secret History,* 289) Thus it was that Smith became—apparently in all innocence—a key actor in the events covered under AR-NOLD'S TREASON. In this matter Van Doren says he "actually deserved his country's thanks for his unintentional share in André's capture and the discovery of Arnold's plot." (*Ibid.,* 428) His country did not see it that way. Although acquitted on 26 Oct. '80, he was imprisoned by the state authorities as a suspected Tory. In May '81 he escaped from the Goshen jail ("in woman's dress," according to Appleton's), reached N.Y.C. the next month, and was given a stipend of $1 a day by the British. Late in Nov. '83 he went to England, and in 1801 he returned to the U.S., going first to S.C. (his wife's home) and then to N.Y.C. Although his property had not been confiscated, "he lost most of his fortune in the confusion caused by his long absence... and died obscure...." (Van Doren, *op. cit.,* 428) His *Authentic Narrative of the Causes which led to the Death of Major André* (London, 1808, N.Y., 1809) is called "loose and untrustworthy" by Van Doren (*op. cit.,* 498) and "not worthy of the least credit except when the statements are corroborated by other authorities" by Jared Sparks (quoted in Appleton's).

SMITH, William (I). 1697–1769. Colonial jurist. N.Y. Son of a tallow chandler who brought his family from England to N.Y. in 1715, William graduated from Yale in 1719 and three years later received his M.A. degree. He remained at Yale as a tutor until

Apr. '24, was admitted that year to the bar, went to England to continue his legal training (Gray's Inn [of Court]), and returned to become a prominent lawyer in N.Y.C. "The most noted cases with which he was associated were those in which he sought to curb the governor's prerogative." (*D.A.B.*) In 1760 he declined the office of chief justice of N.Y., but was associate justice of the supreme court from 1763 until his death. By his first wife, Mary, daughter of René and Blanche (Du Bois) Het, he had 15 children. Two are of interest to us: William (II) and Joshua Hett (*sic*) SMITH.

SMITH, William (II). 1728–1793. Jurist, historian, Loyalist. Eldest son of William SMITH (I), he graduated from Yale in 1745, studied law in his father's office with William Livingston, was admitted to the bar in 1750, and in partnership with Livingston became a highly successful lawyer. At the request of the state authorities, he and Livingston compiled the *Laws of N.Y. from the Year 1691 to 1751, Inclusive* (1752) and *Laws of N.Y. . . . 1752–1762* (1762); these two volumes were the first digest of N.Y. statutes. With Livingston and John Morin Scott he published *A Review of the Military Operations in North America . . . 1753 . . . 1756* in 1757; reprinted in 1801, this was a defense of Gov. William Shirley and a criticism of James De Lancey, Thomas Pownall, and Sir William Johnson. Smith is best known for his *History of the Late Province of N.Y.* (2 vols., N.Y. Hist. Soc., 1829), which evolved from his *History . . . of N.Y.* to the year 1732 (London, 1757), and to which Smith subsequently added a continuation to the year 1762. His "Historical Memoirs," which extend to the year 1783 and exist in six manuscript volumes in the N.Y. Public Library, are described by Richard B. Morris in *D.A.B.* as "indispensable to an understanding of New York's position during the Revolution."

Chief Justice of N.Y. from 1763 to 1782 (nominally), and his father's successor on the Council in 1767, Smith had a career during the Revolution that Professor Morris describes as politically unique: "When violence broke out, he appears to have taken a position on the fence, gradually leaning toward the Loyalist side, never completely repudiated by the patriots, never completely accepted by his own party." (*Ibid.*) When in 1777 he refused to give the TEST OATH he was ordered to Livingston Manor on the Hudson, and when he again refused, the next year, he was banished to British-occupied N.Y.C.

He left with the British in 1783, remained in England until 1786, and then went to Canada to take up the post of chief justice, to which he had been appointed 1 Sept. '85. He held this office until his death. In 1752 Smith had married Janet Livingston, first cousin of James LIVINGSTON ("of Canada"). Their only surviving son (of 11 children) was William (1769–1847), the Canadian jurist and author of *History of Canada . . .* (2 vols., 1815).

Joshua Hett SMITH was a brother of William (II).

SMITH'S POINT, L.I., N.Y. See FORT GEORGE.

SOLEMN LEAGUE AND COVENANT. Led by Joseph Warren, the Mass. patriots struck back at the Intolerable Acts with a document of this name which was produced on 5 June '74. It pledged all signers to boycott British imports after 1 Oct. Boston merchants who protested against this "base, wicked, and illegal measure" were dubbed "Protesters" and marked for persecution by the radical Whigs.

SOMERSET COURTHOUSE (Millstone), N.J. On the Millstone River about halfway between Morristown and Trenton, Somerset C. H. (now Millstone) figured prominently in N.J. military operations. Washington's army spent the night there after the Princeton victory (3 Jan. '77), skirmishes took place there while the rebels were in their Morristown Winter Quarters (Jan.–May. '77), and British forces occupied the village during their perplexing "June Maneuvers" of the PHILADELPHIA CAMPAIGN (1777). The *A. A.*–Heitman list of battles and skirmishes shows actions at this place on 20 and 22 Jan. and 17 June '77. Israel Putnam reported a British advance to Somerset on 20 Jan. (Freeman, *Washington*, IV, 383 *n.*) and *D.A.B.* gives this same date for the exploit of Philemon DICKINSON; hence the events of 20–22 Jan. undoubtedly are related to this single action. The action of 17 June '77 would have involved the harassment by Morgan's riflemen and other light troops of the British redoubts being built at that time. (See PHIL. CAMP'N.)

John SIMCOE conducted a successful raid against this place but was captured, 17 Oct. '79, as he withdrew. (Clinton, *Amer. Reb.*, 147–48)

SONS OF LIBERTY. Secret colonial societies that sprang up in 1765 to protest and nullify the Stamp Act took their name from Isaac Barré's speech opposing that act in the House of Commons; Barré had closed this speech with a reference to the colonists as "these sons of liberty." "During the course of the Revolution they assumed many different names, but whether they called themselves committees of correspondence, committees of safety, or 'true-born Whigs,'" they were "the radicals who led the colonies into revolution against the mother country." (Miller, *Sam Adams*, 51)

In the name of "Liberty" they were responsible for many' acts of mob violence against Loyalists. TAR AND FEATHERS were the fate of those whose conception of liberty did not suit their own. Sam Adams' group, "recruited largely from the wharfingers, artisans and shipyard workers of North Boston" (*ibid.*), on 26 Aug. '65 burned the records of the vice-admiralty court, ransacked the home of the comptroller of the currency, and looted the fine home and library of Thomas Hutchinson. Their effectiveness is shown by the fact that all stamp agents in the colonies had resigned before the Stamp Act was supposed to become law (1 Nov. '65).

Committees of Correspondence were created in 1772 to coordinate activities of colonial agitators and to organize public opinion against the British ministry. The first committee was established in Boston at the urging of Sam Adams. Patrick Henry and Thomas Jefferson led the movement for their establishment in Va.

Committees of Safety were organized in 1775. Mass. again led the way, establishing the first committee in Feb. '75; composed of 11 men, it had authority to mobilize the militia and seize military stores. Other colonies followed suit, their committees generally being appointed by popular conventions. The second Cont'l. Cong. on 18 July '75 issued official support for establishment of such committees of safety to exercise the functions of government. Until 1776, when new state constitutions were adopted, the committees acted as state governments, at least to the extent of keeping order and furnishing men and supplies to the Cont'l. Army. In N.H. and Conn. the committees functioned until after the war.

SOURBADER DE GIMAT. Although this is his correct family name (Lasseray, *passim*) and he should properly be indexed under *S*, this officer appears in English works as GIMAT.

SOUTH AMBOY, N.J. See AMBOY.

SOUTHERN CAMPAIGNS OF NATHANAEL GREENE. Dec. '80–Dec. '81. After three of their own selections in a row had proved spectacular failures (Robt. Howe at Savannah, Lincoln at Charleston, Gates at Camden), Congress let Washington pick a commander for the Southern Dept. Washington's immediate nomination was Nathanael Greene, who reached Charlotte, N.C., on 2 Dec. and took command from Gates the next day. (For intervening events, see SOUTHERN THEATER, Mil. Opns. in.)

GREENE SPLITS HIS FORCES

Paper strength of Greene's army was 2,457, of whom fewer than 800 were properly clothed and equipped. Discipline and morale were poor, and his hungry soldiers were terrorizing the impoverished neighborhood. Greene was therefore faced with the dilemma of building an effective fighting force—which would require time and security—but also of making some show of offensive action that would win him the support he needed from demoralized Southern patriots. In a solution that showed military genius, he adopted the unorthodox plan of splitting his puny forces in the face of a superior enemy: while he moved with 1,100 men to a camp selected by Kosciuszko near Cheraw, he sent Morgan with 600 men to circle the 4,000-man field army of Cornwallis and conduct operations with the militia of the Catawba district. (Many accounts say Morgan's mission was to attack Ninety-Six and Augusta; although such a threat was implicit in Morgan's orders, his initial directive from Greene—as will be seen below—was not this specific.)

In a move that was to prove decisive in subsequent operations, Greene ordered Edward CARRINGTON to continue the mission Gates had previously given him to reconnoiter routes back to Va. (see cross reference for details). Kosciuszko and Edward Stevens were ordered to reconnoiter and map the Yadkin and Catawba Rivers, and these two officers were further instructed to collect or construct boats that could be moved by wagon from one river line to another. (Greene may have gotten this last idea from Jefferson. It is certain that Jefferson wrote Greene to describe such an operation, but Greene may have known that such "bridge trains" had long been used in war.)

When this strategy revealed itself to Cornwallis, the British general was smart enough to see dangers in Greene's unorthodoxy that were not apparent to such subordinates as Tarleton—or to modern military pedagogues. The Napoleonic solution might seem to be for Cornwallis to use his INTERIOR LINES for a DEFEAT IN DETAIL of Greene's forces, which were eventually separated by about 120 miles (Cheraw to Cowpens). But if Cornwallis moved in force against Cheraw, Morgan could attack Ninety-Six and Augusta; if Cornwallis moved in force against Morgan, Greene could attack Charleston. If Cornwallis ignored Greene and Morgan to resume his invasion north, they would be a threat to his flanks and rear. If Cornwallis sat in Winnsboro and did nothing—which was highly unlikely—Greene's dual tasks of rehabilitation and harassment would be simplified. (This "estimate of the situation" is Greene's own, as quoted in G. W. Greene, *Greene*, III, 131.) Although Greene, who died in 1786, would never hear of Napoleon, who was born in 1769, he was taking advantage of his superior mobility to observe Napoleon's principle that an army must separate to live (off the country) but unite to fight.

Greene left Charlotte with Huger's Div. on 20 Dec. and reached Cheraw on the 26th. His troops included 650 Cont'ls., 303 Va. and 157 Md. militia. They were soon reinforced by 400 Va. militia under Col. John Greene. Lee's Legion arrived 13 Jan. '81 and was detached to support Marion (who raided GEORGETOWN, S.C., 24 Jan.).

Morgan left Charlotte on 21 Dec. with 320 Md. and Del. Cont'ls., 200 Va. riflemen—all the infantry under John Howard—and about 80 light dragoons under Wm. Washington. With instructions to act cautiously, he was to join the N.C. militia of Gen. Wm. Davidson and operate between the Broad and Pacolet rivers to protect patriots of the region, harass the enemy, and gather supplies. Morgan had orders to rejoin the main army or harass the enemy's flank and rear if Cornwallis should advance in the direction of Greene's wing.

CORNWALLIS REACTS

At Winnsboro, where he had been reinforced to a strength of 4,000 men with whom he could operate in the field —about the same number were holding his scattered posts—Cornwallis began getting disturbing intelligence of American troop movements. Although he tended to discredit the early reports, by 26 Dec. he was sufficiently alarmed to write Tarleton, who was about 20 miles west on Broad River, to say that "Morgan and Washington have passed Broad river" and asking that he "try to get all possible intelligence of Morgan." (Quoted in Bass, *Green Dragoon,* 141) The evening of 1 Jan. '81, the Earl got unnerving reports from two different sources that Morgan was approaching Ninety-Six with 3,000 men. (*Ibid.,* 142–43) Cornwallis ordered

Tarleton to protect this strategically important place and to find Morgan. "Let me know if you think that the moving the whole, or any part of my corps, can be of use." (*Ibid.*)

Morgan had, in fact, reached the Pacolet River on Christmas, after a tough 58-mile march across rain-soaked country. Two days later Washington rode south on his HAMMOND'S STORE RAID, which was the basis of the alarming, but incorrect, reports that Ninety-Six was threatened.

Cornwallis was relieved by Tarleton's reports that although Morgan was not to be found he was not around Ninety-Six. The Earl had confided to Tarleton on 27 Dec. that he planned to resume the offensive north, and Tarleton realized Cornwallis was reluctant to undertake this operation until Morgan was off his mind. On 4 Jan., therefore, Tarleton proposed a plan. He asked for reinforcements with which he would move to destroy Morgan or drive him north toward Kings Mountain; the main army would advance simultaneously toward the latter point from Winnsboro to trap Morgan if he should elude Tarleton. Cornwallis agreed, and the evening of 5 Jan. wrote that he would head north on Sunday, 7 Jan. He also ordered the 1,500 troops of Maj. Gen. Leslie to leave Camden on 9 Jan. to join the main army on its march.

Meanwhile, Morgan had written Greene on 4 Jan. that because of insufficient forage he would have to retreat or move toward Ga., but Greene answered on 13 Jan., "hold your ground if possible." Pointing out the "disagreeable consequences that will result from a retreat," he suggested that Morgan move toward Ninety-Six or elsewhere in the vicinity if this might alleviate his supply problem. (This is apparently the basis for the belief that Morgan's original directive told him to attack

Ninety-Six and Augusta.) "Col. Tarleton is said to be on his way to pay you a visit," Greene concluded cheerily. "I doubt not but he will have a decent reception and a proper dismission." (Bass, *op. cit.*, 146–47)

Rain continued to impede operations, and Tarleton was stopped at Duggin's Plantation on Indian Creek between 6 and 9 Jan. waiting for a chance to continue north across the swollen Enoree. Cornwallis left Winnsboro on the 8th, but took until the 16th to cover 40 miles to Turkey Creek. During the critical period 9–16 Jan. Cornwallis got only one message from Tarleton; as a result he did not know that on the 14th Tarleton had crossed the Enoree, the Tyger, and was in hot pursuit of Morgan. Nor did Tarleton know that Cornwallis had slowed his own advance on the assumption that Tarleton was still being held back by swollen rivers. Too late to remedy matters, Tarleton sent this message from Pacolet at 8 o'clock the morning of 16 Jan.: "My Lord, I have been most cruelly retarded by the waters. *Morgan is in force and gone for Cherokee Ford.* I am now on my march. I wish he would be stopped."

On the 15th, when Morgan had learned that Tarleton had crossed the Tyger with a force reported to number up to 1,200, Morgan wrote Greene: "My force is inadequate to the attempts you have hinted at" (above). During the day of the 15th, Tarleton probed for a place to cross the Pacolet, but found every ford guarded. That night he faked a march up the river toward Wofford's Iron Works, went silently into bivouac, and after the Americans had taken the bait and moved up the river opposite him, Tarleton countermarched and crossed the Pacolet, unopposed, six miles below Morgan at Easterwood Shoals. Morgan's scouts brought him this bad news as the Americans were

preparing breakfast, about 6 A.M. on the 16th, and a half hour later the rebels were streaking north to put Broad River between them and their pursuers. After eating Morgan's breakfast, Tarleton sent the message quoted above. (Bass, *op. cit.*, 150–51)

At COWPENS, 17 Jan., Morgan turned at bay to beat Tarleton in a little jewel of a battle.

HARE AND HOUNDS

Had Cornwallis been at Kings Mountain, as originally planned, Greene's campaigns in the South might end on this page. But he was still at Turkey Creek, 30 miles from Cowpens, when he learned the evening of the 17th that Tarleton had been beaten. He had decided to wait there for Leslie who, ironically, arrived about the time Bloody Tarleton rode in with his 200 surviving dragoons on the 18th. (*Ibid.*, 160)

Morgan wasted no time. Not more than two hours after the battle he marched east, crossed the Broad River, and camped six miles from the scene of his triumph. Early the next morning he was racing toward Ramseur's Mill (now Lincolnton). He crossed Sherrald's (or Sherrill's) Ford the morning of the 23d (*Ibid.*, 163) and went into camp with the Catawba between him and pursuit. (He had unburdened himself of the prisoners by detaching Pickens with most of the militia and Washington's cavalry to escort them to Island Ford on the upper Catawba, where a commissary for prisoners sent them on to Va. Pickens rejoined Morgan's camp behind Sherrald's Ford.)

Cornwallis did not take up the pursuit until 19 Jan. Then, apparently thinking Morgan might still be around Cowpens but having no real knowledge of his location, his force of almost 3,000 trudged N.W. toward Kings Mountain. Two days later, after Tarleton had scouted west of the Broad, Cornwallis corrected his course and picked up the trail. But the trail was two days cold when the British reached Ramseur's Mill about 7 A.M. on the 25th. The frustrated British commander now made the desperate decision to convert his entire command into light troops and run Morgan into the ground. He ordered all impedimenta destroyed, and during the next two days at Ramseur's Mill his troops burned all their tents, all the wagons except those needed for ammunition, salt, medical supplies, and casualties; all the provisions that could not be packed into haversacks were destroyed, and even the rum. Trevelyan says the soldiers accepted this "sadly but passively," but Ward suggests it may explain the 250 desertions at Ramseur's. (Trevelyan, *Amer. Rev.*, VI, 156; Ward, 765)

This dramatic move proved futile and, in the long run, disastrous. "Cornwallis had been outgeneralled," points out Fisher, and he should now have deferred to Clinton's instructions that N.C. was to be invaded only if S.C. and Ga. were properly secured; Cornwallis had abandoned his first invasion when Ferguson was destroyed at Kings Mountain and should again have done so when Tarleton met so similar a fate. (Fisher, *Struggle,* II, 389)

When Greene received word on 23 Jan. of Morgan's victory he was, naturally, delighted, but he also realized the mortal danger his army now faced. You will remember that in conjunction with the unorthodox and hazardous strategy with which Greene opened his Southern campaign he also made certain provisions for the wholesale retreat he now ordered executed. Huger was directed to move his wing of the army from Cheraw toward Salisbury, on Morgan's line of retreat, as soon as possible. Commissaries at Salisbury and Hillsboro were told to get ready to move their prisoners and stores into Va. Carrington was told to assemble boats on the Dan. On 28 Jan. Greene left Cheraw with a small escort for a hazardous cross-country ride of 125 miles to join Morgan on his line of retreat. The same day Huger started his march, having previously sent nonessential baggage, the weakest horses, and the worst wagons to Hillsboro.

Greene joined Morgan in his camp behind the Catawba on 30 Jan. (Ward, 766; Alden, *South,* 255) He found that the Old Wagoner thought the entire army should retreat west into the mountains. But the baggage-burning indicated to Greene that Cornwallis was planning the mad course of pushing north, and Greene decided on the bolder plan of retreating in the same direction, luring him farther from his bases and destroying him. Greene issued orders for Lee's Legion to rejoin him from the lower Peedee, where it had been operating with Marion. He wrote Huger of the ambitious new plan and urged him to hurry to effect a junction with Morgan. Although he first intended using Morgan's Div. to delay the enemy's crossing of the swollen Catawba, when the river started going down he ordered Morgan to continue his retreat to Salisbury, where he hoped Huger would soon arrive.

ACTION ON THE CATAWBA

Gen. Wm. Davidson had turned out 800 N.C. militia and more were supposed to be coming. Greene planned to use these troops to cover the four crossing sites along a 30-mile front where Cornwallis might move. Shortly after 2 P.M. on the 31st, when Morgan's troops had already started toward the Yadkin, Greene met with Davidson, Morgan, and Wm. Washington at Beattie's Ford on the Catawba to plan the defense of that obstacle. The British had been camped across the river for two days waiting for the water to go down, and an advance guard of 400 or 500 men appeared on the hill overlooking the stream as this 20-minute conference started. When the meeting broke up, Morgan and Washington rode off to join their troops (temporarily commanded by Howard), Greene left with one aide to help assemble N.C. militia a few miles behind the river, and Davidson made final arrangements to defend the fords.*

With two other fords obstructed with felled trees and covered by small detachments, Davidson ordered patrols to watch the unguarded stretches of his 40-mile front during the night and concentrated the bulk of his militia around the other two. At Beattie's Ford, the principal crossing, which had not been obstructed since civilian refugees were still using it, he put about 300 men. Four to six miles downstream, at a private crossing called Cowan's, he put about the same number.

Thinking Morgan's troops were around Beattie's, Cornwallis planned a demonstration there, to consist only of an artillery bombardment; Lt. Col. James Webster would command this operation. Cornwallis would lead the main body across Cowan's Ford at dawn and encircle Morgan at the principal ford. The troops turned out at 1 A.M. on 1 Feb. and moved toward the river. The demonstration fizzled out in the rain because the man carrying the firing match was left along the route of march with an abandoned gun. (S. & R., 437) But

* Details of this commanders' conference are given because they clear up considerable confusion as to who was where at this important moment. The account is that of Maj. Joseph GRAHAM (who was there) as quoted in S. & R., 435.

Cornwallis forced a crossing at COWAN'S FORD in which the Guards faced extremely adverse circumstances and added another page to their proud history. Gen. Davidson was killed and the rag, tag militia scattered. Webster crossed later in the day without opposition. At TARRANT'S TAVERN, about 10 miles beyond the river, Tarleton chopped up a large militia force, scattered the rest, and almost captured Greene, who was nearby. Although Cornwallis had not come close to catching Morgan, he temporarily destroyed the N.C. militia that might otherwise have rendered some service during the retreat; Greene wrote on 13 Feb. that all but about 80 had deserted him.

OPERATIONS ON THE YADKIN

From Salisbury, where he arrived alone during the early hours of 2 Feb., Greene sent word to Huger that unless he was within 24 hours of Salisbury to rendezvous with Morgan at Guilford Courthouse. When Morgan reached the Yadkin on 2 Feb. boats were waiting, and he crossed at Trading (Trader's) Ford during the night. The British advance guard under Gen. O'Hara arrived too late to accomplish anything more than rout the militia who were guarding a few wagons left by fleeing civilians.†

Having been frustrated at the Catawba

† I have used the times, dates, and details from Ward, 771. Bass, however, says Cornwallis reached Salisbury "late in the afternoon" of 4 Feb. (having taken more than three days to cover about 23 miles?), that O'Hara (with the Guards, the Bose Regt. of Hessians, and Tarleton's cavalry) did not reach the river until "near midnight," and that "Morgan's rear guard had crossed in the evening [of the 4th]." (*Op. cit.*, 166, 167)

and the Yadkin, Cornwallis still hoped to catch Greene before he could reach the Dan. Greene's movement north from Trading Ford the evening of 4 Feb. supported Cornwallis' belief that the Americans lacked the necessary boats to cross the lower Dan and would head for the fords upstream. But the rebels turned east a few miles before reaching Salem and, after a march of 47 miles in 48 hours, camped near Guilford C. H. on the 7th. (Lee, *Memoirs*, 236) On this day they were joined by Huger and Lee. (*Ibid.*) * Huger's troops had completed a remarkable march under adverse weather conditions and with pitifully inadequate clothing—many of them barefooted—without the loss of a man.

RACE TO THE DAN

Greene studied the ground and gave serious consideration to making a stand at Guilford, but a council of officers persuaded Greene not to do so. "The addition of 1,500 militia would probably have decided the question in favor of fighting," comments Ward. (*Op. cit.*, 772–73) It is ironic that his main reason for wanting to stop the retreat as soon

* Again, there is much disagreement on dates. Ward says Greene reached Guilford on the 6th, Huger on the 7th (Lee joined Huger on the march to Guilford and arrived with him); he also says the rear guard of Otho Williams, which will be mentioned in a moment, left Guilford on the evening of the 8th, whereas Lee—who was with Williams— says it was the 10th, the same day the main body left. Bass says Greene reached Guilford on the 5th; Bass and Fisher say Huger arrived on the 9th! Although Lee could be mistaken as to his dates, I consider him the most reliable source on operations between Guilford and the Dan.

as possible was to encourage the militia to turn out and save their homes from further invasion, yet only 200 neighborhood militia joined him. With fewer than 1,500 reliable Cont'ls. to oppose the enemy's estimated 2,500 troops, Greene had to keep falling back. Harry Lee gives this explanation of Greene's plans for further retreat:

"The British general was 25 miles from Guilford Court-House; equally near with Greene to Dix's Ferry on the Dan, and nearer to the upper shallows or points of that river, which were supposed to be fordable, notwithstanding the late swell of water. Lt. Col. Carrington, quartermaster-general, suggested the propriety of passing at Irwin's Ferry, 17 [this should be 70] miles from Guilford Court-House, and 20 below Dix's. Boyd's Ferry was four miles below Irwin's; and the boats might be easily brought down from Dix's to assist in transporting the army at these near and lower ferries. The plan of Lt. Col. Carrington was adopted, and that officer charged with the requisite preparations." (*Memoirs*, 236)

A 700-man light corps, including all the cavalry and the best infantry troops, was organized to serve as rear guard and also to draw the enemy away from Greene's line of retreat. Wm. Washington commanded the mounted element, 240 men, which included his own dragoons and the cavalry of Lee's Legion. John Howard commanded the infantry element, which included his 280 Cont'ls., the 120 foot troops of Lee's Legion, and 60 Va. riflemen. (Ward, *op. cit.*, 773)

Morgan was asked to command this body, but he declined on grounds of bad health and intimated that he would like to retire. Lee says he was asked to persuade Morgan to "obey the universal wish," and even argued that "the brigadier's retirement at that crisis might induce an opinion unfavorable to his

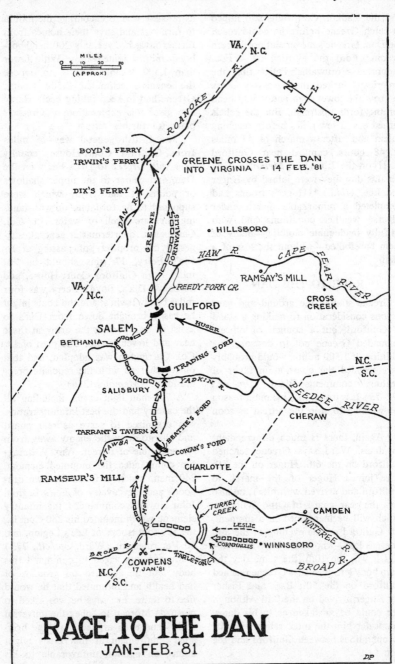

MILES
0 5 10 20 30
(APPROX)

VA.
N.C.

ROANOKE R.

BOYD'S FERRY
IRWIN'S FERRY

GREENE CROSSES THE DAN
INTO VIRGINIA – 14 FEB. '81

DIX'S FERRY

DAN R.

GREENE

CORNWALLIS

• HILLSBORO

HAW R.

CAPE

FEAR

RIVER

RAMSAY'S MILL

REEDY FORK CR.

VA.
N.C.

GUILFORD

CROSS
CREEK

SALEM

HUGER

BETHANIA

TRADING FORD

N.C.
S.C.

SALISBURY

YADKIN R.

PEEDEE RIVER

BEATTIE'S FORD

CHERAW

TARRANT'S TAVERN

CATAWBA R.

COWAN'S FORD

CHARLOTTE

RAMSEUR'S MILL

MORGAN

TURKEY
CREEK

• CAMDEN

LESLIE

WATEREE R.

BROAD R.

CORNWALLIS

• WINNSBORO

BROAD R.

COWPENS
17 JAN '81

TARLETON (?)

N.C.
S.C.

RACE TO THE DAN
JAN–FEB. '81

DP

patriotism." Although this almost swayed the Old Wagoner, on 10 Feb. Greene granted him his requested leave of absence. Morgan was suffering from sciatica, rheumatism, and a less delicate ailment "so that I scarcely can sit upon my horse," as he wrote Greene on the 5th, but at least one historian suspects that his real reason for leaving was to dissociate himself from a strategy he considered too hazardous. (Fisher, *op. cit.,* 398) Command of the rear guard then fell into the capable hands of Otho Williams.

Cornwallis, still blocked at Trading Ford by high water and lack of boats, and with his preconceived idea of Greene's route, sent Tarleton with his cavalry and the 23d Regt. up the Yadkin toward Shallow Ford, 25 miles north. Meeting no resistance, Tarleton crossed on the 6th, Cornwallis left Salisbury with his main body on the 7th, and entered Salem on the 9th. Greene left Guilford with the main body on the 10th and headed for Carrington's crossing sites, 70 miles, bee line, to the N.E. Williams got in front of Cornwallis this same day, with the immediate result that the British checked their advance to close up ranks and reconnoiter. The British then started a vigorous pursuit of Williams, who succeeded for about two days in drawing them in the desired direction. Through intermittent rain and snow, over red clay roads that were churned into mud during the day and frozen into this distorted surface at night, the armies struggled along on three parallel routes. Williams kept on the middle route, with the enemy to his left rear. Lee's cavalry had the particularly exhausting and nerve-racking mission of bringing up the rear and of watching for any indication that Cornwallis might have discovered the true situation. Lee had to keep the enemy advance guard from circling to the right

to get between him and Williams; the latter had to avoid being cut off from Greene by the same maneuver. This meant that half of Lee's troopers were on duty every night and got only six hours' rest out of 48. Lee points out, however, that the enemy cavalry "although more numerous . . . was far inferior in regard to size, condition, and activity of their horses."

Before dawn of the 13th, Tarleton informed Cornwallis that Greene's main body was headed for the lower Dan. Ordering his van to proceed as if the army were still following the former route, Cornwallis started on a forced march and soon found a causeway that led to the road Williams had been following with his infantry. As on previous days, the Americans had broken camp at 3 A.M., marched rapidly, and stopped for their one meal of the day. Mounted outposts covered the rear, and reported that the enemy was moving forward in the normal manner. Having completed his preparations along the Dan, Q.M.G. Carrington was commanding the dragoon detachment in contact with the British van. His periodic reports informed Lee that the enemy was advancing at the usual pace. Suddenly an excited countryman appeared to report that Cornwallis was on the other road and was less than four miles away. Williams had ordered Lee to send a cavalry detachment back with this man to check on this report, and soon after Capt. James Armstrong departed on this mission a report from Carrington, saying that the enemy to his front had slowed down, confirmed the previous intelligence. Williams then ordered Lee to reinforce Armstrong and to take command. This led to a clash in which 18 of Tarleton's troopers were killed. Lee was about to hang the enemy commander, Capt. Thomas Miller, in reprisal for the cold-blooded killing of his un-armed, teenage bugler by Miller's men when the enemy van approached. (The boy, whose name was Gillies, had been ordered to lend his horse to the country-man when the latter was sent forward with a dragoon patrol. Lee then led his detachment off to the side of the high-way and the boy was sent back to tell Williams no contact had yet been made. The dragoon patrol soon reappeared with the enemy hard on their heels. Not seeing Lee's detachment, and unable to overtake the American patrol, some enemy dragoons ran down the unarmed bugler and sabered him as he lay on the ground. Lee then descended on the British, killed 18, and captured Miller and all but two of his men as they tried to escape. Miller argued that since he was on an intelligence mission he had tried to save the boy's life, and he was not hanged.)

The retreat was resumed with Lee bringing up the rear and looking for a chance to chop off the head of Corn-wallis' advance guard if they made the mistake of getting beyond supporting distance. "The skilful enemy never per-mitted any risk in detail, but preserved his whole force for one decisive strug-gle," says Lee. As the day of 13 Feb. wore on—and both sides would approve that choice of the verb—Williams de-cided he had accomplished his mission by luring Cornwallis toward Dix's Ferry. Ordering Lee to continue screening to the rear, he led the main body onto a more direct route toward Irwin's Ferry. Cornwallis soon detected this change of route and came close to surprising Lee's men when they pulled off onto what they hoped was an obscure side road for the breakfast they had missed. A moment's hesitation by the British POINT and the superiority of the Americans' horses enabled them to escape. "Crim-

inal improvidence!" confesses Light-Horse Harry to his momentary but near-fatal lapse of vigilance.

Cornwallis now had the bit in his teeth and pushed his troops on into the night. The Americans had a bad moment about 8 P.M. when they saw camp fires and thought they marked Greene's biv-ouac, but to their immense relief they found he had left this camp two days earlier. ("Friendly hands had kept them alight for the benefit of the light troops," says Ward.) When the British stopped, so did the rebels; but at midnight the race was on again. They were still 40 miles from the Dan, the weather con-tinued wet and cold, the deep mud of the road was incrusted with frost. Dur-ing the morning of the 14th both sides stopped only one hour to rest. About noon there came a message from Greene: "All our troops are over. . . . I am ready to receive you and give you a hearty welcome." It was dated 5:12 P.M. of the preceding day.

O'Hara's vanguard heard the Ameri-cans cheer, but he was pushing his troops forward as he listened and got more determined than ever to trap these miserable rebels against the river in one final rush. But although the British marched 40 miles in those last 24 hours, the Americans covered the distance in 16 hours. (Bass, 168; Ward, 776) Thus Greene was able to drop Lee off at about 3 P.M., some 14 miles from the river, and continue safely to Boyd's Ferry. The infantry reached the bank before sunset to find boats waiting. Lee's cavalry arrived between 8 and 9 P.M. and crossed on the same boats (the horses swimming, as was normal prac-tice). "In the last boat, the quarter-master-general, attended by Lieutenant-Colonel Lee and the rear troop, reached the friendly shore," says Lieutenant-Colonel Lee in his *Memoirs*.

Thus ended Greene's first campaign in the South. Part of his army had won a battle against Tarleton and then all of it had run 200 miles for dear life. Not a single Cont'l. soldier now stood on any of the King's territory south of Virginia. Greene's pleasure over this apparent defeat and Cornwallis' bitter disappointment over this apparent triumph illustrate a fundamental principle of war—no matter how much territory you occupy, you have not won until you destroy the enemy's armed force. Washington had been proving this in the North; Green was now doing it in the South.

If Cornwallis had caught and destroyed Greene's army he would have been able to link up with Benedict Arnold, swell their combined force by liberating the CONVENTION ARMY and the Cowpens prisoners, and all four Southern provinces would have come back under royal authority. It is not inconceivable that Virginia, the Carolinas, and Georgia might have remained a British possession.

WINNING THE CAROLINAS

Now what? Cornwallis lacked the boats to follow Greene. He could not maneuver upstream to cross at the fords because Greene could too easily counter such moves. In straight-line distances he was 250 miles from Winnsboro and another 125 miles from Charleston—every forward step would extend the British further and increase American resistance by compressing them like a spring toward the bases in Va. Cornwallis had no alternative but to withdraw, and on 17 Feb. '81 he started moving slowly toward Hillsboro, N.C. Here he issued a proclamation inviting "faithful and loyal subjects" to escape "the cruel tyranny under which they have groaned for many years"; they could save themselves by rallying around the royal standard with their arms and 10 days' supply of groceries.

Greene's situation was by no means rosy. His 1,430 ill-equipped troops had suffered worse than the enemy during the retreat. The Southern militia was beginning to turn out, however, and Steuben was raising Cont'l. recruits for him in Va., so Greene retreated to Halifax C. H., Va., to reorganize his main body but pushed his advance elements across the Dan a day after the British left it.

On 18 Feb. Lee's Legion and two companies of Md. Cont'ls. crossed the Dan to operate with Pickens and his 700 newly raised militia. Col. Otho Williams crossed two days later with the light infantry who had comprised a rear guard less than a week before. As soon as he was joined by 600 Va. riflemen under Gen. Edward Stevens, Greene himself moved into N.C. His plan was to keep as much pressure on Cornwallis as possible—cut up his foraging parties and discourage the Loyalists from rising—while the rest of his recruits were sent forward. The Dan was falling rapidly and Greene did not want to give his opponent a chance either to resume the offensive or escape.

In an action known as HAW RIVER (PYLE'S DEFEAT), 25 Feb., Lee surprised and brutally chopped up a Loyalist force. This virtually stopped the recruiting of Tory militia. Cornwallis took the field and there was a three-week period of maneuvering as Greene avoided a general engagement. The opposing forces did close in for a sharp skirmish at WETZELL'S MILL, 6 Mar. By mid-March Greene was as ready as he was likely ever to be, and Cornwallis had been ready for some time.

At GUILFORD C. H., 15 Mar. '81, Cornwallis attacked and scored a hard-

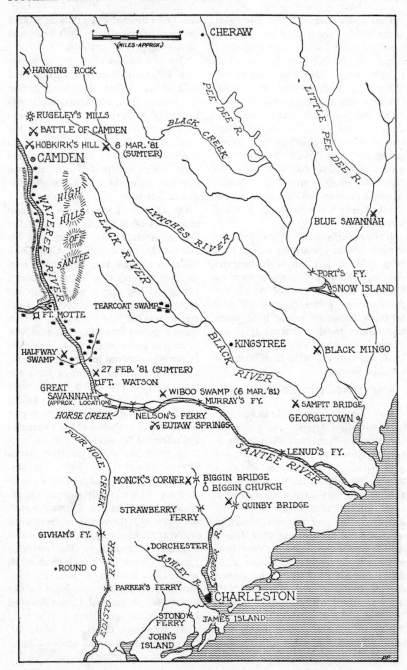

CHERAW

PEE DEE R.

LITTLE PEE DEE R.

✕ HANGING ROCK

BLACK CREEK

☼ RUGELEY'S MILLS
✕ BATTLE OF CAMDEN
✕ HOBKIRK'S HILL ✕ 6 MAR. '81
⊙ CAMDEN (SUMTER)

BLUE SAVANNAH ✕

HIGH HILLS OF SANTEE

WATEREE RIVER

BLACK RIVER

LYNCHES RIVER

✕ PORT'S FY.
🚩 SNOW ISLAND

⬚ FT. MOTTE

TEARCOAT SWAMP

BLACK RIVER

KINGSTREE

HALFWAY SWAMP ✕

✕ BLACK MINGO

27 FEB. '81 (SUMTER)
⬚ FT. WATSON

GREAT SAVANNAH
(APPROX. LOCATION)

✕ WIBOO SWAMP (6 MAR. '81)
✕ MURRAY'S FY.

✕ SAMPIT BRIDGE
GEORGETOWN ⊙

HORSE CREEK
NELSON'S FERRY
✕ EUTAW SPRINGS

FOUR HOLE CREEK

SANTEE RIVER

✕ LENUD'S FY.

MONCK'S CORNER ✕ ✕ BIGGIN BRIDGE
⬚ BIGGIN CHURCH

STRAWBERRY FERRY

✕ ✕ QUINBY BRIDGE

GIVHAM'S FY. ✕

EDISTO RIVER

ASHLEY R.

COOPER R.

• DORCHESTER

• ROUND O

✕ PARKER'S FERRY

CHARLESTON

STONO FERRY
JAMES ISLAND

JOHN'S ISLAND

won tactical victory. But it was a strategic defeat, since it left him with no alternative but retreat.

CORNWALLIS WITHDRAWS TO WILMINGTON

Although Camden, the second most important British post in the South after Charleston, was closer than Wilmington by 40 miles, retreat to Camden would acknowledge failure of Cornwallis' entire campaign. So he headed down the Cape Fear River toward Wilmington. Here he could be supplied by sea. Furthermore, he could hope to draw Greene in that direction, thereby keeping him out of S.C. and Ga. Wilmington had many features of a FLANKING POSITION, but Greene quickly demonstrated that it lacked the essential one.

Giving his men two days' rest and abandoning his wounded, Cornwallis started withdrawing on 18 Mar.; Greene followed immediately. On the 28th, Greene had an opportunity to hit the enemy while they were astride Deep River at Ramsay's Mill, but he lacked the strength to assure success. Cornwallis withdrew unmolested into Cross Creek (now Fayetteville). Since supplies he had ordered sent to this place were not there, he continued on to Wilmington, arriving 7 Apr. (On the 24th he marched north to Va.; see YORKTOWN CAMPAIGN.)

GREENE VERSUS RAWDON

The Va. and N.C. militia had completed their six weeks' service, and Greene released them with thanks; they had run like rabbits at Guilford, but had made that battle possible. After remaining at Ramsay's Mill from 29 Mar. until 5 Apr., Greene headed for S.C.

The failure of Cornwallis' strategy is now apparent, as is the soundness of Greene's. In his determination to re-

place Clinton's defensive policy with an aggressive one, Cornwallis had pyramided his errors; in his unwillingness to face each successive failure in his theater of operations, he went on to lose the war for Britain. As for the immediate strategic situation, however, by his withdrawal to Wilmington—rather than dropping back to Camden, where Rawdon was located with almost 2,000 troops—he had, in effect, abandoned Rawdon. Ramsay's Mill (where Greene stopped his pursuit), Wilmington, and Camden form an equilateral triangle, the points being about 120 miles apart. If Cornwallis had had the strength in Wilmington to threaten Greene's line of communications as he operated toward Camden, then he would have had the flanking position mentioned earlier. But he didn't, and Greene virtually ignored him when he moved against Rawdon.

Greene's army now numbered about 1,500, all of them Cont'ls.: units were the 1st and 2d Va., the 1st and 2d. Md., Lee's Legion, and Washington's dragoons. Partisan forces of Marion, in the Peedee swamps, Sumter, on Broad River, and Pickens, in western S.C., had been harassing the British and could now join forces with Greene.

The youthful but exceptionally capable RAWDON had a paper strength of 8,141 British regulars, German regulars, and Tories with which to hold an area of about 25,000 square miles—that is, a rough parallelogram measuring approximately 120 miles on a side. At Camden, which would inevitably be Greene's first, major objective, and the northernmost point of the parallelogram, Rawdon was located with almost a quarter of his total strength. Along the coast were the major posts of Charleston and Savannah, and the less important one at Georgetown. Far to the interior, where they were important in maintaining Loyalist support, were Augusta, Ninety-Six, and Fort Granby. Orangeburg, Fort Watson, and Fort Motte served as connecting links between Charleston and these more distant strongpoints. (Alden, *South,* 261) (See maps on page 1028 and back endpapers.)

When Greene advanced on Camden he called on the partisan leaders to participate in a coordinated strategy. Pickens was to threaten Ninety-Six and keep reinforcements from being detached from that place. Sumter was asked to join Greene near Camden. Marion was to move out of his Peedee swamps and join Light-Horse Harry Lee in an attack on Ft. Watson if Lee's primary mission of screening against a possible move by Cornwallis from Wilmington could be abandoned.

The siege of FT. WATSON, 15–23 Apr., ended with the capture of that place by Lee and Marion with insignificant losses. The MAHAM TOWER was first used in this operation. The man for whom the fort was named, British Col. John WATSON, had been detached from Camden earlier with 500 of Rawdon's Tory troops to look for Marion in the vicinity of Georgetown (i.e., the Peedee swamps), and uncertainty as to his location played a significant part in the operations around Camden as well as at FT. WATSON.

At HOBKIRK'S HILL, 25 Apr., just outside of Camden, Rawdon outgeneraled and defeated Greene in an action that left him "almost frantic with vexation and disappointment." (Quoted by Alden, *op. cit.,* 263) It was on this occasion that Greene made the statement that summarizes his Southern campaigns: "We fight, get beat, rise, and fight again" (see this entry for exact circumstances). Greene's problems in coordinating his strategy against the various enemy posts, and also of Rawdon's success in making the best of his scattered dispositions, are illustrated in the action around Camden. Pickens' mission, you will remember, was to threaten Ninety-Six; but Rawdon got reinforcements from that place. "The Gamecock," Sumter, was asked to join Greene near Camden, but he simply ignored the request (see below). Marion and Lee were supposed to join Greene, or at least to keep Watson from joining Rawdon; although Watson did not reach Camden until after the battle (7 May), he kept Marion and Lee so busy chasing him that they were not present at the battle of Hobkirk's Hill.

Sumter took ORANGEBURG, 11 May. Marion and Lee took FT. MOTTE, 12 May, and Lee took FT. GRANBY, 15 May. "With his usual rather arrogant independence" (Ward, 801), the Gamecock had gone off to attack Ft. Granby instead of joining Greene outside of Camden; he had then broken off this attack to take Orangeburg, about 30 miles S.S.E.; he then retraced his steps to find that Ft. Granby had already surrendered to Lee.

"Sumter felt that Lee had stolen his glory and complained to Greene of Lee's conduct, stating that he considered it 'for the good of the public to do it without regulars.' Greene replied that Lee had acted in accordance with his orders; whereupon Sumter sent in his resignation. Greene diplomatically persuaded him to withdraw it, and he afterward rendered excellent service, in co-operation with Lee, in the vicinity of Charleston." (F. V. Greene, *Rev. War.,* 249, citing Johnson, *Greene,* II, 122, and G. W. Greene, *Greene,* III, 290, 295, 298)

ROUND TWO

On 10 May, Rawdon abandoned Camden and reached Monck's Corner on the 24th. Georgetown was evacuated on the 23d, by sea, to elude attack by Marion. A better man than Cornwallis at facing military realities, Rawdon had also ordered Ft. Granby and Ninety-Six abandoned, but they did not get the word in time.

Greene moved against Ninety-Six on 9 May and sent Lee with some newly raised militia to join Pickens around Augusta. The siege of AUGUSTA, 22 May–5 June, led to its surrender only after a stout defense by Lt. Col. Thos. Brown's 630-man garrison of regulars and Ga. Tories. The siege of NINETY-SIX, 22 May–19 June, had to be abandoned just as the rebels appeared to be on the point of a hard-won success against the die-hard garrison of Lt. Col. John CRUGER. But, with reinforcements from Ireland, Rawdon mustered a relief column of 2,000, eluded Sumter's delaying force, and moved rapidly to Cruger's support. Greene wisely avoided the risk of a decisive action in the field and retreated on 20 June. Rawdon pursued about 25 miles and then turned back when Greene headed for safety behind the Broad River. Rawdon ordered Ninety-Six abandoned, leaving the place himself on 3 July and withdrawing through Ft. Granby to Orangeburg. Here he was joined by Cruger from Ninety-Six and by Lt. Col. Alexander STEWART and his 3d Regt. from Charleston. Now outnumbered almost two to one, Greene withdrew his Cont'l. regiments into the Santee Hills for a brief rest. Remember, it was July in S.C., and the summer heat was taking its toll. Rawdon left Stewart at Orangeburg and returned to Charleston with 500 men; Marion, Sumter, and Lee dogged his heels to within five miles of the city. This ended the second phase. In less than eight months Greene had reconquered all the South except Savannah and the area around Charleston.

His little army had marched 950 miles, fought three battles and numerous minor engagements, captured nine posts, and taken nearly 3,000 prisoners. (F. V. Greene, *Rev. War*, 253) A point not to be overlooked is the high caliber of his opponents, Cornwallis and Rawdon. The former's strategic blunders were combined with an aggressiveness that permitted Greene no false step. The latter opponent showed good strategic sense along with all Cornwallis' aggressiveness, and made Greene work for his successes.

ROUND THREE

During his six weeks in the Santee Hills, Greene was reinforced to over 2,000. Sumter spent this period around Ft. Granby, Marion was at Nelson's Ferry, and Pickens was in his home territory around Ninety-Six. Rawdon was forced to take sick leave, and command passed to Stewart. The latter moved up from Orangeburg to a position 16 miles from Greene, with the flooded Congaree River between them, and could not be tricked out of position by Greene's raids to the outskirts of Charleston.

On 22 Aug. '81, Greene resumed the offensive. High water of the Santee and Wateree made him take a long detour through Camden to get at Stewart, and the latter withdrew to Eutaw Springs, where he could be supplied better from Charleston. On 7 Sept., Greene was joined by Marion, bringing his strength up to about 2,400. The next morning Stewart was surprised to find Greene on top of him, but he formed in time to meet Greene's attack. The Battle of EUTAW SPRINGS, 8 Sept., left Stewart in possession of the hotly contested field but so weakened that he had to withdraw to Monck's Corner. Greene had lost his fourth battle, but had practically won his campaign.

The little Southern army withdrew into the Santee Hills again for badly needed rest and recuperation. Within 10 days Greene had only 1,000 men fit for duty as sickness and expiration of militia services thinned his ranks. The end of active campaigning gave men time to worry about their arrears in pay, inadequate clothing, and other grievances. A mutiny was brewing when one Timothy Griffin staggered onto the parade ground as the Md. Cont'ls. were being admonished by their officers for recent lax discipline. "Stand to it, boys!" shouted Griffin, full of bottled courage. "Damn my blood if I would give an inch!" This happened on 21 Oct., and the rest of Greene's command watched him shot the next afternoon for encouraging mutiny and desertion, which discouraged the others.

Cornwallis had surrendered three days earlier, and Gen. Arthur St. Clair soon started south with 2,000 regulars to reinforce Greene. Before he could arrive (4 Jan. '82), however, the Southern army had to take the field to quell a Tory uprising that followed Fanning's HILLSBORO RAID, 12 Sept. The attack on DORCHESTER, 1 Dec., forced the last British outpost back into Charleston.

On 9 Dec., Greene joined the rest of his army at the place called Round O, about 35 miles W. of Charleston, and St. Clair's troops arrived there on 4 Jan. '82. Wilmington having been evacuated in Nov., the British in the South were now confined to Charleston and Savannah.

Most accounts of the Revolution in the South end at this point with a general statement that it was all over. The following military events are, however, worth recording: JOHNS ISLAND, 28–29 Dec. '81; the MUTINY OF GORNELL, Apr. '82; the GA. EXPED. of Anthony Wayne; and COMBAHEE FERRY, 27 Aug. '82. The British evacuated Savannah on 11 July '82 and Charleston on 14 Dec., '82.

Greene remained at Charleston until Aug. '83, after news of the peace treaty arrived. He then returned to R.I., being hailed along the way with the respect and admiration he had earned. After two years of getting his tangled personal affairs in order he moved to an estate the Ga. legislature had given him near Savannah. But his days were limited.

The reputation Nathanael Greene won in his Southern campaigns has worn well in the hands of historians, as is indicated in his biographical sketch. Alden points out, however, that some feel the American regulars got too much credit and the irregulars not what they deserve.

"A hot continuing debate sprang up over the question

Who clipped the lion's wings
And flea'd his rump and pared his claws?

It is clear that the patriots of the lower South, although they might have been able to continue guerrilla fighting indefinitely, could hardly have dealt effectively with the British and their Tory allies without the assistance of the regulars from the upper South [Va., Md.] and Delaware. On the other hand, Greene could hardly have kept the field without the aid of Marion, Sumter, Pickens, Clarke, Huger, and the partisans. Those militiamen who so often fled without fighting made their contribution. There was glory enough for all." (Alden, *The South in the Revolution,* 267)

Nor was that glory monopolized by the American patriots: Rawdon, Tarleton, Cruger, Webster, and others had shown magnificent leadership; Camden, Cowan's Ford, and Guilford are names of which the British Army is proud. Cruger's defense of Ninety-Six and

Rawdon's relief of that place were splendid military accomplishments.

SOUTHERN THEATER, Military Operations in. The Revolutionary War was restricted to the North until after the Battle of Monmouth, N.J., 28 June '78. Then it moved south and ended, to all intents and purposes, at Yorktown, Va., 19 Oct. '81.

1775—SOUTHERN REBELS GAIN CONTROL

While major military events were taking place around Boston and in Canada, the British could not spare regulars to support the embattled Loyalists in the South.* The year ended with the rebels generally in control of all four Southern provinces. The Heitman–*Army Almanac* list of battles shows 29 actions in 1775; none took place in N.C. or Ga., and only the following four are listed for all the South: HAMPTON and GREAT BRIDGE, Va., NINETY-SIX and Cane Brake (see REEDY RIVER), S.C. The two actions in S.C. were intramural affairs that gave a preview, albeit a tame one, of the civil war nature of the fighting that was to rage later in the South. Other activities in the South during 1775 are covered under VIRGINIA MILITARY OPERATIONS and two cross references that will be cited below: Moores Creek Bridge, N.C., 27 Feb., and Hutchinson's Island, Ga., 7 Mar. '76.

1776—THE REBELS MAINTAIN CONTROL

The London authorities counted strongly on Loyalist support in putting down the rebellion, and the Loyalists always appeared stronger in areas where

* A minor exception occurred in Va., where a few regulars were called in from the frontier posts and fought at Great Bridge; see below.

the British regulars were not fighting at the moment. Frustrated around Boston and encouraged by reports of the fugitive governors from the Southern provinces, the British launched the CHARLESTON EXPEDITION of Clinton in 1776. But before the British could get going with this operation their hopes for Loyalist support were crushed at NORFOLK, Va., 1 Jan., and MOORES CREEK BRIDGE, N.C., 27 Feb. After a humiliating defeat at Charleston, 28 June, the British expedition limped back to join Howe on Staten Island for the New York Campaign. The only other actions in the South during the year were at HUTCHINSON'S ISLAND, Ga., 7 Mar., GWYNN ISLAND, Va., 8–10 July, Rayborn Creek, S.C., 15 July, and Essenecca Town, S.C., 1 Aug. '76. See also CHEROKEE WAR OF 1776.

1777—QUIET IN THE SOUTH

While decisive events took place in other theaters, armed actions in the South were limited to those at FT. McINTOSH, Ga., 2–4 Feb., and Ft. Henry (see WHEELING), Va., 1 Sept. '77.

1778–1779—THE WAR MOVES SOUTH

The French Alliance, signed in Paris on 6 Feb. '78, changed, *in theory,* the entire complexion of the Revolutionary War since it now challenged the naval supremacy that had given the British such great strategic flexibility: the ability to move large bodies of troops along the coasts and up the rivers of America. *Actually,* the British had not capitalized fully on this advantage, and it was almost three years before the French fleet made any decisive contribution to American strategy, but this new element had been introduced.

Maj. Gen. Robt. Howe was the first commander of the rebel Southern army, and in the spring of 1778 he endeavored to mount an expedition to invade East Florida, where Gen. Augustine Prevost was reported to be receiving British reinforcements. With about 550 Cont'l. troops and the militia commands of Cols. C. C. Pinckney, Bull, Williamson, and Gov. Wm. Houstoun (of Ga.), Howe reached the Altamaha River on 20 May. Here his proposed attack on St. Augustine aborted because Houstoun and Williamson refused to take orders. Dissolution of the expedition was speeded by hunger and sickness.

The British then undertook operations that resulted in the capture of SAVANNAH, 29 Dec. '78, by Col. Archibald Campbell's expedition from N.Y. Prevost marched north to take SUNBURY, 9 Jan. '79, and assume command of British operations in the South.

LINCOLN'S OPERATIONS

Maj. Gen. Benj. Lincoln was appointed commander of the Southern Dept. in Sept. '78 while Howe was operating in Ga. When Howe retreated from Savannah he joined forces with Lincoln, who had moved south to Purysburg, on the S.C. side of the Savannah River. The Americans then numbered 1,121 Cont'ls. and 2,518 militia, but only 2,428 were fit for duty and the militia were substandard in quality. (Ward, *W.O.R.*, 682) Prevost moved up to face Lincoln across the river with 3,000 troops and an unknown number of Tory irregulars. Campbell went inland to take Augusta, 29 Jan., with virtually no opposition.

As the two main armies faced each other across the formidable barrier of the swamp-bordered Savannah River, Prevost capitalized on his available naval forces to make the first move: he sent a force of about 200 men to take Port Royal Island. This turning movement was frustrated by Moultrie at BEAUFORT, 3 Feb. '79.

This success helped to swell Lincoln's ranks with militia reinforcements, and he undertook a counteroffensive to recover Ga. Gen. Andrew Williamson moved with 1,200 men to a position across the river from Campbell's isolated force in Augusta. Gen. Griffith Rutherford led 800 men to Black Swamp, about 10 miles upstream from Purysburg. Gen. John Ashe was then sent with 1,500 to join Williamson opposite Augusta. After Ashe crossed the river and started down the right bank in the tracks of Campbell, who had evacuated Augusta the evening before Pickens won his victory at nearby KETTLE CREEK, Ga., 14 Feb., the British executed a brilliant little operation that destroyed Ashe's column at BRIAR CREEK, Ga., 3 Mar.

This spoiled all chance of recovering Ga. at that time, but "Lincoln, whose courage and determination were perhaps greater than his military skill, did not think so," says F. V. Greene. (*Rev. War*, 195) Leaving Moultrie with 1,000 men at Purysburg and Black Swamp, Lincoln marched up the left bank of the river toward Augusta with the remaining 4,000. Prevost countered with the indirect strategy of pushing through Moultrie's covering force to bring Lincoln back by threatening Charleston. Whereas Lincoln recognized this as a diversion and continued his march toward Augusta, Prevost met so little resistance that he moved on to threaten CHARLESTON, 11–12 May. Lincoln stopped his advance at Silver Bluff, S.C., about 10 miles short of Augusta, and came puffing back toward Charleston. Prevost withdrew by way of the coastal islands. In a mismanaged attempt to destroy the British rear guard of Lt. Col. Maitland, the rebels were beaten at STONO FERRY, 20 June '79. Maitland was left with a strong outpost on Port Royal Island, and Prevost withdrew his main body

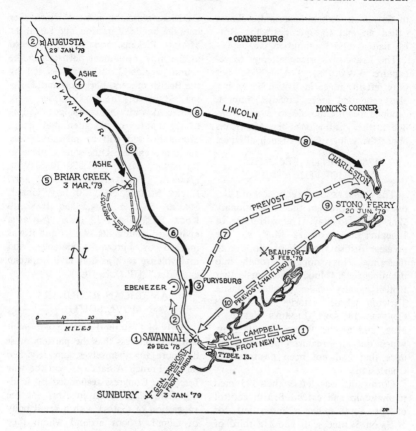

BRITISH CONQUEST OF GEORGIA, DEC. '78—JUNE '79.

1. Campbell captures Savannah. Prevost arrives and assumes command.
2. Prevost masses at Ebenezer, sending Campbell to take Augusta and other interior posts.
3. Lincoln joins Howe at Purysburg with reinforcements from Charleston.
4. Encouraged by successes at Beaufort and Kettle Creek (off map, 50 mi. N.W. of Augusta), Lincoln sends Ashe to liberate the interior posts. The British withdraw toward Savannah, and Ashe follows.
5. Prevost annihilates Ashe at Briar Creek.
6. Lincoln, undaunted, leads another advance toward Augusta.
7. Prevost counters by a raid toward Charleston.
8. Lincoln races back to save the city.
9. Prevost starts a withdrawal along the coast, and his rear guard defeats the Americans at Stono Ferry.
10. Leaving Maitland to outpost Beaufort, Prevost returns to Savannah.

to Savannah. When heat and sickness called an end to operations the British had a solid foothold in Ga.

The Franco-American attempt to recapture SAVANNAH, 9 Oct. '79, not only left the place in British hands but also generated more Loyalist support, dropped patriot morale to a new low, and further disillusioned the Americans about the value of the French alliance.

1780—SOUTH BECOMES MAJOR THEATER

The CHARLESTON EXPEDITION of Clinton in 1780 brought the Revolutionary War south to stay. The surrender of Lincoln's army on 12 May was the greatest British triumph of the war to that time. This campaign brought into prominence a bloody, hell-for-leather British cavalry leader named Banastre Tarleton whose victories at MONCK'S CORNER, 14 Apr., LENUD'S FERRY, 6 May, and at the WAXHAWS, 29 May, wiped out all organized patriot resistance that had not been destroyed at Charleston.

Cornwallis was left with 8,345 men to maintain and extend British control of the South when Clinton left for N.Y. on 5 June with about a third of the troops he had brought on this expedition. With his main body at Charleston, and strong detachments at Savannah, Augusta, and Ninety-Six, Cornwallis established a forward base at Camden and pushed outposts to Rocky Mount, Hanging Rock, and Cheraw. Another post was established at Georgetown, near the mouth of the Peedee River. Within this arc of over 350 miles were many other posts needed to secure lines of communications and rally Loyalists. The latter were counted on heavily to hold this vast area of some 15,000 square miles.

During the three months that followed the surrender of Charleston the Carolinas were the scene of skirmishes between bands of patriots and Loyalists. Marion, Pickens, and Sumter emerged as the most prominent partisans in the actions against Loyalist forces led by the British officers, Ferguson and Tarleton. Many of these skirmishes were connected with the campaigns leading to the battles of Camden and Kings Mountain, and will be mentioned under those entries. Others took place at RAMSEUR'S MILL, N.C., 20 June, WILLIAMSON'S PLANTATION, S.C., 12 July, ROCKY MOUNT, S.C., 30 July, GREEN SPRING, S.C., 1 Aug., and HANGING ROCK, S.C., 6 and 12 Aug. "It was a civil war," comments Ward, "and it was marked by bitterness, violence, and malevolence such as only civil wars can engender." (W.O.R., 704)

AMERICAN REGULARS MOVE SOUTH

Early in 1780 the French government warned Congress that the patriots must do more for themselves and rely less on the French Alliance to win the war for them. Congress responded by sending Gen. Kalb south in Apr. (at the suggestion of Gates) with a small body of Cont'l. troops around whom they hoped the Southern militia would rally. (Fisher, *Struggle*, II, 295) When Lincoln surrendered Charleston, Congress commissioned Gates as commander of the Southern Dept. on 13 July. Washington was not consulted, and was known to oppose the selection of Gates (Washington favored Greene), but Congress obviously hoped Gates would have the same success as he had had in rallying militia to beat Burgoyne. (*Ibid.*)

Kalb, meanwhile, had left Morristown on 16 Apr. with the body of Md. Cont'ls. and the Del. Regt. that were to constitute the main portion of the Southern army throughout most of the subsequent campaigning. For this reason the units should be identified here. The 1st Brig., commanded by Brig. Gen. Wm. Smallwood, was composed of the 1st, 3d, 5th, and 7th Md. The 2d Brig. of Gen. Mordecai Gist comprised the 2d, 4th, and 6th Md., and the Del. Regt. Col. Chas. Harrison's 1st Cont'l. Arty. Regt. (18 guns) completed the contingent. Marching through Philadelphia to Head of Elk, the infantry proceeded by water to Petersburg, Va., and the guns continued by land. From Petersburg Kalb moved at the rate of 15 to 18 miles a day. On 20 June he learned of Charleston's surrender five weeks earlier (12 May). Since the purpose of his expedition was to help defend Charleston, Kalb was faced with a decision as to what he should do next. The hoped-for militia reinforcements failed to arrive in any appreciable numbers while he camped at Parson's Plantation, N.C., about 35 miles N.E. of Hillsboro. Showing initiative and resolution that was lacking in so many native-born patriots of the Revolution, this "foreign adventurer" led his regulars forward. He reached Hillsboro on 22 June. Despite the heat, insects, lack of adequate equipment, and almost total lack of provisions, the expedition struggled on to Buffalo Ford on Deep River, about 50 miles N.N.E. of the enemy post at Cheraw, S.C. Here he was joined by 120 survivors of Pulaski's Legion, now commanded by Armand. But the large force of well-fed N.C. militia under Maj. Gen. Richard Caswell refused to join him, and he was unable to make contact with the Va. forces of Edw. Stevens and Porterfield, who were known to be in the field. During the two weeks he camped at Buffalo Ford, Kalb learned of Gates's appointment. His persevering efforts having gone almost completely unrewarded, the giant Bavarian moved his camp along Deep River to Hollingsworth's Farm (Ward, *W.O.R.,* 717) or Coxe's Mill and surrendered command to Gates on the latter's arrival 25 July.

In the CAMDEN CAMPAIGN, July–Aug. '80, Gates ignored the good advice of Kalb and led the Southern army to an even greater disaster than Lincoln's defeat at Charleston. Kalb died of multiple wounds in the Battle of Camden, 16 Aug., while Gates fled the field and Tarleton wiped out Sumter's detachment at FISHING CREEK, 18 Aug.

REORGANIZATION AFTER CAMDEN

"Having itself chosen the three commanders, Howe, Lincoln and Gates, under whom Savannah and Charleston, Georgia and the two Carolinas had been lost, [Congress] now called upon Washington to select a commander for the Southern army," says F. V. Greene. (*Rev. War,* 220) Nathanael Greene was Washington's immediate choice, and Steuben was selected as second in command.

Before Greene arrived at Charlotte, N.C. (2 Dec.) to take command, however, Gates had reorganized the puny remnants of his army. Of 4,000 that had constituted this force before Camden, only about 700 made their way back to Hillsboro, N.C. Most of them without weapons, they arrived "hungry, fatigued and almost naked." (Schenck, quoted in Ward, *op. cit.,* 732) The militia presented no problem of reorganization since few, if any, of the N.C. irregulars showed up, and the fleetfooted Va. militiamen who found their way to the rendezvous soon went home on termination of enlistments. This left only the regulars, and what was left of two brigades had to be consolidated to form a single regiment of two battalions. A third regiment was constituted a short time later when Col. Abraham

Buford arrived with the portion of his 3d Va. Cont'ls. that had survived the Battle of the WAXHAWS (29 May) plus 200 recruits, and 50 of Porterfield's light infantry also came into camp. Early in Oct., Gates organized a corps of light troops by taking selected men from the regiments; this formed the nucleus of Morgan's division in the operations of Greene that will be mentioned below.

OPERATIONS AFTER CAMDEN

Cornwallis did not wait for Greene's arrival to take the field. Clinton had left Cornwallis with instructions to make the security of S.C. his primary objective, but the ambitious Earl also got authority to communicate directly with the London authorities, and the latter endorsed his more aggressive strategy. On 8 Sept. '80, therefore, he started an offensive.

At KINGS MOUNTAIN, S.C., 7 Oct., the patriots won a victory over Maj. Patrick Ferguson that Clinton later called "the first link of a chain of evils that followed each other in regular succession until they at last ended in the total loss of America."

In response to direction from London, where Cornwallis' strategy was favored over his own, Clinton had ordered Maj. Gen. Leslie to move from N.Y. with 2,500 troops to the Chesapeake; here he was to link up with Cornwallis as the latter pushed into Va., or at least to block movement of American reinforcements south. Leslie sailed from N.Y. on 16 Oct. with the British Guards, 82d and 84th Regts., the Bose Regt., and the units commanded by Edmund Fanning and John Watson. Although the Kings Mountain disaster had already occurred (7 Oct.), Leslie landed at Portsmouth, Va., as originally planned. Here he received orders from Rawdon, who was acting

commander while Cornwallis was incapacitated by fever, to bring his force to Charleston.* Leslie sailed from Portsmouth on 23 Nov., reached Charleston on 16 Dec., and marched inland with 1,500 troops to arrive at Camden on 4 Jan. '81. The 82d and 84th stayed in Charleston, and FANNING went to Georgetown. (Baurmeister, *Journals,* 385, 395, 398, and 414)

Cornwallis, meanwhile, had retreated from Charlotte to Winnsboro, reaching there in late Oct. '80, and while the bulk of his army remained inactive he devoted his attention to suppressing the partisans. Marion's raids on the line of communications between Charleston and Camden were particularly troublesome. The Swamp Fox sallied forth from Snow Island and routed a body of Tory militia under Col. Tynes at Tearcoat Swamp, 28 Oct. Then he materialized out of the Black River swamps to cross the High Hills of Santee and camp astride the British supply line at Singleton's Mills. Cornwallis gave Tarleton permission to take most of his Legion off to catch Marion, but Tarleton was led a merry chase during which he never caught sight of Marion's men. "Come, my boys!" he said finally, "Let us go back and we will find the gamecock [Sumter]. But as for this damned old fox, the devil himself could not catch him." (Quoted in Bass, *Green Dragoon,* 111) The Gamecock, meanwhile, capitalized on blunders of a British force sent out to surprise him—including 40 of Tarleton's cavalry—and repulsed them at FISHDAM FORD, S.C., 9 Nov. '80. This brought swarms of

* This letter was written from Hillsboro by Rawdon, but Professor Rankin comments that Cornwallis actually remained in command and suspects, from the language of the letter, that he dictated it.

patriots to Sumter's camp and seriously alarmed Cornwallis about the safety of his rear area, particularly Ninety-Six. A series of summons went out to bring Tarleton back to meet this menace: "I wish you would get three Legions, and divide yourself in three parts," wrote Cornwallis to his subordinate, "We can do no good without you." (Quoted in *ibid.,* 117) This led to the action at BLACKSTOCKS, S.C., 20 Nov., a hard-fought skirmish between Sumter and Tarleton. You will have to read about this one and form your own opinion as to who won.

GREENE TAKES THE OFFENSIVE

Greene assumed command on 3 Dec. and took the offensive in an extraordinarily unorthodox manner almost immediately. This initial operation and the subsequent events are covered under SOUTHERN CAMPAIGNS OF GREENE. Here we might, however, mention the highlights: Morgan's brilliant victory over Tarleton at the COWPENS, S.C., 17 Jan. '81, Greene's masterful Retreat to the Dan, his return to N.C. and tactical defeat but strategic victory at GUILFORD C. H., 15 Mar., Cornwallis' retreat to Wilmington, Rawdon's victory over Greene at HOBKIRK'S HILL (Camden), S.C., 25 Apr., Greene's mopping up in the Carolinas, and the final major engagement at EUTAW SPRINGS, S.C., 8 Sept. '81.

Meanwhile, Va. was the scene of devastating raids after the stalemate in the North enabled the British to shift strength into that area. Lafayette was sent there with an expeditionary force, and Cornwallis appeared from Wilmington. All these operations are covered under VIRGINIA MILITARY OPERATIONS and the YORKTOWN CAMPAIGN.

SOWER, Christopher. 1754–1799. Loyalist. Pa. In a magnificent under-statement, Appleton's gives this sketch: "... was engaged in business in Philadelphia during the war, and afterward led an unsettled life." He was the grandson of the Christopher Saur or Sauer (1693–1758) who came to Pa. in 1724, settled at Germantown, built a large house, "and in 1738 began his notable career as the first German printer and publisher in America." (*D.A.B.*) In 1743 he published, in German, the first edition of the Bible in America (excepting the Indian translation by John Eliot in 1661–63). The son, also named Christopher, carried on the family business with ability and energy. When the Revolution broke out he was persecuted as a leader of the Dunkers (who refused to take oaths or bear arms), because his two sons were avowed Loyalists, and because he was wealthy. In 1778 all his possessions were confiscated, and for the few remaining years of his life he lived with a daughter at a friend's house at Methacton. In accordance with his religion, he had refused to defend himself in court, and after suffering at the hands of patriot justice he refused to claim redress. Peter MUHLENBERG had secured his release from prison after his arrest and maltreatment on 23 May '78, and Sower's only protest during his persecution was at being called a traitor.

Christopher the third, the subject of this sketch, became a Loyalist primarily because of a congenital antipathy toward the class of men who became patriot leaders, a class that had been hostile to his family on religious grounds. In 1774 his father transferred to him, without legal formalities, the family home and business. Until the British army arrived, he and his brother Peter published the *Germantowner Zeitung* and did all they could to support the Loyalist cause without being put in jail. When the British arrived, he moved to Philadelphia (Sept. '77) and continued his paper under the title of *Staats Courier*. On 5 Dec. '77 he was wounded and captured at Germantown (presumably in connection with the affair of WHITEMARSH), and on 10 Jan. '78 was exchanged. He went to N.Y.C. when the British evacuated Philadelphia (June '78) and in Aug. '78 the family estate, valued at between £10,000 and £30,000, was confiscated and sold. (*D.A.B.*)

In N.Y.C. he became the link between Sir Henry Clinton and the Pa. Loyalists in the frontier counties of Lancaster, Northumberland, and York. During the next three years he was the principal agent for Wm. RANKIN. In the spring of 1781 he went on a secret mission to Va., presumably to rally Loyalist support there. When the British evacuated N.Y.C. in 1783 he went to England, where he was granted £1,289 to cover his war losses by confiscation. Two years later he went to New Brunswick, where he later became king's printer and deputy postmaster general. In 1799 he returned to the U.S., and the same year he died at the home of his brother Samuel in Baltimore. (Van Doren, *Secret History,* many references.)

SPALDING, Simon. 1742–1814. Cont'l. officer. Conn.–Pa. Born in Plainfield, Conn., he moved to the Wyoming Valley in 1772. On 26 Aug. '76 he became a 2d Lt. of Ransom's Wyoming Valley Co. Promoted to 1st Lt. on 1 Jan. '77 (Heitman), he saw action at Bound Brook, N.J., 13 Apr. '77, where "the escape of the Americans with slight loss was largely due to his personal efforts." (Appleton's) Promoted to Capt. on 24 June '78, he led Conn. troops to reinforce the Wyoming Valley but was nearly 50 miles away when the WYOMING VALLEY "MAS-SACRE," 3–4 July '78, took place. He commanded his company with distinc-

tion in Sullivan's Expedition against the Iroquois, 1779. (*Ibid.*) Transferred to the 1st Conn. on 1 Jan. '81, he retired two years later. On 30 May '83 he moved up the Wyoming Valley to settle at Shesequin, where he eventually became B.G. of militia.

SPANGENBERG, Augustus. See MORAVIAN SETTLEMENTS.

SPANISH CONSPIRACY, 1786–1809. Involving a number of Revolutionary War veterans—hence inclusion of this article—this conspiracy was actually a series of related intrigues between Spanish authorities and certain Americans of the Ohio Valley region; they stemmed from a desire of Spain to protect Spanish hold on La. and Fla. by promoting establishment of a Separatist state. The latter was to comprise the vast region bounded by the Illinois, Mississippi, and Tennessee rivers, and including the upper Ohio Valley, that is to say, most of the present states of Ill., Tenn., Ky., Ind., Ohio. W. Va., and western Pa. (Bemis, *Diplomatic Hist. of the U.S.,* map on p. 76) Exploiting sectional antagonism between East and West, using bribery, blocking navigation of the lower Mississippi, and promoting the colonization schemes of speculators, Spain focused her efforts on Ky., where James Wilkinson became the principal American conspirator. At one stage of the dealings the Separatists proposed to guarantee Spanish possession of the eastern Mississippi Valley north of the Illinois River, and the area of modern Ky., Tenn., Miss., Ala., and Ga. bounded on the north by the Tennessee River and on the east by the Flint River. (*Ibid.*)

Gardoqui and James White conducted the first intrigue in 1786. As a result of the deadlock in the Gardoqui-Jay negotiations, in 1786 Congress authorized Jay to abandon the American claim of free navigation on the Mississippi.

This aroused great indignation in the West, and in 1787 James Wilkinson negotiated directly with authorities in New Orleans, becoming the principal agent of Spain in her dealings with the Separatists (or Secessionists). Although the conspiracy was suspected almost from the beginning, and Wilkinson was exposed by Daniel Clark in *Proofs of the Corruption of ... Wilkinson* (1809), the secessionist plan collapsed before any of its principal organizers could be prosecuted. (See also the end of the article on SPANISH PARTICIPATION. ...)

A close associate of Wilkinson in the "Spanish Conspiracy" was Aaron BURR, but the "Burr Conspiracy" was another movement, although WILKINSON was involved.

SPANISH PARTICIPATION IN THE COLONIAL WARS AND THE AMERICAN REVOLUTION, including the postwar period. In the article on the COLONIAL WARS, c. 1560–1763, the role of Spain in this period of American history is outlined. The Treaty of Utrecht, 1713, was the first to rearrange the colonial map of America, and "Some commentators have gone so far as to call it the beginning of the diplomatic history of the United States, because its articles are the root of later important questions of American diplomacy," writes Bemis. (*Diplomatic Hist. of the U.S.,* 7) By this treaty Spanish rights were recognized in Fla. (including most of the southern part of Ga.) and the regions now known as Mexico, Texas, New Mexico, Arizona, and California. The Treaty of Paris, 1763, ending the Colonial Wars, eliminated French holdings in North America, giving Spain the former French possessions west of the Mississippi, and taking from her the Fla. territory, except for the Island of New Orleans (retained by France but ceded immediately to Spain). (See MANCHAC) Spain acknowledged the rights of Britain to maintain her troublesome log-cutting settlements in the regions now known as Honduras and Nicaragua. Britain, in turn, relinquished Cuba to Spain. Bemis writes:

"Another provision of the treaty of Paris that was full of later importance for the diplomatic history of the United States was the regulation of the navigation of the Mississippi River. Because France retained the 'island' of New Orleans as a part of Louisiana, the river flowed between French banks [*sic*] on its last 220 miles to the sea. In order that this might not interfere with the navigation interests of British subjects upstream ... the treaty declared that the navigation of the Mississippi should be 'equally free, as well to the subjects of Great Britain as to those of France. ...'" (*Ibid.,* 10–11)

At the outbreak of the American Revolution Spain shared the French desire to get vengeance on Britain, and her foreign minister, Grimaldi, favored going to war with France against Britain as a pretext for conquering the latter's traditional ally, Portugal. Grimaldi failed to lead his country into this course of action and Spain limited herself to furnishing secret subsidies to the colonists, $200,000 (a million livres) to HORTALEZ & CIE., and another $197,230 in war matériel. In 1778 she *loaned* $74,087 to POLLOCK and Thos. Willing. (Later Spain loaned $174,011 to Jay, bringing her total subsidies and loans to about $645,000, as compared with French subsidies of almost $2,000,000 and loans of over $6,000,000. Bemis, *op. cit.,* 24.) Floridablanca succeeded Grimaldi in 1777 and in a memorandum dated 17 Oct. '77 reviewed the reasons why Spain opposed open war against Britain: Charles III did not wish to appear to be dominated by his nephew Louis XVI, the Spanish gentry liked England and were antipathetic to France, a peaceful settlement had been reached with Portugal and war with Great Britain would interrupt the latter country's extensive trade with the peninsula, and war would jeopardize the vast holdings of Spain in the New World. (Nickerson, *Turning Point*, 408) Spain's objection to the American Revolution from the start was that an independent America would push into her possessions in Louisiana and Mexico (Bemis, *op. cit.*, 11), and that the dangerous notions of independence would spread to Spanish colonies. She was so right.

Floridablanca also hoped to use nonintervention as a weapon to win certain diplomatic goals, while still refraining from assisting the Americans in achieving their dangerous independence. Recovery of Gibraltar and Minorca were Spain's main aspirations; she hoped then to recover Fla., Jamaica, gain full control in Central America (by expelling the British settlements mentioned earlier), and she even aspired to a share in the Newfoundland fisheries. (*Ibid.*, 33) Floridablanca's approach to this problem, which could have resulted in a diplomatic masterpiece, was to threaten Britain with mediation of her dispute with France. His price was Gibraltar. "Really if Great Britain had accepted . . . she would have been left in a position much better than she was forced to accept in her final defeat [comments Bemis].* * * France would have been sorely embarrassed because of her guaranty of the independence of the United States. She would have been obliged either to accept or to refuse. If she had accepted she would have deserted her American alliance. If she had refused she would have abandoned her Spanish affinity." (*Op. cit.*, 33)

George III refused to accept the Spanish offer, fortunately for France and America, and on 12 Apr. '79 Spain allied herself with France by the convention of Aranjuez. The two countries agreed to fight the war until Gibraltar was won for Spain. Other objectives were outlined, and both powers agreed not to make a separate peace. By this treaty Spain did not recognize American independence. Bemis comments that France's alliances with the U.S. (1778) and Spain (1779) insofar as American independence was concerned were "incompatible, almost bigamous." (*Op. cit.*, 34)

On 21 June '79 Spain declared war on Great Britain. Her military efforts were concentrated on an effort to take Gibraltar, a dream that was shattered at Cape St. Vincent, 16 Jan. '81. (See end of article on NAVAL OPERATIONS) Spanish authorities in Havana refused the request of Gov. Rutledge to send a fleet and army for the defense of Charleston in the spring of 1780 (Ward, *W.O.R.*, 698), and Spain declined to join the French in operations against the British in North America. They did, however, show substantial interest in capturing British posts in the West, and in this they were fortunate in having the extremely capable Gen. Gálvez in command at New Orleans. In 1779 Gálvez took the river posts of Manchac, Baton Rouge, and Natchez. The next year he took Mobile, and he forced the surrender of PENSACOLA, 9 May '81. These conquests did little to further the American cause at the time, but they assisted in later diplomatic relations by shifting possession of these places from Britain to Spain. (Bemis, *op. cit.*, 34 *n*.)

A British retaliatory expedition was stopped at ST. LOUIS, 26 May '80. A Spanish expedition against Detroit captured FT. ST. JOSEPH, Jan. '81, and subsequently the Spaniards claimed that by virtue of having held this place (near the S.E. coast of Lake Michigan) for 24 hours they had conquered the St. Joseph and Illinois valleys! Between

Sept. '79 and Oct. '82 the Spanish conducted minor operations in HONDURAS and NICARAGUA, and they captured the undefended Bahamas in May '82. See also JAMAICA and WEST INDIES IN THE REVOLUTION. On the west bank of the Mississippi the Spanish held military posts at St. Louis, New Madrid, and Arkansas. In 1797 they gave up their posts at Memphis (San Fernando) and Confederation (near the junction of the Tombigbee and Black Warrior rivers in Ala.). In 1798 they gave up Vicksburg (Nogales), Natchez, and Ft. St. Stephens (on the Tombigbee, 60 airline miles N. of Mobile). In 1798 they continued to hold New Orleans, Mobile, Pensacola, St. Marks, and St. Augustine. (*Ibid.,* map 6, p. 76; Scribner's *Atlas,* 88–89)

John Jay had been appointed agent to Spain on 27 Sept. '79 and held his post there from Jan. '80 to May '82. Although he failed in his mission of negotiating an alliance—he was not recognized by the government—his presence was useful to Floridablanca,˙ who still was trying to coerce Britain into ceding Gibraltar, and the foreign minister did give Jay a loan of $174,011.

"Floridablanca's persistent flirtations with a British envoy at the Spanish Court, Richard Cumberland, finally drove Vergennes to map out a compromise peace—at the hands of neutral mediators—which would have left the United States in the lurch. Fortunately for American independence George III refused to let Gibraltar go or to recognize any Spanish proposals for the disposition of his colonies. The Cumberland negotiations broke down. The United States and Spain were to come into opposition again in the final peace negotiations. The principal value to the United States or to France of Spain's belligerency was the moral effect of lining up another European country in the war against Great Britain." (*Ibid.,* 35)

Spain had joined the League of ARMED NEUTRALITY in 1781.

Postwar boundary disputes between Spain and the U.S. after 1783 were generally the same as those the new country had with Britain, but they also involved the knotty problem of Mississippi River navigation. Spain refused to recognize the part of the Anglo-American treaty that set the 31st parallel as the northern boundary of Spanish Florida, claiming a line 100 miles northward, at 32° 22' (through Vicksburg), and extending between the Mississippi and the Chattahoochee. In 1784 Spain refused to let American shipping pass freely along the lower Mississippi. On 15 May '85 Don Diego de Gardoqui arrived as minister to the U.S., and he was instructed by his government to make no concessions with respect to navigation of the river. On 20 July Congress authorized John Jay to negotiate with Gardoqui, and on 24 Aug. they instructed him particularly to stipulate the U.S. right to free navigation of the Mississippi. Needless to say, this made a deadlock inevitable, and on 29 Aug. '86 Congress authorized Jay to cede this point in return for a favorable commercial treaty with Spain. This came only after a bitter debate and with a vote of 7–5; since 9 states would have to ratify a treaty that might result from Jay's new instructions, the situation seemed hopeless and negotiations broke down. By the Treaty of San Lorenzo (Pinckney's Treaty), signed at Madrid, 27 Oct. '95, Spain recognized the Mississippi and the 31st parallel as boundaries and gave the Americans free navigation of the river as well as the right for three years to deposit goods at New Orleans; thereafter, if need be, they could deposit goods at another point to be designated. Meanwhile a number of prominent Americans were involved in what generally is known as the SPANISH CONSPIRACY.

SPANISH SUCCESSION, War of the. 1701–14. The Americàn phase, Queen Anne's War (1702–13), is covered under the COLONIAL WARS.

SPECIE. Coin, or "hard money," as opposed to paper money. See CONT'L. CURRENCY and MONEY OF THE 18TH CENTURY. Under NAV. ACTS see "Molasses Act of 1733."

SPENCER, Joseph. 1714–1789. Cont'l general. Conn. Sixty years old when the Revolution started, a militia officer since 1747 and a veteran of the last two Colonial wars, Joseph Spencer was a B.G. of Conn. troops at the start of the BOSTON SIEGE. When Congress ignored his Conn. militia seniority to make him à B.G. on 20 June '75 while appointing Putnam Maj. Gen., the old gentleman simply went home— A.W.O.L. Although some disapproved of this conduct, Spencer had enjoyed an official position in the community throughout his adult life (*D.A.B.*) and the provincial authorities appointed two men to jolly him back into ranks, so to speak. His pride thus salved, he returned to his troops on 18 July, served throughout the rest of the siege, and then went south with the army to N.Y. On 9 Aug. '76 he was promoted to Maj. Gen. The next month he voted with Geo. Clinton and Heath to defend N.Y.C., and he is the first of the triumvirate that Alexander McDougall described years later as "a fool, a knave and an honest, obstinate man." (Freeman, *Washington,* IV, 188 *n.*) In Dec. he was ordered to New England and established his headquarters at Providence. In Sept. '77 he organized an amphibious attack from Tiverton against Rhode Island (Island), but canceled the operation, after the troops had loaded

into boats, when he learned that the plan had been compromised. (Lossing, II, 80) Indignant about a proposed inquiry by Congress into the cause of this failure, Spencer requested a court of inquiry and was exonerated. "No particular regret was recorded when Joseph Spencer resigned the Rhode Island command and his commission as Major General [on 13 Jan. '78]," writes Freeman. (*Op. cit.,* 613) This same authority comments that neither William Heath nor Spencer "had done anything more than discharge routine duties without displaying such scandalous incompetence or sloth as to make their removal a public necessity. Not one flash of shining leadership had come from either of them." (*Ibid.,* 367)

Spencer was immediately appointed to the council of safety and in 1779 was elected to Congress.

SPENCER'S REGT., commanded by Col. Oliver Spencer, was one of the 16 "ADDITIONAL CONT'L. REGTS."

SPENCER'S TAVERN, Va., 26 June '81. (VA. MIL. OPNS.) When reinforcements joined Lafayette, Cornwallis retreated slowly through Richmond to Williamsburg, and Lafayette followed at a respectable distance. Simcoe left on 23 June with his Rangers and some jägers to destroy rebel stores on the Chickahominy. Lafayette detached Col. Richard Butler with his Pa. Regt., Majs. Call and Willis with a body of Va. riflemen, and Maj. Wm. McPherson with 120 mounted troops to intercept Simcoe on his return. After an all-night march they surprised Simcoe at Spencer's Tavern (or Ordinary), six miles N.W. of Williamsburg. At sunrise McPherson had mounted 50 light infantry double with 50 of his dragoons to speed up the pursuit, and this detachment closed in for a brief hand-to-hand action while the main bodies came forward. Simcoe's Rangers drove Mc-Pherson back, but Call and Willis came up and were hotly engaged with Simcoe's infantry when his dragoons hit their flank and pushed them back on Butler's Pa. Cont'ls. Simcoe had the advantage in the confused fighting that followed, but fearing that Lafayette's entire army might be at hand, he took the first opportunity to break off the action and fall back to Williamsburg. Since Cornwallis was moving forward with a strong reinforcement, Butler was equally anxious to see this skirmish end.

The Americans lost nine killed, 14 wounded, and 14 missing. Cornwallis reported 33 casualties; this figure is accepted by historians, although Lafayette thought the enemy lost 60 killed and 100 wounded. "Neither party could fairly claim a victory, though both parties did," says Lossing (II, 465). Simcoe describes the action in detail and claims it was a sizable engagement won by his generalship (Johnston, *Yorktown*, 56 *n.*), yet he left the field and his wounded in the hands of the enemy.

SPLIT ROCK (Lake Champlain), N.Y., 13 Oct. '76. Destruction of Arnold's fleet after the battle of VALCOUR ISLAND. Another Split Rock, a landmark surviving from Colonial history, figured in the action at Pell's Point (now in Pelham Bay Park, The Bronx).

SPONTOON. The espontoon, spontoon, or half pike was a badge of officer's rank that evolved from the halberd, and until a few years before the American Revolution it was carried by all foot officers of all armies. It was replaced by the FUSIL, the change taking place in France in 1754 and in England in 1786. British troops in America started abandoning spontoons much earlier, however: Braddock or-

dered them left behind in 1755 when he left Alexandria, Va., for his defeat in the wilderness, and almost all British regiments abandoned them for active field service during the American Revolution. (Peterson, *Colonial Arms*)

SPRINGFIELD, N.J., RAID of Knyphausen, 7–23 June '80. Prior to the return of Clinton from his Charleston Expedition, Knyphausen (who was temporarily in command in N.Y.) received reports that Washington's army was mutinous and might be won over. (Van Doren, *Secret History*, 270) Being led to believe also that the civil population might rally to support him, Knyphausen organized a force of 5,000 for a large-scale raid, landed them at De Hart's Point, near Elizabethtown, and on 7 June marched toward Morristown. Washington received this disturbing information the evening of the 7th, but when he reached the Short Hills the next day he learned that Col. Dayton's regiment of Maxwell's Brig., promptly reinforced by neighborhood militia, had so successfully blocked the enemy advance that they had gotten only as far as Springfield Bridge and had then pulled back and started entrenching. Knyphausen's position the afternoon of 7 June was on high ground N.W. of Connecticut Farms (now Union, N.J.), a settlement about two and a half miles S.E. of Springfield. (Baurmeister, *Journals*, 352–55; Freeman, *Washington*, V, 169–74; Ward, *W.O.R.*, 621–23)

British intelligence had obviously erred badly: the natives not only were hostile but efficient. Gen. Stirling, who commanded Knyphausen's vanguard, was wounded. "At Connecticut Farms," says Baurmeister, "the Jägers met with unaccustomed resistance, the rebels holding off our vanguard with fixed bayonets." (*Op. cit.*) The invaders burned about 30 buildings in Conn.

Farms and, to the mystification of Washington, withdrew during the night of 8–9 June to De Hart's Point and dug in. It was a peculiar situation: Knyphausen had withdrawn simply because his original mission, based on faulty intelligence, obviously could not be accomplished; Washington, on the other hand, had no way of knowing that the explanation for the enemy's peculiar conduct was this simple—he suspected they were up to something logical, such as feinting in N.J. before making a main effort up the Hudson. " 'Our situation,' said Washington on the 14th, 'is as embarrassing as you can imagine,' and then he had to add: 'When they unite their force, it will be infinitely more so.' " (Freeman, *op. cit.*) He recalled Harry Lee's Light Horse (which had received orders on 30 Mar. to prepare to move to S.C. [*ibid.*, 155 *n.*, 170]), sent for other mounted troops to perform the reconnaissance missions that were now so important, and he organized a force of 500 men under Brig. Gen. Edward Hand to harass the enemy position at De Hart's Point.

When Washington learned on 20 June that six British warships had sailed up the Hudson to Verplancks Point and, "with as little apparent reason for going as for coming, had dropped down the river again" (*ibid.*), he had to redeploy his forces so as to meet an attack against West Point and also to watch for a main effort in N.J. So he moved his main body to Pompton, where it would be closer to West Point yet still within 16 miles of Springfield, and he left Nathanael Greene at the latter place with about 1,000 Cont'l. troops to watch Knyphausen. Militia forces of Gens. Maxwell and Philemon Dickinson were still in the field to support Greene.

Clinton had reached Sandy Hook on 17 June. Learning then of Knyphausen's operation and its lack of success, he also received information from Benedict Arnold (dated 12 June) that the French expeditionary force of Rochambeau would soon reach Newport. The British commander realized that by committing troops to support Knyphausen's stalled offensive against Washington he would leave N.Y.C. open to a possible French attack. The mysterious British movement up the Hudson (see above) had been prompted by Clinton's fear that Washington might try to cross the river and join forces with the French, a movement Washington actually did not make until 31 July. (The French did not actually reach Newport until 12 July, and Clinton did not get word of their arrival until the 18th.)

Meanwhile Clinton prepared to advance into Westchester co., and Knyphausen had built a ponton bridge between Elizabethtown and Staten Island for a rapid junction with the main army when the British learned of Washington's movement toward West Point. Clinton and Knyphausen therefore organized a feint against Springfield and a stronger effort against Morristown on 23 June. Although one reason might have been to save face (C. & M., 728), Knyphausen's new thrust was ordered by Clinton to retard Washington's suspected movement of his entire army up the Hudson and to gain time for the troops just returning from Charleston to be transported up the Hudson to block Washington. (Clinton, *Amer. Reb.*, 193)

At 6 A.M. on 23 June Washington heard the sound of cannon on Greene's front, and in midmorning he received an alarming report from Greene: "The enemy are out on their march towards this place [Springfield] in full force, having received a considerable reenforcement last night." (Quoted in Freeman, *op. cit.*) According to Baurmeister, Knyphausen's original expedition had consisted of the British Guards, the 22d, 37th, 38th, 43d, and 57th Regts., two battalions of Cortland Skinner's West Jersey Vols., two Anspach regiments, the entire Anspach and Hessian Jäger Corps, the 17th Lt. Dragoons, von Diemar's Hussars, the mounted Queen's Rangers (Simcoe's), the Leib Regt., and the Landgraf, Donop, Bünau, and Bose Regts. Brigades were commanded by Gens. von Lossberg, von Hachenberg, Mathew, Skinner, and Thos. Stirling. James Robertson, Commandant of N.Y., and Gov. Tryon accompanied Knyphausen as volunteers. The reinforcements mentioned by Greene were the 42d Regt. and the rest of Simcoe's Rangers; the Leib Regt. and Jäger Corps returned to Staten Island to resupply their ammunition after the action of 7 June and, presumably, returned to N.J.

The enemy's second advance on Springfield was again contested by Maxwell's Brig. Greene positioned his regulars and Dickinson's militia to cover the bridge at Springfield, and Lee's dragoons operated with Maxwell's delaying force. On approaching Springfield, Knyphausen sent half his force to envelop Greene's left by way of the Vauxhall Bridge and to get to his rear at Chatham. Lee's dragoons and Dayton's 3d N.J. delayed the enveloping column under Gen. Mathew at Vauxhall Bridge and then dropped back to hold another position on the Vauxhall Road to protect Greene's left. Knyphausen's frontal attack was held up for 40 minutes by Col. Israel Angell's R.I. Regt., which then dropped back to a new position with Col. Wm. Shreve's N.J. militia. Greene reinforced Lee with two regiments of regulars (Col. Henry Jackson's Mass., and Col. S. B. Webb's Conn.) to block Mathew and concentrated the rest of his command on high ground behind Springfield. Knyphausen

was reluctant to attack Greene and broke off the action. After burning all but four of the 50 houses in Springfield he withdrew during the afternoon and crossed his bridge to Staten Island. Washington had had no alternative but to start back from Pompton to support Greene and to order supplies evacuated from Morristown, but he covered only five or six miles on 23 June and that night received the good news that Greene would not need his help after all. (Freeman, *op. cit.*, 173)

N.J. had once more been cleared of British troops, and the N.Y. Loyalists were "bitter with complaints of what seemed to them Clinton's incomprehensible lack of enterprise." (Van Doren, *op. cit.*, 270–71) Jerseyites, far from being swayed back toward King George, were aroused by the destruction of Connecticut Farms and Springfield. They were particularly outraged by the propaganda that the Rev. James Caldwell's wife, killed at Connecticut Farms on 7 June, had been shot by an enemy soldier as she sat by a window with her children.

Van Doren comments that "Arnold, betraying Washington's secret to the British, unintentionally helped save Washington from further operations in New Jersey." (*Op. cit.*, 271)

NUMBERS AND LOSSES

Patriot losses on 7 June were about 15 killed and 40 wounded, according to Col. Sylvanus Seeley of the N.J. militia. (Diary quoted in C. & M., 728) Baurmeister estimates that the 800 men under Gen. Maxwell in Elizabethtown had been reinforced by militia and regulars to a total of 2,500 by the time they withdrew to Springfield Bridge. (*Op. cit.*) Thacher says the rebels took 20 prisoners in this first action, but enemy killed and wounded are not reported by either side. (*Journal*, 198)

On 23 June the rebels lost 15 killed, 49 wounded, and nine missing. (Freeman, *op. cit.*, 174 *n.* This may, however, be the total casualties for the period 7–23 June, since it bears a strange similarity to the figures already quoted for the 7th, and Ward says American losses for the entire period were 13 killed, 61 wounded, and nine missing. Seeley, however, is specific in saying that 15 were killed and 40 wounded on 7 June.) Knyphausen's losses on the 23d are not known; Thacher says his brigade found 15 bodies, several fresh graves, and that the inhabitants reported seeing eight or 10 wagon loads of dead and wounded. Enemy strength on the 23d was between 5,000 and 6,000. Greene had about 1,000 at Springfield, and Maxwell may have had almost that many militia harassing the enemy's advance.

SPRINGFIELD, N.Y., May '78. In the spring of 1778, after the repulse of St. Leger's Expedition, Joseph Brant returned with his Indians and a large number of Tories to Oquaga. After sending out parties to attack isolated farms, in May he carried out his first large-scale raid. His objective was Springfield, at the head of Lake Otsego, a little less than 10 miles W.N.W. of Cherry Valley and somewhat more than that distance south of Ft. Herkimer. He burned all the houses but one, and moved all women and children into that house for safety. Several men and a considerable amount of property were evacuated to Oquaga.

SPRUCE BEER. Part of the American ration, this was made by boiling an extract from leaves and branches of the spruce fir with sugar or molasses and fermenting with yeast.

SPUYTEN DUYVIL, N.Y. Dutch for "spite the Devil," this creek marks the northern boundary of Manhattan Island. The (Boston) Post Road crossed at Kings Bridge, which made the latter of great strategic importance. Although "there is always a question where Spuyten Duyvil ends and Harlem Creek, now Harlem River, begins" (Freeman, *Washington*, III, 470 *n.*), the two constituted in 1776, as they do today, a continuous waterway between the Hudson and the East River. The British used this route in moving troops from the Hudson into the Harlem River to attack Ft. Washington, 16 Nov. '76.

SQUAW CAMPAIGN, 1778. See Edward Hand.

STAFF OFFICERS. Three military staff concepts were represented by officers of Washington's headquarters. The British, basically unimproved since created by Marlborough (d. 1722), had been known by Americans since the Colonial Wars and was the one they adopted. The Prussian model, which was later to influence all armies, was evolving from the genius of Frederick the Great, and through Steuben was to make itself felt in the Cont'l. Army (see below). The French system influenced the Americans in the establishment of inspectors general (see below). The chief of staff, who had been the key man in the staff of Cromwell's New Model Army, did not figure in the British and American armies of 1775–83. Orders were transmitted through the adjutant, and most of the high-level staff work was done by this officer and the quartermaster general (Q.M.G.). The intermediate echelons of army corps and division not having yet evolved into the form we would recognize today—Napoleon was to develop these organizations—orders went direct from the general commanding the main army or the "grand division" through his adjutant general (A.G.) to the brigade

commander and on to the regimental
(battalion) commander. "General Staff"
planning was done by the A.G., who
was charged with personnel matters,
including the vital problem of musters, and the Q.M.G., who handled
supply, transportation, the organization
of camps, and just about everything
else connected with operations. Food
and forage were the responsibility of
commissaries.

As for these titles, each army, British
and American, had but one A.G.,
Q.M.G., and Commissary General. At
the lower levels they were deputies and
assistant deputies.

Regiments were "brigaded" for specific operations under a B.G., and staffs
at these two echelons were basically the
same: the regimental and brigade majors were charged with operations (that
is to say, with matters pertaining to
combat); the adjutant was the personnel officer, but often was the major's
assistant in combat (Hittle, *post*, 137);
the quartermaster did most of the remaining staff work. See SUPPLY . . . for
his duties in the 18th century. Other
brigade and regimental staff positions
were the commissary, charged with provisions, the paymaster, the surgeon and
surgeon's mate (both of them officers),
and the chaplain. As for the latter, on
29 July '75 the Cont'l. Cong. made provision for the pay of chaplains and "the
chaplaincy evolved from an unplanned
supply of volunteer clergymen to an
organized system of brigade chaplains."
(*A.A.*, 68)

THE CONTINENTAL STAFF

On 16 June '75 the Cont'l. Cong.
created certain staff positions and, except for the Q.M.G., filled them as follows: A.G., Gates (17 June); Commissary Gen. of Stores and Provisions,
Joseph Trumbull (19 July); Paymaster
Gen., James Warren (27 July); Com-

missary Gen. of Musters, Stephen Moy-
lan (11 Aug.); and Chief of Engineers,
Richard Gridley (sometime in June
'75). Washington appointed Thomas
Mifflin Q.M.G. on 14 Aug. (See SUP-
PLY . . . for more about the posts of
Q.M.G. and Commissary Gen.)

On 19 July '75 Congress authorized a Wagonmaster and Commissary
of Artillery Stores, and Washington
appointed John Goddard and Ezekial
Cheever, respectively, to fill them. Dr.
Benj. Church became the first Director
Gen. and Chief of the medical department; see MEDICAL PRACTICE . . . for his
successors.

The Judge Advocate of the Army was
created as an office on 29 July '75, and
Wm. Tudor was appointed to the post.
In 1776 the title was changed to Judge
Advocate General (J.A.G.), and on 11
Apr. '77 Tudor was succeeded by John
LAURANCE. Col. Thomas Edwards was
appointed to the office after the latter's
retirement on 3 June '82.

The Inspector General's Dept. was
created by Congress on 13 Dec. '77.
Washington had felt the need for such
an office, and on 26 Oct. '77 had sent a
circular asking his generals for recommendations on whether an I.G. should
be appointed to establish uniformity in
drill, troop training, and command procedure, "as the time of the Adjutant
General seems to be totally engaged
with other business." The C. in C. visualized the office as being one for a
professionally trained foreign officer.
Prior to this two such officers had been
given such assignments: Col. MOTTIN
DE LA BALME was made I.G. of Cavalry
on 8 July '77, and on 11 Aug. TRONSON
DE COUDRAY had been appointed I.G.
of Ordnance and Military Stores. But
what now was wanted was an over-all
I.G. Col. (Baron) d'Arendt submitted
a plan for a system of inspection that
Washington intended to put into effect,

using "foreign officers who had commissions and no commands and were of ability... particularly the Baron d'Arendt... whose capacity seemed to be well admitted" (quoted in Freeman, *Washington,* IV, 592), but before Washington could find time from the press of field duties to get congressional approval, the delegates acted. On 13 Dec. '77 they created the post of I.G. and directed that this officer report direct to them. Soon thereafter they appointed Gen. Conway "Inspector General of the Army," and the resultant furor is covered under CONWAY CABAL. The French-Irish troublemaker never functioned as I.G., however, and the first man to do so was STEUBEN, whom Congress appointed on 5 May '78.

With Steuben's appointment the American Army began to experience a tenet of Prussian staff doctrine, that of delegated authority. A formal complaint against "the progressive encroachment of a new-fangled power" was submitted by Gen. James M. Varnum, a New Englander who was "filled with horror" when Steuben's inspectors called for reports on men fit for duty. "Steuben made the staff training of the Prussian system available to the Revolutionary leaders, who with the exception of a few such as Washington, Greene, and Wayne, were incapable of comprehending," writes James D. Hittle in *The Military Staff: Its History and Development* (3d ed., Harrisburg, Pa., 1961). "Had our infant army profited... the staff history of the following years would have made more satisfactory reading to a professional soldier. Literally and figuratively, Steuben was the first qualified staff officer of our Army." (Pp. 179–80)

The Northern and Southern military departments had officers corresponding to those on Washington's staff or those answerable direct to Congress. There was a single Q.M.G., and each department had a Deputy Q.M.G.; each brigade had an Assistant Deputy Q.M.G. The same nomenclature applied generally to A.G., I.G., and other staff positions. Although Edward Carrington was a Deputy Q.M.G., as *the* Q.M.G. of Greene's Southern Dept. he can sensibly be referred to as "Greene's Q.M.G."

Robert ERSKINE was commissioned Geographer and Surveyor to the Army on 27 July '77. Other staff titles are mentioned under SUPPLY.... See also ADJUTANTS, ENGINEERS, and MEDICAL PRACTICE....

STAMP ACT (22 Mar. '65–18 Mar. '66) and Stamp Act Congress (7–25 Oct. '65). Designed to raise £60,000 a year in America to pay part of the estimated £350,000 cost of maintaining British troops, the act passed through Parliament with little debate and no suspicion it would meet colonial resistance. Effective 1 Nov. '65, it taxed various types of printed matter (newspapers, broadsides, pamphlets), practically all types of legal documents, and included even dice and playing cards. Taxes were to be paid in specie; transactions in violation of the act were to be invalid; and penalties for infringements could be imposed by Vice-ADMIRALTY COURTS as well as by colonial common law courts. As a palliative, Americans were to be appointed stamp agents; Richard Henry Lee and other prominent colonists eagerly sought the post, which paid £300 a year and offered great patronage possibilities.

Grenville's Stamp Act extended into the colonies an act already existing in England, off and on, since introduced from Holland in 1694 (*E.B.*). N.Y. and Mass. had tried imposing their own stamp acts but had quickly abandoned them.

British justification for the Stamp Act

may be summarized as follows: PON-TIAC'S WAR had showed the unwilling-ness and the inability of the colonists to provide for their own protection; it would cost England about £350,000 a year to maintain the necessary British regulars in America to do the job; the colonists should pay part of the bill.

The Americans first based their objections on inability to pay, but then shifted to the principle of no TAXATION WITH-OUT REPRESENTATION. They viewed the increased jurisdiction of the no-jury Vice Admiralty courts as a threat to civil liberties. The Stamp Act was the first direct tax Parliament had ever tried to levy in America; it came at a time when the colonists were already alarmed by the ending of SALUTARY NEGLECT, and when they were suffering a postwar depression. The act mustered opponents from all geographical sections of America and from diverse influential groups: lawyers (whose business would be particularly hard hit), printers, tavern keepers, land speculators, merchants, and shipowners. The British also made the mistake of allowing the colonists almost a year between passage of the act and its enactment to organize resistance; already aroused by the Sugar Act and the Currency Act, and encouraged by their success in opposing royal prerogatives during the French and Indian War, the colonial assemblies were ready to resist.

The colonists moved swiftly. The SONS OF LIBERTY were organized in 1765 to take direct action; by intimidation and mob action, largely on the part of these "Patriots," all stamp agents were forced to resign. Daniel DULANY published his *Considerations . . .* in a protest against the act's illegality. Patrick HENRY made his famous Treason Speech in introducing the VIRGINIA RESOLVES (of 1765). John ADAMS rose to political prominence in drafting the Instructions to the Town of Braintree, Mass., summarizing colonial objections to the Stamp Act. James OTIS initiated the proposal that led to the Stamp Act Congress, 7–25 Oct. '65, in N.Y.C. This proposal was endorsed by S.C., R.I., Conn., Pa., and Md., in that order, and these colonies sent official delegates. N.J., Del., and N.Y. took no formal action, but sent delegates. Va., N.H., N.C., and Ga. did not participate.

The Stamp Act Congress was distinguished by a tone of moderation. It formulated a 14-resolution Declaration of Rights and Grievances (probably drafted by John Dickinson, or, possibly, by John Cruger [Commager, *Doc.*, 58]); this document denied Parliament's right to tax the colonies, and condemned the Stamp Act's provision that admiralty courts have jurisdiction. The Congress submitted its convictions in the form of an address to the King, a memorial to the Lords, and a petition to the Commons.

Only in Ga., whose Gov. was the remarkable Sir James WRIGHT, was the Stamp Act ever put into effect, and there it was only to a limited degree. Elsewhere, courts closed rather than use the stamps; they later resumed business in open violation of the act by refusing to use stamps. An exception was Rhode Island, where the governor refused to execute the Stamp Act and the courts stayed open.

In England, demand for repeal had been organized even before the act took effect. William Pitt supported the American position and called for repeal. Parliament received numerous petitions for repeal from merchants, whose trade with the colonies had dropped off 25 per cent as a result of NONIMPORTATION and an American austerity program. Grenville advocated enforcement of his act by military force. Benjamin Franklin, then a colonial agent in London, gave Commons cogent testimony that the colonies not only should not but could not pay, and warned that troop intervention might cause rebellion.

Repeal of the Stamp Act received royal assent 18 Mar. and took effect 1 May '66. The news reached America 26 Apr., and colonists in their rejoicing overlooked or ignored the significance of the DECLARATORY ACT, also dated 18 Mar.

See E. S. Morgan, *The Stamp Act Crisis: Prologue to Revolution* (1953).

STANSBURY, Joseph. 1742 o. s. ?–1809. Loyalist secret agent, poet. England–Pa. Son of a London haberdasher, he married a Huguenot and two years later, on 11 Oct. '67, reached Philadelphia. He opened a china store, entered enthusiastically into the social life of the metropolis, and was popular for the humorous and satirical songs that he wrote and sang. Although he sympathized with the patriots he opposed separation from the empire and in 1776 was briefly imprisoned for his loyal sentiments. Basically, he wanted to retain an inoffensive neutrality. He held several minor British posts during the occupation of Philadelphia, signed the oath of allegiance to the patriot cause, paid for substitutes in the Pa. militia, and remained in the city until he was arrested for treason in 1780. On 28 Dec. he was permitted to leave the city with his family, having spent six months in jail (Van Doren, *Secret History,* 407), but still unsuspected for his role in ARNOLD'S TREASON.

Given rations, lodgings, and a stipend of $2 a day as a reward for his services, he continued to write political songs and satirical prose. Unlike the works of ODELL, his writings were "free from hatred or bitterness." (*D.A.B.*) After the war he tried to resume his life in Philadelphia, but he again was imprisoned and forced to return to N.Y.C.

In Aug. '83 he went to Nova Scotia for a year and then to England, where the commission on Loyalist claims disallowed his appeal for £1,000 on the grounds that his loyalty had been too flexible. In Nov. '85 he resumed his business in Philadelphia, but in 1793 he had to give up and move back to N.Y.C. Here he was secretary of the United Insurance Co. for his remaining 16 years. (For his works, see Jonathan ODELL.)

A grandson, Howard Stansbury (1806–1863), became a prominent soldier and explorer of the West. A granddaughter, Caroline Matilda Kirkland (1801–1864), was a prolific author, as was her son, Joseph Kirkland (1830–1894).

STAPLE ACT OF 1663. See NAVIGATION ACTS.

STARK, John. 1728–1822. Cont'l. general. N.H .Son of a Scots–Irishman who came to N.H. in 1720, he was reared as a woodsman and Indian fighter. In 1755 he participated in the operations leading to the defeat of Baron Dieskau and then served as a Lt. and Capt. in Rogers' Rangers. In Jan. '57 he walked 40 miles through deep snow to bring assistance to the wounded, having previously been engaged in a day of fighting and an all-night march. After taking part in Amherst's campaign against Ticonderoga and Crown Point in 1759 he returned to the N.H. grants where he helped establish a new township originally called Starksville and later named Dunbarton.

On 23 Apr. '75 he became Col. of the 1st N.H., and led this militia regiment with conspicuous success at BUNKER HILL, 17 June. Appointed Col. of the 5th Cont'l., a N.H. unit, on 1 Jan. '76, he helped prepare the defenses of N.Y.C. before leaving in May as part of the reinforcements sent to Canada. He became Col. of the 1st N.H. Regt.

on 8 Nov. '76 and was in the battles of Trenton and Princeton. Passed over for promotion, he resigned on 23 Mar. '77 and went home.

At BENNINGTON, Aug. '77, Stark won one of the most spectacular and decisive successes of the Revolution. His insubordination led Congress first to reprimand him and then to appoint him B.G. (4 Oct. 77). In the final stage of BURGOYNE'S OFFENSIVE, he led the force that cut off Gentleman Johnny's last escape route. John Stark had an uncanny way of being at the critical and unexpected place to ruin British plans, first at BUNKER HILL, then at BENNINGTON, and finally at Saratoga. He remained on active duty for the rest of the war, twice commanding the Northern Dept., being involved in the CANADA INVASION (Planned) of 1778, serving under Gates in R.I. in 1779, and taking part in N.J. operations in the summer of 1780. (*D.A.B.*) He sat on André's board of inquiry. Breveted Maj. Gen. on 30 Sept. '83, he retired from the army on 3 Nov. of that year and went home. Unlike other war heroes, he stayed out of public life, finding enough to do in managing his large farm and 11 children. He lived to be 93.

A man of medium height, bold features, keen light blue eyes, and compressed lips (Edward E. Curtis in *D.A.B.*), John Stark was a man who generated legends. Most of them appear to have a kernel of truth. One rare quality that emerges from his picturesque battlefield remarks is an appreciation of the human factor in war. When he refused to hurry his men through an artillery barrage because "one fresh man in action is worth ten fatigued men," he not only was saving energy but was calming down a body of inexperienced officers and men who were on the verge of panic. (See BUNKER HILL). When he said, "Boys, aim at their waistbands," he was enunciating more military wisdom than meets the eye.*

As for the alleged remark at Bennington, "We'll beat them before night, or Molly Stark will be a widow," I will not strain to detect any hidden tactical wisdom. Mrs. Stark's name happened to be Elizabeth, incidentally, so to avoid any question of Gen. Stark's morals we can settle for the fact that although the precise wording of his historic battlefield statements may be questioned, he undoubtedly had a gift for making memorable remarks. (*D.A.B.*) To Stark's discredit it must be said that except at Bunker Hill he showed a consistently insubordinate character; but for incredible luck he would not be the national hero he remains today.

A brother, William (1724–c.1776), served in Rogers' Rangers, fought at Ticonderoga, Louisburg, and Quebec. He defected to the enemy when the Americans would not give him command of a regiment at the start of the Revolution and died after a fall from his horse. A son, Caleb (1759–1838), was a 15-year-old ensign in his father's regiment at Bunker Hill and finished the war as a brigade major. After becoming a Boston businessman, he moved to Ohio in 1828. A grandson, Caleb Stark (1804–1864), was a lawyer before becoming an author (see below).

* European soldiers of this period did not aim at anything, but leveled their muskets and blasted away in the general direction of the enemy. So Stark succinctly suggested that his men should pick a target. Soldiers tend to fire too soon, which Stark's men could not do if they waited until they could see a waistband. For some reason, men tend to shoot too high; Stark told his men, in language they could understand, how to make their "overs" count.

John Stark's letters are in the N.H. Hist. Soc. Coll. His biography, *Memoir and Official Correspondence of . . .* , was published by his grandson in 1860.

STARS AND STRIPES. See FLAG, American.

STATEN ISLAND, N.Y., 22 Aug. '77. Sullivan's raid. (PHILADELPHIA CAMPAIGN) As Washington moved the main portion of his army south on 3 Aug. he ordered Sullivan's Div. to stop at Hanover, N.J. Sir Henry Clinton, British commander in N.Y., received alarming reports on 22 Aug. that the Americans were threatening Kings Bridge, Long Island, and Staten Island. The first two threats turned out to be feints, but a rebel force landed on Staten Island. According to Clinton they "effected an almost total surprise of two provincial battalions belonging to Skinner's Brigade, and after setting fire to the magazines at Decker's Ferry were on their march to Richmond; while another corps, that had landed on the west part of the island for the purpose of cutting off three other provincial battalions, had taken Lt. Col. Lawrence, with the great part of his battalion, prisoners, and only missed the remainder by Lt. Cols. Dongan and Allen having the presence of mind to throw them into some old rebel works at Prince's Bay." (*Amer. Reb.*, 68 *n.*) Clinton had previously reinforced B.G. John Campbell on Staten Island, but Campbell stopped the rebel advance with the 52d Regt., supported by the Waldeck Regt., units already on hand. The Americans withdrew with the loss of 150 captured and 20 wounded, according to Freeman (*Washington*, IV, 464), but Clinton says the British took most of Sullivan's boats and captured 259 officers and men.

Although American histories of the war mention this unsuccessful raid rather casually as an operation for which Sullivan was court-martialed and acquitted, Clinton viewed it as a major part of Washington's strategy, obsessed as he was with the fear that Washington would take advantage of Howe's departure to make a major attack against N.Y.C. or up the Hudson against Burgoyne's Offensive.

STATEN ISLAND EXPEDITION of Alexander, 14–15 Jan. '80. The night of 14–15 Jan., Gen. Wm. Alexander ("Stirling") led 3,000 men across the ice from Elizabethtown Point to surprise the British on Staten Island. The enemy learned of the attack, and after spending a miserable 24 hours in the subzero weather and deep snow, the Americans withdrew with 17 prisoners and a small quantity of loot. In what D. S. Freeman calls "a vain, poorly managed raid" (*Washington*, V, 145), Alexander had six men killed and about 500 "slightly frozen." (Thacher, *Journal*, 188) N.J. civilians who accompanied Alexander as militia engaged in an indiscriminate looting of Staten Island farms and the British retaliated 10 days later by burning the academy at Newark and the courthouse and meeting house at Elizabethtown.

STATEN ISLAND PEACE CONFERENCE, 11 Sept. '76. See PEACE CONFERENCE ON STATEN ISLAND.

STEDMAN, Charles. *c.* 1745–1812. British officer, historian. He served as an officer under Lord Percy at Lexington and Concord, under Gen. Howe in the N.Y., N.J., and Philadelphia Campaigns, and under Cornwallis in the South. His *History of the Origin, Progress, and Termination of the American War* (2 vols., London, 1792; Dublin, 1794) is one of the standard works on the Revolution; "an account by a participant, [it] remains worthy of study

(Alden, *Amer. Rev.*, 278), and is "especially valuable for its military maps." (Appleton's) William Thomas Lowndes (1798–1843), the English bibliographer, ascribes its authorship to Dr. William Thompson. (*Ibid.*) In his later years Stedman was a deputy comptroller of the British stamp office.

STEPHEN, Adam. 1718–1791. Cont'l. general. Va. A long-time associate of Washington in the French and Indian War and subsequently a political opponent in Va., Stephen commanded the Va. Regt. in Amherst's operations against the Cherokees in 1761. (Freeman, *Washington*, III, 10, 61, 69) Appointed Col., 4th Va., on 13 Feb. '76 and B.G. on 4 Sept. '76, he jeopardized Washington's TRENTON RAID by sending an unauthorized patrol across the Delaware on Christmas Day. The leader of this patrol was Capt. Richard Anderson, 5th Va., and the father of the Federal general who defended Ft. Sumter at the start of the Civil War. The son, Robert, is the source of the story that Washington turned on Stephen with one of his occasional bursts of flaming temper. "You, sir," said Washington, "may have ruined all my plans by having put them on their guard." (*Ibid.*, IV, 313 and *n.*)

As early as 1763 Stephen had been suspected of making theatrical moves of no military value (*ibid.*); now as a Maj. Gen. (appointed 19 Feb. '77) he sent troops on missions of his own devising and submitted false reports of their success. On 10 May he attempted to surprise the 42d Highlanders at PISCATAWAY, N.J. Although repulsed and driven back toward his own camp, he reported a gallant success in which at least 200 of the enemy were killed. Washington confirmed his suspicions that Stephen was lying and then wrote him: "Your account ... is favorable, but

I am sorry to add, widely different from those I have had from others, (officers of distinction) who were of the party. ..." (Quoted in *ibid.*, 417) Stephen, undaunted, replied that his account was accurate. After the divisions of Stephen and Wayne collided during the Battle of GERMANTOWN, 4 Oct. '77, a misfortune that probably caused the panic of Washington's attacking force, Stephen was brought before a court of inquiry. The charges investigated were that on three occasions Stephen had acted "unlike an officer." Based on the findings of this group, which met about three weeks after the battle, on 2 Nov. Washington ordered a court-martial. He was convicted of "unofficerlike behavior," "drunkenness," and on 20 Nov. '77 Washington approved the court's recommendation that he be dismissed. Stephen appealed to Congress that "a person of high rank" was out to get him for his honest criticism of the Philadelphia Campaign, but his dismissal was approved. (See Freeman, *op. cit.*, IV, 513 *n.*, 535–36)

STEUBEN, Friedrich Wilhelm Augustus von (or de).* 1730–1794. Inspector General of the Cont'l. Army. His grandfather, Augustin Steube, a minister of the German Reformed Church, inserted the "von" in the family name about 1708. The man who became "the first teacher of the American Army" was born in Magdeburg fortress while his father, an engineer Lt., was stationed there. His early youth was spent in Russia. At the age of 10 he

---

* This is the name by which he was known in America. He was baptized Friedrich Wilhelm Ludolf Gerhard Augustin von Steuben and changed this to Friedrich Wilhelm August Heinrich Ferdinand.

returned to Germany with his father, was schooled by Jesuits in Breslau, and at 17 was a Prussian officer. During the Seven Years' War he served in an infantry unit and as a staff officer. He was then made a member of the General Staff and had a number of confidential military-diplomatic assignments in Russia before being attached to Frederick the Great's headquarters.

"The significance of Steuben's general staff training and service has not been sufficiently appreciated [says John McA. Palmer in *D.A.B.*] It was this specific training for and experience in the duties of the general staff, an agency then little known outside Prussia, that so peculiarly equipped Steuben for his invaluable services to the cause of American independence. He brought to Washington's staff a technical training and equipment that was unknown in either the French or the British armies at that time."

He was discharged as a Capt. in 1763, at the age of only 33, for reasons that are obscure. The next year he became chamberlain (*Hofmarschall*) at the petty court of Hohenzollern-Hechingen, where he attained his title of Baron (*Freiherr*). When his prince had to close the court in 1771 and go incognito to France, where he hoped to borrow money, Steuben was the only courtier to accompany him. In 1775 they were back in Germany, having failed to achieve solvency, and Steuben, seriously in debt, had to seek other employment. After several unsuccessful attempts to enter foreign armies (France, Austria, Baden), he met a friend of Benjamin Franklin who suggested to the latter that Steuben could render valuable service in America. Having pursued this lead to Paris, where he arrived during the summer of 1777, Steuben had the good fortune of being endorsed by the French minister of war,

the Count de St. Germain, who recognized the value of Prussian General Staff training. Beaumarchais advanced travel funds from his Hortalez & Cie. and the resourceful Franklin penned a letter introducing him to Washington as "a Lieutenant General in the King of Prussia's service." With all these bogus credentials Lt. Gen.* the Baron von Steuben left Marseilles on 26 Sept., reached Portsmouth, N.H., on 1 Dec., went to Boston to spend several weeks being royally entertained, and reached York on 5 Feb. Congress promptly accepted his offer to serve for the time being as an unpaid volunteer, and on 23 Feb. '78 he reported to Washington at Valley Forge. Although he spoke no English and his French was limited, Steuben drafted—with the help of Greene and Hamilton—a training program that Washington approved in Mar. In what is "perhaps the most remarkable achievement in rapid military training in the history of the world" (*D.A.B.*), he started with a model company of 100 picked men and spread his instruction in a sort of geometric progression through the little army. An essential element of his successful formula was Steuben's picturesque personality. He stood before the shivering, half-starved provincials in a magnificent uniform and put on a show worthy of paid admission. According to tradition, when he could no longer curse his awkward recruits in German and French he would call on his French-speaking American aide, Capt. Benjamin Walker, to swear for him in English: "*Viens*, Walker, *mon ami....* God-

---

* Lt. Gen. in the Prussian army corresponded to B. G. in the American army, as a Capt.-Lt. in the British army and the American colonial army was the grade just below Capt.

dam de *gaucheries* of dese *badauts.** Je ne puis plus.*" (Montross, *Rag, Tag,* 246, citing Kapp's *Steuben.*)

But the results were solid and rapid, as was shown at BARREN HILL, 20 May, and MONMOUTH, 28 June '78. On 30 Apr. '78 Washington had recommended Steuben's appointment as Maj. Gen. Inspector General and on 5 May Congress confirmed it.

During the Monmouth Campaign the new I.G. served in Washington's headquarters and was the first to report that the enemy army was heading for Monmouth C. H. (*D.A.B.*) In the final phase of the battle of 28 June he was with Washington and Alexander to exert his personal leadership in steadying the Americans' final line of defense. (When Charles Lee referred in his court-martial to Steuben as one of "the very distant spectators of the maneuvers" the Prussian challenged him to a duel but was satisfied when Lee explained that he meant no offense.) The next winter he prepared his *Regulations for the Order and Discipline of the Troops of the United States,* which became known as the "blue book." Continuing his duties of training and instilling discipline, he then set up a badly needed system of property accountability. The winter of 1779–80 he was Washington's representative to Congress on matters of army reorganization. When Greene was given command

* *Badauts*—who operate in the plural —are idlers who wander about at fairs, other exhibitions, or along the book stalls of the Seine, pausing briefly to gaze at one thing before strolling on to find something else that might briefly engage their attention. Steuben's implication was that the recruits looked on him as a sort of sideshow performer whom they would leave for some other attraction when they got bored.

of the Southern Dept., Steuben went along and since most of Greene's support—personnel as well as provisions— would come from Va., he stayed there. In the Old Dominion he was less popular, Freeman points out, being "accused of arrogance, idleness and imperious contempt of natives." (*Washington,* V, 302 *n.*) In the spring of 1781 he took part in the VIRGINIA MILITARY OPERATIONS summarized in the section headed "Cornwallis *vs.* Lafayette," having previously had his task complicated by the raids of Arnold and Phillips. Soon after he delivered his 450 Va. Cont'ls. to Lafayette on 19 June he was forced to take sick leave. He rejoined the army for the YORKTOWN CAMPAIGN, taking command of one of the three divisions of Washington's force and giving the benefit of his experience in siege warfare. This was the closest he came to his cherished desire for a field command. In the spring of 1783 he assisted Washington in planning for the future defense of the U.S. and in demobilizing the Cont'l. Army. In Aug. '83 he went to Canada to receive the surrender of British frontier posts, but found that Haldimand had no authority to treat with him. He was honorably discharged on 24 Mar. '84.

Having become an American citizen by act of the Pa. legislature in Mar. '83 and by the N.Y. authorities in July '86, he established residence in N.Y.C. and became a prominent and popular social figure. He was soon in serious financial straits, however. "Always careless in his business affairs and extravagant in his charities and hospitalities, he went heavily in debt in anticipation of about $60,000 for his military services which he claimed from Congress." In June '90 the new federal government granted him a yearly pension of $2,500 instead of a lump sum and it was only when Alexander Hamilton and other friends got him a "friendly mortgage" on the 16,000 acres given him by N.Y. in 1786 that Steuben's financial affairs were straightened out. The old bachelor spent summers on his Mohawk Valley property north of Utica (near modern Remsen) and his winters in the city. He willed his property to his former aides, Wm. North and Benjamin Walker.

D. S. Freeman expresses the traditional view in the following estimate of Steuben:

". . . he made a sound system of drill and inspection a part of the organism of the armed forces and he contributed in a dozen other ways to the fighting power of Washington's troops. If Washington rightly is venerated as the father of the American Army, Steuben was its first teacher. 'The Baron' was extravagant and he never had for any length of time the extensive line command that probably represented his heart's deepest desire. He had, as he deserved, almost everything else that the affection and gratitude of the American people could bestow." (*Washington*, IV, 617A)

Another historian sounds this note of caution:

"Steuben's considerable services have commonly been overpraised. The army with which he worked was not a rabble in March or a perfect fighting machine in June. * * * The studies of the adventurer-patriot by Friedrich Kapp and Palmer [see below] are by no means exhaustive." (John R. Alden, *Amer. Rev.*, 202 *n.*)

John McA. Palmer's *General von Steuben* (New Haven, Conn., 1937) supersedes the largely apocryphal Kapp's *Steuben* (Berlin, 1858; N.Y., 1859) and Doyle's *Steuben* (1913). Sixteen volumes of Steuben's personal papers are in the library of the N.Y. Hist. Soc. Much valuable material is in the *Washington Papers* and the *Papers of the Cont'l. Congress* in the Library of Congress, and in the Old Records Division of the Department of Defense. (*D.A.B.*)

STEVENS, Gen. No *Cont'l.* general named Stevens existed. As mentioned in the article on militia B.G. Edward STEVENS, some writers may have confused the name Stevens with that of Gen. Adam STEPHEN.

STEVENS, Edward. 1745–1820. Militia general. Va. Born in Culpeper co., he commanded a militia battalion at Great Bridge, Va., Dec. '75, and became Col. of the 10th Va. Cont'ls. on 12 Nov. '76. Joining Washington's army in N.J., he took part in the battles of Brandywine and Germantown. Although Appleton's says he served with credit at both places, D. S. Freeman does not mention him; the index entry "Stevens, Gen., *see* Stephen, Gen. Adam" suggests that Appleton's has confused the two men. (Freeman, *Washington*, IV, 716) Col. Stevens resigned 31 Jan. '78 (Heitman, 59, 519). Appointed B.G. of Va. militia in 1779 (*ibid.*, 519), he joined the army of Gates with 700 militia at Rugeley's Mills on 14 Aug. '80. Although he showed personal courage at the battle of Camden, two days later, his troops disgraced themselves. (Under CAMDEN CAMPAIGN, see section headed "The battle. . . .") After discharging these men on the expiration of their enlistments, he rejoined Greene before the latter retreated across the Dan River and was appointed by Greene to command the Halifax co. militia who started turning out to reinforce the regulars. (Lee, *Memoirs*, 252) He and his irregulars then distinguished themselves at GUILFORD, where he was wounded severely. Three months later he commanded one of the three Va. brigades that joined Lafayette in Va., and he led this brigade of 750 men in the Yorktown Campaign. Promoted to Maj. Gen. of militia, he also served as state senator from adoption of the Va. constitution until 1790. (Appleton's)

STEWART, Alexander. *c.* 1741–1794. British officer in the South. Entering the army as an ensign of the 37th Foot on 8 Apr. '55, he remained with that regiment until promoted to Lt. Col. of the 3d Foot ("Buffs") on 7 July '75 (*Army Lists*). He reached Charleston with his regiment on 4 June '81 and succeeded Rawdon as commander of the field forces at Orangeburg, S.C. In this capacity he was in command at EUTAW SPRINGS, 8 Sept. '81.

Writers commonly make the mistake of calling Rawdon and Stewart the senior British officers in the South when, actually, they commanded only the forces in the field. Col. Paston Gould, who reached Charleston on 3 June '81, was the ranking officer in S.C. He reached Monck's Corner the morning of 12 Sept. with his 30th Regt. and took command of the army under Stewart, and Lt. Gen. Leslie reached Charleston on 8 Nov. '81 to assume over-all command.

The defenses of Charleston after the British army had withdrawn there were commanded by Stewart (across the Neck) and J. Harris CRUGER (at Stono Ferry). Stewart was promoted to Col. on 16 May '82, to Maj. Gen. on 25 Apr. '90 (*Army Lists*), and died four years later.

STEWART, Walter. *c.* 1756–1796. Cont'l. officer. Pa. When the Revolution started he raised a company for the 3d Pa. Bn., was commissioned Capt. on 5 Jan. '76, became A.D.C. to Gates on 26 May, and was promoted to Maj. on 7 June. '76. (Appleton's; Heitman) Commissioned Col. of a Pa. state regiment (militia) on 17 June '77, he left Gates and assumed command on 6 July

to take part in Washington's Philadelphia Campaign. His green regiment distinguished itself at Brandywine, where as part of Weedon's Brig. (with Edw. Stevens' 10th Va.) it held a defile near Dilworth until the main army could make good its retreat. (Ward, *W.O.R.*, 352) In the action at Germantown he fought on Washington's left wing. The next month, 12 Nov. '77, his regiment joined the Cont'l. Army as the 13th Pa. This unit was not with the army in the Valley Forge winter quarters, but was part of Lee's command in the Battle of Monmouth, 28 June '78. Bringing up the rear of the retreat with Ramsey's 3d Md., it was halted by Washington, faced about, and used as a delaying force until the main battle position was organized. (Under MONMOUTH, see "Final Phase....") On 1 July the regiment was merged with the 2d Pa. under Stewart's command.

Col. Stewart is described by Freeman as "an officer of fine presence and persuasive manner." (*Washington,* V, 165) According to Appleton's "He was said to be the handsomest man in the American army." The young colonel also appears to have been an outstanding mediator: in Feb. '78 he intervened to make peace between Gates and Wilkinson (in connection with the Conway Cabal), he stepped in to help dissolve the MUTINY OF THE CONN. LINE, 25 May '80, and he had a prominent part in helping Wayne settle the MUTINY OF THE PA. LINE, 1–10 Jan. '81. He marched south under Wayne to take part in Lafayette's operations against Cornwallis (see Military Operations in VIRGINIA) and was engaged at GREEN SPRING, Va., 6 July '81. He served under Wayne in Steuben's Div. during the Yorktown Campaign. In John Trumbull's painting of the surrender ceremony, "his full-length portrait is ... on the left of the line of the American officers," according to Appleton's. Stewart retired on 1 Jan. '83 and went to Philadelphia. At the insistence of Washington he was recalled as I.G. of the Northern Dept. He agitated the discontent that led to the NEWBURGH ADDRESSES. Breveted B.G. on 30 Sept. '83, he became a prominent merchant in Philadelphia and Maj. Gen. of militia.

STILES, Ezra. 1727–1795. Patriot, scholar, clergyman, Pres. of Yale. Graduating from Yale in 1746, he studied theology and was licensed to preach (30 May '49). Three weeks earlier, however, he had been appointed tutor at Yale, and for a long time he delayed entering actively into the ministry. At Yale he became a friend and scientific collaborator of Franklin. He studied law and was admitted to the bar in 1753. After finally bringing himself to an intellectual acceptance of church dogma he was ordained a Congregational minister in 1755 and for the next 22 years was pastor at Newport, R.I., and Portsmouth, N.H. In the spring of 1778 he accepted the presidency of Yale, an office he held ably during a particularly difficult period. College administrator, intellectual, and minister, the physically delicate Stiles showed tremendous energy and ability in a great variety of pursuits. He died at 68 of "bilious fever." In the main bibliography is a list of his more important works. *The Life of Ezra Stiles, D.D., LL.D.*, was published by his son-in-law, Abiel Holmes, in 1798. Another "Life of Ezra Stiles" was written by J. L. Kingsley for Jared Sparks, *The Library of American Biography,* XVI (1847), including his valuable *Diary.*

STILLWATER, N.Y. On the west bank of the Hudson, about 11 miles below Saratoga, this was the place beyond which Schuyler withdrew his army as Burgoyne's Offensive moved on. After Gates relieved Schuyler as commander of the Northern army (19 Aug. '77) he moved back to Stillwater on 8 Sept. Four days later the Northern army displaced another five miles north to occupy defensive positions at Bemis Heights. The decisive battles that then took place in this area on 19 Sept. and 7 Oct. are known variously by the names of Stillwater, Bemis Heights, Freeman's Farm, and Saratoga. Purely for the purpose of grouping the descriptions and maps of these actions I have called them the first and second battles of SARATOGA.

STIRLING, Lord. See William ALEXANDER.

STOCKTON, Richard. 1730–1781. Signer, lawyer. N.J. His great-grandfather was an English Quaker who settled in Flushing, Long Island, before 1656, and in 1696 Richard's grandfather (also named Richard) acquired a large tract of land around Princeton, where he built an estate he named "Morven." Stockton graduated from the Coll. of N.J. at Newark in 1748, and his father was largely responsible for the school's location being changed to Princeton in 1756. Richard was admitted to the bar in 1754 and within 10 years was recognized as being one of the most eloquent lawyers in the middle colonies. (Richard B. Morris in *D.A.B.*) Among the prominent lawyers trained by him were Elias Boudinot and Joseph Reed. In 1766 he went as a trustee of his alma mater to offer its presidency to John WITHERSPOON. With the assistance of Benjamin Rush, Stockton prevailed on the famous minister of Paisley, Scotland, to accept the post at Princeton.

While in Britain, Stockton was received by the King and Lord Rockingham, and he was given the freedom of the city of Edinburgh. Returning to America in 1767, he entered politics for the first time and the next year was named to the provincial council. He originally advocated conciliation with Great Britain but his feelings then swung toward independence. Late in 1774 he sent Lord Dartmouth a plan for settlement on the basis of continued allegiance to the crown but freedom from Parliamentary control; in this concept he anticipated the scheme under which the Commonwealth was established in modern times. Sent to the Cont'l. Cong., he took his seat on 28 June '76 and signed the Decl. of Indep. On 30 Aug. he tied with Wm. Livingston for Gov. of N.J. and the next day, after the latter was chosen for the office, Stockton declined the post of chief justice to remain in Cong. After serving on many important committees, on 26 Sept. he and George Clymer were appointed to inspect the Northern army, which was then reorganizing after failure of the Canada Invasion. Returning home as the British invaded N.J., he evacuated his family safely to the home of a friend, John Covenhoven, in Monmouth co., but there he was betrayed by a Tory and captured on 30 Nov. '76. Taken first to Perth Amboy and then imprisoned in the infamous Provost Jail in N.Y.C., he was subjected to cruel treatment that broke his spirit and led him to sign the amnesty proclamation. Meanwhile his home had been pillaged and his library burned. On 3 Jan. '77 Cong. formally protested to the British and made efforts to secure his exchange. When he finally was liberated Stockton's health was shattered, his home was destroyed, and he found himself shunned by former friends. He died on 28 Feb. '81 at the age of 51.

The handsome and talented Stockton was a double brother-in-law of Elias Boudinot: he had married the latter's sister Annis, an accomplished poetess, and Boudinot had married Stockton's sister Hannah. Stockton's eldest daughter married Benj. Rush. The Signer's

son, "Richard the Duke," became a famous lawyer and U.S. Senator, and his grandson, Robert Field Stockton (1795–1866), was a naval officer who "liberated" Southern California from the Mexicans in 1846–47.

See W. A. Whitehead, "Sketch of the Life of Richard Stockton," *Proc. N.J. Hist. Soc.*, 2 ser. IV (1849), and T. C. Stockton, *The Stockton Family of N.J.* (1911).

STONE, Thomas. 1743–1787. Signer. Md. Great-great-grandson of the third proprietary Gov. of Md., Thomas received a classical education, studied law in Annapolis, was admitted to the bar in 1764, and four years later married the wealthy Margaret Brown. In 1771 he bought land near Port Tobacco, Charles co., and built "Habre de Venture," which has been described as one of the most beautiful houses in colonial Md. (*D.A.B.*) In 1774 he was one of the sheriff's lawyers against Thos. Johnson, Sam'l. Chase, and Wm. Paca in contesting the legality of poll taxes for supporting the clergy. Although a conservative, Stone sided with the patriots when the break came with England. He served in the Cont'l. Cong. from 13 May '75 until Oct. '78, except for a portion of 1777, when he declined re-election. Fellow Signers from Md. were Chase and Paca, and Johnson was also in Cong. with him. (See above)

"He is the least known of the Maryland signers partly because he seldom spoke either in Congress or the Maryland Senate, and few of his letters have been preserved." (*D.A.B.*) He appears to have retained his mild attitude toward war with England, and one of his few recorded speeches was to advocate making terms with Lord Howe for peace in Sept. '76. Elected to the state senate for a five-year term starting in 1776, and twice re-elected, he also resumed his seat in Cong. on 26 Mar. '84.

Toward the end of this session he was named Pres. pro tempore, but he declined re-election to Cong. and resumed his law practice. He was named to the Fed. Const. Conv. in Philadelphia but declined to serve on account of his wife's illness. She died in June '87, he gave up his work, and four months later he died of melancholy at the age of 44.

STONE ARABIA, N.Y. Mohawk Valley settlement burned 19 Oct. '80 in Tory raid. See FORT KEYSER.

STONO FERRY, S.C., 20 June '79. When Prevost withdrew to Savannah after menacing CHARLESTON, 11–12 May, he left Lt. Col. Maitland in command of a 900-man rear guard on the islands south of the town. To cover Stono Ferry from the mainland —actually, James Island—Maitland had three strong redoubts, an abatis, and a bridge of boats connecting this position with Johns Island.

Lincoln had about 6,500 troops in Charleston and decided to attack this isolated British outpost with a force of 1,200. He personally led the main effort, which crossed the Ashley River about midnight and undertook an eight-mile approach march to hit the enemy position on James Island around dawn. Moultrie was supposed to support this operation by a secondary attack against Johns Island to keep Maitland from moving reinforcements across Stono Inlet to the bridgehead.* Lincoln's main body was organized into a right wing of Carolina militia troops under Jethro

* Authorities disagree as to Moultrie's role in this action. Some, including Ward, indicate that the entire operation was under his command. (*W.O.R.*, 686) I have followed the account of F. V. Greene, who cites Dawson, Lowell, and Henry Lee as his sources. (*Rev War*, 198–99)

Sumner with two guns, a left wing of Cont'l. troops and four guns under Isaac Huger, a Va. militia force with two guns in reserve, light infantry companies covering each flank (Malmedy on the right and John Henderson on the left), and a rear guard of mounted detachments. (Ward, *W.O.R.*, 686)

Henderson's flank patrol made contact first, and shortly before sunrise Lincoln's other columns struggled through the dense woods to open fire at a distance of 300 yards from the British line. An outpost of two Highland companies held their ground against superior numbers until all but 11 were shot down. After a one-hour exchange of small arms and cannon fire the German regiment broke and the Americans pushed forward to the abatis. Part of the 71st was shifted to stop the attack by the American left, and the Hessians were rallied and brought back into action. Maitland then started bringing reserves over from Johns Island and Lincoln ordered a retreat, which was effectively covered by light infantry under Andrew Pickens.

American losses in this poorly conceived operation were heavy: 146 killed or wounded (including 24 officers) and 155 missing. Most of the latter were deserters, since the enemy apparently took no prisoners. (*Ibid.*) The British lost 26 killed, 103 wounded, and one missing.

According to Baurmeister, Maitland had decided on 15 June to withdraw but was delayed by lack of shipping. (*Journals,* 293) The only thing Lincoln achieved by his attack was to speed up the course of action already agreed on by the British commander; Maitland abandoned his bridgehead on the 23d and started a slow retreat to Beaufort (Port Royal Island).

STONY POINT, N.Y., 16 July '79. Anthony Wayne's coup de main. After a quiet winter and spring, on 28 May '79 a British expedition assembled at Kings Bridge and on 1 June they occupied Stony Point and Verplancks Point. These two places secured Kings Ferry, 12 miles by road below West Point. The ferry was strategically important as the closest place on the Hudson to N.Y.C. over which the Americans could easily and safely operate barges to maintain their east-west line of communications. Furthermore, it was at the gateway to the vital HIGHLANDS. Stony Point was taken without a shot, its 40-man garrison having burned a blockhouse and abandoned the unfinished defenses when the enemy flotilla approached. At Ft. Lafayette, a small but completed work on Verplancks Point, the garrison of one officer and 70 N.C. troops was trapped and forced to surrender.

Washington had already moved his available troops to challenge the expected advance on West Point, "key to the Continent." His principal position was in Smith's Clove, about 14 miles west of West Point,* and he established his headquarters here temporarily before moving it to New Windsor. Within a few days the Americans could see that Clinton did not intend to advance up the Hudson but was garrisoning the captured posts and completing the defenses of Stony Point. On 28 June, Washington directed that Anthony Wayne study the possibilities of retaking the positions. He had earlier (15 June) ordered Henry Lee to gather information about enemy strength at Stony Point, and on 2 July Allen MCLANE entered the

place disguised as a countryman. Washington personally reconnoitered Stony Point on 6 July, covered by McLane's partisans (then attached to Lee's Legion). Based largely on McLane's information that the works were incomplete, Washington ordered Wayne to make a surprise night attack and capture Stony Point. It was decided not to complicate matters by attacking Verplancks Point simultaneously but to advance troops toward that place and strike only if the Stony Point operation succeeded. (Freeman, *Washington,* V, 111 ff.)

The sketch shows the main features of the battlefield. Since the Hudson at this point is really an estuary, not a river, the marsh over which the attackers would cross is flooded at high tide. On the 150-foot hill, inside the second abatis, were seven or eight British batteries. Connecting trenches had not been completed, but a semienclosed fort was located on the top. The first abatis was on lower ground, around the base of the hill and about 200 yards west of the other abatis at the point of farthest separation; trees had been cleared in front of this forward barrier and three outworks constructed to cover the most likely avenues of approach. Lt. Col. Henry Johnson † held the position with his 17th Regt., the grenadier company of the 71st Highlanders, a detachment of Loyal Americans, and 15 guns; total strength was about 625.

Wayne's recently formed light infantry brigade of 1,200 men constituted the American force. Col. Febiger com-

* Lossing says "Smith's Clove extends northward from the Ramapo Valley, not far from Turner's station on the Erie rail-road." (II, 176 *n.*) Thacher is authority for the distance from West Point. (*Journal,* 164)

† He is so identified by author and editor in Clinton's *Amer. Reb.,* 132 *n.* and 133 *n.* Although court-martialed after this action, he subsequently became a full general. Meng identifies the British commander as Col. Francis Johnston. (*Gerard,* 802 *n.*)

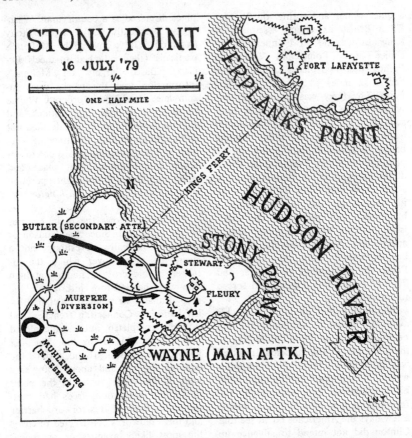

manded the 1st Regt.; his battalion commanders were Lt. Col. Fleury and Maj. Thos. Posey; troops were from Va. and Pa. Col. Richard Butler led the 2d Regt.; battalion commanders were Lt. Col. Samuel Hay and Maj. John Stewart; troops were from Del., Md., and Pa. The 3d Regt., all Conn. men, was commanded by Col. Return Meigs with Lt. Col. Isaac Sherman and Capt. Henry Champion. The 4th Regt., not completely organized, comprised Mass. troops under Maj. Wm. Hull and N.C. men under Maj. Hardy Murfree. Capts. James Pendleton and Thos. Barr accompanied the expedition with 24 gunners

and two small pieces, but did not take part in the attack. Lee's light horse (including McLane's) supported the attack, and 300 men under Gen. Muhlenberg were in reserve.

About noon on 15 July the American light infantry and the two guns started a 15-mile approach march from Sandy Beach (five miles below West Point, near Ft. Montgomery). Their road was so bad that the men had to move single file for part of the distance, but around 8 P.M. they started closing into the final assembly area not more than a mile and a half west of Stony Point (at a place called Springsteel's). Since surprise was essential, Wayne prescribed strict security measures: civilians were cleared from the line of march and ordered to stay home; only a few officers were told of their objective; the final assembly area was "sealed" by guards to keep any traitor from alerting the British.

A dark night favored the attackers as they started forward about 11:30 of the 15th. Orders had been given that weapons would not be loaded (except in Murfree's Bn.—see below), and one soldier is reported to have been killed on the spot by his officer when he persisted in trying to defy this order. (Heath, *Memoirs,* 223; Thacher, *Journal,* 176. The evidence is hearsay, in both instances.) Lossing says all neighborhood dogs had been killed to prevent their alerting the enemy. (II, 176–78)

Wayne planned to penetrate the enemy's defenses at two points, one column hitting on the north, near the ferry landing, and the other to the south, where the defenses were closest to the main enemy works. Both assault columns were preceded by 20-man "forlorn hopes" to knock off sentinels and hack through the abatis; both had advance parties of 150 men under selected officers to exploit the breakthrough; and the third element in each column was a main body that would keep up the momentum of the attack and push on to the objective. As a third force in this plan of attack, Maj. Murfree was to conduct a diversion against the British center, supported by the light horse; his men were the only ones authorized to fire during the operation.

The south column was the main effort; consequently it was stronger, and Wayne was personally in command. Many sketches show the entire American force approaching in a single column across the causeway and bridge that span the marsh about a quarter of a mile from the first abatis (e.g., Lossing, *op. cit.,* 175; Avery's map in F. V. Greene, *Rev. War,* facing p. 158); Freeman, however, says they left the assembly area in three columns and that the main column waded the marsh at a point near the Hudson to attack from the south. (*Op. cit.,* 118) The sketch attached to the 19 July '79 dispatch of French Minister GÉRARD indicates that the left and right American columns *forded* the marsh at points north and south of the causeway; this sketch furthermore shows that Fleury's advance party waded through four feet of water to envelop the most advanced enemy abatis on the south flank of their first line of defense. (Meng, *op. cit.,* following p. 802)

Schematically, the attack formation was as follows:

Col. Butler	Maj. John Stewart		Lt. Gibbons
2d Regt. (–)	150 men; 2/2d Regt.		20 men ↘
(Main Body	(Advance Party)		(Forlorn Hope)
	Maj. Murfree	X	
	&	X	
	Light Horse	X	
	(Demonstration)	X	

Maj. Hull	Col. Meigs	Lt. Col. Fleury	Lt. Knox
1/4th Regt.	3d Regt.	150 men; 1/1st Regt.	20 men ↗
(Main Body)		(Advance Party)	(Forlorn Hope)

Shortly after midnight the two attack columns made contact, almost simultaneously, with the enemy outposts, and the British opened fire. The rebels pressed forward without shooting back. The forlorn hopes chopped and clawed through the first abatis and rushed for the second one while the advance parties pushed forward on their heels. Murfree started his demonstration in the center. Wayne was taken out of action temporarily by a head wound but revived and maintained command. Four other officers of the main column were hit. To the north, Febiger and Hay were wounded.

Lt. Col. Fleury had joined Lt. Knox's party; the fiery Frenchman was the first to enter the British works and he tore down the enemy flag with his own hands. Knox placed second and was followed by a Sgt. Baker of Va., who had been wounded four times in the assault. This sequence is a matter of exact record because cash prizes of $500 to $100 had been announced for the first five to enter the works. Baker was followed by Sgts. Spencer of Va. and Donlop of Pa.

The left column had farther to go, but Lt. Gibbons spearheaded the attack, muddy to the neck from crossing the morass and his clothing torn to shreds in the abatis. Maj. Stewart ordered the forlorn hope to turn right after they got through the second abatis; Gibbons reached the fort with only three of his original 20 men, and Stewart was right behind him with the advance party.

Murfree's demonstration achieved its purpose, and Col. Johnson charged down the hill with half his garrison—six companies of the 17th—to meet what he thought was the main threat. He was cut off and captured by Febiger's regiment when he tried to regain the fort. The others tried to hold out but were isolated into little packets where they vainly tried to resist the bayonets, swords, and spontoons—for about 15 minutes the hilltop was the scene of a mad turmoil, and the British then began to throw down their arms and cry quarter. It is a further tribute to Wayne's discipline that Stony Point did not join the list of Revolutionary War "Massacres." A British officer, Commodore George Collier, entered this comment in his journal:

"The rebels had made the attack with a bravery they never before exhibited, and they showed at this moment a generosity and clemency which during the course of the rebellion had no parallel. There was light sufficient after getting up the heights to show them many of the British troops with arms in their hands; instead of putting them to death, they called to them 'to throw their arms down if they expected any quarter.' " (Quoted in C. & M., 724–25, from Johnston, Stony Point.)

NUMBERS AND LOSSES

Wayne reported 15 killed and 83 wounded. As previously stated, he had 1,200 rank and file in his light infantry brigade; total strength in the action was 1,350, counting officers and musicians (Johnston, Stony Point, cited in Ward, W.O.R., 599). These figures exclude the supporting forces of Lee and Muhlenberg.

The British commander reported 20 killed, 74 wounded, 58 missing, and 472 captured, for a total of 624. American reports that 63 British were killed and about 70 wounded are obviously false. (See CASUALTY FIGURES) Washington approved Wayne's proposal that the captured equipment and stores be appraised and this amount divided among his troops; including the 12 cannon the sum came to $180,655. (Freeman, op. cit., 119 and n.) Collier, quoted above, says most of the captured guns were lost when his ships "luckily sunk" the

American galley carrying them to West Point.

SEQUEL

Clinton reacted swiftly to save Ft. Lafayette, and Washington's failure to plan the capture of this place made it possible for Clinton to succeed. Freeman says:

"Washington may have been correct in deciding that a simultaneous attack on both sides of the river would be too complicated, but after coming to that conclusion he failed to prepare adequately for an undertaking that inevitably would be difficult in daylight, with the British garrison alarmed and certain to receive succor by land and by water in a short time." (*Op. cit.*, 119–20)

This same authority goes on to point out that Washington's other error was his selection of Robt. Howe to command the attempt. An undistinguished general to start with, Howe had been on the scene only a month. "Besides knowing little of the country and scarcely more concerning the officers," says Freeman, "Howe perhaps was made over-cautious by notice from Washington that the command would be transferred to Heath when that officer arrived on the Hudson." (*Ibid.*)

The captured guns of Stony Point were turned on Ft. Lafayette and the sloop *Vulture*. But the *Vulture* dropped down the river to safety, and Ft. Lafayette was reinforced before Howe could get his operation under way. Washington wisely decided the defense of Stony Point would require more men than it was worth, so he ordered the works destroyed, the matériel removed, and on the 18th Wayne's troops were withdrawn. Clinton reoccupied the place the next day; he then established a stronger garrison and rebuilt the defenses.

For this brilliant exploit Wayne was given the thanks of Congress and a gold medal. Fleury and Stewart were voted silver medals. Lts. Gibbons and Knox were commended and given brevet promotions.

COMMENTS

The operation had little strategic value, but it was a morale builder for the American army and people; it had the opposite effect on the British. The latter paid tribute in the *Annual Register* for 1779 by saying, "it would have done honor to the most veteran soldiers." Gérard wrote: "Plan, execution, courage, address and energy, in short, the most rare qualities were found united there, and I am convinced that this action will... elevate the ideas of Europe about the military qualities of the Americans...." (Both passages quoted in Freeman, *op. cit.*, 121)

Another element figured prominently in the operation—luck. It detracts nothing from Wayne's triumph to recognize that the British post was inadequately garrisoned, their intelligence faulty, and their local security measures deficient. (Freeman, *op. cit.*, 115, 113 *n.*, 119 *n.*) Of course the American plan was predicated on the knowledge gained from good intelligence and thorough reconnaissance, but a little bad luck could have turned the attack into a bloody failure, and a little less good luck could have resulted in a tremendous casualty list.

Considering this battle in the context of "Mad Anthony" Wayne's overall career, it is interesting to note that Napoleon would ask this question when called on to evaluate a general: "Is he lucky?"

STORMONT, David Murray, Viscount. As British ambassador to Versailles, Lord Stormont figured prominently as the enemy of Beaumarchais and Vergennes when the latter were sending secret aid to America. Through an efficient net of informers, Stormont repeatedly gained knowledge of covert operations and lodged protests. He also protested the use of French ports by American privateers. When the French Alliance was officially announced in Mar. '78 he was recalled from Versailles.

STRATEGIC ENVELOPMENT. A TURNING MOVEMENT.

STUART, John. British Supt. of Indian Affairs for the South after 1762, succeeding Edmund Atkin of S.C., who had been given the post when established in Feb. '56 (Alden, *Gage,* 84–85), Stuart was in the South what Sir Wm. Johnson and his successor, Guy Johnson, were in the North. Both Sir William and Stuart "knew their business," comments Alden, and both had "considerable latitude in their operations." (*Ibid.,* 86) Surprisingly, Stuart is not in *D.N.B.* Alden, who has written *John Stuart and the Southern Colonial Frontier . . . 1754–1775* (Ann Arbor, 1944), and whose *Gage in America* and *The South in the Revolution* mention Stuart frequently, has this to say about his early life:

"Born in Scotland and descended from the royal Stuarts, the son of a merchant of Jacobite sympathies, he was one of the fortunate survivors of Admiral George Anson's expedition around the world, which brought him a small fortune in prize money. Turning from the sea, he established himself as a merchant in Charleston. He failed, and entered upon a career of arms. As a captain of South Carolina militia he became a hero of the Anglo-Cherokee war." (*South,* 124 and *n.*)

Captured at Fort Loudoun in 1760, in the events that led to the retaliatory CHEROKEE EXPED. OF JAMES GRANT,

1761, he was saved from death by Attakullakulla (Little Carpenter), a principal chief. Stuart and this chief then worked together to promote peace. The Scot's influence with the Cherokee, together with his demonstrated abilities as a leader, led to his appointment in 1762 to the position of Indian Supt. (*Ibid., D.A.B.,* "Oconostota" and "Stuart") Stuart had held his post 13 years when the Revolution started, and figures prominently in Indian affairs during this period. In the summer of 1775 he resisted instructions from Lord Wm. Campbell, royal Gov. of S.C., to turn the Catawba and Cherokee nations against the rebels, replying that "an indiscriminate attack by Indians . . . might do much harm; but I shall dispose them to join in executing any concerted plan, and to act with and assist their well-disposed neighbors," meaning the Loyalists. (Van Doren, *Secret History,* 27)

Stuart was forced to take refuge at St. Augustine when Gov. Campbell fled the province (*ibid.*), but from there and Pensacola he followed out the instructions of Gage to maintain British control over his Indians so they would be ready when needed. (Alden, *Gage,* 259, *South,* 124) He presumably is one of the agents who tried to prevent the abortive CHEROKEE WAR OF 1776. In Feb. '78 he sent deputies to prepare the Cherokee in the mountains and the Seminole in Fla. for hostilities against the patriots of Ga. and the Carolinas, and the next month he established white soldiers and Indians along the lower Mississippi, but the Indians did little damage that year. (Van Doren, *op. cit.,* 121) Subsequent limited operations of the Southern Indians are outlined in the article on INDIANS. . . . Stuart's theater was too far removed from British bases such as Niagara and Detroit, that supported the more active Indian raids in the Old Northwest and in the Border Warfare of N.Y. Another factor, however, was the more virile reaction of the Southern mountaineers to Indian depredations; John Sevier and Andrew Pickens led punitive expeditions that steadily whittled down the power of the savages.

According to Alden, Stuart later became a Charleston aristocrat, but did not marry into the wealthy Fenwick family, as incorrectly held by Charleston tradition and *D.A.B.* The latter authority's statement that he died in 1779 in Pensacola and Appleton's statement that he returned to England in 1779 and died there that year are likewise incorrect. Although he speculated in western lands after the war, he was opposed to immoderate westward expansion. (Alden, *South,* 124 and *n.,* 125)

His son, John Stuart (1759–1815), was born in Ga. (Appleton's, *E.B.*) and sent to school at Westminster, England. According to *E.B.,* he entered the 3d Foot Guards ("Buffs") in 1778 and almost immediately went with them to America. If this was actually his regiment he would have reached Charleston on 4 June '81 and marched under Rawdon to the relief of NINETY-SIX. (Fortescue, *British Army,* III, 382) The Buffs also figured prominently at EUTAW SPRINGS, 8 Sept. '81. If he was with this regiment he was not present at the Yorktown surrender the next month, as stated in *E.B.* A regimental Lt. and army Capt. when the war ended (*ibid.*), he fought on the Continent in 1793, commanded a brigade in Portugal and on Minorca, and as a "substantive Maj. Gen." took part in the Neapolitan operations of Sir James CRAIG, succeeding him as commander in Mar. 1806. After winning the battle of Maida in Calabria over a French force, 4 July, for which he was awarded the Italian title of

Count of Maida, he returned to England in 1806. The next year he was promoted to Lt. Gen. and until 1810 he held the Mediterranean command. During this year he conducted indecisive operations from Sicily against Murat (Napoleon's great cavalry leader and brother-in-law, then King of Naples) on the mainland and at Capri. He returned to England in 1810 and died two months after receiving the G.C.B. in 1815.

SUFFOLK RESOLVES. 17 Sept. '74. (1st Cont'l. Cong.) Drafted by Joseph Warren, adopted by a convention in Suffolk co., Mass., 9 Sept., rushed to Philadelphia by Paul Revere, these resolutions were presented by the radical delegates and endorsed by the 1st Cont'l. Cong. They declared the INTOLERABLE ACTS unconstitutional, urged Mass. to form a government and withhold taxes from the Crown until the said acts were repealed, advised the people to arm, and recommended economic sanctions against Britain. (*E.A.H.*)

SUFFREN DE SAINT TROPEZ, Pierre André de. 1729–1788. French admiral. Born into a noble family in Provence, he entered the *gardes de la marine* in Oct. '43 and served on the *Solide* off Toulon the next year. Aboard the *Pauline* he went to the West Indies, and in 1746 took part in the disastrous attempt of D'Anville to take Cape Breton. The next year he was captured by the British in the Bay of Biscay. After duty with the galleys of the Order of Malta, he was a Lt. in the action against Minorca that resulted in the surrender of the British garrison and the court-martial of Adm. BYNG. In 1757 he again was captured, this time by Boscawen off Lagos. As Capt. of the xebec *Caméléon* he fought the Barbary pirates, returned to the service of the Order of Malta during the period 1767–

71, and became a commander of the Order. He then commanded vessels in the squadron organized to train officers of the revitalized French Navy and gained high praise for his skill and daring.

When France went to war with England Suffren served under d'Estaing in 1778–79. On 5 Aug. '78 he distinguished himself at NEWPORT. In action against Adm. John Byron off Grenada, he held the line despite the loss of 62 men aboard his ship, the *Fantastique* (64). He strongly disapproved of the timid tactics of d'Estaing, and made this known in official communications to his admiral. (David Hannay in *E.B.*) The latter nevertheless recommended that Suffren be given command of the five ships of the line that the French planned to send to help the Dutch defend their Cape of Good Hope colony against an expected British attack. On 22 Mar. '81 Suffren sailed from Brest with Grasse, left the latter at the Azores, and went on to win his name as a great naval commander. On 16 Apr. he found the English expedition under Adm. George Johnstone anchored off the Cape Verde Islands, technically in the neutral waters of Portugal, and remembering how little respect the British had shown for such ·fine points off Lagos in 1757 (see above) he attacked without hesitation. Although even the inept JOHNSTONE was able to inflict as much damage as Suffren's uninspired captains could deliver, the British learned that a new and dangerous type of French admiral had appeared. After going on to save the Cape Colony from capture by Johnstone, Suffren sailed for India where, in a series of four savage actions, he fought Sir Edward Hughes to a standstill. Again it was the indifferent caliber of his captains that kept him from gaining any clean victory. (*E.B., op. cit.*) He was preparing to renew his offensive in India

when news of the peace arrived, and he returned to France for a hero's welcome. A third appointment as Vice-Adm. was created for him. He died suddenly in 1788 just as he prepared to take command of a fleet.

The subject of an admiring sketch in Mahan's *Sea Power,* Suffren is considered a giant among the pygmy admirals in the French Navy of this epoch.

SUGAR ACT of 1764. See NAVIGATION ACTS.

SULLIVAN, John. 1740–1795. Cont'l. general. N.H. Born of parents who had arrived about 1723 as redemptioners from Ireland, he became an "able, if somewhat litigious, lawyer." (Randolph G. Adams in *D.A.B.*) In 1772 he was a Maj. of N.H. militia and in Sept. '74 was seated in the Cont'l. Cong. Home in Dec., he and John Langdon led a group of volunteers that captured Ft. William and Mary at the entrance to Portsmouth harbor. He took his seat in the 2d Cont'l. Cong. on 10 May '75 and was appointed Cont'l. B.G. on 22 June. During the Boston siege he commanded a brigade at Winter Hill except for a period in Oct. '75 when he organized the defenses of Portsmouth. After the British evacuation of Boston he led a column of reinforcements to join the CANADA INVASION. Reaching St. Johns on 1 June '76, he assumed command of the army when Thomas died the next day and after the defeat at Trois Rivières, 8 June, ordered the retreat up Lake Champlain. His army was at Crown Point when Gates superseded him in command. Sullivan left the theater of operations with threats of resignation and took his grievance to Congress. He was prevailed on to remain in service, reached N.Y.C. on 21 July, and was appointed Maj. Gen. on 9 Aug. '76. On 20 Aug. he succeeded Greene as commander on Long Island but four days later he became second in command to Putnam. Captured in the Battle of LONG ISLAND, 27 Aug., he went to Philadelphia with a message from the British that led to the fruitless PEACE CONFERENCE of 11 Sept. '76. He was exchanged for Gen. Richard Prescott about 25 Sept. and was back at Washington's headquarters on the 27th. (Freeman, *Washington,* IV, 217) Given command of a division, he took part in the remaining phase of the N.Y. Camp'n. At the start of the N.J. CAMPAIGN Sullivan's Div. was on the Hudson as part of Lee's command. He succeeded Lee when the latter was captured, and joined Washington south of the Delaware on 20 Dec. with the remaining 2,000 of the 5,000 troops with which Lee had started. At TRENTON he led the right column and rendered valuable service in the American victory. He commanded the main body in the advance on PRINCETON but contributed nothing significant to that success. While the army was in winter quarters around Morristown during the first part of 1776 Sullivan commanded forces on outpost duty and was in the exposed position at Princeton when the British undertook the mystifying "June maneuvers" that started the PHILADELPHIA CAMPAIGN. He led an unsuccessful operation against STATEN ISLAND, 22 Aug., and then hurried south in time to fight at BRANDYWINE, 11 Sept. Meanwhile he had made enemies in Congress by joining Greene and Knox in threatening to resign over the TRONSON DE COUDRAY affair, an action which politicians considered an attempt by generals to "dictate" to civil authority. In Sept. a proposal was advanced in Congress to suspend him from command while an inquiry was made into his failure at Staten Island, and delegate Thos. Burke of N.C. charged him with misconduct at Brandywine. Washington refused to relieve Sullivan,

whom he regarded as one of his most valuable commanders, and he led a column at GERMANTOWN, 4 Oct. No blame has been attached to him for the American failure in this battle. Meanwhile he was cleared of charges in connection with the Staten Island expedition.

He spent the winter at Valley Forge and Bancroft says, "Sullivan's behavior raises a suspicion that he too was more or less involved" in the CONWAY CABAL. Freeman's comment is probably more accurate when he says Sullivan's "love of popularity had led him to seek the good will of parties to the controversy." (*Op. cit.,* IV, 608) Early in 1778 he was named to succeed Spencer as commander in R.I., "not because of any special fitness for the post," comments Freeman, "but because the New Hampshire General happened to be more readily available than any other officer of appropriate rank." (*Ibid.,* 613) He turned out to be singularly unqualified for what this same author calls the "puzzling experiment in cooperation," the Franco-American operation against NEWPORT, 29 July–31 Aug. '78. The latter article covers the military aspects of the Newport fiasco and goes into some detail as to Sullivan's failure as a diplomat. Freeman gives the following evaluation:

"Sullivan had courage and a sense of organization, but he was excessively ambitious and was disposed to be overconfident until some adversity threw him into a desperate mood. Because of unsuppressed love of flattery, he always sought to make himself popular with his troops and with his brother-officers. His record as a military diplomatist was negative, though he had fraternized with some of the French officers in American service and—it was no compliment to his judgment—had formed an amusingly exaggerated opinion of Thomas Conway." (*Op. cit.,* V, 51–52)

Perhaps in testimony to his previously good record, not to mention his political connections in New England, Sullivan's military career survived the Newport affair. In Mar. '79 he left Providence and led SULLIVAN'S EXPEDITION against the Iroquois, one of the largest independent operations of the war. His health impaired by this experience in the out-of-doors, he resigned from the army on 30 Nov. '79. The canny Irishman did not leave his last command without, however, securing a semipolitical indorsement of his Iroquois expedition from his officers. (Elias DAYTON article in D.A.B.)

Sullivan promptly secured re-election to Congress. He was chairman of the committee appointed 3 Jan. '81 to represent Congress in settling the MUTINY OF THE PA. LINE. During this term in Congress his brother Daniel, who was fatally ill from his mistreatment on a British prison hulk, brought him a peace feeler from the enemy. Sullivan refused to have anything to do with the communication but referred it to La Luzerne. Since Sullivan had borrowed money from the French minister, post-mortem charges were made that the general had been paid for this service. This accusation has been completely discredited. (D.A.B.)

In 1782 Sullivan was a member of his state's constitutional convention, was elected Atty. Gen., member of the N.H. Assembly, and was speaker of that body in 1785; he handled the paper money riots of 1786 firmly but coolly. Elected Gov. of N.H. in 1786, 1787, and 1789, he actively supported adoption of the Constitution. The last years of Sullivan's life were spent as a federal judge.

The *Letters and Papers of Maj. Gen. John Sullivan*, 2 vols., edited by O. G. Hammond, were published as Vols. XIII and XIV of the *N.Y.H.S. Colls.*

(1930, 1931). His biography by T. C. Amory, *The Mil. Svcs. and Pub. Life of ...*, must be supplemented by the Letters, according to R. G. Adams (*op. cit.*), and supersedes the sketch in Sparks's *Lib. of Amer. Biog.* (1844). A new biography is Charles P. Whittemore, *A General of the Revolution: John Sullivan of New Hampshire* (N.Y., 1961).

Sullivan's brother James (1744–1808) was one of the most prominent lawyers in Mass. and a political figure of great power and wealth.

SULLIVAN'S EXPEDITION against the Iroquois. May–Nov. '79. Frontier raids from Canada by Tory and Indian forces resulted in mounting pressure against Congress and Washington to do something about this threat. Washington had wisely resisted detaching troops from his meager main army for the protection of frontier settlements, but the WYOMING and CHERRY VALLEY MASSACRES came at a time when the military situation in the North was stalemated, and Washington could therefore alter this policy. Even before Congress directed him to do so (25 Feb. '79), Washington started planning the campaign.

Command of the operation was accepted by Maj. Gen. John Sullivan when Horatio Gates turned it down on the ground that at 57 he was too old. The grand strategy was for Sullivan to lead 2,500 officers and men from Easton, Pa., through Wyoming Valley and rendezvous at Tioga (now Athens, Pa.) with a 1,500-man column that Brig. Gen. James Clinton would lead south from the Mohawk Valley; the combined force would operate along the traditional route to Niagara. BRODHEAD'S EXPEDITION from Ft. Pitt, 600 strong, was to ascend the Allegheny River and join at Genessee (near Cuylerville) for the capture of Niagara. Clark was to continue his WESTERN OPERATIONS against Detroit. As a preliminary move, Col. Gose Van Schaick led a surprise attack against the Onondagas.

Washington assigned Sullivan the mission of "total destruction and devastation" of the Iroquois settlements and "the capture of as many prisoners of every age and sex as possible" to be held as hostages for future good behavior. He specified that the country was not to be "merely overrun but destroyed." (An ingenious plan to furnish Sullivan with a false map was conceived by Samuel WALLIS.)

SULLIVAN'S ADVANCE

The main body assembled at Easton, where some troops had arrived when Sullivan got there on 7 May. But it was 18 June before they started forward, and this column remained in the Wyoming Valley from 23 June until 31 July. By 8 Aug. they had progressed 55 miles when illness forced Sullivan to pass command temporarily to Lt. Col. Daniel Whiting. On 10 Aug., with Sullivan back in command, they reached Tioga. This same day Brodhead left Ft. Pitt (Pittsburgh).

Washington was disgusted with this slow progress, but his own Q.M.G., Gen. Nathanael Greene, attributed part of Sullivan's delays to Washington's inadequate planning. (Freeman, *Washington,* V, 124 and *n.,* 132 and *n.*) Sullivan and Clinton had bickered over their logistics. When Washington expressed dissatisfaction with Clinton's slow movement toward Tioga, saying this column should have moved light instead of burdening itself with a huge supply train, Sullivan pointed out that since his column could not carry supplies for the entire expedition it was necessary for Clinton to bring from the Mohawk everything needed for the entire campaign. Sullivan himself had 120 boats, 1,200 pack

horses, and 700 cattle. Clinton had over 200 bateaux.

CLINTON'S ADVANCE

From his base at Canajoharie on the Mohawk, James Clinton made his preparations somewhat more expeditiously. In a five-and-a-half-day raid that covered 180 miles (Campbell, *Tryon,* 118), Van Schaick led 500 rank and file from Ft. Stanwix into Onondaga country (between Stanwix and Oswego). They destroyed the 50-house settlement of Onondaga on 20 Apr., took 37 prisoners, killed over 20 warriors, and captured 100 muskets. (*Ibid.*)

By 17 June, Clinton started dragging his bateaux across the difficult, 20-mile portage to Lake Otsego, and on the 30th he wrote Sullivan (who was still at Wyoming) that he was ready to start for Tioga. While he waited for orders—which turned out to be seven weeks—he worked out an ingenious solution to the problem of floating his boats down the creek from the lake to the East Branch of the Susquehanna. First moving the boats through the narrow outlet of the lake, he damned the neck, cleared obstructions from the creek and then, when he had orders to move, he broke the dam and floated down on the flood.*

Clinton left the lake on 9 Aug. and joined Sullivan at Tioga the morning of the 19th.

TORY-INDIAN PREPARATIONS

The British in Canada had excellent intelligence of the threat building up against Detroit and Niagara in early 1779. On 2 Apr. the Tory commander

* This brings to mind the Civil War exploit of Col. Joseph Bailey, who used this lumberman's technique to save Adm. David Porter's flotilla in Banks's Red River Campaign of 1864.

at the latter place, John Butler, had the alarming news that Vincennes had surrendered on 25 Feb. (WESTERN OPNS. of Clark) It was rumored that 4,000 French soldiers and all of d'Estaing's artillery were at Vincennes, and the defenders of Detroit were clamoring for reinforcements. The news of Van Schaick's raid signaled danger in another quarter. "I fear they have taken a child of Joseph Brant's," wrote Walter Butler on 10 May to Haldimand. "This stroke of theirs has every appearance as if they mean to take hold of Oswego for by having this Indian in their hands, they conjecture the Indians will not presume to molest them in such an enterprise." (Swiggett, *Niagara*, 179–80) Three days later John Butler got information from a prisoner that indicated an offensive up the Allegheny, and the same day he learned "that a body of the rebels were on their way from Albany to make another attempt against the Indians." (Swiggett, *op. cit.*, 181, quoting Butler's ltr. of 13 May) The Butlers continued to watch and wait while Sullivan tarried at Wyoming. They were tied to their supply point at Genessee, but John Butler's letter of 21 July speaks of strong posts at Cayuga and Chemung, from which places he was ready to oppose Sullivan or move west "should our services be required towards Detroit, Fort Pitt or Venango. . . ." (Swiggett, *op. cit.*, 190, 193) As if to mock the ponderous immobility of the patriot expedition, Brant operated around MINISINK, N.Y., 19–22 July, within 50 miles of West Point, Morristown (G.H.Q.), and Wyoming!

The British high command in Canada could not believe that the patriots were really moving into Iroquois territory with an army of the size that had been reported. On 23 July, Haldimand wrote from Quebec to Lt. Col. Bolton, commander of the Niagara garrison:

"It is impossible the Rebels can be in such force as has been represented by the deserters to Major Butler upon the Susquehanna. He would do well to send out intelligent white men [as opposed to ignorant Indians] to be satisfied of the truth of those reports. If anything is really intended against the Upper Country I am convinced Detroit is the object, and that they show themselves and spread reports of expeditions in your neighborhood merely to divert the Rangers and Indians from their main purpose—Major Butler should be aware of this." (Quoted in Swiggett, *op. cit.*, 191)

The "intelligent white men" sent out in accordance with these instructions were Lt. Henry Hare and Sgt. Wm. Newberry; Hare was executed as a spy and Newberry was hanged for his alleged atrocities at Cherry Valley. On 12 Aug. John Butler wrote his son to march immediately for Tioga with every man fit for duty. There was no longer any doubt about what the rebels were up to. Sullivan had sent a task force ahead to encircle Chemung while the rest of the army moved up to coöperate in a maneuver designed to capture the entire population, but the Indians had plenty of warning and abandoned the place. This settlement of 30 or 40 houses was destroyed on 13 Aug. (Campbell, *Tryon,* 117) in what one incendiary calls "a glorious Bonfire." Having sustained seven casualties on the 12th when attacked by Indians under Brant and Rowland Montour (a brother of Catherine in the complicated MONTOUR FAMILY), and with nothing further to accomplish, this advance column returned to Tioga where work was started on Ft. Sullivan. On 26 Aug. Sullivan advanced from Tioga with all his forces except 250 men left to hold the forward base.

Sullivan's division, about 2,500 officers and men, comprised the brigades

of Wm. Maxwell, Enoch Poor, and Edw.
Hand. The 1st Brig. (Maxwell's) was
made up of the 1st and 2d N.J., and
Oliver Spencer's [N.J.] Regt. The 2d
Brig. included the 1st, 2d, and 3d N.H.,
and the 7th Mass.* Hand's 3d Brig.
comprised the 4th and 11th Pa., Col.
Thos. Proctor's 4th Arty. Regt. (four
3-pdrs., two 6-pdrs., and two howitzers), Maj. James Parr's detachment
of Morgan's Riflemen, Capt. Anthony
Selin's Indep. Rifle Co., and a body of
Wyoming Valley militia.

Clinton's division, about 1,500 strong,
comprised the 2d, 3d, 4th, and 5th N.Y.
and a company of the 2d Arty. Regt.
(two small guns).

The only battle of the campaign took
place before Sullivan had gone 12
cautious and slow miles. Near the village
of NEWTOWN, 29 Aug., six miles from
modern Elmira, N.Y., the Indians and
Tories made a stand and were routed
with a loss of about 12 killed. Sullivan
had about 40 casualties.

The expedition moved slowly on,
burning towns and destroying crops.
Through Catherinetown, north along the
east shore of Seneca Lake, they then
turned west and stopped at Genessee
on 14 Sept.

Walter Butler had been opposed to
making a stand at Newtown, wanting
to fall back to a better position, but
his official report states that the Indians
insisted. On 8 Aug., the day after Sullivan took Seneca Castle (Canadesaga),
Butler reported that he had been unable
to prevail on the Indians to put up a
fight for that place. On the 13th, however, the day before the invaders reached
Genessee, Butler annihilated the advance
guard of 26 men under Lt. Thos. Boyd;

* This was the outfit that had been at
CHERRY VALLEY under Ichabod Alden
and Dan Whiting. Ward calls it the
7th; Swiggett says it was the 6th.

22 men were killed and Boyd was captured along with one other. "The capture
and horrible death of Lieutenant Boyd
on the fourteenth is in a way the most
famous incident of the campaign," says
Swiggett. Boyd was wounded in action,
interrogated by Butler, and then tortured
to death by the Indians. American
tradition is that he was turned over to
the Indians after refusing to talk.
Swiggett shatters this myth by quoting
John Butler's letters of 14 Sept. to
Bolton: "The officer who is a very intelligent person says their army consists
of near 5000 Continental troops. . . .
They have but a month's provision and
intend, according to his account, to come
no further than Genesee." Boyd apparently talked. It is certain that he was
horribly tortured, although accounts
have undoubtedly been embellished, but
the Butlers appear to be guilty of no
greater sin than not assuring that he
was properly guarded after interroga-
tion. (Swiggett, op. cit., 254–55) The
man captured with Boyd was an Oneida
named Hanyerry, who had distinguished
himself at Oriskany and was known to
his Iroquois enemies as a distinguished
marksman; "he was literally hewn to
pieces," according to a rebel officer's
journal quoted by Campbell. (Op. cit.,
124)

Since BRODHEAD'S EXPEDITION had
failed to join him, Sullivan abandoned
all idea of attacking Niagara and started
withdrawing. The ancient Indian town
of Genesee, comprising 128 houses,
was burned. Retracing his steps to
Seneca Castle, Sullivan continued eastward to Cayuga, moved down both
sides of the lake of that name, and
reached Wyoming on 30 Sept. The expedition brought back no hostages, but
Sullivan reported the destruction of 40
towns, "besides scattered houses," an
estimated 160,000 bushels of corn, and
"a vast quantity of vegetables of every

kind." While he and his troops showed no evidence of having learned anything from the savages about the tactics and strategy of frontier warfare, they proved themselves masters of destruction. Not only the well-built houses of the Iroquois and their abundant crops were destroyed, but also their orchards of apple, peach, and pear trees. Not even the Indians had destroyed growing crops, much less orchards.

"It was a ruthless destruction of the greatest advance in civilization that the red men in this country have ever attained.... The Six Nations never recovered. Their organization was destroyed, their empire gone; they had to subsist during the following winter on British charity...." (Fisher, *Struggle*, II, 245)

The irony is that although Sullivan destroyed the Iroquois civilization he did not eliminate their savagery. As outlined under BORDER WARFARE, they struck back in 1780 and '81 with greater frequency and viciousness than ever.

No fewer than 28 officers and men took part in Sullivan's Expedition kept journals or later wrote of the campaign. Of the journals 17 are printed in full in Frederick Cook (ed.), *Journals of the Military Expedition of ... Sullivan ... with Records of Centennial Celebrations* (Auburn, N.Y., 1887).

SULLIVAN'S ISLAND (Charleston Harbor), S.C., June '76 and May '80. The site of Fort Sullivan, which was renamed Fort Moultrie, this island was successfully defended against the CHARLESTON EXPEDITION of Clinton in 1776 and fell to the British without resistance during the CHARLESTON EXPEDITION of Clinton in 1780.

SUMNER, Jethro. *c.* 1735–1785. Cont'l. general. Va.–N.C. Grandson of an English immigrant who reached Va. around 1691, he served throughout the French and Indian War, becoming a Lt. of Va. militia, paymaster, and commander of Ft. Bedford in 1760. Four years later he moved to N.C., married, and with a large inheritance from his wife became a planter and tavern owner at the seat of what became Warren co. He soon became a local leader, holding various public offices, and was elected by his fellow members of the provincial congress of Aug.–Sept. '75 to the rank of Maj. in the Halifax co. minutemen. He went north to support the Virginians at NORFOLK during the last two months of the year, became Col. of the 3d Bn. N.C. Cont'ls. on 15 Apr. '76, and participated in the defense of Charleston in June. In Sept. he was detached from the forces moving toward Fla. and sent to raise supplies in N.C. The next spring he led his unit north, fought at Brandywine and Germantown, and spent the winter at Valley Forge. Early in 1778 he was invalided home and spent the summer recruiting regulars. Promoted to B.G. on 9 Jan. '79, he led his new Cont'l. brigade at STONO FERRY, 20 June '79, according to *D.A.B.*; Ward says he commanded the militia wing in this action. After spending more than a year recruiting in N.C. he commanded a militia brigade in opposing the advance of Cornwallis to Charlotte, N.C., in Sept. '80. When Smallwood was given temporary command of state troops in Oct., Sumner refused to continue serving in the field. (*D.A.B.*) In Feb. '81 he acceded to Greene's request to return to active duty, but Caswell would not give him a command. In July, however, he resumed his recruiting duty and performed his major combat service of the Revolution as commander of three small N.C. Cont'l. Bns. at EUTAW SPRINGS, 8 Sept. '81. Here his men performed with great credit. He was in command of military forces in N.C. for the remainder of the war, taking part in small actions, and on 3 Nov. '83 he retired.

Resuming his life as planter and publican, he died between 15 and 19 Mar. '85. Although his health is said to have suffered during the war, his wealth did not: he left 20,000 acres and 34 slaves. (A. R. Newsome in *D.A.B.*)

SUMTER, Thomas ("Carolina Gamecock.") 1734–1832. Partisan leader. S.C. Son of a Welsh redemptioner, Thomas was born near Charlottesville, Va., and soon was fatherless. Although "better educated and far better read" than Francis Marion (Bass, *Marion*, 201), with whom he was to vie as one of America's most renowned partisans, Sumter's formal schooling was scant. He took part in the expeditions of Braddock and Forbes, was Sgt. of Va. troops in the 1762 campaign against the Cherokees, and then visited England. Soon after his return he was jailed in Staunton. Escaping in 1765, he went to S.C., acquired land near Eutaw Springs, opened a store, became J.O.P., and married in 1767. His wife, a widow eight years his senior, was of the prominent Cantey family. In his adopted state Sumter was elected to the first and second provincial congresses, became Capt. of mounted rangers under Wm. Thompson, and in Mar. '76 was Lt. Col. of the 2d (later 6th) Rifle Regt. (Heitman) Before resigning on 19 Sept. '78 he fought against the Cherokees and in the limited military operations in S.C. and Ga. When his plantation was burned by Capt. Chas. Campbell of Tarleton's Legion, Sumter headed for the Whig stronghold west of the Catawba River and started raising militia. He was soon joined by militia colonels Wm. Bratton, Wm. Hill, Edw. Lacey, Thos. Taylor, and Richard Winn. (Bass, *Green Dragoon*, 88)

His partisans struck first at WILLIAMSON'S PLANTATION, 12 July '80, a victory that brought him more volunteers. Repulsed at ROCKY MOUNT, 1 Aug.,

Sumter was successful at HANGING ROCK, 6 Aug. His lack of strategic sense first showed itself in the CAMDEN CAMPAIGN, and after Gates accepted his request for a reinforcement, just before the main army advanced to defeat at Camden, Sumter was badly beaten by Tarleton at FISHING CREEK, 18 Aug. He soon resumed operations, however, and on 6 Oct. was named senior B.G. of S.C. militia. Although the action at FISHDAM FORD, 9 Nov., was a draw, he foiled an attempt by the notorious Maj. Wemyss to annihilate him and inspired a patriot uprising that panicked Cornwallis. The Gamecock fought Tarleton to a bloody standstill at BLACKSTOCKS, 20 Nov., but was badly wounded.

Sending word for Marion to join forces with him, Sumter started down the Congaree on 16 Feb. '81 with the idea of touching off a *levée en masse* when he pushed on down the Santee. He would support this operation logistically by capturing the enemy base of Ft. Granby. Marion knew that the British were reinforcing the posts along their line of communications and was pessimistic about the success of Sumter's strategy, but being the junior B.G. he started calling his militia and prepared to comply with his orders. (Bass, *Marion*, 141) Sumter reached Ft. Granby on 19 Feb., started his attack before dawn, but had to retreat the next day as Col. Welbore Doyle's N.Y. Vols. approached to relieve the garrison. The partisans moved 35 miles down the river, surprised the post at Belleville, but had to withdraw when enemy forces approached from Camden. (*Ibid.*) On 28 Feb. he launched an attack against Ft. Watson without having properly reconnoitered the place and suffered a costly repulse. When he learned that Col. Watson was preparing to attack him with overwhelming force, Sumter moved to his plantation to pick up his paralytic wife and young son, and started withdrawing northward. After moving some 40 miles to the Bradley Plantation, between the Black and Lynches rivers, he waited until 6 Mar. before giving up hope of seeing Marion and then continued his retreat northward. The same day he was attacked by Maj. Thos. Fraser's Loyal S.C. and escaped with the loss of 10 killed and about 40 wounded. His ill-advised campaign was over, but as Greene's army approached he ignored the latter's requests to join him in an attack on Rawdon's principal post. The Carolina Gamecock wanted to fight his own little war. When Greene needed his support at HOBKIRK'S HILL, Sumter struck at Ft. Granby, gave up, captured ORANGEBURG, 11 May, and then threatened to resign because Henry Lee had taken Granby while he was gone. Greene placated the guerrilla, who then came up with his controversial plan of raising troops by "Sumter's law": to recruit dependable mounted militia for 10 months, he proposed paying them in plunder taken from Loyalists—sort of a pay-as-you-go scheme. He succeeded in assembling men but touched off a renewed wave of vicious civil war and earned himself an evil reputation that dogged him to the grave. When he finally moved south to support Greene his strategic blunders contributed to the American failure at NINETY-SIX.

He then got Marion and Lee put under his command and launched a campaign that ended in the mismanaged attack at QUINBY BRIDGE, 17 July. On the 25th he sent a force to plunder Loyalists in Georgetown, since his troops were clamoring for more booty. The British retaliated by virtually destroying Georgetown on 2 Aug., and the first official act of Gov. Rutledge, who had just arrived to restore civil

government in S.C., was to issue a proclamation that ended "Sumter's law" by prohibiting plundering. This also ended the Gamecock's military career; bothered by his wound, exhausted by his campaigns, his name "almost universally odious" (as Henry Lee put it), he retired to N.C. Command of his brigade passed to Lt. Col. Wm. Henderson, who found "the most discontented set of men I ever saw." (Bass, *Marion*, 210) Sumter was elected senator and sat in the assembly that met 8 Jan. '82 at Jacksonboro. He resigned his military commission the next month.

After the war he was given the thanks of the S.C. senate and a gold medal. He had received the thanks of Congress on 13 Jan. '81. Sumter declined election to Congress but served many terms in the S.C. House. After calling for an investigation of his use of "Sumter's law," he was exonerated, and the legislatures of N.C. and S.C. both forbade state courts to entertain damage suits connected with this matter. (*D.A.B.*) He founded Stateburg, S.C., took out grants of 150,000 acres, experimented with the growth of tobacco and cotton to replace indigo as the staple crop of the region. Elected to the 1st Congress, he had strong antifederalist tendencies and was among the last to be won over by the federalists. Suspected of speculation in government paper, he was defeated for Congress in 1793 but re-elected in 1796. He served in the House until elected to the Senate in Dec. 1801 and resigned from Congress in Dec. 1810. For the next 22 years he was harried by litigation and by creditors. In 1827 the S.C. legislature granted him a lifetime moratorium for his debt to the state bank. He lived to be 98, the oldest surviving general of the war.

As a partisan leader Sumter had

been bold, imaginative, and capable of great physical endurance. As a tactical commander he was poor: he attacked when the odds against him were overwhelming, he failed to reconnoiter thoroughly, he neglected details, and he was unable to coordinate a battle. He has been described as personally brave, but he ran for his life at FISHDAM FORD and FISHING CREEK. He was insubordinate in the most literal meaning of the word and showed a consistently poor strategic sense. "In war he was a politician," says Anne King Gregorie in *D.A.B.*, "and in politics he was an old soldier."

See Gregorie, *Thomas Sumter*, 1931, which includes an extensive bibliography. Manuscript materials, according to the author, are in the Library of Cong., the Clements Library, the Wisconsin State Historical Society, and the N.Y. Historical Library.

SUNBURY (Ft. Morris), Ga., 25 Nov. '78. See John MCINTOSH.

SUNBURY (Ft. Morris), Ga., 9 Jan. '79. British capture. Maj. Joseph Lane was left with 200 Cont'ls. to defend this place when the rest of Robt. Howe's Southern army left for the operation that ended in the British capture of SAVANNAH, 29 Dec. '78. (See this article for other matters of strategy bearing on Lane's situation.) Gen. Prevost left St. Augustine on 23 Dec. with about 2,000 men—including Indians—and attacked Sunbury on 6 Jan. Three days later the British got their artillery into position and Lane surrendered. American casualties were four killed and seven wounded; the British captured 24 guns and a quantity of stores. Their price was one man killed and three wounded.

SUPPLY OF THE CONTINENTAL ARMY. The patriots started the war with almost none of the supplies required to arm, clothe, shelter, or otherwise equip, maneuver, and support army or naval forces. To be more specific, they lacked powder, muskets, cannon, lead, bayonets, cartridge boxes, cartridge paper, textiles, entrenching tools, and such camp equipment as kettles. Food was not a problem while the army was around Boston, but the shortage of SALT meant that meat and fish could not be preserved. MANUFACTURING IN AMERICA was undeveloped when the war started and never was built up to a point where it contributed significantly to the war effort; virtually all the shortages listed above had to be made up from captures, from the French (see HORTALEZ & CIE.), or from purchase abroad on credit.

This article therefore deals primarily with the efforts of the Cont'l. Cong. and the state and military authorities to create and operate supply departments.

On 16 June '75 the delegates provided for the organization of two supply offices: Quartermaster General (Q.M.G.) and Commissary General of Stores and Purchases, both of which would report to Congress. On 19 July they appointed Joseph Trumbull to the later post, but they were not so prompt in naming a Q.M.G. Trumbull's department, charged with feeding the army, functioned well until the war moved from Boston to N.Y. and N.J., so for the moment let us look at the other department.

Until the reorganization of 1780 the American Q.M.G. had duties and responsibilities far beyond those of the modern quartermaster: in addition to the procurement and distribution of supplies other than food and clothing, he was the principal staff officer involved in the movement of troops (route reconnaissance; repair and maintenance of roads and bridges; layout, organization, and construction of camps; supply and maintenance of wagons and teams and of boats for water movement). Washington therefore felt the need for this key staff officer soon after assuming command at Boston and asked for authority to make his own appointment. When this was granted (19 July), Washington named Thomas MIFFLIN for the post on 14 Aug. '75. Stephen MOYLAN took over the office in June '76, but proved unequal to the task, and four months later Mifflin was back. This officer was seldom at Washington's Hq. in 1777 but his duties were performed by three subordinates: Joseph Thornsbury, whom Washington appointed Wagonmaster General in May; Clement Biddle, appointed Commissary General of Forage on 1 July; and Col. Henry Emanuel Lutterloh (or Lutterlough), an officer who had served as a Q.M. in the army of Brunswick, whom (at Washington's suggestion) Mifflin made his deputy.

Quartermaster operations fell apart in 1777, primarily in the field of transportation (i.e., distribution): Mifflin had been detained by Congress in Philadelphia over matters of reorganization; then he had been held there to stimulate recruiting, and later to move stores out of the way of the British threat (see N.J. CAMP'N.). On 8 Oct. '77 he submitted his resignation on grounds of ill health, but Congress, whose indecision and neglect had caused the collapse of supply, did not accept the resignation until 7 Nov. The next day, however, the delegates asked Mifflin to carry on until they could get around to picking his successor. Mifflin, who had been appointed to the new BOARD OF WAR, retaining the rank but not the pay of Maj. Gen., simply told his deputy, Lutterloh, to take over as Q.M.G. He therefore shares with Congress the re-

sponsibility for the army's suffering during the VALLEY FORGE WINTER QUARTERS.

With the lament that "No body ever heard of a quarter Master, in History," the tremendously capable Nathanael Greene reluctantly accepted the noncombatant office of Q.M.G. and held it from 2 Mar. '78 to 5 Aug. '80. Two able men were prevailed on to be his deputies: John Cox was to make all purchases and examine all stores; Charles Pettit would keep the books and the cash. Congress put Greene and his deputies on the "commission system": they could retain one per cent of the money spent by the Q.M. department. The three men agreed to divide this equally.

Trumbull's Commissary Dept., meanwhile, had fed the army well until it moved from the Boston area. (See PAY, BOUNTIES, AND RATIONS) After the disasters of 1776—the loss of N.Y.C. and the retreat through N.J.—Congress was seized by a veritable "rage for reformation" (Ltr. of 20 Nov. '77 from Richard Henry Lee to Washington), and most of this was directed against the Commissary Dept. (Risch, *Quartermaster Support of the Army . . .*, 23, 26) On the recommendation of the Board of War, and in line with Washington's ideas, the delegates split Trumbull's office into a Commissary General of Purchases and a Commissary General of Issues. Fully a year before Congress made the decision Trumbull had wholeheartedly supported this division of his office but made a strong argument that he and his deputies be taken off a fixed salary. He reiterated an earlier proposal that he receive a one-half of one per cent commission of all money passing through his hands, and that two and one half per cent be retained by the deputies purchasing subsistence. The morale of Trumbull's assistants was low because of criticism and because Congress had been so slow to prescribe regulations for the department.

On 10 June '77 Congress finally produced a long, detailed set of regulations, prescribing how records would be kept, how government animals would be branded, and other minutiae. On 18 June they elected the officers for the new organization. Although he apparently was not officially notified until 5 July, Trumbull was retained in the establishment as Commiss. Gen. of Purchases, and his deputies were Wm. Ayless, Wm. Buchanan, Jacob Cuyler, and Jeremiah Wadsworth. The second post was given to Charles Stewart (who retained it until the end of the Yorktown Camp'n.), and his deputies were Wm. Mumford, Matthew Irwin, and Elisha Avery. In this reorganization Congress paid little attention to Trumbull's recommendations, particularly with regard to his proposal about commissions. Trumbull tried to hold his department together while he argued with the Cont'l. Cong. on modification of their plan, but the delegates refused to yield ground and Trumbull's deputies started quitting. On 19 July Trumbull submitted his resignation with the request that it be effective 20 Aug. '77. Buchanan was named (5 Aug.) to succeed him. On the latter's resignation, 20 or 23 Mar. '78, Jeremiah Wadsworth took over the office on 9 Apr. After Wadsworth's resignation on 1 Jan. '80, Ephraim Blaine became Commiss. Gen. of Purchases and held the post until it was abolished after the Yorktown Camp'n., in Oct. '81. (Risch, *op. cit.*, 68; Heitman shows him holding the office until 24 July '82, although Risch says "With no duties left to execute [see below], Blaine submitted his resig-

nation to Congress on 30 July ['81]" but, in the absence of Congressional approval, continued to serve until the fighting ended at Yorktown.)

THE CLOTHIER GENERAL

Although the supply of clothing fell in the domain of the Commiss. Gen., the Q.M.G., Mifflin, had temporarily handled this responsibility in 1775. When Congress got around to reorganizing the supply services after the evacuation of N.Y.C. their first act was to create the office of Commissary of Clothing. This official would submit regimental clothing to the states, receive and pay for deliveries; regimental paymasters then would receive the clothing, make issue to the troops, and deduct the costs from the soldiers' wages. (Risch, 23) George Measam was appointed to this post in the Northern army on 16 Oct. '76, a week after Congress created it, and at the same time Washington was authorized to fill the post in his own army. On 20 Dec., Washington wrote Congress to recommend that a Clothier General for the Cont'l. Army—rather than one for each field army—be appointed, and a week later the delegates agreed, although they did not prescribe his authority. (Bear in mind what was happening about this time: Congress was granting WASHINGTON'S "DICTATORIAL" POWERS.)

James Mease, a Philadelphia merchant and ex-butler, who had been Commiss. to Pa. Troops since 25 Jan. '76 (Heitman) and who had executed supply orders for Congress, asked Washington for this post on 6 Jan. '77 and was given it four days later. He reported to Washington's camp in Feb. '77. Although he "apparently gave the fullest effort to the discharge of his duties" (Freeman, *Washington,* IV, citing 8 *G.W.,* 441) the results were poor.

Shoes were a particular problem, the shortage rendering some organizations "almost entirely incapable of doing duty," in Washington's words (23 June '77 to Mease). Congress had established a "Hide Department" (22 Nov. '76) to take custody of the original wrappings of cattle slaughtered for the army. Now it directed the Commiss. of Hides to exchange these for tanned leather or for shoes; if this were unfeasible the Commiss. of Hides could set up the tanyards, secure the other necessary materials and workmen, and produce the shoes, or he could contract for their manufacture. The Hide Dept. then was put under the Board of War, which directed that it make deliveries of leather to the Commis. of Military Stores for the production of other equipment. Six weeks after the man selected by Congress declined to serve as Commiss. of Hides, George Ewing was appointed to the post on 5 Aug. '77. He resigned on 20 Apr. '79, and the Board of War came up with a new plan under which five commissioners were appointed: Wm. Henry for Pa., Md., and Del.; John Mehelm for N.J.; Moses Hatfield for N.Y.; Robert Lamb for Mass.; and George Starr for Conn. (Risch, 24, 51)

Washington had meanwhile grown increasingly dissatisfied with Mease's performance. In Apr. '78 he asked Congress to make an investigation and on 4 Aug. he wrote that Mease was unfit for the post. Mease's functions were reduced as clothing started arriving from France, the states were directed to supply their own troops, and the Board of War took over the purchase of items for the Cont'l. Army. Late in 1778 Washington told a visiting Congressional Committee that a reorganization of the Clothing Dept. was still necessary, and on 23 Mar. '79 the delegates got around to acting. Mease had submitted his resignation in Dec. '77, offering to stay in office until a successor was named, but on grounds of ill health he left the main army and operated from Lancaster. (Risch, 31) After two others had declined the new office as set up in Mar. '79, James Wilkinson accepted on 24 July. He was to take orders from Washington and the Board of War, and each state would appoint its own clothier.

EXPANSION OF Q.M. DEPT., 1775-80

In 1775 the Q.M.G. had operated with two assistants and some 40 clerks, laborers, wagonmasters, and superintendents. By 1780 the Q.M.G. and his two assistants had 28 deputies and 109 assistant deputies plus many storekeepers, clerks, barrackmasters, express riders, laborers, and superintendents of government property, roads, stables, woodyards, and horseyards. The forage branch had a Commiss. Gen. and assistant, 25 deputies, 128 assistant deputies, as well as clerks, forage masters, measurers, collectors, weighers, stackers, superintendents, and laborers. The wagon branch had a wagonmaster general, 11 deputies, plus many wagonmasters, wagoners, packhorse masters, and packhorsemen. The boat department had superintendents, masters of vessels, mates, and boatmen. In 1780 the Q.M. Dept. employed almost 3,000 people at an estimated monthly payroll of $407,593; this sum excludes the commissions paid to the Q.M.G., his assistants, the Commiss. Gen. of Forage, but includes those paid to some of their deputies, though not all. (Risch, 61)

GREENE AND WADSWORTH RESIGN

In 1779 the operations of the Q.M.G. and the Commiss. Gen. came under mounting criticism. Expenditures of the two departments had gone from $9,272,-534 in 1776 to more than quadruple that amount ($37,202,421) in 1778, and in May '79 the Committee on the Treasury estimated that at least $200,000,000 would be spent by the two departments in that year unless finances could be put on a firmer basis; the problem, of course, was the depreciation of CONT'L. CURRENCY. The extremely severe weather, the suffering of the MORRISTOWN WINTER QUARTERS, 1779–80, and suspicion that all purchasing agents were getting rich on the commission system, all these things brought such animosity against the two department heads that Greene and Wadsworth both threatened to resign. Only a public statement of confidence by Congress kept them in office. In the fall, however, both officials tendered their resignations. Wadsworth's was accepted on 1 Jan. '80 (see above), and Greene's was accepted on 5 Aug. '80. (See GREENE for the circumstances)

Greene's successor, Timothy PICKERING, who held the office until 25 July '85, started operating under the reorganization plan Congress had implemented on 15 July '80. For the first time the duties of the Q.M.G. no longer included the operational functions inherited from the British Army (see above) and retained in the German Army until almost a çentury later. Pickering and subsequent Q.M.G.'s of the American Army have been concerned only with supply. With much noise about "four years of wasteful profusion," Pickering undertook to eliminate the "superfluities" in his department and "lop them off." (Quoted in Risch, 62) But the real thing needed was money to make the supply system work, and this was not available. It was not available to buy food and clothing in sufficient quantities, and it was not available to provide transportation for what little was received. The situation was so desperate that Washington had to dismiss many troops for want of food and clothing when he went into winter quarters in Dec. '80, and Greene's Southern army also was threadbare and hungry. These shortages, plus pay and enlistment grievances, led to troop MUTINIES in 1781.

In the spring of 1781 the New England states again came through with provisions, thanks largely to the efforts of Gen. Wm. HEATH, whom Washington sent to request help. Congress then established a new system whereby private contractors, instead of the states, procured, delivered, and issued the rations. Robert MORRIS, the newly appointed financial dictator, worked out the details and raised the cash. "Through the cooperative efforts of the Quartermaster General, the state deputy quartermasters, and the Superintendent of Finance, Washington performed the prodigious feat of moving the allied forces from the Hudson southward 450 miles to the James River and defeating Cornwallis within the 2-month period between 14 August, when he received the news that Admiral de Grasse had sailed with a French fleet from the West Indies for the Chesapeake Bay, and 15 October 1781, the date set by the Admiral for the departure of the fleet." (Risch, 69–70)

After the victorious Yorktown Camp'n., Q.M.G. Pickering took charge of all arrangements for returning American troops to the North. He took charge of much of the captured British matériel, sending some of it to Greene in the South; he provided wood and straw for the hospitals at Williamsburg and Hanover, Va.; he handled claims for damages and debts incurred by the armies in Va.; and during the winter of 1781–82 he was involved in settling the transportation accounts arising out of the last campaign. (*Ibid.,* 70)

As early as 1781 Morris, whose role as financier of the Revolution caused him to become increasingly prominent in army supply matters, had become responsible for purchasing clothing. Soon he was making all contracts for supplies, and on application of the Clothier Gen. was providing funds to pay for manufacture of clothing. Wilkinson resigned as Clothier Gen. on 27 Mar. '81 and was succeeded by John Moylan, a brother of Stephen (Appleton's).

As the year 1781 ended, Morris had taken over the duties of the Commissary Generals of Purchases and of Issues, both Blaine and Stewart relinquishing their posts without waiting for Congress to accept their resignations. (Risch, 71) Morris, by one means or another, furnished clothes for the army, "not as fully as Washington desired but nevertheless more adequately than in earlier years of the war." (*Ibid.*) Elimination of the Commissary Depts. made it possible to consolidate many supply functions and to reduce overhead, an economy movement that Pickering heartily supported. Congress put other measures into effect, and before the end of 1782 Pickering's staff was reduced to 10 officers. On 25 July '85 the office of the Q.M.G. was abolished.

For the above account of an extremely important but highly involved feature of the American Revolution I am indebted to the first two chapters of *Quartermaster Support of the Army: A History of the Corps, 1775–1939* by Erna Risch (Washington, 1962).

Greene's Q.M.G. in the Southern Dept. and the man nominated by Hamilton to be Q.M.G. of the American Army in the mobilization of 1798 was the remarkable and unsung Edward CARRINGTON.

SUTHERLAND, William (?). British officer. A Lt. William Sutherland of the 38th Foot took part in the expedition to Lexington and Concord, and his account is in the Gage Papers held by the Clements Library at Ann Arbor, Mich. A Capt. William Sutherland of the 55th Foot is identified as Adj. and A.D.C. to Gen. Henry Clinton in 1778; he or a namesake raised and commanded a light infantry unit that may have become the cadre for the BRITISH LEGION, saved Clinton's life at Monmouth (Baurmeister, *Journals,* 187 and *n.*), commanded the corps of INVALIDS that reached Bermuda on 2 Nov. '78 to constitute the first garrison of that place during the Revolution (*ibid.,* 223; Kerr, *Bermuda,* 82), and is identified by Baurmeister as the unlucky commander of PAULUS HOOK, 19 Aug, '79, subsequently court-martialed for his conduct. (*Op. cit.,* 295–96) Other writers are not so sure this was the same Sutherland: Ward so identifies him and adds the further detail that "a part of the Invalid Battalion" was there (*W.O.R.,* 605), but Clinton does not positively indicate that the Maj. Sutherland at Paulus Hook was his former A.D.C., and the index of this work shows him as "Sutherland, William (?)." (*American Rebellion*) Baurmeister mentions a *Capt.* Sutherland of the 55th Foot who reached N.Y.C. from Antigua in Aug. '82 (*op. cit.,* 585); this could be the same officer—having been reduced in grade for his failure at Paulus Hook—or the German journalist could be in error as to name, grade, or organization.

In the final phase of BURGOYNE'S OFFENSIVE a Lt. Col. Sutherland was commanding a force comprising the 9th and 47th Regts.

"SWAMP FEVER." Malaria.

"SWAMP FOX." Francis MARION.

"SWAN SHOT." Large shot, but smaller than buckshot, used for hunting large fowl, small game, and occasionally used in battle.

SWIFT, Heman. Cont'l. officer. Conn. Col. of a Conn. militia regiment from July to Dec. '76, he became Col. of the 7th Conn. Cont'l. Regt. on 1 Jan. '77 and was transferred to the 2d Conn. on 1 Jan. '81. In one of the few references to him in general accounts of the war, Heath mentions that on 28 Sept. '81 he was sent from the Highlands with 300 infantry and some light artillery to Ramapo, N.J., to support the militia against a possible British raid from Staten Island. (*Memoirs,* 326) In June '83 he was retained as Col. of the Consolidated Conn. Regt. On 30 Sept. he was breveted B.G. and in Dec. '83 he left the army. (Heitman)

T

TALLMADGE, Benjamin (Jr.). 1754–1835. Cont'l. officer, manager of Washington's secret service. N.Y. Descended from Thos. Talmadge (*sic*), an early settler of Southampton, L.I., Benjamin was tutored by his father before he entered Yale. Soon after his graduation in 1773 he became Supt. of the high school at Wethersfield, Conn. He left this post to fight in the Revolutionary war, being made Lt. and Adj. in Chester's Conn. State Regt. on 20 June '76, Capt. on 14 Dec. '76, Maj. on 7 Apr. '77, and Bvt. Lt. Col. on 30 Sept. '83. Meanwhile he had seen action at Long Island, White Plains, Brandywine, Germantown, and Monmouth. For his raid to FORT GEORGE, L.I., 21–23 Nov. '80, he was commended by Washington and Congress. During the period 1778–83, after the cessation of major military operations in the North, Tallmadge was primarily occupied with the management of Washington's secret service. (Van Doren, *Secret History,* 237) His initiative after the capture of "John Anderson" led to the exposure of ARNOLD'S TREASON. He was in charge of John André while the latter was a prisoner and developed a deep affection for him.

After the war Tallmadge was a businessman in Litchfield, Conn. In 1800 he was elected as a Federalist to Congress and served from the next year to 1817. He is described as being above average height, well proportioned, and military in bearing. (Ray W. Irwin in *D.A.B.*) His *Memoir* was published in 1858 and reprinted in 1904. See also Charles S. Hall, *Benjamin Tallmadge* (N.Y., 1943).

TAPPAN 'MASSACRE, N.J., 28 Sept. '78. When the British sent large foraging parties up both sides of the Hudson—5,000 men under Cornwallis on the west and 3,000 under Knyphausen on the east—Washington detached small bodies of troops to harass them. Anthony Wayne commanded the forces that were to operate against Cornwallis, and he posted the N.J. militia of Gen. Wm. Winds at New Tappan while the 3d Cont'l. Lt. Dragoons of Lt. Col. George Baylor occupied Old Tappan, two and a half miles away. Cornwallis

saw an opportunity to cut off and annihilate Wayne. Lt. Col. Campbell was
to leave Knyphausen's column, cross
the Hudson, and attack New Tappan
with the 71st Regt. and Simcoe's Rangers. This part of the plan was abandoned, however, when boats failed to
arrive. The other British column was
to attack Baylor at Old Tappan, and
Gen. "No-flint" Grey of PAOLI fame
led what D. S. Freeman says "might be
regarded as a text-book model of the
surprise of a detachment." (Washington, V, 77 n.) After a successful
approach under cover of darkness, undoubtedly with the assistance of Tory
guides, Grey's men silenced a 12-man
guard and surrounded three barns in
which about 100 troopers were sleeping. They then charged in with the
bayonet to kill about 30 and capture 50.
Ten of the prisoners were officers, including Baylor; Maj. Alexander Clough
was mortally wounded. About 40 escaped the initial onslaught, but Baylor's small regiment was destroyed as
a fighting force.

Gen. Winds and his militia had retreated when their position appeared to
be menaced, and Winds' failure to inform Baylor may in some measure account for the latter's lack of security.
An impressive collection of affidavits
was assembled to support the charge
that Grey's officers had ordered their
men to give no quarter. (See Thacher,
Journal, 150 ff.)

TAPPAN SEA (now Tappan Zee,
Hudson R.), N.Y. 12–18 July '76.
(N.Y. CAMPAIGN) On 12 July, 10 days
after the British build-up started on
Staten Island, the warships Phoenix
(40) and Rose (20) with a schooner
and two tenders ran the American batteries that were supposed to be guarding the entrance to the Hudson and
sailed 40 miles up that river to anchor,
virtually unscathed, in Tappan Sea. On

3 Aug. Lt. Col. Benj. TUPPER led five
small boats in a gallant but unsuccessful
attack against the flotilla. On 16 Aug.
an attack by fire rafts also failed, although the Phoenix was seriously threatened and the British commander was
so alarmed by this attempt that he
withdrew; rerunning the gauntlet, he rejoined the fleet on the 18th.

This naval demonstration demoralized
the Americans, showing that British
ships could move at will against the
flanks and rear of the main army in
and around N.Y.C. Washington and his
generals were further bewildered as to
Howe's strategy—where would he move
from Staten Island? As for the immediate purpose of the naval demonstration,
other than testing American defenses,
and preparing for a link-up with Burgoyne's expected advance from Canada,
Washington supposed that it was to cut
the flow of American supplies by water
and land along the Hudson, or to supply
arms to Loyalists in the region. (Freeman, Washington, IV, 136)

One serious aspect of the affair was
the ludicrously poor performance of
many American troops: not more than
half the artillerists went to their guns,
and these scored only a few insignificant hits in firing almost 200 shots at
close range; several men were killed and
wounded because they carelessly failed
to sponge their guns; hundreds of troops
neglected their duties to play spectator.
(Ibid.)

TAR AND FEATHERS. A form of
punishment in which the victim is coated
with molten pitch or tar and then
covered with feathers. Although it was
an official punishment in England as
early as the 12th century, it is associated
in America with mob action. The Sons
of Liberty used the punishment against
Loyalists and Crown officials; a Boston
rebel got the treatment in 1755. In the
opening scenes of Oliver Wiswell, Ken-

neth Roberts gives a vivid and horrible picture of a man tarred, feathered, and ridden on a rail.

TARLETON, Banastre. 1754–1833. British officer. The young man whose name was to become anathema among Southern patriots was born in Liverpool, reared in a wealthy family of high social standing—his father was a merchant who became mayor of the city—and was educated at the University of Liverpool and Oxford. He was preparing to study law when a cornet's commission was purchased for him in the King's Dragoon Guards on 20 Apr. '75. After some training with his regiment he volunteered for service in America, was shown on the muster roll of the 1st Dragoon Guards of 24 Dec. as "absent by King's leave," and on 3 May '76 reached Cape Fear with the forces sent to join the CHARLESTON EXPEDITION of Clinton. Here he had no opportunity to distinguish himself, nor is he mentioned in connection with the operations of the N.Y. Campaign, in which he participated after sailing north with Clinton. When the 16th Light Dragoons arrived from England he was assigned to this unit (Bass, *Green Dragoon*, 18) and took part in the capture of Chas. Lee at BASKING RIDGE, N.J., 13 Dec. '76. During the next month's operations he was promoted to Capt. in Harcourt's cavalry command and appointed Brig. Maj. of the 16th Dragoons. On 8 Jan. '78 he became Capt. in the 79th Foot, and toward the end of the year was named Lt. Col. commandant of the BRITISH LEGION. He led an unsuccessful raid to POUNDRIDGE, N.Y., 2 July '79. Although he had served with sufficient distinction to catch the eye of his military superiors during the Philadelphia and Monmouth campaigns, it was not until he started his operations in the South in 1780 that the stocky little redhead, who at this time was only 26

years old, began to emerge as a legendary leader of light cavalry. Since most of the horses had been lost on the arduous sea voyage from N.Y. to Savannah, Tarleton got Clinton's permission to head for Port Royal with the dismounted troopers of the 17th Light Dragoons and of the British Legion to find mounts. Picking up a few substandard animals on this foray, he joined the column of Paterson as it moved north to reinforce Clinton around Charleston. (See CHARLESTON EXPED. of 1780 for the strategic situation at this time.) Operating as a cavalry screen ahead of Paterson, at Bee's Plantation, 23 Mar. '80, he hit a body of rebel militia and dragoons, killing 10, capturing four, and picking up a few more desperately needed mounts. After linking up with Clinton's main body around Charleston, Tarleton moved against Col. Wm. Washington, but in an action around Gov. Rutledge's plantation, 26 Mar., was driven back with the loss of a few men. The rebels captured Col. Hamilton, commander of the N.C. Royalists, and almost bagged Sir Henry Clinton. (*Ibid.*, 73)

After these preliminaries Tarleton scored his victories at MONCK'S CORNER, 14 Apr., LENUD'S FERRY, 6 May, and the WAXHAWS, 29 May '80. The names "Bloody Tarleton" and "Tarleton's Quarter" had entered the American lexicon.

At CAMDEN, 16 Aug., he was committed to exploit Cornwallis' success and to pursue the shattered force of Gates from the field. Cornwallis then sent him after Sumter, who was trying to escape after conducting his misguided secondary operations. Tarleton trailed the Gamecock, surprised him at FISHING CREEK (Catawba Ford), 18 Aug., and annihilated his force of partisans and regulars.

Tarleton was desperately ill with a

fever soon after the KINGS MOUNTAIN campaign started and his Legion performed poorly under his subordinates. (At WILLIAMSON'S, 12 July '80, WAHAB'S, 21 Sept., and CHARLOTTE, 26 Sept. '80) Before he completely recovered, Tarleton left part of his cavalry with Cornwallis around Winnsboro, S.C., made an unsuccessful attempt to eliminate the threat of Francis MARION to the British supply line, but was called back to meet a more serious menace around Winnsboro (brought on by the British failure at FISHDAM FORD, 9 Nov. '80).

Although Sumter fought him to a standstill at BLACKSTOCKS, 20 Nov. '80, the Gamecock was temporarily eliminated. Bigger things were shaping up, however, and Cornwallis sent Tarleton off to deal with what promised to be a serious threat in another quarter, this time deep to his rear.

At COWPENS, 17 Jan. '81, Tarleton was thoroughly licked when Daniel Morgan suddenly halted a desperate retreat and turned to fight a battle that has been hailed as a military masterpiece. The cocky young commander now found himself the butt of pent-up animosity of British officers in Cornwallis' army, particularly the older ones who, of course, had known all along that Tarleton lacked the "military maturity" to command anything but a partisan raid or a cavalry charge. Some fine officers and veteran troops had been lost, and their surviving messmates held Tarleton personally responsible. He finally submitted his resignation, but this was not accepted by the C. in C. Tarleton's military reputation might well have been lost at the Cowpens, as some writers jumped to conclude, but subsequent events do not support this pat contention. (See also the comments under COWPENS.)

At TARRANT'S TAVERN, N.C., 1 Feb. '81, less than two weeks after Cowpens,

Tarleton was back in form, and little more was seen of the N.C. militia as Greene retreated to the Dan River. At WETZELL'S MILLS, 6 Mar., he performed well in support of the infantry. In the major engagement at GUILFORD C. H., 15 Mar., he had a heavy advance guard action, and despite a wound that cost him two fingers he stayed in the saddle to lead a cavalry attack in the final phase of the battle. He was wounded again.

Marching with Cornwallis to Va., he conducted a long raid to CHARLOTTESVILLE, Va., 4 June, and an even more spectacular—although relatively useless —one covered under TARLETON'S VA. RAID, 9–24 July '81. During the Yorktown siege he was posted across the river from Cornwallis' main body and had a dramatic personal encounter with another *beau sabreur* at GLOUCESTER, 3 Oct. '81.

Early in 1782 he was paroled to England, and on 25 Dec. was appointed Lt. Col. of light dragoons. After an unsuccessful attempt to enter Parliament in 1784, he was returned for Liverpool in 1790 and until 1806 was in and out of Parliament. He had some qualifications as a speaker, but his ignorance of mercantile matters and his pursuit of pleasure made him of little value to his Liverpool constituents. (*D.N.B.*) He formed a liaison with the fascinating Perdita, an author-actress (Mary Robinson) and former mistress of the then 18-year-old Prince of Wales (who became George IV). In 1781 he published his *History . . . ,* which is of considerable value for its details on minor actions in which he participated and for the inclusion of reports and other documents, but "is marred by the author's vanity and by his attacks on Cornwallis." (*E.B.*) Col. Roderick Mackenzie, whose personal experience at COWPENS left him with a low opinion of Tarleton, attacked the History in his *Strictures* ..., also published in 1781. Tarleton published a revised edition in 1787.

Having been a half-pay Lt. Col. since 24 Oct. '83, he returned to the army, was promoted to Col. on 18 Nov. '90, and to Maj. Gen. on 3 Oct. '94. Toward the end of 1798 he went to Portugal but got himself recalled almost immediately when he found his duties too limited. On 25 Sept. 1803 he became commander of the Cork Military District (encompassing much of southern Ireland), and on 23 Feb. '08 became governor in Berwick and Holy Island. On 21 Jan. '12 he was commissioned a full general. Created baronet on 6 Nov. '15, he was knighted on 20 May '20. He married Susan Pricilla, natural daughter of Robert Bertie, fourth duke of Ancaster, but on 25 Jan. '33 died childless.

"As a leader of cavalry," writes Christopher Ward, "he was unmatched on either side for alertness and rapidity of movement, dash, daring and vigor of attack. As a man, he was cold-hearted, vindictive, and utterly ruthless. He wrote his name in letters of blood all across the history of the war in the South." (*W.O.R.*, 701) Virtually forgotten today in England, he is remembered in America.

TARLETON'S LEGION. See BRITISH LEGION.

"TARLETON'S QUARTER." This cynical term for "no quarter" was coined after Tarleton's victory at the WAXHAWS, S.C., 29 May '80.

TARLETON'S VIRGINIA RAID OF 9-24 July '81. (VA. MIL. OPNS.) With orders to destroy public and private stores, Tarleton was directed to ride through Prince Edward C. H. to New London, Va., more than 150 miles west of Cornwallis' new base at Suffolk. Tarleton left Cobham (opposite Jamestown Island) on 9 July and rode through Petersburg, Amelia C. H., Prince Edward C. H., Charlotte, New London, and Bedford. Here he camped in the rich grasslands at the foot of the Blue Ridge for two days and collected some of the finest horses in America. The Va. militia had again proved impotent, and Wayne was sent into Amelia County with his Pa. Cont'ls. to try to intercept Tarleton's return. Dan Morgan was posted with a strong force at Goode's Bridge, near Petersburg, for the same purpose. Warned of this threat, Tarleton burned his three light wagons and returned by a more southerly route through Lunenburg co. Despite intense July heat, which limited his movement to the early morning and late afternoon, Tarleton covered 30 or 40 miles a day and outran all news of his location; he was never in danger. On 24 July he rode into Suffolk, having covered 400 miles in 15 days. It was a remarkable performance, but Tarleton comments in his *Campaigns* that:

"The stores destroyed, either of a public or private nature, were not in quantity or value equivalent to the damage sustained in the skirmishes on the route, and the loss of men and horses by the excessive heat of the climate." (Quoted in Bass, *Green Dragoon*, 182)

TARRANT, Sarah. See SALEM, Mass., 26 Feb. '75.

TARRANT'S TAVERN, N.C., 1 Feb. '81. After Cornwallis crossed the Catawba at Cowan's Ford, Tarleton moved swiftly to this place, about 10 miles from the river, to strike a body of Davidson's militia assembling there. Although outnumbered, Tarleton decided to risk an attack. Stung by their commander's taunt to "Remember the Cowpens," Tarleton's dragoons charged and routed the militia. He claimed to have killed almost 50, wounded many in the pursuit, and to have dispersed more than 500 with a loss of seven men and 20 horses. According to other authorities the militia numbered between 100 and 300, and only 10 dead bodies were seen by a British officer who rode over the battlefield soon after the action. (Ward, *W.O.R.*, 917 *n.*, citing Irving, *Washington*, IV, 251, G. W. Greene, *Greene*, III, 157, and Stedman, II, 329 *n.*) Tarleton may have exaggerated the odds, and he neglects to mention that the weapons of the militiamen had been wet by rain so that few would fire, but history bears out his boast that the action "diffused such a terror among the inhabitants that the King's troops passed through the most hostile part of North Carolina without a shot from the militia." He narrowly missed capturing Gen. Greene in his pursuit immediately after the action. See also TORRENCE'S TAVERN.

TAXATION, external and internal. One of the new political theories advocated by the colonists and their supporters in England (e.g., Wm. Pitt) was a distinction between external and internal taxes. Originally, the Americans conceded that Parliament had the right to lay external taxes, such as customs duties on imports, but had no right to lay internal taxes, such as those prescribed by the Stamp Act. The TOWNSHEND REVENUE ACT cleverly laid no internal taxes, thereby "honoring" the colonists' distinction, while taking advantage of their failure to adopt a strong position prior to 1765 against all forms of parliamentary taxation (Miller, *O.A.R.*, 258). The purpose of the MASSACHUSETTS CIRCULAR LETTER was to organize American resistance to all forms of parliamentary taxation, whether external or internal.

TAXATION WITHOUT REPRESENTATION IS TYRANNY. There was no disagreement either in England or in America as to the truth of this ringing phrase, which had been raised by John Hampden in England in 1637 against Charles I and which, almost a century and a half later, became the watchword of the Revolution. But "in England, that phrase meant only that neither King George nor his ministers could lay a tax without getting the consent of Parliament, while in America only the assembly elected by those to be taxed could exercise such power." (Van Tyne, *England and America,* 103) It was generally accepted in England that the Crown did not have the right to tax the colonies. (Miller, *O.A.R.*, 31) A decision of 1724 established that an English colony could be taxed only by Parliament or by a representative body chosen by the colony. (*Ibid.*) At first, however, the Americans made a distinction between England's rights with respect to external and internal taxation (see entry above).

As for "representation," the English contended that "Parliament represented not men but estates—[meaning such groups as] lawyers, doctors, commercial classes, landed gentry" (Van Tyne, *op. cit.,* 101); hence the colonist had as much "representation" as many other Englishmen. The Americans argued that this was not true representation. Since the representation they wanted was geographically impossible, they were really saying *"taxation* is tyranny."

Despite the decision of 1724, Parliament unwisely waited until 1764 to levy a tax on the colonies; this strengthened the American argument that taxing them was unconstitutional. "The decision of Parliament to hold its hand until after the colonies had become sufficiently strong to offer successful resistance proved one of the cardinal mistakes of British colonial policy." (Miller, *op. cit.,* 31)

"Taxation without representation is

tyranny" became the slogan of the American Revolution, and it deserves recognition as an almost perfect instrument of propaganda. John Adams credits James Otis with coining the phrase in his famous oration against the Writs of Assistance on 24 Feb. '61. Since no formal record was made of this speech, and since the memory of John Adams was notoriously bad (e.g., on the date the Decl. of INDEP. was signed), this evidence of Adams cannot be proved. Although the slogan is generally attributed to Otis, it probably was coined— or popularized—by him in 1764 or 1765. (W. S. Carpenter, *D.A.H.*)

See sketch of Daniel DULANY for more subtle argument.

TAYLOR, George. 1716–1781. Signer. Ireland–Pa. What is reasonably certain about Taylor's early life is that he settled in Chester co., Pa., in 1736, became clerk in an iron works, rose to the position of manager, and in 1742 married a widow whose legacy hastened his "arrival" in the province. (She died in 1768.) Whether he had been a "bound boy" after running away from home, and whether he married the widow of his employer (Appleton's), is not established. In any event, Taylor prospered as a businessman in Chester co. until about 1754 and after that in Bucks co. Much of the time after 1763 he lived in Easton, in Northampton co., but most of his commercial interests remained at Durham in Bucks co. In 1764 he was elected to the first of five one-year terms in the provincial assembly. He opposed the majority, led by Franklin, in advocating overthrow of crown rule. He was a member of the local committee to choose delegates for the Stamp Act Cong., and he later was chairman of the Northampton county meeting to protest the Boston Port Bill in 1774. After being named to the county Comm. of Corresp., in July '75 he became Col. of militia, and on 20 July '76 he became a delegate to the Cont'l. Cong. when it was decided to replace the representatives who refused to sign the Decl. of Indep. He became a Signer on 2 Aug., but resigned from Cong. in Mar. '77 after taking no other part in the business of Cong. other than to treat with the Susquehanna border Indians in Jan. '77. Nor did he take any active part as a militia officer, although he retained the title of Col. He sat briefly in the supreme executive council of his state, but retired for ill health after six weeks. "He had been a moderate radical, whose attitude was largely provincial, and whose interest in politics was never absorbing," writes Joseph E. Johnson in *D.A.B.* He left five illegitimate children by his housekeeper; a legitimate son predeceased his father but left a large family.

TEA ACT. 10 May '73. To save the corrupt and mismanaged East India Tea Co. from bankruptcy, Parliament authorized it to send half a million pounds of tea to America for sale with payment of only the nominal 3d. a pound American duty and with reimbursement for the English duty previously paid. This meant that East India Co. tea could undersell smuggled Dutch tea as well as legally imported tea. Consignees were designated in New York, Charleston, Philadelphia, and Boston to receive the shipment.

The Philadelphia consignees were forced to resign by a committee that had been appointed for this purpose by a mass meeting on 16 Oct. '73. The New York consignees resigned after harbor pilots were warned not to board the tea ships and the Sons of Liberty branded tea importers as enemies of America. The Charleston tea ship arrived 2 Dec., the consignees were forced to resign the next day, and the tea was impounded after lapse of the prescribed 20-day waiting period. In July '76 it was auctioned by the Revolutionary government.

In Boston, a town meeting on 5 and 6 Nov. endorsed the Philadelphia resolves, but the consignees would not resign. This led to the BOSTON TEA PARTY.

TEARCOAT SWAMP, S.C., 25 Oct. '80. With instructions from Gates to continue his harassment of the enemy's rear, Francis MARION called for the militia and established a base at PORT'S FERRY. On 24 Oct. he learned that Col. Samuel Tynes was assembling Tory militia near Tearcoat (or Tarcoat) Swamp, in the vicinity of where U.S. Hwy. 301 now crosses Black River. (Bass, *Swamp Fox*, 254) With the 150 men he now had raised, Marion undertook a fast march, surprised the enemy by an attack shortly after midnight, and routed them with the loss of three dead, 14 wounded, 23 prisoners, 80 good horses captured with their bridles, saddles, and blankets, and 80 new muskets. More important, however, the Tory uprising was completely squelched and many of the Tories joined Marion. There apparently were no patriot casualties. (*Ibid.*, 74–77)

TEISSEDRE DE FLEURY, François Louis. 1749–? French volunteer. Born into a noble Provençal family, he was a volunteer in the infantry regiment of Roergue starting 15 May '68, became a Lt. within five months, and on 5 Feb. '72 was promoted to *sous aide major*. The following information is from a memorandum in the archives of the French War Ministry. The Sieur de Fleury was given a captain's commission in 1776 and authorized leave to serve in America with Coudray. When Congress refused to employ Coudray and his officers, Fleury joined the army as a volunteer. In the affair of Piscataway, N.J., 10 May '77, he distinguished himself and was commissioned Capt. of Engrs. on the 22d. (Date and arm of

service is from Heitman.) Continuing from the French memorandum, Fleury surveyed the area around Philadelphia, sounded the Delaware, fortified Billingsport, and then performed the action described in the following Congressional resolution dated 13 Sept. '77:

"... whereas Congress has received information [from Washington] that Monsieur Lewis de Fleury, during very gallant exertions in the late battle of Brandywine, near Birmingham Meeting-House, had his horse shot under him, resolved that the Quartermaster-General present him with a horse, as a testimonial of the sense Congress have of Monsieur de Fleury's merit." (Quoted in Heitman)

The French source comments that only Benedict Arnold got a similar honor from Congress. This horse was killed under Fleury at Germantown and the officer was wounded in the leg (Heitman does not mention this). The preceding day, 3 Oct. '77, he was appointed Brigade Maj. to Pulaski. He withstood the siege of Ft. Mifflin during six weeks and was wounded on 15 Nov., the day the fort was evacuated. Promoted to Lt. Col. of Engrs. on 26 Nov., he went to work on a project of attacking British shipping on the Delaware with rocket-propelled boats—"*des bâteaux minces qui devaient se mouvoir par la répulsion de fusées à pétard.*" (Lasseray, 428) This scheme was interrupted by orders to join Lafayette for the abortive expedition into Canada, and he spent the rest of the winter training troops. On 27 Apr. '78 Washington appointed him an assistant I.G. to Steuben. During the Monmouth Campaign he was second in command of an elite unit, the chasseurs of Lee's Div. When d'Estaing reached Newport, Fleury was ordered there; he took part in the attack, in the rear guard action, and was commended by the French commander for his ability and personal qualities.

Fleury's performance at STONY POINT eclipsed his other achievements, and he was voted one of only eight Congressional MEDALS bestowed during the nine years of the war. Congress wrote him that they hoped his own country would reward him suitably for this action and also asked La Luzerne to report to the French court on his gallant conduct. On Washington's advice Fleury requested a nine-month leave (to collect his rewards?), but wrote Congress that he hoped this valuable officer would then return to America. On 27 Sept. '79 he was granted this leave (Heitman), on 19 Mar. '80 he was promoted to Maj. in the Saintonge Regt., and he returned with Rochambeau to America (Lasseray). On 22 May Congress extended his leave, a paperwork exercise to enable him to serve with the French forces. His discharge from the American army was dated 1 Jan. '82, according to Lasseray; although Heitman has no information about his return to America from leave, the French military records note: "1781, distinguished himself in the capture of York[town]." Furthermore, he was made Chevalier de Saint Louis for his service at Yorktown.

His subsequent career is outlined as follows in the records: 16 Jan. '84, Col. of Pondichéry Regt.; May–Nov. '85, C. in C. of the Isles of Bourbon and Maurice; Apr. '90, returned to France; 30 June '91, promoted to *maréchal de camp*. In 1791 he fought at Montmédy, Givet, Cambrai, and Valenciennes. In rallying the rear elements of his troop in the retreat from Mons, he was trapped under his wounded horse and trampled by an enemy cavalry charge. After convalescing 18 months he resigned on 24 June '92, two months before his 43d birthday. Appleton's says he was executed in Paris in 1794. The last entry

in the records cited by Lasseray is that he was given a pension of 4,228 francs on 7 June '96.

TERNAY, Charles Louis d'Arsac, Chevalier de. 1722–1780. French Adm. Of an old Breton family with a naval tradition, he entered the French naval school in 1738. After taking part in the unsuccessful defense of Louisburg in 1757 he commanded a division of gunboats on the St. Lawrence. Promoted to Capt., he commanded two frigates in a raid that captured St. John, New Brunswick, 2 June '62, taking several merchant vessels and ruining the cod fisheries along the coast. After the peace of 1763 he served on the Leeward Islands station and later was promoted to B.G. of the naval forces. In 1772 he retired as *chef d'escadre*, was appointed Gov.-Gen. of the island of Bourbon, and left this post in 1779 to re-enter the active service. Early the next year he organized the fleet that was to escort the expeditionary force of Rochambeau to America. With eight ships of the line, two frigates, and two bomb-galliots he arrived off Newport on 10 July '80, just three days before a British fleet under Adm. Thomas Graves arrived off Sandy Hook to give the British an advantage of 13 more powerful ships of the line against Ternay's eight. (One of these was being used as a transport.) The British eventually got around to bottling up Ternay's fleet in Newport, but they have been criticized for failing to move in and destroy it. (See Mahan, *Sea Power,* 394–97) The Americans, on the other hand, were bitterly disappointed to find that they had to spend an inactive season because the French could not achieve the all-important naval superiority. Ternay died on 15 Dec. '80 in Newport of a fever that had not become critical until the last two days. Lafayette wrote that he suspected Ternay's death was caused by the grief of being blockaded. "He was a very rough and obstinate man, but firm and clear in all his views," wrote the Marquis, "and, taking all things into consideration, we have sustained a great loss." (*Memoirs*, ed. 1837, I, 384)

The French fleet was commanded by Adm. Destouches until the arrival of Adm. Barras in May '81.

TEST OATH. To force a declaration of principles from those who were indifferent or were secret enemies of the Revolution, state legislatures enacted "test" laws. The oath demanded by these laws varied in the different colonies that adopted the laws, but in general they prescribed loyalty to the patriot cause, disloyalty to the British government, and a promise not to aid and abet the enemy. In the test acts passed before the Decl. of Indep., "the oath of abjuration and allegiance was omitted." (Van Tyne, *Loyalists*, 131) The British offered various inducements to Americans to swear an oath of allegiance. See PEACE COMMISSION OF THE HOWES for their offer of 30 Nov. '76, and the efforts of Patrick Ferguson during the KINGS MOUNTAIN campaign.

THACHER, James. 1754–1844. Cont'l. surgeon and diarist. Mass. Of an old but undistinguished family in America—Ant[h]ony Thacher or Thatcher came from England in 1635—James was the son of a poor farmer and had no formal education. It was, however, his good fortune to be apprenticed at the age of 16 to Abner Hersey, the leading physician of his home town of Barnstable, and James received five years of arduous training. (*D.A.B.*) According to Heitman his first military appointment was as surgeon's mate of Whitcomb's Mass. Regt. in July '75, but in his own *Military Journal* he records that he applied for assignment to the provincial hospital in Cambridge, was accepted by the medical examiners on the 10th, and started his duties there on 15 July. Writing of this experience he tells of another examination of medical candidates in which one was asked how he would induce a sweat in a patient to remedy rheumatism. "I would have him examined by a medical committee," the candidate replied. (*Op. cit.*, 22, 28–29)

In Feb. '76 young Dr. Thacher was promoted to serve as assistant to David Townsend in Asa Whitcomb's Mass. Regt. on Prospect Hill, according to *D.A.B.*, but Heitman has him assigned as surgeon's mate of this regiment from July '75 to 31 Dec. '76, the unit being designated the 6th Cont'l. Inf. during 1776. He marched with the reinforcements to Canada, took part in the retreat from Ticonderoga (CANADA INVASION), and on 1 Apr. '77 was assigned as hospital surgeon's mate. (Heitman) After a long period in the General Hospital in Albany he returned to the field (*D.A.B.*), being assigned as surgeon of JACKSON'S REGT. on 10 Nov. '78, and remaining with it when it was redesignated the 16th Mass. (23 July 80). On 1 Jan. '81 he transferred to the 9th Mass. During the preceding period he took part in the Penobscot Expedition, spent the arduous winter of 1779–80 in N.J., witnessed the execution of John André, and served in the elite corps of Col. Scammell in the Yorktown Camp'n. Heitman shows 1 Jan. '83 as the date of his retirement; *D.A.B.* says 1 July '83.

Thacher is famous for his *Military Journal during the American Revolutionary War*. This was published in 1823, with a second edition in 1827, was reprinted as *Military Journal* in 1854 and 1862, and as *The American Revolution* at least six times between 1856 and 1862. (*D.A.B.*) The edition at my elbow is the *Military Journal* of 1862, whose page references I have used throughout the present book.

Thacher's *Military Journal* (as it generally is cited) is "a remarkable historical document" (*D.A.B.*), written in a lively style, and valuable for its accurate portrayal of the army and its senior commanders (particularly Washington, Lafayette and Steuben). Since it is not limited to those matters of which Thacher had firsthand knowledge I have specified the phases of the war in which he personally participated. "Unfortunately, Thacher failed to give many details of his hospital experiences, except in regard to smallpox inoculation, which he carried out on a large scale." (*D.A.B.*)

After the war he became a prominent physician in Plymouth, and produced books on medicine and contemporary medical biography (*The American Medical Biography*, 1828). He also wrote on agriculture (*The American Orchardist*, 1822 and 1825; *Management of Bees*, 1829), on *Demonology, Ghosts, and Apparitions* (1831), and the *History of the Town of Plymouth* (1832 and 1835).

He was short, slender, and sociable, but the latter quality did not interfere with his reading and writing.

"THE WORLD TURNED UPSIDE DOWN." The 1828 edition of Garden's *Anecdotes of the Revolution* is responsible for the much-repeated statement that the forces of Cornwallis marched out of Yorktown with their bands playing a piece called "The World Turned Upside Down," and also for the implication that the tune was played repeatedly. The only thing that can be said with certainty is that a piece of music by this name did exist, and that it was popular during the Revolution; as a matter of fact, there were several tunes known by this name. It also seems certain that various pieces of music were played during the surrender ceremonies, and that bands and pipers participated, not just drummers.

"The version which has the strongest support in tradition and which ... we would like to believe was played appeared in the *Gentleman's Magazine* of 1766, beginning 'Goody Bull and her daughter fell out,' " says C. & M. (pp. 1246–48, where the words are reproduced but not the music). Nothing about "the world turned upside down" appears in the words of this song, however. The same authorities (C. & M.) give another song for which a case has been made and in which the words do appear:

If Buttercups buzzed after the bee,
If boats were on land, churches on sea,

***

[If] Summer were spring and the t'other way round,
Then all the world would be upside down.

Freeman has examined this mystery with assistance from the Music Division of the Library of Congress, and he reproduces the score of the piece called "When the King Enjoys His Own Again," from which was adapted (among almost numberless other songs and ballads) one called "The World Turned Upside Down." The Library of Congress says it is generally assumed that this is the tune and Freeman furnishes additional support for this theory. (*Op. cit.*, 388–89)

Bass says the British soldiers were amused by this choice of music, "for they knew the tune as the old Jacobite serenade to Prince Charlie: 'When the King Enjoys His Own Again'!" (*Green Dragoon*, 4) (See CULLODEN) The British are supposed to have played this same tune when they retreated from SALEM, Mass., 26 Feb. '75; if true, this is really stranger than fiction.

THICKETTY FORT, (Fort Anderson), S.C., 30 July '80. In one of the actions that preceded the Battle of KINGS MOUNTAIN, Col. Isaac Shelby led 600 men against the Loyalist post at Thicketty Fort, on the headwaters of the Pacolet, 10 miles S.E. of Cowpens, and without firing a shot succeeded in making the garrison surrender. Although Fisher gives 13 July as the date of this action (*Struggle*, II, 344), more recent authorities give the date of 30 July (A. A.–Heitman; *D.A.B.*, "Shelby").

THOMAS, John. 1724–1776. Cont'l. general. Mass. Grandson of an early settler in Mass., John Thomas was authorized on 1 Mar. '46 by Gov. Shirley to practice medicine in the army, and the next year he served under Gen. Waldo in Nova Scotia. He returned to this region in the operations of 1755 and 1759–60, having meanwhile progressed in military rank from surgeon's mate and Lt. with authority to enlist volunteers (1755) to militia Col. (*D.A.B.*) In 1760 he commanded a regiment in Amherst's advance down Lake Champlain and led the left wing in his capture of Montreal, 8 Sept. '60. (Appleton's) (See COLONIAL WARS) For the next 15 years he was engaged primarily in practicing medicine at Kingston, Mass. In 1770 Gov. Hutchinson appointed him J.O.P. When the revolutionary movement started he joined the Sons of Liberty, raised a volunteer regiment, and on 25 May '75 was notified of his appointment as Lt. Gen. (*sic*) of Mass. troops. (Freeman, *Washington*, III, 478 *n*.)

In his 50th year at this time, he stood an erect six feet tall; he had a distinguished face and a commanding presence. (*Ibid.*) When Congress prepared their 22 June '75 list of B.G.'s they carelessly neglected to consider state military seniority. Among the problems this created was the appointment of the mediocre Heath and the superannuated Pomeroy (who was 69) over the capable Thomas. Washington knew Thomas only by reputation (*ibid.*, 499), but when he wrote Congress his first detailed report of conditions he found on reaching the Boston lines, he hinted broadly that the civil authorities should do something about the blunder they had made in Thomas' case. (*Ibid.*) Since Pomeroy had declined his appointment, Congress was able to solve the problem by making Thomas the senior of the eight new B.G.'s, vice Pomeroy. (*Ibid.*, 501) Meanwhile Thomas had conducted himself with decorum and had demonstrated his superiority as a military leader. He was charged with the critical operation on DORCHESTER HEIGHTS, 2–27 Mar. '76, and gained even higher esteem in the eyes of Washington and the Boston army.

On 6 Mar. '76 Thomas was promoted to Maj. Gen. and ordered north, where disaster had already struck the CANADA INVASION. He left Roxbury on 22 Mar., reached Albany on the 28th, and on 1 May took command of the American army around Quebec. The very next day he got the bad news that a British relief expedition was coming up the St. Lawrence, and on 6 May he had to start a demoralized and disorganized retreat toward Montreal. He came down with the smallpox that was decimating his army and died on 2 June at Sorel.

The Thomas Papers are in the Mass. Hist. Soc. Collections. The standard biography is Charles Coffin, *The Life and Services of Major General John Thomas* (1844).

THOMPSON, Benjamin, Count Rumford. 1753–1814. Colonial administrator, physicist, Loyalist. Mass.–N.H. Justly famous as one of America's leading scientists, he is remembered also as "one who always had a kick ready for the underdog." (Van Tyne, *War of Indep.*, 26–27) Another authority writes: "Throughout his life Thompson seems to have neglected no opportunity for his own advancement. He knew how to ingratiate himself with men of powerful position, and incurred the enmity of those of lesser rank." (T. L. Davis in *D.A.B.*) *Antipathique* as he may have been as a man, however, he is credited with these scientific honors: establishment of the Rumford medals in the Royal Society for work in the field of heat or light, establishment of a similar award for the American Academy of Arts and Sciences, and his founding of the Rumford professorship of physics at Harvard. He developed a nonsmoking and highly efficient fireplace known as the "Rumford Roaster" that came into extensive use in Great Britain and America after its introduction around 1796.

Thompson was descended from James Thompson, who settled in Woburn, Mass., in 1642. Early in his schooling he showed an interest in and aptitude for scientific matters, and in 1771 he started studying medicine. The next year he married Sarah Walker, the wealthy widow of Col. Benj. Rolfe. She was 14 years his senior. Gov. Wentworth was so impressed by his appearance and family connections that he appointed him, over the heads of more qualified persons, to a majority in the 2d Prov. Regt. of N.H. "Thompson's indebtedness to Governor Wentworth committed him in a manner to the British or Loyalist side in the Revolutionary War," writes Davis, though he seems at first to have had no strong inclination toward one side or the other." (*D.A.B.*) In the summer of 1774, however, Thompson faced the first of two inquisitions into his "patriotism." Both times he was cleared for lack of evidence. He associated with patriots of Mass. and is said to have applied for a commission in the Cont'l. army, but, probably because N.H. officers disap-

proved, his application was rejected and he went into the British camp. Leaving his home town of Woburn on 13 Oct. '75, he boarded the frigate *Scarborough* at Newport. The vessel remained in Boston harbor until the British evacuated that place in Mar. '76, and Thompson sailed with her to England. Germain gave Thompson a position in the Colonial Office and then appointed him to the sinecure of Sec. of Ga. In Sept. '80 he became under-secretary of state for the Northern Dept., and later he was commissioned Lt. Col. of cavalry for service in America. He served in America, seeing some action around Charleston in Mar. '82 and commanding a regiment on Long Island, N.Y., until Apr. '83. (*D.A.B.*)

In Aug. '83, having returned to England, he was made Col. of the King's American Dragoons and was retired on half pay. He was knighted on 23 Feb. '84 and for the next 11 years he served the elector of Bavaria as minister of war, minister of police, and grand chamberlain. In 1791 he was made count of the Holy Roman Empire and chose his title of Rumford from the township of his wife, which was later named Concord, N.H. He and his first wife had separated after four years of marriage and never saw each other again. In 1805 he married the widow of Lavoisier, but her predilections for a busy social life and Thompson's love of tranquility led to their separation amicably in 1809. He left England for good, set up his residence outside Paris at Auteuil, and sent for his daughter Sarah (1774–1852). All this while he had continued his scientific studies— working on gunpowder after his first arrival in London in 1776, later becoming interested in heat, and experimenting with traction in Auteuil.

His private papers, including materials for an autobiography, were stolen in 1795 while he was visiting England. His *Complete Works,* 4 vols., were published during the years 1870–75. One biography is *Count Rumford of Mass.* (1935), by J. A. Thompson. Chapters are devoted to him in Bernard Jaffe, *Men of Science in America* ... (1944) and D. S. Jordan (ed.), *Leading American Men of Science* (1910). Using the new evidence of the Gage Papers, Allen French concludes in *General Gage's Informers* that "it seems clear that we have disproved the old story that Thompson was faithful to the provincial cause until forced out of it by his enemies." That he was a paid informer of Gage is suspected but unproved, points out this same author, but there is documentary evidence to establish that he was useful to the British in returning their deserters to Boston in 1774, and that he wrote letters in invisible ink to a correspondent in Boston, giving military information. "After all, if we consider the matter in the light of Thompson's known characteristics, there is nothing surprising in his being a loyalist. The surprise lies in his pretending for so long to be otherwise." (French, *op. cit.,* 115–46)

THOMPSON, William. 1736–1781. Cont'l. general. Pa. Born in Ireland, he settled near Carlisle and became a surveyor and J.O.P. He served as a Capt. under John Armstrong (Sr.) in the expedition of Pa. troops against the Indian settlements at Kittanning, Pa., 8 Sept. '56, and after the French and Indian War took part in locating lands granted to officers on the western frontier of the province. Having been active in patriot politics, he was appointed commander of a rifle battalion raised in southeast Pa. when news of Bunker Hill was received. (Edward E. Curtis in *D.A.B.*) The commission was dated 25 June '75, and his unit was known as Thompson's Pa. Rifle Bn. (or Regt.)

until the reorganization of 1 Jan. '76, when it became the 1st Cont'l. Inf. (Heitman, 47) Although Congress had called for only six rifle companies from Pa., so many volunteers turned out that nine companies were organized with Thompson as Col. and Edward Hand as second in command.

After a remarkable march to join the Boston army and after making an impression on the New England Yankees with their rugged appearance and magnificent marksmanship, the unruly frontiersmen turned out to be more trouble than they were worth in the Boston Siege. (See RIFLEMEN) Thompson commanded the attack on LECHMERE POINT, 9 Nov. '75, and although commended the next day in general orders, Washington subsequently realized that the operation had been less admirable than indicated by the first reports.

Although "Washington privately opposed an excessively responsible assignment for William Thompson, whose seniority seemed to him to be more fortuitously conferred than valiantly earned" (Freeman, *Washington,* IV, 73 and 84), Congress appointed him to B.G. on 1 Mar. '76, before receiving Washington's views. He was named to command the first reinforcements being sent to Canada, and on 21 Apr. he sailed up the Hudson with the regiments of Bond, Greaton, Paterson, and Poor. Thompson commanded the disastrous attack at TROIS RIVIÈRES, 8 June '76, in which hard luck more than poor leadership caused the American defeat. He was captured and although back in Philadelphia on parole two months later, it was four years before his exchange was effected. Meanwhile he became so offensive in accusing Congressman Thos. McKean of hindering his exchange that he was censured by Congress on 23 Nov. '78. Called before this body he apologized, but McKean pressed a libel suit, was awarded damages of £5,700, and then released Thompson from payment. He died on 3 Sept. '81, less than a year after being exchanged for Baron Riedesel. Despite an unruly temperament and Washington's reservations about his fitness for high command, Thompson had showed the qualities of an aggressive combat leader before his career was cut short.

THOMPSON'S PENNSYLVANIA RIFLE BATTALION. Although the Cont'l. Cong. called for only six companies of RIFLEMEN from Pa., so many volunteers presented themselves that they were formed into nine companies and organized as a battalion under the command of Col. William THOMPSON. The unit was created 25 June '75 (Heitman, 47), was reorganized on 1 Jan. '76 as the 1st Cont'l. Inf., and as the 1st Pa. on 1 Jan. '77. Edward Hand was Lt. Col. of the first organization, and Robert Magaw was its Maj.

THORNTON, Matthew. *c.* 1714–1803. Signer. Ireland–Mass.–N.H. Born in Ireland of Scots-Irish ancestry, he came to America with his parents around 1718 and lived in Maine before moving to the neighborhood of Worcester, Mass. He completed his medical studies in 1740 and started a practice in the Scots-Irish colony of Londonderry, N.H. In 1745 he took part in the Louisburg expedition as an "undersurgeon," and for a period of time he was a Col. in the royal militia. In the events leading to the break with England, *D.A.B.* comments that "Thornton's career was a chronicle of revolutionary progress in that part of New England." In 1775 he was elected president of the Prov. Cong. of N.H., and the same year he became chairman of the Comm. of Safety that was, in effect, the local patriot government. In this latter position he showed real statesmanship in calling for disciplined cooperation from

his notoriously unruly people in the prosecution of the war effort. (*Ibid.*) From 1776 to 1782 he was an associate justice of the N.H. superior court, and during the war years he held a number of important posts, including speaker of the house, member of the council, and president of the constitutional convention.

His claim to fame, however, came in Nov. '76 when he belatedly took his seat in the Cont'l. Cong. and was permitted to sign the Decl. of Indep. After serving about a year, and making no other mark as a delegate, Thornton returned to resume his place in state affairs. In 1780 he moved to Merrimack co., where he no longer practiced medicine but remained active in politics. In 1784–86 he was a state senator. He had married Hannah Jack about 1760 and they had five children. After a peaceful old age on his Merrimack farm, Dr. Thornton died at the age of 89 while visiting a daughter in Newburyport, Mass.

THREADWELL'S NECK. See' TREADWELL'S.

THREE RIVERS, Can. See TROIS RIVIÈRES.

"THREE-SIDED STATES" were those which, as colonies, had sea-to-sea charters or some other claim to western land. The four-sided or nonlanded states were N.H., R.I., N.J., Pa., Del., and Md. The latter strongly supported the idea that Congress should have the power to establish the boundaries of the "landed" states; this held up ratification of the ARTICLES OF CONFEDERATION.

THROG'S POINT (Neck), N.Y. 12–18 Oct. '76. (N.Y. CAMPAIGN) To avoid Washington's strong defenses on HARLEM HEIGHTS, Gen. Howe planned an amphibious envelopment with all his forces except one brigade of Hessians and two of British, all under Percy, who would hold the lines around McGown's

Pass to cover N.Y.C. (Fortescue, *Br. Army,* III, 188) At 9 o'clock the morning of 12 Oct. about 4,000 British started landing unopposed at Throg's Point from 80 vessels that had left Kip's Bay the night before. Thick fog in Hell Gate enabled the British to navigate this difficult route unobserved. By afternoon, most of Howe's force was ashore. As soon as the British started inland, however, they found a marshy creek that could be crossed in only two places, a causeway and bridge on one side, and a ford on the other. Col. Edw. Hand's 30-man guard from his 1st Pa. Rifle Regt. (Heath's Div.), firing from concealed positions, stopped them cold. Reinforcements soon arrived to swell the defenders' ranks to 1,800 and bottle up Howe's force. (These reinforcements were Prescott's Mass. Cont'l. Regt. and a 3-pdr. at the causeway, and John Graham's N.Y. Cont'l. Regt. with a 6-pdr. at the ford. McDougall's Brig. arrived the evening of the 12th. [Heath, *Memoirs,* 81].) Frustrated, Howe took six days to prepare for his next move, the landing at PELL'S POINT. It is interesting to speculate on what would have resulted had Howe forced his way through Hand's 30 riflemen and moved against Kings Bridge, eight miles away.

(Throg's Point or Neck, which was virtually an island, being surrounded by water at high tide, was known also as Frog's or Throck's Point. It was apparently named after John Throgmorton —or Throckmorton—who settled there in 1643. Known today as Throg's Neck, it is now Ft. Schuyler Park, in the S.E. corner of the Bronx.)

THRUSTON, Charles Mynn (throo'-ston). 1738–1812. Cont'l. officer. Va. After attending William and Mary he studied theology in England, returned to Gloucester co. for ordination in the Episcopal Church, and soon thereafter moved to the Shenandoah. For his serv-ice as a militia Lt. in 1754 he was later entitled to 2,000 acres in Fincastle co., but in 1770 he became so discouraged about the prospects of actually getting this land that he sold his claim for £10 to a former companion in arms named George Washington (Freeman, *Washington,* III, 246). According to Appleton's the "warrior parson" raised a company at the beginning of the Revolution, was commissioned a Capt., was badly wounded at Trenton, and subsequently was appointed Col. Heitman does not mention this earlier service but says he became Col. of an "ADDITIONAL CONT'L. REGT." on 15 Jan. '77, lost an arm at Amboy, 8 Mar. '77, and resigned 1 Jan. '79.

After the war Thruston was a judge and member of the legislature. In 1808 he moved to La. and died four years later near New Orleans. (Appleton's) His son, Buckner (1763–1845), became a lawyer in Ky., U.S. Senator, and from 1809 until his death was U.S. judge for the D.C. Buckner's son, Charles Mynn (1789–1873), graduated from West Point in 1814, resigned as a Capt. in 1836, became mayor of Cumberland, Md., in 1861, was commissioned B.G. on 7 Sept. of that year, and resigned 17 Apr. '62 to resume his farming.

THRUSTON'S REGT. was one of the 16 "ADDITIONAL CONT'L. REGTS."

TICONDEROGA, N.Y., 1755–59. In Oct. '55 the Marquis de Lotbinière started construction of a fort the French called Carillon at the place later known as Ticonderoga. The fort was an outpost for Ft. St. Frederick (Crown Point). Montcalm was defending Ft. Carillon with 3,600 men on 8 July '58 when Abercromby attacked with 15,000. In one of the costliest failures of British history, Abercromby lost 1,944 while inflicting only 377 casualties. The popular Lord Howe, elder brother of Richard and William, was

to surrender control of its forces to a commander of another service, who might misuse them; the navy, for example, does not trust an army general to take the proper care of an expensive fleet in the support of land operations. Thus there was no unity of command in the allied operations at NEWPORT, 1778, or at Leyte Gulf (Philippine Islands), 1944. There was "cooperation."

V

"VACANT REGIMENT." German regiments (or battalions) were so called when the colonel by whose name they had been known was no longer in command. Baurmeister, for example, refers in a letter of 2 June '77 to "the Regiment vacant Rall." The latter unit was commanded in turn by Rall, Woellwarth, Trumbach, and d'Angelli; it was a "vacant regiment" during the intervening periods.

VALCOUR ISLAND (Lake Champlain), 11–13 Oct. '76. Upon collapse of the ill-fated CANADA INVASION, the British prepared a counteroffensive. Since the critical phase of such an operation was gaining control of Lake CHAMPLAIN, both sides hastened to assemble fleets. For this, see CHAMPLAIN SQUADRONS.

British land forces had been reinforced in June to about 13,000 rank and file, including Maj. Gen. von Riedesel's 5,000 German mercenaries. Carleton could not get his naval commander, Capt. Thomas Pringle, to sail until 4 Oct., but he started land operations on 10 Sept. Leaving four regiments and part of a fifth with some artillery to secure St. Johns and Chambly, he sent a younger brother, Lt. Col. Thomas Carleton, south with 400 Indians in canoes; these were reinforced later with 100 Canadian volunteers and 1,300 Germans. Gen. Simon Fraser went into position about five miles north of the N.Y. state line with the light infantry, grenadiers, and the 24th Foot. Ile aux Noix, which the British had taken in Aug. and later organized into a fortified base, was occupied by Burgoyne with six regiments (9th, 21st, 31st, 47th, Riedesel, and Hanau). On 14 Oct., Burgoyne and Fraser started forward with all but two of Carleton's British regiments (the 20th and 61st garrisoned Ile aux Noix). (All German troops were left in Canada except the Hanau artillery, which was on the *Thunderer.*) Carleton's fleet sailed from St. Johns on 4 Oct.

THE BATTLE

Having left Crown Point on 24 Aug. with the 10 craft that were ready, Arnold moved as far north as Windmill Point, near the Canadian border. Threatened in these narrow waters by some of Carleton's Indians, he withdrew to the vicinity of Cumberland Head by 19 Sept. Then, having taken soundings of the half-mile channel between rocky Valcour Island and the west shore and finding it suited to his needs, Arnold moved his fleet into this anchorage on the 23d. The day of the battle he had 15 vessels under his command: the sloop *Enterprise,* the schooners *Royal Savage* and *Revenge,* the galleys *Congress, Trumbull,* and *Washington,* the cutter *Lee,* and eight gundalows. (The *Gates* galley was not finished in time; the schooner *Liberty* was absent "on command." I subscribe to the opinion of Chapelle that the ninth gundalow, *Success,* was not present—see CHAMPLAIN SQUADRONS for discussion.)

Carleton sailed cautiously south until 10 Oct., when he learned the American fleet was near. The next day he rounded Cumberland Head with a strong wind behind him and had overshot his quarry by two miles before he realized it. The *Revenge* had sighted the oncoming British fleet as they cleared Cumberland Head at 8 A.M., and had scurried into Valcour channel to inform Arnold. Whether the latter decided on his brilliantly unorthodox plan at this time or earlier is not known, but he did have to overrule the proposal of at least one subordinate, Gen. David Waterbury, to leave the anchorage and fight a retreat south. Arnold then issued orders: the *Revenge,* which the British probably had not seen, would sail toward the enemy until spotted, then return and join the line of battle; four of the fastest vessels, *Royal Savage, Congress, Trumbull,* and *Washington,* would sally forth to do what damage they might, but also to draw the enemy into the southern end of the channel and minimize the chance that Carleton might be smart enough to come around the northern end of Valcour; other craft would form line of battle across the channel, facing south.

When Arnold left the channel (he had established his headquarters on the *Congress*) and saw the size of the enemy force, he signaled all his ships back to the line of battle. During this withdrawal, which involved beating back against a wind made treacherous by the cliffs and tall timber of the shore lines, the *Royal Savage* grounded on the S.W. tip of Valcour Island. The British schooner *Carleton* (12 6-pdrs.), aggres-sively leading the attack, blasted the unfortunate *Royal Savage* with a crippling broadside and was passing, with all sails set, along the American front when she was suddenly betrayed by this same wind and whirled straight toward American boats. Under heavy musket and cannon fire, Lt. Dacres, her commander, anchored the *Carleton;* then, with a spring in her cable, he swung her into position to fire broadside. The other British sailing vessels could not get up wind to support Dacres, but 15 or 20 gunboats (Arnold's estimate; Ward says 17) came into line with the *Carleton,* and about 12:30 a general engagement was in progress. At a range of 350 yards, with observation impeded by a haze of gun smoke, the cliffs and tall pines of the confined battleground making "the thunder of the guns ... like a helmet of sound crushed down upon us" (Kenneth Roberts), the two forces hammered away. In the absence of trained gunners, Arnold personally pointed most of the cannon fired from the *Congress.*

After about an hour the spring was shot away from the battered *Carleton,* which then turned on the anchor to face helplessly toward the converging fire of Arnold's fleet. When Pringle signaled her to withdraw, 19-year-old Midshipman Edward Pellew, in command since Dacres and the next-senior officer had been knocked out of action, climbed onto the bowsprit and tried to make a jib draw into the N.E. wind and bring her about to sail away. Unsuccessful, he remained a conspicuous target of massed cannon and musket fire until he could throw a line to two boats that came up to tow the *Carleton* to safety. (Dacres and Pellew went on to distinguished naval careers.)

The chagrined crew of the *Royal Savage* manned her guns until driven off by gunfire. A crew from the *Thun-*

derer boarded her and manned the guns until driven off by American fire. When the Americans tried to return, a crew from the *Maria* beat them to it and set her afire. After dark, the *Royal Savage* exploded when the flames reached her magazine.

The British gunboats withdrew as dusk fell (about 5 o'clock) and continued their fire until dark from a line 600 to 700 yards farther south. About the same time, the *Inflexible* managed to come up and deliver five broadsides that silenced Arnold's guns.

Carleton's Indian auxiliaries had landed on both shores of Valcour channel to deliver a harassing, but generally ineffective, musket fire from the trees.

THE PURSUIT

The British thought they had Arnold trapped and expected to destroy him the next day in Valcour channel, but Arnold had not finished outgeneraling Sir Guy. Aided by a northeast breeze, a dark night, and dense fog, Arnold's battered flotilla sailed single file along the west shore and escaped into the lake. Col. Edw. Wigglesworth led with the *Trumbull* at 7 P.M.; the *Congress* and *Washington* brought up the rear. (Two vessels remained in the channel: the *Royal Savage* and a gundalow, the *Philadelphia,* which sank an hour after the battle ended.) About three hours after the *Trumbull* had started through Carleton's cordon, the last American vessel, the *Congress,* was far enough away from the British to start manning the pumps and oars. Unfortunately, the slight north wind turned, and by dawn their 10 hours of backbreaking rowing and pumping had taken the last five of Arnold's battered craft a mere eight miles. At Schuyler's Island desperate attempts at repair were made. The gundalows *Providence* and *New York* were found to be unsalvageable, so their equipment was removed and they were scuttled in 50 fathoms. The *Jersey* foundered on a rock and, being too waterlogged to burn, had to be abandoned. About 1:30 P.M. the hastily repaired *Congress* and *Washington* started rowing south. Wigglesworth was ahead with the other survivors.

Carleton started south when dawn revealed Arnold's escape. In a nightmare chase, with both sides initially rowing against the wind, the Americans stayed ahead the day of 12 Oct. By dawn of the 13th, after creeping six miles in 16 hours, Arnold and his last two vessels were abreast of Willsborough, 28 miles from Crown Point. But when the wind turned to the south the British benefited first and had closed the gap to within a mile before the sails of the slower moving American vessels began to fill. At 11 A.M., at Split Rock, the end came quickly. The *Maria,* followed by the *Inflexible* and the *Carleton,* forced Waterbury to surrender the *Washington* and his 110 men. The *Lee* ran ashore and was abandoned. The *Congress* and four gundalows (that had fallen back from Wigglesworth's group) kept up a running fight against the three enemy ships, which used their speed and maneuverability to rake them with broadsides at pointblank range. They concentrated their attentions on the *Congress.* In a final act of defiance, the die-hard Arnold signaled his ships to windward, a maneuver the British could not follow, and the Americans rowed for Buttonmould Bay on the east (Vt.) shore. Here he beached and burned his wrecks with their colors still flying. That night he reached Crown Point (10 miles away) with 200 men, having escaped an Indian ambush en route. At Crown Point Arnold found the *Trumbull, Enterprise, Revenge, Liberty,* and (according to some reports) "one gundalow."

Unable to hold Crown Point against

such heavy odds, Arnold burned its buildings and withdrew to Ft. Ti with his survivors of Valcour Island and with Lt. Col. Hartley's garrison of the 6th Pa.

COMMENTS

Actions of the traitor Benedict Arnold on Lake Champlain in 1776 may well have saved the American Revolution. His remarkable accomplishment in building a fleet (see CHAMPLAIN SQUADRONS) did more to gain valuable time for the Americans than did his brilliant generalship at Valcour Island. In the article on the CANADA INVASION, see the paragraph preceding "Comments" for Van Tyne's evaluation.

NUMBERS AND LOSSES

Of the 18 or 19 vessels comprising Arnold's portion of the CHAMPLAIN SQUADRONS, he lost 11 of the 15 that probably were present at Valcour Island. The day of the battle he lost 60 killed and wounded out of some 750 present (assuming absence of the 16th vessel, the *Success*). Two days later, 13 Oct., he had another 20 killed and wounded, and the entire crew of the *Washington* galley was captured; some of the 20 killed and wounded were undoubtedly among the latter. The *Congress* lost 27 out of a crew of 73. Carleton paroled Gen. Waterbury and the rest of the prisoners from the *Washington,* who arrived at Ft. Ticonderoga with such praise of Carleton's generous treatment that they were immediately sent home to prevent their lowering the will of others in the American camp to resist. (Ward, *op. cit.,* 397)

Aside from the *Carleton* and, toward the end, the *Inflexible,* the only British ships engaged in the battle of Valcour Island were the 17 to 20 gunboats. Total British strength, including those on ships that did nothing more than shell from a distance, was 670 seamen and four companies of the 29th Regt. (serving as marines on the four larger vessels). Since the inexperienced American gunners failed to sink any of the gunboats or to damage the *Carleton* enough to keep her out of action on the pursuit, British losses must have been light.

VALENTINE'S HILL, N.Y. Just north of SPUYTEN DUYVIL, this was the site of FT. INDEPENDENCE.

VALLEY FORGE, Pa., 18 Sept. '77. (PHILADELPHIA CAMPAIGN) Advance elements under Knyphausen and Cornwallis captured the rebel depot at this place. According to Montresor the booty included 3,800 barrels of flour, 25 barrels of horseshoes, several thousand tomahawks (!), a quantity of kettles, and other supplies. (Freeman, *Washington,* IV, 564 *n.,* citing *Journal,* 454–55)

VALLEY FORGE WINTER QUARTERS, Pa., 19 Dec. '77–18 June '78. The Philadelphia campaign kept Washington in the field until 11 Dec., when his army started for Valley Forge from Whitemarsh. After a week's delay resulting from the action at MATSON'S FORD the tired, ill-clad, and hungry American troops reached the inhospitable campsite that was to be their home for six months. There was "no village, no plain, and little valley," points out D. S. Freeman, and the reaction of Kalb was that the place must have been selected on the advice of a speculator, a traitor, or a council of ignoramuses. (*Washington,* IV, 565) From the strategic and tactical point of view, however, Valley Forge was a good place for winter quarters. It was only 20 miles from Philadelphia, where the enemy was located, and was between that place and the temporary seat of Congress at York. Located in terrain that favored defense, the site was well drained, close to an abundant water supply, and surrounded by heavy woods that would provide fuel and building material. These sterling military qualities were, of course, lost on the troops who huddled in makeshift shelters until their huts could be completed in mid-Jan., and by this time there had been three complete breakdowns in the supply of food and close to 4,000 men were so destitute of clothing they could not leave their huts. (*Ibid.*, 578)

The horrors of that winter are epitomized by the bald statistic that an estimated 2,500 soldiers out of the 10,000 died during the six-month period. (C. & M., 623) Yet Washington's army left Valley Forge stronger than it entered that Gethsemane. One reason for this is spelled STEUBEN. Another measure, brought on by Thos. Mifflin's miserable failure as Q.M.G., was the appointment of Nathanael Greene to his post and the resultant improvement in this department. Congress also was in a mood to listen to Washington's recommendations for strengthening the officers' corps, assuring recruits for the Cont'l. infantry, improving the quality of the cavalry, and strengthening the army's administrative services. (*Ibid.*, 583)

Although Valley Forge heard the alarming chant, "no pay, no clothes, no provisions, no rum," Washington was never faced with the expected mutiny or mass desertions. Much of this can be attributed to the faith Washington's officers and men had in his leadership. Even as he coped with the CONWAY CABAL, Washington took vigorous action to relieve the suffering of his men: he got food and clothing by forced requisition on the neighboring settlements; he sent his best troops out on long-range foraging expeditions: Anthony Wayne into N.J., Henry Lee into Del., and Allen McLane into the British lines.

The British remained snug in Phila-delphia, but they sent out foraging parties and beat the rebels in small-scale actions at QUINTAN'S BRIDGE, N.J., 18 Mar., HANCOCK'S BRIDGE, N.J., 21 Mar., and CROOKED BILLET, Pa., 1 May '78. News of the French Alliance was celebrated at Valley Forge on 6 May. Lafayette led a detachment out of camp and narrowly escaped annihilation at BARREN HILL, Pa., 20 May, but Steuben's training program bore its first fruit. When the British abandoned Philadelphia in June, Washington led a revitalized army from Valley Forge to chase Clinton across N.J. in the MONMOUTH CAMPAIGN.

Valley Forge has become a sort of national shrine and the most vivid picture of patriot suffering there may well be that of the English historian Trevelyan. (*Amer. Rev.*, III, 294–302) It might be well to remember that the suffering was due to American mismanagement, graft, speculation, and indifference more than to the enemy or the weather. (Wallace, *Appeal*, 169) Actually, the winter was a mild one, and the winter quarters the next year at MORRISTOWN made Valley Forge look like a picnic. While the troops suffered at Valley Forge the farmers of Pa. were selling their produce to the British in Philadelphia, where they could get hard cash; N.Y. grain was going to New England civilians and to British troops in and around N.Y.C.; "private contractors reaped a golden harvest by sending hundreds of government wagons north from Pennsylvania loaded with flour and iron while pork in Jersey awaiting shipment to the army spoiled for lack of transport." (*Ibid.*, citing Miller, *Triumph*, 222–23)

VAN CORTLANDT, Philip. 1749–1831. Cont'l. officer. N.Y. Eldest son of Pierre (d. 1814), who was the first Lt. Gov. of N.Y. (elected 1777 and periodically re-elected for 18 years), he was born in N.Y.C. a few months before his parents moved into the Van Cortlandt manor near Croton. He was privately schooled on the estate (which his father had just inherited) before attending Coldenham Academy for nine months. Having ended his formal education at the age of 16, he spent the 10 years preceding the outbreak of hostilities on the family estate, where he surveyed, disposed of tracts of land that had been part of the original manor, and operated mills for his father. In 1775, when he reached his 26th birthday, he became a radical Whig, attended the Provincial Convention on 20 Apr., and the next month was selected as a representative from Westchester co. to the First Prov. Cong. of N.Y.

Commissioned Lt. Col. of the 4th N.Y. Regt. on 18 June '75, he reached Albany about the end of Aug. with four companies but was prevented by sickness from participating in Montgomery's wing of the Canada Invasion. He served on Washington's staff for a short time before being commissioned Col. of the 2d N.Y. Cont'l. Regt. on 21 Nov. '76. This vacancy resulted from the defection of RITZEMA to the British. (Appleton's) Philip joined his unit at Trenton the day after the battle and commanded it the rest of the war. Ordered to Peekskill, he was moving north to oppose St. Leger's Expedition when Benedict Arnold's success in Aug. '77 led to his being attached instead to the main Northern army. His regiment took part in both battles of Saratoga, coming up among the last to reinforce Arnold at Freeman's Farm, and serving in Poor's Brig. in the battle of 7 Oct. He rejoined the main army for winter quarters at Valley Forge. His regiment was stationed in Ulster co., N.Y., and as part of Clinton's Div. accompanied Sullivan's Expedition against the Iroquois in 1779 He sat on the court-martial of ARNOLD (Dec. '79–26 Jan. '80) and, in disagreement with the majority, felt that he should be dismissed from the service. (John A. Krout in *D.A.B.*) In the spring of 1780 he was sent to Fort Edward, N.Y., and later in the year was ordered to Schenectady, where the 2d, 4th, and 5th N.Y. Cont'ls. were consolidated under his command. (See BORDER WARFARE for situation at this time.) In June '81 he was ordered south to join the forces preparing to march against Cornwallis in Va., and in the Yorktown Campaign he was conspicuous for bravery and resourcefulness while serving in James Clinton's Brig. of Lincoln's Div. He was breveted B.G. on 30 Sept. '83 for his performance at Yorktown. (*D.A.B.*)

As delegate to the Poughkeepsie convention in 1788 Van Cortlandt voted for ratification of the Federal Constitution, but subsequently became anti-Federalist. Twice in the state Assembly (1788, 1790), in the state Senate from 1791 to 1793, he entered the U.S. House of Representatives in Dec. '93 and served 16 years. Undistinguished as a congressman, he became a Jeffersonian until the Republicans came into power and subsequently voted faithfully with them. Withdrawing from public life at the age of 60, he continued the tradition of hospitality for which the Van Cortlandt manor at Croton had long been famous, emerged from retirement to accompany Lafayette on a large part of his triumphal tour in 1824, and died a bachelor on 5 Nov. 1831.

A fragment of his diary was found and printed in the *Magazine of American History*, May 1878.

VAN CORTLANDT FAMILY OF N.Y. Oloff Stevenszen, 1600–1684, was born and reared in the Netherlands. He came to New Amsterdam in 1638 and in 1643 adopted the surname "Van Cortlandt," probably because he came

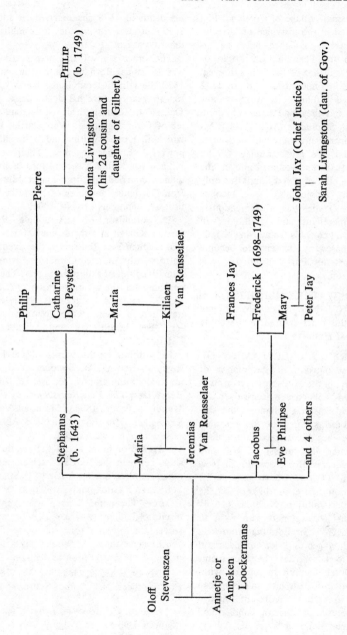

VAN CORTLANDT FAMILY OF NEW YORK

from the small village of Cortlandt that then existed in the province of Utrecht. "No special significance need be attached to the Scandinavian origin of his name and that of his father, Steven, or Stevens," comments *D.A.B.* In 1642 he married a native of what is now Belgium, and they had seven children. The eldest, Stephanus (1643–1700), became a prominent merchant and colonial official; his great-grandson Philip VAN CORTLANDT is sketched above. The youngest child of Oloff, and the only other son (Appleton's), was Jacobus (1658–1739); he was a tremendously wealthy merchant and landholder in Westchester co.; his estate in N.Y.C. was purchased by the city to become "Van Cortlandt Park." John JAY was his grandson.

VANDEWATER'S HEIGHTS (Manhattan), N.Y. Now called Morningside Heights, this place figured in the battle of HARLEM HEIGHTS, 16 Sept. '76.

VAN RENSSELAER FAMILY OF N.Y. First patroon of the manor of Rensselaer on the Hudson River around Albany was Kiliaen van Rensselaer. He and his eldest son, Johannes, the second patroon, spent little or no time in America but did succeed in establishing the first, the largest (*C.E.*), and the only successful patroonship of New Netherland (*D.A.H*). Two sons of the first patroon figure in the era of the American Revolution. Nicholas (1636–1678) was a clergyman who went to N.Y. with Gov. Sir Edmund Andros in 1674 and waged a brief, unsuccessful attempt to administer the sacraments of the Dutch Church in Albany without violating British law and Anglican doctrine. A victim, finally, of bigotry, he was accused of immoral conduct and in 1677 was deposed from his Albany pastorate. Meanwhile, on 10 Feb. 1675 he had married Alida Schuyler. After

his death in 1678 she married (9 July 1679) Robert Livingston to establish the LIVINGSTON FAMILY.

The other son of the first patroon was Jeremias. Born in Holland around 1632, he administered Rensselaerswyck for 16 years before his death there in Oct. 1674. He married Maria, the daughter of Oloff Stevenszen Van Cortlandt, which tied two wealthy and politically powerful families together. Their son Kiliaen (or Killian), second lord of the manor, married his first cousin Maria Van Cortlandt, daughter of his father's brother Stephanus (1643–1700).

The grandson of this couple—the second Kiliaen and the second Maria—was Stephen Van Rensselaer, the seventh patroon, who married Catharine Livingston, daughter of Philip the Signer. Their son Stephen, the eighth patroon (1764–1839), married Margaret Schuyler, daughter of Gen. Philip John Schuyler. (See LIVINGSTON and SCHUYLER FAMILIES)

In addition to the works of Cuyler Reynolds and W. W. Spooner cited in the main bibliography, see M. K. Van Rensselaer, *The Van Rensselaers of the Manor . . .* (copr. 1888), Maunsell Van Rensselaer, *Annals of the Van Rensselaers in the U.S.* (1888).

NOTES. For more about the relationships between the Van Rensselaers and other families, see LIVINGSTON FAMILY, SCHUYLER FAMILY, and VAN CORTLANDT FAMILY. The name Kiliaen was Anglicized to Killian; whereas D.A.B. preserves the original form down to the fourth generation, Appleton's gives the name of the 1st patroon as Killian.

VAN SCHAICK, Gose.* 1736–1789. Cont'l. officer. N.Y. Son of Sybrant Van

---

* Goosen Gerritse Van Schaick (pronounced shake), an Albany brewer in 1649, was his Dutch ancestor. Gose is the spelling of his first name used

Schaick, who was Albany's mayor, 1756–61, he was a Lt. in the Crown Point expedition of 1756 and a militia Capt. with Bradstreet in the capture of Fort Frontenac in 1758. Two years later he was a Lt. Col., and in the final operations of the French and Indian War he served first with the 2d N.Y. Provincials and then with the 1st N.Y. Regt. (*D.A.B.*)

Commissioned Col. of the 2d N.Y. on 28 June '75 (Heitman), he joined Montgomery on Lake Champlain with 400 men in Sept. for the Canada Invasion. The next spring he was stationed at Johnstown in the Mohawk Valley as commander of the 1st N.Y. (appointed 8 Mar. '76). He was wounded at Ticonderoga on 6 July '77. In the Battle of Monmouth, N.J., 28 June '78, he commanded a brigade under Gen. Alexander ("Stirling"). (Appleton's)

The operation for which he is best known is the raid against the Onondagas in Apr. '79, which preceded SULLIVAN'S EXPEDITION. He left Fort Stanwix with 550 men (Swiggett, *op. cit.,* 178) and in a march of 180 miles in five and a half days destroyed the Onondaga Castle of about 50 houses, took 37 prisoners, killed between 20 and 30 warriors, picked up 100 muskets, and returned without losing a man. (Campbell, *Tryon co.,* 117–18) For this achievement he was given the Thanks of Congress on 10 May '79. He was in command at Albany while Gen. James Clinton accompanied Sullivan's Expedition. As part of Clinton's Div. he marched south for the Yorktown Campaign. On 10 Oct. '83 he was breveted B.G., and the next month retired from

by Harold Swiggett (*Niagara,* index). Gozen is the form used by Montross (*Rag, Tag,* 472). *D.A.B.* and most other authorities favor Goose, but other variants are Gosen and Goosen.

the Cont'l. Army. According to the best authorities, he died on 4 July '89. (*D.A.B.*)

VAN WART, Isaac. 1760–1828. Captor of John André. N.Y. A Westchester co. farmer, he took part with Paulding and David Williams in the capture of John André. This exploit and their subsequent awards are covered under ARNOLD'S TREASON.

VARICK, Richard. 1753–1831. Cont'l. officer. N.Y. Great-grandson of Jan van Varick, who came to N.Y. before 1 June 1687, Richard was born in Hackensack, N.J., and moved to N.Y.C. in 1775. (*D.A.B.*) On 28 June '75 he was made Capt. in the 1st N.Y. Regt., a commission he held until 24 Sept. '76. In June '76, however, he became military secretary to Gen. Schuyler. On 25 Sept. he was made deputy Mustermaster General of the Northern army, and during the period 10 Apr. '77–June '80 he was Lt. Col. and Deputy Commiss. Gen. of Musters. (This came as a result of a reorganization of the Muster Dept.) In Aug. '80 he became A.D.C. to Gen. Arnold. (Heitman; *D.A.B.*)

Varick had been a friend of Arnold during the Saratoga campaign, according to Van Doren. (*Secret History,* 286) "Out of active service since the past January, Varick had resumed his interrupted legal studies at his father's house [in Hackensack] but had found himself so often called on for militia duty that he was glad to return to the army as Arnold's writing aide." (*Ibid.*) Both Varick and the other aide, Franks, soon became uneasy about their general's activities as the new commander of West Point, but they thought that he was engaged in nothing more dishonorable than profiteering. Varick's innocent role in ARNOLD'S TREASON is covered in that article (see section

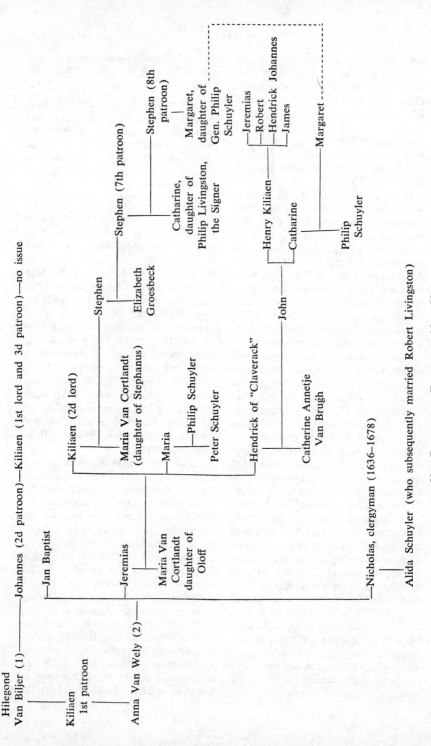

VAN RENSSELAER FAMILY OF NEW YORK

headed "The Climax"). Duped not only by his chief but also by the latter's lovely young wife, Col. Varick was cleared by a court of inquiry that met on 2 Nov. '80 at West Point. He was nevertheless under some suspicion by uninformed persons and, although he wished to remain in the army, he was left without military employment because the Muster Dept. had been abolished. In May '81 he was selected by Washington as his confidential secretary to supervise a staff of writers in the arrangement, classification, and copying of all the correspondence and other papers of the Cont'l. Army located at Washington's Hq. This shut up those who had been whispering their doubts about Varick's loyalty. Establishing his office at Poughkeepsie, Varick and his assistants spent more than two years in compiling the 44 folio volumes known as the Varick Transcripts, now deposited in the Lib. of Cong. Van Doren calls them "an honourable monument to his ability and skill." (Op. cit., 428)

In 1784 Varick became recorder of N.Y.C. With Samuel Jones he codified the N.Y. statutes enacted since the Revolution (2 vols., 1789). Speaker of the N.Y. Assy. in 1787 and 1788, Atty. Gen. in 1788–89, he was Mayor of N.Y.C. from 1789 until 1801, when Aaron BURR's new machine swept the Federalists out of power. He tried with Alexander Hamilton to defend the Jay treaty against the popular tide of disapproval in 1795, but they were unsuccessful. A founder of the American Bible Society, he was its president from 1828 to 1831. In 1817 he was an appraiser for the Erie Canal. (D.A.B.) According to Heitman, he remained Washington's confidential secretary until the latter's death, 14 Dec. '99.

VARNUM, James Mitchell. 1748–1789. Cont'l. general. Mass.–R.I. Son of a prosperous farmer and great-grandson of a man who settled in Mass. about 1635, he graduated with honors from R.I. College (now Brown University) in its first class, 1769. The preceding year he had been expelled from Harvard, probably for participation in student disorders in Apr. '68. (Frederick W. Coburn in D.A.B.) Admitted to the bar in 1771, he rapidly became a successful lawyer famous for his literary form of speech. In Oct. '74 he became Col. of the Kentish Guards, a militia outfit that would not accept his friend Nathanael GREENE as an officer. Before dawn on the day of Lexington and Concord, Varnum was awakened at Dracut, Mass., by the alarm gun at Tewksbury, where Paul Revere's message had been received at 2 A.M. He marched to the Boston Siege and served throughout that operation in the right wing of the army. On 3 May '75 he was commissioned Col. of the 1st R.I., which was known in 1776 as the 9th Cont'l. Inf., and on 21 Feb. '77 Congress appointed him B.G. Meanwhile he had been named B.G. of the R.I. militia 12 Dec. '76. Presumably his command was in the portion of Greene's Div. posted on Governor's Island during the Battle of Long Island. In the reorganization that took place shortly thereafter on Manhattan, Varnum commanded a R.I. brigade in Greene's Div. He had no significant part in the fighting of the N.Y. and N.J. Campaigns. During the winter of 1776–77 he was active in recruiting. (D.A.B.) He had just rejoined Washington's army when the British undertook their perplexing "June maneuvers" of the PHILADELPHIA CAMPAIGN. His brigade of Conn. and R.I. troops was not formally assigned to a division, and he did not receive an order to attack the retreating British forces around Brunswick on 22 June. When the British evacuated N.J. the end of June and it could not be determined whether they were preparing to move by sea against Philadelphia or up the Hudson to link up with Burgoyne's Offensive, the brigades of Varnum and Poor were sent to Peekskill. In Nov., having rejoined Washington, he was put in command of Forts Mercer and Mifflin. He did not personally take part in the defense of either post, but two of his regiments were part of the garrison of Fort Mercer. (See PHILADELPHIA CAMPAIGN for the strategic framework within which Varnum was operating in 1777.)

He took a dim view of Valley Forge. "The situation of the camp is such that in all human probability the army must soon dissolve," he wrote Greene on 12 Feb. '78 from that dismal encampment. "It is unparalleled in the history of mankind to establish winter quarters in a country wasted and without a single magazine." After having an active part in the MONMOUTH CAMPAIGN, serving in Lee's Div., he marched under Lafayette to support Sullivan at NEWPORT, July–Aug. '78. In R.I. he advocated that a Negro unit be raised (Appleton's), and this battalion performed well in the action of 29 Aug. (See NEWPORT)

A mutiny broke out in Varnum's Brig. in early 1779. On 5 Mar. Varnum resigned, "not . . . because of the mutiny," points out Freeman, "but on account of the pressure of private business." (*Washington*, V, 99 *n*.) On 27 Jan. he had been made commander of the Dept. of R.I. He was able to resume his law practice while occupying this position, and in Apr. '79 he became Maj. Gen. of R.I. militia. In this capacity he supported the French army of Rochambeau in July and Aug. '80. He was elected in May '80 to the Cont'l. Cong., where he served in 1780–82 and 1786–87. In Aug. '87 he was appointed judge for the Northwest Territory, hav-

ing shown an interest in the Territory and the Ohio Company. Although in bad health he rode on horseback to (what is now) Marietta, Ohio, arriving 5 June '88. He had an active role in framing a code of territorial laws before his death on 10 Jan. '89. His wife, who had remained in the East, survived him 48 years. (*D.A.B.*)

VAUGHAN, John. ?–1795. British general. Having started his army service in Col. Pawlett's 9th Marine Regt., he became Cornet in the 10th Dragoons on 9 Apr. '48. Promoted to Capt. on 28 Jan. '55, he was with the regiment in Germany for part of the Seven Years' War. On 15 Oct. '59 he left the 10th and was commissioned Maj. to raise a light infantry regiment for American operations. The unit was designated the 94th Regt. (Royal Welsh Volunteers), and on 12 Jan. '60 he was promoted to Lt. Col. commandant. He led the regiment in America until 1761, when he went to the West Indies with Robert Monckton and distinguished himself as commander of the grenadier division at Martinique. On 25 Nov. '62 he became Lt. Col. of the 46th Foot when the 94th was disbanded, and he commanded this regiment in North America until 1767, when it went to Ireland. In May '72 Vaughan was promoted to Col.

With the force under Cornwallis that joined Clinton from Ireland he took part in the Charleston Expedition of 1776. Although *D.N.B.* says he was given "local rank" of Maj. Gen. on 1 Jan. '76, Clinton refers to him as a B.G. during these operations. (*Amer. Reb.*, 31 ff.) Moving to Staten Island with Clinton, Vaughan commanded the grenadiers in the Battle of Long Island, 27 Aug. '76, and had pushed his attack toward the Brooklyn lines when Gen. Howe ordered him to withdraw. (*Ibid.*, 43) At White Plains, 28 Oct., he was wounded in the thigh. (*D.N.B.;* according to Appleton's he was wounded "at the landing at New York.") Returning to England with Cornwallis, he came back to America in 1777 and on 29 Aug. was promoted to Maj. Gen. in the regular establishment, having been given this "local rank" earlier.

In Clinton's Expedition to the Highlands, Oct. '77, Vaughan led the column that captured Ft. Montgomery, 6 Oct., and commanded the 1,700 troops that Sir James Wallace convoyed up the Hudson to burn Kingston (Esopus) on the 16th. When Clinton moved up the Hudson again in 1779, Vaughan captured Verplancks Point on 1 June. This ended his service in North America. He returned to England the end of 1779 and in Dec. was named C. in C. of the Leeward Islands. In 1780 he was appointed Gov. of Berwick, a sinecure worth £600 a year for the rest of his life. In 1781 he and Adm. Rodney made an unsuccessful attack on the island of St. Vincent, but on 3 Feb. '82 they captured St. Eustatius.

Vaughan was knighted in 1793. From 1774 until his death he was M.P. from Berwick, his mother's home. He was in the Irish Parliament from 1776 to 1783. A bachelor, he died suddenly at Martinique on 3 June '95, possibly of poison. (Appleton's)

VENCE, Jean Gaspard. 1747–1808. French privateer, admiral. Son of a merchant marine Capt., he was born in Marseilles. At the age of 15 he sailed for the West Indies to find an elder brother who was a merchant at San Domingo. The next year, in 1763, he served aboard the warship *Protecteur* (74). As 2d Lt. aboard the *Auguste* merchantman in 1767 he survived a shipwreck off the west coast of Africa and the subsequent four-month overland trek. In 1777 he went to Martinique, was commissioned by the Cont'l.

Cong. as a privateer, recruited 120 "pirates," and in May sailed in the *Tigre* (four 6-pdrs.), a one-and-a-half-mast lateen rig.

In 40 actions during the 18 months of Franco-British peace he is credited by his biographer with 211 prizes. (Loir, *Vence.*) On 6 Sept. '78 he took part in the capture of Dominique as *Lt. de frégate.* In Dec. he saw action aboard the *Truite* off St. Lucia. He then served aboard the *Cérès,* then on the *Languedoc,* d'Estaing's flagship. On 4 July '79 he led 80 grenadiers to spearhead the French attack at Grenada, taking the main enemy battery, cutting down the Union Jack, and holding his position against heavy odds until d'Estaing arrived with the main body. Promoted to *Lt. de vaisseau,* he led 80 grenadiers in an attack at Savannah that got into the British works before being driven back.

Made Capt. of the Port of Grenada at the age of 36, he entered into lean years that brought him many lawsuits and personal poverty. On 10 Mar. '93 he was given command of the *Heureux,* and on 16 Nov. of the same year became Vice Adm. Sent to support Napoleon's contemplated cross-channel attack, he made the mistake of pointing out the fallacies of the Emperor's amphibious plans; for being right he was retired on 16 Oct. 1803. Meanwhile he had been made Chevalier of Saint Louis (1780) and a member of the Cincinnati. He died 12 Mar. 1808. ◉

See Maurice Loir, *Vence* (Paris, 1894).

VERGENNES, Charles Gravier, Comte de. 1717–1787. French foreign minister. Born at Dijon, he started his diplomatic career under his uncle, M. de Chavigny, at Lisbon and then served as ambassador at Treves, Constantinople (1755–68), and Stockholm. When Louis XVI ascended the throne Vergennes became foreign minister. With a burning

hatred of England and a desire to revenge his country's humiliation in the
Seven Years' War, he followed the same
general policies of CHOISEUL—who had
started rebuilding French military power
for a war of revenge—but he proceeded
with more caution.

"Devoted to duty, gifted with a subtile intellect, unscrupulous when the
needs of France seemed to require
duplicity, Vergennes hovered on the
fringe of greatness. He had feared that
the crisis in Anglo-American relations
might drive the [inept] North ministry
from power and bring to the British
helm the Earl of Chatham [who had
engineered the recent humiliation of
France]. . . . Hence, he decided to be
most circumspect." (Alden, *American
Revolution*, 180)

Events of 1775 in America led Vergennes to believe that the colonists were
serious about fighting a war for their
independence and that, more important,
they were capable of giving the British
some real trouble. The danger to France
was that after committing themselves
against the British the latter might
quickly settle the problem in America—
by diplomacy or arms—and then turn
their entire strength against France, perhaps in alliance with Spain. Having
previously refused to act on hints from
American agents (e.g.. Arthur Lee in
London) that the colonists would welcome aid from their traditional enemy,
France, should a shooting war develop
with England, Vergennes now agreed to
the exploratory mission of ACHARD DE
BONVOULOIR. At the same time he undertook a study of secret aid that led
to establishment of Beaumarchais' HOR-
TALEZ & CIE.

French statesmen were faced with the
problem of whether it was wise to
fight England, even if that country
was handicapped by its war in America. Turgot, Comptroller General of

Finances, was opposed, and he advanced
a number of very valid reasons. He
finally agreed to secret aid, however.
The other problem was that of getting
support from Spain, a country with
grave fears about how the success of
revolution in the 13 colonies of North
America might inspire Spanish colonies
to revolt.

Vergennes succeeded first in getting his own government and that of
Spain to support the plan for secret
aid through Hortalez & Cie. In the
summer of 1776 Vergennes was ready
to go to war against Britain if Spain
would join in, but when he learned
of the British victory at Long Island
he decided it would be better for
France to restrict her assistance to secret aid until she could be sure the
Americans could continue the war long
enough for open assistance to do them
any good. Two months before Burgoyne's defeat at Saratoga, and influenced largely by Washington's brilliant
riposte in the Trenton-Princeton campaign, in July '77, Vergennes again officially proposed armed intervention by
France and Spain. France had lost the
restraining influence of Turgot, but
Spain had a new foreign minister, Floridablanca, who lacked the enthusiasm
of his predecessor, Grimaldi, for participation in a shooting alliance. Spanish refusal to go along with Vergennes'
plan as well as the reports of Burgoyne's
initial successes in his invasion from
Canada led the French foreign minister
to abandon his schemes for the time being. Lord Stormont, the British ambassador in Paris, had meanwhile succeeded
in seriously embarrassing Vergennes by
finding out details of his secret aid and
making official protests.

The Saratoga Surrender, GERMAN-
TOWN (see end of article), and Franklin's diplomacy in Paris led ultimately to
the FRENCH ALLIANCE, which Congress

ratified 4 May '78. The policy of Vergennes thereby prevailed, to the benefit of the Americans—who probably never could have achieved independence without active French participation in the war in America—but to the eventual distress of the old order in France: "the moral and financial results had not a little to do with the Revolution of 1789." (*E.B.*, "Vergennes")

He was intimately involved in the PEACE NEGOTIATIONS, 1780–84. See also SPANISH PARTICIPATION. . . .

On the eve of the French Revolution, Vergennes intrigued against Necker, "whom he regarded as a dangerous innovator, a republican, a foreigner and a Protestant." (*Ibid.*) He himself was none of these things. He is said to have proposed the meeting of the Assembly of Notables, but he died on 13 Feb. '87 before it took place.

See John J. Meng, *Comte de Vergennes; European Phases of His American Diplomacy.*

VERMONT was an unsurveyed wilderness claimed by N.Y. and N.H. but was not a source of friction between these two provinces until 1749, when Gov. Benning Wentworth of N.H. granted a patent for a township that was named Bennington, in his honor. Despite objections of the Gov. and Council of N.Y., Wentworth continued to issue patents. In 1754, 14 townships were laid out and settled. In 1763, 138 townships were surveyed west of the Connecticut River, and these became known as the "New Hampshire Grants." In 1771 the Green Mountain Boys under Ethan ALLEN started resisting the civil power of N.Y. Gov. TRYON was involved in the boundary dispute, and the rather mild part played by Philip Schuyler was one of the reasons why New Englanders resented being under his command during the Revolution. See also Philip SKENE. In 1777 Ver-

mont declared its independence, in 1790 N.Y. formally relinquished claim to the region, and in 1792 Vermont became the 14th state.

VERPLANCKS POINT (Hudson River), N.Y. On the E. bank of the river, with Stony Point it covered Kings Ferry at the southern approach to the Hudson Highlands. On 1 June '79 the British captured Ft. Lafayette, which had been built on this place, in the operations preceding the action at STONY POINT, 16 July '79.

VERNIER, Pierre-François. 1736 or 1737–1780. Officer in Pulaski's Legion. Born at Belfort, France, he became a volunteer in a mounted corps in 1752, was made Lt. in a regiment of foreign volunteers four years later, took part in the action at St. Cast, 11 Sept. '58, and received a gunshot wound in the thigh at Vildungen, 25 July '60. He was retired on 1 Jan. '68 and assigned to the Invalides in Paris. A note in his records for 1765–66 characterizes him as "a good man, but negligent and unstable" (*dérangé*). As for his American service, Heitman says only that he was Maj., 1st Cav., Pulaski Legion on 23 Feb. '79, and was mortally wounded at MONCK'S CORNER, S.C., 14 Apr. '80. Lasseray, my authority for the spelling of Vernier's name and his pre-Revolutionary record, says nothing of the officer's service in America other than that he was a Maj. under Pulaski. Even more unaccountably, Warrington Dawson's work does not mention him. (*Les 2112 . . .* fails to include Pulaski's Legion among the units in which Frenchmen served in America, and Dawson does not list Vernier among those—including Pulaski—who were killed while "*en mission spéciale*.") He appears in Heitman as "Vernie, Peter J. F. (——)," indicating that this authority did not have any evidence that the officer was of French origin. Ward says "Major Peter

Vernie of Pulaski's Legion" was among those killed or wounded at Monck's Corner. (*W.O.R.*, 701). The incorrect spelling, Vernie, undoubtedly stems from an inaccurate phonetic rendition of the name into English.

VERNON, Edward. 1684–1757. British admiral. As Vice Adm. in the War of Jenkins' Ear (1739–42) (see COLONIAL WARS) he was admired by Lawrence Washington, who named "Mount Vernon" in his honor. He was nicknamed "Old Grog" after 1740 because he ordered rum rations diluted and their issue controlled to reduce drunkenness in his fleet.

VIC GAYAULT. See BOISBERTRAND.

VICE-ADMIRALTY COURTS. See ADMIRALTY COURTS.

VINCENNES, Ind. This French settlement on the Wabash shifted allegiance to Va. on 20 July '78, was retaken by the British on 17 Dec., and capitulated to the Americans on 24–25 Feb. '79. See WESTERN OPERATIONS.

VIRGINIA, Military operations in. Following the lead of Mass. in preparing for armed conflict, on 23 Mar. '75 a Va. convention resolved that the "colony be immediately put into a posture of defense." Patrick Henry delivered his famous "liberty or death" speech on this occasion. The dyspeptic Lord Dunmore, royal governor, immediately assumed his own posture of defiance and undertook a series of actions that built a pyramid of crises. The night of 20–21 Apr. he seized the provincial powder supply at Williamsburg. On 2 May, Patrick Henry assembled the Hanover County militia and marched to right this wrong. Dunmore bellowed that "by the living God if an insult is offered to me or to those who have obeyed my orders, I will declare freedom to the slaves and lay the town in ashes!" But on the 4th he reimbursed the province

£330 for the powder and said he had taken it to prevent a rumored slave uprising. Then he started fulminating again, cried "extortion," and outlawed Henry. On 8 June, however, he fled to the safety of a warship when he got an advance copy of Gage's offer of pardon; since the pardon excluded Sam Adams and John Hancock, Dunmore feared he would be grabbed as a hostage. After the colonists captured, looted, and burned an armed sloop driven ashore during a storm, Dunmore attempted retaliation by sending naval forces to destroy HAMPTON, 24–25 Oct. Frustrated and humiliated by failure, on 7 Nov. he declared martial law and offered to free slaves and indentured servants of rebels. He started assembling armed forces, including an outfit known as Lord Dunmore's Ethiopians.

Col. Wm. Woodford marched on Norfolk with a regiment of Cont'ls. and some militia, defeated the governor's forces at GREAT BRIDGE, 9 Dec., and occupied the town five days later. Crowded aboard ships in the Elizabeth River and unable to get provisions, Dunmore turned the guns of the fleet on NORFOLK, 1 Jan. '76. Destruction of the largest town in Va. (6,000 inhabitants) also wiped out the nucleus of Tory support. Dunmore tried to re-establish a foothold among the ashes, but the rebels kept him from getting supplies from the neighborhood and he was forced to evacuate. His ships crowded with Loyalist refugees and troops, Dunmore attempted to set up a new base in Chesapeake Bay, but was driven from GWYNN ISLAND, 8–10 July '76. With the forces that survived a smallpox epidemic and this last military defeat, the unlovable earl undertook a raid up the Potomac. After burning several plantations and pushing as far as Occoquan Falls, he was forced to retreat. "It is supposed that Dunmore intended to capture Lady Washington, and destroy the estate at Mount Vernon [writes Lossing]. A heavy storm and the Prince William militia frustrated his design." (II, 419 *n.*)

An egregious failure from start to finish, Dunmore took his sorry little armada to Lynnhaven Roads, just west of Cape Henry, Va., and from there sent them off in parcels to Bermuda, St. Augustine, and the West Indies with booty that included almost 1,000 slaves. He went to N.Y., returned to England, and later was "rewarded for his eminent services in America by being appointed governor of the Bahamas." (Ward, *W.O.R.,* 849)

BRITISH RAIDS, 1779–81

Virginia was spared any further military action east of the mountains during the three years following the destruction of Norfolk, although the province supported the SOUTHERN CAMPAIGNS OF GREENE with troops and supplies. Meanwhile, the economy of the Old Dominion played an important role in bolstering the rebel cause, particularly after the fall of Charleston; salt supplies were furnished to the army, and tobacco constituted an important basis of foreign credit. As soon as the British could spare the military means, therefore, they undertook a series of devastating raids. Subsequent events will show that the Va. patriots had gotten soft while the fighting raged north and south of them, and the great Thos. Jefferson was an inept governor during a time when it was necessary to "look to the military for protection."

MATHEW–COLLIER RAID, 1779

On 5 May '79 a British expedition left N.Y. under Adm. Sir John Collier and Maj. Gen. Edward Mathew. Reaching Hampton Roads on 9 May, they took FT. NELSON the same day. On the 11th they moved unopposed into nearby Portsmouth, Norfolk, Gosport, and Suffolk, capturing great quantities of naval supplies, ordnance, and tobacco. The patriots burned a 28-gun warship on the stocks and destroyed two heavily laden French merchantmen. In addition to many privateers, 137 vessels were captured, burned, or destroyed. Without having lost a man, the expedition returned to N.Y. after doing an estimated £2,000,000 worth of damage. (Fisher, *Struggle,* II, 237)

ARNOLD'S RAID, 1781

On 20 Dec. '80 Benedict Arnold sailed from N.Y. with about 1,600 troops, including Simcoe's Rangers, to destroy military stores in Va., rally Loyalists, and stop the support being sent to Greene. This was the first assignment the traitor Arnold was given after going over to the British. Bad weather cost the expedition time and 400 men, but on 30 Dec. they reached Hampton Roads and the resourceful Arnold started up the James River with his remaining 1,200 men in captured American vessels. They took the battery at HOOD'S POINT, 3 Jan. '81, and occupied RICHMOND, 5–7 Jan. After burning tobacco and some buildings in the latter place, Arnold withdrew to Westover. In a night raid Simcoe routed rebel militia at CHARLES CITY C. H., 8 Jan.

LAFAYETTE'S EXPEDITION, 1781

The homegrown patriots, under the inept military leadership of Gov. Jefferson, obviously needed help from outside. It was particularly galling since the man who was running roughshod over them this time was the officer whose military talents had been so little appreciated while he was leading rebel forces. But Washington decided to take advantage of Arnold's isolated position

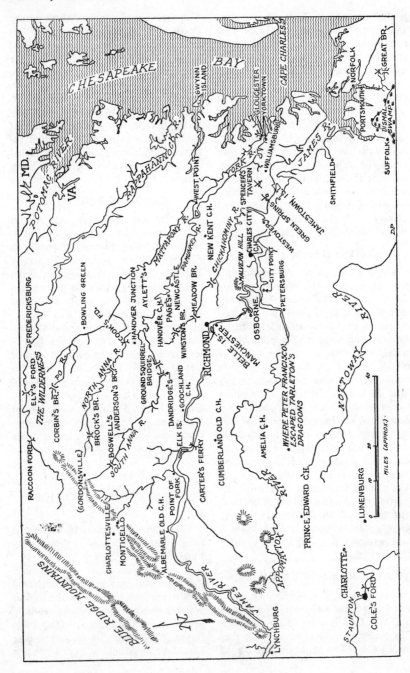

to send an army expedition against him under Lafayette's command and to ask the French fleet to cooperate. With three light infantry regiments drawn from the New England and N.J. Cont'ls., these 1,200 rank and file commanded by Joseph Vose, de Gimat, and Francis Barber, Lafayette started south to link up with a French expedition expected from Newport.

The French fleet kept its unblemished record of failure and hard luck. Although a storm scattered and badly damaged the British squadron blockading Newport, and de Tilly got out on 22 Jan. '81 with the 64-gun *Eveille* and two frigates, the seaman Arnold saved his fleet by moving them up the Elizabeth River to Portsmouth, where the larger French ships could not pursue. Although the French took some British vessels and brought the *Romulus* (44 guns) back to Newport (24 Feb.), this preliminary sally accomplished nothing useful. According to Fisher it had the adverse effect of delaying departure of the entire fleet, which awaited de Tilly's return, and gave the British time to repair the three blockading vessels that had been demasted in the storm of 22 Jan. (*Struggle*, II, 451, 452)

The French expeditionary force left Newport on 8 Mar., five days after Lafayette reached Head of Elk and moved to Annapolis to join forces with them. Adm. Arbuthnot started in pursuit when the French had a 36-hour lead, but actually got ahead of Adm. Destouches and brought on the battle just outside the mouth of CHESAPEAKE BAY, 16 Mar. Destouches emerged from this one-hour fight in slightly better shape than his adversary, but abandoned the expedition, while Arbuthnot limped into the Chesapeake and made contact with Arnold! With the sea routes now open, Clinton sent Maj. Gen. Wm. Phillips with 2,000 more troops to rein-

force Arnold and to take over-all command.

The patriot cause was now at a particularly low ebb. To oppose the threat of some 3,000 high quality troops under Phillips, with such subordinates as Arnold and Simcoe, Va. had only a small force of green Cont'ls. under Steuben and whatever raw militia that Gens. Muhlenberg, Thos. Nelson, and Weedon might hold together. Lafayette was back at Head of Elk, more than 150 miles from Richmond. "Everything now depended on the fleet from France and the loan of hard money," says Fisher. With Washington's main army faced with the possibility of having to disband to search for food, British prospects looked particularly bright for establishing control of Va., consolidating their hold on the other southern provinces, and making some agreement with the rebels to retain these possessions.

While arrangements were made in the North to send some help to the South, Phillips conducted another raid into territory not yet ravaged by preceding forays. Arnold left Portsmouth on 18 Apr. with 2,500 men, the light infantry of the 76th and 80th British regts., the Queen's (Simcoe's) Rangers, the American Legion, and a jäger detachment. They landed at City Point on 24 Apr. and, despite some creditable militia resistance, took PETERSBURG, 25 Apr. Phillips led one column in a pursuit to Chesterfield C. H., while Arnold routed a small flotilla at OSBORNE'S, 27 Apr., and rejoined Phillips. The raiders continued virtually unopposed to Manchester, on the south bank of the James opposite Richmond. The next morning, 30 Apr., they found they were a few hours late to take that place; Lafayette had arrived the evening before with 1,200 Cont'ls.

LAFAYETTE'S MARCH
TO RICHMOND

Failure of the French to reach Va. from Newport had altered the plans of Lafayette's expedition. On 6 Apr., however, he received fresh instructions to march south, and he was almost immediately faced with challenges to his leadership. When his troops started expressing their disapproval of this southern campaign by deserting, Lafayette "encouraged the others" (as the French put it) by hanging one and dismissing another. He then issued an order that any others who wished to abandon what promised to be a tough campaign had only to submit their applications and they would be returned to their units. He received no applications and desertions ceased. (H. P. Johnston, *Yorktown*, 34, citing Lafayette, *Memoirs*.) In Baltimore, Lafayette borrowed £2,000 from the merchants to buy material for summer clothing to replace the winter uniforms of his troops. Expecting the British to head for Richmond, Lafayette left his tents and artillery to follow at their own pace, and moved by forced marches; he left Baltimore on 19 Apr., moved through Alexandria, Fredericksburg, and Bowling Green to reach Richmond the evening of the 29th, a few hours ahead of Phillips. Surprised by this speed, Phillips withdrew to the vicinity of Jamestown Island; learning on 7 May that Cornwallis was moving to join him at Petersburg, Phillips re-entered that place on the 10th. Fisher says Phillips returned to Portsmouth "with immense spoil for his officers to sell for their own profit, leaving behind him burning buildings and scenes of destruction which were hardly equalled in any other British raid during the war." (*Struggle*, II, 453)

CORNWALLIS vs. LAFAYETTE

British strategy in Va. failed in one of its main objectives: to help Cornwallis hold the Carolinas and Ga. In complete defiance of Clinton's instructions to make the security of S.C. and Ga. his primary mission, Cornwallis marched from Wilmington to Petersburg with his 1,500 troops. He arrived on 20 May, and within a few days his ranks were swelled to 7,200 by the arrival of reinforcements from Clinton. (The two Anspach bns., the 17th and 43d Br. regts., totaling 1,200 men.)

The light infantry regiments of Barber, de Gimat, and Vose with which Lafayette marched south were soon reinforced by about 2,000 militia, the 40 dragoons that remained of Armand's Legion, and some volunteer horsemen under John Mercer and Nicholas Moore. Steuben was still organizing some 500 18-months recruits into Va. Cont'l. units. Working to assemble and hold together other militia units were Muhlenberg and Weedon (both Va. Cont'l. officers), and the State Brig. Gens. Lawson, Nelson, and Stevens. Impassioned pleas went to Dan Morgan to come with some of his famous riflemen, but he and Wm. Campbell did not appear until Lafayette's worst crisis was over. The reinforcement whose delayed arrival shaped Lafayette's initial strategy was the body of regulars under Wayne (see below).

"The boy cannot escape me," Cornwallis is alleged to have written as he prepared to undertake his long-cherished operations in Va. (Johnston indicates considerable doubt as to whether he really wrote this phrase. [*Op. cit.*, 38 *n.*] Lafayette mentions it in his *Memoirs*, however. [See C. & M., 1207].) "The boy" was fully aware of his danger. "I am determined to skirmish, but not to engage too far," Lafayette wrote Wash-

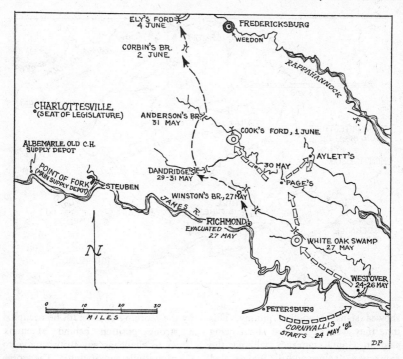

ington on 24 May. "I am not strong enough even to get beaten."

Cornwallis left Petersburg on 24 May, crossed the James at Westover, and camped at Hanover Junction on 1 June. (He was without the services of Phillips, who died of fever in Petersburg, and Arnold, who returned to N.Y.) Lafayette left Winston's Bridge, eight miles north of Richmond, on 28 May and covered 70 miles in seven days. To keep in a position to be reinforced by Wayne and Steuben, he retreated due north through the Wilderness to Ely's Ford on the Rapidan, 20 miles above Fredericksburg. Cornwallis pursued only 30 miles, stopping on the North Anna. He then turned his attention to the destruction of rebel stores. Tarleton led a raid to CHARLOTTESVILLE, 4 June, and Simcoe led another to

POINT OF FORK, 5 June. Cornwallis moved slowly toward the latter place, about 45 miles up the James from Richmond, and established a camp at Elk Hill. His raiders joined him here on the 9th, and he prepared to send Tarleton to raid the supply point at Albemarle Old C. H. (on the James, 20 miles west of Elk Hill) and also to attack Steuben's little band of newly raised regulars.

The last orders were canceled when Cornwallis learned that Wayne had finally joined Lafayette and that the latter was moving toward Elk Hill. Wayne's departure from York, Pa., had been delayed by lack of supplies and unsatisfied payrolls. He was about to start when his troops, most of them Pa. Cont'ls. that had been reorganized after the Mutiny of the Pa. Line,

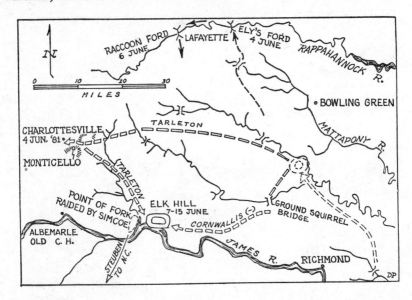

showed signs of another mutiny. This time they were dissatisfied about being paid in Cont'l. currency without the depreciated value added. Wayne had seven of them shot. Leaving York the morning of 26 May, they marched into Lafayette's camp on 10 June. Wayne himself rode ahead to meet Lafayette about three days earlier. Numbering about 1,000 good troops, Wayne's corps consisted of three Pa. regiments under Richard Butler, Walter Stewart, and Richard Humpton, whom Johnston characterizes as "brave and experienced colonels." Proctor's 4th Cont'l. Arty., nine officers, six guns, and 90 men, completed the detachment. (Johnston, *op. cit.*, 45)

Although this reinforcement by no means gave Lafayette the strength to bring on a battle with the British army, it did enable him to move closer and stop the unopposed raiding. The very day Wayne's men arrived, Lafayette therefore moved south from his camp near Raccoon Ford on the Rapidan and

by the morning of the 12th he occupied a strong position behind Mechunk Creek to challenge any British move to Charlottesville and Staunton. The stores had been evacuated by this route from Albemarle Old C. H., and to protect them the rebels had been faced with the difficult problem of moving due west across the enemy's front without exposing themselves to a flank attack; they had solved this by secretly repairing a long abandoned road and had moved along it undetected.

Although not immediately apparent, the tide had turned. On 15 June Cornwallis left Elk Hill and started back to Richmond; he entered that place on the 16th and left four days later to move down the Peninsula to Williamsburg. Lafayette followed cautiously on a parallel course initially 20 miles north of the enemy. He gathered strength as he went: Gen. Wm. Campbell, of Kings Mtn. fame, joined him on the Mechunk with 600 riflemen. Steuben arrived on the 19th with his 450 Va. Cont'ls. This

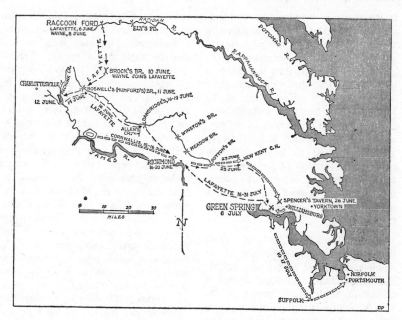

swelled the rebel rolls to 2,000 Cont'ls. and 3,200 militia. (Steuben himself was forced by gout and fatigue to take sick leave.)

Lafayette followed Cornwallis down the Peninsula, wary of bringing on a general engagement but alert to any opportunity to strike at the rear guard. On the 23d, Cornwallis stopped and started to countermarch, but then resumed his retreat. The first skirmish in this campaign of maneuvers and raids took place at SPENCER'S TAVERN, 26 June. When Cornwallis received instructions from Clinton to send about 3,000 men to N.Y. he decided to cross the James. At GREEN SPRING, 6 July, he skilfully lured the rebels into an attempt to catch him astride the river but then missed his opportunity to destroy a sizable portion of Lafayette's army. The Americans withdrew to Malvern Hill; Cornwallis crossed unmolested, and went into camp at Suffolk. (As explained

under YORKTOWN CAMPAIGN, the 3,000-man detachment never was sent.)

TARLETON'S VA. RAID, 9–24 July '81, was a spectacular cavalry operation, but the time had passed when tobacco-burning would beat the revolting colonists. The stage was set for the YORKTOWN CAMPAIGN.

See H. J. Eckenrode, *The Revolution in Virginia,* and Henry P. Johnston, *The Yorktown Campaign.*

VIRGINIA RESOLVES OF 1765. Introduced in the House of Burgesses by Patrick HENRY with his Treason Speech on 29 May, they subsequently were toned down by the elimination of the two most radical resolutions. As finally approved on 31 May they stated that Va. would continue to legislate matters of internal government, and they approved the principle that taxation without representation was illegal.

VIRGINIA RESOLVES OF 1769. Framed by George Mason, introduced in the House of Burgesses by Washington on 16 May, and unanimously adopted the same day, these resolutions asserted that only the governor and the provincial· legislature had the right to lay taxes in Va., they implied censure of the ministry's denunciation of the Va. and MASS. CIRCULAR LETTERS, and they condemned the Parliamentary proposal that an ancient law of Henry VIII be revived to bring American malcontents to England for trial. Gov. Botetourt promptly dissolved the assembly, but the Burgesses met informally and on 18 May adopted the Va. ASSOCIATION.

VIRGINIA RESOLVES OF 1798. In disputing the constitutionality of the Alien and Sedition Acts passed by the Federalists, James Madison drafted a resolution, subsequently passed by the Va. legislature, asserting the right of states, in the last resort, to reject acts of Congress as unconstitutional.

VOLUNTEERS OF IRELAND. Provincial (Tory) Regt. According to Fortescue, this was a regiment "composed entirely of Irish deserters from the American army" (*British Army*, III, 270). Writing of their formation, Clinton has this to say in his memoirs:

"Seeing, therefore, that no very large portion of the friendly colonists who had taken refuge within our posts seemed much inclined to add to their other sufferings those of a military life ... I had recourse to those sources from whence the rebels themselves drew most of their best soldiers—I mean the Irish and other Europeans who had [recently?] settled in America.

"As it was difficult, however, to hold forth terms of sufficient advantage to these emigrants to incite them to quit their present service [i.e., desert] without running a risk of giving umbrage to the natives of America who had, with voluntary zeal, entered into the first provincial corps that had been raised, I made use of another lure, which I thought might prove equally effectual. This was to endeavor to work upon the national attachment of the Irish by inviting them into a regiment whose officers should all be from that country, and placing at its head a nobleman of popular character and ability. Accordingly, before I left Philadelphia [16 June '78], I began to form such a corps, under the title of the Volunteers of Ireland and the command of Lord Rawdon, whose zeal I knew would lead him to spare neither [personal?] expense nor pains to complete its numbers and render it useful and respectable. The foundation of a legionary corps was also at the same time laid.... [See BRITISH LEGION] These two corps afterward filled fast and, being employed on active service the rest of the war, had frequent opportunities of signalizing themselves, as will appear in the sequel of this narrative." (*Amer. Reb.*, 110–11)

In addition to telling us how this unit was formed, the quotation from Clinton's memoirs shows some of his problems of recruiting and reveals the supercilious attitude that helped dismember the British Empire.

In May '79 the Irish Volunteers were part of the expedition sent to Va. for the Mathew–Collier Raid. (See under VA. MIL. OPNS.) (Ward, *W.O.R.*, 867) They arrived with the reinforcements from N.Y. to take part in the final operations of the CHARLESTON CAMPAIGN of 1780. At HOBKIRK'S HILL, S.C., 25 Apr. '81, they particularly distinguished themselves. In his report of this action to Cornwallis, Rawdon wrote (26 Apr. '81):

"We were so fortunate in our march [against Greene's position] that we were not discovered till the flank companies of the Volunteers of Ireland, which led our column, fell in with Greene's pickets. The pickets, though supported, were instantly driven in and followed to their camp.* * * I had ordered . . . Campbell to lead the attack with the Sixty-third and King's American Regiments, which he performed with great spirit. The extent of the enemy's line soon obliged me to throw forward the Volunteers of Ireland also. Those three corps quickly gained the summit of the hill; and, giving room for the rest of our force to act, the rout of the enemy was immediately decided. (*Amer. Reb.*, 514)

The Irish Volunteers are not mentioned in connection with other operations in the South.

VON STEUBEN. See STEUBEN.

VOSE, Joseph. 1738–1816. Cont'l. officer. Mass. From May to Dec. '75, Heath's Mass. Regt. included Lt. Bill Vose, Capt. Elijah Vose, and Maj. Joseph Vose. The senior brother distinguished himself in the raid on GREAT BREWSTER ISLAND, 21 July, and his promotion to Lt. Col. was backdated to 1 July. (Heitman) In the reorganization of 1 Jan. '76 he became Lt. Col. of Greaton's 24th Cont'l. Inf., and on 1 Jan. '77 he took command of the 1st Mass. as full Col. His brother Elijah was promoted to Lt. Col. of this regiment on 21 Jan., and Bill's status

changed from Lt. and Regt'l. Q.M. of the 24th Cont'l. to Paymaster of the 1st Mass. on 1 Jan. '77. (The latter, whom Heitman lists as Bill, not William, resigned 1 Apr. '79.) Joining Washington's army in N.J., Vose took part in the Monmouth Campaign of June–July '78 and marched north for the operations under Sullivan at Newport the next month.

On 17 Feb. '81, "the eight eldest companies" of the Mass. line were formed into a battalion under Joseph Vose, and Maj. Galvan was named second in command. (Heath, *Memoirs,* 288) This unit formed part of Lafayette's force that marched south from West Point for Military Operations in VIRGINIA, and during the Yorktown Campaign was in Muhlenberg's Brig. of Lafayette's Lt. Inf. Div. In the reorganization of 13 June '83 Joseph Vose was given command of one of the four Mass. regiments formed of men whose enlistments had not expired (*ibid.,* 400), and he led it into N.Y.C. on Evacuation Day, 25 Nov. '83. (The Cont'l. Army having been disbanded, Vose's regiment was no longer the 1st Mass. he had commanded from 1 Jan. '77 to 3 Nov. '83. Although his new unit is referred to as the 2d Mass., this was not the 2d Mass. of the war. See Heitman, 36–37, and Freeman, *op. cit.,* V, 462 *n.*)

W

WADSWORTH, Jeremiah. 1743–1804. Commissary general of Cont'l. Army, congressman. Conn. Going to sea at the age of 18 to improve his health, he started as a common sailor aboard one of the ships owned by his

uncle, Matthew Talbott, and rose to the rank of Capt. In Apr. '75 he became commissary of Conn. forces, and on 18 June '77 Congress elected him deputy commissary general of purchases. He resigned this post in Aug. '77. When

Congress re-established the previous system under which Joseph TRUMBULL had operated, Wadsworth became Commiss. Gen. and held this post from Apr. '78 until he resigned on 4 Dec. '79. Washington commended him for keeping the army amply supplied. He was commissary for Rochambeau's army until the close of the war, and in the summer of 1783 went to Paris to report on his transactions. Like Robert Morris, Wadsworth made a good profit from his activities. (See work by R. A. East cited under MORRIS) He was a pioneer in American business, banking, insurance, and cattle breeding.

"WAGONER, Old." Nickname of Daniel MORGAN.

WAHAB'S PLANTATION, N.C., 21 Sept. '80. As outlined under the article on KINGS MOUNTAIN, Tarleton's Legion, reinforced, moved on the left of the British army that advanced toward Charlotte. During this advance Tarleton came down with yellow fever and command passed to Maj. Geo. Hanger. Acting on information from natives, about sunrise on 21 Sept., Col. Wm. Davie approached Wahab's with 80 mounted partisans and 70 riflemen in two small companies under Maj. Geo. Davidson. (This was about the only body of armed patriots left in the field after the events covered under the CHARLESTON EXPED. of 1780.) Oblivious that any enemy troops were near, the British had called in their sentries and more than 60 men were sitting their horses on a road near one of the plantation houses. Davie's force was hidden by a cornfield that came to the very edge of the house. Col. Davie explains his plan as follows:

"A company of infantry were detached thro' the corn with orders to take possession of the houses and immediately fire on the enemy. The cavalry were sent round the corn field with directions to gain the other end of the lane and charge the foe as soon as the fire commenced at the houses, while the Colonel [Davie] advanced to receive them with about 40 riflemen." (Quoted in C. & M., 1137)

The British were surprised and routed with a loss of 15 or 20 killed and about 40 wounded. (*Ibid.*) There was only one American casualty, and this man was wounded during the pursuit when mistaken for an enemy. Having expected to make this attack at night, Davie had ordered that no prisoners be taken. "These orders in the hurry of the morning were not revoked," he says. The rebels carried off 96 fully equipped horses and 120 stand of arms, returning to their camp after covering 60 miles in less than 24 hours. Since Capt. James Wahab (or Wauchope) was known to belong to Davie's command, the British burned his plantation.

Davie and Hanger met next at CHARLOTTE, 26 Sept.

WALLABOUT BAY, Brooklyn, N.Y. Site of today's N.Y. Naval Shipyard, this is where the *Jersey* and other British prison ships were moored. See PRISONS AND PRISON SHIPS.

WALLACE, James. 1731–1803. British naval officer. He entered the Royal Naval Academy at Portsmouth in 1746 and was a Capt. commanding the *Rose* (20) in Nov. '71. In 1774 he sailed this ship to North America, and was stationed at Newport. Here he became extremely unpopular with the Americans for his doing his duty as he saw it. In July '76 he assumed command of the *Experiment* (50) and after taking home the dispatches in Jan. '77 he was knighted on 13 Feb. He was in CLINTON'S EXPEDITION to the Highlands in Oct. '77, including the burning of KINGSTON, 16 Oct. He took part in the relief of Newport in the summer of 1778. On 20 Aug. he escaped capture

by the French off Newport by moving
down Long Island Sound and taking
his ship through Hell Gate, "a piece
of bold navigation previously supposed
impossible for a ship of that size."
(*D.N.B.*) In Dec. his ship suffered storm
damage off the Va. coast and returned
to England for major repairs. Early in
1779 he served under Arbuthnot in the
relief of the Island of Jersey, and in
May he sailed with him to N.Y. Sent
south with pay for the troops in Ga.,
Wallace had the misfortune of being
captured by the French off SAVANNAH.
He was acquitted by a court-martial of
misconduct. In Mar. '80 he took command of the *Nonsuch* (64) and commanded her in operations off the coasts
of Europe and in the West Indies. On
1 Jan. 1808 he was promoted to Adm.
He was a son in-law of Gov. Sir James
WRIGHT of Ga.

WALLIS, Samuel. d. 1798. Loyalist
secret agent. Pa. Although never suspected during his life and his treachery
not known until certain of the Arnold
and Clinton papers came to light in the
20th century, Wallis served the British
during their occupation of Philadelphia,
assisted the Tories in their frontier
raids, and was Benedict Arnold's agent
when the latter went over to the enemy.
Born in Md. of Quaker stock, he had
long been established in Philadelphia
as a shipper and speculator when the
British arrived. After the Treaty of Ft.
Stanwix (1768) opened frontier lands
for settlement he built a stone house at
Muncy in Northumberland co. on the
west branch of the Susquehanna. In
straight-line distances Muncy is about
25 miles due north of Sunbury, where
the important frontier post of Ft.
Augusta was located, and about the
same distance west of the Wyoming
Valley. An Indian raid in the summer
of 1778, just before the Wyoming
Valley "Massacre" and in an event still

remembered in Pa. as the Big Runaway,
settlers took refuge in Wallis' house
before continuing on to Sunbury.
Wallis urged that regulars be stationed
in the region for protection, the militia
having proved itself unworthy, and in
Aug. '78 a detachment of the 6th Pa.
was posted near his house. It was
Wallis' custom to spend only the summer in his frontier home and to live the
rest of the time in Philadelphia.

When Sullivan's Expedition against
the Iroquois was being planned, Wallis
came up with what Van Doren calls
"one of the most extraordinary schemes
ever contrived by a loyalist." (*Secret
History*, 219) Called on by state authorities to draw up a map of the Iroquois
country and to assist in planning the
expedition, Wallis is said to have produced a false map that would lead Sullivan 100 miles to the southwest of
Tioga, which was the place where forces
of Clinton (from upstate N.Y.) and
Sullivan were to join for the campaign.
A correct map was to be furnished to
the British. Van Doren points out that
these maps have never been found and
it is certain that they had no effect on
Sullivan's Expedition, but the idea was
ingenious. Wallis volunteered the use of
his house as a rendezvous for enemy
agents of the frontier.

In the opening stages of ARNOLD'S
TREASON, André dealt with both Wallis
and Arnold. He was named by George
Beckwith, another man involved with
the British secret service, for important
duties in attempting to exploit the
Mutiny of the Pa. Line, but Wallis
realized that the patriots had the situation under control before the British
could act. (*Ibid.*, 410) He managed to
maintain strong personal connections
with the Cont'l. Cong. and successfully
posed as a Whig while profiting from
his shipment of food to the British army
and supplying them with military in-

formation. He was sure to be on the winning side, whichever it turned out to be. After remaining safely and profitably in Philadelphia until 1782, he then moved to Muncy, built his local holdings to about 8,000 acres, and—particularly as a representative of the Holland Land Company—engaged in land speculation to the west. He died of smallpox in Philadelphia in 1798 during the financial crisis that wiped out other speculators (including Robert Morris), and after his death his large fortune was entirely lost.

This little-known figure looms large in Van Doren's *Secret History of the American Revolution,* although he actually appears to have done the patriot cause little real damage. One of Van Doren's sources, other than the papers of the Clements Collection (see main bibliography), is the magazine *Now and Then,* first published at Muncy, Pa., in 1868 and recently edited (1941) by T. Kenneth Wood.

WALPOLE, Horatio or Horace. 1717–1797. English politician and writer. Youngest child of Sir Robert WALPOLE, he entered Parliament in 1754 but paid little attention to politics; he is remembered as a brilliant man of letters, diarist, and historian. Of interest to us here are the diaries he kept during the period 1750–83; in these he records the chief incidents and analyzes the main personalities in this critical span of British politics. Edited by various authorities, these works appeared posthumously as *Memoirs of the Last Ten Years of the Reign of George II* (1846), *Memoirs of the Reign of King George III* (4 vols., 1845; re-edited in 1894), and *Journal of the Reign of George III from 1771 to 1783* (2 vols., 1859; re-edited in 1909). His *Reminiscences,* written in 1788, were published in two volumes in 1819. Walpole has been called the best letter writer in the English lan-

guage; the standard collection of his *Letters* is that published 1903–5 by Mrs. Paget Toynbee. For a specimen, see end of article on TOWNSHEND.

WALPOLE, Robert. First of the true PRIME MINISTERS of Britain (*E.B.,* "Orford, Robert Walpole"), he had passed from the scene before the era of the American Revolution started. An important chronicler of that era, however, was his son, Horace WALPOLE. See also SALUTARY NEGLECT.

WALTON, George. 1741–1804. Signer, Gov. of Ga. Va.–Ga. Grandson of an Englishman who reached the colonies in 1682, he was orphaned and apprenticed to a carpenter. At the end of his term, in 1769, he moved to Savannah, studied law, and was admitted to the bar in 1774. As early as July of that year he was one of the local patriots urging action against Britain, and he had a leading role in putting Ga. in the patriot camp. Named a delegate to the Cont'l. Cong. on 2 Feb. '76, he sat for the periods 1776–77 and 1780–81. He, Lyman Hall, and Button Gwinnett were the Signers from Ga. when the Decl. of Indep. was approved. In the muddled politics of his state he was leader of the conservatives, while Gwinnett led the radicals. After the latter was killed in a duel by Lachlan McIntosh, Walton sent Cong. a forged letter that caused the transfer of McIntosh from the state. In 1783 the legislature censured Walton for this deed and ordered suit brought against him, but on the preceding day this same body had elected him chief justice. (F. M. Green in *D.A.B.*)

On 9 Jan. '78 he had been named Col. of militia and in the unsuccessful defense of SAVANNAH, 29 Dec. '78, he was severely wounded in the thigh and captured. He was exchanged in Sept. '79. Patriot factions elected two governors of the state, and Walton, the

choice of the stronger group, served
from Nov. '79 to Jan. '80 before returning to Cong. He later was chief
justice of the state for six years, and
again was elected Gov. in 1789. From
1790 until his death 14 years later he
had three terms as judge of the state
supreme court and filled an unexpired
U.S. Senate term. He has been described
as being small, handsome, self-impor-
tant, and hot tempered. (*Ibid.*)

WARD, Artemas. 1727–1800. American politician and general. Mass. Of
Pilgrim stock and a believer that Providence had blessed his state and its
inhabitants as the chosen people (Edward E. Curtis in *D.A.B.*), Artemas
Ward was appointed the senior Maj.
Gen. of the Cont'l. Army and second
in command (17 June '75) when Washington was appointed C. in C. A Harvard graduate (1748) and prominent in
colonial affairs, he had risen to the
grade of militia Col. during the French
and Indian War, serving under Abercromby in the unfortunate attack on
Ticonderoga in 1758 and returning from
that campaign with his health permanently impaired. In 1775 he was a
stern-looking man of medium height,
heavy in body and slow of speech
(Freeman, *Washington,* III, 477). Sick
in bed when news of the "Lexington
alarm" (19 Apr.) reached him, he rode
at dawn the next day to assume command of the forces around Boston and
directed operations until Washington
arrived on 2 July. On 19 May he had
been formally commissioned Gen. and
C. in C. of Mass. troops and exercised
some authority over the contingents
from other colonies. (See BOSTON
SIEGE) He directed the Battle of BUN-
KER HILL from his headquarters at
Cambridge. Representing alien cultures,
Washington and Ward worked together
with mutual antipathy. Ward, understandably, was disappointed about being

superseded as C. in C. He resented
Washington's evident conviction that
troops of the Boston army, including
those from Mass., left something to be
desired in the way of military proficiency. (*D.A.B.*) "Although no clash
occurred," writes Freeman, "neither
man cared for the other." (*Op. cit.,*
495A)

When American forces occupied Boston, Ward submitted his resignation
(22 Mar.), withdrew it, and then resub-
mitted it on 12 Apr. On 23 Apr.
Congress accepted it with little appearance of reluctance (*ibid.,* IV, 92), but
at Washington's request Ward retained
his post until the end of May while the
problem of a replacement could be
solved. Sparks flew during this period
when Washington wrote Ward that he
had been informed that troops performing outpost duty on Bunker Hill
and Dorchester Neck were being excused from work on the city's fortifications. Ward fired back that this information was "injurious falsehood" and
complained that "because 1500 men
could not throw up the works as fast
as 6000 or 7000 had done in time past,
there appeared to some an unaccountable
delay." Ward inspired some fine damning
from the pen of Washington. When he
learned that Ward had withdrawn his
original resignation, Washington wrote
Charles Lee that Ward probably wanted
to get away "from the smoke of his own
chimney." The Mass. authorities had
begun to indicate some dissatisfaction
with Ward's performance, and when this
was reported to Washington he asked,
"If General W is judged an improper
person to command five Regiments in
a peaceful camp or garrison... why
was he appointed to the first military
command in the Massachusetts government?" (This and preceding quotations
are from Freeman, *op. cit.,* 92–93.)

After leaving his post at Boston, Ward remained as commander of the Eastern Dept. until succeeded by Wm. Heath on 20 Mar. '77. Meanwhile he also was executive head of Mass. and a member of Congress. In 1798 illness compelled him to resign, and he died of paralysis. His homestead is the property of Harvard and is kept as a memorial. Ward's papers are scattered, but among the principal collections are those of the M.H.S., the Mass. State Archives, and the American Antiquarian Society (Worcester, Mass.). (*D.A.B.*)

Of this austere, unsympathetic Yankee who might well have had Washington's task, Freeman has this epitaph:

"Perhaps he deserved more credit than he received. He kept the Army together in front of Boston until Washington came, and after that, however much he felt aggrieved, he did not add to his successor's difficulties by organizing the discontented. Charles Lee laughed at Ward's generalship and sneeringly termed him a church warden. Perhaps it was a compliment. Had Ward possessed the spirit [and the health?] of the man who assailed him, he might have ruined Washington" [and American independence]. (*Op. cit.*, III, 495A)

WARD, Samuel. 1725–1776. Gov. of R.I., congressman. Son of a prosperous Newport merchant who was Gov. of R.I. from 1740 to 1742, Samuel himself was elected Gov.—in 1762, 1765, and 1766. In R.I. politics Ward was leader of the conservative group, the merchants of Newport, while Stephen HOPKINS was the more successful champion of the Providence radicals. What amounted almost to a tribal feud ended in 1768, when they agreed on a coalition Gov. In 1774 the former political enemies were united as delegates to the 1st Cont'l. Cong. In the 2d Cong. he presided frequently over the Comm. of the Whole. "It was his fortune to pro-

pose and to help secure the appointment of George Washington as commander-in-chief...." (Marguerite Appleton in *D.A.B.*) While he had come around to favoring independence, he died of smallpox on 26 Mar. '76 and, hence, was not a "signer."

Father of Sam'l. WARD (Jr.).

WARD, Samuel (Jr.). 1756–1832. Cont'l. officer. R.I. Second son of Sam'l. WARD, he graduated with honors in 1771 from what is now Brown University. On 3 May '75 he was commissioned Capt. in the 1st R.I. Regt., and on 31 Dec. he was taken prisoner at Quebec. Exchanged in Aug. '76, he returned from Canada and 12 Jan. '77 was promoted to Maj., 1st R.I. He was with the main army at Morristown and then went north to oppose Burgoyne's Offensive. After spending the winter at Valley Forge, he fought at Newport (July–Aug. '78), and on 12 Apr. '79 he was promoted to Lt. Col. (*D.A.B.*; Heitman says this promotion was dated 26 May '78) He retired from the army 1 Jan. '81 and started a business career that took him all over the world: he was one of the first American merchants to visit the Far East (1788), and he was in Paris when Louis XVI was sentenced to death (Jan. '93). His son, Sam'l. (1786–1839), was the father of Julia Ward Howe.

WARNER, Seth. 1743–1784. Militia officer. Vt. Born in Woodbury (now Roxbury), Conn., he moved with his family to Bennington in 1763 and became a leader of the GREEN MOUNTAIN BOYS. On 9 Mar. '74 he was outlawed by N.Y. and a reward offered for his arrest. He took part in the capture of TICONDEROGA, 10 May '75, occupied CROWN POINT two days later, and at a council held here the next month he and Ethan Allen were named to procure incorporation of a Green Mountain regiment in the Cont'l. Army. Their mission was successful, and on 26 July Warner was elected Lt. Col. commandant. Returning to Lake Champlain, he joined Montgomery's wing of the Canada Invasion and fought at LONGUEUIL. In the retreat from Canada he commanded rear guard actions and also raised reinforcements in Vt. At HUBBARDTON, 7 July '77, his rear guard was surprised and defeated in an action that reflects no credit on Warner's tactical ability. He arrived for the final and decisive phase of the battle of BENNINGTON, 16 Aug. '77. (See section headed "Breymann's Defeat") "Although Warner's movements during the action have been much debated, it is generally agreed that the timely arrival of his regiment in the latter part of the battle turned the tide in favor of the yeomanry of New England." (Edward E. Curtis in *D.A.B.*) On 20 Mar. '78 he was promoted to B.G. of Vt. militia, having been given the grade of Col. of one of the "ADDITIONAL CONTINENTAL REGIMENTS" on 5 July '76.

Because of failing health he saw little more active service, although he continued to command his regiment until his retirement on 1 Jan. '83 at the age of 40. He died on 26 Dec. '84. Warner was over six feet tall and is said to have been modest and unassuming.

See Daniel Chipman, *Memoir of Col. Seth Warner* (1848).

WARNER'S REGT. was organized 5 July '76 and in 1777 became one of the 16 "ADDITIONAL CONT'L. REGTS."

"WARRANT MEN." Six fictitious persons in almost all British foot regiments whose pay was distributed as follows: pay of two men went to widows of regimental officers; pay of the others went to reimburse the Col. for deserters' clothing, for recruiting, and for the personal use of the Col. and regimental agent. (Curtis, 24) See also "CONTINGENT MEN."

WARREN, James. 1726–1808. Political leader. Mass. A descendant of Richard Warren of the *Mayflower* and the eldest son of James and Penelope (Winslow) Warren, he was not related to Joseph and John WARREN. (The ancestor of these brothers, John Warren, came over on the *Arbella*, docking at Salem on 12 June 1630.) Born at Plymouth, James graduated from Harvard in 1745, succeeded his father as county sheriff in 1757 (when the father died), and pursued the career of merchant and gentleman farmer. In 1754 he married the sister of James Otis, who as Mercy Otis Warren (1728–1814) is remembered as a famous authoress and "historical apologist for the patriot cause." (*D.A.B.*)

James sat in the lower house of the Mass. General Court and the Prov. Cong. from 1766 until 1778. He was a close friend of the two Adamses and succeeded Joseph Warren as Pres. of the Prov. Cong. On dissolution of that body he became Speaker of the House of Representatives in the new General Court. Between 27 July '75 and 19 Apr. '76 he was Paymaster Gen. of the Cont'l. Army, and from 1776 to 1781 he was on the Navy Board for the Eastern Dept. When the General Court designated him one of three major generals in Sept. '76 to lead a force into R.I. he was unwilling to serve under a Cont'l. officer of lesser rank and excused himself on the grounds of a recent illness. The next year he resigned his commission to avoid another such embarrassment, and his political enemy, John Hancock, used this to undermine his reputation to such a degree that Warren failed to be re-elected in 1778 to the legislature. In 1779 he won re-election, but then was unable to win again until 1787. He held a number of offices after the war, but his individualistic views prevented his massing the political power needed to compete with such antagonists as Hancock. "I am content to move in a small sphere," he had written to John Adams in 1775. "I expect no distinction but that of an honest man who has exerted every nerve." Yet when he later sought and failed to achieve such distinction as the office of Lt. Gov. and member of Congress he was resentful. "His mind has been soured, and he became discontented and querulous," wrote John Quincy Adams.

WARREN, John. 1753–1815. Cont'l. surgeon. Mass. After studying under his elder brother, Joseph WARREN, John became a successful doctor in Boston. In 1773 he joined Col. Pickering's Regt. as a surgeon, and on hearing of his brother Joseph's death at Bunker Hill he gave up his practice and volunteered for service in the ranks. (*D.A.B.*) At the age of only 22 he became senior surgeon of the hospital at Cambridge. In 1776 he was transferred to N.Y. and was appointed surgeon of the general hospital on Long Island. After seeing service with the army at Trenton and Princeton he returned to Boston in Apr. '77 to resume his practice but he also continued to perform the duties of military surgeon in the army hospital there. He became the leading New England surgeon of his day, performing one of the first abdominal operations in America, and was founder of the Harvard Medical School.

WARREN, Joseph. 1741–1775. Patriot leader killed at Bunker Hill. Mass. Born at Roxbury, he distinguished himself at Harvard—graduating in 1759— and became an exceptionally successful doctor in Boston. He got to know John Adams after the latter had been his patient, and he was closely associated with Sam Adams during the Stamp Act crisis. In the political foment of pre-Revolutionary Boston he distinguished himself as a political writer, orator, and organizer, teaming up with Sam Adams, John Hancock, and James Otis. In 1770 he was on the committee to demand removal of British troops after the Boston "Massacre," and on the first two anniversaries of this event he delivered celebrated commemorative addresses. He drafted the SUFFOLK RESOLVES, and succeeded Sam Adams as head of the comm. of safety. On the eve of LEXINGTON AND CONCORD he remained in Boston, despite the danger to himself, and it was he who sent out his friend Paul REVERE (and Wm. Dawes) to warn the patriots. He then took an active part in the next day's fighting. Succeeding John Hancock as Pres. of the Mass. Prov. Cong. on 23 Apr. '75, on 20 May he became head of the committee to organize the army in Mass. On 14 June he was elected Maj. Gen. of militia, having declined the post of physician general. The night of 16–17 June he sat with the provincial congress at Watertown, the morning of the 17th he met with the comm. of safety at Cambridge, and that afternoon he went out to Bunker Hill, where the battle was about to start. Putnam offered to turn over command to Warren, but the latter said he had come as a volunteer to serve where he would be most useful. Sent to the redoubt at Breed's Hill, Warren again declined to assume command.* In the final phase of the action he was shot through the face and killed, one of only 30 Americans who died in the redoubt.

* There was something more than mere modesty involved. Although Warren had been *appointed* Maj. Gen., he had not yet been given a *commission*. "He had no command, nothing but the title," explains Esther Forbes. (*Revere,* 279)

Warren had been buried on Bunker Hill with the other dead in an unmarked grave. When the British left Boston, nine months after the battle, his body was positively identified by the two artificial teeth Revere had made for his friend shortly before he died. This is probably the first recorded instance of what has since become the standard procedure of identifying corpses by their dental records. (Forbes, *Revere,* 302) It was obvious from the path of the bullet that Warren died instantly, without such speeches invented by his contemporaries as "I am a dead man, fight on, my brave fellows, for the salvation of your country." (*Ibid.,* 301, 464) Only 34 years old, Warren was "a leader of great promise, whose loss was heavy to bear." (Van Tyne, *War of Independence,* 48)

The best biography remains that published by Frothingham in 1865, *The Life and Times of Joseph Warren* (Lib. of Cong., *Guide,* 342).

WARREN OR WHITE HORSE TAVERN, Pa., 16 Sept. '77. (PHILADELPHIA CAMPAIGN) Five days after the Battle of the Brandywine the opposing armies converged on White Horse Tavern (in present village of Planebrook, not White Horse, as many authorities err in saying) and on the Admiral Warren Tavern (three miles east in today's Malvern).

Each commander learned early in the day of the other's approach, and both prepared for a major engagement. Pulaski was sent forward with the American cavalry and 300 supporting infantry as a delaying force, but the infantry ran as soon as fired on and the enemy advanced unimpeded.

About 1 P.M. the brigades of Wayne and Maxwell met Knyphausen's column near Boot Tavern and almost cut off a reconnaissance party of jägers commanded by Col. von Donop, but the

Americans were soon forced back by jäger reinforcements and Hessian grenadiers. The main bodies were squaring off for action when nature intervened.

"I wish I could give a description of the downpour which began during the engagement and continued until the next morning [wrote a Hessian officer]. It came down so hard that in a few moments we were drenched and sank in mud up to our calves." (Baurmeister, *Journals,* 114)

Because of defective cartridge boxes —the leather tops did not extend sufficiently to turn the rain—the Americans lost tens of thousands of rounds, and many regiments were unable to fire a shot. (Freeman, *Washington,* IV, 494) The British, on the other hand, lost little ammunition. (*Ibid.*)

Henry Knox wrote his wife on 24 Sept.:

"...nearly all the musket cartridges of the army that had been delivered to the men were damaged, consisting of about 400,000. This was a most terrible stroke to us, and ... obliged us to retire, in order to get supplied with so essential an article as cartridges...." (Drake, *Knox,* quoted by C. & M., 619) Since each man carried 40 rounds in his cartridge box, and Washington had about 10,000 rank and file in his army, Knox's figure of total ammunition loss results from straight multiplication. Although many historians have apparently concluded from the above statement that Washington retreated because the rain had ruined 400,000 rounds, Freeman does not mention this as being the determining factor. (Freeman speaks of "tens of thousands of rounds" being ruined.) (*Op. cit.,* 493–94) See PHIL. CAMP'N. for more about the subsequent retreat and its causes.

WARWARSING, N.Y. See WAWARSING.

WASHINGTON, George. 1732–1799. Commander in chief of Cont'l. Army, first U.S. president. Va. Great-grandson of an Englishman who settled in Va. in 1658, and son of Augustine (1694–1743) by his second wife, Mary Ball (m. 1730), George Washington had an undistinguished and uneventful youth. His elder half-brother, Lawrence, inherited on his father's death the estate he later named Mount Vernon, and young George lived here from 1735 to 1739. After this he lived at the other family estate, on the Rappahannock nearly opposite Fredericksburg, which had been willed to him. His formal schooling ended when he was 15, and although Lawrence guided his efforts at self-education, he remained seriously deficient in all fields of learning except mathematics. (Wm. MacDonald in *E.B.*) He was never an assiduous reader, he lacked facility as a public speaker, and although he did acquire "a dignified and effective English style" such compilers of his writings as Jared Sparks have heavily edited them to enhance their literary quality. (*Ibid.*) It must also be mentioned at this point that the quality of his youth also was enhanced by biographers. The cherry tree story was almost assuredly invented by "Parson" Weems. There is no proof that he had to turn down a midshipman's commission in the British navy because his mother would not consent.

In 1748, when he was living again at Mount Vernon with his brother and guardian, Lawrence, he was appointed surveyor of the Fairfax property, and he soon became a public surveyor. In 1751 he accompanied Lawrence to the West Indies, where the latter hoped to recover from consumption. George caught smallpox on this trip, remaining permanently marked but acquiring a valuable immunity. Lawrence died in 1752, making George executor of his will and residuary heir of Mount Vernon. On the eve of the last COLONIAL WAR, Gov. Dinwiddie sent Washington on the dangerous and arduous mission of warning the French to give up their new posts in the northwest. Appointed Lt. Col. of Va. militia soon after his return, in Apr. '54 he led two companies back into this same region, defeated a French and Indian force at Great Meadows (28 May), but was surrounded and forced to surrender at Ft. Necessity, 3 July. As Braddock's A.D.C. he survived the Battle of the Wilderness, 9 July '55, and the next month was made commander of the Va. militia, although he was then only 23 years old. For the next two years he coped with the problems of commanding 700 irregulars in the defense of a 350-mile frontier. He took part in the Forbes expedition of 1758 to Ft. Duquesne. (See COLONIAL WARS) Resigning his commission the end of 1759, he emerged from his first military service with a fine reputation and with some sound training under BOUQUET and Forbes. (See FORBES EXPEDITION.)

In Jan. '59 he married Martha Dandridge (1732–1802), widow of Daniel Parke Custis, and with her property of about $100,000 added to his own inheritance he was one of America's richest men. Making his home at Mt. Vernon, which became his in 1761, Washington spent 15 years as a prosperous planter of the ruling class in the Old Dominion. He served repeatedly in the House of Burgesses, but was by no means a leader in local politics. "His diaries show a minutely methodical conduct of business, generous indulgence in hunting, comparatively little reading and a wide acquaintance with the leading men of the colonies, but no marked indications of what is usually considered to be 'greatness,'" comments MacDonald. (*Op. cit.*)

As the Revolutionary movement gathered way, however, he was prominently identified with the patriot element. When the House of Burgesses was dissolved in May '70 he was among the members who met at the Raleigh Tavern and adopted a nonimportation agreement. Siding with the radicals, he opposed making petitions to the king and parliament not only because he felt they would be scorned but because he did not believe in begging for what the colonists considered to be rights. His letters show that he clearly comprehended the political course the patriots were taking, and while more sophisticated minds remained cloudy about the alternatives, Washington recognized that the course led to war with England. (*Ibid.*)

On 5 Aug. '74 he was appointed a delegate to the 1st Cont'l. Cong., where his participation was not remarkable. Back in Va. he urged that military preparations get under way, personally drilled volunteers, and was conspicuous in the 2d Cong. as the only member habitually appearing in uniform. On 15 June '75, on the motion of John Adams, Washington was unanimously selected C. in C. This fortunate choice was dictated by elementary politics: if the New Englanders who had hatched the Revolution were to get the support of the most powerful colony to the south they could best do this by naming a Virginian C. in C.

Commissioned on 17 June '75, Washington took command of the Boston army on 3 July. His military service for the next seven years is marked by character and fortitude but a lack of real genius. His biggest battles were little more than skirmishes: the Cont'l. Army never numbered over 35,000 (*A.A.,* 411); Washington never had more than about a third of this total under his personal direction; and in about his only flash of strategic genius, at Trenton and Princeton, his total command was about 6,000, of whom fewer than half were actually engaged.

After the successful termination of the Boston Siege, where his problems were mainly administrative—all he had to do was to organize one army, demobilize it in the face of the enemy, and mobilize a new one!—Washington faced a strategic challenge in the N.Y. Campaign that would have taxed a Napoleon. He showed that he was distinctly no Napoleon—scattering his forces so as to subject them to Defeat in Detail, but achieving a remarkable evacuation from Long Island, from Manhattan, and pulling his army back to White Plains and escaping annihilation. He shares with Nathanael Greene the guilt for the disaster at Fort Washington, 16 Nov. '76, a blow that almost was fatal to the American cause.

Washington's greatness shone through in his brilliant riposte at the end of the N.J. Campaign—Trenton, 26 Dec. '76, and Princeton, 3 Feb. '77. Few commanders could have achieved offensive maneuvers of this type in the dead of winter with demoralized, starved, and almost naked troops. Continuing to hold his little army together in the face of incredible difficulties—public apathy, inadequate state support, impotent Congressional assistance—Washington survived a series of frustrations and defeats in the Philadelphia Campaign before the ordeal of Valley Forge Winter Quarters, Dec. '77–June '78. During this period he exhibited ability of an unexpected sort in facing the threat generally known as the Conway Cabal.

The Monmouth Campaign, June '78, ended major operations in the theater where Washington personally directed the war, but with the supporting French army he moved south three years later for the Yorktown Campaign, May—

Oct. '81. Before the Cont'l. Army was disbanded, 3 Nov. '83, Washington skilfully handled the dangerous problem of the NEWBURGH ADDRESSES and summarily stopped a movement, whose spokesman was Col. Nicholas NICOLA, to make him king. After bidding farewell to his officers at Fraunces Tavern in N.Y.C. (4 Dec. '83) the very day the British fleet finally sailed from the harbor, on 23 Dec. '83 he returned his commission as C. in C. to Congress.

Washington was not able to retire from public life very long. He was involved in shaping the Ordinance of 1787. Mount Vernon was the site of a meeting between Va. and Md. commissioners to work out a code for use of the Chesapeake and Potomac; this meeting led to the Annapolis Convention and the Federal Convention to revise the Articles of Confederation (Philadelphia, 1787). Washington was Va. delegate to the latter and, much against his will, became presiding officer. When the new government was organized he was unanimous choice for president. He took the oath of office on 30 Apr. '89 in N.Y.C., was re-elected for a second term in 1792, and refused to serve a third term. During his presidency he supported the financial plans of Alexander Hamilton, maintained U.S. neutrality despite Jefferson's urging that the country adhere to the 1778 treaty with France in 1793, upheld and strengthened federal authority during the Whiskey Insurrection (1794), upheld Jay's treaty with England (1795), and ended the Indian troubles of the Old Northwest by appointing Anthony Wayne to command army forces in that region. His two terms as president were by no means serene, nor did his great reputation protect him from personal criticism. Unable to grasp the need for party politics in a republic, he attempted to balance one against the other in his cabinet. "The consequence was that . . . Alexander Hamilton and Thomas Jefferson, exponents for the most part of diametrically opposite political doctrines, soon occupied the position, to use the words of one of them, of 'two gamecocks in a pit.' " (E.B.) Although tremendously popular to the end with the vast majority of the people—"his election would have been unanimous in 1796, as in 1792 and 1789, had he been willing to serve"—he was embittered by vicious and scurrilous attacks by those politicians who disapproved of his stand on such issues as neutrality and the Whiskey Insurrection.

Delivering his famous "Farewell Address" on 17 Sept. '96, he retired from the presidency in 1797 and resumed his life at Mount Vernon. In 1798 he was made C. in C. of the provisional army raised for the expected war with France. After an illness of only a day—an infection of the windpipe brought about by a long ride in a snowstorm and complicated by the ministrations of Dr. James Craik—he died at Mount Vernon on 14 Dec. '99, where he was buried. He was childless.

Of Washington at the start of the Revolution, D. S. Freeman says, "Everything about him suggested the commander—height, bearing, flawless proportions, dignity of person, composure, and ability to create confidence by calmness and by unfailing, courteous dignity. The only personal quality of command that he lacked in 1775 was the dramatic sense. He was a bit too cool to fire the imagination of youth." (Washington, III, 445) According to measurements sent to his London tailor, Washington was 6 feet 3 inches tall. (E.B.) He weighed about 220 pounds. Except for bad teeth he enjoyed remarkably vigorous health.

Freeman's seven-volume biography supersedes all others. Recommended shorter biographies are by Marcus Cunliffe (1958), Shelby Little (1929), and N. W. Stephenson and W. H. Dunn (2 vols. 1940). Major sources are those compiled by Burnett, Fitzpatrick, Force, and Sparks, and the *Journals of the Cont'l. Cong.*, all identified in the main bibliography.

WASHINGTON, William. 1752–1810. Cont'l. officer. Va. A kinsman of the C. in C.,* he was studying for the ministry when the Revolution started. On 25 Feb. '76 he was commissioned Capt., 3d Va. Cont'ls., in which he served during the N.Y. and N.J. Campaigns. He was severely wounded at Long Island. Leading the attack on cannon in King Street with Lt. James Monroe at Trenton, he was wounded in the hand by a musket ball. (Lee, *Memoirs*, 587) Promoted to Maj. 4th Cont'l. Dragoons on 27 Jan. '77, he advanced to Lt. Col. of the 3d Dragoons (of Geo. Baylor) on 20 Nov. '78. (Heitman) Col. Washington escaped the TAPPAN MASSACRE, N.Y., 28 Sept. '78, according to Henry Lee (*ibid.*), which would indicate that he had joined Baylor's Regt. before 20 Nov., the date Heitman gives for his promotion.

Late in 1779 or early in 1780 Col.

* Appleton's says he was the son of Bailey Washington. *D.A.B.* identifies Baily Washington, the father of John Macrae Washington (1797–1853), as a second cousin of George Washington. It is possible but not likely that this Baily or Bailey would have sons 45 years apart. If so, and if Appleton's data are otherwise correct, then our William was George Washington's second cousin once removed. Heitman notes that William also was known as William Augustine Washington, which was the name of a son of George Washington's brother John Augustine. (Appleton's, "George Corbin Washington")

Washington moved south with remnants of Baylor's, Bland's, and Moylan's Regts. During the initial phase of the Charleston campaign Washington was beaten in a skirmish with TARLETON at Bee's Plantation, 23 Mar. '80, but got the better of Tarleton in another small action around Gov. Rutledge's plantation, 26 Mar. (Appleton's says Washington defeated Tarleton on 23 Mar. at a place called Rantowles.) By this time Tarleton was starting to get some of his men properly mounted, and Washington was lucky to escape with his life at MONCK'S CORNER and LENUD'S FERRY a few weeks later. Washington and Lt. Col. Anthony White (of Moylan's Regt.) withdrew into eastern N.C. to recover and recruit.

Washington scored a clever victory at RUGELEY'S MILLS, S.C., 4 Dec. '80, and struck next in his HAMMOND'S STORE RAID, 27–31 Dec. This was the start of operations that led to Morgan's victory at COWPENS, 17 Jan. '81, where Washington distinguished himself in the battle and closed the action with a dramatic personal encounter with Tarleton. In the "Race to the Dan" and Greene's counteroffensive, Washington's horse were prominent, bringing up the rear of the retreat or leading the advance. After performing with valor at GUILFORD and HOBKIRK'S HILL (where only 56 of his remaining 87 men were mounted), he was wounded and captured in the battle of EUTAW SPRINGS, 8 Sept. '81. "While a prisoner in Charleston," writes Henry Lee in prose (and punctuation) that must be preserved, "Washington became acquainted with Miss Elliot, a young lady, in whom concentrated the united attractions of respectable descent, opulence, polish, and beauty. The gallant soldier soon became enamored of his amiable acquaintance, and afterward married her." (*Op. cit.*, 588)

Settling in Charleston, he served in the legislature but refused to consider running for Gov. "because he could not make a speech." (Quoted in Appleton's) On 19 July '98 he was ccmmissioned B.G. and served until 15 June 1800. As characterized by Henry Lee:

"He possessed a stout frame, being six feet in height, broad, strong, and corpulent. His occupations and his amusements applied to the body, rather than to the mind; to the cultivation of which he did not bestow much time or application. . . . In temper he was good-humored. . . .

"His military exploits announce his grade and character in arms. Bold, collected, and persevering, he preferred the heat of action to the collection and sifting of intelligence, to the calculations and combinations of means and measures. . . . Kind to his soldiers, his system of discipline was rather lax, and sometimes subjected him to injurious consequences, when close to a sagacious and vigilant adversary." (*Ibid.*)

WASHINGTON'S "DICTATORIAL" POWERS, 27 Dec. '76–27 June '77. When the British advance reached the Delaware River in Dec. '76 (NEW JERSEY CAMP'N.) Congress had started fleeing to Baltimore and the fate of the Revolution appeared to rest solely in military hands. Writing on 20 Dec. that "ten days more will put an end to the existence of our army" unless drastic measures were accepted, he asked for sufficient authority to deal with the military emergency. He pointed out that if "every matter that in its nature is self-evident is to be referred to Congress, at a distance of one hundred and thirty or forty miles [to Baltimore], so much time must necessarily elapse, as to defeat the end in view. It may be said, that this is an application for powers that are too dangerous to be entrusted. I can only add that, desperate

diseases require desperate remedies and I with truth declare, that I have no lust after power. . . ." (Montross, *Reluctant Rebels,* quoting from Ford, *Writings of Washington,* V, 114)

On 21 Dec. Congress appointed Robt. Morris, Geo. Clymer, and Geo. Walton as a three-man committee "with powers to execute such continental business as may be proper and necessary to be done at Philadelphia." (Actually, Morris had been carrying the burden of the administration before this formal action was taken on 21 Dec. Freeman, *Washington,* IV, 298 and *n.*) Washington had been dealing with this "rump" Congress as he planned his counteroffensive resulting in the brilliant victories at Trenton and Princeton. On the evening of 31 Dec. an express reached his headquarters with a Congressional resolution adopted in Baltimore on 27 Dec.:

"This Congress, having maturely considered the present crisis; and having perfect reliance on the wisdom, vigour, and uprightness of General Washington, do, hereby,

"*Resolve,* That General Washington shall be, and he is hereby, vested with full, ample, and complete powers to raise and collect together, in the most speedy and effectual manner, from any or all of these United States, sixteen battallions of infantry, in addition to those already voted by Congress; to appoint officers for the said battallions; to raise, officer, and equip three thousand light horse; three regiments of artillery, and a corps of engineers, and to establish their pay; to apply to any of the states for such aid of the militia as he shall judge necessary; to form such magazines of provisions, and in such places, as he shall think proper; to displace and appoint all officers under the rank of brigadier general, and to fill up all vacancies in every other department in the American armies; to take, wherever he may be, whatever he may want for the use of the army, if the inhabitants will not sell it, allowing reasonable price for the same; to arrest and confine persons who refuse to take the continental currency, or are otherwise disaffected to the American cause; and return to the states of which they are citizens, their names, and the nature of their offences, together with the witnesses to prove them:

"That the foregoing powers be vested in General Washington, for and during the term of six months from the date hereof, unless sooner determined by Congress." (Freeman, quoting *J.C.C.*, VI, 1045–46)

The delegates were obviously breathing more easily in Baltimore after Washington's Trenton victory when they felt some further statement as to their position was in order. In a circular letter of 30 Dec. '76 they informed the 13 states that:

"Congress would not have Consented to the Vesting of such Powers . . . if the Situation of Public Affairs did not require at this Crisis a Decision and Vigour, which Distance and Numbers Deny to Assemblies far Remov'd from each other, and from the immediate Seat of War." (*J.C.C.*, VI, 1053)

It is evident from the wording of the 27 Dec. resolve that the powers granted Washington were far from "dictatorial." When he used his authority to make all citizens who had taken the British offer of protection surrender the papers they had accepted or move within the British lines, Congress violently criticized this policy. He has been criticized by historians for failing to use fully his power to take provisions for his army from the profiteering inhabitants of N.J. Yet in Jan. '77, thanks largely to his new, temporary authority, Washington was able to start building a real army.

(J. C. Fitzpatrick in *D.A.B.,* article on Washington)

When the British army again approached Philadelphia, in the fall of 1777 (PHILADELPHIA CAMP'N.), Congress again evacuated the capital, heading through Lancaster to York, Pa., and again they gave Washington "dictatorial" powers. This time it was for a six-day period only, and he used the authority sparingly. (*Ibid.*)

WASHINGTON'S GUARD. See LIFE GUARD.

WATEREE FERRY, S.C., 15 Aug. '80. As explained under CAMDEN CAMPAIGN, Sumter got the approval of Gates for a secondary effort against the British line of communications between Camden and Charleston. Although the plan violated two of Napoleon's most cherished maxims ("No detachment should be made on the eve of battle. . . ." "When a commander intends to give battle, he should collect all his forces, and overlook none; a battalion sometimes decides the day"), Gates reinforced Sumter with 100 Md. Cont'ls., two guns, and 300 N.C. militia. The detachment was commanded by Lt. Col. Thos. Woolford, C.O., 5th Md.

The British had built a small redoubt on the west side of Wateree Ferry, which was called Fort Carey, after the name of the British colonel who commanded it. On 15 Aug., the day after Woolford joined him, Sumter sent Col. Thos. Taylor * with his regiment to surprise Ft. Carey. Taylor captured Col. Carey, 30 troops, and 36 wagons loaded with clothing, food, and rum. Later in the day he took 50 wagons that were

---

* Bass indicates in the index to his *Green Dragoon* that this was *Thomas* Taylor. Heitman identifies such an officer merely as a Col., S.C. militia, 1779–83.

coming from Ninety-Six with supplies, six wagons loaded with baggage, 300 head of cattle, and some sheep. Sumter started retreating up the Wateree when he learned that the enemy was preparing to cross the river and retrieve their prisoners and stores. Hearing the firing of the Battle of Camden, 16 Aug., and learning later in the day of Gates's defeat, the Gamecock attempted to escape north but was surprised and his command annihilated by Tarleton at FISHING CREEK, 18 Aug.

WATSON, John Watson Tadwell. 1748–1826. British officer. Born in London, he entered the 3d Foot Guards in Apr. '67 and on 20 Nov. '78 became Capt. and Lt. Col. of that regiment. (Appleton's; *Army List*) On 16 Oct. '80 he sailed from N.Y. in the expedition of Gen. Leslie that was diverted from Va. to reinforce Cornwallis in the Carolinas; he commanded a force made up of "the wing companies of the several volunteer corps," having in the spring of 1779 commanded the "wing companies of the Guard regiments" (note of editor Uhlendorf in Baurmeister, *Journals*, 385 *n.*). When Cornwallis went chasing into N.C. and then retreated to Wilmington, rather than to Camden,

"Lord Rawdon...had happened to weaken his post [at Camden] by detaching a considerable part of his best troops, under...Watson, for the purpose of dispersing the plunderers that infested the eastern frontier and co-operating with Lord Cornwallis wherever he might be engaged. And, though His Lordship [Rawdon] had sent orders to recall Colonel Watson immediately upon hearing of Greene's advance, this [latter] officer's movements were too rapid to admit of his joining him before His Lordship found himself under a necessity of repelling the enemy's attack in the best manner he could with the small force he had. And indeed the

position which Marion had taken near the high hills of Santee now precluded all hopes of the detached corps' being able to get to him." (Clinton, *Amer. Reb.*, 295)

Watson left Ft. Watson on 5 Mar. '81 and started down the Santee, but in a brilliant series of little guerrilla actions MARION blocked Watson's advance into the Swamp Fox's district and drove him into the British base at Georgetown. Marion then joined "Light Horse Harry" Lee to capture FORT WATSON, 15–23 Apr. His force much weakened by battle losses, sickness, and detachment of troops to strengthen the Georgetown garrison, Watson rejoined Rawdon at Camden on 7 May. (Clinton, *op. cit.*, 521) He was too late to take part in the battle of HOBKIRK'S HILL, 25 Apr., but incorrect information about his movements had had an effect on that action.

He was promoted to Col. in 1783 and became a full Gen. in Apr. 1808 (Appleton's). The form of his name used at the head of this article is that given in the *Army List*. Appleton's calls him John Tadwell Watson. In Clinton's *American Rebellion* he is indexed as John W. F. Watson, the *F* presumably being a typographical error.

WAUCHOPE. See WAHAB'S PLANTATION, N.C., 21 Sept. '80.

WAWARSING, N.Y., 22 Aug. '81. (BORDER WARFARE) About 400 Tories and Indians under Capt. Wm. Caldwell appeared in Ulster county and destroyed isolated settlements before the militia under Col. Albert Pawling turned out and drove the raiders off with considerable losses. The principal action took place at Wawarsing, on the southern edge of the Catskills about 20 miles west of the Hudson.

WAXHAWS, N.C., 21 Sept. '80. See WAHAB'S PLANTATION.

WAXHAWS, S.C., 29 May '80. Marching to reinforce Charleston during Clinton's siege of 1780, Col. Abraham Buford's 3d Va. Cont'ls. could not get closer than Lenud's Ferry (Santee River), since British forces under Cornwallis had already established control of the intervening 40 miles. (See MONCK'S CORNER, 14 Apr., and LENUD'S FERRY, 6 May.) When Charleston surrendered, 12 May, Buford's regiment and a few cavalry survivors of these last two skirmishes were the only organized American military troops left in S.C. Huger therefore ordered Buford to withdraw to Hillsboro, and Cornwallis started in pursuit. With 2,500 men and five guns Cornwallis left Huger's Bridge on 18 May, cleared Lenud's Ferry on the 22d, and marched rapidly up the Santee toward Nelson's Ferry. He soon realized, however, that his foot troops could not overcome Buford's 10-day lead and Cornwallis then decided to turn this mission over to Tarleton, whose dragoons had been sweeping the country toward Georgetown.

On 27 May Tarleton with 40 men of the 17th Dragoons, 130 cavalry and 100 infantry of the Legion (many of them riding double with the horsemen) left the main body of Cornwallis' command at Nelson's Ferry and started in hot pursuit. Although the weather was oppressively hot and the men and horses already tired from vigorous campaigning, Tarleton's Tories and British dragoons had covered the 60 miles to Camden by the next afternoon. They already knew that Gov. Rutledge was traveling with Buford's command, and at Camden they learned that on 26 May Buford had left Rugeley's Mill, only 12 miles away. Tarleton rested his troops and mounts until 2 A.M. on the 29th, and by early afternoon his leading element had closed in on the tail of Buford's column. The British had covered 105 miles in 54 hours, although they had ridden many horses to death and Tarleton's column was badly strung out.

Warned of this pursuit, Rutledge had ridden away from his escort for safety. Buford's supply train and field guns were also ahead of the column, and his 350 or so Va. Cont'ls. were moving on the double. Tarleton first sent an officer forward under a flag of truce to demand surrender; this, he says candidly, was a stratagem "which, by magnifying the number of the British, might intimidate him into submission, or at least delay him whilst he deliberated on an answer. Colonel Buford, after detaining the flag for some time, without halting his march, returned a defiance." (Tarleton, History, quoted in C. & M., 1113–14)

About 3 P.M., the British advance guard attacked and badly chopped up the small rear guard commanded by Lt. PEARSON, and Buford turned at bay. Holding out a small reserve, he formed his available infantry and cavalry in a single line near the road in an open wood. Tarleton deployed in three elements: Maj. Cochrane with 60 dragoons and about 50 infantry on his right to move forward first and "gall the enemy's flank"; 30 selected dragoons and some infantry constituted Tarleton's left wing, which he would personally lead against Buford's right and rear; and the 17th Dragoons with the rest of the available infantry to attack the American center. The British commander, with an eye not only for sound tactical deployment but also for psychological effect, selected a small hill opposite the enemy center, in plain view of it, and ordered the rest of his command to form there as they reached the battlefield; this, he explains, "afforded the British light troops an object to rally to, in case of repulse, and made no inconsiderable impression on the minds of their opponents." (C. & M., 1114)

Since the American artillery was not in position (see CARTER, John C.), the British were able to form within 300 yards of Buford's line without drawing any fire. Tarleton then launched his attack. When his troopers had charged to within 50 paces they were astounded to hear Cont'l. officers order their men to hold their fire until the British were nearer! "The mistake though gallant was fatal," comments Fortescue. "The volley was fired too late to check the rush of the horses, and in an instant the American battalion was broken up and the sabres were at work." (*British Army,* III, 311) The bayonets followed within a matter of minutes.

"TARLETON'S QUARTER"

The British commander had circled the American flank and charged for the colors that had been posted in the center of the line. Ensign Cruit was just raising a white flag when Tarleton arrived to cut him down. (Bass, *Green Dragoon,* 81) Tarleton then went down himself, his horse killed under him, and before he could mount another one "a report amongst the cavalry that they had lost their commanding officer ... stimulated the soldiers to a vindictive asperity not easily restrained." (Tarleton, *op. cit.,* 1115)

Here is part of an American account that appears to be the basis of most modern versions of the "massacre":

"The demand for quarters ... was at once found to be in vain; not a man was spared, and it was the concurrent testimony of all the survivors that for fifteen minutes after every man was prostrate they went over the ground plunging their bayonets into every one that exhibited any signs of life, and in some instances, where several had fallen

one over the other, these monsters were seen to throw off on the point of the bayonet the uppermost, to come at those beneath." (W. D. James, *Marion,* quoted in C. & M., 1112)

The same author tells how Capt. John Stokes received 23 wounds, one of which cut off his sword hand, and the last four of which were bayonet thrusts through the body; Stokes not only refused to surrender but lived.

NUMBERS AND LOSSES

American losses were 113 killed and 203 captured; 150 of the latter were too badly wounded to be moved, and most of the other 53 prisoners were wounded. Buford and a few other mounted men escaped from the battlefield. The only other survivors were 100 infantry who had been at the head of the retreat and were not in the action. (Ward, *W.O.R.,* 706)

Tarleton's account indicates that about 200 of his 270 troops were on hand for the attack. He gave his casualties as 19 men and 31 horses killed or wounded.

COMMENT

The propaganda-inspired uproar about a "massacre" has obscured the brilliance of Tarleton's pursuit and attack. With professional detachment he credits his opponent with blunders that made the victory possible. Even allowing for poor discipline and low morale, Buford should have been able to fight off a tired enemy he outnumbered two to one. Although he did not have time to find good defensive terrain, he might have formed his wagons into a defensive perimeter and used his guns and infantry in a "hedgehog" the enemy could not have attacked successfully. Ordering his men to hold their fire was a case of applying a sound military principle at the wrong time. The fire, "when given, had little effect either upon the minds or bodies of the assailants, in comparison with the execution that might be expected from a successive fire of platoons or divisions, commenced at the distance of three or four hundred paces," says Tarleton. (Note Tarleton's awareness of how a soldier's *mind* figures in tactics.)

As for the morality displayed by the victor, a successful cavalry charge exploited by a bayonet attack is bound to be messy (see also PAOLI), and the dividing line between military success and slaughter depends on which side you're on. Back in England the *London Chronicle* (18 July) commented that, "Col. Tarleton knew, that having taken a command of the King's troops, the duty he owed to his country directed him to fight and conquer." (Quoted by Bass, *op. cit.*, 83) Unknown prior to the action at Waxhaws, he was now a British hero. But to the American army "Tarleton's quarter" became a synonym for the butchery of surrendered men, and "Bloody Tarleton" is a name more familiar in America today than it is in England.

WAYNE, Anthony. 1745–1796. Cont'l. general. Pa. Son of a prosperous tanner who had settled in Chester co., Pa., around 1724, the man whose fiery martial exploits were to win him the nickname "Mad Anthony" was a prosperous tanner on the eve of the Revolution. He had received two years of schooling at his uncle's academy in Philadelphia, had spent a year (1765) in Nova Scotia as surveyor and agent for a land company, and had been elected to the Pa. legislature (1774–75) and to the committee of safety. Appointed Col. of the 4th Pa. Bn. on 3 Jan. '76, he marched to Canada

with Wm. Thompson's Brig. and fought at TROIS RIVIÈRES, 8 June. As commandant of strategic Ticonderoga he learned about holding together ill-disciplined troops in a vulnerable outpost at the end of a tenuous supply line, and he got his first experience in handling a mutiny. (Randolph C. Downes in *D.A.B.*) Military recognition came promptly. On 21 Feb. '77 he was promoted to B.G. and on 12 Apr. was ordered to join Washington's army at Morristown. As commander of the Pa. Line he saw heavy action at the BRANDY-WINE, 11 Sept., where he was posted at Chadd's Ford. His camp was surprised at PAOLI, 21 Sept., in a masterful night action in which British Gen. "No-flint" Grey won his nickname. Wayne saved his guns and was acquitted of negligence by the court-martial which he requested. He had a prominent part in the Battle of GERMANTOWN, 4 Oct., and although his collision with Stephen led to the failure of Washington's attack, no valid criticism has been made of Wayne's leadership in this action. At MONMOUTH, 28 June '78, he commanded 1,000 men as part of the force Charles Lee led forward in the opening phase of the action and he held the center of the final American defensive position.

At STONY POINT, 16 July '79, Wayne scored one of the most impressive victories of the Revolution. Here his planning and execution were of the first order, but it is interesting to note that the luck so against him at Paoli (where his bad luck was in being attacked by a man of Charles Grey's caliber) and Germantown (which was just one of those things) was very much with him.

Early in 1780 Wayne conducted raids along the lower Hudson and he was repulsed at BULL'S FERRY, N.J., 20–21 July. In late Sept. '80 he hurried to the Highlands when Arnold's Treason was revealed and it was thought that a British force might be advancing to capture West Point.

The MUTINY OF THE PA. LINE, 1–10 Jan. '81, broke out among his veterans despite his timely efforts to prevent it and despite his courageous efforts to stop it. Yet he showed remarkably good sense in handling its settlement. In the spring of 1781 Wayne organized a force of his veterans to join Lafayette in Va. (See under VA. MIL. OPNS. the section headed "Cornwallis *vs.* Lafayette.") At GREEN SPRING (Jamestown Ford), 6 July '81, his impetuosity got him into a position from which only his calm fearlessness and audacity got him out. As part of Steuben's Div. in the Yorktown Campaign he had little opportunity to distinguish himself. Marching south with Gen. St. Clair to reinforce Greene, Wayne reached the latter's camp on 4 Jan. '82 and almost immediately was detached for the GA. EXPED. In addition to the minor activities covered under that entry, he negotiated treaties of submission with the Cherokees and Creeks. (*D.A.B.*)

With a well-merited brevet of Maj. Gen. dated 30 Sept. '83, Wayne left the army on 3 Nov. '83 and entered a lean period of nine years. He failed as a rice planter on the 800 acres given him by Ga. He represented Chester co. in the Pa. Gen. Assy. in 1784 and '85. Elected representative to Congress from Ga. on 4 Mar. '91, his seat was declared vacant on 21 Mar. '92 because of election irregularities and his residence qualifications. (*D.A.B.*) On 5 Mar. '92, however, he was named Maj. Gen. and C. in C. of the badly mishandled little American army that Harmar and St. Clair had led unsuccessfully against the Indians of the Old Northwest the preceding year. Although Congress gave him many advantages denied Harmar and St. Clair, Wayne conducted a well-

administered, well-planned, and well-executed campaign that finally brought peace to the frontier. Taking the time to train his American Legion adequately at Pittsburgh, he moved them to the site of modern Cincinnati and awaited orders. He then marched north to the place he named Greenville (in honor of Nathanael Greene). On 29 June '94 a detachment from the Legion repulsed the Indians with heavy losses at Ft. Recovery, which they had built at the place where St. Clair had been defeated. After being joined by some mounted Ky. levies he moved on with 2,643 men (only half the strength he was supposed to be furnished) and built Ft. Defiance at the junction of the Maumee and Anglaise rivers. The Indians refused his final offer of peace and he went to meet them in the vicinity of modern Toledo, Ohio. "Mad Anthony" directed his troops to fire once and charge the hidden Indians with the bayonet. While in keeping with his nickname, the order was mad only to somebody who did not know the advantage of trained regular troops against Indians. The Indians had picked for the battlefield a place where a tornado had left a wide path of destruction through the forest, but here at "Fallen Timbers," 20 Aug. '94, they broke and ran before what they later referred to as "the sharp ends of the guns." (Ganoe, *U.S. Army*, 101) A year later the Indians agreed to complete submission and surrender at Greenville. On 15 Dec. '96 Wayne died at Erie on his return from occupying Detroit. (*D.A.B.*)

"Mad Anthony" Wayne deserves his reputation as one of America's great soldiers. Soon after he joined Washington's main army the C. in C. "acquired respect for him as an administrator and as a field commander," writes Freeman. "In Wayne, as Washington appraised him, the spark of daring might flame into rashness, but it was better to have such a leader and occasionally to cool him to caution than forever to be heating the valor of men who feared they would singe their plumes in battle." (*Washington*, IV, 461A) A handsome, self-confident man, he had personal differences with St. Clair, Charles Lee, and James Wilkinson but in the case of the last two this is very much to his credit. (Wilkinson was his scheming second-in-command in 1792–96 and succeeded him.)

Understandably, he has had many biographers. Professor Rankin, who wrote the essay on Wayne in *George Washington's Generals* (a recent work edited by George Billias), says that the old biography by C. J. Stillé, *Wayne and the Pennsylvania Line* (1893), is by far the best. J. H. Preston's *A Gentleman Rebel* (1930) is not recommended. Other biographies are by J. R. Spears (1903) and T. A. Boyd (1929). The standard authority on Wayne's finest action is H. P. Johnston, *The Storming of Stony Point* (1900). His papers are in the Pa. Hist. Soc.

WAYNE'S LIGHT INFANTRY. In constituting his LIGHT INFANTRY corps for 1779, Washington directed Wayne on 21 June to assume command. (Freeman, *Washington*, V, 111 and *n.*) Official orders were not issued until 1 July, or at least it was not until then that Wayne took command of the four battalions that had been assembling under Richard Butler at Ft. Montgomery, N.Y. The composition of his 1,200-man force is given in the article on STONY POINT, 16 July '79. On 30 Nov. orders were issued for the corps to disband but for the companies to be ready on one day's notice to reassemble. Before these orders had been completely executed, however, several companies were retained around West Point to meet any movements the British might make up the Hudson. By 15 Dec. '79 all companies had returned to their parent organization.

WAYNE'S PENNSYLVANIA LINE IN VIRGINIA. After the reorganization following the MUTINY OF THE PA. LINE, Wayne left York, Pa., on 26 May '81 with the 2d, 5th, and 6th Pa. (about 1,000 infantry in all), and Proctor's 4th Cont'l. Arty. (6 guns, 90 men). He joined Lafayette on 10 June '81. (See VIRGINIA, Mil. Opns. in)

WEATHER, Winter of 1779–80. Whereas the battle of Monmouth, 28 June '78, is said to have been fought on "the most scorching summer day ever known in America" (Trevelyan, *American Revolution*, V, 290), the following Jan. '79 has been called "the coldest month recorded ... in Pennsylvania over the space of very nearly two centuries." (*Ibid.*, citing *Pa. Weather Records ..., 1664 and 1835 ...*, compiled by Wm. M. Darlington of the Pa. Hist. Soc.)

Sledges moved regularly across 10 miles of ice between Annapolis and the opposite shore of the Chesapeake. Wild animals were almost exterminated. Gen. Alexander marched over a saltwater channel to make his unsuccessful STATEN ISLAND raid. Washington's main army suffered much more, because of this weather, in their MORRISTOWN WINTER QUARTERS than they had at Valley Forge.

WEATHER GAGE. In the days of fighting sail this was of prime importance in naval engagements, and one finds such statements as, "The day was spent in maneuvering for the weather-gage. ..." (Mahan, *Sea Power*, 378) A ship was said to have the weather-gage, or "the advantage of the wind," when she could steer straight for an opponent while the latter would have to tack against the wind.

WEATHERSFIELD. See WETHERS-FIELD, Conn.

WEBB, Samuel Blatchley. 1753–1807. Cont'l. officer. Conn. Stepson of Silas Deane, he became Deane's private secretary and took part in the political activities of the patriots that preceded the Revolution. He commanded a militia company of Wethersfield, led them to join the Boston army, and was wounded at Bunker Hill. On 22 July '75 he became A.D.C. to Israel Putnam with the grade of Maj. On 21 June '76 he was promoted to Lt. Col. and became A.D.C. and private secretary to Washington. With Reed and Knox he met the British officer who was attempting to deliver the letter addressed to "George Washington, Esq. etc. etc." (See PEACE COMMISSION OF THE HOWES.) He was present in the Battle of Long Island, was wounded at White Plains and Trenton, and was present at Princeton. On 11 Jan. '77 he was commissioned Col. of an "ADDITIONAL CONT'L. REGT." In the three places where Heitman indicates this transfer (pp. 13, 27, 578) there is contradiction as to whether it took place 1 or 11 Jan., but Freeman points out that Fitzpatrick has identified a draft letter for Washington prepared by Webb on 11 Jan. (Freeman, *Washington,* IV, 391 *n.*) He was captured in the unsuccessful attack against LONG ISLAND, N.Y., 10 Dec. '77, and not exchanged until a year later. His regiment was transferred to the Conn. Line on 1 Jan. '81, redesignated the 3d Conn., and he was in command of this unit until it was disbanded in June '83. He left the service on 3 June and was breveted B.G. on 30 Sept. '83. From 1789 until his death he lived at Claverack, N.Y. His grandson, Alexander Stewart Webb (1835–1911), was an outstanding Union general in the Civil War and was Pres. of City College of N.Y. 1869–1902.

The Correspondence and Journals of ... Webb, 3 vols., edited by Worthington C. Ford (New York, 1894), is a highly literate and valuable source.

WEBB'S REGT., under Col. Sam'l. B. Webb, was one of the 16 "ADDITIONAL CONT'L. REGTS."

WEBSTER, James. *c.* 1743–1781. British officer. Son of an eminent Edinburgh minister, Dr. Alexander Webster (Appleton's), he became a Lt. in the 33d Foot on 10 May '60, was promoted to Capt. in 1763, to Maj. in 1771, and to Lt. Col. on 9 Apr. '74. The 33d Foot ("West Riding") was the regiment whose Col. since Mar. '66 had been Cornwallis. The latter was promoted to Maj. Gen. in 1775 and Webster commanded the regiment (as Lt. Col.) when Cornwallis sailed for America in Feb. '76. Thereafter the 33d was one of the regiments under CORNWALLIS in the N.Y. and N.J. campaigns. In the Philadelphia Campaign the 33d was in Grey's Brig. of Cornwallis' command. In the battle of MONMOUTH, 28 June '78, it was Webster who came onto the field in the final stage of the action to make it possible for Clinton to extricate the light infantry. Clinton describes this as follows:

"... as I was looking about me in search of other troops to call to their support ... I perceived the Thirty-third Regiment, with that gallant officer, Colonel Webster, at their head, unexpectedly clearing the wood and marching in column toward the enemy. The First Grenadiers, on this, advanced also on their side; and, both pushing together up to the enemy in order to stop the cannonade from a farm on the hill, their [the American] troops did not wait the shock, but instantly quitted and retired again over the bridge. The First Grenadiers and Thirty-third then put themselves as much under cover as possible (by shouldering the hill on their left) until the light corps, whose usual gallantry and impetuosity had engaged them too forward, were returned. And the whole afterward fell back. . . ." (*Amer. Reb.*, 95)

Within a year after this last major battle in the North, Webster was serving as a brigadier (Baurmeister, *Journals*, 279). When Clinton withdrew forces from the Hudson Highlands and R.I. for Gov. Tryon's Conn. Coast Raid (July '79) he left the 33d Foot, Robinson's Loyal American Regt., and half of Ferguson's Corps to hold Ft. Lafayette at Verplancks Point; this detachment was commanded by Webster (*ibid.*, 289–91), "who was an officer of great experience and on whom I reposed the most implicit confidence," wrote Clinton. (*Op. cit.*, 131)

Sailing south on 26 Dec. '79 with Clinton's Charleston Expedition, Webster commanded a task force of 1,400 men that operated against Lincoln's line of communications from Charleston. (Under CHARLESTON EXPEDITION . . . in 1780 see section headed "Operations Against . . . L. of C.") Commanding a brigade composed of his own regiment, three light infantry companies, and the 23d Fusiliers, he distinguished himself at CAMDEN, where he was slightly wounded. In the unsuccessful pursuit of Greene to the Dan River, Webster commanded the force that conducted the demonstration against Beattie's Ford when Cornwallis made his main crossing of the Catawba at Cowan's Ford, 1 Feb. '81. (See SOUTHERN CAMPAIGNS of Greene) He defied American MARKSMANSHIP to lead his brigade forward at WETZELL'S MILLS, N.C., 6 Mar. '81.

At GUILFORD, 15 Mar. '81, Webster particularly distinguished himself from the opening movement of the battle to the end. Mortally wounded in this action, he died a fortnight later. Of this outstanding officer, Tarleton wrote that he "united all the virtues of civil life to the gallantry and professional knowledge of a soldier." (*History*, 289, quoted in Ward, *W.O.R.*, 796) In summing up British performance in the Revolution, Fortescue mentions O'Hara and Webster as Cornwallis' two outstanding brigadiers. (*British Army*, III, 404)

WEEDON, George. c. 1730–1793. Cont'l. general. Va. A Fredericksburg innkeeper and prewar acquaintance of Washington, he was characterized in 1772 by an English visitor as "very active in blowing the seeds of sedition." (Appleton's) He became Lt. Col. of the 3d Va. on 13 Feb. '76, Col. on 13 Aug., joined Washington's army in mid-Sept. with slightly more than 600 men, and took part in the N.Y. and N.J. campaigns. On 20 Feb. '77 he became acting A.G. to Washington, and on 21 Feb. was promoted to B.G. (Montross, *Rag, Tag,* 471; Heitman's date is 27 Feb.) After a long leave of absence he rejoined the army at Morristown in time for the Philadelphia campaign. Leading Greene's Div., he reached the Plowed Hill at Brandywine just as the American defenses were collapsing; his men calmly opened ranks to let the fugitives pass, and reformed to check the enemy. (Freeman, *Washington*, IV, 482–83) As part of Greene's column he participated in the attack at Germantown and expressed the (questionable) view that the Americans were within 15 minutes of victory when their attack collapsed. (*Ibid.*, IV, 510) He was among the nine B.G.'s who memorialized Congress about Conway's promotion, and is characterized with Muhlenberg and Wm. Woodford as one of the "jealous, ambitious men" competing for promotion. (*Ibid.*, IV, 613 *n.*) On 18 Aug. '78 he appealed to Congress to be put on the inactive list; by Nov. "Weedon had gone home and kept both his complaint and his commission" as a Cont'l. B.G. (*Ibid.,* V, 79) In the VA. MIL. OPNS. that followed, Weedon helped organize military resistance to the British raids and in the Yorktown campaign commanded the militia investing Gloucester.

"Joe Gourd," as the tavernkeeping general was known to his soldiers, idolized the former patron who became C. in C. On 14 Apr. '77 he wrote John Page, "no other man but our present General, who is the greatest that ever did or ever will adorn our earth, could have supported himself under the many disappointments and disgraces he was subjected to from this singular system of carrying on a war against the most formidable enemy in the world. . . ." (*Ibid.,* IV, 411 n., citing Chicago Hist. Soc. MSS.) He died in Nov. '93, according to Heitman. A biographical sketch is in Appleton's. The Weedon Letters and MSS. of the Chicago Hist. Soc. were much used by Freeman in his biography of Washington.

WEEMS, Mason Locke ("Parson"). 1759–1825. Clergyman, bookseller, writer. Born in Md., he left no record of his early life but is known to have been in Europe seeking ordination in 1783. The next year he was ordained deacon of the Anglican church, and from 1784 to 1792 he served in parishes of Md. He then married a sister of James Ewell and settled in Dumfries, Va. Having become an agent for publisher Mathew Carey—a career interrupted only briefly during the rest of his life by his religious calling—he developed into a highly successful editor and writer. His *Life and Memorable Actions of George Washington* appeared anonymously about 1800 and went on to have more than 70 editions. The highly dubious cherry tree story was not inserted into the book until the fifth edition (1806). He wrote biographies of Marion (1809), Franklin (1815), and William

Penn (1822), in addition to such tracts as *The Drunkard's Looking Glass.* See also MARION and WASHINGTON.

"WE FIGHT, get beat, rise, and fight again." This much-quoted phrase sums up the SOUTHERN CAMPAIGNS OF GREENE. Although it is frequently cited so as to imply a sort of simple-minded self-satisfaction with his strategy, Nathanael Greene was "almost frantic with vexation and disappointment" (Alden, *South,* 263) over HOBKIRK'S HILL, 25 Apr. '81, when he wrote this in a letter to LA LUZERNE requesting French assistance.

WELZELL'S MILLS, N.C. See WETZELL'S MILLS.

WEMYSS, James. British officer. An Ensign in the 40th Foot on 6 Apr. '66, he was promoted to Capt. in this regiment on 14 Mar. '71 and commanded the Queen's Tory Rangers at BRANDYWINE, 11 Sept. '77. On 10 Aug. '78 he was promoted to Maj. of the 63d Foot. With the start of major British military operations in the South he became second only to Tarleton as the "most hated man in the British army." (Bass, *Green Dragoon,* 105) He was defeated, wounded, and captured by Sumter at FISHDAM FORD, S.C., 9 Nov. '80. On 22 Aug. '83 he became Maj. in the Army, on 20 Sept. '87 he was promoted to Lt. Col. of the 63d Foot, and two years later he disappeared from the *Army Lists.* See R. H. R. Smythies, *Historical Records of the 40th Regiment* (1894) and James Slack, *The History of the 63rd* (*West Suffolk*) *Regiment* (1884).

WENTWORTH, Paul. d. 1793. Double spy. N.H. Referred to as "my dear relation" by Gov. John Wentworth (1737–1820), the last royal Gov. of N.H. (1767–75), he presumably is a member of that illustrious family, but *D.A.B.* points out that the connection is not traced. In the years preceding the break with England he lived in the West Indies, N.H., Amsterdam, London, and Paris. Talented, apparently well educated, and ambitious, he was supported by the profits of his Surinam plantation and his skill as a stock jobber. He was hungry for status, however. He declined the appointment to the council of N.H. obtained for him in 1770 by Gov. Wentworth, apparently feeling he could not leave his financial affairs for such a minor office, but shortly after this he did become agent for the colony in London.

The expatriate had a low opinion of the patriot leadership, obviously because he applied his own standards. According to Van Doren,

"Wentworth genuinely believed that most of the rebels were activated primarily by envy, ambition, or interest, and that many of them would change sides if it were made worth their while or if they faced no penalty for rebellion. 'The highest degree of political profligacy already prevails,' he had lately written [fall of 1777], 'and perhaps a well-timed offer of indemnity and impunity to these Cromwells and Barebones * may serve, like a strong alkali, to reduce the effervescence in the mass of the people, or turn their fury on their misleaders.' " (*Secret History,* 60)

When, after Burgoyne's surrender, the British felt they could offer the Americans some terms short of complete independence, Wentworth was selected to feel out the American commissioners in Paris. He had to wait almost four weeks in Paris before the suspicious Benjamin Franklin agreed to a meeting on 6 Jan. '78. Secretary Wm. Eden had given Wentworth a letter to show Franklin with the assurance that it was from

a source close to the throne and which said that England would fight another 10 years to prevent American independence. Franklin said that America would fight 50 years to win it, and that both countries would be better off when they were bound only by peaceful commerce. Wentworth's mission not only failed to do any good for England but Vergennes used it to accelerate the French Alliance by pointing out to the kings of France and Spain that the Americans might be making peace with Great Britain. Louis XVI consented to the Franco-American treaty the day after Wentworth saw Franklin. (*Ibid.,* 61)

Although he received only £200 a year for it, Wentworth remained as chief of the Loyalist secret agents in London during the war. He "had become a double-dealer by an agreement with Lord North, and presumably shared the colony's secrets with the minister." (*Ibid.,* 59, citing Stevens, *Facsimiles,* 315) Hoping that a British victory would save him his N.H. estates, and aspiring to a title, a seat in Parliament, and an important office, Wentworth appointed and directed spies, used their reports to furnish military intelligence to the British, and in various disguises made frequent trips to the Continent. After his visit to Franklin, however, he was so well known to French police that he had to remain in London. Here he received the reports of Edward BANCROFT, whose services he had secured and who never was suspected by Franklin and Deane.

Wentworth's rewards were meager: only a seat in Parliament in 1780 and which he held only six weeks. Despite his valuable service, George III had little confidence in his interpretations of reports and disapproved of his stock gambling. (*D.A.B.*) After failing in his political career he retired to his Surinam

---

* The Cont'l. Cong. apparently is being likened to the "Barebones Parliament" of 1653.

plantation and died there three years later. See Einstein, *Divided Loyalties* (1933).

WEST CANADA CREEK, N.Y., Action at. See JERSEYFIELD.

WEST INDIES IN THE REVOLUTION.

"The part played by the West Indian Islands during the American War of Independence has been so little appreciated as to demand particular attention in these pages," wrote Sir John Fortescue in his *History of the British Army* in 1902. (P. 259) Half a century later an American author commented in the introductory note of her book: "Years ago I happened on an article by Professor J. F. Jameson about the role of St. Eustatius in the War of Independence. I had never heard of that tiny island, or realized that the Caribbean was intimately bound up with the struggle on the mainland." (Helen Augur, *The Secret War of Independence,* ix) While both these authors devote considerable space to the subject, it remains neglected by historians. "A start has been made on one island," comments Augur, and she cites the works on Bermuda by W. B. Kerr and H. C. Wilkinson, which I have identified in the main bibliography. Jameson's article, which Augur calls "worth a whole row of books," is cited under ST. EUSTATIUS.

Politically, the West Indian islands did not ally themselves with the 13 Colonies although sympathetic noises were made by certain elements in the Caribbean, and Congress originally believed that the British West Indians (along with the Irish and the Canadians) would join cause with them. (Montross, *Reluctant Rebels,* 82) Bermudians, who stood to be ruined by the economic sanctions put into effect by the mainland colonies, worked out an accommodation:

"In 1775–1776 some islanders pro-cured small quantities of powder, perhaps from neutral colonies, brought it in their sloops to the middle harbors of Bermuda and sent it off when accumulated to the Americans. Twenty sail of Bermuda vessels, nominally engaged in picking up wrecks and turtles at the Bahama banks, sold the revolting colonists ships, salt, cannon and military stores, thus keeping in supplies the American privateers who preyed on the West India trade. In fact, most American privateering ships were Bermuda-built. The salt makers at Turks Islands did a lively trade, exchanging their product for flour and grain." (Kerr, *Bermuda,* 54–55)

Until the autumn of 1778 the Bermudians had no cause for complaint, despite periodic appearances of British warships that temporarily interrupted their business (*ibid.,* 73), but on 2 Nov. the nucleus of a British garrison, two companies, arrived under the command of Maj. Wm. Sutherland. These were reinforced on 1 Dec. '79 by 100 men under Lt. Col. Donkin, and thereafter the British governor was able to exercise more authority. (*Ibid.,* 82)

One consideration in the Caribbean colonies that tended to keep them loyal and that was not a major factor among the 13 colonies was fear of a slave revolt. (Knollenberg, *Origin,* 11) An even more significant one, however, was the Royal Navy: West Indian islands were much more vulnerable to police action by His Majesty's ships than were the Cont'l. colonies. By the same token they were more vulnerable to attack by the navies of hostile nations, and were therefore more dependent on their own mother countries for protection. This brings us to a strategic evaluation of the West Indian theater of war, and here is an analysis by Fortescue:

"In the days of sailing ships all naval operations in the West Indies were nec-

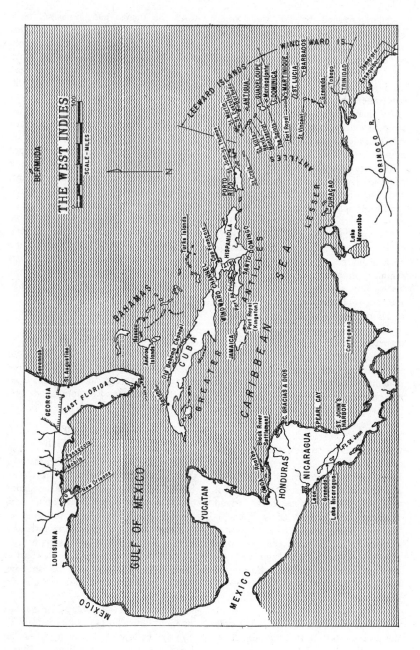

THE WEST INDIES

essarily governed by the trade-wind, which blows, roughly speaking,* from east to west persistently for three parts of the year, and intermittently during the fourth part also. But from the beginning of August to the beginning of November the Archipelago is subject to hurricanes, for which reason it was customary for fleets to desert tropical latitudes during these 'hurricane months.' " (*Op. cit.* 261).

The prevailing trade wind had the effect of dividing the Caribbean islands into what Fortescue calls leeward and windward spheres, generally west and east of Puerto Rico, respectively.

"Practically these two divisions were distinct; for though a ship could be sure of a good passage from Barbados to Jamaica [in about a week], she could be equally sure that a voyage from Jamaica to Barbados would occupy as much time as a voyage from Jamaica to England. In a word, a force once despatched from windward to leeward was to all intent irrecoverable; and this fact was one with which commanders, both naval and military, had always to reckon. The French on their side were in exactly the same case, having their two divisions of territory in St. Lucia, Martinique, and Guadeloupe to windward, and Haiti to leeward. But to leeward they had this advantage, that Haiti, being to windward of Jamaica, and within twenty-four hours' sail of it, was a perpetual menace to that island. Moreover, the harbour of St. Nicholas, which of late had been fortified to great strength, so dominated the Windward Channel between Haiti and Cuba—a very important passage for homeward-bound ships—that it was esteemed the Gibraltar of the West Indies. To wind-

* More precisely S.E. to N.W., notes the author, shifting occasionally in certain months to N.E.

ward, the British had somewhat of a corresponding advantage, Barbados being the most windwardly of the whole of the eastern group. But, on the other hand, Barbados has no safe harbour, nor was there any port in Grenada, St. Vincent, or any of the British islets to northward of it, where British ships could refit, excepting the royal dockyard at English Harbour in Antigua. Barbados, it is true, was an excellent depot for troops and stores, and could be used within certain limits for repair of ships; but the true dockyard . . . was in Antigua, some distance to leeward. The French on the contrary had three admirable harbours in St. Lucia, Martinique, and Guadeloupe, of which Martinique, the principal naval and military centre, was little further distant from France than Barbados from England." (*Op. cit.,* 261–62)

Amid the British, French, and Spanish islands were the Danish island of St. Croix and the Dutch island of St. Eustatius. These two were important supply points and neutral havens for American privateers and smugglers from the start of the Revolution, as was Martinique.

SUMMARY OF MILITARY OPERATIONS

After the French came into the war they seized the initiative in the Caribbean. The Marquis de Bouillé descended on Dominica with about 2,000 men from Martinique and, by the offer of favorable terms, obtained the surrender of the 500 British defenders on 8 Sept. '78. On 4 Nov. d'Estaing left Boston for the West Indies and on the same day Adm. Hotham sailed from N.Y.C. with a fleet escorting a 5,800-man detachment from Clinton's army commanded by Gen. James GRANT. Although slowed by 59 transports, Hotham outsailed d'Estaing, and in a brilliant combined operation the British took and held St. Lucia. See ST. LUCIA . . . , 12–28 Dec.

On 6 Jan. '79 "Foul Weather Jack" Byron reached St. Lucia. Having failed to intercept d'Estaing in the Atlantic, this hard-luck sailor was just too late to intercept the French admiral in his withdrawal to Martinique when he withdrew from St. Lucia.

Trouble now broke out at St. Kitts, where the Assembly refused to pay for militia support and the governor, Burt, clamored for regulars to maintain order. Byron's fleet, though battered in the Atlantic crossing, had sufficed to keep d'Estaing confined to Fort Royal (Martinique), but when Byron gave in to Burt's demands for support and sailed for St. Kitts, a French squadron under De Grasse slipped in to reinforce d'Estaing. In mid-June, Byron had to sail to leeward to convoy some merchant vessels, and d'Estaing took St. Vincent (16 June) and Grenada (4 July '79). On 5 July Byron sailed with 21 ships of the line and 1,000 troops under James Grant to retake the former island, but then decided instead to liberate Grenada. On 6 July the British fleet of 21 ships tied into a French fleet they thought numbered only 16 and continued the attack even after counting an additional nine sail. The action was gallantly pursued by the British but the results were indecisive. (See John BYRON)

Sickness was seriously reducing British strength in the Caribbean, but an even greater enemy was Germain, who insisted with the logic of an amateur strategist that the way to hold the islands was to scatter small detachments throughout them. All surplus troops, wrote Germain to Grant, should be sent back to N.Y.! (Ltr. of 1 Apr. '79) Grant had moral courage as well as the physical variety so common among professional soldiers, and he told

Germain that naval superiority was the key to successful defense of the West Indies possessions, not small army detachments among the islands. (Ltrs. of 8 and 17 July '79) On 29 July he informed Germain that he had made the following dispositions: at St. Kitts were 1,500 men of the artillery, the 15th, 28th, and 55th Foot; at St. Lucia were 1,600 men of the artillery, the 27th, 35th, and 49th; at Antigua were 800 men of the 40th and 60th; serving with the fleet, replacing sick sailors, were 925 soldiers. These were the British defenders of the West Indies when Grant sailed home to England on 1 Aug. '79. By defying the orders of Germain to parcel out his puny forces, Grant had established tenable bases from which the British were able to operate in the last two years of the war to defeat the French in the Caribbean.

Maj. Gen. John Vaughan was put in command of the Leeward Islands in Dec. '79, and on 14 Feb. '80 he reached Barbados with reinforcements to find Adm. Sir Hyde Parker waiting with 16 sail of the line. Adm. George Rodney, who had started from England with Vaughan, had stopped off to whip a Spanish fleet at Cape St. Vincent before continuing on to reach St. Lucia on 22 Mar. with four sail of the line. As evidence of the toll taken by tropical disease, the 1,600 troops left on St. Lucia by Grant in July '79 were by the end of the year reduced to 685 fit for duty and 576 sick. (*Ibid.*, 334 *n.*) Vaughan visited his scattered and demoralized outposts and returned to St. Lucia the last week of Mar. '80 just as Adm. De Guichen reached Martinique with powerful army and navy reinforcements to take command of the French forces in the West Indies. On 23 Mar. the French appeared off St. Lucia with 21 ships of the line but Sir Hyde Parker's 16 ships and Vaughan's strong island defenses caused De Guichen to return to Martinique without risking attack. Rodney had arrived with his four additional ships on the 22d, but in the absence of a promised three more ships of Arbuthnot's fleet from North America, the British navy had to remain on the defensive.

In the action off Martinique, 17 Apr. '80, Rodney gallantly engaged De Guichen at odds of 20 to 23, but the results were inconclusive. (See George RODNEY) In Aug. De Guichen sailed for Europe and Rodney, thinking he was heading for N.Y., left for a futile two months in North America. During his absence a terrible hurricane devastated Barbados and St. Lucia (10 Oct. '80). Operations were resumed in HONDURAS and NICARAGUA about this time and concluded in Nov. '80; they are of interest mainly in that they involved an energetic young British officer named Horatio Nelson.

Rodney returned to St. Lucia early in Dec. '80. On the 16th he sailed for St. Vincent with a force of soldiers under Vaughan, but the French defenses were found to be too strong for any prospect of a successful attack. Adm. Samuel Hood arrived shortly thereafter with a large reinforcement from the 1st, 13th, and 69th Foot. On 27 Jan. '81 Rodney received word that Holland was at war with England, and he celebrated this news by capturing St. Eustatius, on 3 Feb. '81.

De Grasse reappeared in the West Indies, this time as French C. in C. RODNEY failed to reinforce Hood's blockading squadron off Martinique, and De Grasse entered Fort Royal on 29 Apr. with his 20 ships of the line, three frigates, and 150 supply ships to join the four ships that had been bottled up at Martinique. Having gotten his convoy into harbor, De Grasse sallied forth on the 30th to attack Hood but could

not overtake him. The night of 10 May the French landed troops on St. Lucia but the British defensive dispositions were so good that the next day De Grasse re-embarked. A few days later he sent a small squadron and 1,200 troops to Tobago, landing unopposed on 23 May and accepting the surrender of that place on 2 June. '81. Rodney appeared two days later, two days too late. Still the French refused to accept a general naval engagement, despite a superiority of five ships, and on 26 July they anchored off Haiti. Here De Grasse found dispatches that prompted him to move north for operations resulting in the victory at YORKTOWN. Rodney sent Hood north with 14 ships and sailed for England.

The Marquis de Bouillé captured St. Eustatius in a bold surprise attack on 25 Nov. '81, and the next day De Grasse reached Martinique. A joint operation against Barbados was frustrated by weather. De Grasse then captured ST. KITTS, 11 Jan.–12 Feb. '82, despite the attempt of Adm. Samuel Hood to relieve it.

The French took Nevis, Montserrat, and recovered the Dutch settlements of Demerara and Essequibo (taken by British privateers in 1781). (See BRITISH GUIANA) Jamaica now was eyed by the French and Spaniards, but before they could effect a planned concentration of 50 ships of the line and 20,000 troops on Haiti for an invasion Rodney arrived from Europe with 12 ships of the line and, uniting force with the 22 ships of Hood near Antigua (25 Feb. '82), Rodney immediately undertook a pursuit. The French fleet withdrew to Fort Royal (Martinique), anchoring there on the 26th, and the British then took up station at St. Lucia. Reinforcements brought Rodney's total to 37 ships of the line, and on 20 Mar. De Grasse's strength was raised to 33 effective sail of the line and two 50-gun ships. The strategic problem now was this: to launch their invasion of Jamaica, De Grasse had to move from Martinique with all available troops and join forces with the troops and ships already concentrated at Haiti; Rodney had to prevent this link-up. The final, and for the moment decisive, encounter took place in the Battle off Saints Passage, 9–12 Apr. '82, which is located between Guadeloupe and Dominica. De Grasse was captured aboard his gigantic flagship, *Ville de Paris* (110), along with four other ships; ironically, these happened to carry all the siege artillery for the intended invasion of Jamaica. Although the latter place now was saved, Rodney moved there with his fleet. He is criticized for failure to follow up and crush the French fleet, a failure that considerably weakened England's position in the peace negotiations of 1783. (Mahan, *op. cit.*, 498–99)

When Rodney sailed for Jamaica in May '82, the Spanish expeditionary force took the defenseless Bahamas. Operations in the West Indies were ended, although in Oct. a polyglot band regained possession of the British settlement in HONDURAS.

As mentioned at the beginning of this article, there is no good, single, secondary source to which one can turn for an over-all account of the matters outlined above. Fortescue goes into considerable detail, particularly with respect to the army operations, and Mahan gives an excellent coverage of naval operations in his *Sea Power*. In *Secret War*, Helen Augur deals with what her publisher calls "The crucial role of the Caribbean Islands in aiding the War of Independence." On page 405 of his *British Army*, Vol. III, Fortescue cites the official dispatches filed in the Record Office under *America and West Indies* and other headings (including *Military, Promiscuous*). "There is good material also in the *Lives of the Lindsays*," concludes Fortescue.

WEST JERSEY VOLUNTEERS. Another name for SKINNER'S BRIGADE.

WEST POINT, N.Y. Not fortified until after CLINTON'S EXPEDITION ... had showed the inadequacy of existing defenses of the HUDSON RIVER ..., it became, in the words of Washington, the "key to America," and was the price of ARNOLD'S TREASON. "Strategically West Point neutralized New York," wrote Nickerson. "From the moment when its works came into existence [in 1778] the army of Sir Henry Clinton on Manhattan Island was held in a vise.* * * The full effect ... was not at first felt, for in '78 after returning to New York Clinton made no move. In '79 he had to struggle against a breakdown of the British supply system and consequently to put most of his energy into the task of feeding the men.* * * With its difficult communications on the land side, its high cliffs out of reach of the guns of ships in the river below, and its position above a right-angle turn in the river [actually two right angles] which compelled the square-rigged vessels of the time to lose headway by altering their course directly under its batteries, the place was most formidable." (*Turning Point*, 418)

A detachment of the CORPS OF INVALIDS was assigned there in 1781 to instruct officer candidates, but the plan did not materialize. When the CONT'L. ARMY was abolished (2 June '84) West Point was garrisoned by 55 men under a Capt. Later it was home for the "Corps of Artillerists and Engineers" established 9 May '94, and on 4 July 1802 the U.S. Military Academy started operating with 10 cadets present.

West Point is the oldest U.S. military post over which the country's flag has continuously flown. (*Concise D.A.H.*) See also HUDSON RIVER . . . for details on the fortifications.

WESTERN OPERATIONS. Just as Niagara was the British base for raids against American border settlements in N.Y. and Pa., Detroit was headquarters for operations against the frontiers of the central colonies. War in this area did not wait for "the shot heard 'round the world," but had been going on since white settlers started pushing into Indian territory. In defiance of the PROCLAMATION OF 1763, the first settlement in what is now Kentucky was established in 1774 at Harrodsburg. The next year, after DUNMORE'S WAR, Boonesborough and St. Asaph were planted, the three places being about 30 miles from each other. The Cherokees and Shawnees sent their scalping parties into this "DARK AND BLOODY GROUND" in a desperate effort to preserve their hunting area. But the tide could not be stopped. By 1779 there were settlements in what is now N.E. Tenn.—home of the "OVER MOUNTAIN MEN"—and along the Cumberland River—the "Cumberland Settlements"—around French Lick (the site of Nashville).

As an outcome of the COLONIAL WARS the British had scattered posts throughout the Mississippi Valley and in the vast areas claimed by some of the 13 Colonies. French settlers had accommodated themselves to a new allegiance represented by Lt. Gov. Henry Hamilton at Detroit. The British capitalized on Indian hostility toward the American settlers to gain the support of the powerful Illinois confederation and to send them out for scalps. As far away as Williamsburg, Va., Hamilton soon became infamous as the "Hair Buyer." Early in the Revolutionary War a number of Americans proposed attacking Detroit, but Dan'l. Morgan, Edw. Hand, and Lachlan McIntosh suc-

cessively failed to get the operation going. Dan'l. Brodhead was preparing to try his hand at it when George Rogers Clark appeared.

This man was only 23 years old when the war started but was already an experienced woodsman and Indian fighter. He conceived a bold plan, sold it to the authorities, and then put it into execution. "If he was not quite a military genius," comments Howard Peckham, "he remains one of those remarkable and unaccountable products of the frontier." (*War for Indep.*, 107) Clark's idea was to take the French settlements in what is now southern Ill. On the Mississippi and just below the struggling Spanish trading post of St. Louis were the villages of Cahokia, Bellefontaine, Prairie du Rocher, and—most important—Kaskaskia. On the Wabash River, 150 miles to the east, was Vincennes. Clark sent two agents—Ben Lyon and Samuel Moore *—into this region and they brought back the information that the British garrison had been recalled to Detroit from Kaskaskia, that the villages were virtually undefended, and that the *habitants* could be won over. In a letter to Gov. Patrick Henry during the summer or fall of 1777 Clark passed on this intelligence and pointed out the advantages of taking Kaskaskia:

"The remote situation of this town on the back of several of the Western Nations, their being well supplied with goods on the Mississippi, enables them to furnish the different nations, and by presents will keep up a strict friendship with the Indians; and undoubtedly will keep all the nations that lay under their

---

* Clark had actually picked four of his recruits, but they decided that two would do the job more effectively and drew lots. The two who lost out were Si Harland and Simon Kenton.

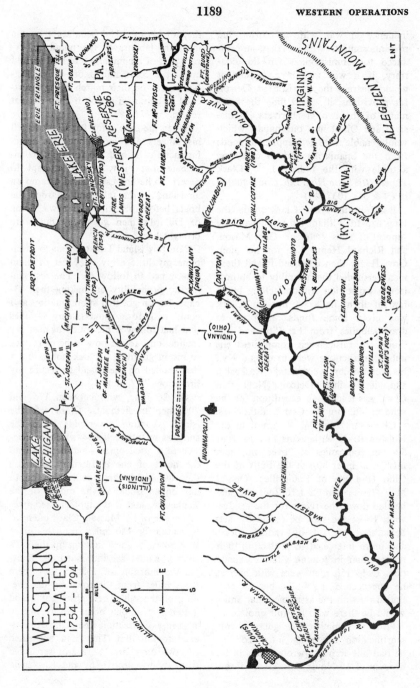

WESTERN
THEATER
1754 – 1794

influence at war with us during the present contest, without they are induced to submission. . . . On the contrary, if it was in our possession it would distress the garrison at Detroit for provisions, it would fling the command of the two great rivers [Mississippi and Ohio] into our hands, which would enable us to get supplies of goods from the Spaniards, and to carry on a trade with the Indians. . . ." (Clark Papers, *Ill. State Hist. Lib. Coll.,* quoted in C. & M., 1037–40)

Later in the year Clark made the long trip to Williamsburg and won the support of Thos. Jefferson, Geo. Mason, and Richard Henry Lee for his plan. Gov. Henry then endorsed it and these men persuaded the assembly to authorize an expedition without telling but a few of them its exact mission. Clark was given some funds, authority to draw supplies from Ft. Pitt, and authority to raise seven companies. His public instructions were to defend Ky.; his secret orders were to take Kaskaskia and, if feasible, Detroit. Note that Clark was leading an expedition for the state of Va., not the Cont'l. authorities.

Clark sent Maj. W. P. Smith to the Holston River settlements to raise four 50-man companies of "over mountain men" and meet him at the Falls of the Ohio (the site of Louisville). On 12 May '78 he himself left Redstone and headed down the rivers for the rendezvous. From the start he found the settlers hard pressed by Indian forays and more interested in protecting their homes than in joining Clark's expedition. Only 150 men were with him as he approached the Falls, but he continued on with the assurance that Smith would be there with his full quota.

"But you may easily guess at my mortification on being informed that he had not arrived; [wrote Clark in his account of 19 Nov. '79 to Geo. Mason]

that all his men had been stopt by the incessant labours of the populace, except part of a company that had arrived under the command of one Capt. Delland, some on their march being threatened to be put in prison if they did not return." (*Ibid.*)

When the time came for Clark to tell his officers and men about his secret instructions he had the foresight to anticipate that many would attempt to desert. So he first established a camp on an island in the falls and guarded the boats before breaking the news. Some of Dillard's men got away but were brought back.

"On this island I first began to discipline my little army. . . . Most of them determined to follow me. The rest seeing no probability of making their escape, I soon got that subordination as I could wish for. About twenty families that had followed me much against my inclination I found now to be of service to me in guarding a block house that I had erected on the island to secure my provisions." (*Ibid.*)

On 26 June, with between 175 and 200 men in flatboats, Clark left the island, shooting the rapids while the sun was in total eclipse—which he considered a good omen—and headed into the heart of enemy territory. Rowing day and night, they landed the fourth day on an island in the mouth of the Tennessee, and that night crossed over to the site of Ft. Massac. Clark intended to march the 120 miles from this place to Kaskaskia, since moving up the Mississippi would sacrifice surprise. Starting the morning of 1 July, they were three miles from the town by the evening of the 4th. Their chief guide had gotten lost at one point but recovered his sense of direction when Clark threatened to kill him. They had not eaten for two days, and were still separated from their objective by the Kaskaskia

River. After dark the Americans captured a farmhouse about a mile above the town. Here Clark learned that the inhabitants "had some suspician of being attacted and had made some prep-arations, keeping out spies [scouts], but they, making no discoveries, had got off their guard." (*Ibid.*)

The commandant of Ft. Gage in Kaskaskia was a French veteran named RASTEL but known in American accounts by his title, Chevalier (or Sieur) de Rocheblave. He had called out the local militia and then disbanded them when his patrols were unable to confirm the report of Clark's approach. The Americans collected enough boats to cross after dark. While one column surrounded the town, Clark led the other to the commandant's quarters, and Rocheblave surrendered the town before a shot was fired.

News of the impending French alliance had reached Clark before he left the Falls of the Ohio, and this helped bring the French over to the American cause. Furthermore, they had been led to expect the worst from the rebels and were favorably impressed by Clark's generous treatment. When Capt. Joseph Bowman was sent with 30 mounted men to secure Prairie du Rocher and Cahokia, Frenchmen accompanied him and entered these places "calling aloud to the people to submit to their happier fate. . . ." (*Ibid.*) Only the ex-commandant failed to enter into the spirit, so he was sent to Va. under guard. Father GIBAULT proved particularly useful. With Dr. Jean Laffont and some other Frenchmen he undertook a trip to Vincennes and returned in early Aug. to report that the town had shifted its allegiance to Va. (20 July). Capt. Leonard Helm promptly marched to occupy the place and take command of the militia.

Although Clark's success was complete, and the *habitants* readily swore allegiance to "The Republic of Virginia," he was in a dangerous situation. Surrounded by Indian tribes allied to Great Britain, he was short of supplies, his force was ridiculously small, and the British were certain to be preparing a counteroffensive from Detroit. He promptly neutralized the Indian threat by a series of conferences in which "he flattered, cajoled, and threatened the savages into promises of good behavior, pledges which were kept for many months." (Ward, *W.O.R.*, 855 *) The supply problem was solved by the remarkable Oliver Pollock, agent for Va. in New Orleans, who shipped enough up the Mississippi for Clark to maintain his position in the Illinois Country.

THE BRITISH
RETAKE VINCENNES

Lt. Gov. Henry Hamilton put on his other hat as Lt. Col. commanding His Majesty's armed forces (for which duties he admitted having "slender knowledge") and prepared to reconquer his lost territory. Because of shortages of supplies, transportation, and troops, he did not get started until 7 Oct. It was to be an arduous, 71-day journey in the dead of winter, and Hamilton showed high qualities of leadership in accomplishing it. Starting with 175 white troops, mostly Frenchmen, and 60 Indians, he picked up Indian allies on the way and finally had at least 500 men under his command. On 17 Dec. he entered Vincennes, virtually unopposed. Capt. Helm had sent out patrols when he learned of the enemy's approach, but Hamilton captured the one heading for Kaskaskia with news of the counter-

* Editor John Richard Alden wrote Ward's chapter on Clark's Western operations and credits James's *Clark* for much of his material.

offensive, and he had also captured an American lieutenant and three men who were reconnoitering along his line of march. The French militia refused to fight, so Helm and the one remaining soldier surrendered.

CLARK TAKES HAMILTON

When Hamilton decided to remain at Vincennes his Indians left him and more than half of the militia were permitted to go home. With his 35 regulars and a slightly larger number of militia, he rebuilt the dilapidated fort and renamed it Ft. Sackville. (Peckham, *War for Indep.*, 108) Clark's command was now reduced by the expiration of enlistments to about 100 riflemen, but he learned that Hamilton did not intend to resume field operations until spring, and once again Clark chose the bold solution. On 3 Feb. '79 he said this in a letter to Gov. Henry:

"Being sensible that without a reinforcement, which at present I have hardly a right to expect, that I shall be obliged to give up this cuntrey to Mr. Hamilton without a turn of fortune in my favour, I am resolved to take advantage of his present situation and risque the whole on a single battle. I shall set out in a few days.... * * * I know the case is desperate but, Sir, we must either quit the cuntrey or attact mr. Hamilton. No time is to be lost. Was I shoer of a reinforcement I should not attempt it. Who knows what fortune will do for us? Great things have been affected by a few men well conducted." (Clark Papers, *op. cit.*)

On 6 Feb. Clark left Kaskaskia with about 200 men (*ibid.*), nearly half of them French volunteers enlisted with the assistance of Father Gibault. The first 100 miles were relatively easy, no serious obstacles being met and an adequate amount of game being available. After crossing the Little Wabash

late 15 Feb., the going got tougher. On the 17th they were stopped by the Embarras River, a mere nine miles from Vincennes and within sound of the reveille gun. But the country was flooded by the early thaw; even game had been driven off by the water, and the men were on starvation rations. The night of 20–21 Feb. they managed to ferry across the Wabash. Wading through icy water that sometimes was shoulder high, they made only three miles the next day, and on the 22d they advanced hardly at all. It was so terrible that Clark skipped the details in his letter to Gov. Henry because he felt they were "too incredible for any person to believe except those that are as well acquainted with me as you are.... I hope you will escuse me until I have the pleasure of seeing you personally," he wrote. The afternoon of 23 Feb. they reached high ground after struggling across two miles of deep water, and Clark's men collapsed to rest and let the sun dry their clothes. They were within two miles of their objective at this point and prisoners said the enemy was still unaware of their presence. While they were resting within sight of the town, a captured *habitant* furnished additional information.

Clark knew he could surprise the town but he lacked the strength to capture the fort quickly. Some of Hamilton's troops had been sent up the Wabash to hurry the movement of supplies; these men could rally Indian reinforcements to raise the siege if it lasted more than a few days. Clark explains his final plan as follows:

"I immediately wrote to the inhabitants in general, informing them where I was and what I determined to do, desiring the friends to the States to keep close in their houses, those in the British interest to repair to the fort and fight for their King: otherways there should be no mercy shewn them etc., etc. . . . I dispatched the prisoner off with this letter, waiting until near sunset, giving him time to get near the town before we marched." (*Ibid.*)

While questioning this last prisoner, Clark had been careful not to let him learn the true strength of the expedition. An important factor in his planning probably was the knowledge that Hamilton had alienated the French in Vincennes by showing his contempt for them as a people. (Peckham, *op. cit.*, 108) Clark's stratagem worked. Marching from the woods across an open plain in two columns, Clark deployed his troops so as to magnify their true number, and he displayed flags "as would be sufficient for a thousand men, which was observed by the inhabitants. . . ." But his arrival also was timed so that darkness would have fallen before the quick-change artists of Vincennes could count his men. The townsmen stayed home or turned out to furnish the Americans badly needed supplies. Hamilton's recently joined Indian allies abandoned him, one chief even offering to join Clark. When the Americans attacked the fort, the British commander thought "some drunken people were amusing themselves."

The long rifles went to work against the gun ports of Ft. Sackville, but inflicted only four casualties. A little before sunrise on the 24th one of Hamilton's patrols returned (under the command of Capt. La Mothe) and achieved the remarkable feat of scaling the 11-foot stockade, weapons in hand, to regain the fort. (Hamilton's *Journal*, quoted in C. & M.) The morning of the 24th, Hamilton refused the first surrender summons at about 9 o'clock. At 11 A.M., however, he sent Capt. Helm out to propose surrender on honorable terms. Clark insisted on unconditional surrender, but offered to parley.

In a bloody bit of showmanship, he then had five captured Indians tomahawked in view of the garrison. Hamilton's French militiamen, half his force, had already indicated a reluctance to join their British colleagues in a defense to the death (*ibid.*), so after further discussion of terms he bowed to the inevitable and signed the capitulation the evening of the 24th. The next day he surrendered the fort and his 79 men. Capt. Helm led a detachment up the Wabash and returned with the 40 men Hamilton had sent for supplies. Hamilton was evacuated to Va. with his regulars and the "Hair Buyer" was put under heavy guard in Williamsburg. (See HAMILTON) Clark released the French militiamen who had come from Detroit and told them to expect him at that place soon.

Although he was able to hold the Illinois Country conquered in this brilliant campaign, Clark's dream of taking Detroit never materialized. He planned expeditions in 1779, 1780, and 1781, and Detroit was practically defenseless, but he was never given the means for the operation and spent the last years of the war trying to counter the renewed wave of Tory-Indian raids against the frontier settlements. After Simon GIRTY surprised and all but wiped out the 70-man supply party of Col. David Rogers on the Ohio and after the KENTUCKY RAID of Henry Bird, Clark retaliated by leading 1,000 Ky. riflemen into Shawnee country to destroy CHILLICOTHE and Piqua in Aug. '80.

Clark's plans for an attack on Detroit in 1781 were spoiled by an enemy offensive along the Ohio. Ft. Jefferson, on the Mississippi below the mouth of the Ohio, had withstood a six-day siege in 1780, but in June '81 it had to be abandoned. Joseph Brant annihilated a force of Pa. militia on the Ohio near the mouth of the Little Miami River as they moved to join Clark. (See LOCHRY's DEFEAT) Brant's Indians and 100 Tories joined 100 British rangers and 300 Indians under Capt. Andrew Thompson and Alexander McKee who were moving from Detroit to attack Clark's 400 as they came down the Ohio from Pittsburgh, but when they were unable to waylay Clark the Indians refused to join in an attack. Clark made his way safely to the Falls of the Ohio where Ft. Nelson had been built to command that strategic point. Although Ky. was being ravaged by continued raids, the settlers refused to support Clark's proposed offensive up the Wabash.

The senseless GNADENHUETTEN MASSACRE, 7–8 Mar. '82, touched off a new wave of Tory-Indian vengeance. After CRAWFORD's DEFEAT, 4–5 June '82, and the rebel disaster at BLUE LICKS, Ky., 19 Aug., Clark led another punitive expedition against the Shawnee and destroyed five towns, including the new CHILLICOTHE, 10 Nov. '82. This was one of the last operations of the Revolution.

In *War Out of Niagara,* Harold Swiggett presents the interesting hypothesis that Clark's Western operations as well as SULLIVAN's and BRODHEAD's EXPEDITIONS were part of Washington's grand design to give America a claim to the Old Northwest. Although this theory has little support, Clark's remarkable achievements with a handful of men in the wilderness certainly strengthened U.S. claims to Ky. and the Illinois Country.

The Harvard Guide to American History has an extensive bibliography under the classification "West in the American Revolution" (pp. 296–97). Among the general works it cites are Turner, *Frontier in American History;* Paxson, *American Frontier;* Parkman, *Pontiac;* Billington, *Westward Expansion;*

Alvord, *Mississippi Valley in British Politics and Centennial History of Illinois;* Beer, *British Colonial Policy;* and Theodore Roosevelt, *Winning of the West.*

Special studies, including biographies, and many identified with their full titles in the main bibliography, are: Abernethy, *Western Lands;* Alden, *Gage, Stuart;* Bakeless, *Clark, Boone;* Carter, *Illinois Country;* Downes, *Council Fires;* English, *Conquest of Northwest;* Hinsdale, *Old Northwest;* James, *Clark, Clark Papers, Pollock;* several works by Kellogg and Thwaites separately and in collaboration; Moore, *Northwest Under Three Flags;* Peckham, *Pontiac;* Phillips, *West in Diplomacy;* Shimmell, *Border Warfare;* and several works by Winsor.

WESTERN RESERVE. About 3,000,-000 acres in the N.E. corner of modern Ohio were reserved by Conn. when that state surrendered claims to all other western lands in 1786. A 500,000-acre tract known as the "Fire Lands" (now the counties of Huron, Erie, and the eastern tip of Ottawa) was used to repay citizens of Danbury, Fairfield, Norwalk, New Haven, and New London for war losses.

WESTMORELAND, Pa. Township into which WYOMING VALLEY settlements were incorporated by Conn. in Jan. '74.

WETHERSFIELD CONFERENCE, Conn., 22 May '81. In a historic meeting here between Washington and Rochambeau a plan was made for a strategic diversion against N.Y.C. (This was not the genesis—except indirectly —of the YORKTOWN CAMPAIGN, as is frequently claimed.)

After meeting at Hartford on the 21st, the two generals rode five miles south to Wethersfield and conferred on the next day. The "Wethersfield Plan" was compromised on 3 June when

Sir Henry Clinton received a captured copy. See YORKTOWN CAMPAIGN for the plan and the effect of its compromise. Wethersfield is the oldest permanently inhabited township in Conn., and is now a suburb of Hartford. A French diarist, almost certainly Cromot du Bourg, wrote: "it would be impossible to find prettier houses and more beautiful view." (Quoted in Freeman, *Washington*, V, 286)

WETZELL'S MILLS (or MILL), N.C., 6 Mar. '81. (SOUTHERN CAMPAIGNS OF GREENE) When Cornwallis started withdrawing from the Dan River toward Hillsboro, N.C. (17 Feb. '81), Greene sent his advance elements over the very next day with the intention of harassing the British until he had received reinforcements and could face Cornwallis in a pitched battle. The opposing forces clashed first at CLAPP'S MILLS, 2 Mar. At 3 o'clock the morning of 6 Mar. Cornwallis undertook a movement by which he hoped to surprise Otho Williams' advance element and draw Greene into a general engagement. By 8 A.M. the British were within two miles of Col. Wm. Campbell's detachment of about 150 Va. militia riflemen when their presence was detected. Sending Lee's Legion and Wm. Washington's dragoons to support Campbell, Williams started withdrawing along Reedy Fork from his camp at High Rock Ford to the ford at Wetzell's Mills.

Tarleton's cavalry and 1,000 infantry of Lt. Col. James Webster's Brig. (23d, 33d, 71st, Lt. Inf. Co. of the Guards, and some jägers) pushed forward aggressively, while Cornwallis followed with the main body. Col. Wm. Preston commanded a covering force of Va. riflemen while Campbell, Lee, and Washington made good their retreat across the ford at Wetzell's Mills. Seeing that the numerically superior enemy

had too many opportunities for turning him out of a defensive position along Reedy Fork, Williams ordered Campbell, Lee, and Washington to delay as long as possible at Wetzell's Mills while the rest of the light corps continued their retreat toward Greene's camp. The delaying force was directed to withdraw when faced with the danger of being overwhelmed.

Lee posted a company of Preston's riflement to cover the ford, deployed the Legion infantry in a line parallel to the creek, and placed Campbell's men and the remainder of Preston's in some heavy woods so that their left flank tied in with the right flank of the Legion infantry. Lee's cavalry were to the rear where they could protect the militia horses and also be prepared to cover the retreat of the first line.

The Guards led Webster's Brig. in an attempt to force a crossing of the creek at the ford. When they were driven back by well-aimed fire from Preston's riflemen, Webster rode up to lead them across. The British infantry then stormed the high bank on which the defenders were deployed, and Tarleton's cavalry splashed across the ford and got into a position to cut off the Americans if they did not withdraw promptly. Covered by the Legion cavalry, the delaying force withdrew five miles while the British maintained pressure. Cornwallis then accepted the fact that his attempt had failed and withdrew. Greene had marched the main body to the ironworks on Troublesome Creek.

Losses were about 50 on each side, according to some sources (Lossing, II, 606; Dawson, *Battles*, 663); Ward says the Americans lost about 20 killed or wounded and that Tarleton "admits" a loss of 21 on his side. (*W.O.R.*, 782) Inability of the Americans to hit Webster is mentioned under MARKS-

MANSHIP. The next encounter between Greene and Cornwallis was the major engagement at GUILFORD C. H., 15 Mar. '81.

"WHALEBOAT WARFARE." This term was applied to water-borne guerrilla operations and small boat privateering in Long Island Sound and along the N.J. coast. (See also "LONDON TRADING") American heroes included Adam Hyler, Wm. MARRINER, R. J. MEIGS, and Benj. TALLMADGE. See also BLUE MOUNTAIN VALLEY.

WHEELING, W. Va., 1 Sept. '77 and 11–13 Sept. '82. This site on the Ohio River was first settled in 1769 by Ebenezer Zane. Ft. Fincastle was built there in 1774 by William CRAWFORD—during Dunmore's War—and the fort was renamed in 1776 for Patrick Henry. The exposed and isolated settlement in the "DARK AND BLOODY GROUND" had often been raided. On the last day of Aug. '77, however, it was hit by almost 400 Indians and besieged for 23 hours. (W. H. Hunter, "The Pathfinders of Jefferson County [Ohio]," *Ohio Arch. and Hist. Soc. Pubs.*, VI, 131) According to Lossing the villagers had sufficient warning to evacuate their 25 log cabins and take refuge in the fort, but 23 of Col. Sheppard's 42-man garrison were killed or captured in preliminary skirmishes. (II, 499) After refusing a summons to surrender, the defenders withstood a six-hour fire delivered from the cover of their abandoned cabins. Lossing's account would indicate that 19 of Col. Sheppard's troops took part in this defense, but Hunter makes reference only to 30 defenders, 12 of whom were men and boys and the rest women and young children. After a lull the Indians resumed their attack at 2:30 P.M. of the first day (31 Aug. or 1 Sept.). The next morning at 4 o'clock Col. Swearingen got into the fort with 14 reinforcements, and Maj. McCulloch

arrived later with 40 mounted men. After burning the settlement and killing what livestock they could find, the Indians withdrew. None of the defenders was killed. Lossing gives the highly improbable figure of 60 to 100 Indians killed. See also "McCULLOCH'S LEAP."

In what may technically be the last battle of the war (*D.A.H.*), Ft. Henry held off 250 Indians and 40 Tories during the period 11–13 Sept. '82. (Hunter, *op. cit.*, 132) It was probably during the latter action that Ebenezer Zane's sister Elizabeth performed her feat of valor: during a lull in the battle she volunteered to leave the fort and get a keg of badly needed powder from her brother's cabin, 60 yards away. It was open ground which no man could safely traverse, but Elizabeth argued that the Indians might be so surprised to see a woman walking out of the fort that they would be slow to fire. She was right; the savages merely gawked as she strolled to the cabin, but when she emerged with the powder keg they recovered their wits and opened up. It was too late, however, and she "sped with the fleetness of a fawn" to reach the fort unscathed. (Lossing, II, 498 *n*.) Lossing says this happened in 1777; in his *D.A.B.* article on Ebenezer Zane, Randolph C. Downes says it happened in 1782. Leadership of both attacks has been attributed to the renegade Simon Girty, but no Girty was fighting against the Americans in 1777 and James Girty was the only member of the notorious family present in the attack of 1782. (See Simon GIRTY for authorities.) Writers disagree also on the exact dates of these actions: I have accepted those of Hunter (*op. cit.*); Lossing says the first attack started on 1 Sept. '77 and that the second action took place during the period 10–11 Sept. '82. As for the dangerous matter of whether this was the "last *battle* of the Revolution," it should be pointed out that the "last *action*" may have been at JOHNS ISLAND, S.C., 4 Nov. '82.

WHIGS AND TORIES. These nicknames were applied contemptuously by opponents of the parliamentary parties that came into existence around 1650, when Parliament started fighting for predominance in England. Origins of the words are obscure, but according to *O.U.D.* "whig" probably comes from "whiggamore," one of a body of Scottish insurgents who marched on Edinburgh in 1648; it also is associated with sour milk ("whey"), horse driving, rustling (to use a purely American word), and with the Scots Covenanters' motto "We' hope in God." (*E.B.*) "Tory" is the Anglicized spelling of an Irish word meaning "pursuer," and was originally (1646) applied to Irish outlaws who preyed on English settlers and soldiers. (*O.U.D.*)

"The persistency of the names of the two parties is mainly owing to their essential unmeaningness," points out *E.B.* "As new questions arose, the names of the old parties were retained, though the objects of contention were no longer the same." The Whigs were the "Country Party" under Shaftesbury; they drew support from the aristocracy, the merchants, and the City of London; they formed a powerful group in the reigns of William III and Anne (1689–1714), backed the winning side in the Hanoverian Succession, and enjoyed a political monopoly during the reigns of George I and II (1714–60). Their power finally broken by GEORGE III, the Whigs divided into the camps of ROCKINGHAM (the larger body) and CHATHAM. Since they generally favored politics popular with the Americans, the Patriot Party in the Thirteen Colonies called themselves Whigs after 1768. (*O.U.D.*) The Whig party in England virtually disappeared after Pitt the

Younger revitalized the Tory party in 1783, but in 1830 they triumphed as the party of Parliamentary reform. By 1868 the name Whig had been replaced in England by that of Liberal. The Whig Party in America after the Revolution was prominent during the period 1824–54. (See REPUBLICAN PARTY)

The Tories upheld hereditary succession and therefore were originally the party of the Royalists and Cavaliers. Tainted with disloyalty after extreme elements championed the Jacobites at the time of the Hanoverian Succession, they were excluded from office during the reigns of George I and II (see above). Although virtually extinct as a political force during the latter period, with the accession of George III the Tories supported the King's right to choose and control his ministers, providing he was supported by a majority in the Commons; the Whigs, on the other hand, contended at this time that Parliament alone should select and control the ministers. After George III broke the power of the Whigs (1770), most of the "King's friends" were Tories.

When Pitt the Younger came to power in 1782 he recreated a liberal party that retained the Tory principle of reliance on the Crown but also attracted the Chatham wing of the Whig party by advocating control of government by the people rather than by the Whig aristocracy. Defeated in 1830 (see above), the Tories began to be known as "Conservatives" and later (after 1886) as "Unionists"; now they are known indiscriminately in Great Britain as Tories or Conservatives. In America after 1775 a loyal colonist was called a Tory. (*O.U.D.*)

It should be made clear that the Whigs and Tories about whom we have been speaking were not organized political parties in the modern sense but were a collection of special-interest groups held together by patronage and personal loyalties rather than by political principles.

WHIPPLE, Abraham. 1733–1819. Cont'l. naval officer. R.I. Descended from John Whipple, one of the original proprietors of the Providence Plantations, and married to a sister of Esek and Stephen HOPKINS, he was appointed commodore of the little R.I. fleet when it was organized in 1775. He had followed the sea from an early age, capturing 23 French vessels while in command of the privateer *Game Cock* in 1759–60, and was considered to be the colony's most experienced sea captain. He also had led the 50-man party in the GASPÉE AFFAIR in 1772. On 15 June '75, the day he received his commission to command the navy of R.I., he captured the tender of the British frigate *Rose,* the first official American prize of the Revolution. One of the first captains of the Cont'l. Navy, he commanded the *Columbus* (20) in the first NAVAL OPERATION of the war. In 1778 he took the *Providence* (12) to Europe, was presented to the French king, and took a few prizes. In mid-July '79, while his *Providence* was cruising with Rathbun's *Queen of France* and the *Ranger,* he had the good fortune of drifting into a British convoy of heavily laden East Indiamen off Newfoundland in a heavy fog. Thanks largely to the initiative of RATHBUN, he cut 11 of the ships out of the convoy and got eight of them safely to Boston. Sold for $1,000,000, they constituted one of the richest single captures of the war.

Later in the year he reached Charleston with four Cont'l. vessels and was given responsibility for the naval defense of the doomed city. He became a prisoner on 12 May '80, when the city was surrendered to Clinton, and for the remainder of the war was on parole at Chester, Pa.

He emigrated to Marietta, Ohio, around 1786, and supported himself by farming until Congress granted him a pension in 1811. In 1801 he made a commercial voyage down the rivers to New Orleans, Havana, and Philadelphia in the *St. Clair.*

WHIPPLE, William. 1730–1785. Signer. Maine–N.H. A descendant of Matthew Whipple, who went to America from England prior to 1638, William was born in Kittery. After attending local schools he went to sea, became master of a vessel while still in his early twenties, and engaged in the "legal if not wholly respectable activity" of slave trading. (Wm. A. Robinson in *D.A.B.*) He left the sea in 1760 and became a business partner of his brother Joseph at Portsmouth, N.H., a short distance from his birthplace. After playing a prominent part in the revolutionary politics of his region he was elected to the Cont'l. Cong. in 1776 and remained a delegate until he declined re-election in 1780. He signed the Decl. of Indep., was active in committees, and showed an exceptionally realistic attitude on such vital matters as the need for heavy taxation to finance the struggle, the need for reforms in the commissary and recruiting systems, the importance of naval operations, and the requirement for military success in America rather than diplomatic cleverness in Europe to win the war. (*D.A.B.*) He left Cong. temporarily to serve as a B.G. in command of state contingents in the two battles of Saratoga (Lossing, II, 868) and in Sullivan's operations around Newport in 1778. He and Gen. Glover commanded the troops that escorted Burgoyne's captured army to Cambridge. (Heath, *Memoirs,* 146) During the period 1780–84 Whipple sat in the state assembly, and from 1782 until his death in 1785 he was associate justice of the N.H. superior court. Only 55 when he died, he had been performing his arduous duties for several years while in bad health and with the belief —confirmed by autopsy—that he was in danger of sudden death. (*D.A.B.*)

WHITCOMB, John. 1713–1785. Militia general. Mass. As a Col. of Mass. militia he took part in operations against Ticonderoga, Crown Point, and Montreal during the French and Indian War. "Though uneducated, and never self-seeking, he became a noted leader of the people," says Appleton's. He was commissioned B.G. of militia by a special resolution of the Mass. Prov. Cong. of 15 Feb. '75, which followed their resolve of 9 Feb. naming Prebble, Ward, Pomeroy, and John Thomas. (Heath, *Memoirs,* 18–19) He participated in the pursuit of the British after Lexington and Concord, 19 Apr., (*ibid.,* 24) and was "elected first major-general of the Massachusetts army" on 3 Feb. '76. (Quoted in Appleton's where, however, the date 3 Feb. '75 is given.) During the Battle of Bunker Hill he had commanded at Lechmere Point. Passed over by Congress in the earlier promotions to general officer, he was appointed B.G. on 5 June '76 (making him Number 20 in order of seniority). He declined the commission on grounds of age.

WHITEFIELD, George. 1714–1770. English evangelist. Closely identified with the Wesleys until 1741, when he espoused Calvinistic views, he made seven trips to America before the Revolution and preached to huge, open-air congregations from Ga. to New England. He was appointed minister of Savannah and in 1739 established an orphanage called Bethesda some 10 miles from the city. A prominent and controversial figure in the history of the church, he is mentioned frequently by Colonial writers. See *D.A.B.* for a long biographical sketch.

WHITE HORSE TAVERN, Pa. In the PHIL. CAMP'N, a major skirmish is known by the names of WARREN or WHITE HORSE TAVERN, 16 Sept., '77.

WHITEHAVEN, England, 27–28 Apr. '78. In command of the sloop *Ranger,* John Paul Jones raided this port on Solway Firth, where he had started his apprenticeship as a seaman. Landing in two boats with about 30 men late 27 Apr. or early the next morning, he spiked the guns of two forts and set fire to three ships. He was unable to carry out his more ambitious plan of destroying all the shipping in the harbor. This raid has been called "the only American operation of war on English soil." (Montross, *Reluctant Rebels,* 254) A contemporary English newspaper account is in C. & M. (pp. 943–45). See also John Paul JONES.

WHITEMARSH, Pa., 5–8 Dec. '77. When Howe learned that Washington was preparing to leave Whitemarsh and take up a new position farther from Philadelphia, he led a sortie to hit the Americans as they changed position. Howe's vanguard reached Chestnut Hill, about four miles from Whitemarsh, at 8 o'clock the morning of the 5th. Brig. Gen. James Irvine, Pa. militia, led an American attack that the British advance guard thought was the beginning of a general attack, but the rebels withdrew after Irvine and about 16 of his men had been captured. The night of 6–7 Dec., Howe led the largest portion of his army from Philadelphia to Germantown and from there to Jenkintown, two and a half miles from the American left, where they arrived at dawn. After pushing in the American outposts and taking position along the high ground around Edge Hill, Howe decided that Washington's defenses were too strong to warrant the risk of a general assault. The British started withdrawing at 3:30 P.M., and were back in Philadelphia by 10:30. Baurmeister, from whom this account is taken, says 10 jägers and 46 British light infantry were killed or wounded (*Journals*, 138). Three days later, Cornwallis led a large foraging expedition that clashed near MATSON'S FORD, 11 Dec., with the forward elements of Washington's army as the latter started for Valley Forge winter quarters.

WHITE PLAINS, N.Y. 28 Oct. '76. (N.Y. CAMPAIGN) Although there was better defensive terrain slightly to the north, Washington deployed his troops on a width of three miles through the village of White Plains; he did this to enable evacuation of valuable supplies, an operation slowed by critical lack of wagons. Alexander ("Stirling") got Washington's order at 2 A.M., 21 Oct., and his first troops were on the ground by 9 o'clock. Washington himself followed the same day with Heath's Div. Although the Americans rushed to secure White Plains before Howe could get there, Howe was in no hurry; he moved slowly forward from Pell's Point and Throg's Point. (See N.Y. CAMPAIGN for background, to include reorganization of patriot forces.)

Howe's main body reached New Rochelle on 21 Oct., where it was reinforced two days later by the second contingent of Germans: almost 4,000 Hessians, 670 Waldneckers, and a company of jägers, all under command of von KNYPHAUSEN. The regulars conducted a number of armed reconnaissances, sustaining a few casualties and capturing some prisoners, during the time Howe's main force remained inactive. On 28 Oct., Howe's 13,000 moved toward White Plains in two columns, led initially by the jägers.

Chatterton's Hill, to the right of the American lines, had not been fortified by the time the enemy advance guard approached on the afternoon of the 27th. Not until the next morning—after his advance guards had been driven back and the general alarm sounded— did Washington decide that this was critical terrain. Col. Joseph Reed was directed to take charge of securing the hill; he started Haslet's veteran Del. Cont'ls. on their way to join the Mass. militia unit of (John?) Brooks already posted there. Reed then instructed Alexander McDougall to move up and construct field fortifications. This put 1,600 troops and two guns on the hill: McDougall's own 1st N.Y., Ritzema's 3d N.Y., Smallwood's Md. Regt., Webb's Conn. Regt., Brooks's militia, and Haslet's Del. Cont'ls. McDougall was in over-all command. (Freeman, *Washington*, IV, 225–29 n.; Ward, *W.O.R.*, 262.)

Meanwhile, Spencer and Wadsworth were sent out to make contact and to delay the enemy. With a mixed force of militia that Freeman puts at between 500 and 600, and that Ward puts at 1,500, contact was made about two miles from White Plains. Freeman dismisses the delaying action with the statement that they "skirmished for an hour, and then retreated on news from a flanking party that the British Light Horse were encircling the force." (*Op. cit.*, 230 n.) The delaying force returned between 9 and 9:30 to report that the enemy was approaching in two columns along the East Chester Road. Spencer retreated to Chatterton's Hill; the Hessians and British pursued across the Bronx River and then withdrew. (S. & R., 195) Having found his adversary, Howe started deploying his regulars in an open area about a mile from and in plain view of the Americans, presenting an awesome spectacle that was dramatized by a bright autumn sun on burnished arms and gaudy uniforms.

Chatterton's Hill, which Howe promptly recognized as critical terrain, and against which he prepared to send eight regiments and a dozen guns, rose 180 feet above the plain on which the attackers formed. The 14-foot-wide Bronx River, swollen by recent rains and obstructed by old tree trunks, ran along the base of the hill to impede the assault column. The top of the hill, on which the British could see the defenders forming, was gently rounded but divided into cultivated fields by stone walls, which would aid the Americans; the sides of the hill were steep and heavily wooded.

THE ATTACK

Three German regiments (Leib, Rall, and von Knyphausen) crossed the Bronx River first and maneuvered onto the ridges that Howe had spotted about half a mile south of Chatterton's Hill and from which McDougall's line could be enfiladed. While these troops fired across the draw and along the American line, other guns fired from the east, and the rest of the attacking force made its way across the river. The Hessians stopped to build a bridge and were attacked by Smallwood and Ritzema. British Gen. Alexander Leslie then learned of a ford downstream and, out to show the Hessians an example of British courage, led the 28th and 35th Regts. across the river and up the steep, wooded hill in a bayonet attack; he was driven back on the 5th and 49th Regts. and the Hessians with heavy losses. Meanwhile, the entire attacking force had crossed the river and marched northward in column to form a line for their final assault.

While Ritzema and Smallwood contested this advance with great gallantry (according to Ward, 265), and the attackers moved through heavy musket fire and grapeshot (Baurmeister, 64), the Americans were quickly routed when the Mass. militia units on the right (Graham and Brooks) were hit first by Rall and then by Birch's Light Dragoons. Haslet's Delawares, their right uncovered by the flight of Graham, Brooks, and Smallwood, fought off two attacks before withdrawing on order. The dragoons pursued the Mass. militia, but the British were content to halt on Chatterton's Hill, where the fighting ended about 5 P.M.

A general attack ordered by Howe for the 31st was postponed because of a heavy storm. When the British advanced the next day they found that Washington had withdrawn north, beyond the Croton River, to a stronger position. Soon thereafter, Howe turned his attention to bypassed FT. WASHINGTON.

COMMENTS

Although the Americans initially put their losses at between 400 and 500, the final estimate was about 150. (Freeman, 230 n.) Fortescue gives Howe's losses as 313: 214 British and 99 Hessians killed and wounded.

Accounts of the action at White Plains show wide disparity. Whereas most secondary works cover tactical details with a broad brush (and "Howe's report [3 Force (5), p. 924–25], is little more than a matter-of-fact summary of an easy assault on a flank position," writes Freeman, 231 n.), Ward and Baurmeister (op. cit.) go into considerable detail. However, the latter two accounts of the action are impossible to reconcile, although they picture American resistance as being admirable. Freeman has a different story:

"Then came silence on the extreme right and a humiliating message to Washington: Hessians and British had stormed Chatterton's Hill; the militia had run away again; Smallwood's men had stood for no longer than a quarter of an hour; Webb's Regiment and part of Haslet's command had held their ground but had to retreat when left alone; some of McDougall's men had not pulled trigger." (*Op. cit.,* 231)

True, Freeman says the above was the "message to Washington" immediately after the action, but he implies that the message was completely accurate. Most accounts mention the rout of Brooks's Regt. in the early stages of the action when one round of artillery wounded one of his men; these militia were rounded up and put on the right flank, behind Smallwood, only to stampede again (see above).

Fortescue comments on Leslie's premature frontal attack, which resulted in unduly heavy casualties (*op. cit.,* 189) and says Howe gained "no solid advantage" in taking Chatterton's Hill. "Howe had ordered a simultaneous attack on the American main position; but this movement, for some unexplained reason, was never executed (Howe, 'for political reasons,' declined to account for this in his examination before the House of Commons [says a footnote]); and indeed it seems that Washington's left was so strongly posted as to insure his retreat to Connecticut with, at any rate, the greater part of his army." (*Op. cit.,* 189–90)

WICKES, Lambert. *c.* 1742–1777. Cont'l. naval officer. Md. Great-grandson of Joseph Wickes, who settled in Md. by 1650, he went to sea early in life. By 1769 he had become a ship's captain, and by Dec. '74 he was part owner of a ship. His courageous devotion to the patriot cause and acquaintance with Robert Morris were factors in his getting command of the Cont'l. armed ship *Reprisal* in Apr. '76. On 3 July he sailed from Cape May after a sharp engagement in which his brother was killed, and on 27 July he appeared off Martinique after sending three prizes back to Philadelphia. Defeating H.M.S. *Shark* outside the harbor of Saint Pierre, he completed his mission by landing Wm. Bingham and on 13 Sept. reached Philadelphia with a valuable cargo of powder, 500 muskets, and clothing. He sailed secretly from Philadelphia on 26 Oct. with Benj. Franklin aboard and reached France on 28 Nov., having taken two English prizes en route. In Jan. '77 he took five British prizes in the Channel. In Apr. the American commissioners in Paris put him in command of a small force comprising his ship and those of Capts. Henry Johnson and Sam'l. Nicholson. Under orders from Franklin and Deane to carry out a naval-privateering cruise in the Irish Sea, Wickes sailed from France on 28 May. Circling around Ireland, they entered the Irish Channel from the north, captured 18 small merchantmen (eight were kept as prizes, the rest destroyed), and escaped through the British forces guarding the south end of the channel. When almost back to France the American raiders sighted a huge enemy warship which turned out to be the *Burford* (74). Wickes signaled for Johnson, Nicholson, and the prizes accompanying them to scatter and fly for safety while he tried to escape from the faster, more heavily armed ship of the line.

The *Reprisal* was a full-rigged ship about 100 feet long, with slender lines from which the famous Yankee clippers evolved, and with an original armament of 18 6-pdrs., 20 swivels, and eight coehorns. (Augur, *Secret War,* 106) She was no match for the 74-gun leviathan, except in speed. The chase started shortly before noon, 27 June '77, and the *Reprisal* managed to keep just out of range until 7 P.M., when the

Burford got close enough to start dropping gunshot on the deck. Even after Wickes had jettisoned all his cannon and swivels the warship continued to narrow the gap, and there was enough remaining light for the kill. When Capt. Bowyer turned to deliver broadsides, however, Wickes countered by turning so that his own side was not exposed. After the desperate step of sawing some beams of the *Reprisal* to increase her resilience, Wickes made a final dash for the rocky coast and Bowyer had to abandon the pursuit. (*Ibid.*, 184)

"The three-ship cruise in the home waters of the British Isles caused great popular alarm, another jump in insurance rates, and the cancellation of the great fair of Chester. Merchants would not trust British bottoms, and forty French ships were soon in the Thames, taking over the carrying trade." (*Ibid.*, 185)

Lord Stormont, already furious over the foray of CONYNGHAM, protested so vigorously that Wickes was detained at St. Malo until 14 Sept., when he sailed for America. His ship foundered off the Banks of Newfoundland on 1 Oct. '77 and only the cook was saved. (L. H. Bolander in *D.A.B.*) Augur says Wickes was "a seasoned commander of thirty-four" when commissioned in 1776; this would mean he was born about 1742; *D.A.B.* gives the date "1735?" "Humane and lovable, he was inarticulate like all his breed, but brilliant and cool in action." (Augur, *op. cit.*, 106)

See William Bell Clark, *Lambert Wickes, Sea Raider and Diplomat* (New Haven, Conn., 1932)

WILKES, John. 1727–1797. British politician. Second son * of a rich Lon-

* The first, Israel (d. 1805), went to America. His son, the grandnephew of John Wilkes, became a prominent naval officer and explorer, Charles Wilkes

don distiller, he was a bright student and went with several other talented young Britishers to study in Leyden. After furthering his education by travel in Europe, he returned to England and in 1749 married a wealthy heiress who was 10 years his senior. The marriage did not last much beyond the birth of a daughter (5 Aug. '50), but Wilkes emerged from the affair with custody of the child and property worth £700 a year. In 1758 the former wife had to seek protection of the law to stop his efforts to extort more money from her.

Although Wilkes has been described as having irregular features to the point of ugliness, with a squint that gave him a sinister expression, he was learned, well mannered, high spirited, fond of society, and possessed of an inexhaustible store of wit and humor. (J. M. Rigg in *D.N.B.*) He soon became a prominent West-end figure of London, his associates being Thos. Potter, son of the archbishop of Canterbury, Sir Francis Dashwood, and Lord Sandwich. In 1749 he was elected a Fellow of the Royal Society. In 1754 he made an unsuccessful attempt to enter Parliament, but in 1757 won a seat with the assistance of Potter and Wm. Pitt. A loyal supporter of Pitt at first, he soon turned rebel because he felt that Pitt's indifference and Lord Bute's hostility were thwarting his admission to the Board of Trade or for the post of ambassador to Turkey or as governor of Quebec. After the success of several of his articles assailing the foreign policies of Bute, he and the poet Charles Churchill founded *The North Briton* as an organ of opposition.

(1798–1877), who discovered Antarctica, 19 Jan. 1840 (*E.B.*), and whose arrest of Confederate commissioners Mason and Slidell on the high seas on 8 Nov. '61 precipitated the *"Trent* Affair" and made him a Union hero.

Issue No. 45 (23 Apr. '63) contained such caustic criticism of the King's message to Parliament that the King and his court were determined to silence him. Lord Halifax, the leading secretary of state, issued a general warrant "to search for authors, printers and publishers" and to bring them before him for examination. (Quoted by Wm. P. Courtney in *E.B.*) Since the offensive articles were anonymous, no grounds existed for arrest warrants. And although the government must have been sure of the author's identity, there existed the further obstacle of Wilkes's parliamentary immunity. On information from the printers, however, Wilkes was grabbed on 30 Apr. and taken before Egremont and Halifax. Lord Temple learned of this almost immediately and applied for a writ of habeas corpus, but Wilkes, meanwhile, after evading the questions put to him, was closely confined in the Tower and his home sacked as agents of the court seized his papers.

On 6 May he was released on the ground of parliamentary privilege and Wilkes took the offensive. In an action against Under Secretary Wood, chief agent in the seizure of his papers, he won £1,000 in damages on 6 Dec. '63. Halifax waged a long and discreditable delaying action against Wilkes's charges, but on 10 Nov. '69 Wilkes won £4,000 damages (*D.N.B.*). General warrants were declared illegal and other law suits against Halifax by others claiming injury from his lawless proceedings eventually cost the ministry at least £100,000. (*E.B.*)

Wilkes had triumphed as a champion of the rights of Englishmen, but he quickly gave his enemies another opportunity. In issue No. 46 of *The New Briton* (12 Nov. '63) he renewed his attacks. He also reprinted the offensive No. 45. But where he came a cropper was in running off 13 copies of an obscene and impious parody of Pope's *Essay on Man* entitled *Essay on Woman*, the latter probably having been written by his friend Potter. (*E.B.; D.N.B.* is less sure, but discredits the theory that Wilkes himself wrote it.) Egremont had died on 21 Aug. '63 and been succeeded by Lord Sandwich, a fellow profligate of Potter and Wilkes in the orgies and black masses of Medmenham Abbey. But something had happened to the contemptible lord since then, because it was he who on 15 Nov. started action against Wilkes in the House of Lords that led to his being charged with printing impious libel. At the same time Lord North moved in the House of Commons that No. 45 be condemned as seditious libel and that proceedings be taken against him. This was pretty impressive competition for a champion of the free press. The next day Wilkes received a serious abdominal wound in a duel with Samuel Martin, an ex-secretary of the treasury, which enabled him to avoid appearance to a citation in Commons. On 4 Dec., in obedience to a royal message, No. 45 was put in the hands of the common hangman and publicly burned in Cheapside. Wilkes's private press reprinted all previous issues of *The North Briton* and about Christmas Wilkes appeared in Paris. He filed a medical certificate of ill health (dated 11 Jan. '64) but Parliament refused to accept its validity and on 19 Jan. '64 expelled him. When he did not appear to receive judgment he was pronounced an outlaw on 1 Nov. '64.

After several years abroad, during which time he traveled and wrote, he was forced by boredom and lack of funds to return. He reached London on 6 Feb. '68, refused to submit a request for pardon in a form the King could honorably accept, was elected by an immense majority to Parliament from Middlesex on 28 Mar., surrendered himself as an outlaw, and on 27 Apr. was sent to prison. It had not taken long for the King to know that Wilkes was back in town and the House of Hanover was in for an airing of English rights that just about blew the roof off. Wilkes's sentence was a £1,000 fine, 22 months' imprisonment, and on release he would have to put up sizable securities for his good behavior during the next seven years.

Even before the authorities could get him to jail he was rescued by the mob and had to escape from them to reach the jail and get on with his role of martyr. Crowds continued to build up until troops had to be used on 10 May to disperse them. On 3 Feb. '69 the House expelled him as a member, Middlesex re-elected him on the 16th, he was pronounced incapable of sitting, the electors returned him again on 16 Mar., and again he was rejected. On 13 Apr., in a fourth election in which he ran against Col. Henry Lawes Luttrell, he won by 1,143 votes to 296 despite all the influence of the court and the Fox family, but two days later the House declared that Luttrell had been elected.

"Wilkes had entered the king's bench prison a ruined man," comments Rigg in *D.N.B.* "He left it [on 17 Apr. '70] free from embarrassment." A committee raised more than £17,000 and discharged his numerous liabilities. Englishmen of all social stations joined the cause of "Wilkes and Liberty!" He was a popular idol whose ugly likeness appeared on trinkets. He was the champion of the bill of rights and of the English constitution. Even before he left prison he had been elected an alderman of the city of London (Jan. '69). On 24 July '71 he was elected sheriff of London and Middlesex. After twice being elected mayor and being rejected by the court of aldermen, on 8 Oct. '74 he attained

this post, and on 29 Oct. '74 he was elected to Parliament. Throughout the Revolution he opposed the government, sharing with Isaac BARRE the distinction of being the men the King most thoroughly disliked. In 1776 he moved for "just and equal representation of the people of England in parliament," but his attempts were premature by at least 50 years. (*E.B.*) In the Gordon Riots (June '80) he played a courageous and effective part in asserting the authority of law. Having been elected chamberlain of the city by a large majority in 1779, with freehold for life, he did not seek re-election to Parliament after 1790. On the day after Christmas, 1797, he died at his house in Grosvenor Square. He was survived less than five years by his daughter Mary, to whom he had shown a tender attachment throughout his stormy career.

The name John Wilkes loomed large in the American Revolution as a symbol of the "rights of Englishmen" on which the colonists so largely based their cause. When Alexander McDOUGALL was imprisoned in N.Y. he was called "the Wilkes of America." A city in Pa. preserves the name Wilkes-Barre. And John Wilkes Booth was not the only American whose parents thus honored the English radical. (The assassin's grandfather was a distant relative of Wilkes's.)

WILKINSON, James. 1757–1825. Cont'l. officer, scoundrel. Md. His "long, checkered, and on the whole dishonorable career" (Nickerson, *Turning Point,* 428) got a good start during the Revolution but reached its flower later. Grandson of an Englishman who had reached America in 1729, James Wilkinson was born at Benedict, Md., was taught by private tutor, and had started to study medicine when the war began. As a volunteer in Thompson's Pa. Bn., 9 Sept. '75–Mar. '76, he and Aaron Burr took part in ARNOLD'S MARCH TO QUE-

BEC. (An interesting collection of scoundrels, but their performance in this expedition was creditable.) Wilkinson remained with Arnold until Dec. '76, when the latter had reached Albany after the retreat from Canada. Meanwhile he had been commissioned Capt. of the 2d Cont'l. Inf. in Mar. '76 with rank from the date he began his volunteer service. (Heitman. This would explain why most writers refer to him as Capt. Wilkinson during the Canada Invasion.) The official records show him as a member of Greene's staff from Nov. '75 to Apr. '76, A.D.C. to Arnold from 2 June to 17 July '76, Brigade Maj. on 20 July and a member of Gates's staff in this capacity from 13 Dec. '76, Lt. Col. of Hartley's Cont'l. Regt. on 12 Jan. '77, Dep. A.G. of the Northern Dept. from 24 May '77 to 6 Mar. '78. (Heitman) He figured in the actions at TICONDEROGA, July '77 and SARATOGA, 7 Oct. '77 (see "Phase Two").

Named by Gates to take the news of the Saratoga Surrender to Congress, Wilkinson did not reach York until 31 Oct. and did not make up his written report until 3 Nov. '77.* The 20-year-old aide had stopped off in Reading, Pa., for some courting and at the headquarters of Gen. Alexander he dropped the bit of gossip that brought the CONWAY CABAL to a head. Wilkinson's

* On 16 Oct. the delegates had received the first incredible news of a victory over Burgoyne (1st Saratoga, 19 Sept.) On the 23d James Adams wrote in a letter, "We have had Rumours, which lifted us up to the Stars," but said in another letter of the same date, "To this moment we have no express from Gates or any authentic confirmation." (Quoted in Montross, *Rebels,* 216)

degree of involvement in the cabal is not known.

Young Wilkinson was an unpopular man in York for having kept Congress writhing on a rack of suspense. They took a dim view of Gates's request that he be breveted B.G., but on 6 Nov. they granted the request and tried to calm the outraged uproar in the army by appointing him immediately to the new board of war. What started as the protest of a few regimental commanders is alleged to have picked up 47 signatures of colonels who objected to Wilkinson's brevet promotion. (At the same time the generals were protesting the promotion of Thos. CONWAY.) He wrote Wayne on 26 Nov. to "assist me by unmasking to me the assassins who dare traduce me." In an effort to vindicate himself from the accusation of betraying the confidence of Gates he threatened to fight a duel with Gen. Alexander, and a duel with Gates was called off at the last minute. (See CONWAY CABAL) Although Gates reportedly refused to accept him on the board of war, Wilkinson actually served (as secretary) until 29 Mar. '78, when he indignantly resigned "in a letter so abusive of Gates that Congress refused to permit the paper to remain among the records." (Freeman, *Washington,* IV, 597 and *n.,* 604 and *n.*) (According to Heitman, Wilkinson resigned as Bvt. B.G. on 6 Mar. and as Sec. of the Bd. of War on 31 Mar. '78.)

Appointed Clothier General of the Cont'l. Army on 24 July '79, he resigned 27 Mar. '81 because of irregularity in his accounts. While in uniform Wilkinson had proved himself guilty of intrigue and excess drinking; now he showed another greed—money. (Isaac J. Cox in *D.A.B.*)

With this wartime preparation Wilkinson entered into intrigue on an interstate, international scale. Moving to Ky.

in 1784, he became prominent in trade and politics, supplanting George Rogers Clark as leader in that region. (*D.A.B.*) In the SPANISH CONSPIRACY—the purpose of which may have been to set up a separate republic in the West allied to Spain, or may have been a plot to force the admission of Ky. to the U.S. (*C.E.*, "Wilkinson")—he appears to have intrigued with and against Spain. (Nickerson, *op. cit.*, 428) Wilkinson did succeed in having Spain open the Mississippi to American traffic after Congress had failed, and this proved of tremendous commercial value to Ky. His various enterprises having failed, he applied for a military commission, was made Lt. Col. commanding the 2d U.S. Inf. on 22 Oct. '91, and served as second-in-command to Anthony Wayne in his operations against the Indians. Appointed B.G. on 5 Mar. '92, he intrigued against Wayne (Nickerson, *op. cit.*, 428), succeeded him as C. in C. when Wayne died in 1796, and managed to retain a Spanish pension. (*Ibid.*) As Gov. of La. (1805) he became involved in the Burr Conspiracy, disclosed the plot in which he was an accomplice if not the originator, evaded the persistent efforts of Congress to prove his implication, and in 1811 won the acquittal of a court-martial. Restored to command, he was made Maj. Gen. on 2 Mar. 1813 but so mishandled the northern campaign of the War of 1812 that he was called before a court of inquiry. In 1815 he was exonerated and on 15 June '15 was honorably discharged (Heitman).

The next year his *Memoirs of My Own Times*, 3 vols., were published in Philadelphia. Needless to say, they are considered unreliable by historians but are much cited. He went to Mexico City, where he was agent for the American Bible Society (!) and where he also hoped to get a land grant. "It is not certain whether the Mexican climate or the use of opium did more to hasten his end." (Nickerson, *op. cit.*, 428) About the only common vice for which Wilkinson was not noted was womanchasing. (He married the girl he had stopped to court at Reading while Congress writhed in 1777.)

See R. O. Shreve, *The Finished Scoundrel* (1933).

WILLETT, Marinus. 1740–1830. Cont'l. officer. N.Y. One of the truly outstanding American leaders of the Revolution, he was the great-grandson of Thos. Willett (1611–1674), who reached Plymouth colony as an English trader and sea captain in 1630. Living most of his life in N.Y.C., Marinus attended Kings College (now Columbia) and became a wealthy merchant and property owner. He was a Lt. in Oliver De Lancey's N.Y. Regt. in 1758 and served on the unfortunate expedition of James Abercromby to Ticonderoga as well as in Bradstreet's capture of Frontenac. During the years leading up to the Revolution he was a fiery and effective Son of Liberty, taking part in the attack on the N.Y.C. arsenal, 23 Apr. '75, and rousing a rabble on Broad Street to prevent the British from evacuating five wagonloads of weapons and ammunition when they left N.Y.C. on 6 June. On the 28th he became Capt. in McDougall's 1st N.Y. Regt., joined Montgomery's wing of the Canada Invasion, and on 3 Nov. '75 was left in command of St. Johns. Holding his original commission until 9 May '76, he became Lt. Col. of the 3d N.Y. on 21 Nov., having meanwhile taken part in skirmishes around N.Y.C. (Appleton's), and was put in command of Ft. Constitution (*D.A.B.*), opposite West Point. See PEEKSKILL RAID, 23 Mar. '77.

On 18 May '77 he was transferred to Ft. Stanwix, where he had served briefly in 1758. Here, as second in command to

Gansevoort, he distinguished himself in stopping ST. LEGER'S EXPEDITION, June–Sept. '77. For his gallant sortie on 6 Aug. he was voted "an elegant sword" by Congress. He served under Charles Scott at Monmouth, June '78, and then took part in the raid against the Onondagas before joining Sullivan's Expedition of May–Nov. '79. On 1 July '80 he was appointed Lt. Col. commanding the 5th N.Y. and in Nov. was promoted to Col. with rank from 22 Dec. '79. When the five N.Y. regiments were consolidated into two on 1 Jan. '81, Willett retired, but soon accepted Gov. Clinton's request to command N.Y. levies and militia in the BORDER WARFARE of 1781. As is described in that article, he did a remarkable job in driving Tory-Indian raiders out of the Mohawk Valley. In Feb. '83 he led an abortive attempt to attack Oswego by a mid-winter advance on snowshoes.

Elected to the state assembly, he vacated his seat to become sheriff of N.Y. City and county, serving seven years in this post during the years 1784–88 and 1792–96. In 1790 he was highly successful as Washington's personal representative in making a peace treaty with the Creeks.

There were many women in this warrior's life. At Ft. Plain, his headquarters 1781–83, he lived with a widow named Seeber and begat Marinus W. Seeber. (Cook, *W.M.O.M.*) His first wife died in 1793 and he married the widow Susannah Vardle (*ibid.*) or Vardill (*D.A.B.*), whom Cook characterizes as the "reigning toast of N.Y. society." She turned out to be a better toast than a wife, and a divorce in 1797 (decree filed in 1805) freed him from this spitfire. Sometime between 1797 and 1800 he married Margaret Bancker, who was 24 when he was 59 (Cook, *op. cit.*), and produced three sons and a daughter. One of these sons, William Marinus

Willett, became a famous author on religious subjects and from his father's manuscripts published *A Narrative of the Military Actions of Col. Marinus Willett* (1831).

See also D. E. Wager, *Col. Marinus Willett: The Hero of Mohawk* (1891) and the chapter devoted to him in Fred J. Cook, *What Manner of Men* (1959).

WILLIAMS, David. 1754–1831. Captor of John André. N.Y. Enlisting in 1775, he served in the operations against St. Johns and Quebec (1775–76). In 1779 he left the army. "During his service his feet were badly frozen, and this partially disabled him for life." (Appleton's) His role in the famous capture of André and his subsequent rewards are covered under ARNOLD'S TREASON. After the war he bought a farm near the Catskill Mountains that had belonged to the leader of Shays's Rebellion.

WILLIAMS, Otho Holland. 1749–1794. Cont'l. general (1782). Md. The man who became one of the outstanding commanders in Greene's Southern campaigns was born a few years after his parents emigrated to America from South Wales. (*D.A.B.*; Appleton's erroneously states he was descended from early settlers under Lord Baltimore.) His father died leaving seven children and a small estate when Williams was 12. The next year the boy got a job in the county clerk's office at Frederick, soon learned to handle the duties by himself, and starting about 1767 was in the county clerk's office at Baltimore. In 1774 he returned to Frederick and started a commercial career. On 22 June '75 he became Lt. in Capt. Thos. Price's Frederick City rifle corps and marched with them to join the Boston army. When the Va. and Md. riflemen were combined to form Col. Hugh Stephenson's regiment on 27 June '76, Williams was made Maj. of that unit, and after Stephenson's death (before Sept., according to Heitman) succeeded him as commander. At Ft. Washington, N.Y., 16 Nov. '76, he received a serious wound in the groin and was taken prisoner. He was initially on parole in N.Y.C., but on suspicion of secretly corresponding with Washington was confined. Sharing a cell with Ethan Allen (*D.A.B.*), he was not exchanged until 16 Jan. '78 and his health was permanently impaired by inadequate food and harsh treatment during this period. Meanwhile, however, he had been promoted to Col. 6th Md. on 10 Dec. '76 and he led them in the Monmouth Campaign.

On 16 Apr. '80 he left Morristown with the force of Cont'l. troops being led by Kalb into the SOUTHERN THEATER. In the CAMDEN CAMPAIGN, July–Aug., Col. Otho Williams made his name well known not only as an outstanding combat commander but also because of his informative and well-written *Narrative,* which is much used and quoted by historians. Serving as A.A.G. to Gates, he performed brilliantly at CAMDEN, 16 Aug. In the reorganization preceding the arrival of Greene, Williams was put in command of a special corps of light troops. Greene made him A.G., however, and Williams was with the left wing of the army at Cheraw when Daniel Morgan led the light troops on the maneuver that resulted in the victory at Cowpens.

When Morgan declined to take command of the rear guard of elite troops that Greene formed to cover his race for the Dan, Otho Williams was given this vital duty. As shown in the section headed "Operations on the Yadkin" in the article on the SOUTHERN CAMPAIGNS OF GREENE, Williams accomplished his hazardous mission well. He then led the return of Greene's army into N.C.,

frustrating an attempt by Cornwallis to surprise and annihilate him at WETZELL'S MILLS, 6 Mar. '81. He played a distinguished part in the battles of GUILFORD, 15 Mar., HOBKIRK'S HILL (Camden), 25 Apr., and EUTAW SPRINGS, 8 Sept. '81. Although he commanded a brigade of Cont'ls. in each of these three major engagements, he was not promoted to B.G. until 9 May '82. He retired on 16 Jan. '83, having been elected naval officer of the Baltimore district on the 6th. He became collector of the port of Baltimore. In May '92 he declined the post of second-in-command of the Army with the rank of B.G.; his reasons were ill health and the need to care for his family. He died 15 July '94 at the age of about 45.

Williams' *Narrative* is an appendix to Wm. Johnson's *Greene* (1822) and also to W. G. Simms's *Greene* (1849). The Md. Hist. Soc. has a large collection of letters and papers having to do with Williams; these are analyzed in the *Calendar of the ... Williams Papers* (Baltimore, 1940). Osmond Tiffany published *A Sketch of the Life and Services of ... Williams* in 1851.

WILLIAMS, William. 1731–1811. Signer. Conn. Descended from Robert Williams, who came to Mass. in 1637, he was born in Lebanon, Conn. In 1751 he graduated from Harvard, studied theology under his father, a Congregationalist minister, and in 1755 he served on the staff of his cousin Ephraim Williams during Sir William Johnson's expedition against Crown Point. Returning home, he went into business and launched upon a long career in public life. He was a selectman of Lebanon, 1760–85; town clerk, 1752–96; state legislator, 1757–76 and 1781–84; member of the governor's council, 1784–1803; county judge, 1776–1806; and probate judge, 1775–1809. Williams was a patriot of the highest type, and on several occasions he volunteered his cash and credit on behalf of the cause. His political career was undoubtedly helped by his marriage in 1771 to Mary, the daughter of Gov. Trumbull and sister of the younger Jonathan Trumbull.

Williams helped his father-in-law with numerous state papers and also contributed to the newspapers. In 1775 he financed on his personal credit the dispatch of Conn. troops to Ticonderoga, and in 1779 he offered a quantity of his own hard cash in exchange for virtually worthless Cont'l. paper money so that supplies could be purchased for the army. Commissioned Col. of the 12th Conn. (militia) Regt. when the war started, he resigned in 1776 to sit in the Cont'l. Cong. As a delegate he signed the Decl. of Indep., helped draft the Articles of Confed., and in 1777 was on the board of war. He remained in Cong. until 1778 and again served in the period 1783–84. Although criticized for resigning his military commission to accept election to Cong., he demonstrated his personal courage by racing 23 miles in three hours to volunteer his services in repelling Benedict Arnold's New London Raid, 6 Sept. '81. (E. E. Curtis in *D.A.B.*)

WILLIAMSON, Andrew. *c.* 1730–1786. Turncoat militia general. S.C. Said to have come to America from Scotland as a child, he probably began earning his living as a cow driver. In 1760 he was commissioned Lt. of militia, and he served in James Grant's CHEROKEE EXPEDITION of 1761. Four years later he was established as a planter on the upper reaches of the Savannah River, and in July '68 he joined other local REGULATORS in a petition. (Alden, *South,* 150) When the Revolution started he was an impressive-looking militia Maj., probably illiterate but highly intelligent and a skilled

woodsman. He owned a plantation, "Whitehall," six miles west of Ninety-Six. He had a key role in the action at NINETY-SIX in Nov. '75, led close to 2,000 militia and Indians in the CHEROKEE WAR OF 1776, and was promoted to state B.G. in 1778 (Andrew Pickens succeeded him as Col.) Taking part in the expedition of Robt. Howe against Fla. in the spring of 1778, his refusal to take orders from Howe contributed to the American failure. In the unsuccessful operations of Lincoln against Prevost, Williamson commanded 1,200 men opposite Augusta and helped force the British from that place (see BRIAR CREEK, 3 Mar. '79), but he is not mentioned again until some six months later, when he took part in the unsuccessful Franco-American assault on Savannah, 9 Oct. '79. During the Charleston campaign next year his militia refused to participate and Williamson himself, with some 300 men, remained idle in the western part of the state. Sir Henry Clinton says in his memoirs: "Lord Cornwallis ... assured me [early in June] that the submission of General Williamson at Ninety-Six had put an end to all resistance in every district of South Carolina," and editor Willcox comments that Williamson's "inactivity and supineness gave rise to suspicion of treason." (*American Rebellion,* 174 n., 176, 223)

While on parole at "Whitehall" Williamson was captured by patriots in the hope that he might consider his parole invalidated and rejoin them. Instead, he escaped and joined the British at Charleston. Recaptured, by Col. Isaac HAYNE, he was promptly rescued by the British. He then is credited with passing information to the Americans, through Col. John Laurens. After the war Gen. Greene, Commodore Alexander Gillon, and Gov. George Mathews supported the movement that resulted in the turncoat's being allowed to remain in S.C. (Alden, *op. cit.,* 328 *n.*) He ended his days comfortably at his new home near Charleston.

WILLIAMSON'S PLANTATION, S.C., 12 July '80. Capt. HUCK was sent from the British post at Rocky Mount with a detachment of Tarleton's cavalry and some Tory troops to destroy the partisan forces being gathered by Sumter in the Catawba District. Starting out with about 35 cavalry, 20 mounted infantry of the N.Y. Vols., and 60 other Loyalists, Huck's force had grown to about 400 when he reached the vicinity of James Williamson's Plantation (now Brattonville). Here, on 11 July, he caught young James McClure and his brother-in-law, Edw. Martin, at Capt. James McClure's house melting pewter dishes to make bullets. He looted the house, announced that he would hang the two rebels the next day, and slapped Mrs. McClure with the flat of his sword when she pleaded for their lives. The raiders then looted the house of Col. Wm. Bratton before camping half a mile away, at Williamson's. Mary Mc-Clure slipped off and rode 30 miles to Sumter's camp where she informed her father of the raid. Bratton and McClure started off with 150 mounted volunteers and were joined by another 350 under Capt. Edw. Lacey Jr., Col. Wm. Hill, and Col. Thos. Neal. By the time they approached Huck's camp, however, all but 90 men had for one reason or another left the column.

During the approach, Capt. Lacey had posted a guard around his own house to keep his Tory father from alerting the enemy; the enterprising old gentleman escaped, was recaptured, and the son ordered him tied in bed. When the column reached Bratton's house, a quarter of a mile from Huck's camp, they learned from Mrs. Bratton that the enemy had pitched their tents between the rail fences that lined the road to Williamson's house.

Taking advantage of Huck's lack of security and his vulnerable situation, the rebels launched a surprise attack at dawn. They approached in two groups from opposite sides so as to cut the enemy off from their horses. Reveille came as the Americans opened fire at 75 yards. The Tories turned out and tried to fight back, but the rail fences kept them from charging with their bayonets and the rebel fire inflicted heavy casualties. Huck was mortally wounded when he rushed from the house and tried to rally his troops. Only 12 of the Legion cavalry and about the same number of others escaped from the force of about 115 Tories in the camp. (Greene, *Rev. War,* 214) Ward says 30 or 40 were killed and about 50 wounded. (*W.O.R.,* 709) The rebels had one man killed. Young Mc-Clure and Martin were found tied in a corncrib and freed.

Tarleton was in Charleston when this action took place. His violent reaction to the misuse of his Legion by Rawdon in such dangerous piecemeal operations led Cornwallis to write the latter a sharp note and was the beginning of Tarleton's bitterness not only toward Rawdon but also toward the C. in C. (Bass, *Green Dragoon,* 90)

This rebel success greatly assisted Sumter's recruiting and enabled him to attack ROCKY MOUNT, 1 Aug. '80.

WILLIAMSON'S PLANTATION, S.C., 29–31 Dec. '80. See HAMMOND'S STORE RAID.

WILMINGTON, N.C., 1 Feb.–18 Nov. '81. British occupation. To provide a closer supply port for his operations into N.C. (see KINGS MTN.) Cornwallis directed Col. Balfour, commandant at Charleston, to send a force to seize and hold this place. Maj. James H. Craig took the town with 400 to 450 regulars on 1 Feb., meeting little resistance. He captured the prominent patriots John Ashe and Cornelius Harnett (both of whom died in captivity)/ and won so much Tory support that the rebel leader, Col. Joseph Hawkins, subsequently found it almost impossible to raise troops or supplies 'in Duplin co. Cornwallis retreated to Wilmington after the Battle of Guilford C. H., arriving 7 Apr. and leaving 18 days later for Va. In July Craig commissioned David Fanning to rally Loyalists and this remarkable partisan leader subsequently used Wilmington as a sort of administrative base. (See HILLSBORO RAID, 12 Sept. '81)

With a well-mounted and well-led body of regulars, mostly from his 82d Regt., and supported by local partisans, Craig himself conducted raids that compared favorably in speed of execution with those of Tarleton. (DeMond, *Loyalists in N.C.*, 138–42) One of the most devastating was against NEW BERN, Aug. '81. During his occupation of Wilmington, Craig converted the Episcopal church into a citadel. (Lossing, II, 780–81) The British commander prudently evacuated the town on 18 Nov. '81 to avoid being cut off by the column of regulars St. Clair was leading south to reinforce Greene after the Yorktown surrender. All the Loyalists of the region who asked to leave with the British were evacuated to the Charleston lines. (See also James H. CRAIG)

WILMOT, William. Cont'l. officer, last casualty of the Revolution? Md. Commissioned 1st Lt. in the 3d Md. on 10 Dec. '76, he was promoted to Capt. on 15 Oct. '77, transferred to the 2d Md. on 1 Jan. '81, and killed at JOHNS ISLAND, S.C., 4 Nov. '82. (Heitman)

WILSON, James. 1742–1798. Signer, jurist, speculator. Scotland–Pa. After studying at St. Andrews, Glasgow, and Edinburgh (1757–65) he had started learning accounting when for some reason he suddenly moved to America. He reached N.Y. in the middle of the Stamp Act crisis. In 1766 he became Latin tutor at the College of Philadelphia but shortly thereafter he started studying law under John Dickinson. Admitted to the bar in 1767, he practiced briefly at Reading before moving to the Scots-Irish community of Carlisle. Here he quickly became the leading lawyer and he also acquired a taste for land speculation. Having also taken an active part in patriot politics, on 12 July '74 he became chairman of the local Comm. of Corresp. and he was also elected to the first Prov. Cong. at Philadelphia. He was nominated to attend the 1st Cont'l. Cong. but not elected.

Before the delegates convened, however, Wilson published a pamphlet concluding that Parliament had no authority of any kind over the colonists and advocating that America be an independent state within the British empire. "Only a few had taken this advanced position as early as 1774," writes Julian P. Boyd in *D.A.B.*, "yet a careful examination of Wilson's original manuscript ... shows that he had arrived at this conclusion ... four years before he revised and published the essay." Published under the title of *Considerations on the Nature and Extent of the Legislative Authority of the British Parliament,* it was widely read on both sides of the Atlantic and "it still has meaning as one of the ablest arguments for what the Britannic Commonwealth of Nations has become." (*Ibid.*)

On 3 May '75 Wilson was elected Col. of the 4th Bn. of Cumberland County associators, and on 6 May he was elected to the Cont'l. Cong. In Aug. and Sept. his duties included 'dealings with the western Indians, but a conference held with them at Pittsburgh was fruitless. The delegates recognized him as what Montross calls one of their "heaviest rhetorical guns" (*Reluctant Rebels,* 107), and he was called on to write a number of papers. Early in 1776 he was directed to draft an address to the people that was to prepare them for the idea of independence, but as mentioned in the article on INDEPENDENCE, Thos. Paine's *Common Sense* made Wilson's task a futile exercise in penmanship and the latter's address was never published. Although Wilson believed in independence for America, he shared the convictions of conservatives John Dickinson, Edward Rutledge, and Robert R. Livingston that neither the American people nor their government were capable at that time of making this jump. Wilson and Duane led the opposition against John Adams and R. H. Lee in the four-day debate on the preamble to the Cong. resolution in favor of independence (May '76). "Before we are prepared to build the new house," said Wilson, "why should we pull down the old one, and expose ourselves to the inclemencies of the season?" After continuing to oppose the Decl. of Indep. in the debate of 8 June, Wilson joined Franklin and John Morton in voting for it on 2 July, while the four other Pa. delegates (including Dickinson) voted against it. Hence the man who had been among the first to advocate independence had been one of the strongest opponents of the Decl. of Indep. but ended by being a Signer. Wilson's heated opposition to the new state constitution resulted in his being removed from the Pa. delegation to Cong. on 4 Feb. '77. Prior to this time he had been on the board of war and was chairman of the standing committee on appeals. Reinstated as a delegate on 22 Feb. because his party could not find a replacement for him,

on 14 Sept. '77 he was again recalled. This ended his congressional career during the war, but he returned to Cong. in 1783 and for the period 1785–87.

His conservative views and his continued opposition to the state constitution—which he considered too "democratic"—made him so unpopular in Philadelphia that he had to spend the winter of 1777–78 in Annapolis, and when he returned to the city he had to barricade his house for protection against the mob. In Oct. '79 "Fort Wilson" was attacked by a militia force in response to a handbill of 4 Oct. calling on them to "drive off from the city all disaffected persons and those who supported them." Wilson and his friends were rescued by the timely arrival of the First City Troop and Pres. Reed (*D.A.B.*)

From June '79 to 1783 Wilson served as *avocat général* for the French government in America. In 1780 he was legal adviser to Robt. Morris in the formation of the Bank of America. According to Appleton's he had been commissioner and superintendent of Indian affairs for the Middle Dept. in 1775, commanded a Pa. militia battalion in the N.J. Campaign of 1776, and was a state B.G. from 23 May '82 until the end of the war. Heitman gives 24 May '82 as the date of the latter commission.

Wilson's postwar congressional career was highlighted by his proposal to erect states in the western lands (9 Apr. '83) and his major part in the adoption of the Constitution. The state constitution of 1790 was his creation. "Modeled precisely on the federal Constitution," comments Boyd, "it represents the climax of his fourteen-year fight against the democratic constitution of 1776." (*Ibid.*)

In the field of law, Wilson was prominently mentioned as a candidate for the office of chief justice of the U.S. in 1789 but ended by being named associate justice (29 Sept.). On 17 Aug. '89 he was appointed to the chair of law at the College of Philadelphia. Alert to the possibilities of establishing a new system of American jurisprudence, he launched into a series of lectures in which he departed from the Blackstonian concept and contended that law was the rule of the individual, "whose obedience the law requires." Blackstone had defined law as the rule of a sovereign superior and maintained that revolution was illegal; Wilson maintained that sovereignty resided in the individual and used this as the basis for legally justifying the American Revolution. Wilson lacked the judicial detachment to succeed in this self-appointed role, however, and his lectures have had no real influence on American jurisprudence.

His early interest in land speculation continued throughout his life and ultimately led to his destruction. Having been interested in various western land companies in 1785—he was president of the Illinois and Wabash Company—in 1792 he involved the Holland Land Company in unwise purchases in Pa. and N.Y. and three years later he bought a large interest in one of the Yazoo companies. In 1797 the bubble of speculation burst as Wilson was launching into a grandiose plan for immigration and colonization. That summer he moved to Burlington, N.J., to avoid arrest for debt, but he retained his supreme court seat despite talk of impeachment. His mind began to break under the stress of this financial and professional failure. Early in 1798 he moved to the home of a friend in Edenton, N.C., and on 21 Aug. he died of what was called a "violent nervous fever."

Julian P. Boyd, whose *D.A.B.* article is the basis of the above sketch, says that Wilson's life was marked by two dominant traits: ambition for place and power, and avid desire for wealth. Although he failed in both, "Yet he was a prophet of both democracy and nationalism."

Wilson's first wife was Rachel Bird of "Birdsboro," near Reading. Their son Bird (1777–1859) became a prominent jurist, Episcopal clergyman, and professor of theology, and he edited the writings of his father (see below). Rachel died in 1786 and in 1793 the 51-year-old widower married the 19-year-old Hannah Gray of Boston. Their son died in infancy, a tragedy that added to the mental burdens of Wilson's last years.

Ten volumes of Wilson's papers are in the Hist. Soc. of Pa. His *Works* were published by his son in three volumes in 1804 and in two volumes by J. D. Andrews in 1896. The most comprehensive biography (*D.A.B.*) is Burton A. Konkle, *James Wilson* (1907).

WITHERSPOON, John. 1723–1794. Signer, clergyman, college president, congressman. Scotland–N.J. Coming from a family that had several Calvinist dominies—though he was not, as alleged, a direct descendant of John Knox —he was the son of a minister and followed his father's calling. At the age of 13 he matriculated at the Univ. of Edinburgh, where he received his M.A. in 1739 and the divinity degree in 1743. Ordained 11 Apr. '45, married to Elizabeth Montgomery in 1748, he left Beith (in Ayrshire) in 1757 to become pastor in Paisley. As one of the leaders of the Popular Party of the Presbyterian Church he strove to maintain the older, conservative doctrine against the efforts of the Moderates to liberalize it. His writings were vigorous and voluminous, and his fame spread from Scotland to

England, the Continent, and America. Richard STOCKTON was sent from N.J. to offer Witherspoon the presidency of the college later called Princeton. Although elected to this post in Nov. '66, he deferred to the objections of his wife, and did not accept until 1768. Meanwhile he had refused calls to Rotterdam and Dublin.

As president of the College of N.J. (Princeton), Witherspoon infused new life into the institution, building up its endowment, its faculty, and its student body until the military events of 1776 interfered. Before the war broke out he had introduced the study of philosophy, French, history, and oratory. Not a profound scholar himself but with the ability of a real educator, he deplored book learning for its own sake, discouraged pure scholarship, and worked on the theory that an education should make a man useful in public life.

Although he disapproved of ministers taking part in politics, he could not help but gravitate into the patriot camp when the rift with the mother country widened. In 1774 he became a county delegate, served on committees of correspondence, and attended provincial conventions. He took a prominent part in the imprisonment of Gov. Wm. Franklin. On 22 June '76 he was chosen as a delegate to the Cont'l. Cong. Although the movement toward independence was nearing a climax, he reached Philadelphia in time to be of real service on 2 July in refuting the arguments of opponents of independence that the country was not ready; "it not only was ripe for the measure but in danger of rotting for the want of it," he contended. (Collins, *President Witherspoon,* I, 217–21, quoted in *D.A.B.*) He remained a delegate from June '76 to Nov. '82, serving on more than 100 committees and being a member of the board of war and the committee on secret correspondence for foreign affairs. With a clearer conception than most native-born Americans of what the conflict with England was about and how to win that conflict, Witherspoon combined brains, patience, and courage to emerge as one of the leaders of the Revolution. (John E. Pomfret in *D.A.B.*) True to his own doctrines of practical education and his philosophy of common sense, he had a way of getting to the root of a problem: opposed to the financial recklessness that had made American currency worthless during and after the Revolution, in 1786 he wrote: "No business can be done, some say, because money is scarce. It may be said, with more truth, money is scarce, because little business is done."

From 1782 until his death in 1794 he worked to rebuild Princeton, but in 1783 and 1789 he also served in the state legislature. He was a member of the N.J. ratifying convention in 1787.

In the religious field he also left his mark. He had reached America at a time when the Presbyterian Church was badly divided, but he brought the New and Old Side elements together and was closely identified with the subsequent growth of Presbyterianism in the Middle Colonies and on the frontier. By 1776, with the help of a large influx of Scots–Irish, the church was firmly entrenched in the new country. From 1785 to 1789 Witherspoon helped organize the church nationwide. "The catechisms, confessions of faith, directory of worship, and the form of government were largely his work." (*D.A.B.*)

In 1791 he married Ann, the 24-year-old widow of Dr. Armstrong Dill. Sixty-eight years old at this time, he fathered two children during the remaining three years of his life. Five of the 10 children of his first marriage survived childhood, and one of his last two children lived past infancy.

In 1800–1 *The Works of John Witherspoon* appeared in four volumes in N.Y.; this set was edited by Rev. Dr. Samuel S. Smith and includes the funeral sermon by the Rev. Dr. John Rogers. Another edition of his works was published in Edinburgh in nine volumes in 1804, and in the same year a two-volume *Select Works* was published in London. The first collection of his writings, *Essays on Important Subjects* ..., was published in three volumes in London in 1764. During his lifetime he published many sermons, letters on philosophy and other subjects, and political essays; among these are his *Essay on Money* (1786) and *Letters on Marriage*. According to *D.A.B.*, the most scholarly biography and the work containing a complete bibliography is V. L. Collins, *President Witherspoon* (2 vols., 1925). Another biography is D. W. Woods, *John Witherspoon* (1906).

WOEDTKE (vet' keh), Frederick William, Baron de. *c.* 1740–1776. Cont'l. general. Prussia. Reaching America with strong letters of recommendation from Franklin (Lossing, II, 329 *n.*), Woedtke is said to have served many years under Frederick the Great and to have attained the rank of Maj. (Appleton's). Congress commissioned him B.G. on 16 Mar. '76 and assigned him to the Northern Army. He is known to have attended the council of war at Crown Point on 5 July (see end of article on CANADA INVASION) and to have died at Lake George on 28 July '76. Kapp quotes a letter from Steuben to von der Goltz that says "our poor Woedtke" was done in by *"la bile et l'eau de vie."* James Wilkinson characterized both FERMOY and Woedtke as worthless drunkards, one of the few subjects on which one feels historically safe in accepting Wilkinson's testimony.

Heitman identifies this officer as *Frederick William* Woedtke (pp. 10, 196), but in his correction and modification of Heitman's list Simon Gratz identifies him merely as "Baron de Woedtke" (*Pa. Mag. of Hist.*, XXVII [1903]—list reproduced in Montross, *Rag, Tag,* 470). Lasseray goes no further than to identify him as "Von Woedtke, former Prussian officer," but mentions that an *Auguste-Henry* Woedtke appears in the 1763 and 1776 rosters of the French infantry regiment of Alsace as a Capt. on 26 Dec. '68; the record notes that he never actually joined the regiment.

WOLCOTT, Erastus. 1722–1793. Militia general, jurist. Conn. Elder brother of Oliver WOLCOTT, he served before 1775 in a number of public offices. In 1775 he was sent to Boston to observe and report on activities of the British garrison, and early the next year he joined Washington in the Boston lines as Col. of a militia regiment. During the summer of 1776 he commanded the New London forts. As B.G. of Conn. troops from Dec. '76 to Jan. '81 he commanded the 1st. Conn. Brig. He was among the multitude elected to the Cont'l. Cong. from Conn. who did not serve. Having risen to the office of chief judge of the county court before the war, he became a judge of the Conn. supreme court after the Revolution.

WOLCOTT, Oliver. 1726–1797. Signer, militia general. Conn. Youngest son of Gov. Roger Wolcott (1679–1767), Oliver was top man in his Yale class for four years. On 1 Jan. '47, prior to his graduation from college, he was commissioned by Gov. Clinton of N.Y. to raise and command a volunteer company in the expedition to Canada. At the conclusion of this unsuccessful campaign he studied medicine with his brother Alexander. He intended to practice at Goshen, but in 1751 he gave up medicine to settle in Litchfield, where his father owned property. This same year he was named sheriff of the new county, and he held this office 20 years. Active in political and militia affairs, he was judge of the court of probate for Litchfield (1772–81), county judge (1774–78), and Col. of militia in 1774.

Wolcott was in his 48th year when the Revolution started and his role in the conflict was varied but relatively unimportant. Sent by the Conn. Assy. to interview Gen. Gage in Boston, he achieved nothing of note. After serving then as Comm. for Conn. forces, in July '75 he was appointed one of the Indian commissioners by Cong. Elected to the Cont'l. Cong. in Oct. '75, he was a delegate until 1783 except for 1779, when he was not elected. Because of sickness he had to leave Philadelphia just before the Decl. of Indep. was signed. On his way home he took with him the equestrian statue of George III that had been thrown over by the N.Y.C. mob; his daughters and other ladies of Litchfield melted the statue into lead for bullets. Although his substitute, William Williams, had signed the Decl. of Indep. for him, Wolcott was permitted to sign the document on 1 Oct. '76 after his return. His work in Cong. was not noteworthy, and he was absent from six to nine months out of every year on other business. In Aug. '76 he commanded the 14 militia regiments sent to reinforce Gen. Putnam on the Hudson. In Dec. '76 he commanded a militia brigade in his county, and in Sept. '77 he led several hundred volunteers off to oppose Burgoyne. Having been a B.G. of militia since 1775 (Heitman), he was promoted to Maj. Gen. in 1779 and commanded a division when the Conn. Coast Raid took place in July of that year.

After the war he served as commissioner at the Treaty of Ft. Stanwix in 1784, and in 1789 he helped negotiate the treaty with the Wyandottes that cleared the title of the Western Reserve for white settlement. Having been chosen Lt. Gov. by the legislature in 1787, he retained that office until succeeding to the governorship when Samuel Huntington died in Jan. '96. Four months later he was elected Gov. After two uneventful years he died in office.

His son and namesake (1760–1833) saw some service as a volunteer in 1777 and 1779. Declining a commission in the army, he took an appointment in the Q.M. Dept. and performed his duties as storekeeper in the depot at Litchfield. Subsequently he served as secretary of the treasury (1795–1800) and as Gov. of Conn. (1817–27).

WOLFE, James. 1727–1759. British general in COLONIAL WARS. Although he died 15 years before the first shot of the Revolution was fired, Wolfe figured prominently in the Colonial Wars and was the associate of many men who were involved in the Revolution. Historians have speculated on how the course of the latter war would have been different if Wolfe had lived to command British forces in America. Tall, slight, redheaded, and exceptionally literate for a soldier—he is alleged to have placed the glory of composing the *Elegy Written in a Country Churchyard* above all military fame (Alden, *Lee,* 6)—Wolfe was of a family originally from Wales. His father, Lt. Gen. Edward Wolfe, was born in 1685 and died six months before his son. James started his military career on 3 Nov. '41 as 2d Lt. in his father's marine regiment, which was then numbered the 44th Foot. Becoming Ensign in the 12th Foot (27 Mar. '42), he was acting Regt'l. Adj. in the battle of Dettingen, 27 June, when only 16 years old. In 1745 he was Brig. Maj., served on the staff in the battle of Culloden, and was wounded at Laeffelt in the Netherlands the same year. During 1748–49 he was Maj. in Geo. Sackville's 20th Foot; Cornwallis was Lt. Col. of this regiment, and Wolfe commanded it much of the time it was on garrison duty in Scotland. Because of his youth he was several times passed over for promotion to Col., but after serving as Q.M. of the British expeditionary force to Rochefort, 20–30 Sept. '57, he was breveted Col. for his energetic performance of duty, although the expedition accomplished nothing more than occupation of the Ile d'Aix. In response to certain criticism of Wolfe's conduct during this operation, the King made his famous comment to Newcastle: "Mad, is he? then I hope he will bite some others of my generals." (*D.N.B.*) Somebody else had noticed the 30-year-old Wolfe: Wm. Pitt (CHATHAM), an associate of Newcastle, had come to power in June '57 and was looking for military talent. Pitt gave Wolfe a brigade under Amherst in the Louisburg expedition. Wolfe distinguished himself in this operation and subsequently was given the local rank of Maj. Gen. and put in command of one of three wings of an offensive against Canada. He was mortally wounded in an audacious and successful attack on Quebec, 13 Sept. '59. He had not reached his 33d year.

See COLONIAL WARS.

WOODFORD, William. 1734–1780. Cont'l. general. Va. Son of Maj. Wm. Woodford, an Englishman who settled in Caroline co., and grandson of Dr. Wm. Cocke, secretary of the colony, he received the normal education for a young Virginian of the better class and served as a militia officer in the French and Indian War. In 1774 he was a member of the county Comm. of Correspondence and of the committee to enforce the "Association." The next year he sat as Edmund Pendleton's alternate in the Va. Convention from 17 July to 9 Aug. On 5 Aug. he was appointed Col. of the 3d Regt. and at HAMPTON, 24–25 Oct. '75, GREAT BRIDGE, 9 Dec., and NORFOLK, 1 Jan. '76, he had a leading role in the fight that drove Lord Dunmore out of the province. On 13 Feb. '76 he became Col. of the 2d Va. Cont'l. Regt., and on 21 Feb. '77 he was promoted to B.G. Commanding the 1st Va. Brig., he was wounded in the hand at the Brandywine but fought at Germantown three weeks later (4 Oct. '77). After the winter at Valley Forge he took part in the Monmouth Campaign and subsequent operations in N.J. On 13 Dec. '79 he received orders to lead 750 Va. Cont'ls. to the relief of Charleston. After marching 500 miles in 28 days during the dead of winter, his column arrived on 6 Apr. '80. (Under CHARLESTON . . . 1780, see end of section headed "Clinton Moves Again." *D.A.B.* says he arrived 17 Apr., which is not supported by the authorities cited in the cross reference just referred to.)

Taken prisoner with the Charleston garrison on 12 May '80 and evacuated to N.Y., Woodford died in captivity on 13 Nov. '80 and was buried in Old Trinity Church Yard. Woodford co., Ky., was named for him in 1789.

In the closing months of 1775, when he was given the mission of opposing Dunmore around Norfolk (see above), Woodford got into a warm dispute with Patrick Henry over the scope of their respective commands. As Col. of the 1st Regt., Henry was the senior officer and would normally have had the honor given to Woodford in making the principal military effort in the colony. (*D.A.B.*, citing Eckenrode, *Rev. in Va.*) During the army's encampment at Valley Forge he quarreled over the relative rank of Muhlenberg, Weedon, and himself in what D. S. Freeman refers to as a "clash of jealous and ambitious men." (*Washington*, IV,˙613 and *n.*)

The biographical sketch by Edward E. Curtis in *D.A.B.*, main source of this article, includes an extensive bibliography.

WOODHULL, Nathaniel. 1722–1776. Militia general. N.Y. During the Colonial Wars he was a Maj. under Abercromby in the Ticonderoga and Crown Point operations of 1758. He accompanied Bradstreet's expedition against Ft. Frontenac, and was a Col. under Amherst in 1760. Active in patriot politics, he was Pres. of the N.Y. Prov. Cong. in 1775 and '76. Appointed B.G. of state troops in Aug. '75, he was surprised at JAMAICA, 28 Aug. '76, and died 20 Sept. (according to *D.A.B.* and Heitman) of wounds received after his surrender. See Oliver DE LANCEY the younger for details. A narrative of his capture and death was published by Henry Onderdonk Jr. (N.Y.C., 1848) and his journal of operations in 1760 appeared in the *Historical Magazine* (N.Y.C., Sept. 1861).

WOOSTER, David. (rhymes with muster.) 1711–1777. Cont'l. general. Conn. Son of a mason, he was a graduate of Yale (1738), became a militia Lt. in 1741, and the next year was captain of the armed sloop *Defense*. In 1745 he served in the Louisburg expedition and on 4 July sailed for France with the prisoners for exchange. He was commissioned Capt. in the new British regiment of Sir Wm. Pepperrell this same year and retired on half pay in 1774. (Appleton's) Meanwhile, he was Col. of a Conn. regiment in all campaigns of the French and Indian War except those of 1755 and 1757, taking part in the attack on Ticonderoga in 1758 and the later operations of Amherst. (*D.A.B.*) In 1763 he became customs collector in New Haven.

At the start of the Revolutionary War the 64-year-old militia veteran was appointed Maj. Gen. of six Conn. regiments. The next month, May '75, he was ordered to N.Y., and during the summer he commanded troops of his state on Long Island and at Harlem. When Congress started commissioning generals, Wooster was named B.G. on 22 June. Although the senior general on this list, he was the only Maj. Gen. of militia not given the equivalent rank in the Cont'l. Army, and was piqued at being passed over by younger men with less military experience. In Sept. he was ordered to the Northern Dept. where, as a New England Yankee, he quarrelled with Schuyler. During the CANADA INVASION he took part in the siege and capture of St. Johns and was left as commandant at Montreal when Montgomery moved against Quebec. On Montgomery's death, 1 Jan. '76, Wooster assumed command in Canada. He reached Quebec on 2 Apr., but was succeeded on 1 May by John Thomas.

Wooster's incompetence, suspected before the war, had now been confirmed. "A general . . . of a hayfield," is J. H. Smith's characterization (*Struggle for the 14th Colony*, quoted in *D.A.B.*) He was "dull and uninspired, garrulous about his thirty years of service . . . tactless, hearty rather than firm with his undisciplined troops who adored him, at times brutal towards the civilian population of Montreal." (Stanley M. Pargellis in *D.A.B.*) The death of Thomas on 2 June again left Wooster as senior officer in Canada but Congress, informed by their committee in Montreal of his incompetence, recalled him immediately.

Although kept on the rolls as a general, he was given no further assignment in the Cont'l. Army. In the autumn of 1776 he was reappointed Maj. Gen. of Conn. militia and that winter commanded a division on the borders of the state. He joined Heath for the mis-

managed diversion against FORT INDE-
PENDENCE, N.Y., 17–18 Jan. '77. Mortally wounded on 27 Apr. while opposing
the DANBURY RAID, he died on 2 May.

Wooster had married the daughter of
Thos. Clap, president of Yale, in 1746;
two of their four children survived him.
In 1750 he had organized in New Haven
one of the first lodges of Free Masons
in Conn. His monument at Danbury
was erected by the Masons in 1854;
Congress had voted him a monument
but never got around to having it built.

WORDS, Archaic. Modern readers
should be warned that the meanings of
many English words have changed since
the time of the American Revolution.
A PRETTY young man meant one who
was "fine, stout." A mechanic was a
skilled laborer in the most common use
of the word at the end of the 18th
century, although it also had the meaning of a low-class person. (Just as
"soldier" had the sense of "to loaf" or
"to make a mere show of working"
within recent years.) See also AMUSE,
DISPLAY.

"WORLD TURNED UPSIDE
DOWN." See "THE WORLD. . . ."

WRIGHT, Gov. Sir James. c. 1714–
1785. Royal Gov. of Ga. S.C.–Ga. Often
confused with his son, Maj. Sir James
Wright (see below), he was born in
Charleston. His father, Robert, had
come from Durham, England, and for
many years was chief justice of S.C.
James probably was educated in England before becoming a lawyer in
Charleston. He was appointed agent of
the province in England, then became
chief justice, and on 13 May '60 was
appointed Lt. Gov. of S.C. In 1764 he
became royal Gov. of Ga., and in Oct.
'64 he reached Savannah to assume his
duties. Alden characterizes Wright as
"wealthy, worthy, and respected" as a
defender of the royal authority and says

that he "retained throughout his stays
in Georgia a certain popularity, in spite
of his steady loyalty to Britain." (South,
95)

Although Ga., newest of the 13 colonies and heavily subsidized by Parliament, could not reasonably maintain
that the Stamp Act was unjust, its
patriot element followed the lead of
their counterparts in the other colonies
in resisting the act. "The usual crowd
destroyed the customary effigy of the
stamp agent on October 25 [1765]; and
three days later a gathering of 'Sons
of Liberty' at Machenry's Tavern in
the capital agreed that the distributor
for the colony must be forced to resign."
(Ibid., 96) Wright did not particularly
approve of the Stamp Act but he courageously and ably attempted to enforce
it, and in this he was loyally supported
by his close friend and president of his
council, James HABERSHAM. On 1 Nov.
he stopped all business requiring the
use of stamps. On 2 Jan. '66 he led a
detachment of mounted rangers to break
up a mob of 200 men in the port who
were threatening to seize and destroy
the recently arrived stamps. On 4 Feb.
he defied a body of 300 armed countrymen who came into Savannah to make
him stop the issue of the stamps, and
public opinion finally rallied to his
defense of law and order.

Gov. Wright performed his duties
capably and without further serious
challenging of his authority until the
news of Lexington and Concord so
aroused public opinion in Ga. that the
"Liberty Boys" of Savannah, now led
by young Joseph Habersham, were emboldened to start defying royal authority. On 11 May they seized 500 pounds
of powder from a provincial magazine;
on 2 June they spiked a battery in
Savannah; three days later they erected
the first liberty pole in the province and
paraded with fixed bayonets. On 4 July

the Prov. Cong. met and took control of the province. Wright remained another six months, hoping for the armed assistance needed to restore his authority, but when two warships and a troop transport arrived in Jan. '76, the patriots promptly arrested Wright to keep him from rallying the Loyalists around this nucleus of regulars. Held incommunicado for a month, he finally escaped and took refuge aboard a warship. He made an unsuccessful attempt to take Savannah by force (see HUTCHINSON'S ISLAND, 7 Mar. '76), but in Feb. '76 he gave up hope of restoring control and sailed for Halifax; two months later he left Halifax for England.

In 1779, after the British had recaptured Savannah, he returned to his former post, arriving 20 July, in time to take part in the defense of the city against the Franco-American assault of 9 Oct. '79. It has been said that without his deciding vote in the council of war the city would have been surrendered. (Appleton's) After the war he returned to England, his extensive properties having been confiscated. He had been created a baronet on 8 Dec. '72. His daughter married James WALLACE.

Jermyn was the brother of Gov. Wright. He commanded a "nest of villains" on the St. Marys River, E. Fla. This was a Tory strongpoint that the patriots attacked several times without success. According to one account, Wright's "garrison" was made up of Negroes. (Ibid.) He was attainted in 1778, losing his estate, and his name is on the S.C. confiscation act of 1782.

Sir James Wright (d. 1816) inherited his title on the death of his father, Gov. Sir James Wright, in 1785. The Ga. Royalists were raised for young James in 1779, and with the grade of Maj. he commanded a redoubt in the defense of Savannah, 9 Oct. '79. He died childless.

Alexander (b. 1751) was another son of Gov. Wright. He married Elizabeth, the heiress of John Izard of S.C., and settled in Jamaica after the Revolution. (*Ibid.*)

WRITS OF ASSISTANCE gave customs officers authority to call on provincial officers for assistance and also authorized them to search private warehouses and homes for contraband. The British authorized their use to combat evasion of the Molasses Act of 1733 (see NAVIGATION ACTS) by widespread smuggling. Although ordered in 1755, they were not widely used until 1760, when customs officers began a wide-scale seizure of illicit cargoes in Boston. James OTIS unsuccessfully argued the illegality of the writs before the Mass. Supreme Court. The British government extended use of the writs to the other colonies after the Boston merchants had asked that they be relieved of the writs or that they be imposed on others.

WYANDOTS (HURONS). The Huron confederacy, which once numbered around 25,000 persons, was virtually destroyed in 1648–50 by the IROQUOIS LEAGUE. One group of 500 survivors moved west until they clashed with the Sioux. After various other troubles the descendants of this band settled around Detroit and Sandusky in 1748 and became known as Wyandots. Although few in number, they gradually acquired a dominant influence in the Ohio Valley. (*Handbook of American Indians,* "Huron") During the Revolution they were among the fiercest enemies of the American patriots. The "Wyandot Panther" is blamed for the McCRAE ATROCITY. Wyandots participated in the defeat and death of Wm. CRAWFORD. See also BRODHEAD EXPEDITION.

WYOMING VALLEY "MASSACRE," Pa., 3–4 July '78. Although the name was sometimes applied to a larger region, the Wyoming Valley of the Revolution was the 25-mile stretch of the Susquehanna River below the mouth of the Lackawanna River, including modern Wilkes-Barre. "Wyoming" comes from the Del. Indian name *M'cheu-wómink,* "upon the great plain." * Conflicting claims of Conn. and Pa. resulted in bloody clashes after the original Conn. settlement in 1753. By 1775 the "Yankees" had the upper hand over the "Pennamites," and the 3,000 inhabitants of the isolated valley started splitting along international lines. In Jan. '74 the Conn. Gen. Assembly incorporated the settlement into a chartered township called Westmoreland, and when the war started, Conn. prohibited further immigration. The original settlers were almost unanimously Whig in sentiment, but Tories started moving in from the Hudson and Mohawk valleys. Prominent among the interlopers was a family from Minisink (now Minisink Ford, N.Y.) named Wintermoot.

Their suspicions aroused by these strangers, who made no apologies for their loyalty to the King, the original settlers formed committees of vigilance. They arrested several of the newcomers and sent them off to Conn. where they probably ended up in the Conn. Mines or Simsbury Prison. "This was an unwise act, although perhaps justifiable," comments Lossing, "and was one cause of subsequent disasters." (I, 350) The Wintermoots had purchased land toward the head of the valley, and proceeded to construct a "fort." This was common sense in a region vulnerable to Indian raids, but under the circumstances the

* *Handbook of American Indians,* II, 978. A "dozen or more places so called" existed in the Union when Wyoming was proposed, "as early as 1865," for what is now the state. (*Ibid.*)

settlers thought it wise to start throwing up some forts of their own. About two miles above the Wintermoots they built Ft. Jenkins. "Forty Fort," a blockhouse whose name came from the first 40 Conn. pioneers, was strengthened. Plans were made to build and renovate others.

Meanwhile, the valley sent off two companies of regulars, 82 men each, to join Washington, and patriot committees continued their "vigilance," sending more Tories to the mines. Howard Swiggett sketches the tense situation that developed:

"Sounds on the roads at night, heard through barred doors and windows, the hooded light in the field, were not friends or neighbors, but a man who lived in a lonely house in bitter loyalty to what cause no one knew. The little knot of men going north in the moonlight was a militia patrol going up the Susquehanna, or secret agents slipping out toward Niagara. There was something fearful in every footfall." (*War Out of Niagara,* 126)

War had lurked around the edges of Wyoming Valley for some months. During ST. LEGER'S EXPED., June–Sept. '77, stray Indians appeared. In Jan. '78, 27 suspected Tories were arrested and 18 were sent to prison in Conn. The other nine fled, probably to Niagara, and were followed by others who subsequently were released in Conn. (Stone, *Border Wars,* I, 299) At Tory headquarters in Niagara, meanwhile, Maj. John Butler was preparing another series of raids. His son, Walter, visited Niagara after his escape from Albany and took Carleton (in Quebec) an outline of his father's plans. In a memorandum dated 4 June '78, Walter Butler wrote:

"... it is his intention to fall on the enemy with the whole body of his Corps and the Warriors of the five Nations, and on such part of the New York

Province as he finds the most likely he will be able to effect joining Sir Henry Clinton . . . and that in the meantime he will break up the back settlements. . . ." (Quoted in Swiggett, *op. cit.*, 118)

An implied mission, common to all Tory raids, was to rescue families of Loyalists who had left their homes. (*Ibid.*)

Butler left Niagara in June with his Rangers, a detachment of Johnson's Royal Greens, and an assortment of volunteers from Pa., N.J., and N.Y. His white contingent numbered about 400, all of them Tories. As "Deputy of the Indian Forces" Butler had succeeded in getting the support of a large number of Iroquois for this operation. About 500 of them, mainly Senecas and Cayugas (*Handbook of American Indians,* II, 979), joined him under the command of a chief named Gi-en-gwah-toh. (Stone, *op. cit.*, 300) As will be explained below, Joseph Brant was long believed to have accompanied Butler, but actually was miles away. Nor did Guy or Sir John Johnson play any part in the operation. The statement by many writers that British regulars were part of Butler's command is probably due to the misconception that his Rangers and the Greens were regulars. Strength estimates vary considerably. The consensus among modern historians is that 1,100 white men and Indians were in the force that reached Wyoming; a good many of these probably joined Butler on the march, and a number of Wyoming Valley settlers came over to his side. Richard Cartwright, who was with the expedition, gives their strength as only 574, of whom 110 were Rangers. (Swiggett, *op. cit.*, 127; "Rangers" presumably is used here to mean "whites," since Swiggett's index refers to this statement as "strength of Loyalists.") Another Tory participant, Richard McGinnis,

whose journal will be quoted below, says only 70 white volunteers and about 300 Indians were present.

The invasion route was east toward Tryon county, southward along Seneca Lake, and on to Tioga. The latter was roughly 50 miles up the Susquehanna River from the head of Wyoming Valley. While waiting for boats and rafts to be built, Butler sent raiding parties to the West Branch of the Susquehanna. On 27 June his entire force reached Wyalusing, and the next day they camped at a rebel mill about 20 miles from their objective. The unschooled McGinnis says:

"About this time we were much distrest for provision. . . . But in the midst of our distress kind Providence was indeed very, very favourable to us. June 30th at night two men, Wintermots by name, hearing of our approach and distress for provision, came to our releif with 14 head of fat cattle.*** The men above mentioned had a fort at Wioming of their own name. . . ." (Quoted in C. & M., 1006)

Indeed they did, and the Wintermoots could tell John Butler a few interesting things about their unfriendly neighbors. Clear warnings of frontier troubles had been reaching the patriots for months. But none of the higher authorities— Schuyler, Gates, Gov. Clinton, Washington, or Congress—felt they could spare the isolated frontier settlement anything but sympathy. A company of "regulars," so called simply because Congress authorized their being raised, assembled at Forty Fort when Butler's approach was detected; they numbered between 40 and 60 and were commanded by Capt. Detrick Hewett. Col. Zebulon Butler, a Cont'l. officer home on leave, was given over-all command of the situation and called on the militia to turn out. But with the inhabitants collecting in the seven or so "forts" that extended 10 miles on both sides of the river, a high percentage of the men, understandably, insisted on staying to protect their families at these places. (Stone, *op. cit.,* 301) Having gathered about 300 militia to support his "regulars," Col. Butler marched up the valley from Forty Fort on 1 July. (*Ibid.*) The preceding day (Ward, *op. cit.,* 630) the Tories entered the valley from the west and quickly took possession of Ft. Jenkins, a little "fort" called Exeter, and established headquarters at Wintermoot's. The patriots clashed with an Indian patrol that had just surprised and murdered some men working in a field near Ft. Jenkins, and the patriot force withdrew to prepare for further action while the Tories camped around Wintermoot's.

THE BATTLE OF WYOMING, 3 JULY '78

According to W. W. Campbell, 368 men were assembled in Forty Fort after Col. Butler withdrew from the initial encounter and his militia had temporarily dispersed to supply themselves. This same author, Campbell, has a long excerpt from a history of Wyoming written by a Judge Isaac Chapman which is obviously the basis for most secondary accounts of the battle (specifically those of Lossing, Stone, and Ward). Here is Chapman's version:

"On the morning of the 3d . . . the officers of the garrison at Forty Fort held a council to determine on the propriety of marching from the fort, and attacking the enemy wherever found. *** On one side it was contended that their enemies were daily increasing in numbers; that they would plunder the settlements of all kinds of property, and would accumulate the means of carrying on the war, while they themselves would become weaker; that the harvest would soon be ripe, and would

be gathered or destroyed by their enemies, and all their means of sustenance during the succeeding winter would fail; that probably all their messengers were killed, and as there had been more than sufficient time, and no assistance arrived, they would probably receive none, and consequently now was the proper time to make the attack. On the other side it was argued, that probably some or all the messengers may have arrived at head-quarters [of the Northern Dept. in Albany?], but that the absence of the commander-in-chief may have produced delay; that one or two weeks more may bring the desired assistance, and that to attack the enemy, superior as they were in number, out of the limits of their own fort, would produce almost certain destruction to the settlement and themselves, and captivity, and slavery, perhaps torture, to their wives and children. While these debates were progressing, five men belonging to Wyoming, but who at that time held commissions in the continental army, arrived at the fort; they had received information that a force from Niagara had marched to destroy the settlements on the Susquehanna, and being unable to bring with them any reenforcements, they resigned their appointments, and hastened immediately to the protection of their families. They had heard nothing of the messengers, neither could they give any certain information as to the probability of relief."

To interrupt Judge Chapman's narrative a moment, Washington and Sir Henry Clinton were involved in the Campaign of MONMOUTH, 16 June–5 July, and Washington could spare no troops for the defense of frontier settlements. Joseph Brant was known to be massing his warriors around Unadilla, 80 miles N.N.E. of Wyoming, and the rebel agent James Deane was warning of raids along the N.Y. frontier, but

Horatio Gates, C.G. of the Northern Dept., was more interested in news of Washington's success in N.J. (Swiggett, *op. cit.*, 114, 123) Chapman's account continues:

"The prospect of receiving assistance became now extremely uncertain. The advocates for the attack prevailed in the council, and at dawn of the day, on the morning of the 3d of July, the garrison left the fort, and began their march up the river, under the command of Col. Zebulon Butler. Having proceeded about two miles, the troops halted for the purpose of detaching a reconnoitering party. . . .

"The scout [patrol] found the enemy in possession of Fort Wintermoot, and occupying huts immediately around it, carousing in supposed security; but on their return to the advancing column, they met two strolling Indians, by whom they were fired upon, and upon whom they immediately returned the fire without effect." (Quoted from W. W. Campbell, *Tryon*, 236–37)

His opportunity for surprise so narrowly lost, Col. Butler pushed forward and deployed for battle in a flat area covered by pine woods and underbrush. He personally commanded the right, and Col. Nathan Denison the left. Hewett's "regulars" were in the center. At a range of 200 yards the rebels opened fire and continued to fire as they advanced. The Tory Butler apparently formed a line parallel to the enemy, anchoring his left flank on Wintermoot's, where he personally commanded his Rangers, deploying the Indians on the opposite flank, and placing the Greens in the center. The eye-witness account of the carpenter Richard McGinnis, however, differs somewhat from those of secondary sources.

"The fort called Wintermot's above mentioned we set on fire to decoy the enemy, they thinking by this that we

were fled. But they soon found it a mistake to their sorrow, for we immediately treed ourselves and secured every spot that was any way advantageous to our designs. When the enemy came within sight of us they fell a-black-guarding of us, calling out aloud, 'Come out, ye villianous Tories! Come out, if ye dare, and show your heads, if ye durst, to the brave Continental Sons of Liberty!' (Remark, I call them Sons of Sedition, Schism and Rebellion.)

"But we came out to their confusion indeed—for the Indians on the right under the command of Col. Butler and their King Quirxhta entirely surrounded the enemy, and the white men under the command of Quiskkal . . . on the left drove and defeated the enemy on every quarter. They fled to the river and many of them even there were pursued by the savages and shared the same fate as those on the land.

" * * * Thus did loyalty and good order that day triumph over confusion and treason, the goodness of our cause, aided and assisted by the blessing of Divine Providence, in some measure help to restore the ancient constitution of our mother country, governed by the best of kings." (Quoted in C. & M., 1007)

Disaster had struck the patriots when Denison tried to turn one company to meet the threatened envelopment. Some of his untrained troops thought he had ordered a retreat, and the right wing was thrown into confusion. About this time the other flank was enveloped and the patriot line collapsed.

Twenty militia officers were killed and three Cont'l. officers. The latter were Hewett, mentioned above, and the two who had led the Cont'l. companies from Wyoming to join Washington in 1776, Capts. Robt. Durkee and Sam'l. Ransom. Only 60 men escaped the vigorous pursuit, and Denison led some of these back to Forty Fort to protect the women and children. Zebulon Butler was less heroic; "with his wife on his horse behind him," says Swiggett, he headed for Wilkes-Barre. Gathering such regulars as he could, the patriot Butler paused at Fort Wyoming (another name for Wilkes-Barre fort) and then withdrew from the valley. Slaughter of fugitives and the torture of prisoners continued through the night of 3–4 July. Some accounts say Hewett, Durkee, and Ransom were killed in action; others say they were captured, thrown into a fire, and held there by pitchforks. "Queen Esther" won infamy as "the fiend of Wyoming." (See MONTOUR FAMILY)

During the night a few reinforcements under John Franklin reached Forty Fort (Swiggett, *op. cit.*, 129), but Denison accepted John Butler's surrender terms the next morning. These terms were that the people of Wyoming Valley not take up arms again during the war; "garrisons" would be demolished; Tories would be spared further persecution and their lost property "made good." Article 4 stipulated "That Major Butler will use his utmost influence that the private property of the inhabitants shall be preserved entire to them."

The Indians got out of control, however, and terrified women, children, and old men started in panic-stricken flight through a swamp known as "The Shades of Death," over wilderness trails, and through the Delaware and Wind gaps. Much of their suffering resulted from their leaving without food or other provision for the arduous trek. Lossing furnishes several accounts of individual tragedy: mothers carrying dead babies, women learning of their widowhood on the trail, children being born and old folks dying. (*Op. cit.*, 360–61) Stone generalizes this phase but dwells on details of the pursuit after the battle —Tories refusing quarter to rebel brothers, and (quoting Dr. THACHER)

the roasting of prisoners, plus several instances of parricide. (*Op. cit.*, 306–7)

Wyoming Valley was destroyed. Maj. Butler withdrew with the greatest portion of his expedition on 8 July after receiving disturbing intelligence. The exact nature of the latter is not known, but he may have feared that rebel forces were coming from the S.E. (Swiggett, *op. cit.*, 132; Lossing, *op. cit.*, 362 *n*.) He reached Tioga on 10 July, and four days later started for Niagara. Small bands of Indians continued to roam the defenseless settlement, however, destroying crops, burning buildings, and menacing the remaining inhabitants.

A relief column of Conn. troops led by a Capt. Simon SPALDING was nearly 50 miles away from Wilkes-Barre the day of the battle. When Spalding got within 12 miles of the valley his scouts reported the enemy was still there in strength, so he wisely withdrew to Stroudsburg. Col. Butler assembled some settlers and troops and returned to Wilkes-Barre on 3 Aug. Col. Thos. Hartley arrived with the 11th Pa. Regt. to protect the valley until the crops were salvaged and the enemy threat was gone. Several militia companies also arrived, and Col. Denison broke his parole to volunteer his services.

In Sept., 130 patriots under Hartley and Denison moved up the East Branch of the Susquehanna destroying several Indian villages, taking a few prisoners, and recovering much loot. They fought an action with the Indians, and withdrew when it was learned that the savages were massing under Joseph Brant around Unadilla. A few settlers strove to get a crop planted even though the season was well advanced, and several were killed by marauding Indians. It was not until 22 Oct. that the rebel dead were collected on the battleground and buried in a common grave.

NUMBERS AND LOSSES

To recapitulate, patriot strength in the battle of 3 July was about 360: 300 militia and Hewett's 60 regulars. No more than 60 escaped. (Ward, *op. cit.*, 631) John Butler said his men took 227 scalps.

Of the 1,000 or so under John Butler's command, he reported two Rangers killed, one Indian killed, and eight Indians wounded. He reported destruction of 1,000 houses, the capture and evacuation of 1,000 head of cattle, as well as large numbers of sheep and pigs. (Ward, *op. cit.*, 631)

COMMENTS

It may appear pedantic to judge this Butler-Butler action first from a purely military point of view when historians for so long limited themselves to the "massacre" aspect. But John Butler deserves his due as a military commander before we investigate his humanity. This 53-year-old Tory leader, "seven years older than Washington, must have been of enormous vitality to come on this raid," says Swiggett. (*Op. cit.*, 127) "The troops' hardships, and those of their leader, were of killing arduousness." (*Ibid.*) After an approach march of almost 200 miles through the wilderness from Niagara they achieved a beautiful example of "strategic surprise," despite the excellent intelligence work of Schuyler's secret agent, James Deane. (*Op. cit.*, 114) Patriot authorities, civil and military, local and elsewhere, failed to do what they could with available resources, and the militia showed no spirit of courage or sacrifice in organizing their own security before John Butler reached Tioga in overwhelming strength. (Once he got this far unchallenged the result was almost inevitable.) Zebulon Butler's handling of the situation on 3 July was singularly inept: he

and Denison herded their troops forward to be slaughtered by an enemy superior in numbers and quality. Denison's error —attempting to maneuver untrained troops in contact with the enemy— merely hastened the inevitable defeat, and John Butler's vigorous pursuit resulted in the strategist's dream: a battle of annihilation. In justice to the officers and men who tried to defend Wyoming Valley on 3 July, it must be reiterated that it was already too late to overcome the "strategic surprise" John Butler had already achieved.

First reports of the disaster were published at Poughkeepsie on 20 July and based exclusively on "monstrous exaggerations ... from the lips of the terrified fugitives. ..." (Stone, *op. cit.*, 307 *n.*) These undoubtedly were embellished by patriot masters of PROPAGANDA, but half a century of historians repeated their errors, and even today it is difficult to know what really happened. "These appear to be the facts," says Swiggett of the events following the battle on 3 July:

"A savage pursuit ... was prosecuted. Practically no quarter was given to men in arms. ... After the surrender Colonel Denison and Colonel John Franklin ... both agreed that the terms were lived up to and that John Butler exerted himself to restrain the savages." (*Op. cit.*, 131)

Stone points out that the Indians were by no means the worst offenders: Wyoming Valley Tories joined John Butler and "exhibited instances of the most savage barbarity against their former neighbors. ..." But he also says, "it does not appear that anything like a massacre followed the capitulation." (*Op. cit.*, 306, 305.)

Using the best "historical" evidence then available, the Scottish poet Thos. Campbell in 1809 published "Gertrude of Wyoming," which Lossing calls a "beautiful poem . . . full of errors of every kind" and which Swiggett refers to as "a long ballad of execration." * Modern authorities have established that Joseph Brant had no part in the expedition, and also that neither Guy nor Sir John JOHNSON was present. Ignoring the written surrender terms, writers have quoted John Butler as offering "the hatchet." Other myths are that he was refused knighthood for his conduct on 3 July and that Haldimand refused to receive him.

John Butler's own report, written 12 July at Tioga, concludes with these words: "But what gives me the sincerest satisfaction is that . . . not a single person was hurt except such as were in arms, to these in truth the Indians gave no quarter." (Quoted in Swiggett, *op. cit.,* 133)

WYTHE (with), George. 1726–1806. Signer, statesman, jurist, law professor. Va. After the death of his wealthy father and the inheritance of the entire estate by his brother Thomas in 1729,

---

* Thos. Campbell (1777–1844) was a poet of some note. Lossing's point may be illustrated from the opening lines of "Gertrude":
"Delightful Wyoming! beneath thy skies/ The happy shepherd swains had naught to do/ But feed their flocks on green declivities,/ Or skim, perchance, thy lake with light canoe." None of these "shepherd swains" ever got to London to look up the author and set him straight, but the son of Joseph Brant did. In a letter dated London, 20 Jan. 1822, the poet explains how he fell into the error of incriminating "the monster Brant" in the Wyoming affair. This letter to "the Mohawk Chief, . . . John Brant, Esq." is an appendix to W. W. Campbell's *Tryon.* It is referred to and parts of "Gertrude" are quoted in Lossing, *op. cit.,* 341, 354 and *n.*

George was tutored by his exceptionally well-educated mother. She died while he was still young. He had little formal schooling, but at 21 he was admitted to the bar. In Dec. '47 he married the daughter of Zachary Lewis, with whose brother, a prominent attorney, he was associated in practice at Spotsylvania. This wife died the next year and George entered an eight-year period of energies squandered in "the amusements and dissipations of society." (Quoted in *D.A.B.*) On the death of his brother in 1755 George inherited a large estate and applied himself to diligent study not only of law but also of the liberal sciences and literature. He moved to Williamsburg, having represented the town in the House of Burgesses (1754–55), and about this time he also remarried. The only child of his union with Elizabeth, daughter of Col. Richard Taliaferro of "Powhatan," died young, and Wythe survived Elizabeth by 19 years.

Wythe's brilliant career was closely related to those of several exceptional men who were his intimate friends or, later, students. In 1758, after being admitted to the bar of the General Court, he started a profitable friendship with the new governor, Francis Fauquier, an exceptionally learned gentleman. Another close friend at this time was Wm. Small, professor of mathematics and natural philosophy at William and Mary. Later he was to be a friend and teacher of Thos. Jefferson, James Monroe, and Henry Clay.

During the years leading up to the break with England, Wythe was a representative in the House of Burgesses (1754–55, 1758–68), and was clerk of that body from 1769 to 1775. He was mayor of Williamsburg in 1768 and on the William and Mary board of visitors in 1769. In the controversy leading to Patrick Henry's triumph in the PARSON'S

CAUSE, Wythe presided over the court that upheld Virginia's action against the claim of the Rev. Thos. Warrington for damages. In 1764 he drafted a protest to the Stamp Act that so far exceeded most of his colleagues' ideas of permissible candor that they toned it down considerably before adoption. When the fiery Patrick HENRY came forth the next year with his famous resolutions, the occasion of his Caesar-Brutus-George III speech, Wythe was one of those who opposed them; he, Richard Bland, and others maintained that Henry's resolutions contained nothing new and should be withheld until the emasculated resolutions of Wythe had been answered.

In 1775 he showed a wisdom surpassing that of the political majority when he recommended that Va. organize a regular army and not a militia. (See VIRGINIA, Mil. Opns. in, for wisdom.) As delegate to the Cont'l. Cong., 1775–76, he ably supported Richard Henry Lee's resolution for independence and became a Signer. He probably designed the Va. state seal with its ominous motto, *Sic Semper Tyrannis* and the conspicuous absence of the traditional shield. (*D.A.B.* The Latin motto, "thus ever to tyrants," is also attributed to George Mason.) With Jefferson and Edmund Pendleton he accomplished the monumental task of revising the laws of Va.; the committee reported 126 bills in 1779. Meanwhile Wythe was speaker in the House of Delegates in 1777 and

the next year assumed the title of Chancellor when he became one of three judges in the state's high court of chancery. The next year, on 4 Dec. '79, he was named to the first chair of law established in an American college, William and Mary, and one that followed the one at Oxford by only 21 years. He then began the part of his remarkable career for which he is most famous. In 1790 he resigned this post to form a small law school in Richmond, where Henry Clay was one of his students. Wythe's opinions were scrupulously honest, learned, and bold. He is credited with making one of the earliest enunciations of "the doctrine of judicial review, America's unique contribution to juridical theory." (*D.A.B.*)

His death was tragic. Wythe left most of his estate to his only sister's grandson, one George Wythe Sweeney, and left a servant a legacy that was to pass to Sweeney if the servant died. Sweeney poisoned some coffee with arsenic with the idea of killing the servant and, possibly, of killing his grand-uncle at the same time. The servant died first, but Wythe lived long enough to disinherit Sweeney. The latter escaped conviction for murder since the testimony of the Negro cook, the principal witness, was not admissible in court. It is ironic that Wythe, like many other eminent Virginians at the time, was opposed to slavery and in his will had emancipated all his servants.

Y

YAGERS. See JÄGERS.

YAMASSEE WAR, 1715–16. See COLONIAL WARS.

"YANKEE DOODLE." Of unknown origin and existing in almost countless versions, it is generally attributed to a British surgeon named Shuckberg, who supposedly wrote it to ridicule provincial troops besieging Boston in 1775. The British played it when they left the surrender field at Saratoga, not in derision but because they had been instructed to play something light.

YANKEE HERO–MELFORD ENGAGEMENT, 7 June '76. Making a run from Newburyport to Boston, the American privateer *Yankee Hero*, commanded by Capt. Tracy and with only a third of her complement on board, was attacked by the British frigate *Melford*, commanded by Capt. John Burr. After a gallant defense of more than two hours, against a crew four times their size, and "with not half the metal [the British] ship had," the critically wounded Tracy struck his colors. (C. & M., 971)

"YEAR OF THE HANGMAN." See "HANGMAN, . . ."

"YELLOWED." See ADMIRALS, "Colored."

YORKTOWN CAMPAIGN, May–Oct. '81. Patriot fortunes were at a particularly low ebb during the spring of 1781. FINANCES had finally collapsed completely. The British were firmly established in the far South, and VIRGINIA MILITARY OPERATIONS had left that state ravaged by enemy raiders. The FRENCH ALLIANCE, now in its third year, was a big disappointment.

In May, however, the picture suddenly brightened. Adm. de Barras arrived from France to take command of the fleet bottled up in Newport. It was hoped that he would break the blockade and get these ships into the war, but the news Barras brought from France was even more exciting: De Grasse was headed for the West Indies with a powerful fleet; and he had 600 troops in vessels that would be diverted en route and sent to reinforce the four regiments at Newport.

Rochambeau was informed that De Grasse had orders to sail north later in the summer from the West Indies to give what support he could in North American waters. Although not yet free to give this last important piece of news to Washington, Rochambeau proposed that the two senior commanders meet to decide what might be done with the forces at hand.

The strategic situation was roughly as follows: Clinton was in and around N.Y.C. with about 10,500 rank and file; Washington had 3,500 Cont'ls. in the Hudson Highlands; the French fleet was bottled up at Newport with about 4,000 French troops. Lafayette was in Va. with a sizable detachment of Cont'l. troops to oppose the British raiding parties in that region, and Anthony Wayne was preparing to follow with more regulars. Greene was doing what he could to contain the forces of Cornwallis in the Carolinas. There was a strong possibility that Cornwallis would be able to push into Va. and join British forces already in that ravaged province. Enemy forces were also known to be coming up Lake Champlain from Canada, and an invasion of northern N.Y. was a possibility.

The WETHERSFIELD CONFERENCE, 22 May '81, was held with this strategic picture as the backdrop but also with the disappointing knowledge that Barras had decided he lacked the naval strength to join in amphibious operations. With Barras unwilling to take French troops into the Chesapeake and then support efforts to drive the British from Virginia, Washington proposed a combined operation against N.Y.C. Barras could take his fleet to Boston for safety when Rochambeau's troops left Newport.

Rochambeau cordially agreed that the proposed plan was the best possible for the time being. But what might be done later, Rochambeau asked, if naval reinforcements from the West Indies happened to become available? (It is important to note that Rochambeau did not at this time inform Washington that De Grasse actually was under orders to effect this cooperation. It is therefore incorrect to say, as many writers have, that the "Wethersfield Plan" visualized the strategy of the Yorktown Campaign. See Freeman, *Washington*, V, 296 *n.* 87 and Higginbotham, *War of Am. Indep.*, 388 *n.* 50.) Washington's restrained reply was that with effective French naval support the strategic possibilities would be almost unlimited. It was decided at Wethersfield that De Grasse should be asked to come north as soon as possible.

Two weeks after the allied commanders returned to their camps to prepare for the coming campaign they learned that Cornwallis had reached Va. This meant Lafayette was in a dangerous position and that plans for the diversion against N.Y.C. would have to be speeded up. But there were other alarming developments. The most serious was that the Wethersfield Plan had been compromised: on 3 June, Clinton received a copy captured in the mails; unless the British commander believed this was a "plant" to deceive him as to the real allied strategy, this compromise would seriously reduce the chances of his withdrawing troops from Cornwallis to reinforce the defenses of N.Y.C. The next bad news came from Adm. Barras: he did not want to move his ships to Boston when the French troops marched from Newport, so additional militia had to be raised for the protection of that harbor. News also was received that British forces had pushed up the lake to Crown Point, and Washington had to resist the proposal that he detach regulars, to meet a possible invasion of northern N.Y.

OPERATIONS AGAINST MANHATTAN

The junction of Rochambeau's forces with those of Washington did not take place until six weeks after plans were made at Wethersfield. The French infantry left Newport on 9 June and moved 25 miles north to Providence. On the 18th they started west. Washington, meanwhile, reorganized his own forces and by 24 June was camped near Peekskill awaiting Rochambeau's arrival. On the 28th, however, he conceived the ambitious plan of capturing the British posts on the north end of Manhattan Island so as to speed up subsequent operations against Clinton. Maj. Gen. Benj. Lincoln was given 800 good troops for this surprise attack: 400 light infantry under Col. Alexander Scammell, the battalion of Lt. Col. Ebenezer Sprout, and a detachment of artillery. They were to descend the Hudson from Peekskill the night of 2–3 July, capture the works around

Kings Bridge, and raid Forts Tryon and Knyphausen (formerly Washington). If this plan did not turn out to be feasible, Lincoln was to land above Spuyten Duyvil and support an attack by Lauzun's Legion, the Conn. militia of Gen. Waterbury, and Sheldon's dragoons against the Tory troops of De-Lancey around Morrisania, N.E. of Kings Bridge. The complicated plan was coordinated with Rochambeau, "who cooperated, as always, with unhesitating heartiness," comments Freeman. (*Op. cit.*, 298) Washington personally supervised most of the preparations, but everything went wrong. Lincoln abandoned his first plan when he saw from Ft. Lee, on the west bank of the Hudson, that a large enemy foraging party had just returned to Ft. Knyphausen from N.J. and that a British warship was in the river below Ft. Knyphausen. When his men crossed the river to undertake the alternate plan they ran into another foraging party and its supporting troops; the alarm was spread, and the enemy outposts were withdrawn across the Harlem River to positions too strong for assault. The Duke de Lauzun's Legion, which had followed a route across Conn. slightly south of the main French column, made a long forced march but the extreme heat exhausted his horses and men; they arrived too late, but surprise had already been lost. "Nothing was gained beyond a good opportunity of close reconnaissance," says Freeman of the entire operation. (*Ibid.*)

Washington had advanced with the rest of his force to Valentine's Hill, four miles above Kings Bridge, to support Lincoln, and Rochambeau was asked to hurry toward the same point. After spending the day of the 3d reconnoitering for further operations against Manhattan, Washington withdrew his entire force to Dobb's Ferry on 4 July,

and the French joined him there on the 6th.

During the four days starting 21 July, 5,000 troops pushed out to form a screen while Washington and Rochambeau, with an escort of 150 Cont'ls., thoroughly reconnoitered the northern defenses of Manhattan. This convinced them that an attack would require formal siege operations, which they lacked the means to undertake.

"But if nothing was accomplished before New York, as no fleet had arrived to co-operate, the very important and expected result was brought about, that Clinton was compelled to call for reenforcements from the Chesapeake, and, for the time being, cripple Cornwallis in Virginia." (Johnston, *op. cit.*, 83)

Allied plans now hung on word from De Grasse. There was still no suspicion that the closing scene of the American Revolution would be enacted at a place called Yorktown, but we might now trace the events that led the British to that place.

When Clinton left Cornwallis to command British forces in the South after the capture of Charleston (12 May '80), Clinton instructed his subordinate to make the security of S.C. his primary concern. Clinton's over-all strategy for the prosecution of the war in America was for the time being defensive: he planned to hold the vital bases at New York, Charleston, and Savannah until the government furnished the reinforcements he considered necessary for further offensive operations. Although Sir Henry has never been called a military genius, his estimate of the situation was sound: in calling for 10,000 more troops and the assurance of continued naval supremacy for operations in 1781, says Johnston, "he but represented . . . the true necessities of the case. England's force in America that year [1780] was inadequate for her purposes." (*Op. cit.,* 29) Most other historians agree.

The ambitious Earl Charles Cornwallis, however, had other ideas. The best way to defend S.C., he proposed, was to attack into N.C. and destroy what little American armed strength was located there. Clinton had no obejction, provided he remember his primary mission. Since New York was too far away for Clinton to control the operations of Cornwallis, the latter received authority to communicate directly with London. So far so good. While the Earl was preparing for his move into N.C. he learned that Gates was advancing against his forward bases. Ignoring the odds, Cornwallis took the offensive and brilliantly defeated Gates at Camden, 16 Aug. '80. It is probably not too much to say that this victory cost the British the war.

"In December Cornwallis's aide-de-camp, Captain Ross, who had carried home the news of Camden, returned to him from England; and from that moment Cornwallis's tone and bearing towards Clinton were completely altered [writes Sir John Fortescue]. The fact was that Germaine, always crooked and purblind, and now dazzled by the success of Cornwallis at Camden, had decided virtually to give him an independent command and to make Clinton's operations subservient to those of his subordinate. In a word, since neither Howe nor Clinton would act upon his insane schemes of conquest without garrisons and of invasions without communications, he took advantage of the ambition and comparative youth of Cornwallis to thrust these disastrous designs upon him." (*British Army,* III, 358)

Despite the British disasters at KINGS MOUNTAIN, 7 Oct. '80, and COWPENS, 17 Jan. '81, and failure of the expected Loyalist support in N.C., Cornwallis followed Greene to the Dan River. He still ignored Clinton's instructions, to make the security of S.C. his primary concern, and refused to withdraw from an untenable position around Hillsboro, N.C. His pyrrhic victory at GUILFORD C. H., 15 Mar. '81, forced him to withdraw, but instead of falling back to Camden, S.C., he moved to Wilmington, N.C. Furthermore, he so misrepresented the facts that Clinton and the London authorities were led to believe he had gained control of N.C. By the time they knew the truth Cornwallis was marching to Va. and Greene was moving against the scattered British forces of Rawdon in S.C.

When Clinton got the incredible news that Cornwallis had abandoned the Carolinas and arrived at Petersburg, Va., he expressed his disapproval but gave him a free hand to conduct such immediate operations as he saw fit, "until we are compelled (as I fear we must be by the climate [*sic*]) to bring them [the British troops in Va.] northward." (Ltr. of 29 May '81 from Clinton to Cornwallis.) Exasperated by Germain's meddling and by the government's support of Cornwallis' strategy in the Carolinas, Clinton had decided to resign "the instant I could with propriety." Professor W. B. Willcox comments that Sir Henry "therefore left his subordinate complete freedom of action. If the government had not taken the stand it did, 'I [Clinton] would have sent His Lordship back by sea' to South Carolina." (Clinton, *The American Rebellion,* edited by Willcox, 525 *n.*) Fortescue says Clinton "kept Cornwallis close at hand in order to resign the command to him, instead of sending him back, as he ought, to Carolina." (*Op. cit.,* III, 391)

After the unsuccessful efforts to trap Lafayette that are covered under VA. MIL. OPNS., Cornwallis reached Williamsburg on 25 June. The next morning he received Clinton's letters of 29 May (quoted above) and those of 11 and 15 June. (Clinton, *op. cit.,* 523, 529, 532, and 535) The second of these said: "I beg leave to recommend it to you, as soon as you have finished the active operations you may be now engaged in, *to take a defensive station in any healthy situation you choose,* be it at Williamsburg or Yorktown. And I would wish *in that case* that, *after reserving to yourself such troops as you may judge necessary for an ample defense and desultory movements by water for the purpose of annoying the enemy's communications, destroying magazines, etc.,* the following corps may be *sent me in succession as you can spare them:* the two battalions of light infantry, Forty-third, Seventy-sixth or Eightieth Regiments, the two battalions of Anspach, Queen's Rangers, [including their] cavalry and infantry, remains of the detachment of Seventeenth Light Dragoons, and such a proportion of artillery as can be spared, particularly men." (*Ibid.,* 530–31) Another letter received this same day, that dated 15 June, added Portsmouth and Port Comfort to possible locations for Cornwallis' base and told him that in view of the possibility that De Grasse was moving his French fleet from the West Indies to attack N.Y., Cornwallis should "immediately embark a part of the troops stated in the letter enclosed [that of 11 June, just quoted], beginning with the light infantry, etc."

The ambitious Earl, who thought operations in Va. were so important that Clinton should abandon N.Y. to provide the necessary strength to support them, now made the startling request that he be allowed to return to Charleston. Meanwhile, he decided he could not hold a position on the Peninsula after this detachment of troops to N.Y. and made plans to cross the James to Portsmouth. He skilfully lured Lafayette into the action at GREEN SPRING, 6 July, but failed to follow up; he might well have crippled the American army to such an extent that he would have been able to maintain his position on the Peninsula. (*Ibid.,* 389) But he crossed the James and immediately (8 July) received instructions from Clinton to send 2,000 or 3,000 troops to Philadelphia, instead of N.Y. On the 12th he got a letter changing the destination of the reinforcements back to N.Y., and on the 20th he was told to keep them all and establish a naval station on the tip of the Peninsula at Old Point Comfort!

This tangle of orders and counterorders resulted from Clinton's efforts to direct Cornwallis with instructions that took eight days to arrive, while Germain was trying to direct both of them from across the Atlantic. All three agreed that major operations should be undertaken in the Chesapeake, but they disagreed on the timing. Clinton wanted to establish a post at the mouth of the Chesapeake that would immediately serve as a base for naval operations and later, when the necessary reinforcements were available, as a base for land operations in the Middle Colonies. Cornwallis wanted the latter strategy undertaken immediately, even if it meant abandoning N.Y. Germain "desired to combine both designs after some incomprehensible fashion of his own," says Fortescue, and he was guilty of an "ill-timed interference . . . in every respect fatal." (*Ibid.,* 391) After Clinton ordered Cornwallis to send reinforcements north he got Germain's letter (of 2 May) prohibiting the withdrawal of a man from the Chesapeake.

"This was nothing less than the rejection of the Commander-in-chief's scheme in favour of his subordinate's;

yet by the irony of fate Clinton had hardly received this order before Germaine repented of it, and wrote again, though of course too late, to approve of Clinton's original plan." (*Ibid.*, 390, citing Germain to Clinton, 7 and 14 July '81)

Clinton's final order telling Cornwallis to establish the base at Old Point Comfort had authorized him to occupy Yorktown also if this would contribute to the security of his main position. But when his engineers advised him that the former site was unsuitable (the channel was too wide to be covered by shore batteries and there would be inadequate protection for shipping) Cornwallis picked Yorktown for his main base and established a supporting position across the York River at Gloucester. Although Clinton later insisted that this was a violation of his orders, he tacitly acquiesced in this arrangement. (Ward, *W.O.R.*, 878; Johnston, *op. cit.*, 69, 70 & *n.*)

Thus, by 22 Aug. Cornwallis had moved his entire command into the two posts they would leave only as prisoners of war.

THE ALLIED CONCENTRATION BEGINS

On 14 Aug. Washington got the news that - shaped the final strategy of the war: De Grasse was sailing for the Chesapeake with 29 warships and more than 3,000 troops; he would remain for combined operations until 15 Oct. and then return to the West Indies. Washington's course of action was now obvious, although by no means without problems. He had only two months in which to effect a concentration 450 miles to the south. There was the distinct possibility that the British Navy would interfere with the planned operation. Barras created a problem by hinting that he would undertake op-

erations at this time against British shipping off Newfoundland (!), and there was some question as to whether he could be prevailed on to waive his seniority and cooperate with De Grasse; Washington and Rochambeau succeeded in persuading him, but there was also some question as to whether this admiral would be able to get through weather and the British squadrons to reach the Peninsula with the French siege artillery and the Americans' reserve of salted provisions from Newport. There was the possibility that if all else went well Cornwallis might escape into the Carolinas before forces could be concentrated against him. German reinforcements reached N.Y. in early Aug. to bring Clinton's total strength to over 15,000 rank and file, and Washington had to worry about securing the line of the Hudson. He had to worry about being attacked from N.Y. as he moved through N.J.

With a decisiveness that does credit to his reputation as a great captain, Washington immediately abandoned his plans for taking N.Y.C. and started planning the strategy dictated by De Grasse. Heath would remain on the Hudson with half the army, covering the passage of the Va. expedition across the river and then withdrawing to deploy as he saw fit to defend the Highlands. With 2,500 Americans and the entire French force, Washington planned to march south.

The Americans crossed by Kings Ferry to Stony Point on 20–21 Aug., and the French completed their crossing on the 25th. Clinton was puzzled by this movement but not worried. He knew De Grasse was expected, but he had been assured that Rodney would trail him from the West Indies with a superior force and he was confident that the British Navy would maintain command of the Atlantic coastal waters.

On the latter assumption, therefore, Clinton ruled out the possibility that Washington would march to Va. Far from concerned about the indications that the Americans were preparing to attack Staten Island—his spies duly reported the presence of boats with the American army—Clinton was planning an attack on R.I.

"It was not until the 2nd of September [when the allied army reached Philadelphia] that Clinton realized that Washington was actually on the march for Virginia, but still he felt little anxiety. He wrote to Cornwallis that Admiral Digby's squadron was expected shortly, and that he himself would send reinforcements and make a diversion from New York, adding, in tragic ignorance of the true state of affairs, that as Graves had sailed Cornwallis need fear nothing." (Fortescue, op. cit., 393. The actual movements of Graves and Digby will be covered below.)

THE ALLIED MARCH SOUTH

After crossing the Hudson the allies followed three roughly parallel routes to Princeton. The American light infantry moved on the left, through Paramus, to simulate an attack in the direction of Staten Island, and the entire army halted in the vicinity of Chatham and Springfield (due west of N.Y.C.) during 28 Aug. to heighten the deception and also to close up the columns. On the 29th the columns still marched as if heading for Sandy Hook to link up with the French fleet, but the next day they abandoned the deception and openly headed for Princeton.*

* Johnston points out an erroneous dating of Washington's journal which apparently escaped Freeman. The latter authority also makes the mistake of writing Sept. when he means Aug., but

The leading elements of Washington's army reached Princeton on the 30th, and Washington rode ahead with Rochambeau to enter Philadelphia the same day. The American troops passed through Philadelphia on the 2d and continued straight on to reach Head of Elk on 6 Sept. They found time, however, to let Congress know that despite the lawmakers' problems of higher finance they wanted a month's pay before they continued their patriotic steps southward, and they wanted it in hard money; Robt. Morris had to raise the funds by borrowing $20,000 from Rochambeau's war chest. French troops entered the American capital in two divisions on 3 and 4 Sept., dazzling the provincials with their brilliant uniforms, their bands, and their military precision.

After struggling with problems of transportation and hoping for news of the two French fleets, Washington left Philadelphia on the 5th. At Chester, that afternoon, he received the joyful news that De Grasse had reached the Chesapeake safely. Now all he had to worry about was whether Barras would get through with the siege guns and whether Lafayette and the troops brought by De Grasse would be able to keep Cornwallis from escaping up the Peninsula and into the Carolinas. While their troops waited at Head of Elk for French transports, Washington and Rochambeau rode ahead with their staffs. Stopping at Mount Vernon, 9–12 Sept. (which Washington had not seen for six years), they reached the Peninsula on 14 Sept. Although Cornwallis had not tried to escape, the naval situation was still fraught with suspense: Washington had learned on the 12th

does comment on Washington's error in saying he reached Philadelphia on the 31st. See Freeman, op. cit., 317 and n.; Johnston, op. cit., 90 and n.

that De Grasse's fleet had disappeared to meet a British fleet approaching the Chesapeake; there was still no news about Barras. By the morning of the 15th, however, word came that De Grasse was back and that Barras had arrived safely.

Washington had achieved an astounding strategic success. While luck figured prominently, the American commander had showed skill of the highest order in planning and executing this concentration.

NAVAL OPERATIONS

Where had the Royal Navy been?

De Grasse left Brest with a powerful French fleet about the time of the Wethersfield conference and (after Suffren left him in the Azores for the East Indies) reached Martinique on 28 Apr., picked up four French ships that had been blockaded by Adm. Hood off Fort Royal, and engaged in some relatively minor operations (see WEST INDIES IN THE REV.) before putting into Cap Haitien on 26 July. Here he found the *Concorde* waiting with dispatches asking for his support in operations either against N.Y.C. or in the Chesapeake. Allen McLANE may deserve credit for convincing the admiral to undertake this mission and that he should head for the Chesapeake. In any event, De Grasse sent the *Concorde* back with word he was coming, and on 13 Aug. he was under way with 3,000 troops borrowed from Haiti, 1,500,000 livres borrowed from Havana, and 34 warships (including six frigates).

Adm. Sir George Rodney, who commanded the British West Indies fleet, warned Adm. Arbuthnot as early as 3 May that De Grasse might come his way. Adm. Thos. Graves, who succeeded the crusty Arbuthnot on 4 July as commander of the fleet supporting Clinton, was notified of De Grasse's arrival at Haiti and advised by Rodney to move his squadron to the Va. coasts and join one Rodney would send north. But Graves never got this message, and De Grasse took an indirect route through the Bahama Channel to conceal his movement as long as possible. On 26 Aug. the French fleet was off the Va. Capes and De Grasse soon made contact with Lafayette; the troops started landing on 2 Sept. and the fleet anchored in Lynnhaven Roads. (Freeman, *op. cit.*, 321 *n.*) Mahan gives this explanation:

"The English were unfortunate in all directions. Rodney, learning of De Grasse's departure, sent fourteen ships-of-the-line under Admiral Hood to North America, and himself sailed for England in August, on account of ill health. Hood, going by the direct route, reached the Chesapeake three days before De Grasse, looked into the bay, and finding it empty went on to New York.* There he met five ships-of-the-line under Admiral Graves, who, being senior officer, took command of the whole force and sailed on the 31st of August for the Chesapeake, hoping to intercept De Barras before he could join De Grasse." (*Sea Power*, 389)

The Battle off the CHESAPEAKE CAPES, 5 Sept. '81, climaxed these wide-ranging fleet movements. Although the superior French fleet was unable to win a clean victory, De Grasse inflicted severe damage on the British and kept them occupied while Barras arrived with his Newport convoy and slipped safely into the Chesapeake on 10 Sept. De Grasse followed him in the next day and on 14 Sept. Graves abandoned the Va.

* I have accepted Freeman's statement that De Grasse arrived on 26 Aug., only a day ahead of Hood. Other authorities have a later date.

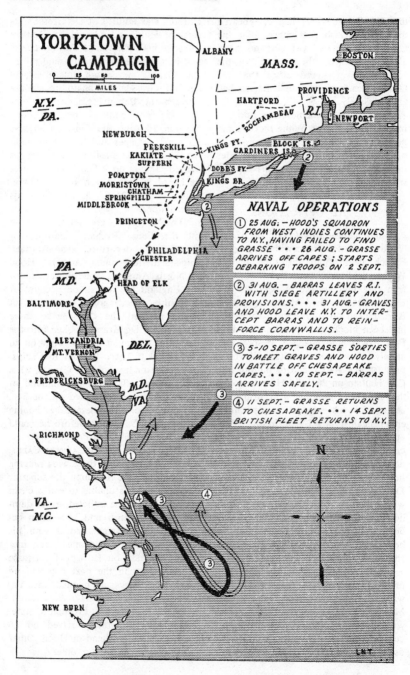

YORKTOWN CAMPAIGN

0 __ 25 __ 50 __ 100
MILES

NAVAL OPERATIONS

① 25 AUG. – HOOD'S SQUADRON FROM WEST INDIES CONTINUES TO N.Y., HAVING FAILED TO FIND GRASSE • • • 26 AUG. - GRASSE ARRIVES OFF CAPES ; STARTS DEBARKING TROOPS ON 2 SEPT.

② 31 AUG. – BARRAS LEAVES R.I. WITH SIEGE ARTILLERY AND PROVISIONS. • • • 31 AUG. - GRAVES AND HOOD LEAVE N.Y. TO INTERCEPT BARRAS AND TO REINFORCE CORNWALLIS.

③ 5-10 SEPT. – GRASSE SORTIES TO MEET GRAVES AND HOOD IN BATTLE OFF CHESAPEAKE CAPES. • • • 10 SEPT. – BARRAS ARRIVES SAFELY.

④ 11 SEPT. – GRASSE RETURNS TO CHESAPEAKE. • • • 14 SEPT. BRITISH FLEET RETURNS TO N.Y.

coast to sail back for repairs in N.Y. The situation of Cornwallis was now hopeless.

From Head of Elk the limited available shipping was used to start the heavy equipment down the Chesapeake while most of the troops marched to Baltimore and Annapolis. Here the latter were picked up by transports that had come from Newport and the captured frigates; leaving on 18 Sept., they arrived to complete the concentration of the allied armies on the Peninsula 26 Sept.

BRITISH DEFENSES

When Saint-Simon's troops were landing on 5 Sept., Cornwallis still had a chance to fight his way up the Peninsula to Richmond and retreat into the Carolinas. Lafayette anxiously deployed the combined forces so as to block this route, but after some probing Cornwallis declined to make the attempt. Confidently expecting that Clinton would soon send him relief, Cornwallis continued to fortify his positions at Yorktown and Gloucester Point.

Yorktown had been established in 1691 on a 35-foot bluff overlooking the York River and separated from Gloucester Point by about half a mile of water. A ferry connected the two places. Yorktown grew to a city of some 300 houses and 3,000 people when it reached its peak in 1750, but as Norfolk and Baltimore were developed and as the center of the tobacco economy moved into southwest Va., Yorktown declined in importance.

Cornwallis established his main line of defense close to the town, with an average depth of only 300 yards between the river and the line of fortifications, and with a width of only 1,000 yards. Yorktown was not selected as a place for withstanding a protracted siege and did not provide good defensive terrain: it was flat, offering little defilade and depriving the defenders of the other advantages of high ground (observation, fields of fire). Yorktown Creek and Wormley Creek would have furnished excellent natural obstacles on which to organize a defense if the British garrison had been large enough to defend such a long perimeter, but this was beyond their capability, particularly in the absence of naval superiority. The inner line of fortifications, mentioned above, comprised 14 batteries, some 65 guns, and 10 redoubts. The principal strongpoint was known as the "horn work," and was located astride the road from Hampton. Forward of this position, to defend the half-mile of flat ground between the heads of the two creeks, were several outworks. This area, part of which was known as Pigeon Quarter, was the principal approach for an attacker. Along the river, west of Yorktown and covering the Williamsburg Road where it entered from that direction, was a strong position called the Fusilier Redoubt, since it was held by a detachment from the Royal Welch Fusiliers (23d Regt.). On the opposite flank were Redoubts 9 and 10.

Gloucester Point was important not only in connection with Cornwallis' original mission of establishing a naval station but also as a base for foraging. The position was commanded by Lt. Col. Thos. Dundas, and its fortifications included four redoubts, three batteries, and a line of entrenchments.

ORDER OF BATTLE

Johnston points out that the armies of Washington and Cornwallis represented a remarkable collection of veteran troops from "four leading groups of people who claim superiority in arms, and each of whom, at different periods of their history, have displayed extraordinary tenacity in supporting their national cause—the English and Germans, the French and Americans." (*Op. cit.,* 108) On 27 Sept. the American Cont'ls. were reorganized into three divisions of two brigades each:

Lafayette's Lt. Inf. Div.

Brig. Gen. Peter Muhlenberg's Brig. was made up of the battalions commanded by Joseph Vose, Jean Gimat, and Francis Barber.

Brig. Gen. Moses Hazen's Brig. comprised the battalions of Ebenezer Huntington, Alexander Hamilton, John Laurens, and Edw. Antill (who commanded Hazen's Canadian Regt.).

Benj. Lincoln's Div.

Brig. Gen. James Clinton's Brig. included the 1st N.Y. Regt. under Gose Van Schaick and the 2d N.Y. Regt. under Philip Van Cortlandt.

Col. Elias Dayton's Brig. was made up of the 1st and 2d N.J. Regts. combined to form the Brig. of Mathias Ogden, and the R.I. Regt. under Jeremiah Olney.

Steuben's Div.

Brig. Gen. Anthony Wayne's Brig. included the 1st Pa. Bn. of Walter Stewart, the 2d Pa. Bn. of Richard Butler, and the Va. Bn. of Thos. Gaskins. Col. Craig's Pa. Bn. arrived just as operations ended.

Brig. Gen. Mordecai Gist's Brig. comprised the 3d Md. under Peter Adams and the 4th Md. under Alexander Roxburg.

Gov. Thos. Nelson's Va. militia were organized into the brigades of Geo. Weedon (1,500 men), Robt. Lawson, and Edw. Stevens (750 each). Other militia troops were the "Va. State Regt." of 200 men under (Chas.?) Dabney and a body of Campbell County, Va., riflemen.

Henry Knox's Arty. Brig. included

John Lamb's 2d Regt. (225 N.Y. and Conn. troops), Capt. Whitehead Coleman's 25-man Co. of Edw. Carrington's 1st Regt., and 60 men of the 4th Regt. under Patrick Duffy, Wm. Ferguson, and James Smith.

Cavalry consisted of 60 troopers of the 4th Dragoon Regt. under Stephen Moylan, and 40 from Armand's Legion.

Sappers and Miners listed in the Order of Battle were a total of 50 men in the detachments commanded by James Gilliland, David Bushnell, and David Kirkpatrick, plus 50 Del. recruits under Wm. McKennan.

Washington's staff was composed of Edw. Hand (A.G.), Timothy Pickering (Q.M.G.), Henry Dearborn (Assist. Q.M.G.), Ephraim Blaine (Commiss. Gen.), Chief Surgeon James Craik, Chief of Engrs. Duportail, and Supt. of Materials Samuel Elbert. Military Secretary was Jonathan Trumbull, Jr. Aides de Camp were Tench Tilghman, David Humphreys, David Cobb, Wm. S. Smith, and John Laurens (until he took command of the 3d Bn. of Hazen's Regt.).

One would have to search long to find another military roster that read so like a roll of honor. A few additional names should be mentioned. Josiah HARMAR was Lt. Col. of Wayne's 2d Bn.; Maj. GALVAN served as Steuben's division inspector, John P. Wyllys was second-in-command to GIMAT in Lafayette's 1st Brig. It is also interesting to note how many of those just named were foreign officers holding Cont'l. commissions; another was Duportail.

THE FRENCH WING

Rochambeau's contingent was made up of the four regiments that had marched from Newport, the three that had come with De Grasse, 600 artillerymen under d'ABOVILLE, Lauzun's Legion of 600 horse and foot (total), and 800 marines detached for operations against Gloucester.

The infantry regiments were named the Bourbonnais, Royal Deux-Ponts, Soissonais, Saintonge, Agenais, Gâtinais, and Touraine. The first four, which had come from Newport, numbered 900 men each; the others were from the West Indies and numbered 1,000 men each. The Gâtinais was Rochambeau's old regiment and had served under d'Estaing at Savannah. Lafayette's father was killed leading the Touraine at MINDEN.

THE ARMY OF CORNWALLIS

To defend Yorktown and Gloucester, Cornwallis had what Johnston terms "the *élite* of the King's army in America." He had brought the following units from the Carolinas: the Brigade of Guards (about 500 men commanded by O'Hara), the 23d, 33d, and 71st Foot (about 670 men in all), the light infantry company of the 82d, Tarleton's British Legion (192 men), Lt. Col. John Hamilton's N.C. Vols. (114 men), and the German Bose Regt. (271 men commanded by Maj. O'Reilly). The other troops had come south with Arnold and Phillips: two battalions of light infantry (about 600 total strength), the 17th (205 men), 43d (307 men), 76th (628), 80th (588 men), the Queen's Rangers (248 men commanded by Simcoe), two Anspach Bns. (948 total), the Hessian Regt. Prince Hereditaire (425), and Capt. John EWALD's Jäger Co. (68 men). Royal Artillery detachments totaled about 200 men; they were supplemented by naval guns and gunners, as was customary in this type of operation. About 800 marines were also on hand, plus 33 pioneers and other detachments.

Johnston points out the dearth of senior officers: O'Hara was the only other general, and among the field grade officers there were only two colonels, 12 lieutenant colonels, and 12 majors.

PRELIMINARY MOVEMENTS

The allies started from Williamsburg at 5 o'clock the morning of 28 Sept. and moved to within a mile of the Yorktown defenses by dark. The light infantry of Lt. Col. Robt. Abercromby on the British right withdrew as the French Wing advanced in that sector, and Tarleton's mounted troops withdrew to the Moore House when the American Wing arrived to the S.E. of Yorktown. The next day Washington and his officers examined the enemy position while their troops deployed to invest Yorktown. Orders were issued for the siege artillery and stores to move up from Trebell's Landing on the James—a difficult operation since sufficient draft animals were not available and the heavy guns had to be moved over six miles of sandy roads.

The morning of Sunday, 30 Sept., the allies were pleasantly surprised to discover that the enemy had abandoned the three outposts covering the approach from the S.W.—the two astride the Goosley Road in the Pigeon Quarter and another one to the north covering a road across the top of Yorktown Creek. Although Cornwallis has been severely criticized for failure to hold these positions to buy time, his decision was sound in the light of the information available to him: he had received word from Clinton on the 29th that a fleet would leave N.Y. for his relief about 5 Oct. Since the three abandoned outposts were vulnerable to envelopment by the superior allied force, Cornwallis believed he could best employ his limited forces in a defense of the inner line during the week or so it would take for relief to arrive. (Johnston, *op. cit.,* 121)

Washington wasted no time undertaking siege operations. While the French pushed forward on the left, driving the pickets into the Fusilier Redoubt and forcing the Royal Welch to make a stubborn defense of their position, 1,200 men worked in the woods gathering wicker material for gabions, fascines, etc. A tragedy of the day was the loss of Alexander SCAMMELL.

Gen. Geo. Weedon's 1,500 Va. militia opposing the British garrison under Lt. Col. Thos. Dundas at Gloucester were reinforced on 28 Sept. by Lauzun's Legion of 600 men. On 1 Oct. Gen. de Choisy assumed over-all command and, about the same time, 800 French marines were detached for service on this front. Tarleton's Legion joined Dundas on 2 Oct. to bring his strength to about 1,000. After a spirited clash at GLOUCESTER, 3 Oct., Choisy kept the British bottled up until the end of the campaign.

REGULAR APPROACHES STARTED

On 6 Oct. the main allied force opposite Yorktown was ready to break ground for their formal siege operations. To divert attention from the main effort, Saint-Simon's troops started a FLYING SAP toward the Fusilier's Redoubt early in the evening. Meanwhile, the trace of the 2,000-yard-long first parallel was staked out by engineers and well-organized work parties moved forward after dark to dig. Favored by a dark, rainy night and sandy soil, some 1,500 men shoveled before daylight enough dirt to have protection in their trench and four redoubts. Saint-Simon's diversion started drawing enemy fire about 9 P.M. (a French deserter had alerted the British), but the working parties were subjected to little shelling during the night. Cornwallis probably did not realize the first parallel had been started until the morning of 7 Oct. when his troops could see

it at a distance of 600 to 800 yards from their positions.

On 9 Oct. the first allied batteries were ready to start the bombardment. Although an American position on the extreme right had 10 pieces ready before noon, Washington gave Saint-Simon the honor of opening the show at 3 P.M. on the opposite flank. Early the next day another four batteries were in action— two French and two American—bringing the total to at least 46 pieces. By 10 A.M. the allied fires had inflicted such damage that the British could return only about six rounds an hour. (Freeman, op. cit., 362–63)

A flag of truce appeared at noon (10 Oct.) and "Secretary" Thos. Nelson, 65-year-old uncle of the Governor, was permitted to leave the embattled city. He brought valuable news: the bombardment, which had severely damaged his own house on the S.E. corner of Yorktown, was so effective that many of the enemy, including Cornwallis, had taken refuge behind the bluffs bordering the river; furthermore, he reported that a small boat had come with word that a British relieving force would arrive within a week.

One legend of the siege must be mentioned here. The battery commanded by Capt. Thos. Machin was one of those opened on the 10th. Here is how Johnston relates the famous story: "On this date Lafayette was general officer of the day, and he invited Governor Thomas Nelson to be present at the opening of the fire from Machin's guns, not only as a compliment, but because of his accurate knowledge of localities in Yorktown. 'To what particular spot,' he asked, 'would your Excellency direct that we should point the cannon?' 'There,' replied Nelson, 'to that house. It is mine, and, now that the Secretary's is nearly knocked to pieces, it is the best one in the town.

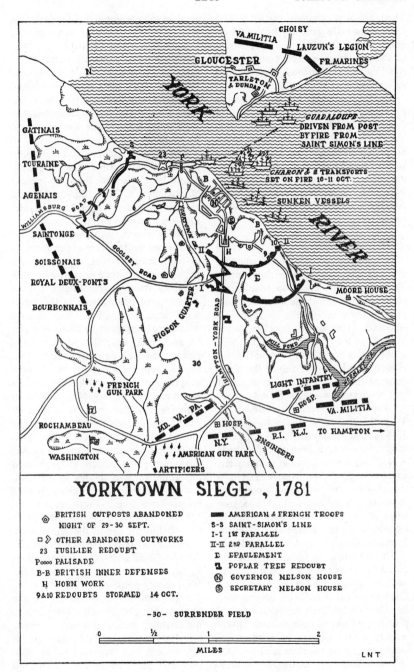

YORKTOWN SIEGE, 1781

◇ BRITISH OUTPOSTS ABANDONED
   NIGHT OF 29-30 SEPT.

□ ◇ OTHER ABANDONED OUTWORKS
23 FUSILIER REDOUBT
Poooo PALISADE
B-B BRITISH INNER DEFENSES
Ⴠ HORN WORK
9 & 10 REDOUBTS STORMED 14 OCT.

▬▬▬ AMERICAN & FRENCH TROOPS
S-S SAINT-SIMON'S LINE
I-I 1ˢᵗ PARALLEL
II-II 2ᴺᴰ PARALLEL
E EPAULEMENT
⚑ POPLAR TREE REDOUBT
Ⓝ GOVERNOR NELSON HOUSE
Ⓢ SECRETARY NELSON HOUSE

-30- SURRENDER FIELD

0   ½   1   2
MILES

LNT

There you will be almost certain to find Lord Cornwallis and the British headquarters.' " (*Op. cit.*, 139–40, citing Custis, *Washington*. The house is still standing and has cannon balls embedded in its east wall.)

The *Charon* (44 guns) was set on fire by French hot shot the night of 10–11 Oct., and another three or four vessels were also destroyed by fire from Saint-Simon's guns. Work was started on the second parallel the next night, but two detached British works, Redoubts Nos. 9 and 10, had to be reduced before the American end of this parallel could be completed.

ASSAULT OF REDOUBTS 9 AND 10

As a preliminary step in the reduction of these two positions, French engineers directed construction of an epaulement on the eastern end of the second parallel as close to the redoubts as this work could be accomplished. Digging started at dusk on the 11th. All possible allied artillery was brought to bear on the two redoubts, and about 2 o'clock the afternoon of the 14th Washington was told that an assault was now feasible.

Since Redoubt No. 10, close to the York River, was in Lafayette's sector he was given responsibility for its capture. He selected Gimat, his former A.D.C. and now a battalion commander, to lead the operation. Alexander Hamilton claimed the honor on grounds of seniority, however, and Washington ruled in his favor. Hamilton's 400-man assault column comprised Gimat's, Hamilton's, and half of Laurens' Bn.

The simultaneous attack on Redoubt No. 9 would be made by 400 grenadiers and chasseurs of the Gâtinais and Royal Deux-Ponts. It would be commanded by Col. Wm. Deux-Ponts with Col. d'Estrade as second in command. Diversionary attacks against the Fusilier Redoubt and across the river at Gloucester were scheduled to precede the two principal assaults, whose signal for departure was to be six guns fired in succession.

Saint-Simon and Choisy started their demonstrations punctually and vigorously at about 6:30 P.M. Half an hour later the signal guns started firing and Hamilton and Deux-Ponts moved forward silently into the darkness; muskets were unloaded, and the works were to be taken by the bayonet.

The French column had advanced about 120 yards when they were challenged by a *Wer da?* from the parapet of Redoubt 9. The 120 British and Hessian defenders under Lt. Col. McPherson then opened fire as the French rushed forward. A strong abatis, 25 yards from the fort, caused the attackers to lose time and men, and they were further delayed, once they reached the ditch, by fraises and palisades. French officers were conspicuous in their personal leadership. While the pioneers worked to chop gaps so that the entire column could scale the parapet, other officers and men went up without waiting for support. Chevalier de Lameth was the first to reach the top, but he was shot down with crippling wounds in both knees. D'Estrade, a veteran of 40 years' service, was knocked from the side of the parapet and into the ditch when a soldier fell on him from above; this unfortunate officer was subjected to the indignity of serving as a human fascine while 200 men charged over his prostrate form. (Freeman, *op. cit.*, 371 *n.*) Deux-Ponts was painfully wounded at the end of the action when a bullet ricocheted close to his face and showered him with sand and gravel as he peered over the parapet toward the main enemy positions.

After inflicting heavy losses on the French before they scaled the parapet, the defenders tried to take refuge behind a line of large casks within the redoubt. The French fired into the huddled mass and then prepared to close with cold steel. British and Hessians threw down their arms and surrendered. Gen. Viomesnil, who had over-all command of the French attack, arrived and ordered Deux-Ponts to consolidate his position and prepare for a counterattack from the main enemy lines; this threat did not, however, materialize.

Hamilton's attack had taken place simultaneously, and the Americans were fired on shortly after the Hessian sentinel challenged the French column, some 200 yards away. Lt. John Mansfield led his forlorn hope of 20 men from the 4th Conn. into the redoubt and was supported immediately by the leading battalion under Gimat. Hamilton's Bn., led by Nicholas Fish, attacked on Gimat's left almost simultaneously, and the two companies under Laurens (80 men) hit the enemy's rear and cut off their escape. The attack was a brilliant success which cost the Americans only nine killed and 25 wounded. (Johnston, *op. cit.*, 147) Although Redoubt 10 was not as strong a fortification as No. 9, and was defended by only 45 men whereas No. 9 had a garrison of 120 (Freeman, *op. cit.*, 371), the American success had a lesson for the French veterans: the former had scrambled through the abatis, ditch, and fraises and into the redoubt without waiting for the pioneers to clear gaps, whereas the French took heavy casualties, "perhaps because they were formalists and, being trained soldiers, insisted upon sending their axmen ahead to clear the way," as Bonsal explains it. (*Op. cit.*, 163–64).

Lafayette had been annoyed a few hours before the attack by Viomesnil's intimation that the Americans might not be up to executing their part of the coordinated attack. When the Americans had captured their redoubt and were evacuating their prisoners some minutes before the French had taken theirs, Lafayette could not resist the opportunity to needle his own countrymen—

he sent a staff officer to ask Deux-Ponts if he wanted any assistance! (Bonsal, *op. cit.*, 163) The French did not need any help, but they had lost 15 killed and 77 wounded. In the two redoubts the enemy had six officers and 67 men captured (Freeman, *op. cit.*, 371); 18 were killed and 50 captured in Redoubt No. 9, according to Johnston. (*Op. cit.*, 143)

Cornwallis did not counterattack, but he massed all possible guns against the captured works. The allies moved working parties out immediately to throw up a protective wall of dirt at the back of the redoubts and to incorporate them into the already completed portion of the second parallel.

ABERCROMBY'S SORTIE

Completion of the second parallel had not only the obvious effect of moving allied guns within closer range of the enemy lines but it also permitted batteries to enfilade them. The standard reaction to such a threat is for the defenders to sally forth and spike the most dangerous guns. About 4 A.M. on 16 Oct., therefore, Lt. Col. Robt. Abercromby led 350 picked British troops out on this mission. Hitting near the boundary between French and American troops in the second parallel and near two unfinished batteries where no working parties were then located, Abercromby led his raid westward along the trench. Pretending to be an American detachment, he surprised an element of the Agenais Regt., most of whom were asleep. (Freeman, *op. cit.*, 373 and *n.*) After spiking four guns he continued down the trench until he sighted another position.

"What troops?" challenged the British commander.

"French," replied a man of Capt. Joseph Savage's American battery.

"Push on, my brave boys, and skin the bastards," shouted Abercromby.

"Vive le Roi!" yelled Count de Noailles to end this international dialogue and start a fight that drove the British back to their lines. Fortunately, he had been nearby with a French covering party, had heard the colloquy, and figured out what was happening. (*Ibid.*) The raiders had meanwhile spiked two of the American guns before withdrawing with a loss of five captured and seven others killed or wounded. Washington reported 17 casualties. Since the guns had been ineffectually spiked with bayonet points, the allies had them back in action within six hours.

The night of 16–17 Oct. Cornwallis tried to ferry his effectives across the river with a view to fighting his way out of the Gloucester lines. Insufficient boats and an exceptionally severe storm frustrated this effort. On 17 Oct., the fourth anniversary of Burgoyne's surrender, the allied artillery started the heaviest bombardment yet delivered; according to some estimates more than 100 pieces were in action.

SURRENDER

Sometime between 9 and 10 A.M. on the 17th a redcoated drummer appeared on the parapet of the horn work. Above the roar of the guns nobody in the allied lines could hear that he was beating a parley, but nobody could fail to guess it. A British officer then came out in front of the lines with a white handkerchief. The guns gradually became silent. An American ran out, blindfolded the officer, and led him into the lines with a message from Cornwallis to Washington proposing surrender.

The British commander asked for a 24-hour truce to work out terms. Washington gave him two hours to submit his proposals. The latter were received about 4:30 P.M., and commissioners met the next morning (18 Oct.) at the Moore House to settle details. Dundas

and Maj. Alexander Ross represented Cornwallis; Noailles and Laurens represented the allies. Washington had stated that "The same Honors will be granted to the Surrendering Army as were granted to the Garrison of Charles Town," but British appeals and objections resulted in a prolonged and heated session at the Moore House. Washington's representatives could show him only a rough draft by midnight, but the morning of the 20th he had written his comments on the draft, had the surrender document transcribed, and sent it to Cornwallis to be signed by 11 A.M. Cornwallis was also informed that Washington expected the garrison to march out at 2 o'clock to surrender. Between 11 and noon the document was back with the signature of Cornwallis and of Capt. Thos. Symonds, senior naval officer present. Washington, Rochambeau, and Barras signed for the allies.

Except for the article based on British precedent at Charleston, that "The troops shall march out, with colors cased, and drums beating a British or a German march," the surrender terms were honorable. Cornwallis and his principal officers could return to Europe on parole or go to an American port in British hands. The sloop *Bonetta* was put at the temporary disposal of Cornwallis "to receive an Aid de Camp to carry dispatches to Sir Henry Clinton; and such soldiers as he may think proper to send to New York...." This last provision was a device for getting rid of American deserters whom Washington could not grant P.O.W. status and with whose disciplining he did not wish to be burdened; troop capacity of the *Bonetta* was 250, and most of those who reached N.Y. on 2 Nov. aboard her were deserters. Surrender terms permitted officers to retain their side arms and all personnel to keep their personal effects. Infantry of the Gloucester garrison would ground their arms there, but the cavalry (Simcoe's and Tarleton's) would proceed to the surrender field outside Yorktown with their swords drawn and their trumpets sounding. Surrendered troops would subsequently be marched to camps in Va., Md., and Pa.

At noon two detachments of 100 men each—one French, one American—occupied two British redoubts S.E. of Yorktown. The rest of the victorious army formed on both sides of the Hampton road along which the vanquished would march to the surrender field, about a mile and a half south of Yorktown. At 2 P.M. the King's troops came slowly down the road, allegedly to the tune of "THE WORLD TURNED UPSIDE DOWN."

The man most intimately responsible for their predicament was not, however, at their head. Earl Cornwallis was "sick," so Gen. O'Hara of the Guards acted as his deputy. An interesting scene of military etiquette resulted when O'Hara asked his French escort to point out Rochambeau and the Guardsman then raced ahead to present himself to this officer. With a devastating *savoir faire* Rochambeau pointed across the road to Washington. The ruddy Irishman bowed and turned about to face Washington, with an apology for his "mistake." "Washington showed neither irritation nor disappointment [at the failure of Cornwallis to appear]," says Freeman, "but, of course, if the British commander acted through a deputy, would General O'Hara be so good as to consult General Lincoln, who was directly at hand?" (*Op. cit.,* 389–90)

A few comments must be made on the above version of this dramatic scene. That O'Hara deliberately sought out Rochambeau is supported by Bonsal, who cites the *Memoirs* of Gen. (then Col.) Mathieu Dumas, the officer sent to escort O'Hara. (*Op. cit.,* 165) The same author (Bonsal) gives many additional instances of British insolence toward the Americans and an attempt to pretend that it was the French who had beaten them at Yorktown. Second, there is much pother about a sword that O'Hara was supposed to be trying to give away—Cornwallis' sword. Dumas and Rochambeau both wrote in their memoirs that O'Hara offered his sword to Rochambeau. Bonsal repeats that Washington refused to accept the sword "from such a worthy hand," and Johnston says Lincoln accepted and returned it. Freeman comments that "no American witness mentioned the tender of the sword [to Rochambeau, or, presumably, to anybody else], which the British officer was entitled to keep under the explicit terms of the capitulation." (*Op. cit.,* 389 *n.*) Another myth that must go is that Lincoln received the surrender in compensation for his surrender at Charleston; "Lincoln was to his chief what O'Hara was to Cornwallis," points out Freeman. "Had Cornwallis sent a Colonel to act for him, Washington would have assigned a Colonel to deal with him." (*Ibid.,* 390 *n.*)

In a field ringed by French hussars the British and German regiments arrived one by one to present arms, ground weapons, accoutrements, and cased colors, and return to Yorktown. Observers commented on the flawless marching of the Germans and the sloppy performance of British troops and their music. Although many British soldiers had on new uniforms made available for the occasion from reserve stocks, many were drunk, and all were carrying stuffed knapsacks on the assumption that they might not return to their camp. Some of the prisoners threw their muskets onto the surrender heaps in an effort to damage them. People of the neighborhood were allowed to witness the surrender ceremonies, and many of Washington's officers excused themselves to watch the events on the surrender field; but Washington apparently remained at his post a few hundred yards away, and the troops, presumably, kept their formations along the road. In the absence of authentic details on the surrender of the colors it is assumed that they were grounded with the weapons. (Freeman, *op. cit.*, 390–91) (See also, James CLINTON.)

NUMBERS AND LOSSES

Of the 20,000 allied forces in Yorktown and Gloucester, casualties did not exceed 400. Cornwallis had a strength of at least 9,750; about 600 were casualties during the siege and 8,081 were surrendered.*

* Here is a more detailed breakdown of these estimates. American army troops included 7,290 Cont'l. inf., 514 arty., and 176 cav. (7,980 total), plus 3,153 militia (11,133 grand total). With 1,000 absent sick and 700 present sick, effective American strength was about 9,500. Rochambeau marched 4,000 from Newport, Saint-Simon landed 3,000, and De Grasse sent 800 "marines" to Gloucester. Counting an additional 1,000 French naval personnel aboard ships directly supporting the siege (and excluding 15,000 on other ships), 19,993 American and French officers and men were on the rolls: 11,133 Americans and 8,800 French.

The Americans lost 23 killed and 65 wounded in the operations up to and including the capture of Redoubt No. 10. Subsequent casualties were few; making generous allowances for militia losses and unreported casualties, Freeman estimates that total American casualties for the entire siege did not exceed 125. Baron Cromot du Bourg, Rochambeau's A.D.C., recorded 253 French

Captured British property included 214 pieces of artillery, 7,320 small arms (1,136 of them damaged), 24 transports,

army casualties, 60 of whom were killed. French naval losses are not known but must have been small.

Cornwallis reported 8,885 land forces at the start of the siege and 552 army casualties during the siege (156 killed, 326 wounded, 70 missing). Surrendered army personnel and camp followers numbered 7,241, and approximately 250 American deserters were evacuated on the *Bonetta*. An additional 840 naval personnel were surrendered to De Grasse, and since the British did not report the number of seamen supporting the land forces, this figure of 840 has been used to establish the minimum army-navy strength of 9,725 British under command of Cornwallis. Cromot du Bourg's estimate that 1,500 seamen supported Cornwallis is reasonable, however, when one considers that 24 transports plus many other naval craft were in the York River. Freeman concludes that 44 naval casualties were sustained; adding these to the 552 army casualties already mentioned, the grand total would be 596. In estimating *effective* British strength, it would be safe to assume that a maximum of 1,500 were sick at any one time.

This summary is based on Freeman, *op. cit.* 513–15, where two minor errors must be noted. Nine lines from the bottom of p. 514, the figure 7,890 is a typographical error that should read 7,980. On line eight of p. 514, Freeman gives 9,725 as the minimum total force under Cornwallis, but on line seven of the next page he erroneously repeats this as 9,775. As a result he gets a figure of 1,142 instead of 1,092 as the unexplained difference between Cornwallis' original strength and his total losses.

many small craft, 40 wagons and teams, 260 horses, a military chest of £2,113, 22 or 24 standards, plus ammunition and stores. Cornwallis had surrendered one fourth of the total British military strength in America, and Freeman comments: "If England had to lose an army, she at least could say she had not stinted it." (*Op. cit.* 516)

SEQUEL

On 24 Sept. Clinton had decided to send a relief expedition to Yorktown, but there were numerous delays even after the arrival of Adm. Digby and repair of damages inflicted by De Grasse off the Chesapeake Capes, 5 Sept. Clinton sighted the capes again on 27 Oct., but as a French officer put it, *"il était trop tard. La Poule était mangée."* ("Too late. The hen had been eaten.") Even if he had arrived earlier, De Grasse's foresight in bringing his entire fleet from the West Indies virtually assured that Graves and Hood would not have been able to fight their way through and land Clinton's 7,000 troops at Yorktown.

Although we know that the Revolution virtually ended at Yorktown, this was by no means obvious at the time. Fisher writes:

"It was the surrender of only the weakest of the three British divisions. It was the loss of only Virginia. . . . They still held New York as strongly as ever; they held Wilmington in North Carolina; Savannah in Georgia; and, most important of all, Charleston, at that time the Capital, and, to a great extent, the strategic position of the South. In the event of mediation of European powers to close the war, England might still claim that having conquered and being still in possession of the South, she could not be required to relinquish it.

"Washington looked forward to at least another year of fighting." (*Struggle,* II, 504)

Washington did his utmost to persuade De Grasse to remain long enough to support operations against the Southern ports. The admiral's reluctant refusal has only recently been fully explained by documents in the French archives: there was a written agreement with the Spanish authorities as to when they might expect his return to the West Indies. (Bonsal, *French,* 171) On 5 Nov. he sailed away, but he promised to be back the following summer.

The siege left Yorktown in a state of ruin from which it never recovered. The surrendered forces remained two days before leaving under militia escort for camps in Md. and Va., and during this time their officers were treated to a series of dinners. Trenches were filled in to prevent their use by a returning enemy force and the allied army was dispersed. Gen. St. Clair started south with 2,000 Pa., Md., and Del. regulars, including Anthony Wayne, to reinforce Greene. Washington led the rest of the Americans back to their posts on the Hudson. Rochambeau's troops remained in Va. until spring, and on 23 June '82 started their march back to Newport.

Congress learned of the victory at Yorktown when Tench Tilghman reached Philadelphia at 3 A.M. on 22 Oct. The bad news arrived in London about noon on Sunday, 25 Nov. Lord North, who had retained his aplomb through previous disasters, is reported to have received this last intelligence with, "Oh God! it is all over!"

BIBLIOGRAPHY

The standard authority has long been Henry P. Johnston, *The Yorktown Campaign and the Surrender of Cornwallis, 1781,* published in 1881, which includes a "List of Original Authorities" and a list of "Maps and Plans of the Siege."

Contemporary sources include Claude Blanchard, Richard Butler, Chastellux, Clinton, Cornwallis, Lafayette, Lauzun, Light-Horse Harry Lee, Simcoe, and Thacher, most of whom were participants. In Ward, *W.O.R.*, editor Alden points out, "On the events and the strategy which led to the siege of Yorktown, the most recent [in 1952] and the best writings are to be found in Gottschalk, *Lafayette and the Close of the American Revolution*, 189–306; Willcox, 'The British Road to Yorktown: A Study in Divided Command' [*Am. Hist. Rev.*, LII (1947)]; and [Randolph G.] Adams, 'A View of Cornwallis's Surrender at Yorktown' [*Am. Hist. Rev.*, XXXVII (1931)]. Among the contemporary accounts on the British side, those published in Stevens [*The Campaign in Virginia, 1781....*] are of the greatest importance." (*Op. cit.*, 924) Freeman, *Washington*, V, and Willcox (ed.), *The American Rebellion* (Clinton's journal) are invaluable works published since Alden listed the authorities above. A recent work is Thomas Fleming, *Beat the Last Drum* (1963), and Willcox has just published a biography of Clinton (1964).

YOUNG'S HOUSE (Four Corners), N.Y., 3 Feb. '80. While the opposing armies were in winter quarters, Lt. Col. Joseph Thompson commanded five Conn. companies—about 250 men—with the mission of patrolling in turbulent Westchester co. According to Heath, Thompson was supposed to move in the region between the Hudson and Bedford, and between White Plains and the Croton River. Although specifically instructed "never to remain long at any

one place," he stopped long enough at Mt. Pleasant for the enemy to send an expedition from Ft. Knyphausen (ex-Washington) to attack him.

Thompson learned of the enemy's advance but, perhaps deceived by the extreme winter weather, thought he had only a mounted patrol to deal with. In reality he was hit by 450 foot troops and 100 mounted men under command of Lt. Col. Chapple Norton, a Guards officer; units were the 1st and 2d Regts. of Guards, 100 Hessian infantry, some mounted and dismounted jägers, and 40 of Col. James de Lancey's Westchester Tories, all mounted. Thompson's Conn. troops were supported in the Mt. Pleasant area by four Mass. companies that brought his total strength to 450. (Ward, *W.O.R.*, 620)

Norton's mounted vanguard cut off and captured a nine-man outpost and opened a long-range fire while waiting for the main body to come up. Around 9 A.M. the opposing forces were in a hot firefight. Within 15 minutes, however, Norton had enveloped Thompson's left and occupied an orchard to his rear. Some of the defenders took refuge in the house of Joseph Young, which was captured and burned by the grenadiers of the Guards. The rest of the defending force retreated and the Tories pursued.

The Americans lost 14 killed, 37 wounded, and 76 captured. (*W.O.R.*, 620) Capt. Moses Roberts, who commanded one of the Mass. companies, was among the dead, and two other commanders of Mass. companies were captured—Capt. Abraham Watson, and Capt.-Lt. Michael Farley. Col. Thompson and four officers in addition to those already named were taken prisoner. Norton had five killed and 18 wounded.

Z

ZANE, Ebenezer. 1747–1812. Pioneer. Va. Born near modern Moorefield, W. Va., the son of an ex-Quaker (*D.A.B.*) of Danish origin (Appleton's), he explored the "dark and bloody ground" with his brothers Silas and Jonathan. In 1770 he established WHEELING. During Dunmore's War he was disbursing agent of Va. militia, and during the Revolution he took part in the defense of WHEELING. Brother Jonathan was present at CRAWFORD'S DEFEAT (1782), and sister Elizabeth became a heroine of the Revolution. (See below) In 1796 Ebenezer got permission from Congress to open a road from Wheeling to Limestone (Maysville), Ky., when southern Ohio was opened for settlement by the Treaty of Greenville (see WAYNE). This became the famous "Zane's Trace," and Zanesville (originally Westbourne) was established on a section of land granted to Zane where his road crossed the Muskingum.

ZANE, Elizabeth. *c.*1759–*c.*1847. Sister of Ebenezer ZANE and heroine of WHEELING. Twice married, she is an ancestress of author Zane Grey.

ZEISBERGER, David. 1721–1808. Moravian missionary. His parents went to Ga. with the first of the MORAVIAN SETTLEMENTS. He followed a few years later, moved with the sect to Pa., and became a missionary among the Indians. After helping the Delawares build Friedenshuetten in the Wyoming Valley after 1763, he established Schoenbrunn in 1771, and within three years had founded Gnadenhuetten, Salem, and Lichtenau in Ohio. After the GNADENHUETTEN MASSACRE he continued to live among the Christian Indians and established new settlements in Michigan, Ohio, and Canada.

ZINZENDORF, Count. See MORAVIAN SETTLEMENTS.

BIBLIOGRAPHY AND SHORT TITLE INDEX

Listed below are full identifications and short titles of works cited frequently in this encyclopedia. Classified bibliographies follow many articles in the book, and if a publication fits under an article it probably is not repeated below. There are a few exceptions: works like Freeman's *Washington* and Gottschalk's *Lafayette* are repeated because of their over-all reference value. In the case of such eminent authorities as J. T. Adams, S. F. Bemis, and Allen French, to indicate the credentials of such scholars I have listed several of their works below, even though these works might be so specialized as to belong only under an article heading if the general rule were followed.

Although depositories are not normally included in a formal bibliography, note the heading MANUSCRIPT COLLECTIONS AND GUIDES and one of its cross references, the CLEMENTS COLLECTION.

A. A.–HEITMAN LIST OF BATTLES. This citation refers to the list of battles and engagements in *The Army Almanac* (Washington, 1950) which, in turn, is an amplification of the list compiled by Heitman for his *Historical Register*.

ADAMS, CHARLES FRANCIS (1807–86). (ed.) *Letters* [of Abigail Adams, the editor's grandmother]. Boston, 1840 and 1848 (4th ed., rev. and enl.).

———. (ed.) *Familiar Letters of John Adams and His Wife, Abigail Adams, During the Revolution.* New York, 1876.

———. *Life of John Adams.* 2 vols. Philadelphia, 1874.

———. (ed.) *The Works of John Adams ... With a Life of the Author....* 10 vols. Boston, 1850–56.

ADAMS, CHARLES FRANCIS (1835–1915; son of preceding). *Studies Military and Diplomatic, 1775–1865.* New York, 1911.

ADAMS, JAMES TRUSLOW. (ed.) *Album of American History.* 5 vols. New York, 1944–49.

———. (ed.) *Dictionary of American History.* 5 vols. 2d ed., rev. New York, 1942. My citations of this work, *D.A.H.*, are to the 1st ed., of 1940. The *Concise D.A.H.* (this is how I cite it), edited by T. C. Cochran and Wayne Andrews, was published in 1961.

———. *The Epic of America.* Boston, 1931.

———. *The Founding of New England.* Boston, 1921.

———. *New England and the Republic, 1776–1850.* Boston, 1926.

———. *Provincial Society.* Boston, 1928.

———. *Revolutionary New England, 1691–1776.* Boston, 1923.

ADAMS, RANDOLPH G. See CLEMENTS COLLECTION, below.

ALDEN, JOHN RICHARD. *The American Revolution.* New York, 1954.

———. *General Charles Lee: Traitor or Patriot?* Baton Rouge, 1951.

———. *General Gage in America.* Baton Rouge, 1948.

———. *John Stuart and the Southern Colonial Frontier ... 1754–1775.* Ann Arbor, 1944.

ALDEN, JOHN RICHARD. *The South in the Revolution, 1763–1789.* Baton Rouge, 1957.

———. (ed.) *The War of the Revolution,* by Christopher Ward, (see below) was edited by Alden after the author's death.

ALLEN, ETHAN. *Narrative....* See biographical sketch.

ALMON, JOHN. (ed.) *The Parliamentary Register; or, History of the Debates and Proceedings of the Houses of Lords and Commons.* 17 vols. London, 1775–80.

———. *The Remembrancer; or Impartial Repository of Public Events.* 17 vols. London, 1775–84. A monthly collection of papers relating to American independence. Almon was a journalist and close friend of John Wilkes, whose *Correspondence* he published in 1805.

AMERICAN HERITAGE PUBLISHING CO., INC. *The American Heritage Book of the Revolution.* New York, 1958.

———. *American Heritage: The Magazine of History.* New York, 1950– .

AMERICAN HISTORICAL ASSOCIATION. *The American Historical Review.* New York etc., 1895– . A quarterly.

———. *Papers.* New York, 1885–91.

———. *Guide to Historical Literature.* New York, 1961.

AMERICAN PHILOSOPHICAL SOCIETY of Philadelphia. Manuscripts include those of Benjamin Franklin, Arthur Lee, Richard Henry Lee, and the Nathanael Greene —George Weedon Papers. The Franklin Papers were analyzed and edited by J. Minis Hays in *Calendar....* (5 vols., Philadelphia, 1906–8).

ANBUREY, THOMAS. *Travels Through the Interior Parts of America.* 2 vols. Boston, 1923.

ANDERSON, TROYER. *The Command of the Howe Brothers During the American Revolution.* New York and London, 1936. See article on WILLIAM HOWE.

ANDREWS, CHARLES MCLEAN. *The Colonial Background of the American Revolution; Four Essays....* Rev. ed. New Haven, 1931.

———. *The Colonial Period of American History.* 4 vols. New Haven, 1934–38.

———. *Guide to the Materials for American History to 1783, in the Public Record Office of Great Britain.* 2 vols., Washington, 1912. Among the important documents in the P.R.O., many of them unpublished, are official reports of military, naval, and civil officers, and copies of instructions sent to them. These are of first importance in the study of the American Revolution.

———. (With FRANCES C. DAVENPORT.) *Guide to the Manuscript Materials for the History of the United States to 1783, in the British Museum, in Minor London Archives, and in the Libraries of Oxford and Cambridge.* Washington, 1908. See also GRACE G. GRIFFIN, *Guide.*

ANDREWS, EVANGELINE MCLEAN. (ed.) In collaboration with CHARLES MCLEAN ANDREWS. *Journal of a Lady of Quality; Being the Narrative of a Journey from Scotland to the West Indies, North Carolina, and Portugal in the Years 1774 to 1776.* New Haven, 1921. Loyalist Janet Schaw, author of the *Journal,* was the sister of a royal official and a highly prejudiced but amusing observer of the revolutionary scene in the Carolinas.

ANDREWS, MATTHEW P. *History of Maryland....* New York, 1929.

THE ANNUAL REGISTER, *or a View of the History, Politics, and Literature for the Year* ———. London. See sketch of Edmund BURKE.

APPLETON'S CYCLOPAEDIA OF AMERICAN BIOGRAPHY. 6 vols. New York, 1886–89.

ARMY LISTS. First published officially in 1754, these registers give the service records of British officers. See work by W. C. FORD, below.

Atlas of American History. JAMES T. ADAMS. (ed.) New York, 1943. Cited as *Scribner's Atlas.*

AUGUR, HELEN. *The Secret War of Independence.* New York, 1955.

BALCH, THOMAS. *The French in America during the War of Independence.* . . . Philadelphia, 1891.

BANCROFT, GEORGE. *History of the United States.* 12 vols. New York, 1834–82.

BAURMEISTER *Journals.* Shortened title for UHLENDORF (ed.), *Revolution in America.* . . .

BEERS, GEORGE L. *British Colonial Policy, 1754–1765.* New York, 1907.

———. *The Origins of the British Colonial System.* New York, 1908.

BEERS, HENRY P. "The Papers of the British Commanders in Chief in North America, 1754–1783." *Military Affairs,* XIII (1949), 79-94. Washington. This article is useful for its comment on location and content of papers.

BELCHER, HENRY. *The First American Civil War.* . . . 2 vols. London, 1911.

BELL, H. C., *et al. Guide to British West Indian Archive Materials in London and in the Islands, for the History of the United States.* Washington, 1926.

BEMIS, SAMUEL FLAGG. (ed.) *The American Secretaries of State and their Diplomacy.* 10 vols. New York, 1927–29. Deals with the period 1789–1925.

———. *A Diplomatic History of the United States.* New York, 3d ed., 1950.

———. *Foundations of American Diplomacy: I, The Revolution.* New York, 1935. This is also identified as *Diplomacy of the American Revolution.*

———. (And GRACE GARDNER GRIFFIN) *Guide to the Diplomatic History of the United States, 1775–1921.* Washington, 1935.

———. *Hussey-Cumberland Negotiations and American Independence.* Princeton, 1931.

———. *Jay's Treaty.* . . . New York, 1923.

———. *John Quincy Adams and the Foundations of American Foreign Policy.* New York, 1949.

———. *Pinckney's Treaty.* . . . Baltimore, 1926.

———. "British Secret Service, and the French-American Alliance." *American Historical Review,* XXIX (1923–24), 474-95.

BEZANSON, ANNE, assisted by BLANCHE DALEY, MARJORIE C. DENISON, and MIRIAM HUSSEY. *Prices and Inflation,During the American Revolution, 1770–1790.* Philadelphia, 1951.

BILLIAS, GEORGE ALLEN. *The American Revolution.* New York, 1964.

———. *The American Revolution: How Revolutionary Was It?* Magnolia, Mass., 1965.

———. (ed.) *George Washington's Generals.* New York, 1964. Interpretive sketches of Washington, Lee, Schuyler, Gates, Greene, Sullivan, Arnold, Lincoln, Lafayette, Knox, Wayne, and Morgan, each by a different historian.

BOLTON, CHARLES K. *The Private Soldier Under Washington.* New York, 1902.

BOUDINOT, ELIAS. His *Journal* (1894) and *Life* (2 vols., 1896) are identified at the end of the biographical sketch in the main body of this work. His "Report on American Prisoners of War in New York," in draft form, is in the *William & Mary Quarterly,* 3d Series, XIII (1956), and an excerpt appears in C. & M., 862-64.

BOWEN, CATHERINE D. *John Adams and the American Revolution.* Boston, 1950.
BROWN, WELDON A. *Empire or Independence. . . . 1774–1783.* Baton Rouge, 1941.
BULLOCK, CHARLES JESSE. *Finances of the United States, 1775–89, with Especial Reference to the Budget.* Madison, Wis., 1895.
BURGOYNE, JOHN. *A State of the Expedition from Canada. . . .* London, 1780.
———. *Orderly Book. . . .* Albany, 1860.
BURNETT, EDMUND CODY. *The Continental Congress.* New York, 1941.
———. (ed.) *Letters of Members of the Continental Congress.* 8 vols. Washington, 1921–36.

The Cambridge History of the British Empire. General editors: J. HOLLAND ROSE, A. P. NEWTON, E. A. BENIANS. Vol. I., *The Old Empire from the Beginnings to 1783.* New York and Cambridge, 1929.
CAMPBELL, WILLIAM W. *The Annals of Tryon County.* 4th ed. New York, 1924.
CARRINGTON, HENRY B. *Battles of the American Revolution.* Rev. ed. New York, 1904.
———. *Battle Maps and Charts of the American Revolution.* New York, 1881.
———. *Washington, the Soldier.* Boston, 1898; New York, 1899.
CHANNING, EDWARD. *A History of the United States.* 6 vols. New York, 1905–25.
CLEMENTS COLLECTION. In the bibliographical notes to his *War for Independence* (Chicago, 1958) Mr. Howard H. Peckham, associate professor of history and director of the William L. Clements Library, University of Michigan, writes:

"Curiously, some of the most pertinent source material [on the American Revolution] did not come to light until the 1920's and early 1930's, when William L. Clements brought to the library he had established at the University of Michigan six great manuscript collections: the papers of Lord George Germain, colonial secretary, 1775–82; of Lord Shelburne, prime minister during the peace negotiations; of General Thomas Gage, British commander-in-chief in North America, 1763–75; of Sir Henry Clinton, commander here, 1778–82; of General Nathanael Greene, American commander in the southern theater; and the letters and diaries of the Hessian officers sent to Baron von Jungkenn, war minister of Hesse-Cassel." (P. 211)

Thus it is that anything written about the Revolution prior to the availability of the Clements Collection must be revised in the light of these new sources. (The papers of Carleton, commander in Canada and last British commander in chief in America, 1782–83, also came to light about the same time as the Clements Collection.) The first historian to use the new sources was Van Tyne, whose *War of Independence* was published in 1929. Troyer Anderson used them for his *Command of the Howe Brothers* (1936). Van Doren's *Secret History of the American Revolution* (1941) and *Mutiny in January* (1943), as well as Allen French's *General Gage's Informers* (1932), all used the Clements Collection to make major revisions in the history of the Revolution. The German papers were used by Bernhard Uhlendorf to cast new light and add significant detail to history of the era (see his works listed below).

Because of this new material the best general histories of the American Revolution are all of recent date: Commager and Morris, *The Spirit of 'Seventy-Six* (1958); John C. Miller, *Triumph of Freedom, 1775–1783* (1948); Willard M. Wallace, *Appeal to Arms* (1951); Lynn Montross, *Rag, Tag and Bobtail* (1952); Edmund S. Morgan, *The Birth of the Republic, 1763–89* (1956); D. S. Freeman,

George Washington (7 vols., 1948–57); John Richard Alden, *The American Revolution* (1954); Howard Peckham, *The War for Independence* (1958); Christopher Ward, *The War of the Revolution* (edited by John R. Alden, 2 vols., 1952); George F. Scheer and Hugh F. Rankin, *Rebels and Redcoats* (1957); and Rankin, *The American Revolution* (1964).

See Howard H. Peckham, *Guide to the Manuscript Collections in the William L. Clements Library* (Ann Arbor, 1942) and the work by the same title by William S. Ewing (Ann Arbor, 1953). The Sir Henry Clinton MSS were calendared by Randolph G. Adams in his *Headquarters Papers of the British Army in North America during the . . . American Revolution* (Ann Arbor, 1926), and this same authority, librarian of the Clements Library, compiled *The Papers of Lord George Germain; a brief description of the Stopford-Sackville papers now in the . . . Clements Library* (Ann Arbor, 1928). See also *Lexington to Fallen Timbers.*

CLINTON, SIR HENRY. *The American Rebellion: Sir Henry Clinton's Narrative of His Campaigns, 1775–1782, with an Appendix of Original Documents.* WILLIAM B. WILLCOX, ed. New Haven, 1954. See CLINTON article for evaluation of this work. The manuscript title of this work was *An Historical Detail of Seven Years Campaigns in North America from 1775 to 1782. . . .* The few historians who had access to the work before its publication in 1954—e.g., Troyer Anderson, author of *Howe Brothers. . . .*—cite it by its manuscript title (i.e., Clinton's *Historical Detail*).

C. & M. See COMMAGER and MORRIS, *Spirit of 'Seventy-Six. . . .*

COBBETT, WILLIAM. *The Parliamentary History of England from the Earliest Period to the Year 1803. . . .* 36 vols. London, 1806–20.

COLLINS, JAMES. *Autobiography of a Revolutionary Soldier.* JOHN M. ROBERTS (ed.). Clinton, La.: *Feliciana Democrat,* 1859.

COLLUM, RICHARD S. *History of the United States Marine Corps.* New York, 1903.

Colonial Arms. See work by H. L. PETERSON, below.

COMMAGER, HENRY STEELE. (ed.) *Documents of American History.* 5th ed. New York, 1949. My page references are to this edition. The 7th ed., revised, was published in 1963.

———. (With S. E. MORISON.) *The Growth of the American Republic.* 2 vols. 5th ed., rev. and enl., New York, 1962.

———. (With R. B. MORRIS.) *The Spirit of 'Seventy-Six: The Story of the American Revolution as told by Participants.* 2 vols. Indianapolis and New York, 1958. Cited as C. & M.

Concise D.A.H. See work mentioned above under J. T. ADAMS (ed.).

COOK, FRED J. *What Manner of Men.* New York, 1959. Sketches of 14 little-known heroes and heroines of the Revolution.

CORWIN, E. S. *French Policy and the American Alliance of 1778.* Princeton, 1916.

CREVECOEUR, HECTOR ST. JOHN DE. *Sketches of Eighteenth Century America.* New Haven, 1925.

CUMMINS, SAXE. (ed.) *Basic Writings of George Washington.* New York, 1948. The 242 items of this work were derived from the 39-vol. collection edited by Fitzpatrick. (See FITZPATRICK, below.)

CURTIS, EDWARD P. *The Organization of the British Army in the Revolution.* New Haven, 1926. See L. C. HATCH for comparable study of American Army.

CUTHBERT, NORMA B. *American Manuscript Collections in the Huntington Library for the History of the Seventeenth and Eighteenth Centuries.* San Marino, Calif., 1941.

D.A.B. See *Dictionary of American Biography,* below.

D.A.H. See J. T. ADAMS (ed.), *Dictionary of American History.*

DANDRIDGE, DANSKE. *American Prisoners of the Revolution.* Charlottesville, Va., 1911.

DARGAN, MARION. *Guide to American Biography* [1607–1933]. 2 vols in one. Albuquerque, 1949–52.

DAWSON, HENRY B. *Battles of the United States....* 2 vols. New York, 1858.

DECKER, MALCOLM. *Benedict Arnold: Son of the Havens.* Tarrytown, N.Y., 1932.

DE FONBLANQUE. See FONBLANQUE, below.

DELAWARE ARCHIVES. 5 vols. Wilmington, 1911–16.

DEMOND, ROBERT O. *The Loyalists of North Carolina During the Revolution.* Durham, N. C., 1940.

DEWEY, DAVIS RICH. *Financial History of the United States.* New York, 1931.

Dictionary of American Biography. 21 vols. New York, 1943. Planned by a committee of six scholars headed by Dr. J. FRANKLIN JAMESON, edited first by ALLEN JOHNSON of Yale (Vols. I–VI) and completed by his assistant, DUMAS MALONE of the U. of Va., this work comprises 13,633 biographies written by 2,243 contributors over a period of 10 years.

Dictionary of American History. See ADAMS, J. T. (ed.).

Dictionary of National Biography. 63 vols. London, 1885–1901. Containing about 30,000 sketches, this is the basic British biographical dictionary; it was published after Appleton's *Cyclopaedia of American Biography* and inspired the *D.A.B.* Many men are covered in all three works, so *D.N.B.* should not be overlooked as a source of data on "Americans."

DODDRIDGE, JOHN. *Notes on the Settlements and Indian Wars of the Western Parts of Virginia and Pennsylvania, 1763–1783.* Albany, 1876.

DONIOL, HENRI. *Histoire de la participation de la France à l'établissement des États-Unis d'Amérique.* 6 vols. Paris, 1884–92.

DOWNES, R. C. *Council Fires on the Upper Ohio.* Pittsburgh, 1940.

———. "Dunmore's War," *Miss. Valley Hist. Rev.,* XXI (1934), 311.

DRAPER, LYMAN C. *King's Mountain and Its Heroes.* Cincinnati, 1881.

DUMBAULD, EDWARD. *The Declaration of Independence and What It Means Today.* Norman, Okla., 1950. A scholarly analysis.

DUPUY, R. ERNEST and TREVOR N. DUPUY. *The Compact History of the Revolutionary War.* New York, 1963.

E.A.H. Short title for R. B. MORRIS (ed.), *Encyclopedia of American History* (see below).

EAST, ROBERT A. *Business Enterprise in the American Revolutionary Era.* New York, 1938. According to Augur (*op. cit.*), "East's meticulous treatment of the commercial activities of the Revolution... stands alone as a general account." Records of the transactions of Robert Morris and Jeremiah Wadsworth are among those examined.

E.B. Short title for *Encyclopaedia Britannica* (see below).

EELKING, MAX VON. *German Allied Troops in the North American War of Independence, 1775–1783.* Albany, 1893. This is the translation by J. G. Rosegarten of the two-volume German work published in Hanover in 1863.

――――. *Memoirs ... of Riedesel. ...* 2 vols. Albany, 1868. See article on RIEDESEL.

EGERTON, H. E. *The Causes and Character of the American Revolution.* Oxford, 1923.

EINSTEIN, LEWIS. *Divided Loyalties: Americans in England during the War of Independence.* Boston, 1933.

The Encyclopaedia Britannica. 29 vols. and index. 11th ed. Cambridge and New York, 1910–11. Unless otherwise specified all my citations of *E.B.* are to this edition.

FAŸ, BERNARD. *The Revolutionary Spirit in France and America ... at the End of the Eighteenth Century.* New York, 1927.

FISHER, SYDNEY GEORGE. *The Legendary and Myth-making Process in Histories of the American Revolution.* Philadelphia, 1912.

――――. *The Struggle for American Independence.* 2 vols. Philadelphia and London, 1908. In his preface the author calls this "a continuation and enlargement" of his *True History of the American Revolution* (Philadelphia, 1902).

FISKE, JOHN. *The American Revolution.* 2 vols. Boston, 1891; Boston and New York, 1898 and 1901.

――――. *The Critical Period of American History, 1783–1789.* Boston and New York, 1898.

――――. *Essays Historical and Literary.* 2 vols. New York, 1907.

FITZPATRICK, JOHN C. (ed.) *The Writings of George Washington from the Original Manuscript Sources 1745–1799.* 39 vols. Washington, 1931–44. Except for the material published separately by Fitzpatrick as *The Diaries of George Washington, 1748–1799* (4 vols., Boston, 1925), this collection of about 17,000 items includes every Washington manuscript known at the time the last volume went to press.

FLEMING, THOMAS J. *Now We Are Enemies: The Story of Bunker Hill.* New York, 1960.

FONBLANQUE, E. B. DE. *Political and Military Episodes ... Derived from the Life and Correspondence of ... Burgoyne.* London, 1876.

FORBES, ESTHER. *Paul Revere and the World He Lived In.* Boston, 1942.

FORCE, PETER. (ed.) *American Archives: Fourth Series, Containing a Documentary History of the English Colonies in North America from the King's Message to Parliament of March 7, 1774, to the Declaration of Independence by the United States.* 6 vols. Washington, 1837–46.

――――. (ed.) *American Archives: Fifth Series, Containing a Documentary History from ... July 4, 1776, to ... September 3, 1783.* 3 vols. Washington, 1848–53.

FORD, WORTHINGTON CHAUNCEY. *British Officers Serving in the American Revolution, 1774–1783.* Brooklyn, 1897. Compiled from the ARMY LISTS (see above), this was published in 250 copies. A comparable work for 1754–74 was published in Boston, 1894, in only 100 copies.

――――. (ed.) *Defenses in Philadelphia.* Brooklyn, 1897.

――――. (ed.) *Letters of William Lee, 1766–1783.* 2 vols. Brooklyn, 1892.

FORD, WORTHINGTON CHAUNCEY. (ed.) *Writings of George Washington*. 14 vols. New York, 1889–93. This was the most useful collection prior to publication of Fitzpatrick's edition, 1931–44.

FORTESCUE, SIR JOHN W. (ed.) *The Correspondence of King George the Third from 1760 to December, 1783*. London, 1927.

————. *A History of the British Army*, 13 vols. London, 1899–1930. Vol. III covers the period 1763–93.

FREEMAN, DOUGLAS SOUTHALL. *George Washington*. 7 vols. New York, 1948–57.

FRENCH, ALLEN. *The Day of Concord and Lexington*. Boston, 1925.

————. *The First Year of the American Revolution*. Boston, 1934.

————. *General Gage's Informers*. Ann Arbor, Mich., 1932.

————. *The Taking of Ticonderoga in 1775: The British Story; A Study of Captors and Captives*. Cambridge, Mass., 1928.

FROTHINGHAM, RICHARD. *The Alarm on the Night of April 18, 1775*. Boston, 1876.

————. *History of the Siege of Boston*. 4th ed. Boston, 1873.

————. *Life and Times of Joseph Warren*. Boston. 1865.

————. *The Rise of the Republic of the United States*. 10th ed. Boston, 1910.

FROTHINGHAM, T. G. *Washington, Commander in Chief*. Boston, 1930.

GANOE, WILLIAM A. *The History of the United States Army*. New York, 1924.

GARDEN, ALEXANDER. *Anecdotes of the American Revolution*. 3 vols. Brooklyn, 1865.

GARDINER, ASA BIRD. *The Order of the Cincinnati in France. Its Origin and History, with the Military or Naval Records of the French Members*. Rhode Island State Society of the Cincinnati, 1905.

GIBBES, R. W. (ed.) *Documentary History of the American Revolution: Consisting of Letters and Papers Relating to the Contest for Liberty, Chiefly in South Carolina*.... 3 vols. New York, 1853–57.

GILMORE, JAMES R. *The Rear-Guard of the Revolution*. New York, 1897.

GIPSON, LAWRENCE HENRY. *The British Empire before the American Revolution: Provincial Characteristics and Sectional Tendencies*.... 9 vols. Caldwell, Idaho, 1936–56.

————. *The Coming of the Revolution, 1763–1775*. New York, 1954.

GORDON, WILLIAM. *History*.... London, 1788; New York, 1789 and 1794. See biographical sketch of author in body of this work.

GOTTSCHALK, LOUIS R. *Lafayette Between the American and the French Revolutions (1783–1789)*. Chicago, 1950.

————. *Lafayette and the Close of the American Revolution*. Chicago, 1942.

————. *Lafayette Comes to America*. Chicago, 1935.

————. *Lafayette Joins the American Army*. Chicago, 1937.

See article on LAFAYETTE MYTH for summary of Gottschalk's conclusions.

GRAHAM, GERALD S. *British Policy and Canada, 1774–1791*.... New York, 1930.

————. *Empire of the North Atlantic; the Maritime Struggle for North America*. Toronto, 1950.

GREENE, EVARTS BOUTELL. *The Foundation of American Nationality*. Rev. ed. New York, 1935. Published in 1922 as Volume I of *A Short History of the American People*.

————. *Provincial America. 1690–1740*. New York, 1905.

GREENE, EVARTS BOUTELL. *The Provincial Governor in the English Colonies of North America*. New York, 1898.

——. With R. B. MORRIS. (eds.) *Guide to the Principal Sources for Early American History (1600–1800) in the City of New York*. New York, 1929; rev. ed., 1952.

GREENE, FRANCIS VINTON. *The Revolutionary War and the Military Policy of the United States*. New York, 1911.

GRIFFIN, GRACE GARDNER. *A Guide to Manuscripts Relating to American History in British Repositories Reproduced for the Division of Manuscripts of the Library of Congress*. Washington, 1946. See also the guides prepared by C. M. ANDREWS.

—— *et al*. (eds.) *Writings on American History*. Princeton, New York, New Haven, Washington, 1904– .

GUTTRIDGE, GEORGE H. *David Hartley, M. P., an Advocate of Conciliation, 1774–1783*. Berkeley, 1926.

HADDEN, JAMES M. *A Journal Kept in Canada and Upon Burgoyne's Campaign in 1776 and 1777. Also Orders kept by Him and Issued by Sir Guy Carleton, Lieut. General John Burgoyne and Major General William Phillips in 1776, 1777, and 1778, with an explanatory chapter and notes by Horatio Rogers*. Albany, 1884.

HAIMAN, MIECISLAUS. *Kosciuszko in the American Revolution*. New York, 1943.

——. *Kosciuszko, Leader and Exile*. New York, 1946.

Handbook of American Indians. See HODGE, F. W., below.

HANDLIN, OSCAR, *et al. Harvard Guide to American History*. Cambridge, Mass., 1954. As evolved from the 1896 Harvard *Guide* of Channing and Hart, this work is in three parts: a series of 66 essays and special lists, a sequence of 211 bibliographical sections covering American history in chronological and topical order, and a detailed index. "The student who can afford only one reference book in general American history would find this his natural choice." (Lib. of Cong., *Guide*.)

Harvard Guide to American History. See HANDLIN, OSCAR, *et al*.

HATCH, LOUIS C. *The Administration of the American Revolutionary Army*. New York, 1904. See E. P. CURTIS on British organization.

HEATH, WILLIAM. *Memoirs of Major-General Heath. Containing Anecdotes, Details of Skirmishes, Battles, and other Military Events During the American War*. Boston, 1798.

——. *Memoirs of Major-General William Heath, by Himself, to which is added the Accounts of the Battle of Bunker Hill by Generals Dearborn, Lee and Wilkinson*. WILLIAM ABBATT (ed.). New York, 1901.

——. *Heath's Memoirs of the American War*. Reprinted from the original edition of 1798 with introduction and notes by RUFUS ROCKWELL WILSON. New York, 1904. My citations are from this edition of the work, whose value is evidenced by the above printing record.

HEITMAN, FRANCIS B. *Historical Register of Officers of the Continental Army....* New, Revised, and Enlarged Ed. Washington, 1914. Containing the Revolutionary War records of 14,000 officers, including many of the militia, this edition supersedes that of 1893. It is based on official Army records, and the short biographical sketches include the name as shown in these records, the state of commission, ranks held, and, in some instances, the date of death. This section of Heitman's work, pages 62 through 611, is invaluable. Other sections include Cont'l. generals in order of seniority (pp. 9-10), the list of military secretaries and A.D.C. to Washington (p. 13), troops at Valley Forge, 1777–78 (pp. 11-12), and a "Chronological Roster of Field Officers of the [Cont'l.] Line . . . arranged by States and Regiments" (pp. 14–61). This last section is extremely valuable not only in double-checking the assignments of FIELD OFFICERS (see article) but also as a roster of regiments. Heitman also includes chronological and alpha-betical lists of "battles, actions, etc." These lists have been slightly amended and republished in the *Army Almanac,* and I have cited the latter authority as "*A. A.*–Heitman list of battles."

HENRY, JOHN JOSEPH. [*Accurate and Interesting*] *Account of Arnold's Campaign Against Quebec.* . . . Lancaster, Pa., 1812, and (with omission of bracketed por-tion of title) Albany, 1877. Son of inventor William Henry (1729–1786) of Lancaster, the author took part in Arnold's March as a rifleman, was captured at Quebec, 1 Jan. '76, and remained a prisoner nine months. After the war he distinguished himself as a jurist.

HIGGINBOTHAM, DON. "American Historians and the Military History of the American Revolution." *American Historical Review,* LXX, No. 1 (October 1964). This article is valuable as a thorough bibliographical essay.

———. *Daniel Morgan: Revolutionary Rifleman.* Chapel Hill, N.C., 1961.

HILL, HELEN. (MILLER, HELEN DAY [HILL]). *George Mason, Constitutionalist.* Cambridge, Mass., 1938.

HODGE, FREDERICK WEBB. (ed.) *Handbook of American Indians, North of Mexico.* 2 vols. Washington, 1907–10. Reprinted, New York, 1960.

HOWARD, GEORGE E. *Preliminaries of the Revolution, 1763–1775.* New York, 1905.

HUFELAND, OTTO. *Westchester County* [N.Y.] *During the American Revolution, 1775–1783.* New York, 1926.

HUNT, GAILLARD. (ed.) See *Journals of the Cont'l. Cong.*

HUNT, GEORGE T. *The Wars of the Iroquois.* . . . Madison, Wis., 1940.

HUNTINGTON LIBRARY COLLECTIONS. See N. B. CUTHBERT.

INSTITUTE OF EARLY AMERICAN HISTORY AND CULTURE. *William and Mary Quar-terly, a Magazine of Early American History.* Third Series. Williamsburg, Va., 1944– . A continuation of the magazine listed under WILLIAM AND MARY COLLEGE, below, and *Williamsburg Restoration Historical Studies* (Williams-burg, 1940–1943), this magazine of scholarly studies on all aspects of American history to 1815 is an indispensable source for students of that period. The in-stitute was established jointly by the college and Colonial Williamsburg, Inc.

JAMES, JAMES ALTON. (ed.) *The Clark Papers,* 2 vols. Springfield, Ill., 1912–26.

———. *The Life of George Rogers Clark.* Chicago, 1928.

See evaluation of these works in article on CLARK.

———. *Oliver Pollock.* . . . New York, 1937.

JAMESON, JOHN FRANKLIN. *The American Revolution Considered as a Social Movement.* Princeton, 1926.

———. (ed.) *Original Narratives.* . . . (See below)

JENSEN, MERRILL. *The Articles of Confederation; an Interpretation of the Social-constitutional History of the American Revolution, 1774–1781.* Madison, Wis., 1948.

——. *The New Nation; a History of the United States during the Confederation.* New York, 1905.

JOHNSTON, HENRY P. *The Battle of Harlem Heights, September 16, 1776, With a Review of the Events of the Campaign.* New York, 1897.

——. "The Campaign of 1776 Around New York and Brooklyn. Including a New and Circumstantial Account of the Battle of Long Island and the Loss of New York, With a Review of Events to the Close of the Year." *Memoirs of the Long Island Historical Society,* Vol. III. Brooklyn: Long Island Historical Society, 1878.

——. *The Storming of Stony Point on the Hudson, midnight, July 15, 1779; its Importance in the Light of Unpublished Documents.* New York, 1900.

——. *The Yorktown Campaign and the Surrender of Cornwallis, 1781.* New York, 1881.

JONES, THOMAS. *History of New York during the Revolutionary War.* Edited by Edward Floyd de Lancey. 2 vols., 1879.

Journals of the Continental Congress, 1774–1789. GAILLARD HUNT (ed.) 34 vols. Washington, 1904–37.

KELLOGG, LOUISE PHELPS, with R. G. THWAITES, co-editor. *Dunmore's War.* Madison, Wisc., 1905.

——. (With R. G. THWAITES.) *The Revolution on the Upper Ohio.* Madison, 1908.

KERR, WILFRED BENTON. *Bermuda and the American Revolution: 1760–1783.* Princeton, 1936.

KNOLLENBERG, BERNHARD. *The Origin of the American Revolution: 1759–1766.* New York, 1960.

——. *Washington and the Revolution.* New York, 1940.

LABAREE, LEONARD WOODS. (ed.) *The Autobiography of Benjamin Franklin.* New Haven, 1964.

——. (ed.) *Franklin Papers.* New Haven, 1959– . Seven vols. published by 1963.

——. *Royal Government in America....* New Haven, 1930.

LAMB, ROGER. *An Original and Authentic Journal of Occurrences During the Late American War from its Commencement to the Year 1783.* Dublin, 1809.

——. *Memoir of His Own Life.* Dublin, 1811.
The famous Sgt. Lamb of the Royal Welch Fusiliers (23rd Foot) was born in Dublin in 1756. He took part in Burgoyne's Offensive, escaped to N.Y.C., carried the regimental colors at Camden, subsequently served temporarily as regimental surgeon (although he had no medical training), saved Cornwallis from capture at Guilford, was surrendered at Yorktown, and escaped with seven men to join Carleton in N.Y.C. His *Journal* and *Memoir* are among the most valuable works on the Revolution.

LASSERAY, ANDRÉ. *Les Français sous les treize étoiles 1775–1783.* 2 vols. Paris, 1935. Biographical sketches of French participants are drawn from archives, official records, and—to a much lesser extent—from family records.

LEARNED, M. D. *Guide to the Manuscript Materials Relating to American History in the German State Archives.* Washington, 1912.

LECKY, W. E. HARTPOLE. *The American Revolution, 1763–1783.* New York, 1898.

LEE, HENRY ("Light Horse"). *Memoirs of the War in the Southern Department of the United States.* Rev. ed. New York, 1869. First published in 1827.

LELAND, WALDO G., and MENG, J. J. *Guide to Materials for American History in the Libraries and Archives of Paris.* 4 vols.

LERWILL, LEONARD L. *The Personnel Replacement System in the United States Army.* Washington, 1954.

Lexington to Fallen Timbers, 1775–1794. Selected and described by RANDOLPH G. ADAMS and HOWARD H. PECKHAM, this 41-page work is subtitled "Episodes from the Earliest History of our MILITARY FORCES. Illustrated by Original Maps and Papers in the Clements Library of the University of Michigan." Ann Arbor, 1942.

LIBRARY OF CONGRESS. *A Guide to the Study of the U.S.A.: Representative Books Reflecting the Development of American Life and Thought.* Washington, 1960.

LIBRARY OF CONGRESS MANUSCRIPTS. Among the tremendously valuable holdings are the George Washington Papers and very important Thomas Jefferson, James Madison, and James Monroe collections. The Papers of the Continental Congress, a gigantic body of documents, were held there until the late 1950's, when they were transferred to the National Archives. The Library also holds reproductions of MSS from British collections: see G. G. Griffin's *Guide.* A *Handbook of Manuscripts in the Library of Congress* was published in 1918, and the American Historical Association's *Annual Report,* 1930 and 1937, contain lists of the MSS collections to July 1938. The Library also has published *Manuscripts in Public Collections in the United States* (Washington, 1924).

LILLARD, RICHARD G. *American Life in Autobiography, a Descriptive Guide.* Stanford, 1956. An annotated bibliography of over 400 entries arranged by occupation and indexed.

LITTLE, SHELBY (MELTON). *George Washington.* New York, 1929.

LOCKE, JOHN. His three principal works on the principles of government are covered in the article LOCKE AND THE AMERICAN REVOLUTION.

LOKKE, CARL L. *France and the Colonial Question: A Study of Contemporary French Opinion, 1763–1801.* New York, 1932.

LOSSING, BENSON J. *The Life and Times of Philip Schuyler.* 2 vols. 1860–73.

——. *The Pictorial Field Book of the Revolution; or, Illustrations, by Pen and Pencil, of the History, Biography, Scenery, Relics, and Traditions of the War for Independence.* 2 vols. New York, 1851.

LOWELL, E. J. *The Hessians . . . in the Revolutionary War.* New York, 1884. See article on GERMAN MERCENARIES.

LUNDIN, LEONARD. *Cockpit of the American Revolution: The War for Independence in New Jersey.* Princeton, 1940.

MACDONALD, WILLIAM. *Documentary Source Book of American History, 1606–1926.* New York, 1926; 3d ed., 1950.

MACKENZIE, FREDERICK. *A British Fusilier in Revolutionary Boston.* Cambridge, Mass., 1926.

——. *Diary of Frederick Mackenzie, Giving a Daily Narrative of his Military Service as an Officer of the Regiment of Royal Welch Fusiliers During the*

Years 1775–1781 in Massachusetts, Rhode Island and New York. 2 vols. Cambridge, Mass., 1930.

The first work, edited by ALLEN FRENCH, deals only with the Boston part of the diary. The 2-vol. *Diary* is the complete work but omits the valuable map by Mackenzie of the Concord fight; French includes it in his *Informers.*

MACKENZIE, RODERICK. *Strictures on Lt. Col. Tarleton's History. . . . To Which is added, a Detail of the Siege of Ninety Six, and the Recapture of the Island of New-Providence* [Bahamas]. London, 1787.

MACKESY, PIERS. *The War for America, 1775–1783.* Cambridge, Mass.: 1964. See also this British author's "British Strategy in the War of American Independence," *Yale Review,* LII (Summer 1963), 539–57.

MAHAN, ALFRED THAYER. *The Influence of Sea Power upon History, 1660–1783.* Boston, 1890 (1st ed.) and 1918 (12th ed.).

———. *The Major Operations of the Navies in the War of American Independence.* London, 1913.

———. *Major Operations of the Royal Navy, 1762–1783.* Boston, 1898.

MALONE, DUMAS, and RAUCH, BASIL. *American Origins, to 1789.* New York, 1960. See also *Dictionary of American Biography.*

MANUSCRIPT COLLECTIONS AND GUIDES. Of first importance are British official records, which have been described in the works of C. M. Andrews (*q.v.*) and many of which have been transcribed for the Library of Congress—see G. G. GRIFFIN, *Guide*—or acquired, as in the case of the Clements Collection (*q.v.*). Next in importance are the Library of Congress Manuscripts (*q.v.*) and those in the National Archives (*q.v.*). Guides to materials in foreign archives bearing on U.S. history have been compiled by H. C. Bell (British West Indies), M. D. Learned (German), Leland and Meng (Paris), D. M. Matteson (European), D. W. Parker (Canadian), J. A. Robertson and W. R. Shepherd (Spanish). All these authors and their works are listed separately. Other guides are listed under the following headings within this bibliography: American Philosophical Society (of Philadelphia), Huntington Library (of San Marino, Calif.), New York Public Library, Pennsylvania Historical Society, Massachusetts Historical Society, Maryland Historical Society, N.C. Historical Commission, S.C. Historical Society, Virginia Historical Society, Williamsburg (Va.) Collections, and Wisconsin State Historical Society. Other collections are held by the Chicago Historical Society, Columbia University, the Houghton Library at Harvard, The Pierpont Morgan Library in N.Y.C., the Morristown National Historical Park (which is building an important collection), and the Philadelphia Free Library (Benjamin Rush Papers).

At the end of biographical articles in the body of this book will be found references to MSS, when such papers are known to exist.

See H. P. BEERS, "The Papers . . . ," above, for guide to papers of British commanders in chief.

MARTIN, JOSEPH PLUMB. *Private Yankee Doodle.* Edited by GEORGE F. SCHEER. Boston, 1962. This is the anonymous *A Narrative of Some of the Adventures, Danger, and Sufferings of a Revolutionary Soldier* (Hallowell, Me., 1830) sometimes attributed to James Sullivan Martin but recently traced by the N.Y. Hist. Soc. to Pvt. Joseph Plumb Martin.

MARYLAND HISTORICAL SOCIETY. See biographical sketch of Otho Holland

WILLIAMS. State documents of the Revolution are catalogued in *Publications of the Hall of Records* (Annapolis, 1942–50).

MASSACHUSETTS HISTORICAL SOCIETY. Founded in Boston in 1791, this society houses the most important collection of American manuscripts outside the Library of Congress. The principal ones are listed in *Handbook of the ... Society, 1791–1948* (Boston, 1949). Serial publications are:

————. *Collections.* Boston, 1792– .

————. *Proceedings.* Boston, 1879– .

MATTESON, D. M. *List of Manuscripts Concerning American History Preserved in European Libraries.* Washington, 1925.

MATTHEWS, WILLIAM. *American Diaries; an Annotated Bibliography of American Diaries Written Prior to the Year 1861.* Berkeley, 1945.

————. *Canadian Diaries and Autobiographies.* Berkeley, 1950.

MCCRADY, EDWARD. *The History of South Carolina in the Revolution, 1775–1780.* New York, 1901.

————. *The History of South Carolina in the Revolution, 1780–1783.* New York, 1902.

MILLER, DAVID HUNTER. (ed.) *Treaties and Other International Acts....* 8 vols. Washington, 1931–48.

MILLER, JOHN C. *Origins of the American Revolution.* Boston, 1943.

————. *Sam Adams, Pioneer in Propaganda.* New York, 1936; Stanford, 1960.

————. *Triumph of Freedom, 1775–1783.* Boston, 1948.

MONAGHAN, FRANK. *French Travellers in the United States, 1765–1932, A Bibliography.* New York, 1933 and reprinted with negligible additions, 1961.

MONTROSS, LYNN. *Rag, Tag and Bobtail: The Story of the Continental Army, 1775–1783.* New York, 1952.

————. *The Reluctant Rebels: The Story of the Continental Congress, 1774–1789.* New York, 1950.

————. *War Through the Ages.* Rev. and enl. ed. New York and London, 1944.

MOORE, FRANK. (comp.) *Diary of the American Revolution.* 2 vols. New York, 1858. Selections primarily from newspapers of 1775–81.

————. (ed.) *Songs and Ballads of the American Revolution.* New York, 1856.

MORGAN, EDMUND S. *The Birth of the Republic, 1763–89.* Chicago, 1956.

————, and MORGAN, HELEN M. *The Stamp Act Crisis; Prologue to Revolution.* Chapel Hill, N.C., 1953.

MORGAN, LEWIS H. *League of the Ho-de-no sau-nee, or Iroquois.* 2 vols. New Haven, reprinted from 1904 edition in 1954. See also, HUNT, GEORGE T., above.

MORISON, SAMUEL ELIOT. (ed.) *Sources and Documents Illustrating the American Revolution, 1764–1788.* 1929.

————. *The Young Man Washington.* Cambridge, Mass., 1932. A 43-page study.

————. (With HENRY STEELE COMMAGER.) *The Growth of the American Republic.* 2 vols. 5th ed., rev. and enl., New York, 1962.

————. (ed.). *The Parkman Reader.* Boston, 1955. See PARKMAN.

MORRIS, RICHARD B. *The American Revolution: A Short History,* Princeton, 1955.

————. (ed.) *Encyclopedia of American History.* Rev. and enl. edition, for which HENRY STEELE COMMAGER was consultant editor. New York, 1961. My citations are to the 1953 edition.

————. (With HENRY STEELE COMMAGER.) *The Spirit of 'Seventy-Six....* See COMMAGER for this work, which I have cited (often) as C. & M. Professor

Morris of Columbia University has recently edited a one-volume edition of Trevelyan, *The American Revolution*. (New York, 1964).

———. (With E. B. GREENE.) *Guide to the Principal Sources for Early American History (1600–1800) in the City of New York*. New York, 1929; rev. ed., 1952.

———. *The Peacemakers: The Great Powers and American Independence*. New York, 1965.

MUMBY, FRANK ARTHUR. *George III. and the American Revolution: The Beginnings*. London, 1923.

MURDOCK, HAROLD. *The Nineteenth of April, 1775*. Boston, 1925. See comment at end of article on LEXINGTON AND CONCORD.

———. *Bunker Hill*. Boston, 1927.

NATIONAL ARCHIVES. The Papers of the Continental Congress have been transferred from the Library of Congress to this depository, and there is some other Revolutionary War material. See *Guide to the Records in the National Archives*, Washington, 1948.

NATIONAL PARK SERVICE. A series of brief, authoritative historical handbooks includes the following titles: *Jamestown, Saratoga, Morristown, Yorktown, Independence, Kings Mountain*, and *Guilford Courthouse*. Designed for use of visitors to these historical sites, the inexpensive pamphlets may be purchased also from the Supt. of Docs., Washington, D.C., 20402.

NEVINS, ALLAN. *The American States During and After the Revolution, 1775–1789*. New York, 1924.

NEW YORK PUBLIC LIBRARY COLLECTIONS. These include the papers of Samuel Adams, Philip Schuyler, the Livingstons, the diary of William Smith, and the Bancroft transcripts of Loyalist documents from the British Public Record Office. These and other N.Y.C. manuscripts are in the *Guide* edited by E. B. GREENE and R. B. MORRIS, which is identified above.

NICKERSON, HOFFMAN. *The Turning Point of the Revolution or Burgoyne in America*. Boston, 1928.

NILES, HEZEKIAH. *Principles and Acts of the Revolution in America: or, An Attempt to Collect and Preserve some of the Speeches, Orations, & Proceedings, with Sketches and Remarks on Men and Things, and other Fugitive or Neglected Pieces....* Baltimore, 1822. The compiler's grandson, SAMUEL V. NILES, brought out a revised edition, *Centennial Offering....* (New York, 1876), which rearranged the contents and resulted in a more conveniently organized book.

NOAILLES, VICOMTE DE. *Marins et soldats français en Amérique pendant la Guerre de l'Indépendance des États-Unis*. Paris, 1872. English translation, Philadelphia, 1895.

NORTH CAROLINA HISTORICAL COMMISSION. DAVID L. CORBITT (ed.), *Calendars of Manuscript Collections....* Raleigh, 1926; *Guide to the Manuscript Collections....* Raleigh, 1942. Other works pertaining to N.C. manuscripts are: *Guide to the Manuscripts in the Southern Historical Collection of the University of North Carolina*, in *James Sprunt Studies...*, XXIV, No. 2, Chapel Hill, 1941; and NANNIE M. TILLEY and NORMA LEE GOODWIN, *Guide to the Manuscript Collections in the Duke University Library*, in Trinity College Historical Society *Papers*, Serial XXVII-XXVIII, Durham, 1947. (Alden, *South*, 401-2) See also

Hugh T. Lefler, *A Guide to the Study and Reading of North Carolina History*, Chapel Hill, 1955.

N.P.S. See NATIONAL PARK SERVICE.

ONDERDONK, HENRY. *Revolutionary Incidents of Suffolk and Kings Counties: With an Account of the Battle of Long Island and the British Prisons and Prison-Ships at New-York*. New York, 1849.

Original Narratives of Early American History. 19 vols. New York, 1906–17. Reproduced under the auspices of the Amer. Hist. Assoc. and edited by JOHN FRANKLIN JAMESON. Most of its volumes were reprinted by Barnes and Noble.

OSGOOD, HERBERT LEVI. *The American Colonies in the Seventeenth Century*. 3 vols. New York, 1930.

———. *The American Colonies in the Eighteenth Century*. 4 vols. New York, 1924.

Oxford Universal Dictionary on Historical Principles. C. T. ONIONS (ed.), 3d edition. Oxford, 1955. Cited as *O.U.D.* The date following this citation is the earliest appearance of the word or term in the sense used.

PARGELLIS, S. M. (ed.) *Lord Loudoun in North America*. New Haven, 1933.

———. *Military Affairs in North America, 1748–1765*. London and New York, 1936.

———, and D. J. MEDLEY. *Bibliography of British History: . . . 1714–1789*. 1951.

PARKER, D. W. *Guide to the Materials for United States History in Canadian Archives*. Washington, 1913.

PARKMAN, FRANCIS. *Works*. 12 vols. New Library ed., Boston, 1902–3. First published during the period 1851–92, and known collectively as *France and England in North America*, these 12 volumes have been condensed into the following books: JOHN TEBBEL, *The Battle for North America* (Garden City, N.Y., 1948) and S. E. MORISON, *The Parkman Reader* (Boston, 1955).

The Parliamentary Register. . . . See JOHN ALMON (ed.).

PAZ, JULIAN. *Catálogo de manuscritos de América existentes en la Biblioteca Nacional*. Madrid, 1933.

PECKHAM, HOWARD H. *The Colonial Wars, 1689–1762*. Chicago, 1964.

———. (co-ed.) *Lexington to Fallen Timbers*. (See entry above.)

———. *Pontiac and the Indian Uprising*. Princeton, 1947.

———. *The War for Independence: A Military History*. Chicago, 1958.

Pennsylvania Archives. SAMUEL HAZARD (ed.). 1st series. 12 vols. Philadelphia, 1852–56.

PENNSYLVANIA, HISTORICAL SOCIETY OF. The Anthony Wayne Papers are among the documents held by this institution and described in *Guide to the Manuscript Collections of the Historical Society of Pennsylvania*. 2d ed., Philadelphia, 1949.

Pennsylvania in the War of the Revolution. . . . JOHN BLAIR LINN and WILLIAM H. EGLE (eds.). 2 vols. Harrisburg, 1880. These volumes are the 2d series of the *Pennsylvania Archives*.

PERKINS, JAMES B. *France in the American Revolution*. Boston, 1911.

PETERSON, HAROLD L. *Arms and Armor in Colonial America 1526–1783*. Harrisburg, Pa., 1956.

PHILLIPS, PAUL C. *The West in the Diplomacy of the American Revolution*. Urbana, 1913.

PONTGIBAUD, CHEVALIER DE. A *French Volunteer in the War of Independence.* Translated from the French. New York, 1898.

P.R.O. Public Record Office. See C. M. ANDREWS, *Guide.* . . . , above.

QUAIFE, MILO M., WEIG, MELVIN J., and APPLEMAN, ROY E. *The History of the United States Flag from the Revolution to the Present.* . . . New York, 1961.

RANKIN, HUGH F. *The American Revolution.* New York, 1964.

———. (with GEORGE F. SCHEER.) *Rebels and Redcoats.* Cleveland and New York, 1957.

The Remembrancer. . . . See John ALMON (ed.).

ROBERTS, KENNETH LEWIS. *The Battle of Cowpens: The Great Morale Builder.* New York, 1958.

———. *March to Quebec.* New York, 1938; revised 1940. This is a valuable collection of journals and documents; see article ARNOLD'S MARCH TO QUEBEC.

ROBERTSON, ARCHIBALD. *Diaries and Sketches in America.* New York, 1930. The author was a British Maj. and Deputy Q.M.G. to Adm. Arbuthnot.

ROBERTSON, J. A. *List of Documents in Spanish Archives Relating to the History of the United States,* . . . *Printed or in American Libraries.* Washington, 1910.

ROBSON, ERIC. *The American Revolution in its Political and Military Aspects, 1763–1783.* London, 1955; Hamden, Conn., 1965.

ROOSEVELT, THEODORE. *The Winning of the West.* 4 vols. New York, 1889–96.

RUTLEDGE, JOSEPH L. *Century of Conflict; the Struggle between the French and British in Colonial America.* Garden City, N.Y., 1956.

RYERSON, EGERTON. *Loyalists of America.* Toronto, 1880.

SABINE, LORENZO. *The American Loyalists, or Biographical Sketches of Adherents to the British Crown in the War of the Revolution; Alphabetically Arranged; with a Preliminary Historical Essay.* Boston, 1847. A 2-vol. edition was published in 1864.

SACHSE, WILLIAM L. *The Colonial American in Britain.* Madison, Wis., 1956.

SAVELLE, MAX. "Nationalism and Other Loyalties in the American Revolution." *American Historical Review,* LXVII, No. 4 (July 1962), 901–23.

SAWYER, CHARLES W. *Firearms in American History, 1600–1800.* Boston, 1910.

SCHAW, JANET. See ANDREWS, E. M. (ed.). *Journal of a Lady.* . . . above.

SCHEER, GEORGE F. (ed.) See J. P. MARTIN, above.

SCHEER, GEORGE F., and RANKIN, HUGH F. *Rebels and Redcoats.* Cleveland and New York, 1957. This is the story of the American Revolution as told by eyewitnesses and participants, famous and obscure, and with their stories tied together by narrative bridges. I cite it as S. & R. This work and C. & M. contain some duplication, but they complement each other remarkably well.

SCHLESINGER, ARTHUR MEIER. *The Colonial Merchants and the American Revolution, 1763–1766.* New York, 1918 and 1939.

Scribner's Atlas. See *Atlas of American History,* above.

SHEPHERD, W. R. *Guide to the Materials for the History of the United States in Spanish Archives.* Washington, 1907. See also JULIAN PAZ, *Catálogo.* . . .

SIMCOE, JOHN GRAVES. *Military Journal.* . . . See biographical sketch.

SMITH, JUSTIN H. *Arnold's March from Cambridge to Quebec.* New York, 1903.

———. *Our Struggle for the Fourteenth Colony.* 2 vols. New York, 1907.

SOMERVELL, D. C. *A History of the United States to 1941*. London, 1942 and 1955.
SOUTH CAROLINA HISTORICAL SOCIETY. HELEN G. MCCORMICK, "A Provisional Guide to the Manuscripts in the South Carolina Historical Society," *S.C. Historical and Genealogical Magazine* (Charleston, 1900—), XLV (1944)—XLVIII (1947). See also JAMES H. EASTERBY, *Guide to the Study and Reading of South Carolina History* (Columbia, 1950), and ROBERT H. WOODY, "The Public Records of South Carolina," in *American Archivist* (Menasha, Cedar Rapids, 1938—), II (1939).

SPARKS, JARED. (ed.). *The Correspondence of the American Revolution: Being Letters of Eminent Men to George Washington.* . . . 4 vols. Boston, 1853.

———. (ed.) *The Diplomatic Correspondence of the American Revolution.* 12 vols. Boston, 1829–30.

———. (ed.) *Library of American Biography.* 25 vols. Boston and London, 1834–48. Sparks contributed several biographies, including that of Arnold (1835).

———. *The Life of Gouverneur Morris.* 3 vols. Boston, 1832.

———. (ed.) *The Works of Benjamin Franklin.* 10 vols. Boston, 1836–40.

———. (ed.) *The Writings of George Washington.* 12 vols. Boston, 1834–37.
See article on BRANDYWINE, second footnote on p. 107.

SPECTOR, MARGARET MARION. *The American Department of the British Government, 1768–1782.* New York, 1940.

S. & R. See SCHEER and RANKIN, above.

STEDMAN, CHARLES. *History of the . . . War* (1792). See biographical sketch.

STEELE, MATTHEW F. *American Campaigns.* Washington, 1909 and 1951.

STEVENS, BENJAMIN FRANKLIN. (ed.) *The Campaign in Virginia 1781, An Exact Reprint of Six Rare Pamphlets on the Clinton-Cornwallis Controversy.* . . . 2 vols. London, 1888. [Binder's title: *Clinton-Cornwallis Controversy.*]

———. (ed.) *Facsimiles of Manuscripts in European Archives Relating to America, 1773–1783.* 26 vols. London, 1889-1895.

STILES, EZRA. *The Literary Diary of Ezra Stiles.* FRANKLIN B. DEXTER (ed.). 3 vols. New York, 1901.

———. *Extracts from the Itineraries and Other Miscellanies of Ezra Stiles . . . with Selections from His Correspondence.* FRANKLIN B. DEXTER (ed.). New Haven, 1916.

———. *Letters & Papers of Ezra Stiles.* ISABEL M. CALDER (ed.). New Haven, 1933.
See biographical sketch of STILES in body of this work.

STONE, WILLIAM LEETE. *Border Wars of the American Revolution.* 2 vols. New York, 1900. First published in 1843; republished 1864.

STRAIT, NEWTON A. *Alphabetical List of Battles, 1754–1900.* Washington, 1900. Compiled by a clerk in the Bureau of Pensions, Department of the Interior, this work is useful despite its many errors since most of the latter can be readily spotted.

STREET, JAMES. *The Revolutionary War, Being a De-Mythed Account.* . . . New York, 1954.

STRYKER, WILLIAM S. *The Battle of Monmouth.* Princeton, 1927.

———. *The Battles of Trenton and Princeton.* Boston and New York, 1898.

———. *The Forts on the Delaware.* Trenton, 1901.

SULLIVAN, KATHRYN. *Maryland and France, 1774–1789.* Philadelphia, 1936.

SWIGGETT, HOWARD. *War out of Niagara: Walter Butler and the Tory Rangers.* New York, 1933.

TARLETON, BANASTRE. *A History of the Campaigns of 1780 and 1781....* See biographical article.

THARP, LOUISE HALL. *The Baroness and the General* [Riedesel]. Boston and Toronto, 1962.

THWAITES, REUBEN GOLD (ed.). *Early Western Travels, 1748–1846.* 32 vols. Cleveland, 1904–7.
   See LOUISE P. KELLOGG (above), with whom he collaborated on two works.

TOLLES, FRED B. "The American Revolution Considered as a Social Movement: A Reevaluation." *American Historical Review,* LX, No. 1 (October 1954).

TOURTELLOT, ARTHUR BERNON. *William Diamond's Drum—The Beginning of the War of the American Revolution.* New York, 1959.

TREVELYAN, GEORGE OTTO. *The American Revolution.* 6 vols., including *George III and Charles Fox,* numbered V and VI. London, 1909–14. A one-volume edition, edited by RICHARD B. MORRIS, is *The American Revolution* (New York, 1964).

TYLER, MOSES COIT. *The Literary History of the American Revolution, 1763–1783.* 2 vols. New York, 1941.

UHLENDORF, BERNHARD A. (ed. and trans.) *Revolution in America: Baurmeister Journals—Confidential Letters and Journals 1776–1784 of Adjutant General Major Baurmeister of the Hessian Forces.* New Brunswick, N.J., 1957.
———. (Ed. and trans.) *The Siege of Charleston, with an Account of the Province of South Carolina: the Von Jungkenn Papers in the Williams L. Clements Library.* Ann Arbor, 1938.

UPTON, EMORY. *The Military Policy of the United States since 1775.* Washington, 1904.

VAN DOREN, CARL. *Mutiny in January; The Story of a Crisis in the Continental Army now for the first time fully told from many hitherto unknown or neglected sources both American and British.* New York, 1943.
———. *Secret History of the American Revolution; an Account of the Conspiracies of Benedict Arnold and Numerous Others drawn from the Secret Service Papers of the British Headquarters in North America now for the first time examined and made public.* New York, 1941.

VAN TYNE, CLAUDE H. *The Causes of the War of Independence.* Boston, 1922.
———. *England and America—Rivals in the American Revolution.* Cambridge, 1927. Six lectures delivered in England; most of the material was incorporated in *The War of Independence* (see below).
———. *The Loyalists in the American Revolution.* New York, 1929. (First published by Macmillan, 1902.) Based on the Loyalist Transcripts in the N.Y. Public Library, "this book did much to contribute to revised opinions regarding the loyalists," writes Van Doren in *Secret History.*
———. *The War of Independence.* Boston, 1929. This work, the first to make use of the Clements Collection (PECKHAM, *War for Indep.,* 211), goes only to the beginning of 1778. See CLEMENTS COLLECTION above.

VIRGINIA HISTORICAL SOCIETY. *Catalogue of Manuscripts....* Richmond, 1901. For other state papers see: University of Virginia Library, *Annual Reports of the Archivist* [Charlottesville], 1930–1940 (I-X), *Annual Reports on Historical Collections* [Charlottesville], 1940–   (XI-   ) and Virginia State Library, *Reports* (Richmond), 1903–1904.

WADE, HERBERT T. *A Brief History of the Colonial Wars in America from 1607 to 1775.* New York, 1948.

WALLACE, WILLARD M. *Appeal to Arms: A Military History of the American Revolution.* New York, 1951.

WALDO, ALBIGENCE. "Valley Forge, 1777–1778: Diary of. . . ." *Historical Magazine,* New York, 1861, and *Pa. Mag. of Hist. and Biog.,* XXI, 1897.

WARD, CHRISTOPHER. *The Delaware Continentals, 1776–1783.* Wilmington, Del., 1941.

——. *The War of the Revolution.* 2 vols. New York, 1952. Ward had nearly completed this history of land operations when he died in 1943. JOHN R. ALDEN (see above) edited the work and contributed the chapter on Western operations.

WHARTON, FRANCIS. (ed.) *The Revolutionary Diplomatic Correspondence of the United States.* 6 vols. Washington, 1889.

WHITTON, F. E. *The American War of Independence.* London, 1931.

WILKIN, W. H. *Some British Soldiers in America.* London, 1914.

WILKINSON, HENRY C. *Bermuda in the Old Empire.* New York, 1950.

WILKINSON, JAMES. *Memoirs of My Own Times.* 3 vols. Philadelphia, 1816. See also biographical article.

WILLCOX, WILLIAM B. (ed.) *The American Rebellion: Sir Henry Clinton's Narrative....* See CLINTON, above.

——. *Portrait of a General, Sir. Henry Clinton in the War of Independence.* New York, 1964.

——. "The British Road to Yorktown," *Am. Hist. Rev.,* LII (1947).

——. "British Strategy in America, 1778," *Jour. of Mod. Hist.,* XIX (June, 1947).

——. "Rhode Island in British Strategy, 1780–81," *Jour. of Mod. Hist.,* XVII (1945).

——. "Why Did the British Lose the American Revolution?" *Mich. Alumnus Quarterly Rev.,* LXII (Aug. 1956).

WILLETT, MARINUS. *Narrative.* See biographical article.

WILLIAM AND MARY COLLEGE. *William and Mary College Quarterly Historical Magazine.* Title varies. Williamsburg, Va., 1892–1942. For its continuation, see INST. OF EARLY AMER. HIST. AND CULTURE.

WILLIAMSBURG (VA.) COLLECTIONS. *A Guide to the Manuscript Collections of Colonial Williamsburg,* compiled by LYNETTE ADCOCK. Williamsburg, Va., 1954.

WINSOR, JUSTIN. *Calendar of the Arthur Lee Manuscripts.* Cambridge, 1882.

——. *Calendar of the Jared Sparks Manuscripts in Harvard College Library.* Cambridge, 1889.

——. *Narrative and Critical History of America.* 8 vols. Boston, 1884–89.

——. *The Reader's Handbook of the American Revolution.* Boston and New York, 1879; Boston, 1880; Boston and New York, 1890, 1895, 1899, and 1910. Still an indispensable bibliography.

WISCONSIN, STATE HISTORICAL SOCIETY OF. Its Lyman Draper Papers, valuable for the history of the Southern frontier and the Revolutionary West, are among the holdings described in Reuben G. Thwaites, *Descriptive List of Manuscript Collections of the State Historical Society of Wisconsin* (Madison, 1906). See also Alice E. Smith, *Guide to the Manuscripts of the Wisconsin State Historical Society* (Madison, 1944).

Wish, Harvey. *The American Historian.* New York, 1960.

————. *Society and Thought in America.* 2 vols. New York, 1950–52.

Wood, W., and Gabriel, R. H. *The Winning of Freedom,* New Haven, 1927.

Woods, Henry F. *American Sayings; Famous Phrases, Slogans and Aphorisms.* Rev. and enl. ed. New York, 1950.

W.O.R. See Ward, *War of the Revolution,* above.

Wright, Louis B. *The Cultural Life of the American Colonies, 1607–1763.* New York, 1957.

ADDENDUM FOR BICENTENNIAL EDITION

As pointed out in the Introduction, new scholarship in the field of the American Revolution continues to be published and should reach a new crest during the bicentennial years now approaching. Any attempt to update my bibliography now would be premature, but I would like to cite a few important new works and mention several scheduled for publication during the bicentennial.

The one national institution that has shown a fitting initiative in preparing for the bicentennial is the Library of Congress, which took timely steps to make its plans for the bicentennial and which started producing results while other organizations were still trying to get organized. One of the first steps taken by the Library was to publish in inexpensive pamphlet form an excellent general bibliography of 340 titles: *The American Revolution: A Selected Reading List* (1968). Another bibliography, for more serious scholars, is *Periodical Literature on the American Revolution* (1971). An annotated list of Revolutionary War maps has been compiled by Walter W. Ristow, chief of the Library's Geography and Map Division. (All can be ordered from the Superintendent of Documents, GPO, Washington, D.C. 20402, who will furnish a current price list.)

An excellent bibliographic essay is included in Don Higginbotham, *The War of American Independence* (1971).

Scheduled for publication in 1973 is a long-needed history of American naval operations in the Revolution, *Sea of Glory: The Continental Navy Fights for Independence, 1775–1783,* by Nathan Miller. Another important reference work compiled since my own research for the first edition of this encyclopedia ended almost a decade ago, and a source I have since found most valuable, is Fred Anderson Berg, *Encyclopedia of Continental Army Units* (Harrisburg, Pa., 1972).

The Atlas of the American Revolution, 1760–1790, is being prepared for the bicentennial by the Newberry Library. It is to include about 175 maps, most of them newly drawn, with a text. The Newberry Library, meanwhile, has been co-sponsor with the Institute of Early American History and Culture in publishing the *Atlas of Early American History.* Figures on enlistments and losses in the Continental Army and state militias during the Revolution are being compiled by The William L. Clements Library at the University of Michigan.

My own *Landmarks of the American Revolution* (Harrisburg, Pa., 1973) is a guide to historic sites that is in many respects a companion volume to *Encyclopedia of the American Revolution.*

INDEX OF MAPS

The following index includes all major place names shown in the maps and endpapers of this book. Not included, because of lack of space, are many houses, fords, streams, and other landmarks in battlefield maps.

ABBREVIATED INDEX OF MAJOR "COVER ARTICLES" AND CERTAIN TOPICAL ARTICLES

NOTES

WESTERN CAROLINAS

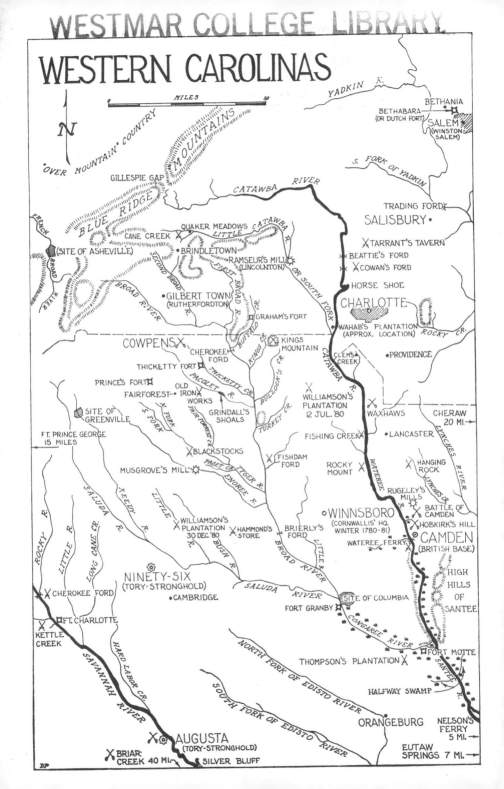

MILES
0 50

N

YADKIN R.

BETHANIA
BETHABARA
(OR DUTCH FORT)
SALEM
(WINSTON-SALEM)

"OVER MOUNTAIN" COUNTRY

MOUNTAINS

S. FORK OF YADKIN

GILLESPIE GAP

CATAWBA RIVER

BLUE RIDGE

TRADING FORD
SALISBURY

QUAKER MEADOWS
CANE CREEK
LITTLE CATAWBA R.
(SITE OF ASHEVILLE)
BRINDLETOWN
RAMSEUR'S MILL
(LINCOLNTON)

TARRANT'S TAVERN
BEATTIE'S FORD
COWAN'S FORD

FRENCH BROAD RIVER

SECOND BROAD R.

FIRST BROAD R.

HORSE SHOE

GILBERT TOWN
(RUTHERFORDTON)
GRAHAM'S FORT

CHARLOTTE

BUFFALO CR.

WAHAB'S PLANTATION
(APPROX. LOCATION)
ROCKY CR.

COWPENS
CHEROKEE FORD
KINGS MOUNTAIN

KINGS CR.

CATAWBA R. OR SOUTH FORK

CLEMS CREEK
PROVIDENCE

THICKETTY FORT

PRINCE'S FORT
FAIRFOREST
OLD IRON WORKS
GRINDALL'S SHOALS

THICKETTY CR.

PACOLET R.

BULLOCK'S CR.

TURKEY CR.

WILLIAMSON'S PLANTATION
12 JUL. '80
WAXHAWS
CHERAW
20 MI.

SITE OF GREENVILLE

FT. PRINCE GEORGE
15 MILES

S. FORK

N. FORK

FAIR FOREST CR.

FISHING CREEK
LANCASTER

BLACKSTOCKS

PAGET CR.
TIGER R.

FISHDAM FORD

ROCKY MOUNT

HANGING ROCK

LYNCHES RIVER

MUSGROVE'S MILL

ENOREE R.

SALUDA R.

REEDY R.

LITTLE R.

WILLIAMSON'S PLANTATION
30 DEC. '80
HAMMOND'S STORE
BRIERLY'S FORD

WINNSBORO
(CORNWALLIS' HQ.
WINTER 1780-81)

RUGELEY'S MILLS
BATTLE OF CAMDEN
HOBKIRK'S HILL

WATEREE FERRY
CAMDEN
(BRITISH BASE)

WATEREE R.

LITTLE R.

BROAD RIVER

NINETY-SIX
(TORY-STRONGHOLD)
CAMBRIDGE

BUSH R.

SALUDA RIVER

SITE OF COLUMBIA
FORT GRANBY

HIGH HILLS OF SANTEE

ROCKY R.

LITTLE R.

LONG CANE CR.

CHEROKEE FORD

FT. CHARLOTTE
KETTLE CREEK

HARD LABOR CR.

CONGAREE RIVER

FORT MOTTE

SANTEE R.

SAVANNAH RIVER

NORTH FORK OF EDISTO RIVER

SOUTH FORK OF EDISTO RIVER

THOMPSON'S PLANTATION

HALFWAY SWAMP

ORANGEBURG

NELSON'S FERRY
5 MI.

AUGUSTA
(TORY-STRONGHOLD)

BRIAR CREEK 40 MI.
SILVER BLUFF

EUTAW SPRINGS 7 MI.

DP